THE INTERNATIONAL
Daffodil Register
- and -
Classified List
1998

Constance G. Oliver
P.O. Box 186
Peterborough NH 03458

THE INTERNATIONAL
Daffodil Register
- and -
Classified List
1998

Compiled by Sally Kington
International Daffodil Registrar

THE ROYAL HORTICULTURAL SOCIETY

Published in 1998 by The Royal Horticultural Society, 80 Vincent Square, London SW1P 2PE

All rights reserved. This book is protected by copyright. No part of it may be reproduced, stored in a retrieval system, or transmitted, in any form or by any means, electronic, mechanical, photocopying, recording or otherwise without written permission from the Publisher.

ISBN 1-874431-69-8

Copyright © The Royal Horticultural Society 1998

Compiled by Sally Kington, International Daffodil Registrar

Cover photograph: *Narcissus* 'Stromboli' at St John's College, Oxford
(by Andrew Lawson)
Line artworks by Rosemary Lindsay and Liz Butler

Cover design by Gail Rose, Clwyd
Printed in Great Britain by Unwin Brothers, Surrey

CONTENTS

Introduction	7
Daffodil Classification	7
Cultivar Registration	8
Scope of the Register	9
Interpreting the Register	10
Illustrations and Glossary of Descriptive Terms	14
Amending the Register	16
Acknowledgements	16
Horticultural Classification	17
Botanical Classification	20
The International Daffodil Register and Classified List	27
Early Divisions and Groups	1147
Originators and Registrants	1148

INTRODUCTION

The International Daffodil Register and Classified List (1998) is the 23rd cumulative list of daffodil names to be published by the Royal Horticultural Society since 1907. The first was simply entitled *List of Daffodil Names*. That was followed by series called *The Classified List of Daffodil Names* and (from 1958) *The Classified List and International Register of Daffodil Names*. A Checklist was published in 1989. The present Register will be updated by annual supplements of newly registered names and periodic lists of amendments.

DAFFODIL CLASSIFICATION

The 1908 List was the first "classified" list, announcing the introduction by the Royal Horticultural Society (RHS) of a new daffodil classification for garden and show purposes, following the "enormous increase of late years in the number of named Daffodils and the crossing and inter-crossing of the once fairly distinct classes of magni-, medio- and parvi-coronati" (p. 1147). Seven arbitrary divisions were adopted, determined chiefly by measurement, but these were said in the 1910 List to have failed to meet with general acceptance. An expanded scheme of 11 divisions was then published which, with some small amendments over the years, served until 1950.

The Revised System of 1950 was designed to make classification more logical, to make it easier to understand and apply, and to provide for the continuing evolution of the daffodil cultivar. In principle and in structure, it remains the basis for the Revised System of 1998 (p. 17). Major developments since 1950 have been the introduction of colour coding, subdividing Division 11, adding a division for Bulbocodium cultivars, and having one division for "daffodils distinguished solely by botanical name" instead of for "species, wild variants and wild hybrids".

Since 1910, Divisions 1 to 3 had carried sub-divisions indicating colour. Then in 1975 Dr Tom Throckmorton of Iowa, USA, devised a more flexible code applicable to all daffodils. It has always been emphasized, however, that colour descriptions could be expected to vary considerably, based as they would be on individual perception, rarely on the RHS or any other recognized colour chart. Also, it is known that the colour of a cultivar can vary according to climate, weather and growing conditions. The colour code would remain only a guide to colour, though potentially a very good guide.

It was at the instigation of the Royal General Bulb Growers' Association of Holland and in subsequent consultation with the national daffodil societies that Collar daffodils were separated from Papillon daffodils in Division 11, the two kinds of split-corona proving to be of consistently different form.

The creation of a division for Bulbocodium hybrids, again after worldwide consultation, reflects the growing number of new registrations in this area.

To limit one division to daffodils distinguished solely by botanical name is to make the difference clear between on the one hand the botanical taxa and on the other hand any selections, whether of wild or cultivated origin, that have been distinguished by a cultivar name. Only the botanical taxa are classified in Division 13. Selections distinguished by a cultivar name, even if they were originally wild plants, are classified in one of Divisions 1-12. Names of botanical taxa are governed by the *International Code of Botanical Nomenclature - 1994* (the Botanical Code), names of cultivars and cultivar-groups by the *International Code of Nomenclature for Cultivated Plants - 1995* (the Cultivated Plant Code).

Horticultural classification

All daffodil cultivars are classified in one of Divisions 1-12 in the horticultural classification (p. 17).

1. The classification of a daffodil cultivar will be that which is submitted by the person registering the cultivar, or will be based on the description and measurements submitted by that person.

2. The classification will consist of a division number (with letters a or b for Division 11) and a colour code.

3. The numbered divisions in which a daffodil cultivar may be placed are defined and illustrated in the horticultural classification (p. 17).

4. Measurements taken in determining between Divisions 1, 2 and 3 will be those of the flower at maturity. The length of the perianth segments (the "petals") is the measurement from the tip of one segment, when flattened out, to the base of the corona (the "trumpet" or "cup"). The length of the corona is the measurement from the base of the perianth segments to the furthest margin of the corona.

5. a) The colours and equivalent code letters which may be used to describe a daffodil cultivar will be those of the flower at maturity, when viewed from the front. They are:

White or Whitish	W
Green	G
Yellow	Y
Pink	P
Orange	O
Red	R

In distinguishing Yellow from Orange in daffodil classification, borderline colours including and on the green side of RHS Yellow-Orange Group 15 on the RHS Colour Chart are said to be Yellow; those including and on the red side of Yellow-Orange Group 16 are Orange.

In distinguishing Orange from Red, borderline colours including and on the yellow side of RHS Orange Group 29 are said to be Orange; those including and on the purple side of Orange-Red Group 30 are Red.

It is at the registrant's discretion to distinguish White from Yellow or Green, Yellow from Green, or Pink from the pale tones of Orange or Red.

b) The colour code will consist of two letters or two groups of letters separated by a hyphen: the letter(s) before the hyphen will describe the perianth segments; the letter(s) following the hyphen will describe the corona. For example: 1 Y-Y, 2 YYW-Y, 3 Y-YYO.

c) For purposes of description the perianth segments are divided into three zones: outer zone, mid-zone and base; and the corona into three zones: base, mid-zone and rim.

d) If the perianth segments are substantially of a single colour, a single code letter will describe them; if they are of more than one colour, three code letters will be used, describing first the outer zone, secondly the mid-zone and lastly the base; or if the colours are non-concentric, describing first the predominant colour, which is followed by an oblique line, then the non-predominant colour. For example: 1 W-Y, 2 YYW-Y, 1 Y/W-W.

e) If the corona is substantially of a single colour, a single code letter will describe it; if it is of more than one colour, three code letters will be used, describing first the base, secondly the mid-zone and lastly the rim; or if the colours are non-concentric, describing first the predominant colour, which is followed by an oblique line, then the non-predominant colour(s) in any order. For example: 2 Y-Y, 3 Y-YYO, 11a W-O/YW.

f) In double daffodils the code letter(s) before the hyphen will describe not only the perianth segments but also any extra petaloid segments, even if they are interspersed with the corona at the centre of the flower; the code letter(s) following the hyphen will describe the corona or the segments of the corona. Multiple letters before or after the hyphen will in doubles as in all other daffodils indicate that there is more than one concentric or non-concentric colour in the perianth and petaloid segments or in the corona or segments of the corona.

Botanical classification

The classification of daffodils distinguished solely by botanical name is summarized under Division 13 in the horticultural classification (p. 17). It is spelt out in full in the botanical classification (p. 20).

CULTIVAR REGISTRATION

Daffodil cultivars are registered first "to prevent, as far as possible, names already appropriated being given to new seedlings" (RHS List 1907), and secondly to prevent the use of names which so closely resemble existing names that they would cause confusion (RHS Classified List 1908). In these and in other ways names must also conform with the *International Code of Nomenclature for Cultivated Plants - 1995*, a basic rule of which is one that was first formulated for daffodil cultivars by the Royal Horticultural Society's Daffodil Conference of 1884, ie that new names should be "fancy names", not botanical names in Latin form.

More than 26,000 cultivar names have accumulated in the RHS files. The majority meet the Society's early strictures about form and largely conform with the International Code.

Unfortunately, however, much duplication has occurred over the years, sometimes accepted by the RHS itself in accordance with contemporary practice. In 1916, for example, it was laid down that unless a cultivar were exhibited for confirmation of name at an RHS meeting within five years of listing, the name would be erased from the Society's list and made available for re-use (though this did not apply to Australian and New Zealand cultivars.) Then in 1955 a quantity of names became available for re-use when some 4,000 cultivars were claimed to have become extinct; and in 1969 a rolling programme of deletion was planned, with the names of cultivars listed before 1930 to be omitted from the next following Register unless still in cultivation or shown to be of historical importance. More recent cultivars were to be similarly sifted in subsequent Registers.

Meanwhile, it was perhaps inevitable that not every daffodil grower the world over would find it easy or even worthwhile to notify the RHS of the cultivar names they chose to use. The chances of duplication were thus increased by the many names that never appeared in the RHS lists at all.

However, a firm stand against further duplication, either through permitted re-use or through failure to register, has once again been taken. The case was put by Dr Alan Leslie, Senior Registrar at the RHS: "Once a name has appeared in print it is there to cause potential confusion for evermore if another plant is allowed to take up the same name" (*Notes RBG Edinb.* **43** (1): 174 (1985)). It is in the interests of the grower, the retailer and the public to ensure that a cultivar name is unique within the genus.

The RHS became International Registration Authority for the genus *Narcissus* in 1955, at the invitation of the 14th International Horticultural Congress. The subsequent (1958) edition of the Classified List was the first to be entitled Classified List and International Register.

The main duties of the International Registration Authority for the genus *Narcissus* are:

(a) to register cultivar and cultivar-group epithets and to ensure their establishment;

(b) to publish full lists of all cultivar and cultivar-group epithets; and

(c) to maintain records, in as great a detail as is practical, of the origin, characteristics and history of each cultivar and cultivar-group.

It is not the duty of the International Registration Authority:

(a) to conduct trials;

(b) to judge whether one cultivar or cultivar-group is more meritorious or more useful than another; or

(c) to judge distinctness of cultivars or cultivar-groups.

There is no charge for daffodil registration; and certificates of registration may be had on request. Registration forms may be obtained from various sources:

The International Daffodil Registrar
Mrs Sally Kington
The Royal Horticultural Society
Vincent Square, London SW1P 2PE, UK

The National Daffodil Registrar (Australia)
Mr Tony Davis
62 Burradoo Road
Bowral, NSW 2576, Australia

The National Daffodil Registrar (Czech Republic)
Ing. Vladimir Domsky
Konevova 40, 400 00 Usti nad Labem
Czech Republic

The National Daffodil Registrar (The Netherlands)
Dr Johan van Scheepen
KAVB
Postbus 175, 2180 Hillegom, Parklaan 5, The Netherlands

The National Daffodil Registrar (New Zealand)
Mr Max Hamilton
Boyd Road
RD1, Hamilton, New Zealand

The National Daffodil Registrar (USA)
Mrs Mary Lou Gripshover
1686 Grey Fox Trails
Milford, Ohio 45150, USA

SCOPE OF THE REGISTER

There are five kinds of name in the Register:

Cultivar names
A name such as *Narcissus* 'King Alfred' is a cultivar name. The epithet 'King Alfred' should appear in single quotation marks, with capital initial letters.

The Register contains every daffodil cultivar name published by the RHS in any of its Lists and Registers since 1907, thus re-instating any that were from time to time deleted. It includes names registered up to 30 June 1997. It also includes many unregistered names gleaned from back numbers of the major daffodil societies' reports and journals, from nursery catalogues, from the American Daffodil Society's Data Bank and from the Tasmanian Seedling Register.

Although new cultivar epithets must be a word or words in a modern language, epithets in Latin form in use before 1959 may continue in use in accordance with Article 17.9 of the Cultivated Plant Code.

Cultivar-group names
A name such as *Narcissus* Incomparabilis is a cultivar-group name, as is *N.* Nylon Group. The epithets Incomparabilis and Nylon Group should have capital initial letters. They do not have quotation marks.

Cultivar-group names are for assemblages of similar plants or cultivars. Cultivar-group names drawn up in 1884 appear in the synonymy of most cultivars of that date. They include Incomparabilis Albidus, Barrii and Backhousei (listed on p. 1147). For the sake of brevity, the word Group is omitted from them when used in cultivar synonymy. Cultivar-group names of more recent date appear in their own right. They include Nylon Group, Double Wintercups Group, Glenbrook Mini-cycla Group and others.

Trade designations
A name such as *Narcissus* JANUARY is a trade designation. In this case it is for the plant with the cultivar epithet 'Rijnveld's Early Sensation'. In the Daffodil Register, trade designations are distinguished by being printed in small capitals, without quotation marks.

Botanical names
A name such as *Narcissus jonquilla* is a botanical name. It should appear in italics. The generic name *Narcissus* may be abbreviated to a capital *N.* where the meaning is unambiguous; the specific epithet *jonquilla* should have a lower-case initial letter.

A name such as *Narcissus × intermedius* is also a botanical name. In this case it is for hybrids between *N. jonquilla* and *N. tazetta*. The cross indicating its hybrid nature is ideally written as a multiplication sign.

The Register contains all currently recognized taxa as set out in the botanical classification (p. 20).

Popular names
A name such as "Angel's Tears" is a popular name. In this case it is for *N. triandrus var. triandrus*. In the Daffodil Register, popular names are distinguished by double quotation marks and capital initial letters.

INTERPRETING THE REGISTER

Order of entries
The Register is arranged alphabetically. The names are sorted letter by letter, ignoring spacing, casing or punctuation, so that 'Glen Isla' is followed by 'Glenlee', 'Glenleslie' and 'Glen Lorne' and 'Mr R.M.Tobin' by 'Mrs Alfred White', 'Mrs Yvonne' and 'Mr Theo A.Havermeyer'. In botanical names, the *N.* for *Narcissus* and the × indicating a hybrid are ignored, so that 'Rupert Brooke' is followed by *N. × rupidulus* and 'Rural Gold'.

Cultivar names, cultivar-group names, trade designations and popular names
Cultivar names, cultivar-group names, trade designations and popular names are accompanied by one or more of the following items of information:

(See under Botanical Names for the information attached to botanical names)

Registration
Names accepted by the Royal Horticultural Society since becoming International Registration Authority in 1955 are registered. Names dated before 1955 are deemed registered. Any other names are unregistered and are marked as such.

Division
Daffodils with cultivar names are assigned to Divisions 1-12 in the horticultural classification (p. 17).

A question mark against the division means that the classification is uncertain, which in many cases is because the cultivar was formerly classified as a Leedsii, a division which until 1950 included cultivars both of Division 2 and Division 3 measurements in today's terms.

Colour code
The letters W, G, Y, O, R and P indicate the colour of the cultivar (see p. 8).

Colours recorded are those that the cultivar displays at maturity in the region where it was bred. However, marked and regularly occurring variation in colour when the same cultivar is grown elsewhere may be noted in the Register. Any case for inclusion of such a note should be sent to the International Registrar (see p. 16, Amending the Register).

Colour sub-division
Until replaced by Dr Throckmorton's system in 1975, a system of colour coding by sub-divisions had been in use since 1950 (replacing a system dating from 1910). The 1950 system applied colour sub-divisions (a), (b), (c) and (d) to Divisions 1-3, with "coloured" meaning yellow or some colour other than white, and "white" meaning white or whitish, as follows:

(a) Perianth coloured: corona coloured, not paler than the perianth
(b) Perianth white; corona coloured
(c) Perianth white; corona white, not paler than the perianth
(d) Any colour combination not falling into (a), (b) or (c)

These sub-divisions have occasionally been retained in the Register. They are a guide to colouring when, for lack of information about a flower, a full interpretation of the sub-division has not been possible under the current scheme. The sub-divisions may all be found in earlier registers and supplements, should today's interpretations be called into question.

Originator's name
A name in brackets is, in the case of pre-1955 cultivars, that of the hybridizer or other introducer; in later cultivars it is almost invariably that of the hybridizer.

Date of first flowering
A date in brackets is the date of first flowering. In the case of pre-1955 cultivars, and of later ones too if they are unregistered, it is usually based either on the earliest reference the RHS has to the cultivar or on the year of death of the originator. It is expressed as "pre" or "c." such and such a date. In registered cultivars it is given only if it is 10 years or more earlier than the date of registration.

Registrant's name
A name outside the brackets is that of the registrant. It is attached to cultivars registered since the RHS became International Registration Authority in 1955.

Date of registration
A date outside the brackets is the date of registration. It is attached to cultivars registered since the RHS became International Registration Authority in 1955.

Parentage
In parentages of cultivars, the seed parent is given before the pollen parent. When it is not known which was which, the parents are in alphabetical order. (Note that the parents of botanical hybrids are always given in alphabetical order; see p. 13.)

Parents given as seedlings under number are the hybridizer's own seedlings unless otherwise stated.

The term Poetaz means that one parent was *N. poeticus* or derived from it and the other *N. tazetta* or derived from it.

Seedling number
Seedling numbers are supplied by the registrant or culled from catalogues.

Description, colour and attributes
Descriptions have been compiled from various sources: registration forms, photographs, paintings, catalogues and personal observation. A number of expressions have had to be ignored, or have been interpreted only from a picture or on the advice of the registrant. For example, the term "flat", which of the perianth segments sometimes seems to have meant "at right angles to the corona", sometimes "not concave" and sometimes both, has not been copied into the present descriptions and has been interpreted only with care. Several terms for corona shape come into this category: eg goblet, vase, chalice.

Colour terms present similar problems. For example, sulphur, primrose, citron, lemon and gold are all open to interpretation, unless there is evidence that they are being used as they were in the Horticultural Colour Chart of 1938, in which case they can be correlated with today's RHS Colour Charts. But many such colour terms have simply been copied into the present descriptions, presuming that they can help differentiate between the many tones of the few full colours in daffodils. They have been interpreted only to the extent of assuming, in the case of sulphur or primrose, for example, that they do mean yellow and do warrant a Y for yellow in the colour code.

Colours that can be identified with a number on the RHS Colour Chart (1966, reprinted 1986, 1995) are given the Colour Chart number (eg 9A) together with a standard colour name drawn up in *A Contribution towards Standardization of Colour Names in Horticulture* published by the American Rhododendron Society in 1984 (the standard colour name for 9A being vivid yellow). A few of the standard colour names are mis-leading as far as daffodils are concerned, in which case they have been altered; the number is then put in brackets.

Descriptions include, in order, one or more of the following items of information. See p. 14 for illustrations and glossary of terms.

About the whole flower: number of flowers per stem (unless single-flowered); outline; width; colour (if self coloured); poise

About the perianth segments: outline; apex; colour*; direction (eg spreading or reflexed); surface direction (eg plane or concave); margins (eg wavy); surface condition (eg smooth); substance (eg strong), relationship (eg separated or overlapping); differences in the inner segments (eg narrower)

About the corona: form; surface (eg ribbed); colour*; axial direction of mouth (eg straight or flared); circumaxial habit of mouth (eg even or frilled); axial direction of rim (eg flanged); circumaxial habit of rim (eg entire or crenate)

* A colour description is usually only included if it adds to the colour code: for example, "fl. white" would not usually be used for a flower coded W-W, but "fl. greenish white" would be. However, an unqualified colour (eg white) would be used in conjunction with a qualified colour (eg bright yellow): for example, "corona white, with a band of bright yellow at rim".

About height: dwarf = less than 32.5 cm or 13 in; tall = more than 67.5 cm or 27 in; no mention = standard (32.5-67.5 cm or 13-27 in) or unknown. Measurements supplied by registrants should be of plants grown in unsheltered conditions in the open air

About flowering season: these are very early, early, mid-season, late, very late. Early to mid-season means early season to mid-season

About weather resistance: although the term sunproof is used, its meaning is probably nearer to sun-resistant in most cases

About chromosome counts: these were assembled by Dr P.E.Brandham, to whom the RHS is indebted. They appear in *Chromosome Numbers in Narcissus Cultivars and their Significance to the Plant Breeder* in *The Plantsman* 14: 133-168 (1992). Where more than one number is quoted for a variety, two or more independent workers have made the count. The differences are probably due to mis-identification.

Estimates of fertility based on chromosomal constitution are indicated in the table. The estimates should be taken only as a rough guide to fertility, since plants with chromosome numbers indicating sterility can produce occasional viable gametes. Other plants with chromosome numbers expected to result in fertility (eg diploids, tetraploids) can sometimes be quite sterile because of genetical imbalance, or absence of pollen as in many double-flowered varieties. Such doubles can nevertheless be female-fertile sometimes.

COUNT	CHROMOSOMAL CONSTITUTION	ESTIMATE OF FERTILITY
2n=14	Diploid	Usually Sterile
2n=17	Diploid hybrid	Sterile
2n=18	Diploid hybrid	Sterile
2n=19	Triploid lacking two chromosomes	Sterile
2n=20	Diploid, except 'Pipers Barn' which is autotriploid	Diploids fertile, triploid sterile
2n=21	Triploid, except 'Sicily White' (?syn. of 'Scilly White') which is diploid	Sterile
2n=22	Aneuploid triploid, except *N. papyraceus*, 'Paper White Grandiflorus' and 'White Pearl' which are diploid	Triploids sterile, diploids fertile
2n=24	Allotriploid	Sterile
2n=26	Tetraploid lacking two chromosomes	Fertile
2n=27	Tetraploid lacking one chromosome	Fertile
2n=28	Autotetraploid, allotetraploid and auto-allotetraploid	Fertile; except 'Silver Chimes' (Allotripoloid) which is sterile
2n=29	Tetraploid with one additional chromosome	Fertile
2n=30	Autotriploid, also tetraploid with two additional chromosomes	Triploids sterile, tetraploids fertile
2n=31	Auto-allotetraploid, except 'Avalanche', 'Compressus' and 'Grand Monarque' which are allotriploid and 'Madame de Graaff' which is tetraploid with three additional chromosomes	Triploids sterile, tetraploids fertile
2n=32	Allotriploid	Sterile
2n=33	Tetraploid with five additional chromosomes	Fertile
2n=34	Allotetraploid	Fertile
2n=35	Pentaploid, also allotetraploid	Slightly fertile
2n=36	Pentaploid	Slightly fertile
2n=37	Pentaploid with two additional chromosomes	Slightly fertile
2n=43	Aneuploid hexaploid	Slightly fertile
2n=45	Allopentaploid	± Sterile
2n=46	Allopentaploid	± Sterile

NOTE Compiling descriptions is an ongoing task. Investigation into particular cultivars will gladly be undertaken on request.

Synonymy
Mis-spellings are included among synonyms. Cultivar epithets treated as synonyms of species bear no classification or colour code

Awards
The awards cited are those of the Royal Horticultural Society, the Koninklijke Algemeene Vereeniging voor Bloembollencultuur (Royal General Bulb Growers' Association) of Holland, the National Daffodil Society of New Zealand and the American Daffodil Society.

Key to RHS awards
*	= award made after trial; trial held at The RHS Garden, Wisley, Surrey unless otherwise indicated (see below)
FCC	= First Class Certificate
AM	= Award of Merit
AGM	= Award of Garden Merit (1992 -)
HC	= Highly Commended
C	= Commended
PC	= Certificate of Preliminary Commendation
PR	= Preliminary Recognition (1915 - 1930)
(a)	= qualified as for the alpine house
(c)	= qualified as for cutting
(e)	= qualified as a show flower
(f)	= qualified as a market cultivar for forcing
(g)	= qualified as for garden decoration
(m)	= qualified as a market cultivar for cutting from the open
(p)	= qualified as for cultivation in pots, pans or bowls
(r)	= qualified as for the rock garden
(s)	= qualified as a species or a variety of a species
(Gulval)	= trial held at Cornwall County Experimental Station, Gulval, Cornwall
(Kirton)	= trial held at Kirton Experimental Horticultural Station, Boston, Lincolnshire

Key to Dutch awards
(distinguished from RHS awards by the addition in brackets of the name Haarlem or Hillegom)
FCC	= First Class Certificate
AM	= Award of Merit
FCEFA	= First Class Early Forcing Award
FCFA	= First Class Forcing Award
EFA	= Early Forcing Award
FA	= Forcing Award
TGA	= Trial Garden Award
(Haarlem)	= award made from Haarlem
(Hillegom)	= award made from Hillegom

Key to New Zealand awards
(distinguished from RHS awards by the addition in brackets of NZ)
All are qualified as awards for show flowers unless otherwise indicated
FCC	= First Class Certificate
AM	= Award of Merit
PC	= Certificate of Preliminary Commendation
(c)	= qualified as for cutting

Key to United States awards
Wister Award = Wister Award for garden merit
Pannill Award = Pannill Award for exhibition

Notes
The word "absorbed" is quoted from an annotated copy of the Barr catalogue of 1884 called *Ye Narcissus or Daffodyl Flowre, and hys Roots*. In what appears to be Peter Barr's own hand many of the daffodils listed are noted as having been "absorbed into" another named variety. It is not known precisely what was implied, but most of the daffodils thus "absorbed" were omitted from the subsequent catalogue.

Botanical names
Botanical names are accompanied by one or more of the following items of information:

Author
A name in roman type following a name in italics is that of the person(s) to whom the name in italics is attributed.

hort.
The abbreviation is for *hortulanorum*, meaning "of gardeners". It identifies certain synonyms or misapplied names that have been regularly used in horticulture.

Division
Daffodils distinguished solely by botanical name are assigned to Division 13 in the horticultural classification (p. 17).

Section
Descriptions of the sections of the genus in the botanical classification are to be found under Division 13 in the horticultural classification (p. 17).

Parentage
The parents of botanical hybrids are given in alphabetical order.

Chromosome count
Chromosome counts attached to botanical names are rendered in the same way and have the same significance as those attached to cultivars (p. 12).

Rank
The abbreviations subsp. (subspecies), var. (varietas) or f. (forma) preceding an epithet indicate the intraspecific rank of the epithet as given in the botanical classification (p. 20).

Synonymy
A selected synonymy is provided, with an emphasis on names that have been used in horticulture. The

equals sign (=) should not be interpreted in its mathematical sense of "being identical with" but often in the sense of "being part of" or "being referred to".

Awards

Awards attached to botanical names are rendered in the same way and have the same significance as those attached to cultivars (p. 13).

ILLUSTRATIONS AND GLOSSARY OF DESCRIPTIVE TERMS

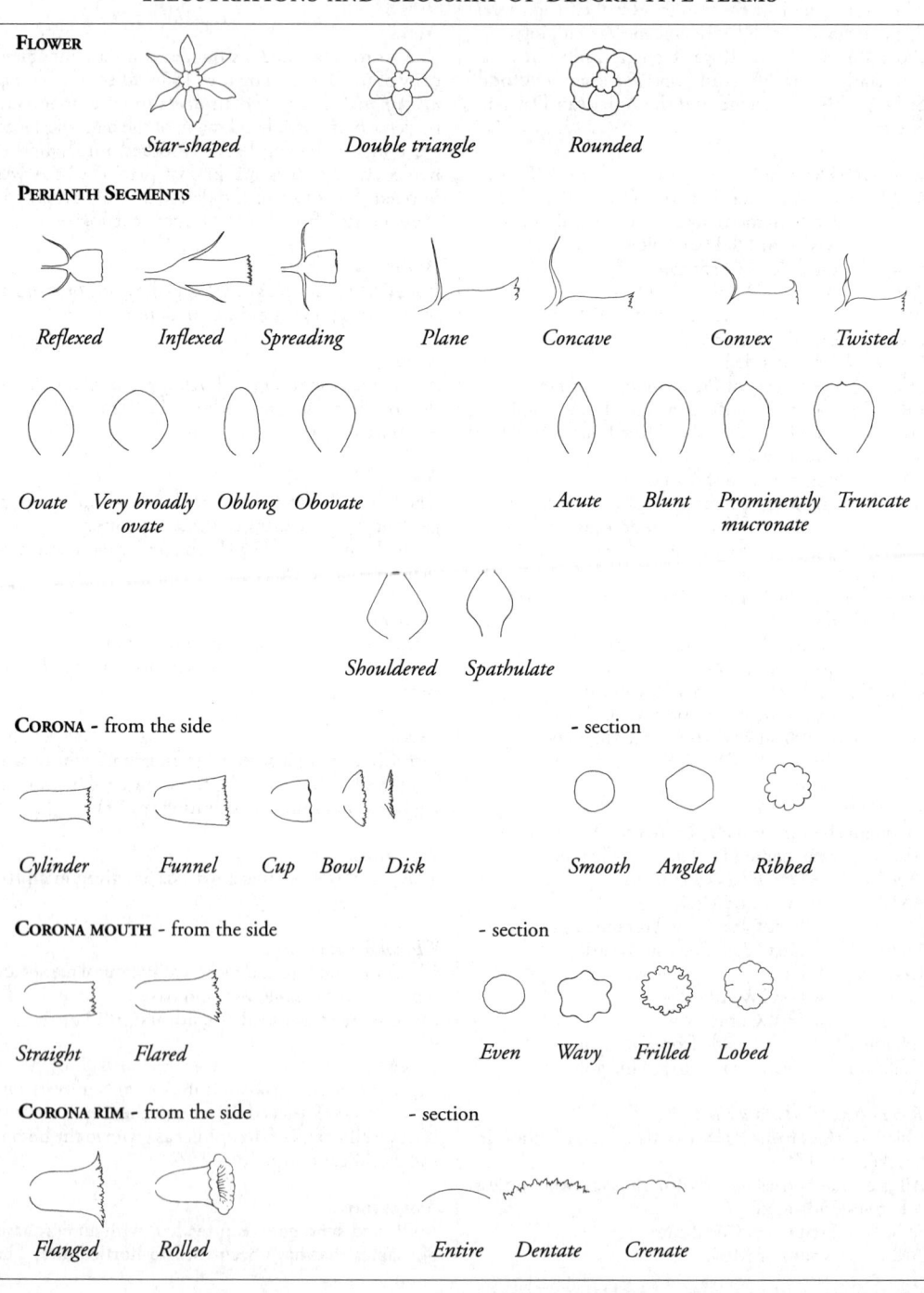

Glossary

above	on the upper or adaxial side of a surface
acute	used of the perianth, petaloid or corona segments; see illustration
abaxial	away from the axis or centre
adaxial	towards the axis or centre
angled	used for the corona; see illustration
anther	the pollen-bearing part of the stamen
ascending	having a direction upwards, with an oblique base
axial	located along the axis
below, beneath	on the lower or abaxial side of a surface
blunt	rounded enough for an angle of 90° to be placed inside. Used of the perianth, petaloid or corona segments; see illustration
bowl-shaped	used of the corona; see illustration
campanulate	bell-shaped
circumaxial	around the axis or centre
concave	used of the perianth, petaloid or corona segments; see illustration
concentric	encircling a common centre
convex	used of the perianth, petaloid or corona segments; see illustration
corona	the "trumpet" or "cup"
crenate	used of the corona rim; see illustration
cultivar which	a taxon of cultivated plants is clearly distinct, uniform and stable in its characteristics and which, when propagated by appropriate means, retains those characteristics
cultivar epithet	the defining part of a name that denotes a cultivar
cup-shaped	used of the corona; see illustration
cylindrical	used of the corona; see illustration
dentate	used of the corona rim; see illustration
disc-shaped	used of the corona; see illustration
dorsifixed	of an anther, attached more or less centrally to the filament
double triangle	used of the outline of the flower; see illustration
entire	used of the corona rim; see illustration
epithet	see cultivar epithet or specific epithet
even	used of the corona mouth; see illustration
exserted	extending beyond surrounding organs
filament	the stalk of the stamen
flanged	used of the corona rim; see illustration
flared	used of the corona mouth; see illustration
forma, f.	botanical rank below variety; see botanical classification (p. 20). Note that the abbreviation f. following the name Schultes means son (*filius*)
frilled	used for the corona mouth; see illustration
funnel-shaped	used of the corona; see illustration
glaucous	covered with a fine bloom the colour of a cabbage leaf
inflexed	used of the perianth segments; see illustration
lanceolate	very narrowly ovate
lobed	used of the corona mouth; see illustration
mucro	the "clasp" or short abrupt point at the apex of a perianth segment
mucronate	used of the perianth or petaloid segments; see illustration
oblong	used of the perianth, petaloid or corona segments; see illustration
obovate	used of the perianth, petaloid or corona segments; see illustration
ovary	the part of the flower enclosing the ovules, developing into the capsule containing the seeds
perianth	collective term for the "petals" (perianth segments)
perianth segments	"petals"
petaloid segments	the extra perianth segments in a Div. 4 (double) daffodil
plane	used of the perianth, petaloid or corona segments; see illustration
Poetaz	with one parent *N. poeticus* or derived from it, the other parent *N. tazetta* or derived from it
POPS	P.Phillips open-pollinated seed
pro parte	in part
rank	any category in the nomenclatural hierarchy in the botanical classification (p. 20)
reflexed	used of the perianth, petaloid or corona segments; see illustration
retuse	terminating in a round end, the centre of which is depressed
ribbed	used largely of the corona; see illustration
rolled	used of the corona rim; see illustration
rounded	used of the outline of the flower: see illustration
saucer-shaped	very shallow bowl-shaped
scarious	of thin dry membranous texture

shouldered	used of the perianth, petaloid or corona segments; see illustration
spathulate	used of the perianth, petaloid or corona segments; see illustration
specific epithet	the defining part of a name that denotes an individual species
species	the basic category in botanical classification; used both as a singular and a plural word
sport	a mutation
spreading	used of the perianth segments; see illustration
stamen	the male part of the flower, consisting of the filament and anther
star-shaped	used of the outline of the flower; see illustration
straight	used of the corona mouth; see illustration
striate	marked with lines
sub-basifixed	attached near the base
subspecies, subsp.	botanical rank between species and variety; see botanical classification (p. 20)
synonym, syn.	name other than the accepted name for an individual taxon
taxon	abbreviation for taxonomic group, a group into which a number of similar individuals may be classified; plural taxa
thumbed	with an excrescence at the margin like a thumb
tone	quality of lightness or darkness
truncate	used of the perianth, petaloid or corona segments; see illustration
tube	the part of the flower between the ovary and the point of divergence of perianth segments and corona
twisted	used of the perianth, petaloid or corona segments; see illustration
varietas, var.	botanical rank between sub species and forma; see botanical classification (p. 20)
wavy	used of the corona mouth; see illustration
whorl	used for the ring of (usually) six perianth segments or for any rings of petaloid segments in a double flower

AMENDING THE REGISTER

Suggestions for alteration or amendment to the entries in the Register should be sent to the International Registrar at the RHS. Changes may be made, but only when sanctioned by the Narcissus Classification Advisory Committee following consultation with the registrant or investigation by the Registrar. Changes to classifications or colour codes will be published periodically, usually in the annual supplements to the Register.

ACKNOWLEDGEMENTS

For their ready co-operation over the years the Royal Horticultural Society is indebted to the Daffodil Society (formerly the Midland Daffodil Society), the Royal General Bulb Growers' Association of Holland, the American Daffodil Society, the National Daffodil Society of New Zealand, the National Daffodil Association of Australia (formerly the Daffodil Society of Australia and before that the Royal Horticultural Society of Victoria) and the Tasmanian Daffodil Council.

For regular and generous support in matters of annual registration the National Registrars are much thanked: Tony Davis of Australia, Ing. Vladimir Domsky of the Czech Republic, Dr Johan van Scheepen of The Netherlands, Max Hamilton of New Zealand and Mary Lou Gripshover of the United States.

In recent work on the Register itself, first thanks go to daffodil people the world over, without whose patient response to a mass of questions about origins, classifications and colour codes there would be no worthwhile Register. It is hoped that they and others will help put in the corrections and amendments that slip through the finest of nets, and will point out any ambiguities or misapprehensions in the descriptions here appearing for the first time.

For sharing their data, a great debt is due to: the American Daffodil Society; the former Experimental Horticultural Station at Rosewarne in the persons of Paul Millett, Mike Pollock, Andrew Tompsett and the late Barbara Fry and F.W.Shepherd; Horticulture Research International at Kirton in the person of Gordon Hanks; and the Horticultural Development Council.

The Rev. D.Pett generously shared his research on Scilly Isles daffodils, as did F.J.Williams on J.C.Williams' daffodils.

John Blanchard gave crucial support in the entering of the botanical names. Peter Brandham ensured that the significance of chromosome numbers was properly explained. Reg Nicholl corrected and updated the list of originators and registrants.

Judy Restall valiantly and meticulously entered descriptions and parentages in the database. Liz Butler renewed the illustrations of divisions and descriptive terms. Mary Pascoe gave doughty assistance in the run-up to publication.

The design and smooth-running of the database, together with the programme for printing, were the work of Robert Hacker. Both he and Philip Gladwin of the IT Department at the RHS have given unfailingly cheerful support.

Much of the proof-reading was undertaken by members of the Narcissus Classification Advisory Committee of the RHS, whose comments then and at all stages have kept the Register on a steady course.

HORTICULTURAL CLASSIFICATION

Whether of wild or cultivated origin, once a selection has been distinguished by a cultivar name it should be assigned to Divisions 1-12. Daffodils distinguished solely by botanical name should be assigned to Division 13.

Notes
1. The characteristics for Divisions 5 to 10 are given for guidance only; they are not all necessarily expected to be present in every cultivar assigned to those divisions
2. Divisions 12 and 13 are not illustrated owing to the wide variation in shape and size between the flowers involved

DIVISION 1 - TRUMPET DAFFODIL CULTIVARS
One flower to a stem; corona ("trumpet") as long as, or longer than the perianth segments ("petals")

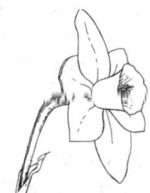

DIVISION 2 - LARGE-CUPPED DAFFODIL CULTIVARS
One flower to a stem; corona ("cup") more than one-third, but less than equal to the length of the perianth segments ("petals")

DIVISION 3 - SMALL-CUPPED DAFFODIL CULTIVARS
One flower to a stem; corona ("cup") not more than one-third the length of the perianth segments ("petals")

DIVISION 4 - DOUBLE DAFFODIL CULTIVARS
One or more flowers to a stem, with doubling of the perianth segments or the corona or both

DIVISION 5 - TRIANDRUS DAFFODIL CULTIVARS
Characteristics of *N. triandrus* clearly evident: usually two or more pendent flowers to a stem; perianth segments reflexed

Division 6 - Cyclamineus Daffodil Cultivars
Characteristics of *N. cyclamineus* clearly evident: one flower to a stem; perianth segments significantly reflexed; flower at an acute angle to the stem, with a very short pedicel ("neck")

Division 7 - Jonquilla and Apodanthus Daffodil Cultivars
Characteristics of Sections Jonquilla or Apodanthi clearly evident: one to five (rarely eight) flowers to a stem; perianth segments spreading or reflexed; corona cup-shaped, funnel-shaped or flared, usually wider than long; flowers usually fragrant

Division 8 - Tazetta Daffodil Cultivars
Characteristics of Section Tazettae clearly evident: usually three to twenty flowers to a stout stem; perianth segments spreading not reflexed; flowers usually fragrant

Division 9 - Poeticus Daffodil Cultivars
Characteristics of the *N. poeticus* group: usually one flower to a stem; perianth segments pure white; corona very short or disc-shaped, usually with a green and/or yellow centre and a red rim, but sometimes of a single colour; flowers usually fragrant

Division 10 - Bulbocodium Daffodil Cultivars
Characteristics of Section Bulbocodium clearly evident: usually one flower to a stem; perianth segments insignificant compared with the dominant corona; anthers dorsifixed (ie attached more or less centrally to the filament); filament and style usually curved

Division 11 - Split Corona Daffodil Cultivars
Corona split - usually for more than half its length

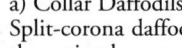

a) Collar Daffodils
Split-corona daffodils with the corona segments opposite the perianth segments; the corona segments usually in two whorls of three

b) Papillon Daffodils
Split-corona daffodils with the corona segments alternate to the perianth segments; the corona segments usually in a single whorl of six

DIVISION 12 - OTHER DAFFODIL CULTIVARS
Daffodil cultivars which do not fit the definition of any other division

DIVISION 13 - DAFFODILS DISTINGUISHED SOLELY BY BOTANICAL NAME

SECTION TAPEINANTHUS
Autumn flowering; one to four flowers to a rounded stem; leaves very narrow, glaucous, not always present on flowering bulbs; flower ascending, yellow; corona absent or rudimentary; anthers widely exserted from the tube, much shorter than the filaments, dorsifixed

SECTION SEROTINI
Autumn flowering; usually one to two flowers to a rounded stem; leaves very narrow, glaucous, not always present on flowering bulbs; perianth segments pure white, usually twisted; corona very short, yellow, orange or green; anthers included in or slightly exserted from the tube, longer than the filaments, dorsifixed; flowers fragrant

SECTION AURELIA
Autumn flowering; three to 12 flowers to a compressed stem; leaves flat not channelled, glaucous; flowers white; corona rudimentary or absent; filaments unequal in length; anthers exserted from the tube, dorsifixed; flowers fragrant

SECTION TAZETTAE
Autumn to Spring flowering; three (rarely two) to 20 flowers to a usually compressed stem; leaves flat or channelled, usually glaucous; flowers white, yellow or bicoloured; anthers included in or slightly exserted from the tube, much longer than the filaments, dorsifixed; flowers fragrant. The rounded stem and green leaves of *N. aureus* atypical, also the orange corona of *N. elegans*

SECTION NARCISSUS
Spring flowering; usually one flower (exceptionally two to four) to a compressed stem; leaves flat not channelled, glaucous; perianth segments pure white; corona disc-shaped or very shallow, sometimes of a single colour, but usually with base green, mid-zone yellow and rim red or orange and often scarious; anthers partly exserted from the tube, much longer than the filaments, dorsifixed; flowers fragrant. Section covers *N. poeticus*

SECTION JONQUILLA
Spring flowering; one to five (rarely eight) flowers to a rounded stem; leaves narrow or semi-cylindrical, green; flowers yellow, never white; perianth segments spreading or reflexed; corona usually cup-shaped, usually wider than long; anthers included in or partly exserted from the tube, much longer than the filaments, dorsifixed; flowers fragrant. The Autumn flowering, green-flowered *N. viridiflorus* is atypical

SECTION APODANTHI
Spring flowering; one flower or two to five to a somewhat compressed stem; leaves narrow, channelled, glaucous; flowers white or yellow, never bicoloured; perianth segments spreading or slightly reflexed; corona cup-shaped, funnel-shaped or flared, usually wider than long; anthers included in the tube or three included and three exserted, much longer than the filaments, dorsifixed

SECTION GANYMEDES
Spring flowering; one flower or two to six to an elliptical or cylindrical stem; flowers pendent, white or yellow or somewhat bicoloured; leaves flat or semi-cylindrical; perianth segments reflexed; corona cup-shaped (rarely campanulate); anthers three included in the tube, three exserted (often beyond the corona), equal to or much shorter than the filaments, dorsifixed. Section covers *N. triandrus*

SECTION BULBOCODIUM
Autumn to Spring flowering; one flower to a rounded stem; leaves narrow, semi-cylindrical; flowers white or yellow; perianth segments insignificant compared with the dominant corona; anthers widely exserted from the tube (often beyond the corona), much shorter than the filaments (which are usually curved), dorsifixed

SECTION PSEUDONARCISSUS
Spring flowering; usually one flower to a more or less compressed or sometimes rounded stem; leaves flat or channelled, usually glaucous; flowers white, yellow or bicoloured; perianth segments usually spreading or

inflexed; corona more or less cylindrical, often flared at mouth, yellow or white (never orange or red); anthers exserted from the tube, equal to or shorter than the filaments, sub-basifixed. The green leaves, rounded stem and strongly reflexed perianth segments of *N. cyclamineus* and the two to four flowers to a stem of *N. longispathus* and *N. nevadensis* are atypical

NOTE Hybrids distinguished solely by botanical name are also assigned to this Division

BOTANICAL CLASSIFICATION

The following classification of the genus *Narcissus* is based on that outlined by A.Fernandes in *The Daffodil and Tulip Year Book* (1968). It is the taxonomy and nomenclature employed by the Royal Horticultural Society in the preparation of *The International Daffodil Register*. It has been revised to take account of the publication of many new taxa since 1968 and some reassessment of the ranks at which to treat those previously recognized.

SECTION TAPEINANTHUS (Herbert) Traub

cavanillesii Barra & López

SECTION SEROTINI Parlatore

serotinus Linnaeus
    var. *serotinus*
    var. *deficiens* (Herbert) Baker
    var. *emarginatus* Chabert

SECTION AURELIA (Gay) Baker

broussonetii Lagasca & Segura
    f. *broussonetii*
    f. *grandiflorus* (Battandier & Trabut) Maire

SECTION TAZETTAE de Candolle

aureus Loiseleur-Deslongchamps
barlae Parlatore
bertolonii Parlatore
    var. *bertolonii*
    var. *algericus* (Roemer) Maire & Weiller
    var. *discolor* Battandier
    var. *primulinus* Maire
canariensis Burbidge
corcyrensis (Herbert) Nyman
cupularis (Salisbury) Schultes
cypri Sweet
dubius Gouan
    var. *dubius*
    var. *micranthus* (Jordan & Fourreau) Ascherson & Graebner
elegans (Haworth) Spach
    var. *elegans*
        f. *elegans*
        f. *auranticoronatus* Maire
    var. *fallax* Font Quer
    var. *flavescens* Maire
    var. *intermedius* Gay
    var. *oxypetalus* (Boissier) Maire
italicus Ker Gawler
pachybolbus Durieu de Maisonneuve
panizzianus Parlatore

papyraceus Ker Gawler
patulus (Loiseleur-Deslongchamps) Baker
polyanthos Loiseleur-Deslongchamps
tazetta Linnaeus
    subsp. *tazetta*
    subsp. *gussonei* (Rouy) A.Fernandes
    subsp. *lacticolor* Baker
    subsp. *ochroleucus* (Loiseleur-Deslongchamps) Baker
tortifolius Fernández Casas

SECTION NARCISSUS

poeticus Linnaeus
    var. *poeticus*
    var. *hellenicus* (Pugsley) A.Fernandes
    var. *majalis* (Curtis) A.Fernandes
    var. *physaloides* Beauverd
    var. *recurvus* (Haworth) A.Fernandes
    var. *verbanensis* Herbert
radiiflorus Salisbury
    var. *radiiflorus*
    var. *exertus* (Haworth) A.Fernandes
    var. *poetarum* (Haworth) Burbidge & Baker
    var. *stellaris* (Haworth) A.Fernandes

SECTION JONQUILLA de Candolle

assoanus Dufour
    var. *assoanus*
    var. *praelongus* Barra & López
cerrolazae J.F.Ureña
cordubensis Fernández Casas
fernandesii Pedro
    var. *fernandesii*
    var. *major* A.Fernandes
gaditanus Boissier & Reuter
jonquilla Linnaeus
    var. *jonquilla*
    var. *henriquesii* Sampaio
    var. *minor* (Haworth) Baker
    var. *stellaris* Baker
marianicus Fernández Casas
minutiflorus Willkomm
× *montsiccianus* Romo (*assoanus* × *palearensis*)
palearensis Romo
rivasmartinezii Fernández Casas
viridiflorus Schousboe
willkommii (Sampaio) A.Fernandes

SECTION APODANTHI A.Fernandes

atlanticus Stern
calcicola Mendonça
cuatrecasasii Fernández Casas, Lainz & Ruiz Rejón
    var. *cuatrecasasii*
    var. *segimonensis* Fernández Casas
rupicola Dufour
    subsp. *rupicola*
    subsp. *marvieri* (Jahandiez & Maire) Maire & Weiller
    subsp. *watieri* (Maire) Maire & Weiller

  scaberulus Henriques

Section Ganymedes (Haworth) Schultes f.

 triandrus Linnaeus
  subsp. *triandrus*
   var. *triandrus*
   var. *concolor* (Haworth) Link
   var. *loiseleurii* (Rouy) A.Fernandes
   var. *pulchellus* (Salisbury) Baker
  subsp. *pallidulus* (Graells) D.A.Webb

Section Bulbocodium de Candolle

 albimarginatus Müller-Doblies
 × *barrae* Fernández Casas (*bulbocodium* × *cantabricus*)
 bulbocodium Linnaeus
  subsp. *bulbocodium*
   var. *bulbocodium*
   var. *citrinus* Baker
   var. *conspicuus* (Haworth) Baker
   var. *ectandrus* Barra & López
   var. *genuinus* Maire
   var. *graellsii* (Webb) Baker
   var. *nivalis* (Graells) Baker
   var. *pallidus* (Gattinger & Weiller) Maire & Weiller
   var. *serotinus* (Haworth) A.Fernandes
   var. *tenuifolius* (Salisbury) Baker
  subsp. *praecox* Gattinger & Weiller
   var. *praecox* (*eu-praecox* in Maire)
   var. *paucinervis* Maire
  subsp. *quintanilhae* A.Fernandes
 cantabricus de Candolle
  subsp. *cantabricus*
   var. *cantabricus*
   var. *eu-albidus* Emberger & Maire
   var. *foliosus* (Maire) A.Fernandes
   var. *kesticus* (Maire & Wilczec) A.Fernandes
   var. *petunioides* A.Fernandes
  subsp. *monophyllus* (Durieu de Maisonneuve) A.Fernandes
  subsp. *tananicus* (Maire) A.Fernandes
 × *carpetanus* (Barra & López) Fernández Casas (*bulbocodium* var. *graellsii* × *bulbocodium* var. *nivalis*)
 hedraeanthus (Webb & Heldreich) Colmeiro
   var. *hedraeanthus*
   var. *luteolentus* Barra & López
 jacquemoudii Fernández Casas
 jeanmonodii Fernández Casas
 juressianus Fernández Casas
 × *magni-antonii* Fernández Casas (published as *cantabricus* × *tenuifolius*)
 × *neocarpetanus* Rivas Ponce, C.Soriano & Fernández Casas (*cantabricus* × *nivalis*?)
   var. *neocarpetanus*
   var. *romanensis* U.Plaza
 obesus Salisbury
 peroccidentalis Fernández Casas
 romieuxii Braun-Blanquet & Maire
  subsp. *romieuxii*
   var. *romieuxii*
   var. *mesatlanticus* Maire
   var. *rifanus* (Emberger & Maire) A.Fernandes
  subsp. *albidus* (Emberger & Maire) A.Fernandes

    var. *albidus*
    var. *zaianicus* (Maire, Weiller & Wilczec) A.Fernandes
subnivalis Fernández Casas
tingitanus Fernández Casas

SECTION PSEUDONARCISSUS de Candolle

abscissus (Haworth) Roemer & Schultes f.
    var. *abscissus*
    var. *graciliflorus* Pugsley
    var. *serotinus* (Jordan) Pugsley
    var. *tubulosus* (Jordan) Pugsley
albescens Pugsley
× *aloysii-villarii* Fernández Casas (*alpestris* × *jacetanus*)
alpestris Pugsley
asturiensis (Jordan) Pugsley
bicolor Linnaeus
    var. *bicolor*
    var. *lorifolius* (Herbert) Pugsley
calcicarpetanus Fernández Casas
confusus Pugsley
cyclamineus de Candolle
× *dichromus* P.D.Sell (*cyclamineus* × *moschatus*)
fontqueri Fernández Casas
gayi Pugsley
genesii-lopezii Fernández Casas
hispanicus Gouan
    var. *hispanicus*
    var. *bujei* (Fernández Casas) Fernández Casas
    var. *concolor* (Jordan) Pugsley
    var. *propinquus* (Herbert) Pugsley
    var. *spurius* (Haworth) Pugsley
jacetanus Fernández Casas
  subsp. *jacetanus*
  subsp. *vasconicus* (Fernández Casas) Fernández Casas
lagoi Merino
longispathus Pugsley
lusitanicus Dorda Alcaraz & Fernández Casas
macrolobus (Jordan) Pugsley
minor Linnaeus
    var. *conspicuus* Haworth
    var. *minimus* (Haworth) Pugsley
moleroi Fernández Casas
× *monochromus* P.D.Sell (*cyclamineus* × *pseudonarcissus*)
moschatus Linnaeus
nanus Spach
nevadensis Pugsley
nobilis (Haworth) Schultes f.
    var. *nobilis*
    var. *leonensis* (Pugsley) A.Fernandes
    var. *primigenius* Fernández Casas & Lainz
obvallaris Salisbury
pallidiflorus Pugsley
    var. *pallidiflorus*
      f. *pallidiflorus*
      f. *asturicus* (Barr) Pugsley
    var. *intermedius* Pugsley
parviflorus (Jordan) Pugsley
perez-chiscanoi Fernández Casas
portensis Pugsley

provincialis Pugsley
pseudonarcissus Linnaeus
    subsp. *pseudonarcissus*
        var. *pseudonarcissus*
        var. *festinus* (Jordan) Pugsley
        var. *humilis* Pugsley
        var. *insignis* Pugsley
        var. *minoriformis* Pugsley
        var. *montinus* (Jordan) Pugsley
        var. *pisanus* (Pugsley) A.Fernandes
        var. *platylobus* (Jordan) Pugsley
        var. *porrigens* (Jordan) Pugsley
    subsp. *eugeniae* (Fernández Casas) Fernández Casas
    subsp. *pugsleyanus* Barra & López
pumilus Salisbury
radinganorum Fernández Casas
tortuosus Haworth
varduliensis Fernández Casas & Uribe-Echebarría

INTERSECTIONAL HYBRIDS

× *abilioi* Fernández Casas (*bulbocodium* × *jonquilla*)
× *alejandrei* (*bulbocodium* subsp. *bulbocodium* var. *citrinus* × *jacetanus* subsp. *vasconicus*)
× *andorranus* Fernández Casas (*nobilis* × *poeticus* var. *poeticus*)
× *aranensis* Fernández Casas (*pallidiflorus* × *poeticus* var. *poeticus*)
× *bakeri* Richter (*bulbocodium* × *pseudonarcissus*)
× *bergidensis* Fernández Casas (*fontqueri* × *triandrus*)
× *bernardii* de Candolle (*hispanicus* × *poeticus*)
× *boutignyanus* Philippe (*moschatus* × *poeticus*)
× *brevitubulosus* A.Fernandes (*asturiensis* × *bulbocodium* var. *nivalis*)
× *buxtonii* Richter (*abscissus* × *assoanus*)
× *carringtonii* Rozeira (*scaberulus* × *triandrus* subsp. *pallidulus*)
× *cazorlanus* Fernández Casas (*hedraeanthus* × *triandrus* subsp. *pallidulus*)
× *chevassutii* Gorenflot, Guinochet & Quézel (*bertolonii* × *serotinus*)
× *christopheri* Blanchard (*assoanus* × *panizzianus*)
× *consolationis* Fernández Casas (*bulbocodium* var. *nivalis* × *triandrus* subsp. *pallidulus*)
× *felineri* Fernández Casas (*bulbocodium* × *nobilis* var. *primigenius*)
× *gracilis* (*jonquilla* × *poeticus* [assumed])
× *gredensis* Fernández Casas (*bulbocodium* var. *nivalis* × *rupicola*)
× *incomparabilis* Miller (*hispanicus* × *poeticus*, or *poeticus* × *pseudonarcissus*)
× *incurvicervicus* Barra & López (*fernandesii* × *triandrus* subsp. *pallidulus*)
× *infundibulum* Poiret (*abscissus* × *jonquilla*)
× *intermedius* Loiseleur-Deslongchamps (*jonquilla* × *tazetta*)
× *johnstonii* (Baker) Pugsley (*pseudonarcissus* × *triandrus* subsp. *pallidulus*)
× *koshinomurae* Fernández Casas (*fernandesii* × *panizzianus*)
× *laetus* Salisbury (*minor* × *jonquilla*)
× *lopezii* Fernández Casas (*bulbocodium* × *obvallaris*)
× *macleayi* Lindley (parentage unknown)
× *maginae* Fernández Casas & Susanna (*cuatrecasasii* × *triandrus* subsp. *pallidulus*)
× *magnenii* Rouy (*assoanus* × *tazetta*)
× *medioluteus* Miller (*poeticus* × *tazetta*)
× *montserratii* Fernández Casas (*abscissus* × *poeticus*)
× *nutans* Haworth (*jonquilla* × *triandrus*)
× *obsoletus* Haworth (*elegans* × *viridiflorus*)
× *odorus* Linnaeus (*jonquilla* × *pseudonarcissus* [or *hispanicus*?])
× *pacensis* Fernández Casas (*confusus* × *triandrus* subsp. *pallidulus*)
× *perezlarae* Font Quer (*cavanillesii* × *serotinus*)
× *petri-mariae* Fernández Casas (*pallidiflorus* × *provincialis*)
× *poculiformis* Salisbury (*dubius* × *moschatus*)
× *ponsii-sorollae* Fernández Casas (*assoanus* × *triandrus* subsp. *pallidulus*)

× *pravianoi* Fernández Casas (*nobilis* var. *primigenius* × *triandrus*)
× *pugsleyi* Fernández Casas (*alpestris* × *assoanus*)
× *pujolii* Font Quer (*assoanus* × *dubius*)
× *rogendorfii* Battandier (*elegans* × *tazetta*)
× *romoi* Fernández Casas (*cantabricus* × *fernandesii*)
× *rupidulus* Fernández Casas (*rupicola* × *triandrus* subsp. *pallidulus*)
× *stenanthus* Fernández Casas (*bulbocodium* var. *nivalis* × *confusus*)
× *susannae* Fernández Casas (*cantabricus* subsp. *monophyllus* × *triandrus* subsp. *pallidulus*)
   var. *susannae*
   var. *toletanus* Fernández Casas & Luceño
× *taitii* Henriques (*pseudonarcissus* × *triandrus* subsp. *pallidulus*)
× *tenuior* Curtis (*jonquilla* × *poeticus* [assumed])
× *trilobus* Linnaeus (*bicolor* × *jonquilla*)
× *tuckeri* Barra & López (*fernandesii* × *hedraeanthus*)

THE INTERNATIONAL DAFFODIL REGISTER AND CLASSIFIED LIST

'A1' 5
(?E.M. Crosfield, pre-1913)

'Aab' 6 Y-Y
(N.H. Anglo) N.H. Anglo, 1988
'Alliance' × 'Charity May'
Fl. yellow; perianth segments smooth; corona funnel-shaped, ribbed, with pale green at base on opening. Dwarf. Mid-season. Windproof. Resembles 'Alliance' but with broader perianth segments

'Aabaknot' 1 W-W
(W.B. Cranfield, pre-1931)

'Aabenraa' 2 Y-O
(P.D. Williams, pre-1931)
Sdlg no. 122
Perianth segments very broadly ovate, blunt or squarish at apex, slightly mucronate, spreading, overlapping one-third to a half; the inner segments more narrowly ovate, angled at shoulder, with margins wavy or incurled; corona broad funnel-shaped, loosely ribbed, orange, paling to base, with mouth straight, lightly frilled. AM(e) 1932

'Aachen' 1 Y-Y
(A.F. Calvert, pre-1928)

'Aala' 2 Y-Y
(W. Jackson Sr, 1949)
'Acca' × 'Guilmette'

'Aard-Wolf' 1 W-W
(W.B. Cranfield, pre-1931)

'Aare' 2 W-P
(R.H.Glover, pre-1989) Unregistered
'Vanessa' × 'Dear Me'
Wrongly named 'Raad'

'Aaron' 1 W-Y
(S.A. Free, 1967) Mrs S.I. Free, 1978
'Saint Saphorin' × 'Preamble'; sdlg no. 67/20
Fl. 100 mm wide; corona lemon yellow. Mid-season

'Aarts Hertogin' 8 W-O
(pre-1851)

'Aashild' 3 W-W
(pre-1938)
?Syn. of 'Aaskild'

'Aaskild' 3 W-W
(W. Jackson Sr, 1934) W. Jackson Jr, 1956
'Mary Blewitt' × 'Virginia'
?The same as 'Aashild'

'Ababa' 2 W-O
(H.A. Brown, 1929) J.N. Hancock & Co., 1960
Sdlg no. 448 23/29
Perianth segments pure white, overlapping at base only; corona bright orange, mouth flared and frilled. Early. 2n=27

'Abacot' 1 W-W
(G.H. Engleheart, pre-1923)

'Abacus' 1 Y-Y
(A.F. Calvert, pre-1929)

'Abadan' 2 W-YRR
(W. Blom & Son, pre-1954)
'John Evelyn' × 'Sender Wallace'

'Abadea' 2 W-W
(W.F.M. Copeland, pre-1920)
Perianth segments fairly smooth; corona creamy white

'Abalone' 2 W-YYP
(G.E. Mitsch) G.E. Mitsch, 1962
Fl. 127 mm wide; corona opening pale lemon yellow, becoming creamy yellow, with buff pink at rim. Mid-season

'Abandon' 2 W-W
(W.A. Bell, pre-1949)

'Abba' 4 W-O
(J.M. van Dijk) J.M. van Dijk, 1984
'Cragford' sport
2n=17

'Abberley' 2 Y-Y
(A.M. Wilson, pre-1944)
Fl. deep golden yellow; corona frilled

'Abbess' 1 W-W
(W.A. Grace, pre-1938)

'Abbeydale' 2 W-W
(F.E. Board) F.E. Board, 1965
'Wedding Bell' × 'Rashee'; sdlg no. 607
Late.

'Abbey Elizabeth' 4 Y-P
(Max Hamilton) Koanga Daffodils, 1989
(O'More sdlg 81/57 × Roblin sdlg 4) × ('Papua' × Heazlewood sdlg); sdlg no. 54-86
Fl. 100 mm wide; perianth and other petaloid segments opening creamy white, maturing to lemon yellow; corona segments pale pink. Mid-season

'Abbey Gold' 1 Y-Y
(J.A.O'More, 1955) P.D.K. Ramsay, 1980

'Cromarty' × 'Billali'; sdlg no. 57/55
Fl. 105 mm wide. Mid-season. Resembles 'Golden Dale'

'Abbey of Egmond' 1 Y-Y
Syn. of 'Abbey of Egmont'

'Abbey of Egmont' 1 Y-Y
(P. van den Berg, pre-1940)
Perianth segments light yellow; corona darker in tone. See also 'Abbey of Egmond'

'Abbotsford' 2 Y-YYR
(D.S. Bell) D.S. Bell, 1977
'Sarcelle' × 'Rupee'
Fl. 110 mm wide; perianth segments deep yellow; corona cup-shaped, with a sharply defined band of red at rim. Mid-season. Resembles 'Rupee' but with a red rim to the corona

'Abbotsley' 2 Y-Y
(R.H. Bath, pre-1933)

'Abbot's Pride' 2 Y-Y
(J.W. Barr, pre-1930)

'Abcal' 5 W-W
(C.A. Nethercote) T. Morrison, 1960
Fl. pure white

'A.B.Cashmore' 2 W-Y
(J.N. Hancock & Co., 1962) J.N. Hancock & Co., 1977
'Euroa' × 'New Light'; sdlg no. 105/56
Fl. 113 mm wide; corona vivid yellow 12A, rim dentate. Mid-season

'Abdiel' 2 Y-? (a)
(Mrs R.O. Backhouse, pre-1921)

'Abebe' 2 W-W
(R.H.Glover, pre-1993) Unregistered

'Abelard' 2 Y-YOO
(Mrs R.O. Backhouse, pre-1921)
Perianth segments rich primrose yellow, overlapping; corona scarlet-orange, shading from golden yellow at base. AM(Haarlem) 1928

'Abel Tasman' 2 W-Y
(Tom Forster, 1960s) Unregistered
Fl. rounded; perianth segments very broad, blunt or squarish at apex, fairly prominently mucronate, slightly reflexed, plane, overlapping half or more; the inner segments more nearly spreading; corona very broad, almost disc-shaped, ribbed, rich golden yellow, with a slightly darker tone at rim, mouth lightly frilled, rim irregularly notched and minutely crenate. Mid-season

'Abel Tasman' 11b W-Y/WO
(?J.W.A.Lefeber, pre-1970) Unregistered
Perianth segments pure white; corona deeply split, the six segments with golden yellow in a longitudinal band flanked by pure white, touched orange at apex, separated. 2n=28

'Aber' 2 Y-? (a)
(W.A. Watts, pre-1927)

'Aberdeen' 1 Y-Y
Syn. of 'Lord Aberdeen'

'Aberfoyle' 2 Y-YOO
(J.S.B.Lea, 1983) Clive Postles Daffodils, 1994
'Loch Lundie' × Lea sdlg 1-9-71; sdlg no. 1-8-78
Fl. forming a double triangle, 100 mm wide; perianth segments ovate; corona funnel-shaped, orange, with yellow at base, mouth flared, rim crenate. Early

'Abessa' 9 W-?
(G.H. Furness, pre-1934)

'A.B.Haggitt' 3 Y-? (a)
(Mrs A.B. Haggitt, pre-1933)

'Abiad' 1 W-? (b)
(de Graaff Bros, pre-1923)

'Abigail' 1 W-W
(A.M. Wilson, pre-1910)

'Abigail' 2 W-P
(c.1975) Unregistered

***N.* × *abilioi* Fernández Casas 13** = *N. bulbocodium* Linnaeus × *N. jonquilla* Linnaeus

'Abinadab' 2 W-W
(R.F. Calvert, pre-1934)

'Abingdon' 3 Y-R
(P.D. Williams, pre-1928)
Perianth segments cream; corona solid red

'Abiqua' 2 Y-Y
(Murray W. Evans, 1966) Murray W. Evans, 1985
'Binkie' × 'Limeade'; sdlg no. J-5/2
Mid-season. Resembles an earlier-flowered 'Dividend' with shorter corona

'Ablaze' 2 Y-? (a)
(A.F. Calvert, pre-1929)

'Ablaze' 2 Y-O
(C.O. Fairbairn, c.1980) Unregistered
Perianth segments broadly ovate, blunt, very slightly mucronate, rich yellow, a little reflexed, smooth and of heavy substance, overlapping one-third to a half; the inner segments not much narrower, square-

shouldered at base, more strongly reflexed; corona long cup-shaped, broadly ribbed, reddish orange, mouth straight, wavy. Tall. Mid-season to late

'Ablon' 1 W-YYO
(J. Gerritsen & Son) J. Gerritsen & Son, 1984
Sdlg × 'Alpine Glow'; sdlg no. 23
Perianth segments ivory white; corona pale yellow 11C, with pale orange (23C) at rim

'Ablush' 2 W-P
Syn. of 'Blush'

'Abo' 2 Y-O
(L. Buckland, pre-1936)
Syn. 'Plurry'

'Abona' 2 Y-Y
(W. Jackson Jr) Jackson's Daffodils, 1979
'Berima' × 'Gold Script'; sdlg no. 50/72
Fl. 104 mm wide. Mid-season

'Aboukir' 3 W-? (b)
(Mrs R.O. Backhouse, pre-1921)

'Abracadabra' 6 Y-Y
(M.G. Temple-Smith) M.G. Temple-Smith, 1985
N. cyclamineus × 'Ristin'; sdlg no. 4/83
Fl. bright butter yellow; perianth segments very broadly ovate, somewhat truncate, with slight white mucro, reflexed, plane, smooth, with midrib faintly showing, overlapping half; the inner segments more narrowly ovate; corona cylindrical, smooth, mouth flared and lightly ribbed, a little frilled, rim crenate. Early. Resembles 'Voodoo' and 'Alacabam'

'Abraz'
(R.H. Bath, pre-1948)

'Abri' 2 Y-Y
(G.J Phillips, 1987) G.J. Phillips, 1994
'Chamkohe' × 'Vixi'; sdlg no. 82-151-1
Fl. 106 mm wide; perianth segments broadly ovate, spreading; corona funnel-shaped, with mouth flared and rim widely dentate. Early

'Abrupt' 3 Y-R
(J.T.Gray) P. Phillips, 1968

'Absalon' 1 Y-Y
(Ken McCombe, 1975) Unregistered
Sdlg no. 89/80
Fl. golden yellow; corona cylindrical, with mouth straight, rim flanged and crenate. Early to mid-season

'Abschied' 3 W-YOO
(A.M. Wilson, pre-1908)
Div.9 sdlg × 'Beacon'

***N. abscissus* (Haworth) Roemer & Schultes f. 13**

Section Pseudonarcissus
var. *abscissus*
var. *graciliflorus* Pugsley
var. *serotinus* (Jordan) Pugsley
var. *tubulosus* (Jordan) Pugsley

'Absegami' 2 Y-YYR
(W.A. Bender) W.A. Bender, 1990
'Sunapee' × 'Zanzibar'; sdlg no. 57
Fl. 100 mm wide; perianth segments broadly ovate, brilliant greenish yellow 4A, spreading, smooth; corona funnel-shaped, vivid yellow 14B, with a broad band of orange-red (33B) at rim. Late. Sunproof

'Abstract' 11a W-YYO
(David L. Sheppard) David L. Sheppard, 1989
('Muscadet' × 'Hillbilly') × 'Honky-Tonk'
Fl. 85 mm wide; perianth segments very broad, blunt or truncate, prominently mucronate, pure white, a little reflexed, somewhat creased, with margins incurling at apex, overlapping half; the inner segments more heavily creased and more nearly spreading; corona split for more than half its length, the six segments one-third the length of the perianth segments and opposite to them, ribbed, clear bright yellow, with orange at rim, spreading, frilled. Mid-season. Sunproof

'Abundance' 2 Y-Y
(Mrs R.O. Backhouse, pre-1921)
Perianth segments lemon yellow; corona large, mouth heavily frilled. AM(Haarlem) 1930

'Abundance' 8 Y-Y
Syn. of 'Helios'

'Acajou' 2 W-? (b)
(Konynenburg & Mark, pre-1953)

'Acapulco' 8 Y-O
(W.G. Pannill) W.G. Pannill, 1992
'Matador' × *N. jonquilla*; sdlg no. 65/98 E
Fl. 45 mm wide. Mid-season

'Acca' 2 Y-Y
(W. Jackson Sr, 1944) W. Jackson Jr, 1956
'Gambrinus' × 'Sir Accolon'

'Accadian' 2 Y-Y
(A.H. Ahrens) J.S. Leitch, 1956

'Acceleration' 7 YYW-W
(R. & E.Havens) R. & E.Havens, 1997
'Hillstar' × 'Quick Step'; sdlg no. Y91/10
Fl. 70 mm wide; perianth segments broad, lemon yellow, with white at base, spreading, plane; corona cup-shaped, with mouth wavy. Late

'Accent' 2 W-P
(G.E. Mitsch) G.E. Mitsch, 1960

'Interim' × 'Interlude'; sdlg no. Q40/1
Fl. 102 mm wide, star-shaped; perianth segments broadly ovate, blunt, only very slightly mucronate, very slightly reflexed, plane, very smooth, and of heavy substance, overlapping one-third; the inner segments a little inflexed, with margins wavy and deeply incurved, nicked at shoulder; corona funnel-shaped, loosely ribbed, deep salmon pink, mouth straight, frilled, with rim crenate. Mid-season. Resembles 'Interlude' but with a broader and smoother perianth and the corona of deeper colour. Wister Award 1987, AGM 1995

'Accident' 1 Y-Y
(Sir C.H. Cave, pre-1928)

'Acclaim' 1 Y-Y
(G.H. Johnstone, pre-1944)

'Acclamation' 4 W-R
(J.L. Richardson) M.J. Jefferson-Brown, 1968
'Gay Time' × 'Arbar'
AM(e) 1968

'Accolade' 3 W-R
(J.L. Richardson) J.L. Richardson, 1956
'Kilworth' × 'Cairo'
Perianth segments pure white; corona cup-shaped, red. 2n=28

'Accomac' 2 Y-O
(E.C. Powell, pre-1949)
('Bernardino' × 'Fortune') × 'Cornish Fire'
Perianth segments rich yellow; corona scarlet-orange

'Accommodate' 2 Y-Y
(Jackson's Daffodils) Jackson's Daffodils, 1993
'Truvius' × 'Barfly'; sdlg no. 63/87
Fl. 112 mm wide; perianth segments very broadly ovate, brilliant yellow 7A; the outer segments overlapping one another; corona funnel-shaped, vivid yellow 9A, with rim flanged and frilled. Early

'Accord' 2 Y-WWY
(W.G. Pannill) W.G. Pannill, 1980
'Bethany' × 'Rus Holland'; sdlg no. PL 66 B
Fl. 97 mm wide. Mid-season

'Accordanto' 2 Y-? (a)
(Konynenburg & Mark, pre-1954)

'Accordanto' 2 Y-O
(Konynenburg & Mark) Konynenburg & Mark, 1960
Fl. 110 mm wide; perianth segments light greenish yellow 5D; corona strong orange 24A

'Accordica' 2 W-? (b or c)
(B. Rowlands, pre-1939)
Syn. 'Artistica'

'Accrual' 2 Y-Y
(Jackson's Daffodils) Jackson's Daffodils, 1986
'Akala' × 'Warcom'; sdlg no. 164/79
Perianth segments broadly ovate, blunt, mucronate, brilliant greenish yellow 5B, incurving, faintly ribbed, overlapping half; the inner segments slightly narrower; corona funnel-shaped, ribbed, darker in tone (9A) than the perianth, with mouth expanded and rim slightly crenate. Early

'Ace' 2 W-PPW
(G.E. Mitsch) G.E. Mitsch, 1979
'Accent' × 'Luscious'; sdlg no. F5/1
Fl. 95 mm wide. Mid-season. Resembles 'Credo' but with the corona lighter in tone and whitish at rim

'Ace High' 1 W-W
(T.H. Piper, c.1966) Unregistered
'Glendermott' × 'Swanlough'

'A Cent Feuilles' 4 Y-Y
Syn. of 'Plenissimus'

'Ace of Diamonds' 9 W-R
(G.H. Engleheart, pre-1921)
Fl. of medium size; perianth segments pure white, smooth and of strong substance, deeply overlapping; corona intense orange-scarlet throughout. Late. Resembles a richer-toned 'Acme' in corona colour. 2n=14

'Ace of Hearts' 3 Y-? (a)
(?T. Buncombe, pre-1933)

'Achates' 1 Y-Y
(Barr & Sons, pre-1923)

'Achduart' 3 Y-O
(J.S.B. Lea) J.S.B. Lea, 1972
Sdlg 2-17-54 ('Spry' × Navarro sdlg) × 'Vulcan'
Fl. 105 mm wide; perianth segments broadly ovate, blunt, only very slightly mucronate, brilliant greenish yellow 5B, spreading, regular, overlapping half; the inner segments a little inflexed, with margins sometimes incurling; corona bowl-shaped, ribbed, vivid orange 28B, with a lighter tone (25A) outside, mouth wavy, rim crenate. Mid-season. AM(e) 1972

'Achelous' 8
(?Dutch origin, pre-1931)
Poetaz

'Achentoul' 4 W-R
(J.S.B. Lea) J.S.B. Lea, 1970
Sdlg 1-34-53 × 'Acropolis'; sdlg no. 1-26-60
Mid-season. Scented

'Achernar' 1 W-W
(J.A. Hunter) J.A. Hunter, 1968

'Cletus' × 'Kanchenjunga'
Fl. 117 mm wide. Mid-season. Resembles 'Cletus'

'Acheron' 1 Y-Y
(W.M. Spry, pre-1975) Unregistered
'Stand By' × 'Golden'
Early

'Achi'
Unregistered
Seed parent of 'Bob Boutcher' and others

'Achievement' 3 Y-O
(Warnaar & Co., pre-1933)
AM(Haarlem) 1936

'Achill' 2 Y-Y
Syn. of 'Kilbride'

'Achilles' 1 Y-Y
(Barr & Sons, pre-1887)
Perianth segments light yellow; corona rich yellow. Early. Variable in form and colour

'Achnasheen' 3 W-GWW
(J.S.B. Lea) J.S.B. Lea, 1964
'Suilven' × 'Hamzali'; sdlg no. 1-38-60
Fl. 85 mm wide; perianth segments broad. Late

'Acis' 3 W-W
(W. Backhouse, pre-1869)
Fl. white; corona opening pale primrose yellow with orange tints, becoming milk white. Syn. Leedsii 'Acis'. "Absorbed" 'Aglaia'

'Ackhill' 2 W-? (b or c)
(A.M. Wilson, pre-1936)
AM(Haarlem) 1936

'A.Cleveland Cox' 9 W-?
(G.P. Haydon, pre-1910)

'Acme' 9 W-R
(G.H. Engleheart, pre-1907)
Fl. rounded; perianth segments very broad, blunt or truncate, prominently mucronate, snow white, a little reflexed, overlapping half or more; the inner segments only very slightly mucronate, with margins recurved at base; corona disc-shaped, closely ribbed, solid brick-red or scarlet. Mid-season

'Acol' 2 W-? (b)
(F.D.B. Cobb, pre-1953)

'Acolyte' 5 W-W
(P.D. Williams, pre-1927)
Large Leedsii sdlg × *N. triandrus*
Fl. 90 mm wide, facing down; perianth segments creamy white, overlapping half; corona cup-shaped, pale cream. Mid-season to late

'Acolyte' 2 Y-O
(West & Fell, pre-1936)
Perianth segments yellow; corona reddish orange

'Aconbury' 2 W-? (b)
(Mrs R.O. Backhouse, pre-1921)
AM(Haarlem) 1936

'Acoustic' 2 Y-? (a)
(A.M. Williams, pre-1948)

'Acropolis' 4 W-O
(J.L. Richardson) J.L. Richardson, 1955
'Falaise' × 'Limerick'; sdlg no. 192
Fl. rounded, 112 mm wide; perianth and other petaloid segments in several whorls, very broad, creamy white, with darker tones at base, overlapping half or more; the outer whorl truncate, slightly mucronate, spreading, concave, with margins a little incurled; the inner whorls successively shorter and narrower, more deeply concave, with margins more deeply incurling; the centre whorl sharply inflexed; corona segments very short, interspersed among the petaloid segments at centre, orange (28A) with brilliant greenish yellow 6A at base, frilled. Mid-season to late. $2n=28$. PC 1955, FCC(e) 1959, AM(Haarlem) 1960, FCC(Haarlem) 1961

'Actaea' 9 W-YYR
(G. Lubbe & Son, pre-1927)
Fl. 87 mm wide; perianth segments broadly obovate, blunt or truncate, prominently mucronate, spreading, somewhat concave, glistening, overlapping half; the inner segments narrower, only very slightly mucronate, with margins sometimes reflexed at base and incurling towards apex; corona very shallow, closely ribbed, yellow, with greenish yellow at base and a band of orange-red (33A or B to 42B) at rim, mouth wavy, rim minutely crinkled. Mid-season. Scented. $2n=28$. AM(Haarlem) 1919, FCC(Haarlem) 1923, *HC(g) 1947, *AM(g) 1950, *FCC(g) 1968, AGM 1993

'Actinica' 2 Y-? (a)
(B. Rowlands, pre-1938)

'Action' 2 W-O
(W.O. Backhouse, pre-1962)

'Actis' 3 W-? (b)
(T. Batson, pre-1914)

'Actor' 2 W-? (b)
(G.T.C. Pearce, pre-1938)
'Call Boy' × 'Suda'

'Actrice' 1 Y-Y
(Konynenburg & Mark, pre-1953)

'Actrice' 2 Y-O
(Konynenburg & Mark) Konynenburg & Mark, 1960
Fl. 120 mm wide

'Acumen' 2 YYW-P
(Jackson's Daffodils) Jackson's Daffodils, 1993
'Euphony' × ('Lalita' × 'Daydream'); sdlg no. 232/87
Fl. 107 mm wide; perianth segments broadly ovate, light greenish yellow 6C with yellowish white 155B at base, glistening; corona cylindrical, orange-pink (22C). Late

'Acushla' 1 W-Y
(Barr & Sons, pre-1923)
Corona rich canary yellow

'Ada' 3 W-Y
(W. Backhouse, pre-1869)
Syn. Barrii Albidus 'Ada'

'Ada' 5 W-W
(G.H. Engleheart, pre-1902)
Fls. usually 2 per stem; perianth segments of waxen texture; corona yellowish white. FCC 1902

'Ada Brooke' 1 W-Y
(de Graaff Bros, pre-1896)
Corona rich orange-yellow. Mid-season

'Ada Finch' 1 W-W
(de Graaff Bros, pre-1927)
Perianth segments narrow, acute, paper white; corona large, opening sulphur yellow, becoming white, mouth heavily frilled. Resembles 'King Alfred' in form. AM(Haarlem) 1927, FCC(Haarlem) 1930

'Adagio' 1 Y-Y
(J. Gerritsen & Son, pre-1941)

'Adallas' 1 W-? (b)
(Barr & Sons, pre-1923)

'Adam' 3 Y-R
(P.D. Williams, pre-1939)
Perianth segments bright primrose yellow; corona shallow bowl-shaped, deep red, tinged terracotta

'Adamant' 2 Y-YYO
(J.C. Williams, pre-1945)
Fl. 100 mm wide; perianth segments broadly ovate, very slightly mucronate, brilliant greenish yellow 6B, spreading or reflexed, plane to twisted, with margins minutely incurling, overlapping one-third to a half; the inner segments a little inflexed, with margins wavy and sometimes strongly recurved; corona somewhat funnel-shaped, smooth or slightly ribbed, much darker in tone (13A) than the perianth, flushed strong orange 24A towards the mouth, mouth slightly expanded, frilled, with rim notched and crenate.

*AM(g) 1952, *FCC(g) 1953

'Adare' 3 Y-R
(J.L. Richardson, pre-1943)
'Seraglio' × 'Varna'

'Adastria'
(?W.E. Weightman, pre-1938)

'Addio' 3 W-Y
(G.L. Wilson, pre-1931)
Perianth segments pure white, slightly reflexed; corona disc-shaped, soft greenish chrome yellow. Very late

'Adela' 2 W-Y
(P.D. Williams, pre-1913)
Perianth segments very broadly ovate, blunt, a little reflexed, overlapping; the inner segments more strongly inflexed, more or less twisted; corona cylindrical, smooth, whitish yellow, with mouth ribbed and flared, lightly frilled, rim regularly crenate. AM 1924

'Adelaide' 1 W-Y
(West & Fell, pre-1935)
Corona cream, almost white. Mid-season

'Adele' 2 W-O
(?New Zealand origin, pre-1996) Unregistered

'Adele Thomson' 3 W-GWY
(D.C. MacArthur) D.C. MacArthur, 1989
Sdlg no. EV88-102
Fl. 90 mm wide; perianth segments greenish white 155C, plane; corona slightly greener in tone (155A), with moderate yellow-green 138C at base and light yellow 162C at rim. Late. Scented

'Adelgar' 1 Y-Y
(C. Dawson, pre-1920)
Perianth soft yellow; corona golden yellow, rim frilled

'Adeline' 2 W-P
(A. Overton) A. Overton, 1960

'Adelong' 1 W-Y
(H.A. Brown, 1936) J.N. Hancock & Co., 1960
Corona soft primrose yellow, with mouth flared

'Aden' 2 W-? (b or c)
(W.A. Watts, pre-1913)

'Aden' 3 W-R
(J.L. Richardson, pre-1937)
Perianth segments broad, milk white; corona small, disc-shaped, intense scarlet

'Aden' 2 W-R
(J.A. O'More) J.A. O'More, 1968

'Kilworth' × 'Arbar'

'Adieu' 9 W-?
(F.H. Chapman, pre-1928)
'Acme' × Div. 9 sdlg

'Adim' 2 W-W
(S.J. Bisdee, 1945)
'White Sentinel' × 'Rosario'

'Adina' 2 W-P
(W. Jackson Jr) W. Jackson Jr, 1968
'Angea' × 'Illinga'

'Adinda' 3 W-? (b)
(de Graaff-Gerharda, pre-1926)
AM(Haarlem) 1926

'Adino' 3 W-? (b)
(W.A. Grace, pre-1938)

'Adios' 2 Y-OOR
(W. Jackson Jr) Jackson's Daffodils, 1980
'Dimity' × sdlg 65/66; sdlg no. 101/72
Fl. 108 mm wide; perianth segments yellow; corona orange, with red at rim. Mid-season

'Adirondack' 2 W-? (b)
(Oregon Bulb Farms, pre-1951)

'Adjutant' 2 W-? (b)
(pre-1907)

'Adler' 2 W-YYO
(de Graaff Bros, pre-1929)
Perianth segments pure white; corona yellow, with orange at rim. AM(Haarlem) 1928

'Administrator' 1 W-? (b)
(J.N. Hancock & Co., pre-1949)

'Admirable' 3 W-? (b)
(A.F. Calvert, pre-1929)

'Admiral' W-R
(pre-1933)
Perianth segments pure white; corona bright red. Late

'Admiral' 3 W-YYR
(Mrs P.E. Speyer) Mrs P.E. Speyer, 1984
'Lynx' × 'Motif'; sdlg no. 2/56
Fl. 105 mm wide

'Admiral Beatty' 1 Y-Y
(G.B. van Rhijn, pre-1936)

'Admiral Bird' 2 W-Y
(M. van Waveren & Sons, pre-1953)

'Admiral Jellicoe' 2 or 3 W-Y
(?West & Fell, pre-1931)
Perianth segments pure white; corona pale primrose yellow

'Admiral Makaroff' 1 Y-Y
(Barr & Sons, pre-1905)
Perianth segments primrose yellow, overlapping; corona cylindrical, soft yellow. Resembles 'Emperor'

'Admiral Nelson' 1 Y-Y
(W. Welchman, pre-1927)

'Admiral of the Fleet' 1 Y-Y
(A.E. Lowe, pre-1927)

'Admiral Togo' 1 Y-Y
(Barr & Sons, pre-1904)
Perianth segments yellow; corona golden yellow

'Admiral Tromp' 2 Y-O
(J.W.A. Lefeber, pre-1968) Unregistered
Breeder's stock destroyed

'Admiration' 8 Y-O
(A. Vis, pre-1912)
Poetaz
Fls many per stem; perianth segments very broad, prominently mucronate, reflexed, with margins strongly waved, and sometimes recurved in the lower half, overlapping; the inner segments more nearly spreading; corona shallow bowl-shaped, ribbed, bright reddish orange. AM(Haarlem) 1913, AM(g) 1914

'Adolphe Menjou' 2 Y-? (a)
(J.W.A. Lefeber, pre-1948)

'Adonia' 8 Y-Y
(pre-1846)
Perianth segments dark primrose yellow; corona rich golden yellow

'Adonia' 3 W-O
(E.M. Crosfield, pre-1909)
Perianth segments creamy white; corona ribbed, scarlet-orange

'Adonis' 2 (b)
(W. Backhouse, pre-1869)
?Syn. of 'Adonis' of Leeds

'Adonis' 2 W-Y
(E. Leeds, pre-1877)
Perianth segments sulphur white; corona yellow. Syn. Incomparabilis Albidus 'Adonis'. ?The same as 'Adonis' of Backhouse

'Adonis' 1 Y-Y
(West & Fell, pre-1927)

'Adonis' 2 W-? (b)
(S.C. Gaspar, 1946) R.J. Abernethy, 1957

'Adorable' 1 W-W
(R.H. Bath, pre-1931)

'Adorable Lass' 6 Y-Y
(J. & E. Frey) J. & E. Frey, 1989
'Wee Bee' × *N. cyclamineus*; sdlg no. PEF9/5
Fl. 35 mm wide; perianth segments broadly ovate, blunt, reflexed, overlapping a quarter; corona cylindrical, narrow, broadly and smoothly ribbed, constricted near mouth, mouth expanded and shallowly lobed. Dwarf. Early

'Adoration' 5 W-W
(W.F.M. Copeland, pre-1927)

'Adoration'
(New Zealand origin, pre-1940)

'Adoration' 4 W-W
(G.E. Mitsch) G.E. Mitsch, 1972
'Cushendall' hybrid; sdlg no. VO3/1
Fl. 60 mm wide; corona sometimes with extra segments clustered within. Late

'Adorn' 2 W-R
(R.H.Glover, pre-1993) Unregistered

'Adorna' 3 Y-GYY
(Barr & Sons, pre-1923)
Perianth segments pale primrose yellow, overlapping; corona rich orange-yellow, with rim frilled

'Adorned' 2 W-P
(C.O. Fairbairn) Unregistered

'Adornica' 2
(B. Rowlands, pre-1938)

'Adornment' 2 Y-O
(H.A. Brown, 1937) J.N. Hancock & Co., 1960
Perianth segments rich golden yellow; corona pale orange, with a deep band of apricot at rim, rim closely and deeply notched, as if fringed

'Adour' 1 Y-Y
(Miss E. Willmott, pre-1903)
Fl. brilliant golden yellow. Late. AM 1903

'Adowa' 3 W-? (b)
(S.J. Bisdee, 1945)
'Hades' × 'Mr Sparks'

'Adrastus' 2 W-GYY
(C. Dawson, pre-1912)
Corona rich golden yellow paling clear yellow at rim, with green at base. Late

'Ad-Rem' 2 Y-Y
(J.H. Rijkelijkhuizen, *c*.1960) Unregistered
Perianth segments broad, vivid yellow 9B, overlapping half; corona brilliant yellow 15C, with orange-yellow at rim when retarded, mouth flared and frilled

'Adri' 1 W-Y
(W. Jackson Sr, 1937) W. Jackson Jr, 1956
'Bianca' × 'Beersheba'

'Adria' 2 W-? (b)
(T. Batson, pre-1914)

'Adria' 3 W-? (b)
(A.H. Ahrens) D.J. Cooper, 1956

'Adriaen Brouwer' 1 Y-Y
(Konynenburg & Mark, pre-1953)

'Adriaen van Ostade' 1 Y-Y
(Konynenburg & Mark, pre-1953)

'Adrian' 2 or 3 W-? (b or c)
(pre-1914)

'Adrian' 2 W-? (b)
(J.T. Gray, pre-1951)

'Adriana' 1 Y-Y
(Barr & Sons, pre-1923)
Fl. large, soft clear yellow

'Adriel' 3 W-? (b)
(J.T. Gray, pre-1939)

'Adrienne' 8 W-Y or O
(pre-1807)

'Adrienne' 2 W-Y
(T. Morrison) T. Morrison, 1961
Perianth pure white; corona lemon yellow

'Adrienne Morris' 2 W-? (b)
(J.A. Morris) J.A. Morris, 1955

'Adsum' 2 W-Y
(A.E. Lowe, pre-1927)
Corona soft yellow

'Adur' 3 W-? (b)
(Sir F.C. Stern, pre-1950)

'Advance' 9 W-OOR
(G.H. Engleheart, pre-1913)
Fl. 70 mm wide; perianth segments overlapping; corona reddish orange, with dull red at rim

'Advance' 1 W-W
(G. Zandbergen-Terwegen) G. Zandbergen-Terwegen, 1962

Fl. 114 mm wide, ivory white. Mid-season. Resembles a more robustly stemmed 'Broughshane' of smoother texture. AM(Haarlem) 1962

'Advance' 8 W-O
Syn. of 'Geranium'

'Advance Guard' 1 Y-Y
(G.H. Engleheart, pre-1923)
'Verona' × 'Angel'; sdlg no. 3.33.80
Fl. 120 mm wide; perianth segments broadly ovate or somewhat oblong, blunt, slightly mucronate, lemon yellow, a little inflexed, with margins wavy or recurved, overlapping one-third; the inner segments more narrowly ovate, with margins more strongly wavy, sometimes twisted; corona cylindrical or somewhat funnel-shaped, smooth, darker in tone than the perianth, mouth 6-lobed, rim very widely rolled, deeply and regularly dentate. Mid-season to late. AM(c)(m) 1926, AM(Haarlem) 1931. See also 'Advance-guard'

'Advance-guard' 1 Y-Y
Syn. of 'Advance Guard'

'Advent' 1 Y-Y
(E.M. Crosfield, pre-1914)

'Adventure' 2 Y-Y
(F.H. Chapman, pre-1927)
'Desperado' × 'Commander in Chief'
Perianth segments broadly ovate, blunt or truncate, slightly mucronate, deep yellow, spreading, overlapping half; the inner segments a little narrower, slightly inflexed; corona funnel-shaped, smooth, darker in tone than the perianth, with mouth expanded, rim slightly rolled and regularly crenate. AM(e) 1929, AM(Haarlem) 1930

'Adversane' 3 W-GWW
(N.A. Burr) N.A. Burr, 1994
'Verona' × 'Angel'; sdlg no. 3.33.80
Fl. rounded, 94 mm wide; perianth segments very broad or roundish, blunt, slightly mucronate, ivory white, spreading, concave towards apex, regular, overlapping half or more; the inner segments more nearly roundish, less noticeably mucronate; corona shallow bowl-shaped, ribbed, pinkish white, with green prominent at base, mouth straight, frilled, occasionally split and slightly overlapping, with rim minutely crenate. Late

'Advocat' 3 Y-GYY
(Brian S. Duncan) Rathowen Daffodils, 1977
'Clogheen' × 'Woodland Prince'; sdlg no. 253
Perianth segments lemon yellow, with a greenish tinge; corona of a deeper tone, with green at base. Mid-season

'Advocate' 2 Y-? (a)
(W. Welchman, pre-1908)

'Advocate' 2 W-O
(G.W.E. Brogden, 1961) Unregistered
Fl. 108 mm wide; corona light orange. Mid-season

'Adwell' 1 W-? (b)
(pre-1913)

'Aeantara'
(pre-1940)

'Aegean Spring' 2 W-W
(D.N.Y. Olson, 1980) D.N.Y. Olson, 1990
'Empress of Ireland' open pollinated; sdlg no. 30/1
Fl. 115 mm wide; perianth segments broadly ovate, a little inflexed, with margins sometimes wavy, sometimes incurled at apex, overlapping half; the inner segments with margins more strongly wavy; corona cylindrical, narrow, loosely ribbed, with mouth expanded and frilled. Mid-season to late. Resembles a smoother 'Empress of Ireland'

'Aegir' 5
(H. Prins, pre-1929)

'Aegis' 2 or 3 (b or c)
(pre-1913)

'Aeglos' 1 W-W
(Brian S. Duncan) Rathowen Daffodils, 1978
'Broughshane' × 'White Prince'; sdlg no. 6
Early mid-season. Resembles a smoother and better-formed 'Broughshane' with a better stem

'A.E.Lowe' 2 W-W
(A.E. Lowe, pre-1925)
Fl. pure white; corona very large, expanded

'Aeolus' 1 W-? (b)
(Barr & Sons, pre-1913)

'Aeolus' 1 W-Y
(M. van Waveren & Sons, pre-1930)
Fl. large; perianth segments very broadly ovate, blunt, only very slightly mucronate, spreading, plane, overlapping half; the inner segments narrower, more nearly acute, somewhat twisted; corona cylindrical, narrow, smooth, mouth ribbed and expanded, split in places and overlapping, loosely frilled, with rim crenate

N. aequilimbus Herbert = *N. tazetta* (wild form from Malta)

N. aequilimbus Nyman = *N. serotinus*

'Aerdenhout' 2 Y-? (a)
(F. Rijnveld & Sons, pre-1939)

'Aerial Light' 3 Y-? (a)
(W.B. Hartland, pre-1907)

'Aerolite' 2 Y-Y
(de Graaff Bros, pre-1923)
Perianth segments primrose yellow, slightly reflexed, overlapping; corona long, slender, bright yellow. Div. 1 until 1941

'Aeronef' 1 W-Y
(J.S. Leitch) J.S. Leitch, 1962
Fl. 45 mm wide; corona lemon yellow. Early

'Aeroplane' 1 W-? (b)
(J. Mallender, pre-1910)

'Aeroplane'
(A.E. Grindrod, pre-1914)

'Aeroplane' 2 Y-? (a)
(R.H. Bath, pre-1927)

'A.F.Barron' 1 Y-Y
(E. Leeds, pre-1877)
Syn. Pseudonarcissus Lorifolius 'A.F.Barron'

'Affable' 4 Y-O
(G.E. Mitsch) G.E. Mitsch, 1977
'Gay Time' × 'Daydream'; sdlg no. H102/1
Fl. rounded, 106 mm wide; perianth and other petaloid segments broad, pale buff apricot; corona segments light orange, frilled. Late

'Affection' 7
(A.H. Ahrens) J.S. Leitch, 1955

'Afficionado' 3 W-O
(Jackson's Daffodils, 1987) Jackson's Daffodils, 1997
Sdlg 155/78 × 'Hartz'; sdlg no. 245/87
Fl. 104 mm wide; perianth segments ovate, yellowish white (155B); corona very small disc-shaped, vivid orange 28B. Mid-season to late

'Affinity' 2 Y-Y
(F.E. Board) F.E. Board, 1965
'Galway' self pollinated
Mid-season. Resembles 'Galway' but with the corona more heavily frilled

'Affluence' 1 Y-Y
(F.E. Board) F.E. Board, 1965
'Kingscourt' × 'Golden Wealth'
Resembles 'Kingscourt' but with the corona more widely flared

'Affray' 3 W-R
(G.A. Uit den Boogaard, pre-1952)

'Afghanistan' 2 W-? (b)
(P.D. Williams, pre-1927)

'Afiena' 2 W-? (b)
(Mrs R.O. Backhouse, pre-1921)

'A Fifth Lancer' 3 W-? (b)
(Miss K. Spurrell, pre-1906)

'Afire' 2 Y-R
(J.N. Hancock & Co., pre-1949)
Perianth segments yellow; corona bright red

'Aflame' 3 W-YOO
(Warnaar & Co., pre-1938)
'Achievement' × 'Hades'
Perianth segments broad, creamy white, of thick substance, overlapping; corona bowl-shaped, deep orange, with gold at base, mouth flared and lobed. 2n=28. AM(Haarlem) 1938, FCC(Haarlem) 1944

'Africander' 1 Y-Y
(Barr & Sons, pre-1932)

'After All' 3 W-YYR
(J. Gerritsen & Son) J. Gerritsen & Son, 1961
Fl. 110 mm wide. Very late. Resembles 'Flower Record'

'Afterglow' 3 Y-YOO
(Barr & Sons, pre-1908)

'Afterglow' 3 Y-YOO
(L. van Leeuwen & Son, pre-1930)
Syn. 'Eventide'

'Afterglow' ?-P
(Alister Clark, pre-1948)

'Aftermath' 3 W-? (a)
(G.H. Engleheart, pre-1901)
Perianth segments creamy white; corona with fiery red at rim. AM 1901

'Afterthot' 2 Y-YYR
(G.E. Mitsch) G.E. Mitsch, 1979
Sdlg Y56/1 × 'Leprechaun'; sdlg no. HH73/2
Fl. 70 mm wide, clear soft lemon yellow; corona with a narrow and well-defined band of orange-red at rim. Dwarf. Mid-season

'Afterthought' 2 W-? (b)
(The Brodie of Brodie, pre-1910)
'Aftermath' × sdlg 662/04 ('Lulworth' × 'Virgil')
Resembles a larger and improved 'Aftermath' with a taller stem

'Agadir' 2 Y-Y
(J.W.A. Lefeber, 1968) J.W.A. Lefeber, 1981
Fl. 90 mm wide; perianth segments brilliant greenish yellow 6B; corona orange-yellow (21A). Early mid-season

'Agag' 2 W-W
(W.A. Bell, pre-1949)

'Aga Khan' 2 Y-? (a)
(G. Lubbe & Son, pre-1938)
AM(Haarlem) 1937, FCC(Haarlem) 1938

'Agamemnon' 2 Y-? (a)
(Sir C.H. Cave, pre-1928)

'Agapenor' 2 Y-? (a)
(Mrs R.O. Backhouse, pre-1921)
Syn. 'Cupido'

'Agate' 2 W-W
(C.E. Radcliff, 1941)
'Nimue' × 'Dawnglow'

'Agatha' 1 W-W
(G.H. Engleheart, pre-1914)
Fl. ivory white; perianth segments narrow, acute; corona slender. Mid-season

'Agathon' 2 Y-Y
(A.M. Wilson, pre-1949)

'Agawam' 1 W-W
(E.C. Powell, pre-1946)
'Nevis' × 'Naxos'

'A.G.Bull' 1 Y-Y
(A.E. Lowe, pre-1925)

'A.G.D.Johnston'
(pre-1913)

'Agena' 3 W-O
(C.R. Wootton) C.R. Wootton, 1968
'Kilworth' × 'Arbar'
Fl. 100 mm wide; corona reddish orange. Early

'Agena' 1 Y-Y
(H.R. Bulman, c.1966) Unregistered
'Vigi' hybrid

'Agheila' 3 W-? (b)
(J.L. Richardson, pre-1945)
'Coronach' × 'Forfar'
Resembles a much later-flowered 'Matapan'

'Agincourt' 1 W-W
(R.C.A. Tombleson) R.C.A. Tombleson, 1972
'Nova' × 'Lochin'
Fl. 105 mm wide

'Aglaia' 3 W-W
(E. Leeds, pre-1877)
Corona opening primrose yellow tinged orange, becoming milk white. Syn. Leedsii 'Aglaia'. Was "absorbed" into 'Acis'

'Aglow' 2 Y-O
(Mrs A.O. Meyrick, pre-1949)
Perianth segments yellow; corona flared, ribbed, orange, with a richer tone at rim

'Agnes' 8 W-Y
(W.J. Eldering & Son, pre-1913)
Perianth segments pure white; corona golden yellow. AM(Haarlem) 1913

'Agnes' 8 W-O
Syn. of 'Saint Agnes'

'Agnes Andreae' 2 W-O
(G.A. Uit den Boogaard, pre-1946)

'Agnes Barr' 3 W-Y
(W. Backhouse, pre-1869)
Perianth segments creamy white. Syn. Burbidgei 'Agnes Barr', Burbidgei 'Delicatus'

'Agnes Bowie' 3 W-? (b or c)
(Mrs R.O. Backhouse, pre-1914)

'Agnes Harvey' 5 W-W
(Miss K. Spurrell, pre-1902)
'Minnie Hume' × *N. triandrus*
Fls 1-3 per stem, facing slightly downwards; perianth segments pure white; corona cup-shaped, white, sometimes flushed soft apricot, with mouth expanded. AM 1902

'Agnes Howell' 9 W-?
(Marsh, pre-1907)

'Agnes Mellish' 1 W-W
(J. Mallender, pre-1910)
Fl. large. Early

'Agnes Montefiore' 2 W-WWY
(N.Y. Lower, pre-1928)
'Cleopatra' × Div. 7 sdlg
Fl. 130 mm wide; perianth segments creamy white, overlapping half; corona almost white, shading to brilliant yellow 8A at rim, with mouth expanded and frilled. 2n=28. *AM(g) 1949

'Agnes Pearson' 3 Y-? (a)
(W.B. Hartland, pre-1908)

'Agnes Webster' 5 W-W
(T. Morrison) T. Morrison, 1960
Fls 1-2 per stem

'Agni' 3 W-? (b)
(de Graaff-Gerharda, pre-1926)
AM(Haarlem) 1926

'Agnostic' 1 Y-Y
(G.H. Engleheart, pre-1927)
Fl. 101 mm wide; perianth segments deep lemon yellow, incurving, irregular, overlapping a quarter; corona buttercup yellow, with mouth expanded and somewhat frilled. Mid-season to late

'Agobard' 2 W-O
(A.M. Wilson, pre-1930)
Perianth segments cream; corona orange

'Agora' 2 W-O
(G.H. Johnstone) G.H. Johnstone, 1959
Fl. 102 mm wide; perianth segments very broad, overlapping half; corona disc-shaped, bright orange, with mouth slightly lobed. Mid-season. 2n=28

'Agra' 2 Y-O
(N.Y. Lower, pre-1927)
Perianth segments large, soft sulphur yellow; corona deep orange, widely expanded. AM(Haarlem) 1927, FCC(Haarlem) 1930

'Agricola' 1 Y-Y
(H.G. Longford, pre-1927)

'Agrippa' 3 W-YYO
(P.J. Worsley, pre-1907)
'Dorothy Wemyss' × 'Poetarum'
Perianth segments creamy white; corona with orange-scarlet at rim

'Agrippa'
(Mrs R.S. Cobley, pre-1937)

'Agrippa' 3 W-?
Syn. of 'Bereby'

'Agrippina'
(P.D. Williams, pre-1914)

'Agrippina' 2 W-P
(A.H. Ahrens, pre-1950)
'Suda' × 'Pink o' Dawn'
Perianth segments very broad, pure white; corona shallow bowl-shaped, pale pink. PC(e)(NZ) 1950. Received PC(NZ) 1950 as 'Georgia'

'Agrippina' 2 W-Y
(Konynenburg & Mark, 1961) Unregistered
'Binkie' × 'Spellbinder'
Fl. 100 mm wide; perianth segments ivory white; corona pale yellow 18C. Mid-season

'Aguila' 2 Y-?
Syn. of 'Aquila'

'Ah Gee' 1 Y-Y
(Glenbrook Bulb Farm, pre-1985) Unregistered
'Golden' × 'Ristin'; sdlg no. 17-85

'Ahjay' 2 W-W
(R.H.Glover, pre-1989) Unregistered
'Lady Slim' × 'Arctic Doric'

'Ahlam' 3 W-W
(D.J. Cooper) D.J. Cooper, 1957

'Ahoy' 2 Y-? (a)
(J.N. Hancock & Co., pre-1949)

'Ahoy' 11a W-Y
(J. Gerritsen & Son) J. Gerritsen & Son, 1960
Fl. 100 mm wide; corona segments pale sulphur yellow, with rim dentate. Mid-season. 2n=28. Resembles an improved 'Evolution'

'Ahuriri' 2 W-GYR
(D.S. Bell) D.S. Bell, 1982
'Huntsman' × 'Masquerade' hybrid
Fl. 95 mm wide; perianth segments pure white; corona very shallow bowl-shaped. Mid-season

'Ahwahnee' 2 Y-YOO
(Brian S. Duncan) Brian S. Duncan, 1992
'Gettysburg' × 'Sportsman'; sdlg no. 1040
Fl. rounded, 108 mm wide; perianth segments very broadly ovate, blunt, fairly prominently mucronate, mid-yellow, faintly tinged green at base, spreading or slightly reflexed, plane, overlapping half; the inner segments rounded at apex; corona funnel-shaped, deep orange, paling to yellow at base, mouth only slightly expanded. Mid-season

'Aida' 3 W-Y
(The Brodie of Brodie, pre-1913)
'Princess Mary' × *N. poeticus*
Perianth segments pure white; corona bright yellow

'Aida' 1 W-W
Syn. of 'Indiana'

'Aide-de-Camp' 3 W-? (b)
(Miss K. Spurrell, pre-1907)

'Aidne' 1 W-W
(W. Jackson Sr, 1944)
'Kanchenjunga' × 'Adri'

'Aigle Blanc' 8 W-O
(pre-1798)

'Aigle d'Or' 8 Y-O
(pre-1792)
Perianth segments yellow; corona rich yellowish orange

'Aigle d'Or' 1 Y-Y
(pre-1907)

'Aileen' 1 Y-Y

(Slieve Donard Nursery Co., pre-1938)
'Magnificence' hybrid
Fl. pure yellow; perianth broad; corona rim flanged. Early. Resembles a stronger and slightly shorter-stemmed 'Magnificence' with the perianth segments more nearly spreading

'Aileen Goodman' 1 W-W
(?Australian origin, pre-1997) Unregistered

'Aileron' 2 W-P
(H.A. Brown, 1941)
Fl. large; corona funnel-shaped

'Ailsa' 1 W-W
(E.M. Crosfield, pre-1907)
Fl. 93 mm wide; perianth segments creamy white, inflexed, overlapping at base only; corona constricted at waist, cream, mouth expanded and frilled, rim reflexed. Mid-season to late. AM 1907

'Aim' 2 Y-O
(Barr & Sons) T.M. Dorrien Smith, 1972
Fl. 100 mm wide

'Aimable' 3 Y-O
Perianth segments smooth; corona large, widely expanded. Syn. of 'Amiable'

'Aimable Jeanne' 8 W-O
(pre-1835)
Early

'Aina Ulmane' 4 W-P
(Vitauts Skuja) Vitauts Skuja, 1966
'Pink Paradise' × 'Coral Ribbon'
Fl. 80 mm wide; perianth and other petaloid segments pure white; corona segments numerous, strong yellowish pink 37B. Late. Sunproof

'Ain Fara' 3 W-Y
(S.J. Bisdee, 1941)
'May Molony' × 'Nautilus'
Corona pale lemon yellow

'Ainsdale' 3 W-? (b)
(P. van Deursen, pre-1920)
Syn. 'Appleby'

'Aintree' 3 W-O
(John T. Williams) John T. Williams, 1994
'Park Springs' × 'Shining Light'; sdlg no. 38
Fl. forming a double triangle, 88 mm wide; perianth segments broadly ovate, blunt, slightly mucronate, chalky white, a little reflexed at maturity, overlapping half or more; corona cup-shaped, dark orange, with a broad band of a darker tone at rim, mouth slightly flared, rim crenate. Mid-season or earlier

'Airborne' 2 W-W
(A.M. Wilson, pre-1948)
Corona opening pale lemon, becoming white

'Aircastle' 3 W-Y
(G.E. Mitsch) G.E. Mitsch, 1958
'Green Island' × 'Chinese White'
Fl. rounded; perianth segments very broad in outline, blunt or rounded at apex, only very slightly mucronate, opening white, becoming yellowish white, spreading or a little reflexed, plane, overlapping half; the inner segments narrower, shouldered at base, spreading or a little inflexed; corona very shallow bowl-shaped, loosely ribbed, pale apricot yellow tinted with whitish yellow, with a darker tone at rim, lightly frilled, rim minutely crenate. Mid-season. PC(e) 1962. Both perianth and corona can vary between white and yellow

'Airline' 3 W-GOO
(S.A. Free, 1955) S.A. Free, 1966
Fl. 102 mm wide; corona orange, shading to a darker tone at rim, with greenish shades at base. Mid-season

'Airman' 1 Y-Y
(A.M. Williams, pre-1948)

'Air Marshal' 2 Y-O
(J.L. Richardson, pre-1953)
'Carbineer' × 'Malta'
Perianth segments very broadly ovate, rounded at apex, brilliant greenish yellow 6A, with paler mucro, spreading, plane or with margins slightly wavy, with broad midrib showing, regular, overlapping half; the inner segments narrower, a little inflexed; corona narrow cup-shaped, orange (near to 28A), slightly paler towards the base, mouth straight, a little frilled. Mid-season to late. 2n=28. AM(e) 1957, *AM(g) 1962

'Air Warden' 2 W-Y
(A.S. Brewster, pre-1950)

'Airway' 2 Y-? (a)
(H.A. Brown, pre-1950)

'Aivenho' 6 W-W
(Jānis Rukšans, 1985) Jānis Rukšans, 1997
'Empress of Ireland' × 'Jenny'; sdlg no. 79-19-1
Fl. 105 mm wide, pure white; perianth segments mucronate, reflexed, smooth, overlapping; corona slightly touched yellowish white at base, with rim flanged. Very early

'Aivita' 1 W-W
(Jānis Rukšans) Jānis Rukšans, 1997
'Churchfield' × 'Birthday Girl'; sdlg no. 85-03-3
Fl. 110 mm wide, pure white; perianth segments mucronate, smooth, deeply overlapping; corona widely expanded, with golden yellow at base, rim flanged. Very early

'Ajana' 1 W-W
(W. Jackson Jr) W. Jackson Jr, 1968
'Seriki' × 'Cardecu'; sdlg no. 45/59

'Akala' 1 Y-Y
(W. Jackson Jr) W. Jackson Jr, 1970
'Jobi' × sdlg 54/61; sdlg no. 93/65
Fl. 135 mm wide, rich warm yellow; corona slender, with rim slightly flanged. Mid-season

'Akaluma' 2 Y-R
(G.J. Phillips, 1984) G.J. Phillips, 1994
'Trelay' × "Tia"; sdlg no. 79-76-3
Fl. 116 mm wide; perianth segments very broadly ovate; the inner segments more narrowly ovate; corona broad and very shallow bowl-shaped, rich orange-red. Tall. Early

'Akaroa' 1 Y-Y
(D.S.Bell, pre-1987) Unregistered

'Akbar' 2 Y-ORR
(A.M. Wilson, pre-1944)
Perianth segments bright yellow; corona yellowish orange, with almost the whole of the upper half deep red

'Akela' 1 Y-Y
(J. Hall, pre-1930)
Fl. yellow; corona expanded, darker in tone than the perianth, frilled

'Akepa' 5 W-P
(G.E. Mitsch) G.E. Mitsch, 1979
'Accent' × *N. triandrus*; sdlg no. HH4/2
Fls usually 2 per stem; perianth segments ovate, blunt, only very slightly mucronate, milk white, spreading, plane, with margins slightly wavy, overlapping one-third to a half; the inner segments a little inflexed, with margins more distinctly wavy; corona cup-shaped, smoothly 6-angled, shell pink, mouth straight, wavy, obscurely 6-lobed, rim entire. Late

'Akin' 2 Y-O
(J.N. Hancock & Co., pre-1949)
Perianth segments rich yellow; corona ribbed, pale orange

'Akinga' 1 Y-Y
(J.N. Hancock & Co., *c.*1981) Unregistered

'Akkad' 1 Y-Y
(W. Jackson Jr, 1967) Unregistered
'Chillion' × 'Tulendena'; sdlg no. 37/67
Fl. large, yellow; perianth segments broad, smooth, of good substance, deeply overlapping; corona deeper in tone than the perianth, with rim rolled and serrate

'Akora' 4 Y-Y
(H.G. Cross) H.G. Cross, 1984
('Kingscourt' × 'Fiji') × 'Fiji'; sdlg no. 24-8
Fl. rounded, rich golden yellow; perianth and other petaloid segments in several whorls, very broadly ovate, with slight white mucro, deeply overlapping; the outer whorl spreading or a little inflexed, a little concave; the inner whorls each a little shorter, more strongly inflexed and more deeply concave; the centre whorl short, crumpled, clustered, strongly inflexed. Early

'Akra' 2 Y-Y
(S.J. Bisdee, 1942)
'Golden Queen' × 'Crocus'

'Akron' 3 W-? (b)
(G.A. Uit den Boogaard, pre-1950)

'Akuna' 2 W-W
(S.J. Bisdee, 1950) S.J. Bisdee, 1956
'Whitefoord' × sdlg B2/45
Div. 3 until 1964

'Akura' 1 Y-Y
(pre-1927)
Fl. golden yellow

'Akura' 2 W-P
(W. Jackson Jr, 1957) W. Jackson Jr, 1968
'Illinga' × 'Dallbro'; sdlg no. 247/57

'Alabama' 3 Y-? (a)
(de Graaff Bros, pre-1927)
Syn. 'Ivanhoe'

'Alabaster' 5 W-W
(H. Backhouse, pre-1912)
'Minnie Hume' × *N. triandrus* var. *loiseleurii*
Perianth segments fairly broad; corona long

'Alabaster' 4 W-W
(G.E. Mitsch, 1952) G.E. Mitsch, 1972
'Cushendall' × 'Cantabile'
Fl. 65 mm wide, pure white; perianth and other petaloid segments in several whorls; the two outer whorls broad, rounded, overlapping; the inner whorls clustered and irregular. Late. Somewhat resembles a later-flowered and more prolific 'Sweet Music'. $2n=14$

'Alacabam' 6 Y-Y
(M.G. Temple-Smith) M.G. Temple-Smith, 1987
N. cyclamineus × 'Ristin'; sdlg no. 2/82
Perianth segments ovate, with prominent white mucro, reflexed, plane, smooth, with midrib faintly showing, overlapping half; the inner segments only slightly narrower; corona cylindrical or somewhat funnel-shaped, very lightly ribbed, with mouth expanded and even, rim minutely notched and

crenate. Early. Resembles 'Abracadabra' and 'Voodoo' but with a shorter corona

'Alachua' 1 W-? (b)
(E.C. Powell, pre-1948)

'Aladale' 2 Y-O
(H.A. Brown, 1931)
Perianth segments rich yellow; corona reddish orange, with mouth frilled

'Aladdin' 2 or 3 W-Y
(E. Leeds, pre-1877)
Fl. 102 mm wide; corona lemon yellow, with rim lightly rolled. Syn. Leedsii 'Aladdin'

'Aladdin's Lamp' 2 Y-O
(G.L. Wilson, pre-1931)
Sdlg × 'Fortune'
Perianth segments yellow, of thick substance; corona clear reddish orange. Syn. 'Alfonso'

'Alamein' 2 Y-O
(J.L. Richardson, pre-1944)
'Trevisky' × 'Marksman'
Fl. 102 mm wide; perianth segments broadly ovate, blunt, slightly mucronate, vivid yellow 9A, spreading or a little inflexed, a little concave, smooth, overlapping half; the inner segments more narrowly ovate, shouldered at base and sometimes "thumbed", more strongly inflexed; corona short funnel-shaped, loosely ribbed, vivid orange 28B, with mouth straight and frilled. Mid-season. AM(e) 1945

'Alamo' 2 Y-R
(G.E. Mitsch) G.E. Mitsch, 1974
Sdlg P50/1 ('Narvik' × 'California Gold') × 'Flaming Meteor'; sdlg no. B45/5
Fl. 105 mm wide; perianth segments rich golden yellow, plane, very smooth; corona rich orange-red, a little frilled. Mid-season

'Alan' 3 W-? (b)
(L. van Leeuwen & Son, pre-1931)
Syn. 'Flamboyant'

'Alan' 1 Y-Y
(P. & G. Phillips) P. Phillips, 1979
Fl. 105 mm wide. Mid-season

'Alana' 1 Y-Y
(J.N.Hancock & Co., 1980) Unregistered
'Toorak Gold' × 'Prince Ki'; sdlg no. 9/80H
Fl. bright orange-yellow; corona widely expanded, ribbed. Tall. Early

'Alan Gibson' 1 Y-Y
(A. Gibson, pre-1950)
'Kingscourt' × 'Goldcourt'
Fl. rounded, soft yellow; perianth segments very broadly ovate, blunt, only very slightly mucronate, plane, very smooth, overlapping half; the inner segments more prominently mucronate, with margins a little incurling; corona mouth ribbed, expanded, loosely frilled. PC(e)(NZ) 1950

'Alannah' 5
(Sir J.A.R. Gore-Booth, pre-1916)

'Alanton' 2 Y-Y
(A. Gibson, pre-1927)

'Alara' 2 W-? (b)
(Barr & Sons, pre-1923)

'Alaric' 3 W-? (b)
(A.M. Wilson, pre-1910)

'Alarm' 2 Y-O
(Warnaar & Co.) Warnaar & Co., 1957
'Bahram' × 'Scarlet Elegance'
AM(Haarlem) 1957, FCC(Haarlem) 1962

'Alaska' 1 Y-Y
(de Graaff Bros, pre-1928)
Syn. 'John Bright'

'Alaskan Forest' 2 W-W
(G.E.Mitsch, 1984) R. & E. Havens, 1994
'Broomhill' × 'Canisp'; sdlg no. TT23/2
Fl. 110 mm wide, smooth and of heavy substance; perianth segments broadly ovate, spreading, plane; corona long, with mouth slightly flared. Mid-season

'Alasnam' 1 Y-Y
(de Graaff Bros, pre-1922)
Perianth segments canary yellow, inflexed; corona broad, rich golden yellow, with mouth expanded and frilled

'Alayne' 2 W-YYO
(C.G. van Tubergen, pre-1947)
Perianth segments snow white; corona yellow, with orange at rim, rim frilled. 2n=28

'Alba' 1 W-W
(Mrs R.O. Backhouse, pre-1921)
Perianth segments creamy white, regular, overlapping one-third; corona deeper in tone, mouth expanded. Mid-season

'Albacore' 2 W-Y
(Murray W. Evans) Murray W. Evans, 1976
('Lunar Sea' × 'Galway') × 'Glenmanus'; sdlg no. K-12
Fl. 105 mm wide. Mid-season

'Albacrest' 3 W-GOW
(T. Bloomer) Rathowen Daffodils, 1985

'Woodland Princess' × 'Woodland Prince'; sdlg no. 411
Corona very shallow bowl-shaped, orange, with green at base and a well-defined band of white at rim. Mid-season

'Alba Dream' 1 W-W
(J.E.Colley) J.E.Colley, 1995
Sdlg F56/5 × 'Alba Pax'; sdlg no. X131/3
Fl. forming a double triangle, 112 mm wide; perianth segments very broadly ovate, blunt, slightly mucronate, spreading, concave, smooth, overlapping half; the inner segments a little narrower, sharply angled at shoulder, very slightly inflexed; corona funnel-shaped, mouth ribbed, frilled, rim flanged and dentate. Late. Resembles 'Alba Pax' but with a smoother perianth

'Alban' 2 W-W
(G.H. Engleheart, pre-1923)

'Albana' 2 Y-YOO
(S.C. Gaspar, 1945) R.J. Abernethy, 1957
Perianth segments yellow, of stiff substance; corona almost cylindrical, deep orange-red, paling to golden yellow at base

'Albania' 8 W-Y
(G. van der Weyden Jobson, pre-1914)
Corona large, deep yellow. AM(Haarlem) 1914

'Albany' 8 W-YOO
(A. Frylink & Sons, pre-1931)
Fls about 3 per stem, medium-sized; perianth segments creamy white; corona orange. 2n=31. AM(Haarlem) 1931

'Alba Pax' 2 W-GWW
(J.E. Colley, 1978) J.E. Colley, 1989
'Greenland' × 'Panache'; sdlg no. F86/3
F. 95 mm wide; pure white; perianth segments broadly ovate, blunt and slightly mucronate, with a touch of green at base, spreading, plane or very slightly concave, with margins incurling at apex, broad midrib showing, regular, overlapping half; the inner segments more narrowly ovate, plane, shouldered at base; corona long, funnel-shaped, with green at base, mouth flared and frilled, rim crenate. Late

'Alba Plena Odorata'
Syn. of 'Albus Plenus Odoratus'

'Albaran' 3 W-? (b)
(Mrs R.O. Backhouse, pre-1921)

'Albast' 1 W-? (c)
(Mrs R.O. Backhouse, pre-1921)

'Albatross' 3 W-YYO
(G.H. Engleheart, pre-1891)

'Ornatus' × 'Empress'; sdlg no. 21
Fl. up to 127 mm wide; perianth segments broadly ovate, rounded or squarish at apex, prominently mucronate, clear white, spreading or slightly inflexed, with margins wavy or incurved, sometimes recurved in lower half, with midrib showing, separated at base, sometimes overlapping at mid-point; the inner segments more narrowly ovate, only very slightly mucronate; corona bowl-shaped, ribbed, very pale lemon yellow, with a well-defined band of orange at rim, mouth straight, loosely frilled, rim notched. Resembles sibling 'Seagull' but with a contrasting colour at corona rim. 2n=28. FCC 1894

'Albemarle' 1 Y-Y
(T.H. Piper, 1954)
'Roundabout' × 'Derflinger'

'Alberich' 1 Y-Y
(P.L.A. Pouw) P.L.A. Pouw, 1983
'Rembrandt' × 'Golden Sunbeam'

'Alberni Beauty' 3 W-GYY
(C.T. Hilton, pre-1930)
Fl. rounded, 89 mm wide; perianth segments very broad, blunt or truncate, slightly mucronate, reflexed, concave, smooth, overlapping half; the inner segments narrower, square-shouldered at base, more nearly spreading, with margins wavy; corona small and very shallow bowl-shaped, closely ribbed, sulphur yellow, with green prominent at base, frilled. Late. *HC(g) 1930, *AM(m)(g) 1931

'Alberni Star' 3 W-GYO
(C.T. Hilton, pre-1930)
Perianth segments white, with lemon at base, separated; corona funnel-shaped, sulphur yellow, with green at base and orange at rim

'Albert' 1 Y-Y
(L. Buckland, pre-1936)

'Alberta' 2 Y-? (a)
(R.H. Bath, pre-1931)

'Albert Cuyp' 1 Y-Y
(G. Lubbe & Son, pre-1927)
AM(Haarlem) 1928

'Albert Elvin' 2 Y-? (a)
(R.H. Bath, pre-1950)

'Albert Haig' 2 Y-O
(West & Fell, pre-1938)
Perianth segments rich yellow; corona expanded, reddish orange. Early

'Albertina' 3 W-Y
(Barr & Sons, pre-1914)
Perianth segments pure white; corona shallow,

ribbed, pale primrose yellow

'Albertina van Kooten' 2 W-P
(L.P.Dettman, 1975) Unregistered
'Creamed Honey' × 'Ellimatta'; sdlg no. 1 CH/E 75

'Alberton' 1 W-P
(C.E. Radcliff, 1942) J.M.Radcliff, 1956
'Fawn' sdlg? × 'Dawnglow'
Corona buff pink

'Albert Rutledge' 2 Y-Y
(J.W. Avery) J.W. Avery, 1959

'Albert Sandler' 3 W-? (b)
(J.W.A. Lefeber, pre-1939)
Syn. 'Chopin'

'Albert Schweizer' 1 Y-Y
(Konynenburg & Mark, pre-1953)
'Adventure' hybrid

'Albert Victor' 2 W-Y
(E. Leeds, pre-1877)
Fl. large; perianth segments sulphur white; corona widely expanded, yellow. Syn. Incomparabilis Albidus 'Albert Victor', Incomparabilis Albidus 'Magnificus'. "Absorbed" 'Partout'

'Albert Vis' 8 W-O
(A. Vis, pre-1912)
'King Edward VII' × 'Staaten Generaal'
Corona rich reddish orange. AM(Haarlem) 1912

N. albescens Pugsley 13 Section Pseudonarcissus

N. albicans hort. = *N. albescens*

N. albicans Sprengel = *N. cantabricus* subsp. *monophyllus*

'Albicans' 1 W-W
(pre-1884)
N. moschatus sdlg
Perianth segments narrowly ovate, acute, reflexed and twisted; corona narrowly funnel-shaped, ribbed, opening primrose yellow, becoming white, lightly frilled, with rim reflexed. 2n=14. Syn. "The Greatest White Spanish Daffodil", Pseudonarcissus Moschatus 'Albicans'

N. albidus Emberger & Maire = *N. romieuxii* subsp. *albidus*

N. albidus Schultes f. = *N.* × *incomparabilis*

'Albidus' 2 W-Y
(E. Leeds, pre-1877)
Perianth segments sulphur white; corona yellow. Syn. Incomparabilis Albidus 'Albidus'

'Albidus' 3 W-Y
(E. Leeds, pre-1877)
Perianth segments sulphur white; corona yellow. Syn. Barrii Albidus 'Albidus'. Was "absorbed" into Barrii Sulphureus 'Sulphureus'

'Albidus' 1 W-Y
A synonym both of 'James Walker' and of 'Hume's Sulphur'

'Albidus Aurantius' 3 Y-O
Syn. of 'Ethel'

'Albidus Paradoxus' 1 W-Y
(?E. Leeds, pre-1877)
N. montanus sdlg
Fl. large; perianth segments sulphur white; corona yellow. Syn. Humei 'Albidus Paradoxus', Humei 'Paradoxus'

'Albiflos' 8 W-W
(pre-1850)

N. albimarginatus Müller-Doblies 13 Section Bulbocodium

'Albingia' 3 W-? (b)
(Mrs R.O. Backhouse, pre-1921)

'Albino' 1 W-W
(H. Backhouse, pre-1910)
Fl. opening creamy white, becoming white. FCC(Haarlem) 1926

'Albion' 3 W-Y
(E. Leeds, pre-1877)
Perianth segments narrow, acute; corona canary yellow. 2n=*c*.14. Syn. 'Delicata', Leedsii 'Albion', Leedsii 'Delicatus'

'Albion Star' 2 W-? (b)
(Mrs R.O. Backhouse, pre-1921)

'Alborado' 4 W-P
(D.S. Bell) D.S. Bell, 1984
From two Div. 4 pink sdlgs

'Alburnia' 3 W-Y
(A.E. Lowe, pre-1927)
Perianth segments pure white; corona shallow, soft yellow. Mid-season

N. albus Haworth = *N. moschatus*

N. albus Miller = *N.* × *medioluteus*

N. albus Spach = *N.* × *incomparabilis*

albus = *N. triandrus*

'Albus' 2 W-Y
(E. Leeds, pre-1877)
Syn. "The Peerless Daffodil", Incomparabilis Albus 'Albus'. "Absorbed" Barrii Albus 'Albus'

'Albus' 3 W-Y
(E. Leeds, pre-1877)
Perianth segments pure white; corona citron yellow. Syn. Barrii Albus 'Albus'. Was "absorbed" into Incomparabilis Albus 'Albus'

'Albus' 1 W-W
(pre-1884)
Syn. Pseudonarcissus Abscissus 'Albus'

'Albus' 1 W-Y
(pre-1884)
Syn. Pseudonarcissus 'Albus'

'Albus' 1 W-W
Syn. of 'Hume's White'

'Albus Multiplex' 4 W-W
(pre-1629)
Perianth and other petaloid segments in successive whorls of more or less the same length, broad, white. Scented. Syn. "The Double White Daffodil"

'Albus Plenus Aurantius' 4 W-O
Syn. of 'Orange Phoenix'

'Albus Plenus Odoratus' 4 W-YYR
See also 'Alba Plena Odorata'. Syn. of Poeticus 'Plenus'

'Albus Plenus Sulphureus' 4 W-Y
Syn. of 'Sulphur Phoenix'

'Albus Stella' 2 W-Y
Syn. of 'Stella Superba'

'Alcaeus' 9 W-?
(G.H. Engleheart, pre-1916)

'Alcanar' 1 Y-Y
(A.M. Wilson, pre-1931)

'Alcantara' 2 W-? (b)
(Mrs R.O. Backhouse, pre-1921)

'Alcatraz' 1 Y-Y
(W.F. Leenen) W.F. Leenen, 1971
Fl. 120 mm wide; perianth segments sulphur yellow; corona buttercup yellow. Mid-season

'Alcazar' 3 Y-? (a)
(Miss G. Evelyn, pre-1930)

'Alceste' 2 W-Y
(C.G. van Tubergen, pre-1922)
Fl. 102 mm wide; perianth segments white, with cream at base, inflexed, with margins incurved, regular, overlapping one-third; corona broad funnel-shaped, rich lemon yellow. AM(Haarlem) 1922, FCC(Haarlem) 1933

'Alcestis' 3 W-W
(S.J. Bisdee, 1938)
'Mary Blewitt' × 'Portia'
Corona cream

'Alchemist' 1 Y-Y
(A.M. Wilson, pre-1908)
Fl. rich yellow; perianth segments acute; corona rim dentate

'Alchemy' 1 Y-Y
(G.E. Mitsch, pre-1952)
'Camberwell King' × 'Galway'; sdlg no. K7/1
Fl. clear rich yellow; perianth segments smooth, overlapping; corona rim neatly flanged. Mid-season. Resembles a stronger-stemmed 'Camberwell King' of more consistent growth and flower

'Alcibiades' 3 Y-? (a)
(de Graaff Bros, pre-1927)

'Alcida' 3 W-O
(Mrs R.O. Backhouse, pre-1921)
'Bernardino' hybrid
Perianth segments pure white; corona bright scarlet-orange. AM(Haarlem) 1921

'Alciette' 2 W-? (b or c)
(W.B. Cranfield, pre-1927)

'Alcinous' 2 W-? (b)
(Mrs R.O. Backhouse, pre-1921)

'Alciphron' 2 Y-? (a)
(R.H. Bath, pre-1931)

'Alcmena' 5
(Barr & Sons, pre-1923)

'Alcomie' 1 W-Y
(Tom Forster, 1960s) Unregistered

'Alconia' 2 W-R
(C.E. Radcliff, pre-1938)
'Alcides' × 'Mrs Fell'

'Alcyone' 2 W-? (b or c)
(C. Dawson, pre-1923)

'Aldabra' 1 W-P
(J.N.Hancock & Co., 1983) J.N.Hancock & Co., 1997
'Beryl Hancock' × 'Jolly Roger'; sdlg no. 22/83H
Perianth segments ovate, blunt, creamy white,

spreading; corona cylindrical, apricot pink, with mouth straight, rim dentate. Early

'Alden' 3 W-? (b)
(J. Pope, pre-1913)

'Aldergrove' 2 W-Y
(W.J. Dunlop, pre-1953)
'White Sentinel' × 'Kanchenjunga'
Perianth segments pure white; corona deep golden yellow. 2n=28

'Alderman' 1 Y-Y
(R.C.A. Tombleson) R.C.A. Tombleson, 1971
Fl. 110 mm wide

'Aldgate' 2 W-O
(H.A. Brown, pre-1936) J.N. Hancock & Co., 1960
Corona pale orange

'Aldhelm' 3 W-G
(Mrs R.S. Cobley, pre-1932)

'Aldie' 2 Y-? (a)
(The Brodie of Brodie, pre-1930)

'Aldor' 1 Y-Y
(H.R. Bulman, c.1967) Unregistered
'Kingscourt' × 'Kalman'

'Aldringham' 2 W-W
(Ballydorn Bulb Farm, 1968) Ballydorn Bulb Farm, 1978
Sdlg × 'Kwannon'
Fl. 100 mm wide. Mid-season. Resembles a whiter 'Kwannon'

'Alec' 1 Y-Y
(W. Poupart, pre-1914)

'Alec Gray' 1 W-W
(Mrs J.B. Capen, 1970) Mrs J.B. Capen, 1987
Gray sdlg open pollinated
Perianth segments ovate, acute, spreading or occasionally slightly reflexed, separated; corona slender, straight-sided, smooth, opening pale yellow, becoming pure white within 2 days, mouth expanded, rim regularly and closely crenate. Dwarf. Early

'Alecto' 2 W-? (b)
(D.J. Cooper) D.J. Cooper, 1956

'Aled' 2 W-? (b)
(W.A. Watts, pre-1923)
'Minnie Hume' × 'Weardale Perfection'

'Alegra' 1 W-? (b)
(Barr & Sons, pre-1929)

N. × *alejandrei* Fernández Casas 13 = *N.* *bulbocodium* Linnaeus var. *citrinus* Baker × *N. jacetanus* subsp. *vasconicus* Fernández Casas

'Alembdar' 2 Y-? (a)
(A.M. Wilson, pre-1944)
'Khamseen' hybrid

'Alembic' 2 Y-R
(A.M. Wilson, pre-1944)
'Khamseen' × P.D.Williams sdlg
Perianth segments deep yellow; corona deep red

'Alembroth' 2 Y-Y
(A.M. Wilson, pre-1944)
Fl. deep yellow

'Alemena' 5
(pre-1936)
'Lord Roberts' × *N. triandrus* var. *loiseleurii*

'Alencon' 2 W-Y
(Barr & Sons, pre-1923)
Perianth segments overlapping; corona long, cylindrical, rich yellow

'Alendale' 2 Y-Y
(Mrs E. Murray)

'Alenmouth' 3 W-Y
(G. Harrison) G. Harrison, 1968
'Chinese White' × 'Clockface'

'Aleppo' 3 W-R
(The Brodie of Brodie, c.1927)
'Bernardino' × 'Sunstar'; sdlg no. 259/B/22
Fl. rounded; perianth segments of great substance, overlapping; corona almost disc-shaped, stained deep red. 2n=28

'Alert' 1 Y-Y
(J.R. Pearson & Sons, pre-1904)
N. obvallaris sdlg
AM 1904

'Aletha' 2 W-YYP
(J.T. Gray, pre-1949)
Corona cylindrical, lemon yellow, with a band of pink at rim

'Alethea Fairbairn' 2 W-W
(H.A. Brown, pre-1936)
Corona opening with citron yellow at rim, gradually becoming self white

'Aletta' 2 Y-? (a)
(Mrs R.O. Backhouse, pre-1921)

'Alexander'
(Sir A.P.W. Thomas, pre-1915)

'Alexander Moissi' 1 Y-Y
(de Graaff Bros, pre-1928)
Syn. 'Xenophon'

'Alexandre' 8
(pre-1938)

'Alexandria' 2 Y-O
(J.L. Richardson, pre-1941)
'Fortune' × 'Marksman'
Perianth segments yellow; corona somewhat cylindrical, orange. Early

'Alexas' 1 W-Y
Syn. of 'Alexis'

'Alex Fleming' 2 W-O
Syn. of 'Doctor Alex Fleming'

'Alexis' 3 W-W
(W. Backhouse, pre-1869)
Corona opening primrose yellow tinged orange, becoming creamy white. Syn. Leedsii 'Alexis'

'Alexis' 1 W-Y
(Barr & Sons, pre-1923)
Fl. 89 mm wide; perianth segments creamy white, regular, overlapping half; corona sulphur yellow. Mid-season to late. See also 'Alexas'

'Alex Kosma' 2 Y-R
(J.N. Hancock & Co., 1965) Unregistered

'Alex Morrison' 1 Y-Y
(T. Morrison, 1950) T. Morrison, 1960
Fl. rich yellow; perianth segments broad, smooth; corona rim flanged

'Alfons Diepenbrock' 2 W-? (b)
(Konynenburg & Mark, pre-1953)

'Alfonso' 1 Y-Y
Syn. of 'Alphonso'

'Alfonso' 2 Y-O
Syn. of 'Aladdin's Lamp'

'Alfred Austin' 9 W-?
(C.L. Adams, pre-1914)

'Alfred Hartley' 1 Y-Y
(G.H. Engleheart, pre-1930)
Fl. 92 mm wide; perianth segments broadly ovate, blunt or squarish at apex, slightly mucronate, bright deep lemon yellow, spreading or a little inflexed, overlapping one-third to a half; the inner segments more narrowly ovate, more strongly inflexed, with margins slightly wavy; corona cylindrical, a little darker than the perianth, with mouth expanded and frilled, rim very deeply crenate, with margins flanged. Mid-season to late. AM(e)(c) 1930

'Alfred Nobel' 2
(G. Lubbe & Son) G. Lubbe & Son, 1955
AM(Haarlem) 1954

'Alfred Noges' 2 W-? (b)
(J.W.A. Lefeber, pre-1945)

'Alfred Parsons' 1 W-Y
(E. Leeds, pre-1877)
Perianth creamy white; corona rich yellow. Dwarf. Syn. Pseudonarcissus Bicolor 'Alfred Parsons'

'Alfresco' 2 W-WWY
(D.S. Bell, 1962) D.S. Bell, 1975
'Papanui Queen' × 'Green Island'
Fl. 106 mm wide; corona almost disc-shaped, white, with a narrow band of yellow at rim, deeply frilled. Resembles 'Green Island' but with a shallower corona and deeper frill. Syn. 'Enid Blyton'

'Alfriston' 2 Y-R
(D.S. Bell) D.S. Bell, 1982
'Checkmate' × 'Falstaff'
Fl. 98 mm wide; perianth segments deep yellow; corona long, red. Resembles 'Checkmate' but with a longer corona. Mid-season

'Algarve' 2 W-GPP
(T. Bloomer) Rathowen Daffodils, 1984
'Simile' × 'Polonaise'; sdlg no. 361
Perianth segments very broadly ovate, truncate, pure white, spreading, regular, overlapping half; the inner segments more narrowly ovate; corona funnel-shaped, lightly ribbed, deep pink, with green at base, mouth lightly frilled

'Algeciras' 3 W-O
(J.L. Richardson) J.L. Richardson, 1956
'Mahmoud' × 'Khartum'
Fl. 77 mm wide; perianth segments very broad, rounded at apex and prominently mucronate, creamy white, slightly reflexed, smooth, overlapping half; the inner segments narrower, ovate, sometimes truncate, only slightly mucronate; corona almost disc-shaped, ribbed, orange, mouth straight and frilled, with lobes sometimes overlapping. AM(e) 1956

algericus = *N. bertolonii*.

'Algernon Livenburg' 9 W-?
(van Zonneveld Bros & Philippo, pre-1931)

'Algernon Swinburne' 9 W-?
(pre-1914)

'Algiers' 3 W-O
(J.L. Richardson, pre-1938)

'Forfar' self pollinated
Perianth segments pure white, slightly incurved; corona very shallow bowl-shaped, bright orange

'Algiers de Waal' 8 W-Y
(pre-1807)

N. algirus Pomel = *N. bertolonii*

'Algitha' 9 W-?
(A.M. Wilson, pre-1914)

'Algonquin' 2 W-W
(E.C. Powell, pre-1946)

'Algor' 2 W-W
(A.M. Wilson, pre-1944)

'Alhambra' 1 Y-Y
(Konynenburg & Mark, pre-1953)

'Alhena' 1 W-? (b)
(R.A. van der Schoot, pre-1930)

'Alicante' 2 W-O
(G.L. Wilson, pre-1954)
'Pierrot' × 'Athlone'
Fl. 111 mm wide; perianth segments white, shading to near brilliant yellow 8A at base, slightly incurving, overlapping; corona ribbed, near strong orange 25A, with streaks of orange-yellow (near 21A) more frequent on the outside, mouth slightly expanded, rim crenate

'Alice' 5
(pre-1913)

'Alice Barr' 3 Y-Y
(W. Backhouse, pre-1869)
Perianth pale primrose yellow; corona expanded, yellow, stained orange, frilled. Syn. Burbidgei 'Alice Barr'

'Alice Knights' 1 W-W
(Barr & Sons, pre-1903)
'Madame de Graaff' × *N. triandrus* subsp. *pallidulus*
Fl. white; perianth segments narrow, slender, acute, somewhat ribbed, with margins incurving, overlapping about one-fifth; corona broad, angled, of a creamier tone than the perianth, mouth expanded, rim broadly recurved and boldly crenate. Early. AM 1905, AM(p) 1915

'Alice Maxwell' 2 W-? (b)
(D.H.L. Corrigan, pre-1949)

'Alice Meyer' 2 W-? (b)
(H.R. Meyer) Hon. Mrs B.B.Ponsonby, 1956

'Alice's Pink' 2 W-P

(Carncairn Daffodils, 1964) Carncairn Daffodils, 1978
Sdlg no. 83X
Fl. 80 mm wide; perianth segments greenish white (155A); corona deep salmon pink (29A), slightly frilled. Late

'Alicia' 2 W-YYW
(Barr & Sons, pre-1922)
Corona large, soft primrose yellow, with creamy white at rim, and rim flanged

'Alicydon' 1 W-W
Syn. of 'Alycidon'

'Alida' 1 Y-Y
(de Graaff Bros, pre-1896)
Perianth segments soft canary yellow, somewhat twisted; corona large, bright yellow

'Alight' 3 Y-O
(P.D. Williams, pre-1933)
Sdlg no. 496
Fl. 70 mm wide; perianth segments broadly ovate or somewhat oblong, blunt or truncate, pale yellow 11D, tinged orange at base, with white mucro, reflexed, overlapping one-third; the inner segments less strongly inflexed, with margins wavy; corona cup-shaped, smooth, orange (28A), mouth only slightly expanded, even, with rim deeply notched. *HC(g) 1952

'Alimony' 3 W-W
(Jackson's Daffodils) Jackson's Daffodils, 1986
'Sea Dream' × sdlg 172/73; sdlg no. 272/78
Fl. greenish white (155A); perianth segments very broadly ovate, blunt, mucronate, spreading, overlapping half; the inner segments only a little narrower, very slightly truncate, somewhat ribbed; corona shallow bowl-shaped, ribbed and heavily frilled. Late

'Aline Skelton' 1 W-W
(pre-1914)

'Alinga' 4 W-Y
(H.G. Cross) H.G. Cross, 1984
'Rhana' × 'Kimellen'; sdlg no. 127-5
Perianth and other petaloid segments greenish white 157D; corona segments closely interspersed among the petaloid segments, light greenish yellow 6D, some with rim more noticeably flanged than others. Late

'Alinta' 3 W-YYO
(H.G. Cross) H.G. Cross, 1984
'Placid' × 'Ariston'; sdlg no. 76-5
Perianth segments very broad, rounded, yellowish white 155D; corona vivid yellow 9A, with vivid orange 28B at rim, and rim tightly frilled. Mid-season

'Alison' 3 W-W
(A.M. Wilson, pre-1931)
'Nelly' hybrid

'Alison' 9 W-GYY
(O.D. Knight) O.D. Knight, 1983
'Cantabile' × 'Portrush'

'Alison' 2 W-P
(J.N. Hancock & Co., c.1984) Unregistered

'Alison Blatch' 2 W-W
(G.L. Wilson, pre-1954)
'Niphetos' × 'Courage'
Corona opening primrose yellow, maturing to pure white

'Alison Johnstone' 2 W-W
(G.H. Johnstone, pre-1941)
'Silver Coin' hybrid
2n=28

'Alison MacDonald' 3 W-GYO
(D.C. MacArthur) D.C. MacArthur, 1989
Rathowen 2 W-GOO sdlg × MacArthur 2 W-GYY sdlg; sdlg no. EV85/29
Fl. 117 mm wide; perianth segments broad, greenish white 155C, overlapping; corona disc-shaped, pale yellow 8D, with very pale green 192B at base and strong orange 169D at rim. Tall. Late

'Alison Wilson' 1 W-? (b)
(A.C. McKillop) A.C. McKillop, 1955

'Alister Clark' 2 Y-Y
(West & Fell, pre-1935)
Fl. pale sulphur yellow; corona rim slightly rolled and regularly dentate. See also 'Alister Clarke'

'Alister Clarke' 2 Y-Y
Syn. of 'Alister Clark'

'Alister Nash' 2 W-?
(Alister Clark) J. Sharp, 1960

'Alitra' 2 W-? (b)
(D.J. Cooper) D.J. Cooper, 1956

'Aljan' 2 Y-? (a)
(J.A. Morris) J.A. Morris, 1955

'Al Johnson' 3 W-? (b)
(J.W.A. Lefeber, pre-1941)

'Alkemade' 2 W-? (b)
(J.A. van der Zwet & Sons, pre-1944)
AM(Haarlem) 1944

'Alkira' 2 Y-Y
(H.G. Cross) H.G. Cross, 1984

'Olympic Gold' × 'Camelot'; sdlg no. 79-6
Fl. mid-yellow; perianth segments very broad; corona slender, with rim ruffled. Mid-season

'Alkmaar' Y-Y
Syn. of 'Marigold'

'Alkoomi' 2 Y-O
(A.O. Roblin, 1945)
'Lilian Murdoch' × 'Cheerio'

'Allafrill' 2 W-P
(G.E. Mitsch) R. Havens, 1980
Fl. 110 mm wide; perianth segments milk white; corona reddish pink, much frilled. Mid-season

'Allalin' 1 W-W
(D. Blanchard, pre-1949)

'Allan-a-Dale' 9 W-YYR
(F.H. Chapman, pre-1914)
Perianth segments broadly ovate; corona pale yellow, with a narrow band of red at rim. See also 'Allen-a-Dale'

'Allanah' 1 W-W
Syn. of 'Joyce MacDonald'

'Allara' 1 W-YPP
(C.E. Radcliff, 1944) J.M.Radcliff, 1956
'Princess Betty' × 'Dawnglow'

'Allard Pierson' 8 W-R
(A. Vis, pre-1939)
AM(Haarlem) 1939, EFA(Haarlem) 1941

'Allawah' 2 W-?
(W.M. Spry, pre-1975) Unregistered
'Margerie' × Ronalds sdlg
Corona green and orange. Late

'All Bright' 2 W-? (b)
(P.L.A. Pouw, pre-1939)
AM(Haarlem) 1939

'Allegheny' 1 W-? (b)
(Oregon Bulb Farms, pre-1951)
'Matlock' × 'Fireguard'

'Allegiance' 2 Y-O
(F.E. Board) F.E. Board, 1965
'Matlock' × 'Fireguard'

'Allegro' 2 Y-YYO
(P. van Deursen, 1943)
Fl. yellow; corona with deep orange at rim.
AM(Haarlem) 1942

'Allen-a-Dale' 9 W-YYR
Syn. of 'Allan-a-Dale'

'Allendale' 3 Y-? (a)
(de Graaff Bros, pre-1927)
Syn. 'Cassiopeia'

'Allendale' 2 W-W
(E.W. Philpott)

'Allen Raine' 9 W-?
(G.H. Engleheart, pre-1913)

'Allen's Beauty' 1 W-Y
(Pyrenean origin)
Selection by J.Allen (c.1890) from wild-collected *N. pseudonarcissus*
Corona funnel-shaped. Dwarf. Very early. Syn. 'Beauty'. AM 1901

'Alley Inn' 4 W-P
(Brian S.Duncan, 1985) Brian S.Duncan, 1995
'Pink Paradise' × sdlg 406 ('Polonaise' × ['Interim' × 'Rose Caprice']); sdlg no. 1026
Fl. 102 mm wide; perianth and other petaloid segments pure white; the outer whorl forming a double triangle, broad and of stiff substance; corona segments regularly interspersed, deep raspberry to watermelon pink. Mid-season to late

'Alleyne' 1 W-W
(D.V. West, pre-1923)
Fl. pure white; corona frilled

'Alley' 1 W-Y
(Jackson's Daffodils) Jackson's Daffodils, 1996
'Hang-five' × sdlg 135/78; sdlg no. 128/89
Fl. 102 mm wide; perianth segments broadly ovate, greenish white (155A); the inner segments more narrowly ovate; corona flared, vivid yellow 9A, frilled. Early

'All Fours' 2 W-? (b)
(G.H. Johnstone, pre-1949)

'All Glory' 1 W-Y
(G.A. Uit den Boogaard, pre-1951)
Corona soft yellow. AM(Haarlem) 1952

'All Gold' 1 Y-Y
(The Brodie of Brodie, pre-1929)

'Alliance' 2 W-Y
(C.E. Radcliff, 1939)

'Alliance' 1 Y-Y
(J.W.A. van der Wereld) J.W.A. van der Wereld, 1983
Fl. white; perianth segments reflexed; corona smooth

'Alliance' 6 Y-Y
Syn. of 'The Alliance'

'Alliance Party' 6 Y-Y
Syn. of 'The Alliance'

'Allison Cayley' 2 W-W
(L.P. Dettman) L.P. Dettman, 1978
'Tablecloth' × 'Arctic Prince'; sdlg no. 17/70
Fl. 92 mm wide; perianth segments greenish white (155A); corona opening lemon, becoming greenish white (150D). Mid-season

'All Round' 11a W-Y
(J. Gerritsen & Son, 1968) J. Gerritsen & Son, 1980
'Sancerre' hybrid
Fl. 110 mm wide; perianth segments ivory white; corona segments greenish yellow (4D), with a darker tone at rim. Mid-season. Resembles a more robust 'Mistral'

'All the Best' 7 Y-GYO
(W.H. Roesé) W.H. Roesé, 1985
'Ceylon' × *N. jonquilla*; sdlg no. R701
Perianth segments becoming rich yellow at maturity; corona shallow, yellow, tinged green on opening, becoming green at base, with yellowish orange at rim. Very early

'Alltruda' 9 W-?
Syn. of 'Altruda'

'Alltrude' 9 W-?
Syn. of 'Altruda'

'Allumette' 8 Y-Y
(pre-1798)
Fl. sulphur yellow

'Allunga' 2 Y-Y
(S.J. Bisdee) S.J. Bisdee, 1956
Sdlg 110/46 × 'Osella'

'Allure' 2 W-? (b)
(L. van Leeuwen & Son, pre-1933)

'Allurement' 2 W-P
(G.E. Mitsch) G.E. Mitsch, 1959
'Glenshane' × 'Mabel Taylor'; sdlg no. AP3/1
Fl. rounded; perianth segments broad, overlapping half; corona widely flared, opening with yellow at base, soon becoming rich salmon pink, frilled. Mid-season. 2n=28

'Alluvial' 1 Y-Y
(A.F. Calvert, pre-1934)

'Alma' 1 Y-Y
(G.H. Engleheart, pre-1900)
'Maximus' hybrid
Fl. 114 mm wide, soft canary yellow; perianth segments twisted; corona broad, with mouth widely expanded, rim flanged. Early. AM 1900

'Alma' 1 W-W
Syn. of 'Alma French'

'Alma French' 1 W-W
(R.H.Glover, pre-1989) Unregistered
'Abebe' × 'Lady Slim'
Syn. 'Alma'

'Alma Glück' 2 W-O
(J.W.A. Lefeber) J.W.A. Lefeber, 1960
Fl. 95 mm wide; corona rich orange. Mid-season

'Almagra' 3 W-? (b)
(N.Y. Lower, pre-1916)

'Almanzor' 2 W-? (b)
(R.H. Bath, pre-1929)

'Almara' 2 W-? (b)
(R. Hyde) R. Hyde, 1955

'Almaranthe' 2 Y-? (a)
(F.H. Chapman, pre-1930)

'Almee' 1 W-W
(van Zonneveld Bros & Philippo, pre-1931)

'Almida'
(?T. Buncombe, pre-1914)

'Almira' 9 W-YYR
(pre-1899)
?Hybrid between 'Ornatus' and *N. radiiflorus* var. *exertus*
Fl. rounded; perianth segments very broad, blunt or shallowly truncate, slightly mucronate, pure white, spreading or a little reflexed, with margins sometimes recurved at base, overlapping one-third to a half or sometimes only at mid-point; the inner segments not noticeably mucronate, with margins more often and more strongly recurved; corona disc-shaped, very closely ribbed, deep yellow, with a narrow band of deep orange-red at rim. Syn. 'King Edward VII', 'King Edward'

'Almoner' 2 Y-R
(P.D. Williams, pre-1939)
Fl. rounded; perianth segments bright yellow, overlapping; corona intense red. Late

'Almora' 2 Y-? (a)
(Mrs R.O. Backhouse, pre-1921)

'Alnilam' 2 W-O
(D.N.Y. Olson, 1967) D.N.Y. Olson, 1987
'Monaco' × 'Ivo Fell'; sdlg no. 19/1
Fl. 94 mm wide; perianth segments opening buff, in two days becoming pure white; corona deep reddish orange. Mid-season. Resembles an 'Arbar' with more orange in the corona

'Aloha' 3 W-? (b)
(Oregon Bulb Farms, pre-1950)

'Aloisis' 1 Y-Y
(J.W. Barr, pre-1930)

'Aloma' 1 W-? (b)
(J.W. Barr, pre-1930)

'Alonnah' 3 W-O
(S.J. Bisdee, 1945)
'Jean Hood' × 'Salvator Rosa'

'Alope' 5 Y-Y
(Barr & Sons, pre-1919)
Perianth segments primrose yellow; corona canary yellow

'Aloquin' 2 W-Y
(Konynenburg & Mark, pre-1953)
'Daisy Schäffer' × 'Fortune'

N. × *aloysii-villarii* Fernández Casas 13 = *N. alpestris* Pugsley × *N. jacetanus* Fernández Casas

'Alpenrose' 2 W-P
(S.J. Bisdee, 1946)
'Birdie' × 'Rosario'

***N. alpestris* Pugsley 13 Section Pseudonarcissus**

'Alpha' 5
(C. Dawson, pre-1905)

'Alpha' 1 Y-Y
(J.W. Jones, pre-1907)

'Alpha' 9 W-YYR
(A.M. Wilson, pre-1915)
Perianth segments very broad, rounded or squarish at apex, mucronate, a little reflexed, plane, overlapping half; the inner segments narrower, spreading, with margins wavy; corona disc-shaped, closely ribbed, pale yellow with a narrow band of red at rim

'Alpha' 1 Y-Y
(W.A. Grace, pre-1927)
Early

'Alpha Centauri' 3 W-?
(A.Wilson, pre-1902)
'Horsfieldii' × *N. poeticus*
Fl. star-shaped; perianth segments ovate, blunt, prominently mucronate, spreading, separated; the inner segments narrower, less noticeably mucronate, a little twisted; corona narrow cup-shaped, closely ribbed, with mouth straight

'Alpha Mayo' 2 W-W
(R.C.A. Tombleson) R.C.A. Tombleson, 1970

'Hawea' × 'Empress of Ireland'

'Alpha of Donard' 1 Y-Y
(Slieve Donard Nursery Co., pre-1927)
'Magnificence' hybrid
Fl. large; perianth broad, spreading, of strong substance; corona funnel-shaped, with rim widely flanged

'Alphons Czybulki' 1 Y-Y
(pre-1950)
Perianth segments golden yellow; corona orange-yellow

'Alphons Diepenbrock' 1 Y-Y
(Konynenburg & Mark) Konynenburg & Mark, 1960
'Rembrandt' × 'Giant General'
Fl. 120 mm wide; perianth segments brilliant yellow 12B; corona slightly darker in tone (9A). Early

'Alphonso' 9
(pre-1907)

'Alphonso' 1 Y-Y
(G. Lubbe & Son, pre-1931)
AM(Haarlem) 1931. See also 'Alfonso'

'Alpine' 7 W-W
(G.E. Mitsch) G.E. Mitsch, 1959
'St. Mary' × *N. jonquilla*; sdlg no. P81/3
Fl. almost pure white; perianth segments of good substance; corona funnel-shaped. Mid-season

'Alpine Crystal' 2 YYW-W
(G.E. Mitsch and R. & E.Havens, 1977) G.E. Mitsch and R. & E.Havens, 1988
'Siletz' open pollinated; sdlg no. MO18/1
Perianth segments broad, mid-lemon yellow, with clean white at base; corona broad, funnel-shaped, pure white, with rim rolled. Mid-season. Resembles 'Sun 'n' Snow' but with a shorter corona

'Alpine Eagle' 1 W-Y
(J.L. Richardson, pre-1953)
'Spitzbergen' × 'Broughshane'
Perianth segments broad, pure white; corona creamy buff yellow, with rim rolled

'Alpine Express' 1 Y-Y
(J.A.Hunter, 1985) J.A.Hunter, 1995
'Temple Gold' × 'King's Ransom'; sdlg no. 10/80C
Fl. rounded, 113 mm wide, brilliant yellow 12B; perianth segments broadly ovate; corona funnel-shaped, with rim notched and flanged. Mid-season

'Alpine Glow' 2 Y-? (a)
(Cartwright & Goodwin, pre-1916)

'Alpine Glow' 1 W-P
(C.E. Radcliff) G. Zandbergen-Terwegen, 1958

'Dawnglow' × 'Rosario'
Perianth segments ivory white; corona yellowish pink (24D). AM(Haarlem) 1958

'Alpine Glow'
(G.T.C. Pearce)

'Alpine Gold' 6 Y-Y
(J.W. Barr, pre-1930)
Fl. golden yellow; perianth segments reflexed; corona ribbed, with rim rolled

'Alpine King' 1 W-W
(Mrs P.M. Davis, pre-1948)

'Alpine Melody' 1 W-W
(G. Lewis) D.S. Bell, 1955

'Alpine Snow' 3 W-W
(G.H. Engleheart, pre-1913)
Fl. rounded, pure white; perianth segments overlapping; corona cup-shaped, neatly frilled

'Alpine Sunset' ?-P
(Alister Clark, pre-1948)

'Alport' 3 Y-R
(D.B. Milne, pre-1950)

'Alray' 1 Y-Y
(J.A. O'More) J.A. O'More, 1968
'Principal' × 'Goldcourt'
Fl. deep gold; corona frilled

'Alroi' 2 Y-Y
(J.L. Richardson, pre-1926)
Fl. forming a double triangle, soft yellow; perianth segments very broadly ovate, blunt, yellow, with slight white mucro, spreading or a little reflexed, plane, with midrib showing, overlapping half; the inner segments more narrowly ovate, more nearly acute, more prominently mucronate, broad-shouldered at base, a little inflexed; corona cylindrical at base, flared from about mid-point, smooth, darker in tone than the perianth, lightly frilled, with rim slightly flanged and broadly and shallowly crenate. AM(e) 1926

'Alsace' 8 W-YYO
(R. van der Schoot & Son, pre-1907)
Poetaz
Fls large, plus or minus 3 per stem; perianth pure white; corona yellow, with orange at rim. 2n=17

'A.L.Scott' 1 Y-Y
(J.N. Hancock & Co., pre-1949)

'Alseba' 2 W-? (b)
(Konynenburg & Mark, pre-1953)

'Alsirat' 2 W-Y
(J.S. Leitch) J.S. Leitch, 1964
Corona primrose yellow

'Al Smith' 1 Y-Y
(G. Haver, pre-1933)

'Alster' 2 W-? (b)
(Mrs R.O. Backhouse, pre-1921)

'Alston' 2 W-P
(Brian S.Duncan) Brian S.Duncan, 1997
'Gracious Lady' × 'Dailmanach'; sdlg no. 1512
Fl. 130 mm wide; perianth segments broadly ovate, slightly reflexed; corona funnel-shaped, deep coral pink, a little paler towards mouth, with rim slightly dentate. Tall. Mid-season to late. Sunproof

'Alswitha' 1 Y-Y
(W. Welchman, pre-1908)

'Altair' 2 Y-? (a)
(de Graaff Bros, pre-1952)
AM(Haarlem) 1951

'Altamont' 1 W-W
(C.E. Radcliff, 1938) C.E. Radcliff, 1956
'Beersheba' × 'Paula'
Probably the same as 'Altimont'

'Altar Cup' 2 W-W
(Mrs P.M. Davis, pre-1948)

'Altavady' 3 Y-YYR
(?New Zealand origin, pre-1990) Unregistered

'Althaea' 3 W-? (b)
(C. Dawson, pre-1916)

'Althea' 1 W-W
(D.V. West, pre-1932)
Perianth segments pure white; corona opening creamy white, becoming almost pure white

'Alt Heidelberg' 2 Y-? (a)
(Konynenburg & Mark, pre-1953)

'Alt Heidelberg' 2 W-?
(Konynenburg & Mark) Konynenburg & Mark, 1960
Fl. 110 mm wide

'Althorpe' 1 W-? (b)
(de Graaff Bros, pre-1928)
Syn. 'Demeter'

'Altimont' 1 W-W
(C.E. Radcliff, pre-1942)
Probably the same as 'Altamont'

'Altofts' 3 W-O
(J.T.E. Akers) J.L. Akers, 1991
'Ringleader' × 'Rockall'; sdlg no. JT 35
Fl. 100 mm wide. Late

'Alton' 2 Y-Y
(J.T. Gray, pre-1949)
Perianth segments buttercup yellow; corona deeper in tone, with rim rolled

'Alton' 1 W-Y
(J.A. O'More, 1954) J.A. O'More, 1971
'Sincerity' × 'Lochin'; sdlg no. 73/54
Corona pale lemon yellow

'Altona' 1 W-? (b)
(J.N. Hancock & Co., pre-1950)

'Alton Locke' 9 W-YYO
(G.H. Engleheart, pre-1908)
'Princess Mary' × ? *N. poeticus* var. *recurvus*

'Altruda' 9 W-?
(G. Lubbe & Son, pre-1927)
See also 'Alltruda' and 'Altrude'

'Altrude' 9 W-?
Syn. of 'Altruda'

'Altruist' 3 O-R
(F.E. Board) F.E. Board, 1965
'Kindled' × 'Alport'
Fl. 80-85 mm wide; perianth segments very broadly ovate, blunt, sometimes truncate, with slight white mucro, opening orange, becoming paler orange at maturity (18A), spreading or a little reflexed, concave or with margins inward rolling, smooth, with margins sometimes notched, overlapping half; the inner segments more narrowly ovate, with margins noticeably wavy; corona shallow bowl-shaped, ribbed, maturing from a darker tone to the lighter orange-red (30B or C), mouth straight, wavy, rim serrate. Mid-season. Resembles 'Ambergate'. AM(e) 1975. Div. 2 until 1972

'Altun Ha' 2 Y-W
(A.J.R. Pearson) A.J.R. Pearson, 1987
'Camelot' × 'Daydream'; sdlg no. 81/13/F1
Fl. rounded; perianth segments very broad, with blunt white mucro, opening brilliant to light greenish yellow 5B-C, becoming darker, with white at base, spreading or inflexed, concave, with margins narrowly incurling, of good substance, overlapping half; the inner segments broad-shouldered at base; corona broad funnel-shaped, smooth or lightly ribbed, opening lemon yellow, maturing to white tinged with pale greenish yellow 1D and sometimes touched with brilliant greenish yellow 5B at rim, mouth straight or a little flared, rim shallowly and irregularly notched and lobed. Mid-season to late. Resembles a whiter

'Daydream' with little or no contrasting colour at corona rim. AM(e) 1989, FCC(e) 1993

'Altyre' 3 W-W
(The Brodie of Brodie, c.1945)
'Nelly' hybrid × 'Chinese White'; sdlg no. 36/C/40
Fl. rounded, about 125mm wide, pure white; perianth segments very broad, blunt or squarish at apex, only slightly mucronate, spreading, of great substance, overlapping half; the inner segments narrower, a little inflexed, with margins wavy, square-shouldered at base; corona narrow bowl-shaped, loosely ribbed, frilled. Mid-season

'Aludra' 2 W-? (b)
(Mrs R.O. Backhouse, pre-1921)
Fl. large. Syn. 'Glory of the Morning'

'Alumna' 2 W-YYP
(Murray W. Evans) Murray W. Evans, 1972
'Green Island' × 'Artist's Model'
Fl. 100 mm wide

'Alva' 5
(E.M. Crosfield, pre-1908)

'Alva Edison' 2 W-O
(J.W.A. Lefeber) J.W.A. Lefeber, 1960
Fl. 90 mm wide; corona deep reddish orange. Early

'Alvanley' 1 W-Y
(C.E. Radcliff, pre-1938)
? The same as 'Avanley'

'Alvara' 1 W-? (b)
(J.T. Gray, pre-1951)

'Alvarez' 1 Y-Y
(de Graaff Bros, pre-1897)
Fl. 150 mm wide. Resembles a shorter-stemmed 'Emperor'

'Alverado' 2 W-Y
(pre-1965) Unregistered

'Alverton' 2 Y-GYY
(R.V. Favell, pre-1946)
Sdlg × 'Fortune'

'Alvie' 2 W-PPY
(W.M. Spry, pre-1975) Unregistered
'Canary Bird' hybrid
Corona peach pink, with yellow at rim, frilled. Late

'Alvis' 2 Y-? (a)
(S.C. Gaspar, 1946) R.J. Abernethy, 1957

'Always' 2 W-P
(W.G. Pannill) W.G. Pannill, 1992
('Interim' × pink sdlg) × 'Keepsake'; sdlg no. 77/9 C
Fl. 71 mm wide. Mid-season

'Alwick' 2 Y-? (a)
(P.D. Williams, pre-1933)

'Alwon' 1 Y-Y
(W. Jackson Jr) Jackson's Daffodils, 1980
'Yarley' × 'Otewa'; sdlg no. 45/73
Fl. 105 mm wide. Mid-season

'Alycidon' 1 W-W
(J.L. Richardson, pre-1949)
'Carmel' open pollinated × 'Broughshane'
Fl. milk white; perianth segments very broadly ovate, slightly mucronate, smooth, with margins sometimes incurving at apex, overlapping half; the inner segments more narrowly ovate, a little twisted and slightly reflexed; corona straight-sided, smooth, mouth expanded and neatly frilled, rim reflexed and dentate. See also 'Alicydon'

'Alys' 5 W-W
(G.H. Engleheart, pre-1913)
Fls one or more per stem, pure white, facing down; perianth segments ovate, blunt, slightly mucronate, a little inflexed, with margins wavy, overlapping at base only; the inner segments narrower and more nearly acute; corona short funnel-shaped, ribbed, mouth straight, a little frilled, rim crenate

'Alzetta' 2 W-P
(J.N.Hancock & Co., 1978) Unregistered
'Winter Hope' × Martin sdlg; sdlg no. 40/78H
Perianth segments milk white, overlapping; corona funnel-shaped, with narrow base, pink, mouth expanded, rim dentate. Early

'Amabilis' 3 W-W
(E. Leeds, pre-1877)
Perianth segments long, narrow, acute; corona long, opening primrose yellow, becoming milk white. Syn. Leedsii 'Amabilis'

'Amabilis Argentius' 2 or 3 W-W
(?E. Leeds, pre-1877)
Syn. Leedsii 'Amabilis Argentius'

'Amabilis Nanus' 2 or 3 W-Y
(?E. Leeds, pre-1877)
Corona pale lemon yellow. Syn. Leedsii 'Amabilis Nanus'

'Amadeus' 2 W-R
(G.E.Mitsch, 1984) R. & E.Havens, 1997
'Precedent' × 'Magician'; sdlg no. TT10/3
Fl. rounded, 105 mm wide; perianth segments very broadly ovate; corona cup-shaped, expanded, deep red, frilled. Mid-season

'Amadis' 1 Y-Y
(Barr & Sons, pre-1924)
Perianth segments primrose yellow; corona broad, rich yellow

'Amador' 2 W-R
(J.L. Richardson, pre-1943)
AM(Haarlem) 1942

'Amalgeste' 2
(G.H. Engleheart, pre-1927)

'Amalie' 2 W-Y
(J.S. Leitch) J.S. Leitch, 1957

'Amana' 2 Y-O
(H.A. Brown, 1937) A. Ladson, 1960
Perianth segments yellow; corona bright reddish orange. Early

'Amanda' 3
(J. Mallender, pre-1914)

'Amanda' 2 Y-Y
(W. Jackson Jr, 1970)
('Haka' × 'Letti') × 'Warbin'; sdlg no. 18/70

'Amanda Jane' 2 W-P
(S.P. Haycock) S.P. Haycock, 1985
'Accent' open pollinated; sdlg no. AW-P-1
Mid-season. Resembles 'Accent' but with a brighter pink in the corona

'Amanda Olsen' 2 W-YYW
(L.P. Dettman) L.P. Dettman, 1979
'Cynthia Dettmann' × 'Aircastle'; sdlg no. CO1/79
Fl. 70 mm wide; perianth segments greenish white 155C; corona light yellow 12C, with yellowish white 155B at rim

'Amante' 8 Y-Y
(pre-1798)

'Amapola' 2 W-GYR
(G. Lewis) G. Lewis, 1955

'Amara' 2 W-? (b)
(J.T. Gray, pre-1933)

'Amarantha' 2 Y-? (a)
(de Graaff Bros, pre-1930)
AM(Haarlem) 1930

'Amarella' 3 W-O
(pre-1950)
Perianth segments snow white; corona very shallow, widely expanded, bright orange, frilled

'Amarillus' 8 W-Y
(pre-1807)

'Amarita' 11b W-O/W
(J.W.A. Lefeber) J.W.A. Lefeber, 1960
Fl. 75 mm wide; perianth segments cream white; corona segments with a longitudinal band of reddish orange flanked by white. Resembles 'Silvester'

'Amaroo' 2 Y-R
(A.O. Roblin, 1948)
'Lillian Murdoch' × 'Dunkeld'

'Amary' 2 Y-YYR
(C.O. Fairbairn, pre-1962) Unregistered
Perianth segments broad, bright rich yellow, spreading; corona widely expanded, yellow, with a broad band of cherry red at rim

'Amaryllis' 3 W-? (b)
(de Graaff Bros, pre-1948)

'Amasis' 2 Y-? (a)
(Mrs R.O. Backhouse, pre-1921)

'Amastris' 1 W-Y
(Barr & Sons, pre-1922)
Perianth segments slightly reflexed; corona lemon yellow, mouth expanded and frilled, rim flanged

'Amateur' 3 W-O
(P. van Deursen, pre-1943)
AM(Haarlem) 1943

'Amazon' 3 W-Y
(C. Smith, pre-1904)
Fls often 2 per stem; corona canary yellow

'Ambassador' 1 W-? (b)
(R.H. Bath, pre-1927)

'Ambassador' 2 or 3 W-? b or c
(pre-1938)

'Ambassador' 1 W-W
(J.L. Richardson) J.L. Richardson, 1956
'Spitzbergen' × 'Broughshane'
Fl. pure white; corona rim rolled and dentate

'Ambell' 1 W-Y
(W.A. Watts, pre-1913)
Fl. 98 mm wide; perianth segments white, tinged green

'Amber' 2 W-Y
(G.H. Engleheart, pre-1901)
'Empress' × 'Ornatus'
Fl. star-shaped, of thick substance; perianth segments ovate, blunt, greenish white, a little inflexed, with margins incurling at apex and sometimes recurved in lower half, irregular, overlapping at base only; the inner segments narrower and sometimes twisted; corona long and broad, rich yellow, sometimes

flushed orange-amber, mouth more or less even, with rim obscurely crenate and slightly notched. Late. AM 1901, *HC(c) 1927

'Amber Castle' 2 YYW-WYY
(Mrs H.K. Richardson) Mrs H.K. Richardson, 1976
'Camelot' × 'Daydream'
Fl. 95 mm wide; perianth segments broadly ovate or roundish, light greenish yellow 5C, with tinges of a darker tone (5B), with white mucro, paling to white at base, reflexed, smooth, overlapping; the inner segments more nearly ovate, square-shouldered at base; corona cylindrical or somewhat funnel-shaped, loosely ribbed, brilliant yellow 14C, paler towards base, the rim flushed with a brighter colour (12B), all parts ageing to buff, mouth more strongly ribbed, straight or slightly expanded, frilled, with rim regularly crenate. Mid-season. 2n=28. Resembles a slightly smaller 'Cairngorm' in colouring with the perianth segments blunter at apex. AM(e) 1981. The predominant colour in the corona may be pinkish

'Amber Flash' 2 W-O
(R.V. Flavell, pre-1946)
'Tunis' × 'Saint Just'
Perianth segments pure white; corona opening pale yellow, becoming amber

'Ambergate' 2 O-O
(D.B. Milne, pre-1950)
Sdlg × 'Cornish Fire'
Perianth segments broadly ovate, blunt, yellow orange, with white mucro, spreading, faintly ribbed, with midrib more prominent, a little concave, with margins incurving at apex, overlapping half; the inner segments narrower, acute, less noticeably mucronate; corona short funnel-shaped, broad, ribbed, orange, with mouth straight and even, rim notched. AM(Haarlem) 1961

'Amberglow' 2 Y-Y
(G.E. Mitsch) G.E. Mitsch, 1969
'Lunar Sea' × 'Daydream'; sdlg no. A26/1
Perianth segments bright lemon yellow, plane, overlapping; corona opening whitish, soon becoming rich amber buff. Mid-season

'Amberjack' 2 Y-Y
(G.E. Mitsch) G.E. Mitsch and T.D.Throckmorton, 1968
Sdlg Y02/4 open pollinated
Fl. opening soft lemon yellow; perianth becoming rich buff yellow; corona bowl-shaped, flared, becoming bronze yellow. Mid-season

'Amberley' 2 Y-Y
(Sir F.C. Stern, pre-1944)
'Saint Egwin' × 'Crocus'
Fl. 117 mm wide; perianth segments broadly ovate, blunt, vivid yellow 9B, with slight white mucro,

spreading, smooth, with midrib showing, overlapping one-third; the inner segments more narrowly ovate, somewhat twisted or with margins incurving; corona funnel-shaped, lightly ribbed, slightly darker in tone (12) than the perianth, with mouth straight and 6-lobed, lightly frilled, rim crenate. PC 1947, AM(e) 1949

'Amber Light' 2 W-Y
(J.L. Richardson) Mrs H.K. Richardson, 1967
'Alpine Eagle' × 'Salmon Trout'
Fl. forming a double triangle; perianth segments very broadly ovate, blunt, pure white, spreading, concave at apex, smooth, overlapping half; the inner segments somewhat reflexed, with margins slightly wavy; corona smooth, buff yellow, with mouth expanded, rim rolled, irregularly and deeply crenate. Mid-season. Resembles 'Careysville'

'Amber Rose' 1 W-P
(H.R. Bulman)

'Amber Sea' 11a W-OOY
(Juris Svarcs) Juris Svarcs, 1992
'Orangery' × 'Professor Einstein'; sdlg no. 84-02-01
Fl. 86 mm wide; perianth segments broadly ovate, prominently mucronate, greenish white (155A), spreading, with margins incurving, overlapping one-third to a half; corona deeply split, the six segments opposite and closely overlying the perianth segments, bi-lobed, strong orange 24A, with vivid yellow 9B at rim flecked white, deeply frilled. Mid-season

'Amber Surprise' 9 W-GOO
(Mrs M.S. Yerger) Mrs M.S. Yerger, 1991
'Quetzal' × 'Ace of Diamonds'; sdlg no. 77 G 1
Fl. 54 mm wide; perianth segments deeply overlapping; the inner segments shorter; corona disc-shaped, strong yellow-green 145A at base, with light orange(23B) at mid-zone suffusing the rim of strong orange 24A. Mid-season

'Amber Tips' 2 W-P
(G. Lewis) G. Lewis, 1955

'Ambition' 3 Y-? (a)
(?Sir C.H. Cave, pre-1914)

'Ambition' 2 W-? (b or c)
(Sir C.H. Cave, pre-1928)

'Amble' 1 W-? (b)
(A.H. Ahrens) J.S. Leitch, 1955

'Amboise' 11a Y-O
(J. Gerritsen & Son) J. Gerritsen & Son, 1983
Sdlg × 'Ambergate'
Perianth segments dark yellow; corona segments orange. Mid-season

'Amboseli' 3 Y-YYR
(Brian S. Duncan) Brian S. Duncan, 1990
'Dilemma' × 'Rotarian'; sdlg no. 989
Fl. rounded, 108 mm wide; perianth segments very broadly ovate, rounded at apex, deep lemon yellow, with slight white mucro, spreading, concave at apex, smooth, overlapping half; the inner segments roundish; corona shallow bowl-shaped, ribbed, yellow, with a clearly defined band of deep orange-red at rim, mouth expanded and loosely frilled. Tall. Mid-season to late

'Amboyna' 1 W-Y
(Barr & Sons, pre-1929)
Perianth segments slightly twisted; corona ribbed, canary yellow, rim ruffled

'Ambrin' 2 Y-Y
(W. Jackson Sr, 1939)
'Golden Queen' × 'Chruseos'

'Ambrosia' 2 Y-P
(A.S. Brewster, pre-1950)

'Ambrosine' 2 W-Y
(W.F.M. Copeland, pre-1913)
'Minnie Hume' × 'Van Waveren's Giant'
Fl. 89 mm wide; perianth segments ivory white, deeply overlapping; corona very widely expanded, bright orange-yellow, mouth lightly frilled. Early

'Ambulc' 2 Y-YYO
(Mrs R.O. Backhouse, pre-1921)
Perianth segments sulphur yellow, overlapping; corona lemon yellow, with a broad band of orange at rim, crenate. 2n=28. *AM(g) 1936

'Ambush' 1 W-? (b)
(Sir C.H. Cave, pre-1928)

'Amelia' 7
(?Barr & Sons, pre-1935)

'Amelia' 2 W-P
(Alister Clark, 1947) A. Ladson, 1960

'Amelia Farmer' 1 W-W
(Ken Farmer Nurseries) Ken Farmer Nurseries, 1978
Fl. 105 mm wide. Early

'Amelia Jane' 2 W-P
(J.N. Hancock & Co., 1973) Unregistered
Sdlg no. 19/73H

'Amelita' 2 W-? (b)
(D.J. Cooper) D.J. Cooper, 1957

'Amen Rā' 1 Y-Y
(H.G. Longford, pre-1927)

'Amense' 2 Y-? (a)
(J.T. Gray, pre-1938)

'Ameola' 3 W-? (b)
(Cartwright & Goodwin, pre-1910)

'A Mere Seedling' 1 Y-Y
(J. Pope, pre-1908)

'America' 1 W-? (b)
(pre-1930)

'American Ace' 1 W-W
(Mrs P.M. Davis, pre-1948)

'American Beauty' 1 Y-Y
(J. Gerritsen & Son, pre-1929)
AM(Haarlem) 1929

'American Classic' 2 Y-WYY
(R. & E.Havens) R. & E.Havens, 1997
'Sun Gem' × 'Lemon Lyric'; sdlg no. XH120/1
Fl. 95 mm wide; perianth segments very broadly ovate, bright lemon yellow, spreading, plane, smooth; corona cylindrical, opening self buff yellow, becoming white at base. Late

'American Dream' 1 Y-P
(R. & E. Havens) R. & E. Havens, 1989
'Memento' × 'Lorikeet'; sdlg no. SEH21/5
Fl. 110 mm wide; perianth segments very broadly ovate, truncate, slightly mucronate, deep lemon yellow, spreading, a little concave, with margins inward rolling at apex, smooth, overlapping half; the inner segments a little inflexed; corona funnel-shaped, smooth, pink, mouth a little flared, slightly frilled, with rim crenate. Mid-season

'American Family' 5 YYW-W
(R. & E. Havens) R. & E. Havens, 1994
'Hillstar' × *N. triandrus* var. *concolor*; sdlg no. Z68/1
Fls 2-3 per stem, 65 mm wide; perianth segments acute, soft lemon yellow, with white at base, reflexed; corona becomes white, with mouth flared. Late. Scented

'American Frontier' 2 Y-P
(R. & E. Havens, 1984) R. & E. Havens, 1994
'Top Notch' × 'Quickstep'; sdlg no. TEH119/1
Fl. 95 mm wide, of heavy substance; perianth segments very broadly ovate, deep lemon yellow; the inner segments no narrower; corona bowl-shaped, mid-pink, with mouth a little frilled. Late. Sunproof

'American Girl' 9 W-GYR
(Mrs M.S. Yerger) Mrs M.S. Yerger, 1992
'Hexameter' × 'Lights Out'; sdlg no. 75 M 5
Fl. 62 mm wide; perianth segments plane; corona very shallow bowl-shaped, greenish yellow (154B), with strong yellow-green 145A at base and red (35A) at

rim. Late. Scented

'American Glory' 1 Y-Y
(G. Lubbe & Son, pre-1929)

'American Heritage' 1 YYW-P
(R. & E. Havens, 1983) R. & E. Havens, 1993
'Memento' × 'Lorikeet'; sdlg no. SEH21/2
Fl. 110 mm wide; perianth segments broadly ovate, slightly mucronate, intense lemon yellow, touched white at base, spreading, plane, with margins incurling at apex, smooth, overlapping half; the inner segments a little inflexed, square-shouldered at base; corona funnel-shaped, smoothly and very broadly ribbed, pink, mouth very slightly flared, split in places and overlapping, with rim notched. Mid-season. Sunproof. Resembles 'American Shores' but with the corona less flared and of a deeper colour

'American Melody' 9 W-GOO
(Mrs M.S. Yerger) Mrs M.S. Yerger, 1993
'Dulcimer' open pollinated; sdlg no. 76 A 22
Fl. forming a double triangle, 48 mm wide; perianth segments deeply overlapping; corona cup-shaped, bright orange (a suffusion of 15B and 31B), with strong yellow-green 144A at base. Mid-season. Strongly scented

'American Robin' 6 Y-O
(John R.Reed) John R.Reed, 1997
'Cock Robin' open pollinated; sdlg no. 83-96-1
Fl. forming a double triangle, 78 mm wide; perianth segments deep yellow, reflexed; the inner segments narrower; corona cup-shaped, mid-orange. Dwarf. Early

'American Shores' 1 Y-P
(R. & E. Havens) R. & E. Havens, 1992
'Memento' × 'Lorikeet; sdlg no. SEH21/20
Fl. forming a double triangle, 90 mm wide; perianth segments broadly ovate, blunt, only very slightly mucronate, clear pale lemon yellow, spreading, a little concave, very smooth, overlapping half; the inner segments somewhat truncate, square-shouldered at base, slightly inflexed; corona funnel-shaped, smooth, pink, mouth expanded and frilled, split in places and overlapping, with rim crenate. Mid-season. Sunproof

'American Songbird' 7 Y-GOO
(Eileen E. Frey, 1976) J. & E. Frey, 1993
'Bantam' × *N. assoanus*; sdlg no. LEE1/5
Fls several per stem, 60 mm wide; perianth segments very broadly ovate, rounded at apex, slightly mucronate, slightly reflexed, overlapping half or more; the inner segments narrower, more nearly spreading; corona bowl-shaped, soft orange, with green at base and bright orange at rim, a little frilled. Dwarf. Very late

'American Triumph' 9 W-GYR
(Mrs M.S. Yerger) Mrs M.S. Yerger, 1992
'Red Rim' × 'Lights Out'; sdlg no. 75 K 1
Corona almost disc-shaped, light yellow 14D, with moderate yellow-green 146D at base and orange-red (33A) at rim. Late

'American Way' 9 W-GGR
(Mrs M.S. Yerger) Mrs M.S. Yerger, 1993
'Quetzal' × 'Ace of Diamonds'; sdlg no. 77 G 9
Fl. 48 mm wide; perianth segments disc-shaped, light yellow-green 145C, with strong yellow-green 145A at base and orange-red (30A) at rim, mouth incurved. Mid-season

'America's Cup' 2 W-W
(Koanga Daffodils) Koanga Daffodils, 1995
'Makapu' × O'More sdlg 12/72 ('Petsamo' × 'Glenshesk'); sdlg no. 20-86
Fl. 115 mm wide; perianth segments very broad; corona broad funnel-shaped, of a purer white than the perianth, rim slightly lobed. Mid-season

'Amethyst' 5
(W.F.M. Copeland, pre-1908)

'Amiable' 3 Y-O
(P. van Deursen, pre-1938)
Perianth segments smooth; corona shallow, widely expanded. AM(Haarlem) 1938. Received AM(Haarlem) 1938 as 'Amie'; see also 'Aimable'

'Amidionette' 3 W-O
Syn. of 'Amidonette'?

'Amidonette' 4
(de Graaff-Gerharda, pre-1936)

'Amidonette' 3 W-? (b)
(J.W.A. Lefeber, pre-1938)
See also 'Amidionette'?

'Amie' 3 Y-O
Syn. of 'Amiable'

'Amiens' 1 Y-GOO
(J. Gerritsen & Son, 1973) J. Gerritsen & Son, 1985
'Alpine Glow' hybrid
Perianth segments pale greenish yellow (4D); corona light orange 29B, with yellowish green darkening in tone towards base. Mid-season. Resembles a more robust 'Alpine Glow'

'Amigo' 2 W-P
(C.E. Radcliff, 1942) J.M.Radcliff, 1956
'Carmoa' × 'Mrs R.O. Backhouse'

'Aminta' 2 W-R
(S.J. Bisdee) S.J. Bisdee, 1956
'White Sentinel' × 'Khartum'

'Amir' 2 Y-O
(Mrs R.O. Backhouse, pre-1921)
Early

'Amity' 2 W-P
(R.V. Favell, pre-1939)
'Mavis' × 'Tunis'
Corona expanded, tinged pink

'Ammon' 1 W-W
(W. Jackson Jr, 1951) W. Jackson Jr, 1966
'Whitemark' × 'Ardclinis'

'Amokura' 3 Y-? (a)
(J.T. Gray, pre-1933)

'Amor' 1 W-? (b)
(Barr & Sons, pre-1923)

'Amor' 3 W-YYO
(W.F. Leenen, 1957) W.F. Leenen, 1971
'Flower Record' hybrid
Fl. 130 mm wide; perianth segments ivory white; corona lemon yellow, with orange at rim. Early to mid-season. 2n=28

'Amora' 4 W-P
(H.G. Cross, 1974) H.G. Cross, 1984
Sdlg no. 69-4
Perianth and other petaloid segments creamy white; corona segments opening apricot yellow, becoming buff pink, frilled, with rim crenate

'Amore' 3 W-Y
(W. Backhouse, pre-1869)
Corona lemon yellow, tinged orange. Syn. Barrii Albus 'Amore'. Was "absorbed" into 'John Bain'

'Amoret' 3 W-Y
(W. Backhouse, pre-1869)
Perianth segments large, pure white; corona citron yellow. Syn. Burbidgei 'Amoret'. Was "absorbed" into 'John Bain'

'Amorica' 1 Y-Y
(B. Rowlands, pre-1938)

'Amory' 3 W-? (b)
(A.H. Ahrens) J.S. Leitch, 1955

'Amourette' 2 W-YYO
(de Graaff Bros, pre-1938)
Perianth segments sulphur white, sprinkled with silver white; corona yellow, shading to reddish orange at rim

'Amoy' 7 Y-Y
(A.J. Bliss, pre-1931)
'Monarch' × *N. jonquilla*; sdlg no. K69(2)
Fl. 67 mm wide; perianth segments bright lemon yellow, separated; corona cylindrical, bright buttercup yellow. Mid-season to late. Syn. 'Sentinel'.
*AM(g) 1931

'Ampere' 2 Y-O
(J.N. Hancock & Co., 1966) Unregistered

'Amphion' 8 Y-O
(pre-1798)
Perianth segments citron yellow; corona orange

'Amphion' 4 Y-YYO
(W.F.M. Copeland, pre-1909)
Perianth segments in 3-4 whorls, creamy lemon yellow; corona segments bright lemon yellow with reddish orange at rim, frilled

'Amphora' 2 W-P
(A.O. Roblin, 1957) Unregistered
Sdlg × 'Karanja'

'Amplicorona' 1 Y-Y
(pre-1884)
Perianth segments pale sulphur; corona yellow. Syn. Pseudonarcissus Lobularis 'Amplicorona'

N. amplus Salisbury = *N.* × *incomparabilis*

'Ampol' 2 Y-YYO
(J.N. Hancock & Co., 1968) Unregistered

'Amrita' 2 Y-? (a)
(Warnaar & Co., pre-1939)

'Amritsar' 1 W-Y
(W.A. Grace, pre-1927)

'Amstel' 4 W-YPP
(Brian S. Duncan) Brian S. Duncan, 1988
'Pink Pageant' × 'Blushing Maiden'; sdlg no. 861
Mid-season. Corona varying from YPP to YYP according to season

'Amsterdam' 2 W-? (b)
(de Graaff Bros, pre-1908)

'Amsterdam' 1 W-Y
(W.F. Leenen) W.F. Leenen, 1970
Perianth segments yellowish white; corona vivid yellow 9A. Early

'Amulet' 3 W-? (b)
(Cartwright & Goodwin, pre-1910)

'Amulet' 2 W-W
(pre-1923)
Fl. milk white; perianth segments somewhat ribbed; corona opening pale primrose yellow, expanded

'Amulette' 2 W-GOO

(D.S. Bell) D.S. Bell, 1960
Fl. 114 mm wide; perianth segments broad, pure white; corona shallow, very wide, orange, shaded amber, with green at base. Late. Resembles 'Papanui Queen'

'Amusement' 4 W-YYO
(J.L. Richardson) C.A. van Paridon, 1962
'Falaise' hybrid
Perianth segments creamy white; corona with outer segments vivid yellow 9A, with pure orange at rim, and with innermost segments solid orange. Resembles 'Eddy Canzony'. AM(Haarlem) 1961

'Amusing' 2 W-Y
(C.E. Radcliff, 1933) J.M.Radcliff, 1956
'Alexus' × sdlg

'Amwell Lady' 6 Y-Y
(Rosewarne EHS) C.M. van Hage, 1986
N. cyclamineus × 'Saint Keverne'; sdlg no. 65/65/2
Fl. yellow. Early

'Amy' 3 W-Y
(W. Backhouse, pre-1869)
Perianth segments long, narrow, acute, opening primrose yellow, becoming sulphur white; corona yellow. Syn. Barrii Sulphureus 'Amy', Barrii Sulphureus 'Stellatus'. ?The same as 'Stellatus Sulphureus'. Was "absorbed" into 'Pericles'

'Amy' 9 W-?
(W. Poupart, pre-1914)

'Amy' 2 W-P
(J.N. Hancock & Co., 1976) Unregistered

'Amyar' 3 W-?
Syn. of 'Amyas'

'Amyas' 3 W-? (b)
(R.O. Backhouse, pre-1938)
See also 'Amyar'

'Amyas Lee'
Syn. of 'Amyas Leigh'

'Amyas Leigh'
(G.H. Engleheart, pre-1908)
See also 'Amyas Lee'

'Amy Belle' 2 Y-? (a)
(Konynenburg & Mark, pre-1953)

'Amy Belle' 2 W-?
(Konynenburg & Mark) Konynenburg & Mark, 1960
Fl. 90 mm wide

'Amy Eleanor Mack' 2 W-Y

(H. Selkirk, pre-1921)

'Amy Johnson' 3 W-? (b)
(P. van Deursen, pre-1930)

'Amy Lemy' 2 or 3 W-? (b or c)
(pre-1913)

'Amynta' 1 W-W
(Barr & Sons, pre-1922)
Fl. white; perianth segments incurving; corona slender, opening pale primrose yellow

'Amy Pierson' 2 W-O
(D.S. Bell) D.S. Bell, 1960
Fl. 114 mm wide; corona reddish orange. Resembles 'Signal Light' but with a bowl-shaped corona

'Anacapri' 3 W-YYO
(D.S. Bell) D.S. Bell, 1960
Fl. rounded, 114 mm wide; perianth segments broad, snow white, of firm substance, overlapping half; corona spreading, apricot yellow at base, shading to reddish orange at rim, with mouth frilled. Midseason. 2n=28. Resembles a larger-flowered 'Corofin'

'Anaconda' 2 Y-? (a)
(Mrs R.O. Backhouse, pre-1921)

'Anacreon' 9 W-GYR
(G.H. Engleheart, pre-1916)
Perianth segments rounded, overlapping; corona saffron yellow, with olive green at base and crimson at rim. Late

'Anadyomene' 2 W-? (b)
(S.A. Morrish, pre-1950)

'Anak' 8 Y-Y
(pre-1927)
Fls 4-5 per stem, clear lemon

'Anak' 1 Y-Y
(Mrs R.S. Cobley, pre-1932)

'Anakim' 1 W-Y
(G.E. Mitsch, pre-1952)
'Ada Finch' × 'Kandahar'; sdlg no. H3/1
Fl. large; corona light yellow, with mouth flared. Midseason

'Anastasia' 1 Y-Y
(C. Dawson, pre-1927)
Perianth segments rich lemon yellow, slightly ribbed, overlapping; corona dark golden yellow, with rim flanged and deeply notched

'Anat' 2 Y-Y
(W. Jackson Jr) W. Jackson Jr, 1966
'Jobi' × sdlg 126/55; sdlg no. 155/61
?Syn. of 'Rodinga'

'Anatolia' 2 YYW-Y
(G.E.Mitsch, 1979) R. & E.Havens, 1995
'Camelot' × 'Symphonette'; sdlg no. 2019/5
Fl. 115 mm wide, smooth and of heavy substance; perianth segments broadly ovate, clear lemon yellow, with white at base, spreading, plane; corona straight-sided, a little darker in tone than the perianth, mouth flared. Late

'Anax'
Unregistered
Pollen parent of 'Samson'

'Anceps' 1 Y-Y
(pre-1883)
Perianth segments sulphur yellow; corona golden yellow. Syn. Pseudonarcissus Bicolor 'Anceps'

N. anceps de Candolle = *N. papyraceus*

'Ancestor' 3 W-YYO
(G.E.Mitsch, 1982) R. & E.Havens, 1997
'Silken Sails' × 'Merlin'; sdlg no. 2R32/20
Fl. 105 mm wide; perianth segments very broadly ovate, pure white, spreading, plane, of heavy substance; corona disc-shaped, pale yellow, with a narrow band of mid-orange at rim and the rim crenate. Late. Sunproof

'Anchorite' 3 W-GYY
(E.M. Crosfield, pre-1910)
Perianth segments spreading or slightly inflexed; corona shallow, widely expanded, soft lemon yellow, with dark green at base, rim frilled. AM(e) 1918

'Ancona' 2 W-? (b)
(Mrs R.O. Backhouse, pre-1921)

'Ancona' 2 W-O
(J.L. Richardson) J.L. Richardson, 1961
'Kilworth' × 'Arbar'
Fl. 105 mm wide; corona reddish orange, with rim dentate and slightly flanged. Mid-season

'Ancore' 2 Y-? (a)
(Konynenburg & Mark, pre-1953)

'Ancore' 2 Y-O
(Konynenburg & Mark) Konynenburg & Mark, 1960
'Aranjuez' × 'Rustom Pasha'
Fl. 105 mm wide; perianth segments brilliant greenish yellow 4A; corona orange (28A). Late

'Andalusia' 6 Y-O
(C.F. Coleman, 1945) C.F. Coleman, 1961
Fl. 95 mm wide; perianth segments ovate, truncate, brilliant greenish yellow 6B-C, reflexed, plane, with margins a little incurving, overlapping one-third; the inner segments only slightly narrower, with margins more markedly inward rolling, sometimes twisted; corona cup-shaped, ribbed, strong orange 25B, mouth straight and frilled, rim crenate. Early. AM(e) 1968, FCC(e) 1969

'Andante' 2 W-? (b or c)
(W.B. Cranfield, pre-1927)

'Andante' 1 W-Y
(J.N. Hancock & Co., 1945) J.N. Hancock & Co., 1965
Perianth segments very broad; corona lemon yellow, with rim widely rolled. Late. Resembles a more refined 'Kanchenjunga'

'Anderida' 1 W-W
(N.A. Burr) N.A. Burr, 1994
'Broomhill' × 'White Star'; sdlg no. 4.21.80
Fl. 115 mm wide; perianth segments broadly ovate, blunt, obscurely mucronate, pure white, slightly reflexed, concave, overlapping half; the inner segments sharply narrowing to base, with margins incurving or wavy towards apex; corona cylindrical, smoothly 6-angled, ivory white, mouth ribbed, straight or very slightly flared, a little wavy, with rim minutely and closely notched. Mid-season

'Andes' 1 W-W
(J.L. Richardson, pre-1953)
'Ardclinis' × 'Broughshane'
Fl 108 mm wide; perianth segments almost triangular in appearance, slightly mucronate, overlapping one-third; the inner segments more narrowly ovate and very slightly twisted; corona mouth expanded, with rim reflexed and irregularly notched. *AM(g) 1966

'Andorra' 2 Y-? (a)
(F. Rijnveld & Sons, pre-1950)
AM(Haarlem) 1950

N. × *andorranus* Fernández Casas 13 = *N. nobilis* (Haworth) Schultes f. × *N. poeticus* Linnaeus var. *poeticus*

'Andover' 1 W-Y
(C.E. Radcliff, 1943) J.M.Radcliff, 1956
Sdlg × 'Bonython'

'André Duran' 2 Y-Y
(Konynenburg & Mark) Konynenburg & Mark, 1960
Fl. 105 mm wide; perianth segments brilliant yellow 8A; corona darker in tone (13A). Early

'Andrew Marvell' 9 W-GYR
(J.M. de Navarro, pre-1950)
'Shanach' × 'Cantabile'
Perianth segments pure white, spreading or slightly reflexed, of thick substance; corona disc-shaped,

greenish yellow, with green at base and a narrow band of red at rim. PC(e) 1957

'Andria' 4 W-O
(J.L. Richardson) D.A. Lloyd, 1962
'Falaise' × 'Arbar'
Fl. 83 mm wide. Late. Resembles a smaller and neater-flowered 'Bali Hai' with the corona segments darker in tone

'Androcles' 1 Y-Y
(W.B. Hartland, pre-1890)
Fl. rich yellow. Very early

'Androcles' 4 W-W
(W.G. Pannill) W.G. Pannill, 1978
'Snowshill' × sdlg; sdlg no. 67/57 B
Fl. 95 mm wide. Mid-season

'Androclese' 2 Y-Y
(pre-1970) Unregistered

'Andromache' 2 W-? (b)
(C. Dawson, pre-1927)

'Andromeda'
(J.C. Williams, pre-1908)

'Andromeda' 1 Y-Y
(Konynenburg & Mark) Konynenburg & Mark, 1964
'Gracious' × 'Daisy Schäffer'
Fl. 135 mm wide; perianth segments brilliant greenish yellow 6C; corona darker in tone (vivid yellow 12A) than the perianth. Mid-season

'Andronicus' 1 Y-Y
(J. Pope, pre-1908)

'Andy' 2 W-P
(Mrs C.O. Fairbairn, c.1950)

'Anetos' 2 W-P
(J.N.Hancock & Co., 1976) Unregistered
Sdlg 106/86H × 'Salad Days'; sdlg no. 60/76H
Mid-season

'Anette' 8 W-W
(pre-1835)
Early

'Angea' 1 (b)
(W.Jackson ?Sr, 1950)
'Morna' × 'Sancia'

'Angel' 3 W-GWW
(G.L. Wilson) G.L. Wilson, 1960
Fl. ice white; corona shades from pale to deep green at base. 2n=28

'Angela' 3 W-? (b)
(Barr & Sons, pre-1908)

'Angela' 1 W-W
Syn. of 'Hugh Aldersey'

'Angela' 1 W-W
(W.M. Spry, pre-1975) Unregistered
'Zero' × Fairbairn sdlg
Mid-season

'Angel Delight' 3 W-Y
(Albert Davis, 1979) Albert Davis, 1991
'Kilworth' × ('Rockall' × 'Woodland Prince'); sdlg no. 409/75
Fl. 90 mm wide; perianth segments roundish, prominently mucronate, pure white; corona bowl-shaped, brilliant greenish yellow 6A, with green noticeable in tube, closely frilled. Mid-season. Resembles 'Woodland Prince' but with the perianth segments more nearly acute and the corona self coloured

'Angeles' 2 W-P
(G.E. Mitsch) G.E. Mitsch, 1962
'Shirley Neale' × 'Pink Lace'
Fl. 108 mm wide

'Angel Eyes' 9 W-GYO
(G.E. Mitsch) G.E. Mitsch, 1976
'Quetzal' × 'Smyrna'; sdlg no. D94/1
Fl. rounded, 72 mm wide; corona small, yellow, with green at base and reddish orange at rim. Late. Resembles a less brightly coloured 'Quetzal'

'Angel Face' 3 W-YYO
(A.J.R. Pearson) A.J.R. Pearson, 1994
'Dell Chapel' × 'Corozal'; sdlg no. 90-35-L15
Fl. rounded, 92 mm wide; perianth segments broadly ovate, blunt, slightly mucronate, greenish white (157B), reflexed, a little concave, with margins a little incurling, overlapping three-quarters; the inner segments only a little narrower; corona disc-shaped, faintly ribbed, light greenish yellow 3C, with a very narrow band of red-orange (28A) at rim, mouth 6-lobed, regularly wavy, with rim entire. Mid-season to late

'Angel Falls' 5 W-W
(E. Longford) E. Longford, 1969
N. triandrus × *N. jonquilla*

'Angelica' 5
(Sir A.P.W. Thomas, pre-1930)

'Angelic Choir' 3 W-GYY
(R. & E.Havens, 1984) R. & E.Havens, 1995
'Alabaster' × sdlg D94/5 ('Quetzal' × 'Smyrna'); sdlg no. TEH91/1
Fl. rounded, 66 mm wide, of heavy substance; perianth segments broadly ovate, pure white; corona

disc-shaped, bright yellow, with deep green at base. Late

'Angeline' 3 W-WWY
(A.M. Wilson, pre-1937)
Corona tinged citron, with golden yellow at rim, frilled

'Angelique' 8 W-GYO
(Mrs G. Link) Mrs G. Link, 1985
'Orange Cup' open pollinated; sdlg no. 21-72
Fls 2 per stem; perianth segments broad in outline, blunt, mucronate, with margins wavy, overlapping; corona shallow, widely expanded, lemon yellow, with a narrow band of rust orange at rim, lightly ruffled. Mid-season. Resembles a large-flowered 'Saint Agnes'

'Angelito' 2 Y-YYO
(Brian S.Duncan) Brian S.Duncan, 1997
'Garden News' × 'Triple Crown'; sdlg no. 1544
Fl. 102 mm wide, deep golden yellow; perianth segments broadly ovate, spreading; corona shallow bowl-shaped, with a band of deep reddish orange at rim. Late

'Angel's Diamond' 2 W-Y
(H. 't Mannetje) H. 't Mannetje, 1961
Fl. 100 mm wide; perianth segments creamy white; corona vivid yellow 12A. Late

'Angels' Dream' 2 Y-O
(Konynenburg & Mark, pre-1953)

'Angel Silk' 2 W-W
(Mrs Ben Robertson) R. & E. Havens, 1987
'Easter Moon' × 'Glenmanus'; sdlg no. 262
Fl. forming a double triangle; perianth segments broadly ovate, blunt, very slightly reflexed, plane, silken smooth and of heavy substance, overlapping half; the inner segments more nearly spreading; corona funnel-shaped, broadly ribbed, with mouth straight and loosely frilled. Mid-season

'Angel's Kiss' ?-P
(Alister Clark, pre-1948)

'Angel's Smile' ?-P
(Alister Clark, pre-1948)

"Angel's Tears"
Syn. of *N. triandrus* var. *triandrus*

'Angel's Whisper' 5 Y-Y
(Glenbrook Bulb Farm) Glenbrook Bulb Farm, 1997
N. triandrus × *N. fernandesii*
Fls 3 or sometimes up to 5 per stem, 27 mm wide; perianth segments oval, light greenish yellow 3D; corona constricted at base, slightly darker in tone (3C) than the perianth, with mouth expanded. Dwarf. Mid-season

'Angel's Wings' 2 W-W
(G. Lubbe & Son, pre-1947)
Fl. ivory white. AM(Haarlem) 1947

'Angelus' 2 W-W
(R.H. Bath, pre-1927)

'Angel Wings' 5 W-W
Syn. of 'Celtic Wings'

'Angenis Christine' 8
(pre-1930)
Poetaz

'Angie' 8 W-Y
(A. Gray, pre-1948)
N. dubius × 'John Evelyn'
Perianth white; corona primrose yellow at maturity, ageing to white

'Angkor' 4 Y-Y
(G.E. Mitsch, 1974) G.E. Mitsch, 1983
'Gay Time' × 'Daydream'; sdlg no. H102/3
Fl. 108 mm wide; perianth and other petaloid segments ivory yellow; corona segments slightly deeper in tone. Mid-season. Formerly named 'Trend'

'Angler' ?-P
(Alister Clark, pre-1948)

'Anglesea' 1 Y-Y
(W.M. Spry, pre-1975) Unregistered
'Tarago' × 'Big Keith'
Fl. lemon yellow. Tall. Early to mid-season

'Anglet' 1 W-W
(pre-1907)

'Angmering' 2 Y-? (a)
(Sir F.C. Stern, pre-1947)
'Killigrew' × 'Rustom Pasha'

'Angola' 1 Y-Y
(Mrs H.K. Richardson) Mrs H.K. Richardson, 1973
'Golden Horn' × 'King's Ransom'
Fl. deep golden yellow; corona long, slender, expanded, with rim dentate

N. angustifolius Haworth = *N. radiiflorus*

'Anhai' 2 W-W
(W. Jackson Sr, 1939)
'Nimue' × 'Pinkeen'

'Anicet' 3 W-WWO
(A.M. Wilson, pre-1913)
Fl. 70 mm wide, pure white; corona with pinkish orange at rim

'Anikawa' 2 W-Y
(Mrs M.M. Comer) Mrs M.M. Comer, 1975
'Golden Cavalcade' × 'High Score'
Fl. 108 mm wide; perianth segments cream; corona yellow. Mid-season. Resembles 'Outward Bound' but with the corona of a clearer yellow

'Animato' 2 Y-? (a)
(van Buggenum Bros) P.J. van den Berg & Sons, 1957

'Anita' 2 W-? (b)
(R.H. Bath, pre-1931)

'Anitra' 1 W-W
(W. Jackson Jr) W. Jackson Jr, 1970
'Tranquil' × sdlg 10/60 × 'Astor'; sdlg no. 20/65

'Anjou' 1 W-W
(J. Gerritsen & Son, pre-1944)

'Anka' 2 Y-YYR
(J.T. Gray, pre-1949)
Perianth segments yellow; corona shallow, expanded, yellow, with a band of bright red at rim

'Ankara' 2 W-O
(Warnaar & Co., pre-1943)
'Fortune' × 'Scarlet Leader'
AM(Haarlem) 1943

'Ann'
(?W.F. Mitchell, pre-1939)

'Anna' 2 W-Y
(J.S. Leitch) J.S. Leitch, 1967
Corona lemon yellow

'Ann Abbott' 2 W-P
(G.H. Johnstone, pre-1947)
'Silver Coin' × 'Mrs R.O. Backhouse'
Perianth segments very broadly ovate, blunt, prominently mucronate, spreading, overlapping one-third to a half; the inner segments twisted or with margins recurved, notched; corona funnel-shaped, pale pink, with a deeper tone at rim and yellow streaks from base to rim, mouth straight, with 6 overlapping lobes, frilled, margins minutely crenate. 2n=28

'Annabel' 2 W-WWY
(H.A. Brown, 1944) J.N. Hancock & Co., 1959
Perianth segments pure white, smooth, deeply overlapping; corona opening lemon yellow, becoming pinkish white, with lemon yellow at rim, mouth expanded and frilled, rim dentate. Late

'Anna Brita' 8 W-R
Syn. of 'Anne-Brita'

'Anna Croft' 3 Y-? (a)
(Mrs R.O. Backhouse, pre-1921)

'Anna Eleanor Roosevelt' 1 Y-Y
Syn. of 'Anna Roosevelt'

'Anna Floor' 11b W-O/W
Syn. of 'Peking'

'Anna Karenina' 2 W-Y
(D.S. Bell) D.S. Bell, 1968
'Green Island' × 'Satin Queen'
Perianth segments pure white; corona very shallow bowl-shaped, apricot yellow

'Annalise' 1 W-W
(G.J. Phillips, 1984) G.J. Phillips, 1994
'Ellanne' × 'Lady Slim'; sdlg no. 79-241-5
Fl. forming a double triangle, 114 mm wide; perianth segments very broad, smooth; corona funnel-shaped, with rim flanged and dentate. Early

'Annalong' 3 W-GWO
(Ballydorn Bulb Farm) Ballydorn Bulb Farm, 1982
'Fairgreen' × 'Capisco'
Fl. 90 mm wide. Mid-season

'Annalra' 2 W-? (b)
(Mrs M.Moorby) Mrs M.Moorby, 1956

'Anna Marie' 8
(G. Zandbergen-Terwegen, pre-1940)

'Anna McMillan'
Unregistered
Seed parent of 'Jilliby'

'Anna Paulowna' 1 Y-O
(de Graaff Bros) J.T. van Oosten & S.A.van Konynenburg, 1979
Perianth segments brilliant yellow 8A; corona orange (23A), with a darker tone at rim

'Anna Pawlona' 8 Y-Y
(pre-1835)
Early

'Annapurna' 1 W-W
(W.J. Dunlop, pre-1953)

'Anna Roosevelt' 1 Y-Y
(M. van Waveren & Sons, pre-1933)
Syn. 'Anna Eleanor Roosevelt', 'Mrs Franklin Roose-velt'. AM(Haarlem) 1943, FCC(Haarlem) 1944

'Anna van Buren' 2 W-? (b)
(F. Rijnveld & Sons, pre-1943)
AM(Haarlem) 1943

'Ann Baird' 1 W-W
(J. MacHardy, pre-1952)

'Ann Brenda' 2 W-GYR
(A.G. Thompson) A.G. Thompson, 1966
'Monique' × 'Kansas'
Fl. 83 mm wide; perianth segments pure white; corona greenish yellow, with a broad band of red at rim. Mid-season. Resembles a more brightly coloured 'Tuskar Light'

'Ann Cameron' 2 W-P
(C.O. Fairbairn, c.1968) Unregistered

'Ann Carter' 2 W-YRR
(R.G.Cull) Hokorawa Daffodils, 1994
'Aden' × 'Rameses'; sdlg no. HC/B46
Corona orange-red (33A), with yellow at base. Mid-season

'Anne' 2 W-? (b or c)
(C.B. Blampied, pre-1929)

'Anne Boleyn' 3 W-? (b)
(Sir C.H. Cave, pre-1908)

'Anne-Brita' 8 W-R
(de Graaff Bros, pre-1943)
Perianth segments broad, pure white; corona bright red, ruffled. AM(Haarlem) 1942. See also 'Anna Brita'

'Annecy' 1 W-PPO
(J. Gerritsen & Son) J. Gerritsen & Son, 1984
Sdlg × 'Alpine Glow'
Perianth segments ivory white; corona light yellowish pink 27B, with light orange 29B at rim. Mid-season

'Anne Frank' 4 W-O
(J.L. Richardson) Warnaar & Co., 1959
'Falaise' × 'Limerick'
Fl. 64 mm wide; perianth and other petaloid segments white; corona segments vivid orange 28B. Late. Resembles 'Mary Copeland' in form. AM(Haarlem) 1959, FCC(Haarlem) 1961

'Anne Holloway' 5 Y-Y
(Mrs R.O. Backhouse, pre-1907)
Fl. pale lemon yellow

'Anne of Cleves'
(Tom Forster, 1960s) Unregistered

'Annepan' 2 W-P
(Mrs C.O. Fairbairn, c.1950)

'Annesbrook' 2 W-O
(J.C. Whibley) J.C. Whibley, 1962
Fl. 120 mm wide; corona rich reddish orange. Mid-season

'Annetta' 2 W-? (b)
(J.S. Leitch) J.S. Leitch, 1956

'Annette' 2 W-? (b or c)
(E.M. Crosfield, pre-1916)

'Annette' 2 W-?
(A. Overton) A. Overton, 1960

'Anne Weston' 6 Y-OOR
(S.P. Haycock) S.P. Haycock, 1986
'Beryl' open pollinated
Perianth segments yellow; corona orange, with a band of red at rim. Mid-season

'Ann Hay' W-Y
Unregistered
Corona pale yellow

'Annie Baden' 2 W-YYO
(E. Leeds, pre-1877)
Perianth segments sulphur white; corona bright golden yellow, stained scarlet-orange at rim. Syn. Incomparabilis Albidus 'Annie Baden', Incomparabilis Albidus 'Aureo-tinctus', Incomparabilis Leedsii 'Aureo-tinctus'. FCC 1878

'Annie Laurie' 1 W-Y
(W.E. Weightman, pre-1933)
Corona clear yellow

'Annie van der Zelm' 3 W-? (b)
(A. Frylink & Sons, pre-1931)

'Annis' 1 Y-Y
(R. Lincoln Lewis, pre-1933)

'Anniversary' 2 W-P
(M.J. Jefferson-Brown, pre-1988) Unregistered
'Infatuation' × 'Debutante'

'Ann Kirton' 3 W-? (b)
(W. Balch, pre-1933)

'Anno Santo' 1 W-Y
(L.van der Brug, pre-1950)

'Ann's Blush' 2 W-GWP
(L.F. Manser) L.F. Manser, 1989
'Easter Moon' × 'Fair Prospect'; sdlg no. 4
Fl. 110 mm wide; perianth segments broadly ovate, clear white, overlapping; corona cup-shaped, opening yellowish, soon becoming creamy white, with grey-green at base and deep pink at rim. Mid-season

'Ann's Cream' 2 W-GYY
(L.F. Manser) L.F. Manser, 1989
'Easter Moon' × 'Verona'; sdlg no. 99
Fl. 105 mm wide; perianth segments broad, clear white, of good substance, overlapping; corona short cup-shaped, pale cream, with green at base, frilled, with rim entire. Mid-season

'Annuity' 3 W-? (b)
(J.E. Exley, pre-1950)

'Annulet' 3 W-? (b)
(E.M. Crosfield, pre-1908)

'Anny Lefeber' 3 W-? (b)
(J.W.A. Lefeber, pre-1945)

'Anny Virginia' 2 Y-O
(D.W. Lefeber & Co., pre-1943)
Perianth segments deep golden yellow; corona expanded, reddish orange. AM(Haarlem) 1954

'Anoka' 2 Y-? (a)
(E.C. Powell, pre-1948)
'Seraglio' × 'Fortune'

'Anouk' 2 W-? (b)
(A.H. Ahrens, pre-1951)

'Ansett' 1 Y-Y
(J.N. Hancock & Co., 1954) J.N.Hancock & Co., 1977
Sdlg 83H × 1963 Div. 1 sdlg; sdlg no. 91/54H
Fl. forming a double triangle, 110 mm wide; perianth segments broadly ovate, blunt, brilliant yellow 13B, with prominent white mucro, spreading, plane, overlapping one-third to a half; the inner segments more narrowly ovate, inflexed and shouldered at base, reflexed towards apex, with margins wavy and sometimes nicked; corona cylindrical, a little darker (13A) than the perianth, with mouth widely expanded and lightly frilled, rim deeply and regularly notched and crenate. Tall. Mid-season

'Answer' ?-P
(Alister Clark, pre-1948)

'Antarctic' 9 W-YYO
(G.H. Engleheart, pre-1923)
Fl. large; perianth segments rounded, overlapping; corona rich yellow, with a broad band of golden orange at rim

'Antarctica' 1 W-W
(D.S. Bell) D.S. Bell, 1978
'Glacier' × 'Ulster Queen'
Fl. 108 mm wide, pure white. Mid-season

'Antares' 2 Y-? (a)
(Mrs F.S. Foote, pre-1941)

'Antares' 2 Y-R
(A.O. Roblin, 1943)
'Killigrew' × 'Market Merry'

'Antelope' 3 Y-? (a)
(C.G. van Tubergen, pre-1914)

'Anteros' 2 W-Y
(Barr & Sons, pre-1920)
Perianth segments creamy white, slightly reflexed, overlapping; corona cup-shaped, yellow, with mouth closely frilled

'Anthea' 3 W-W
(Barr & Sons, pre-1907)
N. × *poculiformis* × *N. poeticus*
Fl. 83 mm wide; perianth segments pure white; corona ribbed, opening creamy yellow, becoming ivory white

'Anthea' 2 W-YRR
(J.L. Richardson) M.J. Jefferson-Brown, 1975
'Kilworth' × 'Arbar'
Perianth segments broad, smooth; corona very shallow bowl-shaped, orange-red, with gold at base. ?See also 'Santhea'

'Anthem' 3 W-YYR
(F.H. Chapman, pre-1930)
'Kestrel' × 'Grand Opera'
Fl. of strong substance; perianth segments ivory white, overlapping; corona disc-shaped, yellow, with deep red at rim. Late

'Anthis' 2 W-Y
(W. Jackson Sr, 1934)
'Mary Blewitt' × 'Mitylene'

'Anthony' 2 W-? (b)
(pre-1939)

'Anthony Meyer' 2 Y-? (a)
(H.R. Meyer, pre-1950)

'Antibes' 2 W-P
(F. Rijnveld & Sons, pre-1950)
Corona pale apricot, shaded salmon pink

'Anticipation' 6 Y-Y
(A. Gray) M.J. Jefferson-Brown, 1975
'Tête-à-Tête' open pollinated
Fls usually one per stem, golden yellow; perianth segments ovate, blunt, fairly prominently mucronate, spreading, overlapping one-third to a half; the inner segments more narrowly ovate; corona short funnel-shaped, ribbed, slightly darker in tone than the perianth, with mouth straight. Dwarf. Mid-season. Resembles a larger and usually single-flowered 'Tête-à-Tête'

'Antics' 2 Y-O
(J.N. Hancock & Co., 1962) Unregistered
Perianth segments broadly ovate, blunt, slightly mucronate, golden yellow, spreading or a little inflexed, slightly concave, with margins sometimes nicked, overlapping one-third; the inner segments narrower, more usually inflexed; corona broad

funnel-shaped, ribbed, glowing red-orange, mouth straight, split in places and overlapping, frilled, with rim notched. Tall. Early

'Antigone' 8
(M. van Waveren & Sons, pre-1916)

'Antiope' 1 W-Y
(Barr & Sons, pre-1923)
Perianth segments creamy white, overlapping; corona soft clear yellow

'Antique' 1 Y-Y
(A.H. Ahrens) J.S. Leitch, 1955

'Antithesis' 1 Y-W
(C.G. van Tubergen, pre-1946)

'Antium' 2 W-? (b)
(A.H. Ahrens, pre-1949)

'Antoine' 2 W-Y
(L. Buckland, pre-1936)
Corona light lemon

'Antoinette Sterling' 1 Y-Y
(?Barr & Sons, pre-1889)
Fl. sulphur yellow; corona mouth flared, with rim recurved

'Antonio' 1 W-Y
(?Barr & Sons, pre-1896)
Corona large, flared, of thick texture. Resembles a large-flowered 'Princeps'

'Antonio' 2 W-? (b or c)
(W.T. Ware, pre-1914)

'Anton Mauve' 2 W-? (b)
(C.G. van Tubergen, pre-1914)

'Antony' 2 Y-Y
(A.M. Wilson, pre-1910)
Fl. 108 mm wide; perianth segments broadly ovate or somewhat oblong, blunt, slightly mucronate, lemon yellow, a little inflexed, plane or with margins sometimes wavy or incurling, overlapping one-third; the inner segments more strongly inflexed, with margins more usually wavy; corona deep bowl-shaped, of a deeper tone than the perianth, with rim slightly flanged and deeply crenate. Resembles 'Magpie' in corona shape

'Antrim' 1 W-? (b)
(G.P. Haydon, pre-1923)

'Antrim Glen' 2 W-W
(A.W. Chappell) A.W. Chappell, 1992
'Easter Moon' × 'White Star'; sdlg no. G-24-1
Fl. white; perianth segments ovate, plane; corona with green in tube, rim flanged. Late

'Antron' 2 Y-? (a)
(Barr & Sons, pre-1954)

'Antwerp' 1 Y-Y
(J.L. Richardson, pre-1945)
'Cromarty' × 'Worlington'
Fl. deep golden yellow; perianth segments broad, spreading, of good substance, overlapping; corona with rim dentate and slightly flanged

'Anubia' 3 W-? (b)
(A.M. Wilson, pre-1913)

'Anukis' 1 Y-Y
(W.Jackson ?Sr, 1950)
'Chromis' × 'Haldor'

'Anvil Chorus' 2 W-O
(R. & E.Havens, 1982) R. & E.Havens, 1997
'Cool Flame' × *N. jonquilla*; sdlg no. REH11/1
Fls very occasionally 2 per stem, rounded, 70 mm wide; perianth segments broadly ovate, white, with undertones of orange; corona cup-shaped, bright orange. Late. Sunproof

'Anytus' 2 W-Y
(W. Jackson Jr) W. Jackson Jr, 1970
'Rowella' × 'Lod'; sdlg no. 15/64

'Anzac' 2 W-? (b)
(R. Crews, pre-1949)

'Anzena' 2 W-Y
(Konynenburg & Mark, pre-1953)
'Gracious' × 'Daisy Schäffer'
AM(Haarlem) 1954

'Anzila'
(A.M. Wilson, pre-1914)

'Anzio' 2 W-O
(J.L. Richardson, pre-1945)
'Clava' × 'Hades'
Fl. rounded; perianth segments very broad in outline, squarish and sometimes truncate at apex, prominently mucronate, pure white, a little reflexed, plane, overlapping half; the inner segments a little narrower, only very slightly mucronate, a little inflexed, creased, with margins wavy; corona very shallow bowl-shaped, broad, loosely ribbed, deep orange. Mid-season. 2n=28

'Aodhan James' 1 W-Y
(Koanga Daffodils) Koanga Daffodils, 1995
'Ebony' × Bramley 1 W-Y sdlg
Fl. 115 mm wide; perianth segments ovate, milk white; corona cylindrical, opening vivid yellow 9A, becoming darker in tone (12A), with the outside

paler, rim flanged and deeply crenate. Late

'Aomarama' 2 W-GWW
(G.C. Graham) G.C. Graham, 1960
Sdlg × 'Ludlow'
Fl. 102 mm wide; corona long, ice white, with sea green at base. Early. Resembles a more vigorous 'Ludlow'

'Aon' 2 W-? (b)
(C. Dawson, pre-1913)

'Aorangi' 1 W-W
(Sir A.P.W. Thomas, pre-1915)

'Aorere' 1 Y-Y
(F.A. Saunders) F.A. Saunders, 1969

'Aoris'
Unregistered
Pollen parent of 'Bene'

'Aosta' 2 W-P
(J.L. Richardson) Mrs H.K. Richardson, 1968
'Cymbeline' × 'Rose Caprice'
Perianth segments snow white, slightly reflexed; corona cup-shaped, deep rose pink. Late

'Aotea' 2 W-? (b or c)
(H.F.E. Cockrell, pre-1936)

'Aotearoa' 1 W-? (b)
(Parr's Nurseries, 1948) Parr's Nurseries, 1958

'Apache'
(P.D. Williams, pre-1908)

'Apache' 2 Y-R
(Elise Havens) G.E. Mitsch, 1979
'Paricutin' × 'Firecracker'; sdlg no. GEJ7/1
Fl. 38 mm wide; corona orange-red. Mid-season

'Apame' 2 W-P
(P. Phillips) P. Phillips, 1967
Fl. 96 mm wide; corona pale pink, shading to bright pink at rim. Mid-season. Resembles a 'Mabel Taylor' of clearer and brighter colour

N. aperticorona Steudel = *N. cupularis*

'Apex' 2 W-W
(J.N. Hancock & Co.) J.N. Hancock & Co., 1955

'Aphrodite' 3 W-? (b or c)
(P.D. Williams, pre-1908)

'Aphrodite' 2 W-O
(de Graaff Bros & van Konynenburg & Co., pre-1931)
Perianth segments opening sulphur yellow, becoming creamy white; corona soft orange, heavily frilled. AM(Haarlem) 1930

'Apia' 1 W-Y
(J.A. O'More, 1961) P.D.K. Ramsay, 1980
'Sincerity' × 'Trousseau'; sdlg no. 13/61
Fl. 99 mm wide; perianth segments broadly or very broadly ovate, blunt, very slightly mucronate, spreading, plane, notched at shoulder, overlapping one-third to a half; corona cylindrical, with mouth straight and rim rolled. Resembles a larger 'Trousseau' with the corona of a stronger colour

'Apiri' 2 W-WWP
(W. Jackson Sr, 1942)
'Charis' × 'Pink of Dawn'

'Aplomb' 1 W-W
(Murray W. Evans, 1981) Estella L. Evans, 1992
'Neahkahnie' × 'Cataract'; sdlg no. Y-3/3
Fl. 120 mm wide; perianth segments very broadly ovate, plane, smooth; corona funnel-shaped, with rim rolled. Mid-season

'Apodanthus' 7 Y-Y
(pre-1884)
Fl. small, yellow. Syn. Odorus 'Apodanthus'

N. apodanthus Boissier & Reuter = *N. rupicola*

'Apogee' 2 W-WRR
(Colin Crotty) Unregistered
Sdlg no. 5-76

'Apollo' 8 Y-Y
(pre-1850)
Fls numerous per stem; perianth segments primrose yellow; corona rich yellow. Syn. Tazetta 'Apollo'. ?The same as 'Apollonia'

'Apollo' 2 W-O
(J.W.A. Lefeber) J.W.A. Lefeber, 1961
Fl. 95 mm wide; corona reddish orange. Late

'Apollonia' 8 Y-Y
(pre-1798)
?The same as 'Apollo'

'Apollyon' 3 W-YYO
(G.H. Engleheart, pre-1916)
Fls sometimes 2 per stem; perianth segments creamy white; corona very shallow, saffron yellow, with a broad band of orange at rim

'Aporima' 2 W-W
(D.S. Bell) D.S. Bell, 1957
Fl. rounded, pure white; perianth segments deeply overlapping; corona short funnel-shaped, with rim entire and flanged

'Apostle' 1 W-Y
(W.G. Pannill) W.G. Pannill, 1978
'Bonnington' × 'Empress of Ireland'
Fl. 110 mm wide

'Apotheose' 4 Y-O
(Oregon Bulb Farms) C. Breed, 1975
'Double Fortune' hybrid
Fl. 105 mm wide; perianth and other petaloid segments in several whorls, brilliant yellow 8A, touched with orange-yellow at midrib; the two outer whorls broadly ovate, with white mucro, spreading, overlapping half or more; the inner whorls inflexed; corona segments interspersed among the inner whorls, appearing to form more than one centre, strong orange 25A, sometimes paler at lower margins; corona occasionally continuous. AM(Hillegom) 1975

'Apotheose' 1 Y-Y
Syn. of 'Apotheosis'

'Apotheosis' 1 Y-Y
(C.G. van Tubergen, pre-1915)
Fl. 114 mm wide; perianth segments sulphur, irregular, overlapping one-third; corona lemon yellow, with mouth expanded and rim deeply crenate. Mid-season to late. AM(Haarlem) 1915. Received AM(Haarlem) 1915 as 'Apotheose'

'Appalachian Star' 2 Y-R
(W.G.Pannill) W.G.Pannill, 1994
('Matlock' × 'Paricutin') × 'Javelin'; sdlg no. 73/19
Mid-season

'Appanoose' 1 W-W
(E.C. Powell, pre-1946)
'Madame de Graaff' × 'White Emperor'

'Appeal' 3 Y-O
(R.V. Favell, pre-1939)
'Peggy' × 'Red Sea'
Perianth segments clear yellow; corona deep orange, slightly frilled

'Appellant' 3 Y-? (a)
(W.B. Cranfield, pre-1923)

'Applause' 1 W-? (b)
(G.H. Johnstone, pre-1953)

'Appleblossom' 2 W-? (b)
(Oregon Bulb Farms, pre-1945)

'Apple Blossom' 2 W-P
Syn. of 'Thelma Gower'

'Appleby' 2 Y-? (a)
(Mrs R.O. Backhouse, pre-1921)

'Appleby' 3 W-?

Syn. of 'Ainsdale'

'Appledew' 2 W-P
(W.A. Noton, 1964) W.A. Noton, 1976
'Passionale' × 'Debutante'; sdlg no. 542
Fl. 90 mm wide. Mid-season

'Appledore' 3 W-? (b)
(P.D. Williams, pre-1939)

'Apple Honey' 1 W-Y
(Clive Postles) Clive Postles Daffodils, 1995
'Panache' × Lea sdlg 3-45-76; sdlg no. 1-38A-82
Fl. 116 mm wide; perianth segments broadly ovate, somewhat inflexed; corona funnel-shaped, clear lemon yellow, with rim rolled and crenate. Mid-season

'Appleshawensis' 2 Y-? (a)
(G.H. Engleheart, pre-1907)

'Appleshaw White' 1 W-W
(G.H. Engleheart, pre-1907)

'Applins' 2 W-P
(J.W.Blanchard) J.W.Blanchard, 1997
'Cherrygardens' × 'Dailmanach'; sdlg no. 83/15E
Fl. 105 mm wide; perianth segments broadly ovate, blunt, slightly mucronate, spreading, with midrib showing, regular, overlapping half; the inner segments more narrowly ovate; corona cup-shaped, ribbed, pink, with a deeper tone in upper third, closely frilled. Mid-season

'Appro' 2 W-Y
(D. Jackson) Jackson's Daffodils, 1983
Sdlg × 'Cyros'

'Approval' 2 Y-OOR
(Warnaar & Co., pre-1952)
'Bahram' × 'Bermuda'
AM(Haarlem) 1952

'Apricot' 1 W-Y
(de Graaff Bros, pre-1897)
'Madame de Graaff' hybrid or *N. abscissus* × *N. albescens*
Perianth segments narrow, creamy white; corona slender, cylindrical, soft yellow, faintly tinged pale amber pink at first. Violet-scented. 2n=14. AM 1898. ?The same as 'Apricot' pre-1902

'Apricot' Y-Y
(Miss F.W. Currey, pre-1902)
Perianth segments creamy primrose; corona long, opening primrose, becoming rosy apricot. Violet scented. ?The same as 'Apricot' pre-1897

'Apricot Attraction' 3 Y-O
Syn. of 'Apricot Distinction'

'Apricot Beauty' 2 W-O
(de Graaff Bros, pre-1954)
AM(Haarlem) 1954

'Apricot Blonde' 2 W-O
(Tom Forster, 1960s) Unregistered
Perianth segments creamy white; corona orange, with mouth expanded, rim dentate. Mid-season

'Apricot Charisma' 6 Y-GYY
(Eileen E. Frey) J. & E. Frey, 1993
Sdlg JEE15/1 × 'Bell Song'; sdlg no. TEF18/1
Perianth segments very broad, squarish at apex, pale lemon yellow, strongly reflexed, overlapping one-third to a half; the inner segments spreading at base, reflexed at apex, with margins wavy; corona funnel-shaped, very broad, opening yellowish white, becoming apricot orange-yellow, with green at base, mouth even and very slightly expanded. Dwarf. Mid-season

'Apricot Distinction' 3 Y-O
(P. van Deursen, pre-1942)
Perianth segments very broad in outline, rounded or squarish at apex, fairly prominently mucronate, pale orange-yellow, spreading, overlapping half; the inner segments shouldered at base, inflexed, with margins wavy and incurving; corona disc-shaped, deeply and closely ribbed, deep orange, mouth 6-lobed, rim minutely dentate. Late. Syn. 'Apricot Attraction'. AM(Haarlem) 1942

'Apricot Frilled' 2 W-O
(W.F.Leenen, 1970s) Unregistered
Corona apricot orange, heavily frilled

'Apricot Gem' 3 W-O
(N.Y. Lower, pre-1934)
Perianth segments pure white; corona pale salmon orange

'Apricot Glow' 2 W-? (b)
(Mrs R.O. Backhouse, pre-1921)

'Apricot Glow' 3 Y-? (a)
(P. van Deursen, pre-1943)

'Apricotine' 2 Y-O
(L. Buckland, pre-1936)
Perianth segments light yellow; corona apricot

'Apricot Phoenix' 4 W-Y
(de Graaff Bros, pre-1905)
Perianth and other petaloid segments in many whorls, decreasing only a little in length towards centre, some ovate and acute, some oblong and blunt, soft sulphury white; the outer whorls inflexed, plane or with margins recurved, sometimes with apex incurved; the inner whorls successively more strongly inflexed, with margins incurved; corona segments short, interspersed among the petaloid segments at centre, pinkish yellow. AM(Haarlem) 1913

'Apricot Pie' 2 W-O
(J.N. Hancock & Co., 1959) Unregistered

'Apricot Queen' 2 W-O
(P.D. Williams, pre-1910)
Perianth segments light sulphur; corona rich apricot

'Apricot Ruffle' 11a W-O
(J.Gerritsen & Son) Mrs E.Bullivant, 1995
Sdlg no. GBS 16
Fl. 85 mm wide; perianth segments broad, slightly mucronate, clear white, somewhat reflexed in upper half; corona deeply split, the six segments opposite the perianth segments and joined to them by the margins at base, ribbed, deep apricot orange, paling to a creamier tone at margins, tightly frilled, with a thick and similarly frilled extra growth beneath the rim. Mid-season

'Apricot Sensation' 2 W-OOY
Syn. of Mother Catherine Grullemans'

'Apricot Sundae' 4 W-P
(Carncairn Daffodils) Carncairn Daffodils, 1984
'Egg Nogg' × 'Little Princess'; sdlg no. 1/2/72
Fl. 100 mm wide; corona soft pink

'Apricot Surprise' 1 Y-O
(W.F. Leenen, pre-1991) Unregistered
Perianth segments broadly ovate, blunt, fairly prominently mucronate, pale primrose yellow, spreading, creased, overlapping half; the inner segments a little inflexed and with margins wavy; corona broad funnel-shaped, opening yellow, with pinkish orange at rim gradually extending to base, mouth ribbed and expanded, frilled, with rim deeply notched.

'April Beauty' 3 W-YYO
(G.H. Rotteveel & Sons) G.H. Rotteveel & Sons, 1982
Perianth segments ivory white; corona vivid yellow 12A, with a broad band of orange at rim

"April Beauty"
Syn. of *N.* × *medioluteus*

'April Change' 2 W-WWY
(V. Brink) V. Brink, 1966
'Wild Rose' × 'Scarlet Leader'
Fl. 76 mm wide; corona opening deep orange, becoming creamy white, with yellow at rim, ageing to all-white. Mid-season. Resembles 'Wild Rose' but with broader perianth segments and different corona colouring

'April Charm' 2 W-WWY
(G.E. Mitsch, 1955) G.E. Mitsch, 1966

'Green Island' × 'Chinese White'; sdlg no. R33/17
Perianth segments of good substance; corona almost disc-shaped, white, with a greenish cast at base and a narrow band of yellow at rim. Mid-season. Resembles 'Green Island' but with a shallower corona

'April Clouds' 3 W-W
(G.E. Mitsch, 1955) G.E. Mitsch, 1966
'Green Island' × 'Chinese White'; sdlg no. R33/3
Fl. rounded; perianth segments pure white, overlapping; corona shallow, small, sometimes opening slightly coloured, becoming white, frilled. Mid-season. Resembles a taller and more robust 'Chinese White' of better poise

'April Dream' 3 Y-O
(G.H. Rotteveel & Sons) G.H. Rotteveel & Sons, 1982
Perianth segments brilliant to light greenish yellow 6C-D; corona vivid orange 28B

'April Fires' 2 Y-O
(T. Bloomer) T. Bloomer, 1964
'Indian Summer' × 'Air Marshal'; sdlg no. 1/67/58

'April Flame' 2 Y-O
(T. Bloomer) T. Bloomer, 1964
'Royal Charger' × 'Border Chief'; sdlg no. 2/29/58

'April Frost' 2 W-W
Syn. of 'April Snow'

'April Gift' 2 Y-? (a)
(H.P. Zwetsloot, pre-1953)
AM(Haarlem) 1953

'April Glow' 9 W-GYR
(Mrs M.S. Yerger) Mrs M.S. Yerger, 1991
'Sea Green' open pollinated; sdlg no. 76 J 10
The inner shorter than the outer perianth segments. Dwarf. Very late

'April Gold' 2 Y-?
(T. Bloomer) T. Bloomer, 1964
'Camelot' × 'Viking'

'April Harvest' 1 W-Y
(T. Bloomer) T. Bloomer, 1962
'Consort' × 'Preamble'; sdlg no. 1/7/54
Corona lemon

'Aprilis' 2 W-W
(G. Lubbe & Son, pre-1944)
AM(Haarlem) 1944

'April King' 1 W-? (b)
(H. Prins, pre-1929)

'April Lass' 2 W-W
(T. Bloomer) T. Bloomer, 1964
'Rashee' × 'Empress of Ireland'; sdlg no. 11/17/58

'April Love' 1 W-W
(Mrs J. Abel Smith) Mrs J. Abel Smith, 1974
'Ave' × 'Empress of Ireland'; sdlg no. L3/01
Fl. 130 mm wide, pure ice white; corona slender, with rim rolled and dentate. Mid-season. Resembles 'Ave' but with a longer and narrower corona

'April Love' 6 W-Y
Syn. of 'Jack Snipe'

'April Magnet' 2 Y-GYR
(T. Bloomer) T. Bloomer, 1964
'Red Ranger' × ('Royal Mail' × 'Narvik')
Perianth segments yellow; corona orange-yellow, with green at base and deep red at rim

'April Merit' 2 W-W
(T. Bloomer) T. Bloomer, 1964
'Ave' × 'Cantatrice'; sdlg no. 15/21/51

'April Message' 1 W-W
(T. Bloomer) T. Bloomer, 1964
'Samite' × 'Cantatrice'; sdlg no. 14/9/51
Perianth segments broadly ovate; corona rim dentate

'April Morn' 5
(W.F.M. Copeland, pre-1916)

'April Parade' 1 W-W
(T. Bloomer) T. Bloomer, 1964
'Glenbush' × 'Empress of Ireland'; sdlg no. 7/20/58
Corona mouth neatly dentate

'April Peach' 7 W-GPP
(J. & E.Frey, 1981) J. & E.Frey, 1996
Sdlg F31/5 × *N. jonquilla*; sdlg no. QEE14/1
Fls 1-3 per stem, 75 mm wide; perianth segments broadly ovate, blunt, creamy white, spreading or slightly reflexed, plane, overlapping half; the inner segments a little inflexed, the margins wavy and sometimes recurved in lower half and incurling near apex; corona broad bowl-shaped, rich peach pink, with green at base and a paler tone of pink at rim, mouth expanded and lightly frilled. Dwarf. Mid-season to late

'April Princess' 7 Y-GYY
(J. & E. Frey, 1976) J. & E. Frey, 1988
'Bantam' × *N. assoanus*; sdlg no. Lee 1/3
Fls sometimes 2 per stem, rounded; perianth segments very broad, rounded at apex, spreading, overlapping half; the inner segments somewhat inflexed; corona very shallow, very broad, darker in tone than the perianth. Late

'April Queen' 2 W-YYO
(P. van Deursen, pre-1938)

AM(Haarlem) 1938

'April Rose' 2 W-PPO
(J.L. Richardson) J.L. Richardson, 1964
'Rose of Tralee' × sdlg 294
Perianth segments pure white; corona pale salmon pink, shading to a band of rich salmon orange at rim, frilled, with rim flanged

'April Showers' 3 W-YYR
(G. Lewis) G. Lewis, 1955

'April Showers' 3 W-W
(pre-1956)
Fl. pure white; corona almost disc-shaped, broad, opening lemon yellow, becoming white

'April Snow' 1 W-W
(Wrigley, pre-1913)

'April Snow' 2 W-W
(G.L. Wilson, pre-1954)
Syn. 'April Frost'

'April Sun' 2 W-YYO
(G.L. Wilson) Mrs D.G. Moore, 1967
Corona deeply ribbed, yellow, with bright orange at rim. Mid-season. Resembles a larger and more brightly coloured 'Duke of Windsor'

'April Sweetheart' 2 W-GPP
(J. & E.Frey, 1981) J. & E.Frey, 1996
'Coral Ribbon' × sdlg FEE5/2; sdlg no. PEF1/3
Fl. 80 mm wide; perianth segments roundish, very smooth, overlapping; corona soft pink, with green at base, lightly frilled. Dwarf to standard. Mid-season to late

'April Symbol' 3 W-? (b)
(A.F. Calvert, pre-1948)

'April Tears' 5 Y-Y
(A. Gray, pre-1939)
N. jonquilla × *N. triandrus* var. *concolor*
Fls 4-5 per stem, 41 mm wide, deep yellow; perianth segments ovate, blunt, reflexed, separated or slightly overlapping; the inner segments a little twisted; corona cup-shaped, loosely ribbed, with mouth straight and even or very slightly wavy, rim entire or occasionally notched. Dwarf. Late. 2n=14. Resembles 'Hawera' but with broader perianth segments. AM(Haarlem) 1954, FCC(Haarlem) 1957, AM(p) 1957, AGM 1996

'Apropos' 2 W-YYP
(W.G. Pannill) W.G. Pannill, 1983
'Green Island' × 'Accent'

'Apsley' 2 Y-YYO
(J.N. Hancock & Co., pre-1949)

Perianth segments yellow; corona deep yellow, with orange at rim

'Apsley' 2 W-P
(W.M. Spry, pre-1975) Unregistered
'Rosy Pink' × 'Inverell'
Corona soft pink. Late

'Aquarius' 3 W-Y
(W.F.M. Copeland, pre-1908)
Fl. large; perianth segments roundish, pure white, of thick substance, overlapping; corona shallow, ribbed, pale creamy yellow, with buff apricot at rim. Mid-season

'Aquarius' 3 W-W
(W.G. Pannill) W.G. Pannill, 1970
'Easter Moon' × 'Chinese White'

'Aquila' 2 Y-? (a)
(Mrs R.O. Backhouse, pre-1921)
Syn. 'Aguila'. AM(Haarlem) 1930, FA(Haarlem) 1936

'Aquila Lyda' 2 W-P
(G. Keasey) G. Keasey, 1984
'Abalone' × 'Carita'
Tall. Mid-season. Weatherproof. Resembles 'Accent' in the perianth segments and 'Pitta' in the corona

'Aquinita' 2 W-P
(J.N. Hancock & Co., pre-1977) Unregistered
See also 'Aquinta'

'Aquinta' 2 W-P
Syn. of 'Aquinita'

'Araba' Y-Y
(pre-1927)
Fl. large, rich yellow

'Arabella' 3 Y-YYO
(W. Backhouse, pre-1869)
Perianth segments short, paling to primrose yellow at maturity. Syn. Burbidgei 'Arabella'. Was "absorbed" into 'Primrose Star'

'Arabella' 8
(pre-1915)

'Arabella Crosbie' 2 W-? (b)
(H.R. Meyer, pre-1927)

'Arabesk' 8
(R.A. van der Schoot, pre-1930)
Poetaz

'Arabesque' 3 W-YYR
(D.S. Bell) D.S. Bell, 1963
Late. Resembles a larger-flowered 'Catherine

Howard' with the corona more heavily frilled

'Arabia' 2 Y-? (a)
(H.G. Longford, pre-1937)

'Arabian King' 2 Y-? (a)
(F.W. Parkinson, pre-1936)

'Arabian Nights' 2 Y-? (a)
(H.B. Shailer, pre-1949)

'Arabis' 2 Y-O
(A.O. Roblin, 1941)
'Scarlet Queen' × 'Lillian Murdoch'

'Araboa' 2 Y-? (a)
(S.C. Gaspar, 1948) R.J. Abernethy, 1957

'Arabon' 1 W-Y
(J.A. O'More) J.A. O'More, 1968
'Bridal Robe' × 'Trousseau'

'Arab Pasha' 2 Y-R
(T.H. Piper, c.1978) Unregistered

'Araby' 7
(G.H. Engleheart, pre-1913)

'Arach Inverse' 2 Y-GWY
(G.E. Mitsch) B.C. Heath, 1977
'Lunar Sea' × 'Daydream'; sdlg no. B 6-1
Fl. 85 mm wide; perianth segments lemon; corona white, with chartreuse green at base and yellow at rim, frilled, with rim dentate. Resembles 'Daydream'

'Arafura' 2 Y-O
(Jackson's Daffodils, 1987) Jackson's Daffodils, 1997
Sdlg no. 120/87
Fl. 107 mm wide; perianth segments broadly ovate, brilliant yellow 7B; the inner segments narrower; corona funnel-shaped, strong orange 25A. Mid-season

'Aragon' 3 W-? (b)
(G.H. Engleheart, pre-1914)

'Arahura' 1 Y-Y
(S.J. Bisdee, 1942)
'Crocus' × 'Robert Montgomery'

'Arakan' 2 Y-O
(C.R. Wootton, pre-1954)
'Tredore' × 'Dunkeld'
Perianth segments yellow; corona very shallow bowl-shaped, scarlet-orange

'Aralia' 2 Y-Y
(H.G.Cross, pre-1997) Unregistered
'Olympic Gold' × 'Camelot'; sdlg no. 79-6

'Araluen' 2 W-Y
(T.H. Piper) T.H. Piper, 1956
'Grayling' × 'Lorinna'
Corona lemon yellow

'Araminta' 2 Y-? (a)
(A.M. Wilson) Mrs R. McConnel, 1956

'Aramis' 2 Y-? (a)
(E.M. Crosfield, pre-1908)

'Aramoana' 2 W-W
(O.R. Marshall) O.R. Marshall, 1963
Fl. 117 mm wide. Mid-season. Resembles 'Ave' but with broader perianth and longer corona. PC(e)(NZ) 1962

'Aran' 2 W-W
(J.S. Leitch, pre-1959)

'Arandora' 2 W-? (b)
(R.F. Calvert, pre-1934)

N. × *aranensis* Fernández Casas 13 = *N. pallidiflorus* Pugsley × *N. poeticus* Linnaeus var. *poeticus*

'Aranjuez' 2 Y-YYO
(Warnaar & Co., pre-1932)
Fl. rounded, 89 mm wide; perianth segments very broad in outline, rounded or somewhat truncate at apex, prominently mucronate, light yellow, spreading, concave, with midrib showing, sometimes creased, regular, overlapping half or more; the inner segments narrower, less prominently mucronate, rounded at shoulder, a little inflexed; corona short funnel-shaped, broad, smooth, deep lemon yellow, shading to reddish orange at rim, mouth lightly ribbed, straight, more or less even. Mid-season. 2n=28. AM(Haarlem) 1932, FCC(Haarlem) 1933, AM(e) 1940

'Aranka' 2 Y-Y
(Lajos Jezerniczky, 1970) Lajos Jezerniczky, 1987
'Adventure' × 'Golden Harvest'; sdlg no. 47/1
Fls 1-2 per stem, 105 mm wide; perianth segments very broadly ovate, blunt, occasionally truncate, very rich golden yellow, with white mucro, spreading, plane, somewhat ribbed or with broad midrib showing, irregular, overlapping one-third to a half; the inner segments more narrowly ovate and slightly inflexed; corona funnel-shaped, large, golden yellow, with mouth expanded, rim flanged and notched. Early

'Aranta' 8
(pre-1939)

'Aranui' 1 W-W
(O.R. Marshall) O.R. Marshall, 1964
Fl. 100 mm wide. Mid-season. Resembles 'Empress of Ireland'

'Arapaho' 2 W-OOY
(Murray W. Evans) Murray W. Evans, 1970
'Blarney' hybrid

'Arapiti' 1 W-GWW
(S.A. Free) S.A. Free, 1963
Fl. 114 mm wide. Mid-season

'Arapuni' 2 Y-? (a)
(R. Hyde) R. Hyde, 1955

'Arastar' 1 Y-Y
(C. Goodson, pre-1936)

'Arawa' 2 Y-YYO
(H.A. Brown, pre-1938)
Perianth segments yellow; corona yellow, with reddish orange at rim

'Arawa' 2 Y-O
(Mrs B.T. Simpson) Mrs B.T. Simpson, 1963
Fl. 108 mm wide; perianth segments vivid yellow 12A; corona strong orange 25A

'Arawannah' 1 Y-Y
(Murray W. Evans) Murray W. Evans, 1976
'Bethany' × 'Daydream'; sdlg no. H-3/1
Fl. 90 mm wide. Mid-season

'A.Rawson' 8 Y-Y
(A. Rawson, pre-1884)
Fls usually 3 per stem; perianth segments overlapping; corona rich yellow. Syn. Tridymus 'A.Rawson'

'Arbalist' 2 Y-? (a)
(A.M. Wilson, pre-1927)
'Hospodar' hybrid

'Arbar' 2 W-O
(J.L. Richardson, pre-1948)
'Monaco' × 'Forfar'; sdlg no. 2064
Fl. 115 mm wide; perianth segments broadly ovate, blunt, very prominently mucronate, pure white, spreading, with margins a little wavy and sometimes nicked, of great substance and with midrib showing, overlapping half; the inner segments more narrowly ovate, a little inflexed; corona shallow bowl-shaped, ribbed, strong orange 25A, mouth expanded, split in places and overlapping, frilled. Mid-season. Somewhat resembles a larger 'Monaco'. AM(e) 1949

'Arbitrary' 1 W-W
(W.A. Bell, pre-1949)

'Arborella' 3 W-GYR
(D.S. Bell) D.S. Bell, 1984
'Masquerade' × 'Arbar'
Fl. 105 mm wide. Mid-season

'Arbourthorne' 2 W-P
(F.E. Board) F.E. Board, 1965
'Pensive' × 'Passionale'; sdlg no. B1646
Late

'Arcadelt' 2 Y-YOO
(Konynenburg & Mark, 1950) Konynenburg & Mark, 1960
'Aranjuez' × 'Rustom Pasha'
Fl. 95 mm wide; perianth segments brilliant greenish yellow 6C; corona vivid orange 28B, with light yellow 17D at base. Mid-season

'Arcadelt' 2 Y-? (a)
(Konynenburg & Mark, pre-1953)

'Arcadia' 1 W-W
(Cartwright & Goodwin, pre-1908)

'Arcadia' 3 W-? (b)
(R.H. Bath, pre-1927)

'Arcadia' 2 W-O
(J.L. Richardson) Warnaar & Co., 1961
Fl. 115 mm wide; perianth segments rounded at apex, creamy white, deeply overlapping; the inner segments more nearly acute, with margins sometimes notched; corona bowl-shaped, orange (28A), with rim crenate. Mid-season. Sunproof. 2n=28. AM(Haarlem) 1961

'Arcadia' 2 Y-O
(W.M. Spry, pre-1975) Unregistered
'Stanley Mann' × 'Golden'

'Arcady' 2 W-YWP
(M.J. Jefferson-Brown) M.J. Jefferson-Brown, 1985
'Rainbow' × 'Highland Wonder'
Perianth segments broad, blunt, sparkling white, very slightly incurving; corona bowl-shaped, expanded, with a broad band of dark pink at rim, frilled. Mid-season. Resembles an improved 'Rainbow'

'Archangel' 2 W-YYW
(J.N.Hancock & Co., 1986) Unregistered
Sdlg 15/82H × 'Convention'; sdlg no. 16/86H
Perianth segments creamy white; corona yellow, with white at rim, mouth widely expanded, rim rolled. Tall. Early to mid-season

'Archdeacon Hockley' 2 Y-O
(R.V. Favell, pre-1939)
'Fortune' hybrid
Perianth segments bright yellow; corona large, rich orange, with mouth frilled

'Archduke' 8 W-Y
(pre-1851)
Corona citron yellow

'Archduke' 2 W-? (b)
(A.M. Wilson, pre-1930)

'Archdutchess' 8 W-Y
(pre-1759)

'Archer' 2 Y-O
(J.S. Leitch) J.S. Leitch, 1968
Fl. 108 mm wide; perianth segments yellow; corona reddish orange

'Archer de Wals' 8 Y-Y
(pre-1798)
Fl. sulphur yellow

'Archeron' 3 W-YOO
(Dutch origin, pre-1930)
Perianth segments cream-white; corona deep orange, with golden yellow at base. AM(Haarlem) 1930

'Archie' 1 Y-Y
(R. Gibson, pre-1927)
Perianth segments lemon; corona a little darker in tone

'Archil' 1 Y-Y
(J.S. Leitch) J.S. Leitch, 1956

'Archimedes' 1 W-? (b)
(de Graaff Bros, pre-1927)

'Arclight' 3 W-GYR
(Barr & Sons, pre-1925)
Perianth segments white, tinged primrose yellow at base, lightly recurving; corona primrose yellow, with a broad band of scarlet at rim

'Arctic Bay' 2 W-GWW
(D. Bramley) D. Bramley, 1978
Sdlg × 'Easter Moon'; sdlg no. 70/221
Fl. 112 mm wide. Mid-season

'Arctic Berg' 1 W-W
(E.G. Taylor) E.G. Taylor, 1956

'Arctic Char' 2 W-P
(Murray W. Evans) Murray W. Evans, 1974
'Accent' × sdlg
Fl. 110 mm wide

'Arctic Chill' 4 W-WWO
(G.E. Mitsch, 1979) R. & E. Havens, 1993
('Gay Time' × 'Silken Sails') × 'Tropic Isle'; sdlg no. 2010/2
Fl. 95 mm wide; perianth segments broad, rounded at apex, smooth; corona segments white, with mid-orange at rim. Late. Sunproof

'Arctic Circle' 2 W-W
(G.H. Johnstone, pre-1949)
'Beersheba' hybrid

'Arctic Circle' 2 W-W
(Carncairn Daffodils, pre-1981) Unregistered
Wootton sdlg 2/439 × 'Ardbane'; sdlg no. W23/1

'Arctic Dawn' 2 W-P
(W.O. Backhouse) E. Longford, 1967
Fl. 97 mm wide; perianth segments pure white; corona opening vivid pink, becoming deep coral pink, paling to base. Mid-season

'Arctic Doric' 2 W-W
(G.L. Wilson, 1950) M.J. Jefferson-Brown, 1960
Sdlg 33/69 × 'Snowline'
Fl. 92 mm wide; perianth segments overlapping; corona mouth straight, with rim slightly crenate. Early. Resembles a cleaner-white 'Purity' with shallower corona. *AM(g) 1967

'Arctic Flame' 2 W-YOO
(J.M. de Navarro) J.M. de Navarro, 1968
'Fermoy' × 'Arbar'
Fl. forming a double triangle, 96 mm wide; perianth segments broad, snow white, smooth, stiff; corona large bowl-shaped, scarlet-orange, paling to orange-yellow at base. Late. Resembles 'Brahms' but with a purer white perianth and the corona of more intense colour at first

'Arctic Gem' 3 W-GWW
(G.L.Wilson, 1945) A.J.R.Pearson, 1991
'Bryher' self pollinated; sdlg no. 45/94
Fl. forming a double triangle, 100 mm wide; perianth segments broadly ovate, prominently mucronate, concave, with margins incurling, smooth and of good substance, overlapping half; the inner segments a little narrower, only very slightly mucronate; corona bowl-shaped, 6-angled and ribbed, opening cream, becoming white, with intense dark moss green at base and touches of light canary yellow at rim, mouth very deeply 6-lobed, with the lobes overlapping, tightly frilled. Late. Resembles an improved 'Bryher'

'Arctic Glow' 2 W-? (b or c)
(G.T.C. Pearce, pre-1938)
'White Sentinel' × 'Eskimo'

'Arctic Gold' 1 Y-Y
(J.L. Richardson, pre-1951)
'Goldcourt' × 'Kingscourt'
Fl. 95 mm wide, vivid yellow; perianth segments very broadly ovate, blunt, only very slightly mucronate, spreading, plane, with margins sometimes slightly incurling, smooth and of waxy texture, overlapping half; the inner segments more narrowly ovate, inflexed at base, recurved towards apex, with margins wavy; corona cylindrical, smooth, a little darker in tone than the perianth, with mouth expanded and heavily ribbed, rim flanged, notched and crenate. Early. 2n=28. AM(e) 1959, FCC(e) 1960, *AM(g) 1963, *FCC(g) 1971, AGM 1993

'Arctic Imp' 3 W-Y
(Mrs H.K. Richardson, 1964) Mrs H.K. Richardson, 1976
'Green Island' × 'Bryher' sdlg
Fl. 80 mm wide; corona pale primrose. Late

'Arctic Jewel' 1 W-W
(R.C.A. Tombleson) R.C.A. Tombleson, 1968
Mid-season

'Arctic King' 1 W-W
(Barr & Sons, pre-1914)

'Arctic King' 1 W-W
(D. Bramley) D. Bramley, 1971
'Lochin' × 'Cinerama'; sdlg no. 60/16
Fl. 115 mm wide. Mid-season. Resembles an all-white 'Cinerama'

'Arctic King' 2 W-W
(Hybrida, 1957) Unregistered
Fl. 125 mm wide; perianth segments creamy white; corona ivory white. Mid-season. Resembles 'Mount Hood'

'Arctic Light' 2 W-GYY
(P.D. Williams, 1911)
Sdlg no. 448
Perianth segments milk white; corona shallow, lemon yellow

'Arctic Mist' 1 W-W
(Mrs H.K. Richardson) Mrs H.K. Richardson, 1977
'Perseus' × 'Ulster Queen'
Fl. 98 mm wide, glistening white; corona widely ribbed, with rim neatly rolled. Mid-season

'Arctic Moon' 2 W-W
(R.V. Favell, pre-1940)

'Arctic Morn' 5 W-W
(A. Gray, pre-1949)
Fls. several per stem, white, with a hint of pink

'Arctic Prince' 1 W-W
(J.L. Richardson) J.L. Richardson, 1955
Sdlg × 'Broughshane'
Corona rim neatly rolled

'Arctic Queen' 2 W-? (b or c)
(Barr & Sons, pre-1913)

'Arctic Queen' 1 W-W
(D. Bramley) D. Bramley, 1959
Fl. 120 mm wide. Mid-season. Resembles a purer white 'Cantatrice' with broader perianth segments and a longer corona

'Arctic Rambler' 2 W-W
(W.A. Noton) W.A. Noton, 1985

'Cold Overton' × 'Easter Moon'
Fl. white; perianth segments broad, of even size, smooth, overlapping; corona slender, tinged green at base. Mid-season. Resembles a whiter and more refined 'Cold Overton'

'Arctic Snow' 2 W-W
(Mrs F.S. Foote, pre-1940)

'Arctic Star'
(?G. Lewis, pre-1939)

'Arctic Star' 2 W-Y
(S.A. Free) S.A. Free, 1961
Fl. 106 mm wide. Mid-season

'Arctic Sun' 2 W-OOY
(J.J. Abernethy, 1950) J.J. Abernethy, 1960
'Blarney' × 'Artist's Model'
Fl. 114 mm wide; perianth segments pure white, of thick substance; corona almost disc-shaped, dark apricot orange, with cream yellow at rim. Mid-season

'Arctic Sunbeam' 2 W-Y
(J.L. Richardson) E. Longford, 1963
'My Love' × 'Tudor Minstrel'
Fl. 112 mm wide; perianth segments pure white; corona vivid yellow. Mid-season. Resembles a more brightly coloured and unfading 'My Love'

'Arctic Sunset' 2 W-GYR
(W.O. Backhouse) E. Longford, 1967
Fl. 92 mm wide; corona yellow, with green at base and a broad band of deep scarlet at rim. Mid-season

'Arctic Tern' 4 W-R
(J.L. Richardson) G. Zandbergen-Terwegen, 1959
'Falaise' hybrid

'Arctic White' 1 W-W
(H.A. Brown, pre-1950)

N. arctuatus Heynhold = *N. triandrus* var. *triandrus*

'Arcturus' 2 W-? (b)
(H. Backhouse, pre-1910)

'Arcturus' 4 W-Y
(R.C. Gordon) R.C. Gordon, 1964
Fl. 114 mm wide. Mid-season. Resembles a larger and stiffer-flowered 'William Copeland'

'Arda' 1 W-W
(W. Jackson Sr, 1946)
'Hothu' × 'Ardclinis'

'Ardara' 2 W-W
(G.L. Wilson) G.L. Wilson, 1956
'Interim' × 'Lisbreen'

'Ardavon' 1 W-Y
(Barr & Sons, pre-1922)
Corona long, slender, pale primrose yellow

'Ardbane' 2 W-W
(G.L. Wilson, pre-1953)
'Saint Brendan' × 'Greenland'
Fl. ice white

'Ardclinis' 1 W-W
(G.L. Wilson, pre-1934)
'Mrs E.H. Krelage' × 'Beersheba'
Fl. white; perianth segments broadly ovate, slightly mucronate, with margins very slightly incurving at apex, smooth, overlapping half; the inner segments more narrowly ovate and acute, with a slight twist; corona cylindrical, mouth expanded and lightly ribbed, with rim deeply rolled. 2n=28

'Ardea' 3 W-? (b)
(Mrs R.O. Backhouse, pre-1910)

'Arden' 2 Y-? (a)
(J.T. Gray, pre-1937)

'Ardent' 2 W-? (b)
(P.D. Williams, pre-1931)

'Ardglass' 3 W-GYR
(Ballydorn Bulb Farm, 1972) Ballydorn Bulb Farm, 1983
'Ballymartin' × sdlg 3B
Fl. 95 mm wide; corona yellow, with a broad band of green at base and a broad band of orange-red at rim. Mid-season

'Ardina' 1 W-Y
(T. Morrison) T. Morrison, 1960
Perianth segments very slightly reflexed; corona lemon yellow. ?The same as 'Diadem'

'Ardis' 7
(de Graaff Bros, pre-1923)

'Ardjuno' 2 Y-O
(S.J. Bisdee, 1939)
'Damson' × 'Lillian Murdoch'

'Ardlussa' 2 Y-R
(D.N.Y. Olson) D.N.Y. Olson, 1988
'Heathcliffe' × ('Baynes' × 'Checkmate'); sdlg no. 77/36
Fl. 84 mm wide; perianth segments very broadly ovate, blunt, fairly prominently mucronate, strong yellow, spreading, smooth, overlapping half or more; the inner segments narrower, a little inflexed, with margins nicked; corona bowl-shaped, smooth, deep orange-red, with mouth expanded and frilled. Mid-season. Sunproof. Resembles a smaller and neater 'Checkmate'

'Ardmillan' 3 W-GWO
(Ballydorn Bulb Farm, 1986) Ballydorn Bulb Farm, 1996
'High Tower' open pollinated
Fl. 95 mm wide; perianth segments broadly ovate, slightly inflexed; corona small bowl-shaped, expanded, opening dark emerald green, becoming whitish yellow, with green at base and bright orange at rim. Late

'Ardmona' 2 Y-R
(J.N. Hancock & Co., 1954)

'Ardmore' 2 Y-? (a)
(J.L. Richardson, pre-1937)

'Ardnaglass' 1 Y-Y
(W.J. Dunlop) W.J. Dunlop, 1963
Fl. deep golden yellow

'Ardour' 3 Y-R
(G.E. Mitsch, pre-1952)
'Cheerio' × 'Market Merry'; sdlg no. 39C29/1
Perianth segments broad, deep yellow, overlapping; corona deep orange-red. Mid-season. 2n=28

'Ardoyne' 1 W-W
(G.L. Wilson, pre-1947)
Sdlg 12/29 × 'Vestal Virgin'

'Ardress' 2 W-GYY
(Brian S. Duncan) Rathowen Daffodils, 1982
'Easter Moon' × 'Knowehead'; sdlg no. 490
Corona greenish lemon yellow, with green at base. Mid-season

'Ard Righ' 1 Y-Y
(pre-1885)
Perianth segments large, full yellow, spreading or a little inflexed, twisted or with margins wavy, overlapping at base only; corona cylindrical, angled, soft rich yellow, mouth expanded and loosely frilled, rim crenate. Early. 2n=14. Syn. 'Golden Dragon', 'Irish King', 'Yellow King', Pseudonarcissus Major 'Spurius Yellow King'. ? Irish origin

'Ardsterdogine'
(pre-1831)

'Ardvarna' 2 W-O
(G.L. Wilson, pre-1947)
Corona pale apricot, ageing to almost pure white, frilled

'Areley Kings' 2 W-GWW
(J.S.B. Lea) Clive Postles Daffodils, 1987
'Misty Glen' × 'Croila'; sdlg no. L1-32-76
Corona slightly expanded. Mid-season

'Arena' 11a Y-O
(J. Gerritsen & Son) J. Gerritsen & Son, 1976
'Colorange' hybrid
Fl. 100 mm wide; perianth segments light greenish yellow 8B; corona segments light orange. Mid-season. Resembles a larger-flowered 'Mondragon' with shorter stem

'Arene' 1 W-? (b)
(W. Jackson Sr, 1944)
'Hothu' × 'Saint Aloysius'

'Arentine' 1 W-W
(C. Kaptein, pre-1945)

'Ares' 1 Y-Y
(J.L. Richardson, pre-1916)
Fl. golden yellow; corona widely expanded, with rim rolled. Early

'Arethusa' 1 W-? (b)
(G.H. Engleheart, pre-1907)

'Arethusa' 1 Y-Y
(W.A. Grace, pre-1936)

'Arethusa' 1 W-? (b)
(J.L. Richardson) J.L. Richardson, 1956
'Spitzbergen' × 'Broughshane'

'Argent' 4 W-Y
(G.H. Engleheart, pre-1902)
'Telamonius Plenus' × 'Ornatus' 'Telamonius Plenus' × 'Ornatus'
Fl. star-shaped; perianth and other petaloid segments narrow, acute, creamy white, twisted; corona shallow funnel-shaped, pale yellow, with mouth straight and loosely frilled, with some segments interspersed among the petaloid segments

'Argentic' 2 W-W
(D.S. Bell) D.S. Bell, 1957
'Slemish' × 'Broughshane'

'Argentina' 1 W-W
(D.S. Bell) D.S. Bell, 1978
'Argentic' self pollinated
Fl. 112 mm wide, pure white; corona with green at base. Mid-season

'Argo' 1 Y-Y
(H.J. Poole Sr, pre-1927)

'Argonaut' 1 W-W
(W.F.M. Copeland, pre-1908)

'Argonaut' 1 W-W
(R.C.A. Tombleson) R.C.A. Tombleson, 1970
'Rostov' × 'Empress of Ireland'

'Argonne' 3 W-O
(Mrs R.O. Backhouse, pre-1921)
AM(Haarlem) 1931

'Argos' 2 W-? (b or c)
(T. Batson, pre-1914)

'Argosina' 3 W-W
(R.H. Bath, pre-1929)

'Argosy' 2 W-W
(Cartwright & Goodwin, pre-1908)

'Argosy' 1 Y-Y
(J.L. Richardson) J.L. Richardson, 1959
'Pretoria' × 'Goldcourt'
Late

'Arguros' 3 W-GOR
(G.A. Uit den Boogaard, pre-1950)

'Argus' 3 W-? (b)
(J.W.A. Lefeber, pre-1938)

'Argyle' 2 W-P
(R.H.Glover, pre-1989) Unregistered
'Vanessa' × 'Sprightly'

'Argyll' 1 Y-Y
(The Brodie of Brodie, c.1932)
'Kandahar' × 'Royalist'; sdlg no. 62/A/27

'Aria' 1 W-W
(M. van Waveren & Sons, pre-1953)

'Aria' 9 W-GYR
(Murray W. Evans, c.1982) Unregistered

'Ariadne' 2 or 3 W-W
(E. Leeds, pre-1877)
Corona opening primrose yellow, tinged orange, becoming sulphur white. Syn. Leedsii 'Ariadne'

'Ariadne' 2 W-W
(G.H. Engleheart, pre-1901)
Fl. becoming creamy white; perianth segments ovate, opening clear white, a little inflexed, somewhat twisted or with margins wavy, overlapping at base only; corona broad and shallow funnel-shaped, closely ribbed, opening ivory white, mouth straight, split in places and overlapping, frilled, with rim crenate. Resembles 'Minnie Hume' but with a larger and more spreading corona. AM 1905

'Ariake' 4 Y-O
(R.C. Gordon) R.C. Gordon, 1964
Also named 'Rubicon'

'Arie Hoek' 2 Y-ORR
(W.J.M. Blom, 1970) W.J.M. Blom, 1984

'Sun Chariot' hybrid; sdlg no. 70-A-2
Early

'Ariel' 3 W-Y
(E. Leeds, pre-1877)
Perianth segments sulphur white; corona canary yellow, tinged orange. Syn. Burbidgei 'Albidus', Burbidgei 'Ariel'. Was "absorbed" into 'Sulphur Star'

'Ariel' 5 W-W
(H. Backhouse, pre-1907)
Resembles a smaller 'Dione'

'Ariel' 5 ?W-W
(Sir A.P.W. Thomas, pre-1926)
'Minnie Hume' × *N. triandrus* var. *loiseleurii*

'Ariel' 3 W-OOY
(J.L. Richardson) J.L. Richardson, 1960
'Blarney's Daughter' × ('Tuskar Light' × 'Green Island')
Corona very shallow bowl-shaped, vermilion orange, with a wide band of pale lemon at rim

'Ariel'
(Dorit Sandler, pre-1996) Unregistered

'Aries' 1 Y-Y
(Barr & Sons, pre-1945)

'Ariki' 1 Y-Y
(H.J. Poole Sr, pre-1927)

'Arilta' 1 W-W
(W. Jackson Sr, 1944)
'Cantatrice' × 'Adri'

'Arion' 2 W-Y
(de Graaff Bros, pre-1915)
'Hera' hybrid
Fl. small; perianth segments rounded, milk white, incurving, of strong substance; corona widely expanded, soft sulphur yellow, with rim tinged apricot yellow, neatly frilled. AM(Haarlem) 1915

'Arion'
(pre-1936)

'Arioso' 2 Y-O
(Konynenburg & Mark) Konynenburg & Mark, 1963
'Firemaster' hybrid
Fl. 110 mm wide. Early. Resembles 'Aranjuez'

'Ariosto' 1 Y-Y
(C. Dawson, pre-1923)

'Arisbe' 2 W-Y
(W. Jackson Jr) W. Jackson Jr, 1970
'Palana' × 'Lod'; sdlg no. 39/65

'Arise' 2 W-O
(J.N.Hancock & Co., 1979) Unregistered
'Toorak Gold' × 'Dreamtime'; sdlg no. 15/79H
Perianth segments ivory white, deeply overlapping; corona opening lemon yellow, becoming glowing apricot orange. Tall. Early

'Arish Mell' 5 W-W
(D. & J.W. Blanchard) D. & J.W. Blanchard, 1961
'Interim' × *N. triandrus* var. *loiseleurii*
Fls 3-4 per stem, 79 mm wide, pure white; perianth segments ovate or broadly ovate, acute, only very slightly mucronate, reflexed, with margins wavy and often incurling at apex, overlapping one-third; the inner segments narrower and less strongly inflexed; corona long cup-shaped, lightly ribbed, mouth straight, more or less even, rim crenate. Mid-season. 2n=21. AM(e) 1961, FCC(e) 1963

'Aristides' 2 W-? (b)
(P. van Deursen, pre-1941)
AM(Haarlem) 1941

'Aristocrat' 2 Y-? (a)
(N.Y. Lower, pre-1914)

'Aristocrat' 1 Y-Y
(G.W.E. Brogden) E.A.K. Lee, 1955

'Ariston' 2 W-R
(W. Jackson Jr) W. Jackson Jr, 1970
'Jo' × 'Arbar'; sdlg no. 1/9/65

'Aristophanes' 9 W-?
(A.M. Wilson, pre-1916)

'Aristoteles' 1 Y-Y
(de Graaff Bros, pre-1927)

'Arizaba' 1 W-? (b)
(J.W. Barr, pre-1930)

'Arizona' 2 Y-? (a)
(Mrs R.O. Backhouse, pre-1921)
Syn. 'Galashy'

'Arizona Sunset' 3 Y-R
(Brian S. Duncan) Brian S. Duncan, 1993

'Arja' 2 W-Y
(G.A. Uit den Boogaard) G.A. Uit den Boogaard, 1950

'Arjay' 2 Y-O
(Miss M. Verry) Miss M. Verry, 1975
Fl. 105 mm wide; perianth segments golden yellow; corona reddish orange. Mid-season. Resembles 'Jaguar' but with a longer, narrower and self coloured corona

'Arjuna' 1 Y-Y
(R.G. Crawford) R.G. Crawford, 1955

'Arkangah' 1 W-W
(A.O. Roblin) A.O. Roblin, 1956
'Bonnington' × 'Kanchenjunga'

'Arkansas' 1 Y-Y
(de Graaff Bros, pre-1927)
Syn. 'Juno'

'Arkansas Traveller' 3 Y-Y
(Mrs R.N. Baughn, 1946) Mrs R.N. Baughn, 1957
Barrii 'Conspicuus' hybrid
Fl. star-shaped, about 160 mm wide; perianth segments narrowly oblong, acute, yellow, inflexed, with margins wavy or incurling, separated; the inner segments twisted; corona cylindrical or somewhat funnel-shaped, slightly darker in tone than the perianth, with mouth straight, closely frilled.

'Arkle' 1 Y-Y
(J.L. Richardson) Mrs H.K. Richardson, 1968
'Yellow Idol' × 'Golden Clarion'
Fl. 125 mm wide, deep golden yellow; perianth segments very broadly ovate, blunt, with white mucro, inflexed, plane or convex, overlapping one-third to a half; the inner segments square-shouldered at base, more usually plane or a little twisted; corona cylindrical, mouth slightly expanded, rim flanged, somewhat irregularly notched and crenate

'Arklow' 2 W-R
(J.L. Richardson, pre-1941)
'Red Sun' × 'Forfar'
Perianth segments milk white; corona vivid brick red

'Arkoola' 1 Y-W
(J.N.Hancock & Co., 1984) J.N.Hancock & Co., 1997
'Convention' × 'Daydream'; sdlg no. 24/84H
Perianth segments ovate, lemon yellow, plane; corona flared, creamy white, with rim rolled and crenate. Mid-season

'Ark Royal' 1 Y-Y
(J.L. Richardson, pre-1945)
'Kilkenny' × 'Goldcourt'
Fl. 102 mm wide, deep golden yellow; perianth segments broadly ovate, blunt, spreading, somewhat ribbed, overlapping half; the inner segments a little twisted; corona funnel-shaped, deeper in tone than the perianth segments, with rim flanged and crenate. *AM(g) 1967

'Arkuna'
Unregistered
Pollen parent of 'Major Luck'

'Arlanza' 2 W-W
(Mrs R.O. Backhouse, pre-1916)
Corona opening sulphur yellow, becoming white

'Arlena' 2 Y-R
(J.T. Gray, pre-1951)

'Arleston' 2 Y-Y
(Brian S.Duncan) Brian S.Duncan, 1996
Sdlg 77/1 ('Golden Jewel' × 'Midas Touch') × 'Barnum'; sdlg no. 1413
Fl. 115 mm wide, deep golden yellow; perianth segments very broadly ovate, mucronate, spreading, plane, with margins slightly incurved at apex; corona funnel-shaped, mouth wavy or a little frilled. Mid-season

'Arletta' 2 W-YYP
(S.J. Bisdee, 1939) S.J. Bisdee, 1956
'May Malony' × 'Portia'

'Arliette' 5
(Cartwright & Goodwin, pre-1910)

'Arline' 2 W-Y
(W.F.M.Copeland, pre-1910)
Perianth segments lemon white, overlapping; corona expanded, soft lemon yellow, frilled. Mid-season

'Arlington' 2 W-YYO
(J.C. Williams, pre-1945)
Fl. rounded; perianth segments broad, creamy white; corona ribbed towards mouth, yellow, with a broad band of orange at rim

'Arlo' 2 Y-Y
(R.H.Glover, pre-1993) Unregistered

'Armacourt' 2 Y-? (a)
(W.A. Grace, 1938)

'Armada' 2 Y-O
(G.L. Wilson, pre-1938)
Sdlg 15/7 × ?'Cornish Fire'
Fl. forming a double triangle, 108 mm wide; perianth segments very broadly ovate, blunt, prominently mucronate, vivid yellow 9A, spreading, a little concave, smooth, with margins minutely incurling at apex, overlapping one-third to a half; the inner segments more narrowly ovate, inflexed at base, reflexed near apex, with margins incurved; corona broad funnel-shaped, lightly ribbed, strong orange 25A, mouth split in places and overlapping, wavy, with rim flanged and crenate. Early. 2n=28. AM(e) 1945, FCC(e) 1947, AM(Haarlem) 1948, FCC(Haarlem) 1955, *AM(g) 1962, *FCC(g) 1968, *AM(p) 1976, *FCC(p) 1977, AGM 1993

'Armagh' 1 Y-Y
(W.J. Dunlop) W.J. Dunlop, 1961
'Cromarty' × 'Principal'

Fl. golden yellow

'Armagnac' 11a W-OOY
(J. Gerritsen & Son) J. Gerritsen & Son, 1981
'Pick Up' hybrid
Fl. 90 mm wide; perianth segments ivory white; corona segments tangerine orange, with buttercup yellow at rim. Mid-season

'A.R.Males' 2 Y-O
(C.O. Fairbairn, pre-1959) Unregistered
Perianth segments deep yellow; corona tangerine orange, with mouth expanded and rim reflexed

'Armanda'
(pre-1915)

'Armathwaite' 2 Y-? (a)
(Mrs R.O. Backhouse, pre-1921)

'Armatroy' 2 Y-R
(G.H. Johnstone, pre-1959) Unregistered
'Armada' × 'Troytown'

'Armeline' 3 W-YYO
(G.H. Engleheart, pre-1913)
Perianth segments almond-shaped, creamy; corona deep lemon, flat, rim orange

'Armell' 2 Y-? (a)
(W.A. Watts, pre-1927)

'Armida' 3 W-YYR
(J. Mallender, pre-1913)
Corona yellow, with scarlet at rim

'Armistice' 1 W-Y
(New Zealand origin, 1930)
Perianth segments pure white; corona yellow, becoming very pale, mouth expanded

'Armley Wood' 2 Y-YOR
(W.A. Noton) W.A. Noton, 1976
'Kilmorack' × 'Pinza'; sdlg no. 603
Fl. rounded, 86 mm wide; perianth segments very broad, overlapping; corona shallow, orange, paling to yellow at base and shading to deep red at rim. Mid-season

'Armorel' 3 W-?O
(G.H. Engleheart, pre-1905)
Perianth segments acute, with margins incurling, overlapping; corona shallow, somewhat ribbed, apricot

'Armoury' 4 Y-R
(R.A.Scamp) R.A.Scamp, 1996
'Paricutin' × 'Tamar Fire'; sdlg no. 483
Fl. 98 mm wide; perianth and other petaloid segments in several whorls, broadly ovate, deep golden yellow, deeply overlapping; the outer whorl spreading; the inner whorls inflexed; corona segments short, interspersed among the petaloid segments, bright red. Mid-season to late

'Armoy' 2 W-Y
(G.L. Wilson, pre-1935)
Perianth segments broad, of strong substance; corona neat, clear yellow. Late

'Armstrong' 2 Y-Y
(W.M. Spry, pre-1975) Unregistered
'Jean Hood' × 'Golden'
Corona dark golden yellow. Tall

'Armynel' 2 Y-Y
(Rosewarne EHS, 1970) Rosewarne EHS, 1985
'Dawley' × 'Saint Keverne'; sdlg no. 65/16/1
Fl. 123 mm wide; perianth segments broadly ovate, blunt, mucronate, brilliant yellow 7A, spreading, plane, finely ribbed, with margins slightly incurling, regular, overlapping one-third; the inner segments more narrowly ovate, more nearly acute and less obviously mucronate; corona broad funnel-shaped, smooth, brighter and darker than vivid yellow 14A, with mouth expanded, rim slightly flanged, deeply notched and crenate. Early. Resembles a larger and earlier-flowered 'Dawley'. Syn. 'King Midas'

'Arndilly' 2 W-R
(J.S.B. Lea) J.S.B. Lea, 1972
Sdlg 1-43-54 × Richardson sdlg 199; sdlg no. 1-32-61
Fl. 95 mm wide

'Arnhem' 3 Y-O
(Warnaar & Co., pre-1947)
Corona brownish orange. AM(Haarlem) 1946

'Arno' 1 W-W
(G.H. Engleheart, pre-1902)
Perianth segments creamy white; corona broad, ivory white. Very late

'Arno' 2 Y-R
(J.A. O'More) J.A. O'More, 1971
'Carbineer' × 'Royal Mail'
Fl. 100 mm wide

'Arnold' 1 W-? (b)
(G.P. Haydon, pre-1908)

'Arnold Neale' 1 W-Y
(H.A. Brown) G.E. Mitsch, 1955

'Arnold Rogers' 2 W-? (b or c)
(R.C. Cartwright, pre-1908)

'Arnold Spoel' 1 W-W
(A. Frylink & Sons, pre-1930)

'Arnor' 1 Y-Y
(W. Jackson Sr, 1940)
'Aurelius' × 'Wattle'

'Arnua'
(J.T.Gray, pre-1931)
AM(e)(NZ) 1931

'Aroagh'
Unregistered
Seed parent of 'Glen Tana'

'Aroha' 2 Y-? (a)
(R. Crews, pre-1949)

'Aroha Nui' 2 W-W
(H. Daines, pre-1951)
'Tenedos' × 'White Nile'
Fl. pure white. AM(e)(NZ) 1958

'Aronda' 2 Y-YYO
(J.T. Gray, pre-1949)
Perianth segments yellow; corona shallow, yellow, with a wide band of scarlet-orange at rim

'Aroonah' 1 W-Y
(W. Jackson Jr) Jackson's Daffodils, 1979
'Narang' hybrid; sdlg no. 34/71
Fl. 132 mm wide

'Arosa' 1 W-Y
(Barr & Sons, pre-1929)
Perianth segments white, tinged sulphur at base; corona large, canary yellow, frilled

'Arosa' 2 W-WWP
(J.L. Richardson, 1959) Mrs H.K. Richardson, 1972
'Interim' × 'Rose Caprice'
Perianth segments ice white, slightly reflexed; corona bowl-shaped, pure white, with a clear-cut band of soft coral pink at rim, frilled, with rim finely dentate. Late. Resembles 'Rainbow' but with a whiter perianth

'Aroya' 2 W-WWO
(A.J. Bliss, pre-1930)
'Albatross' × 'Weardale Perfection' sdlg
Perianth segments pure white; corona opening sulphur white to cream, becoming white, with a fairly narrow band of apricot orange at rim

'Arpad Szandry' 2 Y-Y
(J.W.A. Lefeber) J.W.A. Lefeber, 1960
Fl. 86 mm wide; perianth segments orange-yellow; corona richer in tone. Mid-season

'Arpege' 2 W-W
(F.E. Board) F.E. Board, 1965
'Easter Moon' × 'Homage'
Late. Resembles 'Homage'

'Arpeggio' 2 W-P
(G.E. Mitsch) G.E. Mitsch, 1972
Sdlg R47/6 ('Mabel Taylor' × 'Interim') × 'Accent'; sdlg no. X56/4
Fl. 103 mm wide; perianth segments milk white; corona salmon pink, very heavily ribbed and frilled. Mid-season

'Arquebus' 3 W-? (b)
(G.H. Engleheart, pre-1914)

'Arragon' 2 Y-R
(J.M. de Navarro) J.M. de Navarro, 1958
'Revelry' × 'Ceylon'
Perianth segments broadly ovate, blunt, very slightly mucronate, deep yellow, plane or a little hooded at apex, smooth, with broad midrib showing, of glossy substance, regular, overlapping half; the inner segments more narrowly ovate, shouldered at base, more generally concave; corona cylindrical, short, near blood red, with mouth straight and lightly frilled

'Arran' Y-Y
(pre-1927)
Fl. large, yellow

'Arranbeg' 1 Y-Y
(J.L. Richardson, pre-1951)
'Braemar' × 'Crocus'
Fl. golden yellow; perianth segments very broad, smooth; corona slightly deeper in tone than the perianth, with rim rolled. Mid-season

'Arran Isle' 2 Y-YYP
(Brian S. Duncan) Brian S. Duncan, 1992
'Pismo Beach' × 'High Society'; sdlg no. 1229
Fl. 110 mm wide; perianth segments very broadly ovate, blunt, only very slightly mucronate, opening white, gradually becoming cool lemon yellow, spreading, overlapping one-third to a half; corona bowl-shaped, widely expanded, yellow, with a band of pink at rim, minutely frilled. Mid-season to late

'Arranmore' 1 Y-Y
(W.J. Dunlop, pre-1950)
'Royalist' × 'Crocus'
Fl. deep golden yellow

'Arras' 3 Y-? (a)
(Mrs R.O. Backhouse, pre-1921)

'Arras'
(J.T. Gray, pre-1933)

'Array' 9 W-GYR
(Murray W. Evans) Murray W. Evans, 1984
N. poeticus var. *recurvus* open pollinated; sdlg no. P-18/1
Fl. 70 mm wide. 2n=14

'Arriba' 2 Y-O
(J.M. de Navarro, pre-1954)
('Trevisky' × 'Porthilly' sdlg) × 'Gibraltar'
Perianth segments very broadly ovate, mucronate, deep yellow, slightly concave, overlapping half; the inner segments more narrowly ovate, only slightly mucronate, shouldered at base; corona cup-shaped and smooth, reddish orange, almost crimson, mouth expanded and neatly frilled

'Arrogance' 2 Y-? (a)
(Mrs R.O. Backhouse, pre-1908)

'Arrowette' 3 W-O
(?Australian origin, pre-1997) Unregistered

'Arrowhead' 6 Y-R
(R. & E. Havens) R. & E. Havens
('Jetfire' × 'Trogon') × *N. cyclamineus*
Fl. 80 mm wide; perianth segments ovate, golden yellow, with undertones of red, reflexed; corona cylindrical, deep orange-red, with mouth flared. Dwarf. Early. Sunproof. Resembles 'Jetfire' but with broader perianth segments and 'Emperor's Waltz' but with a shorter and more deeply coloured corona

'Arrowsmith' 3 W-GWY
(E.W. Cotter) E.W. Cotter, 1968
'Tryst' hybrid

'Arsenal' 1 Y-Y
(Konynenburg & Mark) Konynenburg & Mark, 1966
'Trumpet Extra' × 'Bird of Dawning'
Fl. 113 mm wide; perianth segments buttercup yellow; corona lemon yellow. Mid-season

'Arsinoe' 3 W-Y
(E. Leeds, pre-1877)
Corona canary yellow. Syn. Leedsii 'Arsinoë', Leedsii 'Gloriosus Minor'

'Arsinoe' 2 W-W
(A.H. Ahrens, pre-1946)

'Arsinoë' 2 W-W
(A.H. Ahrens, pre-1946)

'Arson' 2 O-O
(Carncairn Daffodils, *c*.1982) Unregistered
'Vulcan' × 'Spelter'

'Artegal' 3 W-YRR
(N.Y. Lower, pre-1930)

'Artemis' 2 W-Y
(G.H. Engleheart, pre-1897)
Corona expanded, yellow. Tall. Early

'Artemis' 2 W-W
(C.E. Radcliff, 1931)
'Pink 'Un' hybrid

'Artemis' 2 W-O
(J.W.A. Lefeber) J.W.A. Lefeber, 1961
Fl. 85 mm wide; corona reddish orange. Mid-season

'Artful' 2 W-P
(Murray W. Evans, 1979) Estella L. Evans, 1992
'Quasar' × sdlg × 'Everpink'; sdlg no. W-2/4
Fl. rounded, 107 mm wide; perianth segments very broad, smooth; corona widely expanded, bowl-shaped, ribbed, deep reddish pink, with rim slightly crenate. Mid-season

'Arthen' 3 W-? (b or c)
(W.A. Watts, pre-1923)

'Arthur' 1 Y-Y
(J.W. Barr, pre-1930)

'Arthur Bowman' 3 W-? (b)
(Mrs R.O. Backhouse, pre-1921)

'Arthur Collins' 9 W-?
(F.H. Chapman, pre-1936)

'Arthurian' 1 Y-Y
(Brian S. Duncan) Rathowen Daffodils, 1986
'Golden Jewel' open pollinated; sdlg no. 719
Fl. golden yellow; perianth segments very broadly ovate, blunt, spreading, overlapping half or more; the inner segments more narrowly ovate, a little inflexed, with margins sometimes wavy; corona cup-shaped, with mouth straight, regularly frilled. Mid-season. Resembles a taller 'Golden Jewel' with broader perianth segments

'Arthur Overton' 2 Y-Y
(L.P. Dettman) L.P. Dettman, 1968
'Galway' × 'Chromis'

'Articol' 11a W-YPP
(J. Gerritsen & Son) J. Gerritsen & Son, 1979
Fl. 100 mm wide; perianth segments ivory white; corona segments orange-pink (29B), with pale greenish yellow 13D at base. Mid-season

'Artificer' 1 Y-Y
(E. & J.C. Martin, pre-1916)

'Artificial' 1 W-Y
(R.H.Glover, pre-1993) Unregistered

'Artificial' 1 W-Y
(T.H. Piper) Unregistered
'Karamudli' × ('Riversdale' × 'Renown')

'Artillery' 3 W-R
(J.L. Richardson) M.J. Jefferson-Brown, 1961

'Kilworth' × 'Arbar'
Corona neatly ribbed

'Artis' 3 W-? (b)
(G. Lubbe & Son, pre-1941)
AM(Haarlem) 1941

'Artist' 3 Y-? (a)
(pre-1915)

'Artist' 3 W-Y
(A.E. Lowe, pre-1927)

'Artist' 2 W-YYO
(West & Fell, pre-1933)
Corona canary yellow, with reddish orange at rim

'Artist' 2 W-YYR
(J.N. Hancock & Co., pre-1949)
Perianth segments creamy white; corona golden yellow, with bright red at rim

'Artist' 9 Y-O
(pre-1968) Unregistered

'Artistic' 2 W-YYO
(West & Fell, pre-1935)

'Artistica' 2 W-?
Syn. of 'Accordica'

'Artistique' 11b W-O/YW
(pre-1962) Unregistered
Fl. rounded; corona segments orange, yellow and white, the colours probably in longitudinal bands with orange predominant, with the base of the segments solid orange

'Artist's Delight' 2 Y-R
(D.S. Bell) D.S. Bell, 1960
'Artist's Model' × 'Union Jack'
Fl. 114 mm wide; corona orange-red. Mid-season. Resembles 'Artist's Model' but with a yellow perianth

'Artist's Glory' 2 W-P
(D.S. Bell) D.S. Bell, 1968
'Artist's Model' × pink sdlg
Corona widely expanded, pinkish buff

'Artist's Model' 2 W-OOY
(G. Lewis, 1939) G. Lewis, 1955
'Nene Beauty' × 'Zillah'
Corona broad, closely overlying the perianth, orange, with a band of yellow at rim. Late

'Artois' 1 Y-Y
(J. Gerritsen & Son, pre-1954)

'Artus' 3 Y-? (a)
(P.D. Williams, pre-1927)

'Aruba' 2 W-YYO
(J.J. Grullemans & Sons) J.J. Grullemans & Sons, 1957
Perianth segments cream white; corona wide-spreading, yellow, with orange at rim, frilled. Syn. 'Broken Tip'

'Aruna' 3 W-YRR
(J.T. Gray, pre-1933)
Perianth segments pure white; corona large, widely expanded, brilliant red, with yellow at base

'Arundel' 2 Y-? (a)
(P.D. Williams, pre-1927)

'Arunta' 1 W-W
(S.J. Bisdee, 1948)
'Tain' × 'Cantatrice'

'Arwenack' 11a Y-YYO
(R.A.Scamp, 1986) R.A.Scamp, 1996
'Brandaris' × 'Paricutin'; sdlg no. 224
Fl. 93 mm wide; perianth segments broad, bright yellow, plane, deeply overlapping; corona deeply split, the six segments opposite and closely overlying the perianth segments, bright yellow, with orange towards rim, lightly frilled. Mid-season. Sunproof

'Arwin' 1 W-? (b)
(pre-1913)
See also 'Arwyn'

'Arwon' 2 W-O
(R.H.Glover, pre-1983) Unregistered
'Ida May' × 'Yin-Nell'

'Arwyn' 1 W-? (b)
Syn. of 'Arwin'

'Aryan' 4 W-O
Syn. of 'Picardy'

'Asa' 8
(C.P. Alkemade, pre-1931)
Poetaz

'Asa Gray' 2 Y-? (a)
(de Graaff Bros, pre-1934)
AM(Haarlem) 1933. Received AM(Haarlem) 1933 as 'Dalila'

'Asante' 1 W-Y
(Brian S. Duncan) Brian S. Duncan, 1992
'Rhinestone' open pollinated; sdlg no. 1085
Fl. 115 mm wide; perianth segments broadly ovate, pure white, faintly tinged green at base, spreading or a little reflexed, with margins lightly wavy, overlapping half; the inner segments squarish and inflexed at base, reflexed at apex, with margins more strongly wavy and sometimes incurved from midrib; corona

narrowly funnel-shaped, ribbed, deep lemon yellow, with mouth widely expanded and even, rim dentate and narrowly rolled. Late

'Ascendant' 1 W-? (b)
(R. Crews, pre-1949)

N. aschersonii Bolle = *N. tazetta* subsp. *lacticolor*

'Ascot' 3 Y-? (a)
(de Graaff Bros, pre-1927)
Syn. 'Lady of the Lake'

'Ascot' 4 Y-O
(J.L. Richardson) Warnaar & Co., 1962
'Falaise' hybrid
Fl. 90 mm wide; perianth and other petaloid segments light greenish yellow 8B; corona segments yellow-orange 17B, with pinkish orange (29A) at rim. Mid-season. 2n=28. AM(Haarlem) 1962

'Ascot Gold' 2 Y-Y
(W.M. Spry, pre-1975) Unregistered
'Brazil' × Fairbairn sdlg
Corona golden yellow, frilled. Tall

'Asgard' 2 W-P
(J.N. Hancock & Co., 1962) Unregistered

'Ashanti' 2 Y-R
(D.S. Bell) D.S. Bell, 1971
'Checkmate' × 'Falstaff'
Fl. 102 mm wide

'Ashavan' 1 W-W
(J.L. Richardson) Mrs H.K. Richardson, 1964
'Spitzbergen' × 'Early Mist'
Corona mouth slightly expanded, with rim rolled and dentate

'Ashbourne' 2 Y-? (a)
(D.B. Milne, pre-1952)
PC(e) 1964

'Ashburton' 4 W-YOO
(Mrs H.K. Richardson) du Plessis Bros, 1989
Sdlg no. ?39
Fl. 105 mm wide, rounded; perianth segments pure white; corona segments lightly frilled. Mid-season

'Ashford' 2 W-R
(F.E. Board) F.E. Board, 1965
JLR sdlg 985 × 'Arbar'
Late

'Ashgard' 9 W-YYR
(E.M. Crosfield, pre-1914)
Perianth segments slightly reflexed, overlapping; corona golden yellow, with madder scarlet at rim

'Ashland' 2 W-Y
(W.G.Pannill) W.G.Pannill, 1994
'Broughshane' × 'Rose Royale'; sdlg no. 72/41
Corona yellow, ageing to white. Mid-season

'Ashlar' 2 Y-R
(J.A. O'More, 1959) R.G. Cull, 1978
Sdlg × 'Armada'; sdlg no. 4/59
Mid-season

'Ashleigh' 3 W-R
(W.J. Dunlop, pre-1947)
'Sunstar' × 'Isola'
Corona deep crimson-red

'Ashmore' 2 W-GWW
(J.W. Blanchard) J.W. Blanchard, 1974
'Easter Moon' × sdlg 53/54B (sdlg 46/62E × 'Chinese White'); sdlg no. 64/25A
Fl. 95 mm wide, greenish white 155C; perianth segments broadly ovate, blunt, slightly mucronate, spreading, with broad midrib showing, overlapping one-third to a half; the inner segments more narrowly ovate, angled at shoulder, slightly inflexed; corona cup-shaped, ribbed, with green prominent at base, mouth straight, rim neatly dentate. Mid-season. Resembles 'Easter Moon' but with broader perianth segments and corona. AM(e) 1977

'Ashover' 3 W-? (b)
(D.B. Milne, pre-1952)

'Ashton Wold' 2 W-W
(A.J.R.Pearson, 1985) A.J.R.Pearson, 1995
'Stoke Charity' × 'Panache'; sdlg no. 86-23-J35
Fl. forming a double triangle, 110 mm wide, greenish white (157C); perianth segments very broadly ovate, spreading, plane, satin smooth and of good substance, very deeply overlapping; corona cylindrical, smooth, with green in tube, mouth lightly ribbed and a little flared, with rim crenate. Mid-season

'Ashwater' 2 W-W
(C.E. Radcliff, pre-1938)
'Mitylene' × 'Margaret H.'

'Ashwell' 1 Y-Y
(R.H. Bath, pre-1933)

'Ashwell' 3 W-WYR
(W.A. Noton) W.A. Noton, 1976
'Benediction' × 'Alport'; sdlg no. 579
Fl. 88 mm wide. Late. PC(e) 1976

'Asila' 2 W-YYP
(Brian S. Duncan) Brian S. Duncan, 1993
'Raspberry Ring' × 'Fragrant Rose'; sdlg no. 1058
Fl. 100 mm wide; perianth segments broad, roundish, mucronate, slightly reflexed, a little concave; the inner segments not noticeably mucronate; corona cup-

shaped, deep lemon yellow, with a broad and clearly defined band of deep pinkish orange at rim, mouth a little expanded, wavy, rim notched. Late

'Asita' 5
(Barr & Sons, pre-1923)

'Askelon' 1 W-W
(The Brodie of Brodie, c.1919)
('Weardale Perfection' × 'Duke of Bedford') × 'Nevis'; sdlg no. 135/A/14
Fl. large, creamy white; perianth segments very broadly ovate, blunt, slightly mucronate, spreading or a little inflexed, with margins wavy, creased, overlapping one-third to a half; the inner segments more narrowly ovate, a little inflexed, somewhat twisted; corona funnel-shaped, smooth, greenish white, with yellow in tube, mouth ribbed and flared, a little frilled, with rim obscurely crenate. AM(e) 1932

'Askival' 1 W-W
(P. Lower) E. Longford, 1964
'Vigil' hybrid
Fl. 114 mm wide; perianth segments broad; corona slender, with rim rolled. Early

'Asknot' 2 W-YOO
(P. & G. Phillips) P. & G. Phillips, 1981
Fl. 100 mm wide; corona orange, paling to yellow at base. Mid-season

'Aslan' 4 Y-Y
(Carncairn Daffodils) Carncairn Daffodils, 1990
'Egg Nogg' × 'Daydream'; sdlg no. 7/11/78
Fl. 90 mm wide; perianth and other petaloid segments very broadly ovate, blunt, light greenish yellow 3C, with margins brilliant greenish yellow 3A, overlapping half or more; the outer whorl spreading, a little concave, smooth; the inner whorl slightly shorter, strongly inflexed, creased, with margins incurled; corona segments two-thirds the length of the inner whorl and regularly arranged beneath it, vivid yellow 14A, with margins wavy or frilled and rim minutely striate. Late

'Asmode' 2 W-? (b)
(de Graaff Bros, pre-1930)
AM(Haarlem) 1930

'Aspasia' 8 W-Y
(R. van der Schoot & Son, pre-1908)
N. poeticus × *N. tazetta*
Fls 3-5 per stem, 64 mm wide; perianth segments very broadly ovate, creamy white, spreading, slightly creased, with margins incurling or more strongly incurved, overlapping half; the inner segments narrower; corona shallow bowl-shaped, ribbed, golden yellow, opening with a narrow band of a deeper tone at rim. Scented. 2n=24. Syn. 'Louise'

'Asphodel' 3 W-? (b)
(P.D. Williams, pre-1948)

'Aspiration' 3 Y-? (a)
(Sir A.P.W. Thomas, pre-1930)

'Aspirin' 2 W-W
(C.E. Radcliff, 1931)
'Lord Kitchener' × 'Silver Dawn'
Corona opening lemon yellow, becoming white

'Aspiring' 1 W-W
(D. Bramley) D. Bramley, 1978
'Perfection' × 'Empress of Ireland'; sdlg no. 59/25
Fl. 100 mm wide. Mid-season

'Asporina' 2 Y-? (a)
(C.G. van Tubergen, pre-1944)

'Aspra' 1 W-W
(G.H. Johnstone, pre-1954)
Sdlg × 'Lady-Day'

'Asprey' 1 Y-Y
(H.A. Brown, 1944)

'Asquith' 8 W-Y
Syn. of 'Mrs Asquith'

'Assam' 2 W-Y
(R.O. Backhouse, pre-1931)
Perianth segments of strong substance; corona large, rich golden apricot yellow

'Assent' 2 W-? (b)
(W.A. Bell, pre-1949)

'Assent' 2 W-YPP
(G.H. Johnstone, pre-1959)

'Assertion' 2 W-P
(Brian S.Duncan) Brian S.Duncan, 1997
'Dailmanach' × 'Quasar'; sdlg no. 1535
Fl. 110 mm wide; perianth segments broadly ovate, blunt, spreading; corona bowl-shaped, expanded, very deep pink, tightly frilled, with rim closely and deeply notched as if fringed. Mid-season to late. Sunproof

'Assini' 2 W-W
(W.A. Grace, 1937) J.A. O'More, 1957
Fl. pure white; perianth segments broad, overlapping; corona large, with rim recurved

'Assisi' 3 W-Y
(J.M. de Navarro) J.M. de Navarro, 1958
'Green Island' × 'Galilee'
Corona buff yellow

N. assoanus Dufour 13 Section Jonquilla. FCC 1865
    var. *assoanus*
    var. *praelongus* Barra & López

N. assoi Dufour = *N. assoanus*

'Assurance' 1 W-? (b)
(W. Welchman, pre-1908)
Mid-season

'Assurance' 1 Y-Y
(F.E. Board) F.E. Board, 1965
'Galway' × 'Kingscourt'
Mid-season

'Assyrian' 2 W-O
(A.M. Wilson, pre-1948)
Perianth segments cream; corona reddish orange. Early

'Astalot' 1 Y-W
(G.E. Mitsch) G.E. Mitsch, 1972
'Rima' open pollinated; sdlg no. YO3/2
Fl. 115 mm wide; perianth segments broad, very pale buff yellow, smooth; corona becoming lighter in tone than the perianth. Mid-season

'Asta Nielsen' 3 W-YYR
(J.W.A. Lefeber, pre-1941)

'Astara' 1 W-W
(pre-1961)

'Astarte' 1 W-Y
(Barr & Sons, pre-1913)
'King Alfred' × 'Peter Barr'
Perianth segments creamy white; corona cylindrical, creamy primrose yellow, the rim flushed with a richer tone

'Astarte' 2 Y-Y
(G.H. Johnstone) G.H. Johnstone, 1959
Sdlg × 'Dunkeld'
Fl. 95 mm wide. Early

'Asteria' 1 W-W
(E.M. Crosfield, pre-1910)

'Asteroid' 2 W-? (b or c)
(H. Backhouse, pre-1908)

'Asteroid' 2 Y-Y
(Elise Havens) G.E. Mitsch, 1977
'Ormeau' × 'Butterscotch'; sdlg no. FEJ7/2
Fl. 115 mm wide, golden yellow; perianth segments broadly ovate, blunt, only very slightly mucronate, slightly reflexed, plane, overlapping half; the inner segments more nearly spreading, creased, sometimes nicked at shoulder; corona funnel-shaped, with mouth ribbed and widely flared, rim crenate and slightly rolled. Mid-season

'Astile' 2 Y-? (a)
(W.A. Grace, pre-1938)

'Astingley' 3 W-YYO
(J.T.E. Akers) J.L. Akers, 1991
'Dell Chapel' × 'Valediction'; sdlg no. JT 15
Fl. 80 mm wide. Mid-season

'Asto' 11a W-W
(?Dutch origin, pre-1994) Unregistered
Perianth segments ovate to broadly ovate, slightly mucronate, a little reflexed, sometimes twisted, with margins nicked, overlapping at base only; corona split to base, the six segments opposite and half the length of the perianth segments, opening cream, becoming pure white, spreading, with margins heavily frilled. Late

'Astonishment' 9 W-?
(G.H. Engleheart, pre-1930)

'Astor' 1 W-W
(W. Jackson Jr, 1950)
'Merri' × 'Ammon'; sdlg no. 99/50

'Astoria' 1 W-Y
(Barr & Sons, pre-1930)
Corona deep primrose yellow, with rim flanged and lightly notched

'Astoria' 2 Y-O
(G. Lewis, 1945) D.S. Bell, 1958
Perianth segments yellow; corona expanded, fiery orange

'Astoria' 8
Syn. of 'Morning Splendour'

'Astra' 3 W-? (b)
(pre-1939)

'Astra' 8
(pre-1939)

'Astraea' 2 Y-YYO
(E. Leeds, pre-1851)
Probably a hybrid between *N. hispanicus* var. *propinquus* and one or other of the two taxa named *calathinus*
Fls. large; perianth segments oblong, acute, sulphur yellow, spreading, with margins wavy, separated; corona cylindrical, short, dark yellow, with a faint tinge of orange in a narrow band at rim. Syn. Incomparabilis Sulphureus 'Astraea', Incomparabilis Sulphureus 'Aureo-tinctus'. "Absorbed" 'Queen Mab'

'Astral Light' 2 W-WWY
(D.S. Bell) D.S. Bell, 1964

Fl. 104 mm wide; perianth segments broad, pure white, smooth, overlapping; corona bowl-shaped, with a broad and clearly defined band of deep golden yellow at rim. Resembles 'Green Island' but with smoother perianth segments and the corona of better form

'Astrardente' 3 W-OOR
(G.H. Engleheart, pre-1903)
'Princess Mary' × *N. poeticus* sdlg
Corona more or less disc-shaped, large, apricot orange, with scarlet at rim. AM 1903

'Astrella' 2 W-P
(R.C.A. Tombleson) R.C.A. Tombleson, 1971
Fl. 110 mm wide

'Astrid' 2 W-W
(W. Jackson Sr, 1931)
'Mary Blewitt' × 'Mrs W. Moodie'
Fl. creamy white; corona long, with mouth frilled and rim rolled

'Astrid Bartlett' 2 W-YYP
(Brian S.Duncan) Mrs J.M.Baker, 1996
'Fragrant Rose' × 'Pol Dornie'; sdlg no. 1451
Fl. rounded, 106 mm wide; perianth segments blunt, slightly inflexed, plane; corona fairly long cup-shaped, lemon yellow, with a band of rich teracotta pink at rim, mouth only slightly expanded, lightly frilled. Late. Sunproof. Scented

'Astrodome' 2 W-PPW
(G.E. Mitsch) G.E. Mitsch, 1984
('Precedent' × 'Debutante') × 'Space Ship'; sdlg no. LL393
Fl. 110 mm wide; corona soft apricot pink, with a narrow band of cream at rim. Mid-season

'Astroite' 3 W-GPP
(S.J. Bisdee, 1937)
'Dactyl' × 'Mystic'

'Astrologer' 3 Y-? (a)
(Mrs R.O. Backhouse)

'Astron' 2 Y-Y
(Slieve Donard Nursery Co., pre-1931)
Fl. star-shaped, of very strong substance

'Astronaut' 1 W-O
(J.W.A. Lefeber) J.W.A. Lefeber, 1968

'Astronoom' 1 Y-Y
(W.F. Leenen) W.F. Leenen, 1982
Perianth segments light greenish yellow 5C; corona brilliant yellow 7B

'Astrophel' 2 W-? (b)
(G.H. Engleheart, pre-1910)

'Astropink' 11a W-P
(G.E. Mitsch, 1981) R. & E. Havens, 1993
('Pink Frost' × 'Accent') × ('Accent' × sdlg Q97/2); sdlg no. 2Q8/2
Fl. 85 mm wide; perianth segments ovate, spreading, more or less plane; corona deeply split, the six segments opposite and closely overlying the perianth segments, mid-pink, with a darker tone at rim. Mid-season. Sunproof

N. asturicus Barr = *N. pallidiflorus* var. *pallidiflorus* f. *asturicus*

***N. asturiensis* (Jordan) Pugsley 13 Section Pseudonarcissus** (?"The Small Clipt Trunk Daffodil"). AM 1981, AGM 1994

'Aswan' 2 W-? (b)
(J.L. Richardson, pre-1937)

'Ata' 3 W-Y
(Barr & Sons, pre-1925)
Fl. small; perianth segments snowy white, slightly reflexed; corona chrome yellow, with apricot at rim, neatly frilled

'Ataahua' 4 W-Y
(R.C. Gordon) R.C. Gordon, 1964
Fl. 102 mm wide; perianth and other petaloid segments white; corona segments lemon yellow. Mid-season. Resembles 'Mrs William Copeland' but with a stronger stem and shorter neck

'Atalanta' 1 W-W
(de Graaff Bros, pre-1905)
'Madame de Graaff' hybrid
Perianth segments pure white; corona creamy white, neatly frilled. AM 1907

'Atanga' 2 W-? (b)
(C.E. Radcliff, 1929)
'War Flame' × ?'Pink'un'

'Ataturk' 2 Y-O
(Sir F.C. Stern, pre-1943)
'Killigrew' × 'Rustom Pasha'
Fl. 89 mm wide; perianth segments brilliant or light greenish yellow 8A or B, with margins very slightly incurving, overlapping half; corona slightly expanded, fairly strongly ribbed, richer in colour than strong orange 25A. Sunproof. *AM(g) 1951, *FCC(g) 1952

'At Dawning' 1 W-P
(G.E. Mitsch) G.E. Mitsch, 1975
'Radiation' × 'Rima'; sdlg no. C38/1
Fl. 90 mm wide; corona pale pink, with creamy tones at base. Mid-season. Resembles a smaller, paler 'Rima'

'Athalia' 1 W-W
(de Graaff Bros, pre-1923)

'Athelstan' 1 W-? (b)
(Barr & Sons, pre-1914)

'Athena' 3 W-O
(J.S. Leitch) J.S. Leitch, 1962
Mid-season

'Athene' 5
(F.H. Chapman, pre-1914)

'Athenian' 9 W-?
(E.M. Crosfield, pre-1914)

'Atherton' 3 W-? (b)
(de Graaff Bros, pre-1927)
Syn. 'Talisman'

'Atherton' 2 W-W
(H.A. Brown, 1945) J.N. Hancock & Co., 1965
Perianth segments plane, of good substance, regular; corona creamy white. Mid-season. Resembles a larger 'Silver Scorn'

'Athford' 1 Y-Y
(G.L. Wilson, pre-1930)
Probably a 'Chloris' hybrid
Fl. broad, golden yellow; perianth segments of great substance; corona rim flanged

'Athilda' 1 W-W
(J.T. Gray, pre-1949)

'Athlone' 2 Y-YYO
(P.D. Williams, pre-1927)
'Clava' × 'Forfar'

'Athol' 1 W-Y
(J.A. O'More) J.A. O'More, 1971
'Kanchenjunga' × 'Trousseau'
Fl. 125 mm wide

'Atholl Palace' 4 W-Y
(Brian S. Duncan) Rathowen Daffodils, 1987
Richardson sdlg 3509 ('Falaise' × 'Debutante') × 'Polonaise'; sdlg no. 703
Fl. rounded; perianth and other petaloid segments in three whorls, white; the outer whorl very broadly ovate, blunt, only very slightly mucronate, spreading, overlapping half or more; the second whorl very little shorter, inflexed; the centre whorl broad, strongly inflexed, deeply concave or with margins incurled; corona segments short, clustered at centre, more loosely arranged among the petaloid segments, lemon yellow, tightly frilled. Mid-season to late. Resembles 'Unique' but with a whiter perianth

'Athor' 3 W-? (b)
(J.T. Gray, pre-1938)

'Athos' 1 Y-Y
(W.B. Hartland, pre-1908)

'Athos' 1 Y-Y
Syn. of 'Hermes'

'Atiamuri' 2 Y-? (a)
(R. Hyde) R. Hyde, 1958

'Atilia' 2 W-P
(C.E. Radcliff, pre-1938)
'Mac' × 'Atanga'

'Atlanta' 4 Y-O
(?Warnaar & Co., c.1962) Unregistered

'Atlantic' 1 W-W
(de Graaff-Gerharda, pre-1930)

N. atlanticus Stern 13 Section Apodanthi. PC 1997

'Atlantis' 2 W-? (b)
(H. Backhouse, pre-1908)

'Atlantis' 1 W-W
(D. Bramley) D. Bramley, 1980
'Cumulus' hybrid; sdlg no. 71/58
Fl. 109 mm. Mid-season. Resembles a larger-flowered 'Cumulus'

'Atlas' 1 Y-Y
(Barr & Sons, pre-1913)

'Atlas' 1 Y-Y
(J.L. Richardson) Warnaar & Co., 1961
Fl. 110 mm wide, vivid yellow 12A. Late. Resembles a darker-coloured 'Irish Luck' of better form. AM(Haarlem) 1961

'Atlas Gold' 10 Y-Y
(Moroccan origin) Potterton and Martin, 1993
Selection from J.C.Archibald's wild-collected *N. romieuxii*; sdlg no. JCA805Y
Fl. 38 mm wide, brilliant greenish yellow 6A; perianth segments narrowly triangular in appearance, a little inflexed, widely separated; corona broad, shallow funnel-shaped, ribbed, with mouth straight, rim irregularly and minutely crenate. Dwarf. Mid-season

'Atom' 6 Y-Y
(G.E. Mitsch) G.E. Mitsch, 1975
'Wee Bee' × *N. cyclamineus*; sdlg no. C47/2
Fl. 40 mm wide, deep yellow; perianth segments strongly reflexed; corona frilled, with rim flanged. Early

'Atom Flash' 3 W-R
(Oregon Bulb Farms, pre-1950)

'Atomic' 2 W-?
(A. Overton) A. Overton, 1960

'Atomy' 3 W-Y
(E. Leeds, pre-1877)
Corona lemon yellow. Syn. Leedsii 'Atomy'

'Atora' 2 W-W
(J.S. Leitch) J.S. Leitch, 1958

'Atranga'
(pre-1959)

'Atreus' 3 W-? (b)
(Mrs R.O. Backhouse, pre-1921)

'Atro' 2 Y-R
(W. Jackson Jr) Jackson's Daffodils, 1979
'Dimity' × sdlg 65/66; sdlg no. 23/73
Fl. 102 mm wide, rounded; perianth segments broad, mid-yellow; corona orange-red. Tall. Mid-season

'Atropos' 1 W-? (b)
(de Graaff Bros, pre-1927)

'Attainment' 2 W-? (b)
(R.H. Bath, pre-1923)

'Attica' 1 Y-Y
(W. Jackson Jr, 1968) Unregistered
'Ilina' × 'King's Ransom'; sdlg no. 56/68

'Attila' 1 W-W
(H. Backhouse, pre 1910)

'Attila' 2 W-O
(J.S. Leitch) J.S. Leitch, 1968

'Attis' 2 W-OOR
(W. Jackson Jr, 1968) Unregistered
Sdlg 86/61 ('Jo' × 'Capella') × 'Arbar'; sdlg no. 127/68

'Attitude' 1 Y-Y
(J.N. Hancock & Co., 1963) Unregistered

'Attraction' 9 W-?
(E.H. Wheadon & Sons, pre-1916)

'Attraction' 1 W-Y
(D. van Buggenum) D. van Buggenum, 1970
'Gold Medal' × 'Victoria'

'Attractive' 1 Y-Y
(pre-1979) Unregistered

'Attrus' 2 O-R
(M.J. Jefferson-Brown) M.J. Jefferson-Brown, 1985
Fl. large; perianth segments broad, rounded, pinkish orange, deeply overlapping; corona neat, orange-red. Mid-season

'Atuaroa' 2 W-W
(Mrs A.R. Simmons) Mrs A.R. Simmons, 1980

Sdlg no. 70-1-76
Fl. 108 mm wide; corona opening cream, becoming white. Mid-season

'Aubade' 2 Y-? (a)
(P. van Deursen, pre-1953)

'Aubrey' 1 Y-Y
(de Graaff Bros, pre-1928)
?The same as 'Superba'

'Auburn' 5 Y-Y
(D. Blanchard, pre-1951)
'Goldbeater' × *N. triandrus* var. *concolor*
2n=21

'Auda' 4 Y-O
(R.H. Bath, pre-1929)
Fl. large; perianth and other petaloid segments white; corona segments soft orange

'Audacious' 2 W-? (b)
(W.F.M. Copeland, pre-1916)

'Audacity' 2 W-Y
(G.E. Mitsch) G.E. Mitsch, 1972
'Green Island' × 'High Life'; sdlg no. Z19/13
Fl. rounded, 100 mm wide; perianth segments plane; corona disc-shaped, large, ribbed, opening soft lemon yellow, becoming white. Mid-season. Resembles a white 'Pinwheel'

'Auden' 9 W-GYR
(E.W. Cotter) D.S. Bell, 1975
'Wordsworth' × 'Sea Green'
Fl. 65 mm wide; corona yellow, with green at base and a band of red at rim. Mid-season. Resembles an earlier-flowered 'Sea Green'

'Auditor' 2 W-? (b)
(Cartwright & Goodwin, pre-1910)

'Audley' 1 Y-Y
(de Graaff Bros, pre-1928)
Syn. 'Isolde'

'Audley' 1 Y-Y
Syn. of 'Herman Gorter'

'Audrey'
(pre-1914)

'Audrey Joan' 2 Y-OYY
(Clive Postles) R.Anderson, 1995
Sdlg 27-79 × 'Badbury Rings'; sdlg no. 45-83
Fl. 80 mm wide; perianth segments lemon yellow, with midrib showing. Mid-season

'Audubon' 2 W-WWP
(G.E. Mitsch, 1955) G.E. Mitsch, 1965

('Interim' × 'Mabel Taylor') × 'Caro Nome'; sdlg no. R110/1A
Fl. 102 mm wide; perianth segments broadly ovate, blunt, fairly prominently mucronate, pure white, spreading, plane, with margins sometimes minutely incurling, of good substance, overlapping one-third to a half; the inner segments a little inflexed, with margins wavy or more strongly incurled; corona bowl-shaped, ribbed, creamy white, with a broad band of coral pink at rim, mouth split in places and overlapping, lightly frilled. Mid-season. Varies between Divs 2 and 3

'Augon' 3 W-? (b)
(G.H. Engleheart, pre-1927)

'Augusta' 1 W-? (b)
(P. van Deursen, pre-1930)
EFA(Haarlem) 1932

'Auguste' 2 Y-YYO
(P.D. Williams, pre-1910)
Fl. facing down; perianth segments broadly ovate, blunt or truncate, spreading, with margins wavy or incurling, with broad midrib showing, overlapping half; the inner segments inflexed, with margins more strongly wavy and more deeply incurled; corona almost disc-shaped, ribbed, greenish yellow, with a broad band of orange at rim, the rim notched and minutely crenate. AM 1924

'August Green' 1 W-Y
(W.M. Spry, pre-1973) Unregistered
'Judy Davidson' × Fairbairn sdlg

'August Moon' 1 Y-Y
(G.L. Wilson, pre-1935)
Sdlg × 'Askelon'

'August Pink' 2 W-P
(O. Ronalds, pre-1967) Unregistered
Corona dark pink

'Auirole' 2 Y-Y
Syn. of 'Auriole'

'Aula' 8 W-Y
(pre-1807)
Early. ?The same as 'Auleus'

'Auleus' 8 W-Y
?Syn. of 'Aula'

'Aulus' 1 Y-Y
(A.H. Ahrens, 1948) D.J. Cooper, 1959
Fl. 95 mm wide; perianth segments sulphur yellow; corona slightly darker in tone. Mid-season

'Auntie Eileen' 2 W-P
(R.A. Scamp) R.A. Scamp, 1993

'Easter Moon' × 'Debutante'; sdlg no. 151
Fl. 90 mm wide; perianth segments very broadly ovate, blunt, slightly mucronate, chalky white, spreading, with margins minutely incurling at apex, smooth, overlapping half or more; the inner segments rounded at apex, shouldered at base; corona broad cup-shaped, broadly and obscurely ribbed, opening pale pink, becoming paler in tone, mouth expanded and lightly frilled. Mid-season

'Aunt Jane' 3 W-Y
(W. Backhouse, pre-1869)
Corona widely expanded, yellow, with tinges of orange. Syn. Burbidgei 'Aunt Jane'. Was "absorbed" into 'Mary'

'Aunt Maria' 1 W-W
(F.H. Chapman, pre-1923)

'Aunt Mary' 2 W-P
(A. Gibson) A. Gibson, 1965
Fl. 102 mm wide. Mid-season

'Auralius' 1 Y-Y
Syn. of 'Aurelius'

'Auramont' 3 W-? (b)
(P.D. Williams, pre-1935)

aurantiacus = *N. triandrus* var. *concolor*

'Aurantiacus' 7 Y-Y
Syn. of 'Orange Queen'

N. auranticoronatus Maire = *N. elegans* var. *elegans* f. *auranticoronatus*

N. auranticoronus Spach = *N. tazetta* subsp. *lacticolor*

N. aurantius hort. = *N.* × *macleayi*

N. aurantius Schultes f. = *N.* × *incomparabilis*

'Aurantius' 2 W-O
(E. Leeds, pre-1877)
Perianth segments pure white; corona ribbed, suffused orange, with mouth expanded. Syn. Nelsonii 'Aurantius'

'Aurantius' 2 or 3 ?-O
(E.Leeds, pre-1877)
Corona stained orange. Syn. Incomparabilis Albidus 'Aurantius'

'Aurantius' 2 or 3 W-R
(E.Leeds, pre-1877)
Perianth segments pure white; corona bright crimson. Syn. Incomparabilis 'Aurantius'

'Aurantius' 2 or 3 Y-YYO
Syn. Incomparabilis 'Aurantius'

'Aurantius' 2 W-Y
Syn. of 'Marmion'

'Aurantius' 3 W-Y
Syn. of 'Cinderella'

'Aurantius Flore Pleno' 4 W-O
Syn. of 'Orange Phoenix'

'Aurantius Grandiflorus' 3? Y-O
(pre-1879)
Syn. Barrii 'Aurantius Grandiflorus'

'Aurantius Plenus' 4 Y-O
Syn. of 'Butter and Eggs'

'Auravale' 1 Y-Y
(J.N.Hancock & Co., 1982) J.N.Hancock & Co., 1997
Sdlg no. 96/82H
Fl. bright yellow; perianth segments broadly ovate, plane; corona cylindrical, with mouth abruptly flared, rim rolled and crenate. Mid-season

'Aureate' 2 Y-? (a)
(F.H. Chapman, pre-1930)

'Aurelia' 7 Y-Y
(Barr & Sons, pre-1913)
Fls 1-2 per stem, 89 mm wide, rich lemon yellow; perianth segments broadly ovate, blunt, with white mucro, spreading, creased, with margins wavy, overlapping half; the inner segments a little inflexed, somewhat twisted; corona funnel-shaped, loosely ribbed, slightly darker in tone than the perianth, mouth straight or a little flared, lightly frilled. Mid-season to late. Scented. 2n=21. *AM(g) 1936

'Aurelius' 1 Y-Y
(W. Jackson Sr, 1926)
'Peter Dawson' × 'Renown'
Early. ?The same as 'Auralius'

'Aureola' 2 Y-?
?Syn. of 'Aureole'

'Aureole' 2 Y-? (a)
(Cartwright & Goodwin, pre-1908)
?The same as 'Aureola'

'Aureo-tinctus' 2 W-Y
(?E.Leeds, pre-1877)
Corona pale yellow, tinged orange. Syn. Incomparabilis Albus 'Aureo-tinctus'

'Aureo-tinctus' 2 Y-YYO
(pre-1877)
Syn. of 'Astraea'

'Aureo-tinctus' 3 W-Y
(pre-1883)
Syn. Barrii Albus 'Aureo-tinctus'

'Aureo-tinctus' 2 W-YYO
(pre-1887)
Syn. of 'Annie Baden'

***N. aureus* Loiseleur-Deslongchamps 13 Section Tazettae**

N. aureus de Candolle = *N. bulbocodium* subsp. *bulbocodium*

'Au Revoir' 3 W-W
(T. Bloomer) T. Bloomer, 1964

'Auric' 1 Y-Y
(A. Sandys-Winsch, pre-1933)

'Auricumus'
(pre-1913)

'Aurie's Star' 2 W-OOG
(W.M. Spry, pre-1975) Unregistered
'Picture' × 'Clinton'
Corona dark honey orange, with creamy green at rim, frilled

'Aurifer' 1 W-? (b)
(T. Batson, pre-1907)

'Auriga'
(pre-1913)

'Auriga' 1 Y-Y
(S.J. Bisdee, pre-1947)
'Golden City' × 'Crocus'

'Auriga' 2 W-P
(W.O. Backhouse) E. Longford, 1967
Pink sdlg × pink sdlg
Fl. 104 mm wide; corona copper pink, paling to base. Mid-season. Resembles 'Inverpolly' in form

'Aurigny' 2 W-? (b)
(Mrs R.O. Backhouse, pre-1921)

'Auriol' 2 Y-O
(J.T. Gray, pre-1949)
Perianth segments buff-coloured, deepening with age; corona straight-sided, reddish orange

'Auriole' 2 Y-Y
(C.E. Radcliff, 1930)
'W.F.Gates' hybrid
See also 'Auirole'

'Aurora' 8 W-Y
(pre-1807)

'Aurora' 2 W-? (b)
(G.H. Engleheart, pre-1902)
AM 1902

'Aurora' 2 W-O
(R.H. Bath, pre-1931)
Perianth segments sulphur white; corona reddish orange, heavily frilled. AM(Haarlem) 1930

'Aurora Borealis' 2 Y-P
(W.A.Bender) W.A.Bender, 1996
Sdlg 91/178 open pollinated
Fl. 90 mm wide; perianth segments broadly ovate, brilliant greenish yellow 4A, spreading, plane, smooth; corona cylindrical, light pink (36A), paling to base (36D), with mouth flared and frilled. Mid-season

'Aurore' 1 Y-Y
Syn. of 'Flavian'

'Aurum' 1 Y-Y
(G.E. Mitsch) G.E. Mitsch, 1971
'Galway' × 'Saint Keverne'; sdlg no. A17/20
Fl. 100 mm wide, golden yellow, velvet smooth; perianth segments plane. Mid-season

'Aurumfino' 1 Y-Y
(W.M. Spry, pre-1975) Unregistered
'Braemar' × 'Golden Valley'
Mid-season

'Au Sable' 2 W-? (b)
(Oregon Bulb Farms, pre-1951)

'Auselmus' 8 W-O
(pre-1798)

'Auspicious' 2 O-O
(Jackson's Daffodils) Jackson's Daffodils, 1986
'Brett' × 'Gunsynd'; sdlg no. 214/77
Perianth segments broadly ovate, blunt, vivid yellow 13A flushed strong reddish orange 32B, with slight white mucro, spreading, with broad midrib slightly paler in tone, overlapping half; the inner segments a little narrower, slightly inflexed, ribbed; corona long cup-shaped, expanded, orange (28A), mouth straight, neatly or sometimes more loosely frilled. Mid-season

'Aussie' 1 Y-Y
(West & Fell, pre-1929)
PC(e)(NZ) 1929

'Australia' 1 Y-Y
(J.N. Hancock & Co., pre-1949) J.N. Hancock & Co., 1960
Fl. yellow; corona with rim widely rolled

'Australian Gold' 1 Y-Y
(D.V. West, pre-1935)
Fl. clear light yellow; perianth segments twisted

'Australind' 1 Y-Y
(J.N. Hancock & Co., pre-1956) Unregistered

'Austral Queen' 1 W-Y
(D.V. West, pre-1927)
Corona canary yellow

'Authentica' 2 Y-? (a)
(B. Rowlands, pre-1938)

'Authority' 1 Y-Y
(J.H. Rijkelijkhuizen) J.H. Rijkelijkhuizen, 1965
Fl. 105 mm wide; perianth segments sulphur; corona deep golden yellow

'Autocrat' 2 Y-Y
(W. Backhouse/E. Leeds, pre-1869)
Fl. large, yellow; corona widely expanded, sometimes stained orange. Syn. Incomparabilis Concolor 'Autocrat', Incomparabilis Concolor 'Expansus'. "Absorbed" 'Eclipse' and 'Provost'

'Automedon' 1 Y-Y
(pre-1886)
Perianth segments yellow; corona very large, full yellow

'Autowin' 3 W-YYR
(G. Lewis) G. Lewis, 1955

N. autumnalis Link = *N. elegans*

AUTUMN GEM 8 W-O
Trade designation for 'Charles Tatham'

'Autumn Gold' 7 Y-Y
(G.E. Mitsch, 1968) G.E. Mitsch, 1979
'Quick Step' × 'Daydream'; sdlg no. D80/13
Fl. 80 mm wide, deep yellow. Late. Resembles a larger and usually single-flowered 'Quail' of darker colour

'Autumn Leaves' 2 W-Y
(D.S. Bell) D.S. Bell, 1963
'Papanui Queen' × 'Green Island'
Fl. 11 mm wide; corona lemon yellow, frilled. Mid-season. Resembles a larger-flowered 'Papanui Queen' with broader perianth segments

'Autumn Sol' 8 Y-Y
(New Zealand origin) F.W. Shepherd, 1961
Fls up to 9 per stem, 35 mm wide; perianth segments ovate, blunt, light greenish yellow 5D, with white mucro, spreading or slightly reflexed, somewhat ribbed, glistening, slightly overlapping; the inner segments not noticeably mucronate; corona cup-shaped, irregular in form, lightly ribbed, vivid yellow 15A, with mouth slightly wavy and rim entire.

Flowering October-November. Strongly scented. Resembles an early-flowered 'Soleil d'Or' of paler colouring

'Auvergne' 5
(Barr & Sons, pre-1923)

'Auxerre' 1 W-O
(J. Gerritsen & Son, 1973) J. Gerritsen & Son, 1984
Sdlg × 'Alpine Glow'
Perianth segments ivory white; corona orange-pink (23D), with bronze yellow at base and touches of a darker pink at rim. Mid-season

'Avalanche' 1 W-W
(de Graaff Bros, pre-1905)
'Madame de Graaff' hybrid
Perianth segments ribbed, snow white; corona long, straight-sided, pure white

'Avalanche' 8 W-Y
(pre-1906) T.M. Dorrien Smith, 1955
Fls about 10 per stem, 33 mm wide; perianth segments broadly ovate, blunt, mucronate, reflexed, concave, ribbed, overlapping half; the inner segments truncate; corona bowl-shaped, brilliant greenish yellow 6C, smooth, mouth straight or slightly constricted, with some shallow lobing, rim entire. Strongly scented. 2n=31+1B. AM(e) 1991, AGM 1995

'Avalon' 3 W-OOR
(A.M. Wilson, pre-1913)
Perianth segments rounded, pure white, overlapping; corona very shallow, lightly frilled. Late. Resembles an improved 'Challenger'

'Avalon' 2 Y-W
(Mrs H.K. Richardson) Mrs H.K. Richardson, 1977
'Camelot' × 'Daydream'; sdlg no. 138
Perianth segments broad, rounded, brilliant yellow, smooth; corona maturing to white throughout. Midseason. Resembles a larger-flowered 'Daydream' of heavier substance and a 'Camelot' with smoother perianth

'Avanley' 1 W-P
(C.E. Radcliff, pre-1938)
'Pink o' Dawn' × 'Beersheba'
?Syn. of 'Alvanley'

'Avanti' 2 Y-OOY
(P.Cleine, 1981) Unregistered
Sdlg no. 27/81C
Perianth segments primrose yellow; corona disc-shaped, regularly ribbed, orange, with yellow at rim. Early

'Ave' 2 W-W
(G.L. Wilson, pre-1935)
Presumed destroyed; replaced by 'Ave' 1942

'Ave' 2 W-W
(G.L. Wilson, 1942)
'Truth' × 'Slemish'; sdlg no. 32/75
Fl. forming a double triangle, large, snow white; perianth segments smooth, of good substance, regular; corona with rim neatly rolled. Replaced 'Ave' pre-1935

'Avebury' 1 W-W
(The Brodie of Brodie, pre-1928)
Sdlg × 'Nevis'

'Aveley' 2 Y-? (a)
(T.A.V. Wood, pre-1949)

'Aveline' 3 W-W
(Barr & Sons, pre-1914)

'Avella' 2 W-W
(G.L. Wilson) G.L. Wilson, 1964
'Dew-pond' × 'Pigeon'

'Ave Maria' 1 W-? (b)
(L. Buckland, pre-1935)

'Avenal Light' 3 W-? (b)
(N. Carter, pre-1949)

'Avenal Plane' 2 W-? (b)
(N. Carter, pre-1949)

'Avenel' 2 W-O
(H.A. Brown, pre-1938)
Corona orange, frilled

'Avenger' 2 W-R
(J.L. Richardson) J.L. Richardson, 1957
'Kilworth' × 'Arbar'
Fl. 90 mm wide; perianth segments very broadly ovate, blunt, slightly mucronate, spreading, a little concave, smooth, with midrib sometimes showing, regular, overlapping half; the inner segments a little more narrowly ovate, shouldered at base, slightly inflexed; corona disc-shaped, loosely ribbed, orange-red (30B), with mouth widely expanded and a little frilled, rim entire. Mid-season. 2n=28. AM(e) 1965, FCC(e) 1969

'Avenir' 1 W-Y
Syn. of 'L'Avenir'

'Aventine' 2 W-Y
(Barr & Sons, pre-1922)
Perianth segments creamy white; corona large, bright yellow. Resembles 'Lady Margaret Boscawen'

'Averil' 1 W-W
(P.D. Williams, pre-1907)
Corona becoming creamy white

'Averill Harriman' 2 Y-O
(H.P. Zwetsloot, pre-1949)
'Aranjuez' hybrid

'Avernus' 2 Y-? (a)
(Mrs R.O. Backhouse, pre-1921)

'Ave Verum' 2 W-? (b)
(M. van Waveren & Sons, pre-1942)

'Aviator' 3 W-? (b)
(W. Welchman, pre-1914)

'Aviemore' 2 Y-YOO
(The Brodie of Brodie, c.1927)
'Beacon' × 'Fortune'
Fl. forming a double triangle, 86 mm wide, facing down; perianth segments broadly ovate, blunt, mucronate, vivid greenish yellow 2A, paler at midrib and apex, spreading or a little inflexed, with margins minutely incurling at apex, creased, overlapping one-third to a half; the inner segments with margins wavy and sometimes more strongly incurling; corona short funnel-shaped, loosely ribbed, strong orange, paling to golden yellow at base, with mouth straight and more or less even, rim irregularly crenate. AM(e) 1931

'Avignon' 1 W-? (b)
(C.E. Radcliff, 1931)

'Avignon' 3 W-GYY
(J.L. Richardson) Mrs H.K. Richardson, 1973
'Dallas' × 'Shagreen'

'Avis' 2 W-YPP
(J.N. Hancock & Co., 1955) Unregistered

'Avoca' 1 Y-Y
(G.L. Wilson, pre-1934)

'Avoca' 9 W-GGR
(C.E. Radcliff, 1938) C.E. Radcliff, 1956
N. poeticus × ?'Dactyl'

'Avocat' 3 Y-? (a)
(W.B. Cranfield, pre-1923)

'Avocet' 8
(C. Dawson, pre-1908)

'Avocet' 7 W-YYW
(G.E. Mitsch) G.E. Mitsch, 1982
('Green Island' × 'Chinese White') × *N. jonquilla*; sdlg no. KK102/3
Fls usually 3 per stem, 64 mm wide; corona buff yellow, paling to white at rim. Late

'Avolet' 2 W-Y
(D.V. West, pre-1935)
Perianth segments pure white; corona canary yellow

'Avon' 1 W-W
Syn. of 'Indiana'

'Avona' 3 Y-R
(D.C. Tongs, pre-1996) Unregistered

'Avondale' 2 W-Y
(H.A. Brown, pre-1936)
Corona rich yellow, with mouth expanded and lightly frilled

'Avondster' 3 W-? (b)
(J.W.A. Lefeber) J.W.A. Lefeber, 1956

'Avonlea' 2 W-O
(H.A. Brown, pre-1938)
Corona reddish orange

'Avonmore' 2 W-GGR
(W.M. Spry, pre-1975) Unregistered
'Chinese White' × 'Revelry'
Corona frilled. Late

'Avril' 2 Y-O
(F. Rijnveld & Sons) F. Rijnveld & Sons, 1959
Fl. 55 mm wide; perianth segments vivid yellow 9a; corona strong orange 30D. Late. Resembles a darker-flowered 'Carbineer'. AM(Haarlem) 1959

'Awadale' 2 Y-? (a)
(Parr's Nurseries, 1946) Parr's Nurseries, 1958

'Awahou' 1 Y-Y
(S.A. Free) S.A. Free, 1966
Mid-season to late

'Awake' 2 W-? (b)
(G.H. Johnstone, pre-1943)

'Awakening' 2 W-?
(C.O. Fairbairn) A. Ladson, 1960

'Awakino' 2 Y-R
(R. Hyde) R. Hyde, 1955

'Awaroa' 2 W-? (b)
(R. Hyde) R. Hyde, 1955

'Awatea' 2 or 3 ?W-P
(J.T. Gray, pre-1949)
'White Sentinel' × 'Pink o' Dawn'
Corona rose pink

'Awatea' 2 Y-?
Syn. of 'Otekura'

'A.W. Tait' 1 Y-Y
(Spanish origin)
Selection by A.W. Tait (c.1917) from wild-collected *N. hispanicus*

Resembles an earlier-flowered *N. hispanicus* of darker colour. Syn. "Extra Early Maximus". *HC(g) 1927

'Awyn' 2 Y-? (a)
(Mrs M.Moorby) Mrs M.Moorby, 1956

'Axedale' 2 W-W
(J.N. Hancock & Co., 1971) Unregistered
'First Frost' hybrid

'Ayacanora' 2 Y-? (a)
(A.R. Goodwin, pre-1908)

'Ayala' 2 Y-O
(J.L. Richardson) Mrs H.K. Richardson, 1963
'Somali' × 'Red Goblet'
Perianth segments slightly rounded, golden yellow; corona deep reddish orange, frilled. Very late. Resembles 'Royal Charger'

'Ayesha' 1 W-W
(pre-1913)

'Ayesha' 1 W-Y
(Barr & Sons, pre-1922)
Perianth segments white, tinged pale primrose yellow at base; corona slender, canary yellow

'Aylmer' 1 Y-Y
(Barr & Sons, pre-1920)
Perianth segments bright yellow, inflexed; corona rich yellow, with rim recurved

'Aylwin' 2 Y-? (a)
(A.H. Ahrens) J.S. Leitch, 1955

'Ayn' 3 W-YYR
(W. Jackson Sr, pre-1948) W. Jackson Jr, 1966
Sdlg 95/50 × 'Estrella'; sdlg no. 73/60
Perianth segmets white; corona deep yellow, with orange-red at rim

'Ayot' 1 W-? (b)
(P. van Deursen, pre-1930)
Syn. 'Edison'. AM (Haarlem) 19??

'Ayston' 2 W-W
(W.A.Noton, pre-1991) Unregistered

'Azalea' 2 W-WPP
(Oregon Bulb Farms, pre-1945)

'Azazel' 3 W-? (b)
(R.O. Backhouse, pre-1930)

'Azie' 3 W-?
(W. Jackson Jr, 1954)
'Oba' × ('Token' × 'Selia')

'Azon' 2 W-YYO
(H.G. Cross) H.G. Cross, 1994
Sdlg no. ESC 90 B
Fl. 98 mm wide; perianth segments very broad in outline, blunt or slightly truncate, only very slightly mucronate, yellowish white 155B, spreading, overlapping half or more; the inner segments with margins wavy; corona widely expanded, lightly ribbed, light greenish yellow 5D, with a broad band of strong orange 25B near the mouth suffusing the yellow at rim, mouth with six deep and overlapping lobes, rim shallowly crenate. Mid-season

'Azrael' 2 W-? (b or c)
(The Brodie of Brodie, pre-1910)
'Una' × 'Madame de Graaff'
Fl. facing down

'Aztec' 2 Y-? (a)
(Oregon Bulb Farms, pre-1946)

'Aztec Chief' 2 Y-? (a)
(A.F. Calvert, pre-1948)

'Aztec Gold' 1 Y-Y
(D.S. Bell) D.S. Bell, 1968
('Ranalagh' × 'Goldcourt') × 'David Bell'
Fl. rich golden yellow, smooth, of strong substance; corona with rim flanged

'Aztec Sun' 2 Y-R
(N.R. McIsaac) N.R. McIsaac, 1978
'Naples' × 'Falstaff'; sdlg no. 82
Fl. 91 mm wide; perianth segments gold; corona deep orange-red. Early

'Azzuro' 3 Y-R
(Jackson's Daffodils) Jackson's Daffodils, 1986
Sdlg 195/67 × 'Brett'; sdlg no. 233/78
Fl. rounded; perianth segments very broad, blunt or shallowly truncate, brilliant greenish yellow 6B, with slight white mucro, spreading, a little concave, smooth, with broad and pale midrib showing, overlapping two-thirds; the inner segments a little inflexed; corona small and shallow cup-shaped, orange-red, with rim minutely crenate. Mid-season to late

B

'Babacott' 2 W-?
Syn. of 'Bovacott'

'Babette' 2 Y-? (a)
(Cartwright & Goodwin, pre-1916)

'Babette' 2 W-P
(J.N. Hancock & Co., 1963) Unregistered

'Babinda' 1 W-P
(Jackson's Daffodils, 1987) Jackson's Daffodils, 1997
'Melancholy' × sdlg 196/75; sdlg no. 106/87
Fl. 105 mm wide; perianth segments ovate, yellowish white (155B); corona cylindrical, pale yellowish pink 29D, frilled, with rim flanged. Mid-season to late

'Babs'
(C. Dawson, pre-1908)

'Baby' 1 W-? (b)
(H.R. Meyer, pre-1927)

'Baby Doll' 6 Y-Y
(M.P. Williams) G. Zandbergen-Terwegen, 1957
Fl. 75 mm wide; perianth segments ovate, vivid yellow 9A, slightly reflexed, overlapping one-third; corona cylindrical, loosely ribbed towards base, of a deeper tone (14B) than the perianth, mouth more strongly ribbed, slightly expanded and a little frilled, rim notched and crenate and sometimes flanged. Dwarf. Resembles a later-flowered and shorter-stemmed 'February Gold'. Syn. 'Cairhayes', 'Cairhays'. AM(Haarlem) 1957, HC 1973, *AM(g) 1977

'Babylon' 3 W-? (h)
(L. van Leeuwen & Son, pre-1950)

'Babylon's Majestic'
(?A. Frylink & Sons, pre-1938)

'Babylon's Sweepstake' 1 W-? (b)
(A. Frylink & Sons, pre-1930)
Syn. 'Luxor'

'Babylon's Treasure' 1 Y-Y
(A. Frylink & Sons, pre-1930)
Syn. 'Treasure'

'Baby Moon' 7 Y-Y
(J. Gerritsen & Son) J. Gerritsen & Son, 1958
N. jonquilla var. *minor* × *N. jonquilla*
Fls 3-5 per stem, canary yellow. Late. Sweetly scented. 2n=14. Resembles *N. jonquilla*. AM(Haarlem) 1958, FCC(Haarlem) 1960

'Baby Pink' 7 W-GWP
(Eileen E. Frey, 1981) J. & E. Frey, 1993
Sdlg F31/5 × *N. jonquilla*; sdlg no. QEE14/8
Fls 1-3 per stem, 68 mm wide; perianth segments roundish, creamy white, slightly reflexed, overlapping half; the inner segments more nearly ovate; corona shallow bowl-shaped, broad, creamy white, with green at base and very soft pink at rim, lightly frilled. Dwarf. Late

'Baby Star' 7 Y-Y
(J. Gerritsen & Son, 1949) J. Gerritsen & Son, 1959
N. jonquilla var. *minor* × *N. jonquilla*
Fl. 35 mm wide; perianth segments vivid yellow 9A; corona of a slightly darker tone (12A). Late. 2n=14. Resembles a smaller and later-flowered 'Baby Moon' of darker colour

'Bacardi' 2 Y-R
(D.S. Bell) D.S. Bell, 1975
'Bengal Tiger' × 'Checkmate'
Fl. 97 mm wide; corona very shallow bowl-shaped, deep red. Mid-season

'Baccante' 2 W-R
(J.L. Richardson)

'Baccarat' 11a Y-Y
(J. Gerritsen & Son, 1950) J. Gerritsen & Son, 1960
Fl. 95 mm wide; perianth segments light greenish yellow 4C, very lightly flushed with a brighter tone (5C), slightly inflexed; corona deeply split, the six segments opposite and closely overlying the perianth segments, rich golden yellow, frilled. 2n=28. *AM(p) 1977

'Bacchanale' 1 Y-Y
(W.B. Cranfield, pre-1930)

'Bacchante' 2 Y-? (a)
(P.D. Williams, pre-1931)

'Bacchante' 2 W-O
(J.L. Richardson, pre-1969) Unregistered
'Kilworth' × ('Kilworth' × 'Arbar')
Corona slightly expanded, reddish orange, frilled. Resembles an improved 'Pirate King'

'Bacchus' 2 Y-O
(Mrs R.O. Backhouse, pre-1921)
Perianth segments pale yellow; corona bowl-shaped, reddish orange. Mid-season

'Bacchus' 1 Y-Y
(Barr & Sons, pre-1923)
Fl. large; perianth segments bright yellow, slightly twisted; corona broad, golden yellow

'Bach' 1 Y-Y
(E.H. Krelage & Son, pre-1930)
Syn. 'Faust'

'Bachelor' 2 Y-? (a)
(Mrs R.O. Backhouse, pre-1921)

'Backchat' 6 Y-Y
(P. Phillips) P. Phillips, 1971
Fl. 82 mm wide, deep gold; perianth segments slightly reflexed; corona funnel-shaped, long

'Backhousei' 2 W-Y

(W. Backhouse, pre-1869)
Hybrid between a variant of *N. bicolor* and *N. poeticus*
Perianth segments broadly ovate, blunt, prominently mucronate, sulphur white, somewhat inflexed, overlapping one-third; the inner segments twisted; corona only a little shorter than the perianth segments, cylindrical, lemon yellow, with mouth straight and loosely frilled, rim deeply crenate. Syn. Backhousei 'Backhousei'. This has also been used as a Group name

'Backhouse's Giant' 2 Y-O
(R.O. Backhouse, pre-1938)
Perianth segments deep yellow, slightly wavy; corona dark reddish orange. AM(Haarlem) 1948

'Backhouse's Queen' 1 Y-Y
(W. Backhouse, pre-1869)
Perianth lemon yellow; corona deep yellow. Syn. Pseudonarcissus Major 'Backhouse's Queen'. Was "absorbed" into 'Mrs J.B.M.Camm'

'Badanloch' 3 W-YYO
(J.S.B. Lea) J.S.B. Lea, 1979
Sdlg 1-19-64 × 'Dalhuaine'; sdlg no. 1-43-71
Fl. 104 mm wide; perianth segments very broadly ovate, blunt or sometimes truncate, fairly prominently mucronate, somewhat concave, overlapping half; the inner segments with margins wavy; corona bowl-shaped, ribbed, yellow, with shades of green at base and a broad band of orange at rim, mouth more closely ribbed, split in places, frilled. Mid-season. *HC(g) 1990

'Badbury Rings' 3 Y-YYR
(J.W. Blanchard) J.W. Blanchard, 1985
'Ferndown' × 'Achduart'; sdlg no. 74/17A
Fl. rounded, 100 mm wide; perianth segments very broadly ovate in outline, rounded or truncate at apex, very slightly mucronate, brilliant yellow 9C, spreading or a little reflexed, plane, smooth, regular, overlapping half; the inner segments narrower, more usually spreading; corona very shallow bowl-shaped, ribbed, brighter than vivid yellow 12A and deeper in tone than the perianth, with a broad and clearly-defined band of bright orange-red at rim, mouth expanded, a little frilled, rim minutely crenate. Mid-season. Slightly scented. Resembles 'Perimeter' but with a more rounded flower. AM(e) 1988

'Badeloch' 8
(J.B. van der Schoot, pre-1931)
*HC(g) 1990

'Baden' 1 Y-Y
(C.E. Radcliff, 1930)
'Michael' × 'Mrs W.Moodie'

'Badger' 2 Y-O
(G.L. Wilson) G.L. Wilson, 1955
'Workman' × 'Carbineer'
Perianth segments bright yellow; corona straight-sided, scarlet-orange

N. baeticus Fernández Casas = *N. assoanus* var. *praelongus*

'Bafflorette' 2 W-W
(de Graaff Bros, pre-1948)

'Bagatelle' 1 Y-Y
(J. Gerritsen & Son) J. Gerritsen & Son, 1965
Fl. 50 mm wide; perianth segments brilliant greenish yellow 6B; corona of a more golden tone (12B). Early. Resembles 'Little Gem' and 'Wee Bee'

'Bagdad' 2 Y-YYR
(The Brodie of Brodie, pre-1934)
Probably a 'Mozart' hybrid
Perianth segments soft yellow; corona very shallow bowl-shaped, yellow with a broad band of scarlet at rim

'Bahram' 2 Y-O
(J.L. Richardson, pre-1935)
'Penquite' × 'Porthilly'
Fl. 111 mm wide; perianth segments broadly ovate, blunt, fairly prominently mucronate, brilliant yellow 8A, spreading, plane, overlapping half; the inner segments more narrowly ovate, slightly truncate, a little inflexed, with margins wavy or incurled; corona bowl-shaped, ribbed, vivid orange 28B, with mouth split in places and overlapping, frilled. Mid-season. 2n=28. PC 1939, AM(Haarlem) 1943, AM(e) 1948, FCC(Haarlem) 1950, FCC(e) 1951

'Bahrein' 2 Y-R
(J.R.Erp) J.R.Erp, 1956
'Diolite' × 'Rustom Pasha'

'Baiba' 11a W-ORR
(Juris Svarcs) Juris Svarcs, 1992
'Professor Einstein' × 'Pomeranza'; sdlg no. 82-12-05
Fl. rounded, 80 mm wide; perianth segments very broadly ovate, greenish white (155A); corona deeply split, the six segments opposite and closely overlying the perianth segments, orange-red (30B), with vivid orange 28B at base and flecks of white at rim, heavily frilled. Mid-season

'Bailey' 2 O-O
(A.E. Robinson) Carncairn Daffodils, 1990
'Bunclody' × 'Fire Raiser'; sdlg no. 2/2/80
Fl. 92 mm wide, orange; perianth segments broadly ovate, blunt, spreading or a little inflexed, plane, smooth, overlapping one-third to a half; the inner segments only a little more narrowly ovate, shouldered at base; corona cup-shaped, smooth, mouth frilled, rim slightly flanged. Early. Sunproof

'Baille' 8 Y-Y
(pre-1807)

'Bainden' 3 W-GYO
(N.A. Burr) N.A. Burr, 1994
'Merlin' × 'Dalhuaine'; sdlg no. 1.69.80
Fl. 110 mm wide; perianth segments broadly ovate in outline, blunt or truncate, white, with prominent yellowish mucro, touched green or yellow at base, spreading, a little concave, regular, overlapping one-third to a half; the inner segments more narrowly ovate; corona broad and very shallow funnel-shaped, greenish yellow, with green prominent below stamens and orange (28A) at rim, mouth straight, with an irregular number of deeply split and overlapping lobes, frilled. Late

'Bairnee' 2 (a or b)
(J.N. Hancock & Co., pre-1949)
'Jean Hood' × 'Fortune'

N. × ***bakeri*** Richter 13 = *N. bulbocodium* Linnaeus × *N. pseudonarcissus* Linnaeus

'Bakewell' 3 Y-? (a)
(D.B. Milne, pre-1950)

'Balaclava' 3 W-? (b)
(The Brodie of Brodie, pre-1930)

'Balalaika' 2 Y-YYR
(J.L. Richardson) J.L. Richardson, 1956
'Aranjuez' × 'Bahram'
Perianth segments bright yellow; corona cup-shaped, bright yellow with a narrow band of deep red at rim

'Balamara' 2 Y-Y
(H.G. Cross) H.G. Cross, 1973
'Butter King' × ('Melissa' × 'Digon')
Fl. 96 mm wide. 2n=28

'Balan' 3 W-Y
(West & Fell, pre-1938)
Corona pale primrose

'Balan' 2 W-P
(J.A. O'More) J.A. O'More, 1972
'Kenmare' hybrid
Fl. 104 mm wide

'Balance' 1 W-? (b)
(A.H. Ahrens) J.S. Leitch, 1955

'Balandra' 4 Y-Y
(H.G. Cross) H.G. Cross, 1984
Sdlg no. 128-5
Perianth and other petaloid segments in several whorls, broadly ovate, blunt or slightly truncate, vivid yellow 9A, with slight white mucro, overlapping half or more; the outer whorl spreading or a little inflexed, slightly concave; the inner whorls shorter, strongly inflexed, clustered at centre, with margins tightly incurled; corona segments broad, shorter than the petaloid segments, interleaved with them, and of a darker tone (14A). Late

'Balboa' 2 Y-? (a)
(D.S. Bell) D.S. Bell, 1955

'Balcairn' 2 W-GPR
(D.S. Bell) D.S. Bell, 1964
Fl. rounded, 96 mm wide; perianth segments broad, smooth; corona salmon, shading to red at rim, with greenish apricot at base

'Balcombe' 2 Y-Y
(W.M. Spry, pre-1975) Unregistered
'Torchlight' × 'Golden Valley'
Late

'Balcourt' 1 Y-Y
(S.C. Gaspar) R.J. Abernethy, 1957
'Balmoral' × 'Kingscourt'
Fl. mid-yellow; corona rim flanged and dentate

'Baldachin' 1 W-Y
(S.J. Bisdee, 1948)
'Whitefoord' × 'Cantatrice'

'Bald Eagle' 2 W-W
(William G. Pannill, 1968) William G. Pannill, 1987
'Arctic Doric' × 'Vigil'; sdlg no. 62/12
Mid-season. Syn. 'Snowdrift'

'Baldhur' 1 W-Y
Syn. of 'Baldur'

'Baldock' 4 Y-P
(M. Hamilton) Koanga Daffodils, 1992

'Baldred' 1 W-W
(G.H. Engleheart, pre-1923)

'Baldur' 1 W-Y
(J.T. Gray, pre-1933)
Perianth segments overlapping; corona lemon yellow, with rim rolled. See also 'Baldhur'

'Baldwin' 1 Y-Y
(C. Dawson, pre-1916)

'Baldza' 2 W-YYO
(D. Blanchard, pre-1947)
'Hymettus' × 'Hades'
Corona large disc-shaped, yellow, with a broad band of reddish orange at rim

'Balgowlah' 2 W-Y
(W.M. Spry, pre-1975) Unregistered
'M.P.Williams' × 'Trousseau'

Corona lemon golden yellow

'Balholmie Gold' 2 Y-Y
(Mrs J. Watson, 1953) Mrs J. Watson, 1963
Fl. 127 mm wide. Early. Resembles a darker-coloured 'Golden Torch' with longer corona

'Bali Hai' 4 W-R
(J.L. Richardson) J.L. Richardson, 1961
'Falaise' × 'Salmon Trout'
Fl. 93 mm wide; perianth and other petaloid segments broad, white; corona segments narrower than the petaloid segments and interspersed among them, orange-red. Late

'Balisand' 2 Y-? (a)
(de Graaff Bros, pre-1927)

'Balkis' 2 Y-? (a)
(W. Jackson Sr, 1928)
'Macebearer' × 'Tamerlane'

'Balkis' 2 W-? (b)
(P.D. Williams, pre-1933)

'Ballad' 9 W-?
(F.H. Chapman, pre-1913)

'Ballade' 1 Y-Y
(D. van Buggenum) D. van Buggenum, 1970
'Dutch Master' × 'Gold Medal'
Mid-season. Syn. ?'Ballart'

'Ballaghtobin' 1 W-W
(J.L. Richardson, pre-1936)

'Ballarat' 2 Y-Y
(L. Buckland, pre-1936)
?The same as 'Ballarto'

'Ballarat Gold' 1 Y-Y
(H.A. Brown, pre-1950)

'Ballart' 2 Y-Y
?See also 'Ballarat' or 'Ballarto'

'Ballarto' 2 Y-? (a)
(L. Buckland, pre-1936)
?The same as 'Ballarat'

'Ballerina' 2 W-O
(Barr & Sons, pre-1936)
Corona lemon yellow, with a band of bright orange at rim, mouth expanded

'Ballet' 2 W-P
(Oregon Bulb Farms, pre-1946)

'Ballet Dancer' 2 W-Y
(A.C. McKillop) A.C. McKillop, 1955
Corona closely overlying the perianth, becoming buff yellow

'Ballet Dancer' 2 W-W
Syn. of 'Virgin Snow'

'Ballet Girl' 2 W-YYR
(Alister Clark, pre-1930) J. Sharp, 1960
Corona flared, bright yellow, with bright red at rim

'Ballet Mandy' 2 W-OOY
(K. McCombe, c.1981) Unregistered

'Balletomane' 4 Y-Y
(D.S. Bell) D.S. Bell, 1982
'Papua' × 'Hicol'
Fl. 102 mm wide, lemon yellow. Resembles 'Evensong' but with a fuller flower

'Ballet Tango' 2 Y-O
(Ken McCombe, pre-1994) Unregistered

'Ballindalloch' 2 Y-Y
(J.S.B. Lea) J.S.B. Lea, 1981
'Arctic Gold' × sdlg 1-1-65; sdlg no. 3-5-72
Fl. 105 mm wide, rich gold

'Ballinode' 2 W-Y
(J.L. Richardson, pre-1927)
Perianth segments pure white; corona golden yellow

'Ballintoy' 2 Y-R
(W.J. Dunlop, pre-1950)
'Carbineer' × 'Porthilly'
Perianth segments golden yellow; corona deep red

'Ball of Gold' 1 Y-Y
(R.A. van der Schoot, pre-1923)

'Ballona'
(pre-1933)

'Balloo' 2 W-W
(G.L. Wilson) F.A.L. Harrison, 1959
Fl. large, pure white; perianth segments broadly ovate, of strong substance; corona of almost Div. 1 proportions, widely expanded

'Ballyarnett' 1 Y-Y
(Carncairn Daffodils) Carncairn Daffodils, 1976
'Goldcourt' × 'Moonstruck'; sdlg no. 4/42/62
Fl. 105 mm wide; perianth segments broadly ovate, truncate, brilliant yellow 9C, tinged green, spreading or somewhat inflexed, plane or a little concave, with margins slightly incurling at apex, overlapping half; the inner segments more strongly inflexed, with margins wavy or incurved; corona funnel-shaped, very broadly ribbed, vivid yellow 9A, with mouth flared and lightly frilled, rim crenate. Early. *HC(g) 1990

'Ballycastle' 3 W-WWO
(W.J. Dunlop, pre-1947)
'Mitylene' × 'Tinsel'
Fl. 95 mm wide; perianth segments overlapping; corona greenish white (4D), with strong orange 25A at rim, mouth expanded and frilled, rim crenate. PC 1949, *AM(g) 1967

'Ballyclare' 2 Y-O
(G.L. Wilson, pre-1947)
'Market Merry' × 'Clackrattle'
Perianth segments deep gold yellow; corona reddish orange

'Ballyferis' 1 W-Y
(J.L. Richardson, pre-1930)
'Effective' × 'Sincerity'
Fl. forming a double triangle; perianth segments very broadly ovate, blunt, slightly mucronate, pure white, spreading, with margins a little wavy, smooth and of great substance, overlapping half; the outer segments overlapping one another; the inner segments more narrowly ovate, square-shouldered at base, a little inflexed, with margins more strongly wavy; corona cylindrical, smooth, clear soft lemon yellow, mouth split in places and overlapping, expanded, lightly frilled, with rim flanged. Mid-season to late. AM(Haarlem) 1950. See also 'Ballyferris'

'Ballyferris' 1 W-Y
Syn. of 'Ballyferis'

'Ballyfrema' 1 W-W
(Carncairn Daffodils) Carncairn Daffodils, 1986
'Empress of Ireland' × 'Arctic Doric'; sdlg no. W5/6
Perianth segments broadly ovate, somewhat inflexed, overlapping half; the inner segments with margins wavy; corona straight-sided, obscurely and widely ribbed, creamy white, with mouth more strongly ribbed, wavy, rim very shallowly crenate. Mid-season

'Ballygarvey' 1 WWY-Y
(W.J. Dunlop, pre-1947)
'Effective' × 'Sincerity'
Fl. 104 mm wide; perianth segments broadly ovate, pure white, shading to brilliant greenish yellow 6B at base, somewhat inflexed, with margins wavy or recurved, deeply overlapping; corona cylindrical, deep golden yellow, slightly paler at base, with rim crenate and widely flanged. Mid-season. *AM(g) 1969

'Ballyglan' 2 W-? (b)
(J.L.Richardson, pre-1953)

'Ballygowan' 3 W-GYO
(Ballydorn Bulb Farm, 1981) Ballydorn Bulb Farm, 1993
'Gransha' × 'Merlin' hybrid
Fl. 90 mm wide; perianth segments broad, glistening white, slightly reflexing; corona saucer-shaped, slightly ribbed, yellow, with green at base and a band of strong orange at rim. Mid-season

'Ballyhoo' 4 W-O
(Jackson's Daffodils, 1982) Jackson's Daffodils, 1995
Evans sdlg × 'Career'; sdlg no. 239/82
Fl. 100 mm wide; perianth segments grenish white (155A); corona segments strong orange 24A. Mid-season

'Ballyhoo' 2 W-YOO
(J.N.Hancock & Co., 1983) Unregistered
'Tangaloa' × 'Orange Monarch'; sdlg no. 104/83H
Perianth segments broad, brilliant white, overlapping; corona very broad and shallow, orange, with yellow at base, heavily frilled. Mid-season

'Ballykinler' 3 W-GYR
(Ballydorn Bulb Farm) Ballydorn Bulb Farm, 1994
'Lisbane' × 'Capisco'
Fl. rounded, 81 mm wide; perianth segments broadly ovate, pure white, plane; corona saucer-shaped, tightly ribbed, yellow, with green at base and a broad band of deep red at rim. Late. Sunproof

'Ballyknock' 1 W-Y
(G.L. Wilson) Guy L.Wilson Ltd, 1961
'Guardian' × 'Empress of Ireland'

'Ballylig' 1 Y-Y
(Carncairn Daffodils, 1981) Carncairn Daffodils, 1992
'Loughanmore' × 'Golden Sovereign'; sdlg no. 23/8/76
Fl. 105 mm wide; perianth segments broadly ovate, brilliant greenish yellow 6A, spreading, overlapping half; corona cylindrical, vivid yellow 14B, with mouth straight, frilled. Tall. Late

'Ballylough' 1 W-W
(Carncairn Daffodils, 1965) Carncairn Daffodils, 1978
'Broughshane' × 'Easter Moon'; sdlg no. 111/1C
Fl. 100 mm wide; corona with a greenish tinge. Mid-season

'Ballymarlow' 2 Y-R
(W.J. Dunlop, pre-1949)
'Varna' × 'Market Merry' hybrid
Perianth segments golden yellow; corona crimson-red

'Ballymartin' 2 W-GYY
(W.J. Toal) Ballydorn Bulb Farm, 1965
'Green Island' × 'Nairobi' hybrid
Perianth segments broad, slightly reflexed, overlapping; corona large, expanded, lemon yellow, with deep green at base and a darker yellow at rim, frilled. Late

'Ballymaster' 2 W-OOR
(Ballydorn Bulb Farm) Ballydorn Bulb Farm, 1967
'Fermoy' open pollinated
Corona orange, shading to orange-red at rim. Late

'Ballymena' 2 Y-? (a)
(The Brodie of Brodie, pre-1944)

'Ballymoney' 1 Y-Y
(W.J. Dunlop) W.J. Dunlop, 1965

'Ballymore' 2 Y-WWY
(Brian S. Duncan) Rathowen Daffodils, 1979
Sdlg × ?'Passionale'; sdlg no. 282
Fl. 110 mm wide; perianth segments lemon yellow 13A; corona white, with a band of deep lemon yellow at rim. Mid-season. Resembles a stronger, larger and more colourful 'Binkie'

'Ballymorran' 1 Y-Y
(Ballydorn Bulb Farm, 1982) Ballydorn Bulb Farm, 1994
'Arctic Gold' × 'Viking'
Fl. 100 mm wide, golden yellow; perianth segments broadly ovate, smooth, plane or with margins slightly wavy; the inner segments more narrowly ovate; corona with straight sides only slightly diverging, rim dentate. Mid-season

'Ballymoss' 2 Y-Y
(J.L. Richardson) Mrs H.K. Richardson, 1964
'Infatuation' × 'Debutante'
Perianth segments broadly ovate, pale yellow; corona darker in tone, with mouth expanded, rim dentate and slightly flanged

'Ballynahinch' 3 W-GYO
(Ballydorn Bulb Farm, 1982) Ballydorn Bulb Farm, 1994
'Lancaster' open pollinated
Fl. rounded, 90 mm wide; perianth segments very broadly ovate, plane; corona saucer-shaped, tightly ribbed, yellow, with green at base and reddish orange towards mouth, lightly suffused with a deeper tone of orange at rim. Mid-season to late. Sunproof

'Ballynichol' 3 W-GYR
(Ballydorn Bulb Farm, 1977) Ballydorn Bulb Farm, 1989
Div. 3 sdlg × Div. 3 sdlg
Fl. 105 mm wide; perianth segments opening pale sulphur white, becoming white, reflexed, plane; corona yellow, with brilliant green at base and orange-red at rim. Mid-season. Sunproof

'Ballyrashane' 2 W-Y
(G.L. Wilson, pre-1938)
Corona golden yellow, frilled, with rim flanged

'Ballyroan' 2 W-P
(Mrs H.K. Richardson) Mrs H.K. Richardson, 1974
'Romance' × 'Rose Royale'
Fl. 100 mm wide; perianth segments broadly ovate, pure white; corona rose pink, with rim dentate

'Ballyrobert' 1 Y-Y
(W.J. Dunlop, c.1968) Jan Dalton, 1991
Sdlg no. 13/12
Fl. golden yellow. Mid-season

'Ballysally' 1 Y-Y
(G.L. Wilson, pre-1932)

'Ballysillan' 3 Y-R
(G.L. Wilson, pre-1947)
'Therm' × 'Bahram'
Perianth segments clear yellow; corona deep red

'Ballyteerim' 2 Y-Y
(G.L. Wilson, pre-1947)
'Fairy King' hybrid
Fl. two shades of gold

'Ballytrim' 2 Y-Y
(Mrs H.K. Richardson) Carncairn Daffodils, 1979
Sdlg no. 3509
Fl. 100 mm wide; perianth segments vivid yellow 9A; corona in some seasons the same colour as the perianth, in others somewhat darker in tone (12A), with the rim slightly dentate and becoming a little flanged with age. Mid-season

'Ballyvoy' 1 Y-WWY
(A.E.Robinson, 1984) Carncairn Daffodils, 1995
'Armagh' × 'Drumnabreeze'; sdlg no. 2/22/79
Fl. forming a double triangle, 95 mm wide; perianth segments broadly ovate, blunt, brilliant yellow 8A, with slight whitish mucro, spreading, or somewhat reflexed in upper half, plane, overlapping one-third to a half; the inner segments more narrowly ovate, more nearly acute, shouldered at base; corona cylindrical, smooth, white, with bright yellow at rim, mouth expanded, rim slightly rolled, regularly notched, crenate. Early

'Ballywalter' 1 W-Y
(W.J. Dunlop, pre-1953)
'Trostan' × 'Kanchenjunga'
Perianth segments pure white; corona deep lemon yellow, with rim rolled

'Ballyward' 2 Y-O
(Ballydorn Bulb Farm) Ballydorn Bulb Farm, 1982
'Torero' × 'Kilmorack'
Fl. 95 mm wide; perianth segments golden yellow; corona reddish orange. Mid-season. Resembles a sunproof 'Pipe Major' with the colour deepening with age

'Balmasque' 4 W-R
(D.S. Bell, 1966) D.S. Bell, 1978
'Falaise' × 'Masquerade'
Fl. 110 mm wide; perianth and other petaloid segments pure white; corona segments interspersed, red. Mid-season

'Balmoral' 1 Y-Y
(The Brodie of Brodie, c1930)
'Hebron' × 'Alchemist'

'Balmoral' 2 Y-Y
(The Brodie of Brodie, pre-1935)
'Pilgrimage' hybrid
Fl. 120 mm wide; perianth segments very broad, blunt or rounded at apex, sometimes slightly truncate, very slightly mucronate, chrome yellow, with a deeper tone at base, spreading, smooth, overlapping half; the inner segments narrower, without apparent mucro, somewhat inflexed, with margins wavy; corona cylindrical, slightly deeper in tone than the perianth, with mouth flared and lightly frilled, rim crenate. AM(e) 1938, AM(Haarlem) 1940

'Balmoral' 2 Y-R
(C.O. Fairbairn, pre-1948)

'Balquhiddar' 1 Y-Y
(pre-1927)

'Balruna' 2 W-W
(C.E. Radcliff, 1940)
'Veronique' × 'Askelon'

'Balthazar' 8
(pre-1939)

'Baltic' 2 W-? (b)
(J.C. Williams, pre-1945)

'Baltic Shore' 3 W-GYR
(Ballydorn Bulb Farm) Ballydorn Bulb Farm, 1991
'Florida Manor' × 'Capisco'
Fl. 105 mm wide; perianth segments slightly reflexed, smooth; corona saucer-shaped, opening orange, becoming yellow, with emerald green at base and deep red at rim, tightly frilled. Mid-season to late. Scented

'Baltimore Beauty' 9 W-GYO
(Mrs M.S. Yerger) Mrs M.S. Yerger, 1992
'Milan' × 'Poet'; sdlg no. 77 D
Fl. forming a double triangle, 55 mm wide, of strong substance; the inner perianth segments as long as the outer segments but less rounded at apex; corona shallow bowl-shaped, light greenish yellow 4B, with light yellow-green 145C at base and orange-red at rim. Late. Scented

'Baltimore's Best' 9 W-GOR
(Mrs M.S. Yerger) Mrs M.S. Yerger, 1993

'Knave of Diamonds' open pollinated; slg no. 76 I 2
Fl. 52 mm wide; the inner a little shorter than the outer perianth segments; corona almost disc-shaped, brilliant orange 29A, with strong yellow-green 144C at base and orange-red (33A) at rim. Very late

'Balvenie' 2 W-GPP
(J.S.B. Lea) J.S.B. Lea, 1976
'Merry Widow' × ('Salmon Trout' × ['Rosedew' × 'Rose Caprice'])
Fl. 104 mm wide; corona pink, with green at base. 2n=28

'Balvraid Lass' 2 O-R
(D.C. MacArthur) D.C. MacArthur, 1990
'Jezebel' × 'Ambergate'; sdlg no. EV4/16
Fl. 94 mm wide; perianth segments broad, vivid yellow 15B with a coppery tinge, plane, overlapping; corona orange-red (30C), mouth straight, frilled. Mid-season. Sunproof. Scented

'Balwyn' 2 Y-YYO
(H.A. Brown, pre-1938)
Perianth segments yellow; corona yellow, with reddish orange at rim, deeply frilled

'Bambalina' 2 Y-R
Syn. of 'Bambalisa'

'Bambalisa' 2 Y-R
(G. Lewis) D.S. Bell, 1955
See also 'Bambalina'

'Bambi' 1 W-Y
(Dutch origin, pre-1948)
Selection from *N. pseudonarcissus*?
Perianth segments blunt, yellowish white (4C), somewhat ribbed and twisted, of thin substance; corona cylindrical, slightly ribbed, vivid yellow 12A, with mouth flared and lobed, closely frilled, rim dentate. Very early. 2n=14

'Bambino' 2 Y-O
(R.V. Favell, pre-1940)
'King Alfred' hybrid

'Bamboozle' 2 W-P
(J.N. Hancock & Co., 1946)
Sdlg × 'Pink o' Dawn'
Perianth segments deeply overlapping; corona opening cream, becoming opalescent and then pink

'Bamboula' 1 W-Y
(Barr & Sons, pre-1930)
Perianth segments creamy white, slightly twisted, overlapping; corona long, pale buttercup yellow, frilled. Mid-season. *C(g) 1936

'Bambro' 1 W-Y
(W.M. Spry, pre-1975) Unregistered

'Constant' × 'Ina Marshall'
Corona cream. Late

'Banallan' 2 Y-Y
(Rosewarne EHS, 1969) Rosewarne EHS, 1985
'Rijnveld's Early Sensation' × 'Finland'; sdlg no. 63/3/7
Perianth segments brilliant greenish yellow 7C; corona of almost Div. 1 proportions, darker than vivid yellow 9A. Very early

'Banbridge' 1 Y-Y
(J.L. Richardson) W.J. Dunlop, 1955
'Kingscourt' × ?'Goldcourt'
Fl. 102 mm wide, deep golden yellow; perianth segments broadly ovate, with white mucro, spreading, smooth, overlapping one-third to a half; the inner segments somewhat twisted; corona cylindrical, lightly ribbed, deeper in tone than the perianth, mouth more strongly ribbed, slightly flared, with rim regularly crenate. Early

'Banchory' 2 W-W
(The Brodie of Brodie, c.1936)
'Naxos' × 'Slemish'
Fl. glistening white; corona of almost Div. 1 proportions, with rim rolled

'Banda' 2 Y-YYO
(G.J.Phillips, pre-1990) Unregistered

'Bandesara' 3 O-R
(Brian S. Duncan) Rathowen Daffodils, 1988
'Altruist' × 'Sabine Hay'; sdlg no. 855
Perianth segments burnt orange; corona disc-shaped, deep red. Mid-season to late

'Bandicoot' 3 W-? (b)
(J.C. Williams, pre-1910)

'Bandit' 3 W-O
(C. Dawson, pre-1908)
Perianth segments acute, creamy white; corona scarlet-orange. Sunproof

'Bandit' 2 W-YYO
(G.W.E. Brogden) G.W.E. Brogden, 1966
'Kowhiri' × 'Green Island'
Fl. rounded, 100 mm wide; perianth segments very broad, spreading, smooth and of heavy substance, overlapping half or more; the inner segments a little narrower and a little inflexed; corona wide-spreading, loosely ribbed, lemon yellow, with pale creamy yellow at base and a broad band of rich yellow or in some seasons golden orange at rim, mouth with six deeply overlapping lobes. Mid-season

'Bandleader' 2 Y-O
(M.J. Jefferson-Brown) M.J. Jefferson-Brown, 1967
Perianth segments golden yellow; corona neat cup-shaped, smooth, deep orange. Resembles 'Falstaff' but with the corona more widely flared. Mid-season

'Band of Gold' 3 W-WWY
(O. Fay) O. Fay, 1959
'Green Island' self pollinated
Corona shallow, opening green-white, becoming pure white, with bright golden yellow at rim. Mid-season

'Bandolier' 2 W-OOY
(T. Bloomer) Rathowen Daffodils, 1977
'Irish Splendour' × 'Orion'; sdlg no. 5/106/65
Fl. 110 mm wide; perianth segments broadly oval; corona orange, with a clearly defined band of gold at rim. Mid-season. Resembles a larger-flowered 'Blarney's Daughter' with a deeper tone to the corona. Sunproof

'Bandolin' 3 W-? (b)
(Barr & Sons, pre-1948)

'Bandon' 2 W-W
(J.L. Richardson, pre-1945)
'Cameronian' × 'Slemish'
Fl. snow white; perianth segments broadly ovate; corona rim slightly flanged

'Bandoo' 2 W-WYY
(W. Jackson Jr) Jackson's Daffodils, 1983
'Bar None' hybrid

'Bandsman' 2 Y-Y
(M.P. Williams, pre-1949)

'Bang' 3 W-YYO
(J.N. Hancock & Co., pre-1974) Unregistered
Perianth segments pure white; corona closely ribbed, yellow, with salmon at rim and a touch of green

'Bang-bang' 2 W-R
(W.M. Spry, pre-1975) Unregistered
'Stanley Mann' × 'Delight'
Corona scarlet

'Bangie' 2 W-P
(G.J. Phillips, 1984) G.J. Phillips, 1994
'Sedate' × 'Eiko'; sdlg no. 79-115-1
Fl. 106 mm wide; perianth segments broadly ovate, smooth; corona narrowly funnel-shaped, with mouth flared. Mid-season

'Bangor' 1 ?-Y (a or b)
?Syn. of 'Bangora'

'Bangora' 1 ?-Y (a or b)
(pre-1913)
?See also 'Bangor'

'Banjo' 2 Y-Y
(J.N. Hancock & Co., pre-1974) Unregistered
Perianth segments yellow; corona gold, with a deeper tone at rim, frilled

'Banjo Paterson' 9 W-?
(J.H. Hinsby, 1920)
'Ornatus' × 'Dante'

'Banker' 2 Y-O
(Jackson's Daffodils) Jackson's Daffodils, 1995
'Scipio' × sdlg 217/82 'Scipio' × sdlg 217/82; sdlg no. 145/89; sdlg no. 145/89
Fl. 110 mm wide; perianth segments broadly ovate, rounded at apex, yellow, with slight white mucro, spreading, a little concave, with margins sometimes incurling at apex, with midrib showing, overlapping half; the inner segments a little narrower, slightly inflexed; corona cylindrical, lightly ribbed, light orange (23A), mouth straight, wavy, rim entire. Mid-season. Sunproof

'Bann' 2 W-P
(G.L. Wilson, pre-1946)
'Gracious' × 'Diva'
Corona biscuit buff or bronzy pink

'Bannatyne' 2 Y-? (a)
(N.Y. Lower, pre-1936)

'Banner' 2 Y-YOO
(G.W.E. Brogden) G.W.E. Brogden, 1966
Fl. 95 mm wide; perianth segments yellow; corona orange, with golden yellow at base. Early

'Banner Cross' 3 W-R
(F.E. Board) F.E. Board, 1965
'Masaka' × 'Arbar'; sdlg no. 552
Late

'Banneret' 3 Y-? (a)
(W.B. Cranfield, pre-1916)

'Bannockburn'
(pre-1913)

'Bannockburn' 1 Y-Y
(H.A. Brown, pre-1938)
Fl. golden yellow; corona frilled

'Banongill' 2 Y-O
(C.O. Fairbairn, pre-1967) Unregistered
Perianth segments yellow; corona reddish orange, with rim tightly frilled

'Banora' 3 W-YYO
(W.M. Spry, pre-1975) Unregistered
'Aldgate' × 'Galilee'
Corona disc-shaped, lemon yellow, with a narrow band of orange at rim, frilled. Late

'Banquet' 2 Y-? (a)
(Mrs R.O. Backhouse, pre-1921)

'Banquet' 1 Y-Y
Syn. of 'Xanthin Gold'

'Banshee' 3 W-? (b or c)
(W.B. Cranfield, pre-1916)

'Banstead Village' 2 Y-O
(John H.J.Goddard, 1985) John H.J.Goddard, 1997
('Richhill' × 'Bunclody') × ('Altruist' × 'Ulster Bank')
Fl. 87 mm wide; perianth segments broadly ovate, blunt, vivid yellow 12A, with very slight white mucro, spreading, concave, with margins minutely incurling, overlapping half; the inner segments narrower, a little inflexed, with margins slightly wavy; corona broad cup-shaped, ribbed, orange (28A), with mouth straight, frilled. Mid-season to late. Sunproof

'Bantam' 2 Y-O
(Barr & Sons, pre-1950)
Fl. 55 mm wide; perianth segments roundish, blunt, slightly mucronate, brilliant greenish yellow 6B, reflexed, with margins incurling, overlapping half; corona bowl-shaped, smooth or lightly ribbed, orange, with yellow at base and sometimes with a darker orange at rim, mouth expanded and 6-lobed, with rim entire or minutely crenate. 2n=27. *AM(p) 1975, *AM(g) 1977, AGM 1993

'Bantling' 2 Y-? (a)
(F.H. Chapman, pre-1930)

'Bantry' 3 W-YYR
(J.L. Richardson, pre-1938)
'Mitylene' × 'Coronach'
Perianth segments snow white; corona pale citron, with a sharply band of bright red at rim

'Banu' 4 Y-R
(W. Jackson Jr, 1959) Unregistered
'Mary Louise' hybrid; sdlg no. 50/59

'Banzai' 1 W-W
(E.M. Crosfield, pre-1905)
Fl. large; perianth segments long; corona expanded, opening soft primrose yellow, becoming sulphur white, with rim rolled. AM 1905

'Bar 20' 3 Y-O
Syn. of 'Bar Twenty'

'Baracuda' 2 Y-O
(G.H. Johnstone, pre-1944)
'Fortune' hybrid

'Baradoc' 1 Y-Y
(W. Jackson Jr) Jackson's Daffodils, 1979
'Berit' × 'Bene'; sdlg no. 17/71

Fl. 102 mm wide. Early

'Baramulla' 2 Y-Y
(W.A. Grace, pre-1927)

'Barass' 1 Y-Y
(Jackson's Daffodils) Jackson's Daffodils, 1986
'Warbin' × 'Comal'; sdlg no. 6/78
Perianth segments vivid yellow 9A; corona darker in tone (14B). Early

'Barbados' 2 W-R
(J.L. Richardson) Mrs H.K. Richardson, 1963
'Kilworth' × 'Avenger'
Perianth segments roundish; corona deep fiery red, with rim neatly dentate

'Barbara' 3 Y-? (a)
(Cartwright & Goodwin, pre-1913)

'Barbara' 2 W-? (b)
(R. Dick, pre-1930)

'Barbara Allen' 2 W-P
(D.S. Bell) D.S. Bell, 1955
Perianth segments broad, pure white, smooth, overlapping; corona deep pink, frilled

'Barbara Ann Scott' 3 W-YYO
(de Graaff Bros, pre-1948)
Syn. 'Daintiness'

'Barbara Cave' 1 W-W
(A.C. McKillop) A.C. McKillop, 1955

'Barbara Daw' 3 W-GWW
(Mrs J. Abel Smith) Mrs J. Abel Smith, 1993
Fl. 95 mm wide; perianth segments broadly ovate, spreading, plane, overlapping half; corona shallow bowl-shaped, smooth, white, with green at base, mouth straight, wavy, with rim crenate. Late

'Barbara Holmes' 3 W-?YYO
Syn. of 'Lady Godiva'

'Barbara Hyde' 2 W-P
(A. Gibson) R. Hyde, 1958
Perianth segments pure white; corona soft coral pink.
PC(e)(NZ) 1960

'Barbara Robinson' 9 W-?
(J.H. Hinsby, 1924)
'Banjo Patterson' hybrid

'Barbarian' 2 Y-R
(J.S. Leitch) J.S. Leitch, 1968

'Barbaric' 3 Y-? (a)
(F.H. Chapman, pre-1927)
'M. J. Berkeley' × 'Socrates'

'Barbary Gold' 2 Y-GYY
(A.J.R.Pearson) A.J.R.Pearson, 1997
'Vulcan' × ([('Home Fires' × 'Ceylon') × 'Court Martial'] × 'Vulcan'); sdlg no. 88-32-M3
Fl. 98 mm wide; perianth segments broadly ovate, rounded at apex, vivid yellow 9A, spreading, plane, smooth, with a silky sheen; corona smooth in lower half, lightly ribbed and a little constricted near mouth, strong orange-yellow 17A, with brilliant yellow-green 149A at base, mouth flared and lobed, rim flanged. Mid-season

'Barbecue' 2 Y-O
(A.G. Thompson) A.G. Thompson, 1961
Perianth segments deep lemon yellow; corona flame orange. Mid-season. Resembles 'Porthilly' but with the corona of a darker tone

'Barbet' 2 W-P
(G.E. Mitsch) G.E. Mitsch, 1975
A5/8 ('Caro Nome' × 'Accent') × A34/10 ('Precedent' × 'Carita'); sdlg no. G36/1
Fl. 85 mm wide; corona rose pink. Mid-season

'Barbican' 2 Y-? (a)
(H.G. Hawker, pre-1928)

'Barbie Doll' 2 W-WWP
(Murray W. Evans) Murray W. Evans, 1980
'Kewpie' × 'Chiquita'; sdlg no. 0-5
Fl. 80mm wide; corona with pink at rim. Mid-season

'Barbizon' 4 W-P
(Brian S. Duncan) Rathowen Daffodils, 1988
'Pink Paradise' × Bloomer pink sdlg
Perianth and other petaloid segments in several whorls, broadly ovate, decreasing in size towards centre; corona segments interspersed, reddish pink. Late to very late

'Barbreck' 1 Y-Y
(D.H.L. Corrigan, pre-1951)

'Barcarolle' 9 W-?
(G.H. Engleheart, pre-1907)
Corona with deep red at rim

'Barcelona' 2 Y-? (a)
(F.H. Chapman, pre-1931)
AM(Haarlem) 1931

'Barchard's Hood' 1 W-W
(Francis Barchard, pre-1935) Mrs E.Bullivant, 1997
Fl. forming a double triangle, 110 mm wide; perianth segments broadly ovate, blunt, slightly inflexed, with margins recurved in lower half, creased, overlapping one-third to a half; the inner segments narrower, acute, twisted; corona cylindrical, loosely ribbed, with light green in tube, mouth expanded and more strongly ribbed, 6-lobed, frilled. Early to

mid-season

'Barclay' 6 Y-Y
(?P.D. Williams, pre-1935)
Fl. golden yellow. Early

'Bard' 6 Y-Y
(G.E. Mitsch) G.E. Mitsch, 1976
('Mitylene' × *N. cyclamineus*) open pollinated; sdlg no. E07/2
Fl. 96 mm wide; perianth segments clear yellow, slightly reflexed, smooth; corona slightly deeper in tone, with mouth flared and frilled. Early

'Bardall' 2 Y-O
(S.A. Free) S.A. Free, 1970
'Dutch Master' × 'Gold Medal'

'Bardelys' 2 Y-? (a)
(A.M. Wilson, pre-1928)

'Bardia' 2 Y-O
(J.L. Richardson, pre-1941)
'Invergordon' × 'Penquite'
Perianth segments soft yellow, thick; corona very shallow bowl-shaped, deep orange

'Bardoe' 2 Y-YYO
(J.T. Gray, pre-1950)
Perianth segments yellow; corona large, yellow, with a broad band of reddish orange at rim, crenate

'Bard of Avon' 9 W-?
(pre-1914)

'Bard of Rotherside' 9 W-?
(F.H. Chapman, pre-1929)

'Bardolph' 1 Y-Y
(Barr & Sons, 1923)

'Bareena' 2 W-Y
(W.M. Spry, pre-1975) Unregistered
'Early Prince' × Fairbairn sdlg
Corona lemon yellow

'Barega' 1 W-W
(S.J. Bisdee, 1948)
'Whitefoord' × 'Poona'

'Barenwyn' 1 Y-Y
(Rosewarne EHS, 1971) Rosewarne EHS, 1985
'Priority' × 'Malvern City'; sdlg no. 66/87/1
Perianth segments broad, acute, vivid yellow, brighter than 9A, overlapping; corona slightly expanded, rich golden yellow, frilled. Very early. Resembles a larger 'Saint Keverne' with a more widely expanded corona

'Bareppa' 1 Y-Y
(Lord Rendlesham, pre-1937)

'Barfly' 1 Y-Y
(W. Jackson Jr) Jackson's Daffodils, 1980
'Comal' × 'Otewa'; sdlg no. 97/74
Fl. forming a double triangle, 100 mm wide, mid-yellow; perianth segments smooth; corona straight-sided, with mouth slightly frilled. Mid-season

'Bargoed' 1 Y-Y
(W.F. Mitchell, pre-1937)

'Barham Court' 2 W-O
(W.A. Noton, pre-1996) Unregistered

'Barin' 2 Y-O
(A.H. Ahrens) J.S. Leitch, 1955
Resembles 'Courtesy'

'Baringa' 1 W-W
(S.J. Bisdee) S.J. Bisdee, 1956
'Whitefoord' × 'Cantatrice'

'Barito' 2 W-? (b)
(G.A. Uit den Boogaard, pre-1950)

N. barlae Parlatore 13 Section Tazettae

'Barland' 2 Y-? (a)
(A.M. Wilson, pre-1950)

'Barlash' 2 Y-O
(G.L. Wilson, pre-1946)
'Sunproof Orange' × 'Fairy King'
Perianth segments rich yellow; corona shallow, reddish orange

'Barley' 2 Y-? (a)
(Barr & Sons, pre-1954)

'Barley Cove' 2 W-Y
(Carncairn Daffodils) Carncairn Daffodils, 1981
'Bizerta' × 'Aircastle'; sdlg no. 1/23/69
Fl. 103 mm wide; perianth segments yellowish white 155B; corona vivid yellow 12A, with mouth tightly frilled

'Barleygold' 2 Y-O
(Ballydorn Bulb Farm, 1980) Ballydorn Bulb Farm, 1990
'Gold Mine' × 'Golden Aura' hybrid
Fl. 90 mm wide; perianth segments golden yellow; corona funnel-shaped, with rim entire. Mid-season. Sunproof

'Barley Sugar' 3 W-YYO
(Carncairn Daffodils) Carncairn Daffodils, 1978
'Bravura' × 'Bushmills'; sdlg no. 3/11/64
Fl. 90 mm wide; perianth segments greenish white (157C); corona brilliant greenish yellow 6A, with strong orange-yellow 17A at rim. Late

'Barleythorpe' 1 W-Y
(F.E. Board, pre-1966) Unregistered
Fl. 92 mm wide; perianth segments very broadly ovate, blunt, mucronate, inflexed, somewhat concave or with margins wavy, smooth, overlapping half; the inner segments more narrowly ovate, with margins more distinctly wavy; corona funnel-shaped, smoothly and widely ribbed, brilliant yellow 7B, mouth widely expanded and more strongly ribbed, wavy, rim flanged, irregularly and shallowly notched. Varies between Divs 1 and 2

'Barleywine' 2 Y-O
(Ballydorn Bulb Farm) Ballydorn Bulb Farm, 1993
'Killeen' × 'Golden Aura'
Fl. 85 mm wide; perianth segments broadly ovate, deep golden yellow, plane; corona with straight sides only slightly diverging, glowing orange, mouth somewhat lobed. Mid-season. Sunproof

'Barlin' 3 Y-? (a)
(C. Goodson, pre-1935) Parr's Nurseries, 1958

'Barlow' 6 Y-Y
(G.E. Mitsch) G.E. Mitsch, 1969
'Cibola' × *N. cyclamineus*; sdlg no. X7/4
Fl. deep yellow; perianth segments only slightly reflexed. Early

'Barmaid' 1 W-W
(F.H. Chapman, pre 1913)

'Barnaby Blatch' 1 Y-Y
(G.L. Wilson, pre-1952)

'Barnard Castle' 2 W-P
(D.S. Bell) D.S. Bell, 1982
Fl. 108 mm wide; perianth segments pure white; corona pink, with green in tube. Mid-season

'Barnby Moor' 3 W-Y
(Mrs J. Abel Smith) Mrs J. Abel Smith, 1979
'Morning Cloud' × 'Jewel Song'; sdlg no. VO/51
Fl. 88 mm wide; perianth segments very broadly ovate, rounded at apex, mucronate, pure white, spreading, plane, overlapping half; the inner segments more narrowly ovate, a little reflexed, with margins sometimes incurved; corona shallow bowl-shaped, minutely ribbed, pale yellow, with a darker tone at rim, mouth expanded, rim dentate. Late. 2n=28

'Barnesgold' 1 Y-Y
(Brian S. Duncan) Brian S. Duncan, 1992
'Golden Jewel' × 'Midas Touch'; sdlg no. 916
Fl. 112 mm wide, deep golden yellow; perianth segments very broadly ovate or roundish, with slight white mucro, slightly inflexed, smooth, of great substance, shallowly concave, with margins sometimes incurling at apex, overlapping half; the inner segments more strongly inflexed; corona cylindrical, loosely ribbed, with mouth straight, lightly frilled. Late

'Barney Gleeson' 1 Y-Y
(C.A. Nethercote) T. Morrison, 1960
Fl. medium yellow

'Bar None' 1 W-Y
(P. Phillips) P. Phillips, 1966
Fl. 115 mm wide; perianth segments broad, spreading, smooth, corona opening pale lemon yellow, becoming pale buff yellow, with mouth slightly flared. Early. Resembles a larger-flowered 'Trousseau' with the the corona rim more nearly rolled

'Barn Owl' 2 Y-O
(G.P. Haydon, pre-1907)
Perianth segments large; corona stained yellowish orange

'Barnsdale' 2 W-P
(K.J. Heazlewood) R. Hyde, 1957

'Barnsdale Wood' 2 Y-R
(W.A. Noton, 1965) W.A. Noton, 1976
'Shining Light' × 'Falstaff'; sdlg no. 503
Fl. 83 mm wide; perianth segments gold; corona red. Mid-season

'Barnstorm' 2 W-W
(Jackson's Daffodils) Jackson's Daffodils, 1986
'Glendermott' × 'Waikato'; sdlg no. 59/77
Fl. forming a double triangle; perianth segments broadly ovate, blunt, mucronate, greenish white (155A), plane or sometimes with margins incurving, smooth, overlapping half; the inner segments more narrowly ovate, acute, square-shouldered at base, a little inflexed; corona funnel-shaped, yellowish white 155D, mouth straight and a little frilled. Late

'Barnum' 1 Y-Y
(Brian S. Duncan) Rathowen Daffodils, 1986
'Golden Jewel' × 'Midas Touch'; sdlg no. 819
Fl. very large, rich golden yellow. Mid-season. Resembles a large-flowered 'Midas Touch'

'Barnwell' 2 W-? (b or c)
(G.H. Furness, pre-1934)

'Barnwell Alice' 2 W-GWW
(Carncairn Daffodils, 1965) Carncairn Daffodils, 1986
'Easter Moon' × ('Fairy Tale' × 'Rashee'); sdlg no. 4/140/60A
Corona cup-shaped, opening with lemon yellow at rim, becoming white, with green at base. Late

'Barobar' 2 W-? (b)
(R. Hyde) R. Hyde, 1957
PC(e)(NZ) 1958

'Baroda' 2 Y-YOR
(S.J. Bisdee, 1939)
'Seraglio' × 'Lillian Murdoch'

'Barok' 11a Y-Y
(J. Gerritsen & Son) J. Gerritsen & Son, 1958
Perianth segments primrose yellow; corona segments deep lemon yellow

'Barometrica' 2 Y-? (a)
(B. Rowlands, pre-1938)

'Baroness Heath' 3 W-O
(W. Backhouse, pre-1869)
Perianth segments opening primrose yellow, becoming sulphur white; corona suffused with scarlet-orange. Syn. Burbidgei 'Baroness Heath'

'Baroness von Krupp' 3 W-? (b)
(R.A. van der Schoot, pre-1923)

'Baronet' 2 Y-? (a)
(P.D. Williams, pre-1916)

'Baronet' 2 Y-YYO
(The Brodie of Brodie, c.1917)
?'King Alfred' × 'Bernardino'
Perianth segments deep yellow; corona yellow, with orange at mouth, frilled. AM(m)(c) 1926

'Baronscourt' 1 Y-Y
(Carncairn Daffodils) Carncairn Daffodils, 1973
'Kingscourt' × 'Prince Igor'
Fl. 110 mm wide; perianth segments yellow; corona becoming slightly deeper in tone

N. × *barrae* Fernández Casas 13 = *N. bulbocodium* Linnaeus × *N. cantabricus* de Candolle

'Barret' 11?a W-Y
(?Australian origin, pre-1993) Unregistered

'Barrett Browning' 3 WWY-O
(J.W.A. Lefeber, pre-1945)
Fl. 89 mm wide; perianth segments broadly ovate, rounded at apex, mucronate, white, with vivid yellow 9A at base, spreading, plane or a little concave, smooth, with broad midrib showing, overlapping half; the inner segments slightly inflexed and somewhat twisted; corona bowl-shaped, ribbed, slightly deeper in tone than strong orange 25A, with mouth expanded, rim closely and minutely frilled. Very early. 2n=27,28. FA(Haarlem) 1957, AM(Haarlem) 1967, *FCC(p) 1977

'Barrier' 1 Y-Y
(J.S. Leitch) J.S. Leitch, 1968

'Barrii' 3 Y-Y
(W. Backhouse, pre-1869)

?(*N.* × *incomparabilis* × *N. poeticus*)
Fl. opening mid-yellow, becoming paler. Syn. Barrii 'Barrii'. This has also been used as a Group name

'Barrii Conspicuus' 3 Y-YYO
Syn. of 'Conspicuus'

'Barrington' 1 Y-Y
(G. Lewis, pre-1939)

'Barrington Gold' 1 Y-Y
(G. Lewis) D.S. Bell, 1955
'Gold Tray' × 'Cromarty'
Fl. deep gold

'Barrister' 3 W-? (b)
(F.H. Chapman, pre-1913)

'Barrow Boy' 3 Y-? (a)
(A.M. Williams, pre-1952)

'Barthold Meryan' 2 W-? (b)
(Mrs R.O. Backhouse, pre-1921)

'Bartizan' 2 Y-O
(Miss G. Evelyn, pre-1928)
AM(Haarlem) 1933, FA(Haarlem) 1936

'Bartley' 6 Y-Y
(J.C. Williams, pre-1934)
N. cyclamineus sdlg
Fl. 83 mm wide; perianth segments ovate, opening vivid yellow 9B, becoming deeper in tone (13A), with slight white mucro, reflexed, overlapping at base only; the inner segments slightly twisted or with margins incurling; corona cylindrical, narrow, smooth, slightly darker in tone than the perianth, with mouth even, rim flanged and regularly crenate. Early to mid-season. 2n=21. *AM(g) 1946, *FCC(g) 1949, AM(p) 1981

'Bartley Cross' 6
(Sir F.C. Stern, pre-1949)

'Barton'
(pre-1899)

'Bar Twenty' 3 Y-O
(A. Overton) T. Morrison, 1961
Perianth segments yellow; corona reddish orange. Syn. 'Bar 20'

'Baruch' 3 Y-? (a)
(G.A. Uit den Boogaard, pre-1950)

'Barwon' 2 Y-O
(?J.N. Hancock & Co., pre-1949)
Perianth segments yellow; corona deep orange, with rim dentate

'Bashbish' 2 Y-? (a)
(E.C. Powell, pre-1946)
'Bernardino' × 'Bokhara'

'Bashful' 2 W-W
(R.V. Favell, pre-1939)
'Niphetos' × 'Adela'
Fl. snow white, of great substance

'Basil' 2 Y-? (a)
(A.M. Wilson, pre-1930)

'Basilia' 2 W-W
(Barr & Sons, pre-1922)
'Maggie May' × 'King Alfred'
Fl. facing down; perianth segments creamy white, irregular, overlapping half; corona large, soft creamy white, with mouth flared and closely frilled

'Basinet' 2 W-? (b or c)
(G.H. Engleheart, pre-1914)

'Baski' 2 Y-R
(J.S. Leitch) J.S. Leitch, 1957

'Baslonica' 1 Y-Y
(B. Rowlands, pre-1938)

'Basra' 3 Y-R
(The Brodie of Brodie, c.1925)
'Beacon' × 'Fortune'; sdlg no. 170/A/20
Perianth segments very broadly ovate, prominently mucronate, creamy yellow, spreading, smooth, overlapping one-third; the inner segments only a little less broad, irregular, with margins nicked; corona red, mouth widely expanded, rim crenate

'Basra' 3 W-R
(J.A. O'More) J.A. O'More, 1971
'Ivo Fell' × 'Matapan'
Fl. 102 mm wide

'Bassanio' 1 Y-Y
(Barr & Sons, pre-1923)

'Bassanio' 1 Y-Y
(de Graaff Bros, pre-1927)

'Basselman Major'
Syn. of *N. tazetta* var. *trewianus*

'Bastemil' 1 Y-Y
(Spanish origin)
Selection by Peter Barr (1888) from wild-collected *N. pseudonarcissus*
Perianth segments sulphur yellow, with some darker tones, twisted; corona large, funnel-shaped, orange-yellow, frilled, with rim rolled

'Bastille Zelotto' 1 Y-Y
(J.W.A. Lefeber) J.W.A. Lefeber, 1968

'Bastion' 1 Y-Y
(G.L. Wilson, pre-1944)
'Counsellor' open pollinated
Fl. 111 mm wide; perianth segments broad, vivid yellow 9A, overlapping; corona straight-sided, of a darker tone (13A) than the perianth, mouth expanded, rim notched. AM(e) 1946, AM(Haarlem) 1948

'Bastoria' 1 Y-Y
(R. Hyde) R. Hyde, 1959
'Pretoria' × 'Bastion'
Perianth segments broad, of good substance, overlapping; corona with rim rolled

'Batavia' 2 W-? (b)
(L. van Leeuwen & Son, pre-1943)

'Batavier' 2 Y-? (a)
(de Graaff Bros, pre-1929)

'Bath's Firefly' 2 Y-? (a)
(R.H. Bath, pre-1931)

'Bath's Flame' 3 Y-YYO
(G.H. Engleheart, pre-1913)
Fl. 102 mm wide, at right angles to the stem or facing slightly downwards; perianth segments broadly ovate, blunt, deep yellow, with prominent white mucro, spreading, overlapping a quarter; the inner segments more narrowly ovate, a little inflexed, touched white at midrib, with margins wavy or incurving, creased at shoulder; corona short broad funnel-shaped, ribbed, deep yellow, with orange at rim, frilled, rim closely and minutely dentate. Early. 2n= 21. Resembles Barrii 'Conspicuus' but with broader and more deeply coloured perianth segments; also resembles 'Brilliancy'. Syn. 'Flame'. AM(m)(g) 1915

'Bathurst' 8 Y-O
(pre-1861)
Fls many per stem; perianth pale primrose yellow; corona orange. Very early. Syn. Tazetta 'Bathurst'

'Batman' 1 Y-Y
(J.L. Richardson) F.E. Board, 1956
('Royalist' × 'Crocus') × 'Goldcourt'

'Batman' 9 W-?
(?Sir J.S. Arkwright)
Perianth segments dull ivory white

'Baton Rouge' 2 Y-? (a)
(Mrs R.O. Backhouse, pre-1921)

'Battleaxe' 2 Y-O
(C. Dawson, pre-1916)
Perianth segments primrose yellow, of thick texture, overlapping; corona straight-sided, bright orange. See

also 'Battle Axe'

'Battle Axe' 2 Y-O
Syn. of 'Battleaxe'

'Battle Cry' 2 Y-R
(T. Bloomer, 1965) Rathowen Daffodils, 1977
'Craigywarren' × 'Air Marshal'; sdlg no. 5/35/58
Perianth segments golden; corona deep orange-red. Mid-season

'Battledore' 3 W-GWW
(F.E. Board) F.E. Board, 1965
Fl. white; corona with sage green at base

'Battler' 2 Y-O
(?New Zealand origin, pre-1990) Unregistered

'Battleship' 2 W-? (b)
(G.L. Wilson, pre-1939)

'Batura' 2 Y-O
(J.T. Gray, pre-1949)
Perianth segments deep golden yellow; corona straight-sided, scarlet-orange

'Baucis' 2 W-? (b)
(Mrs R.O. Backhouse, pre-1921)

'Baveno' 2 Y-? (a)
(A.M. Wilson, pre-1930)

'Bawku' 2 Y-? (a)
(A.M. Wilson, pre-1957)

'Bawnboy' 1 Y-Y
(G.L. Wilson) G.L. Wilson, 1960
'Milanion' × 'Bastion'
Fl. 102 mm wide; perianth segments vivid yellow 9A, slightly recurving, overlapping; corona slightly ribbed, darker in tone (near 14B) than the perianth, with mouth expanded and rim crenate. 2n=28. AM(Haarlem) 1965, *AM(g) 1971, *FCC(g) 1974, *AM(p) 1975, *FCC(p) 1977, AGM 1993

'Baxter' 2 Y-? (a)
(G.L. Wilson, pre-1947)

'Bayard' 3 Y-? (a)
(A.M. Wilson, pre-1908)

'Bayard' 1 Y-Y
(J.L. Richardson) J.L. Richardson, 1956
('Royalist' × 'Crocus') × 'Goldcourt'
Fl. 75 mm wide; perianth segments very broadly ovate, blunt or somewhat truncate, slightly mucronate, vivid yellow 9A, very slightly reflexed, plane, overlapping half; the inner segments more narrowly ovate; corona cylindrical, lightly ribbed, vivid yellow 13A, mouth widely expanded and more heavily ribbed, rim crenate. AM(e) 1958, *AM(g) 1962

'Bayardo' 7 Y-Y
(E.M. Crosfield, pre-1913)
Fl. 83 mm wide, rich yellow; corona rim lightly recurved

'Bayardo' 2 Y-? (a)
(E.M. Crosfield, pre-1927)

'Bayell' 1 Y-Y
(Ken Farmer Nurseries) Ken Farmer Nurseries, 1978
Fl. 120 mm wide

'Bayeux' 1 Y-Y
(J.C. van der Meer, pre-1944)

'Bayham Abbey' 1 W-W
(N.A.Burr) N.A.Burr, 1997
'Broomhill' × 'White Star'; sdlg no. 2.21.80
Fl. forming a double triangle, 112 mm wide; perianth segments broadly ovate, blunt, mucronate, a little inflexed, slightly concave, with margins minutely incurling, overlapping half; the inner segments a little narrower, less prominently mucronate, reflexed in upper half, with margins deeply incurved; corona cylindrical at base, flared from mid-point, lightly ribbed, with mouth even, rim flanged and irregularly crenate

'Baynes' 2 Y-O
(E.W. Cotter) E.W. Cotter, 1968
Perianth segments broad, lemon yellow, of thick substance, smooth; corona expanded, brilliant orange. Mid-season

'Bayonet' 3 Y-? (a)
(A.M. Wilson, pre-1937)

'Bayonne' 10 Y-Y
(French origin) Unregistered
Selection by E.Hodgkin (pre-1964) from wild-collected *N. bulbocodium* var. *citrinus*
Fl. 50 mm wide, light greenish yellow to pale yellow-green 4C-4D, with greenish veins extending from the tube into the perianth segments; perianth segments very narrow, acute, inflexed, separated; corona very broad funnel-shaped, ribbed, mouth straight, more or less even, with rim crenate. Dwarf. Resembles a larger *N. bulbocodium* var. *citrinus*. AM(r)(a) 1964

'Bay Pink' 2 W-P
(R.G. Cull) Hokorawa Daffodils, 1987
'Anne Cameron' open pollinated; sdlg no. R83/4
Perianth segments white; corona strong yellowish pink 37B. Mid-season

'Bay Shore' 2 Y-? (a)
(L. van Leeuwen & Son, pre-1950)

'Bayunga' 1 W-Y
(J.N. Hancock & Co., pre-1962) Unregistered
'Bonnington' × 'Cromarty'
Perianth segments broadly ovate, smooth and of great substance, deeply overlapping; corona large, deep cream yellow, with rim dentate

'Bazaar' 2 Y-OOR
(J. Field) E.W. Cotter, 1968

'Bazarri' 2 Y-R
(R.H.Glover, pre-1993) Unregistered

'Bazelman' 8 Y-Y
(pre-1780)
Fl. pale yellow

'Bazelman Major'
Syn. of *N. tazetta* var. *trewianus*

'Bazelman Medius' 8 W-O
Selection from *N. tazetta*, probably of garden origin
Syn. 'Subcrenatus'

'Bazelman Minor'
Syn. of *N. tazetta* subsp. *lacticolor*

'B.B.'
(pre-1913)

'B.C.Rod' 3 W ? (b)
(E. & J.C. Martin, pre-1931)

'Beach Party' 2 W-GWP
(Brian S.Duncan) Brian S.Duncan, 1996
'Pismo Beach' × 'High Society'; sdlg no. 1391
Fl. forming a double triangle, 106 mm wide; perianth segments broadly ovate, slightly reflexed, plane, smooth; corona broad funnel-shaped, opening yellow, becoming white, with deep green at base and deep pink at rim. Mid-season. Resembles 'Zion Canyon' but with a more clearly defined band of colour at corona rim

'Beachside' 1 W-W
(C.E. Radcliff, 1936) C.E. Radcliff, 1956
'Casinova' × 'Beersheba'

'Beacon' 3 W-R
(G.H. Engleheart, pre-1897)
'Princess Mary' × *N. poeticus* var. *recurvus* sdlg
Fl. rounded; perianth segments sulphur white, of firm texture, deeply overlapping; corona disc-shaped, finely ribbed, brilliant fiery red. 2n=28. FCC 1897

'Beacon Light'
(New Zealand origin, pre-1940)

'Beaconsfield' 1 Y-Y
(W. Backhouse, pre-1869)
Fl. rich primrose yellow. Resembles 'Saint Brigid'. Syn. Pseudonarcissus Major 'Beaconsfield'. Was "absorbed" into 'Saint Brigid'

'Beaconsfield' 1 Y-Y
(C.E. Radcliff, 1944) C.E. Radcliff, 1956
'Bungana' × 'Nangeela'

'Beagle' 3 ?-Y (a or b)
(pre-1914)

'Bealita' 3 Y-O
(pre-1968) Unregistered
2n=28

'Beamlight' 3 W-YYR
(Mrs P.E. Speyer) Mrs P.E. Speyer, 1984
'Lynx' × 'Motif'; sdlg no. 2/56
Fl. 108 mm wide; corona yellow, with orange-red at rim. Resembles 'Motif' but with a more brightly coloured corona. Mid-season

'Beara' 1 W-? (b)
(J. Mallender, pre-1913)

'Bear Springs' 4 Y-O
(Brian S.Duncan) Brian S.Duncan, 1997
('Gettysburg' × 'Barnsdale Wood') × 'Smokey Bear'; sdlg no. 1536
Fl. 110 mm wide; perianth and other petaloid segments broadly ovate, blunt, deep yellow; the outer whorl spreading; corona segments interspersed, deep reddish orange. Early. Sunproof

'Beat-all' 2 Y-Y
(de Graaff-Gerharda, pre-1925)
Perianth segments long, creamy yellow, overlapping; corona widely expanded, buttercup yellow. Mid-season. AM(Haarlem) 1925, *C(g) 1936

'Beaten Gold' 1 Y-Y
(G.L. Wilson, pre-1950)
Fl. golden yellow

'Beatrice' 3 W-W
(W. Backhouse, pre-1869)
Perianth segments narrowly ovate, pure white, with margins wavy or incurved or recurved, spathulate, separated; corona cup-shaped, angled, opening lemon yellow, becoming milk white, with mouth straight, even, rim more or less entire. Syn. Leedsii 'Beatrice'. "Absorbed" 'Purity'

'Beatrice' 3 W-O
(pre-1930)
Barrii 'Conspicuus' sport
Corona reddish orange

'Beatrice' 8
(pre-1938)

'Beatrice Barlow' 1 W-W
(G.P. Haydon, pre-1907)

'Beatrice Corrigan' 2 W-? (b)
(D.H.L. Corrigan, pre-1949)

'Beatrice Hazeltine' 3 W-YYO
Syn. of 'Beatrice Heseltine'

'Beatrice Heseltine' 3 W-YYO
(W. Backhouse, pre-1869)
Perianth segments opening creamy, becoming pure white; corona yellow, with scarlet-orange at rim. Resembles Burbidgei 'Conspicuus' in colour. Syn. Burbidgei 'Beatrice Heseltine'. See also 'Beatrice Hazeltine'

'Beatrice Murray' 3 W-YYO
(W. Backhouse, pre-1869)
Perianth segments creamy white; corona canary yellow. Syn. Barrii Albidus 'Beatrice Murray'

'Beatrice Plumer' 1 W-W
(G.L. Wilson, pre-1946)

'Beatrix' ?-P
(Alister Clark, pre-1948)

'Beatrix Hill-Whetson' 2 W-? (b)
(G.H. Engleheart, pre-1914)

'Beau Bouquet' 8 Y-Y
(pre-1798)

'Beau Brocade' 3 W-? (b)
(Mrs R.O. Backhouse, pre-1921)

'Beau Brummel' 2 Y-? (a)
(J.R. Pearson & Sons, pre-1927)

'Beaucaillou' 2 W-YYO
(H.P. Zwetsloot, pre-1943)
Syn. 'Sunny Girl'. AM(Haarlem) 1942

'Beauclaire' 1 W-W
(G.L. Wilson) F.E. Board, 1962
'White Prince' × 'Vigil'; sdlg no. 475
Early. Resembles a more vigorous 'Vigil'

'Beaudelaire' 2 W-? (b)
(J.W.A. Lefeber, pre-1945)

'Beaufighter' 2 Y-O
(G.H. Johnstone, pre-1944)
'Fortune' hybrid

'Beauform' 2 W-? (b)
(R.P. Cook, pre-1949)

'Beaufort' 1 W-Y
(Jackson's Daffodils, 1978) Jackson's Daffodils, 1989
'Helsal' × 'Cyros'; sdlg no. 113/78
Fl. 110 mm wide; perianth segments broadly ovate, blunt and slightly mucronate, greenish white (155A), a little reflexed, plane, with midrib showing, overlapping half; the inner segments a little more narrowly ovate; corona brilliant greenish yellow 3A, smooth, mouth frilled and slightly expanded, rim dentate. Mid-season

'Beaugarde' 7
Syn. of 'Beauregard'

'Beau Gem' 3 W-W
(C.E. Buckingham, pre-1951)

'Beau Geste' 2 W-? (b)
(Mrs R.O. Backhouse, pre-1921)

'Beau Geste' 1 YYW-Y
(W.F. Leenen, 1966) W.F. Leenen, 1977
Fl. 115 mm wide; perianth segments brilliant greenish yellow 5B, with ivory white at base; corona light greenish yellow 4C, with a darker tone at rim. Mid-season

'Beau Geste' 4 Y-R
(Mrs N.V.Anderson, pre-1962) Unregistered
Perianth segments yellow; corona bright red

'Beaugreen' 2 Y-WWY
(K.J. Heazlewood) K.J. Heazlewood, 1968
'Binkie' × 'Greenore'
Fl. 95 mm wide; perianth segments greenish yellow; corona opening greenish, becoming almost white, with yellow at rim, frilled. Early. Resembles a more deeply coloured 'Binkie'

'Beau Ideal' 1 Y-Y
(D.V. West, pre-1927)
Fl. clear yellow

'Beau Ideal' 2 Y-? (a)
Syn. of 'Salamanca'

'Beaumaris' 1 Y-Y
(A. Gibson, pre-1951)

'Beau Monde' 2 W-O
(Konynenburg & Mark, pre-1953)
Sdlg × 'Sempre Avanti'

'Beau Nash' 3 W-? (b)
(Barr & Sons, pre-1946)

'Beaupré' 2 W-O
(de Graaff Bros, pre-1939)
Perianth segments sulphur white; corona clear orange. AM(Haarlem) 1939

'Beauregard' 7
(Barr & Sons, pre-1927)
See also 'Beaugarde'

'Beaurim' 2 W-YYO
(M.G.Temple-Smith, 1984) M.G.Temple-Smith, 1997
'Mrs David Calvert' × 'Kay'; sdlg no. 24/84
Corona disc-shaped, brilliant yellow 12B, with vivid orange 28B at rim. Mid-season. The corona rim fading with age

'Beaustone' 2 W-R
(C.E. Radcliff, 1942)
'Warflame' × 'Atanga'

'Beaute Nouvelle' 8 W-Y
(pre-1807)

'Beauticol' 11a Y-YYO
(J. Gerritsen & Son) J. Gerritsen & Son, 1980
Sdlg × 'Collarosa'
Fl. 120 mm wide; perianth segments pale greenish yellow; corona pale yellow (18D), with pinkish orange at rim. Early to mid-season. Resembles a larger 'Collarosa'

'Beautiful Dream' 3 W-W
(G.E. Mitsch, 1974) Grant Mitsch Novelty Daffodils, 1985
'Silken Sails' × 'Audubon'; sdlg no. JJ12/20A
Fl. of strong substance; perianth segments very broadly ovate, blunt, only very slightly mucronate, spreading, sometimes creased, overlapping half; the inner segments square-shouldered at base, a little inflexed, with margins wavy; corona very shallow funnel-shaped, very closely ribbed, opening creamy white, becoming white, with mouth straight, densely frilled. Late. Resembles 'Silken Sails' but with much broader perianth segments and a corona of different style

'Beautiful Music' 3 W-GYO
(G.E.Mitsch, 1980) R. & E.Havens, 1997
'Impala' × 'Green Hills'; sdlg no. 2P59/2
Fl. 100 mm wide; perianth segments very broadly ovate, pure white, spreading, plane, smooth; corona disc-shaped. Late. Sunproof

'Beauty' 2 Y-YYO
(W. Backhouse, pre-1869)
Perianth segments long, acute, sulphur yellow, with a darker tone at midrib, twisted, with margins incurved, irregular, only very slightly overlapping; corona long and narrowly cup-shaped, lightly but closely ribbed, yellow, with orange at rim, mouth wavy, rim very slightly notched. Syn. Incomparabilis Sulphureus 'Beauty'. AM 1897

'Beauty' 3 Y-O
(W.Backhouse, pre-1869)

Perianth segments well-formed, clear yellow; corona tinged orange. Syn. Burbidgei 'Beauty'

'Beauty' 1 W-Y
Syn. of 'Allen's Beauty'

'Beauty' 3 W-YYO
Syn. of 'Sensation'

'Beauty Glow' 2 W-P
(Oregon Bulb Farms, pre-1950)

'Beauty of Cambridge' 2 Y-Y
(R.H. Bath, pre-1927)
Fl. deep yellow. AM(e) 1928

'Beauty of Exeter' 3 W-? (b)
(E.T. England, pre-1923)

'Beauty of Kingsland' 2 Y-? (a)
(Guilcher, pre-1933)
Syn. 'Guilcher's Reward'

'Beauty of Radnor' 2 W-YYO
(N.Y. Lower, pre-1923)
'Bernardino' × 'Dragoon'
Perianth segments white; corona lemon yellow, with orange at rim. AM(e) 1923

'Beauty of Stars' 3 W-? (b)
(van Graven Bros, pre-1954)

'Beauty of the Garden'
Unregistered
In parentage of 'Finishing Touch'

'Beauty Point' 4 W-O
(M.G.Temple-Smith, 1983) M.G.Temple-Smith, 1997
'Glowing Red' × 'Challenge'; sdlg no. 18/83
Perianth and other petaloid segments in four whorls, symmetrically arranged; corona segments vivid orange 28B. Mid-season

'Beauty Queen' 2 W-? (b)
(Konynenburg & Mark, pre-1954)

'Beauty Queen' 2 Y-O
(Konynenburg & Mark) Konynenburg & Mark, 1960
'Bertha Aten' × ('Fortune' × 'Memphis')
Fl. 85 mm wide

'Beauty Tip' 2 W-W
(G.E. Mitsch) G.E. Mitsch, 1979
'Easter Moon' × 'Broughshane' hybrid; sdlg no. W65/2/3
Fl. 93 mm wide, ivory white; perianth segments very smooth, deeply overlapping; corona with distinct pink flush on opening. Mid-season

'Beauvallet' 4 Y-R
Syn. of 'Castle Dobbs'

'Beauvallon' 4 Y-ORR
(D.A. Lloyd) D.A. Lloyd, 1969
? × 'Tahiti'
Fl. 90-100 mm wide; perianth and other petaloid segments very broadly ovate, truncate, only very slightly mucronate, brilliant greenish yellow 7C, regular, overlapping half; the outer whorl spreading, with margins incurling; the inner whorl a little shorter, inflexed, with margins more strongly incurling; a single segment at centre; corona segments less than half as long as the petaloid segments, interspersed among them and clustered at centre, red, paling to vivid orange 28B at base, inflexed, heavily frilled. AM(e) 1977

'Beau Vite' 1 W-Y
(G. Lewis) D.S. Bell, 1955
Perianth segments white; corona deep lemon, frilled, with rim dentate

'Beaworthy' 2 Y-? (a)
(T. Batson, pre-1928)

'Bebington Gold' 1 Y-Y
(Clive Postles) Clive Postles, 1995
'Midas Touch' × 'Gold Convention'; sdlg no. 1-50-82
Fl. rounded, 118 mm wide, dark yellow; perianth segments very broadly ovate, with margins slightly incurving; corona cylindrical, with mouth flared and lobed, frilled. Early

'Bebop' 7 Y-Y
(A. Gray, pre-1949)
N. rupicola × *N. poeticus*
Resembles sibling 'Sun Disc' but with a paler perianth. See also 'Beebop'. Perianth paling with maturity, sometimes becoming almost white

'Becard' 1 YYW-Y
(G.E. Mitsch) G.E. Mitsch, 1979
Sdlg B36/3 ('Playboy' × 'Daydream') × sdlg A46/3 (sdlg P39/2 × 'Rima'); sdlg no. II47/1
Fl. 101 mm wide; perianth segments rich lemon gold, with white at base, overlapping; corona rich buff yellow overlying white, with a brighter tone at rim, frilled. Mid-season

'Beckington' 2 W-ORR
(D.N.Y. Olsen) D.N.Y. Olsen, 1978
'Monaco' × 'Ivo Fell'; sdlg no. 19/1
Fl. 92 mm wide; corona bowl-shaped, orange-red, with yellow-orange at base. Mid-season. Sunproof

'Bedale' 3 Y-? (a)
(A.M. Wilson, pre-1948)

'Bedazzled' 2 Y-O
(Tom Forster, 1960s) Unregistered
Perianth segments deep yellow; corona very shallow, bright orange. Early to mid-season

'Bedgebury' 1 YYW-WWY
(Carncairn Daffodils, 1980) Carncairn Daffodils, 1994
'Camelot' × 'Daydream' 'Camelot' × 'Daydream'; sdlg no. 15/51/75; sdlg no. 15/51/75
Fl. 98 mm wide; perianth segments very broadly ovate in outline, rounded at apex, obscurely mucronate, yellow, tinged white at base, spreading, plane, overlapping half; the inner segments narrower, squarish at shoulder, a little inflexed at base, reflexed at apex; corona funnel-shaped, ribbed, yellowish white, with a distinct band of yellow at rim, mouth straight or slightly expanded, tightly frilled. Mid-season

'Bedlam' 3 Y-O
(G.W.E. Brogden) G.W.E. Brogden, 1964
Fl. 89 mm wide; perianth segments yellow; corona reddish orange. Mid-season

'Bedouin' 2 W-YYO
(J.C. Williams, pre-1908)
Fl. more than 100 mm wide; per. segs broadly ovate or oblong in outline, blunt or rounded at apex, prominently mucronate, creamy white, spreading, somewhat creased, with margins slightly wavy and sometimes recurved at base, overlapping up to one-third; the inner segments narrower and a little inflexed, with margins more strongly wavy and recurved, sometimes nicked; corona bowl-shaped, expanded, loosely ribbed, yellow, with a band of reddish orange at rim, mouth straight, frilled. AM(Haarlem) 1912, AM(g)(c) 1914

'Bedouin Bride' 3 W-? (b)
(?M.J. Jefferson-Brown, pre-1950)

'Bedruthan' 2 W-YYR
(R.A.Scamp) R.A.Scamp, 1996
'High Society' × 'Raspberry Ring'; sdlg no. 521
Fl. 100 mm wide; perianth segments broadly ovate, pure white, slightly concave; corona funnel-shaped, opening soft pale yellow, becoming paler in tone, with dark red at rim, neatly frilled. Late

'Beebop' 7 Y-Y
Syn. of 'Bebop'

'Beecher Stowe' 3 W-? (b)
(J.W.A. Lefeber, pre-1945)

'Beechwood' 1 W-P
(C.E. Radcliff, 1942) C.E. Radcliff, 1956
'Carmoa' × 'Dawnglow'

'Beechworth' 1 Y-Y

(J.N. Hancock & Co., pre-1955) Unregistered
Sdlg × 'Hillston'

'Beefeater' 2 Y-O
(Barr & Sons, 1949) Wallace & Barr, 1959
Fl. 110 mm wide; perianth segments broad. Early. Resembles a larger-flowered 'Bahram' with the corona more widely expanded

'Beeley' 3 Y-? (a)
(D.B. Milne, pre-1950)

'Beema' 2 W-P
(W. Jackson Sr, 1946) W. Jackson Jr, 1956
'Leto' × 'Pinka'

'Bee Mabley' 3 W-YYO
(Mrs C.E. Fitzwater) Mrs C.E. Fitzwater, 1973
'Fairy Tale' × 'Matapan'
Fl. 90 mm wide

'Beenak' 2 W-WWY
(C.A. Nethercote, pre-1960) Unregistered
Perianth segments pure white; corona large, lightly ribbed, opening lemon yellow, becoming creamy white, with lemon yellow at rim

'Beersheba' 1 W-W
(G.H. Engleheart, pre-1923)
'White Knight' × Engleheart sdlg
Fl. forming a double triangle, 127 mm wide, ivory white, facing down; perianth segments broadly ovate, blunt, slightly mucronate, spreading or a little inflexed, with margins wavy, overlapping one-third; the inner segments more narrowly ovate, inflexed at base, reflexed towards apex, with margins wavy and sometimes nicked; corona narrowly funnel-shaped, broadly and smoothly ribbed, with mouth expanded and lightly frilled, rim rolled and shallowly crenate. Early. Resembles a 'White Knight' of more than twice the size and of purer white. 2n=28,29. AM(Haarlem) 1925, AM(e) 1925, FCC(Haarlem) 1926, FCC(e) 1926, AM(c) 1929

'Beeswax' 7
(J.C. Williams, pre-1945)

'Bee's Wing' 5
(P.D. Williams, pre-1908)

'Beethoven' 1 Y-Y
(R.A. van der Schoot, pre-1913)
Fl. clear pale yellow; perianth segments slender, somewhat twisted; corona long. Early

'Beethoven' 1 W-W
(Sir C.H. Cave, pre-1928)

'Beevor' 3 W-? (b)
(G.H. Engleheart, pre-1923)

'Bega' 1 Y-Y
(W. Jackson Jr) Jackson's Daffodils, 1982
'Ristin' × 'Otewa'; sdlg no. 96/76
Fl. 98 mm wide. Mid-season

'Begdale' 1 W-O
(?Cross & Co.) Unregistered
Perianth segments creamy white; corona orange

'Beguildy' 3 Y-GGR
(A.M. Wilson, pre-1946)
Perianth segments strong yellow; corona green, with distinct band of red at rim. Very late

'Behold' 3 W-W
(W. Jackson Jr) Jackson's Daffodils, 1979
'Verona' × 'Placid'; sdlg no. 111/74
Fl. 109 mm wide. Mid-season

'Beige Beauty' 3 Y-Y
(G.E. Mitsch, 1955) G.E. Mitsch, 1966
'Green Island' × 'Chinese White'; sdlg no. R33/39
Fl. 105 mm wide; perianth segments rounded, opening ivory white, becoming lemony beige yellow; corona almost disc-shaped, lightly ribbed, chartreuse yellow, sometimes becoming paler in tone. Mid-season. PC(e) 1968

'Beirut' 2 W-YYR
(J.L. Richardson, pre-1944)
'Seraglio' × 'Porthilly'
Fl. rounded; perianth segments very broad, rounded at apex and sometimes truncate, prominently mucronate, ivory white, spreading, of thick substance, overlapping half; the inner segments only a little narrower, with margins wavy, sometimes folded at shoulder; corona shallow bowl-shaped, yellow, with a broad band of bright red at rim, mouth split in places and overlapping, loosely frilled. Tall. Early to mid-season. 2n=28

'Beladar' 1 Y-Y
(D.J. Cooper) D.J. Cooper, 1957

'Belamour' 1 W-W
(G.L. Wilson) F.E. Board, 1956

'Belarius' 2 W-Y
(Barr & Sons, pre-1921)
Perianth segments white; corona long, straight-sided, canary yellow, with mouth frilled. Resembles 'Lady Margaret Boscawen' in form

'Belbroughton' 2 W-WWP
(Clive Postles Daffodils) Clive Postles Daffodils, 1988
'Rainbow' × 'Dailmanach'; sdlg no. 2-48-76
Fl. 90 mm wide; perianth segments broad, rounded, spreading; corona slightly flared, white, with a distinct band of pink at rim. Late. Sunproof

'Belcanto' 11a W-Y
(J. Gerritsen & Son) J. Gerritsen & Son, 1971
'Floralie' × 'President Lebrun'
Fl. 100 mm wide; corona segments spreading, light yellow. Late

'Belconnen' 2 W-P
(W.M. Spry, pre-1975) Unregistered
'Moonstruck' × 'August Pink'
Early

'Belcourt' 1 Y-Y
(C. de Berry) C. de Berry, 1960
Fl. 120 mm wide, canary yellow. Early. Resembles 'Harewood' but with rounder perianth segments

'Beldain' 9 W-?
(A.M. Wilson, pre-1930)
Syn. 'Belinda'

'Beldana' 2 W-? (b)
(Mrs R.O. Backhouse, pre-1921)

'Beleek' 2 W-P
Syn. of 'Belleek'

'Belfast City' 1 W-W
(W.J.E. Dukelow) W.J.E. Dukelow, 1991
'Empress of Ireland' × 'White Star'; sdlg no. 81/16A
Fl. 116 mm wide; perianth segments broadly ovate; corona narrow, with mouth slightly flared. Early. Resembles a 'Silent Valley' of purer white

'Belford' 2 Y-O
(G. Harrison) G. Harrison, 1971
Sdlg × 'Ceylon'
Fl. 89 mm wide

'Belinda' 2 Y-O
(de Graaff Bros, pre-1930)
Perianth segments soft apricot yellow; corona dark reddish orange, frilled. AM(Haarlem) 1930. Received AM(Haarlem) 1930 as 'Bellinde'

'Belinda' 9 W-?
Syn. of 'Beldain'

'Belisana' 2 W-YYO
(C.G. van Tubergen, pre-1946)
Perianth segments very broadly ovate, blunt and mucronate, sometimes truncate, cream white, spreading, plane, overlapping half; the inner segments slightly inflexed, a little narrower, less noticeably mucronate, shouldered at base; corona bowl-shaped, ribbed, orange-yellow, with orange at rim, mouth expanded, split in places and overlapping, lightly frilled, with rim crenate. 2n=28. AM(Haarlem) 1949, FCC(Haarlem) 1952

'Belka' 2 Y-YYO
(J.T. Gray, pre-1949)
Perianth segments yellow; corona wide-spreading, yellow, with a band of reddish orange at rim

'Bella' 2 Y-Y
(E. Leeds, pre-1877)
Fl. small, neat, sulphur yellow. Syn. Incomparabilis Concolor 'Bella', Incomparabilis Concolor 'Minor'. Was "absorbed" into 'Golden Mary'

'Bella' 2 W-?
Syn. of 'D'Artagnan'

'Bella Coola' 2 W-W
(Murray W. Evans) Murray W. Evans, 1987
'Broomhill' × 'Stainless'; sdlg no. U-10/3
Fl. white; perianth segments smooth; corona expanded and ribbed. Late. Resembles a later-flowered 'Stainless' of better quality

'Bella Darwent' 2 W-P
(H. Fell, 1940) R. Hyde, 1958

'Bella Donna' 8
(R.A. van der Schoot, pre-1931)
Poetaz
AM(Haarlem) 1930

'Bella Dron' 3 W-? (b or c)
(R.H. Bath, pre-1923)

'Bellaghy' 2 Y-O
(G.L. Wilson, pre-1944)
'Trevisky' × 'Fairy King'
Perianth segments yellow; corona scarlet-orange

'Bella Marie' 3 W-? (b)
(C.A. van der Wereld) C.A. van der Wereld, 1957

'Bellambi' 1 W-Y
(W.M. Spry, pre-1975) Unregistered
'Marble Queen' × 'Stand By'

'Bellamy' 2 W-? (b)
(Mrs R.O. Backhouse, pre-1921)

'Bellante' 8 W-O
(pre-1851)

'Bellarion' 3 W-? (b)
(de Graaff-Gerharda, pre-1930)

'Bellary' 3 W-? (b)
(N.Y. Lower, pre-1933)

'Bella Vista' 2 W-YYO
(J.W.A. Lefeber) J.W.A. Lefeber, 1959
Fl. very broad; perianth segments ivory white; corona greenish yellow, with a broad band of vivid orange 28B at rim. Very early. The orange rim

dependent on climate

'Bella Vista' 3 W-YYR
Syn. of 'Trident'

'Bellavista' 3 W-YYR
Syn. of 'Trident'

'Bellavista' 3 W-YYR
Syn. of 'Bella Vista'

'Bellbird' 9 W-?
(A.E. Lowe, pre-1925)

'Bell Bird' 9 W-WWR
(pre-1926)
Corona with red at rim

'Bellbird' 1 W-W
(A.H. Ahrens) J.S. Leitch, 1955

'Bellbrae' 1 W-W
(W.M. Spry, pre-1975) Unregistered
'Zero' × Fairbairn sdlg
Tall. Early

'Bellbro' 3 W-? (b)
(Mrs R.O. Backhouse, pre-1921)

'Bellbrook' 2 W-Y
(W.M. Spry, pre 1975) Unregistered
'Morning Glory' × 'Stand By'

'Belle Aire' 2 W-? (b)
(E.C. Powell, pre-1946)

'Belle Aurora' 8 W or Y-O
(pre-1883)

'Belle Chinoise' 3 W-O
(A.M. Wilson, pre-1926)
'Beacon' hybrid
Perianth segments narrow, acute to rounded, rich creamy white, sometimes flushed pink, with margins incurved, slightly ribbed, overlapping at base only; corona small, ribbed, vermilion orange, with mouth a little frilled. AM(Haarlem) 1926

'Belleek' 2 W-P
(G.L. Wilson, pre-1953)
'Rose of Tralee' × 'Evening'
Perianth segments pure white; corona rose pink or in some seasons almost white, with mouth slightly expanded. See also 'Beleek'

'Belleek' 2 W-WWO
Syn. of 'Castlecoole'

'Belle Etoilèe' 8 W-O
(pre-1798)

'Belle Fleur' 4 Y-R
(J.A.O'More, pre-1996) Unregistered

'Belle Forme' 8 W-Y
(pre-1850)
Perianth segments white; corona pale yellow

'Belle Fortuna' 8 W-Y
(pre-1807)
Perianth segments white; corona lemon yellow. Early. See also 'Belle Fortune'

'Belle Fortune' 8 W-Y
Syn. of 'Belle Fortuna'

'Belle Glow' 2 W-P
(J.N. Hancock & Co., 1963) Unregistered
'Pink of Dawn' open pollinated
Perianth segments broadly ovate, blunt, only very slightly mucronate, inflexed, somewhat concave, some with margins incurling, overlapping half; the inner segments more usually plane or with margins slightly wavy; corona cylindrical, obscurely ribbed, deep shrimp pink, mouth a little expanded, even, rim narrowly rolled. Mid-season

'Belle Hative' 8 Y-Y
(pre-1792)

'Belle Jaune' 2 Y-? (a)
(pre-1926)
AM(Haarlem) 1926

'Belle Keller' 1 W-W
(G. Lewis, 1930) Parr's Nurseries, 1958

'Belle Laura' 8 W-Y
(pre-1807)

'Belle Legeoise' 8 W-Y
Syn. of 'Belle Liegeoise'

'Belle Legion' 8
(pre-1883)

'Belle Liegeoise' 8 W-Y
(pre-1798)
Perianth segments white; corona citron yellow. See also 'Belle Legeoise', 'Belle Ligoise'

'Belle Ligoise' 8 W-Y
Syn. of 'Belle Liegeoise'

'Belle Mead' 1 W-Y
(J.W.A. Lefeber) J.W.A. Lefeber, 1968

'Belle Moon' 2 W-Y
(G.J. Phillips) G.J. Phillips, 1987
'Isabella' × 'Killymoon'; sdlg no. 73-107-1
Perianth segments milk white; corona yellow. Early.

Resembles 'Flash Affair'

'Belle of Normandy'
Syn. of 'La Belle de Normandie'

'Belle Pale' 8 Y-Y
(pre-1798)
Fl. sulphur yellow

'Belle Princesse' 8 Y-Y
(pre-1871)

'Bellerephon' 1 Y-Y
(T.H. Piper, 1954)
'Bulwark' × 'Roundabout'

'Belle Rose' 2 W-P
(H.A. Brown, pre-1950)

'Bellever' 2 W-? (b)
(P.D. Williams, pre-1943)

'Bellevue' 2 W-O
(W.J. Dunlop, pre-1952)
'Mitylene' × 'Painted Lady'
Perianth segments white; corona bright orange, with tints of apricot in some lights

'Bellinde' 2 Y-O
Syn. of 'Belinda'

'Bellinzona' 1 W-? (b)
(N.Y. Lower, pre-1934)

'Bellissima' 8 W-O
(pre-1798)

'Bellmont Glory' 1 W-W
(R.H.Glover, pre-1989) Unregistered
'Abebe' × 'Castle of Mey'

'Bellona' 2 W-YYO
(Mrs R.O. Backhouse, pre-1921)
Fl. of great substance and waxy texture; perianth segments pure white, deeply overlapping; corona wide and very shallow bolw-shaped, bright canary yellow, with rim tinged apricot

'Bellringer' 5 Y-Y
(D. Blanchard) M.J. Jefferson-Brown, 1975
Perianth segments pale sulphur cream; corona of a slightly darker yellow

'Bell Rock' 1 W-Y
(R.A.Scamp) R.A.Scamp, 1997
'Cyros' × 'Ben Aligin'; sdlg no. 428
Fl. 90 mm wide; perianth segments broadly ovate, pure white, deeply overlapping; corona funnel-shaped, bright canary yellow, neatly frilled, with rim slightly rolled. Mid-season

'Bellsmith' 2 Y-? (a)
(H.G. Longford, pre-1927)

'Bell Song' 7 W-P
(G.E. Mitsch) G.E. Mitsch, 1971
('Wild Rose' × 'Interim') × *N. jonquilla*; sdlg no. Z46/3
Fls 2-3 per stem, 65 mm wide; perianth segments opening pale buff yellow with a pink tinge at base, becoming ivory white; corona neat, bright pink. Late. $2n=21$

'Belmarino' 1 Y-Y
(D.S. Bell, 1968) D.S. Bell, 1978
'Dawn Patrol' × 'Dawngold'
Fl. 108 mm wide; corona frilled. Mid-season

'Belmont' 1 Y-Y
(C. de Berry, pre-1949)

'Beloved' 2 W-W
(F.E. Board) F.E. Board, 1965
'Wedding Bell' × 'Empress of Ireland'

'Belphoebe'
(A.E. Lowe, pre-1927)

'Belray' 2 Y-? (a)
(Mrs R.O. Backhouse, pre-1921)
Syn. 'Goldcrest'. AM(Haarlem) 1931

'Belshazzar' 1 Y-Y
(G.L. Wilson, pre-1923)
'Glory of Noordwijk' × ('Golden Bell' × 'King Alfred')

'Beltane' 2 Y-? (a)
(Mrs R.S. Cobley, pre-1938)
Early

'Beltany' 1 Y-Y
(G.L. Wilson) G.L. Wilson, 1957
'Kingscourt' × 'Goldcourt'
Fl. deep gold

'Beltrim' 2 W-GPP
(Carncairn Daffodils) Carncairn Daffodils, 1976
'Rosario' × 'Irish Rose'; sdlg no. 136
Fl. 90 mm wide; corona orange-pink (29B), with green at base. Late

'Belushka' 2 W-P
(Jackson's Daffodils) Jackson's Daffodils, 1991
'Madang' × 'Melancholy'; sdlg no. 257/82
Fl. 98 mm wide; perianth segments broad, overlapping; corona with mouth flared and frilled. Mid-season to late

'Belvedere' 1 W-W
(Mrs R.O. Backhouse, pre-1921)

'Belyta' 2 W-? (b)
(de Graaff Bros, pre-1943)
AM(Haarlem) 1942

'Belzone' 2 Y-R
(D.S. Bell) D.S. Bell, 1983
'Irish Light' × 'Ashanti'
Perianth segments yellow, smooth; corona blazing red

'Ben Alder' 1 Y-Y
(The Brodie of Brodie, c.1911)
'King Alfred' × 'Lord Roberts'
Resembles a large-flowered 'King Alfred'

'Ben Aligin' 1 W-GWW
(J.S.B. Lea, 1975) Clive Postles Daffodils, 1986
Sdlg 1-47-64 × sdlg 1-25-62; sdlg no. 2-36-71
Perianth segments broadly ovate, blunt, slightly mucronate, with margins slightly incurving at apex, smooth, overlapping half; the inner segments narrow, acute, slightly reflexed; corona large funnel-shaped, white, with green at base, rim rolled and dentate. Tall. Mid-season

'Benares' 2 Y-? (a)
(The Brodie of Brodie, c.1930)
'Killigrew' × 'Fortune'; sdlg no. 30/A/25

'Ben Armine' 2 Y-YYO
(D.C. MacArthur) D.C. MacArthur, 1994
'Binkie' × 2 W-P; sdlg no. EV35185
Fl. 92 mm wide; perianth segments ovate, mucronate, pale greenish yellow 10D, spreading, glistening; the inner segments not noticeably mucronate; corona funnel-shaped, ribbed, pale greenish yellow 10D, suffused very light orange (23D) at rim, mouth flared and lobed, rim crenate. Dwarf. Late. Sunproof

'Ben Avon' 1 Y-Y
(The Brodie of Brodie, c.1909)
'Emperor' × 'King Alfred'

'Ben Avon' 1 W-W
(J.S.B. Lea) J.S.B. Lea, 1978
'Canisp' × ('Empress of Ireland' × 'Glenshesk'); sdlg no. 2-11-66
Fl. 125 mm wide; Mid-season

'Ben Bhraggie' 2 W-O
(D.C. MacArthur) D.C. MacArthur, 1990
'Trousseau' × 'Preamble'; sdlg no. E502
Fl. 111 mm wide; perianth segments almost triangular in appearance, greenish white (155A), slightly reflexed; corona deep yellow-orange, mouth expanded and frilled. Early. Sunproof

'Benbow' 1 Y-Y
(A.J. Bliss, pre-1930)

'Bencarn' 2 W-?
(A. Overton) A. Overton, 1960

'Benchmark' 3 W-GYR
(T.D. Throckmorton) T.D. Throckmorton, 1974
'Aircastle' × 'Merlin'

'Bendemeer' 3 W-? (b)
(A.M. Wilson, pre-1913)

'Bendigo' 2 Y-Y
(A.M. Wilson, pre-1937)
Fl. deep yellow; corona very heavily frilled. Very early

'Bendigo Gold' 2 Y-Y
(H.A. Brown) J.N. Hancock & Co., 1960

'Bene' 1 Y-Y
(W. Jackson Jr, 1957) Unregistered
'Anukis' × 'Moque'; sdlg no. 2/57

'Benedick' 1 W-? (b)
(Barr & Sons, pre-1923)
'Loveliness' × 'King Alfred'

'Benediction' 3 W-GWW
(J.L. Richardson) J.L. Richardson, 1958
'Chinese White' × 'Bryher'
Perianth segments very broad, snow white, of much substance; corona wide-spreading, white, with deep emerald green at base. Late. 2n=28

'Benefactor' 3 O-O
(Carncairn Daffodils) Carncairn Daffodils, 1988
'Altruist' open pollinated; sdlg no. 7/86/79
Perianth segments peach orange; corona cup-shaped, dark reddish orange, fading in strong sunlight, with rim slightly dentate. Late. Resembles 'Altruist'

'Benen' 1 W-W
(W.A. Watts, pre-1913)

'Benenden' 1 Y-Y
(R.V. Favell, pre-1946)
'Tunis' × 'Tenedos'

'Benevolence' 1 W-? (b)
(J.L. Richardson) F.E. Board, 1955

'Benfica' 3 W-YYO
(G. Kieft, 1918) van Graven Bros, 1962
Fl. 100 mm wide; corona light orange-yellow 16C, with vivid reddish orange 32A at rim. Late

'Bengal' 3 W-O
(Barr & Sons, pre-1934)
Perianth segments white, tinged sulphur yellow at base, of strong substance, overlapping; corona widely expanded, ribbed, dark apricot orange

'Bengal Tiger' 2 Y-O
(D.S. Bell) D.S. Bell, 1965
Sdlg × 'Alamein'
Perianth segments with shades of yellow overlaid with tan; corona reddish orange. Mid-season

'Benghazi' 2 Y-YOO
(J.L. Richardson, pre-1941)
(('Seraglio' × ['Beacon' × 'Fortune']) × 'Porthilly'
Fl. rounded; perianth segments very broadly ovate in outline, rounded at apex, slightly mucronate, rich bright yellow, plane, overlapping half; the inner segments narrower, slightly inflexed, creased, with margin indented at shoulder; corona shallow bowl-shaped, lightly ribbed, bright orange, paling to golden yellow at base, mouth widely expanded, split in places and overlapping, with rim regularly 12-crenate. Mid-season

'Benham' 1 W-Y
(C.E. Radcliff, 1943) J.M.Radcliff, 1956
'Bonnington' × 'Kanchenjunga'
Perianth segments white; corona lemon yellow

'Ben Hart' 1 Y-Y
(H. Hart, pre-1914)
Fl. large, mid-yellow

'Ben Hee' 2 W-GWW
(J.S.B. Lea) J.S.B. Lea, 1964
'Easter Moon' × 'Omeath'
Fl. 102 mm wide, greenish white 155C; perianth segments very broadly ovate in outline, blunt or slightly truncate at apex, very slightly mucronate, spreading, plane, overlapping half or more; the inner segments a little inflexed; corona funnel-shaped, ribbed, with green at base, mouth a little expanded, lightly frilled, with rim crenate. Mid-season. 2n=28. AM(e) 1975, AM(e) 1977, *HC(g) 1990

'Ben Hur' 1 Y-Y
(de Graaff Bros, pre-1927)
AM(Haarlem) 1930

'Benjamin Franklin' 3 W-? (b)
(F. Rijnveld & Sons, pre-1943)
AM(Haarlem) 1943

'Benjamino Gigli' 2 Y-Y
(pre-1950)
Perianth segments rich yellow; corona yellow

'Benjeroop' 1 Y-Y
(C.A. Nethercote) T. Morrison, 1960
Fl. golden yellow; corona heavily dentate

'Ben Jonson' 9 W-R
(G.H. Engleheart, pre-1897)
Sdlg no. 333
Corona suffed deep crimson

'Ben Ledi' 2 W-GWW
(J.S.B. Lea) Clive Postles Daffodils, 1985
'Misty Glen' × 'Croila'
Perianth segments broadly ovate, blunt or a little truncate, slightly mucronate, overlapping one-third to a half; the inner segments a little twisted; corona slender funnel-shaped, lightly ribbed, milk white, with green at base, mouth a little flared and lightly frilled. Mid-season

'Ben Lomond' 1 W-Y
(D.S. Bell, 1965) D.S. Bell, 1975
'Trousseau' open pollinated
Fl. 105 mm wide. Resembles an improved 'Trousseau'

'Ben Loyal' 2 W-O
(J.S.B. Lea) J.S.B. Lea, 1964
Richardson sdlg 647 × sdlg 1-25-56; sdlg no. 2-2-61
Fl. 92 mm wide; perianth segments white; corona dark reddish orange. Late. Resembles a whiter 'Arbar' with the perianth segments more rounded

'Benmore' 2 Y-R
(R. Hyde) R. Hyde, 1957
'Playboy' × 'Narvik'

'Bennett Hale' 2 W-? (b)
(Mrs R.O. Backhouse, pre-1921)

'Bennett-Poë' 5 W-Y
Syn. of 'J.T.Bennett-Pˆe'

'Ben Nevis' 9 W-?
(M. van Waveren & Sons, pre-1943)

'Benois Lovejoy' 2 W-? (b)
(J.W.A. Lefeber, pre-1938)

'Benone' 1 W-? (b)
(G.L. Wilson, pre-1932)

'Benoni' 2 Y-?
Syn. of 'Binge'

'Ben Rinnes' 1 Y-Y
(The Brodie of Brodie, c.1912)
'Duke of Bedford' × 'King Alfred'; sdlg no. 178/A/07
Fl. 101 mm wide; perianth segments broadly ovate, blunt, prominently mucronate, brilliant greenish yellow 5A, somewhat reflexed, overlapping one-third; the inner segments twisted and nicked; corona funnel-shaped, lightly ribbed, richer in tone than vivid yellow 9A, mouth straight, frilled, with six overlapping lobes, rim minutely crenate

'Ben Rinnes' 3 W-R
(J.S.B. Lea) J.S.B. Lea, 1972
'Arbar' × sdlg 1-34-53; sdlg no. 4-43-63
Fl. 93 mm wide; corona frilled. Mid-season

'Ben Simonite'
(pre-1913)

'Benten' 2 W-? (b)
(W. Jackson Sr, 1934)
'Warflame' × 'La Fraicheur'

'Benvarden' 3 W-W
(Carncairn Daffodils) Carncairn Daffodils, 1969
'Chinese White' × G.L.Wilson sdlg
Fl. white; corona with emerald green at abse, frilled. Sweetly scented. 2n=28

'Benventon' 2 W-Y
(pre-1927)
Perianth segments white; corona opening yellow, becoming very pale

'Benvolio' 1 Y-Y
(C. Dawson, pre-1923)

'Ben Vorlich' 2 W-YOO
(J.S.B. Lea, 1970) Clive Postles Daffodils, 1987
Sdlg 1-27-58 × 'Rockall'; sdlg no. 2-34-66
Corona rim widely rolled. Mid-season

'Benvoy' 3 W-GWW
(Mrs H.K. Richardson) Mrs H.K. Richardson, 1977
'Verona' × 'Benediction'; sdlg no. 148
Fl. pure white; perianth segments rounded, smooth, of good substance; corona bowl-shaped, with green at base. Mid-season. 2n=28

'Ben Wyvis' 1 Y-Y
(The Brodie of Brodie, c.1908)
'Emperor' × 'Santa Maria'
Fl. star-shaped, 100 mm wide, brilliant greenish yellow 5A; perianth segments ovate, acute, with white mucro, spreading, a little twisted, overlapping a quarter to one-third; the inner segments more noticeably twisted; corona cylindrical, smoothly 6-angled, with a greater saturation of colour than in the perianth, with mouth expanded, rim flanged, deeply and regularly crenate

'Benzoline' 3 W-? (b)
(pre-1913)

'Beppie' 1 W-Y
Syn. of 'Beppy'

'Beppu' 2 W-W
(H.R. Bulman, c.1966) Unregistered
'Polindra' × 'Whitefoord'

'Beppy' 1 W-Y
(R.V. Hennis or H.Prins, pre-1929)
'Horsfieldii' hybrid
Syn. 'Beppie'

'Bequest' 2 W-W
(R.V. Favell, pre-1940)
Sdlg × 'White Emperor'

'Berceuse' 2 W-P
(G.E. Mitsch) Grant Mitsch Novelty Daffodils, 1984
('Pink Frost' × 'Rose Caprice') × ('Carita' × 'Accent'); sdlg no. KK8/5
Fl. 41 mm wide; perianth segments broadly ovate in outline, blunt or truncate at apex, slightly mucronate, reflexed, smooth, with midrib showing, overlapping half; the inner segments more narrowly ovate, with margins incurling at apex; corona funnel-shaped, smooth, deep rose pink, touched with tones of lavender, mouth straight or a little flared, split in places and overlapping, lightly frilled. Mid-season

'Berdas' 2 Y-? (a)
(W.A. Watts, pre-1923)
'Sir Watkin' × 'Ornatus'

'Berdina' 3 W-? (b)
(Mrs R.O. Backhouse, pre-1921)

'Bereby' 3 W-? (b)
(Mrs R.O. Backhouse, pre-1921)
Syn. 'Agrippa'

'Bere Ferrers' 4 W-O
(Mrs H.K. Richardson) du Plessis Bros, 1979
'Gay Time' × 'Rameses'; sdlg no. 298
Fl. 110 mm wide; perianth and other petaloid segments in several whorls, white, tinged light greenish yellow 4B at base; the outer whorls broadly ovate, blunt or truncate, prominently mucronate, spreading or a little inflexed, with margins incurling, overlapping half; the inner whorls successively shorter and narrower, less regularly arranged, more strongly inflexed, with margins more tightly incurled; corona segments short, interspersed among the inner whorls of petaloid segments, vivid yellow 14A, heavily flushed strong orange 24A, with a paler tone at rim, frilled. Late. Slightly scented. Resembles a more deeply coloured 'Double Event'. AM(e) 1988

'Berenice' 3 Y-? (a)
(W.B. Hartland, pre-1907)

'Berenice' 1 W-W
Syn. of 'Iona'

'Berenson' 2 W-O
(J.W.A. Lefeber) J.W.A. Lefeber, 1968
'Redmarley' hybrid

'Beresford' 1 W-W
(R.H. Bath, pre-1929)

'Bergen' 2 W-W
(J.L. Richardson, pre-1938)

'White Emperor' × 'Beersheba'
Fl. white; perianth segments broadly ovate, of great substance; corona mouth slightly flanged. AM(Haarlem) 1948, FCC(Haarlem) 1950. Div. 1 until 1959

'Bergerac' 11a Y-Y
(J. Gerritsen & Son, 1972) J. Gerritsen & Son, 1984
'Rocky Horror' hybrid; sdlg no. 749
Perianth segments pale yellow; corona segments as long as the perianth segments and at apex broader, ribbed, darker in tone than the perianth segments, sometimes becoming almost white, with bright yellow at rim, often very deeply split and 3-lobed, frilled, with margins strongly recurved. Early

'Bergh'
(?A. Gray, pre-1951)

N. × bergidensis Fernández Casas 13 = N. fontqueri
Fernández Casas × N. triandrus Linnaeus

'Berima' 2 Y-Y
(W. Jackson Jr) W. Jackson Jr, 1968
Sdlg 7/55 × 'Farmington'; sdlg no. 8/60

'Berit' 1 Y-Y
(W. Jackson Jr) W. Jackson Jr, 1968
'Jobi' × sdlg 125/55; sdlg no. 155/61

'Berkeley-Calcott' 2 Y-? (a)
(G.T.C. Pearce, pre-1939)

'Berkeley Court' 4 W-P
(Brian S. Duncan) Rathowen Daffodils, 1987
Sdlg 8/74 (['Falaise' × 'Debutante'] × 'Polonaise') × sdlg 346 ('Polonaise' × 'Violetta'); sdlg no. 813
Perianth and other petaloid segments white; corona segments pink, interpersed among the petaloid segments at centre. Mid-season to late

'Berkshire' 2 Y-? (a)
(T.A.V. Wood, pre-1949)

'Berlin' 2 Y-YYO
(W.F. Leenen) W.F. Leenen, 1980
Fl. 85 mm wide; perianth segments brilliant greenish yellow 6A; corona vivid yellow 13A, with a broad band of orange (30C) at mouth, frilled. Mid-season

'Bermuda' 2 Y-O
(Warnaar & Co., pre-1939)
'Bokhara' × 'Killigrew'
Perianth segments broadly ovate. AM(Haarlem) 1939, FCC(Haarlem) 1944

"Bermuda Jonquil"
Variant of N. tazetta naturalized on Bermuda

'Bernadino' 2 W-Y
Syn. of 'Bernardino'

'Bernadotte' 2 Y-O
(L. van Leeuwen & Son, pre-1947)
AM(Haarlem) 1946

N. × bernardii de Candolle 13 = N. hispanicus
Gouan × N. poeticus Linnaeus ("Straffan Snowdrop")

'Bernardino' 2 W-Y
(P.J. Worsley, pre-1907)
'Lulworth' × 'Duchess of Brabant'
Fl. 103 mm wide; perianth segments broadly ovate, blunt or slightly truncate, prominently mucronate, creamy white, spreading, with margins sometimes incurling, overlapping one-third; the inner segments somewhat inflexed, twisted or with margins wavy; corona short funnel-shaped, ribbed, yellow, deeply tinged orange-apricot, with mouth straight, tightly frilled. 2n=28. AM(Haarlem) 1915. See also 'Bernadino'

'Bernborough' 2 Y-Y
(D.S. Bell) D.S. Bell, 1960
'Igloo' × 'Broughshane'
Fl. 115 mm wide; corona regularly frilled. Mid-season. Resembles 'Galway'

'Bernita' 2 W-? (b)
(P.D. Williams, pre-1939)

'Berringa' 1 W-Y
(W.M. Spry, pre-1975) Unregistered
'Dependable' × 'Wandin Gem'
Corona lemon yellow. Mid-season

'Berry' 3 Y-? (a)
(Mrs R.O. Backhouse, pre-1921)

'Berry Gorse' 3 W-GYY
(W.A. Noton) W.A. Noton, 1985
'Dallas' × 'Woodland Prince'
Corona neat, lemon yellow. Tall. Late

'Berse' 1 Y-Y
(W. Jackson Sr, 1946)
'Saint Aloysius' × 'Mrs R.O. Backhouse'

'Berserker' 1 Y-Y
(A.M. Wilson, pre-1908)

'Bertha' 1 W-W
(W. Poupart, pre-1916)

'Bertha' 1 Y-Y
(H.E. Sharp, pre-1930)

'Bertha Aten' 2 W-O
(R.O. Backhouse, pre-1931)
Perianth segments sulphur white; corona "semi-

'Bernadino' 2 W-Y

double", deep orange. AM(Haarlem) 1931

'Bertie' 2 W-YYO
(E. Leeds, pre-1877)
Perianth segments creamy white. "Absorbed" 'Louis Serres', 'Montrose' and 'Rosa Bonheur'

N. bertolonii **Parlatore 13 Section Tazettae**
    var. ***bertolonii***
    var. ***algericus*** (Roemer) Maire & Weiller
    var. ***discolor*** Battandier
    var. ***primulinus*** Maire

'Bertrand' 1 Y-Y
(A.J. Bliss, pre-1930)
'Glory of Noordwijk' × 'King Alfred'

'Bert Sands' 2 W-? (b)
(J. Pope, pre-1908)

'Berwen' 2 W-WWP
(J.A. O'More, 1960) P.D.K. Ramsay, 1980
'Jean Anderson' hybrid; sdlg no. 64/60
Fl. 95 mm wide

'Berwick' 2 Y-YYR
(S.C. Gaspar, 1951) R.J. Abernethy, 1963
Fl. 102 mm wide; perianth segments soft golden yellow; corona bright yellow, with deep orange-red at rim. Mid-season

'Beryl' 6 W-YYO
(P.D. Williams, pre-1907)
'Chaucer' × *N. cyclamineus*
Fl. 75 mm wide, facing slightly downwards; perianth segments broadly or very broadly ovate, truncate, fairly prominently mucronate, opening brilliant greenish yellow, with white at apex, becoming yellowish white, with tinges of yellow at base, reflexed, with midrib showing, overlapping one-third to a half; the inner segments more narrowly ovate, more nearly acute, with margins wavy or incurved; corona cup-shaped, ribbed, orange-yellow, with a broad band of orange at mouth, mouth straight, even, rim shallowly crenate. Early to mid-season. 2n=21,21+1B. Resembles a smaller-flowered 'Roger'. *AM(g)(?r) 1927, AM(Haarlem) 1934, *AM(g) 1936

'Beryl Dettman' 1 Y-Y
(L.P. Dettman) L.P. Dettman, 1977
'Arctic Gold' × 'Chromis'; sdlg no. 21/76
Fl. 80 mm wide; perianth segments vivid yellow 9A; corona darker in tone (13A). Mid-season. Resembles 'King Kanto' but with a slightly paler perianth and the corona dentate and more widely expanded

'Beryl Dettman' 2 Y-Y
(L.P. Dettman) L.P. Dettman, 1982
'Arctic Gold' × 'Ghana'; sdlg no. 49/75
Fl. 81 mm wide; perianth segments brilliant yellow 7A; corona much darker in tone (15A). Early. Resembles a less regularly formed 'Arctic Gold'

'Beryl Hancock' 1 W-W
(J.N. Hancock & Co., 1973) Unregistered

'Beryl Parr' 2 Y-Y
(The Brodie of Brodie, pre-1931)
Div. 1 sdlg × 'Fortune'
Fl. small, neat, deep gold, of smooth texture. Tall

'Beryl's Little Sister' 6 Y-Y
(?Scottish origin, pre-1936)
Fl. 53 mm wide, facing down; perianth segments ovate, prominently mucronate, greenish yellow (2C), more or less spreading, separated or slightly overlapping at base only; the inner segments more narrowly ovate, only very slightly mucronate; corona cylindrical, short, vivid yellow 12A, with mouth straight, rim obscurely crenate

'Beryl Walker' 1 W-Y
(J.N. Hancock & Co., 1962) J.N. Hancock & Co., 1977
'Zeiss' × 'Trousseau'; sdlg no. 52/57
Fl. 92 mm wide; corona opening brilliant yellow 9C, becoming paler (13D). Early. Resembles a taller and earlier-flowered 'Trousseau' ageing to white

'Bessbrook' 2 W-W
(W.J. Dunlop) W.J. Dunlop, 1960
'Polindra' × 'Kanchenjunga'
Perianth segments white; corona opening pale cream, soon becoming white

'Bessie' 3 W-? (b)
(C. Dawson, pre-1913)

'Bessiebelle' 2 G-G
(W.M. Spry, pre-1975) Unregistered
'Constance' × 'Port Kembla'
Perianth segments creamy green; corona opening apricot, becoming green

'Bessie Beneath' 3 W-GYR
(G.H. Johnstone, pre-1953)
'Silver Coin' hybrid × 'Sunstar'

'Bessie C.Scott' 1 W-Y
Syn. of 'Bessie Scott'

'Bessie Davidson' 1 W-W
(West & Fell, pre-1935)
Fl. white, facing down; corona long, with rim flanged. Early

'Bessie Scott' 1 W-Y
(J.N. Hancock & Co., 1948) R. Hyde, 1958
Perianth segments white; corona rich lemon, with mouth expanded, rim closely and deeply notched, as

if fringed. Syn. 'Bessie C.Scott'

'Bessingham Bouquet' 8
(Miss K. Spurrell, pre-1907)

'Best Man' 2 W-O
(Mrs R.O. Backhouse, pre-1908)
Perianth segments white; corona expanded, reddish orange

'Best of Luck' 3 W-YOR
(Ballydorn Bulb Farm) Ballydorn Bulb Farm, 1983
'Nemo' × 'Strangford'
Fl. 98 mm wide. Mid-season

'Best Regards' 1 YYW-Y
(G.E. Mitsch) Grant Mitsch Novelty Daffodils, 1984
'Arctic Gold' × 'Daydream'; sdlg no. MM14/1
Fl. 98 mm wide; perianth segments golden yellow, with white at base; corona slightly darker in tone. Mid-season

'Best Seller' 1 YYW-Y
(D. van Buggenum) D. van Buggenum, 1970
'Dutch Master' × 'Gold Medal'

'Best Wishes' 2 W-P
(O. Ronalds) O. Ronalds, 1955
'Pink o' Dawn' × 'Mrs Oscar Ronalds'
Corona deep pink to base

'Beta' 2 or 3 W-? (b or c)
(pre-1913)

'Bet-bet' 3 W-YYR
(W.M. Spry, pre-1975) Unregistered
'Nevose' × 'Rethel'
Corona lemon yellow, with red at rim. Late

'Betelgeuse' 2 Y-O
(C.A. van der Wereld, pre-1947)
Perianth segments soft yellow. AM(Haarlem) 1946

'Beth'
(A.E. Lowe, pre-1925)

'Betha' 8 Y-YYO
(W. Welchman, pre-1926)
Fls 1-2 per stem; perianth segments very broad, blunt or truncate, slightly mucronate, sulphur yellow, spreading; the inner segments a little inflexed, with margins wavy or incurled; corona almost disc-shaped, orange-yellow, with green at base and a narrow band of orange at rim, mouth lobed and lightly frilled. AM(e) 1926

'Bethal' 3 Y-Y
(R.A.Scamp) R.A.Scamp, 1997
'Aircastle' × 'Montego'; sdlg no. 342
Fl. rounded, 100 mm wide, opening yellowish white, becoming lemon yellow; perianth segments broadly ovate, very slightly concave, overlapping; corona shallow bowl-shaped, ribbed, with mouth lobed. Mid-season to late

'Bethany' 2 Y-W
(G.E. Mitsch) G.E. Mitsch, 1958
'Binkie' × ('King of the North' × 'Content')
Perianth segments deep lemon; corona long, opening deep lemon, soon becoming near pure white, with a touch of lemon at rim, mouth frilled. Mid-season. 2n=19. Resembles a larger-flowered 'Binkie' sooner becoming white in the corona

'Bethlehem' 2 W-? (b or c)
(Sir F.C. Stern, pre-1938)

'Bethlehem' 8 W-Y
Syn. of 'Nony'

'Betoateione' 1 W-Y
(F.E. Board, pre-1986) Unregistered
'Newcastle' × 'Ballygarvey'

'Betrin' 1 W-Y
(W. Jackson Jr) W. Jackson Jr, 1968
'Maweena' × 'Rowella'; sdlg no. 12/64

'Betrothal' 2 W-O
(F.E. Board) F.E. Board, 1965
'Blarney' × 'Arbar'

'Betsy' 1
(pre-1913)

'Betsy MacDonald' 6 W-P
(R.A. Scamp) R.A. Scamp, 1994
'Foundling' × 'Tangent'; sdlg no. 130
Fl. 75 mm wide, facing down; perianth segments broadly ovate, pure white, reflexed, deeply overlapping; corona funnel-shaped, bright rosy pink, with a slightly paler tone at base, mouth lobed. Dwarf. Mid-season. Sunproof

'Bettatip' 2 W-YYO
(J.N. Hancock & Co., 1953)
Perianth segments glistening white; corona soft yellow, with orange at rim

'Better Half' 2 W-P
(Alister Clark, 1940) R. Hyde, 1958
Fl. small; corona of near Div. 1 proportions, buff pink.

'Better Half' W-P
(C.O. Fairbairn, pre-1956) Unregistered
Clark sdlg × 'Salmon Trout'

'Better Times' 2 Y-YYO
(Warnaar & Co., pre-1944)
Perianth segments clear yellow; corona yellow, with

reddish orange at rim, frilled. AM(Haarlem) 1944

'Bettina' 2 W-Y
(J.N.Hancock & Co., 1983) J.N.Hancock & Co., 1997
Sdlg 30/73H hybrid; sdlg no. 19/83H
Perianth segments ovate, plane; corona bowl-shaped, expanded, bright orange, with rim crenate. Early

'Betty' 1 Y-Y
(G.H. Engleheart, pre-1914)

'Betty Beery' 3 Y-YYO
(L.P. Dettman) L.P. Dettman, 1979
'Janice Dettman' × 'Aircastle'; sdlg no. J/A 1/75
Fl. 83 mm wide; perianth segments light greenish yellow 8C; corona brilliant yellow 13B, with a broad band of strong orange 25B at rim. Mid-season. Resembles 'Janice Dettman' but with shorter and differently coloured perianth segments

'Betty Berkeley' 5 W-W
(G.H. Engleheart, pre-1902)
AM 1902

'Betty Cooper' 2 or 3 W-? (b or c)
(Mrs R.O. Backhouse, pre-1921)

'Betty Crowley' 2 W-? (b)
(W.A. Grace, pre-1938)

'Betty King' 2 W-? (b)
(Mrs R.O. Backhouse, pre-1921)

'Betty MacMullon'
Syn. of 'Betty McMullen'

'Betty McMullen'
(Alister Clark, pre-1910)
See also 'Betty MacMullon'

'Betty Snow' 1 W-W
(O. Ronalds, pre-1949) K. Chandler, 1960
'Beersheba' hybrid

'Beulah' 2 Y-Y
(C.E. Radcliff, 1938)
'Auriole' × 'Fortune'
Fl. rich yellow; corona long, narrowly funnel-shaped, with rim rolled

'Beulah' 1 W-? (b)
(C.A. Latta, 1939) C.A. Latta, 1956

'Beulah Boy' 1 Y-Y
(H.A. Brown) J.N. Hancock & Co., 1960

'Bevera' 2 W-Y
(?Heathcote Bulb Nursery, pre-1960) Unregistered
Perianth segments white; corona rich yellow

'Beverley' 3 Y-? (a)
(G.C. Graham, pre-1953)

'Bevin' 3 W-? (b)
(F. Rijnveld & Sons, pre-1948)
AM(Haarlem) 1956

'Bewdley Belle' 1 W-? (b)
(W.F.M. Copeland, pre-1913)

'Bewdy' 1 W-Y
(D. Jackson) Jackson's Daffodils, 1983
'Helsal' × 'Cyros'; sdlg no. 179/78
Fl. 100 mm wide

'Bewitcher' 2 W-P
(Alister Clark) G.E. Mitsch, 1956
Corona delicate pink

'Bewsher' 1 Y-Y
(W.A. Bell, pre-1949)

'Bezant' 3 W-? (b)
(G.H. Engleheart, pre-1916)

'Bhamo' 2 Y-? (a)
(Mrs R.O. Backhouse, pre-1921)

'Bhutan' 2 Y-O
(G.C. Graham) G.C. Graham, 1960
? × 'Ceylon'
Fl. 102 mm wide; perianth segments pale yellow 12D; corona strong orange 30D. Mid-season. Resembles 'Ceylon' but with the corona more widely expanded

'Bianca' 2 or 3 W-? (b or c)
(W. Backhouse, pre-1869)
Perianth segments sulphur white. Syn. Incomparabilis Albidus 'Bianca', Incomparabilis Albidus 'Expansus'. Was "absorbed" into 'John Bull'

'Bianca' 3? W-GYY
(G.H. Engleheart, pre-1890)
Corona cup-shaped, clear lemon yellow, with dark green at base, ribbed

'Bianca' 1 W-W
(W. Jackson Sr, 1929) W. Jackson Jr, 1956
'Phantasy' × 'Golden Gate'

N. biancae Todaro = *N. tazetta* subsp. *lacticolor*

'Biarritz' 9 W-?
(G.P. Haydon, pre-1908)

'Biarritz' 2 W-P
(pre-1956) Unregistered
Perianth segments white; corona opening pale buttercup yellow, with apricot pink at rim, becoming self apricot pink, frilled

'Bibkie' 2 W-Y
(pre-1968) Unregistered

N. biccianus Parlatore = *N. tazetta* subsp. *lacticolor*

'Bice' 5 Y-Y
(C.E. Radcliff, 1931)
'Ambrosine' × *N. triandrus*

'Bicentennial' 1 W-Y
(W.F. Leenen) W.F. Leenen, 1983

'Bicheno' 2 W-P
(S.J. Bisdee, 1944)
'Birdie' × 'Rosario'

N. bicolor Linnaeus 13 Section Pseudonarcissus
    var. *bicolor*
    var. *lorifolius* (Herbert) Pugsley
        (Pseudonarcissus Lorifolius 'Rugilobus')

'Bicolor King' 1 W-Y
(L. Buckland, pre-1936)

'Bicolor Knight' 1 W-? (b)
(L. Buckland, pre-1936)

'Biffo' 4 Y-O
(R.A.Scamp) R.A.Scamp, 1996
'Saint Keverne' × 'Tamar Fire'; sdlg no. 414
Fl. 86 mm wide; perianth and other petaloid segments in several whorls, broadly ovate, rich golden yellow; corona segments interspersed, dark orange, frilled. Mid-season to late. Sunproof

N. × *biflorus* Curtis = *N.* × *medioluteus*

N. biflorus Schur = *N. radiiflorus*

'Bifrons'
Syn. of *N.* × *intermedius*

N. bifrons Ker Gawler = *N.* × *intermedius*

'Bifrost' 1 W-W
(T.H. Piper, *c.*1966) Unregistered
'Swanlough' × 'Rhana'

'Big Ben' 1 W-Y
(Barr & Sons, pre-1900)
Fl. large; perianth segments opening primrose yellow, becoming sulphur white

'Big Ben' 1 W-Y
(D.S. Bell) D.S. Bell, 1958

'Big Bertha' 1 W-Y
(P. Phillips) P. Phillips, 1968

'Big Boss' 1 Y-Y
(G.B. de Vroomen & Sons, 1950) G.B. de Vroomen & Sons, 1960
Perianth segments sulphur yellow; corona citron yellow. Mid-season. Resembles 'Unsurpassable'. AM(Haarlem) 1960

'Big Boston' 1 Y-Y
(G. Lubbe & Son, pre-1948)
AM(Haarlem) 1948

'Big Boy' 4 W-O
(J.L. Richardson) M.J. Jefferson-Brown, 1969
'Gay Time' × 'Arbar'

'Big Chief' 1 Y-Y
(W.F. Leenen, 1966) W.F. Leenen, 1977
'Amsterdam' hybrid
Fl. 150 mm wide; perianth segments greenish yellow (4D); corona vivid yellow 12A. Early to mid-season. 2n=28

'Big Chimney' 2 Y-YYO
(Curtis Tolley) Curtis Tolley, 1995
'Loch Lundie' × 'Esperanza' 'Loch Lundie' × 'Esperanza'; sdlg no. T88-3-2; sdlg no. T88-3-2
Fl. about 125 mm wide; perianth segments mid-yellow; corona yellow, shading to deep orange at rim. Early. Sunproof

'Big Game' 2 Y-YYO
(J.L. Richardson) J.L. Richardson, 1955
'Porthilly' × 'Rustom Pasha'
Perianth segments deep primrose yellow; corona yellow, with bright red-orange at rim. Sunproof

'Big Gun' 2 W-Y
(W.G. Pannill) W.G. Pannill, 1978
'Court Jester' × 'White Prince'; sdlg no. 64/37
Fl. 110 mm wide. Mid-season

'Big Hunck' 2 Y-Y
(J.W.A. Lefeber) J.W.A. Lefeber, 1984
Sdlg × 'Tinerfe'
Perianth segments brilliant greenish yellow 6C, touched white at apex; corona vivid yellow 14B, with a darker tone (17C) at rim. Mid-season

'Big John' 1 Y-W
(Murray W. Evans) Murray W. Evans, 1975
'Daydream' × 'Bethany'; sdlg no. L-50
Fl. 125 mm wide; perianth segments sulphur yellow. Mid-season

'Big Keith' 1 Y-Y
(O. Ronalds, pre-1973) Unregistered

'Bignor' 2 Y-? (a)
(Sir F.C. Stern, pre-1948)

'Big Norm' 2 Y-Y
(P. & G. Phillips) P. & G. Phillips, 1975
Fl. 110 mm wide, golden; corona with rim strongly rolled. Mid-season

'Big Otter' 2 Y-Y
(Curtis Tolley) Curtis Tolley, 1997
'Loch Lundie' × 'Esperanza'; sdlg no. 88-3-1
Fl. 102 mm wide; perianth segments broadly ovate, brilliant yellow 12B; corona funnel-shaped, darker in tone (14B) than the perianth, lightly frilled. Early

'Big Red' 2 Y-O
(J.L. Martin) J.L. Martin, 1975
'Armada' × 'Apricot Glow'
Fl. 127 mm wide

'Big Sur' 1 W-W
(W.G. Pannill) W.G. Pannill, 1983
'Vigil' × 'Empress of Ireland'

'Big Top' 2 Y-? (a)
(Warnaar & Co., pre-1950)

'Big Wig' 4 W-Y
(Unknown origin) M.J. Jefferson-Brown, 1964
2n=27

'Bijou' 6
(E.H. Chapman, pre-1923)

'Bikkur' 2 W-? (b)
(Mrs R.S. Cobley, pre-1932)

'Bilbo' 6 W-GPP
(Brian S. Duncan) Rathowen Daffodils, 1981
'Roseworthy' × 'Foundling'; sdlg no. 465
Corona constricted at mid-point, flared towards mouth, rose pink, with green at base. Mid-season. Resembles 'Foundling' but with whiter perianth and corona of better form.

'Bilboa' 2 Y-YYO
(S.C. Gaspar) S.C. Gaspar, 1955
'Dunkeld' × 'Carbineer'
Perianth segments golden yellow; corona expanded, gold, shading to a wide zone of reddish orange at mouth. PC(e)(NZ) 1953

'Bilderdijk' 9 W-?
(G. Lubbe & Son, pre-1927)

'Biligaana' 2 W-Y
(Robert Spotts) Robert Spotts, 1993
'Akala' × 'Urbane'; sdlg no. 84-128-1
Fl. 86 mm wide; perianth segments broadly ovate, opening creamy white, becoming pure white; corona slightly flared, opening with a band of orange at rim, becoming clear self yellow, with rim dentate. Early

'Billabong' 1 Y-Y
(J.N. Hancock & Co., 1947)

'Billali' 2 Y-Y
(A.H. Ahrens, pre-1949)
'Royalist' × 'Crocus'

'Bill Blanden' 2 Y-OOR
(L.P. Dettman, 1978) Unregistered
'Vulcan' × 'Spelter'; sdlg no. 4/80

'Billee' 1 Y-Y
(W.M. Spry, pre-1973) Unregistered
'Early Prince' × 'Welcome'
Early

'Billet Doux' ?-P
(Alister Clark, pre-1948)

'Billie Mitchell' 2 W-P
(L.P. Dettman, c.1962) L.P. Dettman, 1977
'Better Half' open pollinated
Fl. 74 mm wide; perianth segments yellowish white 155B; corona light yellowish pink 36A, with a band of pale yellowish pink 36D at rim. Mid-season. Resembles 'Pink Treasure' but with a shorter and more widely expanded corona

'Bill Kelson'
(T.J. McIntyre, pre-1959) Unregistered
PC(e)(NZ) 1959

'Bill Webber' 2 W-?
(W.M. Spry, pre-1973) Unregistered
'Tunis' × 'Trousseau'
Corona honey brown. Early

'Bilyara' 1 Y-Y
(J.N. Hancock & Co., 1980) Unregistered
'Cardinia' × Fairbairn 2 Y-Y; sdlg no. 19/80H
Perianth segments bright yellow; corona cylindrical, narrow, darker in tone than the perianth, with mouth straight. Early

'Bimba' 2 W-P
Syn. of 'Forte'

'Bimbashi' 2 Y-? (a)
(A.H. Ahrens, pre-1946)

'Bimbil' 2 W-Y
(A.O. Roblin, 1946)
'Zamira' × 'Polindra'

'Bimbo' 1 Y-Y
(Mrs R.O. Backhouse, pre-1921)

'Binda' 1 W-P
(W. Jackson Jr) W. Jackson Jr, 1966
Sdlg no. 58A/59

'Binduli' 2 Y-Y
(C.E. Radcliff, 1931)
'Gloriana' × 'Tamerlane'

'Bing Crosby' 3 W-? (b)
(J.W.A. Lefeber, pre-1941)

'Binge' 2 Y-? (a)
(A.H. Ahrens) J.S. Leitch, 1956
Syn. 'Benoni'

'Bingo' 1 Y-Y
(J.T. Gray, 1954) P. Phillips, 1966
Fl. 102 mm wide, lemon yellow. Mid-season. Resembles 'Kanga' but with broader perianth segments and a longer and narrower corona

'Bingo' 2 Y-YOO
(Ken McCombe) Unregistered
Perianth segments roundish, bright golden yellow; corona cylindrical, orange, with yellow at base, mouth straight. Mid-season

'Binkie' 2 Y-W
(G.L. Wilson/W. Wolfhagen, pre-1938)
Fl. 100 mm wide; perianth segments broadly ovate, blunt, light greenish yellow 4C, with a darker tone (4B) at apex, and a prominent white mucro, paling to white at base, spreading or slightly reflexed, somewhat ribbed, overlapping one-third to a half; the inner segments more narrowly ovate, more usually spreading, with margins wavy; corona short funnel-shaped, loosely ribbed, yellowish white, becoming white, with brilliant greenish yellow 6B at rim, mouth straight, widely and shallowly 6-lobed, the lobes often overlapping, rim crenate. 2n=28. AM(Haarlem) 1950, *AM(g) 1952

'Binkiebell' 7 YYW-GWW
(M.G. Temple-Smith) M.G. Temple-Smith, 1997
'Binkie' × *N. fernandesii*; sdlg no. 16/88
Fls 2-3 per stem, 54 mm wide; perianth segments opening brilliant greenish yellow 3B, becoming paler (3C), with a narrow band of white at base; corona cup-shaped, opening deeper in tone (2A) than the perianth, becoming white, with green at base. Early

'Binkie's Brother' 2 Y-Y
(de Graaff Bros) de Graaff Bros & van Konynenburg & Co., 1969
'Binkie' hybrid

'Binkie's Lady' 2 Y-W
(Mrs M.W. Milward) Mrs M.W. Milward, 1964
Fl. 100 mm wide; perianth segments lemon yellow; corona opening lemon yellow, becoming off-white. Mid-season. Resembles 'Binkie' but with shorter and more rounded perianth segments and a more widely expanded corona

'Binnalong' 2 W-W
(K.J. Heazlewood) K.J. Heazlewood, 1968
'Ave' × 'Easter'

'Binsness' 2 W-Y
(Brodie Gardens) Brodie Gardens, 1959
Perianth segments pure white, smooth, overlapping; corona straight-sided, bright golden yellow, with rim rolled

'Binya' 1 W-? (b)
(A.O. Roblin, 1946)
'Cameronian' × 'Adri'

'Biograph' 1 Y-Y
(D. Jackson) Jackson's Daffodils, 1983
Sdlg 1/69 × 'Comal'; sdlg no. 59/78
Fl. 108 mm wide. Mid-season

'Bion' 9 W-?
(G.H. Engleheart, pre-1916)

'Bionic' 2 Y-O
(Jackson's Daffodils) Jackson's Daffodils, 1996
Sdlg 141/80 × 'Rabid'; sdlg no. 227/87
Fl. 110 mm wide; perianth segments broadly ovate, vivid yellow 15A, flushed orange; corona cup-shaped, orange (28A). Mid-season to late

'Birah' 3 W-Y
(A.O. Roblin, 1946)
'Maid of the Mist' × 'Sunstar'

'Birchill' 3 W-WYO
(Mrs J. Abel Smith) Mrs J. Abel Smith, 1974
'Myriantha' × 'Syracuse'; sdlg no. H3/81
Fl. 92 mm wide. Late

'Birchington' 2 Y-? (a)
(F.D.B. Cobb, pre-1953)

'Birchington Glory' 2 Y-? (a)
(J.O. Sherrard) C.M. Sandison, 1955

'Birchover' 1 W-W
(D.B. Milne, pre-1950)

'Birchwood' 3 W-GWW
(Clive Postles) Clive Postles Daffodils, 1993
'Monksilver' × 'Snowcrest'; sdlg no. 3-103-80
Fl. rounded, 95 mm wide, pure white; perianth segments very broadly ovate, with margins slightly incurving; corona bowl-shaped, with dark green prominent at base, mouth slightly lobed. Late

'Birdalone' 2 W-GWW
(J.M. de Navarro) J.M. de Navarro, 1969
Perianth segments white; corona opening primrose yellow, soon becoming white, with sea green at base, mouth a little flared

'Bird Flight' 6 Y-GYY
(G.E.Mitsch, 1978) J. & E.Frey, 1996
Sdlg C47/2('Wee Bee' × *N. cyclamineus*) open pollinated; sdlg no. 2NO3/1
Fl. 45 mm wide; perianth segments narrow, reflexed. Dwarf. Very early

'Birdie' 2 W-WWP
(Alister Clark, 1936) T. Morrison, 1960
Perianth segments milk white; corona large, widely expanded, white, with a broad band of pink at rim, frilled

'Bird Music' 6 Y-Y
(Eileen E.Frey, 1979) J. & E.Frey, 1994
'Wee Bee' × 'Jetfire' 'Wee Bee' × 'Jetfire'; sdlg no. PEF10/1; sdlg no. PEF10/1
Fl. 60 mm wide, yellow; perianth segments becoming somewhat reflexed; corona deeper in tone than the perianth, loosely frilled. Dwarf. Very early

'Bird of Dawning' 1 Y-Y
(Konynenburg & Mark) Konynenburg & Mark, 1960
'Rembrandt' hybrid
Fl. 120 mm wide; perianth segments vivid yellow 9A; corona slightly darker in tone (12A). Early. 2n=28

'Bird of Paradise' 3 W-YYO
(C.G. van Tubergen, pre-1927)
Fl. 89 mm wide; perianth segments white, with sulphur at base, irregular, separated; corona very shallow bowl-shaped, deep sulphur yellow, with a narrow band of orange at rim. Mid-season

'Birdsegg' 2 W-? (b)
(A. Overton) A. Overton, 1960

'Bird's Eye' 8
(A. Vis, pre-1942)

'Birdsong' 3 W-YYR
(Carncairn Daffodils) Carncairn Daffodils, 1978
'Corofin' × 'Tulyar'; sdlg no. 126
Fl. 85 mm wide; perianth segments yellowish white 155B; corona disc-shaped, brilliant greenish yellow 6A, with a band of vivid reddish orange 30B at rim

'Birichen' 2 Y-O
(D.C. MacArthur) D.C.D.C. MacArthur, 1989
'Fireproof' × 'Chungking'; sdlg no. EV82/61
Fl. 82 mm wide; perianth segments prominently mucronate, vivid yellow 12A, of good substance; corona strong orange 25A, with rim dentate. Mid-season. Sunproof. Scented

'Birkasha' 2 W-? (b)
(A.H. Ahrens) D.J. Cooper, 1957
Syn. 'Tamara'

'Birkdale' 2 W-W
(Brian S. Duncan) Rathowen Daffodils, 1981
'Easter Moon' × 'Knowehead; sdlg no. 326
Perianth segments white; corona slightly expanded, of a purer white than the perianth. Mid-season

'Birma' 3 Y-O
(J.W.A. Lefeber, 1938) J.W.A. Lefeber, 1960
Perianth segments broadly ovate in outline, blunt or slightly truncate, yellow, with white mucro, a little reflexed, with broad midrib showing, overlapping half; the inner segments more narrowly ovate, spreading, or sometimes reflexed towards apex; corona long cup-shaped, ribbed, orange, with a paler tone at base, mouth straight, split in places and overlapping, even or slightly frilled, with rim obscurely crenate. 2n=28

'Birma' 2 Y-O
Syn. of 'Dakar'

'Birthday Girl' 2 W-GWW
(Brian S. Duncan) Rathowen Daffodils, 1983
'Easter Moon' × 'Knowehead'; sdlg no. 378
Fl. 63 mm wide. Mid-season. Resembles a smaller-flowered 'Broomhill'

'Birthday's Gift' 3 W-YYO
(Jānis Rukšans, 1980) Jānis Rukšans, 1997
'Enniskillen' open pollinated; sdlg no. 80-15-2
Fl. 110 mm wide; perianth segments roundish, pure white, smooth, overlapping; corona small, vivid yellow 12A, with a greenish tone at base and a broad band of strong orange 25A at rim, mouth deeply frilled. Mid-season

'Birthright' 1 W-W
(G.L. Wilson) F.E. Board, 1956
'Courage' × 'Empress of Ireland'
Fl. snow white; perianth segments very broad, smooth and of firm substance; corona narrow, ribbed

'Biscador' 2 W-OOY
(J.N. Hancock & Co., 1953)

'Biscay' 2 W-Y
(J.N.Hancock & Co., 1982) Unregistered
'Patra' × 'Artist's Model'; sdlg no. 116/82H
Perianth segments roundish, deeply overlapping; corona disc-shaped, yellow. Late

'Biscayne' 1 Y-Y
(P. de Jager & Sons) P. de Jager & Sons, 1966
'Spellbinder' × 'Grapefruit'
Fl. 127 mm wide; perianth segments light greenish yellow 5C, very lightly flushed with a darker tone (5B), with white at apex and base, twisted, overlapping; corona cream, flushed vivid yellow 9A at rim within, flushed brilliant greenish yellow 7C outside and shading to vivid yellow 9A at rim, ribbed and expanded towards mouth, with rim frilled. Mid-

season. 2n=28. *AM(g) 1978, *FCC(g) 1979, AGM 1993

'Bishop Gore' 2 W-W
(G.H. Engleheart, pre-1915)
Fl. milk white; corona flared, rim frilled

'Bishop Mann' 1 W-W
(pre-1886)
Fl. opening greenish white, becoming snow white, of strong substance; perianth segments narrow, inflexed, twisted, separated or very slightly overlapping; corona cylindrical, ribbed, mouth flared, rim crenate. Tall. Syn. ?'Butterfly'

'Bishops Light' 2 Y-R
(R.A.Scamp) R.A.Scamp, 1995
'Torridon' × 'Irish Light' 'Torridon' × 'Irish Light'; sdlg no. S74; sdlg no. 74
Fl. 109 mm wide; perianth segments dark golden yellow, very smooth, deeply overlapping; corona cup-shaped, with rounded sides, dark red, boldly frilled. Mid-season

'Bishopstone' 1 Y-GYY
(Carncairn Daffodils) Carncairn Daffodils, 1989
'Loughanmore' × 'Golden Sovereign'; sdlg no. 3/8/76
Fl. 105 mm wide, deep clear yellow, smooth. Late. Resembles a deeper-coloured 'Loughanmore'

'Bismarck' 1 W-W
(P.D. Williams, pre-1927)

'Bismillah Awan' 2 W-YYO
(Reg Nicholl, 1979) Reg Nicholl, 1995
'Bizerta' × 'Tudor Minstrel' 'Bizerta' × 'Tudor Minstrel'; sdlg no. 14/79; sdlg no. 14/79
Fl. forming a double triangle, 100 mm wide; perianth segments broadly ovate in outline, blunt or rounded at apex, a little reflexed, plane, smooth, with broad midrib showing, overlapping half; the inner segments more narrowly ovate, more nearly spreading; corona bowl-shaped, ribbed, vivid greenish yellow 2A, shading to vivid orange (21A) at rim, mouth straight, more or less even, with rim crenate. Mid-season. Sunproof

'Bitali' 1 W-? (b or c)
(M. Gardiner)

'Bithynia' 3 W-WWO
(G.E. Mitsch, pre-1954)
'Rubra' × 'Sylvia O'Neill'
Fl. rounded; perianth segments slightly reflexed; corona almost disc-shaped. Mid-season

'Bit of Heaven' 2 Y-? (a)
(L. van Leeuwen & Son, pre-1944)

'Bit o' Gold' 2 W-WWY
(G.E. Mitsch) G.E. Mitsch, 1965
'Green Island' × 'Chinese White'; sdlg no. R33/11
Fl. 114 mm wide; perianth segments very broad in outline, rounded at apex and sometimes slightly truncate, very slightly mucronate, slightly reflexed, overlapping half or more; the inner segments narrower, more nearly spreading, with margins wavy; corona almost disc-shaped, heavily ribbed, soft yellow-white, shading to lemon yellow at rim, mouth split in places and overlapping, frilled, rim minutely crenate. Mid-season. Resembles a larger and more vigorous 'Tinsel'

'Bitsy' 6 W-W
(Mrs G. Link) Mrs G. Link, 1988
N. cyclamineus × 'Candlepower'; sdlg no. 677-A
Fl. 25mm wide; perianth segments white; corona opening yellow, becoming white. Tall. Early. Resembles a white-flowered 'Little Miss'

'Bittern' 2 Y-Y
(Mrs R.O. Backhouse, pre-1921)
Fl. ivory lemon yellow. Resembles a small-flowered 'Saint Egwin' in form

'Bittern' 12 Y-O
(G.E. Mitsch) G.E. Mitsch, 1979
'Matador' × *N. cyclamineus*; sdlg no. JJ76/5
Fls 1-2 per stem, 60 mm wide; perianth segments lemon; corona bright orange, with the depth of colour affected by the weather, frilled

'Bitter Sweet' 2 W-GYR
(G. Lewis) D.S. Bell, 1955

'Bittleford' 3 W-YOO
(Brian S. Duncan) du Plessis Bros, 1987
('Kilworth' × 'Rockall') × 'Norval'; sdlg no. 169
Mid-season

'Biway' 1 W-Y
(A.W. Chappell) A.W. Chappell, 1992
'Alton' × 'Lenz'; sdlg no. C-27-1
Fl. 90 mm wide; perianth segments ovate; corona with rim flanged and crenate. Late

'Bixie' 2 Y-YOO
(J.N. Hancock & Co., 1961) Unregistered

'Bizarre' 2 W-W
(C. Goodson, pre-1927)

'Bizerta' 2 W-Y
(J.L. Richardson, pre-1943)
'Niphetos' × 'Kanchenjunga'
Fl. forming a double triangle, 105 mm wide; perianth segments broadly ovate, only very slightly mucronate, pure white, spreading or a little inflexed, of thick and waxy substance, with margins slightly incurling, overlapping half; the inner segments more narrowly ovate, with margins a little wavy; corona

funnel-shaped, smooth, vivid yellow 13A, with a slightly paler tone at rim, mouth straight, frilled, rim crenate. AM(e) 1947, AM(Haarlem) 1949

'Black Prince' 9 W-GYR
(G.H. Engleheart, pre-1913)
Corona with rich crimson at rim

'Blackwell' 2 Y-O
(W. Backhouse, pre-1869)
Fl. 86 mm wide; perianth segments primrose yellow, irregular, separated; corona funnel-shaped, clear yellow heavily stained orange. Mid-season

'Blair Atholl' 2 W-GYP
(Mrs J. Abel Smith) Mrs J. Abel Smith, 1988
'Rufford' hybrid; sdlg no. A2/72
Mid-season

'Blair House' 3 W-O
(G.A. Uit den Boogaard, pre-1950)

'Blaison de Leiden' 8?
(pre-1883)

'Blake'
(pre-1915)

'Blake' 1 Y-Y
(D.H.L. Corrigan, pre-1949)

'Blakeney' 2 W-Y
(J.M. de Navarro) J.M. de Navarro, 1968
'Green Island' × 'Chinese White'

'Blanca' 9 W-?
(pre-1930)

'Blanc de Blancs' 11a W-W
(J. Gerritsen & Son) J. Gerritsen & Son, 1986
'Colblanc' hybrid
Perianth segments ivory white; corona white, with bronzy green at base. Mid-season. 2n=28

'Blanc de Chine' 2 W-W
(G.H. Johnstone, pre-1954)
'Nelamy' × 'Chinese White'

'Blanche' 3 W-Y
(W. Backhouse, pre-1869)
Perianth segments notched at apex, inflexed; corona shallow, primrose yellow. Syn. Burbidgei 'Blanche'

'Blanche' 2 W-Y
(A. Overton) A. Overton, 1960

'Blanche' 9 W-YYO
Syn. of 'Floore'

'Blanche' 11b W-W
(pre-1962) Unregistered
Perianth segments creamy white; corona segments predominantly creamy white

'Blanche Angel' 2 W-? (b or c)
(C.B. Blampied, pre-1929)

'Blanche Barkly' 1 Y-Y
(F. Silcock, 1976) F. Silcock, 1993
'Berit' × 'Daydream'
Fl. of good form, smooth; corona cylindrical. Late

'Blanche Fleur' 2 W-Y
(E.H. Krelage & Son, pre-1915)
'Lady Margaret Boscawen' × 'Madame de Graaff'

'Blanche Fleur' 2 W-W
(de Graaff Bros & van Konynenburg & Co., pre-1918)
AM(Haarlem) 1918

'Blanche Hill' 1 W-? (b)
(G.P. Haydon, pre-1908)

'Blanche L.Case'
(pre-1907)

'Blanchland' 1 W-W
(G. Harrison) G. Harrison, 1968
Sdlg × 'Kanchenjunga'
Fl. 133 mm wide. Mid-season. Resembles a refined 'Broughshane'

'Blanco' 3
(G.H. Engleheart, pre-1914)

'Blancona' 2 Y-Y
(J.L. Richardson, pre-1927)
Fl. yellow; corona widely expanded, mouth frilled

'Blandford' 1 W-Y
(C.E. Radcliff, 1943) J.M.Radcliff, 1956
('Renown' × 'Barbarino') × 'Bonython'
Corona lemon yellow

'Blandfordia' 2 Y-R
(W. Jackson Jr, 1970)
Sdlg 18/60 ('Mars' × 'Ceylon') × sdlg 25/64 ('Ruad' × 'Chitra'); sdlg no. 169/70

'Blandina' 1 W-W
(C.G. van Tubergen, pre-1938)

'Blandine' 2 W-O
(J.W.A. Lefeber, pre-1968) Unregistered

'Blandish' 2 W-?
(Alister Clark, 1930) J. Sharp, 1960

'Blanquet' 4 W-Y
(J. Gerritsen & Son, 1951) J. Gerritsen & Son, 1962
Fl. 100 mm wide; perianth and other petaloid segments sulphur white; corona segments interspersed, greenish yellow. Late. Resembles a well-grown 'White Sail'

'Blaris' 2 W-P
(G.L. Wilson) G.L. Wilson, 1960
('Charis' × 'Foyle') × ('Interim' × 'Wild Rose')
Fl. 90 mm wide; perianth segments broadly ovate, blunt, very pale creamy white with white mucro, spreading or a little reflexed, plane or a little concave, with margins incurling at apex, smooth, with broad midrib showing, overlapping one-third to a half; the inner segments more narrowly ovate, shouldered at base, a little twisted with margins incurved, sometimes notched; corona straight-sided, very lightly ribbed, orange-pink (24C) at mouth, paling to base (20C), mouth straight, with frilled and overlapping lobes, rim entire or minutely dentate. 2n=28. *AM(g) 1971, *FCC(g) 1973

'Blarney' 3 W-OOY
(J.L. Richardson, pre-1935)
'Mitylene' × 'Sunstar'
Fl. 100 mm wide; perianth segments very broadly ovate or somewhat oblong, blunt, prominently mucronate, snow white, spreading, overlapping one-third; the inner segments more narrowly ovate, a little inflexed; corona almost disc-shaped, broad, ribbed, orange, paling to light orange base, with creamy yellow at rim. 2n=28. AM(e) 1939, FCC(e) 1946

'Blarney's Daughter' 2 W-OOY
(J.L. Richardson, pre-1948)
'Blarney' × sdlg 883; sdlg no. 2118
Fl. 100 mm wide; perianth segments broadly ovate, blunt, prominently mucronate, pure white, spreading, very smooth and of good substance, overlapping one-third to a half; the inner segments a little narrower, slightly inflexed; corona bowl-shaped, finely ribbed, near to strong orange 25A, with a clearly defined band of light greenish yellow 8C at rim, mouth widely expanded, lightly frilled, with rim minutely crenate. Closely resembles 'Blarney' but with a larger and deeper corona. Mid-season. PC 1948, AM(e) 1953

'Blayney' 1 Y-Y
(A. Overton) A. Overton, 1959
Fl. 121 mm wide, rich yellow

'Blazaway' 2 Y-O
(J.N. Hancock & Co., 1965) Unregistered

'Blaze' 2 Y-YOR
(R.V. Favell, pre-1939)
'Hospodar' × 'Fortune'

'Blaze' 2 Y-? (a)
(C.G. van Tubergen, pre-1944)

'Blazer' 3 Y-? (a)
(W.F.M. Copeland, pre-1908)

'Blazina' 2 W-? (b)
(Mrs R.O. Backhouse, pre-1921)

'Blazing Fire' 2 Y-? (a)
(A.H. Ahrens) J.S. Leitch, 1955

'Blazing Gold' 7
(G. Lubbe & Son, pre-1937)
AM(Haarlem) 1937

'Blazing Light' 2 Y-? (a)
(R.O. Backhouse, pre-1935)

'Blazing Star' 2 Y-YYR
(G.H. Engleheart, pre-1908)
Fl. large; perianth segments rich yellow; corona large, expanded, rich golden yellow, with a broad band of orange-red at rim

'Blazing Sword' 2 Y-R
(Backhouse, pre-1926)
Perianth segments roundish, opening lemon yellow or sometimes more greenish yellow, becoming paler in tone, with margins wavy, of thick substance, overlapping; corona large, deep orange-red. Resembles 'Merapi'. AM(Haarlem) 1926, FCC(Haarlem) 1930

'Blazoner' 3 W-? (b)
(Mrs P.M. Davis, pre-1948)

'Bleasby Gorse' 1 Y-Y
(Mrs J. Abel Smith) Mrs J. Abel Smith, 1983
'Topnotcher' × 'Brabazon'; sdlg no. C/52
Fl. 95 mm wide; perianth segments broadly or very broadly ovate, mucronate, vivid yellow 9A, slightly inflexed, plane or a little twisted, overlapping half; the inner segments more narrowly ovate and more noticeably twisted; corona cylindrical, ribbed, vivid yellow 14B, with mouth expanded and 6-lobed, rim flanged and deeply notched. Early. Resembles a stronger and earlier-flowered 'Topnotcher'

'Bledfa' 2 W-? (b)
(A.M. Wilson, pre-1950)

'Blenda' 2 W-? (b)
(G.H. Engleheart, pre-1908)

'Blenda' 2 W-Y
(C.E. Radcliff, 1943) C.E. Radcliff, 1956
'Attila' × 'Veronique'
Perianth segments broadly ovate, mucronate, incurved, smooth, semi-transparent, overlapping half; the inner segments a little narrower; corona

funnel-shaped, ribbed, apricot or buff, with mouth straight and frilled

'Blendica' 2 Y-? (a)
(B. Rowlands, pre-1938)

'Blenheim' 2 Y-? (a)
(Miss G. Evelyn, pre-1930)

'Blenheim' 1 Y-Y
(W.J. Dunlop) M.J. Jefferson-Brown, 1963
? × ?'Content'

'Blenheimer' 2 Y-Y
(O.R.Marshall, 1965) P.D.K. Ramsay, 1981
'Easter Moon' × 'Empress of Ireland'; sdlg no. 451
Fl. 96 mm wide, lemon. Mid-season

'Blessing' 2 Y-YWY
(c.1978) Unregistered

'Blimey' 2 Y-W
(?Australian origin, pre-1993) Unregistered

'Blink Bonnie' ?-P
(Alister Clark, pre-1948)

'Blinkbonny' 3 W-R
(The Brodie of Brodie, c.1931)
'Sunstar' × 'Hades'
Perianth segments pure white; corona deep red

'Blinking Billy' 3 W-R
(S.J. Bisdee, 1942)
'Damson' × 'Sunstar'

'Bliss' 2 W-Y
(Alister Clark, pre-1930)
Corona long, cream yellow, widely expanded, rim very frilled. *AM(g) 1934

'Bliss' 1 W-W
(P.D. Williams, pre-1935)
Corona long, expanded, cream, heavily frilled

'Bliss' 2 W-W
(J.N. Hancock & Co., pre-1974) Unregistered
Fl. white; corona long, frilled

'Blithe Spirit' 3 W-R
(F.E. Board) F.E. Board, 1965
Perianth segments white; corona orange-red

'Blitz' 11a W-Y
(Jackson's Daffodils) Jackson's Daffodils, 1993
Sdlg 116/77 × 'King Size'; sdlg no. 40/87

'Blizzard' 1 W-W
(H. Backhouse, pre-1910)

'Blizzard' 2 W-W
(G.H. Engleheart, pre-1927)
Fl. large; perianth segments large, with margins wavy; corona broadly flanged. Late

'Bloden' 1 W-Y
(W.A. Watts, pre-1913)
Perianth segments white; corona pale yellow

'Blodfier' 4 W-R
(W. Jackson Sr, pre-1948) W. Jackson Jr, 1966
'Blodwen' × 'Firenze'

'Blodwen' 2 W-OOR
(W. Jackson Sr, 1927)
'Warflame' × 'Pink'un'
Perianth segments white; corona widely expanded, orange, with a broad band of crimson at rim

'Bloemendaal' 2 W-W
(W.G. Pannill, 1974) W.G. Pannill, 1988
'Broomhill' × 'Cataract'
Fl. 110 mm wide. Mid-season

'Bloemfontein' 2 Y-YYO
(Warnaar & Co., pre-1943)
'Fortune' × 'Aranjuez'
AM(Haarlem) 1943

'Bloemlush' 2 Y-Y
Syn. of 'Bloemlust'

'Bloemlust' 2 Y-Y
(L. van Leeuwen & Son, pre-1931)
Fl. large. AM(Haarlem) 1930, FCC(Haarlem) 1931. See also 'Bloemlush'

'Bloemtuin' 8 W-O
(pre-1798)

'Blond Doré' 1 Y-Y
Syn. of 'Poujastou Blond Doré'

'Blonde' 1 W-W
(T. Morrison) T. Morrison, 1960
Fl. pure white; corona frilled

'Blondel' 2
(W.A. Watts, pre-1916)

'Blond Giant'
Unregistered
Seed parent of 'Dirranbandi'

'Blondie' 2 W-P
(A.O. Roblin, c.1966) Unregistered
'Pink Monarch' × 'Rosegem'

'Blondin' 1 Y-Y
(W.B. Hartland, pre-1885)

Perianth segments ribbed; corona large, rich yellow

'Blondine' 3 W-Y
(de Graaff Bros, pre-1913)
Corona clear citron yellow. AM(Haarlem) 1913

'Blood and Thunder' 3 W-? (b)
(pre-1950)

'Bloodhound' 1 Y-Y
(Sir C.H. Cave, pre-1908)

'Blood Money' 2 Y-? (a)
(Alister Clark) J. Sharp, 1960

'Blood Orange' 3 W-YOO
(G.H. Engleheart, pre-1904)
Fl. large; perianth segments yellowish white, overlapping; corona bright reddish orange, closely frilled

'Blood Red' 3 W-? (b)
(C.L. Adams, pre-1913)

'Blood Red Banner' 2
(C.L. Adams, pre-1913)

'Bloodshot' 3 Y-R
(P. Phillips) P. Phillips, 1971
Fl. 95 mm wide

'Bloodstain' 9 W-?
(F.H. Chapman, pre-1914)

'Bloodstone' 3 W-O
(Sir C.H. Cave, pre-1908)
'Lulworth' × 'Horace'
Perianth segments snow white; corona ribbed, rich orange, tinged green at base

'Bloomfield' 1 W-W
(C.E. Radcliff, 1937)
'Saint Aloysius' × 'Beersheba'

'Bloomfield' 2 W-GRR
(W.J. Dunlop, pre-1969) Unregistered
Perianth segments white; corona disc-shaped, crimson-red, shading into green at base

'Blossom' 1 W-? (b)
(R.H. Bath, pre-1929)

'Blossom' 4 W-O
(J.A. O'More, 1970) P.D.K. Ramsay, 1980
Sdlg 82/58 × sdlg 11/65
Fl. 96 mm wide. Mid-season

'Blossom Time' 1 W-P
(R. Hyde) R. Hyde, 1955
'Woburn Mascot' hybrid

'Blucher' 2 Y-Y
(E. Leeds, pre-1877)
Perianth segments long, narrow, acute. Syn. Incomparabilis Concolor 'Blucher'

'Blue Bird' 2 W-W
(M.J. Jefferson-Brown) M.J. Jefferson-Brown, 1969

'Blue Chip' 4 W-R
(Colin Crotty) Colin Crotty, 1992
'Kinbrace' × 'Eclat'; sdlg no. 112-81
Fl. 110 mm wide, rounded; perianth and other petaloid segments broad, rounded at apex, pinkish white, overlapping; the centre whorl shorter; corona segments shorter than the petaloid segments and clustered among them, deep pinkish red. Late

'Blue Danube' 1 W-W
(G.E. Mitsch, 1981) R. & E. Havens, 1992
Sdlg D68/1 ('Rashee' × 'Knowehead') × 'Cataract'; sdlg no. 2Q29/1
Fl. 110 mm wide, pure white; perianth segments very broadly ovate, blunt, prominently mucronate, slightly reflexed, plane, overlapping half; the inner segments more nearly spreading, with margins wavy; corona narrowly funnel-shaped, smooth, with mouth flared and finely ribbed, lightly frilled, rim minutely crenate. Late

'Blue Glide' 3 W-O
(H.L. Fell, pre-1945)
Perianth segments cream-white; corona very shallow, red-orange

'Blue Horizon' 2 W-GYY
(D.S. Bell) D.S. Bell, 1963
'Invergordon' × 'Papanui Queen'
Perianth segments 101 mm wide; perianth segments white; corona lemon yellow, with base tinted blue with age. Mid-season. Resembles 'Papanui Queen' but with a more widely expanded corona with different colouring at base

'Blue Moon' 2 W-W
(G.H. Johnstone, pre-1949)
'Beersheba' hybrid

'Blue Mountains' 2 W-W
(G.E.Mitsch, 1974) R. & E.Havens, 1997
(Sdlg N6/1 × 'Empress of Ireland') × 'Panache'; sdlg no. JJ55/6
Fl. 110 mm wide, of heavy substance; perianth segments ovate, spreading, plane, smooth; corona cylindrical, yellow, with green at base and a narrow band of orange at rim, with the rim flanged. Mid-season

'Blue Smoke' 1 W-Y
(D.S. Bell) D.S. Bell, 1957
Perianth segments pure white; corona deep lemon yellow, with rim very widely rolled

'Blunder-bore' 1 W-? (b)
(C. Wolley-Dod, pre-1907)
See also 'Blunderbore'

'Blunderbore' 1 W-? (b)
Syn. of 'Blunder-bore'

'Blunderbuss'
(pre-1915)

'Blush' 2 W-P
(G.L. Wilson, pre-1950)
AM(Haarlem) 1950. Received AM 1950 as 'Ablush'
Div. 1

'Blusher' 2 W-P
(Alister Clark, pre-1937) J. Sharp, 1960

'Blushing Beauty' 2 W-P
(G.E. Mitsch) G.E. Mitsch, 1971
'Caro Nome' × 'Accent'; sdlg no. A5/10
Fl. rounded, 127 mm wide; perianth segments deeply overlapping. Mid-season

'Blushing Bride' 2 Y-? (a)
(P.D. Williams, pre-1936)

'Blushing Bride' 1 W-? (b)
(J.W.A. Lefeber, pre-1938)

'Blushing Maiden' 4 W-P
(Murray W. Evans, 1970) David L.Sheppard, 1985
'Pink Chiffon' × 'Accent'; sdlg no. L-43
Fl. 110 mm wide; perianth and other petaloid segments white; corona segments reddish pink. Resembles a shorter 'Replete' with a more loosely arranged flower. Syn. 'West End'

'Blushing Princess' 2 W-? (b)
(L. van Leeuwen & Son, pre-1952)

'Blush Queen' 3 W-P
(de Graaff-Gerharda, pre-1930)
AM(Haarlem) 1930

'Bluster' 2 Y-R
(M.P. Williams, pre-1938)
Perianth segments yellow, smooth; corona scarlet

'Boadicea' 1 W-W
(W. Welchman, pre-1908)
Perianth segments inflexed; corona straight-sided

'Boanerges' 3 W-W
(F.E. Board) F.E. Board, 1965
'Easter Moon' × 'Homage'

'Boastabout' 4 W-O
(Glenbrook Bulb Farm, 1982) Glenbrook Bulb Farm, 1997

'Anne of Cleves' × 'Matapan'
Fl. 75 mm wide; perianth segments very broadly ovate, greenish white (155C); corona segments varying from yellow-orange (18A) to a much darker tone (21A), lightly frilled. Mid-season

'Boatswain'
(pre-1913)

'Bobbin' ?-P
(Alister Clark, pre-1948)

'Bob Boutcher' 1 W-W
(T.H. Piper, c.1966) Unregistered
'Achi' × 'Rhana'

'Bobby Bell' 2 W-Y
(R. Bell, pre-1936)
Perianth segments opening cream, quickly becoming white

'Bobby Shaftoe' 6 W-Y
(G. Harrison) G. Harrison, 1968
'Polindra' × *N. cyclamineus*

'Bobbysoxer' 7 Y-YYO
(A. Gray, pre-1949)
N. rupicola is one parent
2n=22. Resembles a taller 'Sun Disc' with a shallower corona of darker colouring. The corona sometimes more extensively suffused orange

'Bob Minor' 1 Y-Y
(Rosewarne EHS) du Plessis Bros, 1980
'M.J. Berkeley' × 'Tanagra'; sdlg no. 64/26/1
Fl. 65 mm wide. Early

'Bobolink' 2 W-YYO
(G.E. Mitsch, 1951) G.E. Mitsch, 1965
'Galata' × 'Tuskar Light'; sdlg no. M36/1
Fl. rounded, 100 mm wide; perianth segments ovarlapping; corona pale lemon yellow, with a broad band of apricot orange at rim. Very early. Resembles an earlier-flowered 'Coverack Perfection' of stronger colour

'Bobster' 1 W-Y
(Brian S. Duncan) Rathowen Daffodils, 1980
'Ave' × 'Empress of Ireland'; sdlg no. 70
Fl. 115 mm wide; perianth segments pure white; corona cylindrical, mid-yellow, with mouth slightly expanded. Mid-season

'Bobwhite' 7 Y-Y
(G.E. Mitsch) G.E. Mitsch, 1979
'Daydream' × *N. jonquilla*; sdlg no. F72/8
Fls 4-5 per stem, 70 mm wide; perianth segments clear yellow; corona slightly darker in tone. Mid-season. Resembles a multi-flowered 'Quail' of a lighter colour with a differently shaped corona

'Boccaccio' 9 W-?
(de Graaff Bros, pre-1927)

'Boccacio' 2 Y-? (a)
(Alister Clark) J. Sharp, 1960

'Bodilly' 2 W-Y
(P.D. Williams, pre-1925)
Fl. 105 mm wide; perianth segments broadly ovate, mucronate, pure white, slightly inflexed, overlapping one-third; the inner segments narrower, square-shouldered at base, more strongly inflexed, with margins slightly wavy; corona funnel-shaped, lightly ribbed, brilliant greenish yellow 6C, with mouth slightly flared and a little frilled, rim broadly and regularly crenate. 2n=28. AM(e) 1925, FCC(e) 1936, *AM(g) 1946, *FCC(g) 1949

'Bodwannick' 2 W-OOY
(R.A. Scamp, 1983) R.A. Scamp, 1993
'Foresight' × ('Arbar' × 'Signal Light'); sdlg no. 174
Fl. 105 mm wide; perianth segments broad, clear white, with margins sometimes wavy, smooth, deeply overlapping; corona smooth, bright apricot orange, with a narrow band of yellow at rim. Early. Sunproof

'Body-guard' 2 W-? (b)
(G.H. Engleheart, pre-1907)

'Boerhaave' 8 W-Y
(van Zonneveld Bros & Philippo, pre-1928)
Poetaz
Perianth segments pure white; corona sulphur yellow. Tall

'Boforla' 7 W-Y
(M. Fowlds) G.E. Mitsch, 1968
('Bodilly' × 'Fortune') × *N. jonquilla*; sdlg no. F188/2
Fl. 64 mm wide; perianth segments ivory white, plane; corona lemon yellow, with a paler tone at rim. Mid-season

'Bogerman' 8
(C.P. Alkemade, pre-1931)
Poetaz

'Bogla'rka' 2 Y-Y
(Lajos Jezerniczky, 1975) Lajos Jezerniczky, 1987
'Ice Follies' × 'Adventure'; sdlg no. 22/6
Fls 2 per stem, 105 mm wide; perianth segments broadly ovate, blunt or truncate, golden yellow, with slight white mucro, spreading, slightly concave, with margins sometimes wavy, irregular, overlapping one-third; the inner segments somewhat twisted, occasionally notched; corona shallow, deep golden yellow, mouth very widely expanded, frilled. Early

'Bognor' 3 W-? (b)
(P. van Deursen, pre-1930)
Syn. 'Fusilier Grandiflorus'

'Bogota' 2
(?J.L. Richardson, pre-1948)

'Bogside' 3 W-R
(P. & G. Phillips) P. & G. Phillips, 1975
Fl. 86 mm wide; perianth segments broad, rounded; corona rich orange-red, with mouth very widely expanded. Mid-season

'Bohemian' 1 Y-Y
(F.E. Board) F.E. Board, 1965
'Moonstruck' × 'Spellbinder'
Fl. lemon yellow. Mid-season

'Bohemienne' 3 Y-? (a)
(de Graaff Bros, pre-1927)
Syn. 'Ilias'

'Boi' 2 W-YOO
(Jackson's Daffodils) Jackson's Daffodils, 1988
'Toya' × 'Matika'; sdlg no. 260/80
Fl. rounded; perianth segments very broadly ovate, blunt or rounded at apex, prominently mucronate, greenish white (155A), spreading, plane, overlapping half; the inner segments more narrowly ovate; corona very broad disc-shaped, closely ribbed, light orange (21A), paling to vivid yellow 12A at base, lightly frilled, with rim dentate. Mid-season

'Bojangle' 2 Y-YOR
(E.G.B.Jarman) E.G.B.Jarman, 1978
'Border Chief' × 'Majorca'; sdlg no. 5
Fl. 115 mm wide; perianth segments mid-yellow; corona orange, paling to yellow at base and shading to red at rim. Mid-season

'Bokhara' 2 Y-O
(The Brodie of Brodie, *c.*1923)
'Tamerlane' × 'Fortune'; sdlg no. 30/C/18
Perianth segments rich clear yellow; corona opening dull orange, becoming rich reddish orange. Fairly sunproof. 2n=28

'Bolanta' 8
(pre-1939)

'Bold Ben' 1 Y-Y
(W.M. Spry, pre-1975) Unregistered
'Braemar' × 'Golden'

'Bold Effort' 2 W-R
(R.H.Glover, pre-1993) Unregistered

'Bold Lad' 2 Y-O
(Mrs H.K. Richardson) Mrs H.K. Richardson, 1974
'Royal Palace' × sdlg 543 ('Firecracker' × Spelter)
Fl. 88 mm wide; perianth segments broad, deep golden yellow; corona reddish orange

'Boldness' 2 Y-O

(P.D. Williams, pre-1939)

'Bold Venture' 1 W-W
(D.S. Bell) D.S. Bell, 1960
Fl. 114 mm wide, pure white. Mid-season. Resembles a refined 'Broughshane'

'Bolero' 2 Y-? (a)
(P.D. Williams, pre-1935)

'Bolike' 2 Y-O
(J.L. Martin) J.L. Martin, 1982
'Wansea' × 'Bowls'; sdlg no. W/B
Fl. 90 mm wide; perianth segments light greenish yellow 6D; corona orange. Mid-season. Resembles a later-flowered 'Bricsea' of smoother texture and lighter colour

'Bolingbroke' 1 W-? (b)
(Barr & Sons, pre-1923)

'Bolivar' 3 W-YYR
(A.E. Lowe, pre-1927)

'Bolivia' 2 Y-Y
(G. Lewis) D.S. Bell, 1955
Fl. deep golden yellow; corona rim flanged and frilled

'Bolney' 2 W-Y
(Sir F.C. Stern, 1954) Sir F.C. Stern, 1967
Early

'Bolobek' 2 Y-Y
(J.N. Hancock & Co.) J.N. Hancock & Co., 1960
Fl. yellow; corona mouth expanded and tightly frilled

'Bolton' 7 Y-Y
(P.D. Williams, pre-1935)
Late. 2n=21

'Bolventor' 2 Y-O
(G.W. Tarry) du Plessis Bros, 1989
'Red Squirrel' × 'Zanzibar'; sdlg no. 95B
Fl. 109 mm wide; perianth segments yellow, flushed orange; corona bright orange. Late

'Bòlyglan' 2 W-? (b)
(J.L. Richardson, pre-1953)

'Bolzoni' 2 Y-Y
(Konynenburg & Mark) Konynenburg & Mark, 1963
('Aludra' × 'Sara Leander') × ('Killigrew' × 'Porthilly')
Fl. 130 mm wide; perianth segments brilliant greenish yellow 6C; corona vivid yellow 12A. Mid-season

'Boma' 2 W-? (b)
(Mrs R.O. Backhouse, pre-1921)
Syn. 'Dalila'. AM(Haarlem) 1930

'Bombardier'
(?F.H. Chapman, pre-1914)

'Bombardier' 2 Y-? (a)
(A.H. Ahrens, pre-1949)

'Bombastes' 2 W-? (b)
(The Brodie of Brodie, c.1912)
'Lady Margaret Boscawen' × 'King Alfred'

'Bombay' 2 Y-YYR
(J.L. Richardson, pre-1945)
'Diolite' × 'Marksman'
Perianth segments broadly ovate, rounded at apex, prominently mucronate, clear sulphur yellow, spreading, concave either side of prominent midrib, smooth, overlapping half; the inner segments narrower, somewhat oblong, a little inflexed, lightly creased; corona straight-sided, of the same colour as the perianth, with a broad band of bright red at rim, mouth straight, split in places and overlapping, loosely frilled. Mid-season

'Bombo' 1 Y-Y
(A.O. Roblin, c.1966) Unregistered
'Melissa' × 'Kingscourt'

'Bombshell' 2 Y-O
(R.V. Favell, pre-1939)
'Killigrew' × 'Fortune'

'Bomere' 1 W-Y
(J.S. Leitch) J.S. Leitch, 1962
Early

'Bon' 1 W-Y
(P. Phillips) P. Phillips, 1964
Fl. 108 mm wide; perianth segments white; corona lemon yellow. Mid-season. Resembles 'Preamble' with the perianth segments more rounded and the corona unfading

'Bon Accord' 2 W-Y
(D.S. Bell) D.S. Bell, 1975
'My Love' open pollinated
Fl. 101 mm wide; corona lemon. Mid-season. Resembles an earlier-flowered 'My Love' with a longer corona

'Bonamargy' 2 W-YYO
(Carncairn Daffodils, 1975) Carncairn Daffodils, 1986
'Merlin' × ('Seraglio' × 'Signal Light'); sdlg no. W4/11
Perianth segments white, slightly reflexed; corona yellow, with a band of bright reddish orange at rim. Late. Resembles 'Ringleader'

'Bonamble' 2 W-Y
(A. Glover, c.1966) Unregistered
'Bonnington' × 'Preamble'

'Bonamy' 1 Y-Y
(T. Buncombe, pre-1915)
Fl. soft yellow; perianth segments rounded, a little inflexed at apex

'Bonanza' 1 W-Y
(G. Lewis) D.S. Bell, 1955
Corona frilled, with rim dentate

'Bonaparte' 2 Y-Y
(Barr & Sons, pre-1907)
Perianth segments pale creamy sulphur yellow, overlapping; corona large, expanded, bright yellow. Mid-season. AM(p) 1917, *HC(g) 1927, *HC(g) 1936

'Bon Bon' 9 W-OOR
(G.E. Mitsch) G.E. Mitsch, 1976
'Quetzal' × 'Smyrna'; sdlg no. D94/15
Fl. 72 mm wide; corona orange-red. Late. 2n=14. Resembles a larger-flowered 'Tart' of slightly less brilliant colour

'Bondage' 3 W-R
(G.W.E. Brogden)

'Bondi' 2 Y-O
(J.T. Gray, pre-1949)
Perianth segments yellow; corona shallow, reddish orange

'Bondi' 1 Y-Y
(W.M. Spry, pre-1975) Unregistered
'Kingscourt' × 'Golden Valley'
Tall. Mid-season

'Bondsman' 2 Y-? (a)
(W.B. Cranfield, pre-1927)

'Bond Street' 2 WWY-GOO
(M. Veldhuyzen van Zanten, pre-1955) M. Veldhuyzen van Zanten, 1976
Fl. 110 mm wide; perianth segments white, yellowish towards base; corona light orange, with green at base. Early

'Bonfire' 3 Y-O
(P.D. Williams, pre-1910)
Perianth segments yellow; corona shallow, crimson orange. 2n=21. AM(Haarlem) 1918

'Bonga Bonga' 4
(Cartwright & Goodwin, pre-1916)

'Boniface' 1 Y-Y
(J. Pope, pre-1908)

'Bonington' 1 W-Y
Syn. of 'Bonnington'

'Bonita' 2 W-? (b)

(Oregon Bulb Farms, pre-1951)

'Bonjour' 7
(Mrs P.M. Davis, pre-1948)

'Bonne Nuit' 3 W-W
(T. Bloomer) T. Bloomer, 1964

'Bonnet' 3 W-? (b)
(Mrs R.O. Backhouse, pre-1921)

'Bonneville' 2 W-W
(G.E. Mitsch, pre-1954)
'Ada Finch' × 'Fortune'
Fl. up to 152 mm wide; corona opening pale lemon yellow, becoming milk white. Mid-season

'Bonney Gem' 2 W-P
Syn. of 'Bonny Gem'

'Bonnie Bell' 4 W-P
(D.S. Bell) D.S. Bell, 1985
'Takoradi' × 'Bonny Gem'
Fl. 101 mm wide; perianth and other petaloid segments white; corona segments interspersed, pink, with a darker tone at rim. Mid-season. Resembles 'Takoradi' but with pink corona segments

'Bonnie Best' 2 Y-? (a)
(P.D. Williams, pre-1952)

'Bonnie Dundee' 1 Y-Y
(D.N.Y. Olson) D.N.Y. Olson, 1993
'Cardigan Bay' × 'Valley Gold'
Fl. 104 mm wide, deep yellow; perianth segments very broadly ovate, with fairly prominent white mucro, with margins incurling, smooth, of thick substance, square-shouldered at base, overlapping half; the inner segments with margins wavy; corona cylindrical, with mouth a little expanded and lightly frilled, rim crenate. Mid-season

'Bonnie Marie' 9 W-GGW
(L.P. Dettman) L.P. Dettman, 1979
'Greenholm' × 'Sea Green'; sdlg no. GSG 3/75
Fl. 62 mm wide; perianth segments yellowish white 155D; corona moderate bluish green 133B, with yellowish white 155D at rim. Mid-season. Resembles 'Greenholm' but with a rounder perianth

'Bonnie's Gem' 2 Y-YOO
(N.R.McIsaac, pre-1996) Unregistered

'Bonnie's Jewel' 2 Y-YOO
(N.R.McIsaac, 1975) N.R.McIsaac, 1996
'Crescendo' × 'Falstaff'; sdlg no. 174
Fl. about 70 mm wide; perianth segments ovate, vivid yellow 9A, overlapping; corona cup-shaped, orange (28A or B), paling to yellow at base, with rim dentate. Mid-season. Resembles a very small 'Crescendo'

of deeper colour

'Bonniform' 2 W-Y
(R.P. Cook, pre-1949)
Perianth segments white; coriander slender, pale yellow

'Bonnington' 1 W-Y
(C.E. Radcliff, 1932)
'W.F. Gates' × 'Mrs W.Moodie'
Perianth segments white; corona light lemon. See also 'Bonington'

'Bonnivard' 2 Y-? (a)
(H. Backhouse, pre-1910)

'Bonny' 2 W-YYO
(H.A. Brown, pre-1936)
Perianth segments white; corona yellow, with red-orange at rim, frilled

'Bonny Alouise' 2 W-GYO
(D.N.Y. Olson) D.N.Y. Olson, 1988
'Southward' × ('Mataraki' × 'Rockall'); sdlg no. 76/65/1
Perianth segments very broadly ovate in outline, blunt or truncate, prominently mucronate, spreading, with broad midrib showing, overlapping half; the inner segments with margins sometimes folded inwards; corona almost disc-shaped, ribbed, lightly frilled, with rim crenate. Late. Resembles a larger and smoother 'Southward'

'Bonny Bell' 1 W-W
(E.M. Crosfield, pre-1910)

'Bonny Gem' 2 W-P
(E.W. Cotter) E.W. Cotter, 1968
Sdlg × 'Amigo'
Perianth segments pure white, thick; corona rich pink. See also 'Bonney Gem'

'Bonny Glen' 1 Y-Y
(A. Gibson, pre-1927)

'Bonny Jean' 6 W-W
(D.S. Bell) D.S. Bell, 1976
'Jenny' × *N. cyclamineus* sdlg
Fl. 85 mm wide; perianth segments pure white, strongly reflexed; corona white, with rim flanged. Mid-season. Resembles a larger-flowered 'Jenny'

'Bonny Lass' 2 W-P
(O. Ronalds, pre-1955) Unregistered
Perianth segments white; corona soft creamy pink

'Bonnyrig' 2 Y-YYR
(A.M. Wilson, pre-1948)
Perianth segments yellow; corona yellow, with a broad band of red at rim

'Bonny Winkfield' 1 Y-Y
(The Brodie of Brodie, *c*.1923)
Sdlg 147/13 × 'Coolgardie'
Fl. yellow; perianth segments ovate, fairly prominently mucronate, spreading or a little inflexed, margins somewhat wavy, overlapping half; the inner segments more inflexed, twisted or with margins more wavy; corona cylindrical, angled, mouth expanded, rim flanged, notched and crenate

'Bonox' 2 W-? (b)
(Alister Clark, 1932) J. Sharp, 1960

'Bon Rose' 1 W-P
(J.R.Erp) J.R.Erp, 1956
'Glendevie' hybrid
Perianth segments white; corona clear pink

'Bonsall' 1 W-W
(D.B. Milne, pre-1950)
'Cibola' × *N. cyclamineus*
Fl. deep yellow

'Bon Soir' 2 W-P
(D.S. Bell) D.S. Bell, 1978
Sdlg no. 127 N7
Fl. 105 mm wide; perianth segments pure white; corona bright pink. Mid-season

'Bon Ton' 1 Y-Y
(pre-1927)
Fl. golden yellow

'Bon Ton' 2 Y-Y
(G. Lewis) D.S. Bell, 1955
Fl. rich gold

'Bonus' 6 Y-Y
(G.E. Mitsch) G.E. Mitsch, 1972
'Cibola' × *N. cyclamineus*; sdlg no. Z12/14
Fl. 85 mm wide, deep yellow. Early.

'Bonus Bond' 2 W-W
(R.H.Glover, pre-1993) Unregistered

'Bon Voyage' 3 W-W
(W.G. Pannill) W.G. Pannill, 1992
'Cool Crystal' × 'Greenbrier'; sdlg no. 73/23
Fl. 102 mm wide. Late

'Bonython' 1 W-Y
(P.D. Williams, pre-1927)
'King Alfred' × 'Boswin'
Fl. forming a double triangle; perianth segments broadly ovate, acute, only slightly mucronate, sulphur white, spreading, with margins wavy, overlapping one-third; the inner segments more narrowly ovate, a little inflexed, with margins more strongly wavy; corona cylindrical at base, flared from about mid-point, smooth, soft sulphur yellow, rim flanged,

regularly and deeply notched and crenate. AM(e) 1933, *AM(m) 1936

'Bonza' 2 Y-O
(J.N.Hancock & Co., 1978) Unregistered
'Air Marshal' × 'Ablaze'; sdlg no. 89/78H
Perianth segments bright orange-yellow; corona long cup-shaped, deep reddish orange. Mid-season

'Bonzor' 2 W-Y
(A. Gibson, pre-1927)
Perianth segments white; corona yellow

'Boobyalla' 1 W-W
(C.E. Radcliff, pre-1938)
Sdlg × 'Beersheba'

'Book Mark' 2 Y-P
(G.E. Mitsch) G.E. Mitsch, 1977
'Leonaine' × 'Daydream'; sdlg no. F25/21
Fl. 90 mm wide; perianth segments buff lemon, with a touch of white at base; corona apricot salmon, frilled. Mid-season. Resembles 'Sugar Maple' but with the perianth of a darker tone with less white at base

'Booloo' 2 W-P
(A.O. Roblin, 1946) A.O. Roblin, 1956
'Mary Blewitt' × 'Rosario'

'Boom Boy' 2 Y-YOO
(J.N. Hancock & Co., 1955) Unregistered

'Boomerang' 1 Y-Y
(G.H. Engleheart, pre-1914)

'Bootie' 2 W-WWP
(J.N. Hancock & Co., pre-1949)

'Bo Peep' 3 W-O
(pre-1927)

'Bo-Peep' 3 W-? (b)
(Mrs F.S. Foote, c.1940)

'Bo-Peep' 2 W-P
(pre-1964) Unregistered

'Bopeep' 6 Y-Y
(M. Fowlds, c.1965) Unregistered
Sdlg × *N. cyclamineus*

'Border Beauty' 2 Y-R
(Brian S. Duncan) Brian S. Duncan, 1992
'Sunadee' open pollinated; sdlg no. 1123
Fl. 109 mm wide; perianth segments triangular in appearance, spreading, plane, overlapping; corona shallow bowl-shaped, deep orange-red, with mouth wavy, rim reflexed. Mid-season. Sunproof

'Border Chief' 2 Y-O
(J.L. Richardson, pre-1953)
'Carbineer' × 'Bahram'
Fl. 115 mm wide; perianth segments broadly ovate, very slightly mucronate, vivid yellow 9B, smooth, regular, overlapping half; the inner segments more narrowly ovate and very slightly concave; corona bowl-shaped, smooth or slightly ribbed, vivid orange 28B, with mouth expanded and lightly frilled, and rim crenate. 2n=28. AM(e) 1959

'Borderer' 1 Y-Y
(A.M. Wilson, pre-1939)

'Border Flame' 2 Y-YOO
(Mrs H.K. Richardson) Mrs H.K. Richardson, 1972
'Court Martial' × 'Vulcan'
Perianth segments deep golden yellow; corona long cup-shaped, orange, paling to yellow at base

'Border Legend' 2 Y-O
(G.L. Wilson) Guy L.Wilson Ltd, 1963
Sdlg × 'Ceylon'
Perianth segments broadly ovate, yellow, with white mucro, spreading, a little concave, smooth, regular, overlapping half; the inner segments narrower and oval, only very slightly mucronate, with margins sometimes slightly incurling; corona very lightly ribbed, bright reddish orange, with a darker tone at rim, mouth expanded and more heavily ribbed, split in places, a little frilled, with rim crenate. 2n=28

'Border Maid' 2 W-Y
(C. Stuart, pre-1898)
Perianth segments large, pure white, of strong substance; corona long, clear yellow

'Border Minstrel' 9 W-?
(F.H. Chapman, pre-1930)

'Border Queen' 2 Y-YYO
(West & Fell, pre-1935)
Fl. yellow; corona with a broad band of red at rim

'Boreal' 2 W-Y
(C.E. Radcliff, pre-1938)
'Titania' × 'Portia'

'Borealis' 1 W-W
(G.L. Wilson, pre-1940)
'Naxos' × 'Corinth'
Fl. white; corona with touches of pale lemon at rim, flanged and dentate

'Boreas' 1 W-Y
(Barr & Sons, pre-1913)
'Loveliness' × 'King Alfred'
Corona pale citron yellow, with rim rolled

'Boreas' 2 W-? (b)

(de Graaff Bros) de Graaff Bros & van Konynenburg & Co., 1956
AM(Haarlem) 1956

'Borneo' 3 Y-? (a)
(S.C. Gaspar, pre-1949)

'Born Star' 1 Y-Y
(R.H.Glover, pre-1993) Unregistered

'Borodin' 3 W-YYO
(Konynenburg & Mark) Konynenburg & Mark, 1960
'Lady Moore' × ('Carolina' × 'Actaea')
Fl. 90 mm wide; perianth segments cream white; corona light yellow 17D, with orange (28A) at rim. Mid-season

'Boronia' 2 Y-? (a)
(F.W. Parkinson, pre-1936)

'Borrobol' 2 W-R
(J.S.B. Lea) J.S.B. Lea, 1963
'Arbar' × Richardson sdlg 116; sdlg no. 1-12-55
Fl. 111 mm wide; perianth segments white; corona rich orange-red. Mid-season. Resembles 'Arbar' but with a broader and whiter perianth and darker corona

'Borvern' 2 Y-Y
(J.L. Martin) J.L. Martin, 1978
'Wanser' × 'Bowls'; sdlg no. W/B4
Fl. 108 mm wide; perianth segments brilliant greenish yellow 6B; corona vivid yellow 12A. Mid-season. Resembles an earlier-flowered 'Camelot' with a longer stem and smoother texture

'Bosahan' 3 W-WWR
(P.D. Williams, pre-1931)
Perianth segments round, ivory white; corona white, with red at rim

'Bosanketh' 1 W-W
(R.V. Favell, pre-1953)

'Bosavern' 3 W-GYO
(R.V. Favell, pre-1946)
'Silver Coin' × 'Seraglio'

'Bosbigal' 11a Y-O
(R.A. Scamp) R.A. Scamp, 1994
'Brandaris' × 'Paricutin'; sdlg no. 315
Perianth segments very broadly ovate in outline, blunt or rounded at apex, a little inflexed, with margins minutely incurling, overlapping half; the inner segments a little narrower, more usually blunt; corona split to base, the six segments as wide as the perianth segments and two-thirds as long, opposite and closely overlying them, bi-lobed and squarish at apex, smooth, orange, frilled. Early. Sunproof

'Boscastle' 7 Y-Y
(R.A.Scamp) R.A.Scamp, 1996
'Aircastle' × *N. jonquilla*; sdlg no. 111
Fls 2-3 per stem, 80 mm wide; perianth segments broadly ovate, soft golden yellow, deeply overlapping; corona shallow cup-shaped, slightly darker in tone than the perianth. Late. Scented. With many secondary stems

'Boscean' 2 W-? (b)
(R.V. Favell, pre-1953)

'Boscobel' 2 W-W
(C.R. Wootton, 1949) C.R. Wootton, 1960
'Niphetos' × 'Zero'
Fl. 100 mm wide; perianth segments ovate, acute, very slightly mucronate, overlapping half; the inner segments a little narrower; corona opening creamy white, quickly becoming white, with mouth ribbed and expanded, rim dentate and slightly flanged. Early. Resembles an earlier-flowered 'Zero' with a shorter corona. AM(e) 1959

'Boscoppa' 11a Y-O
(R.A.Scamp) R.A.Scamp, 1996
'Obelisk' × 'Tamar Fire'; sdlg no. 293
Fl. 96 mm wide; perianth segments broadly ovate, bright yellow, deeply overlapping; corona deeply split, the six segments almost as long as the perianth segments and opposite and closely overlying them, clear orange. Mid-season. Sunproof

'Boscundle' 2 W-WWR
(G.H. Johnstone, pre-1950)
'Elspeth' hybrid

'Boskenna' 7
(The Brodie of Brodie, pre-1930)
'Pilgrim' × Div. 7 sdlg

'Boskey' 3 Y-O
(S.C. Gaspar) R.J. Abernethy, 1957
Perianth segments deep yellow; corona shallow, expanded, reddish orange, with rim dentate

'Bosloe' 3 Y-O
(R.O. Backhouse, pre-1933)
Perianth segments broad, warm buff yellow, with base stained orange, overlapping; corona soft, rich reddish orange, frilled

'Boslowick' 11a Y-O
(R.A. Scamp) R.A. Scamp, 1991
'Gironde' × 'Paricutin'; sdlg no. 225
Fl. 95 mm wide; perianth segments very broadly ovate in outline, blunt or rounded at apex, prominently mucronate, dark golden yellow, a little reflexed, overlapping half or more; the inner segments narrower, square-shouldered at base, spathulate, more nearly spreading; corona split to base, the six segments

two-thirds the length of the perianth segments, opposite and closely overlying them and joined to them at margins from base to shoulder, squarish at apex, lightly ribbed, vivid orange 28B, a little frilled. Mid-season. Sunproof

'Bosmeor' 2 Y-W
(R.A. Scamp) R.A. Scamp, 1991
'Daydream' open pollinated; sdlg no. 16
Fl. 91 mm wide; perianth segments broadly ovate, soft primrose yellow, overlapping; corona flared, creamy white, with mouth frilled. Early

'Bossa Nova' 3 O-R
(Brian S. Duncan) Rathowen Daffodils, 1983
'Altruist' × 'Ulster Bank'; sdlg no. 628
Perianth segments broadly ovate in outline, blunt or somewhat truncate, evenly flushed orange, paler at apex, with slight white mucro, spreading, plane, overlapping half; the inner segments more narrowly ovate, with a pale tone at midrib; corona bowl-shaped, closely ribbed, deep red, with mouth expanded and lightly frilled. Mid-season

'Bossiney' 11a W-WPP
(R.A.Scamp) R.A.Scamp, 1996
'Pearlax' × 'Audubon'; sdlg no. 333
Fl. 100 mm wide; perianth segments acute, mucronate, pure white, overlapping; corona split, the six segments opposite and closely overlying the perianth segments, bright apple blossom pink, with white at base, slightly frilled. Mid-season. Sunproof

"Bossleman's Narcissus"
Syn. of *N. tazetta* var. *trewianus*

'Boston' 8 W-YYO
(A. Frylink & Sons, pre-1929)
Fls 2-4 per stem; perianth segments sulphur white; corona clear yellow, with bright orange at rim. AM(Haarlem) 1929

'Boston' 11b W-Y/W
(J.W.A. Lefeber) J.W.A. Lefeber, 1983
'Papillon Blanc' × 'Mol's Hobby'

'Bosveal' 2 Y-YYO
(Barr & Sons, pre-1933)

'Bosvigo Gem' 2 Y-? (a)
(E. & J.C. Martin, pre-1931)

'Boswell' 3 W-YYR
(J.L. Richardson, pre-1937)
'Saint Just' open pollinated
Perianth segments very broad in outline, blunt or rounded at apex, fairly prominently mucronate, ivory white, slightly reflexed, plane, overlapping half; the inner segments narrower, square-shouldered at base, a little inflexed; corona shallow bowl-shaped, bright yellow, with a narrow band of orange-red at rim, mouth even, with rim minutely notched and crenate. Tall. Late

'Boswin' 1 W-Y
(P.D. Williams, pre-1927)
Fl. 100 mm wide; perianth segments acute, sulphur white, with margins sometimes incurved, overlapping half; corona funnel-shaped, mouth frilled and slightly expanded, rim flanged. Early. 2n=28. *(Gulval)AM(m) 1935, *AM(g) 1946

'Botallack' 2 W-? (b)
(Warnaar & Co., pre-1930)

'Botanica' 2 Y-? (a)
(B. Rowlands, pre-1938)

'Botany Bay' 2 Y-? (a)
(J.O. Sherrard, pre-1949)

'Botary' 2 W-YYP
(J.L. Richardson, pre-1961) Unregistered

'Bothild' 1 W-W
(W. Jackson Sr, 1934)
'Halfa' × 'Fi-krye'

'Botlar' 3 Y-O
(Jackson's Daffodils) Jackson's Daffodils, 1993
'Tia' × 'Azzuro'; sdlg no. 65/85
Fl. rounded, 104 mm wide; perianth segments very broadly ovate, blunt, only very slightly mucronate, brilliant yellow 7B, spreading, slightly concave, with margins incurling at apex, smooth and of thick substance, overlapping half or more; the inner segments more narrowly ovate, square-shouldered at base, a little inflexed; corona cup-shaped, vivid orange 28B, with mouth straight, minutely frilled. Early to mid-season

'Botticelli' 1 W-? (b)
(E.H. Krelage & Son, pre-1942)

'Boudoir' 1 W-P
(Carncairn Daffodils) Carncairn Daffodils, 1967
'Rose of Tralee' × G.L. Wilson sdlg
Corona rim neatly rolled. Mid-season. Resembles 'Rosario' in colour

'Bougie' 2 W-? (b)
(Mrs R.O. Backhouse, pre-1921)

'Boulder Bay' 2 Y-YYO
(Brian S.Duncan) Brian S.Duncan, 1996
Sdlg 77/1 ('Golden Jewel' × 'Midas Touch') × 'Barnum'; sdlg no. 1351
Fl. 95 mm wide; perianth segments heart-shaped, deep honey yellow, plane, smooth; corona cylindrical, yellow, shading to warm orange at rim, with

mouth wavy and rim rolled. Mid-season. Sunproof

'Boule de Neige' 4
(W.A. Watts, pre-1935)

'Boule d'Or' 8 Y-O
(pre-1792)

'Boule d'Or' 2 Y-O
(F.E. Board) F.E. Board, 1965
'Kilmorack' × 'Kindled'
Perianth segments yellow; corona reddish orange. Early

'Boulevard' 2 W-OOR
(D.S. Bell) D.S. Bell, 1975
'Hampstead' × 'Masquerade'
Perianth segments white; corona apricot, with a narrow band of red at rim. Mid-season

'Bounce' 2 W-? (b)
(C. Smith, pre-1923)

'Boundward' 1 W-Y
(R. Hyde) R. Hyde, 1963
Fl. 123 mm wide; perianth segments white; corona lemon yellow. Mid-season. Resembles 'Outward Bound' with the perianth segments more acute and the corona of a darker colour

'Bounteous' 2 W-! (b)
(F. Rijnveld & Sons, pre-1950)
AM(Haarlem) 1950

'Bountiful' 2 Y-YYO
(C. Smith, pre-1907)
Fl. large; perianth segments yellow, spreading; corona rich yellow, ribbed, with rim flushed orange

'Bounty' 2 Y-O
(Oregon Bulb Farms, pre-1946)

'Bounty' 2 W-YPP
(*c.*1973) Unregistered

'Bouquet' 4 W-P
(J.A. O'More) P.D.K. Ramsay, 1980
Sdlg × 'Fintona'; sdlg no. 51/71
Fl. 84 mm wide. Resembles a lighter-coloured 'Pink Champagne' with rounder perianth segments

'Bouquet Aimable' 8 Y-Y
(pre-1807)

'Bouquet Blanche' 8 W-O
(pre-1835)

'Bouquet de Dames' 8 Y-Y
(pre-1798)

'Bouquet Enorme' 8 W-Y
(M. van Waveren & Sons, pre-1916)
Poetaz
Fl. large; perianth segments broad

'Bouquet Formidable' 8 Y-Y
(pre-1798)

'Bouquet Parfait' 8 W-O
(pre-1829)
See also 'Bouquet Parfaite'

'Bouquet Parfaite' 8 W-O
Syn. of 'Bouquet Parfait'

'Bouquet Roiale' 8 W-O
Syn. of 'Bouquet Royal'

'Bouquet Royal' 8 W-O
(pre-1792)
See also 'Bouquet Roiale'

'Bouquet Sanspareille' 8 W-O
(pre-1846)

'Bouquet Souffre' 8 Y-Y
(pre-1777)

'Bouquet Triomphant' 8 W-O
Syn. of 'Bouquet Triumphant'

'Bouquet Triumphant' 8 W-O
(pre-1792)
See also 'Bouquet Triomphant'

'Bourneville'
(Sir C.H. Cave, pre-1913)

N. × **boutignyanus** Philippe 13 = *N. moschatus* Linnaeus × *N. poeticus* Linnaeus

'Boutique' 1 YYW-WWY
(Jackson's Daffodils) Jackson's Daffodils, 1993
'Tiercel' × Silcock sdlg; sdlg no. 208/87
Fl. rounded, 104 mm wide; perianth segments broadly ovate, brilliant greenish yellow 5B, with yellowish white (11D) at base; the inner segments more narrowly ovate; corona funnel-shaped, yellowish white (11D), with a band of brilliant greenish yellow 5B at rim, mouth flared. Mid-season to late

'Bouzouki' 2 Y-R
(Brian S. Duncan) Brian S. Duncan, 1992
'Red Spartan' × ('Montego' × 'Achduart'); sdlg no. 1024
Fl. 105 mm wide; perianth segments broadly ovate, spreading, deeply overlapping; corona broad funnel-shaped, very deep orange-red, with mouth slightly wavy. Mid-season to late. Sunproof. Resembles a more robust and deeper-coloured 'Red Spartan'

'Bovacott' 2 W-? (b)
(R.O. Backhouse, pre-1938)
See also 'Babacott'

'Bovagh' 2 W-YYO
(Carncairn Daffodils) Carncairn Daffodils, 1975
'Sylvia O'Neill' × G.L. Wilson sdlg; sdlg no. 2/68/60
Fl. 85 mm wide; perianth segments greenish white (157C); corona cup-shaped, brilliant greenish yellow 6B, with a band of strong orange 24A at rim, tightly frilled. Mid-season

'Bow Bells' 5 Y-Y
(James S. Wells) James S. Wells, 1990
Selection from *N. triandrus* × *N. gaditanus*; sdlg no. 84-25
Fl. 30 mm wide, medium clear yellow, facing down; perianth segments reflexed, ovate, separated; corona cup-shaped, lightly ribbed, mouth even, rim obscurely notched. Dwarf. Early

'Bowerbird' 3 W-? (b)
(E. & J.C. Martin, pre-1916)

'Bowles' Early Sulphur' 1 Y-Y
(E.A.Bowles, pre-1954)
Fl. star-shaped, yellow (9C fading to 6D), facing up; perianth segments ovate, acute, with pale mucro, inflexed, plane, overlapping at base only; corona cylindrical in lower two-thirds, flared towards mouth, greenish at base and a darker tone of yellow (7A or 9A) towards mouth, mouth deeply 6-lobed, with the lobes deeply notched and dentate. Early. Resembles a paler and later-flowered 'The O'Mahoney'

'Bowles's Bounty' 1 Y-Y
(E.A. Bowles) A. Gray, 1957
Fl. soft sulphur yellow. Dwarf. Very early. 2n=28

'Bowls' 2 Y-O
(C.O. Fairbairn, pre-1959) Unregistered

'Boxer' 1 W-Y
(P.D. Williams, pre-1930)
Perianth segments creamy white; corona pale primrose

'Boxer' 2 Y-? (a)
(?W.B. Cranfield, pre-1938)

'Boxgrove' 2 Y-R
(Sir F.C. Stern) Sir F.C. Stern, 1961
'Cheerio' × 'Rustom Pasha'
Early. Resembles an improved 'Rustom Pasha'

'Boyet' 2 W-W
(W. Jackson Jr) W. Jackson Jr, 1968
'Whitemark' × 'Colmolhari'; sdlg no. 37/59

'Boz' 3 Y-Y

(W. Backhouse, pre-1869)
Perianth segments sulphur yellow; corona ribbed, lemon yellow. Syn. Burbidgei 'Boz', Burbidgei 'Luteus'

'Bozinov' 1 Y-Y
(G. Lubbe & Son, pre-1930)
AM(Haarlem) 1930

'Bozley' 1 Y-Y
(W. Jackson Jr) Jackson's Daffodils, 1979
'Ristin' × 'Otewa'; sdlg no. 14/73
Fl. 115 mm wide

'Brabançon' 8 W-O
Syn. of 'Medio Luteo Brabançon'

'Brabander' 8 Y-Y
(pre-1798)
Fl. pale yellow

'Brabant' 2 W-? (b)
(de Graaff Bros, pre-1931)
AM(Haarlem) 1930

'Brabazon' 1 Y-Y
(G.H. Johnstone, pre-1950)
'Constantine' × 'King of the North'
Fl. 97 mm wide; perianth segments vivid yellow 9A, overlapping; corona darker in tone (slightly brighter than 14A), mouth slightly expanded, rim flanged and lobed, with margins crenate. Early. 2n=28. *AM(g) 1974, *FCC(g) 1980, AGM 1993

'Bracelet' 3 W-? (b)
(Mrs R.O. Backhouse, pre-1921)

'Bracken' 5
(F.H. Chapman, pre-1913)

'Bracken Hill' 2 Y-GWY
(Carncairn Daffodils) Carncairn Daffodils, 1985
'Daydream' × 'Moonspell'
Fl. opening creamy yellow; perianth segments creamy yellow; corona long, slender, opening creamy yellow, becoming sulphur white, with variable shades of green at base and deep yellow at rim. Mid-season

'Brackenhurst' 2 Y-O
(Mrs J. Abel Smith) Mrs J. Abel Smith, 1977
'Ceylon' × 'Trifine'; sdlg no. M6/11
Fl. 100 mm wide; perianth segments deep yellow; corona bowl-shaped, reddish orange. Early. Sunproof. Resembles 'Trifine' but with the corona of a darker tone

'Braddock' 3 W-GYR
(Ballydorn Bulb Farm) Ballydorn Bulb Farm, 1980
'Strangford' × 'Fermoy'
Fl. 100 mm wide. Mid-season

'Bradley' 2 W-? (b)
(G.A. Uit den Boogaard, pre-1949)

'Bradner Queen' 4 W-Y
(David L. Sheppard) David L. Sheppard, 1994
'Gay Song' × ('Accent' × 'Easter Bonnet')
Fl. 110 mm wide; perianth and other petaloid segments in three whorls, broadly ovate, blunt, pure white, overlapping half; the outer whorl prominently mucronate, spreading; the second whorl shorter, not noticeably mucronate, inflexed, with margins wavy or incurled; the centre whorl irregularly arranged, strongly inflexed, with margins more or less tightly incurled; corona segments crumpled and clustered among the petaloid segments at centre, more loosely arranged between the surrounding whorls, short, broad, bright lemon yellow. Mid-season

'Bradwardine' 2 W-W
(The Brodie of Brodie, c.1923)
'Nevis' × 'Tenedos'
Fl. creamy white; perianth segments broadly ovate, only very slightly mucronate, spreading, overlapping one-third; the inner segments more narrowly ovate, with margins wavy; corona cylindrical, angled, with rim flanged and crenate. AM(e) 1928

'Braemar' 1 Y-Y
(The Brodie of Brodie, c.1933)
'Elgin' × 'Golden Goblet'
Fl. golden yellow; corona with rim rolled

'Braga' 1 Y-Y
(Pouw Bros) Pouw Bros, 1978
'Rembrandt' × 'Golden Sunbeam'
Fl. 125 mm wide; perianth segments brilliant yellow 7A; corona of a brighter tone (12A), with orange-yellow (13A) at rim. Early

'Bragabout' 4 W-O
(Glenbrook Bulb Farm, 1983) Glenbrook Bulb Farm, 1997
'Anne of Cleves' × 'Matapan'
Fl. 88 mm wide; perianth segments ovate, yellowish white (155D); corona segments yellow-orange (14A), frilled. Mid-season

'Braggart' 1 Y-Y
(G.L. Wilson, pre-1931)

'Brahms' 2 W-O
(J.M. de Navarro) J.M. de Navarro, 1957
'Fermoy' × 'Roimond'
Perianth segments roundish; corona bowl-shaped, reddish orange. 2n=28. Resembles a more brightly coloured 'Fermoy'. PC(e) 1957

'Braided Stream' 11a W-YWP
(David Adams) David Adams, 1994
'Ebony' open pollinated; sdlg no. 84/115D
Fl. forming a double triangle, 120 mm wide; perianth segments ovate, plane; the inner segments shorter and acute; corona deeply split, the six segments shorter than the perianth segments and opposite and closely overlying them, deeply bi-lobed, pinkish white, with a sharply defined band of yellow at base, deepening to creamy pink at rim. Early. Sunproof

'Braidwood' 2 Y-Y
(H.M. Barriball, c.1956) Unregistered

'Bramber' 2 W-? (b)
(Sir F.C. Stern, pre-1951)

'Bramble' 2 Y-? (a)
(J.C. Williams, pre-1945)

'Bramble Hill' 2 W-R
(D.S. Bell) D.S. Bell, 1968
('Mannequin' × 'Garland') × 'Arbar'
Corona very shallow bowl-shaped, suffused with red

'Bramble Lady' 3 W-YYO
(P. Fenn) P. Fenn, 1983
'Myriantha' × 'Lichfield'; sdlg no. PF/108/70
Fl. 88 mm wide; perianth segments creamy white, with a hint of green; corona creamy yellow, with green at base and apricot at rim, frilled. Resembles 'Lysander' but with creamier perianth segments and a more distinct rim to the corona

'Brambleton' 3 W-YYR
(Brian S. Duncan) P. Fenn, 1983
'Merlin' × 'Silent Beauty'; sdlg no. 412
Fl. 90 mm wide; corona opening orange, becoming rich yellow, with red at rim. Resembles 'Wetherby' but with larger perianth segments. Mid-season

'Brambling' 3 W-O
(P.D. Williams, pre-1910)
Perianth segments opening creamy, becoming white; corona scarlet-orange

'Brambling' 3 W-? (b)
(J.L. Richardson, pre-1948)

'Brambling' 2 Y-? (a)
(G.H. Johnstone, pre-1951)

'Bramley' 2 W-WWP
(Mrs J. Abel Smith) Mrs J. Abel Smith, 1977
'Lady Jowitt' × 'Famille Rose'; sdlg no. C3/85
Fl. 105 mm wide; corona broad, white, with apple blossom pink at rim, frilled. Resembles 'Famille Rose' but with smoother perianth segments

'Brampton' 3 W-O
(E.F. Hughes) E.F. Hughes, 1962
Fl. 95 mm wide; corona bright scarlet-orange. Mid-season

'Bram Sabelis' 1 Y-Y
(W.J.M. Blom, 1970) W. Blom & Son, 1984
'Arctic Gold' × 'Golden Harvest'; sdlg no. 70-E-21
Fl. dark yellow. Early

'Bram Warnaar' 1 Y-Y
(W.J.M. Blom, 1973) W. Blom & Son, 1984
'Arctic Gold' × 'Golden Harvest'; sdlg no. 73-G-1
Fl. dark yellow. Early

'Brandaris' 11a Y-Y
(J. Gerritsen & Son, 1965) J. Gerritsen & Son, 1976

'Baccarat' hybrid
Fl. 90 mm wide; perianth segments brilliant yellow 8A; corona strong orange-yellow to vivid yellow 17A-B, sometimes tinged orange. Mid-season. Resembles 'Baccarat' but with the corona of a darker tone. Syn. 'Sunburst'

'Brandon' 1 Y-Y
(R.H. Bath, pre-1931)
Perianth segments clear yellow, overlapping; corona bright buttercup yellow, with rim flared and crenate. Early. 2n=28. *AM(g) 1936

'Brandy' 2 Y-Y
(Murray W. Evans) Murray W. Evans, 1977
'Green Island' hybrid
Fl. 110 mm wide; perianth segments yellow-beige at maturity; corona of a deeper tone. Mid-season

'Brandysnap' 2 W-O
(G.H. Johnstone, pre-1952)
'Killifreth' × 'Red Hackle'

'Braniel' 2 Y-O
(G.L. Wilson, pre-1944)
'Hospodar' × 'Fortune'
Perianth segments creamy primrose; corona deep apricot orange. Sunproof

'Brano' 2 W-Y
(W. Jackson Jr, 1945) Jackson's Daffodils, 1979
'Neerim' × 'Gideon'; sdlg no. 88/71
Fl. rounded, 102 mm wide; perianth segments very broadly ovate, blunt, not prominently mucronate, spreading, with margins incurling at apex, overlapping half; corona funnel-shaped, smooth, opening deep clear yellow, becoming deep apricot yellow, tinged green in tube, mouth straight, split and overlapping, frilled, with rim crenate. Mid-season

'Branston' 3 W-YYO
(pre-1903)
Barrii 'Conspicuus' sport
Perianth segments pure white, touched yellow towards base; corona deep yellow, with orange at rim, frilled. Resembles an improved 'Lady Godiva'. AM 1903

'Branta' 2 W-? (b)
(de Graaff Bros, pre-1950)
AM(Haarlem) 1950

'Branwen' 3 W-? (b)
(W. Jackson Sr, 1937) W. Jackson Jr, 1956
'Mountain Pride' × 'Blodwen'

'Brass Band' 1 Y-Y

'Bravado' 2 Y-O
(G.L. Wilson, pre-1950)
'Chungking' × 'Klingo'
Perianth segments yellow; corona shallow bowl-shaped, reddish orange.

'Brave Adventure' 2 W-O
(Ballydorn Bulb Farm) Ballydorn Bulb Farm, 1979
'Bravura' × 'Ballymaster'
Fl. 122 m wide; corona glowing reddish orange. Mid-season. 2n=28. Resembles a better-formed 'Ballymaster'

'Brave Journey' 2 W-YYO
(Carncairn Daffodils) Carncairn Daffodils, 1986
'Merlin' × ('Seraglio' × 'Signal Light'); sdlg no. W4/7
Perianth segments rounded, deeply overlapping; corona closely overlying the perianth, deep chrome yellow, with orange at rim. Very late

'Brave Star' 2 Y-YYO
(J.N. Hancock & Co., pre-1974) Unregistered
Perianth segments bright yellow; corona yellow, with reddish orange at rim

'Bravo' 1 Y-Y
(F.H. Chapman, pre-1923)

'Bravo' 2 W-YYO
(Oregon Bulb Farms) Oregon Bulb Farms, 1958
Perianth segments white; corona lemon yellow, frilled. Very early

'Bravoure' 1 W-Y
(J.W.A.van der Wereld) J.W.A. van der Wereld, 1974
Fl. 120 mm wide; perianth segments broadly ovate, spreading or slightly inflexed, regular, overlapping one-third; the inner segments more narrowly ovate; corona smooth or lightly ribbed, light greenish yellow 5C, paling to 5D at base, with a touch of white at rim, mouth straight or a little expanded, widely and shallowly lobed, with rim entire. 2n=29. AM(e) 1978, AM(p) 1981, *AM(g) 1982, *FCC(g) 1990, AGM 1993

'Bravura' 3 W-O
(G.L. Wilson, pre-1937)
'Folly' × 'Sunstar'
Perianth segments pure white; corona scarlet-orange

'Brazier' 2 Y-? (a)
(R.O. Backhouse, pre-1933)

'Brazier' 2 Y-R
(J.A. O'More, 1962) P.D.K. Ramsay, 1980
'Firemaster' × 'Red Baron'; sdlg no. 71/62
Fl. 96 mm wide; perianth segments rich golden yellow; corona very deep red. Mid-season. Resembles 'Red Coat' but with a spreading corona

'Brazil' 2 Y-? (a)
(A.M. Wilson, pre-1949)

'Bread and Cheese' 2 W-Y
(G.L. Wilson, pre-1938)
'Alburnia' × 'Sincerity'
Perianth segments pure white; corona opening soft yellow, becoming soft rich cheesy buff

'Breage' 2 Y-Y
(R.V. Favell, pre-1940)
'Pilgrimage' × 'Godolphin'

'Breakaway' 2 W-O
(J.N. Hancock & Co., 1959) Unregistered
Perianth segments very broadly ovate, rounded at apex or truncate and split, slightly mucronate, a little reflexed, plane, overlapping half; the inner segments more narrowly ovate, spreading; corona broad disc-shaped, deeply ribbed, creamy orange, with a darker tone at rim, mouth frilled. Early to mid-season

'Break o' Day' 2 W-W
(R.H. Bath, pre-1927)
Fl. snow white, facing slightly downwards; corona frilled. Very early

'Break of Day' 2 Y-R
(T. Bloomer) T. Bloomer, 1962
'Ballintoy' × 'Sun Chariot'; sdlg no. 1/9/53
Perianth segments deep yellow; corona red

'Breakthrough' 2 Y-GYY
(M.J. Jefferson-Brown) M.J. Jefferson-Brown, 1965
'Homage' hybrid
Perianth segments pale butter yellow; corona shallow bowl-shaped, ribbed, pale yellow, with soft green at base, mouth expanded. Mid-season

'Breastplate' 2 W-? (b)
(G.H. Engleheart, pre-1916)

'Breathless' 2 W-O
(Oregon Bulb Farms, pre-1950)
'Fortune' × 'Ada Finch'

'Brecon' 2 Y-O
(pre-1950)
Perianth segments soft yellow; corona dark orange. ?Australian origin or A.M.Wilson sdlg 258

'Breda' 3 W-? (b)
(The Brodie of Brodie, c.1933)
'Beacon' × 'Galopin'

'Bredon' 2 W-GWW
(J.M. de Navarro, 1949) J.M. de Navarro, 1968
'Blakeney' × 'Ice Queen'
PC(e) 1968

'Breeze' 2 W-Y
(J.S. Leitch) J.S. Leitch, 1967
Fl. 114 mm wide; perianth segments white; corona lemon yellow

'Breila' 2 Y-YYO
(W.A. Watts, pre-1923)
'Sir Watkin' × 'Ornatus'
*C(g) 1927

'Brelade' 3 W-? (b)
(N.Y. Lower, pre-1936)

'Bremak'
(New Zealand origin, pre-1942)

'Bremen' 1 Y-Y
(J. Gerritsen & Son, pre-1934)
Perianth segments soft yellow; corona darker in tone

'Brenda' 3 Y-? (a)
(G.H. Engleheart, pre-1930)

'Brenda' 2 W-? (b)
(de Graaff Bros, pre-1943)
AM(Haarlem) 1942

'Brenda Pearl' 2 W-P
(W.G.Pannill) W.G.Pannill, 1996
'Love Boat' × 'Pink Tea'; sdlg no. 81/11
Mid-season to late

'Brenda Troil' 1 Y-Y
(W.B. Hartland, pre-1907)
Dwarf. Early

'Brendon' 2 Y-O
(J.T. Gray, pre-1949)
Perianth segments yellow; corona straight-sided, reddish orange, with rim slightly rolled

'Brenig' 1 W-W
(W.A. Watts, pre-1927)

'Brenin' 2 W-?
Syn. of 'Brennin'

'Brennin' 2 W-? (b or c)
(pre-1928)
See also 'Brenin'

'Brentor' 2 Y-O
(G.W. Tarry) du Plessis Bros, 1989
'Spanish Gold' × 'Craigywarren'; sdlg no. C13C
Fl. 105 mm wide; perianth segments bright yellow; corona cylindrical, orange, with a deeper tone at rim, mouth slightly expanded, with rim rolled. Mid-season. Sunproof

'Brentswood' 8 W-Y
(Cornish origin) du Plessis Bros, 1990
Fls 12-15 per stem, 34 mm wide; perianth segments pure white; corona lemon yellow. Mid-season. Resembles an earlier-flowered 'Grand Primo'. Scented

'Breona' 2 W-O
(S.J. Bisdee, 1942)
'Invergordon' × 'Hades'

'Brer Fox' 1 Y-O
(W.O. Backhouse) W.O. Backhouse, 1959
Fl. rounded, 105 mm wide; perianth segments very broadly ovate in outline, blunt or squarish at apex, rich golden yellow, with prominent white mucro, spreading, ribbed, overlapping half; the inner segments a little narrower, with margins wavy and sometimes nicked; corona funnel-shaped, deep orange, mouth ribbed and widely flared, sometimes deeply split and overlapping, irregularly frilled. Mid-season. Resembles a more upright 'Tidd-Pratt' with rounder perianth segments of deeper colour

'Bret Harte' 9 W-?
(G.H. Engleheart, pre-1910)

'Breton' 1 W-Y
(J. Gerritsen & Son, 1963) J. Gerritsen & Son, 1977
'Sonneclair' × 'President Lebrun'
Fl. 120 mm wide. Resembles a much larger 'President Lebrun'

'Brett' 3 Y-R
(W. Jackson Jr) Jackson's Daffodils, 1979
'Rave' × 'Dimity'; sdlg no. 183/68
Fl. 80 mm wide; perianth segments clear yellow; corona bright red. Mid-season. Resembles an improved 'Dimity' but with smaller and rounder perianth segments and broader inner segments

'Brevan' 2 Y-? (a)
(W.A. Watts, pre-1927)

N. breviflorus Spach = *N. patulus*

N. breviflos Steudel = *N. pseudonarcissus*

N. × brevitubulosus A.Fernandes 13 = *N. asturiensis* (Jordan) Pugsley × *N. bulbocodium* var. *nivalis* (Graells) Baker

'Brian' 1 Y-Y
(C. Dawson, pre-1923)
Perianth segments bright yellow, deeply overlapping; corona golden yellow, with mouth slightly ribbed and well-frilled

'Brian Boru' 1 Y-Y
(Sir J.A.R. Gore-Booth, pre-1916)

'Brian Pink' 2 Y-Y
(L.P. Dettman) L.P. Dettman, 1977
'Jimmy Chandler' × 'Phillus Chidgey'; sdlg no. 8/70
Fl. 98 mm wide; perianth segments vivid yellow 12A; corona darker in tone (15A), with vivid green in tube. Mid-season. Resembles 'Jimmy Chandler' but with a shorter corona

'Bribery'
(Alister Clark, pre-1915)

'Bricsea' 2 Y-R
(J.L. Martin) J.L. Martin, 1973
'Armada' × 'Apricot Glow'
Fl. 83 mm wide

'Bridal Array' 2 W-GWW
(Eileen E. Frey, 1976) J. & E. Frey, 1993
'Old Satin' × 'Cool Crystal'; sdlg no. JEE7/1
Fl. rounded, 100 mm wide; perianth segments roundish, mucronate, slightly reflexed, plane, of good substance, overlapping half; the inner segments narrower, more nearly ovate, more nearly spreading; corona bowl-shaped, small, with green at base, heavily frilled. Late to very late

'Bridal Bouquet' 8 W-O
(pre-1860)

'Bridal Brocade' 2 W-W
(J.A.Hunter, 1987) J.A.Hunter, 1997
'Polar Snow' × ('Glendermott' × 'Kotuku'); sdlg no. 16/82A
Fl. 110 mm wide; perianth segments ovate, spreading, smooth; corona funnel-shaped, heavily frilled and appearing to be in more than one whorl. Mid-season

'Bridal Chorus' 1 W-W
(G.E. Mitsch, 1974) R. & E. Havens, 1992
Sdlg Y16/1 ('Le Cygne' × 'Empress of Ireland') × 'Panache'; sdlg no. 2J54/10
Fl. 110 mm wide, pure white; perianth segments very broadly ovate, blunt, slightly mucronate, spreading, a little concave near apex, of heavy substance, overlapping half; the inner segments slightly inflexed, with margins wavy; corona cylindrical, smooth, with mouth flared and frilled. Late. Resembles a taller 'Chaste' with the corona more heavily frilled

'Bridal Crown' 4 W-Y
(J. Schoorl, pre-1949)
'L'Innocence' sport
Fl. 40 mm wide; perianth and other petaloid segments in several whorls, creamy white; the outer whorl very broad, truncate and mucronate, spreading, sometimes a little twisted, overlapping half; the inner whorls rounded, inflexed, crumpled; those at centre loosely clasped together, usually stained vivid yellow 9A at midrib, with the stained part lifting away from the segment as a flap or spur; corona very short, tightly frilled, darker in tone (brighter than 14A), with rim entire; some corona segments detached and interspersed among the petaloid segments. Strongly scented. 2n=17. AM(Haarlem) 1949, *AM(p) 1985

'Bridal Day' 1 W-W
(O. Ronalds, 1948) T. Morrison, 1960
Fl. white

'Bridal Flower' 2 or 3 W-W
(G.H. Engleheart, pre-1904)
Fl. ivory white, facing down

'Bridal Lace' 11a W-WWY
(J.Gerritsen & Son, 1975) Mrs E.Bullivant, 1995
Sdlg no. GBS 15
Fl. 90 mm wide; perianth segments rounded at apex, prominently mucronate, slightly twisted; corona deeply split, the six segments opposite the perianth segments, deeply bi-lobed, with the lobes wavy or twisted, white, with yellow at rim on opening and again as the flower fades, frilled. Early

'Bridal Morn' 2 W-W
(G.L. Wilson, pre-1923)

'Bridal Robe' 1 W-Y
(G.L. Wilson, pre-1938)
'Sincerity' × 'Slemish'
Perianth segments very broadly ovate, blunt or truncate, prominently mucronate, with margins somewhat wavy, overlapping half; the inner segments with margins more strongly wavy or twisted, shouldered at base; corona pale lemon, mouth expanded and ribbed, rim flanged, irregularly notched and obscurely crenate

'Bridal Rose' 2 W-WWP
(G.L. Wilson) G. Zandbergen-Terwegen, 1965
Fl. 114 mm wide, milk white; corona with soft pink at rim. Mid-season

'Bridal Veil' 3 W-W
(C. Smith, pre-1902)
Fl. facing down; perianth segments long, snow white, twisted; corona long, creamy white

'Bridal Veil' 1 W-W
(G.L. Wilson) G. Zandbergen-Terwegen, 1956
AM(Haarlem) 1956

'Bridara' 2 Y-? (a)
(J.S. Leitch) J.S. Leitch, 1959

'Bride' 2 Y-Y
(E. Leeds, pre-1877)
Perianth segments sulphur yellow; corona expanded. Syn. Incomparabilis Albidus 'Bride'

'Brideburn' 1 W-Y
(D.N.Y. Olson) D.N.Y. Olson, 1988
'Stormy Weather' × 'Malaspina'; sdlg no. 292/8
Fl. 108 mm wide; perianth segments overlapping; corona light yellow, with rim slightly rolled. Mid-season

'Bride Elect' 3 W-? (b or c)
(O. Pease, pre-1927)

'Bridegroom'
(?F.H. Chapman, pre-1913)

'Bridegroom' 3 W-YYO
(The Brodie of Brodie, c.1913)
'Mozart' × 'Gallipoli'
Perianth segments very broad, blunt, prominently mucronate, creamy white, spreading, a little concave, of great substance, overlapping half or more; the inner segments a little inflexed, with margins incurling towards apex or recurving at base; corona expanded, ribbed, yellow, with a narrow band of orange at rim, and with orange suffusing the ribs, mouth sometimes deeply split and overlapping, wavy. Tall. Late. AM(e) 1929

'Bride of Lammermoor' 1 W-W
(Barr & Sons, pre-1913)

'Bridesmaid' 1 W-W
(?Barr & Son, pre-1889)
Perianth segments white; corona opening citron yellow, becoming sulphur white

'Bridesmaid' 3 W-WWY
(C. Smith, pre-1901)
Perianth segments broadly ovate, blunt mucronate, inflexed, with margins recurved, overlapping at base only; corona funnel-shaped, ribbed, with a line of pale primrose yellow at rim, mouth straight, split in places and overlapping, frilled, with rim crenate

'Bridesmaid' 2 W-WPP
(Ballydorn Bulb Farm) Ballydorn Bulb Farm, 1970
Perianth segments ovate, blunt, pure white, inflexed, the margins wavy and often recurved towards base to give a spathulate appearance, overlapping at base only; corona short funnel-shaped, ribbed, white, touched with pale primrose at rim, mouth straight,

split in places and overlapping, frilled, with rim crenate

'Bride's Veil' 1 W-W
(C. Goodson, pre-1927)

'Bridget' 9 W-GYR
(A.M. Wilson, pre-1915)
Perianth segments pure white, smooth, of strong substance; corona with gren at base and a broad and well-defined band of deep red at rim

'Bridget' 1 W-W
(P.D. Williams, pre-1927)

'Bridget Hill' 2 Y-O
(J.L. Richardson, pre-1948)
Fl. 95 mm wide; perianth segments near brilliant greenish yellow 6A, overlapping half; corona orange (28A), paling to vivid orange-yellow 21A at base, mouth frilled and slightly expanded, rim crenate. *AM(g) 1956

'Bridgewater' 1 Y-Y
(C.A. Nethercote) T. Morrison, 1960
Fl. lime yellow; corona deeply flanged and frilled

'Brierglass' 2 W-GWW
(J.S.B. Lea) Clive Postles Daffodils, 1985
'Ashmore' × 'Croila'
Mid-season. Resembles 'Golden Aura' in form

'Brigade' 2 Y-R
(W.M. Spry, pre-1975) Unregistered
'Jean Hood' × 'My Choice'
Corona orange-red

'Brigadier' 2 W-Y
(G.H. Engleheart, pre-1899)
Perianth segments spreading; corona large, deep yellow. Resembles a better-formed 'Sir Watkin' with a white perianth. AM 1899

'Brigadoon' 2 Y-O
(Konynenburg & Mark) Konynenburg & Mark, 1964
'Green Island' × (['Mimosa' × 'David Copperfield'] × ['Pomona' × John Evelyn'])
Fl. 100 mm wide; perianth segments brilliant greenish yellow 6A; corona vivid orange 28B. Mid-season

'Brigand' 1 Y-Y
(W.A. Watts, pre-1923)

'Briged Rossano' 2 W-O
(J.W.A. Lefeber) J.W.A. Lefeber, 1960
Fl. 76 mm wide; perianth segments pure white; corona deep reddish orange

'Bright Angel' 9 W-GOR
(G.E. Mitsch, 1968) R. Havens, 1979
'Quetzal' × 'Smyrna'; sdlg no. D94/3
Fl. rounded, 65 mm wide; perianth segments glistening white; corona orange, with green at base and bright orange-red at rim. Late

'Bright Beauty' 3 W-O
(J.L. Richardson, pre-1939)
AM(Haarlem) 1939

'Bright Bet' 2 W-YYO
(J.N. Hancock & Co., 1954)

'Bright Candle' 2 Y-R
(G.E.Mitsch, 1981) R. & E.Havens, 1997
('Chemawa' × 'Brer Fox') × 'Loch Hope'; sdlg no. 2Q15/5A
Fl. 105 mm wide; perianth segments broadly ovate, clear yellow; corona cup-shaped, orange-red, with mouth slightly flared. Early. Sunproof

'Bright Challenge' 9 W-GGO
(Mrs M.S. Yerger) Mrs M.S. Yerger, 1993
'Felindre' × 'Bon Bon'; sdlg no. 78 D 4
Fl. 55 mm wide; perianth segments white, with margins wavy; corona disc-shaped, brilliant yellow-green 154B suffusing to strong yellow-green 143C at base and orange (28A) at rim. Late

'Bright Charm' 3 W-O
(Warnaar & Co.) Warnaar & Co., 1959
'Win All' × 'Arnhem'
Fl. 89 mm wide; perianth segments cream white; corona vivid orange 28B. Late. AM(Haarlem) 1962

'Bright Circle' 3 W-O
(J.L. Richardson, pre-1939)
AM(Haarlem) 1941

'Bright Dab' 9 W-O
(Mrs M.S. Yerger) Mrs M.S. Yerger, 1994
'Praecox' × 'Lights Out'; sdlg no. 76 D D
Fl. star-shaped, 20 mm wide; perianth segments acute; the inner segments narrower; corona cup-shaped, suffused strong reddish orange, with a darker tone at rim. Dwarf. Early

'Bright Dawn' 2 Y-O
(O. Ronalds) T. Morrison, 1960
Perianth segments broad; corona widely expanded, reddish orange. Early. Syn. 'Rising Sun'

'Bright Delight' 2 W-P
(Colin Crotty) Unregistered
Sdlg no. 46-75

'Brighter Days' 2 Y-? (a)
(G. Lewis) D.S. Bell, 1955

'Brighter London' 3 W-O
(Mrs R.O. Backhouse, pre-1921)
Perianth segments pure white; corona orange. AM(Haarlem) 1937

'Bright Eye' 9 W-?
(G.H. Engleheart, pre-1914)
See also 'Brighteye'

'Bright Eye' 3 W-?
Syn. of 'Eyebright'

'Brighteye' 9 W-?
Syn. of 'Bright Eye'

'Bright Eyes' 2 Y-YYO
(C.M. Grullemans) J.J. Grullemans & Sons, 1959
Fl. 115 mm wide; perianth segments light greenish yellow 4C; corona vivid yellow 13A, with strong orange 25A at rim. Late

'Bright Flame' 2 W-P
(Mrs J. Abel Smith, 1970) Mrs J. Abel Smith, 1986
'Rose of Tralee' hybrid; sdlg no. B5/22
Early. 2n=28

'Bright Gold' 1 Y-Y
(The Brodie of Brodie, pre-1929)

'Bright Gold' 1 Y-Y
(J.A. O'More) J.A. O'More, 1971
'Kingscourt' × 'Bastion'
Fl. 108 mm wide

'Bright Hope' 2 Y-? (a)
(Mrs P.M. Davis, pre-1948)

'Bright Jewel' 3 W-? (b)
(D.S. Bell) D.S. Bell, 1955

'Bright Lad' 2 Y-O
(H.A. Brown, 1944)
Perianth segments deep yellow; corona bright reddish orange

'Bright Lass' 2 Y-YYR
(O. Ronalds, 1950) T. Morrison, 1960

'Bright Lights' 3 W-R
(Oregon Bulb Farms, pre-1950)

'Bright Lights' 2 Y-R
(M.E.Brogden) Unregistered

'Brightling' 2 Y-OOR
(Mrs R.O. Backhouse, pre-1921)
Perianth segments primrose yellow; corona very shallow, ribbed, rich orange, with orange-red at rim, frilled and lobed as if in three whorls. Tall

'Brightmark' 2 W-YOO
(S.C. Gaspar) R.J.Abernethy, 1957
Perianth segments white; corona spreading, tightly ribbed, reddish orange, paling to pale lemon at base

'Brightness' 2 Y-? (a)
(R.H. Bath, pre-1927)

'Brightness' 2 Y-O
(A. Overton) A. Overton, 1960
Perianth segments broad, rich yellow; corona widely expanded, scarlet-orange. Early

'Brighton' 3 Y-R
(C.E. Radcliff, 1937)
'Mayflower' × 'Atanga'

'Brighton' 2 Y-? (a)
(J.T. Gray, pre-1939)

'Brighton' 1 Y-Y
(P.L.A. Pouw) P.L.A. Pouw, 1961
Fl. 125 mm wide; perianth segments broadly ovate, vivid yellow 12A, with white mucro, a little inflexed, somewhat ribbed, overlapping half; the inner segments more strongly inflexed, with margins wavy; corona cylindrical, smooth, slightly darker in tone (13A) than the perianth, with mouth ribbed and expanded, rim rolled and crenate. Mid-season. Resembles an earlier-flowered 'Rembrandt'. AM(Haarlem) 1962

'Brighton' 1 Y-Y
Syn. of 'Brigton'

'Bright Outlook' 9 W-GYO
(Mrs M.S. Yerger) Mrs M.S. Yerger, 1990
'Felindre' × 'Bon Bon'
Fl. 50 mm wide; perianth segments roundish, spreading; the inner segments narrower; corona very shallow bowl-shaped, greenish yellow (154B), with a broad band of brilliant yellowish green (134C) at base, shading to orange (28A) at rim. Dwarf. Late. Scented. Closely resembles 'Felindre'

'Bright Sea' 2 W-? (b)
(P.D. Williams, pre-1948)

'Brightside' 2 Y-? (a)
(Warnaar & Co., pre-1939)

'Bright Side' 2 W-YOO
(J.W.A. Lefeber, pre-1982)
'Barrett Browning' × 'Professor Einstein'

'Bright Spangles' 8 W-O
(Sidney DuBose, 1977) Sidney DuBose, 1996
'Matador' open pollinated; sdlg no. C34-6
Fls 4-6 per stem, 28 mm wide; perianth segments

opening yellow, becoming white; corona orange. Early

'Bright Spark' 3 W-R
(J.M. de Navarro) J.M. de Navarro, 1977
Sdlg no. 428/111
Fl. 85 mm wide; perianth segments very broadly ovate in outline, blunt and mucronate at apex, sometimes truncate, spreading or slightly reflexed, plane, overlapping half; the inner segments more narrowly ovate, slightly inflexed, with margins a little wavy; corona shallow, strongly ribbed, with mouth widely expanded and rim crenate. Late. Resembles a later-flowered 'Parthenia'

'Bright Spark' 2 Y-O
(J.N.Hancock & Co.) Unregistered
Corona expanded, brilliant orange. Tall

'Bright Spot' 8 W-R
(Sidney DuBose) W.R.P. Welch, 1993
'Matador' open pollinated; sdlg no. A16-1
Fls 1-3 per stem, up to 65 mm wide, of very heavy substance; perianth segments opening cream, becoming white; corona bowl-shaped, dark orange-red. Mid-season

'Bright Star' 2 W-P
(Mrs J. Abel Smith) Mrs J. Abel Smith, 1983
'Passionale' hybrid
Perianth segments pure white; corona deep pink

'Bright Tomorrow' 7 W-P
(Eileen E. Frey) J. & E. Frey, 1984
Sdlg × *N. jonquilla*; sdlg no. QEE14/41
Fl. 90 mm wide; corona light pink, with paler tones outside

'Brightwork' 3 W-YYR
(Oregon Bulb Farms, pre-1950)

'Brigitta' 2 W-GPP
(Evalds Paupers) Evalds Paupers, 1986
'Passionale' × Lea sdlg; sdlg no. P-75-69
Perianth segments pure white; corona cup-shaped, light orange-pink (25D), with a darker tone inside (29A). Mid-season

'Brigstock' 2 W-WWP
(E.F. Hughes) E.F. Hughes, 1962
Fl. 111 mm wide; corona opening green white, becoming milk white, with buffy rose pink at rim, frilled. Mid-season

'Brigton' 1 Y-Y
(J.S.B. Lea, 1977) Clive Postles Daffodils, 1988
'Arctic Gold' × (sdlg × 'Capitol Hill')
Fl. forming a double triangle, 100 mm wide; perianth segments vivid yellow 9A, spreading; corona ribbed towards mouth, orange-yellow (14A), mouth flared, with rim dentate. Early. *HC(g) 1991. See also 'Brighton'

'Brilliance' 2 Y-O
(H.A. Brown, 1941)
Corona bright reddish orange, with mouth expanded. Early

'Brilliancy' 3 Y-YYO
(G.H. Engleheart, pre-1906)
'M.J. Berkeley' hybrid
Fl. 108 mm wide; perianth segments narrow, rounded at apex, clear yellow; corona paler in tone, with a well-defined narrow band of reddish orange at rim. Scented. AM 1906, AM(Haarlem) 1915

'Brilliant' 3 Y-? (a)
(Sir C.H. Cave, pre-1905)
Corona richly coloured

'Brilliant' 2 Y-O
(L. Buckland, pre-1933)
Perianth segments yellow; corona bright reddish orange

'Brilliant Eye' 2 W-? (b)
(J. Gerritsen & Son, pre-1931)
Syn. 'Clear Eye', 'Glad Eye'. AM(Haarlem) 1930

'Brilliant Lights' 2 W-O
(J.N. Hancock & Co., pre-1956)
Perianth segments very broadly ovate, rounded and sometimes split at apex, slightly mucronate, spreading or a little reflexed, somewhat concave, overlapping one-third to a half; the inner segments more narrowly ovate, more usually spreading, with margins wavy; corona shallow bowl-shaped, closely ribbed, glowing reddish orange, with darker tones at rim, mouth widely expanded, frilled. Tall. Early. Scented

'Brilliant Star' 3 Y-? (a)
(G.H. Engleheart, pre-1923)

'Brilliant Star' 11b W-O/WY
(J.W.A. Lefeber) J.W.A. Lefeber, 1960
Fl. 87 mm wide; perianth segments very broadly ovate, squarish at apex, very prominently mucronate, yellow-white, with margins wavy, overlapping one-third to a half; the inner segments more narrowly ovate, only very slightly mucronate; corona split to base, the six segments one-third the length of the perianth segments, under half their width and alternate to them, bi-lobed, with deep reddish orange in a broad longitudinal band at midrib touched yellow at border and towards apex, with more or less broad patches of white at margins, spreading, with margins wavy or more strongly incurled, sometimes twisted; some extra growths at centre, alternate to the corona segments, short, strongly inflexed

'Brilliant Star' 2 Y-YRR
Syn. of 'Scarlet Elegance'

'Brimfire' 3 W-GYR
(K. McCombe, c.1981) Unregistered

'Brimstone' 1 Y-Y
(G.H. Engleheart, pre-1923)
Fl. pale sulphur yellow; perianth segments broad; the inner segments narrower, with margins sometimes incurved or twisted; corona long, angled, with rim broadly flanged and deeply and regularly notched. AM(e) 1929, FCC(e) 1936

'Brimstone' 8 W-Y
(de Goede Bros, pre-1927)
Fl. large; corona shallow, canary yellow

'Brindabella' 4 Y-Y
(Jackson's Daffodils) Jackson's Daffodils, 1995
Sdlg 284/80 × sdlg 3/74; sdlg no. 95/87
Fl. 95 mm wide; perianth and other petaloid segments in three whorls, vivid yellow 12A; corona segments of a deeper tone (vivid yellow 14A). Early

'Brindisi' 2 YYW-P
(Brian S. Duncan) Rathowen Daffodils, 1977
Binkie sdlg × sdlg R 3341; sdlg no. 89
Fl. 110 mm wide; perianth segments yellow, with white at base; corona copper pink

'Brindle Pink' 2 Y-P
(Brian S. Duncan) Brian S. Duncan, 1992
'Brindisi' open pollinated × 'Brindisi' open pollinated
Fl. 109 mm wide; perianth segments broadly ovate, rounded at base, mid-yellow, with a tinge of pink, spreading, overlapping; corona funnel-shaped, slightly ribbed, coppery pink, with mouth straight. Mid-season to late. Sunproof

'Brinsonica' 1 Y-Y
(B. Rowlands, pre-1938)

'Brion' 1 W-? (b)
(de Graaff Bros, pre-1943)
AM(Haarlem) 1942

'Brise' 2 Y-? (a)
(J.O. Sherrard) C.M. Sandison, 1955

'Bristol' 2 Y-YYO
(J.N. Hancock & Co., pre-1949)
Fl. yellow; corona with orange at rim

'Bristol' 2 W-W
(R.C.A. Tombleson) R.C.A. Tombleson, 1970
'Killaloe' × 'Ardclinis'

'Britannia' 2 Y-? (a)
(Mrs R.O. Backhouse, pre-1921)

'British Charm' 2 Y-O
(G.L. Wilson, pre-1938)

'British Empire' 1 Y-Y
(pre-1936)

'British Lion'
(pre-1913)

'British Monarch' 1 Y-Y
(pre-1936)
Fl. large, mid-yellow. FA(Haarlem) 1937

'British Queen' 8
(pre-1890)

'Britomark' 1 W-Y
(C.E. Radcliff, 1943) J.M.Radcliff, 1956
('Renown' × 'Barbarino') × 'Bonython'
Perianth segments white; corona lemon yellow

'Briton' 1 Y-Y
(Hon. Sir R.H. Rhodes, pre-1911)
See also 'Britton'

'Brittania' 2 Y-? (a)
(Mrs R.O. Backhouse, pre-1921)
AM(Haarlem) 1933

'Britton' 1 Y-Y
Syn. of 'Briton'

'Brixton' 2 W-Y
(R. Parr) R. Hyde, 1957
Perianth segments white, smooth; corona lemon yellow, with rim neatly rolled

'Broad Acre' 2 W-? (b)
(Mrs M. Moorby) Mrs M. Moorby, 1957

'Broadfield' 2 Y-R
(P. Phillips) P. Phillips, 1968

'Broadford' 1 Y-Y
(The Brodie of Brodie, pre-1913)
'King Alfred' × 'Lord Roberts'

'Broadheath' 2 Y-? (a)
(A.M. Wilson, pre-1950)

'Broadland' 2 W-W
(C. Dye, 1969) P.A. Payne, 1984
'Interim' × 'Lisbreen'
Fl. 120 mm wide, ice white; perianth segments slightly reflexed, regular, overlapping; corona ribbed, with mouth slightly expanded and rim crenate. Resembles a taller 'Canisp' with smoother perianth segments. AM(e) 1985

'Broadlea' 1 W-Y
(M. Gardiner)

'Broadmayne' 2 Y-O
(J.W. Blanchard) J.W. Blanchard, 1974
'Dewlish' × 'Border Chief'
Mid-season

'Broad Oak' 1 Y-Y
(G.P. Haydon, pre-1910)

'Broadside' 2 W-?
(Alister Clark, 1935) J. Sharp, 1960

'Broadstairs' 1 W-? (b)
(F.D.B. Cobb, pre-1953)

'Broadwater' 2 Y-Y
(Sir F.C. Stern, pre-1948)
AM(e) 1950, *AM(g) 1952, *FCC(g) 1953

'Broadway' 2 W-Y
(Barr & Sons, pre-1947)

'Broadway Rose' 2 W-GPP
(J.M. de Navarro) J.M. de Navarro, 1977
'Raspberry Ring' × 'Fair Prospect'; sdlg no. 467/III
Fl. 86 mm wide; corona pale pink, with green at base and a deeper tone of pink at rim. Late. Resembles 'Green Island' but with smoother and whiter perianth segments and a differently coloured corona

'Broadway Star' 11b W-O/W
(J.W.A. Lefeber) J.W.A. Lefeber, 1975
Fl. rounded, 80 mm wide; perianth segments very broad, truncate, prominently mucronate, ivory white, spreading, somewhat concave and with margins incurling at apex, overlapping half or more; the inner segments only very slightly mucronate, with margins wavy; corona split to base, the six segments half as long and less than half as wide as the perianth segments and alternate to them, deeply bi-lobed, vivid orange 28B in a broad band at midrib, with white at margins sometimes veined with light orange, inflexed, with margins frilled and incurling. Late

'Broadway Village' 2 Y-YRR
(Clive Postles Daffodils) Clive Postles Daffodils, 1985
'Stourbridge' × 'Torridon'; sdlg no. 7-42-75
Perianth segments broadly ovate, blunt, slightly mucronate, spreading, a little concave, with margins sometimes slightly incurling, regular, overlapping half; the inner segments more rounded at apex and only very slightly mucronate; corona very shallow bowl-shaped, mouth widely expanded and a little frilled, with rim crenate. Early

'Broadwing' 3 W-O
(G.H. Engleheart, pre-1907)
Perianth segments white; corona reddish orange.
Resembles a larger-flowered 'John Bain'

'Brocade' 5 W-?
(W.B. Cranfield, pre-1930)

'Brocade' 10 W-W
(J.W. Blanchard) J.W. Blanchard, 1974
N. bulbocodium sdlg
Fl. 38 mm wide

'Brockhampton' 2 Y-? (a)
(J. Wilson, pre-1942)

'Brockwell' 2 W-P
(G.L. Wilson) P. de Jager & Sons, 1963
Fl. 100 mm wide; perianth segments ivory white; corona strong yellowish pink 32D. Mid-season

'Brodick' 3 O-R
(Brian S. Duncan) Brian S. Duncan, 1992
Sdlg B.246 ('Rathowen Flame' × 'Shining Light') × 'Sabine Hay'; sdlg no. 990
Fl. 100 mm wide; perianth segments broadly ovate, blunt or somewhat truncate, with slight white mucro, orange, spreading, with margins minutely incurling at apex, overlapping half; the inner segments slightly inflexed; corona bowl-shaped, deep cherry red, with mouth even, rim crenate. Mid-season

'Brodribb' 2 W-O
(W.M. Spry, pre-1975) Unregistered
'Jean Hood' × 'Delight'

'Broere' 9 W-?
(G. Lubbe & Son, pre-1927)

'Brogar' 1 W-? (b)
(J.T. Gray, pre-1929)
PC(e)(NZ) 1929

'Broken Tip' 2 W-YYO
Syn. of 'Aruba'

'Brolga' 2 W-W
(Jackson's Daffodils) Jackson's Daffodils, 1989
'Jonna' × sdlg 102/73; sdlg no. 276/80
Fl. forming a double triangle, 105 mm wide, greenish white (155A); perianth segments very broadly ovate, blunt, spreading, of thick substance, overlapping half; the outer segments overlapping one another; the inner segments square-shouldered at base, more noticeably mucronate; corona only a little shorter than the perianth segments, funnel-shaped, smoothly angled, with mouth expanded and even, rim regularly crenate. Mid-season to late

N. bromfieldii Syme = *N. obvallaris*

'Bromford' 1 Y-Y
(J.C. Whibley) J.C. Whibley, 1959

Fl. sulphur yellow

'Bromley' 4 W-W
(W.G. Pannill) W.G. Pannill, 1982
'Gay Time' × 'Zero'; sdlg no. 66/52 A
Fl. 94 mm wide. Mid-season

'Brompton' 2 W-Y
(Mrs A.R. Simmons, 1970) Mrs A.R. Simmons, 1980
Sdlg no. 101
Fl. 90 mm wide; corona pale lemon, with a darker tone at rim. Mid-season

'Bronte' 1 W-Y
(J.N. Hancock & Co., 1953)

'Bronte' 1 Y-Y
(S.J. Bisdee) S.J. Bisdee, 1956
'Principal' × sdlg B83/43

'Bronte' 1 Y-Y
(W.M. Spry, pre-1975) Unregistered
'Hunter's Moon' × 'Kingscourt'
Late

'Brontes' 9 W-?
(W.B. Hartland, pre-1913)

'Bronwen' 2 W-? (b)
(W.A. Watts, pre-1923)
'Minnie Hume' × 'Duke of Bedford'

'Bronze Eagle' 1 W-Y
(D.S. Bell) D.S. Bell, 1957
'Polindra' sdlg × 'Outward Bound'
Perianth segments pure white, of thick substance

'Bronze Lady' 2 W-? (b)
(Oregon Bulb Farms, pre-1950)

'Bronze Monarch' 1 W-Y
(J.L. Richardson) E. Longford, 1963
'Alpine Eagle' open pollinated
Fl. 120 mm wide; perianth segments white; corona opening lemon yellow, becoming rich buff yellow. Mid-season. Resembles a taller and larger-flowered 'Alpine Eagle' of deeper colour

'Bronze Queen' 3 W-? (b)
(E. & J.C. Martin, pre-1916)

'Bronzette' 3 Y-? (a)
(J.A. Morris) J.A. Morris, 1957

'Bronzino' 2 Y-? (a)
(J.E. Exley, pre-1938)

'Brookdale' 1 W-P
(W.G. Pannill) W.G. Pannill, 1978
'Chivalry' × 'Rima'; sdlg no. 64/35 C

Fl. 101 mm wide. Mid-season

'Brooke Ager' 2 W-P
(Sidney DuBose) Sidney DuBose, 1997
'Pink Ice' × ('Coral Light' × 'My Word'); sdlg no. N16-18
Fl. 74 mm wide; corona deep rose pink. Dwarf. Mid-season

'Brookfield' 2 W-W
(W.J. Dunlop, pre-1947)
'Dava' × 'Justice'
Perianth segments broad, pure white; corona opening cream, becoming white. PC 1948, AM(Haarlem) 1957

'Brooklyn' 3 Y-? (a)
(L. van Leeuwen & Son, pre-1950)
Syn. 'Lynbrook'

'Brookside' 3 W-YYO
(Adrian Frylink) Adrian Frylink, 1958
Perianth segments white; corona deep yellow, with reddish orange at rim

'Brookville' 2 W-Y
(Mrs J. Grullemans van Berghem) J.J. Grullemans & Sons, 1956

'Broomgrove' 1 Y-Y
(F.E. Board) F.E. Board, 1965
'Ormeau' × 'Spanish Gold'; sdlg no. 1127
Perianth segments ovate or broadly ovate, blunt and mucronate, spreading or slightly inflexed, overlapping half; corona cylindrical, smooth, mouth slightly expanded, ribbed, with rim crenate. Late. 2n=28

'Broomhill' 2 W-W
(F.E. Board) F.E. Board, 1965
'Easter Moon' × 'Knowehead'; sdlg no. B455
Fl. 100 mm wide, greenish white (155A); perianth segments broad, overlapping; corona more strongly ribbed inside than out, frilled, with rim crenate and slightly flanged. 2n=28. AM(e) 1971, FCC(e) 1974, AGM 1995

'Bropua' 2 W-YYO
(West & Fell, pre-1938)
Perianth segments pure white; corona spreading, lemon yellow, with reddish orange at rim

'Brotonne' 2 Y-R
(Mrs R.O. Backhouse, pre-1921)
Perianth segments canary yellow; corona dark red. AM(Haarlem) 1926

'Broughshane' 1 W-W
(G.L. Wilson, pre-1938)
'Trostan' × 'Kanchenjunga'; sdlg no. 25/31
Fl. 135 mm wide; perianth segments very broadly

ovate, only slightly mucronate, greenish white, spreading, ribbed, overlapping half; the inner segments more narrowly ovate, inflexed at base, recurved near apex, with margins wavy; corona somewhat funnel-shaped, lightly ribbed, opening with tinges of primrose yellow, becoming amber white, rim widely flanged and deeply dentate. 2n=28. PC 1939, AM(e) 1943, AM(Haarlem) 1948, *AM(g) 1956

N. broussonetii Lagasca & Segura 13 Section Aurelia
    f. ***broussonetii***
        f. ***grandiflorus*** (Battandier & Trabut) Maire

'Brownie' 2 Y-? (a)
(P.D. Williams, pre-1929)

'Browning' 9 W-?
(W. Balch, pre-1933)

'Browning' 2 W-O
(P. Phillips) P. Phillips, 1968

'Brown's Seedling' 2 W-P
(Australian origin, pre-1933)
Corona salmon pink. Resembles 'Bernardino' in form

'Bruce' 1 W-Y
(P. Phillips) P. Phillips, 1964
Fl. forming a double triangle, 108 mm wide; perianth segments very broad; corona long, lemon yellow, mouth widely flared, with rim rolled. Mid-season

'Bruening' 1 Y-Y
(G. Haver, pre-1933)

'Bruges' 1 W-Y
(J.L. Richardson, pre-1945)
'Cromarty' self pollinated
Perianth segments broadly ovate; corona yellow, with a deeper tone at rim, with the rim rolled and dentate

'Bruin' 2 W-O
(F.E. Board) F.E. Board, 1965
'Buncrana' × 'Merryhill'

'Brume' 2 W-W
(Mrs P.M. Davis, pre-1948)

'Bruna Claire' 3 W-? (b)
(J.W.A. Lefeber, pre-1948)

'Brunehilde' 2 W-Y
(Barr & Sons, pre-1913)
Perianth segments white; corona lemon yellow

'Brunette' 3 Y-? (a)
(G.H. Engleheart, pre-1913)

'Brunette' 3 Y-? (a)
(E. & J.C. Martin, pre-1930)

'Bruno' 2 W-? (b)
(A.M. Wilson, pre-1944)

'Brunsica' 2 Y-? (a)
(B. Rowlands, pre-1938)

'Brunswick' 2 W-Y
(P.D. Williams, pre-1931)
Fl. forming a double triangle, 100 mm wide; perianth segments broadly ovate, acute, slightly mucronate, creamy white, spreading, plane or with margins slightly incurling at apex, overlapping half; the inner segments more narrowly ovate, slightly inflexed at base and recurved near apex, with margins wavy, shouldered at base; corona funnel-shaped, smooth, brilliant greenish yellow 4A, paler at base, lightly frilled, with rim rolled and crenate and sometimes notched or split. Early. 2n=28. AM(e) 1934, FCC(e) 1939, *AM(g) 1947

'Brusa'
(The Brodie of Brodie, c.1927)
'Bernardino' × 'Sunstar'

'Brussels' 1 W-W
(J.L. Richardson, pre-1945)
'Ledbury' × 'Broughshane'
Fl. pure white; perianth segments very broadly ovate, blunt, only very slightly mucronate, spreading, plane, of great substance, overlapping one-third to a half; the inner segments more narrowly ovate, a little inflexed, with margins wavy and sometimes nicked; corona funnel-shaped, smooth, with rim rolled and crenate. Early to mid-season. 2n=28

'Brutus' 1 Y-YWW
(Barr & Sons, pre-1913)

'Brutus' 2 Y-? (a)
(H. Homan & Co., c.1931)

'Bryan' 1 W-? (b)
(Trenoweth Valley Flower Farm, pre-1952)

'Bryanston' 2 Y-Y
(J.W. Blanchard) J.W. Blanchard, 1977
'Ormeau' × 'Saint Keverne'; sdlg no. 64/12A
Fl. 95-100 mm wide; perianth segments broadly ovate in outline, blunt or rounded at apex, brilliant yellow 7A, with slight white mucro, spreading, plane, overlapping half; the inner segments a little inflexed; corona funnel-shaped, lightly ribbed, vivid yellow 12A, mouth straight, a little frilled, with rim boldly crenate and very slightly flanged. Early. PC(e) 1976, AM(e) 1978, FCC(e) 1982, *AM(g) 1987

'Bryce Canyon' 2 W-P

(Sidney DuBose, 1975) Sidney DuBose, 1990
'Accent' × 'Salmon Trout'; sdlg no. A4-4
Fl. 100 mm wide. Mid-season

'Bryda' 3 W-? (b)
(J.T. Gray, pre-1938)

'Bryden' 3 W-? (b)
(J.T. Gray, pre-1937)

'Bryher' 2 Y-? (a)
(Trenoweth Valley Flower Farm, pre-1937)

'Bryher' 3 W-GWW
(R.V. Favell, pre-1939)
'Silver Coin' × 'Raeburn'
Fl. white; perianth segments very broadly ovate, blunt, prominently mucronate, spreading or a little reflexed, sometimes concave at apex or with margins minutely incurling, overlapping half; the inner segments inconspicuously mucronate, a little inflexed, with margins wavy; corona bowl-shaped, small, closely ribbed, with green at base, mouth split in places and overlapping, frilled. 2n=28

'Bryn Apricot' 2 W-O
(J. Douglas, pre-1927)
Perianth segments white; corona tightly ribbed, creamy apricot. Mid-season

'Bryn Ellen' 2 (b or c)
(W.A. Watts, pre-1935)
'El Oro' × 'Twinkle'

'Bryn Orange' 2 Y-? (a)
(W.A. Watts, pre-1936)
'Estelle' × 'Fortune'

'Bubbity' 6 W-GPP
(M.J. Ward) M.J. Ward, 1986
'Roseworthy' × 'Foundling'; sdlg no. 76.10.2
Perianth segments reflexed; corona long cup-shaped, pale pink, with green at base and deep coral pink at rim. Mid-season

'Bubbles' 2 Y-R
(C.O. Fairbairn) L.M. Saunders, 1960
'Marksman' × 'Carbineer' sdlg
Perianth segments intense yellow; corona short, intense red

'Bucca' 1 Y-Y
(A. Gray) A. Gray, 1959
Fl. 51 mm wide, golden yellow; perianth segments narrow. Mid-season

'Buccaneer' 2 W-Y
(G.H. Engleheart, pre-1908)
Perianth segments of stiff substance, overlapping; corona large, straight-sided, ribbed, bright yellow.
Varies between Divs 2 and 1

'Buccaneer' 2 Y-Y
(J.N. Hancock & Co., 1970) Unregistered
Corona with rim flanged. Tall. Early

'Bucene' 1 Y-Y
(R.H. Bath, pre-1929)

'Buchan' 1 Y-Y
(Jackson's Daffodils) Jackson's Daffodils, 1991
'Baradoc' × sdlg 3/74; sdlg no. 32/83
Fl. 97 mm wide, vivid yellow 9A; perianth segments broadly ovate, blunt; corona cylindrical, narrow, with mouth straight and slightly frilled. Early

'Bucharest' 2 Y-? (a)
(M.P. Williams, pre-1945)

'Buckland Beauty' 1 W-? (b)
(M.H. Tribe, pre-1937)

'Buckland Boy' 2 Y-? (a)
(M.H. Tribe, pre-1937)

'Buckland Pride' 2 Y-? (a)
(M.H. Tribe, pre-1937)

'Buckland Queen' 2 Y-? (a)
(M.H. Tribe, pre-1937)

'Buckland's Gloaming' 2 W-YYO
(pre-1937)
Perianth segments white; corona lemon, with a broad band of apricot at rim

'Buckland's Yellow Wonder' 1 Y-Y
(L. Buckland, pre-1930)
Fl. dark golden yellow; perianth segments overlapping; corona broad, ribbed, with rim rolled

'Bucklaw' 2 W-Y
(de Graaff Bros, pre-1948)
Perianth segments white; corona sulphur yellow.
AM(Haarlem) 1948

'Bucklen' 2 Y-? (a)
(A. Overton) A. Overton, 1960

'Buckler' 2 W-ORR
(P.D. Williams, pre-1943)

'Buckram' 3 W-? (b)
(P.D. Williams, pre-1910)

'Buckskin' 2 Y-Y
(Murray W. Evans) Murray W. Evans, 1973
'Green Island' × 'Foggy Dew'
Fl. 87 mm wide

'Budock Bells' 5 W-W
(R.A.Scamp) R.A.Scamp, 1995
'Broomhill' × *N. triandrus*; sdlg no. S98
Fl. up to three per stem, 90 mm wide, chalky white, facing down; perianth segments narrow, slightly reflexed, smooth, overlapping; corona cup-shaped, with rounded sides, smooth, with rim neatly crenate. Dwarf. Mid-season to late. With occasional secondary stems

'Buff'
(L. Buckland, pre-1922)
FCC(g) 1922

'Buffalo' 2 W-? (b)
(C.E. Radcliff, 1933)

'Buffawn' 7 Y-Y
(G.E. Morrill, 1961) G.E. Morrill, 1977
Unknown × *N. jonquilla*; sdlg no. 55-5-6
Fls 1-3 per stem, 75 mm wide; perianth segments very broadly ovate, mucronate, light yellow 18B, spreading or a little inflexed, with margins incurling, overlapping half; the inner segments with margins more strongly incurved; corona funnel-shaped, smooth, of a much darker tone (14C) than the perianth, mouth widely and shallowly lobed, straight or a little expanded, rim almost entire. Mid-season. Scented

'Buff Beauty' 2 W-PPY
(Oregon Bulb Farms, pre-1946)

'Buffcoat' 2 W-? (b)
(W.B. Hartland, pre-1913)

'Buffcoat' 2 W-Y
(C.E. Radcliff, pre-1936)

'Buff Cup' 2 W-Y
(C.E. Radcliff, 1929)
'Czarina' hybrid

'Buffette' 1 W-W
(C.E. Radcliff, 1933)
'Buff Cup' × 'Renown'

'Buff Lady' 2 W-?Y
(C. Goodson, pre-1938)
Perianth segments white; corona opening buff, becoming darker in tone. PC(e)(NZ) 1942

'Buffo' 2 W-? (b)
(C. Goodson, 1933) Parr's Nurseries, 1958

'Buff Orpington' 2 W-? (b or c)
(G.H. Johnstone, pre-1959) Unregistered
'White Sentinel' hybrid

'Buff Princess' 2 W-? (b)
(Mrs A.O. Meyrick, pre-1949)

'Buff Queen' 2 W-?Y
(D.V. West, pre-1931)
Perianth segments white; corona buff, frilled

'Buffy' 2 W-? (b)
(P.D. Williams, pre-1948)

'Bugee' 2 Y-O
(J.L. Richardson, pre-1937)

'Buggleskelly' 9 W-GYO
(N.H. Anglo) N.H. Anglo, 1986
'Felindre' × 'Cantabile'
Perianth segments white; corona yellow, shading to green at base, with scarlet-orange at rim, neatly dentate. Late

'Bugle Call' 1 Y-Y
(G. Lewis) D.S. Bell, 1955

'Bugle Major' 2 Y-Y
(A.J.R. Pearson) A.J.R. Pearson, 1994
'Arctic Gold' × sdlg 70-10-C16 ('Fine Gold' self pollinated); sdlg no. 88-5-K19
Fl. forming a double triangle, 115 mm wide; perianth segments very broadly ovate, acute, vivid yellow 9A, spreading, plane, velvet smooth and of great substance, overlapping half; the inner segments only a little narrower; corona cylindrical, lightly ribbed, orange-yellow (14B), with mouth lightly flared, rim flanged and crenate. Early

'Bugler' 1 Y-Y
(G.P. Haydon, pre-1908)

'Bugler Dunne' 3 W-? (b)
(W.B. Hartland, pre-1907)

N. bujei Fernández Casas = *N. hispanicus* var. *bujei*

'Buka' 1 Y-Y
(J.N. Hancock & Co., pre-1974) Unregistered
Fl. deep gold; corona rim tightly frilled

'Bulbarrow' 2 Y-Y
(J.W. Blanchard) J.W. Blanchard, 1985
'Camelot' × 'Golden Aura'; sdlg no. 71/19A
Fl. yellow; perianth segments very broadly ovate, rounded at apex, with slight white mucro, spreading, plane, overlapping half; the inner segments inflexed at base, recurved at apex, with margins somewhat wavy; corona deep bowl-shaped, rim obscurely crenate. Late. Resembles a taller and smoother 'Camelot'

***N. bulbocodium* Linnaeus 13 Section Bulbocodium.** AGM 1994
   subsp. *albidus* Emberger & Maire = *N. romieuxii* subsp. *albidus*.
   subsp. ***bulbocodium*** ("Hoop Petticoat Daffodil", "Medusa's Trumpet", "Trompette de

Meduse")
   var. *bulbocodium*
   var. *citrinus* Baker ('Citrinus'). FCC 1886
   var. *conspicuus* (Haworth) Baker
   var. *ectandrus* Barra & López
   var. *filifolius* (Roemer) hort. = variant of
       N. bulbocodium subsp. *bulbocodium*.
       AM(a) 1946
   var. *genuinus* Maire
   var. *graellsii* (Webb) Baker
   var. *nivalis* (Graells) Baker
   var. *pallidus* (Gattinger & Weiller) Maire &
       Weiller
   var. *serotinus* (Haworth) A.Fernandes
   var. *tenuifolius* (Salisbury) Baker
   subsp. *citrinus* (Baker) Fernández Casas = *N.
       bulbocodium* var. *citrinus*
   subsp. *monophyllus* (Durieu de Maisonneuve)
       Maire = *N. cantabricus* subsp.
       monophyllus
   subsp. *obesus* (Salisbury) Maire = *N. obesus*
   subsp. *praecox* Gattinger & Weiller
     var. *praecox* (*eu-praecox* in Maire)
     var. *paucinervis* Maire
   subsp. *quintanilhae* A.Fernandes
   subsp. *romieuxii* (Braun-Blanquet & Maire)
       Emberger & Maire = *N. romieuxii*
   subsp. *tananicus* Maire = *N. cantabricus* subsp.
       tananicus
   subsp. *vulgaris* (Coutinho) Maire = *N. bulbocodi
       um* subsp. *bulbocodium*

'Bulgaria' 8 Y-O
(G. van der Weyden Jobson, pre-1914)
Perianth segments pale yellow; corona large, rich orange. AM(Haarlem) 1914

'Bulla' 1 W-Y
(H.A. Brown, 1940)

'Bulldog' 1 Y-Y
(The Brodie of Brodie, c.1907)
'Emperor' × 'Mrs F.W.Burbidge'
Perianth segments creamy, of good substance; corona broad, deep yellow

'Bulley' 2 Y-O
(Konynenburg & Mark, 1963) Konynenburg & Mark, 1977
Fl. 95 mm wide; perianth segments light greenish yellow 4B or C; corona vivid orange 28B. Early

'Bullfinch' 3 W-YYO
(G.H. Engleheart, pre-1900)
Fl. symmetrical, of good substance; perianth segments opening lemon yellow, becoming white, overlapping; corona yellow, with a broad band of reddish orange at rim, crenate

'Bullion' 1 Y-Y

(G.L. Wilson, pre-1926)
Fl. golden yellow; corona frilled. Tall. AM(Haarlem) 1926

'Bull's Eye' 8 Y-Y
(R.A. van der Schoot, pre-1923)
Poetaz
Fl. rounded; perianth segments primrose yellow; corona soft orange-yellow

'Bullseye' 3 W-R
(F.E. Board) M.J. Jefferson-Brown, 1975
Perianth segments ivory white

'Bulolo' 2 Y-? (a)
(J.T. Gray, pre-1937)

'Bulwark' 1 Y-Y
(The Brodie of Brodie, pre-1923)
'Ben Alder' × 'Cleopatra'
AM(Haarlem) 1935

'Bunchie' 5 W-W
(H.R. Barr) H.R. Barr, 1972
'Interim' × *N. triandrus* var. *loiseleurii*
Fl. 90 mm wide

'Bunclody' 2 Y-O
(J.S.B. Lea) J.S.B. Lea, 1963
'Revelry' × Richardson sdlg 106 ('Nanking' × 'Ambergate')
Fl. 90 mm wide; perianth segments vivid yellow 9B, with margins incurved, overlapping; corona ribbed, between strong orange 25A and a darker tone (28B), paling towards base, mouth slightly expanded, with rim crenate. Mid-season. *AM(g) 1985

'Bunco' 2 Y-YYR
(Barr & Sons, pre-1954)

'Buncrana' 2 W-O
(J.L. Richardson, pre-1938)
'Carbineer' × 'Porthilly' or 'Therapia' × 'Lidcot'
Fl. 45 mm wide; perianth segments broadly ovate, slightly mucronate, smooth, regular, overlapping half; the inner segments more narrowly ovate, shouldered at base; corona nasturtium orange, paling to base, mouth expanded and closely ribbed, with rim dentate. 2n=28. PC 1941, AM(e) 1942

'Bundarra' 2 W-R
(W.M. Spry, pre-1975) Unregistered
'Jean Hood' hybrid
Corona orange-red

'Bundle of Pink' 4 W-P
(D.S.Bell, 1982) M.J.Brown, 1995
Fl. 95 mm wide; perianth and other petaloid segments broadly ovate, yellowish white 155D; corona segments half as long, clustered at centre, light

yellowish pink 38D, frilled. Mid-season

'Bundoran' 2 W-O
(J.L. Richardson, pre-1945)
'Therapi' × 'Red Sun'
Perianth segments very broadly ovate, blunt, prominently mucronate, spreading, a little concave, of thick substance, overlapping half; the inner segments only slightly narrower, square-shouldered at base, somewhat inflexed; corona funnel-shaped, lightly ribbed, warm pinkish orange, with mouth straight, frilled. Mid-season

'Bundy' 1 W-P
(Jackson's Daffodils) Jackson's Daffodils, 1986
Sdlg 74/70 × 'Verran'; sdlg no. 80/78
Perianth segments greenish white (155A); corona light yellowish pink 27A. Mid-season

'Bunfighter' 2 Y-R
(David Adams) David Adams, 1994
'Air Marshal' × 'Bunclody'; sdlg no. 84/105C
Fl. forming a double triangle, 142 mm wide; perianth segments ovate, acute, golden yellow, plane, very smooth, slightly overlapping; corona cylindrical, smooth, with mouth straight. Late. Sunproof. Resembles 'Bunclody' but with a paler perianth without nicks

'Bungana' 1 Y-Y
(C.E. Radcliff, 1938) J.M.Radcliff, 1956
'The Gift' × 'Golden Legend'
Fl. golden yellow. Early

'Bunillidh Beauty' 2 W-O
(D.C. MacArthur) D.C. MacArthur, 1992
'Preamble' × 2 W-O; sdlg no. EV717
Fl. 121 mm wide; perianth segments triangular in appearance, greenish white (155A), spreading, glistening, of good substance, overlapping; corona narrowly funnel-shaped, angled, orange (17C), with a deeper tone (23A) at base, mouth flared and lobed, rim flanged and crenate. Early. Sunproof

'Bunker Hill' 2 W-YYO
(Warnaar & Co., pre-1935)
AM(Haarlem) 1935

'Bunnies' 5 W-W
(C.A. Nethercote, 1931) T. Morrison, 1961
Fls. usually 2 per stem, pure white; perianth segments slightly reflexed

'Bunny' 3 W-? (b)
(J. Bankhead, pre-1950)

'Bunt' 3 W-W
(Alfred Clark) Alfred Clark, 1955

'Bunthorne' 9 W-?
(F.H. Chapman, pre-1913)

'Bunting' 7 Y-O
(G.E. Mitsch, 1953) G.E. Mitsch, 1965
'Narvik' × *N. jonquilla*; sdlg no. 060/9
Fls 2 per stem, 75 mm wide; perianth segments broadly ovate, rich golden yellow, with white mucro, spreading, concave or with margins incurling, ribbed, overlapping one-third to a half; the inner segments more narrowly ovate, with margins more deeply rolled; corona smooth, orange, mouth straight, very broadly and shallowly lobed, wavy, with rim entire. Mid-season. 2n=22. Resembles a smoother and stronger 'Kinglet'

'Bunyarra' 1 Y-Y
(R. Hyde) R. Hyde, 1959

'Bunyip' 2 W-YYO
(J.N.Hancock & Co., 1983) J.N.Hancock & Co., 1997
Sdlg 72/77H × 'Artist's Model'; sdlg no. 112/83H
Fl. rounded; perianth segments broadly ovate, plane; corona bright orange, with rim regularly crenate. Mid-season

'Buoyant' 2 W-? (b)
(pre-1931)
AM(Haarlem) 1930

'Bura' 2 W-W
(A.O. Roblin, 1944) A.O. Roblin, 1956
'Veronique' × 'Slemish'

'Burbage' 1 Y-Y
(F.E. Board) F.E. Board, 1965
'Kingscourt' × 'Wexford'; sdlg no. B/342
Mid-season

'Burbidgei' 3 W-YYR
(E. Leeds, pre-1877)
(*N.* × *incomparabilis* × *N. poeticus*) × *N. poeticus*
Perianth segments broadly ovate or roundish, prominently mucronate, rich yellow, a little inflexed, with margins incurling, overlapping one-third; the inner segmenst more strongly inflexed; corona small bowl-shaped, yellow, with orange-red at rim. Early. Syn. Burbidgei 'Burbidgei'. This has also been used as a Group name

'Burdett' 2 W-Y
(E. Leeds, pre-1877)
Syn. Incomparabilis Albus 'Burdett'

'Burfa' 2 Y-? (a)
(A.M. Wilson, pre-1950)

'Burgage Hill' 2 W-P
(Mrs J. Abel Smith) Mrs J. Abel Smith, 1978
'Passionale' hybrid; sdlg no. N8/32

Fl. 90 mm wide; perianth segments broad, ice white; corona pink. Late. Resembles 'Passionale' but with more depth of colour to the corona

'Burgemeester Gouverneur' 1 Y-Y
(P. van Deursen, pre-1930)
Fl. 115 mm wide; perianth segments brilliant greenish yellow 5B, flat, of good substance, overlapping half; corona slightly ribbed, vivid yellow 12A, mouth expanded and frilled, with rim flanged and dentate. Dwarf. 2n=28. Syn. 'Mayor Gouverneur'. AM(Haarlem) 1930, FCC(Haarlem) 1938, *AM(g) 1956

'Burgemeester Oude' 2 Y-O
(pre-1951)
Perianth segments rich clear yellow; corona rich reddish orange. Resembles an improved 'Anny Virginia'

'Burgemeester Vosters' 1 Y-Y
(C.A. van der Wereld, pre-1942)

'Burgomaster Max' 1 W-Y
(Barr & Sons, pre-1927)
Perianth segments white; corona widely expanded, primrose, with rim rolled

'Burgonel' 1 W-W
(G.H. Engleheart, pre-1916)

'Burgundy' 2 Y R
(G. Lewis) D.S. Bell, 1955
Perianth segments deep golden yellow; corona very slightly expanded, dark red, frilled

'Burlette' 2 W-Y
(Konynenburg & Mark) Konynenburg & Mark, 1960
('Carolina' × 'Geranium') × 'Sempre Avanti'
Fl. 100 mm wide; corona saffron yellow. Mid-season

'Burley Bushes' 2 Y-O
(W.A. Noton) W.A. Noton, 1976
'Craigywarren' × 'Kilmorack'; sdlg no. 357
Fl. 86 mm wide. Mid-season

'Burlington' 2 W-O
(R.O. Backhouse, pre-1935)
Perianth segments pure white, slightly stained sulphur at base, spreading; corona large, expanded, reddish orange, frilled

'Burma' 2 W-? (b)
(R.O. Backhouse, pre-1921)

'Burma' 2 Y-O
Syn. of 'Dakar'

'Burma Girl' 2 Y-? (a)
(Mrs P.M. Davis, pre-1948)

'Burma Star' 2 Y-GYO
(Carncairn Daffodils) Carncairn Daffodils, 1984
'Vulcan' × 'Spelter'; sdlg no. W19/5
Fl. 92 mm wide; perianth segments deep yellow; corona bright orange, paling to a narrow zone of yellow near base, with green at base. Mid-season

'Burndale' 1 W-W
(J.N. Hancock & Co.) J.N. Hancock & Co., 1955
Fl. becoming almost white

'Burnet' 2 Y-? (a)
(P.D. Williams, pre-1927)
'Beacon' × 'Tamerlane'

'Burnett' 2 Y-O
(pre-1927)
Perianth segments yellow; corona reddish orange

'Burnette' 2 W-W
(L.P. Brumley, c.1948)
Perianth segments white, smooth and of strong substance; corona opening lemon yellow, becoming white

'Burnham' 5 W-W
(W.A. Grace, pre-1927)
Late

'Burnia'
(G. Lewis, pre 1940)

'Burnica' 2 Y-? (a)
(B. Rowlands, pre-1938)

'Burnie' 2 W-R
(C.E. Radcliff, 1942) J.M.Radcliff, 1956
'Cheerio' × 'Blodwen'

'Burning Bush' 3 Y-R
(Brian S. Duncan) Rathowen Daffodils, 1987
('Richhill' × 'Bunclody') × ('Altruist' × 'Ulster Bank'); sdlg no. 982
Fl. rounded; perianth segments very broad, truncate, prominently mucronate, deep golden yellow, spreading, of heavy substance, overlapping half; the inner segments roundish, very slightly mucronate, creased at midrib; corona very shallow bowl-shaped, deep red. Mid-season. Resembles a taller and larger 'Ulster Bank' of deeper colouring

'Burning Heart' 11b Y-O/Y
(J.W.A. Lefeber) J.W.A. Lefeber, 1958
Perianth segments very broadly ovate, rounded at apex, prominently mucronate, creamy yellow, spreading, somewhat concave, overlapping half or more; the inner segments square-shouldered at base, sometimes distorted or curled at shoulder; corona split to base, the six segments half as long as the perianth segments and alternate to them, ovate, sometimes truncate or

bi-lobed, ribbed, orange at base and in a tapering band at midrib, the orange paling to yellow in the upper half and flanked by broad patches of creamy yellow, spreading, with margins wavy and tightly incurled. AM(Haarlem) 1962

'Burning Torch' 2 Y-O
(J.L. Richardson) Mrs H.K. Richardson, 1967
'Cambodia' × 'Vulcan'
Fl. 90 mm wide; perianth segments deep yellow; corona reddish orange. Early

'Burnished Gold' 1 Y-Y
(J.L. Richardson) J.L. Richardson, 1956
('Royalist' × 'Crocus') × 'Goldcourt'
Fl. rounded, deep yellow; perianth segments broadly ovate, rounded or truncate at apex, spreading, overlapping half; the inner segments only a little more narrowly ovate; corona funnel-shaped, with rim dentate and slightly rolled

'Burns' 9 W-?
(G.H. Engleheart, pre-1907)

'Burntollet' 1 W-W
(J.S.B. Lea, 1962) R. Sterling, 1974
'Empress of Ireland' × 'Glenshesk'
Fl. white; perianth segments very broadly ovate, blunt, fairly prominently mucronate, spreading, smooth, overlapping half; the inner segments a little inflexed, with margins wavy; corona funnel shaped, smooth, with mouth flared and even, rim obscurely crenate. Mid-season. 2n=28

'Burpham' 2 Y-? (a)
(Sir F.C. Stern, pre-1950)

'Burradoo' 1 W-Y
(W.M. Spry, pre-1975) Unregistered
Hunter's Moon' × 'Prince'
Corona lemon yellow

'Burrator' 3 W-YYR
(pre-1969) Unregistered

'Burwood' 1 W-Y
(H.A. Brown, pre-1938)

'Bushfire' 2 Y-O
(S.A. Free) S.A. Free, 1961
Fl. 90 mm wide; perianth segments bright yellow; corona reddish orange. Mid-season. Resembles an improved 'Dunkeld'. PC(e)(NZ) 1960

'Bushido' 1 W-? (b)
(W. Welchman, pre-1910)

'Bushmills' 3 W-YYO
(W.J. Dunlop) W.J. Dunlop, 1961
'Portrush' × 'Foggy Dew'

Perianth segments pure white; corona yellow, with a narrow band of pinkish orange at rim. 2n=28

'Bush Queen' 2 W-W
(J.N. Hancock & Co., 1949) J.N. Hancock & Co., 1960
Corona cream white, frilled

'Bushtit' 6 Y-Y
(G.E. Mitsch) G.E. Mitsch, 1960
'Mite' open pollinated; sdlg no. AN11/1
Fl. star-shaped, 70 mm wide, clear yellow. Midseason. 2n=21. Resembles a taller and larger-flowered 'Mite' with the perianth segments less strongly reflexed

'Buster' 2 Y-? (a)
(Barr & Sons, pre-1954)

'Busy Body' 2 Y-Y
(J.N. Hancock & Co., 1970) Unregistered

'Busy Lizzie' 1 Y-Y
(J.N. Hancock & Co., 1978) Unregistered

'Buteo' 7 Y-Y
(E.C. Powell) Mrs G. Link, 1973
Fl. 60 mm wide

'Butta' 2 Y-Y
(W. Jackson Sr, 1943)
'Gisavia' × 'Hymyr'

'Butter and Egg' 4 Y-O
Syn. of 'Butter and Eggs'

'Butter and Eggs' 4 Y-O
(pre-1777)
Perianth and other petaloid segments in several whorls, broadly ovate, blunt, yellow; the outer whorl spreading, with margins wavy, separated; the inner whorls only a little shorter and narrower, inflexed, or at centre strongly inflexed, with margins incurled; corona segments interspersed, very short, broad, orange, or sometimes more nearly yellow. Syn. 'Poached Egg', ?'Golden Phoenix', ?'Golden Rose', ?'Golden Rose', 'Incomparable', 'Luteo-aurantius', 'Queltia Plene', 'Yellow Phoenix', Incomparabilis 'Aurantius Plenus', Incomparabilis 'Fl. Pl. Aur. & Lut.'

'Butter Ball' 2 Y-Y
(W.B. Blanden)

'Butter Bowl' 2 Y-Y
(G.L. Wilson, pre-1931)
'Leontes' × 'Seahorse'
Perianth segments lemon yellow; corona expanded, pale buttercup yellow. Mid-season. *HC(g) 1936

'Butterboy' 1 Y-Y
(R.H. Bath, pre-1927)

'Buttercup' 7
(G.H. Engleheart, pre-1890)
2n=21

'Buttercup' 2 Y-Y
(C. Dawson, pre-1906)
Hybrid between 'Emperor' and *N. × odorus*
Fl. rich deep yellow; perianth segments broadly ovate, blunt, mucronate, spreading or slightly reflexed, with margins wavy, of heavy substance, overlapping one-third to a half; the inner segments with margins incurving or more strongly wavy; corona cylindrical, angled or loosely ribbed, mouth flared and lightly frilled, rim almost entire. Scented. AM 1908. Varies between Divs 2 and 1

'Buttercup' 1 Y-Y
(W.B. Hartland, pre-1907)
Dwarf. Early. Resembles a paler *N. obvallaris*

'Butterflower' 2 Y-Y
(G.E. Mitsch) G.E. Mitsch, 1974
'Alchemy' × 'Butterscotch'; sdlg no. A2/1
Fl. 105 mm wide, soft deep yellow; perianth segments broadly ovate; corona somewhat narrow. Mid-season

'Butterfly' 1 W-W
(W.B. Hartland, pre-1890)
?Syn. of 'Bishop Mann'

'Butterfly' 4 ?W-Y
(pre-1904)
Perianth and other petaloid segments narrow, acute; corona segments interspersed, pale yellow. Syn. 'Double Stella'

'Butterfly' 5 W-Y
(D. & J.W. Blanchard) M.J. Jefferson-Brown, 1968
Fl. 75-100 mm wide; perianth segments white; corona primrose yellow. Mid-season

'Butter King' 1 Y-Y
(S.J. Bisdee, 1941)
'Pilgrimage' × 'Fahan'
2n=28

'Butterlaw' 1 Y-Y
(G. Harrison) G. Harrison, 1968
'Moonstruck' × 'Kingscourt'
Fl. 114 mm wide; perianth segments golden yellow; corona darker in tone. Mid-season

'Butter Mac' 7 Y-Y
(Australian or New Zealand origin, *c.*1927)
Corona large, tightly ribbed. Early. Resembles an improved 'Buttercup'

'Buttermere Lake' 2 W-Y
(Clive Postles, 1985) Clive Postles Daffodils, 1995
Sdlg 1-17-74 × 'Irish Mist'; sdlg no. 1-137-79
Perianth segments broadly ovate, very smooth; corona cylindrical in lower half, flared towards mouth, clear butter yellow, with mouth wavy. Mid-season

'Buttermilk' 2 Y-? (a)
(Cartwright & Goodwin, pre-1910)

'Buttermilk' 4 W-Y
(W.F.M. Copeland, pre-1936)
Perianth and other petaloid segments acute, creamy white; corona segments a quarter the length of the petaloid segments, buffy sulphur yellow. Mid-season. 2n=28. *HC(g) 1936

'Butter Queen' 2 Y-Y
(pre-1965) Unregistered

'Butterscotch' 2 Y-Y
(G.E. Mitsch) G.E. Mitsch, 1962
'Golden Torch' × 'Galway'; sdlg no. 29/1
Fl. 120 mm wide, deep golden yellow; perianth segments plane, very smooth; corona flared and tightly frilled. Mid-season. 2n=28. Resembles a larger-flowered 'Galway' of darker colour

'Butterwells' 1 Y-Y
(J.S. Parker, pre-1927)

'Butterworth' 2
(W.B. Hartland, pre-1914)

'Buttery' 2 Y-Y
(W.M. Spry, pre-1975) Unregistered
'Ferny Creek' × 'Tarago'
Fl. rich yellow. Tall. Late

'Butticion'
(G. Lewis, pre-1940)

'Button' 3 Y-? (a)
(Mrs R.O. Backhouse, pre-1921)

'Buttonhole' 11a W-Y
(Dutch origin, pre-1923)
'Victoria' sport
Perianth segments ovate, inflexed, separated; corona split to base, with the six segments exceeding the perianth segments in size and opposite and closely overlying them, lightly ribbed, very deeply bi-lobed, with the lobes overlapping, loosely frilled. 2n=22. Syn. 'Orchid'

'Buttress' 1 Y-Y
(G.L. Wilson, pre-1927)
Resembles a later-flowered and slightly deeper-coloured 'Bulwark'

'Buxted' 1 Y-Y
(G.P. Haydon, pre-1919)
Fl. golden yellow. AM 1919

'Buxton' 1 W-W
(D.B. Milne, pre-1950)

N. × ***buxtonii*** **Richter 13** = *N. abscissus* (Haworth) Roemer & Schultes f. × *N. assoanus* Dufour

'Buzalong' 2 Y-?
(W.M. Spry, pre-1975) Unregistered
'Green Island' × 'Hunter's Moon'
Corona with green at rim. Late

'Buzzard' 2 W-? (b)
(M.P. Williams, pre-1949)

'By George' 2 Y-Y
(J.N. Hancock & Co., 1947)

'By George' 2 YYW-YPW
(Murray W. Evans) Unregistered

'By Jove' 1 Y-Y
(M.J. Jefferson-Brown) M.J. Jefferson-Brown, 1968
Fl. deep golden yellow. Mid-season

'Bylgia' 1 Y-Y
(W.F. Leenen) W.F. Leenen, 1978
Perianth segments light greenish yellow (4D); corona much darker in tone (7C)

'By Line' 1 Y-Y
Syn. of 'Byline'

'Byline' 1 Y-Y
(J.N. Hancock & Co., 1963) Unregistered
See also 'By Line'

'Byram' 1 Y-Y
(T.H. Piper) T.H. Piper, 1956
'Bungana' × 'Roundabout'

'Byron' 9 W-?
(A.M. Wilson, pre-1908)

'Byron' 9 W-?
(G.H. Engleheart, pre-1927)

'Byton' 2 W-? (b)
(A.M. Wilson, pre-1950)

N. byzantinus hort. = *N. tazetta* subsp. *lacticolor*

C

'Caballero' 1 W-? (b)
(J.L. Richardson, pre-1931)

'Caballero' 4 W-O
(J.L. Richardson) Mrs H.K. Richardson, 1973
'Gay Time' × 'Rainbow'
Perianth and other petaloid segments in several whorls, creamy white, overlapping; corona segments interspersed, smaller, reddish orange

'Cabana' 2 Y-Y
(D.S. Bell) D.S. Bell, 1959
Fl. 102 mm wide; perianth segments broad, rounded

'Cabaret' 2
(pre-1923)

'Cabaret' 2 W-? (b)
(G. Lewis, 1945) D.S. Bell, 1958

'Cabeceiras' 1 W-Y
(Portuguese origin)
Selection by A.W. Tait (*c.*1893) from wild-collected *N.* × *johnstonii*
Perianth segments white, sometimes becoming tinted with primrose yellow; corona rich yellow, frilled

'Caber' 1 W-? (b)
(G.H. Engleheart, pre-1916)

'Cabernet' 2 W-GPP
(Brian S. Duncan) Brian S. Duncan, 1996
'Fragrant Rose' × 'Pol Dornie'; sdlg no. 1516
Fl. forming a double triangle, 105 mm wide; perianth segments broadly ovate, pure white; the inner segments more narrowly ovate, more nearly acute; corona funnel-shaped, slightly ribbed, deep apricot or watermelon pink, with deep green at base and a slightly paler pink at rim, frilled. Mid-season to late

'Cabochon' 2 Y-O
(Murray W. Evans, 1976) Estella L. Evans, 1989
'Carnelian' × 'Falstaff'; sdlg no. T-9
Fl. 90 mm wide; perianth segments golden yellow; corona flared, orange, with rim dentate. Very early

'Cabra' 1 Y-Y
(Carncairn Daffodils) Carncairn Daffodils, 1979
'Kingscourt' × 'Prince Igor'; sdlg no. 159
Fl. 102 mm wide; perianth segments brilliant yellow 7B; corona of a slightly deeper tone (9A). Mid-season. Resembles a smoother 'Prince Igor' with the perianth segments more deeply overlapping

'Cachalot'
(C. Dawson, pre-1907)

'Cacian' 2 W-? (b)
(A.H. Ahrens) J.S. Leitch, 1955

'Cadella' 2 W-Y
(H.A. Brown, 1943)
'Niphetos' × 'Hades'
Perianth segments white, spreading, overlapping; corona long, buffy cheese-coloured. Mid-season

'Cadena' 1 Y-Y
(D. van Egmond & Sons) D. van Egmond & Sons, 1958

'Cadence' 3 W-GYO
(G.E. Mitsch) G.E. Mitsch, 1958
'Galata' × 'Tuskar Light'
Corona yellow, with green at base and reddish orange at rim, broadly crenate

'Cadenza' 9 W-?
(F.H. Chapman, pre-1914)

'Cadfer' 1 W-Y
(Barr & Sons, pre-1920)
Perianth segments slightly twisted; corona long, lemon yellow

'Cadgwith' 2 W-WWP
(R.A.Scamp) R.A.Scamp, 1996
'Rainbow' × 'Dailmanach'; sdlg no. 458
Fl. 122 mm wide; perianth segments very broadly ovate, pure white, deeply overlapping; corona funnel-shaped, becoming whitish, with bright pink at rim, mouth flared, rim neatly dentate. Mid-season to late. Sunproof

'Cadiz' 2 W-WWO
(M.E.Brogden) Unregistered

'Caduceus' 2 W-R
(J.A. Morris) J.A. Morris, 1965
Fl. 108 mm wide. Mid-season. Resembles a darker-coloured 'Arbar' with a longer corona

'Caedmon' 9 W-GYR
(G.H. Engleheart, pre-1913)
Fl. 83 mm wide; perianth segments very broad, somewhat oblong, squarish at apex and obscurely truncate, prominently mucronate, spathulate at base, white, with sulphur yellow at base, spreading, with margins sometimes wavy, overlapping half; the inner segments narrower, more obviously truncate, only very slightly mucronate, with margins more usually wavy; corona small disc-shaped, tightly ribbed, greenish yellow, with dark green at base and a well-defined band of clear dark crimson at rim. Mid-season. 2n=14. AM(Haarlem) 1913, AM 1913, FCC(e) 1915, *C(g) 1931, *C(g) 1936, *HC(g) 1939

'Caelia' 1 W-W
(The Brodie of Brodie, c.1908)
'Florence' × 'Cernuus Pulcher'

'Caerleon' 2 Y-O
(Miss G. Evelyn, pre-1933)
'Hospodar' × A.M. Wilson sdlg
Perianth segments very broad, blunt, pale primrose yellow, spreading, concave at apex, regular, overlapping one-third to a half; the inner segments more narrowly ovate, only very slightly mucronate, with margins a little wavy; corona funnel-shaped, lightly ribbed, orange, mouth straight, more strongly ribbed, even or a little wavy. AM(e) 1935

'Caerphilly' 1 W-W
(S.J. Bisdee, 1948)
'Trostan' × 'Rosemount'

'Caesar' 9 W-YYR
(G.H. Engleheart, pre-1911)
Fl. 75 mm or more wide; perianth segments very broad, round, deeply overlapping; corona large disc-shaped, greenish or lemon yellow, with orange or orange-red at rim

'Caesarine' 2 W-? (b)
(Mrs R.O. Backhouse, pre-1921)

'Caesonia' 2 W-? (b)
(A.H. Ahrens, pre-1949)
PC(e)(NZ) 1958

'Café au Lait' 11a W-Y
(J.Gerritsen & Son) Mrs E.Bullivant, 1997
Sdlg no. GBS 11
Fl. 115 mm wide; perianth segments very broadly ovate, blunt, prominently mucronate, creamy white, spreading or a little inflexed, plane, with margins incurling, creased at midrib, overlapping one-third; the inner segments narrower, more strongly inflexed, ribbed; corona split to base, the six segments two-thirds the length of the perianth segments, opposite and closely overlying them, almost the same width, deeply bi-lobed, with the lobes overlapping, light yellow 10C, with overtones of pink and with bright yellow at base, frilled; the inner corona segments inflexed and ribbed

'Cafe Royal' 4 W-P
(Brian S. Duncan) Rathowen Daffodils, 1987
Sdlg 8/74 × sdlg 346; sdlg no. 888
Perianth and other petaloid segments white; corona segments interspersed, pink. Mid-season to late

'Cahokia' 1 W-PWW
(V. Brink) V. Brink, 1970
'Tintoretto' × 'Rosy Trumpet'
Fl. 93 mm wide

'Cairhayes' 6 Y-Y
Syn. of 'Baby Doll'

'Cairhays' 6 Y-Y
Syn. of 'Baby Doll'

'Cairncairn' 3 W-? (b)
(W.J. Dunlop, pre-1947)
'Folly' × 'Sunstar'
Perianth segments white

'Cairndhu' 2 W-GPP
(Carncairn Daffodils, 1965) Carncairn Daffodils, 1975
Fl. 75 mm wide; perianth segments yellowish white 155B; corona light orange 29B, with olive green at base, frilled. Mid-season

'Cairngorm' 5 Y-Y
(The Brodie of Brodie, c.1908)
'Emperor' × *N. triandrus*
Perianth segments very broad, rounded at apex, primrose yellow; corona rich sulphur yellow, with rim slightly flanged. Mid-season

'Cairngorm'
(C.L. Adams, pre-1910)

'Cairngorm' 2 YYW-WYY
(Mrs H.K. Richardson) Mrs H.K.Richardson, 1974
Fl. 98 mm wide; perianth segments sulphur yellow, with white at base; corona opening orange-yellow, becoming sulphur yellow, with white at base and sometimes with pinkish buff at rim. Resembles a slightly larger and more star-shaped 'Amber Castle'. The predominant colour in the corona may be pinkish

'Cairntoul' 3 W-YOO
(J.S.B. Lea) J.S.B. Lea, 1978
'Merlin' × 'Rockall'; sdlg no. 2-27-67
Fl. 100 mm wide; perianth segments broad, blunt, spreading, regular, overlapping; corona ribbed, orange (28A), with brilliant yellow 10A at base, mouth expanded and frilled, rim crenate. AM(e) 1982

'Cairo' 2 W-R
(J.L. Richardson, pre-1937)
'Seraglio' × 'Red Sun'
Perianth segments milk white; corona very shallow bowl-shaped, brick red

'Caithness' 2 Y-Y
(Clive Postles) Clive Postles Daffodils, 1993
'Golden Jewel' × 'Golden Aura'; sdlg no. 4-64-80
Fl. rounded, 89 mm wide, mid-yellow; perianth segments very broadly ovate, with margins slightly incurving; corona cylindrical, with mouth lobed and rim dentate. Mid-season

'Cajanus' 1 Y-Y
(C.G. van Tubergen, pre-1914)

'Calabar' 2 W-Y
(Angus Wilson) Wallace & Barr, 1957
Perianth segments very broadly ovate, blunt, only very slightly mucronate, opening yellow-white, becoming whiter, spreading, a little concave or with margins incurling at apex, with broad midrib showing, overlapping half; the inner segments more narrowly ovate, slightly inflexed, with margins wavy; corona short funnel-shaped, lightly ribbed, pale yellow, stained orange-yellow, mouth shallowly split in places and overlapping, even, with rim flanged and crenate. AM(Haarlem) 1960

'Caland' 1 Y-Y
(G. Lubbe & Son, pre-1938)
AM(Haarlem) 1938, FCC(Haarlem) 1943

N. calathinus de Candolle = *N. triandrus* var. *loiseleurii*

N. calathinus Linnaeus = *N.* × *odorus*

N. calathinus Loiseleur-Deslongchamps = *N. triandrus* var. *loiseleurii*

'Calchas' 1 Y-Y
(A.M. Wilson, pre-1931)

***N. calcicarpetanus* Fernández Casas 13 Section Pseudonarcissus**

***N. calcicola* Mendonça 13 Section Apodanthi**

'Calcite' 2 W-GWW
(Murray W. Evans, 1972) Murray W. Evans, 1986
'Easter Moon' × 'Castle of Mey'; sdlg no. 0-31/1
Mid-season. Resembles a whiter and more vigorous 'White o' Morn' with the perianth segments more rounded

'Calcot' 2 Y-? (a)
(R.H. Bath, pre-1933)

'Calculus' 2 Y-? (a)
(R. Crews) R. Crews, 1956

'Calcutta' 3 W-O
(Mrs R.O. Backhouse, c.1920)
Perianth segments pure white; corona reddish orange.
Syn. 'Coimbatore'

'Calder Road' 2 W-Y
(Tom Forster, 1960s) Unregistered
Corona broad disc-shaped, orange-yellow. Late

'Caldron' 2 Y-R
(G.E. Mitsch) G.E. Mitsch, 1962

('Market Merry' × 'Carbineer') × 'Armada'; sdlg no. R100/1
Fl. 102 mm wide; perianth segments broad, deep golden yellow, overlapping; corona almost disc-shaped, large, vivid red. Mid-season. Resembles a later-flowered 'Armada' with shallower corona

'Caledonia' 2 W-YYO
(de Graaff Bros, pre-1931)
Perianth segments narrow, acute, cream yellow; corona shallow, widely expanded, yellow, with deep orange at rim, frilled. 2n=28. AM(Haarlem) 1931

'Calendio' 2 Y-? (a)
(Warnaar & Co., pre-1933)
AM(Haarlem) 1936

'Calendula' 2 Y-O
(Mrs R.O. Backhouse, pre-1921)
Perianth segments narrow, acute, clear yellow; corona long, dark orange. AM(Haarlem) 1930

'Caliban' 1 W-Y
(Barr & Sons, pre-1923)
Perianth segments white, tinged yellow at base; corona glowing golden yellow

'Caliban' 2 W-Y
(W. Jackson Jr) W. Jackson Jr, 1966
'Bali' × 'Tudor Minstrel'; sdlg no. 91/58
Perianth segments white; corona lemon yellow

'Calibrate' 1 Y-Y
(A. Gibson, pre-1951)

'Calicé Denté' 2 W-? (b)
(de Graaff Bros & van Konynenburg & Co., pre-1933)

'Calice Orange' 8 W-O
(pre-1798)

'Calico' 2 W-W
(H.A. Brown, 1938)
Corona creamy pink, becoming white, with mouth slightly expanded. Late

'Calicoline' 1 W-W
(R. Hyde) R. Hyde, 1963
Fl. 114 mm wide. Mid-season. Resembles a larger and whiter 'Ardclinis'

'Calif' 2 Y-? (a)
(A.M. Wilson, pre-1927)
'Hospodar' hybrid

'California' 2 Y-Y
Syn. of 'Pentewan'

'California Gold' 2 Y-O
(Barr & Sons, pre-1945)
Syn. 'Commando', 'Corsair', 'Faust'

'California Rose' 4 W-P
(Brian S. Duncan) Rathowen Daffodils, 1987
'Pink Paradise' × Bloomer 2 W-P sdlg; sdlg no. 785
Fl. 102 mm wide; perianth segments very broad, rounded at apex, very slightly mucronate, pure white, spreading, plane, overlapping half or more; the inner segments oblong, truncate; three petaloid segments at centre, white, strongly inflexed, with margins tightly rolled inwards; corona segments one-third the length of the perianth segments and loosely arranged above them, more tightly clustered among the petaloid segments at centre, deep rose pink, closely frilled. Dwarf. Mid-season

'Caligula'
(J.C. Williams, pre-1908)

'Calista' 1 Y-Y
(pre-1910)

'Callander' 2 W-GWW
(J.S.B. Lea) Clive Postles, 1992
'Misty Glen' open pollinated; sdlg no. 1-43-78
Fl. forming a double triangle, 102 mm wide, pure white; perianth segments ovate, with margins slightly incurving; corona funnel-shaped, with mouth flared and rim dentate. Very late. Resembles a later-flowered 'Misty Glen'

'Callaway' 3 W-YYO
(Carncairn Daffodils) Carncairn Daffodils, 1990
'Snow Magic' open pollinated; sdlg no. 1/9/78
Fl. 80 mm wide; perianth segments very broadly ovate, blunt, prominently mucronate, spreading, plane, overlapping half; the inner segments a little more narrowly ovate, only very slightly mucronate, with margins wavy or incurling, shouldered at base; corona yellow, with a well-defined narrow band of soft pinkish orange at rim, mouth expanded and heavily frilled, with rim dentate. Late

'Call Boy' 3 W-GYR
(P.D. Williams, pre-1929)
Perianth segments deeply overlapping; corona disc-shaped, citron yellow, with green at base and dark red at rim

'Calleen' 3 W-Y
(A.O. Roblin, 1945) A.O. Roblin, 1956
'Maid of the Mist' × 'Portia'

'Calleva' 2 W-Y
(W. Jackson Jr, 1968) Jackson's Daffodils, 1979
'Maweena' × 'Lod'; sdlg no. 180/68
Fl. 95 mm wide

'Calliope' 1 Y-Y
(N.F. Lock, pre-1944)

'Callirhoe' 1 W-W
(F.H. Chapman, pre-1923)
'Duke of Bedford' × 'Madame de Graaff'
Perianth segments white; corona sulphur white. AM(e) 1923

'Calm' 2 W-GWY
(J.A. O'More) J.A. O'More, 1968
'Chinese White' × 'Green Island'

'Calo' 2 or 3 W-? (b or c)
(pre-1949)

'Calorama' 2 W-? (b)
(de Graaff Bros, pre-1930)

'Calpurnia' 1 W-Y
(Barr & Sons, pre-1903)
Perianth segments white; corona slender, straight-sided, soft primrose yellow

'Calumet' 2 Y-? (a)
(J.W.A. Lefeber, pre-1945)

'Calvados' 2 Y-? (a)
(A.M. Wilson, pre-1931)

'Calvas Yellow' 1 Y-Y
(Spanish origin)
Selection by Peter Barr (1887) from wild-collected *N. pseudonarcissus*
Perianth segments pale yellow; corona funnel-shaped, darker in tone than the perianth, with rim regularly dentate

'Calvin Coolidge' 2 W-? (b)
(de Graaff Bros, pre-1927)

'Calypso' 2 Y-? (a)
(P.D. Williams) A.M. Williams, 1938

'Camail' 3 W-? (b)
(G.H. Engleheart, pre-1923)

'Camber' 3 W-? (b)
(F.H. Chapman, pre-1910)

'Camber' 1 Y-Y
(H.A. Brown, 1938)

'Camberwell King' 1 Y-Y
(H.A. Brown, pre-1933)
'Beersheba' × 'Golden City'

'Cambisus' 8 Y-Y
(pre-1854)
Fl. yellow. ?The same as 'Cambyses'

'Cambodia' 2 Y-? (a)
(J.L. Richardson) J.L. Richardson, 1956
'Krakatoa' × 'Sun Chariot'

'Camborne' 1 W-W
(A.Gray, pre-1985) Delia Bankhead, 1995
Fl. 42 mm wide, greenish white (155A); perianth segments spreading, almost plane, slightly ribbed, of thin texture, overlapping; corona narrow at base, slightly expanding, lightly ribbed, frilled. Dwarf. Early

'Cambrai' 3 W-? (b)
(Mrs R.O. Backhouse, pre-1921)

'Cambria' 1 Y-Y
(de Graaff Bros) de Graaff Bros, 1963
Perianth segments vivid yellow 9B; corona darker in tone (13B). Early. AM(Haarlem) 1963

'Cambric' 2 W-Y
(A.M. Wilson, pre-1915)
Corona long, pale lemon yellow, frilled

N. cambricus Haworth = *N. obvallaris*

'Cambricus' 1 W-Y
(pre-1884)
Variant of *N. obvallaris* "re-introduced" by Barr & Son
Perianth segments sulphur white. Early. Syn. Pseudonarcissus 'Cambricus'

'Cambridge' 1 Y-Y
(J. Hall, pre-1930)

'Cambridge Bell' 1 W-Y
(A. Hopkirk, pre-1927)
Perianth segments white; corona sulphur yellow

'Cambus More' 1 W-? (b)
(pre-1913)

'Cambyses' 8 W-O
(pre-1798)
?The same as 'Cambisus'

'Camden' 1 W-P
(Jackson's Daffodils, 1974) Jackson's Daffodils, 1986
Sdlg 154/66 × 'Verran'; sdlg no. 61/74
Perianth segments greenish white (155A); corona light yellowish pink 27A. Mid-season

'Camelford' 2 YYW-YPP
(T. Bloomer) du Plessis Bros, 1986
'Rose Caprice' × 'Binkie'; sdlg no. 121
Perianth segments very broadly ovate, pale greenish yellow, paler at midrib, with white at base and white mucro, spreading, a little concave, overlapping half; the inner segments slightly inflexed, shouldered at

base; corona funnel-shaped, pink, with pale yellow at base and sometimes a touch of light yellow 18A at rim, mouth expanded, frilled, with overlapping lobes, rim flanged and minutely crenate. Mid-season

'Camellia' 4 Y-Y
(Messrs van der Zalm, pre-1930)
'Emperor' sport
Fl. creamy yellow. 2n=21. See also 'Cammellia'. ?AM (Haarlem)

'Camelot' 2 W-Y
(R.H. Bath, pre-1927)

'Camelot' 2 Y-Y
(J.L. Richardson) Mrs H.K. Richardson, 1962
'Kingscourt' × 'Ceylon'
Fl. rounded, deep clear yellow; perianth segments very broadly ovate, blunt, with slight white mucro, spreading, plane, of thick substance, with broad midrib showing, overlapping half; the inner segments narrower, roundish and a little inflexed; corona funnel-shaped, lightly ribbed, with mouth flared and loosely frilled, rim regularly crenate. AGM 1995

'Camena' 2 W-W
(C.E. Radcliff, 1940) J.M.Radcliff, 1956
'Astrid' × 'Maid of the Mist'

'Cameo' 2 W-? (b)
(P.D. Williams, pre-1939)

'Cameo Angel' 2 W-WWY
(P.D.K. Ramsay) Koanga Daffodils, 1993
'Angel' × 'Immaculate'; sdlg no. PR2.85
Fl. 120 mm wide; perianth segments very broadly ovate; corona bowl-shaped, white, with yellow at rim or a tinge of orange, rim obscurely crenate. Late

'Cameo Chance' 2 Y-ORR
(P.D.K.Ramsay) Koanga Daffodils, 1996
'Red Cameo' × 'Gambler's Gift'
Fl. 115 mm wide; perianth segments ovate, plane, smooth; corona bowl-shaped, with rim crenate. Mid-season

'Cameo Gold' 1 Y-Y
(D.S. Bell) D.S. Bell, 1975
'Dawngold' × 'Gold Shower'
Fl. 106 mm wide, golden yellow; corona with rim flanged and dentate. Late. Resembles a later-flowered 'Gold Shower' with a longer corona

'Cameo King' 2 W-W
(P.D.K. Ramsay) Koanga Daffodils, 1992
'Cool Crystal' × 'Immaculate'
Fl. forming a double triangle, 115 mm wide; perianth segments ovate, plane; corona short funnel-shaped, irregularly crenate. Tall. Late

'Cameo Knight' 2 Y-O
(Koanga Daffodils) Koanga Daffodils, 1995
('Royal Charger' × 'Cinel') × 'Irish Light'
Fl. 110 mm wide; perianth segments ovate, vivid yellow 9A; corona disc-shaped, reddish orange, with a lighter tone towards base, rim crenate. Early. Sunproof

'Cameo Lord' 2 Y-R
(Koanga Daffodils, pre-1997) Unregistered

'Cameo Prince' 2 W-Y
(P.D.K. Ramsay) Koanga Daffodils, 1992
'Cool Crystal' × 'Immaculate'
Fl. forming a double triangle, 105 mm wide; perianth segments ovate, plane; corona short funnel-shaped, with rim crenate. Tall. Late

'Cameo Queen' 2 W-WPP
(G.E. Mitsch) G.E. Mitsch, 1970
('Wild Rose' × 'Interim') hybrid
Fl. small; Corona very shallow bowl-shaped, deep shell pink, with white at base

'Cameo Rim' 2 W-YYR
(P.D.K.Ramsay) Koanga Daffodils, 1996
'Crimpelene' × 'Cherryrim'
Fl. 100 mm wide; corona cup-shaped, with a broad and well-defined band of brownish pink at rim and the rim dentate. Late

'Cameo Sun' 1 Y-Y
(Koanga Daffodils) Koanga Daffodils, 1995
'Gold Tan' × 'Director'
Fl. 120 mm wide; perianth segments broadly ovate, vivid yellow 12A; corona very broad, darker in tone (13A) than the perianth, with rim flanged. Mid-season

'Cameronian' 1 W-W
(The Brodie of Brodie, c.1930)
'Thira' × 'Askelon'
Fl. 127 mm wide, pure white; perianth segments very broadly ovate, blunt or somewhat truncate, slightly mucronate, a little inflexed, of thick substance, overlapping half; the inner segments square-shouldered at base, more strongly inflexed, with margins incurved to give a narrow appearance; corona funnel-shaped, angled, mouth flared, split in places and overlapping, lightly frilled. Mid-season

'Camilla' 3 W-? (b)
(G.H. Engleheart, pre-1907)

'Camira' 3 W-O
(D. Bramley) D. Bramley, 1986
'Rockall' × 'Envoy'; sdlg no. 77/62
Perianth segments overlapping; corona orange. Mid-season. Resembles an improved 'Envoy'

'Cam Lane' 2 W-Y
(Patrick Kiernan) Patrick Kiernan, 1997
'Tudor Minstrel' × 'Gambler's Gift'; sdlg no. PK1433
Fl. 112 mm wide; perianth segments broadly ovate; corona funnel-shaped, mid-yellow, frilled. Mid-season to late

'Cammellia' 4 Y-Y
Syn. of 'Camellia'

'Camoens' 9 W-?
(Cartwright & Goodwin, pre-1916)

'Camoens' 1 W-Y
(Portuguese origin)
Selection by A.W.Tait (c.1888) from wild-collected *N. bicolor*
Perianth segments creamy white. Syn. Pseudonarcissus Bicolor 'Camoens', Pseudonarcissus Bicolor 'Lusitanicus'

'Camore' 2 W-Y
(D.C. MacArthur) D.C. MacArthur, 1985
'Braniel' × 'Rouge'; sdlg no. E8226
Perianth segments broad, blunt, mucronate, overlapping half; the inner segments narrower, with margins slightly incurved near apex and sometimes irregularly notched; corona shallow, widely expanded, lightly ribbed, vivid yellow 17C, with some white flecks at rim, neatly frilled, the rim in places deeply notched. Mid-season. Scented

'Camoro' 10 WWG-W
(H.Taylor, 1979) H.Taylor, 1994
N. cantabricus subsp. *monophyllus* × *N. romieuxii*
Fl. 35 mm wide; perianth segments creamy white, with green at base and in faint touches at midrib, slightly twisted; corona broad funnel-shaped, pale creamy white. Dwarf. Very early. PC 1995

'Camowen' 1 Y-Y
(Brian S. Duncan) Rathowen Daffodils, 1974
'Kingscourt' self pollinated
Late. 2n=28

'Campanile' 4 Y-O
(G.E. Mitsch) G.E. Mitsch, 1979
'Falaise' × 'Daydream'; sdlg no. F128/2
Fl. 102 mm wide; perianth and other petaloid segments clear lemon yellow; corona segments bright orange. Mid-season.

N. campanulatus Link = *N. triandrus* Linnaeus

'Campari' 3 W-GWR
(D.S. Bell) D.S. Bell, 1983
'Masquerade' × 'Rockall'
Perianth segments pure white; corona white, with green at base and bright red at rim

'Campernelli'
Syn. of *N.* × *odorus*

'Campfire' 3 W-? (b)
(H. Backhouse, pre-1908)

'Campfire' 2 Y-? (a)
(G.L. Wilson) G.E. Mitsch, 1956
'Market Merry' × 'Rustom Pasha'

'Camp Hill' 5 W-Y
(M.W.Spry, c.1970) Unregistered
'Beryl' × *N. triandrus* var. *concolor*
Fl. 66 mm wide; perianth segments ovate, acute, yellowish white 158C, reflexed, somewhat twisted, with margins incurled, separated at base; corona long cup-shaped, brilliant greenish yellow 7C, opening with faint orange at rim, mouth slightly expanded, even, rim crenate. Mid-season

'Campion' 9 W-GYR
(Brian S. Duncan) Rathowen Daffodils, 1980
'Milan' × 'Cantabile'; sdlg no. 504
Fl. forming a double triangle, 68 mm wide; perianth segments very broadly ovate, prominently mucronate, pure white, spreading, concave, overlapping half; the inner segments more narrowly ovate, only very slightly mucronate, with margins wavy and sometimes incurling; corona disc-shaped, ribbed, greenish yellow, with green at base and a very narrow band of red at rim, mouth even, rim minutely notched. Late. 2n=14. AM(e) 1996

'Campsie' 2 W-?
(Alister Clark) J. Sharp, 1960

'Canace' 1 W-? (b)
(W. Jackson Sr, 1935)
'Orange Warley' × 'Golden Gate'

'Canada' 1 Y-Y
(Warnaar & Co., pre-1929)

'Canadel' 3 W-GYR
(D.A. Lloyd) D.A. Lloyd, 1966
'Crete' × 'Corofin'
Fl. 76 mm wide; perianth segments blunt, reflexed, regular, overlapping; corona cup-shaped, ribbed, vivid yellow 9B, with green at base and orange-red (32A) at rim, mouth expanded, frilled, rim crenate. Late. Resembles 'Merlin' but with whiter perianth segments and a shallower corona with a narrower band of colour at rim. AM(e) 1967

'Canadense' 2 W-? (b)
(P.D. Williams, pre-1927)

'Canadian Beauty' 1 Y-Y
(J. Gerritsen & Son, pre-1931)
'King Alfred' hybrid

AM(Haarlem) 1930

N. canaliculatus Gussone = *N. tazetta* subsp. *lacticolor*

'Canaliculatus' 8 W-Y
(Barr & Sons, pre-1915)
Fls several per stem; perianth segments broadly ovate, prominently mucronate, reflexed, creased, overlapping up to one-third; corona cup-shaped, lightly ribbed, golden yellow or darker, mouth somewhat constricted, wavy, with rim entire. Dwarf. Scented

'Canape' 2 W-Y
(Murray W. Evans, 1966) Murray W. Evans, 1977
Sdlg × ('Duke of Windsor' × 'Lady Kesteven'); sdlg no. J-51
Fl. 105 mm wide; perianth segments opening white, becoming creamy; corona opening primrose yellow, becoming peachy buff. Mid-season

'Canara' 1 Y-Y
(Mrs R.O. Backhouse, pre-1921)

N. canariensis Burbidge 13 Section Tazettae

'Canary' 1 Y-Y
(P.D. Williams, pre-1907)

'Canary' 5 ?Y-Y
(Sir J.S. Arkwright, *c.*1930)

'Canary' 1 Y-Y
(G. Lubbe & Son, pre-1931)

'Canary' 7 YYW-W
(G.E. Mitsch) G.E. Mitsch, 1977
'Daydream' × *N. jonquilla*; sdlg no. F72/4

'Canary' 1 Y-Y
(C.O. Fairbairn, *c.*1977) Unregistered

'Canary Bird' 8 Y-O
(?S. Baars, pre-1913)
Perianth segments dark citron yellow; corona mid-orange

'Canarybird' 1 Y-Y
(R.H. Bath, pre-1927)
Fl. opening pale yellow, becoming pale creamy yellow; corona of a darker tone at rim. Resembles 'Citronella'

'Canarybird' 8 Y-GOO
(H. Berghuis) G. Zandbergen-Terwegen, 1959
2n=17

'Canary Eye' 3 W-? (b)
(G.H. Engleheart, pre-1923)

'Canary Lake' 1 Y-Y
(A. Overton, pre-1957) Unregistered

'Canary Queen' 3 W-Y
(C. Smith, pre-1905)
Perianth segments white; corona canary yellow, with a broad band of apricot yellow at rim

'Canasta' 11a W-Y
(J. Gerritsen & Son) J. Gerritsen & Son, 1957
Perianth segments broadly ovate, blunt, not prominently mucronate, pure white, spreading, overlapping one-third to a half; the inner segments more narrowly ovate, more nearly acute, sometimes twisted; corona split to base, the six segments two-thirds the length of the perianth segments, opposite and closely overlying them and joined at margins at base, more or less deeply bi-lobed, bright yellow, heavily frilled, with rim entire. Early. 2n=27

'Canaveral' 1 Y-Y
(J.N. Hancock & Co., 1954)

'Canberra' 8
(H. Selkirk, pre-1913)
'Adonia' × 'Yellow Trumpet'
Fls 3-4 per stem, pale yellow; corona long

'Canby' 2 W-P
(G.E. Mitsch) G.E. Mitsch, 1970
'Precedent' × 'Carita'; sdlg no. A34/11
Perianth segments broad, plane, overlapping; corona salmon pink, suffused lilac. Mid-season

'Can Can Girl' 2 W-Y
(David L. Sheppard) David L. Sheppard, 1977
'Muscadet' × 'Hillbilly'; sdlg no. 70-A-2
Fl. 100-110 mm; perianth segments very broad, blunt, only slightly mucronate, a little reflexed, overlapping half or more; the inner segments creased and with margins wavy or incurled; corona bowl-shaped, ribbed, yellow, occasionally touched white at rim, with mouth 6-lobed and densely frilled. Mid-season

'Candace' 3 W-? (a)
(P.D. Williams, pre-1908)
Perianth segments thicky creamy white; corona tightly ribbed, brightly coloured at rim

'Candace' 2 Y-Y
(P. de Jager & Sons) P. de Jager & Sons, 1963
'Binkie' × 'Pink Gem'
Fl. 95 mm wide; perianth segments light greenish yellow 4C; corona darker in tone (6B). Mid-season

'Candel Menora' 2 Y-YYO
(G.H. Rotteveel & Sons) G.H. Rotteveel & Sons, 1982
Perianth segments light greenish yellow 5C; corona brilliant yellow 13B, with light orange (24C) at rim

'Candent' 2 Y-? (a)
(de Graaff Bros, pre-1948)

N. candicans Haworth = *N. bulbocodium*

'Candid' 2
(P.D. Williams, pre-1931)

'Candida' 1 W-W
(Cartwright & Goodwin, pre-1916)

'Candida' 1 W-W
(A.H. Ahrens, pre-1946)

'Candida' 4 W-Y
(J.L. Richardson) J.L. Richardson, 1956
'Falaise' × 'Petsamo'
Fl. 105 mm wide; perianth and other petaloid segments pure white; the outer whorl very broad; the inner whorls narrower; corona segments interspersed, small, very pale primrose yellow, with a darker tone at rim. 2n=27. AM(e) 1960, AM(Haarlem) 1961, FCC(e) 1961

'Candida' 8
Syn. of 'Papillon'

'Candida Mumford' 4 W-O
(J.L. Richardson) G. Zandbergen-Terwegen, 1964
Perianth and other petaloid segments ivory white; corona segments veined with orange

'Candidata' 3 W-? (b or c)
(J. Mallender, pre-1913)

'Candidate' 3 W-? (b or c)
(Miss K.M. Hinchliff, pre-1933)

N. candidissimus Redouté = *N. moschatus*

'Candleglow' 2 Y-YYP
(P. & G. Phillips) P. & G. Phillips, 1979
Fl. 102 mm wide, pale yellow; corona with pale pink at rim. Mid-season

'Candle-Light' 3 W-GWY
(G.L. Wilson, pre-1935)
'Alburnia' × 'The Admiral'
Perianth segments ivory white; corona widely expanded, creamy white at mid-zone, with a faint ring of sulphur white, with sage green at base and a narrow band of clear lemon yellow at rim, frilled. Late

'Candlelight' 1 Y-Y
(J.N. Hancock & Co., 1947) J.N. Hancock & Co., 1965
'Hunter's Moon' × 'Kingscourt'
Perianth segments soft lime yellow; corona darker in tone, with bright lemon yellow at rim, with the rim rolled and dentate. Mid-season. Resembles a 'Hunter's Moon' of better form

'Candlemas' 3 W-W
(P.D. Williams, pre-1948)

'Candlepower' 1 W-W
(A. Gray) M.J. Jefferson-Brown, 1975
Fl. star-shaped, 39 mm wide; perianth segments narrowly ovate, acute, only very slightly mucronate, pale yellow-green 157C, spreading or a little incurved, overlapping at base only; the inner segments sometimes more nearly oblong; corona cylindrical, smooth, opening light yellow-green 150D, becoming white, with mouth deeply 6-lobed and a little flared, rim minutely dentate and somewhat incurved. AM(e) 1972

'Candlestick' 1 Y-Y
(E.H. Krelage & Son, pre-1931)
AM(Haarlem) 1913

'Candlestick' 1 Y-Y
(G. Lubbe & Son) G. Lubbe & Son, 1956
AM(Haarlem) 1956

'Candour' 2 W-W
(G.L. Wilson, pre-1937)
'Quartz' × 'Naxos'
Perianth segments broad, acute, sulphur white, slightly recurved, with margins sometimes incurving at apex, overlapping two-fifths; corona long, creamy white, rim crenate and widely flanged. AM(e) 1937

'Candy' 2 W-?
(Alister Clark) J. Sharp, 1961

'Candyfloss' 1 W-YPP
(M.J. Jefferson-Brown) M.J. Jefferson-Brown, 1985
Perianth segments broad, overlapping; corona large, glowing rich pink. Mid-season

'Canemah' 2 Y-WWY
(Murray W. Evans) Murray W. Evans, 1978
'Binkie' × (['King of the North' × 'Content'] × 'Suede'); sdlg no. O-25
Fl. 105 mm wide. Mid-season

'Canescent' 2
(P.D. Williams, pre-1931)

'Canford' 3 W-WYO
(J.W. Blanchard, 1973) J.W. Blanchard, 1985
('Hammoon' × 'Irish Minstrel') × 'Ringstead'; sdlg no. 65/15A
Fl. rounded; corona yellow, with white at base and a well-defined band of reddish orange at rim. Mid-season. Resembles 'Ringstead' but with broader perianth segments and a broader and richer band of colour at corona rim

'Canisp' 2 W-W
(J.S.B. Lea) J.S.B. Lea, 1960
'Ave' × 'Early Mist'
Fl. forming a double triangle or sometimes more rounded, 120 mm wide, pale creamy white; perianth segments very broadly ovate, blunt or rounded at apex, more or less prominently mucronate, spreading, plane, with margins incurling at apex, overlapping half; the inner segments more nearly acute, a little inflexed, twisted or with margins wavy; corona cylindrical or somewhat funnel-shaped, lightly angled, with mouth expanded and even, rim shallowly crenate and sometimes rolled. Mid-season. 2n=28. Resembles 'Ave' but with wider perianth and green in tube. PC(e) 1960, AM(e) 1964, FCC(e) 1967

'Cannes' 2 W-YYP
(L. van Leeuwen & Son) P. de Jager & Sons, 1956
Perianth segments white; corona soft canary yellow, with pink at rim, mouth flared and frilled

'Cano' 2 Y-R
(J.S. Leitch) J.S. Leitch, 1957

'Canopus' 1 Y-Y
(Cartwright & Goodwin, pre-1910)

'Canopus' 1 W-W
(J.L. Richardson) J.L. Richardson, 1958
'Spitzbergen' × 'Broughshane'
Fl. 102 mm wide; perianth segments very broadly ovate, blunt, slightly mucronate, pure white, spreading, plane, overlapping half; the inner segments a little inflexed, with margins wavy; corona cylindrical, smooth, opening creamy white, becoming pure white, with rim very widely flanged and deeply notched. Late. *AM(g) 1963

'Canopy' 5
(G.H. Engleheart, pre-1914)

'Canowindra' 1 W-Y
(W.M. Spry, pre-1975) Unregistered
'Morning Glory' × 'Stand By'
Corona dark lemon yellow, flushed orange

'Cansonet' 9 W-?
(G.H. Engleheart, pre-1916)

'Cantabile' 9 W-GYR
(G.L. Wilson, pre-1932)
'Dactyl' hybrid
Perianth segments very broadly ovate, blunt or squarish at apex, sometimes truncate, fairly prominently mucronate, frosty white, reflexed, concave, with margins recurved at base and incurved towards apex, overlapping half; the inner segments more nearly spreading, somewhat twisted; corona disc-shaped, tightly ribbed, with yellow in a narrow band between a very broad band of light bright green at base and a narrower band of orange-red (32A) at rim, mouth split in places and overlapping, rim minutely crenate. Late. 2n=14. AGM 1996

N. cantabricus de Candolle 13 Section Bulbocodium
   subsp. *cantabricus*
      var. *cantabricus.* AGM 1994, AM 1997
      var. *eu-albidus* Emberger & Maire
      var. *foliosus* (Maire) A.Fernandes. AM(a) 1961, AGM 1994
      var. *kesticus* (Maire & Wilczec) A.Fernandes
      var. *petunioides* A.Fernandes. AM(p) 1956, FCC(p) 1960
   subsp. *luteolentus* Barra & López = *N. hedraeanthus* var. *luteolentus*
   subsp. *monophyllus* (Durieu de Maisonneuve) A.Fernandes. FCC 1886
   subsp. *tananicus* (Maire) A.Fernandes

'Cantala' 2 W-W
(Ballydorn Bulb Farm) Ballydorn Bulb Farm, 1968
'Tryst' open pollinated
Fl. 95 mm wide, pure white; corona widely expanded, with rim flanged. Mid-season

'Cantata' 9 W-?
(F.H. Chapman, pre-1913)

'Cantata' 9 W-YYR
(E.W. Cotter, pre-1964) Unregistered
N. poeticus sdlg × 'Sea Green'
Perianth segments pure white, of strong substance; corona disc-shaped, citron yellow, with red at rim

'Cantatrice' 1 W-W
(G.L. Wilson, pre-1936)
Probably 'Beersheba' × 'Eskimo'
Fl. 108 mm wide; perianth segments broadly ovate, acute, slightly mucronate, spreading or a little inflexed, with margins a litle incurved and sometimes wavy, smooth, regular, overlapping one-third; the inner segments more often inflexed, with apex reflexed, only very slightly mucronate, shouldered at base; corona slender, straight-sided, smooth, mouth expanded and loosely frilled, with rim widely and shallowly crenate. 2n=28+1B. FCC(e) 1939, AM(e) 1939, *AM(g) 1956, AM(Haarlem) 1957, *FCC(g) 1958

'Canterbury' 5 Y-Y
(R. & E.Havens) R. & E.Havens, 1995
'Hillstar' × *N. triandrus*; sdlg no. Y93/12
Fl. 74 mm wide; perianth segments ovate, soft yellow, reflexed, smooth; corona slightly lighter in tone. Late

'Canterbury Bell' 2 W-WWO
Syn. of 'Canterbury Belle'

'Canterbury Belle' 2 W-WWO
(H.A. Brown, pre-1930)
Perianth segments white; corona creamy white, with apricot at rim. PC(e)(NZ) 1930. See also 'Canterbury Bell'

'Canterbury Fair' 2 W-OYY
(D.S. Bell) D.S. Bell, 1975
'Papanui Queen' × 'Green Island'
Fl. 99 mm wide; corona very shallow bowl-shaped, golden yellow, with apricot at base. Mid-season. Resembles 'Papanui Queen' but with the corona of 'Green Island'

'Canterbury Queen' 2 W-R
(G. Lewis, 1933) Parr's Nurseries, 1958

'Canticle' 9 W-GYR
(Ballydorn Bulb Farm) Ballydorn Bulb Farm, 1984
'Cantabile' hybrid
Fl. 65 mm wide. Mid-season

'Canto' 9 W-?
(G.H. Engleheart, pre-1914)

'Canton' 2 Y-YYO
(S.C. Gaspar) R.J. Abernethy, 1957
Corona lemon yellow, with a band of reddish orange at rim

'Canton Red' 2 Y-? (a)
(Mrs P.M. Davis, pre-1948)

'Cantru' 2 W-W
(A. Overton) A. Overton, 1959
Fl. 114 mm wide

'Canuda'
(pre-1915)

'Canungra' 2 Y-O
(H.A. Brown, 1941)
Perianth segments pale yellow; corona deep orange, frilled

'Canura' 1 Y-Y
(pre-1927)
Fl. yellow; perianth segments of strong substance. The perianth slightly paler than that of 'Lord Roberts; the corona a little darker

'Canute' 1 Y-Y
(W.A. Watts, pre-1927)
'Emperor' × 'King Alfred'

'Canyon Rim' 3 Y-YYO
(T.D. Throckmorton) T.D. Throckmorton, 1974
'Old Satin' × 'Audubon'

'Capacity' 2 Y-? (a)

(Sir C.H. Cave, pre-1928)

'Caparoe' 3 W-R
Syn. of 'Capparoe'

N. capax (Salisbury) Roemer & Schultes = *N. triandrus* var. *loiseleurii*

'Capax Plenus' 4 Y-Y
Syn. of 'Eystettensis'

'Cape Cool' 2 W-W
(Carncairn Daffodils) Carncairn Daffodils, 1981
'Empress of Ireland' × 'Arctic Doric'; sdlg no. W6/4
Fl. 111 mm wide, yellowish white 155B, tinged green. Mid-season

'Cape Cornwall' 2 Y-R
(R.A.Scamp) R.A.Scamp, 1996
'Golden Aura' × 'Montego'; sdlg no. 423
Fl. rounded, 106 mm wide; perianth segments broadly ovate, golden yellow, slightly concave, smooth; corona cup-shaped, rich red, with rim neatly dentate. Late

'Cape Country' 2 W-O
(Tom Forster, 1960s) Unregistered
Fl. rounded; perianth segments broad; corona disc-shaped, deep orange. Vary late

'Cape Horn' 1 W-Y
(J.L. Richardson, pre-1953)
'Kanchenjunga' × 'Spitzbergen'
Perianth segments white; corona primrose, with rim rolled

'Cape Kennedy' 11b W-R/?W
(J.W.A. Lefeber, *c.*1968) Unregistered
Perianth segments creamy white; corona deeply split, the six segments alternate to the perianth segments, with a longitudinal band of red at midrib. 2n=27

'Capella' 2 W-WYY
(J.R. Pearson & Sons, pre-1909)
'Minnie Hume' × 'Madame de Graaff'
Perianth segments pure white; corona long, primrose yellow, paling to sulphur white at base, neatly frilled

'Capella'
(New Zealand origin, pre-1915)

'Capella' 2 W-OOR
(H.R. Bulman, 1949)
'James Wyness' × 'White Cheerio'

'Cape Point' 2 W-P
(Brian S.Duncan) Brian S.Duncan, 1996
'Gracious Lady' × 'Dailmanach'; sdlg no. 1450
Fl. 125 mm wide; perianth segments broadly ovate, blunt, fairly prominently mucronate, pure white,

spreading, plane, smooth, overlapping half; the inner segments narrower, a little inflexed; corona funnel-shaped, broadly ribbed, apple blossom pink, with shades of lilac, mouth straight, wavy. Tall. Mid-season to late

'Capers' 2 W-YYO
(J.N. Hancock & Co., 1956) Unregistered

'Capisco' 3 W-GYR
(Ballydorn Bulb Farm) Ballydorn Bulb Farm, 1969
Perianth segments pure white; corona very small, yellow, with deep green at base and a band of orange-red at rim. Early. 2n=28

'Capistrano' 2 W-P
(W.G. Pannill) W.G. Pannill, 1985
('Green Island' × 'Interim') × ('Accent' × 'Rose Royale'); sdlg no. 72/23
Mid-season

'Capitol' 3 W-YYR
(Warnaar & Co., pre-1953)
AM(Haarlem) 1953

'Capitol Hill' 2 Y-YYO
(J.S.B. Lea, 1960) W.O. Ticknor, 1979
'Bastion' × ('Nanking' × 'Ambergate'); sdlg no. 106
Fl. 105 mm wide; perianth segments brilliant greenish yellow 6B, flushed with a slightly darker tone (6A), overlapping; corona medium to light orange (17A-C), paling towards base, mouth expanded and frilled, rim flanged and crenate. Mid-season. Slightly scented. 2n=28

'Capoola' 2 Y-Y
(West & Fell, pre-1937)
Perianth segments lemon yellow; corona narrowly expanding, deep yellow, frilled

'Caporal' 3 Y-? (a)
(A.M. Wilson, pre-1908)

'Capparoe' 3 W-R
(G.L. Wilson, 1951) Guy L.Wilson Ltd, 1961
('Merryhill' × ['Aleppo' open pollinated]) × ('Aleppo' × 'Athlone')
2n=27. See also 'Caparoe'

'Cappawhite' 1 W-W
(Slieve Donard Nursery Co., pre-1925)
Fl. broad, pure white, smooth, of strong substance; perianth segments overlapping

'Capper' 3 W-?
(pre-1915)

'Capree Elizabeth' 2 Y-P
(M.E. Brogden) Brogden Bulbs, 1991
'Daydream' × ('Salmon Trout' × 'Vision'); sdlg no.

x142/2
Fl. 100 mm wide; perianth segments light yellow, very smooth; corona deep rosy pink, with rim neatly dentate. Mid-season

'Capri' 1 W-? (b)
(Dutch origin, pre-1926)
AM(Haarlem) 1926

'Capri' 3 W-GGP
(The Brodie of Brodie, c.1926)
'James Hogg' × 'Mystic'
Corona with pink at rim

'Capriano' 3 Y-R
(D.S. Bell) D.S. Bell, 1975
'Indianapolis' × 'Checkmate'
Fl. 116 mm wide. Mid-season

'Caprice' 2 W-? (b)
(R.H. Bath, pre-1927)

'Caprice' 3 W-GOR
(D.S. Bell) D.S. Bell, 1962
Sdlg × 'Green Jade'
Fl. 128 mm wide; corona apricot orange, with green at base and red at rim. Mid-season. PC(e) 1970

'Capricious' 2 W-? (b)
(Barr & Sons, pre-1950)

'Capricorn' 2 W-? (b)
(R. Crews, pre-1949)

'Capstan' 2 Y-? (a)
(R.H. Bath, pre-1929)

'Capstan' 2 W-YYR
(D.S. Bell) D.S. Bell, 1964
Sdlg × 'Judy Andrews'
Fl. 93 mm wide; corona shallow, widely expanded, yellow, with red at rim, frilled

'Captain' 2 Y-? (a)
(W. Balch, pre-1933)

'Captain Carlsen' 2 Y-Y
(Trenoweth Valley Flower Farm, pre-1952)
'Pilgrimage' × N. jonquilla

'Captain Cook' 1 W-W
(G.H. Engleheart, pre-1914)

'Captain Cuttle' 1 Y-Y
(Barr & Sons, pre-1933)
Perianth segments clear yellow, with margins slightly uneven and wavy, overlapping; corona flared, a little darker in tone

'Captain General' 3 W-? (b)
(F.H. Chapman, pre-1913)

'Captain Harvey' 1
(A. Wilson, pre-1901)
? *N. obvallaris* × 'Emperor'
Perianth segments ovate, spreading, separated; the inner segments twisted; corona cylindrical, with mouth ribbed and very widely expanded, loosely frilled, rim notched and crenate

'Captain Kidd' 2 W-WPP
(Oregon Bulb Farms, pre-1946)

'Captain Nelson' 1 Y-Y
(E. Leeds, pre-1877)
Fl. large; perianth clear pale yellow; corona a little darker in tone, long, flared. Syn. Pseudonarcissus Major 'Captain Nelson'. FCC 1887. "Absorbed" 'Lord Mayor' and 'Mrs Nelson'

'Captain Red' 2 Y-? (a)
(H.A. Brown, pre-1950)

'Captain Scott' 1 W-W
(W. Balch, pre-1933)

'Captain Smoolenaars' 1 W-? (b)
(R.A. van der Schoot, pre-1930)

'Captain Smoolenaars' 3 W-?
Syn. of 'MacDonald'

'Captivation' 3 W-? (b)
(P.D. Williams, pre-1939)

'Captivation' 3 W-?
Syn. of 'Virtuoso'

'Captivator' 2 W-Y
(de Graaff Bros) de Graaff Bros & van Konynenburg & Co., 1961
Fl. 127 mm wide; perianth segments ivory white; corona light greenish yellow 8B. Late. AM(Haarlem) 1961

'Captive Glow' 2 W-P
(J.N. Hancock & Co., *c.*1975) Unregistered

'Captive Sun' 2 Y-Y
(V. Brink) V. Brink, 1963
Fl. 110 mm wide; perianth segments pale primrose yellow; corona deep golden yellow, faintly tinged with orange. Mid-season. Resembles an earlier-flowered 'Lothario' with broader perianth segments and the corona more widely expanded and heavily frilled

'Capuchin' 3 Y-? (a)
(A.H. Ahrens, pre-1949)

'Capulet' 3 Y-? (a)
(pre-1914)

'Capulet' 2 W-? (b)
(J.R. Pearson & Sons, pre-1948)

'Caracas' 2 O-O
(J.L. Richardson) Mrs H.K. Richardson, 1963
'Firecracker' × 'Spelter'
Perianth segments coppery orange; corona long cup-shaped, fiery orange

'Caradi' 1 W-P
(S.J. Bisdee, 1948)
'Kehama' × 'Mastercraft'

'Caradoc' 2 W-? (b)
(J.A. Morris) J.A. Morris, 1957

'Caradoc' 1 W-?
Syn. of 'Caradock'

'Caradock' 1 W-? (b)
(H. Backhouse, pre-1910)
See also 'Caradoc'

'Caradon' 2 W-Y
(A.J. Bliss, pre-1931)
'Virgil' × 'Monarch'
Fl. 102 mm wide, facing somewhat downwards; perianth segments creamy white, with lemon at base, irregular, separated; corona funnel-shaped, rich lemon yellow. Mid-season to late

'Caragh' 2 W-GYO
(J.L. Richardson, pre-1941)
'Mitylene' × 'Penquite'
Perianth segments very broadly ovate, blunt or rounded at apex, fairly prominently mucronate, pure white, spreading, plane, of heavy substance, overlapping half; the inner segments more narrowly ovate, a little inflexed, with margins slightly wavy; corona broad bowl-shaped, ribbed, pale citron yellow, with soft sage green at base and a well-defined band of clear golden orange at rim, tightly frilled. Mid-season. 2n=28

'Caralsa' 3 W-YYO
(G.H. Johnstone, pre-1944)
'Silver Coin' hybrid

'Caramba' 2 Y-O
(J.L. Richardson) G. Zandbergen-Terwegen, 1960
Fl. 100 mm wide; perianth segments golden yellow; corona reddish orange. Early. Resembles 'Ceylon' but with broader and longer perianth segments of a darker tone

'Caramel' 9 W-O
(F.H. Chapman, pre-1913)
2n=28

'Caramel' 1 W-Y
(Alister Clark, pre-1956) Unregistered
Perianth segments white; corona opening yellow, becoming cream, with caramel tones at rim. ?The same as 'Carmel'

'Caramel' 2 W-Y
(G.H. Johnstone, pre-1960) Unregistered

'Cara Mia' 2 Y-YYO
(Konynenburg & Mark, 1944) Konynenburg & Mark, 1960
'Gratia' × 'Daisy Schaffer'
Fl. 100 mm wide; perianth segments brilliant greenish yellow 4A; corona vivid yellow 13A, with a narrow band of orange (23A) at rim

'Caraminte' 8 W-O
(pre-1798)

'Caran' 2 Y-? (a)
(W.A. Watts, pre-1927)

'Carara' 1 W-W
Syn. of 'Carrara'

'Caravan' 3 Y-YYR
(G. Lewis, 1940) D.S. Bell, 1958
Fl. bright yellow; perianth segments broadly ovate in outline, blunt or rounded at apex, prominently mucronate, slightly reflexed, of thick substance, overlapping half; the inner segments more nearly spreading, creased; corona shallow bowl-shaped, ribbed, bright yellow, with red at rim. Syn. 'Estrellita'

'Caravelle' 1 Y-Y
(J.L. Richardson) J.L. Richardson, 1959
'Kingscourt' × 'Goldcourt'
Fl. 100 mm wide; perianth segments vivid yellow 12A, overlapping; corona of a slightly darker tone (13A), long, mouth expanded and frilled, with rim flanged and crenate. 2n=27. AM(Haarlem) 1966, *AM(g) 1970

'Carbine' 1 Y-Y
(West & Fell, pre-1931)
Fl. clear yellow. Early to mid-season

'Carbineer' 2 Y-O
(A.M. Wilson, pre-1927)
'Gulliver' hybrid; sdlg no. 477
Fl. 95 mm wide; perianth segments very broadly ovate, blunt or rounded at apex, fairly prominently mucronate, brilliant greenish yellow 6B, spreading, a little concave, overlapping half; the inner segments more narrowly ovate, shouldered at base and sometimes with a "thumb" at the margin, slightly inflexed, somewhat creased; corona bowl-shaped, lightly ribbed, yellow-orange (23A), with a paler tone at base (23B), mouth expanded and loosely frilled, rim crenate. Mid-season. 2n=28. AM(e) 1931, FCC(e) 1938, *AM(m)(g) 1940, AM(Haarlem) 1941, *HC(g) 1946

'Carbis' 2 Y-? (a)
(M.P. Williams, pre-1949)

'Carbon' 2 W-?
(A. Overton) A. Overton, 1960

'Carbrook' 2 W-? (b)
(H.A. Brown, pre-1936)

'Carclew' 6 Y-Y
(R.A. Scamp) R.A. Scamp, 1993
'Saint Keverne' × *N. cyclamineus*; sdlg no. 6
Fl. 68 mm wide, bright yellow; perianth segments narrow, acute, strongly reflexed, overlapping at base only; corona cylindrical, with mouth expanded and neatly frilled. Dwarf. Very early

'Cardecu' 2 W-W
(S.J. Bisdee) S.J. Bisdee, 1956
'Whitefoord' × 'Tain'
Perianth segments almost triangular in appearance, regular; corona rim neatly rolled

'Cardigan' 2 W-Y
(A.M. Wilson, pre-1935)
Sdlg no. 627
Perianth segments broad, overlapping; corona funnel-shaped, light buttercup yellow, with mouth flared. AM(e) 1938. ?The same as 'Cordigan'

'Cardigan Bay' 1 Y-Y
(D.N.Y. Olson, 1978) D.N.Y. Olson, 1988
Sdlg no. 202/1
Perianth segments very broadly ovate, blunt, with white mucro, spreading, overlapping one-third to a half; the inner segments somewhat twisted or with margins wavy; corona cylindrical, smooth, with mouth flared and lightly frilled. Mid-season

'Cardinal' 3 W-O
(G.H. Engleheart, pre-1897)
Perianth segments white; corona large, vivid orange

'Cardinal Queen' 2 W-? (b)
(pre-1914)

'Cardinal Wolsey' 3 W-Y
(G.H. Engleheart, pre-1910)
Perianth segments snowy white, slightly reflexed; corona large, spreading, apricot yellow, flushed orange

'Cardinham' 3 W-O
(T. Bloomer) du Plessis Bros, 1986
'Silent Beauty' × 'Graceful Charmer'; sdlg no. 255
Mid-season

'Cardinia' 2 Y-Y
(J.N.Hancock & Co., 1961) Unregistered
Sdlg no. 8/61H

'Cardona' 2 Y-? (a)
(J.T. Gray, pre-1949)
Perianth segments yellow; corona straight-sided, with orange-scarlet in upper half

'Careen' 2 W-P
(K.J. Heazlewood, c.1966) Unregistered
'Keera' × 'Rosedale'

'Career' 2 Y-OOR
(G.W.E. Brogden) G.W.E. Brogden, 1969

'Carefree' 1 W-? (b)
(G.L. Wilson, pre-1953)

'Carentan' 2 Y-? (a)
(A.M. Wilson, pre-1944)

'Caress' 2 W-? (b)
(A.M. Wilson) Mrs R. McConnel, 1955

'Caresse' 11a W-Y
(J. Gerritsen & Son, c.1978) Unregistered
'Salome' × 'Split'
Corona yellow, tinged pink

'Carey' 2 W-O
(J.N. Hancock & Co.) J.N. Hancock & Co., 1955
Perianth segments white, deeply overlapping; corona almost disc-shaped, ribbed, orange

'Careysville' 2 W-Y
(J.L. Richardson) J.L. Richardson, 1958
'Broughshane' self pollinated
Fl. 108 mm wide; perianth segments creamy white, with margins slightly incurving, overlapping half; corona buff yellow (20C), with brilliant yellow 13C at rim, slightly ribbed, mouth expanded and frilled, with rim rolled and dentate. AM(e) 1958, AM(Haarlem) 1960, FCC(Haarlem) 1961

'Cargan' 2 Y-Y
(G.L. Wilson, pre-1945)
Fl. 88 mm wide; perianth segments vivid to brilliant yellow 12A-B, overlapping half; corona richer in tone, with mouth slightly expanded. AM(e) 1950, *AM(g) 1951, *FCC(g) 1952. See also 'Fargan'

'Cargreen' 9 W-GYR
(Brian S. Duncan) Dan du Plessis, 1993
'Como' open pollinated; sdlg no. 992

'Cariad' 5 Y-Y
(R.A.Scamp, 1984) R.A.Scamp, 1994
'Debutante' × *N. triandrus*; sdlg no. 137
Fl. 70 mm wide, pale golden yellow; perianth segments broadly ovate, reflexed, deeply overlapping; corona cup-shaped, smooth, with mouth slightly expanded and a little wavy. Dwarf. Mid-season to late

'Carib' 6 W-P
(G.E. Mitsch) G.E. Mitsch, 1979
(['Mabel Taylor' × 'Interim'] × 'Rima') × *N. cyclamineus*; sdlg no. bKK105/3
Fl. 82 mm wide, of much substance; perianth segments broadly ovate, blunt, only very slightly mucronate, ivory white, reflexed, with margins wavy, overlapping one-third to a half; the inner segments more nearly spreading at base, reflexed at apex, with margins more heavily wavy or twisted; corona cyindrical, lightly ribbed, peach pink, with a paler tone outside, mouth flared, split in places and overlapping, lightly frilled. Mid-season. Resembles an earlier-flowered 'Cotinga' with a broader and more strongly reflexed perianth

'Caribbean' 2 Y-Y
(D.S. Bell) D.S. Bell, 1963
Fl. 105 mm wide, golden yellow; perianth segments wide; corona frilled. Mid-season. Resembles 'Goldcourt' but with the perianth segments more rounded

'Carib Gipsy' 2 Y-WWY
(A.J.R. Pearson) A.J.R. Pearson, 1987
'Camelot' × 'Daydream'; sdlg no. 81/23/F1
Perianth segments very broadly ovate, opening greeny-lemon yellow, becoming slightly darker in tone, with white at base and touches of white at midrib towards apex, a little concave, with midrib showing, overlapping half; the inner segments a little more narrowly ovate; corona cylindrical, smooth or very lightly ribbed, opening lemon yellow, becoming white, with a broad band of gold at rim, mouth slightly flared, with six shallow and overlapping lobes, rim crenate. Late. Resembles 'Hartgrove' but with a more trumpet-like corona

'Carillon' 2 Y-? (a)
(J.L. Richardson, pre-1938)

'Carina' 2 W-WPP
(J.L. Richardson) Mrs H.K. Richardson, 1963
'Broughshane' × 'Cape Horn'
Perianth segments white; corona flushed pink, with rim flanged

'Carinthia' 3 W-O
(J.M. de Navarro) J.M. de Navarro, 1957
'Folly' × 'Carrowmore'
Fl. 100 mm wide; perianth segments very broadly ovate, blunt, mucronate, white, stained yellow at base, spreading, a little concave, with margins occasionally slightly incurling at apex, smooth, overlapping half; the inner segments more narrowly ovate, truncate, somewhat inward folding, with margins

occasionally more inward rolling and sometimes wavy, shouldered at base; corona ribbed, opening with little colour, with a narrow band of yellow at rim, deepening to self orange, mouth expanded and frilled, with rim crenate. Sunproof. PC(e) 1957, AM(e) 1960

'Carioca' 1 Y-P
(D.S. Bell) D.S. Bell, 1978
'Barbara Allen' × 'Red Conquest'
Fl. 115 mm wide; perianth segments lemon yellow; corona broad, expanding, gradually becoming soft pink, deeply frilled. Mid-season. Resembles a better-formed 'Red Conquest' with the corona of a deeper tone

'Carisbrooke' 1 Y-Y
(H.A. Brown, pre-1935)
Corona with rim closely and deeply notched, as if fringed

'Carissima' 2 W-? (b)
(Cartwright & Goodwin, pre-1910)

'Carissima' 2 Y-YYR
(G. Lewis, 1943) D.S. Bell, 1958

'Carita' 2 W-P
(Oregon Bulb Farms) Oregon Bulb Farms, 1958
'Roman Candle' × 'Pink Diamond'
Perianth segments white; corona opening yellow, becoming deep copper pink. Mid-season

'Carla' 1 Y-Y
(A.C. Paardekooper, pre-1943)

'Carla Maree' 2 W-R
(M.E. Brogden, pre-1996) Unregistered
'Sweet Luck' × 'Bandit'

'Carleen' 3 Y-? (a)
(Mrs R.O. Backhouse, pre-1921)
Perianth segments narrow, cream. AM(Haarlem) 1930

'Carleigh' 2 W-Y
(A.J. Sherriff, 1966) Unregistered
'Preamble' × 'Polindra'

'Carlidnack' 3 Y-? (a)
(P.D. Williams, pre-1937)

'Carlin' 2 W-W
(Mrs F.S. Foote, pre-1941)

'Carlina' 3 W-? (b)
(C. Dawson, pre-1914)

'Carlingford' 2 W-GYW
(Ballydorn Bulb Farm) Ballydorn Bulb Farm, 1992
'Mount Pleasant' open pollinated
Fl. 105 mm wide; perianth segments broadly ovate, pure white, plane; corona bowl-shaped, expanded, pale yellow, with deep green at base and yellow-white at rim, mouth frilled. Late

'Carlisle' 2 W-? (b)
(H.A. Brown, pre-1937)

'Carlisle' 2 Y-? (a)
(A.M. Wilson, pre-1938)

'Carlist' 1 Y-Y
(A.M. Wilson, pre-1937)

'Carlo Perosie' 2 W-O
(J.W.A. Lefeber, 1948) J.W.A. Lefeber, 1960
Fl. 90 mm wide; corona dark reddish orange. Early

'Carlotta' 3 W-? (b)
(F.H. Chapman, pre-1930)

'Carlow' 2 W-? (b or c)
(J.L. Richardson, pre-1937)
Syn. 'Silver Jubilee'

'Carlton' 2 Y-Y
(P.D. Williams, pre-1927)
Fl. 120 mm wide; perianth segments broadly or very broadly ovate, blunt, fairly prominently mucronate, sulphur yellow, spreading, slightly twisted, creased, overlapping one-third to a half; the inner segments with margins wavy; corona broad funnel-shaped, darker in tone than the perianth segments, with mouth expanded and frilled, rim deeply and repeatedly notched and crenate. Mid-season to late. 2n=28. AM(e)(Haarlem) 1930, *AM(g) 1936, *FCC(g) 1939, AGM 1995. ?The same as 'Nimrod'

'Carlyon' 2 Y-? (a)
(P.D. Williams, pre-1927)

'Carl Zeller' 2 Y-O
(Konynenburg & Mark) Konynenburg & Mark, 1961
('Episode' × 'John Evelyn') × ('Frederike' × 'Mimosa')
Fl. 90 mm wide; perianth segments brilliant yellow 12B; corona vivid orange 28B. Mid-season

'Carmand' 2 Y-Y
(G.J. Phillips, 1983) G.J. Phillips, 1994
'Chamkohe' × 'Demand'; sdlg no. 79-45-1
Fl. 108 mm wide; perianth segments broadly ovate, smooth; corona funnel-shaped, with mouth slightly flared and rim obscurely dentate. Early

'Carmat' 2 W-R
(J.A. Morris) J.A. Morris, 1962
'Caradoc' × 'Matapan'
Fl. 114 mm wide; corona deep red. Early

'Carmel' 1 W-Y
(The Brodie of Brodie, c.1919)
'Findhorn' × 'Nevis; sdlg no. 136/A/14
Perianth segments milk white, fairly smooth, overlapping; corona soft yellow, frilled, with rim lightly flanged. Late. AM(e) 1926

'Carmel' 1 W-Y
(Alister Clark, c.1956) Unregistered
?The same as 'Caramel'

'Carmela' 5
(Barr & Sons, pre-1923)

'Carmelite' 1 W-W
(O. Pease, pre-1914)

'Carmelite' 5 W-W
(A.E. Lowe, pre-1927)

'Carmen' 3 W-? (b)
(R.O. Backhouse, pre-1907)

'Carmencita' 2 Y-O
(Mrs R.O. Backhouse, pre-1921)
Perianth segments soft apricot yellow; corona widely expanded, orange. AM(Haarlem) 1928

'Carmen Sylva' 2
(R.H. Bath, pre-1927)

'Carmenta' 1 W-Y
(Barr & Sons, pre-1913)
'Peter Barr' × 'Maggie May'
Fl. 95 mm wide, facing somewhat downwards; perianth segments creamy white, regular, overlapping half; corona broad, soft lemon yellow, mouth widely expanded, with rim neatly frilled. Mid-season to late. Resembles 'Lord Lister'

'Carmenta' 2 Y-R
(W. Jackson Sr, 1944)
'Market Merry' × 'Caerleon'

'Carminea' 3 W-? (b)
(G.H. Engleheart, pre-1914)

'Carminowe' 3 W-R
(P.D. Williams, pre-1927)
Perianth segments of thick substance; corona very shallow, scarlet, flushed with a richer red

'Carmoa' 2 W-YYP
(C.E. Radcliff, 1936) J.M.Radcliff, 1956
'Mitylene' × 'Pink o' Dawn'
Perianth segments white; corona pale citron yellow, with shell pink at rim, frilled

'Carnage' 2 Y-YYO
(Daniel Bellinger) Daniel Bellinger, 1995
'Zeus' × 'Bunclody'; sdlg no. 87-12-4
Fl. 102 mm wide; perianth segments very broad, bright yellow, slightly reflexed, smooth, with a surface sheen, of thick substance; corona cylindrical, bright yellow, with a clearly defined band of dark orange at mouth, mouth even. Late. Sunproof

'Carnalbana' 1 Y-Y
(W.J. Dunlop) W.J. Dunlop, 1967

'Carnalea' 2 W-WWY
(G.L. Wilson, pre-1942)
'Nelly' hybrid
Perianth segments pure white; corona white, with a well-defined band of lemon gold at rim

'Carnation' 4 Y-O
(E. & J.C. Martin, pre-1915)
Fl. large; perianth and other petaloid segments pale buff yellow; corona segments smaller, brilliant orange

'Carnbeg' 2 Y-YOR
(W.J. Dunlop, pre-1964) Unregistered
Fl. up to 127 mm wide; perianth segments broad, deep yellow, flushed orange, smooth, overlapping; corona of the same colour as the the perianth at base, gradually shading to deep red at rim

'Carn Dhu' 2 W-? (b)
(G. Matthews, pre-1951)

'Carne' 1 Y-Y
(The Brodie of Brodie, pre-1930)

'Carnearny' 3 W-Y
(Carncairn Daffodils) Carncairn Daffodils, 1991
'Merlin' × 'Rockall'; sdlg no. 1/60/79
Fl. 102 mm wide; perianth segments very broadly ovate, rounded at apex, only very slightly mucronate, yellowish white 155B, smooth, overlapping half or more; corona disc-shaped, vivid yellow 9A, with faint orange at rim at first, rim dentate. Tall. Late

'Carnelian' 2 Y-R
(Murray W. Evans) Murray W. Evans, 1972
'Paricutin' × ('Ardour' × 'Rustom Pasha')
Fl. 95 mm wide

'Carngham' 2 Y-O
(H.A. Brown, pre-1936)
Perianth segments pale yellow; corona reddish orange, with rim closely and deeply notched, as if fringed

'Carn Glas' 3 W-GGY
(J.M. de Navarro) J.M. de Navarro, 1975
'Verona' × 'Blakeney'; sdlg no. 894
Fl. 81 mm wide; corona pale yellow, shading through grey to green at base. Late. Resembles 'Sacramento' but with a less wide-spreading corona of a different

colour. See also 'Carnglass'

'Carnglass' 3 W-GGY
Syn. of 'Carn Glas'

'Carniola' 2 Y-? (a)
(A.H. Ahrens) J.S. Leitch, 1955

'Carnival' 2 Y-? (a)
(G.H. Engleheart, pre-1923)

'Carnival' 2 W-O
(J.L. Richardson) J.L. Richardson, 1958
'Kilworth' × 'Arbar'; sdlg no. 874
Perianth segments pure white, of thick substance; corona very shallow bowl-shaped, reddish orange, frilled

'Carnival Queen' 2 W-YYO
(G.H. Johnstone, pre-1950)

'Carnival Romaine' 2 Y-O
(D.S. Bell, pre-1971) Unregistered
'Krakatoa' hybrid
Perianth segments broad, overlapping; corona widely expanded, reddish orange, with rim deeply flanged

'Carnkief' 2 W-YYO
(R.A. Scamp) R.A. Scamp, 1993
'Merlin' × 'Tangent'; sdlg no. 148
Fl. 83 mm wide; perianth segments very broadly ovate, rounded or truncate and sometimes split at apex, slightly mucronate, a little reflexed, overlapping half; the inner segments with margins wavy; corona broad, almost disc-shaped, ribbed, soft primrose yellow, with a fine line of orange at rim, mouth split in places and overlapping. Mid-season

'Carnlough' 2 W-WWP
(G.L. Wilson, pre-1934)
Fl. white; corona opening very pale citron, with coral pink at rim, becoming white, with the pink at rim sometimes becoming very faint, frilled

'Carnmoney' 2 W-W
(G.L. Wilson, pre-1944)
'Nelly' × 'Folly'
Corona shallow bowl-shaped

'Carnmoon' 3 W-GWY
(G.L. Wilson, pre-1953)
'Portrush' × 'Green Island'
Perianth segments white; corona shallow, milk white, with green at base and lemon at rim. 2n=28

'Carnsore' 3 W-GRR
(J.L. Richardson, pre-1941)
'Aviemore' × 'Hades'
Perianth segments broadly ovate, blunt or rounded at apex, slightly mucronate, white, slightly flushed yellow at base, spreading, smooth, with margins slightly incurling, overlapping one-third to a half; the inner segments narrower, more nearly acute, angular at base, a little inflexed; corona shallow cup-shaped, loosely ribbed, deep red, shading to a slightly green tone at base, mouth split in places and overlapping, wavy, rim entire. Mid-season

'Carnsulan' 8
(P.D. Williams, pre-1927)

'Carnyorth' 11a Y-O
(R.A.Scamp) R.A.Scamp, 1996
'Brandaris' × 'Paricutin'; sdlg no. 117
Fl. 98 mm wide; perianth segments ovate, somewhat acute, clear golden yellow, deeply overlapping; corona split, the six segments opposite and closely overlying the perianth segments, bright orange, with margins neatly frilled. Early to mid-season. Sunproof

'Caroda' 2 W-P
(J.M.Radcliff, *c.*1966) Unregistered
'Remark' × 'Roselands'

'Carol' 9 W-?
(G.H. Engleheart, pre-1903)
Hybrid between 'Ornatus' and *N. poeticus* var. *recurvus*
Perianth segments pure white; corona with bright red at rim. Scented. Earlier-flowered and more floriferous than *N. poeticus* var. *recurvus*

'Carola' 3 W-? (b)
(W.T. Ware, pre-1914)

'Carola Mills' 1 W-Y
(E.H. Buxton, pre-1923)
Perianth segments white; corona large, pale creamy yellow. AM 1923

'Carol Ann' 2 Y-R
(D.S. Bell) D.S. Bell, 1960
Fl. 120 mm wide; corona shallow, widely expanded, deep red. Early

'Carol Bells' 2 Y-YOO
(Konynenburg & Mark, 1950) Konynenburg & Mark, 1960
'Aranjuez' × 'Rustom Pasha'
Fl. 90 mm wide; perianth segments brilliant greenish yellow 6C; corona strong orange 25A, with vivid yellow 13A at base. Early

'Carole Lombard' 3 W-YYO
(Clive Postles) Clive Postles, 1991
'Purbeck' × 'Estrella'; sdlg no. 4-64-79
Fl. rounded, 84 mm wide; perianth segments very broadly ovate, blunt, spreading, with margins incurling, overlapping half; the inner segments reflexed in upper half, with margins deeply incurved; corona

bowl-shaped, ribbed, yellow, with broad band of orange at rim, mouth compactly frilled. Late

'Carole Nancy' 2 W-P
(A.N. Kanouse) Mrs A.N. Kanouse, 1990
Div 2 or 3 pink sdlg × 'Daydream'
Fl. 130 mm wide; perianth segments broad, roundish; the inner segments narrower, more nearly acute; corona large, widely expanded, soft salmon pink, with a darker tone at rim, heavily frilled. Mid-season to late. Sunproof

'Carolina' 3 W-YYO
(Warnaar & Co., pre-1927)
Seed supplied by Mrs R.O.Backhouse
Perianth segments clear pure white; corona yellow, with dark orange at rim, mouth frilled. AM(Haarlem) 1927

'Caroline' 8 W-O
(pre-1798)

'Caroline' 2 Y-? (a)
(M. van Waveren & Sons, pre-1907)

'Caroline Broom'
(pre-1915)

'Caroline Carver' 2 W-YYO
(Miss K. Spurrell, pre-1903)
Perianth segments creamy white; corona yellow, with orange at rim, frilled. AM 1903

'Caroline Fox' 1 W-Y
(G.H. Johnstone, pre-1952)
'Tunis' × 'Brunswick'
Fl. 102 mm wide; perianth segments white, overlapping; corona slightly ribbed towards mouth, brilliant greenish yellow 5A, paler towards base, mouth straight, frilled. *AM(g) 1978

'Carol Jese' 2 Y-Y
(J.N. Hancock & Co., c.1979) Unregistered

'Carolus' 3 Y-? (a)
(N.Y. Lower, pre-1914)

'Carolyn' 2 W-W
(G.L. Wilson, pre-1950)

'Caron' 1 Y-Y
(J.S. Leitch) J.S. Leitch, 1960
Fl. 108 mm wide

'Caro Nome' 2 W-WPP
(G.E. Mitsch, pre-1954)
'Green Island' × 'Glenshane'; sdlg no. N50/1
Fl. rounded; perianth segments pure white; corona bowl-shaped, small, apple blossom pink to pale apricot salmon. Mid-season

'Caroonboon' 2 Y-O
(J.N. Hancock & Co., pre-1949)
Corona orange apricot, frilled

'Caros' 2 Y-? (a)
(R.H. Bath, pre-1929)

'Carousel' 3 W-OOR
(D.S. Bell) D.S. Bell, 1959
'Monte Carlo' × 'Khartum'
Fl. 114 mm wide; corona apricot orange, with red at rim. Mid-season. Resembles 'Corofin' but with a more intensely coloured corona

'Carpathian' 1 Y-Y
(G.H. Engleheart, pre-1915)
Fl. large. Resembles 'Glory of Leiden' in form

'Carpatica' 3 W-O
(J.L. Richardson, pre-1945)
'Coronach' × 'Forfar'
Perianth segments white; corona almost disc-shaped, tightly ribbed, bright reddish orange

'Carpentaria' 1 W-G
(W.M. Spry, pre-1975) Unregistered
'Hunter's Moon' × 'Oliver'
Corona lemon green

***N.* × *carpetanus* (Barra & López) Fernández Casas**
13 = *N. bulbocodium* Linnaeus var. *graellsii* (Webb) Baker × *N. bulbocodium* Linnaeus var. *nivalis* (Graells) Baker

'Carrara' 5 W-W
(The Brodie of Brodie, c.1912)
'Madame de Graaff' × *N. triandrus*

'Carrara' 1 W-W
(G. Zandbergen-Terwegen, pre-1936)
See also 'Carara'

'Carrara' 3 W-GWW
(Mrs H.K. Richardson) Rathowen Daffodils, 1979
'Benediction' × 'Verona'; sdlg no. R341
Corona very shallow bowl-shaped, opening with pale yellow at rim, soon becoming pure white. Mid-season

'Carrara' 1 W-?
Syn. of 'Jolyon'

'Carrbridge' 1 W-W
(J.M. de Navarro) J.M. de Navarro, 1960
'Preamble' × ('Broughshane' × 'Spitzbergen')
Fl. 95 mm wide, white. Mid-season. Resembles an earlier-flowered and whiter 'Ambassador'

'Carrick' 2 W-P
(J.L. Richardson) Ballydorn Bulb Farms, 1969
'Rose Caprice' × 'Salmon Trout'

Perianth segments white; corona salmon pink, with darker tones at base and lighter at rim

'Carrickbeg' 1 Y-Y
(J.L. Richardson) Mrs H.K. Richardson, 1963
'Titania' × ('Pretoria' × 'Goldcourt' hybrid)
Fl. yellow; perianth segments broad; corona with rim neatly flanged and dentate

'Carrickfergus' 2 W-WWO
(W.J. Dunlop) W.J. Dunlop, 1968
'Castle Coole' × 'Pride of Erin'

'Carrickmannon' 2 W-GPP
(J.L. Richardson) Ballydorn Bulb Farm, 1968
'Rose of Tralee' × 'Lisbreen'
Fl. 102 mm wide; perianth segments white; corona becoming rose pink, paling towards rim. Resembles an improved 'Lisbreen'

'Carrie' 2 W-?
(A. Overton) A. Overton, 1960

'Carrigart' 3 Y-O
(J.L. Richardson, pre-1943)
'Goyescas' × 'Penquite'
Perianth segments soft yellow; corona almost disc-shaped, reddish orange

'Carrigeen' 2 W-W
(Carncairn Daffodils) Carncairn Daffodils, 1967
G.L. Wilson sdlg × 'Fairy Tale'
Fl. 11 mm wide, white, tinged green; corona long cup-shaped. Mid-season

'Carrikore' 1 Y-Y
(D.H.L. Corrigan, pre-1951)

N. × *carringtonii* Rozeira 13 = *N. scaberulus* Henriques × *N. triandrus* Linnaeus subsp. *pallidulus* (Graells) D.A.Webb

'Carronade' 2 Y-? (a)
(W.B. Cranfield, pre-1923)

'Carrowkeel' 2 W-? (b)
(J.L. Richardson, pre-1949)

'Carrowmore' 2 W-R
(J.L. Richardson, pre-1949)
'Carnsore' × 'Arklow'
Perianth segments broad, smooth; corona vivid orange-red. Sunproof

'Carry-on' 2 W-? (b)
(L. van Leeuwen & Son, pre-1932)
AM(Haarlem) 1931

'Carson Pass' 2 W-WWP
(Brian S. Duncan) Brian S. Duncan, 1992

'Pismo Beach' × 'High Society'; sdlg no. 965
Fl. forming a double triangle, 110 mm wide; perianth segments broadly ovate, blunt, slightly mucronate, spreading, plane, with margins incurling at apex, smooth, overlapping half; the inner segments more narrowly ovate, inflexed, with margins more strongly incurling; corona bowl-shaped, white, with grey-green in tube and a band of shell pink at rim, lightly frilled. Mid-season to late. Sunproof. Varying between Divs 2 and 3

'Carte Blanche' 2 W-W
(G.H. Johnstone, pre-1949)

'Carter Bar' 1 W-W
(G. Harrison) G. Harrison, 1968
Sdlg × 'Kanchenjunga'
Fl. 133 mm wide. Mid-season. Resembles 'Broughshane' but with smoother perianth segments

'Carterknowle' 1 W-W
(F.E. Board) F.E. Board, 1965
G.L. Wilson sdlg 38/90 ('Nilkanta' × 'Murmansk') × 'Ardbane'; sdlg no. 460

'Cartertonian' 1 W-Y
(D. Bramley) D. Bramley, 1963
Fl. 120 mm wide; perianth segments white; corona creamy yellow. Mid-season. Resembles a stronger and later-flowered 'Lochin' with unfading corona

'Carthage' 1 W-! (b)
(G.H. Engleheart, pre-1914)

'Carthillian' 3 W-? (b)
(P.D. Williams, pre-1933)
Syn. 'Lizard'

'Cartrefle' 2 Y-R
(A.O. Roblin, 1941)
'Scarlet Queen' × 'Lillian Murdoch'

'Caruna' 2 Y-OOR
(S.J. Bisdee, 1942)
'Gulliver' × 'Sunset Fires'

'Caruso' 2 Y-O
(Konynenburg & Mark) Konynenburg & Mark, 1965
'Queen of Beauties' × 'Red Goblet'
Fl. 110 mm wide; perianth segments vivid yellow 9B; corona orange. Early

'Caruso' 8 W-Y
Syn. of 'Richard Tauber'

'Carveth' 3 W-YYR
(P.D. Williams, pre-1927)
Fl. 79 mm wide; perianth segments pure white, with cream at base, somewhat reflexed, overlapping

two-thirds; corona bowl-shaped, bright sulphur, with bright red at rim. Late. AM(Haarlem) 1930

'Carvozza' 3 W-YYO
(G.H. Johnstone) G.H. Johnstone, 1959
Fl. 89 mm wide. Late

'Caryem' 2 Y-R
(Jackson's Daffodils, 1975) Jackson's Daffodils, 1986
'Duneba' × sdlg 102/65; sdlg no. 52/75
Perianth segments vivid yellow 9A; corona orange-red (30C). Mid-season

'Caryna' 1 Y-Y
(H.A. Brown, pre-1936)

'Casaba' 3 Y-? (a)
(A.H. Ahrens) D.J. Cooper, 1956

'Casabianca' 2 W-Y
(G.E. Mitsch) G.E. Mitsch, 1956
'Tunis' × 'Fortune'
Perianth segments spreading; corona flared, creamy lemon yellow, tightly frilled. Mid-season

'Casablanca' 2 W-Y
(J.L. Richardson, pre-1944)
Division 2 or 3 white or pale-coloured sdlg × 'Trevisky'
Fl. rounded, perianth segments very broad, blunt or squarish at apex, with very slight mucro, pure white, a little inflexed, overlapping half; the inner segments narrower, more strongly inflexed; corona funnel-shaped, soft pale yellow, ribbed, with mouth straight, loosely frilled. Mid-season

'Casa d'Oro' 1 Y-Y
(Konynenburg & Mark) Konynenburg & Mark, 1960
('Aludra' × 'Sara Leander') × ('Killigrew' × 'Porthilly')
Fl. 125 mm wide; perianth segments brilliant greenish yellow 6A; corona vivid yellow 12A. Mid-season

'Cascade' 1 W-W
(N.Y. Lower, pre-1914)

'Cascade' 3 W-W
(J.L. Richardson) J.L. Richardson, 1961
'Altyre' × ('Templemore' × 'Green Island')
Fl. 105 mm wide, pure white; perianth segments very broad, of good substance; corona spreading, ice white, frilled. Mid-season to late

'Cascob' 2 Y-? (a)
(Mrs R.O. Backhouse, pre-1921)

'Cascogne' 1 Y-Y
Syn. of 'Gascogne'

'Cashel' 2 W-W
(J.L. Richardson, pre-1937)
'White Sentinel' × 'Red Sea'
Fl. pure white; perianth segments waxy

'Cashmere Gold' 1 Y-Y
(G. Lewis) D.S. Bell, 1955

'Casilda' 3 W-?
(J. Mallender, pre-1913)

'Casimer' 2 W-Y
Syn. of 'Casimir'

'Casimir' 2 W-Y
(C. Dawson, pre-1921)
Perianth segments acute; corona ribbed, bright yellow, tinged orange. See also 'Casimer'

'Casimir-Perier' 1 W-W
(de Graaff Bros, pre-1923)

'Casino' 2 Y-O
(Mrs R.O. Backhouse, pre-1921)
Perianth segments sulphur white; corona clear orange. AM(Haarlem) 1930

'Casinova' 1 W-W
(C.E. Radcliff, 1931)
'Lemon Star' × 'Mrs W.Moodie'

'Caspary' 2 W-? (b)
(G.A. Uit den Boogaard, pre-1946)

'Casper' 1 W-W
(P. Phillips) P. Phillips, 1964
Fl. 102 mm wide; corona off-white. Mid-season

'Casque' 1 Y-Y
(W.B. Cranfield, pre-1923)

'Casque d'Or' 1 W-? (b)
(Cartwright & Goodwin, pre-1916)

'Cassa' 2 W-W
(R.H.Glover, pre-1983) Unregistered
'Panache' × 'Lady Slim'

'Cassandra' 9 W-GYR
(G.H. Engleheart, pre-1897)
'Ornatus' × *N. radiiflorus* var. *poetarum*; sdlg no. 347
Perianth segments broadly ovate or oblong, squarish at apex, more or less prominently mucronate, spreading, plane or with margins narrowly incurling at apex, overlapping half; the inner segments shouldered at base, a little inflexed, with margins more strongly incurved and giving a narrower appearance; corona very small disc-shaped, ribbed, orange-yellow, more or less heavily tinged green at base, with a clearly defined band of dark red at rim. Mid-season. AM 1899

'Cassanova' 9 W-?
(?H.G. Hawker)

'Cassata' 11a W-W
(J. Gerritsen & Son) J. Gerritsen & Son, 1963
Fl. 100 mm wide; perianth segments very broadly ovate, slightly mucronate, greenish white, reflexed; the inner segments more narrowly ovate, acute; corona split to base, the six segments opposite and closely overlying the perianth segments, bi-lobed, opening greenish yellow (4D), flushed with a brighter tone (4C) towards mouth, becoming white, frilled. Early. Slightly scented. 2n=28. Resembles a larger-flowered 'Split' with the corona less heavily frilled and with no green at corona base. HC(p) 1985

'Cassel'
(pre-1956) Unregistered

'Casselle' 1 W-Y
(C.O. Fairbairn, 1948) P. Phillips, 1966
Fl. 100 mm wide; perianth segments smooth and of good substance, deeply overlapping; corona lemon yellow, mouth frilled, with rim dentate. Mid-season. Resembles a later-flowered 'Preamble' with unfading corona. Syn. 'Pale Moon'

'Cassia' 2 W-? (b)
(Mrs R.O. Backhouse, pre-1921)

'Cassilda'
(J.T. Gray, pre-1933)

'Cassini' 3 W-? (b)
(J.W.A. Lefeber, pre-1943)

'Cassino' 3 W-YYR
(G. Lewis) D.S. Bell, 1955

'Cassiopaeia' 2 or 3 W-? (b or c)
(W.F.M. Copeland, pre-1908)

'Cassiopeia' 3 Y-?
Syn. of 'Allandale'

'Cassowary' 2 W-YPP
(G.E. Mitsch) G.E. Mitsch, 1970
('Mabel Taylor' × 'Green Island') × 'Carita'

'Casta' 3 W-O
(pre-1930)
Perianth segments white; corona very shallow, reddish orange. Resembles 'Firetail'

'Castanets' 8 Y-O
(W.G. Pannill) W.G. Pannill, 1985
'Matador' × 'Grand Soleil d'Or'; sdlg no. 66/49
Fls 4-8 per stem, 50 mm wide; perianth segments broadly ovate, truncate, deep golden yellow, with white mucro, reflexed; the inners egments blunt, only very slightly mucronate, more nearly spreading, with margins reflexed near base and wavy towards apex; corona shallow bowl-shaped, smooth, strong orange 25A, with mouth wavy and rim entire. Mid-season. Scented

'Castaway' 1 W-W
Syn. of 'Treasure Trove'

'Castaway Isle' 4 W-P
(David L. Sheppard) David L. Sheppard, 1987
'Lawali' × 'Replete'
Fl. 90 mm wide; perianth and other petaloid segments in several whorls, symmetrically superimposed, broadly ovate, blunt and mucronate, overlapping two-thirds; the outer whorl spreading, plane; the inner whorls diminishing only a little in size towards centre, gradually becoming more inflexed and concave or crumpled, with margins wavy or inward rolling; corona segments interspersed, short, pink, margins wavy and entire, with those at centre more convoluted and tightly arranged. Resembles 'Tropic Isle'

'Castella' 2 W-W
(H. Leber, pre-1953)
Corona broad, shallow, cream

'Casterbridge' 2 YYW-O
(J.W. Blanchard) J.W. Blanchard, 1986
'Golden Aura' × 'Daydream'; sdlg no. 73/15F
Perianth segments broadly ovate, blunt, greenish yellow, with slight white mucro and with a distinct band of white at base, a little reflexed, plane, smooth, overlapping one-third to a half; the inner segments more narrowly ovate, spreading, with margins slightly wavy; corona cylindrical, constricted near mouth, broadly ribbed, buff orange, mouth straight, split in places and overlapping, frilled, with rim minutely crenate. Mid-season

'Castigate' 2 Y-R
(G. Lewis) D.S. Bell, 1955

'Castile' 3 Y-O
(G.H. Engleheart, pre-1907)
Perianth segments sulphur, tinted white; corona rich orange, with apricot tones

'Castile' 2 Y-R
(J.M. de Navarro) J.M. de Navarro, 1958
('Trevisky' × 'Porthilly') × 'Armada'

'Castlebar' 1 Y-Y
(W.J. Dunlop, pre-1950)
'Cromarty' × 'Crocus'
Fl. deep gold; corona with rim rolled

'Castlecat' 1 Y-Y
(W.J. Dunlop, c.1964) Unregistered

'Castlecoole' 2 W-WWO
(W.J. Dunlop, pre-1953)
Fl. somewhat rounded; perianth segments white; corona large, spreading, corona creamy white, touched orange at rim. Syn. 'Belleek'

'Castledermot' 2 Y-Y
(J.L. Richardson, pre-1951)
'Crocus' × 'Cromarty'
Fl. golden yellow; corona mouth slightly expanded, with rim rolled

'Castle Dobbs' 4 Y-R
(Carncairn Daffodils) Carncairn Daffodils, 1979
'Falaise' self pollinated; sdlg no. 19/67
Fls occasionally 2 per stem, 95 mm wide; perianth and other petaloid segments brilliant yellow 7B; corona segments interspersed, orange-red (30C). Late. Scented. Resembles 'Hawaii' in colour but with fewer segments; resembles a larger and stronger 'Falaise' in form. Syn. 'Beauvallet'

'Castle Dore' 1 Y-Y
(T.A.V. Wood, pre-1949)

'Castlehill' 3 W-YYR
(Ballydorn Bulb Farm, 1971) Ballydorn Bulb Farm, 1981
'Fairmile' × 'Merlin'
Fl. 90 mm wide; corona deep yellow, with a broad band of deep red at rim. Mid-season.

'Castle Howard' 1 W-W
(Clive Postles) Clive Postles Daffodils, 1994
'Ben Avon' × Lea sdlg 35-76; sdlg no. 1-23A-83
Fl. forming a double triangle, 114 mm wide, pure white; perianth segments broadly ovate; corona cylindrical, with mouth flared and rim crenate. Mid-season

'Castle Kennedy' 2 W-WWY
M.J. Jefferson-Brown, 1963

'Castlemaine' 1 W-Y
(D.S. Bell, pre-1961) Unregistered
Perianth segments broad, overlapping; corona deep lemon yellow, with rim frilled and flanged

'Castle of Mey' 2 W-W
(G.L. Wilson, pre-1953)
('Slemish' × 'Broughshane') × 'Murmansk'; sdlg no. 37/38
Fl. pure ice white; perianth segments almost triangular in appearance, mucronate, plane, or a little concave at apex, smooth, overlapping half; the inner segments somewhat narrower, a little twisted, shouldered at base; corona funnel-shaped, ribbed, tinged sea green at base, mouth expanded, with rim flanged and crenate

'Castlepoint' 2 Y-Y
(J.S. Leitch) J.S. Leitch, 1967
Fl. 120 mm wide

'Castlereagh' 1 Y-Y
(G.L. Wilson, pre-1945)

'Castle Regiment' 2 W-Y
(John R.Reed, 1984 or 1985) John R.Reed, 1995
'Royal Regiment' × 'Newcastle'; sdlg no. 79-12-1
Fl. forming a double triangle, 95 mm wide, facing up; perianth segments ovate; corona orange-yellow. Mid-season

'Castlerock' 2 Y-R
(W.J. Dunlop, pre-1947)
'Ballyclare' × 'Bahram'
Perianth segments deep yellow; corona crimson-red

'Castleton' 2 Y-? (a)
(D.B. Milne, pre-1952)

'Castle Upton' 2 Y-R
(Carncairn Daffodils) Carncairn Daffodils, 1970
'Krakatoa' × 'Fury'
Perianth segments deep yellow; corona red

'Castlewellan' 1 Y-Y
(W.J. Dunlop) W.J. Dunlop, 1959
'Cromarty' × 'Crocus'
Fl. clear deep golden yellow, of thick and waxy substance; perianth segments broad, smooth. Mid-season to late

"Castlewellan Daffodil"
See "The Castlewellan Daffodil"

'Castor' 5
(E.T. England, pre-1923)

'Castor' 5 W-W
(D. Blanchard) M.J. Jefferson-Brown, 1975
'Silver Coin' × *N. triandrus* subsp. *pallidulus*
Mid-season

'Castra' 1 W-W
(E.L. Jones, pre-1949)

'Catalina' 5
(Barr & Sons, pre-1923)
'Scarlet Perfection' × 'Diolite'
Perianth segments lemon yellow; corona widely expanded, bright red. Early. Resembles 'Ceylon' but with a larger and more rounded flower

'Catalina' 2 Y-R
(D.S. Bell) D.S. Bell, 1960
Fl. 114 mm wide

'Catalyst' 2 W-R

(G.E.Mitsch, 1984) R. & E.Havens, 1995
'Decoy' × 'Magician'; sdlg no. TT3/1
Fl. 120 mm wide; perianth segments broadly ovate, pure white, spreading, plane; corona straight-sided, deep red, with slight undertones of orange, mouth expanded and frilled. Mid-season. Sunproof

'Catamaran' 1 Y-Y
(S.J. Bisdee, 1951)
'Ranefer' × 'J.P.'

'Catania' 1 W-W
(The Brodie of Brodie, c.1918)
'Morven' × 'Mrs Ernst H. Krelage'
Fl. white; corona broad, frilled

'Cataract' 1 W-W
(Murray W. Evans) Murray W. Evans, 1975
('Zero' × 'Kanchenjunga') × 'Vigil'; sdlg no. M-90
Fl. 120 mm wide. Mid-season

'Catarina' 1 W-W
(E.M. Crosfield, pre-1907)

'Catawba' 9 W-GYO
(E.C. Powell, pre-1948)
'Minuet' × 'Ace of Diamonds'
2n=28

'Catbird' 6 Y-Y
(G.E. Mitsch, 1967) G.E. Mitsch, 1977
'Bushtit' open pollinated; sdlg no. DO1/2
Fl. 95 mm wide; perianth segments soft clear yellow, slightly reflexed, with margins a little wavy; corona long, slightly deeper in tone than the perianth segments. Mid-season. Resembles 'Bushtit' but with broader perianth segments

'Catch Me' 3 W-YOO
(Konynenburg & Mark) Konynenburg & Mark, 1964
'General MacArthur' × (['Frederike' × 'Mimosa'] × ['Dandy Boy'? × 'Red Bird'])
Fl. 100 mm wide; perianth segments ivory white; corona vivid yellow 15A, with orange at rim. Mid-season

'Catchup' ?-P
(Alister Clark, pre-1948)

'Catella' 2 W-? (b)
(A.H. Ahrens) J.S. Leitch, 1956

'Cathal' 1 Y-Y
(Sir J.A.R. Gore-Booth, pre-1916)

'Cathay' 2 W-? (b)
(H. Backhouse, pre-1910)

'Cathay' 2 Y-R
(J.L. Richardson) Mrs H.K. Richardson, 1962
'Air Marshal' × 'Firecracker'
Perianth segments broad, deep yellow; corona deep orange-red. 2n=29

'Cathedral' 5 W-W
(Oregon Bulb Farms, pre-1950)

'Cathedral Hill' 6 W-Y
(W.G. Pannill, 1977) W.G. Pannill, 1990
'Jenny' × (pink sdlg × 'Alpine Glow'); sdlg no. 75/51
Mid-season

'Catherine Grullemans' 2 W-OOY
Syn. of 'Mother Catherine Grullemans'

'Catherine H.Heigham' 1 W-W
(pre-1914)
See also 'Catherine H.Hughan'

'Catherine H.Hughan' 1 W-W
Syn. of 'Catherine H.Heigham'

'Catherine Howard' 3 W-GYO
(G. Lewis) D.S. Bell, 1955
Perianth segments white; corona orange-yellow, with green at base and reddish orange at rim. Spelt 'Cathrine Howard' before 1961

'Catherine Lubbe' 9 W-?
(G. Lubbe & Son, pre-1936)
Syn. 'Madame Lubbe', 'Mrs Lubbe'. AM(Haarlem) 1936

'Catherine MacKenzie' 3 W-GYY
(D.C. MacArthur) D.C. MacArthur, 1988
MacArthur sdlg open pollinated; sdlg no. E8853
Perianth segments white; corona cup-shaped, light yellow 11B, with light yellow-green 145C at base and vivid yellow 17B at rim. Late

'Catherine MacLeod' 2 Y-YYO
(D.C. MacArthur) D.C. MacArthur, 1985
'Chungking' self pollinated; sdlg no. E836
Perianth segments very broad, blunt, brilliant yellow 7A, overlapping; the inner segments much narrower, with margins somewhat uneven and slightly incurved near apex; corona small, shallow, expanded, lightly ribbed, vivid yellow 17C, shading to strong orange 25A at rim, frilled, with rim deeply and irregularly notched. Late. Fairly sunproof

'Catherine Wheel' 2 Y-Y
(Tom Forster, 1960s) Unregistered
Perianth segments soft yellow, deeply overlapping; corona broad disc-shaped, yellow. Mid-season

'Cathlin' 2 W-P
(W. Jackson Jr) W. Jackson Jr, 1968
'Illinga' × 'Dallbro'; sdlg no. 172/57

Corona strong pink

'Cathrine Howard' 3 W-GYO
Syn. of 'Catherine Howard'

'Catlins' 2 W-? (b)
(R. Crews) R. Crews, 1956

'Cato' 1 Y-Y
(Barr & Sons, pre-1923)

'Cato' 1 Y-Y
(C.E. Radcliff, 1932)
'Renown' × 'Billali'

'Catriona' 1 W-W
(E.M. Crosfield, pre-1908)
Perianth segments creamy white, slightly incurved; corona expanded, opening creamy yellow, becoming whiter at maturity, lightly frilled

'Catriona' 2 W-YYW
M.J. Jefferson-Brown, 1963
Perianth segments creamy white, slightly inflexed; corona cream, with mouth expanded and frilled

'Catskill' 2 W-? (b)
(E.C. Powell, pre-1946)
'Bokhara' × 'Sunstar'

'Cattaro' 2 Y-? (a)
(A.H. Ahrens, pre-1949)
Syn. 'Francesca'

'Cattistock' 2 Y-R
(D. Blanchard) D. Blanchard, 1974
'Revelry' × 'Dewlish'
Fl. 95 mm wide; perianth segments deep yellow, a little reflexed; corona solid red. Mid-season

'Catullus' 9 W-?
(de Graaff Bros, pre-1927)

'Cauldron' 2 Y-R
(Brian S. Duncan, 1980) Brian S. Duncan, 1992
'Shining Light' × 'Torridon'; sdlg no. 830
Fl. 104 mm wide; perianth segments broadly ovate, blunt; corona funnel-shaped, with mouth flared. Mid-season. Sunproof

'Causeur' 2 Y-Y
(D. Bramley) D. Bramley, 1978
'Balmoral' × 'Regal Gold'
Fl. 98 mm wide, deep yellow. Mid-season

'Cavalcade' 2 Y-O
(Barr & Sons, pre-1932)
Perianth segments broad, soft primrose yellow, overlapping; corona bright orange

'Cavalcade' 1 Y-Y
(D.S. Bell) D.S. Bell, 1960
Fl. 114 mm wide. Mid-season. Resembles 'Kingscourt' but with a rounder flower and the perianth segments plane

'Cavalier' 3 W-YOO
(pre-1907)
Perianth segments reflexed; corona very shallow, shading to scarlet-orange at rim, with golden yellow at base. Dwarf

'Cavaliero' 2 Y-YOO
(P.D. Williams, pre-1933)
Fl. 101 mm wide; perianth segments brilliant greenish yellow 6C; corona ribbed, strong orange 25A, paling to vivid orange-yellow 21A towards base, mouth slightly expanded, frilled, with rim dentate and slightly flanged. AM(Haarlem) 1933, *AM(g) 1959

'Cavalla' 2 W-O
(de Graaff Bros, pre-1935)
Perianth segments white; corona opening saffron yellow, becoming orange. AM(Haarlem) 1934

'Cavalryman' 3 W-R
(Brian S.Duncan) Brian S.Duncan, 1997
Sdlg 675 ('Arctic Flame' × 'Random Light') × 'Doctor Hugh'; sdlg no. 1401
Fl. 112 mm wide; perianth segments broadly ovate, slightly truncate, mucronate, pure white, spreading, smooth, with margins minutely incurling at apex, overlapping half; the inner segments more narrowly ovate, slightly inflexed, angled at shoulder; corona shallow bowl-shaped, ribbed, deep red, with mouth split in places and overlapping, lightly frilled. Late

N. cavanillesii Barra & López 13 Section Tapeinanthus

'Cavatina' 3 W-? (b)
(F.H. Chapman, pre-1930)

'Cavatina' 2 W-WWP
(J.L. Richardson) Mrs H.K. Richardson, 1967
'Templemore' × 'Rosedew'
Fl. 98 mm wide; perianth segments pure white; corona with a broad band of pale peach pink at rim. Mid-season

'Cave' 3 W-GYR
(J.A. O'More) J.A. O'More, 1968
'Silver Halo' × 'Matapan'
Corona with red at rim

'Cavendish' 4 W-O
(Brian S. Duncan) Rathowen Daffodils, 1987
'Pink Paradise' × sdlg
Fl. rounded; perianth and other petaloid segments in three whorls, very broad, truncate or notched at apex,

only very slightly mucronate, pure white, overlapping half or more; the outer whorl spreading, a little concave; the inner whorl only a little shorter, inflexed, with margins deeply incurling; the centre whorl shorter, irregularly arranged, strongly inflexed, folded inwards along midrib and with margins incurled; corona segments shorter than the centre petaloid segments and clustered among them, more loosely arranged between the surrounding whorls, broad, apricot orange, with a darker tone at rim, tightly frilled. Late

'Cavoda' 1 W-GPP
(J.M.Radcliff, pre-1977) Carncairn Daffodils, 1987
Perianth segments ovate, somewhat inflexed, overlapping one-third; the inner segments with margins wavy; corona funnel-shaped, narrow at base, 6-angled or lightly ribbed, pale yellow-pink, with mouth even and rim regularly crenate. Mid-season. Scented

'Cawdron' 2 Y-O
du Plessis Bros, 1976
Fl. 98 mm wide; corona reddish orange. Mid-season. Resembles a better-quality 'Krakatoa' of stronger colour

'Cawood' 3 W-WWP
(C.E. Radcliff, 1943) C.E. Radcliff, 1956
'Moina' × 'Carmoa'

'Cawsand' 2 W-Y
(Mrs H.K. Richardson) du Plessis Bros, 1978
'Spitzbergen' × 'Rose Caprice'; sdlg no. 396
Fl. 92 mm wide. Mid-season. 2n=28

'Caye Chapel' 3 W-GYO
(A.J.R.Pearson) A.J.R.Pearson, 1995
'Dell Chapel' × 'Corozal'; sdlg no. 89-70-L15
Fl. 98 mm wide; perianth segments broadly ovate, blunt, slightly mucronate, greenish white (157C), a little reflexed, smooth and of heavy substance; the inner segments narrower; corona almost disc-shaped, opening pale primrose yellow (4D), becoming creamy yellow, with grey-green at base and a broad band of vivid orange 28B at rim, mouth lightly ribbed and deeply 6-lobed, closely frilled, with rim entire. Mid-season to late

'Cayuga' 2 W-? (b)
(E.C. Powell, pre-1946)

'Cazique' 6 W-W
(G.E. Mitsch) G.E. Mitsch, 1982
Sdlg × 'Rima' × *N. cyclamineus*; sdlg no. KK105/1
Fl. 78 mm wide; corona opening pale lemon, becoming white. Mid-season

'Cazna' 2 Y-? (a)
(H.A. Brown, pre-1938)

N. × *cazorlanus* Fernández Casas 13 = *N. hedraeanthus* (Webb & Heldreich) Colmeiro × *N. triandrus* Linnaeus subsp. *pallidulus* (Graells) D.A.Webb

'Ceasefire' 2 Y-R
(Brian S.Duncan) Brian S.Duncan, 1995
'Red Spartan' × sdlg 538 ('Montego' × 'Achduart'); sdlg no. 1113
Fl. forming a double triangle, 104 mm wide; perianth segments broadly ovate, strong golden yellow, spreading, smooth; corona broad funnel-shaped, ribbed, deep orange-red, slightly frilled. Mid-season to late. Sunproof

'C.E.Bailey' 2 W-P
Syn. of 'Charles Bailey'

'Cecely Manders' 2 Y-Y
Perianth segments soft yellow; corona darker in tone. Resembles 'Noble' in form and colour. Syn. of 'Cicely Mander'

'Cecile Spitz' 9 W-GWO
(L.P. Dettman) L.P. Dettman, 1979
'Sea Green' × 'Greenholm'; sdlg no. P 1/77
Fl. 55 mm wide; perianth segments greenish white (157B); corona greenish white (157), with brilliant yellowish green 134C at base and a broad band of pinkish orange (29C) at rim. Late

'Cecil Hayward' 1 W-? (b)
(Barton Nurseries, pre-1925)

'Cecilia' 1 W-? (b)
(Barr & Sons, pre-1913)

'Cecilia de Graaff' 1 W-? (b)
(de Graaff Bros, pre-1884)
Perianth segments sulphur white, with yellowish green at midrib beneath; corona funnel-shaped, narrow at base, with mouth widely expanded and rim flanged. Syn. Pseudonarcissus Moschatus 'Cecilia de Graaff'

'Cecil Nice' 6 Y-Y
(English origin) J.W.Blanchard, 1997
Believed to be a chance sdlg from Sheffield Park, Sussex

'Cecil Rhodes' 5
(G.H. Engleheart, pre-1902)
AM 1902

'Cecily Hill' 3 Y-YOR
(Mrs R.O. Backhouse, pre-1899)
Perianth segments soft primrose yellow, with darker tones at base, of strong substance; corona flushed reddish orange, with red at rim. Late

'Cecily O'Rorke' 2 W-P
Syn. of 'Cicely O'Rorke'

'Cedar' 2 W-Y
(S.A. Free) S.A. Free, 1961
Fl. 108 mm wide; corona opening deep yellow, becoming golden yellow, suffused orange. Mid-season

'Cedarbird' 2 W-P
(G.E. Mitsch) Grant Mitsch Novelty Daffodils, 1984
('Precedent' × 'Debutante') × 'Spaceship'; sdlg no. LL39/4
Fl. rounded, 92 mm wide; perianth segments very broad, blunt, irregularly mucronate, spreading, with broad midrib showing, overlapping half; the inner segments narrower, with margins wavy or creased; corona broad, ribbed, clear pink, with rim widely rolled. Mid-season

'Cedar Hills' 3 W-GYY
(G.E. Mitsch and R. & E.Havens, 1975) G.E. Mitsch and R. & E.Havens, 1987
'Impala' × 'Green Hills'; sdlg no. KK87/3A
Perianth segments very broad, rounded at apex, truncate, a little reflexed, smooth, with margins incurling at apex, overlapping half or more; the inner segments spreading, with broad midrib showing and with margins somewhat wavy; corona shallow, closely ribbed, clear yellow, with a broad band of green at base, mouth straight, tightly frilled. Very late

'Cedar Lake' 2 W-P
(Curtis Tolley) Curtis Tolley, 1997
'Dewy Rose' × 'Dailmanach'; 88-6-4
Fl. forming a double triangle, 98 mm wide; perianth segments ovate; corona funnel-shaped, slightly constricted near mouth, strong yellowish pink 32D, with mouth a little expanded, lightly frilled. Mid-season

'Cedric' 2
(W.B. Hartland, pre-1907)

'Cedric' 1 W-Y
Syn. of 'William Baylor Hartland'

'Cedric Graham' 1 Y-Y
(J.N. Hancock & Co., 1963) Unregistered

'Cedric Morris' 1 Y-Y
(Spanish origin)
Selection by Basil Leng (*c.*1956) from wild-collected *N. minor*
Fl. 38 mm wide, lemon yellow; perianth segments ovate or narrowly ovate, blunt, fairly prominently mucronate, strongly inflexed, more or less strongly twisted, separated; corona cylindrical, sometimes slightly constricted near mouth, shallowly ribbed, with mouth widely expanded and even, rim minutely dentate and deeply notched. Dwarf. Very early. AM 1978

'Ceduna' 2 Y-Y
(H.A. Brown, pre-1938)
Fl. rich yellow

'Cedys' 2 or 3 W-? (b or c)
(W.A. Watts, pre-1923)

'Celandine' 2 Y-? (a)
(W.B. Cranfield, pre-1927)

'Celebration' 4 Y-O
(M.J. Jefferson-Brown) M.J. Jefferson-Brown, 1975
Early mid- to mid-season. Resembles a more star-shaped 'Tahiti'

'Celebrity' 1 W-Y
(L. van Leeuwen & Son, pre-1943)
Fl. 101 mm wide; perianth segments creamy white, touched brilliant yellow 9C at base, slightly twisted, overlapping half; corona vivid yellow 9A, mouth expanded and frilled, with rim dentate. *AM(g) 1958

'Celebrity' 2 Y-?
Syn. of 'Guilder'

'Celedon' 2 W-Y
(W.A. Noton) W.A. Noton, 1976
'Homage' × 'Tudor Minstrel'; sdlg no. 516
Fl. 96 mm wide. Mid-season

'Celestan' 2 Y-O
(J.N. Hancock & Co.) J.N. Hancock & Co., 1960
Perianth yellow; corona pale orange

'Celeste' 1 W-W
(A. White, pre-1946)

'Celestial' 5 Y-Y
(Barr & Sons, pre-1950)
2n=21

'Celestial Fire' 2 Y-O
(A.J.R.Pearson) A.J.R.Pearson, 1995
Sdlg 70-8-C2 (['Home Fires' × 'Ceylon'] × 'Court Martial') × 'Loch Lundie'; sdlg no. 90-4-M6
Fl. forming a double triangle, 110 mm wide; perianth segments broadly ovate, acute, yellow (6A), with a golden yellow sheen and undertones of green, with margins very slightly incurving, smooth and of solid waxy substance; the inner segments more nearly ovate; corona funnel-shaped, lightly ribbed, reddish-orange (28A), with a slightly paler tone at base and green in tube, rim flanged and crenate. Mid-season

'Celeus' 3 W-GWY
(J.A. O'More) J.A. O'More, 1968
'Nelly' × 'Chinese White'

'Celia' 1 W-W
(G.H. Engleheart, pre-1907)

'Celia' 2 W-?
(?Guernsey origin, pre-1914)

'Celia' 1 W-W
(J.N. Hancock & Co., 1977) Unregistered

'Celia Rosser' 1 W-W
(J.N. Hancock & Co., c.1975) Unregistered

'Celilo' 1 W-W
(Murray W. Evans, 1957) Murray W. Evans, 1968
'Petsamo' × 'Beersheba'
Fl. 114 mm wide; perianth segments broad; corona narrowly flared. Early. Resembles a taller and more weatherproof 'Cantatrice' of better poise

'Celine' 5 W-W
(T. Morrison) T. Morrison, 1960
Fl. white; corona very shallow bowl-shaped

'Celmesia' 2 W-? (b)
(D.H.L. Corrigan, pre-1949)

'Celtic Chief' 2 Y-Y
(N.A. Burr, 1977) N.A. Burr, 1989
'Golden Aura' × 'Celtic Gold'; sdlg no. 1.5.72
Fl. forming a double triangle, 93 mm wide; perianth segments very broadly ovate, truncate, with slight white mucro, brilliant yellow 7A, spreading, plane, with midrib showing and margins very slightly incurling, regular, overlapping half; corona funnel-shaped, smooth, of a slightly brighter tone (12A) than the perianth, mouth a little frilled, with shallow overlapping lobes, rim flanged and minutely crenate. Mid-season

'Celtic Gold' 2 Y-Y
(J.L. Richardson) Mrs H.K. Richardson, 1974
'Golden Aura' × 'Camelot'
Fl. 100 mm wide, very deep yellow. Resembles a larger-flowered 'Golden Aura'

'Celtic Song' 2 W-WWP
(J.L. Richardson) Mrs H.K. Richardson, 1967
'Interim' × 'Rose Caprice'
Fl. of smooth, waxy texture; perianth segments somewhat rounded, pure white, deeply overlapping; corona creamy white, with a narrow band of buffy pink at rim, dentate

'Celtic Wings' 5 W-W
(John R.Reed, 1982) John R.Reed, 1995
'Angel' × *N. triandrus*; sdlg no. 77-8-1
Fls 2-3 per stem, 68 mm wide; perianth segments broadly ovate, strongly reflexed; corona cup-shaped, small. Late. Syn. 'Angel Wings'

'Cemaes' 2 or 3 W-? (b or c)
(pre-1923)

"Cemetery Ladies"
Syn. of *N.* × *medioluteus*

'Cena' 2 W-W
(W. Jackson Jr, 1967) Unregistered
'Filia' × 'Green Valley'; sdlg no. 61/67
Fl. pure white; perianth segments smooth; corona with green noticeable in tube, mouth slightly expanded, rim dentate

'Cenig' 2 Y-? (a)
(W.A. Watts, pre-1923)

'Cennedy' 1 W-? (b)
(de Graaff Bros, pre-1927)

'Centannées' 11b Y-O
(J. Gerritsen & Son) J. Gerritsen & Son, 1984
Sdlg × 'Tiritomba'
Perianth segments brilliant yellow 11A; corona segments strong orange 24A. Early

'Centaur' 1 W-W
(A.M. Wilson, pre-1915)

'Centaur' 1 Y-Y
(A.M. Wilson, pre-1937)
Fl. white; perianth segments broad; corona flared, with rim crenate and slightly flanged

'Centaurus' 2 W-Y
(J.A. Hunter) J.A. Hunter, 1972
'Bonniform' × 'Kanchenjunga'
Fl. 125 mm wide

'Centenaire' 1 W-Y
(J.B. van der Schoot, pre-1930)
Fl. 100 mm wide; perianth segments cream, with sulphur at base, spreading, with margins recurving, overlapping a quarter; corona bright buttercup yellow, mouth expanded. Syn. 'Purity', 'Rhine'. AM(g) 1930

'Centenary Pride' 4 W-YYO
(Jackson's Daffodils) Jackson's Daffodils, 1989
'Glowing Red' hybrid; sdlg no. 145/84
Fl. 90 mm wide; perianth and other petaloid segments in three whorls, greenish white (155A); corona segments brilliant yellow 13C, with vivid orange 28B at rim. Mid-season

'Centennial'
(G. Lewis, pre-1940)

'Centennial Gold' 2 Y-? (a)
(H.B. Shailer, pre-1949)

'Centerpiece' 4 W-R
(G.E. Mitsch) G.E. Mitsch, 1974
'Falaise' × 'Roimond'; sdlg no. A13/1
Fl. 88 mm wide; corona segments bright orange-red. Mid-season

'Centifolio' 4 Y-Y
?Syn. of 'Telamonius Plenus'

'Central Park' 2
(de Graaff Bros, pre-1930)
AM(Haarlem) 1930

'Central Park' 1 W-Y
(W.G. Pannill) W.G. Pannill, 1972
'Gold Crown' × 'Lapford'
Fl. 107 mm wide

'Centrefold' 3 W-YYR
(G.W.E. Brogden, 1975) Brogden Bulbs, 1991
'Polar Imp' × 'Bandit'; sdlg no. x40/3
Fl. 105 mm wide; perianth segments broad, roundish, truncate, a little concave at margins, smooth and of good substance; the inner segments more nearly ovate; corona very shallow bowl-shaped, yellow, with a broad band of red at rim, mouth sometimes 6-lobed, rim very deeply crenate. Mid-season. Smaller blooms sometimes measuring Div. 2. FCC(e)(NZ) 1991

'Centre Stage' 2 Y-Y
(J.N.Hancock & Co., 1983) Unregistered
'Glorification' open pollinated; sdlg no. 95/83H
Perianth segments roundish, primrose yellow; corona disc-shaped, golden yellow, heavily frilled. Early to mid-season

'Centre Ville' 3 Y-R
(T.D. Throckmorton) T.D. Throckmorton, 1976
'Russet' × 'Altruist'; sdlg no. 67/14
Fl. 95 mm wide; perianth segments yellow, suffused orange-gold; corona small, ribbed, deep red, frilled. Mid-season

'Centrist' 2 W-Y
Syn. of 'Cintrist'

'Centurion' 2 W-Y
(P.J. Worsley, pre-1910)
'Madame de Graaff' self pollinated
Perianth segments ivory white; corona pale yellow. AM(p) 1916

'Century' 2 Y-WWY
(W.G. Pannill) W.G. Pannill, 1980
'Camelot' × 'Daydream'; sdlg no. H 22
Fl. 108 mm wide. Mid-season

'Century Twenty-one' 9 W-GGO
(Mrs M.S.Yerger) Mrs M.S.Yerger, 1996
'Quetzal' × 'Ace of Diamonds'; sdlg no. G 7
Fl. forming a double triangle, 60 mm wide; perianth segments rounded at apex, deeply overlapping; the inner segments narrower, more nearly acute; corona almost disc-shaped, light yellow-green 145B, with strong yellow-green 144C at base and orange (28A) at rim. Tall. Late

'Cephissus' 2 W-?
(Sir J.S. Arkwright, pre-1931)

'Cephus' 3 W-W
(Mrs P.M. Davis, pre-1948)

'C.E.Radcliff' 1 W-P
(J.M.Radcliff, c.1966) Unregistered
'Roseum' × 'Roslyn'

'Ceram' 2 W-P
(W. Jackson Jr, 1949)
'Rosario' × 'Duna'

'Ceramic' 3 W-? (b)
(F.H. Chapman, pre-1930)

'Cerberus' 2 Y-? (a)
(N.Y. Lower, pre-1914)

'Cerberus' 1 W-?
Syn. of 'Jolly'

'Cerebus' 3 ?Y-O
(pre-1948)
Corona tinged reddish orange

'Ceremony' 2 Y-YYO
(Murray W. Evans, 1967) Murray W. Evans, 1979
'Green Island' hybrid; sdlg no. K-27/1
Fl. 110 mm wide, yellow; corona shading to orange at rim. Mid-season

'Ceres' 3 W-YYO
(?W. Backhouse, pre-1869)
Fl. small, neat. Syn. Leedsii 'Ceres'

'Ceres' 8 Y-Y
(pre-1883)
Perianth segments pale yellow; corona slightly darker in tone

'Ceres' 2 W-Y
(G.H.Engleheart, pre-1897)
Sdlg no. 52
Perianth segments ovate, clear white; corona long cup-shaped, luminous yellow

'Ceres' 2 W-WWY
(J.A. O'More) J.A. O'More, 1971
'Green Island' × 'Chinese White'
Fl. 112 mm wide

'Cerimon' 1 W-? (b)
(Barr & Sons, pre-1923)

N. cerinus Schultes = *N. tazetta*

'Cerise Queen' 3 W-?
(de Graaff Bros, pre-1938)
AM(Haarlem) 1937

'Cern' 1 Y-Y
(W.A. Watts, pre-1933)
'Maximus' × 'Duke of Bedford'

N. cernuus Roth = *N. tortuosus*

N. cernuus Salisbury = *N. triandrus* subsp. *pallidulus*

'Cernuus'
Syn. of *N. moschatus*

'Cernuus Bicinctus' 4 W-W
(pre-1884)
Syn. "The Double White Trumpet Daffodil with the Divisions of the Perianth in Duplicate", 'Cernuus Flore Elegantissime Pleno Bicinctus'

'Cernuus Elatus' 1 W-Y
(E. Leeds, pre-1877)
Perianth segments white; corona large, expanded, primrose yellow

'Cernuus Flore Elegantissime Pleno' 4 W-W
Syn. of 'Cernuus Plenus'

'Cernuus Flore Elegantissime Pleno Bicinctus' 4 W-W
Syn. of 'Cernuus Bicinctus'

'Cernuus Plenus' 4 W-W
(pre-1830)
Perianth segments ovate, inflexed, twisted or with margins wavy or recurved, overlapping at base only; corona cylindrical, broad, white or very pale greenish yellow, with mouth lobed, rim flanged and crenate; the corona enclosing numerous segments of more or less the same length and colour, some blunt and some acute; the corona sometimes split to base, with the segments more or less spreading. Syn. "The Double White Trumpet", "The Old English Double White Daffodil", 'Cernuus Flore Elegantissime Pleno', *N. moschatus* 'Plenus', Pseudonarcissus 'Cernuus Plenus'

'Cernuus Pulcher' 1 W-W
(E. Leeds, pre-1877)
Perianth segments silvery white; corona large, opening pale primrose yellow, becoming sulphur white. Syn. Pseudonarcissus Moschatus 'Cernuus Pulcher'

N. cerrolazae J.F.Ureña 13 Section Jonquilla

'Certify' 1 Y-Y
(P. Phillips) P. Phillips, 1966
Fl. 126 mm wide, lemon yellow. Mid-season. Resembles 'Ulster Prince' but with broader perianth segments and the corona more heavily frilled

'Cerubus' 2 W-YOO
(G.A. Uit den Boogaard, pre-1937)
AM(Haarlem) 1936

'Cerva' 2 W-WWY
(pre-1985) Unregistered

'Cervantes' 1 Y-Y
(W.B. Hartland, pre-1907)
Syn. 'Express'. AM(Haarlem) 1922

'Cervinus'
(pre-1915)

'Cethin' 1 W-? (b)
(pre-1913)

'Ceylon' 2 Y-O
(J.L. Richardson, pre-1943)
'Marksman' × 'Diolite'
Fl. 100 mm wide; perianth segments broadly ovate, blunt, vivid yellow 9B, with white mucro, spreading or slightly inflexed, plane, with a metallic sheen, with midrib showing, overlapping one-third to a half; the inner segments a little narrower, sometimes with a "thumb" at the margin, inflexed, a little creased and with margins slightly wavy; corona short funnel-shaped, vivid orange 28B, mouth straight, split in places and overlapping, lightly frilled, with rim crenate. Early to mid-season. Sunproof. 2n=27,28. PC 1945, AM(e) 1946, FCC(e) 1948, *AM(g) 1961, *FCC(g) 1962, *FCC(p) 1974, Wister Award 1994, AGM 1995

'Cezanne' 2 W-P
(S.J. Bisdee, 1946) S.J. Bisdee, 1956
'Rosemount' × sdlg 118/45

'Cezar de Muscow' 8 W-Y
Corona lemon yellow. Early. Syn. of 'Czar of Muscovy'

'C.G.Longmore' 2 W-? (b)
(H.R. Meyer, pre-1927)

'Chablis' 3 W-W
(S.J. Bisdee, 1937)
'Dactyl' × 'Silver Salver'

'Chablis' 11a W-PPY
(J. Gerritsen & Son) J. Gerritsen & Son, 1971
'Split' × 'Silvretta'
Fl. 80 mm wide; perianth segments pure white; corona segments light pink, tinged gold at rim.

Mid-season to late

'Cha-Cha' 6 W-GPP
(Brian S. Duncan) Rathowen Daffodils, 1986
'Roseworthy' × 'Foundling'; sdlg no. 581
Perianth segments broadly ovate, blunt, fairly prominently mucronate, pure white, reflexed, plane, smooth, overlapping half; the inner segments more narrowly ovate, less noticeably mucronate, creased, with margins slightly wavy; corona long cup-shaped, straight-sided, ribbed, warm pink, with green at base, mouth straight, loosely frilled. Mid-season

'Chaconne' 3 W-GWW
(S.J. Bisdee, 1938) S.J. Bisdee, 1956
'Silver Salver' × 'Dactyl'

'Chaconne' 1 W-W
(M. van Waveren & Sons, pre-1954)

'Chadstone' 1 Y-Y
(H.A. Brown, 1948) J.N. Hancock & Co., 1965
Fl. deep golden yellow. Mid-season. Resembles a larger-flowered 'Principal' of better substance

'Chaffinch' 2 W-YOO
(P.D. Williams, pre-1907)
Perianth segments creamy white; corona expanded, rich reddish orange, paling to golden yellow at base

'Chaffinch' 6 Y-Y
(G.E. Mitsch) G.E. Mitsch, 1980
'Vulcan' × *N. cyclamineus*; sdlg no. H37/4
Fl. 90 mm wide; perianth segments rich yellow, reflexed, smooth, only slightly overlapping; corona long, slightly flared, deep gold, tinged with orange. Mid-season

'Chagall' 2 Y-GOO
(Carncairn Daffodils, 1967) Carncairn Daffodils, 1985
'Ballintoy' × 'Ballydorn'; sdlg no. 10/62
Perianth segments vivid yellow 9A; corona long cup-shaped, strong orange 25A, with rim crenate. Mid-season

'Chaka' 1 Y-Y
(G.L. Wilson) G. Zandbergen-Terwegen, 1974
Fl. 110 mm wide

'Chakawana' 4
(Cartwright & Goodwin, pre-1916)

'Chalcedonicus Fimbriatus Multiplex Polyanthos' 4 W-YYP
(pre-1629)
Fls many per stem; perianth and other petaloid segments white; corona segments interspersed, yellow, with purple at rim. Syn. "The Great Double Purple Ringed Daffodil of Constantinople", Tazetta 'Chalcedonicus Fimb. Mult. Polyanthos'

'Chalcedonicus Flore Pleno Albo Polyanthos' 4 W-Y
(pre-1629)
Fls 4-5 or more per stem; perianth and other petaloid segments white, irregularly arranged; corona segments interspersed, small, yellow. Syn. Tazetta 'Chalcedonicus Flore Pleno Albo Polyanthos', Tazetta 'Cypri Plena'

'Chalcedony' 3 W-? (b)
(P.D. Williams, pre-1910)

'Chalcis' 2 W-Y
(J.T. Gray, pre-1949)
Fl. forming a double triangle; perianth segments very broadly ovate, blunt, slightly mucronate, spreading, or slightly reflexed at apex, with margins a little wavy, overlapping half; the inner segments more narrowly ovate, a little inflexed; corona cylindrical, loosely ribbed, mouth notched in places, widely expanded, more or less even, rim slightly rolled, obscurely crenate

'Chalet' 4
(Oregon Bulb Farms, pre-1950)

'Chaliapin' 1 W-? (b)
(J.W. Barr, pre-1930)

'Chalice' 2 W-? (b)
(R.H. Bath, pre-1929)

'Chalim' 1 W-W
(W. Jackson Jr, 1956) Unregistered
'Gwaine' × 'Ammon'

'Challa' 2 W-W
(W. Jackson Jr) W. Jackson Jr, 1968
'Rowella' hybrid; sdlg no. 57/64

'Challenge' 3 W-ORR
(W. Jackson Jr) Jackson's Daffodils, 1979
'Signal Light' × ('Redlands' × ['Magherally' × 'Kai']); sdlg no. 151/70
Fl. 115 mm wide; perianth segments pure white; corona shallow, bright red, with orange at base, with rim heavily dentate. Mid-season

'Challenger' 1 Y-Y
(pre-1886)
Perianth segments sulphur yellow; corona rim crenate

'Challenger' 3 W-YYR
(E.M. Crosfield, pre-1890)
Fl. more than 76 mm wide; perianth segments broadly ovate, blunt or slightly truncate, mucronate, poeticus white, spreading, plane, overlapping half; the inner segments less obviously mucronate, a little

inflexed, with margins wavy; corona shallow, ribbed, soft canary yellow, with a broad band of brilliant fiery red at rim, mouth shallowly 6-lobed, with rim crenate

'Chamar' 3 Y-R
(G.J. Phillips, 1984) G.J. Phillips, 1994
'Trelay' × 'Tia'; sdlg no. 79-76-2
Fl. 118 mm wide; perianth segments very broadly ovate, smooth; corona wide-spreading, with rim dentate. Tall. Early

'Chambord' 11a W-Y
(J. Gerritsen & Son, 1968) J. Gerritsen & Son, 1980
'Floralie' hybrid
Fl. 80 mm wide; perianth segments ivory white; corona segments primrose yellow, with lemon yellow at base. Mid-season. Resembles a 'Cassata' unsuitable for forcing

'Chameleon' 1 Y-YYP
(de Graaff Bros, pre-1911)
?'Apricot' hybrid
Perianth segments acute, pale soft primrose yellow, paling to milk white tinged pink at base, somewhat twisted; corona sulphur yellow, shading to pale shell pink at rim

'Chaminade' 2 Y-? (a)
(A.M. Wilson, pre-1949)

'Chamkohe' 2 Y-Y
(P. & G. Phillips) P. & G. Phillips, 1982
'Roland' × 'Gold Script'; sdlg no. 70-19-4
Fl. 92 mm wide, mid-yellow; perianth segments rounded, spreading, smooth, deeply overlapping; corona mouth slightly flared. Mid-season. Resembles an earlier-flowered 'Gold Bank' with the perianth segments more nearly plane

'Chamois' W-?
(Barr & Sons, pre-1908)
?Syn. of 'Chamois' of pre-1913

'Chamois' 2 or 3 W-GPP
(Barr & Sons, pre-1913)
Fl. 90 mm wide; perianth segments pure white, twisted; corona expanded, ribbed, shaded salmon on a white ground, with pale green at base. ?The same as 'Chamois' pre-1908

'Chamois' 3 W-?
(Sir C.H. Cave, pre-1914)
'Mrs Langtry' × 'Cassandra'

'Chamois' 2 O-O
(G.E. Mitsch) G.E. Mitsch, 1976
'Carita' open pollinated; sdlg no. CS3/1
Fl. 103 mm wide; perianth segments coppery apricot; corona deep copper orange. Mid-season.

'Chamois Beauty' 2 W-Y
(H.P. Zwetsloot, pre-1949)
Corona soft lemon yellow. AM(Haarlem) 1949

'Chamonix' 1 W-W
(J.L. Richardson) J.L. Richardson, 1961
'Broughshane' × 'Alycidon'
Fl. rounded, 104 mm wide, ice white; perianth segments of good substance and texture; corona with rim rolled. Mid-season

'Champ' 1 W-? (b)
(Mrs A.O. Meyrick, pre-1949)
PC(e)(NZ) 1950, PC(e)(NZ) 1952

'Champagne' 2 Y-? (a)
(Cartwright & Goodwin, pre-1916)

'Champagne' 2 W-WWO
(?G. Zandbergen-Terwegen, pre-1950)
Fl. white; corona with rim suffused apricot orange, frilled

'Champagne' 2 W-P
(L. van Leeuwen & Son) J.J. Grullemans & Sons, 1956

'Champagne Magnum' 2 W-GYY
(T.D. Throckmorton) T.D. Throckmorton, 1975
'Easter Moon' × 'Irish Coffee'; sdlg no. 66/3/1
Perianth segments somewhat reflexed; corona greenish yellow, with greenish tones at base. Mid-season. Resembles a taller 'Green Island' with a shorter and broader corona

'Champion' 2 Y-? (a)
(A.M. Wilson, pre-1949)

'Chanak' 1 Y-Y
(S.J. Bisdee, 1951)
'Arahura' × 'Havilah'

'Chance' 3 Y-? (a)
(P.D. Williams, pre-1935)

'Chancellor' 2 W-Y
(G.H. Engleheart, pre-1900)
Perianth segments of stiff substance; corona straight-sided, ribbed, clear light yellow. AM 1900

'Chancellor' 2 W-? (b)
(L. van Leeuwen & Son, pre-1931)
AM(Haarlem) 1930

'Chancellorsville' 2 Y-YYR
(J.M. de Navarro) J.M. de Navarro, 1960
'Carbineer' × 'Majorca'
Fl. 95 mm wide; perianth segments very broadly ovate, mucronate, spreading, plane, smooth, regular, overlapping half; the inner segments more narrowly

ovate, less obviously mucronate, with midrib showing; corona smooth, with a broad band of orange-red at rim, mouth expanded and a little frilled, rim crenate. Mid-season. Resembles a more brightly coloured 'Ringmaster' with smoother perianth segments and a longer corona

'Chanctonbury' 2 Y-? (a)
(Sir F.C. Stern, pre-1950)

'Chanda' 1 W-? (b)
(A.M. Wilson, pre-1914)

'Chandelier' 1 W-W
(J.L. Richardson) Mrs H.K. Richardson, 1964
'White Emperor' self pollinated
Fl. waxy white; perianth segments broadly ovate, of waxy texture; corona with rim widely rolled. Late

'Chandos' 2 W-W
(Barr & Sons, pre-1935)

'Chanelle' 1 W-W
(F.E. Board) F.E. Board, 1965
'Templepatrick' × 'Empress of Ireland'
Mid-season

'Chanford' 2 Y-R
(?New Zealand origin, pre-1990) Unregistered

'Chang' 2 Y-Y
(E. Leeds, pre-1877)
Fl. large. Tall. Syn. Incomparabilis Concolor 'Chang'

'Changing Colors' 11a W-W
(J. Gerritsen & Son) W. Lemmers, 1993
Fl. 105 mm wide; perianth segments very broadly ovate, blunt, prominently mucronate, pale yellow-green to greenish white 157C to D, spreading, overlapping half; the inner segments more narrowly ovate, less prominently mucronate; corona split to base, the six segments half as long as the perianth segments and opposite and closely overlying them, deeply bi-lobed, with the lobes overlapping, opening pale yellow, becoming white, ageing to pink, lightly frilled. Mid-season

'Chango' 2 W-Y
(J.N. Hancock & Co., c.1975) Unregistered

'Chania' 1 W-W
(Carncairn Daffodils) Carncairn Daffodils, 1984
'Empress of Ireland' × 'Arctic Doric'; sdlg no. W6/9
Fl. 100 mm wide; perianth segments tinged green at base. Mid-season. 2n=28

'Channa' 3 W-? (b)
(C. Dawson, pre-1923)

'Chanson' 1 W-P
(Brian S.Duncan) Brian S.Duncan, 1997
'Verran' × 'Algarve'; sdlg no. 1534
Fl. forming a rounded double triangle, 100 mm wide; perianth segments broadly ovate, plane; corona cylindrical, opening apple blossom pink, becoming slightly paler in tone at rim, with mouth expanded. Early to mid-season

'Chansonette' 3 W-YYR
(G. Lewis) D.S. Bell
Corona spreading, yellow, with bright red at rim, frilled. See also 'Chausonette'

'Chantain' 2 W-Y
(P. de Jager & Sons) P. de Jager & Sons, 1963
'Daisy Schaffer' × 'Rosy Sunrise'
Fl. 95 mm wide; perianth segments white, flushed brilliant yellow 12B at base, slightly twisted, overlapping; corona ribbed, vivid yellow 12A, flushed with a darker tone (17C), mouth expanded, margins frilled. 2n=28. *AM(g) 1981

'Chantal' 2 Y-R
(P. Phillips) P. Phillips, 1968

'Chanterelle' 11a Y-Y
(J. Gerritsen & Son) J. Gerritsen & Son, 1962
Fl. 85 mm wide; perianth segments very broadly ovate, prominently mucronate, square-shouldered at base, light greenish yellow 4B, paler at apex, spreading, with margins incurling at apex, overlapping one third to a half; the inner segments a little inflexed; corona split to base, the six segments three-quarters the length of the perianth segments and opposite and closely overlying them, bi-lobed, vivid yellow 9A or 14B, frilled, with rim minutely ribbed and crenate. Mid-season. Scented. Resembles an improved 'Flaneur' more suited to forcing. *HC(p) 1986

'Chanteuse' 2 W-P
(F.E. Board) F.E. Board, 1965
'Irish Rose' × 'Rose Caprice'
Late

'Chanticleer' 1 Y-O
(Barr & Sons, pre-1903)
Perianth segments primrose yellow; corona large, deep golden yellow. Resembles an earlier-flowered 'Emperor'

'Chanticleer' 4 Y-O
(Murray W. Evans) Murray W. Evans, 1979
('Falaise' × ['Craigywarren' × 'Firecracker']) × 'Zanzibar'; sdlg no. N-11
Fl. 105 mm wide. Mid-season

'Chantilly' 2 W-O
(J. Gerritsen & Son, 1952) J. Gerritsen & Son, 1962
Fl. 90 mm wide; perianth segments ivory white; corona strong orange. Mid-season. Resembles a 'Pigalle'

of better form with a more strongly coloured corona

'Chaos' 1 W-W
(W. Jackson Jr, 1976) Unregistered
'Cilla' × 'Glendermott'; sdlg no. 151/76

'Chapeau' 2 W-Y
(Murray W. Evans) Murray W. Evans, 1972
'Wahkeena' × 'Festivity'
Fl. 110 mm wide; corona warm yellow, with mouth closely frilled

'Chapelet' 11?a Y-O
(J. Gerritsen & Son) J. Gerritsen & Son, 1981
Fl. 75 mm wide; perianth segments whitish yellow; corona segments very pale orange, with patches of marigold orange and lemon yellow

'Chaperone' 2 W-O
(Murray W. Evans) Murray W. Evans, 1979
'Hotspur' × ('Green Island' × ['Duke of Windsor' × 'Johann']); sdlg no. N-43/1
Fl. 105 mm wide. Mid-season

'Chaplet' 2 W-?
(W.B. Cranfield, pre-1916)

'Chapman's Peak' 2 Y-YOO
(Brian S.Duncan) Brian S.Duncan, 1996
Sdlg 77/1 ('Golden Jewel' × 'Midas Touch') × 'Barnum'; sdlg no. 1350
Fl. 95 mm wide; perianth segments very broadly ovate, only very slightly mucronate, mid-yellow, spreading, plane, smooth, overlapping half; corona cylindrical, deeper in tone than the perianth at base, shading to glowing orange at rim, lightly frilled, with rim rolled. Early to mid-season. Sunproof

'Chappie' 7 Y-O
(Roberta C.Watrous, 1967) Roberta C.Watrous, 1989
'Ruby' × *N. assoanus*; sdlg no. 611-2
Fl. 40 mm wide; perianth segments light yellow 10C, slightly reflexed; corona bowl-shaped, strong orange 24A. Dwarf. Late

'Character' 2 Y-O
(J.N. Hancock & Co., pre-1949)
Corona pale orange, with rim dentate

'Charade' 2 Y-? (a)
(W.A. Grace, pre-1938)

'Charade' 2 Y-Y
(Murray W. Evans) Murray W. Evans, 1976
'Greenland' × 'Green Island'; sdlg no. K-50
Fl. 97 mm wide; perianth segments opening white, soon becoming greenish beige; corona yellow-beige. Mid-season

'Charbon' 2 W-? (b or c)
(C. Dawson, pre-1923)

'Charborough' 2 W-OOY
(D. Blanchard, pre-1953)
('Mitylene' × 'Treskerby') × 'Penvose'

'Charbury' 2 W-Y
Syn. of 'Charlbury'

'Chardonay' 1 Y-WWY
(J.N.Hancock & Co., 1982) Unregistered
'Daydream' hybrid
Perianth segments sulphur yellow; corona widely expanded, opening citron yellow, becoming creamy white, with yellow at rim, frilled. Late

'Charentais' 3 Y-O
(T.D. Throckmorton) T.D. Throckmortom, 1976
'Old Satin' × 'Altruist'; sdlg no. 67/24/12
Fl. 100 mm wide; perianth segments broadly ovate, tawny suede; corona melon-coloured, with touches of gold at margins, very heavily frilled. Mid-season

'Charioteer' 1 Y-Y
(G.H. Johnstone, pre-1954)
'Constantine' × 'Golden Torch'

'Chariot Wheel' 3 W-YYR
(W.G. Pannill) W.G. Pannill, 1970
'Corofin' × 'Autowin'

'Charis' 2 W-P
(W. Jackson Sr, 1933)
'Mary Blewitt' × 'Mitylene'
Perianth segments white; corona off-white, flushed pale pink, with rim finely frilled

'Charisma' 4 W-R
(D.S. Bell, 1966) D.S. Bell, 1978
'Falaise' × 'Masquerade'
Fl. 108 mm wide; perianth and other petaloid segments in several whorls, pure white; the inner whorls smaller; corona segments interspersed and smaller still, red. Resembles a taller 'Balmasque' with more numerous segments

'Charisse' 2 Y-R
(J.S. Leitch) J.S. Leitch, 1957

'Charity' 9 W-?
(G.H. Engleheart, pre-1930)

'Charity Fair' 6 Y-Y
(Ballydorn Bulb Farm) Ballydorn Bulb Farm, 1983
'Charity May' hybrid
Fl. 80 mm wide; perianth segments gold; corona of a deeper tone, constricted towards mouth, with the mouth expanded. Mid-season

'Charity May' 6 Y-Y
(C.F. Coleman, pre-1948)
'Mitylene' × *N. cyclamineus*
Fl. 89 mm wide; perianth segments ovate to broadly ovate, brilliant yellow 8A, with slight white mucro, strongly reflexed, plane, overlapping one-third to a half; the inner segments a little narrower, with margins wavy and incurved; corona cylindrical, short, ribbed, richer in tone (9A) than the perianth, with mouth expanded and rim crenate. Dwarf. Mid-season. 2n=21. AM(e) 1948, *AM(g) 1952, *FCC(g) 1955, AM(Haarlem) 1961, *FCC(p) 1976, AGM 1993

'Charlbury' 2 W-Y
(J.S.B. Lea, 1982) Clive Postles, 1992
Sdlg 1-29-71 × 'Owston Wood'; sdlg no. 5-20-77
Fl. forming a double triangle, 110 mm wide; perianth segments ovate, pure white; corona mid-yellow, with mouth flared and rim rolled. Mid-season. Mistakenly named 'Charbury'

'Charlemagne' 1 Y-Y
(C.G. van Tubergen, pre-1914)
Fl. 111 mm wide; perianth segments bright rich lemon, irregular, overlapping one-third; corona large, buttercup yellow, mouth expanded and frilled. Mid-season to late. AM(Haarlem) 1914, FA(Haarlem) 1927. Received AM(Haarlem) 1914 as 'Titan' and FA(Haarlem) 1927 as 'Concordia'

'Charles' 3 W-YOO
(W. Polman-Mooy, pre-1913)
Perianth segments narrowly ovate, acute, white, tinged primrose yellow at midrib; corona shallow, rich orange, paling to golden yellow at base. Resembles 'Sunrise'

'Charles I' 1 Y-Y
(P.D. Williams, pre-1908)
Fl. golden yellow; perianth segments overlapping; corona slightly darker in tone than the perianth. Mid-season. 2n=26. *C(g) 1936, *AM(g) 1939

'Charles Bailey' 2 W-P
(C.E. Bailey, pre-1946)
Syn. 'C.E.Bailey'

'Charles Darwin'
(H. Backhouse, pre-1908)

'Charles Dickens' 1 W-Y
(E. Leeds, pre-1877)
Perianth segments pure white, overlapping; corona short, pale yellow. Syn. Pseudonarcissus Bicolor 'Charles Dickens'. Was "absorbed" into Bicolor Group

'Charles Dickens' 8
(pre-1907)

'Charles Dickens' 2 Y-Y
(pre-1938)

'Charles Draper' 1 W-W
(C.A. Nethercote) T. Morrison, 1960
Fl. white; corona heavily frilled, with rim broadly flanged

'Charles Edward' 2 Y-? (a)
(Sir C.H. Cave, pre-1928)

'Charles E. Hammond' 2 Y-? (a)
(Miss K. Spurrell, pre-1907)

'Charles E.Hammond' 2 Y-? (a)
(Miss K. Spurrell, pre-1907)

'Charles Hooper' 2 W-Y
(E. Leeds, pre-1877)
Perianth segments sulphur white; corona flared. Syn. Incomparabilis Albidus 'Charles Hooper'. Was "absorbed" into 'Lorenzo'

'Charles Kuralt' 1 W-Y
(Granville Hall) Granville Hall, 1994
From P.Phillips open-pollinated seed
Fl. 127 mm wide; perianth segments broadly ovate, creamy white, regular, deeply overlapping; corona funnel-shaped, pale lemon yellow, with rim flanged and deeply notched. Early

'Charles R.Fairbairn' 2 Y-? (a)
(C.O. Fairbairn, pre-1952)
'Carbineer' open pollinated

'Charles Sturt' 2 Y-O
(Tom Forster, 1960s) Unregistered
Perianth segments soft yellow, deeply overlapping; corona closely overlying the perianth segments, deep tangerine orange. Mid-season to late

'Charles Surface'
(E.M. Crosfield, pre-1913)

'Charles Tatham' 8 W-O
(T.J.Monkton) T.J.Monkton, 1995
N. tazetta sport
Fls 3-12 per stem, 22mm wide; perianth segments broadly ovate or oblong, blunt, prominently mucronate, creamy white (2C), spreading, with margins incurling, overlapping a quarter; corona cup-shaped, smoothly 6-angled, bright yellow-orange (17B or 24B), mouth straight, shallowly six-lobed, wavy, with rim entire. Very early. Strongly scented. Trade designation AUTUMN GEM

'Charleston' 2 O-R
(Brian S. Duncan) Rathowen Daffodils, 1983
'Altruist' × 'Ulster Bank'; sdlg no. 566
Perianth segments apricot-orange; corona deep red.

Mid-season

'Charles Warren' 1 Y-Y
(A. Gray, pre-1948)
Early. Resembles an earlier-flowered *N. pumilus*

'Charles Wolley-Dod' 2 Y-Y
(Miss E. Willmott, pre-1900)
Syn. 'C.Wolley-Dod', 'Reverend C.Wolley-Dod'.
AM 1900. Variably W-Y

'Charleville' 2 W-O
(W.M. Spry, pre-1975) Unregistered
'Jean Hood' × 'My Choice'

'Charlie's Aunt' 2 Y-R
(C.R. Phillips) C.R. Phillips, 1968
'Red Goblet' × 'Forest Fire'; sdlg no. 39B/44 52
Perianth segments very dark yellow, with traces of red; corona red. Early. Resembles 'Air Marshal' but with a darker-coloured perianth

'Charlotte'
(pre-1913)

'Charlotte' 2 Y-? (a)
(J.W.A. Lefeber, pre-1944)

'Charlotte' 2 W-? (b)
J.W.A. Lefeber, 1960

'Charlotte Baker Farage' 2 W-R
(Brian S.Duncan) Mrs J.M.Baker, 1996
'Young Blood' × 'Doctor Hugh'; sdlg no. 1429
Fl. 106 mm wide; perianth segments broadly ovate, pure white, reflexed, smooth; corona shallow bowl-shaped, deep orange-red, slightly frilled. Mid-season

'Charlotte Bridle' 2 W-Y
(Mrs F.E.W. Hanger, pre-1953)
Fl. 101 mm wide; perianth segments creamy white (near brilliant yellow-green 154B), with margins slightly incurving, overlapping half; corona heavily ribbed, light greenish yellow 8B, mouth widely expanded, frilled, with rim crenate and margins dentate. *AM(g) 1953

'Charlotte Vreeburg' 11b W-O
(J.W.A. Lefeber) J.W.A. Lefeber, 1968
'Papillon' hybrid

'Charlotte Vrieling' 11?b

'Charlton' 2 W-W
(C.E. Radcliff, 1930)
'Lemon Star' × 'Mrs W.Moodie'

'Charlton' 2 W-O
(W.M. Spry, pre-1975) Unregistered
'Torchlight' × 'Delight'

Corona dark orange

'Charm' 3 W-O
(J.C. Williams, pre-1908)
Fl. large; perianth segments snow white; corona large, more or less disc-shaped, glowing reddish orange

'Charm' 2 W-P
(A. Glover, *c.*1978) Unregistered
'Chosen Lady' × 'Verran'

'Charmaine' 3 W-? (b)
(R.O. Backhouse, pre-1930)

'Charmaline' 2 Y-Y
(G. Lewis, 1940) D.S. Bell, 1958

'Charmant' 3 W-R
(de Graaff Bros, pre-1944)
Corona bright scarlet

'Charmant' 3 W-? (b)
(de Graaff Bros, pre-1952)

'Charmant' 8 W-O
Syn. of 'Medio Luteo Charmant'

'Charmante Nyd' 8 W-O
(pre-1798)

'Charmante Plaisante' 8 W-O
(pre-1798)

'Charmer' 2 Y-Y
(M.P. Williams, pre-1938)
Fl. dark yellow

'Charmian Clift' 1 Y-Y
(W.M. Spry, pre-1975) Unregistered
'Golden' × 'Ina Marshall'
Fl. very broad, dark yellow. Late

'Charming' 2 W-W
(G.L. Wilson, pre-1923)

'Charming Yellow' 2 Y-? (a)
(M. van Waveren & Sons, pre-1953)

'Charon' 1 Y-Y
(Cartwright & Goodwin, pre-1916)

'Charter' 3 W-? (b)
(Mrs R.O. Backhouse, pre-1921)

'Charter' 2 Y-WWY
(G.E. Mitsch) M.J. Jefferson-Brown, 1964
'Binkie' × ('King of the North' × Content')
Fl. 108 mm wide; perianth segments broadly ovate, light greenish yellow 4B, with white at base and at midrib near prominent white mucro, spreading, with

margins a little reflexed, overlapping one-third to a half; the inner segments more narrowly ovate, a little inflexed, somewhat twisted or with margins wavy; corona funnel-shaped, smooth, opening yellow, soon becoming white, with light greenish yellow 4B at rim, mouth straight, ribbed, a little frilled, rim notched and crenate. 2n=28. AM(e) 1964, *AM(g) 1968, *FCC(g) 1971, AGM 1993

'Chartres' 2 W-? (b)
(J.W.A. Lefeber, pre-1943)

'Chartreuse' 7
(S.J. Bisdee, 1945) S.J. Bisdee, 1956

'Chartreuse' 2 W-Y
'Content' × 'Rouge'
Syn. of 'Chartwell'

'Chartwell' 2 W-Y
(J.N. Hancock & Co.) J.N. Hancock & Co., 1961
'Content' × 'Rouge'
Perianth segments yellowish white, smooth; corona long, cylindrical, lemon yellow, mouth more or less straight. Syn. 'Chartreuse'. *FCC(g) 1968

'Chasta' 3 W-GWP
(W. Jackson Jr, 1969) Unregistered
'Arbar' × sdlg 79/60; sdlg no. 136/69
Perianth segments rounded, pure white, smooth; corona small, with a narrow band of reddish pink at rim, heavily dentate. ?See also 'Chaste'

'Chaste' 1 W-W
(G.E. Mitsch, 1974) R. & E. Havens, 1988
('Le Cygne' × 'Empress of Ireland') × 'Panache'; sdlg no. JJ54/2
Fl. white, smooth, of heavy substance; perianth segments broadly ovate, with margins slightly incurling at apex, overlapping half; the outer segments overlapping one another; the inner segments almost touching one another at shoulder; corona straight-sided, smooth or lightly ribbed, with mouth flared and a little frilled, rim notched. Mid-season

'Chaste'
(Australian origin, pre-1985) Unregistered
?Syn. of 'Chasta'

'Chastel' 2 W-?
(A.M. Wilson, pre-1930)
'Cicely' × 'Beersheba'

'Chastity' 1 W-W
(C.G. van Tubergen, pre-1931)
2n=30. AM(Haarlem) 1931

'Chat' 7 Y-W
(G.E. Mitsch, 1958) G.E. Mitsch, 1968
'Binkie' × *N. jonquilla*; sdlg no. T6/4

Fls 1-2 per stem, 76 mm wide; perianth segments soft lemon yellow; corona opening yellow, becoming white. Mid-season. Resembles 'Verdin' but with larger and fewer flowers per stem

'Chateau' 2 W-? (b)
(Oregon Bulb Farms, pre-1950)

'Château de Namur' 8 W-O
(pre-1798)

'Chateau Impney' 2 Y-O
(Clive Postles) Clive Postles, 1992
Lea sdlg 2-25-69 × Lea sdlg; sdlg no. 1-71-80
Fl. forming a double triangle, 90 mm wide; perianth segments ovate, deep yellow; corona funnel-shaped, dark orange, with rim dentate. Early. Sunproof

'Chatelaine' 1 W-W
(D.S. Bell, 1968) D.S. Bell, 1978
'Kilsheelan' × 'Broughshane' hybrid
Fl. 112 mm wide, pure white; corona with rim widely frilled. Mid-season. Resembles 'Empress of Ireland' but with the corona more nearly cylindrical

'Chatham' 1 Y-Y
(W.M. Spry, pre-1975) Unregistered
'Kingscourt' × 'Golden Valley'
Fl. lemon yellow

'Chatmoss' 3 W-GWO
(W.G. Pannill) W.G. Pannill, 1978
'Bithynia' × 'Artist's Model'; sdlg no. G 9
Fl. 115 mm wide. Mid-season

'Chatscourt' 1 Y-Y
(R. Hyde) R. Hyde, 1955

'Chatsol' 2 Y-R
(J.N. Hancock & Co.) J.N. Hancock & Co., 1955
'Carbineer' × 'Market Merry'
Perianth segments bright yellow, tinged green; corona almost cylindrical, bright red

'Chatsworth' 1 W-Y
(P.D. Williams, pre-1939)
Fl. 108 mm wide; perianth segments creamy white, overlapping half; corona vivid yellow 9A, with mouth expanded. 2n=28. *AM(g) 1949

'Chatterbox' 2 Y-? (a)
(G.H. Johnstone, pre-1950)

'Chaucer' 9 W-R
(G.H. Engleheart, pre-1897)
'Ornatus' × 'Poetarum'; sdlg no. 367
Corona disc-shaped, rich red. Early

'Chausonette' 3 W-YYR
Syn. of 'Chansonette'

'Chausson' 3 W-? (b)
(G.H. Engleheart, pre-1927)

'Chauvelin' 2 Y-YYO
(Miss G. Evelyn, pre-1930)

'C.H.Curtis' 1 Y-Y
(G.P. Haydon, pre-1904)
Fl. very large; perianth segments deep primrose yellow, smooth; corona golden yellow, with mouth expanded and frilled

'C.H.Dee' 2 Y-YYO
(W. Backhouse, pre-1869)
Perianth segments large, sulphur yellow; corona primrose yellow, with orange at rim. Syn. Incomparabilis Sulphureus 'C.H.Dee'. Was "absorbed" into 'King of the Netherlands'

'Checker' 2 W-R
(C.E. Radcliff, 1931)
'Bernardino' × 'Blodwen'

'Checkmate' 2 Y-R
(D.S. Bell) D.S. Bell, 1957
'Dunkeld' × 'Burgundy'
Corona bowl-shaped, red

'Checkpoint' 2 Y-Y
(P. & G. Phillips) P. & G. Phillips, 1979
Fl. 98 mm wide. Mid-season

'Cheddar' 2 Y-Y
(Murray W. Evans) Murray W. Evans, 1972
'Festivity' hybrid
Fl. 100 mm wide

'Cheek to Cheek' 7 Y-Y
(G. Temple-Smith) G. Temple-Smith, 1993
N. fernandesii × *N. cyclamineus*, sdlg no. M3/90
Fls usually 2 per stem, 33 mm wide, vivid yellow; corona cylindrical, darker in tone than the perianth, with rim slightly dentate. Early

'Cheeky' 7 Y-Y
(L.P. Dettman) L.P. Dettman, 1977
N. obvallaris × 'Tiger Tim'; sdlg no. IM/75
Fl. 51 mm wide; perianth segments brilliant greenish yellow 2B; corona vivid yellow 14A. Early. Resembles a larger *N. minor* with the perianth segments less deeply overlapping

'Cheerful' 2 Y-? (a)
(R.H. Bath, pre-1923)

'Cheerfulness' 4 W-Y
(J.B. van der Schoot, pre-1923)
'Elvira' sport
Fls 3-4 per stem, 57 mm wide; perianth and other petaloid segments white; the outer whorl very broad in outline, rounded or squarish at apex and sometimes truncate, prominently mucronate, spreading, some segments concave, some with margins wavy or incurling, overlapping half or more; the inner segments of the outer whorl not noticeably mucronate; the centre whorl half as long, clustered, strongly inflexed, deeply concave; corona segments very short, interspersed among the petaloid segments at centre, yellow. Mid-season. Scented. 2n=24. AM(Haarlem) 1923, AM(e) 1926, *HC(g) 1927, *AM(g) 1936, *FCC(g) 1939, AGM 1995

'Cheerfulness' 4 W-Y
Syn. of 'Erlicheer'

'Cheerio' 2 Y-O
(The Brodie of Brodie, pre-1932)
Perianth segments soft yellow; corona widely expanded, bowl-shaped, bright reddish orange, paling towards base, frilled. 2n=28. *(Kirton)AM(g)(m) 1941

'Cheer Leader' 3 YYO-R
(Brian S. Duncan) Rathowen Daffodils, 1987
'Ulster Bank' × 'Altruist'; sdlg no. 763
Fl. rounded; perianth segments very broad, deep golden yellow, with slight white mucro, shaded orange at base, spreading, overlapping half; the inner segments broadly ovate, inflexed, with margins minutely incurling at apex; corona bowl-shaped, closely ribbed, red, with mouth expanded and rim crenate. Mid-season

'Cheers' 2 W-? (b)
(F.H. Chapman, pre-1933)
'Kestrel' × 'Fortune'

'Cheersport' 4 W-O
(A. MacFarlane) R.J. Abernethy, 1961
'Cheerfulness' sport
Fl. 64 mm wide; perianth and other petaloid segments white; corona segments interspersed, pale orange. Late

'Cheesburn' 2 Y-YYO
(G. Harrison) G. Harrison, 1968
'Diolite' hybrid
Fl. 127 mm wide; perianth segments yellow, of strong substance; corona darker in tone, with reddish orange at rim. Mid-season. Resembles a larger-flowered 'Diolite' of stronger substance

'Cheesewring' 3 W-WYY
(R.A.Scamp) R.A.Scamp, 1996
'Cool Crystal' × 'Delos'; sdlg no. 486
Fl. 115 mm wide; perianth segments very broadly ovate, pure white, slightly reflexed; corona very shallow bowl-shaped, ribbed, pale primrose yellow, with white at base. Late

'Cheetah' 1 Y-O
(Brian S.Duncan) Brian S.Duncan, 1996
('Midas Touch' × 'Barnsdale Wood') × 'Barnum'; sdlg no. 1419
Fl. 105 mm wide; perianth segments broadly ovate, deep golden yellow, slightly reflexed, smooth; corona cylindrical, opening deep golden yellow, becoming mid-orange, with mouth a little expanded, rim slightly crenate. Early to mid-season. Sunproof

'Chel' 1 W-Y
(W.M. Spry, pre-1975) Unregistered
'Marble Queen' × 'Stand By'
Corona cream

'Chelan' 2 Y-W
(Murray W. Evans, 1964) Murray W. Evans, 1975
'Daydream' × 'Bethany'; sdlg no. H-16
Fl. 92 mm wide; perianth segments sulphur yellow; corona white. Mid-season. Resembles a taller 'Daydream' with paler perianth segments. Syn. 'Vesper'

'Chelsa' 2 W-WWR
(J.T. Gray, pre-1949)
Fl. rounded; perianth segments pure white; corona with a band of red at rim

'Chelsea' 3 W-? (b)
(J.L. Richardson, pre-1939)
AM(Haarlem) 1939

'Chelsea Beauty' 8
(J. Veitch & Sons, pre-1910)

'Chelsea China' 2 W-GPP
(G.H. Johnstone, pre-1954)
'Ann Abbott' × 'Wild Rose'

'Chelsea Derby' 2 W-P
(G.H. Johnstone) Mrs J. Abel Smith, 1968
'Interim' × 'Chelsea China'
Fl. 89 mm wide; corona orange-pink. Late. Resembles a taller 'Chelsea China' of stronger substance with the corona less quickly fading

'Chelsea Gem' 8
(J. Veitch & Sons, pre-1910)

'Chelsea Girl' 2 W-P
(Clive Postles) Clive Postles Daffodils, 1990
'Rose Royale' × 'Dailmanach'; sdlg no. 1-49-76
Fl. 102 mm wide; perianth segments narrowly ovate, slightly reflexed, deeply overlapping; corona slightly flared, neatly ribbed, pink, with shades of lilac, glistening. Mid-season. Sunproof

'Chelsea Gold' 1 Y-Y
(E.G. Taylor) E.G. Taylor, 1956

'Chelsho' 1 Y-Y
(Barr & Sons, pre-1929)
Perianth segments soft yellow, regular, overlapping; corona slightly darker in tone, with mouth widely expanded and rim flanged. 2n=28

'Cheltenham' 2 Y-YOO
(J.S.B. Lea) Clive Postles Daffodils, 1990
Sdlg 1-24-71 × sdlg 1-9-71; sdlg no. 7-3-78
Fl. 80 mm wide; perianth segments very broadly ovate, smooth; corona slightly expanding, neatly ribbed, with rim dentate. Mid-season

'Chelwood' 1 W-P
(C.E. Radcliff, 1943)
('The Fawn' × 'Pink o' Dawn') × 'Dawnglow'

'Chemawa' 2 Y-OOY
(G.E. Mitsch) G.E. Mitsch, 1962
'Narvik' × 'California Gold'
Fl. 102 mm wide; perianth segments deep yellow; corona straight-sided, clear orange, with yellow at rim, frilled, dentate. Mid-season. Resembles 'California Gold' but with yellow in the corona

'Chemeketa' 2 Y-YPP
(Murray W. Evans) Murray W. Evans, 1987
Sdlgs F-243/1 × H-16/1 × Pannill sdlg 70/14; sdlg no. W-5/2
Corona straight-sided, with rim rolled. Mid-season

'Chemere' 1 Y-Y
(E.W. Philpott) E.W. Philpott, 1959
Perianth segments lemon yellow; corona slightly darker in tone. Early. Resembles a larger-flowered 'Royalist'

'Chenango' 2 W-? (b)
(E.C. Powell, pre-1949)

'Chenda' 2 W-O
(J.T. Gray, pre-1949)
Perianth segments ivory white; corona dark reddish orange

'Chenoweth' 2 W-WWP
(Brian S. Duncan) du Plessis Bros, 1980
'Easter Moon' × 'Empress of Ireland'; sdlg no. D.165
Fl. 112 mm wide; corona opening yellow and pink, becoming white, with the pink in a very narrow band at rim. Mid-season

'Cheops' 1 Y-Y
(C.E. Radcliff, 1931)
'Golden City' × 'Gertrude Nethercote'

'Chepstow' 1 Y-Y
(?T. Buncombe, pre-1933)

'Chequers' 2 Y-? (a)

(R.V. Favell, pre-1947)

'Cherana' 2 W-P
(Jackson's Daffodils) Jackson's Daffodils, 1995
'Couth' × sdlg 195/82; sdlg no. 124/89
Fl. 115 mm wide; perianth segments broadly ovate, greenish white (155A); corona orange-pink (29B), with rim broadly flanged. Mid-season to late

'Cherette' 1 Y-Y
(E.W. Philpott) E.W. Philpott, 1959
Fl. lemon yellow. Late. Resembles a larger-flowered 'Chemere' with a shorter and stouter stem

'Cheribon' 1 W-W
(S.J. Bisdee, 1946)
'Whitefoord' × 'Cantatrice'

'Chérie' 7 W-P
(W.F. Mitchell, pre-1935)
'Lord Kitchener' × *N. jonquilla*
Fls 1-3 per stem; perianth segments ivory white; corona smooth, delicate greyish pink, flushed shell pink, mouth a little wavy, rim almost entire. 2n=21. AM(Haarlem) 1962

'Cherie Marie' 2 W-WWP
(H.A. Brown, 1943)
'Pink-a-dell' × 'Bennett's Pink'
Corona pinkish creamy white, with pink at rim, mouth expanded. Mid-season

'Cherish' 2 Y-WWY
(G.E. Mitsch) G.E. Mitsch, 1982
'Aircastle' hybrid; sdlg no. JJ24/6
Fl. 95 mm wide; perianth segments sulphur yellow; corona opening sulphur yellow, becoming near white, with yellow at rim of a deeper tone than the original sulphur. Mid-season

'Cherith' 3 W-Y
(S.J. Bisdee, 1939)
'Mitylene' × 'Portia'

'Chernobyl' 11a W-YPP
(Colin Crotty) Colin Crotty, 1992
Fl. 96 mm wide; perianth segments slightly mucronate, tinged primrose yellow on opening, becoming pure white, overlapping; corona split, the six segments more than three-quarters the length of the perianth segments and opposite and closely overlying them, pure deep pink, with yellowish tones at base, frilled, with rim crenate. Mid-season

'Cherokee' 2 Y-? (a)
(G. Lewis) D.S. Bell, 1955

'Cherokee Maid' 2 Y-? (a)
(Mrs P.M. Davis, pre-1948)

'Cherokee Red' 2 Y-R
(G.E. Mitsch, 1972) R. & E. Havens, 1990
('Armada' × 'Paricutin') × 'Falstaff'; sdlg no. HH74/6
Fl. 90 mm wide; perianth segments deep yellow; corona disc-shaped, deep orange-red. Early

'Cherrie Blyth' 2 W-GYY
(L.P. Dettman) L.P. Dettman, 1974
'Bonnington' × 'Bodilly'
Fl. 105 mm wide

'Cherry' 3 W-? (b)
(Mrs R.O. Backhouse, pre-1921)

'Cherry Bounce' 3 W-R
(T.D. Throckmorton) T.D. Throckmorton, 1975
'Gossamer' × 'Aircastle'; sdlg no. 65/2/8
Perianth segments white; corona cherry red. Mid-season

'Cherrycroft' 2 Y-O
(F.E. Board) F.E. Board, 1965
'Revelry' × 'Hollyberry'; sdlg no. 1131
Late

'Cherrygardens' 2 W-GPP
(N.A. Burr) N.A. Burr, 1978
'Easter Moon' × 'Fair Prospect'; sdlg no. 3.1.69
Fl. 105 mm wide; perianth segments very broad, rounded, only very slightly mucronate, spreading, plane, with midrib showing, overlapping one-third to a half; the inner segments narrower; corona bowl-shaped, smooth, pale pink, with green at base and rich pink at rim, mouth expanded and wavy, rim notched. Mid-season. PC(e) 1989

'Cherry Girl' 2 W-Y
(L.P. Dettman, 1967) L.P. Dettman, 1978
'Lynette Sholl' open pollinated; sdlg no. 2-67
Fl. 87 mm wide; perianth segments yellowish white155B; corona brilliant greenish yellow 4A, with a darker tone (11A) at rim and intense green at base. Mid-season. Resembles a lighter-coloured 'Lynette Sholl' with a slightly longer corona

'Cherry Malotte' 3 Y-? (a)
(Cartwright & Goodwin, pre-1916)

'Cherry Pie' 2 W-R
(G.H. Johnstone, pre-1959) Unregistered

'Cherry Pie' 2 W-P
(C.O. Fairbairn, pre-1964) Unregistered
Perianth segments broadly ovate, blunt, fairly prominently mucronate, spreading, creased, overlapping one-third; the inner segments more narrowly ovate, a little inflexed, with margins wavy; corona funnel-shaped, lightly ribbed, pink, with mouth straight and more heavily ribbed, lightly frilled. Late. Resembles a 'Confusion' two weeks earlier in flower

203

'Cherry Red' 2 Y-?
(A.H. Ahrens) J.S. Leitch, 1955

'Cherryrim' 2 W-YYR
(R. Hyde) R. Hyde, 1963
Fl. 100mm wide, rounded; perianth segments broadly or very broadly ovate, blunt or truncate, sightly mucronate, spreading, plane, smooth and of good substance, overlapping half; the inner segments creased, notched and shouldered at base; corona bowl-shaped, loosely ribbed, brilliant yellow 12B, with a broad band of orange-red (near to 32B) at rim, mouth only a little frilled, rim irregularly notched and obscurely crenate. Mid-season. Resembles 'Interim' but with the corona rim darker in colour or 'Audubon' with the rim lighter. Syn. 'Cherry Rim'

'Cherry Rim' 2 W-YYR
Syn. of 'Cherryrim'

'Cherry Ripe' 3 W-O
(Mrs R.O. Backhouse, pre-1905)
Perianth segments snow white; corona brilliant scarlet-orange

'Cherry Spot' 3 W-O
(G.E. Mitsch) G.E. Mitsch, 1975
'Artillery' × 'Avenger'; sdlg no. F138/4
Fl. forming a double triangle, 102 mm wide; perianth segments broadly ovate, with margins incurved at apex as if acute, only very slightly mucronate, white, with a band of yellow at base, slightly reflexed, overlapping half; the inner segments more nearly spreading, with margins more strongly incurved; corona shallow, wide-spreading, ribbed, vivid reddish orange, with mouth split in places and overlapping. Mid-season. Resembles 'Artillery' but with a whiter perianth

'Cherub' 1 W-W
(J. Mallender, pre-1913)

'Cherub' 1 Y-Y
(J.S. Leitch) J.S. Leitch, 1958

'Cherubino' 3 Y-? (a)
(N.F. Lock, pre-1944)

'Cheryl' 5 Y-Y
(E.F. Hughes) E.F. Hughes, 1962
Fl. 70 mm wide; perianth segments creamy yellow; corona lemon yellow. Mid-season

'Cherylene' 2 W-OOR
(D.S. Bell) D.S. Bell, 1960
'Rosslare' × 'Artist's Model'
Fl. 114 mm wide; corona spreading, apricot orange, shading to red at rim. Mid-season. Resembles an 'Artist's Model' of stronger substance with the corona less widely flared

'Chesalon' 1 Y-Y
(S.J. Bisdee, 1943)
'Principal' × 'Robert Montgomery'

'Chesla' 2 W-WWR
(J.T. Gray, 1930) Parr's Nurseries, 1958

'Chester' 2 Y-? (a)
(Barr & Sons, pre-1945)

'Chesterfield' 2 W-R
(F.E. Board) F.E. Board, 1965
Kilworth' × 'Signal Light'; sdlg no. 1195
Late

'Chester Springs' 2 YYW-Y
(W.,A.Bender, 1984) W.A.Bender, 1996
From P.Phillips open-pollinated seed no. 1978 × 'Lark'
Fl. 85 mm wide, brilliant greenish yellow 6B, with white at base; perianth segments very broadly ovate, plane; corona cylindrical at base, flared from midpoint, with mouth regularly frilled. Mid-season

'Chesterton' 9 W-GYR
(Brian S. Duncan) Rathowen Daffodils, 1979
Fl. rounded, 70 mm wide; perianth segments very broad, prominently mucronate, pure white, reflexed, concave, overlapping half or more; the inner segments narrow and somewhat oblong, only slightly mucronate, more nearly spreading, with margins incurling; corona disc-shaped, ribbed, greenish yellow, with pale green at base and a narrow band of deep red at rim, mouth even, rim minutely notched. $2n=14$

'Chevalier' 1 Y-Y
(W.B. Cranfield, pre-1907)

'Chevalier' 1 Y-Y
(J.L. Richardson) F.E. Board, 1956
'Galway' open pollinated
$2n=28$

N. × chevassutii Gorenflot, Guinochet & Quézel
13 = N. bertolonii Parlatore × N. serotinus Linnaeus

'Cheviot' 2 Y-O
(J.N. Hancock & Co., pre-1949)
Corona deep reddish orange, with rim dentate

'Chevreuse' 11a W-Y
(J. Gerritsen & Son, 1967) J. Gerritsen & Son, 1977
Fl. 100 mm wide; perianth segments ivory white; corona segments light greenish to pale yellow 8B or D, with vivid yellow 12A at base. Mid-season

'Chevron' 2 Y-? (a)
(A.H. Ahrens) J.S. Leitch, 1956

'Chevy Chase' 7 W-W
(Roberta C.Watrous, 1952) Roberta C.Watrous, 1964
'Tunis' × *N. jonquilla*
Fl. creamy white; corona opening yellow, soon becoming white. Early. Scented

'Cheyenne' 7 W-W
(E.C. Powell, pre-1946)

'Chianti' 2 Y-R
(W.G. Pannill) W.G. Pannill, 1970
'Ceylon' × 'Jezebel'
Perianth segments broadly ovate or oblong, vivid yellow, with white mucro, spreading, overlapping one-third to a half; the inner segments narrower; corona short funnel-shaped, ribbed, orange-red, with mouth even and rim irregularly dentate

'Chic' 3 W-? (b)
(N.Y. Lower, pre-1913)

'Chic' 2 W-WWP
(J.N. Hancock & Co., *c.*1957) Unregistered
Fl. white; corona with pink at rim

'Chicago' 1 Y-Y
(M. van Waveren & Sons, pre-1931)

'Chickadee' 6 Y-O
(G.E. Mitsch) G.E. Mitsch, 1959
'Rubra' × *N. cyclamineus*; sdlg no. 085/1
Perianth segments oblong, prominently mucronate, soft yellow, strongly reflexed, overlapping one-third to a half; the inner segments ovate; corona short cylinder-shaped, lightly and broadly ribbed, pale orange, sometimes deeper in tone, mouth straight, wavy, with rim notched. Dwarf. Mid-season. Resembles 'Dove Wings' but with a shorter and more nearly straight-sided corona

'Chickasaw' 1 Y-Y
(E.C. Powell, pre-1946)

'Chickerell' 3 Y-YYR
(J.W. Blanchard) J.W. Blanchard, 1985
'Montego' × ('Hammoon' × ? 'Irish Minstrel'); sdlg no. 71/10A
Fl. primrose yellow; corona with red at rim. Early. Resembles a taller and earlier-flowered 'Perimeter' with the perianth segments more narrowly acute

'Chicopee' 6 Y-Y
(E.C. Powell, pre-1946)
N. obvallaris × *N. cyclamineus*

'Chicot' 9 W-?
(A.M. Wilson, pre-1908)

'Chideock' 2 Y-R
(J.W. Blanchard, 1971) J.W. Blanchard, 1985
('Chungking' × 'Dewlish') × 'Border Chief'; sdlg no. 66/5A
Corona shallow, bright orange-red. Late. Resembles a later-flowered 'Border Chief' with broader perianth segments

'Chief Councillor' 2 W-GYO
(G. Lewis) D.S. Bell, 1955

'Chief Inspector' 1 W-Y
(T. Bloomer) Rathowen Daffodils, 1982
'April Harvest' × 'Newcastle'; sdlg no. 198
Fl. forming a double triangle, 120 mm wide; perianth segments very broadly ovate, triangular in appearance, slightly mucronate, spreading, plane, of good substance, overlapping half; the inner segments much narrower, square-shouldered at base, with margins wavy; corona cylindrical, smooth, deep golden yellow, with mouth expanded and even, rim entire and narrowly rolled. Mid-season. Resembles a larger-flowered 'Newcastle'

'Chief Justice' 1 W-Y
(J.L. Richardson) J.L. Richardson, 1956
'Spitzbergen' × 'Broughshane'
Perianth segments broadly ovate, pure white; corona buffy primrose, becoming whiter, with rim flanged and dentate

'Chief Pilot' 2 Y-YYO
(H.A. Brown, 1939) J.N. Hancock & Co., 1955
Perianth segments rich yellow; corona yellow, with a broad band of orange at rim, mouth flared. Mid-season

'Chief Ruler' 2 Y-Y
(G. Lewis, pre-1940)
'Flash Lightning' × 'Fortune'
Fl. deep golden yellow

'Chieftain' 2 W-Y
(Barr & Sons, pre-1909)
Perianth segments creamy white, overlapping; corona large, expanded, soft lemon yellow, frilled

'Chieftain' 1 W-Y
(O. Ronalds) M. Gardiner, 1956
Perianth segments ivory white, of great substance; corona yellow, with rim flanged

'Chiffon' 2 W-P
(S.J. Bisdee, 1948)
'Alcestis' × 'Wild Rose'
Resembles a taller and much improved 'Wild Rose'

'Chig' 2 W-GWW
(M.J. Jefferson-Brown) M.J. Jefferson-Brown, 1985
'Homage' hybrid
Perianth segments pure white, smooth, of strong

substance; corona very shallow bowl-shaped, ribbed, white, with green at base. Late. PC(e) 1978

'Childe Harold' 9 W-YYR
(G.H. Engleheart, pre-1910)
Perianth segments very broad in outline, squarish and sometimes truncate at apex, prominently mucronate, spreading, overlapping half or more; the inner segments narrower, more usually truncate, not noticeably mucronate, a little inflexed, with margins wavy or incurled; corona disc-shaped, ribbed, yellow, with a very narrow band of light red at rim

'Childeric' 2 W-? (b)
(A.M. Wilson, pre-1937)

'Child of Fortune' 2 Y-? (a)
(S.A. Morrish, pre-1950)

'Child of the Mist' 1 W-W
(de Graaff Bros, pre-1907)
'Madame de Graaff' hybrid
Fl. pure white. Corona rim strongly flanged

'Chili Bean' 2 Y-? (a)
(Oregon Bulb Farms, pre-1945)

'Chilito' 2 Y-R
(W.G. Pannill) W.G. Pannill, 1990
'Torridon' × ('Uncle Remus' × 'Javelin'); sdlg no. 79/13
Mid-season to late

'Chillagoe' 2 W-W
(W.M. Spry, pre-1973) Unregistered
'Zero' × Fairbairn sdlg
Fl. forming a double triangle; perianth segments broadly ovate, acute, slightly mucronate, pure white, spreading, plane, overlapping one-third to a half; the inner segments more narrowly ovate, a little inflexed; corona funnel-shaped, ribbed, opening creamy white, becoming pure white, with mouth flared and more closely ribbed, lightly frilled, rim notched and minutely crenate. Tall. Early

'Chillion' 1 Y-Y
(S.J. Bisdee, pre-1974) Unregistered
Corona deeply frilled, with rim broadly rolled

'Chilmark' 3 Y-O
(J.W. Blanchard, 1978) J.W. Blanchard, 1992
'Lemonade' × 'Achduart'; sdlg no. 73/33A
Fl. forming a double triangle, 100 mm wide; perianth segments broadly ovate, pale mid-yellow, spreading, plane; corona bowl-shaped, strong orange, with a slightly darker tone (25A) at rim, mouth straight, wavy. Early

'Chiloquin' 1 Y-W
(G.E. Mitsch) G.E. Mitsch, 1968

'Bethany' or 'Limeade' open pollinated; sdlg no. Y02/1
Fl. 83 mm wide, clear pale golden yellow; perianth segments ovate, blunt, with slight white mucro, and with white at base, recurved, smooth; the inner segments more narrowly ovate, more strongly recurved, shouldered at base; corona funnel-shaped, smoothly 6-angled, becoming white, with touches of yellow at rim, mouth flared, wavy, with rim irregularly notched and minutely dentate. Mid-season. Resembles a more refined 'Limeade'

'Chiltern' 2 W-? (b or c)
(F.H. Chapman, pre-1927)
Corona cream yellow. Early. Resembles an improved 'Ptolemy'

'Chiltern' 1 W-Y
(J.N. Hancock & Co., 1945) J.N. Hancock & Co., 1965
Perianth segments white; corona creamy yellow. Early. Resembles an improved 'Ptolemy'

'Chimborazo' 1 W-W
(C.E. Radcliff, 1935)
'White Emperor' × 'Darwalla'

'Chimeon' 4 W-P
(W. Jackson Jr) W. Jackson Jr, 1968
('Palin' × 'Dawnglow') × ('Karanja' × 'Brano'); sdlg no. 57/59
Perianth and other petaloid segments white; corona segments pink

'Chimu' 2 W-P
(S.J. Bisdee, 1946) S.J. Bisdee, 1956
'Leto' × 'Rosario'

'China' 2 Y-? (a)
(Mrs F.E.W. Hanger, pre-1950)

'China Boy' 2 W-Y
(D.S. Bell) D.S. Bell, 1983
'Playboy' hybrid
Corona rim slightly rolled. Resembles 'Playboy' but with the corona dark yellow to base

'China Clay' 1 W-W
(The Brodie of Brodie, pre-1928)
'Morven' hybrid × 'Beersheba'

'China Clipper' 1 W-W
(D.S. Bell) D.S. Bell, 1955
Corona frilled, with rim dentate

'China Doll' 2 W-WWP
(Clive Postles) Clive Postles Daffodils, 1985
Lea sdlg × 'Dailmanach'
Perianth segments broadly ovate, blunt, mucronate, pure white, smooth, overlapping half; corona large,

funnel-shaped, ribbed, almost as white as the perianth, with a narrow band of soft shell pink at rim, mouth lightly frilled and shallowly crenate. Late

'China Dragon' 2 W-? (b)
(T.A.V. Wood, pre-1949)

'China Lake' 2 W-YWW
(Elise Havens, 1969) R. Havens, 1979
'Empress of Ireland' × 'Accent'; sdlg no. E64-1/2
Fl. 108 mm wide; perianth segments milk white; corona cream, with a slightly pink cast, with golden yellow at base. Mid-season

"China Lily"
Syn. of *N.tazetta* subsp. *lacticolor*

'China Maid' 2 W-Y
(C.M. Grullemans) J.J. Grullemans & Sons, 1959
Fl. 110 mm wide; perianth segments cream white; corona pale yellow 11D, speckled with strong orange 24A, with a darker yellow at rim. Mid-season

'China Moon' 1 W-? (b)
(K.D. Smith, pre-1951)

'China Pink' 2 W-P
(G.L. Wilson) M.J. Jefferson-Brown, 1960
'Dunaird' × 'Irish Rose'
Perianth segments white; corona rose pink. Mid-season. Resembles a more refined 'Chiffon'

'China Queen' 8
(pre-1892)

'China Town' 2 Y-Y
(Konynenburg & Mark) Konynenburg & Mark, 1965
Fl. 100 mm wide; perianth segments light greenish yellow 5C; corona darker in tone (6A). Mid-season

'Chinaware' 1 W-W
(G.P. Haydon, pre-1908)

'Chinchilla' 2 W-W
(Brian S. Duncan) Rathowen Daffodils, 1983
'Easter Moon' × 'White Star'; sdlg no. 513
Fl. 112 mm wide, pure white; perianth segments broadly ovate, blunt, fairly prominently mucronate, spreading, a little concave, with margins sometimes incurling at apex, of heavy substance, overlapping half; the inner segments more narrowly ovate, only very slightly mucronate, with margins a little wavy and sometimes recurved at base; corona short funnel-shaped, lightly ribbed, with mouth straight, regularly frilled. Mid-season

N. chinensis (Roemer) hort. = *N. tazetta* subsp. *lacticolor*

'Chinese Coral' 1 W-P
(J Gerritsen & Son) Van Eeden Goohof, 1995
Fl. 85 mm wide; perianth segments greenish white (a little paler than 1D); corona orange-pink (26C and 26D), with vivid yellow 12A at base. Dwarf. Mid-season

'Chinese Gordon' 1 Y-Y
(E.Leeds, pre-1877)
Fl. yellow. Syn. Pseudonarcissus Spurius 'Chinese Gordon'

'Chinese Grand Emperor'
Syn. of *N.tazetta* subsp. *lacticolor*

'Chinese Jade' 2 W-? (b)
(D.S. Bell) D.S. Bell, 1955

'Chinese Lantern' 6 Y-Y
(A. Gray) A. Gray, 1955
N. cyclamineus × *N. asturiensis*
Fl. bright yellow, facing down

'Chinese Orange' 2 W-O
(G. Lewis) D.S. Bell, 1955

'Chinese Prince' 5 Y-Y
(Barr & Sons, pre-1935)
Perianth segments pale primrose yellow, recurved, overlapping at base only; corona cylindrical, long, ribbed, dark primrose yellow, lightly frilled

'Chinese Robe' 2 Y-R
(K.J. Heazlewood) K.J. Heazlewood, 1968
'Armada' × 'Tegwith'
Fl. 101 mm wide; perianth segments deep golden yellow; corona brick red. Early. Resembles a more refined 'Armada' of richer colouring

'Chinese Sacred Lily'
Syn. of *N.tazetta* subsp. *lacticolor*

'Chinese White' 3 W-W
(G.L. Wilson, pre-1937)
'Silver Plane' × 'Silver Coin' hybrid
Fl. rounded, 115 mm wide; perianth segments very broad, blunt or truncate, prominently mucronate, greenish white, plane or a little concave, smooth, overlapping one-third to a half or more; the inner segments more nearly ovate, rounded at apex, only very slightly mucronate, with margins wavy, shouldered at base; corona very shallow, widely expanded, ribbed, pale creamy white, with grey-green showing faintly in tube, frilled, with rim minutely crenate. Late. 2n=28. PC(e) 1940, AM(e) 1946, AM(Haarlem) 1948, FCC(e) 1949, FCC(Haarlem) 1950

'Chinita' 8 Y-YYR
(F.H. Chapman, pre-1922)
'Chaucer' × 'Jaune à Merveille'

Fls 1-2 per stem; perianth segments very broad, blunt or truncate, prominently mucronate, straw yellow, a little reflexed; the inner segments roundish, shouldered at base, not noticeably mucronate, spreading or a little inflexed, with margins sometimes incurling; corona disc-shaped, ribbed, yellow, with a narrow band of red at rim, mouth even or wavy. 2n=31. AM 1922, *HC(m)(g) 1927

'Chino' 2 Y-P
(P. Phillips) P. Phillips, 1968

'Chinook' 2 W-Y
(G.E. Mitsch, pre-1952)
'John Evelyn' × 'Fortune'; sdlg no. 37C41/7
Perianth segments milk white; corona very shallow bowl-shaped, broad, varying from salmon orange to yellow. Mid-season. 2n=28

'Chinso' 2 Y-OOR
(A.O. Roblin, 1945)
'Lillian Murdoch' × 'Cheerio'

'Chintz' 3 W-YYO
(E.M. Crosfield, pre-1913)
Perianth segments large, off white; corona yellow, with reddish orange at rim. FCC(Haarlem) 1913

'Chione' 1 W-? (b)
(C. Dawson, pre-1915)

'Chios' 1 W-W
(G.H. Engleheart, pre-1927)

'Chios' 4 W-P
(W. Jackson Jr, 1965) Unregistered
'Lawali' × sdlg 42/61; sdlg no. 222/65

'Chippendale' 3 W-R
(L. van Leeuwen & Son, pre-1926)
Perianth segments white; corona deep red. AM(Haarlem) 1926

'Chipper' 5 Y-Y
(M. Fowlds) G.E. Mitsch, 1971
('Polindra' × 'Tunis') × *N. triandrus*; sdlg no. F180/1
Fl. 68 mm wide; perianth segments narrow, lemon yellow, with a greenish cast, very strongly reflexed; corona pale lemon yellow. Mid-season

'Chippewa' 3 W-YYR
(W.G. Pannill) W.G. Pannill, 1983
'Tuskar Light' × 'Aircastle'

'Chipping Ridgeway' 3 W-W
(F.E. Board) F.E. Board, 1965
'Homage' × 'Chinese White'; sdlg no. 976

'Chips' 2 Y-Y
(R.J. McIlraith) R.J. McIlraith, 1988

'Daydream' × 'Salmon Trout'; sdlg no. S73/5
Fl. 65 mm wide; perianth segments very broadly ovate, blunt, mucronate, pale yellow, faintly tinged pink, spreading, plane, overlapping half; the inner segments shouldered at base; corona short funnel-shaped, smooth, of a deeper yellow than the perianth, a little frilled, with rim flanged, notched and crenate. Dwarf. Mid-season. Resembles 'Salmon Trout'

'Chiquita' 3 Y-? (a)
(A.M. Wilson, pre-1907)

'Chiquita' 2 W-GPP
(Murray W. Evans) Murray W. Evans, 1969
('Interim' × 'Green Island') × 'Caro Nome'

'Chircombe' 3 W-? (b)
(Mrs R.S. Cobley, pre-1937)

'Chiripa'
(C. Dawson, pre-1908)

'Chiron' 5 Y-Y
(Barr & Sons, pre-1923)
Perianth segments primrose yellow; corona canary yellow. See also 'Chirow'

'Chirow' 5 Y-Y
Syn. of 'Chiron'

'Chirrup' 2 W-?
(Alister Clark) J. Sharp, 1960

'Chisholm' 1 Y-Y
(J.N. Hancock & Co., 1978) Unregistered

'Chit Chat' 1 W-Y
(G.L. Wilson, pre-1927)
'King Alfred' hybrid
Perianth segments white, somewhat twisted; corona deep gold, with rim flanged. Tall

'Chit Chat' 7 Y-Y
(M. Fowlds, *c*.1960) G.E. Mitsch, 1975
N. assoanus × *N. jonquilla*
Perianth segments clear yellow; corona yellow. Late. Resembles a more vigorous 'Pixie' or 'Pixie's Sister'. AGM 1996. Mistakenly recorded as 'Heide'

'Chitose' 1 Y-P
(P. & G. Phillips) P. & G. Phillips, 1975
Fl. 106 mm wide; perianth segments primrose, with white at base; corona carrot pink, with rim rolled. Mid-season. Resembles 'Milestone' but with differently shaped perianth segments and the corona more deeply rolled

'Chitra' 2 Y-R
(W. Jackson Jr, 1956) Unregistered
'Kai' × 'Magherally'

'Chittabob' 2 Y-? (a)
(A.M. Wilson, pre-1930)

'Chittagong' 2 W-P
(J.N.Hancock & Co., 1982) Unregistered
'Dame Edith' × ('Pink Pearl' × 'Verran'); sdlg no. 92/82H
Fl. rounded; corona cylindrical, pink, with mouth straight, rim closely and deeply notched, as if fringed, rolled

'Chivalry' 1 W-W
(J.L. Richardson) F.E. Board, 1955
'Broughshane' × 'Brussels'

'Chloe' 5 W-Y
(T. Batson, pre-1908)
'Emperor' × *N. triandrus*
Perianth segments creamy white; corona soft canary yellow

'Chloe' ?-P
(Alister Clark, pre-1948)

'Chloe' 2 W-P
(Murray W. Evans) Murray W. Evans, 1973
'Radiation' × ('Interim' × 'Mabel Taylor')
Fl. 97 mm wide

'Chlora' 2 W-? (b or c)
(T. Batson, pre 1913)

'Chloride' 9 W-?
(F.H. Chapman, pre-1936)
'Distich' × 'Black Prince'

'Chloris' 1 Y-Y
(Barr & Sons, pre-1913)
'Lord Roberts' hybrid
Resembles a more robust 'Lord Roberts'

'Chmoy' 2 W-Y
(R.V. Favell, 1939) R.M. Favell, 1965
Fl. 95 mm wide; corona butter yellow. Mid-season. Resembles 'Preamble' but with a darker-coloured corona

'Chobe River' 1 Y-Y
(Brian S.Duncan, 1985) Brian S.Duncan, 1996
'Verdant' × 'Midas Touch'; sdlg no. 1196
Fl. 113 mm wide, deep yellow; perianth segments broadly ovate, plane, smooth; corona cylindrical, constricted at base, with mouth a little flared. Mid-season. Resembles 'Verdant' in form

'Choice Gift' 3 W-? (b)
(Mrs F.O. Foote, pre-1940)

'Choir Boy' 2 W-O
(J.N. Hancock & Co., 1946)

'Chomolhari' 2 W-W
(A.O. Roblin, 1943) A.O. Roblin, 1956
'Carmel' × 'Askelon'

'Chopin' 8 Y-Y
(pre-1928)
Poetaz
Fl. very pale yellow

'Chopin' 3 W-Y
(J.L. Richardson) Mrs H.K. Richardson, 1973
'Syracuse' open pollinated
Fl. large; corona very shallow bowl-shaped, pale primrose, tinged with lemon yellow, with rim deeply dentate

'Chopin' 3 W-?
Syn. of 'Albert Sandler'

'Chorale' 3 W-YYR
(Murray W. Evans, 1964) Murray W. Evans, 1975
'Falaise' × 'Actaea'; sdlg no. H-53
Fl. 100 mm wide. Mid-season

'Choral Music' 11a W-P
(G.E.Mitsch, 1984) R. & E.Havens, 1997
([('Precedent' × 'Carita') × ('Radiation' × 'Mabel Taylor')] × 'Interim') × 'Phantom'; sdlg no. TT16/2
Fl. 110 mm wide; perianth segments ovate; corona deeply split, the segments opposite and closely overlying the perianth segments, mid-pink, a little frilled. Mid-season. Sunproof

'Choria' 1 W-W
(Barr & Sons, pre-1923)

'Chorine' 2 W-YYW
(Murray W. Evans) Murray W. Evans, 1974
('Content' × ?'Flora's Favourite') × ('Polindra' × ['Lola Prieta' × 'Content'])
Fl. 110 mm wide

'Chorister' 9 W-YYO
(G.H. Engleheart, pre-1913)
Fl. rounded, facing down; perianth segments snowy white, reflexed, overlapping; corona very shallow bowl-shaped, saffron yellow, with a narrow band of orange at rim. Late

'Chortle' 3 Y-W
(Jackson's Daffodils) Jackson's Daffodils, 1993
'Lemonade' × sdlg 249/78; sdlg no. 137/85
Fl. 115 mm wide; perianth segments very broadly ovate, blunt or somewhat truncate, with very slight mucro, light greenish yellow 4B, a little reflexed, glistening, overlapping half; the inner segments more narrowly ovate; corona bowl-shaped, opening light greenish yellow 4B, becoming yellowish white (8D), mouth straight, wavy. Mid-season to late

209

'Chorus Girl' 2 W-P
(J.N. Hancock & Co., 1963) Unregistered

'Chorus Line' 8 W-Y
(W.G. Pannill) W.G. Pannill, 1982
'Matador' × *N. triandrus*; sdlg no. 65/99 B
Fl. 80 mm wide. Mid-season

'Chosen' 2 W-? (b)
(pre-1939)

'Chosen Lady' 2 W-P
(A. Glover, *c*.1965) Unregistered
'Pink Monarch' × 'C.E. Radcliff'

'Chough' 3 W-O
(C. Dawson, pre-1908)
Corona reddish orange

'Chough' 5 Y-Y
(A. Gray) A. Gray, 1958
N. triandrus × *N. scaberulus*
Fl. primrose

'Choysa' 2 W-YYR
(D.S. Bell) D.S. Bell, 1965
'Mannequin' × 'Garland'
Mid-season. Resembles 'Dollar Princess' but with a more widely flared corona

'Chrissie' 2 Y-? (a)
(F.W. Parkinson, pre-1936)

'Christabel' 3 W-? (b)
(A.M. Wilson, pre-1908)

'Christabel' 5 W-W
(L. Buckland, pre-1961) Unregistered
Fls usually 2 per stem, pure white

'Christalla' 2 W-W
(A.R. Goodwin, pre-1910)

'Christella' 2 W-P
(J.N. Hancock & Co., 1979) Unregistered
Early to mid-season

'Christiaan Huygens' 2 Y-? (a)
(J.W.A. Lefeber, pre-1943)
AM(Haarlem) 1943

'Christian' 2 Y-Y
(The Brodie of Brodie, *c*.1935)
'Pilgrimage' × 'Saint Egwin'; sdlg no. 49/A/30
Fl. of strong substance. Tall

'Christie's Companion' 1 Y-Y
(A.G. Thompson) A.G. Thompson, 1966
'Spring Glory' × 'Golden Harvest'
Fl. 95 mm wide, yellow; perianth segments paler than the corona. Early. Resembles a more vigorous 'Christie Shield' with a paler perianth

'Christie Shield' 1 Y-Y
(A.G. Thompson) A.G. Thompson, 1960
'Golden Harvest' × 'Fortune'
Fl. 101 mm wide. Early. Resembles 'Golden Harvest' but with the perianth of stronger substance

'Christina' 2 W-P
(Colin Crotty) Unregistered
Sdlg no. 14-75

'Christina Hooper' 2 W-P
(L.P. Dettman) L.P. Dettman, 1974
'Better Half' × 'Pomeranza'
Fl. 96 mm wide

'Christina Lennett' 2 W-GYO
(L.P. Dettman, 1967) L.P. Dettman, 1979
'Cynthia Dettman' × 'Diane Barker'; sdlg no. 47/68
Fl. 81 mm wide; perianth segments yellowish white 155B; corona brilliant greenish yellow 2B, with green at base and brilliant orange 29A at rim. Mid-season

'Christina Morrison' 2 Y-OOY
(D.C. MacArthur) D.C. MacArthur, 1984
'Rouge' × 'Braniel'; sdlg no. E814
Perianth segments yellow; corona orange, with yellow at rim. Mid-season.

'Christina Rosetti' 9 W-YYR
Syn. of 'Snow King'

'Christine' 5
(Mrs R.O. Backhouse, pre-1921)

'Christine' 1 W-? (b)
(D.V. West, pre-1936)

'Christine Harper' 2 W-P
(L.P. Dettman, *c*.1974) Unregistered

'Christine Miller'
(pre-1933)

'Christine Shankly' 2 W-O
(L.P. Dettman) L.P. Dettman, 1977
'Dame Pattie Menzies' × 'Hugh Dettman'
Fl. 95 mm wide; perianth segments greenish white (157B); corona pale orange (24D). Mid-season. Resembles 'Dame Pattie Menzies' but with a long self pink corona

'Christmas' 8 Y-O
(pre-1969) Unregistered

'Christmas Carol' 1 W-W
(D.S. Bell) D.S. Bell, 1958

Fl. pure white; corona with rim dentate and widely flanged

'Christmas Glory' 1 Y-Y
(W.J. Eldering & Son, pre-1928)
Very early. Resembles a smaller-flowered 'Golden Spur'. EFA(Haarlem) 1927

'Christmas Valley' 4 W-P
(G.E. Mitsch, 1977) R. & E. Havens, 1991
'Pink Chiffon' × sdlg C7/22 ('Carita' × 'Accent'); sdlg no. MM31/10
Fl. symmetrical, 100 mm wide. Mid-season

'Christobel' 2 W-? (b)
(A.M. Wilson, pre-1946)

'Christopher'
(pre-1933)

'Christopher Bowley' 3 W-? (b)
(Bowley, pre-1907)

N. × *christopheri* Blanchard 13 = *N. assoanus* Dufour × *N. panizzianus* Parlatore

'Christopher Marlowe' 9 W-?
(Barr & Sons, pre-1908)

'Chromacolor' 2 W-P
(W,G. Pannill) W.G. Pannill, 1976
'Carita' × 'Accent'; sdlg no. 64/25 FR
Fl. 120 mm wide. Mid-season. Resembles an improved 'Accent' of deeper colour with a more widely expanded corona

'Chrome' 2 Y-? (a)
(G.H. Engleheart, pre-1914)

'Chromis' 1 Y-Y
(W. Jackson Sr, 1939) W. Jackson Jr, 1956
'Chruseos' × 'Crocus'
Fl. soft yellow

'Chromium' 2 W-? (b)
(R. Crews, pre-1949)
'Renown' × 'Fortune'

'Chronique' 2 Y-O
(Konynenburg & Mark) Konynenburg & Mark, 1966
'Red Goblet' × 'Contrapunt'
Fl. 90 mm wide; perianth segments canary yellow; corona marigold orange. Early

'Chruseos' 1 Y-Y
(W. Jackson Sr, 1935) W. Jackson Jr, 1956
'Golden City' × 'Pilgrimage'

'Chrysalie' 2 W-Y
(Mrs M. Moorby) Mrs M. Moorby, 1963
Fl. 88 mm wide; perianth segments white; corona pale lemon yellow. Mid-season

'Chrysanster' 2 W-? (b)
(Lord Rendlesham, pre-1937)

N. chrysanthus de Candolle = *N. bertolonii*

'Chryse' 7 Y-Y
(G.H. Engleheart, pre-1914)
'King Alfred' × *N. jonquilla*
Fl. large, deep yellow; corona widely expanded, with rim crenate. AM(e) 1915

'Chryseis' 2 W-Y
(T. Batson, pre-1907)
Perianth segments creamy white, smooth, overlapping; corona shallow, dark rich yellow, mouth flared and lightly frilled, with rim rolled

'Chrysol' 7
(G.H. Engleheart, pre-1923)

'Chrysolite' 1 Y-Y
(pre-1913)

'Chrysolite' 7
(de Graaff Bros, pre-1927)

'Chrysoprase' 2 Y-? (a)
(A.M. Wilson, pre-1944)

'Chrysos' 1 W-Y
(pre-1913)

'Chrysostom' 1 W-W
(G.H. Engleheart, pre-1907)

'Chukar' 4 W-O
(G.E. Mitsch) G.E. Mitsch, 1982
'Gay Time' × 'Silken Sails'; sdlg no. HH104/2
Fl. 105 mm wide; perianth and other petaloid segments white; corona segments short, orange and amber. Late. Spicily scented. Syn. 'Penguin'

'Chula' 1 W-Y
(Oregon Bulb Farms, pre-1951)

'Chum' 1 Y-Y
(G. Lubbe & Son, pre-1937)
AM(Haarlem) 1937

'Chungking' 3 Y-O
(G.L. Wilson, pre-1942)
'Market Merry' × 'Clackrattle'
Perianth segments golden yellow; corona shallow, orange. AM(Haarlem) 1948, FCC (Haarlem) 1950

'Chunila' 2 Y-? (a)
(A.H. Ahrens) J.S. Leitch, 1957

'Chuploe' 2 Y-O
(West & Fell, pre-1938)
Perianth segments pale yellow; corona bowl-shaped, reddish coppery orange

'Church Bay' 2 W-GWP
(Carncairn Daffodils) Carncairn Daffodils, 1987
'Drumtullagh' × 'Little Princess'; sdlg no. 1/72
Perianth segments very broadly ovate, blunt, fairly prominently mucronate, spreading, with margins sometimes more or less deeply incurling, regular, overlapping half; the inner segments more narrowly ovate, somewhat creased; corona large bowl-shaped, smooth, salmon pink, with white at base and green in tube, mouth strongly ribbed, split in places and overlapping, tightly and irregularly frilled. Late

'Churchfield' 2 W-W
(Carncairn Daffodils) Carncairn Daffodils, 1969
'Easter Moon' hybrid
Resembles 'Easter Moon' but with a more widely expanded corona opening cream and becoming white with green at base

'Churchill' 1 W-W
(J.N. Hancock & Co., 1973) Unregistered

'Churchill Cream' 2 W-?
(Cartwright & Goodwin, pre-1927)

'Churchman' 2 W-W
(Ballydorn Bulb Farm) Ballydorn Bulb Farm, 1968
'Ave' hybrid open pollinated
Fl. 88 mm wide. Mid-season. Resembles 'Ave' but with the corona rim flanged

'Church Town' 2 W-W
(Ballydorn Bulb Farm) Ballydorn Bulb Farm, 1977
'Courage' hybrid
Fl. 110 mm wide. Mid-season. Resembles 'Churchman' but with the corona slightly ribbed

'Churinga' 2 W-? (b)
(R.A. Dunn) R.A. Dunn, 1959

'Churston Ferrers' 4 W-O
(Brian S. Duncan) du Plessis Bros, 1987
'Gay Time' × Duncan sdlg 482
Perianth and other petaloid segments in six whorls. Mid-season

'Chusan' 3 W-O
(S.J. Bisdee) S.J. Bisdee, 1956
'Limerick' × 'Mr Sparks'

'Chutzpah' 2 W-W
(Jackson's Daffodils) Jackson's Daffodils, 1996

'Ragamuffin' × 'Thisbe'; sdlg no. 251/87
Fl. 108 mm wide, greenish white (155A); perianth segments very broadly ovate; the inner segments touching one another at the margins; corona cylindrical, with mouth flared. Mid-season to late

'Chynance' 2 W-? (b)
(R.V. Favell, pre-1953)

'Chyvarrian' 5 Y-Y
(R.V. Favell, 1941) R.M. Favell, 1959
Fl. 88 mm wide, sulphur yellow. Mid-season. Resembles a taller 'Queen of Spain' with broader perianth

'Chyvarton' 5 Y-Y
(R.V. Favell, 1941) R.M. Favell, 1959
Fl. 88 mm wide, sulphur yellow. Resembles a taller and larger-flowered 'Queen of Spain' with the corona rim more deeply rolled

'Cibola' 2 Y-Y
(G.E. Mitsch, pre-1952)
'Malvern Gold' × 'Trenoon'; sdlg no. 148/1
Perianth segments broad, deep golden yellow; corona widely expanded, tightly ribbed. Early. 2n=28

'Cibyn' 5 Y-?
(W.A. Watts, pre-1913)

'Cicely' 7 Y-Y
(A.M. Wilson, pre-1915)
Fl. deep buffy apricot yellow, smooth; corona darker in tone than the perianth

'Cicely' 2 W-W
(A.M. Wilson, pre-1927)
'Fleetwing × 'Mrs Robert Sydenham'
Fl. small, neat, facing slightly downwards; perianth segments overlapping; corona expanded, pale creamy white. Mid-season. 2n=28. *AM(g) 1930, *AM(g) 1936

'Cicely Mander' 2 Y-Y
(R.H. Bath, pre-1915)
Perianth segments soft yellow; corona darker in tone. Resembles 'Noble' in form. See also 'Cecely Manders'

'Cicely O'Rorke' 2 W-P
(Alister Clark, 1935) J. Sharp, 1960
See also 'Cecily O'Rorke'

'Cicero' 8 W-Y
(C.P. Alkemade, pre-1928)
Poetaz
Perianth segments pure white; corona sulphur yellow

'Cicero' 2 W-Y
(J.A. O'More, 1962) P.D.K. Ramsay, 1980
'Trousseau' × 'Lochin'; sdlg no. 3/62

Fl. 99 mm wide; perianth segments spreading; corona large, yellow, with buff overtones, mouth flared. Mid-season. Resembles 'Dunmurry' but with the corona of a different form and colour

'Cicerone' 2 W-W
(Curtis Tolley) Curtis Tolley, 1996
'April Love' × 'Churchman; sdlg no. 88-9-1
Fl. forming a double triangle, 114 mm wide, pure white; perianth segments ovate; corona funnel-shaped, ribbed, with mouth slightly flared. Mid-season

'Cider' 1 Y-Y
(H.A. Brown, 1938) J.N. Hancock & Co., 1960
Fl. soft yellow; perianth segments smooth. Very tall. Early

'Cielette' 1 W-P
(W. Jackson Jr, pre-1952)
'Dawnglow' × 'Palin'

'Cigale' 3 W-O
(R.H. Bath, pre-1929)
Fl. 100 mm wide; perianth segments rounded, creamy white, overlapping; corona brilliant scarlet-orange. Late

'Cigar' 2 Y-O
(W.F.M. Copeland, pre-1909)
Perianth segments soft light yellow, reflexed, of thin substance, overlapping at base only; corona very widely expanded, ribbed, intense orange, heavily frilled

'Cilla' 1 W-W
(W. Jackson Jr, 1966) Unregistered
('Ammon' × 'Merri') × 'Glen Derwent'; sdlg no. 179/66

'Cilldara' 4 W-P
(Brian S. Duncan, 1979) Amisfield, 1992
('Falaise' × 'Debutante') × 'Valinor'; sdlg no. 968
Fl. 102 mm wide; perianth and other petaloid segments white; corona segments interspersed among the petaloid segments at centre, deep pink. Mid-season to late

'Cimarosa' 1 W-Y
(Konynenburg & Mark) Konynenburg & Mark, 1960
'Lord Nelson' hybrid
Fl. 115 mm wide; perianth segments greenish white; corona vivid yellow 9A. Early

'Cimarron' 1 W-? (b)
(K.L. Reynolds, pre-1944)

'Cimba' 2 Y-O
(1945) de Graaff Bros & van Konynenburg & Co., 1959
Perianth segments light greenish yellow 5C; corona strong orange 25A. Late

'Cinder' 2 W-?
(Mrs R.O. Backhouse, pre-1921)

'Cinder' 2 Y-O
(L. Buckland, pre-1930)
Perianth segments yellow; corona expanded, reddish orange

'Cinderella' 3 W-Y
(W. Backhouse, pre-1869)
Perianth segments creamy white; corona sulphur yellow, tinged orange. Syn. Barrii Albidus 'Aurantius', Barrii Albidus 'Cinderella'

'Cinderella' 3 W-? (b)
(Mrs R.O. Backhouse, pre-1921)

'Cinder Hill' 2 W-O
(N.A. Burr, 1980) N.A. Burr, 1992
'Sammy Boy' × 'Rameses'; sdlg no. 2.5.75
Fl. 100 mm wide; perianth segments broadly ovate, blunt or truncate, fairly prominently mucronate, spreading, somewhat concave, overlapping one-third to a half; the inner segments with margins more strongly incurved; corona bowl-shaped, ribbed, vivid orange 28B, mouth straight, deeply 6-lobed, with the lobes overlapping, lightly frilled. Early to mid-season

'Cindywood' 1 Y-W
(Mrs J. Abel Smith) Mrs J. Abel Smith, 1980
'Daydream' × ('Brabazon' × 'Maraval'); sdlg no. MO/42
Fl. 96 mm wide; perianth segments deep yellow; corona becoming white, with rim neatly rolled. Mid-season. Resembles 'Daydream' but with the perianth segments more nearly acute

'Cinel' 2 Y-R
(W. Jackson Jr) W. Jackson Jr, 1970
'Vanity' × 'Freycinet'; sdlg no. 192/65
Fl. 88 mm wide

'Cinerama' 1 W-Y
(D. Bramley) D. Bramley, 1964
Fl. 120 mm wide; perianth segments white; corona creamy yellow. Mid-season. Resembles a larger-flowered and unfading 'Saint Saphorin'

'Cingalee' 5 ?Y-Y
(Mrs R.O. Backhouse, pre-1908)
Perianth segments creamy yellow, spreading; corona long cup-shaped, soft primrose yellow

'Cinna' 2 Y-? (a)
(P.D. Williams, pre-1935)

'Cinnabar' 2 Y-R
(G.L. Wilson) Guy L.Wilson Ltd, 1966
('Indian Summer' × 'Bahram') × ('Klingo' × 'Rustom Pasha')

'Cinnamon' 2 W-? (b)
(Mrs R.S. Cobley, pre-1932)

'Cinque Ports' 2 Y-? (a)
(F.D.B. Cobb, pre-1953)

'Cintra' 3 W-? (b)
(Mrs R.O. Backhouse, pre-1921)

'Cintrist' 2 W-Y
(P. de Jager & Sons) P. de Jager & Sons, 1971
'Polindra' × 'Jules Verne'
Fl. 115 mm wide; perianth segments ivory white; corona pale yellow. See also 'Centrist'

'Cinzano' 2 W-O
(G.L. Wilson, pre-1953)
Perianth segments pure white; corona pale orange

'Circa' 2 W-? (b)
(Mrs R.S. Cobley, pre-1937)

'Circe' 3 W-W
(E. Leeds, pre-1877)
Perianth segments white; corona opening canary yellow, becoming milk white. Syn. Leedsii 'Circe', Leedsii 'Gloriosus'. Was "absorbed" into 'Duchess of Brabant'

'Circlet' 3 W-YYO
(G.H. Engleheart, pre-1907)
'Corofin' self pollinated
Perianth segments pale yellow; corona shallow, bright yellow, with a band of deep reddish orange at rim

'Circlet' 3 Y-YYO
(J.L. Richardson) Mrs H.K. Richardson, 1963
'Corofin' open pollinated
Perianth segments broad, rounded, creamy white, slightly recurved, overlapping; corona almost disc-shaped, bright yellow, with a narrow band of yellowish orange at rim, flanged

'Circuit' 7 Y-Y
(G.E. Mitsch) G.E. Mitsch, 1971
'Aircastle' × *N. jonquilla*; sdlg no. Z2/21
Fls often one per stem, 80 mm wide, rich clear yellow; perianth segments rounded, smooth, overlapping; corona almost disc-shaped, small

'Circumstance' 1 Y-Y
(J.N. Hancock & Co., 1956) Unregistered
Corona cylindrical, with rim slightly flanged. Mid-season

'Circus' 2 Y-O
(?J.N. Hancock & Co., 1960s) Unregistered

'Circus Clown' 2 W-WOO
(Oregon Bulb Farms, pre-1950)

'Cirris' 1 W-W
(J.S. Leitch) J.S. Leitch, 1966
Fl. 115 mm wide. Mid-season

'Cirus' 1 Y-Y
(G.H. Engleheart, pre-1923)

'Cisco' 1 W-WPP
(J.N. Hancock & Co., pre-1967) Unregistered
Perianth segments white; corona funnel-shaped, flushed pink

'Cissbury' 2 Y-O
(Sir F.C. Stern, pre-1949)
'Cheerio' × 'Rustom Pasha'
Perianth segments light yellow; corona deep reddish orange

'Cisticola' 3 W-YYR
(Brian S.Duncan) Brian S.Duncan, 1997
'Mount Angel' × sdlg 675 ('Arctic Flame' × 'Random Light'); sdlg no. 1550
Fl. rounded, 95 mm wide; perianth segments very broadly ovate, pure white, plane, with margins slightly incurved at apex; corona shallow bowl-shaped, slightly ribbed, deep yellow, with a broad and clearly defined band of deep red at rim. Mid-season to late

'Citadel' 1 W-? (b)
(A.M. Wilson, pre-1949)

'Citation' 2 W-W
(Mrs P.M. Davis, pre-1948)

'Citizen' 9 W-?
(W. Welchman, pre-1929)

'Citrina' 8 W-Y
Syn. of 'Grand Primo Citronière'

N. citrinus (Baker) Fernández Casas = *N. bulbocodium* var. *citrinus*

N. citrinus Link = *N. tazetta* subsp. *lacticolor*

'Citrinus'
Syn. of *N. bulbocodium* var. *citrinus*

'Citrinus' 8 W-Y
Syn. of 'Grand Primo Citronière'

'Citriona' 2 Y-Y
(Barr & Sons, pre-1908)
Perianth segments sulphur yellow, irregular; corona a

little darker in tone than perianth, tinged lime green at base

'Citrix' 1 Y-Y
(J. Gerritsen & Son, pre-1953)
Fl. greenish yellow; corona with a darker tone at rim. Very early. 2n=28. AM(Haarlem) 1952. Received AM(Haarlem) 1952 as 'Citrus'

'Citron' 3 W-? (b)
(G.H. Engleheart, pre-1907)

'Citron' 3 Y-WWY
(G.E. Mitsch) G.E. Mitsch, 1982
'Aircastle' hybrid; sdlg no. JJ24/3
Fl. 90 mm wide; perianth segments very pale yellow; corona opening creamy yellow, becoming white, with creamy yellow at rim. Mid-season

'Citron Cup' 8 W-Y
(pre-1881)
Perianth segments white; corona citron yellow

'Citronée' 8 Y-Y
(pre-1798)
Fl. sulphur yellow

'Citronella' 1 Y-Y
(C.G. van Tubergen, pre-1919)
'Sunbeam' hybrid
Perianth segments creamy sulphur, overlapping half; corona pale buttercup yellow, with mouth expanded. AM(Haarlem) 1919, *AM(g) 1930

'Citronier' 8 W-Y
(pre-1851)
Perianth segments white; corona citron yellow

'Citronita' 3 Y-Y
(W.A. Noton) W.A. Noton, 1976
'Lemonade' × 'Perimeter'; sdlg no. 703
Fl. 82-92 mm wide, lemon yellow; corona very shallow bowl-shaped, slightly darker in tone than the perianth. Mid-season

'Citron Queen' 1 Y-Y
(R.H. Bath, pre-1931)

'Citrus' 1 Y-Y
Syn. of 'Citrix'

'City Beautiful' 4 W-R
(D.S. Bell) D.S. Bell, 1982
'Charisma' × 'Gay Challenger'
Perianth and other petaloid segments white; corona segments clustered at centre, red. Mid-season. Resembles a 'Gay Challenger' of whiter appearance

'City Club' 1 Y-Y
(W.G. Pannill, 1971) W.G. Pannill, 1990
'Slieveboy' × 'Arctic Gold'; sdlg no. 64/116

'City Lights' 2 W-YYR
(D.S. Bell) D.S. Bell, 1957
'Fairy Mother' × 'Green Island'
Perianth segments white; corona bowl-shaped, yellow, with red at rim. PC(e) 1970

'City of Haarlem' 1 Y-Y
(C.A. van der Wereld, pre-1936)
AM(Haarlem) 1936

'Civic' 2 Y-YYR
(?New Zealand origin, pre-1990) Unregistered

'Civil Defence' 3 W-YYO
(G.H. Johnstone, pre-1946)

'C.J.Backhouse' 2 Y-O
(W. Backhouse, pre-1869)
Fl. star-shaped; perianth segments ovate, acute, spreading, with margins wavy, overlapping a quarter; corona ribbed, strong orange, with mouth straight, irregularly frilled. 2n=14. Syn. Incomparabilis Leedsii 'C.J.Backhouse', Incomparabilis Leedsii 'Charles James Backhouse'. FCC 1886

'Clackamas' 2 W-YYO
(G.E. Mitsch, pre-1954)
'John Evelyn' × 'Dick Wellband'; sdlg no. 38C43/21
Perianth segments overlapping; corona almost disc-shaped, lemon yellow, with pale orange at rim. Mid-season

'Clackmar' 3 Y-R
(G.L. Wilson, pre-1952)
'Market Merry' × 'Clackrattle'; sdlg no. 27/127

'Clackrattle' 2 Y-O
(P.D. Williams, pre-1932)
Perianth segments deep primrose yellow, smooth; corona reddish orange. AM(e) 1932. Received AM 1932 as 'Crackrattle'

'Claddagh' 1 W-? (b)
(W.B. Hartland, pre-1907)

'Clady Cottage' 2 W-Y
(Carncairn Daffodils) Carncairn Daffodils, 1987
'Folly' open pollinated; sdlg no. 28/75
Perianth segments ovate, acute, spreading at base, reflexed and twisted above near apex, overlapping a quarter; corona short broad funnel-shaped, lightly ribbed, deep yellow, mouth very slightly expanded, even, with rim widely and obscurely crenate. Late

'Clair de Lune' 1 W-W
(G.H. Engleheart, pre-1923)

'Claire' 2 Y-Y
(H. Selkirk, pre-1927)
Perianth segments yellow; corona orange-yellow

'Clairette' 2 W-?
Syn. of 'Claret'

'Clamor' 2 W-YYR
(de Graaff Bros, pre-1936)
AM(Haarlem) 1936

'Clanacombe' 1 W-? (b)
(M.H. Tribe, pre-1937)

'Clanda' 3 Y-? (a)
(J.T. Gray, pre-1951)

'Clandeboye' 1 W-W
(K.B. Burns, 1946) T. Sherriff, 1957
Perianth segments pure white; corona opening lemon, soon becoming creamy white, with mouth expanded

'Clandon' 2 W-W
(Mrs R.O. Backhouse, pre-1913)
Perianth segments acute, of strong substance, overlapping; corona long, opening pale yellow, becoming creamy white, with rim rolled

'Clansman' 3 W-? (b)
(W.B. Cranfield, pre-1916)

'Clarabel' 3 W-Y
Syn. of 'Claribel'

'Clarabella' 2 W-Y
(F.E. Board) F.E. Board, 1965
'Buncrana' × 'Arbar'
Perianth segments white; corona orange-yellow. Late

'Clara Butt' 2 W-?
(J.R. Pearson & Sons, pre-1908)

'Clara Herring' 3 Y-? (a)
(Miss K. Spurrell, pre-1907)

'Claranda' 4
(Alfred Clark) Alfred Clark, 1955

'Clare' 7 Y-Y
(A. Gray, 1958) Broadleigh Gardens, 1968

'Clare' 1 Y-W
(W.M. Spry, pre-1975) Unregistered
'Hunter's Moon' × 'Kingscourt'

'Clareen' 2 W-W
(G.L. Wilson) G.L. Wilson, 1960
'Tryst' × ('Cotterton' × 'Broughshane')

'Claremont' 2 W-R
(C.E. Radcliff, 1940) J.M.Radcliff, 1956
Sdlg × 'Cheerio'

'Clarence' 3 W-? (b)
(de Graaff Bros, pre-1930)

'Clarendon' 2 Y-Y
(C.E. Radcliff, 1939)
'Trenoon' × 'Fortune'

'Clare Park' 2 W-P
(Carncairn Daffodils) Carncairn Daffodils, 1976
'Rosario' × 'Debutante'; sdlg no. 7/96/60
Fl. 110 mm wide; perianth segments greenish white (157B), corona widely expanded, light yellowish pink 29C. Mid-season. Resembles 'Rose Caprice' but with the corona more widely expanded and deeper in colour

'Claret' 2 W-? (b)
(de Graaff Bros, pre-1938)
Syn. 'Clairette'. AM(Haarlem) 1938

'Claret Cup' 2 Y-? (a)
(W.A. Grace, pre-1938)

'Claribel' 2 W-Y
(E. Leeds, pre-1877)
Perianth segments creamy white; corona yellow. Syn. Incomparabilis Albus 'Claribel'

'Claribel' 3 W-Y
Fl. large; perianth segments broad, slightly reflexed; corona widely expanded, yellow, flushed orange, frilled. See also 'Clarabel'

'Clarice' 2 W-W
(R.H. Bath, pre-1927)
Fl. 108 mm wide; perianth segments white, inflexed, irregular; corona broad funnel-shaped, cream. Mid-season

'Claridges' 4 W-P
(Brian S. Duncan) Rathowen Daffodils, 1987
Sdlg 8/74 (['Falaise' × 'Debutante'] × 'Polonaise') × sdlg 346 ('Polonaise' × 'Violetta')
Fl. rounded; perianth and other petaloid segments in two whorls, pure white; the outer whorl very broadly ovate, blunt or truncate, with very slight mucro, spreading, plane, overlapping half or more; the inner whorl a little shorter, broad, strongly inflexed, with margins more or less tightly incurling; corona segments half the length of the inner petaloid segments and clustered among them, more loosely arranged outside them, broad, rose pink, with lilac tones, tightly frilled. Late to very late

'Clarify' 2 W-Y
(T.H. Piper, c.1966) Unregistered

Paringa' × 'Lorinna'

'Clarion' 1 Y-Y
(N.Y. Lower, pre-1914)
'Monarch' × 'King Alfred'
Fl. yellow; perianth segments regular, overlapping; corona rim neatly dentate

'Clarion Call' 2 W-YYP
(Alfred Clark, 1945) R. Hyde, 1958
Perianth segments pure white; corona pale buff, shading to rosy pink at rim

'Clarissa' 3 W-O
(J. Pope, pre-1907)

'Clarissa' 2 Y-YYO
(S.C. Gaspar) S.C. Gaspar, 1955
'Rosslare' × 'Winnipeg'
Perianth segments yellow; corona yellow, with a narrow band of reddish orange at rim, finely dentate

'Clarisse' 8 W-O
(pre-1798)

'Clarity' 2 W-Y
(L. Buckland, pre-1936)
Perianth segments pure white; corona yellow

'Clashmore' 2 Y-Y
(D.C. MacArthur) D.C. MacArthur, 1984
'Rouge' × 'Braniel'
Fl. yellow; corona flecked white at rim. Mid-season

'Class Act' 2 W-GYW
(T.D. Throckmorton) Grant Mitsch Novelty Daffodils, 1987
'Pigeon' × 'Green Hills'; sdlg no. TT2/11/2
Corona very shallow bowl-shaped. Late. Resembles 'Starthroat' but with broad perianth segments

'Classic' 1 W-? (b)
(E.M. Crosfield, pre-1908)

'Classic' 2 W-Y
(G.E. Mitsch, 1966) G.E. Mitsch, 1976
('Broughshane' × 'Cantatrice') × 'Empress of Ireland'; sdlg no. B56/1
Fl. 116 mm wide; corona long, narrow, lemon yellow. Mid-season

'Classic' 2 Y-YYO
Syn. of 'Kudos'

'Classic Delight' 2 YYW-GOO
(J. & E. Frey) J. & E. Frey, 1988
Sdlg JEE8/1 × 'Chiloquin'; sdlg no. DEE3/1
Fl. rounded; perianth segments broad, rounded at apex, yellow, with white at base, slightly reflexed, overlapping half; the inner segments only slightly narrower, a little inflexed; corona long cup-shaped, opening yellow, becoming apricot, with green at base. Dwarf. Mid-season to late. Resembles 'Chiloquin' but with the corona becoming a different colour

'Classic Miss' 2 W-Y
(J.N. Hancock & Co., 1947) J.N. Hancock & Co., 1979
Sdlg no. 885 H
Fl. 102 mm wide; corona brilliant yellow 10B. Mid-season

'Classic Touch' 2 Y-R
(M.E.Brogden, pre-1997) Unregistered
'Trudie May' × 'Torridon'

'Class Ring' 3 W-WWP
(R. & E.Havens, 1984) R. & E.Havens, 1994
'First Formal' × 'Coral Light'; sdlg no. TEH8/1
Fl. rounded, 95 mm wide, of good texture; perianth segments very broad in outline, blunt or squarish at apex, sometimes truncate, only very slightly mucronate, pure white, reflexed, plane or with margins a little incurling, overlapping half or more; corona short bowl-shaped, finely ribbed, pure white, with a broad band of coral pink at rim, mouth straight and minutely frilled. Late. Sunproof

'Claude' 7
(L. Buckland, pre-1936)

'Claudelands' 2 Y-? (a)
(H.M.Hammond) H.M.Hammond, 1955

'Claudia' 2 Y-? (a)
(P.D. Williams, pre-1908)

'Claudia' 2 W-P
(J.N. Hancock & Co., 1969) Unregistered
Perianth segments creamy white; corona narrow, deep amber pink. Tall. Mid-season

'Claudius' 2 Y-O
(J.W.A. Lefeber, pre-1968) Unregistered

'Clava' 2 W-Y
(The Brodie of Brodie, c.1922)
'Beacon' × 'Loch Fyne'
Perianth segments pure white; corona shallow bowl-shaped, large, bright yellow

'Claverack' 3 W-? (b)
(E.C. Powell, pre-1947)
'White Sentinel' × 'Seraglio'

'Claverley' 2 W-P
(Clive Postles) Clive Postles Daffodils, 1993
'Dailmanach' open pollinated; sdlg no. 1-124-79
Fl. forming a double triangle, 102 mm wide; perianth segments broadly ovate, blunt, fairly

prominently mucronate, spreading, with margins slightly incurving, overlapping half; the inner segments narrower, a little inflexed at base and recurved in upper part; corona somewhat funnel-shaped, very broadly ribbed, pale pink, shading to a deeper tone at mouth, mouth flared, almost even, rim irregularly crenate. Late. Sunproof

'Clavier' 6 YYW-WWY
(R. & E.Havens, 1987) R. & E.Havens, 1997
'Owyhee' × *N. cyclamineus*; sdlg no. WH166/1
Fl. 80 mm wide; perianth segments lemon yellow, with white at base, reflexed; corona cylindrical, long, opening lemon, becoming white, with lemon at rim. Mid-season

'Cleanthe' 3 W-? (b)
(C.G. van Tubergen, pre-1930)

'Clearbrook' 2 W-W
(Brian S. Duncan) du Plessis Bros, 1989
'Easter Moon' × 'Knowehead'; sdlg no. 380
Fl. 110 mm wide, pure white; corona cylindrical, mouth slightly expanded and a little frilled. Mid-season to late

'Clear Day' 4 Y-O
(Th. van der Hulst) Th. van der Hulst, 1991
'Orbit' × 'Tahiti' sport
Fl. 92 mm wide; perianth segments brilliant greenish yellow 6B; corona light orange (23A), with strong orange 25A at rim. Early. Sunproof

'Clear Eye'
(pre-1930)

'Clear Eye' 3 W-? (b)
(Warnaar & Co., pre-1940)
AM(Haarlem) 1940

'Clear Eye' 2 W-?
Syn. of 'Brilliant Eye'

'Clear Glow' 4 W-R
(Colin Crotty, pre-1994) Unregistered
'Gay Time' × 'Hotspur'; sdlg no. 4-79

'Clearwater' 2 W-GWW
(G.E. Mitsch, 1973) R. & E. Havens, 1990
'Arctic Doric' × 'Birthright'; sdlg no. II73/1
Fl. 115 mm wide; perianth segments white, with greenish undertones; corona cylindrical, with rim slightly flanged. Early

'Cleda' 2 W-? (b)
(J.T. Gray, pre-1949)

'Cleena' 2 W-OOY
(J.L. Richardson, pre-1939)
'Fortune' × 'Hades'

Perianth segments broadly ovate, blunt, slightly mucronate, white, with a tinge of green at base, spreading, plane, overlapping half; the inner segments more narrowly ovate, more prominently mucronate, a little inflexed; corona funnel-shaped, apricot orange, with pale primrose yellow at mouth and a tinge of green at base, mouth expanded, almost even, with rim crenate. Early to mid-season. 2n=28

'Cleeve Cloud' 2 W-W
(J.M. de Navarro, pre-1951)

'Cleggan' 2 W-WWP
(Carncairn Daffodils) Carncairn Daffodils, 1970
'Templemore' × 'Rose Caprice'

'Clemenceau' 1 Y-Y
(pre-1930)

'Clemenceau' 2 W-? (b)
(Konynenburg & Mark, pre-1953)

'Clemency' 2 W-W
(West & Fell, pre-1935)
Perianth segments white; corona opening with a pinkish tinge, becoming creamy white

'Clementina' 2 W-W
(C.E. Radcliff, 1933)
'Silver Plane' × 'Pink'un'

'Clementine' 2 W-Y
(Konynenburg & Mark) Konynenburg & Mark, 1960
('Invitation' × 'Red Bird') × 'Aloquin'
Fl. 110 mm wide

'Clendinnen' 1 Y-Y
(W.M. Spry, pre-1975) Unregistered
'Braemar' × 'Golden Valley'
Early

'Clent' 1? Y-Y
(The Brodie of Brodie, *c.*1910)
'Glory of Noordwijk' × 'Weardale'
Fl. pale lemon; corona darker in tone than the perianth

'Cleoma' 3 Y-? (a)
(P. van Deursen, pre-1930)

'Cleomenes' 2 W-? (b)
(Barr & Sons, pre-1923)

'Cleon' 1 W-? (b)
(Barr & Sons, pre-1923)

'Cleone' 2 Y-? (a)
(S.C. Gaspar, pre-1949)

'Cleopatra' 8 W-W
(pre-1871)

'Cleopatra' 1 Y-Y
(E. Leeds, pre-1877)
Perianth segments deep primrose yellow; corona darker in tone. Syn. Pseudonarcissus Major 'Cleopatra'. Perhaps the same as 'Cleopatra' pre-1903

'Cleopatra' 1 Y-Y
(Barr & Sons, pre-1903)
Perianth segments broadly ovate, slightly mucronate, yellow, spreading, plane, overlapping one-third to a half; the inner segments more narrowly ovate, a little inflexed, somewhat twisted, corona long, straight-sided, smoothly and broadly angled, deep yellow, mouth expanded, with rim broadly and regularly crenate. Resembles a large-flowered and more refined 'Monarch'. AM 1903, AM(Haarlem) 1913, AM(g) 1914

'Clermont' 3 W-? (b)
(Warnaar & Co., pre-1933)
Syn. 'Martello'

'Cleten' 1 Y-Y
(J.T. Gray, 1930) Parr's Nurseries, 1958

'Cletus' 1 W-W
(J.T. Gray, pre-1949)
'Beersheba' hybrid
Resembles a larger and much improved 'Beersheba'

'Cleverman' 2 W-Y
(J.N. Hancock & Co., 1962) J.N. Hancock & Co., 1977
'Euroa' × 'New Light'; sdlg no. 105/56
Fl. 98 mm wide; corona vivid to brilliant yellow 9A to 10A. Mid-season

'Cliché' 2 Y-Y
(Jackson's Daffodils, 1985) Jackson's Daffodils, 1995
'Scipio' × sdlg 11/77; sdlg no. 100/85
Fl. 115 mm wide; perianth segments vivid yellow 9B, plane, smooth; corona cylindrical, darker in tone (13B) than the perianth, with mouth slightly flared. Mid-season

'Clickety Click' 12 Y-Y
(Brian S. Duncan) Rathowen Daffodils, 1983
'Papua' × ?'Vagabond'; sdlg no. 548
Fl. 85 mm wide. Resembles N. cyclamineus but with occasional extra growths at centre. Mid-season. Varies between Divs 12 and 4

'Clifton' 2 Y-? (a)
(de Graaff Bros, pre-1927)
AM(Haarlem) 1933

'Cliftonville' 2 W-? (b)
(F.D.B. Cobb, pre-1953)

'Climax' 2 W-?
(Sir C.H. Cave, pre-1928)

'Climax' 2 W-YYO
(Warnaar & Co.) Warnaar & Co., 1960
'Sempre Avanti' × 'Mrs Barclay'
Fl. 101 mm wide; perianth segments greenish white; corona canary yellow, with a narrow band of bright orange at rim. Mid-season. AM(Haarlem) 1960

'Climping' 2 Y-?
Syn. of 'Clymping'

'Clinker' 2 Y-OOR
(A.M. Wilson, pre-1948)
Perianth segments yellow; corona orange, with red at rim

'Clinton' 2 Y-? (a)
(pre-1956) Unregistered

'Clio' 1 Y-Y
(S. Morrison, pre-1939)
Fl. yellow; corona of a slightly deeper tone than the perianth, flanged

'Clipper' 2 Y-O
(P.D. Williams, pre-1910)
Perianth segments clear, bright yellow; corona soft scarlet-orange. Tall

'Clipper' 2 W-Y
(P. de Jager & Sons) P. de Jager & Sons, 1963
'Polindra' × 'Jules Verne'
Fl. 120 mm wide; perianth segments ivory white; corona brilliant greenish yellow 6A. Early

'Clipsham' 2 W-Y
(W.A. Noton) W.A. Noton, 1994
Fl. 89 mm wide; perianth segments ovate, blunt, yellowish white, inflexed, overlapping one-third to a half; the inner segments more narrowly ovate, more nearly acute, a little twisted or with margins wavy; corona cylindrical, very lightly ribbed, vivid yellow between 9A and 12A, with mouth flared, rim crenate. Mid-season

'Clique' 2 W-P
(Jackson's Daffodils) Jackson's Daffodils, 1986
'Velask' × 'Dear Me'; sdlg no. 67/78
Perianth segments yellowish white 155B; corona light yellowish pink 36A. Mid-season

'Clisham' 1 W-GWW
(D.C. MacArthur) D.C. MacArthur, 1985
'Ludlow' × ('Braniel' × 'Preamble'); sdlg no. E821
Perianth segments broadly ovate, blunt, mucronate, spreading or a little inflexed, with margins somewhat

wavy, overlapping one-third; the inner segments more strongly inflexed, with margins more markedly wavy; corona funnel-shaped, lightly ribbed, white, with green at base, mouth a little frilled, with rim irregularly notched and sometimes flanged. Mid-season

'Clix' 2 W-YPP
(J.N. Hancock & Co., c.1977) Unregistered

'Clochette' 5
(W.B. Cranfield, pre-1930)

'Clochmerle' 2 W-P
(G.L. Wilson) F.E. Board, 1962
'Irish Rose' × 'Melton'; sdlg no. 46-23
Perianth segments white; corona opening buff, becoming rich pink. Mid-season. Resembles 'Melton' but with the corona of a richer colour

'Clockface' 3 W-YYO
(G.L. Wilson, pre-1947)
Fl. up to 115 mm wide; perianth segments milk white, overlapping; corona disc-shaped, clear yellow, with bright scarlet-orange at rim

'Clodia' 1 W-? (b)
(W. Welchman, pre-1908)

'Clogheen' 3 W-Y
(J.L. Richardson) J.L. Richardson, 1961
'Altyre' × 'Chinese White'
Corona almost disc-shaped, tightly ribbed, pale yellow

'Clogher Park' 2?
(Irish origin, pre-1899)
Resembles a smaller 'Sir Watkin'

'Cloister' 9 W-?
(W. Welchman, pre-1929)

'Clonard' 2 W-O
(G.L. Wilson, pre-1947)
Sdlg 24/109 ('Mitylene' × 'Red Abbot') × 'Painted Lady'
Perianth segments white; corona scarlet-orange

'Clonavon' 1 W-W
(T. Bloomer) T. Bloomer, 1962
'Glenbush' × 'Empress of Ireland'; sdlg no. 10/20/58

'Cloncarrig' 1 Y-Y
(J.L. Richardson, pre-1952)
'Kilkenny' × 'Goldcourt'
Fl. deep gold; corona mouth frilled, with rim rolled. 2n=28. AM(Haarlem) 1960

'Cloncurry' 2
(pre-1907)

'Cloneen' 2 W-W
(G.L. Wilson, pre-1953)
'White Maiden' × 'Greenland'
Perianth segments reflexed; corona cup-shaped

'Cloneytrace' 1 W-W
(Carncairn Daffodils, 1974) Carncairn Daffodils, 1994
'Empress of Ireland' × 'Arctic Doric'; sdlg no. 1/69/69
Fl. forming a double triangle, 100 mm wide, yellowish white 155B; perianth segments regular, overlapping; corona cylindrical, with mouth slightly expanded. Mid-season

'Clonmacnoise' 1 Y-Y
(J.L. Richardson, pre-1954)
'Kingscourt' × 'Goldcourt'
AM(Haarlem) 1965

'Clonmel' 1 Y-Y
(G.L. Wilson, pre-1933)
'King of the North' × 'Sorley Boy'
Perianth segments primrose yellow; corona of a deeper tone, with rim flanged. AM(e) 1933

'Clonmore' 1 Y-Y
(G.L. Wilson, pre-1953)
'Rolled Gold' × 'Bastion'
Fl. 101 mm wide; perianth segments vivid yellow 9B, with margins slightly incurving, overlapping half; corona lightly ribbed, a little darker in tone (12A) than the perianth, mouth widely expanded, frilled, with rim dentate and slightly flanged. *AM(g) 1958, *FCC(g) 1959

'Clontarf' 2 W-O
(G.L. Wilson, pre-1933)
Perianth segments pale creamy buff primrose; corona pale orange

'Cloona' 2 W-YYO
(J.T. Gray, 1930) Parr's Nurseries, 1958
Perianth segments white; corona large, widely expanded, yellow, with reddish orange at rim

'Clorander' 4 W-P
(Alister Clark, pre-1949)

'Close Encounter' 2 W-P
(W.G. Pannill) W.G. Pannill, 1978
'Woodlea' × 'Fintona'; sdlg no. D 50
Fl. 90 mm wide. Mid-season

'Close Harmony' 4 W-Y
(Th.van der Hulst, 1985) Brian S.Duncan and Wim Lemmers, 1997
'Flower Drift' hybrid
Fl. 100 mm wide; corona segments deep yellow. Mid-season

'Clothilda' 3 W-?
(Barr & Sons, pre-1913)

'Clothilde'
(J.T. Gray, pre-1933)

'Clotho' 2 W-Y
(T. Batson, pre-1915)
Fl. facing down; perianth segments ovate, fairly prominently mucronate, ivory white, inflexed, with margins wavy, overlapping about one-third; corona slender, cylindrical and smooth in lower half, flared and lightly ribbed towards mouth, primrose yellow, mouth more or less even, with rim minutely flanged

'Cloth of Gold' 8 Y-Y
(C. Smith, pre-1900)
Fls 3 per stem; perianth segments rich yellow; corona dark golden yellow. Sweetly scented

'Cloth of Gold' 1 Y-Y
(O. Ronalds, pre-1948)
Fl. rich golden yellow; corona long and slender

'Cloth of Gold' 1 Y-Y
Syn. of 'Golden Plover'

'Cloudcap' 2 W-WWP
(G.E. Mitsch, 1956) G.E. Mitsch, 1967
'Mabel Taylor' × 'Interim'; sdlg no. R47/8
Fl. 121 mm wide; perianth segments overlapping; corona bowl-shaped, large, creamy white, with a broad band of salmon pink at rim. Mid-season. Resembles a vigorous 'Rose Ribbon'

'Cloudcuckooland' 3 W-GYO
(J.M. de Navarro) J.M. de Navarro, 1975
('Corofin' × 'Tulyar') × 'Greenfinch'; sdlg no. 877
Fl. 92 mm wide; corona yellow, shading to pinkish orange at rim, with bluish green at base. Mid-season. Resembles 'Audubon' in form

'Clouded Yellow' 2 YYW-Y
(A.J.R. Pearson) A.J.R. Pearson, 1994
Sdlg 81-14-F1 ('Camelot' × 'Daydream') × 'Cool Shades'; sdlg no. 89-47-M15
Fl. rounded, 100 mm wide; perianth segments very broadly ovate, blunt, brilliant greenish yellow 6C, with greenish white (1D) at base and midrib, very slightly concave, silken smooth, with waxy texture and heavy substance, overlapping three-quarters; corona funnel-shaped, lightly ribbed, orange-yellow (14A), with mouth lightly flared, rim flanged and crenate. Mid-season

'Cloudlet' 5
(A. White, pre-1947)

'Cloud Nine' 2 YYW-W
(G.E. Mitsch) G.E. Mitsch, 1972

'Quick Step' × 'Daydream'; sdlg no. D80/8
Fl. 84 mm wide; perianth segments ovate or broadly ovate, clear lemon yellow, with white mucro and with a distinct band of white at base, spreading, overlapping one-third to a half; corona long funnel-shaped, smooth, opening lemon yellow, becoming pure white, with mouth straight, wavy, rim minutely notched and crenate. Mid-season. Resembles 'Step Forward' but with the perianth more prominently mucronate and a narrower corona

'Clouds Hill' 4 W-WPP
(J.W. Blanchard) J.W. Blanchard, 1989
Sdlg 65/51A × sdlg 71/32A; sdlg no. 75/26A
Fl. 100 mm wide; perianth and other petaloid segments in three whorls, white; the outer whorl very broadly ovate, prominently mucronate, reflexed, with midrib showing, overlapping half; the second whorl rounded, not noticeably mucronate, spreading or inflexed; the centre whorl sharply inflexed, with margins folded inwards; corona segments shorter than the two inner whorls of petaloid segments and interspersed among them, broad, smooth, pale pink, with white at base and dark pink at rim, frilled, with rim entire. Late. Formerly named 'Fontmell'

'Clouds Rest' 2 W-P
(Brian S. Duncan) Brian S. Duncan, 1992
'Broadway Rose' × ('Infatuation' × 'Gem of Antrim'); sdlg no. 1149
Fl. 98 mm wide; perianth segments broadly ovate, pinkish white; corona very shallow bowl-shaped, ribbed, pink. Mid-season to late

'Clouds with Pink' 2 W-P
(O.David Niswonger) O.David Niswonger, 1993
'Inverpolly' × 'Impact'; sdlg no. 1-85
Fl. 114.3 mm wide; perianth segments ovate, spreading, plane; corona bowl-shaped, pink, mouth flared and lobed, closely frilled, with rim rolled. Early to mid-season. Sunproof

'Clovelly' 1 W-W
(J.W. Barr, pre-1930)

'Clovelly Gold' 1 Y-Y
(R.M. Miller, pre-1949)

'Clovis' 3 W-?
(W.B. Hartland, pre-1913)

'Clown' 6 Y-O
(C.F. Coleman) M.J. Jefferson-Brown, 1962
'Whang-hi' hybrid

'Cloyfin' 2 Y-Y
(W.J. Dunlop, pre-1970) Unregistered
Fl. soft lemon yellow; perianth segments smooth, overlapping

'Cluan' 2 W-W
(K.J. Heazlewood, 1958) K.J. Heazlewood, 1968
'Petsamo' × 'Kanchenjunga'
Fl. 127 mm wide. Early. Resembles a shorter 'Kanchenjunga' with a shallower and more heavily frilled corona

'Clubman' 1 W-Y
(Jackson's Daffodils, 1984) Jackson's Daffodils, 1995
'Hussy' × 'Helsal'; sdlg no. 28/84
Fl. 103 mm wide; perianth segments broadly ovate, greenish white (155A); corona cylindrical, vivid yellow 9A, with mouth slightly flared, frilled. Early

'Clumber' 3 W-Y
(Mrs J. Abel Smith) Mrs J. Abel Smith, 1975
'Green Howard' × 'Aircastle'; sdlg no. P4/92
Fl. 105 mm wide; perianth segments very broadly ovate, blunt, slightly mucronate, creamy white, spreading, a little concave, with margins slightly incurling at apex, overlapping half; the inner segments more deeply concave; corona shallow bowl-shaped, bright yellow, touched with a darker tone at rim, mouth ribbed and frilled, with three overlapping lobes, rim minutely crenate. Late. 2n=28. Resembles 'Aircastle' but with the corona of a stronger colour

'Cluna' 2 W-? (b)
(J.T. Gray, pre-1949)

'Clunes' 5 Y-Y
(C.A. Nethercote) T. Morrison, 1960
Fl. lemon yellow

N. clusii Dunal = *N. cantabricus* subsp. *cantabricus*

'Clusius' 1 W-Y
(E.H. Krelage & Son, pre-1931)
'King Alfred' × 'Lady Margaret Boscawen'

'Clustine' 5 Y-Y
(Barr & Sons, pre-1933)
Perianth segments acute, soft creamy primrose yellow; corona long, expanded, slightly darker in tone than the perianth, with mouth closely frilled

'Clutha' 3 W-O
(J.T. Gray, pre-1949)
Perianth segments white; corona spreading, deep orange

'Clutha Gold' 1 Y-Y
(D.S. Bell) D.S. Bell, 1977
'David Bell' open pollinated
Fl. 106 mm wide; corona with rim deeply rolled. Mid-season

'Clwyd' 3 W-YYO
(The Brodie of Brodie, c.1925)
'Mozart' × 'Gallipoli'

Perianth segments cream; corona spreading, tightly ribbed, golden yellow, with a broad band of reddish orange at rim. AM(e) 1928

'Clymene' 5
(Barr & Sons, pre-1913)

'Clymping' 2 Y-? (a)
(Sir F.C. Stern) Sir F.C. Stern, 1957
See also 'Climping'

'Clytia' 5
(C. Dawson, pre-1923)

'Clytie' 2 W-W
(H.J. Poole Sr, pre-1927)

'Clyto' 1 W-W
(T. Batson, pre-1914)

'Clytus' 8 Y-Y
(pre-1798)
Fl. pale yellow

'C.M.Owen' 1 W-W

'Coach Horn' 1 Y-Y
(pre-1907)

'Coat of Arms' 2 W-? (b)
(W.B. Hartland, pre-1913)

'Coballero' 1 W-? (b)
(J.L. Richardson, pre-1931)

'Cobden' 2 W-Y
(New Zealand origin, pre-1956) Unregistered
Perianth segments white; corona bright lemon

'Cobham Hall' 2 Y-? (a)
(The Brodie of Brodie, pre-1931)

'Cobweb' 5 W-Y
(A. Gray, pre-1938)
N. triandrus var. *loiseleurii* sdlg
Fls 1-4 per stem, 63 mm wide; perianth segments narrowly ovate, inflexed, twisted, overlapping at base only; corona cylindrical, narrow, smooth, pale yellow, with mouth ribbed and a little expanded, rim crenate

'Coby Henkes' 2 W-O
(G.A. Henkes, pre-1936)
'John Evelyn' sport
Syn. 'Mrs Henkes'. AM(Haarlem) 1936

'Cocarde' 2 Y-? (a)
(L. van Leeuwen & Son, pre-1931)
AM(Haarlem) 1930

'Cockabundu' 2 W-O

(G.H. Johnstone) G.H. Johnstone, 1959
Fl. 95 mm wide; corona bright orange. Late

'Cockade' 2 Y-O
(D. Bramley) D. Bramley, 1980
'Traveller' hybrid; sdlg no. 71/27
Fl. 95 mm wide. Mid-season. Resembles a larger 'Traveller' with broader perianth segments and a more deeply coloured corona

'Cockatiel' 2 W-WPW
(G.E. Mitsch) G.E. Mitsch, 1980
'Precedent' × ('Caro Nome' × 'Carita'); sdlg no. G14/10
Perianth segments white; corona white, with a band of pale pink at mouth and white at rim. Mid-season

'Cockatoo' 3 W-? (b)
(W.B. Hartland, pre-1908)

'Cockatoo' ?-P
(Alister Clark, pre-1948)

'Cockatoo' 2 W-Y
(G.E. Mitsch) G.E. Mitsch, 1975
'Empress of Ireland' × 'White Prince'; sdlg no. B18/1
Fl. 125 mm wide; perianth segments milk white; corona very pale lemon. Mid-season

'Cockatrice' 2 W-W
(G.H. Engleheart, pre-1914)
Fl. large; perianth segments narrow, acute

'Cock Robin' 3 W-? (b)
(W.B. Hartland, pre-1907)

'Cock Robin' 6 Y-R
(C.F. Coleman) C.F. Coleman, 1960
('Seville' hybrid × 'Carbineer') × *N. cyclamineus*
Fl. 76 mm wide. AM(Haarlem) 1962

'Cocktail' 2 Y-W
(G.L. Wilson, pre-1954)
'Binkie' × ?'Spellbinder'
Fl. rounded; perianth segments soft lemon yellow; corona opening yellow, gradually becoming whitish. Mid-season

'Coconut Ice' 2 W-PPW
(J.N. Hancock & Co., 1968) Unregistered

'Codam' 1 Y-Y
Syn. of 'Coham'

'Codlings and Cream' 4 W-Y
Syn. of 'Sulphur Phoenix'

'Codlins and Cream' 4 W-Y
Syn. of 'Sulphur Phoenix'

'Coeur de Lion' 3 Y-O
(P.J. Worsley, pre-1907)
'Princess Mary' × *N. radiiflorus* var. *poetarum*
Perianth segments pale primrose yellow; corona rich scarlet-orange

'Coffeecup' 2 W-?
(W.M. Spry, pre-1975) Unregistered
'Green Island' × 'Hunter's Moon'
Corona coffee brown

'Coham' 1 Y-Y
(T. Buncombe, pre-1934)
See also 'Codam'

'Coho' 1 W-W
(Murray W. Evans) Murray W. Evans, 1974
'Celilo' × 'Vigil'
Fl. 110 mm wide

'Coimbatore' 3 W-O
Syn. of 'Calcutta'

'Coinage' 1 Y-Y
(pre-1965)
Fl. rich yellow; perianth segments very smooth

'Cokefield' 1 W-W
(The Brodie of Brodie, pre-1928)

'Colamore' 11a W-OOP
(J. Gerritsen & Son) J. Gerritsen & Son, 1980
'Frileuse' hybrid
Fl. 80 mm wide; perianth segments ivory white; corona segments pale orange (24D), with coral pink at rim. Early to mid-season

'Colblanc' 11a W-GWW
(J. Gerritsen & Son) J. Gerritsen & Son, 1973
'Cassata' × 'Echo'
Fl. 110 mm wide; perianth segments very broadly ovate, spreading or a little reflexed; the inner segments inflexed and more narrowly ovate; corona split almost to base, the six segments as wide and as long as the perianth segments, opposite and closely overlying them, bi-lobed, with the lobes deeply overlapping, of heavy substance, ivory white, with yellow-green at base, frilled. Early to mid-season

'Col d'Anternes' 1 W-W
(de Graaff Bros, pre-1927)

'Coldbrook' 2 Y-W
(W.A. Bender) W.A. Bender, 1985
'Binkie' × 'Aircastle'; sdlg no. 70/2
Perianth segments light greenish yellow 7D; corona white. Late

'Coldoree' 11a W-OOY
(J. Gerritsen & Son, 1971) J. Gerritsen & Son, 1981

'Pearlshell' × 'Salome'
Fl. 100 mm wide; perianth segments ivory white; corona segments pinkish orange, with amber yellow at rim. Mid-season. Resembles a larger-flowered 'Collarosa'

'Cold Overton' 2 W-GWW
(W.A. Noton, 1965) W.A. Noton, 1976
'Easter Moon' × 'Knowehead'; sdlg no. 550
Fl. 95-100 mm wide; perianth segments broad, overlapping; corona expanded, with green at base, frilled. Mid-season. AM(e) 1976

'Coldstream' 1 W-W
(Heathcote Bulb Nursery, pre-1961) Unregistered

'Col du Moine' 1 W-W
(de Graaff Bros, pre-1927)

'Cold Weather' 2 W-? (b)
(J.W.A. Lefeber, pre-1944)

'Coleridge' 2 W-W
(A. Gibson, pre-1951)

'Coleshill' 3 Y-? (a)
(A.M. Wilson, pre-1950)

'Coletto'
(The Brodie of Brodie, c.1907)
'Madame de Graaff' × *N. triandrus*

'Colibri' 2 Y-Y
(J. Gerritsen & Son) J. Gerritsen & Son, 1968
'Topolino' hybrid
Fl. 82 mm wide; perianth segments greenish yellow (4D); corona vivid yellow 9B. Early. Resembles a much shorter 'Topolino'

'Colin' 1 Y-Y
(N.R. McIsaac) N.R. McIsaac, 1982
'Golden Satin' × 'Iberia'; sdlg no. 289
Fl. 122 mm wide, pale yellow. Mid-season. Resembles a larger and paler 'Golden Satin'

'Colin's Joy' 2 W-GWR
(Colin Crotty) Colin Crotty, 1989
'Cherryrim' × 'Accent'; sdlg no. 4-76
Perianth segments greenish white (155A); corona opening light orange-yellow 22B, becoming whitish, with green at base and deep orange-red (34A) at rim. Mid-season.

'Collarosa' 11a W-YPP
(J. Gerritsen & Son) J. Gerritsen & Son, 1968
'Easter Bonnet' hybrid
Fl. 100 mm wide; perianth segments creamy white; corona pale orange-yellow (near to 21D) at base, opening pale orange towards mouth, becoming pink. Dwarf. Early

'Collector's Choice' 3 W-GOR
(Carncairn Daffodils) Carncairn Daffodils, 1984
Sdlg 2/422 × 'Masaka'; sdlg no. W17/8
Fl. 100 mm wide; corona shallow, orange, with green at base and a broad band of orange-red at rim. Mid-season

'Colleen' 3 W-Y
(G.H. Engleheart, pre-1910)
Perianth segments white; corona greenish yellow. AM 1910

'Colleen Bawn' 1 W-W
(pre-1885)
Fl. pure white, facing down; perianth segments inflexed, symmetrically twisted, overlapping at base only; corona cylindrical, opening greenish white, mouth flared, rim irregularly crenate. Early. Syn. 'The Fair Maid of Erin'

'Colleen Thérèse' 1 W-W
(L.P. Dettman) L.P. Dettman, 1979
'Tablecloth' × 'Glenshesk'; sdlg no. 101/72
Fl. 107 mm wide; perianth segments yellowish white 155B; corona greenish white (155A). Mid-season. Resembles 'Tablecloth' but with the perianth segments broader and more deeply overlapping and the corona longer and more widely expanded

"College Garden Maximus"
Syn. of 'Maximus'

'Collegiate' 3 W-R
(C.E. Radcliff, 1944)
'Cordova' × 'Portia'

'Colley Gate' 3 W-YOR
(J.S.B. Lea, c.1972) Clive Postles Daffodils, 1985
'Rockall' × 'Merlin'; sdlg no. 1-27-67
Mid-season. 2n=28

'Colliford' 2 W-W
(Brian S. Duncan) du Plessis Bros, 1986
'Easter Moon' × 'White Star', sdlg no. 320
Perianth segments broadly ovate, blunt, a little inflexed, plane, overlapping half; the inner segments more strongly inflexed, with margins wavy; corona funnel-shaped, lightly ribbed, with mouth slightly expanded and lightly frilled, rim obscurely crenate. Mid-season

'Collindale' 3 Y-? (a)
(Barr & Sons, pre-1945)

'Collington' 2 W-? (b)
(G.H. Engleheart, pre-1931)

'Collingwood' 2 Y-O
(D.N.Y. Olson, 1983) D.N.Y. Olson, 1993
'Vulcan's Fire' × 'Falstaff'

Fl. forming a double triangle, 100 mm wide; perianth segments broadly ovate, blunt, strong yellow, with slight white mucro, slightly reflexed, overlapping one-third to a half; the inner segments rounded at apex; corona wide funnel-shaped, ribbed, deep orange, with a slightly darker tone towards rim, mouth straight and obscurely lobed, wavy, rim notched. Mid-season. Sunproof

'Collin's Bonnet' 1 W-W
(S.J. Bisdee, 1940)
'Saint Aloysius' × 'Coppice'

'Colloggett' 2 W-Y
(Brian S. Duncan) du Plessis Bros, 1987
'Irish Minstrel' × 'Aldergrove'; sdlg no. 191
Perianth segments white; corona funnel-shaped, deep golden yellow, with mouth expanded. Mid-season. Resembles an improved 'Tudor Minstrel'

'Colmar' 2 Y-?Y
(pre-1939)

'Colmartin' 1 Y-Y
(Miss K.M. Hinchliff, pre-1937)

'Colmolhari' 2 W-W
(A.O. Roblin, c.1950)
'Askelon' × 'Carmel'

'Colmonell' 3 W-GYY
(G.L. Wilson, pre-1948)
'Nelly' × 'Sylvia O'Neill'
Perianth segments white; corona citron yellow, with deep vivid green at base, frilled. Late

'Colna' 1 W-W
(W. Jackson Sr, 1936) W. Jackson Jr, 1956
'Marmora' × 'Beersheba'

'Colombo' 2 Y-? (a)
(Warnaar & Co., pre-1933)
AM(Haarlem) 1933. Received AM(Haarlem) 1933 as 'Target'

'Colona' 2 W-? (b)
(D.J. Cooper) D.J. Cooper, 1957

'Colonel Beck' 2 Y-? (a)
(F. Rijnveld & Sons, pre-1939)

'Colonel Bogey' 2
(Alister Clark, c.1910) J. Sharp, 1960

'Colonel Cotton' 1 Y-Y
(W.A. Watts, pre-1923)

'Colonial Gown' 2 W-? (b or c)
(G.H. Engleheart, pre-1931)
Sdlg no. B26

'Colonial White' 2 W-W
(G.E. Mitsch) R. & E. Havens, 1993
'Panache' × 'Misty Glen'; sdlg no. TT26/1
Fl. 100 mm wide, pure white, with a greenish cast; perianth segments very broadly ovate, blunt, spreading, plane, silken smooth, overlapping half; the inner segments narrower, rounded at base; corona funnel-shaped, loosely ribbed, with mouth straight and a little frilled, rim almost entire. Mid-season

'Colonist' 2 Y-? (a)
(J. Pope, pre-1913)

'Colonnade' 2 W-P
(W.G. Pannill) W.G. Pannill, 1982
'Leonaine' × 'Rose Royal'; sdlg no. 64/79
Fl. 87 mm wide. Mid-season

'Colorable' 1? W-Y
(pre-1933)

'Colorado' 3 W-YRR
(Mrs R.O. Backhouse, pre-1921)
Fl. rounded; perianth segments pure white, smooth, of great substance; corona disc-shaped, tightly ribbed, bright crimson, paling to gold at base, heavily and as if doubly frilled. AM(e) 1931

'Colorama' 11a Y-O
(J. Gerritsen & Son) J. Gerritsen & Son, 1973
Sdlg hybrid
Fl. 90 mm wide; perianth segments very broadly ovate, rounded or sometimes squarish at apex, slightly mucronate, brilliant yellow 12B, spreading, plane, overlapping half; the inner segments more narrowly ovate or roundish; corona very deeply split, the segments in two whorls of three, as broad as the perianth segments and half as long, opposite and closely overlying them, with two overlapping lobes at rim, strong orange 25B, deeply frilled, overlapping; the inner segments themselves overlapping at lobed shoulder. Mid-season

'Colorange' 11a Y-O
(J. Gerritsen & Son, 1950) J. Gerritsen & Son, 1962
Fl. 95 mm wide; perianth segments sulphur yellow; corona segments deep orange. Early. 2n=28

'Coloratura' 3 W-WWO
(G.E. Mitsch) G.E. Mitsch, 1956
'Green Island' × 'Chinese White'; sdlg no. M39/6
Perianth segments rounded, very smooth; corona almost disc-shaped, wihte, with rich apricot at rim, mouth heavily frilled. Mid-season. 2n=27

'Color-bearer' 3 W-? (b)
(A.M. Wilson, pre-1948)

'Colorful' 2 Y-R
(W. Jackson Jr) Jackson's Daffodils, 1979

'Bilboa' × 'Dimity' hybrid; sdlg no. 176/71 Fl. 116 mm wide. Mid-season

'Colorspot' 2 Y-O
(M.G.Temple-Smith, 1982) M.G.Temple-Smith, 1997
'Hot Spot' × 'Colorful'; sdlg no. 18/82
Perianth segments vivid yellow 14A, with overtones of orange; corona broad, orange (28A). Early to mid-season

'Colors Up' 3 W-? (b)
(A.M. Wilson, pre-1948)

'Colossus' 2 Y-Y
(F.H. Chapman, pre-1913)
'King Alfred' hybrid
Perianth segments clear yellow; corona dark yellow. AM(Haarlem) 1912

'Colourful' 2 Y-R
(New Zealand origin, pre-1955) Unregistered
Fl. deep yellow; corona deep red

'Colour Parade' 3 W-YYR
(Tom Forster, 1960s) Unregistered

'Colour Queen' 2 W-P
(Alister Clark, pre-1949)

'Colours' 2 Y-R
(C.O. Fairbairn, pre-1974) Unregistered
Perianth segments yellow; corona red

'Colour Scheme' 2 Y-O
(D.S. Bell) D.S. Bell, 1963
'Balboa' × 'Tamino'
Fl. 102 mm wide; perianth segments yellow; corona orange, with rim dentate. Mid-season

'Colour Sergeant' 2 Y-Y
(Ballydorn Bulb Farm, 1975) Ballydorn Bulb Farm, 1989
'Torch Bearer' × 'Viking'
Fl. 108 mm wide; perianth segments broadly ovate, golden yellow, smooth, deeply overlapping; corona narrow, slightly deeper in tone than the perianth, with rim dentate. Mid-season

'Colourtrue' 4 W-WWP
(D.S. Bell) D.S. Bell, 1985
Fl. 105 mm wide; perianth and other petaloid segments white; corona segments white, with pink at rim tinged orange at maturity. Mid-season. Resembles an orange-tinged 'Temple Maid'

'Colour Wonder' 2 W-O
(D.S. Bell) D.S. Bell, 1977
Fl. 105 mm wide; corona gradually becoming orange, with a pinkish tinge, rim rolled. Late

'Colstar' 11a W-Y
(J. Gerritsen & Son) J. Gerritsen & Son, 1986
'Mondragon' × 'Colorama'
Perianth segments ivory white; corona segments orange-yellow. Mid-season. Resembles 'Mondragon'

'Colston Bassett' 3 W-GWW
(Mrs J. Abel Smith, 1982) Mrs J. Abel Smith, 1992
'Verona' × sdlg K8/31; sdlg no B77/41
Fl. 35 mm wide; perianth segments rounded; corona very shallow bowl-shaped, with green at base. Late

'Columbia' 1 W-? (b)
(R.A. van der Schoot, pre-1923)

'Columbine' 3 W-WWO
(G.L. Wilson, pre-1934)
'Dactyl' × 'Mystic'
Perianth segments broad, pure white, with margins somewhat wavy; corona shallow, wide-spreading, tinged pale greyish green, with a sharply defined band of salmon orange at rim. Late

'Columbus'
(pre-1913)

'Columbus' 2 W-W
(Carncairn Daffodils, 1965) Carncairn Daffodils, 1976
'Easter Moon' × G.L.Wilson sdlg 45/115; sdlg no. 3/140/60
Fl. 105 mm wide, greenish white (155A); corona sometimes opening with yellow at rim, soon becoming white, with greenish grey at base. Mid-season. Resembles 'Easter Moon' but with the corona a little more rounded

'Colville' 9 W-GYR
(R.A. Scamp) R.A. Scamp, 1994
('Corofin' × 'Crenver') × 'Crenver'; sdlg no. 131
Fl. 71 mm wide; perianth segments broadly ovate, slightly mucronate, opening with green undertones, becoming white; corona disc-shaped, bright yellow, with dark green at base and a band of red at rim. Late

'Colwyn' 3 W-?
(W.A. Watts, pre-1923)

'Comal' 1 Y-Y
(W. Jackson Jr) W. Jackson Jr, 1968
'Letti' × 'Zimi'; sdlg no. 41/64
Fl. deep yellow; perianth segments overlapping; corona rim slightly flanged

'Comanche' 1 Y-Y
(K.L. Reynolds, pre-1944)
'Aerolite' × 'Saint Issey'

'Come Again' 2 Y-O
(O. Ronalds) M. Gardiner, 1956

Perianth segments deep yellow; corona reddish orange, frilled

'Comedy' 2 W-? (b)
(G.H. Johnstone, pre-1942)

'Comely' 1 W-? (b)
(G.L. Wilson, pre-1923)

'Comely' ?-P
(Alister Clark, pre-1948)

'Comeragh' 1 Y-Y
(J.L. Richardson, pre-1929)

'Comet' 6
(Mrs R.O. Backhouse, pre-1900)
Hybrid between *N. cyclamineus* and *N. obvallaris*
AM 1900

'Comet' 2 Y-YYR
(D.V. West, pre-1931)
Perianth segments yellow; corona expanded, yellow, with a broad band of bright red at rim

'Comet' 8 Y-Y
Syn. of 'Comete'

'Comete' 8 Y-Y
(pre-1792)
Fl. pale yellow. See also 'Comet'

'Comfort' 2 Y-? (a)
(A.M. Wilson, pre-1938)

'Comic' 1 W-Y
(Glenbrook Bulb Farm, 1984) Glenbrook Bulb Farm, 1997
Fl. 104 mm wide; perianth segments greenish white (155A), spreading, very slightly twisted; corona cylindrical, brilliant greenish yellow 4A, with mouth flared and lightly frilled. Mid-season to late

'Comic Court' 2 W-YYR
(H.A. Brown, 1943)
Perianth segments pure white; corona disc-shaped, bright yellow, rim vivid red. Late

'Commandant' 1 W-? (b)
(R.A. van der Schoot, pre-1923)

'Commander' 2 Y-Y
(Barr & Sons, pre-1891)
Perianth segments pale sulphur yellow, smooth, of thick substance; corona large, straight-sided, yellow, heavily stained scarlet-orange, with rim irregularly dentate

'Commander Byrd' 1 W-Y
(van Zonneveld Bros & Philippo, pre-1930)

Perianth segments sulphur white; corona large, lemon yellow, heavily frilled. AM(Haarlem) 1929

'Commander-in-Chief' 1 Y-Y
(M. van Waveren & Sons, pre-1942)
'Princess Mary' × 'King Alfred'

'Commanding' 1 Y-Y
(D.S. Bell) D.S. Bell, 1961
'Ranalagh' × 'Val d'Or'
Fl. 140 mm wide; corona frilled, with rim dentate. Mid-season. Resembles an improved 'Ranalagh' in form and texture

'Commando' 1 Y-Y
(R.H. Bath, pre-1942)
Resembles an improved 'Golden Spur'

'Commando' 2 Y-O
Syn. of 'California Gold'

'Comment' 2 W-YOO
(M. Fowlds) G.E. Mitsch, 1971
'Rubra' × 'Tuskar Light'
Fl. 110 mm wide; corona disc-shaped, large, reddish orange, with yellow at base, rim flanged with age

'Commissar' 1 Y-Y
(W.A. Noton) W.A. Noton, 1976
'Arctic Gold' × 'Kingscourt'; sdlg no. 542
Fl. 108 mm wide, deep gold; perianth segments broad; corona slightly flared. Tall. Early

'Commodore' 2 Y-YYO
(G.H. Engleheart, pre-1897)
Sdlg no. 47
Fl. rounded; perianth segments very broad, chrome yellow, overlapping; corona expanded, chrome yellow, with a broad band of orange at rim. Early

'Commodore' 2 W-O
(J.L. Richardson) J.L. Richardson, 1956
'Caragh' self pollinated
Perianth segments broadly ovate, pure white, of thick substance; corona deep orange, with mouth expanded and frilled

'Commodore' 2 (a)
Syn. of 'Mrs Mark Perrin'

'Commonwealth' 1 Y-Y
(West & Fell, pre-1936)
Fl. soft yellow

'Commonwealth' 2 W-?
Syn. of 'Longshaw'

'Commotion' 1 Y-Y
(pre-1927)

'Communicant' 2 W-?
(P.D. Williams, pre-1931)

N. commutatus Parlatore = *N. tazetta*

'Como' 9 W-GYR
(D.W. Gourlay) Mrs H.K. Richardson, 1973
Perianth segments round, pure white; corona yellow, with green at base and bright red at rim, frilled. Late. Scented. 2n=14

'Compagnon' 8 Y-Y
(pre-1798)
Fl. golden yellow

'Companion' 2 W-? (b)
(W. Welchman, pre-1930)

'Compare' 3 Y-? (a)
(A.H. Ahrens) J.S. Leitch, 1955

'Compassion' 2 W-P
(J.S.B.Lea, 1981) Clive Postles Daffodils, 1996
'Dailmanach' × sdlg 1-40-67; sdlg no. 1-22-76
Fl. forming a double triangle, 107 mm wide; perianth segments ovate; corona cylindrical, solid pink, with mouth flared and rim dentate. Late. Sunproof

'Compensate' 1 W-W
(D.S. Bell) D.S. Bell, 1963
'Lake Ellesmere' × 'Broughshane'
Fl. 111 mm wide, pure white, corona regularly frilled. Late. Resembles a smoother 'Broughshane'

'Competent' 2 Y-O
(F. Rijnveld & Sons) F. Rijnveld & Sons, 1967
Fl. 100 mm wide; perianth segments brilliant greenish yellow 6C; corona strong orange 25A. Mid-season. Resembles 'Delibes' but with a paler corona

'Competition' 2 Y-? (a)
(Sir C.H. Cave, pre-1928)

'Competitor' 2 Y-YYO
(N. van Reeuwijk) N. van Reeuwijk, 1964
Fl. 110 mm wide; perianth segments brilliant yellow 9C; corona brilliant yellow 13B, with orange at rim. Mid-season.

'Componist' 3 W-? (b)
(de Graaff Bros, pre-1930)

'Composer' 2 W-? (b)
(H.P. Zwetsloot, pre-1943)

'Compressa' 8 Y-Y
Syn. of 'Compressus' pre-1799

'Compressa' 8 W-Y
Syn. of 'Compressus' pre-1926

N. compressus Haworth = 'Compressus'

'Compressus' 8 Y-Y
(pre-1799)
Selection from *N.* × *intermedius*
Fls 2-6 per stem, 25-31 mm wide; perianth segments three times as long as the corona, narrowly ovate, acute, bright lemon yellow, with white mucro, spreading, concave, with margins sometimes wavy or a little twisted, more or less overlapping; corona orange-yellow, mouth expanded, obscurely 3-lobed, with the lobes bi-lobed, a little frilled. Dwarf or standard. Scented. Resembles *N. tazetta* but with narrower perianth segments. Syn. "The Jasmine Jonquil", 'Compressa', *N. compressus* Haworth

'Compressus' 8 W-Y
(?Dutch origin, pre-1926)
Fls up to 13 per stem, 36 mm wide; perianth segments very broad, blunt, prominently mucronate, yellowish white (4D), strongly reflexed, overlapping half; the inner segments not noticeably mucronate, sometimes a little twisted; corona cup-shaped, very broadly and shallowly ribbed, brilliant to light greenish yellow 4A to B, mouth straight, wavy, with rim entire. 2n=31. Resembles a smaller-flowered 'Avalanche' with more flowers per stem or 'Grand Monarque' but with the perianth segments reflexed. Syn. 'Compressa'

'Comptesse' 8 W-W
Syn. of 'Comtesse'

'Comptesse de Hollande' 8 W-Y
Syn. of 'Comtesse d'Hollande'

'Comptoise' 1 Y-Y
(J. Gerritsen & Son) J. Gerritsen & Son, 1984
Perianth segments brilliant greenish yellow 5B; corona vivid yellow 12A. Mid-season

'Compton' 3 W-W
(R.H. Bath, pre-1929)

'Compton Court' 3 Y-GYR
(Brian S.Duncan) Brian S.Duncan, 1997
'Triple Crown' × 'Burning Bush'; sdlg no. 1505
Fl. forming a double triangle, 100 mm wide; perianth segments broadly ovate, deep golden yellow; corona shallow bowl-shaped, ribbed, yellow, with prominent green at base and deep red at rim. Late

'Compton MacKenzie' 2 W-P
(R.V. Favell, pre-1942)
'Suda' × 'Mrs Ernst H.Krelage'
Perianth segments white; corona opening yellow, becoming soft apricot pink

'Compute' 1 W-Y
(Jackson's Daffodils) Jackson's Daffodils, 1986

'Helsal' × 'Lenz'; sdlg no. 36/79
Fl. forming a double triangle; perianth segments broadly ovate, blunt, acute, greenish white (155A), with brighter white mucro, spreading, with midrib showing, overlapping half; the inner segments more narrowly ovate, slightly inflexed, with margins a little wavy; corona funnel-shaped, bright yellow 3B, mouth ribbed and expanded, even, with rim loosely flanged and regularly crenate. Early

'Comrade' 2 W-Y
(W. Welchman, pre-1923)
Corona pale yellow. AM(e) 1928

'Comrie' 2 W-WWY
(Mrs R.S. Cobley, 1948) Seymour Cobley Ltd, 1968
Perianth segments white; corona white, with pale yellow at rim. Mid-season

'Comte d'Artois' 8 Y-Y
(pre-1807)

'Comtesse' 8 W-W
(pre-1831)
See also 'Comptesse'

'Comtesse de Narcisse' 8 W-Y
(pre-1883)
Closely resembles 'Staaten Generaal'

'Comtesse d'Hollande' 8 W-Y
(pre-1835)
Perianth segments white; corona lemon yellow. Early. See also 'Comptesse de Hollande'

'Comus' 9 W-YYR
(G.H. Engleheart, pre-1899)
Corona large, canary yellow, with a narrow band of brilliant red at rim. Sunproof

'Conawarr' 1 W-W
(S.J. Bisdee) S.J. Bisdee, 1956
'Kanchenjunga' × 'Whitefoord'

'Conbeg' 2 W-R
(G.L. Wilson, pre-1944)
'Merryhill' × 'Sunstar'
Perianth segments white, with pale lemon at base; corona deep red

'Con Brio' 2 Y-Y
(P. de Jager & Sons) P. de Jager & Sons, 1966
'Aranjuez' × 'Rococo'
Perianth segments canary yellow; corona lemon yellow. Mid-season

'Concentrate' 1 W-Y
(R.C.A. Tombleson) R.C.A. Tombleson, 1966
Fl. 114 mm wide; perianth segments white; corona deep lemon yellow. Mid-season

'Concertina' 2 W-P
(G.E. Mitsch) Grant Mitsch Novelty Daffodils, 1984
('Precedent' × 'Accent') hybrid; sdlg no. KK25/5
Fl. 102 mm wide; perianth segments white, with a suggestion of pink; corona pink. Mid-season

'Concerto' 2 W-Y
(Oregon Bulb Farms, pre-1950)

'Conchita' 2 W-? (b)
(de Graaff Bros, pre-1944)
AM(Haarlem) 1944

'Conchobar' 2 Y-? (a)
(A.M. Wilson, pre-1944)

N. concolor Bromfield = *N. obvallaris*

N. concolor (Haworth) Link = *N. triandrus* var. *concolor*

N. concolor Jordan = *N. hispanicus* var. *concolor*

'Concolor' 2 Y-Y
(E. Leeds, pre-1877)
Fl. yellow; corona sometimes stained orange. 2n=14.
Syn. Incomparabilis Concolor 'Concolor'

'Concolor Monstrosus' 1 Y-Y
Syn. of 'Hume's Giant'

'Concord' 3 Y-YYO
(G.H. Engleheart, pre-1906)
Perianth segments soft rich primrose yellow, overlapping; corona more or less disc-shaped, golden yellow, with a broad band of intense reddish orange at rim, dentate; corona in some seasons dark copper orange, with green at base. Syn. 'Red Disc'

'Concord' 2 W-W
(C.E. Radcliff, 1940) C.E. Radcliff, 1956
'White Sentinel' × 'Pinkeen'

'Concordat' 1 Y-Y
(G.H. Johnstone) G.H. Johnstone, 1959
'Merrydew' × 'Content'
Fl. 120 mm wide, bright primrose yellow. Mid-season

'Concordia' 2 W-Y
(Barr & Sons, pre-1923)
Fl. large; perianth segments white, incurving; corona primrose yellow, tinged sulphur

'Concordia' 1 Y-Y
Syn. of 'Charlemagne'

'Concurrent' 9 W-?
(P.D. Williams, pre-1942)

'Condesa' 1 W-W
(J.T. Gray, pre-1950)
Syn. 'Egmont'

'Condier' 2 W-? (b or c)
(G.H. Engleheart, pre-1923)

'Condo' 2 Y-Y
(West & Fell, pre-1938)
Perianth segments primrose; corona lemon, with mouth expanded

'Condor' 1 Y-Y
(C.G. van Tubergen, pre-1927)
Fl. 98 mm wide; perianth segments pale sulphur, irregular, overlapping half; corona deep sulphur, with mouth expanded and frilled. Mid-season

'Condor' 1 W-Y
(D.S. Bell) D.S. Bell, 1959
Fl. 127 mm wide. Mid-season. Resembles 'Outward Bound'

'Conestoga' 2 W-GYO
(W.A. Bender, 1967) W.A. Bender, 1985
'Orion' × 'Anacapri'; sdlg no. 67/1
Fl. rounded; perianth segments very broad; corona shallow, ribbed, opening orange, soon becoming apricot yellow, with green at base and orange at rim, crenate. Mid-season. Resembles a 'Stromboli' with more yellow in the corona.

'Confection' 2 W-P
(G.E. Mitsch) G.E. Mitsch, 1974
Probably 'Precedent' × 'Carita'; sdlg no. A34/35?
Fl. rounded, 100 mm wide; perianth segments overlapping; corona almost disc-shaped, large, apricot salmon, paling towards base. Mid-season

'Conference' 2 Y-? (a)
(Sir C.H. Cave, pre-1928)

'Confessor' 1 W-Y
(R.V. Favell, pre-1946)
'Ozan' × 'Tenedos'

'Confetti' 2 W-? (b)
(Mrs M.Moorby) Mrs M.Moorby, 1956

'Confidence' 9 W-?
(G.H. Engleheart, pre-1931)
? × 'Glory of Lisse'

'Confield' 2 W-? (b)
(Mrs R.O. Backhouse, pre-1921)
AM(Haarlem) 1930

'Confuoco' 2 Y-R
(G.A. Uit den Boogaard, pre-1946)

'Confusion' 2 W-P
(C.O. Fairbairn, pre-1964) Unregistered
Perianth segments white, of stiff and velvety substance; corona pink

N. confusus Pugsley 13 Section Pseudonarcissus

'Conglass' 4 W-W
(J.S.B. Lea) J.S.B. Lea, 1983
Sdlg 1-22-69 × 'Croila'; sdlg no. 1-56-73
Fl. 110 mm wide

'Congo' 2 Y-O
(J.L. Richardson) J.L. Richardson, 1958
'Royal Mail' × 'Bahram'
Perianth segments yellow; corona very shallow bowl-shaped, reddish orange

'Congress' 11a Y-O
(J. Gerritsen & Son, 1965) J. Gerritsen & Son, 1976
Fl. 95 mm wide; perianth segments brilliant greenish yellow 7C; corona segments opening with yellow at base, becoming self deep orange. Mid-season. Resembles a smaller-flowered 'Colorama'

'Coniston' 2 Y-? (a)
(Warnaar & Co., pre-1929)

'Conjurer' 1 Y-Y
(G.L. Wilson, pre-1927)
Fl. golden yellow; corona with rim rolled

'Conly' 3 W-GYO
(Ballydorn Bulb Farm, 1978) Ballydorn Bulb Farm, 1995
'Favor Royal' open pollinated
Fl. 95 mm wide; perianth segments broad, prominently mucronate, with margins slightly wavy, overlapping; corona saucer-shaped. Mid-season. Sunproof

'Connemara' 1 W-W
(G.L. Wilson, pre-1930)

'Connie' 2 W-Y
(J.S. Leitch) J.S. Leitch, 1967
Fl. 115 mm wide; perianth segments white; corona lemon yellow

'Connoisseur' 3 W-?
(J.C. Whibley) J.C. Whibley, 1962
Fl. 120 mm wide. Mid-season

'Connor' 2 W-GWW
(Carncairn Daffodils, 1975) Carncairn Daffodils, 1986
'Easter Moon' × 'Rose Caprice'; sdlg no. W9/35
Perianth segments greenish white; corona long cup-shaped, opening cream white, becoming white, with green at base. Very tall. Late

'Conor MacNessa' 2 Y-? (a)
(Sir J.A.R. Gore-Booth, pre-1916)

'Conqueror' 1 W-Y
(P.D. Williams, pre-1907)
Perianth segments acute, overlapping; corona long, pale lemon yellow

'Conquest' 4
(E. & J.C. Martin, pre-1916)
?See also 'Conquet'

'Conquet' 4
?Syn. of 'Conquest'

'Conrad' 8
(P.D. Williams, pre-1913)

'Conrad' 1 W-? (b)
(A.H. Ahrens) D.J. Cooper, 1956

'Conrad Adenhouwe' 2 W-O
(J.W.A. Lefeber) J.W.A. Lefeber, 1968
'Eddy Conzony' hybrid

'Conrad Weiser' 1 Y-Y
(W.A.Bender) W.A.Bender, 1996
Sdlg × 'Glenfarclas'
Fl. 98 mm wide, vivid yellow 14B; perianth segments ovate, plane, smooth; corona cylindrical at base, flared in upper third, with mouth frilled. Tall Mid-season to late

'Consol' 2 W-? (b or c)
(F.H. Chapman, pre-1936)

'Consolation' 3 W-? (b)
(W. Welchman, pre-1913)
'Trostan' × 'Diva' sdlg
Fl. white

N. × consolationis Fernández Casas 13 = *N. bulbocodium* Linnaeus var. *nivalis* (Graells) Baker × *N. triandrus* Linnaeus subsp. *pallidulus* (Graells) D.A.Webb

'Consort' 1 W-Y
(G.L. Wilson, pre-1944)
'Trostan' × ?'Diva'
Perianth segments white; corona pale clear lemon, with rim flanged

N. conspicuus Haworth = *N. bulbocodium* subsp. *bulbocodium* var. *conspicuus*.

N. conspicuus Salisbury = *N. × odorus*

conspicuus = *N. minor* var. *conspicuus*

'Conspicuus' 3 W-YYO
(W. Backhouse, pre-1869)
Perianth segments opening sulphur white, becoming pure white; corona expanded, yellow, with scarlet-orange at rim. Syn. Burbidgei 'Conspicuus'. FCC 1869. "Absorbed" 'Jo'

'Conspicuus' 3 Y-YYO
(W. Backhouse, pre-1869)
Fl. star-shaped; perianth segments ovate, blunt, opening deep yellow, becoming sulphur yellow, with slight white mucro, spreading, overlapping a quarter; corona long cup-shaped, strongly ribbed, yellow, stained orange, with bright scarlet-orange at rim, mouth straight and more or less tightly frilled. 2n=21. Syn. 'Barrii Conspicuus', Barrii 'Conspicuus'. FCC 1886

'Conspicuus Minor' 3
A synonym both of 3Y-YYR 'Orphée' and of 3W-YYO 'May'

'Constance' 3 W-YYO
(W. Backhouse, pre-1869)
Perianth segments broadly obovate, prominently mucronate, creamy white, spreading, with margins a little wavy, separated; corona bowl-shaped, ribbed, yellow, with a broad band of orange at rim, tightly frilled. Syn. Burbidgei 'Joe'

'Constance' 2 Y-O
(Mrs R.O. Backhouse, pre-1914)
Perianth segments soft golden yellow; corona deep orange, frilled. AM (Haarlem). Date of award unknown

'Constance Evelyn' 2 W-? (b)
(H.R. Meyer, pre-1927)

'Constance Lyon' 2 W-Y
(Mrs F. Chatard) Mrs F. Chatard, 1972
'Blarney's Daughter' hybrid
Fl. 74 mm wide

'Constance Mary'
(New Zealand origin, pre-1952)

'Constance Morel' 3 W-? (b)
(Mrs R.S. Cobley, pre-1937)

'Constance Pierpoint' 3 W-?
(W.B. Hartland, pre-1907)

'Constance Spry' 2 W-W
(G.H. Johnstone, pre-1946)

'Constancy' 2 Y-Y
(G.E. Mitsch) G.E. Mitsch, 1979
'Scio' × 'Camelot'; sdlg no. JJ26/7
Fl. 80 mm wide; perianth segments soft yellow; corona slightly deeper in tone. Mid-season. Resembles 'Golden Aura' but with a differently shaped corona

without orange tones

'Constancy' 3 W-?
(G. Lewis, pre-1961) Unregistered
Perianth segments pure white, smooth, overlapping; corona very shallow bowl-shaped, widely expanded, with bright orange-red at rim. Tall

'Constant' 2 W-? (b)
(W. Welchman, pre-1929)

'Constant' 1 Y-Y
(pre-1955)
Fl. yellow; corona of a deeper, golden tone, with mouth flared and frilled

'Constant Fire' 2 W-O
(E.F. Hughes) E.F. Hughes, 1962
Fl. 127 mm wide; perianth segments opening pale yellow, becoming creamy white; corona expanded, bright scarlet-orange, frilled. Mid-season

'Constantia' 8 Y-Y
(pre-1835)
Early

'Constantine' 1 Y-Y
(W.B. Cranfield, pre-1930)
$2n=28$

'Constantinople' 4 W-Y
'Chinese Sacred Lily' sport
Fls numerous per stem; perianth and other petaloid segments white; the outer whorl broadly ovate, spreading, overlapping; the inner whorl(s) strongly inflexed; corona segments very short, clustered among the inner whorl(s) of petaloid segments, yellow. Scented

'Constantinopolitanus' 4 W-O
Syn. of 'Romanus'

N. constantinopolitanus hort. = *N. tazetta* subsp. *lacticolor*

'Constellation' 2 W-YYO
(C. Smith, pre-1900)
Perianth segments large; corona bright yellow, frilled. Tall

'Consul' 2 W-Y
(G.H. Engleheart, pre-1904)
Perianth segments overlapping; corona widely expanded, clear yellow

'Consul' 3 Y-YYO
(S.C. Gaspar) R.J. Abernethy, 1960
Fl. 102 mm wide, rich soft yellow; corona with bright reddish orange at rim. Mid-season. Resembles an improved 'Orissa'

'Consul Crawford' 2 W-Y
(E. Leeds, pre-1877)
Fl. large; perianth segments white, tinged yellow; corona yellow. Syn. Incomparabilis Albus 'Consul Crawford', Incomparabilis Albus 'Crawfordii'. Was "absorbed" into 'Queen Bess'

'Content' 1 W-WWY
(P.D. Williams, pre-1927)
'Lord Antrim' × ? 'Beersheba'
Fl. 120 mm wide, opening pale clear lemon; perianth segments becoming white, spreading, slightly twisted, smooth, deeply overlapping; corona slender, becoming cream, with pale canary yellow at rim, mouth slightly expanded. $2n=28$. Resembles a larger and taller 'Beersheba' in form and poise. AM(e) 1940, AM(Haarlem) 1957

'Contessa' 1 W-? (b)
(A.H. Ahrens) J.S. Leitch, 1956

'Continental' 2 Y-W
(W.G. Pannill) W.G. Pannill, 1982
'Rushlight' × 'Daydream'; sdlg no. 64/110
Fl. 89 mm wide. Mid-season

'Contour' 1 W-W
(G.L. Wilson, pre-1946)
'Askelon' × 'Diva'
Perianth segments white, smooth; corona cream white, with rim deeply and evenly rolled. AM(c) 1950

'Contour' 1 W-Y
(D.S. Bell, pre-1981) Unregistered
'Golden Glisten' open pollinated
Perianth segments white; corona yellow, mouth frilled, with rim dentate

'Contraband' 2 Y-YYR
(E.W. Cotter) E.W. Cotter, 1968
'Firemaster' × 'Fury'

'Contrapunt' 2 Y-O
(Konynenburg & Mark, 1950) Konynenburg & Mark, 1962
'Aranjuez' × 'Red Bird'
Fl. 100 mm wide; perianth segments deep yellow; corona clear orange. Early. $2n=27$

'Contrast' 2 W-? (b)
(R.H. Bath, pre-1913)

'Contravene' 2 Y-O
(Jackson's Daffodils) Jackson's Daffodils, 1993
'Pzaz' × 'Jandra'; sdlg no. 253/87
Fl. 100 mm wide; perianth segments broadly ovate, light greenish yellow 6C; the inner segments more narrowly ovate; corona cup-shaped, vivid orange 28B. Mid-season to late

'Control' 2 Y-? (a)
(A.M. Williams, pre-1948)

'Convair' 1 Y-Y
(H.A. Brown, 1938)
Fl. soft yellow. 2n=27

'Conval' 2 W-WPP
(J.S.B. Lea) J.S.B. Lea, 1973
'Irish Rose' × 'Rose Caprice'; sdlg no. 1-48-58
Fl. 102 mm wide; corona deep clear rosy pink, paling to greenish white at base. Late

'Convention' 1 W-Y
(W.M. Spry, pre-1975) Unregistered
'Gwen Fleming' × 'Zero'
Corona lemon yellow, frilled

'Convoy' 2 W-? (b)
(Oregon Bulb Farms, pre-1942)

'Conway Gold' 1 Y-Y
(D.S. Bell) D.S. Bell, 1955

'Conway Pink' 2 W-P
(D.S. Bell) D.S. Bell, 1959
Fl. 114 mm wide. Mid-season

'Coo-ee' 1 W-? (b)
(?West & Fell, pre-1926)
Fl. pale citron; corona with rim shallowly rolled

'Cooee' 2 Y-R
(C.E. Radcliff, 1939)
'Fortune' × 'Lybster'

'Cooee' 1 Y-Y
(J.N. Hancock & Co., 1970) Unregistered
Sdlg no. 6/70H
Corona frilled, with rim rolled. Early

'Cooinda' 1 Y-Y
(J.N. Hancock & Co., 1980) Unregistered
'Cardinia' × Fairbairn 2 Y-Y; sdlg no. 11/80H
Fl. rich golden yellow; corona narrow, lightly frilled. Early

'Coolah' 2 W-P
(C.E. Radcliff, c.1966) Unregistered
'Roselands' × 'Rosegem'

'Coolattin' 2 W-Y
(Carncairn Daffodils) Carncairn Daffodils, 1969
'Green Island' hybrid
Perianth segments white; corona yellow, with a slightly darker tone at rim and greenish grey tones in tube

'Cool Autumn' 2 W-Y
(W.A. Noton) W.A. Noton, 1976
'Homage' × 'Tudor Minstrel'

Perianth segments white; corona somewhat disc-shaped, greenish yellow. Mid-season

'Cool Charm' 3 W-Y
(R.G.Cull) Hokorawa Daffodils, 1994
'Ceres' × 'Cool Crystal'; sdlg no. HC/B25
Corona pale yellow 8D. Mid-season

'Cool Contrast' 1 W-Y
(T. Bloomer) T. Bloomer, 1970
'Ballygarvey' × 'Preamble'; sdlg no. 1/8/54

'Cool Crystal' 3 W-GWW
(G.E. Mitsch) G.E. Mitsch, 1966
'Chinese White' hybrid; sdlg no. T10
Fl. 107 mm wide; perianth segments white, touched bright green at base, slightly reflexed, regular, overlapping; corona ribbed, white, with light green at extreme base, mouth expanded and frilled, with rim crenate. Mid-season. Resembles 'Wings of Song' but with a more rounded flower and a smaller corona. AM(e) 1985

'Coole' 2 W-W
(J.L. Richardson, pre-1949)

'Cool Evening' 11a W-P
(G.E. Mitsch, 1979) R. & E. Havens, 1991
Sdlg C35/16 ('Precedent' × 'Accent') × 'Phantom'; sdlg no. 206/11
Perianth segments broadly ovate, blunt, slightly mucronate, a little reflexed, overlapping one-third to a half; the inner segments with margins incurling or wavy; corona split to base, the six segments one-third to half as long as the perianth segments and opposite and closely overlying them, bi-lobed, ribbed, delicate pink. Mid-season. Resembles a slightly smaller 'Phantom' of true pink

'Cool Flame' 2 W-P
(G.E. Mitsch) G.E. Mitsch, 1969
'Precedent' × 'Accent'; sdlg no. B37/6
Perianth segments overlapping; corona cup-shaped, ribbed, clear coral pink

'Coolgardie' 1 Y-Y
(G.H. Engleheart, pre-1917)
Fl. rich luminous gold

'Coolgreany' 3 W-GYY
(Carncairn Daffodils) Carncairn Daffodils, 1967
'Sylvia O'Neill' × 'Chinese White'
Fl. 102 mm wide. Mid-season. Resembles a stronger and larger-flowered 'Syliva O'Neill' with the perianth segments more definitely rounded and a more pronounced green at corona base

'Cool Harmony' 1 W-Y
(Mrs H.K. Richardson) Mrs H.K. Richardson, 1972
'Glencairn' open pollinated

Perianth segments pure white; corona primrose yellow, with a paler tone at rim, dentate and widely flanged

'Coolibah' 2 W-OOY
(J.N. Hancock & Co., 1946) J.N. Hancock & Co., 1964
('Glenfern' × 'Lyndale Beacon') × 'Ivo Fell'
Perianth segments broadly ovate, of good substance; corona bowl-shaped, large, rich orange, with yellow at rim and the rim deeply rolled

'Coolin' 1 W-W
(A.M. Wilson, pre-1937)
'Nevis' × 'Beersheba'

'Cooling Spring' 2 W-W
(Mrs P.M. Davis, pre-1948)

'Cool Peppermint' 11a W-P
(G.E. Mitsch, 1979) R. & E. Havens, 1992
'Recital' × 'Phantom'; sdlg no. 205/1A
Fl. 105 mm wide; perianth segments very broadly ovate, clean white; corona split, the six segments opposite and closely overlying the perianth segments, soft pink. Mid-season. Sunproof

'Cool Pink' 2 W-P
(G.E. Mitsch, 1974) R. & E. Havens, 1993
'Quick Step' × 'Cool Flame'; sdlg no. 2J79/1
Fl. 70 mm wide; perianth segments broadly ovate, blunt or truncate, slightly mucronate, pinkish white, with undertones of pink, spreading, plane, smooth, overlapping half; the inner segments more nearly spreading, with margins wavy; corona cup-shaped, smooth, soft apricot pink, with mouth slightly flared and loosely frilled, rim entire. Late. Sunproof. With occasional secondary stems

'Coolport' 2 W-W
(J.N. Hancock & Co.) J.N. Hancock & Co., 1955
Perianth segments white; corona deep cream, frilled

'Cool Shades' 2 Y-Y
(A.J.R. Pearson) A.J.R. Pearson, 1989
'Camelot' × 'Daydream'; sdlg no. 80/16/F1
Fl. 105 mm wide, greenish yellow, faintly touched with white at base; perianth segments very broad, blunt, with slight white mucro, reflexed, convex, smooth, overlapping half; the inner segments more nearly spreading and plane, creased; corona funnel-shaped, smoothly and lightly ribbed, with mouth a little flared and frilled, rim notched and irregularly crenate. Mid-season

'Cool Valley' 2 Y-WWY
(Colin Crotty) Unregistered
Sdlg no. 43-75

'Cool Waters' 2 W-GRR
(T. Bloomer) T. Bloomer, 1964
'Kilworth' × ('Red Hackle' × 'Glenwherry'); sdlg no. 3/57/58

'Cool White' 3 W-W
(G.E. Mitsch, 1978) R. & E. Havens, 1990
'Aircastle' × 'Verona'; sdlg no. NN34/6
Fl. 95 mm wide; corona disc-shaped. Late

'Cooma' 2 W-? (b)
(H.A. Brown) H.A. Brown, 1956
Perianth segments broadly ovate, slightly mucronate, with margins a little incurling and with midrib showing, overlapping half; the inner segments more narrowly ovate, truncate; corona mouth widely expanded, with rim closely and minutely notched

'Coombe' 1 Y-Y
(J. Hall, pre-1930)
Resembles a smaller and slightly later-flowered 'Hallmark'

'Coombe Creek' 6 W-O
(R.A.Scamp) R.A.Scamp, 1997
'Kea' × 'Foundling'; sdlg no. 431
Fl. 85 mm wide; perianth segments broad, ivory white, very strongly reflexed, deeply overlapping; corona funnel-shaped, orange, with undertones of pink, neatly frilled. Dwarf. Mid-season to late. Sunproof

'Coomb Eden' 3 W-? (b)
(Mrs R.O. Backhouse, pre-1921)

'Coonamble' 1 W-Y
(W.M. Spry, pre-1975) Unregistered
'Trousseau' × 'Snow Maid'
Early

'Coonardoo' 2 W-W
(C.E. Radcliff, 1929)
'Pink'un' hybrid

'Coonoor' 2 W-? (b)
(Mrs R.O. Backhouse, pre-1921)

'Coope' 2 Y-R
(Mrs C.O. Fairbairn, c.1950)

'Coosa' 1 W-W
(E.C. Powell, pre-1946)

'Coos Bay' 2 W-? (b)
(Oregon Bulb Farms, pre-1951)

'Copan' 2 Y-R
(W. Jackson Jr, 1961) Unregistered
'Verity' × sdlg 106/55; sdlg no. 106/61

'Copeland's Seedling'
(W.F.M.Copeland, pre-1927)

'Copenhagen'
(pre-1913)

'Copernicus' 4 Y-O
(W.F.M.Copeland, pre-1910)
Perianth and other petaloid segments in three whorls; corona segments interspersed, light orange. Mid-season

'Cophetua' 1 Y-Y
(H.G. Longford, pre-1927)

'Cophetua' 1 Y-Y
(Carncairn Daffodils) Carncairn Daffodils, 1973
'Kingscourt' × 'Goldcourt'
Fl. 115 mm wide. Resembles a larger and later-flowered 'Kingscourt' with the corona mouth narrower and more regularly dentate

'Coppelia' 2 W-P
(Mrs H.K. Richardson) Mrs H.K. Richardson, 1972
'Templemore' × 'Green Island'
Perianth segments white, slightly reflexed, of waxy texture; corona long cup-shaped, pale pink, frilled, with rim dentate

'Copperas' 2 Y-? (a)
(J.E. Exley, pre-1938)

'Copper Bowl' 2 Y-O
(The Brodie of Brodie, c.1925)
'Beacon' × 'Fortune'
Perianth segments very broadly ovate, blunt, clear yellow, slightly incurving, overlapping half; the inner segments ovate, blunt to acute, with margins sometimes slightly incurving; corona shallow bowl-shaped, lightly ribbed towards mouth, copper orange, mouth wavy, rim entire or occasionally notched. AM(e) 1928, AM(Haarlem) 1934

'Copperfield' 2 Y-Y
(Elise Havens) G.E. Mitsch, 1977
'Paricutin' × 'Daydream'; sdlg no. GEJ6/1
Fl. 100 mm wide; perianth segments buff yellow; corona of a deeper bronze or copper-toned yellow

'Copper King' 3 W-? (b)
(Mrs R.O. Backhouse, pre-1910)

'Copper Lustre' 9 W-GOO
(Mrs M.S. Yerger) Mrs M.S. Yerger, 1989
'Quetzal' × 'Ace of Diamonds'; sdlg no. 77 G 2
Fl. 50 mm wide; perianth segments rounded; the inner segments acute; corona very shallow bowl-shaped, strong reddish orange 31B, with strong yellow-green 144A at base. Late

'Copper Nob' 2 O-R
(Ballydorn Bulb Farm, 1980) Ballydorn Bulb Farm, 1991
'Rio Rouge' × 2 O-O
Fl. 100 mm wide; perianth segments flushed copper orange; corona bowl-shaped, red. Mid-season. Sunproof

'Copper Penny' 9 W-GOR
(Mrs M.S. Yerger) Mrs M.S. Yerger, 1991
'Raeburn' open pollinated; sdlg no. 76 G 3
Dwarf. Late

'Copperplate' 2 W-P
(G.H. Johnstone, 1948) G.H. Johnstone, 1959
'Alison Johnstone' × 'Wild Rose'
Fl. 114 mm wide; corona opening copper pink, becoming less orange in tone. Mid-season

'Copper Rings' 3 O-R
(Mrs J. Abel Smith) Mrs J. Abel Smith, 1992
'Rio Rouge' × 'Ambergate'; sdlg no R44/41
Fl. 36 mm wide; perianth segments orange; corona disc-shaped, orange-red. Late

'Coppersmith' 2 Y-O
(G.L. Wilson) G.L. Wilson, 1956
Sdlg × ('Carbineer' × 'Indian Summer')
Perianth segments yellow; corona reddish tangerine

'Coppertint' 4 Y-O
(K.J. Heazlewood) K.J. Heazlewood, 1971
'Tekapo' hybrid
Fl. 90 mm wide, copper-coloured. Late

'Coppertone' 3 O-R
(K.J. Heazlewood) K.J. Heazlewood, 1968
'Tekapo' × 'Chungking'
Perianth segments very broad, rounded at apex and sometimes split, slightly mucronate, spreading, slightly concave, overlapping half or more; the inner segments a little narrower, slightly inflexed; corona very shallow bowl-shaped, heavily ribbed, frilled. Tall. Mid-season. Resembles 'Rouge' but with a shallower corona

'Coppertop' 2 W-P
(A.O. Roblin) A.O. Roblin, 1956
'Mary Blewitt' × ('Pink o' Dawn' hybrid × 'Mrs R.O. Backhouse')
See also 'Copper Top'

'Copper Top' 2 W-P
Syn. of 'Coppertop'

'Coppertop' 2 Y-R
(W.M. Spry, pre-1975) Unregistered
Corona dark copper red

'Coppice' 1 W-W
(F.H. Chapman, pre-1927)

'Coppins' 4 W-Y
(Mrs H.K. Richardson) du Plessis Bros, 1977
Sdlg 604 × 'Debutante'; sdlg no. R612
Fl. 82 mm wide; perianth and other petaloid segments white; corona segments yellow

'Copsana' 2 W-W
(D. Bramley) D. Bramley, 1980
'Easter Moon' hybrid; sdlg no. 70/28
Fl. 97 mm wide

'Coq d'Or' 1 Y-Y
(W.A. Noton) W.A. Noton, 1976
'Golden Rapture' × 'Olympic Gold'; sdlg no. 579
Fl. 114 mm wide. Mid-season

'Coquette' 5
(N.Y. Lower, pre-1913)

'Coquette' 1 W-? (b)
(R. Dick, pre-1930)

'Coquette' 2 Y-Y
(K. McCombe, c.1983) Unregistered
Fl. bright yellow; perianth segments broadly ovate, blunt, slightly mucronate, slightly inflexed, a little concave, overlapping half; the inner segments with margins wavy; corona cylindrical, smooth, with mouth expanded, rim flanged, deeply notched and crenate. Mid-season

'Coquille' 2 W-P
(J.L. Richardson) W. Blom & Son, 1966
'Interim' × 'Rose Caprice'
Fl. 100 mm wide; perianth segments ivory white; corona orange-pink (25D). Mid-season

'Cora' 5
(Barr & Sons, pre-1913)

'Cora' 1 W-Y
(D.V. West, pre-1932)
Corona yellow. Early to mid-season

'Cora' 2 W-YYO
(D.J. Cooper) D.J. Cooper, 1959
Fl. 79 mm wide; corona lemon yellow, with orange at rim. Early

'Cora Ann' 7 W-Y
(W.F. Mitchell, pre-1939)
Perianth segments white; corona pale yellow. 2n=21

'Coral'
(Mrs Lawrenson, pre-1900)

'Coral' 2 W-W
(W.F.M. Copeland, pre-1916)
Perianth segments white; corona creamy white, tightly ribbed. AM(e) 1916

'Coral-beach' 2 W-? (b)
(Mrs P.M. Davis, pre-1948)

'Coral Beach' 4 W-P
(Mrs H.K. Richardson, pre-1977) Unregistered
'Marietta' × 'Irani'
Perianth and other petaloid segments broad, white, deeply overlapping; corona segments coral pink. Very late

'Coral Blush' 2 W-P
(J.N. Hancock & Co., 1982) Unregistered
Fl. rounded; corona cylindrical, pink, with rim dentate. Mid-season

'Coral Charm' 1 W-GWP
(Mrs G. Link, 1980) Mrs G. Link, 1992
'April Rose' × *N. triandrus*; sdlg no. 673
Fl. smooth; corona cylindrical, white, with green at base and apricot pink at rim, the rim flanged. Very late

'Coral Cloud' 4 W-P
(A.N. Kanouse) A.N. Kanouse, 1978
'Pink Chiffon' × 'Mabel Taylor'
Fl. 110 mm wide; perianth and other petaloid segments cream white; corona segments opening coral pink, becoming deeper in tone. Mid-season. Resembles a shorter and slightly later-flowered 'Coral Strand' with the corona segments of a deeper colour

'Coral Dawn' 2 W-Y
(C.M. Grullemans) J.J. Grullemans & Sons, 1957
Corona large, opening orange, gradually becoming lemon yellow, frilled

'Coral Disc' 2 W-WPW
(Colin Crotty, 1980) Colin Crotty, 1995
'Cherryrim' × 'Caro Nome' 'Cherryrim' × 'Caro Nome'; sdlg no. 35-75; sdlg no. 35-75
Fl. 110 mm wide; perianth segments very broadly ovate, blunt, pure white, slightly concave; corona broad disc-shaped, coral pink, paling to creamy white at base, with a narrow band of white at rim, mouth deeply lobed. Mid-season

'Coraleena' 2 W-?
(G.L. Wilson) Mrs D.G. Moore, 1966

'Coral Eye' 3 W-? (b)
(Cartwright & Goodwin, pre-1910)

'Coral Fair' 2 W-P
(Mrs J. Abel Smith) Mrs J. Abel Smith, 1984
Sdlg × 'Fair Prospect'; sdlg no. 00/51

Perianth segments white; corona coral pink. Mid-season

'Coral Gable' 2 W-P
(O.L. Brown) O.L. Brown, 1977
'Carita' × 'Accent'; sdlg no. 67-27-1
Fl. 91 mm wide; corona strong yellowish pink 32C, with vivid orange 28B outside, with a darker pink (40D) at base, mouth expanded and lightly frilled. Early. Resembles an earlier and more orange-toned 'Accent'

'Coral Gem' 9 W-O
(G.H. Engleheart, pre-1931)
Perianth segments white; corona reddish orange. AM(c) 1931

'Coral Glow' 1 W-W
(J.W. Barr, pre-1930)

'Coralie' 2 Y-? (a)
(R.H. Bath, pre-1927)

'Coralie' 2 W-P
(Alister Clark) Oregon Bulb Farms, 1955

'Coral Island' 2 W-GPP
(J.L. Richardson, pre-1938)
'Mitylene' × 'Fortune'
Perianth segments white; corona rosy coral, with tones of sea-green at base

'Coralita' 2 W-YPP
(J.L. Richardson) Mrs H.K. Richardson, 1973
'Infatuation' × 'Debutante'
Perianth segments white; corona deep coral pink, lightening to pale lemon at base, with rim dentate

'Coral Jubilee' 4 W-P
(Mrs H.K. Richardson) Mrs H.K. Richardson, 1977
'Marietta' × 'Irani'
Fl. 95 mm wide; corona segments coral pink. Mid-season

'Coral Light' 2 W-GWP
(A.N. Kanouse) G.E. Mitsch, 1972
'Green Island' × 'Interim'
Fl. rounded, 100 mm wide; perianth segments overlapping; corona opening with a wide band of pink at rim, becoming almost entirely pink, with cool green at base. Mid-season

'Corallina' 3 W-PPY
(G.H. Engleheart, pre-1907)
Perianth segments white, incurving; corona straight, ribbed, pale brick-rose, shading to orange apricot at rim

'Corallina' 3 W-P
(Heathcote Bulb Nursery, pre-1956) Unregistered

'Coralline' 6 W-P
(Brian S. Duncan) Rathowen Daffodils, 1981
Sdlg × ? 'Foundling'; sdlg no. 447
Perianth segments pure white, reflexed; corona pale lilac pink. Mid-season

'Corallite' 2 W-P
(Heathcote Bulb Nursery, pre-1960) Unregistered

'Coral Luster' 2 W-P
(G.E. Mitsch, 1956) G.E. Mitsch, 1967
('Interim' × 'Mabel Taylor') × 'Caro Nome'; sdlg no. R110/5
Fl. 117 mm wide; perianth segments white; corona small, coral salmon pink. Mid-season

'Coral Queen' 3 W-YYP
(G.H. Engleheart, pre-1914)
Fl. 70 mm wide, facing slightly downwards; perianth segments broadly ovate, blunt, fairly prominently mucronate, creamy white, spreading, plane or loosely twisted, overlapping one-third to a half; corona shallow funnel-shaped, soft lemon yellow with pale buffy coral pink at rim, mouth widely expanded, split in places and overlapping, wavy. Mid-season to late

'Coral Reef' 1 W-WWP
(S.J. Bisdee, 1945)
('White Conqueror' × 'Saint Aloysius') × 'Rosario'

'Coral Ribbon' 2 W-WWP
(G.E. Mitsch) G.E. Mitsch, 1964
(Sdlg M45/2 × ['Interim' × 'Mabel Taylor']) × 'Caro Nome'; sdlg no. R110/1
Fl. 95 mm wide; perianth segments rounded; corona creamy white, with coral rose pink at rim. Mid-season. $2n=28$

'Coral Ring' 3 W-YYR
(The Brodie of Brodie, c.1910)
'Dorothy Yorke' × 'White Elephant'
Perianth segments, of good substance, irregular; corona large disc-shaped, yellow, with a well-defined band of bright scarlet at rim

'Coral Ring' 2 W-WWY
(D.S. Bell) D.S. Bell, 1960
Sdlg × 'Green Island'
Fl. 108 mm wide; corona with golden yellow at rim. Mid-season. Resembles 'Green Island'

'Coral Sea' 2 W-? (b)
(J.L. Richardson, pre-1953)

'Coral Springs' 2 W-WWP
(G.E. Mitsch, 1982) R. & E. Havens, 1996
'Coral Light' × 'Delectable'; sdlg no. 2R1/1
Fl. 75 mm wide; perianth segments broadly ovate, pure white, spreading, plane, of heavy substance; corona cup-shaped, pure white, with reddish coral

pink at rim, mouth a little frilled. Late. Sunproof

'Coral Star' 2 W-P
(G.E. Mitsch) G.E. Mitsch, 1959
'Mabel Taylor' × 'Interim'
Perianth segments white; corona reddish pink

'Coral Strand' 4 W-P
(A.N. Kanouse, 1956) A.N. Kanouse, 1976
'Pink Chiffon' × 'Mabel Taylor'
Fl. 102 mm wide; perianth and other petaloid segments cream white; corona segments pale coral pink, frilled. Mid-season. Resembles an improved 'Pink Chiffon'

'Corangamite' 1 Y-Y
(H.A. Brown, 1941)
Fl. golden yellow. Mid-season. See also 'Corongamite'

'Corato' 2 W-GYY
(J.L. Richardson) Mrs B.T. Simpson, 1963
Fl. 95 mm wide; perianth segments white; corona pale buttercup yellow, with green at base and vivid yellow15A at base. Late

'Corban' 2 W-P
(G.L. Wilson, pre-1953)
Perianth segments white; corona blush pink

'Corbel' 10 Y-Y
(J.W. Jones, pre-1926)
Probably a *N. bulbocodium* var. *conspicuus* sdlg
Fl. large, of good substance. With several secondary stems

'Corbiere' 1 Y-YOO
(J.S.B. Lea) Clive Postles Daffodils, 1988
'Gold Convention' × 'Glen Farclas'; sdlg no. L1-13-77
Fl. rounded, 100 mm wide; corona funnel-shaped, opening deep yellow, becoming suffused with glowing orange, mouth slightly flared, with rim denate. Tall. Mid-season

'Corbridge' 2 W-Y
(G. Harrison) G. Harrison, 1968
'Green Island' hybrid
Fl. 115 mm wide; perianth segments white; corona pale yellow, with a slightly darker tone at base and a richer tone at rim. Mid-season. Resembles 'Green Island' but with a longer corona of slightly different colouring

'Corbula' 2 W-? (b)
(Mrs G. Link, pre-1953)
'Sweetheart' × 'Stresa'

'Corby' 2 W-W
(G.L. Wilson, pre-1948)
Perianth segments white; corona opening cream, soon becoming white. Late. Resembles 'Dunlewey'

N. corcyrensis (Herbert) Nyman 13 Section Tazettae

'Cordelia' 1 W-Y
(Barr & Sons, pre-1923)
Perianth segments white, somewhat twisted; corona long, soft primrose yellow. Resembles 'Calpurnia'

'Cordell Hull' 2 W-? (b)
(F. Rijnveld & Sons, pre-1939)
AM(Haarlem) 1940

'Cordial' 2 W-P
(Murray W. Evans) Murray W. Evans, 1970
'Pink Lace' × 'Interim'
Perianth segments white; corona pink, frilled

'Cordigan' 2
?Syn. of 'Cardigan'

'Cordillera' 5
(Oregon Bulb Farms, pre-1951)

'Cordite' 2 W-W
(Jackson's Daffodils) Jackson's Daffodils, 1989
'Sea Dream' × sdlg 212/75; sdlg no. 273/82
Fl. 105 mm wide; perianth segments very broad, blunt, only very slightly mucronate, yellowish white 155B, spreading, plane, overlapping half or more; the inner segments more nearly ovate, with margins a little wavy; corona bowl shaped, shallow, of a creamier tone (155D) than the perianth, tightly frilled, sometimes split and overlappingto give the appearance of a double frill. Late

'Cordon Rouge' 3 W-? (b)
(F.H. Chapman, pre-1923)

'Cordova' 3 Y-R
(The Brodie of Brodie, c.1930)
'Seraglio' × ('Beacon' × 'Fortune'); sdlg no. 139/M/25
Perianth segments overlapping; corona deeply stained with dark rich red. Tall

N. cordubensis Fernández Casas 13 Section Jonquilla

'Coreen' 3 W-GYY
(G.H. Engleheart, pre-1913)
Perianth segments very broad and somewhat oblong, rounded at apex, only very slightly mucronate, creamy white, spreading, overlapping; the inner segments a little inflexed, with margins wavy and incurling; corona wide bowl-shaped, ribbed, pale yellow, with green at base and tints of deep orange on the ribs and at rim. Dwarf

'Coreen' 2 W-PPO
(Carncairn Daffodils) Carncairn Daffodils, 1973

'Rosario' × 'Salmon Trout'; sdlg no. 1/73/60
Fl. 100 mm wide; perianth segments yellowish white 155B; corona deep pink, tinged mauve, with light orange 28D at rim, and with the rim rolled

'Corella' 2 W-Y
(S.J. Bisdee, 1942)
'May Molony' × 'Nautilus'

'Corella' 3 W-WWO
(T. Morrison) T. Morrison, 1960
Corona shallow, white, with salmon orange at rim

'Corfu' 3 W-? (b)
(J.L. Richardson, pre-1945)
'Coronach' × 'Forfar'

'Corgi' 2 Y-? (a)
(Sir J.S. Arkwright, pre-1931)
Perianth segments pale dull orange-yellow

N. corifolius Steudel = *N. bicolor* var. *lorifolius*

'Coringa' 1 W-W
(C.E. Radcliff, 1942) C.E. Radcliff, 1956
'Bonnington' × 'Tain'

'Corinna' 9 W-YYR
(C. Dawson, pre-1925)
Perianth segments white; corona small, orange-yellow, with a narrow band of madder crimson at rim, neatly frilled

'Corinna' 2 W-?
Syn. of 'Phocea'

'Corinne' 2 W-P
(J.N. Hancock & Co., 1953)

'Corinth' 1 W-W
(The Brodie of Brodie, c.1925)
'Nevis' × 'Beersheba'
Perianth segments spreading; corona ivory

'Corinthian' 1 Y-Y
(P.D. Williams, pre-1931)
Fl. yellow; perianth segments somewhat oblong, with apex blunt or squarish, with slight white mucro, spreading, with margins wavy, overlapping one-third; the inner segments narrower, ovate, with margins more strongly wavy and sometimes twisted; corona funnel-shaped, lightly ribbed, with mouth widely expanded, rim deeply and regularly notched and dentate. *(Kirton)AM(g)(m) 1939

'Coriolanus' 2 Y-? (a)
(Barr & Sons, pre-1913)

'Corlo' 1 Y-Y
(W. Jackson Sr, 1939)

'Chruseos' × 'Crocus'
Fl. deep yellow

'Cormac' 1 Y-Y
(S.J. Bisdee) S.J. Bisdee, 1956
'Fahan' × sdlg 30/46

'Cormeen' 1 W-W
(G.L. Wilson) G.L. Wilson, 1960
('Nilkanta' × 'Murmansk') × 'Rashee'

'Cormoran' 1 W-Y
(C. Wolley-Dod, pre-1907)
Perianth segments whitish; corona large, yellow. ?See also 'Cormorant'

'Cormorant' 4 W-R
(J.L. Richardson) G. Zandbergen-Terwegen, 1959
'Falaise' hybrid

'Cormorant' 1 W-?
?Syn. of 'Cormoran'

'Corncrake' 3 W-R
(G.L. Wilson, pre-1947)
Fl. 92 mm wide; perianth segments broad, smooth, overlapping; corona very shallow bowl-shaped, ribbed, orange-red (30C), frilled. AM(e) 1955

'Corndale' 2 Y-Y
(West & Fell, pre-1935)
Perianth segments deep yellow, corona rich yellow, with mouth widely expanded

'Cornelia' 1 Y-Y
(M. van Waveren & Sons, pre-1905)
Perianth segments yellow, fairly smooth; corona expanded, soft yellow. AM 1905

'Cornell' 3 Y-W
(G.E.Mitsch, 1984) R. & E.Havens, 1997
'Limpkin' × 'Wedding Band'; sdlg no. TT47/22A
Fl. rounded, 105 mm wide; perianth segments very broadly ovate, light lemon yellow; corona very shallow bowl-shaped, becoming pure white, frilled. Late

'Cornerstone' 2 Y-O
(M.J. Jefferson-Brown) M.J. Jefferson-Brown, 1984
'Cathay' × 'Royal Charm'
Perianth segments broadly ovate, mucronate, golden yellow, spreading, overlapping half; the inner segments more narrowly ovate; corona cylindrical or somewhat funnel-shaped, smooth, deep tangerine orange, mouth straight, split in places and overlapping, with rim notched. Late to very late

'Cornet' 6 Y-Y
(A. Gray, pre-1953)
N. cyclamineus sdlg
2n=21. Later in flower than sibling 'Jana'

'Cornish Cheer' 2 W-? (b)
(The Brodie of Brodie, pre-1928)

'Cornish Chuckles' 12 Y-Y
(Harry I.Tuggle Jr, 1973) Cornwall Area Bulb Growers Association, 1996
'Matador' × *N. cyclamineus*; sdlg no. USA 66/0/2
Dwarf. Early

'Cornish Cream' 10 Y-Y
(James S. Wells) James S. Wells, 1990
N. obesus × *N. romieuxii*; sdlg no. 82-23B
Fl. 35 mm wide, pale creamy yellow; perianth segments lanceolate, spreading or a little inflexed, somewhat twisted, separated; corona deep bowl-shaped, broad, very lightly ribbed, with mouth straight and even, rim almost entire. Dwarf. Very early

'Cornish Cross' 3 W-WWP
(The Brodie of Brodie, pre-1928)
'The Sahib' × 'Mystic'
Fl. white; corona touched pink at rim

'Cornish Fire' 2 Y-O
(P.D. Williams, pre-1930)
Perianth segments yellow; corona widely expanded, scarlet-orange

'Cornish Gold' 1 Y-Y
(The Brodie of Brodie, pre-1928)
Fl. 88 mm wide; perianth segments broadly ovate, not prominently mucronate, brilliant greenish yellow 5B, spreading, with margins somewhat wavy, finely creased, overlapping one-third; the inner segments inflexed, twisted and more widely creased; corona cylindrical, smooth, vivid yellow 9A, mouth ribbed and a little expanded, split in places and overlapping, frilled, with rim deeply notched

'Cornish Prince' 2 Y-? (a)
(R.F. Calvert, pre-1934)

'Cornish Saint' 2 Y-? (a)
(G.L. Wilson, pre-1928)

'Cornish Star'
(?M.P. Williams, pre-1950)

'Cornish White' 2 W-W
(The Brodie of Brodie, pre-1929)

'Cornopean' 1 W-Y
(P.D. Williams, pre-1910)
Corona lemon

'Cornubia' 3 W-?
(pre-1907)

'Cornubia' 2 W-O
(D. Bramley) D. Bramley, 1980

'Envoy' × 'Signal Light'; sdlg no. 68/51(A)
Fl. 95 mm wide. Mid-season. Resembles a smaller 'Signal Light' with whiter perianth and the corona of different form

'Cornwall' 2 Y-? (a)
(P.D. Williams, pre-1938)

'Corofin' 3 W-YYR
(J.L. Richardson, pre-1943)
'Seraglio' × 'Mr Jinks'
Fl. rounded; perianth segments very broad, rounded at apex and slightly truncate, prominently mucronate, snow white, spreading, a little concave, of waxy substance, overlapping half; the inner segments slightly inflexed; corona bowl-shaped, ribbed, yellow, with a broad band of orange-red at rim, mouth with deep and overlapping lobes, frilled. Mid-season

'Coroglen' 2 W-P
(D.S. Bell) D.S. Bell, 1979
'Red Conquest' × 'Pastel Pink'
Fl. 102 mm wide; corona pale pink, frilled. Mid-season

'Corolet' 2 Y-? (a)
(R.H. Bath, pre-1929)

'Corolet' 2 W-O
(West & Fell, pre-1945)
Perianth segments creamy white; corona long, scarlet-orange

'Corolle d'Orange' 2 W-? (b)
(de Graaff Bros & van Konynenburg & Co., pre-1933)

'Coromandel' 2 Y-Y
(Brian S. Duncan) Rathowen Daffodils, 1987
'Golden Jewel' open pollinated; sdlg no. 751
Fl. forming a double triangle, mid-yellow, with a greenish tinge, very smooth; perianth segments broadly ovate, blunt or truncate, with slight white mucro, a little reflexed, overlapping half; the inner segments more nearly acute, a little inflexed, with margins wavy; corona cylindrical, smooth, mouth slightly expanded, even or a little wavy. Mid-season

'Corona' 8 W-YYO
(A. Frylink & Sons, pre-1933)
N. poeticus × *N. tazetta* × Div. 3 sdlg
Perianth segments snowy white; corona yellow, with rim becoming clear orange. AM(Haarlem) 1932, FCC(Haarlem) 1933

'Coronach' 3 W-R
(Mrs R.O. Backhouse, pre-1921)
Fl. rounded; perianth segments very broad, prominently mucronate, snow white, spreading, with margins incurling at apex, of great substance, overlapping

half or more; the inner segments roundish, a little inflexed; corona disc-shaped, ribbed, deep red, mouth obscurely 6-lobed and a little frilled. Late

'Coronado' 2 Y-P
(G.E. Mitsch, pre-1954)
'Tunis' × 'Mrs R.O. Backhouse'; sdlg no. 39C136/2
Perianth segments creamy yellow with an admixture of buff; corona buff apricot, frilled. Mid-season

'Corona Hibernica' 3 Y-? (a)
(W.B. Hartland, pre-1913)

'Coronation' 9 W-?
(E.M. Crosfield, pre-1913)

'Coronation' 2 W-O
Syn. of 'Royal Orange'

'Coronation Fanfare' 1 Y-Y
(G.L. Wilson, pre-1953)
Syn. 'Royal Daffodil'

'Coronation Year' 2 W-? (b)
(G.H. Engleheart, pre-1902)
AM 1902

N. coronatus de Candolle = *N. hispanicus* var. *concolor*

'Coronatus' 1 Y-Y
Syn. of 'Spurius Coronatus'

'Coronella' 2 W-WWY
(H.A. Brown, pre-1935)
Perianth segments white; corona white, with a distinct band of lemon yellow at rim

'Coronet' 1 W-Y
(G.H. Engleheart, pre-1904)
Perianth segments ivory white; corona very deep golden yellow, mouth boldly frilled. Early to mid-season. Resembles an improved 'Mrs Walter Ware'

'Corongamite' 1 Y-Y
Syn. of 'Corangamite'

'Corot' 2 W-W
(de Graaff Bros, pre-1923)

'Corozal' 3 W-GYO
(A.J.R. Pearson, 1979) A.J.R. Pearson, 1989
'Fairy Tale' × ('Fairy Tale' × 'Corofin'); sdlg no. 79/24/D21
Fl. 100 mm wide; perianth segments very broad, truncate, fairly prominently mucronate, a little reflexed, concave, with broad midrib showing, very smooth and of good substance, overlapping half; corona broad and very shallow bowl-shaped, lightly ribbed, primrose yellow, with green at base and a broad band of solid bright orange at rim, mouth straight, wavy, rim occasionaly notched. Mid-season to late

'Corpach' 2 Y-? (a)
(A.M. Wilson, pre-1951)

'Corporal' 1 Y-Y
(T. Buncombe, pre-1934)

'Corporal Trim' 1 Y-Y
(E. Leeds, pre-1877)
Fl. dark yellow; corona long, rim irregularly and deeply notched. Syn. Pseudonarcissus Major 'Corporal Trim'. Was "absorbed" into Pseudonarcissus Major 'Major'

'Corra'
Unregistered
Seed parent of 'Eric the Red'

'Corra Linn' 2 W-R
(S.J. Bisdee, 1937)
'Margaret H' × 'Sunstar'

'Correct' 3 W-YYR
(P.D. Williams, ?1928)
AM(Haarlem) 1937

'Corregio' 2 W-O
(The Brodie of Brodie, c1916)
'Will Scarlett' × 'Bernardino'
Perianth segments creamy white; corona orange red

'Corrie Plemp' 1 W-Y
(pre-1897)
Perianth segments white; corona opening soft primrose yellow, becoming pale sulphur yellow or almost white

'Corrima' 2 W-O
(J.T. Gray, pre-1949)
Perianth segments broadly ovate; corona straight, deep orange

'Corrisande' 2 Y-? (a)
(J.T. Gray, pre-1933)

N. corrugatus Jordan = *N. tazetta* subsp. *lacticolor*

'Corry' 2 W-? (b)
(de Graaff Bros, pre-1931)
AM(Haarlem) 1930

'Corry Blonk' 2 W-Y
(G.A. Uit den Boogaard, pre-1950)

'Corrymeela' 2 W-Y
(G.L. Wilson, pre-1947)
'Gracious' × 'Broughshane'
Perianth segments white; corona primrose, flushed

with coppery salmon rose, frilled, with rim rolled

'Corsage' 2 W-? (b)
(Nieuwenhuis Bros) Nieuwenhuis Bros, 1956

'Corsair' 1 Y or W-? (a,b or c)
(Mrs R.O. Backhouse, pre-1908)

'Corsair' 2 W-R
(J.L. Richardson) J.L. Richardson, 1959
'Kilworth' × 'Arbar'

'Corsair' 2 Y-O
Syn. of 'California Gold'

'Corsana' 2 W-P
(J.H. Davenport) Mrs E. Milliken, 1974
'Thelrosia' × 'Dreen'
Fl. 106 mm wide

'Corselet' 2 W-?
(G.H. Engleheart, pre-1914)

'Corsica' 2 Y-R
(G. Lewis) D.S. Bell, 1955
Perianth segments deep yellow; corona deep red

'Corsican' 2 or 3 W-? (b or c)
(A.M. Wilson, pre-1916)

'Cortez' 2 Y-O
(G.E. Mitsch and R. & E.Havens) G.E. Mitsch and R. & E.Havens, 1985
'Gay Time' × 'Chiloquin'; sdlg no. LL61/5
Perianth segments broad, acute, clear yellow; corona tangerine orange. Late

'Cortina' 1 W-W
(G.L. Wilson) F.A.L. Harrison, 1956
'Broughshane' × sdlg 28/60
Fl. white, of great substance

'Corton' 2 Y-? (a)
(A.M. Wilson, pre-1944)

'Corvette' 2 Y-O
(F.E. Board) F.E. Board, 1965
'Armada' × 'Straight Flush'
Perianth s egments yellow; corona reddish orange. Early. Resembles a taller 'Armada'

'Corvo' 1 Y-Y
(W. Jackson Jr) Jackson's Daffodils, 1979
Sdlg no. 55/72
Fl. 115 mm wide. Mid-season

'Corycia' 1 W-? (b)
(Barr & Sons, pre-1913)

'Corydon' 5
(Miss E. Willmott, pre-1901)
AM 1901

'Coryn' 2 Y-? (a)
(W.A. Watts, pre-1923)

'Coryphee' 2 W-O
(Konynenburg & Mark) Konynenburg & Mark, 1960
('Invitation' × 'Extase') × ('Bertha Aten' × ['Anaconda' × 'Marion'])
Fl. 105 mm wide; perianth creamy white; corona rich orange. Late

'Corython' 3 W-? (b)
(Mrs R.O. Backhouse, pre-1921)

'Cosmic Dance' 2 O-R
(Brian S. Duncan, 1981) Brian S. Duncan, 1992
(['Ballintoy' × 'Air Marshal'] × 'Shining Light') × 'Sabine Hay'; sdlg no. 1012
Fl. 93 mm wide; perianth segments broadly ovate, blunt, orange, with prominent white mucro, spreading, smooth, overlapping half; the inner segments more narrowly ovate, with less noticeable mucro, a little inflexed, with margins wavy; corona shallow bowl-shaped, deep orange-red, with mouth even and rim crenate. Late. Varies between Divs 2 and 3

'Cosmic Pink' 2 W-P
(G.J. Phillips) G.J. Phillips, 1994
'Dawncrest' × 'My Word'; sdlg no. 81-134-1
Fl. forming a double triangle, 102 mm wide; perianth segments broadly ovate; the inner segments more narrowly ovate; corona funnel-shaped, with mouth lobed and flared. Early

'Cosmos' 1 Y-Y
(P.D. Williams, pre-1935)

'Cossack' 3 W-O
(G.H. Engleheart, pre-1908)
Perianth segments cream, slightly reflexed; corona expanded, intense dark reddish orange

'Cossima' 2 W-O
(J.W.A. Lefeber) J.W.A. Lefeber, 1960
Fl. 71 mm wide; perianth segments snow white; corona reddish orange, frilled. Mid-season

'Costa Rica' 2 Y-? (a)
(A.M. Wilson, pre-1949)

'Costly' 2 Y-Y
(M.P. Williams, pre-1938)
Fl. yellow

'Cosy' ?-P
(Alister Clark, pre-1948)

'Cotehele' 1 W-W
(T. Bloomer) du Plessis Bros, 1981
'Rashee' × 'Empress of Ireland'; sdlg no. 39
Fl. 125 mm wide. Mid-season

N. cothurnalis Salisbury = *N.* × *medioluteus*

'Cotillon' 3 W-? (b)
(F.H. Chapman, pre-1913)

'Cotinga' 6 W-P
(G.E. Mitsch) G.E. Mitsch, 1976
'Mitylene' open pollinated × *N. cyclamineus*; sdlg no. E07/3
Perianth segments ivory white, a little reflexed, with margins wavy; corona flared, apricot pink, with a deeper tone at rim. Mid-season. Somewhat resembles 'Dove Wings' in form

'Cotopaxi' 2 Y-O
(J.L. Richardson, pre-1943)
'Killigrew' × 'Penquite'
Fl. forming a double triangle, just over 100 mm wide; perianth segments broadly ovate, blunt, mucronate, deep mimosa yellow, with margins sometimes slightly incurling at apex, and with midrib showing, overlapping half; the inner segments more narrowly ovate, only slightly mucronate, a little inflexed, with margins slightly wavy; corona cup-shaped, expanded, marigold orange, loosely frilled. 2n=28. AM(e) 1942

'Cotswold' 2 W-?
(F.H. Chapman, pre-1927)

'Cottage Maid' 2 W-? (b)
(Miss K. Spurrell, pre-1927)

'Cottage Maid' 3 W-YYR
Syn. of 'Queen of Narcissi'

'Cottee' 2 Y-O
(A. Overton) A. Overton, 1960
'Skylark' × 'Chungking'

'Cottenham'
(pre-1949)

'Cotterton' 2 W-W
(The Brodie of Brodie, c1936)
'Tain' × 'Evening'
Fl. pure white

'Cottesmore' 2 Y-YOO
(J.O. Sherrard, pre-1948)
Syn. 'Cream Gorse'

'Cotton Candy' 4 W-WYP
(Murray W. Evans) Murray W. Evans, 1979
('Falaise' × ['Snowball' × 'Interim']) × ('Snowball' × 'Interlude'); sdlg no. N-10
Fl. 85 mm wide. Mid-season

'Cotton Puff' 8 W-W
(H.Koopowitz) H.Koopowitz, 1997
N. pannizianus × *N. papyraceus* sdlg
Fls 7-9 per stem, 26 mm wide, pure white; corona cup-shaped. Dwarf. Early

'Coty Prince' 3 W-? (b)
(J.W.A. Lefeber) J.W.A. Lefeber, 1956

'Coulmony' 1 W-Y
(Brodie Gardens) Brodie Gardens, 1957
'Broughshane' × 'Niphetos'
Fl. forming a double triangle, 97 mm wide; perianth segments broadly ovate, blunt, not prominently mucronate, pure white, a little inflexed, concave, with margins incurling, smooth, of great substance, overlapping one-third; the inner segments with margins more strongly incurved; corona cylindrical, smooth, brilliant greenish yellow 2B, mouth ribbed and widely expanded, rim notched and crenate

'Counsel' 2 W-YYR
(P. Phillips) P. Phillips, 1968

'Counsellor' 1 Y-Y
(G.L. Wilson, pre-1935)
Sdlg 13/7 × 'Tipperary Tim'
Fl. large, deep golden yellow; perianth segments somewhat ribbed, with margins a little wavy, overlapping one-third; corona slender, ribbed, with rim widely rolled and deeply crenate. Late. Resembles 'Beersheba' in form

'Count Antonio' 2 Y-? (a)
(W.F.M. Copeland, pre-1910)

'Countess Cadogan' 1 W-W
(pre-1907)

'Countess de Gray' 5 Y-Y
Syn. of 'Countess Grey'

'Countess Grey' 5 Y-Y
(G.H. Engleheart, pre-1900)
'Empress' × *N. triandrus*
FCC 1900. Received FCC 1900 as 'Countess de Grey'

'Countess of Annesley' 1 Y-Y
(Irish origin, pre-1886)
Syn. "The Castlewellan Daffodil"

'Countess of Antrim' 1 W-? (b)
(G.L. Wilson, pre-1927)

'Countess of Desmond' 1 Y-Y
(Irish origin, pre-1889)
Naturally occurring hybrid introduced by Miss

F.W.Currey
Perianth segments narrow, soft primrose yellow, twisted; corona soft yellow, with rim deeply notched. Resembles a dwarf 'Bishop Mann'

'Countess of Mayo' 1 Y-Y
(Hogg & Robertson, pre-1907)

'Countess of Pembroke' 3 W-W
(W.A. Watts, pre-1923)

'Countess of Southesk' 3 W-W
(W.B. Hartland, pre-1908)
Perianth segments white, twisted; corona pale creamy white

'Countess of Stair' 1 W-Y
(G.L. Wilson) M.J. Jefferson-Brown, 1963
'Guardian' × 'Kanchenjunga'

'Countess of Stamford' 1 W-W
(E.M. Crosfield, pre-1905)
Fl. opening cream; corona becoming whiter, with rim flanged. AM 1905

'Countess of Strathmore' 1 W-W
(pre-1907)

'Countess Visconti' 5 W-Y
(G.H. Engleheart, pre-1903)
Perianth segments white; corona light yellow. AM 1903

'Count Palatine' 3 W-? (b)
(Sir C.H. Cave, pre-1913)

'Country Girl' 2 Y-O
(Konynenburg & Mark) Konynenburg & Mark, 1965
'Red Goblet' × 'Contrapunt'
Fl. 90 mm wide; perianth segments brilliant yellow 8A; corona rich orange. Late

'Country Morning' 3 W-GOO
(J.L. Richardson) Carncairn Daffodils, 1985
'Ariel' open pollinated; sdlg no. 246
Fl. rounded; perianth segments white, overlapping; corona very shallow bowl-shaped, peachy orange, fading a little in bright light, with a slightly paler tone at rim, dentate. Late. Resembles a larger-flowered and more robust 'Ariel'

'Count Visconti' 5 Y-Y
(G.H. Engleheart, pre-1903)
Perianth segments soft yellow; corona bright yellow. AM 1903, FCC 1904

'Coupled'
(?W.B. Cranfield, pre-1914)

'Coupon' ?-P
(Alister Clark, pre-1948)

'Courage' 2 W-W
(The Brodie of Brodie, c.1932)
('Nevis' open pollinated × 'Naxos') × 'Askelon'
Fl. large, pure white, of smooth texture and thick substance

'Courageous' 2 Y-? (a)
(A.M. Wilson, pre-1938)

'Courageous' ?-P
(Alister Clark, pre-1948)

'Courago' 1 Y-Y
(J.L. Martin) J.L. Martin, 1978
'Courtill' × 'Tarago'; sdlg no. T/C 1
Fl. 115 mm wide; perianth segments brilliant greenish yellow 3A; corona vivid yellow 9A. Early. Resembles a taller and larger 'Courtill' of greater substance

'Cour de Versailles' 8 W-O
(pre-1798)

'Courier' 3 W-? (b)
(F.H. Chapman, pre-1913)

'Courier' 1 Y-Y
(Brian S. Duncan) Rathowen Daffodils, 1979
'Yellow Idol' hybrid × 'Viking'; sdlg no. 288
Fl. 95 mm wide, mid-yellow; perianth segments reflexed. Mid-season

'Couronne Blanche' 8 W-W
(pre-1846)

'Couronne Blanche' 8 W-Y
(pre-1897)
Fl. large; perianth segments white; corona orange-yellow. Late

'Couronne de Braadenbourg' 8 W-O
(pre-1798)

'Couronne Imperial' 8 Y-O
(pre-1798)

'Court Beauty' 2 W-? (b)
(H. Backhouse, pre-1910)

'Court Beauty' 2 Y-O
(W.O. Backhouse) Mrs W.O. Backhouse, 1964
Fl. 89 mm wide; perianth segments bright yellow; corona deep orange. Late. Resembles 'Reserve'

'Courtcraft' 1 Y-Y
(R.C.A. Tombleson) R.C.A. Tombleson, 1972
'Harewood' × 'Spanish Gold'

Fl. 124 mm wide

'Court Dress' 1 W-? (b)
(D.S. Bell) D.S. Bell, 1955

'Courteous' 1 W-Y
(T.H. Piper, c.1966) Unregistered
'Nagara' × 'Lorinna'

'Courtesy' 2 W-Y
(G.H. Johnstone, pre-1942)

'Courtesy' 2 Y-O
Syn. of 'Metis'

'Court Favourite' 3 W-? (b)
(W.O. Backhouse) W.O. Backhouse, 1956

'Court Herald' 1 Y-Y
(T.H. Piper, c.1966) Unregistered
'Kingscourt' × ('Melissa' × 'Kingscourt')

'Courthill' 1 Y-Y
?Syn. of 'Courtill'

'Courtier' 1 Y-Y
(W. Polman-Mooy, pre-1916)

'Courtier' 1 Y-Y
(A.E. Lowe, pre-1927)

'Courtier' 1 Y-Y
(J.N. Hancock & Co., pre-1974) Unregistered

'Courtill' 1 Y-Y
(C.O. Fairbairn, pre-1968) J.L. Martin, 1978
Fl. 103 mm wide; perianth segments brilliant greenish yellow 3A; corona brilliant yellow 8A. Mid-season. Resembles a taller 'Kingscourt' of smoother texture. Syn. 'Courtship'. ?See also 'Courthill'

'Court Jester' 2 Y-O
(pre-1939)

'Court Jester' 1 W-Y
(Harry I.Tuggle Jr, 1949) Harry I.Tuggle Jr, 1964
'Tunis' × 'Fortune'
Fl. 120 mm wide; perianth segments white; corona ribbed, orange-yellow. Mid-season

'Courtly' 2 Y-Y
(M.P. Williams, pre-1949)
'Havelock' sdlg

'Court Martial' 2 Y-O
(J.L. Richardson) J.L. Richardson, 1956
'Big Game' × 'Narvik'
Fl. 88 mm wide; perianth segments brilliant yellow 7A, slightly flushed orange at base, a little reflexed, overlapping at base only; corona ribbed, on the outside opening light orange (21A), becoming darker in tone (24A), tinged with a yet darker tone (25A), on the inside a richer deeper orange than 25A, paling towards base, mouth a little expanded, with rim slightly flanged and crenate. Mid-season. 2n=28. AM(e) 1957, *AM(g) 1974, *FCC(g) 1977

'Courtney' 2 W-W
(F.J. Klein) F.J. Klein, 1986
'Empress of Ireland' × Culpepper white sdlg
Fl. white. Mid-season. Resembles 'Empress of Ireland'

'Court Queen' 2 W-Y
(D.J. Cooper) D.J. Cooper, 1959
Fl. 114 mm wide; perianth segments off white; corona creamy yellow. Early

'Courtrai' 3 W-? (b)
(Mrs R.O. Backhouse, pre-1921)

'Court Royal' 2 W-W
(G.L. Wilson) F.E. Board, 1957
'Snowline' × 'Empress of Ireland'

'Courtship' 1 W-P
(S.J. Bisdee, 1943) S.J. Bisdee, 1956
'Eskimo' × 'Dawnglow'

'Courtship' 1 Y-Y
Syn. of 'Courtill'

'Couth' 1 W-P
(Jackson's Daffodils) Jackson's Daffodils, 1986
Sdlg 110/70 × 'Dear Me'; sdlg no. 75/78
Perianth segments greenish white 155C; corona light yellowish pink 27A. Mid-season

'Cove' 2 Y-Y
(H.A. Brown, 1939)
Perianth segments wide, lemon yellow, plane; corona large, ribbed, bright orange-yellow, with mouth expanded. Very early. 2n=28

'Covent Garden' 1 Y-Y
(J. Verduyn, pre-1939)

'Coventry Patmore' 9 W-?
(G.H. Engleheart, pre-1910)

'Coverack'
(E.C. Powell)

'Coverack Beauty' 1 W-Y
(The Brodie of Brodie, c.1919)
'Findhorn' × 'Nevis'
Fl. forming a double triangle, 80 mm wide; perianth segments ovate, acute, fairly prominently mucronate, greenish white, a little inflexed, overlapping one-third to a half; corona cylindrical, narrow, smooth, vivid

yellow 9A, with mouth shallowly and regularly 6-lobed, rim widely flanged, entire or obscurely crenate. Very early

'Coverack Cheer' 2 Y-O
(P.D. Williams, pre-1927)
Perianth segments deep primrose; corona only slightly orange

'Coverack Chief' 1 Y-Y
(The Brodie of Brodie, pre-1930)

'Coverack Chimes' 2 W-?
(The Brodie of Brodie, pre-1930)

'Coverack Crest' 2 W-?
(The Brodie of Brodie, pre-1930)
'Nissa' hybrid

'Coverack Cross' 1 W-W
(The Brodie of Brodie, pre-1930)

'Coverack Crown' 2 W-?
(The Brodie of Brodie, pre-1928)
Sdlg hybrid

'Coverack Delight' 2 Y-? (a)
(The Brodie of Brodie, pre-1930)
'White Emperor' × 2 Y-Y

'Coverack Flame' 2 Y-? (a)
(The Brodie of Brodie, pre-1930)

'Coverack Gem' 2 W-? (b)
(The Brodie of Brodie, c.1924)
'Mozart' × 'Gallipoli'
Perianth segments cream. Mid-season. AM(Haarlem) 1930

'Coverack Glory' 2 Y-Y
(P.D. Williams, pre-1927)
Perianth segments clear yellow, overlapping; corona long, slender, pale buttercup yellow, with mouth flared. Mid-season. 2n=28. Resembles 'Pentewan'. *HC(g) 1936

'Coverack Glow' 1 Y-Y
(The Brodie of Brodie, pre-1930)

'Coverack Gold' 2 Y-O
(The Brodie of Brodie, pre-1928)
'King Alfred' × 'Tenedos'
Perianth segments broadly ovate, prominently mucronate, brilliant greenish yellow 2B, with broad midrib paler at apex, spreading, overlapping one-third; the inner segments a little inflexed, somewhat twisted, creased, with margins nicked; corona funnel-shaped, ribbed, vivid orange-yellow 21A, mouth straight, with six slightly overlapping lobes, lightly frilled, rim obscurely crenate

'Coverack Hope' 9 W-?
(The Brodie of Brodie, pre-1930)

'Coverack Knight' 1 W-W
(The Brodie of Brodie, pre-1930)

'Coverack Lad' 2 W-R
(The Brodie of Brodie, pre-1928)
Perianth segments white; corona deep red

'Coverack Perfection' 2 W-YYO
(The Brodie of Brodie, pre-1930)
'Mitylene' × 'Fortune'
Fl. 91 mm wide; perianth segments broadly ovate, blunt, fairly prominently mucronate, greenish white (2D), spreading, a little concave, creased, overlapping one-third; the inner segments a little inflexed and somewhat twisted; corona funnel-shaped, broad and shallow, closely ribbed, brilliant greenish yellow 7C, tinged green in tube, with a narrow band of yellow-orange (17B) in a narrow band at rim and lightly suffusing the ribs, mouth split in places and overlapping, wavy, rim irregularly crenate. AM(e) 1934

'Coverack Pride' 1 Y-Y
(P.D. Williams, pre-1927)
Early. Resembles an improved 'King Alfred'

'Coverack Sister' 2 Y-? (a)
(The Brodie of Brodie, pre-1930)
'Mitylene' × 'Fortune'

'Coverack Star' 2 Y-? (a)
(The Brodie of Brodie, pre-1928)

'Coverack Star' 3 W-? (b)
(The Brodie of Brodie, c.1935)
'Elspeth' × P.D. Williams W-R sdlg

'Coverack Sun' 7
(The Brodie of Brodie, pre-1930)
'Pilgrimage' × *N. jonquilla*

'Cover Girl' 2 W-P
(Oregon Bulb Farms, pre-1950)

'Covina' 2 W-? (b)
(D.J. Cooper) D.J. Cooper, 1956

'Cowani' 1 W-Y
Syn. of 'Mr Cowan'

'Cowboy' 2 Y-O
(D. Jackson, 1975) Unregistered
'Craze' × 'Coope'; sdlg no. 128/75
Perianth segments very broadly ovate, blunt, yellow, with slight white mucro, spreading, smooth, regular, overlapping half or more; the inner segments almost as wide, only very slightly mucronate; corona bowl-shaped, very broad and shallow, ribbed, bright full

orange, with mouth tightly frilled

'Cowfold' 2 W-W
(Sir F.C. Stern, pre-1953)

'Cowley' 1 W-? (b)
(D.B. Milne, pre-1950)
AM(Haarlem) 1956

'Cowslip' 3 Y-R
(W. Backhouse, pre-1869)
Perianth segments primrose yellow; corona red. Syn. Burbidgei 'Cowslip', Burbidgei 'Primulinus'

'Cow-warr' 1 W-Y
(A.O. Roblin, 1939)
'Renee' × 'Carmel'

'Coxwain' 1 W-W
(J. Pope, pre-1908)

'Coylum' 3 W-GWW
(J.M. de Navarro) J.M. de Navarro, 1967
'Frigid' × 'Dallas'
Fl. 88 mm wide. Late. 2n=14. Resembles a larger 'Cushendall'

'Crackajack' 2 Y-? (a)
(G. Lewis, pre-1949)

'Cracker' 2 Y-R
(R.G.Cull, 1984) Hokorawa Daffodils, 1996
Sdlg HC/A6 × 'Falstaff'
Fl. 61 mm wide; perianth segments vivid yellow 12A; corona red (40A). Dwarf. Mid-season

'Crackington' 4 Y-O
(D. Lloyd) J.W. Blanchard, 1986
'Golden Aura' × 'Beauvallon'; sdlg no. 75/35A
Perianth and other petaloid segments in several whorls; the outer whorls of almost equal length, very broadly ovate, slightly mucronate, rounded at apex, yellow, spreading or a little inflexed, with margins incurling; the centre whorl shorter, more strongly inflexed, with margins wavy and folding inwards; corona segments half the length of the centre petaloid segments and interspersed among them, opening orange, becoming paler, frilled. Mid-season

'Crackrattle' 2 Y-R
(G.H. Johnstone, pre-1947)

'Crackrattle' 2 Y-O
Syn. of 'Clackrattle'

'Cracksman' 2 Y-? (a)
(W.A. Grace, pre-1938)

'Cradle Song' 3 W-W
(D.S. Bell) D.S. Bell, 1959

'Verona' hybrid
Fl. 112 mm wide. Late. Resembles a 'Chinese White' of better poise and texture

'Cradle Time' 3 W-GWW
(D.S. Bell, 1970) D.S. Bell, 1985
'Verona' sdlg
Fl. 94 mm wide. Mid-season. Resembles 'Verona' but with the perianth segments less rounded

'Craftsman' 2 Y-? (a)
(Cartwright & Goodwin, pre-1910)

'Craftsman' 1 W-Y
(R.C.A. Tombleson) R.C.A. Tombleson, 1972
'Ardclinis' × 'Glenshesk'
Fl. 107 mm wide

'Craganour' 1 W-? (b)
(de Graaff Bros, pre-1927)

'Cragford' 8 W-O
(P.D. Williams, pre-1930)
'Gloriosus' hybrid
Fls 4-6 per stem, 53 mm wide; perianth segments very broadly ovate, blunt or sometimes truncate, fairly prominently mucronate, white, flushed vivid yellow 14B at base, spreading, a little concave, overlapping one-third; the inner segments more narrowly ovate, angled at shoulder, a little inflexed, with margins wavy or incurled; corona very shallow bowl-shaped, ribbed, vivid orange 28B, with mouth wavy, rim indented. Very early. Scented. 2n=17. FCEFA(Haarlem) 1939, EFA(Haarlem) 1939, AM(f) 1946, FCC(f) 1947, *AM(p) 1975, *FCC(p) 1977

'Craig' 1 Y-Y
(R.H. Glover) R.H. Glover, 1972
'Melissa' × 'Molong'
Fl. 114 mm wide

'Craigarusky' 2 W-Y
(Ballydorn Bulb Farm) Ballydorn Bulb Farm, 1992
'Mount Pleasant' open pollinated
Fl. 115 mm wide; perianth segments broadly ovate, pure white, smooth; corona straight-sided, creamy yellow, with rim crenate. Mid-season

'Craigavon' 1 W-Y
(T. Bloomer) T. Bloomer, 1973
'Alpine Eagle' × 'Downpatrick'

'Craigdun' 2 W-OOY
(Carncairn Daffodils) Carncairn Daffodils, 1979
'Tryst' × ('Kilworth' × 'Pirate King'); sdlg no. W3/5
Fl. 90 mm wide; perianth segments greenish white (157B); corona light orange (21A), with brilliant yellow 13B at rim. Very tall. Mid-season. Sunproof. 2n=28

'Craigieburn' 3 W-O
(E.W. Cotter, pre-1978) Unregistered
Perianth segments broadly ovate, pure white; corona very shallow bowl-shaped, deep reddish orange

'Craignair' 1 Y-Y
(Mrs E. Murray)
'Balmoral' × 'Kingscourt' hybrid

'Craig's Emperor'
(pre-1940)

'Craig Stiel' 2 O-O
(J.S.B.Lea, 1978) Clive Postles Daffodils, 1986
'Bunclody' × 'Torridon'; sdlg no. 1-52-73
Perianth segments flushed orange; corona cylindrical, with mouth straight. Mid-season

'Craigtara' 2 Y-O
(Carncairn Daffodils) Carncairn Daffodils, 1975
'Virtue' × 'Fury'; sdlg no. 2/57/59
Fl. 94 mm wide; perianth segments deep yellow; corona orange

'Craigwen' 2 Y-Y
(R.J. Ralph, 1946)
'Saint Egwin' × ?'Bungana'

'Craigywarren' 2 Y-R
(W.J. Dunlop, pre-1949)
'Dunkeld' × 'Bahram'
Perianth segments very broadly ovate, blunt, slightly mucronate, deep yellow, spreading, plane, with margins minutely incurling at apex, waxy smooth, of good substance, overlapping half; the inner segments more narrowly ovate, a little inflexed, with midrib showing and margins wavy, spathulate; corona cup-shaped, red, with mouth widely expanded, split in places and overlapping, loosely and irregularly folded

'Cranborne' 2 Y-O
(J.W. Blanchard, 1971) Unregistered
('Chungking' × 'Dewlish') × 'Border Cheif'; sdlg no. 66/5A
Fl. 95 mm wide; perianth segments broad, rounded, medium to deep yellow; corona funnel-shaped, reddish orange, with rim slightly crenate. Late

'Cranbourne' 1 Y-Y
(G.P. Haydon, pre-1910)

'Cranbourne' 2 Y-YOO
(H.A. Brown, pre-1938)
Perianth segments yellow; corona light orange, with yellow at base, frilled

'Cranbrook' 5 W-W
(W.A. Grace, pre-1927)

'Cranda' 2 Y-? (a)
(West & Fell, pre-1938)

'Cranfield' 1 W-Y
(G.P. Haydon, pre-1914)
Corona expanded, pale yellow

'Cranford' 2 W-W
(G.C. Graham, pre-1949)

'Crannog' 1 Y-Y
(G.L. Wilson, pre-1931)

'Crannuibh' 2 W-? (b)
(P.D. Williams, pre-1931)

'Cranreuch' 2 W-?
(P.D. Williams, pre-1931)

'Cranstoun' 2 W-? (b)
(N.Y. Lower, pre-1936)

'Craskin' 1 Y-Y
(P.D. Williams, pre-1927)

'Craster' 3 W-YOO
(G. Harrison) G. Harrison, 1968
Sdlg × 'Mahmoud'
Mid-season

'Crater' 3 W-O
(F.H. Chapman, pre-1914)
Fl. small; perianth segments ovate, slightly mucronate, golden yellow, spreading, loosely ribbed, somewhat uneven; the inner segments more narrowly ovate, somewhat inflexed and twisted; corona proportionately large, shallow, very widely expanded, densely ribbed, reddish orange, broadly crenate, with rim dentate

'Crater' 2 Y-GRR
(J.M. de Navarro) J.M. de Navarro
Perianth segments broadly ovate, blunt, slightly mucronate, deep gold, plane, smooth, regular, overlapping one-third; the inner segments more narrowly ovate, a little inflexed, with margins wavy or inward folding, shouldered at base; corona smooth, red, with dark green at base, mouth ribbed, a little expanded and lightly frilled, rim crenate. PC(e) 1961

'Crater Lake' 3 Y-? (a)
(Oregon Bulb Farms, pre-1950)

'Crawford Barlow' 1 W-? (b)
(G.P. Haydon, pre-1908)

'Crawfordii' 2 W-Y
Syn. of 'Consul Crawford'

'Craze' 2 Y-P

(W. Jackson Jr) W. Jackson Jr, 1966
'Verity' × 'Ceylon'; sdlg no. 101/61

'Creag Dubh' 2 O-R
(J.S.B. Lea) J.S.B. Lea, 1978
(['Chungking' × 'Spry'] × 'Home Fires') × 'Vulcan'; sdlg no. 2-26-69
Fl. 100 mm wide; perianth segments pale orange, sometimes with a lighter tone the length of the midrib; corona deep red. Mid-season

'Creagh Castle Seedling' 1 Y-Y
(Irish origin, c.1887)
Fl. yellow; perianth segments ovate or oblong, spreading or inflexed, sometimes twisted or with margins wavy, overlapping at base only; corona funnel-shaped, ribbed, with mouth flared, rim closely and deeply dentate. Dwarf. Very early. Resembles *N. minor*. ?The same as 'Dorothy Bucknall'

'Cream Bell' 1 W-Y
(H.A. Brown, 1943)
Perianth segments very broad, smooth; corona large, creamy yellow. Mid-season to late

'Cream Cloud' 2 W-WWY
(G.E. Mitsch, 1953) G.E. Mitsch, 1965
'Polindra' × 'Green Island'
Fl. 108 mm wide; perianth segments milk white; corona opening pale lemon yellow, becoming ivory white, with lemon yellow at rim, frilled. Mid-season. Resembles a smoother-textured 'Oratorio' with the margins of the perianth segments less often nicked

'Cream Cone' 4 W-Y
(J.A.Hunter, 1986) J.A.Hunter, 1997
'Blossom' × 'Virma'; sdlg no. 13/81C
Fl. 110 mm wide; perianth and other petaloid segments white; the outer whorl ovate, smooth; the inner whorls tightly arranged within the corona; corona flared, yellow, with additional segments interspersed among the petaloid segments within

'Cream Cornet' 1 W-Y
(A.G. Thompson) A.G. Thompson, 1965
'Beersheba' × 'Imperator'
Fl. 108 mm wide; perianth segments creamy white; corona deep yellow. Mid-season. Resembles 'Imperator' but with a darker-coloured corona

'Cream Crest' 1 W-Y
(J.N. Hancock & Co., 1963) Unregistered
Sdlg no. 356/63H

'Cream Crinoline' 2 W-?
(C. Goodson, pre-1939)

'Cream Cup' 1 W-W
(J. Kouwenhoven, pre-1914)
Fl. large; perianth segments white; corona creamy white. AM(Haarlem) 1915

'Cream Cup' 2 W-Y
(G.E. Mitsch, pre-1952)
'Beersheba' × 'Killigrew'; sdlg no. 37C17/1
Perianth segments overlapping; corona opening light lemon yellow, becoming cream. Mid-season

'Cream Dawn' 1 W-Y
(J.M. Walker, pre-1949)
Perianth segments white; corona pale lemon yellow

'Creamed Honey' 1 Y-W
(L.P. Dettman) L.P. Dettman, 1968
'Content' × 'Spellbinder'
Fl. opening dirty yellow; corona usually becoming pure white

'Cream Gorse' 2 Y-YOO
Syn. of 'Cottesmore'

'Cream Lily' 2 W-?
(Mrs R.O. Backhouse, pre-1901)

'Cream Pearl' 2 W-? (b)
(E.H. Krelage & Son, pre-1942)

'Cream Puff' 1 W-W
(Oregon Bulb Farms, pre-1946)

'Cream Wave' 1 W-W
(Unknown origin) M. Gardiner, 1956
Perianth segments white; corona widely expanded, cream

'Creation' 1 W-W
(G.E.Mitsch, 1982) R. & E.Havens, 1997
('Trousseau' × 'Paradise') × (sdlg A39/1 × 'Panache'); sdlg no. 2R26/1
Fl. 105 mm wide; perianth segments broad, spreading, plane; corona cylindrical, with rim flanged. Early

'Crebilly' 2 W-WWY
(W.J. Dunlop, pre-1949)
'Mitylene' × 'Dunkeld'
Corona spreading, creamy white, flushed pale greenish lemon at rim

'Credit' 2 Y-? (a)
(Sir C.H. Cave, pre-1928)

'Credo' 2 W-P
(G.E. Mitsch) G.E. Mitsch, 1977
'Accent' × 'Rima'; sdlg no. F6/1
Fl. 43 mm wide; corona deep rose pink. Mid-season. Resembles 'Accent' but with broader perianth segments and a more deeply coloured corona

'Creme de Menthe' 2 W-GWW
(Carncairn Daffodils) Carncairn Daffodils, 1976

'Chinese White' × sdlg 11/39/59 (G.L.Wilson sdlg × 'Cotterton'); sdlg no. 2/63
Fl. 105 mm wide; perianth segments greenish white (155A); corona expanded, tightly ribbed, pure white, with emerald green at base. Late

'Cremona' 1 Y-Y
(C.G. van Tubergen, pre-1929)

'Cremorne' 2 W-?
(L.P. Brumley) A. Overton, 1960

'Crene' 2 Y-? (a)
(West & Fell, pre-1938)

'Crenelet' 2 W-W
(Brian S. Duncan) Rathowen Daffodils, 1977
'Interim' × 'Aosta'; sdlg no. 31
Fl. 124 mm wide; perianth segments spreading; corona funnel-shaped, broad, opening yellow, with a paler tone at rim, becoming pinkish white, mouth straight, deeply lobed, with rim crenate. Mid-season

N. crenulatus Haworth = *N. tazetta* subsp. *lacticolor*

'Crenulatus'
Syn. of *N. tazetta* subsp. *lacticolor*

'Crenver' 3 W-GYR
(P.D. Williams, pre-1927)
Perianth segments very broad, pure white, more or less spreading, with margins sometimes wavy, sometimes incurling at apex, overlapping half; the inner segments square-shouldered at base, with margins more usually wavy; corona almost disc-shaped, broad, yellow, with green at base and orange-red at rim. AM(Haarlem) 1931, FCC(Haarlem) 1936

'Creole' 3 W-O
(The Brodie of Brodie, *c.*1909)
'Princess Mary' × 'Will Scarlett'
Perianth segments creamy white; corona deep reddish orange

'Creon' 8
(M. van Waveren & Sons, pre-1916)

'Crêpe de Chine' 1 W-? (b)
(J.L. Richardson) Mrs A.O. Meyrick, 1957

'Crepel' 1 Y-Y
(J.L. Martin) J.L. Martin, 1982
'Tarago' × 'Courtill'; sdlg no. T/C11
Fl. 100 mm wide; perianth segments brilliant greenish yellow 3B; corona vivid yellow 9B. Mid-season. Resembles 'Tarago' but with broader perianth segments

'Crepello' 3 W-GWY
(J.L. Richardson) J.L. Richardson, 1957

'Bryher' × 'Chinese White'
Fl. 87 mm wide; perianth segments white, slightly incurved, overlapping; corona white, with green at base, the rim opening light greenish yellow 8B touched brilliant yellow 8A and becoming paler (9D), mouth expanded, frilled, with rim crenate. 2n=28. *AM(g) 1967

'Cresalla' 2 Y-R
(D.S. Bell) D.S. Bell, 1968
('Crescendo' × 'Alamein') × 'Checkmate'
Perianth segments yellow; corona expanded, shaded red to base

'Crescendo' 9 W-?
(pre-1914)

'Crescendo' 2 Y-YYO
(J.C. Williams, pre-1945)
Fl. 89 mm wide; perianth segments brilliant greenish yellow 6B, overlapping half; corona ribbed, vivid yellow 15B, deepening to orange (28A) at rim, mouth straight, frilled, rim dentate. 2n=28. *AM(g) 1952

'Crescent' 2 Y-R
(P.D. Williams, pre-1938)

'Crescent Queen' 1 Y-Y
(Konynenburg & Mark, pre-1953)

'Cresset' 3 W-YYR
(G.H. Engleheart, pre-1902)
'Princess Mary' × *N. radiiflorus* var. *poetarum*
Corona shallow, widely expanded, golden yellow, with vivid scarlet at rim. AM 1902

'Cressida' 1 Y-Y
(W. Wilks, pre-1888)
'Troilus' hybrid
Fl. yellow; perianth segments broadly ovate, a little inflexed, with margins wavy, overlapping one-third to a half; corona very broad funnel-shaped, with mouth expanded and frilled, rim deeply notched. Resembles a larger-flowered 'Troilus'

'Cressy' 2 Y-R
(S.J. Bisdee) S.J. Bisdee, 1956
'Dunkeld' × 'King of Hearts'

'Crest'
(W.D. Burns, pre-1927)

'Cresta' 5 W-W
(Mrs R.O. Backhouse, pre-1921)
Fls more than one per stem; perianth segments ovate, blunt, fairly prominently mucronate, spreading, with midrib showing, overlapping one-third; corona long cup-shaped, mouth straight, more or less even, rim crenate

'Crested Crown' 2 Y-O
(pre-1950)
Perianth segments clear yellow; corona widely expanded, orange, frilled

'Creston' 1 Y-Y
(J.T. Gray, pre-1951)

'Crete' 2 Y-? (a)
(Mrs M. Moorby, pre-1942)

'Crete' 3 W-GYR
(J.L. Richardson, pre-1945)
'Seraglio' × 'Sunstar'
Fl. rounded; perianth segments very broad, somewhat raggedly truncate, prominently mucronate, snow white, spreading, overlapping half or more; the inner segments a little narrower, slightly inflexed and creased; corona bowl-shaped, ribbed, golden yellow, with rich green at base, shading to deep red at rim, mouth expanded, often deeply split and overlapping, frilled. Late

'Creusa' 1 W-Y
(Barr & Sons, pre-1913)
Perianth segments white; corona sulphur primrose, neatly frilled. Resembles 'J.B.M. Camm' in form

'Crevette' 8 W-O
(J.W. Blanchard, 1967) J.W. Blanchard, 1992
'Mahmoud' × *N. dubius*; sdlg no. 61/44A
Fls 2 or occasionally 3 per stem, forming a double triangle, 35 mm wide; perianth segments broadly ovate, blunt, not prominently mucronate, spreading, plane, with margins incurling, overlapping one-third; the inner segments with margins wavy; corona cup-shaped, loosely ribbed, opening pale orange, becoming paler, sometimes with yellow at base, mouth straight, even or a little wavy, with rim entire. Dwarf. Mid-season

'Crewenna' 1 W-Y
(Rosewarne EHS) Rosewarne EHS, 1985
'Rijnveld's Early Sensation' × 'Foresight'; sdlg no. 63/1/3
Perianth segments greenish white (155A); corona vivid yellow 9A, mouth deeply lobed, with 6 fairly regularly spaced white flecks. Very early

'C.R.Garlick' 1 W-Y
(H.T. Dettmann, pre-1952)

'Cricket' 2 Y-? (a)
(pre-1947)
Perianth segments yellow; corona flushed red

'Cricket' 5 Y-Y
(Roberta C.Watrous, 1957) Roberta C.Watrous, 1974
N. triandrus × *N. jonquilla*; sdlg no. TA-J 3

Fl. 31 mm wide, light greenish yellow 5D. Mid-season. Resembles a smaller and earlier-flowered 'April Tears'

'Crimea' 2 W-Y
(The Brodie of Brodie, pre-1930)
AM(Haarlem) 1930

'Crimpelene' 3 W-O
(P. Phillips) P. Phillips, 1968
Perianth segments rounded; corona widely expanded, ribbed, burnt orange

'Crimson Braid' 3 W-YYR
(F.H. Chapman, pre-1918)
N. poeticus var. *hellenicus* × 'Will Scarlett'
Perianth segments slightly reflexed; corona almost disc-shaped, large, yellow, with a broad band of crimson at rim. FCC(e) 1918, AM(e) 1918

'Crimson Chalice' 3 W-GRR
(Brian S. Duncan) Rathowen Daffodils, 1987
'Irish Splendour' × Bloomer sdlg ('Mahmoud' × ['Bravura' × 'Glenwherry']); sdlg no. 677
Perianth segments broadly ovate, somewhat truncate, slightly mucronate, spreading, a little concave, very smooth, overlapping half; the inner segments more narrowly ovate, with margins a little wavy; corona narrow bowl-shaped, ribbed, very deep red, with green prominent at base, mouth neatly frilled. Late to very late. Resembles 'Rockall' but with a deeper-coloured corona

'Crimson Comet' 3 W-? (b)
(G.H. Engleheart, pre-1913)

'Crimson Coronet' 2
(C.L. Adams, pre-1913)

'Crimson Emblem' 3 W-? (b)
(Mrs R.O. Backhouse, pre-1921)

'Crimson Eye' 3 W-? (b)
(Cartwright & Goodwin, pre-1908)

'Crimson King' 3 Y-? (a)
(Cartwright & Goodwin, pre-1908)

'Crimson Queen' 3 Y-? (a)
(The Brodie of Brodie, *c.*1908)
'Princess Mary' × 'Lady of the Lake'
Perianth segments pale yellow; corona with crimson at rim

'Crinkle' 2 W-? (b)
(pre-1937)

'Crinklecut' 4 Y-O
(M.E.Brogden, pre-1996) Unregistered
Sdlg no. 137/1

'Crinkled Ice' 1 W-W
(J.N. Hancock & Co., 1968) Unregistered

'Crinoline' 1 Y-Y
(Wrigley, pre-1913)

'Crinoline' 2 Y-? (a)
(?New Zealand origin) Parr's Nurseries, 1958

'Crinoline' 2 W-P
(J.N. Hancock & Co., 1956) Unregistered

'Crinoline' 2 W-W
(G.L. Wilson, pre-1962) Unregistered
Fl. white; perianth segments very broad; corona flared

'Criole' 8 Y-Y
(pre-1798)

'Crisis' 2 W-P
(Jackson's Daffodils, 1973) Jackson's Daffodils, 1986
'Solinus' × 'Verran'; sdlg no. 18/73
Early

'Crispa' 1 W-Y
(R.A. van der Schoot, pre-1923)
Perianth segments opening pale primrose yellow, becoming white, overlapping; corona ribbed, canary yellow, neatly frilled

N. crispicorona Spach = *N. tazetta* subsp. *lacticolor*

'Crispin' 8 Y-Y
(pre-1798)

'Crispin' 7 Y-GYO
(Roberta C.Watrous) Roberta C.Watrous, 1974
'Ruby' × *N. juncifolius*; sdlg no. 611-1
Fl. 40 mm wide; perianth segments pale greenish yellow 2D, or in some climates near to white; corona vivid yellow 12A, with green at base and strong orange 25A at rim. Late. Resembles a smaller 'Lintie' with proportionately longer perianth segments

'Crispin' 1 Y-Y
(W.M. Spry, pre-1975) Unregistered
'Golden Valley' self pollinated
Corona frilled. Early

'Criss Cross' 2 W-W
(David Adams) David Adams, 1996
Sdlg no. 86/108I
Fl. forming a double triangle, 100 mm wide, whitish; perianth segments very broadly ovate, plane; the inner segments more narrowly ovate; corona funnel-shaped, ribbed, with mouth straight and frilled, rim dentate. Mid-season to late

'Cristata' 2 W-? (b)
(M. van Waveren & Sons, pre-1907)

'Cristobal' 1 W-Y
(J.L. Richardson) Mrs H.K. Richardson, 1968
'My Love' open pollinated
Perianth segments broadly ovate; corona deep lemon yellow, with rim rolled and dentate. Mid-season. Resembles 'Newcastle'

'Criterion' 2 W-OOY
(de Graaff-Gerharda, pre-1930)
Perianth segments white; corona orange, with a band of dark yellow at rim. AM(Haarlem) 1930

'Critic' 2 Y-R
(G.W.E. Brogden) G.W.E. Brogden, 1963
Fl. 95 mm wide; perianth segments golden yellow; corona brick red. Mid-season

'Crito' 8 Y-Y
(pre-1798)
Fl. pale yellow

'Criton' 2 W-? (b)
(Mrs R.O. Backhouse, pre-1921)
Syn. 'Derwent'

'Croceo-cinctus' 9 W-?
(pre-1629)
Corona yellow, shaded with orange at rim. Syn. "The Dwarf Saffron Rimmed", Poeticus 'Croceo-cinctus'

'Crock of Gold' 1 Y-Y
(G.L. Wilson, pre-1948)
('Van Waveren's Giant' hybrid × 'Magnificence') × 'Hebron'
Fl. 115 mm wide; perianth segments brilliant yellow 12B, fairly smooth; corona deeper in tone, with rim notched and slightly flanged. AM(e) 1947

'Crocus' 2 Y-Y
(P.D. Williams, pre-1927)
Fl. 102 mm wide; perianth segments broadly or very broadly ovate, blunt, only very slightly mucronate, vivid yellow 9B, spreading or somewhat inflexed, concave or with margins incurling at apex, overlapping half; the inner segments more narrowly ovate, more definitely inflexed, with margins slightly wavy; corona cylindrical, smooth, very slightly brighter in tone (12A) than the perianth, with mouth ribbed and widely expanded, rim flanged, notched and crenate. 2n=28. AM(e) 1935, AM(Haarlem) 1936, FCC(e) 1936, *AM(g) 1947, FCC(Haarlem) 1948

'Croesus' 2 Y-YYO
(J.C. Williams, pre-1912)
Fl. 78 mm or more wide; perianth segments very broad, rounded, mucronate, light yellow 12C or paler, of firm texture, regular, overlapping half; the inner segments more nearly ovate, less noticeably mucronate, with margins sometimes incurling; corona shallow, deeply ribbed, orange (23A), paling

slightly towards base (17B), mouth widely expanded, split in places and overlapping, lightly frilled. 2n=21. FCC 1912, AM(Haarlem) 1914, AM(g) 1914, FA(Haarlem) 1933

'Croila' 2 W-GWW
(J.S.B. Lea) J.S.B. Lea, 1978
'Pitchroy' × ('Salmon Trout' × 'Rose Royal'); sdlg no. 1-25-68
Fl. 100 mm wide; perianth segments broad, slightly mucronate, plane; corona expanded, with rim flanged. Mid-season

'Crom-a-Boo' 1 Y-Y
Syn. of 'Croom Frilled'

'Cromarty' 1 Y-Y
(The Brodie of Brodie, c.1930)
'Hebron' × 'Alchemist'; sdlg no. 53/A/25
Fl. 100 mm wide; perianth segments brilliant yellow 13B, spreading, plane, smooth, overlapping half; corona slightly darker in tone (13A) than the perianth segments, with mouth expanded, rim flanged and serrate. Dwarf. Mid-season. 2n=28. AM(e) 1938, *AM(g) 1949

'Cromford' 2 Y-? (a)
(D.B. Milne, pre-1950)

'Cromla' 1 Y-Y
(W. Jackson Sr, 1944)
'Chromis' × 'Vuster'

'Cromwell' 1 Y-Y
(Barr & Sons, pre-1916)
Fl. yellow; perianth segments ovate, acute, inflexed, often twisted or reflexed at apex, uneven, overlapping at base only; corona narrowly funnel-shaped, ribbed, darker in tone than the perianth, rim flanged and deeply and somewhat irregularly notched

'Cronos' 2 W-YYO
(D.J. Cooper) D.J. Cooper, 1960
Fl. 108 mm wide; corona shallow, creamy yellow, with soft buff apricot orange at rim. Mid-season

'Cronulla' 2 W-YYP
(A.O. Roblin, 1945)
Maid of the Mist' × 'Luther'

'Cronulla' 1 Y-Y
(W.M. Spry, pre-1975) Unregistered
'Early Wonder' × 'Golden'
Tall

'Croom-a-Boo' 1 Y-Y
Syn. of 'Croom Frilled'

'Croom Frilled' 1 Y-Y
(pre-1886)

'Ard Righ' sport
Perianth segments ovate, greenish chrome yellow, inflexed, twisted or with margins wavy or incurled, overlapping; corona funnel-shaped, with six extra growths from base to rim on outer surface lobed like acanthus leaves, pure chrome yellow, mouth straight or with rim slightly rolled, rim deeply notched and crenate, Very early. Syn. "Frilled Trunk Daffodil", 'Crom-a-Boo', 'Croom-a-Boo'

'Crosol' 2 Y-Y
(T.H. Piper) T.H. Piper, 1956
'Solleret' × 'Crocus'

'Crossbow' 9 W-YYO
(G.H. Engleheart, pre-1913)
Perianth segments rounded, of strong substance; corona rim reddish orange. Tall

'Crossfell' 2 W-? (b)
(M. van Waveren & Sons, pre-1953)

'Cross Roads' 2 Y-W
(W.G. Pannill, 1979) W.G. Pannill, 1996
'Camelot' × 'Daydream'; sdlg no. H 22 A
Mid-season

'Crowle' 2 Y-YYO
(J.S.B. Lea, 1983) Clive Postles Daffodils, 1996
Sdlg 1-24-71 × sdlg 1-9-71; sdlg no. 3-3-78
Fl. rounded, 85 mm wide; perianth segments broadly ovate; corona funnel-shaped, with rim dentate. Early

'Crowndale' 4 Y-O
(Clive Postles) Clive Postles Daffodils, 1995
'Loch Lundie' × 'Flying Colours'; sdlg no. 4-16-82
Fl. 94 mm wide; perianth and other petaloid segments in three whorls, clear medium yellow; the outer whorls broadly ovate, spreading; the centre whorl smaller, less formally arranged; corona segments interspersed, bright orange. Early. Sunproof

'Crown Derby' 3 W-YYO
(The Brodie of Brodie, c.1935)
'White Sentinel' × 'Sunstar'; sdlg no. 57/B/30
Fl. large; perianth segments pure white, deeply overlapping; corona clear yellow with scarlet-orange at rim

'Crowned Beauty' 3 Y-O
(de Graaff Bros, pre-1930)
Perianth lemon yellow; corona deep orange, frilled. AM(Haarlem) 1930

'Crown Gold' 2 W-O
(R. & E. Havens, 1982) R. & E. Havens, 1994
'Gold Crown' × 'Paricutin; sdlg no. REH25/1
Fl. 105 mm wide; perianth segments broadly ovate, white, touched yellow at base, spreading, plane;

corona cylindrical, bright orange, with mouth slightly flared. Mid-season. Sunproof

'Crown Imperial' 2 Y-O
(C.G. van Tubergen, pre-1947)
Perianth segments yellow; corona deep orange

'Crowning Glory' 1 Y-Y
(G. Zandbergen-Terwegen, pre-1936)

'Crown Jewel'
(W. Backhouse, pre-1869)

'Crown Jewel' 9 W-?
(G.H. Engleheart, pre-1914)

'Crown Jewel' 2 W-O
(J.J. Grullemans & Sons, c.1966) Unregistered

'Crown of Victory' 2 Y-? (a)
(G. Zandbergen-Terwegen, pre-1937)

'Crown Point' 2 W-P
(Murray W. Evans, 1972) William F. Tribe, 1989
'Caro Nome' × 'Gypsy Princess'; sdlg no. P-10
Fl. 120 mm wide; perianth segments broad, pure white; the inner segments reflexed; corona expanded, pale pink, paling with age at base, lightly frilled. Mid-season

'Crown Prince' 3 W-YYO
(W. Backhouse, pre-1869)
Perianth segments ovate, blunt or more usually acute, prominently mucronate, creamy white, spreading, with margins wavy or incurling, overlapping at base only or up to one-third; the inner segments more narrowly ovate, not noticeably mucronate; corona cup-shaped, ribbed, canary yellow, with golden orange at rim, neatly frilled. Syn. Burbidgei 'Crown Prince'

'Crown Princess' 3 W-YYO
(W. Backhouse, pre-1869)
Perianth segments white; corona canary yellow, with orange at rim. Syn. Burbidgei 'Crown Princess'

'Crown Royalist' 2 W-YYO
(Ballydorn Bulb Farm) Ballydorn Bulb Farm, 1976
'Nemo' × 'Lysander'
Fl. 98 mm wide; corona pale cream, with a broad band of gold at rim. Mid-season

'Crown Star' 2 Y-R
(A.W. Chappell) A.W. Chappell, 1992
'Rabid' × 'Cresalla'; sdlg no. C-2-1
Fl. 90 mm wide; perianth segments very broadly ovate; corona funnel-shaped, ribbed. Mid-season

'Croxley' 2 W-W
(R.C.A. Tombleson) R.C.A. Tombleson, 1971
'Namsos' hybrid

Fl. 100 mm wide

'Croydon' 2 W-? (b)
(Warnaar & Co., pre-1929)

'Crozier' 1 Y-Y
(S.J. Bisdee, 1946)
'Crocus' × 'Robert Montgomery'

'Cruacau' 2 W-R
(R. Hyde) R. Hyde, 1959

'Crucial Point' 1 W-O
(J.M. Radcliff) J.M. Radcliff, 1987
Sdlg 27/76 × sdlg 26/75; sdlg no. 53/83
Perianth segments very broadly ovate, blunt, slightly mucronate, plane, smooth, with broad midrib showing, regular, overlapping half; the inner segments shouldered at base; corona long, straight-sided, bright orange, with a lighter tone at base and rim, mouth straight, rim notched. Late

'Crucible' 3 W-? (b)
(Barr & Sons, pre-1928)
Perianth segments pure white; corona flushed and rimmed deep red

'Cruiser' 2 Y-? (a)
(Mrs R.O. Backhouse, pre-1921)

'Crumlin' 1 Y-Y
(W.J. Dunlop) W.J. Dunlop, 1958
'Cromarty' × 'Principal'
Fl. clear yellow

'Crusader' 2 W-R
(P.J. Worsley, pre-1907)
'Princess Mary' × *N. radiiflorus* var. *poetarum*
Perianth segments white; corona deep red

'Crusader' 3 Y-?Y
(pre-1934)

'Crusader' 2 W-? (b)
(West & Fell, pre-1936)

'Crusader' 2 W-O
(Warnaar & Co.) Warnaar & Co., 1958
Perianth segments ivory white; corona frilled. AM(Haarlem) 1958

'Crusader' 2 W-WWR
(G. Lewis, pre-1960) Unregistered
Perianth segments pure white; corona opening buffy apricot yellow, becoming pure white, with brilliant red at rim, frilled

'Crushed Strawberry' 2 W-? (b)
(Mrs F.S. Foote, pre-1940)

'Crusoe' 9 W-YYR
(E.M. Crosfield, pre-1921)
Fl. facing slightly downwards; perianth segments overlapping; corona shallow, buffy sulphur yellow, with scarlet at rim, mouth widely expanded. Mid-season. *HC(g) 1936

'Crusta' 1 W-W
(W. Jackson Jr) Jackson's Daffodils, 1980
'Saroya' × 'Mercedes'; sdlg no. 54/73
Fl. 110 mm wide. Mid-season

'Cryptic' 1 W-P
(W. Jackson Jr) Jackson's Daffodils, 1983
'Salome' × 'Verran'; sdlg no. 268/76
Fl. 99 mm wide; corona pastel pink, with rim rolled. Mid-season. Varies between Divs 1 and 2

'Crys Martin' 2 W-YYP
(J.L. Martin) J.L. Martin, 1973
'Pink o' Dawn' × 'Pink Bonnet'
Fl. 95 mm wide

'Crystal' 3 W-?Y
(The Brodie of Brodie, pre-1928)
'Tenedos' × 'Fortune'

'Crystal Blanc' 2 W-GWW
(W.G. Pannill) W.G. Pannill, 1980
'Easter Moon' × 'Pristine'; sdlg no. 66/60 L
Fl. 91 mm wide. Mid-season

'Crystal Bowl' 1 W-W
(J.R. Byfield, pre-1936)

'Crystal Cameo' 2 W-WWP
(J.N.Hancock & Co., 1980) Unregistered
Corona expanded, white, with a well-defined band of pink at rim. Late

'Crystal Chalice' 2 W-WWY
(Sidney DuBose, 1975) Sidney DuBose, 1990
'Pretender' × 'Salmon Trout'; sdlg no. A28-20
Fl. 102 mm wide. Mid-season

'Crystal Chimes' 1 W-? (b)
(New Zealand origin, pre-1939)

'Crystal Clear' 3 W-GWW
(W.G. Pannill) W.G. Pannill, 1978
'Benediction' × 'Tobernaveen'; sdlg no. 64/13
Fl. 100 mm wide. Late

'Crystal Cup' 2 W-? (b or c)
(Sir A.P.W. Thomas, pre-1930)

'Crystal Hour' 2 or 3 W-? (b or c)
(Cartwright & Goodwin, pre-1910)

'Crystal Lake' 2 W-W
(C. Goodson, 1935) Parr's Nurseries, 1958

'Crystal Langham' 4 W-Y
(G.L. Wilson) Mrs D.G. Moore, 1967
Fl. 102 mm wide; perianth and other petaloid segments creamy white; corona segments smaller than the petaloid segments and interspersed among the outer whorls, pale lemon yellow. Mid-season. Resembles 'Double Event' but with the corona segments more regularly distributed

'Crystalline' 2 W-W
(Mrs R.O. Backhouse, pre-1914)
Fl. pure white; perianth segments a little reflexed; corona long, narrow, lightly ribbed, with mouth deeply frilled. Somewhat resembles 'The Fawn'

'Crystal Pink' 2 W-P
(G.E. Mitsch and R. & E.Havens, 1970) G.E. Mitsch and R. & E.Havens, 1986
'Accent' × 'Debutante'; sdlg no. F3/7
Perianth segments glistening white; corona soft clear pink. Late

'Crystal Queen' 2 W-W
(R.H. Bath, pre-1913)
Fl. forming a double triangle, 89 mm wide, pure white, of great substance; perianth segments broadly ovate, blunt, not noticeably mucronate, somewhat inflexed, plane, overlapping one-third to a half; the inner segments narrower, slightly inflexed at base and recurved in upper part; corona funnel-shaped, widely expanded, opening pale yellow, lightly frilled, with rim crenate. Tall. Resembles 'White Queen' but with a longer corona

'Crystal River' 3 W-W
(G.E. Mitsch, 1957) G.E. Mitsch, 1967
'Green Island' × 'Chinese White'; sdlg no. R33/14
Fl. 102 mm wide; perianth segments rounded; corona almost disc-shaped, opening with a touch of colour at rim, soon becoming self white, tightly frilled. Mid-season. Resembles 'Dream Castle' but with the corona shallower, more widely expanded and more heavily frilled

'Crystal Springs' 2 YYW-GWW
(G.E. Mitsch and R. & E.Havens, 1975) G.E. Mitsch and R. & E.Havens, 1987
'Quick Step' open pollinated; sdlg no. K04
Perianth segments lemon yellow, with white at base, smooth; corona white, with green at base. Late

'Crystal Star' 2 Y-Y
(G.E. Mitsch, 1978) R. & E. Havens, 1990
'Camelot' × 'Aurum'; sdlg no. 2015/20
Fl. forming a double triangle, clear yellow; perianth segments broadly ovate, blunt, slightly mucronate, spreading, plane, smooth and of heavy substance, overlapping half; the inner segments narrower, a

little inflexed, with margins sometimes wavy or incurved; corona cylindrical, smooth, with mouth flared, rim irregularly and shallowly crenate. Mid-season

'C.S.Titheradge' 2 Y-? (a)
(West & Fell, pre-1934)

'Cuan' 1 W-W
(W. Jackson Jr, 1955) Unregistered
'Pax' × 'Merri'

'Cuan Gold' 1 Y-Y
(Ballydorn Bulb Farm, 1982) Ballydorn Bulb Farm, 1993
'Golden Aura' × 'Arctic Gold'
Fl. 100 mm wide, deep golden yellow; perianth segments broadly ovate, with margins very slightly wavy; corona with straight sides widely diverging. Mid-season

N. cuatrecasasii Fernández Casas, Lainz & Ruiz Rejón 13 Section Apodanthi. PC(s) 1968, AM 1969, PC 1989, AM(a)(r) 1991. Received PC 1968 and AM 1969 as *N. rupicola* subsp. *pedunculatus*
    var. *cuatrecasasii*
    var. *segimonensis* Fernández Casas

'Cuba' 2 Y-O
(J.L. Richardson) Mrs H.K. Richardson, 1962
'Narvik' × 'Sun Chariot'
Perianth segments deep golden yellow; corona expanded, bowl-shaped, reddish orange. Mid-season

'Cuckmere' 1 W-W
(N.A.Burr, 1985) N.A.Burr, 1996
'Panache' × 'White Star'; sdlg no. 2.19.80
Fl. 110 mm wide; perianth segments very broadly ovate, only very slightly mucronate, tinged green at base, inflexed, overlapping half or more; the inner segments more narrowly ovate; corona cylindrical, smooth, with green in tube, mouth expanded and wavy, rim slightly notched in places. Mid-season to late

'Cuckoo' 3 W-Y
(Mrs R.O. Backhouse, pre-1907)
Perianth segments white; corona bright yellow

'Cuckoo' 2
(G.E.Mitsch) Unregistered
'Wild Rose' × 'Hillbilly'
Varies between Divs 2 and 11

'Cuddles' 2 W-P
(J.N. Hancock & Co., c.1980) Unregistered

'Cue Ball' 2 W-W
(P.Cleine, 1981) Unregistered
Fl. ivory white; perianth segments broadly ovate, deeply overlapping; corona cylindrical, with mouth a little expanded. Early

'Cuesta' 2 W-GYP
(Brian S. Duncan) Brian S. Duncan, 1992
('Lilac Charm' × ['Interim' × 'Aosta']) × 'Valinor'; sdlg no. 1097
Fl. 92 mm wide; perianth segments broadly ovate, spreading, plane; corona funnel-shaped, with mouth flared and rim crenate. Late to very late. Sunproof

'Cuirass' 1 W-? (b)
(G.H. Engleheart, pre-1914)

'Culbann' 2 W-? (b or c)
(G.L. Wilson, pre-1937)

'Cul Beag' 3 W-R
(J.S.B. Lea) J.S.B. Lea, 1971
Navarro sdlg 2(b) × sdlg 1-1-55; sdlg no. 3-41-62
Fl. rounded, 108 mm wide; perianth segments broad, pure white; corona orange-red (30B). Mid-season

'Culbin' 1 Y-Y
(Brodie Gardens) Brodie Gardens, 1957
Hybrid between 'Golden Torch' and 'Hebron'
Fl. very large; perianth segments clear yellow, spreading, plane, smooth; corona funnel-shaped, deep golden yellow, with mouth expanded

'Culfind' 2 Y-YOO
(J.A.Hunter) J.A.Hunter, 1995
'Excalibur' × 'Kasia'; sdlg no. 36/84A
Fl. forming a double triangle, 110 mm wide; perianth segments ovate, vivid yellow 9B; corona funnel-shaped, vivid orange 28B, with yellow at base, frilled. Mid-season

'Cullen' 2 W-Y
(Mrs R.S. Cobley, 1948) Seymour Cobley Ltd, 1968
Perianth segments white; corona lemon yellow. Late

'Cullercoats' 3 W-O
(G. Harrison) G. Harrison, 1968
'Arbar' × 'Signal Light'
Fl. 115 mm wide. Mid-season. Resembles 'Arbar'

'Culliamurra' 1 Y-Y
(J.N. Hancock & Co., pre-1949) J.N. Hancock & Co., 1960
'Trawalla' × 'Mortlake'
Early

'Cullinan' 2 Y-? (a)
(de Graaff Bros, pre-1931)
Fl. large; corona flared and frilled. AM(Haarlem) 1930

'Culloden' 2 Y-? (a)
(Barr & Sons, pre-1932)

'Cullybacky' 1 Y-Y
(Mrs M.Moorby) Mrs M.Moorby, 1956

'Culmination' 2 W-P
(G.E. Mitsch) G.E. Mitsch, 1982
'Romance' × 'Cool Flame'; sdlg no. LL14/1
Fl. 115 mm wide; perianth segments ivory white; corona salmon rose. Mid-season. 2n=28. Resembles a taller 'Romance' of deeper colour with fewer blemishes

'Culmore' 2 W-W
(G.L. Wilson, pre-1944)
'Nelly' × ('Eskimo' × 'Tenedos')
Perianth segments white; corona opening pale primrose, becoming cream

'Culrathain' 2 Y-? (a)
(The Brodie of Brodie, pre-1932)
Probably 'Seraglio' × 'Fortune'

'Cultured Pearl' 2 W-W
(Clive Postles) Clive Postles Daffodils, 1989
'Pitchroy' × 'Misty Glen'; sdlg no. 1-30-76
Fl. 94 mm wide; perianth segments ovate, deeply overlapping; corona straight-sided, opening cream, becoming pure white. Tall. Very late

'Culverin' 3 W-? (b)
(F.H. Chapman, pre-1923)

'Cumberland' 1 W-W
(Brian S. Duncan) J.R. Reed, 1985
'Knowehead' × 'White Star'; sdlg no. D.511
Perianth segments greenish white (157C); corona deeper in tone (157B), frilled. Mid-season. Resembles an improved and taller 'Rashee'

'Cum Laude' 11a W-P
(J. Gerritsen & Son) J. Gerritsen & Son, 1984
Sdlg × 'Easter Bonnet'
Perianth segments ivory white; corona segments pale orange-pink (24C to 19C). Early

'Cumulus' 1 W-W
(G.H. Engleheart, pre-1923)
Fl. 95 mm wide, creamy white; perianth somewhat incurving, regular, overlapping half; corona with mouth slightly expanded, frilled. Mid-season to late

'Cumulus' 2 W-W
(D. Bramley) D. Bramley, 1973
Sdlg × 'Lucille'
Fl. 105 mm wide

N. cuneiflorus Link = *N. pseudonarcissus*

N. cuneiflorus Willkomm & Lange = *N. pumilus*

N. cupanianus Gussone = *N. elegans*

'Cupid' 2 Y-Y
(E. Leeds, pre-1877)
Perianth segments long, narrow, acute, primrose yellow. Syn. Incomparabilis Albidus 'Cupid', Incomparabilis Albidus 'Stellatus'. Was "absorbed" into 'Gil Blas'

'Cupid' 2 W-Y
(M. Leichtlin, pre-1884)
Perianth segments sulphur white; corona flushed apricot yellow. Late. Sweetly scented. Syn. Backhousei 'Cupid'

'Cupid' 2 or 3 W-? (b or c)
(W.T. Ware, pre-1914)

'Cupid' 12 Y-Y
(D.J. Cooper) D.J. Cooper, 1959
N. cyclamineus × *N. jonquilla*
Fls 2-5 per stem, golden yellow; perianth segments narrowly ovate or oblong, blunt, strongly reflexed, separated or very slightly overlapping; corona cylindrical, ribbed, with mouth straight and even. Dwarf. Early. Scented

'Cupida' 3 Y-? (a)
(W.B. Hartland, pre-1907)

'Cupido' 1 Y-Y
(M. van Waveren & Sons, pre-1949)

'Cupido' 2 Y-?
Syn. of 'Agapenor'

'Cupid's Blush' 1 W-? (b)
(S.J. Bisdee, 1942) S.J. Bisdee, 1956
'Eskimo' × 'Dawnglow'

'Cupid's Eye' 3 Y-GYP
(Brian S. Duncan) Rathowen Daffodils, 1987
Varies between Divs 3 and 2, with perianth opening white

'Cup o' Cheer' 7
(P.D. Wilson, pre-1931)

'Cuprona' 2 W-O
(C.E. Radcliff, 1934)
'Croesus' × 'Blodwen'

N. cupularis (Salisbury) Schultes 13 Section Tazettae

'Curaçao' 3? Y-? (a)
(F.H. Chapman, pre-1915)
'Princess Mary' × 'Acme'
Perianth segments pale yellow; corona large, shallow, with rim rolled and crenate

'Curacoa' 2 Y-? (a)
(A.M. Wilson, pre-1938)

'Curana' 2 W-W
(C.E. Radcliff, 1947)

'Curds and Whey' 4
(W.F.M. Copeland, pre-1914)

'Curena' 2 or 3 W-W
(C.E. Radcliff, pre-1947)
'Courage' × 'Swanlea Peerless'

'Curfew' 2 W-Y
(A.M. Wilson, pre-1915)
Perianth segments broad; the inner segments narrower and acute; corona flared, pale lemon yellow

'Curfew' 9 W-GYO
(G.H. Engleheart, pre-1916)
Fl. rounded, 89 mm wide; perianth segments snowy white, smooth, overlapping; corona large, almost disc-shaped, saffron yellow, with green at base and a broad band of orange at rim

'Curie'
(pre-1913)

'Curio' 3 W-? (b)
(F.H. Chapman, pre-1914)

'Curium' 3 W-? (b)
(G. Lubbe & Son, pre-1943)

'Curlew' 2 W-Y
(Mrs R.O. Backhouse, pre-1907)
Fl. 83 mm wide; perianth segments creamy white, irregular, overlapping half; corona funnel-shaped, bright lemon

'Curlew'
(G.H. Engleheart, pre-1908)

'Curlew' 7 W-W
(G.E. Mitsch) G.E. Mitsch, 1972
'Killaloe' × *N. jonquilla*; sdlg no. V22/1
Fls 1-3 per stem, 75 mm wide; corona long, ivory white. Mid-season

'Curlew' 1 Y-Y
(Heathcote Bulb Nursery, pre-1961) Unregistered
Perianth segments broad, rich yellow, smooth; corona long, slender, with rim rolled. Late

'Curley' 1 W-P
(C.O. Fairbairn)

'Curly' 2 Y-Y
(J.W.A. Lefeber) A.C. van der Schoot Jr, 1968
Fl. rounded, 85 mm wide; perianth segments very broad, rounded at apex, pale yellow, overlapping half or more; corona bowl-shaped, brighter than vivid yellow 14B, very heavily and closely frilled and appearing to be double. 2n=28

'Curlylocks' 7 Y-Y
(Roberta C.Watrous) Roberta C.Watrous, 1964
'Seville' × *N. assoanus*
Perianth segments pale yellow; corona bright yellow. Mid-season. Resembles 'Bobbysoxer'

'Curly Top' 4
(pre-1940)

'Curraghmore' 2
(?J.L. Richardson, pre-1939)

'Currawong' 1 W-Y
(T. Morrison, pre-1961) Unregistered
Perianth segments pure white; corona primrose yellow, with rim flanged

'Currie' 2 Y-? (a)
(C.E. Radcliff, 1931)
'Pink'un' × 'Harpagon'

'Curtain' 2 W-? (b)
(Mrs R.O. Backhouse, pre-1921)

N. curtisii Spach = *N.* × *odorus*

'Curtisii'
Syn. of *N.* × *odorus*

'Curvaceous' 10 Y-Y
(James S. Wells) James S. Wells, 1993
'Julia Jane' × 'February Gold'; sdlg no. 82-52-4
Fl. 35 mm wide, pale yellow; perianth segments lanceolate; corona more than half as long as the perianth segments, widely expanded, lightly ribbed, with rim rolled and irregularly dentate. Early

N. curvilobus Salisbury = *N. poeticus* var. *recurvus*

'Curwood' 1 Y-Y
(Sir C.H. Cave, pre-1941)

'Cushendall' 3 W-GWW
(G.L. Wilson, pre-1931)
'Emerald Eye' × 'Dactyl'
Perianth segments pure white, overlapping; corona almost disc-shaped, ribbed, pale creamy white, with rich dark green at base, frilled. Late. 2n=14. AM(e) 1936, AM(Haarlem) 1949

'Cushendun' 3 W-Y
(Ballydorn Bulb Farm, 1968) Ballydorn Bulb Farm, 1980
'Cushendall' open pollinated
Fl. 50 mm wide. Mid-season. 2n=14

'Cushie' 2 W-P
(J.N.Hancock & Co., 1982) Unregistered

Corona funnel-shaped, with rim dentate. Early

'Cushie Butterfield' 1 W-W
(G.L. Wilson) M.J. Jefferson-Brown, 1975
Fl. white. Mid-season

'Cushlake' 3 W-W
(G.L. Wilson, pre-1934)
'Mystic' × 'Fairy Circle'
Fl. white; corona opening pale pink orange at rim, soon becoming self white. 2n=14

'Custis' 2 W-Y
(W. Jackson Jr) W. Jackson Jr, 1966
'Sari' × 'Capella'; sdlg no. 99/58

'Customer' 1 Y-Y
(?J.N. Hancock & Co., pre-1949)

'Cutie' 2 W-YYO
(M.Boyd) Unregistered
Sdlg no. 5/70/27
Mid-season

'Cutie Pie' 2 W-P
(J.N.Hancock & Co., 1975) Unregistered
Sdlg 2 W-P × 'My Word'; sdlg no. 26/75H
Perianth segments pure white; corona pink, neatly frilled

'Cutty Sark' 7 Y-Y
(R.V. Favell, pre-1939)
Fl. lemon yellow; perianth segments pale sulphur yellow, becoming creamy sulphur, spreading, ribbed, often creased at midrib, overlapping; corona sulphur yellow. Scented

'C.W.Cowan' 1 W-Y
(E. Leeds, pre-1877)
Perianth segments white; corona sulphur. Probably the same as 'Mr Cowan'

'Cwm' 2 Y-? (a)
(A.M. Wilson, pre-1933)

'C.Wolley-Dod' 2 Y-Y
Syn. of 'Charles Wolley-Dod'

'Cyane' 1 W-Y
(Barr & Sons, pre-1921)
Perianth segments white, smooth, overlapping; corona soft primrose yellow

'Cybele' 3 W-Y
(E. Leeds, pre-1877)
Perianth segments white, incurving; corona opening soft orange, becoming primrose yellow. Syn. Leedsii 'Cybele'

'Cybele' 2 W-Y
(Barr & Sons, pre-1922)
Perianth segments creamy white; corona long, straight, delicate primrose yellow

'Cybelle' 2 W-YYO
(W. Jackson Jr, c.1974) Unregistered
Sdlg 59/60 × 'Arbar'
Perianth segments broad, smooth and of good substance, deeply overlapping; corona large, bowl-shaped, rich yellow, tinged orange in a narrow band at rim, mouth expanded, rim dentate

'Cyclades' 6 Y-Y
(D. Blanchard, pre-1948)
'Goldbeater' × *N. cyclamineus*
Fl. bright yellow; perianth segments narrowly ovate, blunt, slightly mucronate, reflexed, with margins inward folding or twisted, overlapping a quarter; corona cylindrical, smooth, with rim deeply and irregularly notched, loosely and widely flanged. AM(Haarlem) 1960

'Cyclahyd' 1 Y-Y
(?P.D. Williams, pre-1913)

'Cyclak' 6 Y-Y
(S. Morrison) T. Morrison, 1960
Fl. rich yellow; corona cylindrical, long

N. cyclamineus de Candolle 13 Section Pseudonarcissus. FCC 1887, AGM 1993

'Cyclataz' 8 Y-O
(A.W. Tait, pre-1922)
Hybrid between *N. cyclamineus* and 'Soleil d'Or'
Fls 2-3 per stem; perianth segments ovate, blunt, deep yellow, spreading or reflexed, with margins incurling, overlapping at base only; corona cylindrical or somewhat funnel-shaped, ribbed, bright orange, mouth straight, wavy, rim entire. Dwarf. 2n=17

'Cyclax' 1 W-W
(J.A. Morris) J.A. Morris, 1955

'Cycle' 9 W-?
(G.H. Engleheart, pre-1907)

'Cyclone' 6 Y-Y
(D. & J.W. Blanchard) D. & J.W. Blanchard, 1960
Fl. 102 mm wide, rich yellow. Early. 2n=28. Resembles a taller 'Cyclades' with the perianth segments larger and less sharply reflexed and the corona more widely flared

'Cyclope' 1 Y-Y
(P.L.A. Pouw) P.L.A. Pouw, 1974
'Rembrandt' × 'Golden Sunbeam'
Fl. 125 mm wide. 2n=28

'Cyclops' 3 W-Y
(G.H. Engleheart, pre-1904)
Perianth segments overlapping; corona large disc-shaped, bright yellow. Resembles 'Egret'

'Cydonia' 2 W-YYO
(Mrs R.O. Backhouse, pre-1921)

'Cygnet' 1 W-Y
(G.P. Haydon, pre-1902)
'Monarch' × 'Madame de Graaff'
Perianth segments spreading, twisted, overlapping at base only; corona soft canary yellow, with rim rolled. AM 1902

'Cygnus' 1 W-W
(A. White, pre-1946)

'Cyleen' 1 W-W
(pre-1913)

'Cylgad' 9 W-YYR
(C. Dawson, pre-1924)
Perianth segments white, overlapping; corona creamy yellow, with a narrow band of crimson at rim

'Cymbal' 3 W-? (b)
(R.H. Bath, pre-1929)

'Cymbeline' 1 W-W
(G.H. Engleheart, pre-1907)

'Cymbeline' 2 W-P
(J.L. Richardson) J.L. Richardson, 1958
'Wild Rose' × 'Rose Caprice'

'Cymric Queen' 2 W-? (b)
(de Graaff Bros, pre-1929)
AM(Haarlem) 1929

'Cymry' 1 Y-Y
(T. Batson, pre-1907)
AM(g) 1916

'Cynan' 2 W-? (b)
(pre-1913)

'Cynara' 3 W-YYR
(G.W.E. Brogden) G.W.E. Brogden, 1966
Perianth segments white; corona green-yellow, with orange-red at rim. Late. Resembles a smaller and later-flowered 'Tongahoe' with whiter perianth

'Cynisia' 1 W-Y
(pre-1914)

'Cynosure' 2 W-YYO
(E. Leeds, pre-1877)
Fl. large; perianth segments opening primrose yellow, becoming white; corona large, deep greenish yellow, stained scarlet-orange at rim. Syn. Incomparabilis Albidus 'Cynosure', Incomparabilis Albidus 'Leedsii'. "Absorbed" 'H.C.Smith'

'Cynthia' 3 W-? (b)
(Sir C.H. Cave, pre-1908)

'Cynthia' 1 W-W
(P. Phillips) P. Phillips, 1968

'Cynthia Dettman' 2 W-YYR
(L.P. Dettman) L.P. Dettman, 1968
'Jean Hood' × 'Nevose'

'Cypher' 6 Y-Y
(G. Temple-Smith) G. Temple-Smith, 1993
N. fernandesii × *N. cyclamineus*; sdlg no. M2/90
Fl. vivid yellow 9A; perianth segments reflexed, overlapping; corona cylindrical. Early

'Cypher' 2
(J.A.O'More, pre-1996) Unregistered

N. cypri Sweet 13 Section Tazettae. 2n=30

'Cyprian' 5
(pre-1907)

'Cyprian' 1 Y-Y
(P.D. Williams, pre-1927)

'Cypri Plena' 4 W-Y
Syn. of 'Chalcedonicus Flore Pleno Albo Polyanthos'

'Cypri Semiplena' 4 W-Y
Syn. of 'Medio-luteus Corona Duplici'

'Cyprius Flore Pleno Luteo Polyanthos' 4 Y-Y
(pre-1604)
Fls 4-5 per stem, pale yellow. Syn. "The Double Yellow Daffodil of Cyprus", Tazetta 'Cyprius Flore Pleno Luteo Polyanthos', Tazetta 'Deflexicaulis Plenus'

'Cyprus' 2 W-? (b or c)
(G.H. Engleheart, pre-1936)

'Cyrano' 1 Y-Y
(M. van Waveren & Sons, pre-1938)

'Cyrene' 2 Y-? (a)
(Barr & Sons, pre-1914)

'Cyrene' 1 W-Y
(D.V. West, pre-1932)
Perianth segments creamy white; corona citron yellow

'Cyrette' 2 W-WWP
(J.N. Hancock & Co.) J.N. Hancock & Co., 1960

Perianth segments white; corona cream, flushed inside and at rim with pink

'Cyrilla' 2 Y-? (a)
(C. Dawson, pre-1938)

'Cyrille'
(New Zealand origin, pre-1940)

'Cyril Price' 3 W-? (b)
(G.H. Engleheart, pre-1916)

'Cyros' 1 W-Y
(W. Jackson Jr, 1966) Unregistered
'Lod' × 'Rowella'; sdlg no. 217/66
Varies between Divs 1 and 2

'Cyrus' 8 Y-Y
(pre-1792)
Fl. sulphur yellow

'Cyrus' 1 W-? (b)
(Barr & Sons, pre-1923)

'Cyrus' 1 Y-Y
(P. Phillips) P. Phillips, 1968

'Cythereia'
(C. Dawson, pre-1908)

'Czar Alexander' 8 Y-O
(pre-1861)
Perianth primrose yellow

'Czar de Moscovie' 8 W-Y
Syn. of 'Czar of Muscovy'

'Czarina' 8 W-Y
(pre-1759)

'Czarina' 2 W-Y
(Mrs R.O. Backhouse, pre-1908)
'Sir Watkin' × 'Perfection'
Fl. facing somewhat downwards; perianth segments ovate, milk white, slightly inflexed, ribbed, with margins recurved and sometimes notched; corona broad, ribbed, soft primrose yellow, mouth widely expanded and lightly frilled. Tall

'Czar Monarque' 8 W-Y
Syn. of 'Grand Monarque'

'Czar of Muscovy' 8 W-Y
(pre-1759)
Perianth segments white; corona citron yellow. Early. See also 'Cezar de Muscow', 'Czar de Moscovie', 'Le Czar de Moscovie'

'Czarwitz' 1 W-W
(W. Welchman, pre-1908)

D

'Daali' 3 W-GWW
(A.M. Wilson, pre-1938)
'Nelly' × 'Folly'
Perianth segments white, overlapping; corona white, faintly tinged yellow, with green at base

'Dab-chick' 3 W-? (b)
(Sir C.H. Cave, pre-1908)

'Dabster' 1 W-Y
(Jackson's Daffodils) Jackson's Daffodils, 1986
'Lod' × sdlg 73/69; sdlg no. 36/78
Early to mid-season

'Dace' 2 W-GOO
(Jānis Rukšans) Jānis Rukšans, 1987
'Verona' × 'Kilworth'; sdlg no. R-79-14/6
Perianth segments milky white; corona funnel-shaped, opening orange with yellow at rim, becoming orange with yellow at base, maturing to light orange (22A) with yellow-green at base and strong orange 25A at rim. Mid-season. Sunproof

'Da Costa' 4
(Dutch origin, pre-1936)
'Laurens Koster' sport

'Dactyl' 9 W-GYR
(G.H. Engleheart, pre-1923)
? 'Glory of Lisse' hybrid
Perianth segments broad, squarish at apex and slightly truncate, prominently mucronate, snow white, spreading, plane, of thick substance, overlapping half; the inner segments narrower, ovate, not noticeably mucronate, a little inflexed, the margins wavy and sometimes nicked near the apex; corona disc-shaped, tightly ribbed, citron yellow, with green at base and a sharply defined band of deep red at rim, the rim minutely notched and crenate. Tall. Late. 2n=14. AM(Haarlem) 1929, AM(e)(c) 1931

'D'Admirable' 8 Y-O
(pre-1798)

'Dafila' 2 Y-? (a)
(F.H. Chapman, pre-1928)

'Dageraad' 8 Y-Y
(pre-1851)

'Dagmar' 3 Y-? (a)
(A.M. Wilson, pre-1908)

'Dagnia' 2 W-YWY
(Jānis Rukšans) Jānis Rukšans, 1987
'Knowehead' × 'Green Island'; sdlg no. R-79-12/6
Perianth segments milky white; corona cup-shaped,

mid-zone opening pale yellow 8D, becoming almost white, with brilliant greenish yellow 6A at base and vivid yellow 9A at rim. Mid-season

'Dagonet' 3 W-GYY
(A.M. Wilson, pre-1914)
Perianth segments white; corona shallow, buff yellow, shading to green at base

'Dagrena' 1 Y-Y
(J.N. Hancock & Co., pre-1956) Unregistered

'Dahlonega' 1 Y-Y
(V. Brink) V. Brink, 1969
'Late Sun' × 'Backhouse's Giant'

'Dahomey' 2 W-? (b)
(Mrs R.O. Backhouse, pre-1921)

'Dailmanach' 2 W-P
(J.S.B. Lea) J.S.B. Lea, 1972
'Inverpolly' × Navarro sdlg 797 (['Interim' × 'Salmon Trout'] × 'Rosedew')
Fl. 115 mm wide; perianth segments very broadly ovate in outline, blunt or rounded at apex, very slightly mucronate, spreading, smooth, plane, with margins sometimes minutely incurling, overlapping half; the inner segments more narrowly ovate, sharply angled from shoulder to narrow base, a little inflexed, with margins slightly wavy; corona funnel-shaped, pink, with mouth heavily ribbed and widely expanded, loosely frilled, rim deeply crenate and slightly rolled

'Daina' 1 W-W
(W. Jackson Sr, 1943) W. Jackson Jr, 1956
'Dava' × 'Tain'

'Daintee' 2 W-?
(A. Overton) A. Overton, 1960

'Daintiness' 2 W-? (b)
(Mrs M. Moorby, pre-1937)

'Daintiness' 3 W-YYO
Syn. of 'Barbara Ann Scott'

'Dainty' 5 Y-Y
(Mrs R.O. Backhouse, pre-1907)
Perianth segments pale primrose yellow; corona broad, expanded, darker in tone than the perianth

'Dainty Bell' 1 W-W
(E.M. Crosfield, pre-1910)

'Dainty Belle' 8 W-Y
(pre-1938)
'Canaliculatus' hybrid
Fls 3-4 per stem, 150 mm wide; perianth segments white, corona golden yellow

'Dainty Dianne' 3 W-W
(T.H. Piper, c.1966) Unregistered
'Swanley Peerless' × 'Portia'

'Dainty Lady' 1 W-P
(S.J. Bisdee, 1942)
'Eskimo' × 'Dawnglow'

'Dainty Lady' 3 W-? (b)
(Oregon Bulb Farms, pre-1946)

'Dainty Lass' 1 W-Y
(Barr & Sons, pre-1923)
Perianth segments pure white; corona citron yellow

'Dainty Lilian' 5
(R. Dick, pre-1933)
See also 'Dainty Lillian'

'Dainty Lillian' 5
Syn. of 'Dainty Lilian'

'Dainty Maid' 1 W-W
(Barr & Sons, pre-1890)

'Dainty Maid' 2 W-YYO
(R.H. Bath, pre-1923)
Perianth segments white; corona lemon yellow, with dull orange at rim. AM(e) 1923

'Dainty Maiden' 2 Y-Y
(M.P. Williams, pre-1949)
Fl. lemon yellow

'Dainty Miss' 7 W-GWW
(G.E. Mitsch) G.E. Mitsch, 1966
('Rubra' × 'Coverack Perfection') × *N. rupicola* subsp. *watieri*; sdlg no. V96/1
Fl. 57 mm wide, glistening white; perianth segments overlapping; corona very shallow bowl-shaped, small. Mid-season. Resembles a larger-flowered 'Xit' with the perianth segments more rounded

'Dainty Nell' 3 W-YYW
(Barr & Sons, pre-1925)
Perianth segments narrow, with margins wavy; corona tightly ribbed, chamois yellow, with a broad band of white at rim

'Dainty Queen' 3 W-? (b)
(de Graaff Bros, pre-1938)
AM(Haarlem) 1938

'Dainty Ring' 2 Y-OOR
(A.G. Thompson) A.G. Thompson, 1961
Fl. 89 mm wide; perianth segments lemon yellow; corona orange, with flame at rim. Mid-season

'Daiquiri' 3 Y-Y
(W.G. Pannill) W.G. Pannill, 1978

'Lemnos' × 'Lemonade'; sdlg no. D 26
Fl. 103 mm wide. Mid-season

'Dairy' 2 W-W
(The Brodie of Brodie, pre-1940)
'White Sentinel' self pollinated

'Dairy Maid' 2 W-? (b)
(G.H. Engleheart, pre-1910)
See also 'Dairymaid'

'Dairymaid' 2 W-? (b)
Syn. of 'Dairy Maid'

'Dairyman' 2 W-? (b)
(pre-1914)

'Daisy' 2 W-Y
(M. Leichtlin, pre-1884)
Perianth segments sulphur white. Syn. Backhousei 'Daisy'

'Daisy Bell' 1 W-W
(E.M. Crosfield, pre-1910)

'Daisy Cumberlege' 1 W-W
(N.Y. Lower, pre-1916)
'Madame de Graaff' × 'Cleopatra'

'Daisy Dee' 3 W-? (b)
(J.E. Exley, pre-1950)

'Daisy Hellings' 3 W-? (b)
(W.F.M. Copeland, pre-1925)

'Daisy Hill' Y-O
(Thomas Smith, pre-1902)
'Sir Watkin' hybrid
Perianth segments deep primrose yellow; corona intense orange

'Daisy Jean' 2 W-O
(O. Ronalds, 1947) T. Morrison, 1960
Perianth segments pure white; corona reddish orange. Resembles 'Jean Hood' in form and colour

'Daisy Pied' 2 Y-? (a)
(W.B. Hartland, pre-1914)

'Daisy Schäffer' 2 W-WYY
(de Graaff Bros, pre-1925)
Fl. forming a double triangle; perianth segments broadly ovate, blunt, slightly mucronate, greenish white, spreading, a little concave and with margins wavy, overlapping half; the inner segments a little narrower, slightly inflexed, with margins more strongly wavy; corona funnel-shaped, lightly ribbed, pale sulphur yellow, paling to whitish at base, mouth more heavily ribbed, widely expanded, irregularly and deeply split, with lobes overlapping, loosely frilled. AM(Haarlem) 1925, FCC(Haarlem) 1929, AM(e) 1933, FA(Haarlem) 1936, FCFA(Haarlem) 1937

'Daisy Willes' 2 W-O
(Alister Clark, 1935) T. Morrison, 1960
Perianth segments pure white; corona buffy orange

'Dakar' 2 Y-O
(J.W.A. Lefeber, pre-1949)
Perianth segments clear yellow, slightly reflexed, very smooth, overlapping half; corona vivid orange-scarlet. Syn. 'Burma', 'Birma'

'Dakota' 3 W-YYO
(Mrs R.O. Backhouse, pre-1921)
Perianth segments creamy white; corona large, expanded, rich golden yellow, with a broad band of scarlet-orange at rim, frilled

'Daladier' 2 Y-Y
Syn. of 'Makassar'

'Dalai' 2 Y-Y
(E.W. Philpott)

'Dalboyne' 2 Y-O
(G.L. Wilson, pre-1947)
2n=28

'Dalcharn' 2 W-P
(J.S.B. Lea) Clive Postles Daffodils, 1988
('Inverpolly' × 'Rose Royale') × 'Dailmanach'
Perianth segments broad, blunt, mucronate; corona clear pink, shading to a darker tone at mouth, rim dentate

'Dalefield' 1 Y-Y
(J.S. Leitch) J.S. Leitch, 1967
Fl. 118 mm wide

'Dalham' 2 Y-? (a)
(R.H. Bath, pre-1933)

'Dalhauine' 3 W-R
(J.S.B. Lea) J.S.B. Lea, 1971
('Green Island' × ['Easter Moon' × 'Homage']) × sdlg 1-1-55 ('Arbar' self pollinated); sdlg no. 1-26-61
Fl. 105 mm wide; perianth segments white; corona deep red, frilled. 2n=28

'Dalila' 2 W-?
Syn. of 'Boma'

'Dalila' 2 Y-?
Syn. of 'Asa Gray'

'Dalinda' 1 Y-O
(W.O. Backhouse) W.O. Backhouse, 1956

'Dallas' 3 W-GWW
(The Brodie of Brodie, c.1942)
'Cushendall' × 'Silver Salver'; sdlg no. 87/A/37
Fl. 89 mm wide; perianth segments very broadly ovate, rounded, slightly mucronate, a little reflexed, overlapping half; the inner segments only very slightly mucronate, sometimes more narrowly ovate, sometimes roundish; corona very shallow, closely ribbed, white, with pale green at base, mouth expanded and regularly frilled. Very late. 2n=14. AM(e) 1956

'Dallbro' 2 W-P
(W. Jackson Jr, 1951) W. Jackson Jr, 1966
'Hothu' × 'Mena'

'Dalliance' 2 YYW-GWY
(Carncairn Daffodils, 1974) Carncairn Daffodils, 1985
Probably 'Daydream' × 'Moonspell'; sdlg no. 5/8/69
Perianth segments brilliant greenish yellow 5A, with sulphur white at base; corona opening yellow, becoming white, with yellow at rim. Mid-season. Resembles a later-flowered and more robust 'Daydream'

'Dalliance' 1 Y-Y
(J.N. Hancock & Co., 1956) Unregistered

'Dalmore' 2 Y-O
(H.A. Brown, 1931)
Perianth segments rounded, bright yellow; corona very shallow bowl-shaped, intense reddish orange. Very early

'Dalmore' 2 Y-? (a)
(The Brodie of Brodie, c.1931)
('Tenedos' × 'White Emperor') × 'Hades'; sdlg no. 123/A/26

'Dalray' 2 Y-YYO
(J.N. Hancock & Co.) J.N. Hancock & Co., 1955
'Valerie' × 'Carbineer'
Perianth segments golden yellow; corona short, straight, gold, with a band of bright orange at rim

'Dalriada' 2 Y-? (a)
(G.L. Wilson, pre-1939)

'Dalveen' 2 W-WWO
(H.A. Brown, pre-1938)
Perianth segments white; corona cream, with apricot at rim, frilled

'Dalvey' 1 W-W
(Brodie Gardens) Brodie Gardens, 1957
Hybrid between 'Kanchenjunga' and 'Naxos'
Fl. of strong substance; corona funnel-shaped, opening lemon yellow, soon becoming pure white, mouth flared, rim flanged and dentate. Early

'Dalvui' 2 W-P

(J.M. Radcliff, 1953) P. Phillips, 1966
Fl. 105 mm wide; perianth segments white; corona pale pink. Late

'Damaris' 1 Y-Y
(D.S. Bell) D.S. Bell, 1979
'Surrey Gold' self pollinated; sdlg no. 572/78
Fl. 109 mm wide, golden yellow; corona with rim rolled and slightly dentate. Mid-season

'Damascene' 2 Y-? (a)
(A.M. Wilson, pre-1948)

'Damascus' 3 W-R
(P.D. Williams, pre-1939)

'Damask' 5
(W.B. Cranfield, pre-1930)

'Dame Edith' 2 W-P
(J.N. Hancock & Co., 1964) Unregistered

'Dame Pattie' 2 W-P
(J.N. Hancock & Co., pre-1988) Unregistered

'Dame Pattie Menzies' 2 W-P
(Mrs C.O. Fairbairn, pre-1974) Unregistered
Corona deep pink

'Dame Primrose' 5
(Barr & Sons, pre-1923)

'Dame Royal' 8 W-Y
Syn. of 'Dame Royale'

'Dame Royale' 8 W-Y
(pre-1777)
Perianth segments creamy; corona orange-yellow. See also 'Dame Royal'

'Damocles' 1 Y-Y
(J.L. Richardson) J.L. Richardson, 1956
'Pretoria' × 'Goldcourt'

'Damon' 1 Y-Y
(Barr & Sons, pre-1931)

'Dampier' 1 Y-Y
(J.N. Hancock & Co., 1975) Unregistered

'Dampier' 2 Y-R
(?New Zealand origin, pre-1990) Unregistered

'Damsel' 2 W-W
(M.P. Williams, pre-1949)

'Damsel' 2 Y-O
Syn. of 'Imago'

'Damson' 2 WWY-R

(P.D. Williams, pre-1925)
Perianth segments broadly ovate, blunt, fairly prominently mucronate, spreading, opening primrose yellow, becoming creamy white, with a suffusion of primrose yellow at base, overlapping one-third to a half; the inner segments a little inflexed, with margins wavy; corona funnel-shaped, loosely ribbed, red, with mouth straight and loosely frilled. AM(e) 1925, AM(Haarlem) 1930

'Dan' 2 W-? (b)
(Mrs R.O. Backhouse, pre-1921)

'Danaë' 8
(H.H.B. Bradley, pre-1909)

'Danae' 2 Y-O
(Mrs H.K. Richardson) Ken Farmer Nurseries, 1978
'Patagonia' × 'Firecracker'; sdlg no. 551
Fl. 110 m wide; perianth segments gold; corona reddish orange. Mid-season

'Dancer' 2 W-GYO
(M.J. Jefferson-Brown) M.J. Jefferson-Brown, 1984
'Pontresina' self pollinated
Corona very shallow, pale primrose, with pinkish orange at rim. Mid-season

'Dan Chaucer'
(Mrs R.S. Cobley, pre-1936)

'Dancing Aurora' 4 W-Y
(Tom Forster, 1960s) Unregistered
Fl. rounded; perianth and other petaloid segments creamy white; corona segments interspersed, deep golden yellow. Early

'Dancing Fairies' 5 Y-Y
(S.J. Bisdee, 1943) S.J. Bisdee, 1956
'Robert Berkeley' × *N. triandrus*

'Dancing Fairy' 5 W-Y
(S.S. Berry, pre-1937)
N. triandrus × 'Bernardino'
Fls 2 per stem, facing down; perianth segments ovate, mucronate, reflexed in upper half, often twisted, overlapping one-third; corona bowl-shaped, ribbed, with mouth straight and a little frilled

'Dancing Flame' 2 Y-O
(J.L. Richardson) J.L. Richardson, 1968
'Mazurka' × 'Firecracker'
Perianth segments deep golden yellow, of good substance; corona reddish orange, with rim neatly dentate. Early

'Dancing Girl' 11a W-Y
(Jānis Rukšans, 1986) Jānis Rukšans, 1997
'Canasta' hybrid; sdlg no. 81-12-2
Fl. 103 mm wide; perianth segments pure white, spreading, smooth, overlapping; corona segments opposite and closely overlying the perianth segments, vivid yellow 12A, paling to 12D at rim, frilled. Early

'Dancing Light' 9 W-GYO
(Mrs M.S. Yerger) Mrs M.S. Yerger, 1992
'Red Rim' × 'Lights Out'; sdlg no. 75 K 4
Fl. forming a double triangle, 55 mm wide; perianth segments white, overlapping at base only; corona very shallow bowl-shaped, vivid yellow 9A, with light yellow-green 145B at base and orange (28A) at rim. Late

'Dancing Partner' 2 W-P
(M.J. Jefferson-Brown, pre-1969) M.J. Jefferson-Brown, 1985
?'Rose of Tralee' × 'Passionale'
Late. Resembles a later-flowered 'Passionale'

'Dandelion' 2 Y-? (a)
(Mrs R.S. Cobley, pre-1938)

'Dandenong' 1 Y-Y
(H.A. Brown, 1938) J.N. Hancock & Co., 1964
Fl. rounded, soft yellow; perianth segments smooth. Mid-season. Resembles a more refined 'Godolphin'

'Dandula' 1 Y-Y
(C.E. Radcliff, pre-1936)
'The Gift' hybrid

'Dan du Plessis' 8 Y-O
(Rosewarne EHS) Cornwall Area Bulb Growers Association, 1996
'Matador' × *N. jonquilla*; sdlg no 77/72/4
Fls 3-6 per stem, 50 mm wide; perianth segments broadly ovate, brilliant greenish yellow 6B, with white mucro, spreading or sometimes reflexed, concave, smooth, overlapping half or more; the inner segments spreading or sometimes inflexed, with margins wavy or incurling; corona bowl-shaped, ribbed, strong orange 25B. Mid-season

'Dandy' 3 W-Y
(E. Leeds, pre-1877)
Corona ribbed. Syn. Burbidgei 'Dandy', Burbidgei 'Stellatus'

'Dandy' 1 Y-Y
(?J. Kouwenhoven, pre-1913)
'King Alfred' hybrid
Perianth segments citron yellow; corona darker in tone. AM(Haarlem) 1913

'Dandy' 2 (b or c)
(Mrs E. Murray)

'Dandy Boy' 1 Y-Y
(G.H. Engleheart, pre-1931)
Fl. 102 mm wide; perianth segments bright golden yellow, overlapping; corona more or less cylindrical,

a little darker in tone than the perianth. Mid-season. 2n=28. *AM(g) 1947

'Dandy Dick' 2 Y-YYO
(C. Smith, pre-1903)
Perianth segments overlapping; corona bright yellow, with dark reddish orange at rim, mouth expanded and lightly frilled

'Danegeld' 2 W-? (b)
(F.D.B. Cobb, pre-1953)

'Danehill' 1 Y-Y
(N.A. Burr) N.A. Burr, 1990
'Celtic Gold' × 'Arctic Gold'; sdlg no. 1.10.80
Fl. 96 mm wide, yellow; perianth segments very broadly ovate, blunt, with white mucro, spreading, with margins incurling at apex, overlapping half or more; the inner segments more narrowly ovate, shouldered a base; corona funnel-shaped, smoothly and broadly ribbed, mouth more strongly ribbed, wavy, rim a little reflexed, shallowly notched and crenate. Early

'Danes Balk' 2 W-W
(F.E. Board) F.E. Board, 1965
'Easter Moon' × 'Homage'; sdlg no. 683
Fl. pure white. Late

'Danesfield' 1 W-Y
(Barr & Sons, pre-1919)
Fl. large; perianth segments overlapping; corona canary yellow, with mouth expanded and frilled

'Danger' 3 Y-O
(Mrs R.O. Backhouse, pre-1921)
Perianth segments soft yellow; corona disc-shaped, deep reddish orange, heavily frilled

'Danger' 2 Y-R
(G.W.E. & M.E.Brogden) G.W.E. & M.E.Brogden, 1980
'Feature' × 'Falstaff'; sdlg no. T80
Fl. 100 mm wide; perianth segments broad, rounded at apex, deep yellow; corona very deep red

'Danger Signal' 2
(C.L. Adams, pre-1913)

'Daniel Boone' 1 W-? (b)
(L. van Leeuwen & Son, pre-1931)

'Daniel Dewar' 1 W-Y
(Spanish origin, pre-1888)
Selection by Peter Barr (c.1888) from wild-collected *N. pseudonarcissus*
Perianth segments ovate, sulphur white, stained yellow at base, a little inflexed, twisted or with margins wavy, separated; corona cylindrical, smooth, orange-yellow, with mouth slightly expanded and very deeply lobed, rim crenate

'Danny' 2 W-Y
(?New Zealand origin, pre-1996) Unregistered

'Danny Boy'
(?Sir J.S. Arkwright, pre-1936)

'Danseuse' 3 W-? (b)
(Mrs P.M. Davis, pre-1948)

'Dante' 2 W-?Y
(E. Leeds, pre-1877)
Perianth segments sulphur white; corona very large, with mouth expanded. Syn. Incomparabilis Albidus 'Dante'

'Dante' 9 W-YYR
(G.H. Engleheart, pre-1896)
'Ornatus' × *N. radiiflorus* var. *poetarum*
Fl. 75 mm wide; perianth segments greenish white (155A), of good substance, deeply overlapping; corona brilliant yellow 15C, with vivid red 45A at rim. FCC 1896

'Danton' 1 Y-Y
(C.E. Radcliff, 1930)
'Golden City' × 'Gertrude Nethercote'

'Danube' 2 W-? (b)
(E.H. Krelage & Son, pre-1942)

'Daphne' 3 Y-? (a)
(Sir C.H. Cave, pre-1908)

'Daphne' 4 W-W
(F. Culpin, pre-1914)
'Ornatus' sport
Fl. rounded; perianth and other petaloid segments in several whorls, broad in outline, rounded at apex, very slightly mucronate, slightly concave, with midrib showing; the outer whorl spreading; the inner whorls a little inflexed; the centre whorl narrower, strongly inflexed, with margins deeply incurled. Scented. 2n=14. Earlier-flowered than Poeticus 'Plenus'. Syn. 'Spalding Queenie'. AM(m)(e) 1917, FCC(c) 1924, AM(Haarlem) 1928, FCC(Haarlem) 1929

'Dapper' 2 Y-? (a)
(F.H. Chapman, pre-1938)

'Darby' 1 W-? (b)
(J.H. Hinsby, 1924)
'Empress' × 'Silvester'

'Dardanus' 1 Y-Y
(A.E. Lowe, pre-1927)

'Daric' 1 W-Y
(W. Jackson Jr, 1967) Unregistered

'Rowella' × 'Lod'; sdlg no. 32/67

'Daring' 2 W-P
(Oregon Bulb Farms, pre-1950)

'Darite' 3 W-O
(T. Bloomer) du Plessis Bros, 1986
'Graceful Charmer' hybrid; sdlg no. 417
Mid-season

'Darius' 1 Y-Y
(G.L. Wilson, pre-1923)
'Grandee' × 'Emperor'
Perianth segments broad, the outer segments often touching one another, soft primrose yellow; corona soft clear yellow

'Dark Lochnagar' 2 Y-R
(D.N.Y. Olson) D.N.Y. Olson, 1989
'Checkmate' × 'Heathcliffe'; sdlg no. 77/29/4
Fl. 84 mm wide; perianth segments broadly ovate, blunt, fairly prominently mucronate, mid- to dark yellow, spreading, somewhat concave, overlapping half; the inner segments a little inflexed; corona funnel-shaped, smooth, strong dark red, with mouth widely expanded and more or less even, rim obscurely dentate. Early to mid-season. Sunproof

'Dark Ronald' 2 W-O
(W.M. Spry, pre-1975) Unregistered
'Jean Hood' × 'My Choice'

'Dark Victory' 1 W-? (b)
(D.S. Bell) D.S. Bell, 1955
Perianth segments very broadly ovate, spreading; the inner segments more narrowly ovate, reflexed

'Darley' 1 Y-Y
(D.B. Milne, pre-1950)
AM(Haarlem) 1956

'Darling' 2 Y-YYO
(E. Leeds, pre-1877)
Perianth segments sulphur yellow; corona yellow, with orange at rim. Syn. Incomparabilis Sulphureus 'Darling', Incomparabilis Sulphureus 'Marginatus'

'Darlington' 2 Y-O
(Warnaar & Co., pre-1943)
'Fortune' × 'Scarlet Leader'
AM(Haarlem) 1943

'Darllen' 3 W-? (b or c)
(?W.A. Watts, pre-1930)

'Darlow Dale' 2 Y-O
(W.A. Noton) W.A. Noton, 1994
Fl. 94 mm wide; perianth segments broadly ovate, rounded at apex, slightly mucronate, vivid yellow 9A, spreading, a little concave, regular, overlapping half; the inner segments square-shouldered at base, more nearly plane; corona funnel-shaped, lightly ribbed, orange (23A), intensifying in tone towards the rim, mouth 6-lobed, rim shallowly crenate. Mid-season

'Darnaway' 1 Y-Y
(The Brodie of Brodie, c.1939)
'Royalist' × 'Slemish'
Perianth segments acute, mid-yellow

'Dārta' 2 W-WWY
(Jānis Rukšans, 1987) Jānis Rukšans, 1997
'Knowehead' × 'Bit o' Gold'
Fl. 105 mm wide, pure white; perianth segments roundish, deeply overlapping; corona almost disc-shaped, with a distinct narrow band of vivid yellow 13A at rim, frilled. Mid-season to late

'D'Artagnan' 2 W-? (b)
(Mrs R.O. Backhouse, pre-1921)
Syn. 'Bella'

'Darven' 2 Y-YYO
(H.A. Brown, pre-1938)
Perianth segments soft yellow; corona yellow, with reddish orange at rim, frilled

'Darwalla' 1 W-W
(C.E. Radcliff, 1929)

'Darwin' 2 Y-Y
(?J.N. Hancock & Co., pre-1949)

'Daspyl' 2 Y-? (a)
(C.E. Radcliff, 1939) C.E. Radcliff, 1956
'Wingeen' × 'Cheerio'

'Dateline' 3 Y-O
(Brian S. Duncan) Rathowen Daffodils, 1986
'Montego' × 'Achduart'; sdlg no. 525
Fl. 98 mm wide; perianth segents broadly ovate, blunt, bright greenish yellow 6B, with very slight white mucro, spreading, slightly concave, with margins sometimes incurling at apex, overlapping half; the inner segments not much narrower, a little inflexed, with margins slightly wavy; corona bowl-shaped, ribbed, yellow-orange (21A) at base, shading to deep orange (28A) at mouth, with mouth expanded and lightly frilled. Mid-season. Resembles a more consistent and vigorous 'Achduart'. AM(e) 1986

'Datsun' 3 W-WWO
(J.N. Hancock & Co., 1955) Unregistered
Perianth segments cream; corona with orange at rim. Scented

'Dauntless' 1 Y-Y
(G.H.Engleheart, pre-1897)
N. obvallaris sdlg
Corona frilled. Early

'Dauntless' 2 W-W
(F.E. Board) F.E. Board, 1965
G.L.Wilson sdlg 38/74 × 'Glendermott'
Late. Resembles 'Glendermott' but with the perianth segments more rounded

'Dauphin' 2 W-YOO
(Konynenburg & Mark) Konynenburg & Mark, 1969
'Limerick' × 'Handel'

'Dauphine'
(pre-1831)

'Daura' 1 W-W
(W. Jackson Sr, 1937)
'Canace' × 'White Emperor'

'Dava' 2 W-W
(The Brodie of Brodie, c.1929)
'Nissa' × 'White Emperor'
Perianth segments broadly ovate, blunt, mucronate, spreading at base, slightly inflexed near apex, plane, with broad midrib showing, overlapping half; the inner segments more narrowly ovate, slightly inflexed, somewhat twisted; corona cylindrical, smoothly angled, with mouth expanded and even, rim crenate. 2n=28. AM(e) 1937

'Davara' 2 W-Y
(W. Jackson Jr, c.1960) Unregistered
'Faralong' × 'Sari'

'Dave' 2 Y-Y
(P. & G. Phillips) P. & G. Phillips, 1981
Fl. 100 mm wide. Mid-season.

'Davenport' 2 W-R
(J.A. Morris) J.A. Morris, 1965
Fl. 105 mm wide. Mid-season. Sunproof. Resembles 'Signal Light' but with a whiter perianth and darker corona

'Daventry' 2 Y-? (a)
(W.F.M. Copeland, pre-1927)

'David' 1 W-W
(J.T. Gray, pre-1933)

'David Alexander' 1 Y-Y
(R.A.Scamp) Mrs Angela Fowler, 1995
'Arkle' × 'Viking'; sdlg no. 309
Fl. 100 mm wide, rich golden yellow; perianth segments broadly ovate, plane, deeply overlapping; the inner segments slightly narrower and a little twisted; corona long, smooth, with rim neatly crenate. Mid-season to late

'David Bell' 1 Y-Y
(D.S. Bell) D.S. Bell, 1955
('Belle Keller' × 'Askelon') × 'King of the North' hybrid
Fl. golden yellow; corona cylindrical, with mouth frilled

'David Black's Memory' 2 Y-O
(G. Lubbe & Son) G. Lubbe & Son, 1963
Fl. 80 mm wide; perianth segments light yellow. Mid-season

'David Gower' 2 W-P
(D.S. Bell) D.S. Bell, 1984
'Alfresco' hybrid
Fl. 112 mm wide. Resembles 'Alfresco' but with a differently coloured corona

'David Griffiths' 1 Y-Y
(E.C. Powell, pre-1946)

'David Meyer' 1 Y-Y
(H.R. Meyer) J.P. Izzard, 1955

'David's Gold' 1 Y-Y
(R.J. Abernethy) R.J. Abernethy, 1991
'Sun Gold' open pollinated; sdlg no. 359
Fl. deep golden yellow, smooth and of heavy substance; perianth segments very broadly ovate, blunt; the inner segments more narrowly ovate; corona funnel-shaped, with rim lightly rolled. Mid-season. Resembles an improved 'Sun Gold'

'David Spry' 1 Y-Y
(W.M. Spry, pre-1973) Unregistered
'Royal Armour' × 'Julius Caesar'
Early

'David Walker' 1 W-Y
(E. Leeds, pre-1877)
Perianth segments sulphur white, overlapping. Syn. Pseudonarcissus Bicolor 'David Walker'. Was "absorbed" into 'James Walker'

'David West' 2 W-W
(West & Fell, pre-1935)
Corona opening pale primrose, becoming pure white

'Daviot' 2 W-OOY
(The Brodie of Brodie, c.1943)
'Sea Shell' × 'Ischia'; sdlg no. 24/A/38
Fl. 102 mm wide; perianth segments greenish white, very smooth, overlapping; corona pale orange (24D), with a paler tone at base and pale yellow at rim, rim slightly notched. AM(e) 1953

'Davlyn' 2 W-YPP
(M.J. Jefferson-Brown) M.J. Jefferson-Brown, 1985
Perianth segments acute, pure white; corona orange-pink, with a brighter tone at rim. Mid-season. Resembles an earlier-flowered 'Holiday Fashion' with the perianth segments more narrowly acute

'Davochfin Lass' 1 W-Y
(D.C. MacArthur) D.C. MacArthur, 1990
'Ludlow' × ('Braniel' × 'Preamble'); sdlg no. E855A
Fl. 104 mm wide; perianth segments greenish white (155A), glistening, of strong substance, overlapping; corona narrowly funnel-shaped, light greenish yellow 4B, paling to a creamier tone (4D) at base and rim, with mouth widely flared. Mid-season

'Dawley' 2 Y-Y
(F.E. Gibbs, pre-1948)

'Dawn' 1 W-WWY
(A.Wilson, pre-1902)
'Princeps' × 'Albicans'
Perianth segments narrow, slightly inflexed, twisted, separated; corona funnel-shaped, white, with a narrow band of lemon yellow at rim, mouth expanded and 6-lobed, lightly frilled, with rim minutely crenate

'Dawn' 5 W-Y
(G.H. Engleheart, pre-1907)
Fls 2 per stem, star-shaped, facing down; perianth segments ovate, acute, some reflexed, some more nearly spreading, sometimes with margins incurling, overlapping at base only; corona disc- or very shallow bowl-shaped, lemon yellow, mouth even, with rim crenate. Tall

'Dawn'
(W.Jackson Sr, pre-1936)

'Dawn' 3 Y-? (a)
(?H. Prins, pre-1938)

'Dawn Blush' 2 W-P
(Elise Havens) G.E. Mitsch, 1975
'Precedent' × 'Carita'; sdlg no. FEJ8/5
Fl. 112 mm wide; corona bowl-shaped, rich pink. Mid-season

'Dawn Chorus' 1 Y-Y
(Rosewarne EHS) Cornwall Area Bulb Growers Association, 1985
'Rijnveld's Early Sensation' × *N. asturiensis*; sdlg no. 65-90-3
Perianth segments lemon yellow, with a paler tone at base; corona darker in tone than the perianth. Very early

'Dawncrest' 2 W-PPW
(G.E. Mitsch, 1967) G.E. Mitsch, 1978
'Carita' × 'Accent; sdlg no. C7/22
Fl. 103 mm wide; corona deep salmon pink, paling to cream at rim. Early

'Dawn Frost' 2 W-WPP
(J.A.Hunter, 1987) J.A.Hunter, 1997
'Precedent' × 'Verran'; sdlg no. 38/82G

Fl. 109 mm wide; perianth segments ovate, smooth; corona flared, pink, with white at base and a darker tone of pink at rim, with mouth wavy. Mid-season

'Dawnglow' 1 W-P
(C.E. Radcliff, 1935)
Rosary' × 'Pink o' Dawn'
Perianth segments broad, pure white, overlapping; corona opening salmon yellow with buff yellow at rim, becoming deep salmon pink

'Dawngold' 1 Y-Y
(D.S. Bell) D.S. Bell, 1962
('Braemar' × 'Barrington') × ('Braemar' × Gold Court')
Fl. 102 mm wide, golden yellow; corona regularly frilled. Early

'Dawn Light' 5
(Cartwright & Goodwin, pre-1910)
See also 'Dawnlight'?

'Dawn Light' 1 Y-W
(Murray W. Evans) Murray W. Evans, 1970
'Lunar Sea' × 'Bethany'

'Dawnlight' 2 W-? (b)
(J.R. Byfield, pre-1936)

'Dawnlight' 1 W-P
(C.E. Radcliff, pre-1940)
'Pink o' Dawn' × 'Rosary'

'Dawnlight' 5?
Syn. of 'Dawn Light'?

'Dawn Mist' 2 W-WWP
(G.Barr, 1954)
'Maiden's Blush' × 'White Sentinel'; sdlg no. 4054
Perianth segments broadly ovate, truncate, slightly mucronate, creamy white, spreading, somewhat concave, overlapping a quarter to one-third; corona short funnel-shaped, ribbed, creamy white, with pink at rim, mouth flared, 6-lobed, lightly frilled, with rim flanged and minutely crenate. Resembles an improved 'Maiden's Blush'

'Dawn Patrol' 1 Y-Y
(D.S. Bell) D.S. Bell, 1957
('Alroi' × 'Kanchenjunga') × 'Pre-eminent'
Fl. soft bright yellow

'Dawn Run' 2 O-R
(Brian S. Duncan) Brian S. Duncan, 1992
('Rathowen Flame' × 'Shining Light') × 'Sabine Hay'; sdlg no. 971
Fl. 105 mm wide; perianth segments broadly ovate, blunt or rounded at apex, evenly flushed orange, with white mucro, slightly reflexed, overlapping half; the inner segments more narrowly ovate, more nearly

spreading; corona shallow bowl-shaped, loosely ribbed, deep orange-red, with mouth widely expanded and lightly frilled. Mid-season to late

'Dawn's Delight' 2 W-? (b)
(Oregon Bulb Farms, pre-1950)

'Dawn Shower' 1 Y-Y
(D.S. Bell, 1965) D.S. Bell, 1975
'Dawngold' × 'Gold Shower'
Fl. 109 mm wide. Mid-season

'Dawn Sky' 2 W-GWP
Syn. of 'Tykky-dew'

'Dawn Star' 2 W-W
(Mrs P.M. Davis, pre-1948)

'Dawson City' 1 Y-Y
(C.G. van Tubergen, pre-1920)
Fl. 98 mm wide; perianth segments broadly ovate, fairly prominently mucronate, golden yellow, spreading or slightly inflexed, somewhat creased and with margins incurlng, smooth, overlapping one-third to a half; the inner segments a little more narrowly ovate, with margins wavy; corona cylindrical, smooth, darker in tone than the perianth, mouth flared and lightly frilled, with rim irregularly crenate. AM(Haarlem) 1920, FCC(Haarlem) 1923, AM(e) 1925, *AM(g) 1930

'Dayan' 1 Y-Y
(W. Jackson Jr, 1967) Unregistered
'Jobi' × 'Chillion'; sdlg no. 57/67

'Day-a-peep' 2 Y-? (a)
(Miss K.M. Hinchliff, pre-1939)

'Day Break' 2 Y-O
(J.N. Hancock & Co., pre-1949)

'Daybreak' 2 Y-YYO
(M. van Waveren & Sons, pre-1907)

'Daybreak' 2 W-P
(J.L. Richardson) J.L. Richardson, 1961
Fl. 106 mm wide; perianth segments acute; corona flushed deep rosy pink, with mouth expanded and frilled. Late

'Daydawn' 2 W-O
(P.D. Williams, pre-1929)
Corona pinkish orange

'Day Dream' 2 W-O
(J.N. Hancock & Co., pre-1949)
Corona reddish orange

'Day Dream' 3 W-O
Syn. of 'Daydream'

'Daydream' 3 W-O
(W. Welchman, pre-1910)
Perianth segments white; corona reddish orange. See also 'Day Dream'

'Daydream' 2 Y-W
(G.E. Mitsch) G.E. Mitsch, 1960
'Binkie' × ('King of the North' × 'Content'); sdlg no. P5/6
Fl. rounded, 81 mm wide; perianth segments very broad, rounded at apex, brilliant greenish yellow 4A, with slight white mucro, touched creamy white at base, spreading, plane or with margins incurling at apex, smooth, overlapping half or more; the inner segments a little narrower, more nearly ovate, rounded at base, somewhat inflexed, with margins sometimes wavy; corona cylindrical, smooth, opening pale yellow (4D), soon becoming white, with the rim touched yellow, mouth expanded, deeply ribbed, lightly frilled, rim irregularly and more or less deeply notched and crenate. Mid-season. 2n=28. PC(e) 1962, AM(e) 1963, FCC(e) 1966, AGM 1995

'Daylight' 2 W-? (b)
(H.R. Meyer, pre-1945)
Syn. 'Kiss-in-the-Ring'

'Dayspring' 2 W-? (b)
(Mrs R.S. Cobley, pre-1937)

'Day Star' 3 W-? (b)
(G.H. Engleheart, pre-1901)
'Princess Mary' × 'Ornatus'
Corona flushed orange. AM 1901

'Day Star' 1 Y-Y
(Australian or New Zealand origin, pre-1927)
Fl. large; perianth segments overlapping; corona frilled

'Daytime' 2 Y-? (a)
(A.H. Ahrens) J.S. Leitch, 1955

'Daytona' 3 W-O
(J.L. Richardson, pre-1937)
'Mitylene' × 'Sunstar'
Fl. 9 mm wide; perianth segments broadly or very broadly ovate, blunt, slightly mucronate, white, suffused pale yellow at base, spreading, plane, with margins narrowly incurlng, regular, overlapping one-third to a half; the inner segments only a little narrower, a little inflexed, with margins wavy; corona disc-shaped, heavily ribbed, orange, with mouth frilled and rim closely and minutely notched. Mid-season. AM(e) 1937

'Dayton Lake' 2 Y-W
(John R.Reed, 1985) John R.Reed, 1997
'Festivity' × 'Easter Moon'; sdlg no. 79-165-1
Fl. 90 mm wide; perianth segments blunt, dull white,

spreading, smooth; corona butter yellow. Mid-season

'Daze' 2 W-R
(J.T. Gray, 1954) P. Phillips, 1964
Fl. 89 mm wide; perianth segments off white; corona saturn red. Mid-season to late. Resembles 'Vieva' but with the perianth segments more rounded and the corona mouth more widely expanded

'Dazzle' 2 Y-Y
(J.N. Hancock & Co., pre-1949)
Fl. rich golden yellow; corona frilled

'Dazzler' 3 Y-O
(G.H. Engleheart, pre-1913)
Perianth segments narrow, acute, primrose yellow; corona shallow, glowing orange, with mouth widely expanded

'Dazzler' 2 Y-R
(G.E. Mitsch) G.E. Mitsch, 1976
'Matlock' × 'Falstaff'; sdlg no. 2I62/1
Fl. 106 mm wide; perianth segments broadly ovate in outline, blunt or truncate at apex, slightly mucronate, intense golden yellow, spreading, somewhat creased, overlapping half; the inner segments a little inflexed, with margins wavy or incurved; corona almost disc-shaped, more than half as long as the perianth segments and closely overlying them, ribbed, fiery orange-red, with mouth split in places and overlapping, frilled. Mid-season

'Dazzling Beauty' 3 W-? (b)
(W. Welchman, pre-1913)

'D.C.Stewart' 1 W-W
(J.W. Barr, pre-1930)

'Dead White' 1 W-W
(Miss K.M. Hinchliff, pre-1943)

'Dean' 2 W-YOO
(R.V. Favell, pre-1946)
'Treskerby' × P.D.Williams sdlg

'Dean Herbert' 1 W-Y
(E. Leeds, pre-1877)
Fl. large; perianth segments opening clear primrose yellow, becoming sulphur white; corona rich yellow. Syn. Pseudonarcissus Bicolor 'Dean Herbert', Pseudonarcissus Bicolor 'Primulinus'

'Deanna Durbin' 2 W-O
(de Graaff Bros, pre-1939)
2n=28. AM(Haarlem) 1943

'Dearborn' 3 W-? (b)
(J.E. Exley, pre-1950)

'Dear Love' 11a W-YPP

(D.S. Bell) D.S. Bell, 1980
'Perlax' × 'Accent'
Fl. 106 mm wide; perianth segments smooth; corona segments pink, with yellow at base and touches of creamy white at rim. Mid-season. Resembles 'Perlax' but with a differently coloured corona

'Dear Me' 2 W-P
(T.H. Piper, 1965) D.H. Butcher, 1977
'Keera' × 'Bon Rose'
Fl. 98 mm wide; corona bright pink

'Debate' 2 Y-R
(H.G. Cross) H.G. Cross, 1991
Fl. 100 mm wide; perianth segments broadly ovate, blunt, with blunt, yellow, with white mucro, spreading, with white midrib showing, regular, overlapping half; the inner segments roundish, only very slightly mucronate, occasionally nicked; corona widely expanded, red, touched orange-yellow at base and rim, mouth deeply 6-lobed, the lobes alternate to the perianth segments, bi-lobed, wavy. Early

'Debbie Joan' 2 W-GWR
(Colin Crotty, 1980) Colin Crotty, 1990
'Cherryrim' × 'Caro Nome'; sdlg no. 34-75
Fl. 104 mm wide; perianth segments roundish, smooth, overlapping; corona opening yellowish, quickly becoming white, with green at base and a narrow band of pinkish red at rim, mouth frilled. Mid-season. Sunproof

'Debbie Rose' 2 W-P
(Brian S. Duncan) Rathowen Daffodils, 1976
'Rosewell' × 'Debutante'
Perianth segments pure white, slightly reflexed; corona narrow at base, deep salmon, with mouth expanded and rim dentate. Mid-season. Resembles a more vigorous 'Debutante'

'Debenture' 4 W-P
(D. Jackson) Jackson's Daffodils, 1983
Sdlg 66/70 × sdlg 64/70; sdlg no. 212/78
Fl. 90 mm wide. Mid-season

'Debir' 3 W-? (b)
(M. Zandbergen, pre-1944)

'Debonair' 3 W-Y
(G.H. Engleheart, pre-1913)
Perianth segments smooth and of thick substance; corona disc-shaped, chrome yellow

'Debonair' 2 (b)
(R. Dick, pre-1930)

'Debonair' 2 W-W
(D.S. Bell) D.S. Bell, 1964
'Kilsheelan' × 'Outward Bound'
Fl. 105 mm wide. orona with green at base. Resembles

'Ludlow' but with the perianth segments more rounded and of smoother texture

'Debora' 2 W-Y
(de Graaff Bros, pre-1917)
Perianth segments rounded at apex; corona pure yellow. AM(Haarlem) 1917, FCC(Haarlem) 1950

'Deborah Blake' 2 W-W
(D.H.L. Corrigan, pre-1949)

'Debra' 2 W-W
(R.H.Glover, pre-1993) Unregistered

'Debrett' 2 W-WWP
(Brian S. Duncan) Rathowen Daffodils, 1987
'Rainbow' open pollinated; sdlg no. 687
Corona deep bowl-shaped. Mid-season to late. Resembles a taller and stronger 'Rainbow'

'Debussy' 2 Y-? (a)
(Mrs R.O. Backhouse, pre-1921)

'Debutante' 3 W-? (b)
(F.H. Chapman, pre-1923)

'Debutante' 2 W-P
(J.L. Richardson) J.L. Richardson, 1956
'Wild Rose' × 'Rose Caprice'; sdlg no. 220
Perianth segments very broadly ovate, rounded at apex and slightly mucronate, pure white, a little concave, with margins incurling at apex, smooth, with midrib showing, overlapping half; the inner segments more narrowly ovate, truncate; corona bowl-shaped, smooth, rich pink, with green at base, mouth expanded and loosely frilled. PC 1956, AM(e) 1959

'Decade' 2 Y-O
(J.S. Leitch) J.S. Leitch, 1968

'Decamerone' 9 W-?
(de Graaff Bros, pre-1927)

'Decapolis' 5 W-W
(W.F.M. Copeland)

'December Bride' 11a W-P
(R. & E. Havens, 1980) R. & E. Havens, 1993
('Precedent' × ['Caro Nome' × 'Carita']) × ('Accent' × sdlg Q97/2); sdlg no. PEH28/1
Fl. 100 mm wide; perianth segments ovate; corona split, the six segments opposite and closely overlying the perianth segments, deep pink, sometimes with undertones of lavender. Mid-season. Sunproof

'Decency' 1 Y-Y
(P. van Deursen, pre-1930)
Fl. facing down; perianth segments clear pale yellow, overlapping; corona slightly darker in tone, with rim crenate. 2n=28. AM(Haarlem) 1930, *AM(g) 1936,
*FCC(g) 1944

'Decimal Currency' 2 W-O
(Tom Forster, 1960s) Unregistered
Fl. rounded; perianth segments milk white; corona orange, flared. Early to mid-season

'Declare' 2 W-P
(P. Phillips) P. Phillips, 1968

'Decor' 2 Y-YOO
(H.P. Zwetsloot, pre-1939)
'Fortuna' × 'Orange Glow'
AM(Haarlem) 1939, FCC(Haarlem) 1944, FA(Haarlem) 1953

'Decor' 2 W-P
(pre-1965) Unregistered
Corona pure pink

'Decora' 1 Y-Y
(R.A. van der Schoot, pre-1910)

'Decorator' 1 Y-Y
(R.H. Bath, pre-1916)

'Decorous' 2 W-Y
(G.L. Wilson, pre-1940)
'Niphetos' × 'Naxos'

'Decorum' 2 Y-? (a)
(R. Crews, pre-1949)

N. decorus Spach = *N. tazetta* subsp. *lacticolor*

'Decoy' 2 W-R
(G.E. Mitsch) G.E. Mitsch, 1979
Sdlg Y43/1 (sdlg × 'Caro Nome') × 'Cool Flame'; sdlg no. JJ17/1
Fl. forming a double triangle, 95 mm wide; perianth segments broadly ovate, spreading, concave near apex and with margins incurled, overlapping half; the inner segments square-shouldered at base, a little inflexed, creased, with margins wavy or incurved; corona short funnel-shaped, ribbed, deep rose red, with mouth straight and closely frilled. Mid-season. Resembles 'Cool Flame' but with the corona red on opening

'Decree' 2 W-P
(P. Phillips) P. Phillips, 1968

'Decumen' 2 W-? (b or c)
(J.L. Richardson, pre-1931)

'Dederang' 1 W-Y
(H.A. Brown, 1938) J.N. Hancock & Co., 1964
Corona creamy yellow, flecked white at rim, rim dentate. Mid-season

'Deemat' 7 Y-Y
(S.J. Bisdee, 1942)
'Golden Queen' × Jonquilla 'Plenus'

'Deemster' 2 Y-O
(F.E. Board) F.E. Board, 1965
'Workman' × 'Dunkeld'
Corona reddish orange. Mid-season

'Deenavee' 2 W-GYY
(M. Valois) D.F. Lee, 1973
Fl. 88 mm wide

'Deen Day' 1 W-W
(W.G. Pannill, 1981) W.G. Pannill, 1993
'Big Sur' × 'Canisp'
Early

'Deepdale' 2 W-? (b or c)
(W.A. Milner, pre-1916)

'Deep Freeze' 1 W-W
(J.A. Morris) J.A. Morris, 1962
Fl. 118 mm wide. Mid-season. Resembles 'Empress of Ireland' but with whiter perianth segments

'Deep Water' 2 W-W
(M.E. Brogden, pre-1993) Unregistered
'Easter Moon' × 'Empress of Ireland'

'Deerfin' 2 Y-Y
(W.J. Dunlop, pre-1969) Carncairn Daffodils, 1987
Fl. opening lime or lemon yellow, becoming darker in tone; corona with mouth expanded and frilled. Mid-season

'Deerfin' 2 Y-Y
(J.A. Morris, c.1987) Unregistered

'Deerlands' 1 W-W
(F.E. Board) F.E. Board, 1965
'Glenshesk' × 'Cantatrice'; sdlg no. 328

'Defender' 2 Y-? (a)
(L. van Leeuwen & Son, pre-1932)
AM(Haarlem) 1931

'Deference' 2 Y-Y
(R. & E. Havens, 1984) R. & E. Havens, 1994
'On Edge' × 'Kingbird'; sdlg no. TEH110/1
Fl. 75 mm wide; perianth segments broadly ovate, clear yellow, slightly reflexed; corona bowl-shaped, darker in tone than the perianth, with mouth wavy. Mid-season

'Defiance' 1 Y-Y
(C. Smith, pre-1906)
Perianth segments light yellow, twisted; corona golden yellow, with rim flanged

'Défiance' 2 Y-O
(Konynenburg & Mark) Konynenburg & Mark, 1960
'Aranjuez' × 'Beauty of the Garden'
Fl. 100 mm wide; perianth segments brilliant greenish yellow 6C; corona orange (28A). Late

N. deficiens Herbert = *N. serotinus* var. *deficiens*

'Deflexicaulis Plenus' 4 Y-Y
Syn. of 'Cyprius Flore Pleno Luteo Polyanthos'

'Defoe' 1 Y-Y
(R.C.A. Tombleson) R.C.A. Tombleson, 1972
'Kanga' × 'Kingscourt'
Fl. 115 mm wide

'Degrena' 1 Y-Y
(W. Jackson Sr, 1937) W. Jackson Jr, 1956
'Golden City' × 'Pilgrimage'

'Degryn' 1 W-W
(W.A. Watts, pre-1930)

'Deidre' 2 W-? (b or c)
(Sir J.A.R. Gore-Booth, pre-1916)

'Deirdre' 3 W-?
M.J. Jefferson-Brown, 1963

'Déjà Vu' 3 W-W
(T.D. Throckmorton, 1977) R. & E. Havens, 1989
'Easter Moon' × 'Snowshill'; sdlg no. 72/14/4
Fl. 115 mm wide; perianth segments white; corona bowl-shaped, opening ivory white, becoming pure white. Late. Resembles a larger 'Easter Moon'

'Deko' 2 Y-O
(J.N. Hancock & Co., 1949)

'Delabole' 2 Y-YOO
(Mrs H.K. Richardson) du Plessis Bros, 1986
'Teheran' × 'Ceylon'; sdlg no. 2929
Corona shallow. Mid-season

'De Lacey' 11a W-WWP
(D.S. Bell, pre-1986) Unregistered
'Perlax' × 'Accent'

'Delamont' 2 W-P
(Carncairn Daffodils) Carncairn Daffodils, 1971
Fl. 112 mm wide; corona expanded, pink, slightly frilled

'Delaware' 2 W-? (b)
(de Graaff Bros, pre-1927)

'Delaware' 2 W-P
(A. Overton) A. Overton, 1960

'Delectable' 2 W-? (b or c)
(F.H. Chapman, pre-1923)

'Delectable' 2 W-WWP
(G.E. Mitsch) G.E. Mitsch, 1972
'Pigeon' × 'Carnmoon'; sdlg no. B34/2
Fl. 82 mm wide; corona almost white, with a narrow band of bright pink at rim

'Delectus' 2 W-W
(G.L. Wilson) F.E. Board, 1962
'Killaloe' × 'Empress of Ireland'; sdlg no. 47-17
Resembles a Div. 2 'Empress of Ireland' with taller stem and whiter flower. Mid-season

'Deleena' 2 W-W
(Jackson's Daffodils) Jackson's Daffodils, 1991
'Scope' × sdlg 186/76; sdlg no. 286/82
Fl. forming a double triangle, 104 mm wide; perianth segments very broadly ovate, blunt, only very slightly mucronate, greenish white (155A), very slightly inflexed, plane, glistening, overlapping half or more; the outer segments overlapping one another; the inner segments more narrowly ovate, with margins sometimes wavy; corona funnel-shaped, usually shorter than the perianth segments, lightly ribbed, yellow-white (4D), with mouth flared and lightly frilled, rim crenate and narrowly rolled. Mid-season

'Delegate' 6 W-Y
(M. Fowlds) G.E. Mitsch, 1971
'Green Island' × *N. cyclamineus*; sdlg no. F378/9
Fl. 95 mm wide; perianth segments ovate, blunt, prominently mucronate, strongly reflexed, a little twisted, overlapping one-third; corona cylindrical, smooth, opening pale lemon yellow, fading almost to pure white, mouth slightly flared, frilled. Dwarf or standard. Mid-season

'Delegate' 2 Y-Y
(G.W.E. Brogden)

'Delhi' 2 W-O
(Mrs R.O. Backhouse, pre-1921)
Perianth segments pure white; corona reddish orange

'Delhi' 1 Y-Y
(J.N. Hancock & Co., 1957) Unregistered

'Delia' 3
(G.P. Haydon, pre-1914)

'Delia' 6 W-YWP
(Brian S. Duncan) Rathowen Daffodils, 1984
('Interim' × 'Aosta') × 'Foundling'; sdlg no. 563
Perianth segments broadly ovate, blunt, pure white, strongly reflexed, with margins recurved at base and incurved at apex, overlapping one-third; corona cylindrical, ribbed, a little constricted below mouth, white, with yellow at base and a band of soft pink at rim broadening with maturity, closely and minutely frilled. Mid-season to late

'Delibes' 2 Y-YYO
(F. Rijnveld & Sons, pre-1950)
Fl. 95 mm wide; perianth segments very broad, squarish at apex and sometimes truncate, brilliant greenish yellow 6C flushed with a darker tone (6B), with slight white mucro, spreading, plane, overlapping half or more; the inner segments narrower, slightly inflexed, with margins wavy and sometimes recurved; corona shallow bowl-shaped, very widely expanded, lightly ribbed, vivid yellow 14B shading to orange (near to 26B) at mouth, with mouth frilled, rim crenate. Early. 2n=29. AM(Haarlem) 1950, *HC(p) 1978

'Delicacy'
(pre-1913)

'Delicata' 3 W-? (b or c)
(G.H. Engleheart, pre-1907)

'Delicata' 3 Y-O
(Australian or New Zealand origin, pre-1927)
Perianth segments primrose yellow; corona deep reddish orange

'Delicata' 3 W-Y
Syn. of 'Albion'

'Delicato' 2 Y-W
(Konynenburg & Mark) Konynenburg & Mark, 1966
'Spellbinder' × 'Binkie'
Fl. 95 mm wide; perianth segments light greenish yellow 4C; corona creamy white. Mid-season

'Delicatus' ?-Y
(?E. Leeds, pre-1877)
Corona citron yellow. Syn. Incomparabilis Albus 'Delicatus'

'Delicatus' 3 W-Y
Syn. of 'Agnes Barr'

'Delicatus' 3 W-Y
Syn. of 'Albion'

'Delicia' 3 W-? (b)
(J.L. Richardson, pre-1939)
'Hospodar' × 'Sunstar'

'Delicious' 2 W-P
(Alister Clark, 1935) T. Morrison, 1960
Corona bright pink. Mid-season

'Delid' 2 Y-? (a)
(W.A. Watts, pre-1927)
See also 'Deud'

'Delight' 3 W-? (b)
(C.G. van Tubergen, pre-1914)

'Delight' 2 W-YYO
(Australian or New Zealand origin, pre-1951)

'Delight' 1 W-GWW
(W. Jackson Jr, 1968) Jackson's Daffodils, 1979
('Carcedu' × 'Seriki') × 'Empress of Ireland'; sdlg no. 172/68
Fl. 118 mm wide. Mid-season

'Delightful' 3 W-GYY
(G.E. Mitsch) G.E. Mitsch, 1969
'Cushendall' open pollinated; sdlg no. V03/2
Fl. rounded; perianth segments pure white, deeply overlapping; corona yellow, with green at base, frilled. Late. 2n=14. Resembles 'Grace Note' in colouring

'Delilah' 5
(H. Prins, pre-1929)

'Delissaville' 1 W-Y
(W.M. Spry, pre-1975) Unregistered
'Marble Queen' × 'Stand By'
Corona lemon yellow

'Delius' 2 W-? (b)
(R.H. Bath, pre-1933)

'Dell' 3 W-GYY
(E.M. Crosfield, pre-1910)
Fl. rounded; perianth segments deeply overlapping; corona tightly ribbed, bright lemon yellow, with olive green at base, rim lightly frilled

'Dellan' 2 Y-Y
(Rosewarne EHS, 1971) Rosewarne EHS, 1989
'Brandon' × 'Saint Keverne'; sdlg no. 65/7/2
Fl. 111 mm wide; perianth segments vivid yellow 9A, overlapping; corona expanded, slightly darker in tone (12A) than the perianth, with rim flanged and crenate. Early

'Dell Chapel' 3 W-WWO
(J.S.B. Lea) J.S.B. Lea, 1970
'Suilven' × 'Hamzali'; sdlg no. 2-48-57
Perianth segments very broadly ovate, truncate, only very slightly mucronate, spreading or a little reflexed, somewhat concave at apex; the inner segments less broadly ovate, slightly twisted, with margins strongly incurved at apex; corona bowl-shaped, ribbed, white, with pinkish orange at rim, mouth frilled, rim dentate. Mid-season

'Del Mar' 2 W-WWY
(G.H. Wayne) G.H. Wayne, 1981
'Aircastle' × 'Pontsiana'; sdlg no. A-1/4
Fl. 100 mm wide. Mid-season

'Delmar' 2 Y-O
(J.N. Hancock & Co., 1986) Unregistered
'Marilyn' × 'Artist's Model'; sdlg no. 25/86H
Perianth segments soft lemon yellow, deeply overlapping; corona disc-shaped, ribbed, deep bright orange. Late

'Delmont' 2 W-GWW
(W. Jackson Jr) Jackson's Daffodils, 1979
'Rashee' × ('Empress of Ireland' × 'Ammon'); sdlg no. 146/70
Fl. 125 mm wide. Mid-season

'Delnashaugh' 4 W-P
(J.S.B. Lea) J.S.B. Lea, 1978
'Kinbrace' × 'Romance'; sdlg no. 3-39-68
Fl. 105 mm wide. Late. *HC(g) 1990

'Delos' 3 W-? (b or c)
(W.B. Hartland, pre-1907)

'Delos' 3 W-GWW
(J.M. de Navarro) J.M. de Navarro, 1968
'Tobernaveen' × 'Verona'

'Delphi' 3 W-GWP
(G.H. Johnstone, pre-1960)

'Delphi' 1 W-W
(J.M. de Navarro) J.M. de Navarro, 1975
'Glendermott' open pollinated; sdlg no. 61/III
Fl. 90 mm wide. Mid-season. Resembles 'Matterhorn' but with the inner perianth segments broader

'Delphine' 2 W-P
(J.M. Radcliff, 1953) P. Phillips, 1964
F. 102 mm wide. Mid-season

'Delphin Hill' 4 W-W
(Ballydorn Bulb Farm, 1976) Ballydorn Bulb Farm, 1989
'Silver Spell' hybrid × Div. 3 sdlg with green corona
Fl. 60 mm wide, pure white; perianth segments very broadly ovate, plane; corona segments with green at base. Late

'Del Rey' 1 W-P
(W.G. Pannill) W.G. Pannill, 1979
('Interim' × 'Rose of Tralee') × 'Alpine Glow'; sdlg no. F 16 A
Fl. 110 mm wide. Mid-season

'Delrobin' 2 Y-O
(H.A. Brown, 1936) J.N. Hancock & Co., 1960
Corona reddish orange. Mid-season

'Del Rose' 2 W-P
(J.N. Hancock & Co.) J.N. Hancock & Co., 1955
Corona pink, frilled

'Delta' 1 Y-Y
(pre-1913)

'Delta' 8 Y-O
(Mrs R.O. Backhouse, pre-1921)
Poetaz
Perianth segments buff; corona reddish orange

'Delta' 11b W-O/YW
(W.F. Leenen) W.F. Leenen, 1983
Sdlg × 'Nippon'

'Delta Flight' 6 W-W
(Brian S. Duncan, 1980) Brian S. Duncan, 1992
'Lilac Charm' × 'Lavender Lass'; sdlg no. 630
Fl. 85 mm wide, glistening; perianth segments broadly ovate, blunt, slightly mucronate, pure white, reflexed, with margins wavy, overlapping half; the inner segments almost as wide; corona cylindrical or somewhat funnel-shaped, lightly ribbed, constricted near mouth, opening pale lilac pink, becoming pure white, with mouth flared and loosely frilled, rim minutely crenate. Dwarf. Early to mid-season

'Delta Queen' 2 W-P
(W.G. Pannill) W.G. Pannill, 1985
'Interim' × 'Fintona'; sdlg no. I 9 A
Mid-season

'Delta Wings' 6 W-P
(Brian S. Duncan) Rathowen Daffodils, 1977
Sdlg no. 75
Fl. 115 mm wide; perianth segments narrow, slightly reflexed; corona deep rosy pink, with rim slightly dentate. Mid-season. 2n=28

'De Luxe' 2 W-P
(G.E. Mitsch) G.E. Mitsch, 1971
'Accent' × 'Pink Monarch'; sdlg no. Z64/4
Fl. 112 mm wide; perianth segments very deeply overlapping; corona deep rose pink, heavily frilled. Mid-season

'Demand' 2 Y-Y
(P. & G. Phillips) P. & G. Phillips, 1975
Fl. 110 mm wide; perianth segments broadly ovate, rounded and very slightly inward curving at apex, vivid yellow 13A, smooth and of heavy substance; corona slightly darker in tone (14A), with mouth a little flared, rim shallowly dentate. Mid-season. Resembles 'Gold Bank' but with a more funnel-shaped corona

'Demelza' 2 Y-? (a)
(P.D. Williams, pre-1938)

'Demeter' 2 W-? (b)
(T. Batson, pre-1914)

'Demeter' 1 W-?
Syn. of 'Althorpe'

'Demitasse' 12 W-Y
(W.G. Pannill) W.G. Pannill, 1980
'Jenny' × *N. jonquilla*; sdlg no. G20C
Fls 2 per stem, 50 mm wide. Mid-season

'Demmo' 2 Y-O
(Jackson's Daffodils) Jackson's Daffodils, 1993
Sdlg 5/77 × Silcock sdlg RW2/761; sdlg no. 33/87
Fl. rounded, 102 mm wide; perianth segments ovate, vivid yellow 9A; corona cylindrical, strong orange 25A. Early. Sunproof

'Democlites' 8? ?-Y
Corona yellow. Syn. of 'Democlitus'

'Democlitus' 8? ?-Y
(pre-1881)
Syn. 'Democlites'

'Democrat' 1 W-Y
(J.N. Hancock & Co., pre-1949)
Corona lemon

'Demophon' 1 Y-Y
(Barr & Sons, pre-1929)
Perianth segments bright lemon yellow, overlapping; corona expanded, lightly ribbed, slightly darker in tone than the perianth, neatly frilled

'Dempo' 4
(pre-1934)

'Demure' 7 W-Y
(A. Gray, pre-1953)
N. rupicola subsp. *watieri* sdlg
Corona small, pale yellow

'Demure' 3 Y-O
Syn. of 'Dimity'

'Denali' 1 W-W
(R. & E. Havens, 1981) R. & E. Havens, 1992
'Empress of Ireland' × (['Virgil' × 'Empress of Ireland'] × 'Panache'); sdlg no. QEJ30/3
Fl. forming a double triangle, 110 mm wide, pure white; perianth segments broadly ovate, blunt, spreading, smooth, overlapping half; the inner segments a little inflexed; corona narrowly funnel-shaped, smooth, with mouth flared and very lightly frilled, rim crenate. Late

'Denbeam' 2 W-O
Syn. of 'Denbeau'

'Denbeau' 2 W-O
(J.N. Hancock & Co.) J.N. Hancock & Co., 1955
Perianth segments of good substance, deeply overlapping; corona apricot orange. See also 'Denbeam'

'Denham' 2 Y-O
M.J. Jefferson-Brown, 1964

'Denia' 2 Y-? (a)
(Mrs R.S. Cobley, pre-1937)

'Denise' 3 W-OOR
(J.S. Leitch) J.S. Leitch, 1962
Fl. 89 mm wide. Mid-season

'Dent Blanche' 1 W-W
(R.H. Bath, pre-1931)
Syn. 'Yungfrau'

'Dent-de-Lion' 2 W-W
(F.D.B. Cobb, pre-1953)

'Denys Meyer' 2 W-WYY
(H.R. Meyer, pre-1927)
'Bernardino' hybrid
Fl. 102 mm wide; perianth segments creamy white, overlapping half; corona light yellow 11B, paling to creamy white at base. 2n=28. *AM(g) 1947

'Deodolus' 2 W-? (b)
(W.F.M. Copeland, pre-1908)

'Deodora' 2 W-WWY
(J.L. Richardson, pre-1951)
'Green Island' × 'Greenore'
Fl. 117 mm wide; perianth segments very broadly ovate, blunt, mucronate, pure white, of thick substance, overlapping half; the inner segments more narrowly ovate, blunt or very slightly mucronate, with margins a little inward rolling; corona opening pale primrose, becoming white, with green at base and very pale primrose at rim, mouth very widely expanded, minutely ribbed and frilled. 2n=28. AM(e) 1959, AM(Haarlem) 1960

'Dependable' 1 W-Y
(O. Ronalds) T. Morrison, 1960
Perianth segments smooth; corona rim flanged. Syn. 'Stand By'

'Derby' 11?b W-O/Y
(?Dutch origin, pre-1990) Unregistered

'Derek' 1 Y-Y
(H.R. Meyer, pre-1938)
'Walter Fitch' × 'Golden Emperor'
Syn. ?'Derek Meyer'

'Derek Meyer' 1 Y-Y
?Syn. of 'Derek'

'Derflinger' 1 Y-Y
(T.H. Piper, 1946) T.H. Piper, 1956
'Bulwark' × 'Duddington'

'Derg Valley' 1 Y-Y
(Brian S. Duncan) Rathowen Daffodils, 1978
Richardson sdlg 3329 × 'Viking'; sdlg no. 147
Fl. forming a double triangle, mid-yellow, smooth; perianth segments broadly ovate, blunt, with slight white mucro, spreading, plane, overlapping; the inner segments inflexed at base, recurved near apex; corona funnel-shaped, narrowly based, with mouth expanded and rim notched. Mid-season. Resembles 'Golden Rapture'

'Dermot' 3 W-? (b)
(P.D. Williams, pre-1916)

'Derrinal' 1 Y-Y
(T. Morrison, 1939) T. Morrison, 1960
Perianth segments primrose yellow; corona darker in tone

'Derring' 2 W-R
(A.O. Roblin, 1945)
'Mr. Jinks' × 'Hades'

'Derrybann' 2 Y-? (a)
(G.L. Wilson, pre-1932)

'Derryboy' 3 W-YYO
(Ballydorn Bulb Farm) Ballydorn Bulb Farm, 1990
'Irish Minstrel' × 'Gransha'
Fl. 90 mm wide; perianth segments broadly ovate, pure white, overlapping; corona small bowl-shaped, golden yellow, with reddish orange at rim. Mid-season

'Dersingham'
(R.H. Bath, pre-1948)

'Dervish' 2 Y-O
(G.L. Wilson, pre-1937)
'Fortune' × 'Cornish Fire'
Fl. 102 mm wide; perianth segments ovate, acute, mucronate, lemon yellow, faintly suffused reddish orange, a little inflexed, smooth, with margins sometimes slightly incurving, overlapping one-third; the inner segments a little twisted; corona cup-shaped, marigold orange, with mouth straight and lightly frilled, rim crenate. AM(e) 1940, AM(Haarlem) 1949

'Derwent' 3 Y-YYO
(G.H. Cammell, pre-1907)

'Derwent' 2 W-P
(Campbell Duncan) Campbell Duncan, 1956
'Rosario' × 'Roselands'

'Derwent' 2 W-?
Syn. of 'Criton'

'Derwin' 2 Y-? (a)
(W.A. Watts, pre-1923)
'Sir Watkin' × 'Ornatus'

"Derwydd Daffodil"
See "The Derwydd Daffodil"

'Descanso' 1 W-Y
(Murray W. Evans) G.E. Mitsch, 1965
'Polindra' × 'Frolic'
Fl. 115 mm wide; perianth segments smooth, overlapping; corona slender, opening clear lemon yellow, becoming a little paler. Mid-season. 2n=28. Resembles a taller 'Frolic'

'Descartes' 2 Y-? (a)
(J.W.A. Lefeber, pre-1945)

'Deschutes' 2 Y-? (a)
(Oregon Bulb Farms, pre-1951)

'Desdemona' 3 W-Y
(W. Backhouse, pre-1869)
Corona expanded. Syn. Barrii Albus 'Desdemona'

'Desdemona' 2 W-Y
(E. Leeds, pre-1877)
Perianth segments white; corona expanded, clear yellow. Syn. Incomparabilis Albus 'Desdemona'. Was "absorbed" into Incomparabilis 'Albus'

'Desdemona' 3 W-? (b)
(C. Dawson, pre-1916)

'Desdemona' 2 W-W
(G.L. Wilson) Guy L. Wilson Ltd, 1964
('Courage' × 'Broughshane') × 'Rashee'
Perianth segments very broadly ovate, blunt, mucronate, spreading, plane, smooth, overlapping half; the inner segments shouldered at base, with margins wavy or slightly incurved; corona funnel-shaped, loosely ribbed, mouth flared and very lightly frilled, rim minutely and irregularly notched. 2n=28

'Deseado' 1 Y-O
(W.O. Backhouse) W.O. Backhouse, 1956
PC(e) 1967

'Desert Bells' 7 W-Y
(G.E. Mitsch, 1973) Grant Mitsch Novelty Daffodils, 1984
'Quick Step' × *N. assoanus*; sdlg no. II134/1
Fls 2-3 per stem, 43 mm wide; perianth segments broadly ovate, blunt, prominently mucronate, opening yellow, becoming almost white, spreading or slightly reflexed, plane, overlapping one-third to a half; corona cup-shaped, lightly ribbed, opening yellow, becoming pale lemon yellow, with mouth straight and wavy. Dwarf. Late

'Desert Cloud' 1 Y-Y
(H. Homan, pre-1933)

'Desert Dream' 1 Y-Y
(R.G. Cull) Hokorawa Daffodils, 1987
'Showtime' open pollinated; sdlg no. 78/3
Fl. vivid yellow 9B. Mid-season

'Desert Fox' 1 Y-YOR
(W.O. Backhouse) E. Longford, 1966
'Brer Fox' hybrid [probably]
Fl. 102 mm wide; perianth segments yellow; corona deep yellow at base, shading to fiery red rim. Early to mid-season

'Desert Gold' 7
(Mrs P.M. Davis, pre-1948)

'Desert Orchid' 2 Y-W
(Mrs J. Abel Smith) Mrs J. Abel Smith, 1989
'Grand Prospect' hybrid; sdlg no. G44/91
Perianth segments pale yellow. Late

'Desert Rose' 2 W-P
(Mrs H.K. Richardson) Carncairn Daffodils, 1979
'Daybreak' × 'Romance'; sdlg no. 399
Fl. 105 mm wide; perianth segments greenish white (155A); corona pink (29B). Late

'Desert Song' 2 Y-? (a)
(Mrs R.O. Backhouse, pre-1921)

'Desert Storm' 2 Y-ORR
(Clive Postles) Clive Postles, 1991
'Torridon' × 'Loch Hope'; sdlg no. 1-77-79
Fl. 96 mm wide; perianth segments ovate, somewhat concave at margins, smooth; corona funnel-shaped, with mouth straight and rim slightly dentate. Early

'Desert Sun' 2 Y-R
(Mrs R.O. Backhouse, pre-1921)
Perianth segments pale yellow; corona red

'Desert Sunrise' 2 W-PPY
(Sidney DuBose, 1977) Sidney DuBose, 1990
'Salome' × 'Carita'; sdlg no. C48-8
Fl. 108 mm wide. Mid-season

'Desert Victory' 2 Y-O
(G. Lewis) D.S. Bell, 1955
Corona reddish orange

'Design' 2 Y-O
(Warnaar & Co., pre-1952)
'Carbineer' × 'Westminster'
AM(Haarlem) 1952

'De Sion' 4 Y-Y
Syn. of 'Van Sion'

'Desirade' 2 W-? (b)
(Mrs R.O. Backhouse, pre-1921)

'Desiré' 2 W-O
(Barr & Sons, pre-1941)

'Desiree' 2 W-W
(J.N.Hancock & Co., 1984) Unregistered
'Chillagoe' × 'Beryl Hancock'; sdlg no. 4/84H
Fl. pure white; perianth segments deeply ovate; corona cylindrical, with rim neatly dentate. Early to midseason

'Desna' 9 W-?
(A.M. Wilson, pre-1913)

'Des Oldham' 2 W-P
(D.T. Oldham) P.J. Radcliff, 1990
Fl. 95 mm wide; perianth segments very broadly ovate, blunt, obscurely mucronate, clear white, with margins sometimes notched, smooth, regular, overlapping half; the inner segments almost as wide; corona clear mid-pink, with mouth expanded and wavy. Very late. Sunproof

'Desperado' 1 Y-Y
(H. or R.O. Backhouse, pre-1936)
'King Alfred' × 'Harvest'

'Dessert' 2 W-Y
(G.E. Mitsch) G.E. Mitsch, 1972
'Oratorio' × 'Pretender'; sdlg no. B32/3
Fl. rounded, 105 mm wide; perianth segments somewhat concave; corona bowl-shaped, pale lemon yellow, paling to base. Mid-season

'Destiny' 3 W-? (b)
(A.M. Wilson, pre-1930)

'Detention' 2 Y-YOO
(C.E. Radcliff, 1938) J.M.Radcliff, 1956
'Malvern Gold' × 'Fortune'

'Detroit' 1 W-? (b)
(G. Haver, pre-1930)
AM(Haarlem) 1930

'Deud' 2 Y-?
Syn. of 'Delid'

'De Valera' 2 Y-YYR
(pre-1926)
Perianth segments primrose yellow; corona deep yellow, with scarlet at rim

'Devenagh' 2 W-W
(G.L. Wilson, pre-1942)
'Niphetos' × 'Scapa'

'Dever' 2 W-? (b)
(H.P. Zwetsloot, pre-1939)
AM(Haarlem) 1939

'Devilry' 2 Y-O
(J.L. Richardson) M.J. Jefferson-Brown, 1961
'Sun Chariot' × 'Narvik'
Corona reddish orange

'Devils Pool' 2 Y-O
(J.N. Hancock & Co., c.1977) Unregistered

'Devon' 2 Y-? (a)
(Mrs R.S. Cobley, pre-1937)

'Devon Loch' 1 W-W
(J.L. Richardson) J.L. Richardson, 1956
'Ardclinis' × 'Kanchenjunga'
Fl. pure white; corona mouth frilled, with rim flanged. See also 'Devon Lough'

'Devon Lough' 1 W-W
Syn. of 'Devon Loch'

'Devonshire' 2 Y-R
(F.E. Board) F.E. Board, 1965
'Kindled' × 'Alport'; sdlg no. 1251
Late

'Devonshire Cream' 2 W-? (b)
(Cartwright & Goodwin, pre-1910)

'Devora' 2 W-Y
(D.J. Cooper) D.J. Cooper, 1959
Corona lemon yellow. Early

'Devotion' 1 Y-Y
(G. Lewis, pre-1940)
'Renown' × 'Beersheba'
Resembles a larger-flowered 'Royalist'

'Devotion' 1 W-W
(H.A. Brown) H.A. Brown, 1956

'Devoto' 1 Y-Y
(J. Gerritsen & Son, pre-1934)
Fl. soft yellow; corona slightly darker in tone

'Dewdrop' 3 W-? (b or c)
(Mrs R.O. Backhouse, pre-1904)
Corona sulphur. AM 1904

'Dewess' 5
(pre-1913)

'Dewlish' 2 Y-O
(D. & J.W. Blanchard) D. & J.W. Blanchard, 1955
'Penquite' × ('Aviemore' × 'Trevisky')

'Dew-pond' 2 W-W
(G.L. Wilson) G.L. Wilson, 1955

'White Maiden' × 'Greenland'
Corona bowl-shaped

'Dewy' 3 Y-? (a)
(A.H. Ahrens) J.S. Leitch, 1956

'Dewy Rose' 2 W-WPP
(Murray W. Evans) Murray W. Evans, 1976
'Cordial' × 'Caro Nome'; sdlg no. L-30
Fl. 95 mm wide. Mid-season

'D.Haring' 8 W-Y
(de Goede, pre-1927)
Perianth segments pure white; corona bright yellow, tinged orange at rim. Resembles a more refined 'Elvira' with a smaller flower

'Dhulin' 2 W-? (b)
(A. White, pre-1946)

'Diablo' 2 W-GYR
(W.G. Pannill) W.G. Pannill, 1980
'Roimond' × 'Corsair'; sdlg no. 64/106
Fl. 98 mm wide. Mid-season

'Diadem' 8 W-Y
(pre-1850)
Corona rich yellow

'Diadem' 3 W-YYR
(G.H. Engleheart, pre-1898)
Perianth segments creamy yellow; corona very shallow, yellow, with a sharply defined band of bright red at rim. AM 1898

'Diadem' 1 W-?
?Syn. of 'Ardina'

'Diamanté' 3 W-?
(pre-1950)

'Diamantina' 2 W-W
(W.M. Spry, pre-1975) Unregistered
'Chinese White' × Ronalds sdlg
Mid-season

'Diamond' 5 W-W
(W.F.M. Copeland, pre-1906)
Hybrid between 'Minnie Hume' and *N. triandrus* var. *loiseleurii*
Fls often 2 per stem, pure white; perianth segments spreading, overlapping; corona with mouth incurved

'Diamond' 2 or 3 W-W
(pre-1927)
Fl. pure white; corona mouth incurved

'Diamond Beauty' 1 W-W
(N.H. Anglo) N.H. Anglo, 1988
'Rashee' × 'Queenscourt'

Fl. pure ice white; perianth segments smooth; corona large, with rim flanged. Mid-season

'Diamond Cut' 2 W-W
(N.H. Anglo) N.H. Anglo, 1988
'Easter Moon' × 'Worcester'
Fl. pure white; corona bowl-shaped, with rim dentate. Mid-season. Resembles 'Diamond Edge' but with the perianth segments more narrowly acute

'Diamond Edge' 2 W-W
(N.H. Anglo) N.H. Anglo, 1988
'Easter Moon' × 'Worcester'
Fl. pure white; perianth segments smooth; corona bowl-shaped, with rim neatly dentate. Mid-season. Resembles 'Diamond Cut' with the perianth segments more rounded

'Diamond Finish' 2 W-GWW
(N.H. Anglo) N.H. Anglo, 1988
'Misty Glen' × 'Worcester'
Fl. icy white; perianth segments very smooth; corona cup-shaped, with mouth widely expanded and rim regularly dentate. Mid-season

'Diamond Head' 2 W-W
(W.G. Pannill) W.G. Pannill, 1972
'Easter Moon' × 'Vigil'
Fl. 132 mm wide

'Diamond Jubilee' 2 W-? (b)
(J.J. Grullemans & Sons) J.J. Grullemans & Sons, 1956

'Diamond King' 2 Y-R
(G. Lewis) D.S. Bell, 1955
Perianth segments soft yellow; corona dark red

'Diamond Lass' 2 W-P
(D. Bramley, 1970) D. Bramley, 1984
Sdlg × 'Mrs Oscar Ronalds'; sdlg no. 61/35
Fl. 110 mm wide; corona light pink

'Diana' 3 W-Y
(G.H. Engleheart, pre-1900)
Fl. large, rounded; perianth segments creamy white; corona large disc-shaped, pale cowslip yellow. AM 1900

'Diana' 8
Syn. of 'Diane'

'Diana Kasner' 3 Y-YYR
(Mrs R.O. Backhouse, pre-1921)
Perianth segments pure white; corona ribbed, yellow, with blood red at rim, frilled

'Diana Mary' 2 Y-? (a)
(de Graaff Bros, pre-1937)

'Diane' 8
(pre-1798)
Fl. pale yellow or white. See also 'Diana'

'Diane' 6 W-GPP
(Brian S. Duncan) Rathowen Daffodils, 1983
('Roseworthy' × 'Rosedew') × 'Foundling'; sdlg no. 547
Fl. 85 mm wide; perianth segments pure white, strongly reflexed; corona cylindrical, narrow, ribbed, deep pink, with green at base. Mid-season

'Diane Barker' 3 W-YYO
(L.P. Dettman) L.P. Dettman, 1972
'Jean Hood' × 'Nevose'
fl. 94 mm wide

N. dianthos Haworth = *N.* × *medioluteus*

'Diapason' 1 W-W
(G.L. Wilson) F.E. Board, 1962
'White Prince' × 'Vigil'; sdlg no. 47-6
Early. Resembles 'Vigil' but with broader perianth segments

'Diaphenia' 2 or 3 W-? (b or c)
(Cartwright & Goodwin, pre-1908)

'Diarmuid' 2 Y-? (a)
(Sir J.A.R. Gore-Booth, pre-1916)

'Diatone' 4 W-P
(Brian S. Duncan) Brian S. Duncan, 1992
'Quickstep' × sdlg 8/74 (['Falaise' × 'Debutante'] × 'Polonaise'); sdlg no. 977
Fls 2 per stem, 90 mm wide; perianth and other petaloid segments very broad, rounded at apex, white; the outer whorl spreading, plane, with midrib showing, deeply overlapping; the inner whorl a little shorter, strongly inflexed, with margins deeply incurling; corona segments short, clustered among the inner whorl of petaloid segments, pale pink. Mid-season to late. Sunproof. Jonquil scented

N. × *dichromus* P.D.Sell 13 = *N. cyclamineus* de Candolle × *N. moschatus* Linnaeus

'Dick' 1 W-Y
(de Graaff Bros, pre-1908)
FCC(Haarlem) 1908, FA(Haarlem) 1925

'Dickcissel' 7 Y-W
(G.E. Mitsch) G.E. Mitsch, 1963
'Binkie' × *N. jonquilla*; sdlg no. T6/11
Fls 1-3 per stem, 70 mm wide; perianth segments luminous lemon yellow, a little inflexed; corona somewhat flared, ribbed, opening yellow, becoming white. Mid-season. 2n=21

'Dick Sartoris' 1 W-Y
(pre-1893)
Perianth segments sulphur white, flushed pale orange at base; corona rich orange-yellow

'Dick Turpin' 3 W-R
(E.M. Crosfield, pre-1913)
Perianth segments ivory white; corona rich red, with a slightly paler tone at base. AM(Haarlem) 1937

'Dick Wellband' 2 W-O
(Mrs R.O. Backhouse, pre-1921)
Corona large, bright reddish orange. 2n=28. AM(Haarlem) 1931

'Dick Wilden' 4 Y-Y
(P.Th.Zwetsloot) G.B. de Vroomen & Sons, 1962
'Carlton' sport
Fl. 50 mm wide; perianth segments fairly broadly ovate, brilliant greenish yellow 6A, with slight white mucro, spreading, plane or sometimes concave at apex, overlapping a quarter; the inner segments narrowly spathulate, with margins nicked in places and wavy; corona funnel-shaped, smooth, orange-yellow, deeply split, sometimes to base, the segments broad, sometimes spreading, frilled; many corona segments tightly clustered within; a number of petaloid segments interspersed, longer than the corona segments, of the same colour as the perianth segments, those at centre with margins tightly incurled as if tubular, those in a surrounding whorl of six ovate, plane. Early

'Dictator' 2 W-? (b)
(W. Welchman, pre-1908)

'Dictum' ?-P
(Alister Clark, pre-1948)

'Dido' 3 W-R
(W.F.M. Copeland, pre-1908)
Perianth segments rounded; corona dark orange-red

'Dido' 7
(J.C. Williams, pre-1930)
Sdlg no. 764

'Dido' ?-P
(Alister Clark, pre-1948)

'Dieppe' 3 W-R
(J.L. Richardson, pre-1945)
'Coronach' × 'Forfar'
Fl. rounded; perianth segments very broadly ovate, blunt, prominently mucronate, pure white, spreading, of thick and waxy substance, overlapping half; the inner segments rounded at apex, only very slightly mucronate, a little inflexed; corona shallow bowl-shaped, heavily ribbed, intense deep red, mouth split in places and overlapping, with rim crumpled. Late

'Dierdre' 9 W-GOR
Syn. of 'Sidelight'

'Dignity' 1 W-W
(W. Welchman, pre-1908)

'Dignity' 1 W-? (b)
(A.M. Wilson) Mrs R. McConnel, 1956

'Digon' 1 Y-Y
(W. Jackson Sr, 1943) W. Jackson Jr, 1956
'Djaro' × 'Sir Accolon'

'Di-hard' 1 W-P
(Jackson's Daffodils) Jackson's Daffodils, 1996
Sdlg 42/76 × sdlg 268/76; sdlg no. 128/88
Fl. 105 mm wide; perianth segments broadly ovate, greenish white (155A); corona cylindrical, narrow, moderate yellowish pink 31D, with mouth slightly flared. Mid-season

'Dik Dik' 2 Y-R
(G.E. Mitsch) G.E. Mitsch, 1971
(['Market Merry' × 'Carbineer'] × 'Armada') × *N. cyclamineus*; sdlg no. A52/6
Fl. 62 mm wide; perianth segments broadly ovate, blunt, deep golden yellow, with white mucro, spreading, somewhat concave, with margins incurling at apex, a little creased, of good substance, regular, overlapping half; the inner segments more narrowly ovate, shouldered at base, more heavily creased; corona cylindrical, opening very deep golden yellow, becoming brilliant orange-red, mouth straight, regularly frilled. Dwarf to standard. Early

'Dilemma' 3 Y-YYO
(Brian S. Duncan) Rathowen Daffodils, 1983
'Aircastle' hybrid; sdlg no. 351
Fl. 112 mm wide; perianth segments primrose yellow; corona deep yellow, with orange at rim. Mid-season

'Diligence' 1 Y-Y
(G.L. Wilson) F.E. Board, 1956
'Crocus' × 'Golden Hind'

'Dillenburg' 2 Y-R
(Warnaar & Co., pre-1938)
AM(Haarlem) 1937

'Dilly' 5 W-W
(A. Gray) A. Gray, 1958
N. cyclamineus × *N. triandrus* var. *loiseleurii*
Fl. cream, of much substance. Dwarf

'Dilston' 2 W-? (b)
(C.E. Radcliff, 1930)

'Dim' 2 W-Y
(L.P. Dettman) L.P. Dettman, 1984

'Lemonade' × 'Cynthia Dettman'; sdlg no. 8/79
Fl. 84 mm wide; perianth segments greenish white (155A); corona greenish yellow, with light greenish yellow 1C at rim. Early. Resembles 'Cynthia Dettman' but with a more widely expanded corona mouth

'Dimity' 2 W-? (b or c)
(Mrs R.S. Cobley, pre-1932)

'Dimity' 3 Y-O
(W. Jackson Sr) W. Jackson Jr, 1968
'Vanity' × ('Narvik' × 'Kalit'); sdlg no. 15/60
Corona bright orange. Formerly named 'Demure'

'Dimple' 9 W-O
(Brian S. Duncan) Brian S. Duncan, 1992
Sdlg no. 1242
Fl. star-shaped, 68 mm wide; perianth segments ovate, blunt, only very slightly mucronate, pure white, spreading, plane, regular, overlapping one-third to a half; corona very short, solid brownish orange, with three yellow anthers prominent. Late to very late. Scented

'Dimpsey' 1 W-W
(G.L. Wilson) L. Major, 1965
Mid-season. Resembles 'Empress of Ireland'

'Dinah' 2 W-O
(Tom Forster, 1960s) Unregistered
Fl. rounded; perianth segments very broadly ovate, blunt, slightly mucronate, milk white, spreading, wih broad midrib showing, overlapping half; the inner segments a little inflexed. with margins wavy; corona very broad disc-shaped, closely ribbed, dark apricot orange, with rim irregularly notched and minutely crenate. Tall. Mid-season

'Dinard' 2 W-? (b)
(Barr & Sons, pre-1939)

'Dinas' 2 Y-? (a)
(A.M. Wilson, pre-1950)

'Dinedor Hall'
(pre-1935)

'Ding Dong' 1 W-W
(M.P. Williams, pre-1937)

'Dingle' 3 W-? (b)
(J.L. Richardson, pre-1938)
'White Sentinel' × 'Coronach'

'Dingle Dell' 6 W-W
(P. & G. Phillips) P. & G. Phillips, 1979
N. cyclamineus sdlg
Fl. 48 mm wide. Mid-season

'Dingo' 2 Y-Y
(G.L. Wilson, pre-1923)
Fl. bright yellow; corona expanded

'Dink' 2 W-YYO
Syn. of 'Elmira'

'Dinkie' 3 Y-GYR
(F.H. Chapman, pre-1927)
'Princess Mary' × 'Crimson Braid'
Perianth segments very broad, truncate, slightly mucronate, pale greenish yellow, spreading or a little reflexed, with margins narrowly incurlng at apex, of waxy substance, overlapping half; the inner segments narrower, more nearly ovate, spreading, with margins wavy or slightly incurved; corona bowl-shaped, narrowly ribbed, darker in tone than the perianth, with green at base and a well-defined narrow band of red at rim, mouth split in places and overlapping, frilled, rim minutely crenate. Mid-season. 2n=21. AM(c) 1930, FCC(e) 1935, *AM(g) 1936

'Dinkie Di' 3 Y-? (a)
(J.R. Byfield, 1932)

'Dinkie Duffle' 7 Y-R
(J.S. Leitch) J.S. Leitch, 1956

'Dinofor' 2 Y-? (a)
(Miss K.M. Hinchliff, pre-1935)

'Dinton Giant' 1 W-Y
(G.H. Engleheart, pre-1930)
Fl. rounded, very wide; perianth segments cream white, overlapping; corona yellow, with mouth expanded, with rim flanged. AM(Haarlem) 1938, FCC(Haarlem) 1940

'Dinton Leedsii' 2 or 3 W-? (b or c)
(G.H. Engleheart, pre-1914)

'Dinton Red' 9 W-OOR
(G.H. Engleheart, pre-1923)
Fls. occasionally 2 per stem, 76 mm wide; perianth segments clear white, reflexed, overlapping half; corona very shallow bowl-shaped, dark greenish orange, shading to dark red at rim. Mid-season to late. AM(e) 1923

'Dinton Sulphur' 1 Y-Y
(G.H. Engleheart, pre-1936)
Fl. sulphur yellow; corona rim dentate

'Diogenes' 1 W-Y
(P.D. Williams, pre-1907)
Fl. 95 mm wide, creamy white; corona opening pale lemon yellow

'Diolite' 2 Y-YYO
(A.M. Wilson/Miss G.Evelyn, pre-1930)

'Hospodar' × A.M.Wilson sdlg
Fl. more than 108 mm wide; perianth segments broadly ovate, rounded at apex, fairly prominently mucronate, primrose yellow, spreading, smooth, overlapping one-third to a half; the inner segments reflexed in upper half, somewhat creased, with margins wavy and sometimes nicked; corona bowl-shaped, ribbed, golden yellow, with a band of brownish orange at rim, mouth a little frilled, rim crenate and slightly flanged. Early to mid-season. AM(e) 1932, AM(Haarlem) 1938

'Diomed' 1 Y-Y
(Cartwright & Goodwin, pre-1923)

'Dione' 5 W-W
(H. Backhouse, pre-1913)
'Minie Hume' × *N. triandrus* var. *loiseleurii*
Fl. 89 mm wide, snowy white; corona expanded and ribbed

'Dionysius' 1 Y-Y
(de Graaff Bros, pre-1927)

'Diorama' 3 Y-YYR
(Brian S. Duncan) Rathowen Daffodils, 1987
'Dilemma' × 'Rotarian'; sdlg no. 937
Corona with a clearly defined band of orange-red at rim. Mid-season. Resembles a larger and taller 'Badbury Rings'

'Diotima' 1 Y-Y
(de Graaff Bros, pre-1927)

'Diploma' 2 Y-Y
(Elise Havens) R. Havens, 1979
'Paricutin' × 'Daydream'; sdlg no. GEJ6/2
Fl. 105 mm wide; perianth segments pale lemon, slightly tinged white at base, smooth; corona yellow, shading to pale orange gold at rim. Mid-season

'Diplomacy' 2 W-P
(G.L. Wilson) R.W. Ward & Sons, 1960
Mid-season

'Diplomat' 2 W-Y
(A.M. Wilson, pre-1937)
Sdlg no. 446
Fl. 95 mm wide; perianth segments very broadly ovate, fairly prominently mucronate, greenish white, a little inflexed, smooth, overlapping one-third to a half; corona cylindrical, smooth, lemon yellow, faintly flushed apricot orange, mouth flared, even, with rim more or less entire. AM(e) 1937

'Dipper' 6 W-Y
(M. Fowlds) G.E. Mitsch, 1971
'Green Island' × *N. cyclamineus*; sdlg no. F378/7
Fl. 92 mm wide; corona light yellow. Mid-season

'Direct Issue' 2 Y-? (a)
(J.A. Morris) J.A. Morris, 1957

'Director' 1 Y-Y
(G.W.E. Brogden) G.W.E. Brogden, 1968
Fl. 118 mm wide; perianth segments medium yellow; corona darker in tone. Mid-season

'Dirk Lubbe' 1 Y-Y
(W.J.M. Blom, 1970) Walter Blom & Son, 1984
'Arctic Gold' × 'Golden Harvest'; sdlg no. 70-E-12
Perianth segments clear yellow; corona dark yellow.
Early

'Dirranbandi' 1
(W.M. Spry, pre-1975) Unregistered
'Blond Giant' × 'Clare'
Fl. golden brown, flushed pink

'Disc' 3 W-? (b or c)
(G.H. Engleheart, pre-1903)
AM 1903

'Discipline' 3 W-Y
(F.E. Board) F.E. Board, 1965
Milne sdlg 1152 × G.L.Wilson sdlg 36/190
Corona lemon yellow

'Disco' 9 W-GGR
(Mrs M.S. Yerger) Mrs M.S. Yerger, 1988
'Sonata' open pollinated; sdlg no. 76 H 2
Perianth segments very smooth, overlapping; corona disc-shaped, yellow-green (151C), with a much darker tone at base and orange-red (33B) at rim. Dwarf. Mid-season. Scented. Resembles 'Sonata'

'Discoed' 9 W-?
(N.Y. Lower, pre-1921)
'Almira' × 'Will Scarlett'
?See also 'Discord'

discolor = *N. bertolonii* var. *discolor*

'Discord' 9 W-?
?Syn. of 'Discoed'

'Discovery' 1 W-? (b)
(W. Welchman, pre-1908)

'Discovery' 4 Y-O
(G.E. Mitsch) G.E. Mitsch, 1976
'Gay Time' × 'Daydream'; sdlg no. G69/1
Fl. 95 mm wide; perianth and other petaloid segments very broad, lemon yellow, deeply overlapping; corona segments interspersed, pale orange. Late

'Discretion' 3 W-Y
(F.E. Board) F.E. Board, 1965
'Gallilee' × 'Chinese White'
Corona lemon yellow

'Discus' 3 W-GYY
(H. Backhouse, pre-1913)
Perianth segments ivory white, overlapping; corona very shallow, citron yellow, with dull green at base and a suffusion of buffy apricot yellow towards rim. Tall

'Disky' 2 W-YYO
(S.C. Gaspar, 1950) R.J. Abernethy, 1960
Fl. 108 mm wide; corona shallow, orange-yellow, with mid-orange at rim. Mid-season

'Dispatch Box' 1 Y-Y
(Brian S. Duncan) Rathowen Daffodils, 1988
'Golden Jewel' × 'Midas Touch'; sdlg no. 820
Fl. very large; corona cylindrical, with mouth expanded. Early to mid-season. Resembles an 'Olympic Gold' of more deeply golden tone

'Display' 2 Y-? (a)
(Sir C.H. Cave, pre-1928)

'Disquiet' 1 Y-Y
(Jackson's Daffodils) Jackson's Daffodils, 1993
'Scipio' × 'Odin'; sdlg no. 254/87
Fl. 102 mm wide; perianth segments broadly ovate, vivid yellow 9A; corona cylindrical, slightly lighter in tone (12A) than the perianth, with rim rolled. Late

'Disraeli' 1 Y-Y
(G.L. Wilson, pre-1931)
'Madame de Graaff' × 'King Alfred'

'Distant Drums' 2 Y-R
(G.E. Mitsch, 1978) R. & E. Havens, 1992
'Zuni' × 'Vertex'; sdlg no. NN27/11
Fl. 120 mm wide, of heavy substance; perianth segments very broadly ovate, blunt, clear medium yellow; corona flared, brilliant orange-red, with rim deeply notched. Early. Sunproof

'Distich' 9 W-YYO
(F.H. Chapman, pre-1914)
Perianth segments rich creamy white; corona with a broad rim of scarlet-orange. AM(e) 1915

'Distinction' 3 Y-Y
(W. Backhouse, pre-1869)
Perianth segments primrose yellow. Syn. Barrii 'Distinction'. "Absorbed" 'Superbus'

'Distinction' 2 Y-Y
(G.H. Engleheart, pre-1890)
Fl. rich yellow; corona rim flanged

'Distinction' 1 W-W
(F.E. Board) F.E. Board, 1965
'Queenscourt' × 'Glendermott'
Mid-season. Resembles a large-flowered 'Queenscourt'

'Distingué' 3 W-W
(H. Backhouse, pre-1923)
Fl. white; corona slightly tinged pale lemon. Tall

'Ditty' 9 W-GYR
(F.H. Chapman, pre-1914)
'Socrates' × 'Acme'
Perianth segments very broadly ovate, mucronate, spreading, with margins incurling, overlapping half; the inner segments square-shouldered at base, with margins sometimes more strongly incurling; corona disc-shaped, narrowly ribbed, greenish yellow, with green at base and a broad band of brownish red at rim, mouth more or less even, rim minutely crenate. AM(e) 1926

'Diva' 2 W-Y
(G.L. Wilson, pre-1935)
'Madame de Graaff' hybrid × 'Naxos'

'Diversion' 3 W-GYR
(Carncairn Daffodils, 1970) Carncairn Daffodils, 1983
'Bravura' × 'Bushmills'; sdlg no. 4/11/64
Fl. 82 mm wide; perianth segments pure white; corona brilliant yellow 13B, with dark yellowish green 139A at base and a narrow band of orange-red (33A) at rim. Mid-season. 2n=28

'Divertimento' 7 W-P
(G.E. Mitsch) G.E. Mitsch, 1967
('Wild Rose' × 'Radiation') × *N. jonquilla*; sdlg no. V74/1
Fl. 67 mm wide; perianth segments ivory white; corona pale pink. Mid-season. Resembles a shorter and more floriferous 'Chérie' with the corona of a richer tone. 2n=21

'Dives' 1 Y-Y
(E.M. Crosfield, pre-1908)

'Dividend' 1 Y-Y
(Murray W. Evans) Murray W. Evans, 1975
'Lunar Sea' × 'Bethany'; sdlg no. F-266/8
Fl. 100 mm wide. Mid-season

'Divine' 2 W-P
(P. Phillips) P. Phillips, 1968
Corona opening bright pink, becoming more intense in tone

'Divot' 2 W-Y
(P.D. Williams, pre-1935)

'Dixie Dan' 11a Y-O
(?New Zealand origin) Unregistered

'Dixie Glory' 2 W-O
(Doornbosch Bros, 1948) Doornbosch Bros, 1960
Fl. 127 mm wide; corona reddish orange. Mid-season. Resembles 'Amateur'

'Dixieland' 4 W-P
(W.G.Pannill) W.G.Pannill, 1996
('Pink Chiffon' × 'Rima') × 'Pipestone'; sdlg no. 81/19
Fl. 90 mm wide; perianth and other petaloid segments white; corona segments pink. Late

'Dixie Lass' 2 W-? (b)
(de Graaff Bros, pre-1948)

'Dix Memory' 1 Y-Y
(G.H. Rotteveel & Sons, 1967) G.H. Rotteveel & Sons, 1989
'Louis Armstrong' sport; sdlg no. 6714
Fl. 120 mm wide; perianth segments pale greenish yellow; corona light greenish yellow 3D, with a much darker tone at base (9B) but only a slightly darker tone at rim (3C). Mid-season. Resembles 'Louis Armstrong'

'Djaro' 1 Y-Y
(W. Jackson Sr, 1938)
'Sir Gareth' × 'Golden City'

'Doak's Stand' 2 W-Y
(T.E. Snazelle) T.E. Snazelle, 1988
'Wahkeena' × 'Festivity'; sdlg no. 74/1/3
Mid-season

'Doctor Adenauer' 2 Y-Y
(L. Steenvoorden) L. Steenvoorden, 1958

'Doctor Alex Fleming' 2 W-O
(J.W.A. Lefeber, pre-1948)
Fls occasionally 2 per stem, rounded; perianth segments very broad, prominently mucronate, somewhat inflexed, overlapping half or more; the inner segments only very slightly mucronate, with margins sometimes wavy or recurved; corona bowl-shaped, orange, mouth deeply 6-lobed, heavily frilled, with rim crenate; the mouth sometimes widely expanded, with lobes opposite and closely overlying the perianth segments. 2n=28. Syn. 'Alex Fleming'

'Doctor Bruning' 2 W-? (b)
(pre-1953)

'Doctor Dentz' 1 Y-Y
(J.A. van Gent, pre-1944)

'Doctor Donald Rosanove' 1 Y-Y
(J.N. Hancock & Co., 1963) Unregistered

'Doctor Eckener' 1 W-? (b)
(W.J. Eldering & Son, pre-1930)

'Doctor E.van Slogteren' 1 Y-Y
(pre-1925)
AM(Haarlem) 1925

'Doctor Fell' 3 W-O
(W. Backhouse, pre-1869)
Perianth segments off white; corona scarlet-orange. Early

'Doctor Gorman' 2 W-Y
(pre-1884)
Syn. "The Great White", 'Great White', 'Queltia Alba', Incomparabilis Albus 'Dr Gorman'

'Doctor Hogg' 1 W-W
(W. Backhouse, pre-1869)
Corona long, smooth, opening pale primrose yellow, becoming creamy white, with rim flanged. Syn. Pseudonarcissus Moschatus 'Doctor Hogg'

'Doctor Hugh' 3 W-GOO
(Brian S. Duncan) Rathowen Daffodils, 1975
'Mahmoud' × 'Don Carlos'; sdlg no. 41
Fl. 110 mm wide; perianth segments very broadly ovate, truncate, prominently mucronate, pure white, spreading, shallowly concave, with margins minutely incurling at apex, smooth, regular, overlapping half; the inner segments more narrowly ovate, only very slightly mucronate, slightly inflexed, with margins a little wavy; corona disc-shaped, ribbed, opening deep orange (28A), becoming yellow-orange (23A), with green at base, mouth lightly frilled, deeply split, with overlapping lobes. Mid-season. Resembles a larger-flowered 'Omagh' of heavier substance with purer white perianth. AM(e) 1986

'Doctor James Parkinson' 2 WYY-YYO
(P. de Jager & Sons) J.W.A. van der Wereld, 1980
Fl. forming a double triangle, 105 mm wide; perianth segments broadly ovate, blunt, prominently mucronate, white, lightly flushed brilliant greenish yellow 6C at base, spreading, plane, overlapping half; the inner segments more narrowly ovate, less prominently mucronate, somewhat creased; corona cylindrical, lightly ribbed, vivid yellow, with yellow-orange (17A to B) at rim, mouth slightly expanded, frilled, rim loosely flanged. Mid-season. Syn. 'Professor Parkinson'. AM(p) 1981

'Doctor Jazz' 2 Y-ORR
(A.J.R. Pearson) A.J.R. Pearson, 1992
'Vulcan' × (['Home Fires' × 'Ceylon'] × 'Court Martial'); sdlg no. 88-34-M2
Fl. forming a double triangle, 105 mm wide; perianth segments ovate, blunt, vivid yellow 14B, spreading, plane, smooth; corona cylindrical, ribbed, orange-red (30C), paling to light orange at base, with mouth lobed and slightly flared. Mid-season. Resembles a later-flowered 'Vulcan' with a more cylindrical corona

'Doctor Johannes Beijer' 2 W-O
(J.W.A. Lefeber, 1940) J.W.A. Lefeber, 1961
Fl. 60 mm wide; perianth segments pure white; corona deep reddish orange. Mid-season. Resembles 'Smiling Mary'

'Doctor Johnson'
(?H.B.J. Bull, pre-1914)

'Doctor Kumura' 1 W-W
(G.P. Haydon, pre-1908)
Perianth segments pure white, somewhat twisted; corona opening creamy white, becoming milk white, lightly frilled

'Doctor Laumonier' 7
(Laumonier, pre-1897)
AM 1897

'Doctor Margaret' 12 W-Y
(David Salter) David Salter, 1997
Fl. 75 mm wide; perianth segments narrowly ovate, acute, reflexed; corona disc-shaped, plane, with mouth even. Dwarf. Mid-season

'Doctor Masters' 3 W-W
(J.G. Nelson, pre-1882)
Fls 2-3 per stem, silver white. Syn. Poculiformis 'Doctor Masters'

'Doctor Nansen' 1 Y-Y
(M. van Waveren & Sons, pre-1930)
Fl. large; corona slightly darker in tone than the perianth

'Doctor Peron' 2 W-GOO
(J.W.A. Lefeber, pre-1954)

'Doctor Primrose' 1 Y-Y
(G.H. Engleheart, pre-1913)

'Doctor Roseby' 2 Y-O
(O. Ronalds) M. Gardiner, 1956
Perianth segments near to orange-yellow; corona pale orange, frilled. Early

'Doctor Scott-Moncrieff' 1 W-Y
(J. Mallender, pre-1910)

'Doctor Valentine' 2 W-? (b)
(G.A. Uit den Boogaard, pre-1950)

'Doctor van Schelven' 2 Y-? (a)
(P.D. Williams, pre-1936)

'Doctor Verhage' 1 Y-Y
(G. Lubbe & Son, pre-1937)
AM(Haarlem) 1936

'Doctor Willem de Mol' 11a Y-Y
(J.W.A. Lefeber, 1948) J.W.A. Lefeber, 1961
Fl. 90 mm wide. Mid-season

'Dodman' 1 Y-Y
(The Brodie of Brodie, pre-1930)

'Doe Ross' 1 Y-Y
(W.M. Spry) W.M. Spry, 1979
'Marble Queen' × 'Big Keith'
Fl. 95 mm wide; perianth segments brilliant yellow 7A; corona slightly darker in tone (12A). Early. 2n=28

'Doette' 4 W-W
(W. Jackson Jr, 1955) W. Jackson Jr, 1966
'Kanchenjunga' × 'Fierenz'
Fl. cream and white

'Doily' 9 W-GYR
(Murray W. Evans, 1970) Murray W. Evans, 1982
N. poeticus var. *recurvus* × 'Dallas'; sdlg no. N-25/2
Fl. 53 mm wide. Late

'Dolce' 5 W-W
(A.E. Lowe, pre-1927)

'Dolce Vita' 4 Y-O
(Th. van der Hulst) Th. van der Hulst, 1989
'Orbit' × 'Tahiti'
Fl. 85 mm wide, of firm substance; perianth segments vivid yellow 9B; corona segments vivid orange 28B. Early to mid-season

'Dolina' 2 Y-Y
(D.C. MacArthur) D.C. MacArthur, 1985
'Kingscourt' open pollinated; sdlg no. F8330
Perianth segments very broad, blunt, vivid yellow 12A, a little ribbed, with margins slightly incurved, overlapping half; the inner segments much narrower; corona cup-shaped, lightly ribbed, darker in tone (14B) than the perianth, rim crenate, with some deeper notches. Mid-season. Scented

'Dollar' 3 W-YYR
(pre-1918)
Perianth segments pure white; corona yellow, with red at rim

'Dollar Princess' 2 W-? (b)
(G. Lewis) D.S. Bell, 1955
Corona very wide, with a broad band of red at rim

'Doll Baby' 7 W-P
(Mrs J.B. Capen) Mrs J.B. Capen, 1985
Fls sometimes 2 per stem. Mid-season. Scented. Resembles 'Demure' but with a clear pink corona

'Doll Dance' 11a W-W
(A.N. Kanouse, 1957) A.N. Kanouse, 1976
'Hillbilly' × 'Mabel Taylor'
Fl. 89 mm wide. Mid-season

'Dolly' 5 Y-Y
(Sir F.C. Stern) Sir F.C. Stern, 1960

Fl. pale yellow. Early. Resembles *N. triandrus*. PC(p) 1960

'Dolly Mollinger' 3 W-? (b)
(J.W.A. Lefeber, pre-1941)

'Dolly Mollinger' 11b W-O/W
(J.W.A. Lefeber) J.W.A. Lefeber, 1958
Perianth segments very broad, blunt, prominently mucronate, spreading, somewhat creased, overlapping half or more; the inner segments only a little narrower, only very slightly mucronate; corona segments six, half as long as the perianth segments and alternate to them, broad, ribbed, orange at base and in a wide longitudinal band at midrib, with white at margins in upper half, spreading or a little inflexed, with margins wavy and sometimes incurled. 2n=28

'Dolly Pentreult' 1 Y-Y
(G.H. Johnstone, pre-1960) Unregistered

'Dolly Warden' 2 W-? (b)
(Mrs R.O. Backhouse, pre-1921)

'Dolomite' 1 W-W
(J.N. Hancock & Co., 1971) Unregistered

'Dolores' 2 Y-? (a)
(Cartwright & Goodwin, pre-1910)

'Dominant' 1 W-W
(Australian or New Zealand origin, pre-1927)
Fl. 120 mm wide; perianth segments regular, overlapping; corona ivory white, with green at base

'Dominator' 1 Y-Y
(G. Lubbe & Son, pre-1948)
'Hindenburg' × 'Unsurpassable'
2n=28. AM(Haarlem) 1948

'Dominica' 1 W-W
(Donna C.Dietsch) Donna C.Dietsch, 1995
'Silent Valley' × 'Faro'; sdlg no. 86/11
Fl. 98 mm wide; perianth segments broadly ovate; corona cylindrical, slightly constricted towards mouth, with mouth ribbed and flared. Mid-season

'Dominick' 2 Y-Y
(P.D. Williams, pre-1925)
Fl. soft yellow; corona widely expanded, with rim rolled. AM(e) 1925

'Dominion' 2 Y-Y
(F.H. Chapman, pre-1914)

'Dominion' 1 W-W
(W. Welchman, pre-1923)

'Dominion Monarch' 1 Y-Y
(D.S. Bell) D.S. Bell, 1955

'Kingscourt' × 'Pre-eminent'
Fl. pure golden yellow; corona rim rolled

'Domino' 3 W-Y
(Mrs R.O. Backhouse, pre-1921)

'Domino' 1 Y-WWY
(G.H. Johnstone) G.H. Johnstone, 1959
Fl. 115 mm wide; corona opening very pale yellow, becoming white, with bright yellow at rim. Mid-season

'Donacloney' 2 W-R
(W.J. Dunlop, c.1964) Unregistered
Corona dark red

'Donald' 1 Y-Y
(W. Poupart, pre-1914)

'Donald Richardson' 2 W-? (b)
(Miss K.M. Hinchliff, pre-1941)

'Donatello' 2 Y-? (a)
(de Graaff Bros, pre-1927)

'Donation' 2 Y-W
(G.H. Johnstone, pre-1950)

'Donation' 2 Y-Y
(?New Zealand origin) Unregistered

'Donax' 2 Y-O
(Mrs R.O. Backhouse, pre-1910)
Perianth segments bright golden yellow; corona large, expanded, reddish orange

'Don Brockwell' 2 GGP-P
(L.P. Dettman) L.P. Dettman, 1976
'Arctic Gold' × 'Creamed Honey'; sdlg no. 45/75
Fl. 89 mm wide; perianth segments light yellow-green 145D, with a band of pale yellowish pink 29D at base; corona pale yellowish pink 29D, with yellow on the outside, rim dentate. Mid-season. Resembles 'Creamed Honey' but with a differently coloured perianth and longer corona

'Don Camillo' 2 W-? (b)
(J.H. Rijkelijkhuizen, pre-1953)

'Don Carlos' 8 W-O
(pre-1777)
See also 'Don Charlos'

'Don Carlos' 2 W-O
(J.L. Richardson) Mrs H.K. Richardson, 1962
'Kilworth' × 'Arbar'
Fl. 105 mm wide; perianth segments very broadly ovate, blunt, mucronate, creamy white, tinged yellow at base, spreading, slightly concave, with margins incurling at apex and sometimes notched, overlap-

ping half; the inner segments a little narrower, shouldered at base; corona very shallow bowl-shaped, widely expanded, loosely ribbed, vivid orange 25B, tinged vivid orange-yellow 21A and 23A, mouth deeply 3-lobed, lightly frilled, the lobes shallowly bi-lobed and overlapping, rim minutely and irregularly crenate. Late. AM(e) 1964, *AM(g) 1971

'Doncella' 1 W-W
(A. Gray) A. Gray, 1967
Very early. Resembles an earlier-flowered *N. alpestris* of better constitution

'Don Charlos' 8 W-O
Syn. of 'Don Carlos'

'Dondrosa' 2 W-Y
(W. Blom & Son) W. Blom & Son, 1959
Fl. 95 mm wide; corona lemon yellow. Late. Resembles 'Mitylene'

'Donegal' 2 W-WWR
(C. Dawson, pre-1908)
Corona with a sharply defined band of red at rim

'Donegal Beauty' 2 Y-? (a)
(G.L. Wilson, pre-1935)

'Donegal Glory' 1 Y-Y
(G.L. Wilson, pre-1935)

'Donis' 3 Y-? (a)
(A.H. Ahrens) J.S. Leitch, 1955

'Donizetti' 2 W-Y
(Konynenburg & Mark) Konynenburg & Mark, 1961
('Daisy Schäffer' × 'Fortune') × ('Daisy Schäffer' × 'Gracious')
Fl. 120 mm wide; perianth segments greenish white; corona light yellow 10B. Mid-season

'Don Juan' 1 Y-Y
(The Brodie of Brodie, c.1908)
'Santa Maria' × 'King Alfred'; sdlg no. 66/B/06
Fl. very deep yellow; perianth segments twisted

'Donlia' 4 W-P
(D.S. Bell) D.S. Bell, 1982
Sdlg × 'Accent'
Fl. 107 mm wide. Mid-season

'Don Lorenzo' 2 W-O
(J.W.A. Lefeber) J.W.A. Lefeber, 1960
Fl. 95 mm wide; perianth segments pure white; corona deep reddish orange. Early

'Donna'
(New Zealand origin, pre-1940)

'Donna Bella' 11b W-O/Y
(J.W.A. Lefeber, 1943) J.W.A. Lefeber, 1960
Fl. 75 mm wide; corona deeply split, the segments alternate to the perianth segments, with a longitudinal band of orange at centre shaded with red and flanked by yellow. Late

'Donna Buang' 1 Y-Y
(Heathcote Bulb Nursery, pre-1960) Unregistered

'Donna Maria' 6 W-GPP
(D.S. Bell) D.S. Bell, 1984
'Eastern Dawn' × 'Jenny' hybrid
Fl. 85 mm wide; perianth segments strongly reflexed. Mid-season

'Donore' 1 Y-Y
(G.L. Wilson) G.L. Wilson, 1956
'Bastion' × 'Goldcourt'
Fl. dark gold. Late

'Don Pedro' 1 Y-Y
(Barr & Sons, pre-1923)

'Don Philippe' 8 W-O
(pre-1798)

'Don Quixote' 1 W-? (b)
(Barr & Sons, pre-1908)

'Don Quixotte' 1 W-Y
Syn. of 'Princeps Maximus'

'Donside' 2 (a)
(Seymour Cobley Ltd, pre-1954)

'Donwal' 1 W-Y
(W. Jackson Sr, 1944)
'Thubui' × 'Dawnglow'
See also 'Donwall'

'Donwall' 1 W-Y
Syn. of 'Donwal'

'Dookie' 2 Y-O
(J.N. Hancock & Co., 1954)

'Doomben' 1 Y-Y
(H.A. Brown, pre-1938)
Mid-season

'Dora' 3 W-? (b or c)
(pre-1908)

'Dora' 2? W-?
?Syn. of 'Dora Fell'

'Dora Allum' 2 W-WWP
(R.A.Scamp) S.Holden, 1997
'Chenoweth' × 'Premier'; sdlg no. 84
Fl. 96 mm wide, chalky white; perianth segments broadly ovate, smooth, deeply overlapping; corona slightly flared, with bright rosy pink at rim, neatly frilled. Early to mid-season. Sunproof

'Dorada Dawn' 2 W-PPW
(T. Bloomer) Rathowen Daffodils, 1985
'Passionale' × ('Interim' × 'Rose Caprice' hybrid); sdlg no. 376
Perianth segments broadly ovate, smooth, overlapping; corona clear apple blossom pink, with emerald green at base and white at rim, mouth expanded, slightly frilled. Mid-season. Tall

'Dorade' 8 Y-Y
(pre-1798)

'Dorade' 2 W-W
(W. Jackson Jr, 1956) Unregistered
'Whitemark' × 'Ludlow'

'Dorado' 2 W-? (b)
(W.A. Grace, pre-1938)

'Dorado' 2 Y-Y
(S.J. Bisdee, 1940)
'Golden Queen' × 'Kallista'

'Dora Fell' 2 W-R
(West & Fell, pre-1935)
Perianth segments creamy white; corona frilled, brilliant red. Syn. ?'Dora'

'Dorcas' 1 W-Y
(Barr & Sons, pre-1908)
Perianth segments creamy white, slightly twisted; corona expanded, pale canary yellow, frilled

'Dorcas' 7 Y-Y
(A.M. Wilson, pre-1915)
Perianth segments rich deep yellow; corona a little darker in tone

'Dorcas' 1 Y-Y
(D.S. Bell) D.S. Bell, 1979
'David Bell' × 'Dawngold'
Fl. 98 mm wide; corona frilled

'Dorchester' 4 W-P
(Brian S. Duncan) Rathowen Daffodils, 1987
Evans sdlg H22/1 ('Pink Chiffon' × ['Rosegarland' × pink sdlg]) × 'Pink Pageant'; sdlg no. 898
Fl. rounded; perianth and other petaloid segments in several whorls, white; the two outer whorls of about equal length, regularly superimposed, very broadly ovate, spreading or slightly inflexed, overlapping half or more; those at centre irregularly arranged, broad, strongly inflexed, with margins tightly incurled; corona segments short, clean pink, tightly frilled, clustered among the centre petaloid segments and more

loosely arranged between the outer whorls. Late to very late

'Doré' 3 W-Y
(A.E. Lowe, pre-1927)

'Doreen' 3 W-? (b)
(C. Dawson, pre-1908)

'Doreen' 1 Y-Y
(?W.F. Mitchell, pre-1935)

'Doreen Eblen' 2 Y-Y
(L.P. Dettman) L.P. Dettman, 1975
'Creamed Honey' × 'Binkie'; sdlg no. 20/68
Fl. 77 mm wide. Mid-season. Resembles 'Ellimatta' but with a paler corona

'Dorelia' 2 W-? (b)
(Mrs R.O. Backhouse, pre-1921)

'Dorette' 1 W-Y
(W.Jackson Sr, 1944)
'Alope' × 'Dawnglow'

'Dorian' 2 W-? (b)
(Barr & Sons, pre-1952)

'Dorinda' 3 W-R
(J.T. Gray, pre-1949)
Corona deep brick red

'Dorine' 2 W-O
(van Zonneveld Bros & Philippo, pre-1923)
Perianth segments creamy white; corona large, expanded, reddish orange. AM(Haarlem) 1923, FCC(Haarlem) 1924

'Dorion' 1 W-Y
(W. Jackson Sr, 1944)
'Thubui' × 'Dawnglow'

'Doris' 2 Y-? (a)
(G.H. Engleheart, pre-1907)

'Doris' 9 W-?
(pre-1915)

'Doris Mathew' 2 W-Y
(Miss K.M.Hinchliff, pre-1941)
See also 'Doris Matthew'

'Doris Matthew' 2 W-Y
Syn. of 'Doris Mathew'

'Doris May'
Pollen parent of 'Rahiti'

'Dorothea' 2 W-P
(?Campbell Duncan, c.1959) Unregistered
'Rosario' × Pink Monarch'

'Dorothea Gertrude' 8 W-Y
(J.J. Nieuwland, pre-1949)
TGA(Haarlem) 1949

'Dorothy' 3 W-O
(A.R. Goodwin, pre-1910)
Fl. facing down; perianth segments creamy white, separated; corona cup-shaped, dark reddish orange. Resembles an improved 'Firebrand'

'Dorothy B.'
Unregistered
Pollen parent of 'Trifo'

'Dorothy Bucknall' 1 Y-Y
(Irish origin, pre-1930)
Fl. bright golden yellow; perianth segments twisted; corona deeper in tone than the perianth. Dwarf. Very early. ?The same as 'Creagh Castle Seedling'

'Dorothy Carter' 2 W-? (b)
(Mrs R.O. Backhouse, pre-1921)
Syn. 'Miss D.Carter'

'Dorothy E.Wemyss' 3 W-YYO
(W. Backhouse, pre-1869)
Perianth segments large, pure white; corona expanded, canary yellow, with scarlet-orange at rim. Syn. Barrii Albus 'Dorothy E.Wemyss'. AM 1901. See also 'Dorothy Wemyss'

'Dorothy Ford' 2 W-W
(E.W. Philpott) Unregistered

'Dorothy Heath' 2 W-Y
(G.E. Mitsch) B.C. Heath, 1977
('Mabel Taylor' × 'Interim') × 'Rima'; sdlg no. Y36/3
Fl. 90 mm wide; perianth segments pure white; corona opening orange, becoming light apricot

'Dorothy Hector' 8 W-R
(W.J.G. Hector) W.J.G. Hector, 1965
Fl. 65 mm wide. Mid-season. Resembles 'Saint Keyne'

'Dorothy J.Speck' 2 W-? (b)
(W.A. Grace, pre-1938)

'Dorothy Kingsmill' 5 W-Y
(G.H. Engleheart, pre-1899)
'Grandis' × N. triandrus
Perianth segments broadly ovate, pure white, spreading or a little inflexed, with margins wavy, overlapping at base only; corona cylindrical, long, lightly ribbed, greenish yellow, with mouth flared and a little frilled. AM 1899, FCC 1900

'Dorothy Osborne' 2 W-Y

(D.N.Y. Olson) D.N.Y. Olson, 1978
'Greenore' × 'Pink Isle'; sdlg no. 84/1
Fl. 118 mm wide; corona opening pale yellow, rapidly becoming buff white, faintly touched gold at rim. Mid-season

'Dorothy Pearson' 2 W-O
(G.H. Engleheart, pre-1907)
Fl. rounded; corona bright orange

'Dorothy Priestley' 3 W-YYO
(Mrs R.O. Backhouse, pre-1921)
Perianth segments pure white; corona bright canary yellow, with a broad band of scarlet-orange at rim

'Dorothy Rogerson' 2 W-P
(Alister Clark, 1940) J. Sharp, 1960

'Dorothy Simmons' 1 G-G
(W.M. Spry, pre-1975) Unregistered
'Judy Davidson' × Fairbairn sdlg
Fl. lemon green; corona frilled. Early

'Dorothy Strom' 2 W-? (b)
(?W.M. & A.P. Spry, pre-1955) Unregistered

'Dorothy Vernon' 2 or 3 W-? (b or c)
(J.R. Pearson & Sons, pre-1910)

'Dorothy Wemyss' 3 W-YYO
Syn. of 'Dorothy E.Wemyss'

'Dorothy Yorke' 2 W-YYO
(G.H. Engleheart, pre-1897)
Sdlg no. 40
Perianth segments more or less broadly ovate, blunt, prominently mucronate, spreading, overlapping at base only; corona large cup-shaped, loosely ribbed, bright yellow, with a reddish orange stain deepening to a solid colour at rim, mouth frilled. Mid-season. Resembles a larger and firmer-flowered 'Lulworth'

'Dorrien Smith' 1 W-Y
Syn. of 'T.A.Dorrien Smith'

'Dorset' 1 Y-Y
(H.J. Poole Sr, pre-1927)

'Dorset Beauty' 2 W-? (b or c)
(J.W. Barr, pre-1930)

'Dorus' 2 W-O
(W. Jackson Jr, 1966) Unregistered
'Jo' × 'Arbar'; sdlg no. 159/66

'Dosoris' 3 W-O
(P.D. Williams, pre-1910)
Fls 2 per stem; perianth segments slightly reflexed; corona shallow, salmon orange, tinged scarlet. Syn. 'Mahdi'. AM(Haarlem) 1914

'Dosorus' 2
(?G. Lubbe & Son, pre-1930)

'Doss Cowie' 2 W-P
(H.T. Dettmann)
Fl. large; perianth segments white, of good substance; corona deep lavender pink

'Dossier' 2 Y-YOO
(G.W.E. Brogden) G.W.E. Brogden, 1963
Fl. 102 mm wide; perianth segments pale yellow; corona orange, with lighter tones at base. Mid-season

'Dot' 1 Y-Y
(R. Gibson, pre-1931)

'Dotteral' 2 Y-WWY
(G.E. Mitsch) G.E. Mitsch, 1975
'Aircastle' × 'Daydream'; sdlg no. F136/2
Fl. 95 mm wide; perianth segments lemon, slightly inflexed; corona bowl-shaped, deep, opening lemon, becoming white, with a narrow band of lemon at rim, frilled. Mid-season

'Dottie' 3 W-YYP
(R.H. Glover) R.H. Glover, 1973
'Marilyn' × 'Estrella'
Fl. 83 mm wide

'Double Blush' 4 W-P
(Carncairn Daffodils) Carncairn Daffodils, 1987
'Egg Nog' × 'Little Princess'; sdlg no. 2/2/72
Perianth and other petaloid segments white; the outer whorl very broadly ovate, truncate, spreading, a little concave, with broad midrib showing, of good substance, overlapping half; the inner whorl inflexed, with margins deeply incurved, more or less regularly arranged, overlapping; corona segments clustered at centre, more loosely arranged between the petaloid segments, pink (29A), sometimes splashed yellow. Late

'Doublebois' 5 W-W
(A. Gray) A. Gray, 1962
N. triandrus var. *loiseleurii* sdlg
Fls 2 per stem, 80 mm wide. Late. Resembles a late and larger-flowered 'Tristesse'

"Double Border"
?Syn. of Poeticus 'Plenus'

'Double Campernelle' 4
(Mauger & Son, pre-1900)
2n=14. Syn. 'Plenus'. AM 1900

'Double Chance' 4
(J.M. de Navarro, pre-1949)

'Double Chance' 4 Y-O
(Tom Forster, 1960s) Unregistered

Probably a 'Telamonius Plenus' hybrid
Fl. rounded; perianth and other petaloid segments in several whorls, very broadly ovate, primrose yellow, with slight white mucro, overlapping; the outer whorl spreading; the inner whorls shorter, inflexed, successively more crumpled and with margins inrolling; corona segments shorter still, clustered among the inner whorls of petaloid segments, bright orange, frilled. Mid-season

'Double Cream' 4 W-Y
(W.G. Pannill) W.G. Pannill, 1987
'Snowshill' × Richardson white/yellow double sdlg; sdlg no. 67/57 B
Late

'Double Crest' 4 W-R
(J.L. Richardson) G. Zandbergen-Terwegen, 1959
'Falaise' hybrid
AM(Haarlem) 1959

'Doubledale' 4 W-Y
(J.J. Abernethy, 1953) R.J. Abernethy, 1963
Perianth and other petaloid segments milky white; corona segments rich deep creamy yellow. Mid-season. 2n=28. See also 'Double Dale'

'Double Dale' 4 W-Y
Syn. of 'Doubledale'

'Doubleday' 4 Y/W-W/Y
(J.W.Blanchard, 1985) J.W.Blanchard, 1996
'Daydream' × sdlg 71/32A (sdlg 59/45C × 'Irani'); sdlg no. 80/33A
Fl. rounded, 90 mm wide; perianth and other petaloid segments in three whorls, broad in outline, round or squarish at apex, pale yellow, with white mucro and with a more or less broad band of white at midrib, overlapping; the outer whorl spreading or a little inflexed, with margins slightly wavy; the inner whorl more strongly inflexed, with margins more heavily wavy or recurved; the centre whorl shorter, strongly inflexed, tightly clustered, with margins infolded; corona segments two-thirds the length of the two outer whorls of petaloid segments and interspersed among all three, white, sometimes touched with yellow, loosely frilled. Mid-season to late

'Double Decker' 4 Y-Y
(Tom Forster, 1960s) Unregistered
Perianth and other petaloid segments creamy yellow; corona segments interspersed, deep golden yellow. Tall. Late

'Double Desire' 4 Y-P
(D.S. Bell) D.S. Bell, 1983
'Papua' × 'Hicol'

'Double Diamond' 4 Y-Y
(J. Valkering & Sons) J. Valkering & Sons, 1972
'Youth' sport

'Double Diamond' 4 W-Y
(pre-1987) Unregistered

'Double Dividend' 4 Y-Y
(D.S. Bell) D.S. Bell, 1957
Fl. primrose yellow

'Double Eagle' 4 W-O
(J.L. Richardson) G. Zandbergen-Terwegen, 1960
Fl. white and orange. 2n=27. Resembles an improved 'Mary Copeland'. AM(Haarlem) 1959

'Double Event' 4 W-Y
(J.L. Richardson, pre-1952)
'Falaise' × 'Green Island'
Fl. rounded, 90 mm wide; perianth and other petaloid segments very broad, rounded at apex and truncate, very deeply overlapping; the outer whorl mucronate, spreading; the inner whorl slightly shorter, not noticeably mucronate, inflexed, with margins incurling; three segments at centre strongly inflexed, with margins deeply incurling; corona segments very short, clustered among the petaloid segments at centre, brilliant yellow 13B, frilled. 2n=29. AM(e) 1952, FCC(e) 1956, *AM(g) 1981, *FCC(g) 1982, AGM 1993

'Double Fashion' 4 Y-O
(J.L. Richardson) G. Zandbergen-Terwegen, 1965
'Falaise' hybrid
Fl. rounded, 102 mm wide; perianth and other petaloid segments very broad, light yellow; the outer whorl blunt or truncate, slightly mucronate, spreading; the inner whorls only a little shorter, truncate, not noticeably mucronate, successively more strongly inflexed; corona segments one-quarter the length of the petaloid segments and interspersed among them, yellow-orange, shading to deep orange at rim, frilled. Mid-season. Resembles 'Extol'

'Double Fortune' 4 Y-Y
(G. Zandbergen-Terwegen, pre-1954)
'Fortune' sport
Syn. ?'Fortune's Double'. AM(Haarlem) 1956

'Double Gold' 4 Y-Y
(?New Zealand origin, pre-1996) Unregistered

'Double Golden Dawn' 4 Y-Y
(Tom Forster, 1960s) Unregistered
Perianth and other petaloid segments in many whorls, lemon yellow; corona segments shorter, interspersed, golden yellow. Tall. Early

"Double Golden Trumpet"
Syn. of 'Maximus Flore Pleno'

'Double Gold Medal' 4 Y-Y

(Koopman-Laan) Koopman-Laan, 1994
'Gold Medal' sport
Fl. 110 mm wide; perianth segments vivid yellow 9A; corona segments a little darker in tone. Mid-season

'Double Happy' 4 Y-R
(G.J. Phillips) G.J. Phillips, 1987
2 Y-R sdlg × 'Warne'; sdlg no. 75-32-2
Fl. yellow and orange-red. Early. Resembles 'Beauvallon'

"Double Italian"
?Syn. of 'Romanus'

'Double Lemon' 1 W-Y
(J.N. Hancock & Co., 1968) Unregistered
Sdlg no. 178/68H
Fl. large; perianth segments broad, creamy white; corona bright lemon yellow, heavily frilled, occasionally enclosing white petaloid segments. Early to mid-season

"Double Marsellian"
Syn. of 'Romanus'

'Double Ming' 4 W-W
(A.M. Wilson, pre-1950)
Perianth segments in a single whorl; corona segments tinged green

'Double Perfection' 4 Y-Y
(G.H. Rotteveel & Sons) G.H. Rotteveel & Sons, 1975
'Emperor' sport

"Double Pheasant Eye"
Syn. of Poeticus 'Plenus'

"Double Poeticus"
Syn. of Poeticus 'Plenus'

"Double Roman"
Syn. of 'Romanus'

'Double Sir Watkin' 4 Y-O
(English origin, pre-1916)
'Sir Watkin' sport
Syn. 'Sir Watkin, Double'. AM(e) 1916

'Double Stella' 4 ?W-Y
Syn. of 'Butterfly'

'Doublet' 4
(W.A. Watts, pre-1929)

'Doublet' 4 W-Y
(J. Gerritsen & Son) J. Gerritsen & Son, 1961
Fl. 100 mm wide; perianth and other petaloid segments pure white; corona segments pale yellow. Late. 2n=14. Resembles a larger-flowered 'Medina'.

AM(Haarlem) 1961

"Double Tags"
Syn. of 'Flore Pleno'

'Double Triumph' 4 W-O
(J.L. Richardson) G. Zandbergen-Terwegen, 1965
'Falaise' hybrid
Fl. 114 mm wide; perianth and other petaloid segments milky white; corona segments clear orange. Late

"Double Trumpet Major"
Syn. of 'Maximus Flore Pleno'

'Double Vision' 4 Y-R
(J.L. Richardson) R.W. Ward & Sons, 1973

'Double White' 4
Syn. of 'Tamar Double White' and 'Spalding Double White'

"Double White Polyanthus"
Syn. of 'Romanus'

"Double White Sweet Scented"
?Syn. of 'Romanus'

Double Wintercups Group
Commercial name for a group of several different cultivars specially forced for early flowering

'Double Youth' 4 Y-Y
(J. Valkering & Sons, 1952) J. Valkering & Sons, 1963
'Youth' sport
Fl. 102 mm wide. Mid-season. Resembles a larger-flowered 'Telamonius Plenus' of a clearer yellow. TGA(Haarlem) 1963

'Doubloon' 4
'Telamonius Plenus' × 'Ornatus'
Syn. of 'Dubloon'

'Doubtful' 3 Y-O
(J.L. Richardson, pre-1953)
'Bahram' × 'Sun Chariot'
Perianth segments clear yellow, spreading, smooth; corona intense reddish orange

'Douceur' 2 W-? (b or c)
(P.D. Williams, pre-1931)

'Douglasbank' 1 Y-Y
(W. Buchanan) Alan M. Edwards, 1993
Selection from *N. minor*
Fl. 40 mm wide, yellow; perianth segments touched paler yellow at base, with whitish mucro, a little inflexed, somewhat twisted, overlapping at base only; corona cylindrical, constricted near mid-point,

slightly darker in tone than the perianth, with mouth expanded and deeply 6-lobed, heavily frilled. Dwarf. Early. PC 1993

'Douglas Dick' 2 Y-? (a)
(R. Dick, pre-1930)

'Doule' 2 W-? (a)
(West & Fell, pre-1938)

'Doumer' 1 Y-Y
(J. Verduyn, pre-1944)

'Doushinka' 3 W-? (b)
(R. & G. Cuthbert, pre-1938)

'Doutrice Triumphante' 8 Y-Y
(pre-1798)
Fl. pale yellow

'Dove' 2? W-Y
(E. Leeds, pre-1877)
Dwarf. Syn. Incomparabilis Albus 'Dove', Incomparabilis Albus 'Nanus'

'Dove' 7 W-Y
(C.F. Coleman) M.J. Jefferson-Brown, 1962
'Mitylene' × N. jonquilla
Fls 2-3 per stem; perianth segments rounded, smooth; corona cream. Scented

'Dovedale' 2 W-? (b or c)
(C.B. Blampied, pre-1929)

'Dovekie' 12 Y-Y
(G.E. Mitsch) G.E. Mitsch, 1980
'Matador' × N. cyclamineus; sdlg no. HH133/6
Fls 1-4 per stem, 70 mm wide; perianth segments light lemon; corona deeper in tone. Mid-season. Resembles 'Quince'

'Dove of Peace' 6 W-O
(Ballydorn Bulb Farm) Ballydorn Bulb Farm, 1980
'Buncrana' hybrid
Fl. 45 mm wide. Mid-season

'Dover' 2 W-W
(F.A. Secrett, pre-1948)

'Dover' 2 Y-R
(W. Jackson Jr, pre-1949)
'Caerleon' × 'Market Merry'

'Dover Cliffs' 2 W-W
(F.E. Board) F.E. Board, 1956
'Brookfield' hybrid
Fl. chalk white; corona with yellow in tube

'Dove Song' 2 W-WWP
(Sidney DuBose, 1977) Sidney DuBose, 1990

'Rainbow' × 'Carita'; sdlg no. C43-8
Fl. 95 mm wide. Mid-season

'Dove Wings' 6 W-Y
(C.F. Coleman, pre-1949)
'Mitylene' × N. cyclamineus
Fl. 76 to 85 mm wide; perianth segments broadly ovate or somewhat oblong, blunt or squarish at apex, prominently mucronate, creamy white, reflexed, plane, with midrib showing, overlapping one-third to a half; the inner segments more narrowly ovate, not noticeably mucronate, with margins slightly wavy; corona cylindrical or narrowly funnel-shaped, loosely ribbed, between brilliant yellow 9C and vivid yellow 9B, mouth very slightly expanded, frilled, with rim crenate. Early. 2n=21. AM(e) 1949, *AM(g) 1954, AM(Haarlem) 1961, *FCC(g) 1973, *AM(p) 1985, AGM 1993

'Downas' 2 Y-? (a)
(The Brodie of Brodie, pre-1930)
'Sunstar' hybrid

'Downcast' 1 W-W
(G.P. Haydon, pre-1914)

'Downham' 1 W-? (b)
(R.H. Bath, pre-1950)

'Downhill' 3 W-W
(W.J. Dunlop) W.J. Dunlop, 1960
'Portrush' × 'Chinese White'
Perianth segments pure white, smooth; corona shallow, white, tinged green towards base. 2n=28

'Downlands' 3 W-Y
(G.J. Phillips) G.J. Phillips, 1992
'Modulux' × 'Flash Affair'; sdlg no. 82-13-1
Fl. 108 mm wide; perianth segments roundish, pure white; corona rich yellow, with mouth lobed and widely expanded. Tall. Late

'Downpatrick' 1 W-Y
(W.J. Dunlop) W.J. Dunlop, 1959
'Guardian' × 'Broughshane'
Fl. 110-115 mm wide; perianth segments blunt, greenish white (155A), inflexed, slightly twisted, regular, overlapping; corona slightly ribbed, greenish yellow (4C), mouth expanded, with rim flanged and crenate. 2n=28. AM(e) 1971

'Draco' 2 Y-? (a)
(R.O. Backhouse, pre-1934)

'Dracula' 2 Y-? (a)
(W.A. Grace, pre-1938)

'Dragoman' 3 W-R
(J.L. Richardson) J.L. Richardson, 1956
'Mahmoud' × 'Matapan'

Corona ribbed, red

'Dragon Fly' 5
(W.F.M. Copeland, pre-1908)

'Dragon Fly' 4
(?J.N. Hancock & Co., pre-1949)

'Dragonfly' 6 OOR-R
(H. Koopowitz) H. Koopowitz, 1979
'Beryl' × 'Ambergate'; sdlg no. A573/1
Fl. 64 mm wide; perianth segments pinkish beige, flushed red, with a band of more solid red at base; corona deep orange-red. Mid-season

'Dragon Run' 2 W-R
(R.A.Scamp, 1986) R.A.Scamp, 1997
'Hotspur' × 'Saint Anns'; sdlg no. 147
Fl. 83 mm wide; perianth segments very broadly ovate, pure white, concave; corona very shallow bowl-shaped, dark red, with mouth lobed. Mid-season

'Dragoon' 3 W-R
(J.C. Williams, pre-1913)
Corona large, expanded, bright vermilion red. Tall

'Dragos' 2 Y-O
(D. Blanchard, pre-1949)
'Seraglio' × ?'Hades'

'Drake' 1 Y-Y
(P.D. Williams, pre-1927)
Fl. rich yellow; perianth segments deeply overlapping; corona rim widely flanged

'Drama' 2 W-P
(Alister Clark, 1945) J. Sharp, 1960
Corona deep pink, with rim flanged

'Dramatis' 9 W-YYR
(Brian S. Duncan) Rathowen Daffodils, 1987
'Pantomine' open pollinated
Perianth segments recurved. Late to very late. Resembles a larger and neater *N. poeticus* var. *recurvus*

'Drapeau de France' 8 W-Y
(pre-1792)

'Dreadnought' 1 Y-Y
(M. van Waveren & Sons, pre-1908)

'Dream' 1 W-W
(R.H. Bath, pre-1908)

'Dreamboat' 2 W-YYO
(Murray W. Evans, 1970) Murray W. Evans, 1980
'Marshfire' × 'Hotspur'; sdlg no. N-36/3
Fl. 95 mm wide. Mid-season

'Dream Castle' 3 W-W
(G.E. Mitsch) G.E. Mitsch, 1963
'Green Island' × 'Chinese White'; sdlg no. R33/49
Fl. rounded, 108 mm wide; perianth segments pure white; corona opening cream, becoming whitish. Mid-season. 2n=28. Resembles a larger-flowered 'Chinese White' of somewhat rougher surface

'Dreamgift' 3 W-? (b)
(J.E. Exley, pre-1950)

'Dream Girl' 2 W-YYO
(Warnaar & Co.) Warnaar & Co., 1957

'Dreamland' 1 W-Y
(W. Welchman, pre-1908)
Perianth segments narrow, acute, tinged green at base; corona pale yellow, with rim rolled

'Dreamland' 9 W-GYR
(J.S. Leitch) J.S. Leitch, 1962
Fl. 51 mm wide; corona lemon yellow, with green at base and orange-red at rim. Late

'Dreamlight' 3 W-GWR
(G.L. Wilson, pre-1934)
'Dactyl' × 'Mystic'
Perianth segments very broad, rounded, pure white; corona white, tinged soft greenish grey, with greenish white at base and a narrow band of orange-red at rim. Late. 2n=14. AM(e) 1938, AM(Haarlem) 1949

'Dreamlike' 2 W-P
(Mrs C.O. Fairbairn)

'Dreamlover' 6 YYW-W
(M.G.Temple-Smith) M.G.Temple-Smith, 1995
'Daydream' × *N. cyclamineus*; sdlg no. 26/89
Fl. 62 mm wide; perianth segments narrow, yellow, with a broad band of white at base, reflexed, separated; corona funnel-shaped, opening lemon yellow, becoming white, with mouth slightly flared. Mid-season

'Dream of Beauty' 5 W-W
(Sir A.P.W. Thomas, pre-1912)
N. × *johnstonii* sdlg
Fls often 2 per stem, large, pure white. Tall

'Dream Pool' 2 Y-O
(J.N. Hancock & Co., 1965) Unregistered

'Dream Prince' 2 Y-Y
(R.H.Glover, pre-1993) Unregistered

'Dream Queen' 3 W-GYW
(Mrs G. Link, 1983) Mrs G. Link, 1993
'Pewee' × ('Sweet Music' × 'Pewee'); sdlg no. 17-78
Fl. 70 mm wide; perianth segments white, spreading, smooth, glistening, deeply overlapping; corona spreading, ribbed, yellow, with deep green at base and

a band of white at rim, mouth frilled. Very late

'Dream Rocks' 2 W-YYO
(J.N. Hancock & Co., pre-1956)
Corona bright golden yellow, with pinkish apricot orange at rim

'Dreamthorpe' 2 W-P
(Mrs E. Murray)

'Dreamtime' 1 W-Y
(J.N. Hancock & Co., 1956)
Perianth segments smooth, of good substance; corona cylindrical, opening soft yellow, becoming rosy cream, with rim regularly dentate. See also 'Dream Time'

'Dreamtime' 3 W-?
(Mrs B.A. Woods) Mrs B.A. Woods, 1968

'Dream Time' 1 W-Y
Syn. of 'Dreamtime'

'Dream World' 11a W-PPY
(David L. Sheppard) David L. Sheppard, 1987
'Travertine' × 'Gypsy Princess'
Fl. 100 mm wide; perianth segments very broadly ovate, blunt, mucronate, spreading, very slightly concave at apex, overlapping one-third; the inner segments more narrowly ovate, inflexed, with margins incurling; corona split to base, the six segments half the length of the perianth segments and opposite to them, with many deeply overlapping lobes at apex, smooth, pink, with soft pinkish yellow at rim, inflexed, heavily frilled. Resembles 'Travertine' in colour

'Dreen' 2 W-P
(W.J. Dunlop, pre-1949)
'White Sentinel' × 'Evening'
Perianth segments pure white; corona pale pink

'Drenagh' 2 W-P
(Carncairn Daffodils) Carncairn Daffodils, 1969
G.L.Wilson sdlg × 'Rose Royale'

'Dresden' 9 W-O
(G.H. Engleheart, pre-1910)
Perianth segments broad and roundish, only slightly mucronate, milk white, spreading, plane, overlapping half; the inner segments a little inflexed; corona very shallow, orange, with a broad band of scarlet-orange at rim

'Dresden' 3 W-YYR
(S.A. Free) S.A. Free, 1960
Fl. 89 mm wide; perianth segments pure white; corona tightly ribbed, yellow, with red at rim. Mid-season

'Dresden China' 2 W-YPY

(S.J. Bisdee, 1943)
'Mitylene' × 'Dawnglow'

'Dresden China' 2 W-P
(G.S. Young) G.S. Young, 1956
Perianth segments slightly mucronate, pure white, translucent, overlapping half; the inner segments more narrowly ovate, shouldered at base; corona cup-shaped, smooth, clear shell pink, mouth widely expanded and a little frilled, rim notched and flanged

'Dress Circle' 3 W-YYR
(T. Bloomer, 1964) Rathowen Daffodils, 1976
'Corofin' × 'Hamzali'; sdlg no. 19/78/58
Perianth segments white; corona deep yellow, with a narrow band of deep red at rim. Resembles 'Silent Grace' but with a larger and smoother perianth

'Dressy Bessy' 2 W-GYO
(W.G. Pannill, 1976) W.G. Pannill, 1990
'Hotspur' × 'Larry'; sdlg no. 70/13
Late

'Drew Stewart' 1 W-P
(Brian S.Duncan) Mrs J.M.Baker, 1996
1 W-P sdlg × 'Parkfields Beauty'; sdlg no. EV88331
Fl. forming a double triangle, 112 mm wide; perianth segments broadly ovate, mucronate, yellowish white 158C, concave; corona narrowly funnel-shaped, ribbed, light yellowish pink 27A, with mouth straight and regularly frilled, rim crenate. Mid-season

'Dreyfus'
(Davies, pre-1901)

'Drift' 1 W-W
(R.V. Favell, pre-1940)
'Irish Pearl' × 'Gyrfalcon'

'Drina' 2 W-? (b)
(Mrs R.O. Backhouse, pre-1921)

'Driven Snow' 1 W-W
(G.L. Wilson, pre-1923)
Corona opening faint primrose ivory, becoming white

'Dromalga' 2 W-GWW
(M.J. Ward, 1972) M.J. Ward, 1986
'Verona' × 'Stainless'; sdlg no. 67.9.1
Perianth segments very broadly ovate, blunt or rounded at apex, slightly mucronate, spreading, plane, smooth, overlapping half; the inner segments more narrowly ovate, a little inflexed; corona broad bowl-shaped, loosely ribbed, with mouth lightly frilled. Mid-season. Resembles 'Verona' in perianth and 'Stainless' in corona

'Dromina' 1 W-W
(pre-1914)

'Dromona' 2 W-Y
(Carncairn Daffodils) Carncairn Daffodils, 1973
'Fairy Tale' hybrid
Fl. 100 mm wide; corona butter yellow. 2n=28

'Dromore' 2 W-Y
(W.J. Dunlop) W.J. Dunlop, 1959
Perianth segments broad; corona opening pale creamy yellow, becoming paler in tone. Late

'Drongo' 4 W-Y
(G.E. Mitsch) Grant Mitsch Novelty Daffodils, 1984
'Gay Time' × 'Stainless'; sdlg no. LL66/20
Fl. 100 mm wide; perianth and other petaloid segments broadly ovate, inflexed, overlapping; the outer and the inner whorls of more or less equal length; some shorter segments at centre strongly inflexed, with margins tightly incurled; corona segments very short, clustered among the centre petaloid segments and more loosely interspersed among the surrounding segments, opening white and yellow, becoming creamy yellow. Late

'Droplet' 5 W-W
(Don Bramley) Don Bramley, 1989
'Lunar Ring' × *N. triandrus*; sdlg no. 79/44
Fl. 55 mm wide; perianth segments a little reflexed; corona cup-shaped. Mid-season. Resembles an earlier-flowered 'Rippling Waters' with broader perianth segments and the corona mouth more strongly incurved

'Dropmore' 1 W-W
(G.P. Haydon, pre-1908)
'Monarch' × 'Madame de Graaff'
ad

'Drop o' Gold' 5 Y-Y
(James S. Wells) James S. Wells, 1990

'Druid' 9 W-?
(A.M. Wilson, pre-1908)

'Druid' 9 W-?
(G.L. Wilson, pre-1934)

'Druim' 1 Y-Y
(Brodie Gardens) Brodie Gardens, 1957
'Naviston' hybrid × 'Golden Torch'
Fl. opening deep golden yellow, the corona becoming orange-yellow; perianth segmnts very broad, spreading, plane, smooth; corona long, of thick substance, with rim flanged

'Drumadarragh' 1 Y-Y
(Carncairn Daffodils) Carncairn Daffodils, 1971
'Kingscourt' × 'Prince Igor'
Fl. 105 mm wide. Resembles a slightly deeper-toned 'Kingscourt' with the corona rim more heavily rolled

'Drumadoon' 2 W-O
(Carncairn Daffodils) Carncairn Daffodils, 1981
'Home Fires' × 'Armada'; sdlg no. 102/60
Fl. 105 mm wide; perianth segments broadly ovate, greenish white (155A); corona slightly expanded, light orange (23A), with darker tones in some environments, rim dentate

'Drumard' 1 W-?
(T. Bloomer) T. Bloomer, 1962

'Drumawillan' 2 Y-W
(Carncairn Daffodils) Carncairn Daffodils, 1970
'Cantatrice' × 'Content'
Resembles a Div. 2 'Spellbinder' with no roll at corona rim

'Drumbeg' 2 W-Y
(Ballydorn Bulb Farm, 1983) Ballydorn Bulb Farm, 1994
'Mount Pleasant' × 'Dundrod'
Fl. 97 mm wide; perianth segments very broadly ovate, pale milk white; corona expanded, somewhat ribbed, orange-yellow, with rim widely rolled. Mid-season

'Drumboe' 2 W-WWP
(G.L. Wilson) G.L. Wilson, 1960
'Tryst' × ('Cotterton' × 'Broughshane')
Corona rim pale pink

'Drumcairne' 2 W-PPR
(Carncairn Daffodils) Carncairn Daffodils, 1970
'Irish Rose' × Radcliff sdlg
Perianth segments pure white, creased opening, becoming plane. Sunproof

'Drumfearn' 2 W-P
(J.L. Richardson) E. Longford, 1963
'Rose Caprice' × 'Salmon Trout'
Fl. 102 mm wide; perianth segments white; corona salmon pink. Mid-season. Resembles 'Salmon Trout' but with broader perianth segments and a deeper colour to the corona

'Drumlin' 1 W-Y
(Ballydorn Bulb Farm, 1981) Ballydorn Bulb Farm, 1993
'Dundrod' × 'Preamble' hybrid
Fl. 112 mm wide; perianth segments very broadly ovate, opening milky white, becoming pure white; corona deep yellow, with mouth flared at maturity and rim rolled. Mid-season

'Drummer Boy' 1 Y-Y
(G.P. Haydon, pre-1910)

'Drummer Boy' 2 Y-Y
(W.G. Pannill) W.G. Pannill, 1970
'Saint Keverne' × 'Golden Rapture'

'Drumnabreeze' 2 Y-WWY
(Carncairn Daffodils) Carncairn Daffodils, 1978
'Daydream' × 'Moonspell'; sdlg no. 1/9/69
Fl. 112 mm wide; perianth segments acute, brilliant greenish yellow 3A, slightly reflexed; corona quickly becoming greenish white (157C), with deep lemon at rim, tightly frilled. Mid-season

'Drumnasole' 3 W-Y
(Carncairn Daffodils) Carncairn Daffodils, 1970
'Sylvia O'Neill' × G.L.Wilson sdlg
Perianth segments opening yellow, becoming white; corona yellow

'Drumragh' 1 Y-Y
(Brian S. Duncan) Rathowen Daffodils, 1979
'Yellow Idol' self pollinated × 'Viking'; sdlg no. 97
Fl. 110 mm wide, deep golden yellow; perianth segments slightly reflexed; corona slender. Mid-season

'Drum Roll' 1 Y-Y
(D.S. Bell) D.S. Bell, 1963
Fl. 106 mm wide, deep yellow. Early. Resembles 'Kingscourt' but with the perianth segments more rounded

'Drumrunie' 2 Y-O
(J.S.B. Lea) J.S.B. Lea, 1971
Sdlg 2-17-54 ('Spry' × Navarro sdlg) × 'Vulcan'; sdlg no. 2-41-63
Fl. 110 mm wide; perianth segments rich gold; corona vivid reddish orange. Early

'Drumtullagh' 2 W-GWW
(Carncairn Daffodils) Carncairn Daffodils, 1971
'Easter Moon' × G.L.Wilson sdlg
Fl. 110 mm wide; perianth segments pure white; corona opening with pink at rim, soon becoming pure white, with green at base

'Drusiform' 2 W-? (b or c)
(P.D. Williams, pre-1931)

'Drusilla' 1 W-W
(Barr & Sons, pre-1914)
Fl. 82 mm wide; perianth segments creamy white, with margins recurved, overlapping at base only; corona opening creamy white, becoming milk white, mouth expanded and frilled, with rim flanged. Mid-season to late

'Drusilla' 2 Y-? (a)
(A.H. Ahrens, pre-1946)

'Dryad' 3 W-W
(G.H. Engleheart, pre-1903)
Fl. large, ivory white; perianth segments broad. Resembles a larger 'Mrs Langtry'

'D.S.West' 2 W-O
(West & Fell, pre-1935)
Perianth segments opening pale yellow, becoming white; corona widely expanded, scarlet-orange, frilled

'Duala' 2 Y-R
(J.S. Leitch) J.S. Leitch, 1958

'Dual Gift' 2 W-P
(J.N. Hancock & Co., 1949) J.N. Hancock & Co., 1960
Corona pink, frilled

N. dubius Gouan 13 Section Tazettae
    var. ***dubius***
    var. ***micranthus*** (Jordan & Fourreau) Ascherson & Graebner

'Dubloon' 4 Y-Y
(G.H. Engleheart, pre-1907)
'Telamonius Plenus' × 'Ornatus'
Fl. bright yellow; corona segments darker in tone than the perianth or petaloid segments. See also 'Doubloon'

'Ducat' 1 Y-Y
(G.H. Engleheart, pre-1907)

'Ducat d'Or' 8 Y-Y
(pre-1851)

'Ducaton' 1 Y-Y
(C.G. van Tubergen, pre-1931)
AM(Haarlem) 1930

'Duc d'Ahremberg' 8 W-O
(?Dutch origin, pre-1777)
See also 'Duc d'aremberg'

'Duc d'aremberg' 8 W-O
Syn. of 'Duc d'Ahremberg'

'Duchanel' 1 Y-Y
(de Graaff Bros, pre-1923)

'Duchess de Braband' 8 Y-Y
(pre-1798)

'Duchess of Abercorn' 3 W-GWW
(T. Bloomer) Omagh & District Horticultural Society, 1973
'Chinese White' × 'Bryher'; sdlg no. 9/81/58

'Duchess of Albany' 8 Y-Y
(W. Backhouse, pre-1869)
Fls 2-3 per stem; perianth segments sulphur yellow; corona darker in tone. Syn. Tridymus 'Duchess of Albany'

'Duchess of Brabant' 3 W-Y
(W. Backhouse, pre-1869)

'Minnie Hume' hybrid
Corona canary yellow. Syn. Leedsii 'Duchess of Brabant', Leedsii 'Vincenti'. "Absorbed" 'Circe', 'Favourite' and 'Queen of England'

'Duchess of Cambridge' 1 W-W
(R.H. Bath, pre-1929)

'Duchess of Connaught' 1 W-Y
(W. Backhouse, pre-1869)
Fl. small; perianth segments sulphur white. Syn. Pseudonarcissus Moschatus 'Duchess of Connaught'

'Duchess of Edinburgh' 1 Y-Y
(W. Backhouse, pre-1869)
Perianth segments sulphur yellow; corona canary yellow. Syn. Pseudonarcissus Bicolor 'Duchess of Edinburgh'

'Duchess of Hatton' 1 W-? (b)
(?Mrs D. Duff, pre-1951)

'Duchess of Kent' 1 Y-Y
(G.P. Haydon, pre-1908)

'Duchess of Normandy' 1 W-W
(C. Smith, pre-1901)
Perianth segments somewhat shouldered at base, milk white, twisted; corona long, ribbed, with mouth expanded and rim flanged. Early. Faintly scented

'Duchess of Orange' 8
(W.A. Grace, pre-1936)

'Duchess of Rutland' 2 or 3 W-? (b or c)
(J.R. Pearson & Sons, pre-1914)

'Duchess of Sparta' 3 W-? (b)
(Mrs R.O. Backhouse, pre-1921)

'Duchess of Wellington' 1 W-W
(pre-1907)

'Duchess of Westminster' 2 W-W
(W. Backhouse, pre-1869)
Perianth segments ovate to narrowly ovate or oblong, blunt, not prominently mucronate, spreading or somewhat inflexed, with margins sometimes wavy or sometimes recurved at base, overlapping at base only; corona cylindrical or somewhat funnel-shaped, closely ribbed, opening canary yellow with a tinge of orange towards mouth, becoming pure white, mouth straight, lightly frilled. Syn. Leedsii 'Duchess of Westminster'. FCC 1886. "Absorbed" 'Flora MacDonald'

'Duckwing'
(Thompson, pre-1908)

'Duddingston' 1 Y-Y
(W.B. Cuthbertson, pre-1927)
'Glory of Leiden' × 'King Alfred'
Fl. 89 mm wide; perianth segments sulphur, with margins incurved, overlapping half; corona pale buttercup yellow, with mouth somewhat expanded. Mid-season to late

'Duessa' 2 W-Y
(A.M. Wilson, pre-1914)
Corona rich yellow

'Duessa' 2 Y-Y
(W. Jackson Jr, 1968) Unregistered
'Illinga' × 'King's Ransom'; sdlg no. 55/68

'Duet' 4 W-OYY
(P.B. van Eeden) P.B. van Eeden, 1980
'Golden Castle' sport
Fl. 105 mm wide; perianth segments ivory white; corona segments vivid yellow 15A, with light orange (23A) at base. Early

'Duet' 5 W-W
(Heathcote Bulb Nursery, pre-1961) Unregistered
Fls 2 per stem, pure white

'Duiker' 6 Y-Y
(Brian S.Duncan) Brian S.Duncan, 1997
'Elfin Gold' × *N. cyclamineus*; sdlg no. 1406
Fl. 61 mm wide, deep golden yellow; perianth segments ovate, blunt, reflexed; corona cylindrical, with mouth straight. Dwarf. Very early

'Duke of Albany' 8 Y-O
(W. Backhouse, pre-1869)
Fls 2-3 per stem; perianth segments sulphur yellow; corona orange. Syn. Tridymus 'Duke of Albany'

'Duke of Anjou' 1 W-Y
(Barr & Sons, pre-1923)
Fl. 95 mm wide; perianth segments creamy white, flushed pale sulphur yellow at base, regular, overlapping half; corona lemon yellow, mouth somewhat expanded, frilled. Mid-season to late

'Duke of Bedford' 1 W-Y
(Barr & Sons, pre-1899)
Fl. 114 mm wide; perianth segments broadly ovate, blunt, not noticeably mucronate, pure white, spreading, twisted, overlapping one-third; the inner segments inflexed; corona cylindrical, smooth, soft yellow, with mouth ribbed and rim widely flanged and boldly crenate. Early. AM 1899

'Duke of Buccleuch' 2 W-Y
(E. Leeds, pre-1877)
Fl. large. Tall. Syn. Incomparabilis Albus 'Duke of Buccleuch', Incomparabilis Albus 'Elatus'. Was "absorbed" into 'Magog'

'Duke of Cambridge' 1 W-? (b)
(W. Welchman, pre-1908)

'Duke of Clarence' 1 Y-Y
(C.B. Blampied, pre-1929)

'Duke of Cornwall' 1 Y-Y
(C.B. Blampied, pre-1928)

'Duke of Edinburgh' 1 W-Y
(W. Backhouse, pre-1869)
Corona canary yellow. Syn. Pseudonarcissus Bicolor 'Duke of Edinburgh'

'Duke of Kent' 1 Y or W-Y
(G.P. Haydon, pre-1908)
'Madame de Graaff' × 'Monarch'
Corona bright yellow

'Duke of Lancaster' 1 Y-Y
(C.B. Blampied, pre-1929)

'Duke of Leinster' 2 W-R
(G.H. Engleheart, pre-1907)
Perianth segments creamy white; corona expanded, brilliant red

'Duke of Marlborough' 2 W-? (b)
(de Graaff Bros, pre-1927)

'Duke of Norfolk' 1 Y-Y
(C.B. Blampied, pre-1929)

'Duke of Normandy' 1 Y-Y
(C.B. Blampied, pre-1926)
AM(m)(c) 1926

'Duke of Rutland' 1 W-W
(W.H. Divers, pre-1914)

'Duke of Wellington' 1 Y-Y
(J. Kendall, pre-1907)

'Duke of Windsor' 2 W-OOY
(G.A. Uit den Boogaard, pre-1936)
'John Evelyn' hybrid
Perianth segments very broad, truncate, spreading or slightly reflexed, a little concave, with margins slightly incurling, overlapping half; the inner segments a little narrower, more often inflexed, with margins incurved and wavy; corona cup-shaped, apricot orange, flushed pale yellow at rim, mouth expanded, split, with six overlapping lobes, closely frilled, with some smaller lobes sometimes occurring on the outside. 2n=28. Syn. 'Walhalla'. AM(Haarlem) 1936, FCC(Haarlem) 1938

'Duke of York' 2 Y-? (a)
(C.B. Blampied, pre-1928)

'Duke of York' 1 Y-Y
(M. van Waveren & Sons, pre-1930)

'Dulce'
(E.M. Crosfield, pre-1914)

'Dulcetta' 8
(G.H. Johnstone, pre-1949)
'Dulcimer' × *N. tazetta*

'Dulcianna' 2 W-Y
(John Gray, pre-1948)

'Dulcie' 2 W-W
Syn. of 'Dulsie'

'Dulcie Joan' 2 W-WWP
(Mrs J. Abel Smith) Mrs J. Abel Smith, 1972
'Ethyl' × 'Syracuse'
Fl. 100 mm wide; corona white, with pink at rim

'Dulcie May' 1 Y-Y
(L.P. Dettman, 1969) L.P. Dettman, 1979
'Creamed Honey' × 'Moonstruck'; sdlg no. S5/78
Fl. 105 mm wide; perianth segments greenish yellow; corona a tone paler. Mid-season. Resembles a 'Moonstruck' of improved substance with no green at corona rim

'Dulcimer' 9 W-GYO
(G.H. Engleheart, pre-1913)
Perianth segments squarish at apex, prominently mucronate, milk white, spreading, plane, regular, overlapping half; the inner segments narrower; corona small disc-shaped, ribbed, deep yellow, with green at base and a broad band of orange at rim. Tall. Late. 2n=28. AM(g)(c) 1923, AM(Haarlem) 1927

'Dulcinea' 5
(Sir A.P.W. Thomas, pre-1930)

'Dulnan' 3 W-GWW
(J.M. de Navarro, 1956) J.M. de Navarro, 1968
'Portrush' × 'Galilee'
Fl. 83 mm wide. Late

'Dulsie' 2 W-W
(The Brodie of Brodie, c.1932)
'Everest' × 'White Emperor'
Fl. pure white; perianth segments spreading, plane, smooth; corona slender, smooth, with rim narrowly flanged. See also 'Dulcie'

'Dulve' 1 W-W
(P.D. Williams, pre-1930)

'Dulverton' 1 W-P
(C.E. Radcliff, 1942) J.M.Radcliff, 1956
'Saint Aloysius' × 'Dawnglow'

'Dumbarton' 1 W-W
(D.S. Bell) D.S. Bell, 1963
Fl. 105 mm wide, pure white; corona rim neatly frilled. Mid-season. Resembles 'Broughshane' but with smoother perianth segments

'Dumbleton' 1 Y-Y
(J.M. de Navarro) J.M. de Navarro, 1959
'Braemar' × 'Arctic Gold'
Fl.102 mm wide, deep yellow; corona slightly deeper in tone than the perianth, with mouth flared and rim dentate. Mid-season. Resembles 'Kingscourt'. PC(e) 1967

'Dumbo' 1 Y-Y
(G. Lewis) D.S. Bell, 1955
Fl. gold; perianth segments of great substance; corona rim widely flanged

'Duna' 8
(R.A. van der Schoot, pre-1931)
Syn. 'Lady Boreel'

'Duna' 2 W-P
(W. Jackson Sr, 1945)
'Leto' × 'Dawnglow'

'Dunadry' 1 W-Y
(W.J. Dunlop) W.J. Dunlop, 1957
Perianth segments pure white; corona lemon yellow

'Dunadry Inn' 4 W-P
(Brian S. Duncan) Rathowen Daffodils, 1988
Evans sdlg N22/1 × 'Pink Pageant'; sdlg no. 1011
Perianth and other petaloid segments white; corona segments tightly interspersed among the petaloid segments at centre, deep pink. Late

'Dunain Park' 3 W-GWO
(Mrs J. Abel Smith, 1978) Mrs J. Abel Smith, 1989
Corona with a narrow band of orange at rim. Mid-season

'Dunaird' 2 W-P
(G.L. Wilson) Unregistered
'Mitylene' × 'Evening'

'Dunbar' 1 W-Y
(Ken Farmer Nurseries) Ken Farmer Nurseries, 1978
Fl. 107 mm wide. Mid-season

'Dunbrody' 1 W-WWY
(J.L. Richardson) J.M. de Navarro, 1968
'My Love' × 'Tudor Minstrel'

'Duncairn' 1 Y-Y
(G.L. Wilson, pre-1945)
Fl. deep gold; corona rim flanged and dentate

'Duncan' 2 Y-Y

(P.D. Williams, pre-1927)
Fl. large, facing slightly downwards; perianth segments sulphur yellow, deeply overlapping; corona primrose yellow, frilled, with rim loosely rolled.
*AM(g)(m) 1927, *(Gulval)AM(m) 1935

'Duncan Gray' 3 W-? (b)
(H.R. Meyer, pre-1946)

'Dundarave' 2 Y-R
(Carncairn Daffodils) Carncairn Daffodils, 1969
'Market Merry' × 'Fury'
Perianth segments deep yellow; corona red

'Dundee' 3 Y-? (a)
(P.D. Williams, pre-1935)

'Dundonald' 1 Y-Y
(G.L. Wilson, pre-1945)

'Dundrod' 2 W-Y
(Ballydorn Bulb Farm) Ballydorn Bulb Farm, 1979
'Preamble' × ?'Candour'
Fl. 112 mm wide; corona lemon yellow, with some orange at base. Mid-season. Varies between Divs 2 and 1

'Dundrum' 1 Y-Y
(J.L. Richardson) W.J. Dunlop, 1957
Fl. mid-yellow

'Duneba' 2 Y-R
(W. Jackson Jr) W. Jackson Jr, 1966
'Ceylon' × 'Mars'

'Dunedin Gem' 2 Y-W
(J.A. Morris) J.A. Morris, 1968

'Dunfane' 2 W-W
(W.J. Dunlop, pre-1950)
'Niphetos' × 'Truth'
Fl. pure white

'Dungannon' 1 Y-Y
(W.J. Dunlop, pre-1949)
'Principal' × 'Crocus'
Fl. mid-yellow; corona frilled

'Dungiven' 1 Y-Y
(G.L. Wilson, pre-1937)
'Clarion' × 'Lord Roberts'
Fl. 118 mm wide; perianth segments broad, acute, brilliant yellow 12B, slightly inflexed, smooth, overlapping half; corona straight-sided, brighter in tone (12A) than the perianth, mouth expanded and lightly ribbed, rim flanged and deeply notched. AM(e) 1951, *AM(g) 1952

'Dunhelved'
Syn. of 'Dunheved'

'Dunheved' 2 Y-O
(G.L. Wilson) G. Zandbergen-Terwegen, 1963
Fl. 102 mm wide; perianth segments vivid yellow 9A; corona strong orange 25A. Early. AM(Haarlem) 1963. ?See also 'Dunhelved'

'Duniwassal' 2 W-? (b)
(P.D. Williams, pre-1931)

'Dunkeld' 2 Y-O
(The Brodie of Brodie, c.1934)
'Seraglio' × 'Killigrew'; sdlg no. 114/E/29
Fl. 95 mm wide; perianth segments broadly ovate, blunt or rounded at apex, slightly mucronate, between light greenish yellow 5C and the even lighter 5D, tinged with a darker tone (5B), spreading, concave either side of the broad midrib, smooth, overlapping half; the inner segments more narrowly ovate, a little inflexed, with margins recurved in lower third; corona short broad funnel-shaped, ribbed, between vivid orange 28B and a darker tone (28A), paling to yellow-orange (23A) towards base, mouth straight, split in places and overlapping, loosely frilled, with rim irregularly notched and crenate. Mid-season. 2n=28. *HC(p) 1986

'Dunkery' 4 Y-O
(Brian S.Duncan, pre-1997) Unregistered

'Dunkirk' 2 W-? (b)
(Barr & Sons, pre-1937)

'Dunlambert' 2 W-Y
(Ballydorn Bulb Farm) Ballydorn Bulb Farm, 1975
'Preamble' open pollinated
Fl. 112 mm wide; corona pale yellow. Mid-season. Resembles a bolder 'Downpatrick' in form but with a more widely expanded corona mouth. Varies between Divs 2 and 1

'Dunlavin' 2 W-W
(J.L. Richardson, pre-1945)
'Niphetos' × 'Kanchenjunga'
Fl. forming a double triangle; perianth segments broadly ovate, blunt, prominently mucronate, pure white, spreading, plane, overlapping half; the inner segments more narrowly ovate, more nearly acute, somewhat creased; corona funnel-shaped, opening pale primrose yellow, becoming almost white, mouth expanded, ribbed, frilled, rim crenate and widely flanged. Mid-season

'Dunlewey' 2 W-W
(G.L. Wilson, pre-1934)
'Mitylene' × 'Kantara'
Fl. 108 mm wide, white, tinged green; perianth segments somewhat twisted, overlapping one-third; corona ribbed, mouth slightly expanded, frilled, rim flanged and dentate. 2n=28. AM(e) 1938, *HC(g) 1952, *AM(g) 1953

'Dunley Hall' 3 W-GYY
(J.S.B. Lea, 1971) Clive Postles Daffodils, 1986
'Loch Assynt' × Blanchard sdlg 68/15A; sdlg no. 4-37-76
Fl. 108 mm wide; perianth segments very broadly ovate, rounded at apex, only very slightly mucronate, spreading, a little concave, of good substance, regular, overlapping half; the inner segments only a little narrower, plane; corona shallow bowl-shaped, closely ribbed, brilliant greenish yellow 6C, with green at base and a deeper tone of yellow at rim (6A), mouth with six overlapping lobes, frilled, rim minutely crenate. Scented. AM(e) 1988

'Dunlin' 3 W-? (b)
(G.L. Wilson) G. Zandbergen-Terwegen, 1959

'Dunloe' 2 W-P
(J.L. Richardson, pre-1937)
'White Sentinel' self pollinated
Perianth segments very broadly ovate, blunt or squarish at apex, slightly mucronate, spreading, with margins sometimes incurling, overlapping one-third to a half; the inner segments more narrowly ovate, inflexed at base, recurved in upper part; corona cylindrical, ribbed, very pale pink, mouth expanded, even, broadly and obscurely lobed, rim striate and widely rolled. Mid-season

'Dunloy' 2 W-P
(G.L. Wilson, pre-1945)
'Mitylene' × 'Evening'
Perianth segments pure white; corona pale shell pink

'Dunluce' 1 W-W
(G.L. Wilson, pre-1937)
'Beersheba' × ?'White Knight'
Fl. ice white; corona with green tones at base. Syn. 'Glenariff'

'Dunminning' 2 Y-R
(W.J. Dunlop) W.J. Dunlop, 1959
Sdlg × 'Porthilly'
Perianth segments clear yellow; corona rich red

'Dunmore' 2 W-Y
(J.L. Richardson, pre-1941)
'Bodilly' × 'Crocus'
Perianth segments white; corona deep lemon yellow, frilled

'Dunmurry' 1 W-Y
(W.J. Dunlop) W.J. Dunlop, 1958
'Niphetos' × 'Kanchenjunga'
Corona deep golden yellow. Resembles 'Newcastle' in colour but with a shorter corona. Varies between Divs 1 and 2

'Dunphail' 3 W-? (b)
(The Brodie of Brodie, c.1938)

'Mozart' × 'Galopin'

'Dunraven' 1 Y-Y
(R.C.A. Tombleson) R.C.A. Tombleson, 1970
'Faris' × 'Arctic Gold'

'Dunrobin' 1 Y-Y
(West & Fell, pre-1935)

'Dunrod' 1 Y-Y
(Ballydorn Bulb Farm, c.1980) Unregistered
'Preamble' hybrid

'Dunsany' 1 W-? (b)
(R.H. Bath, pre-1929)

'Dunseverick' 2 W-W
(G.L. Wilson, pre-1940)
'Still Waters' × 'Dava'
Corona ribbed, opening ivory, becoming white, with rim somewhat flanged. AM(Haarlem) 1948

'Dunsilly' 2 Y-R
(W.J. Dunlop, c.1968) Unregistered

'Dunskey' 3 W-R
(Brian S. Duncan) Rathowen Daffodils, 1977
'Enniskillen' × 'Don Carlos'; sdlg no. 80
Perianth segments white; corona deep orange-red. Mid-season. Resembles 'Rockall' but with broader perianth segments

'Duntroon' 2 Y-WWY
(Mrs J. Abel Smith) Mrs J. Abel Smith, 1984
'Daydream' × 'Langwith'; sdlg no. C9/71
Perianth segments yellow; corona opening yellow, becoming white, with yellow at rim. Mid-season

'Dunvegan' 3 Y-O
(Mrs R.S. Cobley, 1948) Seymour Cobley Ltd, 1968
Perianth segments pale primrose yellow; corona reddish orange. Mid-season

'Dunwel' 2 W-O
(S.C. Gaspar, 1949) R.J. Abernethy, 1960
Fl. 102 mm wide; perianth segments milk white, of thick and waxy texture; corona spreading, deep reddish orange. Mid-season. PC(c)(NZ) 1958

'Dunwold' 2 W-? (b)
(A.C. McKillop) A.C. McKillop, 1955

'Duopoly' 7 W-YYW
(M.G. Temple-Smith, 1987) M.G. Temple-Smith, 1997
'Jo' × *N. jonquilla*; sdlg no. 45/87
Fls 2 per stem, rounded; perianth segments greenish white (155A); corona brilliant greenish yellow 6B, with green at base and a line of white at rim. Mid-season

'Duplex' 8 Y-Y
(Dutch origin, pre-1922)
Poetaz
Perianth segments opening sulphur yellow, becoming light yellow; corona light yellow

'Durango' 6 W-W
(W.G. Pannill) W.G. Pannill, 1977
'Jenny' × 'Empress of Ireland'; sdlg no. 64/68
Fl. 75 mm wide. Early

'Durbar' 1 Y-Y
(N.Y. Lower, pre-1913)
'Glory of Noordwijk' × 'Cleopatra'

'Durbar' 2 Y-YOO
(D.S. Bell) D.S. Bell, 1979
'Ceylon' × 'Rupee'
Fl. 104 mm wide; corona stained reddish orange, with yellow at base. Mid-season

'Durgan' 1 Y-Y
(R.F. Calvert, pre-1935)

'Duriel' 1 W-W
(W.A. Grace, pre-1936)

'Durness' 1 Y-Y
(J. Hall, pre-1930)

'Dusart' 1 Y-Y
(M. van Waveren & Sons, pre-1907)

'Dusk' 2 W-? (b)
(H.A. Brown, pre-1938)

'Dusk' 1 W-W
(G.L. Wilson, 1950) G. Zandbergen-Terwegen, 1961
'Broughshane' × 'Candour'

'Dusky'
(pre-1913)

'Dusky Princess' 2 W-? (b)
(A. Gibson, pre-1950)

'Dusky Rose' 2 W-P
(J.N. Hancock & Co., 1980) Unregistered
Perianth segments broadly ovate, blunt, slightly mucronate, brilliant white, spreading, plane, overlapping half; the inner segments a little inflexed, with margins wavy; corona cylindrical, smoothly 6-angled, deep rose pink, with mouth flared and a little frilled, rim minutely crenate. Mid-season to late

'Dusty Pink' 2 W-P
(J.S. Leitch) J.S. Leitch, 1966
Fl. 102 mm wide

'Dutch Delight' 2 Y-R
(Brian S.Duncan, 1982) Brian S.Duncan, 1997
'Hero' × 'Gold Convention'; sdlg no. 1636
Fl. 100 mm wide; perianth segments broadly ovate, deep yellow; the inner segments a little narrower; corona cylindrical, with mouth flared and rim notched. Early to mid-season. Sunproof

'Dutch Girl' 2 W-W
(Alister Clark) A. Ladson, 1960
Perianth segments pure white; corona opening pale lemon, becoming white

'Dutch Gold' 1 Y-Y
(M. van Waveren & Sons, pre-1933)
'King Alfred' hybrid
FA(Haarlem) 1933

'Dutchman' 1 Y-Y
(Cartwright & Goodwin, pre-1916)

'Dutchman' 2 Y-O
(S. Clay) S. Clay, 1964
Fl. large; perianth segments rich yellow; corona dark reddish orange. Mid-season. Resembles an improved 'Royal Orange'

'Dutch Master' 1 Y-Y
(pre-1938)
Fl. 109 mm wide; perianth segments ovate, very slightly mucronate, brilliant greenish yellow 5A, slightly inflexed, plane or a little concave, overlapping one-third; the inner segments a little reflexed, with margins slightly incurving; corona cylindrical, smooth, vivid yellow (richer in tone than 12A), with mouth expanded, rim rolled and deeply and regularly notched. 2n=28. AM(p) 1948, *FCC(p) 1976, AGM 1995

'Dutch Pale Moon' 2 W-GYY
(Tom Forster, 1960s) Unregistered
Corona closely overlying the perianth, soft creamy yellow

'Dutch Quince' 5 Y-Y
(?A.Gray, pre-1986) Unregistered

'Dutch Rocket' 1 Y-Y
(L.J. Steenvoorden, 1948) L.J. Steenvoorden, 1959
Fl. golden yellow. Mid-season

'Dutch Victoria'
?Syn. of 'Victoria'

'Duyf' 8 W-W
(pre-1807)

'Dwarf Golden Mary' 3 Y-Y
(E. Leeds, pre-1877)
Perianth segments opening clear yellow, becoming primrose yellow. Syn. Barrii 'Dwarf Golden Mary', Incomparabilis 'Nanus', Incomparabilis Concolor 'Nanus'. Was "absorbed" into 'Golden Mary'

'Dyak' 2 Y-R
(P. & G. Phillips) P. & G. Phillips, 1975
Fl. 95mm wide; perianth segments deep yellow, flushed with orange; corona narrow, vivid red. Mid-season

'Dymphnia' 2 W-? (b)
(Mrs M.Moorby) Mrs M.Moorby, 1956

'Dynamic' 2 Y-YYO
(W. Jackson Jr) Jackson's Daffodils, 1979
'Dimity' hybrid × 'Bilboa'; sdlg no. 205/71
Fl. 103 mm wide. Mid-season

'Dynamite' 2 W-O
(M.J. Jefferson-Brown) M.J. Jefferson-Brown, 1964
('Kilworth' × 'Arbar') × ('Arbar' × 'Signal Light')

'Dynamo' 3 W-? (b)
(de Graaff Bros, pre-1930)
AM(Haarlem) 1934. Div. 2 until 1935

'Dynamo Beat' 2 Y-R
(N.H. Anglo) N.H. Anglo, 1988
Sdlg × 'Bunclody'
Perianth segments glowing yellow; corona bowl-shaped, opening orange and yellow, with red at base, becoming self red. Mid-season. Sunproof

'Dynast' 2 W-W
(G.L. Wilson) G. Zandbergen-Terwegen, 1963
Fl. 110 mm wide, ivory white; corona creamy white. Mid-season. AM(Haarlem) 1963

E

'Eager Beaver' 2 Y-O
(J.N. Hancock & Co., 1960) Unregistered

'Eagle' 9 W-R
(E.H. Wheadon & Sons, pre-1916)
Mid-season

'Eagle Rose' 2 W-YYP
(W.O. Backhouse) E. Longford, 1967
Fl. 114 mm wide; perianth segments white; corona long, pale amber yellow, with a broad band of deep pink at rim. Mid-season

'Eagle Stone' 2 W-? (b or c)
(G.H. Engleheart, pre-1927)

'Eaglet' 4
(E. & J.C. Martin, pre-1916)

'Earani' 2 W-? (b)
(A.H. Ahrens, pre-1949)

'Earendil' 2 W-YPP
(Brian S. Duncan) Brian S. Duncan, 1992
'Pismo Beach' × 'High Society'; sdlg no. 1062
Fl. 106 mm wide; perianth segments broad, rounded and sometimes truncate at apex, prominently mucronate, pure white, a little reflexed, slightly concave, regular, overlapping half; the inner segments more nearly ovate, more nearly spreading, with margins slightly wavy; corona funnel-shaped, orange-pink, with golden buff yellow at base, mouth flared and frilled, rim crenate. Mid-season to late. Sunproof

'Earl Goodwin' 1 W-Y
(G.P. Haydon, pre-1913)
Perianth segments creamy white, somewhat ribbed; corona canary yellow, frilled. Resembles an improved 'Weardale Perfection'

'Earl Grey' 5 Y-Y
(G.H. Engleheart, pre-1901)
'Emperor' × *N. triandrus*
Perianth segments pale primrose yellow, spreading; corona long, soft primrose yellow. FCC 1901

'Earl Harold' 3 W-? (b)
(W. Welchman, pre-1910)

'Earlicheer' 4 W-Y
Syn. of 'Erlicheer'

'Earlichere' 4 W-Y
Syn. of 'Erlicheer'

'Earliest of All' 9 W-?
(G. Lubbe & Son, pre-1927)

'Earlish' 1 Y-Y
(Mrs R.S. Cobley, 1948) Seymour Cobley Ltd, 1968
Fl. golden yellow. Early. Resembles a smaller-flowered 'Golden Harvest' of improved substance

'Earl Leofric' 2 Y-? (a)
(R.H. Bath, pre-1931)

'Earl Marshal' 2 Y-O
(F.H. Chapman, pre-1938)

'Earl of Morley' 5
(G.H. Engleheart, pre-1908)

'Earl Winterton' 2 Y-YYO
(P. van Deursen, pre-1953)
Perianth segments clear yellow; corona widely expanded, with a broad band of bright orange at rim

'Early Alfred' 1 Y-Y
(Miss K.M. Hinchliff, pre-1930)
'King Alfred' hybrid

'Early Arrival' 6 Y-Y
(J. & E.Frey, *c*.1977) J. & E.Frey, 1988
?'Goldette' hybrid; sdlg no. B
Very early

'Early Attraction' 2 Y-? (a)
(P. van Deursen, pre-1953)

'Early Beauty' 1 Y-Y
(E.H. Krelage & Son, pre-1914)

'Early Bird' 1 Y-Y
(W.B. Hartland, pre-1907)

'Early Bird' 3 Y-? (a)
(G.B. de Vroomen & Sons) G. de Vroomen & Sons
2n=28

'Early Bird' 2 W-W
(J.M.Radcliff, pre-1996) Unregistered

'Early Blackwell' 2
(pre-1914)

'Early Blossom' 1 W-P
(Mrs J. Abel-Smith) Mrs J. Abel-Smith, 1980
'Famille Rose' hybrid
Fl. 85 mm wide; perianth segments broadly ovate, slightly mucronate, inflexed, a little concave, overlapping half; the inner segments only a little narrower, with margins a little incurved and sometimes wavy; corona finely ribbed, pink, mouth expanded and frilled, rim notched and minutely crenate. Early. Resembles a much stronger 'Famille Rose'

'Early Bride' 2 W-YOO
(N. van Reeuwijk, 1943) N. van Reeuwijk, 1961
Fl. 100 mm wide; perianth segments ivory white, plane or twisted; corona strongly ribbed, light orange (21A), paling to brilliant yellow 7A at base and touched 7A at rim, with mouth expanded and much frilled. Early. 2n=28. FA(Haarlem) 1964, EFA(Haarlem) 1965, *AM(p) 1978

'Early Dawn' 1 W-W
(Barr & Sons, pre-1913)

'Early Dawn' 2 Y-R
(D.S. Bell) D.S. Bell, 1962
'Jansen' × 'Ceylon'
Fl. 95 mm wide

'Early Easter' 2 Y-? (a)
(W. Backhouse, pre-1869)

'Early Entry' 6 W-Y
(J.W. Blanchard) M.J. Jefferson-Brown, 1975
'White Sentinel' × *N. cyclamineus*
Perianth segments white; corona primrose, sometimes becoming pinky buff. Early

'Early Gem' 2 Y-O
(G.H. Johnstone, pre-1949)

'Early Giant' 1 Y-Y
(pre-1926)
AM(Haarlem) 1926

'Early Glory' 1 Y-Y
(J.C.van der Meer, pre-1942)

'Early Gold' 1 Y-Y
(Miss K.M. Hinchliff, pre-1927)

'Early Gold' 2 Y-Y
(C.R. Wootton, 1949) C.R. Wootton, 1960
'Leinster' × 'Saint Issey'
Fl. 108 mm wide, golden yellow. Early. Resembles an earlier-flowered 'Saint Issey' with broader perianth segments

'Early Grand Primo' 8 W-Y
Unregistered
Fls 12-15 per stem, star-shaped, 25-32 mm wide; perianth segments ovate, blunt, prominently mucronate, spreading, overlapping one-third; the inner segments acute; corona cup-shaped. Very early

'Early Highness' 1 W-Y
(C.W. Culpepper, pre-1980) Unregistered

'Early Lemon' 1 Y-Y
(Miss A.E. Wood, pre-1943)

'Early Light' 2 Y-O
(Warnaar & Co., pre-1953)
'Hollywood' hybrid
AM(Haarlem) 1953

'Early Love' 2 W-P
(J.N. Hancock & Co.) J.N. Hancock & Co., 1960
Corona pale pink

'Early Mist' 2 W-W
(J.L. Richardson, pre-1953)
'Glendalough' × 'Ardclinis'
Fl. pure white; perianth segments ovate, blunt, very slightly mucronate, flat, smooth, regular, overlapping one-third; the inner segments more narrowly ovate and acute; corona trumpet-shaped, lightly flanged at expanded mouth, rim notched and rolled

'Early Morn' 2 W-WWP
(H.R. Meyer, pre-1932)

'Leslie Hulbert' × 'Fortune'
Fl. ivory white; corona with a sharply defined band of deep dull pink at rim, frilled

'Early Mystic' 2 W-O
(J.L. Richardson, pre-1948)
Corona with orange gold at rim

'Early Orange' 3 Y-? (a)
(pre-1936)

'Early Paper White' 8 W-W
(pre-1872)
Fl. pure white. ?The same as 'Early Pure White' and 'Early Silver Cup'

'Early Pearl' 8 W-W
(W.R.P. Welch) W.R.P. Welch, 1984
Selection from 'Grand Primo'
Fl. 35 mm wide; corona opening cream, becoming white. Tall. Early. 2n=32. Syn. "Florida White"

'Early Perfection' 8 W-Y
(R.A. van der Schoot, pre-1924)
Poetaz
Fls 4-6 per stem; perianth segments very broad, almost white, spreading, concave, overlapping half or more; corona bowl-shaped, clear yellow, mouth tightly frilled. Early. FA(Haarlem) 1924, EFA(Haarlem) 1929

'Early Pioneer' 1 Y-Y
(D.S. Bell) D.S. Bell, 1959
'Ranalagh' × 'Goldcourt'
Fl. 114 mm wide. Early. Resembles a larger-flowered 'Kingscourt'

'Early Prince' 1 Y-Y
(Mrs R.O. Backhouse, pre-1914)

'Early Prince' 1 W-Y
(O. Ronalds) M. Gardiner, 1956
Corona sulphur, deeply frilled. 2n=28

'Early Pure White' 8 W-W
(pre-1877)
?The same as 'Early Paper White' and 'Early Silver Cup'

'Early Queen' 8
(A. Vis, pre-1942)

'Early Red' 2 W-R
(E.F. Hughes) E.F. Hughes, 1962
Fl. 95 mm wide; perianth segments greenish white; corona scarlet, with a slightly paler tone at rim. Very early

'Early Riser' 1 Y-Y
(Slieve Donard Nursery Co., pre-1933)

'Magnificence' × 'Van Waveren's Giant'
Fl. pale yellow. Early. Weatherproof

'Early Roman' 8
(pre-1938)
?The same as 'Romanus' pre-1576

'Early Seedling'
(pre-1935)

'Early Sensation' 1 Y-Y
(A.C. van der Schoot, pre-1954)
Very early. 2n=28

'Early Sensation' 1 Y-Y
Syn. of 'Rijnveld's Early Sensation'

'Early Silver Cup' 8 W-W
(pre-1881)
?The same as 'Early Paper White' and 'Early Pure White'

'Early Snowflake' 8 W-W
Syn. of 'Paper White Grandiflorus'

'Early Splendour' 8 W-O
(A.C. van der Schoot, pre-1938)
Poetaz
Fl. 60 mm wide; perianth segments ovate, mucronate, cream, flushed yellow at base, spreading, twisted, with margins incurling, overlapping one-quarter; corona bowl-shaped, ribbed, light orange (23B), flushed strong orange 25A, mouth expanded, deeply split, with three overlapping lobes, lightly frilled, rim entire. 2n=17. *FCC(p) 1978

'Early Spring' 9 W-?
(Mrs R.O. Backhouse, pre-1914)

'Early Spring' 2 Y-O
(O. Ronalds, 1947) T. Morrison, 1960
Corona reddish orange. Early

'Early Sunrise' 2 Y-O
(G.E. Mitsch) G.E. Mitsch, 1959
'John Evelyn' × 'Fortune'

'Early Surprise' 3 W-YYO
(W. Polman-Mooy, pre-1927)
Fl. small; perianth segments broadly ovate, prominently mucronate, yellowish white, spreading, creased or with broad midrib showing, overlapping a quarter; the inner segments narrower, a little inflexed, with margins wavy; corona bowl-shaped, ribbed, orange-yellow, with a broad band of orange at rim, tightly frilled

'Early Surprise' 8 W-Y
(pre-1927)
Poetaz

'Early Tenby' 1 Y-Y
(Miss K.M. Hinchliff, pre-1927)

'Early to Rise' 2 W-Y
(O. David Niswonger, 1981) O. David Niswonger, 1995
'Ice Follies' × 'Carita'; sdlg no. 2-86
Fl. 107.95 mm wide; perianth segments ovate, plane; corona bowl-shaped, light yellow, ageing to white, frilled. Very early

'Early Treasure' 1 Y-Y
(D.S. Bell) D.S. Bell, 1964
'Treasure Trove' × 'Treasure'
Fl. 113 mm wide, deep gold; corona frilled. Early. Resembles 'Kingscourt'

'Early White' 1 W-W
(G. Lubbe & Son, pre-1927)

"Early White"
?The same as "Ragged White"

'Early Wonder' 2 Y-? (a)
(R.H. Bath, pre-1932)

'Earthlight' 3 Y-WWY
(T.D. Throckmorton) T.D. Throckmorton, 1976
Fl. 92 mm wide

'East Anglia's Queen' 3 W-? (b)
(W. Welchman, pre-1927)

'Eastbourne' 2 W-Y
(Hokorawa Daffodils, 1974) R.G. Cull, 1988
'Green Island' × 'Empress of Ireland'; sdlg no. HC/A123
Fl. 115 mm wide; corona brilliant greenish yellow 5A. Tall. Mid-season

'Eastcott' 2 Y-Y
(T. Bloomer) du Plessis Bros, 1989
'Camelot' × 'Arctic Gold'; sdlg no. 3/72/65A
Fl. 95 mm wide, deep yellow; corona mouth expanded. Late

'Easter' 9 W-?
(Barr & Sons, pre-1907)

'Easter' 3 W-Y
Syn. of 'Eoster'

'Easter Attire' 2 Y-GWY
(J. & E. Frey, 1974) J. & E. Frey, 1988
'Silken Sails' × 'Easter Time'; sdlg no. JEE14/4
Perianth segments lemon yellow; corona wide, opening lemon yellow, becoming white, with yellow at rim, heavily frilled. Mid-season

'Easter Bonnet' 2 W-YYP
(H.R. Meyer) Hon. Mrs B.B.Ponsonby, 1956
Perianth segments ivory white; corona large, creamy yellow at base, becoming paler, with a more or less broad band of pink at rim. Early

'Easter Bride' 1 W-W
(G.L. Wilson) G. Zandbergen-Terwegen, 1957
AM(Haarlem) 1957

'Easter Dawn' 2 W-P
Perianth segments very broadly ovate, blunt, only very slightly mucronate, reflexed, convex, overlapping half; corona loosely ribbed, orange-pink (24D) at base, shading to a deeper tone at rim (24C), mouth wavy, rim slightly flanged, minutely notched and crenate. ?Syn. of 'Eastern Dawn'

'Easter Day' 2 Y-? (a)
(?H.Backhouse, pre-1916)

'Easter Dress' 2 W-GWP
(J. & E.Frey, 1981) J. & E.Frey, 1996
'Coral Ribbon' × sdlg FEE5/2; sdlg no. PEF1/7
Fl. 80 mm wide; perianth segments roundish, creamy white; corona yellowish white, with green at base and rich watermelon pink at rim. Dwarf or standard. Mid-season

'Easter Flower' 1 Y-Y
(H. Zeestraten, pre-1944)
TGA(Haarlem) 1955

'Easter Glow' 2 Y-O
(J.W.A. Lefeber, 1950) J.W.A. Lefeber, 1960
Fl. 95 mm wide; perianth segments deep canary yellow. Late

'Easter Hero' 1 W-W
(J.L. Richardson, pre-1929)
Fl. pure white; corona mouth expanded, with rim dentate

'Easter Joy' 1 Y-Y
(pre-1953)
AM(Haarlem) 1953, TGA(Haarlem) 1956

'Easter Moon' 2 W-GWW
(G.L. Wilson, pre-1954)
'Tryst' × 'Greenland'
Fl. 100 mm wide, ice white; perianth segments very broadly ovate, blunt, mucronate, spreading, a little concave each side of midrib, smooth, regular, overlapping one-third; the inner segments more narrowly ovate, only very slightly mucronate, shouldered at base, with margins somewhat inward curving; corona lightly ribbed, tinged sage green at base, mouth expanded, wavy. 2n=28. *AM(g) 1979

'Easter Morn' 2 W-W
(G.H. Engleheart, pre-1931)
Corona tinged pink

'Eastern Belle' 1 W-? (b)
(A.S. Brewster, pre-1936)

'Eastern Dawn' 2 W-P
(G.L. Wilson) G.L. Wilson, 1964
'Irish Rose' hybrid
Fl. 88 mm wide; perianth segments ovate, blunt, mucronate, cream, a little reflexed, very slightly concave, with margins occasionally incurling, overlapping one-third; corona cylindrical, lightly angled, orange-pink (24C), with a paler tone towards base (23D), mouth slightly expanded and a little frilled, rim minutely and unevenly notched and crenate. Mid-season. 2n=28. *HC(p) 1986. ?See also 'Easter Dawn'

'Eastern Glory' 2 Y-? (a)
(Mrs R.O. Backhouse, pre-1921)

'Eastern Glow' 3 Y-? (a)
(Mrs R.O. Backhouse, pre-1921)

'Eastern King' 1 Y-Y
(R.L. Thornton, pre-1930)

'Eastern Maid' 2 Y-Y
(P.D. Williams, pre-1914)
Fl. pale primrose yellow, tinged green; perianth segments slightly reflexed; corona darker in tone than the perianth. AM(e) 1914

'Eastern Monarch' 1 Y-Y
(W.M. Spry, pre-1975) Unregistered
'Royal Armour' × 'Dependable'
Tall. Early

'Eastern Prince' 2 W-? (b)
(Mrs R.O. Backhouse, pre-1921)

'Eastern Promise' 2 W-WPP
(Clive Postles, 1982) Clive Postles Daffodils, 1994
Lea sdlg 1-39-66 × 'Dailmanach'; sdlg no. 2-8-76
Fl. forming a double triangle, 112 mm wide; perianth segments broadly ovate, slightly reflexed; corona funnel-shaped, very deep reddish-pink, with white at base, mouth flared, rim crenate. Mid-season. Sunproof

'Eastern Sun' 2 W-O
(R.H. Bath, pre-1929)
Perianth segments rounded, creamy white; corona widely expanded, reddish orange

'Easter Parade' 3 W-? (b)
(F.H. Chapman, pre-1938)

'Easter Queen' 1 W-W
(J.L. Richardson, pre-1932)

'Easter Sunday' 2 W-GPP
(J. & E. Frey) J. & E. Frey, 1988
Sdlg LEE4/1 × sdlg D95/1; sdlg no. QEE7/2
Corona long cup-shaped, soft pink. Mid-season. Resembles a taller 'Rima' in corona colouring

'Easter Sunrise' 7 W-GPP
(J. & E.Frey, 1981) J. & E.Frey, 1996
Sdlg F31/5 × *N. jonquilla*; sdlg no. QEE14/4
Fl. 70 mm wide; perianth segments creamy white, with tints of pink at base stronger on opening; corona opening yellow, with green at base and pink at rim, becoming rich pink, with green at base. Dwarf. Mid-season to late. Resembles an earlier-flowered 'Pink Hummer'

'Easter Surprise' 2 W-GPP
(J. & E.Frey, 1981) J. & E.Frey, 1996
Sdlg LEE4/1 × sdlg D95/1; sdlg no. QEE7/1
Fl. 105 mm wide; perianth segments very broad, opening creamy white touched yellow-green at base, becoming white, spreading, plane, overlapping half; the inner segments inflexed at base, recurved in upper part, with margins wavy; corona funnel-shaped, ribbed, salmon pink, with green at base, mouth very widely expanded, loosely frilled. Dwarf. Mid-season to late. Somewhat resembles a deeper-coloured 'Rima' in corona shape

'Eastertide' 4 Y-Y
(M. Zandbergen) G. Zandbergen-Terwegen, 1959
'Easter Joy' sport

'Easthope' 2 W-? (b)
(R.H. Bath, pre-1933)

'East Lynne' 2 W-? (b)
(G. Lewis) D.S. Bell, 1955

'East Wind' 1 W-W
(D.S. Bell, 1968) D.S. Bell, 1978
'Glacier' × 'Ulster Queen'
Fl. 110 mm wide, ice white; corona expanded and deeply frilled

'Eastwood' 2 W-O
(W.M. Spry, pre-1975) Unregistered
'Aldgate' × 'Delight'
Corona buff orange. Late

'Eaton Park' 3 W-R
(T. Bloomer) Rathowen Daffodils, 1984
('Irish Charm' × sdlg R202) × 'Royal Regiment; sdlg no. 250
Fl. 110 mm wide; corona deep orange-red. Mid-season. Resembles a taller and neater 'Royal Regiment'

'Eaton Song' 12 Y-O
(Harry I. Tuggle Jr, 1973) Rosewarne EHS, 1989
'Matador' × *N. cyclamineus*; sdlg no. USA 66/0/1
Fls usually 3 per stem, 68 mm wide; perianth segments ovate, blunt, only very slightly mucronate, opening sulphur yellow, becoming a little paler, reflexed, sometimes twisted and with margins incurved or recurved, overlapping a quarter to one-third; corona cylindrical, short, strongly ribbed, opening yellow-orange, becoming bright orange, sometimes with a paler tone at rim, mouth straight, frilled, rim crenate. Dwarf. Early. With secondary stems of 1-2 fls

'Eau de Nil' 2 W-? (b or c)
(Mrs R.O. Backhouse, pre-1914)

'Ebb Tide' 1 W-Y
(D.S. Bell) D.S. Bell, 1958
'Royalist' × 'Broughshane'
Fl. 120 mm wide; corona deep lemon, with rim rolled. Mid-season

'Ebonite' 1 W-Y
(David Adams) David Adams, 1994
'Ebony' open pollinated; sdlg no. 84/115I
Fl. 115 mm wide; perianth segments ovate, blunt, whitish, plane, with a sheen on opening; the outer segments almost overlapping one another; the inner segments narrower; corona cylindrical, opening pale yellow, becoming whitish yellow, with mouth flared and frilled. Tall. Mid-season

'Ebony' 1 W-Y
(D.S. Bell) D.S. Bell, 1977
'David Bell' open pollinated
Fl. 106 mm wide; corona frilled. Mid-season

'Eccellenza' 2 W-? (b)
(Cartwright & Goodwin, pre-1914)

'Eccles' 3 W-Y
(W. Backhouse, pre-1869)
Perianth segments sulphur white; corona tinged orange. Syn. Barrii Albidus 'Eccles'

'Echelon' 2 Y-YYO
(G.E. Mitsch) G.E. Mitsch, 1979
('Playboy' × 'Ardour') × ('Aranjuez' × 'Tamino'); sdlg no. JJ63/1
Fl. 100 mm wide; perianth segments broad, golden yellow, sometimes somewhat reflexed, overlapping; corona slightly deeper in tone, with a narrow band of orange at rim, frilled. Mid-season

'Echo' 1 W-W
(de Graaff Bros, pre-1910)

'Echo' 2 Y-YRR
(G. Lewis, pre-1940)

'Moonfleet' × 'Fortune'

'Echo' 2 W-? (b)
(G.L. Wilson) G. Zandbergen-Terwegen, 1957
AM(Haarlem) 1957

'Echuca' 1 W-Y
(H.A. Brown, 1940) J.N. Hancock & Co., 1964
Perianth segments of thick substance, deeply overlapping; corona large, orange-yellow. Mid-season to late

'Eckener' 1 Y-Y
(G. Haver, pre-1930)
AM(Haarlem) 1930

'Eclair' 3 W-? (b)
(Mrs R.O. Backhouse, pre-1921)

'Eclat' 2 W-YPP
(G.E. Mitsch) G.E. Mitsch, 1970
'Caro Nome' × 'Accent'; sdlg no. A5/5
Fl. rounded; perianth segments overlapping; corona almost disc-shaped, large, opening pale lemon, with a band of coral pink at rim, gradually becoming almost entirely pink, or in damp seasons near to red. Mid-season

'Eclatant' 1 Y-Y
(P.L.A. Pouw) P.L.A. Pouw, 1974
'Rembrandt' × 'Golden Sunbeam'
Fl. 125 mm wide

'Eclipse' 2 Y-Y
(W. Backhouse or E. Leeds, pre-1869)
Syn. Incomparabilis Concolor 'Eclipse', Incomparabilis Concolor 'Grandiflorus'. Was "absorbed" into 'Autocrat'

'Eclipse' 2 W-? (b)
(A.H. Ahrens) J.S. Leitch, 1955

'Ecola' 2 Y-? (a)
(E.C. Powell, pre-1949)
'Dawson City' self pollinated × 'Saint Egwin'

'Ecru' 2 W-? (b or c)
(E.M. Crosfield, pre-1907)

'Ecru' 2 W-WYP
(T.D. Throckmorton) T.D. Throckmorton, 1974
'Easter Moon' × 'Rose Caprice'

'Ecstasy' 9 W-?
(pre-1914)

'Ecstasy' 2 W-W
(Oregon Bulb Farms, pre-1946)

'Ecstasy' 1 W-W
?Syn. of 'Ecstatic'

'Ecstasy' 3 Y-?
Syn. of 'Nuance'

'Ecstatic' 1 W-W
(H.A. Brown, 1941) J.N. Hancock & Co., 1960
Syn. ?'Ecstasy'

ectandrus = *N. bulbocodium* var. *ectandrus*

'Ecuador' 2 Y-? (a)
(A.M. Wilson, pre-1947)

'Edda' 2 W-R
(Mrs R.O. Backhouse or de Graaff Bros, pre-1930)
AM(Haarlem) 1930

'Eddington' 2 W-? (b or c)
(pre-1913)

'Eddy Canzony' 2 W-YYO
(J.W.A. Lefeber, pre-1952)
Fl. 95-102 mm wide; perianth segments slightly reflexed, somewhat twisted, regular, overlapping; corona spreading, closely overlying the perianth, ribbed, vivid yellow 12A, shading to vivid orange 28B at mouth, mouth straight, frilled, rim crenate. 2n=28.
AM(Haarlem) 1952, FCC(Haarlem) 1961, AM(p) 1967

'Eddystone' 3 W-? (b)
(A.M. Wilson, pre-1938)

'Edelweiss' 5
(C.G. van Tubergen, pre-1914)

'Edelweiss' 3 W-? (b)
Syn. of 'Show Bride'

'Eden'
(?Sir A.P.W. Thomas, pre-1915)

'Eden' 1 W-Y
(Mrs R.S. Cobley, 1948) Seymour Cobley Ltd, 1968
Corona opening pale primrose yellow, becoming paler in tone. Mid-season

'Edenbank' 3 W-R
(W.J. Dunlop) W.J. Dunlop, 1961
Corona dark crimson

'Edenhope' 1 W-Y
(West & Fell, pre-1935)
Corona lemon yellow

'Edenmore' 2 W-O
(Mrs H.K. Richardson) Carncairn Daffodils, 1973
'Kilworth' × 'Norval'
Fl. 98 mm wide

'Edensor' 3 Y-? (a)
(D.B. Milne, pre-1952)

'Edgar Thurston' 1 Y-Y
(G.H. Engleheart, pre-1930)
Fl. 114 mm wide; perianth segments lemon yellow, inflexed, somewhat twisted, with margins recurved, overlapping at base only; corona buttercup yellow, mouth expanded and somewhat frilled. Mid-season. AM(c) 1930, *AM(m)(g) 1931

'Edgbaston' 2 Y-YOO
(A.J.R.Pearson, 1986) A.J.R.Pearson, 1996
Sdlg 72-9-C16 ('Fine Gold' self pollinated) × 'Capitol Hill'; sdlg no. 86-44-K18
Fl. forming a double triangle, 105 mm wide; perianth segments broadly ovate, rounded at apex, brilliant greenish yellow 5A, spreading, plane, smooth, of stiff substance, overlapping two-thirds; the inner segments more nearly acute; corona cylindrical, smooth, opening vivid yellow 12A, usually becoming yellow-orange 17A, with yellow at base, with mouth ribbed and flared, rim rolled and crenate. Mid-season. Sunproof

'Edge Grove' 2 W-Y
(Carncairn Daffodils) Carncairn Daffodils, 1990
Sdlg no. 1/18/79
Fl. 91 mm wide; perianth segments spreading, smooth; corona cylindrical, with rim dentate. Mid-season

'Edge of Dawn' 2 W-WWP
(G.H. Wayne) G.H. Wayne, 1981
'Aircastle' × 'Pontsianna'; sdlg no. A-1.6
Fl. 80 mm wide. Mid-season

'Edgerton' 2 Y-? (a)
(Warnaar & Co., pre-1943)
AM(Haarlem) 1943

'Edgeworth' 1 Y-Y
(G.H. Furness, pre-1934)

'Ediba' 1 W-? (b)
(Mrs R.O. Backhouse, pre-1921)

'Edile' 2 W-Y
(J.S. Leitch) J.S. Leitch, 1956

'Edinonstone' 1 (c)
(Australian or New Zealand origin, pre-1927)

'Edipus' ?-P
(Alister Clark, pre-1948)

'Edison' 1 W-Y
(R.A. van der Schoot, pre-1913)
Perianth segments pure white; corona rich yellow. AM(Haarlem) 1913

'Edison' 1 W-?
Syn. of 'Ayot'

'Edith' 3 W-? (b)
(Mrs R.O. Backhouse, pre-1921)
AM(Haarlem) 1928

'Edith Amy' 1 W-W
(Mrs F.E.W. Hanger, pre-1952)
Fl. 108 mm wide; perianth segments overlapping half; corona creamy white, with rim flanged and dentate. *AM(g) 1952

'Edith Barber' 1 Y-Y
(W. Backhouse, pre-1869)
Perianth segments primrose yellow; corona darker. Dwarf. Syn. Pseudonarcissus Lorifolius 'Edith Barber'

'Edith Bell' 3 W-YYO
(W. Backhouse, pre-1869)
Perianth segments opening alabaster white, becoming pure white; corona canary yellow. Syn. Burbidgei 'Edith Bell'

'Edith Carter' 3 W-Y
(de Graaff Bros, pre-1933)
Perianth segments sulphur white; corona widely expanded, heavily frilled. AM(Haarlem) 1932

'Edith Cavell' 2 W-W
(R.H. Bath, pre-1927)

'Edith Clark' 2 W-?
(Alister Clark, 1935) J. Sharp, 1960

'Edith Piaff' 3 W-O
(G.H. Rotteveel & Sons, 1946) G.H. Rotteveel & Sons, 1961
Fl. 100 mm wide; perianth segments creamy white. Mid-season

'Edith Sitwell' 3 W-GGY
(R.V. Favell, pre-1943)
'Silver Coin' × 'Raeburn'

'Edith Willkie' 2 W-? (b)
(G.A. Uit den Boogaard, pre-1950)

'Edition' 2 Y-YOO
(G.W.E. Brogden) G.W.E. Brogden, 1969

'Edmondale' 1 W-? (b)
(Mrs M. Moorby) Mrs M. Moorby, 1957

'Edmond's White' 2 W-Y
Syn. of 'Maggie May'

'Edmunds' White' 2 W-Y
Syn. of 'Maggie May'

'Edmund's White' 2 W-Y
Syn. of 'Maggie May'

'Edna' 9 W-YYR
(G.H. Engleheart, pre-1913)
Fl. small; perianth segments rounded at apex; corona bright yellow, with glowing scarlet at rim

'Edna Dunlop' 2 W-WWO
(J.N. Hancock & Co., 1959) Unregistered

'Edna Earl' 3 W-OOR
(G.A. Uit den Boogaard, pre-1950)

'Edna Gibbs' 2 Y-? (a)
(C. de Berry) C. de Berry, 1956

'Edna Jones' 2 ?-R
(J.N. Hancock & Co., pre-1949)
Corona rich red

'Edna Lee Ismay' 2 W-Y
(A.L. Ismay) A.L. Ismay, 1970
'Ada Finch' hybrid

'Edna Rose' 3 Y-? (a)
(N.Y. Lower, pre-1934)

'Edna's Memory' 2 W-Y
(L.P. Dettman) L.P. Dettman, 1974
'Bonnington' open pollinated
Fl. 105 mm wide

'Edom' 2 Y-R
(A.O. Roblin, c.1966) Unregistered
'Tegwith' × 'Keren'

'Edric' 2 W-? (b or c)
(R.H. Bath, pre-1933)

'Edwalton' 2 W-YYO
(W.A. Noton, 1974) W.A. Noton, 1985
'Arpege' × 'Avenger'
Perianth segments very broad, rounded at apex, mucronate, spreading, a little concave, with raised midrib, overlapping half; the inner segments only slightly narrower, blunt, somewhat twisted; corona bowl-shaped, lightly ribbed, mouth widely expanded, 6-lobed, lightly frilled. Late

'Edward Buxton' 3 Y-YYO
(A. Sandys-Winsch, pre-1932)
Flower rounded; perianth segments broadly ovate, pale creamy primrose yellow with a paler tone at apex, overlapping; corona ribbed, dark yellow, with a broad band of orange at rim, rim dentate. Sunproof. 2n=27,28. AM(Haarlem) 1933

'Edward Crouch' 1 W-? (b)
(H.R. Meyer, pre-1927)

'Edward Grieg' 2 W-Y
(Konynenburg & Mark, pre-1953)
'Invitation' × 'Extase'

'Edward Hart' 2 Y-Y
(E. Leeds, pre-1877)
Fl. rich yellow. Syn. Incomparabilis Concolor 'Edward Hart'

'Edward Heath' 2 W-P
(G.E. Mitsch) B.C. Heath, 1977
'Precedent' × 'Carita'; sdlg no. A34/8
Fl. 100 mm wide; perianth segments pure white; corona pink, with rosy pink at base, shading to salmon at outside rim, heavily frilled

'Edward Leeds' 1 Y-Y
(E. Leeds, pre-1877)
Resembles an inferior 'Golden Spur'. "Absorbed" *N. hispanicus* var. *propinquus*, 'Mrs Gladstone', 'President Lincoln'

'Edward Stewart' 1 Y-Y
(J.W. Barr, pre-1930)

'Edwina' 9 W-YYR
(de Graaff Bros, pre-1927)
Corona with bright red at rim. AM(Haarlem) 1926

'Edwinstowe' 3 W-YYR
(Mrs J. Abel Smith) Mrs J. Abel Smith, 1992
'Winkburn' × 'Lichfield'; sdlg no. T44/31
Fl. 34 mm wide; perianth segments acute; corona pale yellow, with a narrow band of intense red at rim. Mid-season

'E.E.Morbey' 2 Y-O
(West & Fell, pre-1938)
Perianth segments golden yellow; corona spreading, bright reddish orange

'Eeyeuk Sunset' 2 Y-O
(D.J.A. Dennis) J.L. Martin, 1982
'Sunpool' × 'Hugh Poate'
Fl. 100 mm wide; perianth segments vivid yellow 9A; corona brilliant orange 25C to strong orange 25A. Mid-season. Resembles a later-flowered 'Lemcut' of deeper colour

'Effect' 2 Y-O
(Mrs R.O. Backhouse or de Graaff Bros, pre-1930)
Perianth segments soft yellow; corona deep orange. AM(Haarlem) 1930

'Effective' 1 WWY-Y
(G.L. Wilson, pre-1931)
'Jack Spratt' open pollinated
Perianth segments broad, sulphur white, stained yellow at base, overlapping; corona long, chrome yellow, with rim flanged and regularly notched. AM(e) 1935

'Effendie' 2 W-? (b)
(G.A. Uit den Boogaard, pre-1937)
Syn. 'Isolde'

'Effie' 3 Y-? (a)
(Mrs R.O. Backhouse, pre-1921)

'Effingham' 1 Y-Y
(Mrs F.E.W. Hanger, pre-1953)

'E.F.Prentis' 5
(?H.G.Hawker, pre-1936)

'Egard' 11a W-Y
(J. Gerritsen & Son) J. Gerritsen & Son, 1973
Fl. 90 mm wide

'Egberdina' 2 W-? (b)
(Mrs R.O. Backhouse, pre-1921)

'Egeria' 2 or 3 W-W
(G.H. Engleheart, pre-1901)
Perianth segments pale ivory white, slightly reflexed; corona long cup-shaped, constricted below mouth, darker in tone than the perianth, with mouth a little incurved at rim

'Eggishorn' 1 W-W
(de Graaff Bros, pre-1927)

'Egg Nogg' 4 W-Y
(Mrs J.L.K. Richardson) Carncairn Daffodils, 1975
'Gaytime' × 'Rose Caprice'
Fl. 90 mm wide; perianth segments white and yellow; corona brilliant yellow 7A. Late. 2n=28

'Eggs and Bacon' 4 W-O
Syn. of 'Orange Phoenix'

'Eggshell' 2 Y-Y
(Murray W.Evans) Murray W.Evans, 1976
'Oneonta' × 'Protege'; sdlg no. K-7/1
Fl. 100 mm wide. Mid-season

'Egina' 1 W-P
(W. Jackson Jr) W. Jackson Jr, 1966
'Imp' × 'Pink Monarch'; sdlg no. 76/59

'Eglinton' 2 W-? (b)
(G.L. Wilson, pre-1923)

'Egmond' 3 W-? (b)
(de Graaff Bros, pre-1931)
AM(Haarlem) 1930

'Egmont' 2 Y-YYO
(Sir A.P.W. Thomas, pre-1926)
Perianth segments yellow; corona with a broad band of scarlet-orange at rim

'Egmont' 1 W-W
Syn. of 'Condesa'

'Egmont Charm' 2 W-YYO
(M.E.Brogden, pre-1995) Unregistered
'Conquest' × 'Bandit'

'Egmont Gold' 2 Y-Y
(G.W.E. Brogden, 1979) Brogden Bulbs, 1991
'Gold Bank' × 'Daydream'; sdlg no. x74/1
Fl. 105 mm wide, deep golden yellow; perianth segments broadly ovate, acute, plane, smooth; corona funnel-shaped, with mouth wavy, rim crenate and lightly rolled. Mid-season

'Egmont King' 2 Y-YOR
(G.W.E. Brogden) Brogden Bulbs, 1991
'Orator' × 'Loch Hope'; sdlg no. x95/2
Fl. 115 mm wide; perianth segments broad, mid-yellow, smooth; corona slightly expanding, with yellow at base shading to orange at mid-zone and red at rim, rim dentate. Early to mid-season

'Egmont Princess' 2 W-Y
(M.E.Brogden, pre-1993) Unregistered
'Hostage' × 'Bandit'

'Egmont Queen' 2 W-W
(J.Gibson, pre-1927)
Corona creamy white, frilled. AM(e)(NZ) 1928

'Egmont Snow'
Unregistered
Seed parent of 'Snowy River'

'Ego Flos' 1 Y-Y
(M. van Waveren & Sons, pre-1942)

'E.G.Quick' 2 Y-Y
(C. Dawson, pre-1924)
Perianth segments primrose yellow, twisted; corona ribbed, bright yellow, frilled. Resembles a larger-flowered 'Frank Miles'

'Egret' 3 W-Y
(G.H. Engleheart, pre-1902)
Corona large, shallow, ribbed, lemon yellow, shading to golden yellow at rim

'Egrin' 2 Y-Y
(W.A. Watts, pre-1927)
*HC(g) 1927

'Egwin' 2 Y-Y
Syn. of 'Saint Egwin'

'Egypt' 1 Y-Y
(J.L. Richardson, pre-1928)
Fl. soft yellow; perianth segments broadly ovate; corona slightly deeper tone than the perianth, with rim

dentate and widely flanged. Resembles 'Countess of Annesley'

'E.H.Jenkins' 1 W-? (b)
(Barr & Sons, pre-1908)

'E.H.Krelage' 1 Y-Y
(pre-1908)
Perianth segments light yellow; corona pure yellow. AM(Haarlem) 1908. ?The same as 'J.H.Krelage'

'E.H.Wilson' 2 W-Y
(de Graaff Bros, pre-1945)

'Eider' 2 W-W
(G.E. Mitsch) G.E. Mitsch, 1970

'Eifell' 1 W-P
(P. & G. Phillips) P. & G. Phillips, 1982
Fl. 98 mm wide. Mid-season

'Eifina' 3 W-? (b)
(Mrs R.O. Backhouse, pre-1921)
AM(Haarlem) 1936. Div. 9 until 1957

'Eiko' 1 W-P
(P. Phillips) P. Phillips, 1977
Fl. forming a double triangle, 100 mm wide; perianth segments very broadly ovate, prominently mucronate, spreading, overlapping half; corona funnel-shaped, smooth, pink, with mouth wavy and a little expanded, rim crenate and lightly rolled. Mid-season. Resembles 'Vision' but with a whiter perianth and the corona of a different pink

'Eildon' 2 W-WWY
(J.A. O'More) J.A. O'More, 1968
'Chinese White' × 'Green Island'
Perianth segments rounded; corona widely expanded, closely ribbed, becoming pastel yellow towards mouth, with orange tones

'Eileen' 9 W-?
(Sir J.A.R. Gore-Booth, pre-1908)

'Eileen' 2 W-P
(Australian origin, 1945) R. Hyde, 1958
Corona clear pink, frilled

'Eileen' 3 W-YYO
Syn. of 'Evelyn Aldersey'

'Eileen Mitchell' 5 W-W
(Barr & Sons, pre-1906)
N. triandrus sdlg
Fls usually 3 per stem; corona opening primrose yellow, becoming milk white, frilled

'Eileen Patterson' 3 Y-? (a)
(W.A. Grace, pre-1938)

'Eileen Squires' 2 W-GPP
(R.E. Jerrell) R.E. Jerrell, 1984
'Precedent' × ('Melody Lane' × 'Rima'); sdlg no. 69-28-1
Corona deep pink. Mid-season

'Eilwier' 1 W-W
(J.L. Richardson, pre-1948)

'Einig' 3 W-? (b)
(G.L. Wilson, pre-1947)

'Eion' 2 W-R
(W. Jackson Jr, 1966) Unregistered
'Jo' × 'Arbar'; sdlg no. 183/66

'Eireanne' 2 Y-W
(Mrs M. Moorby) Mrs M. Moorby, 1956

'Eire Gem' 2 Y-? (a)
(J.L. Richardson, pre-1938)

'Eisty' 2
(G.H. Johnstone, pre-1960) Unregistered
?The same as 'Elsty'

'Ekron' 1 Y-Y
(J.T. Gray, pre-1951)

'Elaborate' 2 Y-?
(H.A. Brown, 1937) J.N. Hancock & Co., 1960
Perianth segments golden; corona deep cup shaped, with orange at rim, frilled

'Elaine' 3 W-YWW
(G.H. Engleheart or W.B. Hartland, pre-1901)
Fl. silvery white; corona cup-shaped, ribbed, shading to citron yellow at base. FCC 1901

'Elan' 6 Y-R
(G.E. Mitsch) G.E. Mitsch, 1979
('Armada' × 'Paricutin') × *N. cyclamineus*; sdlg no. JJ93/1
Fl. 90 mm wide; perianth segments golden yellow, reflexed; corona orange-red. Mid-season. Resembles a larger 'Jetfire' of heavier substance with a broader perianth

'Elana' 1 W-Y
(J.S. Leitch) J.S. Leitch, 1964
Corona lemon yellow

'Eland' 7 W-W
(G.E. Mitsch) G.E. Mitsch, 1968
'Aircastle' × *N. jonquilla*; sdlg no. Z2/14
Fls 2-3 per stem, rounded, 76 mm wide; perianth segments very broadly ovate, only very slightly mucronate, pure white, spreading, plane, with midrib showing, overlapping half; the inner segments a little inflexed, with margins wavy; corona shallow bowl-

shaped, opening pale lemon yellow, becoming white, with mouth lightly frilled. Late. 2n=21

'Elanora' 2 W-R
(W.M. Spry, pre-1975) Unregistered
'Stanley Mann' × 'Delight'
Corona dark orange-red. Late

'El Arish' 2 Y-? (a)
(G.C. Graham, pre-1951)

'Elation' 3 W-? (b)
(R. Crews) R. Crews, 1956

N. elatior Haworth = *N.* × *odorus*

'Elatior'
(pre-1915)

N. elatus Gussone = *N. tazetta* subsp. *lacticolor*

'Elatus' 2 W-Y
Syn. of 'Duke of Buccleuch'

'Elba' 9 W-?
(F.H. Chapman, pre-1929)

'El Banco' 1 Y-Y
(J.N. Hancock & Co.) J.N. Hancock & Co., 1955
'Hallmark' × 'Camberwell King'
Corona rim neatly rolled

'Elbee' 2 W-Y
(T. Morrison) T. Morrison, 1960
Corona ribbed, rich yellow

'Elburton' 2 Y-O
(T. Bloomer) du Plessis Bros, 1989
('Ballintoy' × 'Air Marshal') × 'Shining Light'; sdlg no. 325
Fl 108 mm wide; perianth segments golden yellow, very smooth; corona deep orange, with rim dentate. Mid-season

'El Camino' 6 Y-Y
(G.E. Mitsch) W.H. Roesé/Brian S. Duncan, 1978
'Honey Bells' × *N. cyclamineus*; sdlg no. E09
Mid-season. Resembles a deeper-coloured 'Charity May' with a taller and stronger stem

'Elcana' 3 W-? (b)
(Mrs D. Duff, pre-1951)

'Elcano' 1 W-W
(S.J. Bisdee, 1948)
'Beachside' × 'Cantatrice'

'El Capitan' 1 Y-Y
(G.H. Engleheart, pre-1913)

'El Capitan' 1 W-Y
(G.E. Mitsch) G.E. Mitsch, 1972
'Cibola' open pollinated; sdlg no. A53/3
Fl. 112 mm wide; corona pale lemon yellow, tightly frilled, with rim flanged. Early

'Elderslie' 2 Y-R
(C.E. Radcliff, 1939) J.M.Radcliff, 1956
'Red Torch' hybrid × ?'Miss Beatty'

'Eldon' 1 Y-Y
(J.T. Gray, pre-1951)

'El Dorado' 1 Y-Y
(C. Smith, pre-1910)
See also 'Eldorado'

'El Dorado' 2 Y-O
(P.D. Williams, pre-1933)
Perianth segments golden yellow; corona frilled. AM(Haarlem) 1933. See also 'Eldorado'

'Eldorado' 1 Y-Y
Syn. of 'El Dorado'

'Eldorado' 2 Y-O
Syn. of 'El Dorado'

'Eldred' 1 W-Y
(Barr & Sons, pre-1920)
Fl. 95 mm wide; perianth segments creamy white, overlapping half; corona bright sulphur yellow, with mouth expanded and frilled. Mid-season

'Eleanor' 1 Y-W
(T.A.V. Wood) T.A.V. Wood, 1972
Sdlg 4/42 × 'Spellbinder'
Fl. 98 mm wide; perianth segments lemon yellow; corona opening lemon yellow, becoming white. Mid-season. Resembles a Div. 1 'Handcross'

'Eleanora' 8
(pre-1883)

'Eleanor Bennett'
(pre-1914)

'Eleanor Berkeley' 5
(G.H. Engleheart, pre-1900)
AM 1900

'Eleanor Harris' 2 Y-? (a)
(The Brodie of Brodie, pre-1931)

'Eleanor May' 4 W-R
(H.E. Reeve) W. Jackson Jr, 1970
'Insulinde' × 'Rouge'
Perianth and other petaloid segments white; corona segments symmetrically interspersed, red

'Eleanor Rose' 2 W-P
(Mrs J. Abel Smith) Mrs J. Abel Smith, 1992
'Rose Royale' × 'Bright Flame'; sdlg no. J44/32
Fl. 36 mm wide; corona solid deep pink. Mid-season

'Eleazar' 2 Y-Y
(G.J. Phillips, 1977) G.J. Phillips, 1992
'Camelot' × 'Golden Aura'; sdlg no. 72-102-6
Fl. 112 mm wide; perianth segments broadly ovate, of good substance. Mid-season

'Elector' 1 W-? (b)
(L. van Leeuwen & Son, pre-1931)

'Elector' ?-P
(Alister Clark, pre-1948)

'Electra' 2 Y-Y
(G.H. Engleheart, pre-1901)
Fl. opening small, becoming larger after several days; perianth segments soft canary yellow; corona of a slightly darker tone

'Electra' 3 Y-? (a)
(Mrs M. Moorby, pre-1949)

'Electra' 2 Y-O
(J.N. Hancock & Co., 1968) Unregistered

'Electric' 3 W-? (b)
(de Graaff Bros, pre-1930)
AM(Haarlem) 1931

'Electric Pink' 11a W-P
(R. & E.Havens, 1980) R. & E.Havens, 1996
Sdlg F67/1 (['Precedent' × 'Carita'] × ['Radiation' × ('Mabel Taylor' × 'Interim')]) × sdlg D7/12 ('Accent' × sdlg Q97/2 ['Wild Rose' × 'Hillbilly'])
Fl. 95 mm wide; perianth segments broad; corona split, the six segments opposite the perianth segments, reddish pink, deeply frilled. Late. Sunproof

'Elegance' 3 W-? (b or c)
(G.H. Engleheart, pre-1908)

'Elegance' 2 W-W
(R.H. Bath, pre-1923)
AM(e) 1926

N. elegans (Haworth) Spach 13 Section Tazettae. PC 1995
    var. *elegans*
        f. *elegans*
        f. *auranticoronatus* Maire
    var. *fallax* Font Quer
    var. *flavescens* Maire
    var. *intermedius* Gay
    var. *oxypetalus* (Boissier) Maire

'Elegans' 3 W-WWY
(W. Backhouse, pre-1851)
Corona expanded, white, with saffron yellow at rim.
Syn. Burbidgei 'Elegans'. Was "absorbed" into 'Lottie Simmons'

'Elegans' 3 W-Y
(E. Leeds, pre-1851)
N. × *poculiformis* × *N. radiiflorus*
Fl. large; perianth segments narrowly ovate, creamy white, twisted or with margins incurved, separated; corona straight-sided, primrose yellow, sometimes quite heavily stained pinkish orange at rim, mouth straight, with rim minutely crenate. Syn. Leedsii 'Elegans'. ?"Absorbed" 'Juno'

'Elegantea' 5
(C.G. van Tubergen, pre-1914)

'Elegant Lady' 1 W-Y
(Mrs Ben Robertson, 1970) Mrs Ben Robertson, 1980
('Corinth' × 'Kanchenjunga') × 'Empress of Ireland'; sdlg no. 199
Fl. 110 mm wide; corona lemon yellow. Mid-season. Resembles 'Willow Green' but with whiter perianth and narrower corona

'Elegy' 9 W-GRR
(F.H. Chapman, pre-1910)
'Horace' × 'Almira'

'Elegy' 3 W-WOR
(D.S. Bell) D.S. Bell, 1962
Fl. 156 mm wide; corona apricot orange, becoming white at base, with orange-red at rim. Mid-season. Resembles a larger-flowered 'Corofin' with white at corona base

'Elena' 2 Y-? (a)
(R.H. Bath, pre-1933)

'Eleonora' 8
(pre-1883)
Resembles 'La Citronière'

'Eleonora Duse' 2 Y-? (a)
(M. van Waveren & Sons, pre-1937)

'Eleonor's Pride' 2 W-O
(J.W.A. Lefeber) J.W.A. Lefeber, 1968
'Professor Einstein' hybrid

'Elevato' 2 W-YOO
(Konynenburg & Mark, 1950) Konynenburg & Mark, 1962
'Aranjuez' × 'Rustom Pasha'
Fl. 115 mm wide; perianth segments creamy white; corona orange, with deep yellow at base. Early

'Elf' 2 Y-WWP

(Barr & Sons, 1948) Wallace & Barr, 1959
'Frilled Beauty' × 'Mrs R.O.Backhouse'
Perianth segments white, with shades of sulphur yellow; corona creamy white, flushed shell pink at rim. Mid-season

'Elfcap' 6
(Mrs R.S. Cobley, pre-1932)

'Elfhorn' 10 Y-Y
(A.Gray, pre-1941)
Closely resembles 'Elfhorn' pre-1948

'Elfhorn' 10 Y-Y
(A. Gray, pre-1948)
Fl. bright yelllow. Dwarf. Late. Closely resembles 'Elfhorn' pre-1941. Listed by Gray under Bulbocodium

'Elfin' 2 Y-Y
(A.M. Wilson, pre-1914)
Fl. yellow; perianth segments very broadly ovate, blunt, not prominently mucronate, spreading, plane, overlapping; the inner segments with margins a little wavy and sometimes nicked; corona shallow and wide-spreading, deeply ribbed, rim boldly notched and crenate

'Elfin' 6
(A.M. Wilson, pre-1948)
N. rupicola × *N. cyclamineus*

'Elfin Gold' 6 Y-Y
(Brian S. Duncan) Rathowen Daffodils, 1983
'Golden Joy' open pollinated; sdlg no. 654
Fl. deep golden yellow, of polished texture; perianth segments broadly or very broadly ovate, blunt or truncate, not prominently mucronate, reflexed, plane, overlapping half; the inner segments a little less strongly reflexed, somewhat twisted or with margins wavy or incurved; corona cylindrical, broadly ribbed, a little constricted below mouth, mouth even. Mid-season

'Elfin Moon' 2 W-W
(J.A.Hunter) J.A.Hunter, 1995
O'More sdlg ('Easter Moon' × [('Bodilly' × 'Clonmell') × 'Petsamo']) × ('Easter Moon' × ['Daisy Schäffer' × 'Carnlough']); sdlg no. 5/82A
Fl. forming a double triangle, 74 mm wide; perianth segments ovate; corona funnel-shaped, with mouth wavy. Mid-season

'Elfin Queen' 5
(H.G. Longford, pre-1927)

'Elfrida Pearson' 2 W-Y
(J.R. Pearson & Sons, pre-1910)
'Minnie Hume' × 'Madame de Graaff'
Corona deep yellow

'Elfride' 2 Y-? (a)
(van Zonneveld Bros & Philippo, pre-1931)

'Elgar' 2 Y-? (a)
(Mrs R.O. Backhouse, pre-1914)

'Elgeman' 2 W-P
(H.G. Cross) H.G. Cross, 1984
'Accent' × 'Verran'
Mid-season

'Elgin' 1 Y-Y
(The Brodie of Brodie, *c*.1927)
('Ben Alder' × 'Broadford') × 'Yukon'
Fl. about 127 mm wide; perianth segments ovate, acute, mucronate, canary yellow, slightly inflexed, overlapping one-third; the inner segments narrower, more strongly inflexed in lower half, reflexed towards apex; corona cylindrical, smooth, chrome yellow, with mouth ribbed and expanded, rim deeply crenate and widely flanged. AM(e) 1940

'Elgiva' 3 W-O
(P.D. Williams, pre-1914)
Perianth segments cream; corona large, spreading, ribbed, deep apricot orange

'E.Lial'
(?Slieve Donard Nursery Co., pre-1927)

'Elica' 3 W-R
(A.H. Ahrens) J.S. Leitch, 1956

'Elida' 2 W-? (b)
(J.T. Gray, pre-1950)

'Elinor' 2 Y-? (a)
(Mrs R.O. Backhouse, pre-1921)

'Elinor Cowdall' 1 W-? (b)
(T. Buncombe, pre-1934)

'Elinor M.G.Angus' 3 W-Y
(J. Mallender, pre-1912)
'White Lady' hybrid
Perianth segments pure white, overlapping; corona small, yellow

'Elisabeth Bas' 11a W-Y
(J.W.A. Lefeber) J.W.A. Lefeber, 1958
Corona segments lemon yellow, heavily frilled

'Elisabeth Nobel' 1 W-O
(J.W.A. Lefeber) J.W.A. Lefeber, 1968

'Elisabeth van Ginhoven' 1 W-W
(A. Frylink & Sons, pre-1931)
AM(Haarlem) 1930. Received AM(Haarlem) 1930 as 'Lohengrin'

'Elisabeth Wijkmans' 2 Y-O
(F. Rijnveld & Sons, pre-1951)
'Fortune' × 'Scarlet Elegance'

'Elisa Volta' 2 Y-YYO
(Konynenburg & Mark) Konynenburg & Mark, 1960
('Frederike' × 'Mimosa') × ('Aranjuez' × 'Beauty of the Garden')
Fl. 95 mm wide; perianth segments light greenish yellow 4C; corona vivid yellow 17B, with strong orange 25A at rim

'Elise' 2 W-? (b)
(J. Mallender, pre-1932)

'Elissa' 3 W-? (b)
(Cartwright & Goodwin, pre-1910)

'Elite' 8 Y-Y
(pre-1792)
Fl. golden yellow

'Elite' 2 Y-O
(J.N. Hancock & Co., pre-1949)
Corona reddish orange

'Elixir' 4 Y-Y
(G.E. Mitsch) G.E. Mitsch, 1976
'Gay Time' × 'Daydream'; sdlg no. G69/2
Fl. 95 mm wide; perianth and other petaloid segments deep lemon; corona segments yellow. Late. Resembles 'Discovery'

'Elizabeth' 5 Y-Y
(P.D. Williams, pre-1907)
Fl. pale lemon yellow; corona darker in tone

'Elizabeth' 1 W-W
Syn. of 'Elizabeth Arden'

'Elizabethan' 1 Y-Y
(Hon. Sir R.H. Rhodes, pre-1914)

'Elizabeth Ann' 6 W-GWP
(Brian S. Duncan) Rathowen Daffodils, 1983
Sdlg × 'Foundling'; sdlg no. 419
Fl. 85 mm wide; perianth segments very broadly ovate, blunt, prominently mucronate, pure white, reflexed, plane, very smooth, overlapping half; the inner segments twisted or with margins wavy or incurved; corona broad bowl-shaped, lightly ribbed, white, with green at base and a well-defined band of rose pink at rim, mouth lightly frilled. Mid-season

'Elizabeth Arden' 1 W-W
(J.W. Barr, pre-1930)
Syn. 'Elizabeth'

'Elizabeth Bandon' 2 W-R
(J.O. Sherrard, pre-1949)

'Elizabeth Beaty' 2 Y-YYO
(H.A. Brown, pre-1935)
Corona yellow, with orange at rim, frilled

'Elizabeth Bowen' 2 Y-YOO
(R.V. Favell, pre-1942)
'Pentreath' × 'Penquite'

'Elizabeth Browning' 3 W-? (b)
(G.H. Engleheart, pre-1927)
Fls sometimes 2 per stem

'Elizabeth F.Prentis' 5 W-W
(P.D. Williams, pre-1927)
Fls 1-2 per stem, 82 mm wide, facing down; perianth segments broadly ovate, blunt, prominently mucronate, more or less spreading, somewhat concave or with margins incurling, with broad midrib showing, overlapping half; the inner segments sometimes more strongly inflexed; corona cup-shaped, broadly ribbed, creamy white, with mouth straight, even, rim minutely notched and crenate. Late. Syn. 'Elizabeth Prentis', 'Mrs Prentis'. See also 'Elizabeth S.Prentis'

'Elizabeth Herbert' 1 W-W
(W.F. Mitchell, pre-1935)

'Elizabeth Jane' 6 W-P
(D.S. Bell) D.S. Bell, 1982
'Red Conquest' hybrid × 'Jenny' hybrid
Fl. 88 mm wide. Mid-season. Resembles 'Jenny' but with a pink corona

'Elizabeth Ladson' 1 W-P
(A. Overton) A. Overton, 1959
Perianth segments white; corona soft pink

'Elizabeth Pownall' 1 W-W
(C.A. Nethercote) T. Morrison, 1960
F. pure white

'Elizabeth Prentis' 5 W-W
Syn. of 'Elizabeth F.Prentis'

'Elizabeth S.Prentis' 5 W-W
Syn. of 'Elizabeth F.Prentis'

'Eliza Turck' 1 Y-Y
(W. Backhouse, pre-1869)
Fl. deep canary yellow. Syn. Pseudonarcissus Major 'Eliza Turck'

'El Jourdan' 2 W-W
(L. Buckland, pre-1936)
Corona with green at base

'Elka' 1 W-W
(A. Gray, c.1967) Mrs J.B. Capen, 1989
Fl. star-shaped, 33 mm wide; perianth segments narrowly ovate, opening pale yellow, becoming white, spreading, with margins somewhat wavy, slightly overlapping at base; the inner segments more narrowly ovate, twisted or with margins more wavy; corona cylindrical, smooth, opening yellow, becoming white, with mouth ribbed and a little expanded, lightly frilled, rim crenate. Dwarf. Early. Resembles 'Snipe'

'Ella' 2 W-? (b)
(Barr & Sons, pre-1914)

'Ella Guthrie' 2 W-?
(Alister Clark, 1935) J. Sharp, 1960

'Ellangowan' 2 Y-? (a)
(The Brodie of Brodie, pre-1934)
'Killigrew' × 'Marquis'

'Ellanne' 2 W-W
(Miss M. Verry) Miss M. Verry, 1974
'Vigil' × 'Empress of Ireland'
Fl. 104 mm wide

'Ellbridge' 3 W-ORR
(Mrs H.K. Richardson) du Plessis Bros, 1977
'Matapan' × 'Toreador'; sdlg no. 263
Fl. 75 mm wide. Mid-season

'Ellen' 2 W-Y
(L. Buckland, pre-1936)

'Ellen' 2 W-W
(A.Ladson, 1960s) Unregistered
Fl. ivory white; corona flared and heavily frilled

'Ellen Barr' 3 W-YYR
(W. Backhouse, pre-1869)
Corona primrose yellow, with scarlet at rim. Syn. Burbidgei 'Ellen Barr'

'Ellenese' 2 W-O
(J.N. Hancock & Co.) J.N. Hancock & Co., 1955
Perianth segments creamy white; corona spreading, deep orange, dentate

'Ellen Graham' 2 W-? (b)
(G.C. Graham, pre-1949)

'Ellen Isabel' 2 W-PWW
(L.P. Dettman) L.P. Dettman, 1979
'Chartwell' × 'Isobel Chaplin'; sdlg no. 54/77
Fl. 76 mm wide; perianth segments greenish white (155A); corona yellowish white (158B), with orange-pink (29C) at base. Mid-season. Resembles a better-proportioned 'Ann Cameron'

'Ellen Lee' 2 W-? (b)
(Mrs F.S. Foote, pre-1941)

'Ellen Mann'
(pre-1960) Unregistered

'Ellen Ney' 3 W-R
Syn. of 'Elly Ney'

'Ellen Terry' 1 W-Y
(C.G. van Tubergen, pre-1927)
Perianth segments acute, pure white, overlapping; corona rich canary yellow, frilled

'Ellen Willmott' 1 W-Y
(G.H. Engleheart, pre-1897)
Perianth segments broadly ovate, blunt, fairly prominently mucronate, spreading or a little inflexed, with margins slightly wavy and sometimes incurled at apex, of great substance, overlapping half; corona broad, cylindrical, angled, deep golden yellow, lightly frilled, with rim widely flanged. FCC 1897

'Ellery' 2 Y-R
(G.L. Wilson) Guy L.Wilson Ltd, 1964

'Ellesmere' 2 Y-YOO
(P.D. Williams, pre-1939)
Fl. 89 mm wide; perianth segments light greenish yellow 4C, with a darker tone at margins, with margins incurved to give a star-shaped appearance; corona ribbed, brilliant yellow 13B at base, shading to near strong orange 25A at rim, mouth widely expanded and frilled, rim dentate. *AM(g) 1953

'Ellie Ney' 3 W-R
Syn. of 'Elly Ney'

'Ellimatta' 1 Y-W
(L.P. Dettman) L.P. Dettman, 1968
'Spellbinder' × 'La La'
Fl. 120 mm wide, opening lime yellow; corona passing to white, flushed sulphur yellow outside, off white inside. Mid-season. Resembles an improved 'La La'

'Ellimatta Gold'
(L.P. Dettman, c.1977) Unregistered

'Ellimatta Midnight' 2 Y-Y
(L.P.Dettman, 1975) Unregistered
'Arctic Gold' × 'Gahna'; sdlg no. 1/76

'Ellimatta Reversed' 2 YYW-WWY
(L.P. Dettman) L.P. Dettman, 1978
'Ellimatta' × 'Binkie'; sdlg no. E1/74
Fl. 77 mm wide; perianth segments vivid greenish yellow 2A, with yellowish white 155B at base; corona yellowish white 155B, with vivid greenish yellow 2A at rim, mouth slightly expanded, with rim dentate

'Elloe' 2 Y-O
(M. van Waveren & Sons, pre-1930)
Perianth segments bright yellow; corona reddish orange. Resembles 'Killigrew'

'Elly Ney' 3 W-R
(de Graaff Bros, pre-1925)
AM(Haarlem) 1925. 'Ellen Ney','Ellie Ney'

'Elma MacLeod' 2 W-YYO
(D.C. MacArthur) D.C. MacArthur, 1988
Rathowen pink sdlg × MacArthur sdlg; sdlg no. E8807
Corona pale yellow 11D, with light orange-yellow at rim. Mid-season

'Elmara' 4 Y-Y
(H.G. Cross) H.G. Cross, 1984
'Camelot' × ('Kingscourt' × 'Fiji'); sdlg no. 61-6
Perianth segments vivid yellow 9A; corona segments densely arranged, orange-yellow (14A), lightly frilled. Late

'Elmbridge' 1 W-Y
(J.S.B. Lea) Clive Postles Daffodils, 1990
Sdlg 1-29-71 × 'Owston Wood'; sdlg no. 1-20-77
Fl. 115 mm wide; perianth segments broadly ovate, smooth; corona slightly expanding, deep yellow, with mouth flared and rim neatly dentate. Mid-season

'Elmer' 2 Y-?
(J.T. Gray, pre-1949)
Perianth segments rounded, smooth; corona with red at rim

'Elmer' 2 Y-YYR
(P. & G. Phillips) P. & G. Phillips, 1981
Fl. 103 mm wide. Mid-season

'Elmira' 2 W-YYO
(J.T. Gray, pre-1951)
Perianth segments pure white; corona lemon yellow, with orange at rim. Syn. 'Dink'

'El Misti' 2 W-WWP
(S.J. Bisdee, 1951)
'The Stork' × 'Rosario'

'Elmley Castle' 1 Y-Y
(J.M. de Navarro, pre-1949)
'Royalist' × 'Arctic Gold'
Perianth segments broadly ovate; corona cylindrical or slightly expanding, with rim dentate

'Elm Park' 2 Y-Y
(P. Phillips) P. Phillips, 1968

'Elmwood' 2 Y-R
(W.J. Dunlop) W.J. Dunlop, 1958
'Workman' × 'Craigywarren'

Corona crimson-red

'Elnia' 2 Y-OOP
(J.T. Gray, pre-1949)
? × 'Suda'
Perianth segments white, spreading, smooth, overlapping; corona straight-sided, yellowish amber orange, with pink at rim, rim rolled

'Elnith' 2 W-? (b)
(H.R. Meyer, pre-1927)

'Elongatus' 1 Y-Y
(E. Leeds, pre-1877)
Syn. Humei 'Elongatus'

'Elongatus' 2 or 3
(E. Leeds, pre-1877)

'Elongatus' 2 W-?YYO
Syn. of 'Fair Helen'

'Eloquence' 2 Y-? (a)
(Mrs P.M. Davis, pre-1948)

'El Oro' 2 (a)
(Mrs R.O. Backhouse, pre-1921)

'El Paso' 2 Y-O
(Warnaar & Co., pre-1936)

'Elpenor' 2 W-? (h)
(Mrs R.O. Backhouse, pre-1921)

'Elphin' 4 W-P
(J.S.B. Lea, 1968) Unregistered
('Falaise' × 'Rose Caprice') × 'Fionn'; sdlg no. 1-61-62
Late

'Elrick'
(?R.H. Bath, pre-1948)

'Elrond' 2 W-W
(Brian S. Duncan) Rathowen Daffodils, 1981
'Stainless' × 'Foundling'; sdlg no. 350
Fl. pure white; corona faintly touched green at base. Mid-season. 2n=28

'Elsa' 2 Y-YOO
(H.A. Brown, 1941)
Perianth segments broadly ovate, pale yellow, with slight white mucro, spreading, plane, overlapping half; the inner segments shouldered at base, a little inflexed, with margins wavy or incurved; corona cup-shaped, ribbed, bright reddish orange, with yellow at base, mouth frilled. Very late

'Else' 3 W-YYR
(T.H. Piper, 1949) T.H. Piper, 1956

'Elspeth' × 'Gyda'

'Elsewhere' 2 W-Y
(J.N.Hancock & Co., 1984) J.N.Hancock & Co., 1997
Sdlg 30/73H (2 W-P) hybrid; sdlg no. 17/84H
Perianth segments ovate; corona apricot yellow, with rim deeply crenate. Mid-season

'Elsie' 9 W-?
(W. Poupart, pre-1913)

'Elsie Gott' 2 or 3 W-? (b or c)
(pre-1913)

'Elsie Gunter' 2 W-Y
(R.W. Ward & Son) R.W. Ward & Son, 1973
'Blarney' × 'Heaven'

'Elsie Stewart' 2 W-? (b or c)
(J.W. Barr, pre-1930)

'Elsmaree' 1 W-Y
(J.N. Hancock & Co., 1968) Unregistered
'Narrewarren' × 'Hoyle'

'Elspeth' 3 W-YYO
(P.D. Williams, pre-1913)
Fl. rounded, 76 mm wide; perianth segments very broad, rounded at apex, slightly mucronate, creamy white, spreading, plane, with broad midrib faintly showing, overlapping half or more; the inner segments narrower, slightly truncate, shouldered at base, a little inflexed; corona bowl-shaped, lightly ribbed, pale yellow, with a narrow band of orange at rim, frilled. *AM(g) 1933. Div. 2 from 1930 to 1935

'Elstree' 2 W-? (b)
(R. Crews, pre-1949)

'Elsty' 2
(G.H. Johnstone, pre-1960) Unregistered
'Elspeth' × 'Laity'
?The same as 'Eisty'

'Elta' 7
(de Graaff Bros, pre-1930)
AM(Haarlem) 1930

'Elton Legget' 2 W-Y
(J.W.A. Lefeber) J.W.A. Lefeber, 1958
Perianth segments creamy white; corona light yellow 10C. AM(Haarlem) 1960

'El Toro' 2 W-Y
(A. Money) David L.Sheppard, 1970

'Elusive' 3 W-R
(Jackson's Daffodils, 1983) Jackson's Daffodils, 1997
'Dorus' × 'Challenge'; sdlg no. 26/83

Fl. 100 mm wide; perianth segments ovate, yellowish white; corona bowl-shaped, orange-red (32A). Mid-season

'Elva' 2 W-? (b or c)
(Mrs R.O. Backhouse, pre-1921)

'Elven Lady' 2 W-WWP
(Brian S. Duncan) Brian S. Duncan, 1992
'Pismo Beach' × 'High Society'; sdlg no. 1227
Fl. 95 mm wide; perianth segments very broadly ovate, rounded at shoulder, with margins slightly incurved; corona short, constricted below the mouth, white, with a well-defined band of lilac pink at rim, mouth flared. Late. Sunproof

'Elvira' 8 W-YYO
(R.A. van der Schoot, pre-1902)
'Ornatus' × Div. 8 hybrid
Fls 3-4 per stem, 46-59 mm wide; perianth segments very broadly ovate, broadly spathulate, blunt, prominently mucronate, pure white, flushed greenish yellow at base, spreading, creased, with margins incurling, overlapping one-third; the inner segments truncate, not noticeably mucronate, a little inflexed, with margins wavy or more strongly incurling, sometimes notched; corona very shallow bowl-shaped, closely ribbed, vivid yellow 9B, with a very narrow band of reddish orange at rim, mouth expanded, wavy, with rim minutely dentate. Tall. Lightly scented. 2n=24. AM 1904

'Elwing' 2 W-W
(Brian S. Duncan) Rathowen Daffodils, 1981
'Stainless' × 'Foundling'; sdlg no. 461
Mid-season

'Elwood Drive' 1 Y-Y
(H.G. Cross) H.G. Cross, 1984
'Chillion' × 'Warbin'; sdlg no. 28-5
Fl. clear golden yellow; perianth segments broad, with white mucro; corona flared, deeply frilled. Early

'Elysée' 11a W-Y
(J. Gerritsen & Son) J. Gerritsen & Son, 1973
'Valdrome' × 'Fondant'
Fl. 90 mm wide; perianth segments pure white; corona segments creamy yellow. Mid-season to late

'Elysian' 2 W-? (b)
(A.O. Roblin, 1943)
'Maid of the Mist' × 'Gyda'

'Elysian' 2 W-P
Syn. of 'Elysian Fields'

'Elysian Fields' 2 W-P
(M.J. Jefferson-Brown) M.J. Jefferson-Brown, 1985
'Rose Caprice' hybrid
Perianth segments broad, snow white; corona

widely expanded, vivid deep pink. Mid-season. Syn. 'Elysian'

'Elysium' 1 W-W
(A.M. Wilson, pre-1950)

'Elysium' 2 W-? (b)
(G.A. Uit den Boogaard, pre-1950)

emarginatus = *N. serotinus* var. *emarginatus*

'Embassy' 1 W-? (b)
(G.H. Engleheart, pre-1914)

'Embassy' ?-P
(Alister Clark, pre-1948)

'Embassy' 3 Y-YYR
(E.W. Cotter) E.W. Cotter, 1968
'Artist's Model' hybrid

'Embee' 9 W-GOR
(M.F. Butcher) A.W. Chappell, 1990
Poeticus sdlg 5/9 × sdlg P3 ('Cantata' × 'Rondo'); sdlg no. P-2
Fl. 55 mm wide; perianth segments roundish; corona disc-shaped. Mid-season

'Ember' 3 W-? (b)
(G.H. Engleheart, pre-1913)

'Ember' 2 Y-O
(G.L. Wilson, 1950) G. Zandbergen-Terwegen, 1961
Fl. rounded; perianth segments very broadly ovate, rounded at apex, rich golden yellow, with prominent white mucro, spreading, plane, overlapping half; the inner segments more narrowly ovate, a little inflexed, with margins wavy; corona short funnel-shaped, fiery reddish-orange, with coppery overtones, mouth a little flared, wavy, rim obscurely crenate. Mid-season

'Emberglow' 6 Y-O
(V. Brink) V. Brink, 1964
'February Gold' × 'Rouge'
Perianth segments deep golden yellow, flushed red; corona yellow-orange. Mid-season

'Embia' 2 W-? (b)
(Mrs R.O. Backhouse, pre-1921)

'Emblaze' 2 Y-R
(R.H.Glover, pre-1993) Unregistered

'Emblem' 3 W-? (b)
(G.H. Engleheart, pre-1916)

'Emblem' 1 W-Y
(pre-1927)

Perianth segments creamy white; corona pale yellow. Early

'Emblem' 2 W-W
(G.L. Wilson) G. Zandbergen-Terwegen, 1963
Fl. 119 mm wide; perianth segments ivory white; corona creamy white. Early. AM(Haarlem) 1963

'Emblyn' 2 Y-Y
(Rosewarne EHS, 1970) Rosewarne EHS, 1989
'Dutch Master' × 'Saint Keverne'; sdlg no. 66/37/1
Fl. 124 mm wide; perianth segments vivid yellow 9A, overlapping; corona expanded, slightly darker in tone (12A) than the perianth, frilled, with rim flanged. Early

'Embo' 2 Y-Y
(D.C. MacArthur) D.C. MacArthur, 1984
'Rouge' × 'Golden Harvest'
Mid-season

'Emerald' 3 W-GWW
(Barr & Sons, pre-1907)
N. × *poculiformis* × *N. poeticus*
Perianth segments pure white; corona small, with darke green at base. Late

'Emerald' 9 W-GOR
(G.E. Mitsch, 1968) G.E. Mitsch, 1979
'Quetzal' × 'Smyrna'; sdlg no. 94/6
Fl. 80 mm wide; perianth segments pure white; corona green, with red at rim, and with a narrow band of orange between the green and the red. Late

'Emerald' 2 W-Y
(J.J. Grullemans & Sons, pre-1955) Unregistered
Corona widely expanded, lemon yellow, heavily frilled. ?The same as 'Green Emerald'

'Emerald Eye' 3 W-GWW
(G.H. Engleheart, pre-1913)
?'Moonbeam' × *N. poeticus*
Fl. 83 mm wide, pure white; corona with distinct green at base. Late. Syn. ?'Emerald Gem'

'Emerald Gem' 3 W-GWW
?Syn. of 'Emerald Eye'

'Emerald Isle' 3 W-GYR
(D.S. Bell) D.S. Bell, 1959
Fl. 115 mm wide; perianth segments broad, rounded, overlapping; corona spreading, yellow, strongly shaded emerald green at base, with bright red at rim. Resembles 'Autowin' but with green more conspicuous in the corona

'Emerald Pink' 3 W-GWP
(R. & E. Havens, 1984) R. & E. Havens, 1994
'Ever Pink' × 'Jewel Song'; sdlg no. TEH6/31
Fl. 90 mm wide; perianth segments broadly ovate,

pure white, glistening; corona bowl-shaped, white, with green at base and a band of bright pink at rim, mouth slightly wavy. Late. Sunproof

N. × *emeritensis* Fernández Casas 13 (parentage: *N. bulbocodium* Linnaeus var. *tenuifolius* (Salisbury) Baker × *N. triandrus* Linnaeus subsp. *pallidulus* (Graells) D.A.Webb) = *N.* × *consolationis*

'Emerson' 9 W-?
(A.M. Wilson, pre-1908)

'Emerson' 1 Y-Y
(M. van Waveren & Sons, pre-1931)
Fl. rich yellow; corona slightly darker in tone. Tall

'Emilea' ?-P
(Alister Clark, pre-1948)

'Emilena' 1 Y-GPP
(D.S. Bell) D.S. Bell, 1984
('Red Conquest' × 'Golden Fortune') × 'Barbara Allen' hybrid
Fl. 109 mm wide

'Emile Plessow' 2 Y-? (a)
(J.W.A. Lefeber, pre-1944)

'Emile Zola' 2 Y-O
(J.W.A. Lefeber) J.W.A. Lefeber, 1960
Fl. 76 mm wide; perianth segments deep yellow; corona orange, shading to a darker tone at rim. Midseason

'Emily' 9 W-?
(W. Poupart, pre-1916)

'Emily' 2 Y-Y
(Mrs J. Abel Smith) Mrs J. Abel Smith, 1974
'Green Howard' × 'Aircastle'; sdlg no. P4/91
Fl. 90 mm wide; perianth segments pale lime yellow; corona of a deeper tone. Late. Resembles a smaller-flowered 'Aircastle'

'Eminent' 1 Y-Y
(?T. Buncombe, pre-1933)

'Eminent' 3 W-GYY
(G.E. Mitsch) G.E. Mitsch, 1963
'Green Island' × 'Bithynia'; sdlg no. P32/1
Fl. 92 mm wide; perianth segments blunt, greenish white (157C), slightly inflexed, overlapping; the inner segments narrower; corona ribbed, light greenish yellow 5C, tinged green at base, mouth straight, frilled, rim crenate. Resembles a more vigorous 'Bithynia' with a smoother and whiter perianth. AM(e) 1968

'Emir' 1 W-? (b)
(T. Buncombe, pre-1931)

'Emita' 2 Y-Y
(S.J. Bisdee, pre-1939)
Sdlg × 'Loxton'

'Emita' 2 W-W
(R.H.Glover, pre-1989) Unregistered
'Empress of Ireland' × 'Ace High'

'Emma' 2 Y-? (a)
(G.A. Uit den Boogaard, pre-1944)

'Emma' 2 W-W
(J.N. Hancock & Co., 1959) Unregistered
Perianth segments pale cream; corona with rim rolled

'Emmerich Kalman' 2 Y-? (a)
(J.W.A. Lefeber, pre-1951)

'Emneth' 3 W-? (b)
(R.H. Bath, pre-1933)

'Emperor' 1 Y-Y
(W. Backhouse, pre-1869)
Hybrid between *N. bicolor* and *N. pseudonarcissus*
Perianth segments broadly ovate, blunt, slightly mucronate, brilliant greenish yellow 6C, with a darker tone at midrib beneath, somewhat inflexed, plane, overlapping one-third; the inner segments with margins wavy; corona cylindrical at base, flared in upper part, loosely ribbed, vivid yellow 9A, with mouth expanded and lightly frilled, rim flanged, notched and crenate. 2n=21. Resembles a *N. bicolor* var. *lorifolius* of almost twice the size. Syn. 'The Emperor', Pseudonarcissus Lorifolius 'Emperor', Pseudonarcissus Lorifolius 'Maximus'

'Emperor Frederick' 1 Y-Y
(Barr & Sons, pre-1913)

'Emperor of India' 2 Y-? (a)
(W. Welchman, pre-1923)

'Emperor's Waltz' 6 Y-YOO
(G.E. Mitsch) G.E. Mitsch, 1985
'Resplendent' × *N. cyclamineus*; sdlg no. NN42/1
Perianth segments broadly ovate, blunt, golden yellow, with slight white mucro, strongly reflexed, plane, overlapping half or more; the inner segments somewhat creased; corona cylindrical, shorter than the perianth segments, constricted near mouth, smooth, orange, paling to deep golden yellow at base and shading to rich orange at rim, with mouth flared, rim closely notched. Early to mid-season. Syn. 'Rivoli'

'Emphasis' 2 W-P
(G.E. Mitsch) G.E. Mitsch, 1982
'Precedent' × 'Accent'; sdlg no. D17/30
Fl. 104 mm wide; corona orange-pink, with a deeper tone at rim, the colours intensifying with age

'Emphatic' 1 W-W
(R.C.A. Tombleson) R.C.A. Tombleson, 1967
Fl. 108 mm wide. Mid-season. Resembles an improved 'White Prince' with a shorter neck

'Empire' 2 W-WYY
(E.M. Crosfield, pre-1908)
Perianth segments creamy white, overlapping; corona large, expanded, lemon yellow, paling to sulphur white at base, neatly frilled. 2n=28. FA(Haarlem) 1926

'Empire' 2 W-? (b)
(R.G. Berkeley, pre-1933)
Resembles 'Mitylene'

'Empire Champion' 2 Y-? (a)
(G. Zandbergen-Terwegen, pre-1937)

'Empire Rose' 2 W-P
(D.N.Y. Olson) D.N.Y. Olson, 1989
'Kuprena' × 'Fintona'; sdlg no. 77/27/2
Fl. 92 mm wide; perianth segments broadly ovate, slightly mucronate, spreading, with margins sometimes incurling near apex, of good substance, overlapping; the inner segments a little inflexed; corona cylindrical, or very slightly flared towards mouth, lightly ribbed, soft pink, with rim shallowly notched and a little flanged. Early to mid-season. Sunproof. Resembles a shorter-stemmed 'Verran' with the perianth segments of a different form at base

'Empress' 1 W-Y
(W. Backhouse, pre-1869)
Fl. 103 mm wide; perianth segments ovate, only very slightly mucronate, spreading, of great substance, overlapping one-third; the inner segments a little inflexed, with margins wavy; corona narrowly funnel-shaped, ribbed, rich yellow, with mouth expanded and 6-lobed, lightly frilled, rim flanged and crenate. 2n=21+1B,22. Resembles a larger and later-flowered 'Horsfieldii' of greater substance and more rapid increase. Resembles a smaller 'Emperor' in form. Syn. 'The Empress', Pseudonarcissus Bicolor 'Empress', Pseudonarcissus Bicolor 'Maximus'

'Empress Eugenie' 3 W-Y
(W. Backhouse, pre-1869)
Perianth segments creamy white; corona yellow. Syn. Burbidgei 'Empress Eugenie'. ?"Absorbed" into 'Lottie Simmons'

'Empress of Ireland' 1 W-W
(G.L. Wilson, pre-1952)
'Guardian' × 'Kanchenjunga'
Fl. forming a double triangle, 100-120 mm wide, creamy white; perianth segments very broadly ovate, slightly mucronate, spreading, plane or a little concave, smooth, overlapping half or more; the inner segments more narrowly ovate, shouldered at base, inflexed at base, reflexed towards apex, with margins wavy or incurved; corona cylindrical, very lightly ribbed, appearing to be of a darker tone than the perianth, with mouth expanded and lightly frilled, rim widely rolled and shallowly crenate. 2n=28. PC 1952, AM(e) 1956, *AM(g) 1970, *FCC(g) 1971, AGM 1993

'E.M.R.'
Unregistered
Seed parent of 'Red Ruff'

'Em's Pride' 2 Y-Y
(K. McCombe) J.N. Hancock & Co., 1979
'Crocus' × 'Julius Caesar'
Fl. 110 mm wide; perianth segments broadly ovate, blunt, brilliant greenish yellow 3A, with white mucro, spreading, plane, overlapping a quarter; the inner segments narrower, inflexed at base, reflexed towards apex, with margins wavy and incurling; corona cylindrical, angled, darker in tone (13A) than the perianth, with a band of brownish yellow at base, mouth heavily ribbed and very widely expanded, rim irregularly and very deeply notched. Early. Resembles a larger and improved 'Julius Caesar'

'Ena' 2 W-R
(G. Lubbe & Son, pre-1931)
Perianth segments pure white; corona brilliant orange-red. AM(Haarlem) 1931

'Ena Fisher' 2 Y-? (a)
(W.A. Grace, pre-1938)

'Enamel' 2 W-? (b)
(F.H. Chapman, pre-1927)

'Enchanted Elf' 3 W-GYO
(Mrs G. Link) Mrs G. Link, 1989
'Pewee' × 'Perdita'; sdlg no. 177
Perianth segments glistening white; corona straight-sided, frilled. Very late. Resembles a more colourful 'Pewee'

'Enchantment' 1 W-W
(pre-1937)

'Enchantment' 1 Y-Y
(F. Rijnveld & Sons, pre-1950)

'Enchantment' 3 W-OOR
Syn. of 'Kindergarten'

'Enchantress' 1 W-? (b)
(W. Welchman, pre-1908)

'Enchantress' 2 W-P
(J.L. Richardson) Mrs H.K. Richardson, 1962
('Rose of Tralee' × 'Lisbreen') × ('Templemore' × 'Green Island')

Perianth segments pure white; corona rose pink, with rim flanged and dentate

'Encore' 2 Y-YYO
(G. Lewis) D.S. Bell, 1955
'Militant' × 'Fortune'
Perianth segments yellow; corona disc-shaped, yellow, with a broad band of orange at rim

'Endeavour' 3 W-? (b or c)
(P.D. Williams, pre-1934)

'Endeavour' 1 Y-Y
(J.W.A. Lefeber) J.W.A. Lefeber, 1968
'Golden Harvest' × 'Golden Triumphator'

'Endor' 1 Y-Y
(The Brodie of Brodie, c.1921)
Cross 207/09 × 'White Emperor'; sdlg no. 16/A/16
Fl. pale sulphur lemon

'Endowment' 1 W-W
(D.S. Bell) D.S. Bell, 1979
'Treasure Chest' self pollinated
Fl. 110 mm wide, pure white; corona cylindrical, with rim rolled. Mid-season

'Endurance' 2 or 3 W-? (b or c)
(pre-1913)

'Endurance' 2 Y-Y
(C.E. Webster, 1930)
'Osiris' × 'Wheel of Fortune'

'Endymion' 3 W-W
(H. Backhouse, pre-1908)
'Minnie Hume' × *N. radiiflorus* var. *poetarum*

'Energy' 2 W-? (b)
(P. van Deursen, pre-1938)
AM(Haarlem) 1938

'Enez' 2 W-Y
(W.F.M. Copeland, pre-1921)
Perianth segments white; corona widely expanded, greenish primrose yellow, with rim frilled. AM 1921

'Enfield' 2 Y-R
(Mrs H.K. Richardson) du Plessis Bros, 1987
'Border Chief' × 'Heath Fire'; sdlg no. 166
Corona cup-shaped, straight-sided. Late to very late. Sunproof. Resembles a later-flowered 'Falstaff'

'Engadine' 3 W-W
(J.L. Richardson) J.L. Richardson, 1956
'Altyre' × 'Chinese White'
Fl. white; corona tinted green at base, and with rim finely dentate

'Engagement Ring' 3 W-WWY
(Grant E. Mitsch, 1982) R. & E. Havens, 1994
'Silken Sails' × 'Merlin'; sdlg no. 2R32/14
Fl. 100 mm wide; perianth segments very broadly ovate, pure white, of heavy substance; corona disc-shaped, pure white, with a band of lemon yellow at rim, mouth ribbed. Late

'Engaging' 2 W-P
(H.A. Brown, 1937) J.N. Hancock & Co., 1960
Corona rim dentate. Mid-season

'Enghus' 2 Y-Y
(W. Jackson Jr) Jackson's Daffodils, 1979
'Haka' hybrid × 'Ristin'; sdlg no. 56/72
Fl. 100 mm wide. Mid-season

'Englander' 6 Y-Y
(Unknown origin) Potterton & Martin, 1992
N. cyclamineus sdlg
Fl. 63 mm wide, vivid or brilliant yellow 12A or B; perianth segments narrowly ovate, reflexed, a little twisted, separated; corona cylindrical, ribbed, very slightly darker in tone than the perianth, mouth narrowly flared and even, rim slightly flanged and regularly crenate. Dwarf. Early. Syn. 'The Usurper'

'Engleheart's Carnation' 4 W-W
(G.H. Engleheart, pre-1933)
Fl. rounded, sulphur white; perianth and other petaloid segments in about five whorls, compactly arranged, very broad, rounded at apex, sometimes obscurely truncate, a little concave, with margins incurling, deeply overlapping; the outer whorls spreading or a little inflexed; the inner whorls successively shorter and more strongly inflexed; the centre whorl very strongly inflexed, with margins incurled or more tightly folded inwards. AM(e) 1933

'Engleheart's White Rose' 4 W-W
(G.H. Engleheart, pre-1927)
N. poeticus sdlg
Fl. snow white; perianth and other petaloid segments in about five whorls, regularly superimposed and loosely arranged, broadly ovate, concave, overlapping half; the outer whorl sometimes prominently mucronate, spreading; the inner whorls successively a little shorter and more strongly inflexed, with margins wavy or incurled or folded inwards from the midrib; the centre whorl short, very strongly inflexed, contorted. Scented. Syn. 'White Rose'. PR(e) 1927, FCC(e) 1933

'Engleheart Yellow' 1 Y-Y
(pre-1930)

'English Caye' 1 YYW-WWY
(A.J.R.Pearson) A.J.R.Pearson, 1997
('Camelot' × 'Daydream') × 'Gin and Lime'; sdlg no. 92-24-Q28
Fl. 110 mm wide; perianth segments broadly ovate,

rounded at apex, gold, with undertones of vivid greenish yellow 2A, with a narrow band of white at base, slightly reflexed, of much substance, smooth, glistening; the inner segments a little more nearly acute; corona cylindrical, slightly constricted near mid-point, smooth at base, lightly ribbed towards mouth, pale greenish yellow 1D, with green in tube and vivid greenish yellow at rim, mouth expanded, rim flanged and crenate. Early to mid-season. Resembles 'Lighthouse Reef' in colour but with the perianth segments slightly narrower and the corona proportionately longer

'Enid' 3 W-W
(G.H. Engleheart, pre-1903)
Perianth segments ivory white; corona long cup-shaped, creamy white. Tall. Resembles an improved 'Mrs Langtry'

'Enid Blyton' 2 W-WWY
Syn. of 'Alfresco'

'Enid Dorothea' 2 Y-? (a)
(Mrs R.O. Backhouse, pre-1921)

'Enid Kirby' 2 Y-? (a)
(W.A. Grace, pre-1938)
Syn. 'Marara'

'Enid Marian' 2 or 3 W-W
Syn. of 'Enid Marion'

'Enid Marion' 2 or 3 W-W
(W.B. Hartland, pre-1913)
Fl. pure white; perianth segments inflexed. See also 'Enid Marian'

'Enigma' 2 W-? (b)
(Mrs D. Duff, pre-1951)

'Eniko' 2 W-Y
(Lajos Jezerniczky, 1975) Lajos Jezerniczky, 1987
'Ice Follies' × 'Adventure'
Fl. 100 mm wide; perianth segments very broadly ovate, truncate, prominently mucronate, slightly reflexed, plane, ocasionally lightly ribbed, overlapping one-third; the inner segments more narrowly ovate, acute, slightly inflexed, with margins incurved and wavy; with an extra whorl of short white segments at base; corona smooth, yellow, with darker tones at base and rim, mouth expanded and frilled, often split, with lobes overlapping and slightly recurved, rim dentate. Dwarf. Resembles a larger-flowered 'Ice Follies'

'Enlil' 2 Y-Y
(W. Jackson Sr, 1935)
'Pilgrimage' × 'Renown'

'Enmore' 1 Y-Y

(J.M. Radcliff, c.1967) Unregistered
'Principal' × 'Roundabout'

'Ennerdale' 1 W-W
(G.L. Wilson) E. Longford, 1966
?'Empress of Ireland' hybrid
Fl rounded, 108 mm wide, white. Mid-season. Resembles a smaller and better proportioned 'Empress of Ireland'

'Enniskillen' 3 W-R
(W.J. Dunlop, pre-1952)
'Folly' × 'Hades'
Perianth segments pure white; corona deep crimson-red. 2n=28

'Ennismore' 1 Y-Y
(J.L. Richardson) Mrs H.K. Richardson, 1964
'Rio d'Oro' open pollinated
Fl. deep golden yellow; perianth segments wide, spreading, overlapping; corona with rim dentate and widely flanged

'Enosis' 2 W-? (b)
(Mrs R.O. Backhouse, pre-1921)

'Enquilla' 8 Y-O
Syn. of 'Enquille'

'Enquille' 8 Y-O
(pre-1883)
Resembles 'Grand Soleil d'Or'. Syn. 'Enquilla'

'En Route' 2 W-P
(G.E. Mitsch) G.E. Mitsch, 1976
'Passionale' × 'Accent'; sdlg no. D60/3
Fl. 120 mm wide; perianth segments roundish, deeply overlapping; corona light apricot pink. Mid-season

'Ensemble' 4 Y-Y
(Murray W. Evans, 1974) Murray W. Evans, 1986
(4Y-Y × 'Dawnlight') × ('Daydream' × 'New Era'); sdlg no. Q-23/1
Mid-season

'Ensign' 2 W-? (b)
(G.H. Engleheart, pre-1907)
AM 1906

'Ensign Ewart' 2 Y-R
(W.M. Spry, pre-1975) Unregistered
'Winsome' × Ronalds sdlg
Corona frilled. Late

'Ensor Doone' 1 Y-Y
(G.H. Engleheart, pre-1914)

'Entally' 2 Y-Y
(S.J. Bisdee, 1948)
'Trostan' × 'Cantatrice'

'Entente' 2 Y-O
(Jackson's Daffodils) Jackson's Daffodils, 1996
'Mattara' × 'Gallactica'; sdlg no. 259/88
Fl. 110 mm wide; perianth segments very broadly ovate, vivid yellow 9A, slightly concave; corona funnel-shaped, strong orange 25A. Mid-season

'Enterprise' 3 W-? (b)
(G.H. Engleheart, pre-1913)

'Enterprise' ?-P
(Alister Clark, pre-1948)

'Enterprise' 4 Y-O
(Oregon Bulb Farms) Oregon Bulb Farms, 1958
'Fortune' sport or self pollinated
Fl. large, rounded; perianth and other petaloid segments in several whorls, bright yellow; the outer whorls broadly ovate, blunt, slightly mucronate, more or less spreading, plane or a little concave, overlapping half; the inner whorls shorter, inflexed or strongly inflexed, with margins incurled; corona segments not much shorter than the inner petaloid segments and interspersed among them, broad, bright orange, frilled. Tall. Mid-season. 2n=28

'Entice' 2 Y-? (a)
(A.H. Ahrens) J.S. Leitch, 1955

'Entr' Acte' 2 Y-O
(Konynenburg & Mark) Konynenburg & Mark, 1964
Fl. 110 mm wide; perianth segments vivid yellow 9B; corona orange (28A). Mid-season

'Entrancement' 1 Y-W
(G.E. Mitsch) G.E. Mitsch, 1958
'King of the North' × 'Content'
Perianth segments very broadly ovate or almost triangular in appearance, blunt, slightly mucronate, soft greenish lemon yellow, spreading, plane, smooth, with broad midrib sometimes showing, overlapping half; the inner segments a little more narrowly ovate, with margins occasionally wavy, shouldered at base; corona opening greenish lemon yellow, becoming almost white, mouth ribbed, expanded and a little frilled, rim flanged, notched and crenate. Early. 2n=28

'Entreaty' 2 W-OOY
(F.E. Board) F.E. Board, 1965
'Blarney's Daughter' × 'Arbar'
Resembles a more deeply coloured 'Blarney's Daughter'

'Envoy' 3 W-? (b)
(F.H. Chapman, pre-1930)

'Envoy' 1 W-W
(G.L. Wilson) Unregistered

'Envy' 3 W-W
(A.M. Wilson, pre-1947)

'Envy' 2 W-P
Syn. of 'Mangatoki'

'Enya' 2 W-P
(J.N.Hancock & Co., 1983) J.N.Hancock & Co., 1997
Sdlg no. 73/83H
Perianth segments ovate, blunt, plane; corona funnel-shaped, true pink, with mouth flared. Early

'Enzed' 2 W-W
(W.A. Grace, pre-1927)
Corona creamy white

'Enzed' 1 Y-Y
(P. & G. Phillips) P. & G. Phillips, 1973
Fl. 105 mm wide

'Eochy' 2 Y-? (a)
(Sir J.A.R. Gore-Booth, pre-1916)

'Eos' 3 W-? (b)
(pre-1907)

'Eoster' 3 W-Y
(G.H. Engleheart, pre-1906)
Fl. rounded; perianth segments deeply overlapping; corona cup-shaped, light clear lemon yellow. AM 1906. See also 'Easter'. Formerly named 'Oberon'

'Eothen' 3 W-? (b)
(Seymour Cobley Ltd, pre-1935)

'Epaminondas' 1 W-? (b)
(de Graaff Bros, pre-1927)

'Epaulet' 2 W-? (b)
(W.B. Hartland, pre-1913)

'Epaulier' 2 Y-? (a)
(W.B. Cranfield, pre-1923)

'Ephesus' 2 W-? (b)
(A.H. Ahrens, pre-1949)

'Ephraim' 5 W-W
(W.A. Grace, pre-1927)
Corona cream white

'Epic' 9 W-YOR
(G.H. Engleheart, pre-1898)
Fl. rounded; perianth segments of heavy substance, overlapping; corona disc-shaped, large, heavily suffused with red at rim

'Epic' 1 W-W
(J.N. Hancock & Co., c.1975) Unregistered

'Epicure' 2 or 3 W-Y
(?G. Zeestraten, pre-1914)
Perianth segments creamy white; corona widely expanded, deep yellow. AM(Haarlem) 1914

'Epicure' 1 W-W
(G.L. Wilson, pre-1930)
'White Emperor' self pollinated

'Epigram' 9 W-?
(Mrs R.S. Cobley, pre-1938)

'Epilogue' 1 Y-Y
(G.H. Engleheart, pre-1908)

'Epilogue' 2 Y-R
(Mrs A.O. Meyrick) Mrs B.T. Simpson, 1963
Fl. 102 mm wide, vivid yellow 9B; corona rim orange-red (30B). Late. Resembles 'Park Royal'

'Epimetheus' 2 W-? (b)
(de Graaff Bros, pre-1927)

'Episode' 2 Y-YYO
(Warnaar & Co., pre-1951)
'Carbineer' × 'Rosslare'
AM(Haarlem) 1951

'Epitome' 1 Y-WWY
(Murray W. Evans) Murray W. Evans, 1974
'Daydream' × 'New Era'
Fl. 105 mm wide

'Epoch' 1 W-W
(J. Bankhead, pre-1950)

'Epona' 3 W-GRR
(W. Jackson Jr) Jackson's Daffodils, 1979
Sdlg 87/63 × sdlg 79/65; sdlg no. 66/72
Fl. 97 mm wide. Mid-season

'Epsom' 1 W-? (b)
(Sir A.P.W. Thomas, pre-1930)

'Equation' 11a Y-O
(R. & E.Havens, 1985) R. & E.Havens, 1997
('Chemawa' × 'Party Dress') × 'Tiritomba'; sdlg no. UH63/1
Fl. 80 mm wide; perianth segments broadly ovate, deep yellow; corona deeply split, the six segments opposite and closely overlying the perianth, tangerine orange, frilled. Mid-season. Sunproof

'Equator' 2 Y-O
(A. Robert, 1956) A. Robert, 1966
'Dunkeld' × 'Rustom Pasha'
Fl. 99 mm wide; perianth segments golden yellow; corona becoming bright reddish orange

'Equerry' 1 Y-Y

(F.E. Board) F.E. Board, 1965
'Kingscourt' × 'Goldcourt'
Mid-season

'Equinox' 3 W-? (b)
(F.H. Chapman, pre-1910)

'Equity' 1 W-W
(G.L. Wilson) G. Zandbergen-Terwegen, 1966

'Erasmus' 1 W-? (b)
(de Graaff Bros, pre-1927)

'Erastus' 2 W-P
(A.O. Roblin, 1958) Unregistered
'Rosaline' × 'Pink Monarch'

'Erda' 2 Y-? (a)
(N.F. Lock, pre-1944)

'Erebus' 2 Y-R
(S.J. Bisdee, 1940)
'Popinjay' × 'Twinkle'
Perianth segments pale yellow; corona deep red

'Erebus' 2 W-O
(S.A. Free) S.A. Free, 1976
Sdlg × 'Arbar'; sdlg no. 67/56
Fl. 100 mm wide; corona reddish orange, with yellow at rim on opening. Mid-season

'Erebus' 1 W-W
(J.L. Richardson, pre-1961) Unregistered
'Spitzbergen' × 'Broughshane'
Fl. snowy white; corona mouth widely expanded, frilled

'Erewhon' 2 W-Y
(A.E. Lowe, pre-1927)
Perianth segments white; corona soft yellow

'Eribol' 2 W-R
(J.S.B. Lea) J.S.B. Lea, 1964
'Arbar' × 'Kilworth'
Fl. 89 mm wide. Late. Resembles an 'Orion' with greater contrast of colour

'Eric' 3 W-? (b)
(N.Y. Lower, pre-1931)

'Erica Jean' 4 Y-O
(A.O. Roblin, 1956) Unregistered
'Cartrefle' × 'Telamonius Plenus'

'Eric the Red' 2 W-R
(T.H. Piper, c.1966) Unregistered
'Corra' × 'Nerissa'

'Eridanus' 2 W-W
(J.A. Hunter, 1981) J.A. Hunter, 1992

('Easter Moon' × 'Glendermott') × ('Glendermott' × 'Floris Selina'); sdlg no. 1/76A
Fl. 113 mm wide; corona mouth slightly expanded, with rim dentate. Mid-season

'Erie' 2 Y-O
(F. Rijnveld & Sons, pre-1939)

'Erin' 1 W-? (b)
(G.H. Engleheart, pre-1916)

'Erini' 4
(W.B. Hartland, pre-1907)
? *N.* × *incomparabilis* sdlg

'Erin's Isle' 11a W-W
(A.N. Kanouse, 1980) Mrs A.N. Kanouse, 1991
Fl. 80 mm wide, pure white; perianth segments broad, rounded at apex; the inner segments narrower; corona deeply split, the six segments opposite and closely overlying the perianth segments, opening creamy yellow, becoming white, heavily frilled. Early

'Erinvale' 2 W-W
(W.J. Dunlop) W.J. Dunlop, 1962
Fl. forming double triangle; perianth segments broadly ovate, broad-shouldered; corona opening creamy yellow, gradually becoming whitish

'Eriskay' 4 W-Y
(J.S.B. Lea) J.S.B. Lea, 1979
Sdlg no. 1-37-72
Fl. 115 mm wide. Mid-season

'Eritana' 3 W-GYR
(D.S. Bell) D.S. Bell, 1979
'Masquerade' × 'Rockall'
Fl. 111 mm wide; perianth segments pure white; corona very shallow bowl-shaped. Mid-season

'Erk' 2 Y-? (a)
(A.M. Williams, pre-1948)

'Erlicheer' 4 W-Y
(M. Gardiner, pre-1934)
?'White Pearl' sport
Fls 6-12 or more per stem; perianth and other petaloid segments in four whorls, broadly ovate, yellowish white (2D), a little concave, with midrib showing, overlapping; the outer whorl prominently mucronate, a little inflexed; the inner whorls only slightly mucronate, successively more strongly inflexed and more deeply overlapping; corona segments short, opposite and regularly arranged between the petaloid segments, very broad, brilliant greenish yellow 3B, with rim wavy and entire. Very early. Scented. 2n=32. Syn. 'Cheerfulness', 'Gaiety'. See also 'Earlichere', 'Earlicheer'

'Erlirose' 2 W-P
(G.E. Mitsch) G.E. Mitsch, 1972
'Precedent' × 'Accent'; sdlg no. C37/9
Fl. 105 mm wide; perianth segments slightly reflexed; corona bowl-shaped, large, rose pink. Mid-season

'Erl King' 1 Y-Y
(Hon. Sir R.H. Rhodes, pre-1912)

'Erl King' 2 or 3 W-? (b or c)
(A.M. Wilson, pre-1916)

'Ermenilda' 1 W-? (b)
(W. Welchman, pre-1907)

'Ermine' 3 W-W
(G.H. Engleheart, pre-1907)
Corona ivory, tinged yellow

'Ermington' 2 Y-? (a)
(H.G. Hawker, pre-1939)

'Erminie' 2 W-P
(Alister Clark, 1935) J. Sharp, 1960

'Ernani' 2 W-YYO
(Konynenburg & Mark) Konynenburg & Mark, 1963
'Gratia' × 'Daisy Schäffer' hybrid
Fl. 100 mm wide; perianth segments greenish white; corona vivid yellow 13A, with strong orange 24A at rim. Mid-season

'Erna Rubinstein' 1 Y-Y
(M. van Waveren & Sons, pre-1930)
Fl. deep yellow

'Ernest H.Wilson' 2 W-Y
(Oregon Bulb Farms, pre-1945)
Syn. ?'Silver Pink'

'Ernevale' 3 W-GWY
(Brian S. Duncan) Rathowen Daffodils, 1983
'Woodland Prince' × 'Crepello'; sdlg no. 459
Fl. 102 mm wide; perianth segments pure white; corona tightly ribbed, white, with green at base and yellow at rim. Mid-season. Resembles 'Rimmon' but with a more rounded flower of deeper colour at corona rim

'Ernie Gibson' 1 W-W
(L.P. Dettman) L.P. Dettman, 1977
'Glenshesk' × 'Tablecloth'; sdlg no. 14/74
Fl. 97 mm wide; perianth segments yellowish white 155B; corona greenish white (155A). Mid-season. Resembles 'Tablecloth' but with the corona mouth more widely expanded and the rim less noticeably dentate

N. × *ernii* Fernández Casas 13 (parentage: *N. bulbocodium* Linnaeus subsp. *bulbocodium* ×

N. triandrus Linnaeus var. *triandrus*) = *N.* × *consolationis*

'Eroica' 2 W-? (b)
(J.N. Hancock & Co.) J.N. Hancock & Co., 1959

'Eros' 3 W-OOR
(G.H. Engleheart, pre-1909)
Fl. 89 mm wide; perianth segments broadly ovate, rounded at apex, creamy white, spreading, overlapping one-third; the inner segments slightly inflexed, with margins sometimes wavy; corona very shallow bowl-shaped, ribbed, golden orange, shading to fiery scarlet at rim

'Eros' 2 Y-R
(J.S. Leitch) J.S. Leitch, 1960
Fl. 114 mm wide. Late

'Errigal' 2 W-W
(G.L. Wilson, pre-1948)
'White Sentinel' × 'Pink o' Dawn'
Fl. pure white

'Errol' 3 W-? (b or c)
(W.A. Grace, pre-1938)

'Erudycie' 3 W-? (b)
Syn. of 'Eurydice'

'Eryl' 2 Y-? (a)
(C. Dawson, pre-1938)

'Escalus' 1 W-Y
(Barr & Sons, pre-1927)
Perianth segments creamy white, overlapping; corona rich yellow, with mouth expanded and frilled, rim flanged

'Escamillo' 2 W-YYO
(The Brodie of Brodie, *c.*1911)
'Crown Prince' × 'Virgil'
Fl. 97 mm wide; perianth segments broadly ovate, blunt, prominently mucronate, creamy white, spreading, with broad midrib showing, regular, overlapping one-third to a half; the inner segments a little inflexed, with margins very slightly wavy; corona cylindrical, smooth, brilliant greenish yellow 6A, touched pinkish orange (near to 16B) at rim, mouth expanded and loosely frilled, rim crenate and irregularly notched

'Escapade' 1 W-Y
(J.S. Leitch) J.S. Leitch, 1962
Fl. 115 mm wide. Early

'Eschscholtzia'
(pre-1915)

'Escort' 2 Y-O
(J.N. Hancock & Co., pre-1950)
Perianth segments yellow; corona orange, with a deeper tone at rim, frilled

'Escort' 3 Y-O
(J.S. Leitch) J.S. Leitch, 1968

'Esk' 1 W-W
(J.N.Hancock & Co., 1983) Unregistered
'Chillagoe' × 'Beryl Hancock'; sdlg no. 12/83H
Perianth segments acute, milk white; corona creamy white, with mouth expanded and frilled. Early

'Eskdale' 2 W-W
(Barr & Sons, pre-1952)

'Eskimo' 2 W-W
(The Brodie of Brodie, pre-1927)
2W-? × 'Mrs Ernst H.Krelage'
Fl. 89 mm wide, facing down; perianth segments creamy white, overlapping half; corona opening very pale primrose, becoming faintly pink and then snowy white, mouth somewhat expanded and frilled. Midseason to late. AM(e) 1927, *C(g) 1936. Div. 1 until 1965

'Eskylane' 2 Y-Y
(Carncairn Daffodils) Carncairn Daffodils, 1975
'Maviston' × 'Kingscourt'; sdlg no. 2/36/62
Fl. 90 mm wide, clear yellow. Mid-season. Resembles a Div. 2 'Kingscourt'

'Esme' 9 W-?
(D.V. West, pre-1935)
Corona large disc-shaped, with a broad band of crimson-red at rim

'Esmeralda' 3 W-? (b)
(Mrs R.O. Backhouse, pre-1907)

'Esmeralda' 3 W-GYY
(J.L. Richardson, pre-1961) Unregistered
'Syracuse' × 'Cascade'

'Esopus' 2 W-? (b)
(E.C. Powell, pre-1946)
'Hera' × 'Fair Bostonian'

'Espada' 2 Y-O
(A.M. Wilson, pre-1930)
Perianth segments light yellow; corona widely expanded, pinkish apricot. AM(Haarlem) 1931

'España' 1 Y-Y
(D.S. Bell) D.S. Bell, 1984
'Iberia' hybrid
Fl. 110 mm wide. Resembles 'Iberia' but with a rounder flower

'Espartero' 8
(pre-1883)
Resembles 'Gloriosa'

'Esperance' 3 W-Y
(S.J. Bisdee) S.J. Bisdee, 1956
'Limerick' × 'Palana'
Corona lemon yellow, flushed orange

'Esperanza' 2 Y-R
(W.H. Roesé, 1972) W.H. Roesé, 1984
'Burning Torch' × 'Heathfire'; sdlg no. 72/15/2
Fl. 103 mm wide; corona straight-sided, with mouth slightly flared and frilled. Mid-season

'Esse' 1 Y-Y
(J.N. Hancock & Co., 1968) Unregistered

'Essie McKinley' 1 W-? (b)
(J. Flemming, pre-1938)

'Estafette' 1 Y-Y
(Warnaar & Co., pre-1930)

'Estate' 3 W-R
(S.A. Free) Mrs S.I. Free, 1968

'Este' 3 W-R
(J.M. de Navarro) J.M. de Navarro, 1968
('Bravura' × ['Coronach' × 'Hades']) × 'Matapan'
Perianth segments very broad, rounded; corona very shallow bowl-shaped, red

'Esteemed' 2 Y-?
(Alister Clark, 1935) J. Sharp, 1960

'Estella de Mol' 11a W-Y
(J.W.A. Lefeber, 1948) J.W.A. Lefeber, 1960
Fl. 70 mm wide; perianth segments somewhat oblong in outline, squarish or truncate at apex, prominently mucronate, more or less spreading, overlapping half; the inner segments narrower and more nearly ovate, with margins wavy; corona split to base, the six segments half as long as the perianth segments and opposite and closely overlying them, smooth, brighter than vivid yellow 14B, deeply frilled. Late

'Estella's Favourite' 11b ?-Y
(J.W.A. Lefeber) J.W.A. Lefeber, 1968
'Lemon Beauty' hybrid

'Estelle' 2 Y-O
(Mrs R.O. Backhouse, pre-1907)
Perianth segments lemon yellow; corona deep orange, heavily frilled. AM(Haarlem) 1929

'Estelle' 2 Y-? (a)
(P.D. Williams, pre-1915)

'Esterelle' 9 W-?
(A.M. Wilson, pre-1927)

'Ester Fay' 1 W-O
(J.W.A. Lefeber) J.W.A. Lefeber, 1968

'Esteven' 4 W-W
(K.J. Heazlewood) K.J. Heazlewood, 1971
'Glowing Red' × 'Stromboli'
Fl. 100 mm wide

'Esther' 1 Y-Y
(J.H. Mander, pre-1933)

'Estimate' 2 Y-? (a)
(Sir C.H. Cave, pre-1928)

'Estio Pinza' 2 Y-O
(J.W.A. Lefeber, pre-1977) Unregistered
Perianth segments ovate, acute, yellow, with white mucro, spreading, a little concave or with margins wavy, overlapping one-third; the inner segments narrower, with margins wavy and recurved; corona broad funnel-shaped, ribbed, orange, deepening in tone towards rim, mouth slightly expanded and closely frilled, rim notched

'Estrella' 1 Y-Y
(W.A. Grace, pre-1936)

'Estrella' 3 W-YYR
(H.R. Bulman) H.R. Bulman, 1956
'Seraglio' × 'Moina'
Perianth segments very broad in outline, rounded or truncate at apex, more or less prominently mucronate, a little reflexed, somewhat concave, overlapping half or more; the inner segments angled at shoulder, spreading or a little inflexed, creased; corona small, shallow bowl-shaped, ribbed, orange-yellow, with a broad band of red at rim. 2n=28

'Estrellita' 6 Y-Y
(G.E. Mitsch, pre-1954)
'Mite' × 'Malvern Gold'
Fl. 70 mm wide; perianth segments broad, slightly reflexed, overlapping. Early

'Estrellita' 3 Y-YYR
Syn. of 'Caravan'

'Estremadura' 2 Y-O
(J.M. de Navarro) J.M. de Navarro, 1967
'Castile' × 'Caramba'
Perianth segments very broadly ovate, rounded at apex, rich yellow, with small white mucro, spreading, overlapping half; corona broad funnel-shaped, lightly ribbed, stained orange, shading to a deeper tone at rim, mouth straight and a little frilled, with rim notched and crenate. Early. Sunproof. PC(e) 1967

'Estuary' 2 W-GWW
(Murray W. Evans) Murray W. Evans, 1987
'Broomhill' × 'Stainless'; sdlg no. U-10/2
Perianth segments pure white, very smooth; corona mouth expanded and regularly frilled. Mid-season

'Etat General' 8 W-Y
Syn. of 'States-General'

'Etawah' 2 Y-? (a)
(G. Lewis) D.S. Bell, 1955
See also 'Etaway'

'Etaway' 2 W-? (a)
Syn. of 'Etawah'

'E.T.Cook' 1 W-Y
(G.P. Haydon, pre-1905)
Corona rich chrome yellow

'Etendart' 8 Y-Y
(pre-1798)
Fl. pale yellow. ?The same as 'Grand Etandart'

'Eterna' 1 W-W
(Konynenburg & Mark) Konynenburg & Mark, 1966
'Lord Nelson' × 'Soirée'
Fl. 120 mm wide wide, ivory white. Early

'Ethel' 3 Y-O
(W. Backhouse, pre-1869)
Perianth segments primrose yellow; corona suffused scarlet-orange. Syn. Burbidgei 'Albidus Aurantius', Burbidgei 'Ethel'

'Ethel'
(A.M. Wilson, pre-1914)

'Ethel' 3 W-Y
(G.H. Johnstone, 1943) G.H. Johnstone, 1959
'Elspeth' hybrid
Fl. 90 mm wide. Mid-season. Resembles a stronger-stemmed 'Elspeth' with a shorter neck

'Ethelbad' 1 Y-Y
(Barr & Sons, pre-1923)

'Ethelbert' 3 W-YYO
(Mrs R.O. Backhouse, pre-1904)
Periath segments white; corona canary yellow, with a broad band of orange at rim

'Ethel Breen' 2 W-P
(J.N. Hancock & Co., 1977) Unregistered

'Ethelburga' 9 W-GYR
(G.H. Engleheart, pre-1913)
Perianth segments snow white, overlapping; corona lemon yellow, shading to green at base, with a broad band of dark madder red at rim

'Etheldreda' 1 W-W
(de Graaff Bros, pre-1916)

'Ethel M.Allen' 2 W-YYR
(J.H. Hinsby, 1928)
'Bernardino' hybrid

'Ethel Rayner' 2 Y-? (a)
(Mrs R.O. Backhouse, pre-1921)

'Ethelred' 2 Y-R
(Colin Crotty) Unregistered
Sdlg no. 25-75

'Ethel Wightman' 1 W-? (b)
(H.R. Meyer, pre-1927)

'Ethereal' 2 W-W
(H. Backhouse, pre-1908)

'Ethereal Angel' 3 W-GWW
(N.H. Anglo) N.H. Anglo, 1986
'Verona' × 'Angel'
Perianth segments white; corona white, with emerald green at base, rim dentate. Mid-season to late

'Ethereal Beauty' 2 W-WWP
(Brian S. Duncan) Brian S. Duncan, 1993
'Pismo Beach' × 'High Society'; sdlg no. 1228
Fl. rounded, 105 mm wide; perianth segments very broadly ovate, blunt or rounded at apex, prominently mucronate, snow white, spreading, very smooth, overlapping half; the inner segments more nearly roundish, less obviously mucronate, a little inflexed; corona bowl-shaped, smooth, snow white, with dark greyish green in tube and a narrow band of apple blossom pink at rim, mouth expanded, even, rim shallowly crenate. Late

'Ethna' 2 W-? (b)
(J.T. Gray, pre-1951)

'Ethni' 3 W-YRR
(W. Jackson Sr, 1945)
'Evening' × 'Noevia'
Perianth segments white; corona red, paling to lemon at base

'Ethos' 1 Y-Y
(Brian S. Duncan, 1983) Brian S. Duncan, 1993
'Golden Jewel' × 'Midas Touch'; sdlg no. 840
Fl. forming a double triangle, 110 mm wide, deep yellow; perianth segments broadly ovate, blunt, slightly mucronate, a little reflexed, plane, very smooth, regular, overlapping one-third; the inner segments more narrowly ovate, more nearly spreading, with margins somewhat wavy; corona cylindrical in lower third, slightly expanding towards mouth, with

mouth straight, rim entire or obscurely crenate. Mid-season

'Ethwald' 1 Y-Y
(Barr & Sons, pre-1923)

'Etienne van Este' 2 Y-O
(J.W.A. Lefeber) J.W.A. Lefeber, 1960
Fl. 95 mm wide; perianth segments deep yellow; corona deep reddish orange. Early

'Etincelante' 11a W-WPP
(J. Gerritsen & Son) J. Gerritsen & Son, 1981
Sdlg × 'Salome'
Fl. 90 mm wide; perianth segments ivory white; corona segments pink, tinged yellow at first, orange later, with ivory white at base. Mid-season

'Etna' 2 Y-? (a)
(R.H. Bath, pre-1907)

'Etoile d'Or' 8 Y-Y
(pre-1798)
Syn. ?'L'Etoile d'Or'

'Etoile d'Or'
Syn. of *N. × intermedius*

'Etoile du Nord' 2 Y-? (a)
(P.D. Williams, pre-1908)

'Etoile du Nord' 1 W-W
(J. Gerritsen & Son, 1948) J. Gerritsen & Son, 1959
Fl. 90 mm wide, creamy white; corona slightly darker in tone. Late. Resembles a robust 'Beersheba'

'Etos' 1 W-? (b)
(West & Fell, pre-1938)

N. etruscus Parlatore = *N. patulus*

'Etta' 3 W-O
(?Barr & Sons, pre-1887)
Corona small, stained orange

'Ettie Kaye' 2 W-?
(Alister Clark, 1942) J. Sharp, 1960

'Ettrick' 2 W-W
(The Brodie of Brodie, pre-1923)
'Pilgrim' × 'Mrs Robert Sydenham'
Corona yellowish white. AM 1924

'Etude' 1 W-Y
(J. Gerritsen & Son, 1948) J. Gerritsen & Son, 1959
Fl. 100 mm wide; perianth segments creamy white; corona vivid yellow 13A. Early. Resembles a much improved 'Queen of Bicolors'

eu-albidus = *N. cantabricus* var. *eu-albidus*

'Eucharis' 2 W-W
(G.P. Haydon, pre-1907)

'Euclid' ?-P
(Alister Clark, pre-1948)

'Eucumbine' 2 Y-O
(J.N. Hancock & Co., 1946)
'Trenoon' × 'Fortune'
Resembles 'Fortune'

N. eugeniae Fernández Casas = *N. pseudonarcissus* subsp. *eugeniae*

'Eukareena' 2 W-O
(W.M. Spry, pre-1975) Unregistered
'Aldgate' × 'Delight'

'Eulaine' 3 W-? (b)
(P.D. Williams, pre-1948)

'Eulogy' 2 W-? (b)
(A.M. Wilson, pre-1944)
'Lavino' hybrid
Corona rim orange-pink, deeply notched

'Eunice' 1 W-? (b)
(de Graaff Bros, pre-1907)

'Eunice' 1 W-W
(West & Fell, pre-1936)
Perianth segments ivory white; corona creamy white, with rim rolled

'Eunice Stares' 1 W-W
(West & Fell, pre-1935)

'Euphemus' 2 Y-O
(A.M. Wilson, pre-1948)
Perianth segments clear yellow; corona vivid reddish orange, slightly paling towards base

'Euphonic Grace' 2 Y-W
(G.E. Mitsch and R. & E.Havens, 1972) G.E. Mitsch and R. & E.Havens, 1987
'Euphony' open pollinated; sdlg no. HO13/1
Perianth segments soft lemon, smooth; corona opening soft lemon, becoming white. Mid-season. Resembles a 'Euphony' becoming whiter in the corona

'Euphonium' 1 W-? (b)
(G.P. Haydon, pre-1927)

'Euphony' 2 Y-Y
(G.E. Mitsch) G.E. Mitsch, 1968
'Leonaine' × ?'Daydream'; sdlg no. AS11/2
Fl. 102 mm wide, soft creamy lemon yellow. Mid-season

'Euphoria' 2 Y-P
(Ben Hager, 1984) Ben Hager, 1996
DuBose sdlg A3-6 ('Accent' × 'Daydream') × DuBose sdlg C12-2 ('Bethany' × 'Rosedew'); sdlg no. D53-3
Fl. 90 mm wide. Mid-season

'Euphrosyne' 1 W-Y
(G.P. Haydon, pre-1907)
Perianth segments creamy white; corona cylindrical, soft citron yellow

eu-praecox = *N. bulbocodium* var. *praecox*

'Eureka' 8 W-Y
(pre-1928)
Poetaz
Corona pale yellow

'Eureka' 2 W-? (b or c)
(S.L. Danby, pre-1936)

'Eurelia' 2 Y-YOO
(J.T. Gray, pre-1949)
Perianth broadly ovate, yellow; corona reddish orange, paling to yellow at base

'Euroa' 2 Y-?
(Alister Clark, 1930) J. Sharp, 1960

'Euroa' 2 W-Y
(H.A. Brown, 1941)
'Miss Glory' × 'Carbineer'
Fl. large; perianth segments white, of good substance, deeply overlapping; corona buff, mouth widely expanded, with rim closely and deeply notched, as if fringed. Mid-season

'Europa' 1 W-Y
(G.P. Haydon, pre-1913)
Corona pale yellow, with a darker tone at rim, frilled. AM 1913

'Eurovisie' 2 Y-Y
(L. Steenvoorden) L. Steenvoorden, 1970
'John Evelyn' × 'Carlton'

'Euryalus' 1 Y-Y
(R.A. Scamp) R.A. Scamp, 1993
'Saint Keverne' × 'Ristin'; sdlg no. 283
Fl. 109 mm wide, dark golden yellow; perianth segments broadly ovate, smooth, deeply overlapping; corona narrow funnel-shaped, mouth only a little expanded, frilled. Early

'Euryclea' 3 W-? (b)
(C. Dawson, pre-1914)

'Eurydice' 9 W-?
(G.H. Engleheart, pre-1910)

'Eurydice' 8 W-Y
(pre-1927)
Poetaz

'Eurydice' 3 W-? (b)
(New Zealand origin, 1934) Parr's Nurseries, 1958
See also 'Erudycie'

'Euterpe' 1 W-W
(Barr & Sons, pre-1923)

'Eva' 2 W-YYO
(de Graaff Bros, pre-1930)
Sdlg no. 54
Fl. 115 mm wide; perianth segments very broadly ovate, blunt, prominently mucronate, a little reflexed, regular, overlapping one-third to a half; the inner segments more narrowly ovate, only very slightly mucronate, more nearly spreading, sometimes creased, with margins nicked and somewhat wavy; corona broad funnel-shaped, smooth or lightly ribbed, clear yellow, with a well-defined band of deep orange at rim, mouth more closely ribbed, straight, split in places and overlapping, wavy, with rim minutely crenate. Mid-season. 2n=28. AM(e) 1930, AM(f)(p)(c) 1933, *AM(g) 1936

'Evadne' 9 W-?
(Mrs R.O. Backhouse, pre-1921)
Corona rim deep red

'Evander' 9 W-?
(A.M. Wilson, pre-1908)

'Evangeline' 3 W-Y
(G.H. Engleheart, pre-1908)
Fl. large; perianth segments broadly ovate or somewhat oblong in outline, blunt or squarish at apex, prominently mucronate, pure white, smooth and of solid texture, with midrib showing, overlapping one-third; the inner segments a little inflexed, not noticeably mucronate, with margins wavy; corona bowl-shaped, ribbed, clear yellow, lightly frilled. Tall. 2n=21. AM 1913

'Evangelist' 9 W-?
(G.H. Engleheart, pre-1930)

'Evansford' 2 W-? (b)
(H.A. Brown, pre-1938)

'Eve' 2 W-W
(de Graaff Bros, pre-1928)
Syn. 'Mount Everest'

'Eve Cecil' 1 W-W
(T. Buncombe, pre-1931)

'Eve Daly' 1 W-Y
(J.N. Hancock & Co.) J.N. Hancock & Co., 1955

('Nevis' × 'Beersheba') × 'Carisbrooke'
Corona creamy yellow, frilled. Early

'Evelina' 5
(Sir A.P.W. Thomas, pre-1930)

'Eveline' 1 W-W
(Barr & Sons, pre-1907)
Corona rim neatly crenate

'Evelix' 2 W-O
(D.C. MacArthur, 1971) D.C. MacArthur, 1990
Sdlg no. E5016
Fl. 90 mm wide; perianth segments broad, greenish white (155A), glistening, plane, deeply overlapping; corona disc-shaped, pale orange (17D), with a darker tone at rim (23A), densely and minutely notched. Late. Sunproof

'Evelyn Aldersey' 3 W-YYO
(H. Aldersey, pre-1931)
Fl. 79 mm wide; perianth segments white, irregular, separated; corona very shallow bowl-shaped, sulphur, with orange at rim, frilled. Mid-season to late. Syn. 'Eileen'

'Evelyn Hodge' W-?
(?Barr & Sons, pre-1908)
$N. \times poculiformis \times N. \times medioluteus$

'Evelyn Lloyd' 1 W-? (b)
(T. Buncombe, pre 1931)

'Evelyn Mary' 1 W-W
(J. Wilson & Sons, pre-1931)

'Evelyn Mellish' 1 W-W
(?J. Mallender, pre-1914)

'Evelyn Murray' 2 W-P
(H.T. Dettmann, pre-1979) Unregistered

'Evelyn Snell' 2 W-? (b)
(Miss K.M. Hinchliff, pre-1937)

'Evendine' 2 W-GWW
(M.J. Jefferson-Brown) M.J. Jefferson-Brown, 1985
'Pontresina' self pollinated
Fl. 82 mm wide, opening soft yellow, becoming white, sometimes touched yellow at corona rim; perianth segments very broadly ovate, blunt or rounded at apex, only very slightly mucronate, spreading, plane, with margins sometimes incurling at apex, of good substance, overlapping half or more; the inner segments a little inflexed, with margins incurved; corona bowl-shaped, widely expanded, narrowly ribbed, mouth sometimes split and overlapping, lightly frilled, with rim dentate. Mid-season to late

'Evening'
(pre-1913)

'Evening' 2 W-W
(G.L. Wilson, pre-1935)
'Blizzard' hybrid
Fl. 94 mm wide; perianth segments slightly reflexed; corona opening yellow, becoming white. 2n=28

'Evening Dew' 2 or 3 W-? (b or c)
(Cartwright & Goodwin, pre-1916)

'Evening Glow' 1 W-P
(G.H. Engleheart, pre-1931)
Perianth segments creamy white; corona widely flared. rich pink, flushed beige

'Evening Grosbeak' 6 YYW-W
(Eileen E. Frey) J. & E. Frey, 1993
Sdlg JEE15/1 × 'Cotinga'; sdlg no. TEF19/3
Fl. 80 mm wide; perianth segments broadly ovate, blunt, opening yellow, becoming soft lemon yellow, tinged white at base, reflexed, overlapping half; the inner segments creased; corona cylindrical, opening yellow, becoming creamy white, with mouth flared and slightly frilled. Dwarf. Early

'Evening Mist' 2 W-P
(J.N. Hancock & Co., pre-1962) Unregistered
Perianth segments pure white, smooth; corona long funnel-shaped, clear pink

'Evening Peal' 2 W-RRY
(D.S. Bell) D.S. Bell, 1965
'Papanui Queen' × 'Sir Heaton Rhodes'
Perianth segments white; corona bright red, with light golden yellow at rim, frilled. Mid-season. Resembles an 'Artist's Model' of more regular form and better texture

'Evening Pink' 2 W-P
(J.A. O'More, 1961) R.G. Cull, 1978
'Vasey' × 'Salmon Trout'
Fl. 90 mm wide. Mid-season

'Evening Rose' 2 W-P
(G.H. Johnstone, pre-1960) Unregistered

'Evening Shadows' 1 W-Y
(D.S. Bell) D.S. Bell, 1958
Fl. 115 mm wide. Mid-season

'Evening Sky' 3 Y-? (a)
(R.O. Backhouse, pre-1932)

'Evening Star' 1 Y-Y
(E. Leeds, pre-1877)
Perianth segments long, narrow, acute; corona darker in tone than the perianth. Syn. Pseudonarcissus Major 'Evening Star'. "Absorbed" 'G.H.Engleheart'

'Evening Star' 1 W-W
(T. Bloomer) T. Bloomer, 1962

'Evening Sun' 2 W-OOR
(G.H. Johnstone, pre-1944)
'Clava' × 'Hades'

'Evenlode' 2 W-WWY
(J.M. de Navarro, pre-1949)
'Green Island' × 'Chinese White'
Fl. 90-92 mm wide; perianth segments very broadly ovate, blunt and slightly mucronate, spreading, a little concave, with margins slightly incurling at apex, overlapping half; the inner segments a little more narrowly ovate, more rounded at apex, slightly inflexed, with margins somewhat wavy, shouldered at base; corona lightly ribbed, greenish yellow (4D), touched vivid yellow 15A at rim, mouth expanded and densely frilled, rim crenate. PC(e) 1964, AM(e) 1965

'Evensong' 2 W-? (b)
(G.H. Engleheart, pre-1913)

'Evensong' 1 W-W
(C.E. Radcliff, 1931)

'Evensong' 4 Y-Y
(D.S. Bell, 1968) D.S. Bell, 1978
'Papua' × 'Hicol'
Fl. 98 mm wide, lemon yellow. Mid-season

'Evensong' 2 W-?
Syn. of 'Mount Tacoma'

'Even Stevens' 1 Y-Y
(R. Hyde) R. Hyde, 1963
Fl. 115 mm wide, golden yellow. Mid-season. Resembles a larger-flowered 'Maurice Hyde' of darker colour

'Even Stevens' 1 W-Y
(J.N. Hancock & Co., pre-1974) Unregistered
Perianth segments white; corona pale yellow, with rim deeply dentate

'Eventide' 1 W-? (b)
(W. Welchman, pre-1908)

'Eventide' 1 W-? (b)
(D.S. Bell) D.S. Bell, 1957

'Eventide' 3 Y-?
Syn. of 'Afterglow'

'Evenus'
(Barr & Sons, pre-1915)

'Everdina' 2 W-? (b)
(G.A. Uit den Boogaard, pre-1944)

'Everelda' 1 Y-Y
(J.W. Barr, pre-1930)

'Everell' 3 W-? (b)
(J.L. Richardson, pre-1944)
'Clava' × 'Sunstar'
Perianth segments very broad in outline, squarish at apex and slightly truncate, prominently mucronate, a little reflexed, plane, overlapping half; the inner segments only very slightly mucronate, more nearly spreading, with margins wavy, sometimes nicked at shoulder; corona broad disc-shaped, lightly ribbed, with a broad band of dark colour at rim, mouth regularly 6-lobed, with rim minutely crenate

'Everest' 1 W-W
(E.M. Crosfield, pre-1910)
AM(e) 1924

'Everest' 1 W-W
(Thomas Smith, pre-1920)

'Everest' 1 W-W
(G.L. Wilson, pre-1924)
AM(e) 1924, AM(e) 1926

'Everest Peak' 2 W-W
(G.L. Wilson) R.W. Ward & Son, 1960
Mid-season. Resembles an improved 'Ludlow'

'Everest Snow' 1 W-W
(D.S. Bell) D.S. Bell, 1955

'Everglades' 4 W-O
(Brian S. Duncan) Rathowen Daffodils, 1988
Richardson sdlg 3509 ('Falaise' × 'Debutante') × sdlg 704 ('Passionale' × 'Polonaise')
Fl. large; perianth segments in a single whorl, broad, milk white, spreading; corona segments numerous, rich apricot orange. Tall. Mid-season to late

'Everglaze' 2 Y-R
(S.A. Free)

'Evergold' 1 Y-Y
(Murray W. Evans) Murray W. Evans, 1980
'Enmore' × 'Fiji'; sdlg no. 0-12
Fl. 100 mm wide. Mid-season. Resembles a taller and more deeply coloured 'Enmore' with broader perianth segments

'Evergreen' 2 W-? (b)
(D.S. Bell) D.S. Bell, 1955

'Everjack' 2 Y-Y
(M. Valois) D.F. Lee, 1973
Fl. 92 mm wide

'Everlasting' 2 W-Y
(G.H. Engleheart, pre-1930)

Fl. facing slightly downwards; perianth segments creamy white, sulphur at base, overlapping half; corona funnel-shaped, very bright deep buttercup yellow. Mid-season to late. *AM(m) 1930

'Evermore' 2 W-? (b)
(pre-1944)
AM(Haarlem) 1944

'Everpink' 2 W-P
(Murray W. Evans) Murray W. Evans, 1970
'Wild Rose' × 'Interim'

'Everton' 2 Y-? (a)
(F. Rijnveld & Sons, pre-1948)
AM(Haarlem) 1956

'Evertsen' 2 Y-? (a)
(P.J. Ruigrok, pre-1946)

'Evert van Dijk' 2 W-? (b)
(P. van Deursen, pre-1930)

'Evesham' 3 W-GYY
(J.S.B. Lea) Clive Postles Daffodils, 1990
'Loch Assynt' × sdlg 68/15A; sdlg no. 1-37-76
Fl. 113 mm wide; perianth segments very broadly ovate, smooth; corona very shallow bowl-shaped, with rim neatly dentate. Tall. Mid-season

'Evewin Joy' 2 Y-? (a)
(G.C. Gaspar, pre-1949)

'Evita' 1 W-Y
(J.N. Hancock & Co., pre-1988) Unregistered

'Evita Peron' 2 W-O
(Konynenburg & Mark, 1950) Konynenburg & Mark, 1963
('Flaming Torch' × 'Extase') × ('Frederike' × 'Mimosa')
Fl. 105 mm wide; perianth segments creamy white; corona strong orange 25A. Mid-season

'Evocation' 4 W-P
(D.S. Bell) D.S. Bell, 1979
Fl. 108 mm wide. Mid-season

'Evolution' 5
(W.B. Cranfield, pre-1930)

'Evolution' 11a Y-Y
(J. Gerritsen & Son) J. Gerritsen & Son, 1957
2n=28. AM(Haarlem) 1961

'Ewen McIntyre' 4 Y-O
(M.Hamilton) Koanga Daffodils, 1996
Sdlg hybrid
Fl. 95 mm wide; perianth and other petaloid segments broadly ovate, vivid yellow 12A; corona segments neatly arranged, orange (28A). Mid-season

'Exaltation' 1 Y-Y
(G.E.Mitsch, 1978) R. & E.Havens, 1996
'Aurum' × 'Arctic Gold'; sdlg no. 2N19/3
Fl. 100 mm wide, golden yellow; perianth segments broadly ovate, smooth and of heavy substance; corona cylindrical, with mouth straight, very slightly frilled. Mid-season

'Exalted' 2 O-R
(W.G. Pannill) W.G. Pannill, 1972
'Vulcan' × 'Zanzibar'
Fl. 96 mm wide

'Excalibur' 1 Y-Y
(W.B. Cranfield, pre-1930)

'Excalibur' 2 Y-O
(J.A. Hunter) J.A. Hunter, 1982
'Swordsman' × 'Air Marshal'
Fl. 108 mm wide. Mid-season. PC(e)(NZ) 1984

'Excellent' 2 Y-? (a)
(T. MacLaren) Holland Bulb Co., 1959

'Excellente' 8 W-O
(pre-1846)

'Excellentie' 3 Y-? (a)
(J.W.A. Lefeber, pre-1938)

'Excelsior' 1 Y-Y
(?Barr & Sons, pre-1906)
Fl. dark golden yellow. Resembles a darker-coloured 'Golden Spur'

'Excelsior' 8
(R.A. van der Schoot, pre-1929)
AM(Haarlem) 1929

'Excelsum' 2 Y-O
(Warnaar & Co., pre-1930)
AM(Haarlem) 1930

'Exception' 1 Y-Y
(D. van Buggenum) D. van Buggenum, 1971
'Dutch Master' × 'Gold Medal'
Fl. 103 mm wide; perianth segments very broadly ovate, blunt, with white mucro, spreading or a little inflexed, plane, overlapping one-third; the inner segments more usually inflexed, twisted; corona cylindrical or somewhat funnel-shaped, with mouth expanded, rim flanged, deeply and regularly notched and crenate. Early

'Exchequer' 1 Y-Y
(R.H. Bath, pre-1930)

'Exchequer' 2 Y-Y
(J.N. Hancock & Co., 1970) Unregistered

'Excite' 2 Y-? (a)
(A.H. Ahrens) J.S. Leitch, 1955

'Exclaim' 1 Y-Y
(G.H. Johnstone, pre-1958) Unregistered
Perianth segments spreading; corona large, with rim widely flanged and deeply dentate

'Exclusive' 2 W-P
(C.E. Radcliff, 1940) J.M.Radcliff, 1956
'Glendevie' × 'Dawnglow'

'Executive' 2 Y-Y
(G.E. Mitsch) G.E. Mitsch, 1972
'Playboy' × 'Daydream'; sdlg no. B36/28
Fl. 100 mm wide, deep rich yellow. Mid-season

'Executive Pink' 2 W-P
(G.E.Mitsch, 1976) R. & E.Havens, 1997
(['Mabel Taylor' × 'Green Island'] × 'Caro Nome') × 'Space Ship'; sdlg no. LL20/25
Fl. 95 mm wide; perianth segments broadly ovate, spreading, plane; corona cylindrical, rosy pink, with mouth straight, frilled. Mid-season. Sunproof

'Exemplar' 1 Y-Y
(F.E. Board) F.E. Board, 1965
'Kingscourt' × 'Golden Rapture'
Fl. forming a double triangle, yellow; perianth segments very broadly ovate, blunt, with slight white mucro, spreading, overlapping half; the inner segments more narrowly ovate, more nearly acute, more prominently mucronate; corona mouth widely expanded. Mid-season

N. exertus (Haworth) Pugsley = *N. radiiflorus* var. *exertus*

'Exeter' 2 Y-YOO
(R.V. Favell, pre-1947)
'Hospodar' × 'Fortune'
Perianth segments clear yellow; corona flushed orange towards mouth

'Exhibition' 2
(pre-1979) Unregistered

N. exiguus Salisbury = *N. minor*

'Exile' 2 Y-Y
(J.S. Leitch) J.S. Leitch, 1967
Fl. 108 mm wide

'Exon' 2 Y-Y
(J.N. Hancock & Co., 1973) Unregistered

'Exotica' 2 Y-Y
(de Graaff Bros) de Graaff Bros & van Konynenburg & Co., 1960
Fl. 115 mm wide; perianth segments vivid yellow 12A; corona shallow, of a slightly darker tone (13A) than the perianth. Early. AM(Haarlem) 1960

'Exotic Pink' 2 W-P
(J.N. Hancock & Co., 1964) Unregistered
Fl. forming a double triangle; perianth segments broadly ovate, blunt, fairly prominently mucronate, creamy white, spreading, plane, smooth, overlapping half; the inner segments a little inflexed, with margins wavy; corona funnel-shaped, pink, with bronze overtones, mouth expanded, lightly frilled, rim notched and crenate. Late. Scented

'Expansus' 2 W-Y
(E. Leeds, pre-1877)
Corona with mouth expanded. Syn. Nelsonii 'Expansus'

'Expansus' 2 or 3 W-Y
(?E. Leeds, pre-1877)
Syn. Leedsii 'Expansus'

'Expansus' 3? Y-Y
(pre-1879)
Syn. Barrii 'Expansus'

'Expansus' 3? W-Y
(pre-1882)
Syn. Barrii Albus 'Expansus'

'Expansus' 2
Syn. of 'Roland' 2W-Y, 'Vivian' 2W-Y, 'John Bull' 2Y-?, 'Autocrat' 2Y-Y and 'Figaro' 2Y-YYO

'Expansus' 2 or 3 W-?
Syn. of 'Bianca'

'Expansus' 3 W-Y
Syn. of 'Mary'

'Expansus Aureo-tinctus' 2 or 3
(?E. Leeds, pre-1877)
Corona expanded, tinged orange. Syn. Incomparabilis Albidus 'Expansus Aureo-tinctus'

'Expectation' 3 W-O
(A. Frylink & Sons, pre-1931)
Corona rim neatly frilled

'Experiment' 2 Y-? (a)
(Sir C.H. Cave, pre-1928)

'Explorer' 1 Y-Y
(Doornbosch Bros) Doornbosch Bros, 1958
AM(Haarlem) 1959

'Explosion' 8 Y-O
(W.G. Pannill) W.G. Pannill, 1978
'Matador' × *N. jonquilla*; sdlg no. 65/98 C
Fl. 55 mm wide. Mid-season

'Explosion' 2
(C.O. Fairbairn, pre-1974) Unregistered

'Expo' 11a Y-Y
(J. Gerritsen & Son) J. Gerritsen & Son, 1958
Perianth segments sulphur yellow; corona segments mimosa yellow

'Express' 1 Y-Y
Syn. of 'Cervantes'

'Expressive' 1 Y-Y
(Konynenburg & Mark) Konynenburg & Mark, 1963
'Lord Nelson' × ('Killigrew' × 'Porthilly')
Fl. 120 mm wide; perianth segments vivid yellow 9B; corona slightly darker in tone (12A). Early

'Exquisite' 1 W-W
(E. Leeds, pre-1882)
Perianth segments sulphur white; corona opening primrose yellow, becoming white. Syn. Pseudonarcissus Moschatus 'Exquisite'

'Exquisite' W-P
(pre-1927)

'Exquisite' 2 Y-? (a)
(L. van Leeuwen & Son, pre-1931)

'Extase' 2 W-? (b)
(de Graaff Bros, pre-1931)
AM(Haarlem) 1930

'Exter' 1 W-Y
(C.E. Radcliff, 1938)
'Effective' hybrid

'Extol' 4 Y-R
(J.L. Richardson) G. Zandbergen-Terwegen, 1959
'Falaise' × 'Ceylon'
2n=27

'Exton' 2 W-P
(W.A. Noton, 1967) W.A. Noton, 1977
'Passionale' × 'Debutante'; sdlg no. 544
Fl. 88 mm wide. Mid-season

'Exton Park' 2 W-P
(W.A. Noton) W.A. Noton, 1985
'Passionale' × 'Fair Prospect'
Fl. 116 mm wide; perianth segments broadly ovate, spreading, overlapping half; the inner segments somewhat inflexed, with margins wavy or twisted; corona broadly funnel-shaped, very lightly ribbed, deep pink, with mouth flared and wavy, rim crenate. Mid-season

'Extortioner' 3 Y-? (a)
(G.P. Haydon, pre-1908)

"Extra Early Maximus"
Syn. of 'A.W. Tait'

'Extravaganza' 4 W-P
(Brian S. Duncan) Rathowen Daffodils, 1983
('Pink Chiffon' × 'Accent') × 'Polonaise'; sdlg no. 698
Perianth and other petaloid segments white; the inner whorls within the corona; corona rose pink, with numerous segments intermingled with the petaloid segments within. Mid-season

'Extrovert' 1 YYW-WWY
(Jackson's Daffodils) Jackson's Daffodils, 1993
'Daydream' × 'Comal'; sdlg no. 66/87
Fl. 102 mm wide; perianth segments roundish, slightly mucronate, vivid yellow 9A, with yellowish white (4D) at base, spreading, plane, overlapping half; the inner segments more nearly ovate, with margins slightly wavy; corona cylindrical, smoothly angled, yellowish white (4D), with a narrow band of vivid yellow 9A at rim, mouth flared, a little frilled, rim notched and minutely crenate. Early to mid-season

'Exuberance' 2 W-W
(F.E. Board) F.E. Board, 1965
'Green Island' × 'Wedding Bell'

'Exultation' 2 W-W
(F.E. Board) F.E. Board, 1965
'Topic' × 'Vigil'

'Eyam' 3 Y-? (a)
(D.B. Milne, pre-1952)

'Eyebright' 3 W-? (b)
(G.H. Engleheart, pre-1907)
Syn. 'Bright Eye'

'Eyecatcher' 3 W-GYO
(Carncairn Daffodils) Carncairn Daffodils, 1982
'Bravura' × 'Bushmills'; sdlg no. 14/11/64
Fl. 95 mm wide; perianth segments pure white; corona vivid yellow 16A, with strong yellow-green 144A at base and light orange (23A) at rim, with the rim dentate. Late

'Eye Catcher' 2 W-PPW
(G.E. Mitsch, c.1983) Unregistered
('Precedent' × 'Debutante') × 'Space Ship'

'Eyeglow' 2 Y-O
(pre-1967) Unregistered
Perianth segments bright yellow; corona reddish orange

'Eye Level' 9 W-YYO
(Ballydorn Bulb Farm, 1983) Ballydorn Bulb Farm, 1994
'Frost in May' × Div. 9 hybrid
Fl. 78 mm wide; perianth segments ovate, with

margins wavy; corona disc-shaped, greenish yellow, with a narrow band of strong reddish orange at rim. Very late

'Eystettensis' 4 Y-Y
(pre-1601)
N. triandrus sdlg?
Fl. 60 mm wide, clear pale sulphur yellow; perianth and other petaloid segments in six whorls regularly superimposed, ovate, acute; the outer whorl spreading; the inner whorls successively shorter, narrower and more strongly inflexed. Syn. "Queen Anne's Daffodil", "Queen Anne's Double Daffodil", "Robinus his Daffodil", "The Lesser French Double Bastard Daffodil", 'Gallicus Minor Flore Pleno', 'Pleno Flore', 'Sylvestris Stellatus', 'Trilobus Plene', Pseudonarcissus 'Capax Plenus'

'Ezra' 2 Y-R
(P. & G. Phillips) P. & G. Phillips, 1975
Fl. 85 mm wide; perianth segments yellow; corona solid red. Mid-season. Resembles a later-flowered 'Falstaff' with a neater and less noticeably lobed corona

F

'Fabia' 2 W-W
(J.S. Leitch) J.S. Leitch, 1967
Fl. 115 mm wide, pure white

'Fabiola' 1 W-? (b)
(R. van der Schoot & Son, pre-1907)

'Fabulous' 2 W-O
(G.W.E. Brogden) G.W.E. Brogden, 1963
Fl. 102 mm wide; perianth segments white; corona reddish orange, with a paler tone at base. Late

'Face Me' 2 Y-O
(O. Ronalds) T. Morrison, 1960
Perianth segments rich yellow; corona reddish orange

'Face to Face' 5 W-Y
(K. van der Veek) K. van der Veek, 1994
Sdlg × *N. triandrus*
Fl. 85 mm wide; perianth segments greenish white (155A, with margins in lower half touched with the colour of the corona; corona brilliant greenish yellow 6A. Late

'Facile' 1 W-?
(pre-1961) Unregistered

'Faction' 2 W-Y
(E.M. Crosfield, pre-1909)

Corona widely expanded, citron yellow

'Factor' 2 W-? (b)
(Mrs R.O. Backhouse, pre-1921)
AM(Haarlem) 1938

'Fad' 1 Y-Y
(P. Phillips) P. Phillips, 1964
Fl. 99 mm wide, pale primrose. Mid-season

'Faenza' 2 Y-? (a)
(A. Gibson, pre-1951)

'Fafnir' 2 Y-? (a)
(N.F. Lock, pre-1944)

'Fahan' 1 Y-Y
(C.E. Radcliff, pre-1937)
'Renown' × 'Golden Legend'
Fl. rich dark yellow; corona short, frilled, with rim rolled

'Fairbanks' 2 W-W
(C.E. Radcliff, 1929)
'Pink'un' × 'Pedestal'

'Fair Bett' 1 YYW-WYW
(R.G. Cull) Hokorawa Daffodils, 1992
'Daydream' × 'Camelot'; sdlg no. HC/1188
Fl. light yellow 10B; perianth segments with white at base; corona with white at base and rim. Mid. Resembles a Div. 1 'Daydream'

'Fair Bostonian' 1 W-Y
(M. van Waveren & Sons, pre-1930)
Fl. large; perianth segments pure white

'Fairbourne' 2 W-Y
(P. de Jager & Sons) P. de Jager & Sons, 1963
'Pink Fancy' × 'Carnlough'
Fl. 115 mm wide; perianth segments white, flushed light yellow 10C at base, a little twisted, overlapping; corona slightly ribbed, vivid yellow 12A, paler towards base, with a tinge of light orange (23C) inside and a slightly paler tone (22C) outside, paler towards base, mouth expanded and frilled. Mid-season.
*AM(g) 1979

'Fairbridge' 1? W-Y
(G.H. Engleheart, pre-1927)
Syn. . ?Syn. of 'Kingsley Fairbridge'

'Fair Chance' 2 W-? (b)
(Mrs A.O. Meyrick) Mrs A.O. Meyrick, 1958

'Fair Colleen' 3 W-OOY
(J.L. Richardson, pre-1953)
'Blarney' × ('Seraglio' × 'Aviemore')
Perianth segments pure white; corona shallow, salmon orange, with yellow at rim

'Fair Dame' 2 W-? (b)
(Mrs R.O. Backhouse, pre-1921)

'Fairday' 3 W-Y
(Ballydorn Bulb Farm) Ballydorn Bulb Farm, 1967
'Tryst' open pollinated

'Fair Edith' 2 W-Y
(Barr & Sons, pre-1910)
'Honourable Mrs Jocelyn' × *N. poeticus*
Perianth segments white, flushed pale primrose yellow at base, reflexed, overlapping; the inner segments spreading; corona straight, ribbed, bright yellow, with rim tinged orange

'Fairest Love' 1 W-P
(J.N.Hancock & Co., 1982) Unregistered
'Dame Edith' × ('Pink Pearl' × 'Verran'); sdlg no. 91/82H
Perianth segments pure white; corona cylindrical, pink, with mouth straight, rim closely and deeply notched, as if fringed. Late

'Fairey's Flight' 2 W-? (b)
(J.N. Hancock & Co., pre-1955)

'Fairfax' 2 Y-? (a)
(Barr & Sons, pre-1949)

'Fairfield' 1 W-Y
(W.M. Spry, pre-1975) Unregistered
'Highland Chief' × 'Hercami'
Corona lemon yellow. Late

'Fairgreen' 3 W-GYO
(Ballydorn Bulb Farm) Ballydorn Bulb Farm, 1965
'Portrush' sdlg
Fl. of good substance; perianth segments broadly ovate, pure white; corona small, with deep green at base. Tall. Late. 2n=28. See also 'Fair Green'

'Fair Green' 3 W-GYO
Syn. of 'Fairgreen'

'Fairhaven' 1 W-Y
(D. Bramley) D. Bramley, 1980
Sdlg 64/2 × 'Newcastle'; sdlg no. 70/12/B
Fl. 104 mm wide. Mid-season. Resembles 'Newcastle' but with rounder perianth segments and paler corona

'Fair Head' 9 W-GYP
(Ballydorn Bulb Farm) Ballydorn Bulb Farm, 1982
'Cantabile' hybrid
Fl. 75 mm wide; corona with coral pink at rim. Late. 2n=14

'Fair Helen' 2 W-Y
(E. Leeds, pre-1877)
Perianth segments creamy white; corona bright yellow. Syn. Incomparabilis Albus 'Elongatus', Incomparabilis Albus 'Fair Helen'

'Fairhope' 1 Y-Y
(J.N. Hancock & Co., pre-1949)
Corona with rim rolled

'Fairies Kiss' ?-P
(Alister Clark, pre-1948)

'Fair Isle' 2 W-? (b)
(D.S. Bell) D.S. Bell, 1955
Corona flared, tinted pink, with dark amber at rim

'Fair Lady' 5 Y-Y
(?C. Dawson, pre-1907)
N. triandrus sdlg
Fl. soft creamy yellow, of good substance. See also 'Fair Ladye'

'Fair Lady' 9 W-YYR
(G.H. Engleheart, pre-1923)
Fl. 64 mm wide; perianth segments white, with cream at base, somewhat reflexed, overlapping one-third; corona very shallow bowl-shaped, broad, sulphur, with scarlet at rim. Mid-season to late. 2n=14. *AM(g) 1931, *HC(g) 1936

'Fair Ladye' 5 Y-Y
Syn. of 'Fair Lady'

'Fair Lass' 3 W-Y
(C. Dawson, pre-1912)
Corona citron yellow

'Fairlie' 3 W-O
(R.C.A. Tombleson) R.C.A. Tombleson, 1968
Fl. 100 mm wide. Mid-season. Resembles a larger-flowered 'Envy' with the corona more richly coloured

'Fairlight' 1 Y-Y
(W.M. Spry, pre-1973) Unregistered
'Stand By' × 'Golden Valley'
Early

'Fairlight Glen' 2 W-YYO
(N.A. Burr, 1981) N.A. Burr, 1991
'Homage' × 'Irish Minstrel'; sdlg no. 8.2.75
Fl. rounded, 91 mm wide; perianth segments very broadly ovate, blunt, fairly prominently mucronate, sparkling white, spreading, somewhat concave, regular, overlapping half; the inner segments square-shouldered at base, more nearly plane, with margins occasionally nicked; corona shallow funnel-shaped, ribbed, vivid yellow 12A, with dark green noticeable in tube and a line of light orange (23A) at rim, mouth straight, rim minutely frilled. Mid-season

'Fairmaid' 3 W-GYY
(Ballydorn Bulb Farm, 1970) Ballydorn Bulb Farm, 1980
'Fairgreen' hybrid
Fl. 95 mm wide; perianth segments broadly ovate, blunt, only very slightly mucronate, a little inflexed, plane, overlapping half; the inner segments more narrowly ovate, square-shouldered at base, more strongly inflexed, with margins wavy; corona cylindrical, smooth, yellow, flushed orange, with deep green at base. Mid-season. 2n=28. Resembles 'Fairgreen' but with the corona only flushed with orange and with the base of a deeper green

'Fair Maiden' 3 W-YYO
(Barr & Sons, pre-1908)
Perianth segments pure white, overlapping; corona expanded, ribbed, yellow, with orange buff at rim. Resembles a 'Seagull' of better form

'Fairmile' 3 W-GYO
(Ballydorn Bulb Farm) Ballydorn Bulb Farm, 1969
'Lough Areema' × 'Cantabile'
Corona pale yellow, with green at base and orange at rim

'Fairness' 4 W-O
(C. Dekker Jr, pre-1949)
Poetaz
Fls 2 per stem; perianth and other petaloid segments pale yellow; corona segments interspersed, orange and scarlet

'Fair Pauline' 2 W-W
(R.H. Bath, pre-1931)

'Fairplay' 2 Y-Y
(M.P. Williams, pre-1949)

'Fair Prospect' 2 W-GPP
(J.L. Richardson) Mrs H.K. Richardson, 1962
'Infatuation' × 'Debutante'
Perianth segments very broadly ovate or almost triangular in appearance, blunt, only very slightly mucronate, spreading, a little concave, with margins incurling at apex, smooth, regular, overlapping half; the inner segments more narrowly ovate, not noticeably mucronate, a little inflexed; corona bowl-shaped, smooth, coral pink, with a well-defined zone of green at base, mouth widely expanded, loosely frilled, occasionally split and overlapping, with rim somewhat flanged and minutely dentate. PC(e) 1966

'Fair Rosamund' 3 W-? (b)
(F.H. Chapman, pre-1923)

'Fair Rosmarin' 2 Y-GPP
(D.S. Bell) D.S. Bell, 1984
'Red Conquest' hybrid × 'Hicol'
Fl. 110 mm wide. Resembles 'Hicol' but with an improved perianth

'Fairsel' 3 W-GYO
(Ballydorn Bulb Farm, 1968) Ballydorn Bulb Farm, 1978
'Lough Areema' × 'Cantabile'
Fl. 80 mm wide. Mid-season. Resembles 'Fairmile' but with deep green at corona base

'Fairs Fair' 2 W-P
(R.C.A. Tombleson) R.C.A. Tombleson, 1966
Fl. 108 mm wide. Late

'Fair Trial' 1 W-Y
(J.L. Richardson) J.L. Richardson, 1956
'Ardclinis' × 'Kanchenjunga'
Perianth segments white; corona widely expanded, pale yellow, unfading, with rim flanged

'Fairview' 2 or 3 W-? (b or c)
(C.G. van Tubergen, pre-1914)

'Fairview' 1 W-W
(G.L. Wilson) Mrs D. Rend, 1956

'Fairway' 3 W-? (b)
(Mrs R.O. Backhouse, pre-1921)

'Fair William' 2 W-P
(Mrs J. Abel Smith, 1975) Mrs J. Abel Smith, 1987
Sdlg × 'Fair Prospect'; sdlg no. 00/52
Perianth segments broad, pure white; corona rose pink, mouth expanded and frilled, rim dentate. Mid-season

'Fair Wind' 2 Y-Y
(J.N.Hancock & Co., 1977) Unregistered
'Fastnet' × Forster sdlg; sdlg no. 22/77H
Fl. deep golden yellow; corona with mouth expanded, rim broadly crenate. Tall. Early

'Fair Wind' 2 W-P
(J.N.Hancock & Co., pre-1977) Unregistered
Perianth segments rounded; corona funnel-shaped, deep watermelon pink, with mouth flared

'Fairy' 2 Y-YYO
(E. Leeds, pre-1877)
Fl. small; corona rim scarlet-orange. Syn. Incomparabilis Leedsii 'Fairy', Incomparabilis Leedsii 'Marginatus Minor'

'Fairy' 1 Y-Y
(R. van der Schoot & Son, pre-1913)

'Fairy' 2 W-? (b or c)
(L. Buckland, pre-1936)

'Fairy Bells' 5 W-Y
(A.E. Lowe, pre-1927)

Periath segments cream white

'Fairy Charm' 2 W-WWP
(G.W.E. Brogden, 1980) Brogden Bulbs, 1991
Sdlg T38 (sdlg × 'Fintona') × 'Cool Flame'; sdlg no. ×89/8
Fl. 95 mm wide; perianth segments ovate, plane, very smooth; corona cup-shaped, white, with a very narrow band of deep rosy pink at rim, mouth straight, rim neatly crenate. Mid-season

'Fairy Chimes' 5 Y-Y
(G.E. Mitsch, 1966) G.E. Mitsch, 1976
N. jonquilla × *N. triandrus*; sdlg no. C76/1
Fl. 44 mm wide, pale yellow. Mid-season. Resembles an earlier and more prolific 'April Tears' with taller stem

'Fairy Circle' 3 W-P
(The Brodie of Brodie, *c.*1910)
Engleheart *N. poeticus* sdlg × 'Mrs C.Bowley'
Fl. rounded; perianth segments creamy white; corona small, suffused strawberry pink

'Fairy Circle' 3 W-WWP
(The Brodie of Brodie, *c.*1919)
'Pinkie' × 'Hypatia'; sdlg no. 185/A/14
Fl. rounded; perianth segments broadly ovate, blunt, spreading, regular, overlapping one-third to a half; the inner segments with margins sometimes wavy; corona broad disc-shaped, closely ribbed, white, with a broad band of light green at base and a well-defined narrow band of vivid yellowish pink 30C at rim, minutely frilled. Dwarf. 2n=14. AM(e) 1926

'Fairy Cup' 5 W-Y
(T. Morrison) T. Morrison, 1960
Fls 2-3 per stem; perianth segments ovate, blunt, spreading, overlapping at base only; corona cylindrical, short, lemon yellow, with mouth straight or somewhat incurved, even, rim almost entire. Dwarf. Mid-season to late

'Fairy Dell' 2 Y-? (a)
(A. Gibson, pre-1951)

'Fairy Dream' 1 W-W
(G.E. Mitsch, pre-1952)
'Nevis' × 'Beersheba'; sdlg no. 36C29/1
Perianth segments overlapping. Mid-season

'Fairy Footsteps' 3 W-GGW
(Ballydorn Bulb Farm) Ballydorn Bulb Farm, 1982
'Cushendall' × 'Silver Spell'
Fl. 68 mm wide; corona with white at rim. Late. 2n=14

'Fairy Frills' 2 W-GPP
(J.N. Hancock & Co., 1962) Unregistered

'Fairy Frolic' 7 Y-R
(J.S. Leitch) J.S. Leitch, 1956

'Fairy Glen' 3 W-GWW
(Ballydorn Bulb Farm) Ballydorn Bulb Farm, 1991
'Cushendun' × 'Jamestown'
Fl. 75 mm wide; perianth segments slightly reflexed; corona opening pale emerald green to more or less half its length, becoming white, with emerald green at base, rim dentate. Late

'Fairy Herald' 6
(C.R.L. Scowen) C.R.L. Scowen, 1961
N. cyclamineus × 'Goldcourt'
PC(r)(a) 1961

'Fairyhill' 2 W-O
(W.M. Spry, pre-1975) Unregistered
'Aldgate' × 'Delight'

'Fairy Island' 3 W-GOO
(C.R. Wootton, 1975) Carncairn Daffodils, 1990
Sdlg × 'Hamzali'; sdlg no. 15/10
Fl. 104 mm wide; perianth segments very broadly ovate, blunt, only very slightly mucronate, spreading, concave, smooth, regular, overlapping half; the inner segments truncate, shouldered at base; corona very shallow bowl-shaped, ribbed, mouth widely expanded, split in places and overlapping, wavy, with rim minutely crenate. Late to very late

'Fairy King' 2 Y-O
(A.M. Wilson, pre-1933)
'Gulliver' hybrid
Fl. small; perianth segments golden yellow, overlapping; corona neat, glowing scarlet-orange, with rim flared. AM(e) 1936

'Fairyland' 2 W-? (b)
(Sir C.H. Cave, pre-1928)

'Fairy Lantern' 7 Y-O
(S.J. Bisdee, 1946) S.J. Bisdee, 1956
'Dunkeld' × Jonquilla 'Plenus'

'Fairy Light' 3 W-?
(G.H. Johnstone, pre-1943)

'Fairy-light' 3 W-P
(G.H. Johnstone, pre-1943)
Corona coral pink

'Fairy Maid' 2 W-WWO
(H.A. Brown, 1930)
Perianth segments broad, snow white; corona creamy white, with salmon orange at rim, mouth expanded. Late

'Fairy Meadow' 1 W-Y
(W.M. Spry, pre-1975) Unregistered

'Moonstruck' × Fairbairn sdlg
Corona creamy lemon yellow, frilled. Late

'Fairymine' 3 W-? (b)
(A. Gibson, pre-1951)

'Fairy Moon' 3 W-GWP
(G.L. Wilson, pre-1954)
'Cantabile' × 'Cushendall'

'Fairy Mother' 2 W-O
(G. Lewis) D.S. Bell, 1955
Corona apricot

'Fairy Nymph' 7 W-Y
(Barr & Sons, pre-1923)
'Maggie May' × *N. jonquilla*
Fls usually 2 per stem; perianth segments white; corona pale creamy primrose yellow

'Fairy Queen' 3 W-W
(C. Smith, pre-1903)
Perianth segments pure white; corona broad, straight, ribbed, creamy white

'Fairy Ring' 2 W-? (b)
(W.B. Hartland, pre-1913)

'Fairy's Flight' 2 W-P
(H.A. Brown, 1931) J.N. Hancock & Co., 1955
Corona pink amber, heavily frilled

'Fairy Snow' 3 W-W
(G.H. Engleheart, pre-1927)

'Fairy Spell' 3 W-GWW
(Ballydorn Bulb Farm) Ballydorn Bulb Farm, 1991
'Cushendun' × 'Jamestown'
Fl. 65 mm wide; perianth segments very smooth, overlapping; corona opening emerald green almost to three-quarters of its length, rapidly becoming almost white, with a distinct band of pure white at rim. Late. Scented

'Fairy Tale' 3 W-YYO
(G.L. Wilson, pre-1952)
'Portrush' × 'Green Island'
Fl. about 90 mm wide; perianth segments very broadly ovate, prominently mucronate, spreading, overlapping half; the inner segments more narrowly ovate, sometimes roundish, with margins a little wavy; corona bowl-shaped, more or less smooth, creamy white, with a well-defined band of vivid orange 28B at rim, mouth slightly frilled, with rim shallowly crenate. AM(e) 1955

'Fairy Trace' 7
(Mrs P.M. Davis, pre-1948)

'Fairy Wings' 6 W-Y
(G.S. Crouch, pre-1938)
? × *N. poeticus*
Fl. 50 mm wide; perianth segments broadly ovate, blunt or truncate, creamy white, stained yellow at base, reflexed, overlapping two-thirds; the inner segments twisted or with margins wavy; corona cylindrical, short, ribbed, brilliant yellow 12B, mouth straight, even, with rim crenate. 2n=14. AM(a) 1938

'Fairy Wings' 5
(S.J. Bisdee, 1939)

'Fairy Wonder' 2 W-P
(C. Goodson) R. Hyde, 1958
Perianth segments opening lime, becoming white; corona rich salmon pink

'Faith' 2 W-? (b or c)
(W. Balch, pre-1933)

'Faithful' 2 Y-Y
(G.L. Wilson, pre-1927)
'Princess Mary' hybrid × 'King Alfred' hybrid
Fl. of great substance; perianth segments smooth. Tall. Early

'Fakir' 1 Y-Y
(C.G. van Tubergen, pre-1925)
AM(Haarlem) 1925

'Falada' 1 Y-Y
(D.J. Cooper) D.J. Cooper, 1956

'Falaise' 4 W-O
(J.L. Richardson, pre-1945)
'Mary Copeland' × ? *N. poeticus*; sdlg no. 427
Perianth segments long, pure white; corona reddish orange. Very late. Scented. 2n=26

'Falamai' 3 W-? (b)
(A. Gibson, pre-1951)

'Falchion' 2 W-? (b or c)
(G.H. Engleheart, pre-1923)

'Falcon' 2 or 3 W-? (b or c)
(Sir C.H. Cave, pre-1908)
'Mrs Langtry' × *N. poeticus*

'Falcon' 1 Y-Y
(J.J. Abernethy) R.J. Abernethy, 1961
Fl. 115 mm wide, bright golden yellow. Mid-season

'Falconer' 3 W-? (b)
(R.O. Backhouse, pre-1934)

'Falconet'
(?W.B. Cranfield, pre-1914)

'Falconet' 8 Y-O

(G.E. Mitsch) G.E. Mitsch, 1979
'Matador' × *N. jonquilla*; sdlg no. G82/5
Fls 3-5 or occasionally more per stem, 40 mm wide; perianth segments deep yellow, overlapping; corona bright orange. Mid-season. Resembles a smaller and more brightly coloured 'Hoopoe'

'Falkland' 2 W-? (b)
(J.L. Richardson, pre-1942)
'Mitylene' × 'Sunstar'

'Fallacy' 2 W-YYP
(R.C.A. Tombleson, pre-1987) Unregistered
Corona yellow, with a narrow band of pink at rim

fallax = *N. elegans* var. *fallax*

'Fallen Star' 3 Y-? (a)
(G.P. Haydon, pre-1908)

'Falling Star' 6 Y-O
(D. Bramley) D. Bramley, 1965
Fl. 70 mm wide. Mid-season. Resembles a shorter and more refined 'Marcellos'

'Falmouth' 3 Y-? (a)
(E. & J.C. Martin, pre-1931)

'False Heart' 11?b W-OYO
(?Australian origin, pre-1990) Unregistered

'False Measure' 1 Y-WWY
(G.W.E.Brogden) A.W. Chappell, 1992
'Topmark' × 'Daydream'
Fl. 95 mm wide; perianth segments lemon yellow; corona white, with yellow at rim. Mid-season

'False Pride' 1 Y-Y
(Wrigley, pre-1913)

'Falstaff' 3 W-YYO
(W. Backhouse, pre-1869)
Perianth segments broadly ovate, prominently mucronate, somewhat spathulate, pure white, spreading or a little inflexed, separated at base, sometimes overlapping at shoulder; the inner segments more narrowly spathulate, with margins wavy; corona small bowl-shaped, ribbed, lemon yellow, with a band of pale orange at rim, lightly frilled

'Falstaff' 2 Y-O
(J.L. Richardson) J.L. Richardson, 1960
'Ceylon' × ('Narvik' × 'Marksman')
Fl. 90 mm wide; perianth segments very broad, rounded or squarish at apex, slightly mucronate, vivid yellow 9B, spreading, plane, regular, overlapping half; the inner segments narrower, more usually rounded at apex; corona cup-shaped, smooth, vivid orange 28B, mouth slightly expanded, lightly frilled, with rim crenate and a llittle flanged. Sunproof. AM(e) 1963, FCC(e) 1968

'Fame' 8 W-O
(Oregon Bulb Farms) Oregon Bulb Farms, 1958
?'Admiration' open pollinated
Fls 3-4 per stem; corona bright orange. Early

'Famille Rose' 2 W-P
(G.H. Johnstone, pre-1942)
('Suda' × ['Albino' × 'Taranto']) × 'Rose of Brodie'

'Fanad Head' 9 W-GGR
(Ballydorn Bulb Farm, 1973) Ballydorn Bulb Farm, 1987
('Cantabile' hybrid) open pollinated
Corona disc-shaped, opening green, with orange-red at rim, becoming pale sage green, with a broad band of brick red at rim. Dwarf. Late

'Fancheon' 2 W-YOR
(F. Rijnveld & Sons, pre-1939)

'Fancy' 3 W-? (b)
(Sir C.H. Cave, pre-1908)

'Fancy Free' 2 W-YYP
(G.L. Wilson) G.L. Wilson, 1960
'Mabel Taylor' × 'Interim'

'Fancy Frills' 2 W-YYP
(G.E. Mitsch, 1956) G.E. Mitsch, 1968
'Mabel Taylor' × 'Caro Nome'; sdlg no. R49/10
Fl. 102 mm wide; corona lemon yellow, becoming buff pink at rim, frilled. Mid-season

'Fancy Girl' 2 W-P
(Brian S. Duncan, 1978) David L. Sheppard, 1989
'Passionale' × 'Polonaise'
Fl. 120 mm wide; perianth segments very broadly ovate, blunt, prominently mucronate, pure white, spreading, concave, with broad midrib showing, regular, overlapping one-third to a half; the inner segments more narrowly ovate, a little inflexed, shouldered at base; corona funnel-shaped, closely ribbed, pure pink, mouth expanded and lobed, with some lobes overlapping, frilled, with rim minutely crenate. Sunproof

'Fancy Lad' 2 Y-O
(P. de Jager & Sons) Unregistered P.de Jager & Sons, 1971
'Armada' × 'Mary Roozen'
Fl. 115 mm wide; perianth segments vivid yellow 12A, overlapping; corona ribbed, light orange (21A), slightly flushed with a darker tone (23A) towards mouth, mouth expanded and frilled

'Fandango' 1 Y-Y
(pre-1913)

'Fandango' 2 W-P
(Oregon Bulb Farms, pre-1950)

'Fanfare' 1 Y-Y
(P.D. Williams, pre-1927)

'Fanflare' 10 G-Y
(H. Koopowitz) H. Koopowitz, 1979
N. bulbocodium var. *conspicuus* × ? 'Gaytime'; sdlg no. D.977/1
Fl. 33 mm wide; perianth segments grass green; corona strongly ribbed, rich lemon, with rim crinkled. Early

'Fania' 2 W-P
(Kate Reade) Carncairn Daffodils, 1995
'Dailmanach' × 'Quiet Day'; sdlg no. 5/11/86
Fl. 87 mm wide; perianth segments broadly ovate, blunt, only very slightly mucronate, yellowish white 155B, spreading, with margins minutely incurling, overlapping half; the inner segments a little narrower, shouldered at base, lightly creased; corona somewhat funnel-shaped, light yellowish pink 29C, with mouth wavy, rim slightly rolled, notched and shallowly crenate. Mid-season

'Fanita'
(C. Dawson, pre-1908)

'Fanline' 11a W-Y
(J. Gerritsen & Son, *c.*1974) Unregistered
Fl. 95 mm wide; perianth segments ivory white; corona segments opening greenish yellow, becoming pale orange-yellow. Early

'Fanmore' 2 Y-YYO
(D.C.MacArthur) D.C.MacArthur, 1996
'Embo' hybrid; sdlg no. EV89016
Fl. 95 mm wide; perianth segments very broad, triangular in appearance, mucronate, brilliant yellow 8A, spreading; corona large funnel-shaped, angled, vivid yellow 13A, with a lighter tone (9A) at base and yellow-orange (17B) at rim, mouth straight and frilled. Mid-season. Sunproof. Scented

'Fanny Currey' 2 W-YYP
(J.L. Richardson, pre-1925)
'Lord Kitchener' × 'Bernardino'
Corona expanded, creamy white, tinged apricot pink at rim, dentate. PC(e) 1925, AM(e) 1929

'Fanny Haydon'
(G.P. Haydon, pre-1908)

'Fanny Hill' 3 W-GYR
(T.D. Throckmorton) T.D. Throckmorton, 1974
'Irish Coffee' × 'Gossamer'

'Fanny Mason' 3 W-Y
(E. Leeds, pre-1877)
Corona canary yellow. Syn. 'Vincenti Gloriosus', Leedsii 'Fanny Mason', Leedsii 'Vincenti Gloriosa'. "Absorbed" 'Mignonne' and 'Silver King'

'Fanta' 2 W-GYO
(Mrs B.T. Simpson) Mrs B.T. Simpson, 1963
Fl. 90 mm wide; corona lemon yellow, with green at base and a broad band of clear orange at rim. Early

'Fantail' 2 W-? (b)
(A.H. Ahrens) J.S. Leitch, 1955

'Fantasia' 3 W-YYP
(S.J. Bisdee, 1937)
'Mystic' × 'Dactyl'

'Fantasie' 3 W-Y
(G.P. Haydon, pre-1907)
N. × *poculiformis* × *N. poeticus*
Corona disc-shaped, bright yellow

'Fantasma' 2 W-O
(Mrs R.O. Backhouse, pre-1921)
Corona shallow, reddish orange, mouth widely expanded, frilled. AM(Haarlem) 1932

'Fantastique' 3 W-? (b)
(J.W.A. Lefeber, pre-1948)

'Fantasy' 2 W-O
(J.W.A. Lefeber) J.J. Grullemans & Sons, 1959
Fl. 120 mm wide; perianth segments creamy white; corona opening brilliant yellow 15C, becoming strong orange 25B, flecked with creamy white and golden yellow. Mid-season

'Fantasy Isle' 2 W-P
(David L. Sheppard) David L. Sheppard, 1987
'Madang' × 'Accent'
Fl. 90 mm wide; perianth segments very broadly ovate, blunt, slightly mucronate, a little concave, with margins sometimes incurling, overlapping one-third to a half; the inner segments more narrowly ovate, acute, somewhat twisted; corona broad funnel-shaped, delicate lilac pink, mouth straight, split in places and overlapping, lightly frilled, with rim unevenly notched and crenate. Mid-season. Resembles 'Accent' but with the corona of a different pink and wider at the mouth

'Fantée' 1 Y-Y
(G.L. Wilson) R.W. Ward & Son, 1959

'Fantin Latour' 1 Y-Y
(de Graaff Bros, pre-1915)
Fl. large; perianth segments lemon yellow; corona broad, rich golden yellow, with mouth expanded and neatly frilled. AM(Haarlem) 1915

'Farabo' 1 W-Y

(J.J. Abernethy) R.J. Abernethy, 1957
Perianth segments broadly ovate, of thick substance; corona lemon yellow, with rim flanged and dentate

'Faraday' 1 Y-Y
(H.L. Jones, pre-1908)

'Faralong'
Unregistered
Seed parent of 'Davura'; pollen parent of 'Gideon'

'Farandole' 9 W-?
(F.H. Chapman, pre-1923)

'Faraway' 3 W-GRR
(Ballydorn Bulb Farm) Ballydorn Bulb Farm, 1976
'Corncrake' × 'Fairgreen'
Fl. 93 mm wide; corona red, with green prominent at base and with red at rim becoming darker with age. Late. Resembles 'Favor Royal' but without yellow in the corona

'Far Country' 2 W-GWP
(Carncairn Daffodils, 1976) Carncairn Daffodils, 1986
Sdlg no. CP76
Corona white, with green at base and a suffusion of pink towards rim, slightly frilled. Late

'Farewell' 2 W-Y
(M.P. Williams, pre-1938)
Fl. 111 mm wide; perianth segments rounded, creamy white, smooth, overlapping half; corona neat, funnel-shaped, light greenish yellow 6D, with mouth a little expanded and lightly frilled. 2n=28. AM(e) 1948, FCC(e) 1949, *HC(g) 1950, *AM(g) 1953, *FCC(g) 1954

'Far Fetched' 1 W-W
(W. Jackson Jr) Jackson's Daffodils, 1980
Sdlg no. 54/74
Fl. 95 mm wide. Mid-season

'Fargan' 2 Y-Y
Syn. of 'Cargan'

'Farida' 2 W-YYR
(S.J. Bisdee, 1939)
'Warflame' × 'Seraglio'

'Farin' 2 W-? (b)
(A.H. Ahrens) D.J. Cooper, 1956

'Faris' 1 Y-Y
(S.J. Bisdee) S.J. Bisdee, 1955
'J.P.' × 'Ysbryn'
Fl. forming a double triangle; perianth segments very broadly ovate, blunt, slightly mucronate, spreading, plane, regular, overlapping half; the inner segments narrower, a little inflexed, with margins very slightly wavy; corona mouth widely expanded, ribbed and frilled

'Farmington' 1 Y-Y
(W.Jackson Jr, 1951)
'Chromis' × 'La La'

'Farndale' 1 Y-Y
(F.H. Chapman, pre-1935)

'Farnsfield' 1 W-P
(Mrs J. Abel Smith) Mrs J. Abel Smith, 1979
'Rima' × 'Geisha'; sdlg no. D5/11
Fl. 98 mm wide. Late. Resembles 'Rima' but with more substance to the perianth

'Faro' 1 W-W
(Ballydorn Bulb Farm) Ballydorn Bulb Farm, 1965
'Broughshane' hybrid
Perianth segments broadly ovate, pure white; corona widely expanded. Tall. Mid-season

'Farrago' 3 W-W
(D.J. Jackson) Jackson's Daffodils, 1989
'Verona' × 'Placid'; sdlg no. 287/80
Fl. 93 mm wide; perianth segments rounded, greenish white (155A), smooth; corona opening slightly yellow, becoming creamy white. Mid-season

'Farranfad' 2 W-YYO
(Ballydorn Bulb Farm) Ballydorn Bulb Farm, 1988
'Mount Pleasant' × 'Noble'
Fl. 100 mm wide; perianth segments broadly ovate, plane; corona disc-shaped, deep primrose yellow, with a broad band of golden orange at rim. Late

'Farrney Fox' 2 Y-O
(W.O. Backhouse) E. Longford, 1963
Fl. 114 mm wide; perianth segments lemon yellow; corona long, tangerine orange. Early to mid-season

'Farro' 1 Y-Y
(C.E. Radcliff, 1931)
'Golden City' × 'Gertrude Nethercote'

'Farthingale' 2 Y-Y
(G.H. Engleheart, pre-1923)
Fl. 102 mm wide; perianth segments clear lemon, regular, overlapping half; corona cylindrical, buttercup yellow. Mid-season to late

'Far West' 3 Y-OOR
(Helen A.Grier) Helen A.Grier, 1964
'Dervish' × 'Mexico'
Fl. 90 mm wide, chrome yellow, with stains of reddish orange at base becoming darker in tone and more extensive with age; corona deep orange, with a narrow band of reddish orange at rim becoming broader with age. Early. Resembles 'Dervish'

'Fascile' 1 W-? (b)
(A.H. Ahrens) J.S. Leitch, 1955

'Fascination' 1 W-? (b)
(W. Welchman, pre-1908)

'Fascination' 3 W-YYR
(G. Lewis) D.S. Bell, 1955

'Fascination' 4 Y-Y
Syn. of 'Pride of Heemstede'

'Fasgadh' 1 Y-Y
(D.C. MacArthur) D.C. MacArthur, 1992
'Golden Harvest' × 'Sundance'; sdlg no. EV78242
Fl. 114 mm wide; perianth segments broadly ovate, vivid yellow 9A, slightly concave, of great substance; the inner segments less broad, slightly twisted; corona broad funnel-shaped, ribbed, darker in tone (13A) than the perianth, with mouth flared and deeply lobed. Very early. Scented

'Fashion' 4 W-O
(R.H. Bath, pre-1927)

'Fashion' 11b Y-Y/O
(W.F. Leenen, 1966) W.F. Leenen, 1977
'Nippon' hybrid
Fl. 100 mm wide; perianth segments light greenish yellow 4C; corona deeply split, the six segments three-quarters the length of the perianth segments and alternate to them, light greenish yellow, with darker yellow at midrib and marigold orange at apex. Early

'Fashion' 2 W-P
Corona pale pink. Syn. of 'Mark Time'

'Fashionette' 3 W-W
(Mrs M. Moorby, pre-1949)

'Fashion Parade' 4 Y-Y
(Th. van der Hulst) Th. van der Hulst, 1989
'Festivity' × 'Tahiti' hybrid
Fl. 140 mm wide; perianth and other petaloid segments brilliant to light greenish yellow 5B/C; corona segments vivid yellow 14B. Mid-season

'Fashion Plate' 2 W-YYO
(G. Lewis, pre-1940)
'Burgundy' × 'Encore'
Perianth segments creamy white; corona yellow, with reddish orange in a broad band at rim and suffusing the mid-zone

'Fastidious' 2 W-W
(G.E. Mitsch) G.E. Mitsch, 1971
'Pigeon' × 'Empress of Ireland'; sdlg no. Z30/1
Fl. 95 mm wide, pure white. Mid-season

'Fastnet' 2 W-YYO
(J.L. Richardson, pre-1953)
'Tuskar Light' × 'Green Island'
Perianth segments pure white; corona very shallow bowl-shaped, very pale yellow, with a narrow band of biscuit orange at rim

'Fata Morgana' 1 Y-OOY
(W.F. Leenen) W.F. Leenen, 1982
Perianth segments light greenish yellow 6D; corona strong orange 24A, with lemon yellow at rim

'Father Christmas' 1 W-W
(G.L. Wilson, pre-1946)

'Fatima' 1 W-W
(G.L. Wilson, pre-1953)
AM(Haarlem) 1953

'Faust' 2 Y-Y
(Barr & Sons, pre-1945)

'Faust' 1 Y-Y
Syn. of 'Bach'

'Faust' 2 Y-O
Syn. of 'California Gold'

'Faustina' 3 W-? (b)
(Cartwright & Goodwin, pre-1910)

'Favel' 11?a W-GPP
(?Dutch origin, pre-1975) Unregistered

'Favell Lee' 2 W-Y
(H.R. Meyer, pre-1944)
Fl. 95 mm wide; perianth segments creamy white, overlapping two-thirds; corona vivid yellow 9A, with mouth expanded. 2n=28. *HC(g) 1947

'Faveur' 2 Y-? (a)
(pre-1953)

'Favorite' 8 Y-Y
(pre-1835)
Early

'Favorite Bulliux' 8 Y-Y
(pre-1851)

'Favorite de Voorhelm' 8 Y-O
(pre-1798)

'Favor Royal' 3 W-GYR
(Ballydorn Bulb Farm) Ballydorn Bulb Farm, 1976
'Corncrake' × 'Fairgreen'
Fl. 100 mm wide; corona yellow, with green at base and bright red at rim. Late

'Favourite' 2? W-Y
(E. Leeds, pre-1884)

Corona canary yellow. Syn. Leedsii 'Favourite'. Was "absorbed" into 'Duchess of Brabant'

'Favourite' 1 Y-Y
(R.H. Bath, pre-1907)

'Favourite' 2 W-Y
(F.E. Board) M.J.Jefferson-Brown, 1965
'Castle Coole' × 'Irish Rose'
Corona pale yellow

'Fawcett Clapperton' 1 W-? (b)
(R. Dick, pre-1930)

'Fawnglo' 2 Y-Y
(G.E. Mitsch) G.E. Mitsch, 1960
'Binkie' × ('King of the North' × 'Content')
See also 'Fawnglow'

'Fawnglow' 2 Y-Y
Syn. of 'Fawnglo'

'Fawzy' 2 W-P
(J.L. Martin) J.L. Martin, 1982
'Ann Cameron' × 'Jill Bolte'; sdlg no. AC/JB 12
Fl. 100 mm wide; corona orange-pink (33B). Early to mid-season

'Fay' 2 W-W
(L. Buckland, pre-1936)

'Fay' 2 W-R
(R.H. Glover, pre-1993) Unregistered

'Fay Diane' 2 W-O
(J.N. Hancock & Co., pre-1949)
Perianth segments broad; corona widely expanded

'Faye Haynes' 1 W-Y
(L.P. Dettman) L.P. Dettman, 1975
'Spellbinder' × 'Bonnington'; sdlg no. 3/66
Fl. 89 mm wide; perianth segments yellowish white 155D; corona vivid yellow 9A. Mid-season. Resembles 'Bonnington' but with the corona of a deeper yellow

'Faye Norman' 2 W-W
(D.S. Bell) D.S. Bell, 1985
Fl. 115 mm wide; corona opening yellow, becoming milk white, with rim neatly rolled. Late

'Fay MacLure' 3 W-W
(Campbell Duncan, 1950)
'Nervose' × 'Chinese White'

'Fay Mark' 2 W-O
(J.W.A. Lefeber, 1945) J.W.A. Lefeber, 1960
Fl. 90 mm wide; corona frilled. Early. Resembles a more strongly coloured 'Smiling Queen'

'Faymelthea' 2 Y-YYR
(L.J. Chambers) L.J. Chambers, 1982
'Masai King' × 'Royal George'; sdlg no. 66/142
Fl. 115 mm wide. Mid-season

'Fayum' 3 W-O
(J.M. de Navarro, pre-1953)
'Monaco' × 'Matapan'
Perianth segments broadly ovate, prominently mucronate, snow white, smooth, regular, overlapping half; the inner segments slightly narrower, less obviously mucronate; corona orange, mouth widely expanded and frilled, with rim flanged

'F.C.J.Spurrell' 3 W-? (b)
(Miss K. Spurrell, pre-1923)

'F.D.C.Godman' 1 Y-Y
Syn. of 'F.Du Cane Godman'

'F.Du Cane Godman' 1 Y-Y
(W. Backhouse, pre-1869)
Perianth segments pale sulphur yellow; corona rich yellow. Syn. Pseudonarcissus 'F.Du Cane Godman'. See also F.D.C.Godman. Was "absorbed" into 'Wolley Dod'

'Fearless' 2 W-Y
(G.H. Engleheart, pre-1904)
Perianth segments creamy white, of strong substance, overlapping; corona very large, rich yellow, with mouth tightly frilled

'Fearless' 1 Y-Y
Syn. of 'Frontline'

'Feastentide' 2 Y-? (a)
(G.H. Johnstone, pre-1947)

'Feature' 2 Y-YYR
(G.H. Johnstone, pre-1960)

'Feature' 3 Y-O
(G.W.E. Brogden) G.W.E. Brogden, 1968
Fl. 108 mm wide; perianth segments clear yellow; corona light orange, with a darker tone at rim. Mid-season

'February Bicolor' 2 W-Y
(C.W. Culpepper, c.1970) Unregistered
Corona funnel-shaped, clear lemon yellow. Early

'February Gold' 6 Y-Y
(de Graaff Bros, pre-1923)
'Golden Spur' × *N. cyclamineus*
Fl. 75 mm wide; perianth segments ovate, brilliant greenish yellow 6B, with slight white mucro, reflexed, with margins wavy and incurved, overlapping at base only; the inner segments twisted; corona cylindrical, ribbed, vivid yellow 14B, paling slightly to base,

mouth 6-lobed and a little expanded, rim deeply and regularly notched and dentate. Very early. 2n=21. EFA(Haarlem) 1928, EFA(Haarlem) 1943, *AM(g) 1973, *FCC(g) 1974, *AM(p) 1977, AGM 1993

'February Silver' 6 W-Y
(de Graaff Bros, pre-1949)
Perianth segments broadly ovate, greenish white, reflexed, with margins wavy, creased, overlapping one-third; the inner segments more narrowly ovate, twisted; corona cylindrical, broadly ribbed, mouth expanded, with six overlapping lobes, rim crenate. 2n=35. Resembles 'February Gold' in form

'Fedelta' 2 Y-W
(S.J. Bisdee, 1945) S.J. Bisdee, 1956
Richardson sdlg 312 × 'Binkie'
Fl. opening lemon yellow; corona becoming off-white

'Federation'
(W. Welchman, pre-1910)

'Fedora' 2 W-? (b)
(de Graaff Bros, pre-1943)
AM(Haarlem) 1943, FCC(Haarlem) 1950, TGA(Haarlem) 1956

'Feeling Lucky' 2 Y-R
(J.L. Richardson) M.J. Jefferson-Brown, 1969
'Patagonia' × 'Firecracker'
Fl. 90 mm wide; perianth segments broadly ovate, blunt, fairly prominently mucronate, brilliant greenish yellow 6 or 7C, spreading, with margins sometimes nicked, overlapping one-third to a half; the inner segments only slightly narrower, not noticeably mucronate, sometimes a little creased, with margins wavy; corona shallow, very widely expanded, orange-red, mouth ribbed, split in places and overlapping, loosely frilled. Mid-season. *AM(g) 1981, *FCC(g) 1982, AGM 1993

'Feena' 2 Y-Y
(Rosewarne EHS) Rosewarne EHS, 1985
'Rijnveld's Early Sensation' × 'Victorious'; sdlg no. 63/2/4
Perianth segments light greenish yellow 7D; corona brighter and darker than vivid yellow 12A. Very early

'Felicity' 1 Y-Y
(W. Welchman, pre-1908)
Perianth segments acute; corona expanded, soft pale yellow, a little darker in tone than the perianth, lightly frilled, with rim rolled

'Felicity' 1 W-Y
(D.V. West, pre-1932)
'Weardale Perfection' hybrid
Perianth segments white; corona light canary yellow

'Felicity' 2 W-? (b)

(Mrs M.Moorby) Mrs M.Moorby, 1956

'Felicity' 2 W-?
Syn. of 'Hostess'

'Felicity' 2 W-P
(J.N. Hancock & Co., 1976) Unregistered
Corona true pink, frilled. Mid-season

'Felicity Sarah' 3 W-GWW
(Mrs H. Oxton) Mrs H. Oxton, 1985
'Verona' × 'Homage'
Fl. 83 mm wide. Late. Resembles a Div. 3 'Homage'

'Felika' 1 W-P
(S.J. Bisdee) S.J. Bisdee, 1956
'Pentavalon' × 'Rosario'

'Felindre' 9 W-GYR
(A.M. Wilson, pre-1930)
Corona disc-shaped, closely ribbed, yellow, shading to green at base, with near crimson at rim, rim densely and irregularly notched. Very late. 2n=14

N. × felineri Fernández Casas 13 = *N. bulbocodium* Linnaeus × *N. nobilis* (Haworth) Schultes f. var. *primigenius* Fernández Casas & Lainz

'Felix' 1 W-Y
(The Brodie of Brodie, c.1910)
'Jeannie Woodhouse' × 'King Alfred'

'Felix' 5
(Sir A.P.W. Thomas, pre-1937)

'Felix' 2 Y-R
(J.N. Hancock & Co., 1973) Unregistered

'Felix Schwab' 2 W-? (b or c)
(G.L. Wilson, pre-1932)

'Fellowship' 2 Y-? (a)
(W.B. Cranfield, pre-1930)

'Fellowship' 2 W-YYP
(Brian S. Duncan) Rathowen Daffodils, 1978
'Mary Queen' × sdlg R.3341; sdlg no. 142
Fl. 98 mm wide; perianth segments broadly ovate, milk white; corona mid-yellow, with bright pink at rim. Mid-season

'Felspar' 2 W-Y
(W.F.M. Copeland, pre-1911)

'Felstar' 2 W-O
(pre-1965) Unregistered
Corona bright reddish orange

'Felsted' 3 W-? (b)
(F.H. Chapman, pre-1929)

'Felucca' 2 W-? (b)
(Alister Clark, pre-1914)

'Felucca' 2 Y-? (a)
(Alister Clark, 1935) J. Sharp, 1960

'Femina' 2 Y-O
(Konynenburg & Mark) Konynenburg & Mark, 1967
'Carol Bells' × 'Revelry'
Fl. 100 mm wide; perianth segments vivid yellow 9A; corona strong orange 25A

'Fenella' 1 W-Y
(D.V. West, pre-1927)
Perianth segments pure white; corona pale canary yellow

'Fenella Place' 3 W-? (b)
(R.O. Backhouse, pre-1938)

'Fenella's Finesse' 2 Y/W-WWY
(Albert Davis, 1978) Albert Davis, 1995
'My Love' × 'Irish Mist'; sdlg no. 401/74
Fl. 89 mm wide; perianth segments broadly ovate, slightly mucronate, brilliant greenish yellow 6C, with a broad band of white from base to apex at midrib; corona straight-sided, slightly expanding towards the mouth, whitish, with a broad band of greenish yellow at rim and with the rim minutely dentate. Mid-season. Resembles a paler 'Daydream' in form with the perianth segments longitudinally rather than horizontally banded white

'Fengold' 1 Y-Y
(J.A. van der Zwet & Sons, pre-1950)
AM(Haarlem) 1950

'Fenlan' W-Y
(R.V. Favell, pre-1940)
Fl. rounded, of good substance; perianth segments clean white; corona pale primrose yellow

'Fenland' 1 W-? (b)
(W. Welchman, pre-1908)

'Fenland Gem' 2 Y-? (a)
(R.H. Bath, pre-1927)

'Fenton Fire' ?-R
(R. Lincoln Lewis, pre-1940)

'Feock' 3 W-YYR
(R.A. Scamp) R.A. Scamp, 1991
'Corofin' × 'Kimmeridge'; sdlg no. 93
Fl. 87 mm wide; perianth segments broadly ovate, slightly inflexed; corona bowl-shaped, ribbed, bright yellow, with a well-defined band of bright red at rim. Mid-season

'Ferdie' 6 Y-Y
(Glenbrook Bulb Farm, pre-1992) Unregistered
N. rupicola × *N. cyclamineus*; sdlg no. 46/88

'Ferdinand' 2 Y-O
(P.D. Williams, pre-1939)
Corona deep reddish orange

'Fergie' 2 Y-R
(M.J. Jefferson-Brown) M.J. Jefferson-Brown, 1985
'Tambourine' × 'Falstaff'
Perianth segments broad, golden yellow; corona very large, fiery orange-red, mouth widely expanded. Early

'Ferida' 3 W-R
(J.T. Gray, pre-1936)
Corona dark red

'Fermain' 2 W-? (b or c)
(C.B. Blampied, pre-1929)

'Fermoy' 2 W-YOO
(J.L. Richardson, pre-1938)
'Niphetos' × sdlg 263
Fl. 116 mm wide; perianth segments very broadly ovate in outline, blunt and sometimes truncate at apex, very slightly mucronate, pure white, spreading, plane, of great substance, overlapping half; the inner segments a little inflexed, with margins wavy; corona broad bowl-shaped, narrowly ribbed, glowing orange, pulling to golden yellow at base, mouth somewhat incurved, split in places and overlapping, lightly and unevenly frilled. Mid-season to late. 2n=28. PC 1941, AM(e) 1943, AM(Haarlem) 1949, FCC(Haarlem) 1951

N. *fernandesii* Pedro 13 Section Jonquilla.
AM(a)(r) 1991
    var. ***fernandesii***
    var. ***major*** A. Fernandes

'Fernando' 8 W-O
(pre-1883)
Perianth segments pale sulphur; corona orange. Resembles a less distinctive 'Grand Alexander'

'Ferndown' 3 Y-Y
(J.W. Blanchard, 1971) J.W. Blanchard, 1990
'Lemonade' × sdlg 59/33C; sdlg no. 66/13A
Fl. rounded, 85 mm wide; perianth segments very broadly ovate, rounded at apex or slightly truncate, light greenish yellow 5D, a little reflexed, with margins slightly incurving, regular, overlapping half or more; the inner segments more nearly spreading or a little inflexed; corona funnel-shaped, ribbed, darker in tone (12B flushed 15A) than the perianth, with yet darker tones at rim, mouth even, rim minutely notched. Mid-season. AM(e) 1979

'Ferness' 2 W-YYO
(Brodie Gardens) Brodie Gardens, 1959
('Coronach' × 'Folly') × 'Red Hackle'
Perianth segments very broad, smooth and of good substance, overlapping; corona wide bowl-shaped, golden yellow, with a broad band of reddish orange at rim, frilled. Tall

'Ferney Creek' 1? Y-Y
Syn. of 'Ferny Creek'

'Fernglen' 1 W-Y
(D.S. Bell) D.S. Bell, 1982
Sdlg 34-80 open pollinated
Fl. 104 mm wide; corona with rim somewhat rolled. Mid-season

'Fernhill' 2 W-Y
(W.M. Spry, pre-1975) Unregistered
'Full Moon' × 'Hereami'
Corona broad, lemon yellow. Late

'Fernie' 3 W-? (b)
(J.O. Sherrard, pre-1954)

'Fernisky' 2 W-W
(W.J. Dunlop) W.J. Dunlop, 1962
Corona opening cream, soon becoming white

'Ferny Creek' 1? Y-Y
(O. Ronalds or W.M. & A.P.Spry, pre-1955) Unregistered
Perianth segments broadly ovate, medium yellow; corona dark gold, with rim slightly rolled. See also 'Ferney Creek'

'Feronia' 2 W-WWY
(Barr & Sons, pre-1915)
Fl. large; perianth segments white, tinged sulphur yellow at apex, overlapping; corona creamy white, shading to pale lemon yellow at rim

'Ferral' 4 Y-O
(Jackson's Daffodils, 1981) Jackson's Daffodils, 1997
H.E.Reeve Div. 4 sdlg × sdlg 69/70; sdlg no. 174/81
Fl. 105 mm wide; perianth and other petaloid segments very broadly ovate, brilliant yellow 7B; corona segments light orange (23A). Late

'Ferrara' 3 W-R
(J.M. de Navarro) J.M. de Navarro, 1958

'Ferring' 3 W-? (b)
(Sir F.C. Stern, pre-1949)

'Fervent' 2 Y-? (a)
(P.D. Williams, pre-1931)

'Fervent Hope' 1 Y-Y
G. Zandbergen-Terwegen, 1969

'Fervid' 2 W-OOR
(Parr's Nurseries) Parr's Nurseries, 1958

N. festalis Salisbury = *N. pseudonarcissus*

N. festinus Jordan = *N. pseudonarcissus* var. *festinus*

'Festival' 2 Y-? (a)
(A.M. Wilson, pre-1951)

'Festive' 2 W-O
(Mrs R.O. Backhouse, pre-1921)
Perianth segments cream, overlapping; corona long, scarlet-orange

'Festive' 2 Y-?
(Mrs C.O. Fairbairn)

'Festive' 4 W-O
(Tom Forster, 1960s) Unregistered
Perianth and other petaloid segments opening creamy white, becoming white; corona segments interspersed, bright orange, lightly frilled. Mid-season to late

'Festivity' 2 W-Y
(G.E. Mitsch, pre-1954)
?'Bodilly' × ?'Brunswick'
Perianth segments broadly ovate, blunt, mucronate, somewhat shouldered at base, spreading, plane or a little concave, smooth, overlapping half; the inner segments more narrowly ovate, with margins somewhat inward rolling or wavy; corona cup-shaped, smooth, clear yellow, mouth expanded, ribbed, lightly frilled, rim crenate. Mid-season. Somewhat resembles 'Tudor Minstrel' but with a longer and less widely expanded corona

'Festone'
(New Zealand origin, pre-1940)

'Feston Fire' 2 W-O
(R.Lincoln Lewis, pre-1940)
PC(e)(NZ) 1940

'Festoon' 2 Y-YYO
(G.W.E. Brogden) G.W.E. Brogden, 1967
Fl. 102 mm wide; corona with a narrow band of clear orange at rim. Early

'Fettle' 1 Y-Y
(Murray W. Evans) Murray W. Evans, 1977
('Binkie' × 'Daydream') × 'Protege'; sdlg no. L-22
Fl. 105 mm wide; perianth segments primrose beige, slightly reflexed; corona slightly darker in tone, with mouth flared and rim regularly dentate. Mid-season

'Feu Ardent' 3 W-? (b)
(P. van Deursen, pre-1938)
AM(Haarlem) 1938

'Feu de Joie' 4 W-O
(W.F.M. Copeland, pre-1927)
Perianth and other petaloid segments opposite one another and of more or less equal length, ovate, blunt, creamy white, with margins recurved and wavy or twisted, separated; the outer whorl spreading; the inner whorl more or less strongly inflexed; corona segments short, interspersed, pale orange, with a darker tone at rim, frilled, the whorl at centre continuous. Mid-season. 2n=21. AM(Haarlem) 1929, *HC(g) 1936, *AM(g) 1944

'Fez' 3 Y-YYR
(Mrs R.O. Backhouse, pre-1921)
Perianth segments primrose yellow, flushed creamy yellow; corona large, canary yellow, with a broad band of fiery scarlet at rim, mouth expanded

'Ffitch's Ffolly' 2 Y-O
(R. Ffitch) R.A. Scamp, 1993
'Tanera' × 'Gold Convention'; slg no. 341
Fl. 110 mm wide; perianth segments broad, golden yellow, spreading; corona cylindrical, bright orange, with rim regularly crenate. Mid-season

'Fiancee' 2 W-WPP
(G.E. Mitsch) G.E. Mitsch, 1970
'Precedent' × 'Carita'

'Fiancée' 3 W-?
Syn. of 'Morpheus'

'Fickle' 3 Y-? (a)
(P.D. Williams, pre-1930)

'Fida' 3 Y-R
(W.Jackson, 1946)
'Market Merry' × 'Hakon'

'Fiddleedee' 3 W-W
(W. Jackson Jr) Jackson's Daffodils, 1980
'Placid' × 'Romney'; sdlg no. 72/73
Fl. 95 mm wide. Mid-season

'Fiddlers Choice' 2 W-P
(Mrs J.Abel Smith) David Townley, 1996
'Pink Shadow' × 'Fidelity'
Fl. 70 mm wide; perianth segments slightly mucronate, off white, overlapping; corona opening yellow, becoming pale coppery pink. Dwarf. Mid-season

'Fideles' 1 W-Y
(W.A. Grace, pre-1927)

'Fidelia' 3 W-Y
(Barr & Sons, pre-1907)
N. × *poculiformis* × *N. poeticus*
Corona primrose yellow, shading to sulphur yellow at rim. Sweetly scented

'Fidelis' 2 W-W
(Alister Clark) G.E. Mitsch, 1956

'Fidelity' 1 W-W
(R.H. Bath, pre-1929)

'Fidelity' 1 Y-P
(G.E. Mitsch) G.E. Mitsch, 1982
'Gloriola' × 'Rima'; sdlg no. KK4/4
Fl. 100 mm wide; perianth segments pale sulphur yellow; corona flared, apricot pink, with rim rolled. Mid-season

'Fides' 1 W-W
(W. Backhouse, pre-1869)
Corona expanded, opening primrose yellow, becoming white. Syn. Leedsii 'Fides'. Was "absorbed" into 'Grand Duchess'

'Fides' 1 W-Y
(Barr & Sons, pre-1915)
Fl. 108 mm wide; perianth segments white, spreading, deeply overlapping; corona yellow, with rim widely flanged

'Fiducia' 3 W-R
(W.A. Grace, pre-1927)

'Fieldfare' 3 Y-R
(A.E. Robinson) Carncairn Daffodils, 1993
'Montego' × ('Red Bay' × 'Circlet'); sdlg no. 2/36/79
Fl. 83 mm wide, perianth segments vivid yellow 9B; corona orange-red (30C), with a slightly darker (30B) at rim. Mid-season

'Field Marshal' 3 W-? (b)
(H. Backhouse, pre-1910)

'Field Marshal' 1 Y-Y
(pre-1914)

'Field Marshal' 2 Y-O
(J.L. Richardson) J.L. Richardson, 1956
'Narvik' × 'Alamein'
Perianth segments clear yellow; corona reddish orange, frilled

'Fiery Chariot' 2 Y-R
(T. Bloomer) T. Bloomer, 1962
'Chungking' × 'Air Marshal'; sdlg no. 16/67/58
Corona deep red

'Fiery Contrast' 2 W-?
(T. Bloomer) T. Bloomer, 1970
'Fastnet' × G.L.Wilson sdlg 40/78; sdlg no. 2/52/58

'Fiery Cross' 3 W-YYR
(C.G. van Tubergen, pre-1907)
'Ornatus' × 'Will Scarlet'
Perianth segments creamy white, a little reflexed;

corona expanded, ribbed, brilliant yellow, with bright fiery red at rim

'Fiery Flame' 2 O-O
(J.L. Richardson) Mrs H.K. Richardson, 1962
'Vulcan' × 'Firecracker'
Perianth segments coppery orange; corona deep reddish orange, dentate

'Fiery Furnace' 3 Y-R
(S.J. Bisdee, 1940)
'Pink'un' × 'Killigrew'

'Fiery Knight' 4 Y-R
(Mrs R.O. Backhouse, pre-1921)
Perianth and other petaloid segments in 2-3 whorls, deep yellow; the two outer whorls broadly ovate, spreading or inflexed, with margins wavy; the centre whorl with fewer than six segments, narrower, more strongly inflexed; corona segments less than half the length of the petaloid segments and clustered among them at centre, ribbed, scarlet. ?See also 'Fiery Night'

'Fiery Lad' 2 Y-O
(T. Bloomer) T. Bloomer, 1972
'Red Ranger' × ('Royal Mail' × 'Narvik'); sdlg no. 4/34/58
Corona deep orange

'Fiery Monarch' 2 W-O
(Mrs R.O. Backhouse, pre-1921)
Perianth segments creamy, faintly flushed lemon yellow at base, overlapping; corona very large, rich reddish orange

'Fiery Night' 4 Y-R
Perianth and other petaloid segments deep yellow; corona segments short, scarlet. ?Syn. of 'Fiery Knight'

'Fiesta' 2 Y-? (a)
(Oregon Bulb Farms, pre-1946)

'Fifer' 1 Y-Y
(G.P. Haydon, pre-1908)

'Fi Frye'
See 'Fi-krye'

'Fifth Avenue' 1 W-O
(J.W.A. Lefeber) J.W.A. Lefeber, 1968

'Figaro' 2 Y-YYO
(W. Backhouse or E.Leeds, pre-1869)
N. hispanicus? × *N. poeticus*
Fl. large; corona widely expanded, rich yellow, stained orange at rim. Syn. Incomparabilis Leedsii 'Expansus', Incomparabilis Leedsii 'Figaro'. "Absorbed" 'Nabob'

'Figurant' 2 Y-YYO
(F. Rijnveld & Sons, 1957) F. Rijnveld & Sons, 1967
Fl. 120 mm wide, vivid yellow 9B; corona with vivid orange 28B at rim. Mid-season. Resembles a more vigorous 'Tannhauser'. AM(Haarlem) 1967

'Figurehead' 1 W-W
(W.G. Pannill) W.G. Pannill, 1970
'Broughshane' × 'Vigil'

'Fiji' 4 Y-Y
(J.L. Richardson) J.L. Richardson, 1956
'Falaise' × 'Ceylon'
Fl. rounded; perianth and other petaloid segments in 2-3 whorls, deep yellow; the outer whorl very broadly ovate, blunt or slightly truncate, with white mucro, a little concave, of thick substance, overlapping half; the inner whorl(s) shorter but not much narrower, inflexed or strongly inflexed, with margins incurved; corona segments shorter than the petaloid segments and darker in tone, interspersed among them and clustered at centre, roundish, frilled, with rim split and overlapping. Mid-season to late

'Fi Krye'
Syn. of 'Fi-krye'

'Fi-krye'
Unregistered
Pollen parent of 'Shirin'. See also 'Fi Krye'

'Filia' 2 W-W
(W. Jackson Jr, 1953)
'Pydna' × 'Nabis'

'Filibuster' 2 Y-O
(R.O. Backhouse, pre-1931)
Perianth segments bright yellow, overlapping; corona large, bright scarlet-orange

N. filifolius Roemer = variant of *N. bulbocodium* subsp. *bulbocodium*

'Filigree' 2 Y-? (a)
(W. Sutherland, pre-1930)
PC(e)(NZ) 1930

'Filigree' 2 Y-Y
(J.N. Hancock & Co., 1954)
Sdlg × 'Shanghai' × 'Shanghai'
Fl. soft yellow; corona broad, heavily frilled

'Fillan' 2 W-ORR
(W. Jackson Jr, 1966) Unregistered
'Beirut' × 'Capella'

'Filly' 2 W-YYP
(J.W.A.van der Wereld) Tom Parker Farms, 1984
Sdlg no. Z422
Fl. 63 mm wide; perianth segments broadly ovate, blunt, fairly prominently mucronate, spreading,

plane, lightly ribbed, with margins sometimes notched, regular, overlapping one-third to half; the inner segments more narrowly ovate, slightly twisted or with margins wavy; corona cylindrical, loosely ribbed, opening pink, becoming yellow, with pink at rim, ageing to white, mouth straight or slightly expanded, wavy or lightly frilled, rim minutely notched and crenate. 2n=28

'Film Queen' 2 Y-YYR
(S.C. Gaspar) S.C. Gaspar, 1955
Perianth segments deep yellow, of thick and velvety texture; corona shallow, with a broad band of scarlet at rim. 2n=27

'Film Star' 2 Y-R
(G. Lewis, 1935) Parr's Nurseries, 1958
Corona very shallow bowl-shaped, red

'Film Star' 2 W-Y
(pre-1987) Unregistered

'Filoli' 1 Y-YPP
(J.S.B. Lea) Clive Postles, 1991
Navarro sdlg × 'Pol Voulin'; sdlg no. 2-23-80
Fl. 94 mm wide; perianth segments ovate, concave at margins, very smooth; corona funnel-shaped, buff pink, with yellow tones at base, mouth widely flared. Late. Sunproof

'Filou' 1 Y-Y
(J.T.Gray, 1954) P. Phillips, 1966
Fl. 102 mm wide. Mid-season. Resembles a darker-coloured 'Royalist' with a more widely expanded corona

'Final Curtain' 3 W-GYY
(Mary Lou Gripshover, 1980) Mary Lou Gripshover, 1995
'Grace Note' open pollinated; sdlg no. 73-36-7
Fl. forming a double triangle, 72 mm wide; perianth segments broadly ovate, blunt or truncate, only very slightly mucronate, pure white, slightly reflexed, with margins incurved, overlapping half; the inner segments shouldered at base, more strongly reflexed, with margins wavy or incurling; corona very short cup-shaped, ribbed, yellow, with green at base, frilled, with rim dentate. Very late

'Finale' 3 W-? (b)
(G.H. Furness, pre-1949)

'Finality' 1 Y-Y
(pre-1927)
Fl. golden yellow

'Finality' 9 W-YYR
(G.H. Engleheart, pre-1930)
Perianth segments slightly reflexed; corona yellow, with red at rim. AM(c) 1929

'Finch' 7 Y-O
(G.E. Mitsch, 1954) G.E. Mitsch, 1966
'Narvik' × *N. jonquilla*
Fl. 76 mm wide; perianth segments clear yellow; corona bright orange. Mid-season. Resembles a larger and taller 'Kinglet' usually with one flower stem

'Fincham' 2 Y-? (a)
(R.H. Bath, pre-1931)

'Finchcocks' 2 Y-R
(N.A. Burr) N.A. Burr, 1986
Perianth segments broadly ovate, blunt, yellow, with slight white mucro, spreading, overlapping one-third to a half; the inner segments with margins recurved at base; corona funnel-shaped, very broadly ribbed, orange-red, loosely frilled, with rim notched. Early

'Fincool' 1 W-W
(Ballydorn Bulb Farm) Ballydorn Bulb Farm, 1965
'Broughshane' hybrid
Fl. of good substance; perianth segments broadly ovate, pure white; corona widely expanded, opening pale creamy white, becoming white. Tall. Mid-season.

'Find' 1 W-Y
(P. Phillips) P. Phillips, 1964
Fl. 102 mm wide; corona pale creamy yellow. Mid-season

'Findhorn' 1 W-Y
(The Brodie of Brodie, *c*.1911)
'Madame de Graaff' × 'Lady Margaret Boscawen'

'Findon' 3 W-? (b)
(Sir F.C. Stern, pre-1946)

'Fine Art' 2 Y-O
(J.A. Morris) J.A. Morris, 1957

'Fine Fashion' 2 Y-YYR
(D.S. Bell) D.S. Bell, 1968
'Burgundy' × 'Encore'
Corona with broad and sharply defined band of red at rim

'Fine Gold' 1 Y-Y
(G.L. Wilson, pre-1946)
'Fahan' × 'Golden Melody'
Fl. golden yellow; corona mouth expanded

'Finella' 3 W-Y
(Barr & Sons, pre-1907)
Perianth segments snowy white, spreading; corona ribbed, bright lemon yellow. Tall. Late

'Fine Romance' 2 W-WPP
(A.J.R. Pearson) A.J.R. Pearson, 1991
'Stoke Charity' × 'Romance'; sdlg no. 87-50-J33
Fl. 95 mm wide; perianth segments very broad in out-

line, rounded at apex, spreading, plane, smooth and of good substance, overlapping half or more; the inner segments roundish; corona cylindrical or somewhat funnel-shaped, bright rose pink, paling to pinkish white at base, with green noticeable in tube, shading to a darker tone of pink at rim, mouth lightly ribbed, straight or a little expanded, even, rim irregularly and very shallowly notched. Mid-season. Resembles 'Fragrant Rose' but with shorter perianth segments and longer corona

'Finery' 2 W-Y
(G.E. Mitsch) G.E. Mitsch, 1972
('Shirley Neale' × ['Shirley Wyness' × 'Pink-a-dell']) × 'Caro Nome'; sdlg no. Y53/1
Fl. rounded, 102 mm wide; corona very shallow bowl-shaped, pale lemon yellow, with shades of buff, frilled, with rim deeply incised

'Finespun' 2 Y-Y
(Cartwright & Goodwin, pre-1908)
Fl. rich deep yellow

'Finesse' 9 W-?
(G.H. Engleheart, pre-1930)

'Finestra' 2 W-R
(D.S. Bell) D.S. Bell, 1962
Fl. 102 mm wide. Late. Resembles an 'Artist's Model' with self coloured corona

'Fine Style' 2 W-W
(J.N.Hancock & Co., 1984) J.N.Hancock & Co., 1997
Sdlg 9/77H × 'Immaculate'; sdlg no. 26/84H
Fl. pure white; perianth segments broadly ovate, plane; corona funnel-shaped, smooth, with mouth slightly flared and rim crenate. Mid-season

'Fingal' 1 W-Y
(R.H. Bath, pre-1929)
Fl. 108 mm wide; perianth segments creamy white, overlapping half; corona brilliant yellow 9C. *AM(g) 1946

'Fingal's Cave' 2 Y-W
(Campbell Duncan) Campbell Duncan, 1956
'Fingal' × 'Binkie'
Perianth segments champagne yellow

'Finglas' 3 W-WWY
(G.L. Wilson) G.L. Wilson, 1956
'Portrush' × 'Green Island'
Corona white, with pale gold at rim

'Finishing Touch' 2 Y-O
(Konynenburg & Mark) Konynenburg & Mark, 1964
'Aranjuez' × ('Beauty of the Garden' × 'Hit Parade')
Fl. 115 mm wide; perianth segments pale yellow 11D;
corona brilliant orange 29A. Early

'Finisterre' 2 Y-? (a)
(A.M. Wilson, pre-1930)

'Finland' 2 W-Y
(R.V. Favell, pre-1940)
'Tunis' × 'Saint Just'
Perianth segments broadly ovate, blunt or slightly truncate, creamy white, very slightly inflexed, plane, overlapping one-third; the inner segments more narrowly ovate, slightly reflexed, occasionally twisted and with margins incurved; corona cylindrical, smooth, opening light lemon yellow, becoming primrose yellow, mouth expanded, with rim rolled and crenate. $2n=28$

'Finlandia' 1 W-Y
(G. Lewis) D.S. Bell, 1955
'Belle Keller' × 'Kanchenjunga'

'Fin Mac Cumhal' 2 W-Y
(Sir J.A.R. Gore-Booth, pre-1914)

'Finmacool' 2 W-W
(Ballydorn Bulb Farm) Ballydorn Bulb Farm, 1975
'Cortina' open pollinated
Fl. 125 mm wide. Early to mid-season

'Finn' 2 W-W
(C.E. Radcliff, 1933)
'Phyllida' × 'Buff Cup'

'Finnebrogue' 2 W-P
(Carncairn Daffodils) Carncairn Daffodils, 1971
'Broughshane' × Radcliffe sdlg
Fl. 110 mm wide; corona opening white, becoming flushed with pink

'Finola' 1 W-W
(G.L. Wilson) G.L. Wilson, 1957
'Dunluce' × ?'Broughshane'
Fl. ice white; corona with green at base, rim flanged

'Fintona' 2 W-P
(G.L. Wilson) G.L. Wilson, 1956
('Nautilus' × 'Lisbreen') × ('Suda' × 'Evening')
Corona opening pale chrome yellow, quickly becoming strong rosy pink

'Finvola' 3 W-? (b)
(G.L. Wilson, pre-1939)

'Fiona' 1 W-W
(E.M. Crosfield, pre-1907)

'Fiona' 2 W-W
(Mrs M. Moorby, pre-1946)

'Fiona' 2 W-P

(J.N. Hancock & Co., pre-1967) Unregistered
Perianth segments white, spreading, smooth; corona pink

'Fiona Jean' 7 Y-GYY
(G.E. Morrill) G.E. Morrill, 1979
'Fruit Cup' hybrid
Fls 1-2 or sometimes 3 per stem, 55 mm wide; perianth segments brilliant greenish yellow 6B; corona brilliant yellow 7A. Scented. Resembles a self yellow 'Fruit Cup'

'Fiona MacKillop' 2 W-Y
(Frank Verge) Frank Verge, 1987
'Empress of Ireland' hybrid
Perianth segments very broadly ovate, blunt or truncate, mucronate, smooth, overlapping half; the inner segments square-shouldered at base; corona cylindrical, smooth, vivid yellow, with mouth ribbed and flared, lightly frilled. Mid-season

'Fiona Macleod' 9 W-?
(J.R. Pearson & Sons, pre-1927)

'Fionn' 2 W-P
(J.S.B. Lea) J.S.B. Lea, 1962
Sdlg 2-34-49 × 'Rose Caprice'; sdlg no. 1-33-54
Fl. 102 mm wide. Late. Resembles 'Rose Caprice' and 'Debutante' but with broader perianth segments

'Fiorella' 3 W-YYO
(J.L. Richardson) Mrs H.K. Richardson, 1963
'Galilee' × 'Hamzali'
Perianth segments long, acute, pure white; corona disc-shaped, pale yellow, with reddish orange at rim. 2n=28

'Fire' 2 Y-O
(pre-1965) Unregistered
Perianth segments deep golden yellow, of good substance; corona scarlet-orange

'Fire Alarm' 2 Y-R
(W.G. Pannill) W.G. Pannill, 1972
'Vulcan' × 'Paricutin'
Fl. 97 mm wide

'Fire and Ice' 9 W-GGR
(Mrs M.S. Yerger) Mrs M.S. Yerger, 1991
'Felindre' open pollinated; sdlg no. 76 N 3
Dwarf. Very late

'Fireball' 3 W-R
(N.Y. Lower, pre-1907)
Perianth segments creamy white; corona disc-shaped, red

'Fireball' 2 Y-R
(D.S. Bell) D.S. Bell, 1980
('Sabre Dance' × 'Alemein') × 'Ashanti'

Fl. 100 mm wide; corona very shallow bowl-shaped, red. Mid-season. Resembles 'Ashanti' but with a narrower corona

'Fireball' 2 Y-R
(W.M. Spry, pre-1975) Unregistered
'Narvik' × 'Port Kembla'
Corona dark flame red

'Fire Ban' 2 Y-O
(J.N. Hancock & Co., 1963) Unregistered

'Firebell' 2 Y-O
(Alister Clark, c.1915) T. Morrison, 1960

'Firebird' 3 W-O
(Mrs F.S. Foote, pre-1940)

'Fireblaze' 2 Y-? (a)
(Mrs R.O. Backhouse, pre-1921)

'Firebrand' 3 WWY-R
(G.H. Engleheart, pre-1897)
'Princess Mary' × *N. radiiflorus* var. *poetarum*; sdlg no. 481
Fl. star-shaped; perianth segments ovate, acute, not prominently mucronate, creamy white, shaded lemon yellow at base, spreading or a little inflexed, with margins wavy and sometimes incurling, overlapping at base only; corona cup-shaped, ribbed, brilliant orange-red, with mouth straight and even, rim crenate. Mid-season. 2n=14

'Firebrand' 2 Y-?
Syn. of 'Moindah'

'Fire Brigade' 2 Y-YYR
(D.S. Bell) D.S. Bell, 1980
Sdlg 109 × 'Ceylon'
Fl. 110 mm wide; corona bowl-shaped. Resembles a brighter-coloured 'Ceylon'. Mid-season

'Firebubbles' 2 Y-O
(Mrs C.O. Fairbairn)

'Fire Chief' 2 Y-R
(G.E. Mitsch, pre-1954)
'Damson' × 'Fortune'; sdlg no. 38C19/2
Corona flared, brilliant orange-red. Mid-season. 2n=28

'Fire Chief' 2 Y-O
(G.L. Wilson, pre-1962)

'Firecracker' 2 Y-O
(J.L. Richardson, pre-1953)
'Narvik' × 'Ceylon'
Corona intense reddish orange, becoming fully coloured after some days, frilled

'Firecrest' 2 Y-R
(Sir C.H. Cave, pre-1907)
Perianth segments yellow; corona scarlet

'Firecrest' 2 Y-? (a)
(S.J. Bisdee, 1947)
'Dunkeld' × 'Red Mantle'

'Fire Crown' 2 Y-R
(C. Goodson, pre-1927)

'Firecrown' 2 Y-R
(J.N. Hancock & Co., pre-1974) Unregistered

'Firedance' 2 Y-R
(D.S. Bell) D.S. Bell, 1960
Fl. 115 mm wide. Early. Resembles 'Ceylon' but with the perianth segments more regularly arranged

'Fire Dart' 3 W-? (b)
(Sir C.H. Cave, pre-1913)

'Fire Dome' 2 W-YYO
(G.H. Engleheart, pre-1910)
Perianth segments creamy white, with a longitudinal band of sulphur yellow at midrib, reflexed, twisted; corona widely expanded, ribbed, brilliant yellow, shading to light light scarlet-orange at rim, frilled

'Fire Drake' 2 W-O
(R.V. Favell, pre-1946)
? × 'Hades'

'Firefall' 2 W-? (b)
(Oregon Bulb Farms, pre-1951)

'Fireflame' 2 Y-O
(Mrs R.O. Backhouse, pre-1908)
N. radiiflorus var. *poetarum* × *N. obvallaris*
Perianth segments rich yellow; corona straight, ribbed, fiery scarlet-orange. Early

'Fireflame' 2 Y-R
(G.E. Mitsch) G.E. Mitsch, 1976
'Firecracker' × 'Brer Fox'; sdlg no. F103/3
Fl. 100 mm wide; perianth segments intense gold; corona fiery red. Mid-season. Sunproof. Resembles a larger and taller 'Firecracker'

'Fire Flash' 2 O-O
(Mrs H.K. Richardson) Mrs H.K. Richardson, 1976
'Air Marshal' × 'Vulcan'
Fl. 90 mm wide, coppery orange; perianth segments broadly ovate; corona expanded. Mid-season

'Firefly' 3 W-? (b)
(Mrs R.O. Backhouse, pre-1894)

'Firefly' 2
(G.H.Engleheart, pre-1897)

'Firefly' 3 W-R
(L. Buckland, pre-1930)
Corona disc-shaped, red

'Firefly' 2 W-? (b)
(de Graaff Bros, pre-1931)
AM(Haarlem) 1930

'Fire Gleam' 2 Y-O
(G. Lewis, pre-1940)
See also 'Firegleam'

'Fire Gleam' 2 W-R
(de Graaff Bros, pre-1950)
AM(Haarlem) 1950, FCC(Haarlem) 1955

'Firegleam' 2 Y-O
Syn. of 'Fire Gleam'

'Fireglobe' 2 Y-? (a)
(de Graaff Bros, pre-1936)
AM(Haarlem) 1936

'Fireglow' 2 W-YYO
(Barr & Sons, pre-1900)
Fl. 89 mm wide, facing down; perianth segments pale sulphur, irregular, separated; corona funnel-shaped, lemon, shading to bright orange at rim. Mid-season to late. See also 'Fire Glow'

'Fireglow' 2 Y-O
(J.W.A. Lefeber) J.W.A. Lefeber, 1958
Perianth segments broadly ovate, blunt, prominently mucronate, pale yellow 11D, spreading, a little concave, somewhat creased, overlapping half; the inner segments slightly inflexed, more heavily creased and with margins wavy; corona bowl-shaped, strong orange 25A, with mouth loosely and regularly frilled

'Fire Glow' 2 W-YYO
Syn. of 'Fireglow'

'Fire-god' 2 Y-? (a)
(Mrs P.M. Davis, pre-1948)

'Fire Grenade' 3 Y-? (a)
(P.D. Williams, pre-1910)

'Fire Grenade' 2 W-O
(pre-1911)

'Fire Guard' 2 Y-O
(G.L. Wilson, pre-1944)
'Carbineer' × 'Rosslare'
Fl. of great substance; perianth segments golden yellow; corona reddish orange. Late

'Firehills' 2 Y-O
(N.A. Burr) N.A. Burr, 1991
Lea sdlg 1-18-66 × 'Loch Hope'; sdlg no. 1.9.80

Fl. forming a double triangle, 93 mm wide; perianth segments broadly ovate, blunt, only very slightly mucronate, vivid yellow 9A, spreading, plane, smooth, regular, overlapping one-third to a half; corona funnel-shaped, smooth or loosely ribbed, vivid orange 28B, mouth 6-lobed, straight, wavy, with rim entire. Early. Sunproof

'Fire Island' 2 Y-O
(J.L. Richardson) J.L. Richardson, 1958
'Hong Kong' × 'Ceylon'
Perianth segments deep gold; corona somewhat expanded, reddish orange

'Fire King' 3 Y-? (a)
(R.H. Bath, pre-1908)

'Fire King' 2 W-R
(Australian or New Zealand origin, pre-1927)
Perianth segmens overlapping; corona large, red

'Fireking' 2 Y-R
(Mrs C.O. Fairbairn)

'Firelight' 2 Y-YYO
(Mrs R.O. Backhouse, pre-1903)
N. poeticus × *N. obvallaris*
Fl. 73 mm wide, facing down; perianth segments pale bright lemon, with margins incurved, irregular, separated; corona funnel-shaped, lemon, with a broad band of reddish orange at rim. Mid-season. AM 1903

'Fire Lily' 3 Y-? (a)
(Cartwright & Goodwin, pre-1916)

'Fireman' 3 W-? (b)
(W. Balch, pre-1933)

'Fireman' 2 O-O
(Carncairn Daffodils) Carncairn Daffodils, 1982
'Vulcan' × 'Spelter'; sdlg no. W24/2
Fl. 90 mm wide; perianth segments opening light orange (21A), becoming strong orange 24A; corona vivid orange 28B. Mid-season

'Firemaster' 2 Y-O
(J.L. Richardson, pre-1948)
'Zariba' open pollinated
Fl. 102 mm wide; perianth segments very broadly ovate, rounded at apex, vivid yellow 12A, flat, smooth, overlapping half; the inner segments narrower and roundish; corona chalice-shaped, mouth straight, slightly expanded, closely ribbed and tightly ribbed. AM(e) 1950

'Firemist' 2 O-O
(Colin Crotty) Unregistered
Sdlg no. 18-76

'Firenze' 4 W-Y
(W.F.M. Copeland, pre-1910)
Perianth and other petaloid segments white; the outer whorl broadly ovate, blunt, mucronate, spreading, with margins slightly wavy, overlapping one-third; the inner whorl narrower, not noticeably mucronate, inflexed, with margins more strongly wavy; corona segments less than half the length and forming an almost continuous whorl between the outer and inner whorls, with many additional segments clustered at centre, lemon, frilled

'Fire Opal' 2 W-? (b)
(Mrs R.S. Cobley, pre-1937)

'Fireproof' 2 Y-O
(G.L. Wilson, pre-1952)
('Sunproof Orange' × 'Trevisky') × 'Rustom Pasha'
Fl. 95 mm wide; perianth segments vivid yellow 9B, overlapping half; corona long, ribbed, strong orange 25A, mouth slightly expanded, frilled, with rim dentate and slightly flanged. *HC(g) 1959

'Fire Queen' 3 W-YYR
(C.G. van Tubergen, pre-1909)
Perianth segments broadly ovate, prominently mucronate, snowy white, spreading or a little reflexed, somewhat ribbed, overlapping one-third; the inner segments narrower, more usually spreading, with margins sometimes recurved in lower half; corona bowl-shaped, ribbed, rich orange-yellow, with a band of fiery red at rim

'Fire Raiser' 2 O-O
(Carncairn Daffodils) Carncairn Daffodils, 1981
'Vulcan' × 'Spelter'; sdlg no. 1/75/OR
Fl. 76 mm wide; perianth segments light orange (23B); corona vivid orange 28B. Mid-season

'Fire Rim' 2 W-GYR
(G.E. Mitsch and R. & E.Havens) Grant Mitsch Novelty Daffodils, 1984
'Tigard' × 'Snow Gem'; sdlg no. 2H95/3
Fl. 87 mm wide; perianth segments pure white; corona clear yellow, with a band of orane-red at rim. Mid-season. Resembles an earlier-flowered and somewhat larger 'Snowgem'

'Fire Rocket' 2 W-O
(J.L. Richardson) Mrs H.K. Richardson, 1967
'Kilworth' × 'Avenger'
Fl. 97 mm wide; perianth segments broadly ovate; corona reddish orange, dentate. Mid-season. Resembles 'Rameses'

'Fireside' 2 Y-?
(A. Overton) A. Overton, 1960

'Fire Song' 3 W-O
(W.G. Pannill) W.G. Pannill, 1982
'Enniskillen' × 'Hotspur'; sdlg no. 64/45A

Fl. 95 mm wide. Mid-season

'Fire Spark' 2 Y-R
(C. Goodson, pre-1927)

'Firestar' 2 W-P
(R. & E.Havens) R. & E.Havens, 1994
'Pink Valentine' × 'Pink Flame'; sdlg no. VH20/4
Fl. 80 mm wide; perianth segments ovate or somewhat roundish; corona very shallow bowl-shaped, pinkish lavender at base, shading to reddish pink at rim, heavily frilled. Late. Sunproof

'Firestone' 2 Y-? (a)
(de Graaff Bros, pre-1940)
AM(Haarlem) 1940

'Firestorm' 2 Y-R
(Ballydorn Bulb Farm) Ballydorn Bulb Farm, 1979
'Vulcan' open pollinated
Fl. 110 mm wide. Mid-season. Resembles a sunproof and more brightly coloured 'Vulcan'

'Firestreak' 11b W-R/OW
(J.W.A. Lefeber) J.J. Grullemans & Sons, 1959
Perianth segments very broad, blunt, prominently mucronate, spreading, overlapping half; the inner segments only very slightly mucronate, sometimes truncate; corona split, the six segments half as long as the perianth segments and alternate to them, broadly ovate, usually orange-red at base and in longitudinal bands at midrib and margins, paling to yellow-orange at apex and shoulder, with white at margins towards apex, spreading or a little inflexed, with margins wavy and sometimes incurling, overlapping, sometimes with a shallow "thumb" at margin at shoulder. Corona colour variable

'Firetail' 3 W-R
(E.M. Crosfield, pre-1910)
'Mrs C.Bowley' hybrid
Perianth segments broadly ovate, blunt, prominently mucronate, creamy white, spreading, plane, somewhat ribbed, regular, overlapping one-third to a half; the inner segments more narrowly ovate, only very slightly mucronate; corona small, very shallow bowl-shaped, closely ribbed, brilliant deep orange-red. 2n=21. AM 1920, FCC(e) 1922, AM(Haarlem) 1924, FCC(Haarlem) 1925

'Firewater' 3 W-YYO
(The Brodie of Brodie, c.1937)
'Nelly' × 'Hades'; sdlg no. 147/A/32
Perianth segments pure white, with margins slightly incurved; corona citron yellow, with deep reddish orange at rim

'Firework' 2 Y-O
(G.H. Johnstone, pre-1946)
'Marksman' hybrid

'Firgrove' 3 W-YYR
(Carncairn Daffodils) Carncairn Daffodils, 1971
'Matapan' × 'Tulyar'
Fl. 75 mm wide. Resembles 'Merlin' but with a slightly wider band of red at corona rim

'First Blush' 2 W-?P
(Alister Clark, 1919) J. Sharp, 1960

'First Born' 6 YYW-GYP
(John R.Reed) John R.Reed, 1995
'Milestone' × 'Foundling'; sdlg no. 81-60-1
Fl. 71 mm wide; perianth segments broadly ovate, honey yellow, reflexed, plane; corona funnel-shaped, honey yellow, with green at base and light reddish pink in upper half. Mid-season. Sunproof

'First Class' 3 W-OOY
(W.G.Pannill) W.G.Pannill, 1994
'Artist's Model' × 'Avenger'; sdlg no. 66/80A
Corona orange and yellow. Mid-season to late

'First Dance' 11a Y-Y
(Jānis Rukšans) Jānis Rukšans, 1997
'Obelisk' × 'Jumbo Gold'; sdlg no. 85-57-2
Fl. 115 mm wide; perianth segments vivid yellow 9A, spreading, overlapping; corona deeply split, the six segments opposite and closely overlying the perianth segments, slightly darker in tone (between 12A and 13A), frilled. Early. Resembles a taller and stronger-stemmed 'Obelisk' of deeper colour

'First Date' 3 W-Y
(Carncairn Daffodils) Carncairn Daffodils, 1982
'Tryst' × 'Portrush'; sdlg no. 3/146/60
Fl. 90 mm wide; perianth segments greenish white (155A); corona brilliant greenish yellow 6A, with rim dentate. Late

'First Fiddle' 2 W-P
(J.N. Hancock & Co., 1945) J.N. Hancock & Co., 1965
Perianth segments overlapping; corona pinkish amber, frilled

'First Formal' 3 W-YWP
(T.D. Throckmorton) T.D. Throckmorton, 1974
'Aircastle' × 'Gossamer'; sdlg no. T66/21/1
Fl. 110 mm wide; perianth segments very broad, blunt, slightly mucronate, spreading, sometimes concave at apex, overlapping more than half; the inner segments a little narrower, somewhat twisted; corona very shallow bowl-shaped, broad, ribbed, yellowish white, with pale yellow at base and a narrow band of orange-pink at rim, mouth deeply split in places and overlapping, frilled, rim minutely dentate. Mid-season. Resembles 'Aircastle' but with a pink rim to the corona

'First Frost' 2 W-W

(J.N. Hancock & Co., 1945) E.W.Philpott, 1959
Fl. forming a double triangle; perianth segments broadly ovate, blunt, slightly mucronate, a little inflexed, overlapping half; the inner segments more narrowly ovate, square-shouldered at base, more strongly inflexed, with margins wavy; corona cylindrical, narrow, very lightly ribbed, yellow-white, mouth straight, even or a little wavy, rim irregularly and shallowly crenate. Mid-season

'First Hope' 6 Y-Y
(Rosewarne EHS) Cornwall Area Bulb Growers Association, 1985
'Jana' × 'Rijnveld's Early Sensation'; sdlg no. 65-38-1
Perianth segments bright lemon yellow; corona darker in tone, with rim flecked white in places. Very early. Trade designation JANUARY GOLD

'First Impression' 2 Y-R
(Grant E. Mitsch, 1981) R. & E. Havens, 1994
('Chemawa' × 'Brer Fox') × 'Loch Hope; sdlg no. 2Q15/10
Fl. 95 mm wide, of heavy substance; perianth segments broadly ovate, bright golden yellow; corona bowl-shaped, deep orange-red. Early. Sunproof

'First Kiss' 6 Y-Y
(Mrs G. Link) Mrs G. Link, 1992
'Mite' × *N. cyclamineus*; sdlg no. 3379
Fl. 38 mm wide, clear deep yellow; perianth segments somewhat narrow, reflexed. Very early. Weatherproof

'First Lady' 11b W-R/W
(J.W.A. Lefeber) J.W.A. Lefeber, 1960
Fl. 58 mm wide; perianth segments broadly ovate, creased, overlapping one-third to a half; corona deeply split, the six segments about half as long as the perianth segments and alternate to them, strong red, with white at margins, spreading. Mid-season. Syn. 'Moulin Rouge'

'First Lady' 1 W-P
(J.N. Hancock & Co., 1965) Unregistered

'First Light' 1 Y-O
(R. Hyde) R. Hyde, 1957
Gibson sdlg × 'Krakatoa'
Perianth segments broad; corona mouth widely expanded

'First Love' 2 W-P
(S.A. Free) S.A. Free, 1961
Fl. 102 mm wide. Early

'First Snow' 2 W-W
(M.E.Brogden, pre-1996) Unregistered
'Guiding Light' × 'Silver Convention'; sdlg no. 263/3

'First Step' 6 W-O

(John R.Reed, 1987) John R.Reed, 1997
'Kilworth' × 'Dove Wings' hybrid; sdlg no. 81-23-1
Fl. 75 mm wide; perianth segments obovate, reflexed; corona cup-shaped, strong orange, paling in lower quarter towards base. Dwarf. Late. Sunproof

'First Tango' 11a W-WWY
(Jānis Rukšans) Jānis Rukšans, 1997
'Bit o' Gold' × 'Fresco'; sdlg no. 85-18-1
Fl. 100 mm wide; perianth segments pure white, spreading, smooth, overlapping; corona segments opposite and closely overlying the perianth segments, white, with greenish tones at base, a distinct band of brilliant greenish yellow 3B at rim becoming paler (3C) with age. Early. Resembles a taller 'Goldband' with greater colour contrast

'First Waltz' 11a W-WWY
(Jānis Rukšans) Jānis Rukšans, 1997
Gerritsen sdlg 729 × 'Egard'; sdlg no. 85-25-1
Fl. 115 mm wide; perianth segments acute, pure white, regular; corona segments shorter than the perianth segments, opposite and closely overlying them, creamy white, touched brilliant greenish yellow 1A-B at base, with an indistinct narrow band of creamy yellow (4C) at rim becoming paler with age, frilled. Early

'Firvale' 1 Y-Y
(F.E. Board) F.E. Board, 1965
'Cloncarrig' × 'Prince Igor'; sdlg no. 544
Late

'Fisherman' 2 W-P
(Alister Clark, 1935) R.A. Dunn, 1960

'Fisherwick' 3 W-GWW
(W.J. Dunlop) W.J. Dunlop, 1963
'Downhill' × ('Portrush' × 'Chinese White')
Fl. white; corona very shallow bowl-shaped, with a touch of green at base

'Fistral' 1 Y-W
(J.N. Hancock & Co., 1976) Unregistered
Sdlg no. 72/76H

N. fistulosus Schultes = *N. tazetta*

'Fitzjames' 2 W-Y
(W. Backhouse, pre-1869)
Perianth segments creamy white; corona expanded. Syn. Incomparabilis Albidus 'Fitzjames'. Was "absorbed" into 'Princess Mary'

'Fitz Richard' 1 Y-Y
(R. Freer, pre-1916)

'Fitzwater's Green' 3 W-GGY
(Mrs C.E. Fitzwater) Mrs C.E. Fitzwater, 1973
'Bithynia' × 'Portrush'

Fl. 70 mm wide

'Five Ashes' 2 W-W
(N.A.Burr) N.A.Burr, 1997
'Broomhill' × 'White Star'; sdlg no. 3.21.80
Fl. 118 mm wide; perianth segments very broadly ovate, blunt, mucronate, spreading, slightly concave in upper half, sometimes creased, overlapping half; the outer segments touched grey-green at base; the inner segments slightly inflexed at base and reflexed at apex, with margins wavy; corona funnel-shaped, very lightly ribbed, with mouth even, rim slightly flanged and obscurely crenate. Mid-season

'Fix' 8
(J.W.A. Lefeber) J.W.A. Lefeber, 1943

'Fixit' 2 W-R
(P. & G. Phillips) P. & G. Phillips, 1979
Fl. 85 mm wide. Mid-season

'Flag' 2 Y-? (a)
(A.M. Wilson, pre-1944)

'Flag of Truce' 5 W-W
(G.H. Engleheart, pre-1904)
AM 1904

'Flag of Truce'
(A.E. Lowe, pre-1925)

'Flag Ship' 2 W-P
(W.G.Pannill, 1976) W.G.Pannill, 1996
'Salome' × 'High Tea'; sdlg no. 70/23
Mid-season

'Flagstaff' 1 Y-Y
(F.H. Chapman, pre-1918)
Tall

'Flair' 2 W-YYP
(G.A. Challies) G.A. Challies, 1976
Fl. 100 mm wide; corona primrose, with pink at rim. Mid-season. Resembles 'Coral Ribbon' but with the corona of different form

'Flamante' 1 Y-Y
(Oregon Bulb Farms, pre-1951)

'Flambard' 2 W-? (b)
(H. Backhouse, pre-1908)

'Flambeau' 2 Y-O
(G.H. Engleheart, pre-1899)
Perianth segments yellow; corona golden orange. AM 1899

'Flambent' 3 W-? (b)
(W.B. Cranfield, pre-1930)

'Flamborough' 2 Y-YYR
(S.C. Gaspar) S.C. Gaspar, 1955
Perianth segments deep yellow, of thick substance; corona golden yellow, with red at rim

'Flamboyant' 2 Y-O
(Mrs R.O. Backhouse, pre-1921)
Perianth segments dark primrose yellow; corona scarlet-orange, heavily frilled

'Flamboyant' 2 Y-O
(J.L. Richardson) Mrs H.K. Richardson, 1963
'Air Marshal' × 'Vulcan'
Fl. 95 mm wide; perianth segments very broadly ovate, blunt, slightly mucronate, vivid yellow 13A, with an orange tinge most noticeable at the overlap of the segments, slightly inflexed, a little concave, smooth, with broad midrib sometimes showing, regular, overlapping half; the inner segments more narrowly ovate, rounded at base; corona cup-shaped, smooth, orange, with mouth a little expanded, rim notched, crenate, slighty flanged. Syn. 'Tangerine'. AM(e) 1966

'Flamboyant' 3 W-?
Syn. of 'Alan'

'Flame' 3 W-? (b)
(G.H. Engleheart, pre-1913)

'Flame' 3 Y-O
Syn. of 'Bath's Flame'

'Flamenco' 2 W-O
(J.L. Richardson, pre-1935)
'Hospodar' × 'Sunstar'
Fl. 102 mm wide; perianth segments very broad, blunt or truncate, prominently mucronate, creamy white, spreading, overlapping half; the inner segments broadly ovate, angled at shoulder, a little inflexed, with margins wavy; corona broad disc-shaped, loosely ribbed, strong orange 24A, with mouth irregularly frilled. Mid-season. Sunproof. 2n=28. *AM(g) 1949, *FCC(g) 1952

'Flame Opal' 2 W-WWR
(Colin Crotty) Colin Crotty, 1992
'Debutante' open pollinated
Fl. 96 mm wide; perianth segments roundish, strong white, smooth, overlapping; corona bowl-shaped, white, with a very broad band of deep pink-red at rim and the rim slightly dentate. Mid-season

'Flaminaire' 2 W-O
(J.L. Richardson) Mrs H.K. Richardson, 1964
'Kilworth' × 'Matapan'
Perianth segments rounded, pure white, deeply overlapping; corona very shallow bowl-shaped, reddish orange

'Flaming Halo' 2 W-? (b)
(S.S. Berry, pre-1937)
Syn. 'Wedding Ring'

'Flaming Heart' 2 W-? (b)
(F.H. Chapman, pre-1931)

'Flaming Jewel' 3 W-R
(D.S. Bell) D.S. Bell, 1975
'Masquerade' × 'Arbar'
Fl. 92 mm wide. Mid-season

'Flaming Meteor' 2 Y-R
(G.E. Mitsch) G.E. Mitsch, 1962
'Armada' × 'Ceylon'; sdlg no. R4/1
Fl. 127 mm wide; perianth segments clear deep yellow; corona orange-red. Early. Resembles a larger-flowered 'Ceylon'

'Flaming Morn' 2 Y-? (a)
(J.L. Richardson, pre-1938)

'Flamingo' 2 Y-R
(G.H. Engleheart, pre-1907)
Corona scarlet

'Flamingo' 2 W-P
(G.E. Mitsch) G.E. Mitsch, 1958
'Coralie' × 'Dawnglow'; sdlg no. O16/1
Perianth segments overlapping; corona flared, deep pink. Mid-season

'Flaming Spring' 2 Y-O
(J.L. Richardson) Mrs H.K. Richardson, 1967
'Patagonia' × 'Firecracker'
Fl. 90 mm wide; perianth segments deep golden yellow; corona rich reddish orange. Mid-season

'Flaming Star' 2 Y-? (a)
(Mrs R.O. Backhouse, pre-1921)

'Flaming Sun' 2 Y-? (a)
(L. van Leeuwen & Son, pre-1948)

'Flaming Sword' 3 W-ORR
(Mrs R.O. Backhouse, pre-1921)
Perianth segments creamy white; corona brick red, paling to golden orange at base

'Flaming Torch' 2 Y-O
(Mrs R.O. Backhouse, pre-1921)
'Ladybird' hybrid
Perianth segments rich golden yellow; corona bright reddish orange. AM(Haarlem) 1931

'Flammarion' 3 W-? (b)
(J.W.A. Lefeber, pre-1941)

'Flamwen' 2 Y-O
(W. Jackson Sr, 1930)
'Pink'un' × 'Warflame'
Perianth segments sulphur; corona small, reddish orange

'Flan' 2 Y-R
(W. Jackson Jr, 1952)
'Kai' × 'Kalit'

'Flandria' 2 W-? (b)
(Mrs R.O. Backhouse, pre-1921)

'Flaneur' 11a Y-Y
(J. Gerritsen & Son, 1948) J. Gerritsen & Son, 1959
Fl. 90 mm wide; perianth segments sulphur yellow; corona segments deep yellow. Early. 2n=28

'Flap Jack' 2 Y-R
(J.N. Hancock & Co., c.1983) Unregistered

'Flare' 9 W-?
(F.H. Chapman, pre-1928)
'Bloodstain' × 'Ecstasy'

'Flare' 3 Y-? (a)
(E. & J.C. Martin, pre-1930)

'Flare Path' 2 W-? (b)
(G.H. Johnstone, pre-1944)

'Flash' 2 Y-? (a)
(G.H. Engleheart, pre-1916)

'Flash' 2 Y-? (a)
(Barr & Sons) Wallace & Barr, 1957

'Flash' 2 Y-O
(O. Ronalds, pre-1956) Unregistered
Perianth segments yellow; corona reddish orange

'Flash Affair' 2 W-Y
(R.H. Glover) R.H. Glover, 1973
'Lady Slim' × 'Easter Moon'
Fl. 102 mm wide

'Flashback' 6 Y-Y
(Brian S. Duncan) Brian S. Duncan, 1992
N. cyclamineus open pollinated; sdlg no. 1098
Fl. 70 mm wide, yellow; perianth segments narrowly ovate, acute, yellow, with white mucro, strongly reflexed, concave, overlapping at base only; corona cylindrical, constricted near mouth, lightly ribbed, slightly darker in tone than the perianth, with mouth flared and rim deeply notched. Dwarf. Very early. Resembles a larger and more robust *N. cyclamineus*

'Flash Harry' 2 Y-O
(J.N.Hancock & Co., 1982) Unregistered
'Ablaze' × 'Redeem'; sdlg no. 64/82H
Perianth segments overlapping; corona bright orange. Tall. Mid-season. Sunproof

'Flashlight' 3 W-? (b)
(C. Dawson, pre-1914)
Resembles 'Dorothy'

'Flashlight' 2 Y-? (a)
(S.C. Gaspar, 1946) R.J. Abernethy, 1957

'Flash Lightning' 2 Y-R
(C. Goodson, pre-1927)
'Tamerlane' × 'Gloria Mundi'
Perianth segments rich yellow; corona red, frilled. Resembles 'Killigrew'. AM(e)(NZ) 1927, FCC(e)(NZ) 1931

'Flattery' 7 Y-Y
(P.D. Williams, pre-1913)
Fl. yellow; corona large, slightly darker in tone than the perianth, with mouth widely expanded

'Flava' 2 Y-Y
(G.L. Wilson, pre-1927)
'Leontes' hybrid
Fl. clear rich yellow

N. flaveolus Spach = *N. aureus*

flavescens = *N. elegans* var. *flavescens*

'Flavia' 8 Y-Y
(pre-1798)
Fl. pale yellow

'Flavian' 1 Y-Y
(L. van Leeuwen & Son, pre-1931)
Syn. 'Aurore'

'Flavinius' 5
(C.G. van Tubergen, pre-1945)

N. flavus Lagasca & Segura = *N. jonquilla*

'Fledgling' ?-P
(Alister Clark, pre-1948)

'Fledgling' 7 Y-Y
(*c*.1978) Unregistered
N. jonquilla or *N. assoanus* × *N. rupicola*

'Fleetwing' 2 W-Y
(J.C. Williams, pre-1907)
Perianth segments pure white; corona primrose yellow

'Fleetwood' 1 Y-W
(J.N.Hancock & Co., 1983) Unregistered
'Moonstruck' × 'Daydream'; sdlg no. 82/83H
Perianth segments sulphur yellow, of good substance; corona cylindrical, opening citron yellow, becoming white, with mouth straight, rim rolled and dentate. Tall. Early to mid-season

'Fleur' 3 W-O
(Mrs R.O. Backhouse, pre-1921)
Perianth segments pure white, overlapping; corona disc-shaped, reddish orange. AM(Haarlem) 1927

'Fleur de Lys' 5
(Cartwright & Goodwin, pre-1908)

'Fleurimont' 3 W-O
(de Graaff Bros, pre-1939)
Corona deep orange. AM(Haarlem) 1939

'Fleurimont' 2 Y-YYR
(P.D. Williams, pre-1948)
AM(Haarlem) 1948, FCC(Haarlem) 1950

'Fleurs d'Oranger' 2 Y-? (a)
(P. van Deursen, pre-1930)

'Flevo' 1 Y-Y
(J. Gerritsen & Son, pre-1954)

N. flexiflorus Spach = *N. tazetta* subsp. *lacticolor*

'Flicka' 3 Y-? (a)
(A.M. Wilson, pre-1948)

'Flickering Light' 9 W-GGR
(Mrs M.S. Yerger) Mrs M.S. Yerger, 1991
'Praecox Grandiflorus' × 'Lights Out'; sdlg no. 75 N 4
Fl. 60 mm wide; corona strong yellow-green 144C, with a paler tone (145A) at base and orange-red (30A) at rim. Mid-season

'Flight' 2 W-GWW
(T.D. Throckmorton) T.D. Throckmorton, 1977
'Easter Moon' × 'Irish Coffee'; sdlg no. T66/3/2
Fl. 86 mm wide; corona opening soft fawn, gradually becoming whiter than the perianth, with greenish tones at base. Late

'Flintstone' 3 W-? (b)
(G.H. Engleheart, pre-1923)

'Flippant' 2 W-? (b)
(G.H. Johnstone, pre-1944)

'Flirt' 6 Y-Y
(Mrs H.K. Richardson) Carncairn Daffodils, 1985
'Jenny' self pollinated; sdlg no. R699
Fl. sulphur yellow. Mid-season

'Flirtation' 2 Y-R
(G. Lewis) D.S. Bell, 1955

'Flitfor' 2 Y-O
(C.A. Nethercote, 1950) T. Morrison, 1960
Perianth segments rich yellow; corona reddish orange, frilled

'Flitter' 2 W-O
(L. Buckland, pre-1936)

'Flomay' 7 W-WWP
(A. Gray, pre-1946)
N. rupicola subsp. *watieri* sdlg
Perianth segments broadly ovate, blunt, a little reflexed, overlapping; the inner segments somewhat twisted or with margins incurving; corona bowl-shaped, white, with a faint band of pink at rim. Dwarf. The corona sometimes more or less suffused pink

'Floodlit' 2 W-W
(J.N. Hancock & Co.) J.N. Hancock & Co., 1960
Corona opening with a touch of pink at rim, becoming self white

'Floore' 9 W-YYO
(Miss R. Thornton, pre-1939)
Perianth segments very broad in outline, blunt or squarish at apex, prominently mucronate, creamy white, tinged sulphur yellow at base, a little reflexed, overlapping half; the inner segments more nearly spreading, with margins recurved at base; corona small bowl-shaped, very shallow, ribbed, creamy sulphur yellow, with a narrow band of scarlet-orange at rim. Mid-season. 2n=28. Syn. 'Blanche'. *AM(g) 1939

'Flopper Newman' 2 YYW-WWY
(L.P. Dettman) L.P. Dettman, 1977
'Spellbinder' × 'Ellimatta'; sdlg no. 147/70
Fl. 122 mm wide; perianth segments light greenish yellow 4B, with a broad band of greenish white (155A) at base; corona greenish white 155C, with a band of brilliant greenish yellow 1B at rim and the dentate. Mid-season. Resembles a lighter-coloured 'Spellbinder' of better substance with the corona more widely expanded

'Flora' 3 W-Y
(E. Leeds, pre-1877)
Fl. facing down on opening; perianth segments broadly ovate, spreading, overlapping one-third; corona bowl-shaped, broad, lemon yellow, stained apricot yellow, with mouth wavy. Syn. Leedsii 'Flora', Leedsii 'Galanthiflorus'

'Flora' 3 W-Y
(Sir C.H. Cave, pre-1913)
?'Flora Wilson' × 'Lulworth'

'Floral Beauty' 2 Y-O
(J.W.A. Lefeber, 1948) J.W.A. Lefeber, 1960
Fl. 80 mm wide. Mid-season

'Floral Dance' 2 Y-? (a)
(M.P. Williams) V.M. Dickinson, 1955

'Floralie' 11a W-W

(J. Gerritsen & Son) J. Gerritsen & Son, 1963
Fl. 102 mm wide; perianth segments creamy white; corona segments opening creamy yellow, becoming white. Early. Resembles a larger and more refined 'Split'

'Flora MacDonald' 3 W-Y
(W. Backhouse, pre-1869)
Perianth segments large; corona canary yellow. Syn. Leedsii 'Flora MacDonald'. Was "absorbed" into 'Duchess of Westminster'

'Flora Ornatus'
(pre-1885)

'Flora's Beauty' 4 W-W
(C.A. van der Wereld, 1951) C.A. van der Wereld, 1961
Fl. 95 mm wide, greenish white. Mid-season. AM(Haarlem) 1961

'Flora's Favourite' 2 W-Y
(C.G. van Tubergen, pre-1944)
Perianth segments silver white; corona sulphur yellow. AM(Haarlem) 1944, FCC(Haarlem) 1949

'Flora Tristan' 2 Y-O
(J.W.A. Lefeber) W. Blom & Son, 1955
Perianth segments clear soft yellow; corona widely expanded, deep orange

'Flora Wilson' 3 W-YYR
(W. Backhouse, pre-1869)
Perianth segments large, pure white; corona canary yellow, with scarlet at rim. Syn. Barrii Albus 'Flora Wilson'

'Flore Multiplici' 4 W-W
Syn. of 'Romanus'

'Florence' 1 W-W
(G.H. Engleheart, pre-1901)
Sdlg no. 242
Fl. rounded; perianth segments ivory, twisted at apex; corona long, ivory maize. AM 1901

'Florence Austral' 1 W-Y
(W.M. Spry, pre-1975) Unregistered
'Dependable' × 'Big Keith'
Early

'Florence Barclay' 1 Y-Y
(G. Lubbe & Son, pre-1927)

'Florence Cook' 2 Y-O
(J.N. Hancock & Co., pre-1949)
Perianth segments pale yellow; corona light orange, frilled

'Florence Crimp' 3 W-? (b)

(J. Flemming, pre-1938)

'Florence Davey' 3 W-? (b)
(Mrs R.O. Backhouse, pre-1921)

'Florence Dettman' 1 W-W
(L.P. Dettman) L.P. Dettman, 1977
'Tablecloth' × 'Glenshesk'; sdlg no. 15/74
Fl. 93 mm wide; perianth segments greenish white 155C; corona yellowish white 155B. Mid-season. Resembles a much whiter 'Empress of Ireland'

'Florence Edna Foote' 2 W-? (b or c)
(G.H. Engleheart, pre-1931)

'Florence Joy' 2 W-W
(G.W.E. Brogden, 1980) Brogden Bulbs, 1991
'Guiding Light' × 'Verona' hybrid; sdlg no. x88/1
Fl. 105 mm wide, milk white; of good substance; perianth segments very broadly ovate, of good substance, very smooth, deeply overlapping; corona cup-shaped, with mouth straight, rim lightly dentate. Early to mid-season

'Florence Nightingale' 8 W-O
(?Barr & Sons, pre-1861)
Syn. 'Miss Nightingale'

'Florence Pearson' 1 W-W
(J.R. Pearson & Sons, pre-1902)
'Emperor' × 'Madame de Graaff'
Perianth segments broadly ovate, inflexed, creased, overlapping; the inner segments more strongly inflexed, with margins wavy or recurved; corona cylindrical, yellowish white, with mouth ribbed and widely expanded, rim dentate

'Florentia' 2 W-W
(L. van Leeuwen & Son, pre-1931)
Syn. 'Le Printemps'

'Florentian'
(C. Dawson, pre-1907)

'Florentina' 8 W-O
(pre-1846)

'Florentine Gold' 1 Y-Y
(D.N.Y. Olson, 1975) D.N.Y. Olson, 1988
'David Bell' × 'Highway'; sdlg no. 151/10
Corona narrow, frilled. Early. Resembles a more elegant 'Highway'

'Flore Pleno' 4 Y-Y
(pre-1611)
Variant of *N. jonquilla*
Perianth and other petaloid segments in numerous whorls of more or less equal length, ovate, acute, yellow, overlapping at base only; the outer whorl reflexed; the inner whorls inflexed; corona segments variably shorter than the petaloid segments and interspersed among them, darker in tone, inflexed. Syn. "Double Tags", "Queen Anne's Double Jonquil", "Queen Anne's Jonquil", 'Juncifolius Luteus Flore Pleno', Odorus 'Minor Plenus' (misapplied), Odorus 'Plenus' (misapplied)

'Flore Pleno' 4 W-YYR
Syn. of Poeticus 'Plenus'

'Flore Pleno' 4
Syn. Tazetta 'Flore Pleno'. FCC 1874. Name used at one time to cover any double variants of *N. tazetta*

'Florestan' 4 W-R
(D.A. Lloyd) D.A. Lloyd, 1962
'Matapan' hybrid
Fl. 76 mm wide; corona segments cherry red. Late. Resembles a more compact 'Acropolis' with paler corona segments

'Floria' 2 Y-? (a)
(G. Lubbe & Son, pre-1950)
AM(Haarlem) 1950

'Floriade' 2 Y-O
(Warnaar & Co.) Warnaar & Co., 1960
'Fortune' × 'Sempre Avanti'
Fl. 127 mm wide; perianth segments clear yellow; corona clear orange, with a darker tone at rim. Early

'Florian' 2 W-? (b or c)
(H. Mitchell, pre-1942)

'Floria Tosca' 1 Y-Y
(R.A. van der Schoot, pre-1930)

'Floribunda' 1 Y-Y
Syn. of 'Saragossa'

'Floribunda' 8 W-Y
Syn. of 'Grand Monarque'

N. floribundus Schultes = *N. tazetta* subsp. *lacticolor*

'Floribundus' 8 W-Y
Corona citron yellow. Syn. of 'Grand Monarque'

'Florida' 2 Y-? (a)
(Mrs R.O. Backhouse, pre-1921)
AM(Haarlem) 1931

'Florida Manor' 3 W-GYO
(Ballydorn Bulb Farm) Ballydorn Bulb Farm, 1979
'Clockface' hybrid
Fl. 100 mm wide. Late. Resembles 'Clockface' but with the bands of colour in the corona more clearly defined

"Florida White"
Syn. of 'Early Pearl'

'Florimel' 1 W-W
(W.A. Grace, pre-1936)

'Floriment'
Unregistered
In parentage of 'Lady's Desire'

'Florin' 3 W-? (b)
(G.H. Engleheart, pre-1907)

'Florinda' 2 Y-? (a)
(J.C. Williams, pre-1931)
Syn. 'Goldelse'

'Florinda' 2 W-R
(G. Lewis, pre-1962)

'Florissant' 2 W-YYW
(C.A. van der Wereld, pre-1953)
AM(Haarlem) 1953

'Floris Selina' 2 W-W
(J.A. Hunter) J.A. Hunter, 1963
Fl. 124 mm wide. Mid-season. Resembles 'Cletus' but with a shorter and smoother corona. PC(e)(NZ) 1962

'Florists' Delight' 1 Y-Y
(G.L. Wilson, pre-1923)
Corona with rim dentate and widely flanged. *HC(g) 1927

'Florists' Fancy' 2 W-YYO
(J.J. Abernethy) R.J. Abernethy, 1960
Fl. 115 mm wide; corona bright yellow, with clear orange at rim, frilled. Mid-season

'Florists' Favourite' 1 Y-Y
(G.H. Engleheart, pre-1914)
Fl deep rich yellow; perianth segments regular; corona lightly ribbed, with rim rolled and deeply and regularly notched

'Florizel' 3 W-YYO
(C. Dawson, pre-1912)
'Lulworth' × 'Horace'
Perianth segments creamy white, with cream at base, overlapping; corona expanded, ribbed, rich golden yellow, with a broad band of reddish orange at rim, deeply frilled

'Florizel' 3 W-YYO
(J.L. Richardson) Mrs H.K. Richardson, 1964
'Kilworth' × 'Tulyar'
Perianth segments broadly ovate; corona disc-shaped, yellow, shading to deep orange at rim

'Flosshilde' 2 Y-? (a)
(N.F. Lock, pre-1944)

'Flossie' 2 W-P
(J.N. Hancock & Co., 1957) Unregistered

'Flossie C.Cook' 3 W-O
(?Heathcote Bulb Nursery, pre-1961) Unregistered
Perianth segments smooth; corona widely expanded, reddish orange. Tall

'Flotina' 1 W-W
(W.A. Grace, pre-1936)

'Floton' 2 Y-O
(Konynenburg & Mark) Konynenburg & Mark, 1960
('Episode' × 'John Evelyn') × ('La Charmante' × 'John Evelyn')

'Flounce'
(pre-1914)

'Flounder' 2 Y-O
(Tom Forster, 1960s) Unregistered
Perianth segments soft yellow; corona closely overlying the perianth segments, vivid orange, ribbed. Tall. Mid-season to late

'Flourish' 2 W-O
(M.P. Williams, pre-1949)
Fl. of good substance; perianth segments ivory white; corona orange

'Flovette' 2 W-R
(J.S. Leitch) J.S. Leitch, 1956

'Flower Carpet' 1 Y-Y
(pre-1948)
Resembles 'King Alfred'

'Flowerdale' 2 W-? (b)
(C.E. Radcliff, pre-1938)
Sdlg × 'Portia'

'Flower Drift' 4 W-OYO
(C.A. van Paridon) C.A. van Paridon, 1966
'Flower Record' sport
Fl. 105 mm wide; perianth and other petaloid segments cream, flushed brilliant greenish yellow 6C at base; the outer whorl very broadly ovate, usually truncate, spreading, plane; the inner whorl inflexed, with margins recurved; corona brilliant yellow 7A, flushed orange (28A), mouth split in places and overlapping, tightly frilled; segments within the corona short, yellow. Early. 2n=28

'Flower Festival' 1 W-? (b)
(C.S. van Dobben de Bruyn Jr, pre-1953)

'Flowering Gold' 1 Y-Y
(J.A. O'More) J.A. O'More, 1968
?The same as 'Flowing Gold'

'Flower-Parade' 4 GGY-YOO
(Th. van der Hulst) Th. van der Hulst, 1991
'Flower Drift' × 'Tahiti'
Fl. 100 mm wide; perianth and other petaloid segments in several whorls, broadly ovate, blunt or truncate, slightly mucronate, light yellow-green 150D, with brilliant greenish yellow 3B at base; the outer whorl spreading or a little inflexed; the inner whorls successively more strongly inflexed, a little shorter, with margins wavy or incurved; the centre whorl strongly inflexed, with margins tightly incurled; corona segments very short, clustered among the petaloid segments at centre, broad, vivid orange 28B, with vivid yellow 14B at base, frilled. Mid-season. Sunproof

'Flower Power' 4 W-O
(Th. van der Hulst) Th. van der Hulst, 1991
'Flower Drift' × 'Acropolis'
Fl. 105 mm wide; perianth segments greenish white (155A); corona orange (28A) to vivid orange 28B. Mid-season. Sunproof

'Flower Record' 2 W-YYO
(J.W.A. Lefeber, pre-1943)
Perianth segments broadly ovate, mucronate, greenish white, tinged yellow at base, slightly inflexed, with margins incurling, overlapping one-third; corona cup-shaped, ribbed, yellow, with a broad band of orange at rim, mouth straight, closely frilled. Dwarf. Strongly scented. 2n=28. EFA(Haarlem) 1948

'Flowersong' 2 Y-YYO
(Warnaar & Co.) Warnaar & Co., 1960
'Aranjuez' × 'Westminster'
Fl. 115 mm wide; perianth segments brilliant greenish yellow 6B; corona vivid orange-yellow 21A, with strong orange 25A at rim. Mid-season. 2n=28. AM(Haarlem) 1960

'Flower Waltz' 6 Y-O
(G.E. Mitsch, 1973) R. & E. Havens, 1993
'Ardour' × *N. cyclamineus*; sdlg no. II122/1
Fl. 90 mm wide; perianth segments fairly broad, acute, bright mid-yellow, strongly reflexed, smooth; corona funnel-shaped, opening reddish orange, becoming mid-orange. Early. Sunproof. Syn. 'Vicksburg'

'Flower Wealth' 8
(A.C. van der Schoot, pre-1939)
Syn. 'Orange Queen'

'Flowing Bowl'
(A.E. Lowe, pre-1925)

'Flowing Gold' 1 Y-Y
(J.A.O'More, *c.*1968) Unregistered
'Kingscourt' × 'Bastion'
?The same as 'Flowering Gold'

'Fl. Pl. Aur. & Lut.' 4 Y-O
Syn. of 'Butter and Eggs'

'Flush' 2 W-P
(R.V. Favell, pre-1939)
'Avanley' × 'Rosario'

'Flush' 2 W-YPP
(S.J. Bisdee, 1945)
'Tunis' × 'Tenedos'
Fl. star-shaped; corona flushed pink

'Flushing' 1 W-W
(The Brodie of Brodie, pre-1930)
1W-W sdlg × 'Beersheba'

'Flute' 6 Y-Y
(A. Gray) A. Gray, 1957
'Tangra' × *N. cyclamineus*
Fl. deep yellow

'Flyaway' 12 Y-Y
(Roberta C.Watrous, 1950) Roberta C.Watrous, 1964
N. cyclamineus × *N. jonquilla*
Fls usually 3 per stem, golden yellow; perianth segments narrowly ovate or oblong, blunt, strongly reflexed, separated; corona short cylinder-shaped, smoothly angled, mouth straight, wavy, rim entire. Dwarf. Early. Scented

'Fly Beam' 2 W-P
(J.N. Hancock & Co.) J.N. Hancock & Co., 1955
Perianth segments broad, spreading, smooth; corona creamy pink

'Flycap' 6 Y-Y
(Mrs R.O. Backhouse, pre-1921)
Perianth segments opening canary yellow, becoming creamy yellow, reflexed; corona ribbed, canary yellow

'Flycatcher' 7 Y-Y
(G.E. Mitsch) G.E. Mitsch, 1970
('Playboy' × 'Firecracker') × *N. assoanus*; sdlg no. E38/1
Fls usually 2 per stem, rounded; perianth segments broadly ovate, blunt or truncate, clear yellow, spreading or a little reflexed, plane, overlapping half; the inner segments more nearly spreading, sometimes creased; corona short funnel-shaped, smooth, somewhat deeper in tone than the perianth, mouth straight, wavy, rim minutely crenate. Late

'Flyer' 11a Y-Y
(J. Gerritsen & Son) J. Gerritsen & Son, 1978
'Moonbird' hybrid
Fl. 95 mm wide; perianth segments broadly ovate, vivid yellow 9A, spreading, with margins irregularly and slightly notched, somewhat ribbed, overlapping; corona deeply split, the six segments whitish yellow,

with vivid yellow 9A at rim and margins and in tube, inflexed, overlapping, heavily frilled, with margins deeply and regularly notched. Mid-season

'Fly Half' 2 Y-R
(T. Bloomer) Rathowen Daffodils, 1984
('Ballintoy' × 'Air Marshal') × 'Shining Light'; sdlg no. 247
Fl. 105 mm wide; perianth deep golden yellow; corona deep orange-red. Mid-season

'Flying Cloud' 2 YYW-WWY
(D.N.Y. Olson) D.N.Y. Olson, 1990
Sdlg × 'Camelot'
Fl. forming a double triangle, 100 mm wide; perianth segments broadly ovate, blunt, prominently mucronate, medium bright yellow, with stronger yellow towards base and a well-defined band of white at base, spreading, plane, regular, overlapping one-third to a half; the inner segments slightly twisted, rounded at shoulder; corona cylindrical, white, with a very narrow band of golden yellow at rim, mouth a little expanded, rim shallowly notched and slightly rolled. Mid-season

'Flying High' 3 W-R
(Brogden Bulbs, pre-1996) Unregistered

'Flying Mist' 1 W-W
(G. Lewis, 1940) D.S. Bell, 1958

'Flying Nun' 3 W-W
(W.G. Pannill) W.G. Pannill, 1985
'Pristine' × *N. triandrus*
Fls 2-3 per stem. Mid-season

'Flying Saucer' 2 W-Y
(G.E. Mitsch, pre-1954)
'John Evelyn' × 'Fortune'
Perianth segments yellowish white; corona very shallow bowl-shaped, very large, light yellow. Mid-season

'F.Moore' 1 W-? (b)
Syn. of 'F.W.Moore'

'Foam' 3 W-? (b or c)
(N.Y. Lower, pre-1916)

'Foaming Seas' 1 W-W
(G.L. Wilson) Guy L.Wilson Ltd, 1963
('Nilkanta' × 'Murmansk') × ('Courage' × 'Zero')

'Focal Point' 2 Y-W
(G.E. Mitsch) G.E. Mitsch, 1972
'Rus Holland' × 'Entrancement'; sdlg no. Z35/1
Fl. 95 mm wide, becoming self white with age, facing up. Mid-season

'Focus' 2 Y-R
(G.W.E.Brogden, pre-1992) Unregistered
'Torridon' × 'Jetsetter'; sdlg no. x107/7

'Foeman' 1 Y-Y
(Mrs R.O. Backhouse, pre-1921)

'Foggy Dew' 3 W-GWW
(G.L. Wilson, pre-1941)
'Silver Plane' × 'Silver Coin' hybrid
Corona with deep sage green at base, frilled

'Foible' 4 W-Y
(W. Jackson Jr) Jackson's Daffodils, 1980
'Lawali' × 'Chimeon'; sdlg no. 4/74
Fl. 95 mm wide; corona segments pale yellow, slightly tinged pink. Mid-season

'Folio' 2 Y-Y
(Murray W. Evans, 1975) Murray W. Evans, 1986
'Bridal Rose' × 'Chiloquin'; sdlg no. S-7
Mid-season

foliosus = *N. cantabricus* var. *foliosus*

'Folk Lore' 1 W-P
(J.M. Radcliff, 1953) P. Phillips, 1966
Fl. 99 mm wide. Mid-season. Resembles 'Roseum' but with broader perianth segments and a more widely expanded corona

'Folk Song' 2 W-P
(J.S. Leitch) J.S. Leitch, 1966
Fl. 108 mm wide

'Folly' 2 W-O
(P.D. Williams, pre-1926)
Fl. 95 mm wide; perianth segments broadly ovate in outline, blunt or squarish at apex, prominently mucronate, creamy white, recurved, overlapping half; the inner segments more narrowly ovate, with margins wavy and incurved; corona bowl-shaped, ribbed, yellow-orange, shading to red-orange at rim, with mouth expanded and distinctly 6-lobed. Mid-season. Sunproof. 2n=28. AM(e) 1926, *FCC(g) 1936

'Fon' 1 Y-Y
(T.H. Piper, *c*.1966) Unregistered
'Goldbridge' × 'Melissa'

'Fondant' 2 W-Y
(J. Gerritsen & Son) J. Gerritsen & Son, 1967
'Alpine Glow' hybrid
Fl. 110 mm wide; perianth segments greenish white; corona pale orange-yellow. Mid-season

'Fond Memories' 2 W-P
(Tom Forster, 1960s) Unregistered
Perianth segments acute; corona clear apricot pink, frilled. Late

'Fontanalis' 2 W-P
(Alfred Clark) Alfred Clark, 1955
Perianth segments pure white; corona expanded, deep pink, frilled. PC(e)(NZ) 1951

'Fontmell' 1 W-Y
(R.C.A. Tombleson) R.C.A. Tombleson, 1966
'Preamble' hybrid
Fl. 108 mm wide; corona deep lemon yellow. Late. Resembles a later-flowered 'Preamble' with a deeper-toned and unfading corona

'Fontmell' 4 W-WWP
Syn. of 'Clouds Hill'

N. fontqueri Fernández Casas 13 Section Pseudonarcissus

'Fooklan' 2 Y-R
(A.O. Roblin, 1946) A.O. Roblin, 1956
'King of Hearts' × 'Lillian Murdoch'

'Fools Gold' 4 Y-WWY
(Carncairn Daffodils) Carncairn Daffodils, 1984
'Daydream' × 'Egg Nogg'; sdlg no. 3/74
Fl. 80 mm wide; corona segments opening lime yellow, becoming white, with gold at rim

'Footlight' 2 Y-? (a)
(Alister Clark, pre-1936)

'Foray' 2 W-WWP
(G.E. Mitsch, 1953) G.E. Mitsch, 1964
'Mabel Taylor' × 'Interim'; sdlg no. O49/4
Fl. 105 mm wide; corona large, pale yellow, with a broad band of rich orange salmon at rim. Mid-season. Resembles 'Rose Ribbon' but with a larger corona of darker tone. First distributed as 'Procession'

'Forber' 2 Y-? (a)
(E.C. Powell, pre-1946)
'Bernardino' × 'Fortune'

'Ford' 2 Y-Y
(West & Fell, pre-1938)
Perianth segments pale primrose; corona deep yellow, frilled

'Fordham' 1 W-? (b)
(R.H. Bath, pre-1933)

'Forecast' 3 W-? (b)
(F.H. Chapman, pre-1930)

'Foreland' 1 W-W
(F.H. Chapman, pre-1927)

'Forelli' 1 Y-Y
(Miss K.M. Hinchliff, pre-1937)

'Foremost' 2 W-YYO
(G.W.E. Brogden) G.W.E. Brogden, 1963
Corona with golden orange at rim. Late

'Forensic' 2 W-? (b)
(W.A. Bell, pre-1949)

'Forerunner' 1 Y-Y
(G.H. Engleheart, pre-1927)
Fl. 104 mm wide, of good substance; perianth segments fairly broadly ovate, brilliant greenish yellow 6B, spreading or a little inflexed, often twisted or with margins wavy and recurved, separated; corona funnel-shaped, vivid yellow 9A, paler at base, with mouth expanded and frilled, rim widely flanged and deeply and regularly notched. Very early. AM(c) 1930, *(Gulval)AM(m) 1934, *(Gulval)FCC(m) 1935

'Foresail' 9 W-?
(G.H. Engleheart, pre-1927)

'Forescate' 1 Y-Y
(J. Gerritsen & Son, pre-1951)

'Foresight'
(?F.A. Secrett, pre-1936)

'Foresight' 1 W-Y
(G.L. Wilson, pre-1944)
'Bonython' open pollinated
Fl. 100 mm wide; perianth segments very broadly ovate, blunt, milk or amber white, spreading, plane, sometimes a little concave at apex, smooth, overlapping half; the inner segments more narrowly ovate, a little twisted; corona widely angled, brilliant yellow 8A, lightly frilled, with rim dentate and neatly flanged. 2n=28. AM(e) 1945

'Forest Fire' 2 Y-O
(The Brodie of Brodie, c.1936)
'Invergordon' × ('Fortune' × 'Gulliver')
Resembles a larger and improved 'Porthilly'

'Forest Park' 2 W-W
(W.G. Pannill) W.G. Pannill, 1978
'Vigil' × 'Empress of Ireland'; sdlg no. 64/119 A
Fl. 130 mm wide. Mid-season

'Forestvale' 1 G-?
(W.M. Spry, pre-1975) Unregistered
'Brazil' × 'Clare'

'Forever Amber' 2 W-PPY
(Oregon Bulb Farms, pre-1946)

'Forfar' 3 W-O
(The Brodie of Brodie, pre-1930)
('Beacon' × 'Fortune') × 'Sunstar'
Perianth segments broadly ovate, rounded at apex, prominently mucronate, pale sulphury white,

spreading, smooth and of good substance, overlapping one-third to a half; the inner segments sometimes truncate, only very slightly mucronate, a little inflexed; corona broad and shallow bowl-shaped, loosely ribbed, reddish orange, mouth widely expanded, split in places and overlapping, lightly frilled. Mid-season to late. AM(e) 1932

'Forge' 3 W-? (b)
(G.H. Engleheart, pre-1907)

'Forgeman' 4 W-O
(L.T. Allen, 1977) L.T. Allen, 1992
'White Lion' × 'Rose Royale'; sdlg no. 1.5.72
Fl. 107 mm wide; perianth and other petaloid segments in four whorls decreasing in length towards centre, very broadly ovate, white, with margins incurling, overlapping half; the centre whorl with margins strongly incurled; corona segments opposite to and interspersed among the petaloid segments, brilliant orange-yellow 21B, touched white at margins, wavy or frilled. Early

'Forge Mill' 2 Y-GOO
(Carncairn Daffodils, 1976) Carncairn Daffodils, 1986
'Vulcan' × 'Spelter'; sdlg no. W24/8
Perianth segments rounded, vivid yellow 9A; corona straight, reddish orange. Mid-season

'Forgotten' 2 Y-Y
(J.M. Radcliff, 1981) D.J. & K.D. Radcliff, 1993
Sdlg no. 29/81
Fl. forming a double triangle, brilliant yellow 7B; perianth segments broadly ovate, blunt, with slight white mucro, spreading, plane or with margins incurling a little at apex, smooth, overlapping half; the inner segments with margins a little wavy; corona funnel-shaped, smooth, with mouth even, rim flanged and crenate. Mid-season to late

'Formby' 2 W-R
(P. Phillips) P. Phillips, 1975
Sdlg no. 2BR-17
Fl. 95 mm wide; perianth segments very broad, rounded, somewhat slow to become white, of good substance; corona shallow, tightly ribbed, fiery red. Mid-season. Resembles 'Avenger' but with a broader corona

'Formidable' 2 Y-Y
(R.H.Glover, pre-1993) Unregistered

'Form Master' 1 W-Y
(Brian S. Duncan) Rathowen Daffodils, 1977
'Joybell' × 'Empress of Ireland'; sdlg no. 113
Perianth segments white; corona yellow. Mid-season. Resembles a much larger 'Joybell'

'Formosa' 8 W-Y or O
(pre-1807)

'Formosa' 2 W-? (b)
(P.D. Williams, pre-1937)

'Formosa' 2 Y-R
(C.E. Radcliff, 1938)
'Fortune' × 'Damson'

'Formosus' 2 W-Y
(W. Backhouse, pre-1869)
Perianth segments sulphur white. Syn. Incomparabilis Albus 'Formosus'

'Formula' 1 Y-Y
(F.H. Chapman, pre-1914)

'Forte' 2 W-P
(Jackson's Daffodils) Jackson's Daffodils, 1986
'Tim' × 'Verran'; sdlg no. 58/78
Perianth segments ovate, yellowish white 155B, the outer segments touching one another; corona light yellowish pink 36A. Mid-season. 2n=28. Syn. 'Bimba'

'Fortescue' 4 W-R
(Jackson's Daffodils) Jackson's Daffodils, 1992
'Glowing Red' × 'Potent'; sdlg no. 147/84
Fl. rounded, 95 mm wide; perianth and other petaloid segments in several whorls regularly superimposed, very broadly ovate, whitish, spreading, with broad midrib showing, overlapping half, the whorls successively a little shorter towards the centre and becoming inflexed; the centre whorl of fewer than six segments strongly inflexed, with margins tightly incurled; corona segments very short, clustered among the petaloid segments, bright red, tightly frilled. Mid-season

'Fort George' 1 W-? (b)
(The Brodie of Brodie, c.1910)
'Jenny Woodhouse' × 'King Alfred'
Corna with rim flanged

'Forthel' 2 Y-YYO
(West & Fell, pre-1938)
Perianth segments deep yellow; corona yellow, with a band of reddish orange at rim, rim flanged

'Forthright' 2 Y-Y
(The Brodie of Brodie, pre-1949)
'Trenoon' × 'Carbineer'; sdlg no. 11/A/39
Fl. 115 mm wide; perianth segments broadly ovate, slightly mucronate, yellow, spreading, with margins sometimes minutely incurling at apex, very smooth, with broad midrib showing, overlapping half; the inner segments narrower, a little inflexed; corona deep cup-shaped, vivid yellow 15A, mouth only a little expanded, rim crenate and narrowly flanged. AM(Haarlem) 1954, AM(e) 1954

'Fortilly' 2 Y-YYR
(G.H. Johnstone, pre-1960)
'Fortune' × 'Porthilly'

'Fortissimo' 1 W-Y
(J. Gerritsen & Son, pre-1934)
Corona soft yellow

'Fortissimo' 2 Y-O
(de Graaff Bros) de Graaff Bros & van Konynenburg & Co., 1964
Fl. 120 mm wide; perianth segments oblong, blunt, prominently mucronate, brilliant greenish yellow 6C, spreading, overlapping one-third; the inner segments more nearly ovate, a little twisted; corona funnel-shaped, lightly ribbed, strong orange 25B, lightly frilled, with rim deeply notched and crenate. Mid-season

'Fortitude' 2 Y-O
(Mrs R.O. Backhouse, pre-1921)
Perianth segments pale creamy yellow; corona large, reddish orange, flecked with gold

'Fortitude' 2 Y-GYY
(Brian S. Duncan) Rathowen Daffodils, 1977
Sdlg × 'Viking'; sdlg no. 59
Fl. deep golden yellow; corona with green at base. Late. Mid-season

'Fort Knox' 1 Y-Y
(M.J. Jefferson-Brown) M.J. Jefferson-Brown, 1975
'Arctic Gold' × 'Burnished Gold'
Fl. forming a double triangle, vivid yellow 12A; perianth segments broadly ovate, blunt, mucronate, with margins incurving, smooth, regular, overlapping half; corona cylindrical, smooth, darker in tone than the perianth, mouth flared, with rim notched and crenate

'Fortress' 1 Y-Y
(G.L. Wilson, pre-1927)
'King of the North' × 'Sorley Boy'
Resembles a larger and improved 'Bulwark'

'Fortrose' 2 W-P
(E.F. Hughes) E.F. Hughes, 1962
Fl. 121 mm wide; corona pale pink, with a darker tone at rim, frilled. Mid-season. Resembles a later-flowered 'Rose of Tralee'

'Fortuity' 2 W-? (b)
(R. Crews, pre-1949)

'Fortuna' 8 W-O
(pre-1846)

'Fortunatus' 3 W-? (b)
(F.H. Chapman, pre-1927)
'Kestrel' × 'Fortune'

'Fortune' 2 Y-O
(W.T. Ware, pre-1917)
Possibly 'M.J. Berkeley' × ('C.J. Backhouse' or 'King Alfred'); or 'Sir Watkin' × 'Blackwell'
Fl. 108 mm wide; perianth segments broadly ovate, blunt, slightly mucronate, brilliant yellow 8A, spreading, overlapping half; the inner segments a little inflexed, somewhat creased and with margins nicked; corona short funnel-shaped, broad, smooth, strong orange 24A, paler towards base, mouth straight, finely ribbed, with deeply overlapping lobes, lightly frilled. Early. 2n=28. PC 1923, FCC 1924, AM(Haarlem) 1926, FCC(Haarlem) 1927, FA(Haarlem) 1934, FCFA(Haarlem) 1935, *AM(g) 1947

'Fortune Finder' 2 Y-? (a)
(J.E. Exley, pre-1938)

'Fortune Hunter' 2 Y-? (a)
(J.E. Exley, pre-1938)

'Fortune's Accountant' 2 Y-? (a)
(J.E. Exley, pre-1938)

'Fortune's Arrow' 2 Y-? (a)
(The Brodie of Brodie, pre-1930)

'Fortune's Attendant' 2 Y-? (a)
(J.E. Exley, pre-1938)

'Fortune's Beacon' 2 Y-? (a)
(The Brodie of Brodie, pre-1930)
'Beacon' × 'Fortune'

'Fortune's Beauty' 2 Y-O
(The Brodie of Brodie, pre-1928)
'Bernardino' × 'Fortune'
Fl. 89 mm wide; perianth segments broadly ovate, blunt, fairly prominently mucronate, primrose yellow, a little inflexed, somewhat ribbed, overlapping one-third to a half; the inner segments twisted or with margins wavy, appearing to be acute, more strongly ribbed; corona short and broad funnel-shaped, strongly ribbed, bright orange, with mouth straight, tightly frilled. AM(c) 1934

'Fortune's Blaze' 2 Y-O
(The Brodie of Brodie, c.1930)
'Fortune' × 'Gulliver'; sdlg no. 38/H/26
Corona rich reddish orange

'Fortune's Bowl' 2 Y-O
(The Brodie of Brodie, pre-1930)
Fl. 83-102 mm wide; perianth segments very broadly ovate, blunt, fairly prominently mucronate, brilliant greenish yellow 4A, more or less spreading, concave, with margins a little incurling, overlapping half or more; the inner segments inflexed, with margins strongly incurling to give a narrow appearance with

apex acute; corona short funnel-shaped, ribbed, strong orange, paling slightly to base, with mouth expanded and even, rim crenate, irregularly notched, sometimes slightly flanged. *(Gulval)AM(m) 1940

'Fortune's Boy' 2 Y-? (a)
(The Brodie of Brodie, pre-1930)

'Fortune's Caretaker' 2 Y-? (a)
(J.E. Exley, pre-1938)

'Fortune's Champion' 2 Y-O
(The Brodie of Brodie, pre-1933)
Corona rich reddish orange

'Fortune's Charmer' 2 Y-? (a)
(J.E. Exley, pre-1938)

'Fortune's Cheer' 2 Y-O
(The Brodie of Brodie, c.1927)
'Fortune' × 'Robin Redbreast'
Fl. 83 mm wide; perianth segments very broadly ovate, brilliant greenish yellow, paling at midrib near apex, with prominent white mucro, concave near apex, overlapping one-third to a half; the inner segments more narrowly ovate, creased and with margins occasionally incurling; corona funnel-shaped, ribbed, strong orange 25A, mouth sometimes split and obscurely 6-lobed, straight, with rim notched

'Fortune's Chief' 2 Y-? (a)
(The Brodie of Brodie, pre-1930)

'Fortune's Chimes' 2 Y-? (a)
(The Brodie of Brodie, pre-1930)

'Fortune's Circle' 2 Y-? (a)
(The Brodie of Brodie, pre-1930)
'Seraglio' × 'Fortune'

'Fortune's Coronet' 2 Y-? (a)
(The Brodie of Brodie, pre-1930)

'Fortune's Credentials' 2 Y-? (a)
(J.E. Exley, pre-1938)

'Fortune's Credit' 2 Y-? (a)
(J.E. Exley, pre-1938)

'Fortune's Crest' 2 Y-O
(The Brodie of Brodie, pre-1930)
'Seraglio' × 'Fortune' or 'Fortune' × 'Robin Redbreast'
Fl. about 93 mm wide; perianth segments very broadly ovate, blunt, prominently mucronate, light greenish yellow, paling at midrib towards apex, somewhat reflexed, concave, creased, overlapping one-third to a half; the inner segments inflexed, more narrowly ovate, with margins nicked; corona funnel-shaped, loosely 6-ribbed, strong orange 25A, paling towards base, mouth straight, with six deeply overlapping lobes, rim more or less crenate. AM(e) 1931

'Fortune's Cross' 2 Y-? (a)
(The Brodie of Brodie, pre-1930)

'Fortune's Crown' 2 Y-? (a)
(The Brodie of Brodie, pre-1928)
'Tamerlane' × 'Fortune'

'Fortune's Dame' 2 Y-? (a)
(The Brodie of Brodie, pre-1930)

'Fortune's Delight' 2 Y-? (a)
(The Brodie of Brodie, pre-1930)

'Fortune's Display' 2 Y-? (a)
(J.E. Exley, pre-1938)

'Fortune's Double' 4 Y-?
(Spalding Bulb Co., pre-1957) Unregistered
AM(Haarlem) 1957. ?The same as 'Double Fortune'

'Fortune's Dream' 2 Y-? (a)
(J.E. Exley, pre-1938)

'Fortune's Emblem' 2 Y-? (a)
(The Brodie of Brodie, pre-1930)

'Fortune's Ensign' 2 Y-? (a)
(The Brodie of Brodie, pre-1930)
'Fortune' × 'Galopin'

'Fortune's Factor' 2 Y-? (a)
(J.E. Exley, pre-1938)

'Fortune's Fame' 2 Y-? (a)
(J.E. Exley, pre-1938)

'Fortune's Fancy' 2 Y-? (a)
(The Brodie of Brodie, pre-1934)

'Fortune's Favour' 2 Y-? (a)
(J.E. Exley, pre-1938)

'Fortune's Flag' 2 Y-? (a)
(The Brodie of Brodie, pre-1930)
'Knipp' × 'Fortune'

'Fortune's Flame' 2 Y-? (a)
(The Brodie of Brodie, pre-1930)
'Killigrew' × 'Fortune'

'Fortune's Foundation' 2 Y-? (a)
(J.E. Exley, pre-1938)

'Fortune's Foundling' 2 Y-? (a)
(J.E. Exley, pre-1938)

'Fortune's Friendship' 2 Y-? (a)
(J.E. Exley, pre-1938)

'Fortune's Gain' 2 Y-? (a)
(J.E. Exley, pre-1938)

'Fortune's Gem' 2 Y-? (a)
(The Brodie of Brodie, pre-1928)

'Fortune's Giant' 2 Y-? (a)
(The Brodie of Brodie, pre-1930)

'Fortune's Gift' 2 Y-O
(The Brodie of Brodie, pre-1930)
'Fortune' × 'Robin Redbreast'
Fl. large; perianth segments broadly or very broadly ovate, rounded at apex, fairly prominently mucronate, pale yellow, spreading, smooth, overlapping one-third; the inner segments a little inflexed and sometimes creased; corona broad funnel-shaped, rich reddish orange, mouth ribbed and widely expanded, wavy. AM(e) 1930

'Fortune's Gleam' 2 Y-? (a)
(The Brodie of Brodie, pre-1928)

'Fortune's Glory' 2 Y-? (a)
(The Brodie of Brodie, pre-1928)

'Fortune's Glow' 2 Y-? (a)
(The Brodie of Brodie, pre-1930)
'Mozart' × 'Fortune'

'Fortune's Greeting' 2 Y-? (a)
(J.E. Exley, pre-1938)

'Fortune's Guardian' 2 Y-? (a)
(J.E. Exley, pre-1938)

'Fortune's Help' 2 Y-? (a)
(J.E. Exley, pre-1938)

'Fortune's Hero' 2 Y-? (a)
(J.E. Exley, pre-1938)

'Fortune's Hireling' 2 Y-? (a)
(J.E. Exley, pre-1938)

'Fortune's Holdings' 2 Y-? (a)
(J.E. Exley, pre-1938)

'Fortune's Hope' 2 Y-? (a)
(The Brodie of Brodie, pre-1930)
'Red Sea' × 'Fortune'

'Fortune's Idol' 2 Y-? (a)
(The Brodie of Brodie, pre-1930)

'Fortune's King' 2 Y-? (a)
(The Brodie of Brodie, pre-1930)

'Fortune's Knight' 2 Y-O
(The Brodie of Brodie, pre-1930)

Fl. 85 mm wide; perianth segments ovate, blunt, fairly prominently mucronate, brilliant greenish yellow 5A, creased, overlapping one-third; the inner segments a little twisted; corona funnel-shaped, smooth, yellow-orange (23A), mouth expanded, split in places and overlapping, with rim notched and irregularly crenate

'Fortune's Late' 2 Y-R
(A. Overton) A. Ladson, 1960
Perianth segments rich yellow; corona expanded, red

'Fortune's Leader' 2 Y-? (a)
(J.E. Exley, pre-1938)

'Fortune's Legacy' 2 Y-? (a)
(J.E. Exley, pre-1938)

'Fortune's Mantle' 2 Y-? (a)
(J.E. Exley, pre-1938)

'Fortune's Overlord' 2 Y-? (a)
(J.E. Exley, pre-1938)

'Fortune's Patriot' 2 Y-? (a)
(J.E. Exley, pre-1938)

'Fortune's Pearl' 2 Y-? (a)
(The Brodie of Brodie, pre-1930)

'Fortune's Perfection' 2 Y-? (a)
(The Brodie of Brodie, pre-1930)

'Fortune's Prestige' 2 Y-? (a)
(J.E. Exley, pre-1938)

'Fortune's Pride' 2 Y-R
(The Brodie of Brodie, pre-1928)
'Beacon' × 'Fortune'
Perianth segments yellow; corona bright red

'Fortune's Protégé' 2 Y-? (a)
(J.E. Exley, pre-1938)

'Fortune's Queen' 2 W-O
(Mrs R.O. Backhouse, pre-1921)
Perianth segments creamy white, flushed pale lemon yellow at base; corona large, flared, apricot orange, frilled. AM(Haarlem) 1930

'Fortune's Royalties' 2 Y-? (a)
(J.E. Exley, pre-1938)

'Fortune's Ruler' 2 Y-? (a)
(J.E. Exley, pre-1938)

'Fortune's Sceptre' 2 Y-? (a)
(The Brodie of Brodie, pre-1930)

'Fortune's Sentinel' 2 Y-O

(The Brodie of Brodie, c.1930)
'Fortune' × P.D. Williams red and yellow sdlg; sdlg no. 12/K/26
Perianth segments broadly ovate, blunt or rounded at apex, pale sulphur yellow, spreading or a little inflexed, with margins sometimes incurling, somewhat irregular, overlapping one-third to a half; the inner segments more narrowly ovate, more strongly inflexed, with margins slightly wavy; corona long cup-shaped, lightly ribbed, rich orange, mouth straight and even, with rim shallowly crenate. AM(e) 1935

'Fortune's Shield' 2 Y-? (a)
(The Brodie of Brodie, pre-1930)

'Fortune's Shrine' 2 Y-? (a)
(J.E. Exley, pre-1938)

'Fortune's Sister' 2 Y-? (a)
(The Brodie of Brodie, pre-1930)

'Fortune's Smile' 2 Y-? (a)
(The Brodie of Brodie, pre-1929)
'Mozart' × 'Fortune'

'Fortune's Song' 2 Y-? (a)
(The Brodie of Brodie, pre-1930)

'Fortune's Star' 2 Y-? (a)
(The Brodie of Brodie, pre-1928)
Sdlg × 'Fortune'

'Fortune's Start' 2 Y-? (a)
(J.E. Exley, pre-1938)

'Fortune's Strike' 2 Y-? (a)
(J.E. Exley, pre-1938)

'Fortune's Successor' 2 Y-? (a)
(J.E. Exley, pre-1938)

'Fortune's Sun' 2 Y-O
(The Brodie of Brodie, c.1930)
'Fortune' × P.D. Williams red and yellow sdlg; sdlg no. 12/G/26
Corona rich reddish orange

'Fortune's Thriller' 2 Y-? (a)
(J.E. Exley, pre-1938)

'Fortune's Trustee' 2 Y-? (a)
(J.E. Exley, pre-1938)

'Fortune's Vendetta' 2 Y-? (a)
(J.E. Exley, pre-1938)

'Fortune's Welcome' 2 Y-? (a)
(J.E. Exley, pre-1938)

'Fortune's Wheel' 2 Y-Y
(West & Fell, pre-1936)

'Fortune's Windfall' 2 Y-? (a)
(J.E. Exley, pre-1938)

'Fortune's Wonder' 2 Y-? (a)
(The Brodie of Brodie, pre-1930)

'Fortune Teller' 2 Y-? (a)
(J.E. Exley, pre-1938)

'Fortune Winner' 2 Y-? (a)
(J.E. Exley, pre-1938)

'Fortwilliam' 1 Y-Y
(W.J. Dunlop) W.J. Dunlop, 1960
'Cromarty' × 'Kingscourt'
Fl. mid-yellow. 2n=28

'Fortwyn' 2 W-Y
(S.C. Gaspar) R.J. Abernethy, 1962
Fl. 102 mm wide; perianth segments creamy white; corona pale lemon yellow. Mid-season. Resembles a shorter 'Tirpitz' of paler colour

'Forty-Niner' 5 Y-Y
(Oregon Bulb Farms, pre-1950)
Resembles a shorter 'Thoughtful' with more flowers per stem. See also 'Fortyniner'

'Fortyniner' 5 Y-Y
Syn. of 'Forty-Niner'

'Forum' 1 Y-Y
(J. Gerritsen & Son) J. Gerritsen & Son, 1961

'Forward' 1 W-? (b)
(W. Welchman, pre-1908)

'Fotis' 2 Y-R
(W. Jackson Sr, 1928)
'Bernardino' × 'Tamerlane'

'Foundation' 2 W-W
(W.G. Pannill, 1978) W.G. Pannill, 1990
'Panache' × 'Canisp'; sdlg no. 72/15

'Foundling' 2 Y-? (a)
(W.B. Cranfield, pre-1930)

'Foundling' 6 W-P
(Carncairn Daffodils) Carncairn Daffodils, 1969
'Irish Rose' × 'Jenny'
Fl. 72 mm wide; perianth segments broadly ovate, blunt, mucronate, greenish white (157C), reflexed, regular, overlapping; the inner segments more narrowly ovate, square-shouldered at base, sometimes a little twisted, with margins wavy and sometimes incurved; corona short cylinder-shaped, closely

ribbed, pink (33D), shading to a darker tone at rim, mouth straight, even or a little wavy, rim irregularly notched. 2n=27. AM(e) 1972, AGM 1995

'Fount' 2 W-P
(Murray W. Evans) Murray W. Evans, 1976
'Interim' hybrid; sdlg no. L-2
Fl. 110 mm wide. Mid-season

'Fountain' 1 W-W
(G.L. Wilson, pre-1935)
'Eskimo' × 'Tenedos'

'Fountain's Glory'
(R.Fountain, pre-1931)
PC(e)(NZ) 1931

'Fourboro' 2 Y-? (a)
(G.H. Johnstone, pre-1949)

'Fourways' 3 W-GYR
(Ballydorn Bulb Farm) Ballydorn Bulb Farm, 1979
Fl. 95 mm wide; corona mid-zone suffused orange-yellow. Mid-season

'Four Winds' 2 W-W
(J.S. Leitch) J.S. Leitch, 1966
Fl. 115 mm wide

'Fourwy' 4 W-Y
(?Australian origin, pre-1990) Unregistered

'Fowey' 3 W-YYO
(Brian S. Duncan) du Plessis Bros, 1989
'Green Island' × 'Merlin'; sdlg no. 583
Fl. 100 mm wide; corona disc-shaped, with a narrow band of orange at rim. Late

'Foxfire' 2 W-GWO
(Murray W. Evans) Murray W. Evans, 1968
'Limerick' × ('Shirley Neale' × 'Chinese White')
Fl. 95 mm wide. Mid-season. 2n=28. Resembles a smaller-flowered 'Redstart' with a whiter perianth and a broader band of colour at corona rim

'Foxhunter' 2 Y-O
(G.L. Wilson, pre-1953)
'Armada' × 'Saltash'
Perianth segments broadly ovate, blunt, slightly mucronate, clear rich yellow, spreading, overlapping one-third to a half; the inner segments more narrowly ovate, a little inflexed, somewhat creased; corona narrow, rich reddish orange, with mouth straight, neatly frilled. Early. Resembles an improved 'Saltash'

'Foxley' 2 Y-?O
(R.O. Backhouse, pre-1937)

'Fox Moon' 2 YYW-W
(Donna C.Dietsch) Donna C.Dietsch, 1997

'Epitome' × 'Young American'; sdlg no. 89/63
Fl. 92 mm wide; perianth segments ovate, deep golden yellow, with a narrow band of white at base; corona constricted near mouth, with mouth expanded and lightly frilled. Mid-season

'Fox Trot' 11a W-YYW
(A.N. Kanouse, 1965) A.N. Kanouse, 1978
'Hillbilly' × 'Mabel Taylor'
Fl. 105 mm wide; corona split, the six segments lemon, with some white at rim. Mid-season

'Foyle' 2 W-P
(G.L. Wilson, pre-1940)
'Nevis' x' White Nile' × 'Cameronian'
Corona very pale creamy primrose, faintly flushed with rose pink

'Fra Angelico' 2 Y-O
(J.W.A. Lefeber, 1945) J.W.A. Lefeber, 1960
Fl. 76 mm wide; perianth segments pale citron yellow, smooth; corona large, dark orange, frilled

'Fra Diavolo' 1 Y-Y
(Konynenburg & Mark) Konynenburg & Mark, 1962
'Rembrandt' hybrid
Fl. 110 mm wide; corona deep yellow. Mid-season

'Fragrance' 7
(W.F.M. Copeland, pre-1913)

'Fragrance' 8
(E.L. Jones, pre-1946)

'Fragrant' 2 Y-Y
(R.V. Favell, pre-1946)
'Havelock' × ? *N. jonquilla*

'Fragrant Breeze' 2 W-O
(W.F. Leenen & Sons, 1976) O.A. Taylor & Sons, 1993
Fl. 110 mm wide. Mid-season. Sunproof. Scented

'Fragrant Rose' 2 W-GPP
(Brian S. Duncan) Rathowen Daffodils, 1978
'Roseworthy' hybrid × ?'Merlin'; sdlg no. 143
Fl. 95 mm wide; perianth segments broadly ovate, blunt, slightly mucronate, spreading, a little concave, smooth and of waxy substance, regular, overlapping half; the inner segments only a little narrower, slightly inflexed; corona long cup-shaped, deep reddish pink, paling towards base and with green prominent at base, mouth straight, wavy, rim obscurely crenate. Mid-season. Raspberry or rose-scented. 2n=28

'Frailty' 3 W-YYR
(G.P. Haydon, pre-1904)
N. × poculiformis × *N. poeticus*
Fl. facing down; perianth segments snow white, twist-

ed; corona expanded, with bright red at rim

'Framton' 1 W-Y
(C.E. Radcliff, 1942) J.M.Radcliff, 1956
'Avanley' × 'Dawnglow'

'Frances' 2 W-W
(Campbell Duncan) Campbell Duncan, 1956
'Omaroe' × 'Broughshane'
See also 'Francis'

'Francesca' 1 W-W
(de Graaff Bros, pre-1907)
'Madame de Graaff' hybrid

'Francesca' 2 Y-?
Syn. of 'Cattaro'

'Frances Christie' 2 Y-? (a)
(J.A. Christie, pre-1943)

'Frances Diana' 2 Y-YYO
(Albert Davis) Albert Davis, 1991
'Perimeter' × 'Shining Light'; sdlg no.191/77
Fl. 90 mm wide; perianth segments very broadly ovate, prominently mucronate, pale greenish yellow 9D; corona shallow, vivid yellow 15A, with a broad band of strong orange 25A at rim, mouth regularly frilled. Late

'Frances I'Anson' 2 Y/W-WPP
(Jan Dalton, 1906) Jan Dalton, 1997
'Jewel Song' × 'Daydream'; sdlg no. 811/1
Perianth yellow, with a longitudinal band of white at midrib. Mid-season to late

'Franceska' 2 W-R
(G. Lewis) D.S. Bell, 1955

'Frances Lyster' 2 W-? (b)
(H.R. Meyer, pre-1927)

'Frances Patterson' 2 W-W
(Mrs C.E. Fitzwater, 1966) Mrs C.E. Fitzwater, 1986
'Easter Moon' × 'Panache'; sdlg no. 43/1
Mid-season. Resembles a Div. 2 'Panache' with stronger stem

'Frances Taylor' 2 Y-? (a)
(J.R. Byfield, pre-1936)

'Franchot Tone' 2 W-YYO
(F. Rijnveld & Sons, pre-1943)
AM(Haarlem) 1943

'Francis' 2 W-W
Syn. of 'Frances'

'Francis Bacon' 9 W-YYR
(A.M. Wilson, pre-1914)

Fl. large; perianth segments rounded, inflexed; corona citron yellow, with dark red at rim

'Franciscus Drake' 2 W-YYO
(Mrs R.O. Backhouse, pre-1921)
Perianth segments pure white, tinted gold at base; corona golden yellow, shading to orange at rim, with mouth densely frilled. AM(Haarlem) 1926

'Francis Thomson' 9 W-?
(G.H. Engleheart, pre-1927)

'Francoise' 1 W-W
(T. Buncombe, pre-1931)

'Francolin' 1 Y-Y
(Brian S.Duncan, 1983) Brian S.Duncan, 1996
'Golden Jewel' × 'Midas Touch'; sdlg no. 925
Fl. 95 mm wide, deep golden yellow, shiny; perianth segments broadly ovate, plane; corona cylindrical, with mouth expanded, rim dentate. Early to mid-season

'Frank Fairbairn' 2 Y-O
(C.O. Fairbairn, 1945) R. Hyde, 1958

'Frank Galsworthy' 3 W-? (b)
(G.H. Engleheart, pre-1910)

'Franklin' 2 Y-Y
(A.M. Wilson, pre-1931)
'Havelock' hybrid
Perianth segments broad, rich primrose yellow; corona expanded, dark canary yellow, lightly frilled, with rim flanged. AM(e) 1936, AM(Haarlem) 1938

'Franklin Mead' 2 Y-? (a)
(The Brodie of Brodie, pre-1931)

'Frank Miles' 2 Y-Y
(E. Leeds, pre-1877)
Fl. star-shaped, soft clear yellow; perianth segments narrowly ovate, acute, with very slight white mucro, spreading, twisted, with margins incurling, separated; corona cup-shaped, loosely ribbed, darker in tone than the perianth, with mouth straight, a little frilled, rim crenate. Syn. Incomparabilis Concolor 'Frank Miles'

'Frankness' 2 W-? (b or c)
(G.H. Johnstone, pre-1941)

'Frank Penn' 3 W-? (b)
(A. Gibson, pre-1933)

'Frank's Fancy' 9 W-GGR
(Ballydorn Bulb Farm) Carncairn Daffodils, 1979
'Cantabile' hybrid
Fls usually 2 per stem, 60 mm wide; corona green, with a narrow band of orange-red at rim. Scented

'Frans Hals' 1 Y-Y
(E.H. Krelage & Son, pre-1913)

'Frans Hals' 8 W-Y
(pre-1927)
Poetaz

'Franz Liszt' 3 W-? (b)
(J.W.A. Lefeber, pre-1941)

'Franz Schubert' 2 Y-YYO
(Konynenburg & Mark) Konynenburg & Mark, 1960
'Aranjuez' × 'Red Bird'
Fl. 75 mm wide

'Frater Casimirus' 9 W-?
(van der Poel Bros) van der Poel Bros, 1955

'Frau Margarethe Hohmann' 3 W-? (b)
(de Graaff Bros, pre-1928)
Perianth segments acute, pure white; corona with red at rim, frilled

'Fred'
(pre-1914)

'Freda' 1 W-W
(W.A. Grace, pre-1936)

'Freda O'Neill' 2 W-? (b)
(J.A. O'Neill, pre 1949)

'Freddie Silcock' 2 Y-WWY
(L.P. Dettman) L.P. Dettman, 1973
'Creamed Honey' × 'Ellimatta'
Fl. 109 mm wide

'Freddie Watts' 2 Y-O
(L.P.Dettman, 1974) Unregistered
'Bubbles' × 'Fireking'; sdlg no. BF 1/74

'Frederica' 8 W-Y
(pre-1850)
Corona citron yellow

'Frederic Chopin' 2 W-O
(J.W.A. Lefeber) J.W.A. Lefeber, 1960
Fl. 85 mm wide; corona reddish orange. Mid-season

'Frederike'
Unregistered
In parentage of 'Carl Zeller' and others

'Fred Marks' 2 Y-GYO
(L.P. Dettman) L.P. Dettman, 1979
'Vulcan' × 'Spelter'; sdlg no. 8/74
Fl. 79 mm wide; perianth segments brilliant yellow 13B; corona with strong to vivid reddish orange 32C-32C at rim. Mid-season. Resembles 'George Tindale'
but with a lighter-coloured corona

'Fred Moore' 1 Y-Y
(de Graaff Bros, pre-1890)
Perianth segments primrose yellow; corona large, rich golden yellow, frilled. AM 1897

'Fred van Eden' 9 W-?
(G. Lubbe & Son, pre-1927)

'Freeby Wood' 1 Y-Y
(W.A. Noton) W.A. Noton, 1976
'Kingscourt' × 'King's Ransom'; sdlg no. 509
Fl. 106 mm wide. Mid-season

'Free Choice' 2 W-W
(S.A. Free) S.A. Free, 1966
Fl. 108 mm wide. Mid-season

'Freedom' 1 Y-Y
(J.R. Pearson & Sons, pre-1923)

'Freedom' 2 Y-R
(S.A. Free) Mrs S.I. Free, 1978
'Bushfire' hybrid; sdlg no. 69/1
Fl. 107 mm wide; perianth segments deep yellow; corona orange-red. Mid-season

'Freedom Rings' 2 Y-P
(R. & E. Havens) R. & E. Havens, 1994
'Widgeon' × 'Memento'; sdlg no. VH18/7
Fl. 80 mm wide; perianth segments ovate, lemon yellow, slightly reflexed, smooth; corona apricot pink, with rim flanged. Mid-season. Sunproof

'Freedom Stars' 11a W-YWW
(Jānis Rukšans) Jānis Rukšans, 1997
'April Tears' × 'Canasta'; sdlg no. 85-22-5
Fls 3-5 per stem, 60 mm wide, facing slightly downwards; perianth segments pure white, a little reflexed, smooth, deeply overlapping; corona deeply split, closely overlying the perianth, smooth, white, shading to brilliant greenish yellow 6B at base, with rim very slightly frilled. Dwarf. Late to very late. Resembles a much earlier-flowered 'Tripartite' of different colouring

'Freelance' 2 Y-O
(H.A. Brown, 1931) R. Hyde, 1958
Perianth segments broad, rich yellow, spreading; corona large, orange, frilled

'Freeman' 1 W-Y
(F.E. Board) F.E. Board, 1965
'Aldergrove' × 'Preamble'
Corona orange-yellow. Mid-season

'Freemason' 1 W-? (b)
(Hon. Mrs Petre, pre-1934)

'Freesia' 1 W-W
(D.H.L. Corrigan, pre-1949)

'Free Spirit' 2 W-W
(W.G. Pannill) W.G. Pannill, 1980
'Verona' × 'Stainless'; sdlg no. 66/43
Fl. 100 mm wide. Mid-season

'Freestyle' 1 W-W
(S.A. Free) Mrs S.I. Free, 1968

'Freeway' 1 Y-Y
(J.S. Leitch) J.S. Leitch, 1968

'Freia' 2 W-Y
(N.F. Lock, pre-1944)
Fl. 105 mm wide; perianth segments smooth, overlapping; corona funnel-shaped, vivid yellow 9B. AM(e) 1948

'Freifrau von Friesen' 3 W-? (b)
(Mrs R.O. Backhouse, pre-1921)
Corona with red at rim

'Fremeaux'
(Miss R. Thornton, pre-1936)

'French Kiss' 2 W-P
(John R.Reed, 1984) John R.Reed, 1995
'Passionale' × 'Accent'; sdlg no. 79-21-1
Fl. 100 mm wide; perianth segments ovate; corona funnel-shaped, opening pale yellow, quickly becoming deep glowing pink, with a slight tint of orange. Mid-season. Sunproof

'French Monarque' 8 W-Y
? The same as 'Grand Monarque'

'French Prairie' 2 W-P
(G.E.Mitsch, 1980) R. & E.Havens, 1997
'At Dawning' × 'C.E.Radcliff'; sdlg no. 2P4/2
Fl. 100 mm wide; perianth segments broadly ovate, spreading, plane; corona intense mid-pink, with mouth flared and frilled. Early to mid-season. Sunproof

'French Sol' 8 Y-Y
(French origin) Rosewarne EHS, 1979
Fl. 40 mm wide; perianth segments vivid yellow 9A; corona darker in tone (13A). Flowering October-December. Resembles 'Newton'

'Frenzi' 4 Y-O
(J.N.Hancock & Co., 1987) J.N.Hancock & Co., 1997
('Falaise' × 'Ceylon') × 'Jezebel'; sdlg no. 6/87H
Perianth and other petaloid segments bright yellow; corona segments interspersed, numerous, bright orange. Mid-season

'Fresco' 11a W-GYY
(J. Gerritsen & Son) J. Gerritsen & Son, 1976
'Canasta' hybrid
Fl. 90 mm wide; perianth segments ivory white; corona segments brilliant yellow 10A, with tints of green at base. Early. Resembles 'Canasta' but with the corona of a darker tone

'Fresco' 1
(W.M. Spry, pre-1975) Unregistered
'Hunter's Moon' × 'Tunis'
Fl. buff. Late

'Fresh Lime' 1 YYW-Y
(A.J.R. Pearson) A.J.R. Pearson, 1994
('Fine Gold' self pollinated × 'Camelot') × 'Daydream'; sdlg no. 89-59-M14
Fl. forming a rounded double triangle, 98 mm wide; perianth segments broadly ovate, blunt, light greenish yellow 4B, with greenish white (1D) at base, spreading, plane, smooth and with good substance, overlapping two-thirds; the inner segments more narrowly ovate; corona cylindrical, lightly ribbed, light greenish yellow 4B becoming paler with age, with a slightly darker tone (5A) at rim, mouth lightly flared, lobed, with rim flanged and crenate. Mid-season

'Freshman' 2 W-GPP
(Brian S. Duncan) Rathowen Daffodils, 1977
Sdlg 3341 × 'Passionale'; sdlg no. 53
Fl. 110 mm wide; corona salmon pink, with green at base. Late. Resembles 'Rosedew' but with a much whiter, broader and smoother perianth and the corona of a deeper tone

'Fresh Season' 10 Y-Y
(James S. Wells) James S. Wells, 1990
Hybrid between selections from *N. bulbocodium* var. tenuifolius and *N. romieuxii*; sdlg no. 83-16
Fl. bright chrome yellow; perianth segments lanceolate, with white mucro, inflexed, separated; corona funnel-shaped, smooth or lightly ribbed, with mouth straight and irregularly frilled. Dwarf. Very early

'Freshwater' 1 W-W
(G.L. Wilson, pre-1944)
'Tain' hybrid
Perianth segments white; corona opening very pale lemon, becoming white in a day or two, with rim flanged and dentate

'Fresno' 3 W-R
(Brian S. Duncan) Brian S. Duncan, 1993
'Red Rooster' × 'Verve'; sdlg no. 1047
Fl. 90 mm wide; perianth segments white; corona shallow bowl-shaped, ribbed, deep orange-red, with mouth frilled. Mid-season

'Fresoe' 3 W-? (b)
(pre-1914)

'Freya' 2 W-Y
(Colin Crotty, 1981) Colin Crotty, 1995
'Eminent' × 'Lysander'; sdlg no. 36-76
Fl. forming a double triangle, 112 mm wide, of glistening texture; perianth segments ovate, acute, pure white, smooth; corona bowl-shaped, pale yellow at base, shading to a darker tone towards mouth, with mouth wavy. Mid-season

'Freya' 2 W-P
(J.N.Hancock & Co., 1976) Unregistered
'Greta' × 'My Word'; sdlg no. 51/76H
Perianth segments roundish, ice white; corona cylindrical, strong yellowish pink 38A, with mouth straight. Tall. Mid-season

'Freyberg' 2 Y-R
(Mrs B.T. Simpson) Mrs B.T. Simpson, 1963
Fl. 95 mm wide; corona with rim frilled. Mid-season

'Freycinet' 2 Y-R
(S.J. Bisdee, 1945) S.J. Bisdee, 1956
'Dunkeld' × 'Sunset Fires'

'Friar' 3 W-Y
(Mrs R.O. Backhouse, pre-1921)
Perianth segments sulphur white; corona small, frilled. AM(Haarlem) 1929

'Friar Tuck' 2 W-? (b)
(E.T. England, pre-1923)

'Fricka' 2 W-? (b)
(N.F. Lock, pre-1944)

'Fricklestin V.C.' 2 W-Y
Syn. of 'Frickleton V.C.'

'Frickleton V.C.' 2 W-Y
(pre-1927)
Corona rich yellow, frilled, with rim flanged. See also 'Fricklestin V.C.'

'Fried Egg' 2 Y-YYO
(?Tom Forster) Unregistered
Fl. rounded; perianth segments primrose yellow; corona very broad disc-shaped, orange-yellow, with a band of orange at rim. Mid-season

'Fried Eggs' 4 W-O
Syn. of 'Orange Phoenix'

'Friend' 2 W-Y
(J.T. Gray) P. Phillips, 1968

'Friend Jim' 2 Y-Y
(J.A. O'More, 1975) Koanga Daffodils, 1990
'Camelot' × 'Director'; sdlg no. 21/75
Fl. 115 mm wide; perianth segments broadly ovate, vivid yellow 9B; corona narrow, a little brighter in tone (12A) than the perianth, with mouth slightly expanding. Late

'Friendly' 2 Y-? (a)
(M.P. Williams, pre-1949)

'Friendship' 2 W-? (b or c)
(W. Welchman, pre-1908)

'Friendship' 2 W-W
(G.L. Wilson) F.E. Board, 1962
'Knowehead' × ('Murmansk' × 'Broughshane'); sdlg no. 46-83
Mid-season

'Friesland' 2 W-? (b)
(de Graaff Bros, pre-1930)

'Frigid' 3 W-GGW
(G.L. Wilson, pre-1935)
'Emerald Eye' × 'Dactyl'
Fl. forming a double triangle, 83 mm wide, ice white; perianth segments broadly ovate, very slightly mucronate, spreading, plane, with margins incurling at apex, overlapping half; the inner segments spathulate, a little inflexed, with margins wavy; corona very small bowl-shaped, with emerald green at base, tightly frilled. Late. Scented. 2n=14. AM(e) 1947, AM(Haarlem) 1949, FCC(e) 1950

'Frileuse' 11a W-Y
(J. Gerritsen & Son) J. Gerritsen & Son, 1964
Fl. 65 mm wide; perianth segments opening yellow, becoming white; corona segments yellow. Early

'Frillbelow' 2 W-W
(A.E. Lowe, pre-1925)

'Frill Buff' 2 W-? (b)
(?W.M. & A.P. Spry, pre-1955) Unregistered

'Frilled Beauty' 2 Y-Y
(Mrs R.O. Backhouse, pre-1900)
Perianth segments cream, slightly flushed apricot; corona large, darker in tone than the perianth, also flushed apricot, mouth strongly ribbed, frilled

'Frilled Champion' 3 W-? (b)
(F. Rijnveld & Sons, pre-1939)

'Frilled Gem' 3 W-? (b)
(C. Dawson, pre-1923)

'Frilled Robin' 2 W-O
(Mrs R.O. Backhouse, pre-1921)

"Frilled Trunk Daffodil"
Syn. of 'Croom Frilled'

'Frilled White' 1 W-W

(G.H. Engleheart, pre-1907)

'Frillity Frill'
(Sir C.H. Cave, pre-1913)

'Frill Prince' 1 W-Y
(H.A. Brown, 1949) J.N. Hancock & Co., 1960
Corona with deep buff at rim, frilled

'Frills' 1 W-W
(The Brodie of Brodie, c.1911)
'Mrs H.D.Betteridge' × 'Monarch'
Fl. pale cream; corona heavily frilled

'Frilly Pink' 2 W-P
(Campbell Duncan) Campbell Duncan, 1956
'Shirley Wyness' × 'Karanja'; sdlg no. 502

'Frimley' 2 W-O
(D. Bramley) D. Bramley, 1987
Sdlg 68/51 × 'Rockall'; sdlg no. 79/19
Perianth segments broad, clear white, overlapping. Mid-season. Resembles an improved sdlg 68/51 with broader perianth segments and a more evenly coloured corona

'Fringed Benefit' 2 W-YYO
(?Canadian origin, pre-1983) Unregistered

'Frisbee' 2 Y-Y
Syn. of 'Frisby'

'Frisby' 2 Y-Y
(P. & G. Phillips) P. & G. Phillips, 1980
Fl. rounded, 105 mm wide; perianth segments broad, mid-yellow, spreading; corona almost disc-shaped, wide-spreading, rich golden yellow, with a darker tone at rim. Mid-season. Syn. 'Frisbee'

'Frisco' 2 Y-? (a)
(G. Lewis, 1945) D.S. Bell, 1958

'Frisia' 2 Y-? (a)
(Mrs R.O. Backhouse, pre-1921)

'Frisky' 2 W-? (b)
(M.P. Williams, pre-1938)

'Fritton Decoy' 2 W-YYO
(French origin)
Selection by H.E.Buxton (c.1881) from wild-collected N. × bernardii
Corona yellow, with orange at rim. Resembles a smaller and more abundantly flowered N. × bernardii with more numerous leaves. Syn. Bernardii 'Fritton Decoy'

'Frivolity'
(Thomas Smith, pre-1904)
N. moschatus sdlg

Corona deeply split, with the four segments heavily frilled

'Frivolity' 2 W-OOY
(G.L. Wilson, pre-1950)
'White Sentinel' × 'Hades'
Perianth segments pure white; corona bright salmon orange, with a narrow band of bright yellow at rim

'Frivolous' 2 W-Y
(J.N.Hancock & Co., 1982) Unregistered
'John Evelyn' × 'Rococo'; sdlg no. 97/82H
Corona deep yellow, heavily frilled. Late

'Frizette' 2 W-P
(Alister Clark, 1945) J. Sharp, 1960

'Frobisher' 2 Y-? (a)
(Barr & Sons, pre-1942)

'Frodo' 1 Y-Y
(D.N.Y. Olson) D.N.Y. Olson, 1979
'Saint Keverne' × 'Ark Royal'
Fl. 103 mm wide, medium dark yellow; perianth segments very broadly ovate, blunt, fairly prominently mucronate, spreading, plane, overlapping one-third to a half; the inner segments more narrowly ovate, square-shouldered at base, somewhat creased; corona with mouth only a little expanded. Mid-season

'Froggatt' 1 W-? (b)
(D.B. Milne, pre 1952)

'Frohsinn' 2 Y-O
(Konynenburg & Mark) Konynenburg & Mark, 1965
'Blarney' hybrid
Fl. 90 mm wide; perianth segments brilliant yellow 8A; corona strong orange 30D. Late

'Frolic' 2 W-? (b)
(Sir C.H. Cave, pre-1908)

'Frolic' 2 Y-?
(M.P. Williams, pre-1949)
Corona a little frilled

'Frolic' 1 W-Y
(G.E. Mitsch) G.E. Mitsch, 1958
('Beersheba' × 'Kandahar') × 'Kanchenjunga'
Perianth segments pure white, deeply overlapping; corona flared, clear lemon yellow, frilled, with rim crenate. Mid-season

'Frolic' 2 W-YYR
(G.H. Johnstone, pre-1960)

'Frontal' 1 W-W
(E.W. Philpott)

'Frontier' 1 Y-Y
(G.L. Wilson, pre-1944)
'King of the North' × 'Content'
Fl. soft primrose yellow

'Frontispiece' 2 Y-? (a)
(G.H. Johnstone, pre-1946)
('Havelock' × 'Fortune') × 'Saint Issey'

'Frontline' 1 Y-Y
(M.J. Jefferson-Brown) M.J. Jefferson-Brown, 1985
Fl. rich golden yellow; corona rim flanged and dentate. Syn. 'Fearless'

'Front Royal' 2 Y-YYO
(J.M. de Navarro) J.M. de Navarro, 1958
'Carbineer' × 'Majorca'
Perianth segments dark yellow; corona mouth only slightly expanded, dark yellow at base, shading to orange at rim. Mid-season

'Frontrunner' 2 Y-W
(H. Koopowitz) H. Koopowitz, 1981
'Binkie' × ('Daydream' × *N. cyclamineus*); sdlg no. C473/4
Fl. 90 mm wide; perianth segments bright lemon; corona white, frilled. Early. Resembles an earlier and smaller-flowered 'Snow Frills'

'Frore' 2 W-? (b or c)
(J.L. Richardson, pre-1931)

'Frosta' 1 W-W
(W. Jackson Jr, 1954)
'Bonnington' × 'Tamara'

'Frost and Flame' 3 W-R
(G.L. Wilson) Guy L.Wilson Ltd, 1964
'Flamenco' × 'Rockall'

'Frostbite' 4 W-W
(Ballydorn Bulb Farm) Ballydorn Bulb Farm, 1994
'Silver Spell' × Div. 9 hybrid
Fl. rounded, 70 mm wide, pure white; perianth segments very broad, somewhat ovate; corona segments six or more, one-third the length of the perianth segments, spreading. Very late

'Frostbound' 1 W-Y
(E.M. Crosfield, pre-1913)
Fl. 95 mm wide, facing down; perianth segments, creamy white, inflexed, irregular, overlapping at base only; corona sulphur, with mouth expanded. Mid-season to late

'Frost-Cave' 2 or 3 W-? (b or c)
(E. & J.C. Martin, pre-1916)

'Frostflower' 2 W-W
(Mrs P.M. Davis, pre-1948)

'Frosting' 1 W-YYW
(H.A. Brown, 1936) J.N. Hancock & Co., 1960
Perianth segments smooth; corona straight-sided, soft yellow, with flecks of white at rim. Mid-season

'Frost in May' 9 W-GGY
(Ballydorn Bulb Farm) Ballydorn Bulb Farm, 1981
'Frigid' × 'Cantabile'
Fl. 35 mm wide. Late. 2n=14

'Frostkist' 6 W-W
(G.E. Mitsch) G.E. Mitsch, 1968
'Charity May' open pollinated; sdlg no. W01/1
Fl. 102 mm wide; perianth segments reflexed; corona opening pale lemon yellow, becoming white. Mid-season. Resembles a white 'Charity May' with larger flowers

'Frost Star' 2 W-W
(J.L. Richardson, pre-1948)

'Frosty' 2 W-W
(G.L. Wilson, pre-1952)

'Frosty' 3 W-GWY
(Ken McCombe) Unregistered
Perianth segments roundish, deeply overlapping; corona disc-shaped, ribbed, white, with green at base and pale yellow at rim. Late

'Frosty Lace' 11a W-WWY
(?New Zealand origin) Unregistered

'Frosty Morn' 5 W-W
(A. Gray, pre-1941)
N. triandrus var. *loiseleurii* sdlg
Fls 1-3 per stem

'Frothblower' 1 W-? (b)
(H. Prins, pre-1929)

'Froth 'n Bubble' 2 W-Y
(J.N. Hancock & Co., c.1975) Unregistered

'Frothy Ale' 2 W-?
(Miss K.M. Hinchliff, pre-1935)

'Frou-Frou' 4 W-W
(Carncairn Daffodils) Carncairn Daffodils, 1984
'Frigid' × 'Silver Chimes'; sdlg no. 20/19/74
Fl. 75 mm wide. Late. 2n=14. Resembles a larger and stronger 'Rose of May'

'Frozen' 2 W-W
(G.L. Wilson, pre-1950)
'Nelly' hybrid × 'Greenland' hybrid; sdlg no. 28/65

'Fruit Cup' 7 W-Y
(G.E. Morrill, 1966) G.E. Morrill, 1977
'Green Island' × *N. assoanus*; sdlg no. 61-1-1

Fls 1-2 or occasionally 3 per stem, rounded, 55 mm wide; perianth segments greenish white (157C); corona light greenish yellow 8C. Late. Slightly scented

'Fruition' 2 W-W
(P. Phillips) P. Phillips, 1971
Fl. forming a double triangle, 120 mm wide; perianth segments blunt, spreading; corona opening pale lemon yellow, becoming white, with mouth widely expanded and rim dentate

'Frumerty' 2 W-? (b)
(J.E. Exley, pre-1938)

'Frylink' 3 W-W
(A. Frylink & Sons, pre-1921)
Corona opening pale citron yellow, becoming sulphur white, neatly frilled. AM(Haarlem) 1921

'Fuco' 1 W-W
(J. Gerritsen & Son, 1979) J. Gerritsen & Son, 1988
Perianth segments ivory white; corona darker in tone. Early. Resembles 'Minor'. Formerly named 'Little Pearl'

'Fuego' 2 Y-O
(Mrs H.K. Richardson) Carncairn Daffodils, 1976
'Cathay' × sdlg 475 ('Patagonia' × 'Firecracker')
Fl. 80 mm wide; perianth segments vivid yellow 9A, slightly flushed red; corona opening yellow, becoming orange (28A), a little frilled. Mid-season. Sunproof. 2n=29

'Fuga' 3 W-? (b)
(de Graaff Bros, pre-1929)

'Fujiyama' 1 W-W
(J.R. Pearson & Sons, pre-1927)

'Fulgent' 1 Y-R
(W.O. Backhouse) W.O. Backhouse, 1959
Fl. 102 mm wide. Mid-season

'Full Circle' 10 Y-Y
(James S. Wells) James S. Wells, 1993
'Julia Jane' × 'February Gold'; sdlg no. 83-52
Fl. 35 mm wide, medium yellow; corona about three times as long as the perianth segments, spreading, ribbed, with rim dentate. Dwarf. Early

'Full Fashion' 2 W-P
(W.G. Pannill) W.G. Pannill, 1970
'Rosario' × 'Carita'

'Full Measure' 2 W-? (b)
(J.L. Richardson, pre-1944)

'Full Moon' 2 Y-? (a)
(Cartwright & Goodwin, pre-1916)

'Full Moon' 2 W-W
(J.M. de Navarro) J.M. de Navarro, 1958

'Full Moon' 2 W-Y
(O. Ronalds, pre-1956) Unregistered
Corona lemon yellow

'Full Sail' 2 W-W
(C.R. Runyan, pre-1952)

'Full Value' 1 W-? (b)
(L. van Leeuwen & Son, pre-1933)

'Fullwell' 4 W-R
(Brian S. Duncan) Rathowen Daffodils, 1987
'Monterrico' × 'Doctor Hugh'; sdlg no. 756
Perianth and other petaloid segments in two or three whorls, very broadly ovate, blunt or somewhat truncate, white, overlapping half; the outer whorl prominently mucronate, spreading; the inner whorls a little shorter, inflexed, with margins wavy or incurled, sometimes longitudinally creased or folded; the centre whorl strongly inflexed, with margins deeply incurled; corona segments very short, interspersed among the petaloid segments at centre, deep orange-red, tightly frilled. Mid-season to late

'Fulman' W-O
(West & Fell, pre-1927)
Perianth segments ivory white; corona largely orange

'Fulmar' 2 W-W
(J.L. Richardson) J.L. Richardson, 1959
'Green Island' × 'Ludlow'

'Fulmen' 2? W-Y
(P.D. Williams, c.1915)
Perianth segments very broadly ovate, blunt, mucronate, ivory white, spreading, plane, overlapping one-third to a half; the inner segments narrower, somewhat truncate, inflexed, twisted; corona cup-shaped, orange-yellow, mouth straight, frilled

'Fulvia' 5
(Barr & Sons, pre-1923)

'Fulvous' 1 Y-Y
(A.O. Roblin, pre-1940)
'Golden City' × 'Matchless'

'Fulwood' 3 W-R
(F.E. Board) F.E. Board, 1965
'Bella Vista' × 'Matapan'; sdlg no. 946
Late

'Funchal' 9 W-?
(A.M. Wilson, pre-1932)

'Funface' 2 Y-YYO
(G.H. Johnstone, pre-1960)

'Mozart' × 'Fortune'

'Funny Face' 2 Y-Y
(Brian S. Duncan) Rathowen Daffodils, 1977
'Break of Day' × 'Dinkie'; sdlg no. 275
Fl. 93 mm wide; perianth segments acute, deep yellow, slightly reflexed; corona deeper in tone, with rim flanged. Scented

'Furbelow' 1 Y-Y
(Mrs R.O. Backhouse, pre-1914)

'Furbelow' 4 Y-O
(J.L. Richardson, pre-1961) Unregistered
'Falaise' hybrid
2n=27

'Furious' 2 W-? (b)
(R.O. Backhouse, pre-1935)

'Furnace' 3 Y-R
(G.H. Engleheart, pre-1908)
Fl. large; perianth segments pale canary yellow; corona expanded, ribbed, deep fiery red, tinged crimson, frilled

'Furnace Creek' 2 Y-R
(Brian S. Duncan, 1983) Brian S. Duncan, 1993
'Bunclody' open pollinated; sdlg no. 873
Fl. 108 mm wide; perianth segments broadly ovate, blunt, deep golden yellow, plane, overlapping; the inner segments more narrowly ovate; corona narrow funnel-shaped, smooth, orange-red, with rim crenate. Mid-season. Sunproof

'Furore' 2 Y-O
(Konynenburg & Mark) Konynenburg & Mark, 1965
'Green Island' hybrid
Fl. 95 mm wide; perianth segments brilliant yellow 8A; corona strong orange 25A

'Furstin Maria Oettingen' 1 W-W
(pre-1907)

'Further-on' 1 Y-Y
(G.H. Johnstone, pre-1960)
'New Horizon' hybrid

'Fury' 2 Y-O
(G.L. Wilson, pre-1940)
'Workman' × 'Carbineer'
Perianth segments deep gold; corona vivid reddish orange

'Fury' 2 W-P
(Mrs C.O. Fairbairn)

'Furze Bloom' 2 Y-? (a)
(Cartwright & Goodwin, pre-1910)

'Fushimi'
(pre-1939)

'Fusilier' 3 Y-? (a)
(G.H. Engleheart, pre-1907)
2n=14,28

'Fusilier Grandiflorus' 3 W-?
Syn. of 'Bognor'

'Future' 2 W-? (b)
(de Graaff Bros, pre-1930)

'Future' 2 Y-Y
(R.H. Glover) R.H. Glover, 1972
'Noble Prince' × 'Gold Script'
Fl. 114 mm wide

'F.W.Burbidge' 1 W-W
(W. Backhouse, pre-1869)
Fl. facing down; perianth segments ovate, strongly inflexed, twisted; corona cylindrical, opening sulphur yellow, becoming milk white, with mouth a little flared and rim deeply and irregularly notched. Resembles an inferior 'Mrs Thompson'. Syn. Pseudonarcissus Moschatus 'F.W.Burbidge'

'F.W.Moore' 1 W-? (b)
(Hogg & Robertson, pre-1913)
See also 'F.Moore'

'Fynbos' 3 W-YOR
(Brian S.Duncan) Brian S.Duncan, 1996
'Mount Angel' × 'Doctor Hugh'; sdlg no. 1262
Fl. rounded, 102 mm wide; perianth segments broadly ovate; corona shallow bowl-shaped, slightly ribbed, orange, paling to yellow at base, shading to red at rim. Mid-season to late

'Fyno' 10 W-W
(Glenbrook Bulb Farm, 1987) Glenbrook Bulb Farm, 1997
Nylon Group × *N. cantabricus* var. *foliosus*
Fl. 30 mm wide, yellowish white (155D); perianth segments very narrowly ovate, acute; corona widely flared, with rim lightly crenate. Dwarf. Very early

G

'Gabor' 2 W-? (b)
(A.M. Wilson, pre-1930)

'Gabriel' 2 W-? (b)
(R.O. Backhouse, pre-1937)

'Gabriël Kleiberg' 11a W-WWR
(J. Gerritsen & Son) J. Gerritsen & Son, 1973

'Cassata' hybrid
Fl. rounded, 90 mm wide; perianth segments very broad, blunt, very slightly mucronate, creamy white, spreading, with margins minutely incurling, overlapping half or more; the inner segments a little narrower, with margins somewhat wavy; corona split, the six segments three-quarters the length of the perianth segments, opposite to them and joined at the margins in lower half, sometimes with two deep lobes overlapping at rim, ribbed, opening yellowish, becoming white, usually with a broad band of orange-red at rim, closely frilled, overlapping

'Gabriel's Trumpet' 1 Y-Y
M. Gardiner, 1956

'Gaby' 3 W-? (b)
(Mrs R.O. Backhouse, pre-1921)

'Gadabout' 2 Y-O
(J.N.Hancock & Co., 1984) J.N.Hancock & Co., 1997
Sdlg no. 16/84H
Perianth segments ovate, lemon yellow, spreading; corona bowl-shaped, expanded, bright reddish orange, frilled. Mid-season

'Gaddesby' 2 W-? (b)
(J.O. Sherrard, pre-1949)

'Gadfly' 2 W-YOR
(J.C. Williams, pre-1910)
Fl. facing slightly downwards; perianth segments ivory white, flushed pale sulphur yellow at base, reflexed; corona shallow, widely expanded, buff yellow at base, shading to rich orange-scarlet at rim

N. gaditanus Boissier & Reuter 13 Section Jonquilla

N. gaditanus Boissier & Reuter subsp. *minutiflorus* Willkomm = *N. minutiflorus*

'Gael' 2 W-? (b)
(Parr's Nurseries, 1943) Parr's Nurseries, 1958

'Gael Erica' 2 Y-OOY
(J.N.Hancock & Co., 1983) Unregistered
'Mao' × 'Artist's Model'; sdlg no. 96/83H
Perianth segments roundish, pale lemon yellow; corona disc-shaped, ribbed, bright yellow-orange, with touches of yellow at rim, tightly frilled. Mid-season

'Gaelic Rose' 2 W-P
(G.L. Wilson) E. Longford, 1965
('Charis' × 'Irish Rose') × 'Passionale'; sdlg no. 50/17
Fl. 95 mm wide; corona deep pink, occasionally paler at rim. Mid-season

'Gahana'
(pre-1973) Unregistered
?Syn. of 'Gahna'

'Gahna' 2 Y-?
(Mrs C.O. Fairbairn, pre-1972) Unregistered
?See also 'Gahana' and 'Ghana'

'Gaiety' 2 Y-O
(pre-1905)
Perianth segments narrow, pale primrose yellow; corona ribbed, brilliant fiery orange

'Gaiety' 2 Y-O
(R.H. Bath, pre-1923)
'Honourable Mrs Jocelyn' × *N. poeticus*
Fl. 108 mm wide; perianth segments ovate or somewhat oblong, blunt, sulphur, spreading, with margins sometimes notched, separated; the inner segments narrower and more usually ovate, with margins wavy; corona funnel-shaped, widely expanded, bright orange, heavily frilled. Mid-season

'Gaiety' 9 W-R
(pre-1927)

'Gaiety' 4 W-Y
Syn. of 'Erlicheer'

'Gaiety Girl' 2 W-? (b)
(D.H.L. Corrigan, pre-1949)

'Gail O'Kahn' 2 W-Y
(G.A. Ult den Boogaard) Warnaar & Co., 1965
Fl. 120 mm wide; perianth segments ivory white; corona vivid yellow 12A. Mid-season

'Gaily Clad' 2 W-P
(G.E. Mitsch) G.E. Mitsch, 1974
'Precedent' × 'Carita'; sdlg no. A34/16
Fl. 100 mm wide; perianth segments ivory white; corona disc-shaped, large, ribbed, buff apricot, touched with pink. Mid-season

'Gainsborough' 2 W-? (b)
(de Graaff Bros, pre-1927)

'Gainsborough' 2 W-P
(Carncairn Daffodils, 1964) Carncairn Daffodils, 1975
'Irish Rose' hybrid; sdlg no. 1/8/59
Fl. 88 mm wide; perianth segments greenish white (155A); corona pale yellowish pink 29D. Late

'Gairloch' 3 W-Y
(The Brodie of Brodie, *c.*1913)
'Marina' × 'Acme'
Perianth segments creamy white; corona very large and shallow, citron yellow

'Gajo' 2 Y-Y
(H. Aldersey, pre-1931)

Fl. 95 mm wide, facing down; perianth segments sulphur, regular, overlapping one-third; corona funnel-shaped, pale buttercup yellow. Mid-season

'Gala' 2 W-O
(G.L. Wilson, pre-1940)
'Folly' × 'Red Abbott'
Perianth segments pure white; corona shallow bowl-shaped, scarlet-orange, with a touch of green at base, frilled

'Gala Chief' 2 W-YYR
(J.N. Hancock & Co., 1948) J.N. Hancock & Co., 1965
Perianth segments ice white; corona with bright red at rim. Late. Resembles 'Khartum' but with a whiter perianth

'Gala Choice' 2 W-P
(R.H.Glover, pre-1993) Unregistered

'Galactic' 2 W-YYW
(Mrs G. Link) Mrs G. Link, 1985
'Easter Moon' × 'Wild Rose'; sdlg no. 12/72
Perianth segments very broad, blunt, of silken texture, overlapping; corona shallow, straw yellow, with rim usually becoming sulphur white, lightly frilled. Very late

'Gala Day' 2 Y-O

'Gala Gold' 2 Y-Y
(J.A. O'More, 1967) P.D.K. Ramsay, 1984
'Saint Keverne' open pollinated; sdlg no. 16/67

'Galah' 2 W-Y
(S.J. Bisdee, 1942)
'Eskimo' × 'Dawnglow'

'Galahad' 1 Y-Y
(T. Bloomer) Rathowen Daffodils, 1978
'Camelot' × 'Arctic Gold'; sdlg no. 5/72/65
Fl. 108 mm wide, deep gold; corona expanding slightly from base to mouth, with rim slightly flanged and dentate. Mid-season. Resembles a Div. 1 'Golden Jewel'. Varies between Divs 1 and 2

'Gala King' 2 Y-O
(Mrs H.K. Richardson) Mrs H.K. Richardson, 1974
'Tambourine' × 'Falstaff'
Fl. 97 mm wide

'Galalis' 2 W-? (b)
(S.A. Morrish, pre-1950)

N. galanthifolius Schultes f. (?'Galanthiflorus') = *N.* × *poculiformis*

'Galanthiflorus' 2 W-W
(pre-1884)

Syn. Poculiformis 'Galanthiflorus'. ?The same as *N. galanthiflorus*

'Galanthiflorus' 3 W-Y
Syn. of 'Flora'

'Galanthiflorus Aurantius' ?-Y
(?E. Leeds, pre-1877)
Corona citron yellow, tinged orange. Syn. Leedsii 'Galanthiflorus Aurantius'

'Galanthiflorus Major' 3 W-W
Syn. of 'Juno'

'Galanthiflorus Minor' 2 W-W
Syn. of 'Venus'

'Galanthiflorus Stellatus' 2? W-W
Syn. of 'Leda'

'Galashiels' 1 Y-Y
(W.M. Spry, pre-1973) Unregistered
'Early Prince' × 'Welcome'
Corona broad, lemon yellow. Tall. Very early

'Galashy' 2 Y-?
Syn. of 'Arizona'

'Galata' 3 W-YYR
(The Brodie of Brodie, *c.*1922)
'Mozart' × 'Gallipoli'; sdlg no. 40/B/17
Perianth segments ivory white; corona very shallow bowl-shaped, expanded, clear yellow, with a band of red at rim

'Galatea' 1 W-W
(J.G. Nelson, pre-1882)

'Galatea' 2 W-? (b)
(C.E. Radcliff, 1939)
'Meryl' × 'Kallista'

'Galaxy' 8
(E.H. Wheadon & Sons, pre-1914)

'Galaxy' 2 W-P
(G.L. Wilson, 1950) L. Major, 1965
Corona shell pink. Late

'Galaxy Prince' 2 YYW-W
(G.W.E. Brogden, 1980) Brogden Bulbs, 1991
'Gold Bank' × 'Daydream'; sdlg no. x74/G4
Fl. 110 mm wide; perianth segments broad, mid-lemon yellow, touched white at base, slightly twisted, very smooth; corona broad, mouth straight, with rim slightly dentate and lightly rolled. Early to mid-season

'Galbrina' 3 W-YYR
(W. Jackson Sr, pre-1945)

'Branwen' × 'Gwillian'

'Galcador' 2 Y-O
(J.L. Richardson, pre-1951)
'Sudan' × 'Penquite'
Perianth segments soft golden yellow; corona very shallow bowl-shaped, deep reddish orange

N. × *galdoanus* Fernández Casas 13 (parentage: *N. nobilis* (Haworth) Schultes f. × *N. triandrus* Linnaeus) = *N.* × *pravianoi*

'Galena' 2 W-GWY
(J.A. O'More) J.A. O'More, 1968
'Green Island' × 'Best Wishes'

'Galgorm' 1 Y-Y
(T. Bloomer) T. Bloomer, 1962
'Camelot' × 'Arctic Gold'
Fl. clear lemon

'Galil' 8 W-W
Syn. of 'Galilee'

'Galilee' 3 W-GWO
(G.L. Wilson, pre-1950)
'Nelly' × 'Chinese White'
Fl. forming a double triangle; perianth segments very broadly ovate, blunt, slightly mucronate, spreading, a little concave, smooth and of good substance, overlapping half; the inner segments more narrowly ovate, shouldered at base, a little inflexed, with margins slightly wavy; corona shallow, expanded, lightly ribbed, white, with green at base and a band of soft salmon orange at rim, neatly frilled, with rim crenate

'Galilee' 8 W-W
(Herut Yahel, pre-1988) Unregistered
Selected from French *N. papyraceus*
Fls 10-15 per stem; perianth segments ovate, fairly prominently mucronate, spreading or a little inflexed, with margins slightly incurling, overlapping one-third to a half; the inner segments more narrowly ovate, with midrib showing; corona cup-shaped, ribbed, with some green at base, mouth straight, wavy, rim crenate. Dwarf. Very early. Strongly scented. Resembles 'Ziva'. See also 'Galille', 'Galil'

'Galileo' 1 Y-Y
(C.G. van Tubergen, pre-1931)
Syn. 'Primavera', 'Sindbad'

'Galille' 8 W-W
Syn. of 'Galilee'

'Galipot' 1 Y-Y
(Cartwright & Goodwin, pre-1916)

'Gallactica' 2 Y-YOO
(Jackson's Daffodils) Jackson's Daffodils, 1993
'Sansui' × sdlg 290/70; sdlg no. 66/83
Fl. 107 mm wide; perianth segments broadly ovate, blunt or somewhat truncate, very slightly mucronate, brilliant yellow 13B, spreading, smooth and of thick substance, overlapping half; the inner segments more narrowly ovate, a little inflexed, with margins wavy; corona funnel-shaped, orange (28A) with brilliant orange-yellow at base, mouth straight and frilled. Mid-season. See also 'Gallatica'

'Gallant' 1 Y-Y
(F.G. Lawson, pre-1947)

'Gallantry' 2 Y-O
(S.J. Bisdee, 1948)
'Caruna' × 'Royal Mail'

'Gallantry' 2 W-? (b)
(G.A. Uit den Boogaard, pre-1954)

'Gallatica' 2 Y-YOO
Syn. of 'Gallactica'

'Galleon' 1 Y-Y
(G.L. Wilson, pre-1943)

'Gallery' 2 W-W
(W.G. Pannill) W.G. Pannill, 1980
'Vigil' × 'Empress of Ireland'; sdlg no. 62/31 A
Fl. 120 mm wide. Mid-season

'Gallia' 2 Y-? (a)
(M. van Waveren & Sons, pre-1938)

'Galliard' 2 Y-Y
(A.M. Wilson, pre-1928)
'Calif' hybrid

'Gallicus Major Flore Pleno' 4 Y-Y
(pre-1629)
Fl. pale whitish yellow or lemon; segments somewhat irregularly arranged; the outer whorl recurved at apex, touched with green below. Syn. "The Great Double French Daffodil", ? 'Scoticus Plenus', Pseudonarcissus 'Gallicus Major Flore Pleno'

'Gallicus Minor Flore Pleno' 4 Y-Y
Syn. of 'Eystettensis'

'Gallina' 2 W-YYR
(S.J. Bisdee) S.J. Bisdee, 1956
'Limerick' × 'Bishop'

'Gallipoli' 2 Y-O
(The Brodie of Brodie, *c*.1916)
'Bernardino' × 'Will Scarlett'
Fl. large; perianth segments ovate, blunt or truncate, only slightly mucronate, pale yellow, spreading, plane, overlapping one-third; the inner segments a little twisted; corona flushed deep glowing reddish

orange, mouth expanded and frilled, rim minutely crenate. Late

'Gallopade' 3? W-WWR
(?Sir J.S. Arkwright, pre-1931)
Fl. pure white; perianth segments slightly reflexed; corona with a narrow band of cinnamon red at rim

'Galmara' 2 W-Y
(A.O. Roblin, 1944)
'Arion' × 'Bonnington'

'Galopia' 2 W-R
(c.1934)

'Galopin' 2 W-O
(Mrs R.O. Backhouse, pre-1921)
Fl. forming a double triangle; perianth segments broadly ovate, blunt, with slight or sometimes prominent mucro, pure white, spreading, occasionally creased, of great substance, overlapping one-third to a half; the inner segments more narrowly ovate, twisted at apex; corona bowl-shaped, smooth orange, suffused with red, mouth expanded, deeply, broadly and somewhat irregularly lobed. Mid-season

'Galore' 2 W-O
(W.M. Spry, pre-1975) Unregistered
'Torchlight' × 'Lochin'
Corona broad, brownish orange. Mid-season

'Galtonia' 3 W-? (b)
(P. van Deursen, pre-1930)

'Galveston' 3 W-? (b)
(G. Lewis) D.S. Bell, 1955
Corona with a band of reddish orange at rim

'Galway' 2 Y-Y
(J.L. Richardson, pre-1943)
'Royalist'? × 'Crocus'?
Fl. forming a double triangle, 114 mm wide; perianth segments broadly ovate, blunt, not prominently mucronate, vivid yellow 9B, spreading, smooth, with midrib showing, overlapping one-third to a half; the inner segments a little narrower, somewhat inflexed, twisted or with margins wavy; corona funnel-shaped, lightly ribbed, a little brighter in tone (12A) than the perianth, mouth expanded and more strongly ribbed, rim notched and crenate. Mid-season. 2n=28. AM(e) 1942, AM(Haarlem) 1948, FCC(e) 1948, FCC(Haarlem) 1954, *AM(g) 1961, *FCC(g) 1962

'Gamay' 11a W-Y
(J. Gerritsen & Son) J. Gerritsen & Son, 1984
'Belcanto' × 'Mistral'; sdlg no. 36
Perianth segments ivory white; corona segments mimosa yellow, with bronze yellow at base. Mid-season. 2n=28

'Gambaga' 2 Y-? (a)
(A.M. Wilson) L.A. Hagen, 1957

'Gambas' 1 Y-Y
(A. Gray) A. Gray, 1964
Fl. 35 mm wide; perianth segments vivid yellow 9A; corona of a brighter tone (12A). Early. Resembles a larger and better-formed *N. asturiensis*

'Gambetta' 3 W-? (b)
(de Graaff Bros, pre-1938)
AM(Haarlem) 1937

'Gambit' 1 Y-Y
(A.M. Wilson, pre-1950)
Fl. dark yellow

'Gamble' 1 Y-Y
(C.E. Radcliff, 1938)
('Lord Roberts' × 'Cutty Sark') × 'Gambrinus'

'Gambler's Gift' 2 Y-O
(J.L. Richardson) Mrs H.K. Richardson, 1968
'Cambodia' × 'Vulcan'
Perianth segments deep gold; corona fiery orange, with rim neatly dentate

'Gambrina' 3 W-? (b)
(W. Jackson Sr, 1944) W. Jackson Jr, 1956

'Gambrinus' 1 Y-Y
(W. Jackson Sr, 1930)
'Eoster' × 'Swanley Perfection'

'Gamecock' 2 Y-? (a)
(Mrs R.O. Backhouse, pre-1921)

'Gamma' 2 W-? (b)
(?T. Buncombe, c.1936)

'Gamut' 1 YYW-W
(Jackson's Daffodils) Jackson's Daffodils, 1989
'Daydream' × sdlg 70/76; sdlg no. 179/84
Fl. 100 mm wide; perianth segments very broadly ovate, blunt or somewhat truncate, with slight white mucro, brilliant greenish yellow 3B, with yellowish white 155D at base and at midrib near apex, slightly reflexed, plane, smooth, overlapping half; the outer segments overlapping one another; the inner segments more nearly spreading; corona funnel-shaped, yellowish white 155D, with a narrow band of yellow at rim, mouth expanded and frilled. Mid-season to late

'Ganaway' 3 W-YOO
(Ballydorn Bulb Farm) Ballydorn Bulb Farm, 1984
'Strangford' × 'Northern Sceptre'
Fl. 110 mm wide. Mid-season

'Ganesh' 2 or 3

(?A.M. Wilson, c.1933)

'Ganges' 2 Y-? (a)
(Mrs P.M. Davis, pre-1948)

'Ganilly' 2 Y-Y
(P.D. Williams, pre-1931)
Perianth segments greenish yellow, spreading or a little inflexed, overlapping one-third; the inner segments sometimes twisted; corona funnel-shaped, narrow, smooth, slightly darker in tone than the perianth, with shades of orange, rim sharply flanged, regularly and deeply notched and crenate

'Ganimedes' 8 Y-Y
(pre-1807)
Fl. sulphur yellow

'Gannet' 2 Y-YYR
(P.D. Williams, pre-1923)
Perianth segments lemon; corona yellow, with bright red at rim

'Gannet' 2 W-? (b)
G. Zandbergen-Terwegen, 1959

'Ganymedes' 3 W-? (b)
(Mrs R.O. Backhouse, pre-1921)

"Ganymede's Cup"
Syn. of *N. triandrus*

ganymedioides = *N. tazetta*

'Garden Beauty' 8 W-Y
(R. van der Schoot & Son, pre-1931)
Poetaz
AM(Haarlem) 1930

'Garden Charm' 2 Y-O
(Warnaar & Co.) L. Schoorl, 1983

'Garden City' 3 Y-? (a)
(L. van Leeuwen & Son, pre-1950)

'Gardeners' Pride' 8 ?-YYO
(A.C. van der Schoot, pre-1926)
Poetaz
Corona deep golden yellow, with orange at rim. FA(Haarlem) 1926. Received FA(Haarlem) 1926 as 'Sensation'

'Garden Flame' 2 Y-O
(?Heathcote Bulb Nursery, pre-1951)
Perianth segments creamy yellow; corona rich reddish orange

'Garden Giant' 2 Y-? (a)
(de Graaff Bros, pre-1950)
AM(Haarlem) 1950

'Garden Gold' 2 Y-? (a)
(A.M. Wilson, pre-1948)

'Gardenia' 4 W-W
(pre-1914)
?Syn. of Poeticus 'Plenus'

'Garden Jewel' 8 W-Y
(A.C. van der Schoot, pre-1937)
Poetaz
Dwarf

'Garden Love' 1 Y-Y
(pre-1936)
Syn. 'King Edward VIII'

'Garden Magic' 2 Y-YYO
(J.N. Hancock & Co.) J.N. Hancock & Co., 1960
Corona with reddish orange at rim

'Garden News' 3 Y-ORR
(Brian S. Duncan) Brian S. Duncan, 1990
'Sun Magic' × ('Montego' × 'Achduart'); sdlg no. 891
Fl. forming a double triangle, 99 mm wide; perianth segments very broadly ovate, obscurely truncate, with slight white mucro, deep canary yellow, spreading, somewhat concave, with margins incurling at apex, smooth, regular, overlapping half; the inner segments a little more narrowly ovate; corona short broad funnel-shaped, ribbed, opening self orange-red (32A), becoming yellow-orange at base, mouth straight, split in places and overlapping, filled, with rim minutely crenate. Late

'Garden of Allah' 9
(pre-1907)

'Garden Officer' 3 W-YYR
(J.W.A. Lefeber, pre-1938)

'Garden Prayer' 7 W-GYP
(J. & E.Frey, 1981) J. & E.Frey, 1996
Sdlg F31/5 × *N. jonquilla*; sdlg no. QEE14/30
Fls 1-2 per stem, 75 mm wide when one fl. only, 60 mm when two; perianth segments white; corona creamy yellow shading to shell pink at rim, with green at base. Dwarf or standard. Mid-season

'Garden Princess' 6 Y-Y
(de Graaff Bros, pre-1938)
Perianth segments ovate, brilliant yellow 8A, strongly recurved, overlapping up to one-third; corona somewhat funnel-shaped, short, richer in tone (13A) than the perianth, with mouth slightly expanded. 2n=28. Resembles a better-formed 'February Gold' of stronger substance. TGA(Haarlem) 1956

'Garden Queen' 1 Y-Y
(G.B. van Rhijn, pre-1937)
AM(Haarlem) 1939

'Garden Song' 2 W-GWP
(J. & E.Frey)
'Coral Ribbon' × sdlg FEE5/2; sdlg no. PEF1/5
Fl. 90 mm wide; perianth segments roundish; corona creamy white, with green at base, shading to soft salmon pink at rim. Dwarf. Mid-season

'Garden Sun' 1 Y-Y
(de Graaff Bros) de Graaff Bros, 1962
Perianth segments brilliant greenish yellow 6B; corona vivid yellow 13A. Mid-season. AM(Haarlem) 1962

'Gardenvale' 2 W-OOY
(Carncairn Daffodils) Carncairn Daffodils, 1969
'Kilworth' × 'Roimond'
Perianth segments milk white; corona expanded, orange, paling through orange-yellow to green at base, with orange-yellow at rim, rim flanged

'Gardoon' 2 Y-? (a)
(A.H. Ahrens) J.S. Leitch, 1956

'Garforth' 1 Y-Y
(Mrs M.Moorby) Mrs M.Moorby, 1956

'Gargleblaster' 1 Y-Y
(Glenbrook Bulb Farm, 1983) Glenbrook Bulb Farm, 1997
'Golden' × 'Heart of Gold'
Fl. 102 mm wide; perianth segments ovate, brilliant yellow 12B, spreading; corona funnel-shaped, slightly darker in tone (12A) than the perianth, with mouth flared and frilled. Mid-season

'Garian' 2 Y-OOR
(W. Jackson Jr, 1970) Unregistered
('Mars' × 'Ceylon') × 'Janz'; sdlg no. 36/70

'Garibaldi' 8 W-O
(pre-1863)

'Garibaldi' 2 Y-O
(A.M. Wilson, pre-1931)
'Hospodar' hybrid; sdlg no. 491
Perianth segments narrow, lemon yellow, with margins sometimes notched, overlapping at base only; corona rich orange. Mid-season. 2n=28. AM(c) 1931, *(Kirton)AM(g) 1934

'Garland' 2 Y-YOO
(The Brodie of Brodie, c.1938)
'Seraglio' × 'Copper Bowl'; sdlg no. 81/E/33
Perianth segments very broad, waxy, of good substance; corona very shallow, dark orange, paling to gold at base. AM(Haarlem) 1955

"Garland"
See "The Garland"

'Garlidna' 3 Y-O
Syn. of 'Garlidna'

'Garlidna' 3 Y-O
(P.D. Williams, pre-1927)
Perianth segments creamy yellow; corona reddish orange. See also 'Garlidina'

'Garlinge' 2 Y-? (a)
(F.D.B. Cobb, pre-1953)

'Garnet' 3 W-? (b)
(N.Y. Lower, pre-1916)

'Garos' 1 Y-Y
(W. Jackson Sr, 1946)
'Shirin' × 'Gorm'

'Garrick' 3 W-YYR
(J.L. Richardson, pre-1947)
'Mitylene' × 'Coronach'
Perianth segments pure white; corona very shallow bowl-shaped, yellow, with red at rim

'Garron' 1 Y-Y
(G.L. Wilson, pre-1934)
'King of May' hybrid
Fl. 128 mm wide; perianth segments broad, brilliant yellow 9C, slightly twisted, smooth, of good texture, overlapping half; corona almost cylindrical, of a brighter tone (12A) than the perianth, mouth expanded. 2n=28. AM(e) 1944, *AM(g) 1946, AM(Haarlem) 1948

'Gartan' 2 Y-O
(G.L. Wilson) Guy L.Wilson Ltd, 1961

'Garter King' 2 Y-Y
(F.E. Board) F.E. Board, 1965
'Galway' × 'Golden Rapture'
Mid-season

'Garth' 1 Y-Y
(?New Zealand origin, pre-1990) Unregistered

'Gascogne' 1 Y-Y
(J. Gerritsen & Son, pre-1944)
See also 'Cascogne'

'Gascon' 2 Y-OOR
(A.M.Wilson, pre-1913)
'Princess Mary' hybrid
Fl. large; perianth segments very broad, primrose yellow, with a darker stain at base, reflexed, smooth; corona widely expanded, reddish orange, shading to orange-red at rim

'Gasparilla' 2 Y-WPY
(W.G.Pannill, 1986) W.G.Pannill, 1996
'Keepsake' × ('Camelot' × 'Daydream'); sdlg no.

80/2 C
Mid-season

'Gateway' 2 W-YYO
(G.E. Mitsch) G.E. Mitsch, 1972
'Pretender' × 'High Life'; sdlg no. Z60/1
Fl. rounded, 90 mm wide; perianth segments milk white, overlapping; corona very shallow bowl-shaped, pale lemon yellow, with a band of orange at rim. Mid-season

'Gath-a-Bawn' 2 W-W
(G.L. Wilson, pre-1956) Unregistered
(['Okapi' × 'Samite'] × 'Evening') × 'Greenland'

'Gaucho' 2 Y-O
(G.L. Wilson, pre-1953)
Perianth segments deep yellow; corona deep scarlet-orange. 2n=29

'Gaudeamus' 11a W-Y
(Juris Svarcs) Juris Svarcs, 1992
'Semiramis' × 'Orangery'; sdlg no. 84-01-03
Fl. 90 mm wide; perianth segments very broad, not prominently mucronate, greenish white (157C), spreading, somewhat creased, overlapping half; the inner segments a little inflexed, with margins wavy, prominently shouldered at base; corona split to base, the six segments half to two-thirds the length of the perianth segments, opposite to them and joined at margins in lower half, deeply bi-lobed, pale greenish yellow, with brilliant yellow 10A towards rim, spreading, heavily frilled. Mid-season

'Gaultier' 2 Y-? (a)
(J.L. Richardson) Sir A.T.C. Neave, 1957

'Gauntlet' 3 W-O
(G.W.E. Brogden) G.W.E. Brogden, 1964
Fl. 115 mm wide; corona reddish orange. Mid-season. Resembles 'Arbar' but with the perianth segments more nearly acute

'Gavotte' 9 W-?
(F.H. Chapman, pre-1913)

'Gavotte' 2 Y-R
(J.S. Leitch) J.S. Leitch, 1956

'Gawkabout' 4 W-Y
(Glenbrook Bulb Farm, 1982) Glenbrook Bulb Farm, 1997
'Anne of Cleves' × 'Matapan'
Fl. 92 mm wide; perianth segments broadly ovate, greenish white (155A); corona segments brilliant yellow 13B, lightly wavy. Late

'Gay Bachelor' 2 Y-? (a)
(R.O. Backhouse, pre-1937)

'Gay Ballad' 2 W-WWY
(P. de Jager & Sons) P. de Jager & Sons, 1963
'Criterion' × 'Pink Fancy'
Fl. 92 mm wide; perianth segments ivory white; corona with light yellow 10B at rim. Mid-season

'Gay Bandit' 3 W-? (b)
(P.D. Williams, pre-1948)

'Gay Banner' 2 W-? (b)
(Mrs R.O. Backhouse, pre-1908)

'Gaybird' 2 W-? (b)
(E.M. Crosfield, pre-1914)

'Gay Boa'
(New Zealand origin, pre-1940)

'Gay Bowness' 9 W-?
(P.D. Williams, pre-1943)

'Gay Boy' 2 Y-R
(M.P. Williams, pre-1949)

'Gay Brano' 2 W-GPP
(W. Jackson Jr, c.1978) Unregistered
'Neerim' × 'Gideon'

'Gaybrook' 2 W-YYO
(Carncairn Daffodils) Carncairn Daffodils, 1973
'Blarney' × 'Killala'
Fl. 89 mm wide

'Gay Buccaneer' 4 Y-O
(J.L. Richardson) Mrs H.K. Richardson, 1968
'Gay Time' × 'Vulcan'
Perianth and other petaloid segments in several whorls, pale golden yellow; the inner whorls shorter; corona segments shorter still, interspersed among the inner whorls of petaloid segments, reddish orange

'Gay Cavalier' 4 Y-O
(J.L. Richardson) Mrs H.K. Richardson, 1967
'Gay Time' × 'Vulcan' or 'Golden Rapture'
Perianth and other petaloid segments in several whorls, pale lemon; corona segments smaller, interspersed, bright orange. Very late

'Gay Challenger' 4 W-O
(J.L. Richardson) Mrs H.K. Richardson, 1962
'Gay Time' × 'Arbar'
Fl. 117 mm wide; perianth and segments very broadly ovate, pure white, a little concave, overlapping half; the outer whorl truncate, prominently mucronate, spreading; the inner whorl a little shorter, blunt, only very slightly mucronate, inflexed, with margins wavy; a number of segments at centre strongly inflexed, twisted or with margins deeply incurling or folded inwards; corona segments very short, interspersed among the petaloid segments at centre, brilliant

orange 29A, tightly frilled. Mid-season. AM(e) 1964, FCC(e) 1972

'Gay Charm' 2 Y-R
(J.A. Morris) J.A. Morris, 1957

'Gay Colours' 2 W-R
(T. Bloomer) T. Bloomer, 1962
'Fermoy' × 'Arbar'; sdlg no. 1/39/54
Corona deep red

'Gay Comedy' 2 W-YYR
(H.A. Brown, 1939) J.N. Hancock & Co., 1960
Perianth segments broadly ovate, blunt, fairly prominently mucronate, creamy white, spreading, overlapping one-third; the inner segments inflexed, with margins wavy; corona shallow funnel-shaped, golden yellow, with a broad band of tomato red at rim, mouth widely expanded, ribbed and a little frilled, rim notched and minutely crenate. Tall. Late

'Gay Crest' 2 W-O
(R.C.A. Tombleson) R.C.A. Tombleson, 1964
Fl. 108 mm wide; corona tangerine orange. Mid-season. Resembles a smaller and earlier-flowered 'Arbar'

'Gay Crusader' 1 Y-Y
(G.H. Johnstone, pre-1949)

'Gay Dancer' 3 W-? (b)
(K.L. Reynolds, pre-1937)

'Gay Dawn' 4
(J.L. or Mrs Richardson, pre-1978) Unregistered

'Gay Day' 3 W-? (b)
(F.H. Chapman, pre-1930)

'Gay Deceiver' 3 W-? (b)
(Barr & Sons, pre-1946)

'Gay Delight' 2 W-ORR
(Tom Forster, 1960s) Unregistered
Fl. rounded; corona very shallow bowl-shaped, widely expanded, fiery red, with brilliant orange at base. Early to mid-season

'Gay Fantasy' 2 W-O
(J.S. Leitch) J.S. Leitch, 1964

'Gay Fiesta' 2 W-R
(G. Lewis) D.S. Bell, 1955
Perianth segments broadly ovate, blunt, mucronate, pure white, spreading, smooth, overlapping half; corona broad disc-shaped, ribbed, with a band of bright red at rim

'Gay Flinger' 4
(J.L. or Mrs Richardson, pre-1978) Unregistered

'Gay Glorious' 4 Y-O
(Tom Forster, 1960s) Unregistered
Fl. rounded; perianth and other petaloid segments broadly ovate; the inner whorls of a richer yellow than the outer; corona segments interspersed, mid-orange. Tall. Early

'Gay Gold' 1 Y-Y
(J.N. Hancock & Co., 1963) Unregistered

'Gay Gordon' 2 Y-O
(G. Lewis, 1935) Parr's Nurseries, 1958
Corona scarlet-orange

'Gay Heart' 9 W-?
(G.H. Engleheart, pre-1916)

'Gay Hussar' 3 Y-O
(Barr & Sons, pre-1918)
Perianth segments primrose yellow; corona shallow, widely expanded, rich scarlet-orange

N. gayi Pugsley 13 Section Pseudonarcissus (?'Princeps')

'Gay King' 4
(J.L. or Mrs Richardson) Unregistered

'Gay Knight' 2 Y-? (a)
(S.C. Gaspar, 1946) R.J. Abernethy, 1957

'Gay Kybo' 4 W-O
(Mrs H.K. Richardson) du Plessis Bros, 1980
'Gay Time' × 'Rameses'
Fl. 105 mm wide; perianth and other petaloid segments blunt, slightly mucronate, inflexed, overlapping; the outer whorl sometimes more than six in number; corona segments interspersed, nearest to strong orange 25A, with rim crenate. Mid-season. AM(e) 1987, FCC(e) 1992, AGM 1995

'Gay Lad' 8
(Cartwright & Goodwin, pre-1910)

'Gay Lad' 2 Y-YYO
(J.N. Hancock & Co., 1949) J.N. Hancock & Co., 1960
Perianth segments primrose; corona with orange at rim

'Gaylee' 2 W-W
(G. Lewis, 1940) D.S. Bell, 1958

'Gay Light' 2 Y-? (a)
(Warnaar & Co., pre-1933)

'Gay Look' 3 W-O
(Konynenburg & Mark) Konynenburg & Mark, 1964
'Binkie' × 'Spellbinder'

Perianth segments ivory white; corona strong orange 30D, with a paler tone at base. Early

'Gaylord' 2 Y-YOO
(D.F. Lee) D.F. Lee, 1979
Fl. 91 mm wide; perianth segments vivid yellow 9B; corona strong orange 25A, with a darker yellow than the perianth at base. Early. 2n=28

'Gay Lover' 2 Y-YYR
(H.A. Brown, 1937)
Perianth segments broad, primrose yellow; corona large, expanded, lemon yellow, with bright red at rim. Mid-season to late. Syn. 'Glover'

'Gay Masquerade' 4 W-R
(D.S. Bell) D.S. Bell, 1982
('Falaise' × ' Masquerade') × 'Gay Challenger'
Fl. 104 mm wide. Mid-season. Resembles 'Gay Challenger' but with the corona segments of a purer colour

'Gay Mood' 2 W-P
(G.E. Mitsch) G.E. Mitsch, 1962
'Green Island' × (['White Sentinel' × 'Mrs R.O.Backhouse'] × 'Wild Rose')
Fl. 102 mm wide; corona rose pink. Mid-season. Resembles 'Leonaine' but with a darker-toned and more heavily frilled corona

'Gaynelle' 3 W-? (b)
(Mrs F.S. Foote, pre-1940)

'Gayness' 2 W-WWP
(J.N. Hancock & Co., pre-1950)
Corona flushed pink

'Gaynor' 2 W-P
(C.E. Radcliff, 1940) J. Radcliff, 1956
'White Sentinel' × 'Princess Betty'

'Gaynor' 2 Y-? (a)
(S.C. Gaspar, 1948) S.C. Gaspar, 1957

'Gay Note' 2 Y-R
(J.A. Morris) J.A. Morris, 1960
Fl. 115 mm wide. Mid-season. Resembles 'Revelry' but with the perianth segments of a clearer yellow

'Gay Pinkie' 2 W-? (b)
(pre-1955)

'Gay Pride' 2 W-P
(R.C.A. Tombleson) R.C.A. Tombleson, 1966
Late

'Gay Reaper' 2 Y-O
(J.N. Hancock & Co., 1946)

'Gay Record' 4 W-O
(J.L. Richardson) Mrs H.K. Richardson, 1964
'Gay Time' × 'Tulyar'
Perianth and other petaloid segments white; corona segments deep orange. 2n=28

'Gay Rose' W-P
(Australian origin, pre-1950)

'Gay Ruler' 4 W-O
(Mrs H.K. Richardson) Mrs H.K. Richardson, 1974
'Gay Time' × 'Matapan'
Fl. 90 mm wide

'Gay Salute' 2 Y-O
(J.N. Hancock & Co.) J.N. Hancock & Co., 1960
Corona widely expanded, soft deep orange

'Gay Side' 4
(J.L. or Mrs Richardson, pre-1978) Unregistered

'Gay Sol' 2 Y-R
(J.N. Hancock & Co., 1959) Unregistered
Perianth segments slightly mucronate, golden yellow, of good substance; corona expanded, intense orange-red, frilled

'Gay Song' 4 W-W
(J.L. Richardson) Mrs H.K. Richardson, 1968
'Gay Time' × 'Brussells'
Fl. large; perianth and other petaloid segments in several whorls, broadly ovate, blunt or truncate, slightly mucronate, pure white, inflexed, overlapping half or more; the inner whorls more strongly inflexed, with margins wavy or incurled; corona segments short, clustered among petaloid segments at centre, white, faintly touched with lemon yellow. Late. Scented. 2n=28

'Gay Sonnet' 2 Y-? (a)
(J.A. Morris) J.A. Morris, 1957

'Gay Spring' 2 Y-YYO
(G. Lubbe & Son, pre-1947)
Perianth segments lemon yellow; corona shallow. AM(Haarlem) 1946

'Gay Stroller' 1 Y-Y
(A. Gibson, pre-1951)

'Gay Sun' 2 Y-R
(S.A. Free) S.A. Free, 1961
Fl. 102 mm wide. Mid-season

'Gay Symphony' 4 W-Y
(J.L. Richardson) Mrs H.K. Richardson, 1973
'Gay Time' × 'Brussels'
Fl. large; perianth and other petaloid segments in several whorls, pure white; the outer whorl very broad, deeply overlapping; the inner whorls neatly arranged; corona segments interspersed, smaller, pale lemon.

Mid-season. 2n=28

'Gay Tabor' 4 W-O
(?Dutch origin, pre-1996) Unregistered

'Gay Time' 4 W-R
(J.L. Richardson, pre-1952)
'Falaise' × 'Limerick'
Fl. 108 mm wide; perianth and other petaloid segments in three whorls, broadly ovate, blunt or squarish at apex, creamy white, smooth, overlapping half; the outer whorl prominently mucronate, a little inflexed, with midrib showing; the inner whorls only very slightly mucronate; the second whorl a little shorter than the outer and more strongly inflexed; the centre whorl shorter still, strongly inflexed, crumpled and with margins incurling; corona segments very short, tightly frilled and clustered among the petaloid segments at centre, or more loosely frilled and interspersed among the surrounding whorls, orange-red (30B). Late. 2n=28. AM(e) 1955

'Gayton' 2 W-? (b)
(R.H. Bath, pre-1931)
Perianth segments broadly ovate, blunt or squarish at apex, slightly mucronate, spreading, a little creased, overlapping one-third to a half; the inner segments narrower and slightly inflexed; corona deep bowl-shaped, loosely ribbed, mouth more tightly ribbed, straight, split in places and overlapping, even, with rim notched. Syn. 'Saint Germans'

'Gay Trip' 4 W-R
(J.L. Richardson) Mrs H.K. Richardson, 1970
'Gay Time' × 'Arbar'

'Gay Vagabond' 2 W-YYO
(Tom Forster, 1960s) Unregistered
Perianth segments very broad, only very slightly mucronate, creamy white, spreading or somewhat reflexed, overlapping half or more; corona very broad disc-shaped, ribbed, soft lemon yellow, shading to golden orange at rim, rim unevenly and deeply dentate. Mid-season

'Gay Vienna' 2 Y-O
(G. Lewis) D.S. Bell, 1955

'Gaywood' 2 Y-Y
(R.H. Bath, pre-1933)

'Gaza' 1 W-W
(G.H. Engleheart, pre-1923)
Fl. large, of strong substance; corona tinged green at base

'Gazana' 2 Y-? (a)
(R.H. Bath, pre-1931)

'Gazelle' 3 W-Y
(W. Backhouse, pre-1869)
Perianth segments creamy white; corona canary yellow, tinged orange. Syn. Barrii Albidus 'Gazelle'. Was "absorbed" into 'Piccio'

'Gazelle' 2 W-? (b or c)
(Mrs R.O. Backhouse, pre-1921)

'Gazelle' 7 Y-Y
(G.E. Mitsch) G.E. Mitsch, 1970
'Aircastle' × ? *N. jonquilla*; sdlg no. Z2/40
Fl. rounded; perianth segments pale lemon yellow; corona opening lemon yellow, becoming paler, with amber tones at base. Mid-season

'Gazelon' 2 Y-R
(A.M. Wilson, pre-1948)
Perianth segments yellow; corona deep red

'Geddes' 1 W-W
(Brodie Gardens) Brodie Gardens, 1959
'Kanchenjunga' × 'Nevis'

'Gedonia' 2 Y-? (a)
(Mrs R.O. Backhouse, pre-1921)

'Geehi' 2 Y-O
(J.N. Hancock & Co., 1955) Unregistered

'Geele Hofnagel' 8 Y-Y
(pre-1798)
Fl. pale yellow

'Geertruida Carelsen' 2 Y-Y
(E.H. Krelage & Son, pre-1938)
'King Alfred' × 'Lady Margaret Boscawen'
AM(Haarlem) 1937

'Gee Tee' 2 Y-Y
(G.W. Tarry) Koanga Daffodils, 1992
Fl. 105 mm wide, rounded; perianth segments very broadly ovate, vivid yellow 9A, plane; corona funnel-shaped, darker in tone (15A) than the perianth, mouth flared, rim flanged. Mid-season

'Geevor' 4 Y-YYO
(R.A.Scamp) R.A.Scamp, 1994
'Saint Keverne' × 'Tamar Fire'; sdlg no. S274
Fl. 100 mm wide; perianth and other petaloid segments in several whorls, broadly ovate, blunt, very slightly mucronate, golden yellow, smooth, overlapping half; the two outer whorls of about equal length, spreading or a little inflexed, more or less plane; the inner whorls shorter, strongly inflexed, with margins incurling; corona segments shorter still, broad, yellow, touched with orange at rim, frilled. Early to mid-season. Sunproof

'Geewizz' 11a W-P
(M.G.Temple-Smith) M.G.Temple-Smith, 1997

'Valdrome' × 'Dear Me'; sdlg no. 49/88
Fl. 90 mm wide; corona deeply split, the six segments opposite and closely overlying the perianth segments, becoming inflexed with age, sometimes bi-lobed, moderate yellowish pink, with a line of a deeper tone at base, fading to white at rim with age, frilled. Mid-season to late

'Geheimniss' 3 W-? (b or c)
(A.M. Wilson, pre-1908)

'Gehema' 2 Y-Y
(de Graaff Bros, pre-1936)
Perianth segments soft sulphur yellow; corona widely expanded, chrome yellow, with a darker tone at rim. AM(Haarlem) 1935

'Geisha' 3 Y-? (a)
(H.G. Longford, pre-1927)

'Geisha' 2 W-P
(G.L. Wilson) G.L. Wilson, 1960
('Gracious' × 'Evening') × 'Irish Rose'

'G.E.Lane' 2 Y-? (a)
(Mrs R.O. Backhouse, pre-1921)

'Gelria' 1 Y-Y
(de Graaff Bros, pre-1929)

'Gelwil' 1 W-W
(G.L. Wilson, pre-1938)

'Gem' 3 W-W
(W. Backhouse, pre-1869)
Perianth segments ovate, fairly prominently mucronate, pure white, slightly inflexed, separated; the inner segments with margins sometimes incurved or recurved; corona cup-shaped, straight-sided, lightly ribbed, opening greenish yellow, becoming white, mouth straight, rim irregularly and slightly dentate. Mid-season or earlier. Syn. Leedsii 'Gem'

'Gemini' 5
(?F.H. Chapman, pre-1915)

'Gemini Girl' 2 W-P
(R.A.Scamp) Mr & Mrs R.A.Hough, 1996
'Chenoweth' × 'Kirklington'; sdlg no. 371
Fl. 100 mm wide; perianth segments ovate, pure white, deeply overlapping; corona funnel-shaped, clear pink, with mouth slightly flared. Early to mid-season. Sunproof

'Geminy' 3 W-? (b)
(A.H. Ahrens) J.S. Leitch, 1956

'Gemma' 2 W-? (b)
(Papendrecht-Vandervoet, pre-1939)

'Gem Major' ?-Y
(?W. Backhouse, pre-1869)
Corona long, lemon yellow

'Gem of Antrim' 2 W-P
(T. Bloomer) T. Bloomer, 1964
'Interim' × 'Rose Caprice'; sdlg no. 1/47/58
$2n=28$

'Gem of Spring' 2 W-P
(T. Bloomer) T. Bloomer, 1970
'Salome' × 'Debutante'

'Gem of Ulster' 2 W-P
(T. Bloomer) T. Bloomer, 1964
'Interim' × 'Rose Caprice'; sdlg no. 4/47/58
Corona pink, shading to deep pink at rim, with rim dentate. $2n=28$

'General' 2 Y-Y
(P. Phillips) P. Phillips, 1968

'General Allenby' 2 W-? (b or c)
(J.R. Pearson & Sons, pre-1923)

'General Allenby' 1 W-Y
(pre-1927)

'General Baden Powell' 1 Y-Y
(pre-1908)

'General Buller' 2 or 3 W-? (b or c)
(P.D. Williams, pre-1907)

'General Byrd' 2 Y-? (a)
(L. Steenvoorden) L. Steenvoorden, 1957
TGA(Haarlem) 1957

'General Eisenhower' 2 Y-O
(H.P. Zwetsloot, pre-1945)
AM(Haarlem) 1948

'General French' 1 Y-Y
(Barr & Sons, pre-1923)

'General Gordon' 1 Y-Y
(E.H.Krelage & Son, pre-1885)
Fl. bright yellow; corona large, mouth very widely expanded. Syn. Pseudonarcissus Major 'Chinese Gordon'. FCC 1885. At one time identified (probably wrongly) with 'Spurius Coronatus'. Received FCC 1885 as 'Spurius Coronatus' . Was "absorbed" into 'Thomas Moore'

'General Gordon' 4
(W.B. Hartland, pre-1885)
N. pseudonarcissus × *N.* × *incomparabilis*

'General Gorgas' 3 W-? (b)
(L. van Leeuwen & Son, pre-1931)

'General Gruenther' 2 W-? (b)
(M. van Waveren & Sons, pre-1954)

'Generaliffe' 3 Y-O
(G. Lubbe & Son, 1950) G. Lubbe & Son, 1960
Fl. 85 mm wide; perianth segments pale buttercup yellow; corona deep orange. Mid-season. AM(Haarlem) 1960

'General Joffre' 1 Y-Y
(C. Dawson, pre-1923)

'General Jurgens'
(pre-1939)

'General Leman' 1 Y-Y
(A.E. Lowe, pre-1927)

'General MacArthur' 2 Y-Y
(Oregon Bulb Farms, pre-1942)

'General Murray' 3 W-? (b)
(W. Backhouse, pre-1869)
Perianth segments creamy white, overlapping. Resembles an inferior 'Maurice Vilmorin'. Syn. Barrii Albidus 'General Murray'. "Absorbed" 'Mrs Horace Darwin' and 'Mrs Murray'

'General Patton' 1 W-Y
(J.W.A. Lefeber, 1944) J.F. Prins, 1959
Perianth segments creamy white; corona sulphur yellow. Resembles a larger-flowered 'President Lebrun'. TGA(Haarlem) 1960

'General Pershing' 7 Y-Y
(de Graaff Bros, pre-1923)
'Rugulosus Maximus' hybrid

'General Philip Curtis' 1 Y-Y
(J.B. van der Schoot, pre-1954)

'General Roberts' 1
(pre-1901)
Fl. large, symmetrical. FCC 1901

'General Sarrail' 2 W-? (b)
(Barr & Sons, pre-1923)
'Maggie May' × 'Weardale Perfection'

'General Smuts' 2 Y-O
(J.L. Richardson, pre-1947)

'General Townsend' 1 Y-Y
(J.R. Pearson & Sons, pre-1923)

'General Windham' 8 Y or W-Y
(pre-1861)
See also 'General Wyndham'

'General Wyndham' 8 Y or W-Y

Syn. of 'General Windham'

N. genesii-lopezii Fernández Casas 13 Section Pseudonarcissus

'Genevieve' 3 W-? (b)
(A.M. Wilson, pre-1908)

'Genevra' 1 W-? (b)
(J.W. Barr, pre-1930)

'Genial Star' 3 W-YYR
(W.F.M.Copeland, pre-1910)
Hybrid between 'Homer' and 'Siddington'
Perianth segments pure white, of good substance, overlapping; corona disc-shaped, heavily ribbed, brilliant lemon yellow, with a broad band of intense orange-red at rim

'Genii' 2? W-W
(W. Backhouse, pre-1869)
Corona silver white. Syn. Leedsii 'Genii'

N. gennarii Parlatore = *N. papyraceus*

'Genoa' 1 W-W
(G.H. Engleheart, pre-1907)

'Genteel' 1 W-W
(W.G. Pannill) W.G. Pannill, 1978
'Vigil' × 'Empress of Ireland'; sdlg no. 64/119 K
Fl. 120 mm wide. Mid-season

'Gentility' 2 W-W
(G.L. Wilson, pre-1947)
'White Sentinel' × 'Evening'
Perianth segments broadly ovate; corona rim slightly flanged

'Gentle Giant' 2 W-O
(J.W.A.Lefeber) Van Eeden Goohof, 1995
Fl. 120 mm wide; perianth segments greenish white (between 155A and 1D), touched brilliant greenish yellow 6B at base; corona orange (between 28A and B), paling to yellow-orange (23A) below. Mid-season

'Genuine' 1 Y-Y
(R.W. Ward) M.J. Jefferson-Brown, 1975
Mid-season. Syn. 'Penbearth'

genuinus = *N. bulbocodium* var. *genuinus*

'Geoffrey' 1 W-Y
(R. Gibson, pre-1927)

'Geoffrey Hay' 2 W-? (b)
(H.R. Meyer, pre-1927)

'Geometrics' 2 W-Y
(Sidney DuBose, 1979) Sidney DuBose, 1990

'Precedent' × 'Camelot'; sdlg no. MS42-30
Fl. 95 mm wide; corona light yellow. Mid-season

'George' 9 W-?
(?van Zonneveld Bros & Philippo, pre-1930)

'George' 1 W-Y
(H.M. Hammond, 1950) P. Phillips, 1964
Fl. 102 mm wide; corona primrose yellow. Mid-season

'George Armstrong' 11b Y-O/?Y
(J.W.A. Lefeber) J.W.A. Lefeber, 1958
Corona segments with orange and ?yellow in longitudinal bands

'George Bass' 2 W-Y
(Tom Forster, 1960s) Unregistered
Fl. rounded; perianth segments milk white; corona disc-shaped, opening bright lemon yellow, becoming buff yellow, frilled. Early

'George Davidson'
(pre-1951)

'George Engleheart' 8 W-Y
(G.H. Engleheart, pre-1890)
'Bazelman Major' × 'Ornatus'
Corona pale yellow, with a brighter tone at rim. AM 1890. Mis-named 'G.H.Engleheart'

'George H.Barr' 1 W-Y
(E. Leeds, pre-1877)
Syn. Pseudonarcissus Bicolor 'George H.Barr'

'George Herbert' 9 W-?
(G.H. Engleheart, pre-1913)

'George Jones' 2 W-YYO
(H.A. Brown, 1941)
Corona widely expanded, soft lemon yellow, with yellow-orange at rim, frilled. Late

'George Leak' 2 W-O
(J.L. Richardson) J.L. Richardson, 1960
'Kilworth' × 'Arbar'
Fl. 87 mm wide; perianth segments broadly ovate, prominently mucronate, snow white, spreading, with margins incurling at apex, smooth, of thick substance, overlapping half; the inner segments more narrowly ovate, with margins wavy or more strongly incurled; corona shallow broad funnel-shaped, ribbed, yellow-orange (14A tinged 21A or 23A), mouth more strongly ribbed, wavy, deeply split and overlapping. Sunproof. 2n=28. AM(Haarlem) 1969

$N. \times geogemawii$ Fernández Casas 13 (parentage: $N.$ $elegans$ (Haworth) Spach × $N. viridiflorus$ Schousboe) = $N. \times obsoletus$

'George Moran' 2 W-WWY
(L.P. Dettman, 1968) L.P. Dettman, 1979
'Content' × 'Ellimatta'; sdlg no. L3/69
Fl. 98 mm wide; perianth segments greenish white (2D); corona paler (155A), with a yellowish tone at rim. Mid-season. Resembles 'Daisy Schäffer' but with the perianth segments paler and the corona rim more heavily dentate

'George Nicholson' 2 W-Y
(Barr & Sons, pre-1893)
Perianth segments pure white; corona clear yellow. Late

'George Philip Haydon' 1 Y-Y
(G.P. Haydon, pre-1905)
Perianth segments primrose yellow; corona canary yellow, with mouth expanded and ribbed

'George R.Barr' 1 W-? (b)
(Barr & Sons, pre-1890)

'George Rogers Clark' 2 W-W
(L. van Leeuwen & Son, pre-1931)
Corona widely expanded, greenish, paling to cream at base, frilled. AM(Haarlem) 1931

'George Sand' 2 W-O
(J.W.A. Lefeber) J.W.A. Lefeber, 1960
Fl. 85 mm wide; perianth segments pure white; corona reddish orange. Mid-season

'George's Pink' 2 W-GPP
(G.W. Tarry) Carncairn Daffodils, 1989
'Ann Cameron' × 'Dailmanach'; sdlg no. 1/67/76
Fl. 106 mm wide; perianth segments slightly reflexed; the inner segments a little narrower; corona long, with mouth expanded and rim rolled. Mid-season

'George Tindale' 2 Y-GRR
(L.P. Dettman) L.P. Dettman, 1978
'Vulcan' × 'Spelter'; sdlg no. 61/75
Fl. 89 mm wide; perianth segments vivid yellow 14A, with a coppery sheen; corona orange-red, with green at base. Mid-season. Resembles 'Coope' but with a paler perianth

'Georgette' 2 W-? (b)
(R. & G. Cuthbert, pre-1938)

'Georgia' 2 Y-? (a)
(de Graaff Bros, pre-1928)
Syn. 'Leander'

'Georgia' 2 W-P
Syn. of 'Agrippina'

'Georgia Moon' 2 Y-Y
(Warnaar & Co.) Warnaar & Co., 1962
'Riva' × 'Truth'

Fl. 110 mm wide, primrose yellow. Mid-season. AM(Haarlem) 1965

'Georgiana' 2 W-? (b or c)
(Mrs R.O. Backhouse, pre-1913)
See also 'Georgina'

'Georgie Girl' 6 W-GWP
(Brian S. Duncan) Brian S. Duncan, 1989
'Sputnik' × 'Foundling'; sdlg no. 749
Fl. 85 mm wide; perianth segments very broadly ovate, blunt, prominently mucronate, pure white, reflexed, overlapping half; the inner segments more narrowly ovate, somewhat twisted, sometimes creased; corona short, straight-sided, ribbed, opening pale yellow, becoming white, with sage green at base and a broad band of deep reddish pink at rim, mouth straight, tightly frilled. Dwarf. Mid-season. Sunproof

'Georgina' 2 W-? (b or c)
Syn. of 'Georgiana'

'Georgina Clogstoun' 1 W-W
(N.Y. Lower, pre-1928)
'Hamlet' × 'White Knight'

'Geotia' 1 Y-Y
(de Graaff Bros, pre-1929)
AM(Haarlem) 1931

'Gerald' 3 W-? (b)
(P. van Deursen, pre-1930)

'Geraldine' 3 WWY-O
(pre-1908)
Fl. large; perianth segments white, shading to sulphur yellow at base; corona intense scarlet-orange. ?The same as 'Geraldine Cremer'

'Geraldine Cremer'
(pre-1907)
?The same as 'Geraldine'

'Geranium' 8 W-O
(J.B. van der Schoot, pre-1930)
Poetaz
Fls up to 6 per stem, 57 mm wide; perianth segments very broad in outline, truncate or squarish at apex, fairly prominently mucronate, spreading or a little reflexed, plane or slightly concave, overlapping half or more; the inner segments narrower, more usually spreading, sometimes recurved either side of the midrib, with margins wavy and incurling; corona shallow bowl-shaped, ribbed, yellowish orange, overlaid with strong orange 25A, irregularly frilled, with rim crenate. Scented. 2n=17. Syn. 'Advance'.
AM(Haarlem) 1931, *FCC(g) 1952, *AM(p) 1975, *FCC(p) 1977, AGM 1995

"Gerard's Double Daffodil"
Syn. of Pseudonarcissus 'Plenus'

'Gerbrandt Kieft' 2 W-Y
(L. Onderwater) L. Onderwater, 1967
Perianth segments ivory white; corona primrose yellow

'Gerda' 2 W-? (b)
(D.J. Cooper) D.J. Cooper, 1956

'Germaine' 2 W-? (b)
(Mrs R.O. Backhouse, pre-1921)
AM(Haarlem) 1931

'Germoc' 2 Y-? (a)
Syn. of 'Germoe'

'Germoe' 2 Y-? (a)
(P.D. Williams, pre-1927)
AM(Haarlem) 1926. See also 'Germoc'

'Geronimo' 2 Y-? (a)
(K.L. Reynolds, pre-1944)

'Geronimo'
(E.C. Powell, pre-1945)
'Pilgrimage' × 'White Emperor'

'Geronte' 1 W-W
(W.A. Grace, pre-1936)

'Gertia' 2 Y-? (a)
(Mrs R.O. Backhouse, pre-1921)

'Gertie Gotto' 2 W-? (b)
(A.M. Williams, pre-1952)

'Gertie Millar' 2 W-Y
(de Graaff Bros, pre-1927)
AM(Haarlem) 1930

'Gertrude' 3 W-? (b)
(G.H. Engleheart, pre-1916)

'Gertrude' 5
Syn. of 'Lorna'

'Gertrude Bell' 9 W-?
(Miss K.M. Hinchliff, pre-1931)

'Gertrude Gubbin' 1 W-W
(H.R. Meyer, pre-1927)

'Gertrude Hastings' 2 W-? (b)
(pre-1930)

'Gertrude Jekyll' 1 Y-Y
(J.G. Nelson, pre-1882)
Fl. soft lemon yellow, of waxy texture, at an acute angle to the stem; perianth segments broadly ovate,

inflexed, with margins wavy, overlapping at base only; corona cylindrical, mouth straight or very slightly flared, rim regularly notched and crenate. Early to mid-season. Syn. Pseudonarcissus Major 'Gertrude Jekyll'

'Gertrude Nethercote' 7 Y-Y
(C.A. Nethercote, pre-1927)
Resembles an earlier-flowered 'Buttercup' with a wider perianth and more widely expanded corona

'Gertrude Ray' 1 Y-Y
(J.W. Barr, pre-1930)

'Gertrude S.Mott' 3 W-? (b)
(Miss K. Spurrell, pre-1907)

'Gertrude Wills' 1 W-W
(M.H. Tribe, pre-1937)

'Gerunuk' 2 Y-? (a)
(E.M. Crosfield, pre-1914)

'Gervo' 2 W-W
(J. Gerritsen & Son, pre-1944)
2n=30. AM(Haarlem) 1944

'Gesture' 2 Y-? (a)
(Warnaar & Co., pre-1930)
AM(Haarlem) 1930

'Getaway' 3 Y-GYY
(Jackson's Daffodils) Jackson's Daffodils, 1989
'Sea Dream' × sdlg 242/75; sdlg no. 205/81
Fl. 100 mm wide; perianth segments very broadly ovate, rounded or truncate at apex and sometimes split, Greenish yellow (4D), somewhat concave, overlapping half; the inner segments more narrowly ovate, very slightly inflexed, with margins sometimes incurling at apex; corona vivid yellow, with green at base, mouth ribbed and frilled, rim closely and deeply notched, as if fringed. Late

'Gettysburg' 2 Y-GYR
(J.M. de Navarro) Rathowen Daffodils, 1979
('Teheran' × 'Ceylon') × 'Majorca'; sdlg no. 718
Perianth segments deep gold; corona golden yellow, with green at base and red at rim. Mid-season

'Gezelle' 9 W-?
Syn. of 'Guido Gezelle'

'G.F.Hemerick' 1 Y-Y
(G. Lubbe & Son, pre-1931)
Syn. 'Mr G.F.Hemerik'

'G.F.Loder' 1 W-? (b or c)
(Loder, pre-1884)

'G.F.Wilson' 2 W-O
(W. Backhouse, pre-1869)
Corona large, stained orange. Syn. Incomparabilis Albus 'G.F.Wilson'. "Absorbed" 'Mrs G.F.Wilson'. Was "absorbed" into 'John Stevenson'

'Ghana' 2 Y-Y
(pre-1971) Unregistered
?Syn. of 'Gahna'

'Ghandi' 2 Y-? (a)
(Mrs R.O. Backhouse, pre-1921)

'G.H.Davison' 1 Y-Y
(G.H. Davison, pre-1916)

'G.H.Engleheart' 1 Y-Y
(E. Leeds, pre-1884)
Corona long, flared, darker in tone than the perianth. Syn. Pseudonarcissus Major 'G.H.Engleheart'. Was "absorbed" into 'Evening Star'

'G.H.Engleheart' 8 W-Y
(G.H. Engleheart, pre-1890)
AM 1890. Syn. of 'George Engleheart'

'Ghost' 1 W-W
(Murray W. Evans) Murray W. Evans, 1974
'Celilo' × ('Petsamo' × 'Zero')
Fl. 110 mm wide

'Ghost Dancer' 3 W-YOY
(T.D. Throckmorton) T.D. Throckmorton, 1975
'Old Satin' × 'Green Howard'; sdlg no. 68/19/2
Corona orange, with greeny yellow at base and yellow gold at rim. Late

'Ghurka' 1 W-W
(C.E. Radcliff, pre-1936)
'Golden City' × 'Gertrude Nethercote'

'G.H.van Waveren' 1 Y-Y
(M. van Waveren & Sons, pre-1924)
Perianth segments pale yellow; corona golden yellow. Tall. Early. AM(Haarlem) 1924

'Giant' 1 W-Y
(pre-1908)
Fl. large; perianth segments creamy white; corona broad. AM(Haarlem) 1908

'Giant' 7 Y-Y
(?de Graaff Bros, pre-1913)
Perianth segments clear sulphur yellow; corona darker in tone. AM(Haarlem) 1913

'Giant' 1 Y-Y
(H.F. Fletcher, pre-1939)

'Giant' 1 Y-Y
Syn. of 'Wavertree'

'Giant Attraction' 2 or 3 W-Y
(de Graaff Bros, pre-1939)
Perianth segments acute; corona sulphur yellow, frilled. AM(Haarlem) 1939

'Giant Cup' 8 W-Y
(A.C. van der Schoot, pre-1931)
Poetaz
Corona large, lemon yellow

"Giant Daffodil"
Syn. of 'Sir Watkin'

'Giant General' 1 Y-Y
(G. Vink, pre-1939)
FA(Haarlem) 1939

'Giant Killer' 1 Y-Y
(de Graaff Bros, pre-1927)

'Giant Muticus' 1 Y-Y
(G.L. Wilson, pre-1927)
N. abscissus sdlg
Fl. large; corona slender. Late

'Giant Perfection' 1 Y-Y
(J. Gerritsen & Son, pre-1930)
AM(Haarlem) 1930

'Giant Queen' 2 or 3 W-? (b or c)
(pre-1927)

'Giant Santa Maria' 1 Y-Y
(G.L. Wilson, pre-1949)
'King Alfred' × 'Santa Maria'

'Giant Split' 11a Y-Y
(J. Gerritsen & Son) P.Q.M.Pennings, 1988
'Belcanto' × 'Obelisk'; sdlg no. 211
Fl. 100 mm wide; perianth segments light greenish yellow 3D, shiny; corona brilliant greenish yellow 5B, with a creamier tone (8B) at margins and rim. Very early. Resembles 'Sancerre' and 'Printal'

'Giant Spur' 1 Y-Y
(W.T. Ware, pre-1914)

'Giant Van Sion' 4
(G. Rijk, pre-1951)
'Telamonius Plenus' sport

'Gibraltar' 2 Y-O
(J.L. Richardson, pre-1937)
'Carbineer' × 'Porthilly'
Fl. rounded, of very strong substance; perianth segments very broad, rounded at apex, slightly mucronate, rich yellow, spreading, concave near apex, overlapping half; the inner segments roundish, only very slightly mucronate, a little inflexed; corona short broad funnel-shaped, ribbed, orange, mouth straight, lightly frilled. Mid-season

'Gibsonii' 2 Y-R
(R. Gibson, pre-1927)

'Giddygert' 4 W-Y
(Glenbrook Bulb Farm, 1983) Glenbrook Bulb Farm, 1997
'Gay Time' × 'Lawali'
Fl. 90 mm wide; perianth segments broadly ovate, greenish white (155A); corona segments brilliant yellow 7A, frilled. Late

'Gideon' 8 Y-Y
(pre-1798)
Fl. pale yellow

'Gideon' 2 W-P
(W. Jackson Jr) W. Jackson Jr, 1968
'Buncrana' × 'Sari'; sdlg no. 156/61

'Gidget' 3 W-GGY
(Mrs G. Link) Mrs G. Link, 1990
'Pewee' open pollinated; sdlg no. 75-A
Fl. 60 mm wide; perianth segments white, suffused green at base, spreading, plane, deeply overlapping; corona ribbed, dark green, with light greenish yellow at rim. Very late

'Gift' 8
(P.D. Williams, pre-1931)

'Gigantea' 2 Y-Y
(R. Gibson, pre-1927)

'Gigantic' 2 W-Y
(de Graaff Bros, pre-1930)
Perianth segments acute, sulphur white; corona large, soft yellow. AM(Haarlem) 1930

'Gigantic Orchidflower' 11a Y-Y
(W.E. de Mol, pre-1922)
'King Alfred' × 'Buttonhole'
Perianth segments broadly ovate, blunt, only very slightly mucronate, pale yellow, a little inflexed, separated at base, sometimes overlapping at shoulder; the inner segments half as wide; corona split to base, the six segments almost as long as the perianth segments, opposite and closely overlying them, of more or less the same width, with the inner corona and perianth segments joined at the margins from base to shoulder, deeply bi-lobed, loosely ribbed, of a much darker yellow than the perianth, frilled, with the inner segments inflexed at apex. Resembles a larger and better-formed 'Buttonhole'

'Gigantic Star' 2 Y-Y
(G. Helmus) G. Helmus, 1960
'Magnificence' × 'Carlton'
Fl. 127 mm wide; perianth segments broadly ovate,

slightly mucronate, brilliant greenish yellow 4A, a little inflexed, regular, overlapping one-third; corona vivid yellow 9A, with mouth expanded and frilled, rim notched and crenate. TGA(Haarlem) 1962, AM(p)(f) 1967, FA(Haarlem) 1968, FCFA(Haarlem) 1969

'Giggles' 9 W-GYR
(Mrs M.S. Yerger) Mrs M.S. Yerger, 1993
N. poeticus var. *hellenicus* × 'Lights Out'; sdlg no. 75 H 2-1
Fl. rounded, 36 mm wide; perianth segments broad, overlapping; the inner segments no less broad than the outer; corona bowl-shaped, light greenish yellow 4B, with dark bluish green 133A at base and red (40A) at rim. Late

'Gigi' 2 W-OOY
(J.N. Hancock & Co., 1947) J.N. Hancock & Co., 1964
'Carey' × 'Jillian'
Corona shallow, widely expanded, deep apricot orange, with creamy yellow at rim, deeply frilled

'Gigolo' 2 Y-Y
(Murray W. Evans) Murray W. Evans, 1977
'Aircastle' × 'Protege'; sdlg no. J-45
Fl. 90 mm wide. Mid-season

N. gigus Steudel = *N. bulbocodium*

'Gilberte'
(R.Fountain, pre-1931)
PC(e)(NZ) 1931

'Gil Blas' 2 Y-?Y
(E. Leeds, pre-1877)
Perianth segments narrow, acute, sulphur yellow; corona large, flared. Syn. Incomparabilis Sulphureus 'Gil Blas', Incomparabilis Sulphureus 'Stellatus'. "Absorbed" 'Cupid'

'Gilda' 2 Y-Y
(Ballydorn Bulb Farm) Ballydorn Bulb Farm, 1988
'Golden Aura' × 'Golden Amber'
Fl. 110 mm wide; perianth segments broadly ovate; corona large, slightly flared, with mouth expanded and rim crenate. Mid-season

'Gilded' 1 Y-Y
(F.H. Chapman, pre-1928)

'Gilfach' 2 W-WWO
(A.M. Wilson, pre-1951)
Corona slightly ribbed, white, with tawny beige at rim

'Gilford' 3 W-O
(W.J. Dunlop) W.J. Dunlop, 1958
'Folly' × 'Sunstar'

Corona reddish orange, shading to green at base

'Gilgandra' 1 Y-Y
(W.M. Spry, pre-1975) Unregistered
'Early Wonder' × 'Golden'
Late

'Gilgold' 1 Y-Y
(G. Errey) G. Errey, 1962
Fl. 115 mm wide; perianth segments vivid yellow 12A; corona of a slightly darker tone (13A). Early. Resembles 'Forerunner' but with the perianth segments overlapping

'Gilia' 3 W-? (b)
(A.H. Ahrens) D.J. Cooper, 1956

'Gill' 9 W-GYO
(Mrs M.S. Yerger) Mrs M.S. Yerger, 1994
'Mrs Weightman' × 'Praecox'; sdlg no. 84 E 4
Fl. 16 mm wide; perianth segments white; the inner segments narrower; corona brilliant yellow 7A, with light yellow-green 145B at base and strong reddish orange at rim. Dwarf. Very early

'Gillan' 11a Y-YOO
(R.A.Scamp) R.A.Scamp, 1996
'Brandaris' × 'Falstaff'; sdlg no. 411
Fl. 78 mm wide; perianth segments rich yellow; corona split, the six segments opposite and closely overlying the perianth segments, rounded at apex, ribbed, orange, with yellow tones towards base, frilled. Mid-season to late

'Gillian' 3 Y-? (a)
(G.H. Furness, pre-1934)

'Gilt Complex' 2 Y-Y
(Sidney DuBose, 1975) Sidney DuBose, 1990
'Aircastle' × 'Salmon Trout'; sdlg no. A14-1
Fl. 100 mm wide; perianth segments lemon yellow; corona deep yellow. Mid-season

'Gilt-edge' 3 W-GYY
(F.H. Chapman, pre-1927)
'Moonbeam' × 'Allan-a-Dale'
Perianth segments overlapping; corona opening white, becoming yellow, with green at base and a different tone of yellow at rim, neatly frilled. Late

'Gilt Edge' 2 W-WWY
(J.M. de Navarro) J.M. de Navarro, 1977
'Blakeney' hybrid; sdlg no. 252/III
Fl. 106 mm wide; corona with yellow at rim. Late. Resembles 'Evenlode' but with a larger and less rounded perianth

'Giltol' 1 W-Y
(G. Errey, 1950) G. Errey, 1962
Fl. 115 mm wide; perianth segments pale greenish

yellow (4D), becoming white; corona brilliant greenish yellow 6A. Early. Resembles an earlier-flowered and more brightly coloured 'Ptolemy'

'Gilwin' 2 Y-Y
(G. Errey, 1944) G. Errey, 1962
Fl. 115 mm wide; perianth segments opening brilliant yellow 9C, becoming paler (9D); corona much darker in tone (13A). Very early. Resembles an earlier-flowered 'Magnificence' with paler perianth

'Gimli' 2 W-P
(Brian S. Duncan) Rathowen Daffodils, 1981
'Roseworthy' × 'Foundling'; sdlg no. 463
Perianth segments pure white, reflexed; corona very deep pink, tinged orange. Mid-season. 2n=27

'Gimu' 4 W-Y
(W. Jackson Jr, 1969) Unregistered
'Mrs W.Copeland' × ('Chimeon' × 'Lawali'); sdlg no. 206/99
Perianth and other petaloid segments in several whorls, white; corona segments interspersed, cream

'Gina' 2 W-P
(J.N. Hancock & Co., 1975) Unregistered

'Gina' 2 Y-YOR
(M.E.Brogden) Unregistered

'Gin and Lime' 1 Y-WWY
(Carncairn Daffodils) Carncairn Daffodils, 19/3
'Goldcourt' × 'Moonstruck'; sdlg no. 2/42/62
Fl. forming a double triangle, 115 mm wide; perianth segments broadly ovate, blunt, slightly mucronate, greenish lemon yellow, becoming darker in tone, with whitish yellow at base, spreading, with margins slightly wavy, overlapping one-third to a half; the inner segments more narrowly ovate, narrowing sharply from shoulder to base, creased, with margins more heavily wavy or twisted; corona cylindrical, narrow, angled, opening yellow, becoming white, with a band of yellow at rim, mouth expanded, rim deeply and regularly notched and crenate. Early to mid-season. 2n=28

'Ginger' 2 Y-Y
(Murray W. Evans) Murray W. Evans, 1974
'Aircastle' × 'Protege'
Fl. 95 mm wide

'Ginger Head' 2 Y-O
(S.J. Bisdee, 1945)
'Market Merry' × 'Erebus'

'Ginger Lee' 7 Y-O
(E. Zinkowski) E. Zinkowski, 1984
'Ceylon' × *N. jonquilla*; sdlg no. 80-4N
Fl. 55 mm wide; perianth segments deep yellow; corona orange. Mid-season. Resembles a scented and better-formed 'Suzy' of deeper colour with a single flower per stem

'Ginjulla' 2 W-WWP
(A.O. Roblin, 1946)
'Maid of the Mist' × 'Luther'

'Gioconda' 3 W-? (b)
(C.G. van Tubergen, pre-1914)

'Gioconda' 2 W-YYO
(Mrs R.O. Backhouse, pre-1921)
Fl. star-shaped; perianth segments sulphur white; corona large, yellow, with a broad band of orange at rim. AM(Haarlem) 1930

'Gionesius' 3 Y-? (a)
(de Graaff Bros, pre-1927)

'Giovanni' 9 W-?
(G.H. Engleheart, pre-1914)

'Giovanni' 2 W-O
(G.H. Johnstone, 1948) G.H. Johnstone, 1959
'Seraglio' hybrid
Fl. 102 mm wide; corona bright orange. Mid-season. Resembles a larger-flowered 'Seraglio' with the perianth segments more rounded

'Giovanni' 2 Y-?
Syn. of 'Golden Dragon'

'Gipsy' 3 Y-? (a)
(W.F.M. Copeland, pre-1908)

'Gipsy Lad' 2 Y-YYO
(C. Smith, c.1904)
Perianth segments primrose yellow; corona large, with intense reddish orange at rim

'Gipsy Moth' 2 W-W
(Carncairn Daffodils) Carncairn Daffodils, 1967
G.L.Wilson sdlg × 'Cotterton'
Fl. 88 mm wide, pure white, of good substance. Mid-season. 2n=29

'Gipsy Queen' 3 W-? (b)
(G.H. Engleheart, pre-1908)
Perianth segments creamy white; corona with orange at rim

'Gipsy Queen' 1 YYW-WWY
(A. Gray) Broadleigh Gardens, 1969
Selection from *N. minor* × *N. asturiensis*
Fl. 30 mm wide; perianth segments narrowly ovate, acute, light greenish yellow 3C, whitish at base and with white mucro, inflexed, plane, overlapping at base only,; the inner segments a little twisted; corona cylindrical, slightly constricted below mouth, lightly 6-ribbed, opening light greenish yellow 3C, soon

paling to whitish, flecked yellow at base, with a narrow band of bright greenish yellow 2B at rim, mouth flared and deeply 6-lobed, rim dentate. Dwarf. Early

'Gipsy Tap' 3 W-O
Syn. of 'Gypsy Tap'

'Giraffe' 2 Y-Y
(E.M. Crosfield, pre-1910)
'Princess Mary' × 'Madame de Graaff'

'Giralda' 3 Y-? (a)
(J.T. Gray, pre-1933)
Perianth segments pale yellow, of strong substance; corona with a narrow band of orange-red at rim

'Girasol' 1 Y-P
(Murray W. Evans, 1975) Murray W. Evans, 1986
'Salome' × ('Binkie' × 1YYW-W) × 'Suede'

'Girdle' 2 W-Y
(W.A. Watts, pre-1914)
'Minnie Hume' × 'Weardale Perfection'
Fl. facing slightly downwards; perianth segments rounded at apex, creamy white, overlapping; corona slender, pale yellow, with mouth flared. Tall. *C(g) 1936, *HC(g) 1939

'Girl Friend' 2 W-O
(A.G. Thompson) A.G. Thompson, 1965
'Daisy Schäffer' × 'Carbineer'
Fl. 89 mm wide; perianh segments creamy white; corona deep orange. Mid season. Resembles 'Daisy Schäffer' but with a darker-toned corona

'Girl James' 2 W-OOR
(H.A. Brown, 1949) J.N. Hancock & Co., 1960
Perianth segments pure white; corona orange, with crimson at rim

'Gironde' 11a Y-Y
(J. Gerritsen & Son) J. Gerritsen & Son, 1977
'Gold Collar' hybrid
Fl. 95 mm wide; perianth segments very broadly ovate, blunt, slightly mucronate, brilliant yellow 7A, spreading, plane or a little concave, overlapping half or more; the inner segments slightly inflexed, sometimes twisted; corona split to base, the six segments three-quarters the length of the perianth segments, opposite and closely overlying them, of the same width and joined at margins in lower half, squarish at apex, heavily ribbed and frilled, darker in tone (14A) than the perianth. Late

'Girrahween' 2 W-Y
(A.O. Roblin, 1941) A.O. Roblin, 1956
'Nelly' × 'Loila'

'Girton Girl' 2 Y-? (a)
(R.H. Bath, pre-1933)

'Gisavia' 2 Y-? (a)
(W. Jackson Sr, 1937)
'Mary Blewitt' × 'Astrid'

'Gisela' 2 W-P
(S.J. Bisdee) S.J. Bisdee, 1956
'Pink Princess' × 'Mastercraft'
Corona buff pink

'Gitana' 1 W-W
(de Graaff Bros, pre-1950)
AM(Haarlem) 1950

'Giuseppe Verdi' 1 W-? (b)
(H. Bader) N. Liefting, 1956
Syn. 'Verdi'

'Given Fleming' 1 Y-Y
(O. Ronalds)

'Givon' 1 W-W
(G.H. Engleheart, pre-1923)

'G.J.Diekema' 2 Y-? (a)
(Warnaar & Co., pre-1930)

'G.K.Veitch' 1 W-Y
(West & Fell, pre-1935)
Perianth segments pure white, deeply overlapping; corona creamy lemon, with rim rolled

'Glacier' 2 W-? (b or a)
(Mrs R.O. Backhouse, pre-1908)

'Glacier' 4? Y-Y
(?R.H. Beerhorst & Son, pre-1912)
Fl. citron yellow; perianth and other petaloid segments and the corona with a narrow band of clear yellow at rim. AM(Haarlem) 1912

'Glacier' 1 W-W
(J.L. Richardson) J.L. Richardson, 1956
'Killaloe' × 'Broughshane'
Fl. 127 mm wide; perianth segments broadly ovate, only very slightly mucronate, spreading or a little inflexed, concave, overlapping half; the inner segments more narrowly ovate, more strongly inflexed; corona funnel-shaped, lightly ribbed, with rim widely flanged and irregularly notched and crenate. Scented. AM(e) 1960, *AM(g) 1962, *AM(p) 1986

'Glacier des Bossons' 1 W-W
(de Graaff Bros, pre-1928)

'Glad Boy' 3 Y-? (a)
(Mrs R.O. Backhouse, pre-1921)

'Glad Day' 2 Y-O
(G.E. Mitsch) G.E. Mitsch, 1974
'Bahram' × 'Ardour'; sdlg no. L3/1

Fl. rounded, 38 mm wide; perianth segments soft light yellow, overlapping; corona bowl-shaped. Mid-season

'Glad Days' 2 Y-O
(H.A. Brown, pre-1946)
Perianth segments bright yellow; corona expanded, golden orange, frilled. Very early

'Glad Eye' 2 W-YYO
(Mrs R.O. Backhouse, ?pre1913)
N. poeticus × 'Will Scarlett'

'Glad Eye' 2 W-?
Syn. of 'Brilliant'

'Glad Eye' 2 W-R
Syn. of 'Hades'

'Gladiator' 2 W-YYO
(Mrs R.O. Backhouse, pre-1914)
Perianth segments creamy white; corona shallow, expanded, golden yellow, shading to reddish orange at rim, frilled. AM(Haarlem) 1915

'Gladness' 2 Y-? (a)
(P.D. Williams, pre-1932)

'Gladsome' 2 Y-? (a)
(G. Zandbergen-Terwegen, pre-1937)

'Gladstone' 1 Y-Y
(E. Leeds, pre-1877)
Fl. pale yellow. Syn. Pseudonarcissus Major 'Gladstone'

'Gladstone' 8 Y-O
(pre-1883)
Perianth segments bright sulphur yellow; corona bright orange

'Gladstone' 2 Y-? (a)
(H. Homan, pre-1933)

'Gladwin' 2 W-R
(W. Jackson Jr, 1961) Unregistered
'Capella' × 'Jo'; sdlg no. 86/61

'Gladys' 1 W-W
(pre-1887)
Resembles a large-flowered 'Minnie Hume'

'Gladys' 3 Y or W-? (a or b)
(pre-1913)

'Gladys' 1? Y-Y
(Hawes, pre-1914)
Resembles 'Androcles'

'Gladys' 1 W-? (b)

(Barr & Sons, pre-1927)

'Gladys Bibby' 2 W-? (b or c)
(W.A. Watts, pre-1923)

'Gladys Dettman' 2 Y-?
(H.T. Dettmann) H.T. Dettmann, 1960

'Gladys Dobie' 9 W-?
(de Graaff Bros, pre-1927)
?The same as 'Gladys Doby'

'Gladys Doby'
?The same as 'Gladys Dobie'

'Gladys Harper' 2 Y-Y
(L.P.Dettman, 1969) Unregistered
'Keith Trevan' × 'Creamed Honey'; sdlg no. 67/70

'Gladys Hartland' 1 W-W
(Irish origin, pre-1907)
Div. 2 until 1931

'Gladys Meadors' 2 W-? (b)
(Mrs Ben Robertson, pre-1950)

'Gladys Moncrieff' 2 W-O
(H.A. Brown, pre-1938)
Perianth segments pure white; corona deep reddish orange, with rim closely and deeply notched, as if fringed

'Glamis' 2 W-W
(Barr & Sons, pre-1939)

'Glamis' 2 W-WYP
(C.E. Radcliff, 1943)
'Veronique' × 'Keridwen'

'Glamor' 2 W-WWY
(C.E. Radcliff, 1943) J.M.Radcliff, 1956
'Veronique' × 'Keridwen'

'Glamorous' 2 W-Y
(G.E. Mitsch, 1956) G.E. Mitsch, 1967
'Green Island' × 'Chinese White'; sdlg no. R33/45
Fl. 115 mm wide; perianth segments very broad, rounded at apex; corona almost disc-shaped, large, pale lemon yellow, with a darker tone at rim. Mid-season. Resembles 'Bit o' Gold' but with a shallower and more widely flared corona

'Glamour' 2 Y-? (a)
(R.H. Bath, pre-1927)

'Glamour Girl' 3 W-R
(Brogden Bulbs, pre-1966) Unregistered

'Glandore' 8 W-Y
(Miss F.W. Currey, pre-1907)

Fls 5-7 per stem; perianth segments roundish, pale primrose, overlapping; corona widely expanded, deep primrose. Scented

'Glandore' 2 W-W
(Ballydorn Bulb Farm) Ballydorn Bulb Farm, 1972
'Cortina' × 'Green Island'
Fl. 116 mm wide

'Glanmire' 2 W-Y
(J.L. Richardson, pre-1937)
('Killigrew' × 'Damson')?
Perianth segments pure white; corona pale lemon

'Glare' 3 W-R
(pre-1927)
Perianth segments creamy white; corona red. Sunproof

'Glare of the Garden' 1 W-Y
(R.A. van der Schoot, pre-1923)
Fl. large; perianth segments overlapping; corona large, canary yellow, deeply frilled

'Glaring Star' 2 Y-? (a)
(G. Zandbergen-Terwegen, pre-1937)

'Glaslyn' 1 W-W
(pre-1913)

'Glasnevin' 2 W-W
(Carncairn Daffodils) Carncairn Daffodils, 1993
'Polar Circle' × 'Soledad'; sdlg no. 1/12/82
Fl. forming a double triangle, 105 mm wide; perianth segments broadly ovate, blunt, prominently mucronate, a little inflexed, regular, with margins sometimes wavy, overlapping one-third to a half; the inner segments more narrowly ovate, less prominently mucronate; corona short funnel-shaped, ribbed, mouth straight, split in places and overlapping, lightly frilled, with rim irregularly notched and minutely dentate. Standard or tall. Mid-season

'Glaspel' 2 W-? (b or c)
(A.M. Wilson, pre-1937)

'Glaston' 2 W-ORR
(P. Phillips) P. Phillips, 1966
Fl. 110 mm wide; corona bowl-shaped, red, with rich orange at base. Mid-season. Resembles 'Arbar' but with broader perianth segments and a more widely expanded corona

'Glastonbury' 3 W-? (b)
(P.D. Williams, pre-1939)

'Glata' 3
(pre-1934)

'Glaucus' 9 W-?
(pre-1914)

'Glaucus' 1 Y-Y
(S. Morrison, pre-1939)

'Glayne' 1 Y-Y
(Mrs M.Moorby) Mrs M.Moorby, 1956

'Gleam' 3 Y-? (a)
(G.H. Engleheart, pre-1907)

'Gleam' 2 Y-YYO
(S.C. Gaspar, 1946) R.J. Abernethy, 1957

'Gleaming' 2 Y-O
(M.P. Williams, pre-1941)

'Gleeful' 2 Y-W
(G.E. Mitsch) G.E. Mitsch, 1962
'Binkie' × 'Content'; sdlg no. N3/1
Fl. 102 mm wide; perianth segments clear sulphur lemon; corona opening the same colour as the perianth, becoming near pure white. Mid-season. Resembles 'Binkie' but with a darker perianth and a whiter and more heavily frilled corona

'Glee Maiden' 2 W-WWY
(W.F.M. Copeland, pre-1911)
Fl. 95 mm wide; perianth segments broadly ovate, glistening white, overlapping; corona closely ribbed, lemon white, flushed greenish lemon yellow at base, with rim peach-coloured. Mid-season

'Gleeman' 9 W-?
(W. Balch, pre-1936)

'Glenacre' 2 W-Y
(D.S. Bell) D.S. Bell, 1960
Fl. 115 mm wide; corona bowl-shaped, deep yellow. Mid-season. Resembles 'Polindra' but with the corona of better form and richer colour

'Glenaire' 1 W-W
(Mrs M.Moorby) Mrs M.Moorby, 1956

'Glenalbyn' 2 Y-R
(H.A. Brown, pre-1938)
Perianth segments primrose yellow; corona spreading, mouth expanded, red, with a darker tone at rim. See also 'Glen Albyn'

'Glen Albyn' 2 Y-R
Syn. of 'Glenalbyn'

'Glen Alladale' 3 W-WYO
(J.S.B. Lea) Clive Postles, 1991
('Loch Assynt' × 'Achnasheen') × ('Rockall' × 'Merlin'); sdlg no. 4-28-78
Fl. rounded, 104 mm wide; perianth segments very broadly ovate, pure white; corona disc-shaped, with

a well-defined band of bright orange at rim. Mid-season

'Glenally' 1 Y-Y
(A. Overton) A. Overton, 1960

'Glenalmond' 1 W-W
(F.E. Board) F.E. Board, 1965
'Riber' × 'Glendermott'; sdlg no. 1109
Mid-season

'Glen Alvie' 2 Y-OOR
(J.N. Hancock & Co., pre-1950)
Perianth segments golden yellow; corona orange, with bright orange-red at rim

'Glenamoy' 1 W-Y
(Carncairn Daffodils) Carncairn Daffodils, 1979
'Preamble' × sdlg 1/59/59; sdlg no. 1/11/67
Fl. 110 mm wide; perianth segments greenish white 155C; corona vivid yellow 9A, with rim rolled. Mid-season

'Glenara Bendigo' 2 Y-?
(Alister Clark, 1926) J. Sharp, 1960

'Glenara Bermuda' 2 Y-?
(Alister Clark, 1932) J. Sharp, 1960

'Glenara Bliss' 2 W-W
(Alister Clark, 1926) J. Sharp, 1960

'Glenara Caramel' 1 W-WWY
(Alister Clark, 1930) U.L. Daly, 1960

'Glenara Comely' 2 W-?
(Alister Clark, 1935) J. Sharp, 1960

'Glenara Day Dream' 2 W-?
(H.A. Brown) J.N. Hancock & Co., 1961

'Glenara Derrick' 2 Y-?
(Alister Clark) J. Sharp, 1961

'Glenara Derwent' 2 W-?
(Alister Clark) J. Sharp, 1961

'Glenara Enterprise' 2 W-?
(Alister Clark) J. Sharp, 1961

'Glenara Glamour' 2 Y-Y
(Alister Clark, 1947) J. Sharp, 1961
Fl. deep yellow. Tall

'Glenara Guinea' 2 Y-?
(Alister Clark, 1930) J. Sharp, 1960

'Glenara Ingot' 2 Y-?
(Alister Clark, 1930) J. Sharp, 1960

'Glenara Proverb' 2 Y-?
(Alister Clark) J. Sharp, 1961

'Glenara Quest' 2 W-?
(Alister Clark, 1950) J. Sharp, 1960

'Glenara Warning' 2 W-?
(Alister Clark, 1935) J. Sharp, 1960

'Glenariff' 1 W-W
Syn. of 'Dunluce'

'Glenarm' 2 W-W
(G.L. Wilson, pre-1933)
(['Minnie Hume' × 'Pearl of Kent'] × 'Mrs Robert Sydenham') × ' Tenedos'
Fl. large, pure white; perianth segments broad; corona widely expanded, frilled

'Glenavon' 1 W-W
(A.M. Wilson, pre-1931)

'Glenavy' 2 W-W
(J.L. Richardson, pre-1937)
'Mitylene' × 'Sunstar'
Fl. chalk white; corona shallow, widely expanded. Resembles 'Mitylene' in form

'Glenbane' 1 W-W
(G.L. Wilson) G.L. Wilson, 1956
('Truth' × 'Kanchenjunga') × 'Greenland'

'Glenbar' 1 W-W
(S.A. Free) S.A. Free, 1966
Fl. 102 mm wide. Mid-season

Glenbrook Minicycla Group 6 Y-Y
(Glenbrook Bulb Farm, 1987) Glenbrook Bulb Farm, 1997
N. asturiensis × *N. cyclamineus*
Fl. 44 mm wide, brilliant yellow 7A; perianth segments narrow; corona slender, frilled, with rim dentate. Dwarf. Very early

Glenbrook Ta-Julia Group 10 Y-Y
(Glenbrook Bulb Farm, pre-1994) Unregistered
'Tarlatan' × 'Julia Jane'
Fl. creamy lemon yellow; corona widely flared, with the rim sometimes rolled. Very early

'Glenburn' 2 Y-? (a)
(H.A. Brown, pre-1936)

'Glenburvie' 2 W-OOR
(W. Jackson Jr) W. Jackson Jr, 1966
'Capella' × 'Wyena'
Corona deep orange, shading to red at rim

'Glenbush' 2 W-W
(G.L. Wilson, pre-1952)

'Contour' × 'Samite'
Fl. 121 mm wide, greenish white; perianth segments broad, smooth, overlapping; corona somewhat slender, regularly ribbed, with rim flanged and dentate. AM(e) 1953

'Glencairn' 1 W-Y
(J.L. Richardson) J.L. Richardson, 1955
'Spitzbergen' × 'Broughshane'
Perianth segments broadly ovate; corona chrome yellow, with rim rolled and dentate

'Glencalvie' 2 W-W
(D.C.MacArthur) D.C.MacArthur, 1996
'Kathleen Munroe' × 'Margaret Joyce'; sdlg no. EV8726
Fl. forming a double triangle, 102 mm wide; perianth segments broadly ovate, mucronate, greenish white (155A), plane, smooth; corona funnel-shaped, smooth, greenish white, with a stronger saturation of green towards mouth, mouth flared, rim crenate. Early

'Glen Cassley' 3 W-W
(J.S.B. Lea, 1977) Clive Postles Daffodils, 1988
'Achnasheen' × 'Loch Assynt'

'Glen Clova' 2 Y-ORR
(J.S.B. Lea) J.S.B. Lea, 1978
Sdlg 1-39-63 × 'Arctic Gold'; sdlg no. 2-19-65
Fl. 95 mm wide. Sunproof

'Glencoe' 2 W-W
(R.H. Bath, pre-1941)
Fl. 102 mm wide; perianth segments creamy white, overlapping a quarter; corona opening pale greenish yellow 9D, becoming creamy white, with rim crenate. Syn. 'Vespa'. *PC(g) 1941

'Glen Cove' 8
(A. Frylink & Sons, pre-1933)
AM(Haarlem) 1933

'Glencraig' 2 Y-R
(Ballydorn Bulb Farm) Ballydorn Bulb Farm, 1977
'Craigywarren' × 'Gaucho'
Fl. 105 mm wide; perianth segments golden yellow; corona orange-red. Mid-season. Resembles a deeper-coloured 'Craigywarren' of greater substance

'Glendale' 1 W-Y
(1948) Seymour Cobley Ltd, 1968
Corona lemon yellow. Late

'Glendale' 2 W-W
(W.M. Spry, pre-1975) Unregistered
'Trousseau' × 'Snowflake'
Mid-season

'Glendalough' 2 W-GWW
(J.L. Richardson, pre-1938)
'Cameronian' × 'Slemish'
Fl. about 127 mm wide, snowy white; perianth segments broadly ovate, blunt or truncate, fairly prominently mucronate, spreading, plane, smooth, overlapping half; the inner segments a little inflexed, with margins wavy; corona funnel-shaped, smooth, slightly whiter than the perianth, with green shading at base, mouth only a little expanded, lightly frilled, rim more or less entire. Mid-season. PC 1939

'Glendarroch' 3 W-YOO
(J.S.B. Lea) Clive Postles Daffodils, 1987
'Loch Assynt' × 'Purbeck'; sdlg no. 1-26-74
Perianth segments very broadly ovate, truncate, slightly mucronate, spreading, a little concave, smooth, overlapping half; the inner segments more narrowly ovate, shouldered at base, a little reflexed and very slightly twisted; corona ribbed, pale orange, with mouth widely expanded and lightly frilled. Late

'Glendawr' 3 Y-? (a)
(H.G. Longford, pre-1927)

'Glendermid' 1 W-Y
(G.H. Brownlee, pre-1939)

'Glendermott' 2 W-GWW
(G.L. Wilson) G.L. Wilson, 1957
'Truth' × 'Broughshane'
Fl. 102 mm wide, greenish white (155A); perianth segments slightly inflexed, overlapping; corona slightly ribbed, with green at base, mouth expanded and frilled, rim flanged and crenate. AM(e) 1969

'Glen Derwent'
Unregistered
In parentage of 'Cilla'

'Glendevie' 2 W-WWP
(C.E. Radcliff, 1935) J.M.Radcliff, 1956
Sdlg × 'Pink o' Dawn'

'Glendora' 1 W-Y
(G. Lewis, pre-1940)

'Glendoveer' 2 W-O
(S.J. Bisdee, 1947)
Corona apricot orange. Early. Sunproof

'Glendower' 4 Y-O
(D.S. Bell, 1968) D.S. Bell, 1978
'Papua' × 'Hicol'
Fl. 106 mm wide; perianth and other petaloid segments yellow; the inner whorl(s) shorter; corona segments interspersed, orange

'Glendun' 3 W-GYR
(Kate Reade) Carncairn Daffodils, 1995
'Red Cottage' open pollinated; sdlg no. 3/47/82

Fl. rounded, 92 mm wide; perianth segments very broadly ovate, rounded at apex, prominently mucronate, a little reflexed, overlapping half; the inner segments narrower, only very slightly mucronate; corona shallow bowl-shaped, ribbed, yellow, with dark green at base and a broad band of orange-red at rim, tightly frilled. Late

'Glendwen' 2 W-YYR
Syn. of 'Glendwin'

'Glendwin' 2 W-YYR
(W. Jackson Sr, 1927)
'War Flame' × 'Pink'un'
Perianth segments ivory white, overlapping; corona flared, with a broad band of red at rim. See also 'Glendwen'

'Gleneagles' 2 W-? (b)
(P.D. Williams, pre-1933)

'Glen Echo' 2 W-W
(W.G. Pannill) W.G. Pannill, 1985
'Easter Moon' × 'White Prince'; sdlg no. 64/40 D
Mid-season

'Glen Eden' 1 W-? (b)
(R.G. Sharp, pre-1930)

'Glenelg' 1 W-Y
(pre-1927)

'Glenelg' 1 W-Y
(A.C. McKillop) A.C. McKillop, 1955

'Glenfalloch' 1 Y-Y
(E.W. Cotter) E.W. Cotter, 1957
'Gold Tray' hybrid × 'Milson'
Fl. rich gold; perianth segments broadly ovate; corona straight-sided, with mouth flared and rim dentate

'Glenfarclas' 1 Y-O
(J.S.B. Lea) J.S.B. Lea, 1976
Sdlg 1-6-60 × 'Vulcan'; sdlg no. 1-10-68
Fl. 101 mm wide; perianth segments broadly ovate, deep gold, with slight white mucro, spreading, with margins a little incurling at apex, overlapping one-third; corona funnel-shaped, smooth, reddish orange, loosely frilled, with rim crenate and slightly rolled. Varies between Divs 1 and 2

'Glenfern' 1 W-Y
(H.A. Brown, pre-1936)
Perianth segments white; corona rich lemon, with mouth expanded

'Glen Fire' 2 W-O
(de Graaff Bros & van Konynenburg & Co., pre-1940)
AM(Haarlem) 1940

'Glenganagh' 4 Y-R
(Carncairn Daffodils) Carncairn Daffodils, 1991
'Castle Dobbs' × sdlg 1/14/64 ('Falaise' open pollinated); sdlg no. A31/79
Fl. 88 mm wide; perianth and other petaloid segments in 2-3 whorls, very broadly ovate, blunt, yellow; the outer whorl with prominent white mucro, slightly inflexed, somewhat concave, with margins incurling at apex, smooth, overlapping half; the inner segments of the outer whorl no less broad, rounded at apex, only very slightly mucronate; the second whorl shorter, more strongly inflexed, with margins more deeply incurling; an incomplete whorl at centre irregularly arranged; corona segments short, clustered at centre, more loosely interspersed among the surrounding petaloid segments, red, touched yellow at rim, frilled. Late. Weatherproof

'Glengaree'
(pre-1940)

'Glengarriff' 1 W-YYW
(J.L. Richardson, pre-1937)
'White Emperor' × 'Beersheba'
Perianth segments acute, pure white; corona primrose, with cream at rim, rim widely flanged

'Glengarry' 2 Y-O
(The Brodie of Brodie, c.1930)
('Bernardino' × 'Fortune') × 'Basra'; sdlg no. 49/A/25
Perianth segments soft yellow; corona reddish orange, frilled

'Glengormley' 2 W-OOY
(W.J. Dunlop, pre-1952)
'White Sentinel' × 'Hades'
Corona deep salmon orange, with a narrow band of lemon yellow at rim

'Glen Hope' 2 W-GWW
(J.A. O'More) P.D.K. Ramsay, 1980
'Snowshill' × 'Empress of Ireland'; sdlg no. 47/73
Fl. 90 mm wide

'Glen Isla' 1 W-GWW
(J.S.B. Lea) J.S.B. Lea, 1981
Hybrid between ('Inverpolly' × 'Rose Royale') hybrids; sdlg no. 1-45-71
Fl. 112 mm wide

'Glen Lake' 2 W-WWO
(Patrick Kiernan) Patrick Kiernan, 1997
'Highland Wedding' × 'Merlin'; sdlg no. PK1429
Fl. 110 mm wide; perianth segments broadly ovate, acute, plane, smooth; corona funnel-shaped, slightly ribbed, whitish, with a band of orange at rim. Mid-season to late. Sunproof

'Glenlee' 2 W-W
(J.A. O'More) J.A. O'More, 1968

'Bridal Robe' × 'Petsamo'

'Glenleslie' 2 W-W
(W.J. Dunlop, pre-1949)
'White Sentinel' × 'Evening'
Corona opening cream, soon becoming white

'Glen Lorne' 2 W-P
(Mrs J. Abel Smith, 1975) Mrs J. Abel Smith, 1986
'Knightwick' hybrid; sdlg no. L0/81
Corona clear pink. Late

'Glenluce' 1 W-Y
(H.A. Brown, pre-1936)
Corona rich lemon

'Glenlusk' 2 Y-YYR
(C.E. Radcliff, 1937)
('Red Torch' × 'Tamerlane') × 'Malvern Gold'

'Glenlyn' 2 W-P
(H.G. Cross) H.G. Cross, 1986
'Dear Me' × 'Vahu'; sdlg no. 5050
Fl. forming a double triangle; perianth segments broadly ovate, blunt, only very slightly mucronate, milk white, spreading, plane, overlapping half; the inner segments a little inflexed; corona funnel-shaped, angled, creamy salmon pink, with mouth flared and loosely frilled. Early

'Glenmanus' 2 W-W
(W.J. Dunlop, pre 1949)
'Dava' × 'Justice'
Perianth segments broad, pure white; corona opening cream, soon becoming white. PC 1949

'Glenmorangie' 2 W-W
(D.C. MacArthur) D.C. MacArthur, 1992
2 W-W sdlg × 'Preamble'; sdlg no. EV8290/1
Fl. 91 mm wide; perianth segments broadly ovate, prominently mucronate, greenish white (155A), of great substance, deeply concave, overlapping; corona funnel-shaped, ribbed, opening light greenish yellow at base and pale yellow-green at rim, maturing to yellowish white, mouth flared and lobed, rim rolled and crenate. Early

'Glen Moray' 1 W-? (b)
(A. Gibson) R. Hyde, 1955

'Glenmore' 2 Y-? (a)
(The Brodie of Brodie, c.1931)
'Therapia' × 'Fortune'; sdlg no. 167/A/26
Perianth segments yellow; corona tinged orange

'Glenmore' 2 W-Y
(J.A. O'More) J.A. O'More, 1973
'Kingdom' × 'Invergordon'
Fl. 102 mm wide

'Glenocum' 2 W-W
(G.L. Wilson, pre-1949)
'White Sentinel' × 'Kanchenjunga'
Fl. 118 mm wide, greenish white; perianth segments broad, smooth, overlapping; corona mouth slightly expanded, with rim finely dentate. AM(e) 1949

'Glenora' 3 W-WWY
(J.T. Gray, pre-1949)
Perianth segments pure white, of thick substance; corona opening pale citron, becoming white, faintly flushed pink in some seasons, with lemon at rim

'Glenorchy' 1 WWY-Y
(D.N.Y. Olson) D.N.Y. Olson, 1989
'Red Conquest' × 'Green Island'
Fl. 110 mm wide; perianth segments broadly ovate, blunt, not prominently mucronate, opening pale yellow, becoming white with a halo of dark yellow at base, spreading a little inflexed, smooth, overlapping one-third; the inner segments more strongly inflexed, with margins somewhat wavy, rounded at base; corona funnel-shaped, smooth, dark yellow, mouth expanded and loosely frilled, rim crenate. Early to mid-season. Resembles a more reliable and slightly larger 'Stormy Weather'

'Glenore' 2 W-YYR
(S.C. Gaspar, 1951) R.J. Abernethy, 1961
Fl. 95 mm wide. Mid-season

'Glenravel' 1 W-Y
(G.L. Wilson, pre-1934)
'Mrs Ernst H.Krelage' hybrid
Fl. 92 mm wide; perianth segments creamy white, overlapping half; corona cream, with rim flanged. 2n=28. *HC(g) 1946

'Glen Rosa' 1 W-Y
(Barr & Sons, pre-1930)
Perianth segments of strong substance; corona soft lemon yellow

'Glenrose' 2 W-P
(C.E. Radcliff, 1942) J.M.Radcliff, 1956
Sdlg × 'Dawnglow'

'Glen Rossie' 2 W-R
(G. Lewis) D.S. Bell, 1955
See also 'Glenrossie'

'Glenrossie' 2 W-R
Syn. of 'Glen Rossie'

'Glen Rothes' 2 W-P
(J.S.B. Lea) J.S.B. Lea, 1976
'Inverpolly' × 'Fionn'; sdlg no. 2-25-65
Fl. 103 mm wide; perianth segments somewhat reflexed; corona pink. Mid-season

'Glissando' 2 Y-Y
(G.E. Mitsch) G.E. Mitsch, 1982
'Scio' × 'Camelot'; sdlg no. JJ26/8
Fl. 100 mm wide, bright medium yellow. Mid-season. Resembles a larger and later-flowered 'Constancy'

'Glisten' 2 Y-W
(G.E. Mitsch) G.E. Mitsch, 1979
('Playboy' × 'Dreamboat') hybrid; sdlg no. JO9/2
Fl. 100 mm wide; perianth segments bright lemon; corona becoming white. Mid-season

'Glister' 2 W-? (b)
(P.D. Williams, pre-1931)

'Glitter' 3 Y-YYO
(G.H. Engleheart, pre-1904)
Perianth segments rounded at apex, rich lemon yellow, of strong substance; corona shallow, neatly ribbed, with a broad band of intense reddish orange at rim. Dwarf. Mid-season. Scented

'Glittering' 2 Y-? (a)
(G. Zandbergen-Terwegen, pre-1937)

'Glitterwax' 2 W-O
(G.H. Johnstone, pre-1949)

'Glitz' 9 W-GYO
(Mrs M.S. Yerger) Mrs M.S. Yerger, 1990
'Praecox Grandiflorus' × 'Lights Out'; sdlg no. 75 N 5
Fl. 62 mm wide; perianth segments ovate, acute, spreading; the inner segments a little shorter; corona cup-shaped, light orange-yellow 16B, shading to strong yellow-green 145A at base, with vivid orange 28B at rim. Dwarf. Late. Resembles 'Lights Out' in corona colouring

'Gloaming' 5 W-W
(The Brodie of Brodie, c.1912)
'Minnie Hume' × *N. triandrus*
Fls sometimes 2-3 per stem, of good substance

'Gloaming' 2 Y-Y
(A.E. Lowe, pre-1927)

'Globemaster' 2 W-Y
(D.S. Bell) D.S. Bell, 1961
'Green Island' × 'Satin Queen'
Fl. 113 mm wide; perianth segments broad; corona almost disc-shaped, very broad, deep yellow

'Gloire de Nantes' 2 Y-? (a)
(C.M. Grullemans) J.J. Grullemans & Sons, 1956

'Gloria' 8 W-Y
(pre-1913)
Poetaz
AM(Haarlem) 1913

'Gloria' 3 W-O
(de Graaff Bros, pre-1931)
Perianth segments cream white; corona reddish orange. AM(Haarlem) 1931

'Gloria' 1 W-W
(G. Lubbe & Son, pre-1947)
Fl. ivory white

'Gloria' 8 W-O
Syn. of 'Gloriosus'

'Gloria Mundi' 8 W-O
(pre-1793)

'Gloria Mundi' 2 Y-YOR
(W. Backhouse, pre-1869)
Perianth segments ovate or broadly ovate, blunt, not noticeably mucronate, clear rich yellow, spreading, overlapping one-third; the inner segments a little inflexed, with margins wavy; corona shallow funnel-shaped, broad, orange, paling to yellow at base and shading to rich orange-scarlet at rim, mouth straight, lightly frilled. 2n=21. Syn. Incomparabilis Leedsii 'Gloria Mundi'. FCC 1887. "Absorbed" 'J.T.D.Llewelyn'

'Gloriana' 8 Y-Y
(pre-1829)
?The same as 'Gloria Narcisses'

'Gloriana' 2 Y-O
(L. Buckland, pre-1936)

'Gloria Narcisses' 8 Y-Y
(pre-1807)
?The same as 'Gloriana'

'Gloribee' 2 Y-O
(J.N. Hancock & Co., pre-1967) Unregistered
Corona large, expanded, reddish orange, frilled. Early

'Glorietta' 2 W-?
(G.L. Wilson) D.G. Moore, 1966

'Glorieuse' 8 Y-Y
(pre-1835)
?The same as 'Glorieux'

'Glorieuse' 8 W-W
(pre-1835)
?The same as 'Glorieuse' 8 W- Y or O

'Glorieuse' 8 W-Y or O
?The same as 'Glorieuse' 8 W-W, 'Gloriosa' 8 W-O

'Glorieux' 8 Y-Y
(pre-1851)
?The same as 'Glorieuse' 8 Y-Y

'Glenrowan' 1 Y-Y
(A. Overton) A. Overton, 1960

'Glenroy' 1 W-Y
(H.A. Brown, pre-1938)
Perianth segments opening pale yellow, quickly becoming white; corona rich lemon, with mouth expanded

'Glenshane' 2 W-W
(G.L. Wilson, pre-1941)
'Silver Plane' × ? 'Rinsey'
Perianth segments pure white; corona shallow, cream, faintly touched gold at rim, frilled

'Glenshee' 2 W-Y
(J.J. Abernethy) R.J. Abernethy, 1960
Fl. 115 mm wide; perianth segments broadly ovate; corona lemon yellow, with rim dentate. Mid-season

'Glenshesk' 1 W-W
(G.L. Wilson, pre-1950)
'Courage' × 'Kanchenjunga'
Fl. 102 mm wide, creamy white; perianth segments broadly ovate, slightly mucronate, smooth, overlapping half; the inner segments more narrowly ovate, slightly twisted; corona mouth widely expanded, with rim flanged and crenate. AM(e) 1950, *FCC(g) 1971

'Glenside' 2 W-GWW
(F.E. Board, 1963) Rathowen Daffodils, 1976
'Easter Moon' × 'Pigeon'; sdlg no. 837
Fl. icy white; corona slender, with green at base. Mid-season. Resembles a stronger and taller 'Misty Glen' with slightly broader perianth segments

'Glen Springs' 2 W-YYO
(de Graaff Bros, pre-1939)
Corona shallow, widely expanded, deep yellow, with soft orange at rim. AM(Haarlem) 1939

'Glen Tana' 1 Y-Y
(R.H. Glover) R.H. Glover, 1975
'Aroagh' × 'Melissa'; sdlg no. 1209
Fl. 110 mm wide; corona frilled. Mid-season. Resembles a larger-flowered 'Ardagh' with the inner perianth segments broader

'Glenties' 2 W-O
(W.J. Dunlop) W.J. Dunlop, 1961
Perianth segments pure white, slightly reflexed; corona orange

'Glentui' 2 W-Y
(E.W. Cotter) E.W. Cotter, 1968
'Monte Carlo' hybrid
Perianth segments pure white, of thick substance; corona deep lemon, with rim flanged and dentate

'Glenvar' 3 W-R
(J.L. Richardson, pre-1950)
'Forfar' × 'Lady Kesteven'
Perianth segments white, with margins slightly incurved; corona tightly ribbed, deep red

'Glenville' 3 W-R
(W.J. Dunlop, pre-1947)
'Folly' × 'Sunstar'
Perianth segments snow white; corona deep crimson-red

'Glenwherry' 3 W-R
(W.J. Dunlop, pre-1947)
'Sunstar' × 'Isola'
Perianth segments snow white; corona crimson-red

'Glenwood' 2 Y-? (a)
(C. de Berry, pre-1943)

'Glenwynne' 2 W-GWP
(D.S. Bell) D.S. Bell, 1982
('Fontanalis' × 'Barbara Allen') × 'Iridescent'
Fl. 103 mm wide; corona very shallow bowl-shaped, with a narrow band of bright pink at rim. Mid-season

'Glenys' 2 Y-OOY
(G.W.E. Brogden) M.E. Brogden, 1959

'Glider' ?-P
(Alister Clark, pre-1948)

'Glider' 2 Y-Y
(W. Jackson Jr) Jackson's Daffodils, 1979
Sdlg 128/65 × 'Ristin'; sdlg no. 47/72
Fl. 106 mm wide. Mid-season

'Glimmer' 9 W-GYO
(Mrs M.S. Yerger) Mrs M.S. Yerger, 1986
'Praecox Grandiflorus' × 'Lights Out'; sdlg no. 75 Q 3
Perianth segments white, of good substance; corona brilliant greenish yellow 2B, with vivid yellow-green 154A at base and vivid reddish orange 32A at rim. Mid-season to late. Scented. Resembles 'Praecox' in form and 'Lights Out' in colour

'Glint' 9 W-GGO
(Mrs M.S. Yerger) Mrs M.S. Yerger, 1987
'Praecox Grandiflorus' × 'Lights Out'; sdlg no. 75 O 2
Fl. 68 mm wide; perianth segments spreading, overlapping; corona cup-shaped, closely ribbed, yellow-green (145B), with a darker tone at base (145A) and strong reddish orange 31B at rim, with a line of white between green and orange at maturity, rim dentate

'Glint of Gold' 1 Y-Y
(W. Balch, pre-1933)

'Glorification' 2 W-YOO
(pre-1944)
Perianth segments very broad, blunt, only very slightly mucronate, white or yellowish white, spreading, with margins nicked at apex, overlapping half or more; the inner segments more nearly ovate, slightly inflexed, with margins wavy; corona shallow bowl-shaped, very broad, ribbed, orange, with a more or less narrow band of yellow at base, mouth heavily frilled. Mid-season. AM(Haarlem) 1944. Corona variably YYO

'Gloriola' 2 Y-W
(G.E. Mitsch) G.E. Mitsch, 1969
('Shirley Wyness' × 'Pink-a-dell') × 'Dawnglow' × 'Lunar Sea'

'Gloriole' 2 W-P
(G.H. Johnstone, pre-1960)

'Gloriosa' 8 W-O
(pre-1852)
Probably the same as 'Gloriosus'. ?The same as 'Glorieuse' 8 W-Y or O, also 'Gloriosa' 8 W-Y and 8 W-W

'Gloriosa' 8 W-Y
(pre-1884)
?The same as 'Gloriosa' 8 W-O

'Gloriosa' 8 W-W
(pre-1897)
?The same as 'Gloriosa' 8 W-O

'Gloriosa Superba' 8 W-O
Syn. of 'Gloriosus'

'Gloriosus' 8 W-O
(pre-1883)
Fls. many per stem; perianth segments very broadly ovate, white, with prominent mucro of a brighter white, spreading, with margins wavy and incurling, overlapping half; corona cup-shaped, shallowly 6-ribbed, light orange (23A), tinged green in tube, mouth straight, wavy, somewhat 3-angled, rim entire. Scented. 2n=20. Syn. 'Gloriosa Superba', 'Gloria', Tazetta 'Gloriosus'. Probably the same as 'Gloriosa' 8 W-O

'Gloriosus' 3 W-W
Syn. of 'Circe'

'Gloriosus Major' 2 or 3 ?-Y
(?E. Leeds, pre-1877)
Corona canary yellow. Syn. Leedsii 'Gloriosus Major'

'Gloriosus Minor' 3 W-Y
Syn. of 'Arsinoë'

'Glorious' 8 W-O
(J.C. Williams, pre-1923)
Poetaz
Fls 2-3 per stem, rounded, 65-70 mm wide; perianth segments very broadly ovate or almost roundish, blunt or truncate, prominently mucronate, white, touched orange-yellow at base, spreading or slightly inflexed, concave, with margins incurling, overlapping one-third; the inner segments more narrowly ovate, not noticeably mucronate, often twisted, with margins more strongly incurled; corona shallow bowl-shaped, ribbed, deep orange, with a darker tone at rim. Mid-season. Scented. 2n=24. AM(c)(g) 1923, AM(Haarlem) 1926, FCC(c)(m) 1926, *KirtonHC(g)(m) 1927, *KirtonAM(g)(m) 1934, *AM(g) 1936

'Glorious Dawn' 2 Y-? (a)
(R.O. Backhouse, pre-1932)

'Glorious Devon' 2 Y-? (a)
(R.O. Backhouse, pre-1934)

'Glorita' 3 Y-Y
(Erle Randall) Erle Randall, 1994
Thought to be a hybrid between *N. poeticus* and *N. triandrus*
Fl. star-shaped, 60-65 mm wide; perianth segments very narrow, pale greenish yellow (4D), with margins sometimes recurved, separated; corona short funnel-shaped, slightly ribbed, opening darker in tone than the perianth, becoming as pale as the perianth, with the darker tone at base, a little frilled. Mid-season. Slightly scented

'Glory' 8 W-?
Poetaz

'Glory' 9 W-YYR
Syn. of 'Glory of Lisse'

'Glory Be' 2 W-P
(R.H.Glover, pre-1989) Unregistered
'Mirra Donna' × 'Vahu'

'Glory of Haarlem' 1 Y-Y
(E.H. Krelage & Son, pre-1913)

'Glory of Hillegom' 1 W-Y
(M. van Waveren & Sons, pre-1930)

'Glory of Leiden' 1 Y-Y
(de Graaff Bros, pre-1887)
'Emperor' hybrid or *N. abscissus* × 1 W-W
Flower very large, yellow; perianth segments ovate, blunt, a little inflexed, with margins sometimes incurling, overlapping a quarter to one-third; the inner segments somewhat twisted; corona cylindrical, smooth, darker in tone than the perianth, with mouth flared and a little frilled, rim notched and shallowly and unevenly crenate. Resembles a large-

flowered 'Emperor' of slightly lighter colour. FCC 1887. See also 'Glory of Leyden'

'Glory of Leyden' 1 Y-Y
Syn. of 'Glory of Leiden'

'Glory of Limmen' 1 W-W
(W.J. Eldering & Son, pre-1928)
AM(Haarlem) 1937

'Glory of Lisse' 9 W-YYR
(J. Segers, pre-1901)
'Poetarum' hybrid
Fl. rounded; perianth segments pure white, of good substance, overlapping; corona large, citron yellow, with red at rim. 2n=14. Syn. 'Glory'. AM(Haarlem) 1908

'Glory of Noordwijk' 1 W-Y
(J. de Groot & Sons, pre-1902)
'Madame de Graaff' × 'Victoria'
Corona neatly frilled. AM 1902

'Glory of Oegstgeest' 1 Y-Y
(G. Lubbe & Son, pre-1929)
AM(Haarlem) 1929

'Glory of Sassenheim' 1 W-Y
(S.A. van Konynenburg & Co., pre-1922)
Perianth segments broadly ovate, inflexed, somewhat twisted, often with margins recurved, overlapping at base only; corona funnel shaped, frilled, with rim deeply notched. Syn. 'Samson'. FA(Haarlem) 1921

'Glory of the Morning' 2 W-?
Syn. of 'Aludra'

'Glory of Voorhout' 2 W-? (a)
(P. van Deursen, pre-1930)
AM(Haarlem) 1930

'Glory of Warmond' 1 Y-Y
(?J. Kouwenhoven, pre-1913)
Fl. dark yellow. AM(Haarlem) 1913

'Glory of Warmond' 1 W-? (b)
(G.B. de Vroomen & Sons, pre-1934)

'Glory of Wassenar' 1 Y-Y
(Dutch origin, pre-1916)

'Gloucester Point' 2 W-P
(W.G. Pannill) W.G. Pannill, 1985
('Rose of Tralee' × 'Interim') × 'Fintona'; sdlg no. J 24 B
Mid-season

'Glover' 2 Y-YYR
Syn. of 'Gay Lover'

'Glow' 2 Y-YYO
(E. Leeds, pre-1877)
Corona with scarlet-orange at rim. Syn. Incomparabilis Leedsii 'Glow', Incomparabilis Leedsii 'Marginatus'. "Absorbed" 'Mrs Meston'

'Glowing' 2 Y-O
(C.O. Fairbairn, 1945) R. Hyde, 1958

'Glowing Ember' 2 W-R
(Mrs H.K. Richardson) Carncairn Daffodils, 1973
'Kilworth' × 'Arbar'
Fl. 110 mm wide; corona orange-red

'Glowing Gold' 2 Y-Y
(T. Bloomer) T. Bloomer, 1970
'Chungking' × 'Galway'; sdlg no. 1/51/54
Fl. deep golden yellow; corona rim dentate

'Glowing Morn' 2 Y-O
(T. Bloomer) T. Bloomer, 1962
'Red Ranger' × ('Royal Mail' × 'Narvik'); sdlg no. 3/34/58
Corona orange

'Glowing Phoenix' 4 Y-O
(R.O. Backhouse, pre-1930)
Fl. rounded, 100 mm wide; perianth and other petaloid segments primrose yellow, the two outer whorls symmetrically arranged, separated; the centre whorl fewer than six in number, short, twisted; corona segments interspersed, glowing orange. Early or very early

'Glowing Red' 4 W-R
(K.J. Heazlewood, 1958) K.J. Heazlewood, 1968
'Mary Copeland' hybrid
Early. 2n=28. Resembles a brighter-coloured 'Eleanor May'

'Glowing Sands' 11a Y-YOO
(W. & J. Munro, 1971) W. & J. Munro, 1985
'Naples' × 'Baccarat'; sdlg no. 66/06
Perianth segments butter yellow. Mid-season. AM(c)(NZ) 1984. Received AM(c)(NZ) 1984 as 'Golden Sands'

'Glowing Torch' 2 Y-R
(T. Bloomer) T. Bloomer, 1964
'Red Ranger' × 'Air Marshal'; sdlg no. 1/32/58
Perianth segments deep yellow; corona very deep red

'Gloworm' 3 W-YYR
(J.J. Abernethy, 1949) R.J. Abernethy, 1962
Fl. 95 mm wide; perianth segments whitish. Mid-season

'Glowworm' 3 W-? (b)
(Sir C.H. Cave, pre-1908)

'Glyce' 1 W-W
(W.Jackson Sr, 1937)
'Bianca' × 'Beersheba'
Seed parent of 'Sigval'

'Glycon' 2 W-W
(A.M. Wilson, pre-1948)

'Glynde' 2 W-WWP
(N.A.Burr) N.A.Burr, 1996
'Rainbow' × 'Cherrygardens'; sdlg no. 1.11.82
Fl. 108 mm wide; perianth segments very broadly ovate, blunt or somewhat truncate, only very slightly mucronate, spreading, overlapping half; the inner segments narrower, with margins incurved; corona short funnel-shaped, loosely ribbed, white, with a band of pink at rim, mouth straight, frilled, shallowly lobed. Mid-season. Sunproof

'Glyngarth' 2 Y-Y
(Carne-Ross, pre-1913)
Fl. pale yellow; corona shallow, widely expanded. Resembles 'Homespun'. AM 1913

'Glynis' 2 Y-Y
(J.S. Leitch) J.S. Leitch, 1960
Fl. 115 mm wide, lemon yellow. Late. Resembles a brighter-flowered 'Tiki'

'Glynn Wye' 4 W-Y
(E.W. Cotter) E.W. Cotter, 1968
'Mary Copeland' × 'Bryher'

'Glynver' 3 W-O
(Mrs R.O. Backhouse, pre-1921)
Perianth segments white, smooth; corona light orange. Mid-season. 2n=28. AM(e) 1936

'Gnome' 6 Y-Y
(A. Gray) Broadleigh Gardens, 1967
N. cyclamineus × 1Y-Y
Fl. 65 mm wide. Early

'Gnomon' 2 W-Y
(A.H. Ahrens) J.S. Leitch, 1956

'Gobi' 1 Y-Y
(S.J. Bisdee, 1939)
'Mortlake' × 'Golden City'

'Goblet' 1 W-Y
(G.B. van Rhijn, pre-1952)
AM(Haarlem) 1961

'Goblet of Gold' 1 Y-Y
(W.B. Hartland, pre-1907)

'Goblin' 1 Y-Y
(pre-1896)
Corona large, rich golden yellow

'Goblin' 3 W-? (b)
(Mrs F.S. Foote, pre-1941)

'Goddess' 2 W-Y
(J.W. Barr, pre-1931)

'Godolphin' 1 Y-Y
(P.D. Williams, pre-1925)
'Maximus' hybrid
Fl. 102 mm wide, lemon yellow; perianth segments broadly ovate, blunt, very slightly mucronate, a little inflexed, with margins wavy, overlapping one-third; the inner segments narrower, more strongly inflexed, twisted; corona cylindrical at base, a little flared towards mouth, slightly darker in tone than the perianth, with rim widely flanged and broadly crenate. Mid-season. 2n=28. AM(m)(g) 1925, AM(e) 1927, AM(Haarlem) 1930, FA(Haarlem) 1936, FCFA(Haarlem) 1937, *AM(g) 1949

'Godrevy' 1 Y-Y
(P.D. Williams, pre-1925)
Fl. small; corona broad, with rim flanged. AM(e) 1925

'Goethe' 9 W-?
(W.J. Eldering & Son, pre-1930)

'Goff's Caye' 2 YYW-W
(A.J.R. Pearson) A.J.R. Pearson, 1992
'Daydream' × ('Camelot' × 'Daydream'); sdlg no. 88-26 L5
Fl. forming a double triangle, 103 mm wide; perianth segments broadly ovate, blunt, not noticeably mucronate, brilliant greenish yellow 3B, touched pale yellowish white (4D) at base and at midrib towards apex, spreading, plane, smooth, overlapping one-third to a half; the inner segments with margins wavy; corona funnel-shaped, lightly ribbed, pale yellowish white (4D), mouth flared, more strongly ribbed, frilled, rim notched and crenate, with margins minutely crenate. Mid-season to late. Resembles 'Grand Prospect' but with the corona of purer white

'Goforit' 2 Y-O
(Jackson's Daffodils, 1983) Jackson's Daffodils, 1993
Sdlg no. 56/75 × 'Caryem'; sdlg no. 20/83
Fl. rounded, 102 mm wide; perianth segments very broadly ovate, rounded at apex or somewhat truncate, vivid yellow 14A, with very slight white mucro, faintly flushed red, a little reflexed, plane, smooth, overlapping half; the inner segments narrower, more nearly spreading; corona funnel-shaped, smooth, orange (28A), with mouth a little flared, finely ribbed, loosely frilled. Early to mid-season

'Gog' 2 W-Y
(W. Backhouse, pre-1869)
Fl. large; perianth segments creamy white. Syn. Incomparabilis Albidus 'Gog', Incomparabilis

Albidus 'Grandiflorus'. "Absorbed" 'Sylvia'

'Gog' 1 Y-Y
(G.H. Engleheart, pre-1919)
Early

'Golconda' 8 Y-O
(pre-1882)
Resembles 'Grand Soleil d'Or'

'Golconda' 2 W-? (b)
(N.Y. Lower, pre-1928)
'Lord Roberts' × 'Fireball'

'Golconda' 1 Y-Y
Perianth segments acute, overlapping. Syn. of 'Monterey'

'Gold' 1 Y-Y
(C.E. Radcliff, 1929)
'Volunteer' hybrid

'Gold' 2 Y-Y
(L. Buckland, pre-1936)

'Gold Ader' 1 Y-Y
(Konynenburg & Mark) Konynenburg & Mark, 1970
'Golden Robes' × 'Rembrandt' hybrid

'Gold Aura' 2 Y-Y
Syn. of 'Golden Aura'

'Goldball' 2 Y-?
(de Graaff Bros, pre-1954)
AM(Haarlem) 1954

'Gold Band' 1 Y-Y
(The Brodie of Brodie, c.1909)
'Glory of Noordwijk' × 'King Alfred'; sdlg no. 42/A/04

'Goldband' 11a W-WWY
(J. Gerritsen & Son, pre-1977) Unregistered
Corona segments silvery, with gold at rim. Mid-season to late

'Gold Bank' 2 Y-Y
(G.W.E. & M.E.Brogden, pre-1987) Unregistered
'Gold Script' × 'Arctic Gold'
Fl. self yellow; perianth segments rounded and with margins a little incurling at apex, spreading, overlapping

'Gold Bar' 1 Y-Y
(H.A. Brown, pre-1950)
'Gold Tray' × 'Cromarty'

'Gold Beach' 2 Y-Y
(G.E. Mitsch, 1979) R. & E. Havens, 1993

'Camelot' × 'Aurum'; sdlg no. 2015/2
Fl. 105 mm wide, deep golden yellow; perianth segments broadly ovate, of heavy substance; corona funnel-shaped, with mouth slightly flared. Mid-season

'Goldbeater' 1 Y-Y
(G.L. Wilson, pre-1923)
'Maximus' hybrid
Fl. orange-gold; perianth segments twisted; corona with mouth expanded, rim dentate. Very tall. Early

'Goldberg' 2 Y-? (a)
(L. van Leeuwen & Son, pre-1937)
AM(Haarlem) 1937

'Gold Bond' 2 Y-Y
(Brian S. Duncan) Rathowen Daffodils, 1983
'Golden Jewel' open pollinated; sdlg no. 650
Fl. deep golden yellow; perianth segments very broad in outline, rounded at apex and with margins sometimes incurling, with slight white mucro, spreading, plane, smooth, regular, overlapping half or more; the inner segments more nearly ovate, square-shouldered at base, a little inflexed, with pale midrib showing; corona cylindrical, smooth, with mouth slightly expanded, loosely frilled. Mid-season. AM 1997

'Gold Brocade' 1 W-Y
(S.J. Bisdee, 1946)
'Kurana' × 'Rosario'

'Gold Bullion' 1 Y-Y
(Carncairn Daffodils) Carncairn Daffodils, 1982
'Kingscourt' × 'Prince Igor'; sdlg no. 5/152/60
Fl. 105 mm wide, vivid yellow 12A. Mid-season. Resembles a deeper-coloured 'Prince Igor'

'Gold Bullion' 1 Y-Y
(pre-1972) Unregistered

'Goldburn' 1 Y-Y
(C. de Berry) C. de Berry, 1956

'Gold Cache' 11a Y-PPY
(Colin Crotty, 1985) Colin Crotty, 1996
'Honeybird' open pollinated; sdlg no. 25-80
Fl. 100 mm wide; perianth segments broadly ovate, lemon yellow; the inner segments smaller and more nearly acute; corona deeply split, the the six segments almost as long as the perianth segments and opposite and closely overlying them, deeply bi-lobed, opening yellow, becoming amber pink, with creamy pink at base and yellow at rim. Early to mid-season. Sunproof

'Gold Cameo' 1 Y-Y
(J.A. O'More, 1967) P.D.K. Ramsay, 1984
'Belmont' hybrid; sdlg no. 25/67

'Gold Chain' 7 Y-Y
(G.E. Mitsch and R. & E.Havens, 1975) G.E. Mitsch

and R. & E.Havens, 1985
'Top Notch' × *N. jonquilla*; sdlg no. 2K99/5
Fls usually 2 per stem, deep golden yellow. Late. Scented. Resembles a larger and later-flowered 'Quail'

'Gold Chalice' 2 Y-? (a)
(G.H. Engleheart, pre-1914)

'Gold Charm' 2 Y-Y
(Brogden Bulbs, pre-1995) Unregistered

'Gold Chrome' 2 W-Y
(Tom Forster, 1960s) Unregistered
Corona disc-shaped, warm yellow. Tall. Mid-season

'Gold Coast' 2 Y-?
(Alister Clark, 1930) J. Sharp, 1960

'Goldcoast' 1 Y-Y
(C.G. van Tubergen, pre-1945)

'Gold Cockade' 2 W-Y
(S.J. Bisdee, 1941)
Sdlg × 'Kallista'

'Gold Coin' 3 W-? (b)
(E.M. Crosfield, pre-1910)

'Gold Coin' 2 Y-Y
(Elise Havens) G.E. Mitsch, 1979
'Ormeau' × 'Butterscotch'; sdlg no. FEJ7/9
Fl. 103 mm wide, deep yellow; corona almost straight-sided, slightly frilled. Mid-season

'Gold Collar' 11a Y-Y
(J. Gerritsen & Son) J. Gerritsen & Son, 1956
Perianth segments yellow; corona segments orange-yellow (17C). 2n=28. AM(Haarlem) 1956

'Gold Convention' 2 Y-Y
(J.S.B. Lea) J.S.B. Lea, 1978
Fl. 110 mm wide; perianth segments very broadly ovate in outline, blunt or rounded at apex, slightly mucronate, vivid yellow 9A, spreading, somewhat concave, overlapping half or more; the inner segments more or less truncate, shouldered at base; corona ribbed, orange-yellow (15A), with a slightly darker tone at mouth, mouth expanded, lightly frilled, rim crenate. Mid-season. *HC(g) 1990, *AM(g) 1991, AGM 1995. Varies between Divs 2 and 1

'Goldcourt' 1 Y-Y
(J.L. Richardson, pre-1937)
'Crocus' × 'Cromarty'
Fl. forming a double triangle, 108 mm wide; perianth segments broadly ovate, blunt, mucronate, vivid yellow 9A, spreading, with margins incurling, smooth, overlapping half; the inner segments a little inflexed, somewhat twisted; corona cylindrical, smooth below, ribbed towards mouth, vivid yellow 12A, with rim flanged and shallowly crenate. AM(e) 1946, FCC(e) 1947, *FCC(g) 1962. See also 'Gold Court'

'Gold Court'
Syn. of 'Goldcourt'

'Goldcraft' 1 Y-Y
(D.S. Bell) D.S. Bell, 1961
'Val d'Or' × 'Treasure'
Fl. 102 mm wide, golden yellow; corona frilled, with rim flanged. Mid-season. Resembles 'Kingscourt' but with rounder perianth segments

'Gold Crest' 2 Y-? (a)
(Sir C.H. Cave, pre-1908)

'Gold Crest' 2 Y-O
(R.O. Backhouse, pre-1931)
AM(Haarlem) 1931

'Goldcrest' 2 Y-?
Syn. of 'Belray'

'Gold Crown' 2 Y-P
(A.E. Lowe, pre-1927)
Corona salmon pink

'Gold Crown' 2 W-Y
(G.E. Mitsch, 1940) G.E. Mitsch, 1965
'Nevis' × 'Fortune'
Fl. 95 mm wide; corona deep golden yellow. Mid-season

'Gold Cup' 8 W-Y
(pre-1872)
Perianth segments pure white; corona golden yellow

'Gold Cup' 1 Y-Y
(G.H. Engleheart, pre-1907)
Fl. brilliant golden yellow

'Gold-digger' 1 Y-Y
(J.L. Richardson, pre-1941)
'Crocus' × 'Cromarty'
Fl. golden; corona small, with rim neatly rolled

'Gold Digger'
Unregistered
Seed parent of 'Golden Falcon'

'Gold Dust' 2 Y-Y
(R.V. Favell, pre-1939)
'Alroi' × 'Fortune'
Fl. golden yellow; corona with rim lightly rolled

'Gold Dust' 8
(pre-1942)

'Goldella' 1 Y-Y
(Barr & Sons, pre-1929)

'Gold Else' 8
(pre-1930)

'Goldelse' 2 Y-?
Fls 2-3 per stem, bright yellow. Syn. of 'Florinda'

'Golden' 1 Y-Y
(O. Ronalds, pre-1955)
Fl. forming a double triangle; perianth segments very broadly ovate, with slight white mucro, spreading, with margins minutely incurling at apex; the inner segments more narrowly ovate, somewhat creased; corona mouth expanded, lightly frilled, rim notched and broadly crenate

'Goldena' 3 Y-? (a)
(R.H. Bath, pre-1929)

'Goldena' 1 Y-Y
(G.W.E. Brogden) C.W. Johnson, 1956

'Golden Ace' 2 Y-Y
(S.A. Free) S.A. Free, 1960
Fl. 108 mm wide. Mid-season. Resembles a darker-coloured 'Golden Robe' of greater substance

'Golden Acre' 2 Y-Y
(?S.A. Free, pre-1960) Unregistered
Fl. deep golden yellow; perianth segments spreading, of thick substance; corona cup-shaped. PC(e)(NZ) 1958

'Golden Advance' 1 Y-Y
(Messrs Turnhout, pre-1947)
FA(Haarlem) 1955

'Golden Age' 1 Y-Y
(Barr & Sons, pre-1929)
Perianth segments soft yellow; corona broad, expanded, rich yellow, frilled

'Golden Age' 1 Y-Y
(J.L. Richardson, pre-1964) Unregistered
'Goldcourt' self pollinated
Corona with rim rolled and dentate

'Golden Aides' 1 Y-Y
(E.W. Philpott)

'Golden Amber' 3 Y-? (a)
(Sir C.H. Cave, pre-1908)

'Golden Amber' 2 Y-OOY
(Ballydorn Bulb Farm) Ballydorn Bulb Farm, 1975
'Kilmorack' open pollinated
Fl. forming a double triangle, 96 mm wide; perianth segments very broad, blunt, fairly prominently mucronate, sandy yellow, or almost white if forced, spreading, overlapping half; the inner segments less noticeably mucronate, square-shouldered at base; corona strong orange, touched golden yellow at rim, or entirely yellow if forced, mouth lightly frilled, with rim crenate. Mid-season. $2n=28$

'Golden Apple' 1 Y-Y
(The Brodie of Brodie, c.1908)
'Emperor' × 'King Alfred'
Fl. very large

'Golden Apricot' 2 W-Y
(Mrs R.O. Backhouse, pre-1914)
Perianth segments tinged green at base; corona rich apricot yellow, with buff yellow at rim

'Golden Arrow' 6 Y-Y
(Barr & Sons, pre-1913)
'Monarch' × *N. cyclamineus*
Perianth segments acute, primrose yellow, reflexed, lightly twisted; corona slender, ribbed, darker in tone than the perianth, mouth slightly flared, with rim crenate

'Golden Attraction' 2 Y-Y
(G.L. Wilson, pre-1933)
Fl. deep golden yellow; perianth segments narrow, acute. AM(Haarlem) 1933

'Golden Aura' 2 Y-Y
(J.L. Richardson) Mrs H.K. Richardson, 1964
'Halo' open pollinated
Fl. 95 mm wide, deep golden yellow; perianth segments broadly ovate, blunt, with slight white mucro, spreading, plane, regular, overlapping half; the inner segments a little narrower, slightly inflexed; corona long cup-shaped, darker in tone than the perianth, with mouth expanded and lightly frilled. Mid-season. $2n=28$. AGM 1995. See also 'Gold Aura'

'Golden Ballot' 2 Y-? (a)
(W.B. Cranfield, pre-1927)

'Golden Banner' 1 Y-Y
(L. Marchand, pre-1937)

'Golden Bantam' 2 Y-Y
(L. van Leeuwen & Son, pre-1929)
Fl. yellow, ageing to near orange

'Golden Bay' 1 Y-Y
(R.P. Cook) R.P. Cook, 1955

'Golden Beach' 1 Y-Y
(G. Lubbe & Son, pre-1939)
AM(Haarlem) 1939

'Golden Beam' 2 Y-? (a)
(W. Balch, pre-1936)

'Golden Bear' 4 Y-Y
(Brian S. Duncan) Brian S. Duncan, 1992
'Smokey Bear' × 'Sportsman'; sdlg no. 1039
Fl. 112 mm wide; perianth segments deep golden yellow; corona segments orange-yellow. Mid-season to late

'Golden Beauty' 8 Y-Y
(pre-1867)
Fl. golden yellow

'Golden Beauty' 1 Y-Y
(Barr & Sons, pre-1910)
Fl. brilliant yellow; perianth segments somewhat twisted; corona ribbed, a little darker in tone than the perianth, with rim deeply crenate

'Golden Beauty' 1 W-Y
(van Zonneveld Bros & Philippo, pre-1930)
Perianth segments creamy white

'Golden Beauty' 1 Y-Y
(G. Lewis, 1945) D.S. Bell, 1958
'Gold Tray' × 'Cromarty'
Fl. dark bronzy yellow; corona frilled

'Golden Bell' 1 Y-Y
(G.H. Engleheart, pre-1892)
'Emperor' × 'Egypt'
Fl. facing slightly downwards; perianth segments pale yellow, somewhat twisted; corona funnel-shaped, clear soft yellow, with mouth widely expanded, frilled, rim deeply notched. Tall. FCC 1892

'Golden Bells' 10 Y-Y
(Tesselaar Group, pre-1995) Unregistered
N. bulbocodium sport
Fl. rich golden yellow, facing up; perianth segments very narrow, acute, inflexed, separated; corona funnel-shaped, narrow at base, mouth wavy, rim entire. Dwarf. With up to 15 secondary stems. Syn. 'Silvania'

'Golden Blaze' 1 Y-Y
(K.J. van der Veek) K.J. van der Veek, 1984
Perianth segments vivid yellow 12A; corona a little paler in tone (12B). Resembles a shorter 'Gold Medal' with a larger flower

'Golden Bough' 2 Y-? (a)
(Parr's Nurseries, 1947) Parr's Nurseries, 1958

'Golden Bounty' 1 Y-Y
(Warnaar & Co., pre-1939)
'Godolphin' × 'Golden Harvest'
AM(Haarlem) 1939

'Golden Bowl' 1
(A. Wilson, pre-1902)
'Emperor' hybrid
Perianth segments rounded at apex, inflexed, overlapping; the inner segments more nearly ovate, creased; corona cylindrical, broad, with mouth heavily ribbed and widely expanded, lightly frilled, with rim crenate

'Golden Bowl' 7 Y-Y
(G.H. Engleheart, pre-1923)
Fl. jonquil yellow; corona long, funnel-shaped

'Golden Boy' 1 Y-Y
(The Brodie of Brodie, pre-1928)

'Golden Boy' 2 WWY-Y
(G.N. Rees) G.N. Rees, 1963
'Pink Fancy' × ?'Mrs R.O.Backhouse'
Fl. 95 mm wide; perianth segments acute, white, with yellow at base; corona lemon yellow. Mid-season

'Golden Bracelet' 2 Y-O
(C.G. van Tubergen, pre-1954)
AM(Haarlem) 1954

'Golden Brilliant' 1 Y-Y
(G. Vink, pre-1936)
AM(Haarlem) 1936, FA(Haarlem) 1938

'Golden Brocade' 1 Y-Y
(D.S. Bell) D.S. Bell, 1969
Corona frilled, with rim dentate

'Golden Butterfly' 2 Y-Y
(S.J. Bisdee, 1941)
'Golden Queen' × 'Fahan'
Syn. 'The Golden Butterfly'

'Golden Carbineer' 2 Y-? (a)
(H.M. Hammond) H.M. Hammond, 1955
PC(e)(NZ) 1952

'Golden Casquet' 1 Y-Y
(The Brodie of Brodie, *c.*1909)
'Big Ben' × 'King Alfred'
Perianth segments deep yellow, reflexed

'Golden Castle' 4 Y-O
(Warnaar & Co., pre-1947)
'Decency' sport
Perianth segments broadly ovate, blunt, golden yellow, with slight white mucro, spreading, with margins sometimes incurling, overlapping a quarter to one-third; the inner segments with margins wavy or recurved; corona cylindrical, smooth, golden orange, loosely frilled, with rim rolled and crenate; the corona enclosing many segments of similar length and colour, tightly clustered, lightly frilled. AM(Haarlem) 1947, FCC(Haarlem) 1950

'Golden Cavalcade' 1 Y-Y
(D.S. Bell) D.S. Bell, 1955
Fl. deep golden yellow; corona regularly frilled, with

rim dentate

'Golden Cavalier' 1 Y-Y
(D.S. Bell) D.S. Bell, 1968
'Val d'Or' × 'Treasure' hybrid
Fl. golden yellow

'Golden Century' 2 Y-Y
(N.A.Burr) Daffodil Society, 1997
'Celtic Chief' × 'Gold Convention'; sdlg no. 4-17-83
Fl. more than 100 mm wide; perianth segments very broad in outline, blunt or rounded at apex, with slight white mucro, a little reflexed, plane, overlapping half; the inner segments slightly truncate, more nearly spreading; corona funnel-shaped, slightly darker in tone than the perianth, lightly frilled. Mid-season

'Golden Champion' 1 Y-Y
(A.F. Calvert, pre-1928)

'Golden Chance' 2 Y-Y
(Mrs H.K. Richardson) Mrs H.K. Richardson, 1972
'My Love' open pollinated
Fl. golden yellow; corona with rim rolled

'Golden Chariot' 1 Y-Y
(J.L. Richardson, pre-1923)
Fl. deep golden yellow; corona widely expanded, frilled

'Golden Charm' 1 Y-Y
(R. Crews, pre-1949)

'Golden Cheer' 2 Y-? (a)
(P.D. Williams, pre-1938)

'Golden Chief' 1 Y-Y
(C.A. van Paridon, pre-1914)
Fl. 114 mm wide or more, dark golden yellow; corona mouth expanded, with rim flanged. AM(Haarlem) 1931, FA(Haarlem) 1931

'Golden Chimes' 6 Y-Y
(S.S. Berry, pre-1937)
N. jonquilla × *N. cyclamineus*
Perianth segments ovate, blunt, only very slightly mucronate, strongly reflexed, with margins a little incurved, overlapping one-third; corona cylindrical, long, with mouth straight and rim crenate

'Golden Chord' 1 Y-Y
(W.G. Pannill) W.G. Pannill, 1970
'Arctic Gold' × 'Royal Oak'

'Golden Circle' 1 W-? (b)
(W.B. Hartland, pre-1908)

'Golden Circle' 2 Y-? (a)
(?New Zealand origin) Parr's Nurseries, 1958

'Golden City' 1 Y-Y
(D.V. West, pre-1923)
Fl. golden yellow

'Golden City' 2 Y-R
(?West & Fell, *c*.1933)
Perianth segments rich golden yellow; corona shallow, widely expanded, brilliant red

'Golden Clarion' 1 Y-Y
(?Australian origin, pre-1955)

'Golden Clarion' 1 Y-Y
(Mrs H.K. Richardson) Ballydorn Bulb Farm, 1968
Fl. 99 mm wide, golden yellow. Late. Resembles a more refined and vigorous 'Kingscourt'

'Golden Cloud' 1 Y-Y
(H. Backhouse, pre-1910)

'Golden Cloud' 1 Y-Y
(H.J. Poole Sr, pre-1927)

'Golden Cloud' 1 Y-Y
(J.L. Richardson, 1952) Mrs H.K. Richardson, 1962
'Spanish Gold' × 'King's Ransom'
Fl. golden yellow; corona with rim rolled. Mid-season

'Golden Clown' 1 Y-Y
(G.E. Morrill) G.E. Morrill, 1979
N. asturiensis × 'Small Talk'; sdlg no. 72-2-2
Fl. 23 mm wide; perianth segments brilliant greenish yellow 7C, twisted; corona of a slightly darker tone (7A)

'Golden Cockerel' 1 Y-Y
(J.L. Richardson) G.L. Wilson, 1955
'Kilkenny' × 'Goldcourt'
Fl. bright golden yellow

'Golden Coin' 1 Y-Y
(O. Ronalds, 1945) R. Hyde, 1958
Fl. rich yellow

'Golden Comet' 1 Y-Y
(C. Dawson, pre-1923)

'Golden Coronet' 1 Y-Y
(C. Dawson, pre-1923)

'Golden Cross' 1 Y-Y
(The Brodie of Brodie, pre-1928)
'Morven' hybrid

'Golden Crown' 1 Y-Y
(Warnaar & Co., pre-1927)

'Golden Crown' 1 Y-Y
(West & Fell, pre-1936)

'Golden Cups' 8 W-Y
(W.R.P. Welch) W.R.P. Welch, 1984
'Avalanche' sport
Fls up to 23 per stem, 37 mm wide; corona deep yellow. Mid-season

'Golden Cycle' 6 Y-Y
(H.G. Hawker, pre-1916)
Hybrid between *N. cyclamineus* and 'Golden Spur'
Fl. golden yellow, facing down; perianth segments narrowly ovate, acute, with white mucro, reflexed, somewhat twisted or with margins wavy or incurving, overlapping at base only; corona cylindrical, lightly ribbed, with mouth flared and rim deeply notched. Dwarf. Very early. 2n=21. AM(p)(r) 1919

'Golden Dale' 1 Y-Y
(R.H. Bath, pre-1927)

'Golden Dale' 1 Y-Y
(J.A. O'More) J.A. O'More, 1968
'Goldcourt' × 'Kingscourt'

'Golden Dawn' 1 Y-Y
(C. Goodson, pre-1927)

'Golden Dawn' 1 Y-Y
(West & Fell, pre-1936)

'Golden Dawn' 8 Y-O
(Oregon Bulb Farms) Oregon Bulb Farms, 1958
Fls several per stem, 45 mm wide; perianth segments broadly to very broadly ovate, brilliant greenish yellow between 5A and 5B, with prominent white mucro, spreading, with margins incurved, overlapping half or more; the inner segments less noticeably mucronate, with margins more strongly wavy or incurved, sometimes twisted; corona bowl-shaped, ribbed, deep orange, becoming darker in tone with age, lightly frilled. Late. Scented. With secondary stems. 2n=24. *AM(g) 1988, *FCC(g) 1990, AGM 1993

'Golden Day' 1 Y-Y
(C.W. Culpepper, pre-1980) Unregistered

'Golden Days' 1 Y-Y
(E.W. Cotter) E.W. Cotter, 1968
'Glenfalloch' × 'Arctic Gold'
Fl. bright gold; corona with rim rolled and dentate

'Golden Delight' 2 Y-Y
(A. Gibson, pre-1933)

'Golden Dew' 2 Y-? (a)
(A.H. Ahrens) J.S. Leitch, 1955

'Golden Dollar' 1 Y-Y
(W.J. Dunlop, pre-1953)
'Principal' × 'Cromarty'

Fl. deep gold

'Golden Dragon' 2 Y-? (a)
(Barr & Sons, pre-1931)
Syn. 'Giovanni'

'Golden Dragon' 1 Y-Y
Syn. of 'Ard Righ'

'Golden Dream' 1 Y-Y
(M. Veldhuyzen van Zanten & Sons, pre-1937)
'Van Waveren's Giant' hybrid
FA(Haarlem) 1938

'Golden Drop' 6 Y-Y
(Barr & Sons, pre-1929)

'Golden Ducat' 4 Y-Y
(Speelman & Sons, pre-1947)
'King Alfred' sport
Fl. rounded, 110 mm wide; perianth and other petaloid segments in several whorls, regularly superimposed, vivid yellow 9A, overlapping, of waxy texture; the outer whorls broadly ovate, spreading; the inner whorls successively narrower, shorter, more strongly inflexed; the centre whorl contorted and sharply inflexed; corona segments shorter than the petaloid segments and interspersed among them, broad, slightly darker in tone (12A), with rim crenate. 2n=28. Closely resembles a less readily forced 'Planet'. AM(Haarlem) 1946, FCC(Haarlem) 1950, AM(e) 1950, FCC(e) 1952, *AM(p) 1978

'Golden Dustman' 1 Y-Y
(R.H. Bath, pre-1914)

'Golden Eagle' 1 Y-Y
(E.H. Krelage & Son, pre-1907)

'Golden Eagle' 1 Y-Y
(P. van Deursen, pre-1931)
AM(Haarlem) 1931

'Golden East' 1 Y-Y
(R.H. Bath, pre-1916)

'Golden Edris' 2 Y-? (a)
(T. Slee, pre-1937)

'Goldene Geige' 1 Y-Y
(H. Wentink, 1978) Thoolen International, 1994
Hybrid between 'Goblet' and 'Gold Medal'
Fl. 100 mm wide; perianth segments vivid yellow 12A; corona a little darker in tone. Late. Resembles 'Gold Medal'

'Golden Elegance' 1 Y-Y
(T. Bloomer) T. Bloomer, 1970
'Kingscourt' × 'Standard Bearer'; sdlg no. 2/8/58

'Golden Emblem' 1 Y-Y
(R.H. Bath, pre-1923)

'Golden Emperor' 1 Y-Y
(J.R. Pearson & Sons, pre-1923)
'Lord Roberts' × 'King Alfred'
Early

'Golden Empire' 1 Y-Y
(Barr & Sons, pre-1923)

'Golden Empire' 1 Y-Y
(O. Ronalds, pre-1967) Unregistered
Fl. forming a double triangle, golden yellow; perianth segments broadly ovate, with slight white mucro, spreading, plane, or with margins a little wavy, overlapping half; the inner segments slightly inflexed, with margins more heavily waved or twisted; corona funnel-shaped, broadly ribbed, with mouth flared and even, rim notched. Tall. Mid-season. 2n=28

'Golden Empress' 1 Y-Y
(de Graaff Bros, pre-1923)
Perianth segments broadly ovate or oblong, usually acute, sometimes mucronate, rich yellow, somewhat ribbed, with margins a little wavy, overlapping one-third to a half; the inner segments smaller, a little twisted; corona angled, rich golden yellow, with mouth expanded, rim crenate and very widely flanged. AM(e) 1923

'Golden Ensign' 7 Y-Y
(G.H. Engleheart, pre-1912)
Perianth segments overlapping; corona slender, rich golden yellow. Scented

'Golden Era' 1 Y-Y
(J.A. O'More, 1961) P.D.K. Ramsay, 1980
'Braemar' × 'Golden Dale'; sdlg no. 71/61
Fl. 113 mm wide

'Golden Essence' 7 Y-Y
(E. Zinkowski) E. Zinkowski, 1981
'Saint Keverne' × *N. jonquilla*; sdlg no. 80-5N
Fl. 67 mm wide, intense golden yellow. Mid-season. Resembles a larger-flowered and more intensely coloured 'Sweetness'

'Golden Excelsior' 8
(A. Vis, pre-1942)

'Goldeneye' 3 W-Y
(Mrs H.K. Richardson) Mrs H.K. Richardson, 1974
'Syracuse' open pollinated
Fl. 98 mm wide

'Golden Fairy' 1 Y-Y
(M. van Waveren & Sons, pre-1942)

'Golden Falcon' 1 Y-Y
(W.G. Pannill) W.G. Pannill, 1972
'Gold Digger' × 'Arctic Gold'
Fl. 105 mm wide

'Golden Favourite' 1 Y-Y
(J.W.A. van der Wiel, pre-1953)

'Golden Fires' 2 Y-O
(T. Bloomer) T. Bloomer, 1970
'Chungking' × 'Air Marshal'
Perianth segments deep gold; corona reddish orange

'Golden Flag' 1 Y-Y
(G.L. Wilson, pre-1923)
'Monarch' × 'King Alfred'
Fl. rich golden yellow

'Golden Flake' 1 Y-Y
(Warnaar & Co., pre-1927)

'Golden Flame' 2 Y-? (a)
(P.D. Williams, pre-1940)

'Golden Flame' 2 Y-O
(T. Bloomer) T. Bloomer, 1970
'Craigywarren' × 'Air Marshal'; sdlg no. 2/35/58
Corona straight, deep reddish orange

'Golden Flash' 2 Y-O
(H.A. Brown, 1938) J.N. Hancock & Co., 1960
Corona reddish orange, with rim rolled

'Golden Fleece' 1 Y-Y
(H.J. Poole Sr, pre-1927)

'Golden Fortune' 1 Y-Y
(D.S. Bell) D.S. Bell, 1962
'Ranalagh' × 'Val d'Or'
Fl. 128 mm wide; corona frilled. Mid-season. Resembles 'Kingscourt' but with the perianth segments less strongly reflexed

'Golden Frill' 1 Y-Y
'Golden Spur' sport
Fl. rich yellow; corona deeply frilled. ?The same as 'Golden Frilled'

'Golden Frilled' 2 Y-Y
(pre-1928)
Perianth segments primrose yellow, overlapping; corona chrome yellow, with a darker tone at rim, with the rim closely and deeply notched, as if fringed. Syn. ?'Golden Frill'. FA(Haarlem) 1931, AM(p) 1934, *C(g) 1936

'Golden Future' 2 Y-? (a)
(pre-1937)
AM(Haarlem) 1937

'Golden Future' 1 Y-Y
(O. Ronalds) O. Ronalds, 1955

'Golden Gain' 1 Y-Y
(G.L. Wilson, pre-1943)
Fl. deep gold

'Golden Gala' 1 Y-Y
(Brian S.Duncan) Brian S.Duncan, 1997
Sdlg 77/1 ('Golden Jewel' × 'Midas Touch') open pollinated; sdlg no. 1533
Fl. forming a double triangle, 110 mm wide, golden yellow; perianth segments spreading; corona cylindrical, with rim widely rolled. Mid-season

'Golden Galaxy' 1 Y-Y
(D.S. Bell) D.S. Bell, 1983

'Golden Gate' 1 Y-Y
(D.V. West, pre-1923)
Fl. light yellow; perianth segments slightly reflexed

'Golden Gate' 2 Y-Y
(W.H. Roesé, 1968) W.H. Roesé, 1982
'Camelot' × 'Daydream'; sdlg no. 68/6/?
Fl. 117 mm wide. Mid-season

'Golden Gem' 3 Y-YYO
(W. Backhouse, pre-1869)
Perianth segments opening rich yellow, becoming primrose yellow. Syn. Barrii 'Golden Gem'

'Golden Gem' 1 Y-Y
(C. Dawson, pre-1927)

'Golden Giant' 1 Y-Y
(Warnaar & Co., pre-1927)

'Golden Gift' 1 Y-Y
(G.H. Johnstone, pre-1952)
Fl. golden yellow; corona with rim heavily rolled. AM(Haarlem) 1962

'Golden Girl' 1 Y-Y
(Kate Reade, 1981) Carncairn Daffodils, 1995
'Loughanmore' × 'Golden Sovereign'; sdlg no. 32/8/76
Fl. forming a double triangle, 120 mm wide; perianth segments broadly ovate, blunt, vivid yellow 9A, with slight white mucro, spreading, plane, overlapping half; the inner segments with margins a little wavy; corona narrowly funnel-shaped, lightly ribbed, darker in tone (14B) than the perianth, rim slightly flanged, crenate. Late

'Golden Gleam' 1 Y-Y
(R.H. Bath, pre-1923)

'Golden Gleam' 1 Y-Y
(G.H. Johnstone, pre-1960)

'Stronghold' × 'Maviston'

'Golden Glen' 1 Y-Y
(J.A. O'More) P.D.K. Ramsay, 1983
'Principal' × 'Kingscourt'

'Golden Glisten' 1 Y-Y
(D.S. Bell) D.S. Bell, 1968
Fl. glistening yellow

'Golden Glory' 1 Y-Y
(de Graaff Bros, pre-1913)

'Golden Glory' 1 Y-Y
(R.H. Bath, pre-1923)

'Golden Glow' 2 Y-? (a)
(C. Smith, pre-1910)

'Golden Glow' 1 Y-Y
(G. Lewis, 1945) D.S. Bell, 1958

'Golden Glow' 2 Y-Y
(L.P.Dettman, 1974) Unregistered
'Arctic Gold' × 'Gahna'; sdlg no. 45/75

'Golden Goblet' 1 Y-Y
(C. Dawson, pre-1916)

'Golden Goblet' 7 Y-Y
(C.G. van Tubergen, pre-1927)
1 Y-Y × *N. jonquilla*
Fl. large, deep yellow; perianth segments of great substance, overlapping; corona expanded, with rim widely flanged. AM(e) 1928

'Golden Goddess' 1 Y-Y
(F. Rijnveld & Sons, pre-1947)
Fl. golden yellow. AM(Haarlem) 1946, FCC(Haarlem) 1951

'Golden Grandeur' 1 Y-Y
(T. Bloomer) T. Bloomer, 1970
'Kingscourt' × 'Standard Bearer'; sdlg no. 3/8/58
Perianth segments deep gold; corona slightly deeper in tone, with rim dentate and slightly rolled

'Golden Guinea' 2 Y-Y
(G.H. Johnstone, pre-1954)

'Golden Hades' 1 Y-Y
(F.H.Chapman, pre-1931)
Fl. golden yellow; corona flared. AM(Haarlem) 1931

'Golden Halo' 1 W-? (b)
(J.W. Barr, pre-1930)

'Golden Halo' 2 Y-WWY
(Ballydorn Bulb Farm) Ballydorn Bulb Farm, 1983
'Daydream' × 'Moonspell'

Fl. 94 mm wide; perianth segments deep yellow; corona becoming white, with yellow at rim. Mid-season

'Golden Harbinger' 1 Y-Y
(Barr & Sons, pre-1927)
Fl. yellow, perianth segments ovate, blunt, slightly mucronate, spreading, more or less plane, overlapping one-third; the inner segments with margins wavy; corona cylindrical, smooth, mouth flared and ribbed, rim widely flanged and deeply notched

'Golden Harvest' 1 Y-Y
(Warnaar & Co., pre-1920)
'Golden Spur' × 'King Alfred'
Fl. 113 mm wide; perianth segments broadly ovate, blunt, slightly mucronate, brilliant yellow 7A, often inflexed at base and reflexed at apex, overlapping one-third; the inner segments ribbed and twisted; corona cylindrical or somewhat funnel-shaped, narrow, ribbed, of a much deeper tone (14B) than the perianth, mouth widely expanded and more strongly ribbed, with rim deeply notched and crenate. Early. 2n=27,28. AM(Haarlem) 1920, FCC(Haarlem) 1923, EFA(Haarlem) 1928, *FCC(p) 1975

'Golden Haze' 1 Y-Y
(G.H. Johnstone, pre-1953)
'Overseer' × 'Garron'

'Golden Herald' 1 Y-Y
(Mrs R.O. Backhouse, c.1921)
Corona a little darker in tone than the perianth, neatly frilled. Early. AM(g) 1923

'Golden Hind' 1 Y-Y
(G.L. Wilson, pre-1938)
'Hebron' × 'Crocus'
Fl. deep gold; corona with rim flanged

'Golden Hope' 1 Y-Y
(Barr & Sons, pre-1928)

'Golden Hope' 2 Y-Y
(J.A. O'More, 1964) P.D.K. Ramsay, 1980
'Gold Script' × 'Mulrany'; sdlg no. 29/64
Fl. 85 mm wide. Mid-season. Resembles a much improved 'Mulrany'

'Golden Horn' 1 Y-Y
(H. Backhouse, pre-1910)

'Golden Horn' 1 Y-Y
(J.L. Richardson) J.L. Richardson, 1958
'Kingscourt' self pollinated
Fl. 106 mm wide; perianth segments richer and deeper in tone than vivid yellow 12A, a little inflexed, overlapping; corona lightly ribbed, darker in tone (14A) than the perianth, mouth slightly expanded, with rim crenate. 2n=28. *AM(g) 1971

'Golden Hour' 4 Y-R
(J.R.Erp) J.R.Erp, 1956
'Killigrew' × 'Telamonius Plenus'

'Golden Hue' 2 (a)
(W. Jackson Jr, 1950)
'J.P.' × 'Hymyr'

'Golden Idol' 1 Y-Y
(G.P. Haydon, pre-1913)
Fl. soft yellow

'Golden Image' 2 Y-Y
(S.J. Bisdee, 1942)
'Golden Queen' × 'Fahan'
Syn. 'The Golden Image'

'Golden Incense' 7 Y-Y
(C.R. Wootton) G.L. Wilson, 1957
'Gulliver' × *N. jonquilla*
Scented. 2n=21

'Golden Ingot' 2 Y-Y
(J.L. Richardson, pre-1923)
Fl. deep gold; perianth segments smooth; corona deeper in tone than the perianth, frilled. AM(e) 1929

'Golden Jewel' 2 Y-GYY
(T. Bloomer) T. Bloomer, 1973
'Camelot' × 'Arctic Gold'; sdlg no. 8/72/65
Fl. deep golden yellow; perianth segments broadly ovate, blunt, with slight white mucro, a little inflexed, smooth, slightly concave, overlapping one-third to a half; the inner segments a little narrower, square-shouldered at base, more strongly inflexed, with margins slightly wavy; corona cylindrical or somewhat funnel-shaped, loosely ribbed, with green at base, mouth straight and frilled. Mid-season. 2n=29. AGM 1995

'Golden Joy' 2 Y-Y
(T. Bloomer) T. Bloomer, 1973
'Camelot' × 'Arctic Gold'; sdlg no. 10/72/65
Fl. deep gold; perianth segments very broadly ovate, rounded at apex, slightly mucronate, spreading, smooth, of heavy substance, overlapping half; the inner segments narrower, more nearly oval, blunt; corona nearly cylindrical, mouth a little expanded, with rim crenate. 2n=28

'Golden Jubilee' 1 Y-Y
(de Graaff Bros, pre-1910)

'Golden King' 1 Y-Y
(J.C. Williams, pre-1913)
Fl. 95 mm wide, rich golden yellow; corona neatly frilled

'Golden Kiwi' 2 Y-Y
(S.A. Free) S.A. Free, 1964

Mid-season

'Golden Knight' 1 Y-Y
(G.P. Haydon, pre-1913)

'Golden Lacquer' 6 Y-Y
(de Graaff Bros, pre-1949)
Fl. golden yellow. 2n=28. AM(Haarlem) 1949

'Golden Leader' 1 Y-Y
(J.R. Pearson & Sons, pre-1933)

'Golden Legend' 2 Y-Y
(J.H. Hinsby, 1928) RHS(Victoria), 1956
'Yellow Aster' × Jonquilla 'Plenus'
Fl. deep yellow; corona frilled

'Golden Legend' 1 Y-Y
(Barr & Sons, pre-1929)
'King Alfred' hybrid
Perianth segments rich buttercup yellow, fairly smooth; corona dark golden yellow, with rim deeply crenate

'Golden Legion' 1 Y-Y
(F.H. Chapman, pre-1930)

'Golden Light' 2 W-?
(Mrs R.O. Backhouse, pre-1921)

'Golden Link' 1 Y-Y
(Stevens & Son, pre-1930)
'King Alfred' hybrid

'Golden Lion' 1 Y-Y
(E.H. Krelage & Son, *c.*1912)
'King Alfred' × 'Big Ben'
Fl. golden yellow; corona with rim lightly rolled. Resembles 'Glory of Haarlem' in form. AM(Haarlem) 1912. Some 'McIvor' stock sold as this

'Golden Lotus' 1 Y-Y
(J.A. O'More) P.D.K. Ramsay, 1983
'Cromarty' × 'Wexford'

'Golden Luck' 2 Y-Y
(T. Bloomer) Unregistered
'Golden Torch' × 'Galway'; sdlg no. 2/23/54

'Golden Majesty' 2 Y-Y
(G.A. Uit den Boogaard, pre-1948)

'Golden Mantle' 2 Y-Y
(J.N. Hancock & Co.) J.N. Hancock & Co., 1960
Fl. yellow; corona slightly darker in tone than the perianth, frilled. Early

'Golden Marvel' 1 Y-Y
(Warnaar & Co., pre-1938)
Fl. golden yellow; corona slender. AM(Haarlem) 1938, FCC(Haarlem) 1950

'Golden Mary' 3 Y-Y
(E. Leeds, pre-1877)
"Absorbed" 'Dwarf Golden Mary' and 'Tall Golden Mary'

'Golden Mary' 3 ?-O
(pre-1902)
Corona scarlet-orange. ?The same as 'Golden Mary' pre-1877

'Golden Master' 1 Y-Y
(J.T. Gray) P. Phillips, 1959

'Golden Measure' 2 Y-? (a)
(R.H. Bath, pre-1923)

'Golden Melody' 1 Y-Y
(G.L. Wilson, pre-1930)
'Royalist' × 'Godolphin'
Fl. lemon gold

'Golden Memories' 1 W-? (b)
(H.J. Gooding, pre-1927)

'Golden Mile' 1 Y-Y
(D.S. Bell) D.S. Bell, 1964
Fl. 107 mm wide, golden yellow; perianth segments broad, of good substance; corona frilled, with rim flanged. Resembles 'Kingscourt' but with larger and smoother perianth segments

'Golden Milestone' 1 Y-Y
(Leone Y. Low) Leone Y. Low, 1993
'Strathkanaird' × 'Gold Convention'; sdlg no. SGC-N2E
Fl. glistening; perianth segments broadly ovate, vivid yellow 9A; the inner segments blunt and almost as broad; corona cylindrical, smooth, orange-yellow (14A or 15A) or lighter in tone in a warm season, mouth slightly flared, rim regularly crenate. Mid-season

'Golden Miller' 1 Y-Y
(Slieve Donard Nursery Co., pre-1934)
Fl. large, golden yellow; perianth segments broad, spreading; corona expanded, with rim flanged. Early

'Golden Mist' 1 Y-Y
(The Brodie of Brodie, *c.*1909)
'Florence' × 'Coronatus'
Fl. pale yellow. Early

'Golden Model' 7 Y-Y
(Barr & Sons, pre-1923)
'Monarch' × Div. 7

'Golden Monarch' 1 Y-Y
(Barr & Sons, pre-1923)

'Weardale Perfection' × 'C.H.Curtis'

'Golden Moon'
(C.Goodson, pre-1930)
PC(NZ) 1930

'Golden Moon' 1 Y-Y
(N.Y. Lower, pre-1930)

'Golden Morning' 2 Y-O
(G.H. Rotteveel & Sons) G.H. Rotteveel & Sons, 1980
Perianth segments light yellow 14D; corona vivid orange 28B, with a paler tone at base

'Golden Mydon' 1 YYW-WWY
(M.Hamilton) D. & M.Stuart, 1996
('Honeybird' × 'Daydream') × 'Lemon Candy'
Fl. 110 mm wide; perianth segments ovate, vivid yellow 9A, with a broad band of white at base, plane, smooth; corona cylindrical, white, with vivid yellow 9A at rim and the rim flanged. Mid-season

'Golden Myth' 1 Y-Y
(A.O. Roblin, pre-1940)

'Golden Noon' 3 W-? (b)
(Miss E. Willmott, pre-1907)

'Golden Nugget' 1 Y-Y
(W. Backhouse, pre-1869)
Corona rich golden yellow, frilled

'Golden Nugget' 1 Y-Y
(D.S. Bell) D.S. Bell, 1957

'Golden Orb' 2 Y-? (a)
(C.M. Doyne, pre-1914)

'Golden Orb' 2 Y-Y
(J.A. Hunter) J.A. Hunter, 1982
'Crescendo' hybrid
Fl. 110 mm wide. Mid-season

'Golden Orbit' 4 Y-Y
(K.J.Heazlewood) P.D.K. Ramsay, 1981
'Glowing Red' × 'Rouge'; sdlg no. E1
Fl. 55 mm wide; perianth and other petaloid segments opening rich yellow, becoming a little paler; corona segments deeper in tone. Dwarf. Early

'Golden Orchid' 11a Y-Y
(A.C. van der Schoot) A.C. van der Schoot, 1959
Fl. 102 mm wide, pale golden yellow; perianth segments with white mucro, reflexed, with margins nicked, separated; corona split to base, the six segments opposite the perianth segments and joined to them at margins in lower two-thirds, ribbed, bilobed, darker in tone than the perianth, with margins wavy. Syn. 'Jester', 'Spring Festival'

'Golden Oriole' 2 Y-? (a)
(P.D. Williams, pre-1907)

'Golden Oriole' 2 Y-R
(J.A. Morris) J.A. Morris, 1965
Fl. 100 mm wide. Mid-season. Resembles 'Royal Charger' but with a richer-coloured corona

'Golden Pedestal' 2 Y-Y
(J.L. Richardson, pre-1922)
Fl. forming a double triangle, 115 mm wide, clear golden yellow; perianth segments broadly ovate, blunt, only very slightly mucronate, spreading, plane, of good substance, overlapping one-third to a half; the inner segments more narrowly ovate, a little inflexed, with margins wavy; corona funnel-shaped, lightly ribbed, with mouth straight and loosely frilled. Tall. Early. AM(e) 1922

'Golden Perfection' 7 Y-Y
(de Graaff Bros, pre-1925)
Fls 2-3 per stem, 92 mm wide; perianth segments very broadly ovate, blunt or squarish at apex, sometimes truncate, with slight white mucro, brilliant greenish yellow 5B, spreading, plane, overlapping one-third to a half; the inner segments more narrowly ovate, shouldered at base, somewhat inflexed, with margins wavy; corona short funnel-shaped, lightly ribbed, vivid yellow 13A, mouth widely expanded and wavy, with rim notched and crenate. Scented. 2n=31. AM(Haarlem) 1925, FCC(Haarlem) 1926, *HC(g) 1941, *AM(g) 1944

'Golden Perfection' 2 Y-Y
(pre-1927)
Fl. rich golden yellow; perianth segments very broad, overlapping; corona mouth expanded

'Golden Perfection' 8 Y-Y
(pre-1930)
Poetaz

'Golden Phoenix' 4 Y-O
(pre-1888)
Corona segments deep orange. ?Syn. of 'Butter and Eggs'

'Golden Plover' 1 Y-Y
(W.B. Hartland, pre-1885)
Early. 2n=14. Resembles 'Princeps' but with the corona more deeply dentate and widely flanged. Syn. 'Cloth of Gold', 'Golden Princeps', 'Single Cloth of Gold', 'Tanist'

'Golden Pond' 3 Y-YYO
(T.D. Throckmorton) T.D. Throckmorton, 1982
('Oasis' × 'Green Island') × ('Aircastle' × 'Irish Coffee'); sdlg no. 70/2/10
Fl. rounded; perianth segments very broad, rounded at apex, somewhat truncate, luminous pale yellow,

spreading, slightly concave at apex, with a silken sheen, overlapping two-thirds; the inner segments a little inflexed; corona wide-spreading, almost disc-shaped, ribbed, slightly darker in tone than the perianth, touched pale orange at rim, mouth split in places and overlapping, frilled. Mid-season

'Golden Prince' 1 Y-Y
(W. Backhouse, pre-1869)
Fl. rich bright yellow, of slender proportions. Resembles a small-flowered 'Maximus'. Syn. Pseudonarcissus Major 'Golden Prince'

'Golden Prince' 1 Y-Y
(Mrs H.K. Richardson) Mrs H.K. Richardson, 1974
'Yellow Idol' × 'King's Ransom'
Fl. 103 mm wide

'Golden Princeps' 1 Y-Y
Syn. of 'Golden Plover'

'Golden Princess' 7 Y-?
(Barr & Sons, pre-1923)

'Golden Produce' 1 Y-Y
(van Zonneveld & Co., pre-1944)
'Golden Harvest' × 'Producer'

'Golden Prospect' 1 Y-Y
(J.L. Richardson, pre-1923)

'Golden Queen' 1 Y-Y
(M. van Waveren & Sons, pre-1897)
Corona large, flared, rich yellow. Resembles 'Maximus'

'Golden Queen' 2 Y-Y
(J.H. Hinsby, 1928)
'Homespun' hybrid

'Golden Quest' 2 Y-Y
(S.J. Bisdee, 1940)
'Golden Queen' × 'Crocus'

'Golden Quince' 12 Y-Y
(J.W.A. van der Wereld, 1982) J.W.A. van der Wereld, 1992
'Quince' sport
Fl. 45 mm wide; perianth segments ovate, vivid yellow 9A, reflexed, overlapping at base only; corona cylindrical or narrowly funnel-shaped, richer in tone (14B) than the perianth, with mouth straight

'Golden Radiance' 1 Y-Y
(Ballydorn Bulb Farm) Ballydorn Bulb Farm, 1974
'Golden Rapture' hybrid
Fl. 110 mm wide

'Golden Rain' 2 Y-? (a)
(G.H. Engleheart, pre-1910)

'Golden Rain' 4 Y-O
(L. Bernard) J. Voges & Co., 1968
'Soleil d'Or' hybrid
Fls many per stem

'Golden Rally' 1 Y-Y
(Warnaar & Co.) Warnaar & Co., 1969
'Dominator' × 'Royal Gold'
AM(Haarlem) 1969

'Golden Ranger' 2 Y-Y
(Mrs H.K. Richardson) Mrs H.K. Richardson, 1976
'Camelot' × 'Daydream'
Fl. 110 mm wide, golden yellow; corona with a hint of green at base. Mid-season. 2n=29+1B

'Golden Rapture' 1 Y-Y
(J.L. Richardson, pre-1952)
'Pretoria' × 'Goldcourt'
Fl. 127 mm wide; perianth segments broadly ovate, blunt, very slightly mucronate, vivid yellow 9A, plane or a little concave, with margins slightly incurling at apex, smooth, overlapping half; corona smoothly angled, darker in tone (13A) than the perianth, mouth ribbed and expanded, lightly frilled, rim flanged and irregularly notched. Mid-season. Scented. FCC(e) 1959, AM(Haarlem) 1962, *AM(g) 1984, *FCC(g) 1985, *AM(p) 1986, AGM 1993

'Golden Ray' 1 Y-Y
(Warnaar & Co., pre-1920)
Fl. bright golden yellow; perianth segments overlapping; corona cylindrical, slightly darker in tone than the perianth, with rim flared. Mid-season. 2n=28. AM(Haarlem) 1920, FA(Haarlem) 1933, *C(g) 1936, *HC(g) 1939, *AM(g) 1947

'Golden Realm' 1 Y-Y
(D.S. Bell, 1965) D.S. Bell, 1975
'Dawngold' × 'David Bell'
Fl. 103 mm wide, golden yellow; corona frilled, with rim rolled. Mid-season

'Golden Record' 2 Y-Y
(J.H. Rijkelijkhuizen) J.H. Rijkelijkhuizen, 1973
'Carlton' hybrid
Fl. 115 mm wide

'Golden Reflection' 9 WWY-GOR
(Mrs M.S. Yerger) Mrs M.S. Yerger, 1990
'Praecox Grandiflorus' × 'Lights Out'
Fl. 65 mm wide; perianth segments ovate, acute, with yellow at base; the inner segments a little shorter; corona long cup-shaped, orange (28B), with strong yellow-green 145A at base and shading to orange-red at rim. Late. Resembles 'Praecox Grandiflorus' in form and 'Lights Out' in corona colouring

'Golden Riches' 1 Y-Y
(D.S. Bell) D.S. Bell, 1985

('Red Conquest' × 'Golden Fortune') × 'Salome'
Fl. 100 mm wide. Mid-season. Resembles a more strongly coloured 'Golden Fortune'

'Golden Ring' 1 Y-Y
(D.H.L. Corrigan, pre-1933)

'Golden Riot' 1 Y-Y
(G.L. Wilson, pre-1948)
'Counsellor' × 'Golden Hind'
Fl. golden; corona with rim dentate. AM(Haarlem) 1950

'Golden River' 1 Y-Y
(G. Lubbe & Son, pre-1936)
Syn. 'Gold River', 'Golden Wonder'. AM(Haarlem) 1936

'Golden Road' 2 Y-Y
(The Brodie of Brodie, c.1931)
'Tashkend' × 'Golden Pedestal'

'Golden Road' 1 Y-Y
(D.S. McLenaghan) H. Dyer, 1972
'Tashkend' × 'Golden Pedestal'; sdlg no. 50/26
Fl. 103 mm wide

'Golden Robe' 2 Y-Y
(C.E. Buckingham, pre-1938)

'Golden Robes' 2 Y-Y
(Konynenburg & Mark, pre-1953)
'Adventure' hybrid

'Golden Robin' 1 Y-Y
(O. Ronalds) T. Morrison, 1960
2n=28. Syn. 'Golden Valley'

'Golden Rod' 1 Y-Y
(F.W. Parkinson, pre-1936)

'Golden Rogue' 1 Y-Y
(Miss K.M. Hinchliff, pre-1943)

'Golden Rose' 4 Y-O
(pre-1904)
Fl. very large, rounded; perianth segments rich sulphury yellow; corona segments orange. AM(Haarlem) 1913. ?Syn. of 'Butter and Eggs'

'Golden Royal' 8 Y-?
(pre-1759)

'Golden Rule' 1 Y-Y
(Barr & Sons, pre-1929)
'King Alfred' hybrid
Perianth segments dark golden yellow, slightly twisted; corona ribbed, rich yellow, with rim deeply crenate

'Golden Rupee' 1 Y-Y
(W.A. Noton, pre-1985) Unregistered

'Golden Sand' 1 Y-Y
(The Brodie of Brodie, c.1909)
'King Alfred' × 'Glory of Noordwijk'; sdlg no. 43/A/04
Perianth segments bright yellow; corona rich golden yellow, frilled. ?See also 'Golden Sands'

'Golden Sands' 1 Y-Y
?Syn. of 'Golden Sand'

'Golden Sands' 11a Y-YOO
Syn. of 'Glowing Sands'

'Golden Satin' 1 Y-Y
(Mrs A.O. Meyrick, pre-1947)

'Golden Sceptre' 8 Y-O
(pre-1759)

'Golden Sceptre' 7 Y-Y
(de Graaff Bros, pre-1914)
'Monarch' × ? *N. jonquilla*
Fl. 70 mm wide, bright buttercup yellow; perianth segments overlapping half; corona cylindrical. Mid-season to late. Scented. 2n=21. AM(e) 1914, *C(g) 1931, *FCC(g) 1936

'Golden Sea' 1 Y-Y
(G.L. Wilson, pre-1937)
Fl. golden yellow

'Golden Seal' 2 Y-? (a)
(P.D. Williams, pre-1938)

'Golden Sensation' 1 Y-Y
(P.J. de Groot, pre-1942)

'Golden Sentinel' 1 Y-Y
(R.H. Bath, pre-1927)
Syn. 'Sentinel'

'Golden Shadow' 1 Y-Y
(R. Crews, pre-1949)

'Golden Shape' 1 Y-Y
(Van Paridon's Bloembollenbedrijf) Van Paridon's Bloembollenbedrijf, 1986
Fl. small; perianth segments canary yellow; corona lemon yellow. Mid-season

'Golden Sheaf' 1 Y-Y
(pre-1930)

'Golden Sheen' 2 Y-Y
(Brian S. Duncan) Rathowen Daffodils, 1988
'Golden Jewel' open pollinated; sdlg no. 691
Fl. shining golden yellow; perianth segments

broadly ovate, blunt, sightly mucronate, a little inflexed, with broad midrib showing , overlapping half; the inner segments more narrowly ovate, squarish at shoulder and almost touching one another; corona cylindrical or somewhat funnel-shaped, short, with mouth straight and lightly frilled. Mid-season

'Golden Shield' 1 Y-Y
(G.H. Engleheart, pre-1913)

'Golden Showers' 1 Y-Y
(Mrs J. Abel Smith) Mrs J. Abel Smith, 1982
'Arctic Gold' × 'Welbeck'; sdlg no. F9/41
Fl. 85 mm wide. Mid-season. Resembles a later-flowered 'Arctic Gold'

'Golden Sidewinder' 2 Y-Y
(N.H. Anglo) N.H. Anglo, 1986
'Golden Aura' × 'Camelot'
Fl. of good substance; perianth segments golden yellow; corona large, expanded, yellow. Mid-season

'Golden Silk' 1 Y-Y
(Mrs A.O. Meyrick) Mrs A.O. Meyrick, 1957

'Golden Slipper' 2 Y-Y
(G. Lewis) D.S. Bell, 1955

'Golden Smile' 1 Y-Y
(C.M. Grullemans, pre-1949)

'Golden Song' 1 Y-Y
(Barr & Sons, pre-1926)
Perianth segments bright yellow, overlapping; corona straight, ribbed, golden yellow, frilled

'Golden Sovereign' 1 Y-Y
(C. Dawson, pre-1916)
Fl. of medium size, dark golden yellow

'Golden Sovereign' 1 Y-Y
(Ballydorn Bulb Farm) Ballydorn Bulb Farm, 1975
'Golden Rapture' × ?'Golden Clarion'
Fl. 120 mm wide, deep gold. Mid-season. Resembles a 'Golden Rapture' of better substance

'Golden Spider'
(pre-1914)

'Golden Splendour' 1 Y-Y
(W.J. Dunlop, pre-1952)
'Royalist' × 'Crocus'
Fl. deep golden yellow

'Golden Spray' 2 Y-Y
(Konynenburg & Mark, pre-1953)
'Toscanini' × 'Diorama'

'Golden Spring' 1 Y-Y
(Warnaar & Co., pre-1930)

AM(Haarlem) 1930

'Golden Sprite' 7 Y-Y
(?Australian origin, pre-1997) Unregistered

'Golden Spur' 1 Y-Y
(Dutch origin, pre-1885)
Fl. 107 mm wide, yellow; perianth segments narrowly ovate, acute, with white mucro, inflexed, overlapping at base only; the inner segments somewhat twisted; corona cylindrical, smooth, slightly deeper in tone than the perianth, the mouth ribbed, flared, 6-lobed, with rim deeply notched. Early. 2n=14,21,30. Resembles larger-flowered *N. hispanicus* vars *propinquus* or *spurius*. Syn. 'Spur'

'Golden Standard' 1 Y-Y
(R.H. Bath, pre-1927)

'Golden Star' 8 Y-?
(pre-1759)
Sdlg no. 1/24/58

'Golden Star' 3 W-Y
(W. Backhouse, pre-1869)
Corona yellow, stained orange. Syn. Barrii Albus 'Golden Star'. "Absorbed" 'S.A.de Graaff'

'Golden Star' 1 Y-Y
(Warnaar & Co., pre-1930)
Fl. golden yellow; corona widely expanded, with rim dentate.

'Golden Star' 1 Y-Y
(T. Bloomer) T. Bloomer, 1970
'Cargan' × 'Golden Rapture'
Fl. golden yellow; corona a little deeper in toner, frilled. 2n=28

'Golden Starlight' 1 Y-Y
(C.W. Culpepper, c.1976) Unregistered

'Golden State' 1 W-Y
(J.M. Esseveld, pre-1949)
'Victoria' × 'Golden Harvest'
Perianth segments creamy white; corona soft yellow. TGA(Haarlem) 1949

'Golden Statue' 1 Y-Y
(C. Brunting, pre-1931)
Fl. golden yellow; perianth segments narrow, acute; corona flared. AM(Haarlem) 1931

'Golden Stinze' 1 Y-Y
(K. van der Veek) K. van der Veek, 1994
2 Y-O × 'Golden Amber'
Fl. 105 mm wide; perianth segments vivid yellow 9A; corona darker in tone (14A or B). Mid-season

'Golden Strand' 2 Y-O

(Ballydorn Bulb Farm) Ballydorn Bulb Farm, 1988
Fl. 90 mm wide; perianth segments broadly ovate, pale creamy gold; corona straight-sided, deep orange, with a paler tone at rim, rim lightly dentate. Mid-season

'Golden Sun' 1 Y-Y
(C. Dawson, pre-1923)
Fl. of medium size; perianth segments bright yellow; corona dark golden yellow, neatly frilled

'Golden Sun' 8 Y-Y or O
Syn. of 'Soleil d'Or'

'Golden Sunbeam' 1 Y-Y
(P.L.A. Pouw, pre-1949)

'Golden Sunlight' 1 Y-Y
(Barr & Sons, pre-1923)

'Golden Sunrise' 1 Y-Y
(R.H. Bath, pre-1916)
Perianth segments slightly reflexed. Early. Resembles 'Golden Harvest'. AM(c)(g) 1923, AM(Haarlem) 1930

'Golden Sunset' 1 Y-Y
(R.H. Bath, pre-1916)

'Golden Sunset' 8 Y-?
(pre-1935)

'Golden Sunset' 2 Y-R
(W.A. Noton) W.A. Noton, 1976
'Border Chief' × 'Revelry'; sdlg no. 210
Fl. 85 mm wide. Mid-season

'Golden Supreme' 1 Y-Y
(G.B. de Vroomen & Sons, pre-1934)

'Golden Supreme' 1 Y-Y
(Konynenburg & Mark) Konynenburg & Mark, 1964
'Soirée' × 'Albert Schweitzer'
Fl. 115 mm wide; perianth segments brilliant yellow 13B; corona slightly darker in tone (13A). Early

'Golden Surprise' 1 Y-Y
(G. Vink, pre-1931)
Fl. star-shaped; corona narrow. AM(Haarlem) 1930, FA(Haarlem) 1937

'Golden Thought' 1 Y-Y
(Slieve Donard Nursery Co., pre-1932)

'Golden Thread' 2 Y-O
(O. Ronalds) T. Morrison, 1960
Perianth segments rich yellow; corona bright reddish orange. Tall. Early

'Golden Top' 1 Y-Y
(G.A. Verdegaal, pre-1953)
AM(Haarlem) 1959, FA(Haarlem) 1961, FCC(Haarlem) 1962

'Golden Topaz' 2 Y-O
(Ballydorn Bulb Farm) Ballydorn Bulb Farm, 1990
2 Y-O × 'Golden Amber'
Fl. rounded, 100 mm wide; perianth segments broadly ovate, very smooth; corona flushed orange gold, with mouth slightly lobed and rim entire. Mid-season. Sunproof

'Golden Torch' 2 Y-Y
(The Brodie of Brodie, c.1938)
'Golden Road' × ('Samarkand' × G.L Wilson Div. 1 sdlg)
Fl. about 100 mm wide, vivid yellow 9A; perianth segments broadly ovate, fairly prominently mucronate, spreading, plane, smooth, overlapping one-third to a half; the inner segments creased and somewhat twisted; corona broad funnel-shaped, smooth or slightly ribbed, a little deeper in tone than the perianth, rim widely flanged, deeply and regularly crenate. 2n=27. AM(e) 1947, AM(Haarlem) 1949, FCC(e) 1949, FCC(Haarlem) 1954, *AM(g) 1956

'Golden Treasure' 2 Y-O
(G. Lewis, pre-1940)
'Tamerlane' × 'Fortune'
Perianth segments golden yellow, velvet smooth; corona reddish orange, frilled. Sunproof. AM(e)(NZ) 1940. Perhaps the same as 'Leader'

'Golden Treasure' 1 Y-Y
(G. Lubbe & Son, pre-1944)
AM(Haarlem) 1944

'Golden Tribune' 2 Y-? (a)
(J.A. van der Zwet & Sons, pre-1943)
AM(Haarlem) 1943

'Golden Triumphator' 2 Y-Y
(J.W.A. Lefeber, pre-1944)
AM(Haarlem) 1952, FCC(Haarlem) 1955

'Golden Trophy' 1 Y-Y
(J.L. Veldhuyzen van Zanten, pre-1931)
'Golden Spur' sport
EFA(Haarlem) 1931, FA(Haarlem) 1932

'Golden Trumpet' 1 Y-Y
(J.R. Pearson & Sons, pre-1910)

'Golden Vale' 1 Y-Y
(F.E. Board) W.A. Noton, 1976
'Golden Rapture' × 'Olympic Gold'
Fl. 120 mm wide, vivid yellow; perianth segments broadly ovate, blunt, with very slight white mucro, spreading, somewhat concave, smooth, overlapping

one-third to a half; corona cylindrical in lower half, flared towards mouth, broadly and lightly ribbed, darker in tone than the perianth, with mouth lightly frilled and rim crenate. Mid-season. 2n=28. AGM 1995

'Golden Valley' 3 Y-? (a)
(Mrs R.O. Backhouse, pre-1921)

'Golden Valley' 1 Y-Y
Syn. of 'Golden Robin'

'Golden Vanity'
(C. Dawson, pre-1907)

'Golden Vase' 1 Y-Y
(G.H. Engleheart, pre-1890)
Fl. rich golden yellow; corona ribbed and frilled

'Golden Venture' 1 Y-Y
(J.A. O'More) P.D.K. Ramsay, 1981
'Darnaway' × 'Mulrany'; sdlg no. 13/62
Fl. 80 mm wide, gold. Mid-season

'Golden Vest' 2 Y-Y
(S.C. Gaspar) S.C. Gaspar, 1955
Perianth segments gold; corona expanded, deeper in tone than the perianth, with rim dentate

'Golden Victor' 2 Y-? (a)
(Konynenburg & Mark, pre-1953)

'Golden Victor' 1 Y-Y
(Konynenburg & Mark) Konynenburg & Mark, 1960
('Toscanini' × 'Extase') hybrid
Fl. 120 mm wide; perianth segments vivid yellow 9A; corona slightly darker in tone (12A). Mid-season

'Golden Vintage' 2 Y-Y
(J.N. Hancock & Co., 1948) J.N. Hancock & Co., 1965
Perianth segments broadly ovate, blunt, deep yellow, with slight white mucro, spreading, plane or with margins a little wavy, smooth, overlapping half; the inner segments inflexed at base, reflexed at apex, with margins more strongly wavy and sometimes twisted; corona funnel-shaped, loosely ribbed, darker in tone than the perianth, mouth straight, tightly frilled, rim crenate. Early

'Golden Vision' 2 Y-O
(H.A. Brown, 1936) J.N. Hancock & Co., 1960
Perianth segments acute, golden yellow; corona orange, frilled. Early

'Golden Wand' 1 Y-Y
(Barr & Sons, pre-1931)

'Golden Wealth' 1 Y-Y
(G.L. Wilson, pre-1941)
'Hebron' open pollinated
Fl. intense gold

'Golden Wedding' 2 Y-Y
(G.L. Wilson, pre-1935)
'White Emperor' hybrid
Perianth segments acute, pale chrome yellow, overlapping; corona ribbed, slightly darker in tone than the perianth, neatly frilled. AM(e) 1935

'Golden West' 1 Y-Y
(W.J. Eldering & Son, pre-1926)
AM(Haarlem) 1926

'Golden Wings' 1 Y-Y
(R.A. van der Schoot, pre-1923)

'Golden Wings' 6 Y-Y
(Ballydorn Bulb Farm) Ballydorn Bulb Farm, 1977
'Charity May' open pollinated
Fl. 90 mm wide; perianth segments golden yellow; corona deeper in tone. Mid-season

'Golden Wonder' 1 Y-Y
(R.H. Bath, pre-1933)

'Golden Wonder' 1 Y-Y
Syn. of 'Golden River'

'Golden Years' 6 Y-Y
(G.E. Mitsch, 1979) R. & E. Havens, 1991
Sdlg F91/1 ('Focal Point' × 'Salem') × *N. cyclamineus*; sdlg no. 0047/20
Fl. clear yellow; perianth segments broadly ovate, blunt, with slight white mucro, strongly reflexed, with margins slightly incurling at apex, smooth, overlapping half or more; corona narrowly funnel-shaped, smooth, with mouth straight and lightly frilled, rim irregularly notched and crenate. Early. Resembles 'Rapture' but with broader perianth segments and a differently shaped corona

'Goldette' 6 Y-Y
(M. Fowlds, 1950) G.E. Mitsch, 1965
Dwarf 1 Y-Y × *N. cyclamineus*
Fl. 64 mm wide. Dwarf. Early

'Goldex' 2 Y-Y
(David Adams) David Adams, 1994
'Golden Aura' × 'Daydream'; sdlg no. 81/03F
Fl. forming a double triangle, 100 mm wide, deep golden yellow; perianth segments broadly ovate, plane; the inner segments more narrowly ovate; corona slightly constricted below mouth, mouth flared and frilled. Early. Resembles a golden yellow 'Daydream'

'Gold Eye' 3 W-YYO
(G.H. Engleheart, pre-1904)

Perianth segments snow white, of good substance; corona large, disc-shaped, golden yellow, with reddish orange at rim. See also 'Gold-Eye'

'Gold-Eye' 3 W-YYO
Syn. of 'Gold Eye'

'Goldfield' 1 Y-Y
(T. Batson, pre-1927)

'Goldfinch' 1 Y-Y
(M. van Waveren & Sons, pre-1907)

'Goldfinch' 6 Y-Y
Syn. of 'Little Goldfinch'

'Goldfinch' 7 Y-O
Syn. of 'Pet Finch'

'Goldfinder' 1 Y-Y
(W.B. Hartland, pre-1890)
Fl. rich orange-yellow; corona with rim flanged and dentate. Tall. Resembles a larger *N. obvallaris*

'Goldfinger' 1 Y-Y
(Brian S. Duncan) Rathowen Daffodils, 1983
'Golden Jewel' open pollinated; sdlg. 651
Fl. forming a double triangle, deep golden yellow; perianth segments very broadly ovate, spreading, plane, smooth and of good substance, overlapping half; the inner segments more narrowly ovate, sometimes creased at margin, corona cylindrical, mouth very slightly expanded, even, with rim dentate. Mid-season. AM 1997

'Goldfire' 2 Y-R
(J.S. Leitch) J.S. Leitch, 1960
Fl. 114 mm wide. Late

'Gold Fish' 1 Y-Y
(Dutch origin, pre-1914)

'Gold Flag' 1 Y-Y
(?T. Buncombe, pre-1933)

'Goldflake' 2 Y-YYO
(H.P. Zwetsloot, pre-1947)
Perianth segments golden yellow. AM(Haarlem) 1947, FCC(Haarlem) 1950, FA(Haarlem) 1957, FCFA(Haarlem) 1959, FA(Haarlem) 1959

'Gold Flood' 1 Y-Y
(P.J. de Groot, pre-1942)

'Gold Flush' 1 Y-Y
(J.A. O'More, 1957) R.G. Cull, 1978
'Integrity' × 'Goldcourt'; sdlg no. 17/57
Fl. 123 mm wide. Mid-season

'Gold Frills' 3 W-WWY
(G.E. Mitsch) G.E. Mitsch, 1966
'Chinese White' hybrid; sdlg no. T10/2
Fl. rounded, 108 mm wide; corona ribbed, with golden yellow at rim, frilled. Mid-season. Resembles 'Procession' but with a brighter-coloured and more heavily frilled corona rim

'Gold Gem' 2 Y-Y
(G.W.E. & M.E.Brogden) G.W.E. & M.E.Brogden, 1980
'Bayard' hybrid; sdlg no. T 81
Fl. 102 mm wide. Mid-season

'Gold Gleam' 3 (a)
(Barr & Sons, pre-1913)

'Goldhanger' 2 Y-Y
(A.J.R. Pearson, 1981) A.J.R. Pearson, 1993
'Camelot' self pollinated; sdlg no. 85-48-F30
Fl. forming a rounded double triangle, 95 mm wide; perianth segments very broadly ovate, rounded at apex, buttercup yellow, spreading, plane, smooth, of thick substance and velvet texture; corona straight-sided, lightly ribbed, golden yellow and darker than the perianth, mouth straight, with rim lightly crenate. Mid-season

'Goldhawk' 1 Y-Y
(H.G. Longford, pre-1927)

'Goldia Vernia' 3 W-YOR
(Jack Schlitt) Betty Beery, 1993
'Merlin' × Evans sdlg N-36 ('Marshfire' × 'Hotspur'); sdlg no. 1-JS-2
Fl. 75 mm wide; perianth segments broadly or very broadly ovate, blunt or truncate, slightly mucronate, spreading, with margins incurling at apex, overlapping half; the inner segments more narrowly ovate; corona very shallow bowl-shaped, loosely ribbed, lightly frilled. Late

'Goldie Hugh' 3 W-? (b)
(E. & J.C. Martin, pre-1916)

'Goldilocks' 7 Y-Y
(J.C. Williams, pre-1937)
Fl. soft yellow; corona shallow, expanded, ribbed

'Gold Imp' 2 Y-O
(Colin Crotty, 1981) Colin Crotty, 1996
'Johore' × 'Falstaff'; sdlg no. 40-76
Fl. forming a double triangle, 67 mm wide; perianth segments acute, bright yellow; corona cup-shaped, short, light yellow-orange, with a deeper tone at rim, frilled. Mid-season to late

'Goldina' 2 Y-O
(Mrs R.O. Backhouse, pre-1921)
Perianth segments narrow, acute, soft yellow; corona deep orange. AM(Haarlem) 1931

'Golding' 1 Y-Y
(N.A.Burr, 1984) N.A.Burr, 1997
'Celtic Gold' × 'Arctic Gold'; sdlg no. 2-12-79
Fl. deep gold; perianth segments broadly ovate, blunt, with slight white mucro, spreading, slightly concave near apex, smooth, overlapping half or more; the inner segments a little narrower, slightly inflexed, with margins very slightly wavy; corona cylindrical, with rim minutely flanged and obscurely crenate. Mid-season

'Gold Ingot' 2 Y-Y
(Brian S.Duncan) Brian S.Duncan, 1996
Sdlg 77/1 ('Golden Jewel' × 'Midas Touch') × 'Barnum'; sdlg no. 1345
Fl. 110 mm wide, deep golden yellow; perianth segments very broadly ovate, plane, with margins slightly incurving at apex, smooth; corona broad funnel-shaped, smooth, sometimes faintly tinged orange at rim, with mouth slightly flared. Mid-season

'Goldish' 1 Y-Y
(O. Ronalds, pre-1960) Unregistered
Perianth segments broadly ovate, clear yellow; corona rich golden yellow

'Gold Lace' 2 Y-? (a)
(L. van Leeuwen & Son, pre-1943)

'Gold Lap' 2 Y-? (a)
(Parr's Nurseries, 1946) Parr's Nurseries, 1958

'Goldleaf' 1 Y-Y
(G.H. Johnstone, pre-1960)
'Hebron' × 'Acclaim'

'Gold Light' 2 Y-Y
(R.J. Abernethy) R.J. Abernethy, 1991
'First Light' × 'Masked Light'; sdlg no. 444
Fl. bright golden yellow; corona funnel-shaped, with mouth only slightly flared. Mid-season

'Gold Link' 1 Y-Y
(D.V. West, pre-1936)
Fl. pale yellow

'Goldlip' 3 W-? (b)
(P.D. Williams, pre-1927)

'Gold Lure' 2 Y-Y
(G.C. Graham, pre-1951)

'Gold Mark' 1 Y-Y
(The Brodie of Brodie, pre-1929)
'Hebron' × 'Solleret'

'Goldmark' 1 Y-Y
(D.S. Bell) D.S. Bell, 1975
'Dawngold' × 'Gold Shower'
Fl. golden yellow; corona frilled. Mid-season. Resembles a later-flowered 'Gold Shower' with a longer corona

'Gold Mark' 1 Y-Y
(D.S. Bell, c.1975) Unregistered
'Dawngold' × 'Gold Shower'

'Gold Medal' 1 Y-Y
(G. Lubbe & Son, pre-1938)
2n=28. AM(Haarlem) 1938, FCC(Haarlem) 1944

'Gold Medallion' 1 Y-Y
(Mrs J. Abel Smith, 1982) Mrs J. Abel Smith, 1992
'Great Expectations' × 'Ormeau'; sdlg no. A77/41
Fl. 38 mm wide, deep yellow. Mid-season

'Gold Merit' 1 Y-Y
(D.S. Bell) D.S. Bell, 1961
Fl. 108 mm wide. Mid-season. Resembles 'Goldcourt' but with broader perianth segments

'Gold Mine' 1 Y-Y
(N.Y. Lower, pre-1916)

'Gold Mine' 2 Y-Y
(Ballydorn Bulb Farm) Ballydorn Bulb Farm, 1983
'Golden Amber' × 'Golden Aura'
Fl. 104 mm wide, gold. Mid-season. See also 'Goldmine'

'Goldmine' 1 Y-Y
(R.H. Bath, pre 1923)

'Goldmine' 2 Y-Y
(G.W.E. Brogden) G.W.E. Brogden, 1981
'Gold Script' × 'Reward'
Fl. rich yellow; perianth segments rounded at apex, spreading, smooth, deeply overlapping; corona mouth flared. AM(e)(NZ) 1975

'Goldmine' 2 Y-O
(W.M. Spry, pre-1975) Unregistered
'Hunter's Moon' × 'Port Kembla'
Late

'Goldmine' 2 Y-Y
'Golden Amber' × 'Golden Aura'
Syn of 'Gold Mine'

'Gold Mist' 2 Y-Y
(J.A. O'More, 1955) P.D.K. Ramsay, 1981
'Cromarty' × 'Billali; sdlg no. 30/55
Fl. 76 mm wide, gold. Mid-season. Resembles 'Gold Plate'

'Gold Mohur' 7
(N.Y. Lower, pre-1929)
Fls usually 2 per stem. Resembles a deeper-coloured 'Buttercup'

'Goldmore' 1 Y-Y
(Mrs C.O. Fairbairn)

'Gold Nut' 1 Y-Y
(P. van Deursen, pre-1931)

'Gold of Ophir' 1 Y-Y
(J.R. Pearson & Sons, pre-1929)

'Goldona' 2 W-? (b)
(Mrs R.O. Backhouse, pre-1921)

'Gold Phantom' 1 Y-Y
(J.L. Richardson) Mrs H.K. Richardson, 1968
'Arctic Gold' open pollinated
Fl. uniform deep gold

'Gold Piece' 1 Y-Y
(P.L.A. Pouw Bros, pre-1953)
AM(Haarlem) 1953, FCC(Haarlem) 1959

'Gold Plane' 2 W-Y
(A.E. Lowe, pre-1927)
Perianth segments acute; corona golden yellow, with mouth expanded

'Gold Plate' 1 Y-Y
(J.A. O'More, 1967) P.D.K. Ramsay, 1980
'Belmont' × 'Golden Dale'; sdlg no. 24/67
Fl. 118 mm wide. Mid-season

'Gold Poppa' 1 Y-Y
(R.H. Glover, pre-1993) Unregistered

'Goldpore' 2 Y-? (a)
(M.P. Williams, pre-1946)

'Gold Quest' 1 Y-Y
(J.A. O'More) P.D.K. Ramsay, 1983
'Belmont' hybrid

'Goldrau' 2 Y-? (a)
(West & Fell, pre-1938)
Perianth segments golden yellow; corona tinged orange, with rim closely and deeply notched, as if fringed

'Gold Reef' 2 Y-Y
(G.L. Wilson, pre-1930)
'Leontes' × 'Seahorse'
Fl. golden yellow. See also 'Goldreef'

'Goldreef' 2 Y-Y
Syn. of 'Gold Reef'

'Gold Reign' 2 Y-Y
(Colin Crotty, pre-1997) Unregistered

'Gold Reserve' 1 Y-Y
(S.J. Bisdee, 1940)

'Pilgrimage' × 'Fahan'

'Gold Rim' 2 Y-Y
(L. van Leeuwen & Son, pre-1933)
Perianth segments dark yellow, somewhat tinged orange; corona broad, yellow

'Gold River' 1 Y-Y
Syn. of 'Golden River'

'Gold Rush' 2 Y-? (a)
(Warnaar & Co., pre-1939)
AM(Haarlem) 1939

'Gold Rush' 2 Y-Y
(J.N. Hancock & Co., 1953)

'Gold Rush' 11b Y-O/Y
(J. Gerritsen & Son, pre-1968) Unregistered
Perianth segments creamy yellow; corona segments with orange and yellow in longitudinal bands. See also 'Goldrush'

'Goldrush' 2 Y-Y
(F.H. Chapman, pre-1939)

'Goldrush' 11b Y-O/Y
Syn. of 'Gold Rush'

'Gold Sails' 2 Y-Y
(G.E. Mitsch, 1979) R. & E. Havens, 1993
'Camelot' × 'Rich Reward'; sdlg no. 2017/1
Fl. 116 mm wide; perianth segments broadly ovate, soft clear yellow, spreading, with margins slightly wavy, smooth; corona cylindrical, deeper in tone than the perianth, with mouth slightly flared. Mid-season

'Gold Salute' 1 Y-Y
(pre-1956) Unregistered

'Gold Sand' 1 Y-Y
(Barr & Sons, pre-1929)

'Goldsborough' 1 Y-Y
(J.L. Richardson, pre-1950)
Sdlg 176 × 'Goldcourt'
Fl. bright gold; corona with rim rolled and dentate

'Gold Script' 2 Y-Y
(Parr's Nurseries, 1946) Parr's Nurseries, 1958
Fl. deep yellow. PC(e)(NZ) 1952, FCC(e)(NZ) 1954

'Goldseeker' 1 Y-Y
(C. Dawson, pre-1910)
'Santa Maria' hybrid
Fl. small, golden yellow

'Goldshell' 2 W-? (b)
(Mrs R.O. Backhouse, pre-1921)

'Gold Shower' 2 Y-Y
(D.S. Bell) D.S. Bell, 1965
'David Bell' × 'Bernborough'
Fl. 109 mm wide; corona neatly frilled. Mid-season. Resembles 'Galway' but with a smoother perianth

'Goldsithney' 2 Y-Y
(A. Gray, pre-1949)
Fl. 81 mm wide

'Goldsmith' 1 Y-Y
(Mrs R.O. Backhouse, pre-1908)

'Goldsmith' 1 Y-Y
(G.H. Johnstone, pre-1960)

'Goldspinner' 2 Y-? (a)
(W. Balch, pre-1933)

'Gold Split' 11a Y-Y
(Jackson's Daffodils) Jackson's Daffodils, 1995
Sdlg 116/77 × 'King Size'; sdlg no. 76/87
Fl. 126 mm wide; perianth segments brilliant greenish yellow 6B; corona split, the six segments vivid yellow 14A. Early to mid-season

'Gold Sprite' 7 Y-Y
(C.A. Nethercote) T. Morrison, 1960
Fls 2 or more per stem, rich yellow

'Gold Standard' 2 Y-? (a)
(G.H. Johnstone, pre-1942)

'Gold Standard' 2 Y-Y
(S.J.Bisdee, pre-1943)
'Golden Queen' × 'Crocus'

'Gold Standard' 2
Syn. of 'Tutanekai'

'Gold Star' 2 Y-? (a)
(F.W. Parkinson, pre-1936)

'Gold Sterling' 1 Y-Y
(pre-1955)
Fl. rich golden yellow

'Goldstream' 2 Y-? (a)
(L. van Leeuwen & Son, pre-1938)

'Goldstream' 1 Y-Y
(D.S. Bell) D.S. Bell, 1957
Corona with rim flanged

'Gold Strike' 1 Y-Y
(Carncairn Daffodils) Carncairn Daffodils, 1984
1Y-Y × 'Tittle-Tattle'; sdlg no. 2/10/75
Fl. 90 mm wide, deep gold; corona with rim slightly rolled. Scented. 2n=28

'Gold Tan' 1 Y-Y
(J.A. O'More) P.D.K. Ramsay, 1983
Fl. deep yellow; perianth segments spreading, overlapping; corona mouth flared, with rim dentate. Mid-season

'Gold Target' 9 W-GOR
(Mrs M.S. Yerger) Mrs M.S. Yerger, 1984
Lights Out' × 'Perdita'; sdlg no. 73 3
Fl. 61 mm wide; corona vivid reddish orange 30A, with brilliant yellow-green 154B at base and red (42B) at rim. Scented

'Gold Tip' 2 W-?
(Alister Clark, 1935) J. Sharp, 1960

'Gold Tit' 5 Y-Y
(C. Dawson, pre-1912)
Perianth segments light yellow, slightly reflexed, overlapping; corona cup-shaped, ribbed, golden yellow

'Goldtone' 6 W-YOO
(G.E. Mitsch) G.E. Mitsch, 1979
('Playboy' × 'Daydream') × *N. cyclamineus* sdlg; sdlg no. JO9/3
Fl. 70 mm wide; perianth segments chalky white, reflexed; corona opening lemon, becoming orange, with orange-yellow at base. Early

'Gold Top' 2 Y-Y
(Rosewarne EHS, 1970) M. Verdegaal (Peterborough), 1986
'Saint Keverne' × 'Rijnveld's Early Sensation'; sdlg no. 65/67/1
Perianth segments bright lemon yellow; corona expanded, darker in tone than the perianth, lightly frilled. Early

'Gold Trail' 1 Y-Y
(R.C.A. Tombleson) R.C.A. Tombleson, 1964
Fl. 124 mm wide. Mid-season. Resembles a large and earlier-flowered 'Kanga'

'Gold Tray'
(G. Lewis, pre-1962)
'Huia' × 'Golden Glory'

'Gold Tray' 1 Y-Y
(J.A. O'More) P.D.K. Ramsay, 1981
'Braemar' hybrid; sdlg no. 77/61
Fl. 78 mm wide, gold. Mid-season

'Gold Velvet' 1 Y-Y
(G.E. Mitsch, 1978) R. & E. Havens, 1991
'Aurum' × 'Arctic Gold'; sdlg no. NN19/2
Perianth segments deep yellow, very smooth; corona cylindrical, deep yellow with orange undertones. Mid-season

'Gold Venture' 2 Y-? (a)
(S.C. Gaspar, 1945) R.J. Abernethy, 1957

'Goldwell' 2 Y-Y
(New Zealand origin, pre-1927)
Corona suffused rich orange, with mouth expanded

'Gold Wolf' 1 Y-Y
(G.H. Engleheart, pre-1914)
Fl. golden yellow

'Goldwyn' 1 Y-Y
(J.A. Morris) J.A. Morris, 1957

'Goldy Locks' 2 Y-GYY

'Golford' 1 Y-Y
(The Brodie of Brodie, c.1930)
'Hebron' × 'Yukon'
Fl. deep yellow

'Goliard' 2 Y-R
(A.H. Ahrens) J.S. Leitch, 1956

'Goliath' 2 W-Y
(E. Leeds, pre-1877)
Perianth segments ovate, blunt, mucronate, white, with touches of yellow, a little inflexed, with margins wavy, separated; the inner segments twisted; corona funnel-shaped, not much expanding, yellow, with mouth straight and frilled. Syn. Incomparabilis Albus 'Goliath'

'Goliath' 1 Y-Y
(P. van Deursen, pre-1931)
Fl. large; corona flared. AM(Haarlem) 1931

'Golitha Falls' 2 W-W
(R.A.Scamp) R.A.Scamp, 1997
'Pitchroy' × 'Dailmanach'; sdlg no. 71
Fl. 120 mm wide, pure white; perianth segments broadly ovate, deeply overlapping; corona with mouth flared and neatly frilled. Mid-season to late

'Golly' 4 W-Y
(J.L. Richardson) M.J. Jefferson-Brown, 1968
Fl. 133 mm wide; perianth segments very broadly ovate, snow white, very smooth; corona segments interspersed, golden yellow, sometimes quite deeply tinged orange. Mid-season. PC 1967

'Gollywog' 4 Y-YYO
(W.F.M. Copeland, pre-1909)
Fl. large; perianth and other petaloid segments in 5 or 6 whorls, lemon yellow, of strong substance; corona segments light yellow, with orange at rim

'Golyer' 1 Y-Y
(G.H. Johnstone, pre-1947)
'Grenadier' hybrid

'Gonard' 1 W-Y
(S.J. Bisdee, pre-1946)
'Kanchenjunga' hybrid

'Gonaro' 1 W-Y
(S.J. Bisdee, 1953)

'Gondolier' 3 W-? (b)
(F.H. Chapman, pre-1913)

'Gondolier' 1 W-? (b)
(M.P. Williams, pre-1938)

'Gonfalon' 2 Y-? (a)
(E.H. Wheadon & Sons, pre-1914)

'Good Cheer' 2 Y-Y
(G.L. Wilson, pre-1944)
('Fortune' × 'Gulliver') × 'Rustom Pasha'
Perianth segments golden yellow; corona old gold

'Good Dawning' 2 Y-O
(O. Ronalds) T. Morrison, 1960
Perianth segments broad, clear yellow; corona reddish orange. Syn. 'Good Morning'

'Goodenough' 2 Y-? (a)
(J.E. Exley, pre-1950)

'Good Fishing' 2 W-YOO
(David Adams) David Adams, 1996
Sdlg 75/04B ('Fastnet' × 'Gay Fiesta') × 'Merridee'; sdlg no. 85/106H/93
Fl. rounded, 93 mm wide; perianth segments very broadly ovate, blunt, plane or sometimes concave at margins; the outer segments touching one another; corona bowl-shaped, ribbed, orange, with light yellow at base touched with yellow between the ribs and frills, mouth 6-lobed and deeply frilled, rim crenate. Mid-season. Sunproof

'Good Hope' 2 Y-? (a)
(G. Zandbergen-Terwegen, pre-1945)

'Good Idea' 2 Y-OYY
(J.N. Hancock & Co.) J.N. Hancock & Co., 1955
Perianth segments yellow, of good substance; corona widely expanded, yellow, with orange at base, heavily frilled

'Good Life' 1 W-Y
(W.G. Pannill) W.G. Pannill, 1992
'Jet Set' × 'Spartan'; sdlg no.74/28
Fl. 104 mm wide. Mid-season

'Good Luck' 2 W-OYY
(Mrs F.S. Foote, pre-1941)

"Good Luck Lily"
Syn. of *N.tazetta* subsp. *lacticolor*

'Good Measure' 2 W-W
(M.J. Jefferson-Brown) M.J. Jefferson-Brown, 1975
Fl. forming a double triangle; perianth segments broadly ovate, blunt, very slightly mucronate, spreading, plane, smooth, regular, overlapping half; the inner segments a little narrower, shouldered at base, with margins a little wavy; corona cup-shaped, opening pale cream, becoming white, mouth slightly expanded, neatly frilled

'Good Morning' 2 W-? (b or c)
(G.H. Engleheart, pre-1931)

'Good Morning' 2 Y-O
Syn. of 'Good Dawning'

'Goodness' 2 Y-R
(P. Phillips) P. Phillips, 1967
Fl. 115 mm wide; perianth segments lemon yellow; corona widely expanded, bright red. Mid-season. Resembles 'Pillar Box' but with a larger and darker-coloured corona

'Good Oh' 2 Y-Y
(R.H.Glover, pre-1993) Unregistered

'Goodson's Choice' 2 W-W
(C. Goodson, pre-1927)

'Goodson's Star' 1 W-Y
(C. Goodson, pre-1927)
Corona light yellow

'Good Tidings' 2 Y-P
(D.S. Bell) D.S. Bell, 1982
'Red Conquest' × 'Golden Fortune'
Fl. 106 mm wide; corona strongly flushed pale pink. Mid-season. Resembles a better-formed 'Red Conquest'

'Goodwill' 2 Y-O
(G.L. Wilson, pre-1935)
'Copper Bowl' × 'Killigrew'
Perianth segments clear lemon; corona scarlet-orange

'Goodwood' 1 W-Y
(J.N. Hancock & Co., 1971) Unregistered

'Goodyear' 3 W-? (b)
(J.E. Exley, pre-1950)

'Goola' 2 Y-Y
(W. Jackson Jr) Jackson's Daffodils, 1979
Hybrid between ('Demure' × (['Tando' × 'Chungking']) and ('Teg' × 'Keren'); sdlg no. 156/70
Fl. 110 mm wide. Mid-season. Resembles a smoother 'Camelot' of deeper colour. Syn. 'Gwynne'

'Goonhilly' 2 W-Y
(L. Major) L. Major, 1962
Perianth segments pure white; corona deep saffron yellow, with a paler tone at rim. Resembles a stronger 'Blarney's Daughter'

'Goonvean' 2 Y-? (a)
(P.D. Williams, pre-1927)

'Goornong' 1 W-Y
(H.A. Brown, pre-1938)
Perianth segments pale yellow; corona deep lemon

'Goose Green' 3 W-GYR
(Ballydorn Bulb Farm) Ballydorn Bulb Farm, 1983
Div. 9 × Div. 9
Fl. 90 mm wide. Mid-season. Scented

'Gordon' 9 W-?
(D.V. West, pre-1923)
Corona with deep red at rim

'Gordon Grace' 2 Y-? (a)
(W.A. Grace, pre-1938)

'Gorgeous' 1 Y-Y
(G.H. Engleheart, c.1920)

'Gorgeous' 2 W-? (b)
(R.H. Bath, pre-1927)

'Goring' 2 Y-YYO
(Sir F.C. Stern, pre-1947)
Fl. 102 mm wide; perianth segments vivid yellow 9B to brilliant yellow 9C; corona vivid orange-yellow 21A, shading to light orange (23A) at rim. 2n=28. Resembles 'Fortune'. *AM(g) 1949

'Gorkeith' 2 W-? (b)
(Tasmanian origin, 1945) R. Hyde, 1958

'Gorm' 1 Y-Y
(W. Jackson Sr, 1937) W. Jackson Jr, 1956
'Golden City' × 'Gambrinus'

'Gorran' 3 W-YYR
(R.A.Scamp) R.A.Scamp, 1996
'Corofin' × 'Kimmeridge'; sdlg no. 196
Fl. 102 mm wide; perianth segments ovate, acute, pure white, deeply overlapping; corona shallow bowl-shaped, bright yellow, with dark red at rim and the rim dentate. Mid-season to late

'Gosford' 2 W-Y
(W.M. Spry, pre-1975) Unregistered
'Snowflake' × 'Carnlough'
Corona pale lemon yellow. Mid-season

'Gosh' 2 G-Y
(W.M. Spry, pre-1975) Unregistered
'Green Island' × 'Hunter's Moon'
Perianth creamy green; corona lemon yellow, frilled

'Goshen Cloud' 4 W-Y
(Greg Thomson) Greg Thomson, 1997
'Blushing Maiden' × 'Ragbag'; sdlg no. 26A/92
Fl. 100 mm wide; perianth and other petaloid segments in about seven whorls, broadly ovate, slightly mucronate, pure white, overlapping; the outer whorls more or less spreading; the inner whorls successively more strongly inflexed, often folded along midrib and with margins incurled; corona segments shorter, interspersed, orange-yellow. Mid-season.

'Goshen Duat' 4 W-Y
(Greg Thomson) Greg Thomson, 1997
'Blushing Maiden' × 'Ragbag'; sdlg no. 26B/92
Fl. 100 mm wide; perianth and other petaloid segments in about five whorls, broadly ovate, slightly mucronate, pure white, overlapping; the outer whorl more or less spreading, blunt, plane or slightly concave; the inner whorls successively slightly shorter, more strongly inflexed, more deeply concave, with margins incurved, appearing to be acute at apex; corona segments much shorter, interspersed, orange-yellow. Mid-season. Slightly scented

'Goshen Heat' 4 O-O
(Greg Thomson) Greg Thomson, 1997
'Glowing Red' × Jackson sdlg 61/83; sdlg no. 18B/92
Fl. 100 mm wide; perianth and other petaloid segments in 2-3 whorls, very broadly ovate, flushed orange, deeply overlapping; the outer whorl blunt, with prominent white mucro, more or less spreading, a little concave; the inner whorl strongly inflexed, truncate, not noticeably mucronate, deeply concave each side of the midrib; the centre whorl incomplete, shorter, irregularly arranged, strongly inflexed; corona segments about the same length as the petaloid segments at centre, interspersed, deep orange. Late

'Goshen Sokar' 4 W-P
(Greg Thomson) Greg Thomson, 1997
'Blushing Maiden' × 'Ragbag'; sdlg no. 26C/92
Fl. 100 mm wide; perianth and other petaloid segments in about four whorls, roundish, truncate, pure white, with margins nicked, irregular, deeply overlapping; the outer whorl slightly reflexed; the inner whorls successively more strongly inflexed; the centre whorl with margins strongly incurled, appearing to be acute at apex; corona segments shorter, interspersed, broad, dark pink, frilled. Late. Resembles 'Ragbag' in form

'Goshen Stargate' 4 W-P
(Greg Thomson) Greg Thomson, 1997
'Blushing Maiden' × 'Pink Blush'; sdlg no. 11B/92
Fl. 80 mm wide; perianth and other petaloid segments in about seven whorls, ovate, mucronate, white, overlapping one-third; the outer whorls blunt, a little inflexed, with margins a little wavy; the inner whorls successively more strongly inflexed, with margins more strongly incurled, appearing to be acute at apex; corona segments half the length, regularly interspersed, soft pink, broad, only slightly wavy. Dwarf. Late

'Gossamer' 3 W-YYP
(G.E. Mitsch) G.E. Mitsch, 1962
'Rubra' × 'Foggy Dew'
Fl. 102 mm wide; perianth segments slightly reflexed; corona cup-shaped, pale yellow, with a narrow band of pink at rim. Mid-season

'Gossamer Gold' 3 Y-? (a)
(H.G. Longford, pre-1927)

'Gossip' 3 W-? (b)
(M.P. Williams, pre-1938)

'Gotcha' 3 W-O
(D. Jackson, 1970) Jackson's Daffodils, 1983
'Motif' hybrid; sdlg no. 175/58
Fl. 100 mm wide. Mid-season

'Gothelney' 3 W-O
(A.M. Wilson, pre-1914)
Perianth segments narrow; corona very shallow, cinnamon orange. See also 'Gotholney'

'Gotholney' 3 W-O
Syn. of 'Gothelney'

'Gouache'
(W.F.Leenen, pre-1993) Unregistered

N. gouanii Roth = *N.* × *incomparabilis*

'Goude Kroon' 8 Y-Y
(pre-1798)

'Gouden Arend' 8 Y-Y
(pre-1835)
Early

'Goud Geel van den Ende' 8 Y-Y
(pre-1777)

'Gourmet' 2 W-WWP
(J.J. Grullemans & Sons) P.Q.M. Pennings, 1983
Perianth segments broadly ovate, blunt, prominently mucronate, creamy white, spreading, with margins sometimes creased, overlapping one-third to a half; the inner segments somewhat inflexed and with margins distinctly wavy; corona funnel-shaped, loosely ribbed, creamy white, with a band of orange-pink at rim, mouth more or less straight, split in places and overlapping, frilled, with rim crenate. Resembles 'Pink Fancy'

'Govert Flink' 3 W-GYO
(de Graaff Bros, pre-1931)
AM(Haarlem) 1930

'Goviley' 3 W-YOO
(P.D. Williams, pre-1928)
Perianth segments snow white; corona reddish orange, with yellow at base. See also 'Govilly'

'Govilly' 3 W-YOO
Syn. of 'Goviley'

'Gowo' 3 W-R
(W. Jackson Jr, 1949) W. Jackson Jr, 1966
'Gyda' × 'Owo'

'Gowrie' 1 W-?
(Mrs B.A. Woods) Mrs B.A. Woods, 1968

'Goyescas' 3 Y-YYO
(The Brodie of Brodie, c.1930)
'Seraglio' × ('Beacon' × 'Fortune')
Perianth segments pale yellow; corona bright yellow, with reddish orange at rim

'G.P.Haydon'
(pre-1924)

'Gracchus' 2 Y-O
(de Graaff Bros, pre-1929)
AM(Haarlem) 1928

'Grace' 3 W-? (b)
(R.H. Bath, pre-1930)

'Grace' 1 W-W
(R.C.A. Tombleson) R.C.A. Tombleson, 1968

'Grace Cobley' 2 W-? (b)
(Miss K.M. Hinchliff, pre-1937)

'Gracedale' 2 Y-Y
(H.A. Brown, pre-1936)
Early

'Grace Darling' 3 W-YYO
(W. Backhouse, pre-1869)
Corona canary yellow, with orange at rim. Syn. Barrii Albus 'Grace Darling'

'Grace Darling' 1 W-W
(de Graaff Bros, pre-1897)
Perianth segments broadly ovate, inflexed, twisted, overlapping one-third; corona cylindrical, narrow, ribbed, opening pale primrose yellow, becoming milk white, with mouth widely expanded and rim deeply crenate

'Gracefield' 2 W-GWY
(E.F. Hughes) E.F. Hughes, 1962
Fl. 108 mm wide; corona widely expanded, ribbed, with apricot yellow at rim, frilled. Mid-season

'Grace Forbes' 8 W-Y
(M. van Waveren & Sons, pre-1925)
Fl. large; perianth segments pure white; corona orange-yellow

'Graceful' 1 W-Y
(W.A. Grace, pre-1927)

'Graceful Charmer' 3 W-R
(T. Bloomer) T. Bloomer, 1962
'Irish Charm' × Richardson sdlg 202; sdlg no. 1/3/60

'Grace Gardiner' 2 Y-? (a)
(W.A. Grace, pre-1938)

'Gracehill' 2 W-W
(G.L. Wilson, pre-1940)
(Sdlg × 'Vestal Virgin') × ('Madame de Graaff' hybrid × Beersheba')
Fl. pure white

'Graceland' 3 W-GWY
(T. Bloomer) Rathowen Daffodils, 1982
'Woodland Grace' × 'Woodland Prince'; sdlg no. 205
Fl. 100 mm wide; corona slightly frilled. Mid-season

'Grace Moffat' 2 Y-O
(G.H. Johnstone, pre-1939)
Perianth segments rounded at apex, canary yellow; corona cup-shaped, marigold orange. AM(e) 1939

'Grace Note' 3 W-GGY
(G.E. Mitsch, 1952) G.E. Mitsch, 1966
Probably 'Cushendall' × 'Cantabile'
Fl. 83 mm wide; perianth segments broadly ovate, blunt or truncate, prominently mucronate, pure white, spreading or somewhat inflexed, with margins incurved, overlapping half; the inner segments a little reflexed, with margins wavy; corona very shallow bowl-shaped, small, closely ribbed, vivid emerald green, with lemon yellow at rim, frilled. Late

'Gracieuse' 8 Y-Y
(pre-1798)
Fl. pale yellow

graciliflorus = *N. abscissus* var. *graciliflorus*

N. × *gracilis* Sabine 13 = *N. jonquilla* Linnaeus × *N. poeticus* Linnaeus (assumed) (Poeticus 'Planicorona', "The Slender Flat Crowned")

'Gracilis' 3 W-?Y
(W. Backhouse, pre-1869)
Perianth segments sulphur white. Syn. Burbidgei 'Gracilis'. This has also been used as a Group name. Was "absorbed" into 'Mrs Krelage'

'Gracious' 2 W-? (b)
(L. van Leeuwen & Son, pre-1931)

'Gracious' 2 Y-Y
(W. Jackson Jr, 1970) Unregistered
'Vixi' × 'Oriel'; sdlg no. 5/70
Fl. clear golden yellow; perianth segments broadly ovate, rounded at apex, of good substance; corona slightly deeper in tone, with rim dentate. Syn. 'Gratia'

'Gracious Lady' 2 W-P
(Mrs H.K. Richardson) Mrs H.K. Richardson, 1974
'Romance' × 'Rose Royale'
Fl. 112 mm wide; perianth segments large, pure white; corona bright pink, with green at base, rim slightly dentate. PC(e) 1974

'Grackle' 2 Y-O
(P.D. Williams, pre-1929)
Perianth segments broadly ovate, blunt or squarish at apex, fairly prominently mucronate, bright yellow, plane or with margins slightly wavy, overlapping one-third; the inner segments a little inflexed, creased, with margins more strongly waved; corona bowl-shaped, loosely ribbed, reddish orange, with mouth even, rim notched and slightly flanged. Early to mid-season

'Graduate' 2 W-GPP
(Brian S. Duncan) Rathowen Daffodils, 1977
Rathowen sdlg 3341 × 'Passionale'; sdlg no. 105
Fl. 114 mm wide; perianth segments broadly ovate; corona deep pink, with mouth expanded and rim flanged. Mid-season. Resembles 'Passionale' but with a smoother and whiter perianth and a deeper-coloured corona. Formerly named 'Graduation'

'Graduation' 2 W-WWP
(Elise Havens) G.E. Mitsch, 1975
'Empress of Ireland' × 'Accent'; sdlg no. E64-1/1
Fl. 100 mm wide; perianth segments very broadly ovate, blunt, slightly mucronate, spreading, a little concave, overlapping half; the inner segments slightly inflexed, with margins wavy; corona narrowly funnel-shaped, smooth, white, shading to pure pink at rim, with mouth flared and heavily frilled. Mid-season

'Graduation' 2 W-GPP
Syn. of 'Graduate'

N. graellsii Webb = *N. bulbocodium* subsp. *bulbocodium* var. *graellsii*

'Graeme Dettman' 2 Y-O
(L.P. Dettman) L.P. Dettman, 1982
'Chemawa' × 'Torridon'
Fl. 76 mm wide; perianth segments vivid yellow 9A; corona yellow-orange (17A), with a lighter tone (13A) at rim. Early

'Graeme's Memory' 2 Y-W
(L.P. Dettman) L.P. Dettman, 1982

'Binkie' × 'Beaugreen'; sdlg no. B/B 72
Fl. 89 mm wide; perianth segments pale greenish yellow 1D; corona greenish white 157D. Resembles 'Beaugreen'

'Graffiti' 2 W-YYO
(Jackson's Daffodils) Jackson's Daffodils, 1986
Sdlg 170/67 × 'Challenge'; sdlg no. 66/77
Perianth segments yellowish white 155D; corona vivid yellow 9B, with orange at rim. Mid-season. Syn. 'Mithra'

'Graf Zeppelin' 2 Y-? (a)
(R.A. van der Schoot, pre-1931)

'Graham Hyde' 2 Y-? (a)
(W.F.M. Copeland, pre-1910)

'Grail' 3 W-? (b)
(F.H. Chapman, pre-1930)

'Gramercy' 2 W-?
(Alister Clark, 1940) J. Sharp, 1960

'Gramophone' 1 Y-Y
(Hon. Sir R.H. Rhodes, pre-1913)

'Granada' 2 Y-R
(A.M. Wilson, pre-1927)
'Hospodar' hybrid
Perianth segments ivory yellow; corona bright red

'Granat' 2 W-? (b)
(Mrs R.O. Backhouse, pre-1921)
AM(Haarlem) 1930

'Grand' 2 W-Y
(R. Gibson, pre-1927)
Perianth segments creamy white

'Grand Alexander' 8 W-Y or O
(pre-1807)

"Grandalla"
Variant of *N. poeticus*

'Grand Bouquet' 8 W-O
(pre-1846)
Syn. ?'Le Grand Bouquet'

'Grand Cañon' 2 W-? (b or c)
(de Graaff Bros, pre-1927)

'Grand Cesar' 8 Y-O
(pre-1850)
Perianth segments citron yellow

'Grand Charteux' 8 Y or W-Y
Syn. of 'Grand Chartreux'

'Grand Chartreux' 8 Y or W-Y
(pre-1777)
Corona citron yellow. See also 'Grand Charteux', 'Grand Chartrieux'

'Grand Chartrieux' 8 Y or W-Y
Syn. of 'Grand Chartreux'

'Grand Citron' 1 Y-Y
(F. Rijnveld & Sons, pre-1939)

'Grand Dorothé' 8 W-Y
(pre-1835)
Corona lemon yellow. Early

'Grand Duc' 8 ?W-Y or O
(pre-1798)
Syn. 'Grand Duke'

'Grand Duchess' 3 W-W
(W. Backhouse, pre-1869)
Perianth segments narrow, acute; corona expanded, opening primrose yellow with a tinge of orange, becoming creamy white. Syn. Leedsii 'Grand Duchess'. "Absorbed" 'Fides'

'Grand Duke' 2? W-Y
(W. Backhouse, pre-1869)
Corona fawn yellow. Syn. Leedsii 'Grand Duke'

'Grand Duke' 8 ?W-Y or O
Syn. of 'Grand Duc'

'Grand Duke of Hesse' 8 W-Y
(W. Backhouse, pre-1869)
Perianth creamy white. Syn. Tridymus 'Grand Duke of Hesse'

'Grandee' 1 W-Y
Syn. of 'Grandis'

'Grand Emperor'
Syn. of *N.tazetta* subsp. *lacticolor*

'Grand Emperor of China'
2n=30. Probably syn. of *N.tazetta* subsp. *lacticolor*

'Grandesse' 1 W-? (b)
(J.W.A. Lefeber, pre-1941)

'Grand Etandart' 8 Y-Y
(pre-1807)
Fl. sulphur yellow. ?The same as 'Etendart'

'Grandeur' 2 W-? (b)
(G.H. Engleheart, pre-1910)

'Grand Final' 2 W-YYO
(Tom Forster, 1960s) Unregistered
Perianth segments broad, ice white; corona disc-shaped, bright lemon yellow, with bright orange at rim, frilled. Tall. Late

'Grandfinale' 1 Y-Y
(1960) G. Zandbergen-Terwegen, 1979
Fl. golden yellow. Resembles a slightly lighter-coloured 'Golden Harvest'

'Grand Gala' 1 Y-Y
(J. Gerritsen & Son) J. Gerritsen & Son, 1971
Perianth segments vivid yellow 12A; corona slightly darker in tone

'Grand Goliath' 8 Y-Y
(pre-1777)

N. grandicrenatus Parlatore = *N. tazetta* subsp. *lacticolor*

N. grandiflorus Battandier & Trabut = *N. broussonetii* f. *grandiflorus*

N. grandiflorus Sabine = *N. radiiflorus* var. *poetarum*

N. grandiflorus Salisbury = *N. hispanicus*

'Grandiflorus' 9 W-?
(pre-1873)
Fl. apt to go green; perianth segments very large, pure white; corona more or less suffused crimson. Mid-season. Syn. Poeticus 'Grandiflorus'

'Grandiflorus' 2 W-Y
(?E. Leeds, pre-1877)
Syn. Incomparabilis 'Grandiflorus'

'Grandiflorus' 1 Y-Y
Syn. of 'Maximus'

'Grandiflorus' 2
Syn. of 'Magog' or 'Eclipse' ?Y-Y, also of 'Titan' Y-YYO and of 'Gog' W-Y

'Grandiflorus' 3 W-Y
Syn. of 'John Bain'

'Grandiflorus Aurantius' 3 ?-O
(pre-1879)
Corona stained scarlet-orange. Syn. Burbidgei 'Grandiflorus Aurantius'

'Grandiflorus Elatus' 2 or 3
(?E. Leeds, pre-1877)
Fl. large. Tall

'Grandiflorus Expansus' 3 W-Y
Syn. of 'Thomas Moore Absolon'

'Grandiose' 2 Y-? (a)
(G. Zandbergen-Terwegen, pre-1939)

'Grandiplenus' 4 Y-Y
(pre-1873)
?Variant of *N. minor* var. *conspicuus*
Fl. very large; perianth and other petaloid segments in many whorls, ovate, light yellow, with some green segments interspersed; the outer whorls spreading or a little inflexed; the inner whorls successively more strongly inflexed; corona segments shorter than the petaloid segments and interspersed among them, orange-yellow, broad, lightly frilled, with rim crenate; the petaloid and corona segments at centre sometimes in several separate clusters. Resembles a shorter 'Plenissimus'. Syn. Pseudonarcissus Lobularis 'Grandiplenus'

'Grandis' 1 W-Y
(E. Leeds, pre-1877)
Hybrid between *N. bicolor* and 'Maximus' or *N. hispanicus* var. *propinquus*
Fl. large; perianth segments oblong, blunt, prominently mucronate, white or pale yellow, spreading, overlapping one-third; the inner segments somewhat inflexed; corona cylindrical, strongly ribbed, deep yellow, mouth flared and lobed, frilled, with rim crenate. Late. 2n=22. Resembles an earlier-flowered 'Empress' of less refinement and stronger substance. Syn. 'Grandee', Pseudonarcissus Bicolor 'Grandis', Pseudonarcissus Bicolor 'Maximus'

'Grandissima' 8 Y-O
(pre-1850)
Perianth segments citron yellow

'Grand Maître' 1 Y-Y
(G. Lubbe & Son, pre-1927)
AM(Haarlem) 1926

'Grand Maitre' 8 W-O
Syn. of 'Princess of Holland'

'Grand Marnier' 3 W-? (b)
(F.H. Chapman, pre-1923)

'Grand Master' 1 Y-Y
(G. Davison, pre-1929)
Fl. 114 mm wide, golden yellow, facing up; perianth segments broadly ovate, blunt, slightly mucronate, a little inflexed, with margins wavy, overlapping at base only; corona funnel-shaped, smooth, with mouth expanded and strongly ribbed, rim deeply notched. AM(c) 1930, *(Kirton)HC(g) 1935

'Grand Monarch' 8 W-Y
Syn. of 'Grand Monarque'

'Grand Monarque' 8 W-Y
(?Dutch origin, pre-1798)
Variant of *N. tazetta* subsp. *lacticolor*
Fls many per stem; perianth segments broadly ovate, blunt, prominently mucronate, spreading, somewhat concave, with margins wavy or incurled, overlapping one-third to a half; the inner segments a little inflexed; corona shallow cup-shaped, broadly and shallowly ribbed, brilliant greenish yellow 6A, with mouth straight or a little incurved, rim entire. Mid-season. 2n=31+1B. Syn. "Nosegay", "The Nosegay", 'Czar Monarque', 'Floribunda', 'Floribundus', 'French Monarque', 'Grand Monarch', 'Grand Monarque de France', 'Monarch', ?'Le Grand Monarque', Tazetta 'Grand Monarque'

'Grand Monarque de France' 8 W-Y
Syn. of 'Grand Monarque'

'Grand Monarque Jaune' 8 Y-O
(pre-1852)

'Grandmother Grullemans' 2 W-OOY
Syn. of 'Mother Catherine Grullemans'

'Grand National' 2 Y-R
(M.P. Williams, pre-1938)
Perianth segments yellow; corona scarlet. AM(Haarlem) 1950

'Grand National' 8 W-Y
(New Zealand origin, pre-1990) Unregistered
Corona orange-yellow

'Grand Opening' 4 W-R
(W.G. Pannill) W.G. Pannill, 1985
'Kingfisher' x 'Gay Challenger'; sdlg no. 66/17 G
Mid-season

'Grand Opera' 3 W-YYR
(F.H. Chapman, pre-1929)
'Kestrel' hybrid
Perianth segments pure white; corona disc-shaped, citron, with a broad band of deep red at rim. Div. 9 until 1940

'Grand Parade' 2 Y-YYR
(G. Lewis) D.S. Bell, 1955

'Grand Patriarch' 8 W-Y
(pre-1850)
Corona pale yellow

'Grand Phoenix' 8 W-O
(pre-1798)

'Grand Primo' 8 Y-Y
(pre-1807)
Syn. ?'Primo Luteo', Tazetta 'Grand Primo'

'Grand Primo' 8 W-Y
Syn. of 'Grand Primo Citronière'

'Grand Primo Citronière' 8 W-Y
(pre-1780)

Fls many per stem, large; perianth segments broadly ovate, blunt, fairly prominently mucronate, spreading, incurved in upper third, overlapping half; corona shallow cup-shaped, obscurely ribbed, light greenish yellow 4C, mouth straight and even, with rim entire. Jasmine scented. $2n=30,32$. Syn. 'Primo Citronier', ?'La Citronière', 'Citrina', 'Citrinus', 'Grand Primo', 'Primo Citronière', 'Primo'

'Grand Prince' 8 Y-Y
(pre-1851)
Corona lemon yellow

'Grand Prix' 4
(J.L. Richardson) G. Zandbergen-Terwegen, 1964

'Grand Prospect' 2 Y-W
(Mrs H.K. Richardson) Mrs J. Abel Smith, 1974
'Camelot' × 'Daydream'
Fl. 104 mm wide; perianth segments broadly ovate in outline, blunt or roundish at apex, yellow, with a paler tone at midrib and a slight white mucro, spreading, with margins slightly incurling at apex, regular, overlapping half; the inner segments a little narrower, with margins wavy; corona funnel-shaped, opening sulphur yellow, becoming white, with mouth straight, loosely frilled. Late. Resembles a stronger 'Daydream' of more refined form

'Grand Seigneur' 11a W-Y
(J. Gerritsen & Son) J. Gerritsen & Son, 1971
'Baccarat' × 'Norwind'
Fl. 90 mm wide

'Grandsire' 1 Y-Y
(F.H. Chapman, pre-1915)

'Grand Slam' 2 W-? (b)
(Mrs R.O. Backhouse, pre-1921)

'Grand Soleil d'Or' 8 Y-O
(?Dutch origin, pre-1770)
Fls 10-20 per stem, 43 mm wide; perianth segments very broadly ovate, brilliant yellow 7A or a little deeper in colour than vivid yellow 12a, with long white mucro, spreading, plane, overlapping half; the inner segments only very slightly mucronate, sharply narrowing from mid-point to base, with margins a little wavy; corona cup-shaped, smooth, yellow-orange (17A or 21A), mouth straight or a little incurved, even or somewhat 3-angled, rim entire. Very early. Scented. $2n=20,30$. Resembles a larger-flowered 'Soleil d'Or' with a more vividly coloured corona. Syn. Tazetta 'Grand Soleil d'Or'. *AM(p) 1977

'Grand Souverain' 8 W-Y or W
(pre-1851)
Syn. ? 'Le Grand Souverain'

'Grand Style' 1 Y-Y
(P.L.A. Pouw) J.H. Rijkelijkhuizen, 1960

'Grand Sultan' 8
(pre-1915)

'Grange Beauty' 3 W-R
(New Zealand origin, pre-1956) Unregistered
Corona scarlet

'Grania' 7 Y-Y
(S.J. Bisdee, 1946)
Sdlg × Jonquilla 'Plenus'

'Gransha' 3 W-GYR
(Ballydorn Bulb Farm) Ballydorn Bulb Farm, 1977
'Merlin' open pollinated
Fl. 95 mm wide; corona golden yellow, with green at base and scarlet at rim. Mid-season

'Grantulla' 1 Y-Y
(J.N. Hancock & Co., c.1982) Unregistered

'Granvelle' 2 W-O
(G.A. Uit den Boogaard, pre-1944)

'Grape Fruit' 1 Y-Y
(G. Lubbe & Son, pre-1939)
Fl. pale lemon. AM(Haarlem) 1939, FCC(Haarlem) 1944

'Graphic' 1 W-W
(R.H. Bath, pre-1931)
AM(Haarlem) 1938

'Grapillon' 11a W-Y
(J. Gerritsen & Son, 1957) J. Gerritsen & Son, 1968
'Valdrome' hybrid
Fl. 115 mm wide; perianth segments creamy white; corona segments light greenish yellow 5D. Mid-season. Resembles a larger-flowered 'Valdrome'

'Grasmere' 1 Y-Y
(J.S.B.Lea, 1984) Clive Postles Daffodils, 1994
Lea sdlg 7-76 × 'Glen Clova'; sdlg no. 1-5-80
Fl. forming a double triangle, 102 mm wide; perianth segments ovate, concave at margins; corona funnel-shaped, with mouth flared and frilled. Tall. Very early

'Grasse Daffodil' 1 ?Y-Y
(Spanish origin)
Selection by Peter Barr (c.1887) from wild-collected *N. pseudonarcissus*
Fl. small; perianth segments creamy white or pale yellow; corona funnel-shaped, canary- or orange-yellow. Dwarf. Early

'Grasshopper' 3 W-? (b)
(W.F.M. Copeland, pre-1908)

'Gratia' 2 W-? (b)
(de Graaff Bros, pre-1938)
AM(Haarlem) 1938

'Gratia' 2 Y-Y
Syn. of 'Gracious'

'Gratitude' 2 Y-Y
(M.P. Williams, pre-1938)
Fl. dark yellow

'Gravinne' 8 Y-Y
(pre-1798)
Fl. pale yellow

'Gravity' 2 W-W
(M.P. Williams, pre-1938)

'Graybird'
(pre-1913)

'Grayling'
(C. Dawson, pre-1908)

'Grayling' 2 W-YYW
(P.D. Williams, pre-1927)
'The Fawn' × 'Maximus'
Fl. 108 mm wide, of much substance; perianth segments creamy white, spreading, overlapping half; corona funnel-shaped, clear sulphur yellow, paling with age, whitish at rim. Mid-season. 2n=28. *AM(g) 1931, *AM(g) 1936

'Graywoods' 2 Y-? (a)
(The Brodie of Brodie, pre-1930)

'Great Ace' 2 W-Y
(A.E. Lowe, pre-1927)
Corona expanded, clear yellow

'Great Algiers' 8 Y-?
(pre-1759)

'Great Arthur' 2 Y-? (a)
(P.D. Williams, pre-1931)

'Great Blaze' 2 Y-R
(D.S. Bell) D.S. Bell, 1964
('Seraglio' × 'Encore') × 'Tamino'
Fl. 106 mm wide; perianth segments rich yellow; corona red

'Great Circle' 2 Y-YYR
(D.S. Bell) D.S. Bell, 1964
Fl. 103 mm wide; perianth segments pale yellow; corona shallow, widely expanded, yellow, with a narrow band of red at rim

'Great Dane' 1 Y-Y
(E. & J.C. Martin, pre-1916)

Fl. golden yellow; corona frilled. AM(e) 1923

'Greater Bell' 8 Y-?
(pre-1759)

'Great Expectations' 2 Y-Y
(Mrs H.K. Richardson) Mrs J. Abel Smith, 1977
'Golden Aura' × 'Camelot'; sdlg no. 3982
Fl. 93 mm wide, deep golden yellow. Mid-season. Resembles 'Golden Aura' but with a narrower corona

'Great Gatsby' 2 Y-R
(W.G. Pannill) W.G. Pannill, 1992
'Vulcan' × 'Fire Alarm'; sdlg no. 75/14
Fl.115 mm wide. Mid-season

'Great Harry' 1 W-W
(E.H.G. Thurston, pre-1930)

'Great Heart' 9 W-?
(G.H. Engleheart, pre-1930)

'Great Hope' 1 Y-Y
(Hon. Mrs Petre, pre-1934)

'Great Jewel' 2 Y-O
(S.C. Gaspar, 1944) R.J. Abernethy, 1957
Perianth segments soft yellow; corona orange

'Great Leap' 4 Y-Y
(E. & J.C. Martin, pre-1923)
'Telamonius Plenus' hybrid
Fl. buttercup yellow and sulphur yellow; perianth, petaloid and corona segments densely arranged. 2n=21

'Great Northern' 2 WWY-Y
(R. & E.Havens, 1984) R. & E.Havens, 1995
'Gold Crown' × 'Trogon'; sdlg no. TEH57/1
Fl. 110 mm wide; perianth segments broadly ovate, white, with yellow at base, spreading, plane; corona golden yellow bordering on orange, mouth slightly expanded and a little frilled. Mid-season

'Great Tom' 2 W-? (b or c)
(J.R. Pearson & Sons, pre-1927)

'Great Warley' 2 W-Y
(G.H. Engleheart, pre-1904)
'Horsfieldii' × 'Ornatus'
Perianth segmens broad, creamy white; corona widely expanded, clear citron yellow. 2n=29,36. Resembles a large-flowered 'Lady Margaret Boscawen'. FCC 1904, FCC(Haarlem) 1912

'Great White' 2 W-Y
Syn. of 'Doctor Gorman'

'Greatwood' 1 Y-Y
(R.A.Scamp) R.A.Scamp, 1997

'Ormeau' × ('Saint Keverne' × 1Y-Y); sdlg no. 305
Fl. rounded, 97 mm wide, dark golden yellow; perianth segments very broad, slightly inflexed; corona cylindrical, neatly frilled. Mid-season

'Great Work' 1 W-W
(M.P. Williams, pre-1937)

'Greave' 1 W-? (b)
(G.H. Engleheart, pre-1916)

'Greba'
(pre-1935)
'Bernardino' hybrid
Corona faintly tinged pink

'Grebe' 4 Y-O
(G.E. Mitsch) G.E. Mitsch, 1979
Sdlg R63/1 ('Playboy' hybrid) × 'Enterprise'; sdlg no. F133/1
Fl. 95 mm wide; perianth and other petaloid segments in several whorls, very broadly ovate, clear mid-yellow, with slight white mucro, plane, overlapping half or more; the outer whorl spreading or a little inflexed; the inner whorls successively slightly shorter and narrower and more strongly inflexed; the centre whorl strongly inflexed, with margins tightly incurled; corona segments clustered among the petaloid segments at centre, more loosely arranged among the surrounding whorls and half their length, broad, yellow, with more or less heavy touches of orange at margins, frilled. Mid-season. Resembles sibling 'Oregon Beauty' but with more numerous petaloid segments

'Grecian Beauty' 3 W-? (b)
(Mrs R.O. Backhouse, pre-1921)

'Grecian Maid' 2 or 3 W-? (b or c)
(pre-1949)

N. × **gredensis** Fernández Casas 13 = *N. bulbocodium* Linnaeus var. *nivalis* (Graells) Baker × *N. rupicola* Dufour

'Greek Column' 1 W-Y
(Grant E. Mitsch, 1972) R. & E. Havens, 1994
'Wahkeena' × (sdlg AM29/1 × 'Preamble'); sdlg no. HH122/2
Fl. 105 mm wide, of thick substance; perianth segments ovate, white, with yellow at base, spreading, plane; corona flared, rich mid-yellow. Mid-season

'Greek Fire' 2 Y-R
(D.S. Bell, pre-1981) Unregistered
('Sabre Dance' × 'Alamein') × 'Ashanti'
Perianth segments broad; corona frilled

'Greek God' 1 W-W
(Cartwright & Goodwin, pre-1916)

'Greek Gold' 1 Y-Y
(G. Lewis, 1935) Parr's Nurseries, 1958

'Greek Key' 1 W-Y
(G.E. Mitsch & R.& E.Havens, 1974) G.E. Mitsch & R.& E.Havens, 1988
'Spitzbergen' × 'Prologue'; sdlg no. JJ42/1
Corona long, narrow, deep lemon yellow, with rim rolled. Mid-season. Resembles a later-flowered 'Prologue' with a differently shaped corona

'Greek Slave' 5
(Barr & Sons, pre-1923)
'Cleopatra' × *N. triandrus* var. *loiseleurii*

'Green Back' 1 Y-Y
(E. Leeds, pre-1877)
Perianth segments suffused green below. Syn. Pseudonarcissus Major 'Green Back'

'Greenback' 2 Y-Y
(J.N. Hancock & Co., 1959) Unregistered

'Greenbank' 2 G-Y
(W.M. Spry, pre-1975) Unregistered
'Highland Chief' × 'Port Kembla'
Perianth segments greenish white; corona lemon yellow. Tall. Late

'Green Beauty' 9 W-GGR
(Mrs M.S. Yerger) Mrs M.S. Yerger, 1989
'Sea Green' open pollinated; sdlg no. 77 H 1
Fl. 52 mm wide; corona disc shaped, light yellow-green 145C, with strong yellow-green 144B at base and orange-red (31A) at rim. Mid-season

'Greenbelt' 9 W-GGR
(Mrs M.S. Yerger) Mrs M.S. Yerger, 1993
'Sea Green' open pollinated; sdlg no. 76 J 3
Fl. 65 mm wide; perianth segments white; the inner segments narrower and a little shorter; corona almost disc-shaped, yellow-green (151A) with a broad band of orange-red (32B) at mouth and a narrow band of darker red (35A) at rim. Late

'Green Bridge' 3 W-GYO
(Carncairn Daffodils, 1984) Carncairn Daffodils, 1994
'Merlin' × 'Rockall'; sdlg no. 3/60/79
Fl. 108 mm wide; perianth segments yellowish white 155B, smooth, overlapping; corona 6-angled, vivid yellow 13A, with green at base and a broad band of vivid orange 28B at rim, closely frilled. Late

'Greenbrier' 3 W-GWW
(W.G. Pannill) W.G. Pannill, 1978
'Pigeon' × 'Tobernaveen'; sdlg no. 64/92 C
Fl. 103 mm wide. Late

'Greencastle' 3 W-GGO

(W.J. Dunlop, pre-1952)
'Folly' × 'Sunstar'
Corona disc-shaped, deep mossy green, with a broad band of orange at rim

'Green Chartreuse' 2 W-GGY
(A.J.R. Pearson) A.J.R. Pearson, 1993
'Easter Moon' × 'Cloneen'; sdlg no. 87-83-K39
Fl. forming a double triangle, 105 mm wide; perianth segments broadly ovate, acute and prominently mucronate, greenish ivory white becoming greener with age, slightly reflexed, plane, or sometimes a little concave at apex, smooth and of good substance, with broad midrib showing, overlapping half; corona short funnel-shaped, angled and lightly ribbed, pale lime green (145C), with moss green (144B) at base and brilliant greenish yellow 5B at rim, mouth slightly wavy, rim regularly crenate. Mid-season to late

'Green Cove' 9 W-GGR
(Mrs M.S. Yerger) Mrs M.S. Yerger, 1993
'Sea Green' open pollinated; sdlg no. 76 J 8
Fl. forming a double triangle, 46 mm wide; perianth segments white; the inner segments a little shorter; corona brilliant yellow-green 150B, with strong yellow-green 144A at base and a broad band of orange-red (31A) at rim. Late

'Greendel' 8 W-Y
(J.J. Abernethy, 1949) R.J. Abernethy, 1960
Fls 2 per stem, 70 mm wide; corona lemon yellow, shaded green. Mid-season. Resembles a later-flowered 'Green Goddess' with a darker-coloured corona

'Green Delight' 9 W-GGR
(Mrs M.S. Yerger) Mrs M.S. Yerger, 1989
'Milan' open pollinated; sdlg no. 75 C 2
Fl. 48 mm wide; perianth segments ovate, acute; corona very shallow bowl-shaped, brilliant yellow-green 154C, with strong yellow-green 144B at base and orange-red (33A) at rim. Mid-season

'Green Disc' 3 W-? (b)
(C. Dawson, pre-1908)

'Green Elf' 3 W-GYO
(H.A. Brown, 1942) J.N. Hancock & Co., 1955
Perianth segments greenish white, heavily marked with bright green, twisted at apex; corona very shallow, opening green, becoming yellow, with orange at rim. Late

'Green Emerald' 2 W-? (b)
(pre-1955)
?Syn. of 'Emerald'

'Green Eye' 3 Y-GYY
(G.H. Engleheart, pre-1907)
Perianth segments creamy; corona bright yellow, with dark green at base

'Green Eyes' 1 Y-Y
(Konynenburg & Mark) Konynenburg & Mark, 1964
'Spellbinder' × 'Binkie'
Fl. 47 mm wide; perianth segments light greenish yellow 4B; corona slightly darker in tone (4A)

'Greenfinch' 3 W-? (b)
(pre-1907)

'Greenfinch' 2 W-GYY
(G.H. Johnstone, pre-1960)

'Greenfinch' 3 W-GWO
(J.L. Richardson) Mrs H.K. Richardson, 1962
'Corofin' × 'Tulyar'
Fl. 80 mm wide. Late

'Green Gables' 2 W-GWY
(D.S. Bell) D.S. Bell, 1957
'Green Island' hybrid
Corona bowl-shaped, with green at base and a broad band of deep gold at rim. Syn. 'Green Mountain'

'Green Ginger' 7 Y-Y
(A. Gray) M.J. Jefferson-Brown, 1975
Fls 1-3 per stem; perianth segments opening darker in tone than the corona, becoming primrose yellow; corona disc-shaped, yellow, tinged with green. Dwarf. Very late. Scented. Resembles 'Skiffle' but with the perianth slightly lighter in tone and a shallower corona

'Green Glens' 2 W-GYY
(Carncairn Daffodils) Carncairn Daffodils, 1981
Sdlg W2/857 × 'Shantallow'; sdlg no. W1/19
Fl. 100 mm wide; perianth segments yellowish white 155B; corona ribbed, with the moderate olive green 137A at base slightly suffusing the mid-zone, with vivid yellow 9A at rim. Late

'Green Glow' 9 W-GGR
(Mrs M.S. Yerger) Mrs M.S. Yerger, 1989
'Sea Green' open pollinated; sdlg no. 76 J 21
Fl. 50 mm wide; perianth segments rounded, deeply overlapping; corona very shallow bowl-shaped, brilliant yellow-green 154B, with a much darker tone (144C) at base and orange-red (31A) at rim. Late

'Green Goddess' 8 W-GYY
(E. James, pre-1949)
Corona lemon yellow. PC(e)(NZ) 1947

'Green Gold' 2 Y-WWY
(G.E. Mitsch) G.E. Mitsch, 1975
'Playboy' × 'Daydream'; sdlg no. B36/13
Fl. 115 mm wide, greenish lemon; corona becoming whitish at base, with rim neatly flanged. Mid-season

'Greenheart' 12 W-GYY
(Barr & Sons, pre-1907)
N. × *medioluteus* × *N. poeticus*
Fl. 2 per stem; perianth segments usually acute, spreading, twisted, with margins recurved, overlapping at base only; corona very small, olive yellow, with dark green at base. Tall. Late. Richly scented

'Green Hills' 3 W-GGY
(G.L. Wilson) M.J. Jefferson-Brown, 1960
'Moyness' × 'Portrush'
Fl. 102 mm wide; perianth segments satin smooth and of great substance; corona green, with lemon or pale gold at rim, frilled

'Greenholm' 2 W-GWW
(Brian S. Duncan) Rathowen Daffodils, 1981
'Easter Moon' × 'Knowehead'; sdlg no. 325
Perianth segments broadly ovate. Mid-season

'Green Holm' 9 W-GYO
Syn. of 'Greenholm'

'Greenholm' 9 W-GYO
(K.J. Heazlewood, pre-1971) Unregistered
'Milan' × 'Moina'; sdlg no. B14
Perianth segments reflexed, smooth; corona disc-shaped, greenish yellow (4D), with pale green at base and vivid orange 28B at rim. See also 'Green Holm'

'Green Howard' 3 W-GYY
(G.H. Johnstone, pre-1944)
'Elspeth' × 'Laity'
Fl. opening pale lime green; corona becoming bright yellow

'Green Ice' 2 W-GWW
(Brian S. Duncan) Rathowen Daffodils, 1981
'Easter Moon' × 'Knowehead'; sdlg no. 327
Resembles 'Broomhill' but with green at corona base and rim rolled. Mid-season

'Green Ice' 2 W-GWW
(pre-1968) Unregistered

'Green Island' 2 W-GWY
(J.L. Richardson, pre-1938)
'Gracious' × 'Seraglio'
Fl. rounded, 100 mm wide; perianth segments very broad, blunt or rounded at apex, slightly mucronate, spreading, concave at apex or with margins incurling, waxy smooth and of heavy substance, overlapping half or more; the inner segments roundish, somewhat truncate, only very slightly mucronate, a little inflexed; corona shallow, ribbed, creamy white, greenish at base, with a broad band of brilliant greenish yellow 6C at rim, mouth widely expanded, split in places and overlapping, closely frilled. Mid-season. *(Gulval)PC(m) 1940, AM(e) 1946, AM(Haarlem) 1965

'Green Jacket' 3 W-GYR
(J.L. Richardson) Mrs H.K. Richardson, 1968
'Corofin' × 'Tulyar'
Perianth segments ice white; corona opening yellow, becoming green at base, with a band of dark cherry red at rim, frilled

'Green Jade' 3 W-? (b)
(G. Lewis) D.S. Bell, 1955

'Green Joy' 9 W-GYR
(Mrs M.S. Yerger) Mrs M.S. Yerger, 1987
'Milan' open pollinated; sdlg no. 75 C 1
Fl. 58 mm wide; perianth segments reflexed; corona very shallow bowl-shaped, ribbed, brilliant greenish yellow 1B, with yellow-green (151A) at base and orange-red (30B) at rim, with the rim crenate. Mid-season. Resembles a smaller and earlier-flowered 'Milan' of stronger colouring

'Greenland' 2 W-W
(G.L. Wilson, pre-1949)
('Quartz' × 'Naxos') × 'Chinese White'
Corona with a hint of green at base

'Greenlet' 6 W-GWY
(M. Fowlds) G.E. Mitsch, 1969
'Green Island' × *N. cyclamineus*
Perianth segments broad, reflexed; corona opening pale lemon, becoming ivory, with green at base and lemon at rim, frilled. Mid-season

'Green Light' 2 Y-? (a)
(R.M. Miller, pre-1949)

'Green Linnet' 3 W-GGO
(J.L. Richardson) Mrs H.K. Richardson, 1967
'Corofin' × 'Tulyar'
Fl. 73 mm wide; corona disc-shaped, bright green, with a band of deep orange at rim, frilled. Late

'Green Lodge' 9 W-GGO
(Ballydorn Bulb Farm) Ballydorn Bulb Farm, 1992
'Moyle' × sdlg with green corona
Fl. 75 mm wide; perianth segments ovate, plane; corona shallow bowl-shaped, ribbed, opening green, with orange towards mouth, becoming orange-yellow, with a deeper tone at rim. Late

'Green Mantle' 3 W-YWY
(Slieve Donard Nursery Co., pre-1932)
Fl. white; perianth segments of great substance; corona shallow, white, with shades of pale clear lemon yellow at base and rim, mouth expanded and frilled. Late. See also 'Greenmantle'

'Greenmantle' 3 W-YWY
Syn. of 'Green Mantle'

'Green Meadows' 3 W-GOR
(D.S. Bell) D.S. Bell, 1960
Sdlg × 'Green Jade'
Fl. 108 mm wide; corona apricot orange, with green at base and red at rim. Mid-season. Resembles 'Green Jade' but with the perianth segments more rounded

'Green Mint' 3 W-W
(J.O. Sherrard, pre-1943)

'Greenmount' 3 W-Y
(W.J. Dunlop) W.J. Dunlop, 1957
'Chinese White' × 'Foggy Dew'
Corona pale greeny lemon, with a very narrow band of clear lemon at rim. 2n=28

'Green Mountain' 2 W-GWY
Syn. of 'Green Gables'

'Green Mountaineer' 3 W-YYG
(Mrs C.E. Fitzwater) Mrs C.E. Fitzwater, 1973
'Bithynia' × 'Portrush'
Fl. 83 mm wide; perianth segments roundish, slightly mucronate, opening pale yellow, becoming white, with tinges of yellow at base, spreading, overlapping half; corona narrow cup-shaped, ribbed, opening green, soon becoming yellow, with a broad band of green at rim

'Greenodd' 3 W-YYW
(Reg Nicholl) R.A. Scamp Daffodils, 1991
'Easter Moon' × 'Cool Crystal'; sdlg no. 17/86
Fl. 102 mm wide; perianth segments broadly ovate, blunt, sometimes slightly truncate, fairly prominently mucronate, spreading, slightly concave near apex, overlapping half; the inner segments a little narrower, not noticeably mucronate, with broad midrib showing; corona disc-shaped, deeply ribbed, brilliant to light greenish yellow 3, with dark green noticeable in tube and touches of white at rim, frilled. Tall. Late

'Greenore' 2 W-WWY
(J.L. Richardson, pre-1937)
'White Sentinel' × 'Fortune'
Perianth segments very broadly ovate, rounded at apex, spreading, regular, overlapping half; the inner segments only a little narrower; corona cup-shaped, pale primrose, with greenish lemon at rim, mouth slightly expanded

'Greenpark' 9 W-GGO
(Ballydorn Bulb farm) Ballydorn Bulb Farm, 1988
'Moyle' sport
Fl. 75 mm wide; perianth segments broadly ovate; corona disc-shaped, lightly ribbed, dark emerald green, with yellow-orange at rim and some flecks of red. Very late. Scented

'Green Pastures' 3 W-GWW
(Mrs Vyner Ellis, pre-1950)

'Green Peace' 3 W-GGY
(Ballydorn Bulb Farm) Ballydorn Bulb Farm, 1984
'Frigid' hybrid
Fl. 75 mm wide; corona green, with yellow at rim. Late. 2n=14

'Green Pearl' 9 W-GWW
(P. de Jager & Sons) P. de Jager & Sons, 1974

'Green Pond' 9 W-GGR
(Mrs M.S. Yerger) Mrs M.S. Yerger, 1986
'Lights Out' × 'Perdita'; sdlg no. 73 B 5
Perianth segments white; the inner segments narrower; corona strong yellow-green 144C, with a much darker tone at base and orange-red (30A) at rim. Resembles a smaller and daintier 'Perdita' in form. Mid-season to late

'Greenpool' 9 W-GGR
(Mrs M.S. Yerger) Mrs M.S. Yerger, 1984
'Lights Out' × 'Perdita'; sdlg no. 73 B 4
Fl. 57 mm wide; corona brilliant yellow-green 154B, with green at base and orange-red (33B) at rim. Mid-season

'Green Quest' 3 W-GWW
(G.E. Mitsch, 1956) G.E. Mitsch, 1968
'Chinese White' × 'Autowin'; sdlg no. R12/3
Corona creamy, with green at base. Mid-season. Resembles 'Foggy Dew' but with a smaller and more persistently creamy white corona

'Green Ray' 3 W-? (b or c)
(W.F.M. Copeland, pre-1936)

'Green Rising' 3 W-WWR
(S.J. Bisdee, 1940) S.J. Bisdee, 1956
'Atanga' × 'Sunstar'

'Green Rival' 2 Y-W
(Konynenburg & Mark) Konynenburg & Mark, 1962
'Binkie' × 'Spellbinder'
Fl. 110 mm wide; perianth segments broad, bright greenish yellow, with white at base; corona yellowish white, flushed green, with a darker tone towards the mouth, touched with the perianth colour at rim. Mid-season

'Green Scene' 9 W-GGR
(Mrs M.S. Yerger) Mrs M.S. Yerger, 1988
'Sea Green' open pollinated; sdlg no. 76 J 24
Perianth segments broadly ovate, rounded at apex; the inner segments more narrowly ovate; corona very shallow bowl-shaped, brilliant yellow-green 150B, with a darker tone at base (145B) and orange-red (33A) at rim. Dwarf. Very late

'Greenshank' 6 Y-Y
(A.M. Wilson, pre-1948)

?'W.P. Milner' × ? *N. cyclamineus*
Fl. golden yellow. See also 'Greenshanks'

'Greenshanks' 6 Y-Y
Syn. of 'Greenshank'

'Green Silver' 2 Y-W
(A. Gibson, pre-1950)

'Greensleeves' 2 W-W
(Mrs R.S. Cobley, pre-1932)

'Greensleeves' 2 Y-WWY
(J.N. Hancock & Co., *c*.1979) Unregistered

'Greenspan' 9 W-GYO
(Mrs M.S. Yerger) Mrs M.S. Yerger, 1988
'Sea Green' open pollinated; sdlg no. 76 J 17
Corona disc-shaped, greenish yellow (154D), with light yellow-green 145B at base and brilliant orange 29A at rim. Late to very late. Scented

'Greenspring' 9 W-GGR
(Mrs M.S. Yerger) Mrs M.S. Yerger, 1984
'Sea Green' open pollinated; sdlg no. 76 J 14
Fl. 50 mm wide; corona light yellow-green 145B, with green at base and orange-red (30A) at rim. Mid-season

'Greenstar' 4 G-G
(Scottish origin, pre-1956) Unregistered
Perianth and other petaloid segments in several whorls, green, touched yellowish green at margins and midrib, fading to yellow when past maturity; the outer whorl oblong, acute, more or less spreading, separated; some inner whorls almost as long as the outer, narrower, inflexed; some only half as long and strongly inflexed. Resembles 'Rip van Winkle' but with narrower segments in fewer whorls and with no noticeable corona. ?Syn. of 'Whiteadder'

'Greenvale' 2 W-GWW
(Brian S. Duncan) Rathowen Daffodils, 1981
'Easter Moon' × 'Empress of Ireland'; sdlg no. 434
Fl. icy white. Early to mid-season. Resembles a taller and stronger-stemmed 'Ave'

'Green Valley' 2 W-GWW
(S.J. Bisdee, 1951)
'Saint Finbar' × 'Whitefoord'

'Green Woodpecker' 2 W-GYO
(J.M. de Navarro, pre-1954)
'Folly' × 'Coronach' open pollinated
Perianth segments broad, snow white, slightly reflexed, smooth; corona very shallow bowl-shaped, with a narrow mid-zone of orange-yellow, deep moss green at base and reddish orange at rim. Sunproof. 2n=28. PC(e) 1960

'Greetham' 2 Y-Y
(W.A. Noton) W.A. Noton, 1994
Fl. 98 mm wide; perianth segments very broadly ovate, blunt, slightly mucronate, light greenish yellow 4B, spreading or somewhat inflexed, concave, regular, overlapping half; the inner segments with margins incurling at apex; corona shallow bowl-shaped, loosely ribbed, vivid yellow 9A, touched with orange-yellow at rim, mouth straight, more or less deeply 3-lobed, frilled, rim crenate. Mid-season

'Greeting' 2 W-Y
(P.D. Williams, pre-1934)
Fl. large; perianth segments acute, with margins sometimes recurved, of strong substance; corona cup-shaped, clear lemon yellow, with rim flared. 2n=28. AM(e) 1939

'Gregalach' 1 W-Y
(J.L. Richardson, pre-1930)
?'Lady Primrose' hybrid
Perianth segments broadly ovate, fairly prominently mucronate, spreading, overlapping one-third to a half; the inner segments a little inflexed and with margins wavy; corona funnel-shaped, soft yellow, mouth expanded and loosely frilled

'Gregory' 1 W-Y
(W.M. Spry, pre-1975) Unregistered
Corona lemon yellow

'Gremlin' 2 W-YYP
(Oregon Bulb Farms, pre-1946)

'Grenade' 2 Y-Y
(G.H. Engleheart, pre-1916)
Perianth segments deep sulphur yellow, with margins recurved, overlapping; corona long, slender, bright orange-yellow, frilled. Very tall. Mid-season. AM(c)(m) 1926, *AM(g) 1927, *AM(g) 1936

'Grenadier' 1 Y-Y
(Sir C.H. Cave, pre-1908)
Fl. 99 mm wide; perianth segments lemon yellow, overlapping half; corona deep lemon yellow, with mouth somewhat expanded and rim reflexed. Mid-season to late. *HC(g) 1930, *AM(g)(m) 1931

'Grenadier' 2 Y-YYO
(H.A. Brown, 1941)

'Grenfel' 3 W-YYR
(W.M. Spry, pre-1975) Unregistered
'Aldgate' hybrid
Corona lemon yellow, with scarlet at rim

N. × *grenieri* Richter = *N.* × *medioluteus*

'Grenoble' 2 Y-Y
(J.N. Hancock & Co., 1946)

Perianth segments yellow; corona expanded, deeper in tone than the perianth, frilled

'Grenoble' 2 W-OOY
(D.S. Bell) D.S. Bell, 1960
'Green Island' hybrid
Fl. 105 mm wide; corona apricot, with a band of yellow at rim. Mid-season. 2n=29. Resembles 'Green Island' but with a bowl-shaped corona

'Grenofen' 2 W-W
(G.L. Wilson, pre-1943)

'Gresham' 4 W-P
(Brian S. Duncan) Rathowen Daffodils, 1987
'Blushing Maiden' × 'Polonaise'; sdlg no. 872
Perianth segments very broadly ovate, white, spreading, smooth, overlapping half; a few white petaloid segments at centre very little shorter, broad, strongly inflexed, with margins deeply incurling; corona segments half as long as the petaloid segments at centre and loosely arranged among them, broad, brilliant reddish pink, frilled. Mid-season to late

'Gressenhall' 2 W-W
(H. Wormald, pre-1940)

'Greta' 2 W-P
(J.N. Hancock & Co., 1964) Unregistered

'Greta Garbo' 2 Y-O
(J.W.A. Lefeber, pre-1938)

'Gretchen' 8 W-Y
(pre-1928)
Poetaz
Perianth segments white; corona lemon yellow

'Gretel' 2 Y-P
(J.A.O'More) Mrs B.T. Simpson, 1963
'Kenmare' × 'Yantara'
Fl. 102 mm wide; perianth segments lemon yellow; corona salmon pink. Mid-season

'Gretel' 2 W-Y
(J.N. Hancock & Co., 1955) Unregistered
Fl. forming a double triangle; perianth segments broadly ovate, with blunt mucro, pure white, spreading, with broad midrib showing, overlapping half; the inner segments inflexed, with margins wavy or incurved; corona funnel-shaped, lightly ribbed, deep lemon yellow, frilled, with rim minutely crenate and narrowly flanged. Late. Resembles 'Bodilly'

'Gretna' 1 W-W
(P.D. Williams, pre-1927)

'Gretna Green' 2 Y-? (a)
(G. Zandbergen-Terwegen, pre-1939)

'Grey Dawn' 1 W-Y
(D.S. Bell) D.S. Bell, 1959
Fl. 115 mm wide. Mid-season. Resembles a more deeply frilled 'Outward'

'Grey Lady' 3 W-WWP
(G.L. Wilson, pre-1935)
'Dactyl' × 'Mystic'
Fl. 70 mm wide; perianth segments very broad, blunt or slightly truncate, prominently mucronate, slightly reflexed, overlapping half; the inner segments more nearly spreading, somewhat twisted at apex or with margins wavy; corona disc-shaped, greenish white, with a narrow band of vivid yellowish pink 30C at rim, tightly frilled. AM(e) 1940

'Grey Steel' 1 W-?
Syn. of 'Greysteel'

'Greysteel' 1 W-? (b)
(P.D. Williams, pre-1927)
See also 'Grey Steel'

'Greywoods' 2 or 3 Y-R
(R.F. Calvert, pre-1934)
Perianth segments broad, clear yellow; corona widely expanded

'Grianan' 1 W-Y
(T. Bloomer) T. Bloomer, 1964
'Rashee' × 'Empress of Ireland'; sdlg no. 4/19/58
Perianth segments pure white; corona pale lemon

'Gribben Head' 4 Y-O
(R.A.Scamp) R.A.Scamp, 1994
'Obelisk' × 'Tamar Fire'; sdlg no. 251
Fl. 89 mm wide; perianth segments ovate, golden yellow, deeply overlapping; corona segments three-quarters the length of the perianth segments, bright yellow-orange. Early to mid-season. Sunproof

'Grieve' 2 W-O
(J.A. Morris) J.A. Morris, 1964
Fl. 108 mm wide; perianth segments broad, milky white; corona reddish orange. Early. Resembles 'Signal Light' but with a darker-coloured corona

'Griffa' 2 W-OOR
(W. Jackson Jr, 1967) Unregistered
'Jo' × 'Arbar'; sdlg no. 221/67

'Grimoral' 2 Y-? (a)
(Mrs A.O. Meyrick) Mrs A.O. Meyrick, 1957

'Grindleford' 1 W-Y
(F.E. Board) F.E. Board, 1965
'Ballygarvey' × 'Preamble'; sdlg no. 366
Early

'Griselda' 2 W-Y
(A.H. Ahrens) J.S. Leitch, 1957

'Groenloo' 3 W-GWW
(G.A. Uit den Boogaard, pre-1946)

'Groote van Nek' 8 W-Y or O
(pre-1807)

'Grootvorst' 8 W-W
(pre-1851)
Corona opening citron yellow, becoming creamy white. Very early. Syn. Tazetta 'Grootvorst'. See also 'Groot Vorst'

'Groot Vorst' 8 W-W
Syn. of 'Grootvorst'

'Grosbeak' 2 Y-W
(M. Fowlds) G.E. Mitsch, 1970
('Fortune's Sun' × 'Cheerio') × 'Binkie'; sdlg no. F195/2
Perianth segments broad, lemon yellow; corona widely flared, opening yellow, becoming almost pure white. Mid-season

'Grossfürstin' 8 W-W
(pre-1850)

'Gross Glockner' 1 W-W
(J.W.A. Lefeber) J.W.A. Lefeber, 1984
Sdlg × 'Queen Juliana'
Fl. 115 mm wide; perianth segments ivory white; corona opening yellowish white (4D), becoming white, with flecks of yellow at rim. Mid-season

'Grosvenor' 4 W-P
(Brian S. Duncan) Rathowen Daffodils, 1987
'Pink Pageant' × 'Replete'; sdlg no. 754
Fl. 105 mm wide; perianth and other petaloid segments in three whorls, white; the outer whorl very broad, somewhat truncate, spreading; the second whorl shorter, inflexed, with margins incurling or folded inwards; the centre whorl fewer than six in number, strongly inflexed, with margins deeply incurled; corona segments shorter, clustered among the petaloid segments at centre and more loosely interspersed among the surrounding whorls, pink, frilled. Mid-season. Resembles 'Pink Pageant' but with corona segments of a deeper tone

'Grotto' 2 W-W
(J.S. Leitch) J.S. Leitch, 1968

'Gruinard' 2 W-Y
(J.M. de Navarro) J.M. de Navarro, 1968

'Grullemans' Giant' 2 W-YYO
(J.J. Grullemans & Sons, pre-1951)

'Grullemans Senior' 2 W-Y
(G.A. Uit den Boogaard, pre-1951)

'Gruno' 2 W-? (b)
(Mrs R.O. Backhouse, pre-1921)

'G.S.Titheradge' 2
(R.M. Pitt, pre-1914)

'Guane' 2 W-YYO
(Australian origin, 1945) R. Hyde, 1958
Perianth segments pure white; corona bright yellow, with reddish orange at rim

'Guardee' 2 O-O
(F.E. Board) F.E. Board, 1965
'Kindled' × 'Alport'
Perianth segments tangerine orange; corona reddish orange. Late

'Guardian' 2 W-Y
(G.L. Wilson, pre-1942)
('Niphetos' × 'Trostan') × 'Kanchenjunga'
Fl. 115 mm wide; perianth segments overlapping half; corona lightly ribbed, pale cream, mouth ribbed and expanded, with rim slightly dentate. AM(Haarlem) 1949, *AM(g) 1952

'Guardsman' 1 Y-Y
(Sir C.H. Cave, pre-1908)

'Gubbah' 2 Y-YOO
(A.O. Roblin, 1942)
Sdlg × 'Market Merry'

'Gudgeon' 1 Y-Y
(pre-1933)
Perianth segments clear lemon yellow; corona very pale sulphur yellow, with a narrow band of intense lemon yellow at rim

'Gudrid' 2 W-? (b)
(Mrs R.O. Backhouse, pre-1921)

'Guenda' 2 W-? (b)
(C.E. Radcliff, pre-1936)

"Guernsey Cabbage Daffodil"
Syn. of 'Telamonius Plenus'

'Guernsey Gold' 8 Y-?
(E.H. Wheadon & Sons, pre-1916)

'Guida'
(R.Fountain, pre-1931)
PC(e)(NZ) 1931

'Guide' 2 Y-O
(A.M. Wilson, pre-1944)
'Fortune' hybrid

Corona vivid reddish orange

'Guiding Light' 2 W-W
(G.W.E. Brogden)

'Guiding Star' 2 W-O
(Warnaar & Co.) Warnaar & Co., 1962
Fl. 120 mm wide; perianth segments ivory white; corona vivid orange 28B. Mid-season. AM(Haarlem) 1962

'Guido Gezelle' 9 W-?
(G. Lubbe & Son, pre-1926)
Syn. 'Gezelle'

'Guilcher's Reward' 2 Y-?
Syn. of 'Beauty of Kingsland'

'Guilder' 2 Y-? (a)
(R. Crews, pre-1949)
Syn. 'Celebrity'

'Guildhall' 2 Y-?
(T.A.V. Wood) T.A.V. Wood, 1960
Early. Resembles an earlier-flowered 'Ladbroke' with smoother perianth segments and a larger corona

'Guildhall' 1 Y-Y
(J.L. Richardson) T.A.V. Wood, 1963
'King's Ransom' × 'Ark Royal'

'Guile' 1 Y-Y
(G.L. Wilson) R.W. Ward & Son, 1959

'Guilmette' 2 Y-Y
(W. Jackson Sr, 1943)
'Gisavia' × 'Hymyr'

'Guinea Gold' 1 Y-Y
(G.P. Haydon, pre-1908)
'Glory of Leiden' × Nelsonii 'Aurantius'
Perianth segments inflexed; corona cylindrical, rich golden yellow

'Guinea Gold' 1 Y-Y
(T.H. Piper, 1955) Unregistered
'Bulwark' × 'Roundabout'

'Guinever' 3 W-Y
(W. Backhouse, pre-1869)
Corona canary yellow, frilled. Syn. Burbidgei 'Guinever'. "Absorbed" 'Wallace'

'Guinevere' 2 Y-Y
(W.H. Roesé) W.H. Roesé, 1982
'Camelot' × 'Golden Aura'; sdlg no. 70/20/3
Fl. 100 mm wide. Mid-season. Resembles an improved and earlier-flowered 'Camelot' of smoother texture and lighter colour

'Gulbrock' 4
Syn. of 'Gullrock'

'Gules' 3 W-? (b)
(G.H. Engleheart, pre-1927)

'Gull' 2 W-GWW
(G.E. Mitsch) G.E. Mitsch, 1979
'Easter Moon' × 'Broughshane' hybrid; sdlg no. Wootton65/2/7
Fl. forming a double triangle, 117 mm wide, clean white, satin smooth; perianth segments ovate or broadly ovate, blunt, spreading, with margins incurling, overlapping one-third; the inner segments more narrowly ovate, with margins wavy and more strongly incurved; corona funnel-shaped, shaded green at base, with mouth straight and loosely frilled. Mid-season. Resembles 'Broomhill' but with longer perianth segments and more green in the corona. Pannill Award 1997

'Gulliver' 3 Y-YYO
(P.D. Williams, pre-1927)
Fl. 90 mm wide; broadly ovate, not prominently mucronate, light greenish yellow 5C, paling to white at upper midrib and apex, spreading or a little reflexed, overlapping one-third to a half; the inner segments more narrowly ovate, more nearly spreading, with broad midrib showing and margins wavy; corona bowl-shaped, closely ribbed, vivid yellow 12A, with a broad band of vivid orange 12B at rim, mouth widely expanded, even, rim irregularly notched. $2n=28$. AM(Haarlem) 1938, *C(g) 1941, *AM(g) 1947

'Gullrock' 4
(E. & J.C. Martin, pre-1931)
See also 'Gulbrock'

'Gulvain' 2 W-W
(de Graaff Bros, pre-1950)
AM(Haarlem) 1950

'Gulval' 2 Y-YOO
(C. Dawson, pre-1925)
Perianth segments sulphur yellow, somewhat inflexed; corona scarlet-orange, paling to bright yellow at base

'Gundagai' 2 Y-O
(J.N. Hancock & Co., pre-1949)
Perianth segments pale yellow; corona with reddish orange at rim

'Gunnerside' 3 Y-O
(Jan Dalton, 1985) Jan Dalton, 1997
'Revelry' × 'Achduart'; sdlg no. 794/1
Mid-season

'Gunners Mate' 1 Y-Y
(Jackson's Daffodils, 1976) Jackson's Daffodils, 1986

'Otewa' × 'Ristin'; sdlg no. 51/76
Perianth segments vivid yellow 9A; corona slightly brighter in tone (12A). Mid-season

'Gunsmoke' 1 W-Y
(D.S. Bell) D.S. Bell, 1982
Fl. 100 mm wide; corona funnel-shaped, regularly frilled. Mid-season

'Gunsynd' 2 Y-ORR
(W. Jackson Jr, 1966) Unregistered
Sdlg 111/57 × sdlg 110/56; sdlg no. 65/66

'Gunthorpe Belle' 2 W-? (b)
(J.R. Pearson & Sons, pre-1935)
'Will Scarlett' × 'Elfrida Pearson'

'Gunwalloe' 11a Y-R
(R.A.Scamp) R.A.Scamp, 1996
'Brandaris' × 'Falstaff'; sdlg no. 291
Fl. 95 mm wide; perianth segments broad, rich golden yellow, deeply overlapping; corona split, the six segments opposite and closely overlying the perianth segments, bright red. Mid-season to late

'Gunyak' 2 Y-Y
(A.O. Roblin, 1942)
'Golden Legend' × 'Marengo'

N. gussonei Rouy = *N. tazetta* subsp. *gussonei*

'Gustav Doré' 3 W-? (b)
(J.W.A. Lefeber, pre-1943)

'Gustav Mahler' 2 W-Y
(Konynenburg & Mark, pre-1953)
'Toscanini' × 'John Evelyn'

'Gustavus Adolphus' 8 W-Y or O
(Dutch origin, pre-1807)

'Gusto' 2 Y-Y
(G.L. Wilson, pre-1944)
'Hopeful' × 'Havelock'
Fl. buttercup yellow

'Guthers' 2 Y-? (a)
(P.D. Williams, pre-1931)

'Guthrum' 1 Y-Y
(T. Buncombe, pre-1934)

'Guvezne' 2 W-O
(D. Blanchard, pre-1947)
'Mitylene' × 'Hades'

'Guy Gibson' 2 Y-O
(F. Rijnveld & Sons, 1950) F. Rijnveld & Sons, 1962
Perianth segments deep yellow. Mid-season. Resembles a large and earlier-flowered 'Scarlet Elegance'

'Guy's Gift' 1 Y-Y
(G.L. Wilson) C.R. Wootton, 1958
'Kingscourt' × ('Rolled Gold' × 'Bastion')

'Gwaine' 1 W-W
(W. Jackson Jr, 1950)
'Sancia' × 'Colmolhari'

'Gweal' 9 W-YYR
(Ken Farmer Nurseries) Ken Farmer Nurseries, 1978
Fl. 88 mm wide; corona whitish yellow, with red at rim. Mid-season

'Gweek' 2 Y-Y
(R.V. Favell, pre-1940)
'Goldbeater' × 'Fortune'

'Gweleath' 2
(P.D. Williams, pre-1927)

'Gwen Best' 1 Y-WWY
(F. Silcock, 1981) F. Silcock, 1993
Seedling hybrid
Perianth segments lemon yellow, deepening with age, with white at base, the colour deepening with age; corona narrow at base, whitish, with lemon yellow at rim, frilled. Early

'Gwenda' 2 W-WWR
(C.E. Radcliff, 1931)
'Pink'un' × 'Fotis'

'Gwendal' 1 Y-Y
(W.A. Watts, pre-1927)

'Gwendalin' 1 W-Y
Syn. of 'Gwendolin'

'Gwendolin' 1 W-Y
(G.P. Haydon, pre-1905)
Perianth segments broadly ovate, somewhat truncate, very slightly mucronate, ivory white, spreading, ribbed and a little twisted, overlapping one-third to a half; the inner segments more strongly twisted; corona cylindrical, pale primrose yellow, with mouth ribbed and widely expanded, rim very deeply notched and crenate, with margins flanged. See also 'Gwendalin'

'Gweneth' 2 W-YOR
(G. Lewis) D.S. Bell, 1955
See also 'Gwineth'

'Gwen Fleming' 1 Y-Y
(?W.M. Spry, pre-1960) Unregistered
Perianth segments broad, rich yellow; corona narrow, deeper in tone than the perianth, with rim slightly rolled. ?The same as 'Gwen Flemming'

'Gwen Flemming' 2 W-?

(O. Ronalds)
?The same as 'Gwen Fleming'

'Gwennap' 1 Y-Y
(R.A. Scamp) R.A. Scamp, 1991
'Empress of Ireland' × 'Fine Gold'; sdlg no. 136
Fl. 108 mm wide, vivid yellow 12A; perianth segments broadly ovate; corona smooth, mouth a little expanded, neatly and regularly frilled. Mid-season

'Gwen Nash' 2 W-?
(Alister Clark, 1940) J. Sharp, 1960

'Gwennie' 3 W-W
(Campbell Duncan, 1950)
'Mr Jinks' × 'Moina'

'Gwen Sampson' 2 W-P
(J.N. Hancock & Co., 1965) Unregistered

'Gwenter' 2 W-W
(P.D. Williams, pre-1927)
Corona with rim rolled. See also 'Gwinter'

'Gwills' 3 W-GWO
(P.D. Williams, pre-1927)

'Gwinear' 2 Y-Y
(R.A. Scamp) R.A. Scamp, 1993
'Saint Keverne' × 'Golden Aura'; sdlg no. 308
Fl. rounded, 102 mm wide, rich golden yellow; perianth segments broadly ovate, blunt, slightly mucronate, spreading, smooth, with broad midrib sometimes showing, overlapping half; the inner segments roundish, a little inflexed; corona with mouth expanded, regularly and tightly frilled. Mid-season

'Gwineth' 2 W-YOR
Syn. of 'Gweneth'

'Gwinter' 2 W-W
Syn. of 'Gwenter'

'Gwlyfa' 2 W-? (b)
(W.A. Watts, pre-1931)

'G.W.Miller' 2 W-? (b)
(Miller, pre-1907)

'Gwyn' 1 W-W
(A.O. Roblin, c.1966) Unregistered
('Bura' × 'Karanja') × 'Mowbray'

'Gwynne' 2 Y-Y
Syn. of 'Goola'

'Gwyrif' 2 W-YYR
(G.H. Johnstone, pre-1943)

'Gwyther' 3 Y-O

(E. Leeds, pre-1877)
Perianth segments ovate, blunt, yellow, slightly reflexed, with margins wavy or recurved, occasionally twisted, overlapping at base only; corona cup-shaped, ribbed, suffused orange, with mouth straight and a little frilled

'Gyda' 3 W-YYR
(W. Jackson Sr, 1936)
'Mountain Pride' × 'Blodwen'
Perianth segments broad, pure white, deeply overlapping; corona lemon yellow, with bright red at rim

'Gydene' 1 W-? (b)
(W.A. Bell, pre-1949)
PC(e)(NZ) 1951

'Gyges' 8 Y-Y
(pre-1798)

'Gypsum' 5
(?E.M. Crosfield, pre-1913)

'Gypsy' 2 O-R
(J.L. Richardson) M.J. Jefferson-Brown, 1964
Perianth segments suffused with orange tan; corona brick red

'Gypsy Lad'
(pre-1915)

'Gypsy Maid' 2 W-Y
(R.C.A. Tombleson) R.C.A. Tombleson, 1959

'Gypsy Princess' 2 W-P
(Murray W. Evans, 1970) David L.Sheppard, 1982
'Cordial' × 'Accent'
Mid-season. Resembles a more brightly coloured and longer-lasting 'Accent'

'Gypsy Rose' 2 W-YYP
(J.N. Hancock & Co., 1965) Unregistered

'Gypsy Tap' 3 W-O
(S.C. Gaspar) R.J. Abernethy, 1960
Fl. rounded, 89 mm wide; perianth segments white, with the corona colour radiating slightly from base; corona apricot orange, paling towards base, frilled. See also 'Gipsy Tap'

'Gyre' 2 W-W
(A.O. Roblin, 1940)
'Suda' × 'Finn'

'Gyrfalcon' 2 W-Y
(E.M. Crosfield, pre-1913)
Fl. 108 mm wide; perianth segments white, tinged green; corona pale primrose yellow, with a faint greenish cast. Tall. *C(g) 1930

H

'Haagdis' 8 Y-Y
(pre-1798)
Fl. sulphur yellow

'Haarlem' 1 Y-Y
(J. de Groot & Sons, pre-1913)

'Habit' 1 Y-Y
(Jackson's Daffodils) Jackson's Daffodils, 1996
'Ricom' × sdlg 3/74; sdlg no. 3/89
Fl. 111 mm wide; perianth segments broadly ovate, vivid yellow 9A; the outer segments overlapping one another; corona funnel-shaped, darker in tone (13B) than the perianth, with mouth flared and frilled. Early

'Hacienda' 1 Y-YOO
(Murray W. Evans, 1975) Murray W. Evans, 1985
'Arctic Gold' × 'Brer Fox'; sdlg no. Q-20/1
Corona reddish orange. Mid-season

'Haddon' 2 W-W
(F.E. Board) F.E. Board, 1965
('Nilkanta' × 'Murmansk') × 'Knowehead'; sdlg no. 1067
Late

'Hades' 2 W-R
(Mrs R.O. Backhouse, pre-1921)
Perianth segments broadly ovate, blunt, prominently mucronate, creamy white, spreading, with incurled margins reducing the apparent width, overlapping one-third; the inner segments a little inflexed, with margins sometimes nicked at shoulder; corona broad and shallow bowl-shaped, ribbed, deep cherry red, with mouth even and rim raggedly crenate. Mid-season. Syn. 'Glad Eye'. PC(e) 1925, AM(e) 1928

'Hadley' 3 W-O
(de Graaff Bros, pre-1931)
Perianth segments pure white; corona deep orange. AM(Haarlem) 1931

'Hadlow Down' 1 Y-Y
(N.A.Burr, 1985) N.A.Burr, 1996
'Camelot' × 'Ballyrobert'; sdlg no. 2.1.79
Fl. 97 mm wide; perianth segments broadly ovate, vivid yellow 9A, with slight white mucro, spreading, with margins sometimes a little recurved, overlapping half; the inner segments square-shouldered at base, somewhat inflexed, with margins a little wavy; corona cylindrical, smooth, darker in tone than the perianth, with mouth lightly ribbed and a little expanded, even, rim very slightly flanged and shallowly crenate. Late

'Hadrada' 3 W-? (b)
(H. Backhouse, pre-1910)

'Hadrian' 1 Y-Y
(S.J. Bisdee, pre-1939)
('Victor' × 'Renown') hybrid

'Hadspen' 2 W-W
(C.E. Radcliff, 1937)
Sdlg × 'Nymphea'

'Haemon' 8
(M. van Waveren & Sons, pre-1916)
Poetaz

'Haeremai' 2 Y-YYR
(W.E. Weightman, pre-1936)
Perianth segments broad, lemon yellow; corona large, shallow, with cinnabar red at rim

'Hafey' 1 Y-Y
(D. Jackson) Jackson's Daffodils, 1983
'Ristin' × 'Berit'; sdlg no. 5/77
Fl. 112 mm wide. Mid-season

'Hafiz' 9 W-OOR
(G.H. Engleheart, pre-1914)
Fl. small; perianth segments rounded at apex, pure white; corona with a narrow band of red at rim

'Hagar' 2 W-GYY
(J.N. Hancock & Co., pre-1988) Unregistered

'Hagar' 1 Y-Y
(R.H.Glover, pre-1989) Unregistered
'Dream Prince' × 'Warbin'

'Hagen' 1 Y-Y
(G.L. Wilson, pre-1932)

'Hagley' 1 Y-Y
(C.E. Radcliff, 1943) J.M.Radcliff, 1956
'Wang' × 'Fahan'

'Hailstone' 2 W-? (b or c)
(Papendrecht-Vandervoet, pre-1939)

'Hailstone' 5 W-W
Syn. of 'Hailstorm'

'Hailstorm' 2 or 3 W-? (b or c)
(?J. Wilson, pre-1933)

'Hail Storm' 1 W-W
(J.N. Hancock & Co., 1946)
Fl. rounded; perianth segments very broad; corona opening very pale lemon, becoming white, with rim dentate and widely flanged

'Hailstorm' 5 W-W
(D. & J.W. Blanchard, 1955) D. & J.W. Blanchard, 1968
N. triandrus var. *loiseleurii* × *N. rupicola*

Fl. 21 mm wide; perianth segments strongly reflexed, overlapping at base only; the inner segments slightly narrower; corona greenish white (155A), with mouth constricted and slightly frilled, rim entire. Mid-season. Resembles 'Icicle'. AM(p) 1968. Shown 1968 as 'Hailstone'

'Haitana' 1 W-P
(R. Hyde) R. Hyde, 1957
'New Idea' self pollinated

'Haka' 1 Y-Y
(W. Jackson Jr, 1956) Unregistered
'Moque' × 'Jobi'

'Hakon' 2 Y-? (a)
(W. Jackson Sr, 1938)
('Fortune' × 'Beacon') × 'Flamwen'

'Hakone' 3 Y-YYR
(P. Phillips) P. Phillips, 1971

'Halak' 1 W-W
(A.O. Roblin, 1958) Unregistered
'Mowbray' × 'Truth'

'Halberd' 1 W-W
(G.H. Engleheart, pre-1914)

'Halcyon' 2 W-? (b)
(R.H. Bath, pre-1933)

'Halcyon' 2 W-PPY
(F.E. Board) F.E. Board, 1965
Richardson sdlg × G.L.Wilson sdlg
Corona flanged

'Halcyone'
(pre-1914)

'Haldor' 1 Y-Y
(W. Jackson Sr, 1947)
'Vuster' × 'Han'

'Halesowen' 2 W-YOO
(Horace Goodwin) Horace Goodwin, 1992
'Ringleader' × 'Ben Vorlich'; sdlg no. G7-1-83
Fl. 88 mm wide; perianth segments broadly ovate, deeply overlapping; corona bowl-shaped, frilled. Mid-season

"Hales' Vase of Beaten Gold"
?Variant of Pseudonarcissus Major 'Maximus'

'Halfa' 1 W-Y
(The Brodie of Brodie, c.1920)
'Queen of the West' × 'White Emperor'
Perianth segments broadly ovate, fairly prominently mucronate, creased, overlapping one-third to a half; the inner segments twisted and with margins nicked; corona cylindrical, broadly ribbed, soft yellow, rim notched and tightly rolled. Early

'Half Moon' 5 Y-Y
(de Graaff Bros) de Graaff Bros & van Konynenburg & Co., 1956
'Moonshine' sport
AM(Haarlem) 1956

'Half Pint' 6 Y-Y
(James S. Wells) James S. Wells, 1993
'Little Beauty' × *N. cyclamineus*; sdlg no. 83-58
Fl. 50 mm wide. Dwarf. Early. Resembles a half-sized 'February Gold'

'Half Tone' 3 W-Y
(Sidney DuBose, 1977) Sidney DuBose, 1997
'Olivet' self pollinated; sdlg no. E71-1
Fl. 65 mm wide, ageing to Y-W. Mid-season. Varies between Divs 3 and 2

'Halgarry' 3 W-YYR
(J.S.B. Lea) Clive Postles Daffodils, 1985
Sdlg 1-27-67 × Blanchard sdlg 68/15A; sdlg no. 1-25-76
Perianth segments broadly ovate, truncate, margins sometimes slightly incurving near apex, overlapping two-thirds; corona very shallow bowl-shaped, rich orange-yellow, ribbed, with a well-defined narrow band of orange-red at rim, lightly but closely frilled. Mid-season

'Halidom' 2 W-W
(A.M. Wilson, pre-1947)

'Halima' 2 Y-O
(J.T. Gray, pre-1949)
Corona deep reddish orange

'Halingy' 8 W-Y
(A. Gray, pre-1949)
'Scilly White' hybrid
Corona pale yellow

'Halkett' 3 W-YRR
(J.A. Morris) J.A. Morris, 1964
Fl. 108 mm wide. Mid-season. Resembles a large and earlier-flowered 'Marewa'

'Hallali' 4 W-O
(J.L. Richardson) Mrs H.K. Richardson, 1964
'Gay Time' × 'Tulyar'
Perianth and other petaloid segments in many whorls, pure white; the outer whorl broad and rounded; the inner whorls narrower; corona segments smaller than the petaloid segments and interspersed among them, bright reddish orange. Scented. Resembles a smaller 'Acropolis'

'Hallamshire' 1 Y-Y
(F.E. Board) F.E. Board, 1965
'Ormeau' × 'Arctic Gold'; sdlg no. 486
Late

'Hall Caine' 2 Y-? (a)
(M. van Waveren & Sons, pre-1910)
Fl. tinted sulphur yellow

'Halleluliah' 2 Y-? (a)
(de Graaff Bros, pre-1948)

'Halley' 2 Y-? (a)
(Mrs R.O. Backhouse, pre-1921)
AM(Haarlem) 1932

'Halley's Comet' 3 W-GYY
(Mrs J. Abel Smith) Mrs J. Abel Smith, 1986
'Verona' × 'Thoresby'; sdlg no. I44/91
Fl. smooth and of strong substance; corona very shallow bowl-shaped, deep yellow, with green at base. Late

'Hallmark' 1 Y-Y
(J. Hall, pre-1927)
Fl. rich yellow; corona expanded and frilled

'Halloween' 1 Y-Y
(Oregon Bulb Farms, pre-1946)

'Hallworthy' 2 W-Y
(Mrs J. Abel Smith) du Plessis Bros, 1989
'Green Island' × 'Ave'; sdlg no. 3/01
Fl. 130 mm wide; perianth segments narrowly ovate, pure white; corona broad, with rim rolled. Mid-season

'Halo' 3 W-? (b)
(F.H. Chapman, pre-1913)

'Halo' 2 Y-R
(J.L.Richardson, pre-1957) Unregistered
'Carbineer' × 'Sun Chariot'; sdlg no. 122

'Halolight' 2 Y-W
(G.E. Mitsch) G.E. Mitsch, 1960
'Binkie' × ('King of the North' × 'Content'); sdlg no. P5/21
Fl. 115 mm wide, opening sulphur lemon yellow; corona becoming white. Mid-season. Resembles 'Daydream' but with longer and more acute perianth segments and a longer and narrower corona

'Halos' 2 Y-? (a)
(A.H. Ahrens) J.S. Leitch, 1955

'Halskraag' 11a W-W
(?Dutch origin, pre-1959) Unregistered

'Halstock' 2 Y-W
(J.W. Blanchard) J.W. Blanchard, 1986

'Golden Aura' × 'Daydream'; sdlg no. 73/15J
Corona white, with pale yellow outside. Mid-season

'Halvasso' 6 W-W
(R.A.Scamp, 1985) R.A.Scamp, 1997
'Knowehead' × *N. cyclamineus*; sdlg no. 138
Fl. 70 mm wide, pure white; perianth segments narrow, plane, strongly reflexed; corona cylindrical, with mouth frilled. Dwarf. Early to mid-season

'Halvose' 8 Y-O
(P.D. Williams, pre-1927)
Poetaz
Fls 2-3 per stem, 45 mm wide; perianth segments broadly ovate, truncate, very prominently mucronate, clear yellow, flushed coppery orange at base, spreading or a little inflexed, with margins incurling, overlapping; the inner segments a little narrower, more nearly spreading, creased; corona shallow bowl-shaped, ribbed, vermilion orange, very deeply 3-lobed, with the lobes overlapping and wavy. AM(Haarlem) 1926. See also 'Helvose'

'Halwyn' 1 Y-Y
(P.D. Williams, pre-1927)

'Hambledon' 2 YYW-Y
(J.W. Blanchard) J.W. Blanchard, 1985
'Golden Aura' × 'Daydream'; sdlg no. 73/15E
Perianth segments very broadly ovate, brilliant greenish yellow 4A, with a narrow band of sulphur white at base; corona opening brilliant yellow 13B, flushed buff yellow, becoming yellow. Mid-season. Resembles a far smoother-textured 'Amber Castle'. AM(e) 1982

'Hambleton' 2 W-R
(W.A. Noton, pre-1991) Unregistered
'Rockall' × 'Avenger'
Perianth segments deeply overlapping; corona expanded, orange-red. Mid-season

'Hamelin' 2 W-Y
(Mrs B.T. Simpson) Mrs B.T. Simpson, 1966
Fl. 127 mm wide; corona clear yellow. Mid-season

'Hamilton' 2 W-YYO
(West & Fell, pre-1935)
Perianth segments pure white; corona lemon, with a broad band of apricot at rim

'Hamings'
(pre-1913)

'Hamish' 1
(pre-1913)

'Hamish' 2 Y-? (a)
(J.L. Richardson) V.M. Dickinson, 1955
PC(e)(NZ) 1949

'Hamish' 2 Y-R
(?New Zealand origin, pre-1990) Unregistered

'Hamlet' 1 Y-Y
(Barr & Sons, pre-1905)
Perianth segmens broad, primrose yellow; corona darker in tone. Early. Resembles 'Emperor'

'Hammerfest' 2 W-W
(A.M. Wilson, pre-1951)

'Hammoon' 3 W-Y
(D. & J.W. Blanchard, 1952) D. & J.W. Blanchard, 1968
'Hamzali' × 'Green Island'
Fl. 108 mm wide; perianth segments very broad, rounded at apex, mucronate, spreading, plane, overlapping half; the inner segments more narrowly ovate, with margins incurling or wavy; corona very shallow bowl-shaped, lightly ribbed, pale primrose yellow, with green at base and a narrow band of darker yellow at rim, mouth expanded and lightly frilled, rim densely and minutely notched. Mid-season. Resembles 'Green Island' but with a longer, wider and more lightly frilled corona

'Hampstead' 3 W-YYR
(Alfred Clark) Alfred Clark, 1955
Perianth segments white, of thick substance; corona almost disc-shaped, yellow, with a broad band of red at rim. AM(e)(NZ) 1957

'Hampton Court' 2 Y-YOO
(Clive Postles, 1984) Clive Postles Daffodils, 1994
Sdlg 47-75 (sdlg × 'Bunclody') × 'Torridon'; sdlg no. 1-94-80
Fl. rounded, 90 mm wide; perianth segments blunt; corona funnel-shaped, with mouth wavy and rim crenate. Early

'Hamzali' 3 W-WYR
(D. Blanchard, pre-1948)
'Marco' × ('Silver Plane' × ?'Rinsey')
Fl. rounded, 90 mm wide; perianth segments snow white, plane, with margins slightly incurving, overlapping half; corona disc-shaped, ribbed, citron yellow, with creamy white at base and a narrow band of orange-red (33B at rim, mouth straight, expanded and frilled, rim finely dentate. AM(e) 1957

'Han' 1 Y-Y
(W. Jackson Sr, 1941)
'Lao-tzu' × 'Crocus'

'Hanbury' 2 W-W
(Clive Postles, 1985) Clive Postles Daffodils, 1995
'Ben Avon' × 'Panache'; sdlg no. 1-43-80
Fl. 115 mm wide; perianth segments very broadly ovate, pure white, with margins slightly incurving; corona cylindrical, touched green at base, mouth flared and wavy. Early

'Handcross' 2 Y-Y
(Sir F.C. Stern) Sir F.C. Stern, 1957
'Binkie' × 'New Timber'
Fl. 115 mm wide; perianth segments light greenish yellow 5C, overlapping half; corona slightly ribbed, paler than the perianth, with mouth expanded and frilled, rim dentate. AM(e) 1957

'Händel' 2 W-O
(Konynenburg & Mark, pre-1953)
'Frederike' × 'Mimosa'

'Handicap' 1 W-W
(Sir C.H. Cave, pre-1928)

'Handmaiden' 2 W-W
(F.E. Board) F.E. Board, 1965
'Killaloe' × 'Empress of Ireland'

'Handsome' 2 or 3 Y-O
(F.H. Chapman, pre-1937)
'Fortune' × 'Kestrel'
Perianth segments creamy yellow; corona expanded, reddish orange

'Handsome' 1 Y-Y
Syn. of 'Royal Oak'

'Handsome Lake' 2 W-Y
(W.A. Bender) W.A. Bender, 1996
'Flash Affair' × 'Lod'
Fl. 92 mm wide, of good substance; perianth segments broadly ovate, spreading, plane; corona cylindrical, vivid yellow 14B, with mouth straight and lightly frilled. Tall. Mid-season

'Haneda' 2 Y-Y
(P. & G. Phillips) P. & G. Phillips, 1975
Fl. 115 mm wide. Mid-season. Resembles a slightly lighter-coloured 'Galway' with smoother and broader perianth segments and a less deeply rolled corona rim

'Hang-five' 1 W-Y
(W. Jackson Jr) Jackson's Daffodils, 1983
'Daric' × 'Nala'; sdlg no. 130/77

'Hanibal' 8 Y-Y
(pre-1807)
Fl. sulphur yellow

'Hanibal' 11b Y-O/Y
Syn. of 'Hannibal'

'Hanley Swan' 1 W-W
(J.S.B. Lea) Clive Postles Daffodils, 1990
'Panache' × sdlg 1-11-71; sdlg no. 1-11-76
Fl. 112 mm wide; perianth segments broadly ovate,

smooth, deeply overlapping; corona narrowly funnel-shaped, with mouth flared and rim neatly dentate. Early

'Hanmer' 2 W-Y
(?New Zealand origin, pre-1990) Unregistered

'Hannah Langhorn'
(pre-1913)

'Hannah More' 9 W-?
(pre-1914)

'Hanneke' 1 Y-Y
(R.H.Glover, pre-1993) Unregistered

'Hannibal' 1 Y-Y
(P.D. Williams, pre-1907)

'Hannibal' 11b Y-O/Y
(J.W.A. Lefeber, c.1968) Unregistered
Perianth segments yellow; corona segments with orange in a longitudinal band at midrib and yellow at margins. 2n=28. See also 'Hanibal'

'Hanover' 2 Y-W
(P. Phillips) P. Phillips, 1966
Fl. 125 mm wide, opening lemon yellow; corona becoming white, flushed primrose yellow. Mid-season

'Hans Andersen' 2 Y-? (a)
(Konynenburg & Mark, pre-1954)

'Hans Christian Andersen' 1 Y-Y
(Konynenburg & Mark) Konynenburg & Mark, 1960
Fl. 115 mm wide; perianth segments brilliant greenish yellow 6C; corona vivid yellow 12A. Mid-season

'Han van Meegeren' 2 Y-? (a)
(J.W.A. Lefeber, pre-1949)
Corona large, with a broad band of red at rim, frilled

'Hanya' 2 W-P
(C.R. Wootton) C.R. Wootton, 1958
'Evening' × 'Salmon Trout'
Perianth segments ivory white; corona copper pink

'Happiness' 2 W-? (b)
(P. van Deursen, pre-1930)

'Happiness' 2 Y-R
(J.L. Richardson) G. Zandbergen-Terwegen, 1960
Fl. 100 mm wide; perianth segments deep golden yellow; corona rich orange-red. Very early. Resembles a darker-coloured 'Ceylon'

'Happy Birthday' 3 Y-YYR
(David Karnstedt) David Karnstedt, 1992

Sdlg no. 83-32-13
Fl. rounded, 82 mm wide; perianth segments ovate to very broadly ovate, vivid greenish yellow 2A, very slightly reflexed, satin smooth; the inner segments spreading; corona bowl-shaped, vivid greenish yellow 2A, with deep moss green noticeable in tube and a narrow band of orange-red (33A) at rim, mouth straight and frilled, rim crenate. Mid-season

'Happy Day' 2 W-? (b)
(Mrs F.S. Foote, pre-1940)

'Happy Easter' 5
(?R.H. Bath, c.1936)
2n=21

'Happy Elf' 6
(S.S. Berry, pre-1937)

'Happy Ending' 4 W-W
(Mary Lou Gripshover, 1982) Mary Lou Gripshover, 1997
'White Sail' × 'Glory of Lisse'; sdlg no. 75-17
Fl. 55 mm wide; perianth and other petaloid segments white; the outer whorl broadly ovate; the inner whorls more narrowly ovate; corona segments minute. Very late. Resembles a more robust 'White Sail'. Varies between Divs 4 and 3

'Happy Event' 2 Y-ROO
(J.L. Richardson) M.J. Jefferson-Brown, 1964
'Sun Chariot' × 'Ceylon'

'Happy Face' 2 W-O
(Carncairn Daffodils, 1968) Carncairn Daffodils, 1979
'Chinese White' × 'Fermoy'; sdlg no. 1/63
Fl. 110 mm wide; perianth segments yellowish white 155B; corona expanded, buff orange (16A). Mid-season. Resembles 'Tudor Minstrel' but with the perianth more rounded and the corona more widely expanded and of a different colour

'Happy Fellow' 2 Y-YOO
(A.J.R. Pearson) A.J.R. Pearson, 1994
'Camelot' × 'Hot Gossip'; sdlg no. 85-18-J11
Fl. forming a double triangle, 110 mm wide; perianth segments very broadly ovate, blunt, vivid yellow 9A, spreading, plane, smooth and of great substance, overlapping two-thirds; the inner segments only a little narrower, more nearly acute; corona bowl-shaped, ribbed, opening yellow, becoming orange (23A) after several days, with yellow at base, mouth flared, rim lightly crenate. Early to mid-season. Sunproof

'Happy Hour' 7 Y-O
(Roberta C.Watrous) Roberta C.Watrous, 1974
'Sun Chariot' × *N. jonquilla*; sdlg no. 633-6
Fl. 55 mm wide; perianth segments vivid yellow 12A; corona strong orange 25A. Early

Fls 1-3 per stem, 76 mm wide, clear yellow, at an acute angle to the stem; perianth segments broadly ovate, reflexed, plane, overlapping; corona cylindrical or somewhat funnel-shaped, short, darker in tone than the perianth, with mouth a little expanded and rim crenate. Mid-season. Resembles a shorter-stemmed and more floriferous 'King's Sutton'

'Harmony Bells' 5 Y-Y
(J.N. Hancock & Co., pre-1988) Unregistered

'Harold Alston' 2 Y-R
(West & Fell, pre-1935)
Perianth segments very broadly ovate, truncate, deep yellow, smooth, overlapping half; the inner segments more narrowly ovate, with margins incurling and midrib showing; corona widely expanded, ribbed, orange-red, with a broad band of scarlet at rim, closely frilled

'Harold Beale' 1 Y-Y
(M. van Waveren & Sons, pre-1930)
Perianth segments pale yellow; corona flared

'Harold Everwyn' 1 Y-Y
(A. Frylink & Sons, pre-1930)
AM(Haarlem) 1930

'Harold Finn' 3 W-O
(F.H. Chapman, pre-1908)
Perianth segments pure white; corona bright reddish orange. See also 'Harold Fynn', 'Harold Linn'

'Harold Fynn' 3 W-O
Syn. of 'Harold Finn'

'Harold Hodge' 1 W-W
Syn. of 'Lieut.H.Hodges'

'Harold Hodge' 3 W-YYR
Syn. of 'Harold Lodge'

'Harold Hodges' 1 W-W
Syn. of 'Lieut.H.Hodges'

'Harold Linn' 3 W-O
Syn. of 'Harold Finn'

'Harold Lodge' 3 W-YYR
(Mrs R.O. Backhouse, pre-1904)
See also 'Harold Hodge'

'Harold Low' 6 Y-Y
(L.P. Dettman) L.P. Dettman, 1979
'Charity May' × 'Harmony Bells'; sdlg no. HB 1/74
Fl. 78 mm wide; perianth segments brilliant greenish yellow (2B); corona darker in tone (7A). Mid-season. Resembles a larger and lighter-coloured 'Harmony Bells'

'Harold's Favorite' 2 W-PPW
(John R.Reed, 1985) John R.Reed, 1997
'Precedent' × 'Vahu'; sdlg no. 79-26-1
Fl. rounded, 89 mm wide; perianth segments broadly ovate, of great substance, overlapping; the inner segments almost touching one another; corona bowl-shaped, ribbed, deep strawberry pink, with a line of white at rim, with the rim deeply and narrowly notched. Mid-season. Sunproof

'Haros' 2 W-R
(pre-1960) Unregistered
Perianth segments creamy white; corona intense bright red

'Harpagon' 3 Y-YYO
(A.M. Wilson, pre-1913)
Fl. 89 mm wide; perianth segments pale primrose yellow, with margins lightly incurved, overlapping; corona very shallow, expanded, shading to bright reddish orange at rim

'Harperrig' 2 Y-Y
(A.M. Wilson, pre-1948)
Fl. clear yellow; corona wide, shallow, frilled

'Harpeth Hills Moon' 1 Y-Y
(Mrs P.M. Davis, pre-1948)

'Harpist' 1 Y-Y
(W.B. Cranfield, pre-1926)
PC(c) 1926

'Harpton' 1 Y-Y
(A.M. Wilson, pre-1950)

'Harpur Crewe' 2 W-Y
(E. Leeds, pre-1877)
Fl. very large. Syn. Incomparabilis Albus 'Harpur Crewe'. Was "absorbed" into 'Queen Bess'

'Harrier' 2 Y-O
(J.L. Richardson, pre-1948)
'Porthilly' × 'Rustom Pasha'
Perianth segments golden; corona scarlet-orange

'Harriet' 2 W-GWY
(J.M. de Navarro) J.M. de Navarro, 1977
'Syracuse' × 'Tobernaveen'
Fl. 88 mm wide; corona white, with green at base, the rim maturing from pale biscuit to yellow and ageing to white. Mid-season. Resembles a stronger-stemmed 'Evenlode' with a whiter and smoother perianth and the corona rim of a different tone

'Harriet Beecher Stowe' 2 W-R
(pre-1965) Unregistered
Corona bright red

'Happy Miss' 7 Y-?
(Mrs P.M. Davis, pre-1948)

'Happy Moments' 2 Y-YYR
(G. Lewis, 1940) D.S. Bell, 1958

'Happy Prince' 2 W-O
(J.N. Hancock & Co., 1968) Unregistered

'Happy Prospect' 2 W-? (b)
(J.P. Wesselman, pre-1943)
AM(Haarlem) 1943

'Happy Sentinel' 3 W-Y
(G.L. Wilson, pre-1949)
'Nelly' × 'Chinese White'

'Happy Smiles' 2 W-WYO
(M.E.Brogden, pre-1995) Unregistered
'Conquest' × 'Bandit'

'Happy Talk' 2 WWG-P
(Sidney DuBose, 1982) Sidney DuBose, 1996
'Precedent' × 'Salome'; sdlg no. G67-11
Fl. 85 mm wide. Mid-season

'Happy Thought' 9 W-GYR
(Mrs M.S. Yerger) Mrs M.S. Yerger, 1989
'Quetzal' × 'Ace of Diamonds'; sdlg no. 77 G 5
Fl. 52 mm wide; corona very shallow bowl-shaped, brilliant greenish yellow 3B, with strong yellow-green 144A at base and orange-red (33A) at rim. Mid-season

'Harbinger' 1 Y-Y
(Barr & Sons, pre-1900)
Perianth segments sulphur yellow; corona darker in tone. Early

'Harbinger' 1 W-Y
(R.A. van der Schoot, pre-1923)
Corona very large, widely expanded. Syn. 'Magnificent'. FA(Haarlem) 1927

'Harbinger of Spring' 1 Y-Y
(pre-1979) Unregistered
2n=27

'Harborne'
(pre-1915)

'Harbour Lights' 8 W-O
(A.E. Lowe, pre-1915)
Fls 4-5 per stem; corona large, orange

'Harcourt' 2 Y-Y
(R. Hyde) R. Hyde, 1959
'Kingscourt' × 'Ohakea'
Fl. rounded; perianth segments plane, smooth; corona with rim rolled

'Hardy' 3 W-O
(F. Rijnveld & Sons, pre-1943)
Perianth segments sulphur white; corona orange, with a narrow band of a lighter tone at rim, densely frilled. AM(Haarlem) 1942

'Hardy Lee' 4
(K.van der Veek, pre-1994) Unregistered

'Harebell' 2 W-? (b or c)
(P.D. Williams, pre-1927)

'Harewood' 1 Y-Y
(A. Gibson, pre-1949)
'Kingscourt' × 'Royalist'
Fl. deep yellow. PC(e)(NZ) 1949, AM(e)(NZ) 1951

'Hari Hari' 1 Y-Y
(D.van Buggenum) Jac J.van der Berg, 1995
Fl. 100-110 mm wide; perianth segments brilliant yellow 7A to B; corona broad, broghter in tone (a little darker than 12A). Late

'Harina' 2 W-P
(J.N. Hancock & Co., 1959) Unregistered

'Harlaw' 2 Y-O
(A.M. Wilson, pre-1948)
Perianth segments soft yellow; corona deeply ribbed, reddish orange

'Harleman' 8 Y-Y
(pre-1807)

'Harlequin' 2 Y-? (a)
(Mrs R.O. Backhouse, pre-1908)

'Harlequin' 2 W-YOO
(E.F. Hughes) E.F. Hughes, 1962
Fl. 121 mm wide; perianth segments stained yellow at base; corona brilliant scarlet-orange, shading to yellow at base, with flecks of white at rim, heavily frilled. Early

'Harlestone' 2 W-O
(E.F. Hughes) E.F. Hughes, 1962
Fl. 108 mm wide; corona apricot orange. Mid-season

'Harmodius' 2 W-? (b)
(Mrs R.O. Backhouse, pre-1921)

'Harmony' 1 W-? (b)
(R.H. Bath, pre-1908)

'Harmony' 2 W-? (b)
(A.H. Ahrens) J.S. Leitch, 1956

'Harmony Bells' 5 Y-Y
(M. Fowlds) G.E. Mitsch, 1962
'Whiteley Gem' × *N. triandrus*

'Harriet Horn' 1 W-W
(H.R.Meyer, pre-1927)

'Harriet Lady Birkin' 3 Y-? (a)
(J.L. Richardson, pre-1938)

'Harrison Weir' 1 W-Y
(W. Backhouse, pre-1869)
Perianth segments ovate, inflexed, twisted or with margins wavy, separated; corona funnel-shaped, smooth, with mouth flared, rim flanged and crenate. Syn. Pseudonarcissus Bicolor 'Harrison Weir'. "Absorbed" 'Lorifolius'

'Harrogate' 2 Y-YYR
M.J. Jefferson-Brown, 1963

'Harry Brown' 2 W-YYO
(J.N. Hancock & Co., 1949) J.N. Hancock & Co., 1964
Corona widely expanded, lemon yellow, with orange at rim, heavily frilled. Late. Resembles an improved 'Walter J.Smith'

'Harry Veitch' 8
(de Graaff Bros, pre-1907)

'Hartford' 1 Y-Y
(R.C.A. Tombleson) R.C.A. Tombleson, 1968

'Hartgrave' 2 Y-W
Syn. of 'Hartgrove'

'Hartgrove' 2 Y-W
(J.W. Blanchard, 1975) Unregistered
'Lemonade' × 'Daydream'
See also 'Hartgrave'

'Harting' 3 W-GOO
(Sir F.C. Stern, pre-1954)
Perianth segments broad, rounded, pure white; corona coral orange, with green at base, frilled. Mid-season to late. Scented

'Hartington' 2 W-P
(F.E. Board) F.E. Board, 1965
'Rose of Tralee' × 'Irish Rose'; sdlg no. 1267
Late

'Hartland's Leda' 1 W-W
(W.B. Hartland, pre-1884)
Perianth segments pure white, inflexed, usually twisted, separated, shorter than corona; corona cylindrical, pale sulphur yellow becoming snow white, mouth only slightly flared, rim flanged and crenate. Oak scented. Syn. 'Tortuosus Tenuifolius'

'Hartlebury' 3 W-ORR
(J.S.B. Lea) Clive Postles Daffodils, 1987
Sdlg 2-4-69 × Blanchard sdlg 68/15A;

sdlg no. 1-24-76
Perianth segments broadly ovate, blunt, mucronate, pure white, with margins slightly incurling at apex, smooth, overlapping half; the inner segments more narrowly ovate, somewhat truncate, only very slightly mucronate, with margins a little wavy; corona disc-shaped, red, with orange at base, ribbed. Tall. Late

'Hartsdown' 1 W-W
(F.D.B. Cobb, pre-1953)
AM(Haarlem) 1956

'Hartside' 2 Y-? (a)
(R.O. Backhouse, pre-1934)

'Hartz' 3 W-O
(D. Jackson) Jackson's Daffodils, 1982
Sdlg 227/67 × 'City Lights'; sdlg no. 243/75

'Harvest' 1 Y-Y
(Mrs R.O. Backhouse, pre-1908)

'Harvester' 1 Y-Y
(P.D. Williams, pre-1927)
*C(g) 1927

'Harvest Gold' 1 Y-Y
(J.A. O'More) P.D.K. Ramsay, 1983
'Cromarty' × 'Kingscourt'

'Harvest Home' 1 Y-Y
(F.E. Board) F.E. Board, 1965
'Moonstruck' hybrid × 'Galgorm'
Fl. lemon yellow. Mid-season

'Harvest Moon' 5 Y-Y
(G.H. Engleheart, pre-1913)
N. triandrus var. loiseleurii × 'King Alfred'
Fl. 83 mm wide, soft sulphur yellow, of great substance, facing down; perianth segments slightly reflexed, overlapping a quarter; corona funnel-shaped. Mid-season to late. *HC(g) 1930

'Harvest Star' 2 Y-Y
(D.N.Y. Olson, 1982) D.N.Y. Olson, 1993
'Spanish Gold' × 'Harewood'; sdlg no. 76/68
Fl. 111 mm wide, of good substance; perianth segments very broad, blunt, mid-yellow, with slight white mucro, slightly concave, overlapping half; the inner segments with margins somewhat wavy; corona more or less cylindrical, lightly ribbed, a little darker in tone than the perianth, with mouth ribbed and a little expanded, rim crenate. Late

'Harvest Time' 1 Y-Y
(W. Balch, pre-1933)

'Hasbury' 2 W-YYO
(Horace Goodwin) Horace Goodwin, 1994
'Ringleader' × 'Ben Vorlich'; sdlg no. G1-1-83

Fl. forming a double triangle, 97 mm wide; perianth segments broadly ovate, whitish, deeply overlapping; corona bowl-shaped, yellow, with green at base and a broad band of orange at rim, mouth expanded. Late

'Hassan' 2 Y-? (a)
(A.M. Wilson, pre-1948)

'Hassle' 2 W-Y
(Jackson's Daffodils) Jackson's Daffodils, 1986
'Jolly Roger' × 'Gideon'; sdlg no. 269/80
Perianth segments broadly or very broadly ovate, blunt, mucronate, spreading, greenish white (155A), slightly ribbed, overlapping half; the inner segments more narrowly ovate, slightly inflexed; corona cup-shaped, expanded, opening brilliant orange-yellow 21B, becoming apricot yellow, loosely frilled

'Haste' 1 Y-Y
(R.H.Glover, pre-1989) Unregistered
'Dream Prince' × 'Warbin'

'Hastings' 1 Y-Y
(C.A. Latta) C.A. Latta, 1960
Fl. 108 mm wide, lemon yellow; corona very slightly darker than the perianth. Early to mid-season

'Hatfield Beauty' 1 Y-Y
(G.P. Haydon, pre-1905)
'Madame de Graaff' × 'Monarch'
Perianth segments pale creamy yellow; corona bright canary yellow, with mouth expanded and rim flanged

'Hathersage' 3 W-? (b)
(G.H. Cammell, pre-1907)

'Hathor' 7 Y-Y
(Barr & Sons, pre-1952)

'Hatsheput' 2 W-GOO
(J.L. Richardson, pre-1937)

'Hatteras Light' 9 W-OOR
(Mrs M.S. Yerger) Mrs M.S. Yerger, 1994
N. poeticus var. *hellenicus* open pollinated
Fl. 52 mm wide; perianth segments broad, rounded at apex, deeply overlapping; corona almost disc-shaped, bright orange, with red at rim. Very late

'Haughtiness' 1 W-W
(pre-1927)

'Hauraki' 2 W-? (b)
(S.L. Danby, pre-1936)

'Haurangi' 1 W-Y
(D. Bramley, 1967) D. Bramley, 1978
'Lochin' hybrid; sdlg no. 60/17
Fl. 100 mm wide; corona medium yellow. Mid-season

'Haute Couture' 1 W-W
(G.L. Wilson) F.E. Board, 1962
('Murmansk' × 'Broughshane') × 'White Prince'; sdlg no. 47/1
Early. Resembles 'White Prince' but with broader perianth segments

'Havana' 2 Y-? (a)
(P.D. Williams, pre-1935)

'Havelock' 1 Y-Y
(E. Leeds, pre-1877)
Perianth segments pale yellow, recurved; corona darker in tone. Syn. Pseudonarcissus Major 'Havelock'

'Havelock' 2 Y-Y
(P.D. Williams, pre-1927)
Perianth segments broadly ovate, blunt or truncate, pale primrose yellow, touched white at apex, smooth, with margins very slightly incurving; the inner segments more narrowly ovate and slightly twisted; corona funnel-shaped, ribbed, orange-yellow, mouth lightly frilled, with rim notched. Mid-season. 2n=28. AM(e) 1927, AM(Haarlem) 1930, AM(c) 1931, FCC(Haarlem) 1933, *AM(g) 1933, FA(Haarlem) 1936, *FCC(g) 1936, FCFA(Haarlem) 1938

'Havemeijer' 3 W-? (b)
(M. van Waveren & Sons, pre-1942)

'Havilah' 1 Y-Y
(S.J. Bisdee, 1944)

'Havilah' 5 W-W
(E.C. Powell, pre-1948)

'Havildar' 2 Y-? (a)
(G.H. Johnstone, pre-1943)

'Havoc' 1 Y-Y
(J.O. Sherrard, pre-1943)

'Hawaii' 4 Y-O
(J.L. Richardson) J.L. Richardson, 1956
'Falaise' × 'Ceylon'
Fl. rounded, 79 mm wide; perianth and other petaloid segments in three whorls, roundish, brilliant greenish yellow 6B-C, with very slight white mucro, a little concave, overlapping; the outer whorl spreading; the second whorl superimposed, very little smaller, a little inflexed; the centre whorl irregularly arranged, with some segments fused, inflexed, with margins wavy; corona segments interspersed among the petaloid segments at centre, short, orange (28A), frilled. 2n=27. AM(e) 1963

'Hawaiian Pink' 2 W-P
(G.E. Mitsch and R. & E.Havens, 1965) G.E. Mitsch and R. & E.Havens, 1989
'Precedent' × 'Carita'; sdlg no. A34/21

Fl. 110 mm wide; corona flared, pink, frilled. Mid-season. Lightly scented. Resembles a less formal 'Confection'

'Hawangi' 3 W-R
(Brian S.Duncan, 1985) Brian S.Duncan, 1996
'Cul Beag' × 'Doctor Hugh'; sdlg no. 1130
Fl. 115 mm wide; perianth segments broadly ovate, pure white, plane, smooth; corona shallow bowl-shaped, slightly ribbed, deep orange-red. Mid-season to late

'Hawberk' 1 Y-Y
(G.H. Engleheart, pre-1929)
'Maximus' hybrid
Fl. large, bright clear yellow; perianth segments somewhat twisted; corona expanded, with rim deeply and unevenly notched. Early

'Hawea' 2 W-W
(A. Gibson, pre-1950)
'Ludlow' × 'Whitehouse'
Perianth segments pure white; corona a little frilled. FCC(e)(NZ) 1954, AM(e)(NZ) 1954

'Hawera' 5 Y-Y
(W.M. Thomson, pre-1928)
N. jonquilla × *N. triandrus*
Fls 6-8 per stem, pale canary yellow; perianth segments ovate or oblong, blunt, prominently mucronate, reflexed, plane, overlapping at base only; the inner segments less noticeably mucronate, less strongly reflexed, with margins wavy or incurved; corona cup-shaped, very broadly and shallowly ribbed, paler in colour than the perianth, mouth even, with rim broadly and obscurely crenate. Dwarf. Scented. With occasional secondary stems. 2n=14. Resembles an 'April Tears' of slower increase. AM(a) 1938, AGM 1995

'Hawk Eye' 3 W-YYR
(W.G. Pannill) W.G. Pannill, 1972
'Aircastle' × 'Merlin'
Fl. 90 mm wide

'Hawkins' 11a W-YWY
(David Adams) David Adams, 1994
'Ebony' open pollinated; sdlg no. 84/115C
Fl. 80 mm wide; perianth segments ovate, blunt, plane, overlapping one-third; corona split, the six segments opposite the perianth segments and three-quarters their length, creamy white, with a distinct band of yellow at base and shading to light yellow at rim; the outer three corona segments broad, smooth, overlapping the inner perianth segments; the inner three ribbed and inflexed. Early

'Hawlet'
(pre-1913)

'Hawley Flame' 1 W-O
(J.M.Radcliff) Radcliff Daffodils, 1995
Sdlg 68/81 × sdlg 76/81; sdlg no. 31/86
Fl. 95 mm wide; perianth segments very broad, rounded at apex and only very slightly mucronate, spreading, slightly concave, smooth, overlapping half; the inner segments a little narrower, square-shouldered at base; corona funnel-shaped, smooth in lower half, loosely ribbed towards mouth, strong orange 26A, with yellow-orange (21C) at base and a slightly darker yellow-orange (23B) at rim, mouth straight, frilled. Late. Sunproof

'Hawley Gold' 1 W-YOO
(J.M.Radcliff) Radcliff Daffodils, 1995
Silcock sdlg × sdlg 40/81; sdlg no. 39/90
Fl. 105 mm wide; perianth segments very broad, blunt, slightly mucronate, spreading, slightly concave, with midrib sometimes showing, overlapping half; the inner segments with margins slightly wavy; corona cylindrical and smooth in lower half, slightly flared and closely ribbed towards mouth, yellow-orange 23A, with brilliant yellow 10A at base and creamy orange at rim (16C), mouth straight and a little frilled. Late. Sunproof

'Hawley Pink' 1 W-P
(J.M.Radcliff) Radcliff Daffodils, 1996
Sdlg 46/77 × 'Alana'; sdlg no. 19/88
Fl. 92 mm wide; perianth segments very broadly ovate, blunt, only very slightly mucronate, spreading, plane or with margins sometimes incurling at apex, overlapping half; the inner segments a little inflexed; corona cylindrical, smooth, strong yellowish pink 37B, with mouth flared, ribbed on the inside, even, rim somewhat unevenly crenate. Mid-season to late. Sunproof

'Hawley Rose' 1 W-P
(J.M.Radcliff) Radcliff Daffodils, 1996
Sdlg × 'Obsession'; sdlg no. 19/90
Fl. 100 mm wide; perianth segments very broad in outline, blunt or roundish at apex, only very slightly mucronate, spreading, plane, overlapping half; the inner segments slightly inflexed; corona somewhat funnel-shaped, ribbed, strong yellowish pink 31C, paling to whitish pink at mouth (23D), mouth straight, frilled. Mid-season. Sunproof

'Hawley Sunset' 2 W-O
(J.M.Radcliff, 1980) Radcliff Daffodils, 1996
Sdlg no. 42/81
Fl. 100 mm wide; perianth segments very broadly ovate, blunt, only very slightly mucronate, spreading or slightly reflexed, overlapping; the inner segments a little narrower and more nearly spreading, with margins incurved; corona funnel-shaped, very broadly ribbed, strong orange 24A, mouth straight, finely ribbed on the inside, wavy, rim shallowly crenate. Late. Sunproof

N. haworthii G.Don = *N. triandrus*

'Hawthorn' 1 W-Y
(F.H. Chapman, pre-1927)
*C(g) 1927

'Hawthorn Belle' 1 Y-Y
(H.A. Brown, pre-1936)

'Haydee' 1 W-W
(D.V. West, pre-1923)

'Hay Dixie' 2 Y-O
(J.N.Hancock & Co., 1980) J.N.Hancock & Co., 1997
'Air Marshal' × 'Ablaze'; sdlg no. 60/80H
Perianth segments acute, golden yellow, spreading; corona bowl-shaped, bright orange, with mouth wavy. Mid-season

'Haye' 2 Y-O
(Mrs H.K. Richardson) du Plessis Bros, 1977
'Air Marshal' × 'Border Chief'; sdlg no. 380
Fl. 99 mm wide. Mid-season. 2n=28. Resembles 'Air Marshal' but with a paler corona

'Hayle' 2 Y-? (a)
(pre-1949)

'Hayle' 2 Y-YOO
(pre-1966) Unregistered

'Hayley Green' 3 O-R
(Horace Goodwin) Horace Goodwin, 1992
'Arriba' × 'Altruist'; sdlg no. G3-2-78
Fl. forming a double triangle, 83 mm wide; perianth segments orange; corona bowl-shaped, red, with mouth a little frilled. Late

'Hay Maker' 2 Y-YOO
(J.N. Hancock & Co., 1957) Unregistered

'Hazard' 1 Y-Y
(Jackson's Daffodils) Jackson's Daffodils, 1986
'Warbin' × 'Ristin'; sdlg no. 25/78
Perianth segments vivid yellow 9A; corona darker in tone (14A). Early

'Hazel' 2 W-YOO
(J.N. Hancock & Co., 1953)

'Hazel Brilliant' 2 Y-O
(C.W. Culpepper, *c.*1973) Unregistered

'Hazel Jones' 1 W-W
(W.A. Grace, pre-1936)

'Hazel Rutherford' 2 W-Y
(D.C. MacArthur) D.C. MacArthur, 1988
MacArthur 2 W-W open pollinated; sdlg no. E8545

Perianth segments very broadly ovate, blunt, mucronate, spreading, fairly smooth, overlapping half; the inner segments more narrowly ovate, less prominently mucronate, shouldered at base, slightly inflexed, occasionally a little twisted; corona narrow cup-shaped, a little expanded, smooth, mouth straight, with rim densely and irregularly notched. Mid-season. Scented

'Hazel Winslow' 2 W-P
(Brian S. Duncan) Rathowen Daffodils, 1983
'Simile' × 'Passionale'; sdlg no. 279
Fl. 105 mm wide; perianth segments very broadly ovate, blunt, slightly mucronate, pure white, spreading, smooth, overlapping half; the inner segments more narrowly ovate, a little inflexed; corona funnel-shaped, deep salmon pink, mouth widely expanded, even, with rim rolled and crenate. Mid-season

'Hazelwood' 3 W-WWY
(W.J. Dunlop) W.J. Dunlop, 1957
'Tinsel' × 'Chinese White'
Perianth segments pure white; corona shallow, white, flushed and rimmed with lemon

'H.B.May' 2 W-? (b)
(W. Poupart, pre-1914)

'H.Camp' 3 O-O
(pre-1977) Unregistered

'H.C.Bowles' 2 W-Y
(C.G. van Tubergen, pre-1912)
Perianth segments broadly ovate, spreading or a little inflexed, with margins wavy or recurved, overlapping a quarter; the inner segments more strongly inflexed; corona somewhat funnel-shaped, smooth or lightly ribbed, pale greenish yellow, ageing to whitish yellow, mouth flared, frilled, rim notched. Late. Resembles a larger 'White Queen'

'H.C.Smith' 2 W-Y
(E. Leeds, pre-1877)
Syn. Incomparabilis Albus 'H.C.Smith'. Was "absorbed" into 'Cynosure'

'H.D.van Waveren' 1
(pre-1933)

'Head Hunt' 2 Y-O
(Jackson's Daffodils) Jackson's Daffodils, 1993
'Mattara' × 'Colorful'; sdlg no. 51/87
Fl. forming a double triangle, 107 mm wide; perianth segments broadly ovate, blunt, slightly mucronate, vivid yellow 9A, spreading, smooth and of thick substance, overlapping half; the inner segments a little inflexed; corona cup-shaped, strong orange 25A, with mouth straight and wavy. Mid-season

'Headlight' 2 Y-O
(D.W. Gourlay) D.W. Gourlay, 1958
Sdlg × 'Armada'
Perianth segments vivid yellow 9B; corona vivid orange 28B, frilled

'Headliner' 2 Y-YYO
(N. Burn, 1950) F.A. Saunders, 1961
Fl. 95 mm wide; perianth segments yellow, shaded copper orange; corona with a broad band of reddish orange at rim. Mid-season

'Headway' 1 Y-Y
(Murray W. Evans, 1972) Murray W. Evans, 1985
'Spanish Gold' × 'Dividend'; sdlg no. N-61
Late. Resembles a later-flowered 'Spanish Gold'

'Heamoor' 4 Y-Y
(R.A.Scamp) R.A.Scamp, 1996
'Saint Keverne' × 'Tamar Fire'; sdlg no. 278
Fl. 96 mm wide; perianth and other petaloid segments rich golden yellow; corona segments slightly darker in tone. Early to mid-season

'Heartland' 3 W-Y
(R. & E. Havens) R. & E. Havens, 1993
'Merlin' × 'Gold Frills'; sdlg no. TEH107/1
Fl. rounded, 90 mm wide; perianth segments very broadly ovate, spreading, plane; corona cylindrical, short, ribbed, deep yellow, with mouth frilled. Late

'Heart of Fire' 3 W-O
(The Brodie of Brodie, c.1910)
'Princess Mary' × *N. poeticus*
Perianth segments creamy or pale yellow; corona small, very shallow bowl-shaped, bright reddish orange

'Heart of Gold' 2 W-O
(Hon. Sir R.H. Rhodes, pre-1912)
Perianth segments creamy white; corona golden orange. Resembles a much improved 'Victory'

'Heart's Delight' 2 Y-Y
(H. Homan & Co., pre-1933)

'Heart's Desire' 9 W-YYR
(S.J. Bisdee, 1945)
'Dactyl' × 'Minuet'

'Heart's Desire' 4 W-Y
(J.L. Richardson) M.J. Jefferson-Brown, 1969
'Gay Time' × 'Salmon Trout'

'Heartstring' 2 Y-P
(W. Gould Jr) W. Gould Jr, 1992
'Rubythroat' × 'Widgeon'; sdlg no. 83-13-C
Fl. 125 mm wide. Early to mid-season

'Heart Throb' 2 W-GWP
(Murray W. Evans) Murray W. Evans, 1976
'Everpink' × (['Caro Nome' × ('Mabel Taylor' × 'Rosario')] × 'Interim'); sdlg no. L-39
Fl. 90 mm wide. Mid-season

'Heat Haze' 2 Y-R
(Carncairn Daffodils, 1967) Carncairn Daffodils, 1978
'Revelry' × 'Kindled'; sdlg no. 1/40/62
Fl. 100 mm wide; perianth segments brilliant yellow 10A, flushed red; corona orange-red (30C). Late

'Heathcliffe' 2 Y-YYR
(D.S. Bell) D.S. Bell, 1975
'Air Marshal' × 'Checkmate'
Fl. 113 mm wide; perianth segments rich yellow; corona yellow, with orange-red at rim. Mid-season

'Heather Jenkins' 2 W-? (b)
(J.H. Hinsby, 1927)
'Bernardino' hybrid

'Heather Joy' 1 Y-Y
(P. & G. Phillips, 1967) P. & G. Phillips, 1977
Fl. forming a double triangle, 105 mm wide, clear lemon yellow; perianth segments very broad. Mid-season

'Heather Storey' 2 W-P
(L.P.Dettman, 1974) Unregistered
'Peggy Dettman' × 'Most Delicious'; sdlg no. P/M 4/75

'Heath Fire' 2 Y-O
(J.L. Richardson) Mrs H.K. Richardson, 1964
'Air Marshal' × 'Firecracker'
Perianth segments golden yellow; corona reddish orange, frilled. Sunproof

'Heathmont' 2 W-W
(H.A. Brown, pre-1936)

'Heatwave' 2 Y-R
(W.M. Spry, pre-1975) Unregistered
'Port Kembla' × 'Gibraltar'
Corona flame red. Late

'Heaven' 2 W-OOY
(A.M. Wilson, pre-1944)
Fl. 108 mm wide; perianth segments broadly ovate, prominently mucronate, with margins slightly incurving, waxy smooth, of thick substance, overlapping half; the inner segments more narrowly ovate, shouldered at base, inflexed and twisted; corona cup-shaped, light orange (23B), with a slightly brighter tone outside, paling to yellow and white at rim, mouth loosely ribbed, straight, a little frilled. AM(e) 1951

'Heavenly Gift' 2 W-O
(Tom Forster, 1960s) Unregistered
Perianth segments creamy white; corona disc-shaped, opening bright lemon yellow, becoming apricot orange. Mid-season

'Hebe' 1 W-W
(W. Welchman, pre-1910)

'Hebe' 2 Y-? (a)
(Sir A.P.W. Thomas, pre-1930)

'Hebe Too' 2 W-YYO
(A.O. Roblin, 1939)
'Queen of Hearts' × 'Pink'un'

'Hebron' 1 Y-Y
(The Brodie of Brodie, c.1921)
'White Emperor' × 'King Alfred'; sdlg no. 16/A/16
Fl. dark bright golden yellow; perianth segments fairly even and of smooth texture; corona ribbed, with rim recurved

'H.E.Buxton' 2 W-O
(French origin)
Selection by H.E.Buxton (c.1881) from wild-collected *N. × bernardii*
Perianth segments white; corona suffused scarlet-orange. Resembles *N. × bernardii* but with smaller and more abundant flowers. Syn. Bernardii 'H.E.Buxton'

'Hecate' 1 W-Y
(Barr & Sons, pre-1907)
Perianth segments incurving; corona pale creamy primrose yellow

'Hecla' 2 W-O
(Mrs Lawrenson, pre-1913)
Corona large, expanded, rich reddish orange. Resembles 'Lucifer'

'Hecoma' 3 W-? (b)
(P. van Deursen, pre-1930)

'Hector' 2 Y-Y
(E. Leeds, pre-1877)
Perianth segments narrow, acute, pale yellow; corona tinged orange. Syn. Incomparabilis Concolor 'Hector'. Was "absorbed" by 'Mrs A.F.Barron'

'Hector' 1 W-? (b)
(G.H. Engleheart, pre-1907)

'Hector Treub' 1 Y-Y
(de Graaff Bros, pre-1923)

'Hecuba' 8 W-Y or O
(pre-1807)

'Hecuba' 2 W-Y
(C.E. Radcliff, 1934)
'Pedestal' hybrid

'Hedi' 2 W-WWY
(W.Jackson Sr, 1940) W.Jackson Jr, 1956
'Veronique' × 'Nimue'

'Hedley Hancock' 2 Y-Y
(L.P. Dettman) L.P. Dettman, 1979
'Spanish Gold' × 'Arctic Gold'; sdlg no. 84-AG1/79
Fl. 99 mm wide; perianth segments brilliant yellow 7B; corona darker in tone (13A). Mid-season. Resembles a Div. 2 'Spanish Gold' of paler colour

'Hedley Reeve' 4 Y-Y
(H.E. Reeve) W. Jackson Jr, 1970
'Magherally' × 'Fiery Knight'

N. hedraeanthus **(Webb & Heldreich) Colmeiro**
13 Section Bulbocodium. AM 1977
    var. ***hedraeanthus***
    var. ***luteolentus*** Barra & López

'Heemskirk' 1 W-W
(C.E. Radcliff, pre-1938)
'Saint Aloysius' × 'Beersheba'

'Hegar' 2 W-W
(G.H. Johnstone, pre-1960)
'Silver Coin' × 'Beersheba'

'Hegira' 2 Y-R
(C.E. Radcliff, 1944) J.M.Radcliff, 1956
'Marksman' × 'Formosa'

'Heide' 7 Y-Y
Syn. of 'Chit Chat'

'Heidi' 6 Y-Y
(M. Fowlds, c.1965) J. & E. Frey, 1982
Sdlg no. 268/1
Fl. 51 mm wide

'Heidi' 2 Y-YOO
(J.N. Hancock & Co.) Unregistered

'Heir Apparent' 1 Y-Y
(Wrigley, pre-1913)

'Heir Apparent' 1 Y-Y
(E.W. Philpott)

'Heiress' 2 YYW-P
(Murray W. Evans, 1978) Estella L. Evans, 1992
('Daydream' × ['Green Island' × 'Accent']) × ('Daydream' × 'Gypsy Princess'); sdlg no. V-3/2
Fl. 105 mm wide, rounded; perianth segments ovate, medium yellow, touched white at base; corona funnel-shaped, light salmon pink, with a paler tone

outside, frilled. Mid-season

'Heirloom' 1 Y-Y
(Wrigley, pre-1913)

'Heirloom' 2 W-P
(D.S. Bell) D.S. Bell, 1961
'White Sentinel' × 'Seraglio' hybrid
Fl. 102 mm wide; perianth segments overlapping; corona long, funnel-shaped, deep pink. Mid-season. Resembles 'Salmon Trout' but with the perianth segments more nearly acute and the corona more widely flared

'Heirloom' 1 Y-Y
(D.S. Bell, c.1961) Unregistered
'Rabaul' × 'Crocus'

'Heir Presumptive' 1 Y-Y
(Wrigley, pre-1913)

'Heka' 1 W-W
(S.J. Bisdee, 1942)
'Mrs Ernst Krelage' × 'Nautilus'

'Hela' 3 W-YYR
(E.M. Crosfield, pre-1913)
Fl. 89 mm wide; perianth segments creamy white; corona deep yellow, with a well-defined band of rich madder red at rim

'Helada' 2 W-W
(A. Gray) A. Gray, 1961
Fl. 40 mm wide, ice white. Early. Resembles 'Shangri-La'

'Heldinne' 8 W-Y or O
(pre-1807)

'Helen' 1 Y-Y
(Miss F.W. Currey, pre-1907)

'Helen' 5
(Sir F.C. Stern) Sir F.C. Stern, 1961
N. cantabricus subsp. *monophyllus* × *N. triandrus* var. *concolor*
Perianth segments oblong, acute, reflexed, separated; corona cup-shaped, lightly ribbed, mouth straight, wavy, with rim entire. PC(p) 1961

'Helen, Countess of Radnor' 1 W-W
(Miss E. Willmott, pre-1905)
Corona frilled. AM 1905

'Helena' 3 W-? (b)
(C. Dawson, pre-1916)

'Helena Maria' 8 W-Y
Syn. of 'Princess Yolande'

'Helen Buncombe' 1 W-? (b)
(T. Buncombe, pre-1931)

'Helen Falconer' 1 W-W
(pre-1907)

'Helen F.Ohms' 2 Y-W
(Warnaar & Co.) Warnaar & Co., 1956
'Carbineer' × 'Amarantha'

'Helen Gay' 9 W-?
(Miss K. Spurrell, pre-1907)

'Helen Gibson' 2 W-P
(Alister Clark, 1940) J. Sharp, 1960

'Helen Madison' 2 Y-? (a)
(P.D. Williams, pre-1942)

'Helen Mary' 2 W-? (b)
(W.A. Grace, pre-1938)

'Helen of Troy' 2 W-? (b or c)
(J.H. Mander, pre-1933)

'Helen O'Hara' 1 W-W
(J.L. Richardson, pre-1926)
Fl. ivory white; perianth segments broadly ovate, blunt, very slightly mucronate, strongly inflexed, with margins wavy, recurved and sometimes nicked, overlapping one-third to a half; corona cylindrical, smooth, opening pale primrose yellow, soon becoming white, mouth expanded and lightly frilled, rim flanged and broadly crenate. Syn. 'Miss Helen O'Hara'. AM(e) 1923

'Helen O'More' 4 Y-O
(J.A.O'More, 1984) Koanga Daffodils, 1996
Richardson sdlg 123 × 'Red Coat'
Fl. 95 mm wide; perianth and other petaloid segments in several whorls, broadly ovate, vivid yellow 12A, slightly concave; corona segments regularly interspersed among the petaloid segments, strong orange 25A. Mid-season to late.

'Helen's Tower' 2 W-W
(Ballydorn Bulb Farm, 1987) Ballydorn Bulb Farm, 1994
'Churchman' × 'April Love'
Fl. 125 mm wide; perianth segments broadly ovate, smooth; the inner segments a little more narrowly ovate; corona cylindrical, with olive green at base, mouth flared and shallowly lobed. Mid-season

'Helen Thompson' 2 W-P
(Campbell Duncan) Campbell Duncan, 1956
('Mitylene' × 'Pink o' Dawn') × ('Dawnglow' × 'Karanja')

'Helen Wills' 2 W-O
(E.H. Krelage & Son, pre-1929)
Perianth segments creamy white; corona long and slender. AM(Haarlem) 1929

'Helford' 1 Y-Y
(P.D. Williams, pre-1939)
Perianth segments slightly twisted; corona deep golden yellow, with rim rolled and slightly dentate. *GulvalAM(m) 1939

'Helford Dawn' 2 Y-W
(R.A.Scamp) R.A.Scamp, 1996
'Sophia' × 'Grand Prospect'; sdlg no. 430
Fl. 96 mm wide; perianth segments broadly ovate, soft golden yellow, deeply overlapping; corona straight-sided, opening soft golden yellow, becoming white, with mouth slightly flared and rim crenate. Mid-season

'Helga' 2 W-W
(G.H. Engleheart, pre-1927)

'Helga' 2 W-W
(A.M. Wilson) D.W. Gourlay, 1959
'Tambov' × 'Ludlow'
Fl. large; perianth segments pure white, of heavy texture; corona shallow, tinged yellowish green at base, frilled. Tall

'Helianthus' 3 Y-? (a)
(J.W.A. Lefeber, pre-1938)

'Helice' 1 W-Y
(Barr & Sons, pre-1919)
Corona expanded, pale creamy yellow, lightly frilled

'Helicon' 2 W-? (b)
(R.H. Bath, pre-1930)

'Heliog' 1 Y-Y
(S.J. Bisdee, 1942)
'Golden City' × 'Lyndale Gold'

'Helios' 2 Y-O
(G.H. Engleheart, pre-1912)
Fl. 98 mm wide; perianth segments broadly ovate, soft clear yellow, with white mucro, somewhat creased, with margins recurved, overlapping; the inner segments a little twisted or with margins wavy; corona cylindrical, very lightly ribbed, opening clear buttercup yellow, becoming rich golden yellow, tinged coppery orange, mouth expanded, split in places and overlapping, frilled, with rim regularly notched and crenate. Mid-season. AM 1912, AM(Haarlem) 1921, FCC(Haarlem) 1926, *KirtonAM(g) 1934, *AM(g) 1936

'Helios' 8 Y-Y
(?M. van Waveren & Sons, pre-1917)

Poetaz
Fls several per stem; perianth segments very broad, blunt or squarish at apex, sometimes truncate, only very slightly mucronate, creamy yellow, spreading or a little reflexed, with margins wavy or incurling, overlapping half; the inner segments more usually spreading, with margins more heavily waved; corona shallow bowl-shaped, ribbed, pure yellow, mouth split in places and overlapping, more or less even, with rim crenate. 2n=21. Syn. 'Abundance'. AM(Haarlem) 1917

'Hellcat' 2 Y-? (a)
(M.P. Williams, pre-1938)

N. hellenicus Pugsley = *N. poeticus* var. *hellenicus*

'Helles' 2 W-O
(The Brodie of Brodie, c.1921)
'Madame de Graaff' × 'Gallipoli'
Corona light orange

'Hellespont' 2 W-Y
(W.M. Spry, pre-1975) Unregistered
'Green Island' × Ronalds sdlg
Corona lemon yellow. Late

'Hellfire' 2 W-O
(G.L. Wilson, pre-1953)

'Helloa' 4
(Cartwright & Goodwin, pre-1916)

'Helma' 1 W-? (b)
(de Graaff Bros, pre-1941)
AM(Haarlem) 1941

'Helmet' 2 W-GWW
(G.H. Engleheart, pre-1914)
Fl. very large; perianth segments creamy white, overlapping; corona expanded, opening pale lemon yellow, becoming milk white, frilled. AM(e) 1917

'Helmi Elegance' 2 Y-O
(G. Helmus) G. Helmus, 1965
Fl. 95 mm wide; perianth segments vivid yellow 9A; corona strong orange 25A. Mid-season

'Helmsdale' 2 W-? (b)
(A.M. Wilson, pre-1951)

'Heloise' 1 Y-Y
(de Graaff Bros, pre-1927)

'Helper' ?-P
(Alister Clark, 1940) J. Sharp, 1960

'Helsal' 1 W-Y
(W. Jackson Jr, 1969) Unregistered
('Ammon' × 'Merri') × ('Rowella' × 'Maweena');

sdlg no. 73/69

'Helston' 3 W-? (b or c)
(The Brodie of Brodie, c1924)
'White Emperor' hybrid × 'Ringdove'

'Helva' 2 W-? (b)
(J.O. Sherrard, pre-1947)

'Helvellyn' 1 W-W
(W. Markham) E. Longford, 1966
'Peeress' × 'Kanchenjunga'
Fl. 120 mm wide. Tall. Mid-season.

'Helvetia' 2 Y-? (a)
(Mrs R.O. Backhouse, pre-1921)
AM(Haarlem) 1930

'Helvick' 2 W-P
(J.L. Richardson, pre-1938)
'Hera' × 'Penquite'
Corona pinkish apricot, frilled. Resembles an improved 'Rewa'

'Helvin' 2 Y-YYO
(S.J. Bisdee, 1942)
Sdlg × 'Kallista'

'Helvose' 8 Y-R
Syn. of 'Halvose'

'Helzephron' 1 W-W
(G.L. Wilson, pre-1935)

N. heminalis Schultes f. = *N.* × *infundibulum*

'Heminalis'
Syn. of *N.* × *infundibulum*

'Hemlock' 1 Y-Y
(C.E. Radcliff, 1934)
Sdlg × 'Golden Legend'

'Hemploe' 3 W-GWO
(A.M. Wilson, pre-1948)
'Ming' hybrid
Perianth segments of thick substance; corona with green at base and orange at rim

'Hemsworth' 3 W-?
(F.E. Board) F.E. Board, 1965
'Pride of Erin' × Richardson sdlg 985 ('Fermoy' × 'Roimond'); sdlg no. 616

'Hena' 3 W-YYO
(S.J. Bisdee, 1945)
'Hades' × 'Red Crusader'

'Henchman' 2 W-? (b)
(G.H. Engleheart, pre-1907)

'Hendrick Hudson' 1 Y-Y
(F. Rijnveld & Sons, pre-1936)
AM(Haarlem) 1936

'Hendrik Ibsen' 1 Y-Y
(de Graaff Bros, pre-1927)

'Henfield' 2 Y-GOO
(N.A. Burr) N.A. Burr, 1989
'Achduart' × 'Loch Stac'; sdlg no. 1.17.80
Fl. forming a double triangle, 93 mm wide; perianth segments broadly ovate, blunt, slightly mucronate, spreading, regular, overlapping one-third to a half; the inner segments a little narrower; corona very short funnel-shaped, widely expanded, smooth, mouth lobed and a little frilled, the lobes shallow and occasionally overlapping. Early to mid-season. Sunproof

'Hengan' 2 Y-? (a)
(W.A. Watts, pre-1923)

'Hengist' 1 Y-Y
(H. Backhouse, pre-1908)

'Hengrove' 3 W-Y
(G.L. Wilson, pre-1942)
'Silver Plane' × 'Silver Coil' hybrid

'Henna' 2 Y-O
(Mrs R.O. Backhouse, pre-1921)
Perianth segments deep lemon yellow; corona cylindrical, clear orange. AM(Haarlem) 1920

'Hennie' 3 W-R
(T.H. Piper) T.H. Piper, 1956
('Elspeth' × 'Ngaere') × 'Portia'

'Henny' 9 W-?
(van Zonneveld Bros & Philippo, pre-1920)
AM(Haarlem) 1920, AM(Haarlem) 1930. Received AM(Haarlem) 1920 as 'Nelly'

'Henrietta' 2 Y-Y
(W.F.M. Copeland, pre-1920)
Perianth segments becoming twisted. Early

'Henriette Gerrevink' 2 Y-? (a)
(G. Lubbe & Son, pre-1931)
Syn. ? 'Mevrouw Gerrevink'. AM(Haarlem) 1931

'Henri le Grand' 8? W-Y
(pre-1883)
Fl. small. Somewhat resembles 'La Pucelle'

henriquesii = *N. jonquilla* var. *henriquesii*

'Henri Vilmorin' 1 W-W
(G.P. Haydon, pre-1903)
'Monarch' × 'Madame de Graaff'
Fl. 114 mm wide; perianth segments broadly ovate,

opening creamy white, becoming white, a little inflexed, slightly twisted, overlapping a quarter; the inner segments narrower and more noticeably twisted; corona cylindrical, lightly ribbed, opening primrose yellow, becoming white, with mouth expanded and frilled, rim shallowly crenate. AM 1904

'Henry' 2 W-Y
(J.M. de Navarro) J.M. de Navarro, 1956
'Waterville' × 'Chinese White'

'Henry Blair' 7 Y-Y
(H. Blair) F.A. Saunders, 1968
Fls usually 3 per stem, rounded, 32 mm wide. Mid-season. Resembles 'Trevithian' but with the corona of better form and more heavily frilled

'Henry Blake' 3 W-? (b)
(Miss K. Spurrell, pre-1923)

'Henry Boyce' 1 Y-Y
(C.A. Nethercote) T. Morrison, 1960
Fl. rich yellow

'Henry Burra' 1 Y-Y
(F.H. Chapman, pre-1927)

'Henry Deterding' 1 W-Y
(A. & P. Nijssen Bros, pre-1939)
'Victoria' × 'King Alfred'
Syn. 'Sir Henry Deterding'

'Henry Dyer' 2 W-P
(Alfred Clark) Alfred Clark, 1955
Corona strong pink. PC(e)(NZ) 1956

'Henry Fitzgerald' 2 W-? (b)
(H. Fitzgerald, 1933)
'Isis' × 'Blodwen'

'Henry Fletcher' 2 W-? (b)
(W.A. Watts, pre-1939)

'Henry Ford' 1 Y-Y
(W.J. Eldering & Son, pre-1928)

'Henry Hellyer' 2 W-O
(Tom Forster, 1960s) Unregistered
Perianth segments broad; corona very shallow bowl-shaped, bright orange. Tall. Early to mid-season

'Henry Irving' 1 Y-Y
(Dutch origin, pre-1885)
Selection from *N. hispanicus* var. *spurius*
Fl. yellow; perianth segments broadly ovate, blunt, spreading, ribbed, with margins wavy or recurved, overlapping one-third; corona funnel-shaped, mouth widely flanged, rim deeply and irregularly notched and crenate. 2n=14. Syn. 'Irving', 'Sir Henry Irving',
Pseudonarcissus Major 'Spurius Henry Irving'. FCC 1886

'Henry James' 3 W-? (b)
(F.H. Chapman, pre-1910)

'Henry Lawson' 9 W-GYR
(T. Morrison) T. Morrison, 1960
Fl. 67 mm wide; perianth segments broad, pale yellow-green 155A, smooth, overlapping; corona saucer-shaped, light yellow 15D, with strong yellow-green 143B at base and a narrow band of vivid red 45C at rim

'Henry Vaughan' 9 W-?
(J.M. de Navarro, pre-1950)
Incorrectly registered 'Herbert Vaughan'

'Henty' 2 W-Y
(West & Fell, pre-1935)
'White Emperor' hybrid
Corona lemon, with rim flanged

'Heptamerone' 9 W-?
(de Graaff Bros, pre-1927)

'Hera' 2 W-WWY
(de Graaff Bros, pre-1914)
Perianth segments broadly ovate, blunt, very slightly mucronate, pure white, spreading, a little creased, with margins sometimes incurling, overlapping half; the inner segments narrower, a little inflexed, more heavily creased, very slightly twisted; corona bowl- or short funnel-shaped, widely expanded, ribbed, opening creamy yellow, becoming creamy white, with faint apricot yellow at rim, lightly frilled. Mid-season. Tall. 2n=28. AM(Haarlem) 1915, *AM(g) 1936

'Heraclitus' 2 Y-R
(A.M. Wilson, pre-1944)
Perianth segments yellow; corona red

'Herald' 1 Y-Y
(pre-1907)

'Herald' 1 Y-Y
(D.V. West, pre-1932)
Perianth segments primrose yellow

'Herald' 3 W-O
(G.W.E. Brogden) G.W.E. Brogden, 1966
Fl. 89 mm wide; corona deep reddish orange. Early

'Heralding' 1 W-W
(R.H. Glover) R.H. Glover, 1975
'Glenshesk' × 'Gwyn'; sdlg no. 1210
Fl. 114 mm wide. Mid-season. Resembles a larger-flowered 'Gwyn' with a narrower corona

'Herbert Barr' 1 Y-Y
(Barr & Sons, pre-1923)

'Herbert Beadle' 2 W-? (b)
(H.R. Meyer, pre-1927)

'Herberton' 2 Y-YOO
(J.N. Hancock & Co., 1966) Unregistered

'Herbert Smith' 1 Y-Y
(M. van Waveren & Sons, pre-1916)
Perianth segments large, light yellow; corona deep yellow

'Herbert Vaughan' 9 W-?
Syn. of 'Henry Vaughan'

'Herbert von Bismarck' 3 W-Y
(M. Leichtlin, pre-1884)
Perianth segments sulphur white. Syn. Barrii Sulphureus 'Herbert von Bismarck'

'Hercules' 2 Y-Y
(pre-1889)
Perianth segments opening clear yellow, becoming sulphur yellow, overlapping; corona large, dark yellow

'Hercules' 1 Y-Y
(G.H. Engleheart, pre-1907)

'Hercules' 0
(van Zonneveld Bros & Philippo, pre-1930)
Poetaz

'Hercules' 2 W-Y
(C.M. Grullemans) J.J. Grullemans & Sons, 1959
Fl. 120 mm wide; perianth segments greenish white; corona vivid yellow 9A. Mid-season

'Hereami' 1 Y-Y
(O. Ronalds, pre-1948)

'Hereford' 2 W-P
(Alister Clark, 1943) J. Sharp, 1960

'Hereward' 1 Y-Y
(W. Welchman, pre-1908)
Fl. 102 mm wide, rich yellow; corona rim almost entire

'Her Grace' 2 W-YYW
(C.G. van Tubergen, pre-1914)

'Her Grace' 9 W-?
(G.H. Engleheart, c.1920)

'Heritage' 1 W-W
(G.H. Engleheart, pre-1931)

'Her Ladyship' 3 W-? (b or c)
(W.F.M. Copeland, pre-1937)

'Her Majesty' 8 W-O
(?Dutch origin, pre-1871)
Fl. large. Syn. Tazetta 'Her Majesty'

'Her Majesty' 1 Y-Y
(E. Leeds, pre-1877)
Fl. clear pale yellow; perianth segments somewhat twisted; corona flared. Syn. Pseudonarcissus Major 'Her Majesty'. "Absorbed" 'John Bright'

'Her Majesty Queen Alexandra' 2 W-Y
(W.A. Watts, pre-1923)
'Minnie Hume' × 'Weardale Perfection'
*AM(g) 1927

'Herman Gorter' 1 Y-Y
(de Graaff Bros, pre-1927)
Syn. 'Audley', 'Socrates'

'Hermanse' 2 W-? (b)
(A.H. Ahrens, pre-1950)
Syn. 'Hestea'

'Hermes' 1 Y-Y
(The Brodie of Brodie, c.1917)
('King Alfred' × 'Weardale') × 'Windmill'
Fl. 127 mm wide or more, deep yellow. Early. Syn. 'Athos'

'Hermia' 1 Y-Y
(W. Jackson Jr) Jackson's Daffodils, 1979
'Haka' hybrid × 'Warbin'; sdlg no. 20/71
Fl. 115 mm wide. Mid-season

'Hermina' 2 W-? (b or c)
(A.H. Ahrens, pre-1939)

'Hermina' 1 W-?
Syn. of 'Jolanda'

N. herminiens Link = N. assoanus Dufour

N. × herminii Fernández Casas 13 (parentage: N. bulbocodium Linnaeus subsp. bulbocodium var. nivalis (Graells) Baker × N. nobilis (Haworth) Schultes f. var. primigenius Fernández Casas & Lainz) = N. × felineri

'Herminius' 1 Y-Y
(Sir A.P.W. Thomas, pre-1930)

'Hermione' 8 Y-Y
(pre-1798)

'Hermione' 1 W-W
(J.M. de Navarro, pre-1949)
(['Sincerity' × 'Carmel'] × 'Murmansk') × 'Broughshane'

'Hermione Floribunda' 8 W-Y
Syn. of 'Grand Monarque'

'Hermit' 2 Y-? (a)
(Sir C.H. Cave, pre-1908)

'Hermitage' 1 Y-Y
(G.L. Wilson, pre-1931)

'Hero' 1 Y-O
(M.J. Jefferson-Brown) M.J. Jefferson-Brown, 1984
Sdlg × 'Brer Fox'
Perianth segments ovate, acute, slightly mucronate, very slightly inflexed, smooth, overlapping half; the inner segments a little narrower; corona bright mid-orange, mouth ribbed and slightly expanded, a little frilled, with rim notched and slightly flanged

'Herod' 1 W-Y
(E.M. Crosfield, pre-1907)
Fl. facing down; perianth segments creamy white, with lemon at base, smooth, overlapping; corona large, expanded, lightly ribbed, clear yellow, a little frilled, with rim flanged

'Heroic' 1 W-? (b)
(G.H. Engleheart, pre-1914)

'Heroine' 2 W-YYO
(G.H. Engleheart, pre-1906)
Perianth segments broad at base, snow white, spreading; corona expanded, citron yellow, with apricot orange at rim, frilled

'Heroine' 2 W-P
(F.E. Board) F.E. Board, 1965
'Saintfield' × 'Irish Rose'

'Heron' 2 Y-? (a)
(P.D. Williams, pre-1927)

'Heron' 2 W-P
(G.E. Mitsch) G.E. Mitsch, 1977
'Magic Dawn' × 'Carita'; sdlg no. D95/1
Fl. 123 mm wide; perianth segments deeply overlapping; corona light pink. Mid-season

'Herrick' 9 W-R
(G.H. Engleheart, pre-1897)
Fl. large, of strong substance; perianth segments pure white, slightly reflexed; corona disc-shaped, deep red. AM 1901

'Hersham Glory' 9 W-?
(G.H. Engleheart, pre-1930)

'Herzogin Cecilie' 2 W-? (b)
(M.H. Tribe, pre-1937)

'H.E.Sharp' 1 W-W
(H.E. Sharp, pre-1930)

'Hesione' 1 W-W
(Barr & Sons, pre-1923)

'Hesla' 7 Y-Y
(P.D. Williams, pre-1908)
Fls sometimes 2 per stem, clear rich primrose yellow; perianth segments overlapping; corona shallow, expanded, a little darker in tone than the perianth. Mid-season. 2n=21. AM 1924, *AM(g) 1936

'Heslington' 3 W-YYR
(Clive Postles Daffodils) Clive Postles Daffodils, 1985
'Accolade' × 'Aircastle'
Perianth segments blunt, mucronate, pure white, with margins sometimes slightly incurving near apex, overlapping half to two-thirds; corona small, bowl-shaped, rich lemon yellow, with sulphur lemon yellow at base and a narrow, well-defined band of orange-red at rim, lightly and neatly frilled. Late

'Hesperus' 2 Y-O
(G.H. Engleheart, pre-1889)
Perianth segments creamy buff; corona deep apricot orange. AM 1899

'Hessary Tor' 2 W-W
(G.H. Johnstone) G.H. Johnstone, 1959
'Zero' × 'Blue Moon'
Fl. 102 mm wide. Mid-season

'Hessenford' 2 Y-R
(Mrs H.K. Richardson) du Plessis Bros, 1981
'Flaming Spring' × 'Royal Palace'; sdlg no. 4039
Fl. 112 mm wide. Late

'Hestea' 2 W-?
Syn. of 'Hermanse'

'Hester' 8 Y-O
(H. Selkirk, pre-1927)

'Hestia' 2
(P.D. Williams, pre-1908)

'Heston' 1 W-W
(G.C. Graham, pre-1949)

'Heston Beauty' 2 Y-Y
(S.J. Bisdee) S.J. Bisdee, 1956
'Dorado' × sdlg 3/44

'Hetepheres' 1 Y-Y
(R.F. Calvert, pre-1935)

'Hetty Alper' 3 W-O
(pre-1950)

'Hever' 4 Y-Y
(N.A.Burr) N.A.Burr, 1996
'Golden Aura' × 'Tonga'; sdlg no. 1.19.82
Fl. rounded, 92 mm wide; perianth and other petaloid segments in more than three whorls, regularly arranged opposite one another, decreasing slightly in size towards the centre, brilliant greenish yellow 5A; the three outer whorls broadly or very broadly ovate, blunt, with white mucro, a little concave; the outer whorl spreading, the second and third whorls a little inflexed; the whorls at centre sharply inflexed, with margins tightly infolded; corona segments in several whorls, opposite and a little more than half as long as the petaloid segments and interspersed among them, broad, vivid yellow 14A, tinged with a darker tone at rim, frilled. Mid-season

'Hexagon' 2 W-W
(G.L. Wilson, pre-1923)
'Madame de Graaff' hybrid
Corona opening faint citron or cream, soon becoming white. Mid-season to late

'Hexameter' 9 W-GYR
(The Brodie of Brodie, c.1923)
'Raeburn' × 'Dactyl'; sdlg no. 156/D/18
Perianth segments very broadly ovate, truncate, slightly mucronate, pure white, a little reflexed, smooth, overlapping half; the inner sements more narrowly ovate, more nearly spreading, twisted or with margins wavy; corona disc-shaped, closely ribbed, citron yellow, with bright green at base and a band of dark red at rim. 2n=14

'Hexangularis' 1 Y-Y
(pre-1629)
Perianth segments pale yellow; corona long, 6-angled, slightly deeper in tone than the perianth. Syn. "The Six-angled Clipt Trunk Daffodil", Pseudonarcissus Abscissus 'Hexangularis'

'Hexham' 3 W-YOO
(G. Harrison) G. Harrison, 1971
'Otterburn' × 'Signal Light'
Fl. 89 mm wide

'Hexworthy' 3 W-GWO
(Ballydorn Bulb Farm) du Plessis Bros, 1985
probably 'Cushendall' × 'Lough Areema'; sdlg no. H22
Late. 2n=28

'Heyday' 2 W-? (b)
(R.H. Bath, pre-1929)

'Hey Jude' 2 W-WPW
(Colin Crotty) Colin Crotty, 1995
'Telita' × 'Accent'; sdlg no. 160-81
Fl. 110 mm wide; perianth segments ovate, smooth, overlapping; corona straight-sided, pure pink, paling to white at base and with a narrow band of white at rim, slightly frilled. Mid-season. Sunproof

'H.G.Seyler' 2 Y-? (a)
(L. van Leeuwen & Son, pre-1930)
AM(Haarlem) 1930

'H.H.B.Bradley' 2
(R.M. Pitt, pre-1914)
'Emperor' × 'Poetarum'

'Hiawassee' 8 W-W
(E.C. Powell, 1943) E.C. Powell, 1956
'Cassandra' × 'Paper White'
2n=18

'Hiawatha' 3 Y-? (a)
(P.D. Williams, pre-1927)

'Hiawatha' 1 Y-Y
(Frank Verge) Frank Verge, 1971
'Cromarty' × 'Galway'
Fl. 105 mm wide

'Hicol' 2 Y-P
(D.S. Bell) D.S. Bell, 1971
'Red Conquest' self pollinated

'Hidalgo' 2 Y-? (a)
(G.H. Engleheart, pre-1904)

'Hidcote' 2 Y-R
(Clive Postles) Clive Postles Daffodils, 1996
'Loch Lundie' × Lea sdlg 2-27-74; sdlg no. 2-12A-82
Fl. forming a double triangle, 95 mm wide; perianth segments ovate; corona funnel-shaped, with rim crenate. Early

'Hifi' 7 Y-Y
(A. Gray) A. Gray, 1959
N. calcicola sdlg
Fl. 32 mm wide; corona lighter in tone than the perianth. Early. Resembles a shorter and darker-coloured 'Rugulosus' with a larger corona

'High Bank' 1 W-Y
(G. Lewis) D.S. Bell, 1955

'Highbury' 2 W-R
(W.A. Noton) W.A. Noton, 1985
'Rockall' × 'Avenger'
Corona intense red. Mid-season

'High Cadenza' 2 Y-R
(D.S.Bell, pre-1986) Unregistered

'High Church' 2 W-GWW
(Ballydorn Bulb Farm) Ballydorn Bulb Farm, 1986
'Church Town' open pollinated
Corona funnel-shaped. Very tall. Mid-season.

Resembles a larger and much improved 'Courage'

'High Cotton' 3 W-W
(W.G. Pannill) W.G. Pannill, 1985
'Dreamcastle' × 'Stainless'; sdlg no. 67/28
Late

'Highcourt' 1 Y-Y
(R.C.A. Tombleson) R.C.A. Tombleson, 1968

'Highcroft' 2 W-W
(C.E. Radcliff, 1942)
'Nautilus' × 'Naxos'

'Highdown' 2 W-W
(Sir F.C. Stern, pre-1948)

'Highdown Bells' 12 W-W
(Sir F.C. Stern) Lady Stern, 1969
N. cantabricus × *N. triandrus* var. *concolor*
Fl. 35 mm wide; perianth segments slightly reflexed, irregular, widely separated; corona cup-shaped, ribbed, with mouth straight, rim entire. AM(p) 1969

'Highfield Beauty' 8 Y-YYO
(H.R. Mott) H.R. Mott, 1964
Fl. 63 mm wide; perianth segments very broad, blunt and prominently mucronate, brilliant greenish yellow 6C, spreading, somewhat concave or with margins incurved, with midrib showing, overlapping; the inner segments a little inflexed and somewhat twisted; corona large, shallow bowl-shaped, lightly ribbed, vivid yellow 13A with a narrow band of orange (23A) at rim, sometimes opening with green at base, mouth loosely frilled, split in places and overlapping, with rim almost entire. Slightly scented. 2n=31. AM(e) 1985, *HC(g) 1991

'Highfire' 2 Y-R
(D.S. Bell) D.S. Bell, 1968
Perianth segments deep yellow; corona red. PC(e) 1970

'High Glory' 2 Y-? (a)
(Parr's Nurseries, 1946) Parr's Nurseries, 1958

'High Jinks' 3 W-? (b)
(N.Y. Lower, pre-1936)

'Highland Bard' 9 W-?
(Cartwright & Goodwin, pre-1910)

'Highland Castle' 1 W-Y
(G.L. Wilson) Guy L.Wilson Ltd, 1964
('Guardian' × 'Kanchenjunga') × 'Preamble'

'Highland Chief' 1 W-Y
(The Brodie of Brodie, pre-1928)

'Highlander' 1 Y-Y
(W. Welchman, pre-1908)

'Highlander' 2 W-O
(O. Ronalds) M. Gardiner, 1956
Perianth segments broad, smooth; corona apricot orange. Tall. Early. Syn. 'Highlight'

'Highland Fling' 11a Y-WWY
(A.N. Kanouse) A.N. Kanouse, 1978
'Daydream' × 'Lemon Ice'
Fl. 97 mm wide; perianth segments soft lemon; corona segments opening soft yellow, becoming cream white, with lemon at rim, frilled. Mid-season. Resembles 'Three Cheers' but with a contrasting colour at corona rim

'Highland Globe' 2 W-Y
(D.S. Bell) D.S. Bell, 1964
'Papanui Queen' × 'Green Island'
Fl. 54 mm wide; corona chrome yellow

'Highland Rose' 2 W-P
(The Brodie of Brodie, *c*.1943)
'Wild Rose' × 'Pink Mitylene'

'Highland Spring' 2 W-WWP
(Mrs J. Abel Smith) Mrs J. Abel Smith, 1990
'Jewel Song' hybrid; sdlg no. Q55/32
Fl. 83 mm wide. Late

'Highland Wedding' 2 W-GWP
(J.L. Richardson) Mrs H.K. Richardson, 1969
'Interim' × 'Rose Caprice'
Fl. 109 mm wide; perianth segments broadly ovate, blunt or truncate, prominently mucronate, pure icy white, spreading, plane, overlapping; the inner segments more narrowly ovate, with margins wavy; corona funnel-shaped, ribbed, white, greenish at base, with a very broad band of bright coral pink at rim, mouth frilled, deeply and irregularly lobed, the lobes often overlapping

'High Life' 2 W-OOY
(G.A. Uit den Boogaard, pre-1951)
'Duke of Windsor' × 'Fortune'
Perianth segments pure white, of thick substance; corona orange, with golden yellow at rim, with the rim closely and deeply notched, as if fringed. AM(Haarlem) 1951, FCC(Haarlem) 1953

'Highlight' 2 W-R
(S.J. Bisdee, 1944)
'Hades' × 'Red Crusader'

'Highlight' 2 W-O
Syn. of 'Highlander'

'Highlite' 2 Y-YPP
(W.G. Pannill) W.G. Pannill, 1978
'Lemnos' × 'Kilkenny; sdlg no. 64/77

Fl. 100 mm wide. Mid-season

'High Noon' 1 Y-Y
(M.P. Williams, pre-1950)

'High Note' 7 Y-W
(G.E. Mitsch) G.E. Mitsch, 1974
'Quick Step' × 'Daydream'; sdlg no. D80/16
Fls 1-3 per stem, 90 mm wide; perianth segments rich yellow; corona flared, becoming almost white. Mid-season

'Highpeak' 2 Y-YYO
(J.N. Hancock & Co., 1954)
Corona gold, with deep orange at rim, frilled

'High Perch' 2 W-W
(P. de Jager & Sons) P. de Jager & Sons, 1963
'Polindra' × 'Jules Verne'
Fl. 125 mm wide, ivory white; corona richer in tone than the perianth. Mid-season

'Highpoint' 2 Y-Y
(Eileen E. Frey) J. & E. Frey, 1984
'Playboy' × 'Chiloquin'; sdlg no. JEE8/10
Fl. 110 mm wide; corona almost apricot-coloured, with lighter yellow at base, slightly frilled. Mid-season

'High Repute' 2 W-P
(G.E. Mitsch) G.E. Mitsch, 1975
'Precedent' × 'Accent'; sdlg no. B37/11
Fl. rounded, 108 mm wide; corona very shallow bowl-shaped, salmon pink, slightly suffused with orange. Resembles a slightly larger 'Precedent' with a self coloured corona. Mid-season

'High Road' 7 Y-O
(W.H. Wheeler, 1972) W.H. Wheeler, 1985
'Binkie' × *N. jonquilla*
Corona funnel-shaped, pale orange. Early. Resembles a taller and larger-flowered 'Quail' with the perianth segments more wavy

'High School' 2 W-P
(Alister Clark, pre-1949)
Fl. large; perianth segments broad; corona pale pink, frilled. Early

'High Score' 1 Y-Y
(D.S. Bell) D.S. Bell, 1962
'Treasure Trove' × 'Treasure'
Fl. 107 mm wide, golden yellow; corona frilled. Mid-season. Resembles 'Kingscourt'

'High Seas' 1 W-Y
(G.W. Tarry) Carncairn Daffodils, 1991
'Dunmurry' × 'Stormy Weather'; sdlg no. 3/36/82
Fl. 112 mm wide; perianth segments very broadly ovate, blunt, not prominently mucronate, spreading or a little inflexed, with broad midrib showing, overlapping one-third to a half; the inner segments with margins wavy or incurved; corona cylindrical, smooth, vivid yellow 9A, mouth flared and loosely ribbed, rim shallowly crenate. Early

'High Sherriff' 1 W-Y
(J.L. Richardson) Mrs H.K. Richardson, 1964
('Spitzbergen' × 'Broughshane') × 'Broughshane'
Corona buffy primrose, ageing to near white, with rim dentate and widely flanged

'High Sierra' 1 W-W
(Oregon Bulb Farms, pre-1951)

'High Society' 2 W-GWP
(Brian S. Duncan) Rathowen Daffodils, 1979
'May Queen' × ? Richardson sdlg 3341; sdlg no. 262
Fl. 112 mm wide; perianth segments very broadly ovate, slightly mucronate, spreading, a little concave, with margins sometimes incurling, smooth, regular, overlapping half; the inner segments more narrowly ovate, shouldered at base, a little inflexed; corona cup-shaped, smooth, white, ageing to lemon yellow, with green at base and deep rose pink at rim, mouth expanded, with rim widely crenate and slightly flanged. Mid-season. Resembles a taller and larger-flowered 'Bridesmaid' of better colour

'High Style' 9 W-GYR
(Mrs G. Link, 1980) Mrs G. Link, 1991
'Perdita' × 'Sidelight'; sdlg no. 1675
Fl. rounded, 75 mm wide; perianth segments broad, snow white, spreading, very smooth, of thick substance, deeply overlapping; corona rim brilliant red, loosely dentate. Very late. Sunproof. Scented

'High Tea' 2 W-P
(W.G. Pannill) W.G. Pannill, 1970
'Caro Nome' × 'Accent'

'High Tide' 1 Y-Y
(E.L. Agee) E.L. Agee, 1965
'Cantatrice' sport
Fl. 108 mm wide; corona darker in tone than the perianth. Mid-season

'High Title' 1 W-Y
(W.M. Spry, pre-1975) Unregistered
'Hunter's Moon' × 'Prince'
Corona lemon yellow. Late

'High Tor' 2 Y-? (a)
(Oregon Bulb Farms, pre-1951)

'High Tower' 3 W-GWY
(Ballydorn Bulb Farm) Ballydorn Bulb Farm, 1982
Fl. 98 mm wide; perianth segments glistening white; corona white, with green at base and yellow at rim. Mid-season. 2n=28

'High Value' 2 W-YYO
(J.N. Hancock & Co., c.1980) Unregistered

'Highway' 1 Y-Y
(R.C.A. Tombleson) R.C.A. Tombleson, 1968
Fl. 124 mm wide. Mid-season. Resembles 'Golden Rapture' but with broader perianth segments

'Highway Song' 2 W-GYO
(Carncairn Daffodils, 1970) Carncairn Daffodils, 1987
'Kilworth' × 'Matapan'; sdlg no. 8/22/64
Corona cup-shaped, chrome yellow, with green at base and deep reddish orange at rim, slightly dentate. Late. Resembles 'Matapan'

'Hijack' 2 W-R
(Jackson's Daffodils, 1986) Jackson's Daffodils, 1996
Sdlg 216/75 × sdlg 243/75; sdlg no. 56/86
Fl. 105 mm wide; perianth segments broadly ovate, greenish white (155A); corona disc-shaped, orange-red (30C). Mid-season to late

'Hi Jinks' 2 Y-R
(J.N. Hancock & Co., 1963) Unregistered

'Hiker' 1 W-? (b)
(J.L. Richardson, pre-1938)

'Hi King' 1 Y-Y
(C.O. Fairbairn) J.L. Martin, 1978
Fl. 100 mm wide; perianth segments brilliant greenish yellow 6A; corona darker in tone (9A). Mid-season. Resembles a taller and more robust 'Kingscourt'

'Hikurangi' 1 W-W
(R.C.A. Tombleson) R.C.A. Tombleson, 1966
Fl. 114 mm wide. Mid-season. Resembles a smaller-flowered 'Empress of Ireland' with the corona rim less deeply rolled

'Hilarion' 1 Y-Y
(D.J. Cooper) D.J. Cooper, 1957

'Hilarity' 2 Y-OOY
(G.E. Mitsch) G.E. Mitsch, 1974
Sdlg × 'Flaming Meteor'; sdlg no. B45/7
Fl. 110 mm wide; perianth segments broadly ovate, soft clear yellow; corona orange, paling to yellow at rim. Early

'Hilda' 3 W-? (b)
(G.H. Engleheart, pre-1914)

'Hilda' 1 W-W
(Sir A.P.W. Thomas, pre-1937)

'Hilda Camp' 3 Y-O
(L.P. Dettman, 1968) L.P. Dettman, 1978

'Rouge' × 'More So'; sdlg no. 1/69
Fl. 82 mm wide; perianth segments pale yellow 20C; corona orange (28A). Resembles a Div. 3 'Rouge'

'Hilda Denroche' 1 Y-Y
(W.B. Hartland, pre-1907)

'Hilda Mary' 2 W-O
(Hilda M.C.Jeffrey) Hilda M.C.Jeffrey, 1995
'Pontresina' × ?'Irish Minstrel'
Fl. 76 mm wide; perianth segments broadly ovate; corona disc-shaped, yellow-orange (17A), with mouth deeply lobed and rim crenate. Late. Sunproof

'Hildebrand' 2 W-? (b)
(H. Backhouse, pre-1936)

'Hildegard' 1 W-W
(?J. Mallender, pre-1914)

'Hildegarde' 9 W-YYR
(G.H. Engleheart, pre-1910)

'Hilden' 1 W-Y
(W.J. Dunlop) W.J. Dunlop, 1962

'Hilford' 2 W-O
(Ballydorn Bulb Farm, 1967) Ballydorn Bulb Farm, 1979
?'Buncrana' hybrid
Fl. 90 mm wide; corona deep apricot. Mid-season. Resembles a deeper-coloured 'Buncrana' with improved perianth

'Hilite' 2 W-R
(M.E.Brogden, pre-1997) Unregistered
'Rockall' × 'Gauntlet'; sdlg no. T31

'Hillary' 2 W-P
(J.N. Hancock & Co., 1955) Unregistered
('Kenmare' × 'Pink o' Dawn') × 'Marlene'
Corona expanded, heavily frilled

'Hillbilly' 11a Y-Y
(Jac Lefeber, pre-1950s)
Perianth segments creamy yellow; corona segments yellow

'Hillbilly's Sister' 11a Y-Y
(Jac Lefeber, pre-1950)
Early. Resembles a deeper-coloured 'Hillbilly'

'Hillburn' 2 Y-R
(C.E. Radcliff, 1943) J.M.Radcliff, 1956
Sdlg × 'Fortune'

'Hillcrest' 1 W-? (b)
(R. Crews, pre-1949)

'Hill Head' 9 W-GGR
(Ballydorn Bulb Farm) Ballydorn Bulb Farm, 1990
'Cantabile' open pollinated
Fl. 75 mm wide; perianth segments slightly reflexed; corona disc-shaped, jade green, with a broad band of red at rim. Late

'Hill House' 3 W-YYO
(Jan Dalton, 1984) Jan Dalton, 1997
'Pontresina' × 'Estrella'; sdlg no. 7829/1
Mid-season

'Hillinen' 2 Y-YYO
(F. Rijnveld & Sons, pre-1944)
'Aranjuez' × 'Reginald Dixon'
EFA(Haarlem) 1949

'Hillmount' 2 W-R
(W.J. Dunlop, pre-1949)
'Aleppo' × 'Hades'
Perianth segments pure white; corona dark crimson-red

'Hillsborough' 1 W-Y
(W.J. Dunlop) W.J. Dunlop, 1955
'Sincerity' × 'Cantatrice'
Corona pale lemon, with rim rolled

'Hillside Daffodil' 1 Y-Y
(pre-1899)
Fl. rich golden yellow; corona expanded, frilled

'Hillstar' 7 YYW-YWW
(G.E. Mitsch) G.E. Mitsch, 1979
'Daydream' × *N. jonquilla*; sdlg no. F72/6
Fl. 2-3 per stem, 68 mm wide; perianth segments broadly ovate, bright lemon yellow, with a broad band of white at base and a white mucro, spreading or a little reflexed, with margins incurved or more strongly incurling, overlapping one-third; the inner segments inflexed, sometimes reflexed in upper part; corona funnel-shaped, short and broad, very loosely ribbed, ivory white, shaded with buff yellow at base and tinted with a clearer white at rim, mouth flared and frilled, split in places and overlapping. Mid-season. 2n=28

'Hillston' 1 Y-Y
(J.N. Hancock & Co.) J.N. Hancock & Co., 1955
'Hebron' × 'Mortlake'
Fl. deep yellow; perianth segments plane, deeply overlapping. Very early. 2n=28

'Hilltown' 2 W-W
(Ballydorn Bulb Farm, 1975) Ballydorn Bulb Farm, 1991
'Fincool' × 'Church Town'
Fl. 110 mm wide; perianth segments broadly ovate, overlapping; the inner segments more narrowly ovate; corona cylindrical, with mouth slightly flared. Mid-season. Varies between Divs 2 and 1. Varies between Divs 2 and 1

'Hiltruda' 1 W-?Y
(Barr & Sons, pre-1913)
'Madame de Graaff' × 'White Queen'

'Himalaya' 1 W-W
(J.L. Richardson, pre-1953)
'Spitzbergen' × 'Kanchenjunga'
Fl. 118 mm wide; perianth segments broad, smooth, overlapping; the inner segments slightly inflexed; corona slightly expanded, mouth ribbed and frilled, with rim flanged. AM(e) 1953

'Hina' 1 Y-Y
(W. Jackson Sr, 1944)
'Principal' × 'Hymyr'

'Hinahina' 3 W-YYR
(R. Crews) R. Crews, 1962
Fl. 95 mm wide; corona lemon yellow. Mid-season

'Hinchinbrook' 2 Y-Y
(W.M. Spry, pre-1975) Unregistered
'Torchlight' × 'Golden Valley'
Tall

'Hind' 2 W-? (b or c)
(P.D. Williams, pre-1938)

'Hindenburg' 1 Y-Y
(G. Lubbe & Son, pre-1933)
AM(Haarlem) 1932

'Hindostan' 1 W-W
Syn. of 'Hindustan'

'Hindu' 1 Y-Y
(C.G. van Tubergen, pre-1931)
AM(Haarlem) 1931

'Hindustan' 1 W-W
(J.L. Richardson, pre-1949)
'Thurso' × 'Broughshane'; sdlg no. 153
Fl. pure white; perianth segments very broad, blunt, spreading, somewhat creased, overlapping half; the inner segments narrower, shouldered at base, a little inflexed; corona funnel-shaped, with rim widely rolled and deeply dentate. See also 'Hindostan'

'Hinemoa' 1 W-? (b)
(A.M. Wilson, pre-1916)

'Hineroto' 2 Y-YYO
(A. Gibson, pre-1951)

'Hinscup' 3 Y-Y
(T.H. Piper) T.H. Piper, 1956
'Saint Egwin' × 'Paula'

'Hippolyta' 3 W-? (b)
(Barr & Sons, pre-1913)

'Hirlas' 1 Y-Y
(W.A. Watts, pre-1916)
'Maximus' × 'Henry Irving'

'Hiromi' 2 Y-R
(P. Phillips, 1964) P. Phillips, 1977
'Pillar Box' × 'Arakan'
Fl. 108 mm wide; perianth segments bright lemon yellow, of good substance; corona rich red, with mouth widely expanded. Resembles an improved 'Pillar Box'

'His Excellency' 8
(C. Dawson, pre-1907)

'His Excellency' 1 Y-Y
(G.L. Wilson, pre-1931)
'King Alfred' × 'Honey Boy'
Fl. 115 mm wide; perianth segments brilliant yellow 13B, overlapping half; corona very slightly darker in tone (13A). 2n=28. *HC(g) 1950

'His Lordship' 11b W-Y/OW
(J.W.A. Lefeber) J.J. Grullemans & Sons, 1959
Fl. 110 mm wide; corona deeply split, the six segments alternate to the perianth segments, brilliant yellow 12B, with longitudinal bands of orange and with patches of white at apex. Scented

'His Majesty' 1 Y-Y
(R.H. Bath, pre-1918)
FCC 1918

'His Majesty' 1 Y-Y
(L. Buckland, pre-1930)

N. hispanicus Gouan 13 Section Pseudonarcissus
var. **_hispanicus_**
var. **_bujei_** (Fernández Casas) Fernández Casas
var. **_concolor_** (Jordan) Pugsley
var. **_propinquus_** (Herbert) Pugsley
(Pseudonarcissus Major 'Propinquus', Pseudonarcissus Major 'Luteus')
"Absorbed" into 'Edward Leeds'
var. **_spurius_** (Haworth) Pugsley
(Pseudonarcissus Major 'Spurius')

'Hispar' 2 W-W
(The Brodie of Brodie, pre-1948)
('Askelon' × 'Beersheba') × ('Naxos' × 'Corinth')

'Hissar' 2 Y-O
(J.N. Hancock & Co., 1963) Unregistered

'Historic' 2 Y-R
(G. Lewis, 1935) Parr's Nurseries, 1958
'Seraglio' × 'Wellington'

Perianth segments soft yellow; corona brick red

'Hitch-hiker' 1 Y-Y
(Jackson's Daffodils) Jackson's Daffodils, 1986
'Otewa' × 'Ristin'; sdlg no. 25/79
Early

'Hitchy Koo'
(Sir C.H. Cave, pre-1913)

'Hit Parade' 2 W-Y
(Konynenburg & Mark, pre-1953)
'Frederike' × 'Mimosa'

'Hiyo Silver' 2 W-W
(W.H. Roesé) W.H. Roesé, 1985
'Easter Moon' × 'Castle of Mey'
Corona long. Mid-season

'H.J.Elwes' 2 Y-Y
(W. Backhouse, pre-1869)
Fl. large; corona dark yellow. Syn. Backhousei 'H.J.Elwes'

'Ho' 2 Y-O
(H.A. Brown, 1931)

'Hoarfrost' 2 or 3 W-? (b or c)
(pre-1914)

'Hobart' 1 Y-Y
(C.E. Radcliff, 1932)
'Renown' × ('King Alfred' × 'Lord Roberts')
Fl. pale yellow

'Hobbema' 1 W-? (b)
(R.A. van der Schoot, pre-1923)

'Hoboken' 1 Y-Y
(?R. van der Schoot & Son, pre-1914)
Fl. dark rich yellow

'Hodsock's Pride' 1 W-? (b)
(J. Mallender, pre-1894)
AM 1894

'Hogan' 2 Y-O
(J.N. Hancock & Co., 1968) Unregistered

'Hogarth' 2 Y-Y
(W. Backhouse, pre-1869)
Perianth segments primrose yellow; corona large, expanded. Syn. Incomparabilis Sulphureus 'Hogarth'

'Hohenlinden'
(?F.H. Chapman, pre-1914)

'Hohere' 2 W-Y
(R.C.A. Tombleson) R.C.A. Tombleson, 1959

'Hokio' 1 W-Y
(A.B. Davey) A.B. Davey, 1975
'Sincerity' × 'Kanchenjunga'; sdlg no. 8/60
Corona lemon. Mid-season. Resembles a larger-flowered 'Sincerity'

'Hokitika' 2 W-YYR
(G. Lewis) D.S. Bell, 1955
Corona widely expanded, with brilliant red at rim. See also 'Hokitiki'

'Hokitiki' 2 W-YYR
Syn. of 'Hokitika'

'Hokorawa' 2 Y-YYR
(R.G.Cull) Hokorawa Daffodils, 1996
'Film Queen' × O'More sdlg 2/70
Fl. 110 mm wide; perianth segments vivid yellow 12A; corona vivid yellow 12A, with a broad band of orange-red (32B) at rim. Mid-season

'Hokus' 1 Y-Y
(W.F. Leenen) W.F. Leenen, 1982
Perianth segments brilliant greenish yellow 6C; corona darker in tone (12A)

'Holbeck' 4 W-P
(Brian S. Duncan) Rathowen Daffodils, 1988
Sdlg 8174 (['Falaise' × 'Debutante'] × 'Polonaise') × sdlg 346 ('Polonaise' × 'Violetta'); sdlg no. 904
Fl. rounded; perianth and other petaloid segments white; the outer whorl very broad, rounded at apex, spreading, overlapping half or more; the inner whorl two-thirds the length, irregularly arranged, with some segments spreading and plane, others strongly inflexed, with margins folded inwards and deeply incurled; some corona segments more or less the same length as the inner petaloid segments, broad, spreading, wavy, with rim notched, some half the length and clustered among them, rose pink, deeply frilled. Late

'Holbein' W-Y
(C.G. van Tubergen, pre-1912)
Perianth segments creamy white; corona citron yellow. AM(Haarlem) 1912

'Holdfast' 2 W-? (b)
(G.H. Engleheart, pre-1907)

'Holiday' 2 W-? (b)
(Mrs F.S. Foote, pre-1940)

'Holiday Fashion' 2 W-WPP
(G.E. Mitsch, 1956) G.E. Mitsch, 1967
'Mabel Taylor' × 'Interim'; sdlg no. R47/12
Fl. 120 mm wide; perianth segments broad, overlapping; corona widely expanded, somewhat ribbed, deep salmon pink, with creamy pinkish white at base, frilled. Mid-season. Resembles 'Cloudcap' but with a larger and more heavily frilled corona with a deeper band of pink at rim

'Holiday-Inn International' 11a Y-Y
(J. Gerritsen & Son) J. Gerritsen & Son, 1968
'Baccarat' hybrid
Fl. 125 mm wide; perianth segments light greenish yellow 4C, with small white mucro; corona segments vivid yellow 13A. Mid-season

'Holiday Moon' 2 W-Y
(W.M. Spry, pre-1975) Unregistered
'Full Moon' × 'Hereami'
Late

'Holland' 2 Y-O
(W. Blom & Son, pre-1951)
AM(Haarlem) 1951

'Holland Express' 2 W-Y
(G. Lubbe & Son) G. Lubbe & Son, 1960
Fl. 115 mm wide; perianth segments greenish white; corona mimosa yellow. Mid-season

'Holland Festival' 1 W-W
(M. van Waveren & Sons, pre-1953)
'Beersheba' × 'Wedding March'
Syn. 'Josephine'. AM(Haarlem) 1953

'Hollandia' 2 Y-? (a)
(Dutch origin, pre-1926)
AM(Haarlem) 1926

'Hollandia' 4 Y-O
(Warnaar & Co., pre-1943)
AM(Haarlem) 1943

'Holland's Delight' 2 W-? (b)
(pre-1939)

'Holland Sensation' 1 W-Y
(G. Lubbe & Sons) G. Lubbe & Sons, 1984
Perianth segments yellowish white (4D); corona vivid yellow 9B

'Holland's Glory' 4 Y-Y
(L. van Leeuwen & Son, pre-1913)
Fl. buff yellow; perianth and other petaloid segments in several whorls, with more or less prominent white mucro; the two outer whorls opposite and closely overlying one another, broadly ovate, inflexed, overlapping; the centre whorls tightly clustered within the corona; corona shorter, smooth. FCC(Haarlem) 1915, AM(e) 1927

'Hollingdale' 2 W-O
(J.N.Hancock & Co., 1983) Unregistered
Sdlg no. 15/83H
Perianth segments broadly ovate, milk white; corona long cup-shaped, yellow-orange, with a darker tone at rim. Tall. Very early

'Hollingworth' 2 W-? (b or c)
(W.A. Grace, pre-1927)

'Holly Berry' 2 Y-R
(W.J. Dunlop, pre-1950)
'Trevisky' × 'Sun Chariot'
Perianth segments golden yellow; corona deep crimson-red. See also 'Hollyberry'

'Hollyberry' 2 Y-R
Syn. of 'Holly Berry'

'Hollypark' 3 W-GYR
(Ballydorn Bulb Farm, 1975) Ballydorn Bulb Farm, 1989
('Fairgreen' × sdlg) × Div. 3 sdlg
Fl. 90 mm wide; the inner perianth segments ovate; corona ribbed, with dark emerald green at base and dark orange-red at rim, mouth expanded and lobed. Mid-season to late

'Hollythorpe' 3 W-R
(F.E. Board) F.E. Board, 1965
'Chinese White' × 'Alport'; sdlg no. 1655
Corona cherry red. Late

'Hollywood' 2 Y-O
(Warnaar & Co., pre-1939)
'Fortune' hybrid
Perianth segments lemon yellow, ribbed; corona yellow-orange. 2n=28. AM(Haarlem) 1949

'Holmdale' 2 W-W
(F.H. Chapman, pre-1927)
'Phantasy' × 2 W-W
AM(e) 1928

'Holme Fen' 2 W-Y
(A.J.R. Pearson) A.J.R. Pearson, 1993
('Easter Moon' × 'Rashee') × 'Fair Prospect'; sdlg no. 87-32-K29
Fl. forming a double triangle, 110 mm wide; perianth segments very broadly ovate, acute, clear off-white, with no staining at base, spreading, plane, with margins slightly incurving, of thick and waxy texture, overlapping two-thirds; the inner segments less broadly ovate; corona cylindrical, ribbed, strong chrome yellow, with mouth flared and lightly frilled, rim crenate. Mid-season to late

'Holroyd' 1 Y-Y
(J.N. Hancock & Co., 1946) J.N. Hancock & Co., 1964
Perianth segments smooth. Late. Resembles a paler-flowered 'Rabaul'

'Holywell' 3 W-R
(W.J. Dunlop, c.1955) Unregistered
Corona deep crimson-red

'Homage' 2 W-W
(G.L. Wilson) F.E. Board, 1955
('Nelly' × 'Chinese White') × ('Tryst' × 'Foggy Dew')
PC(e) 1963

'Homage' 3 W-Y
(?Australian origin, pre-1989) Unregistered

'Homai' 2 W-? (b)
(J.H. Braithwaite, 1933) Parr's Nurseries, 1958

'Homecoming' 2 W-GWP
(Eileen E. Frey, 1980) J. & E. Frey, 1993
'Coral Ribbon' × sdlg FEE5/2; sdlg no. PEF1/4
Fl. 95 mm wide; perianth segments very broadly ovate, very slightly reflexed, overlapping half; the inner segments with margins slightly wavy; corona bowl-shaped, white, with green at base and a broad band of watermelon pink at rim. Late

'Home Fires' 2 Y-O
(G.L. Wilson, pre-1950)
('Bokhara' × 'Porthilly') × 'Armada'
Fl. 111 mm wide; perianth segments broad, vivid yellow 9B, with margins very slightly incurved, overlapping; corona ribbed, vivid orange 28B, mouth expanded, rim regularly dentate. Scented. 2n=28. AM(e) 1956, *AM(p) 1985

'Home Fires' 2 Y-O
Syn. of 'Kilmorack'

'Home Guard' 2 Y-? (a)
(A. Gray, pre-1941)

'Homeland' 1 W-? (b)
(R.H. Bath, pre-1929)

'Homer' 2? W-W
(W. Backhouse, pre-1869)
Perianth segments narrow, acute; corona opening primrose yellow, becoming sulphur white. Syn. Leedsii 'Homer'

'Homer' 9 W-OOR
(G.H. Engleheart, pre-1897)
'Ornatus' × *N. radiiflorus* var. *poetarum*
Perianth segments of firm substance; corona orange, with a very broad band of clear deep crimson at rim. 2n=14. Resembles *N. radiiflorus* var. *poetarum* but with a much larger perianth. Flowering at the same time as 'Ornatus'. FCC 1898

'Homer Biflorus'
(J.L. Richardson, pre-1914)
'Homer' sport
Fls 2 per stem

'Homespun' 2 Y-Y
(G.H. Engleheart, pre-1905)

'Golden Spur' × 'Ornatus'
Perianth segments ovate, rounded at apex, light yellow, overlapping; corona rich yellow, frilled. Resembles 'Sir Watkin' but with the perianth segments of a deeper tone. AM 1907, EFA(Haarlem) 1925

'Homestead' 2 W-W
(W.G. Pannill) W.G. Pannill, 1972
'Easter Moon' × 'White Prince'
Fl. 94 mm wide, pure white; perianth segments broadly ovate, plane, with slight midrib showing

'Home Truth' 2 Y-? (a)
(E.M. Crosfield, pre-1908)

'Hometruth' 2 Y-Y
(pre-1927)
Fl. soft yellow; perianth segments broadly ovate; corona of great substance, frilled

'Home Vale' 4 Y-R
(H.G. Cross, 1975) H.G. Cross, 1985
Mid-season

'Homeward Bound' 1 W-W
(K.B. Burns) Mrs E. Milliken, 1969

'Hondoman' 2 Y-Y
(W. Jackson Jr) Jackson's Daffodils, 1979
Sdlg 128/65 × 'Ristin'; sdlg no. 9/72
Fl. 110 mm wide. Mid-season

'Honduras' 2 W-O
(J.L. Richardson) Mrs H.K. Richardson, 1968
'Kilworth' × 'Rockall'
Perianth segments broadly ovate, slightly reflexed; corona expanded, orange, with rim dentate

'Hone Heke' 2 Y-? (a)
(J.H. Braithwaite, pre-1930)

'Honest' 9 W-?
(G.H. Engleheart, pre-1930)

'Honesty' 2 W-? (b)
(Mrs R.O. Backhouse, pre-1921)

'Honey' 3 W-W
(Mrs R.O. Backhouse, pre-1921)

'Honey Bells' 5 Y-Y
(M. Fowlds) G.E. Mitsch, 1963
? × *N. triandrus*
Fl. 64 mm wide, clear yellow. Mid-season. Resembles a darker-flowered 'Yellow Warbler' of better substance

'Honeybird' 1 Y-W
(G.E. Mitsch, 1950) G.E. Mitsch, 1965
'King of the North' × 'Content'; sdlg no. K43/2

Fl. 103 mm wide; perianth segments broadly or very broadly ovate, blunt, mucronate, brilliant greenish yellow 3B, a little inflexed, plane, smooth, overlapping; the inner segments more narrowly ovate, shouldered at base, more strongly inflexed, with margins wavy; corona cylindrical, lightly ribbed, becoming white, mouth expanded and more strongly ribbed, rim notched and crenate. Mid-season. Resembles a more vigorous 'Entrancement' with a flower of better substance. AM(e) 1967

'Honeybourne' 2 W-Y
(Clive Postles, 1982) Clive Postles Daffodils, 1994
'Cristobal' × 'Pennine Way'; sdlg no. 4-35-77
Fl. forming a double triangle, 116 mm wide; perianth segments broadly ovate, pure white; corona funnel-shaped, opening yellow, deepening to amber yellow (15C-D), mouth flared, rim crenate. Early

'Honey Boy' 1 Y-Y
(G.L. Wilson, pre-1923)
'Madame de Graaff' × 'King Alfred'
Corona soft lemon, with rim slightly rolled

'Honey Bun' 2 Y-Y
(Mrs B.T. Simpson) Mrs B.T. Simpson, 1966
Fl. 115 mm wide, pale yellow. Late

'Honeycomb' 4 W-Y
(W.F.M. Copeland, pre-1920)
Perianth and other petaloid segments cream white; corona segments light yellow, frilled. AM(e) 1920

'Honey Cup' 2 W-? (b)
(C.G. van Tubergen, pre-1944)
AM(Haarlem) 1948

'Honeydew' 1 Y-Y
(Barr & Sons, pre-1932)
Perianth segments acute, golden lemon yellow, of smooth texture; corona slightly darker in tone than the perianth. AM(e) 1932

'Honeydrop' 5
(E.M. Crosfield, pre-1908)

'Honeyeater' 2 Y-Y
(J.L. Martin) J.L. Martin, 1978
Sdlg × 'Ellimatta'; sdlg no. 22/ED1
Perianth segments brilliant yellow 10A; corona paler in tone (11C), with pink undertones. Mid-season. Resembles a pinkish 'Honeybird' opening with the corona whitish

'Honey Gem' 1 Y-GYP
(D.S. Bell) D.S. Bell, 1980
'Barbara Allen' self pollinated
Fl. 105 mm wide; perianth segments soft yellow; corona with green at base and pale pink at rim, with rim flanged and dentate. Mid-season

'Honey Gold' 2 Y-Y
(de Graaff Bros) de Graaff Bros, 1961
Fl. 102 mm wide; perianth segments vivid yellow 9A; corona slightly brighter in tone (12A). Late. AM(Haarlem) 1961

'Honey Guide' 5 Y-Y
(G.E. Mitsch, 1971) G.E. Mitsch, 1982
'Quickstep' × *N. triandrus* var. *concolor*; sdlg no. G90/5
Fl. 62 mm wide; perianth segments soft lemon; corona slightly deeper in tone. Late

'Honey King' 1 Y-Y
(C. Goodson, 1935) Parr's Nurseries, 1958

'Honey Lou' 1 Y-Y
(D.S. Bell) D.S. Bell, 1975
'Trousseau' open pollinated
Fl. 108 mm wide, lemon yellow. Mid-season. Resembles 'Trousseau' in form

'Honeymaid' 5
(pre-1913)
See also 'Honey Maid'

'Honey Maid' 5
Syn. of 'Honeymaid'

'Honeymoon' 3 Y-? (a)
(H.G. Longford, pre-1927)

'Honeymoon' 1 Y-Y
(Murray W. Evans) Murray W. Evans, 1969
'Trousseau' × 'Cantatrice'
Fl. pale yellow; perianth segments ageing to white at base; corona ageing to white, with yellow at rim

'Honeyorange' 2 O-R
(Brian S.Duncan) Brian S.Duncan, 1997
'Rezare' × 'Cheer Leader'; sdlg no. 1495
Fl. rounded, 109 mm wide; perianth segments broadly ovate, blunt, burnt orange; corona shallow bowl-shaped, slightly ribbed, deep orange-red. Mid-season

'Honeypie' 6 YYW-Y
(M.G.Temple-Smith) M.G.Temple-Smith, 1995
Sdlg 12/84 ('Honeybird' × 'Chartwell') × sdlg 4/80 (*N. obvallaris* × *N. cyclamineus*); sdlg no. 9/90
Perianth segments narrow, brilliant greenish yellow 5B, with a band of white at base, reflexed; corona long cup-shaped, constricted near mouth, slightly lighter in tone (5C) than the perianth, with mouth flared and rim dentate. Dwarf. Early

'Honey Pink' 2 Y-P
(G.E. Mitsch, 1975) R. & E. Havens, 1991
'Euphony' × 'Amberjack'; sdlg no. KK40/1
Fl. smooth; perianth segments creamy lemon yellow, of heavy substance; corona bowl-shaped, creamy pastel pink, with mouth slightly flared and a little frilled. Mid-season

'Honey Queen' 1 Y-Y
(C. Goodson, 1935) Parr's Nurseries, 1958

'Honey Warbler' 7 W-Y
(Eileen E. Frey, 1981) J. & E. Frey, 1993
Sdlg F33/37 open pollinated; sdlg no. QEE4/1
Fl. 45 mm wide; perianth segments opening lemon yellow, becoming white, slightly reflexed; corona very bright yellow. Late

'Honeywood' 2 W-?
(W.M. Spry, pre-1975) Unregistered
'Green Island' × 'Hunter's Moon'
Corona light honey brown

'Hong Kong' 2 Y-O
(J.L. Richardson, pre-1939)
'Fortune' × 'Penquite'
Perianth segments lemon yellow; corona bright reddish orange, slightly frilled. AM(Haarlem) 1950

'Honiset' 1 Y-YYP
(J.N.Hancock & Co., 1983) Unregistered
'Winter Hope' × 'Mulatto'; sdlg no. 28/83H
Perianth segments soft lemon yellow; corona opening golden yellow, becoming flushed with apricot pink, shading to pure pink at rim, with mouth flared and frilled. Early

'Honkey' 2 W-O
(W.F.Leenen, pre-1995) Unregistered
Perianth segments creamy white; corona disc-shaped, creamy yellow-orange, heavily frilled. Mid-season

'Honky-Tonk' 11a W-YYO
(David L. Sheppard) David L. Sheppard, 1977
'Muscadet' × 'Hillbilly'; sdlg no. 69-A-2
Fl. 90-95 mm wide; perianth segments very broadly ovate, truncate, prominently mucronate, spreading, plane, overlapping half; the inner segments more narrowly ovate, creased; corona deeply split, the six segments one-third to half the length of the perianth segments, opposite and closely overlying them and of the same width, appearing to be continuous, strongly ribbed, yellow, shading to orange at rim, mouth with numerous overlapping lobes, irregularly frilled. Mid-season

'Honolulu' 4 W-R
(J.L. Richardson) J.L. Richardson, 1956
'Falaise' × 'Arbar'

'Honoria' 2 Y-O
(J.W.A. Lefeber) J.W.A. Lefeber, 1960
Perianth segments canary yellow; corona deep reddish orange. Mid-season

'Honour' 1 W-Y
(The Brodie of Brodie, c.1918)
'Empire' × 'Miss Clinch'

'Honour' 1 W-W
(H.J. Poole Sr, pre-1930)

'Honourable J.R.Seddon' 1 or 2 Y-Y
(Biggs, pre-1913)
Fl. 105 mm wide; perianth segments narrow, acute, primrose yellow; corona deep yellow. See also 'Honourable R.J.Seddon'

'Honourable Mrs Barton' 3 W-W
(W. Backhouse, pre-1869)
Corona opening primrose yellow, becoming sulphur white. Syn. Leedsii 'Honourable Mrs Barton'

'Honourable Mrs J.F.Franklin' 2 W-W
Syn. of 'Honourable Mrs J.L.Francklin'

'Honourable Mrs J.L.Francklin' 2 W-W
(J.R. Pearson & Sons, pre-1907)
'Minnie Hume' × 'Madame de Graaff'
Perianth segments milk white, overlapping; corona large, opening soft primrose yellow, becoming silvery white, with rim flanged. Tall. See also 'Honourable Mrs J.F.Franklin'

'Honourable Mrs Jocelyn' 2 Y-Y
(G.P. Haydon, pre-1901)
Fl. star shaped, rich golden yellow, perianth segments ovate, mucronate, spreading, twisted, overlapping at base only; corona cylindrical, smooth, darker in tone than the perianth, with rim flanged and crenate

'Honourable R.J.Seddon' 1 or 2 Y-Y
Syn. of 'Honourable J.R.Seddon'

'Honour Bright' 2 W-O
(J.L. Richardson) F.E. Board, 1962
'Kilworth' × 'Rockall'; sdlg no. 646
Corona reddish orange. Late. Resembles 'Avenger' but with a paler corona

'Hoodsport' 11a W-W
(M.B. Hatch) M.B. Hatch, 1977
'Mount Hood' sport
Fl. 85 mm wide; corona segments opening pale yellow, quickly becoming white. Mid-season. Resembles a split-corona 'Mount Hood'

'Hoo Ha' 2 Y-Y
(J.N.Hancock & Co., 1986) J.N.Hancock & Co., 1997
'Glorification' × 'Mrs David Calvert'; sdlg no. 41/86H
Perianth segments ovate, spreading; corona bowl-shaped, ribbed, heavily frilled. Late

'Hookah' 1 W-Y
(A.O. Roblin, 1946) A.O. Roblin, 1956
'Sincerity' × 'Kanchenjunga'

'Hoopoe' 8 Y-O
(G.E. Mitsch) G.E. Mitsch, 1977
'Matador' × *N. jonquilla*; sdlg no. JJ77/2
Fls 2-3 per stem, 54 mm wide; perianth segments rounded; corona orange. Mid-season. Scented

"Hoop Petticoat Daffodil"
Syn. of *N. bulbocodium*

'Hoosac' 2 Y-? (a)
(E.C. Powell, pre-1946)
'Golden Beauty' × *N. jonquilla*

'Hope' 1 W-? (b)
(Cartwright & Goodwin, pre-1916)

'Hope' 4 W-Y
(J.L. Richardson) M.J. Jefferson-Brown, 1971
'Falaise' × 'Rose Caprice'
AM(e) 1971

'Hope' 1 W-GWW
Syn. of 'Scope'

'Hopeful' 2 Y-Y
(G.L. Wilson, pre-1927)
'Bernardino' × 'King Alfred'
Fl. rich yellow, perianth segments very broadly ovate; corona with rim somewhat flanged

'Hope of Holland' 1 Y-Y
(E.H. Krelage & Son, pre-1913)
Fl. 121 mm wide, rich butter yellow; corona broad, flared, ribbed, with rim widely rolled

'Hopesay' 2 W-YYO
(C.B. Habershon, pre-1947)
'Mitylene' × 'Hades'
Fl. 121 mm wide; perianth segments broad, smooth, overlapping; corona very shallow bowl-shaped, ribbed, light greenish yellow 6D, with a well-defined band of orange (28A) at rim. AM(e) 1951

'Horace' 9 W-GOR
(G.H. Engleheart, pre-1894)
'Ornatus' × *N. radiiflorus* var. *poetarum*
Fl. 73 mm wide; perianth segments roundish, fairly prominently mucronate, snow white, spreading, a little concave, margins recurved at base, wavy, separated at base, touching or slightly overlapping at midpoint; the inner segments with margins more strongly waved and more deeply recurved at base; corona disc-shaped, closely ribbed, orange, with greenish tones at base and a broad band of brilliant red at rim, with the rim notched and minutely dentate. Tall. 2n=14

'Horace Daines' 1 Y-Y
(H. Daines) H. Daines, 1964
Mid-season

'Horace Shailer' 1 Y-Y
(A. Gibson, pre-1951)
'Kingscourt' × 'Goldcourt'
Corona deeper in tone than the perianth, with rim rolled

'Horace Wright' 3 W-? (b)
(Barr & Sons, pre-1908)

'Horatio' 2 W-? (b)
(M. van Waveren & Sons, pre-1954)

'Horatius' 2 W-Y
(E.M. Crosfield, pre-1909)
Perianth segments overlapping; corona ribbed, clear yellow, with rim broadly crenate. Resembles an improved 'Lady Margaret Boscawen'

'Horatius' 1 Y-Y
(Sir A.P.W. Thomas, pre-1915)

'Horizon' 3 W-GOO
(G.H. Engleheart, pre-1910)
Fl. small; perianth segments reflexed, overlapping; corona shallow, ribbed, reddish orange

'Horizon' 1 Y-Y
(W. Jackson Jr, 1956) W. Jackson Jr, 1968
'Kalman' × 'Kingscourt'; sdlg no. 97/56

'Hornblower' 1 W-Y
(J.N. Hancock & Co., c.1983) Unregistered

'Horndon' 2 Y-Y
(J.W. Avery) J.W. Avery, 1959

'Hornet' 3 Y-? (a)
(P.D. Williams, pre-1908)

'Horn Mill' 2 W-R
(W.A.Noton, pre-1996) Unregistered

'Horn of Plenty' 5 W-W
(C.G. van Tubergen, pre-1947)
? × *N. triandrus*
Fls 3 per stem, 62 mm wide, greenish white, facing down; perianth segments ovate, blunt, fairly prominently mucronate, spreading, plane, overlapping a quarter; the inner segments a little narrower; corona cylindrical or slightly funnel-shaped, smooth, mouth even, obscurely lobed, rim slightly flanged and minutely notched. 2n=21. AM(Haarlem) 1957

'Horoscope' 2 W-OOY
(D.S. Bell) D.S. Bell, 1963

'Mannequin' × 'Garland'
Fl. 111 mm wide; corona carrot orange, with a narrow band of yellow at rim, frilled. Mid-season. Resembles 'Blarney's Daughter' but with a rounder flower and darker-coloured corona

'Horris Hill' 2 W-P
(Mrs J.Abel Smith) M.W.Baxter, 1996
Sdlg × 'Jewel Song'
Fl. 92 mm wide; perianth segments broadly ovate, truncate, with margins incurved, overlapping one-third; the inner segments a little narrower, inflexed at base, recurved towards mouth; corona bowl-shaped, lightly ribbed, apple blossom pink, mouth straight, more closely ribbed, obscurely 6-lobed and very lightly frilled. Late

'Horsa' 1 Y-Y
(H. Backhouse, pre-1908)

'Hors d'Oeuvre' 8 Y-Y
(A. Gray, 1949) A. Gray, 1959
'Canaliculatus' × *N. minor*
Fl. 25 mm wide. Dwarf. Early or very early. 2n=17

'Horsfield' 1 W-Y
Syn. of 'Horsfieldii'

'Horsfieldii' 1 W-Y
(J. Horsefield, c.1845)
N. pseudonarcissus × *N. bicolor*
Fl. 104 mm wide; perianth segments broadly ovate, mucronate, spreading, somewhat creased, overlapping one-third; the inner segments a little inflexed at base and reflexed at apex; corona cylindrical, rich yellow, with rim flanged and crenate. Early. 2n=22. Syn. 'Horsfield', Pseudonarcissus Bicolor 'Horsfieldii'. "Absorbed" 'Mrs Harrison Weir', 'President Garfield' and 'Sir Robert Peel'

'Horton' 1 Y-Y
(J.W. Barr, pre-1930)

'Hortulanus Witte' 1 Y-Y
Syn. of 'Unsurpassable'

'Hortus' 2 Y-YYO
(R.H. Bath, pre-1928)
Perianth segments yellow; corona deeper in tone than the perianth, with a broad band of scarlet-orange at rim. Early

'Horus' 2 Y-? (a)
(Barr & Sons, pre-1945)

'Hosanna' 2 Y-Y
(W. Jackson Jr) Jackson's Daffodils, 1979
Sdlg 128/65 × 'Ristin'; sdlg no. 48/72
Fl. 105 mm wide. Mid-season

'Hospoda' 2 Y-O
Syn. of 'Hospodar'

'Hospodar' 2 Y-O
(J.C. Williams, pre-1914)
'Firebrand' × 'King Alfred'
Fl. 95 mm wide; perianth segments ovate, acute, rich primrose yellow, with white mucro, a little inflexed, with margins sometimes notched in upper third, overlapping one-third; the inner segments more narrowly ovate, with margins incurved and more frequently and deeply notched; corona funnel-shaped, ribbed, opening light orange, becoming darker in tone, mouth straight, a little wavy, with rim notched. Mid-season. Sunproof. 2n=28. *C(g) 1936. See also 'Hospoda'

'Hostess' 2 W-? (b)
(R. Crews, pre-1949)
Syn. 'Felicity'

'Hostile' 2 W-O
(W.M. Spry, pre-1975) Unregistered
'Jean Hood' × 'My Choice'
Corona dark reddish orange

'Hot Dot' 2 Y-R
(Colin Crotty) Unregistered
Sdlg no. 9-75

'Hot Gossip' 2 Y-O
(A.J.R. Pearson) A.J.R. Pearson, 1987
('Home Fires' × 'Ceylon') × 'Vulcan'; sdlg no. 79/9/E8
Fl. forming a double triangle; perianth segments broadly ovate, blunt, golden yellow, with slight white mucro, spreading, with margins incurling at apex, smooth, regular, overlapping one-third to a half; corona broad funnel-shaped, strong orange 25A paling slightly to base, mouth even, rim regularly crenate and slightly flanged. Early to mid-season. Resembles a 'Ceylon' of better form and colour

'Hotham' 2 W-W
(C.A. Nethercote, pre-1961) Unregistered
Fl. pure white; perianth segments broad and smooth

'Hothu' 1 W-W
(W. Jackson Sr, 1938) W. Jackson Jr, 1956
'Canace' × 'White Emperor'
Fl. pure white; corona with rim slightly rolled

'Hot Ice' 2 W-R
(J.S. Leitch) J.S. Leitch, 1956

'Hot Idea' 2 Y-OOR
(M.E.Brogden) Unregistered

'Hot Line' 2 Y-R
(P. Phillips) P. Phillips, 1966
Fl. 92 mm wide; perianth segments yellow, suffused red at base; corona intense red. Mid-season. Resembles a more strongly coloured 'Hot Line' with the corona more deeply rolled at rim

'Hot Lips' 2 W-P
(John R.Reed) John R.Reed, 1995
'Arctic Char' × 'Dear Me'; sdlg no. 83-87-2
Fl. 98 mm wide, facing up; perianth segments smooth; corona broad funnel-shaped, intense deep rose pink. Mid-season

'Hot Pink' 2 W-P
(O.David Niswonger) O.David Niswonger, 1993
'Precedent' × Evans sdlg N-81/1 ('Chiquita' × 'Tyee'); sdlg no. 7-86
Fl. 98.43 mm wide; perianth segments ovate, pure white, plane; corona funnel-shaped, deep pink, with the base lighter in colour and the rim darker, frilled, with rim flanged. Mid-season. Sunproof

'Hot Point' 2 Y-O
Syn. of 'Hotpoint'

'Hotpoint' 2 Y-O
(S.J. Bisdee, 1942)
'Killigrew' × 'Red Morn'
See also 'Hot Point'

'Hot Spot' 3 W-? (b)
(G.H. Engleheart, pre-1923)

'Hot Spot' 2 Y-O
(J.N. Hancock & Co., 1965) J.N. Hancock & Co., 1977
'Excellent' hybrid; sdlg no. 138/60
Fl. 93 mm wide; perianth segments vivid yellow 12A; corona orange (28A). Mid-season

'Hotsprings' 2 Y-O
(G.L. Wilson, pre-1943)
Resembles a smaller 'Fortune' with a brighter-coloured corona

'Hotspur' 3 Y-Y
(E. Leeds, pre-1877)
Perianth segments primrose yellow; corona tinged orange. Syn. Barrii Albidus 'Hotspur'. Was "absorbed" into 'John Stevenson'

'Hotspur' 2 W-O
(J.L. Richardson) J.L. Richardson, 1959
'Kilworth' × 'Arbar'
Perianth segments smooth, deeply overlapping; corona deep reddish orange, with mouth expanded and rim dentate

'Hot Stuff' 2 Y-R
(J.T.Gray, 1954) P. Phillips, 1964
Fl. 105 mm wide; perianth segments broad, rounded, smooth and of good substance; corona

bowl-shaped, deep red. Mid-season

'Hot Sun' 3 W-GYR
(W.A. Noton, 1972) W.A. Noton, 1985
Sdlg × 'Matapan'
Late

'Hot Toddy' 4 Y-O
(Carncairn Daffodils) Carncairn Daffodils, 1983
'Egg Nogg' × 'Little Princess'; sdlg no. 3/2/72
Fl. 110 mm wide; perianth and other petaloid segments vivid yellow 16A; the outer whorl very broad in outline, blunt or truncate at apex, mucronate, reflexed, a little concave; the inner whorls narrow, irregularly shaped, crumpled, touched with dark yellow, decreasing in size and becoming more contorted towards centre; corona segments interspersed, short, smooth, vivid reddish orange 32A, frilled and minutely crenate. Mid-season

'Houipapa' 3 W-Y
(R. Crews) R. Crews, 1962
Fl. 108 mm wide; corona lemon yellow. Mid-season

'House of Orange' 2 Y-O
(G.A. Uit den Boogaard) C.W. Oudshoorn, 1960
'High Life' × 'Duke of Windsor'
Perianth segments sulphur yellow; corona shallow, orange. Mid-season. AM(Haarlem) 1960

'Howard's Way' 3 W-GYR
(Mrs J. Abel Smith) Mrs J. Abel Smith, 1987
'Verona' × ('Hamzali' × 'Aircastle'); sdlg no. R33/21
Perianth segments broad, rounded, overlapping; corona disc-shaped. Late

'Howard Thomas' 6 Y-Y
(H. Thomas) F.A. Saunders, 1966
Fl. 76 mm wide, golden yellow; corona darker in tone. Early

'Howzat' 2 W-R
(P. & G. Phillips) P. & G. Phillips, 1978
Fl. 93 mm wide. Mid-season. Resembles 'Aden' with a more rounded perianth and broader corona

'Hoyle' 1 W-Y
(J.N. Hancock & Co.) J.N. Hancock & Co., 1955
Perianth segments of good substance, deeply overlapping; corona ageing to near white, with the outside remaining yellow

'Hoylyn' 2 W-P
(J.N. Hancock & Co., c.1955) Unregistered
'Pink Pearl' × 'Rose Bay'

'Hubert Cuijpers' 2 W-? (b)
(pre-1953)

'Hudibras' 1 Y-Y

(E. Leeds, pre-1877)
Fl. large; perianth segments overlapping; corona darker in tone than the perianth. Syn. Pseudonarcissus Major 'Hudibras'

'Huesca' 3 W-R
(The Brodie of Brodie, c.1928)
'Kaffir' × 'Dactyl'
Corona red

'Hugh Aldersey' 1 W-W
(H. Aldersey, pre-1917)
Fl. 95 mm wide, facing down; perianth segments creamy white, regular, overlapping at base only; corona pale creamy sulphur, with creamy white at rim, mouth expanded. Mid-season. Syn. 'Angela'

'Hugh Dettman' 2 W-?
(J. Sharp, pre-1935)
Perianth segments broadly ovate, blunt, slightly mucronate, pure white, smooth, overlapping one-third to a half, with one margin of one outer segment lying over not under the inner segment; the inner segments more narrowly ovate and a little inflexed; corona deep bowl-shaped, with a distinct band of pink at rim, mouth straight, regularly frilled

'Hugh Didit' 2 YYW-WWP
(P. & G. Phillips) P. & G. Phillips, 1978
Fl. 110 mm wide; perianth segments lemon, with white at base; corona whitish, with pale pink at rim. Mid-season

'Hugh Evans' 2 Y-? (a)
(H.G. Longford, pre-1937)

'Hugh Mermagen' 2 W-? (b)
(Mrs R.O. Backhouse, pre-1921)

'Hugh Morbey' 2 Y-O
(A. Overton) A. Overton, 1960
Perianth segments broad, rich yellow; corona large, deep orange. Early

'Hugh Poate' 2 Y-O
(The Brodie of Brodie, pre-1931)
'Fortune' hybrid
Perianth segments broad, deep yellow, overlapping; corona rich orange

'Hugh Ramsay' 3 W-R
(W.M. Spry, pre-1975) Unregistered
'Aldgate' × 'Delight'
Corona scarlet, frilled

'Hugh Town' 8 Y-O
(Harry I. Tuggle Jr, 1974) Rosewarne EHS, 1987
'Matador' × 'Grand Soleil d'Or'; sdlg no. USA 66/49/12
Fls 4-6 per stem; perianth segments broadly ovate,

prominently mucronate, vivid yellow 9B, a little inflexed, with margins incurling, overlapping half; corona bowl-shaped, loosely ribbed, more intense in colour than light orange (23A), tinged green at base, frilled. Very early

'Huguenot' 2 W-? (b)
(Mrs R.S. Cobley, pre-1932)

'Huia'
(H.E. Sharp, pre-1915)

'Huia' 1 or 2 Y-Y
(G. Lewis, c.1933)

'Huia' 1 W-Y
(J.S. Leitch) J.S. Leitch, 1968
'Leontes' × 'Sunwell'
Fl. 111 mm wide; corona lemon yellow

'Hukarere' 2 W-R
(A.B. Davey) A.B. Davey, 1978
'Nearula' hybrid; sdlg no. 1/10/65
Fl. 82 mm wide. Mid-season

'Hula Girl' 11a Y-YWY
(A.N. Kanouse) Mrs A.N. Kanouse, 1991
'Daydream' × 'Lemon Ice'
Fl. 85 mm wide; perianth segments broad, soft light yellow, overlapping; the inner segments less broad; corona split, the six segments opposite the perianth segments, soft white, with light yellow at base and rim, spreading, frilled, with rim minutely and densely notched. Early

'Hulda' 1 W-Y
(Barr & Sons, pre-1904)
Fl. 102 mm wide; perianth segments broadly ovate, blunt, mucronate, inflexed, somewhat creased and with margins incurling, overlapping one-third to a half; the inner segments squarish at apex, only very slightly mucronate, somewhat twisted; corona funnel-shaped, angled, soft primrose yellow, with mouth expanded and heavily ribbed, rim crenate

'Hulta' 2 W-O
(J.T. Gray, pre-1938)
Perianth segments pure white; corona buff apricot, with rim flanged

'Humber' 2 Y-?
(R.C.A. Tombleson) R.C.A. Tombleson, 1971
'Harewood' × 'Spanish Gold'
Fl. 119 mm wide

'Humdinger'
(?H.M. & D.W. Gourlay, pre-1950)

'Humei' 1 Y-Y
(E. Leeds, pre-1877)

Perianth segments sulphur yellow; corona darker in tone. This has also been used as a Group name

'Hume's Concolor' 1 Y-Y
(E. Leeds, pre-1877)
Syn. Humei 'Hume's Concolor'

'Hume's Giant' 1 Y-Y
(E. Leeds, pre-1877)
Fl. large; perianth segments opening mid-yellow, becoming sulphur yellow. Syn. Humei 'Concolor Monstrosus', Humei 'Hume's Giant', Humei 'Monstrosus'

'Hume's Sulphur' 1 W-Y
(E. Leeds, pre-1877)
$N. \times poculiformis$ sdlg
Perianth sulphur white. Syn. Humei 'Albidus', Humei 'Hume's Sulphur'

'Hume's White' 1 W-W
(E. Leeds, pre-1877)
Fl. silvery white. Syn. Humei 'Albus', Humei 'Hume's White'

N. humilis (Cavanilles) Traub = *N. cavanillesii*

humilis = *N. pseudonarcissus* var. *humilis*

'Humility' 2 W-P
(F.E. Board) F.E. Board, 1965
'Lunar Rainbow' × 'Irish Rose'
Corona with rim rolled

'Humming Bird' 9 W-?
(E. Oostdam, pre-1939)

'Hummingbird' 6 Y-Y
(G.E. Mitsch) G.E. Mitsch, 1975
([('Market Merry' × 'Carbineer') × 'Armada'] × *N. cyclamineus*) open pollinated; sdlg no. FO15/2
Fl. 60 mm wide, clear deep yellow, of good substance; perianth segments ovate, acute, with slight white mucro, reflexed, with margins wavy, overlapping at base only; the inner segments twisted or with margins more strongly waved; corona cylindrical, lightly ribbed, with mouth very slightly flared, rim notched. Early

'Humoresque' 2 W-R
(D.S. Bell) D.S. Bell, 1959
'Mannequin' × 'Garland'
Fl. 115 mm wide; corona very shallow bowl-shaped, red. Mid-season. Resembles 'Salmon Trout' but with the perianth white on opening and the corona richer in colour. PC(e)(NZ) 1961

'Humorist' 2 W-? (b)
(H.A. Brown, pre-1950)

'Humpty Dumpty' 5 W-W
(C.A. Nethercote) T. Morrison, 1960
Perianth segments pure white, slightly reflexed

'Hungarian Rhapsody' 11a W-P
(G.E.Mitsch, 1984) R. & E.Havens, 1997
([('Precedent' × 'Carita') × ('Radiation' × 'Mabel Taylor')] × 'Interim') × 'Phantom'; sdlg no. TT16/4
Fl. 110 mm wide; perianth segments broadly ovate; corona segments opposite and closely overlying the perianth segments, deep apricot pink, frilled. Mid-season to late. Sunproof

'Huntercombe' 2 W-Y
(Mrs R.S. Cobley, pre-1938)
Perianth segments ovate, blunt, slightly mucronate, sulphur white, spreading, overlapping one-third to a half; the inner segments a little inflexed and very slightly twisted; corona cup-shaped, pale amber yellow, shading to rich yellow at base, mouth straight, wavy, rim notched and crenate. AM(e) 1938

'Hunterlea' 3 W-WWR
(W.J. Dunlop) W.J. Dunlop, 1968

'Hunters Bar' 2 Y-Y
(F.E. Board) F.E. Board, 1965
'Galway' × 'Arctic Gold'; sdlg no. 475
Late

'Hunters Gold' 1 Y-Y
(J.A.Hunter) J.A.Hunter, 1997
'Temple Gold' × ('Spellbinder' × ['Hunter's Moon' × 'Content']); sdlg no. 21/84E
Fl. 113 mm wide, at right angles to the stem; perianth segments ovate, vivid yellow 9B, spreading, plane, smooth; corona flared, very slightly darker in tone (9A) than the perianth, with rim rolled and crenate. Very early

'Hunters Luck' 2 W-P
(C.L. Andrews)

'Hunter's Moon' 1 Y-Y
(The Brodie of Brodie, c.1936)
'Brimstone' × 'Moongold'
Fl. 102 mm wide; perianth segments light greenish yellow 8B, overlapping half; corona ribbed, slightly darker in tone (6B) than the perianth, with a brighter tone at rim, mouth expanded and frilled, with rim crenate. AM(e) 1943, AM(Haarlem) 1950, *AM(g) 1953

'Hunthawang' 1 Y-Y
(J.N. Hancock & Co.) J.N. Hancock & Co., 1959
Perianth segments broadly ovate, bright yellow; corona deeper in tone, with rim rolled

'Hunting Caye' 2 Y-GYY
(A.J.R. Pearson) A.J.R. Pearson, 1989

'Camelot' × 'Daydream'; sdlg no. 80/19/F1
Fl. rounded, 98 mm wide; perianth segments very broad, rounded at apex, golden yellow, with slight white mucro, spreading or very slightly inflexed, plane or concave, smooth, overlapping half; the outer segments overlapping one another; the inner segments broad-shouldered at base; corona cylindrical, broad, lightly ribbed, slightly darker in tone than the perianth, with green at base, rim loosely flanged and lightly crenate

'Huntingtower' 1 Y-Y
(D.N.Y. Olson) D.N.Y. Olson, 1978
'Horace Shailer' × 'Goldcourt'; sdlg no. 30/1
Fl. 108 mm wide, mid-yellow; perianth segments broadly ovate, fairly prominently mucronate, spreading, overlapping half; the inner segments sometimes inflexed, somewhat creased and with margins wavy; corona cylindrical, smooth, mouth flared and a little frilled, rim notched. Mid-season. Resembles a deeper-coloured 'Slieveboy'

'Huntley' 2 G-G
(W.M. Spry, pre-1975) Unregistered
'Hunter's Moon' × 'Tunis'
Fl. lemon green, with overtones of buff

'Huntsman' 3 Y-? (a)
(E. & J.C. Martin, pre-1916)

'Huntsman' 2 W-R
(J.L. Richardson) Mrs H.K. Richardson, 1963
'Kilworth' × 'Signal Light'
Perianth segments broadly ovate, pure white; corona very shallow bowl-shaped, orange-red, slightly frilled

'Huon' 9 W-YYO
(G.H. Engleheart, pre-1927)
Perianth segments white, with lemon at base, overlapping two-thirds; corona yellow, with reddish orange at rim. AM(c) 1929, AM(Haarlem) 1930, *AM(m) 1930, FCC(c) 1931

'Huon Chief' 4 W-Y
(Jackson's Daffodils) Jackson's Daffodils, 1986
'Tavelle' × 'Blodfier'; sdlg no. 305/78
Perianth and other petaloid segments in several whorls, broadly ovate, blunt, greenish white (155A), deeply overlapping; the outer whorls prominently mucronate, spreading or a little inflexed, with margins wavy; the inner whorls only very slightly mucronate, successively a little shorter, more strongly inflexed, with margins more heavily waved; the centre whorl strongly inflexed, with margins tightly incurled; corona segments interspersed, short vivid yellow 9A, frilled. Late

'Huon Glow' 4 W-Y
(D. Jackson) Jackson's Daffodils, 1989
'Tavelle' × 'Signal Light'; sdlg no. 306/80

Fl. 90 mm wide; perianth and other petaloid segments in four layers whorls, greenish white (155A); corona segments brilliant yellow 7A, touched light orange (23A). Late

'Huon Lass' 4 W-P
(Jackson's Daffodils) Jackson's Daffodils, 1986
Sdlg 66/70 × sdlg 64/70; sdlg no. 216/78
Perianth segments greenish white (155A); corona pale orange (29C). Mid-season. Scented

'Huon Pride' 4 W-W
(D.J. Jackson, 1976) Jackson's Daffodils, 1989
'Tavelle' × 'Chimeon'; sdlg no. 300/76
Fl. 93 mm wide; perianth segments greenish white (155A); corona segments opening yellow, becoming pinkish white (159D). Late

'Huron' 1 W-? (b)
(E.C. Powell, pre-1946)
'Aeolus' × 'White Emperor'

'Hurrah' 2 Y-Y
(W.G.Pannill) W.G.Pannill, 1994
'New Penny' × ('Lemonade' × 'Lemnos'); sdlg no. 81/2
Mid-season

'Hurricane' 2 Y-? (a)
(G.H. Johnstone, pre-1944)

'Hurunui' 2 WWY-YYO
(L.C.Palmer, c.1980) M.E.Rollinson, 1994
'Jaguar' × 'Vulcan'; sdlg no. H21
Fl. forming a double triangle; perianth segments very broadly ovate, blunt, only very slightly mucronate, white, touched light greenish yellow 8B at base, a little inflexed, overlapping half; the inner segments more narrowly ovate; corona vivid yellow 9A, shading to yellow-orange (16A) at rim, mouth expanded, even, rim obscurely crenate. Mid-season to late

'Hush' 2 W-GWW
(J.N.Hancock & Co., 1978) Unregistered
'My Word' × 'Glenshesk'; sdlg no. 93/78H
Fl. pure white, glistening; perianth segments deeply overlapping; corona funnel-shaped, with green at base, rim rolled. Tall. Mid-season

'Huskie' 2 W-W
(G.C. Yeates) G.C. Yeates, 1968
PC(e)(NZ) 1972

'Husky' 3 Y-YOR
(P.D. Williams, pre-1927)
Early. Resembles a more brightly coloured 'Bath's Flame' in the corona

'Hussar' 2 Y-? (a)
(P.D. Williams, pre-1931)

'Hussar' 2 Y-YYR
(J.L. Richardson) J.L. Richardson, 1959
'Benghazi' × 'Ceylon'
Perianth segments broadly ovate, deep yellow; corona opening orange, becoming bright yellow, with a broad band of almost cherry red at rim, frilled. Late. Sunproof

'Hussy' 1 W-Y
(Jackson's Daffodils, 1975) Jackson's Daffodils, 1986
'Jacobar' × 'Bruce'; sdlg no. 36/75
Perianth segments broadly ovate, blunt, mucronate, greenish white (155A), faintly ribbed, overlapping half; the inner segments more narrowly ovate, acute, slightly mucronate; corona funnel-shaped, vivid yellow 9A, mouth expanded, frilled with rim rolled. Early

'Hustler' 2 Y-O
(J.S. Leitch) J.S. Leitch, 1967
Fl. 102 mm wide; corona reddish orange

'H.W.Curtis' 2 W-? (b)
(West & Fell, pre-1938)

'Hwyfa'
(C. Wolley-Dod, pre-1907)

'Hyacinth' 3 W-Y
(G.H. Engleheart, pre-1904)
Perianth segments snow white; corona large, disc-shaped, pale lemon yellow. Hyacinth-scented

'Hydra' 3 W-? (b)
(G.A. Uit den Boogaard, pre-1950)

'Hyglow' 2 W-P
(A. Gibson) A. Gibson, 1965
Fl. 95 mm wide; perianth segments off-white; corona strong pink. Mid-season

'Hylas' 1 W-Y
(W. Jackson Jr) W. Jackson Jr, 1968
'Rowella' × 'Lod'; sdlg no. 66/64

'Hylena' 2 W-P
(J.N.Hancock & Co., pre-1974) Unregistered

'Hymen' 1 W-Y
(Barr & Sons, pre-1919)
Corona broad, opening soft primrose yellow, becoming creamy yellow then almost white, rim flared and frilled

'Hymettus' 2 W-WWY
(The Brodie of Brodie, c.1916)
Sdlg 633/05 × 'Bernardino'
Perianth segments ovate, white, spreading, overlapping one-third; the inner segments slightly inflexed and a little twisted; corona broad funnel-shaped,

ivory white, with clear lemon yellow at rim when fully developed, mouth widely expanded, frilled. AM(Haarlem) 1931

'Hymis' 2 Y-Y
(W. Jackson Sr, 1946)
'Hymyr' × 'Matoome'

'Hymyr' 2 Y-Y
(W. Jackson Sr, 1936) W. Jackson Jr, 1956
'Thyl' × 'Pilgrimage'

'Hypatia' 3 W-GYY
(J.C. Williams, pre-1910)
Perianth segments creamy white; corona canary yellow, with green at base

'Hyperion' 3 Y-? (a)
(Cartwright & Goodwin, pre-1908)

'Hyperion' 2 Y-Y
(J.J. Grullemans & Sons) J.J. Grullemans & Sons, 1956

'Hypnos' 1 Y-Y
(Sir J.S. Arkwright, pre-1931)

'Hythe' 2 Y-Y
(W. Jackson Jr, 1967) Unregistered
Sdlg 28/56 × 'Lyetta'; sdlg no. 180/70

I

'Iambic' 9 W-?
(G.H. Engleheart, pre-1914)

'Ian' 1 W-W
(T. Buncombe, pre-1934)

'Iana' 1 W-W
(E.C. Powell, pre-1946)
'Mrs Ernst H. Krelage' × 'Tenedos'

'Ian Patterson' 2 Y-? (a)
(H.R. Meyer, pre-1946)

'Ian Secrett' 9 W-O
(G.H. Engleheart, pre-1933)
Perianth segments rounded, creamy white, deeply overlapping; corona shallow, widely expanded, ribbed, with rim crenate. *GulvalAM(m) 1935

'Ian Shankley' 2 Y-Y
(L.P. Dettman) L.P. Dettman, 1975

'Creamed Honey' open pollinated; sdlg no. 7/71
Fl. 87 mm wide; perianth segments vivid yellow 9A, with greenish white (155A) at base; corona light yellow 20B, with a broad band of a darker tone (22C) at rim. Mid-season

'Ianthe' 3 W-Y
(E. Leeds, pre-1877)
Perianth segments sulphur white; corona canary yellow. Syn. 'Vincenti Delicatus', Leedsii 'Ianthe', Leedsii 'Vincenti Delicata'

'Ianthe' 3 W-? (b)
(W.A. Bell, pre-1949)

'Iatros' 2 Y-R
(W. Jackson Jr, c.1965) Unregistered
Sdlg × 'Dimity'

'Ibanez' 1 W-Y
(M. van Waveren & Sons, pre-1930)
Perianth segmens broad; corona flared. Early

'Ibberton' 3 W-YYO
(J.W. Blanchard) J.W. Blanchard, 1974
'Roimond' × 'Arbar'
Fl. 90 mm wide

'Iberia' 1 Y-Y
(D.S. Bell) D.S. Bell, 1964
'Ranalagh' × 'Val d'Or'
Fl. 110 mm wide; corona flanged and regularly frilled. Resembles 'Kingscourt' but with the perianth segments more rounded

'Ibex' 3 W-? (b)
(E.M. Crosfield, pre-1913)

'Ibis' 9 W-?
(P.D. Williams, pre-1907)
Perianth segments reflexed, overlapping; corona with a broad band of scarlet at rim

'Ibis' 6 W-Y
(G.E. Mitsch) G.E. Mitsch, 1972
'Trousseau' × *N. cyclamineus*; sdlg no. Z39/1
Fl. star-shaped, 80 mm wide; perianth segments broadly ovate, fairly prominently mucronate, milk white, spreading or more or less strongly reflexed, plane, overlapping a quarter to one-third; the inner segments only very slightly mucronate; corona cylindrical, narrow, lightly ribbed, pale lemon yellow, with mouth slightly expanded, rim regularly crenate. Dwarf. Early. Resembles a shorter-stemmed 'Perky' of purer white with the perianth segments less strongly reflexed

'Ibis' 3 W-GOR
Syn. of 'Icon'

'Ibycus' 9 W-GYR
(A.M. Wilson, pre-1930)
Corona yellow, with olive green at base, shading to scarlet at rim

'Icarus' 1 Y-Y
(M. van Waveren & Sons, pre-1942)

'Ice Age' 2 W-W
(Murray W. Evans) Murray W. Evans, 1976
'Zero' × ('Zero' × 'Kanchenjunga'); sdlg no. F-268
Fl. 110 mm wide. Early

'Iceberg' 1 W-W
(E.M. Crosfield, pre-1907)

'Iceberg' 1 W-W
(G.L. Wilson) Harry I. Tuggle Jr, 1962
'Broughshane' × 'Cotterton'
Fl. 130 mm wide. Mid-season

'Icebound' 2 W-W
(J.A. Hunter) J.A. Hunter, 1997
'Penguin' × ('Glendermott' × 'Kotuku'); sdlg no. 34/83G
Fl. 106 mm wide, pure white; perianth segments ovate; corona funnel-shaped, with mouth wavy. Mid-season

'Ice Cap' 2 W-W
(G.L. Wilson) Guy L. Wilson Ltd, 1967
('Tryst' × ['Greenland' × 'Saint Mary']) × 'Glendermott'
Mid-season

'Ice Cavern' 1 W-W
(J.N. Hancock & Co., 1963) Unregistered

'Ice Chimes' 5 Y-Y
(G.E. Mitsch & R. & E. Havens, 1970) G.E. Mitsch & R. & E. Havens, 1988
'Silver Bells' × *N. triandrus* var. *concolor*; sdlg no. F153/1
Fls 3-4 per stem; perianth segments ivory yellow; corona light yellow. Dwarf. Mid-season. 2n=22. The perianth is sometimes whitish

'Ice Circle' 11a W-W
(J. Gerritsen & Son, c.1979) Unregistered

'Ice Cream' 2 Y-W
(Konynenburg & Mark, c.1966) Unregistered
'Spellbinder' × 'Binkie'

'Ice Crystal' 11a W-W
(J. Gerritsen & Son) J. Gerritsen & Son, 1965
Fl. large; perianth segments pure white; corona segments blush white. Tall. Early

'Ice Curtain' 1 W-W
(G.L. Wilson, pre-1937)

'Ice Dancer' 2 W-GWP
(Brian S. Duncan) Brian S. Duncan, 1996
'Pismo Beach' × 'High Society'; sdlg no. 1307
Fl. 108 mm wide; perianth segments broadly ovate, pure white, glittering, plane; corona deep bowl-shaped, pure white, with green at base and deep rose pink at rim, mouth slightly lobed, rim entire. Mid-season

'Ice Diamond' 4 W-W
(G.E. Mitsch, 1976) R. & E. Havens, 1990
'Gay Time' × 'Stainless'; sdlg no. LL66/1
Fl. 100 mm wide; perianth segments in three whorls symmetrically arranged, broadly ovate, blunt, slightly mucronate, white, plane, smooth, overlapping half; the outer whorl spreading; the second whorl slightly shorter, inflexed; the centre whorl fewer than six in number, more strongly inflexed, with margins incurling; corona segments clustered at centre, very short, opening creamy yellow, becoming pure white. Late. Seed set

'Iced Lemon' 2 Y-WWY
(J.N. Hancock & Co., 1982) Unregistered
'Daydream' hybrid; sdlg no. 76/82H
Perianth segments sulphur yellow; corona opening sulphur yellow, becoming white, with orange-yellow at rim. Tall. Early to mid-season

'Ice Fall' 2 W-W
(R.C.A. Tombleson) R.C.A. Tombleson, 1964
Mid-season

'Icefield' 1 W-W
(W. Balch, pre-1933)

'Icefirth' 1 W-W
(D.N.Y. Olson, 1972) D.N.Y. Olson, 1988
'Ave' × 'Empress of Ireland'; sdlg no. 64/1
Mid-season. Resembles a Div. 1 'Canisp'

'Icefloe' 2 W-Y
(W.B. Cranfield, pre-1923)
Perianth segments pure white, overlapping; corona straight, lemon yellow

'Ice Follies' 2 W-W
(Konynenburg & Mark, pre-1953)
Fl. 95 mm wide; perianth segments broadly ovate, truncate, only very slightly mucronate, spreading or a little reflexed, overlapping half; the inner segments more usually spreading, with margins wavy; corona shallow, very widely expanded, heavily ribbed, opening light greenish yellow with tints of a lighter tone (6D), becoming white, frilled, with rim deeply notched and minutely crenate. Mid-season. 2n=14,28. *FCC(p) 1975, *FCC(g) 1978, Wister Award 1992, AGM 1993

'Icegleam' 3 W-W
(C. Dawson, pre-1922)
Corona very shallow, creamy white, flushed apricot yellow

'Ice House' 2 W-W
(G.W.E. Brogden, 1981) Brogden Bulbs, 1991
'Guiding Light' × ('Empress of Ireland' × 'Canisp'); sdlg no. X91/2
Fl. forming a double triangle, 110 mm wide, ice white; corona cylindrical, mouth straight, wavy, rim lightly dentate. Early

'Ice King' 4 W-Y
A.P. van den Berg-Hytuna, 1984
'Ice Follies' sport
Perianth and other petaloid segments ivory white; the outer whorl broadly ovate, blunt or truncate, slightly mucronate, spreading or a little reflexed, overlapping one-third; the inner whorls shorter than the corona and clustered within it, of irregular shape, frilled and crumpled; corona deeply and irregularly split, spreading to half as long as the outer whorl of petaloid segments, sulphur yellow, with a broad band of white at rim, frilled, rim notched and minutely crenate. Mid-season

'Iceland' 2 W-W
(A.M. Wilson, pre-1939)

'Icelandic Pink' 2 W-P
(G.E. Mitsch and R. & E.Havens, 1971) G.E. Mitsch and R. & E.Havens, 1987
'Precedent' × 'Eclat'; sdlg no. G13/29A
Fl. rounded; perianth segments very broadly ovate, slightly reflexed, overlapping half; the inner segments more nearly spreading, creased; corona wide bowl-shaped, ribbed, deep apricot pink, mouth straight and more closely ribbed, frilled. Mid-season. Resembles a larger-flowered 'Pink Ice'

'Icelette' 2 W-P
(A.W. Chappell) A.W. Chappell, 1990
'Inverpolly' × 'Recital'; sdlg no. C-12-1
Fl. rounded, 105 mm wide; perianth segments very smooth; corona bright pink. Late

'Ice Maiden' 1 W-W
(pre-1907)

'Ice Maiden' 1 W-W
(G.L. Wilson, 1946) Mrs D.G. Moore, 1960

'Ice Peak' 3 W-GWW
(C. Dawson, pre-1910)
Fl. small; perianth segments pure white, smooth; corona long, straight, creamy white. Tall. See also 'Icepeak'

'Icepeak' 3 W-GWW
Syn. of 'Ice Peak'

'Ice Queen' 2 W-W
(J.M. de Navarro) J.M. de Navarro, 1958
'Caragh' × 'Chinese White'
Perianth segments rounded; the inner segments more nearly ovate and acute; corona bowl-shaped, ribbed, with blue-green at base, rim dentate. PC(e) 1965

'Ice Rim' 7 W-YYW
(G.E. Mitsch & R.& E.Havens, 1975) G.E. Mitsch & R.& E.Havens, 1986
('Green Island' × 'Chinese White') × *N. jonquilla*; sdlg no. KK102/1
Perianth segments broad, rounded; corona butterscotch yellow. Late

'Icerna' 2 (b or c)
(pre-1926)
Fl. pale mauve or lilac, sometimes tinged pale apricot; corona with a darker tone at rim

'Icevus' 2 W-W
(G. Lewis) D.S. Bell, 1955
'Lowcliffe' × 'Beersheba'

'Ice Wings' 5 W-W
(C.F. Coleman) C.F. Coleman, 1958
'Ischia' × *N. triandrus*
Fls 2-3 per stem, pure white; perianth segments ovate, blunt, slightly mucronate, more or less strongly reflexed, plane, overlapping one-third to a half; the inner segments with margins slightly wavy; corona two-thirds the length of the perianth segments, cylindrical, lightly ribbed, mouth straight and wavy, rim shallowly crenate. Mid-season. PC(e) 1964

'Icicle' 3 W-? (b or c)
(P.D. Williams, pre-1907)

'Icicle' 5
(?L. Buckland, pre-1914)

'Icicle' 1 W-W
(?J.C. Wister, pre-1936)
Fl. pure white

'Icicle' 5 W-W
(D. & J.W. Blanchard) D. & J.W. Blanchard, 1962
N. dubius × *N. triandrus* var. *loiseleurii*
Fls 2-4 per stem, 30 mm wide; perianth segments broadly ovate, blunt, reflexed, with margins inward curving or twisted, overlapping half; corona cup-shaped, smooth, with mouth straight or slightly constricted, rim entire. Dwarf. Early. Resembles an earlier-flowered and smoother-textured 'Raindrop'. AM(p) 1962

'Icilinda' 2 W-W
(W.F.M. Copeland, pre-1929)

Corona creamy white, frilled. AM(e) 1928

'Icon'
(pre-1915)

'Icon' 3 W-GOR
(W. Jackson Jr, 1970) Jackson's Daffodils, 1980
Sdlg 67/69 × 'Arbar'; sdlg no. 117/70
Fl. 100 mm wide, rounded; perianth segments pure white, of good substance, overlapping; corona frilled. Mid-season. Syn. 'Ibis'

'Idah'
(New Zealand origin, pre-1940)

'Ida May' 2 W-OOY
(R.H. Glover) R.H. Glover, 1968
'Arbar' × 'Old Faithful'
Perianth segments very broadly ovate, blunt, prominently mucronate, pure white, smooth, overlapping half; the inner segments narrower, not noticeably mucronate, creased; corona shallow funnel-shaped, widely expanded, narrowly ribbed, opening intense apricot orange, becoming slightly paler at base, with a well-defined narrow band of a more creamy tone at rim, mouth irregularly and more or less deeply split

'Ida Pope' 3 W-R
(J. Pope, pre-1904)
Corona with mouth expanded

'Idas' 2 W-O
(J.T. Gray, pre-1937)
Corona deep reddish orange

'Ida Triomphant' 8 W-W
(pre-1777)

'Ideal' 8 W-O
(R. van der Schoot & Son, pre-1906)
Poetaz
Fls 4-6 per stem; corona deep orange. 2n=17+1B

'Ideal' 2 W-Y
(pre-1929)
Perianth segments opening cream yellow, becoming pure white. Resembles a much improved 'Sir Watkin'

'Idealism' 2 W-W
(G.E.Mitsch, 1984) R. & E.Havens, 1995
'Broomhill' × 'Credo'; sdlg no. TT1/1
Fl. 105 mm wide; perianth segments broadly ovate, spreading, plane; corona straight-sided, pinkish white. Mid-season

'Idler' 1 Y-Y
(J.S. Leitch) J.S. Leitch, 1968

'Idless' 1 W-W
(R.A. Scamp) R.A. Scamp, 1991

'Sateen' self pollinated; sdlg no. 12
Fl. forming a double triangle, 104 mm wide, clear white; perianth segments broadly ovate, blunt, fairly prominently mucronate, spreading, plane, overlapping half; the inner segments with margins slightly wavy; corona narrow, mouth expanded, rim notched and widely flanged. Early

'Idlewild' 3 W-GYY
(Murray W. Evans) Murray W. Evans, 1969
'Alberni Beauty' × *N. poeticus* var. *recurvus* × 'Carolina'

'Idris' 2 W-Y
(W.A. Watts, pre-1913)
Perianth segments snow white; corona deep lemon

'Idris Watts'
(pre-1948)

'Iduna' 3 W-Y
(de Graaff Bros, pre-1931)
Perianth segments sulphur white; corona sulphur yellow, lightly frilled. AM(Haarlem) 1931

'Idwal' 1 Y-Y
(W.A. Watts, pre-1935)

'Idyll' 2 Y-? (a)
(G. Zandbergen-Terwegen, pre-1939)

'Idyllic' 2 W-P
(J.N.Hancock & Co., 1980) Unregistered
Corona long cup-shaped, deep apricot pink, with mouth expanded and frilled. Tall. Mid-season

'If Only' 2 Y-R
(M.E.Brogden, pre-1996) Unregistered
'Torridon' × 'Jetsetter'

'Igerna' 2 W-WWP
(A.M. Wilson, pre-1916)
Corona with a distinct band of pink at rim

'Igloo' 2 W-W
(Oregon Bulb Farms, pre-1946)

'Igloo' 1 W-Y
(G. Lewis, pre-1962)
Perianth segments broad, snow white, very smooth, overlapping; corona somewhat long, lemon, with rim neatly flanged

'Ikebana' 2 W-P
(W.F. Leenen) W.F. Leenen, 1970

'Ilah' 3 Y-? (a)
(J.T. Gray, pre-1950)

'Ildiko' 2 W-YYO
(Lajos Jezerniczky, 1975) Lajos Jezerniczky, 1987

'Flower Record' × 'Manco'
Fl. 95 mm wide; perianth segments very broad, rounded at apex, prominently mucronate, spreading, a little concave, with margins incurling, somewhat creased, overlapping half; the inner segments broadly ovate, shouldered at base, a little inflexed, with margins wavy; corona large, shallow, yellow, with a darker tone at base and a broad band of orange at rim, mouth very widely expanded, split or folded into overlapping lobes, frilled, with rim minutely dentate. Dwarf. Mid-season

'Ile de France' 2 W-Y
(C.M. Grullemans) J.J. Grullemans & Sons, 1956
Perianth segments broad, pure white; corona yellow ochre, mouth widely expanded, frilled

'Iliad' 9 W-YYR
(G.H. Engleheart, pre-1913)
Perianth segments overlapping; corona orange-yellow, with a broad band of madder crimson at rim

'Ilias' 3 Y-?
Syn. of 'Bohemienne'

'Ilina' 1 Y-Y
(W.Jackson Jr, 1959) Unregistered
'Kingscourt' × 'Jobi'; sdlg no. 16/59

'Ilione' 2 W-W
(A.M. Wilson, pre-1948)

'Illawarra' 1 Y-Y
(W.M. Spry, pre-1975) Unregistered
'Braemar' × 'Golden Valley'

'Illinga' 2 W-P
(W. Jackson Jr, 1950) W. Jackson Jr, 1966
'Rosario' × 'Duna'

'Illini' 2 W-Y
(V. Brink) V. Brink, 1968
'Polindra' open pollinated
Fl. 120 mm wide; corona bright orange-yellow. Mid-season

'Illinois' 1 Y-Y
(W.J. Eldering & Son, pre-1930)

'Illinos' 8
(pre-1934)

'Illowra' 2 W-P
(S.J. Bisdee) S.J. Bisdee, 1956
'Courtship' × sdlg 123/43

'Illuminate' 2 Y-R
(G. Lewis, 1940) G. Lewis, 1956
'Flash Lightning' × 'Fortune'
Perianth segments golden yellow; corona scarlet. Early. FCC(e)(NZ) 1941

'Illuminator' 2 Y-? (a)
(J.L. Richardson, pre-1945)

'Illusion' 2 Y-PPY
(J.A. Hunter) J.A. Hunter, 1992
'Rich Reward' × 'Vahu'; sdlg no. 13/80C
Fl. 105 mm wide; perianth segments broadly ovate, lemon yellow; corona pink, with lemon yellow at rim, mouth frilled and slightly expanded. Early to mid-season

'Illusion' 1 W-W
(P.Cleine, 1981) Unregistered
Sdlg no. 12/81C
Perianth segments ice white, regular; corona cylindrical, opening soft yellow, becoming creamy white, with rim dentate. Tall. Early

'Illustrious' 2 W-? (b or c)
(W. Welchman, pre-1908)

'Illustrious' 2 W-?
(G.L. Wilson) F.E. Board, 1962
('Dunluce' × 'Ardclinis') × 'Knowehead'; sdlg no. 46-46
Corona creamy yellow. Mid-season

'Ilma' 3 W-? (b)
(J.T. Gray, pre-1936)

'Iluka' 2 W-YWW
(W. Jackson Jr) Jackson's Daffodils, 1979
('Caprice' × 'Joningham') × 'Empress of Ireland'; sdlg no. 163/70
Fl. 120 mm wide. Mid-season

'Ilze' 3 W-GWW
(Jānis Rukšans) Jānis Rukšans, 1987
'Angel' × 'Verona'; sdlg no. R-80-11/2
Perianth segments very bright white; corona funnel-shaped, pure white, with a broad band of bright emerald green at base. Late

'Imagery' 1 W-W
(J.L. Richardson, pre-1948)

'Imagine' 3 W-YYR
(J.A.Hunter, 1986) J.A.Hunter, 1997
('Rockall' × 'Corofin') × 'Placid'; sdlg no. 35/81B
Fl. 95 mm wide; perianth segments broadly ovate, smooth; corona bowl-shaped, yellow, with a broad band of red at rim, with mouth wavy. Mid-season

'Imago' 2 Y-O
(R. Crews, pre-1949)
Corona pale orange, neatly frilled. Syn. 'Damsel'

'Imari' 2 W-? (b)
(P.D. Williams, pre-1907)
Corona widely expanded, tightly ribbed, with cerise at rim

'Imbros' 2 W-W
(The Brodie of Brodie, c.1916)
'Minnie Hume' × 'Lemon Star'

'Imbros' 2 W-?
(Alister Clark, 1929) J. Sharp, 1960

'Imelda' 1 Y-Y
(G.A. Challies) G.A. Challies, 1966
Fl. 115 mm wide, pale yellow. Mid-season

'Imirsti' 2 W-W
(A.M. Wilson, pre-1938)

'Immaculate' 1 W-W
(G.L. Wilson, pre-1923)

'Immaculate' 2 W-W
(W. Jackson Jr, 1971) Unregistered
Hybrid between('Green Valley' × 'Tetecta') and ('Tudor Minstrel' × 'Amorette'); sdlg no. 167/71
Fl. pure white; perianth segments very broad, rounded at apex, slightly mucronate, spreading, plane, overlapping half; the inner segments ovate, angled at shoulder; corona cup-shaped, with green prominent in tube, mouth loosely frilled. Mid-season

'Immemorial' 2 Y-? (a)
(W.A. Bell, pre-1949)

'Immense' 1 W-? (b)
(L. van Leeuwen & Son, pre-1933)

'Imogen' 3 Y-Y
(W. Backhouse, pre-1869)
Perianth segments sulphur yellow. Syn. Barrii Sulphureus 'Imogen'. "Absorbed" 'Liz', 'Lucy'. See also 'Imogene'

'Imogen' 3 W-YYO
(G.H. Engleheart, pre-1907)

'Imogen' 2 Y-R
(S.J. Bisdee, 1950)
'Market Merry' × sdlg 62/45

'Imogen' 2 W-P
(J.L. Richardson) J.L. Richardson, 1958
'Rose Caprice' × 'Salmon Trout'
Corona clear pink, mouth slightly expanded, frilled

'Imogene' 3 Y-Y
Syn. of 'Imogen'

'Imola' 2 W-W
(A.M. Wilson, pre-1948)
Corona faintly tinged buff at rim. Very late

'Imp' 2 W-? (b)
(A.H. Ahrens) J.S. Leitch, 1955

'Imp' W-P
(W. Jackson Jr, pre-1955) Unregistered
'Duna' × 'Rosario'

'Impact' 2 W-P
(G.E. Mitsch) G.E. Mitsch, 1969
'Precedent' × 'Carita'; sdlg no. A34/24
Corona somewhat funnel-shaped, rich pink. Mid-season

'Impala' 3 W-GYY
(G.E. Mitsch) G.E. Mitsch, 1966
'Chinese White' hybrid; sdlg no. T10/1
Fl. 115 mm wide; perianth segments opening greenish white, becoming pure white, reflexed; corona pale lemon yellow, with a darker tone at rim. Mid-season

'Impeccable' 2 Y-Y
(Jackson's Daffodils) Jackson's Daffodils, 1992
'Abona' × sdlg 3/74; sdlg no. 85/84
Fl. 100 mm wide, golden yellow; perianth segments very broadly ovate, blunt, with slight white mucro, spreading, plane, very deeply overlapping; the outer segments overlapping one another; the inner segments rounded at apex, slightly inflexed; corona almost as long as the perianth segments, darker in tone, cylindrical, lightly ribbed, with mouth a little flared and lightly frilled, rim crenate. Early to mid-season

'Imperator' 8 W-O
(pre-1835)
Early

'Imperator' 1 W-W
(de Graaff Bros, pre-1915)
Fl. large; perianth segments pure white; corona creamy white. AM(Haarlem) 1915

'Imperial' 8 W-Y
(pre-1777)

'Imperial' 1 Y-Y
(E.M. Crosfield, pre-1913)
Fl. 114 mm wide, deep yellow

'Imperial' 1 W-? (b)
(F.H. Chapman, pre-1927)

'Imperial' 2 Y-Y
(G.E. Mitsch) G.E. Mitsch, 1972
'Playboy' × 'Daydream'; sdlg no. B36/16
Fl. rounded, 100 mm wide; perianth segments bright yellow, with white at base, very deeply overlapping;

corona bowl-shaped, deeper in tone than the perianth. Mid-season

'Imperial' 4 Y-Y
Syn. of 'Imperial Crown'

'Imperial Crown' 4 Y-Y
(M.J. Jefferson-Brown) M.J. Jefferson-Brown, 1985
'Gay Time' × 'Camelot'
Fl. of medium size, neat; perianth and other petaloid segments loosely arranged, rich yellow; corona segments interspersed, deep golden yellow. Tall. Syn. 'Imperial'

'Imperialist' 3 W-? (b)
(G.H. Engleheart, pre-1913)

'Imperial Lady' 2 Y-O
(G. Lewis) D.S. Bell, 1955

'Imperium' 2 Y-? (a)
(G. Zandbergen-Terwegen, pre-1937)

'Impetuous' 4 W-R
(G.E.Mitsch, 1980) R. & E.Havens, 1995
'Gay Time' × 'Green Hills'; sdlg no. 2P68/10A
Fl. 90 mm wide; perianth and other petaloid segments pure white; corona segments orange-red. Late. Sunproof

'Impish Empress' 2 W-W
(M.L. Summerell) M.L. Summerell, 1978
'Empress of Ireland' × 'Polar Imp'
Fl. 108 mm wide. Mid-season

'Imposant' 1 Y-Y
(M. van Waveren & Sons, pre-1953)

'Impresario' 1 Y-Y
(F.H. Chapman, pre-1913)
Fl. 102 mm wide; perianth segments slightly inflexed, deeply overlapping

'Impresario' 2 Y-WWY
(G.E. Mitsch) G.E. Mitsch, 1975
Sdlg P5/8 × 'Lunar Sea' × 'Salem'; sdlg no. F88/2
Fl. 100 mm wide; perianth segments pale lemon, becoming deeper in tone, slightly reflexed; corona narrow, opening pale lemon, becoming white, with gold at rim. Mid-season

'Impressive' 8
(A. Vis, pre-1942)

'Impressive Dream' 2 YYW-W
(John R.Reed) John R.Reed, 1995
'Daydream' × 'Impresario'; sdlg no. 81-44-1
Fl. 95 mm wide; perianth segments broadly ovate, yellow, becoming deep yellow, with white at base; corona funnel-shaped, creamy white.

Mid-season. Resembles a smoother 'Impresario' of deeper colour

'Impretty' 3 W-W
(Mrs B.A. Woods) Mrs B.A. Woods, 1968

'Imprint' 2 W-Y
(W.G. Pannill) W.G. Pannill, 1970
'Green Island' × 'Festivity'

'Impromptu' 2 W-GYY
(Konynenburg & Mark) Konynenburg & Mark, 1960
Sdlg × 'Daisy Schäffer'
Fl. 120 mm wide, ivory white; corona brilliant yellow 8A. Mid-season

'Impudence' 3 W-? (b)
(Mrs F.S. Foote, pre-1941)

'Impulse' 2 Y-? (a)
(A.H. Ahrens) J.S. Leitch, 1955

'Ina' 3 W-O
(de Graaff Bros, pre-1930)
AM(Haarlem) 1930

'Ina Marshall' 1 W-W
(J.N. Hancock & Co.) J.N. Hancock & Co., 1955
Perianth segments very broadly ovate; corona expanded, opening pale cream, becoming sparkling white, with rim slightly dentate

'Inamorata' 2 W-? (b)
(F.H. Chapman, pre-1913)
'King Alfred' × 'Minnie Hume'

'Inanda' 1 Y-Y
(A.J. Bliss, pre-1930)

'Inara' 4 W-Y
(H.G. Cross, 1974) H.G. Cross, 1984
'Irish Minstrel' × 'White Lion'; sdlg no. 114-4
Fl. rounded; perianth and other petaloid segments in three whorls, greenish white (157C); the outer whorl very broadly ovate, spreading, a little concave, overlapping half or more; the second whorl a little shorter, inflexed, more deeply concave; the centre whorl clustered together, contorted, with margins tightly inward rolling; corona segments interspersed among the petaloid segments at centre, very short, light greenish yellow 5C. Late

'Inauguration' 2 Y-Y
(G.E. Mitsch) G.E. Mitsch, 1974
'Galway' × 'Saint Keverne'; sdlg no. A17/21
Fl. 100 mm wide; perianth segments golden yellow; corona deeper in tone. Early. Resembles 'Aurum' but with the corona more widely flared

'Inbal'
(Dorit Sandler, pre-1996) Unregistered

'Inca' 9 W-GRR
(F.H. Chapman, pre-1929)
'Socrates' × 'Acme'
Corona brick red, with green at base

'Inca' 6 YYW-WWY
(G.E. Mitsch) G.E. Mitsch, 1979
'Barlow' open pollinated; sdlg no. JO1/1
Fl. 78 mm wide; perianth segments broadly ovate, blunt, slightly mucronate, brilliant greenish yellow 5B, touched white at base, strongly reflexed, slightly twisted, glistening, overlapping a quarter to one-third; the inner segments more gently reflexed, creased and more distinctly twisted; corona cylindrical, lightly ribbed, becoming greenish white, touched brilliant greenish yellow 5B at rim, mouth flared, even, rim regularly crenate. Dwarf. Very early

'Inca Gold' 1 Y-Y
(A.N. Kanouse) G.E. Mitsch, 1965
Fl. 134 mm wide, rich golden yellow. Mid-season

'Incanto' 3 W-Y
(T.D. Throckmorton) T.D. Throckmorton, 1974
'Old Satin' × 'Beige Beauty'

'Incarnation' 9 W-?
(pre-1939)

'Incemore' 3 W-? (b)
(R.H. Bath, pre-1933)

'Inchbonnie' 2 YYW-WWY
(D.N.Y. Olson) D.N.Y. Olson, 1991
'Bethany' × 'Honeybird'; sdlg no. 76/8/1
Fl. 89 mm wide; perianth segments broad, rounded at apex, only very slightly mucronate, mid-yellow, with white at base, spreading; corona cylindrical, white, with golden yellow outside and in a narrow band at rim, mouth slightly expanded and occasionally a little frilled, rim dentate. Resembles 'Silken Thomas' but with more contrast in colour between perianth and corona. Mid-season

'Incognita' 3 W-YYO
(G.H. Engleheart, pre-1902)
Fl. star-shaped; perianth segments ovate, blunt, not prominently mucronate, spreading, overlapping a quarter; corona more or less disc-shaped, large, bright yellow, touched apricot orange at rim, mouth frilled, rim crenate. AM 1902

N. × *incomparabiliformis* Rouy = *N.* × *incomparabilis*.

N. × *incomparabilis* **Miller 13** = *N. hispanicus* Gouan × *N. poeticus* Linnaeus or *N. poeticus* Linnaeus × *N. pseudonarcissus* Linnaeus (Macleayi 'Major', Macleayi 'Parkinsonii', Macleayi 'Sabinii', ?'No. 1', ?"The Great Late Flowering White Daffodil with a Long Cup", ?"The Small Early White Daffodil with a Long Cup")

'Incomparabilis Plena' 4 W-O
Syn. of 'Orange Phoenix'

'Incomparable' 8 Y-Y
(pre-1850)

'Incomparable' 4 Y-O
Syn. of 'Butter and Eggs'

N. × *incurvicervicus* **Barra & López 13** = *N. fernandesii* Pedro × *N. triandrus* Linnaeus subsp. *pallidulus* (Graells) D.A. Webb

'Indamora' 1 W-W
(E.M. Crosfield, pre-1907)
Resembles a whiter 'Madame de Graaff'

'Independence' 4
(J. Gerritsen & Son, pre-1934)
'Emperor' sport

'Independence Day' 4 W-R
(G.E. Mitsch, 1976) R. & E. Havens, 1990
'Gay Time' × 'Bantam'; sdlg no. LL60/1
Fl. 100 mm wide, of heavy substance. Petaloid and corona segments regularly arranged. Late. Scented

'Indiana' 1 W-W
(de Graaff Bros, pre-1928)
Syn. 'Aida', 'Avon', 'Leda'

'Indianapolis' 2 Y-R
(D.S. Bell) D.S. Bell, 1957
'Indian Summer' × 'Rosslare'
Corona bowl-shaped, red

'Indian Brave' 2 Y-O
(Mrs Ben Robertson, 1954) Mrs Ben Robertson, 1965
'Dunkeld' × 'Fortune'
Fl. 115 mm wide; perianth segments deep yellow; corona reddish orange. Mid-season

'Indian Chief' 4 Y-O
(Mrs R.O. Backhouse, pre-1921)
Perianth and other petaloid segments in three whorls; the outer whorl broadly ovate, mucronate, spreading, separated; the second whorl regularly superimposed on the outer, a little narrower and shorter, slightly inflexed; the centre whorl shorter, strongly inflexed, with margins incurling or more sharply infolded, overlapping; corona segments shorter than the petaloid segments and interspersed among them, broad, with rim crenate. AM(Haarlem) 1925

'Indian Dawn' 3 Y-R
(D.S. Bell) D.S. Bell, 1964
'Rosslare' × 'Indian Summer'
Fl. 90 mm wide; perianth segments deep yellow; corona very shallow bowl-shaped, red

'Indian Maid' 7 O-R
(W.G. Pannill) W.G. Pannill, 1972
'Jezebel' × *N. jonquilla*; sdlg no. B 33/1
Fls 2-3 per stem, 76 mm wide; perianth segments orange, spreading, with margins incurling; the inner segments a little inflexed and somewhat twisted; corona very shallow funnel-shaped, loosely ribbed, red, mouth straight, regularly and loosely frilled, with rim entire. Resembles 'Suzy' but with the perianth of deeper colour

'Indian Prince' 2 Y-? (a)
(Barr & Sons, pre-1936)

'Indian Ruler' 2 Y-O
(P. de Jager & Sons) P. de Jager & Sons, 1971
'Armada' × 'Mary Roozen'
Fl. 126-130 mm wide; perianth segments broadly ovate, vivid yellow 9B, spreading, overlapping one-third to a half; the inner segments sometimes notched, somewhat twisted or with margins wavy; corona broad funnel-shaped, ribbed, slightly brighter in tone than strong orange 25A, mouth straight, frilled, rim deeply notched. *AM(g) 1978

'Indian Summer' 2 Y-O
(G.L. Wilson, pre-1940)
'Market Merry' × 'Clackrattle'
Fl. 92 mm wide; perianth segments broad, vivid yellow 9A, smooth, overlapping; corona neat, shallow, strong orange 30D, with paler tones towards base, rim dentate. AM(e) 1946, AM(Haarlem) 1948, FCC(Haarlem) 1955

'Indian Sunset' 2 Y-R
(R. Hyde) R. Hyde, 1955
'Klingo' hybrid
PC(e)(NZ) 1954

'Indiscreet' 1 W-P
(Oregon Bulb Farms) Oregon Bulb Farms, 1955

'Indoline' 1 Y-Y
(P.D. Williams, pre-1938)

'Indomitable' 2 Y-? (a)
(G.H. Engleheart, pre-1907)

'Indonesia' 2 Y-O
(G. Lubbe & Son, pre-1942)
Syn. 'Pace'. AM(Haarlem) 1942

'Indora' 4 W-P
(H.G. Cross, 1974) H.G. Cross, 1984

'Rhana' × 'Kimellen'; sdlg no. 73-4
Perianth and other petaloid segments pale greenish white 157A; corona segments interpersed, buff pink, frilled. Late

'Indulgence' 3 W-? (b)
(W. Welchman, pre-1910)

'Indulgence' 1 W-W
(F.E. Board) F.E. Board, 1965
'Vigil' × 'Empress of Ireland'
Mid-season

'Indus' 2 Y-Y
(Sir C.H. Cave, pre-1930)
Fl. large; perianth segments overlapping; corona expanded, bright yellow. AM(e) 1932

'Industry' 2 W-? (b or c)
(Sir C.H. Cave, pre-1928)

'Inelae' 1 Y-Y
(G. Errey, 1941) G. Errey, 1963
Fl. 115 mm wide; vivid yellow 13A. Early

'Inessa' 2 YYW-YYP
(Jānis Rukšans) Jānis Rukšans, 1986
'Chiffon' × 'Daydream'; sdlg no. R-79-10/1
Perianth segments vivid yellow 9B, with white at base; corona funnel-shaped, expanded, light greenish yellow 8B, with rim flushed apricot pink. Mid-season

'Inez' 2 Y-Y
(W.F.M. Copeland, pre-1927)
Perianth segments creamy primrose yellow; corona broad, very shallow bowl-shaped, slightly darker in tone than the perianth, frilled. See also 'Innes'

'Infanta' 5
(T. Batson, pre-1914)

'Infanta' 6 Y-Y
(Sir A.P.W. Thomas, pre-1931)

'Infatuation' 2 W-YYP
(J.L. Richardson, pre-1954)
'Glenshane' × 'Waterville'
Perianth segments pure white, waxy; corona pale primrose yellow, with reddish pink at rim, frilled

'Inferno' 9 W-?
(de Graaff Bros, pre-1927)

'Inferno' 2 Y-O
(J.L. Richardson) J.L. Richardson, 1959
'Ceylon' × 'Narvik'
Perianth segments deep golden, of thick texture; corona very shallow bowl-shaped, orange

'Inflammable' 2 Y-O
(O. Ronalds, c.1961) Unregistered
Fl. large; perianth segments broad; corona widely expanded, intense scarlet-orange. Early

'Inflammable' 2 Y-O
(G.L. Wilson, pre-1972) Unregistered

N. inflatus Haworth = *N. bulbocodium*

'Infra Red' 2 Y-YYO
(J.N. Hancock & Co., 1963) J.N. Hancock & Co., 1977
Sdlg × 'Kai'; sdlg no. 89/57
Fl. 95 mm wide; perianth segments brilliant yellow 12B; corona darker in tone (13A), with strong orange 25A at rim. Mid-season. Sunproof

N. × ***infundibulum*** **Poiret 13** = *N. abscissus* (Haworth) Roemer & Schultes f. × *N. jonquilla* Linnaeus (Odorus 'Heminalis', ?'Orange Queen', "The Narrow Cupped")

'Inga' 3 W-Y
(P.D. Williams, pre-1907)
Perianth segments overlapping; corona large, rich apricot yellow, tinged orange. Resembles an improved 'Incognita'. See also 'Ingar'

'Ingar' 3 W-Y
Syn. of 'Inga'

'Ingenleur K.Volkersz' 1 Y-Y
(Belle & Teeuwen, pre-1928)
Perianth segments canary yellow; corona dark yellow, with rim widely flanged. AM(Haarlem) 1928. See also 'Ir.K.Volkersz', 'Mr K.Volkersz', 'Volkersz', 'Volkerz'

'Ingle' 2 W-W
(D. Jackson) Jackson's Daffodils, 1982
'Challa' × 'Arctic Doric'; sdlg no. 225/75
Fl. 104 mm wide. Mid-season

'Ingleburn' 1 G-?
(W.M. Spry, pre-1975) Unregistered
'Brazil' × 'Clare'

'Inglescombe' 4 Y-Y
(J. Walker, pre-1912)
Fl. rounded, 70 mm wide; perianth and other petaloid segments in many whorls, regularly superimposed, broadly ovate, blunt or truncate, only very slightly mucronate, light greenish yellow 5C; the outer whorls spreading, plane, overlapping one-third; the inner whorls each a little shorter and increasingly inflexed, with margins sometimes rolled inwards, sometimes recurved; corona segments very small, darker in tone than the petaloid segments and interspersed among them. Mid-season to late. 2n=14. Syn. 'Inglescombe Phoenix', 'Inglescombe Yellow'. AM(c) 1914, *AM(m) 1931

'Inglescombe Phoenix' 4 Y-Y
Fl. primrose yellow. Syn. of 'Inglescombe'

'Inglescombe Yellow' 4 Y-Y
Syn. of 'Inglescombe'

'Inglesport' 4
(W.W. Avery, pre-1937)

'Inglewood' 2 G-W
(W.M. Spry, pre-1975) Unregistered
'Hunter's Moon' hybrid

'Ingoldsby' 9 W-?
(G.H. Engleheart, pre-1914)

'Ingot' 1 Y-Y
(A.J. Bliss, pre-1930)
'King Alfred' × 'Monarch'

'Ingram' 2 W-W
(S.J. Bisdee, 1945)
'Nelly' × 'Whitefoord'

'Ingrid' 2 W-YYO
(Warnaar & Co., pre-1943)
AM(Haarlem) 1943

'Ingrid Evensen' 2 W-P
(Peter Royles) du Plessis Bros, 1990
'Dailmanach' hybrid; sdlg no. 76-1-1
Fl. 115 mm wide; perianth segments pure white; corona bright pure pink

'Ingrid Valberg' 11b Y-O
(J.W.A. Lefeber) J.W.A. Lefeber, 1971
Fl. 115 mm wide; perianth segments brilliant greenish yellow; corona light orange (23B). Mid-season

'Ingrid Weldon' 2 W-Y
(J.W.A. Lefeber) J.W.A. Lefeber, 1958
Perianth segments ivory white; corona brilliant yellow 8A

'Inheritance' 2 Y-? (a)
(W.A. Bell, pre-1949)

'Inishkeen' 1 W-Y
(G.L. Wilson, 1951) Guy L.Wilson Ltd, 1961
'Guardian' × 'Kanchenjunga'
Fl. 99 mm wide; perianth segments creamy white, overlapping; corona brilliant yellow 7A, mouth expanded and lobed, with rim dentate and slightly reflexed. 2n=28. AM(Haarlem) 1965, *AM(g) 1970

'Inishmaan' 2 W-YPP
(Mrs H.K. Richardson) Mrs H.K. Richardson, 1972

'Interim' × 'Rose Caprice'
Perianth segments very broadly ovate, overlapping; corona slightly expanded, reddish pink, paling to pale lemon at base, with rim deeply dentate

'Inishmore' 2 W-GWW
(Mrs H.K. Richardson) Mrs H.K. Richardson, 1976
'Verona' × 'Stainless'
Fl. 85 mm wide, pure white; corona with bluish green at base

'Inishowen Head' 9 W-GGO
(Ballydorn Bulb Farm, 1985) Ballydorn Bulb Farm, 1996
'Cantabile' × 'Moyle'
Fl. 74 mm wide; perianth segments opening ivory, becoming white; corona small saucer-shaped, tightly ribbed, emerald green, with deep yellow near mouth and a line of orange at rim. Dwarf. Late

'Initiation' 1 W-W
(Carncairn Daffodils) Carncairn Daffodils, 1969
'Cotterton' × 'Broughshane'
Corona with green at base, frilled, the rim becoming rolled. 2n=28

'Inner Circle' ?-P
(Alister Clark, pre-1948)

'Inner Ring' 9 W-GYR
(Mrs M.S. Yerger) Mrs M.S. Yerger, 1988
'Praecox Grandiflorus' × 'Lights Out'; sdlg no. 75 N 2
Perianth segments regular, of good substance, overlapping; the inner segments narrower; corona strong yellow 153D, with strong green 132B at base and red (42B) at rim. Dwarf. Early

'Innes' 2 Y-Y
Syn. of 'Inez'

'Innis' 3 Y-? (a)
(A.M. Wilson, pre-1943)

'Innis Beg' 2 W-GWW
(Carncairn Daffodils, 1965) Carncairn Daffodils, 1976
Sdlg no. 199
Fl. 95 mm wide, yellowish white 155B. Mid-season

'Inniscorrig' 1 Y-Y
(D.H.L. Corrigan, pre-1949)

'Innisfail' 2 W-P
(O. Ronalds, c.1960) Unregistered
Perianth segments broad; corona large, opening rich pink, becoming clear shell pink

'Innisfallen' 2 W-Y
(J.L. Richardson, pre-1943)

'White Emperor' × 'Gracious'
Perianth segments very broadly ovate, blunt, slightly mucronate, pure white, spreading, a little concave, satin smooth, overlapping half; the inner segments a little narrower, somewhat inflexed, with margins wavy; corona funnel-shaped, ribbed, clear yellow, with mouth straight and slightly frilled. Mid-season

'Innisfree' 2 W-W
(A.M. Wilson, pre-1944)

'Innisfree' 3 W-WWY
(Carncairn Daffodils, pre-1976) Unregistered
Perianth segments white, of good substance; corona small, with yellow at rim, frilled. Sweet scented

'Innisidgen' 8 Y-O
(Rosewarne EHS) Rosewarne EHS, 1982
'French Sol' × 'Autumn Sol'; sdlg no. 69/305/11
Fls 9 per stem, 40 mm wide; perianth segments vivid yellow 12A, tinged pale orange; corona light orange (23A) to strong orange 25A. Very early

'Inniswood' 1 W-W
(Carncairn Daffodils, 1965) Carncairn Daffodils, 1978
'Cotterton' × 'Kanchenjunga'; sdlg no. 1/26/59
Fl. 100 mm wide, greenish white (155A); corona with mouth slightly expanded. Mid-season. 2n=28

'Innocence' 8 W-Y
(W. Backhouse, pre-1869)
Perianth segments sulphur white. Syn. Tridymus 'Innocence'. "Absorbed" 'Princess Alice'

'Innocence' 1 W-W
(W. Welchman, pre-1910)

'Innocence' 9 W-O
(G.L. Wilson) G. Milner, 1958
'Cantabile' × 'Cushendall'

'Innovation' 1 Y-Y
(W.J. Eldering & Son, pre-1928)
EFA(Haarlem) 1932

'Innovator' 4 Y-O
(Th. van der Hulst) Th. van der Hulst, 1992
'Ambergate' × 'Tahiti'
Fl. 110 mm wide; perianth and other petaloid segments light greenish yellow 8C, touched with light orange-yellow 22B; corona segments vivid orange 28B. Mid-season

'Inny River' 1 Y-Y
(Patrick Kiernan) Patrick Kiernan, 1997
'Lancelot' × 'Golden Sovereign'; sdlg no. PK1430
Fl. rounded, 115 mm wide, deep golden yellow; perianth segments very broadly ovate, blunt, plane, smooth; corona cylindrical, with mouth only

slightly expanded. Mid-season to late

'Ino' 3 W-R
(W. Jackson Jr, 1962) Unregistered
'Matapan' × 'Jo'; sdlg no. 4/62

'In Pursuit' 1 W-Y
(A.W. Chappell) A.W. Chappell, 1992
'Lenz' × 'Cristobal'; sdlg no. C-29-1
Fl. 97 mm wide; perianth segments ovate; corona with rim flanged and crenate. Late

'Inshan Rahaman' 2 W-P
(Brian S. Duncan) L. Rahaman, 1991
Sdlg 247 ('Lilac Charm' × ['Roseworthy' × 'Minerva']) × 'Valinor'
Fl. 106 mm wide; perianth segments ovate, pure white, slightly reflexed; corona cylindrical, narrow, deep cherry pink, with mouth slightly expanded and rim crenate. Mid-season to late

'Insignia' 3 W-? (b)
(R. Crews, pre-1949)
Syn. 'Kewpie'

insignis = *N. pseudonarcissus* var. *insignis*

'Inspiration' 2 W-W
(Konynenburg & Mark, pre-1953)
'Copper Bowl' × 'Furore'

'Inspiration' 2 W-?
Syn. of 'Nita'

'Inspire' 1 W-Y
(P. & G. Phillips) P. & G. Phillips, 1981
Fl. 105 mm wide; perianth segments milky white; corona pale lemon. Mid-season

'Instow' 2 Y-? (a)
(Miss K.M. Hinchliff, pre-1937)

'Insulinde' 8 W-Y
(pre-1915)
Corona orange-yellow

'Insulinde' 4 W-O
(Mrs R.O. Backhouse, pre-1921)
Perianth and other petaloid segments in several whorls, opening pale greenish yellow, becoming creamy white; the outer whorl broadly ovate, blunt, only very slightly mucronate, spreading, overlapping half; the inner whorls as broad as the outer whorl, a little shorter, slightly inflexed, creased or with margins incurling; the centre whorl fewer than six in number, much shorter, narrow, strongly inflexed; the corona segments one-third the length of the inner whorls of petaloid segments and loosely interspersed among them, more tightly clustered at centre, deep vivid reddish orange, deeply frilled. Sunproof. 2n=21.

AM(Haarlem) 1923, FCC(Haarlem) 1934, FA(Haarlem) 1934

'Insurance' 2 Y-? (a)
(Sir C.H. Cave, pre-1928)

'Insurpassable' 1 Y-Y
Syn. of 'Unsurpassable'

N. integer Spach = *N. viridiflorus*

'Integer' 11a W-WWP
(G.E.Mitsch, 1984) R. & E.Havens, 1997
([('Precedent' × 'Carita') × ('Radiation' × 'Mabel Taylor')] × 'Interim') × 'Phantom'; sdlg no. TT16/12
Fl. 115 mm wide; perianth segments ovate; corona deeply split, closely overlying the perianth, white, with pink at rim. Mid-season. Sunproof

'Integrity' 1 Y-Y
(G.L. Wilson, pre-1936)
'Bulwark' × 'Sorley Boy'
Corona mouth expanded

'Intensity' 9 W-R
(G.H. Engleheart, pre-1923)
AM(e) 1923

'Interflora' 1 Y-Y
(J.A. O'More) P.D.K. Ramsay, 1983
'Principal' × 'Kingscourt'

'Interim' 2 W-YYO
(G.L. Wilson, pre-1944)
'Cushlake' × 'Dava'
Fl. 94 mm wide; perianth segments ovate, fairly prominently mucronate, greenish white, spreading or slightly reflexed, with margins sometimes incurling, overlapping a quarter to a half; the inner segments with margins wavy or more strongly incurved; corona broad funnel-shaped, loosely ribbed, brilliant greenish yellow 6A, touched strong orange 30D at rim, mouth straight, frilled, rim crenate. 2n=28

N. interjectus Schultes f. = *N.* × *odorus*

'Interjectus'
Syn. of *N.* × *odorus*

'Interloper' 6 W-O
(Brian S.Duncan, 1984) Brian S.Duncan, 1994
Sdlg no. 890
Fl. 81 mm wide; perianth segments ovate, strongly reflexed; corona broad funnel-shaped, terracotta orange, with mouth slightly frilled. Dwarf. Mid-season to late

'Interlude' 2 W-P
(G.E. Mitsch) G.E. Mitsch, 1958
'Tunis' × 'Shadeen'

Corona salmon pink. Mid-season

N. × intermedius Loiseleur-Deslongchamps 13 = *N. jonquilla* Linnaeus × *N. tazetta* Linnaeus ('Etoile d'Or', Tazetta 'Bifrons', Tazetta 'Primulinus', "Texas Star", "The Cowslip Cupped"). 2n=17

intermedius = *N. elegans* var. *intermedius*

intermedius = *N. pallidiflorus* var. *intermedius*

'Intermezzo' 2 W-WWR
(D.S. Bell) D.S. Bell, 1968
'Mannequin' × 'Garland'
Corona very shallow bowl-shaped, with a broad band of red at rim

'Interval' 2 W-GYP
(Ballydorn Bulb Farm, 1975) Ballydorn Bulb Farm, 1986
'Interim' × 'Dove Wings'
Mid-season

'Intrepid' 2 Y-? (a)
(P.D. Williams, pre-1948)

'Intrigue' 7 Y-W
(W.G. Pannill) W.G. Pannill, 1970
'Nazareth' × *N. jonquilla*
Fls 2-3 per stem, varying in size, the largest about 70 mm wide; perianth segments sometimes more than six in number, broadly ovate, blunt or squarish at apex, prominently mucronate, brilliant greenish yellow 6A, with a broad band of white at base of some mature flowers, spreading, with margins incurling, overlapping half; the inner segments sometimes inflexed and twisted; corona shallow funnel-shaped, finely ribbed, opening yellow, becoming white, with mouth straight or a little flared, rim crenate and sometimes rolled. Scented. Wister Award 1998

'Intrinsic' 2 W-P
(J.N.Hancock & Co., 1977) Unregistered
Corona funnel-shaped, deep watermelon pink. Early

'Intrude' 3 Y-O
(G. Lubbe & Son, pre-1947)
Perianth segments lemon yellow; corona frilled. AM(Haarlem) 1947

'Intuition' 2 Y-P
(J.N.Hancock & Co., 1986) Unregistered
Sdlg no. O/86H

'Invader' 4 Y-R
(Mrs H.K. Richardson, 1968) P. & G. Phillips, 1978
'Gay Time' × 'Border Chief'
Fl. 96 mm wide. Mid-season

'Invention' 1 W-W
(Sir C.H. Cave, pre-1928)

'Inver' 1 Y-Y
(G.L. Wilson) G.L. Wilson, 1956
'King of the North' × 'Content'
Fl. brilliant greenish yellow 5A

'Invercassley' 3 W-R
(J.S.B. Lea) Clive Postles Daffodils, 1989
'Colley Gate' × sdlg 68-15A; sdlg no. 4-25-76
Fl. 114 mm wide; perianth segments very broadly ovate, overlapping; corona very shallow bowl-shaped, dark red, with rim regularly dentate. Late

'Invercauld' 1 W-W
(W.G. Pannill) W.G. Pannill, 1987
'Canisp' × 'Cataract'; sdlg no. 74/44A
Mid-season

'Inverell' 2 W-W
(Australian origin, pre-1967) Unregistered

'Invergordon' 2 Y-O
(The Brodie of Brodie, c.1929)
'Therapia' × ('Beacon' × 'Fortune')
Perianth segments rounded, soft yellow; corona shallow, intense orange, with a paler tone at base, mouth expanded. AM(e) 1933

'Invermark' 3 W-? (b)
(Warnaar & Co., pre-1933)

'Invermay' 2 Y-O
(R. Crews, 1944) R. Crews, 1958
Fl. 89 mm wide; perianth segments pale yellow; corona reddish orange. Mid-season. Resembles 'Luminary' but with a shallower and more widely expanded corona

'Inverness' 2 Y-YOO
(The Brodie of Brodie, pre-1930)
'Seraglio' × 'Fortune'; sdlg no. 167/B/24
Perianth segments pale sulphur yellow; corona funnel-shaped, yellow-orange, paling to yellow at base. AM(e) 1932

'Inverpolly' 2 W-W
(J.S.B. Lea, c.1961) J.S.B. Lea, 1980
'Easter Moon' × 'Omeath'
Fl. 120 mm wide, greenish white 157D; perianth segments broadly ovate, blunt, mucronate, spreading or very slightly inflexed, plane or a little concave, with margins sometimes incurling at apex, smooth, with midrib showing, overlapping half; the inner segments more narrowly ovate, acute, more strongly inflexed; corona narrow, straight-sided and only slightly expanding, lightly ribbed, opening buffy pink, soon becoming white, mouth straight and lightly frilled, with rim crenate. PC(e) 1961, AM(e) 1972

'Invershin' 2 Y-? (a)
(P.D. Williams, pre-1930)

'Inverurie' 2 Y-? (a)
(Mrs R.S. Cobley, pre-1954)

'Investment' 1 Y-Y
(P.L.A. Pouw, 1945) van Graven Bros, 1961
Fl. 75 mm wide. Early. 2n=28. Resembles 'Dutch Master' but with the corona more widely flared

'Invicta' 1 Y-Y
(J.L. Richardson, pre-1948)
Fl. 108 mm wide; perianth segments vivid yellow 9B, overlapping half; corona slightly ribbed, a little brighter in tone (12A), mouth expanded and frilled, with rim flanged and dentate. *AM(g) 1956

'Invincible' 2 W-YYO
(C.G. van Tubergen, pre-1916)
'Will Scarlett' × 'Miss Willmott'
Perianth segments very broad, rounded and sometimes nicked at apex, prominently mucronate, spreading, slightly creased, overlapping half; the inner segments apparently longer, slightly truncate, only very slightly mucronate, with margins recurved in lower half; corona disc-shaped, ribbed, mouth with six overlapping lobes, minutely frilled. AM(Haarlem) 1916, FCC(Haarlem) 1918

'Invitation' 3 W-GYY
(M.J. Jefferson-Brown) M.J. Jefferson-Brown, 1975
'Easter Moon' × 'Homage'
Perianth segments ivory white; corona lemon, with green at base. Mid-season

'Inwood' 2 W-P
(G.L. Wilson) Guy L.Wilson Ltd, 1966
'Roseyards' × 'Passionale'

'Iny' 2 W-R
(A.M. Wilson, pre-1944)
Perianth segments creamy; corona red

'Inzell' 2 W-GYY
(J.W.A. Lefeber) J.W.A. Lefeber, 1975
Fl. 110 mm wide; perianth segments ivory white; corona light greenish yellow 4C or paler, with pale green at base. Mid-season

'Io' 3 W-W
(E. Leeds, pre-1877)
Perianth segments narrow, acute; corona opening primrose yellow, becoming sulphur white. Syn. Leedsii 'Io', Leedsii 'Stellatus'

'Io' 3 W-Y
(J. Mallender, pre-1910)
'White Lady' hybrid
Perianth segments pure white, overlapping; corona small, yellow

'Iolanthe' 1 W-? (b)
(Barr & Sons, pre-1907)
'Czarina' × 'Peter Barr'

'Iolanthe' 1 W-W
(R. Dick, pre-1931)
'Mrs Robert Sydenham' hybrid

'Iolanthe' 2 W-P
(T. Morrison, pre-1961) Unregistered

'Ion' 3 W-? (b or c)
(T. Batson, pre-1913)

'Iona' 1 W-W
(A.J. Bliss, pre-1931)
'Madame de Graaff' × 'Duke of Bedford'
Fl. 95 mm wide, facing down; perianth segments creamy white, with margins recurved, overlapping a quarter; corona opening sulphur, becoming paler, with mouth expanded. Mid-season to late. Syn. 'Berenice'

'Ione' 1 W-? (b)
(W.B. Hartland, pre-1907)

'Iorane' 2 Y-R
(J.S. Leitch) J.S. Leitch, 1957

'Ios' 1 Y-Y
(G.H. Johnstone, pre-1954)

'Iota' 9 W-GYO
(Mrs M.S. Yerger) Mrs M.S. Yerger, 1994
Evans sdlg N-25 × 'Lyric'; sdlg no. 80 D 3
Fl. 20 mm wide; perianth segments white, deeply overlapping; corona almost disc-shaped, brilliant yellow 7A, with light yellow-green 145B at base and strong reddish orange at rim. Dwarf. Very early

'Iphigenia' 2 W-? (b)
(G.H. Engleheart, pre-1916)

'Iphigenia' 4 W-Y
(W.F.M. Copeland, pre-1931)
Perianth and other petaloid segments white; centre segments golden apricot, with yellow at rim

'Ipi Tombi' 2 Y-O
(W.F. Leenen, 1964) W.F. Leenen, 1977
Sdlg × 'Grand Soleil d'Or'
Fl. 80 mm wide; perianth segments broadly ovate, prominently mucronate, brilliant greenish yellow 6A, spreading or slightly inflexed, creased; corona broad funnel-shaped, lightly ribbed, vivid orange 28B, mouth straight, with six deep and overlapping lobes. Dwarf. Early. Sunproof

'Irala' 2 or 3 W-? (b or c)
(Cartwright & Goodwin, pre-1916)

'Irani' 4 W-Y
(J.L. Richardson) Mrs H.K. Richardson, 1964
'Gay Time' × 'Arbar'
Fl. 88 mm wide; perianth and other petaloid segments in two or more whorls, greenish white; the outer whorl very broadly ovate, blunt, prominently mucronate, spreading, a little concave, with margins slightly incurling, overlapping half; the inner segments of the outer whorl truncate, only very slightly mucronate, inflexed; the inner whorls successively more strongly inflexed, decreasing only slightly in size, somewhat twisted, with margins more deeply incurling; corona segments clustered at centre and among inner petaloid segments, short, with margins wavy, light greenish yellow 4B, becoming paler. AM(e) 1966

'Iras' 3 W-YYR
(pre-1938)
Perianth segments pure white; corona pale citron, with bright red at rim

'Ireland's Eye' 3 W-? (b)
(pre-1910)

'Ireland's Eye' 9 W-GYR
(Ballydorn Bulb Farm) Ballydorn Bulb Farm, 1979
'Cantabile' × probably 'Fairgreen'
Fl 75 mm wide; perianth segments sparkling white; corona small, yellow, shading to olive green at base, with a broad band of red at rim. Late

'Irene' 8 Y-Y
(R. van der Schoot & Son, pre-1906)
Poetaz
Fls 5-6 per stem; perianth segments pale primrose yellow; corona ribbed, deep golden yellow. 2n=17

'Irene Bordoni' 2 W-O
(J.L. Richardson, pre-1930)
Perianth segments sulphur white, stained yellow at base; corona shallow. AM(Haarlem) 1930

'Irene Copeland' 4 W-Y
(W.F.M. Copeland, pre-1915)
Fl. 85 mm wide; perianth and other petaloid segments in up to 5 whorls, broadly ovate, snow white, overlapping; the outer whorl spreading, plane; the inner whorls becoming successively shorter, more inflexed, with margins incurved; corona segments opposite the petaloid segments, two-thirds their length and interspersed among them, oblong, rounded at apex, brilliant greenish yellow 6B, with margins tightly incurled. 2n=14. AM(e) 1925, AM(Haarlem) 1926, FCC(Haarlem) 1929

'Irene Keeley' 2 W-W

(H.A. Brown, 1943) J.N. Hancock & Co., 1955
'Niphetos' × 'Del Rose'
Corona very frilled

'Iridescent' 2 W-P
(G.A. Challies) G.A. Challies, 1963
Corona bright pink, becoming paler, tinged green at base, with rim dentate. Mid-season

'Irina' 8
(pre-1939)

'Iris' 3 W-? (b)
(Mrs R.O. Backhouse, pre-1921)

'Iris' 3 W-YYO
(H.J. Poole Sr, pre-1927)

'Irish Affair' 2 W-Y
(John R.Reed) John R.Reed, 1995
'Irish Mist' × 'Flash Affair'; sdlg no. 84-34-1
Fl. forming a double triangle, 93 mm wide; perianth segments broadly ovate, bright white, with a slight yellow stain at base; corona long funnel-shaped, bright yellow. Mid-season

'Irish Belle' 1 W-W
(G.L. Wilson, pre-1948)

'Irish Charm' 2 W-OOY
(W.J. Dunlop, pre-1952)
'White Sentinel' × 'Mulberry'
Perianth segments broad, pure white, plane, smooth

'Irish Coffee' 3 Y-YYO
(G.E. Mitsch, 1957) G.E. Mitsch, 1967
'Green Island' × 'Chinese White'; sdlg no. R33/41
Fl. 101 mm wide; perianth segments very broad, opening ivory white, becoming yellow; corona pale yellow, with orange at rim, becoming almost white in warmer climates. Mid-season

'Irish Colleen' 2 W-Y
(G.L. Wilson) E.G. Hayes, 1958
Fl. 102 mm wide; corona vivid yellow 9A, with mouth widely expanded, rim frilled

'Irish Cream' 3 Y-Y
(John R.Reed, 1984) John R.Reed, 1995
'Irish Coffee' × 'Moonfire'; sdlg no. 79-27-2
Fl. rounded, 82 mm wide; whitish yellow, facing slightly downwards, very smooth; perianth segments broadly ovate; corona bowl-shaped. Mid-season

'Irish Elegance' 2 W-W
(G.L. Wilson) F.E. Board, 1956
'Guardian' × 'Saint Andrew'

'Irish Fire' 2 Y-R
(John R.Reed, 1985) John R.Reed, 1995

'Vulcan' × 'Rio Rouge'; sdlg no. 80-18-3
Fl. 95 mm wide; perianth segments blunt, light yellow; corona cylindrical, intense red. Mid-season

'Irish Flame' 2 Y-R
(T. Bloomer) T. Bloomer, 1972
'Red Ranger' × ('Royal Mail' × 'Narvik'); sdlg no. 1/34/58

'Irish Gift' 4 W-R
(J.L. Richardson, pre-1961) Unregistered
Fl. rounded; perianth and other petaloid segments in several whorls, broadly ovate, blunt, fairly prominently mucronate, white, overlapping half; the outer whorl spreading or a little inflexed; the inner whorls becoming more inflexed towards the centre; the centre whorl(s) narrower, strongly inflexed, with margins incurled; corona segments short, clustered among petaloid segments at centre, orange-red, tightly ribbed. Tall. Late to very late

'Irish Gold' 1 Y-Y
(A.F. Calvert, pre-1929)

'Irish Grace' 2 Y-?
(T. Bloomer) T. Bloomer, 1972
'Richhill' × 'Masai King'; sdlg no. 1/31/65

'Irish Guard' 1 Y-Y
(W.B. Hartland, pre-1908)

'Irish Jig' 11a W-YWW
(A.N. Kanouse) Mrs A.N. Kanouse, 1991
'Fox Trot' × pink sdlg
Fl. 100 mm wide; perianth segments broad, rounded at apex, overlapping; the inner segments more nearly acute; corona split, the six segments opening creamy white, becoming white, with light yellow at base. Mid-season

'Irish King' 1 Y-Y
Syn. of 'Ard Righ'

'Irish Legend' 2 W-O
(J.L. Richardson) Mrs H.K. Richardson, 1964
'Kilworth' × 'Tulyar'
Perianth segments round, pure white; corona deep reddish orange, dentate. 2n=28

'Irish Light' 2 Y-O
(Mrs H.K. Richardson) Mrs H.K. Richardson, 1972
'Patagonia' × 'Border Chief'
Fl. 105 mm wide; perianth segments broadly ovate, blunt, slightly mucronate, vivid yellow 12A, spreading, plane, smooth, overlapping one-third; the inner segments not much narrower, a little inflexed, with margins sometimes incurling; corona short funnel-shaped, ribbed, orange (28A), lightly frilled, with rim crenate and very slightly flanged. Mid-season. 2n=28. AM(e) 1970

'Irish Linen' 3 W-GWW
(Carncairn Daffodils) Carncairn Daffodils, 1979
Wootton sdlg 866 × 'Hamzali'; sdlg no. W15/4
Fl. yellowish white 155B or D. Scented

'Irish Lizard' 2 W-W
(J.L. Richardson, pre-1953)
'Templemore' × 'Ludlow'

'Irish Love' 2 W-YYO
(Mrs H.K. Richardson) Mrs H.K. Richardson, 1976
'Irish Minstrel' × 'My Love'
Fl. 110 mm wide; corona pale lemon, with deep orange at rim. Mid-season

'Irish Luck' 1 Y-Y
(G.L. Wilson, pre-1948)
'Counsellor' × 'Goldcourt'
Perianth segments ovate, blunt, inflexed, slightly concave, smooth, overlapping one-third; corona smooth at base, lightly ribbed towards mouth, with mouth expanded, rim crenate and slightly flanged. 2n=28. AM(Haarlem) 1948, FCC(Haarlem) 1950

'Irish Maximus' 1 Y-Y
(W.M. & A.P. Spry, pre-1955) Unregistered

'Irish Minstrel' 2 W-Y
(J.L. Richardson) J.L. Richardson, 1958
'Green Island' × 'Tudor Minstrel'
Fl. 102 mm wide, of great substance; perianth segments very broadly ovate, blunt, slightly mucronate, creamy white, spreading, plane, or slightly concave at apex, with margins minutely incurling, smooth, overlapping half; the inner segments more narrowly ovate, somewhat rounded at apex, shouldered at base, a little inflexed; corona bowl-shaped, smooth, vivid yellow 12A, loosely frilled. 2n=28. AM(e) 1960, *AM(g) 1968, *FCC(g) 1976, AGM 1993

'Irish Mint' 3 W-GGW
(John R.Reed) John R.Reed, 1995

'Irish Mist' 2 W-Y
(Mrs H.K. Richardson) Mrs H.K. Richardson, 1972
'Irish Minstrel' open pollinated
Corona deep orange-yellow, with rim dentate. 2n=28

'Irish Nymph' 3 W-GYO
(Carncairn Daffodils) Carncairn Daffodils, 1981
Wootton sdlg 86 × 'Hamzali'; sdlg no. W15/2
Fl. 77 mm wide; perianth segments pure white; corona brilliant greenish yellow 6C, shading through brilliant yellow-green 142B to deep yellowish green 141B at base, with light orange (23A) at rim. Late. Scented

'Irish Pearl' 2 W-W
(G.L. Wilson, pre-1923)
'Minnie Hume' × 'Pearl of Kent'

Corona opening primrose, soon becoming white, frilled

'Irish Prince' 1 Y-Y
(G.L. Wilson, pre-1930)
'Goldbeater' × 'Belshazzar'
Corona with rim flanged and dentate

'Irish Princeps' 1 W-Y
Syn. of 'Princeps'

'Irish Queen' 2 W-W
(G.L. Wilson, pre-1927)
Syn. 'Mavourneen'. *AM(g) 1927

'Irish Ranger' 3 W-O
(Carncairn Daffodils) Carncairn Daffodils, 1975
'Kilworth' × Richardson sdlg 260; sdlg no. 1/104/60
Fl. forming a double triangle, 100 mm wide; perianth segments broadly ovate, greenish white; the inner segments more narrowly ovate, with margins incurved or wavy; corona broad, very shallow bowl-shaped, closely ribbed, glowing reddish orange, mouth straight and 6-lobed, with lobes sometimes deeply overlapping, rim irregularly crenate. Resembles a 'Rockall' less prone to disease

'Irish Rhapsody' 1 W-W
(G.L. Wilson) Guy L.Wilson Ltd, 1964
'Ardbane' × 'Santa Lucia'

'Irish Romance' 1 Y-Y
(A.F. Calvert, pre-1929)

'Irish Rose' 2 W-P
(G.L. Wilson, pre-1953)
'Interim' × 'Evening'
Fl. 115 mm wide; perianth segments pure white, overlapping half; corona slightly ribbed, near to light yellowish pink 36C, frilled, with rim crenate. PC 1955, AM(e) 1957

'Irish Rover' 2 W-OOY
(J.L. Richardson) Mrs H.K. Richardson, 1967
'Kilworth' × 'Rockall'
Fl. 89 mm wide; perianth segments blunt, white, flushed yellow at base, slightly reflexed, overlapping; corona very shallow, ribbed, vivid orange 28B, with orange-yellow at rim, frilled, with rim crenate. AM(e) 1967

'Irish Rum' 2 Y-O
(John R.Reed, 1983) John R.Reed, 1995
'Red Rum' × 'Irish Light'; sdlg no. 78-1-1
Fl. 90 mm wide; perianth segments very broadly ovate, light yellow; corona bowl-shaped, orange

'Irish Splendour' 3 W-R
(W.J. Dunlop) W.J. Dunlop, 1962
'Red Hackle' hybrid

Perianth segments snow white; corona small, crimson-red

'Irish Treasure' 2 W-P
(Mrs H.K. Richardson) Mrs H.K. Richardson, 1977
'Romance' × 'Rondetto'
Fl. 106 mm wide; corona very shallow bowl-shaped, deep salmon pink, with mouth widely expanded and rim dentate. Mid-season

'Iris Humphrey' 1 W-? (b)
(pre-1913)

'Irish Wedding' 2 W-GWW
(John R.Reed, 1987) John R.Reed, 1997
'Misty Glen' × 'Immaculate'; sdlg no. 81-30-1
Fl. 100 mm wide, crystalline white; perianth segments ovate, slightly concave; corona funnel-shaped, with sage green at base. Mid-season

'Ir.K.Volkersz' 1 Y-Y
Syn. of 'Ingenieur K.Volkersz'

'Irma' 2 Y-O
(de Graaff Bros, pre-1927)
Perianth segments broadly ovate, blunt, fairly prominently mucronate, sulphur yellow, slightly reflexed, plane or with margins sometimes incurling, overlapping a quarter; the inner segments a little twisted or with margins incurved; corona clear orange, with mouth expanded, lightly frilled. AM(Haarlem) 1927

'Irmelin' 8 W-O
(R.A. van der Schoot, pre-1930)
Poetaz
Fls up to 6 per stem, 57 mm wide; perianth segments very broadly ovate, truncate, mucronate, spreading or a little reflexed, overlapping half; the inner segments a little inflexed, with margins wavy or incurled; corona bowl-shaped, tightly ribbed, clear orange, mouth with six lobes sometimes deeply split and overlapping. AM(Haarlem) 1929

'Iron Duke' 1 Y-Y
(E. & J.C. Martin, pre-1916)

'Iroquois' 2 Y-? (a)
(E.C. Powell, pre-1949)
'Prosperity' × 'Fortune'

'Iroquois' 2 YYW-O
(R. & E.Havens, 1976) R. & E.Havens, 1995
Sdlg GEJ6/ ('Paricutin' × 'Daydream') × sdlg F107/3 ('Red Marley' × 'Brer Fox'); sdlg no. LEJ28/1
Fl. 104 mm wide; perianth segments ovate, lemon yellow, with white at base, spreading, plane, smooth; corona straight-sided, bright tangerine orange, with mouth frilled. Mid-season. Sunproof

'Irresistible' 2 Y-P
(G.E. Mitsch) G.E. Mitsch, 1979
'Milestone' × 'Sugar Maple'; sdlg no. LL8/2
Fl. 92 mm wide; perianth segments pale buffy lemon; corona buff pink, with a creamier tone outside and apricot pink at rim, frilled. Mid-season

'Irving' 1 Y-Y
Syn. of 'Henry Irving'

'Irvington' 3 W-R
(W.G. Pannill) W.G. Pannill, 1976
'Merlin' × 'Hotspur'; sdlg no. 64/84 B
Fl. 87 mm wide; corona red

'Irwin Hunter' 2 W-R
(West & Fell, pre-1935)
Corona pinkish red, frilled

'Isaac Beckman' 3 W-OOR
(J.W.A. Lefeber) W. Blom & Son, 1955
Perianth segments snow white; corona reddish orange, with scarlet at rim

'Isabel' 2 Y-? (a)
(Cranwell, pre-1910)

'Isabella' 8 Y-O
(pre-1850)

'Isabella' 2 W-W
(J.N. Hancock & Co.) E.W. Philpott, 1959
Sdlg 89H (1W-Y) × 'Truth'; sdlg no. 21/53H
Corona slightly expanded, creamy white, with rim dentate. Mid-season. See also 'Isobella'

'Ischia' 2 W-PPY
(The Brodie of Brodie, pre-1932)
'Penwith' × 'Suda'
Corona long, opening coral pink, with a narrow band of creamy yellow at rim, becoming paler, frilled

'Ishbel' 3 W-? (b)
(R.H. Bath, pre-1927)

'Ishtar' 2 W-? (b)
(D.J. Cooper) D.J. Cooper, 1957

'Isidoor' 2 W-? (b)
(Mrs R.O. Backhouse, pre-1921)
See also 'Isidor', 'Isodor', 'Isodoor'

'Isidor' 2 W-? (b)
Syn. of 'Isidoor'

'Isis' 3 Y-YYR
(C.G. van Tubergen, pre-1908)
'Ornatus' × 'Will Scarlett'
Perianth segments pale primrose yellow, overlapping; corona widely expanded, ribbed, soft citron yellow, with dark madder scarlet at rim. AM(Haarlem) 1912

'Isis' 2 Y-Y
(Angus Wilson) Wallace & Barr, 1959
Fl. 100 mm wide; perianth segments pale sulphur yellow; corona darker in tone, with lemon yellow at rim. Mid-season. Resembles a lighter-coloured and somewhat taller 'Binkie'

'Isita' 8
(R.H. Bath, pre-1923)

'Island' 1 Y-Y
(E.W. Philpott)

'Island Dream' 4 Y-YOO
(David Adams) David Adams, 1996
Sdlg 80/19B (4 Y-Y × 'Daydream') × 'Tahiti'; sdlg no. 85/27B
Fl. 93 mm wide; perianth segments broadly ovate, blunt, light yellow, whitish at base; the inner segments more narrowly ovate; corona segments in two whorls of three, bright orange, with strong yellow at base; the inner whorl almost continuous, cup-shaped. Mid-season. Sunproof

'Islander' 4 Y-Y
(Carncairn Daffodils, 1980) Carncairn Daffodils, 1993
'Fiji' open pollinated; sdlg no. 1/44/75
Fl. 90 mm wide; perianth and other petaloid segments light yellow, Irregular; the outer whorl very broad in outline, blunt or truncate at apex, with white mucro, overlapping half or more; the inner whorl shorter, inflexed, with margins sometimes incurved or more tightly incurling; corona segments shorter than the inner petaloid segments, clustered at centre and more loosely arranged between the petaloid segments, broad, dark yellow, loosely frilled. Late. Resembles 'Fiji' but with the corona segments of a deeper tone

'Islandhill' 3 W-YYO
(Ballydorn Bulb Farm) Ballydorn Bulb Farm, 1984
'Strangford' × 'Fermoy' hybrid
Fl. 92 mm wide. Mid-season

'Islandreagh' 2 W-Y
(Carncairn Daffodils) Carncairn Daffodils, 1969
'Guardian' × 'Preamble'
Perianth segments white; corona yellow, with near to orange-brown at base and a darker tone of yellow at rim

'Isle of Bute' 1 Y-Y
(A.G. Thompson) A.G. Thompson, 1965
'Fortune' × 'Imperator'
Fl. 108 mm wide; corona darker in tone than the perianth. Mid-season

'Isle of Ely' 2 W-? (b)
(W. Welchman, pre-1923)

'Ismailia' 2 W-W
(J.L. Richardson) J.L. Richardson, 1963
'Empress of Ireland' × 'Early Mist'

'Ismaris' 1 Y-Y
(West & Fell, pre-1935)

'Iso' 3 Y-? (a)
(J.L. Richardson, pre-1937)

'Isobel Chaplin' 2 W-R
(L.P. Dettman) L.P. Dettman, 1971
'Better Half' × 'Annette'
Fl. 91 mm wide

'Isobeline' 2 W-P
(G.H. Johnstone) G.H. Johnstone, 1959
Fl. 95 mm wide. Mid-season

'Isobell' 2 W-?
(A. Overton) A. Ladson, 1960

'Isobella' 2 W-W
Syn. of 'Isabella'

'Isodoor' 2 W-? (b)
Syn. of 'Isidoor'

'Isodor' 2 W-?
Syn. of 'Isidoor'

'Isola' 3 W-YYO
(J.T. Gray, pre-1936)
'Kestrel' hybrid
Perianth segments ivory white; corona yellow, with a broad band of reddish orange at rim

'Isolde' 1 Y-Y
(G.P. Haydon, pre-1905)
'Weardale Perfection' × 'Madame de Graaff'
Fl. 127 mm wide; primrose yellow; perianth segments inflexed; corona softer in tone than the perianth

'Isolde'
(Alister Clark, pre-1915)

'Isolde' 1 Y-WWY
(Konynenburg & Mark) Konynenburg & Mark, 1964
'Spellbinder' × 'Binkie'
Fl. 95 mm wide; perianth segments brilliant greenish yellow 6B; corona greenish white, with brilliant greenish yellow 6A at rim. Late

'Isolde' 1 Y-Y
Syn. of 'Audley'

'Isolde' 2 W-?
Syn. of 'Effendie'

'Isoline' 2 W-? (b)
(R.H. Bath, pre-1927)

'Ispahan' 2 Y-? (a)
(A.M. Wilson, pre-1948)

'Israel' 8 W-Y
Syn. of 'Omri'

'Isrid' 1 W-W
(W. Jackson Jr, 1957) Unregistered
'Merri' × 'Ammon'; sdlg no. 301/57

'Istar' 7 Y-?
(de Graaff Bros, pre-1923)

'Istria' 1 W-W
(The Brodie of Brodie, c.1920)
'White Emperor' × 'Trappist'; sdlg no. 5/A/15

'Istria' 2 W-? (b)
(A.H. Ahrens) D.J. Cooper, 1957

'Ita' 2 W-P
(Brian S.Duncan) Brian S.Duncan, 1996
'Gracious Lady' × 'Dailmanach'; sdlg no. 1469
Fl. forming a double triangle, 105 mm wide; perianth segments broadly ovate, pure white; corona funnel-shaped, slightly ribbed, deep apple blossom pink, with mouth a little flared. Mid-season

N. italicus Ker Gawler 13 Section Tazettae

'Italicus Plenus' 4 W-O
Syn. of 'Romanus'

'Itasca'
(E.C. Powell)
'Nevis' × 'Godolphin'

'Ithaca' 2 W-? (b)
(The Brodie of Brodie, c.1921)
'Nevis' × 'Loch Fyne'; sdlg no. 3/A/16
Corona shallow, expanded

'Ithica' 2 Y-GRR
(J.N. Hancock & Co., 1965) Unregistered

'Itika' 2 W-? (b)
(Warnaar & Co., pre-1930)

'Itonus' 1 Y-Y
(D.V. West, pre-1935)
Perianth segments primrose; corona rich yellow

'It's True' 1 W-W
(M.J. Jefferson-Brown) M.J. Jefferson-Brown, 1968

Sdlg × 'Empress of Ireland'
Perianth segments rounded; corona narrow, mouth expanded, with rim flanged. PC(e) 1968

'Itzim' 6 Y-R
(G.E. Mitsch) Rathowen Daffodils, 1982
'Vulcan' sdlg × *N. cyclamineus*; sdlg no. H.137/5
Perianth segments ovate, prominently mucronate, deep yellow, sharply reflexed, plane, overlapping a quarter or less; corona cylindrical, loosely ribbed, deep orange-red, mouth straight or a little expanded, split in places and overlapping, with rim irregularly dentate. Early to mid-season. 2n=21. Resembles a taller 'Jetfire' with narrower perianth segments and a larger corona. AGM 1995

'Ivanhoe' 2 W-O
(J. Veitch & Sons, pre-1898)
AM 1898

'Ivanhoe' 1 Y-Y
(W.B. Hartland, pre-1910)

'Ivanhoe' 2 Y-O
(West & Fell, pre-1933)
Corona reddish orange

'Ivanhoe' 3 Y-?
Syn. of 'Alabama'

'Iveridge' 4 W-Y
(K.J. Heazlewood) R. Hyde, 1959
'Nautilus' × 'Royal Sovereign'
Perianth and other petaloid segments pure white, overlapping; corona segments lemon yellow

'Ivernia' 2 W-? (b)
(R.H. Bath, pre-1908)

'Iverson' 2 Y-O
Syn. of 'Ivoson'

'Ives' 2 Y-Y
(?Australian origin, pre-1996) Unregistered

'Ivo Fell' 2 Y-O
(West & Fell, 1940) R. Hyde, 1958
Fl. large, of good substance; perianth segments pale primrose; corona reddish orange

'Ivor' 9 W-?
(W. Poupart, pre-1914)

'Ivorine' 3 W-W
(P.D. Williams, pre-1910)
? × 'Lulworth'
Perianth segments silvery white, overlapping; corona shallow, opening pale yellow, becoming ivory white. AM(e) 1914

'Ivory' 3 W-? (b)
(J.W.A. Lefeber, pre-1938)

'Ivory Beauty' 4
(P. Heemskirk, pre-1946)

'Ivory Bowl'
(A.E. Lowe, pre-1927)

'Ivory Crown' 2 W-YOY
(F.E. Board, pre-1965) Unregistered
Perianth segments pure white; corona bowl-shaped, peachy orange, with yellow at base and rim

'Ivory Crown' 2 W-O
(W.A. Noton, pre-1986) Unregistered
Corona shallow, salmon orange

'Ivory Eye' 3 W-Y
(W.F.M. Copeland, pre-1923)
Perianth segments pure glistening white, very deeply overlapping; corona heavily ribbed, pale ivory white. Mid-season

'Ivory Fashion' 1 Y-Y
(J.N. Hancock & Co., 1984) Unregistered
'Rich Strike' × 'Standard Bearer'; sdlg no. 46/84H
Fl. pale parchment yellow; perianth segments deeply overlapping; corona narrow, lightly frilled, with rim rolled. Tall. Mid-season to late

'Ivory Gate' 5 W-W
(A. Gray, pre-1949)
? × *N. triandrus* var. *loiseleurii*
Fls 2 per stem, ivory white; corona frilled

'Ivory Glory' 1 W-W
(D. van Egmond & Sons) D. van Egmond & Sons, 1959
Fl. 115 mm wide, creamy white; corona darker in tone. Mid-season. AM(Haarlem) 1959

'Ivory Gull' 5 W-W
(G.E. Mitsch, 1967) R. Havens, 1980
'Quick Step' × *N. triandrus*; sdlg no. C52/28
Fl. 70 mm wide, ivory white. Late. Resembles 'Petrel' but with a larger and longer corona

'Ivory King' 1 W-W
(G.H. Engleheart, pre-1914)
Fl. ivory white, of strong substance; corona flared

'Ivory Star' 1 W-W
(The Brodie of Brodie, pre-1929)

'Ivory Tower' 1 W-W
(Campbell Duncan) Campbell Duncan, 1956
'Ardclinis' × 'Broughshane'

'Ivory Yellow' 3 W-? (b)
(G. Lubbe & Son, pre-1944)
AM(Haarlem) 1944

'Ivoson' 2 Y-O
(A. Overton) A. Overton, 1960
Corona large, widely expanded. Resembles 'Ivo Fell' in colour but with a more sunproof corona. Syn. 'Winterset'. See also 'Iverson'

'Ivy Diamond' 2 Y-? (a)
(H. Daines) H. Daines, 1957

'Ivy League' 1 W-Y
(Murray W. Evans) Murray W. Evans, 1972
'Effective' × 'Festivity'
Fl. 100 mm wide; perianth segments becoming white only with sun

'Ixion' 2 Y-YOO
(Barr & Sons, pre-1915)
Perianth segments canary yellow; the inner segments narrower, slightly twisted; corona large, orange, paling to rich yellow at base, shading to dark orange at rim, with mouth flared. Resembles 'Helios'

'Ixion' 2 W-R
(R.H.Glover, pre-1993) Unregistered

'Izard' 3 W-YYR
(Barr & Sons, pre-1907)
Perianth segments ivory white, reflexed; corona expanded, golden yellow, with intense orange-red at rim

'Izarra' 3 W-? (b or c)
(Barr & Sons, pre-1927)

'Izebel'
(G. Zandbergen-Terwegen, pre-1954)

J

'Jabiru' 2 Y-O
(J.N. Hancock & Co., 1979) Unregistered
Sdlg no. 49B/79H
Fl. forming a double triangle; perianth segments broadly ovate, blunt, bright yellow, with white mucro, spreading, somewhat creased, overlapping half; the inner segments a little inflexed, with margins wavy; corona broad funnel-shaped, vivid orange, mouth straight, ribbed, a little frilled, with rim crenate. Midseason

'Jabot' 3 W-Y
(T.D. Throckmorton) T.D. Throckmorton, 1974

'Old Satin' × 'Arbar'

'Jacana' 1 W-W
(S.J. Bisdee, pre-1950)
'Kanchenjunga' × 'Ardclinis'

N. jacetanus Fernández Casas 13 Section Pseudonarcissus. PC 1996
    subsp. *jacetanus*
    subsp. *vasconicus* (Fernández Casas) Fernández Casas

'Jacinta Marto' 2 W-O
(W. Blom & Son, pre-1954)
'John Evelyn' × 'Peggy'
Resembles a more prolific 'John Evelyn'

'Jacinth' 2 Y-? (a)
(A.H. Ahrens) J.S. Leitch, 1955

'Jack' 1 Y-Y
(G.P. Haydon, pre-1908)

'Jackadee' 2 Y-R
(Brian S.Duncan) Brian S.Duncan, 1996
'Garden News' × ('Bunclody' × 'Barnsdale Wood'); sdlg no. 1312
Fl. forming a double triangle, 100 mm wide; perianth segments broadly ovate, deep golden yellow, plane; corona expanded, bowl-shaped, intense orange-red, with mouth a little frilled. Late. Sunproof

'Jack and Jill' 8
(E. & J.C. Martin, pre-1916)

'Jack Bateman' 2 Y-? (a)
(Warnaar & Co., pre-1951)
'Carbineer' × 'Amarantha'

'Jack-be-Nimble' 6
(K.L. Reynolds, pre-1939)

'Jack-be-Quick' 6 Y-Y
(K.L. Reynolds, pre-1939)
'Lady Hillingdon' × *N. cyclamineus*
Fl. very deep yellow

'Jack Charrington'
(G.H. Engleheart, pre-1907)

'Jackdaw' 3 Y-? (a)
(Sir C.H. Cave, pre-1908)

'Jack Deller' 2 Y-O
(L.P. Dettman) L.P. Dettman, 1976
'Bubbles' × 'Coppertone'; sdlg no. 5/75
Fl. 84 mm wide; perianth segments vivid yellow 15A, touched green at base; corona strong orange 24A, with green at base. Early. Resembles 'Coppertone' but with perianth segments of thicker substance

'Jack Dennis' 1 Y-Y
(W.M. Spry, pre-1975) Unregistered
'Braemar' × 'Golden'

'Jack Frost' 2 W-W
(P.D.L. Hudden) P.D.L. Hudden, 1955

'Jack Goldsmith' 4 W-O
(W.J.M. Blom, 1968) W. Blom & Son, 1984
'Anne Frank' × 'Coquille'; sdlg no. 68-F-1
Fl. rounded; perianth and other petaloid segments in several whorls, white; the outer segments of the outer whorl prominently mucronate, others truncate; the outer whorl more or less spreading and plane; the inner whorls successively slightly shorter, more strongly inflexed, concave; the centre whorl narrow, strongly inflexed, with margins tightly incurled; corona segments one-third the length of the petaloid segments and interspersed among them, pale orange, frilled. Late

'Jack Horner' 1 W-Y
(J.L. Richardson, pre-1927)
'Cleopatra' × 'White Knight'
Perianth segments very broad, pure white; corona pale lemon, with rim flanged

'Jackie' 7 Y-Y
(S. Morrison) T. Morrison, 1960

'Jackie Jones' 1 Y-GYY
(L.P. Dettman, 1967) L.P. Dettman, 1904
'Arctic Gold' × 'King Kanto'; sdlg no. A-K 17/69
Fl. 80 mm wide; perianth segments brilliant yellow 13B; corona slightly darker in tone, with green at base

'Jack Kavanaugh' 2 Y-OOR
(L.P.Dettman, 1977) Unregistered
'Vulcan' × 'Spelter'; sdlg no. V/S 1/77

'Jack Point' 9 W-YYR
(G.H. Engleheart, pre-1910)

'Jackpot' 2 Y-R
(W.O. Backhouse) M.J. Jefferson-Brown, 1964
2n=28

'Jackpot' 2 Y-O
(Tom Forster, 1960s) Unregistered
Perianth segmens roundish, mid-yellow; corona broad disc-shaped, mid-orange, with a brighter tone at rim. Early to mid-season

'Jack Schlitt' 1 Y-Y
(Betty Beery) Betty Beery, 1987
'Ormeau' × 'Slieveboy'; sdlg no. JS-20-FR
Perianth segments very broadly ovate, rounded at apex, slightly mucronate, spreading, with margins occasionally incurling at apex, smooth, overlapping half; the inner segments rounded at base; corona smooth, darker in tone than the perianth, with mouth expanded and a little frilled, rim crenate and loosely flanged. Dwarf. Early

'Jack Snipe' 6 W-Y
(M.P.Williams, pre-1951)
Fl. 70 mm wide, at an acute angle to the stem; perianth segments ovate, mucronate, creamy white, flushed pale yellow at base, reflexed, with margins incurved, overlapping a quarter; corona cylindrical, ribbed, vivid yellow 13a, with a brighter tone (9A) at rim, mouth very slightly expanded and a little frilled, with rim notched and crenate. Tall. Early. 2n=21.
AM(Haarlem) 1956, HC(p) 1985, AGM 1995

'Jack Spratt' 1 W-Y
(G.L. Wilson, pre-1927)
Corona bright clear yellow

'Jack Wood' 11a Y-YYO
(R.A.Scamp) R.A.Scamp, 1997
'Saint Keverne' × 'Tiritomba'; sdlg no. 540
Fl. 100 mm wide; perianth segments broad, acute, golden yellow, spreading, smooth, deeply overlapping; corona regularly split, the six segments opposite and closely overlying the perianth segments, slightly darker in tone, with orange at rim. Midseason. Sunproof

'Jacoba' 1 W-W
(de Graaff Bros, pre-1923)

'Jacobar' 1 W-Y
(W. Jackson Jr) W. Jackson Jr, 1968
'Lod' × 'Palana'; sdlg no. 37/65

'Jacobin' 1 Y-Y
(Brian S.Duncan, 1985) Brian S.Duncan, 1996
'Midas Touch' open pollinated; sdlg no. 1121
Fl. 100 mm wide, deep golden yellow; perianth segments broadly ovate, plane, smooth; corona cylindrical, slightly frilled, with rim broadly flanged. Late

'Jacob Maris' 1 Y-Y
Syn. of 'Rembrandt'

'Jacopo' 2 Y-O
(P.D. Williams, pre-1933)
'Tredore' hybrid
Perianth segments acute; corona reddish orange, frilled

'Jacqueline' 2 W-O
(pre-1927)
Perianth segments clear white; corona pure deep orange, frilled. AM(Haarlem) 1927

'Jacqueline' 2 W-Y
(C.E.Kitchin, pre-1927)
Fl. 95 mm wide, facing down; perianth segments

creamy white, separated; corona funnel-shaped, primrose. Mid-season

'Jacqueline' 2 W-? (b)
(D.J. Cooper) D.J. Cooper, 1956

'Jacqueline Kay' 2 W-P
(G.N. Rees) G.N. Rees, 1963
'Pink Fancy' × 'Mrs R.O.Backhouse'
Fl. 95 mm wide; corona opening apricot pink, becoming clear pink. Mid-season. Scented

'Jacqueline Morris' 2 W-R
(J.A. Morris) J.A. Morris, 1960
Fl. 112 mm wide; corona tomato red. Mid-season

N. jacquemoudii Fernández Casas 13 Section Bulbocodium

'Jacquenetta' 3 W-? (b)
(Barr & Sons, pre-1923)

'Jacques' 2 W-? (b)
(Barr & Sons, pre-1923)

'Jacques Lefeber' 11b W-O
(J.W.A. Lefeber) J.W.A. Lefeber, 1968
'Papillon' hybrid

'Jade' 3 W-GWW
(G.E. Mitsch) G.E. Mitsch, 1972
'Cushendall' × 'Cantabile'
Fl. 65 mm wide, pure white; corona with vivid green at base. Late. Resembles 'Tern'

'Jaffa' 3 W-? (b)
(Mrs R.O. Backhouse, pre-1921)

'Jago' 2 Y-O
(J.N. Hancock & Co., 1965) Unregistered
Perianth segments very broadly ovate, blunt, slightly mucronate, deep yellow, a little inflexed, overlapping half; the inner segments sometimes more strongly inflexed, with margins a little wavy; corona bowl-shaped, ribbed, intense red-orange, frilled, with rim minutely notched and crenate. Tall. Mid-season

'Jaguar' 2 Y-O
(J.L. Richardson, pre-1951)
'Bahram' × 'Ceylon'
Perianth segments deep golden yellow; corona bowl-shaped, reddish orange

'Jake' 3 Y-GOO
(Brian S.Duncan) Brian S.Duncan, 1997
'Garden News' × 'Triple Crown'; sdlg no. 1577
Fl. 105 mm wide; perianth segments broadly ovate, mid-yellow, spreading, plane, smooth; corona shallow bowl-shaped, rich reddish orange, with olive green at base. Late

'Jalna' 2 Y-R
(A.M. Wilson, pre-1930)
'Granada' hybrid
Perianth segments golden yellow; corona vivid orange-red. FA(Haarlem) 1942

'Jamage' 8 W-Y
(G.W. Tarry) G.W.Tarry & du Plessis Bros, 1990
?'Grand Primo' × 'Green Island'
Fls 2-4 per stem, 63 mm wide; perianth segments creamy white; corona lemon yellow. Mid-season. Scented. 2n=46

'Jamaica' 3 W-R
(J.L. Richardson, pre-1941)
'Clava' × 'Forfar'
Perianth segments pure white; corona very shallow bowl-shaped, scarlet

'Jamaica inn' 4 W-YOO
(Brian S. Duncan) Dan du Plessis, 1993
Sdlg no. 874 × sdlg no. 346; sdlg no. 948
Fl. 90 mm wide; perianth and other petaloid segments white; the outer whorl broadly ovate; the inner whorls within the corona; corona deep apricot orange, yellow at base, with pink overtones when young. Late

'Jamal' 2 Y-R
(J.S. Leitch) J.S. Leitch, 1958

'Jambart' 2 Y-? (a)
(G.H. Englehcart, pre-1923)

'Jambo' 2 Y-R
(Brian S. Duncan) Brian S. Duncan, 1990
'Shining Light' × 'Torridon'; sdlg no. 1002
Fl. 98 mm wide; perianth segments very broadly ovate, blunt, only very slightly mucronate, deep golden yellow, spreading, very smooth, overlapping half; the inner segments more narrowly ovate, square-shouldered at base, a little inflexed; corona cup-shaped, very broadly ribbed, deep orange-red, mouth straight, even or very lightly frilled, rim entire and occasionally split. Early to mid-season. Sunproof

'Jamboree' 2 Y-? (a)
(F.H. Chapman, pre-1923)

'Jamboree' 1 Y-O
(W.G. Pannill) W.G. Pannill, 1982
'Kingscourt' × 'Chemawa'; sdlg no. E 11
Fl. rounded, 90 mm wide; perianth segments very broad, blunt or truncate, spreading, smooth, overlapping half or more; the inner segments square-shouldered at base, with margins slightly wavy; corona cylindrical, lightly ribbed, mouth straight, minutely and closely ribbed, with many overlapping lobes, rim minutely crenate. Mid-season. Varies between Divs 1 and 2

'James' 2 W-Y
(R. Gibson, pre-1927)
Corona creamy yellow

'James Bateman' 2 W-Y
(W. Backhouse, pre-1869)
Perianth segments pure white; corona large, expanded, clear yellow. Syn. Incomparabilis Albus 'James Bateman'

'James Boyd' 2 Y-? (a)
(C.E. Buckingham, pre-1936)

'James Bray' 2 Y-? (a)
(W.B. Hartland, pre-1912)

'James Dickson' 2 Y-Y
Syn. of 'Sir Watkin'

'James Douglas' 3 W-YYO
(F.H. Chapman, pre-1913)
Fl. 76 mm wide, facing down; perianth segments creamy white, overlapping half; corona very shallow bowl-shaped, greenish lemon, with orange at rim, frilled. Late

'James Hogg' 9 W-YYR
(The Brodie of Brodie, c.1913)
'Oliver Goldsmith' × 'Hildegarde'
Corona with crimson at rim

'James Ianson'
(W.Backhouse, pre-1869)

'James Pierson' 1 Y-Y
(D.S. Bell) D.S. Bell, 1984
'David Bell' × 'Red Conquest'
Fl. 102 mm wide, lemon yellow. Mid-season

'James River' 2 Y-P
(W.G. Pannill) W.G. Pannill, 1982
'Bethany' hybrid; sdlg no. J 74
Fl. 88 mm wide. Mid-season

'James Stuart' 2 W-W
(Mrs F.S. Foote, pre-1941)

'Jamestown' 3 W-GYY
(Ballydorn Bulb Farm) Ballydorn Bulb Farm, 1978
'Ballymartin' × 'Irish Minstrel'
Fl. 85 mm wide; corona frilled. Mid-season

'James Veitch' 1 Y-Y
(Dutch origin, pre-1890)

'James Walker' 1 W-Y
(E. Leeds, pre-1877)
Perianth segments sulphur white, overlapping; corona golden yellow. Very early. Syn. Pseudonarcissus Bicolor 'Albidus', Pseudonarcissus Bicolor 'James Walker'. "Absorbed" 'David Walker' and 'Prince of Wales'. ?Syn. of 'Mrs James Walker'

'James Wyness' 2 W-OOR
(West & Fell, pre-1935)
Corona orange, with a very broad band of scarlet at rim

'Jamie' 4
(C.E. Radcliff, pre-1938)
'Rheban' × 'Telamonius Plenus'

'Jamie C.' 2 Y-Y
(D.S.Bell, pre-1987) Unregistered

'Jamore' 2 Y-R
(J.A.O'More, 1977) J.A.Hunter, 1997
'Air Marshal' × 'Falstaff'; sdlg no. 28/77
Fl. forming a double triangle, 107 mm wide; perianth segments ovate, very smooth; corona cup-shaped, with mouth wavy. Mid-season

'Jana' 6 Y-Y
(A. Gray, pre-1949)
Fl. clear yellow; perianth segments ovate, acute, more or less spreading, overlapping a quarter or less; the inner segments a little twisted or with margins wavy; corona cylindrical, smooth, darker in tone than the perianth, with mouth ribbed and even, rim flanged and regularly and deeply dentate. 2n=21. Variable in height

'Jan de Geer' 2 W-? (b)
(J.W.A. Lefeber, pre-1944)

'Jandra' 2 Y-R
(W. Jackson Jr) Jackson's Daffodils, 1979
'Dimity' hybrid × 'Jaguar'; sdlg no. 41/73
Fl. 115 mm wide. Mid-season

'Jane Adams' 2 Y-? (a)
(D.S. Bell) D.S. Bell, 1958

'Jane and Mary' 1 (a)
Syn. of 'Robust'

'Jane Biggio' 2 W-WWP
(Oregon Bulb Farms, pre-1950)

'Jane-Elizabeth' 3 W-GYR
(L.P. Dettman) L.P. Dettman, 1984
'Janice Dettman' × 'Nancy Havergal'; sdlg no. 104/75
Fl. 76 mm wide; perianth segments yellowish white 155B; corona vivid greenish yellow 2A, with brilliant yellow-green 149A at base and orange-red (40D) at rim. Mid-season

'Jane Eyre' 2 W-R
(G. Lewis) D.S. Bell, 1955

'Jane Frances' 1 W-W
(D.C. MacArthur) D.C. MacArthur, 1987
'Ludlow' hybrid open pollinated; sdlg no. E8702
Fl. greenish white (155A); corona neatly frilled. Mid-season

'Jane Furse' 5
(H.R. Meyer, pre-1927)

'Jane Kolle' 2 W-Y
(W. Backhouse, pre-1869)
Perianth segments sulphur white; corona yellow, with mouth expanded. Syn. Incomparabilis Albidus 'Jane Kolle'. Was "absorbed" into 'Surprise'

'Jane MacDonald' 4 Y-O
(D.C. MacArthur) D.C. MacArthur, 1988
Rathowen hybrid open pollinated; sdlg no. E8805
Perianth segments vivid yellow 9B, flushed strong yellow-green 144C; corona light orange (23A), shading to reddish orange at rim. Very late. Scented

'Jane MacLennan' 4 W-Y
(D.C. MacArthur) D.C. MacArthur, 1987
Sdlg open pollinated; sdlg no. E8704
Perianth and other petaloid segments yellowish white 155D; corona segments interspersed, between vivid yellow 13A and a creamier tone (11A). Late

'Jane Sinclair' 2 W-? (b)
(D.H.L. Corrigan, pre-1949)

'Janet' 2 Y-?
(Barr & Sons, pre-1903)

'Janet Cox' 2 W-P
(Alister Clark, 1937) L.P. Dettman, 1960

'Janet Fairclough' 2 W-? (b)
(A.C. McKillop) A.C. McKillop, 1955

'Janet Image' 2 Y-Y
(Barr & Sons, pre-1903)
Perianth segments pale sulphur yellow; corona large, straight, clear light yellow. AM 1903

"Janette des Contois"
Syn. of *N. poeticus*

'Jane van Kralingen' 3 W-GOY
(D.C. MacArthur) D.C. MacArthur, 1989
Sdlg 2W-GYO × sdlg 2W-GYY; sdlg no. EV88/100
Fl. 108 mm wide; perianth segments greenish white (155A), of good substance, overlapping; corona disc-shaped, strong orange 25B, with greyish yellow-green 194B at base and light orange-yellow 19A at rim. Late. Scented

'Jane Vleek' 2 Y-GYO
(L.P. Dettman, 1971) Unregistered

'Coope' × 'Langley Gold Dust'; sdlg no. 19/73

'Janice' 2 W-? (b)
(D.J. Cooper) D.J. Cooper, 1956

'Janice Dettman' 2 W-YYR
(L.P. Dettman) L.P. Dettman, 1968
'Buncrana' × 'Jean Hood'

'Janice Leam' 2 W-Y
(A. Overton) A. Overton, 1960
Perianth segments pure white; corona yellow, ribbed, lightly frilled

'Janice Page' 8
(H. Frylink, c.1900)

'Janice Shakespeare' 1 Y-Y
(D.S. Bell) D.S. Bell, 1955

'Janine' 2 Y-YOO
(J.N. Hancock & Co.) J.N. Hancock & Co., 1955
Perianth segments yellow; corona deep orange, paling to yellow at base

'Janis Babson' 2 W-WWP
(Murray W. Evans) Murray W. Evans, 1968
('Pink Lace' × 'Interim') × 'Caro Nome'
Fl. 102 mm wide; perianth segments pure white. Mid-season. Resembles 'Audubon' but with a whiter and more heavily frilled corona with a clearer pink at rim

'Janitor'
(pre-1950)

'Janka' 1 W-? (b)
(C. Alkemade, pre-1944)

'Jan Lambert' 2 W-PPW
(L.P. Dettman) L.P. Dettman, 1975
'Better Half' × 'Hugh Dettman'; sdlg no. 72/70
Fl. 78 mm wide; perianth segments greenish white 157D; corona light yellowish pink 27A, with a narrow band of pale greenish white (155A) at rim. Mid-season

'Jan Maree' 2 W-P
(R.H. Glover) R.H. Glover, 1971
'Nina' × 'Pink Monarch'
Fl. 108 mm wide

'Jan Masaryk' 3 W-? (b)
(F. Rijnveld & Sons, pre-1948)

'Janole' 2 W-P
(J.N. Hancock & Co., 1982) J.N. Hancock & Co., 1997
'Glorification' × 'Mrs David Calvert'; sdlg no. 119/82H

Perianth segments ovate, spreading; corona funnel-shaped, deep bronze pink, with mouth neatly flared and rim crenate. Late

'Jansen' 2 O-R
(D.S. Bell) D.S. Bell, 1958
Perianth segments peach-coloured; corona bowl-shaped, coppery orange-red

'Jan Steen' 1 Y-Y
(G. Lubbe & Son, pre-1927)

'Jan Toorop' 3 Y-? (a)
(G. Lubbe & Son, pre-1937)
AM(Haarlem) 1936

JANUARY 1 Y-Y
Trade designation for 'Rijnveld's Early Sensation'

JANUARY GOLD 6 Y-Y
Trade designation for 'First Hope'

JANUARY SILVER 2 W-Y
Trade designation for 'Melyor'

'Janus' 2 W-? (b)
(Mrs R.O. Backhouse, pre-1921)

'Janus' 1 Y-Y
(H.J. Poole Sr, pre-1927)

'Janus' 2 Y-Y
(J.N. Hancock & Co., pre-1956) Unregistered
Perianth segments very broadly ovate, blunt, rich yellow, with slight white mucro, spreading, plane, somewhat creased, overlapping half; the inner segments a little inflexed, with margins wavy and sometimes nicked; corona very broad funnel-shaped, golden yellow, mouth straight, tightly frilled. Early

'Jan Vermeer' 1 Y-Y
(pre-1953)

'Janz' 2 Y-R
(W. Jackson Jr, 1964) Unregistered
'Chitra' × 'Ruad'; sdlg no. 25/64

'Japaddy' 2 W-O
(H.A. Brown, 1943) J.N. Hancock & Co., 1955
'Melva Fell' × 'Cordova'
Perianth segments smooth, deeply overlapping; corona disc-shaped, deep reddish orange, with rim dentate. Sunproof

'Japonaise' 2 or 3 W-? (b or c)
(Cartwright & Goodwin, pre-1916)

'Japonica'
(pre-1913)

'Jardine' 2 Y-O
(J.N. Hancock & Co., 1961) Unregistered

'Jarjik' 1 Y-Y
(A.M. Wilson, pre-1938)

'Jarnac' 2 Y-? (a)
(Miss G. Evelyn, pre-1930)

'Jarrah' 2 W-OOR
(S.J. Bisdee, 1952)
'Limerick' × 'Palana'

'Jas. Ianson'
(W.Backhouse, pre-1869)

'Jasione' 2 Y-? (a)
(A.M. Wilson, pre-1948)

'Jaslin' 2 Y-Y
(W. Jackson Jr, 1955)
'Moque' × 'Vigi'

'Jasmanian'
(?J.L. Richardson, *c.*1959)

'Jasmin' 2 Y-R
(The Brodie of Brodie, *c.*1910)
'M.J.Berkeley' × *N. poeticus*
Perianth light yellow; corona heavily suffused with red

"Jasmine Jonquil"
See "The Jasmine Jonquil"

N. jasmineus Schultes f. = *N. papyraceus*

'Jason' 8 Y-Y
(pre-1798)
Fl. pale yellow

'Jason' 1 W-Y
(A.M. Wilson, pre-1908)
Perianth segments lightly inflexed, with margins wavy; corona pale lemon yellow

'Jason' 1 W-? (b)
(Sir A.P.W. Thomas, pre-1930)

'Jason' 3 (a)
Syn. of 'Sunion'

'Jaspar' 3 Y-O
Syn. of 'Jasper'

'Jasper' 3 Y-O
(P.D. Williams, pre-1908)
Perianth segments very pale primrose yellow; corona almost disc-shaped, rich scarlet-orange. Mid-season. See also 'Jaspar'

'Jasperina' 1 W-Y
(D. van Buggenum) D. van Buggenum, 1969
'Dutch Master' × 'Gold Medal'

'Jassy' 8 Y-Y
(pre-1846)

'Jauinata' 2 W-W
(R.H. Bath, pre-1933)

'Jaune à Merveille' 8 Y-YYO
(R. van der Schoot & Son, pre-1906)
Poetaz
Fls 4-6 per stem; perianth segments soft primrose yellow, overlapping; corona bright yellow, with a narrow band of orange at rim. 2n=17

'Jaune Belle' 8 Y-Y
(pre-1798)

'Jaune d'Or' 8
(pre-1938)

'Jaune Elegant' 8 Y-Y
(pre-1846)

'Jaune Pure' 8 Y-Y
(pre-1846)

'Jaune Supreme' 8 Y-Y
(pre-1871)
Fls many per stem; perianth segments buffy primrose yellow; corona orange-yellow. Syn. Tazetta 'Jaune Supreme'

'Jaunty' 2 W-Y
(J.J. Abernethy) R.J. Abernethy, 1961
Fl. 83 mm wide; corona tightly ribbed, bright yellow. Mid-season

'Java' 2 Y-Y
(Warnaar & Co, pre-1939)
'Fortune' × 'Golden Harvest'

'Javelin' 3 W-? (b)
(F.H. Chapman, pre-1913)

'Javelin' 2 Y-R
(W.G. Pannill) W.G. Pannill, 1970
'Paricutin' × 'Vulcan'

'Jaypin' 2 W-P
(J.R.Erp) J.R.Erp, 1956
Corona orange-pink

'Jazz' 11?b W-?
(R.O. Backhouse, pre-1934)
Corona regularly split, the six segments "striped" orange

'Jazzmin Baker Farage' 2 W-P
(Brian S.Duncan, 1986) Mrs J.M.Baker, 1996
'Gracious Lady' × Bloomer sdlg ('Infatuation' × 'Gem of Antrim'); sdlg no. 1274
Fl. 110 mm wide; perianth segments broadly ovate, pure white, plane, smooth; corona funnel-shaped, deep rosy pink, with a paler tone at base, frilled. Mid-season

'J.B.M.Camm' 1 W-Y
(W. Backhouse, pre-1869)
N. albescens × *N. bicolor*
Perianth segments ovate to broadly ovate, blunt, slightly mucronate, inflexed at base, reflexed towards apex, with margins wavy, overlapping a quarter; corona cylindrical, lightly ribbed, soft primrose yellow, mouth expanded and tightly frilled. Syn. Pseudonarcissus Bicolor 'J.B.M.Camm'. FCC 1884

'Jealousy'
(pre-1913)

'Jealousy' 3 W-? (b or c)
(G.H. Johnstone, pre-1938)

'Jealousy' 2 W-WWY
(G.L. Wilson) G. Milner, 1958
'Portrush' × 'Sylvia O'Neill'
Perianth segments pure white; corona opening greenish white, becoming whiter, with pale yellow at rim

'Jean' 3 W-? (b)
(J.W. Barr, pre-1930)

'Jean' 2 Y-WWY
(D.J. Cooper) D.J. Cooper, 1960
Fl. 111 mm wide, opening self sulphur yellow; corona becoming off white, with pale sulphur yellow at rim. Mid-season. Resembles a taller and larger-flowered 'Binkie'

'Jean Anderson' 2 W-W
(A.G. Bull, 1935) Parr's Nurseries, 1958
Fl. ice white; perianth segments broadly ovate, blunt, very slightly mucronate, spreading, of good substance, with midrib showing, overlapping half; the inner segments more narrowly ovate, more nearly acute, shouldered at base, a little inflexed, with margins slightly wavy; corona bowl-shaped, with mouth straight and lightly frilled, rim minutely dentate. Resembles a less robust 'Ludlow'

'Jean Colette' 2 W-O
(J.W.A. Lefeber) J.W.A. Lefeber, 1958
Corona orange (28A)

'Jean Cox' 3 W-P
(Alister Clark, pre-1949)

'Jeanette' 1 W-Y
(E. Leeds, pre-1877)
Fl. neat; perianth segments overlapping. Syn. Pseudonarcissus Bicolor 'Jeanette'. Was "absorbed" into 'Murrell Dobell'

'Jeanette' 2 Y-Y
(W.F.M. Copeland, pre-1907)
Corona lemon yellow, frilled. AM(e) 1918

'Jeanette Gower' 6 Y-Y
(D.S. Bell) D.S. Bell, 1982
'Charity May' × *N. cyclamineus* sdlg
Fl. 77 mm wide; perianth segments reflexed. Mid-season. Resembles a darker-coloured 'Charity May'

'Jean Flagler Matthews' 3 W-YYO
(Adrian Frylink) Adrian Frylink, 1958
Corona deep yellow, with a broad band of reddish orange at rim

'Jean Haynes' 2 W-P
(L.P.Dettman, 1971) Unregistered
'Peggy Dettman' × 'Pink Treasure'; sdlg no. 28/72

'Jean Hood' 2 W-OOR
(West & Fell, pre-1935)
'Bernardino' × 'Horace'
Perianth segments broadly ovate, blunt or squarish at apex and sometimes nicked, slightly mucronate, pure white, spreading, a little concave near apex, somewhat creased, overlapping half or more; the inner segments more narrowly ovate, a little inflexed, with margins wavy, sometimes nicked at mid-point; corona bowl-shaped, orange, with red at rim, mouth straight, ribbed, tightly frilled, with rim minutely crenate. Tall. Mid-season

'Jean Ingelow' 9 W-YYR
(G.H. Engleheart, pre-1923)

'Jean Ladson' 1 Y-WWY
(A. Ladson, *c*.1965-70)
'Rus Holland' × 'Spellbinder'
Perianth segments green-yellow; corona opening green-yellow, becoming white, with lemon yellow at rim. Mid-season

'Jean Lurcat' 2 Y-O
(Konynenburg & Mark, 1950) Konynenburg & Mark, 1960
'Aranjuez' × 'Brilliant Star'
Fl. 100 mm wide; perianth segments light greenish yellow 5B; corona strong orange 25A. Mid-season

N. jeanmonodii Fernández Casas 13 Section Bulbocodium

'Jeanne d'Arc' 11b W-Y/W
Syn. of 'Light Star'

'Jeanne Désor' 2 W-Y
(G.A. Uit den Boogaard, pre-1948)
'John Evelyn' hybrid

"Jean(n)ette Blanche"
Syn. of *N. poeticus* var. *recurvus*

'Jeannie Woodhouse' 1 W-?
Syn. of 'Jenny Woodhouse'

'Jeannine Hoog' 1 Y-Y
(Michael H. Hoog, 1968) Michael H. Hoog, 1988
'Rembrandt' × 'Youth'
Fl. 110 mm wide. Early to mid-season

'Jean Rudd' 2 W-GYR
(L.P. Dettman) L.P. Dettman, 1984
'Janice Dettman' × 'Jennifer Sholl'
Fl. 92 mm wide; perianth segments greenish white (155A); corona brilliant greenish yellow, with light yellow-green 145B at base and red (40C) at rim. Mid-season

'Jean Turnbull' 2 W-?
(Alister Clark, 1935) J. Sharp, 1960

'Jean Venn' 2 W-W
(Ken Farmer Nurseries) Ken Farmer Nurseries, 1978
Fl. 110 mm wide

'Jeb' 3 W-YYR
(W. Jackson Jr, 1954) W. Jackson Jr, 1966
'Token' × 'Ethni'

'Jecunda' 2 W-? (b)
(Mrs R.O. Backhouse, pre-1921)
AM(Haarlem) 1928

'Jedda' 1 Y-Y
(S.J. Bisdee, 1953)
'Kingscourt' × 'Auriga'

'Jedda' 1 Y-Y
(W. Jackson Jr) Jackson's Daffodils, 1979
'Otewa' × 'Ristin'; sdlg no. 67/73
Fl. 95 mm wide. Mid-season

'Jedna' 2 Y-Y
(Rosewarne EHS) Rosewarne EHS, 1985
'Forerunner' × 'Rijnveld's Early Sensation'; sdlg no. 63/4/1
Corona brighter than vivid yellow 12A. Very early

'Jeepers' 2 W-R
(J.N. Hancock & Co., 1963) Unregistered

'Jefferson Davis' 2 W-? (b)
(Mrs R.O. Backhouse, pre-1921)

'Jefta' 1 W-? (b)

(de Graaff Bros, pre-1927)

'Jehol' 5 Y-Y
(Barr & Sons, pre-1933)
Perianth segments straw yellow, overlapping; corona slightly darker in tone than the perianth, frilled

'Jemima' 2 Y-? (a)
(G.H. Johnstone, pre-1949)

'Jennie Tair' 2 Y-O
(Kate Reade) Carncairn Daffodils, 1995

'Jennie Tait' 2 Y-O
(Kate Reade) Carncairn Daffodils, 1995
'Zeus' × 'Bunclody'; sdlg no. 6/3/82
Fl. rounded, 100 mm wide; perianth segments broadly ovate, rounded or truncate at apex, only very slightly mucronate, yellow, somewhat reflexed, smooth, with sparkling surface, overlapping half; the inner segments more nearly spreading, with margins a little wavy; corona cup-shaped, orange, with mouth expanded, rim rolled, notched and crenate. Midseason. Sunproof

'Jennie Woodhouse' 1 W-? (b)
Syn. of 'Jenny Woodhouse'

'Jennifer' 3 W-YYO
(Miss G. Evelyn, pre-1930)
Perianth segments pure white; corona with deep apricot orange at rim

'Jennifer' 2 W-YYO
(H.A. Brown, 1936)

'Jennifer Balmer' 1 W-Y
(L.P. Dettman) L.P. Dettman, 1984
'Content' × 'Pearl Schubert'; sdlg no. CP 1/83
Fl. 96 mm wide; perianth segments greenish white (155A); corona light greenish yellow 3D. Early. Resembles 'Content'

'Jennifer Mary' 2 W-WWO
(J.N. Hancock & Co.) J.N. Hancock & Co., 1960

'Jennifer Milliken' 3 W-YYR
(K.B. Burns) K.B. Burns, 1964
Fl. 102 mm wide; corona lemon yellow, with rich red at rim. Mid-season

'Jennifer Ruth' 1 W-W
(G.H. Johnstone, pre-1954)
'Nuage' × 'Kanchenjunga'
Fl. forming a double triangle, 127 mm wide; perianth segments broadly ovate, very slightly mucronate, spreading, plane or a little twisted, overlapping half; the inner segments more narrowly ovate, shouldered at base, inflexed in lower half, reflexed towards apex, with margins wavy; corona cylindrical, mouth widely expanded, rim flanged, deeply notched and crenate. AM(e) 1957

'Jennifer Sholl' 2 W-YYR
(L.P. Dettman) L.P. Dettman, 1968
'Buncrana' hybrid

'Jennifer Susan' 2 W-? (b)
(N.F. Lock, pre-1942)

'Jenny' 6 W-W
(C.F. Coleman, pre-1943)
'Mitylene' × *N. cyclamineus*
Fl. 90 mm wide; perianth segments ovate, blunt, slightly mucronate, reflexed, a little twisted and with margins incurved, smooth, overlapping one-third; the inner segments only very slightly mucronate, more strongly twisted; corona cylindrical, lightly ribbed, opening pale yellow (4C or 4D), becoming white, mouth more heavily ribbed and a little flared, loosely frilled, rim crenate and minutely dentate. Scented but unpleasant. 2n=21. AM(e) 1948, FCC(e) 1950, *AM(g) 1973, *FCC(g) 1974, *AM(p) 1985, AGM 1993

'Jenny Deans' 3 W-YYO
(W. Backhouse, pre-1869)
Perianth segments opening sulphur white, becoming white. Syn. Burbidgei 'Jenny Deans'

'Jenny Largo' 6 W-W
(J.L. Richardson) Ballydorn Bulb Farm, 1969
'Jenny' hybrid
Resembles a larger-flowered 'Jenny' in colour

'Jenny Lind' 2 Y-Y
(E. Leeds, pre-1877)
Perianth segments slightly reflexed; corona expanded. Syn. Incomparabilis Concolor 'Jenny Lind'. Was "absorbed" into 'John Bull'

'Jenny Woodhouse' 1 W-? (b)
(W.B. Hartland, pre-1908)
See also 'Jeannie Woodhouse'; 'Jennie Woodhouse'

'Jenny Wren' 3 W-? (b)
(Mrs R.O. Backhouse, pre-1921)

'Jephta' 8 Y-Y
(pre-1798)

'Jerboa' 2 W-O
(G. Milner) G. Milner, 1958
Perianth segments pure white; corona salmon orange. Sunproof

'Jeremy' 2 Y-GOO
(R.V. Favell, pre-1946)
'Killigrew' × 'Penquite'

'Jericho' 3 W-YYO
(J.L. Richardson, pre-1938)
'Beacon' × 'Red Sun'
Corona yellow, with reddish orange at rim

'Jerpoint' 2 Y-YYO
(J.L. Richardson, pre-1943)
'Aviemore' × 'Trevisky'
Fl. rounded; perianth segments very broad, blunt, fairly prominently mucronate, clear yellow, spreading, very smooth and of great substance, a little concave at apex, overlapping half; the inner segments slightly inflexed, with midrib showing; corona bowl-shaped, very loosely ribbed, rich yellow, with a well-defined band of brilliant scarlet-orange at rim. Mid-season

'Jersey Beauty' 2 Y-O
(Warnaar & Co.) Warnaar & Co., 1962
Fl. 110 mm wide; perianth segments vivid yellow 9B; corona orange (28A). Early. Resembles 'Orange Bell' but with a darker-coloured corona. AM(Haarlem) 1962, FCC(Haarlem) 1967

'Jersey Cream' 1 W-Y
(The Brodie of Brodie, pre-1923)
Perianth segments somewhat inflexed, of waxy texture; corona opening with a faint flush of pink, becoming rich cream or almost fawn, with rim flanged

'Jerusalem' 8 W-W
Syn. of 'Sheleg'

'Jervis Bay' 1 Y-Y
(J.O. Sherrard, pre-1943)

'Jess' 3 W-? (b)
(A.M. Wilson, pre-1950)

'Jessamy' 10 W-W
(D. Blanchard, pre-1952)
N. romieuxii × *N. cantabricus* var. *foliosus*
Fl. opening greenish yellow, becoming ice white, with many faint and narrow streaks of green beneath; perianth segments strongly inflexed; corona a little shorter than the perianth segments, funnel-shaped, with mouth wavy and rim entire. 2n=28

'Jessica' 1 W-W
(G.H. Engleheart, pre-1907)

'Jessica' 2 W-Y
(W. Jackson Sr, 1942)
'Portia' × 'Gyda'

'Jessie' 5
(Barr & Sons, pre-1927)

'Jessiman' 3 W-YYO
(Mrs J. Abel Smith) Mrs J. Abel Smith, 1971
'Chinese White' × 'Ethel'
Fl. 84 mm wide; perianth segments pure white

'Jess Johnston' 1 W-? (b)
(Alister Clark, pre-1954)

'Jessonda' 2 W-YYP
(G.L. Wilson, pre-1953)

'Jest' 2 Y-Y
(G.E. Mitsch, 1942) G.E. Mitsch, 1962
'John Evelyn' × 'Fortune'
Fl. 102 mm wide; perianth segments light yellow; corona darker in tone. Mid-season. Resembles a less vigorous 'Pinwheel' with a paler perianth

'Jester' 2 Y-? (a)
(de Graaff Bros, pre-1923)

'Jester' 2 Y-?
(J.S. Leitch) J.S. Leitch, 1962

'Jester' 11a Y-Y
Syn. of 'Golden Orchid'

'Jeta' 1 W-Y
(de Graaff Bros, pre-1928)
'King Alfred' hybrid

'Jetage' 6 Y-Y
(A. Gray) A. Gray, 1957
Fl. vivid yellow 9A; perianth segments ovate, blunt, yellow, with white mucro, strongly reflexed, convex, overlapping one-third to a half; the inner segments narrower; corona cylindrical, smooth, with mouth flared, lightly ribbed, loosely frilled, rim notched and crenate. Dwarf

'Jetfire' 6 Y-O
(G.E. Mitsch) G.E. Mitsch, 1966
('Market Merry' × 'Carbineer') × 'Armada'; sdlg no. A52/1
Fl. 75 mm wide; perianth segments ovate, vivid yellow 9A, with slight white mucro, strongly reflexed, creased, with margins wavy, overlapping one-third; the inner segments more heavily creased and with margins more strongly waved; corona cylindrical, loosely ribbed, constricted near mouth, strong orange 24A, with mouth slightly expanded and rim regularly crenate. Dwarf. Early. Slightly scented. With many secondary stems. 2n=21. AM(e) 1987, *HC(g) 1990, AGM 1995

'Jethan' 7 Y-Y
(A. Gray) A. Gray, 1967
N. rupicola × sdlg 56D
Fl. 33 mm wide; perianth segments vivid yellow 12A; corona slightly darker in tone (13A). Early. Resembles an earlier-flowered 'Stella Turk' with the corona frilled

and more widely expanded

'Jet Set' 1 W-Y
(Murray W. Evans) Murray W. Evans, 1972
'Effective' × 'Festivity'
Fl. 105 mm wide

'Jetsetter'
Unregistered
Pollen parent of 'If Only'

'Jetstream' 2 Y-R
(D.S. Bell) D.S. Bell, 1960
'Burgundy' × 'Diamond King'
Fl. 118 mm wide; perianth segments deep yellow; corona very shallow bowl-shaped, red. Mid-season. Resembles 'Ceylon' but with the corona mouth more widely expanded

'Jewel' 3 Y-Y
(W. Backhouse, pre-1869)
Perianth segments sulphur yellow. Syn. Barrii Albidus 'Jewel'

'Jewel' 3 W-? (b)
(Mrs R.O. Backhouse, pre-1921)

'Jewel' 3 Y-O
(?Dutch origin, pre-1950)
Perianth segments acute, deep golden yellow; corona intense scarlet-orange

'Jewel' 2 W-P
(J.A. O'More) J.A. O'More, 1971
'Suda' hybrid × 'Mrs Oscar Ronalds'
Fl. 95 mm wide

'Jewelite' 2 W-W
(J.N. Hancock & Co., 1980) Unregistered
'Kathryn Breen' × 'Glenshesk'; sdlg no. 82/80H
Fl. ice white; corona with rim rolled. Mid-season

'Jewelled Lady' 3 W-YOR
(S.J. Bisdee, 1939)
'Atanga' × 'Sunstar'

'Jewel of Spring' 2 W-YYO
(T. Bloomer) T. Bloomer, 1970
'Fastnet' × G.L. Wilson sdlg 40/78 ('Seraglio' × 'Sylvia O'Neill'); sdlg no. 1/52/58
Corona deep yellow, with very bright red at rim, rim dentate

'Jewel Song' 2 W-P
(J.L. Richardson) Mrs H.K. Richardson, 1967
'Infatuation' × 'Debutante'
Corona rich pink. Mid-season

'Jezebel' 3 Y-R
(A.M. Wilson, pre-1948)

'Khamseen' × 'P.D. Williams sdlg
Perianth segments deep reddish gold; corona shallow, deep brick red. 2n=28. AM(Haarlem) 1956, FCC(Haarlem) 1957

'J.F. Meston' 2 Y-O
(W. Backhouse, pre-1869)
Perianth segments sulphur yellow; corona large, expanded, stained orange. Syn. Incomparabilis Sulphureus 'J.F. Meston'

'J.G. Baker' 1 Y-Y
(E. Leeds, pre-1877)
Fl. rich primrose yellow; perianth segments twisted; corona large, ribbed, frilled. Syn. Pseudonarcissus Major 'J.G. Baker', Pseudonarcissus Major 'Volutus'

'Jhelum' 1 Y-Y
(N.Y. Lower, pre-1933)
'King Alfred' × 'Cleopatra'

'J.H. Krelage' 1 Y-Y
(pre-1912)
Perianth segments primrose yellow; corona large, ribbed, rich yellow. ?The same as 'E.H. Krelage'

'J.H. Piper' 2 W-R
(C.E. Radcliff, 1934)
'Paula' × 'Atanga'

'Jiemba' 1 W-P
(H.G. Cross) H.G. Cross, 1985
'Bon Rose' × 'Dear Me'; sdlg no. 36-7
Perianth segments broadly ovate, blunt, slightly mucronate, spreading, plane, overlapping half; the inner segments a little more narrowly ovate, shouldered at base, a little inflexed, slightly concave; corona funnel-shaped, soft salmon pink, closely frilled

'Ji Ju' 2 W-Y
(W. Jackson Sr, 1936) W. Jackson Jr, 1956
'Mary Blewitt' × 'Una Dunbar'

'Jill' 2 W-YYO
(Barr & Sons, pre-1941)

'Jill' 7 W-W
(Heathcote Bulb Nursery, c.1956) Unregistered
Fl. opening creamy yellow, becoming creamy white

'Jill Bolte' 2 W-P
(Mrs C.O. Fairbairn, c.1950)

'Jillian' 2 W-WWO
(H.A. Brown, 1940) J.N. Hancock & Co., 1961
Perianth segments pure white; corona expanded, tightly ribbed, opening cream, becoming white, with pale apricot at rim. Mid-season

'Jilliby' 1 G-G
(W.M. Spry, pre-1975) Unregistered
'Anna McMillan' × Fairbairn sdlg
Fl. green. Late

'Jim' 1 W-W
(de Graaff Bros, pre-1927)
'Daisy Schäffer' × 'Tunis'
AM(Haarlem) 1927

'Jimdic' 2 Y-YOO
(J.M.Radcliff, pre-1990) Unregistered

'Jimmy Chandler' 2 Y-O
(L.P. Dettman) L.P. Dettman, 1973
'Hymyr' open pollinated
Fl. 103 mm wide

'Jimmy Rogers' 3 W-R
(W.M. Spry, pre-1975) Unregistered
'Aldgate' × 'Delight'
Corona frilled

'Jimmy Speed' 1 Y-Y
(L.P. Dettman) L.P. Dettman, 1970
'Arctic Gold' open pollinated

'Jimmy Taylor' 2 Y-Y
(Mrs R.S. Cobley, 1948) Seymour Cobley Ltd, 1968
Mid-season

'Jimpy' 7
(S. Morrison) T. Morrison, 1960

'Jim's Gold' 2 Y-Y
(J.A. O'More, 1976) J.A. O'More, 1993
'Golden Aura' × 'Bawn Boy'; sdlg no. 32
Fl. 110 mm wide; perianth segments very broadly ovate, vivid yellow 9B; corona funnel-shaped, slightly lighter in colour (12A) than the perianth, mouth slightly flared. Mid-season

'Jindalee' 2 W-Y
(W.M. Spry, pre-1973) Unregistered
'Torchlight' × 'Lochin'
Corona creamy lemon yellow. 2n=28

'Jindivik' 1 W-Y
(S.J. Bisdee) S.J. Bisdee, 1956
'Sincerity' × 'Summerleas'
Corona lemon yellow

'Jingellic' 2 W-P
(W.M. Spry, pre-1972) Unregistered
'Soft Moonlight' × 'Ina Marshall'
Mid-season to late

'Jingle' 3 W-YYO
(Mrs R.O. Backhouse, pre-1921)
Perianth segments broadly ovate, blunt, slightly mucronate, spreading, creased, overlapping one-third; the inner segments a little narrower; corona disc-shaped, ribbed, deep yellow, with a narrow band of orange at rim. Div. 2 until 1936

'Jingle' 6 Y-Y
(P. & G. Phillips) P. & G. Phillips, 1975
Fl. 65 mm wide; perianth segments pale lemon, reflexed; corona opening pale lemon, becoming cream. Mid-season. Resembles 'Binkie' but with a reflexed perianth

'Jingle Bells' 2 W-? (b or c)
(K.L. Reynolds, pre-1944)

'Jingle Bells' 5 W-Y
(W.G. Pannill) W.G. Pannill, 1983
'Fair Colleen' × *N. triandrus*

'Jingle Jangles' 5 Y-Y
(J.N. Hancock & Co., 1979) Unregistered
Fls up to 3 per stem, soft lime yellow; perianth segments broadly ovate, slightly mucronate, spreading or a little inflexed, overlapping one-third; corona short cylinder- or somewhat funnel-shaped, obscurely ribbed, mouth straight, rim sometimes slightly flanged, minutely crenate. Late

'Jingling Gate' 9 W-YYR
(G. Harrison) G. Harrison, 1968
Fl. 95 mm wide. Mid-season

'Jingo' 1 Y-Y
(J.N. Hancock & Co., 1965) Unregistered

'Jinjai' 2 W-P
(H.G. Cross) H.G. Cross, 1985
'Nina' × 'Rose Royale'; sdlg no. 91-6
Fl. forming a double triangle; perianth segments broadly ovate, blunt, mucronate, ivory white, spreading or a little inflexed, concave, with margins incurling, overlapping half; the inner segments square-shouldered at base, more strongly inflexed; corona cylindrical, smooth, creamy salmon pink, with mouth straight or very slightly expanded, even, rim almost entire. Late

'J.K.Ramsbottom' 3 W-O
(P.D. Williams, pre-1928)
Perianth segments pure white; corona very shallow, orange, with a deeper tone at rim. AM(e)(c) 1928, AM(Haarlem) 1929

'Jo' 3 W-YYR
(W. Jackson Jr, 1955) W. Jackson Jr, 1966
Sdlg 61/50 × 'Ethni'

'Joan' 2 W-O
(E. Leeds, pre-1877)
Perianth segments sulphur white; corona suffused

orange. Syn. Incomparabilis Albidus 'Joan'. Was "absorbed" into 'John Stevenson'

'Joan' 1 W-Y
(J.H. Hinsby, 1924)
'Empress' × 'Silvester'

'Joan' 8 W-Y
(H. Selkirk, pre-1927)
Early

'Joan Auton' 2 W-W
(A. Gibson) A. Gibson, 1965
Fl. 95 mm wide. Early

'Joan Burness' 2 W-P
(D.C. MacArthur) D.C. MacArthur, 1987
Pink sdlg open pollinated
Perianth segments greenish white (157B); corona pink (23D). Mid-season

'Joan Christie' 3 W-? (b)
(J.A. Christie, pre-1943)

'Joan Clarke' 3 W-W
(D.S. Bell) D.S. Bell, 1968
'Mannequin' × 'Garland'
Perianth segments pure white; corona very shallow bowl-shaped, frilled

'Joan Comeadow' 2 Y-O
(H.A. Brown) Parr's Nurseries, 1958
Perianth segments soft yellow; corona deep orange

'Joan Hanright' 2 W-? (b or c)
(J. Flemming, pre-1939)

'Joan Moffat' 2 W-P
(L.P. Dettman, 1975) Unregistered
'Verran' × 'Silhouette'; sdlg no. V/S 2/76

'Joanne' 7 Y-Y
(J.N. Hancock & Co., 1949) J.N. Hancock & Co., 1960
Fls 1-3 per stem, deep yellow

'Joanne d'Arc' 2 W-YWY

'Joan of Arc' 3 Y-O
(G.H. Engleheart, pre-1908)
Perianth segments creamy yellow; corona expanded, ribbed, bright reddish orange

'Joan Rush' 2 W-? (b or c)
(J. Flemming, pre-1939)

'Joan White' 2 Y-O
(J.N. Hancock & Co., pre-1949)
Perianth segments pale yellow

'Jobelle' 1 Y-WWY
(J.N. Hancock & Co., 1980) Unregistered
Sdlg no. 112/82H
Perianth segments broad, sulphur yellow; corona funnel-shaped, white, with yellow at rim, frilled. Tall. Mid-season

'Jobi' 1 Y-Y
(W. Jackson Jr, 1951) W. Jackson Jr, 1966
'Winston' × 'Chromis'

'Jocasta' 2 Y-? (a)
(Mrs R.O. Backhouse, pre-1921)

'Jocelyn' 2 Y-? (a)
(Mrs R.O. Backhouse, pre-1921)

'Jocelyn Hyde' 2 W-W
(A. Gibson, pre-1951)

'Jocelyn Thayer' 3 W-YYO
(Clive Postles) Clive Postles Daffodils, 1990
'Avenger' × 'Ben Loyal'; sdlg no. 2-58-76
Fl. rounded, 100 mm wide; perianth segments broadly ovate, prominently mucronate, pure white; corona cylindrical, with rim neatly dentate. Mid-season

'Joconde' 8 Y-Y
(M. van Waveren & Sons, pre-1916)
Poetaz
Perianth segments pale yellow; corona deep golden yellow

'Jocose' 2 Y-? (a)
(A.H. Ahrens) J.S. Leitch, 1955

'Jocular' 2 W-? (b)
(Mrs R.O. Backhouse, pre-1921)

'Jocunda' 2 W-R
(pre-1937)

'Joe' 3 W-YYO
Was "absorbed" into Burbidgei 'Conspicuus'. Syn. of 'Constance'

'Joe Brearley' 2 Y-W
(L.P. Dettman, 1975) Unregistered
'Ellimatta' × 'Spellbinder'; sdlg no. E1/68

'Joe Dunstone' 2 Y-Y
(L.P. Dettman) L.P. Dettman, 1979
'Arctic Gold' × 'Gahna'; sdlg no. 60/75
Fl. 90 mm wide; perianth segments brilliant yellow 12B; corona slightly darker in tone (13B). Resembles a deeper-coloured 'Gahna' with a broader perianth

'Joe Fraser' 1 Y-W
(L.P. Dettman) L.P. Dettman, 1975
'Ellimatta' × 'Daydream'; sdlg no. 5/71

Fl. 93 mm wide; perianth segments brilliant greenish yellow 2B, with a broad band of a brighter tone (3B) at the margin; corona greenish white (150D). Mid-season. Resembles 'Creamed Honey'

'Joffre' 1 Y-Y
(R.H. Bath, pre-1915)
Fl. pale yellow; corona flared

'Johann'
Unregistered
In parentage of 'Chaperone'

'Johanna' 3 W-? (b)
(W. Backhouse, pre-1869)
Corona spreading, stained orange. Syn. Burbidgei 'Johanna'

'Johanna' 5 Y-Y
(A. Gray, pre-1950)
Corona large, pale yellow. 2n=21

'Johannesburg' 4 W-O
(W.A. Watts, pre-1930)
Perianth segments pure white; corona in three continuous whorls, reddish orange, frilled. AM(Haarlem) 1937

'Johann Strauss' 3 Y-? (a)
(Papendrecht-Vandervoet, pre-1939)

'Johann Strauss' 2 W-O
(J.W.A. Lefeber) J.W.A. Lefeber, 1968

'Johan Vermeer' 8 W-Y
(de Goede, pre-1927)
Corona expanded, canary yellow. Resembles a more floriferous 'Alsace'

'John Alistair' 2 Y-? (a)
(G.C. Graham, pre-1949)

'John Bain' 3 W-Y
(W. Backhouse, pre-1869)
Fl. star-shaped; perianth segments ovate, blunt, spreading, sometimes twisted, with margins wavy, or sometimes recurved in lower half, separated; corona cup-shaped, ribbed, citron yellow, tinged orange, with mouth straight and frilled. Syn. Burbidgei 'Grandiflorus', Burbidgei 'John Bain'. "Absorbed" 'Amore', 'Amoret'

'John Ballance' 1 W-Y
(Ballydorn Bulb Farm, 1972) Ballydorn Bulb Farm, 1989
'Candour' hybrid
Fl. 120 mm wide; perianth segments very broadly ovate, smooth; corona deep primrose yellow, mouth widely flared. Early

'John Bendall' 1 Y-Y
(L.P. Dettman, 1973) L.P. Dettman, 1984
'Arctic Gold' × 'Gahna'; sdlg no. K-80
Fl. 84 mm wide; perianth segments brilliant yellow 13B; corona slightly brighter in tone (14B). Resembles an 'Arctic Gold' of greater substance

'John Bright' 1 Y-Y
(E. Leeds, pre-1877)
Fl. light clear yellow; perianth segments twisted; corona rim flanged. Syn. Pseudonarcissus Major 'John Bright'. Was "absorbed" into 'Her Majesty'

'John Bright' 3 Y-? (a)
(E. & J.C. Martin, pre-1930)

'John Bright' 1 Y-Y
Syn. of 'Alaska'

'John Bull' 2 Y-? (a)
(E. Leeds, pre-1877)
Fl. large; perianth segments sulphur yellow; corona widely expanded. Syn. Incomparabilis Sulphureus 'Expansus', Incomparabilis Sulphureus 'John Bull'. "Absorbed" 'Bianca', 'Jenny Lind' and 'Miss Neilson'

'John Bunyan' 9 W-?
(G.H. Engleheart, pre-1931)
AM(Haarlem) 1930

'John Bushby' 2 W-? (b)
(F.H. Chapman, pre-1927)

'John Cairns' 1 Y-Y
(M. van Waveren & Sons, pre-1931)
Fl. clear yellow

'John Copeland' 4 W-Y
(W.F.M.Copeland, pre-1925) Mrs E.Bullivant, 1997
Fl. 92 mm wide; perianth and other petaloid segments in three whorls opposite one another, ovate, blunt, white, slightly twisted, with margins recurved, overlapping at base only; the inner whorls creased, apparently narrower, successively more twisted; corona segments one-third to a half as long as the petaloid segments, bi-lobed, brilliant greenish yellow, touched white at the margins; the outer whorls opposite and interspersed among the petaloid segments, loosely frilled; the centre whorl continuous and tightly frilled. Mid-season

'John Daniel' 4 Y-Y
(R.A. Scamp) R.A. Scamp, 1993
'Saint Keverne' × 'Tamar Fire'; sdlg no. 295
Fl. 90 mm wide; perianth and other petaloid segments very broad in outline, blunt or rounded at apex, yellow, with white mucro, plane, smooth, overlapping half or more; the outer whorl spreading; the inner whorl not much shorter, inflexed; corona segments regularly arranged between the petaloid segments,

roundish, orange-yellow, smooth; corona continuous at centre, funnel-shaped, closely ribbed, with a line of orange at rim, frilled, with rim entire. Mid-season

'John Davidson' 1 W-Y
(de Graaff Bros, pre-1897)
Perianth segments creamy white; corona clear yellow, mouth flared and frilled

'John Dawson' 1 Y-Y
(C.E. Radcliff, 1929)
'Peter Dawson' × 'Golden City'

'John Dettman' 1 Y-PPY
(L.P. Dettman) L.P. Dettman, 1979
'Creamed Honey' × 'Spellbinder'; sdlg no. 38/72
Fl. 91 mm wide; perianth segments brilliant greenish yellow 3B; corona buff pink (159A), with a band of vivid yellow 12A at rim. Mid-season. Resembles a lighter-coloured 'Ian Shankley'

'John Dix' 3 W-R
(P. van Deursen, pre-1927)
Perianth segments creamy white, overlapping; corona orange, frilled. AM(Haarlem) 1927. Received AM(Haarlem) 1927 as 'Mr Dix'

'John Dory' 2 or 3 W-WWY
(Sir J.S. Arkwright, pre-1934)
Perianth segments broad; corona shallow, widely expanded, rich creamy white, with pale golden yellow at rim, frilled

'John Drinkwater' 9 W-?
(pre-1927)

'John D.Rockefeller' 2 W-? (b)
(de Graaff Bros, pre-1938)

'Johneen' 1 W-? (b)
(G.L. Wilson, pre-1932)

'John Evelyn' 2 W-O
(W.F.M. Copeland, pre-1920)
'Tunis' × 'Therapia'
Fl. 94 mm wide; perianth segments very broadly ovate, blunt or truncate, fairly prominently mucronate, creamy white, spreading, with margins somewhat wavy, overlapping half; the inner segments less obviously mucronate, with margins nicked and more strongly wavy; corona broad and shallow, heavily ribbed, apricot orange, with a darker tone at rim, mouth with deep and overlapping lobes heavily frilled; a number of short strap-shaped growths irregularly placed on the outside of the corona. 2n=28. AM(e) 1920, AM(Haarlem) 1921, FCC(Haarlem) 1924

'John Farquhar' 1 Y-Y

(M. van Waveren & Sons, pre-1930)
Fl. large, clear yellow. AM(Haarlem) 1931

'John Fenton' 2 Y-YOO
(L.P. Dettman) L.P. Dettman, 1982
'Vulcan' × 'Spelter'; sdlg no. 62/75
Fl. 94 mm wide; perianth segments vivid yellow 15B; corona strong orange 25A, with a very broad band at base of a slightly darker tone (15A) than the perianth. Mid-season. Resembles 'George Tindale' but with a lighter-coloured corona

'John Forsyte' 1 Y-Y
(D.S. Bell) D.S. Bell, 1968
Corona cylindrical, narrow, frilled

'John Gay' 9 W-YYR
(pre-1913)

'John Gay' 2 W-? (b)
(J.W.A. Lefeber, pre-1943)

'John Gilpin' 7 Y-Y
(C.A. Nethercote) T. Morrison, 1960
Resembles a richer-coloured 'Buttercup'. Scented

'John Glenn' 2 W-?
(Warnaar & Co., c.1962) Unregistered

'John Greenway' 2 W-WWY
(pre-1964) Unregistered

'John Henry' 2 W-O
(W.M. Spry, pre-1975) Unregistered
'Aldgate' × Ronalds sdlg
Corona brilliant apricot orange. Tall. Late

'John Henry Taylor' 3 Y-? (a)
(Mrs R.S. Cobley, pre-1943)

'John Izzard' 2 Y-? (a)
(H.R. Meyer) Hon. Mrs B.B.Ponsonby, 1956

'John Kennedy' 1 Y-Y
(G. Lubbe & Son) G. Lubbe & Son, 1961
Fl. 110 mm wide; perianth segments brilliant yellow 9C; corona much darker in tone (13A). Early. AM(Haarlem) 1961

'John Knox' 1 W-? (b)
(van Zonneveld Bros & Philippo, pre-1931)

'John Kropholler' 2 Y-? (a)
(Papendrecht-Vandervoet, pre-1939)

'John Masefield' 9 W-YYR
(G.H. Engleheart, pre-1920)
Perianth segments snow white; corona disc-shaped, with red at rim. AM 1920

'John Morris' 1 Y-Y
(J.A. Morris) J.A. Morris, 1960
Fl. 120 mm wide, soft yellow; corona slender, with mouth slightly flared. Mid-season. Resembles 'Kingscourt'

'John Nelson' 1 Y-Y
(E. Leeds, pre-1877)
Fl. large, golden yellow, facing down; perianth segments ovate, blunt, slightly mucronate, inflexed, somewhat twisted, overlapping at base only; corona cylindrical, with mouth flared and lightly frilled, rim crenate. Syn. Pseudonarcissus Major 'John Nelson'

'Johnnie Boy' 2 Y-? (a)
(A.M. Williams, pre-1951)

'Johnnie Walker' 3 Y-Y
(T.D. Throckmorton) T.D. Throckmorton, 1977
'Aircastle' × 'Irish Coffee'; sdlg no. 66/12/6
Fl. 95 mm wide. Late

'Johnny Belinda' 3 W-YYR
(G. Lewis) D.S. Bell, 1955
Corona spreading, bright yellow, with broad band of red at rim

'Johnny Kigarrow' 5
(pre-1907)

'Johnny Ray' 1 Y-Y
(C.S. van Dobben de Bruyn Jr, pre-1953)

'Johnny Sands' 2 Y-?Y
(E. Leeds, pre-1877)
Perianth segments sulphur yellow; corona expanded. Syn. Incomparabilis Sulphureus 'Johnny Sands'. Was "absorbed" into 'Magog'

'John of Gaunt' 1 Y-Y
(Cartwright & Goodwin, pre-1910)
Fl. 133 mm wide, deep yellow; perianth segments acute, somewhat twisted

'John of Salisbury' 2 W-Y
(M.J. Jefferson-Brown) M.J. Jefferson-Brown, 1975
Corona pale buff

'John Parkinson' 1 W-Y
(pre-1891)

'John Pearce' 1 Y-Y
(J.N. Hancock & Co., 1946) J.N. Hancock & Co., 1964
('Cromarty' × 'Crocus') × 'Principal'
Fl. rich golden yellow; perianth segments smooth and of good substance; corona almost cylindrical, with rim regularly dentate. Late. Resembles a 'Principal' of better form and deeper colour

'John Peel' 3 Y-R
(N.Y. Lower, pre-1928)
'Dorothy' × 'Sheba'
Perianth segments pinkish yellow; corona brick red

'John Philip Sousa' 2 W-O
(John R.Reed) John R.Reed, 1995
'Preamble' × 'Poet's Dream'; sdlg no. 81-125-3
Fl. 104 mm wide; perianth segments ovate, corona broad funnel-shaped, light carrot orange. Mid-season. Sunproof

'John Ridd' 1 W-? (b)
(W.B. Hartland, pre-1913)

'John's Delight' 3 W-YYR
(R.A.Scamp) River Gardeners Association, 1995
'Corofin' × 'Kimmeridge'; sdlg no. 316
Fl. 96 mm wide; perianth segments broadly ovate, pure white, spreading, plane; corona almost disc-shaped, ribbed, bright yellow, with dark red at rim and the rim dentate. Mid-season

'John Sheppard' 4 W-Y
(D.S. Bell) D.S. Bell, 1985
'Candida' hybrid
Fl. 101 mm wide. Mid-season. Resembles a more fully double 'Candida'

'John Silver' 1 W-W
(T.H. Piper, c.1966) Unregistered
'Swanlough' × 'Rhana'

'John's Pink' 2 W-GPP
(Carncairn Daffodils) Carncairn Daffodils, 1973
'Irish Rose' hybrid
Fl. 80 mm wide; perianth segments roundish; corona dusty pink, with rim rolled

'John Stevenson' 3 W-Y
(E. Leeds, pre-1877)
Perianth segments sulphur white; corona large, widely expanded, stained scarlet-orange. Syn. Barrii Albidus 'John Stevenson'. "Absorbed" 'G.F.Wilson', 'Hotspur', 'Joan'

N. × *johnstonii* (Baker) Pugsley 13 = *N. pseudonarcissus* Linnaeus × *N. triandrus* Linnaeus subsp. *pallidulus* (Graells) D.A.Webb. FCC 1884

"John Tradescant's Great Rose Daffodil"
Syn. of 'Plenissimus'

'John Vincent' 1 Y-Y
(W. Backhouse, pre-1869)
Fl. canary yellow; perianth segments twisted; corona slender. Syn. Pseudonarcissus Major 'John Vincent'

'John Wall' 6 Y-Y
(John Wall, ?1940s) Mrs Margaret Owen, 1997

Perianth segments reflexed. Very early

'John Willis' 2 W-YYW
(Tom Forster, 1960s) Unregistered
'Artist's Model' × 'Green Island'
Fl. rounded; perianth segments pure white; corona disc-shaped, lemon yellow, with white at rim, lightly frilled. Late

'Johore' 2 Y-O
(J.L. Richardson) Mrs H.K. Richardson, 1968
'Cambodia' × 'Firecracker'
Perianth segments golden yellow; corona reddish orange, frilled

'Joie de Vie' 2 W-WWY
(G.H. Wayne) G.H. Wayne, 1981
'Bithynia' × ('Cordial' × 'Caro Nome'); sdlg no. A-2/4
Fl. 96 mm wide; corona with yellow at rim

'Joke Fulmer' 2 W-YOO
(J.W.A. Lefeber, pre-1948)

'Joker' 11?a Y-?
(Mrs R.O. Backhouse, pre-1921)
AM(Haarlem) 1930

'Jolanda' 1 W-? (b)
(C. Alkemade, pre-1944)
Syn. 'Hermina'

'Joli-Coeur' 11a W-O
(J. Gerritsen & Son) J. Gerritsen & Son, 1962
Fl. 90 mm wide; perianth segments pure white; corona split, the six segments pure orange, deeply frilled. Late

'Joliette' 2 W-Y
(J.N. Hancock & Co., 1946)
'Polindra' × 'Chandler's Red Cup'
Resembles 'Polindra'

'Jolity' 2 W-Y
(M.J. Jefferson-Brown) M.J. Jefferson-Brown, 1985
Sdlg × 'Debutante'
Fl. of smooth texture; perianth segments broad at base, snow white; corona rich primrose yellow, with rim flared. Tall. Mid-season. Resembles 'My Love'.
Syn. 'Joy'

'Jolly' 1 W-? (b)
(de Graaff Bros, pre-1928)
Syn. 'Cerberus'

'Jolly Boy' 2 Y-? (a)
(G.L. Wilson, pre-1942)

'Jolly Friar' 3 W-? (b)
(Barr & Sons, pre-1935)

'Jolly Giant' 4 W-W
(David L. Sheppard) David L. Sheppard, 1994
'Gay Song' × ('Accent' × 'Easter Bonnet')
Fl. 140 mm wide; perianth and other petaloid segments in several whorls, pure white; the outer whorl very broadly ovate, fairly prominently mucronate, spreading, overlapping half or more; the inner whorls narrowly ovate, only very slightly mucronate, inflexed, with margins wavy or incurled; corona segments short, loosely interspersed among the inner whorls of petaloid segments and clustered at centre, broad, opening very pale creamy yellow, soon becoming pure white, loosely frilled. Mid-season

'Jolly Good' 2 Y-YOO
(Jackson's Daffodils) Jackson's Daffodils, 1993
Sdlg 26/75 × 'Caryem'; sdlg no. 32/84
Fl. 105 mm wide; perianth segments ovate, vivid yellow 9A; corona funnel-shaped, mid-orange, yellow at base and shading to a deeper tone of orange (28A) at rim. Early

'Jollyman' 2 W-? (b)
(Mrs F.S. Foote, pre-1940)

'Jolly Roger' 2 W-Y
(Murray W. Evans) Murray W. Evans, 1969
'Wahkeena' × 'Bread and Cheese' hybrid

'Jolyon' 1 W-? (b)
(de Graaff Bros, pre-1928)
Syn. 'Carrara'

'Jonah' 2 W-? (b)
(W.A. Watts, pre-1933)

'Jonathan' 2 Y or W-? (a,b or c)
(pre-1915)

'Jonathan' 2 W-? (b)
(S.A. Morrish, pre-1950)

'Jones' 1
(pre-1913)

'Joningham' 1 W-W
(W. Jackson Jr, 1950)

'Jonkheer Ruys de Berenbrouck' 1 W-W
(A. Frylink & Sons, pre-1930)

'Jonkheer van Doorn' 9 W-YYR
(G. Lubbe & Son, pre-1935)
AM(Haarlem) 1936

'Jonkheer van Tets' 1 Y-Y
(G. Lubbe & Son, pre-1939)

'Jonlyn' 2 W-? (b)
(A.F. Blakeman, pre-1946)

'John Evelyn' hybrid

'Jonna' 1 W-W
(W. Jackson Jr, 1968) Unregistered
Sdlg 45/59 × 'Empress of Ireland'; sdlg no. 75/68

'Jonnie' 7
(L. Buckland, pre-1939)

'Jonno' 7 Y-Y
(?Australian origin, pre-1997) Unregistered

N. jonquilla Linnaeus **13 Section Jonquilla**
("Jonquil single", "Simplex", "Sweeties"). AGM 1994
    var. *jonquilla*
    var. *henriquesii* Sampaio
    var. *minor* (Haworth) Baker (Odorus 'Minor',
       Odorus 'Pseudo-juncifolius')
    var. *stellaris* Baker

N. jonquilloides Willkomm = *N. willkommii*

"Jonquil single"
Syn. of *N. jonquilla*

'Joop Terheul' 3 W-? (b)
(J.W.A. Lefeber, pre-1948)

'Joppa' 7 Y-YYO
(du Plessis Bros) du Plessis Bros, 1987
Sdlg no. J101
Fls 2 per stem, 63 mm wide; perianth segments reflexed; corona cup-shaped, small. Mid-season

'Jordan' 3 W-YYR
(C.E. Radcliff, 1937)
'Mayflower' × 'Pink'un'

'Jorinda' 2 Y-? (a)
(D.J. Cooper) D.J. Cooper, 1956

'Jorinde' 2 W-? (b)
(G.A. Uit den Boogaard, pre-1937)

'Jorrocks' 2 Y-? (a)
(Mrs R.O. Backhouse, pre-1921)
AM(Haarlem) 1925

'Josef van Fraunhofer' 3 W-? (b)
(J.W.A. Lefeber, pre-1941)

'José Iturbi' 2 W-? (b)
(J.W.A. Lefeber, pre-1948)

'Joselito' 2 Y-YOO
(S.J. Bisdee, 1946)
'Ardjuno' × 'Red Mantle'

'Joseph Banks' 2 Y-YYO
(Tom Forster, 1960s) Unregistered

'Fried Egg' hybrid
Perianth segments very broad in outline, blunt or truncate, mid-yellow, with white mucro, spreading or a little inflexed, creased, overlapping half or more; the inner segments inflexed, more heavily creased; corona very shallow, very wide-spreading, ribbed, golden yellow, with a distinct band of orange at rim, mouth more closely ribbed, split in places and overlapping, wavy, with rim crenate. Early

'Joseph Chamberlain' 1 Y-Y
(W. Backhouse, pre-1869)
Resembles 'Lord Derby'. Syn. Pseudonarcissus Major 'Joseph Chamberlain'

'Josephine' 1 W-W
(J.N. Hancock & Co.) J.N. Hancock & Co., 1955
'Token' × 'Saint Cecilia'
Perianth segments broad, spreading, overlapping; corona creamy white

'Josephine' 1 W-W
Syn. of 'Holland Festival'

'Josephine Gundry' 1 W-? (b)
(Barr & Sons, pre-1916)

'Joseph Lakin' 2? Y-Y
(?Barr & Sons, pre-1896)
Perianth segments sulphur yellow; corona darker in tone

'Joseph MacLeod' 1 Y-Y
(Warnaar & Co., pre-1946)
Fl. 108 mm wide; perianth segments broadly ovate, vivid yellow 9B, overlapping half; corona slightly ribbed, a little brighter in tone (12A) than the perianth, mouth expanded and frilled, with rim dentate. Early. 2n=28. AM(Haarlem) 1946, FCC(Haarlem) 1956, *AM(g) 1956, *FCC(g) 1959

'Joseph Sangster' 2 W-? (b)
(Sir J.A.R. Gore-Booth, pre-1908)

'Josette' 5 Y-Y
(W.F.M. Copeland, pre-1913)
Fl. soft primrose yellow; perianth segments slightly twisted; corona a little darker in tone than the perianth, with rim slightly rolled and indented. Midseason

'Joshua Braithwaite'
(pre-1960) Unregistered

'Josiana' 3 W-W
(W. Jackson Jr) W. Jackson Jr, 1966
'Nevose' sdlg; sdlg no. 286/57

'Josine' 1 W-W
(Krelage & Son, pre-1914)

'King Alfred' × 'Madame de Graaff'
Corona opening very pale primrose yellow, becoming white, frilled. AM(g) 1914

"Joss Lily"
Syn. of *N.tazetta* subsp. *lacticolor*

'Jostle' 2 Y-? (a)
(A.H. Ahrens) J.S. Leitch, 1955

'Jotun' 2 Y-? (a)
(A.H. Ahrens) J.S. Leitch, 1955

'Jo van der Zwet' 2 W-? (b)
(J.A. van der Zwet & Sons, pre-1954)
AM(Haarlem) 1954

'Jove' 1 Y-Y
(W. Balch, pre-1933)

'Jove' 1 Y-YRR
(W.O. Backhouse) W.O. Backhouse, 1959
Fl. 103 mm wide; perianth segments yellow, with a darker tone at base; corona orange-red, paling to orange-yellow at base. Early

'Jovial' 2 W-? (b)
(Mrs R.O. Backhouse, pre-1921)

'Jovial' 5 Y-O
(W.G. Pannill) W.G. Pannill, 1970
'Narvik' × *N. triandrus* var. *concolor*

'Jo Vincent' 2 W-? (b)
(H.P. Zwetsloot, pre-1948)
AM(Haarlem) 1948

'Joy'
(A.E. Lowe, pre-1927)

'Joy' 2 W-Y
Syn. of 'Jolity'

'Joyance'
(Mrs R.S. Cobley, pre-1938)

'Joyant' 2 W-O
(de Graaff Bros) de Graaff Bros & van Konynenburg & Co., 1960
Perianth segments ivory white; corona large, shallow, light orange (22D), heavily ruffled. Mid-season. AM(Haarlem) 1960

'Joy Bartlett' 1 YYW-WYY
(Ken McCombe) A.W.Bartlett, 1994
Fl. 90-95 mm wide, yellow, with perianth segments and corona tinged white in a broad band at base; perianth segments very broad, with white mucro; corona glistening inside, with mouth frilled and rim slightly flanged. Mid-season

'Joybell' 6 W-Y
(J.L. Richardson) Mrs H.K. Richardson, 1969
'Jenny' open pollinated
Perianth segments broadly ovate, blunt, prominently mucronate, reflexed, concave near apex, overlapping one-third to a half; the inner segments more narrowly ovate, more nearly spreading, creased; corona short funnel-shaped, bright yellow, with mouth very slightly flared and lightly frilled, rim minutely crenate

'Joy Bells' 1? W-W
(New Zealand origin, *c.*1895)
Fls sometimes 2 per stem. Resembles 'Princess Ida'

'Joy Bells' 5
(W.F.M. Copeland, pre-1937)

'Joy Bishop' 10 Y-Y
(Moroccan origin) K.N. Dryden, 1985
Selection by J.C.Archibald (1966) from wild-collected *N. romieuxii*; from collection no. JCA805
Perianth segments very narrow, yellow, a little inflexed, widely separated; corona funnel-shaped, very widely expanded on maturity, light greenish yellow 4B, mouth straight, shallowly and distinctly 6-lobed, rim more or less entire. Very early

'Joy Boy' 2 Y-OYO
(J.N. Hancock & Co., *c.*1979) Unregistered

'Joyce' 2 W-O
(C.G. van Tubergen, pre-1949)
Perianth segments creamy white. AM(Haarlem) 1949

'Joyce Burton' 2 W-? (b)
(W.A. Grace, pre-1938)

'Joyce Fair' 2 W-? (b or c)
(F.H. Chapman, pre-1938)

'Joyce MacDonald' 1 W-W
(W.A. Grace, pre-1938)
Syn. 'Allanah'

'Joyce Rihill' 9 W-GYO
(S. Dudman) S. Dudman, 1957
See also 'Joyce Rihll'

'Joyce Rihll' 9 W-GYO
Syn. of 'Joyce Rihill'

'Joycette' 3 W-? (b)
(Mrs F.S. Foote, pre-1941)

'Joyfair' 2 Y-Y
(Mrs C.O. Fairbairn) J.L. Martin, 1982
Fl. 97 mm wide; perianth segments brilliant greenish yellow 6A; corona brighter in tone (9A). Mid-

season. Resembles a Div. 2 'Courtill'. Syn. 'Joyous'

'Joyful' 4
(W.A. Watts, pre-1927)

'Joyful' 4 W-O
(?New Zealand origin, pre-1996) Unregistered

'Joyful Day' 7 Y-Y
(G.E. Morrill) G.E. Morrill, 1979
'Rubra' × *N. jonquilla*; sdlg no. RJ-9
Fl. 56 mm wide; perianth segments brilliant greenish yellow 3B; corona darker in tone (7A). Mid-season.

'Joy Gray' 2 W-YYO
(L.P. Dettman) L.P. Dettman, 1977
'Glamour' × 'Gladys Dettman'; sdlg no. 107/74
Perianth segments greenish white (157D); corona light greenish yellow 5C, with a broad band of yellow-orange (14B) at rim. Mid-season. Resembles 'Glamour' but with a paler-coloured corona

'Joyita' 2 Y-ORR
(W. Jackson Jr) Jackson's Daffodils, 1979
Sdlg 152/65 × sdlg 101/65; sdlg no. 165/71
Fl. 104 mm wide. Mid-season

'Joyland' 2 Y-GYY
(Brian S. Duncan) Rathowen Daffodils, 1977
'Joybell' × 'Empress of Ireland'; sdlg no. 129
Fl. mid-yellow; perianth segments with greenish undertones; corona straight, with green at base. Mid-season

'Joyous' ?-P
(Alister Clark, pre-1948)

'Joyous' 2 W-Y
(G.E. Mitsch) G.E. Mitsch, 1963
'Polindra' × 'Ludlow'; sdlg no. P62/4
Fl. 102 mm wide; perianth segments pure white, deeply overlapping; corona opening pale lemon yellow, becoming creamy yellow. Mid-season. Resembles a neater and earlier-flowered 'My Love'

'Joyous' 2 Y-Y
Syn. of 'Joyfair'

'Joyous Cavalier' 2 W-? (b)
(Mrs F.S. Foote, pre-1940)

'Joy Stream' 2 W-YYP
(J.N. Hancock & Co., 1949) J.N. Hancock & Co., 1960
Corona widely expanded

'J.P.' 1 Y-Y
(C.E. Radcliff, 1940)
'Principal' × 'Mortlake'

'J.R.Bill' 2 (b)
(Australian or New Zealand origin, pre-1927)
Corona with red at rim

'J.S.Bach' 2 W-W
(E.H. Krelage & Son, pre-1952)

'J.T.Bennett-Poë' 5 W-Y
(G.H. Engleheart, pre-1904)
'Emperor' × *N. triandrus*
Perianth segments creamy white, reflexed; corona long, straight, primrose yellow. AM 1904. See also 'Bennett-Poë'

'J.T.D.Llewelyn' 2 Y-O
(W. Backhouse, pre-1869)
Perianth segments pale yellow; corona expanded, orange. Syn. Incomparabilis Sulphureus 'J.T.D.Llewelyn'. Was "absorbed" into 'Gloria Mundi'

'Juanita' 5
(pre-1933)

'Juanita' 2 Y-O
(de Graaff Bros, pre-1952)
'Fortune' hybrid
Perianth segments broadly ovate, blunt, fairly prominently mucronate, somewhat inflexed, a little twisted, with margins wavy, incurved at apex, overlapping one-third; the inner segments more strongly inflexed and twisted, with margins sometimes notched at overlap; corona closely ribbed, yellowish orange, with a darker tone at rim, tightly frilled, mouth lobed, the lobes overlapping and appearing to be in more than one whorl, touched at apex with yellowish orange or white

'Juba' 4 W-W
(?Australian origin, pre-1990) Unregistered

'Jubilant' 2 Y-Y
(P.D. Williams, pre-1925)
Fl. rich golden yellow, of strong substance; perianth segment with margins incurved, overlapping; corona expanded. Mid-season. 2n=28. AM(e) 1925, *HC(g)(m) 1927, AM(Haarlem) 1930, *AM(g) 1936, *FCC(g) 1944

'Jubilant Spirit' 2 W-P
(Sidney DuBose, 1986) Sidney DuBose, 1996
Sdlg 53-6 ('Precedent' × 'Cordial') × 'Dailmanach'; sdlg no. M73-3
Fl. 90 mm wide; perianth segments broadly ovate, blunt, slightly mucronate, spreading, plane, with broad midrib showing, overlapping half; the inner segments narrower, square-shouldered at base, with margins a little wavy; corona pink, mouth slightly flared, frilled, with rim dentate. Mid-season

'Jubilata' 2 Y-O
(Mrs C.O. Fairbairn) J.L. Martin, 1982
Fl. 95 mm wide; perianth segments vivid yellow 12A; corona orange. Mid-season

'Jubilation' 2 W-Y
(G.E. Mitsch) G.E. Mitsch, 1959
Linn' × 'Green Island'
Corona shallow, widely expanded, lemon yellow, frilled

'Jubilee'
(de Graaff Bros, pre-1914)

'Jubilee' 1 W-Y
(D.V. West, pre-1935)
'Stoic' × 'Carbineer'
Corona golden yellow

'Judas' 2 Y-R
(J.S. Leitch) J.S. Leitch, 1957

'Judea' 2 W-P
(J.A. O'More) J.A. O'More, 1968
'Kenmare' hybrid

'Judge Bird' 1 W-? (b)
(G.H. Engleheart, pre-1910)

'Judgement' 2 W-Y
(G.L. Wilson, pre-1946)
'White Sentinel' × 'Kanchenjunga'
Perianth segments broadly ovate; corona bright yellow

'Judith' 2 W-Y
(?A.M.Wilson, pre-1913)
Fl. more than 75 mm wide; corona light sulphur yellow, with a darker tone at rim, frilled. Somewhat resembles an improved 'White Queen'. AM 1913

'Judith' 3 W-W
(R.H. Bath, pre-1931)
Corona opening pale lemon, becoming white

'Judy' 2 Y-GYY
(G.H. Johnstone, pre-1949)

'Judy Andrews' 3 W-YYR
(G. Lewis, 1943) D.S. Bell, 1958

'Judy Cotter' 4 W-W
(E.W. Cotter, c.1964) Mrs C. Cotter, 1978
Sdlg no. 8/55
Fl. 50 mm wide, pure white. Late. Scented. Resembles 'Daphne' but with more numerous petaloid segments

'Judy Davidson'
Unregistered
Seed parent of 'August Green'

'Judy Main' 2 Y-O
(?Heathcote Bulb Nursery, pre-1960) Unregistered
Perianth segments rich yellow; corona widely expanded, bright orange

'Juel' 2 Y-ORR
(W. Jackson Jr, 1969) Unregistered
Sdlg 18/60 × 'Tanais'; sdlg no. 72/69

'Julep' 2 W-GWP
(Murray W. Evans) Murray W. Evans, 1974
('Interim' × 'Mabel Taylor') × ('Loch Maree' × 'Mabel Taylor')
Fl. 98 mm wide

'Jules Verne' 2 W-Y
(D.W. Lefeber & Co., pre-1949)
Perianth segments sulphur white; corona narrow, creamy yellow, frilled, with rim flanged. AM(Haarlem) 1949

'Julia' 8 Y-Y
(pre-1798)
Fl. sulphur yellow

'Julia' 3 W-? (b)
(C. Dawson, pre-1923)

'Julia Culp' 2 W-? (b)
(J.W.A. Lefeber) W. Blom & Son, 1955

'Julia Dodd' 1 W-W
(G.H. Engleheart, pre-1931)

'Julia Jane' 10 Y-Y
(Moroccan origin) Unregistered
Selection by J.C.Archibald (1966) from wild-collected *N. romieuxii*; from collection no. JCA805
Fl. large, light greenish yellow (2C or 3C); perianth segments very narrow, tapering to apex, acute, with green at midrib, spreading or slightly reflexed, twisted, separated; corona disc-shaped or very broad and shallow funnel-shaped, lightly ribbed, paler in tone than the perianth, sometimes touched with darker yellow at base and rim, mouth a little wavy, sometimes obscurely lobed, rim irregularly and shallowly crenate, sometimes recurved or rolled. Dwarf. Later-flowered than others in same group, eg 'Joy Bishop'. Resembles *N. cantabricus* var. *petunioides*

'Julia Minden' 2 W-? (b)
(D.H.L. Corrigan, pre-1949)

'Juliana' 1 W-Y
(J. Mallender, pre-1913)
Corona very pale creamy yellow

'Julia Ward Howe' 9
(?G.P. Haydon, pre-1910)

'Julie' 2 W-P
(J.N. Hancock & Co., c.1970) Unregistered
Corona mauve pink

'Juliet' 9 W-YYR
(G.H. Engleheart, pre-1906)
Perianth segments overlapping; corona canary yellow, with a narrow band of madder red at rim. 2n=14

'Juliette' 2 W-Y
(C.M. Grullemans) J.J. Grullemans & Sons, 1956
Perianth segments pure white; corona bright yellow ochre, with creamy yellow at rim, frilled

'Juliette Dunbar' 1 W-? (b)
(T. Buncombe, pre-1938)

'Julius Caesar' 8?
(?French or Dutch origin, pre-1831)

'Julius Caesar' 1 Y-Y
(A.C. Paardekooper, pre-1944)

'Julius Caesar' 1 Y-Y
(G. Errey, 1945) G. Errey, 1962
Fl. 127 mm wide; perianth segments brilliant yellow 9C; corona much darker in tone (13A). Early

'July' 1 Y-Y
(O. Ronalds, 1950) T. Morrison, 1960
Resembles 'King Alfred'

'Julyan' 1 Y-Y
(J.C. Whibley) J.C. Whibley, 1963
Fl. 102 mm wide; corona darker in tone than the perianth. Very early. Resembles an earlier-flowered 'Forerunner' of better form

'July Gold' 1 Y-Y
(J.C. Whibley) J.C. Whibley, 1963
Fl. 99 mm wide, golden yellow. Very early

'July Sun' 2 Y-Y
(H.A. Brown, 1932)

'Jumblie' 12 Y-O
(A. Gray, pre-1952)
'Cyclataz' hybrid or self pollinated
Fls 2-3 per stem; perianth segments ovate or oblong, blunt, deep golden yellow, with prominent white mucro, more or less strongly reflexed, overlapping up to a half; the inner segments less strongly reflexed; corona cylindrical, sometimes constricted near mouth, ribbed, orange, with rim irregularly crenate. Mid-season. 2n=24+1B. Smaller than sibling 'Tête-à-Tête'; more nearly resembles sibling 'Quince'. With occasional secondary stems. AM(Haarlem) 1959, AGM 1995

'Jumbo' 1 W-W
(pre-1908)

'Jumbo Gold' 1 Y-Y
(Brian S. Duncan) Rathowen Daffodils, 1979
'Yellow Idol' self pollinated × 'Spanish Gold'; sdlg no. 92
Fl. 112 mm wide, deep yellow; perianth segments very broad; the outer segments touching one another; the inner segments more nearly ovate. Mid-season

'Jumbuck' 1 Y-Y
(J.N.Hancock & Co., 1980) Unregistered
Hancock sdlg 38/61H × Fairbairn 2Y-Y; sdlg no. 21/80H
Fl. golden yellow; corona neatly frilled. Tall. Early to mid-season

'Jumna' 1 Y-Y
(N.Y. Lower, pre-1933)

'Jumping-Jack' 2 Y-GYO
(T.D. Throckmorton) T.D. Throckmorton, 1976
'Old Satin' × 'Arbar'; sdlg no. 67/6/2
Perianth segments golden fawn, with shiny yellow overtones, of thick substance; corona bright yellow, with olive green at base and orange with flecks of gold and white at rim

'Jump-Up' 1 Y-O
(M.G.Temple-Smith, 1986) M.G.Temple-Smith, 1997
'Trumpet Call' × ('Burnished Gold' × 'Janz' hybrid); sdlg no. 27/86
Perianth segments brilliant yellow 13B, very smooth; corona straight-sided, slightly expanded, light orange (21B) at base, shading towards mouth to strong orange 24A. Mid-season. Immature flowers sometimes measuring Div. 2

N. juncifolius Lagasca & Segura = *N. assoanus*

N. juncifolius Lagasca & Segura subsp. *gaditanus* (Boissier & Reuter) Baker = *N. gaditanus*

N. juncifolius Lagasca & Segura subsp. *minutiflorus* (Willkomm) Baker = *N. minutiflorus*

N. juncifolius Lagasca & Segura subsp. *rupicola* Dufour = *N. rupicola*

N. juncifolius Salisbury = *N. jonquilla*

'Juncifolius Luteus Flore Pleno' 4 Y-Y
Syn. of 'Flore Pleno'

'Junco' 1 W-W
(A.O. Roblin, 1944) A.O. Roblin, 1956
'Nautilus' × 'Tain'
2n=28

'June' 3 Y-? (a)
(Mrs R.O. Backhouse, pre-1921)

'June' 2 W-P
(L.P.Dettman, 1965) Unregistered
'Creamed Honey' × 'Nelle Worth'; sdlg no. 16/72

'June Allyson' 2 W-O
(J.W.A. Lefeber, pre-1948)
Corona shallow

'June Baker' 2 W-P
(Brian S.Duncan, 1985) Mrs J.M.Baker, 1996
'Gracious Lady' × Bloomer sdlg ('Infatuation' × 'Gem of Antrim'); sdlg no. 1128
Fl. 120 mm wide; perianth segments broadly ovate, spreading, smooth; corona broad funnel-shaped, deep apple blossom pink, with rim entire. Mid-season to late. Sunproof

'June Bride' 11a W-P
(R. & E. Havens, 1983) R. & E. Havens, 1994
(Sdlg D17/18 × 'Spaceship') × 'Mission Impossible'
Fl. 110 mm wide; perianth segments broadly ovate; corona deeply split, the six segments just under half as long as the perianth segments and opposite to them, pure pink, spreading, heavily frilled. Mid-season. Sunproof

'June Christy' 2 W-P
(Reg Nicholl) Reg Nicholl, 1995
'Broomhill' × 'Shell Bay'; sdlg no. 19/90
Fl. 110 mm wide; perianth segments broadly ovate, blunt, only very slightly mucronate, ivory white, spreading, slightly concave, overlapping half; the inner segments only a little narrower, slightly inflexed, more nearly plane, somewhat creased; corona cylindrical, moderate yellowish pink 33D, paling at base, mouth straight, wavy, rim minutely crenate. Mid-season. Sunproof

'June Collins' 2 W-P
(L.P. Dettman, 1965) L.P. Dettman, 1984
'Creamed Honey' × 'Nelle Worth'; sdlg no. 16/72
Fl. 95 mm wide; perianth segments yellowish white 155D; corona light yellowish pink 36A. Mid-season. Resembles 'Nelle Worth' but with unfading corona colour

'June Lake' 2 W-GYP
(Brian S. Duncan) Brian S. Duncan, 1990
'Fellowship' × 'High Society; sdlg no. 1161
Fl. rounded, 114 mm wide; perianth segments very broadly ovate, blunt, pure white, spreading, overlapping half; the inner segments more narrowly ovate; corona bowl-shaped, deep lemon yellow, with green at base and a broad and well-defined band of rich pink at rim, mouth expanded, loosely frilled. Mid-season to late

'Jungfrau' 1 W-W
(de Graaff Bros, pre-1927)

'Jungle' 3 W-? (b)
(Mrs R.O. Backhouse, pre-1921)

'Jungle Cock' 1 W-? (b)
(E.G. Taylor) E.G. Taylor, 1956

'Jungle Fire' 2 W-O
(Mrs R.O. Backhouse, pre-1921)
Perianth segments creamy white; corona reddish orange, frilled

'Junia' 2 W-? (b)
(A.H. Ahrens, pre-1949)

'Junia-Too' 2 W-P
(A.O. Roblin, 1959) Unregistered
'Lisdillon' × ('Mena' × 'Hothu')

'Junior Miss' 12 W-Y
(W.G. Pannill) W.G. Pannill, 1977
'Jenny' × *N. jonquilla*; sdlg no. G20
Fls more than one per stem, 22 mm wide; perianth segments ovate, acute, somewhat reflexed, plane, overlapping a quarter; the inner segments spreading or a little inflexed; corona short cylinder-shaped, smooth, yellow at maturity, becoming white with age, slightly constricted near mouth or with mouth straight, rim shallowly notched and crenate. Dwarf. Early to mid-season

'Junior Prom' 4 Y-R
(R. & E.Havens, 1984) R. & E.Havens, 1994
'Gypsy' × red Div. 4; sdlg no. TEH77/1
Fl. symmetrical, 85 mm wide; perianth and other petaloid segments broadly ovate, light yellow, in some climates tinged with buff; corona segments orange-red. Late. Sunproof

'Juniper' 2 Y-? (a)
(Mrs R.O. Backhouse, pre-1921)

'Junius'
(pre-1933)

'Junket' 4
(W.A. Watts, pre-1935)

'Junne Johnsrud' 2 Y-WWY
(W.G. Pannill) W.G. Pannill, 1985
'Rushlight' × 'Daydream'; sdlg no. 64/110
Mid-season

'Juno' 8 Y-Y
(pre-1798)

'Juno' 3 W-W
(W. Backhouse, pre-1869)

Perianth segments inflexed; corona opening primrose yellow, becoming white. Syn. Leedsii 'Galanthiflorus Major', Leedsii 'Juno'. Was "absorbed" into ?Leedsii 'Elegans'

'Juno' 2 W-YOY
(Carncairn Daffodils) Carncairn Daffodils, 1978
Fl. 108 mm wide; perianth segments greenish white (155A); corona slightly expanded, strong orange 24A, with vivid yellow 9A at base and rim

'Juno' 1 Y-Y
Syn. of 'Arkansas'

'Juno's Kar' 8 Y-Y
(pre-1798)

'Juno's Tempel' 8 Y-Y
(pre-1798)

'Junta' 2 Y-O
(G.J. Phillips) G.J. Phillips, 1992
Sdlg no. 2YR-23
Fl. 106 mm wide; perianth segments broad, blunt, mid-yellow; the inner segments more nearly ovate; corona funnel-shaped, rich orange, with mouth moderately flared. Late

'Jupita' 2 W-O
(?Tom Forster) Unregistered
Perianth segments rounded; corona disc-shaped, ribbed, orange, with flecks of white at rim

'Jupiter' 8 Y-O
(pre-1798)

'Jupiter' 3 Y-R
(A.M. Wilson, pre-1908)

'Jupiter' 1 Y-Y
(J.L. Richardson) J.L. Richardson, 1956
'Kingscourt' × 'Goldcourt'

'Jupiter' 2 Y-O
Syn. of 'Marion Cran'

'Jupiter' 2 Y-YRR
Syn. of 'Scarlet Elegance'

N. × *juratensis* Rouy = *N.* × *incomparabilis*

N. juressianus Fernández Casas 13 Section Bulbocodium

'Juryman' 1 Y-Y
(G.L. Wilson, pre-1945)
'Hebron' × 'Crocus'
Fl. deep gold; corona with rim flanged and finely dentate

'Jussy Björling' 2 Y-Y
(J.W.A. Lefeber, 1950) J.W.A. Lefeber, 1960
Fl. 83 mm wide; perianth segments dark yellow; corona orange-yellow. Mid-season

'Just-a-dash' 2 Y-R
(J.M.Radcliff, pre-1996) Unregistered

'Just Fred' 1 YYW-WWY
(Mrs E.Murray) Unregistered
Fl. opening strong citron yellow; perianth segments becoming white at base; corona funnel-shaped, becoming white, with citron at rim. Early

'Justice' 2 W-W
(G.L. Wilson, pre-1935)
'Quartz' × 'Naxos' or 'Askelon'
Perianth segments broad, pure white; corona opening primrose yellow, becoming ivory white, with rim flanged. AM(e) 1939

'Justicia' 1 W-? (b)
(Barr & Sons, pre-1913)

'Just Molly' 2 W-P
(?Australian origin, pre-1990) Unregistered

'Just Ruth' 2 W-WPP
(S.P. Haycock) S.P. Haycock, 1984
'Accent' open pollinated; sdlg no. AW-WP-1
Fl. 90 mm wide; corona salmon pink, paling to near white at base. Mid-season. Resembles 'Accent' but with a brighter-coloured corona

'Just So' 2 W-P
(G.E. Mitsch) G.E. Mitsch, 1968
'Green Island' × 'Accent'; sdlg no. Z20/2
Fl. 99 mm wide, of good form and substance; perianth segments very broad, overlapping; corona bowl-shaped, widely flared, clear salmon pink. Mid-season

'Juvenal' 9 W-YYR
(G.H. Engleheart, pre-1910)

'Juventus' 1 W-Y
(Konynenburg & Mark) Konynenburg & Mark, 1960
'Lord Nelson' × 1W-Y sdlg
Fl. 105 mm wide; perianth segments greyish white; corona brilliant yellow 12B. Early

'Juweeltje' 3 Y-O
(D.W. Lefeber & Co., pre-1947)
Perianth segments acute; corona widely expanded. AM(Haarlem) 1946

'J.W.H.Barr' 1 Y-Y
(W. Backhouse, pre-1869)
Perianth segments sulphur yellow, overlapping. Dwarf. Syn. 'Willie Barr', Pseudonarcissus Lorifolius

'J.W.H.Barr'

'J.W.Winson' 2 W-?
Syn. of 'Wildwood'

'Jylda' 2 W-P
(S.J. Bisdee, 1949)
'Leto' × 'Rosario'

K

'Kabi' 2 W-YYR
(W. Jackson Jr, 1966) Unregistered
'Jo' × 'Arbar'; sdlg no. 159/66

'Kabonova' 2 Y-P
(D.S. Bell) D.S. Bell, 1982
'Red Conquest' × 'Qantasia'
Fl. 98 mm wide. Mid-season. Resembles a smoother-flowered 'Red Conquest'

'Kader' 1 W-Y
(J.S. Leitch) J.S. Leitch, 1960
Fl. 114 mm wide; corona lemon yellow

'Kadina' 2 W-? (b)
(H.A. Brown, pre-1938)

'Kadisha' 2 Y-W
(D.J. Cooper) J.S. Leitch, 1956
Perianth segments pale yellow, with shades of lime green

'Kaffir' 3 W-R
(The Brodie of Brodie, c.1916)
('Cassandra' × Bernardii hybrid) × Engleheart Div. 3 red sdlg
Perianth segments round, very white; corona of darkest red, almost black

'Kai' 2 Y-O
(W. Jackson Sr, 1945)
'Caerleon' × 'Dunkeld'
Perianth segments clear yellow; corona orange

'Kaiapo' 1 W-Y
(Jackson's Daffodils) Jackson's Daffodils, 1989
'Helsal' × sdlg 116/74; sdlg no. 67/80
Fl. 105 mm wide; perianth segments very broadly ovate, blunt, greenish white (155A); corona brilliant greenish yellow 5B, with mouth expanded and slightly frilled. Late

'Kaidu' 1 W-W
(S.J. Bisdee) S.J. Bisdee, 1956
Sdlg 32/43 × 'Tain'

'Kairouan' 3 W-R
(J.L. Richardson, pre-1944)
'Folly' × 'Sunstar'
Perianth segments snow white; corona ruby red, with mouth frilled

'Kaiser' 1 Y-Y
(C.J. Backhouse, pre-1908)

'Kaitaia' 1 W-W
(F. Bloomfield, pre-1949)

'Kaiteriteri' 2 (a)
(R.P. Cook) R.P. Cook, 1957

'Kaituna' 2 W-W
(J.S. Leitch) J.S. Leitch, 1968

'Kaka' 2 W-O
(D. Bramley) D. Bramley, 1980
'Envoy' × 'Signal Light'; sdlg no. 68/51
Fl. 100 mm wide. Mid-season. Resembles 'Signal Light' but with whiter perianth and shorter corona

'Kakoda' 2 W-P
Syn. of 'Kokoda'

'Kalahari' 1 Y-Y
(S.J. Bisdee, 1942)
'Mortlake' × 'Gambrinus'

'Kalamazoo' 2 or 3 W-Y
(pre-1927)
Corona expanded, citron yellow

'Kalamazoo' 1 W-? (b)
(L. van Leeuwen & Son, pre-1950)

'Kalami' 1 Y-Y
(H.G. Cross) H.G. Cross, 1986
'Chillion' × 'Balamara'; sdlg no. 10-1
Perianth segments broadly ovate, blunt, mucronate, inflexed, very smooth, overlapping half; corona straight, darker in tone than the perianth, with mouth very slightly expanded and lightly frilled. Early

'Kalang' 3 W-YYR
(A.O. Roblin, 1944) A.O. Roblin, 1956
'Maid of the Mist' × 'Lady Derby'

'Kalangadoo' 2 W-P
(J.N.Hancock & Co.) J.N.Hancock & Co., 1997
Sdlg no. 29/88H
Perianth segments ovate, plane; the inner segments no narrower; corona funnel-shaped, bronze pink, with mouth neatly flared. Mid-season

'Kaleidoscoop' 1 Y-YYO
(J.W.A. Lefeber) J.W.A. Lefeber, 1980
Fl. 100 mm wide; perianth segments vivid yellow 9B;

corona saffron yellow, with strong orange 25B at rim. Mid-season

'Kalgoorlie' 1 Y-Y
(G.L. Wilson, pre-1947)
'King of the North' × 'Content'
Fl. 108 mm wide; perianth segments brilliant yellow 8A to light greenish yellow 8B, almost white at apex, slightly twisted, overlapping half; corona slightly ribbed, brilliant yellow 8A, shading to brilliant greenish yellow 6A at rim, mouth expanded and frilled, rim flanged and slightly crenate. *HC(g) 1959, *AM(g) 1968

'Kalimna' 1 W-P
(H.G. Cross) H.G. Cross, 1985
'Verran' × 'Dear Me'; sdlg no. 49-8
Perianth segments broadly ovate, blunt, slightly mucronate, inflexed, concave, with midrib showing, overlapping half; the inner segments more strongly inflexed; corona funnel-shaped, smooth, flushed salmon pink, mouth straight and lightly frilled, with rim shallowly notched and crenate. Mid-season

'Kalinda' 1 Y-Y
(S.J. Bisdee, 1951)
Sdlg × 'Clonmel'

'Kalit' 2 Y-O
(W. Jackson Sr, 1941) W. Jackson Jr, 1956
'Killigrew' × 'Market Merry'
Perianth segments roundish, yellow. Resembles 'Indian Summer'

'Kallala' 2 Y-Y
(W.M. Spry, pre-1975) Unregistered
'Torchlight' × 'Golden Valley'
Corona golden yellow

'Kallikrates' 4
(W.F.M. Copeland, pre-1916)

'Kallista' 2 Y-? (a)
(C.E. Radcliff, 1935)
'Pilgrimage' hybrid

'Kalman' 1 Y-Y
(W. Jackson Sr, 1945) W. Jackson Jr, 1956
'Hymyr' × 'Matoome'

'Kaloola' 1 W-? (b)
(J. Hall, pre-1930)

'Kamadeva' 2 Y-O
(S.J. Bisdee, 1946)
'Caruna' × 'Royal Mail'

'Kamahl' 2 Y-Y
(R.H.Glover, pre-1993) Unregistered

'Kamala' 2 Y-OOY
(D.J. Cooper) D.J. Cooper, 1959
Fl. 102 mm wide; perianth segments golden yellow; corona clear orange, tinged red, with golden yellow at rim. Early. Resembles 'Crocus' but with better substance and a darker corona

'Kamalight' 2 Y-Y
(R.J. Abernethy) R.J. Abernethy, 1991
Fl. golden yellow, smooth; corona funnel-shaped, only slightly expanded. Early to mid-season

'Kamau' 9 W-GYR
(Brian S. Duncan) Brian S. Duncan, 1990
'Como' open pollinated; sdlg no. 910

'Kamelin' 3 W-? (b)
(P.D. Williams, pre-1948)

'Kamera' 2 W-R
(J.S. Leitch) J.S. Leitch, 1956

'Kamila' 2 Y-R
(S.J. Bisdee, 1942)
'Gulliver' × 'Sunset Fires'

'Kamona' 2 Y-R
(C.E. Radcliff, 1938)
'Atanga' hybrid

'Kampo' 2 Y-R
(G.J. Phillips, 1982) G.J. Phillips, 1992
'Tokonui' × 'Hiromi'; sdlg no. 77-264-1
Fl. 102 mm wide; perianth segments broadly ovate; corona disc-shaped, wide-spreading, rich orange-red. Mid-season

'Kamura' 2 W-P
(H.G. Cross) H.G. Cross, 1984
'Lawali' × 'Nina'; sdlg no. 90-5
Perianth segments broadly ovate, blunt, very slightly mucronate, inflexed, concave, overlapping half; the inner segments shouldered at base, more strongly inflexed, with margins more deeply incurved; corona funnel-shaped, loosely angled, mid-pink, mouth straight, finely ribbed, even or slightly wavy, with rim minutely notched

'Kanapa' 2 Y-YYR
(G.W.E. Brogden) M.E. Brogden, 1959

'Kanawha' 2 YYW-WWY
(Curtis Tolley) Curtis Tolley, 1995
'Euphony' × 'Dalliance'; sdlg no. T88-17-5
Perianth segments yellow, with white at base, plane; corona funnel-shaped, opening yellow, quickly becoming white, with yellow at rim. Early

'Kanchenjunga' 1 W-W
(G.L. Wilson, pre-1934)

('White Knight' × 'Conqueror') × 'Askelon'; sdlg no. 19/59
Fl. about 130 mm wide, of great substance; perianth segments very broad, smooth or slightly ribbed, overlapping; corona broad, with yellow at base, mouth expanded, rim flanged and deeply notched. 2n=28. AM(e) 1940, AM(Haarlem) 1949

'Kandahar' 1 Y-Y
(The Brodie of Brodie, c.1923)
'Ben Alder' × 1Y-Y sdlg
F. 105 mm wide, vivid yellow 13A; perianth segments overlapping half; corona mouth expanded. 2n=28.
*AM(g) 1947

'Kandi' 2 W-R
(J.S. Leitch) J.S. Leitch, 1956

'Kandos' 2 Y-R
(W.M. Spry, pre-1975) Unregistered
'Port Kembla' × 'Red Poppett'
Corona orange-red, with dark red at rim. Tall. Late

'Kanga' 1 Y-Y
(J.T. Gray, pre-1949)
?'Sir Nigel' × ?'Cleopatra'
Corona slightly darker in tone than the perianth

'Kanierie Gold' 1 Y-Y
(J.A. Hunter) J.A. Hunter, 1973
'Wexford' × 'Kings' Ransom'
Fl. 110 mm wide

'Kano' 1 Y-Y
(S.J. Bisdee, 1948)
'Koranga' × 'Mahu'

'Kansas' 3 W-GYO
(F. Rijnveld & Sons, pre-1939)

'Kanshara' 8
(New Zealand origin, pre-1933)

'Kantaka' 2 Y-? (a)
(Barr & Sons, pre-1929)

'Kantara' 1 W-W
(G.H. Engleheart, pre-1927)
Fl. very wide; corona of very thick substance and marble-like texture, with mouth widely expanded

'Kanton' 1 W-Y
(C.E. Radcliff, 1944) J.M.Radcliff, 1956
'Bonnington' × 'Kanchenjunga'

'Kaoota' 2 Y-Y
(S.J. Bisdee, pre-1939)
'Damson' × 'Lillian Murdoch'

'Kaos' 4 Y-O

(J.L.Richardson) J.N.Hancock & Co., 1997
'Falaise' × 'Ceylon'
Perianth and other petaloid segments warm lemon yellow; corona segments interspersed, bright reddish orange. Mid-season to late

'Kapai' 1 W-W
(A. Hopkirk, pre-1933)

'Kapimana' 1 Y-Y
(S.A. Free) S.A. Free, 1963
Fl. 118 mm wide, deep yellow. Mid-season

'Kapinda' 2 W-? (b)
(Mrs R.O. Backhouse, pre-1921)

'Kapitah' 1 W-W
(W. Jackson Jr, 1950)
? × 'Pella'

'Kapital' 1 Y-Y
(W. Jackson Jr) Jackson's Daffodils, 1980
'Carrickbeg' × 'Comal'; sdlg no. 116/75
Fl. 110 mm wide. Mid-season

'Kapiti' 1 W-W
(J.S. Leitch) J.S. Leitch, 1958

'Kapiti Mayflower' 8 Y-Y
(A.W.A.Walls) J.F.McLennan, 1996
'Soleil d'Or' hybrid
Fls 3-16 per stem, rounded; perianth segments very broadly ovate, prominently mucronate, mid-yellow, spreading, a little concave, with margins incurling near apex, overlapping half; the inner segments only very slightly mucronate, a little inflexed; corona bowl-shaped, broad, lightly ribbed, darker in tone than the perianth, with mouth slightly wavy, rim entire. Very early. Scented

'Kapuni' 1 Y-Y
(G.C. Yeates) G.C. Yeates, 1968
AM(e)(NZ) 1976

'Kara' 3 W-? (b)
(J.T. Gray, pre-1939)

'Kara' 1 W-P
Syn. of 'Petina'

'Kara' 1 W-P
(W. Jackson Jr, 1966) Unregistered
'Illinga' × 'Telita'

'Karachi' 2 Y-YYR
(J.L. Richardson, pre-1943)
'Diolite' × 'Carbineer'
Perianth segments lemon yellow; corona slightly deeper in tone, with a narrow band of deep red at rim, frilled. Div. 3 until 1965

'Karaka' 1 Y-Y
(J.S. Leitch) J.S. Leitch, 1966
Fl. 114 mm wide. Mid-season

'Karakorum' 1 W-W
(C.G. van Tubergen, pre-1938)

'Karamea' 1 Y-Y
(D.S. Bell) D.S. Bell, 1983

'Karaminor' 7 Y-O
(J.H.Davenport) Unregistered

'Karamudli' 1 W-Y
(D. Blanchard, 1944)
'Beersheba' × 'Likovan'
Perianth segments glistening white; corona narrow, soft yellow

'Karanja' 1 W-P
(C.E. Radcliff, 1942)
'Kene' hybrid × 'Dawnglow'
Perianth segments broadly ovate, blunt, very slightly mucronate, pure white, of good substance, overlapping half; the inner segments only slightly narrower; corona deep coppery pink, mouth expanded, ribbed, lightly frilled, with rim notched and flanged

'Karapiro' 2 Y-R
(A. Gibson, c.1925)

'Kardoris' 2 Y-O
(H. Daines, pre-1949)
PC(e)(NZ) 1947, PC(e)(NZ) 1949

'Kareela' 1 W-W
(W. Jackson Jr, c.1965) Unregistered

'Kareen Veronica' 1 W-PPW
(L.P. Dettman) L.P. Dettman, 1979
'Pink Delight' × 'Pink Treasure'; sdlg no. 41/71
Fl. 67 mm wide; perianth segments yellowish white 155B; corona light yellowish pink 29D, with yellowish white (155A) at rim. Mid-season

'Karel' 1 W-W
(W. Jackson Jr) W. Jackson Jr, 1968
'Astor' hybrid
Perianth segments deeply overlapping; corona rim flanged and slightly dentate

'Karelia' 1 W-Y
(Konynenburg & Mark) Konynenburg & Mark, 1962
'Gracious' × 'Daisy Schäffer' hybrid
Fl. 120 mm wide; perianth segments ivory white; corona vivid yellow 12A. Early

'Karen' 2 W-WWO
(T. Morrison) T. Morrison, 1960

'Carbineer' hybrid
Perianth segments pure white; corona with apricot orange at rim

'Karena' 2 W-P
(W. Jackson Jr, 1953)
'Palin' × 'Rosario'

'Karen Anne' 2 W-P
(?Australian origin, pre-1996) Unregistered

'Karen Leake' 2 Y-O
(Australian origin) Parr's Nurseries, 1958
Perianth segments lemon yellow; corona spreading, orange, heavily frilled

'Karen Lee' 2 W-WWY
(L.P. Dettman) L.P. Dettman, 1975
'Glamour' × 'Guardian'; sdlg no. 50/68
Fl. 85 mm wide; perianth segments greenish white (157C); corona paler in tone, with brilliant yellow 20A at rim. Mid-season

'Karen Mumford' 4 Y-O
(J.L. Richardson) G. Zandbergen-Terwegen, 1964
Fl. 95 mm wide. Mid-season

'Kareno' 2 Y-R
(J.S. Leitch) J.S. Leitch, 1956

'Karenza'
(A.T. Boscawen, pre-1937)
Dwarf

'Karessa' 2 W-Y
(J.N. Hancock & Co.) Unregistered
'Joan White' × 'Yolande'

'Karima' 2 W-Y
(D.J. Cooper) D.J. Cooper, 1959
Fl. 99 mm wide; perianth segments off-white; corona creamy yellow. Early

'Karimata' 2 Y-? (a)
(C.E. Radcliff, 1939)

'Karimata' 2 Y-? (a)
(E. Oostdam, pre-1940)

'Karina' 1 W-? (b)
(Barr & Sons, pre-1923)

'Karinga' 1 W-W
(H.A. Brown, pre-1936)
Perianth segments pure white; corona mouth expanded and frilled

'Karin Weisbeck' 2 W-O
(J.W.A. Lefeber, 1948) J.W.A. Lefeber, 1960
Fl. 85 mm wide; corona frilled. Mid-season

'Karisma' 2 W-WWP
(J.N.Hancock & Co., 1978) Unregistered
'Pink Pearl' × 'Verran'; sdlg no. 111/78H
Perianth segments pure white; corona funnel-shaped, delicate pink. Mid-season to late

'Karlene' 2 W-P
(J.N. Hancock & Co.) Unregistered

'Karl Stern' 2 W-? (b)
(J.W.A. Lefeber, pre-1954)

'Karmsea' 2 Y-YOO
(J.L. Martin) J.L. Martin, 1982
'Wansea' × 'Kai'; sdlg no. W/K 17
Fl. 97 mm wide; perianth segments brilliant greenish yellow 3A; corona light orange, with vivid yellow 12A at base. Late. Resembles 'Wansea' but with the colours more distinct

'Karnak' 2 Y-YOO
(S.J. Bisdee, 1946)
'King of Hearts' hybrid

'Karo' 1 W-W
(S.J. Bisdee, 1942)
'Eskimo' × 'Darwalla'

'Karoola' 2 W-WWY
(S.J. Bisdee, 1939)
'Mitylene' × 'Portia'

'Karoon' 1 Y-Y
(S.J. Bisdee, 1949)
'Mortlake' × 'Fahan'

'Karu' 3 W-R
(A.B. Davey) A.B. Davey, 1978
'Masaka' hybrid; sdlg no. 5.1.65
Fl. 120 mm wide. Mid-season

'Kasha' 2 Y-? (a)
(D.J. Cooper) D.J. Cooper, 1957

'Kashgar' 2 W-? (b)
(Mrs R.O. Backhouse, pre-1921)

'Kashmir' 2 W-? (b)
(Mrs R.O. Backhouse, pre-1921)

"Kashmir Local"
2n=30. Syn. of *N. tazetta* from Kashmir

'Kasia' 2 Y-OOR
(W. Jackson Jr) W. Jackson Jr, 1971
Sdlg 187/53 × sdlg 15/60; sdlg no. 113/65
Fl. 115 mm wide; perianth segments bright yellow, of good substance; corona deep orange, shading to bright red at rim

'Kasota' 7 Y-O
(E.C. Powell, pre-1949)
'Trevisky' × *N. jonquilla*

'Kassels Gold' 1 Y-Y
(N. Dofferhof, 1967) C.J. Dobbe Export, 1984
'Dominator' × 'Golden Harvest'; sdlg no. 32
Perianth segments brilliant greenish yellow 5B; corona vivid yellow 12A, with a slightly darker tone (13A) at rim. Mid-season

'Katanga' 11b Y-Y
(J.W.A. Lefeber, 1943) J.W.A. Lefeber, 1960
Fl. 90 mm wide. Mid-season

'Katea' 3 W-? (b)
(R. Crews) R. Crews, 1956

'Kate Fraser' 2 Y-GOO
(D.C.MacArthur) D.C.MacArthur, 1997
'Birichen' × 2 Y-GGO; sdlg no. EV61289
Fl. rounded, 76 mm wide; perianth segments very broadly ovate, vivid yellow 14B, spreading; corona broad funnel-shaped, smooth, vivid orange 28B, with yellow-green (153D) near base and a much stronger green (143B) at base, mouth straight, lobed, with rim crenate. Mid-season. Sunproof

'Kate Greenaway' 2 W-WWP
(G.H. Johnstone, pre-1960) Unregistered

'Kathadin' 2 Y-? (a)
(E.C. Powell, pre-1949)
'Robin Hood' × 'Fortune'

'Katharine' 2 Y-? (a)
(J.W.A. Lefeber) W. Blom & Son, 1955

'Katherine Spurrell' 3 W-Y
(E. Leeds, pre-1877)
Fl. large; perianth segments broadly ovate or oblong, prominently mucronate, spreading, of good substance, overlapping one-third; the inner segments more nearly ovate, a little inflexed, with margins wavy, recurved at base; corona cup-shaped, ribbed, soft canary yellow, mouth straight, wavy, rim crenate. Syn. Leedsii 'Katherine Spurrell', Leedsii 'Vincenti Katherine Spurrell'

'Kathkenny' 1 W-? (b)
(G.L. Wilson, pre-1939)
Corona creamy white

'Kathleen' 2 Y-? (a)
(G.H. Engleheart, pre-1916)

'Kathleen' 2 Y-O
Syn. of 'Redfast'

'Kathleen' 2 W-WWO
(Heathcote Bulb Nursery, pre-1960) Unregistered
Perianth segments pure white; corona with a broad band of copper orange at rim. Tall. Late

'Kathleen' 1 W-Y
(pre-1967) Unregistered

'Kathleen Dryden' 3 Y-O
(Mrs J. Abel Smith) Martin Harwood, 1993
'Altruist' × 'Minster Lodge'
Fl. 80 mm wide; perianth segments very broad, rounded at apex, fairly prominently mucronate, opening bright primrose yellow (4A), becoming whitish yellow, slightly reflexed, somewhat concave, smooth, overlapping half; the inner segments more nearly ovate and spreading; corona bowl-shaped, closely ribbed, strong orange 24A, with a broad band of a darker tone at rim, mouth lightly frilled, occasionally split and overlapping. Late

'Kathleen Ferrier' 2 W-Y
(G.A. Uit den Boogaard, pre-1954)
AM(Haarlem) 1954

'Kathleen Leaper' 2 W-? (b)
(W. Dent, pre-1948)

'Kathleen Mavourneen' 2 W-R
(G. Lewis) D.S. Bell, 1955
Perianth segments pure white; corona fiery red

'Kathleen Munro' 2 W-Y
(D.C. MacArthur) D.C. MacArthur, 1990
Evelix 2 W-Y sdlg × 'Preamble'; sdlg no. EV90/12
Fl. 107 mm wide; perianth segments broad, greenish white (155A), of great substance, overlapping; corona broad, ribbed, light greenish yellow 3C, mouth even. Mid-season. Scented

'Kathleen Poole' 1 W-PPY
(L.P.Dettman, 1974) Unregistered
'Peggy Dettman' × 'Pink Treasure'; sdlg no. PD/PT 1/75

'Kathleen Ross' 3 W-GWW
(D.C. MacArthur) D.C. MacArthur, 1987
Sdlg open pollinated; sdlg no. E8706
Fl. greenish white (157C); corona cup-shaped, with moderate yellow-green 138B at base. Late. Scented

'Kathleen Simpson' 2 W-GPY
(L.P. Dettman) L.P. Dettman, 1979
Sdlg × 'Pink Treasure'; sdlg no. P1-79
Fl. 86 mm wide; perianth segments yellowish white 155D; corona orange-pink (29A), with a narrow band of brilliant yellow 11A at rim. Late. Resembles 'Pink Treasure' but with a differently shaped corona of deeper colour

'Kathryn Breen' 2 W-W
(J.N.Hancock & Co., 1971) Unregistered
Sdlg no. 101/71H

'Kathryn Joy' 2 W-W
(J.N. Hancock & Co., 1971) Unregistered

'Kathryn Mae' 2 W-P
(Max Hamilton) Koanga Daffodils, 1989
'Vahu' × 'Melancholy'; sdlg no. 33-85
Fl. 115 mm wide; perianth segments broadly ovate, pure white; corona pale pink. Mid-season

'Kathy' 4 W-P
(A.N. Kanouse) Mrs A.N. Kanouse, 1990
Div. 4 pink sdlg × Div. 2 or 3 pink sdlg
Fl. 105 mm wide; perianth and other petaloid segments in several whorls, pure white; the outer whorls broad; the inner whorls smaller; corona segments interspersed among the petaloid segments and more clustered at centre, pure pink, frilled. Mid-season. Sunproof

'Katie Campbell' 12 W-Y
(L.P. Dettman) L.P. Dettman, 1976
'Beryl' × 'Jenny'; sdlg no. M1/75
Fls 2 per stem, 55 mm wide; perianth segments greenish white 157D; corona light greenish yellow 4B. Mid-season. Resembles a twin-flowered 'Beryl' of different colouring

'Katinka' 2 W-? (b)
(A.H. Ahrens) J.S. Leitch, 1955

'Katonah' 1 Y-Y
(E.C. Powell, pre-1946)
'King Alfred' hybrid

'Katreena' 2 W-P
(C.R.Best, pre-1988) Unregistered

'Katrina' 3 Y-? (a)
(W.A. Grace, pre-1936)

'Katrina' 2 W-Y
(J.N. Hancock & Co., 1968) Unregistered

'Katrina Rea' 6 W-WOO
(A.J.R.Pearson) A.J.R.Pearson, 1997
'Foundling' × ('Easter Moon' × 'Romance'); sdlg no. 92-4-P57
Fl. 80 mm wide; perianth segments ovate, blunt, greenish white, very strongly reflexed, smooth and with much substance; corona short funnel-shaped, slightly constricted near mid-point, flared towards mouth, opening red-orange, becoming pinkish orange, with white at base, rim crenate. Dwarf. Early to mid-season

'Katru' 1 W-W
(S.J. Bisdee) S.J. Bisdee, 1956
'Tain' × 'Cantatrice'

'Katuma'
?Syn. of 'Katuna'

'Katuna' 2 Y-ORR
(S.J. Bisdee, 1942)
'Invergordon' × 'Red Morn'
?See also 'Katuma'

'Katy' 6 Y-Y
(D. Bramley) D. Bramley, 1978
Sdlg × 'Falling Star'; sdlg no. 68/23
Fl. 77 mm wide; perianth segments lemon; corona gold. Early

'Kavi' 2 Y-R
(W. Jackson Jr, 1968) Unregistered
'Rave' × 'Dimity'; sdlg no. 58/68

'Kawa Kawa' 12 Y-Y
(Robin Brown) Robin Brown, 1995
N. jonquilla var. *henriquesii* × *N. cyclamineus*; sdlg no. JH/C 2
Fls 2 per stem, 37 mm wide, mid-yellow, facing down; perianth segments reflexed; corona cylindrical, smooth, with mouth straight and lobed. Dwarf. Very early

'Kawal' 2 Y ? (a)
(Mrs M.Moorby) Mrs M.Moorby, 1956

'Kawarau' 1 Y-Y
(J.T. Gray, pre-1937)

'Kawau' 4 W-O
(Mrs H.K. Richardson, 1967) P. Phillips, 1977
'Gay Time' × 'George Leake'; sdlg no. 118
Fl. 75 mm wide; perianth and other petaloid segments whitish; corona segments orange. Mid-season

'Kawerau' 2 W-W
(R. Hyde) R. Hyde, 1957

'Kay' 1 W-? (b)
(N.Y. Lower, pre-1931)

'Kay' 2 W-GYR
(W. Jackson Jr, 1970) Unregistered
'Jo' × 'Arbar'; sdlg no. 45/70

'Kayak' 2 W-P
(A.O. Roblin, 1941) A.O. Roblin, 1956
'Eskimo' × 'Pinkeen'

'Kaydee' 6 W-P
(Brian S. Duncan) Rathowen Daffodils, 1984
'Foundling' × 'Delta Wings'; sdlg no. 662

Perianth segments broadly ovate, blunt, prominently mucronate, pure white, reflexed, plane or with margins incurved, glistening, overlapping one-third; the inner segments more narrowly ovate, twisted; corona cylindrical, short, lightly ribbed, fiery pink, with mouth widely expanded and even, rim shallowly crenate. Mid-season

'Kay Elizabeth' 2 W-YPP
(J.N. Hancock & Co., 1964) Unregistered
Perianth segments broadly ovate, blunt, slightly mucronate, spreading, plane, with broad midrib showing, overlapping one-third; the inner segments inflexed at base, recurved towards apex, with margins wavy and sometimes nicked; corona narrowly funnel-shaped, deeply ribbed, smoother towards base, clear pink, with yellow at base, mouth straight and frilled, rim notched and crenate. Tall. Mid-season to late

'Kayena' 2 Y-R
(C.E. Radcliff, 1939)
'Marengo' × 'Killigrew'

'Kay Francis' 2 Y-? (a)
(?J.R.Byfield, pre-1936)

'Kayoko' 11a W-Y
(Jackson's Daffodils) Jackson's Daffodils, 1993
Sdlg 116/77 × 'King Size'; sdlg no. 92/88
Fl. 110 mm wide; perianth segments broadly ovate, greenish white (155A); corona split to base, the six segments in two whorls of three, opposite the perianth segments and joined to them at the margins at base, vivid yellow 12A. Early

'Kaz' 6 Y-O
(P. & G. Phillips) P. & G. Phillips, 1979
Fl. 75 mm wide. Mid-season. Resembles a deeper-coloured 'Jetfire' with the corona more deeply rolled

'Kazan' 2 Y-O
(D.N.Y. Olson, 1973) D.N.Y. Olson, 1987
'Armada' × ('Kingscourt' × 'Crescendo'); sdlg no. 60/1
Fl. 90 mm wide; perianth segments golden yellow, slightly inflexed; corona medium orange, with a somewhat deeper tone at rim. Early

'Kazuko' 3 W-R
(J.A. O'More, 1963) P. & G. Phillips, 1975
'Vieva' × 'Matapan'
Fl. 98 mm wide; perianth segments very broadly ovate, prominently mucronate, opening clean white, becoming whitish, spreading or a little reflexed, with broad midrib showing, overlapping half; the inner segments shouldered at base; corona very short funnel-shaped, widely expanded, ribbed, deep red, mouth straight, even or somewhat wavy, with rim minutely dentate. Mid-season. Resembles a larger and taller-flowered 'Vieva' of smoother texture

'Kea' 6 W-P
(R.A. Scamp) R.A. Scamp, 1994
'Jenny' × 2 W-P sdlg; sdlg no. 217
Fl. 90 mm wide, facing down; perianth segments narrow, acute, chalky white, reflexed; corona cylindrical, opening yellow, becoming buff pink, mouth flared and a little wavy. Dwarf. Mid-season

'Kea Mary' 3 W-? (b)
(Van 't Hof & Blokker, pre-1952)

'Keats' 4 W-Y
(A. Gray, 1958) Broadleigh Gardens, 1968
Fl. 71 mm wide; perianth segments, ovate, blunt, with very slight mucro, white, with a broad band of green at midrib beneath, with margins recurved at base, slightly overlapping; the inner segments wholly white; six petaloid segments within the corona, half as long as the perianth segments and opposite to them, oblong or lanceolate, white, with green at midrib beneath; corona very shallow, widely expanded, with three deeply overlapping lobes, bright yellow, tinged with green; four or five corona segments among the petaloid segments within. Very late. 2n=14

'Kebaya' 2 W-YYP
(Brian S. Duncan) Brian S. Duncan, 1992
'Pismo Beach' × 'High Society'; sdlg no. 1181
Fl. 105 mm wide; perianth segments ovate, spreading, plane; corona shallow bowl-shaped, with mouth straight. Late. Sunproof

'Kedah' 2 Y-? (a)
(A.M. Wilson, pre-1950)

'Kedron' 2 W-P
(S.J. Bisdee, 1939)
'Mary Blewitt' × 'Pinkeen'

'Kedron' 7 Y-O
(W.H. Wheeler) W.H. Wheeler, 1974
N. jonquilla × 'Apricot Distinction'; sdlg no. 27/59/1
Fls usually 2 per stem, 70 mm wide; perianth segments light apricot yellow; corona dark orange. Mid-season

'Keelita' 2 W-R
(K.J. Heazlewood, *c.*1950)
'Koomela' × 'Signal Light'

'Keeper' 1 Y-Y
(J.N. Hancock & Co., 1976) Unregistered

'Keepsake' 8
(W. Welchman, pre-1908)

'Keepsake' 2 W-P
(W.G. Pannill) W.G. Pannill, 1980
'Green Island' × 'Leonaine'; sdlg no. PK 9
Fl. 110 mm wide. Mid-season

'Keera'
Unregistered
Seed parent of 'Dear Me'

'Kef' 3 W-Y
(S.J. Bisdee, 1937) S.J. Bisdee, 1956
'Silver Plane' × 'Portia'

'Kehama'
(pre-1945)
'White Conqueror' × 'Saint Aloysius'

'Kehelland' 4 Y-Y
(A. Gray, pre-1946)
N. minor var. *conspicuus* sport
Fl. soft yellow

'Keith'
(pre-1915)
Resembles a small-flowered 'Lord Roberts'

'Keith' 1 Y-Y
(R.G. Sharp, pre-1930)

'Keith Trevan' 2 Y-Y
(L.P. Dettman, 1967) L.P. Dettman, 1978
'Amberley' open pollinated
Fl. 92 mm wide; perianth segments brilliant greenish yellow 3A; corona slightly brighter in tone (2A). Mid-season. Resembles a lighter-coloured 'Amberley' with the perianth segments more deeply overlapping

'Keizer's Kroon' 3 Y-? (a)
(J. Pope, pre-1908)

'Kelanne' 2 YYW-P
(T. Bloomer) Rathowen Daffodils, 1982
('Rose Caprice' × 'Binkie') × 'Daydream'; sdlg no. D211
Fl. 110 mm wide; perianth segments deep sulphur yellow, paling to white at base; corona cylindrical, salmon pink, with mouth slightly expanded. Mid-season

'Kelburn' 1 W-Y
(D.S. Bell) D.S. Bell, 1983
'Caribbean' × 'David Bell'

'Kellswater' 2 Y-R
(W.J. Dunlop, pre-1947)
'Ballyclare' × 'Bahram'
Perianth segments deep old gold; corona deep red

'Kellva' 2 W-R
(J.S. Leitch) J.S. Leitch, 1956

'Kelmont' 1 W-? (b)
(A. Gibson, pre-1951)

'Kelpie' 6 W-P
(J.L. Richardson) Mrs H.K. Richardson, 1968
'Cymbeline' × 'Debutante'

'Kelsall' 1 Y-Y
(E.L. Jones, pre-1949)

'Kelso' 1 W-P
(S.J. Bisdee, 1947)
'Rochelle' × 'Pink o' Dawn'

'Kelso' 1 Y-Y
(C.A. Latta) C.A. Latta, 1960
Fl. 108 mm wide. Early. Resembles an improved 'Kanga'

'Kelston' 1 W-Y
(C.E. Radcliff, pre-1949)

'Kelton' 1 W-Y
(H.R. Bulman) H.R. Bulman, 1956
'Leslie Fell' × 'Bonnington'
Corona lemon yellow

'Kembla' 1 W-W
(D.J. Jackson, 1978) Jackson's Daffodils, 1989
Sdlg 172/65 × 'Mercedes'; sdlg no. 15/78
Fl. 103 mm wide, yellowish white 155D & B; perianth segments broadly ovate, rounded at apex; corona darker in tone than the perianth. Early

'Kemel' 2 Y-R
(T.H. Piper, 1952)
'Killigrew' × 'Rustom Pasha'

'Kemil' 2 Y-? (a)
(J.T. Gray, pre-1939)

'Kempton' 3 W-Y
(S.J. Bisdee, 1945) S.J. Bisdee, 1956
'Loila' × 'Fay'
Corona lemon yellow

'Kenbane' 1 W-W
(G.L. Wilson, pre-1927)
('Madame de Graaff' × 'King Alfred') self pollinated
Perianth segments broadly ovate, blunt, slightly mucronate, spreading in lower half, reflexed towards apex, with margins wavy, overlapping one-third; the inner segments more strongly reflexed; corona cylindrical, 6-angled, ivory white, with mouth widely expanded, rim deeply notched and crenate. Late

'Kenbane Head' 9 W-GYR
(Ballydorn Bulb Farm, 1973) Ballydorn Bulb Farm, 1989
'Cantabile' hybrid open pollinated
Fl. 90 mm wide; perianth segments very broadly ovate, rounded at apex; corona ribbed, with orange-red at rim. Late. Sunproof

'Kencott' 2 W-W
(J.L. Richardson, pre-1935)
'White Sentinel' open pollinated
Corona opening pale primrose, becoming white, frilled

'Kendal' 1 W-Y
(H.R. Bulman) H.R. Bulman, 1956
'Moongold' × 'Bonnington'

'Kenebri' 2 Y-R
(W.M. Spry, pre-1975) Unregistered
'Ivo Fell' × 'Revelry'
Corona brick red

'Kenellis' 10 W-Y
(A. Gray, pre-1948)
N. bulbocodium var. *citrinus* × 'Snowflake'
Fl. star-shaped; perianth segments narrowly ovate or oblong, acute, spreading or a little inflexed, only very slightly overlapping; corona narrow funnel-shaped, lightly ribbed, brilliant greenish yellow 5A, ageing to white, mouth closely ribbed, straight, obscurely lobed, wavy, with rim minutely crenate. Dwarf. Early. With secondary stems

'Ken Farmer' 2 Y-YYR
(Ken Farmer Nurseries) Ken Farmer Nurseries, 1978
Fl. 115 mm wide

'Kenilworth' 2 Y-O
(G. Lewis, 1945) D.S. Bell, 1958
See also 'Kennilworth'

'Kenmare' 2 W-P
(J.L. Richardson, pre-1937)
'White Sentinel' self pollinated
Perianth segments very broadly ovate, blunt, pure white, a little inflexed, plane or concave, smooth, overlapping half; the inner segments more narrowly ovate, square-shouldered at base, more strongly inflexed; corona funnel-shaped, smooth, flushed pale rose pink, tinged green at base, mouth straight, wavy, rim more or less entire. Mid-season. Resembles a later-flowered 'Dunloe' of deeper colour with a straighter corona

'Kenna' 2 Y-? (a)
(G.H. Furness, pre-1934)

'Kennach' 2 W-O
Syn. of 'Kennack'

'Kennack' 9 W-YYR
(Sir A.P.W. Thomas, pre-1915)

'Kennack' 2 W-O
(P.D. Williams, pre-1927)
'Oriflamme' hybrid
Fl. 82 mm wide; perianth segments creamy white, of

good substance, overlapping half; corona funnel-shaped, yellow-orange, becoming deeper in tone, frilled. Mid-season to late. See also 'Kennach'

'Kennegie' 3 W-YYR
(P.D. Williams, pre-1927)
Perianth segments very broad, ivory white; corona disc-shaped, yellow, with deep red at rim

'Kenneth' 1 Y-Y
(R.H. Bath, pre-1929)

'Kennilworth' 2 Y-O
Syn. of 'Kenilworth'

'Kenrose' 2 W-P
(Brian S. Duncan) Rathowen Daffodils, 1987
'Fragrant Rose' × 'Ken's Favorite'; sdlg no. 933
Mid-season

'Ken's Favorite' 2 W-P
(Murray W. Evans, 1968) Murray W. Evans, 1978
'Cordial' × 'Caro Nome'; sdlg no. L-30/1
Fl. 110 mm wide; perianth segments very broad in outline, rounded or squarish at apex, sometimes truncate, mucronate, spreading, slightly concave, overlapping half; the inner segments inflexed, more narrowly ovate, sometimes twisted or with margins incurved; corona cup-shaped, smooth, deep rose pink, touched white between crenations at rim, mouth slightly expanded, occasionally split and overlapping, rim irregularly crenate

'Kensho' 2 W-P
(C.O. Fairbairn, c.1950)

'Ken's Memory' 2 W-GWW
(K.J. Heazlewood) L.P. Dettman, 1984
'Empress of Ireland' hybrid × 'Lady Slim'
Fl. 114 mm wide; perianth segments yellowish white 155D; corona slightly darker in tone (155B). Mid-season

'Kensole' 2 W-? (b or c)
(J.L. Richardson, c.1950)
'White Sentinel' open pollinated

'Kent'
(G.P. Haydon, pre-1914)

'Kentish Maid' 2 W-W
(K.B. Burns) K.B. Burns, 1964
Fl. 102 mm wide; corona opening primrose yellow, becoming white. Mid-season. Resembles 'Greenore' in form

'Kentucky' 3 W-YYR
(de Graaff Bros, pre-1928)
Div. 9 until 1959

'Kentucky Cardinal' 2 W-R
(J.M. de Navarro) J.M. de Navarro, 1966
'King Cardinal' × 'Brahms'
Fl. 98 mm wide; corona very shallow bowl-shaped, red

'Kenwyn' 3 W-? (b)
(P.D. Williams, pre-1927)

'Kenya' 2 Y-? (a)
(A.M. Wilson, pre-1937)

'Kepler' 2 W-? (b)
(G. Lubbe & Son, pre-1943)
AM(Haarlem) 1943

'Kerabin' 2 W-YYP
(S.J. Bisdee, 1944)
Sdlg × 'Rosario'

'Kerak' 1 Y-Y
(D.N.Y. Olson, 1972) D.N.Y. Olson, 1988
'Wexford' × 'Kingscourt'; sdlg no. 195/1
Perianth segments very smooth. Resembles a Div. 1 'Strines'

'Kerami' 2 Y-YYO
(J.N. Hancock & Co., pre-1949)
Fl. yellow; corona with reddish orange at rim

'Keras' 1 W-W
(S.J. Bisdee, 1942)
'Eskimo' × 'Dawnglow'

'Keremoana' 2 W-R
(A.B. Davey) A.B. Davey, 1978
'Nevose' × 'Arbar'; sdlg no. 3/11/65
Fl. 96 mm wide. Mid-season

'Keren' 2 Y-YYO
(S.J. Bisdee, 1945) S.J. Bisdee, 1956
'Carbineer' × 'Erebus'

'Kerensa' 1 Y-Y
(Rosewarne EHS, 1969) Rosewarne EHS, 1989
'Saint Keverne' × 'Malvern City'; sdlg no. 65/68/3
Fl. 105 mm wide; perianth segments broadly ovate, vivid yellow 12A, deeply overlapping; corona expanded, darker in tone (14A) than the perianth, with rim flanged and crenate. Early

'Keridwen' 2 W-YYR
(W. Jackson Sr, 1932)
'Bernardino' × 'Warflame'

'Kerlew' 2 Y-WWY
(J.N. Hancock & Co., 1980) Unregistered
'Chartwell' × 'Daydream'; sdlg no. 75/80H
Perianth segments bright citrus yellow; corona long, constricted near mouth, becoming white, with yel-

low at rim, frilled. Mid-season

'Kernow' 2 Y-WWY
(R.A. Scamp) R.A. Scamp, 1993
'Grand Prospect' × 'Daydream'; sdlg no. 67
Fl. 95 mm wide; perianth segments very broadly ovate, blunt, only very slightly mucronate, pale golden yellow, a little reflexed, smooth, overlapping half; the inner segments more nearly spreading, with margins a little wavy; corona funnel-shaped, smooth, white, with a narrow band of pale golden yellow at rim, neatly frilled. Mid-season

'Kerrabee' 1 Y-O
(W.M. Spry, pre-1975) Unregistered
'Morning Glory' × 'Golden Valley'
Early

'Kerri' 2 W-Y
(pre-1927)

'Kerri' 2 Y-? (a)
(J. Hall, pre-1930)
Perianth segments creamy white, veined green at base; corona expanded, yellow

'Kerry' 3 Y-R
(G. Lewis, 1945) D.S. Bell, 1958

'Kerry Dance' 2 W-W
(D.S. Bell) D.S. Bell, 1961
'White Sentinel' hybrid × 'Regency Lace'
Fl. 108 mm wide. Mid-season. Resembles a 'Killaloe' of better poise and smoother texture

'Kerry Piper' 1 Y-Y
(J.L. Richardson) F.E. Board, 1956
('Royalist' × 'Crocus') × 'Kingscourt'

'Kerry Werry' 2 Y-O
(G.H. Johnstone, pre-1950)

'Kerstin' 3 W-WPP
(S.J.Bisdee, c.1960) H.G.Cross, 1995
'Chinese White' × 'Chiffon'
Fl. 80 mm wide; perianth segments very broadly ovate, blunt or truncate, not prominently mucronate, greenish white, concave, with margins incurling at apex, overlapping half; the inner segments creased; corona very shallow bowl-shaped, lightly ribbed, light yellowish pink 36A, with white at base becoming pink with age, mouth wavy, shallowly 6-lobed, rim irregularly notched and minutely crenate. Very late. Varies between Divs 3 and 2. See also 'Kirsten'

'Kerta' 2 Y-R
(W. Jackson Jr) W. Jackson Jr, 1966
'Magherally' × 'Chungking'; sdlg no. 117/57

'Keshcarrigan' 2 Y-? (a)
(J.M. de Navarro) J.L. Richardson, 1956
'Royal Mail' × 'Narvik'

N. kesticus Maire & Wilczec = *N. cantabricus* var. *kesticus*

'Kestrel' 9 W-GOR
(P.D. Williams, pre-1907)
Fl. rounded, 63 mm wide; perianth segments rounded at apex, overlapping one-third; corona almost disc-shaped, ribbed, orange, with a greenish colour at base and bright red at rim. Mid-season to late. Tall

'Keswick' 3 W-? (b)
(Warnaar & Co., pre-1929)

'Keven' 2 Y-? (a)
(A.M. Wilson, pre-1927)
AM(Haarlem) 1930. Received AM(Haarlem) 1930 as Div. 3

'Keverne' 3 Y-YYO
(P.D. Williams, pre-1930)
Perianth segments lemon yellow; corona widely expanded. AM(Haarlem) 1930

'Kevin Wise' 2 W-P
(Tom Forster, 1960s) Unregistered
Perianth segments roundish; corona widely expanded, ribbed, deep rose pink, heavily frilled. Tall. Late

'Kewpie' 3 W-R
(C.E. Radcliff, 1943)
'Portia' × 'Hades'

'Kewpie' 2 W-P
(Murray W. Evans) Murray W. Evans, 1974
Fl. 70 mm wide

'Kewpie' 3 W-?
Syn. of 'Insignia'

'Kewpie Sprite' 9 W-GYO
(Mrs M.S. Yerger) Mrs M.S. Yerger, 1993
N. poeticus var. *hellenicus* × 'Lights Out'; sdlg no. 75 H 3-3
Fl. star-shaped, 25 mm wide; perianth segments mucronate; the inner segments a little narrower; corona cup-shaped, green-yellow (154B), with green at base and orange at rim. Dwarf. Very late

'Key Largo' 2 Y-Y
(W.G. Pannill) W.G. Pannill, 1980
'Kingscourt' × 'Royal Oak'; sdlg no. D 23/4
Fl. 104 mm wide. Mid-season

'Keynote' 2 W-P
(E.F. Hughes) E.F. Hughes, 1962
Fl. 108 mm wide; corona narrow, pale pink, frilled. Mid-season

'Keystone' 2 Y-W
(Murray W. Evans, 1968) Murray W. Evans, 1979
'Pinkie' × ('Bethany' × 'Daydream'); sdlg no. L-10
Fl. 95 mm wide. Mid-season

'Keziah' 1 W-W
(Barr & Sons, pre-1923)

'Khaki' 2 Y or W-? (a or b)
(pre-1915)

'Khalasa' 2 Y-? (a)
(G.C. Graham, pre-1949)
Syn. 'Rocliffe'

'Khaled' 3 W-YYO
(R.V. Favell, pre-1946)
'Firetail' × 'Warlock'

'Khamseen' 2 Y-? (a)
(A.M. Wilson, pre-1930)
'Calif' hybrid
Perianth segments acute; corona with red at rim

'Khancoban' 1 W-W
(J.N. Hancock & Co., pre-1988) Unregistered

'Khanwin' 2 W-P
(J.L. Martin, 1972) J.L. Martin, 1982
'Ann Cameron' × 'Jill Bolte'; sdlg no. AC/JB 7
Fl. 102 mm wide; corona light yellowish pink 36C to a darker tone (38B). Mid-season. Resembles an earlier-flowered 'Lynny' with a longer and narrower corona

'Khartum' 3 W-R
(J.L. Richardson, pre-1938)
'Coronach' × 'Hades'
Fl. rounded; perianth segments very broadly ovate, rounded at apex, prominently mucronate, spreading, plane, overlapping half; the inner segments roundish, somewhat truncate, only very slightly mucronate, a little inflexed; corona broad disc-shaped, loosely ribbed, vivid red, rim entire, in places split and overlapping. Late

'Khatmandu' 3 W-GWW
(F.H. Chapman, pre-1929)
Corona shallow, frilled. AM(e) 1929

'Khedive' 1 Y-Y
(E. Leeds, pre-1877)
Fl. pale yellow. Syn. Pseudonarcissus Major 'Khedive'. Was "absorbed" into 'Mrs H.J.Elwes'

'Khedive' 3 W-? (b)
(P.D. Williams, pre-1914)

'Khem' 2 Y-Y
(W. Jackson Sr, pre-1948)

'Khemmel' 2 Y-Y
(T.H. Piper, c.1966) Unregistered
'Khem' × 'Melissa'

'Khiva' 2 W-Y
(The Brodie of Brodie, c.1925)
'Beacon' × 'Tenedos'

'Khroma' 3 W-R
(S.J. Bisdee, 1937) S.J. Bisdee, 1956
Sdlg × 'Dactyl'

'Khyber' 7
(The Brodie of Brodie, pre-1930)

'Kialoa' 2 W-W
(W. Jackson Jr) Jackson's Daffodils, 1979
'Mercedes' × sdlg 15/65; sdlg no. 29/74
Fl. 114 mm wide. Mid-season

'Kiama' 2 W-O
(W.M. Spry, pre-1975) Unregistered
'Narvik' × 'Stand By'

'Kiandra' 2 Y-YYO
(H.A. Brown, 1941) J.N. Hancock & Co., 1964
Perianth segments broadly ovate, rich yellow, with white mucro, spreading, a little concave, overlapping half; the inner segments more narrowly ovate, somewhat inflexed, with margins wavy; corona cup-shaped, yellow, with a broad band of reddish orange at rim, frilled mouth. Early

'Kia Ora' 2 W-W
(J.S. Leitch) J.S. Leitch, 1968

'Kiara' 2 W-W
(A.O. Roblin, 1945)
'Zamira' × 'Portia'

'Kibitzer' 6 Y-Y
(Roberta C.Watrous) Roberta C.Watrous, 1968
N. minor × *N. cyclamineus*
Fl. 32 mm wide, vivid yellow 9B; corona very slightly darker in tone (9A). Very early

'Kibo' 2 W-W
(G.L. Wilson, pre-1948)
'Gracious' × 'Broughshane'
Corona very widely expanded, with rim deeply dentate. AM(Haarlem) 1950

'Kidling' 7 Y-Y
(A. Gray, pre-1951)
N. jonquilla and *N. assoanus*
Fls 1-2 per stem, yellow; perianth segments broadly ovate, slightly reflexed, overlapping; corona bowl-shaped, darker in tone than the perianth segments. Dwarf. Late. Scented

'Kiev' 1 W-P
(G.E.Mitsch, 1974) R. & E.Havens, 1995
Sdlg C38/2 ('At Dawning' sibling) × 'C.E.Radcliff'; sdlg no. JJ22/6
Fl. 90 mm wide; perianth segments broadly ovate; corona straight-sided, clear pink, with mouth slightly flared. Early. Sunproof

'Kiewa' 1 W-W
(S.J. Bisdee, 1945)
'Askelon' × 'Cantatrice'

'Kilamanjaro' 2 W-YOO
Syn. of 'Kilimanjaro'

'Kilbarry' 2 Y-? (a)
(J.L. Richardson, pre-1929)

'Kilbride' 2 Y-Y
(J.L. Richardson, pre-1938)
'Saint Egwin' × 'Penquite'
Fl. pale yellow. 2n=28. Syn. 'Achill', 'Moonshine', 'Rathlin'

'Kilclief' 3 W-GYR
(Ballydorn Bulb Farm, 1980) Ballydorn Bulb Farm, 1995
'Strangford' open pollinated
Fl. rounded, 110 mm wide; perianth segments broadly ovate, smooth, overlapping; corona bowl-shaped, golden yellow, with green at base and a band of orange-red at rim. Mid-season to late

'Kilcohen' 2 W-YYR
(Mrs R.O. Backhouse, pre-1921)
Perianth segments pure white; corona yellow, with a broad band of red at rim

'Kilcoo' 2 W-O
(Ballydorn Bulb Farm) Ballydorn Bulb Farm, 1968
'Kilworth' × 'Signal Light'
Fl. 95 mm wide; perianth segments ivory white; corona reddish orange, with a deeper tone at base, frilled. Mid-season

'Kilcool' 2 W-YYO
(Ballydorn Bulb Farm, pre-1968) Unregistered
'Kilworth' × 'Arbar'
Fl. 89 mm wide; perianth segments creamy white; corona expanded, yellow, with reddish orange at rim. Late

'Kilcoran' 2 W-YYO
(J.L. Richardson) J.L. Richardson, 1956
'Blarney' × 'Coverack Perfection'

'Kilcroney' 2 Y-O
(Mrs R.O. Backhouse, pre-1921)
Perianth segments bright yellow; corona very widely expanded, reddish orange, with rim dentate

'Kildare' 1 Y-Y
(J.L. Richardson, pre-1938)
'Royalist' × 'Crocus'
Fl. golden; corona widely expanded

'Kildavin' 2 W-P
(J.S.B. Lea) J.S.B. Lea, 1963
'Psddionslr' × 'Fionn'; sdlg no. 3-19-62
Corona china pink. Late. Resembles 'Irish Rose' in form

'Kilderkin' 3 W-WWY
(F.E. Board) F.E. Board, 1965
Corona with lemon yellow at rim

'Kildonan' 2 W-O
(J.S.B. Lea) J.S.B. Lea, 1962
'Arbar' × Richardson sdlg 247
Fl. 99 mm wide; corona reddish orange. Mid-season. Resembles 'Arbar' but with broader perianth segments and darker-coloured corona

'Kildowney' 2 Y-Y
(W.J. Dunlop) W.J. Dunlop, 1963
Fl. greenish lemon

'Kildrum' 3 W-R
(W.J. Dunlop, pre-1950)
'Sunstar' × 'Isola'
Corona disc-shaped, crimson-red

'Kilfinnan' 2 Y Y
(J.L. Richardson, pre-1943)
'Stirling' × 'Saint Egwin'
Fl. soft yellow; corona rim slightly dentate. Resembles a much improved 'Saint Egwin'

'Kiligrew' 2 Y-O
Syn. of 'Killigrew'

'Kilimanjaro' 2 W-YOO
(G.L. Wilson, pre-1938)
'Clara' × 'Hades'
Perianth segments pure white; corona deep reddish orange, with citron at base. See also 'Kilamanjaro'

'Kilkeel' 3 W-O
(W.J. Dunlop, pre-1952)
'Folly' × 'Sunstar'
Corona reddish orange

'Kilkenny' 1 Y-Y
(J.L. Richardson, pre-1938)
'Royalist' × 'Trenoon'
Fl. forming a double triangle, golden yellow; perianth segments very broadly ovate, blunt, slightly mucronate, spreading, plane, smooth and of heavy substance, overlapping half; the inner segments a little inflexed and slightly twisted; corona cylindrical, smooth, with mouth expanded, rim crenate and

widely rolled. Mid-season

'Killala' 2 W-YYO
(J.L. Richardson, pre-1948)
'Therapia' × 'Red Sun'
Perianth segments creamy white; corona straight-sided, lemon yellow, with reddish orange at rim, with the rim flanged and dentate. AM(Haarlem) 1949. See also 'Killalla'

'Killalla' 2 W-YYO
Syn. of 'Killala'

'Killaloe' 2 W-W
(J.L. Richardson, pre-1937)
'Cameronian' × 'Slemish'
Fl. forming a double triangle, 117 mm wide; perianth segments very broadly ovate, blunt, slightly mucronate, pure white, spreading, plane, of good substance, overlapping half; the inner segments more narrowly ovate, only very slightly mucronate, a little inflexed and very slightly twisted; corona funnel-shaped, mouth ribbed, widely expanded, lightly frilled, rim flanged. Mid-season. 2n=28. *(Gulval)PC(m) 1940, AM(e) 1948, FCC(e) 1951, *AM(g) 1962

'Killara' 8 W-Y
(H. Selkirk, pre-1910)
'Grand Monarque' × 'Empress'
Fls 3-4 per stem, 75 mm wide. 2n=45+1B. ?The same as 'Sanda' 8

'Killara Pink' 2 W-P
(M.G.Temple-Smith, 1983) M.G.Temple-Smith, 1997
'Dear Me' × 'My Word'; sdlg no. 6/83
Corona green at base, with rim flanged. Early

'Killarney' 2 W-? (b or c)
(G.L. Wilson, pre-1927)

'Killarney Sunset' 2 W-O
(W.B. Hartland, pre-1912)
Corona scarlet-orange

'Killdeer' 6 Y-Y
(G.E. Mitsch) G.E. Mitsch, 1970
('Green Island' × 'Chinese White') × *N. cyclamineus*; sdlg no. C55/1
Perianth segments broad, soft greenish yellow, paler at base, reflexed, with margins wavy; corona very pale, with mouth expanded. Mid-season

'Killearnan' 9 W-GYR
(J.S.B. Lea) Clive Postles Daffodils, 1985
'Andrew Marvel' × 'Greenfinch'; sdlg no. 5-80-74
Corona very shallow, closely and unevenly ribbed, mouth tightly frilled, with overlapping lobes. Late. Scented

'Killeen' 2 Y-O
(Ballydorn Bulb Farm) Ballydorn Bulb Farm, 1980
'Kilmorack' open pollinated
Fl. 115 mm wide; perianth segments yellow gold; corona reddish orange. Mid-season. Sunproof

'Killiecrankie' 1 W-Y
(E.M. Crosfield, pre-1912)
Perianth segments creamy; corona yellow. AM 1912

'Killifreth' 3 W-? (b)
(M.P. Williams, pre-1937)

'Killigenz' 2
Syn. of 'Pirate's Gold'

'Killigrew' 2 Y-O
(P.D. Williams, pre-1907)
Fl. forming a double triangle, 97 mm wide; perianth segments very broadly ovate, blunt or acute, prominently mucronate, bright yellow, spreading, plane, with broad midrib showing, overlapping half; the inner segments more narrowly ovate, angled at shoulder, only very slightly mucronate, a little inflexed, concave and with margins wavy or incurled; corona cup-shaped, lightly ribbed, bright orange, paling towards base, mouth straight, loosely frilled. Mid-season. Sunproof. 2n=28. AM 1924, AM(Haarlem) 1930, FCC(e) 1930, *AM(g) 1936. See also 'Kiligrew'

'Killinchy' 2 Y-O
(G.L. Wilson, pre-1947)
'Market Merry' × 'Porthilly'
Perianth segments yellow; corona scarlet-orange

'Killirose' 3 W-? (b)
(M.P. Williams, pre-1937)

'Killite'
(New Zealand origin, pre-1940)

'Killwater' 2 Y-? (a)
(pre-1949)
'Ballyclare' × 'Bahram'

'Killycowan' 1 Y-Y
(W.J. Dunlop) W.J. Dunlop, 1962

'Killyleagh' 3 W-GOR
(Ballydorn Bulb Farm, 1986) Ballydorn Bulb Farm, 1994
'Florida Manor' × 'Capisco'
Fl. 90 mm wide; perianth segments very broadly ovate, opening creamy white, rapidly becoming pure white, plane; corona saucer-shaped, tightly ribbed, suffused orange, with dark emerald green at base and a band of dark red at rim. Mid-season to late

'Killymoon' 2 W-W
(S.J. Bisdee, 1950)
'Pinkeen' × 'Whitefoord'

'Killymoon' 2 W-W
(A. Pye) A. Pye, 1966
Fl. 100 mm wide; perianth segments broad, smooth; corona with green at base, mouth expanded, rim dentate. Mid-season. Resembles 'Ludlow' but with a differently shaped corona

'Killynure' 1 W-Y
(G.L. Wilson, pre-1948)
'Justice' × 'Truth'
Perianth segments pure white; corona golden

'Kilmood' 2 Y-R
(Ballydorn Bulb Farm) Ballydorn Bulb Farm, 1988
'Golden Amber' hybrid
Fl. 90 mm wide; perianth segments broadly ovate, golden yellow, very smooth; corona small, deep red, with rim entire. Mid-season. Sunproof

'Kilmorack' 2 Y-O
(The Brodie of Brodie, c.1944)
'Trevisky' × 'Fairy King' hybrid; sdlg no. 52/A/39
Fl. 91 mm wide; perianth segments broadly ovate, blunt, mucronate, brilliant greenish yellow 6B, slightly reflexed, overlapping half; the inner segments more narrowly ovate or oval, only very slightly mucronate, slightly inflexed, with midrib showing; corona cylindrical, narrowly ribbed, strong orange 24A, with mouth straight and rim slightly dentate. 2n=28. AM(e) 1956, *AM(g) 1959. Formerly named 'Home Fires'

'Kilmore' 3 W-O
(J.L. Richardson) Mrs H.K. Richardson, 1962
'Kilworth' × 'Signal Light'
Fl. 80 mm wide; perianth segments white, shading to near brilliant yellow 12B at extreme base, slightly inflexed, overlapping; corona ribbed, near vivid orange 28B, with mouth straight and a little wavy, rim entire. Late. 2n=28

'Kilmorna' 2 W-Y
(J.L. Richardson, pre-1945)
'Aranjuez' open pollinated
Fl. 108 mm wide; perianth segments roundish, smooth, overlapping; the inner segments slightly narrower; corona funnel-shaped, light greenish yellow 6D, slightly darker without, mouth expanded and frilled, rim slightly flanged. Resembles a later-flowered 'Brunswick'. AM(e) 1948

'Kilmurry' 3 W-O
(J.L. Richardson) Mrs H.K. Richardson, 1967
'Kilworth' × 'Arbar'
Fl. 102 mm wide; perianth segments greenish white (155A), slightly inflexed, with margins notched, overlapping; corona ribbed, strong orange 25A, with rim crenate. AM(e) 1969

'Kilnagross' 2 Y-O
(P.D. Williams, pre-1929)
Perianth segments pale yellow, of good substance

'Kilndown' 2 W-YYO
(N.A.Burr, 1987) N.A.Burr, 1997
'Ringleader' × 'Edwalton'; sdlg no. 1.2.82
Fl. 92 mm wide; perianth segments very broadly ovate, blunt or somewhat truncate, prominently mucronate, spreading, with margins minutely incurling, overlapping half or more; the inner segments a little inflexed; corona shallow, widely expanded, ribbed, dark yellow, with a broad band of bright orange at rim and the rim slightly crenate. Late

'Kilo' 2 Y-O
(Heathcote Bulb Nursery, pre-1956) Unregistered
Perianth segments smooth, overlapping; corona reddish orange

'Kilpa' 1 W-W
(A.O. Roblin, 1945) A.O. Roblin, 1956
'Pepin' × 'Kanchenjunga'

'Kilpatrick' 1 Y-Y
(D.N.Y. Olson, 1980) D.N.Y. Olson, 1993
'Wexford' × 'Highway'
Fl. forming a double triangle, 95 mm wide, mid- to deep yellow; perianth segments broad, blunt, slightly mucronate, plane, overlapping; corona cylindrical, smooth, mouth flared, rim crenate and slightly rolled. Very early

'Kilrane' 3 W-? (b)
(The Brodie of Brodie, c.1929)
('Beacon' × 'Fortune') × 'Sunstar'; sdlg no. 108/B/24
Perianth segments creamy white; corona disc-shaped, with a broad band of reddish orange at rim

'Kilrea' 2 W-W
(W.J. Dunlop, pre-1952)
'White Sentinel' × 'Cantatrice'
Corona opening cream, soon becoming white. 2n=28+1B

'Kilroot' 2 Y-R
(W.J. Dunlop) W.J. Dunlop, 1965

'Kilrush' 2 Y-Y
(J.L. Richardson, pre-1945)
'Stirling' × 'Saint Egwin'
Resembles a darker-coloured 'Kilfinnan'

'Kilsheelan' 2 W-W
(J.L. Richardson, pre-1937)
'White Sentinel' self pollinated
Fl. pure white; perianth segments very broadly ovate,

blunt or squarish at apex, slightly mucronate, plane, overlapping half; the inner segments more narrowly ovate, angled at shoulder, a little inflexed, with margins wavy; corona cylindrical, smooth, mouth expanded, ribbed, even, rim crenate and narrowly rolled. Mid-season

'Kilsyth' 1 Y-Y
(H.A. Brown, 1926)

'Kilter' 3 W-R
(P.D. Williams, pre-1927)
Perianth segments creamy white, overlapping; corona disc-shaped, deep brilliant red. AM(Haarlem) 1927

'Kiltie' 3 W-? (b)
(The Brodie of Brodie, c.1943)
('Sunstar' × 'Warlock') × 'Blinkbonny'

'Kiltonga' 2 W-YYR
(Ballydorn Bulb Farm) Ballydorn Bulb Farm, 1990
Hybrid between Ballydorn sdlgs
Fl. 78 mm wide; perianth segments broadly ovate, deeply overlapping; corona very shallow bowl-shaped, yellow, with red at rim extending into the mid-zone. Mid-season to late

'Kilver'
(New Zealand origin, pre-1940)

'Kilwinning' 2 Y-? (a)
(S.C. Gaspar) R.J. Abernethy, 1957

'Kilworth' 2 W-YOO
(J.L. Richardson, pre-1938)
'White Sentinel' × 'Hades'
Fl. 108 mm wide; perianth segments very broadly ovate, blunt or truncate, slightly mucronate, creamy white, tinged yellow at base, spreading, a little concave, overlapping half; the inner segments a little inflexed, with margins wavy or incurled; corona deep bowl-shaped, lightly ribbed, vivid orange 28B, with deep yellow at base and a touch of dark green in tube, mouth straight or a little incurved, split in places and overlapping, slightly frilled. Mid-season. 2n=28. FCC(e) 1946, AM(e) 1946, AM(Haarlem) 1948, FCC(Haarlem) 1950, *FCC(g) 1952

'Kim' 4 W-Y
(D.S. Bell) D.S. Bell, 1982
'Mount White' open pollinated
Fl. 105 mm wide. Mid-season

'Kim' 1 Y-Y
(T.H. Piper, c.1966) Unregistered
'Golden Cockerel' × 'Khem'

'Kimange' 1 Y-Y
(W. Jackson Jr) W. Jackson Jr, 1971

'Jobi' × sdlg 8/62; sdlg no. 31/66
Fl. 95 mm wide. Early

'Kimba'
(H.A. Brown, pre-1955)

'Kimba' 2 W-O
(J.N. Hancock & Co., 1961) Unregistered

'Kimberley' 1 Y-Y
(C.G. van Tubergen, pre-1927)
AM(Haarlem) 1926

'Kimberley Ann' 2 W-P
(Colin Crotty, 1984) Colin Crotty, 1994
'Caro Nome' open pollinated; sdlg no. 13-79
Fl. 105 mm wide; perianth segments very broadly ovate, pure white, spreading, smooth and of heavy substance, overlapping; corona almost disc-shaped, mid-pink at base shading to a deeper tone towards mouth, mouth heavily frilled. Mid-season

'Kimbolton' 2 Y-? (a)
(S.C. Gaspar) R.J. Abernethy, 1957

'Kimellen' 4 W-P
(W. Jackson Jr, 1965)
'Lawali' hybrid; sdlg no. 77/65

'Kimi' 2 W-P
(W. Jackson Jr, 1956) Unregistered
Sdlg 86/51 × 'Ceram'
2n=28

'Kimmeridge' 3 W-YYO
(D. & J.W. Blanchard) D. & J.W. Blanchard, 1966
'Portrush' × 'Pretty Polly'
Fl. 95 mm wide; corona pale yellow, with orange at rim. Mid-season. Resembles a Div. 3 'Pretty Polly' with a differently coloured corona. AM(e) 1975

'Kimono' 3 W-W
(F.E. Board) F.E. Board, 1965
Milne sdlg 1152 × G.L. Wilson sdlg 36/190

'Kimsey' 3 W-YYO
(G.C. Yeates) G.C. Yeates, 1974
Fl. 85 mm wide

'Kin' 3 W-? (b or c)
(W. Jackson Jr, 1955) Unregistered
'Ethni' hybrid

'Kinard' 2 W-Y
(G.L. Wilson) G.L. Wilson, 1959
('Portrush' × 'Green Island') × 'Silver Coin'
Perianth segments broad, of good substance; corona shallow, widely expanded, tinted pale lemon yellow. Resembles a much improved 'Green Island'

'Kinbrace' 4 W-P
(J.S.B. Lea) J.S.B. Lea, 1968
('Falaise' × 'Rose Caprice') × 'Fionn'; sdlg no. 1-54-62
Fl. 108 mm wide; corona segments bright pink. PC(e) 1968

'Kincaid' 1 Y-Y
(A.H. Ahrens) D.J. Cooper, 1956

'Kinco' 1 Y-Y
(H.R. Bulman, c.1966) Unregistered
'Kingscourt' × ('Fahan' × 'Corlo')

'Kincorth' 3 W-GWW
(Brodie Gardens) Brodie Gardens, 1957
Hybrid between 'Chinese White' and 'Pucelle'
Fl. 115 mm wide or more; perianth segments very broad, blunt, fairly prominently mucronate, spreading or reflexed, plane, smooth, overlapping half; the inner segments more nearly oblong or ovate; corona almost disc-shaped, ribbed, white, tinged with pale yellow and shading to green at base, mouth straight, frilled, rim crenate. AM(e) 1959

'Kindee' 1 W-GWW
(W. Jackson Jr) Jackson's Daffodils, 1979
'Kareela' × 'Karel'; sdlg no. 209/71
Fl. 98 mm wide. Mid-season

'Kindergarten' 3 W-OOR
(D.S. Bell, 1947) D.S. Bell, 1958
Perianth segments pure white; corona disc-shaped, apricot, with red at rim. Syn. 'Enchantment'

'Kindershot' 2 Y-O
(J.N. Hancock & Co., pre-1967) Unregistered

'Kindled' 2 Y-R
(G.L. Wilson, pre-1950)
'Indian Summer' × ('Workman' × 'Trevisky'); sdlg no. 27/183
Perianth segments golden, flushed reddish with age; corona dark red

'Kindly' ?-P
(Alister Clark, pre-1948)

'Kindly Light' 2 Y-O
(F.E. Board) F.E. Board, 1965
'Spry' × 'Craigywarren'
Corona reddish orange

'Kindred' 1 Y-Y
(J.R.Erp) J.R.Erp, 1956
'Bungana' × 'Corlo'

'Kindred' 1 Y-Y
(G.L. Wilson, pre-1962) Unregistered
Corona with rim flanged

'King Albert' 1 Y-Y
(A. Frylink & Sons, pre-1938)
Fl. large; perianth segments clear golden yellow; corona a little darker in tone. 2n=28. AM(Haarlem) 1937

'King Alfred' 1 Y-Y
(J. Kendall, pre-1899)
'Maximus' hybrid
Fl. 98 mm wide, vivid yellow 9A; perianth segments oblong, blunt, inflexed, of strong substance, somewhat twisted, overlapping a quarter; the inner segments ovate, more nearly acute, more strongly twisted; corona cylindrical, smooth, slightly deeper in tone than the perianth, with mouth expanded, rim widely flanged and regularly and deeply notched. 2n=28. FCC 1899, FA(Haarlem) 1921

'King Arthur' 1 Y-Y
(de Graaff Bros, pre-1923)

'King Arthur' 1 Y-Y
(Sir A.P.W. Thomas)

'Kingbird' 2 Y-Y
(G.E. Mitsch) G.E. Mitsch, 1969
('Narvik' × 'Playboy') × 'Velvet Robe'; sdlg no. Y51/4
Perianth segments clear soft yellow, overlapping; corona cup-shaped, deeper in tone than the perianth. Mid-season

'King Bran' 1 Y-Y
(S.J. Bisdee, 1943)
'Crocus' × 'Robert Montgomery'

'King Canute' 4 W-O
(W.F.M. Copeland, pre-1909)
Hybrid between *N. radiiflorus* var. *poetarum* and 'Telamonius Plenus'
Perianth segments pure white; corona segments brilliant orange

'King Cardinal' 2 W-R
(J.L. Richardson, pre-1951)
'Tebourba' × 'Carnsore'
Perianth segments broadly ovate, truncate, slightly mucronate, pure white, a little reflexed, plane, smooth, overlapping one-third; the inner segments more narrowly ovate, more nearly spreading, with margins wavy; corona very shallow bowl-shaped, broad, strongly ribbed, intense bright red, mouth deeply lobed, rim unevenly crenate. Late. 2n=28

'King Christian' 1 Y-Y
(The Brodie of Brodie, pre-1943)
'Ben Alder' × 1Y-Y sdlg
Fl. deep yellow; corona large, expanded, heavily frilled

'King Cole' 1 Y-Y
(L. Buckland, pre-1936)

'King Connor' 1 Y-Y
(G.L. Wilson, pre-1928)
Fl. deep gold; corona with rim flanged and dentate.

'Kingcraft' 8 W-O
(P.D. Williams, pre-1915)
Fls usually 2 per stem; perianth segments very broad, ivory white, deeply overlapping; corona shallow, lightly ribbed, reddish orange. 2n=24. AM(m) 1925, AM(Haarlem) 1926, *AM(g) 1930

'Kingcup' 2 Y-? (a)
(C.L. Adams, pre-1908)
'Golden Spur' × 'Ornatus'
See also 'King Cup'

'King Cup' 2 Y-?
Syn. of 'Kingcup'

'Kingcup' 1 Y-Y
(W.A. Noton) Unregistered

'King Cyrus' 3 W-? (b)
(W. Welchman, pre-1913)

'King David' 1 W-W
(W.A. Grace, pre-1936)

'King Dick' 1 W-? (b)
(R. Dick, pre-1930)

'Kingdom' 2 W-WWY
(W.A. Milner, pre 1913)
Fl. 89 mm wide, creamy white; perianth segments overlapping; corona with rim becoming pale sulphur yellow, mouth widely expanded, rim lightly flanged. Resembles a tall 'Lord Kitchener'. AM(Haarlem) 1914

'Kingdom' 2 W-Y
(?West & Fell, pre-1927)
Corona bright lemon yellow

'King Edgar' 2 Y-? (a)
(W. Welchman, pre-1927)

'King Edward' 9 W-YYR
Syn. of 'Almira'

'King Edward VII' 9 W-YYR
Syn. of 'Almira'

'King Edward VIII' 1 Y-Y
Syn. of 'Garden Love'

'King Ellimatta' 1 Y-Y
(L.P. Dettman) L.P. Dettman, 1977
'Arctic Gold' × 'King Kanto'; sdlg no. 3/73
Fl. 101 mm wide; perianth segments vivid yellow 13A; corona cylindrical, slightly darker in tone (15A)

than the perianth. Early. Resembles a larger and more deeply coloured 'King Kanto'

'King Emperor' 1 Y-Y
(W. Welchman, pre-1913)
Fl. 102 mm wide, soft yellow

'King Ethelbert' 1 W-W
(F.D.B. Cobb, pre-1953)

'Kingfisher' 5
(pre-1907)

'Kingfisher' 3 W-GYR
(J.L. Richardson) J.L. Richardson, 1958
'Corofin' × 'Mahmoud'
Perianth segments roundish, snowy white; corona yellow, with green at base and cherry red at rim

'King Frost' 3 W-? (b or c)
(Sir A.P.W. Thomas, pre-1930)

'King George' 1 Y-Y
(R.A. van der Schoot, pre-1923)

'King George' 9 W-YYR
(J. Segers, pre-1930)
'Poetarum' hybrid
Resembles an improved 'Ornatus'. Mid-season

'King George V' 3 W-YYO
(C.G. van Tubergen, pre-1913)
'Ornatus' × 'Gloria Mundi'
Fl. 76 mm wide; perianth segments white, overlapping two-thirds; corona very shallow bowl-shaped, sulphur yellow, with a very narrow band of reddish orange at rim. Mid-season to late

'King Haakon' 1 Y-Y
(C.J. Stijnman, pre-1952)
TGA(Haarlem) 1952

'King Hal' 1 Y-Y
(G.H. Engleheart, pre-1910)

'Kingham' 1 Y-Y
(Clive Postles, 1981) Clive Postles Daffodils, 1995
'Golden Vale' × 'Camelot'; sdlg no. 1-17-76
Fl. forming a double triangle, 120 mm wide; perianth segments deep yellow, with margins slightly incurving; corona funnel-shaped, slightly darker in tone than the perianth and becoming near orange at maturity, mouth lobed and frilled, rim rolled. Mid-season

'King Harold' 1 Y-Y
(C. Dawson, pre-1915)
Fl. golden yellow, of good substance; perianth segments slightly twisted; corona slender, neatly frilled, with rim rolled. Resembles 'King Alfred'

'King Harold' 9 W-YYR
(J. Segers, pre-1930)
'Poetarum' hybrid

'King Hit' 2 Y-YOO
(D.J. Jackson, 1979) Jackson's Daffodils, 1989
'Ra' × 'Yoone'; sdlg no. 119/79
Fl. 100 mm wide; perianth segments broadly ovate, rounded at apex, brilliant greenish yellow 6A, with slight white mucro, spreading, smooth, overlapping half or more; the inner segments truncate and only very slightly mucronate, shouldered at base, a little inflexed, with margins slightly wavy; corona bowl-shaped, orange (28A) paling to yellow at base, lightly frilled. Early to mid-season

'Kinghorn' 1 Y-Y
(D.S. Bell) D.S. Bell, 1979
'David Bell' self pollinated
Fl. 103 mm wide; perianth segments broad; corona expanded, frilled, with rim dentate. Mid-season

'King Kanto' 1 Y-Y
(Mrs C.O. Fairbairn, c.1960) Unregistered

'King Ki' 1 Y-Y
(pre-1971) Unregistered

'Kinglake' 1 Y-Y
(H.A. Brown, 1943)
Fl. forming a double triangle, clear golden yellow; perianth segments broadly ovate, with white mucro, spreading, with upper half somewhat incurved, plane, smooth, overlapping half; the inner segments a little inflexed, with margins wavy; corona cylindrical, mouth flared and even, rim notched and crenate. Late

'King Lear' 1 Y-Y
(de Graaff Bros, pre-1914)
Perianth segments clear canary yellow; corona darker in tone, with rim frilled. AM(Haarlem) 1915

'King Lear' 1 W-W
(Barr & Sons, pre-1923)

'King Lemon' 2 Y-O
(pre-1932)
Perianth segments lemon yellow; corona shallow, widely expanded, scarlet-orange. AM(Haarlem) 1932

'King Leo' 1 Y-Y
(pre-1927)

'Kinglet' 7 Y-O
(G.E. Mitsch) G.E. Mitsch, 1959
'Narvik' × *N. jonquilla*; sdlg no. O60/5
Fls 1-3 per stem; perianth segments ovate, acute, bright yellow, spreading, plane or occasionally slightly twisted, overlapping at base only; the inner segments more often and more markedly twisted; corona cup-shaped, loosely ribbed, with mouth straight and rim widely crenate

'King Louis' 1 Y-Y
(C. Dawson, pre-1916)

'King Lud' 1 Y-Y
(G.L. Wilson, pre-1932)
Fl. dark golden yellow

'Kingly Pride' 1 Y-Y
(Wrigley, pre-1913)

'King Max' 1 Y-Y
(T. Batson, pre-1928)
?'Maximus' × 'King Alfred'

'King Midas' 2 Y-Y
Syn. of 'Armynel'

'King of Clubs' 3 W-R
(Mrs R.O. Backhouse, pre-1921)
Perianth segments very broad, squarish at apex, prominently mucronate, snow white, spreading, with margins slightly incurling at apex, smooth, overlapping half; the inner segments sometimes truncate, only very slightly mucronate, inflexed, sometimes with lower margin notched and "thumbed"; corona small bowl-shaped, ribbed, deep cherry red, mouth split in places and overlapping, frilled. Mid-season to late

'King of Diamonds' 9 W-R
(G.L. Wilson, pre-1935)
'Dactyl' × 'Ace of Diamonds'
Perianth segments pure white; corona vivid red

'King of Fire' 2 Y-R
(C. Goodson, pre-1927)

'King of Hearts' 2 Y-R
(A.M. Wilson, pre-1935)
'Damson' hybrid
Perianth segments rich yellow; corona red. Resembles 'Damson' in corona colour

'King of May' 1 Y-Y
(G.L. Wilson, pre-1923)
'Preston' hybrid × 'King Alfred'
Fl. large, golden yellow. Late

'King of Poets' 9 W-YYR
(J.H. Hinsby, 1928)
'Banjo Patterson' hybrid

'King of Spain' 5
(Spanish origin)
Selection by Peter Barr (c.1898) from wild-collected material

Resembles 'Queen of Spain' but with the corona mouth expanded. A name that cannot be applied with any certainty to any one of several clones of *N. x johnstonii*

'King of the Netherlands' 2 Y-O
(W. Backhouse, pre-1869)
Perianth segments ovate, sulphur yellow, twisted or with margins incurled or wavy, separated; corona broad funnel-shaped, stained orange, mouth straight, lightly frilled. Syn. Incomparabilis Sulphureus 'King of the Netherlands'. "Absorbed" 'C.H.Dee'

'King of the North' 1 Y-Y
(The Brodie of Brodie, *c*.1909)
'King Alfred' × 'Glory of Noordwijk'

'King of the Poets' 9 W-YYR
(W.B. Hartland, pre-1913)

'King of the Poets' 9 W-YYR
(L. Buckland, pre-1914)

'King of the West' 2 W-? (b)
(E. & J.C. Martin, pre-1931)

'King Peter' 2 Y-? (a)
(Miss K.M. Hinchliff, pre-1941)
'Golden Pedestal' × 'Fortune'

'King Pin' 2 Y-OOR
(R.C.A. Tombleson) R.C.A. Tombleson, 1966
Fl. 115 mm wide. Mid-season. Resembles 'Playboy' but with the perianth segments slightly reflexed and the corona less widely expanded

'King Priam' 1 W-Y
(Barr & Sons, pre-1913)
Perianth segments creamy white, stained canary yellow at base; corona flared, golden yellow, with rim frilled

'King Robert' 1 Y-Y
(J.E. Exley, pre-1938)

'King's Bowl' 2 W-Y
(A.E. Lowe, pre-1927)
Corona bowl-shaped, deep golden yellow

'King's Bridge' 1 Y-Y
(Brian S. Duncan) Rathowen Daffodils, 1980
'Kingscourt' × 'Banbridge'; sdlg no. 76
Fl. 120 mm wide, deep golden yellow. Mid-season

'King's Counsel' 1 Y-Y
(J.E. Exley, pre-1938)

'Kingscourt' 1 Y-Y
(J.L. Richardson, pre-1938)
'Royalist' × 'Crocus'

Fl. 111 mm wide; perianth segments broadly ovate, blunt, vivid yellow 9A, slightly inflexed, smooth, overlapping half; the inner segments more narrowly ovate, shouldered at base, inflexed and slightly twisted; corona ribbed, rich golden yellow, with mouth expanded and lightly frilled, rim flanged, deeply notched and crenate. Mid-season. 2n=28. PC 1941, AM(e) 1942, FCC(e) 1947, AM(Haarlem) 1949, *AM(g) 1968, *FCC(g) 1977, AGM 1993

'King's Cross' 2 Y-? (a)
(H.P. Zwetsloot, pre-1948)
AM(Haarlem) 1948

'King's Crown' 1 Y-Y
(Mrs F.S. Foote, pre-1940)

'Kingsdown' 2 W-W
(F.D.B. Cobb, pre-1954)

'King's Dream' 2 W-P
(R.C.A. Tombleson) R.C.A. Tombleson, 1966
Late

'King's Favourite' 1 Y-Y
(W. Balch, pre-1933)

'Kingsford Smith' 2 W-? (b)
(P. van Deursen, pre-1930)

'King's Gold' 1 Y-Y
(W. Balch, pre-1933)

'King's Grove' 1 Y-O
(Brian S. Duncan) Rathowen Daffodils, 1987
'Bunclody' open pollinated
Corona opening yellowish orange, becoming deep orange. Mid-season

'King Size' 11a Y-Y
(J. Gerritsen & Son) J. Gerritsen & Son, 1969
'Gold Collar' × 'Golden Harvest'
Perianth segments broadly ovate, blunt, only very slightly mucronate, light greenish yellow 4B, spreading or a little reflexed, plane, overlapping one-third; corona split to base, the six segments two-thirds the length of the perianth segments, opposite and overlying them and equally broad, vivid yellow 14A; the outer three segments smooth, deeply bi-lobed, with the lobes overlapping, wavy; the inner three segments ribbed, frilled. Early to mid-season

'Kingsley' 9 W-GYR
(G.H. Engleheart, pre-1910)

'Kingsley Fairbridge' 1 W-Y
(G.H. Engleheart, pre-1927)
Fl. 114 mm wide; perianth segments creamy white, overlapping half; corona sulphur yellow, with mouth

somewhat expanded. Mid-season to late. ?See also 'Fairbridge'

'Kingsmill' 1 Y-Y
(du Plessis Bros) du Plessis Bros, 1976
Fl. 115 mm wide, golden yellow. Resembles a larger-flowered 'Golden Top'

'Kingsnorth Reeve' 1 Y-Y
(F.H.Chapman, pre-1913)
See also 'Kingsnorth Rex'

'Kingsnorth Rex' 1 Y-Y
Syn. of 'Kingsnorth Reeve'

'King's Norton' 1 Y-Y
(J. Pope, pre-1903)
Fl. large, rich golden yellow; corona with mouth frilled. AM 1903, FCC 1905

'King Sol' 2 Y-? (a)
(Mrs R.O. Backhouse, pre-1921)

'King Solomon' 1 Y-Y
(W.F.M. Copeland, pre-1913)
Fl. 89 mm wide, very pale sulphur yellow. Resembles 'J.B.M.Camm' in form

'Kings Pipe' 2 Y-P
(R.A. Scamp) R.A. Scamp, 1994
'Daydream' open pollinated; sdlg no. 13
Fl. rounded, 85 mm wide; perianth segments broadly ovate, pale yellow, smooth; corona smooth, opening buff pink, becoming deeper in tone, frilled. Mid-season

'King's Pirate' 3 W-O
(Mrs R.O. Backhouse, pre-1921)
Perianth segments slightly reflexed; corona mid-orange, shading to bright reddish orange at rim

'King's Ransom' 1 Y-Y
(J.L. Richardson, pre-1950)
'Kingscourt' × 'Goldcourt'
Fl. forming a double triangle; perianth segments very broadly ovate, blunt, slightly mucronate, spreading, smooth, concave, overlapping half; the inner segments more narrowly ovate, square-shouldered at base, with margins wavy; corona cylindrical, smooth, mouth ribbed and widely expanded, rim regularly and very deeply notched and crenate, the crenations each folded back at the margins and appearing to be dentate. PC 1950

'King's Robe' 2 Y-? (a)
(D.S. Bell) D.S. Bell, 1957

'King's Stag' 1 Y-Y
(J.W. Blanchard) J.W. Blanchard, 1974
'Tollard Royal' × 'Arctic Gold'

Fl. 110 mm wide. Mid-season

'King's Sutton' 5 Y-Y
(Alister Clark, pre-1949)
? × *N. triandrus* var. *loiseleurii*

'Kingston' 2 W-Y
(Sir F.C. Stern, pre-1948)
*AM(g) 1951

'Kingston Flyer' 1 Y-Y
(D.S. Bell, 1965) D.S. Bell, 1978
Fl. 110 mm wide, deep gold; corona frilled. Mid-season. Resembles 'David Bell' but with a longer corona

'King Sualtach' 3 W-? (b)
(J.W.A. Lefeber, pre-1943)

'Kingsworthy' 2 Y-Y
(J.L. Richardson) Mrs H.K. Richardson, 1963
'Kingscourt' × 'Ceylon'
Fl. deep golden yellow; perianth segments very broad; corona mouth expanded, with rim flanged and deeply dentate

'King Tut' 2 W-P
(Mrs H.K. Richardson) M.J. Jefferson-Brown, 1975
Sdlg × 'Rose Caprice'
Corona salmon and pink. Mid-season

'King Umberto'
Syn. of *N. pseudonarcissus* subsp. *pseudonarcissus*

'Kingurra' 1 W-W
(D.J. Jackson, 1977) Jackson's Daffodils, 1989
Sdlg 19/70 × 'Mercedes'; sdlg no. 67/77
Fl. 107 mm wide; perianth segments broadly ovate, acute, greenish white 155C; corona cylindrical, with mouth straight and slightly frilled. Mid-season

'King Volmer' 1 Y-Y
(A.M. Wilson, pre-1908)

'King William' 1 Y-Y
(Barr & Sons, pre-1913)

'Kinleith' 3 W-W
(R. Hyde) R. Hyde, 1957

'Kinloch' 1 Y-Y
(A. Hopkirk, pre-1927)
Fl. primrose yellow; corona darker in tone than the perianth

'Kinross' 1 W-? (b)
(W. Balch, pre-1933)

'Kinsale' 2 W-W
(J.L. Richardson, pre-1937)

'White Sentinel' self pollinated
Fl. snow white; perianth segments broad; corona with rim rolled and regularly dentate

'Kinsman' 3 Y-YYO
(S.A. Free) S.A. Free, 1976
'Merry King' hybrid; sdlg no. 69-12
Fl. 100 mm wide; perianth segments yellow; corona yellow, shading to deep orange at rim. Mid-season. Resembles a deeper-coloured 'Merry King'

'Kintamani' 1 W-Y
(A.H. Ahrens) J.A.O'More, 1957
'Sincerity' × 'Crocus'

'Kintessack' 3 W-W
(Brodie Gardens) Brodie Gardens, 1959
'Pucelle' × 'Chinese White'
Perianth segments broadly ovate, slightly reflexed, smooth; corona ice white, neatly frilled. Tall

'Kiowa' 7 W-W
(E.C. Powell, pre-1946)

'Kipi' 3 Y-R
(W. Jackson Jr, c.1964) Unregistered
Sdlg × 'Dimity'

'Kipling' 3 W-GYR
(Brian S. Duncan) Rathowen Daffodils, 1978
'Merlin' open pollinated; sdlg no. 104
Fl. 94 mm wide. Mid-season. Scented. Resembles 'Merlin' but with a more clearly defined band of red at corona rim

'Kiri' 2 W-YYO
(P. Phillips) P. Phillips, 1971
Fl. 103 mm wide; corona spreading, lemon yellow, with orange at rim. Mid-season

'Kirkinriola' 3 W-GYO
(Carncairn Daffodils) Carncairn Daffodils, 1986
'Merlin' × 'Fairmile'; sdlg no. 1/7/73
Perianth segments opening creamy white, becoming whiter; corona with rim dentate. Late

'Kirklington' 2 W-P
(Mrs J. Abel Smith) Mrs J. Abel Smith, 1979
'Chelsea China' × 'Maiden's Blush'; sdlg no. E3/82
Fl. 115 mm wide; corona deep rose pink. Mid-season. Resembles a much larger-flowered 'Chelsea China'

'Kirri billy' 1 Y-Y
Syn. of 'Kirribilly'

'Kirribilly' 1 Y-Y
(Mrs E. Murray, c.1974) Unregistered
See also 'Kirri billy'

'Kirsten' 3 W-WPP
Syn. of 'Kerstin'

'Kirwee' 3 W-R
(G. Lewis) D.S. Bell, 1955

'Kiskadee' 3 W-YYW
(Mrs H.K. Richardson) Mrs H.K. Richardson, 1972
'Crepello' open pollinated

'Kismet' 2 W-? (b)
(G.H. Engleheart, pre-1914)

'Kismet' 2 Y-R
(T.H. Piper, 1953)
'Royal Mail' × 'Carbineer' hybrid

'Ki Son' 1 Y-Y
(E.W. Philpott) E.W. Philpott, 1959
Perianth segments pale yellow; corona lemon yellow. Early. Resembles 'Royalist' but with longer and broader perianth segments

'Kiss-in-the-Ring' 2 W-?
Syn. of 'Daylight'

'Kissproof' 2 Y-O
(Warnaar & Co.) Warnaar & Co., 1964
Perianth segments greenish yellow (4D); corona vivid reddish orange. Late. Sunproof. AM(Haarlem) 1964

'Kitcat' 3 W-? (h)
(A.M. Wilson, pre-1948)

'Kite' 5 W-Y
(M. Fowlds) G.E. Mitsch, 1971
N. poeticus × *N. triandrus*
Fl. 70 mm wide; perianth segments with margins wavy; corona yellow, with a darker tone at rim. Late

'Kit Halford' 2 W-Y
(W.M. Spry, pre-1975) Unregistered
'Dependable' × 'Big Keith'
Corona creamy yellow. Tall. Early

'Kithara' 9 W-YYR
(S.J. Bisdee, 1938) S.J. Bisdee, 1956
'Pierre Loti' × 'Minuet'

'Kit Hill' 7 Y-YWW
(R.A.Scamp) R.A.Scamp, 1995
'Aircastle' × *N. jonquilla*; sdlg no. S107
Fl. usually 2 per stem, 64 mm wide; perianth segments broad, roundish, soft pale yellow; the inner segments with slight midrib showing; corona cup-shaped, small, with rounded sides, opening soft pale yellow, becoming ivory white with yellow at base, rim neatly crenate. Late. Scented. With many secondary stems

'Kitiwa' 2 W-Y
?Syn. of 'Kittiwake'

'Kit Marlowe' 9 W-YYR
(Cartwright & Goodwin, pre-1908)

'Kitrina' 3 W-R
(H.R. Bulman) H.R. Bulman, 1956
'Rethel' × 'Wonderlight'

'Kitten' 6 Y-O
(C.F. Coleman) M.J. Jefferson-Brown, 1962
'Alight' × 'Charity May'
Perianth segments oval, reflexed; corona broad, shallow

'Kittiwake' 2 W-Y
(P.D. Williams, pre-1907)
Corona light lemon yellow, a little frilled. ?See also 'Kitiwa'

'Kitty' 6 W-Y
(C.F. Coleman, pre-1942)
'Mitylene' × *N. cyclamineus*
Perianth segments ovate, ivory white, a little reflexed, with margins lightly incurved, overlapping a quarter; corona cylindrical, short, smooth at base, ribbed towards mouth, light greenish yellow 3D, paling to ivory white at base, mouth straight or a little flared, rim irregularly and minutely notched

'Kitty' 2 W-O
?Syn. of 'Kitty Campbell'

'Kitty Campbell' 2 W-O
(J.N. Hancock & Co., pre-1949)
Corona with rim closely and deeply notched, as if fringed. Syn. ? 'Kitty'

'Kitty Crowley' 2 W-? (b or c)
(Miss K.M. Hinchliff, pre-1941)

'Kitty Hawk' 3 W-? (b)
(Warnaar & Co., pre-1930)

'Kitty Lapp' 9 W-YYR
(W.A.Bender, 1980) W.A.Bender, 1996
'Milan' × 'Cantabile'
Fl. 65 mm wide; perianth segments broadly ovate, slightly reflexed, with margins incurling; the outer segments touching one another at margin; corona very shallow bowl-shaped, brilliant greenish yellow 6C, with a narrow band of orange-red (41A) at rim, mouth frilled. Late

'Kiwanis' 1 Y-Y
(G.L. Wilson, 1956) G. Zandbergen-Terwegen, 1966
Mid-season. Resembles 'Dutch Master'

'Kiwi Boy' 1 W-? (b)
(A.H. Ahrens) J.S. Leitch, 1955

'Kiwi Charm' 2 WWY-W
(M.E.Brogden) Unregistered

'Kiwi Gal' 2 Y-Y
(R.G. Cull) Hokorawa Daffodils, 1987
'Showtime' × 'Galway'; sdlg no. R79/1
Fl. vivid yellow 9A. Mid-season

'Kiwi Gold' 1 Y-Y
(J.S. Leitch) J.S. Leitch, 1965
Fl. 115 mm wide

'Kiwi Gold' 2 Y-Y
(R.G.Cull, pre-1996) Unregistered

'Kiwi Invader'
Unregistered
Seed parent of 'Stardom'

'Kiwi Magic' 4 W-Y
(Max Hamilton) Koanga Daffodils, 1989
'Windblown' hybrid × (sdlg 115-58 × sdlg 4); sdlg no. 43-86
Fl. 110 mm wide; perianth and other petaloid segments in several whorls, very broadly ovate, slightly mucronate, white, plane or a little concave, overlapping half; the three outer whorls more or less spreading; the inner whorls strongly inflexed; corona segments not much shorter than the petaloid segments and interspersed among all but the two outer whorls, opening lemon yellow, becoming creamy yellow, with margins wavy. Mid-season. FCC(e)(NZ) 1991

'Kiwi Mist' 1 W-W
(R.G. Cull) Hokorawa Daffodils, 1987
'Ave' × 'Snowdean'; sdlg no. R83/3
Mid-season

'Kiwi Moon' 2 Y-Y
(G.W.E. Brogden, 1981) Brogden Bulbs, 1991
('Park Royal' × 'Dunkeld') × 'Loch Hope'; sdlg no. NT41
Fl. 100 mm wide; perianth segments very broad, roundish, mid-yellow, smooth and of strong substance; corona more-or-less cylindrical, slightly deeper in tone than the perianth and touched orange with age, rim entire

'Kiwi Red' 2 Y-R
(A.W. Chappell) A.W. Chappell, 1992
'Belzone' × 'Salute'; sdlg no. F-1-1
Fl. 90 mm wide; perianth segments ovate; corona flared, with rim crenate. Mid-season

'Kiwi Ruler' 3 W-O
(M.E.Brogden, pre-1995) Unregistered
'Sweet Luck' × 'Bandit'

'Kiwi Solstice' 4 Y-R
(M. Hamilton) Koanga Daffodils, 1993
Fl. 85 mm wide; perianth and other petaloid segments very broadly ovate, brilliant yellow 12B; corona segments interspersed, orange-red (30B). Mid-season

'Kiwi Sunrise' 2 Y-YOO
(G.J.Phillips) J.N.Hancock & Co., 1997
Sdlg no. 78-11-2
Perianth segments spreading, plane; corona orange, shading to a darker tone towards mouth, with mouth expanded and frilled. Early

'Kiwi Sunset' 4 Y-R
(Koanga Daffodils) Koanga Daffodils, 1995
Fl. 95 mm wide; perianth and other petaloid segments in four whorls, broadly ovate, brilliant yellow 12B; corona segments orange-red (30B). Mid-season

'K.J.H.' 2 W-P
(G.C.Yeates, pre-1987) Unregistered

'K.J.Heazlewood' 2 W-P
(R.H.Glover, pre-1993) Unregistered

'Klamath' 2 W-Y
(G.E. Mitsch) G.E. Mitsch, 1960
'Tunis' × 'Penvose'
Fl. 115 mm wide; perianth segments ivory white; corona opening pale lemon yellow, becoming buff yellow. Mid-season. Resembles a large-flowered 'Penvose'

'Klaxon' 2 Y-R
(W.M. Spry, pre-1975) Unregistered
'Winsome' × Ronalds sdlg

'Klingo' 2 Y-R
(G.L. Wilson, pre-1941)
'Rosslare' open pollinated

'Klondyke' 8 Y-Y
(R. van der Schoot & Son, pre-1907)
Poetaz
Fls up to 7 per stem; corona rich golden yellow, darker in tone than the perianth

'Klondyke Gold' 1 Y-Y
(G. Lewis) D.S. Bell, 1955
'Gold Tray' × 'Cromarty'

'Kluto' 1 W-? (b)
(de Graaff Bros, pre-1927)

'Knapdale' 1 W-W
(G.L. Wilson) E. Longford, 1969
'Empress of Ireland' × 'Knowehead'

'Knave of Diamonds' 9 W-R
(G.L. Wilson, pre-1935)
'Dactyl' × 'Ace of Diamonds'
Fl. rounded; perianth segments snow white; corona deep red. Resembles a taller and more vigorous 'Ace of Diamonds'

'Knave of Hearts' 3 W-? (b)
(G.H. Engleheart, pre-1913)

'Knight Errant' 1 W-Y
(G.P. Haydon, pre-1907)
'Monarch' × 'Madame de Graaff'
Corona lemon yellow

'Knight Errant' 1 Y-Y
(R.H. Bath, c.1933)

'Knight Errant' 2 Y-OOR
(F.E. Board) F.E. Board, 1965
'Craigywarren' × 'Air Marshal'
Mid-season

'Knighton' 2 Y-O
(A.M. Wilson, pre-1933)
Perianth segments with margins slightly incurved; corona reddish orange, with rim dentate

'Knight Royal' 1 Y-Y
(R.H. Glover) R.H. Glover, 1968
'Melissa' × 'Golden Rapture'

'Knightsbridge' 1 Y-O
(J.S.B. Lea, 1983) Clive Postles Daffodils, 1993
'Ballindalloch' × 'Glen Clova'; sdlg no. 1-7-78
Fl. forming a double triangle, 90 mm wide; perianth segments ovate, deep yellow, spreading; corona cylindrical, orange, with mouth flared and rim crenate. Early. Sunproof

'Knight Templar' 2 W-? (b)
(H. Backhouse, pre-1908)

'Knight Templar' 2 W-Y
(A.G. Thompson) A.G. Thompson, 1960
'John Evelyn' × 'Daisy Schäffer'
Fl. 102 mm wide; perianth segments narrow, acute; corona sulphur yellow. Mid-season. Resembles 'Daisy Schäffer' but with a more widely expanded corona

'Knightwick' 2 W-P
(J.L. Richardson) M.J. Jefferson-Brown, 1963
'Rosewell' × 'Rose Caprice'
Fl. forming a double triangle; perianth segments broadly ovate, blunt, slightly mucronate, spreading; the inner segments more narrowly ovate, shouldered at base, with margins a little wavy; corona funnel-shaped, smooth or lightly ribbed, rich rose pink, paler towards base, mouth straight and frilled, with rim irregularly notched

'Knill' 3 W-? (b)
(A.M. Wilson, pre-1950)

'Knipp' 2 Y-YOO
(P.D. Williams, pre-1927)

'Knockanure' 2 O-R
(Carncairn Daffodils) Carncairn Daffodils, 1994
'Glencraig' × 'Fireraiser'; sdlg no. 2/11/80
Fl. rounded, 84 mm wide; perianth segments very broadly ovate, blunt or somewhat truncate, orange, with white mucro, spreading, smooth, overlapping one-third to a half; the inner segments rounded at apex, a little inflexed; corona narrow bowl-shaped, ribbed, orange-red (33B), mouth straight, split in places and overlapping, neatly frilled. Mid-season

'Knockbane' 2 W-W
(G.L. Wilson) G.L. Wilson, 1960
'Tryst' × ('Greenland' × 'Saint Mary')

'Knockboy' 1 Y-Y
(G.L. Wilson, pre-1927)
'King of the North' × 'Sorley Boy'
Fl. rich yellow; corona with rim flanged and frilled

'Knockdolian' 1 W-W
(A.M. Wilson, pre-1948)
Sdlg × 'Samaria' or 'Samite'
Early

'Knocklayde' 3 W-GWW
(A.E.Robinson) Carncairn Daffodils, 1994
'Cool Crystal' × 'Delos'; sdlg no. 3/51/79
Fl. 98 mm wide, greenish white (155A); perianth ovate, blunt, fairly prominently mucronate, spreading, concave and with margins sometimes incurling at apex, overlapping half; the inner segments only a little more narrowly ovate, sightly inflexed; corona shallow bowl-shaped, strongly ribbed, with moderate yellowish green 138A in the tube, mouth tightly frilled. Late. Resembles a better-poised 'Cool Crystal' with the corona more tightly frilled

'Knockmoroon' 3 W-? (b)
(R.V. Favell, pre-1946)

'Knockomie' 2 W-P
(Brodie Gardens) Brodie Gardens, 1957
Hybrid between 'Loch Maree' and 'Scotch Rose'
Perianth segments pure white; corona funnel-shaped, rich apricot yellow, tinged with rosy salmon pink, mouth flared and frilled

'Knockstacken' 1 Y-Y
(W.J. Dunlop, c.1965) Jan Dalton, 1991
('Goldcourt' × 'Kingscourt') self pollinated
Fl. deep golden yellow. Mid-season

'Knoll Hill' 2 W-Y
(D.A.B. Harries) D.A.B. Harries, 1969
'Easter Moon' × 'Tudor Minstrel'

'Knowehead' 2 W-W
(G.L. Wilson, pre-1954)
'Cotterton' × 'Broughshane'
Fl. 97 mm wide, greenish white (155A); perianth segments very broadly ovate, blunt, slightly mucronate, spreading, plane or a little concave, smooth, overlapping half; the inner segments more narrowly ovate, shouldered at base, slightly inflexed, with margins slightly wavy; corona cylindrical, angled, mouth expanded, with rim rolled, widely and very shallowly crenate. 2n=28. AM(e) 1969, *AM(g) 1970

'Knoydart' 1 W-W
(G.L. Wilson) E. Longford, 1966
Sdlg 33/51 ('Courage' × 'Broughshane') × 'Empress of Ireland'
Fl. 102 mm wide

'Knut Hamsun' 1 Y-Y
(de Graaff Bros, pre-1928)
Syn. 'Yellow Hammer'

'Koa'
(W.D. Burns, pre-1927)

'Koa' 1 W-? (b or c)
(N.R.W. Thomas, c.1930)

'Koala' 2 W OOR
(W. Jackson Jr, 1970) Unregistered
Sdlg 83/14 × ('Signal Light' × 'Jo'); sdlg no. 41/70

'Kobie' 2 Y-O
(K.B. Burns, 1954) K.B. Burns, 1964
Mid-season. Resembles 'Tamino' but with broader perianth segments and an orange corona

'Kodiak' 2 W-P
(Elise Havens) G.E. Mitsch, 1979
'Precedent' × 'Carita'; sdlg no. FEJ8/1
Fl. 114 mm wide; corona lavender pink at base, with coppery pink at rim. Mid-season

'Koh-i-noor' 3 W-? (b)
(Mrs R.O. Backhouse, pre-1921)

'Koh-i-noor' 2 W-GOO
Syn. of 'Oranje Bruid'

'Koko' 1 Y-Y
(J.L. Richardson, pre-1927)
Fl. yellow; corona widely expanded, slightly deeper in tone than the perianth

'Koko' 2 Y-R
(J.S. Leitch) J.S. Leitch, 1957

'Koko' 2 Y-R
(R.H.Glover, pre-1993) Unregistered

'Kokoda' 2 W-P
(H.A. Brown, 1941) J.N. Hancock & Co., 1955
Perianth segments cream; corona long, pinky orange buff, heavily frilled. Late. Syn. 'Kakoda'

'Kokoda' 2 W-YYO
(S.J. Bisdee, 1944)
'Mitylene' × 'Jean Hood'
Perianth segments creamy; corona pinky apricot buff, heavily frilled

'Kokopelli' 7 Y-Y
(Robert Spotts) Robert Spotts, 1993
'Sundial' open pollinated; sdlg no. 84-87
Fls 2-4 per stem, rounded, 37 mm wide; corona opening with green at base, becoming self yellow, darker in tone than the perianth. Resembles a 'Sundial' of heavier substance

'Kolo' 5 Y-Y
(S.J. Bisdee, 1943) S.J. Bisdee, 1956
'Robert Berkeley' × *N. triandrus*

'Kona' 3 W-O
(J.T. Gray, pre-1949)
Corona very shallow bowl-shaped, reddish orange

'Konia' 2 W-W
(A.M. Wilson, pre-1931)
'Albatross' × 'Mrs Robert Sydenham'

'Koning David' 8 W-O
(pre-1798)

'Koningin Astrid' 3 W-? (b)
(G. Lubbe & Son, pre-1935)
Syn. 'Queen Astrid'. AM(Haarlem) 1935

'Koningin Nedelander' 8 Y-O
(pre-1885)
Fls large, of good substance; perianth segments clear yellow; corona bright orange

'Konings Wapen' 8 Y-Y
(pre-1807)
Fl. sulphur yellow

'Konini' 2 W-W
(J.S. Leitch) J.S. Leitch, 1967
Fl. 124 mm wide

'Kontiki' 2 W-P
(J.N. Hancock & Co., c.1968) Unregistered

'Kookaburra' 2 W-Y
(O. Ronalds) M. Gardiner, 1956
Perianth segments pure white; corona golden, with rim dentate

'Koolite' 2 YYW-WWY
(J.N.Hancock & Co., 1977) Unregistered
'Chartwell' × 'Rushlight'; sdlg no. 41/77H
Perianth segments bright sulphur yellow, with dwhite at base; corona opening sulphur yellow, becoming white, with yellow at rim and with the rim dentate. Tall. Mid-season

'Koomela' 2 W-YOO
(S.J. Bisdee, 1945) S.J. Bisdee, 1956
'Hades' × 'Red Crusader'

'Koomooloo' 2 W-W
(Jackson's Daffodils, 1985) Jackson's Daffodils, 1995
Sdlg 120/79 × 'Who's Who'; sdlg no. 115/85
Fl. 120 mm wide; perianth segments yellowish white 155B, spreading, plane; corona cylindrical, narrow, very slightly darker in tone than the perianth (155A). Mid-season to late

'Koonya' 2 W-ORR
(S.J. Bisdee, 1953)
'Kilworth' × 'Nacooma'

'Koonya' 2 W-W
(J.N. Hancock & Co., c.1966) Unregistered
Corona somewhat pinkish. Mid-season to late

'Koonya' 2 Y-WWY
(J.N.Hancock & Co., pre-1995) Unregistered

'Kootara' 1 W-P
(S.J. Bisdee) S.J. Bisdee, 1956
'Galah' × 'Rosario'

'Kooyong' 2 W-W
(H.A. Brown, 1938) J.N. Hancock & Co., 1960
Fl. pure white. Mid-season

'Kopi' 3 W-? (b)
(The Brodie of Brodie, pre-1930)
'Bernardino' × 'Sunstar'

'Kopi' 3 Y-ORR
(W. Jackson Jr) W. Jackson Jr, 1968
'Dimity' × sdlg 187/52; sdlg no. 42/64
Perianth segments deep yellow; corona bright red, paling to orange at base

'Kopriva' 2 W-O
(D. Blanchard, 1936)
'Fortune' × Copeland sdlg 31/44A
Corona reddish orange

'Koranga' 1 Y-Y
(S.J. Bisdee, 1940)
'Pilgrimage' × 'Fahan'

'Korea' 1 Y-Y
(Mrs F.E.W. Hanger, pre-1950)
Fl. 115 mm wide; perianth segments vivid yellow 9B, smooth or slightly ribbed; corona slightly ribbed, a little darker in tone (12A) than the perianth, mouth expanded and frilled, with rim flanged and dentate. *AM(g) 1955

'Korenne' 2 W-O
(P. van Deursen, pre-1953)

'Koritza' 2 W-Y
(S.J. Bisdee, 1945)
'Hades' × 'Red Crusader'

'Koroline Kroow' 2
(pre-1915)

'Koromiko' 1 W-? (b)
(New Zealand origin) Parr's Nurseries, 1958

'Koromo' 1 Y-Y
(H.G. Cross) H.G. Cross, 1984
'Chillion' × 'Warbin'; sdlg no. 23-5
Fl. golden yellow; perianth segments broadly ovate, blunt, with white mucro, spreading, plane, overlapping half; the inner segments a little more narrowly ovate, slightly inflexed, with margins wavy; corona funnel-shaped, with mouth slightly flared and deeply frilled. Early

'Kortright' 2 W-P
(Alister Clark, 1929) T. Morrison, 1960
Corona pale pink. Early. See also 'Kortwright'

'Kortwright' 2 W-P
Syn. of 'Kortright'

N. × *koshinomurae* Fernández Casas 13 = N. *fernandesii* Pedro × N. *panizzianus* Parlatore

'Kostock' 2 Y-YYO
(S.C. Gaspar, pre-1949)
Perianth segments golden yellow; corona deep yellow, with a band of reddish orange at rim, tightly frilled

'Kotick' 1 W-W
(G.H. Engleheart, pre-1923)
Fl. 86 mm wide, facing down; perianth segments creamy white, irregular, overlapping half; corona opening pale cream, becoming creamy white, mouth expanded and somewhat frilled. Mid-season to late

'Kotiro' 2 W-? (b)
(A. Gibson, pre-1932)
PC(e)(NZ) 1932

'Kotuku' 2 W-W
(A.B. Davey) A.B. Davey, 1974
'Kanchenjunga' × 'Carnlough'

Fl. 116 mm wide

'Kowhai' 1 Y-Y
(W.E. Weightman, pre-1936)

'Kowhiri' 2 W-Y
(G.W.E. Brogden) M.E. Brogden, 1959
Corona lemon yellow

'Krain' 1 Y-Y
(W. Jackson Sr, 1944)
'Crocus' × 'Hymyr'

'Kraka' 1 Y-Y
(J.N.Hancock & Co., 1980) Unregistered
Sdlg 38/61H × Fairbairn 2Y-Y; sdlg no. 21B/80H
Fl. rich yellow; corona cylindrical, with mouth frilled, rim rolled. Early to mid-season

'Krakatoa' 2 Y-O
(J.L. Richardson, pre-1937)
'Garibaldi' × 'Fortune'
Fl. 121 mm wide; perianth segments ovate, blunt, slightly mucronate, vivid yellow 9A, slightly ribbed, overlapping half; the inner segments inflexed and slightly twisted; corona funnel-shaped, strong orange 25A, mouth ribbed and widely expanded, with rim flanged and crenate. Sunproof. 2n=27. AM(e) 1945, FCC(e) 1947, AM(Haarlem) 1950, FCC(Haarlem) 1955

'Krelagem' 1 W-W
(C.L. Adams, pre-1927)

'Krevin' 1 W-W
(New Zealand origin, pre-1948)

'Kris' 1 Y-Y
(G.H. Engleheart, pre-1923)

'Krishna' 3 W-? (b)
(C. Dawson, pre-1923)

'Kristin' 2 Y-R
(W. Jackson Jr, 1966) Unregistered
'Mars' × sdlg 38/59; sdlg no. 180/66

'Kronestein' 2 W-Y
(J. van Velzen) J. van Velzen, 1981
'Daisy Schäffer' × 'Carlton'
Fl. 95 mm wide; perianth segments ivory white; corona lemon yellow. Early

'Kros' 3 Y-R
(D.J. Jackson) Jackson's Daffodils, 1989
'Kopi' × 'Tia'; sdlg no. 233/80
Fl. 90 mm wide; perianth segments broadly ovate, rounded at apex, vivid yellow 9B, overlapping; corona orange-red (30B). Mid-season to late

'Kruger Rand' 11a W-Y
(?New Zealand origin) Unregistered

'Kubelik' 2 W-R
(C.E. Radcliff, 1934)
'Atanga' × 'Scarlet Queen'
Perianth segments creamy white; corona intense red

'Kubor' 1 Y-Y
(W. Jackson Jr, 1953)
'Chromis' × 'Moque'

'Kuching' 2 W-YPP
(J.N. Hancock & Co., 1947) J.N. Hancock & Co., 1964
'Pink o' Dawn' hybrid
Perianth segments of thick substance, deeply overlapping; corona large, expanded, frilled

'Kuckri' 2 Y-Y
(G.H. Engleheart, pre-1923)

'Kudos' 2 Y-O
(Sir J.S. Arkwright, pre-1931)
Perianth segments acute, clear yellow; corona clear orange, frilled

'Kudos' 5 Y-YYO
(W. Jackson Jr, c.1978) Unregistered
('Dimity' × 'Rave') × 'Bilboa'
Perianth segments broad, rounded at apex, golden yellow, smooth, of good substance; corona orange-yellow, touched orange at rim, frilled. Syn. 'Classic'

'Kukim' 1 W-Y
(D.J. Jackson, 1979) Jackson's Daffodils, 1989
'Helsal' × 'Daric'; sdlg no. 234/79
Fl. 104 mm wide; perianth segments greenish white 155C; corona cylindrical or somewhat funnel-shaped, brilliant greenish yellow 7C, with mouth slightly flared. Mid-season

'Kukri' 2 Y-Y
(G.H. Engleheart, pre-1923)
Fl. soft yellow; perianth segments overlapping; corona large

'Kulki' 2 Y-Y
(R.H. Glover, pre-1993) Unregistered

'Kumarra' 1 Y-Y
(S.J. Bisdee) S.J. Bisdee, 1956
'Fahan' × sdlg 32/46

'Kumbra' 4 W-Y
(H.G. Cross) H.G. Cross, 1984
'Kilpa' × 'Glowing Red'; sdlg no. 112-5
Fl. rounded; perianth and other petaloid segments in three or more whorls, broadly ovate, white, overlapping; the two outer whorls slightly inflexed, plane; the inner whorls strongly inflexed, concave or with margins deeply incurled; corona segments shorter, interspersed among the inner whorls of petaloid segments and clustered at centre, apricot yellow, frilled. Late

'Kumiss' 3 W-O
(R.H. Glover, pre-1990) Unregistered
'Ida May' × 'Yin Nell'

'Kumsong' 2 W-P
(J.N. Hancock & Co., 1947)
Corona pinkish

'Kunama' 1 W-W
(S.J. Bisdee) S.J. Bisdee, 1956
'Kanchenjunga' × 'Whitefoord'

'Kunega' 2 W-R
(S.J. Bisdee, 1953)
'The Bishop' × 'Lacroma'

'Kung Fu' 2 Y-R
(R.H. Glover, pre-1993) Unregistered

'Kunjo' 2 W-P
(J.L. Martin) J.L. Martin, 1982
'Lynny' × 'Zanglo'; sdlg no. LZ3
Fl. 95 mm wide; corona light yellowish pink 38C. Late. Resembles 'Longeray' but with a deeper-coloured corona

'Kuprena' 2 W-P
(S.J. Bisdee) S.J. Bisdee, 1956
'Rosario' × 'Mastercraft'

'Kurana' 1 W-YPP
(S.J. Bisdee, 1938)
'Dawn' × 'Eskimo'

'Kure' 3 W-YOO
(Mrs B.T. Simpson) Mrs B.T. Simpson, 1966
Fl. 95 mm wide; corona reddish orange, with rich yellow at base. Mid-season

'Kuripuni' 1 W-Y
(J.S. Leitch) J.S. Leitch, 1966
Fl. 115 mm wide; corona lemon yellow

'Kuroki' 1 Y-Y
(G.P. Haydon, pre-1908)

'Kurrewa' 1 W-W
(Jackson's Daffodils) Jackson's Daffodils, 1995
'Delight' × 'Far Fetched'; sdlg no. 88/87
Fl. 110 mm wide, greenish white (155A); perianth segments broadly ovate, plane; corona cylindrical, with mouth flared and frilled. Mid-season

'Kurrilee' 2 W-P
(S.J. Bisdee) S.J. Bisdee, 1956
'Lisbreen' × 'Lady Binney'

'Kusum' 2 Y-R
(W. Jackson Jr, pre-1952)
'Redlands' × 'Dunkeld'

'Kwannon' 2 W-Y
(G.L. Wilson, pre-1947)
'Silver Plane' × ('Askelon' × 'Samite')
Corona narrow at base, flaring towards mouth, yellow, becoming flushed with creamy buff

'Kwasind' 2 Y-? (a)
(J.R. Pearson & Sons, pre-1927)
'Van Waveren's Giant' × 'Romance'

'Kwinana' 1 W-Y
(J.N. Hancock & Co.) J.N. Hancock & Co., 1960
('Nevis' × 'Beersheba') × 'Carisbrooke'
Perianth segments of good substance; corona medium yellow, with rim closely and deeply notched, as if fringed, slightly rolled

'Kyema' 2 W-W
(S.J. Bisdee, 1936)
'Sunrise' × ('Warflame' × ['Puzzle' hybrid])

'Kykyu' 1 W-W
(J,M,Radcliff, 1948)
'Pink o' Dawn' × 'Moray'

'Kyle' 3 W-R
(J.A. O'More) P.D.K. Ramsay, 1983
'Matapan' × 'Signal Light'

'Kylemore' 2 W-W
(J.L. Richardson, pre-1937)
'White Sentinel' × 'Red Sea'

'Kylie' 2 W-WWP
(J.N. Hancock & Co., 1965) Unregistered

'Kynance' 9 W-YYR
(P.D. Williams, pre-1927)

'Kynaston' 2 W-? (b)
(E.A.K. Lee) E.A.K. Lee, 1955

'Kyoto' 3 W-GRR
(Mrs B.T. Simpson) Mrs B.T. Simpson, 1966
Fl 102 mm wide. Mid-season

'Kyria' 1 W-W
(Miss K.M. Hinchliff, pre-1939)

'Kyzer Karel' 8 W-Y or O
(pre-1807)

L

'La Argentina' 2 W-O/WY
(P. van Deursen, pre-1953)
Perianth segments very broad, blunt or truncate, promimently mucronate, pure white, somewhat reflexed, overlapping half; the inner segments more nearly spreading, square-shouldered at base, creased; corona widely expanded, very deeply 6-lobed, the lobes alternate to the perianth segments, with a broad longitudinal band of orange tapering from base to rim, touched with white and flanked by yellow

'La Argentina' 8 W-O

'La Beauté' 3 W-R
(P. van Deursen, pre-1938)
Corona deep red. AM(Haarlem) 1937

'La Belle' 7 Y-O
(Barr & Sons, pre-1937)
N. assoanus × ? *N. poeticus*
Fls 2-3 per stem; perianth segments deep yellow; corona reddish orange

'La Belle Aurore' 8 W-O
(pre-1798)

'La Belle de Normandie'
(pre-1885)
Syn. 'Belle of Normandy'

'La Belle Liègeoise' 8?
(pre-1820)

'La Bohéme' 2 W-? (b)
(J.O. Sherrard, pre-1943)

'Labour' 2 Y-? (a)
(Sir C.H. Cave, pre-1928)

'Labrador' 1 W-W
(J.L. Richardson, pre-1939)
'Slemish' × 'Cameronian'

'Laburnum' 2 Y-Y
(J.H. Hinsby, 1931)
'Homespun' × 'Tamerlane'

'Laburnum' 2 Y-? (a)
(E.W. Philpott)

'Lac du Chêne' 2 W-? (b)
(Oregon Bulb Farms, pre-1951)

'La Charmante' 2 W-? (b)
(Mrs R.O. Backhouse, pre-1921)
AM(Haarlem) 1930

'Lachlan' 2 W-Y
(E.M. Crosfield, pre-1920)
Perianth segments creamy white; corona bright yellow, deeply frilled

'Lachlan' 1 W-G
(W.M. Spry, pre-1975) Unregistered
'Hunter's Moon' × 'Prince'
Corona lemon green

'Lachryma'
(pre-1914)

'La Cigne' 3 W-W
(S.J. Bisdee, 1939)
'Mitylene' × 'Portia'

'La Citronière' 8 Y-Y
(pre-1927)
Poetaz
Fl. light yellow. ?The same as 'Grand Primo Citronière'

'Lackey' 2 Y-O
(Konynenburg & Mark, 1951) Konynenburg & Mark, 1964
Fl. 95 mm wide; perianth segments brilliant yellow 9C; corona orange. Mid-season

'Lacklay' 1 W-P
(K.J. Heazlewood, c.1970) Unregistered
'Lanena' × 'Roselands'

'La Comtesse' 8 Y-Y
(pre-1897)
Perianth segments pale primrose yellow; corona darker in tone

'La Corona' 3 W-? (b)
(Mrs R.O. Backhouse, pre-1921)

'Lacquer' 9 W-GOO
(G.L. Wilson, pre-1935)
'Dactyl' × 'Mystic'
Corona disc-shaped, reddish orange, with green at base

'Lacroma' 2 W-R
(S.J. Bisdee, 1946) S.J. Bisdee, 1956
'Hades' × 'Mr Sparks'

N. lacticolor Steudel = *N. tazetta* subsp. *lacticolor*

'La Dauphine' 1 W-W
(Barr & Sons, pre-1929)

'Ladbroke' 2 Y-Y
(P.D. Williams, pre-1930)
Fl. dark yellow

'Laddie' 2 Y-Y
(Warnaar & Co., pre-1940)
AM(Haarlem) 1940

'Ladies' Choice' 7 W-W
(Brian S.Duncan) Brian S.Duncan, 1995
'Quick Step' open pollinated; sdlg no. 1336
Fls 2-3 per stem, 79 mm wide, pure white; perianth segments ovate, spreading; corona cylindrical, smooth, with dark grey-green at base, mouth even. Late. Scented

'Ladies First' ?-P
(Alister Clark, pre-1948)

'Ladies Nosegay' 8 Y-?
(pre-1759)

'Ladock' 2 W-? (b)
(P.D. Williams, pre-1933)

'La Donna' 1 W-W
(pre-1913)

'Ladrus' 2 Y-? (a)
(A.H. Ahrens) J.S. Leitch, 1955

'Lady A.Currie'
Unregistered
Seed parent of 'Loyola' and others

'Lady Angliss' 2 W-?
(Alister Clark, 1935) J. Sharp, 1960

'Lady Ann' 2 W-GPP
(Brian S. Duncan) Brian S. Duncan, 1992
'Fragrant Rose' × 'Ken's Favorite'; sdlg no. 975
Fl. 100 mm wide; perianth segments very broad, rounded at apex, prominently mucronate, pure white, a little reflexed, glistening, overlapping half or more; the inner segments broadly ovate, truncate, with margins very slightly wavy; corona bowl-shaped, deep pink (31A and B). Mid-season to late

'Lady Arnott' 2 Y-? (a)
(W.B. Hartland, pre-1907)

'Lady Astor' 1 Y-Y
(G. Lubbe & Son, pre-1939)
AM(Haarlem) 1939

'Lady Audrey' 1 W-W
(Barr & Sons, pre-1903)
Fl. opening pale creamy primrose, becoming white; perianth segments broadly ovate, inflexed, more strongly so towards rim, with margins recurved, overlapping; corona cylindrical, angled, mouth widely expanded, split in places and overlapping, almost even, with rim minutely crenate

'Lady Backhouse' 2 W-W

'Lady Baltimore' 9 W-GOR
(Mrs M.S. Yerger) Mrs M.S. Yerger, 1993
'Phebe' open pollinated; sdlg no. 79 H 7
Fl. rounded, 60 mm wide; perianth segments very broad, slightly reflexed, overlapping; the inner segments slightly shorter; corona disc-shaped, strong orange 25B, suffused with the orange-red (30A) of the rim, with strong yellowish green 141C at base. Late

'Ladybank' 1 W-W
(Brian S. Duncan) Rathowen Daffodils, 1981
'Empress of Ireland' × 'White Star'; sdlg no. 321
Fl. pure white; corona with green at base. Mid-season. Resembles a larger-flowered and stronger 'Rashee'

'Lady Beatrice Pole-Carew' 1 W-W
(W.B. Hartland, pre-1914)

'Lady Bee' 2 W-P
(Barr & Sons, pre-1929)
Corona small, pale coral pink. 2n=14

'Lady Betty' 2 W-W
(N.Y. Lower, pre-1933)
Fl. pure white, facing slightly downwards; corona ribbed, with rim flared and rolled. 2n=28

'Lady Binney' 2 W-P
(S.J. Bisdee, 1946) S.J. Bisdee, 1956
'White Sentinal' × 'Rosario'

'Ladybird' 2 Y-YOO
(Mrs R.O. Backhouse, pre-1910)
N. radiiflorus var. poetarum × N. obvallaris
Fl. small; perianth segments bright yellow, with white mucro, somewhat twisted; corona ribbed, scarlet-orange, paling to golden yellow at base, frilled. Very early. 2n=14. Resembles 'Firelight'. See also 'Lady Bird'

'Lady Bird' 2 W-O
(L. van Leeuwen & Son, pre-1947)
Perianth segments creamy white; corona apricot orange, shading to a darker tone at base, paler outside. AM(Haarlem) 1946

'Lady Bird' 2 Y-?YOO
Syn. of 'Ladybird'

'Lady Blanche' 1 W-W
(C.G. van Tubergen, pre-1929)
AM(Haarlem) 1928

'Lady Bona' 5
(Barr & Sons, pre-1923)

'Lady Bonython' 1 W-W

(H.A. Brown, pre-1938)

'Lady Boreel' 1 W-W
(C.G. van Tubergen, pre-1916)

'Lady Boreel' 2 W-O
(J.W.A. Lefeber, 1944) J.W.A. Lefeber, 1960
Fl. 95 mm wide; corona deep orange. Early

'Lady Boreel' 8
Syn. of 'Duna'

'Lady Boscawen' 2 W-Y
Syn. of 'Lady Margaret Boscawen'

'Lady Boss' 2 W-Y
(J.N. Hancock & Co., 1956) Unregistered

'Ladybower' 1 W-W
(F.E. Board) F.E. Board, 1965
'Vigil' × 'White Prince'; sdlg no. 524
Late

'Lady Brilliant' 3 W-OOR
(Mrs R.O. Backhouse, pre-1921)
Corona very shallow, mid-orange, shading to bright crimson at rim

'Lady Caro' 2 W-P
(Colin Crotty, 1981) Colin Crotty, 1996
'Telita' × 'Accent'; sdlg no. 80-81
Fl. forming a double triangle, 112 mm wide; perianth segments ovate, slightly mucronate; corona cylindrical, pink, a little paler in tone at rim, with mouth neatly wavy. Mid-season. Sunproof

'Lady Chamberlain' 3 W-Y
(G. Lubbe & Son, pre-1929)
Corona primrose, frilled. AM(Haarlem) 1928

'Lady Charlotte' 2 Y-? (a)
(M.P. Williams) R.W. Ward & Son, 1959

'Lady Chauvel' 2 W-P
(Alister Clark, 1935) J. Sharp, 1960

'Lady Chesterfield'
(Barr & Sons, pre-1908)

'Lady Churchill' 2 W-? (b)
(Cartwright & Goodwin, pre-1927)

'Lady Clare' 2 W-? (b)
(R.H. Bath, pre-1929)

'Lady Cross' 2 Y-? (a)
(A.M. Williams, pre-1951)

'Lady Curzon' 3 W-? (b)
(de Graaff Bros, pre-1931)

'Lady Darnley' 2 Y-R
(Mrs R.O. Backhouse, pre-1921)
Perianth segments yellow; corona bowl-shaped, red

'Lady-Day' 1 W-W
(G.H. Johnstone, pre-1942)

'Lady de Bathe' 2 Y-Y
(G.H. Engleheart, pre-1913)

'Lady de Chair' 5 W-W
(H. Selkirk, pre-1927)
Fl. creamy white

'Lady Dell'
(pre-1914)

'Lady Derby' 3 W-R
(Warnaar & Co., pre-1925)
Perianth segments snow white; corona very shallow, fiery red. AM(Haarlem) 1925

'Lady Di' 2 W-Y
(J.A. O'More, 1955) R.G. Cull, 1987
'White House' × 'Trousseau'; sdlg no. 33/55
Corona light greenish yellow 4C. Mid-season

'Lady Diana' 2 W-W
(Broadfield's Daffodils, pre-1996) Unregistered

'Lady Diana Manners' 3 W-YYR
(Mrs R.O. Backhouse, pre-1921)
Fl. rounded; perianth segments very broad, roundish, slightly reflexed, with margins wavy and midrib showing, overlapping one-third to a half; the inner segments narrower, sometimes obovate, more nearly spreading; corona shallow bowl-shaped, ribbed, rich yellow, with a narrow band of deep red at rim. AM(Haarlem) 1924, AM(g)(m) 1925

'Lady Doneraile' 1 Y-Y
(E. Leeds, pre-1877)
Fl. pale yellow. Syn. Pseudonarcissus Major 'Lady Doneraile'

'Lady Dorothy' 1 Y-Y
(E. Leeds, pre-1877)
Perianth segments primrose yellow; corona pale yellow. Syn. Pseudonarcissus Lorifolius 'Lady Dorothy'

'Lady Dorothy' 1 W-Y
(Broadfield's Daffodils, pre-1989) Unregistered

'Lady Edith Foljambe' 1 Y-Y
(G.H. Engleheart, pre-1914)

'Lady Ellen Stewart' 1 Y-Y
(Barr & Sons, pre-1898)
AM 1898

'Lady Emily' 2 Y-O
(Ballydorn Bulb Farm) Ballydorn Bulb Farm, 1988
'Emily' × ?'Golden Wings'
Fl. 95 mm wide; perianth very broadly ovate, very smooth; corona bowl-shaped, orange-gold, with green at base and a darker tone of orange at rim, mouth even. Mid-season

'Lady Fair' 2 W-YYO
(Barr & Sons, pre-1933)
Perianth segments of thick texture, overlapping; corona expanded, bright yellow, with rich orange at rim

'Lady Fair' 2 W-W
(K.J. Heazlewood, c.1967) Unregistered
'Petsamo' × 'Kanchenjunga'

'Lady Fargoe' 2 W-? (b or c)
(C. Goodson, pre-1927)

'Lady Fenwick'
(H. Hart, pre-1930)

'Lady Friend' 2 W-P
(Tom Forster, 1960s) Unregistered
Corona deep salmon pink, frilled. Tall. Mid-season

'Lady Godiva' 3 W-?YYO
(pre-1900)
Barrii 'Conspicuus' sport
AM 1903. Received AM 1903 as 'Barbara Holmes'

'Lady Gore-Booth' 2 Y-Y
(Sir J.A.R. Gore-Booth, pre-1903)
Perianth segments creamy yellow; corona lemon yellow. AM 1903

'Lady Gowrie' 2 Y-R
(H.A. Brown, 1938) J.N. Hancock & Co., 1960
'Red Radiance' × 'Fortune'
Perianth segments pale yellow; corona red

'Lady Gray' 3 W-Y
(W. Backhouse, pre-1869)
Perianth segments pure white. Syn. Barrii Albus 'Lady Gray'. Was "absorbed" into 'Prince Teck'

'Lady Gregory' 3 W-? (b)
(W.B. Hartland, pre-1907)

'Lady Grosvenor' 1 W-Y
(W. Backhouse, pre-1869)
Corona sulphur yellow, with rim flanged. Syn. Pseudonarcissus Moschatus 'Lady Grosvenor'

'Lady Hamilton' 3 Y-? (a)
(A.S. Brewster, pre-1950)

'Lady Helen Ferguson' 1 W-? (b)
(Barr & Sons, pre-1907)

'Lady Helen Vincent' 1 Y-Y
(pre-1898)
Fl. soft clear yellow, of strong substance. Resembles 'Emperor' in form. AM 1898

'Lady Hilda' 1 W-Y
(Barr & Sons, pre-1927)
Perianth segments spreading; corona soft clear yellow, frilled, with rim rolled. Tall

'Lady Hillingdon' 7 Y-Y
(de Graaff Bros, pre-1927)
Fls 2-3 per stem; perianth segments deep primrose yellow; corona golden yellow

'Lady Ilse' 1 W-? (b)
(K.D. Smith, pre-1951)

'Lady-in-Waiting' 3 W-? (b)
(C.A. van Paridon, pre-1951)
AM(Haarlem) 1951. Div. 9 until 1957

'Lady in White' 1 W-W
(Barr & Sons, pre-1908)

'Lady Irene Denison' 1 W-? (b)
(G.P. Haydon, pre-1913)

'Lady Isabel' 2 Y-? (a)
(W.B. Hartland, pre-1907)

'Lady Ivor' 2 W-P
(J.O. Sherrard, pre-1949)

'Lady Jane' 2 W-Y
(pre-1889)
Perianth segments of strong substance; corona clear yellow

'Lady Jane' 2 W-WWO
(S.P. Haycock) S.P. Haycock, 1985
'Audubon' open pollinated; sdlg no. AW-WWP-1
Corona rim opening soft clear pink, becoming pale orange. Mid-season

'Lady Jane Grey' 5
(H.G. Longford, pre-1927)

'Lady Jane Jodrell' 3 W-W
(Miss K. Spurrell, pre-1906)
Fls sometimes 2 per stem, small; perianth segments pure white; corona ribbed, opening milk white, becoming purer white. See also 'Lady Janet Jodrell'

'Lady Janet Jodrell' 3 W-W
Syn. of 'Lady Jane Jodrell'

'Lady Jane Trefusis'
(?Miss E. Willmott, pre-1907)

'Lady Jean Rankin' 2 W-W
M.J. Jefferson-Brown, 1963

'Lady Jellicoe' 3 W-? (b)
(G.H. Engleheart, pre-1910)

'Lady Jenkins' 1 W-W
(H.T. Dettmann) H.T. Dettmann, 1960

'Lady Jinks' 2 W-O
Syn. of 'Merryhill'

'Lady Jowitt' 2 W-P
(G.T.C. Pearce, pre-1939)

'Lady Kenyon' 1 W-W
(W.A. Watts, pre-1923)
'Madame de Graaff' × 'Weardale Perfection'

'Lady Kesteven' 3 W-O
(Mrs R.O. Backhouse, pre-1921)
Perianth segments broadly ovate, blunt or slightly truncate, slightly mucronate, spreading, somewhat creased, overlapping one-third; the inner segments narrower, a little inflexed, very slightly twisted; corona almost disc-shaped, irregularly ribbed, deep orange, frilled. AM(Haarlem) 1931

'Lady Kestive' 3
(?Lord Rendlesham, pre-1936)

'Lady Ki' 1 W-W
(E.W. Philpott) E.W. Philpott, 1959
'Altamont' × 'Quartz'
Early

'Ladykin' 2 W-W
(A.E. Lowe, pre-1927)

'Lady Lace' 2 W-OOW
(J.N. Hancock & Co., 1968) Unregistered
Sdlg no. 117/68H
Perianth segments broadly ovate, blunt or slightly truncate, slightly mucronate, creamy white, spreading, plane, with margins sometimes minutely incurling near apex, overlapping half; the inner segments a little inflexed, twisted or with margins wavy; corona broad cup-shaped, smooth, opening deep orange-yellow, becoming deep apricot orange, with flecks of white at rim, mouth widely expanded, loosely frilled, rim irregularly notched and crenate. Tall. Early

'Lady Lilford' 3 W-? (b)
(Mrs R.O. Backhouse, pre-1921)
Corona with a broad band of red at rim

'Lady Love' 2 W-W
(R.H. Bath, pre-1927)

'Lady Love' 2 W-GPP
(Brian S. Duncan) Brian S. Duncan, 1990

'Lady Luck' 2 Y-O
(Warnaar & Co., pre-1951)
AM(Haarlem) 1951

'Lady Macbeth' 9 W-YYR
(W. Welchman, pre-1907)

'Lady Margaret Boscawen' 2 W-Y
(G.H. Engleheart, pre-1898)
Fl. star-shaped, 90 mm wide, facing slightly upwards; perianth segments broadly ovate or somewhat oblong, blunt, fairly prominently mucronate, milk white, slightly stained at base, a little inflexed, with margins incurved, ribbed, of somewhat thin substance, overlapping one-third; the inner segments a little more narrowly ovate, with margins wavy; corona funnel-shaped, ribbed, primrose yellow, mouth straight, lightly frilled, with rim crenate. 2n=29. Resembles 'Sir Watkin' in form. Syn. 'Lady Boscawen'. FCC 1898, *C(g) 1931

'Lady Marjorie Manners'
(pre-1914)

'Lady Mary' 2
(pre-1915)

'Lady May' 2 Y-R
(S.C. Gaspar) R.J. Abernethy, 1957

'Lady Mayoress' 2 W-W
(G.H. Engleheart, pre-1913)
Fl. facing down; perianth segments narrow, acute, pure white; corona opening cream, becoming white. Resembles 'Crystalline'

'Lady McCalmont' 3 W-? (b)
(W.B. Hartland, pre-1907)

'Lady McKenzie' 1 W-Y
(pre-1926)
Perianth segments white; corona creamy yellow, with mouth expanded and frilled

'Lady Millicent Taylor' 2 W-?
(J.L. Richardson, pre-1927)

'Lady Mine' 1 W-? (b)
(J.R. Pearson & Sons, pre-1923)
'Great Warley' × 'Van Waveren's Giant'
*C(g) 1931

'Lady Moore' 3 W-YYO
(W. Polman-Mooy, pre-1913)
Perianth segments broadly or very broadly ovate, blunt or truncate, fairly prominently mucronate, ivory white to creamy yellow, with margins sometimes incurling, overlapping one-third to a half; the inner segments more narrowly ovate, truncate, with margins wavy and sometimes nicked; corona shallow funnel-shaped, ribbed, citron yellow, with a well-defined narrow band of bright reddish orange at rim and the rim minutely crenate. AM(Haarlem) 1923, FA(Haarlem) 1924

'Lady Northcote'
(Alister Clark, pre-1915)

'Lady of Cambridge' 2 Y-? (a)
(R.H. Bath, pre-1929)

'Lady of Shalott' 5 W-Y
(E.M. Crosfield, pre-1909)
Fls usually 2 per stem; perianth segments narrowly ovate, acute, milk white, reflexed, with margins sometimes incurving, overlapping; corona large, widely expanded, ribbed, soft creamy lemon yellow, lightly frilled. Tall

'Lady of the Isle' 3 W-? (b)
(W. Welchman, pre-1927)

'Lady of the Lake' 9 W-YOR
(G.H. Engleheart, pre-1899)
Fl. broad, rounded

'Lady of the Lake' 3 Y-?
Syn. of 'Ascot'

'Lady of the Lea' 9 W-YYR
(pre-1907)

'Lady of the Manor' 3 W-?
(J. Mallender, pre-1912)

'Lady of the Snows' 1 W-W
(de Graaff Bros, pre-1905)
'Madame de Graaff' hybrid
Fl. pure white; corona frilled, with rim flanged

'Lady Ogilviy Dalgleish' 2 or 3 W-?
(Miss K.Spurrell, pre-1923)
See also 'Lady Ogilvy Dalgleish'

'Lady Ogilvy Dalgleish' 2 or 3 W-?
Syn. of 'Lady Ogilviy Dalgleish'

'Lady Orlay' 1 W-W
(Cartwright & Goodwin, pre-1916)

'Lady Penrhyn' 2 Y-YYO
(A.M. Wilson, pre-1937)

'Lady Primrose' 1 W-Y
(G.H. Engleheart, pre-1923)
Perianth segments ivory white; corona primrose yellow, with mouth expanded

'Lady Rendlesham' 5
(Barr & Sons, pre-1927)

'Lady Rhana' 1 W-W
(R.H.Glover, pre-1993) Unregistered

'Lady Rhodes' 1 Y-Y
(Australian or New Zealand origin, c.1927)
Fl. golden yellow. Resembles a larger and later-flowered 'King Alfred' of better form

'Lady Roberts' 1 Y-Y
(C. Goodson, pre-1927)
Fl. mid-yellow

'Lady Rona' 2 W-P
(S.W. Gower) P.D.K. Ramsay, 1980
Fl. 80 mm wide. Mid-season

'Lady Ruffles' 1 W-W
(Oregon Bulb Farms, pre-1946)

'Lady Sackville' 3 Y-? (a)
(Mrs R.O. Backhouse, pre-1921)

'Lady's Desire' 2 Y-O
(Konynenburg & Mark) Konynenburg & Mark, 1963
'Etude' × ('David Copperfield' × 'Floriment')
Fl. 110 mm wide; perianth segments brilliant greenish yellow 6A; corona orange. Early

'Lady Serena' 9 W-GYR
(P.D. Williams) Mrs M.S. Yerger, 1976
Sdlg no. 101
Fl. 66 mm wide; corona ribbed, greenish yellow, with green at base and red at rim, with a line of white between the yellow and the red on ageing. Mid-season. 2n=28. Resembles 'Perdita' but with the corona less widely flared

'Lady Slim' 1 W-W
(C.O. Fairbairn, c.1968) Unregistered

'Lady's Maid' 2 W-? (b)
(Mann, pre-1910)

'Lady Somerset' 1 W-W
(pre-1897)
Perianth segments twisted

'Lady Superior' 3 W-YYR
(Mrs R.O. Backhouse, pre-1914)
Perianth segments large; corona yellow, with crimson at rim. Somewhat resembles 'Albatross'. AM(e) 1914

'Lady Sweers' 2 Y-R
(J.W.A. Lefeber) J.W.A. Lefeber, 1960
Fl. 76 mm wide; perianth segments canary yellow; corona deep orange-red. Mid-season

'Lady Sybil' 1 Y-Y
(Barr & Sons, pre-1903)
Fl. primrose yellow; corona with mouth expanded and rim flanged. Dwarf

'Lady Sylvia' 3 W-R
(pre-1945)
Div. 9 and named 'Resplendent' until c.1945

'Lady Theodora' 2 Y-? (a)
(Mrs R.O. Backhouse, pre-1921)

'Ladytide' 2 or 3 W-? (b or c)
(F.H. Chapman, pre-1914)

'Lady Warren' 1 W-? (b or c)
(pre-1936)
'Weardale Perfection' × 'Madame de Graaff'

'Lady Watkin' 2 Y-? (a)
(T. Walker, pre-1890)

'Lady Willes' 1 Y-Y
(de Graaff Bros, pre-1899)
Perianth segments primrose yellow; corona flared, ribbed

'Lae' 2 W-? (b)
(Mrs M. Moorby, pre-1942)

'Laetare' 2 Y-? (a)
(P.D. Williams, pre-1943)
AM(Haarlem) 1943

'Laetitia' 8 Y-YYO
(pre-1963) Unregistered

N. × *laetus* Salisbury 13 = *N. minor* Linnaeus × *N. jonquilla* Linnaeus (Odorus 'Laetus')

'Laetus'
Syn. of *N.* × *laetus*

'La Favorite' 8 W or Y-O
(pre-1798)

'Lafayette' 2 W-O
(Barr & Sons, pre-1934)
Perianth segments creamy white, spreading, of thick substance; corona large, bowl-shaped, intense scarlet-orange. Tall

'La Fayette' 9 W-YYR
(J.R. Byfield, pre-1938)

'La Fée' 2 Y-? (a)
(L. van Leeuwen & Son, pre-1931)
AM(Haarlem) 1930

'La Fiancée' 8 W-O

(pre-1932)
Poetaz
Fls up to 6 per stem; perianth segments very broadly ovate in outline, blunt or squarish at apex, sometimes truncate, mucronate, pure white, spreading, deeply overlapping; the inner segments roundish, with margins wavy; corona almost disc-shaped, ribbed, yellow. EFA(Haarlem) 1932

'La Fiancée' 9 W-YYR
(R.H. Bath, pre-1932)
2n=24

'La Fontaine' 2 Y-? (a)
(Mrs R.O. Backhouse, pre-1921)

'La Fontaine' 9 W-YYR
(J.R. Byfield, 1931)
'King of Poets' × 'Banjo Patterson'

'La Fraicheur' 2 W-W
(L. Buckland, pre-1915)
FCC 1918

'Lagado' 1 Y-Y
(G.H. Furness, pre-1934)

'La Gaieté' 3 W-? (b)
(P. van Deursen, pre-1933)
AM(Haarlem) 1932

'La Gama' 2 W-? (b)
(Miss K.M. Hinchliff, pre-1937)

'Lagan' 2 Y-R
(West & Fell, pre-1935)
Perianth segments deep yellow; corona red

'Lagana' 2 W-P
(C.E. Radcliff, pre-1944)
'Rosary' × 'Pink o' Dawn'

***N. lagoi* Merino 13 Section Pseudonarcissus**

'Lagonda' 2 W-YYW
(Barr & Sons, pre-1933)

'Lagos' 2 Y-? (a)
(Barr & Sons, pre-1949)

"La Grandalla"
See "Grandalla"

'La Grandeur' 2 W-? (b)
(G.H. Engleheart, pre-1914)

'Laguna' 2 Y-YYR
(G. Lewis) D.S. Bell, 1955
Perianth segments deep yellow; corona very shallow bowl-shaped, bright yellow, with red at rim

'Lahana' 1 Y-Y
(D. Blanchard, pre-1947)
'Clarion' × 'Kandahar'

'Laibach' 3 W-? (b)
(G.A. Uit den Boogaard, pre-1950)

'Laida' 2 Y-? (a)
(pre-1928)
See also 'Zaida'

'L'Aiglon' 2 W-? (b)
(Mrs R.O. Backhouse, pre-1921)

'Lainee' 2 W-R
(W. Jackson Jr) W. Jackson Jr, 1973
'Jo' × 'Arbar'; sdlg no. 253/67

'Laira' 1 W-W
(J.T. Gray, pre-1949)
Fl. pure white; corona mouth slightly expanded

'Laird of Killilan' 2 Y-? (a)
(M.H. Tribe, pre-1937)

'Laity' 3 W-? (b)
(P.D. Williams, pre-1930)

'La Jolla' 2 W-Y
(G.H. Wayne) G.H. Wayne, 1981
'Aircastle' × 'Pontsiana'; sdlg no. A-1/5
Fl. 80 mm wide; corona pale lemon. Mid-season

'La Joyeuse' 1 W-? (b)
(R.A. van der Schoot, pre-1923)

'La Joyeuse' 3 W-? (b)
(L. van Leeuwen & Son, pre-1930)
AM(Haarlem) 1930

'Lake Ellesmere' 1 W-W
(G. Lewis) D.S. Bell, 1955

'Lake George' 2 W-W
(J.M. de Navarro, c.1968) Unregistered
'Samite' × 'Chinese White'

'Lakehurst' 2 W-? (b)
(Warnaar & Co., pre-1930)

'Lakeland Fair' 2 W-GPP
(M.W. Baxter) M.W. Baxter, 1994
'Coral Fair' × 'Rainbow'; sdlg no. 87-10
Fl. forming a double triangle, 107 mm wide; perianth segments broadly ovate, blunt, only very slightly mucronate, spreading, a little concave, overlapping half; the inner segments more narrowly ovate, square-shouldered at base; corona funnel-shaped, lightly ribbed, pale pink shading to strong yellowish pink 32D at rim, with light bright green prominent at base,

mouth straight, more strongly ribbed, a little frilled, with rim minutely and irregularly notched. Mid-season. Sunproof

'Lake Linden' 1 W-W
(G. Lewis) D.S. Bell, 1955
Fl. pure white; corona with rim flanged and frilled

'Lake Louise' 2 W-W
(K.J. Heazlewood) K.J. Heazlewood, 1968
'Vigil' × 'Empress of Ireland'
Fl. 95 mm wide. Mid-season. Resembles 'Ulster Queen' but with a shallower corona

'Lake Moana' 1 W-Y
(G. Lewis) D.S. Bell, 1955

'Lake Placid' 2 Y-YYO
(G.H. Rotteveel & Sons) G.H. Rotteveel & Sons, 1980
Perianth segments brilliant greenish yellow 4A; corona lemon yellow, with strong orange 25A at rim

'Lakeside' 2 W-W
(C.E. Radcliff, 1930)
'Pedestal' × 'Pink'un'

'Lake Tahoe' 2 W-GWP
(Brian S. Duncan) Brian S. Duncan, 1993
'High Society' × 'Valinor'; sdlg no. 1160
Fl. 102 mm wide; perianth segments white; corona broad funnel-shaped, opening pink, becoming white, with deep salmon pink at rim, with green at base at all times, mouth slightly wavy. Mid-season to late

'La La' 1 Y-Y
(C.E. Radcliff, 1943)
'Fahan' × 'Sir Accolon'
Perianth segments broadly ovate, blunt, slightly mucronate, spreading, plane, smooth, overlapping half; the inner segments a little narrower, more prominently mucronate, shouldered at base, slightly inflexed; corona smooth, mouth ribbed, expanded, a little frilled, rim notched and dentate, loosely flanged

'Lalage' 3 W-? (b)
(G.L. Wilson, pre-1937)

'Lalique' 3 Y-GYY
(T.D. Throckmorton) T.D. Throckmorton, 1975
'Gossamer' × 'Aircastle; sdlg no. T/65/2/1
Perianth segments opening white, becoming greenish beige; corona opening yellow, becoming white. Resembles 'Aircastle' or 'Beige Beauty'. Varies between Divs 3 and 2

'Lalita' 2 W-P
(W. Jackson Jr, 1966) Unregistered
'Kimi' × 'Egina'; sdlg no. 47/66

'Lalla' 2 (a)
(J.T. Gray, pre-1938)

'Lalla Rookh' 1 (a)
(H. Backhouse, pre-1908)

'Lalli' 1 W-? (b)
(W. Jackson Sr, 1938)
'White Emperor' × 'Saint Aloysius'
Corona buff

'La Lune' 4
(G.H. Engleheart, pre-1913)

'La Lune' 2 W-Y
(H. Selkirk, pre-1927)
Perianth segments creamy white

'La Mancha' 2 Y-Y
(A.M. Wilson, pre-1914)
Fl. large; perianth segments clear pale yellow; corona flared, rich yellow

'La Mancha' 2 W-W
(W.G. Pannill) W.G. Pannill, 1970
'Easter Moon' × 'Pristine'

'Lamanva' 2 W-WWP
(R.A. Scamp) R.A. Scamp, 1993
'Ben Hee' × 'Romance'; sdlg no. 168
Fl. 95 mm wide; perianth segments ovate, white, smooth, deeply overlapping; corona pure white, with a band of clear pink at rim, mouth neatly frilled. Mid-season. Sunproof

'Lambeg' 2 W-? (b)
(W.J. Dunlop, pre-1950)

'Lambessow' 3 (a)
(P.D. Williams, pre-1930)

'Lambourn' 1 Y-Y
(R.C.A. Tombleson) R.C.A. Tombleson, 1970
'Faris' × 'Spanish Gold' hybrid

'Lambriggan' 2 (a)
(P.D. Williams, pre-1930)

'Lamellyn' 3 (a)
(P.D. Williams, pre-1930)

'Lamerton' 2 Y-R
(Mrs H.K. Richardson) du Plessis Bros, 1985
'Air Marshal' × 'Royal Jester'; sdlg no. 174
Mid-season

'La Merveilleuse' 8 Y-O
(pre-1798)

'Lamia' 1 W-P
(W. Jackson Sr, 1944)
'Dawnglow' × 'Lalli'

'La Mignonne' 8 Y-Y
(pre-1851)

'Lamington' 2 Y-O
(J.L. Richardson, pre-1951)
'Krakatoa' × 'Ceylon'
Perianth segments deep gold; corona reddish orange, with rim dentate and widely flanged

'La Minuette' 2 W-WPP
(David Adams) David Adams, 1996
Sdlg 79/14A ('Easter Moon' × Brogden sdlg T19) × 'Dear Me'; sdlg no. 85/04A
Fl. forming a double triangle, 100 mm wide; perianth segments ovate, blunt, pure white, plane; corona funnel-shaped, ribbed, pink, with white at base, shading to mid-pink at rim, mouth flared and frilled, rim crenate. Early to mid-season. Sunproof

'Lamira' 2 (a)
(G.H. Furness, pre-1934)

'Lammermuir' 1 Y-Y
(The Brodie of Brodie, c.1909)
'Glory of Noordwijk' × 'King Alfred'
Fl. very deep glowing yellow

'Lamond' 1 Y-Y
(Barr & Sons, pre-1919)
Perianth segments creamy white, suffused pale sulphur yellow; corona ribbed, primrose yellow, tinged sulphur yellow, frilled

'La Monnoye' 8 Y-Y
(pre-1798)
Fl. pale yellow

'Lamorna' 3 W-O
(P.D. Williams, pre-1927)
AM(Haarlem) 1931

'Lamorna' 1 Y-Y
Syn. of 'Sulphur'

'L'Amour' 2 W-? (b)
(D.S. Bell) D.S. Bell, 1955

'L'Amour' 2 W-P
Syn. of 'Madelaine'

'Lamplight' 2 Y-R
(New Zealand origin, pre-1962)
Fl. large; perianth segments broad, golden yellow, smooth; corona deep red, frilled. Tall

'Lamplighter' 9 W-R
(G.L. Wilson, pre-1936)
Perianth segments pure white, of strong substance; corona dark red. Late

'Lampra' 3 (a)
(P.D. Williams, pre-1933)

'Lana' 1 W-P
(J.N. Hancock & Co., c.1977) Unregistered
Corona cream pink

'Lanarth' 7 Y-O
(P.D. Williams, pre-1928)
Fls 2 per stem, rounded; perianth segments very broad, somewhat oblong, rounded at apex, mucronate, deep golden yellow, spreading, sometimes a little reflexed towards apex, plane, overlapping one-third; the inner segments narrower, ovate, a little inflexed, with margins wavy and sometimes incurved; corona broad and shallow bowl-shaped, orange-yellow, flushed orange. Scented. 2n=21. AM(e) 1927, *AM(g) 1930, AM(Haarlem) 1931, *FCC(g) 1936

'Lancarrow' 3 (a)
(P.D. Williams, pre-1930)

'Lancaster' 1 W-? (b)
(J.O. Sherrard, pre-1943)

'Lancaster' 3 W-GYO
(Ballydorn Bulb Farm) Ballydorn Bulb Farm, 1977
'Clockface' open pollinated
Fl. rounded, 94 mm wide; perianth segments very broad, truncate, very slightly mucronate, a little reflexed, with margins incurling at apex, overlapping half or more; the inner segments spreading; corona very shallow bowl-shaped, narrow, tightly ribbed and frilled, yellow, with deep green at base, with a faint flush of orange at rim on opening, mouth sometimes deeply split and overlapping. Mid-season. 2n=28

'Lancefield' 1 W-Y
(?Australian origin) Unregistered

'Lancelot' 3 W-? (b or c)
(Mrs R.O. Backhouse, pre-1907)

'Lancelot' 1 Y-Y
(T. Bloomer) Rathowen Daffodils, 1979
'Camelot' × 'Arctic Gold'; sdlg no. 6/72/65
Fl. 110 mm wide. Mid-season. Resembles a Div. 1 'Golden Jay'

'Lancer' 3 (a)
(G.H. Engleheart, pre-1907)

'Lancing' 2 (a)
(Sir F.C. Stern, pre-1949)

'Lander' 3 (a)
(E. & J.C. Martin, pre-1931)

'Landewednack' 1 W-W
(P.D. Williams, pre-1930)

'Landfall' 1 Y-Y
(D.S. Bell) D.S. Bell, 1960
Fl. 108 mm wide, pure yellow; corona with rim flanged. Mid-season

'Land Girl' 3 W-YOO
(A. Gray, pre-1944)
'John Evelyn' × 'Red Cross'

'Landglow' 2 W-Y
(J.N. Hancock & Co., c.1966) Unregistered
Perianth segments smooth; corona long, cylindrical, opening golden yellow, becoming creamy yellow

'Landithy' 2 Y-Y
(P.D. Williams, pre-1933)
Fl. deep yellow; perianth segments broad, of good substance; corona with rim flanged and dentate

'Landmark' 2 W-O
(G.W.E. Brogden) G.W.E. Brogden, 1963
Fl. 108 mm wide; corona disc-shaped, reddish orange, with a paler tone at base. Mid-season. Resembles an earlier-flowered 'Tongahoe' with a whiter perianth

'Landrake' 3 (a)
(P.D. Williams, pre-1933)

'Landrivick' 2 (a)
(P.D. Williams, pre-1930)

'Landseer' 3 W-? (b or c)
(A.M. Wilson, pre-1937)

'Landulph' 2 Y-Y
(P.D. Williams, pre-1930)

'Lane' 1 W-? (b)
(pre-1913)

'Laneast' 3 (a)
(P.D. Williams, pre-1933)

'La Neige' 5 W-W
(G.H. Engleheart, pre-1936)

'Lanena' 1 W-P
(C.E. Radcliff, 1942) J.M.Radcliff, 1956
('Mitylene' × 'Pink o' Dawn') × 'Dawnglow'

'Langara' 1 W-Y
(J.N.Hancock & Co., 1983) J.N.Hancock & Co., 1997

Sdlg 1/70H (2 Y-Y) × 'Artist's Model'; sdlg no. 2/83H
Perianth segments ovate, spreading; corona cylindrical, warm yellow, with rim crenate. Early

'Langdale' 2 W-O
(C.A. Nethercote) T. Morrison, 1960
Perianth segments creamy white; corona widely expanded, reddish orange, frilled. Tall

'Langford' 2 W-? (b or c)
(P.D. Williams, pre-1930)

'Langford Grove' 3 W-YYO
(Mrs J. Abel Smith) Mrs J. Abel Smith, 1977
'Hamzali' × 'Aircastle'; sdlg no. Q4/15
Fl. 90 mm wide; perianth segments slightly reflexed; corona disc-shaped, yellow, with reddish orange at rim. Mid-season. 2n=29. Resembles a smaller-flowered 'Thoresby' with a more reflexed perianth

'Langley' 2 W-P
(Mrs E. Murray)

'Langley Dandy' 3 W-GYR
(Mrs E.Murray) Unregistered
Perianth segments roundish, ice white; corona disc-shaped, ribbed, yellow, with green at base and a well-defined band of orange-red at rim. Mid-season to late

'Langley Gold Dust' 2 Y-? (a)
(Mrs E. Murray)

'Langley Surprise' 2 W-P
(Mrs E. Murray)

'Langley Vale' 2 W-?
(Alister Clark, 1937) J. Sharp, 1960

'Langlo' 1 Y-Y
(W.M. Spry, pre-1973) Unregistered
'Russ Holland' × 'Spellbinder'
Early. 2n=28

'Langton' 2 Y-O
(Barr & Sons) Wallace & Barr, 1959
Fl. 76 mm wide; perianth segments canary yellow; corona light orange, with golden orange at rim, frilled. Mid-season. Resembles 'California Gold'

'Langwith' 2 W-Y
(Mrs J. Abel Smith) Mrs J. Abel Smith, 1969
'Trousseau' × 'Winter'
Fl. 103 mm wide; perianth segments creamy white, with margins incurved and recurved, overlapping; corona very slightly ribbed, vivid yellow 12A, paling to light yellow 10C at base, with mouth expanded and frilled. Late

'Lanherne' 1 W-W
(P.D. Williams, pre-1933)

'Lanivet' 1 (a)
(P.D. Williams, pre-1933)

'Lanka' 2 W-P
(W.Jackson Sr, 1947)
'Leto' × 'Pinka'

'Lanlivery' 2 W-? (b or c)
(P.D. Williams, pre-1933)

'La Noblesse' 8 W-Y or O
(pre-1807)

'Lanoma' 2 Y-YYO
(S.C. Gaspar) R.J. Abernethy, 1961
Fl. 102 mm wide; perianth segments bright yellow; corona very shallow bowl-shaped, golden yellow, with bright orange at rim, tightly frilled. Mid-season

'Lanreath' 2 W-P
(Brian S. Duncan) du Plessis Bros, 1989
'Simile' × 'Violetta'; sdlg no. 578
Fl. 100 mm wide; perianth segments pure white; corona mouth expanded. Late

'Lansallos' 2 Y-YRR
(T. Bloomer) du Plessis Bros, 1986
'Fiery Chariot' × 'Shining Light'; sdlg no. 436
Mid-season

'Lansdowne' 2 W-YRR
(D.S. Bell) D.S. Bell, 1961
Fl. 105 mm wide. Mid-season. Resembles an improved 'Tuskar Light' in form and texture

'Lantana' 1 W-Y
(Warnaar & Co., pre-1949)

'Lanteglos' 2 (a)
(P.D. Williams, pre-1933)

'Lantern' 1 (a)
(R.H. Bath, pre-1927)

'Lantern' 1 Y-Y
(Murray W. Evans, c.1985) Unregistered
'Spanish Gold' × 'Dividend'

'Lantwit' 2 Y-Y
(P.D. Williams, pre-1927)
Fl. yellow; corona shading to orange. Early

'Lantyne' 2 (a)
(T.A.V. Wood, pre-1949)

'Lanyon' 1 W-W
(The Brodie of Brodie, pre-1930)
? × 'Fortune'

N. lanzae Lojacono Pojero = *N. tazetta* subsp. *lacticolor*

'Lanzarote' 2 W-O
(Mrs H.K. Richardson) Mrs H.K. Richardson, 1977
'Lorenzo' × 'Hotspur'
Fl. 86 mm wide; corona scarlet-orange. Mid-season.

'Laomedon' 8 Y-Y
(pre-1798)
Fl. golden yellow

'Lao Tza' 1 Y-Y
Syn. of 'Lao Tzu'

'Lao-Tze' 1 Y-Y
Syn. of 'Lao Tzu'

'Lao-Tzu' 1 Y-Y
(W. Jackson Sr, 1934)
'Golden City' × 'Pilgrimage'
See also 'Lao-Tze', 'Lao Tza'

'La Paille' 8 Y-Y
(pre-1777)

'La Paloma' 1 W-W
(A.S. Brewster, pre-1936)

'La Paloma' 3 W-GYR
(W.H. Roesé, 1968) Unregistered W.H.Roesé, 1982
'Estrella' × 'Merlin'
Fl. rounded, 83 mm wide. Mid-season. Resembles an earlier-flowered 'Estrella' with a whiter perianth

'Lapford' 1 W-Y
(G.L. Wilson, pre-1952)
?'Nevis' hybrid
Fl. 108 mm wide; perianth segments very broad, rounded at apex, smooth, overlapping; corona brilliant greenish yellow 6C, rim flanged and slightly dentate. Early. AM(e) 1954

'Laphroaig' 2 Y-R
(D.N.Y. Olson) D.N.Y. Olson, 1988
'Heathcliffe' hybrid; sdlg no. 78/12/1
Fl. 92 mm wide; perianth segments mid-yellow; corona bowl-shaped, ribbed, very dark red, frilled, with rim deeply notched. Early to mid-season. Sunproof

'Lapine' 3 Y-YYO
(G.E. Mitsch) G.E. Mitsch, 1982
'Aircastle' × 'Ardour'; sdlg no. II88/1
Fl. 90 mm wide; perianth segments bright yellow; corona deeper in tone, with orange at rim. Mid-season. 2n=28

'Lapland' 1 W-W
(J.L. Richardson) J.L. Richardson, 1958

'Spitzbergen' × 'Broughshane'
Fl. pure white; corona mouth expanded, with rim dentate and widely flanged

'La Plus Belle' 8 Y-Y
(pre-1792)
Fl. golden yellow

'Lapthorne' 2 (a)
(P.D. Williams, pre-1930)

'Lapwing' 2 W-? (b or c)
(Sir C.H. Cave, pre-1908)

'Lapwing' 5 W-Y
(G.E. Mitsch) G.E. Mitsch, 1975
'Silver Bells' open pollinated; sdlg no. CO11/1
Fls 1-2 per stem, 80 mm wide; corona lemon. Mid-season

'Lara' 2 W-O
(W.G. Pannill) W.G. Pannill, 1977
'Roimond' × 'Corsair'; sdlg no. 64/106 B
Fl. 100 mm wide. Mid-season

'Larapinta' 1 W-Y
(A.O. Roblin, c.1966) Unregistered
'Taran' × 'Rhana'

'Larch Mountain' 1 Y-Y
(Murray W. Evans, pre-1989) Unregistered

'La Reine' 8 W-Y
(pre-1850)

'La Reine de France' 8
(pre-1820)

'La Reine de Perse' 8
(pre-1793)

'Largess' 1 W-W
(J.L. Richardson, pre-1948)

'Largo' 8
(J.B. van der Schoot, pre-1931)

'Largo' 2 Y-YYO
(Konynenburg & Mark) Konynenburg & Mark, 1960
'Aranjuez' × ('Kimono' × 'Memphis')
Fl. 100 mm wide; perianth segments canary yellow; corona vivid yellow 17C, with strong orange 26B at rim. Mid-season

'La Riante' 3 W-YOO
(P. van Deursen, pre-1931)
Fl. rounded, 79 mm wide; perianth segments very broadly ovate or roundish, truncate, prominently mucronate, opening creamy white, becoming pure white, spreading, a little concave, somewhat creased or with midrib showing, overlapping half; the inner segments rounded at base; corona shallow bowl-shaped, closely ribbed, reddish orange, with greenish yellow at base, mouth expanded, with up to six deeply split and overlapping lobes. Early. 2n=28.
AM(Haarlem) 1931

'Lariat' 2 W-GYP
(W.G. Pannill, 1980) W.G. Pannill, 1996
'Coral Ribbon' × ('Green Island' × 'Accent'); sdlg no. I 42
Mid-season

'Larinna' 1 W-Y
(pre-1960) Unregistered
Perianth segments broad, pure white, smooth; corona clear lemon yellow

'Larissa' 3 W-R
(R.H. Bath, pre-1908)
Perianth segments snow white; corona brilliant red

'Larissa' 2 W-R
(pre-1927)
Corona brilliant scarlet

'Lark' 2 Y-WWY
(G.E. Mitsch) G.E. Mitsch, 1976
'Irish Coffee' × Richardson 3 Y-W sdlg; sdlg no. H123/1
Fl. 90 mm wide; perianth segments broadly ovate, blunt, spreading or a little reflexed, soft lemon yellow, a little concave, overlapping one-third to a half; the inner segments more usually spreading, with margins wavy; corona widely expanded, almost disc-shaped, closely ribbed, opening lemon yellow, becoming almost white, with lemon yellow at rim. Mid-season

'Larkelly' 6 Y-O
(P.D. Williams, pre-1930)
? × *N. cyclamineus*
Corona reddish orange. 2n=36

'Larkfield' 2 W-O
(W.J. Dunlop, c.1969) Unregistered
Perianth segments broad, pure white, smooth, overlapping; corona salmon orange

'Larkhill' 2 W-Y
(John T. Williams) John T. Williams, 1992
'Daviot' open pollinated
Fl. 102 mm wide, forming a double triangle; perianth segments broadly ovate, blunt, fairly prominently mucronate, spreading, plane, smooth, with midrib showing, of thick substance, overlapping half; the inner segments more narrowly ovate, less prominently mucronate, with margins slightly incurving; corona cylindrical, lightly ribbed, vivid yellow 9A,

mouth straight, more strongly ribbed, wavy, with rim crenate. Mid-season.

'Larkwhistle' 6 Y-Y
(L. Palmer) L. Palmer, 1960
Fl. 76 mm wide; perianth segments broadly ovate, vivid yellow 9B, reflexed, overlapping at base only; corona cylindrical, richer in tone (between 14A and 17B), with base paler than rim, mouth slightly expanded, with rim flanged and dentate. Early. 2n=21. *AM(g) 1967, *FCC(g) 1970, AGM 1993

'Larnaca' 1 (a)
(Seymour Cobley Ltd, pre-1935)

'Larne' 2 W-Y
(G.L. Wilson, pre-1934)
Perianth segments broad, acute, pure white, sometimes tinged green; corona ribbed, clear lemon yellow, with mouth flared and frilled. AM(e) 1938

'La Rochelle' 2 W-P
(S.A. Free) Mrs S.I. Free, 1969

'La Ronde' 3 Y-OOR
(T.H. Piper, 1954)
'Sunset Fires' × 'Playboy'

'La Ronde' 3 W-R
(D.S. Bell) D.S. Bell, 1963
'Mannequin' × 'Garland'
Late

'Larool' 2 W-P
(J.N. Hancock & Co., 1953)
Sdlg no. 139/53H
Perianth segments broadly ovate or oblong, blunt, slightly mucronate, creamy white, spreading or a little inflexed, plane, with margins sometimes nicked, smooth, overlapping half; the inner segments ovate, inflexed, with margins wavy or fairly deeply incurved, with some nicks and "thumbs"; corona funnel-shaped, smooth, deep apricot pink, mouth split in places and overlapping, densely frilled. Tall. Mid-season

'Larrerpy' 1 Y-Y
(K.J. Heazlewood) K.J. Heazlewood, 1970
'Melissa' × 'Kingscourt'

'Larrerpy' 4 Y-R
(K.J. Heazlewood, c.1970) Unregistered
'Glowing Red' × 'Carbineer'

'Larrigan' 2 (a)
(P.D. Williams, pre-1930)

'Larry' 3 W-GYO
(F.E. Board) Mrs H. Bloomer Jr, 1976
('Fermoy' × 'Roimond') × 'Arbar'; sdlg no. 361

Fl. 97 mm wide; corona almost disc-shaped, yellow, with deep green at base and reddish orange at rim. Mid-season. Resembles a more brightly coloured 'Fermoy'

'Laser' 2 W-R
(G.E. Mitsch) G.E. Mitsch, 1979
('Precedent' × 'Accent') × 'Space Ship'; sdlg no. KK32/10
Fl. 120 mm wide, frequently with one perianth segment twisted; corona intense rose red, with a narrow band of deeper red above the green at base. Late

'La Sirenne' 8 W-Y or O
(pre-1807)

'Lasseter' 1 Y-Y
(J.N. Hancock & Co., 1984) Unregistered
'Convention' × 'Daydream'; sdlg no. 40/84H
Fl. mid-yellow; perianth segments broad; corona funnel-shaped, neatly frilled. Tall. Early

'Lassie' 9
(P.D. Williams, pre-1937)

'Lass o' Gowrie' 3 Y-Y
(W. Backhouse, pre-1869)
Perianth segments narrow, acute, sulphur yellow. Syn. Barrii 'Lass o' Gowrie', Barrii 'Stellatus'. "Absorbed" 'Major' and 'Sycorax'

'Lasswade' 1 W-P
(C.E. Radcliff, 1943) J.M. Radcliff, 1956
'Dawnglow' × 'Rosario'

'Last Chance' 11a W-P
(David L. Sheppard) David L. Sheppard, 1977
'Canasta' × 'Easter Bonnet'; sdlg no. 73-D-1
Fl. 100 mm wide; perianth segments broadly ovate, spreading, overlapping one-third; the inner segments more narrowly ovate, somewhat inflexed; corona split to base, the six segments more than half as long as the perianth segments and opposite and closely overlying them, ribbed, opening pink, becoming deeper in tone, deeply frilled. Mid-season

'Laster' 1 Y-Y
(Alister Clark) T. Morrison, 1960

'Last Out' 2 or 3 W-? (b or c)
(pre-1913)

'Last Out' 1 Y-Y
(G.L. Wilson, pre-1931)
Fl. large, clear yellow. Very late

'Last Promise' 1 Y-Y
(Carncairn Daffodils) Carncairn Daffodils, 1991
'Loughanmore' × 'Golden Sovereign'; sdlg no. 33/8/76

Fl. 105 mm wide, yellow; perianth segments broadly ovate, blunt, with white mucro, spreading, a little concave, with margins incurling at apex, regular, overlapping half; the inner segments more narrowly ovate, truncate, somewhat creased, with margins incurved; corona cylindrical, with mouth flared and frilled. Late

'Last Say' 2 W-P
(J.N. Hancock & Co.) J.N. Hancock & Co., 1960
Corona large, pale pink

'Last Shot' 2 W-WWP
(Alister Clark, pre-1960) Unregistered
Corona with bright pink at rim

'Last Word' 3 W-GYY
(M.J. Jefferson-Brown) M.J. Jefferson-Brown, 1985
'Portrush' × 'Cantabile'
Perianth segments broadly ovate, white, tinged green and yellow at base, slightly inflexed, overlapping half; the inner segments with margins incurling; corona bowl-shaped, very shallow, primrose yellow, with green at base. Very late. Resembles 'Portrush in form but with the corona of a different colour

'La Superbe' 8 W or Y-Y or O
(pre-1798)

'La Surpassante' 8
(pre-1820)

'Las Vegas' 1 W-Y
(D. van Buggenum) J. Duindam, 1981
Perianth segments ivory white; corona vivid yellow 9B

'Latchley' 2 Y-O
(Brian S. Duncan) Dan du Plessis, 1993
'Gettysburg' × 'Barnsdale Wood'; sdlg no. 744
Fl. forming a double triangle, 105 mm wide; perianth segments ovate; corona cup-shaped, orange, with mouth flared. Late

'Late Call' 3 W-GYR
(Ballydorn Bulb Farm) Ballydorn Bulb Farm, 1984
'Corncrake × 'Clockface'
Fl. 98 mm wide. Mid-season

'Late Gold' 1 Y-Y
(G.L. Wilson) L. van Leeuwen Jr, 1960
Fl. deep yellow. Late. Resembles a small 'Irish Luck'.
AM(Haarlem) 1960

'Late Love' 2 Y-O
(Jānis Rukšans) Jānis Rukšans, 1997
Sdlg no. 94-12
Fl. 85 mm wide; perianth segments vivid yellow 9A, plane, smooth, overlapping; corona orange (28A), suffused yellow towards base, with yellow-orange (23A) at base, slightly frilled. Late. Sunproof

'La Tendresse' 8 Y-Y
(pre-1798)
Fl. sulphur yellow

'La Tendresse' 2 W-? (b)
(L. van Leeuwen & Son, pre-1931)
AM(Haarlem) 1930. Received AM(Haarlem) 1930 as 'Puck'. ?See also 'Latendresse'

'Latendresse' 2 W-?
(P. van Deursen)
?The same as 'La Tendresse' of van Leeuwen

'Late Present' 2 W-O
(G.H. Rotteveel & Sons) G.H. Rotteveel & Sons, 1981
Fl. 100 mm wide; perianth segments ivory white, with flecks of buttercup yellow; corona vivid orange 28B

'Later Date' 2 Y-O
(J.N. Hancock & Co., c.1977) Unregistered
Perianth segments creamy yellow; corona reddish orange

'Late Snow' 3 W-GWW
(T.D. Throckmorton) T.D. Throckmorton, 1975
'Old Satin' × 'Bryher'; sdlg no. T66/3
Fl. 100 mm wide; corona with green at base

'Late Sol' 8 Y-O
Unregistered
Fls 8-10 per stem, 25-32 mm wide; perianth segments light yellow; corona fairly broad, orange

'Latest of All' 3
(G.P. Haydon, pre-1908)

'Late Success' 2 (a)
(F. Rijnveld & Sons) F. Rijnveld & Sons, 1956
AM(Haarlem) 1956

'Late Sun' 1 Y-Y
(G.E. Mitsch, pre-1954)
'Aerolite' × 'Sorley Boy'; sdlg no. A38C1/1
Perianth segments deep yellow; corona narrow. Mid-season

'Latifa' 2 W-O
(de Graaff Bros, pre-1950)
AM(Haarlem) 1950

N. latifolius Schultes f. = *N. cupularis*

'Latimer' 2 (a)
(van Zonneveld Bros & Philippo, pre-1931)

'Latona' 1 Y-Y
(Barr & Sons, pre-1923)
Fl. butter yellow; corona with rim rolled

'Latonia' 1 W-? (b)
(de Graaff Bros, pre-1914)

'Latonia' 3 W-R
(P. van Deursen, pre-1928)
Mid-season. AM(Haarlem) 1928

'Latony' 1 W-? (b)
(W. Balch, pre-1928)

'La Tosca' 2 W-YYR
(The Brodie of Brodie, c.1915)
'Bernardino' × *N. poeticus*
Corona pale yellow, with red at rim

'La Tosca' 2 Y-Y
(Konynenburg & Mark) Konynenburg & Mark, 1960
'Mimosa' hybrid
Fl. 115 mm wide; perianth brilliant greenish yellow 6B; corona much darker in tone (13A). Late

'La Traviata' 3 Y-YYR
(R. & E.Havens, 1982) R. & E.Havens, 1997
'Bantam' × 'Kindled'; sdlg no. REH7/1A
Fl. 75 mm wide; perianth segments broadly ovate, bright yellow, smooth; corona cup-shaped, bright yellow, with a clearly-defined band of brilliant orange-red at rim. Late. Sunproof

'Latrobe' 1 Y-Y
(J.N. Hancock & Co., 1947) J.N. Hancock & Co., 1964
Fl. mid-yellow; corona darker in tone than the perianth. Early. Resembles an earlier-flowered 'Mortlake'

'Lattice' ?-P
(Alister Clark, pre-1948)

'Lattoon' 2 (a)
(J.L. Richardson, pre-1949)
'Cromarty' × 'Goldcourt'

'Latvia' 2 YOO-O
(Jānis Rukšans) Jānis Rukšans, 1987
'Kissproof' × 'Altruist'; sdlg no. R-77-05/2
Perianth segments brilliant yellow 21C at rim, shading to light orange 23A below; corona funnel-shaped, orange (28A). Late. Fairly sunproof

'Laughing Lady' 2 W-P
(J.N. Hancock & Co., 1955) Unregistered
Corona light orange-pink

'Laughing Water' 3 W-Y
(The Brodie of Brodie, c.1908)
'Minnie Hume' × 'Stella Superba'
Fl. 89 mm wide; perianth segments mucronate, creamy white, overlapping half; corona funnel-shaped, clear sulphur yellow, becoming paler, frilled

'Laughter' 3 W-YYO
(Mrs R.O. Backhouse, pre-1921)
Fl. 76 mm wide, facing down; perianth segments creamy white, reflexed, overlapping half; corona broad funnel-shaped, sulphur yellow, with a broad band of bright reddish orange at rim, frilled. Mid-season to late. Div. 2 until 1945

'Launcells' 7
(P.D. Williams, pre-1930)

'Launy' 4 Y-Y
(?Australian origin, pre-1996) Unregistered

'Laur' 1 W-P
(W. Jackson Sr, 1946)
'Dawnglow' × 'Lalli'

'Laura' 8 Y-O
(Dutch origin, pre-1884)
Perianth segments primrose yellow. Syn. Tazetta 'Laura'. ?The same as 'Laura' 8W-O of Vandervoort

'Laura' 9
(G.H. Engleheart, pre-1890)

'Laura' 2
(pre-1902)
Perianth segments ovate, spreading or a little inflexed, with margins incurled or slightly wavy, overlapping a quarter; corona broad funnel-shaped, much darker in tone than the perianth, mouth expanded, rim loosely flanged and unevenly notched

'Laura' 1 Y-Y
(R.A.van der Schoot, pre-1929)
Corona golden yellow, somewhat darker in tone then the perianth

'Laura' 8 W-O
(J.A. Vandervoort, pre-1931)
?The same as 'Laura' 8Y-O of pre-1884

'Laura' 5 W-W
(L.P. Dettman) L.P. Dettman, 1979
N. triandrus × 'Agnes Webster'
Fls 2 per stem, rounded, 55 mm wide, creamy white, facing down; perianth segments reflexed. Dwarf. Early. Syn. 'Laura Lee'. The colour code W-W is deduced from the originator's records; some stock of apparently good provenance would however be coded W-Y

'Laura David' 2 (a)
(R.O. Backhouse, pre-1931)

'Laura Lee' 5 W-W
(W.O. Ticknor, 1973) W.O. Ticknor, 1986
'Quickstep' × *N. triandrus*; sdlg no. M M-1
Fls usually 3 per stem; perianth segments strongly

reflexed; corona bowl-shaped. Mid-season to late. Resembles a taller 'April Tears' with larger and smoother flowers

'Laura Lee' 5 W-W
Syn. of 'Laura' (Dettman)

'Laura Manser' 3 W-GYY
(Frank Verge) Frank Verge, 1987
'Aircastle' × 'Green Island'
Perianth segments broadly ovate, smooth; corona lemon yellow, mouth slightly flared, wavy. Late

'Laureate' 9 W-YYR
(G.H. Engleheart, pre-1903)
Corona bright yellow, with bright crimson at rim

'Laurens Koster' 8 W-Y
(A. Vis, pre-1906)
'Ornatus' × *N. tazetta*
Fls. 4-5 per stem; perianth segments very broad, rounded or truncate at apex, prominently mucronate, creamy white, spreading, with margins sometimes incurling, overlapping one-third; the inner segments not noticeably mucronate, spathulate, with margins wavy and sometimes recurved; corona shallow bowl-shaped, ribbed, bright orange-yellow, with mouth wavy. 2n=17. AM(Haarlem) 1912

'Laurentia' 5
(J.D. van den Burg, pre-1938)

'Laurentic' 2 W-? (b)
(R.H. Bath, pre-1931)

'Lauretta' 1 W-? (b)
(Barr & Sons, pre-1923)

'Lauriston' 1 W-P
(T. Morrison, pre-1961) Unregistered
Perianth segments broad, pure white, smooth; corona amber pink, with rim flanged

'Lausanne' 1 Y-Y
(P. van Deursen, pre-1933)
AM(Haarlem) 1933

'Lava' 3 W-? (b)
(E.M. Crosfield, pre-1910)

'Lavalier' 5 YYW-W
(G.E. Mitsch) G.E. Mitsch, 1979
'Nazareth' × *N. triandrus* var. *concolor*; sdlg no. G79/3
Fls usually one per stem, 85 mm wide, facing down; perianth segments ovate, bright lemon yellow, with slight white mucro and with a narrow band of white at base, reflexed, overlapping at base only; corona funnel-shaped, lightly ribbed, opening lemon yellow, becoming ivory white, mouth straight, even, with rim obscurely crenate. Mid-season

'La Vella' 2 Y-R
(Brian S. Duncan, 1981) Brian S. Duncan, 1992
'Bunclody' open pollinated; sdlg no. 688
Fl. 97 mm wide; perianth segments broadly ovate, blunt, only very slightly mucronate, golden yellow, tinged green at base, spreading, smooth, overlapping half; the inner segments a little inflexed; corona long cup-shaped, a little constricted near mouth, lightly ribbed, deep orange-red, with mouth straight. Mid-season to late

'Lavender' 3 W-GWP
(P.D. Williams, pre-1908)
Fl. small; corona very shallow, white, with tints of pink, with soft emerald green at base and a stain of soft orange or cerise pink at rim

'Lavender Hope' 2 W-P
(John R.Reed) John R.Reed, 1995
'Melody Lane' × 'Dailmanach'; sdlg no. 81-1-2
Fl. 90 mm wide; perianth segments ovate, dull white, spreading; corona cylindrical, lavender pink. Mid-season to late. Sunproof

'Lavender Lass' 6 W-GPP
(Brian S. Duncan) Rathowen Daffodils, 1976
'Roseworthy' × sdlg R562 × 'Rose Caprice'
Perianth segments ovate, truncate, reflexed, with margins deeply incurved, overlapping one-third; corona lightly ribbed, pale lavender pink, mouth expanded, rim densely and minutely crenate, slightly flanged. Mid-season. Resembles 'Lilac Charm' in colour

'Lavender Mist' 2 W-WPP
(A.J.R.Pearson) A.J.R.Pearson, 1997
Noton sdlg 297 ('Easter Moon' × 'Pigeon') × 'Dailmanach'; sdlg no. 90-24-N41
Fl. forming a double triangle, 110 mm wide; perianth segments broadly ovate, very slightly mucronate, greenish white (157C), slightly reflexed, satin smooth; corona funnel-shaped, opening pale purplish pink 56D, with white at base, the pink becoming paler in tone, mouth ribbed and lobed, rim flanged. Mid-season

'L'Avenir' 1 W-Y
(Mauger & Son, pre-1907)
Sdlg no. 3/4/02
Fl. 127 mm wide; perianth segments deeply overlapping; corona bright yellow, with mouth widely expanded. Closely resembles 'Duke of Bedford'. Syn. 'Avenir'

'Laverna' 2 (a)
(A.M. Wilson, pre-1916)

'La Vestale' 1 W-W
(de Graaff Bros, pre-1927)

'La Victoire' 3 W-YYR
(Mrs R.O. Backhouse, pre-1921)
Corona canary yellow, with orange-red at rim

'Lavington' 2 (a)
(Sir F.C. Stern, pre-1952)

'Lavinia' 8 Y-Y
(pre-1798)
Fl. sulphur yellow

'Lavinia Bingham' 3 W-? (b)
(G.H. Engleheart, pre-1916)

'Lavino' 2 W-? (b)
(A.M. Wilson, pre-1930)
Perianth segments off white; corona with pink at rim

'Lawali' 4 W-P
(W. Jackson Jr) W. Jackson Jr, 1966
'Hugh Dettman' × sdlg 113/51; sdlg no. 6/58
Fl. sometimes measuring Div. 2. 2n=28

'Lawful' 2 W-R
(Sir J.S. Arkwright, pre-1934)
Resembles 'Folly'

'Lawhill' 2 Y-? (a)
(R.V. Favell, pre-1940)
'Fortune' open pollinated

'Lawhitton' 2 Y-O
(G.W. Tarry) du Plessis Bros, 1989
'Red Squirrel' × 'Zanzibar'; sdlg no. G 5 C
Fl. 80 mm wide; perianth segments bright yellow; corona very bright orange. Mid-season

'Lawless' 2 W-P
(Jackson's Daffodils) Jackson's Daffodils, 1987
'Accent' × 'Verran'; sdlg no. 129/78
Perianth segments very broadly ovate, blunt or rounded at apex, slightly mucronate, greenish white (155A), a little concave, overlapping half; the outer segments overlapping one another; the inner segments square-shouldered at base; corona funnel-shaped, smooth, pale yellowish pink 29D, mouth widely expanded, wavy, with irregular lobes sometimes overlapping, rim almost entire. Early

'Laxton Beauty' 3 W-WYY
(Mrs J.Abel Smith) M.W.Baxter, 1996
'Jessiman' hybrid; sdlg no. L33/91
Fl. 90 mm wide; perianth segments roundish, reflexed, somewhat concave, with midrib showing, overlapping half or more; the inner segments narrower and more nearly ovate, more nearly spreading; corona disc-shaped, ribbed, whitish, with vivid yellow 9A at rim, mouth lightly frilled, rim minutely crenate. Late

'Layette' 5
(F.H. Chapman, pre-1927)

'Layonah' 7 Y-Y
(V. Brink) V. Brink, 1970
'Gold Digger' × *N.* × *odorus*
Fl. 70 mm wide

'Laza' 1 W-P
(W. Jackson Sr, 1944)
'Leto' × 'Dawnglow'

'Leader' 2 Y-O
M.J. Jefferson-Brown, 1975
Perianth segments gold; corona orange and gold. Early. Perhaps the same as 'Golden Treasure'

'Leading Lady' 3 W-? (b)
(Cartwright & Goodwin, pre-1910)

'Leading Lady' 3 Y-YYR
(G. Lewis) D.S. Bell, 1955

'Leading Light' 2 Y-R
(Malcolm S. Bradbury, *c.*1979) Malcolm S. Bradbury, 1994
'Shining Light' × 'Torridon'
Fl. 95 mm wide; perianth segments broadly ovate, blunt, with slight white mucro, vivid yellow 9A-B, spreading, a little concave at apex, overlapping half; corona cup-shaped, strongly ribbed, orange-red (30B), mouth straight, even, rim shallowly and irregularly crenate and occasionally notched. Early

'Leah' 2 W-W
(W.F.M. Copeland, pre-1927)
Corona opening creamy white, becoming pure white

'Leal' 2 W-P
(Campbell Duncan) Campbell Duncan, 1956
'Rose of Tralee' × 'Mabel Taylor'

'Leam' 2 W-W
(H.R. Bulman, *c.*1966) Unregistered
'Kendal' × 'Whitemark'

'Leander' 8 Y-Y
(pre-1798)
Fl. golden yellow

'Leander' 2 or 3 W-? (b or c)
(W.B. Hartland, pre-1907)

'Leander' 2 Y-O
(J.L. Richardson) J.L. Richardson, 1961
'Sun Chariot' × 'Ceylon'
Fl. 93 mm wide; perianth segments deep yellow; corona deep reddish orange, with rim slightly flanged. Early

'Leander' 2 Y-?
Syn. of 'Georgia'

'Leanne's Choice' 2 W-GWW
(L.P. Dettman) L.P. Dettman, 1984
'Janice Dettman' × 'Amanda Olsen'; sdlg no. JD-AO 1/80
Fl. 90 mm wide; perianth segments yellowish white 155D; corona darker in tone (155B), with green at base. Mid-season

'Leaping Salmon' 2 W-P
(J.L. Richardson) M.J. Jefferson-Brown, 1964
'Rosewell' × 'Rose Caprice'

'Leara'
(pre-1960) Unregistered

'Least Coin' 9 W-GGR
(Mrs M.S. Yerger) Mrs M.S. Yerger, 1991
'Raeburn' open pollinated; sdlg no. 76 G 5
Late

'Lea Valley' 1 Y-Y
(Mrs J.Abel Smith, pre-1984) M.W.Baxter, 1996
Rogue from among stock of 'Loch Naver'
Fl. 110 mm wide; perianth segments very broadly ovate, blunt, vivid yellow 9A, with whitish mucro, spreading, concave at apex, somewhat creased, overlapping half; the inner segments more narrowly ovate and sometimes slightly twisted; corona cylindrical, very slightly expanding towards the mouth, lightly ribbed, darker in tone than the perianth, mouth straight, even, rim notched and crenate. Early

'Leawood' 2 W-P
(?Australian origin, pre-1997) Unregistered

'Lebanon' 2 Y-Y
(J.N. Hancock & Co., 1954)

'Lebanon' 2 W-Y
(G.E. Mitsch) G.E. Mitsch, 1956
'John Evelyn' × 'Fortune'
Corona almost disc-shaped, large, ribbed, with rim closely and deeply notched, as if fringed. Mid-season. 2n=28

'Le Beau' 6 Y-Y
(Barr & Sons, pre-1925)
N. cyclamineus sdlg
Fl. soft yellow, facing slightly downwards; perianth segments ovate, with slight white mucro, spreading, twisted, overlapping one-eighth; corona cylindrical, smooth, mouth ribbed and a little expanded, with rim crenate. Dwarf to standard. Early. Resembles a taller 'Golden Cycle'

'Le Bouquet Royal' 8
(pre-1793)

'Lebrina' 2 W-O
(S.J. Bisdee, 1944)
'Blodwen' × 'Corra Linn'

'Le Citronniere' 8 Y-Y
(pre-1887)
Perianth segments primrose yellow; corona orange-yellow

'Le Cygne' 1 W-W
(G.E. Mitsch) G.E. Mitsch, 1959
'Fairy Dream' × 'Cantatrice'

'Le Czar de Moscovie' 8 W-Y
Syn. of 'Czar of Muscovy'

'Leda' 2? W-W
(E. Leeds, pre-1877)
Perianth segments narrow, acute; corona opening canary yellow, becoming sulphur white. Scented. Syn. Leedsii 'Galanthiflorus Stellatus', Leedsii 'Leda'

'Leda' 1 W-W
Perianth segments long, narrow, acute; corona opening canary yellow, becoming sulphur white. Scented. Syn. of 'Indiana'

'Ledbury' 1 W-W
(A.M. Wilson, pre-1937)
Sdlg no. 71
Corona with rim rolled

'Ledesma' 1 W-? (b)
(A.M. Wilson, pre-1931)

'Leedsii' 2 Y-YYO
(E. Leeds, pre-1851)
'Major' × *N. poeticus*
Fl. large; perianth segments ovate, yellow, spreading, plane, only slightly overlapping; corona short funnel-shaped, ribbed, deep yellow, heavily stained bright scarlet-orange at rim, mouth straight, wavy, indistinctly lobed. Syn. Incomparabilis Leedsii 'Leedsii'. This has also been used as a Group name

'Leedsii' 2 W-O
(1851)
This has also been used as a Group name. Syn. of 'Cynosure'

'Leedsii' 2 Y-O
(?E. Leeds, pre-1877)
Corona scarlet-orange. Syn. Incomparabilis Sulphureus 'Leedsii'. This has also been used as a Group name

'Leedsii' 3 W-W
(E. Leeds, pre-1877)
Perianth segments long, narrow, acute; corona opening lemon yellow, becoming silvery white. Syn.

Leedsii 'Leedsii'. This has also been used as a Group name

'Lee Mill' 2 Y-O
(J.S.B. Lea) du Plessis Bros, 1989
Sdlg no. 1-1-79
Fl. 105 mm wide; perianth segments deep yellow; corona deep orange. Mid-season. Sunproof

'Lee Moor' 1 Y-Y
(J.S.B. Lea) du Plessis Bros, 1989
'Daydream' × sdlg 2-29-62; sdlg no. 4-40-75
Fl. 80 mm wide; perianth segments lemon yellow; corona cylindrical, opening lemon yellow, touched with pink, becoming paler, with mouth slightly expanded. Late

'Leenan' 5 Y-W
(A. Gray, pre-1952)
Perianth segments primrose

'Leesburg' 2 W-W
(W.G.Pannill) W.G.Pannill, 1994
'Glendermott' × 'Starmount'; sdlg no. J3G
Mid-season

'Leesthorpe' 3 W-Y
(W.A. Noton, 1965) W.A. Noton, 1976
Sdlg no. 619
Fl. 89 mm wide. Mid-season

'Leeston' 1 W-Y
(J. Field) E.W. Cotter, 1968
Corona deep lemon

'Leeuwenhorst' 2 W-YYO
(Papendrecht-Vandervoet, pre-1938)
AM(Haarlem) 1938

'Legacy' 2 W-? (b or c)
(P.D. Williams, pre-1932)

'Legacy' 1 Y-Y
(J.N. Hancock & Co., pre-1974) Unregistered
Corona mouth expanded

'Legal Tender' 1 Y-Y
(F.E. Board) F.E. Board, 1965
'Kingscourt' × 'Wexford'
Mid-season

'Legana' 1 W-P
(C.E. Radcliff, 1942) J.M.Radcliff, 1956
'Rosary' × 'Pink o' Dawn'

'Legato' 2 Y-WWY
(J.N.Hancock & Co., 1982) Unregistered
'Galway' × sdlg 1/70H; sdlg no. 55/82H
Perianth segments strong citron yellow; corona opening yellow, becoming white, with yellow at rim, rolled and dentate. Tall. Early to mid-season

'Legend' 2 (a)
(Sir C.H. Cave, pre-1928)

'Legend' 2 Y-R
(F.E. Board) F.E. Board, 1965
'Ceylon' × 'Royal Charger'
Corona orange-red. Mid-season. Resembles a large flowered 'Ceylon'

'Legionair' 2 W-YYR
(Albert Davis, 1978) Albert Davis, 1989
'Kilworth' × 'Arbar'; sdlg no. 101/75
Fl. 96 mm wide; perianth segments broad, overlapping; corona very shallow bowl-shaped, vivid yellow 9B, with orange-red (30B) at rim, mouth expanded and frilled. Mid-season. Closely resembles 'Ringleader' but with a purer white perianth and a broader rim to the corona

'Le Grand Bouquet' 8
?Syn. of 'Grand Bouquet'

'Le Grand Citronier' 8
(pre-1820)

'Le Grand Monarque' 8
(pre-1820)
?Syn. of 'Grand Monarque'

'Le Grand Souverain' 8
(pre-1820)
?Syn. of 'Grand Souverain'

'Lehiam' 2 Y-GYY
(Colin Crotty) Colin Crotty, 1990
'Golden Aura' × 'Camelot'; sdlg no. 29-75
Fl. 86 mm wide, bright yellow; perianth segments very smooth, overlapping. Mid-season

'Leicester Square' 2 W-P
(Alister Clark, 1945) J. Sharp, 1960

'Leiden Jar' 1 (a)
(G.P. Haydon, pre-1908)

'Leigh' 1 Y-Y
(pre-1951)
Fl. deep gold

'Leila Carew' 2 W-W
(J.L. Richardson, pre-1923)

'Leila Mitchell' 2 (a)
(W.F. Mitchell, pre-1942)

'Leilani' 1 W-W
(H. Daines) H. Daines, 1956

'Leinster' 1 Y-Y
(G.L. Wilson, pre-1934)
'King of the North' × 'Sorley Boy'
Fl. deep lemon yellow; perianth segments overlapping; corona frilled, with rim flanged

'Leith' 1 (a)
(V. Dickinson) Miss M. Verry, 1956

'Leitrim' 2 Y-Y
(J.L. Richardson, pre-1950)
'Royalist' × 'Crocus'
Fl. 108 mm wide, golden yellow; perianth segments broad, slightly acute, vivid yellow 12A, smooth, overlapping; corona vivid yellow 13A, with mouth expanded, rim deeply dentate. AM(e) 1951

'Lelant' 1 W-W
(P.D. Williams, pre-1927)

'Lelo' 2 W-W
(J.S. Leitch) J.S. Leitch, 1967
Fl. 121 mm wide

'Lemberg' 1 Y-Y
(Barr & Sons, pre-1932)
Fl. lemon yellow, of strong substance; corona with rim flanged

'Lembet' 1 Y-Y
(D. Blanchard, pre-1947)
'Clarion' × 'Kandahar'

'Lemcot' 2 Y-O
(J.L. Martin) J.L. Martin, 1973
'Wansea' × 'Kai'
Fl. 100 mm wide

'Lemnos'
(The Brodie of Brodie, c.1916)
'Great Warley' × 'Lord Kitchener'

'Lemnos' 2 Y-Y
(A.H. Ahrens, pre-1949)
Fl. primrose lemon; corona shallow, bowl-shaped. PC 1955

'Le Mogul' 1 (a)
(M. van Waveren & Sons, pre-1942)

'Lemonade' 1 Y-Y
(The Brodie of Brodie, c.1921)
'Nevis' × 'Morven'
Fl. pale citron

'Lemonade' 3 Y-Y
(J.L. Richardson) J.L. Richardson, 1959
'Green Island' × 'Chinese White'
Fl. rounded, 83 mm wide, green-yellow (near to 149D); perianth segments very broad, rounded or squarish at apex, slightly mucronate, opening white, spreading, plane, smooth, with broad midrib showing, overlapping half or more; the inner segments narrower, not noticeably mucronate, slightly truncate, with margins recurved at base and incurled towards apex; corona small bowl-shaped, loosely ribbed, with a deeper tone of yellow at base, mouth split in places and overlapping, frilled, with rim crenate. AM(e) 1961

'Lemonaire' 1 Y-Y
(D.S. Bell) D.S. Bell, 1977
'David Bell' × 'Red Conquest'
Fl. 105 mm wide, creamy lemon; corona narrow, with mouth expanded and shallowly frilled

'Lemonalla' 4 Y-Y
(D.S. Bell) D.S. Bell, 1983
'Papua' × 'Red Conquest' hybrid
Fl. lemon yellow

'Lemon Beauty' 11b W-Y/W
(J.W.A. Lefeber, 1948) J.W.A. Lefeber, 1962
Fl. 100 mm wide; perianth segments very broad in outline, blunt or truncate at apex, prominently mucronate, spreading, concave, overlapping half; the inner segments only very slightly mucronate, with margins wavy; corona split to base, the six segments half as long as the perianth segments and alternate to them, ovate, truncate or sometimes deeply bi-lobed, yellow at base and in a longitudinal band at midrib narrowing towards the apex, with the yellow sometimes touched orange and with broad patches of white at margins, spreading or a little inflexed, with margins wavy or incurled, overlapping, with some short extra growths at the overlap. AM(Haarlem) 1962

'Lemon Belle' 5
(G.H. Engleheart, pre-1913)

'Lemon Bird' 11a Y-Y
(?New Zealand origin) Unregistered

'Lemon Brook' 2 YYW-W
(G.E. Mitsch, 1979) R. & E. Havens, 1991
'Euphony' open pollinated; sdlg no. 2002/
Perianth segments broadly ovate, deep lemon yellow, with white at base; corona cylindrical, becoming pure white at maturity, mouth straight and frilled. Late

'Lemon Candy' 2 YYW-WWY
(Mrs H.K. Richardson) Mrs H.K. Richardson, 1977
'Camelot' × 'Daydream'
Fl. 100 mm wide; perianth segments sulphur yellow, with white at base; corona pale sulphur, with lemon yellow at rim. Mid-season

'Lemon Chiffon' 2 W-GYY
(K. van der Veek) K. van der Veek, 1991
Fl. 110 mm wide; perianth segments between

greenish white 157D and C; corona light greenish yellow 8B with brilliant yellow-green 150B at base. Late

'Lemon Chintz' 2 Y-Y
(W.F.M. Copeland, pre-1914)
Fl. 89 mm wide; perianth segments oval, soft lemon yellow, overlapping; corona of a deeper tone, with mouth flared and frilled. Mid-season

'Lemon Circle' 3 W-OOY
(A.G. Thompson) A.G. Thompson, 1965
'Duke of Windsor' × 'Tuskar Light'
Fl. 89 mm wide; corona deep orange, with a well-defined band of lemon yellow at rim. Mid-season. Resembles 'Tuskar Light' but with a differently coloured corona

'Lemon Cloud' 1 Y-Y
(M.J. Jefferson-Brown) M.J. Jefferson-Brown, 1969
'Spellbinder' × 'Moonstruck'

'Lemon Cooler' 9 W-GYO
(Mrs M.S. Yerger) Mrs M.S. Yerger, 1987
'Sea Green' open pollinated; sdlg no. 76 J 20
Fl. 65 mm wide, of strong substance; perianth segments very broadly ovate; corona very shallow bowl-shaped, brilliant greenish yellow 1A, with strong yellow-green 145A at base and a narrow band of vivid reddish orange 33A at rim, frilled. Late

'Lemon Cremes' 2 YYW-W
(G.E. Mitsch, 1979) R. & E. Havens, 1990
'Top Notch' × 'Chiloquin'; sdlg no. NN23/2
Fl, 90 mm wide, of very heavy substance; perianth segments deep creamy yellow, with white at base; corona cylindrical, opening buff, becoming pure white, neatly frilled. Mid-season

'Lemon Crinkles' 2 W-? (b)
(Mrs M. Moorby) Mrs M. Moorby, 1957

'Lemon Cup' 2 W-Y
(G.A. Uit den Boogaard, pre-1944)
Sdlg no. GBS 10
Perianth segments creamy white, spreading, deeply creased, often twisted, overlapping; corona deeply ribbed, opening golden yellow, becoming pale apricot yellow, with a narrow band of primrose yellow at rim

'Lemoncurd Cream' 11a W-Y/W
(J.Gerritsen & Sons) Mrs E.Bullivant, 1997
Sdlg no. GBS 10
Fl. 96 mm wide; perianth segments very broad, slightly mucronate, square-shouldered at base, creamy white, reflexed, plane, creased at shoulder, overlapping one-third; the inner segments strongly inflexed at base, reflexed towards apex; corona split to base, the six segments as long and broad as the perianth segments and opposite to them, very deeply 2- or 3-lobed, with margins particularly of a middle lobe tightly folded back, ribbed, light yellow 3C, with creamy white at margins, inflexed, deeply frilled

'Lemon Delicious' 2 YYW-WWY
(Ken Farmer Nurseries) Ken Farmer Nurseries, 1978
Fl. 115 mm wide. Mid-season

'Lemon Delight' 11a W-Y
(J. Gerritsen & Son) J. Gerritsen & Son, 1981
'Riesling' hybrid
Fl. 100 mm wide; perianth segments ivory white; corona primrose yellow. Mid-season

'Lemon Doric' 2 Y-W
(G.L. Wilson) F.E. Board, 1955
'Binkie' × 'Spellbinder'
2n=27. Resembles a stronger and taller 'Binkie' with a longer corona; resembles both parents in colouring

'Lemon Drop' 2 (a)
(G.H. Engleheart, pre-1907)
See also 'Lemondrop'

'Lemondrop' 2 (a)
Syn. of 'Lemon Drop'

'Lemon Drops' 5 Y-Y
(G.E. Mitsch) G.E. Mitsch, 1956
'Fortune' × *N. triandrus*
Fls often 3 per stem, soft lemon, facing down

'Lemon Empress' 1 Y-W
(Brian S. Duncan) Brian S. Duncan, 1989
? 'Amber Castle' hybrid; sdlg no. 1042
Perianth segments broadly ovate, pale greenish yellow, spreading; corona cylindrical, opening pale greenish yellow, becoming almost pure white, mouth widely expanded, with rim lightly crenate

'Lemonetta' 2 (a)
(Barr & Sons, pre-1937)

'Lemon Eye' 8 W-Y
(A.C. van der Schoot, pre-1931)
Poetaz
Corona long, lemon yellow

'Lemon Fancy' 1 Y-Y
(W.J. Dunlop) W.J. Dunlop, 1958
'King of the North' × 'Content'
Fl. of varying tones of lemon

'Lemon Flash' 2 W-Y
(Tom Forster, 1960s) Unregistered
'Artist's Model' hybrid
Perianth segments snow white; corona broad disc-shaped, bright lemon yellow, frilled. Late

'Lemon Frill' 3 W-Y
(Sir C.H. Cave, pre-1913)
'Mabel Cowan' × 'Lulworth'
Corona pale lemon, tinged cream, frilled

'Lemon Giant' 1 Y-Y
(J.R. Pearson & Sons, pre-1923)
'Florence Pearson' hybrid

'Lemon Glow' 1 Y-Y
(G. Lubbe & Son) G. Lubbe & Son, 1958
Fl. primrose yellow; the corona lighter in tone, with primrose yellow at rim. AM(Haarlem) 1958, FCC(Haarlem) 1961

'Lemon Grey' 3 W-Y
(Brian S.Duncan) Brian S.Duncan, 1997
(['Dallas' hybrid × 'Cool Crystal'] × 'Vernal Prince') × sdlg 349 ('Aircastle' × 'Woodland Prince'); sdlg no. 1517
Fl. rounded, 95 mm wide; perianth segments very broad, roundish, blunt; corona shallow, slightly ribbed, lemon yellow, with grey at base, lightly frilled. Mid-season to late

'Lemon Haze' 2 Y-GWY
(D.S. Bell) D.S. Bell, 1982
'Riptide' × 'Qantasia'
Fl. 104 mm wide, of firm substance; corona pure white, with green at base, with gold at rim in early stages. Mid-season. Resembles 'Riptide' but with colour at corona rim

'Lemon Heart' 5 W-W
(Barr & Sons, pre-1952)
Fls up to 4 per stem; perianth segments white; corona cream. 2n=21. Syn. 'White Heart'

'Lemon Heart' 2 Y-Y
Syn. of 'Tiki'

'Lemonia' 2 (a)
(C.G. van Tubergen, pre-1944)

'Lemon Ice' 11a W-Y
(A.N. Kanouse, 1956) A.N. Kanouse, 1976
'Hillbilly' × 'Lisbreen'
Fl. 89 mm wide; corona lemon, with a lighter tone at base, frilled. Mid-season

'Lemon Ice' 2 G-G
(W.M. Spry, pre-1975) Unregistered
'Hunter's Moon' × 'Tunis'
Fl. lemon green

'Lemonick' 2 Y-Y
(M.P. Williams, pre-1949)
Fl. 89 mm wide; perianth segments brilliant greenish yellow 6B, overlapping; corona ribbed, vivid yellow 13A, with mouth expanded and frilled

'Lemon Lantern' 1 W-Y
(V. Brink) V. Brink, 1966
'Quip' open pollinated
Fl. 102 mm wide; corona flared, clear lemon yellow. Mid-season

'Lemon Light' 2 Y-Y
(D. Bramley) D. Bramley, 1962
Fl. 102 mm wide, lemon yellow. Late. Resembles 'Lemnos' but with broader and smoother perianth segments and with the corona mouth straight

'Lemon Lyric' 2 YYW-Y
(G.E. Mitsch, 1979) R. & E. Havens, 1992
'Top Notch' × 'Camelot'; sdlg no. 2027/10
Fl. 100 mm wide, very smooth; perianth segments broad, rounded at apex, deep lemon yellow, with a band of white at base, spreading; corona long, pinkish buff yellow. Late. Somewhat resembles a larger-flowered 'Top Notch' with a longer corona

'Lemon Meringue' 1 Y-Y
(G.E. Mitsch, pre-1954)
'King of the North' × 'Content'
Fl. sulphur lemon. Mid-season

'Lemon Mist' 1 Y-Y
(D.S. Bell) D.S. Bell, 1984
'Red Conquest' hybrid × 'Golden Fortune'
Fl. 107 mm wide, lemon yellow. Mid-season

'Lemon Moon' 2 Y-GYY
(Mrs G. Link) Mrs G. Link, 1979
'Beige Beauty' × 'Limeade'; sdlg no. 1067
Fl. 85 mm wide; perianth segments light yellow; corona deeper in tone, with green at base, frilled. Mid-season

'Lemonora' 1 Y-Y
(The Brodie of Brodie, c.1932)
'Corinth' × 'Naxos'; sdlg no. 70/A/27
Fl. very pale sulphur, almost white

'Lemon Phoenix' 4 W-Y
Syn. of 'Sulphur Phoenix'

'Lemon Pie' 1 (a)
(Oregon Bulb Farms, pre-1946)

'Lemon Punch' 6 W-Y
(Jānis Rukšans, 1985) Jānis Rukšans, 1997
'Jenny' × 'Empress of Ireland'; sdlg no. 79-19-5
Fl. 80 mm wide; perianth segments narrow, pure white, strongly reflexed; corona cylindrical, light greenish yellow 4B, with a paler tone at base, becoming almost self white with age. Dwarf. Very early. Resembles a more floriferous 'Toby' with slightly narrower perianth segments and a differently shaped corona with greener tones at base

'Lemon Queen' 2 Y-Y
(G.H. Engleheart, pre-1907)
Perianth segments soft yellow; corona deeper in tone

'Lemon Queen' 11?b
(J.W.A. Lefeber)

'Lemon Rim' 1 W-W
(D. Bramley) D. Bramley, 1963
Fl. 102 mm wide; corona creamy white, with lemon yellow at rim. Mid-season

'Lemon Sails' 2 Y-Y
(G.E. Mitsch, 1978) R. & E. Havens, 1991
Sdlg B36 ('Playboy' × 'Daydream') open pollinated; sdlg no. MO25/20
Perianth segments broad, lemon yellow, waxen smooth and of heavy substance; corona buff yellow. Mid-season

'Lemon Sherbet' 2 W-GYY
(Carncairn Daffodils) Carncairn Daffodils, 1979
Probably 'Aircastle' × 'Green Island'; sdlg no. 151
Fl. 110 mm wide; perianth segments greenish white 157D; corona expanded, slightly ribbed, light greenish yellow 6D, with moderate yellowish green 139B at base and a brighter tone of yellow (6A) at rim. Mid-season

'Lemon Silk' 6 YYW-W
(G.E. Mitsch & R.& E.Havens, 1971) G.E. Mitsch & R.& E.Havens, 1987
'Nazareth' × *N. cyclamineus*; sdlg no. G78/2
Perianth segments narrowly ovate, soft lemon, with white at base, more or less reflexed, very smooth, separated or slightly overlapping; corona cylindrical, lightly and broadly ribbed, white, with mouth straight, rim irregularly and minutely notched and crenate. Early

'Lemon Snow' 2 YYW-WWY
(G.E. Mitsch & R.& E.Havens, 1970) G.E. Mitsch & R.& E.Havens, 1986
'Lunar Sea' hybrid; sdlg no. F88/1
Perianth segments lemon yellow, with sulphur white at base; corona opening lemon yellow, becoming sulphur white, with lemon yellow remaining at rim. Mid-season. Resembles 'Impresario' but with the rim more deeply rolled

'Lemon Sorbet' 1 Y-WWY
?Syn. of 'Touch of Silver'

'Lemon Soufflé' 3 W-Y
(G.L. Wilson) Guy L.Wilson Ltd, 1967
'Easter Moon' × 'Shantallow'
Corona rich lemon yellow, slightly frilled. Mid-season

'Lemon Sparks' 4 Y-Y
(G.E. Mitsch, 1976) R. & E. Havens, 1990
'Gay Time' × 'Chiloquin'; sdlg no. LL61/1
Fl. 100 mm wide; corona segments slightly deeper in tone than the perianth. Late. Resembles 'Moonflight' but with the segments more regularly arranged

'Lemon Sprite' 7 YYW-W
(G.E. Mitsch and R. & E.Havens, 1970) G.E. Mitsch and R. & E.Havens, 1988
'Daydream' × *N. jonquilla*; sdlg no. F72/25
Fls 2-3 per stem; perianth segments lemon yellow, white white at base; corona bowl-shaped, becoming white. Mid-season. Resembles 'Pipit' but with a broader and darker-coloured perianth and a more regularly formed corona

'Lemon Squash' 2 W-?W
(Miss K.M. Hinchliff, pre-1941)
Corona opening pale lemon yellow, becoming creamy white

'Lemon Squash' 1 Y-Y
(Mrs A.R. Simmons) Mrs A.R. Simmons, 1980
Fl. 90 mm wide, sulphur lemon. Mid-season

'Lemon Star' 2 W-Y
(W.F.M. Copeland, pre-1907)
Fl. large; perianth segments yellowish white, spreading, overlapping; corona expanded, opening lemon yellow, becoming whitish

'Lemon Tarts' 7 YYW-W
(G.E. Mitsch, 1968) G.E. Mitsch, 1979
'Quick Step' × 'Daydream'; sdlg no. D80/11
Fls 1-3 per stem, 80 mm wide; perianth segments lemon with white at base; corona becoming white. Late. Resembles 'Wishing Well' but with more sharply contrasting colours

'Lemon Tree' 3 W-YYO
(G.E. Mitsch, 1960) G.E. Mitsch, 1979
'Cushendall' open pollinated; sdlg no. VO3/3
Fl. 72 mm wide; corona yellow, with a narrow band of orange at rim in damp climates. Late

'Lemon Trim' 3 W-WWY
(D. Bramley) D. Bramley, 1968
Fl. 108 mm wide; corona creamy white, with a broad band of bright lemon yellow at rim. Late. Resembles 'Green Island' but has no green at corona base

'Lemon Weardale' 1 Y-Y
(G.L. Wilson, pre-1935)
'Weardale Perfection' hybrid

'Lemon Weargraaff' 1 (a)
(C.L. Adams, pre-1913)

'Lemrose' 2 W-YYP
(J.L. Martin, 1972) J.L. Martin, 1982
'Del Rose' hybrid; sdlg no. DR/B 18

Fl. 100 mm wide; corona lemon yellow, with strong yellowish pink 32D at rim. Mid-season

'Lemstar' 1 Y-Y
(Barr & Sons, pre-1929)
Perianth segments deep lemon yellow; corona deeper in tone than the perianth, with rim notched and flanged

'Lena' 1 Y-Y
(pre-1890)
Perianth segments primrose yellow; corona lemon yellow

'Lena' 2 W-W
(C.A. Latta) C.A. Latta, 1956

'Lena' 1 W-Y
Syn. of 'Little Dancer'

'Lena Parker' 2 W-? (b)
(G.H. Engleheart, pre-1907)

'Lenarda' 2 (a)
(Parr's Nurseries, 1948) Parr's Nurseries, 1958

'Lendra' 3 (a)
(P.D. Williams, pre-1933)

'Lenna' 2 Y-R
(C.E. Radcliff, 1936)
('Warflame' × 'Puzzle') × 'Blodwen'

'Lennox' 2 (a)
(A.M. Wilson, pre-1931)

'Lennox Milne' 3 W-W
(Brodie Gardens) Brodie Gardens, 1959
'Chinese White' × 'Alltyre'
Perianth segments broad; corona tinged green at base, frilled. Resembles a small flowered 'Alltyre'

'Lennymore' 2 Y-R
(Brian S. Duncan) Rathowen Daffodils, 1983
'Shining Light' × 'Torridon'; sdlg no. 721
Perianth segments very broadly ovate, blunt, deep golden yellow, with slight white mucro, spreading, plane, overlapping half; the inner segments more narrowly ovate, rounded at apex, slightly inflexed; corona bowl-shaped, ribbed, orange-red, mouth expanded, lightly frilled, shallowly 6-lobed. Mid-season. Resembles a larger 'Shining Light' of better substance and deeper colour. AM 1997

'Lenore Nethercote' 2 Y-YYO
(H.A. Brown, 1931) R. Hyde, 1958
Perianth segments golden yellow; corona with bright orange at rim, frilled

'Len's Legacy' 2 Y-R
(L.J. Chambers) Koanga Daffodils, 1992
Sdlg 66/135 × 'True Orbit'
Fl. 105 mm wide; perianth segments very broadly ovate, rounded at apex, vivid yellow 12A; corona bowl-shaped, orange-red (30C). Mid-season

"Lent Lily"
See "The Lent Lily"

'Lenz' 1 W-Y
(L.J. Chambers) L.J. Chambers, 1972
Fl. 102 mm wide; perianth segments smooth; corona straight-sided, lemon yellow

'Lenzburg' 2 Y-R
(J.M. de Navarro) J.M. de Navarro, 1968
Sdlg × 'Majorca'

'Leo' 1 W-? (b)
(E.M. Crosfield, pre-1908)

'Leominster' 3 W-? (b)
(P.D. Williams, pre-1928)

'Leonaine' 2 W-P
(G.E. Mitsch) G.E. Mitsch, 1959
'Green Island' hybrid; sdlg no. P36/3
Perianth segments smooth, overlapping; corona bowl-shaped, pink, with a distinct band of lavender midway between base and rim. Mid-season

'Leonard' 1 W-W
(P.D. Williams, pre-1910)

'Leonard Buckland' 2 Y-O
(West & Fell, pre-1935)
Perianth segments rich yellow; corona expanded, rich reddish orange, frilled

'Leonard Montgomerie' 2 Y-Y
(L.P. Dettman) L.P. Dettman, 1978
'Arctic Gold' × 'Ghana'; sdlg no. 34/75
Fl. 95 mm wide; perianth segments brilliant yellow 7A; corona darker in tone (14A). Resembles 'Ghana' but with the inner perianth segments slightly inflexed and a narrower corona

'Leonardo da Vinci' 2 W-O
(J.W.A. Lefeber) J.W.A. Lefeber, 1968
'Redmarley' hybrid

N. leonensis Pugsley = *N. nobilis* var. *leonensis*

'Leonia'
(pre-1914)

'Leonidas' 3 W-? (b)
(W.B. Hartland, pre-1907)

'Léonie' 2 Y-Y
(R.van der Schoot & Son, pre-1907)
Fl. soft yellow; corona short, expanded

'Leonie' 3 W-Y
(E.W. Cotter) E.W. Cotter, 1968
Sdlg × 'Rosewell'

'Leonora' 2 (a)
(W.B. Hartland, pre-1914)

'Leonora' 3 W-OOY
(J.L. Richardson) Mrs H.K. Richardson, 1963
'Kilworth' × 'Rockall'
Fl. 102 mm wide; perianth segments roundish, greenish white 155A, slightly reflexed, overlapping; corona ribbed, strong orange 24A, with yellow at rim, dentate. 2n=28. AM(e) 1969

'Leonta' 2 W-O
(J.T. Gray, pre-1949)
Perianth segments ivory white; corona spreading, deep apricot

'Leontes' 2 Y-Y
(A.M. Wilson, pre-1913)
'Beacon' × 'Lord Roberts'
Fl. 82 mm wide; perianth segments lemon, overlapping half; corona shallow funnel-shaped, expanded, buttercup yellow

'Leontine' 2 W-O
(J.W.A. Lefeber) J.W.A. Lefeber, 1968
'Redmarley' hybrid

'Lepena' 3 W-YRR
(S.J. Bisdee, pre-1938)
'Margaret H.' × 'Sunstar'

'Le Phare' 3 W-? (b)
(pre-1913)
'White Knight' × 'Tenedos'
Fl. pure white, of thick and waxy texture

'Le Phare' 1 W-W
(J.L. Richardson, pre-1930)

'Leprechaun' 2 Y-R
(P.D. Williams, pre-1939)
Perianth segments deep lemon gold; corona ruby red

'Le Printemps' 1 (a)
(G.H. Engleheart, pre-1916)

'Le Printemps' 2 W-W
Syn. of 'Florentia'

'Lerida' 8
(F. Rijnveld & Sons, pre-1939)

'Leroy' 3
(?F.H. Chapman, pre-1913)

'Lerryn' 1 (a)
(P.D. Williams, pre-1930)

'Lesbia' 1 W-W
(Sir A.P.W. Thomas, pre-1930)

'Lesley Barbara' 1 Y-Y
(L.P. Dettman, 1966) L.P. Dettman, 1979
'Galway' × 'Yellow Moon'; sdlg no. 1-66
Fl. 109 mm wide; perianth segments brilliant yellow 7A; corona darker in tone (14A). Mid-season. Resembles a larger-flowered 'Galway'

'Leslie Dudley' 3 W-O
(H.G. Longford, pre-1928)
Perianth segments ivory; corona orange

'Leslie Hill' 1 W-GWW
(Carncairn Daffodils, 1969) Carncairn Daffodils, 1985
'Chinese White' × 'Ave'; sdlg no. 1-8-64
Fl. forming a double triangle; perianth segments broadly ovate, blunt, very slightly mucronate, spreading or slightly inflexed, plane, overlapping one-third; the inner segments more narrowly ovate, more strongly inflexed at base, reflexed towards apex, with margins wavy; corona cylindrical, smooth, with mouth expanded and even, rim minutely notched. Early

'Leslie Hulbert' 2 W-Y
(H.R. Meyer, pre-1927)
'Lucifer' hybrid
Fl. 115 mm wide; perianth segments pure white, overlapping half; corona slender, brilliant yellow 9C, with mouth expanded. 2n=28. *AM(g) 1946

'Lesneague' 3 (a)
(P.D. Williams, pre-1933)

'Le Soleil d'Or' 8 Y-Y or O
Syn. of 'Soleil d'Or'

'Les Preludes' 2 W-W
(G.E.Mitsch, 1974) R. & E.Havens, 1997
'Celilo' × 'Paradise'; sdlg no. 2J49/1
Fl. 100 mm wide, pure white; perianth segments very broadly ovate; corona with mouth slightly flared and frilled. Early

'Lester' 2 (a)
(L. Buckland, pre-1936)

'Letchmoor' 3 W-? (b)
(R.O. Backhouse, pre-1930)

'Lethen' 2 Y-O
(Brodie Gardens) Brodie Gardens, 1957
Hybrid between 'Garland' and ('Invergordon' × 'Damson')
Fl. rounded; perianth segments clear yellow, waxen smooth and of great substance; corona very shallow bowl-shaped, bright reddish orange

'Leti' 2 Y-Y
(W. Jackson Jr, 1957) Unregistered
'Kalman' × 'Vigi'

'Leticia' 2 W-P
Syn. of 'Letticia'

'Letitia' 2 W-P
Syn. of 'Letticia'

'Leto' 9
(pre-1907)

'Leto' 2 W-P
(W. Jackson Sr, 1938) W. Jackson Jr, 1956
'Pink o' Dawn' × 'Pinkeen'

'L'Etoile d'Or' 8 Y-Y
Syn. of 'Etoile d'Or'

'Le Torch' 4 Y-R
(Brian S.Duncan) Brian S.Duncan, 1997
Sdlg 633 ('Gettysburg' × 'Barnsdale Wood') × 'Smokey Bear'; sdlg no. 1318
Fl. 110 mm wide; perianth and other petaloid segments deep golden yellow; the outer whorls ovate; the inner whorls smaller, irregularly arranged; corona segments interspersed, deep red. Mid-season to late. Sunproof

'Letsee' 2 Y-R
(Jackson's Daffodils) Jackson's Daffodils, 1989
'Rabid' × 'Blandfordia'; sdlg no. 43/84
Fl. forming a double triangle, 105 mm wide; perianth segments rounded at apex, vivid yellow 9B; corona orange-red (30C), slightly frilled. Mid-season

'Let's Go' 2 W-? (b)
(L. van Leeuwen & Son, pre-1942)

'Letterkenny' 1 Y-Y
(W.J. Dunlop) W.J. Dunlop, 1957
'Hebron' × 'Crocus'
Fl. golden yellow

'Lettice Harmer' 1 W-Y
(G.H. Engleheart, pre-1897)
Perianth segments flushed yellow at base; corona canary yellow, with rim flanged. Very early. AM 1897

'Letticia' 2 W-P
(Alister Clark, 1945) J. Sharp, 1960

Syn. 'Leticia', 'Letitia'

'Letty' 9
(A.G. Bull, pre-1933)

'Leura' 1 Y-Y
(A.O. Roblin, pre-1936)
'La La' × 'Melissa'

'Levada' 9
(A.M. Wilson, pre-1932)

'Levant' 1 W-W
(The Brodie of Brodie, pre-1930)
'Tenedos' × 'White Knight'

'Leven' 2 W-Y
(W. Jackson Jr) Jackson's Daffodils, 1979
Sdlg 156/61 × 'Neerim'; sdlg no. 175/71
Fl. 102 mm wide. Mid-season

'Leverington' 1 W-W
(R.H. Bath, pre-1929)

'Levi' 1 (a)
(G.P. Haydon, pre-1908)

'Leviathan' 2 Y-? (a)
(de Graaff Bros & van Konynenburg & Co., pre-1927)
Fl. large; perianth segments sulphur yellow; corona very shallow, flecked with colour. AM(Haarlem) 1927, FCC(Haarlem) 1932

'Leviathan' 2 Y-Y
(West & Fell, pre-1936)
Perianth segments pale yellow

'Levity' 2 W-? (b or c)
(A.M. Wilson, pre-1927)

'Le Voleur' 1 W-Y
(J.L. Richardson, pre-1930)
'Cleopatra' × 'White Knight'
Perianth segments pure white, deeply overlapping; corona soft lemon yellow, frilled

'Levona' 3 W-W
(A.M. Wilson, pre-1949)

'Lewannick' 2 W-WWY
(Mrs H.K. Richardson) du Plessis Bros, 1987
'Stainless' × 'Verona'; sdlg no. 888
Late

'Lewarne' 2 (a)
(P.D. Williams, pre-1933)

'Lewdown' 2 Y-O
(Brian S. Duncan) du Plessis Bros, 1989

'Richhill' × 'Bunclody'; sdlg no. 464
Fl. 95 mm wide; perianth segments satin smooth; corona deep orange. Mid-season. Sunproof

'Lewis Butler' 2 W-? (b)
(H.R. Meyer, pre-1927)

'Lewis Carroll' 9 W-YYR
(Mrs R.O. Backhouse, pre-1908)
Fl. 90 mm wide, rounded; perianth segments slightly inflexed; corona canary yellow, with a distinct band of dark madder red at rim

'Lewis George' 1 Y-Y
(R.A.Scamp) S.Holden, 1996
'Viking' × 'Ristin'; sdlg no. 55
Fl. 93 mm wide, dark golden yellow; perianth segments ovate, smooth, deeply overlapping; corona cylindrical. Early to mid-season

'Lewis Palmer' 2 W-GYY
(L. Palmer) Mrs L. Palmer, 1973
Sdlg no. 6
Fl. 114 mm wide, facing up; perianth segments broadly ovate, creamy white, spreading, creased, overlapping; the inner segments inflexed; corona funnel-shaped, broad, strongly ribbed, vivid yellow 16A, flushed light orange (21A), paling to creamy yellow in lower part, with green at base and pale yellow outside, mouth straight, rim shallowly crenate. Early.
*HC(g) 1973

'Lexington Green' 2 W-GWW
(R. & E.Havens) R. & E.Havens, 1996
'Misty Glen' × 'Angel'; sdlg no. Y149/4
Fl. 105 mm wide, pure white; perianth segments broadly ovate, spreading, plane, of heavy substance; corona bowl-shaped, with a large patch of intense green at base, mouth slightly frilled. Late

'Leyton' 2 W-? (b)
(R.H. Bath, pre-1933)

'L.F.M.'
(pre-1913)

'Lhasa' 1 W-W
(pre-1968) Unregistered

'Liapoota' 4 W-O
(K.J. Heazlewood) K.J. Heazlewood, 1968
'Glowing Red' × 'Rouge'
Fl. 102 mm wide; corona segments apricot orange. Mid-season

'Libby Holman' 1 W-W
(G.L. Wilson) Warnaar & Co., 1959
Fl. 89 mm wide. Mid-season

'Libelle' 2 W-? (b)
(de Graaff Bros, pre-1936)
AM(Haarlem) 1936

'Liberator' 1 (a)
(J.O. Sherrard, pre-1943)

'Libertine' 2 O-O
(F.E. Board) F.E. Board, 1965
'Makassar' × 'Golden Torch'
Mid-season

'Liberty' 3 (a)
(Sir C.H. Cave, pre-1908)

'Liberty' 1 (a)
(Speelman, c.1930)
?The same as Hemerick's cv. of the same name

'Liberty' 1 Y-Y
(G.F. Hemerick, pre-1931)
Fl. large, rich golden yellow. Tall. Early. ?The same as Speelman's cv. of the same name

'Liberty' 2 W-Y
(G.W.E. Brogden) G.W.E. Brogden, 1963
Fl. 102 mm wide; corona lemon yellow. Late

'Liberty Bells' 5 Y-Y
(F. Rijnveld & Sons, pre-1950)
Fls usually 2 per stem, 90 mm wide, brilliant greenish yellow 6A; perianth segments prominently mucronate, spreading, overlapping one-third; corona very broadly ribbed, mouth constricted and slightly wavy, very shallowly 6-lobed, touched white between lobes. 2n=21. AM(Haarlem) 1950, *AM(g) 1974, *FCC(p) 1976

'Liberty Light' 2 W-YYO
(J.L. Richardson, pre-1952)
'Coral Island' open pollinated
Perianth segments pure white; corona pale yellow, with pinkish orange at rim

'Libido' 3 W-YOO
(W. Jackson Jr) Jackson's Daffodils, 1979
'Placid' × 'Altyre'; sdlg no. 115/73
Fl. 98 mm wide. Mid-season

'Libra' 2 W-Y
(W.F.M. Copeland, pre-1908)
'Minnie Hume' × 'Madame de Graaff'
Fl. of heavy substance; perianth segments ivory white, overlapping; corona large, light yellow, with mouth expanded and frilled

'Libya' 2 W-O
(J.L. Richardson) J.L. Richardson, 1959
'Kilworth' × 'Cairo'
Corona deep orange-red, frilled

'Lichfield' 3 W-GYR
(C.R. Wootton) C.R. Wootton, 1956
Corona greenish primrose, with a broad band of red at rim

'Licinius' 2 (a)
(de Graaff Bros, pre-1928)

'Lickety Split' 11a W-Y
(N.H. Anglo) N.H. Anglo, 1988
'Cassata' × 'Egard'
Perianth segments creamy white; corona regularly split, the six segments yellow, spreading. Mid-season

'Licon' 2 Y-R
(W. Jackson Jr) W. Jackson Jr, 1970
Sdlg 187/53 × 'Dimity'; sdlg no. 120/65

'Lidcot' 3 W-YYO
(Mrs R.O. Backhouse, pre-1921)
?'Will Scarlett' hybrid
Perianth segments broadly ovate, rounded at apex, slightly mucronate, pure white, spreading, with margins sometimes wavy or incurled, overlapping half; the inner segments slightly inflexed, not noticeably mucronate, somewhat truncate, asymmetrically shouldered at base; corona disc-shaped, ribbed, pale bright yellow, shading to intense yellow-orange at rim, with the rim closely and minutely dentate. AM(Haarlem) 1932, AM(e) 1933

'Liddon' 2 W-Y
(W.G.Pannill) W.G.Pannill, 1994
('Bizerta' × 'Festivity') × 'Downpatrick'; sdlg no. 70/35A
Early to mid-season

'Lido' 2 W-W
(The Brodie of Brodie, c.1923)
'Imbros' × 'Tenedos'; sdlg no. 108/B/18
Corona opening primrose, becoming white

'Lieberstraume' 2 W-P
(D.S. Bell) D.S. Bell, 1957
'Salmon Trout' × pink sdlg
Corona clear pink. AM(e)(NZ) 1976

'Liebeslied' 3 W-WWP
(R. & E.Havens, 1984) R. & E.Havens, 1995
'Ever Pink' × 'Jewel Song'; sdlg no. TEH6/14
Fl. 90 mm wide; perianth segments ovate, pure white, spreading, plane; corona cup-shaped, white, with reddish pink at rim, mouth wavy. Late. Sunproof

'Liège' 1 W-Y
(D.V. West, pre-1923)
Perianth segments creamy white; corona rich creamy yellow

'Liena' 2 W-P
(C.E. Radcliff, 1944)
'Pinkeen' × 'Dawnglow'

"Lien Chu Lily"
Syn. of *N.tazetta* subsp. *lacticolor*

'Lieutenant N.R.W.Thomas' 1 W-Y
Syn. of 'Norman Thomas'

'Lieutenant Sorby' 1 Y-Y
(D.S. Bell, pre-1931)
Early

'Lieut. H.Hodges' 1 W-W
(H.R. Meyer, pre-1927)
Fl. 102 mm wide, creamy white; perianth segments overlapping half; corona mouth expanded. Syn. 'Harold Hodge', 'Harold Hodges'. *HC 1949

'Life' 7 YYW-Y
(G.E. Mitsch) G.E. Mitsch, 1979
'Top Notch' × *N. jonquilla*; sdlg no. KK99/2
Fl. 80 mm wide; perianth segments lemon yellow, touched white at base; corona lemon, with undertones of pink in favourable conditions. Mid-season

'Lifeguard' 1 W-? (b)
(F.H. Chapman, pre-1927)

'Light Brigade' 2 W-R
(G. Lewis, 1945) D.S. Bell, 1958
Corona deep red

'Light Fantastic' 9 W-GYO
(Mrs M.S. Yerger) Mrs M.S. Yerger, 1992
'Red Rim' × 'Lights Out'; sdlg no. 75 K 3
Fl. rounded; perianth segments opening ivory white, becoming pure white; corona almost disc-shaped, brilliant greenish yellow 3A, with moderate yellow-green 138B at base and pinkish orange (32D) at rim. Late. Resembles sibling 'Light Touch'

'Lightheart' 1 W-Y
(G.L. Wilson, pre-1935)
Perianth segments broad, pure white; corona clear bright lemon yellow, with rim flanged

'Lighthouse' 3 W-? (b)
(G.H. Engleheart, pre-1916)

'Lighthouse' 2 W-? (b)
(West & Fell, pre-1936)
Sdlg no. 109

'Lighthouse' 3 W-R
(Brian S. Duncan) Rathowen Daffodils, 1981
'Avenger' × 'Merlin'; 109
Perianth segments broadly ovate, blunt, very slightly mucronate, spreading, concave at apex, smooth, overlapping half; the inner segments more narrowly ovate,

sometimes truncate, a little inflexed, with margins sightly wavy or incurved, sometimes creased at shoulder; corona disc-shaped, loosely ribbed, deep orange-red, mouth even, obscurely lobed, rim entire. Mid-season. Resembles a larger 'Mahmoud' of more vigorous habit

'Lighthouse Reef' 1 YYW-WWY
(A.J.R.Pearson) A.J.R.Pearson, 1995
'Daydream' × 'Gin and Lime'; sdlg no. 89-24-M12
Fl. forming a double triangle, 100 mm wide; perianth segments broadly ovate, blunt, opening brilliant greenish yellow 1A, becoming deeper in tone (5A), with greenish white (2D) at base, a little reflexed, smooth and of heavy substance, very deeply overlapping; the inner segments acute and more nearly spreading; corona cylindrical, broad, lightly ribbed, opening brilliant greenish yellow 1A, becoming creamy white (4C), with ochre yellow (7B) at rim, mouth flared, rim flanged and crenate. Mid-season

'Lightning' 2 (a)
(G.H. Johnstone, pre-1944)

'Light of America' 9 W-GYP
(Mrs M.S. Yerger) Mrs M.S. Yerger, 1993
'Lights Out' × 'Ace of Diamonds'; sdlg no. 75 L 8
Fl. forming a double triangle, 55 mm wide; perianth segments acute; the inner segments narrower and a little shorter; corona almost disc-shaped, yellow, with brilliant yellow-green 154B at base and pink (38A) at rim. Late

'Light o' Morn' 9 W-OOR
(Mrs M.S. Yerger) Mrs M.S. Yerger, 1994
'Tart' × 'Lights Out'; slg no. 78 A 4
Fl. forming a double triangle, 47 mm wide; perianth segments acute, reflexed; corona almost disc-shaped, strong orange 25A, with orange-red (32A) at rim. Very late

'Lightsome' 2 (a)
(Cartwright & Goodwin, pre-1908)

'Lights On' 2 (a)
(J.A. Morris) J.A. Morris, 1957

'Lights Out' 9 W-OOR
(G.L. Wilson, pre-1939)
'Dactyl' × Engleheart Poeticus sdlg
Perianth segments pure white, of good substance; corona vivid deep orange-scarlet. Resembles an improved 'Lamplighter'. Very late

'Light Star' 11b W-Y/W
(J.J.Grullemans & Sons, 1965) P.Q.M.Pennings, 1988
Sdlg no. 212
Fl. 95 mm wide; perianth segments greenish white (155A); corona split to three-quarters or more, the six segments a little over half as long as the perianth segments and alternate to them, bi-lobed, ribbed, light yellow at base and in a broad longitudinal band at midrib, touched with golden yellow at apex, white at margins, frilled. Late. Resembles 'Marie José' and 'Lemon Beauty'. Syn. 'Jeanne d'Arc'

'Light Touch' 9 W-GRR
(Mrs M.S. Yerger) Mrs M.S. Yerger, 1986
'Red Rim' × 'Lights Out'; sdlg no. 75 K 2-2
Corona orange-red (32A), with moderate yellow-green 138B at base. Mid-season to late. Faintly lemon scented

'Light Up' 2 W-YYO
(A. Glover)

'Liguria' 1 (a)
(Mrs R.O. Backhouse, pre-1921)

'Likely Lad' 1 Y-Y
(1978) Unregistered

'Like Wise' 2 W-P
(J.N. Hancock & Co., 1955) Unregistered

'Likovan' 1 Y-Y
(D. Blanchard, pre-1947)
'Clarion' × 'Kandahar'
Fl. about 111 mm wide; perianth segments light yellow 12C, slightly inflexed, smooth, overlapping; corona slightly deeper in tone (12A) than the perianth, with mouth expanded and frilled. AM(e) 1949

'Lil' 2 (a)
Parr's Nurseries, 1958

'Lila' 5
(G.H. Engleheart, pre-1913)

'Lilac Charm' 6 W-GPP
(Brian S. Duncan) Brian S. Duncan, 1973
'Roseworthy' × Richardson sdlg 3339/3; sdlg no. 42
Fl. 85 mm wide; perianth segments ovate, blunt, prominently mucronate, reflexed, plane or with margins wavy or incurved, overlapping one-third; the inner segments only very slightly mucronate, spreading at base, strongly recurved at apex, twisted; corona cylindrical, lightly ribbed, lilac pink, with deep green at base, rim flanged and deeply crenate. Mid-season. 2n=21,27

'Lilac Delight' 2 W-P
(G.E. Mitsch) G.E. Mitsch, 1968
'Precedent' × 'Carita'; sdlg no. R34/10
Fl. rounded, 108 mm wide; corona very shallow bowl-shaped, salmon pink, tinged lilac pink. Mid-season

'Lilac Hue' 6 W-P
(Brian S. Duncan, 1978) Rathowen Daffodils, 1987

Corona cylindrical, medium lilac pink, with rim flanged. Mid-season. Resembles a sturdier and more robustly stemmed 'Lilac Charm'

'Lilac Shadows' 2 W-P
(T.D. Throckmorton) T.D. Throckmorton, 1975
'Easter Moon' × 'Rose Caprice'; sdlg no. 67/7/4
Fl. 82 mm wide; corona lila*c*. Mid-season

'Lilac Time' 2 W-P
(S. Clay) S. Clay, 1964
Fl. 102 mm wide; corona opening lilac pink, becoming buff pink, with clear pink at rim. Late

'Lila McFarlane' 2 W-P
(West & Fell, pre-1933)
Syn. 'Mrs C.McFarlane'

'Lil Crewes' 3 W-? (b)
(N. Carter, pre-1949)

'Lilian' 2 W-Y
(G.H. Engleheart, pre-1903)
Perianth segments creamy white; corona sulphur yellow, frilled. AM 1903

'Lilian Duff' 2 W-? (b or c)
(Hon. Mrs Petre, pre-1934)

'Liliane' 9
(de Graaff Bros, pre-1937)
AM(Haarlem) 1937

'Lilian Magee' 1 W-Y
(pre-1956) Unregistered
Perianth segments pure white; corona deep yellow, with rim rolled

'Lilian McLean' 3 W-O
(W.D. Burns, pre-1927)
Corona apricot orange

'Lilian Murdoch' 2
Syn. of 'Lillian Murdoch'

'Lilian Sydenham' 3 W-? (b)
(G.H. Engleheart, pre-1916)

'Lilibet' 2 (a)
(Mrs R.S. Cobley, pre-1937)

'Lili Marlene' 1 W-? (b)
(D.S. Bell) D.S. Bell, 1955

'Lilink' 1 W-?
(A. Overton) A. Overton, 1960

'Lilith' 2 W-? (b)
(de Graaff Bros, pre-1938)
AM(Haarlem) 1938

'Lilith' 2 Y-R
(W. Jackson Jr, *c.*1956) Unregistered
'Redlands' × 'Dover'

'Lillah McCarthy' 9
(T.A.V. Wood, pre-1949)

'Lillande' 4 W-W
(Carncairn Daffodils) Carncairn Daffodils, 1991
'Egg Nogg' × 'Castle Dobbs'; sdlg no. 9/66/79
Fl. 95-100 mm wide, white; perianth and other petaloid segments in more than one whorl; the outer whorl very broadly ovate, very prominently mucronate, spreading; the inner whorl(s) inflexed, roundish, with margins wavy; corona segments half or more as long as the petaloid segments and interspersed among them, broad, closely frilled, with margins striate. Late

'Lillian Murdoch' 2 Y-O
(J.H. Hinsby, 1929)
'Homespun' hybrid
Perianth segments deep golden yellow, overlapping; corona widely expanded, reddish orange. See also 'Lilian Murdoch'

'Lilliput' 3 W-Y
(W. Backhouse, pre-1869)
Perianth segments creamy white; corona tinged orange. Syn. Barrii Albus 'Lilliput'

'Lilliput' 1 W-Y
(J. Gerritsen & Son) J. Gerritsen & Son, 1965
Fl. 127 mm wide; perianth segments yellowish white; corona brilliant yellow 8A. Early. Resembles 'Little Beauty' but with a paler corona

'Lilydale' 2 W-W
(C.E. Radcliff, 1935) J.M.Radcliff, 1956
'Silver Plane' × 'Titania'

'Lilydale' 1 W-Y
(J.J. Brown)
Perianth segments pure white; corona deep yellow, with rim flanged

'Lily Langtry' 3 W-W
Syn. of 'Mrs Langtry'

'Lily May' 2 W-P
(pre-1960) Unregistered
Fl. small; perianth segments broad, smooth; corona rich pink

'Lily May Curtis' 3 W-YYO
(L.P. Dettman) L.P. Dettman, 1968
'Jean Hood' open pollinated
Fl. rounded; perianth segments broadly ovate, pure white; corona very shallow bowl-shaped, lemon yellow, with a narrow band of orange at rim

'Lily of Laguna' 2 W-Y
(S.J. Bisdee, 1942)
'Mitylene' × 'Dawnglow'

'Lily of Rotherside' 2 W-W
(F.H. Chapman, pre-1936)
'Lowdham Beauty' × 'Crimson Braid'
Perianth segments broad, overlapping; corona shallow, expanded, lightly ribbed, frilled. Mid-season. AM(e) 1936

'Lily Ronalds' 2 W-GYO
(H.A. Brown, 1936)
Corona semi-double, primrose yellow, greenish at base, with apricot at rim, frilled. Early to mid-season

'Lily White' 1 W-W
(G. Lewis, pre-1939)
Sdlg × 'Kantara'
Fl. clear white; perianth segments broad, of good substance, overlapping

'Lima' 2 W-? (b)
(A.M. Wilson, pre-1933)

'Limberlost' 3 W-YYW
(Murray W. Evans) Murray W. Evans, 1969
'Carolina' × 'Lady Kesteven'
Fl. 100 mm wide; perianth segments broadly ovate, blunt, slightly mucronate, concave and with margins incurling, overlapping half; the inner segments truncate, with margins indented at overlap; corona sometimes deeply split, light yellow, with white towards mouth

'Limbet' 1 Y-Y
(pre-1949)
'Clarion' × 'Kandahar'

'Limbo' 2 O-R
(Brian S. Duncan) Rathowen Daffodils, 1984
'Altruist' × 'Ulster Bank'; sdlg no. 592
Fl. 98 mm wide; perianth segments very broadly ovate, blunt or sightly truncate, flushed orange, paling towards apex, with white mucro, spreading, smooth, regular, overlapping half; the inner segments a little more narrowly ovate, slightly inflexed; corona shallow bowl-shaped, closely ribbed, deep orange-red, mouth widely expanded, split in places and overlapping, even. Mid-season

'Limeade' 2 Y-W
(G.E. Mitsch) G.E. Mitsch, 1962
'Binkie' × ('King of the North' × 'Content'); sdlg no. P5/4
Fl. 115 mm wide; perianth segments broadly ovate, lemon yellow, with white mucro, plane, with margins sometimes nicked, overlapping one-third to a half; the inner segments more narrowly ovate, with margins wavy; corona cylindrical, 6-angled, opening lemon yellow, becoming white, with yellow-white outside, mouth straight, frilled. Mid-season. Resembles 'Bethany' but with the perianth segments narrower at apex and the corona somewhat narrower

'Lime Beauty' 2 (a)
(Mrs M.Moorby) Mrs M.Moorby, 1956

'Lime Chiffon' 1 Y-GWW
(Elise Havens) G.E. Mitsch, 1975
'Daydream' × 'Empress of Ireland'; sdlg no. E64-6/1
Fl. 95 mm wide; perianth segments ivory yellow; corona ivory white, tinged green at base, with mouth flared and frilled, rim closely notched. Mid-season

'Limegrove' 3 Y-GYY
(C.R. Wootton) Rathowen Daffodils, 1985
'Aircastle' hybrid; sdlg no. 169
Perianth segments bright greenish lemon yellow; corona dark lemon yellow

'Limehurst' 2 YYW-W
(T. Bloomer) Rathowen Daffodils, 1982
'Daydream' × ('Rose Caprice' × 'Binkie'); sdlg no. 390
Fl. 98 mm wide; corona opening deep lemon, quickly becoming white. Mid-season. Resembles 'Daydream' but with a more rapidly changing corona colour

'Lime Ice' 9 W-GGP
(Mrs M.S. Yerger) Mrs M.S. Yerger, 1988
'Dulcimer' open pollinated; sdlg no. 76 A 4
Fl. rounded; corona light yellow-green 145D, with a darker tone at base and pale yellowish pink 27D at rim. Dwarf. Mid-season. Citrus scented

'Limelight' 1 Y-Y
(J. Hall, pre-1930)
Fl. pale yellow

'Limelight' 1 Y-Y
(W.J. Dunlop) W.J. Dunlop, 1958
'King of the North' × 'Content'
Fl. 112 mm wide; perianth segments very pale yellow, flushed with darker tones (5D and 6C), with near-white at base, slightly reflexed, a little twisted; corona almost white, touched with brilliant yellow at rim, with pale greenish yellow 2D outside, flushed with much darker tones (7C and 7D), mouth straight and frilled, rim flanged and crenate. 2n=28

'Lime Love' 2 W-Y
(Ken McCombe) Unregistered
Perianth segments broadly ovate; corona cylindrical, lemon yellow, rim rolled and broadly crenate. Tall. Mid-season to late

'Lime Mist' 2 Y-GYY
(Mrs G. Link) Mrs G. Link, 1979

'Green Quest' × 'Beige Beauty'; sdlg no. 1669
Fl. 90 mm wide; perianth segments greenish yellow; corona yellow, with green at base and a deeper tone of yellow at rim, frilled. Mid-season

'Lime Queen' 2 Y-Y
(Mrs M. Moorby) Mrs M. Moorby, 1963
Fl. lime yellow; corona darker in tone. Mid-season

'Limequilla' 7 W-W
(R. & E. Havens) R. & E. Havens, 1989
'Lime Chiffon' × *N. jonquilla*; sdlg no. QEJ55/1
Fls 2-3 per stem, 70 mm wide, greenish white; corona long, straight-sided. Late. 2n=28

'Lime Regent' 2 Y-Y
(Ballydorn Bulb Farm) Ballydorn Bulb Farm, 1975
'Tibet' × 'Candour'
Fl. 115 mm wide, sulphur lemon; corona with a deeper tone at rim. Mid-season

'Limerick' 1 Y-Y
(*c*.1927)

'Limerick' 3 W-R
(J.L. Richardson, pre-1938)
'Folly' × 'Hades'
Fl. about 90 mm wide; perianth segments broadly ovate, blunt or truncate, prominently mucronate, white, with slight shading of pale yellow-green 4D, smooth, with midrib showing, overlapping half; the inner segments only slightly mucronate, with margins a little wavy; corona broad disc-shaped, closely ribbed, orange-red (near 32A), with mouth obscurely 6-lobed and rim unevenly crenate. Mid-season. Sunproof. AM(e) 1943, FCC(e) 1946, *AM(g) 1952

'Lime Sherbet' 9 W-GGP
(Mrs M.S. Yerger) Mrs M.S. Yerger, 1988
'Dulcimer' open pollinated; sdlg no. 76 A 14
Perianth segments slightly reflexed, overlapping; corona disc-shaped, light yellow-green 145D, with a darker tone (145B) at base and light yellowish pink 27A at rim. Dwarf. Mid-season. Resembles 'Lime Ice' but with a more intense peach colour at rim

'Limestone' 1 W-W
(D. Bramley) D. Bramley, 1978
'Tararua' × 'Snowcraft'; sdlg no. 64/2
Fl. 110 mm wide. Mid-season. Resembles a large and earlier-flowered 'Tararua' with differently shaped perianth segments

'Limey' 2 Y-Y
(pre-1960) Unregistered
Fl. clear lime yellow

'Limey Circle' 3 W-WWY
(Mrs Ben Robertson) Mrs Ben Robertson, 1979
'Carnmoon' × 'Green Island'; sdlg no. 192 A

Fl. 103 mm wide; corona white, with limey yellow at rim, frilled. Mid-season. Resembles 'Carnmoon' but with shorter and wider perianth segments and a more greenish tone to the corona rim

'L'Immaculee' 1 W-Y
(G. Lubbe & Son, pre-1930)

'L'Immaculée' 8 W-Y
(A. Frylink & Sons, pre-1930)
Fls several per stem, compactly arranged; perianth segments pure white, overlapping; corona clear yellow. FA(Haarlem) 1930

'Limondi' 2 (d)
(Mrs M. Moorby) Mrs M. Moorby, 1956

'Limone' 1 Y-Y
(J. Gerritsen & Son, pre-1949)
Fl. lemon yellow; corona rim darker in tone. Early. 2n=28

'Limora' 2 (d)
(Mrs M. Moorby) Mrs M. Moorby, 1956

'Limpkin' 2 W-WWY
(G.E. Mitsch) G.E. Mitsch, 1975
'Aircastle' × 'Homage'; sdlg no. D21/2
Fl. rounded, 102 mm wide; perianth segments very broad, rounded at apex, only very slightly mucronate, ivory white, spreading, concave, overlapping half or more; the inner segments a little inflexed; corona shallow bowl-shaped, ribbed, ivory white, with a narrow band of golden yellow at rim, mouth straight, sometimes deeply split and overlapping, frilled. Mid-season. 2n=28. Resembles a whiter 'Aircastle' with a slightly larger corona

'Limpopo' 3 W-GYY
(Brian S.Duncan) Brian S.Duncan, 1997
(['Dallas' hybrid × 'Cool Crystal'] × 'Vernal Prince') × sdlg 349 ('Aircastle' × 'Woodland Prince'); sdlg no. 1518
Fl. 98 mm wide; perianth segments very broadly ovate; corona shallow, lemon yellow, slightly frilled. Mid-season to late

'Limurr' 2 (d)
(Mrs M. Moorby) Mrs M. Moorby, 1956

'Lina Pott' 2 W-? (b)
(Miss K.M. Hinchliff, pre-1937)

'Linatora' 1 (a)
(R.H. Bath, pre-1933)

'Lincolnshire Yellow' 1 Y-Y
(pre-1885)
Fl. rich yellow

'Linda' 2 W-? (b)
(R.H. Bath, pre-1929)

'Linda Betz' 2 W-YYO
(L.P.Dettman, 1975) Unregistered
'Ogeesan Wally' × 'Trumpet Call'; sdlg no. 80/75

'Linda Lovatt' 3 W-O
(R.J. Ralph, 1945) R.J. Ralph, 1956
'Moina' × 'Elspeth'
Corona reddish orange

'Linda Pope' 3 W-? (b)
(G.H. Engleheart, pre-1904)
Perianth segments white; corona finely marked with red

'Linden' 2 Y-Y
(J.N. Hancock & Co., pre-1950)
Perianth segments rich yellow; corona deeper in tone

'Linden Lea' 2 W-? (b)
(G. Matthews, pre-1951)

'Lindess'
(?G. Lewis, pre-1940)

'Lindis' 6 Y-YOO
(D. Bramley) D. Bramley, 1978
Sdlg × 'Beryl' hybrid; sdlg no. 59/17
Fl. 80 mm wide; perianth segments mid-yellow; corona orange, paling to yellow at base. Resembles a larger and improved 'Beryl' with differently shaped perianth segments

'Lindis' 1 Y-Y
(?New Zealand origin, pre-1990) Unregistered

'Lindisfarne' 3 W-YYO
(G. Harrison) G. Harrison, 1971
'Otterburn' × 'Signal Light'
Fl. 89 mm wide

'Lindrick' 2 Y-Y
(F.E. Board) F.E. Board, 1965
'Galway' × 'Golden Rapture'; sdlg no. 735
Mid-season

'Lindsay Gordon'
(pre-1910)

'Lindsay Joy' 2 W-WWP
(R.A.Scamp) Roger Henry, 1995
'Foundling' × 'Raspberry Ring'; sdlg no. S349
Fl. 96 mm wide; perianth segments broadly ovate, pure white, slightly reflexed, deeply overlapping; corona cup-shaped, with rounded sides, smooth, opening buff, paling to white, with bright pink at rim and the rim neatly crenate. Mid-season to late. Sunproof

'Lindy Lou' 2 Y-R
(G. Lewis) D.S. Bell, 1955

'Lineage' 2 W-W
(F.E. Board) F.E. Board, 1965
'Wedding Bell' × 'Empress of Ireland'
Early.

'Linesman' 2 W-? (b)
(G.H. Engleheart, pre-1907)

'Linette'
(?W.F.M. Copeland, pre-1937)

'Linga Longa' 2 W-R
(pre-1962) Unregistered
Perianth segments pure white; corona disc-shaped, deep red

'Lingen' 2 (a)
(A.M. Wilson, pre-1950)

'Lingerie' 4 W-Y
(Murray W. Evans) Murray W. Evans, 1977
('Falaise' × ['Shirley Neale' × 'Chinese White']) × 'Dawnlight'; sdlg no. L-42/2
Fl. 105 mm wide. Mid-season

'Lingering Light' 2 W-P
(G.L. Wilson, pre-1950)
'White Sentinel' × 'Carnlough'
Corona shallow, bowl-shaped, pale apricot pink

'Lingi' 1 W-W
(W. Jackson Jr, 1958) Unregistered
'Kapitah' × 'Zaire'; sdlg no. 3/58

'Linkboy' 3 W-? (b)
(R.O. Backhouse, pre-1930)

'Linkfield' ?-P
(Alister Clark, pre-1948)

'Linkinhorne' 3 W-O
(P.D. Williams, pre-1930)
Fl. of strong substance; perianth segments pure white, overlapping; corona shallow, expanded, golden orange below, shading to reddish orange at rim

'Linkman' 1 Y-Y
(pre-1914)

'Linksfield' 2 Y-Y
(F.D.B. Cobb, pre-1952)

'Linley Dettmann' 2 W-YYO
(L.P.Dettman, 1972) Unregistered
'Janice Dettman' × 'Jennifer Sholl'; sdlg no. 58/74

'Linn' 2 W-Y
(G.E. Mitsch, pre-1952)
'John Evelyn' × 'Fortune'; sdlg no. 37C41/1
Corona very shallow bowl-shaped, very large, apricot yellow. Mid-season

N. linnaeanus Rouy
   subsp. *dubius* (Gouan) Rouy = *N. dubius*
   subsp. *ganymedioides* Rouy = *N. tazetta*
   subsp. *gussonei* Rouy = *N. tazetta* subsp. *gussonei*
   subsp. *intermedius* (Loiseleur-Deslongchamps)
        Rouy = *N.* × *intermedius*
   subsp. *italicus* (Ker Gawler) Rouy = *N. italicus*
   subsp. *ochroleucus* (Loiseleur-Deslongchamps)
        Rouy = *N. tazetta* subsp. *ochroleucus*
   subsp. *papyraceus* (Ker Gawler) Rouy =
        N. papyraceus
   subsp. *polyanthos* (Loiseleur-Deslongchamps)
        Rouy = *N. polyanthos*
   subsp. *pseuditalicus* Rouy = *N. italicus*
   subsp. *redoutei* (Rouy) = *N. tazetta* subsp.
        lacticolor
   subsp. *rempolensis* (Pannizi) Rouy = *N. tazetta*
   subsp. *subalbidus* (Loiseleur-Deslongchamps)
        Rouy = *N. italicus*
   subsp. *tazetta* (Linnaeus) Rouy = *N. tazetta*

'Linnet' 3 W-? (b)
(A.M. Wilson, pre-1937)

'L'Innocence' 1 W-W
(de Graaff Bros, pre-1898)
'Madame de Graaff' hybrid
Corona opening pale primrose yellow, becoming sulphur white

'L'Innocence' 8 W-Y
(C.P. Alkemade, pre-1930)
Poetaz
2n=17

'L'Innocence' 2 W-?
Syn. of 'Maritza'

'Linors' 2 W-W
(W. Jackson Sr, 1938) W. Jackson Jr, 1956
'Helles' × 'Damson'

'Linred' 2 Y-O
(R.C.A. Tombleson) R.C.A. Tombleson, 1968
Fl. 81 mm wide; perianth segments slightly reflexed. Mid-season. Resembles a large and earlier-flowered 'Anita' with broader perianth segments

'Lintie' 7 Y-YYO
(Barr & Sons, pre-1937)
N. assoanus × *N. poeticus*
Fl. 53 mm wide; perianth segments brilliant greenish yellow 6B, paling slightly towards midrib, overlapping at base only; corona ribbed, vivid yellow 12A, with vivid orange 28B at rim, mouth expanded and frilled, with rim crenate. 2n=21. Resembles an earlier-flowered 'La Belle'. *AM(g) 1974

'Linton' 2 Y-O
(J.N. Hancock & Co., pre-1949)
Corona pale orange, with rim closely and deeply notched, as if fringed

'Lioba' 2 (a)
(C.G. van Tubergen, pre-1930)

'Lion d'Or' 8 Y-Y
(pre-1798)
Fl. golden yellow

'Lionel' 2 W-? (b)
(H.G. Longford, pre-1930)

'Lionel Richardson' 2 W-P
(W.J.M. Blom, 1970) W. Blom & Son, 1984
'Trousseau' × 'Coquille'; sdlg no. 70-D-2
Perianth segments pure white; corona salmon pink, frilled. Early

'Lionheart' 4 W-Y
(Mrs H.K. Richardson) M.J. Jefferson-Brown, 1975
'Falaise' × 'Imogen'
Corona segments amber. Resembles 'Hope' but with more buff coloured corona segments

'Lion's Cub' 2 (a)
(Miss K.M. Hinchliff, pre-1941)
'Leontes' × 'Fortune'

'Lipstick' 2 Y-R
(Murray W. Evans) Murray W. Evans, 1979
'Multnomah' × 'Firecracker'; sdlg no. N-66
Fl. 110 mm wide. Mid-season

'Lipstick Pink' 2 W-P
(A. Glover)

'Liquid Amber'
(pre-1914)

'Liquid Gold' 2 (a)
(E.G. Taylor) E.G. Taylor, 1956

'Liriope' 9
(Sir J.S. Arkwright, pre-1931)

'Lisanore' 2 W-P
(Carncairn Daffodils) Carncairn Daffodils, 1973
'Pink o' Dawn' × 'Rose Royale'
Fl. 87 mm wide; corona rose pink, paling to near white with age, frilled, with rim flanged

'Lisbane' 3 W-GYR
(Ballydorn Bulb Farm) Ballydorn Bulb Farm, 1975

'Clockface' open pollinated
Fl. 100 mm wide; corona with deep red at rim. Mid-season

'Lisbarnett' 3 W-GRR
(Ballydorn Bulb Farm) Ballydorn Bulb Farm, 1984
'Faraway' × 'Lisbane'
Fl. 110 mm wide. Mid-season. Resembles a larger 'Faraway' of better colour

'Lisboa' 2 W-? (b)
(Mrs R.O. Backhouse, pre-1921)

'Lisbon' 5 Y-Y
(pre-1961) Unregistered
Perianth segments lemon yellow; corona small, clear yellow. Tall

'Lisbreen' 2 W-GPP
(G.L. Wilson, pre-1940)
'Mitylene' × 'Evening'
Fl. about 115 mm wide; perianth segments broad, greenish white, slightly inflexed, overlapping; corona funnel-shaped, orange-pink (24D), with rim dentate. 2n=28. AM(e) 1944

'Lisburn' 3 W-R
(Ballydorn Bulb Farm, 1985) Ballydorn Bulb Farm, 1995
'Woodland Star' × 'Lisbane'
Fl. 90 mm wide; perianth segments white, plane, smooth; corona saucer-shaped, lightly ribbed, deep red. Mid-season. Sunproof

'Liscarton' 3 Y-O
(P.D. Williams, pre-1927)

'Lisdillon' 1 W-P
(C.E. Radcliff, 1943) J.M.Radcliff, 1956
'Nautilus' × 'Dawnglow'

'Lisette' 3
(pre-1926)

'Lisette' 7 Y-GYR
(A.H. Ahrens, pre-1951)

'Lisheen' 2 W-Y
(A.M. Wilson, pre-1931)
'Nelly' hybrid
Perianth segments acute

'Lismore' 1 W-Y
(Miss F.W. Currey, pre-1899)
Perianth segments faintly tinged moss green; corona opening milky white, becoming very pale primrose yellow

'Lismore' 1 Y-Y
(J.L. Richardson) Mrs H.K. Richardson, 1963

'Rio d'Oro' self pollinated
Fl. golden yellow; perianth segments broadly ovate; corona slender, with rim flanged and dentate

'Lisnamulligan' 3 W-R
(Ballydorn Bulb Farm, 1980) Ballydorn Bulb Farm, 1990
'Woodland Star' × 'Faraway Cross' hybrid
Fl. 95 mm wide; perianth segments pure white, plane; corona disc-shaped, ribbed, deep red, with green noticeable in tube. Mid-season to late

'Lisnamurrican' 2 W-P
(G.W.Tarry) Carncairn Daffodils, 1996
'Ann Cameron' × 'Quiet Day'; sdlg no. 18/5/85
Fl. 85 mm wide; perianth segments broadly ovate, blunt, mucronate, spreading, plane, overlapping half; the inner segments a little inflexed; corona cylindrical or very slightly expanded, smooth, pink, with mouth straight and more or less even, rim entire or with some shallow and irregularly spaced notches. Late

'Lisrenny' 1 W-Y
(Carncairn Daffodils) Carncairn Daffodils, 1973
'Sincerity' × 'Preamble'
Fl. 99 mm wide; corona lemon yellow, with rim rolled

'Lisroan' 2 (a)
(G.L. Wilson, pre-1937)

'Lissa' 3 W-? (b)
(J.T. Gray, pre-1949)
Corona expanded, with a band of reddish orange at rim

'Lissadell' 3 Y-YOO
(D.N.Y. Olson) D.N.Y. Olson, 1993
'Trelay' × 'Achduart'
Fl. rounded, 80 mm wide; perianth segments broadly ovate, medium yellow, slightly reflexed, concave near apex, overlapping; corona bowl-shaped, straight-sided, orange, with yellow at base, with a deeper tone of orange outside, mouth flared and frilled. Late

'Lissome' 2 W-W
(Murray W. Evans) Murray W. Evans, 1986
'Broomhill' × 'Stainless', sdlg no. U-10/1
Perianth segments broadly ovate, prominently mucronate, spreading, regular, overlapping half; corona cup-shaped, with mouth straight and lightly frilled. Mid-season. Resembles 'Stainless'

'Listerdale' 2 W-? (b)
(F.E. Board) F.E. Board, 1965
'Daviot' × 'Buncrana'; sdlg no. 522

'Lita' 2 (a)
(J.T. Gray, pre-1936)

'Little Audrey' 2 W-GYO
(J.L. Richardson, pre-1937)

'Little Barry' 12 W-Y
(H.Koopowitz, 1979) H.Koopowitz, 1997
'Lilac Delight' × *N. serotinus*
Fl. 56 mm wide; perianth segments broadly ovate; corona cup-shaped, straight-sided, ribbed, opening lemon yellow, becoming buff then white, with a paler tone at rim, slightly frilled. Dwarf. Very early

'Little Beauty' 1 W-Y
(J. Gerritsen & Son, pre-1953)
Perianth segments ovate, blunt, greenish white, a little inflexed, twisted or with margins recurved, overlapping a quarter; the inner segments more narrowly ovate, more distinctly twisted; corona cylindrical, smooth, vivid yellow, paling to the perianth colour towards base, mouth ribbed, rim flanged and deeply and closely notched. Dwarf. 2n=14. AM(Haarlem) 1953

'Little Becky' 12 Y-Y
(?New Zealand origin, pre-1996) Unregistered

'Little Bell' 5 Y-Y
(Murray W. Evans) Murray W. Evans, 1986
N. triandrus open pollinated; sdlg no. W-8
Fls 5-10 per stem, very pale yellow. Mid-season. Resembles *N. triandrus* var. *concolor*

'Little Big Horn' 8 W-W
(H. Koopowitz) H. Koopowitz, 1981
'Paper White' × 'Accent'; sdlg no. B373/1
Fl. 57 mm wide; corona sometimes tinged pink. Early. Resembles a larger-flowered 'Paper White' with a longer corona

'Little Bo-peep' 5
(F.H. Chapman, pre-1913)
See also 'Little Bopeep'

'Little Bopeep' 5
Syn. of 'Little Bo-peep'

'Littlebourne' 2 (a)
(F.D.B. Cobb) F.D.B. Cobb, 1956

'Little Carla' 6 Y-Y
(F.R. Waley) F.R. Waley, 1984
N. cyclamineus open pollinated
Fl. 37 mm wide, bright yellow. Mid-season

'Little Charley' 11b W-R/?W
(J.W.A. Lefeber) J.J. Grullemans & Sons, 1959
Fl. rounded; perianth segments silver white; corona segments with a longitudinal band of strong red

'Little Dancer' 1 W-Y
(A. Gray, 1960) Broadleigh Gardens, 1977

N. asturiensis × 'Little Beauty'; sdlg no. 138B
Fl. 65 mm wide; perianth segments ovate, inflexed, a little twisted or with margins wavy or incurved, overlapping at base only; corona cylindrical or somewhat funnel-shaped, ribbed, with mouth a little flared, rim deeply notched. 2n=14. Resembles a taller and later-flowered 'Tosca' with the corona mouth more distinctly flared. Syn. 'Lena'

'Little Dawn' 1 W-Y
(A. Gray), 1977
N. asturiensis × 'Little Beauty'

'Little Diamond' 3 Y-O
(F. Rijnveld & Sons, pre-1950)
AM(Haarlem) 1951

'Little Dirk' 3 W-YYO
(W. Backhouse, pre-1869)
Fl. small; perianth segments opening pale yellow, becoming creamy white; corona with scarlet-orange at rim. Syn. Burbidgei 'Little Dirk'

'Little Doll' 3 W-Y
(M.E.Brogden, pre-1995) Unregistered
'Sea Dream' × 'Verona'

'Little Dorrit' 3 W-O
(Mrs R.O. Backhouse, pre-1904)
Fl. small; corona almost disc-shaped, reddish orange

'Little Duke' 1 W-? (b)
(Cartwright & Goodwin, pre-1916)

'Little Echo' 2 W-P
(Alfred Clark) D.S. Bell, 1963
Fl. 66 mm wide; corona bright pink. Mid-season

'Little Emma' 12 Y-Y
(?New Zealand origin, pre-1996) Unregistered
N. cyclamineus × *N. jonquilla* var. *henriquesii*

'Little Flirt' 2 W-WWP
(J.N. Hancock & Co., *c.*1970) Unregistered

'Little Fortune' 2 (a)
(A.W. Bull, pre-1939)

'Little Gem' 3 (a)
(?E. & J.C. Martin, pre-1907)

'Little Gem' 1 Y-Y
(J. Gerritsen & Son, 1938) J. Gerritsen & Son, 1959
Selection from *N. minor*
Fl. 40 mm wide, vivid yellow 9B; perianth segments fairly broadly ovate, with slight white mucro, strongly inflexed, overlapping a quarter to one-third; the inner segments with margins wavy; corona cylindrical, sometimes constricted near mid-point, slightly ribbed, with a darker tone of yellow at rim, mouth

flared, 6-lobed, even, with rim notched. Dwarf. Early. 2n=14. Resembles 'Bagatelle' and 'Wee Bee', also a more floriferous *N. nanus*. AGM 1997

'Little Gentleman' 6 Y-Y
Syn. of 'The Little Gentleman'

'Little Goldfinch' 6 Y-Y
(Muriel Davison) Muriel Davison, 1994
N. cyclamineus × *N. nanus*
Fl. 65 mm wide, yellow; perianth segments narrowly oblong, blunt, with slight white mucro, reflexed, separated; corona cylindrical, very lightly ribbed, with mouth flared and more strongly ribbed, rim deeply and closely notched. Dwarf. Very early. Resembles a shorter and much earlier-flowered 'Mite' with the flower facing further down. Syn. 'Goldfinch'

'Little Herald' 1 Y-Y
(J. Gerritsen & Son) J. Gerritsen & Son, 1967
'Little Gem' self pollinated
Fl. 35 mm wide; perianth segments brilliant greenish yellow 6C; corona vivid yellow 9A. Early

'Little Hobo' 8 W-R
(K. McCombe, *c*.1983) Unregistered
'Medusa' hybrid
Fls 2 per stem; perianth segments broadly to very broadly ovate, prominently mucronate, spreading, somewhat creased, with margins wavy or incurling, overlapping half; the inner segments less noticeably mucronate, a little inflexed; corona narrow bowl-shaped, ribbed, orange-red, mouth straight, wavy. Early to mid-season. Scented

'Little Honey' 1 W-W
(Mrs A.O. Meyrick) Mrs A.O. Meyrick, 1957

'Little Imp' 6 Y-O
(R.E. Parsons) R.E. Parsons, 1967
'Chungking' × *N. cyclamineus*; sdlg no. 60/6/3
Perianth segments clear yellow; corona intense orange. Early. Resembles 'Satellite' but with broader and smoother perianth segments which are reflexed

'Little Jazz' 6 W-WRR
(Reg Nicholl) Reg Nicholl, 1994
'Delia' × 'Raspberry Ring'; sdlg no. 27/91
Fl. 70 mm wide; perianth segments ovate, blunt, only slightly mucronate, reflexed, with margins incurling at apex, wavy, overlapping half; corona short cylinder-shaped, loosely ribbed, with the band of white at base only slightly less broad than the band of red at rim, mouth straight, more closely ribbed. Dwarf. Mid-season

'Little Jewel' 3 W-P
(J.A. O'More, 1971) R.G. Cull, 1985
Sdlg 45/62 × sdlg 34/65; sdlg no. 50/71
Corona light yellowish pink 38D. Mid-season

'Little Jill' 6 Y-Y
(S. Dudman) S. Dudman, 1959
Fl. 80 mm wide; perianth segments primrose yellow; corona golden yellow. Early. Resembles 'Le Beau' but with paler perianth and darker corona and with the corona rim more heavily frilled and deeply rolled

'Little Joan' 3 W-? (b or c)
(G.H. Engleheart, pre-1913)

'Little John' 3 W-Y
(W. Backhouse, pre-1869)
Perianth segments sulphur white; corona ribbed, tinged orange. Syn. Burbidgei 'Little John', Burbidgei 'Minor'

'Little John' 2 W-R
(A.E. Lowe, pre-1927)

'Little John Walker' 6 Y-Y
(John Walker) K.N. Dryden, 1993
N. cyclamineus × *N. asturiensis*
Fl. 15 mm wide, chrome yellow; perianth segments ovate, reflexed, overlapping at base only; corona cylindrical, or slightly flaring towards mouth, faintly ribbed, slightly darker in tone than the perianth, with rim flanged and deeply notched. Dwarf. Early. Resembles a slightly larger 'Minicycla' flowering two weeks later

'Little Karoo' 3 Y-O
(Brian S.Duncan) Brian S.Duncan, 1997
'Triple Crown' × 'Burning Bush'; sdlg no. 1594
Fl. rounded, 85 mm wide; perianth segments very broadly ovate, lemon to mid-yellow, spreading, plane, smooth; corona shallow bowl-shaped, orange, with mouth straight and rim entire. Late

'Little King' 1 W-W
(J. Kerkhof) J. Kerkhof, 1982
Fl. star-shaped, 65 mm wide; perianth segments ovate, acute, ivory white, with touches of yellow, spreading, plane, overlapping at base only; the inner segments very slightly inflexed, with margins a little wavy; corona cylindrical, smooth, slightly constricted at mid-point, opening brilliant greenish yellow 7C, with ivory white at rim, becoming self greenish white, mouth expanded, rim regularly crenate

'Little Lady' 3 W-? (b)
(F.H. Chapman, pre-1913)

'Little Lady' 2 W-W
(J.N. Hancock & Co.) J.N. Hancock & Co., 1959

'Little Lass' 5 W-W
(M. Fowlds) G.E. Mitsch, 1969
N. cyclamineus sdlg × *N. triandrus*
Fls usually 2 per stem, facing down; perianth segments narrow, strongly reflexed. Mid-season

'Little Miss' 6 Y-Y
(Mrs G. Link) Mrs G. Link, 1988
N. cyclamineus × 'Candlepower'
Fl. 25mm wide. Very early. Tall. Resembles a yellow flowered 'Dewdrop'

'Little Missus' 7 Y-Y
(Glenbrook Bulb Farm, pre-1992) Unregistered
N. fernandesii × *N. cylamineus*; sdlg no. 1/88

'Little Nell' 1 W-W
(Irish origin, pre-1912)

'Little Nell' 3 W-Y
(C. Dawson, pre-1912)
Fl. small; perianth segments creamy white; corona ribbed, lemon yellow, with golden yellow at rim. Late

'Little Pal'
(pre-1940)

'Little Peach' 2 W-? (b)
(G.L. Wilson, pre-1950)

'Little Pearl' 1 W-W
(C. Goodson, pre-1927)

'Little Pearl' 1 W-W
Syn. of 'Fuco'

'Little Prince' 7 Y-O
(Barr & Sons, pre-1937)
Resembles a smaller and very late flowered 'La Belle'

'Little Princess' 1 Y-Y
(E. Leeds, pre-1877)
Fl. sulphur yellow. Resembles 'Gertrude Jekyll' in colour. Syn. Pseudonarcissus Major 'Little Princess'

'Little Princess' 6 W-P
(Mrs H.K. Richardson) Carncairn Daffodils, 1978
Sdlg no. 3618 II
Fl. 85 mm wide; perianth segments grenish white (155A); corona strong yellowish pink 32C. Late

'Little Queen' 5 Y-W
(F.H. Chapman, pre-1912)
N. triandrus var. *loiseleurii* × *N. asturiensis*
Fls usually 2 per stem; perianth segments primrose yellow; corona milk white. Dwarf

'Little Rusky' 7 Y-GYO
(Roberta C.Watrous, 1974) Roberta C.Watrous, 1989
'Ruby' × *N. scaberulus*; sdlg no. 691-1
Fls usually 2 per stem, 32 mm wide; perianth segments ovate, acute, spreading; corona shallow bowl-shaped, ribbed, a little darker in tone than the perianth. Dwarf. Mid-season

'Little Sentry' 7 Y-Y
(A. Gray) Broadleigh Gardens, 1984
N. rupicola × *N. poeticus*
Fl. 32 mm wide; perianth segments spreading, opening vivid yellow 9A, soon becoming light greenish yellow 3C; corona vivid yellow 9A, minutely touched with a darker tone at rim. Dwarf. Mid-season. Closely resembles a 'Sun Disc' flowering about ten days earlier. Syn. 'Sentry'

'Little Soldier' 10 Y-Y
(J.S. Romine, 1973) J.S. Romine, 1984
N. obesus × 'Chemawa'; sdlg no. 73-1
Fl. star-shaped, 44 mm wide, yellow; perianth segments ovate, blunt, with slight white mucro, and with a faintly paler tone of yellow at midrib, spreading, with margins slightly wavy or incurved, overlapping at base only; the inner segments a little narrower, less prominently mucronate; corona broad funnel-shaped, lightly ribbed, darker in tone than the perianth, with mouth straight and wavy, rim entire. Early to mid-season

'Little Spell' 1 Y-Y
(C.A.van der Wereld, pre-1990) Unregistered
Fl. pale greenish yellow; perianth segments oblong, with white mucro, strongly inflexed, twisted, overlapping at base only; the inner segments a little narrower, more nearly ovate; corona narrowly funnel-shaped, smooth, becoming very pale, touched with darker tones at rim, mouth slightly flared and deeply 6-lobed, rim crenate

'Little Star' 6 Y-Y
(Eileen E.Frey, 1983) J. & E.Frey, 1994
Sdlg no. TEF31/1
Fl. 37 mm wide; perianth segments very soft lemon yellow, strongly reflexed; corona soft yellow at base shading to dark yellow at rim, mouth frilled. Dwarf. Very early

'Little Sunshine' 6 Y-Y
(Eileen E. Frey) J. & E. Frey, 1989
'Wee Bee' × *N. cyclamineus*; sdlg no. PEF9/2
Fl. 25 mm wide; perianth segments ovate, with white mucro, strongly reflexed, overlapping at base only; corona cylindrical, with mouth expanded and rim deeply notched. Dwarf. Early. Resembles *N. cyclamineus* but with shorter and broader perianth segments and a slightly broader corona

'Little Tich' 3
(?F.H. Chapman, pre-1914)

'Little Tim' 6 Y-Y
(J.H. Walker) J.H. Walker, 1990
N. cyclamineus open pollinated
Fl. 51 mm wide; perianth segments narrowly ovate, with white mucro, slightly reflexed, overlapping at base only; the inner segments with margins somewhat

inward folding; corona cylindrical, ribbed, slightly darker in tone than the perianth, with mouth flared, rim notched and dentate. Dwarf. Very early. Resembles 'February Gold' in colour

'Little Trophy' 1 Y-Y
(C.A. van der Wereld) C.A. van der Wereld, 1963
Fl. 60 mm wide, light greenish yellow 6D. Early

'Little Witch' 6 Y-Y
(Mrs R.O. Backhouse, pre-1921)
Fl. yellow; perianth segments ovate, blunt or squarish at apex, with slight white mucro, reflexed, plane or with margins slightly incurved, separated; the inner segments more narrowly ovate, more nearly acute, sometimes twisted, with margins incurled; corona cylindrical, strongly ribbed, darker in tone than the perianth, with mouth straight and rim crenate. Dwarf. 2n=21. AM(Haarlem) 1957

'Litton' 3 W-? (b)
(A.M. Wilson, pre-1950)

'Lively Lady' 5 W-W
(A. Gray) Broadleigh Gardens, 1969
N. triandrus var. *loiseleurii* × *N. rupicola* subsp. *watieri*
Fl. 65 mm wide; perianth segments white; corona cream. Dwarf. Late. Resembles a later-flowered and more vigorous 'Frosty Morn'

'Liverpool Festival' 2 Y-O
(J.S.B. Lea, 1974) Clive Postles Daffodils, 1985
('Tanera' × 'Sheildaig') × 'Vulcan'; sdlg no. 2 25 69
2n=28

'Live Wire' 2 Y-YYR
(J.N. Hancock & Co., pre-1950)
Perianth segments yellow; corona with red at rim

'Livia' 4 Y-O
(Mrs R.O. Backhouse, 1929)
AM(Haarlem) 1930

'Livingstone' 3 W-? (b)
(E. & J.C. Martin, pre-1916)

'Livingstone' 1 W-? (b)
(pre-1930)

'Livonia' 2 W-Y
(Mrs R.O. Backhouse, pre-1921)
Fl. large; perianth segments with margins wavy; corona flared, rich buffy apricot yellow

'Livonia' 2 or 3 W-? (b or c)
(pre-1931)

'Liz' 3 Y-Y
(W. Backhouse, pre-1869)
Perianth segments sulphur yellow; corona stained orange. Syn. Barrii Albidus 'Liz'. Was "absorbed" into 'Imogen'

'Lizard' 1 W-W
(The Brodie of Brodie, pre-1928)
'Mrs Ernst H.Krelage' hybrid × 'Beersheba'

'Lizard' 3 W-?
Syn. of 'Carthillian'

'Lizard Light' 2 Y-O
(M.P. Williams, pre-1947)
Perianth segments broadly ovate, with prominent white mucro, spreading, somewhat concave, especially near apex, overlapping half; the inner segments not much narrower, more nearly plane, with margins nicked; corona short funnel-shaped, ribbed, orange, shading to strong orange 25A at rim, mouth straight, frilled, rim deeply notched, with lobes overlapping. 2n=27

'Lizelle' 1 W-Y
(J.N. Hancock & Co., *c*.1977) Unregistered

'Lizette' 3 W-? (b)
(C. Dawson, pre-1927)

'Lizzie Hop' 1 Y-Y
(W.G. Pannill) W.G. Pannill, 1976
'Arctic Gold' × 'Fine Gold'; sdlg no. 64/38
Fl. 108 mm wide, gold. Mid-season

'Llanberis' 2 W-O
(S.J. Bisdee, 1939)
'Mitylene' × 'Portia'

'Llandaff' 2 W-R
(A.O. Roblin, 1940)
'Alcides' hybrid

'Llewlyn' 2 (a)
(pre-1934)

'Llinos' 4 Y-O
(W.A. Watts, pre-1914)
'Beacon' × 'Telamonius Plenus'
Fl. 102 mm wide; perianth and other petaloid segments broadly ovate, primrose yellow; the outer whorl spreading; the inner whorl opposite, not much shorter, a little inflexed, folded or creased along midrib, with margins wavy or sometimes tightly incurled; corona one-third the length of the petaloid segments, orange, frilled; a few petaloid segments within the corona short, narrow, buff, convoluted

'Lloyd George' 1 Y-Y
(G. Lubbe & Son, pre-1927)
AM(Haarlem) 1926

'Llysdulas' 2 (a)
(J.L. Richardson) Sir A.T.C. Neave, 1958

N. × *lobatus* Poiret = *N.* × *infundibulum*

'Lobster' 2 Y-O
(G.H. Engleheart, pre-1898)
Corona large, heavily stained brilliant reddish orange. Tall

N. lobularis hort. = *N. nanus*

N. lobularis Schultes = *N. obvallaris*

N. lobulatus Haworth = *N. bulbocodium*

'Locarno' 1 W-Y
(K. Oudshoorn, pre-1926)
'King Alfred' × 'Weardale Perfection'
AM(Haarlem) 1926, FA(Haarlem) 1927

'Loch Achray' 2 Y-ORR
(J.S.B. Lea) Clive Postles, 1992
'Loch Loyal' × 'Loch Carron'; sdlg no. 4-3-78
Fl. forming a double triangle, 90 mm wide; perianth segments ovate, deep yellow; corona flared, red, with orange at base, mouth lobed, rim flanged. Early

'Loch Alsh' 3 W-YYO
(J.S.B. Lea) Clive Postles Daffodils, 1988
'Loch Assynt' × Sdlg 68/15A; sdlg no. 2-37-76
Fl. rounded, 109 mm wide; perianth segments pure white; corona very shallow bowl-shaped, yellow, with a distinct band of orange at rim fading to yellow with age, the rim dentate. Mid-season. Resembles a larger 'Loch Assynt' with a more rounded perianth

'Loch Alvey' 2 Y-YYO
(J.M. de Navarro) J.M. de Navarro, 1975
'Falstaff' × 'Estremadura'; sdlg no. 369
Fl. 86 mm wide; corona yellow, with orange at rim. Mid-season. Resembles a stronger-coloured 'Front Royal' with a broader band of colour at corona rim

'Loch Assynt' 3 W-YYO
(J.S.B. Lea) J.S.B. Lea, 1963
'Syracuse' × sdlg 1-1-55 ('Arbar' self pollinated); sdlg no. 3-44-61
Fl. 87 mm wide; perianth segments very broad, rounded at apex, spreading, a little concave, smooth, with broad midrib showing, overlapping half; the inner segments a little narrower, more nearly ovate, very slightly inflexed; corona shallow, closely ribbed, yellow, with orange at rim and with a paler tone at margin at maturity, mouth widely expanded and tightly frilled

'Lochavich' 2 W-W
(G.C. Graham) G.C. Graham, 1961
? × 'Ludlow'
Fl. 115 mm wide. Early. Resembles an earlier-flowered and more robust 'Ludlow'

'Loch Broom' 2 or 3 W-? (b or c)
(The Brodie of Brodie, *c.*1913)
'Madame de Graaff' × *N. poeticus*
Corona narrow, pale lemon

'Loch Broom' 3 W-ORR
(J.S.B. Lea) J.S.B. Lea, 1979
Sdlg × 'Ohio'; sdlg no. 1-24-67
Fl. 104 mm wide

'Loch Brora' 2 W-O
(J.S.B. Lea) J.S.B. Lea, 1979
'Arbar' self pollinated × sdlg × 'Brahms'; sdlg no. 1-31-64
Fl. 100 mm wide

'Loch Carron' 2 Y-O
(J.S.B. Lea) J.S.B. Lea, 1980
('Capitol Hill' × 'Vulcan') self pollinated; sdlg no. 1-24-71
Fl. rounded, 95 mm wide; perianth segments broadly ovate, blunt, brilliant greenish yellow 5A, with white mucro, spreading, smooth, overlapping half; corona cylinder-shaped, short, lightly ribbed, brighter than vivid orange 28B, touched yellow at rim, mouth straight and 6-lobed, with rim obscurely crenate. Early to mid-season

'Loch Coire' 3 W-R
(J.S.B. Lea) J.S.B. Lea, 1983
Sdlg 1-20-67 ([sdlg 3-44-61 × 'Loch Assynt'] × 'Merlin') × 'Purbeck'; sdlg no. 2-20-74
Fl. 105 mm wide

'Loch Fada' 2 Y-R
(J.S.B. Lea) J.S.B. Lea, 1972
'Tanera' × 'Loch Stac'; sdlg no. 1-40-61
Fl. 89 mm wide. Late

'Loch Fleet' 2 Y-O
(D.C. MacArthur) D.C. MacArthur, 1990
'Jezebel' × 'Fireproof'; sdlg no. E314
Fl. 92 mm wide; perianth segments brilliant yellow 9C, spreading; corona narrow, strong orange 25A, with mouth even. Late. Sunproof

'Loch Fyne' 2 W-Y
(The Brodie of Brodie, *c.*1911)
'Minnie Hume' × 'Lady Margaret Boscawen'
Perianth segments ivory white, overlapping; corona spreading, ribbed, pale lemon yellow

'Loch Garvie' 2 Y-O
(J.S.B. Lea) J.S.B. Lea, 1971
Sdlg 1-19-55 × 'Caramba'; sdlg no. 1-13-61
Fl. 98 mm wide; periant segments rich deep yellow; corona reddish orange. Mid-season

'Loch Hope' 2 Y-R
(J.S.B. Lea) J.S.B. Lea, 1970
Sdlg 1-32-57 × 'Vulcan'; sdlg no. 1-6-62
Fl. 100 mm wide; perianth segments very broadly ovate, blunt, only very slightly mucronate, brilliant greenish yellow 6A, spreading, with margins minutely incurled, overlapping half; the inner segments a little narrower, slightly inflexed; corona cylindrical, short, loosely ribbed, vivid orange 28B, with mouth straight and frilled. Early. 2n=28. AM(e) 1978, FCC(e) 1981

'Lochiel' 3 W-Y
(E.W. Cotter) E.W. Cotter, 1968

'Lochin' 1 W-W
(J.T. Gray, pre-1949)
Fl. forming a double triangle; perianth segments very broadly ovate, blunt, slightly mucronate, spreading, with margins a little wavy, overlapping half; the inner segments narrower, slightly inflexed at base and reflexed at apex, shouldered at base; corona funnel-shaped, broadly ribbed, with mouth widely expanded, rim flanged and deeply and irregularly notched. AM(Haarlem) 1956

'Lochinch' 2 Y-O
(pre-1963) Unregistered

'Lochindorb' 2 (a)
(R. Crews, pre-1949)

'Lochinvar' 2 or 3 W-? (b or c)
(A.M. Wilson, pre-1916)

'Lochinvar' 2 W-O
(J.L. Richardson) J.L. Richardson, 1959
'Kilworth' × 'Arbar'
Fl. 88 mm wide; perianth segments overlapping; corona vivid orange 28B, tinged with a darker tone (28A) and touched towards mouth with brilliant orange-yellow 21B, mouth straight, widely lobed and frilled, with rim dentate

'Loch Katrine' 2 Y-YOO
(J.S.B. Lea) Clive Postles Daffodils, 1987
Sdlg 62/10A × 'Torridon'; sdlg no. 2-27-74
Perianth segments broadly ovate, blunt, with slight white mucro, spreading or very slightly inflexed, smooth, with broad and shallow midrib showing, overlapping half; the inner segments more narrowly ovate, very slightly reflexed; corona narrow, straight-sided, ribbed, reddish orange, paling to yellow at base, mouth straight and a little wavy, with rim entire. Mid-season. Sunproof

'Lochlee' 1 W-W
(H.A. Brown, 1942) J.N. Hancock & Co., 1965
'Lyndale Giant' × 'Kanchenjunga'
Fl. large, marble white, of heavy substance; perianth segments rounded at apex, deeply overlapping; corona with rim rolled and dentate. Late

'Loch Leven' 2 O-ORR
(J.S.B. Lea, 1983) Clive Postles Daffodills, 1993
'Creag Dubh' × sdlg L1-26-73; sdlg no. 1-11-78
Fl. 104 mm wide; perianth segments very broadly ovate, clear orange, smooth, with margins slightly incurving; corona cup-shaped, orange-red, with clear orange at base, mouth even, rim crenate. Tall. Mid-season

'Loch Lomond' 2 or 3 W-W
(The Brodie of Brodie, c.1913)
'Weardale Perfection' hybrid
Fl. pure white

'Loch Loyal' 2 Y-R
(J.S.B. Lea) J.S.B. Lea, 1980
('Vulcan' × 'Achduart') × sdlg 38/66; sdlg no. 1-9-71
Fl. 100 mm wide; perianth segments deep chrome yellow. Mid-season

'Loch Lundie' 2 Y-O
(J.S.B. Lea) J.S.B. Lea, 1978
Sdlg 1-8-58 (sdlg × 'Tanera') × sdlg 1-63-53 ('Chungking' × 'Spry'); sdlg no. 1-38-66
Fl. 105 mm wide; perianth segments broadly ovate in outline, blunt or rounded at apex, brilliant yellow 7A, with slight white mucro, a little reflexed, concave, with margins sometimes incurling, overlapping half; the inner segments a little narrower, more nearly spreading; corona cup-shaped, straight-sided, ribbed towards mouth, slightly darker in tone than strong orange 25A, flushed towards mouth with a darker tone (28B), mouth straight, neatly frilled. AM(e) 1980

'Loch Maberry' 2 Y-O
(J.S.B. Lea) J.S.B. Lea, 1983
'Torridon' × sdlg 1-38-66; sdlg no. 2-11-74
Fl. 95 mm wide; perianth segments very broadly ovate, rounded at apex, yellow, slightly stained orange at base, spreading, a little concave, overlapping half; corona funnel-shaped, loosely ribbed, reddish orange, a little frilled, with rim split in places

'Loch Maree' 2 W-P
(The Brodie of Brodie, c.1940)
'Easter Morn' × 'Riva'
Corona opening almost pure white, gradually becoming soft rose pink. 2n=28. See also 'Lough Maree'

'Loch Meadie' 2 Y-O
(J.S.B. Lea) J.S.B. Lea, 1979
'Drumrunie' × 'Torridon'
Fl. 115 mm wide. Mid-season

'Loch More' 2 Y-R
(J.S.B. Lea) J.S.B. Lea, 1981

Sdlg 1-38-66 × 'Torridon'; sdlg no. 2-3-73
Fl. 92 mm wide

'Loch Naver' 2 Y-ORR
(J.S.B. Lea) J.S.B. Lea, 1963
Sdlg 1-58-53 ('Dunkeld' × ['Green Island' × 'Ambergate']) × 'Tanera'; sdlg no. 1-50-59
Fl. 95 mm wide; perianth rich yellow; corona rich orange-red. Mid-season. Resembles 'Revelry' with larger and darker flowers

'Loch Nell' 1 W-Y
(G.C. Graham) G.C. Graham, 1960
Fl. 108 mm wide; corona light greenish yellow 6D. Early. Resembles 'Trousseau' but with the corona rim more deeply rolled

'Loch Ness' 2 Y-YYO
(J.L. Richardson, pre-1933)
Perianth segments creamy yellow; corona widely expanded, with a narrow band of deep reddish orange at rim

'Lochness'
(The Brodie of Brodie)
'Seraglio' × sdlg 30/A/18

'Loch Owskeich' 2 Y-O
(J.S.B. Lea) J.S.B. Lea, 1971
Sdlg 1-19-55 × 'Caramba'; sdlg no. 2-13-61
Fl. 100 mm wide; perianth segments slightly brighter than brilliant greenish yellow 6A, overlapping; corona strong orange 24A, flushed with a darker tone (slightly brighter than 25A), a little paler towards base, mouth ribbed, straight, slightly lobed. Mid-season. *AM(g) 1981, *FCC(g) 1982, AGM 1993

'Loch Poulary' ?-P
(Alister Clark, pre-1948)

'Lochranza' 9 W-YYR
(E.M. Crosfield, pre-1927)
Fl. 70 mm wide; perianth segments snow white, somewhat reflexed, overlapping at base only; corona almost disc-shaped, sulphur, greenish at base and shading to red at rim. Mid-season to late

'Loch Rimsdale' 2 Y-YRR
(J.S.B. Lea) Clive Postles Daffodils, 1985
Sdlg 1-18-66 × 'Torridon'
Perianth segments broadly ovate, blunt, mucronate, smooth, overlapping half; corona cup-shaped, very lightly ribbed, a little frilled. Mid-season

'Loch Roag' 3 W-R
(J.S.B. Lea, 1976) Clive Postles Daffodils, 1988

'Loch Scridain' 2 Y-Y
(D.C. MacArthur) D.C. MacArthur, 1989
'Rouge' × 'Chungking'; sdlg no. EV85/412
Fl. 90 mm wide; perianth segments light greenish yellow 7D, spreading, plane, deeply overlapping; corona vivid yellow 9A, with a darker tone at base (21B) and creamier tone at rim (13B), mouth wavy, rim deeply dentate. Mid-season. Sweetly scented

'Loch Seaforth' 2 WWY-O
(D.C. MacArthur) D.C. MacArthur, 1989
'Kilworth' hybrid; sdlg no. EV87/9
Fl. 103 mm wide; perianth segments broad, greenish white (155A), suffused brilliant yellow 9C at base, of good substance, overlapping; corona orange (28A), intricately frilled. Mid-season. Sunproof. Slightly scented

'Loch Stac' 2 Y-R
(J.S.B. Lea) J.S.B. Lea, 1961
'Air Marshal' × Richardson sdlg 852; sdlg no. 8-29-55
Fl. 85 mm wide; perianth segments deep golden yellow; corona rich orange-red. Mid-season. Resembles a darker-coloured 'Revelry' with smaller and broader perianth segments. Mid-season

'Loch Tarbert' 2 Y-Y
(D.C. MacArthur) D.C. MacArthur, 1992
'Kingscourt' × 2 Y-O; sdlg no. EV8346
Fl. 107 mm wide; perianth segments broadly ovate, with prominent white mucro, vivid yellow 12A, tinged bronze, spreading; the inner segments narrower and only slightly mucronate; corona funnel-shaped, ribbed, deeper in tone (14A) than the perianth, mouth flared and frilled, rim flanged and crenate. Late

'Loch Trool' 3 W-YRR
(J.S.B. Lea) J.S.B. Lea, 1983
('Merlin' × 'Rockall') × 'Purbeck'; sdlg no. 1-21-74
Fl. 100 mm wide. Div 2. until 1987

'Loch Turnaig' 2 W-R
(J.S.B. Lea) J.S.B. Lea, 1979
'Eribol' × ('Rockall' × ['Matapan' × 'Loch Crewe']); sdlg no. 1-41-68
Fl. 110 mm wide. Mid-season

'Locksley' 2 W-YYR
(A.E. Lowe, pre-1927)

'Loco' 2 W-?
(Alister Clark) J. Sharp, 1960

'Locust' 3 W-? (b)
(pre-1910)

'Lod' 1 W-Y
(W. Jackson Jr) W. Jackson Jr, 1966
'Mitanni' × 'Preamble'; sdlg no. 57/58
Perianth segments rounded at apex, smooth, deeply overlapping; corona broad, deep rich yellow. 2n=28

'Lodear' 2 (a)
(A.H. Ahrens) J.S. Leitch, 1955

'Lodestar'
(pre-1913)

'Lodestar' 1 W-W
(D.S. Bell, 1947) D.S. Bell, 1958

'Lodestone' 3 W-? (b)
(W.B. Hartland, pre-1907)

'Lodore' 9
(pre-1914)

'Lodore' 3 W-? (b)
(R.H. Bath, pre-1929)

'Loftus' 1 Y-Y
(J.N.Hancock & Co., 1982) Unregistered
Sdlg no. 52/82H
Fl. rounded, golden yellow; perianth segments deeply overlapping; corona with rim dentate. Tall. Early to mid-season

'Lofty' 6 Y-O
(R.E. Parsons) R.E. Parsons, 1967
'Chungking' × *N. cyclamineus*
Fl. 82 mm wide; perianth segments clear yellow, neatly reflexed, smooth; corona light orange, with a paler tone at base. Early

'Logan Rock' 7 Y-Y
(R.V. Favell, pre-1953)
Perianth segments somewhat reflexed; corona smoothly angled, mouth slightly split in places and overlapping, wavy, with rim entire. Resembles 'Sweetness'

'Loge' 2 W-? (b)
(Mrs R.O. Backhouse, pre-1921)

'Logie' 3 Y-YYR
(Brodie Gardens) Brodie Gardens, 1957
Hybrid between 'Carbineer' and 'Market Merry'
Fl. clear yellow; corona with a broad band of near scarlet at rim

'Lohengrin' 3 W-Y
(G.H. Engleheart, pre-1908)
Fl. broad, rounded; corona expanded, deeply ribbed, canary yellow

'Lohengrin' 2 W-O
(J.W.A. Lefeber, 1945) J.W.A. Lefeber, 1960
Fl. 85 mm wide. Mid-season

'Lohengrin' 1 W-?
Syn. of 'Vermont'

'Lohengrin' 1 W-W
Syn. of 'Elisabeth van Ginhoven'

'Loila' 2 W-? (b)
(S.J. Bisdee, 1939)

'Loira' 1 W-P
(C.E. Radcliff, 1941)
('Mitylene' × 'Pink o' Dawn') × 'Dawnglow'

loiseleurii = *N. triandrus* var. *loiseleurii*

'Loki' 2 Y-Y
(E.M. Crosfield, pre-1913)
Fl. 102 mm wide, pale yellow. Resembles an improved 'Frank Miles'

'Lola' 1 W-W
(E.M. Crosfield, pre-1908)
'Madame de Graaff' × 'Weardale Perfection'
Perianth segments slightly inflexed; corona creamy white, with mouth expanded and frilled. ?See also 'Lolah'

'Lola Anderson' 2 W-? (b)
(pre-1956) Unregistered
Corona biscuit-coloured

'Lolah' 1 W-W
?Syn. of 'Lola'

'Lola Leak' 1 W-Y
(R.H. Bath, pre-1930)
Perianth segments creamy; corona primrose yellow. AM(e) 1930

'Lolan'
(pre-1915)

'Lola Prieta'
Unregistered
In parentage of 'Chorine'

'Lolette' 1 W-W
(D.V. West, pre-1923)
Corona narrow. Mid-season

'Lolita' 2 W-YOO
(S.J. Bisdee, 1945)
'Hades' × 'Red Crusader'

'Lolita' 2 W-?
(J.S. Leitch) J.S. Leitch, 1960
Fl. 114 mm wide

'Lollipop' 2 W-P
(Mrs E.Murray, pre-1955)
Corona smooth, soft pink, with mouth slightly expanding

'Lollipop' 3 W-Y
(Murray W. Evans, 1966) Murray W. Evans, 1976
'Green Island' × 'Actaea'; sdlg no. J-16
Fl. 85 mm wide. Mid-season

'Lombard' 2 Y-Y
(P.D. Williams, pre-1933)
Fl. 102 mm wide; perianth segments vivid yellow 9B, with margins slightly incurving, overlapping half; corona lightly ribbed, darker in tone (13A) than the perianth, with mouth a little expanded, rim dentate.
*AM(g) 1952

'London Pride' 2 W-? (b)
(F.E. Gibbs, pre-1948)

'Londontown Lass' 9 W-GGR
(Mrs M.S. Yerger) Mrs M.S. Yerger, 1996
Poeticus hybrid open pollinated; sdlg no. A 2-1
Fl. 65 mm wide; perianth segments white; corona brilliant yellow-green 150B, with light yellow-green 145B at base and orange-red (30A) at rim. Dwarf. Mid-season

'Loner' 6 Y-Y
(Broadleigh Gardens, pre-1993) Unregistered

'Lonesome Dove' 2 W-W
(W.G. Pannill) W.G. Pannill, 1992
'Starmount' × 'Panache'; sdlg no. 74/27
Fl. 95 mm wide. Mid-season

'Lone Star' 3 W-Y
(Barr & Sons, pre-1908)
N. × *poculiformis* × *N. poeticus*
Fl. small; perianth segments of smooth texture, overlapping; corona clear lemon yellow. Sweetly scented

'Lone Star' 2 W-W
(W.G. Pannill) W.G. Pannill, 1982
'Easter Moon' × 'Cataract'; sdlg no. 74/41
Fl. 95 mm wide. Mid-season

'Longbow' 3 W-? (b)
(G.H. Engleheart, pre-1923)

'Long Branch' 3 W-R
(J.M. de Navarro, pre-1949)
'Red Hackle' × 'Signal Light'
Perianth segments creamy white; corona orange-red

'Long Champs' 2 Y-?
(Konynenburg & Mark) Konynenburg & Mark, 1963
'Mimosa' hybrid
Mid-season

'Longeray' 2 W-P
(A. Overton) A. Overton, 1959
'Grayling' sdlg × 'Grayling' sdlg

Fl. 114 mm wide; corona broad, dusty lavender pink

'Longfellow' 2 W-Y
(W.F.M. Copeland, pre-1907)
Perianth segments deep ivory white, overlapping; corona short broad funnel-shaped, bright yellow

'Longford' 1 W-W
(W.J. Dunlop) W.J. Dunlop, 1957
'Kanchenjunga' × 'Cantatrice'
Fl. pure white; perianth segments somewhat acute; corona with rim flanged

'Longhorn' 1 Y-O
(V. Brink) V. Brink, 1966
'Quip' open pollinated
Fl. 127 mm wide; perianth segments acute, pale yellow; corona narrowly ribbed, opening tawny orange, becoming paler buff orange. Mid-season

N. longiflorus Willdenow = *N.* × *intermedius*

N. longipetalus Schleicher = *N. radiiflorus* var. *exertus*

N. longispathus Pugsley 13 Section Pseudonarcissus

N. longispathus Pugsley var. *bujei* Fernández Casas = *N. hispanicus* var. *bujei*

'Long Ridge' 6 Y-Y
(Curtis Tolley) Curtis Tolley, 1996
'Backchat' × 'Akala'; sdlg no. 89-40-1
Fl. clear mid-yellow; perianth segments ovate, reflexed, slightly overlapping; corona cylindrical, with mouth slightly flared, even. Mid-season

'Longshanks' 2 Y-Y
(E. Leeds, pre-1877)
Perianth sulphur yellow. Tall. Syn. Incomparabilis Sulphureus 'Longshanks'

'Longshaw' 2 W-? (b or c)
(W.A. Milner, pre-1931)
Syn. 'Commonwealth'

'Longships' 2 (a)
(G.L. Wilson, pre-1937)
'Fortune' sdlg
Resembles 'Fortune' in colour but with a longer and narrower corona

'Long Span' 1 (a)
(Mrs R.O. Backhouse, pre-1908)

'Longspur' 5 W-W
(G.E. Mitsch) G.E. Mitsch, 1979
'Easter Moon' × *N. triandrus*; sdlg no. F152/9
Fl. 56 mm wide, pure white; perianth segments slightly reflexed. Mid-season. Resembles 'Saberwing' but with more flowers per stem and a longer and less

widely flared corona

'Longstander' 1 (a)
(W.B. Hartland, pre-1913)

'Longstone' 2 Y-O
(F.E. Board) F.E. Board, 1965
'Missouri' × 'Craigywarren'; sdlg no. 1000
Mid-season

'Long Tom' 2 W-Y
(W.F.M. Copeland, pre-1913)
Perianth segments overlapping; corona cylindrical, light yellow. Mid-season

'Longun' ?-P
(Alister Clark, pre-1948)

'Longview' 1 W-W
(S.A. Free) Mrs S.I. Free, 1968

'Longwood Court' 1 Y-Y
(F.E. Board) F.E. Board, 1965
'Stronghold' × 'Kingscourt'
Mid-season

'Looe' 3 Y-O
(P.D. Williams, pre-1937)

'Looking Good' 2 W-Y
(J.N. Hancock & Co., c.1975) Unregistered

'Lookout' 9 W-GGO
(Mrs M.S. Yerger) Mrs M.S. Yerger, 1991
'Sea Green' open pollinated; sdlg no. 77 H 3
Fl. 50 mm wide; the inner shorter than the outer perianth segments; corona with a wide band of orange at rim. Late

'Loongana' 1 W-W
(K.J. Heazlewood) K.J. Heazlewood, 1968
'Glenshesk' × 'Castle of Mey'

'Loophole' 2 W-W
(W. Jackson Jr) Jackson's Daffodils, 1983
'Saroya' × Sdlg 200/68; sdlg no. 33/75
Fl. 115 mm wide. Mid-season

'Lopez' 3 (a)
(A.M. Wilson, pre-1931)

N. × *lopezii* Fernández Casas 13 = *N. bulbocodium* Linnaeus × *N. obvallaris* Salisbury

'Lord Aberdeen' 1 Y-Y
(de Graaff Bros, pre-1897)
Perianth segments primrose yellow, of strong substance; corona bright golden yellow. Syn. 'Aberdeen'

'Lord Antrim' 1 Y-Y
(G.L. Wilson, pre-1927)
'Lord Roberts' × 'King Alfred'
Corona rim flanged and dentate. Mid-season to late

'Lord Balfour' 1 W-Y
(R.A. van der Schoot, pre-1923)
Perianth segments very broad; corona golden yellow

'Lord Beaconsfield' 1 (a)
(W. Welchman, pre-1923)

'Lord Bledisloe'
(New Zealand origin, pre-1940)

'Lord Canning' 8 Y-Y
(pre-1861)
Perianth segments primrose yellow; corona darker in tone. Syn. Tazetta 'Lord Canning'

'Lord Carrington' 8
(pre-1915)

'Lord Chancellor' 1 W-Y
(J.L. Richardson) J.L. Richardson, 1956
'Spitzbergen' × 'Kanchenjunga'
Perianth segments very broadly ovate, of great substance; corona deep primrose, with rim dentate and widely rolled

'Lord Clive' 3 W-? (b)
(W. Welchman, pre-1908)

'Lord Cromer' 1 (a)
(W. Welchman, pre-1907)

'Lord Curzon' 1 (a)
(W.J. Eldering & Son, pre-1928)

'Lord Derby' 1 Y-Y
(W. Backhouse, pre-1869)
Perianth segments dark primrose yellow, of thick texture, overlapping; corona dark rich yellow. Resembles 'Joseph Chamberlain'. Syn. Pseudonarcissus Lorifolius 'Lord Derby'

'Lord Gort' 1 Y-Y
(S.J. Bisdee, pre-1940)
'Michael Forth' × 'Gambrinus'

'Lord Ivor'
(pre-1940)

'Lord Kenyon' 4 Y-O
(Mrs R.O. Backhouse, pre-1921)
Perianth and other petaloid segments in three whorls, broadly ovate, blunt, yellow, with slight white mucro, overlapping one-third to a half; the outer whorls of about equal length, spreading or a little inflexed, plane or with margins a little wavy; the centre whorl shorter, more strongly inflexed and with margins deeply

incurled; corona segments shorter still, clustered at centre and interspersed among the petaloid segments, reddish orange, frilled. Mid-season. AM(Haarlem) 1930

'Lord Kitchener' 2 W-Y
(Mrs R.O. Backhouse, pre-1905)
'Minnie Hume' × 'Weardale Perfection'
Fl. facing slightly downwards; perianth segments broadly ovate, usually acute, sometimes mucronate, somewhat ribbed, with margins often incurving towards apex, overlapping half; corona angled, pale primrose yellow, sometimes tinged yellowish pink, with mouth expanded, deeply and somewhat irregularly frilled. 2n=28. AM 1905

'Lord Lister' 1 W-W
(W. Welchman, pre-1908)
Fl. 102 mm wide; perianth segments with margins incurved; corona broad, opening very pale yellow, becoming milk white, with rim rolled

'Lord Louis Mountbatten' 1 W-W
(de Graaff Bros, pre-1926)
Fl. large; perianth segments overlapping; corona creamy white. AM(Haarlem) 1926

'Lord Mayor' 1 Y-Y
(E. Leeds, pre-1877)
Fl. large, soft pale yellow. Syn. Pseudonarcissus Major 'Lord Mayor'. Was "absorbed" into 'Captain Nelson'

'Lord Medway' 1 Y-Y
(G.P. Haydon, pre-1910)
'Monarch' hybrid

'Lord Melbourne' 1 Y-Y
(H.A. Brown, pre-1938)

'Lord Milner' 1 W-W
(G.P. Haydon, pre-1908)

'Lord Muncaster' 1 Y-Y
(Miss A.M. Crellin, pre-1907)

'Lord Munster' 1 W-W
(A.M. Williams, pre-1951)

'Lord Nelson' 1 Y-Y
(G.B. van Rhijn, pre-1936)
2n=28. AM(Haarlem) 1936

'Lord of the Manor' 1 Y-Y
(F.H. Chapman, pre-1927)
Late. AM(Haarlem) 1937

'Lord Rendlesham' 2 W-O
(Mrs R.O. Backhouse, pre-1921)
Perianth segments creamy white; corona rich reddish orange, frilled

'Lord Revel' 1 (a)
(E.N. Amoore) J.A.O'More, 1957

'Lord Roberts' 1 Y-Y
(Barr & Sons, pre-1901)
Fl. golden yellow; perianth segments broadly ovate, blunt, inflexed, sometimes a little reflexed towards apex, overlapping half; the inner segments narrower, more strongly inflexed, twisted; corona cylindrical, angled, mouth ribbed, widely expanded, with rim deeply crenate. FCC 1901

'Lord Russell' 1 Y-Y
(pre-1896)
Perianth segments soft clear yellow; corona darker in tone

'Lord Selborne' 2 W-? (b or c)
(Mrs R.O. Backhouse, pre-1914)

'Lordship' 1 Y-Y
(Miss M. Verry) Miss M. Verry, 1966
Fl. 115 mm wide, deep golden yellow. Mid-season. Resembles a larger-flowered and darker-coloured 'Royalist'

'Lord Tedder' 2 W-GYY
(G.A. Uit den Boogaard, pre-1946)

'Lord Trent' 1 (a)
(J.R. Pearson & Sons, pre-1933)

'Lord Warden' 1 Y-Y
(F.H. Chapman, pre-1915)
Resembles a larger-flowered and darker-coloured 'Lord Roberts'

'Lord Wellington' 1 Y-Y
(G.H. Engleheart, pre-1914)
Fl. large, golden yellow; corona mouth widely expanded. Resembles an improved 'King Alfred'. AM(Haarlem) 1923, FA(Haarlem) 1929

'Lore' 1 Y-Y
(R.H. Glover, pre-1993) Unregistered

'Lorelei' 2 W-P
(R.V. Favell, pre-1939)
Corona ribbed, soft salmon pink

'Loreley' 3 W-? (b or c)
(G.H. Engleheart, pre-1910)

'Lorentz' 1 Y-Y
Syn. of 'Sassenheim's Gold'

'Lorenzo' 2 W-Y
(E. Leeds, pre-1877)
Fl. large; perianth segments irregularly notched at apex, opening soft primrose, becoming sulphur

white, inflexed. Resembles an inferior 'Stella Superba'. Syn. Incomparabilis Albidus 'Lorenzo'. "Absorbed" 'Charles Hooper' and 'Themistocles'

'Lorenzo' 2 W-O
(J.L. Richardson) J.L. Richardson, 1959
'Kilworth' × 'Arbar'
Perianth segments somewhat acute, pure white; corona deep orange, frilled. 2n=28

N. × *loretii* Rouy = *N.* × *medioluteus*

'Loretto Lotto' 2 W-O
(J.W.A. Lefeber) J.W.A. Lefeber, 1968
'Redmarley' hybrid

N. lorifolius Gillot = *N. abscissus*

N. lorifolius Herbert = *N. bicolor* var. *lorifolius*

N. lorifolius Rouy = *N. abscissus*

N. lorifolius Schultes f. = *N. bicolor* var. *lorifolius*

'Lorifolius' 1
Was "absorbed" into 'Harrison Weir'

'Lorikeet' 1 Y-P
(G.E. Mitsch) G.E. Mitsch, 1979
'Rima' open pollinated; sdlg no. HO9/3
Fl. 95 mm wide; perianth segments soft lemon yellow; corona flared, apricot pink. Mid-season

'Lorinna' 1 W-Y
(C.E. Radcliff, 1939) J.M.Radcliff, 1956
'Effective' × 'Bonnington'

'Lorna' 5
(van Zonneveld Bros & Philippo, pre-1914)
AM(Haarlem) 1922. Received AM(Haarlem) 1922 as 'Gertrude'

'Lorna Bell' 4 W-P
(D.S. Bell) D.S. Bell, 1986
Fl. 104 mm wide. Mid-season. Resembles 'Templeton Rose' but with the corona segments of a richer and brighter tone

'Lorna Doone' 1 Y-Y
(W.B. Hartland, pre-1907)
Corona dark yellow

'Lorna Doone' 2 W-?
(Alister Clark, 1929) J. Sharp, 1960

'Lornaeve' 3 W-YYO
(L.P. Dettman) L.P. Dettman, 1979
'Lynette Sholl' × 'Lily May Curtis'; sdlg no. LS 5/77
Fl. 75 mm wide; perianth segments greenish white (155A); corona vivid yellow 13A, with a narrow band of strong orange 24A at rim. Late. Resembles 'Lily May Curtis' but with improved substance and a deeper corona

'Lorna Hymus' 2 W-Y
(L.P. Dettman) L.P. Dettman, 1976
'Tudor Minstrel' × 'Irish Minstrel'; sdlg no. 57/73
Fl. 94 mm wide; perianth segments greenish white (155C); corona vivid yellow 9B. Mid-season. Resembles an earlier-flowered 'Tudor Minstrel' with the flower at right angles to the stem

'Lorne' 1 (a)
(R. Dick, pre-1930)

'Lorraine' 2 W-W
(C.A. Latta) C.A. Latta, 1956

'Lorris' 3 (a)
(J.T. Gray, pre-1950)

'Los Angeles' 9
(de Graaff Bros, pre-1928)
Syn. 'Shelley'

'Los Flamencos' 1 (a)
Syn. of 'Royal Spain'

'Lostine' 3 W-GWW
(Murray W. Evans) Murray W. Evans, 1969
'Chinese White' × *N. poeticus* var. *recurvus* × 'Carolina'

'Lost Legend' 2 W-? (b)
(A.H. Ahrens) J.S. Leitch, 1955

'Lostwithiel' 2 Y-O
(Brian S. Duncan) du Plessis Bros, 1989
'Altruist' × 'Ulster Bank'; sdlg no. 551
Fl. 105 mm wide; perianth segments very smooth; corona bowl-shaped, deep orange. Mid-season

'Lothario'
(J. Pope, pre-1913)

'Lothario' 2 W-Y
(P. van Deursen, pre-1938)
AM(Haarlem) 1938

'Lotherio' 2 Y-O
(pre-1987) Unregistered
Very late

'Loth Lorien' 3 W-GYY
(Brian S. Duncan) Rathowen Daffodils, 1981
Sdlg R3546 ('Pontresina' open pollinated) × 'Woodland Prince'; sdlg no. 331
Fl. 120 mm wide; corona very shallow bowl-shaped, lemon yellow, with green at base

'Lotta Svärd' 1 W-Y
(J. Prins & Son, pre-1944)
FA(Haarlem) 1944

'Lottery' 2 W-O
(G.W.E. Brogden) G.W.E. Brogden, 1966
Corona salmon orange. Early

'Lottie' 9
(W. Poupart, pre-1914)

'Lottie Simmons' 2 W-YYO
(W. Backhouse, pre-1869)
Perianth segments sulphur white; corona canary yellow, with orange at rim. Syn. Burbidgei 'Lottie Simmons'. "Absorbed" Burbidgei 'Elegans' and ? 'Empress Eugenie'

'Lotus' 1 W-W
(E.M. Crosfield, pre-1908)

'Lotus' 2 W-P
(J.N. Hancock & Co., 1968) Unregistered

'Loudon' 8
(van Zonneveld Bros & Philippo, pre-1931)
Poetaz

'Loud Speaker' 2 W-Y
(Mrs R.O. Backhouse, pre-1921)
Perianth segments sulphur white; corona expanded, orange yellow

'Lough Allen' 2 W-W
(G.L. Wilson, pre-1949)
'Dava' × 'Ischia'
Fl. pure white

'Loughanisland' 1 Y-Y
(Ballydorn Bulb Farm) Ballydorn Bulb Farm, 1986
'Viking' open pollinated
Early. Resembles an improved 'Viking'

'Loughanmore' 1 Y-Y
(Carncairn Daffodils) Carncairn Daffodils, 1969
'Kingscourt' × 'Antwerp'
Fl. bright yellow. Resembles 'Kingscourt' but with the corona rim more prominently dentate

'Lough Areema' 3 W-GWO
(G.L. Wilson, pre-1950)
Fl. 90 mm wide; perianth segments somewhat oblong, slightly mucronate, a little truncate, slightly reflexed, plane, overlapping half; the inner segments narrower, more nearly spreading, with margins recurved at base as if spathulate, folded at midrib near apex, with margins wavy; corona disc-shaped, ribbed, cream, shading to green at base and vivid reddish orange 33B at rim, with the rim minutely incised. AM(e) 1951

'Lough Bawn' 2 Y-R
(Carncairn Daffodils, 1975) Carncairn Daffodils, 1986
Wootton sdlg × 'Spelter'; sdlg no. W19/11
Perianth segments broadly ovate or roundish, prominently mucronate, vivid yellow 9A, overlapping half; the inner segments more narrowly ovate; corona short funnel-shaped, orange-red, sometimes more nearly orange, with mouth straight and 6-lobed, rim irregularly dentate. Early

'Lough Crew' 2 W-R
(J.L. Richardson, pre-1952)
'Laverick' × 'Coronach'; sdlg no. 578
Perianth segments somewhat acute

'Lough Cuan' 1 Y-Y
(Ballydorn Bulb Farm, 1973) Ballydorn Bulb Farm, 1984
'Viking' × 'Torchbearer' sdlg
Fl. 105 mm wide. Mid-season. Resembles a 'Viking' of improved colour

'Lough Erne' 3 W-YYR
(W.J. Dunlop) W.J. Dunlop, 1955
'Isola' × 'Sunstar'
Perianth segments snow white, of thick and waxy texture; corona with deep red at rim

'Loughgall' 2 W-P
(W.J. Dunlop) W.J. Dunlop, 1965

'Lough Gowna' 1 Y-Y
(Patrick Kiernan) Patrick Kiernan, 1997
'Verdant' × 'Arkle' or 'Golden Sovereign'; sdlg no. PK1434
Fl. 124 mm wide, deep yellow; perianth segments very broadly ovate, blunt, plane, smooth; corona cylindrical, with mouth slightly expanded and rim crenate. Mid-season to late

'Lough Maree' 2 W-P
Syn. of 'Loch Maree'

'Lough Neagh' 3 W-Y
(G.L. Wilson) G.L. Wilson, 1957
'Nelly' × 'Chinese White'
Perianth segments pure white; corona pale primrose, touched green at base, frilled

'Lough Ree' 2 W-W
(G.L. Wilson, pre-1949)
'Pinkeen' × 'Smyrna'

'Lough Ryan' 1 Y-Y
(Ballydorn Bulb Farm) Ballydorn Bulb Farm, 1987
'Viking' × 'Moon Goddess'
Fl. golden yellow. Early

'Louisa Alexandra' 2 Y-GYO
(L.P. Dettman) L.P. Dettman, 1978
'Vulcan' × 'Spelter'; sdlg no. 40/75
Fl. 92 mm wide; perianth segments vivid yellow 13A; corona vivid orange-yellow 23A, with green at base and orange (28A) at rim. Mid-season

'Louisa de Vries' 2 W-O
Syn. of 'Louise de Vries'

'Louis Armstrong' 1 Y-Y
(G.H. Rotteveel & Sons) G.H. Rotteveel & Sons, 1961
Fl. 130 mm wide; perianth segments light greenish yellow 5C; corona vivid yellow 9B. Mid-season. AM(Haarlem) 1962

'Louis Bouwmeester' 1 (a)
(P. van Deursen, pre-1930)

'Louis Capet' 2 W-? (b)
(de Graaff Bros, pre-1927)

'Louis d'Or' 2 Y-Y
(Konynenburg & Mark) Konynenburg & Mark, 1963
'Mimosa' hybrid
Fl. 95 mm wide; perianth segments brilliant yellow 12B; corona darker in tone (15B). Mid-season

'Louise' 2 W-Y
(M. van Waveren & Sons, pre-1900)
Corona canary yellow, faintly tinged orange at rim, frilled

'Louise' 8 W-Y
Fls 4-5 per stem; perianth segments pure white, overlapping; corona golden yellow. Syn. of 'Aspasia'

'Louise' 2 W-W
(?New Zealand origin, pre-1996) Unregistered

'Louise de Coligny' 2 W-YYP
(L. van Leeuwen & Son, pre-1940)
Fl. 95 mm wide; perianth segments broadly ovate, squarish at apex, prominently mucronate, clear white, slightly reflexed, with margins wavy, overlapping one-third to a half; the inner segments more narrowly ovate, blunt, more nearly spreading at base, more or less strongly reflexed in upper half, often nicked or "thumbed" at shoulder; corona funnel-shaped, smooth, light yellow, shading to apricot pink (28C or D) at rim, mouth straight, with six deeply overlapping lobes, frilled. Sweetly scented. AM(Haarlem) 1940

'Louise de Vries' 2 W-O
(J.W.A. Lefeber) J.W.A. Lefeber, 1960
Fl. 95 mm wide; corona deep orange. Early. See also 'Louisa de Vries'

'Louise L.Linton' 2 W-Y
(J.R. Pearson & Sons, pre-1914)
'Minnie Hume' × 'Madame de Graaff'

'Louis le Grand' 8 W-W
(pre-1850)
Corona opening primrose or sulphur yellow, becoming creamy white. Syn. Tazetta 'Louis le Grand'. ?The same as 'White Pearl'

'Louis Pasteur' 2 W-GYO
(J.W.A. Lefeber, pre-1945)

'Louis Serres' 2 W-YYO
(W. Backhouse, pre-1869)
Corona expanded. Syn. Incomparabilis Albus 'Louis Serres'. Was "absorbed" into 'Bertie'

'Louisville' 2 W-R
(J.M. de Navarro, pre-1949)
'Folly' × 'Flamenco'

'Louky' 3 W-? (b)
(G.A. Uit den Boogaard, pre-1950)
AM(Haarlem) 1951

'Lourae' 9 W-GGR
(Mrs M.S. Yerger) Mrs M.S. Yerger, 1993
'Caedmon' open pollinated; sdlg no. 79 A 1
Fl. 65 mm wide; perianth segments slightly reflexed; the inner segments shorter; corona almost disc-shaped, brilliant yellow-green 154B, with strong yellow-green 145A at base and a band of orange-red (35A) at rim. Late

'Lourdes' 2 Y-O
(C.M. Grullemans) J.J. Grullemans & Sons, 1956
Perianth segments pale yellow; corona frilled

'Lou Rosa' 2 W-W
(R.C.A. Tombleson) R.C.A. Tombleson, 1966
Fl. 118 mm wide. Mid-season. Resembles 'Glacier' but with a longer corona

'Lovable' 3 W-W
(G.E. Mitsch, 1957) G.E. Mitsch, 1967
'Green Island' × 'Chinese White'; sdlg no. R33/60
Perianth segments sparkling white, spreading. Mid-season. Resembles a purer white 'Easter Moon' with more rounded perianth segments and a shallower corona. See also 'Loveable'

'Lovacott' 3 W-? (b)
(R.O. Backhouse, pre-1938)

'Lovat Scout' 3 W-? (b)
(The Brodie of Brodie, c.1929)
('Beacon' × 'Fortune') × 'Sunstar'; sdlg no. 108/A/24

'Loveable' 3 W-W

Syn. of 'Lovable'

'Love Affair' 1 W-Y
(J.A. Hunter, 1976) J.A. Hunter, 1989
'My Love' × 'Centaurus'; sdlg no. 8/70A
Fl. 112 mm wide; perianth segments broadly ovate, smooth, of good substance; corona cylindrical, light greenish yellow 4C, with mouth straight. Early to mid-season

'Love Boat' 2 W-P
(W.G. Pannill) W.G. Pannill, 1978
'Knightwick' × 'Caro Nome'; sdlg no. 65/87
Fl. 103 mm wide. Mid-season

'Love Call' 11a W-OOY
(J. Gerritsen & Son) J. Gerritsen & Son, 1977
'Orangery' × 'Chantilly'
Perianth segments very broadly ovate, rounded at apex, prominently mucronate, spreading or a little reflexed, overlapping half; the inner segments a little inflexed, spathulate, with margins incurling; corona split to base, the six segments half as long as the perianth segments, opposite and closely overlying them and joined at margins below the shoulder, deeply bi-lobed, strong orange 25B, with lemon yellow at rim, frilled. Mid-season

'Love Child' 2 W-Y
(J.A. O'More) P.D.K. Ramsay, 1983
'My Love' open pollinated

'Loveday' 2 Y-O
(Rosewarne EHS, 1971) Rosewarne EHS, 1985
'Scorpion' × 'Armada'; sdlg no. 65/72/1
Fl. of strong substance; perianth segments broad, acute, brilliant greenish yellow 6B, with a slightly paler tone at apex, with margins slightly incurved, overlapping; corona bowl-shaped, brighter and darker than strong orange 25A, frilled. Early. Trade designation ORANGE APPEAL

'Love Desire' 2 Y-GYO
(C.M. Grullemans) J.J. Grullemans & Sons, 1959

'Love Dream' 3 W-O
(P. van Deursen, pre-1943)
AM(Haarlem) 1943

'Love in Idleness' 2 W-P
(W.M.Spry, pre-1987) Unregistered
Perianth segments broad; corona cylindrical, deep pink, with mouth a little flared. Late. 2n=28

'Loveit' 4 Y-Y
(M.E.Brogden, pre-1993) Unregistered
'Double Event' × 'Lemonade'; sdlg no. R2/6

'Lovejoy' 2 W-YPP
(Murray W. Evans, 1971) Jean E. Driver, 1993

Dwarf pink Div. 2 × ([sdlg 112 × 'Caro Nome'] × ['Interim' × 'Green Island']); sdlg no. 05-1
Fl. 100 mm wide; perianth segments broad, white, with a satin sheen, overlapping; corona cup-shaped, ribbed, peach pink, with yellow at base and a darker tone of pink at rim, mouth expanded. Late. Sunproof

'Lovelace' 9
(G.H. Engleheart, pre-1897)

'Lovelace' 3 W-GYO
(W.B.Blanden, 1970s) Unregistered
Perianth segments ivory white; corona ribbed, creamy yellow, with a broad band of bright tangerine orange at rim. Mid-season

'Lovelight' 2 W-? (b)
(Oregon Bulb Farms, pre-1950)

'Loveliness' 1 W-W
(de Graaff Bros, pre-1903)
?'Madame de Graaff' self pollinated
Fl. large; perianth segments snow white; corona slender, with mouth expanded

'Loveliness' 3 W-Y
(G. Lewis, pre-1956) Unregistered
Perianth segments white; corona widely expanded, very pale gold, with a brighter tone at rim and the rim dentate

'Lovellia' 3 W-WWO
(?Australian origin, pre-1997) Unregistered

'Lovelock' 2 W-P
(O. Ronalds, pre-1955)
'Wild Rose' × 'Mrs Oscar Ronalds'

'Lovely' 3 W-Y
(W. Backhouse, pre-1869)
Corona lemon yellow, frilled. Syn. Burbidgei 'Lovely'

'Lovely Lady' 2 W-? (b)
(A.H. Ahrens) J.S. Leitch, 1955

'Love Lyric' 2 W-P
(E.F. Hughes) E.F. Hughes, 1962
Fl. 102 mm wide; corona salmon pink. Late

'Lovenest' 2 W-Y
(Mrs R.O. Backhouse, pre-1921)
Corona primrose yellow, tinged pink. Resembles 'Suda'

'Loveny' 2 W-W
(Brian S. Duncan) du Plessis Bros, 1989
'Easter Moon' × 'Knowehead'; sdlg no. 317
Fl. 100 mm wide; perianth segments pure white, of good substance; corona touched with pale pink on opening, becoming pure white. Mid-season

'Love Parade' 2 W-YYO
(Konynenburg & Mark) Konynenburg & Mark, 1960
('Flaming Torch' × Mimosa') × ('Dick Wellband' × 'Bertha Aten')
Fl. 90 mm wide; perianth segments creamy white; corona canary yellow, with vivid orange 28B at rim. Late

'Love Potion' 2 W-P
(W. Gould Jr) W. Gould Jr, 1992
'Watercolour' × 'Dailmanach'; sdlg no. 83-18-E
Fl. 105 mm wide. Mid-season

'Love's Fire' 3 W-? (b)
(P.D. Williams, pre-1937)
AM(Haarlem) 1937

'Love Song' 2 W-OOY
(C.M. Grullemans) J.J. Grullemans & Sons, 1957
Corona opening canary yellow, becoming tangerine orange, with canary yellow at rim, frilled. 2n=28

'Love Sonnet' 2 W-P
(Sidney DuBose, 1982) Sidney DuBose, 1996
Sdlg B39-6 ('Magic Dream' × 'Salome') × 'Verran'; Sdlg no. H68-3
Fl. 92 mm wide. Mid-season

'Love Story' 1 Y-Y
(P.L.A. Pouw) N. Blokker, 1971
'Rembrandt' × 'Golden Sunbeam'
Fl. 123 mm wide

'Lovette' 2 YYW-GWY
(Mrs G. Link) Mrs G. Link, 1988
'Euphony' × 'Golden Aura'; sdlg no. 78-D-1
Perianth segments yellow, with white at base, spreading, smooth, of good substance; corona bowl-shaped. Dwarf. Late. Resembles a smaller-flowered 'Euphony'

"Loving Couples"
Syn. of *N. × medioluteus*

'Lowanna' 2 Y-YRR
(A.O. Roblin, 1944)
'Market Merry' × 'Lillian Murdoch'

'Lowcarn' 2 W-?
(A. Overton) A. Overton, 1960

'Lowcliffe' 2 W-W
(G. Lewis, 1935) Parr's Nurseries, 1958
'White Emperor' × 'A.E.Lowe'

'Lowdham Beauty' 2 W-W
(J.R. Pearson & Sons, pre-1907)
'Minnie Hume' × 'Madame de Graaff'
Fl. milk white; perianth segments overlapping; corona opening pale creamy yellow, frilled. Tall

'Lowdina' 1 W-P
(C.E. Radcliff, 1941)
'Glendevie' × 'Dawnglow'

'Lowestoft' 2 (a)
(J.L. Richardson, pre-1938)

'Lowlander' 1 (a)
(W. Welchman, pre-1908)

'Loxton' 1 Y-Y
(C.E. Radcliff, 1930)
'Yellow Aster' hybrid

'Loyal' 2 W-? (b)
(?T. Buncombe, pre-1933)

'Loyal Chief' 1 Y-Y
(Miss M. Verry) Miss M. Verry, 1966
Fl. 107 mm wide, medium yellow. Mid-season. Resembles a smaller-flowered and darker-coloured 'Crocus'

'Loyalist' 1 Y-Y
(J.L. Richardson, pre-1923)
Fl. forming a double triangle; perianth segments broadly ovate, fairly prominently mucronate, overlapping one-third to a half; corona golden yellow, darker in tone than the perianth, with mouth widely expanded and loosely frilled, rim deeply notched and crenate. AM(e) 1926

'Loyalty' 1 W-Y
(Sir A.P.W. Thomas, pre-1914)

'Loyalty' 1 (a)
(R.H. Bath, pre-1923)

'Loyce' 7 Y-YYO
(Roberta C.Watrous, ?1972) Roberta C.Watrous, 1989
'Ruby' × *N. assoanus*
Fls 1-2 per stem, 40 mm wide; perianth segments light greenish yellow 8C, spreading, overlapping; corona bowl-shaped, vivid yellow 9A, with vivid orange 28B at rim. Dwarf. Late

'Loyola' 2 Y-R
(C.E. Radcliff, 1939)
'Lady A.Currie' × 'Fortune'

'Luala' 3 W-? (b)
(A.M. Wilson, pre-1931)

'Luan' 2 Y-R
(W. Jackson Jr, 1969) Unregistered
'Vulcan' × 'Dimity'; sdlg no. 39/69

'Luana' 2 Y-YOO
(S.J. Bisdee, 1946)
Sdlg × 'Red Morn'

'Lubbe Senior' 1 (a)
(G. Lubbe & Son, pre-1936)
AM(Haarlem) 1936. Received AM(Haarlem) 1936 as 'Rising Sun'

'Lubbe's Favourite' 1 (a)
(G. Lubbe & Son, pre-1933)
AM(Haarlem) 1933

'Lube' 2 W-OOW
(R.H.Glover, pre-1990) Unregistered
'Ida May' × 'Dorus'

'Lubomir' 3 W-? (b)
(A.M. Wilson, pre-1930)

'Lucania' 2 (a)
(J.T. Gray, pre-1949)

'Lucasta' 8 W-O
(P.D. Williams, pre-1914)
Poetaz
Corona rich reddish orange

'Lucca' 1 W-? (b)
(G.H. Engleheart, pre-1907)

'Luccombe' 2 Y-O
(P.D. Williams, pre-1933)
Corona deep reddish orange. 2n=28

'Luce' 2 W-P
(W. Jackson Jr) W. Jackson Jr, 1966
'Illinga' × Bisdee sdlg 253/53; sdlg no. 61/59

'Lucerne' 8
(pre-1907)

'Lucetta' 1 W-W
(T.H. Piper) T.H. Piper, 1956
'White Knight' × 'Cantatrice'

'Lucia' 2 or 3 W-Y
(G.H. Engleheart, pre-1906)
Fl. 102 mm wide; corona straight-sided, ribbed, citron yellow. Resembles an improved 'Katherine Spurrell'

'Lucia' 8 W-Y
(pre-1909)
Poetaz
Fl. large; corona golden yellow

'Lucia di Lammermoor' 1 W-? (b)
(de Graaff Bros, pre-1927)

'Luciana' 3 W-? (b)
(C. Dawson, pre-1914)

'Lucida' 1 W-? (b)
(Slieve Donard Nursery Co., pre-1931)

'Lucien Manceau' 2 Y-YYO
(Konynenburg & Mark) Konynenburg & Mark, 1964
Fl. 95 mm wide; perianth segments brilliant greenish yellow 6A; corona vivid yellow 17C, with a broad band of orange at rim. Mid-season

'Lucienne' 2 W-YOO
(de Graaff Bros, pre-1930)
Perianth segments overlapping. 2n=28. AM(Haarlem) 1930

'Lucienne Boyer' 2 (a)
(M. van Waveren & Sons, pre-1937)

'Lucifer' 2 W-YOO
(Mrs Lawrenson, pre-1890)
'Princeps' × *N. radiiflorus* var. *poetarum*
Fl. star-shaped, 98 mm wide; perianth segments ovate, creamy white, with greenish yellow at base, spreading or a little inflexed, lax, twisted, with margins wavy and often incurved or recurved, overlapping at base only; corona short funnel-shaped, ribbed, glowing reddish orange, with greenish yellow at base, mouth straight, loosely frilled, rim crenate. 2n=14,28. AM 1898, FCC 1901

'Lucifer' 3 W-O
(G.H. Engleheart, pre-1897)

'Lucille' 2 Y-Y
(C. Dawson, pre-1925)
Fl. 82 mm wide; perianth segments soft primrose yellow, faintly streaked with white, overlapping half; corona broad funnel-shaped, bright yellow, closely frilled. Dwarf to standard. Mid-season to late. Resembles 'Homespun' in colour

'Lucille' 2 W-Y
(A.H. Ahrens) J.S. Leitch, 1957
PC(e)(NZ) 1958

'Lucinda' 5
(Barr & Sons, pre-1923)
'Albatross' × *N. triandrus* var. *loiseleurii*

'Lucinda' 2 W-P
(J.N. Hancock & Co., 1968) Unregistered

'Lucinius' 2 Y-Y
(L. van Leeuwen & Son, pre-1928)
Fl. 115 mm wide; perianth segments clear lemon, spreading, overlapping; corona buttercup yellow. Mid-season to late. *AM(g) 1936

'Lucius' 1 (a)
(J. Pope, pre-1908)

'Luckett' 3 W-O
(Brian S. Duncan) du Plessis Bros, 1989
'Dragoman' × 'Silent Beauty'; sdlg no. 371
Fl. rounded, 89 mm wide; perianth segments snow white; corona cup-shaped, deep orange. Late

'Lucks Way' 3 W-YYR
(J.A. Morris) J.A. Morris, 1962
Fl. 108 mm wide; corona citron yellow, with a broad band of deep red at rim. Mid-season. Resembles 'Hampstead' but with a smoother perianth

'Lucky Charm' 2 Y-YYR
(A.H. Ahrens) J.S. Leitch, 1955

'Lucky Dip' 2 (a)
(A.H. Ahrens) J.S. Leitch, 1955

'Lucky Lad' 2 W-?
(T. Bloomer) T. Bloomer, 1973
'Deodora' × 'Debutante'

'Lucky Lady' 3 W-?
(T. Bloomer) T. Bloomer, 1973
'Enniskillen' × 'Orion'

'Lucky Lass' 2 W-W
(T. Bloomer) T. Bloomer, 1973
'Rashee' × 'Empress of Ireland'

'Lucky Me' 3 W-?
(T. Bloomer) T. Bloomer, 1973
('Pride of Erin' × 'Wedding Bell') × 'Woodland Prince'

'Lucky Number' 1 Y-Y
(K.van der Veek) K.van der Veek, 1995
Seedling hybrid
Fl. 115 mm wide; perianth segments brilliant greenish yellow 6A; corona as long as the perianth segments and very broad, darker in tone (vivid yellow between 9A and 12A) then the perianth. Dwarf. Mid-season

'Lucky Star' 2 W-R
(H.P. Zwetsloot, pre-1938)
Perianth segments narrow, acute, milk white; corona widely expanded, orange-red

'Lucky Star' 3 W-R
(T. Bloomer) T. Bloomer, 1973
'Irish Splendour' × 'Orion'; sdlg no. 4/106/65
Fl. 100 mm wide; corona intense orange-red. Mid-season to late. Resembles 'Cul Beag' but with a more rounded flower

'Lucky Strike' 3 (a)
(L. van Leeuwen & Son, pre-1925)
AM(Haarlem) 1925

'Lucky Tune' 2 Y-YYR
(Barbara Rupers) Barbara Rupers, 1993
'Fortune' open pollinated; sdlg no. 85-1
Fl. 90 mm wide; perianth segments overlapping; corona widely expanded and regularly frilled. Early to mid-season. Sunproof

'Lucky You' 3 W-?
(T. Bloomer) T. Bloomer, 1973
'Carnmoon' × 'Woodland Prince'

'Lucrèce' 8 W-O
(M. van Waveren & Sons, pre-1916)
Poetaz
Fl. large; perianth segments pure white; corona rich orange

'Lucretia' 2 W-W
(R. Crews, pre-1949)

'Lucullus' 1 (a)
(de Graaff Bros, pre-1927)

'Lucy' 3 W-Y
(W. Backhouse, pre-1869)
Perianth segments sulphur white; corona expanded, stained orange. Syn. Barrii Albidus 'Lucy'. Was "absorbed" into 'Imogen'

'Lucy Buxton' 2 W-? (b)
(H.R. Meyer, pre-1927)

'Lucy Gilbert' 1 W-W
(G.H. Engleheart, pre-1907)

'Lucy Gray' 6 Y-Y
(A. Gray) A. Gray, 1974
N. cyclamineus × 'Soleil d'Or'
Fls more than one per stem, 40 mm wide; perianth segments brilliant greenish yellow 6A; corona vivid yellow 13A. Dwarf. Early to mid-season. Resembles a paler 'Jumblie'

'Lucy Jane' 9 W-GYR
(Mrs G. Link) Mrs G. Link, 1975
'Milan' × 'Sea Green'; sdlg no. 1962/1
Fl. 73 mm wide. Late

'Lucy Locket' 2 W-P
(J.N. Hancock & Co., 1980) Unregistered

'Ludgvan' 4 Y-Y
(Mrs H.K. Richardson) du Plessis Bros, 1989
Sdlg no. 606
Fl. 130 mm wide. Late

'Ludlow' 2 W-W
(A.M. Wilson, pre-1937)
'Naxos' × 'Lysywern'
Fl. 111 mm wide, pure white; perianth segments

broadly ovate, slightly mucronate, spreading, plane, with midrib showing, sometimes creased, overlapping half; the inner segments a little inflexed at base and reflexed at apex, with margins wavy and sometimes incurved; corona funnel-shaped, lightly ribbed, with greenish yellow at base, mouth expanded and frilled, rim irregularly and sometimes deeply notched. PC 1939, FCC(e) 1940, AM(Haarlem) 1944

'Lufo' 2 Y-Y
(West & Fell, pre-1938)
Perianth segments primrose; corona flared, deep yellow, frilled

'Lugano' 1 YYW-W
(J. Gerritsen & Son) J. Gerritsen & Son, 1981
'Reverbera' × 'Spellbinder'
Fl. 115 mm wide; perianth segments primrose yellow, with white at base; corona whitish. Early

'Luina' 3 W-Y
(S.J. Bisdee, pre-1939)
'Mitylene' × 'Portia'

'Luisillo' 2 W-O
(H.A. Brown, 1943)
Perianth segments pure white, smooth; corona deep apricot buff. Mid-season

'Luiva' 7 Y-Y
(S.J. Bisdee, 1955) Unregistered
'Keren' × *N. jonquilla*

'Lulea' 2 (a)
(A.H. Ahrens) J.S. Leitch, 1955

'Lullaby' 9 W-GRR
(G.H. Engleheart, pre-1913)

'Lullaby' 2 (a)
(A.H. Ahrens) J.S. Leitch, 1956

'Lully' 1 W-W
(van Zonneveld & Philippo, pre-1930)

'Lulworth' 2 W-YOO
(W. Kendall, pre-1886)
Perianth segments ovate or oblong, prominently mucronate, more or less spathulate, opening pale sulphur white, becoming pure white, spreading, with midrib showing, sometimes twisted, with margins wavy, separated at base, sometimes overlapping at mid-point; corona deep cup-shaped, bright reddish orange, with yellow at base, mouth straight or slightly flared, a little frilled, rim crenate. Syn. 'Vicar of Lulworth'. FCC 1894

'Luma' 2 or 3 W-? (b or c)
(?A.M. Wilson, pre-1914)

'Lumeah' 1 Y-Y
(S.J. Bisdee, 1955) Unregistered
'J.P.' hybrid

'Lumina' 2 W-? (b)
(J.W.A. Lefeber, pre-1938)

'Luminary' 2 (a)
(R. Crews, pre-1949)

'Luminous' 3 W-YYR
(E.M. Crosfield, pre-1914)
Perianth segments pure white, with margins wavy; corona with deep red at rim

N. luna Schultes f. = *N. polyanthos*

'Luna' 3 W-? (b)
(pre-1907)

'Luna Chance' 2 Y-W
(A.W. Chappell) A.W. Chappell, 1992
'Entrancement' × 'Gin and Lime'; slg no. EGL-2
Flower forming a double triangle; corona with rim flanged. Mid-season

'Lunalight' 1 W-Y
(T.H. Piper, *c.*1966) Unregistered
'Glendermott' × 'Swanlough'

'Luna Moth' 1 Y-Y
(G.E. Mitsch, pre-1954)
'King of the North' × 'Content'; sdlg no. K43/15
Fl. sulphur lemon; perianth segments broad, spreading, overlapping; corona fairly narrow. Mid-season. See also 'Lunar Moth'

'Lunar Glow' 2 Y-WWO
(J.N. Hancock & Co., 1978) Unregistered
'Chartwell' × 'Daydream'; sdlg no. 77/78H
Fl. rounded; perianth segments strong sulphur yellow; corona cylindrical, opening lemon yellow, becoming white, yellow-orange at rim, frilled. Tall

'Lunar Light' 3 W-WWY
(D. Bramley) D. Bramley, 1968
Fl. 108 mm wide; corona creamy white, with lemon yellow at rim. Late

'Lunar Moth' 1 Y-Y
Syn. of 'Luna Moth'

'Lunar Rainbow' 2 W-Y
(G.L. Wilson, pre-1949)
('Clava' × 'Evening') × 'Moylena'
Perianth segments white, slightly reflexed; corona expanded, bowl-shaped, opening soft primrose, developing with tints of cool primrose, faint rose pink and almost grey

'Lunar Ring' 3 W-GWY
(D. Bramley) D. Bramley, 1968
Fl. 89 mm wide; corona with bright lemon yellow at rim. Late

'Lunar Sea' 1 Y-W
(G.E. Mitsch, pre-1954)
'King of the North' × 'Content'
Perianth segments greenish yellow; corona opening yellow, becoming almost white. 2n=28

'Lunar Spell' 2 Y-WWY
(Ballydorn Bulb Farm) Ballydorn Bulb Farm, 1968
'Moon Boy' hybrid open pollinated
Fl. 95 mm wide; perianth segments lime sulphur yellow; corona opening paler in tone, becoming pale ivory, with lemon yellow at rim. Mid-season. 2n=29

'Lunawanna' 3 W-WWO
(S.J. Bisdee, 1939) S.J. Bisdee, 1956
'Silver Plane' × 'Portia'

'Lundy Light' 2 Y-R
(R.A.Scamp) R.A.Scamp, 1996
'Polbathic' × 'Loch Lundie'; sdlg no. 377
Fl. 112 mm wide; perianth segments ovate, rich golden yellow, deeply overlapping; corona cup-shaped, bright red, with mouth flared and rim crenate. Late

'Lune de Miel' 4 W-Y
(R.O. Backhouse, pre-1928)
N. × *incomparabilis* sdlg
Perianth and other petaloid segments pure white, broadly ovate, blunt, only very slightly mucronate, spreading, or a little inflexed, overlapping one-third; the second whorl of uneven length a little shorter than the perianth segments, ovate, inflexed, sometimes recurved at apex, creased or folded at midrib, overlapping a quarter to one-third; a few short segments at centre, narrow, strongly inflexed, with margins tightly rolled inwards; corona segments very short, clustered among the petaloid segments at centre, opening apricot yellow, becoming creamy yellow, frilled. Early to mid-season

'Lune Star' 1 W-? (b)
(A. White, pre-1946)

'Lunette' 2 (a)
(P.D. Williams, pre-1948)

'Luprena' 1 W-W
(Jackson's Daffodils) Jackson's Daffodils, 1988
Sdlg 301/69 × sdllg 54/74; sdlg no. 124/79
Fl. forming a double triangle, greenish white (155A); perianth segments very broadly ovate, blunt, fairly prominently mucronate, spreading, plane, overlapping one-third to a half; the inner segments more narrowly ovate, square-shouldered at base, with margins wavy; corona narrowly funnel-shaped, smooth, with mouth ribbed and expanded, rim crenate and slightly rolled. Mid-season

'Lurgain' 1 Y-Y
(J.S.B. Lea) J.S.B. Lea, 1957
'Kingscourt' × 'Cromarty'; sdlg no. 113-41-49
Fl. 117 mm wide; perianth segments broadly ovate, blunt, vivid yellow 9B, with white mucro, spreading or a little inflexed, with margins incurled, overlapping half; the inner segments narrower, more definitely inflexed, twisted; corona cylindrical, lightly ribbed, darker in tone (13A) than the perianth, mouth more strongly ribbed, expanded, a little frilled, with rim flanged and dentate. 2n=28. AM(e) 1961, *AM(g) 1982. See also 'Lurgan'

'Lurgan' 1 y-Y
Syn. of 'Lurgain'

'Lurig' 2 Y-R
(Carncairn Daffodils) Carncairn Daffodils, 1993
'Bunclody' × 'Zeus'; sdlg no. 9/11/82
Fl. star-shaped, 100 mm wide; perianth segments ovate, blunt, slightly mucronate, golden yellow, spreading, overlapping one-third; the inner segments a little inflexed; corona short cylinder-shaped, orange-red (30B), with mouth a little expanded and rim crenate. Mid-season

'Lurline' 2 W-? (b)
(C. Dawson, pre-1907)

'Lurline' 2 Y-? (a)
(C.E. Radcliff, 1930)
'Molly' × 'Warflame'

'Luscious' 2 W-P
(G.E. Mitsch) G.E. Mitsch, 1962
'Rose of Tralee' × 'Mabel Taylor'; sdlg no. R70/2
Fl. 115 mm wide; perianth segments clean white; corona clear deep pink. Mid-season. Resembles 'Flamingo' but with flowers of better substance and poise and the perianth segments more nearly acute

'Luscon' 2 W-? (b)
(A.H. Ahrens) J.S. Leitch, 1956

N. lusitanicus Dorda Alcaraz & Fernández Casas
13 Section Pseudonarcissus

'Lusitanicus' 1 W-Y
Syn. of 'Camoens'

'Lusky Mills' 3 W-GYO
(Ballydorn Bulb Farm) Ballydorn Bulb Farm, 1978
'Clockface' × 'Ballymartin'
Fl. 95 mm wide. Mid-season. 2n=29

'Lussalite' 2 (a)
(P.D. Williams, pre-1948)

'Lusterous Jade' 3 W-? (b)
(Mrs P.M. Davis, pre-1948)

'Lustra' 3 (a)
(P.D. Williams, pre-1931)

'Lustre' 5
(G.H. Engleheart, pre-1910)

'Lustre' 2 W-? (b)
(L. van Leeuwen & Son, pre-1931)

'Lustre' 2 W-P
(Alister Clark) T. Morrison, 1960
'Rosario' × 'Palin'
Fl. large; perianth segments broad, creamy white; corona large, apricot pink. Perhaps the same as 'Lustre' pre-1956

'Lustre' 1 ?-P
(W. Jackson Jr, pre-1956) Unregistered
'Rosario' × 'Palin'
Perhaps the same as 'Lustre' pre-1960

'Lustre de Soleil' 8 Y-Y
(pre-1807)
Early. Syn. 'Lustre du Soleil'

'Lustre du Soleil' 8 Y-Y
Early. Syn. of 'Lustre de Soleil'

'Lutana' 2 W-O
(J.M. Radcliff) P.J. Radcliff, 1992
Sdlg 42/81 × sdlg 48/76
Fl. forming a double triangle, 98 mm wide; perianth segments very broadly ovate, blunt, spreading, smooth, overlapping half; the inner segments square-shouldered at base, with margins wavy; corona cylindrical, ribbed, strong orange near to 26A, with mouth a little expanded and slightly frilled, rim crenate. Mid-season to late. Sunproof

'Lutea' 1 (a)
(G.H. Brownlee, pre-1930)

'Lutea' 1 (a)
(D.V. West, pre-1936)

'Luteo-aurantius' 4 Y-O
Syn. of 'Butter and Eggs'

luteolentus = *N. hedraeanthus* var. *luteolentus*

N. luteolus Jordan = *N. tazetta* subsp. *lacticolor*

'Lutetia' 2 or 3 W-? (b or c)
(R. Freer, pre-1916)

'Luteus' 1 Y-Y
(pre-1884)
Corona deep yellow, deeper in tone than the perianth. Syn. Pseudonarcissus 'Luteus'

'Luteus'
Syn. of *N. hispanicus* var. *propinquus*

'Luteus' 3 Y-Y
Syn. of 'Boz'

'Luther' 2 W-YYP
(C.E. Radcliff, pre-1938)
'Mary Blewitt' × 'Imbros'
Corona with a band of pink at rim

'Luther' 2 W-? (b)
(C.E. Radcliff, 1945) R. Hyde, 1958

'Lutine' 1 (a)
(A. Frylink & Sons, pre-1944)
AM(Haarlem) 1939

'Lux' 1 W-W
(H.A. Brown, 1933)
Fl. large; perianth segments broadly ovate, blunt, slightly mucronate, spreading, somewhat creased, overlapping one-third; the inner segments inflexed, twisted or with margins wavy; corona funnel-shaped, lightly ribbed, opening creamy white, becoming ivory white, mouth straight, split in places and overlapping, loosely frilled, with rim crenate. Mid-season

'Lux' 2 W-? (b)
(L. Buckland, pre-1936)

'Luxembourg' 8 W-O
Syn. of 'Medio Luteo Luxembourg'

'Lux Mundi' 2 W-? (b or c)
(G. Lubbe & Son, pre-1931)

'Luxor' 1 Y-Y
(J.L. Richardson, pre-1923)
Fl. soft yellow. Early

'Luxor' 1 W-?
Syn. of 'Babylon's Sweepstake'

'Luxulyan' 2 W-Y
(T. Bloomer) du Plessis Bros, 1986
('Whitehead' × 'Rose Caprice') × 'Festivity'; sdlg no. 320
Perianth segments white; corona expanded, opening yellow, becoming buff. Mid-season

'Luxury' 1 Y-Y
(M.P. Williams, pre-1938)

'Lyada' 2 W-P
(P. Phillips) P. Phillips, 1971
Fl. 96 mm wide

'Lyaece' 2 Y-Y
(W. Jackson Sr, 1939)
?See also 'Lycaea'

'Lybster' 2 Y-R
(C.E. Radcliff, 1933)
'Croesus' × 'Blodwen'
Perianth segments broad, overlapping

'Lycaea' 2 Y-Y
(W. Jackson Sr, 1939)
'Matchless' × 'Laburnum'
?Syn. of 'Lyaece'

'Lycidas' 9 W-R
(G.H. Engleheart, pre-1908)
Corona scarlet, with a line of madder red at rim

'Lydia' 2 (a)
(P. Lower, pre-1937)

'Lydia Purser' 2 Y-O
(Albert Davis, 1983) Albert Davis, 1995
'Vulcan' × 'Armada'; sdlg no. 52/78
Fl. 108 mm wide; perianth segments broad, roundish, slightly mucronate, brilliant yellow 8A; the inner segments a little more narrowly ovate; corona cup-shaped, orange (24A), with rim minutely dentate. Mid-season. Resembles 'Vulcan' but with a paler corona

'Lydwells' 2 W-GYY
(N.A. Burr) N.A. Burr, 1986
'Homage' × 'Irish Minstrel'; sdlg no. 1.2./5
Perianth segments broadly ovate, blunt, only very slightly mucronate, spreading, a little concave, overlapping half; corona short funnel-shaped, lightly ribbed, mouth straight, a little frilled, rim minutely notched. Mid-season. Resembles a more rounded 'Irish Minstrel' with a purer white perianth

'Lyestra' 2 W-Y
(Mrs M. Moorby) Mrs M. Moorby, 1963
Fl. 102 mm wide; corona pale lemon yellow. Early

'Lyetta' 2 Y-Y
(W. Jackson Jr, 1954) W. Jackson Jr, 1968
'Kalman' × 'Vigi'

'Lyles' 2 Y-Y
(L.G. McNairy) W.O. Ticknor, 1974
'Sligo' × 'Saint Egwin'
Fl. 105 mm wide

'Lyme Regis' 1 W-Y
(W.M. Spry, pre-1975) Unregistered
'Hunter's Moon' × 'Kingscourt'

'Lynbrook' 3 Y-?
Syn. of 'Brooklyn'

'Lynchburg' 2 W-YOO
(W.G. Pannill) W.G. Pannill, 1978
'Enniskillen' × 'Hotspur'; sdlg no. 64/45 B
Fl. 118 mm wide. Mid-season

'Lyndale' 2 Y-YYR
(H.A. Brown, pre-1930)
Perianth segments rich yellow; corona with red at rim, frilled. PC(e)(NZ) 1930

'Lyndale Beacon'
(H.A. Brown)

'Lyndale Beauty' 2 Y-R
(H.A. Brown, pre-1936)
Corona shallow, bright red

'Lyndale Gem' 2 (a)
(H.A. Brown, pre-1936)

'Lyndale Gold' 1 Y-Y
(H.A. Brown, pre-1933)
Fl. rich yellow; corona frilled

'Lyndale Lady' 2 W-W
(H.A. Brown, pre-1936)

'Lyndale Star' 2 Y-Y
(H.A. Brown, 1923)
Late

'Lyndhurst' 9
(G.H. Engleheart, pre-1914)

'Lyndhurst Beauty' 9 W-R
(H.J. Poole Sr, pre-1927)

'Lyndhurst Gem' 2 W-W
(pre-1926)
Fl. large, pure white

'Lynell' 2 W-YYR
(P. & G. Phillips) P. & G. Phillips, 1973
Fl. 110 mm wide; perianth segments smooth, deeply overlapping; corona narrow, with bright orange at rim

'Lynette' 7
(Cartwright & Goodwin, pre-1916)
'Empire' × 'Pink'un'

'Lynette' 2 W-W
(C.E. Radcliff, 1930)

'Lynette Sholl' 3 W-OOR
(L.P. Dettman) L.P. Dettman, 1968
'Jean Hood' × 'Nevose'

'Lynette Wise' 2 W-YYO
(Tom Forster, 1960s) Unregistered
Fl. rounded; perianth segments creamy white;

corona disc-shaped, ribbed, yellow, with a well-defined band of orange at rim. Early to mid-season

'Lynholm' 2 W-YOO
(J.J. Abernethy, 1948) R.J. Abernethy, 1960
Fl. 108 mm wide; perianth segments pure white, of heavy substance; corona yellow-orange, with greenish lemon yellow at base. Mid-season

'Lynick' 2 W-? (b)
(Mrs M.Moorby) Mrs M.Moorby, 1956

'Lynmouth' 2 W-? (b)
(R.H. Bath, pre-1933)

'Lynn's Delight' 1 Y-Y
(L.C.Palmer) M.E.Rollinson, 1994
(['Kingscourt' × sdlg 61/47] × 'Valley Gold') × 'Temple Gold'
Fl. vivid yellow 12A, very smooth. Very early

'Lynn's Joy' 2 WWG-Y
(L.C.Palmer) M.E.Rollinson, 1994
'Turakina' × sdlg I81; sdlg no. N61
Fl. forming a double triangle; perianth segments broadly ovate, acute, only very slightly mucronate, white, tinged green at base, spreading, with margins minutely incurling, overlapping one-third to a half; the inner segments squarish at shoulder, a little inflexed, with margins wavy; corona funnel-shaped, smooth, pale greenish yellow 10D, mouth expanded and even, rim obscurely crenate and narrowly rolled. Mid-season to late

'Lynny' 2 W-YYP
(J.L. Martin) J.L. Martin, 1968
'Mabel Taylor' × 'Pink-a-dell'
Fl. 102 mm wide; corona creamy lemon yellow, with a broad band of bright coral pink at rim. Mid-season. Resembles 'Mabel Taylor' but with broader and smoother perianth segments and a larger corona with paler tones at base and darker at rim

'Lyn Parker' 2 Y-Y
(W.M. Spry, pre-1973) Unregistered
'Julius Caesar' × 'Early Prince'
Corona broad, frilled

'Lyn's Fancy' 3 W-WWO
(Colin Crotty, 1981) Colin Crotty, 1995
'Eminent' × 'Lysander'; sdlg no. 44-76
Fl. 104 mm wide; perianth segments very broadly ovate, pure white, plane, smooth and of heavy substance, overlapping; corona cup-shaped, white, with greenish tones at base and a narrow band of bright orange at rim, heavily frilled, with rim notched. Late

'Lynton' 2 (a)
(Barr & Sons, pre-1945)

'Lynwood' 1 W-W
(Carncairn Daffodils, 1963) Carncairn Daffodils, 1975
'Cotterton' × 'Broughshane'; sdlg no. 3/30/59
Fl. 100 mm wide. Mid-season

'Lynx' 9
(G.H. Engleheart, pre-1914)

'Lynx' 3 W-YYR
(P. Phillips) P. Phillips, 1964
Fl. 108 mm wide; corona primrose yellow, with a narrow band of red at rim. Mid-season. Resembles 'Anacapri' but with a better formed corona with a richer colour at rim

'Lynxhall' 2 Y-YYR
(?O.R. Marshall)

'Lyon' 2 W-OOY
(C.M. Grullemans) J.J. Grullemans & Sons, 1956
Corona disc-shaped, orange, with pale yellow at rim

'Lyonesse' 1 Y-Y
(R.V. Favell, pre-1939)
'Bonython' × 'Godolphin'
Fl. clear yellow

'Lyra' 2 W-? (b)
(E.M. Crosfield, pre-1908)

'Lyrebird' 3 W-? (b)
(E. & J.C. Martin, pre-1916)

'Lyrebird' 3 Y-GWW
(G.E. Mitsch) G.E. Mitsch, 1975
'Irish Coffee' × Richardson 3Y-W sdlg; sdlg no. H123/3
Fl. 93 mm wide; perianth segments very broad, pale lemon yellow, reflexed, overlapping half; the inner segments ovate, with margins wavy; corona wide-spreading, closely ribbed, opening pale lemon yellow, becoming almost pure white, with grey-green at base, mouth straight, even, rim minutely crenate. Mid-season

'Lyric' 9
(G.H. Engleheart, pre-1907)

'Lyric' 2 (a)
(R.H. Bath, pre-1925)

'Lyric' 2 W-P
(J.N. Hancock & Co., 1953)

'Lyric' 9 W-GYR
(Brian S. Duncan) Rathowen Daffodils, 1977
'Milan' × 'Cantabile'; sdlg no. 272
Mid-season. Resembles a smoother and more formally shaped 'Milan'

'Lysander' 1 Y-Y
(A.M. Wilson, pre-1908)

'Lysander' 2 W-YYO
(The Brodie of Brodie, pre-1913)

'Lysander' 3 W-OOR
(P.D. Williams, pre-1913)
Fl. 86 mm wide; perianth segments spreading; the inner segments slightly inflexed; corona deep orange, with red at rim

'Lysander' 2 W-YYO
(J.L. Richardson) J.L. Richardson, 1959
'Green Island' × 'Chinese White'
Fl. rounded; perianth segments very broad in outline, rounded at apex and sometimes slightly truncate, only very slightly mucronate, pure white, spreading, somewhat concave, overlapping half or more; the inner segments a little inflexed, with margins incurling; corona shallow bowl-shaped, pale clear yellow, touched with bright orange at rim, mouth densely frilled, rim minutely notched

'Lysimachus' 1 Y-Y
(Barr & Sons, pre-1925)
Perianth segments ovate, canary yellow, inflexed, ribbed, somewhat twisted, overlapping one-third; the inner segments more strongly twisted; corona rich yellow, with mouth expanded, rim rolled and crenate

'Lyspwern' 1 W-W
(The Brodie of Brodie, pre-1943)
'White Emperor' × 'Beersheba'

'Lyttelton' 1 W-? (b)
(New Zealand origin, pre-1962) Unregistered

M

'Maatsuyker' 3 W-? (b)
(S.J. Bisdee, 1942)

'Mabel' 2 W-YYO
(de Graaff Bros, pre-1930)
Perianth segments sulphur white, shaded yellow; corona frilled. AM(Haarlem) 1930

'Mabel Cowan' 2 W-YYO
(M. Leichtlin, pre-1890)
Perianth segments broadly ovate in outline, blunt or squarish at apex, prominently mucronate, spreading, with midrib showing, overlapping one third; the inner segments a little narrower and inflexed, with margins wavy, the margins sometimes recurved between shoulder and base; corona short funnel-shaped, loosely ribbed, yellow, with a band of scarlet-orange at rim, mouth straight, lightly frilled, with rim crenate

'Mabel Grey' 2 W-WYY
(M. Grey) M. Grey, 1958
Fl. 102 mm wide; perianth segments creamy white, overlapping one-third; corona ribbed, brilliant yellow 12B, paling to creamy white at base, mouth expanded and frilled, rim dentate. *AM(g) 1958

'Mabella' 2 W-P
(D.S. Bell) D.S. Bell, 1984
'Mabel Taylor' × 'Lieberstraume'
Fl. 100 mm wide. Mid-season. Resembles a 'Mabel Taylor' of improved colour and texture

'Mabel Lean' 2 Y-R
(G.L. Wilson, pre-1954)
Perianth segments golden; corona ruby red

'Mabel Taylor' 2 W-WPP
(Alister Clark) Oregon Bulb Farms, 1955
Corona large, rosy salmon pink, usually with white at base, in some weather conditions without, heavily frilled

'Mabon'
(Thompson, pre-1908)

'Mabs' 2 W-?
(A. Overton) A. Overton, 1960

'Mac' 2 W-WWP
(C.E. Radcliff, 1928)
'White Queen' hybrid
Corona with copper pink at rim

'Macauly' 2 W-? (b)
(J.W.A. Lefeber, pre-1945)

'Macaw' 2 Y-O
(G.E. Mitsch) G.E. Mitsch, 1969
('Marvik' × 'California Gold') × ('Playboy' × 'Alamein'); sdlg no. X42/3
Fl. rounded; perianth segments deep yellow, overlapping; corona widely flared, reddish orange, frilled, with rim crenate. 2n=27

'Macca' 1 Y-Y
(W. Jackson Jr) Jackson's Daffodils, 1979
Sdlg no. 169/71
Fl. 92 mm wide. Mid-season

'MacDonald' 3 W-? (b)
(J.W.A. Lefeber, pre-1939)
Syn. 'Captain Smoolenaars'

'MacDuff' 2 (a)
(Barr & Sons, pre-1923)

'Mace' 3 W-? (b)
(G.H. Engleheart, pre-1923)

'Macebearer' 2 W-YYO
(P.D. Williams, pre-1910)
Perianth segments creamy white, overlapping; corona expanded, pale yellow, with reddish orange at rim

'Macedonia' 2 W-? (b)
(R.H. Bath, pre-1931)

'Macfin' 2 (a)
(G.L. Wilson, pre-1945)

'Machan' 2 Y-Y
(Jackson's Daffodils) Jackson's Daffodils, 1991
Sdlg 58/73 ('Gold Script' × 'Berima') × 'Gratia'; sdlg no. 48/84
Fl. 108 mm wide; perianth segments triangular in appearance, vivid yellow 9A, spreading, plane, smooth and of good substance; corona cylindrical, slightly darker in tone (12A) than the perianth, with mouth straight. Early

'Machete' 2 W-? (b)
(G.H. Engleheart, pre-1923)

'Maciste' 1 (b)
(pre-1927)

'Mackerel' 1 W-? (b)
(Cartwright & Goodwin, pre 1916)

'Mackinac' 2 W-OOR
(E.C. Powell, pre-1947)
'John Evelyn' × 'Fortune's Crest'

'Macleai'
Syn. of *N.* × *macleayi*

N. × *macleayi* Lindley 13 Parentage unknown
(Macleayi 'Macleayi', see also 'Macleai')

'Macleayi'
Syn. of *N.* × *macleayi*

'MacMahon' 1 (a)
(de Graaff Bros, pre-1927)

'Mac Meiere' 1 W-W
P. van Deursen, 1960
Mid-season

'Macquarie' 1 W-W
(J.N. Hancock & Co., *c.*1972) Unregistered

'Macro' 2 W-W
(D.S. Bell) D.S. Bell, 1975
'Grenoble' open pollinated
Fl. 113 mm wide; corona frilled. Mid-season.

Resembles 'Grenoble' but with a white corona

N. macrolobus (Jordan) Pugsley 13 Section Pseudonarcissus

'Macushla' 2 or 3 ?-R (a or b)
(W.E. Weightman, pre-1935)

'Macushla' 2 W-P
(G.E. Mitsch) Grant Mitsch Novelty Daffodils, 1984
'Precedent' × 'Spaceship'; sdlg no. LL13/1
Fl. 110 mm wide; corona soft pink, with a deeper tone at rim, frilled. Mid-season

'Madagascar' 2 Y-R
(J.L. Richardson, pre-1943)
'Killigrew' × 'Carbineer'

'Madame Barrois' 2 W-? (b)
(de Graaff Bros, pre-1927)

'Madame Butterfly' 11b W-O/YW
(J.J. Grullemans & Sons, 1955) J.J. Grullemans & Sons, 1966
Fl. 76 mm wide; perianth segments creamy white; corona deeply split, the six segments alternate to the perianth segments, with a longitudinal band of reddish orange at midrib flanked by yellow, with white at margins. Late

'Madame Curie' 8
(J.B. van der Schoot, pre-1931)

'Madame de Graaff' 1 W-W
(de Graaff Bros, pre-1887)
N. albescens × 'Empress'
Perianth segments ovate or oblong, not prominently mucronate, creamy white, spreading, with margins recurved, overlapping a quarter; the inner segments more nearly ovate, twisted; corona cylindrical, smooth or lightly ribbed, opening pale primrose yellow, becoming waxy white, with mouth even, rim flanged and crenate. 2n=31. FCC 1887

'Madame de Maintenon' 2 W-? (b)
(de Graaff Bros, pre-1927)

'Madame du Barry' 2 W-? (b)
(Mrs R.O. Backhouse, pre-1921)

'Madame Krelage' 1 (a)
(pre-1910)

'Madame Kuroda' 1 W-W
(G.P. Haydon, pre-1908)

'Madame Lubbe' 9 W-?
Syn. of 'Catherine Lubbe'

'Madame Melba' 3 W-? (b or c)
(W.B. Hartland, pre-1913)

'Madame Patti' 3 W-Y
(W. Backhouse, pre-1869)
Corona canary yellow. Syn. Leedsii 'Madame Patti'

'Madame Plemp' 1 W-Y
(de Graaff Bros, pre-1890)
'Empress'? × 'Madame de Graaff'
Perianth segments ovate, blunt, prominently mucronate, spreading or a little inflexed, with margins recurved, overlapping a quarter; the inner segments twisted; corona of strong substance, cylindrical, smooth or lightly ribbed, golden yellow, with mouth flared and more or less even, rim notched and crenate. Resembles a large-flowered 'Horsfieldii'

'Madame R^ell' 2 Y-YYO
(P. van Deursen, pre-1942)
AM(Haarlem) 1946. ?See also 'Mademoiselle Roell'

'Madame Roiale' 8 Y-Y
(pre-1807)
Fl. pale yellow. Syn. 'Madame Royale'

'Madame Roland' 1 W-W
(Mrs R.O. Backhouse, pre-1921)

'Madame Royale' 8 Y-Y
Syn. of 'Madame Roiale'

'Madame Sans Gêne' 9
(de Graaff Bros, pre-1927)

'Madame Speelman' 1 W-Y
(M. van Waveren & Sons, pre-1930)
Fl. large; perianth segments creamy white; corona flared. Tall

'Madame van Waveren' 1 W-Y
(M. van Waveren & Sons, pre-1930)
Perianth segments pure white; corona large, golden yellow. Syn. 'Mrs Laxton'. AM(Haarlem) 1930

'Madang' 1 W-P
(W. Jackson Jr) W. Jackson Jr, 1970
'Philo' × 'Remis'; sdlg no. 191/61

'Madcap' 3 (a)
(Sir C.H. Cave, pre-1908)

'Madeira' 2 Y-O
(J.L. Richardson) J.L. Richardson, 1956
'Sun Chariot' × 'Bahram'
Perianth segments yellow; corona very shallow bowl-shaped, reddish orange

'Madelaine' 2 W-P
(Mrs H.K. Richardson) M.J. Jefferson-Brown, 1975
'Salmon Trout' × 'Rose Caprice'
Syn. 'L'Amour'

'Madeleine' 8 W-O
(pre-1835)
Early

'Madeline' 2 W-W
(Barr & Sons, pre-1922)
Perianth segments inflexed; corona long, slender, milk white, tinged pale creamy yellow, neatly frilled

'Madelon' 2 Y-O
(G.A. Uit den Boogaard, 1950) P. Ciggaar, 1961
Perianth segments greenish yellow (4D); corona strong orange 25A. Mid-season

'Mademoiselle Roell' 2 Y-YYO
?Syn. of 'Madame R^ell'

'Madena' 2 W-Y
(S.J. Bisdee, 1942)
'Nautilus' × 'Rewa'

'Madge' 2 W-?
(A. Overton, 1950) A. Overton, 1960

'Madge Anderson' ?-P
(Alister Clark, pre-1948)

'Madge Buckland' 2 W-P
(Alister Clark, 1939) J. Sharp, 1960

'Madge Matthew' 3 W-Y
(W. Backhouse, pre-1869)
Perianth segments large; corona opening canary yellow, becoming primrose yellow. Syn. Leedsii 'Madge Matthew'

'Madge Titheradge' 8
(H.H.B. Bradley, pre-1914)
'Minnie Hume' × 'Grand Monarque'

'Madonna' 1 W-W
(W. Backhouse, pre-1869)
Fl. facing down; corona sulphur white. Syn. Pseudonarcissus Bicolor 'Madonna'. Was "absorbed" by 'Mrs Vincent'

'Madonna' 5 W-W
(H. Backhouse, pre-1913)
N. triandrus var. *loiseleurii* sdlg
Perianth segments slightly reflexed; corona expanded

'Madonna' 5
(G.H. Engleheart, pre-1914)

'Madonna' 2 or 3 W-W
(pre-1927)
Perianth segments white; corona ivory white, with a

slightly darker tone at rim, with the rim closely and deeply notched, as if fringed

'Madonna' 1 W-W
(S.A. Free) S.A. Free, 1963
Fl. 115 mm wide, pure white. Mid-season

'Madouce' 8 Y-Y
(pre-1835)
?The same as 'Madouse'

'Madouse' 8 Y-?
(pre-1759)
?The same as 'Madouce'

'Madras' 2 W-? (b)
(Mrs R.O. Backhouse, pre-1921)

'Madrid' 2 Y-R
(J.L. Richardson, c.1971) Unregistered
'Cambodia' × 'Vulcan'

'Madrigal' 9 W-YYO
(G.H. Engleheart, pre-1913)

'Madrigal' 2 W-WWY
(G.E. Mitsch) G.E. Mitsch, 1956
'Chinese White' × 'Green Island'; sdlg no. M11/1
Corona almost disc-shaped, white, with yellow at rim, frilled. Mid-season

'Madron' 2 Y-? (a)
(The Brodie of Brodie, c.1930)
'Fortune' × P.D. Williams red and yellow sdlg; sdlg no. 12/C/29

'Madruga' 1 Y-Y
(W. Jackson Jr) Jackson's Daffodils, 1979
('Haka' × ['Melissa' × 'Jobi']) × 'Ristin'; sdlg no. 22/71
Fl. 106 mm wide. Mid-season

'Madura' 2 W-O
(S.J. Bisdee) S.J. Bisdee, 1956
Khartum' × 'Ivo Fell'

'Mae Gibson Foster' 2 W-GWP
(R.E. Jerrell) R.E. Jerrell, 1984
'Precedent' × ('Rima' × 'Melody Lane'); sdlg no. 69-28-2
Corona white, with green at base and a broad band of red-pink at rim. Mid-season. Resembles a more deeply coloured 'Coral Ribbon'

'Maelee' 2 W-P
(R.J. McIlraith) R.J. McIlraith, 1988
'Waikato' × 'Salmon Trout'; sdlg no. S75/3
Fl. 98 mm wide; perianth segments broadly ovate, blunt, slightly mucronate, spreading, a little concave, overlapping half; the inner segments slightly inflexed, a little twisted; corona light pink, shading to a deeper tone at rim, mouth expanded, lightly frilled, rim flanged, crenate, minutely dentate. Dwarf. Mid-season

'Maenporth' 1 W-W
(The Brodie of Brodie, pre-1930)

'Maestro' 8 W-O
(Dutch origin, pre-1897)
Corona rich orange. Dwarf. Sometimes with extra segments, as if Div. 4

'Mae Toney' 2 W-YYW
(A.L. Ismay, 1950) A.L. Ismay, 1964
?'Ada Finch' × 'Mrs Ernst H.Krelage'
Fl. 95 mm wide; corona lemon yellow, with irregular white markings at rim. Mid-season. Resembles a less vigorous 'Ada Finch'

'Mae West' 2 W-Y
(J. van Velzen) J. van Velzen, 1981
'John Evelyn' × 'Magnificence'
Fl. 100 mm wide; perianth segments ivory white; corona canary yellow, with orange-yellow at rim

'Magdalene' 2 W-? (b)
(Barr & Sons, pre-1937)

'Magellan' 4 Y-O
(G.E.Mitsch, 1980) R. & E.Havens, 1994
'Grebe' × 'Matlock'; sdlg no. 2P70/
Fl. 110 mm wide; perianth and other petaloid segments in three whorls, broadly ovate, bright yellow, overlapping half or more; the outer whorl spreading, plane; the inner whorl of about the same length, inflexed, sometimes folded along midrib; the centre whorl shorter, strongly inflexed, with margins tightly incurled; corona segments shorter than the centre petaloid segments and thickly clustered around and among them, more loosely arranged between the surrounding whorls, bright orange, frilled. Mid-season. Sunproof

'Maggie May' 2 W-Y
(E. Edmunds, pre-1899)
Perianth segments broadly ovate, blunt, pure white, inflexed, with margins often recurved at base, overlapping at base only; the inner segments narrower, with margins wavy or more strongly recurved; corona broad funnel-shaped, smooth, lemon yellow, with mouth expanded and tightly frilled, rim crenate. Syn. 'Edmond's White', 'Edmunds' White', 'Edmund's White'. FCC 1899

'Maggie West' 2 W-YYO
Syn. of 'Margaret Fell'

'Magherally' 2 Y-O
(G.L. Wilson, pre-1944)
?'Fairy King' hybrid

Perianth segments golden. AM(Haarlem) 1948

'Magic' 3 (a)
(Sir C.H. Cave, pre-1908)

'Magic' 4 W-Y
(J.L. Richardson) G. Zandbergen-Terwegen, 1962
'Falaise' hybrid
Perianth and other petaloid segments creamy white; corona segments pale orange-yellow

'Magic Circle' 2 W-YYR
(J.L. Richardson, pre-1938)
AM(Haarlem) 1940

'Magic Circle' 2 Y-R
(W.M. Spry, pre-1975) Unregistered
'Stanley Mann' × Ronalds sdlg
Corona orange-red, frilled. Late

'Magic Dawn' 2 W-P
(G.E. Mitsch) G.E. Mitsch, 1963
'Loch Maree' × 'Radiation'; sdlg no. Q52/4
Fl. 108 mm wide; corona bowl-shaped, intense apricot pink. Mid-season. Resembles a more vigorous 'Carita' of more rapid increase

'Magic Dream' 2 W-Y
(F. Rijnveld & Sons, 1941) F. Rijnveld & Sons, 1961
Fl. 110 mm wide; perianth segments creamy white; corona brilliant yellow 13C. Mid-season. Resembles a darker-coloured 'Queen of Bicolors'

'Magic Eye' 2 W-YOO
(Jānis Rukšans, 1987) Jānis Rukšans, 1997
Sdlg no. 82-43-26
Fl. 110 mm wide; perianth segments pure white; corona almost disc-shaped, strong orange 25A, with vivid yellow 15A at base and a paler orange at rim, frilled. Mid-season

'Magic Fire' 3 W-WWR
(Oregon Bulb Farms, pre-1946)

'Magic Flute' 2 W-GWP
(Carncairn Daffodils) Carncairn Daffodils, 1984
'Easter Moon' × 'Rose Caprice'; sdlg no. W9/24
Fl. 90 mm wide; corona opening pink, soon becoming white, with pink at rim, slightly frilled. 2n=28

'Magician' 3 W-R
(J.C. Williams, pre-1927)
Perianth segments pure white; corona disc-shaped, brick red. Late

'Magician' 2 W-R
(G.E. Mitsch) G.E. Mitsch, 1979
('Accent' × 'Rose Caprice') × 'Cool Flame'; sdlg no. JJ16/1
Fl. 120 mm wide; perianth segments of good substance; corona bowl-shaped, ribbed, red (42B), paler at base, with mouth flared. Mid-season

'Magic Light' 2 W-Y
(J.N. Hancock & Co., 1955) Unregistered
Corona expanded, deep yellow

'Magic Maiden' 2 W-R
(T. Bloomer) Rathowen Daffodils, 1982
'Spring Magic' × 'Maid of Ulster'; sdlg no. 293
Perianth segments broadly ovate, pure white, spreading; corona deep orange-red. Mid-season

'Magic Moment' 3 Y-YYO
(Clive Postles, 1984) Clive Postles Daffodils, 1994
Richardson sdlg 132 × 'Ferndown'; sdlg no. 3-22-79
Fl. rounded, 94 mm wide; perianth segments very broadly ovate, concave at margins; corona bowl-shaped, yellow, with orange at rim. Mid-season

'Magic Pink' 2 W-P
(Oregon Bulb Farms, pre-1945)
? × 'Mrs R.O.Backhouse'

'Magic Step' 2 w-P
(R. & E.Havens, 1986) R. & E.Havens, 1996
'Quick Step' × 'Magician'; sdlg no. VH85/1
Fl. 82 mm wide; perianth segments broadly ovate, white, with undertones of pink, more or less spreading and plane, of heavy substance; corona cup-shaped, deep pink. Mid-season. Sunproof

'Magic Waters' 2 W-?
(T. Bloomer) T. Bloomer, 1970
('Red Hackle' × 'Arbar') × Richardson sdlg 202

'Magill' 2 Y-Y
(W. Jackson Jr) Jackson's Daffodils, 1979
Sdlg 107/76 × 'Comal'; sdlg no. 11/74
Fl. 110 mm wide. Mid-season

N. × *maginae* Fernández Casas & Susanna 13 = *N. cuatrecasasii* Fernández Casas, Lainz & Ruiz Rejón × *N. triandrus* subsp. *pallidulus* (Graells) D.A.Webb

'Magis' 2 W-W
(C.E. Radcliff, 1930)

'Magistrate' 1 Y-Y
(Slieve Donard Nursery Co., pre-1935)
'Magnificence' hybrid
Early. Syn. 'Magnet'

'Magma' 2 Y-O
(J.N.Hancock & Co., 1982) J.N.Hancock & Co., 1997
'Ablaze' × 'Redeem'; sdlg no. 62/82H
Perianth segments ovate, deep yellow, plane; corona vivid reddish orange, with rim neatly dentate. Mid-season

'Magna Carta' 2 W-O
(Brian S. Duncan) Rathowen Daffodils, 1987
'Arctic Flame' or 'Spring Magic' open pollinated; sdlg no. 720
Fl. forming a double triangle; perianth segments very broadly ovate, blunt, slightly mucronate, pure white, spreading, smooth, overlapping half; the inner segments more narrowly ovate, a little inflexed, with margins sometimes incurved; corona bowl-shaped, ribbed, deep orange, lightly frilled, with rim deeply crenate. Mid-season to late

'Magnate' 1 W-? (b)
(G.H. Engleheart, pre-1910)

'Magnates' 8 Y-Y
(pre-1792)
Fl. pale yellow

'Magna Vista' 6 W-W
(W.G. Pannill, 1980) W.G. Pannill, 1990
'Jenny' × 'Panache'; sdlg no. 74/31
Fl. about 90 mm wide; perianth segments slightly reflexed; corona expanded, with rim deeply dentate. Mid-season

N. × *magnenii* Rouy 13 = *N. assoanus* Dufour × *N. tazetta* Linnaeus

'Magnet' 1 W-Y
(H. Backhouse, pre-1908)

'Magnet' 1 W-Y
(L. van Leeuwen & Son, pre-1931)
Perianth segments creamy white, flushed yellow at base; corona yellow, distinctly darker in tone than the perianth. 2n=27

'Magnet' 1 Y-Y
Syn. of 'Magistrate'

'Magnetic' 2 (a)
(A.M. Williams, pre-1948)

N. × *magni-antonii* Fernández Casas 13 = *N. bulbocodium* Linnaeus var. *tenuifolius* (Salisbury) Baker × *N. cantabricus* de Candolle

'Magnificence' 1 Y-Y
(G.H. Engleheart, pre-1914)
'Maximus' hybrid
Fl. 115 mm wide, rich golden yellow, of good poise; perianth segments oblong, blunt, slightly mucronate, a little inflexed, overlapping at base only; the inner segments recurved; corona ribbed, mouth expanded and deeply 6-lobed, rim reflexed and deeply and densely crenate. Early. 2n=21. AM 1920, FCC 1921, EFA(Haarlem) 1932, FCEFA(Haarlem) 1934, *(Gulval)AM(m) 1934

'Magnificent' 1 W-Y
Syn. of 'Harbinger'

'Magnificus' 2 W-Y
Syn. of 'Albert Victor'

'Magnificus' 2 W-Y
Syn. of 'Queen Bess'

'Magnifique' 1 Y-Y
(?Australian origin, 1950s)

'Magnitude' 1 (a)
(Cartwright & Goodwin, pre-1916)

'Magnolia' 2 W-W
(The Brodie of Brodie, c.1918)
'Felspar' × 'Empire'
Perianth segments broadly ovate, fairly prominently mucronate, inflexed, wavy, creased, overlapping one-third to a half; the inner segments somewhat twisted; corona funnel-shaped, smooth, mouth flared and frilled, rim irregularly notched and crenate. AM(e) 1922

'Magnum Bonum' 2 W-? (b)
(Miss K.M. Hinchliff, pre-1937)

'Magnus' 1 Y-Y
(E.C. Powell, pre-1948)
'Apotheosis' × 'Pilgrimage'

'Magog' 2 Y-Y
(W. Backhouse and E. Leeds, pre-1869)
Fl. large; perianth segments sulphur yellow. Syn. Incomparabilis Sulphureus 'Grandiflorus', Incomparabilis Sulphureus 'Magog'. "Absorbed" 'Johnny Sands', 'Sir Christopher Wren', 'Vesta' and 'Duke of Buccleuch'

'Magog' 1 Y-Y
(G.H. Engleheart, pre-1907)
Fl. soft golden yellow; corona large, frilled. AM(m) 1922
'Magog Improved' 2 Y-O
(pre-1914)
Perianth segments pale sulphur yellow; corona expanded, pale orange

'Magpie' 2 W-YYO
(G.H. Engleheart, pre-1907)
Perianth segments creamy white; corona ribbed, bright yellow, shaded bright orange at rim

'Mahal' 1 Y-Y
(P. Phillips) P. Phillips, 1966
Fl. 108 mm wide, sulphur yellow. Mid-season

'Maharajah' 1 W-Y
(N.Y. Lower, pre-1928)

'Victoria' × 'Weardale Perfection'
Perianth segments pure white; corona primrose

'Mahdi' 3 W-O
Syn. of 'Dosoris'

'Mahee' 1 Y-Y
(G.L. Wilson) G.L. Wilson, 1955
?'Golden Hind' × ?'Rumpelstiltskin'
Corona with rim flanged and dentate

'Mahia' 3 W-ORR
(D. Bramley) D. Bramley, 1987
Sdlg 68/51 × 'Rockall'; sdlg no. 77/57
Perianth segments broad, overlapping. Mid-season. Resembles an earlier-flowered 'Rockall' with more rounded perianth segments and orange at corona base

'Mahjong' 1 Y-Y
(G.H. Johnstone) G.H. Johnstone, 1959
'Funface' × 'Content'
Fl. 121 mm wide, primrose yellow. Early

'Mahmoud' 3 W-R
(J.L. Richardson, pre-1937)
Fl. 89 mm wide; perianth segments very broad, rounded or squarish at apex, sometimes truncate, prominently mucronate, snow white, spreading, a little concave either side of the lightly raised midrib, of waxy texture, overlapping half; the inner segments ovate or roundish, a little inflexed, with margins wavy; corona almost disc-shaped, ribbed, orange-red, mouth with six lobes sometimes overlapping. Mid-season to late. *(Gulval)PC(m) 1940, AM(e) 1947, FCC(e) 1951

'Mahogany' 1 W-Y
(D.S. Bell) D.S. Bell, 1982
Fl. 100 mm wide; corona with rim rolled. Mid-season. Resembles 'Burntollet' but with a yellow corona

'Mahu' 1 Y-Y
(S.J. Bisdee, 1943)
'Mortlake' × 'Elgin'

'Maia' 1 Y-Y
(H.H.B. Bradley, pre-1910)
'M.J.Berkeley' hybrid

'Maiden' 3
(G.P. Haydon, pre-1908)

'Maiden Bower' 3 W-? (b)
(Barr & Sons, pre-1943)
Formerly named 'Maiden's Bower'

'Maiden Flight' 2 W-W
(M.J. Jefferson-Brown)
'Chinese White' hybrid × 'Verona'

'Maidenhood' 3 W-? (b or c)
(Cartwright & Goodwin, pre-1916)

'Maiden Over' 2 W-P
(W.A. Noton, pre-1988) Unregistered
Corona rich pink. Late

'Maiden's Blush' 2 W-P
(H.R. Meyer, pre-1945)
Fl. facing down; perianth segments broadly ovate, blunt, slightly mucronate, plane or with margins incurling at apex, overlapping half; the inner segments a little narrower, with margins wavy and sometimes nicked; corona cylindrical, soft yellow-pink, with mouth slightly expanded, rim irregularly notched and crenate. 2n=29

'Maiden's Bower' 3 W-?
Syn. of 'Maiden Bower'

'Maiden's Prayer' 2 W-O
(G.A. Uit den Boogaard, pre-1954)

'Maid Marian' 1 W-? (b)
(E.M. Crosfield, pre-1907)
Fl. 79 mm wide; corona pale yellow. See also 'Maid Marion'

'Maid Marian' 2 W-W
(W.M. Spry, pre-1975) Unregistered
'Chinese White' × Ronalds sdlg

'Maid Marion' 8 Y-Y
(W.M. Thomson) A.E. White, 1972
Fls 2 per stem, 67 mm wide; perianth segments light greenish yellow 5C, flushed with a brighter tone (6B), twisted, overlapping; corona ribbed, darker in tone than the perianth (13B), with mouth expanded. *AM(g) 1978

'Maid Marion' 1 W-?
Syn. of 'Maid Marian'

'Maid Monica' 5 W-W
(H. Backhouse, pre-1913)
N. triandrus var. *loiseleurii*
Fl. 76 mm wide; perianth segments faintly tinged cream, inflexed, overlapping half; corona cup-shaped, with darker shades of cream than the perianth. Late

'Maid of Athens' 3 W-WWY
(G.H. Engleheart, pre-1914)
Perianth segments with apex sometimes notched, inflexed; corona sulphur white, with buff yellow at rim. Early

'Maid of Honour' 1 W-Y
(G.P. Haydon, pre-1913)

'Maid of Honour' 1 W-Y
(G. Lewis) D.S. Bell, 1955
Fl. small; corona very pale primrose yellow

'Maid of the Mist' 5
(H. Backhouse, pre-1910)

'Maid of the Mist' 3 W-W
(J.H. Hinsby, 1927) RHS(Victoria), 1956
Corona opening lemon, becoming white

'Maid of Ulster' 2 W-YYR
(T. Bloomer) T. Bloomer, 1964
'Fermoy' × 'Arbar'; sdlg no. 13/15/53
Fl. forming a double triangle; perianth segments pure white; corona deep yellow, with a broad band of deep red at rim

'Maidstone Ruby' 2 (a)
(J.C. Whibley) J.C. Whibley, 1957
PC(e)(NZ) 1960

'Maimie' 2 W-P
(J.N. Hancock & Co., c.1980) Unregistered

'Main' 1 Y-Y
(G. Milner) G. Milner, 1959

'Mainsail' 9 W-YYR
(G.H. Engleheart, pre-1923)
AM(e) 1923

'Mairead' 2 Y-Y
(D.C. MacArthur) D.C. MacArthur, 1987
'Spellbinder' open pollinated; sdlg no. E8705
Perianth segments vivid yellow 9B; corona pale greenish yellow 10D, with the perianth colour (9B) at rim. Mid-season

'Maisie Roach' 2 W-P
(L.P.Dettman, 1972) Unregistered
'Creamed Honey' × 'My Word'; sdlg no. 121/74

'Maitai' 2 W-WWP
(J.A. Hunter) J.A. Hunter, 1989
'Rainbow' × 'Leonaine'; sdlg no. 12/78B
Fl. 102 mm wide; perianth segments smooth; corona only slightly wider at mouth than at base, near to vivid yellowish pink 30C at rim, a little frilled. Mid-season

'Maitland' 1 (a)
(R.H. Bath, pre-1929)

'Maître Blanc' 8 W-O
(pre-1850)

'Maiva' 1 (a)
(J.W. Barr, pre-1930)

'Maiveroe' 1 W-W
(G.L. Wilson, pre-1935)
'Quartz' × 'Beersheba'
Fl. ice white

'Maja' 2 (a)
(C.A. van der Wereld, pre-1954)

N. majalis Curtis = *N. poeticus* var. *majalis*

N. majalis var. *exertus* Haworth = *N. radiiflorus* var. *exertus*

'Majarde' 2 Y-O
(G.A. Uit den Boogaard, pre-1944)

'Majella' 2 W-R
(S.J. Bisdee, 1945) S.J. Bisdee, 1956
'Jean Hood' × 'Red Crusader'

'Majella' 5 W-W
(pre-1956) Unregistered
Fls 2 per stem, pure white. Resembles 'Christabel' but with a slightly shorter corona

'Majestic' 1 W-W
(E.M. Crosfield, pre-1914)

'Majestic' 8 W-Y
(Dutch origin, pre-1922)
Poetaz
Perianth segments pure white

'Majestic' 1 Y-Y
(pre-1930)
Fl. large, golden yellow. Early

'Majestic Gold' 1 Y-Y
(Malcolm S. Bradbury, 1984) Malcolm S. Bradbury, 1994
'Golden Vale'? × 'Gold Convention'
Fl. 113 mm wide; perianth segments very broad or roundish, vivid yellow 9A, with slight whitish mucro, very slightly reflexed, overlapping half; the inner segments more nearly ovate; corona narrowly funnel-shaped, smooth at base, ribbed towards mouth, darker in tone (14B) than the perianth, with mouth slightly flared and a little wavy, rim irregularly crenate. Mid-season to late

'Majestic Star' 1 W-W
(T. Bloomer) Rathowen Daffodils, 1982
'White Majesty' × 'White Star'; sdlg no. 240
Fl. 120 mm wide. Mid-season. Resembles a better-poised 'White Star' of less oily texture with the corona rim less deeply rolled

'Majesty' 1 Y-Y
(W.O. Backhouse) W.O. Backhouse, 1959
Fl. 105 mm wide; perianth segments orange-yellow;

corona yellow. Late. Resembles 'Tidd-Pratt' but with the corona more widely flared and heavily frilled

'Majolica' 1 W-W
(Konynenburg & Mark, pre-1953)

'Majolica' 2 Y-Y
(Konynenburg & Mark) Konynenburg & Mark, 1960
('Uhu' × 'Covent Garden') × ('Fortune' × 'Flaming Torch')
Fl. 115 mm wide; perianth segments greenish yellow (4D); corona pale orange-yellow 24D. Early

N. major Curtis = *N. hispanicus*

N. major hort. = *N. hispanicus* var. *propinquus*

major = *N. fernandesii* var. *major*

'Major' 1 Y-Y
(pre-1873)
Fl. almost self coloured, rich deep yellow; perianth segments a little twisted; corona distinctly 6-lobed. Resembles a smaller-flowered 'Maximus' with paler perianth segments. Syn. Pseudonarcissus Major 'Major'. "Absorbed" 'Corporal Trim'

'Major' 2 W-Y
(?E. Leeds, pre-1877)
Fl. large. Syn. Incomparabilis Albus 'Major'

'Major' 2 W-Y
(E. Leeds, pre-1877)
Perianth segments ovate, a little inflexed, with margins wavy, separated; corona cylindrical, ribbed, yellow, often suffused orange on opening, with mouth straight and even, rim crenate. 2n=14. Resembles a later-flowered *N. bicolor*. Syn. Nelsonii 'Major'. "Absorbed" 'Nelsonii'

'Major' 2 or 3 ?-Y
(?E. Leeds, pre-1877)
Syn. Incomparabilis Albidus 'Major'

'Major' 3 Y-Y
(pre-1879)
Perianth segments sulphur yellow. Syn. Barrii 'Major'. Was "absorbed" into 'Lass O'Gowrie'

'Major' 3? ?-Y
(pre-1880)
Fl. small; corona expanded. Syn. Barrii Sulphureus 'Major'

'Major' 1 W-Y
(pre-1882)
Perianth segments sulphur white; corona large, golden yellow. Syn. Pseudonarcissus Bicolor 'Major'

'Major'
Syn. of *N.* × *incomparabilis*

'Major' 8 W-O
Syn. of 'Medio Luteo Major'

'Majorca' 2 Y-YYO
(J.L. Richardson) J.L. Richardson, 1956
'Royal Mail' × 'Malta'
Perianth segments yellow; corona slightly deeper in tone, with a broad band of orange at rim

'Major Crenulatus' 1 Y-Y
(E. Leeds, pre-1877)
Fl. rich golden yellow

'Majorette' 1 Y-Y
(J. Gerritsen & Son) J. Gerritsen & Son, 1967
'Reverbera' hybrid
Fl. 112 mm wide, brilliant greenish yellow 6B; corona with vivid yellow 9B at rim. Mid-season. Resembles a deeper toned 'Reverbera'

'Major Luck' 2 W-W
(A. Glover, 1978) Unregistered
'Gwyn' × 'Arkuna'

'Major Seagrave' 1 (a)
(P. van Deursen, pre-1930)

'Major Spurrell' 3 W-YYO
(Miss K.Spurrell, pre-1901)
Fl. broad; perianth segments snowy white; corona expanded, yellow, with a broad band of dark reddish orange at rim. AM 1901

'Majuba' 1 (a)
(J.W.A. Lefeber, pre-1949)
Syn. 'Mon Trésor'

'Makalu' 1 W-W
(Mrs H.K. Richardson) Mrs H.K. Richardson, 1972
'Ambassador' × 'Himalaya'

'Makanda' 1 Y-W
(V. Brink) V. Brink, 1970
'Broughshane' × 'Spellbinder'
Fl. 98 mm wide

'Makapu' 2 W-W
(M.Hamilton, 1972) Koanga Daffodils, 1996
'Glendermott' × 'Empress of Ireland'; sdlg no. 3-72
Fl. 115 mm wide; perianth segments very broadly ovate, clean white, slightly concave; corona cylindrical, of a purer white than the perianth, with rim flanged. Mid-season

'Makasa Sun' 2 W-P
(Brian S.Duncan, 1986) Brian S.Duncan, 1996
'Fragrant Rose' × 'Mentor'; sdlg no. 1403

Fl. 112 mm wide; perianth segments broadly ovate, blunt, white, with undertones of apricot pink; corona narrowly funnel-shaped, apricot pink, with mouth even or slightly wavy, rim entire. Late. Sunproof

'Makassar' 2 Y-Y
(F. Rijnveld & Sons, pre-1939)
AM(Haarlem) 1940, FCC(Haarlem) 1946, PC 1946. Received FCC(Haarlem) 1946 as 'Daladier'

'Maker' 2 Y-Y
(J.N. Hancock & Co.) du Plessis Bros, 1989
? × 'Fortune'; sdlg no. 781
Fl. 105 mm wide; corona bright yellow, tinged with golden yellow. Very early

'Make Up' 2 W-WWY
(Alister Clark, 1930) T. Morrison, 1960
Perianth segments pure white, of good substance; corona widely expanded, with lemon yellow at rim, frilled. Early

'Makita' 1 W-W
(J.N.Hancock & Co., 1974) Unregistered
Sdlg no. 32/78H
Perianth segments creamy white, smooth; corona narrow, opening deep creamy yellow, becoming white, with rim lightly flanged. Very early

'Makkeda' 2 W-? (b)
(G.A. Uit den Boogaard, pre-1944)

'Mala' 3 W-? (b)
(A.H. Ahrens) D.J. Cooper, 1956

'Malabella' 2 W-? (b)
(D.S. Bell, 1947) D.S. Bell, 1958

'Malachy' 1 (a)
(Sir J.A.R. Gore-Booth, pre-1916)

'Malaga' 2 W-O
(J.L. Richardson, pre-1931)
Perianth segments creamy white; corona long, deep orange. AM(Haarlem) 1931

'Malaga' 2 W-? (b)
(R.O. Backhouse, pre-1933)

'Malakka' 1 Y-Y
(L. Steenvorden, 1951) L. Steenvorden, 1961
Fl. 105 mm wide; perianth segments light greenish yellow 8C; corona orange-yellow (15B). Mid-season

'Malando' 2 Y-YYO
(G.H. Rotteveel & Sons) G.H. Rotteveel & Sons, 1981
Fl. 90 mm wide; perianth segments sulphur yellow; corona lemon yellow, with marigold orange at rim. Early to mid-season

'Malane' 1 Y-Y
(J.S. Leitch) J.S. Leitch, 1956

'Malaspina' 1 W-Y
(D.N.Y. Olson) D.N.Y. Olson, 1978
'Rosario' × 'Rose of Sharon'; sdlg no. 50/3
Fl. 110 mm wide; corona fairly dark yellow. Resembles 'Stormy Weather' but with a whiter perianth and a lighter-coloured corona

'Malaya' 2 W-? (b)
(R.O. Backhouse, pre-1935)

'Malcolm' 2 W-Y
(Barr & Sons, pre-1919)
Perianth segments creamy white, paling to primrose yellow at base; corona ribbed, bright yellow

'Malheur' 2 W-Y
(G.E. Mitsch) G.E. Mitsch, 1960
'Bread and Cheese' × 'Penvose'; sdlg no. AN2/1
Fl. 102 mm wide; perianth segments ivory white; corona opening lemon yellow, becoming rich buffy yellow. Mid-season. Resembles 'Penvose' but with broader perianth segments and a larger and darker-coloured corona

'Malibu' 4 Y-R
(Clive Postles) Clive Postles Daffodils, 1993
'Torridon' × 'Tahiti'; sdlg no. 3-9-80
Fl. 104 mm wide; perianth and other petaloid segments very broadly ovate, mid-yellow, the outer whorl slightly convex, corona segments of regular form and arrangement, bright red. Early. Sunproof

'Malinda' 2 W-GYR
(D.S. Bell) D.S. Bell, 1982
'Huntsman' × 'Masquerade' hybrid
Fl. 105 mm wide; corona very shallow bowl-shaped, yellow, with green at base and bright red at rim. Mid-season

'Malin Head' 9 W-GWO
(Ballydorn Bulb Farm) Ballydorn Bulb Farm, 1993
'Cantabile' hybrid × 'Cantabile' hybrid
Fl. 70 mm wide; perianth segments reflexed; corona small saucer-shaped, ribbed, opening yellow, becoming whitish, with jade green at base and a band of strong coral red at rim. Late

'Malit' 2 Y-Y
(W. Jackson Sr, 1937) W. Jackson Jr, 1956
'Aurelius' × 'Golden City'

'Mallala' 2 Y-R
(C.E. Radcliff) J.M.Radcliff, 1956
'Lady A. Currie' × 'Sunset Fires'

'Mallard' 9
(A.M. Wilson, pre-1927)

'Malleny' 2 (a)
(A.M. Wilson, pre-1930)

'Mallock' 1 Y-Y
(Warnaar & Co, pre-1933)

'Malmesbury' 1 (a)
(J.W. Barr, pre-1930)

'Malm^' 3 W-YYO
N. Zandbergen, 1959
Corona greenish yellow, with orange at rim

'Malone' 2 W-? (b or c)
(J.W. Barr, pre-1930)

'Malone' 1 Y-Y
(W.J. Dunlop) W.J. Dunlop, 1956
'Golden Hind' × 'Cromarty'
Fl. deep golden yellow; corona with rim rolled

'Malory' 3 W-? (b or c)
(Mrs R.S. Cobley, pre-1937)

'Malou' 2 Y-R
(W. Jackson Sr, 1944) W. Jackson Jr, 1956
'Market Merry' × 'Hakon'

'Malta' 2 Y-O
(J.L. Richardson, pre-1938)
'Killigrew' × 'Carbineer'
Perianth segments clear yellow; corona narrow, reddish orange. 2n=29

'Maltimo' 2 W-P
(pre-1957) Unregistered
Perianth segments broad, smooth; corona large, opening pink, becoming darker in tone

'Malvern City' 1 Y-Y
(C.W. Pierson, pre-1951)
2n=28

'Malvern Gold' 2 Y-Y
(H.A. Brown, pre-1933)
?'King Alfred' hybrid
Perianth segments vivid yellow 9B; corona expanded, darker in tone (13B), frilled. 2n=28. *HC(g) 1939

'Malvina' 1 W-W
(Barr & Sons, pre-1927)

'Mammoth' 1 W-? (b)
(R.A. van der Schoot, pre-1923)

'Mamouth' 3 W-R
(pre-1968) Unregistered

'Mamselle' 2 W-O
(G. Lewis) D.S. Bell, 1955

'Mam Tor' 1 W-W
(F.E. Board) Unregistered F.E. Board, 1965
'Kilrea' × 'Broughshane'; sdlg no. 437
Mid-season

'Manaccan' 1 W-W
(R.A.Scamp, 1986) R.A.Scamp, 1997
'Pitchroy' × 'Dailmanach'; sdlg no. 33
Fl. 94 mm wide, pure white; perianth segments ovate, deeply overlapping; corona funnel-shaped, sometimes opening with buff undertones, neatly frilled. Mid-season to late

'Manacles' 1 W-W
(The Brodie of Brodie, pre-1928)
'Nevis' hybrid × 'Naxos'

'Manaia' 2 Y-Y
(pre-1926)
Corona darker in tone than the perianth, with mouth expanded, rim closely and deeply notched, as if fringed

'Manaia' 2 (a)
(M.E. Brogden) M.E. Brogden, 1956

'Manapouri' 1 W-Y
(G. Lewis) D.S. Bell, 1955
Perianth segments pure white; corona deep lemon

'Manawapou' 2 Y-YYO
(pre-1949)
Perianth segments yellow; corona lemon, with a broad band of tangerine at rim

'Manchu' 2 W-Y
(Barr & Sons, pre-1947)
Perianth segments pure white; corona opening yellow, becoming apricot buff

'Mancia' 3 W-W
(A.M. Wilson, pre-1948)

'Manco' 2 W-YYO
(G.A. Uit den Boogaard, pre-1944)

'Mandalay' 3 W-O
(N.Y. Lower, pre-1916)
'Harold Finn' × 'Ethelbert'
Corona fiery orange, frilled

'Mandarin' 9
(G.H. Engleheart, pre-1907)

'Mandarin' 3 W-OOY
Syn. of 'Mandrake'

'Mandarine' 2 Y-O
(J.N. Hancock & Co., 1955) Unregistered

'Mandate' 1 W-W
(G.L. Wilson) G.L. Wilson, 1956
'Broughshane' × 'Trousseau'
Corona opening cream, becoming white

'Mando' 1 Y-Y
(G.L. Wilson) R.W. Ward & Son, 1959

'Mandolin' 2 W-GPP
(G.L. Wilson) F.A.L. Harrison, 1959
Fl. large, of good substance; perianth segments pure white; cylindrical, deep rose pink, with mouth expanded and rim slightly notched

'Mandrake' 3 W-OOY
(New Zealand origin, pre-1961) Unregistered
Corona slightly ribbed, deep orange, with gold at rim. Syn. 'Mandarin'

'Mandy' 2 W-R
(A.H. Ahrens) J.S. Leitch, 1956

'Mandy' 1 W-P
(pre-1974) Unregistered

'Manet' 3 W-WWO
(W.G. Pannill, 1970) W.G. Pannill, 1987
'Tobernaveen' × 'Verona'; sdlg no. 64/118
Very late

'Manfred' 3 (a)
(A.M Wilson, pre-1930)

'Manfred Gravina' 2 W-O
(J.W.A. Lefeber, 1950) J.W.A. Lefeber, 1960
Fl. 90 mm wide; corona frilled. Early

'Mangahao' 2
(R. Hyde) R. Hyde, 1955

'Mangakino' 2 (a)
(A. Gibson, pre-1951)

'Manganui'
(pre-1927)

'Mangatoki' 2 W-P
(Mrs N.V. Anderson, pre-1948)
Corona salmon pink. Syn. 'Envy'. PC(e)(NZ) 1947, PC(e)(NZ) 1949. Received PC(NZ) 1947 and 1949 as 'Envy'

'Mangaweka' 6 Y-Y
(M. Hamilton) Koanga Daffodils, 1993
'Ristin' × *N. cyclamineus*; sdlg no 14-86
Fl. 78 mm wide; perianth segments ovate, vivid yellow 12A, reflexed; corona funnel-shaped, darker in tone (15A) than the perianth, with mouth flared. Early

'Mangere' 1 Y-Y
(A. Gibson, pre-1950)
'Kingscourt' × 'Goldcourt'

'Mangosteen' 3 Y-O
(A.M. Wilson, pre-1933)
Sdlg no. 895
Fl. forming a double triangle; perianth segments very broadly ovate, blunt, prominently mucronate, pure yellow, spreading, overlapping half; the inner segments a little inflexed, with margins sometimes incurling; corona deep bowl-shaped, lightly ribbed, deep orange, with mouth expanded and frilled. Mid-season. AM(Haarlem) 1933

'Manhar' 2 W-? (b)
(A.H. Ahrens) J.S. Leitch, 1955

'Manhattan' 2 W-GYO
(J.M. de Navarro) J.M. de Navarro, 1968
'Fermoy' × ('Limerick' × 'Signal Light')

'Manifest' 3 W-W
(W.G. Pannill) W.G. Pannill, 1970
'Easter Moon' × 'Chinese White'

'Manifesto' 1 (a)
(R.H. Bath, pre-1927)

'Manila' 2 W-O
(J.T. Gray, pre-1950)
Corona apricot orange

'Manilla' 2 Y-O
(pre-1950)
Perianth segments golden yellow; corona reddish orange

'Manitoba' 2 W-? (b)
(Barr & Sons, pre-1945)

'Manly' 4 Y-O
(J.L. Richardson) W. Blom & Son, 1972
Fl. 50 mm wide; perianth and other petaloid segments in several whorls, broadly ovate, prominently mucronate, greenish yellow (4D), overlapping half or more; the outer whorls spreading or a little inflexed, plane; the inner whorls successively shorter and more strongly inflexed, concave; the centre whorls very strongly inflexed, with margins tightly incurled; the corona segments shorter than the petaloid segments and interspersed among them, strong orange 25B. Mid-season. *AM(p) 1986

'Manna' 1 W-Y
(J.L. Richardson, pre-1927)
'Cleopatra' × 'White Knight'
Corona clear yellow, with rim slightly rolled

'Manna' 2 W-GWW
(Murray W. Evans) Murray W. Evans, 1982
'White o' Morn' × ('Duke of Windsor' × 'Green Island'); sdlg no. 0-7/1
Fl. 100 mm wide. Mid-season

'Mannequin' 8 W-O
(A.C. van der Schoot, pre-1925)
Poetaz
Fl. large; perianth segments white; corona reddish orange. Syn. 'Oranje Nassau'. AM(Haarlem) 1925

'Mannequin' 2 W-WWP
(G. Lewis, pre-1962)
'Border Queen' × 'Pink'un'
Corona opening soft primrose, becoming white, with salmon pink at rim

'Manon' 2 (a)
(J.O. Sherrard, pre-1943)

'Manon' 2 Y-O
(Konynenburg & Mark) Konynenburg & Mark, 1960
'Covent Garden' × 'Brilliant Star' hybrid

'Manon Lescaut' 2 W-YYO
(Konynenburg & Mark) Konynenburg & Mark, 1960
'Blarney' × (['Actaea' × 'Glorious'] × ['Frederike' × 'Mimosa'])
Fl. 115 mm wide; corona light yellow 10B, with a narrow band of brilliant orange-yellow 23B at rim. Mid-season

'Manora' 1 W-W
(A.J. Bliss, pre-1927)
Corona very pale yellow. PC(e) 1927

'Manresa' 1 W-P
(W. Jackson Jr) W. Jackson Jr, 1966
'Dawnglow' × 'Palin'
Corona deep pink

'Manta' 2 W-O
(D. Jackson, 1972) D. Jackson, 1983
'Bondage' × sdlg 128/69; sdlg no. 63/72

'Mantle' 2 W-GPP
(Brian S. Duncan) Rathowen Daffodils, 1987
Sdlg R.3341 (2W-P) × 'Fellowship'
Corona cylindrical, mouth flared, tangerine pink. Late to very late

'Mantovani' 1 Y-Y
(Konynenburg & Mark) Konynenburg & Mark, 1960
'Lady Moore' × 'Orange Cup'
Fl. 110 mm wide; perianth segments vivid yellow 9B;
corona darker in tone (13A). Mid-season

'Mantua' 2 Y-R
(D.J. Cooper) J.S. Leitch, 1956

'Manu' 2 W-P
(J.A. O'More) J.A. O'More, 1968
'Kenmare' × 'Tarago Pink'

'Manuella' 2 Y-Y
(W. Jackson Jr, 1960) Unregistered
'Kala' × sdlg 123/53; sdlg no. 28/60

'Manuel Lima' 2 W-YYO
(L.P. Dettman) L.P. Dettman, 1978
'Mabel Taylor' × 'Salmon Trout'; sdlg no. 85/73
Fl. 93 mm wide; perianth segments greenish white 155C; corona light yellow 15D, with a broad band of light orange 29B at rim. Mid-season

'Mao' 2 W-R
(J.N. Hancock & Co., 1956) Unregistered

'Maonia' 2 W-? (b)
(Mrs R.O. Backhouse, pre-1921)

'Maori'
(G.H. Engleheart, pre-1908)

'Maori Belle' 2 (a)
(C.E. Buckingham, pre-1936)

'Maori Chief' 1
(pre-1913)

'Maplebeck' 2 W-WWP
(Mrs.J Abel Smith) Mrs.J Abel Smith, 1978
'Infatuation' × 'Chelsea Derby'; sdlg no. U4/91
Fl. 80 mm wide; corona with deep pink at rim. Mid-season. Resembles a smaller-flowered 'Infatuation' with a darker colour at corona rim

'Mara' 9 W-YYO
(de Graaff Bros, 1950) de Graaff Bros, 1961
Fl. 89 mm wide; perianth segments pure white; corona vivid yellow 17B, with orange at rim and the rim notched. Late. 2n=28

'Marabella' 2 W-? (b)
(de Graaff Bros, pre-1953)
AM(Haarlem) 1953

'Marabou' 4 W-P
(Murray W.Evans) Murray W.Evans, 1984
'Pink Chiffon' hybrid × 'Rosegarland' hybrid; sdlg no. N-22/4
Fl. 112 mm wide; perianth and other petaloid segments in several whorls, pure white; corona segments interspersed, deep reddish pink. Early to mid-season. See also 'Maribou'

'Maraetai' 2 Y-YYR
(A. Gibson, pre-1951)

'Maragon' 9 W-YYR
(S.J. Bisdee) S.J. Bisdee, 1956
'Chaconne' × 'Sea Green'

'Marakeesh' 2 W-R
(C.E. Radcliff, 1932)
'Pink'un' × 'Fotis'

'Marala' 2 Y-O
(J.T. Gray, 1935) Parr's Nurseries, 1958
Perianth segments broad; corona large, bright reddish orange. Early

'Maralinga' 2 Y-O
(S.J. Bisdee) S.J. Bisdee, 1956
Sdlg 53/42 × 'Morello'

'Maralyn' 2 W-? (b)
(Barr & Sons, pre-1950)

'Marama' 2 W-? (b)
(Cartwright & Goodwin, pre-1916)

'Marama' 3 W-? (b or c)
(Sir A.P.W. Thomas, pre-1930)

'Maramax' 1 (a)
(de Graaff Bros)

'Maranae' 2 W-W
(Mrs M.Moorby) Mrs M.Moorby, 1956

'Maranoa' 2 Y-R
(C.E. Radcliff, 1940)
'Garibaldi' × 'Lilian Murdoch'

'Maranon' 1 (a)
(Warnaar & Co., pre-1933)
AM(Haarlem) 1933

'Maraquita' 3 W-? (b)
(Barr & Sons, pre-1927)

'Marara' 2 Y-?
Syn. of 'Enid Kirby'

'Mararoa' 2 W-Y
(Hon. Sir R.H. Rhodes, pre-1914)
Perianth segments pure white

'Marathon' 4 Y-Y
(C.E. Radcliff, pre-1938)
'Rheban' × 'Telemonius Plenus'

'Marathon' 2 W-?
(W.B. Blanden)

'Maraton' 3 W-O
(W.F. Leenen, c.1970) Unregistered

'Marauder' 4 Y-Y
(C.E. Radcliff, 1940)
2 W-Y hybrid × 'Telemonius Plenus'

'Marauder' 3 W-YYR
(K.J. Heazlewood) K.J. Heazlewood, 1971
?'Calleen' hybrid
Fl. 100 mm wide

'Maraval' 1 Y-Y
(G.L. Wilson, pre-1945)
'King of the North' × 'Content'
Fl. soft sulphur lemon; perianth segments broad; corona rim flanged

'Marazion' 3 W-? (b)
(Lord Rendlesham, pre-1937)

'Marble Arch' 2 W-? (b or c)
(Papendrecht-Vandervoet, pre-1939)

'Marble Hill' 1 W-W
(G.L. Wilson, pre-1950)
'Nilkanta' × 'Broughshane'

'Marble Queen' 1 W-Y
(O. Ronalds) M. Gardiner, 1956
'Sincerity' × 'Oliver'
Corona pale yellow, with rim rolled

'Marcata' 2 W-YYO
Syn. of 'Mercato'

'Marcel' 1 W-W
(G.H. Engleheart, pre-1923)

'Marcella' 3 W-YYO
(Barr & Sons, pre-1919)
Perianth segments creamy white, flushed sulphur at base; corona bright yellow, shading to reddish orange at rim

'Marcellos' 2 (a)
(A.H. Ahrens, pre-1950)

'March Beauty' 1 (a)
(Cartwright & Goodwin, pre-1916)

'March Bells' 1 (a)
(C.S. van Dobben de Bruyn Jr, pre-1953)

'March Breeze' 6 Y-O
(A. Gray, pre-1954)
N. cyclamineus sdlg
Resembles a taller 'March Sunshine' with a deeper-coloured corona

'Märchenland' 2 W-Y
(Konynenburg & Mark) Konynenburg & Mark, 1967
'Spellbinder' × 'Binkie'
Fl. 95 mm wide; perianth segments ivory white; corona light yellow

'Märchenland' 2 Y-R
(Konynenburg & Mark, pre-1983) Unregistered
'Firemaster' × 'Contrapunt'
Perianth segments ivory white; corona heavily creased, rose red

'March Glory' 1 (a)
(E.H. Krelage & Son, pre-1912)
Fl. large, clear yellow; corona with rim neatly rolled. AM(Haarlem) 1912

'March Hare' 6
(F.R. Waley, pre-1950)

'Marchioness of Anglesey' 1 W-? (b)
(W.A. Watts, pre-1923)

'Marchioness of Headfort' 1
(Irish origin, 1894)
Resembles a larger and more shapely 'Glory of Leiden'

'Marchioness of Lorne' 1 W-W
(W. Backhouse, pre-1869)
Perianth segments sulphur white; corona opening primrose yellow, becoming white. Resembles a more refined 'Exquisite'. Syn. Pseudonarcissus Moschatus 'Marchioness of Lorne'

'Marchioness Oyama' 1 W-W
(G.P. Haydon, pre-1907)

'March Madness' 2 Y-R
(Carncairn Daffodils) Carncairn Daffodils, 1976
'Armada' × 'Fury'; sdlg no. 114/60
Fl. 84 mm wide; perianth segments brilliant greenish yellow 6A; corona orange-red (30C). Early. 2n=28. Resembles 'Armada' but with a better-shaped perianth and more brilliantly coloured corona

'March Sunshine' 6 Y-Y
(de Graaff Bros, pre-1923)
Perianth segments oblong, blunt, mucronate, brilliant greenish yellow 5A, reflexed, plane, somewhat creased, separated; corona long, narrow, ribbed, orange-yellow (14A), mouth straight, with deeply overlapping lobes, rim minutely crenate. 2n=21

'March White' 1 W-Y
(G.P. Haydon, pre-1913)
Perianth segments narrow, twisted; corona sulphur yellow. AM(f) 1927

'March Wind' 1 (a)
(G.L. Wilson, pre-1923)

'Marchwood' 1 (a)
(R.P. Cook) R.P. Cook, 1957
PC(e)(NZ) 1957

'Marcia' 5
(H. Backhouse, pre-1929)

'Marcius' 1 W-? (b)
(J.W. Barr, pre-1930)

'Marco'
(pre-1913)

'Marco' 3 W-WWO
(The Brodie Of Brodie, pre-1929)
'Dactyl' hybrid
Perianth segments pure white; corona disc-shaped, white, with pinkish apricot at rim

'Marcoa' 2 Y-O
(G.H. Johnstone, pre-1960) Unregistered
'Marksman' × 'Curacoa'

'Marcola' 2 W-P
(G.E. Mitsch, c.1969) Unregistered
'Interim' × 'Shot Tower'; sdlg no. P37/3
Corona salmon pink. Mid-season

'Marconi' 1 W-Y
(?J. Prins, pre-1913)
'Victoria' × 'Empress'
FCC(Haarlem) 1913

'Marconi' 1 W-Y
(A.E. Lowe, pre-1927)

'Marco Polo' 4
(Mrs R.O. Backhouse, pre-1921)
AM(Haarlem) 1930

'Marcos' 1 W-Y
(W. Jackson Sr, 1945) W. Jackson Jr, 1956
'Morna' × 'Napé'
Corona lemon yellow

'Marcura' 2 Y-R
(G.H. Johnstone, pre-1960) Unregistered

'Marcus Allen' 2 W-? (b)
(Miss K. Spurrell, pre-1908)

'Mardi Gras' 3 W-? (b)
(Oregon Bulb Farms, pre-1950)

'Maréchal Ney' 2 W-? (b)
(F. Rijnveld & Sons, pre-1940)
AM(Haarlem) 1940

'Maréchal Niel' 3 W-? (b)
(Warnaar & Co., pre-1935)
AM(Haarlem) 1935

'Mareea' 1 W-Y
(Miss M. Verry) Miss M. Verry, 1974
'Verlene' × 'Trousseau'
Fl. 100 mm wide

'Mareeba' 1 W-Y
(Jackson's Daffodils, 1979) Jackson's Daffodils, 1991
'Wilbur' × 'Aroonah'; sdlg no. 151/79
Fl. forming a double triangle, 115 mm wide; perianth segments very broadly ovate, blunt, only very slightly mucronate, greenish white (155A), spreading, smooth and of thick substance; the inner segments more narrowly ovate, very slightly inflexed; corona cylindrical, lightly ribbed, light greenish yellow 3C, mouth straight, very finely ribbed, even, with rim rolled and crenate. Early to mid-season

'Marelon' 2 W-O
(W.F. Leenen) W.F. Leenen, 1970

'Marena' 2 W-R
(J.S. Leitch) J.S. Leitch, 1956

'Marengo' 2 Y-YYO
(C.E. Radcliff, 1931)
'Gloriana' × 'Tamerlane'
Corona with deep orange at rim

'Marengo' 2 W-Y
(W.M. Spry, pre-1975) Unregistered
'Green Island' × Ronalds sdlg
Corona buff lemon yellow, frilled

'Marenka' 2 W-P
(J.N. Hancock & Co., 1962) Unregistered

'Marentha' 2 Y-YOO
(Warnaar & Co., pre-1933)
AM(Haarlem) 1933, *(Kirton)AM(m)(g) 1942

'Marewa' 3 W-? (b)
(D.S. Bell) D.S. Bell, 1958
Corona almost disc-shaped, with red at rim

'Marfort' 2 (a)
(C.W. Pierson, pre-1949)

'Margaret' 1 W-W
(H. Hart, pre-1906)
'Madame de Graaff' × 'J.B.M.Camm'
Fl. pure white, of waxy texture

'Margaret' 1 W-W
(de Graaff Bros, pre-1907)

'Margaret' 2 W-P
(A. Overton, 1950) A. Overton, 1960

'Margaret Bishop' 2 W-YYR
(J.W.A. Lefeber, 1945) J.W.A. Lefeber, 1960
Fl. 90 mm wide. Mid-season

'Margaret Buckley' 1 (a)
(Barr & Sons, pre-1907)

'Margaret Chapman' 2 W-? (b or c)
(W. Balch, pre-1933)

'Margaret Clare' 2 W-GPP
(Mrs J. Abel Smith) Mrs J. Abel Smith, 1973
'Infatuation' × 'Chelsea China'
Fl. 88 mm wide; corona pink, tinged sea green at base

'Margaret Crooks' 1 W-W
(?New Zealand origin, pre-1990) Unregistered

'Margaret Cutler' 1 W-W
(Miss K.M. Hinchliff, pre-1941)

'Margaret D.' 1 W-W
(R. Dick, pre-1930)

'Margaret Fell' 2 W-YYO
(West & Fell, pre-1935)
Corona lemon, with a broad band of reddish orange at rim. Syn. 'Maggie West', 'Mrs H.L.Fell'

'Margaret Garlick' 2 W-?
(H. Dettmann) H. Dettmann, 1960

'Margaret H.' 2 W-R
(C.E. Radcliff, 1932)
'Warflame' × 'Ruby'

'Margaret Hartup' 2 W-GPW
(L.P. Dettman) L.P. Dettman, 1979
'Peggy Dettman' × 'Doss Cowie'; sdlg no. 85/75
Fl. 86 mm wide; perianth segments greenish white (155A); corona moderate pink 35D, with buff white (159B) at rim. Mid-season. Resembles 'Peggy Dettman' but with a more softly coloured corona

'Margaret Isabel Barker' 2 W-P
(Clive Postles, 1984) Joyce Tunley, 1994
Richardson sdlg 283 × 'Dailmanach'; sdlg no. 14-79
Dwarf. Late. Sunproof

'Margaret Jones' 2 W-Y
(M. Leichtlin, pre-1884)
'Empress' × Poeticus 'Grandiflorus'
Perianth segments sulphur white, with margins wavy. Syn. Nelsonii 'Margaret Jones'

'Margaret Joyce' 2 W-W
(D.C. MacArthur) D.C. MacArthur, 1987
('Ludlow' × white sdlg) open pollinated; sdlg no.

E8703
Fl. yellowish white 155D; corona disc-shaped. Late

'Margaret Kneebone' 2
(pre-1949)

'Margaret Mann' 3 W-R
(West & Fell, pre-1935)
Perianth segments creamy white; corona fiery red

'Margaret McDonald' 2 W-P
(D.S. Bell) D.S. Bell, 1982
Fl. 105 mm wide. Mid-season. Resembles 'Salmon Trout' but with a differently shaped corona

'Margaret Mitchell' 3 W-YYR
(G. Lubbe & Son, pre-1943)
'Actaea' hybrid
2n=28. AM(Haarlem) 1942, FCC(Haarlem) 1947. Formerly Div.9

'Margaret Selkirk' 2 W-WWY
(G. Errey, 1948) G.Errey, 1962
Fl. 108 mm wide; corona with a broad band of canary yellow at rim. Late

'Margaret Sharp' 2 W-? (b or c)
(R.G. Sharp, pre-1930)

'Margaret Simson' 2 W-? (b or c)
(W. Balch, pre-1933)
Perianth segments broad, blunt, overlapping

'Margaret Stares' 2 W-O
(West & Fell, pre-1948)
Perianth segments broad, rounded, creamy white; corona bright reddish orange

'Margaretta' 2 W-O
(pre-1964) Unregistered
Corona reddish orange, frilled

'Margaret Waterfield' 3 W-? (b)
(G.H. Engleheart, pre-1910)

'Margaron' 9 W-YYR
(S.J. Bisdee, 1948)
'Chaconne' × 'Sea Green'

'Marga's Dream' 3 Y-O
(G.H. Rotteveel & Sons, pre-1945) G.H.Rotteveel & Sons, 1961
Fl. 95 mm wide; perianth segments greenish yellow (4D); corona strong orange 25A. Mid-season

'Margate' 1 W-W
(Campbell Duncan, 1953)
'Hothu' × 'Broughshane'

'Marg. Durand' 2 Y-Y
Syn. of 'Marguerite Durand'

'Marge Riche' 3 W-O
(Ken Farmer Nurseries) Ken Farmer Nurseries, 1978
Fl. 87 mm wide; corona reddish orange

'Margerie' 2 W-? (b)
(pre-1955)

'Margie' 3 W-? (b)
(C.L. Adams, pre-1908)

'Marginatus' 2 Y-YYO
Syn. of 'Darling'

'Marginatus' 2 Y-YYO
Syn. of 'Glow'

'Marginatus' 3 W-YYO
Syn. of 'Robin Hood'

'Marginatus Minor' 2 W-Y
Syn. of 'Queen Mab'

'Marginatus Minor' 2 Y-YYO
Syn. of 'Fairy'

'Margola' 3 W-? (b)
(Mrs R.O. Backhouse, pre-1921)

'Margory' 3 W-? (b)
(J.W.A. Lefeber, pre-1944)

'Margot' 3 W-YYR
(G.H. Engleheart, pre-1908)
Perianth segments creamy white; corona broad disc-shaped, soft canary yellow, with light scarlet at rim, tightly frilled

'Margot Blampied' 2 W-? (b or c)
(C.B. Blampied, pre-1927)

'Margot Fonteyn' 2 W-? (b)
(G.H. Johnstone, pre-1953)

'Margot Wates' 2 W-GYR
(Brian S. Duncan) P. Fenn, 1983
'Merlin' × 'Silent Beauty'; sdlg no. 410
Fl. 90 mm wide; perianth segments of thick substance; corona yellow, with green at base and deep orange-red at rim. Late. Resembles 'Green Woodpecker' but with a smaller corona and a deeper colour at rim

'Margot Young' 3 W-? (b)
(F.W. Young, pre-1948)

'Margrew' 2 Y-R
(C.E. Radcliff, 1939)
'Marengo' × 'Killigrew'

637

'Margriet' 2 W-? (b)
(G.A. Uit den Boogaard, pre-1944)

'Marguerite Durand' 2 Y-Y
(J.R. Pearson & Sons, pre-1907)
Fl. soft primrose yellow. Syn. 'Marg. Durand'

'Margy Ginny' 9 W-GGR
(Mrs M.S. Yerger) Mrs M.S. Yerger, 1993
'Praecox Grandiflorus' × 'Lights Out'; sdlg no. 75 O 3-1
Fl. 70 mm wide; perianth segments acute; the inner segments of the same length; corona bowl-shaped, brilliant yellow-green 150B, with a deeper tone (145A) at base and a band of orange-red at rim (32A). Mid-season

'Maria' 8 W-Y
(pre-1850)
Corona citron yellow

'Maria' 1 W-W
(C. Alkemade, pre-1944)

'Maria Anna' 8 W-?
(pre-1807)

'Maria Edgworth' 1 (a)
(W.B. Hartland, pre-1913)

'Maria Magdalene de Graaff' 3 W-O
Syn. of 'Maria Magdaline de Graaff'

'Maria Magdalina de Graaff' 3 W-O
Syn. of 'Maria Magdaline de Graaff'

'Maria Magdaline de Graaff' 3 W-O
(W. Backhouse, pre-1869)
Fls sometimes 2 per stem; perianth segments broadly obovate, rounded or squarish at apex, mucronate, spreading, plane, overlapping a quarter; the inner segments ovate, a little inflexed, somewhat twisted; corona cup-shaped, narrowly ribbed, suffused orange, with mouth straight, rim slightly indented. Syn. 'M.M.de Graaff', 'M.Magdalina de Graaff', 'Maria M.de Graaff', 'Maria Magdalene de Graaff', 'Maria Magdalina de Graaff', 'Mary Magdelen de Graaff', Leedsii 'Maria Magdalina de Graaff'. "Absorbed" 'Maude' and 'Modesty'

'Maria M.de Graaff' 3 W-O
Syn. of 'Maria Magdaline de Graaff'

'Marian' 9
(R.H. Bath, pre-1908)

'Marian' 2 W-O
(D. van Buggenum) van Graven Bros, 1958
Corona deep orange

'Mariana' 2 (a)
(G.H. Engleheart, pre-1931)

'Marian Cran' 2 Y-O
Syn. of 'Marion Cran'

'Mariandel' 3 W-R
(J.W.A. Lefeber, pre-1951)

N. marianicus Fernández Casas 13 Section Jonquilla

'Marianne Karsh' 2 Y-Y
(P. de Jager & Sons) P. de Jager & Sons, 1967
Fl. 90 mm wide; perianth segments pale primrose yellow; corona pale orange-yellow 24D

'Marianne Lefeber' 3 W-? (b)
(J.W.A. Lefeber, pre-1948)

'Marianne van Herwerden' 7
(G. Lubbe & Son, pre-1935)
AM(Haarlem) 1934

'Maria Stuard' 8 W-?
(pre-1807)

'Maribou' 4 W-P
Syn. of 'Marabou'

'Marie' W-W
(Irish origin, pre-1902)
Hybrid between *N. bicolor* and *N. triandrus* subsp. *pallidulus*

'Marie' 1 W-? (b)
(van Zonneveld Bros & Philippo, pre-1930)

'Marie' 2 W-W
(P. & G. Phillips) P. & G. Phillips, 1981
Fl. 102 mm wide. Mid-season

'Marie Antoinette' 3 W-? (b)
(E.A.K. Lee) E.A.K. Lee, 1955

'Marie Brizard' 2 W-Y
(D.S. Bell) D.S. Bell, 1963
'Gweneth' × 'Satin Queen'
Fl. 116 mm wide; corona very shallow bowl-shaped, lemon yellow. Mid-season

'Marie Curie' 1 Y-Y
(D.C. MacArthur) D.C. MacArthur, 1991
'Golden Harvest' × 'Sundance'; sdlg no. EV80-7
Fl. 114 mm wide; perianth segments ovate, slightly mucronate, vivid yellow 9A, spreading; the inner segments more narrowly ovate; corona funnel-shaped, ribbed, darker in tone (14B) than the perianth, with mouth flared and more strongly ribbed, rim notched and crenate and deeply rolled. Very early. Scented

'Marie Hall' 5 Y-Y
(C.G. van Tubergen, pre-1905)
'Grandis' × variant of *N. triandrus*
Perianth segments pale primrose; corona funnel-shaped, soft yellow, mouth straight. Resembles 'Princess Ena'. AM 1905

'Marie-José' 11b W-Y/OW
(J.W.A. Lefeber) J.W.A. Lefeber, 1974
'Papillon Blanc' × 'Eddy Canzony'
Fl. 95 mm wide; perianth segments broadly ovate, blunt, fairly prominently mucronate, greenish white 155C, spreading or a little reflexed, somewhat creased, overlapping half or more; corona split to base, the six segments two-thirds the length of the perianth segments, alternate to them and more narrowly ovate, sometimes two- or three-lobed, with yellow at base and in a broad longitudinal band at midrib flecked with orange, white at margins, the margins wavy or incurling and sometimes twisted, overlapping. Mid-season. Syn. 'White Butterfly'

'Marieke' 1 Y-GYY
(A. van Rijn, 1960) A. van Rijn, 1986
Perianth segments vivid yellow 12A; corona darker in tone (15A). Mid-season. Resembles an earlier-flowered and more refined 'Unsurpassable'. Syn. 'Maskerade', 'Snowdrift', 'Stargazer', 'Yellow Star'

'Marie Lacoo' 2 W-P
(A.O. Roblin, *c*.1966) Unregistered
'Pink Princess' × ('Pink Monarch' × 'Rosegem')

'Marielle' 3 W-YYO
(H A. Brown, 1942) J.N. Hancock & Co., 1964
Perianth segments broad, rounded; corona clear yellow, with bright orange at rim. Mid-season to late

'Marie Louise' 1 Y-Y
(W. Backhouse, pre-1869)
Perianth segments canary yellow; corona flared. Resembles Pseudonarcissus Major 'Maximus' in form. Syn. Pseudonarcissus Major 'Marie Louise'. Was "absorbed" into 'Townshend Boscawen'

'Marie Louise' 3 W-R
(C. Dawson, pre-1907)
Corona large, rich scarlet

'Marie Louise' 2 W-WWO
(G. Lewis, pre-1940)
Corona disc-shaped, opening apricot, becoming white, with light amber at rim

'Marie Lubbe' 2 W-? (b)
(G. Lubbe & Son, pre-1937)
AM(Haarlem) 1936

'Marie Temple' 2 (a)
(R. & G. Cuthbert, pre-1938)

'Marietta' 2 W-P
(J.L. Richardson) Mrs H.K. Richardson, 1963
'Rosewell' × 'Rose Caprice'
Perianth segments very broadly ovate in outline, blunt or truncate at apex, slightly mucronate, pure white, tinged vivid yellow 9A at base, spreading, with margins sometimes nicked at apex, overlapping half; the inner segments narrower and a little inflexed; corona short funnel-shaped, orange-pink, with mouth flared and loosely frilled

'Mariette' 3 W-YYO
(G.H. Engleheart, pre-1910)
Fl. 51 mm wide; perianth segments broadly ovate, blunt, fairly prominently mucronate, clear white, spreading, somewhat creased, overlapping one-third; the inner segments more narrowly ovate, slightly inflexed; corona disc-shaped, ribbed, orange-yellow, with a suffusion of scarlet at rim, mouth more or less obscurely lobed

'Mariette' 1 W-? (b)
Syn. of 'Roberta'

'Marie Wilson' 2 W-? (b or c)
(Miss K.M. Hinchliff, pre-1944)
'Irish Pearl' hybrid

'Marigold' 2 (a)
(G.H. Engleheart, pre-1910)
Syn. 'Marygold'

'Marigold' 7 Y-Y
(de Graaff Bros, pre-1913)
'Monarch' × *N. jonquilla*
Perianth segments broadly ovate, blunt, prominently mucronate, inflexed, overlapping one-third; the inner segments more strongly inflexed, with margins wavy; corona funnel-shaped, smooth, mouth lightly ribbed, very slightly flared, even, rim obscurely crenate, notched in places. Syn. 'Alkmaar'

'Marigold'
(G.H. Johnstone, pre-1960)

'Marilyn' 3 W-YYO
(H.R. Bulman) H.R. Bulman, 1956
'Seraglio' × 'Moina'
Perianth segments very broad, rounded at apex, prominently mucronate, a little reflexed, plane, overlapping half; the inner segments more nearly spreading, with margins wavy; corona almost disc-shaped, lightly ribbed, lemon yellow, with a narrow band of bright orange at rim, mouth split in places and overlapping, wavy, with rim minutely crenate. Late

'Marilyn Anne' 2 Y-ORR
(N.R.McIsaac, 1978) N.R.McIsaac, 1996
'Marshal' × 'Falstaff'; sdlg no. 346
Fl. rounded, 107 mm wide; perianth segments

brilliant greenish yellow 6A, overlapping; corona bowl-shaped, broad, orange-red (30A), paling to orange at base, with rim crenate. Mid-season. Resembles a larger and much improved 'Marshal' of a slightly deeper colour

'Marilyn Monroe' 2 W-OOR
(D.S. Bell) D.S. Bell, 1959
Fl. 115 mm wide; corona widely expanded, apricot orange, with red at rim. Mid-season. Resembles 'Tuskar Light' but with a broader band of colour at corona rim

'Marimba' 2 Y-YYO
(Murray W.Evans, 1962) N. van der Bruggen, 1973
'Sacajawea' × 'Armada'; sdlg no. F-260
Fl. 110 mm wide; corona yellow, with reddish orange at rim. Early. Resembles a taller and earlier-flowered 'Sacajawea'. Syn. 'Shriner'

'Marin' 1 W-? (b)
(G.H. Brownlee, pre-1930)

'Marina' 2 W-Y
(G.H. Engleheart, pre-1899)
Perianth segments cream; corona shallow, pale lemon. AM 1899

'Marinez' 2 W-WWO
(R.J. Ralph, 1946)
'Rubra' × 'Painted Lady'
Perianth segments very broadly ovate, truncate, plane or slightly concave, very smooth, regular, overlapping half; the inner segments narrower, shouldered at base; corona expanded, smooth, with a narrow band of orange at rim, mouth straight and slightly frilled. Resembles a better formed 'Painted Lady' with a clearer white to the perianth

'Marinka' 3 W-O
(S.J. Bisdee) S.J. Bisdee, 1956
'Limerick' × sdlg 137/45
Corona reddish orange

'Mario' 1 (a)
(J.W. Barr, pre-1930)

'Mario Lanza' 2 W-? (b)
(J.W.A. Lefeber) Unregistered J.W.A. Lefeber, 1955
AM(Haarlem) 1955

'Marion' 2 Y-O
(pre-1928)
Perianth segments sulphur yellow; corona widely expanded, deep orange. AM(Haarlem) 1928

'Marion Cran' 2 Y-O
(P.D. Williams, pre-1931)
Perianth segments broadly ovate, blunt, slightly mucronate, clear lemon yellow, spreading, with margins a little wavy, overlapping one-third; the inner segments narrower, a little inflexed at base, somewhat reflexed in upper part; corona bowl-shaped, very closely and finely ribbed, bright orange, with paler tones at base, mouth straight, even, rim notched and crenate. Mid-season. 2n=28. Syn. 'Jupiter'. *AM(g) 1936. See also 'Marian Cran'

'Marionette' 2 Y-YYO
(A. Gray, pre-1946)
N. asturiensis × *N. poeticus*
Perianth segments bright yellow; corona with reddish orange at rim

'Marion Morrison' 2 W-W
(S. Morrison) T. Morrison, 1960
Fl. pure white; corona ribbed

'Marion Pearce' 11a Y-YYO
(Reg Nicholl) Reg Nicholl, 1997
'Achduart' × 'Congress'; sdlg no. 17/91
Fl. rounded, 85 mm wide; perianth segments ovate, rounded at apex, smooth; corona split, the six segments opposite the perianth segments, deeply truncate, ribbed, frilled. Mid-season

'Marion Studd' 2 W-? (b)
(H.A. Brown)

'Mariposa' 2 W-W
(K.L. Reynolds, pre-1944)

'Marita' 2 Y-O
(J.T. Gray, pre-1949)
Fl. large; perianth segments broad, smooth; corona bright reddish orange. Early

'Marita' 2 W-P
(S.J. Bisdee) S.J. Bisdee, 1956
'Courtship' × 'Rosario'

'Maritoma' 8
(pre-1939)

'Maritza' 2 W-? (b or c)
(R.A. van der Schoot, pre-1931)
Syn. 'L'Innocence'

'Marjorie' 1 (a)
(W.A. Milner, pre-1907)

'Marjorie' 4 Y-Y
Syn. of 'Marjorie Treveal'

'Marjorie Brown' 2 Y-Y
(Ken Farmer Nurseries) Ken Farmer Nurseries, 1978
Fl. 130 mm wide, gold. Mid-season

'Marjorie Hill-Whetson' 3 W-? (b)
(G.H. Engleheart, pre-1914)

'Marjorie Hine' 2 W-YYO
(H.A. Brown, 1943) J.N. Hancock & Co., 1955
Sdlg no. 397H
Perianth segments broadly or very broadly ovate, blunt, prominently mucronate, pure white, spreading, with margins a little wavy, smooth, overlapping one-third; the inner segments more narrowly ovate, with margins nicked and more strongly wavy, creased; corona broad cup-shaped, ribbed, creamy lemon yellow, with a broad band of reddish orange at rim, mouth expanded and tightly frilled. Early

'Marjorie Jones' 2 (a)
(P.D. or J.C.Williams, pre-1938)

'Marjorie Kingsmill' 3 W-? (b)
(G.H. Engleheart, pre-1913)

'Marjorie Muir' 7 Y-Y
(L.P. Dettman) L.P. Dettman, 1973
'Trevithian' × 'Tiger Tim'
Fl. 69 mm wide

'Marjorie Treveal' 4 Y-Y
(R.W. Ward) R.A. Scamp, 1991
'Papua' hybrid
Fl. 90 mm wide; perianth and other petaloid segments symmetrically arranged, brilliant yellow 13B; the outer whorl broadly ovate, blunt, prominently mucronate, spreading, overlapping half or more; the inner whorl shorter, not much narrower, inflexed, sometimes with margins strongly incurled; a few segments at centre very strongly inflexed, deeply concave, with margins incurved; corona segments half as long as the inner whorl of petaloid segments, interspersed among them and of a darker yellow, broad, loosely frilled. Syn. 'Marjorie'

'Marjorie White' 2 W-W
(E.H.G. Thurston, pre-1930)

'Marjory's Luck' 2 W-? (b)
(A.M. Wilson, pre-1938)

'Markant' 3 W-R
(A.M. Wilson, pre-1938)
Perianth segments broad, pure white, overlapping; corona shallow. Mid-season.

'Mark Antony' 1 (a)
(Barr & Sons, pre-1913)

'Market Favourite' 8
(J.H. Stevens & Son, pre-1930)
Syn. 'Stevens' Market Favourite'

'Market Gem' 2 W-Y
(G.H. Engleheart, pre-1923)
Perianth segments creamy white

'Market Glory' 2 Y-O
(Mrs R.O. Backhouse, pre-1921)
Perianth segments clear yellow; corona large, flushed rich reddish orange, frilled

'Market Gold' 1 Y-Y
(R.H. Bath, pre-1930)
Perianth segments broadly ovate, blunt, rich yellow, with paler mucro, a little inflexed, plane, overlapping a quarter; the inner segments narrower, more strongly inflexed at base, reflexed towards apex, twisted or with margins wavy; corona cylindrical, smooth, of a somewhat deeper tone than the perianth, mouth expanded and ribbed, lightly frilled, rim minutely crenate. AM(c) 1930

'Markethill' 1 Y-Y
(W.J. Dunlop) W.J. Dunlop, 1959
'Cromarty' × 'Crocus'
Fl. clear mid-yellow. Late

'Market King' 9
(Warnaar & Mark, pre-1936)
AM(Haarlem) 1936

'Market Merry' 3 Y-O
(The Brodie of Brodie, c.1930)
'Seraglio' × ('Tamerlane' × 'Fortune')
Fl. 105 mm wide; perianth segments brilliant yellow 8A, overlapping half; corona very shallow bowl-shaped, orange (28A). Mid-season. 2n=28. AM(e) 1933, *AM(g) 1949, *FCC(g) 1950

'Market Pride' 3 W-? (b)
(P.D. Williams, pre-1928)

'Market Surprise' 2 (a)
(P. van Deursen, pre-1939)
AM(Haarlem) 1939

'Marko Spade' 2 W-W
(Konynenburg & Mark) Konynenburg & Mark, 1963
Corona creamy white. Mid-season

'Mark Proof' 2 W-YYR
(J.N. Hancock & Co., c.1955) Unregistered

'Marksman' 2 Y-O
(A.M. Wilson/Miss G.Evelyn, pre-1930)
'Hospodar' × A.M.Wilson sdlg; sdlg no. 184
Fl. 108 mm wide; perianth segments broadly ovate or somewhat oblong, blunt or squarish at apex, slightly mucronate, brighter than brilliant yellow 8A, slightly inflexed, plane, with margins minutely incurling at apex, overlapping half; the inner segments narrower, with no noticeable mucro, a little more strongly inflexed, creased; corona broad and deep cup-shaped, loosely ribbed, orange (28A), suffused with yellow at base, mouth straight, slightly

frilled, with rim almost entire. 2n=28. AM(e)(c) 1933, *AM(g) 1947, *FCC(g) 1949

'Marksman' 2 Y-O
(H.A. Brown, 1941)

'Marktime' 2 W-?
(A. Overton) A. Overton, 1960
?The same as 'Mark Time'

'Mark Time' 2 W-P
(A. Overton, pre-1950) Unregistered
Perianth segments smooth; corona pale pink. Syn. 'Fashion'. ?The same as 'Marktime'

'Mark Twain' 2 (a)
(?R. van der Schoot & Son, pre-1913)

'Marland' 4 Y-Y
(C.E. Radcliff, 1938)
'Rheban' × 'Telemonius Plenus'

'Marlborough' 2 W-P
(R.A. Scamp) R.A. Scamp, 1991
'Dailmanach' × 'Accent'; sdlg no. 150
Fl. 115 mm wide; perianth segments ovate, pure white, deeply overlapping; corona funnel-shaped, clear pink, with mouth wavy, rim neatly crenate. Early to mid-season.

'Marlborough Freya' 2 W-GPP
(R.A.Scamp) J,Money, 1997
'Chenoweth' × 'Premier'; sdlg no. 426
Fl. 99 mm wide; perianth segments very broadly ovate, chalky white, slightly concave; corona funnel-shaped, bright pink, with green at base, mouth slightly flared, rim neatly crenate. Mid-season. Sunproof

'Marlene' 3 W-R
(J.S. Leitch) J.S. Leitch, 1962
Fl. 95 mm wide. Mid-season

'Marloch' 2 (a)
(Mrs M. Moorby) Mrs M. Moorby, 1957

'Marlock' 2
(?Lord Rendlesham, pre-1934)

'Marloe' 2 W-W
(J.S. Leitch) J.S. Leitch, 1960
Fl. 114 mm wide

'Marmagay' 2 Y-O
(J.L. Martin, 1964) J.L. Martin, 1982
'Shanghai' × 'Ivo Fell'; sdlg no. S.I.F4
Fl. 110 mm wide; perianth segments greenish yellow (4D); corona orange (26B to 30C). Mid-season. Resembles a taller and larger 'Hugh Poate' with a brighter-coloured corona

'Marmalade' 2
(Alister Clark) A. Overton, 1960

'Marmion' 2 W-Y
(E. Leeds, pre-1877)
Corona stained orange. Syn. ?Incomparabilis Pallidus 'Aurantius', Incomparabilis Albus 'Aurantius', Incomparabilis Albus 'Marmion'. Was "absorbed" into 'Mary Anderson'

'Marmion' 2 W-W
(G.L. Wilson, pre-1916)

'Marmora' 2 W-W
(The Brodie of Brodie, c.1919)
'Minnie Hume' × 'Mrs Ernst H.Krelage'
Fl. ivory white, facing slightly downwards; perianth segments very broadly ovate, not prominently mucronate, a little inflexed, with margins slightly wavy, very smooth, overlapping half; the inner segments twisted; corona cylindrical, angled, rim flanged, notched, minutely crenate. Mid-season. 2n=28. *FCC(g) 1936

'Marmoset' 2 W-P
(G.L. Wilson) Guy L.Wilson Ltd, 1963
'Rosario' × 'Roslyn'
Perianth segments very smooth; corona with rim rolled

'Marong' 2 W-? (b)
(H.A. Brown, pre-1938)

'Maroth' 2 Y-YYO
(S.J. Bisdee, 1942)
'Bokhara' × 'Sunset Fires'

'Marotz' 1 W-W
(pre-1914)

'Maroubra' 1 Y-Y
(S.J. Bisdee, 1941)
'Golden Queen' × 'Fahan'

'Marpessa' 1 (a)
(Cartwright & Goodwin, pre-1916)

'Marque' 3 Y-ORR
(T.D. Throckmorton) T.D. Throckmorton, 1974
'Old Satin' × 'Russet'

'Marquis' 3 Y-O
(Mrs R.O. Backhouse, pre-1921)
Perianth segments pale yellow; corona deep orange. Resembles an improved 'Firetail'

'Marquis de Westerlo' 8 Y-O
(pre-1798)
?The same as 'Marquiss de Westerio' and 'Marquise de Westerade'

'Marquis de Westrode'
(pre-1885)
Probably the same as 'Marquise de Westerade'

'Marquise de Westerade' 8 Y-Y
(pre-1885)
Perianth segments straw yellow, with a darker tone at midrib; corona bright golden yellow. Probably the same as 'Marquis de Westrode'

'Marquis of Headfort' 1 W-Y
(J.L. Richardson, pre-1923)
Perianth segments pure white, spreading; corona long, pale primrose, with mouth widely expanded

'Marquiss de Westerio' 8 Y-Y
(pre-1780)
?The same as 'Marquis de Westerlo' and 'Marquise de Westerade'

'Marquita' 2 W-? (b)
(J.L. Richardson) F.E. Board, 1956
'Nairobi' × 'Arbar'

'Marrakesh' 2 W-W
(J.L. Richardson) Mrs H.K. Richardson, 1968

'Marrawah' 2 Y-R
(C.E. Radcliff, 1939)
'Marengo' × 'Fortune'

'Marrinook' 2 Y-OOR
(S.J. Bisdee, 1939)
'Seraglio' × 'Lilian Murdoch'

'Mars' 3 W-O
(G.H. Engleheart, pre-1904)
Corona large, expanded, rich reddish orange

'Mars' 2 Y-R
(W. Jackson Jr, 1954) W. Jackson Jr, 1968
'Kalit' × 'Fooklan'
2n=28

'Marseillaise' 9 W-YYO
(F.H. Chapman, pre-1915)
Perianth segments of good substance, with margins wavy; corona large, pale lemon yellow, with a narrow band of crimson orange at rim. AM(e) 1915

'Marsena' 2 W-P
(A.O. Roblin, 1957) Unregistered
'Beema' × 'Salmon Trout'

'Marshal' 2 Y-R
(G.W.E. Brogden) G.W.E. Brogden, 1963
Perianth segments light yellow; corona orange-red. Mid-season

'Marshal Foch' 1 W-Y
(A.E. Lowe, pre-1927)

'Marshall Tweedie' 2 Y-YOO
(H.A. Brown) J.N. Hancock & Co., 1955
'Carbineer' hybrid
Perianth segments broad, golden yellow, plane, smooth; corona bright orange, paling to gold at base. Mid-season

'Marshal Pétain' 1 (a)
(P. van Deursen, pre-1930)
AM(Haarlem) 1930

'Marshal Tsjoekof' 2 W-OOR
(J. Berbee, pre-1945)
2n=28. EFA(Haarlem) 1948

'Marshfire' 2 W-YOR
(Murray W.Evans) Murray W.Evans, 1970
'Limerick' × 'Bithynia'
Corona coral red

'Marshlight' 2 W-O
(P.D. Williams, pre-1907)
'Princeps' × *N. radiiflorus* var. *poetarum*
Perianth segments creamy; corona bright orange

'Marsh Maiden'
(pre-1913)

'Marston Moor' 1 (a)
(pre-1913)

'Martel' 2 Y-Y
(G.H. Engleheart, pre-1914)
Fl. 102 mm wide; perianth segments broadly ovate, blunt, very slightly mucronate, spreading, plane, overlapping one-third to a half; the inner segments more narrowly ovate, inflexed, twisted or with margins wavy; corona funnel-shaped, dark yellow, with mouth finely ribbed and widely expanded, rim flanged and crenate

'Martello' 2 W-? (b or c)
(The Brodie of Brodie, *c.*1919)
('Minnie Hume' × 'King Alfred') × 'Nevis'; sdlg no. 138/B/14

'Martello' 3 W-?
Sdlg no. 138/B/14
Syn. of 'Clermont'

'Martha' 2? Y-YYR
(A.M. Wilson, pre-1914)
Fl. primrose yellow; corona with a narrow band of bright red at rim

'Martha' 1 W-? (b)
(L. van Leeuwen & Son, pre-1928)

'Martha Clark' 2 W-? (b)
(West & Fell, pre-1935)
'Livonia' hybrid
Corona widely expanded, buff, with pink at rim, frilled

'Martha Smith' 2 W-P
(Mrs C.E. Fitzwater) Mrs C.E. Fitzwater, 1986
'Easter Moon' × 'Panache'; sdlg no. 43/3
Corona very pale pink. Resembles a more floriferous 'Lingering Light' of stronger substance with more rounded perianth segments and a paler-coloured corona

'Martha Washington' 8 W-O
(A. Frylink & Sons, pre-1927)
Poetaz
Fls 2-3 per stem, 83 mm wide; perianth segments sulphur white, slightly twisted, overlapping two-thirds; corona ribbed, strong orange 25A, paling to yellow-orange (15B) at extreme base, mouth straight, frilled, rim slightly dentate. Late. 2n=31. AM(Haarlem) 1927, *AM(g) 1953

'Marti' 2 W-P
(W. Jackson Jr, 1950)
'Carnlough' × 'Rosario'

'Marti' 2 Y-R
(J.S. Leitch) J.S. Leitch, 1956

'Martial' 9 W-R
(A.M. Wilson, pre-1915)
Perianth segments narrow, acute; corona deep red

'Martian' 1 (a)
(Barr & Sons, pre-1927)

'Martian Sunbeam' 1 Y-R
(W.O. Backhouse) E. Longford, 1966
'Red Curtain' hybrid
Fl. 114 mm wide; perianth segments golden yellow, of thick substance; corona red. Early to mid-season. Resembles 'Golden Rapture' in form

'Martigny' 1 W-W
(J.L. Richardson) Mrs H.K. Richardson, 1968
'Ambassador' × 'Himalaya'
Fl. ice white; corona rim slightly rolled, dentate. Early

'Martinette' 7 Y-O
(H.I. Tuggle Jr) Cornwall Area Bulb Growers Association, 1985
'Matador' × *N. jonquilla*; sdlg no. USA 66-72-2
Fls 4-5 per stem; perianth segments lemon yellow, stained pale orange at base; corona bright, dark orange. Early

'Martini' 1 (a)
(R.H. Bath, pre-1929)

'Martinsville' 8 Y-O
(Harry I. Tuggle Jr, 1974) Rosewarne EHS, 1987
Fls 4-6 per stem; perianth segments brilliant yellow 8A; corona darker than vivid orange-yellow 23A, with a tinge of green at base. Very early

'Martinus Nyhoff' 3 W-? (b)
(C.A. van der Wereld) C.A. van der Wereld, 1956

'Martius' 1 (a)
(J. Pope, pre-1908)

'Martlet' 5
(F.H. Chapman, pre-1923)

'Martona' 2 Y-R
(A. Gibson, pre-1927)
Perianth segments bright yellow; corona bright red, shading to a deeper tone at base, frilled

'Marton Beacon' 2 Y-R
(A. Gibson, pre-1927)

'Martonii' 2 Y-R
(R. Gibson, pre-1927)

'Marton Memory' 2 W-W
(H.J. Shailer) R.C.A. Tombleson, 1966
Fl. 115 mm wide. Mid-season

'Maru'
(S.A. Free, pre-1958) Unregistered
PC(c)(NZ) 1958

'Marvel' 3 W-YYO
(W. Backhouse, pre-1869)
Perianth segments pure white; corona with saffron at rim and the rim somewhat irregularly notched. Syn. Burbidgei 'Marvel'. Div.9 until 1931. Was "absorbed" into 'Saint John's Beauty'

'Marvel' 4 Y-O
Syn. of 'Texas'

'Marvel' 9 W-GYO
Syn. of 'Stellaris'

'Marvellous' 1 W-Y
(C. Alkemade, pre-1929)
Perianth segments sulphur white, of firm substance; corona very large, golden yellow. AM(Haarlem) 1929

'Marven' 8 W-O
(J.S. Leitch) J.S. Leitch, 1960
Fl. 85 mm wide; corona reddish orange. Late

N. marvieri Jahandiez & Maire = *N. rupicola* subsp. *marvieri*

'Mary' 3 W-Y
(W. Backhouse, pre-1869)
Corona citron yellow, tinged orange. Resembles 'Pearl'. Syn. Burbidgei 'Expansus', Burbidgei 'Mary'. "Absorbed" 'Aunt Jane' and 'Thomas Moore Absolon'

'Mary Anderson' 2 W-O
(pre-1884)
Fl. star-shaped; perianth segments ovate, acute, pure white, spreading, with margins wavy, separated or only slightly overlapping; corona short broad funnel-shaped, bright scarlet-orange, with mouth straight and even, rim notched. Syn. "Single Orange Phoenix", Incomparabilis Albus 'Mary Anderson'. "Absorbed" 'Marmion'

'Mary Ann' 2 W-W
(G.L. Wilson) M.J. Jefferson-Brown, 1975
Early to mid-season

'Mary Baldwin' 3 W-W
(W.G. Pannill) W.G. Pannill, 1977
'Syracuse' × 'Verona'
Fl. 105 mm wide; corona with green at base. Late

'Mary Beirne' 2 W-W
(C.G. van Tubergen, pre-1916)
Fl. pure white; perianth segments broadly ovate, blunt, spreading, somewhat creased, overlapping one-third; the inner segments a little inflexed, more heavily creased, with margins nicked; corona funnel-shaped, smooth, with mouth flared and frilled

'Mary Blewett' 2 W-Y
Syn. of 'Mary Blewitt'

'Mary Blewitt' 2 W-Y
(D.V. West, pre-1935)
'Bernardino' hybrid
Corona lemon yellow, frilled. See also 'Mary Blewett'

'Mary Blonk' 2 W-YOO
(G.A. Uit den Boogaard, pre-1944)

'Mary Bohannon' 2 Y-O
(M.P. Williams) G. Zandbergen-Terwegen, 1957
Perianth segments broadly or very broadly ovate, blunt, yellow, with white mucro, a little reflexed, the inner segments more nearly spreading, slightly creased; corona funnel-shaped, 6-angled, orange, with mouth flared and frilled, rim deeply notched and crenate

'Mary Boogaard' 3 W-YYO
(G.A. Uit den Boogaard) G.A. Uit den Boogaard, 1958
Corona lemon yellow

'Mary Booth' 2 W-? (b)
(W.E. Weightman, pre-1936)

'Mary Carvell'
(pre-1914)

'Marychild' 12 Y-Y
(A. Gray) A. Gray, 1956
N. triandrus × *N. bulbocodium*
Intermediate between parents

'Mary Clark' 2 W-O
(Alfred Clark, pre-1949)
Corona deep apricot orange. AM(c)(NZ) 1959

'Mary Cobley' 2 W-? (b)
(Miss K.M. Hinchliff, pre-1941)

'Mary Cook' 2 W-WRR
(D.S. Bell) D.S. Bell, 1965
'Papanui Queen' × 'Invergordon'
Mid-season

'Mary Copeland' 4 W-O
(W.F.M. Copeland, pre-1913)
Div. 9 sdlg × 'Orange Phoenix'
Fl. 95-100 mm wide; perianth and other petaloid segments broadly ovate, blunt or somewhat truncate, glistening white, with creamy sulphur yellow at base, overlapping; the outer whorl spreading or a little inflexed, mucronate; the inner whorl of about the same length, less noticeably mucronate, a little inflexed, with margins incurling; three white segments at centre shorter, strongly inflexed, with margins deeply incurled; corona segments very short, some interspersed among the petaloid segments, some clustered at centre and almost continuous, orange, with a broad suffusion of scarlet-orange at rim, frilled. Mid-season to late. Scented. 2n=21. AM(e) 1915, AM(Haarlem) 1925, FCC(e) 1925, FCC(Haarlem) 1926, *AM(g) 1936

'Mary Dudgeon' 1 Y-Y
(D.C. MacArthur) D.C. MacArthur, 1984
'Sun Dance' × 'Magnificence'
Fl. yellow. Early. Scented

'Mary Florence' 2 Y-O
(P.D. Williams, pre-1930)

'Mary Fuller' 2 (a)
(D.S. Bell) D.S. Bell, 1955
Perianth segments broadly ovate, a little inflexed, concave, with midrib showing; the inner segments more rounded at apex

'Marygold' 2 (a)
Syn. of 'Marigold'

'Mary Gowing' 2 (a)
(S.A. Morrish, pre-1950)

'Mary Horn' 1 W-? (b)
(H.R. Meyer, pre-1927)

'Mary Horsham' 2 W-W
(Broadfield's Daffodils, pre-1985) Unregistered
'Easter Moon' × 'Rhapsody'

'Mary Housley' 2 W-YYO
(J.W.A. Lefeber, pre-1951)

'Mary Isabel' 3 W-WWY
(Mrs J. Abel Smith, 1968) Mrs J. Abel Smith, 1982
'Ethel' × 'Syracuse'; sdlg no. Q3/91
Fl. 94 mm wide; corona with yellow at rim. Mid-season. Resembles a taller and later-flowered 'Ethel'

'Mary Jane Brookfield' 2 W-W
(Berkeley Nurseries, pre-1938)

'Mary J.Gibson' 2 W-W
(A. Gibson, pre-1927)
Corona pale cream white

'Mary Kate' 2 W-GWP
(Brian S. Duncan) Rathowen Daffodils, 1983
Sdlg × 'Foundling'; sdlg no. 460
Fl. 83 mm wide; perianth segments broadly ovate, blunt, prominently mucronate, reflexed, plane or with margins incurving, smooth, overlapping one-third to a half; the inner segments more narrowly ovate, with margins more strongly incurved and occasionally wavy; corona cylindrical, smooth or loosely ribbed, white, with green at base and a broad band of apple blossom pink at rim, mouth more tightly ribbed, straight, regularly frilled, with rim minutely notched. Mid-season. 2n=27. Resembles 'Elizabeth Ann' but with the perianth segments more prominently mucronate and a longer corona

'Mary Kathleen' 2 W-O
(J.N. Hancock & Co., 1953)
('Valerie May' × 'Carbineer') × 'Carbineer'
Corona bright yellow

'Maryland' 1 (a)
(de Graaff Bros, pre-1928)
Syn. 'Oberon'

'Maryland Beauty' 9 W-GYR
(Mrs M.S. Yerger) Mrs M.S. Yerger, 1990
'Lamplighter' open pollinated
Fl. rounded, 50 mm wide; perianth segments rounded at apex, deeply overlapping; corona very shallow bowl-shaped, brilliant greenish yellow 2B, with strong yellow-green 145A at base and a narrow band of orange-red (33A) at rim. Late. Musty scented

'Mary Lefeber' 2 (a)
(J.W.A. Lefeber, pre-1938)

'Mary Longstreet' 2 (a)
(Mrs R.O. Backhouse, pre-1921)
AM(Haarlem) 1934

'Mary Lou' 6 W-Y
(Brian S. Duncan) Rathowen Daffodils, 1984
'Lilac Charm' × 'Lavender Lass'; sdlg no. 664
Fl. 30 mm wide; perianth segments broadly ovate, blunt, fairly prominently mucronate, pure white, strongly reflexed, plane, glistening, somewhat creased, overlapping half; the inner segments a little twisted, or with margins wavy; corona cylindrical, very lightly ribbed, opening pale lilac pink, becoming pure white, with mouth expanded and even, rim minutely notched. Dwarf. Mid-season

'Mary Louise' 4 Y-R
(R.J. Ralph, 1945)
'Killigrew' × 'Telemonius Plenus'

'Mary Lyne' 2 W-? (b)
(A.M. Wilson, pre-1938)

'Mary Magdalen de Graaff' 3 W-O
Syn. of 'Maria Magdaline de Graaff'

'Mary Millicent' 3 W-R
(A. Hopkirk, pre-1927)

'Mary Morris' 2 Y-R
(J.A. Morris) J.A. Morris, 1960
Fl. 108 mm wide; perianth segments deep yellow. Mid-season. Resembles 'Ceylon' but with broader perianth segments

'Mary Oliver' 9 W-GOR
(Daniel Bellinger) Daniel Bellinger, 1997
'Felindre' open pollinated; sdlg no. 87.27.3
Fl. forming a double triangle, 56 mm wide, facing up; perianth segments acute, pure white, slightly reflexed, smooth and of thick substance; corona broad disc-shaped, mid-orange, with deep green at base and a broad band of red at rim. Late

'Mary Parkinson' 2 W-W
(F. Parkinson) T. Morrison, 1960
Corona opening primrose, becoming white

'Mary Pickford' 2 Y-YYO
(de Graaff Bros, pre-1931)
Perianth segments clear lemon yellow, corona frilled.
AM(Haarlem) 1931

'Mary Plumstead' 5 Y-Y
(A. Gray, pre-1954)
N. jonquilla × *N. triandrus* var. *loiseleurii*
Fl. creamy; perianth segments ovate, blunt, prominently mucronate, strongly reflexed, somewhat twisted, separated or slightly overlapping; corona cup-shaped, smooth, with mouth straight and even,

rim notched in places

'Mary Quarles' 9 W-YYR
(W.A.Bender, 1980) W.A.Bender, 1996
'Milan' × 'Cantabile'
Fl. 64 mm wide; perianth segments broadly ovate, very slightly reflexed, with margins incurved; corona very shallow bowl-shaped, light greenish yellow 6C, with a narrow band of orange-red (42B) at rim, frilled. Late

'Mary Robinson' 2 Y-Y
(Kate Reade, 1987) Carncairn Daffodils, 1997
'Ballytrim' × 'Golden Aura'; sdlg no. 9/9/82
Fl. 100 mm wide, deep yellow; perianth segments broad in outline, rounded or squarish at apex, sometimes truncate, with slight white mucro, spreading, plane, smooth, regular, overlapping half; the inner segments narrower, nicked near apex, with margins very slightly wavy; corona short, with rim neatly dentate. Mid-season

'Mary Roozen' 2 Y-O
(P. van Deursen, pre-1938)
AM(Haarlem) 1937, FCC(Haarlem) 1949

'Mary Rose' 2 W-? (b)
(R.H. Bath, pre-1927)

'Mary Schouten' 2 Y-Y
(D.C. MacArthur) D.C MacArthur, 1989
'Binkie' open pollinated; sdlg no. EV87/406
Fl. 87 mm wide; perianth segments light yellow 10C, spreading; corona large, flared, of good substance, of a slightly darker tone (10A). Dwarf. Mid-season. Scented

'Mary Searby' 2 Y-O
(C.O. Fairbairn, pre-1945)

'Mary's Pink' 2 W-P
(Carncairn Daffodils) Carncairn Daffodils, 1975
Sdlg no. 4/46/59
Fl. 94 mm wide; perianth segments greenish white (155A); corona light orange 29B, with green at base. Mid-season

'Mary Sumner' 1 W-Y
(Carncairn Daffodils) Carncairn Daffodils, 1975
Sdlg no. 100/59
Fl. 105 mm wide; perianth segments greenish white (157C); corona opening yellow, becoming greenish yellow (4D), with a darker tone outside (4C), rim rolled. Mid-season

'Mary Veronica' 3 W-YYO
(A.J.R. Pearson) A.J.R. Pearson, 1994
'Tryst' × 'Dell Chapel; sdlg no. 85-35-H32
Fl. forming a star-shaped double triangle, 95 mm wide; perianth segments ovate, acute, mucronate, greenish ivory white (150D), spreading, plane, satin smooth and of good substance, overlapping half; the inner segments more narrowly ovate; corona cup-shaped, angled and lightly ribbed, light greenish yellow 3D, with a very narrow band of strong orange 24A at rim, mouth frilled, rim dentate. Mid-season

'Mary West' 2 W-W
(D.V. West, pre-1923)
Perianth segments white, inflexed; corona opening citron, becoming white

'Marzali' 3 W-?
(Mrs B.A. Woods) Mrs B.A. Woods, 1968

'Marzo' 7 Y-Y
(J.W.Blanchard, 1985) J.W.Blanchard, 1996
'Falstaff' × *N. cordubensis*; sdlg no. 80/1F
Fl. 1-2 per stem, 60 mm wide; perianth segments very broadly ovate, rich butter yellow, with white mucro, spreading, with margins incurved, deeply overlapping; the inner segments a little narrower and slightly inflexed; corona bowl-shaped, slightly darker in tone than the perianth, with mouth straight and even, rim very broadly and shallowly crenate. Very early

'Masai King' 2 Y-O
(J.L. Richardson, pre-1953)
'Bahram' × 'Alamein'
Fl. 102 mm wide; perianth segments very broadly ovate, blunt, slightly mucronate, vivid yellow 9A, spreading, a little concave, with margins slightly incurling, smooth, overlapping half; the inner segments more narrowly ovate, rounded at shoulder; corona short funnel-shaped, lightly ribbed, strong orange 25A, with mouth straight and a little frilled. AM(e) 1960

'Masai Mara' 2 W-GYP
(Brian S. Duncan) Brian S. Duncan, 1990
'Pismo Beach' × 'High Society'; sdlg no. 1070
Fl. 110 mm wide; perianth segments broadly ovate, blunt, prominently mucronate, pure white, spreading, smooth, with broad midrib showing, regular, overlapping half; corona deep bowl-shaped, opening deep yellow, becoming whitish lemon, with green at base and a distinct band of pink at rim, mouth even, rim crenate. Tall. Mid-season to late

'Masaka' 3 W-R
(J.L. Richardson, pre-1948)
'Coronach' × 'Forfar'
Corona disc-shaped, tightly ribbed, deep red

'Masala' 1 Y-Y
(H.R. Bulman) H.R. Bulman, 1956
'Royalist' × 'Crocus'

'Mascotte' 3 W-YYO
(C. Dawson, pre-1907)

Perianth segments slightly reflexed; corona with a broad band of scarlet-orange at rim

'Mascotte' 2 W-YYR
(West & Fell, pre-1936)
Corona expanded, yellow, with a broad band of scarlet at rim

'Mascotte' 2 W-YYR
(Alister Clark) A. Ladson, 1960
Perianth segments broad, pure white; corona widely expanded, with a broad band of scarlet at rim

'Mascotte Powell' 2 W-Y
(L.P. Dettman) L.P. Dettman, 1971
'Bodilly' × 'Bonnington'
Fl. 104 mm wide

'Mascoutah' 2 W-? (b)
(E.C. Powell, pre-1949)
'Pinkeen' × 'Mrs R.O.Backhouse'

'Masefield' 9 W-YYR
Syn. of 'Rupert Brooke'

'Masked Light' 2 Y-O
(J.L. Richardson, pre-1951)
'Narvik' × 'Ceylon'
Perianth segments broadly ovate, blunt, slightly mucronate, deep greenish golden yellow, spreading or reflexed, plane or a little convex, somewhat creased, with margins sometimes nicked, overlapping one-third to a half; the inner segments only a little narrower, spreading or inflexed, with margins lightly recurved at base; corona deep cup-shaped, loosely ribbed, reddish orange, with a darker tone at mouth, the mouth straight, 6-lobed, frilled, with rim crenate. Tall. Mid-season

'Maskerade' 1 Y-GYY
Syn. of 'Marieke'

'Maslyn' 4 W-P
(W. Jackson Jr, 1968) Unregistered
'Lawali' × 'Chimeon'; sdlg no. 185/68

'Masport' 2 W-Y
(P. Phillips) P. Phillips, 1978
Fl. 94 mm wide; corona lemon. Mid-season

'Masquerade' 2 W-R
(D.S. Bell) D.S. Bell, 1955
'Mannequin' × 'Garland'
Corona bowl-shaped, deep red. AM(e)(NZ) 1963, FCC(e)(NZ) 1970

'Massasoit' 2 Y-YYO
(E.C. Powell, pre-1946)
'Hera' × 'Fair Bostonian'

'Masserate' 4 W-Y
(Jackson's Daffodils) Jackson's Daffodils, 1989
'Tavelle' × 'Nala'; sdlg no. 187/84
Fl. 108 mm wide; perianth and other petaloid segments greenish white (155A); corona segments almost as long, vivid yellow 9B, with those at centre slightly tinged pink. Mid-season

'Massive Gold' 1 Y-Y
(pre-1914)

'Master-at-Arms' 2 W-Y
(G.H. Engleheart, pre-1901)
AM 1901

'Mastercraft' 1 W-P
(S.J. Bisdee, 1943)
'Eskimo' × 'Dawnglow'

'Master Floris' 1 W-Y
(de Graaff Bros, pre-1939)
AM(Haarlem) 1939, TGA(Haarlem) 1956

'Master of Balliol' 1 (a)
(Cartwright & Goodwin, pre-1910)

'Masterpiece' 3 W-OOR
(G.H. Engleheart, pre-1906)
Fl. rounded; perianth segments very broad, somewhat obovate, blunt or squarish at apex, sometimes truncate, mucronate, creamy white, a little reflexed, ribbed, overlapping half; the inner segments a little narrower, more nearly ovate and spreading; corona more or less disc-shaped, closely ribbed, intense reddish orange, shading to vermilion at rim, tightly frilled. 2n=28. AM 1906

'Master Robert' 1 Y-Y
(J.L. Richardson, pre-1927)
Fl. golden yellow; perianth segments broadly ovate, blunt, with slight white mucro, spreading, a little twisted, overlapping a quarter; the inner segments inflexed at base, reflexed at apex, more strongly twisted; corona cylindrical, smooth, with rim crenate and broadly rolled

'Mastiff' 1 W-? (b)
(R. Dick, pre-1930)

'Matador' 2 W-Y
(C. Goodson, pre-1927)

'Matador' 8 Y-O
(Oregon Bulb Farms) Oregon Bulb Farms, 1958
?'Admiration' open pollinated
Fls 3-5 per stem; perianth segments broadly ovate, blunt, prominently mucronate, sulphur yellow, spreading, overlapping one-third to a half; the inner segments a little inflexed, with margins wavy; corona shallow, expanded, closely ribbed, bright orange,

with mouth frilled. Tall. Early. 2n=34

'Mata Hari' 2 W-O
(J. Berbee, pre-1944)
'John Evelyn' × 'Elly Ney'

'Matahina' 2 Y-ORR
(C.A. Latta) C.A. Latta, 1964
Fl. 95 mm wide; perianth segments crocus yellow. Mid-season. Resembles an improved 'Invergordon'

'Matakana' 4 W-P
(D.S. Bell) D.S. Bell, 1980
'Mount White' × 'Sleeping Beauty'
Fl. 106 mm wide; perianth and other petaloid segments white; corona segments interspersed, pink. Mid-season

'Matala' 2 W-R
(A.H. Ahrens, 1947) D.J.Cooper, 1959
Fl. 102 mm wide; corona strong orange-red. Mid-season

'Matamata' 2 W-P
(R. Hyde) R. Hyde, 1959

'Matamax' 1 (a)
(de Graaff Bros, pre-1923)

'Matamix' 1 Y-Y
(pre-1937)

'Matangi' 1 Y-Y
(D.S. Bell) D.S. Bell, 1975
'Dawngold' × 'Gold Shower'
Fl. 108 mm wide. Mid-season. Resembles a later-flowered 'Gold Shower' with a longer corona

'Matapan' 3 W-R
(J.L. Richardson, pre-1941)
'Coronach' × 'Forfar'
Fl. 81 mm wide; perianth segments very broadly ovate, truncate, prominently mucronate, pure white, a little concave, very smooth and of thick substance, with midrib showing, ribbed, overlapping half; the inner segments more narrowly ovate, only slightly mucronate; corona orange-red (30B), mouth widely expanded and frilled, with three overlapping lobes. AM(e) 1957

'Matapeake' 2 W-OOR
(E.C. Powell, pre-1946)
'Will Scarlett' × 'Warlock'

'Matapu' 2 (a)
(M.E. Brogden) M.E. Brogden, 1956

'Mataranka' 2 Y-Y
(J.N. Hancock & Co., 1954)

'Matariki' 2 W-O
(G.W.E. Brogden) C.W. Johnson, 1955

'Matawhero' 3 W-R
(A.E. Lowe, pre-1927)
Corona ruby red. Resembles *N. poeticus* in perianth shape

'Matchless' 2 W-? (b)
(G.H. Engleheart, pre-1923)

'Matchless' 2
(New Zealand origin, pre-1936)

'Matchless' 2 W-O
(C.M. Grullemans) J.J. Grullemans & Sons, 1959
Fl. 115 mm wide; perianth segments creamy white; corona strong orange 25A. Mid-season

'Mate' 2 Y-O
(D. Jackson) Jackson's Daffodils, 1983
'True Orbit' × 'Gunsynd'; sdlg no. 110/78
Fl. 96 mm wide. Early to mid-season

'Mathinna' 7 Y-Y
(S.J. Bisdee, 1937)
'Osiris' × *N. jonquilla*

'Matika' 2 W-R
(W. Jackson Jr) W. Jackson Jr, 1971
'Jo' × 'Signal Light'; sdlg no. 96/66
Fl. 100 mm wide; perianth segments very broadly ovate, rounded at apex, prominently mucronate, pure white, with some yellow staining at base, slightly reflexed, overlapping half; corona bowl-shaped, ribbed, vivid red, with mouth frilled

'Matinée' 2 W-Y
(J.S. Leitch) J.S. Leitch, 1960
Fl. 108 mm wide; corona lemon yellow. Late

'Matisse' 2 W-Y
(Konynenburg & Mark) Konynenburg & Mark, 1963
'Mimosa' × ('Gratia' × 'Daisy Schäffer')
Fl. 100 mm wide; perianth segments silver white; corona light greenish yellow 8C. Mid-season

'Matlock' 2 Y-R
(D.B. Milne, pre-1950)

'Matoome' 1 Y-Y
(W. Jackson Sr, 1939)
'Chruseos' × 'Crocus'

'Matron' 1 W-W
(G.L. Wilson, pre-1923)

'Matson Vincent' 1 W-W
(W. Backhouse, pre-1869)

Fl. small, pure white; corona flared, with rim crenate. Dwarf

'Mattara' 2 Y-OOR
(W. Jackson Jr, 1970) Unregistered
('Mars' × 'Ceylon') × 'Tanais'; sdlg no. 2/70
Perianth segments deep yellow, smooth; corona narrow, orange, shading to orange-red at rim, dentate. Sunproof

'Matterhorn' 1 W-W
(de Graaff Bros, pre-1927)

'Matterhorn' 1 W-W
(J.L. Richardson) J.L. Richardson, 1958
'Petsamo' self pollinated
Fl. 119 mm wide, ice white; perianth segments broadly ovate, blunt, slightly mucronate, slightly inflexed, plane, with margins occasionally a little incurling, overlapping half; the inner segments more narrowly ovate, more nearly acute, square-shouldered at base, inflexed at base, slightlyreflexed at apex, a little concave; corona funnel-shaped, ribbed, with mouth expanded, rim widely rolled and minutely crenate. AM(e) 1962

'Matthew Arnold' 9 W-YYR
(G.H. Engleheart, pre-1910)
AM 1910

'Matthew Arnold' 9 W-OOR
(?Australian origin, pre-1997) Unregistered

'Matthew Flinders' 2 Y-?
(Alister Clark) H.T. Dettmann, 1960

'Matthew Henry' 2 or 3 W-? (b or c)
(pre-1913)

'Matthew Holmes' 3
(pre-1914)

'Mattie' 9
Syn. of 'Matty'

'Mattsuyker' 3 W-YOR
(S.J. Bisdee, pre-1943)
'Mitylene' × 'Hades'

'Matty' 9
(pre-1913)
See also 'Mattie'

'Matula' 1 Y-Y
(C.E. Radcliff, 1943) J.M.Radcliff, 1956
'Nangeela' × 'Fahan'

'Maud' 9
(G.H. Engleheart, pre-1910)

'Maude' 3 W-? (b)
(W. Backhouse, pre-1869)
Corona tinged orange. Syn. Leedsii 'Maude'. Was "absorbed" into 'Maria Magdaline de Graaff'

'Maude' 2 W-W
(R. Gibson, pre-1927)

'Maude' 2 W-W
(P. & G.Phillips) P. & G.Phillips, 1979
Fl. 102 mm wide. Mid-season

'Maude Adams' 2
(pre-1939)

'Maud Miller' 1 W-W
Syn. of 'Maud Muller'

'Maud Muller' 1 W-W
(A.M. Wilson, pre-1908)
See also 'Maud Miller'

'Maud West' 3 W-W
(W.B. Hartland, pre-1908)
Resembles a large flowered 'Fairy Queen'

'Maui' 1 W-? (b)
(Hon. Sir R.H. Rhodes, pre-1914)

'Mauna Loa' 2 Y-OOR
(G.E. Mitsch, pre-1952)
'Market Merry' × 'Carbineer'; sdlg no. K48/2

'Maunganui' 1 W-Y
(A.E. Lowe, pre-1927)

'Maura' 2 W-YOO
(J.T. Gray, pre-1937)
Corona reddish orange, paling to yellow at base

'Maureen' 3 W-Y
(G.H. Engleheart, pre-1923)
Fl. 76 mm wide, facing down; perianth segments creamy white, with cream at base, with margins recurved, overlapping; corona cylindrical, sulphur, frilled. Late

'Maurice Bevan' 2 W-? (b)
(H.R. Meyer, pre-1927)

'Maurice Hyde' 1 Y-Y
(R. Hyde) R. Hyde, 1957
Perianth segments acute; corona with rim evenly rolled

'Maurice Vilmorin' 3 W-YYO
(W. Backhouse, pre-1869)
Perianth segments ovate, acute, creamy white, tinged yellow at base, a little inflexed, with margins wavy, the margins sometimes recurved between shoulder

and base; corona short funnel-shaped, smooth at base, ribbed towards mouth, lemon yellow, shading to scarlet-orange at rim, with mouth straight, a little frilled. Syn. Barrii Albidus 'Maurice Vilmorin', Incomparabilis Albidus 'Maurice Vilmorin'

'Mausolies' 2 W-W
Syn. of 'Mausolus'

'Mausolus' 2 W-W
(G.H. Engleheart, pre-1948)
See also 'Mausolies'

'Maverick' 3 Y-R
(W.G. Pannill) W.G. Pannill, 1970
'Ceylon' × 'Jezebel'

'Maverick' 2 Y-O
(J.N.Hancock & Co., 1984) Unregistered
'Tangaloa' × 'Marjorie Hine'; sdlg no. 39/84H
Perianth segments mid-yellow; corona disc-shaped, bright orange, neatly frilled. Early

'Mavis' 3 Y-? (a)
(P.D. Williams, pre-1927)

'Mavis' 3 W-R
(A.E. Lowe, pre-1928)

'Maviston' 2 Y-Y
(The Brodie of Brodie, pre-1933)
'Pilgrimage' hybrid
Perianth segments broadly ovate

'Mavourneen' 2 W-? (b or c)
(J.R. Pearson & Sons, pre-1913)

'Mavourneen' 1 W-W
(G.L. Wilson, pre-1930)
Sdlg × 'Antrim'

'Mavourneen' 2 W-W
Syn. of 'Irish Queen'

'Maweena' 1 W-? (b or c)
(W. Jackson Jr, 1956) Unregistered
'Tamara' × 'Preamble'

'Mawhero' 2 W-P
(Koanga Daffodils) Koanga Daffodils, 1995
Fl. 120 mm wide; perianth segments very smooth; corona broad, ribbed, light yellowish pink 36B, with rim slightly rolled. Late

'Mawnan' 2 (a)
(P.D. Williams, pre-1936)

'Max' 11a Y-YRR
(R.A.Scamp) R.A.Scamp, 1994
'Gironde' × 'Falstaff'; sdlg no. S412

Fl. 95 mm wide; perianth segments broadly ovate, rounded at apex, slightly mucronate, bright yellow, spreading, overlapping half; the inner segments narrower, inflexed at base, a little reflexed towards apex, with margins wavy; corona split to base, the six segments half the length of the perianth segments and opposite and closely overlying them, deeply ribbed, dark orange-red, with yellow at base, tightly frilled. Mid-season. Sunproof

'Max Havelaar' 2 W-OOR
(J.W.A. Lefeber) W. Blom & Son, 1955
Perianth segments narrow, acute, pure white; corona widely expanded, vivid yellowish orange, with scarlet at rim

'Maxim' 1 W-? (b)
(Mrs R.O. Backhouse, pre-1921)

N. maximus Haworth = *N. obvallaris*

N. maximus hort. = 'Maximus'

'Maximus' 1 Y-Y
(pre-1576)
Considered to be a variant of *N. hispanicus*
Fl. 90 mm wide; perianth segments ovate, rich yellow, somewhat inflexed, twisted, with margins recurved, overlapping at base only; corona cylindrical or somewhat funnel-shaped, smooth, darker in tone than the perianth, with mouth expanded and ribbed, rim widely flanged and deeply notched. Tall, Early. 2n=21. Syn. "College Garden Maximus", "TCD Maximus", "Trinity College (Dublin) Maximus", 'Grandiflorus', 'Maximus Superbus Longivirens', 'Trumpet Major', *N. maximus* hort., Pseudonarcissus Major 'Maximus'. *C(g) 1936. "Hales' Vase of Beaten Gold" and 'Maximus Laetevirens' are thought to be variants of this

'Maximus' 8 Y-Y
(pre-1792)
Fl. sulphur yellow

'Maximus' 2 Y-Y
(?E. Leeds, pre-1877)
Syn. Incomparabilis Sulphureus 'Maximus'

'Maximus' 2 W-W
(?E.Leeds, pre-1877)
Syn. Incomparabilis Albus 'Maximus'

'Maximus' 1 Y-Y
Syn. of 'Emperor'

'Maximus' 1 W-Y
Syn. of 'Grandis'

'Maximus' 1 W-Y
Syn. of 'Empress'

'Maximus Crenulatus' 1 Y-Y
(E. Leeds, pre-1877)
Fl. rich golden yellow

'Maximus Flore Pleno' 4 Y-Y
(pre-1870)
Fl. large, deep golden yellow. Syn. "Double Golden Trumpet", "Double Trumpet Major", Pseudonarcissus Major 'Maximus Flore Pleno'. ?The same as 'Plenissimus'

'Maximus Grandiplenus' 4 Y-Y
Syn. of 'Plenissimus'

'Maximus Laetevirens' 1 Y-Y
?Variant of Pseudonarcissus Major 'Maximus'

'Maximus Superbus' 1 Y-Y
(E. Leeds, pre-1851)
'Maximus' hybrid
Fl. golden yellow, facing up; perianth segments somewhat oblong, blunt, with slight white mucro and with green at midrib beneath, spreading or a little inflexed, often twisted or with margins recurved, margins notched, overlapping up to a quarter; the inner segments ovate, acute; corona cylindrical, broadly ribbed, darker in tone than the perianth, tinged orange with age, mouth abruptly expanded and more closely ribbed, deeply 6-lobed, with rim deeply notched and dentate, margins flanged. 2n=21

'Maximus Superbus Longivirens' 1 Y-Y
Syn. of 'Maximus'

'Maxina' 2 W-P
(?New Zealand origin, pre-1997) Unregistered

'Maxine Elliott' 2 W-? (b)
(W.B. Hartland, pre-1913)

'Maxwell' 2 W-? (b)
(R.H. Bath, pre-1931)

'May' 3 W-YYO
(E. Leeds, pre-1877)
Syn. Burbidgei 'Conspicuus Minor', Burbidgei 'May'

'May' 2 W-W
(W.A. Watts, pre-1907)
Fl. creamy white, facing slightly downwards; perianth segments overlapping; corona with a tinge of sulphur yellow at rim, frilled. Mid-season. *C(g) 1936. Formerly Div. 1

'Maya' 2 W-Y
(A.E. Lowe, pre-1927)

'Maya' 2 W-? (b or c)
(de Graaff Bros, pre-1937)
AM(Haarlem) 1937

'Maya Angelou' 9 W-GOO
(Donna C.Dietsch) Donna C.Dietsch, 1995
'Como' × 'Glory of Lisse'; sdlg no. 86/44
Fl. 58 mm wide; perianth segments obovate, blunt; the inner segments broadly ovate; corona broad disc-shaped, yellow-orange, green at base, shading to deep orange at rim, with the rim dentate. Very late. Scented

'Maya Dynasty' 2 Y-Y
(G.E. Mitsch, 1979) R. & E. Havens, 1993
'Camelot' × 'Chiloquin'; sdlg no. 2016/9
Fl. 90 mm wide, clear mid-yellow; perianth segments broadly ovate, spreading, plane, smooth; corona funnel-shaped, with mouth slightly flared. Late

'Mayan Chief' 1 Y-Y
(G.E. Mitsch, 1957) G.E. Mitsch, 1967
'Galway' × 'Kingscourt'; sdlg no. S9/4
Fl. 111 mm wide, golden yellow. Mid-season

'Mayan Gold' 1 Y-Y
(Ballydorn Bulb Farm) Ballydorn Bulb Farm, 1988
'Golden Clarion' × 'Mayo Gold'
Fl. 110 mm long, golden yellow; perianth segments "shovel-shaped", spreading, overlapping; corona long, straight-sided, mouth slightly expanded, with dark yellow at base, rim dentate. Mid-season

'May Be' 2 W-P
(J.N. Hancock & Co., 1953)
'Fairy's Flight' hybrid
Corona frilled

'May Beauty' 3 W-? (b)
(H.P. Zwetsloot, pre-1938)
AM(Haarlem) 1938

'May Bibby' 2 W-? (b)
(Mrs R.O. Backhouse, pre-1921)
AM(Haarlem) 1930

'May Blossom' 2 W-? (b or c)
(G.L. Wilson, pre-1927)
Corona creamy, faintly flushed peach pink

'May Burgh' 2 W-Y
(L.P. Dettman) L.P. Dettman, 1979
'Tudor Minstrel' open pollinated
Fl. 93 mm wide; perianth segments yellowish white 155B; corona brilliant yellow 7A. Mid-season. Resembles 'Tudor Minstrel' but with the flower at right angles to the stem

'May Day' 9
(G.H. Engleheart, pre-1916)

'May Day' 3 W-YYR
(Murray W.Evans) Murray W.Evans, 1970
'Rubra' × 'Seraglio'

'May Dew' 3 W-Y
(G.P. Haydon, pre-1907)
N. × medioluteus × N. poeticus
Fl. rounded; perianth segments of great substance, overlapping; corona pale lemon yellow, frilled. Tall. Late. Scented. See also 'Maydew'

'Maydew' 3 W-Y
Syn. of 'May Dew'

'May Fair' 2 W-? (b or c)
(Mrs R.O. Backhouse, pre-1908)

'Mayfair' 1 W-Y
(Australian or New Zealand origin, pre-1927)
Corona mouth expanded, frilled

'Mayfair' 4 W-P
(E.W. Cotter, 1970) D.S. Bell, 1980
'Mount White' × 'Debutante'
Fl. 105 mm wide; perianth and other petaloid segments white; corona segments interspersed, pinkish buff. Mid-season. Resembles a pinker 'Mount White'

'Mayfield' 3 W-? (b)
(P.D. Williams, pre-1928)

'Mayfield' 1 Y-Y
(R.J. McIlraith) R.J. McIlraith, 1982
'Hereami' × 'Arctic Gold'; sdlg no. 68/2
Fl. 95 mm wide. Early. Resembles a deeper-coloured 'Arctic Gold' with a green tinge at corona base

'May Fisher' 2 W-? (b)
(N.Y. Lower, pre-1928)
'Saint Olaf' × 'Mrs Ernst H.Krelage'

'Mayflower' 3 W-O
(Mrs R.O. Backhouse, pre-1921)
Perianth segments creamy white, flat, overlapping half; corona broadly funnel-shaped, orange, rim scarlet. AM(e) 1927

'Mayfly' 2 W-YYW
(G.L. Wilson) Mrs D.G. Moore, 1967
Fl. 95 mm wide; perianth segments pale creamy white, slightly reflexed; corona lemon yellow, rim creamy white. Late

'May Glory' 9 W-O
(G.H. Engleheart, pre-1930)
Corona reddish orange. AM(e) 1929

'May Hanson' 5 W-W
(H. Backhouse, pre-1913)
Hybrid between 'Minnie Hume' and N. triandrus var. loiseleurii
Fl. pure white. Mid-season

'May Johnston' 2 Y-Y
(L.P.Dettman, 1972) Unregistered
'Foresight' × 'Glenara Caramel'; sdlg no. 172

'Maylene' 2 W-P
(J.N. Hancock & Co.) J.N. Hancock & Co., 1955
'Cherie Marie' × 'Pink o' Dawn'
Corona glowing pink

'May Massey' 2 W-O
(pre-1930)
Corona glowing reddish orange

'May Molony' 2 W-Y
(G.L. Wilson, pre-1927)
Engleheart sdlg 633 open pollinated
Perianth segments pure white, smooth; corona clear lemon yellow. AM(e) 1929

'May Moon' 3 W-? (b or c)
(C.T.D. Digby, pre-1913)
See also 'Maymoon'

'Maymoon' 3 W-?
Syn. of 'May Moon'

'May Morning' 3 W-YOO
(A.G. Thompson) A.G. Thompson, 1965
'Desire' × 'Kansas'
Fl. 89 mm wide; corona with creamy yellow at base. Late. Resembles 'Desiré' in form

'May Muriel' 2 W-Y
(J.J. Grullemans & Sons) J.J. Grullemans & Sons, 1957
Perianth segments pure white; corona large, creamy yellow, with rim rolled. 2n=28

'Maymyo' 2 Y-O
(R.V. Favell, pre-1940)

'Mayo Gold' 1 Y-Y
(J.A. O'More) J.A. O'More, 1968
'Integrity' × 'Goldcourt'

'Mayon' 2 W-W
(J.S. Leitch) J.S. Leitch, 1958

'Mayora' 1 (a)
(J.T. Gray, pre-1949)

'Mayor Gouverneur' 1 Y-Y
Syn. of 'Burgemeester Gouverneur'

'May Prince' 2 (a)
(G.P. Haydon, pre-1907)

'May Queen' 1 W-Y
(Barr & Sons, pre-1907)
Perianth segments overlapping; corona opening pale canary yellow, becoming creamy yellow

'May Queen' 2 W-GYY
(J.L. Richardson) Brian S.Duncan, 1973
Sdlg 562 × 'Rose Caprice'
Fl. 114 mm wide; corona opening deep lemon, gradually becoming pinkish buff

'May Star' 3 (a)
(Miss K. Spurrell, pre-1907)

'Maytime' 3 W-? (b)
(Mrs F.S. Foote, pre-1940)

'May White' 2 W-W
(G.L. Wilson, pre-1932)

'Maywin' 2 (a)
(S.C. Gaspar) R.J. Abernethy, 1957

'Mazaka'
Unregistered
Seed parent of 'Sword Play'

'Mazarin' 3 W-? (b)
(Cartwright & Goodwin, pre-1908)

'Mazda' 1 Y-Y
(W.Jackson Jr, 1973) Unregistered
Sdlg 35/65 × 'Warbin'; sdlg no. 8/73

'Mazeppa' 2 Y-OOR
(A.M. Wilson, pre-1930)
Perianth segments pale yellow; corona orange, rim orange-red, frilled. Late

'Mazurka' 2 Y-? (a)
(J.L. Richardson) J.L. Richardson, 1956
'Narvik' × 'Alamein'

'M.Bluett'
Unregistered
Seed parent of 'Aaskild'

'M.Boardman' 2 W-? (b)
(L. van Leeuwen & Son, pre-1931)
AM(Haarlem) 1930

'McIvor' 1 Y-Y
(pre-1960)
Fl. rich yellow; corona mouth expanded, rim deeply dentate. Very late. Some stock sold as 'Golden Lion'

'McRob' 1 Y-Y
(J.N. Hancock & Co., 1955) Unregistered
Fl. rich golden yellow; perianth segments rounded; corona long, much frilled. Tall. Mid-season to late

'M.Dobell' 1 W-Y
Syn. of 'Murrell Dobell'

'Meadow Gold' 2 Y-Y
(D.S. Bell) D.S. Bell, 1959
Fl. 108 mm wide; corona neatly rimmed. Mid-season. Resembles a darker 'Saint Egwin' of stronger substance

'Meadowhead' 2 W-W
(F.E. Board) F.E. Board, 1965
Sdlg WJD 9/9 × 'Empress of Ireland'; sdlg no. 737
Early

'Meadow Lake' 2 Y-Y
(Elise Havens) G.E. Mitsch, 1979
'Nazareth' × 'Butterscotch'; sdlg no. FEJ6/6
Fl. forming a double triangle, 100 mm wide, clear yellow; perianth segments broadly ovate, blunt, with slight white mucro, spreading, plane, overlapping half; the inner segments narrower and somewhat twisted; corona cylindrical, smooth, with mouth ribbed and even, rim rolled and crenate. Early. Resembles a lighter-coloured 'Asteroid'

'Meadowlark' 2 W-Y
(G.E. Mitsch) G.E. Mitsch, 1956
'Tunis' × 'Fortune'; sdlg no. 38C90/2
Perianth segments creamy white; corona buff yellow, paling towards base. Mid-season

'Meander' 4 Y-R
(K.J. Heazlewood) K.J. Heazlewood, 1968
'Mary Copeland' × 'Dunkeld'
Fl. 89 mm wide. Late. Resembles 'Livia' but with more densely arranged petaloid and corona segments

'Meavy' 1 W-W
(Mrs H.K. Richardson) du Plessis Bros, 1978
Sdlg no. 130
Fl. 100 mm wide. Mid-season

'Mecca' 3 W-? (b)
(A.M. Wilson) Mrs R. McConnel, 1955

'Mecklenberg' 1 (a)
(A. Frylink & Sons, pre-1938)
AM(Haarlem) 1937

'Medaillon' 2 Y-O
(J. Gerritsen & Son) J. Gerritsen & Son, 1960
Fl. 80 mm wide; perianth segments primrose yellow; corona dark orange. Mid-season. 2n=28. Resembles 'Carbineer' but with a more strongly coloured corona of firmer texture

'Medalist' 2 W-YPP
(G.E. Mitsch, 1956) G.E. Mitsch, 1967
'Mabel Taylor' × 'Caro Nome'; sdlg no. R49/1
Fl. rounded, 108 mm wide, of good poise; perianth segments deeply overlapping; corona bowl-shaped, large, creamy yellow, with pink and lilac shading. Mid-season

'Medallion' 2 W-? (b)
(F.H.Chapman, pre-1928)

'Medan' 11?b Y-Y
(J.W.A. Lefeber, 1969) J.W.A. Lefeber, 1980
'Papillon Blanc' hybrid
Fl. 75 mm wide; perianth segments light greenish yellow 4B; corona segments with light greenish yellow 4B and vivid yellow 13A probably in longitudinal bands. Early

'Medea' 1 W-W
(E.H. Krelage & Son, pre-1915)
Perianth segments narrow; corona creamy white, rim frilled. AM(Haarlem) 1915

'Medford' 1 W-? (b)
(de Graaff Bros, pre-1926)
Syn. 'Vesta'. AM(Haarlem) 1926

'Media' 3 W-OOR
(W. Jackson Jr, 1967) Unregistered
'Jo' × 'Arbar'; sdlg no. 112/67
Perianth segments pure white, of good substance; corona deep orange becoming red at broadly banded rim, neatly dentate

'Media Girl' 2 W-WWP
(Brian S.Duncan) Brian S.Duncan, 1997
'Dailmanach' × 'Gracious Lady'; sdlg no. 1462
Fl. forming a double triangle, 110 mm wide; perianth segments broadly ovate; corona broad funnel-shaped, opening lilac pink, becoming almost white, with lilac pink at rim, mouth straight and slightly frilled. Mid-season to late

'Medichina' 2 (a)
(A. Gibson, pre-1951)

'Medici' 2 W-W
(R.H.Glover, pre-1993) Unregistered

'Medina' 4 W-W
(J. Gerritsen & Son, pre-1954)
TGA(Haarlem) 1954

'Medio Luteo Brabançon' 8 W-O
(pre-1798)
Perianth segments white; corona orange. Syn. 'Brabançon'

'Medio Luteo Charmant' 8 W-O
(pre-1798)
Perianth segments white; corona orange. Syn. 'Charmant'

'Medio Luteo de Brande' 8 W-O
(pre-1798)
Perianth segments white; corona orange

'Medio Luteo de Duffel' 8 W-O
(pre-1798)
Perianth segments white; corona orange

'Medio Luteo de France' 8 W-O
(pre-1807)
Perianth segments white; corona orange

'Medio Luteo de Munk' 8 W-O
(pre-1798)
Perianth segments white; corona orange

'Medio Luteo d'Harlem' 8 W-O
(pre-1807)
Perianth segments white; corona orange

'Medio Luteo Luxembourg' 8 W-O
(pre-1798)
Perianth segments white; corona orange. Syn. 'Luxembourg'

'Medio Luteo Major' 8 W-O
(pre-1798)
Perianth segments white; corona orange. Syn. 'Major'

'Medio Luteo Mignonne' 8 W-O
(pre-1798)
Perianth segments white; corona orange. Syn. 'Mignonne'

'Medio Luteo Minor' 8 W-O
(pre-1798)
Perianth segments white; corona orange. Syn. 'Minor'

'Medio Luteo Pamela' 8 W-O
(pre-1798)
Perianth segments white; corona orange. Syn. 'Pamela'

'Medio Luteo Superbe' 8 W-O
(pre-1798)
Perianth segments white; corona orange. Syn. 'Superbe'

'Medio Luteo Van Dyk' 8 W-O
(pre-1807)
Perianth segments white; corona orange. Syn. 'Van Dyk'

N. × *medioluteus* Miller 13 = *N. poeticus* Linnaeus × *N. tazetta* Linnaeus ("April Beauty", "Cemetery Ladies", "Loving Couples", "Primrose Peerless", "Twin Sisters"). 2n=17, 24

'Medio-luteus Corona Duplici' 4 W-Y
(pre-1629)
Syn. "The Turkie Daffodil with a Double Crown", Tazetta 'Cypri Semiplena' Haw., Tazetta 'Medio-luteus Corona Duplici'

'Medio-purpureus Multiplex' 4 W-YYR
(pre-1629)
Fls 1-2 per stem; perianth and other petaloid segments in three successively shorter whorls, white; the centre whorl with fewer than six segments; corona segments short, interspersed, yellow, with purple at rim. Early. Scented. Syn. "The Double Purple Ring Daffodil"

'Meditate' 2 W-YYR
(D.S. Bell) D.S. Bell, 1968

'Meditation' 2 W-? (b or c)
(pre-1933)

'Meditation' 2 W-YWP
(G.E. Mitsch) G.E. Mitsch, 1979
'Precedent' × 'Eclat'; sdlg no. G13/2
Fl. 108 mm wide; perianth segments broadly ovate, blunt, mucronate or prominently mucronate, clean white, very sightly reflexed, with margins incurling at apex, of heavy substance, overlapping half; the inner segments with margins wavy, somewhat creased and with broad midrib showing; corona short funnel-shaped, smooth, creamy white, with yellow at base and a broad band of bright pink at rim, mouth straight and tightly frilled. Mid-season. Resembles a larger 'Spring Song' of improved form and substance

N. medius Roemer = *N. jonquilla*

'Medora' 1 W-W
(G.H. Furness, pre-1934)

'Medusa' 8 W-O
(P.D. Williams, pre-1907)
Poetaz
Fls 2-3 per stem, 60 mm wide; perianth segments very broadly ovate, truncate, prominently mucronate or with margins a little incurling at apex, milk white, flushed primrose yellow at base, spreading, slightly concave, somewhat ribbed, overlapping up to one-third; the inner segments shouldered at base, somewhat inflexed, twisted or with margins inward rolling; corona bowl-shaped, ribbed, opening yellow-orange, becoming scarlet-orange, with faint green at base, mouth straight or a little expanded, slightly wavy, with rim minutely notched. Early. Scented. 2n=24. AM(Haarlem) 1925, AM(m)(g) 1925, FCC(m)(g) 1926

"Medusa's Trumpet"
Syn. of *N. bulbocodium*

'Medway' 2 Y-? (a)
(The Brodie of Brodie, c.1929)
'Bokhara' × 'Knipp'; sdlg no. 45/B/24

'Meerrust' 1 (a)
(G.B. de Vroomen & Sons, pre-1934)

'Meersbrook' 2 (a)
(pre-1910)

'Meeting' 4 Y-Y
(P.B. van Eeden) P.B. van Eeden, 1980
'Golden Castle' sport
Fl. 100 mm wide; perianth segments light greenish yellow 5D; corona vivid yellow 13A

'Meg' 2 W-? (b)
(pre-1950)

'Mega' 9 W-GYR
(G.A. Uit den Boogaard, pre-1950)
AM(Haarlem) 1957

N. megacodium Durieu de Maisonneuve = *N. bulbocodium*

'Megalith' 2 W-Y
(T. Bloomer) Rathowen Daffodils, 1984
(('Fermoy' × ['Red Hackle' × 'Glenwherry']) × 'Festivity'; sdlg no. 292
Perianth segments very broad, rounded at apex and with margins sometimes incurling, mucronate, spreading, plane, smooth, overlapping half; the inner segments narrower, somewhat truncate, minutely mucronate, shouldered at base; corona funnel-shaped, rich golden yellow, mouth widely expanded, finely ribbed, a little frilled, rim crenate. Tall. Mid-season

'Megan' 2 W-P
(J.N. Hancock & Co., 1979) Unregistered

'Megaphone' 1 (a)
(de Graaff Bros, pre-1929)

'Megaroma' 9 W-GYR
(Mrs M.S. Yerger) Mrs M.S. Yerger, 1988
'Mega' open pollinated; sdlg no. 75 E 2
The inner perianth segments narrower than outer; corona almost disc-shaped, yellow, with yellow-green (2B) at base and orange-red (33A) at rim. Mid-season. Resembles 'Mega' and 'Meggy' but is more prolific than the latter and taller and larger-flowered than both

'Meggy' 9 W-YYO
(Mrs M.S. Yerger) Mrs M.S. Yerger, 1987
'Mega' open pollinated; sdlg no. 75 E 3
Fl. 75 mm wide; the inner perianth segments narrower than the outer; corona almost disc-shaped, brilliant yellow 7A, with a narrow band of reddish orange 40A at rim and a line of white between the yellow and the orange at maturity. Mid-season. Resembles an earlier-flowered 'Mega' and a much earlier 'Stilton' or 'Lady Serena'

'Megola' 9 W-GGR
(Mrs M.S. Yerger) Mrs M.S. Yerger, 1992
'Mega' open pollinated; sdlg no. 75 E 1
Perianth segments white; corona bowl-shaped, brilliant yellow-green 150C, with a darker tone (151A) at base and red (42A) at rim, with the rim dentate. Mid-season. Resembles sibling 'Meggy'

'Mehades'
(W. Welchman, pre-1914)

'Mehela'
(W. Welchman, pre-1935)

'Meijerbeer' 2 Y-O
(J.W.A. Lefeber, 1945) J.W.A. Lefeber, 1960
Fl. 85 mm wide; perianth segments deep yellow; corona reddish orange. Mid-season

'Meiling' 1 W-Y
(J.S. Leitch) J.S. Leitch, 1966
Fl. 108 mm wide; corona lemon yellow

'Meissen' 2 W-P
(Clive Postles, 1984) Clive Postles Daffodils, 1996
Richardson sdlg 283 × 'Dailmanach'; sdlg no. 7/96/80
Fl. forming a double triangle, 110 mm wide; perianth segments ovate, with margins slightly incurved; corona cylindrical, with mouth flared and rim crenate. Late. Sunproof

'Mekkeda' 2 (a)
(pre-1955)

'Melancholy' 1 W-P
(W. Jackson Jr) Jackson's Daffodils, 1980
'Egina' × 'C.E.Radcliff'; sdlg no. 74/72
Fl. 95 mm wide; perianth segments broad, pure white, smooth; corona clear pink, with rim flanged and dentate. Mid-season

'Melania' 2 W-? (b)
(J.T. Gray, pre-1949)
Perianth segments pure white; corona spreading, with a broad band of pinkish apricot at rim and paler tones towards base

'Melanie' 3? W-W
(A.M. Wilson, pre-1914)
Fl. pure white; the inner perianth segments inflexed; corona with green at base

'Melanite' 3 W-YYO
(P.D. Williams, pre-1927)
Fl. 76 mm wide; perianth segments white, with yellow at base, overlapping half; corona very shallow bowl-shaped, lemon yellow, with a broad band of reddish orange at rim. Mid-season to late. *AM(m) 1930

'Melany' 2 W-P
(J.N.Hancock & Co., 1975) Unregistered
'My Word' hybrid; sdlg no. 39B/78H
Perianth segments almost acute, glistening white; corona cylindrical, deep shell pink, lightly frilled. Tall. Early

'Melbil' 3 W-YYR
(H.G. Cross) H.G. Cross, 1984
'Marilyn' × 'Estrella'; sdlg no. 130-5
Perianth segments very broad in outline, squarish at apex and slightly truncate, mucronate, greenish white (155A), spreading, overlapping half or more; the inner segments narrower, not noticeably mucronate, with midrib showing; corona small bowl-shaped, vivid yellow 9A, with orange-red (30B) at rim, mouth with six very deeply overlapping lobes, tightly frilled. Late

'Melbury' 2 W-P
(J.W. Blanchard) J.W. Blanchard, 1977
(['Green Island' × 'Roseworthy'] × 'Debutante') × 'Romance'; sdlg no. 66/34A
Fl. 95 mm wide. Resembles 'Romance' but with larger and broader perianth segments and a darker-coloured corona

'Melchior' 3 W-? (b)
(Barr & Sons, pre-1923)

'Meldrum' 1 Y-Y
(J.S.B. Lea) J.S.B. Lea, 1976
'Arctic Gold' × sdlg 2-13-61; sdlg no. 3-5-67
Fl. forming a double triangle, 100 mm wide, deep yellow; perianth segments broadly ovate, with slight white mucro, spreading or a little inflexed, smooth, regular, overlapping one-third to a half; corona with rim flanged, deeply and regularly crenate

'Meleager' 1 (a)
(Cartwright & Goodwin, pre-1916)

'Meledor' 2 W-? (b)
(G.H. Johnstone, pre-1953)

'Melford' 1 (a)
(E.M. Crosfield, pre-1934)

'Meliades' 3 W-YYO
(W. Welchman, pre-1913)
Perianth segments slightly reflexed; corona yellow, with a broad band of reddish orange at rim, frilled. AM(e) 1930

'Melicoma' 2 W-Y
(W. Jackson Sr, 1935)
'Mary Blewitt' × 'Nursemaid'

'Melina' 2 W-YOR
(W. Jackson Jr, 1967) Unregistered

'Jeb' × 'Arbar'; sdlg no. 168/67

'Melinda' 3 W-WWR
(K.J. Heazlewood, c.1967) Unregistered
'Galilee' self pollinated

'Melinde' 9
(de Graaff Bros, pre-1927)

'Melini' 1 (a)
(R.H. Bath, pre-1933)

'Melisa Corrius' 2 (a)
(J.W.A. Lefeber, pre-1945)

'Mélisande' 7
(Cartwright & Goodwin, pre-1916)

'Melisande' 2 Y-? (a)
(C.E. Radcliff, 1931)
'Gloriana' × 'Tamerlane'

'Melisma' 2 (a)
(Konynenburg & Mark, pre-1954)

'Melisma' 2 W-Y
(Konynenburg & Mark) Konynenburg & Mark, 1960
'Libelle' × 'Zuiderkruis'
Fl. 90 mm wide; corona brilliant yellow 8A. Early

'Melissa' 5
(T. Batson, pre-1914)

'Melissa' 1 Y-Y
(A.O. Roblin, pre-1949)
'Corlo' × 'Woorak'

'Melisse' 8 Y-Y
(pre-1798)
Fl. sulphur yellow

'Melita' 2 Y-Y
(J.T. Gray, pre-1949)
Fl. deep golden yellow; corona large, slightly darker in tone than the perianth

'Melito' 2 W-P
(W. Jackson Sr, 1940)
'Nissa' × 'Benten'

'Melitza' 2 W-? (b or c)
(J.N. Hancock & Co., c.1958)
'Show Princess' × 'Penquite'

'Melling' 2 W-W
(Wilson Stewart) John T. Williams, 1992
'Simile' × 'Rose Royale'; sdlg no. W 39
Fl. forming a double triangle, 107 mm wide; perianth segments broadly ovate, blunt, fairly prominently mucronate, spreading, plane, smooth, regular, overlapping about three-fifths; the inner segments only a little more narrowly ovate, only very slightly mucronate; corona cup-shaped, angled, opening pale yellow, becoming white, mouth straight, ribbed, wavy, with rim notched. Mid-season

'Mellon Park' 3 W-O
(T. Bloomer) Rathowen Daffodils, 1984
('Irish Charm' × sdlg R.202) × 'Royal Regiment'; sdlg no. 218
Fl. 111 mm wide; perianth segments very broad, rounded and with margins sometimes a little incurling at apex, truncate, spreading, slightly concave, smooth, of heavy substance, overlapping half; the inner segments ovate, slightly inflexed, with margins lightly incurved; corona ribbed, opening yellow, with green at base and orange at rim, becoming orange, with yellow at base, then self bright orange, mouth widely expanded and lightly frilled. Mid-season

'Mellow' 1 Y-Y
(G.L. Wilson, pre-1935)
'Cleopatra' × ('Monarch' × 'King Alfred')
Fl. medium yellow; corona with rim neatly flanged

'Mellow Dawn' 1 Y-Y
(D. Bramley) D. Bramley, 1966
Fl. 102 mm wide, mid-yellow; perianth segments broad, overlapping. Mid-season

'Mellow Glow' 2 (a)
(Mrs Ben Robertson, pre-1950)

'Mellow Gold' 1 Y-Y
(D. Bramley) D. Bramley, 1973
'Palmino' hybrid
Fl. 112 mm wide

'Mellow Mist' 7 Y-YYO
(G.E. Morrill) G.E. Morrill, 1979
'Bithynia' × *N. assoanus*; sdlg no. 63/2/2
Fls 1-2 per stem, 65 mm wide; perianth segments brilliant greenish yellow 6B, slightly reflexed; corona darker in tone (12A), with orange at rim. Scented

'Mellow Moon' 1 W-? (b)
(J. Boot, pre-1949)
AM(Haarlem) 1949

'Mellowtint' 2 W-P
(A.O. Roblin) A.O. Roblin, 1956
'Nautilus' × 'Pinka'
Perianth segments rich cream; corona cream, flushed apricot pink

'Mellow Yellow' 1 Y-W
(J.N.Hancock & Co., 1979) Unregistered
'Convention' × 'Daydream'; sdlg no. 65/82H
Perianth segments broadly ovate, blunt, very slightly

mucronate, sulphur yellow, spreading, plane, overlapping half; the inner segments a little inflexed, with margins wavy; corona cylindrical, smooth, opening sulphur yellow, becoming pinkish white, touched yellow at rim, with mouth flared and lightly frilled, rim deeply notched and crenate. Mid-season

'Mello Yello' 2 Y-Y
(Colin Crotty) Unregistered
Sdlg no. 50-75

'Melmos' 2 W-W
(J.T. Gray, pre-1949)

'Melodia' 2 W-Y
(J.N. Hancock & Co., 1983) Unregistered
Sdlg 13/75H × sdlg 7/70J; sdlg no. 7/83H
Fl. rounded; corona long cup-shaped, deep bronze, with a pinkish tone. Very early

'Melodious' 2 Y-Y
(G.E. Mitsch) G.E. Mitsch, 1984
'Jetfire' open pollinated; sdlg no. KK2/9
Fl. 84 mm wide; perianth segments light lemon yellow; corona deeper in tone. Mid-season

'Melody' 3 W-? (b)
(Sir C.H. Cave, pre-1908)

'Melody' 1 Y-Y
(D.V. West, pre-1915)
Fl. rich yellow

'Melody' 2 Y-R
(J.S. Leitch) J.S. Leitch, 1957

'Melody Lane' 2 W-P
(G.E. Mitsch) G.E. Mitsch, 1962
'Loch Maree' × 'Radiation'
Fl. 102 mm wide; corona pink, with overtones of lila*c*. Mid-season

'Melone' 2 W-W
(J.W. Barr, pre-1930)
Perianth segments pure white, overlapping; corona ribbed, opening creamy white, becoming milk white, frilled

'Melorna' 2 (a)
(H.A. Brown) H.A. Brown, 1956

'Melpomene' 8 Y-Y
(pre-1835)
Early

'Melpomene' 2 W-O
(T. Batson, pre-1913)
Fl. 95 mm wide; perianth segments ivory white, overlapping; corona pale orange, heavily frilled. Formerly Div.3

'Melrose' 3 W-? (b)
(P.D. Williams, pre-1934)

'Melrose' 2 W-WWY
(J.N. Hancock & Co., pre-1949)
Perianth segments broad, pure white, overlapping; corona creamy white, with lemon yellow at rim, frilled

'Melton' 1 W-P
(C.E. Radcliff, 1946) J.M. Radcliff, 1956
'Rosario' × 'Dawnglow'
Corona pale creamy pink

'Meltonia' 1 W-? (b)
(J.A. O'Neill, pre-1949)

'Melusina' 5 W-W
(Barr & Sons, pre-1923)
'Albatross' × *N. triandrus* var. *loiseleurii*
Fls usually 2 per stem; perianth segments silvery white; corona milk white

'Melva' 1 (a)
(C. Dawson, pre-1927)

'Melva Fell' 2 W-YYR
(West & Fell, pre-1935)
Perianth segments very broad, rounded at apex, prominently mucronate, spreading, smooth, with margins very slightly incurving, overlapping half; the inner segments narrower, variable in width, slightly inflexed, with margins wavy and sometimes nicked, with midrib showing; corona shallow, widely expanded, ribbed, bright yellow, with orange-red at rim, tightly frilled

'Melvin'
(New Zealand origin, pre-1948)

'Melyn' 2 W-? (b)
(W.A. Watts, pre-1913)

'Melyn'
(G.H. Johnstone, pre-1960)

'Melyor' 2 W-Y
(Rosewarne EHS) Rosewarne EHS, 1985
'Rijnveld's Early Sensation' × 'Foresight'; sdlg no. 63/1/14
Perianth segments greenish white (157A); corona slender, brilliant greenish yellow 6A, with a paler tone at base. Very early. Trade designation JANUARY SILVER

'Melzar' 1 Y-Y
(G.L. Wilson, pre-1927)
Fl. golden yellow; corona with rim flanged and dentate

'Memento' 3 W-? (b)
(F.H. Chapman, pre-1913)

'Memento' 1 YYW-P
(G.E. Mitsch) G.E. Mitsch, 1979
'Gloriola' × 'Rima'; sdlg no. KK4/2
Fl. 95 mm wide; perianth segments pale lemon, paling to ivory at base, overlapping; corona apricot pink. Mid-season

'Memo' 2 Y-Y
(P. & G. Phillips) P. & G. Phillips, 1979
Fl. 90 mm wide

'Memoir' 2 Y-WWY
(Murray W. Evans, 1978) Estella L. Evans, 1989
('Daydream' × ['Green Island' × 'Accent']) × ('Daydream' × 'Gypsy Princess'); sdlg no. V-3/6
Fl. 100 mm wide; perianth segments light yellow; corona ivory white, with light yellow at rim. Mid-season

'Memorable' 8 Y-Y
(pre-1798)
Fl. golden yellow. Early

'Memorial' 2 (a)
(H.A. Brown, pre-1950)

'Memories' 2 (a)
(A.H. Ahrens) J.S. Leitch, 1955

'Memories' 1 W-O
(J.N. Hancock & Co., 1972) Unregistered

'Memory' 9 W-GYO
(Sir C.H. Cave, pre-1912)
'Almira' × 'Horace'
Corona yellow, tinged olive green at base, with reddish orange at rim

'Memory' 2 W-W
(W.G. Bond, pre-1963) Unregistered
Perianth segments smooth, of good substance; corona funnel-shaped, with green at base, slightly frilled

'Memphis' 3 Y-? (a)
(P.D. Williams, pre-1939)

'Mem Sahib' 2 W-P
(Alister Clark, 1935) H.T. Dettmann, 1960

'Mem Sahib' 2 Y-Y
(T.H. Piper, 1953)
'Carbineer' × 'Bungana'

'Mena' 1 (a)
(O. Pease, pre-1927)

'Mena' 1 W-W

(W. Jackson Sr, 1944) W. Jackson Jr, 1956
'Kanchenjunga' × 'Tain'

'Menabilly' 4 O-O
(R.A. Scamp) R.A. Scamp, 1994
'Ocarino' × 'Ambergate'; sdlg no. 205
Fl. 95 mm wide; perianth and other petaloid segments in three whorls, broadly ovate, clear apricot orange; the outer whorl spreading, a little concave, overlapping half; the inner whorls shorter, inflexed or strongly inflexed, with margins tightly incurling; corona segments interspersed among the inner petaloid segments, darker in tone, frilled. Late

'Menadne' 3 W-GYP
Syn. of 'Menadue'

'Menadue' 3 W-GYP
(P.D. Williams, pre-1927)
See also 'Menadne'

'Měn-an-Tol' 2 Y-YYR
(R.A. Scamp) R.A. Scamp, 1994
'Golden Aura' × 'Montego'; sdlg no. 422
Fl. 93 mm wide; perianth segments broadly ovate, bright yellow, slightly concave, smooth, deeply overlapping; corona slightly expanded, bright yellow, with clear red at rim, mouth wavy. Mid-season to late. Sunproof

'Mencius' 2 (a)
(A H. Ahrens) D.J. Cooper, 1956

'Mendel' 2 Y-Y
(G. Lubbe & Son, pre-1935)
AM(Haarlem) 1934

'Mendelssohn Bartholdy' 2 W-O
(J.W.A. Lefeber) J.W.A. Lefeber, 1960
Fl. 90 mm wide; corona reddish orange. Mid-season

'Mendip' 1 W-W
(F.H.Chapman, pre-1927)
*C(g) 1927

'Mendoza' 2 Y-O
(Barr & Sons, pre-1932)
Perianth segments creamy primrose yellow; corona ribbed, golden yellow, frilled

'Menehay' 11a Y-O
(R.A. Scamp) R.A. Scamp, 1991
'Paricutin' × 'Top Hit'; sdlg no. 133
Fl. forming a double triangle, 85 mm wide; perianth segments broadly ovate, blunt, slightly mucronate, deep yellow, spreading, overlapping one-third to a half; the inner segments narrower, spathulate, square-shouldered at base; corona split to base, the six segments half as long as the perianth segments, opposite and closely overlying them and joined to them at the

margins from base to shoulder, bi-lobed, bright reddish orange, lightly frilled. Mid-season. Sunproof

'Menelik' 1 (a)
(Mrs R.O. Backhouse, pre-1908)

'Mengelberg' 1 (a)
?Syn. of 'Willem Mengelberg'

'Menton' 2 W-P
(L. van Leeuwen & Son, pre-1943)
Corona very pale shell pink, with a deeper tone at rim, frilled. AM(Haarlem) 1943

'Mentone' 2 Y-YYO
(H.A. Brown, 1946) A. Ladson, 1960
Perianth segments creamy yellow; corona bright gold, with orange at rim

'Mentor' 2 W-GPP
(T. Bloomer) Rathowen Daffodils, 1982
'Passionale' × ('Interim' × 'Rose Caprice'); sdlg no. 384
Perianth segments very broadly ovate, blunt, slightly mucronate, spreading, a little concave, with margins sometimes incurling at apex, overlapping half; the inner segments more narrowly ovate, a little inflexed, with margins wavy; corona funnel-shaped, deep rose pink, with mouth flared and lightly frilled, rim crenate. Mid-season. Resembles a taller and stronger 'Romance' with the perianth segments less frequently nicked at the margins

'Menucha' 2 W-GWW
(Carncairn Daffodils) Carncairn Daffodils, 1984
Wootton sdlg × 'White Prince'; sdlg no. W22
Fl. 112 mm wide; corona with green at base. Resembles 'Easter Moon' but with a longer corona

'Menuet' 3 W-? (b)
(Mrs R.O. Backhouse, pre-1921)
AM(Haarlem) 1930

'Meoble' 2 W-W
(A.M. Wilson, pre-1949)

'Mepal' 2 W-? (b)
(R.H. Bath, pre-1933)

'Mephisto' 2 Y-O
(P.D. Williams, pre-1927)
Fl. rounded; perianth segments bright yellow; corona bright reddish orange, ageing to yellow at base. AM(e) 1927

'Mephistopheles' 3 W-? (b)
(W.B. Hartland, pre-1904)
See also 'Mephistophiles'

'Mephistopheles' 9

Fl. 100 mm wide; perianth segments pale yellow, becoming white, somewhat twisted and ribbed; corona funnel-shaped, rich chestnut in colour. Syn. of 'Sylvania'

'Mephistophiles' 3 W-? (b)
Syn. of 'Mephistopheles'

'Mera' 2 W-? (b)
(J.T. Gray, pre-1938)

'Merapi' 2 Y-R
(Mrs R.O. Backhouse, pre-1921)
Perianth segments sulphur yellow; corona very widely expanded, deep orange-red. Resembles 'Blazing Sword'. AM(Haarlem) 1925

'Mercato' 2 W-YYO
(J. Berbee, pre-1945)
'John Evelyn' × 'Elly Ney'
Corona widely expanded. Syn. 'Marcata', 'Mercator'. EFA(Haarlem) 1946

'Mercator' 8
(pre-1939)

'Mercator' 2 W-YYO
Syn. of 'Mercato'

'Mercedes' 3 W-?
(G.P. Haydon, pre-1904)
Fl. small, facing down; perianth segments snow white, twisted; corona expanded, with bright red at rim

'Mercedes' 1 W-W
(W. Jackson Jr) W. Jackson Jr, 1970
'Kapitah' × sdlg 28/59; sdlg no. 30/65
Fl. 110 mm wide

'Mercia' 9
(W. Welchman, pre-1907)

'Mercian' 2 Y-R
(A.H. Ahrens, pre-1949)
PC(e)(NZ) 1950

'Mercurius' 8 Y-O
(Dutch origin, pre-1884)
Somewhat resembles Tazetta 'Apollo' but with a differently shaped corona. Syn. Tazetta 'Mercurius'

'Mercurius' 1 Y-Y
(J.W.A. van der Wereld) J.W.A. van der Wereld, 1973
'City of Haarlem' × 'Dutch Master'
Fl. 110 mm wide

'Mercurius' 2 Y-O
Syn. of 'Pyroantha'

'Mercury' 2 W-? (b)
(W.A. Watts, pre-1913)

'Mercy' 9
(G.H. Engleheart, pre-1930)

'Mercy Foster' 3 W-Y
(W. Backhouse, pre-1869)
Perianth segments alabaster white; corona canary yellow, frilled. Syn. Burbidgei 'Mercy Foster'

'Meredith' 3 Y-YYO
(Carncairn Daffodils) Carncairn Daffodils, 1993
Wootton sdlg × 'Pale Sunlight'; sdlg no. 13/19/82
Fl. rounded, 180 mm wide; perianth segments very broad in outline, blunt or rounded at apex, prominently mucronate, whitish yellow, a little reflexed, smooth, overlapping half or more; the inner segments more nearly spreading, shouldered at base; corona shallow, minutely ribbed, orange-yellow, with a line of orange at rim, mouth split and overlapping, wavy, with rim minutely crenate. Mid-season to late

'Meretrix' 2 W-O
(F.E. Board) F.E. Board, 1965
'Buncrana' × 'Merryhill'

'Mereworth' 3
(pre-1933)

'Mereworth' 2 W-Y
(Frank Verge) Frank Verge, 1975
'Glenocum' × 'Newcastle'; sdlg no. D-6-6
Fl. 105 mm wide; corona deep yellow. Mid-season

'Merida' 2 Y-R
(Ballydorn Bulb Farm) Ballydorn Bulb Farm, 1992
'Mexico City' × 2 Y-R sdlg
Fl. 105 mm wide; perianth segments broad, golden yellow, plane, smooth; corona cup-shaped, opening bright red, becoming deeper in tone. Early. Sunproof

'Meridian' 2 Y-YYO
(G.L. Wilson, pre-1950)
'Magherally' × 'Sudan'
Corona with reddish orange at rim

'Meriel' 2 W-W
(A.M. Wilson, pre-1944)
Perianth segments pure white; corona cream, frilled

'Merinda' 2 W-YYO
(A.O. Roblin, 1945) A.O. Roblin, 1956
Perianth segments pure white, of great substance; corona pale yellow, with reddish orange at rim

'Meriones' 2 W-? (b)
(Mrs R.O. Backhouse, pre-1921)

'Merit' 2 Y-? (a)

(P.D. Williams, pre-1927)
'Pilgrim' hybrid

'Merivale' 2 W-W
(G.L. Wilson, pre-1943)
Fl. opening very pale cream, becoming pure white. Early

'Merkara' 2 Y-O
(Mrs R.O. Backhouse, pre-1921)
Perianth segments soft yellow; corona large, expanded, glowing reddish orange. AM(Haarlem) 1926. See also 'Merkera'

'Merkera' 2 Y-O
Syn. of 'Merkara'

'Merle' 2 W-? (b or c)
(W.F. Mitchell, pre-1936)

'Merlin' 2 (a)
(pre-1907)

'Merlin' 3 W-YYR
(J.L. Richardson) J.L. Richardson, 1956
'Mahmoud' self pollinated
Fl. 74 mm wide; perianth segments very broad in outline, rounded at apex and sometimes truncate, mucronate, spreading or a very slightly inflexed, concave, smooth, with margins occasionally incurling at apex; the inner segments a little narrower, minutely mucronate, rounded at shoulder; corona almost disc-shaped, lightly ribbed, brilliant yellow 8A, with orange-red (32B) at rim, mouth with six deeply overlapping lobes, with margins wavy. Mid-season. Scented. 2n=28. AM(e) 1962, *AM(g) 1970, *FCC(g) 1976, AGM 1993

'Merlin'
(W. Jackson Jr, pre-1975) Unregistered
'Dimity' hybrid

'Merlin's Castle' 3 W-GYO
(Carncairn Daffodils, 1975) Carncairn Daffodils, 1989
('Corofin' × 'Merlin') × 'Aircastle'; sdlg no. 5/30/69
Fl. 89 mm wide; perianth segments roundish, glistening white, regularly overlapping; corona very shallow bowl-shaped, chrome yellow, with emerald green at base and orange at rim, mouth even, with rim slightly dentate

'Mermaid' 2 W-W
(E.M. Crosfield, pre-1905)
Perianth segments broadly ovate, mucronate, spreading, plane, smooth, overlapping one-third; the inner segments more nearly acute, slightly inflexed, with margins a little wavy; corona deep bowl-shaped, opening pale creamy primrose, becoming milk white, with mouth expanded and loosely frilled. Resembles

a taller and more refined 'White Queen'

'Mermaid's Spell' 2 W-GWY
(Carncairn Daffodils, 1975) Carncairn Daffodils, 1985
Wootton sdlg × 'Shantallow'
Corona with lemon yellow at rim. Tall. Late

'Merodach' 9
(A.M. Wilson, pre-1908)

'Merri' 1 W-W
(W. Jackson Jr, 1950)
'Sancia' × 'Colmolhari'

'Merridee' 2 W-Y
(Brogden Bulbs) Unregistered
'Kowhiri' hybrid
Perianth segments reflexed

'Merrilyn' 1 W-P
(H.A. Brown) J.N. Hancock & Co., 1955
Perianth segments plane; corona salmon pink, frilled. Mid-season to late

'Merriment' 2 Y-YOO
(S.C. Gaspar) R.J. Abernethy, 1957
'Onawe' × 'Dunkeld'
Perianth segments golden yellow, of good substance; corona shallow, reddish orange, with a distinct band of gold at base

'Merrivale' 1 W-Y
(J.N.Hancock & Co., 1983) Unregistered
'Beryl Hancock' × 'Jolly Roger'; sdlg no. 13/83H
Perianth segments broadly ovate, creamy white, regular; corona creamy yellow, with lime yellow at rim, mouth expanded and frilled. Tall. Very early

'Merriwa' 2 W-? (b)
(Mrs M.Moorby) Mrs M.Moorby, 1956

'Merry' 3 (a)
(pre-1955)

'Merry Amber' 2 W-P
(J.N. Hancock & Co., c.1966) Unregistered
Sdlg × 'Tea Cake'

'Merry Bells' 5 W-Y
(Oregon Bulb Farms) Oregon Bulb Farms, 1958
Fls 2-3 per stem; perianth segments broadly ovate or oblong, prominently mucronate, pure white, spreading, overlapping one-third; the inner segments more nearly ovate, less obviously mucronate; corona short funnel-shaped, lemon yellow, with mouth straight and sometimes 3-lobed, even, rim crenate

'Merry Child' 8 Y-Y
(Helen A. Grier, 1968) Helen A. Grier, 1980

'Helios' 8 Y-Y × *N. jonquilla*; sdlg no. 63/2/68
Fl. 45 mm wide; perianth segments light canary yellow; corona deep yellow or light orange. Early to mid-season. Scented. Resembles an earlier-flowered 'Canary Bird'

'Merrydew'
(G.H. Johnstone, pre-1960) Unregistered

'Merry Dick' 3 W-? (b)
(C. Dawson, pre-1926)

'Merry England' 3 W-? (b)
(G. Zandbergen-Terwegen, pre-1936)

'Merry-go-round'
(C. Dawson, pre-1908)

'Merry-go-round'
(G. Lewis, pre-1940)

'Merryhill' 2 W-O
(Mrs R.O. Backhouse, pre-1921)
Corona rich apricot orange. Mid-season. Syn. 'Lady Jinks'. AM(Haarlem) 1935

'Merry King' 3 Y-R
(S.A. Free) S.A. Free, 1961
'Market Merry' × 'Chungking'
Fl. 95 mm wide; corona orange-red, frilled. Mid-season

'Merry Lass' 2 W-? (b)
(Cartwright & Goodwin, pre-1910)

'Merry Mac' 2 Y-O
(J.N. Hancock & Co., 1968) Unregistered
Fl. large; perianth segments vivid yellow, smooth; corona orange (28A). Mid-season

'Merry Maid' 3 W-YYO
(Barr & Sons, pre-1907)
Corona deeply ribbed, bright yellow, with dark orange at rim. Tall. Late. Sweetly scented

'Merry Maidens' 6 Y-Y
(R.V. Favell, 1941) R.M. Favell, 1959
Fl. 70 mm wide. Early. Resembles a smaller-flowered *N. cyclamineus*

'Merrymaker' 4 Y-O
(M.J. Jefferson-Brown, pre-1978) M.J. Jefferson-Brown, 1985
Perianth and other petaloid segments rich golden yellow; corona segments glowing orange. Resembles 'Celebration' but with the segments more nearly acute

'Merryman'
(?C. Bourne, pre-1914)

'Merrymeet' 4 Y-YOO
(Mrs H.K. Richardson) du Plessis Bros, 1989
'Falaise' × 'King's Ransom'; sdlg no. 698
Fl. 105 mm wide. Late

'Merry Mood' 2 W-? (b)
(A.H. Ahrens) J.S. Leitch, 1955

'Merry Pilgrim' 2 W-Y
(D.V. West, pre-1935)

'Merry Princess' 2 W-W
(R.H.Glover, pre-1993) Unregistered

'Merry Princess'
Unregistered
Pollen parent of 'Olive Horsham'

'Merry Thought' 1 W-W
(Sir C.H. Cave, pre-1928)

'Merry Widow' 2 W-P
(J.L. Richardson) J.L. Richardson, 1958
'Templemore' × 'Salmon Trout'
Fl. 92 mm wide; perianth segments very broadly ovate, blunt and slightly mucronate, spreading or very slightly reflexed, plane, smooth, overlapping half or more; the inner segments narrower, slightly inflexed, lightly ribbed; corona funnel-shaped, loosely ribbed, soft salmon pink (28D), very lightly frilled, with rim crenate and narrowly flanged. AM(e) 1962

'Merton' 2 W-Y
(C.E. Radcliff, 1942) J.M.Radcliff, 1956
'Mitylene' × 'Dawnglow'
Perianth segments pure white, of thick substance; corona bowl-shaped, yellow

'Merula' 2 Y-O
(de Graaff Bros, pre-1932)
Perianth segments soft yellow; corona widely expanded, frilled. AM(Haarlem) 1932

'Mervyn' 1 Y-Y
(Cartwright & Goodwin, pre-1908)
'Emperor' × *N. obvallaris*
Fl. soft yellow; perianth segments of firm substance; corona cylindrical, with rim flanged

'Merwestein' 2 Y-Y
(G. Lubbe & Sons) G. Lubbe & Sons, 1985
Perianth segments primrose yellow; corona widely expanded, buttercup yellow, with lemon yellow at rim. Mid-season

'Meryl' 2 Y-R
(C.E. Radcliff, 1932)
'Pink'un' × 'Fotis'

mesatlanticus = *N. romieuxii* var. *mesatlanticus*

'Mesdag' 1 (a)
(G. Lubbe & Son, pre-1927)

'Mesdag' 9
(G. Lubbe & Son, pre-1927)

'Mesha' 1 W-W
(Barr & Sons, pre-1920)
Perianth segments somewhat twisted; corona creamy white, frilled

'Message' 1 Y-Y
(de Graaff Bros) de Graaff Bros & van Konynenburg & Co., 1959
Fl. 114 mm wide. AM(Haarlem) 1959

'Messale' 2 W-? (b)
(J.W.A. Lefeber, pre-1938)

'Messenger' 2 Y-O
(A.M. Wilson, pre-1944)
Perianth segments deep yellow; corona expanded, reddish orange, frilled. Mid-season

'Messier' 2 (a)
(G. Lubbe & Son, pre-1943)

'Messina' 3 W-R
(P.D. Williams, pre-1908)
Fl. rounded, more than 83 mm wide; perianth segments broadly ovate, blunt, snow white, spreading, overlapping half; the inner segments spathulate; corona almost disc-shaped, scarlet, with rim crenate. Resembles an improved 'Lucifer'. *(Gulval)AM(m) 1935

'Meta' 2 W-? (b or c)
(J.R. Pearson & Sons, pre-1933)

'Metaphor' 3 Y-YYO
(Alister Clark, pre-1936)
Corona paler than the perianth, with reddish orange at rim

'Meteor' 3 W-YYR
(H.J. Poole Sr, pre-1927)
Corona with scarlet at rim

'Meteorite' 2 (a)
(R. Crews, pre-1949)

'Metherell' 4 W-Y
(Mrs H.K. Richardson) du Plessis Bros, 1989
Sdlg no. 624
Fl. 95 mm wide. Late

'Methven' 9 W-YYR
(A.G. Bull, pre-1927)

'Metis' 2 Y-O
(A.H. Ahrens, pre-1949)
Syn. 'Courtesy'

'Metresse' 8 W-?
(pre-1807)

'Metrolite' 2 Y-R
(J.N. Hancock & Co., 1963) Unregistered
Perianth segments rounded, light yellow; corona bright orange-red. Mid-season

'Metropole' 1 Y-Y
(pre-1927)
Perianth segments rich primrose; corona deep orange gold. Resembles 'Milana' in form

'Metropolis' 1 Y-Y
(pre-1950)
Early

'Metropolis' 1 W-W
(D.S. Bell) D.S. Bell, 1957
'Big Ben' × 'Petsamo'
Fl. pure white

'Metropolitan' 8 Y-Y
(pre-1846)

'Metropolitan' 2 W-O
(G.A. Uit den Boogaard) Warnaar & Co., 1958
Perianth segments very broadly ovate, blunt, prominently mucronate, spreading, overlapping half or more; the inner segments less prominently mucronate, with margins wavy; corona widely expanded, narrowly ribbed, light orange, with mouth split in places and overlapping, rim irregularly and closely notched and crenate. AM(Haarlem) 1957, FCC(Haarlem) 1958

'Metta' 2 W-WWP
(C.E. Radcliff, 1941) R. Hyde, 1958
Sdlg × 'Dawnglow'

'Metua' 2 (a)
(C.A. Latta) C.A. Latta, 1956

'Meursault' 11a W-W
(J. Gerritsen & Son, 1974) J. Gerritsen & Son, 1986
'Sancerre' hybrid
Perianth segments ivory white; corona opening yellowish white, becoming paler in tone. Early. Resembles an earlier-flowered 'Sancerre'

'Meus' 1 Y-Y
(Sir J.S. Arkwright, pre-1934)
Fl very pale clear primrose yellow, tinged green

'Mevrouw Gerrevink' 2 Y-O
(G. Lubbe & Son, pre-1931)
Perianth segments clear yellow; corona deep orange, frilled. AM(Haarlem) 1931. ?The same as 'Henriette Gerrevink'

'Mew Stone' 2 W-O
(Mrs H.K. Richardson) du Plessis Bros, 1989
'Rose Caprice' open pollinated; sdlg no. 141
F. 108 mm wide; corona opening yellow-orange, becoming rich buff orange. Late. Sunproof. Resembles 'Romance' in corona shape

'Mexico' 2 Y-O
(J.L. Richardson, pre-1943)
'Alight' × 'Rustom Pasha'
Fl. about 105 mm wide; perianth segments ovate, blunt, slightly mucronate, brilliant yellow 8A, spreading, sometimes reflexed in upper half, with margins slightly wavy, overlapping one-third; the inner segments narrower, slightly inflexed; corona long cup-shaped, lightly ribbed, vivid orange 28B, with mouth straight, minutely frilled. AM(e) 1949

'Mexico City' 2 Y-O
(W.J. Toal) Ballydorn Bulb Farm, 1967
'Mexico' × 'Ceylon'

'Mezzo' 1 (a)
(R.H. Bath, pre-1931)

'Mia' 2 W-P
(J.N.Hancock & Co., 1984) J.N.Hancock & Co., 1997
Sdlg no. A/84H
Perianth segments ovate; corona funnel-shaped, delicate pink, with mouth flared. Late

'Miami' 3 Y-Y
(A.M. Wilson, pre-1913)
Fl. 83 mm wide; perianth segments pale primrose yellow, smooth; corona very shallow, lemon yellow

'Mi-Carême' 2 (a)
(Mrs R.O. Backhouse, pre-1921)

'Michael' 1 Y-Y
(?P.D. Williams, pre-1907)
Fl. large; perianth segments soft yellow, slightly inflexed; corona slender, richer in tone than the perianth. AM 1917

'Michaela' 2 Y-YRR
(G. Lewis) D.S. Bell, 1955
Perianth segments bright yellow; corona deep red, paling to gold at base, frilled. See also 'Mickaela'

'Michael Angelo' 2 W-YYO
(P.D. Williams, pre-1910)
Perianth segments overlapping half; corona expanded, ribbed, canary yellow, with reddish orange at rim, frilled

'Michael Forth'
Unregistered
Seed parent of 'Lord Gort'

'Michael Foster' 1 W-Y
(E. Leeds, pre-1877)
Perianth segments sulphur white; corona large, rich yellow, of thick texture. Syn. Pseudonarcissus Bicolor 'Michael Foster', Pseudonarcissus Bicolor 'Sulphurescens'

'Michael Mee' 3 W-? (b)
(J.E. Exley, pre-1950)

'Michael Morris' 6 W-YYP
(J.A. Morris) J.A. Morris, 1963
Fl. 67 mm wide; corona pale citron yellow, with a narrow band of pink at rim, frilled. Mid-season

'Michael P.Williams' 2 Y-YYO
(Alister Clark, pre-1940)
Fl. large, of smooth texture; perianth segments pale yellow; corona golden yellow, with orange at rim. Syn. 'M.P.Williams'

'Michaels Gold' 2 Y-Y
(A.J.R. Pearson, 1980) A.J.R. Pearson, 1990
'Camelot' × 'Daydream'; sdlg no. 81/20/F1
Fl. rounded, 105 mm wide, golden yellow; perianth segments very broad, rounded at apex, with slight white mucro, spreading, plane or concave, smooth and of good substance, overlapping half or more; the inner segments more often plane, very broad-shouldered at base; corona cylindrical or somewhat funnel-shaped, lightly ribbed, darker in tone than the perianth, with green noticeable in tube, mouth more strongly ribbed, straight, a little frilled, rim irregularly crenate and slightly flanged. Mid-season. Varies between Divs 2 and 1

'Michael Spry' 2 W-YYP
(J.N. Hancock & Co., c.1958) Unregistered
'Jean Anderson' × 'Mabel Taylor'

'Michelle' 2 W-WWP
(Brian S. Duncan) R.A. Brand, 1993
'Coral Light' × 'High Society'; sdlg no. 1165
Fl. 105 mm wide; corona bowl-shaped, white, with a broad band of deep pink at rim. Mid-season

'Michigan' 2 (a)
(Mrs R.O. Backhouse, pre-1921)
Syn. 'Norma'

'Michilinda' 2 W-? (b)
(Mrs F.S. Foote, pre-1941)

'Mickaela' 2 Y-YRR
Syn. of 'Michaela'

'Mickey' 6 Y-Y
(Glenbrook Bulb Farm) Glenbrook Bulb Farm, 1997
N. rupicola × *N. cyclamineus*
Fl. 30 mm wide, brilliant yellow 7B; perianth segments narrowly oval, slightly reflexed; corona cylindrical, with mouth 6-lobed and rim very slightly flanged. Dwarf. Mid-season

'Mico' 2 Y-O
(J.N. Hancock & Co., 1959) Unregistered

micranthus = *N. dubius* var. *micranthus*

'Midas' 3 W-YYR
(J.C. Williams, pre-1913)
Fl. rounded; perianth segments ivory white; corona shallow, widely expanded, bright yellow, with brilliant red at rim

'Midas Gold' 1 Y-Y
(John R.Reed) John R.Reed, 1995
'Temple Gold' × 'Midas Touch'; sdlg no. 83-36-1
Fl. 96 mm wide, intense golden yellow; perianth segments broadly ovate; corona with rim slightly flanged. Early

'Midas Touch' 1 Y-Y
(T. Bloomer) Rathowen Daffodils, 1977
Probably 'Camelot' × 'Arctic Gold'; sdlg no. 1/119/65
Fl. deep gold; perianth segments broadly ovate; corona with rim dentate and slightly flanged. Mid-season. Resembles a larger-flowered 'King's Ransom' of deeper colour and smoother texture

'Midday' 1 Y-Y
(O. Ronalds, pre-1955) Unregistered

'Midday Sun' 3 Y-R
(T. Bloomer) Rathowen Daffodils, 1982
'Perimeter'? × ('Chungking' × 'Air Marshal'?); sdlg no. 287
Perianth segments deep golden yellow; corona deep orange-red. Mid-season

'Middleton Favourite' 1 W-W
(J. Pope, pre-1913)

'Middlewood' 1 W-W
(F.E. Board) F.E. Board, 1965
'Petsamo' × 'Rashee'; sdlg no. 617

'Mider' 3 W-? (b)
(M.P. Williams, pre-1949)

'Midget' 3 W-? (b)
(Sir C.H. Cave, pre-1908)

'Midget' 7 W-W
(A.M. Wilson, pre-1915)
N. jonquilla × 'The Fawn'

Fl. pure white

'Midget' 1 Y-Y
G.J. Mooyman, 1984
Selection from *N. nanus*
Perianth segments narrowly ovate, light greenish yellow 5C, with slight white mucro, inflexed or somewhat spreading, overlapping at base only; corona cylindrical, smooth, vivid yellow 12A, mouth flared, ribbed, rim irregularly and deeply notched and a little incurved. Very early

'Midia' 3 W-YYR
(The Brodie of Brodie, *c*.1927)
'Lady Superior' × 'Sunstar'
Perianth segments pure white; corona yellow, with vivid scarlet at rim

'Midinette' 7
(A.H. Ahrens, pre-1951)

'Midlothian' 2 Y-R
(G. Lewis) D.S. Bell, 1955
Corona deep red, mouth expanded, rim frilled

'Midnight' 3 Y-R
(Clive Postles, 1980) Clive Postles, 1992
'Sabine Hay' × 'Achduart'; sdlg no. 3-35-76
Fl. 105 mm wide; perianth segments ovate, dark yellow, flushed orange; corona bowl-shaped, red, with rim dentate. Mid-season. Resembles a much deeper-coloured 'Achduart'

'Mid-Season Gold' 1 Y-Y
(?P. van Deursen, pre-1936)

'Midshipman' 3 (a)
(P.D. Williams, pre-1931)

'Mid Way' 3 W-? (b or c)
(Mrs E. Murray)

'Mifanwy' 3 W-WWO
(G.H. Engleheart, pre-1923)
Fl. 82 mm wide, facing slightly downwards; perianth segments creamy white, regular, overlapping a quarter; corona very shallow bowl-shaped, pale cream, faintly tinged blue at base, with apricot at rim. Mid-season to late

'Migdale' 2 Y-O
(D.C. MacArthur) D.C. MacArthur, 1985
'Chungking' self pollinated; sdlg no. E838
Perianth segments broadly ovate, blunt, brilliant yellow 9C, spreading, with margins sometimes "thumbed", overlapping half; the inner segments a little inflexed, with margins slightly wavy; corona shallow, widely expanded, finely ribbed, light orange (23A), with mouth straight, frilled. Mid-season. Scented

'Mighty Atom' 3 (a)
(Cartwright & Goodwin, pre-1916)

'Mighty Atom' 2 Y-R
(G. Lewis) D.S. Bell, 1955

'Mighty Fine' 2 W-P
(J.M. Radcliff, 1953) P. Phillips, 1966
Fl. 108 mm wide; corona bright pink. Mid-season

'Mignon' 8 Y-?
(pre-1759)

'Mignon' 8 W-WWO
(M. van Waveren & Sons, pre-1913)
Poetaz
Fl. rounded; perianth segments very broad, white, spreading or slightly reflexed; corona shallow, creamy white, with deep scarlet-orange at rim

'Mignonne' 8 Y-Y
(pre-1798)
Fl. golden yellow

'Mignonne' 2? W-Y
(W. Backhouse, pre-1869)
Perianth segments narrow, acute, pure white; corona canary yellow. Syn. Leedsii 'Mignonne'. Was "absorbed" into 'Fanny Mason'

'Mignonne' 8 W-O
Syn. of 'Medio Luteo Mignonne'

'Migoelet' 2 W-? (b)
(de Graaff Bros, pre-1936)
AM(Haarlem) 1936

'Migoli' 3 W-?O
(J.L.Richardson, pre-1946)
'Carnsore' × 'Arklow'
Late

'Mikado' 1 Y-Y
(Barr & Sons, pre-1905)
Fl. golden yellow; perianth segments twisted; corona large, expanded, ribbed. Resembles a refined 'M.J.Berkeley'

'Mikado' 2 W-O
(J.L. Richardson) J.L. Richardson, 1959
'Kilworth' × 'Arbar'
Corona very shallow bowl-shaped, reddish orange

'Mike Pollock' 8 Y-O
(Rosewarne EHS) Cornwall Area Bulb Growers Association, 1996
'Matador' × *N. jonquilla*; sdlg no. 77/72/2
Fls 4-8 per stem, 50 mm wide; perianth segments broadly ovate, brilliant greenish yellow 6B, with slight white mucro, spreading, a little concave, overlapping

half; the inner segments a little narrower, somewhat inflexed, with margins wavy; corona bowl-shaped, ribbed, deep orange. Mid-season

'Mikie' 3 W-GYR
(M.A. de Navarro) M.A. de Navarro, 1959
'Picador' × 'Thomas Hardy'
Fl. 64 mm wide. Late. Resembles a large-flowered 'Sea Green'

'Milady' 2 Y-Y
(D.S. Bell, 1965) D.S. Bell, 1975
'Barbara Allen' self pollinated
Fl. 117 mm wide, greenish lemon yellow. Mid-season

'Milan' 9 W-GYR
(A.M. Wilson, pre-1932)
Fl. 83 mm wide; perianth segments very broad in outline, blunt or rounded at apex, prominently mucronate, spreading, concave, with margins incurling at apex; the inner segments truncate, only very slightly mucronate, slightly inflexed, somewhat uneven of surface and creased at margin, sometimes folded along midrib; corona almost disc-shaped, closely ribbed, brilliant yellow 9C, with green at base and red (35A) at rim, mouth split in places and overlapping, wavy, with rim closely and minutely notched. 2n=14. AM(e) 1953

'Milana' 1 Y-Y
(Australian or New Zealand origin, pre-1927)
Fl. deep velvety gold; perianth segments broad

'Milang' 2 (a)
(H.A. Brown, pre-1938)

'Milanion' 1 Y-Y
(G.L. Wilson, pre-1935)
Parentage involving 'Tipperary Tim' and 'Royalist'
Fl. 115 mm wide; perianth segments broad, brilliant yellow 12B, spreading, smooth, overlapping half; corona cylindrical, slightly ribbed, a little darker in tone (12A) than the perianth, mouth expanded and frilled, rim flanged and dentate. Late. PC 1947, AM(e) 1949, *AM(g) 1956

'Milant' 1 Y-Y
(Australian or New Zealand origin, pre-1942)

'Mild' 1 W-Y
(P. Phillips) P. Phillips, 1968

'Mildred' 2 or 3 W-? (b or c)
(pre-1910)

'Milemcro' 2 Y-O
(Colin Crotty, 1980) Colin Crotty, 1990
'Checkmate' × 'Falstaff'; sdlg no. 12-75
Fl. 100 mm wide; perianth segments roundish, deep yellow, smooth, deeply overlapping; corona bowl-shaped, bright orange. Early

'Milend' 2 Y-O
(A. Overton) A. Overton, 1960
Fl. rounded; corona reddish orange, frilled. See also 'Millend'

'Milestone' 2 Y-P
(G.E. Mitsch) G.E. Mitsch, 1968
'Leonaine' open pollinated; sdlg no. AS11/3
Fl. 89 mm wide; perianth segments soft pale lemon yellow; corona salmon apricot. Mid-season

'Milete' 1 (a)
(de Graaff Bros, pre-1927)

'Milford' 2 W-O
(Mrs J. Abel Smith) Mrs J. Abel Smith, 1978
'Kilworth' × 'Arbar'; sdlg no. I5/12
Fl. 102 mm wide; perianth segments very broadly ovate, slightly mucronate, spreading, a little concave, with midrib showing, overlapping half; corona cup-shaped, closely ribbed, mouth expanded, rim minutely dentate. Late. Sunproof. Resembles a neater-flowered 'Kilworth' with a whiter perianth

'Milford Haven' 2 W-Y
(Mrs R.O. Backhouse, pre-1921)

'Militant' 2 Y-R
(L. Buckland, pre-1930)
Perianth segments dark yellow; corona expanded, red, frilled. AM(Haarlem) 1931

'Miliza' 2 (a)
(A.H. Ahrens, pre-1949)

'Milk and Apricots' 2 W-YYO
(O.David Niswonger) O.David Niswonger, 1996
'Precedent' × Evans sdlg N81-1 ('Chiquita' × 'Tyee'); sdlg no. 9-87
Fl. about 98 mm wide, facing down; perianth segments ovate, plane; corona bowl-shaped, pale yellow, with apricot orange at rim, frilled. Mid-season. Sunproof

'Milk and Cream' 2 W-Y
(P. van Deursen, pre-1943)
AM(Haarlem) 1943

'Milk and Honey' 4 W-Y
(W.F.M. Copeland, pre-1919)
Perianth and other petaloid segments slightly twisted; corona segments short, sulphur yellow. Mid-season. *C(g) 1936

'Milkmaid' 2 W-W
(P.D. Williams, pre-1907)
'The Fawn' × 'Maximus'
Perianth segments tinged creamy white, overlapping;

corona expanded, opening rich creamy white, becoming milk white. Mid-season. 2n=28. AM(e) 1925, *HC(g) 1930, *HC(g) 1936

'Milky Way' 1 Y-? (a or b)
(pre-1905)
Corona large, pale yellow

'Milky Way' 3 W-? (b or c)
(Cartwright & Goodwin, pre-1914)

'Milky Way' 2 W-W
(J.N. Hancock & Co., 1947) J.N. Hancock & Co., 1964
Fl. large, opening pale lime yellow, becoming creamy white

'Millais' 3 W-YYR
(A.E. Lowe, pre-1927)

'Millbrook' 2 W-YPP
(A. Robert) A. Robert, 1966
'Green Island' × 'Interim'
Fl. 108 mm wide; perianth segments pure white, with margins wavy, of good substance; corona opening clear yellow in lower half, with bright rosy salmon pink towards mouth, becoming salmon, with lighter base. Mid-season

'Millend' 2 Y-O
Perianth segments yellow; corona reddish orange, frilled. Syn. of 'Milend'

'Millenium' 1 (a)
(F.H. Chapman, pre-1923)

'Millennium' 1 Y-Y
(A. Gray) Lord Skelmersdale, 1972
'Rockery Gem' × 'Jana'
Fl. 65 mm wide; perianth segments ovate, blunt, whitish yellow, with white mucro, lightly reflexed, with margins wavy, overlapping one-third; the inner segments with margins more distinctly wavy; corona cylindrical, smooth, slightly darker in tone (9A) than the perianth, with pale tones at base, mouth with six shallow and overlapping lobes, rim flanged and obscurely crenate. Dwarf. Early. With several secondary stems. 2n=28. Resembles 'Bambi' in form

'Miller' 2 (a)
(W.A. Watts, pre-1933)

'Millerick' 1 Y-Y
(R.M. Miller) S.A. Free, 1966
Fl. 121 mm wide, deep yellow. Early

'Miller's Daughter' 1 W-? (b)
(W. Balch, pre-1933)

'Millford Haäkon' 2 (a)
(Dutch origin, pre-1926)
AM(Haarlem) 1926

'Mill Gold' 1 Y-Y
(J.A. O'More, c.1970) L.J. Chambers, 1984
'Integrity' × 'Goldcourt'; sdlg no. 72/57
Fl. 120 mm wide. Mid-season

'Millgreen' 1 Y-Y
(Rosewarne EHS, 1964) Gee Tee Bulb Co., 1985
'Golden Marvel' × 'Mulatto'; sdlg no. 64/21/1
Perianth segments acute, opening pale greenish yellow, becoming creamier in tone, slightly twisted and with margins lightly incurved, overlapping; corona brilliant greenish yellow 5B, paler at base (5C), with mouth expanded and rim deeply crenate.

'Mill Grove' 2 Y-R
(W.A. Noton) W.A. Noton, 1976
'Revelry' × 'Craigywarren'; sdlg no. 620
Fl. 85 mm wide; corona dark red. Mid-season. Resembles 'Graigywarren' in colour but with broader and smoother perianth segments

'Millicent' 5
(J.W. Barr, pre-1930)

'Millie Galyon' 2 W-R
(Frank B.Galyon) Frank B.Galyon, 1997
'Dewy Rose' × 'Pipestone'; sdlg no. DR-2-P
Fl. 95 mm wide; perianth segments broadly ovate, plane; corona straight-sided, pinkish red, frilled. Mid-season. Sunproof

'Millie Gibson' 2
(Alister Clark, 1930) J. Sharp, 1960

'Millie Price' 9 W-YYR
(G.H. Engleheart, pre-1913)
Fl. large; perianth segments overlapping; corona primrose yellow, with a narrow band of orange-red at rim. See also 'Minnie Price'

'Millionnaire' 1 (a)
(M. van Waveren & Sons, pre-1942)

'Millisle' 3 W-W
(W.J. Dunlop) W.J. Dunlop, 1957
'Portrush' × 'Foggy Dew'
Fl. white; corona almost disc-shaped, with deep green at base

'Mill Reef' 1 Y-Y
(J.L. Richardson) Mrs H.K. Richardson, 1973
'Rio d'Oro' open pollinated
Fl. deep golden yellow; perianth segments broadly ovate; corona with rim dentate and slightly rolled

'Mill Street' 3 W-? (b)
(P. van Deursen, pre-1930)
AM(Haarlem) 1930

'Mill Wheel' 1 (a)
(E.L. Jones, pre-1949)

'Milneri' 1 W-W
Syn. of 'W.P.Milner'

'Milneri' 2 W-O
Syn. of 'William Ingram'

'Milo' 1 W-W
(G.H. Engleheart, pre-1923)
Fl. white; perianth segments broadly ovate, tinged green below; corona with green at base, mouth expanded and frilled, rim widely flanged

'Milofor' 2 W-? (b)
(Miss K.M. Hinchliff, pre-1935)

'Milora' 1 W-W
(C.E. Radcliff, 1931)

'Milsom' 1 Y-Y
Syn. of 'Milson'

'Milson' 1 Y-Y
(A. Gibson, pre-1945)
'Kingscourt' × 'Goldcourt'
Fl. bright deep yellow; corona rim slightly rolled. PC(e)(NZ) 1945. See also 'Milsom'

'Miltiades' 2 Y-Y
(pre-1889)
Perianth segments clear sulphur yellow, overlapping; corona pale yellow, tinged orange

'Miltie' 1 W-Y
(Campbell Duncan) Campbell Duncan, 1956
'Sincerity' × 'Bonnington'

'Milton' 3 Y-Y
(W. Backhouse, pre-1869)
Perianth sulphur yellow. Syn. Barrii Sulphureus 'Milton'

'Milton' 9
(G. Lubbe & Son, pre-1907)

'Mimas' 3 (a)
(L. van Leeuwen & Son, pre-1931)

'Mimi' 1 W-W
(van Meerbech, pre-1925)
Perianth segments somewhat twisted, inflexed; corona creamy white, lightly frilled

'Mimi' 2 W-P
(Alister Clark, 1935) J. Sharp, 1960

'Mimico' 2 Y-Y
(pre-1885)
Perianth segments sulphur yellow

'Mimie'
(pre-1915)

'Mina' 1 W-W
(W. Jackson Sr, 1944)
'Sancia' × 'Tatia'

'Minafon' 3 (a)
(Mrs R.O. Backhouse, pre-1921)
See also 'Minaton'

'Minallo' 2 Y-R
(C.E. Radcliff, 1940)
'Lady A.Currie' × 'Cheerio'

'Minalto' 1 W-Y
(R.V. Favell, pre-1946)
'Beersheba' × 'Tunis'

'Minard' 4 W-R
(M. Zandbergen) du Plessis Bros, 1978
Fl. 86 mm wide. Mid-season. Resembles a more brightly coloured 'Gay Time'

'Minaret' 1 W-Y
(Hon. Sir R.H. Rhodes, pre-1914)
Corona pale canary yellow

'Minaret' 3 W-YYR
(D.S. Bell) D.S. Bell, 1977
'Hampstead' × 'Masquerade'
Fl. 101 mm wide; perianth segments pure white; corona very shallow bowl-shaped, with red at rim

'Minaton' 3 (a)
Syn. of 'Minafon'

'Mincarlo' 1 (a)
(A.A. Dorrien Smith, pre-1949)
Resembles 'Emperor' but is of improved substance

'Mindai' 2 (a)
(H.A. Brown, pre-1936)

'Minder' 1 Y-Y
(Jackson's Daffodils) Jackson's Daffodils, 1986
'Yarley' × 'Comal'; sdlg no. 33/77
Perianth segments vivid yellow 9A; corona cylindrical, slightly darker (14B) than the perianth, with mouth more or less even. Early

'Minder' 1 Y-Y
(J.N. Hancock & Co., 1973) Unregistered

'Mindful' 1 W-W
(M.P. Williams, pre-1938)

'Mindie' 3 W-? (b)
(T. Batson, pre-1914)

'Mine d'Or' 8 Y-Y
(pre-1798)
Fl. golden yellow

'Mineola' 1 W-W
(E.C. Powell, pre-1948)
? × 'Corinth'

'Minerva' 8 W-W
(pre-1829)
Syn. ?'Minerve'

'Minerva' 8 Y-O
(pre-1850)
Corona bright orange

'Minerva' 9 W-YYR
(G.H. Engleheart, pre-1910)
Perianth segments reflexed; corona pale chrome yellow, with cinnabar red at rim

'Minerva' 2 W-P
(J.L. Richardson) Mrs H.K. Richardson, 1968
'Rose Caprice' × 'Infatuation'

'Minerve' 8 W-W
(pre-1835)
Early. ?The same as 'Minerva'

'Mineus' 6 W-W
(E.H.G. Thurston, pre-1933)

'Ming' 3 W-Y
(R.O. Backhouse, pre-1930)
Perianth segments deeply overlapping; corona expanded, pale creamy yellow. Mid-season. 2n=28. *HC(g) 1936

'Minglow' 1 (a)
(Barr & Sons, pre-1943)

'Mingrelienne' 8 Y-Y
(pre-1798)
Fl. golden yellow

'Mingy' 3 W-? (b)
(C.E. Radcliff, 1930) Parr's Nurseries, 1958

'Minicycla' 6 Y-Y
(F.H. Chapman, pre-1912)
N. cyclamineus × *N. asturiensis*
Fl. 40 mm wide, golden yellow; perianth segments narrowly ovate or oblong, with white mucro, a little reflexed, slightly overlapping; corona cylindrical, smooth, mouth lightly ribbed and a little flared, 6-lobed, with rim closely notched. Dwarf. 2n=14. AM 1913. See also 'Minicycle'

'minicycle' 6 Y-Y
Syn. of 'Minicycla'

'Minidaf' 1 Y-Y
(J. Gerritsen & Sons) J. Gerritsen & Sons, 1970

'Minikin' 3 W-R
(A.O. Roblin, 1942)
'Minuet' × 'Seville

'Minikin' 2 (a)
(D.H.L. Corrigan, pre-1949)

'Minikin' 3 W-GYR
(Murray W.Evans) Murray W.Evans, 1969
?'Snowball' × 'Interim'
Perianth segments slightly reflexed; corona small, with a fine line of red at rim

N. minimus Haworth = *N. minor* var. *minimus*

N. minimus hort. = *N. asturiensis*

'Minion' 2 W-W or Y
(A.O. Roblin, 1938)
'Mary Blewitt' hybrid

'Miniskirt' 7 Y-Y
(A. Gray) A. Gray, 1967
N. rupicola × sdlg 95F (6 Y-Y)
Fl. 25 mm wide; perianth segments greenish yellow (4D); corona darker in tone (4B). Mid-season

'Minister Colijn' 1 Y-Y
(E.H. Krelage & Son, pre-1925)
AM(Haarlem) 1925, FA(Haarlem) 1927

'Minister Karnebeek' 1 (a)
Syn. of 'Minister van Karnebeek'

'Minister Pierson' 8
(R.A. van der Schoot, pre-1930)
AM(Haarlem) 1931

'Minister Ruys' 1 W-? (b)
(H. Prins, pre-1929)

'Minister Talma' 1 Y-Y
(A. Philippo & Sons, pre-1920)
Fl. bright yellow; corona expanded, ribbed, frilled, with rim flanged. Syn. 'Talma'

'Minister van Karnebeek' 1 (a)
(Warnaar & Co., pre-1930)
Syn. 'Minister Karnebeek'

'Minister Verschuur' 2 W-O
(P. van Deursen, pre-1933)
Perianth segments sulphur white; corona heavily frilled. AM(Haarlem) 1933

'Miniver' 2 W-W
(A.M. Wilson, pre-1940)

'Minkie' 1 (a)
(R.H. Bath, pre-1923)

'Minna Watson' 2 W-? (b)
(pre-1955)

'Minnehaha' 9
(G.H. Engleheart, pre-1923)

'Minnie' 2 W-? (b)
(M. van Waveren & Sons, pre-1900)
AM 1900

'Minnie' 6 Y-Y
(Glenbrook Bulb Farm, pre-1992) Unregistered
N. rupicola × *N. cyclamineus*; sdlg no. 44/88

'Minnie Hume' 3 W-W
(W. Backhouse, pre-1869)
'Albicans' × N. radiiflorus
Fl. white; perianth segments ovate, blunt, prominently mucronate, spreading, with midrib showing, overlapping at base only; the inner segments only very slightly mucronate, with margins wavy; corona short funnel-shaped, ribbed, opening lemon yellow, becoming white, with mouth straight and frilled. Resembles 'Queen of England'. Syn. Leedsii 'Minnie Hume', Leedsii 'Vincenti Minnie Hume'. "Absorbed" 'Queen of England'

'Minnie Price' 9 W-YYR
Syn. of 'Millie Price'

'Minnie Warren' 1 W-W
(pre-1886)
Variant of *N. nanus*
Fl. creamy white; perianth segments narrowly ovate, inflexed, twisted, overlapping at base only; corona cylindrical, with mouth flared and shallowly lobed, rim notched . Dwarf. Slightly scented

'Minnis Bay' 3 W-? (b)
(J.O. Sherrard) C.M. Sandison, 1955

'Minnow' 8 Y-Y
(A. Gray) A. Gray, 1962
Fls 2 or more per stem, 27 mm wide; perianth segments very broadly ovate, rounded at apex, mucronate, light greenish yellow 4C, spreading, plane, regular, overlapping one-third to a half; the inner segments somewhat inflexed, with margins recurved; corona shallow cup-shaped, smooth, vivid yellow 9A, with mouth straight, rim lightly crenate. Dwarf. Mid-season. 2n=18. Resembles 'Canaliculatus' in habit and a dwarf Poetaz in form and colour. A variant now widely cultivated has whitish perianth segments at maturity and should probably receive a distinct cultivar name

'Minola' 5
(Barr & Sons, pre-1923)

N. minor Linnaeus 13 Section Pseudonarcissus
(?'The Lesser Clipt Trunk Daffodil"). AGM 1994
    var. ***minor***
    var. ***conspicuus*** Haworth
    var. ***cuneiflorus*** Willkomm & Lange =
        N. pumilus
    var. ***minimus*** (Haworth) Pugsley
    var. ***nanus*** Herbert = *N. nanus*
    var. ***parviflorus*** (Jordan) A.Fernandes =
        N. parviflorus
    var. ***provincialis*** (Pugsley) A.Fernandes =
        N. provincialis
    var. ***pumilus*** (Salisbury) A.Fernandes =
        N. pumilus

N. minor Brotero = in part *N. pumilus*, in part *N. asturiensis*

N. minor Haworth = *N. jonquilla* var. *minor*

'Minor' 2
(E. Leeds, pre-1877)
Syn. Incomparabilis Albidus 'Minor'

'Minor' 2 ?-O
(E.Leeds, pre-1877)
Corona rich yellow, stained orange. Syn. Incomparabilis Leedsii 'Minor'

'Minor' 2 Y-Y
(E.Leeds, pre-1877)
Syn. Incomparabilis Sulphureus 'Minor'

'Minor' 2 W-Y
(E.Leeds, pre-1877)
Perianth segments ovate, reflexed at base, inflexed towards apex, with margins wavy, sometimes twisted, separated; corona cylindrical, short, ribbed, mouth more strongly ribbed, straight or a little incurved, even, with rim minutely crenate. Syn. Nelsonii 'Minor'

'Minor' 3 ?-Y
(?E. Leeds, pre-1877)
Corona lemon yellow. Syn. Leedsii 'Minor'

'Minor' 3 Y-Y
(pre-1882)
Perianth segments sulphur yellow. Syn. Barrii Sulphureus 'Minor'

'Minor'
Syn. of *N. jonquilla* var. *minor*

'Minor' 2 Y-Y
Syn. of 'Bella'

'Minor' 3 W-Y
Syn. of 'Little John'

'Minor' 8 W-O
Syn. of 'Medio Luteo Minor'

'Minore' 1 W-W
(A.O. Roblin) A.O. Roblin, 1956
'Bonnington' × 'Tain'

minoriformis = *N. pseudonarcissus* var. *minoriformis*

'Minor Monarque' 8 W-Y
N. papyraceus sdlg?
Fls 8-13 per stem, star-shaped, 28-38 mm wide, of poor substance; perianth segments narrowly ovate, prominently mucronate, spreading, overlapping at base only; the inner segments less prominently mucronate, with margins wavy or incurved; corona cup-shaped, with mouth straight and wavy. Very early. Syn. "Straws", 'Stars'

'Minor Plenus' 4 Y-Y
Syn. of 'Flore Pleno'

'Minoru' 1 W-? (b)
(Cartwright & Goodwin, pre-1916)

'Minster' 1 W-W
(F.D.B. Cobb, pre-1953)

'Minster Lodge' 3 Y-Y
(Mrs J. Abel Smith) Mrs J. Abel Smith, 1977
'Green Howard' × 'Aircastle'; sdlg no. P4/02
Fl. 82 mm wide, pale yellow; perianth segments broadly ovate, rounded at apex, slightly truncate, a little reflexed, overlapping half; the inner segments only slightly narrower; corona shallow bowl-shaped, densely ribbed, with mouth expanded and in places split and overlapping, rim notched and crenate. Late. 2n=27. Resembles 'Green Howard' but with the perianth remaining yellow

'Minster Lovell' 3 W-? (b)
(J.M. de Navarro, pre-1952)
'Corofin' × 'Matapan'
Perianth segments very broadly ovate, rounded at apex, mucronate, spreading, a little concave, smooth, with midrib showing, overlapping half or more; the inner segments narrower, somewhat truncate, minutely mucronate, a little inflexed, with margins sometimes incurled at apex; corona very shallow bowl-shaped, lightly ribbed, with a broad band of colour at rim, mouth with three overlapping lobes, loosely frilled

'Minstrel' 5
(G.H. Engleheart, pre-1910)

'Minstrel' 2 Y-Y
(pre-1939)

'Minstrel Boy' 1 W-W
(J.L. Richardson, pre-1937)

'Mint Cup' 3 W-GWY
(Carncairn Daffodils) Carncairn Daffodils, 1983
Wootton sdlg × 'Shantallow'; sdlg no. W1/2
Fl. 85 mm wide; corona white, with grey-green at base and yellow at rim. Late

'Minter' 2
(Alister Clark, 1950) J. Sharp, 1960

'Mint Julep' 3 Y-GYY
(Brian S. Duncan) Rathowen Daffodils, 1981
'Pontresina' open pollinated × 'Woodland Prince'; sdlg no. 345
Perianth segments greenish yellow; corona yellow, with green at base

'Mint Mist' 9 W-GGR
(Mrs M.S. Yerger) Mrs M.S. Yerger, 1987
'Sea Green' open pollinated; sdlg no. 76 J 6
Fl. 72 mm wide; corona disc-shaped, brilliant yellow-green 150B, with a slightly brighter tone at base (154B) and a broad band of orange-red (32B). Late. Sweetly scented. Resembles a larger-flowered 'Andrew Marvel' or a large and earlier-flowered 'Sea Green' or 'Perdita' without the line of white between green and red in the corona

'Minuet' 9 W-R
(F.H. Chapman, pre-1923)
'Kingsley' × 'Socrates'
Corona dark red. 2n=21

'Minute Waltz' 6 YYW-WWY
(G.E. Mitsch, 1977) R. & E. Havens, 1992
'Killdeer' open pollinated; sdlg no. MO11/2
Fl. 30 mm wide; perianth segments broad, lemon yellow, with a band of white at base, reflexed; corona cylindrical, becoming whitish, with lemon yellow at rim, mouth slightly flared and a little frilled. Midseason

***N. minutiflorus* Willkomm 13 Section Jonquilla**

'Minx' 2 W-YYO
(C. Smith, pre-1907)
Perianth segments creamy white; corona large, ribbed, with a broad band of intense reddish orange at rim

'Minx' 3 W-GYR
(Murray W.Evans) Murray W.Evans, 1969
'Snowball' × 'Interim'

'Mio Asklon' W-W
(pre-1953)

'Mirabeau' 2 W-P
(H.R. Bulman, pre-1962) Unregistered
Perianth segments of strong substance; corona large, coppery pink. Early

'Mirabel' 2 W-W
(R.H. Bath, pre-1907)

'Mirabelle' 3 W-YYO
(J. Gerritsen & Son) J. Gerritsen & Son, 1969
'Petillant' hybrid

'Mirabilis' 8 W-O
(pre-1850)

'Miracle' 2 Y-R
(Barr & Sons, pre-1932)
Perianth segments clear deep lemon yellow, overlapping; corona large, vivid orange-red, frilled

'Miracle' 2 Y-YYO
(G. Lewis, 1935) Parr's Nurseries, 1958
Corona shallow, expanded, with deep reddish orange at rim

'Mirage' 2 W-W
(J.L. Richardson, pre-1937)
HC(p) 1986

'Miralgo' 2 Y-O
(J.L. Richardson) Mrs H.K. Richardson, 1963
('Narvik' × 'Ceylon') × 'Firecracker'
Corona deep reddish orange, frilled. Sunproof

'Miramar' 3 Y-R
(The Brodie of Brodie, c.1930)
'Beacon' × 'Sunstar'
Perianth segments pale yellow; corona deep red

'Miramare' 2 or 3 W-W
(E.H. Krelage & Son, pre-1927)
Fl. large; perianth segments pure white; corona creamy white. Tall. AM(Haarlem) 1927

'Miranda' 1 W-W or Y
(Barr & Sons, pre-1907)
Coona opening primrose yellow, becoming milk white, with rim crenate

'Miranda' 9
(G.H. Engleheart, pre-1908)

'Miranda' 2 Y-R
(J.S. Leitch) J.S. Leitch, 1957

'Mirandella' 2 (a)
(Mrs R.O. Backhouse, pre-1921)

'Mirbon' 3 W-YYP
(G.J. Phillips, 1981) G.J. Phillips, 1992
'Cherryrim' × 'Audubon'; sdlg no. 76-18-5
Fl. 95 mm wide; corona lemon yellow, with a narrow band of rich pink at rim, mouth widely expanded. Tall. Late

'Mireen' 2 Y-Y
(W. Jackson Jr) W. Jackson Jr, 1968
'Kala' × ('Butta' × 'Hymis'); sdlg no. 76/60

'Mireille' 2 W-? (b)
(M. van Waveren & Sons, pre-1938)

'Miriam' 2 W-? (b or c)
(P.D. Williams, pre-1907)

'Miriam Barton' 3 Y-Y
(E. Leeds, pre-1877)
Perianth segments pale primrose yellow; corona canary yellow. Syn. 'Vincenti Miriam Barton', Barrii Albidus 'Miriam Barton'

'Mirka' 1 (a)
(C.G. van Tubergen, pre-1947)

'Miro' 2 Y-O
(J.T. Gray, pre-1949)
Corona shallow, widely expanded, deep reddish orange

'Miro' 2 Y-O
(Konynenburg & Mark, 1957) Konynenburg & Mark, 1965
'Etude' × ('David Copperfield' × 'Floriment')
Fl. 90 mm wide; perianth segments brilliant yellow 8A; corona strong orange 25A. Early

'Mirova' 3 W-? (b)
(D. Blanchard, pre-1948)

'Mirra' 2 W-W
(W. Jackson Jr, 1958) Unregistered
'Kapitah' × 'Zaire'; sdlg no. 36/58

'Mirrabooka' 2 W-W
(Jackson's Daffodils, 1981) Jackson's Daffodils, 1992
'Immaculate' × 'Rhapsody'; sdlg no. 81/81
Fl. forming a double triangle, 110 mm wide, greenish white (155A); perianth segments broadly ovate in outline, blunt or slightly truncate, only very slightly mucronate, spreading, sometimes creased at midrib, overlapping half; the inner segments more narrowly ovate; corona funnel-shaped, smooth, with yellowish green in tube, mouth flared and

loosely frilled. Mid-season

'Mirra Donna' 2 W-P
(A. Glover)
'Pink Treasure' × 'Dear Me'

'Mirralaiur' 2 W-? (b)
(Mrs M. Moorby) Mrs M. Moorby, 1957

'Mirren' 3 Y-R
(G.W.E. Brogden) M.E. Brogden, 1959

'Mirri' 2 W-Y
(New Zealand origin, pre-1955) Unregistered 'Kingdom' hybrid
Perianth segments white, of thick texture; corona pale citron buff

'Mirth' 1 W-Y
(G.E. Mitsch, pre-1952)
Sdlg no. 37S1/1
Perianth segments milk white, overlapping; corona rich yellow. Early

'Mirza' 2 W-O
(J.T. Gray, pre-1949)
Perianth segments pure white; corona straight, deep apricot

'Mischief' 2 Y-O
(H.A. Brown, 1936) J.N. Hancock & Co., 1960
Corona reddish orange, frilled

'Misdemeanour' 2 W-W
(G.L. Wilson, pre-1952)

'Mishelle' 2 Y-R
(J.S. Leitch) J.S. Leitch, 1956

'Mishra' 11a W-P
(D.Munro, 1982) J.N.Hancock & Co., 1997
'My Word' × 'Giltol'
Perianth segments acute, creamy white, spreading; corona split, the six segments overlying and almost covering the perianth segments, biscuit pink. Mid-season

'Mismay' 3 Y-R
(G.L. Wilson, 1950) R.W. Ward & Son, 1960
Corona deep red. Late. Resembles 'Market Merry' but with a paler perianth

'Misquote' 1 Y-Y
(Jackson's Daffodils, 1979) Jackson's Daffodils, 1989
'Akala' × 'Warcom'; sdlg no. 14/79
Fl. forming a double triangle, 105 mm wide, vivid yellow 12A; perianth segments very broadly ovate, blunt, with prominent white mucro, spreading, smooth, overlapping half; the inner segments a little inflexed, with margins slightly wavy; corona cylindrical, narrow, smooth, shading to a darker yellow at mouth (14B), with mouth slightly flared and lightly frilled. Early

'Miss Alice' 1 (a)
(S.A. van Konynenberg & Co., pre-1907)

'Miss Aukland' 2 (a)
(J.H. Braithwaite, pre-1930)

'Miss Barklay' 3
(pre-1930)
?The same as 'Mrs Barclay'

'Miss Beatty' 2 Y-O
(H.A. Brown, pre-1933)
Perianth segments slightly reflexed; corona shallow, widely expanded, bright reddish orange, frilled

'Miss Clinch' 1 W-W
(Cartwright & Goodwin, pre-1907)
Late

'Miss Dainty' 5
(Sir A.P.W. Thomas, pre-1930)

'Miss D.Carter' 2 W-?
Syn. of 'Dorothy Carter'

'Miss Deloraine' 1 W-Y
(T.H. Piper, 1951)
'Grayling' × 'Lorinna'

'Miss Earhardt' 2 W-? (b)
(P. van Deursen, pre-1942)

'Miss Ellen Terry' 1 W-Y
(S.A. van Konynenberg & Co., pre-1907)
Corona clear yellow. AM(Haarlem) 1908

'Miss E.M.Bowling' 2 W-O
(W.B. Cranfield, pre-1918)
'Anthea' × 'Lord Kitchener'
Corona soft apricot orange, flushed pink. AM(e) 1918

'Miss Furbelow' 3?
(pre-1948)

'Miss Glory' 2 W-Y

'Miss Helen O'Hara' 1 W-W
Syn. of 'Helen O'Hara'

'Miss H.M.White' 8 W-W
Syn. of 'Miss White'

'Miss Hutchinson'
(A.W. Tait, pre-1907)

'Mission' 3 W-O
(J.S. Leitch) J.S. Leitch, 1968
Fl. 95 mm wide; corona reddish orange

'Mission' 2 W-W
(R.H.Glover)
'Easter Moon' × 'Lady Slim'

'Mission Bells' 5 W-W
(G.E. Mitsch, 1971) Grant Mitsch Novelty Daffodils, 1984
'Silver Bells' open pollinated; sdlg no. GO27/1
Fls 1-3 per stem, 75 mm wide, ivory white; perianth segments broadly ovate, spreading or a little reflexed, somewhat creased, overlapping one-third; the inner segments with margins wavy; corona long cup-shaped, with yellow-green showing in tube, mouth straight, wavy. Mid-season. Resembles a healthier and more readily propagated 'Silver Bells'

'Mission Impossible' 11a W-P
(G.E. Mitsch, 1976) R. & E. Havens, 1987
('Accent' × ['Wild Rose' × 'Hillbilly']) × ('Pink Frost' × 'Accent'); sdlg no. 2L34/1
Perianth segments very broadly ovate, fairly prominently mucronate, slightly reflexed, creased, overlapping half; the inner segments smoother; corona split to base, the six segments half as long as the perianth segments and opposite and closely overlying them, deeply bi-lobed, bright pink, thickly frilled. Mid-season

'Miss Julia Hill' 2 W-? (b or c)
(Australian or New Zealand origin, pre-1927)

'Miss Kitty' 2 W-P
(G.W.Tarry) Carncarin Daffodils, 1995
'Vital' × 'Sweet Georgia'; sdlg no. 1/8/85
Fl. 110 mm wide; perianth segments very broadly ovate in outline, blunt or rounded at apex, slightly mucronate, creamy white, spreading, smooth, overlapping half; the inner segments more narrowly ovate, shouldered at base; corona light yellowish pink, with mouth ribbed and widely expanded, rim shallowly crenate. Mid-season

'Miss Lanyon' 3 W-? (b)
(E & J.C. Martin, pre-1931)

'Miss Leeds' 2 (a)
(P.D. Williams, pre-1907)

'Miss Lilian Cave' 4
(W. & J. Brown, pre-1907)

'Miss Marton' 2
(pre-1942)

'Miss Mary' 2 or 3 W-W
(P.D. Williams, pre-1907)

Perianth segments acute; corona widely expanded, with rim closely and deeply notched, as if fringed

'Miss Matty' 2 W-? (b or c)
(E.H.G. Thurston, pre-1935)
Dwarf. See also 'Miss Natty'

'Miss Natty' 2 W-? (b or c)
Syn. of 'Miss Matty'

'Miss Neilson' 2 Y-Y
(E. Leeds, pre-1877)
Perianth segments sulphur yellow; corona pale yellow. Syn. Incomparabilis Sulphureus 'Miss Neilson'. Was "absorbed" into 'John Bull'

'Miss New Zealand' 2 W-Y
(C. Goodson, pre-1927)
Perianh segments white; corona pale buff yellow

'Miss Nightingale' 8 W-O
Syn. of 'Florence Nightingale'

'Miss Nina Cave' 4
(pre-1908)

'Missouri' 2 Y-O
(G. Zandbergen-Terwegen, pre-1945)
AM(Haarlem) 1949

'Miss Prim' 2 W-W
(G.L. Wilson, pre-1923)

'Miss Prim' 2 Y-Y
Syn. of 'Miss Primm'

'Miss Primm' 2 Y-Y
(C.K.Dorwin, 1976) Unregistered
'Arctic Gold' × 'Fine Gold'
Fl. brilliant greenish yellow 3A; perianth segments smooth; corona cylindrical, with mouth slightly expanded and rim entire. Early. See also 'Miss Prim'

'Miss Rose Bedford' 3 W-?
(W.B.Hartland, pre-1907)
Syn. 'Rosa Bedford'

'Miss Ruffles' 1 W-W
(Oregon Bulb Farms, pre-1946)

'Miss Sato' 1 W-W
(G.P. Haydon, pre-1908)

'Miss Swanwick' 1 W-W
(pre-1915)

'Miss Ulverstone' 1 W-W
(T.H. Piper, 1953)
'White Knight' × 'Cantatrice'

'Miss Weisse' 3 W-W
(W.B. Hartland, pre-1907)
'Praecox' hybrid

'Miss White' 8 W-W
(de Graaff Bros, pre-1890)
Fls 3-4 per stem, silvery white. See also 'Miss H.M.White'

'Miss Wilcox' 1 W-? (b)
(pre-1938)

'Miss Willmott' 3 W-YYO
(C.G. van Tubergen, pre-1907)
'Ornatus' × 'Will Scarlett'
Corona large, lemon yellow, with bright reddish orange at rim. AM 1907, FCC 1911

'Missy' 5 W-GYY
(Mrs G. Link) Mrs G. Link, 1988
'Dinkie' × *N. triandrus*; sdlg no. 773-A
Corona cup-shaped, frilled. Dwarf. Late

'Mist' 2 W-W
(A.M. Wilson, pre-1930)

'Mist Glow' 2 W-P
(J.N. Hancock & Co.) J.N. Hancock & Co., 1955
Corona straight, soft pink

'Mistinguett' 2 W-? (b)
(P.D. Williams, pre-1933)

'Mistique' 2 W-W
(G.E. Mitsch) G.E. Mitsch, 1979
'Pigeon' × 'Wings of Song'; sdlg no. HH84/3
Fl. 91 mm wide; perianth segments broadly ovate, slightly truncate, minutely mucronate, reflexed, overlapping one-third to a half; the inner segments more narrowly ovate, with margins wavy; corona short funnel-shaped, ribbed, with green showing in tube, mouth straight and frilled. Late

'Mistletoe' 2 (a)
(Mrs R.O. Backhouse, pre-1921)

'Mistral' 9
(Cartwright & Goodwin, pre-1923)

'Mistral' 11a W-Y
(J. Gerritsen & Son) J. Gerritsen & Son, 1965
Perianth segments broadly ovate, slightly inflexed; corona split to base, the six segments broader than the perianth segments and almost as long, closely overlying them, ribbed, brilliant greenish yellow 5A, sometimes touched white at shoulder, bi-lobed and frilled. Early. 2n=28

'Mistress Mine' 2 W-P
(D.N.Y. Olson) D.N.Y. Olson, 1993
'Easter Moon' × 'Immaculate'; sdlg no. 82/14/1
Fl. forming a double triangle, 110 mm wide; perianth segments very broadly ovate, spreading, plane or somewhat concave, rounded at base, overlapping half; the inner segments narrower, a little inflexed; corona short funnel-shaped, very pale rose pink, fading a little with age, mouth straight, wavy, shallowly lobed, rim crenate. Late. Sunproof

'Mistress Mine' 2 W-P
Syn. of 'Shady Lady'

'Mistress Prue' 9
(pre-1908)

'Misty Dawn' 3 W-Y
(Ballydorn Bulb Farm, 1976) Ballydorn Bulb Farm, 1989
'Golden Amber' × 'Misty Glen'
Fl. 97 mm wide; perianth segments broadly ovate, acute, deeply overlapping; corona expanded, closely ribbed, pale yellow, with a darker tone at rim. Mid-season

'Misty Glen' 2 W-GWW
(F.E. Board) W.A. Noton, 1976
'Easter Moon' × 'Pigeon'; sdlg no. 294
Fl. 85 mm wide; perianth segments broadly ovate in outline, rounded at apex and slightly mucronate, spreading, sometimes creased, overlapping half; the inner segments angled at shoulder, a little inflexed, with margins wavy; corona long cup-shaped, bluish white, with green prominent at base, mouth straight, loosely frilled. Mid-season. AM(e) 1982, AGM 1995

'Misty Meadow' 7 YYW-W
(G.E. Mitsch) R. Havens, 1980
'Quick Step' × ?'Daydream'; sdlg no. H08/
Fl. 85 mm wide; perianth segments deep lemon yellow, with white at base. Late. Scented. Resembles 'High Note' but with the colours more clearly contrasting

'Misty Moon' 3 W-WOO
(G.L. Wilson, pre-1936)
'Mystic' hybrid
Perianth segments very broad in outline, blunt or squarish at apex, slightly mucronate, pure white, a little reflexed, plane, with margins sometimes munutely incurling, overlapping half; the inner segments narrower, roundish, sometimes truncate or with margins nicked at apex, spreading; corona shallow bowl-shaped, narrow, ribbed, soft pale salmon orange, with grey-white in lower half, mouth even. Late or very late. 2n=14

'Misty Morning' 2 Y-P
(G.E. Mitsch, 1978) R. & E. Havens, 1993
'Bookmark' × 'Daydream' open pollinated; sdlg no. 2N14/1

Fl. 95 mm wide; perianth segments broadly ovate, rounded at apex, soft lemon yellow, spreading, plane, smooth; corona funnel-shaped, pale pink, with mouth frilled. Mid-season. Sunproof

'Mitanni' 1 W-? (b or c)
(W. Jackson Jr, 1950)
'Leto' × 'Pinkess'

'Mitchell' 9 W-YYR
(W.F. Mitchell) A. Gray, 1973
Fl. 65 mm wide, of good substance; perianth segments somewhat reflexed, with margins incurved

'Mite' 6 Y-Y
(Sir J.A.R. Gore-Booth, c.1935) G.E. Mitsch, 1965
? *N. obvallaris* × *N. cyclamineus*
Fl. 57 mm wide; perianth segments strongly reflexed. Very early

'Mite'
(?W. Wheeler, pre-1959) Unregistered

'Mithian' 3 W-YYR
(P.D. Williams, pre-1927)
Corona yellow, with dark red at rim

'Mithra' 2 W-YYO
Syn. of 'Graffiti'

'Mithras' 2 Y-Y
(C.G. van Tubergen, pre-1929)
Fl. 108 mm wide; perianth segments sulphur yellow, overlapping half; corona buttercup yellow, with mouth expanded and frilled. Mid-season

'Mitra' 2 W-? (b)
(Barr & Sons, pre-1933)
AM(Haarlem) 1936

'Mitsuko' 2 W-P
(P. Phillips, 1964) P. Phillips, 1977
Fl. 102 mm wide; corona carrot pink. Resembles a deeper-coloured 'Profusion' of greater substance

'Mittagong' ?-P
(Alister Clark, pre-1948)

'Mitylene' 2 W-Y
(G.H. Engleheart, pre-1923)
'Beacon' hybrid
Fl. 107 mm wide; perianth segments broadly ovate, blunt, slightly mucronate, milk white, spreading, with margins a little wavy, overlapping one-third; the inner segments more narrowly ovate, acute, a little inflexed, with margins more strongly wavy; corona widely expanded, narrowly ribbed, primrose yellow, with mouth straight and wavy. 2n=28. AM(e) 1926, FCC(e) 1927, *HC(g) 1930, *AM(g) 1931, AM(Haarlem) 1933, *AM(g) 1936

'Mitzi' 6 W-W
Syn. of 'Mitzy'

'Mitzy' 6 W-W
(A. Gray) A. Gray, 1955
N. cyclamineus × 'Rockery White'
Perianth segments narrowly ovate or oblong, fairly prominently mucronate, yellowish white, reflexed, with margins incurved, very slightly overlapping at base; the inner segments narrowly ovate, a little twisted; corona cylindrical, narrow, lightly ribbed, opening primrose yellow, becoming white or yellowish white, mouth slightly flared, more strongly ribbed, 6-lobed, the lobes notched and dentate. See also 'Mitzi'

'Mizuda' 3 Y-O
(Mrs B.T. Simpson) Mrs B.T. Simpson, 1966
Fl. 108 mm wide; corona reddish orange. Mid-season. Resembles 'Rangitane' in colour

'Mizzen Head' 9 W-GYY
(Ballydorn Bulb Farm, 1985) Ballydorn Bulb Farm, 1996
'Cantabile' × 'Moyle'
Fl. 75 mm wide; perianth segments opening greenish ivory, becoming white; corona small, lemon yellow, with green at base. Late

'M.J.Berkeley' 1 Y-Y
(W. Backhouse, pre-1869)
'Maximus' hybrid
Fl. rich deep yellow; perianth segments ovate, acute, not noticeably mucronate, inflexed, with margins wavy or twisted, overlapping at base only; the inner segments sometimes more strongly inflexed towards apex, with margins recurved; corona cylindrical, mouth very widely expanded, heavily ribbed, 6-lobed, with rim deeply notched and crenate. Early. 2n=14. Resembles a large-flowered 'Maximus'. Syn. Pseudonarcissus Major 'M.J.Berkeley'

'Mlas' 3 W-Y
(J.M. Radcliff, 1974) Mr & Mrs P.J. Radcliff, 1988
Sdlg no. 26
Perianth segments very broadly ovate, blunt, slightly mucronate, spreading, somewhat concave, with margins incurling at apex, smooth, with midrib showing, overlapping half; the inner segments a little inflexed; corona ribbed, mouth expanded and frilled, with very deeply overlapping lobes. Very late. Resembles 'Pacific Lady' but is of better substance and has a smoother perianth

'M.Magdalina de Graaff' 3 W-O
Syn. of 'Maria Magdaline de Graaff'

'M.M.de Graaff' 3 W-O
Syn. of 'Maria Magdaline de Graaff'

'Moa' 1
(pre-1914)

'Moana' 2 (a)
(S.C. Gaspar) R.J. Abernethy, 1957

'Moana Marie' 2 Y-R
(D.S. Bell) D.S. Bell, 1979
'Checkmate' × 'Rupee'
Fl. 115 mm wide; corona bowl-shaped, red. Mid-season. Resembles an improved and larger-flowered 'Checkmate'

'Moanaroa' 2 Y-R
(A.B. Davey, 1966) A.B. Davey, 1978
'Sun Chariot' × 'Malta'; sdlg no. 1/13/61
Fl. 91 mm wide. Mid-season. Resembles a larger 'Narvik' with a better flower

'Moawhanga' 4 W-Y
(Koanga Daffodils, pre-1997) Unregistered

'Moawhango' 4 W-Y
(Koanga Daffodils) Koanga Daffodils, 1995
Fl. 90 mm wide; perianth and other petaloid segments broadly ovate, milk white; corona segments brilliant yellow 15C. Early

'Mobjack Bay' 1 Y-Y
(Raymond W. Lewis) Mrs Raymond W. Lewis, 1989
'Arctic Gold' open pollinated; sdlg no. FR75/27
Fl. clear yellow. Mid-season. Resembles 'Arctic Gold'

'Moby Dick' 11a W-GWW
(John R.Reed) John R.Reed, 1997
'Panache' × 'Colblanc'; sdlg no. 84-140-1
Fl. 117 mm wide, pure white; perianth segments ovate, smooth; corona split to base, the six segments opposite and closely overlying the perianth segments, with green at base. Dwarf. Mid-season

'Moccas' 1 W-? (b)
(Mrs R.O. Backhouse, pre-1921)

'Mockingbird' 7 Y-W
(G.E. Mitsch) G.E. Mitsch, 1971
'Binkie' × *N. jonquilla*
Fl. 70 mm wide; perianth segments lemon gold. Mid-season. 2n=21. Resembles 'Dickcissel' but with broader perianth and flared corona

'Mod' 2 Y-R
(P. & G. Phillips) P. & G. Phillips, 1978
'Border Chief' × 'Hot Stuff'
Fl. 108 mm wide. Early to mid-season. Resembles a more strongly coloured 'Border Chief'

'Modbury' 2 Y-O
(Brian S. Duncan) du Plessis Bros, 1989
'Richhill' × 'Border Chief'; sdlg no. 421
Fl. 106 mm wide; perianth segments saffron yellow; corona frilled. Early. Sunproof

'Mode' 2 Y-R
(Colin Crotty) Unregistered
Sdlg no. 24-75

'Model' 2 or 3 W-Y
(W. Backhouse, pre-1869)
Perianth segments sulphur white; corona canary yellow, stained orange. Syn. Barrii Albidus 'Model'

'Model' 3 W-YYO
(W. Backhouse, pre-1869)
Fl. rounded; perianth segments broadly ovate or somewhat roundish in outline, blunt or rounded at apex, mucronate, clear white, spreading, with midrib showing, overlapping one-third; the inner segments only very slightly mucronate, a little inflexed; corona bowl-shaped, ribbed, lemon yellow, with a narrow band of orange at rim, frilled. Syn. Burbidgei 'Model', Burbidgei 'Sulphureus Model'. "Absorbed" 'Topsy'

'Model' 3 W-? (b or c)
(F.W. Parkinson, pre-1936)

'Modern Art' 2 Y-O
(W.F. Leenen) W.F. Leenen, 1973
Fl. rounded, 90 mm wide; perianth segments very broad, truncate, prominently mucronate, whitish yellow, spreading or slightly reflexed, overlapping two-thirds; the inner segments equally broad, less prominently mucronate; corona broad, shallow, with many shorter extra growths beneath, often split to base, with the segments deeply bi-lobed, tightly frilled. Late. Sunproof

'Modern Time' 1 Y-Y
(W.F. Leenen) W.F. Leenen, 1971
Fl. 120 mm wide. Mid-season to late

'Modern Times' 2 (a)
(L. van Leeuwen & Son, pre-1938)

'Modesta' 11a Y-Y
(J. Gerritsen & Son, 1951) J. Gerritsen & Son, 1961
Fl. 90 mm wide; perianth segments pale yellow; corona primrose yellow. Mid-season. 2n=30

'Modest Maid' 2 W-? (b)
(R.H. Bath, pre-1931)

'Modest Maiden' 2 W-P
(Brian S. Duncan) Rathowen Daffodils, 1976
'Rosario' × 'Rose Royale; sdlg no. 44
Corona deep pink, with a paler tone outside. Mid-season. Resembles 'Rose Royale'. Syn. 'Modesty'

'Modesty' 3 W-Y
(W. Backhouse, pre-1869)

Perianth segments inflexed; corona lemon yellow. Syn. Leedsii 'Modesty'. Was "absorbed" into 'Maria Magdaline de Graaff'

'Modesty' 2 W-? (b or c)
(Australian or New Zealand origin, pre-1927)

'Modesty' 2 W-P
Syn. of 'Modest Maiden'

'Modish' 4 W-R
(E.W. Cotter) E.W. Cotter, 1968
'Gay Time' × 'Bryher'
Fl. rounded, about 100 mm wide; corona vivid scarlet

'Modoc' 1 Y-Y
(G.E. Mitsch) G.E. Mitsch, 1971
'Galway' × 'Saint Keverne'
Fl. 103 mm wide

'Modulation' 2 Y-P
(G.E. Mitsch) G.E. Mitsch, 1976
'Accent' × 'Daydream'; sdlg no. 2H1/2
Fl. 103 mm wide; perianth segments pale lemon; corona apricot pink. Mid-season. Resembles 'Milestone' but with more evenly distributed colour and the corona more widely flared

'Modulux' 2 W-Y
(P. & G. Phillips, 1968) P. & G. Phillips, 1978
Sdlg no. 2B-12.
Fl. forming a double triangle, 98 mm wide; perianth segments very broadly ovate, blunt, fairly prominently mucronate, a little reflexed, concave, smooth, regular, overlapping half; the inner segments spreading; corona shallow funnel-shaped, smooth or lightly ribbed, pale yellow, with a grey-green cast at base and brilliant yellow 9C at rim, mouth widely expanded, 3-lobed, frilled. Mid-season. Resembles 'Ceres' but with a less obviously lobed corona

'Moe' 3 W-R
(C.A. Nethercote) T. Morrison, 1960
Perianth segments ivory white; corona ruby red

'Mogador' 2 W-W
(G.H. Engleheart, pre-1914)
Fl. pure white; perianth segments ovate, blunt, a little inflexed, overlapping at base only; the inner segments more nearly acute; corona funnel-shaped, creamy white on opening, with mouth slightly flared and loosely frilled

'Mogul' 2 Y-O
(J.T. Gray, pre-1937)

'Mohave' 2 (a)
(A.M. Wilson, pre-1948)

'Mohawk' 3 W-? (b)
(pre-1910)

'Mohawk' 1 (a)
(J.T. Gray, pre-1938)

'Mohawk' 2 W-Y
(Murray W.Evans, 1967) Murray W.Evans, 1977
Sdlg × 'Accent'; sdlg no. K-38/2
Fl. 105 mm wide. Mid-season

'Mohican' 3 W-YYO
(Mrs R.O. Backhouse, pre-1903)
Perianth segments with a stain of lemon yellow at midrib becoming stronger towards base; corona expanded, rich golden yellow, with scarlet-orange at rim. Somewhat resembles sibling 'Sunrise'. AM 1903

'Mohua' 2 (a)
(J.T. Gray, pre-1951)

'Moidore' 2 (a)
(G.H. Engleheart, pre-1913)

'Moidore' 4 Y-Y
(R.C. Gordon) R.C. Gordon, 1964
Fl. 115 mm wide; perianth segments light yellow; corona golden yellow. Mid-season. Resembles 'Golden Ducat' in form

'Moiki' 2 W-Y
(J.S. Leitch) J.S. Leitch, 1968
Fl. 115 mm wide; corona bright lemon yellow

'Moina' 3 W-WWO
(C.E. Radcliff, pre-1938)
'Mystic' × 'Pink'un'
Fl. about 95 mm wide; perianth segments roundish, sulphur white, smooth, overlapping; corona bowl-shaped, white, tinged yellow, with greenish tones at base and reddish orange at rim (30B and 30C), tightly frilled. 2n=28. AM(e) 1945

'Moindah' 2 (a)
(R.M. Miller, pre-1951)
Syn. 'Firebrand'

'Moira' 3 (a)
(G.H. Engleheart, pre-1916)

'Moira O'Neill' 1 W-Y
(G.H. Engleheart, pre-1923)
Fl. 100 mm wide; perianth segments creamy white, spreading, overlapping one-third; corona lemon yellow, with mouth somewhat expanded and rim rolled

'Moira Shearer' 2 W-YYO
(Konynenburg & Mark) Konynenburg & Mark, 1963
'General MacArthur' × (['Frederike' × 'Mimosa'] ×

['Dandy'? × 'Red Bird'])
Fl. 95 mm wide; perianth segments greenish white; corona vivid yellow 13A, rim with strong orange 25A at rim. Late

'Mokalua' 1 W-W
(J.L. Richardson, pre-1961) Unregistered
'Ambassador' × 'Himalaya'

'Moldau' 3 W-Y
(Konynenburg & Mark) Konynenburg & Mark, 1962
'Cleopatra' hybrid
Fl. 105 mm wide; corona vivid orange-yellow 21A. Mid-season

'Molenaar' 8 Y-Y
(de Goede, pre-1927)
Perianth segments primrose yellow; corona canary yellow, neatly frilled

N. moleroi Fernández Casas 13 Section Pseudonarcissus

'Moliagul' 1 Y-Y
(T. Morrison) T. Morrison, 1960
Fl. rich yellow; corona rim flanged and dentate

'Moliere' 8 W-O
(pre-1835)
Early

'Molière' 9
(The Brodie of Brodie, pre-1916)
Corona very pale, with a narrow band of red at rim

'Molly' 2 Y-Y
(W.F.M.Copeland, pre-1914)
'Minnie Hume' × 'Monarch'
Fl. rounded, bright lemon yellow; perianth segments overlapping; corona widely expanded, frilled. Mid-season

'Molly Bawn' 3 W-? (b)
(G.L. Wilson, pre-1923)

'Molly Bryan' 1 W-? (b)
(West & Fell, pre-1938)

'Molly Ryley' 2 W-?W
(D.R. Acheson, pre-1937)
Corona slender

'Molly Walsh' 2 Y-O
(C.O. Fairbairn, 1948) L.M. Saunders, 1960
'Stoic' × 'Aranjuez'

'Molong' 1 Y-Y
(C.E. Radcliff, *c.*1966) Unregistered
'Golden Torch' × 'Roundabout'

'Mol's Hobby' 11a Y-Y
(J.W.A. Lefeber, 1947) J.W.A. Lefeber, 1960
Fl. 95 mm wide; perianth segments very broad in outline, rounded at apex or sometimes truncate, overlapping half; corona deeply split, the six segments half the length of the perianth segments and opposite and closely overlying them, ribbed, bi-lobed, heavily frilled. Mid-season

'Molski' 1 (a)
(G.T.C. Pearce, pre-1939)

'Moltema' 1 W-P
(C.E. Radcliff, 1941) J.M.Radcliff, 1956
'Pinkie' × 'Dawnglow'

'Molten Gold' 1 Y-Y
(S.J. Bisdee, pre-1939)

'Molten Lava' 3 Y-YYR
(G.E. Mitsch and R. & E.Havens, 1977) G.E. Mitsch and R. & E.Havens, 1987
'Merlin' open pollinated; sdlg no. MO13/1
Fl. rounded; perianth segments very broad, truncate, clear yellow, with slight white mucro, reflexed, smooth, overlapping half; the inner segments narrower, rounded at shoulder, less strongly reflexed; corona shallow bowl-shaped, lightly ribbed, yellow, with a broad band of bright red at rim, mouth straight, split in places and overlapping, frilled, with rim crenate. Late. Resembles 'Merlin' in corona

'Mombassa' 2 (a)
(Mrs R.O. Backhouse, pre-1921)

'Momentum' 3 W-YYR
(D.S. Bell) D.S. Bell, 1979
'Bramble Hill' × 'Norval'
Fl. 102 mm wide; corona very shallow bowl-shaped, yellow, with a broad band of red at rim. Mid-season

'Momus' 1 Y-Y
(P.L.A. Pouw & Sons) P.L.A. Pouw & Sons, 1987
'Carlton' × 'Raffael'
Perianth segments vivid yellow 12A; corona broad, darker in tone (7A) than the perianth. Early

'Mona' 9
(G.H. Engleheart, pre-1914)

'Monaco' 2 W-O
(J.L. Richardson, pre-1937)
Perianth segments very broadly ovate, blunt, prominently mucronate, pale creamy white, stained yellow at base, spreading, plane, with margins sometimes incurling at apex, smooth, overlapping one-third; the inner segments more narrowly ovate, angled at shoulder, only very slightly mucronate, a little inflexed, with margins wavy; corona shallow bowl-shaped, ribbed, deep apricot orange, with mouth expanded

and loosely frilled. Mid-season. AM(e) 1938

'Mona Davis' 2 Y-O
(de Graaff Bros, pre-1931)
Corona deep orange. AM(Haarlem) 1931

'Monaghan' 1 Y-Y
(W.J. Dunlop) W.J. Dunlop, 1965
Fl. dark golden yellow

'Mona Kenny' 2 W-P
(Brian S.Duncan) Mrs J.M.Baker, 1996
'Gracious Lady' × Bloomer sdlg ('Infatuation' × 'Gem of Antrim'); sdlg no. 1277
Fl. 108 mm wide; perianth segments ovate, slightly reflexed; corona funnel-shaped, apple blossom pink, with a paler tone at rim, mouth expanded, rim entire. Mid-season to late. Sunproof

'Monal' 2 Y-R
(G.E. Mitsch) G.E. Mitsch, 1976
('Armada' × 'Paricutin') × 'Falstaff'; sdlg no. G65/3
Fl. 108 mm wide; perianth segments broadly ovate, blunt, rich golden yellow, with slight white mucro, spreading, concave, with margins incurling at apex, somewhat creased, overlapping one-third to a half; the inner segments a little narrower, slightly inflexed, more strongly creased; corona funnel-shaped, smooth or lightly ribbed, deep orange-red, with mouth straight and a little frilled, rim crenate. Early. Resembles a much larger 'Falstaff'

'Mona Lisa' 1 W-W
(R.H. Bath, pre-1923)

'Mona Lisa' 2 W-W
(F.E. Board) M.J. Jefferson-Brown, 1965
'Chinese White' × 'Pigeon'
Corona pure white. Mid-season

'Monalto' 2 (a)
(H.A. Brown, pre-1939)

'Mon Ami' 3 W-YYO
(J.N. Hancock & Co.) J.N. Hancock & Co., 1977
Sdlg no. 65/68
Fl. 150 mm wide; corona brilliant yellow 13C, with orange-yellow (17B) at rim. Early to mid-season

'Monarch' 1 Y-Y
(Barr & Sons, pre-1891)
'Emperor' hybrid
Fl. rich yellow; perianth segments broadly ovate, blunt, mucronate, a little inflexed, twisted or with margins wavy, overlapping one-third; the inner segments narrower, more strongly inflexed; corona cylindrical, broad, with mouth expanded and strongly ribbed, rim flanged and deeply crenate

'Monarch' 8 W-Y
Syn. of 'Grand Monarque'

'Monarchist' 1 W-? (b)
(D.H.L. Corrigan, pre-1949)

'Monash' 1 Y-Y
(J.N. Hancock & Co., 1947) J.N. Hancock & Co., 1964
'Carisbrooke' × 'Cloth of Gold'
Fl. golden yellow. Mid-season. Resembles a paler 'Carisbrooke'

'Monaster' 2 (a)
(F.H. Chapman, pre-1933)

'Monaughty' 2 (a)
(A.M. Wilson, pre-1950)

'Monaveen' 2 (a)
(R. Hyde) R. Hyde, 1957

'Mon Cheri' 2 W-P
(P.Q.M.Pennings) P.Q.M. Pennings, 1983
Perianth segments very broad, blunt, fairly prominently mucronate, creamy white, spreading, a little concave, overlapping half; the inner segments narrower and more nearly ovate, somewhat creased, with margins wavy and sometimes nicked; corona very widely expanded, smooth, orange-pink, mouth loosely ribbed, sometimes deeply split and deeply overlapping, irregularly frilled, with rim crenate

'Moncorvo' 7 Y-Y
(J.W. Blanchard, 1976) J.W. Blanchard, 1986
N. jonquilla × *N. rupicola* subsp. *watieri*; sdlg no. 71/3B
Fls 2-3 per stem; perianth segments pale yellow; corona slightly darker in tone. Late. Dwarf

'Mondaine' 2 W-P
(G.L. Wilson) F.E. Board, 1956
(['Mitylene' × 'Evening'] × 'Foyle') × 'Irish Rose'

'Mon Désir' 1 Y-Y
(C.J. Stijnman, pre-1952)
TGA(Haarlem) 1952

'Mondial' 11a W-YYW
(J. Gerritsen & Son) J. Gerritsen & Son, 1984
Perianth segments ivory white; corona segments light greenish yellow 4C, with ivory white at rim. Mid-season

'Mondo' 1 W-Y
(West & Fell, pre-1938)
Perianth segments pure white

'Mondragon' 11a Y-O
(J. Gerritsen & Son) J. Gerritsen & Son, 1973
Fl. 105 mm wide; perianth segments very broadly

ovate, blunt, brilliant greenish yellow 6C, with prominent white mucro, spreading or somewhat reflexed, plane, overlapping half; the inner segments more usually spreading, with margins wavy and sometimes distorted at shoulder; corona split to base, the six segments half as long as the perianth segments and opposite and closely overlying them, squarish at apex, ribbed, orange, deeply frilled. Mid-season

'Monee' 2 W-W
(J.N. Hancock & Co., c.1965) Unregistered
'Truth' × 'Engaging'

'Moneyglass' 3 W-O
(W.J. Dunlop, pre-1949)
'Isola' × 'Sunstar'
Corona deep reddish orange. Late

'Moneymaker' 1
(pre-1930)

'Moneymaker' 2 Y-Y
(W.F. Leenen) W.F. Leenen, 1980
Fl. 120 mm wide; perianth segments light greenish yellow 4C; corona vivid yellow 14B. Early

'Money Moon' 4 Y-Y
(J.B. Roozen, pre-1943)
?'Van Waveren's Giant' sport
AM(Haarlem) 1943

'Moneymore' 2 Y-R
(W.J. Dunlop) W.J. Dunlop, 1960
'Workman' × 'Kellswater'
Perianth segments golden yellow; corona dark crimson-red

'Mongleath' 2 W-P
(R.A.Scamp) R.A.Scamp, 1994
'Dailmanach' × 'Accent'; sdlg no. 149
Fl. 105 mm wide; perianth segments very broadly ovate, chalky white, slightly convex; corona rosy pink, paling to base, mouth flared and frilled. Early

'Mongolia' 1 (a)
(C.G. van Tubergen, pre-1929)
AM(Haarlem) 1929

'Monica' 2 Y-R
(D.S. Bell) D.S. Bell, 1955
Perianth segments golden yellow; corona expanded, opening glowing red, becoming deeper in tone

'Monica King' 2 W-YYO
(C.A. Nethercote, pre-1957) Unregistered
Perianth segments snow white; corona yellow, with a broad band of bright orange at rim. Late

'Monique' 2 W-OOR
(Mrs R.O. Backhouse, pre-1921)

Perianth segments overlapping. AM(Haarlem) 1936, FA(Haarlem) 1939

'Monitor' 2 W-WWR
(G.E. Mitsch, 1971) G.E. Mitsch, 1982
'Precedent' × 'Audubon'; sdlg no. G10/1
Fl. 90 mm wide; corona opening yellow, becoming white, with tomato red at rim, frilled

'Monksilver' 3 W-W
(F.E. Board) W.A. Noton, 1976
'Easter Moon' × 'Pigeon'
Fl. 108 mm wide; corona pure white, with dark green at base. Mid-season

'Monkstown' 2 Y-?
(Ballydorn Bulb Farm) Ballydorn Bulb Farm, 1970

'Monkton' 2 (a)
(F.D.B. Cobb, pre-1954)

'Monocacy' 1 W-Y
(E.C. Powell, pre-1946)
'Royalist' × 'Godolphin'

N. × *monochromus* P.D.Sell 13 = *N. cyclamineus* de Candolle × *N. pseudonarcissus* Linnaeus

'Monogram' 2 (d)
(R. Crews, pre-1949)
Syn. 'Tasman'

N. monophyllus (Durieu de Maisonneuve) T..Moore = *N. cantabricus* subsp. *monophyllus*

'Monopole' 1 W-Y
(G. Lewis, pre-1940)
'Lemon Giant' × 'Beersheba'
Corona soft lemon

'Monopoly' 1 W-Y
(D.S. Bell) D.S. Bell, 1980
'David Bell' × 'Dawn Gold'
Fl. 105 mm wide, opening self yellow; perianth segments soon becoming pure white. Early

'Mon Plaisir' 8 W-Y
(van Zonnefeld Bros & Philippo, pre-1928)
Poetaz
Perianth segments pure white

'Mons'
(?Sir A.P.W. Thomas, pre-1915)

'Monseigneur Poels' 2 W-? (b)
(J.W.A. Lefeber, pre-1940)

'Monseigneur Westerwoudt' 2 W-? (b)
(E. Oostdam, pre-1939)

'Monsignor' 1 (a)
(R.H. Bath, pre-1927)

'Monsoon' 1 W-Y
(D.S. Bell) D.S. Bell, 1962
Fl. 110 mm wide; corona narrow, with mouth widely expanded and regularly frilled. Mid-season. Resembles 'Sincerity' but with the perianth segments more rounded

N. monspeliensis Jordan & Fourreau = *N. tazetta* subsp. *lacticolor*

'Monstrosus' 1 Y-Y
Syn. of 'Hume's Giant'

'Montagna' 2
(pre-1926)

'Montague' 3 (a)
(pre-1914)

'Montalto' 2 Y-R
(Carncairn Daffodils) Carncairn Daffodils, 1971
'Chungking' × 'Fury'
Fl. 92 mm wide; perianth segments deep yellow; corona deep red

'Montalto' 4 W-Y
(D.S. Bell, 1976) D.S.Bell, 1981
'Mount White' open pollinated
Fl. 105 mm wide; perianth and other petaloid segments white; corona segments interspersed among the centre whorls of petaloid segments, yellow. Mid-season. Resembles 'Mount White' but with differently coloured corona segments

'Montana' 1 Y-Y
(C.E. Radcliff, pre-1938)
'Golden City' × 'Gertrude Nethercote'

'Montana' 1 W-W
(J.L. Richardson) Mrs H.K. Richardson, 1969
'Canopus' × 'Queen's Counsel'
Perianth segments very broadly ovate; corona with rim rolled and dentate

'Montana' 2 W-?
Syn. of 'Montmartre'

N. montanus Ker Gawler = *N.* × *poculiformis*

'Montanus'
Syn. of *N.* × *poculiformis*

'Montaval' 1 Y-Y
(J.L. Richardson) Mrs H.K. Richardson, 1964
'Golden Rapture' open pollinated
Fl. deep golden yellow; perianth segments of thick substance; corona expanded, frilled, with rim deeply dentate. Late

'Montaz' 12
(M. Foster, pre-1905)
N. bulbocodium × *N. tazetta*

'Mont Blanc' 1 W-W
(de Graaff Bros, pre-1927)

'Mont Blanc' 1 W-W
(G.H. Johnstone) G.H. Johnstone, 1959
'Slemish' × 'Zero'
Fl. 121 mm wide; corona greenish white. Mid-season

N. × *montcaunicus* Fernández Casas 13 (parentage: *N. bulbocodium* Linnaeus × *N. pseudonarcissus* Linnaeus subsp. *eugeniae* Fernández Casas) = *N.* × *bakeri*

'Mont Cenis' 8 W-O
(Dutch origin, pre-1890)
Dwarf

'Montclair' 2 W-YYP
(Mrs J. Abel Smith, 1967) Mrs J. Abel Smith, 1985
'Dulcie Joan' hybrid; sdlg no. R2/73
Corona shallow, yellow, with pink at rim. Mid-season. 2n=28

'Monte Bello' 2 Y-O
(D.S. Bell) D.S. Bell, 1958
Fl. 108 mm wide; perianth segments rich yellow, of thick substance; corona deep red. Mid-season. Resembles 'Ceylon' but with rounder perianth segments

'Monte Carlo' 2 Y-? (a)
(P.D. Williams, pre-1928)
AM(Haarlem) 1928

'Monte Cassino' 2 W-GRR
(J.W.A. Lefeber, pre-1945)

'Montego' 3 Y-YYO
(J.L. Richardson) Mrs H.K. Richardson, 1968
'Merlin' open pollinated
Fl. small; perianth segments roundish, deep golden yellow, plane, overlapping; corona broad disc-shaped, yellow, sometimes flushed orange, with a broad band of intense orange at rim and a tinge of green at base

'Montello' 2 W-? (b)
(C.E. Radcliff, 1941)

'Montenegro' 8 W-O
(?G. van der Weyden Jobson, pre-1914)
Perianth segments creamy white; corona large. AM(Haarlem) 1914

'Monterey' 1 Y-Y
(de Graaff-Gerharda, pre-1931)
Syn. 'Golconda'. AM(Haarlem) 1930

'Monte Rosa' 1 W-W
(W.J. Eldering & Son, pre-1925)
AM(Haarlem) 1925, FA(Haarlem) 1934

'Monterrico' 4 W-O
(J.L. Richardson) Mrs H.K. Richardson, 1962
'Falaise' × 'Arbar'
Fl. large; perianth and other petaloid segments in several whorls, broadly ovate, blunt or truncate, only very slightly mucronate, pure white, of strong substance, overlapping half; the outer whorl spreading, plane; the inner whorls inflexed, with margins strongly incurled; corona segments very short, clustered among petaloid segments at centre, orange. Late. 2n=28

'Montevideo' 2 W-O
(J.L. Richardson) Mrs H.K. Richardson, 1968
'Kilworth' × 'Arbar'
Corona reddish orange

'Montezuma' 1 (a)
(K.L. Reynolds, pre-1944)

'Monticello' 1 W-Y
(W.G. Pannill) W.G. Pannill, 1977
'Ballygarvey' × 'Preamble'; sdlg no. B28/1
Fl. 105 mm wide

N. montinus Jordan = *N. pseudonarcissus* var. *montinus*

'Montlea' 1 W-W
(S.J. Bisdee, 1948)
Sdlg × 'Tain'

'Montmartre' 2 W-? (b)
(Warnaar & Co., pre-1936)
Syn. 'Montana'

'Montpellier' 2 (a)
(P.D. Williams, pre-1932)
AM(Haarlem) 1931

'Montpier' 3 W-Y
(Mary Lou Gripshover) Mary Lou Gripshover, 1997
'Angel' × 'Fellowship'; sdlg no. 84-3-G
Fl. 105 mm wide; perianth segments broadly ovate, truncate, reflexed, with broad midrib showing, overlapping half; the inner segments a little narrower, less strongly reflexed, very slightly twisted; corona bowl-shaped, loosely ribbed, light greenish yellow 3C, with a darker tone (3A) at base and rim, with the rim dentate. Late

'Mon Trésor' 8
(G. Zandbergen-Terwegen, pre-1938)

'Mon Trésor' 1 (a)
Syn. of 'Majuba'

'Montreux' 2 (a)
(pre-1954)

'Montrose' 2 W-Y
(W. Backhouse, pre-1869)
Perianth segments creamy white; corona orange-yellow. Syn. Incomparabilis Albus 'Montrose'. Was "absorbed" into 'Bertie'

'Montrose' 4 W-Y
(J.J. Abernethy, 1950) R.J. Abernethy, 1961
Fl. 102 mm wide; corona segments buff creamy yellow. Mid-season

'Montserrat Caballé' 2 W-P
(W.P.van Eeden, pre-1993) Unregistered

N. × *montserratii* Fernández Casas & Rivas Ponce 13 = *N. abscissus* (Haworth) Roemer & Schultes f. × *N. poeticus* Linnaeus

N. × *montsiccianus* Romo 13 = *N. assoanus* Dufour × *N. palearensis* Romo

'Monty' 2 Y-O
(Sir F.C. Stern, pre-1943)
Perianth segments broadly ovate, blunt, sometimes truncate, spreading, concave, sometimes with midrib raised, overlapping half; the inner segments narrower, a little inflexed, with margins wavy and sometimes nicked near mid-point; corona bowl-shaped, expanded, ribbed, reddish orange, mouth straight, tightly frilled

'Monument' 8 W-O
(pre-1829)

'Monument' 2 W-? (b)
(Sir C.H. Cave, pre-1928)

'Monument' 2 Y-Y
(Murray W.Evans) Murray W.Evans, 1969
'Festivity' × Evans sdlg (2 W-Y)

'Monyash' 2 W-? (b)
(D.B. Milne, pre-1950)

'Monza' 4 Y-R
(Brian S. Duncan) Rathowen Daffodils, 1986
'Smokey Bear' × 'Barnsdale Wood'; sdlg no. 812
Fl. rounded; perianth and other petaloid segments deep golden yellow, with slight white mucro; the outer whorl broadly ovate, spreading, overlapping half; the inner whorl almost as long, inflexed, with margins strongly incurling; corona segments short,

clustered at centre and more loosely arranged between the petaloid segments, deep orange-red, touched with yellow, frilled. Mid-season. Resembles a deeper-coloured 'Tahiti'

'Moogara' 1 W-W or Y
(C.E. Radcliff, pre-1938)
'Buttercup' × 'Renown'

'Mooltan' 3 W-Y
(pre-1949)
Corona pale lemon

'Moomba' 3 W-YYO
(Jackson's Daffodils, 1977) Jackson's Daffodils, 1987
'Placid' × 'Verona'; sdlg no. 272/77
Fl. rounded; perianth segments smooth, of good substance; corona small bowl-shaped, light yellow-green 154D, with brownish orange (163B) at rim. Late

'Moonah' 2 W-? (b)
(C.E. Radcliff, 1945) J.M.Radcliff, 1956
'Atilia' × 'Seraglio'

'Moonara' 1 Y-Y
(R. Hyde) R. Hyde, 1963
Fl. 115 mm wide; corona golden yellow. Mid-season. Resembles 'Palmino' but with a paler corona

'Moonbeam' 3 W-W
(Mrs R.O. Backhouse, pre-1901)
'Mrs Barton' × *N. poeticus* var. *recurvus*
Fl. rounded; perianth segments pure white, spreading, deeply overlapping; corona ribbed. FCC 1901

'Moonbird' 11a Y-Y
(J. Gerritsen & Son) J. Gerritsen & Son, 1969
Sdlg × 'Silvretta'
Perianth segments lemon yellow; corona deeply split, the six segments lemon yellow, with gold at rim, deeply frilled. Mid-season to late

'Moonborn' 2
(C.L. Adams, pre-1913)

'Moon Boy' 2 Y-Y
(G.L. Wilson, pre-1953)
'Binkie' hybrid

'Moon Burst' 4 Y-W
(John R.Reed) John R.Reed, 1997
'Spun Honey' × 'Bethany'; sdlg no. 82-121-1
Fl. rounded, 90 mm wide; perianth and other petaloid segments mid-yellow; corona segments interspersed, dull white. Mid-season

'Moonchild' 1 W-WYY
(J.N. Hancock & Co., 1963)

'Mooncrest' 2 W-WWY
(D.S. Bell) D.S. Bell, 1963
'Papanui Queen' × 'Green Island'
Fl. 110 mm wide; perianth segments pure white; corona shallow, widely expanded, opening apricot yellow, becoming off white, with a broad band of deep golden yellow at rim. Mid-season. Syn. 'Moon Crest'

'Moon Crest' 2 W-WWY
Syn. of 'Mooncrest'

'Moondance' 3 W-W
(G.L. Wilson, pre-1937)
('Silver Plane' × 'Distingué') × 'Rinsey'
Corona shallow

'Moon-dawn' 2 W-W
(Mrs P.M. Davis, pre-1948)

'Moon Dream' 1 Y-Y
(J.A. Hunter) J.A. Hunter, 1973
'Royalist' × 'Ulster Prince'
Fl. 115 mm wide

'Moondust' 1 Y-Y
(J.S. Leitch) J.S. Leitch, 1964

'Moon Empress' 1 Y-Y
(Ballydorn Bulb Farm, pre-1970) Unregistered
'Moon Goddess' open pollinated
Fl. 115 mm or more wide, pale sulphur yellow; perianth segments broadly ovate, overlapping; corona flared, with rim flanged. Resembles a larger 'Moon Goddess'

'Moon Empress' 2 W-W
(Broadfield's Daffodils, pre-1990) Unregistered
'Easter Moon' × 'Empress of Ireland'

'Moon-Fairies' 7 Y-Y
(S.J. Bisdee) S.J. Bisdee, 1956
'Carbineer' × *N. jonquilla*

'Moonfire' 3 Y-W
(G.E. Mitsch) G.E. Mitsch, 1972
'Aircastle' × Richardson sdlg; sdlg no. B2/1
Fl. 100 mm wide; perianth segments pale lemon, with a greenish cast; corona small, opening yellow, becoming white, with a touch of yellow at rim, frilled. Mid-season

'Moonfleet'
(?G. Lewis, pre-1940)
'Border Queen' × 'Zillah'

'Moonflight' 4 Y-Y
(G.E. Mitsch) G.E. Mitsch, 1979
'Gay Time' × 'Daydream'; sdlg no. G69/6
Fl. 96 mm wide; perianth and other petaloid segments broadly ovate, soft lemon yellow, overlapping half; the outer whorl spreading; the inner whorl usually

inflexed, sometimes with some segments more nearly spreading, with margins incurved or strongly incurved; corona segments short, deep lemon yellow, clustered at centre and among inner whorl of petaloid segments. Late. Resembles a shorter 'Discovery' with the corona segments more yellow than orange

'Moonflower' 2 Y-Y
(J.S. Leitch) J.S. Leitch, 1960
Fl. 115 mm wide, lemon yellow; perianth segments smooth, overlapping; corona slightly expanded, with rim neatly rolled. Late. Resembles 'Lemnos'

'Moongate' 6 Y-Y
(G.E. Mitsch, 1955) G.E. Mitsch, 1965
'Trousseau' × *N. cyclamineus*; sdlg no. R82/1
Fl. 89 mm wide, pale lemon yellow, becoming paler with age. Very early. Resembles 'Content' in colour

'Moonglade' 2 W-Y
(de Graaff Bros, pre-1935)
Corona shallow, widely expanded, sulphur yellow, with apricot yellow at rim. AM(Haarlem) 1935

'Moongleam' 2 W-Y
(D.S. Bell) D.S. Bell, 1959
'Idealist' × 'Artist's Model'
Fl. 108 mm wide; corona shallow, bright yellow. Mid-season

'Moonglow' 1 Y-Y
(Oregon Bulb Farms, pre-1945)

'Moon Goddess' 1 Y-Y
(G.L. Wilson, pre-1953)
'King of the North' × 'Content'
Fl. soft sulphur lemon

'Moongold' 1 Y-Y
(G.L. Wilson, pre-1929)
'Ben Alder' × 'White Knight'
Fl. deep soft lemon yellow, of waxy substance; perianth segments smooth; corona with rim rolled. Mid-season. 2n=28

'Moongold' 1 Y-Y
(D.S. Bell) D.S. Bell, 1977
'David Bell' open pollinated
Fl. 107 mm wide; corona with rim rolled. Mid-season

'Moongreen' 2 Y-Y
(Ballydorn Bulb Farm) Ballydorn Bulb Farm, 1974
'Moon Goddess' × 'Tibet'
Fl. 112 mm wide

'Moonie' 2 W-GWW
(J.N. Hancock & Co., *c*.1965) Unregistered
'Truth' hybrid
Perianth segments pure white; corona narrow, slightly frilled

'Moon Jade' 3 W-GWY
(Ballydorn Bulb Farm) Ballydorn Bulb Farm, 1983
'Moondance' hybrid
Fl. 92 mm wide. Mid-season. Resembles a better-formed 'Moondance' of stronger substance

'Moon Lady' 2 W-? (b)
(Mrs A.O. Meyrick, pre-1949)

'Moonlight' 5
(pre-1907)

'Moonlight' 1 W-Y
(P. van Deursen, pre-1922)
Resembles 'King Alfred' in form and size. FA(Haarlem) 1922

'Moonlight Sonata' 1 Y-W
(G.E. Mitsch) G.E. Mitsch, 1960
'Binkie' × ('King of the North' × 'Content'); sdlg no. P5/7
Fl. 102 mm wide, opening self sulphur yellow; corona becoming off-white, frilled. Mid-season. Resembles a later-flowered 'Spellbinder' with broader perianth segments

'Moon-Maiden' 2 W-W
(de Graaff Bros, pre-1948)

'Moonmist' 1 Y-Y
(G.E. Mitsch) G.E. Mitsch, 1958
'King of the North' × 'Content'; sdlg no. EE

'Moon Moth' 5 W-W
(Mrs G. Link) Mrs G. Link, 1986
'Green Hills' × *N. triandrus*; sdlg no. 2470-2
Fls usually 2-3 per stem; corona lemon yellow. Mid-season. Resembles a much larger and more graceful 'Dawn' of improved form

'Moon Mountain' 2 W-Y
(W.M. Spry, pre-1975) Unregistered
'Frances' × 'Stand By'
Corona creamy lemon yellow

'Moon Orbit' 2 Y-Y
(Warnaar & Co.) Warnaar & Co., 1969
'Calabar' × 'Rushlight'
Perianth segments broad, rounded at apex, greenish yellow (2C); corona brighter in tone (5D), regularly frilled. AM(Haarlem) 1969. Varies between Divs 2 and 1

'Moon Probe' 1 Y-Y
(Mrs B.T. Simpson) Mrs B.T. Simpson, 1966
Fl. 102 mm wide. Early

'Moon-raker' 3 W-? (b)
(J.R. Pearson & Sons, pre-1948)

'Moon Raker' 8 Y-YYO
(J.N.Hancock & Co., 1978) Unregistered
'Corofin' × 'Geisha'; sdlg no. 108/78H
Fls 1-2 per stem, rounded; soft sulphur yellow; corona small, yellow, with deep orange at rim. Late

'Moon Ranger' 3 Y-YYO
(Ballydorn Bulb Farm, 1975) Ballydorn Bulb Farm, 1990
Fl. 75 mm wide; perianth segments broadly ovate, sulphur yellow; corona yellow, with a wide band of reddish orange at rim and the rim entire. Mid-season to late

'Moonray' 5
(Miss E. Willmott, pre-1902)
AM 1902

'Moon Rhythm' 3 Y-O
(Ballydorn Bulb Farm, 1970) Ballydorn Bulb Farm, 1980
Fl. 105 mm wide; perianth segments lime sulphur yellow, becoming paler with age; corona reddish orange. Mid-season

'Moonrise' 1 Y-Y
(G. Lubbe & Son, pre-1947)
Fl. sulphur yellow. AM(Haarlem) 1947, FCC(Haarlem) 1948

'Moonrise' 2 W-W
(J.N. Hancock & Co., pre-1949)

'Moon River' 1 Y-Y
(J.A. Hunter) J.A. Hunter, 1970
'Kingscourt' hybrid
Perianth segments broadly ovate, blunt, yellow, with slight white mucro, spreading, overlapping half; the inner segments a little inflexed, with margins very slightly wavy; corona funnel-shaped, smooth, darker in tone than the perianth, with mouth a little expanded and wavy, rim crenate. AM(e)(NZ) 1984

'Moon Rose' 2 W-P
(L.P. Dettman) L.P. Dettman, 1982
'Langley' × 'Ann Cameron'; sdlg no. L/AC 1/81
Fl. 91 mm wide; perianth segments greenish white 155C; corona light yellowish pink 36A. Mid-season. Resembles 'Ann Cameron' but with a proportionately longer corona

'Moon Runner' 2 W-W
(Broadfield's Daffodils, pre-1990) Unregistered
'Easter Moon' × 'Rhana'

'Moon Shadow' 3 W-GYY
(Clive Postles) Clive Postles, 1992
'Goldeneye' × Lea sdlg 2-4-69; sdlg no. 3-78-79
Fl. 110 mm wide, rounded; perianth segments very broadly ovate, rounded at apex, fairly prominently mucronate, creamy white on opening, soon becoming pure white, spreading, smooth, with margins slightly incurving, and with midrib showing, overlapping half; the inner segments only a little narrower; corona broad, shallow, unfading citron yellow, with green at base, mouth loosely frilled, with deeply overlapping lobes. Mid-season

'Moonshine' 5 W-W
(de Graaff Bros, pre-1927)
N. triandrus sdlg
Fls 1-3 per stem; perianth segments ovate, acute, only very slightly mucronate, spreading or a little inflexed, overlapping a quarter; the inner segments with margins sometimes recurved at base; corona funnel-shaped, ribbed, with mouth straight, rim obscurely crenate. 2n=21. AM(Haarlem) 1930

'Moonshine' 2 Y-Y
Syn. of 'Kilbride'

'Moonshot' 1 Y-Y
(G.E. Mitsch, 1951) G.E. Mitsch, 1963
'King of the North' × 'Content'; sdlg no. M49/35
Fl. 108 mm wide, creamy lemon yellow; corona darker in tone, sometimes tinged pink, with rim dentate and slightly flanged. Mid-season

'Moonsilver' 2 W-O
Fl. 110 mm wide; perianth segments creamy white; corona vivid yellow 16A. Mid-season. Syn. of 'Silver Moon'

'Moonsong' 2 W-? (b)
(de Graaff Bros) de Graaff Bros & van Konynenburg & Co., 1956
AM(Haarlem) 1956

'Moonspell' 2 Y-W
(Ballydorn Bulb Farm) Ballydorn Bulb Farm, 1972
'Moon Boy' open pollinated
Fl. 102 mm wide

'Moonstone' 5 W-W
(Miss E. Willmott, pre-1903)
Fls facing slightly downwards; corona frilled. AM 1903. Received AM 1903 as 'The Moonstone'

'Moonstone' 2 W-? (b or c)
(D.V. West, pre-1936)
Corona becoming white with age

'Moonstruck' 1 Y-Y
(G.L. Wilson, pre-1944)
'King of the North' × 'Content'
Fl. 127 mm wide; perianth segments very broadly ovate, blunt, slightly mucronate, greenish yellow (4D), a little reflexed, plane or very slightly twisted, overlapping half; the inner segments rounded at shoulder, a little inflexed at base and reflexed towards

apex; corona cylindrical, greenish yellow (4D), with a deeper tone (4A) at rim, mouth ribbed and expanded, rim flanged and deeply notched. Resembles a larger and more striking 'Content'

'Moonta' 2 (a)
(H.A. Brown, pre-1938)

'Moon Tide' 3 Y-YOO
(Ballydorn Bulb Farm, 1970) Ballydorn Bulb Farm, 1984
Fl. 90 mm wide; perianth segments pale sulphur yellow; corona reddish orange, with a broad band of yellow at base. Mid-season. Resembles sibling 'Moon Rhythm' but with a rounded flower

'Moontide' 2 W-?
(W.M. Spry, pre-1975) Unregistered
'Green Island' × 'Hunter's Moon'
Late

'Moonvale' 1 Y-Y
(S.A. Free) Mrs S.I. Free, 1968

'Moon Valley' 2 W-GWW
(Brian S. Duncan) Rathowen Daffodils, 1983
'Easter Moon' × 'Silent Valley'; sdlg no. 528
Fl. forming a double triangle, 110 mm wide; perianth segments broadly ovate, blunt, prominently mucronate, slightly reflexed, somewhat concave, very smooth, overlapping one-third to a half; the inner segments more narrowly ovate, without apparent mucro, with margins wavy; corona cup-shaped, ice white, with green at base, mouth straight or a little expanded, neatly frilled. Mid-season

'Moonwhite' 1 W-W
(S.A. Free) S.A. Free, 1966
Fl. 102 mm wide; corona creamy white. Mid-season. Resembles 'Snowcraft' but with the corona broader at base and more creamy in tone

'Moon Wood' 2 (a)
(Mrs R.O. Backhouse, pre-1921)

'Mooreanus' 1 Y-Y
Syn. of 'Thomas Moore'

'Moorfoot' 1 W-W
(The Brodie of Brodie, c.1910)
'Madame de Graaff' × 'Weardale Perfection'

'Moorhouse' 1 W-W
(K.B. Burns, 1950) K.B. Burns, 1960
Fl. 121 mm wide, pure white; corona with rim rolled. Mid-season. Resembles a smoother textured 'Broughshane' with a narrower corona

'Moorland' 1 Y-Y
(J.N. Hancock & Co., pre-1949)

Corona deeper in tone than the perianth, with rim dentate

'Mooroopna' 2 Y-O
(J.N. Hancock & Co., 1946)

'Moorpark' 2 W-P
(C.E. Radcliff, 1944)

'Moorpark' 2 W-O
(W.M. Spry, pre-1975) Unregistered
'Aldgate' × Ronalds sdlg
Corona apricot orange. Late

'Moppet' 7
(Mrs P.M. Davis, pre-1948)

'Mopsa' 3 W-YYR
(C. Dawson, pre-1921)
Perianth segments creamy white, slightly reflexed; corona lemon yellow, with fiery red at rim

'Moque' 1 Y-Y
(W. Jackson Sr, 1946)
'Principal' × 'Matoome'

'Morag' 3 W-? (b)
(G.H. Engleheart, pre-1923)

'Morag' 1 Y-Y
(W. Jackson Sr, 1944)
'Principal' × 'Matoome'

'Morag MacDonald' 2 Y-O
(D.C. MacArthur) D.C. MacArthur, 1984
'Chungking' open pollinated
Perianth segments vivid yellow 12A; corona strong orange 24A. Mid-season

'Moralee' 4 Y-R
(Brian S. Duncan) Rathowen Daffodils, 1983
'Smokey Bear' × 'Altruist'; sdlg no. 667
Fl. 112 mm wide; perianth and other petaloid segments broadly ovate, blunt or truncate, yellow, overlapping half; the outer whorl with slight white mucro, spreading; the inner whorl a little shorter, with less noticeable mucro, inflexed; segments at centre not much shorter, irregularly arranged, strongly inflexed, with margins tightly or very tightly incurled; corona segments half the length of the petaloid segments and clustered among them at centre, more loosely arranged between the surrounding whorls, frilled. Mid-season

'Moralis' 3 W-? (b)
(J.W.A. Lefeber, pre-1938)

'Moran' 2 Y-Y
(W. Jackson Jr, 1964) Unregistered
('Moque' × 'Bene') × sdlg 16/59; sdlg no. 36/64

'Moray' 1 W-W
(The Brodie of Brodie, c.1922)
'Nevis' × 'Tenedos'; sdlg no. 68/A/18

'Morea'
(pre-1913)

'Morea' 2 Y-O
(Mrs R.O. Backhouse, pre-1921)
Perianth segments soft lemon yellow; corona frilled. AM(Haarlem) 1930

'Moree' 1 Y-Y
(A.O. Roblin, c.1966) Unregistered
'Kingscourt' × 'Melissa'

'Moreland Memory' 2 W-YYP
(S.W. Gower, pre-1960)
Corona yellow, with a line of strong yellowish pink 33C at rim. PC(e)(NZ) 1960

'Morello' 2 Y-R
(S.J. Bisdee, 1944)
'Marengo' hybrid

'Moresby' 2 W-O
(J.N. Hancock & Co., 1950) J.N. Hancock & Co., 1960
Corona reddish orange

'More So' 3 Y-R
(Mrs E. Murray)

'Moreton' 1 W-Y
(K.J. Heazlewood) K.J. Heazlewood, 1968
'Bonnington' × 'Karamudli'
Fl. 127 mm wide; corona lemon yellow. Early

'Morgan le Fay' 1 W-W
(pre-1907)

'Morgenstern' 8 W-W
(pre-1851)

'Morge Zon' 8 W-?
(pre-1807)

'Moriarty' 12 Y-Y
(M.G.Temple-Smith) M.G.Temple-Smith, 1995
'Jetfire' × *N. bertolonii*; sdlg no. 1/89
Fl. rounded, 53 mm wide; perianth segments brilliant greenish yellow 6A, overlapping; corona cup-shaped, orange-yellow, with mouth incurved, rim entire. Early

'Morinnis' 8 Y-Y
(pre-1798)
Fl. pale yellow

'Morla' 2 Y-Y
Syn. of 'Norla'

'Morlaix' 2 W-W
(A.M. Wilson, pre-1948)
Leedsii sdlg × 'Broughshane'
Corona shading to gold at base

'Morna' 2 W-W
(W. Jackson Sr, 1938) W. Jackson Jr, 1956
'Veronique' × 'Finn'

'Morning Cloud' 3 W-Y
(Mrs J. Abel Smith) Mrs J. Abel Smith, 1973
'Chinese White' × 'Trudy'
Fl. 93 mm wide; corona sometimes faintly flushed pink

'Morning Dew' 1 W-? (b)
(A.H. Ahrens) J.S. Leitch, 1955

'Morning Flame' 3 W-? (b)
(P.D. Williams, pre-1942)

'Morning Glory' 2 Y-Y
(The Brodie of Brodie, c.1910)
'Gold Cup' × Engleheart red Poeticus sdlg
Fl. 70 mm wide; perianth rich clear lemon yellow, regular, overlapping one-third; corona cylindrical, pale buttercup yellow, neatly frilled. Dwarf. Mid-season

'Morning Glow' 2 W-? (b)
(de Graaff Bros, pre-1930)
AM(Haarlem) 1930

'Morning Light' 1 W-W
(D.S. Bell, 1965) D.S. Bell, 1975
('Kilsheelan' × ['Broughshane' hybrid]) × 'Empress of Ireland'
Fl. 104 mm wide. Mid-season

'Morning Mists' 2 W-? (b or c)
(Sir A.P.W. Thomas, pre-1930)

'Morningside' 2 W-YYP
(Oregon Bulb Farms, pre-1950)

'Morning Splendour' 8
(J.B. van der Schoot, pre-1931)
Syn. 'Astoria'

'Morning Star' 8 W-O
(pre-1851)

'Morning Star' 1 Y-Y
(E. Leeds, pre-1877)
Perianth segments narrow, acute, pale yellow; corona darker in tone. Syn. Pseudonarcissus Major 'Morning Star', Pseudonarcissus Major 'Stellatus'. "Absorbed" 'Seraph'

'Morning Star' 1 W-? (b)
(L. van Leeuwen & Son, pre-1931)

'Morning Sun' 2 Y-O
(A.H. Ahrens) J.S. Leitch, 1956
Perianth segments broad, rounded at apex; corona widely expanded, intense coppery orange. Tall

'Morning Wings' 2 W-W
(G.L. Wilson, pre-1947)
('Silver Coin' × 'Sea Shell') × 'Chinese White'
Perianth segments pure white, slightly reflexed; the inner segments spreading; corona opening with faint lemon at rim, soon becoming self white, with rim closely and deeply notched, as if fringed

'Morocco' 3 W-O
(The Brodie of Brodie, c.1919)
'Hildegarde' × 'Oiseau de Feu'
Perianth segments rounded, of great substance; corona disc-shaped, dark orange. Late. AM(e) 1925

'Morpeth' 2 W-Y
(G. Harrison) G. Harrison, 1968
'Geen Island' hybrid
Fl. 108 mm wide; corona pale yellow. Mid-season

'Morpheus' 3 W-? (b)
(R. Crews, pre-1949)
Syn. 'Fiancée'

'Morro Bay' 2 W-WWY
(G.H. Wayne) G.H. Wayne, 1981
'Bithynia' × ('Cordial' × 'Caro Nome'); sdlg no. A-2/3
Fl. 85 mm wide. Mid-season

'Mortlake' 1 Y-Y
(D.V. West, pre-1935)
PC(e)(NZ) 1929. Received PC(e)(NZ) 1929 as 'Renown II'

'Morton' 11a Y-O
(Tom Forster, 1960s) Unregistered
Perianth segments mid-yellow; corona deeply split, the six segments spreading, bright orange. Tall. Late

'Morvah' 1 W-W
(The Brodie of Brodie, pre-1930)

'Morven' 1 W-Y
(The Brodie of Brodie, c.1911)
'Victoria' × 'Madame de Graaff'
Perianth segments pure white; corona pale lemon yellow, frilled. Somewhat resembles 'J.B.M.Camm'. AM(e) 1914

'Morwenna' 2 Y-Y
(R.O. Backhouse, pre-1938)

'Morwenstow' 9
(G.H. Engleheart, pre-1914)

'Moscar' 3 W-? (b)
(G.H. Cammell, pre-1907)

N. moschatus Linnaeus 13 Section Pseudonarcissus (Pseudonarcissus Moschatus 'Cernuus', 'Silver Trumpet', "The Drooping White Spanish Daffodil", "The Swan's Neck Daffodil")

N. moschatus Haworth = *N. alpestris*

'Mosel' 1 Y-Y
(J.M. de Navarro) J.M. de Navarro, 1956
'Moongold' × 'Maraval'
Fl. pale yellow; perianth segments very broad, smooth and of waxy substance; corona straight-sided and somewhat narrow, with rim neatly flanged

'Mosquito' 3 W-W
(J.O. Sherrard, pre-1943)

'Mossman' 1 W-P
(Jackson's Daffodils, 1982) Jackson's Daffodils, 1993
'Madang' × 'Melancholy'; sdlg no. 90/82
Fl. 105 mm wide; perianth segments very broadly ovate, blunt, greenish white (155A), spreading, with margins deeply incurved towards apex, overlapping half or more; the inner segments more narrowly ovate, plane, lightly creased; corona cylindrical, very broadly ribbed, yellowish pink (20D), with mouth expanded and more finely ribbed, even, rim minutely crenate. Mid-season

'Moss Trooper' 3 (a)
(Mrs R.O. Backhouse, pre-1908)

'Moss Vale' 2 G-G
(W.M. Spry, pre-1975) Unregistered
'Hunter's Moon' × Ronalds sdlg
Fl. lime green

'Mossy Face' 3 W-GGO
(R.V. Favell, pre-1946)

'Most Beautiful' 8 Y-?
(pre-1759)

'Most Delicious' 1 W-P
(C.O. Fairbairn)

'Moth' 3 W-? (b)
(Miss K. Spurrell, pre-1907)

'Mother' 1 (a)
(G. Lubbe & Son, pre-1937)
AM(Haarlem) 1937

'Mother Catherine Grullemans' 2 W-OOY
(J.J. Grullemans & Sons, pre-1951)
Fl. 100 mm wide; perianth segments very broad, blunt, ivory white, spreading or a little inflexed, concave, of good substance, overlapping half; the inner segments with margins sometimes incurling; corona funnel-shaped, broad or very broad, closely ribbed, light orange-yellow 22C, with a stain of strong orange-yellow 24B becoming darker towards the mouth, and with a distinct band of light greenish yellow 4C at rim, mouth straight, with six deep and overlapping lobes, frilled, with rim minutely crenate. Scented. Syn. 'Apricot Sensation', 'Catherine Grullemans', 'Mother Grullemans', 'Grandmother Grullemans'

'Mother Grullemans' 2 W-OOY
Syn. of 'Mother Catherine Grullemans'

'Motherland' 2 W-? (b or c)
(W. Welchman, pre-1910)

'Mother Lode' 2 W-? (b)
(Oregon Bulb Farms, pre-1946)

'Mother of Pearl' 1 W-W
(W.B. Hartland, pre-1914)

'Mothers' Day' 3 W-? (b)
(J.W.A. Lefeber, pre-1941)

'Mother's Day' 4 W-Y
(C.A. van der Wereld, 1953) C.A. van der Wereld, 1964
Fl. 70-80 mm wide; perianth and other petaloid segments creamy white; corona segments pale yellow. Late. Resembles 'White Sail' but with paler corona segments. AM(Haarlem) 1964

'Mother's Favourite' 2 W-? (b)
(J.W.A. Lefeber, pre-1938)

'Motif' 3 W-YYO
(G.W.E. Brogden) G.W.E. Brogden, 1969

'Motmot' 8 Y-R
(G.E. Mitsch) G.E. Mitsch, 1979
'Matador' × *N. jonquilla*; sdlg no. G82/1
Fls up to 6 or more per stem, rounded, 43 mm wide; perianth segments bright yellow; corona bright orange-red, frilled. Mid-season. Scented. Resembles a smaller-flowered 'Hoopoe' with a frilled corona

'Motto' 3 W-YYO
(Murray W.Evans, 1972) Murray W.Evans, 1982
'Marshfire' × 'Hotspur'; sdlg no. N-36/5
Fl. 90 mm wide. Mid-season

'Mottoo' 2 W-OOW
(H.R.Mott) Unregistered

Perianth segments overlapping; corona disc-shaped, ribbed, creamy orange, with creamy white at rim, frilled. Mid-season to late

'Motts Mill' 2 Y-O
(N.A. Burr) N.A. Burr, 1988
'Border Chief' × 'Front Royal'; sdlg no. 1.9.75
Perianth segments broadly or very broadly ovate, blunt, mucronate, spreading, plane, with margins sometimes incurling at apex, smooth, with midrib showing, of good substance, regular, overlapping half; corona long cup-shaped, lightly ribbed, light orange, shading to a darker tone at rim, mouth straight, wavy, 6-lobed, with rim entire. Mid-season

'Mougli'
(pre-1913)
?Syn. of 'Mowgli'

'Moulin Rouge' 4 Y-R
(Mrs R.O. Backhouse, pre-1921)
AM(Haarlem) 1926

'Moulin Rouge' 11b W-R/W
Syn. of 'First Lady'

'Moulton' 2 (a)
(Mrs R.O. Backhouse, pre-1921)

"Mountain Daffodil"
Syn. of 'Sir Watkin'

'Mountain Dew' 1 W-W
(W.G. Pannill) W.G. Pannill, 1970
'White Prince' × 'Empress of Ireland'

'Mountaineer' 1 Y-Y
(G.H. Engleheart, pre-1922)
Fl. 89 mm wide; perianth segments lemon yellow, somewhat inflexed, overlapping half; corona deep lemon yellow, with mouth expanded and rim flanged. Mid-season. AM(e) 1922

'Mountain Frost' 9 W-GYR
Syn. of 'Mountain Poet'

'Mountain Gnome' 3 W-? (b)
(pre-1915)

'Mountain Maid' 3 W-W
(C. Smith, pre-1901)
Fl. facing down; perianth segments snow white; corona pure white

'Mountain Mist' 1 W-W
(W. Balch, pre-1933)

'Mountain Music' 2 Y-R
(G.E. Mitsch) G.E. Mitsch, 1981
'Chemawa' × 'Brer Fox'; sdlg no. HH59/3

Fl. 90 mm wide; perianth segments deep golden yellow, overlapping; corona intense orange-red. Mid-season

'Mountain Poet' 9 W-GYR
(G.E. Mitsch and R. & E.Havens, 1968) G.E. Mitsch and R. & E.Havens, 1987
'Quetzal' × 'Smyrna'; sdlg no. D94/3A
Perianth segments very broad; corona yellow, with green at base and bright red at rim. Very late. Resembles 'Angel Eyes' but with a slightly more disc-shaped corona. Syn. 'Mountain Frost'

'Mountain Pride' 3 W-YYO
(Mrs R.O. Backhouse, pre-1921)
Perianth segments tinged canary yellow at base; corona widely expanded, ribbed, bright canary yellow, with a broad band of scarlet-orange at rim

'Mountain Queen'
(C.Goodson, pre-1930)
PC(e)(NZ) 1930

'Mount Ajax' 1 W-Y
(Mrs H.K. Richardson) Mrs H.K. Richardson, 1972
'Canopus' × ('Spitzbergen' × 'Broughshane')
Corona pale primrose, with rim dentate and widely rolled

'Mount Angel' 3 W-YYR
(Brian S. Duncan) Rathowen Daffodils, 1978
'Merlin' open pollinated; sdlg no. 190
Fl. rounded, 100 mm wide; perianth segments very broad, mucronate, pure white, slightly reflexed, plane, smooth, overlapping half or more; the inner segments broadly ovate, not noticeably mucronate, spreading, with broad midrib showing; corona disc-shaped, finely ribbed, yellow, with a broad and clearly defined band of deep red at rim, mouth split in places and overlapping, tightly frilled. Mid-season. 2n=28

'Mount Ararat' 1 W-W
(R. Dick, pre-1933)

'Mount Arthur' 1 W-W
(R.P. Cook) R.P. Cook, 1957

'Mount Aspiring' 2 W-W
(H.T. Trevena, pre-1949)

'Mount Baker' 2 or 3 W-? (b or c)
(pre-1927)

'Mount Baker' 2 W-Y
(Mrs H.H. Simmons) Mrs H.H. Simmons, 1975
'Duke of Windsor' hybrid; sdlg no. D.W.69
Fl. 105 mm wide. Late

'Mount Cargill' 1 W-Y
(J.A. Morris) J.A. Morris, 1960
Fl. 111 mm wide; corona lemon yellow. Mid-season. Resembles 'Preamble' but with broader perianth segments

'Mount Cenis' 8 W-Y
(pre-1897)
Corona deep golden yellow

'Mount Cheam' 4 W-Y
(David L. Sheppard) David L. Sheppard, 1982
'Unique' × 'Saint Brendan'
Fl. 100 mm wide; perianth and other petaloid segments very broadly ovate in outline, blunt or rounded at apex, slightly mucronate, white, overlapping half; the outer whorl spreading, plane; the inner whorl a little shorter, inflexed, concave, some with margins deeply incurling; corona segments half the length of the petaloid segments and clustered among them, lemon yellow, frilled. Mid-season. Resembles 'Unique' but with paler corona segments becoming almost white

'Mount Cloyd' 2 W-? (b)
(C.M. Grullemans) J.J. Grullemans & Sons, 1959

'Mount Curl' 1 W-? (b)
(A. Gibson, pre-1951)

'Mount Edgecumbe' 2 W-WPP
(Brian S. Duncan) du Plessis Bros, 1989
Sdlg no. 860
Fl. 92 mm wide; perianth segments pure white, very smooth; corona pink, with white at base and a darker tone of pink at rim, mouth expanded, with rim dentate. Mid-season

'Mount Erebus' 2 W-W
(C.G. van Tubergen, pre-1913)
'Minnie Hume' × 'Madame de Graaff'
Perianth segments pure white, separated; corona funnel-shaped, opening pale citron yellow, becoming ivory white. AM(Haarlem) 1912, *AM(g) 1931

'Mount Ernsclough' 1 W-W
(G.H. Brownlee) G.H. Brownlee, 1964
Fl. 121 mm wide; corona opening creamy yellow, becoming milk white. Mid-season. Resembles a better poised 'Kanchenjunga' of improved texture

'Mount Etna' 2 Y-Y
(Albert Davis, 1979) Albert Davis, 1991
'Camelot' × 'Arctic Gold'; sdlg no. 146/74
Fl. 123 mm wide, vivid yellow 13A; perianth segments broadly ovate, smooth; corona cylindrical, smooth, frilled, with rim rolled. Mid-season

'Mount Evelyn' 1 W-Y
(A. Overton, pre-1957) Unregistered
Perianth segments broad, smooth; corona lemon

yellow. Late

'Mount Everest' 2 W-W
Syn. of 'Eve'

'Mount Faber' 1 W-W
(J.A. O'More) J.A. O'More, 1968
'Sincerity' × 'Carnlough'

'Mount Fuji' 2 W-W
(Brian S. Duncan) Rathowen Daffodils, 1987
'Easter Moon' × 'Silent Valley'; sdlg no. 619
Fl. forming a double triangle; perianth segments broadly ovate, blunt, prominently mucronate, slightly reflexed, plane, with broad midrib showing, overlapping half; the inner segments more narrowly ovate, spreading; corona funnel-shaped, lightly ribbed, bluish white, with mouth straight and neatly frilled. Mid-season

'Mount Hector' 1 W-W
(S.A. Free) Mrs S.I. Free, 1968

'Mount Holyoke' 9 W-GYR
(Mrs M.S.Yerger) Mrs M.S.Yerger, 1996
'Dulcimer' open pollinated; sdlg no. A 10
Fl. 54 mm wide; perianth segments ovate; corona bowl-shaped, greenish yellow (154C), with strong yellow-green 144B at base and red (41A) at rim. Mid-season

'Mount Hood' 1 W-W
(P. van Deursen, pre-1938)
Fl. 102 mm wide, creamy white; perianth segments broadly ovate, blunt, only very slightly mucronate, inflexed, with margins incurling at apex, overlapping one-third to a half; the inner segments more narrowly ovate, more nearly acute, angled at shoulder, reflexed towards apex, with margins wavy; corona cylindrical, smooth, opening light greenish yellow 6D, mouth ribbed and expanded, with rim flanged and regularly notched and crenate. Dwarf. Mid-season. 2n=28,29. AM(Haarlem) 1937, PC 1946, *AM(g) 1951, *FCC(g) 1955, *AM(p) 1975, *FCC(p) 1977, AGM 1995

'Mount Hutt' 1 W-Y
(R.J. McIlraith) R.J. McIlraith, 1982
'Empress of Ireland' × 'Trousseau'; sdlg no. 71/3
Fl. 90 mm wide; perianth segments overlapping; corona yellowish. Early to mid-season

'Mount Ida' 2 W-GYO
(Ballydorn Bulb Farm, 1976) Ballydorn Bulb Farm, 1987
'Mount Pleasant' × 'Notable'
Corona saucer-shaped, opening with mid-zone yellowish white, becoming very pale yellow, with pale orange at rim. Mid-season

'Mount Isa' 2 W-P
(pre-1965) Unregistered
Corona large, frilled

'Mount Jefferson' 1 W-W
(G.E. Mitsch) G.E. Mitsch, 1956
'Kanchenjunga' × 'Ada Finch'; sdlg no. J37/5
Corona with rim closely and deeply notched, as if fringed. Mid-season. Resembles 'Kanchenjunga' but with narrower perianth segments

'Mountjoy' 7 Y-Y
(Barr & Sons, pre-1950)

'Mountjoy' 2 W-WWY
(W.J. Dunlop, pre-1969) Unregistered
Corona opening pale primrose, becoming white, with greenish lemon at rim

'Mount Kosciusko' 1 W-W
(H.A. Brown, 1931) J.N. Hancock & Co., 1960
'Tenedos' × 'Kantara'
Fl. large, opening creamy white, becoming ivory. Early to mid-season

'Mount Lassen' 2 W-? (b)
(Oregon Bulb Farms, 1951)

'Mount Logan' 2 W-GWO
(Betty Beery) Betty Beery, 1988
'Salome' × 'Green Island'; sdlg no. S-27-F
Perianth segments very broadly ovate, somewhat truncate, mucronate, spreading or a little reflexed, concave either side of prominent midrib, overlapping one-third to a half; the inner segments more narrowly ovate, a little inflexed, somewhat twisted; corona shallow bowl-shaped, lightly ribbed, white, with green at base and with pale orange at rim fading with age, mouth expanded and more heavily ribbed, tightly frilled, with rim dentate. Mid-season. Resembles 'Green Island'

'Mount Major' 1 Y-Y
(J.N. Hancock & Co., c.1979) Unregistered

'Mountnorris' 2 W-Y
(Ballydorn Bulb Farm) Ballydorn Bulb Farm, 1968
'Coverack Perfection' × 'Green Island' hybrid
Fl. 95 mm wide; corona deep buff yellow, with overtones of pale orange and with grey-green at base. Mid-season. 2n=28

'Mount Oriel' 2 W-Y
(Ballydorn Bulb Farm, 1979) Ballydorn Bulb Farm, 1991
'Mount Pleasant' open pollinated
Fl. 110 mm wide; perianth segments shouldered at base, deeply overlapping; corona bowl-shaped, opening with orange tints, becoming deep yellow, mouth widely expanded, with rim

closely dentate. Mid-season

'Mount Peel' 1 W-Y
(J.H.Davenport) Mrs E. Milliken, 1974
'Alpine Eagle' hybrid
Fl. 105 mm wide

'Mount Pleasant' 2 W-Y
(Ballydorn Bulb Farm) Ballydorn Bulb Farm, 1968
'Coverack Perfection' × 'Green Island' hybrid
Fl. 102 mm wide; corona deep yellow, flushed orange. Late. 2n=28. See also 'Mountpleasant'

'Mountpleasant' 2 W-Y
Syn. of 'Mount Pleasant'

'Mount Rainier' 1 W-W
(J.W.A. Lefeber) J.W.A. Lefeber, 1983
'Queen Juliana' hybrid

'Mount Ross' 1 Y-Y
(G. Lewis) D.S. Bell, 1955

'Mount Sandel' 1 (a)
(G.L. Wilson, pre-1937)

'Mount Shasta' 1 W-? (b)
(H. Prins, pre-1934)

'Mount Somers' 4
(Alfred Clark) Alfred Clark, 1955

'Mount Tacoma' 2 W-? (b)
(de Graaff Bros, pre-1938)
AM(Haarlem) 1938. Received AM(Haarlem) 1938 as 'Evensong'

'Mount Thomas' 1 W-Y
(G. Lewis, pre-1940)

'Mount Todden' 2 Y-Y
(R.W. Ward, 1947) R.W. Ward & Son, 1960
Early. Resembles an improved 'Magnificence'

'Mount Vernon' 2 W-P
(G.E. Mitsch) G.E. Mitsch, 1968
('Shirley Wyness' × 'Mabel Taylor') × 'Caro Nome'; sdlg no. V58/1
Fl. 115 mm wide; perianth segments deeply overlapping; corona bowl-shaped, opening salmon pink, becoming paler. Mid-season. Resembles 'Caro Nome' but with a shallower and paler corona

'Mount White' 4 W-P
(E.W. Cotter) E.W. Cotter, 1968
'Mrs William Copeland' × 'Roselene'

'Mount Whitney' 2 W-W
(Oregon Bulb Farms, pre-1951)

'Mourne' 1 Y-Y
(T. Bloomer) T. Bloomer, 1964
'Cargan' × 'Golden Rapture'; sdlg no. 2/24/58

'Mourneview' 1 W-W
(Ballydorn Bulb Farm) Ballydorn Bulb Farm, 1991
Sdlg hybrid
Fl. 120 mm wide; perianth segments shouldered at base, tinged green at base; corona flared and frilled. Mid-season

'Mousquetaire' 1 (a)
(M. van Waveren & Sons, pre-1938)

'Moustache' 11a W-OOY
(J. Gerritsen & Son) J. Gerritsen & Son, 1984
'Pick Up' × 'Sovereign'; sdlg no. 915
Perianth segments ivory white; corona segments strong orange 25A, with patches of lemon yellow at rim. Mid-season

'Movie Star' 2 W-YYP
(Brian S. Duncan) Brian S. Duncan, 1993
('Lilac Charm' × ['Interim' × 'Aosta']) × 'Valinor'; sdlg no. 1076
Fl. rounded, 103 mm wide; perianth segments very broad in outline, blunt or rounded at apex, slightly mucronate, pure white, spreading, a little concave, smooth, overlapping three-quarters; the inner segments roundish, with margins somewhat wavy; corona deep bowl-shaped, chrome yellow, with a broad and clearly defined band of deep rose pink at rim, mouth expanded, very lightly frilled, lobed. Mid-season to late. Resembles 'Bandit' in form

'Moville' 2 W-W
(The Brodie of Brodie, c.1940)
'Nelly' × 'Banchory'
Fl. 127 mm wide; perianth segments broad, smooth, overlapping; corona cup-shaped, frilled. AM(Haarlem) 1948, AM(e) 1948

'Mowana' 2 W-GPP
(Brian S.Duncan, 1985) Brian S.Duncan, 1996
'Gem of Ulster' × 'Fragrant Rose'; sdlg no. 1092
Fl. 96 mm long; perianth segments very broadly ovate, truncate and slightly mucronate, white, with a hint of pink, spreading, with broad midrib showing and with margins incurling, overlapping half; the inner segments narrower and a little inflexed; corona broad funnel-shaped, closely ribbed, deep reddish pink, with deep green at base, mouth straight, minutely frilled. Dwarf. Late or very late. Sunproof

'Mowbray' 1 W-W
(C.E. Radcliff, 1944)
'Tain' × 'Whitefoord'
Fl. pure white

'Mowequa' 1 W-Y
(V. Brink) V. Brink, 1967
Fl. 102 mm wide; corona clear bright yellow. Mid-season. Resembles 'Festivity'

'Mowgli' 3 W-R
(E.M. Crosfield, pre-1914)
Corona disc-shaped, red. ?The same as 'Mougli' of pre-1913

'Mowser' 7 Y-R
(R.A.Scamp) R.A.Scamp, 1997
'Altruist' × *N. jonquilla*; sdlg no. 557
Fls up to 4 per stem, rounded, 55 mm wide; perianth segments very dark yellow, slightly concave, deeply overlapping; corona very shallow bowl-shaped, red. Mid-season to late

'Moya' 2 (a)
(J.T. Gray, pre-1933)

'Moya Newman' 2 W-Y
(L.P. Dettman) L.P. Dettman, 1975
'Bonnington' open pollinated; sdlg no. 10/70
Fl. 99 mm wide; perianth segments yellowish white 155B; corona light greenish yellow 7D. Mid-season. Resembles 'Bonnington' but with the corona deeply frilled and more widely expanded

'Moyard' 2 W-GWW
(G.L. Wilson) Guy L.Wilson Ltd, 1961
(['Evening' × 'Dava'] × ['Silver Coin' × 'Dava']) × 'Snowline'

'Moyarget' 3 W-Y
(Carncairn Daffodils) Carncairn Daffodils, 1993
'Merlin' × 'Rockall'; sdlg no. 3/65/79
Perianth segments broadly ovate, blunt or minutely truncate, yellowish white 155B, spreading, concave or with margins incurling at apex, overlapping half; the inner segments square-shouldered at base; corona very shallow funnel-shaped, ribbed, light greenish yellow 5D, shading to brilliant greenish yellow 6B at rim, with the rim occasionally touched vivid orange 28B, mouth usually with six overlapping lobes, frilled. Mid-season

'Moyasta' 1 W-?
(J.L. Richardson) Mrs H.K. Richardson, 1963
('Rose of Tralee' × 'Lisbreen') × 'Salmon Trout'

'Moyle' 9 W-GYO
(Ballydorn Bulb Farm) Ballydorn Bulb Farm, 1982
'Cantabile' × 'Cushendall'
Fl. 68 mm wide; corona deep yellow, with green at base and orange at rim. Late

'Moylena' 2 W-P
(G.L. Wilson, pre-1944)
'Mitylene' × 'Evening'

Corona strong pink

'Moylough' 3 W-YYR
(J.L. Richardson, pre-1948)
'Coronach' × 'Forfar'
Perianth segments snow white; corona disc-shaped, pale yellow, with a broad band of red at rim

'Moyness' 2 Y-GYO
(The Brodie of Brodie, *c.*1932)
('White Sentinel' × 'Gallipoli') × 'Raeburn'
Perianth segments lemon primrose; corona shallow, citron yellow, with green at base and reddish orange at rim

'Moyola' 2 W-P
(Carncairn Daffodils) Carncairn Daffodils, 1976
'Templemore' × 'Rose Caprice'; sdlg no. 3-90-60
Fl. 95 mm wide; perianth segments greenish white (157A); corona peach (16C), with green-grey at base. Late

'Moyra' 2 W-W
(P. Phillips) P. Phillips, 1968

'Mozart' 8 W-O
(pre-1880)
Fls many per stem. Probably the same as 'Muzart Orientalis'

'Mozart' 2 Y-YYR
(The Brodie of Brodie, *c.*1911)
'Princess Mary' hybrid; sdlg no. 0/A/06
Fl. 76 mm wide; perianth segments primrose yellow, deeply overlapping; corona widely expanded, deep yellow, with a broad band of red at rim, mouth with several very deep and overlapping lobes

'Mozart's' 8 W-O
Syn. of 'Muzart Orientalis'

'M.P.Williams' 2 Y-YYO
Perianth segments broad, rich yellow, smooth; corona golden yellow, with orange at rim. Syn. of 'Michael P.Williams'

'Mr Bowles' 1 W-Y
(R.A.van der Schoot, pre-1929)
Corona widely expanded, deep yellow

'Mr Churchill' 1 (a)
(W.J. Eldering & Son, pre-1928)

'Mr Cowan' 1 W-Y
(W. Backhouse, pre-1869)
N. minor × *N. moschatus*
Corona sulphur yellow. Syn. Pseudonarcissus Moschatus 'Cowani', Pseudonarcissus Moschatus 'Mr Cowan'. Probably the same as 'C.W.Cowan'

'Mr C.R.Hamilton'
?Syn. of 'Mrs C.R.Hamilton'

'Mr Dix' 3 W-R
Syn. of 'John Dix'

'Mr Everwijn' 1 ?-Y
(pre-1930)
Perianth segments narrow, acute; corona golden yellow. AM(Haarlem) 1930

'Mr F.Eugene Dixon' 8
(P.D. Williams, pre-1928)

'Mr G.F.Hemerik' 1 Y-Y
Syn. of 'G.F.Hemerik'

'Mr Gladstone' 1 Y-Y
(pre-1884)
Fl. pale yellow. Resembles 'Mrs Gladstone' but with a shorter corona

'Mr Harold Irving Pratt' 3 W-? (b)
(P.D. Williams, pre-1928)

'Mr H.D.Betteridge' 1 W-W
Syn. of 'Mrs H.D.Betteridge'

'Mr Henderson' 1 (a)
(G. Lubbe & Son, pre-1930)

'Mr Hilterman' 2 W-R
(J.W.A. Lefeber, c.1968) Unregistered

'Mr Jinks' 3 W-YOO
(The Brodie of Brodie, c.1928)
'Bernardino' × 'Sunstar'
Fl. about 89 mm wide; perianth segments very broad in outline, rounded or squarish at apex, prominently mucronate, pure white, spreading, concave, smooth and of good substance, overlapping half; the inner segments broadly ovate, square-shouldered at base, a little inflexed; corona bowl-shaped, ribbed, fiery orange, with yellow at base, mouth loosely and unevenly frilled. Late. 2n=29. AM(e) 1936

'Mr John Pierpoint Morgan' 3 W-? (b)
(P.D. Williams, pre-1928)

'Mr K.Volkersz' 1 Y-Y
Perianth segments canary yellow; corona deep yellow, with rim flanged. Syn. of 'Ingenieur K.Volkersz'

'Mr Milner' 1 W-W
Syn. of 'W.P.Milner'

'Mr Nijgh' 3 W-YOO
(Mrs R.O. Backhouse, pre-1921)
Perianth segments clear white; corona deep orange, with yellow at base, frilled. AM(Haarlem) 1929

'Mr R.M.Tobin' 2 W-? (b)
(Warnaar & Co., pre-1927)

'Mrs A.E.Lowe' 9 W-YYR
(A.G. Bull, pre-1927)

'Mrs A.F.Barron' 2 Y-YYO
(W. Backhouse, pre-1869)
Corona slender, with bright scarlet-orange at rim. Syn. Incomparabilis Leedsii 'Mrs A.F.Barron'. "Absorbed" 'Hector'

'Mrs Alfred Pearson' 8 W-Y
(de Graaff Bros, pre-1923)

'Mrs Alfred White' 2 W-? (b)
(Mrs R.O. Backhouse, pre-1921)

'Mrs Alister Clark' ?-P
(Alister Clark, 1948) J. Sharp, 1960

'Mrs Asquith' 8 W-Y
(A. Vis, pre-1923)
 Poetaz
Corona deep yellow. Syn. 'Asquith'

'Mrs Backhouse' 2 W-Y
Syn. of 'Mrs C.J.Backhouse'

'Mrs Barclay' 3 W-W
(W. Backhouse, pre-1869)
Corona large, opening canary yellow, becoming sulphur white. Syn. Leedsii 'Mrs Barclay'

'Mrs Barclay' 3 Y-YYO
(W. Polman-Mooy, pre-1927)
Perianth segments very broadly ovate or roundish, rounded at apex, not prominently mucronate, pale primrose, with margins sometimes incurling, overlapping half; the inner segments more narrowly ovate, blunt; corona large, very shallow, ribbed, bright yellow, with a distinct narrow band of bright scarlet-orange at rim, mouth split in places and overlapping, lightly frilled, with rim closely and minutely crenate. Resembles an improved 'Lady Moore'. See also 'Mrs Berkley'. ?The same as 'Miss Barklay'

'Mrs Barton'
(pre-1936)

'Mrs Ben Hart' 1 W-Y
Syn. of 'Mrs B.Hart'

'Mrs Berkeley' 2 W-W
(G.H. Engleheart, pre-1900)
N. triandrus × 'Minnie Hume'
FCC 1900

'Mrs Berkley' 3 Y-YYO
Syn. of 'Mrs Barclay'

'Mrs Betteridge' 1 W-W
Syn. of 'Mrs H.D.Betteridge'

'Mrs B.Farmer' 1 W-W
Syn. of 'Mrs Bretland Farmer'

'Mrs B.Hart' 1 W-Y
(H. Hart, pre-1914)
Perianth segments pure white; corona pale primrose yellow. Also named 'Mrs Ben Hart'

'Mrs Bowley' 3 W-O
Syn. of 'Mrs C.Bowley'

'Mrs Bretland Farmer' 1 W-W
(de Graaff Bros, pre-1910)
Also named 'Mrs B.Farmer'

'Mrs Brett' 9
(G.H. Engleheart, pre-1915)

'Mrs Brewster' 3
Syn. of 'Mrs Walter Brewster'

'Mrs Brice' 9
(Mrs R.O. Backhouse, pre-1910)

'Mrs Buchanan' 1 W-Y
(A.W. Tait, pre-1905)
Perianth segments creamy white, inflexed, slightly twisted; corona expanded, ribbed, soft primrose yellow

'Mrs Burbidge' 1 W-W
Syn. of 'Mrs F.W.Burbidge'

'Mrs Camm' 1 W-W
Syn. of 'Mrs Camm'

'Mrs C.Bowley' 3 W-O
(W. Backhouse, pre-1869)
Corona glowing reddish orange. Also named 'Mrs Bowley'

'Mrs C.E.Shea'
(pre-1914)

'Mrs Chambers' 1 W-?
(A. Overton) A. Overton, 1960

'Mrs Chester J.Hunt' 3 W-YYR
(M. van Waveren & Sons, pre-1931)

'Mrs C.J.Backhouse' 2 W-Y
(W. Backhouse, pre-1869)
Perianth segments ovate, pure white, spreading or a little inflexed, with margins wavy or recurved, separated; corona straight-sided, lightly ribbed, clear yellow, with mouth straight and loosely frilled. Syn. 'Mrs Backhouse', Incomparabilis Albus 'Mrs C.J.Backhouse', Nelsonii 'Mrs Backhouse'

'Mrs Clementi Smith' 3
(G.H. Engleheart, pre-1913)

'Mrs C.McFarlane' 2 W-P
Syn. of 'Lila McFarlane'

'Mrs C.O.Fairbairn' ?-P
(Alister Clark, 1948) J. Sharp, 1960

'Mrs C.R.Hamilton' 2 W-? (b)
(G.H. Engleheart, pre-1914)
?See also 'Mr C.R.Hamilton'

'Mrs Crosfield' 1 W-W
Syn. of 'Mrs Ernest Crosfield'

'Mrs C.W.Earle' 1 W-Y
(Barr & Sons, pre-1905)
Perianth segments pure white; corona pale citron yellow

'Mrs David Calvert' 3 W-GRR
(C.O. Fairbairn, c.1968) Unregistered
'Limerick' hybrid
Corona very shallow bowl-shaped, blood red, with green at base. 2n=28

'Mrs David Walker' 2 Y-O
(Mrs R.O. Backhouse, pre-1914)
Perianth segments sulphur yellow; corona reddish orange. See also 'Mrs D.Walker'

'Mrs D.F.Pont' 2 Y-YYO
Syn. of 'Mrs D.J.Pont'

'Mrs D.J.Pont' 2 Y-YYO
(F. Rijnveld & Sons, 1936) F. Rijnveld & Sons, 1955
AM(Haarlem) 1936. See also 'Mrs D.F.Pont', 'Mrs Pont'

'Mrs D.V.West' 1 W-W
(D.V. West, pre-1911)
'Weardale Perfection' × 'Madame de Graaff'
Fl. 102 mm wide, facing slightly downwards; perianth segments creamy white, inflexed, irregular, overlapping half; corona large, opening pale primrose yellow, becoming creamy white, mouth expanded, with rim flanged and crenate. Mid-season

'Mrs D.Walker' 2 Y-O
Syn. of 'Mrs David Walker'

'Mrs E.C.Mudge' 1 W-Y
(Mrs R.O. Backhouse, pre-1921)
Perianth segments broadly ovate, blunt, slightly mucronate, creamy white, a little inflexed, plane, overlapping one-third to a half; the inner segments more strongly inflexed, a little twisted; corona

funnel-shaped, soft primrose yellow, with mouth expanded and broadly ribbed, rim crenate. Mid-season. 2n=28. *AM(g) 1936

'Mrs E.Crosfield' 1 W-W
Syn. of 'Mrs Ernest Crosfield'

'Mrs E.E.Morbey'
Unregistered
Seed parent of 'Sphere'

'Mrs E.G.Knights' 2 W-Y
(pre-1898)
Perianth segments of strong substance; corona bright yellow

'Mrs E.Harvey' 3 W-? (b)
(Miss K. Spurrell, pre-1910)

'Mrs E.H.Krelage' 1 W-W
Syn. of 'Mrs Ernst H.Krelage'

'Mrs Elisabeth Palmer' 2 (a)
(pre-1937)
AM(Haarlem) 1937

'Mrs E.Martin' 4 W-?
(E. & J.C. Martin, pre-1923)
Corona segments with some reddish orange colouring

'Mrs E.M.Crosfield' 1 W-W
Syn. of 'Mrs Ernest Crosfield'

'Mrs E.M.Wingate' 1 W-W
(Barr & Sons, pre-1914)
Perianth segments milk white; corona expanded, ribbed, rich creamy white, neatly frilled

'Mrs Eric Jeffrey' 2 W-YYR
(J.H. Hinsby, 1928)
'Bernardino' × 'Pink'un'

'Mrs Ernest Crosfield' 1 W-W
(E.M. Crosfield, pre-1907)
Also named 'Mrs Crosfield'; 'Mrs E.Crosfield'; 'Mrs E.M.Crosfield'

'Mrs Ernst H.Krelage' 1 W-W
(E.H. Krelage & Son, pre-1912)
Fl. 102 mm wide, creamy white, of great substance; perianth segments broadly ovate, blunt, slightly mucronate, inflexed, plane or a little concave, sometimes with raised midrib, with margins minutely incurling at apex, overlapping one-third; the inner segments more narrowly ovate, a little twisted, with margins sometimes nicked; corona cylindrical, smooth, opening creamy yellow, mouth 6-lobed and lightly frilled, rim crenate and widely rolled. Mid-season. 2n=28. AM 1912, FCC 1913, *AM(g) 1944.

Also named 'Mrs E.H.Krelage'

'Mrs F.G.Lawson' 1 W-? (b)
(F.G. Lawson, pre-1936)

'Mrs Francis King' 2 W-? (b)
(Mrs R.O. Backhouse, pre-1921)
AM(Haarlem) 1925

'Mrs Frank Barclay' 3 W-? (b or c)
(Miss K. Spurrell, pre-1908)

'Mrs Franklin Roosevelt' 1 Y-Y
Syn. of 'Anna Roosevelt'

'Mrs F.W.Burbidge' 1 W-W
(W. Backhouse, pre-1869)
Corona opening primrose yellow, becoming milk white. Resembles 'F.W.Burbidge'. Syn. Pseudonarcissus Moschatus 'Mrs F.W.Burbidge'. Also named 'Mrs Burbidge'

'Mrs F.W.Moore' 1 W-W
(de Graaff Bros, pre-1913)

'Mrs F.W.Parkinson' 2 W-? (b or c)
(F.W. Parkinson, pre-1936)

'Mrs Galton' 1 W-W
(J. Pope, pre-1907)

'Mrs Gamp' 1 W-W
(?E.M. Crosfield, pre-1913)

'Mrs George Cammell' 1 Y-Y
(Spanish origin)
Selection by Peter Barr (1888) from wild-collected *N.* × *johnstonii*
Syn. "The Great Spanish Beauty"

'Mrs George Chandler' 2 Y-Y
(de Graaff Bros, pre-1927)
Perianth segments butter yellow, somewhat reflexed; corona funnel-shaped, orange-yellow, with mouth widely expanded and heavily frilled. AM(Haarlem) 1927

'Mrs G.F.Brooke' 2 (a)
(Hogg & Robertson, pre-1907)

'Mrs G.F.Wilson' 2 W-? (b)
(W. Backhouse, pre-1869)
Corona expanded. Syn. Incomparabilis Albus 'Mrs G.F.Wilson'. Was "absorbed" into 'G.F.Wilson'

'Mrs G.H.Barr' 1 W-W
(de Graaff Bros, pre-1903)
Perianth segments snow white, inflexed; corona expanded, creamy white, frilled. AM 1903

'Mrs Gladstone' 1 Y-Y
(E. Leeds, pre-1877)
Fl. pale yellow. Resembles 'Mr Gladstone' but with a longer corona. Syn. Pseudonarcissus Major 'Mrs Gladstone'. Was "absorbed" into 'Edward Leeds'

'Mrs Gordon Pirie' 5
(P.D. Williams, pre-1927)

'Mrs Guy Fairfax Cary' 3 W-? (b)
(P.D. Williams, pre-1928)

'Mrs H.A.Debenham' 1 W-W
(N.Y. Lower, pre-1916)

'Mrs Harding' 1 (a)
(G. Vink, pre-1931)
AM(Haarlem) 1930, FA(Haarlem) 1937

'Mrs Harrison Smith'
(J.H. Padley, pre-1914)

'Mrs Harrison Weir' 1 W-Y
(W. Backhouse, pre-1869)
Corona with rim flanged. Syn. Pseudonarcissus Bicolor 'Mrs Harrison Weir'. Was "absorbed" into 'Horsfieldii'

'Mrs Harry J.Veitch' 1 Y-Y
(pre-1912)
Perianth segments pale yellow, overlapping; corona golden yellow. Also named 'Mrs H.J.Veitch', 'Mrs Veitch'

'Mrs H.D.Betteridge' 1 W-W
(de Graaff Bros, pre-1905)
'Madame de Graaff' hybrid
Corona expanded, creamy white, with rim crenate. See also 'Mrs Betteridge', 'Mr H.D.Betteridge'

'Mrs Heman' 9
Syn. of 'Mrs Hemans'

'Mrs Hemans' 9
(T. Buncombe, pre-1918)
See also 'Mrs Heman'

'Mrs Henkes' 2 W-O
Syn. of 'Coby Henkes'

'Mrs Henry Buckley' 2 W-? (b)
(Barr & Sons, pre-1905)

'Mrs Henry R.Rea' 2 (a)
(P.D. Williams, pre-1927)
?The same as 'Mrs H.Ray' and 'Mrs R.H.Rea'

'Mrs Herbert Smith' 1 W-W
(F.H. Chapman, pre-1923)

'Mrs H.E.Sharp' 2 W-W
(H.E. Sharp, pre-1930)

'Mrs Hillhouse'
(J.D. Pearson, pre-1896)

'Mrs H.J.Elwes' 1 Y-Y
(E. Leeds, pre-1877)
Fl. soft clear yellow; corona flared. Syn. Pseudonarcissus Major 'Mrs H.J.Elwes'. "Absorbed" 'Khedive'

'Mrs H.J.Veitch' 1 Y-Y
Syn. of 'Mrs Harry J.Veitch'

'Mrs H.L.Fell' 2 W-YYO
Syn. of 'Margaret Fell'

'Mrs Horace Darwin' 3 W-YYO
(W. Backhouse, pre-1869)
Perianth segments creamy white; corona canary yellow, with orange at rim. Syn. Barrii Albidus 'Mrs Horace Darwin'. Was "absorbed" into 'General Murray'

'Mrs H.Pratt' 3 W-? (b)
(P.D. Williams, pre-1927)
AM(Haarlem) 1936

'Mrs H.Ray' 3 W-YYR
(P.D. Williams, pre-1929)
Perianth segments creamy white; corona yellow, with a broad band of red at rim. ?The same as 'Mrs Henry R.Rea'

'Mrs Hugh Campbell' 1 W-W
(J. Hall, pre-1930)
Corona opening creamy, becoming almost white, frilled

'Mrs Iwasa Masako' 2 W-Y
(?Dutch origin, pre-1995) Unregistered

'Mrs J.A.Cooper' 3 W-? (b)
(G.H. Engleheart, pre-1914)

'Mrs James A.Burden' 2 (a)
(P.D. Williams, pre-1928)

'Mrs James Bateman' 1 W-W
(W. Backhouse, pre-1869)
Perianth segments of strong substance; corona slender, creamy white. Syn. Pseudonarcissus Moschatus 'Mrs James Bateman'. Was "absorbed" into 'Mrs Vincent'

'Mrs James H.Veitch' 1 Y-Y
(M. van Waveren & Sons, pre-1907)
Perianth segments pale yellow; corona golden yellow

'Mrs James Walker' 1 W-Y
(E. Leeds, pre-1877)
Perianth segments of strong substance, overlapping. Resembles 'James Walker'. Syn. Pseudonarcissus Bicolor 'Mrs James Walker'. ?Mis-quoted as 'James Walker'

'Mrs J.B.M.Camm' 1 W-W
(W. Backhouse, pre-1869)
Perianth segments broadly ovate, fairly prominently mucronate, a little inflexed, with margins wavy, overlapping at base only; the inner segments narrower and sometimes twisted; corona cylindrical, ribbed, greenish white, with rim flanged and crenate. Syn. ?'Paul Engleheart', Pseudonarcissus Bicolor 'Mrs J.B.M.Camm'. FCC 1888. Also named 'Mrs Camm'. "Absorbed" 'Backhouse's Queen'

'Mrs Jezerniczky' 2 W-YOR
(Lajos Jezerniczky) Lajos Jezerniczky, 1987
'Dick Wellband' × 'Manco'; sdlg no. 914
Fl. 110 mm wide; perianth segments broadly ovate, truncate, spreading, plane, with margins sometimes incurling at apex, overlapping one-third; the inner segments a little inflexed, with margins wavy; corona broad, shallow, finely ribbed, mouth widely expanded, with six deeply overlapping lobes, margins wavy. Mid-season to late. Resembles 'Dick Wellband'

'Mrs J.G.Weightman' 9 W-GYR
(pre-1926)
Syn. of 'Mrs Weightman'

'Mrs J.Kirker' 2 Y-Y
(New Zealand origin, c.1895)
Fls occasionally 2 per stem

'Mrs John Bodger' 1 W-W
(de Graaff Bros, pre-1927)

'Mrs John Hoog' 1 W-Y
(C.G. van Tubergen, pre-1914)
Fl. 95 mm wide; perianth segments creamy white, with cream at base, inflexed, with margins incurving, irregular, overlapping half; corona lemon yellow, with mouth expanded and frilled. Mid-season. AM(Haarlem) 1915, FCC(Haarlem) 1920

'Mrs John Martin' 2 or 3 W-?
(pre-1927)
Corona expanded and frilled

'Mrs John Robinson' 9 W-YYR
(A. Robinson, pre-1925)
Corona yellow, with crimson at rim. AM(e) 1925

'Mrs John T.Scheepers' 9
(P.D. Williams, pre-1927)

'Mrs J.Thorley' ?-O
(pre-1915)

'Mrs J.W.Boys' 2 W-? (b or c)
(pre-1949)

'Mrs Krelage' 3 Y-Y
(W. Backhouse, pre-1869)
Perianth segments primrose yellow; corona widely expanded, tinged orange. Syn. Burbidgei 'Mrs Krelage'. "Absorbed" 'Gracilis'

'Mrs Langtry' 3 W-W
(W. Backhouse, pre-1869)
Fl. star-shaped, 83 mm wide; perianth segments ovate, blunt, not prominently mucronate, spreading or a little inflexed, somewhat twisted or with margins incurling or wavy, overlapping one-third; the inner segments more strongly twisted or with margins more strongly wavy or incurved; corona short funnel-shaped, ribbed, yellowish white, with canary yellow at rim, mouth straight and occasionally split, frilled, with rim minutely crenate. 2n=14. Syn. 'Lily Langtry', Leedsii 'Mrs Langtry'

'Mrs Laxton' 1 W-Y
Syn. of 'Madame van Waveren'

'Mrs L.Breck' 1? W-W
(?de Graaff Bros, pre-1912)
Perianth segments pure white; corona milk white. FCC(Haarlem) 1912

'Mrs Lefebre' 3 W-? (b)
(pre-1930)

'Mrs Leonard Harrison' 7 Y-Y
(L.F. Harrison, pre-1920)
N. jonquilla × *N. triandrus*
Fl. sulphur yellow. Resembles *N. triandrus* var. *pulchellus*. AM(r) 1920

'Mrs Limrick' 1 Y-Y
(Australian or New Zealand origin, pre-1927)

'Mrs Lloyd George' 2 W-? (b or c)
(W.A. Watts, pre-1923)

'Mrs Lower' 1 W-W
(N.Y. Lower, pre-1928)
'Cleopatra' × 'Clarion'

'Mrs Lubbe' W-W
Syn. of 'Catherine Lubbe'

'Mrs Lyall Gillespie' 3 Y-YRR
(W.M. Spry, pre-1975) Unregistered
'Calleen' × 'Matapan'
Corona lemon yellow, with red at rim

'Mrs Mackinnon' 1 W-? (b)
(Barr & Sons, pre-1927)

'Mrs Margaret Erskine' 2 Y-Y
(M. van Waveren & Sons, pre-1942)

'Mrs Mark Perrin' 2 Y-YYO
(Hogg & Robertson, pre-1923)
Syn. 'Commodore'

'Mrs Meston' 2 Y-?Y
(W. Backhouse, pre-1869)
Perianth segments sulphur yellow; corona large. Syn. Incomparabilis Sulphureus 'Mrs Meston'. Was "absorbed" into 'Glow'

'Mrs M.Foster' 1 W-Y
(E. Leeds, pre-1877)
Perianth segments sulphur white. Syn. Pseudonarcissus Bicolor 'Mrs M.Foster'. Was "absorbed" into 'Murrell Dobell'

'Mrs Moodie' 1 W-W
Syn. of 'Mrs W.Moodie'

'Mrs Moody' 1 W-W
Syn. of 'Mrs W.Moodie'

'Mrs Morland Crosfield' 1 W-Y
(Barr & Sons, pre-1898)
Perianth segments broadly ovate, pure white, touched yellow at base, inflexed, with margins wavy or incurled, overlapping at base only; corona cylindrical, smooth, clear yellow, mouth expanded and ribbed, lightly frilled, with rim crenate

'Mrs Murray' 3 W-YYO
(W. Backhouse, pre-1869)
Perianth segments creamy white; corona canary yellow, with scarlet-orange at rim. Syn. Barrii Albidus 'Mrs Murray'. Was "absorbed" into 'General Murray'

'Mrs Nelson' 1 Y-Y
(W. Backhouse, pre-1869)
Fl. pale yellow. Dwarf. Syn. Pseudonarcissus Major 'Mrs Nelson'. Was "absorbed" into 'Captain Nelson'

'Mrs Nette O'Melveny' 3 W-GYY
(Mrs R.O. Backhouse, pre-1921)
'Hera' hybrid

'Mrs Norman Cookson' 2 W-W
(N. Cookson, pre-1910)
AM 1910

'Mrs Nott' 3 W-? (b)
(E. & J.C. Martin, pre-1931)

'Mrs Oscar Ronalds' 2 W-P
(O. Ronalds) O. Ronalds, 1956

Perianth segments very broad, rounded or squarish at apex, fairly prominently mucronate, pure white, spreading or a little reflexed, plane, of papery texture, overlapping half or more; the inner segments narrower, with margins wavy; corona funnel-shaped, closely ribbed, deep clear pink, paler at base, mouth straight, split in places and overlapping, frilled, with rim minutely crenate. Tall. Late

'Mrs Pankhurst' 8
(R.A. van der Schoot, pre-1930)

'Mr Sparks' 3 W-R
(S.J. Bisdee, 1940)
'Atanga' × 'Sunstar'

'Mrs Percy Foster' 3 W-W
(G.H. Engleheart, pre-1914)
'Princess Mary' × *N. poeticus*

'Mrs Percy Neale' 2 W-Y
(W.F.M. Copeland, pre-1923)
Fl. rounded; corona broad, soft creamy yellow, frilled

'Mrs Pont' 2 Y-YYO
Perianth segments lemon yellow; corona widely expanded. Syn. of 'Mrs D.J.Pont'

'Mrs Pope' 1 W-W
(de Graaff Bros, pre-1904)

'Mrs Prentis' 5 W-W
Syn. of 'Elizabeth F.Prentis'

'Mrs P.W.Dyson' 2 Y-R
(L. Buckland, pre-1936)
Perianth segments yellow; corona deep red

'Mrs R.C.Notcutt' 3 W-O
(Barr & Sons, pre-1905)
Perianth segments snow white; corona ribbed, buff orange

'Mrs R.H.Rea'
(pre-1934)
?The same as 'Mrs Henry R.Rea'

'Mrs R.J.Lambert' 1 W-P
(pre-1956) Unregistered
Corona ribbed, pale pink, with rim rolled. Tall

'Mrs R.O.Backhouse' 2 W-P
(Mrs R.O. Backhouse, pre-1921)
Fl. 97 mm wide; perianth segments broadly ovate in outline, rounded or somewhat squarish at apex, prominently mucronate, spreading, slightly twisted, overlapping half; the inner segments more or less inflexed; corona cylindrical, pale apricot pink, shading to a deeper tone at rim, with mouth slightly expanded and loosely frilled, rim crenate. 2n=28

'Mrs Robert Sydenham' 1 W-W
(de Graaff Bros, pre-1906)
?'Madame de Graaff' self pollinated
Fl. 89 mm wide, creamy white, facing down; perianth segments overlapping half; corona mouth very slightly expanded, frilled. Mid-season. AM 1906, *C(g) 1930, *AM(g) 1931. See also 'Mrs R.Sydenham'

'Mrs R.Sydenham' 1 W-W
Syn. of 'Mrs Robert Sydenham'

'Mrs Samuel Wallrock' 2 W-? (b)
(Mrs R.O. Backhouse, pre-1921)

'Mrs Sharman Crawford' 5 W-W
(Portuguese origin)
Selection by Mrs Sharman Crawford (c.1884) from wild-collected *N. triandrus*
Fl. variable in width; perianth segments sharply reflexed; corona about three-quarters the length of the perianth segments. Syn. Calathinus 'Mrs Sharman Crawford', Triandrus 'Mrs Sharman Crawford'

'Mrs Shirley Hibberd' 1 Y-Y
(W. Backhouse, pre-1869)
Corona darker in tone than the perianth, with rim flanged. Syn. Pseudonarcissus Major 'Mrs Shirley Hibberd'

'Mrs Syme' 2 W-? (b or c)
(W. Backhouse, pre-1869)
Perianth segments sulphur white; corona widely expanded. Tall. Syn. Incomparabilis Albidus 'Mrs Syme'

'Mrs Thompson' 1 W-W
(?Dutch origin, pre-1891)
Perianth segments ovate, strongly inflexed, twisted or with margins wavy, overlapping at base only; corona narrowly funnel-shaped, lightly ribbed, yellowish white, with mouth expanded and rim crenate. Early. See also 'Mrs Thomson'

'Mrs Thomson' 1 W-W
?Syn. of 'Mrs Thompson'

'Mrs Thorley' 2 (a)
(Hogg & Robertson, pre-1923)

'Mrs T.Philipson' 2 W-W
(A.Gibson, pre-1927)
AM(e)(NZ) 1927

'Mrs Veitch' 1 Y-Y
Syn. of 'Mrs Harry J.Veitch'

'Mrs Vincent' 1 W-W
(W. Backhouse, pre-1869)
Fl. of strong substance. "Absorbed" 'Madonna', 'Mrs James Bateman'

'Mrs Vyner Ellis' 3 W-YYO
(Mrs R.O. Backhouse, pre-1921)
Perianth segments milk white, of strong substance; corona very shallow, expanded, bright yellow, with a broad band of bright reddish orange at rim. Late

'Mrs Wakefield Christie-Miller' 1 W-Y
(J.L. Richardson, pre-1923)
Perianth segments deeply overlapping; corona expanded, primrose yellow

'Mrs Walter Brewster' 3
(pre-1939)
Syn. 'Mrs Brewster'

'Mrs Walter T.Ware' 1 W-Y
Syn. of 'Mrs Walter Ware'

'Mrs Walter Ware' 1 W-Y
(de Graaff Bros, pre-1890)
Perianth segments broadly ovate, blunt, mucronate, inflexed, twisted, overlapping one-third; corona cylindrical, smooth, golden yellow, with rim regularly crenate and widely rolled. Also named 'Mrs W.Ware', 'Mrs Walter T.Ware', 'Mrs W.T.Ware'

'Mrs Walter Wright' 5
(G.H. Engleheart, pre-1913)

'Mrs W.A.Milner'
(W.Backhouse, pre-1869)

'Mrs Warnaar' 1 Y-Y
(Warnaar & Co., pre-1930)
AM(Haarlem) 1930, FA(Haarlem) 1939

'Mrs Watts' 2 W-? (b)
(Mrs R.O. Backhouse, pre-1921)
AM(Haarlem) 1930

'Mrs W.D.Burns' 1 W-W
(W.D. Burns, pre-1927)
Corona creamy white

'Mrs Weightman' 9 W-GYR
(A.E. Lowe, pre-1927)
Corona greenish yellow (154B), with strong yellow-green 144A at base and orange-red (31A). Also named 'Mrs J.G.Weightman'

'Mrs W.Goldring' 1 Y-Y
(W. Backhouse, pre-1869)
Perianth segments sulphur yellow; corona pale yellow. Syn. Pseudonarcissus Lorifolius 'Mrs W.Goldring'

'Mrs Willard'
(pre-1933)

'Mrs William Copeland' 4 W-W
(W.F.M. Copeland, pre-1930)
'Venus' × Div. 4 sdlg of pale colouring
Fl. 95 mm wide; perianth and other petaloid segments in several whorls, creamy white; the outer whorls ovate or broadly ovate, only very slightly mucronate, spreading or a little inflexed, with margins sometimes nicked, overlapping one-third; the inner whorls shorter and narrower, inflexed or strongly inflexed; a few segments at centre; corona segments shorter than the inner whorls of petaloid segments and interspersed among them, opening yellow, becoming creamy white and darker in tone than the petaloid segments, frilled; some segments sometimes continuous at centre, encircling the centre petaloid segments. 2n=21. AM(e) 1930, AM(Haarlem) 1940, *AM(g) 1944, *FCC(g) 1949

'Mrs William Miles' 2 Y-O
(W.F.M.Copeland, pre-1913)
'M.J.Berkeley' × 'Gloria Mundi'
Fl. 102 mm wide; perianth segments broadly ovate, deep yellow, overlapping; corona large, very widely expanded, closely ribbed, rich pure orange. Early. Also named 'Mrs W.Miles'

'Mrs Wilson' 1 W-? (b)
(van Zonneveld Bros & Philippo, pre-1931)

'Mrs W.Miles' 2 O-O
Syn. of 'Mrs William Miles'

'Mrs W.Moodie' 1 W-W
(D.V. West, pre-1927)
Corona creamy white, with a semblance of pink, frilled. See also 'Mrs Moodie', 'Mrs Moody'

'Mrs W.O.Wolseley' 2 W-W
(P.D. Williams, pre-1913)

'Mrs W.T.Ware' 1 W-Y
Syn. of 'Mrs Walter Ware'

'Mrs W.Ware' 1 W-Y
Syn. of 'Mrs Walter Ware'

'Mrs Yvonne' 2 (a)
(Mrs R.O. Backhouse, pre-1921)

'Mr Theo A.Havermeyer' 3 W-YOO
(pre-1939)
Fl. about 80 mm wide; perianth segments broadly ovate, blunt, fairly prominently mucronate, pure white, stained yellow at base, somewhat creased and with midrib showing, overlapping one-third; the inner segments more strongly inflexed, a little more narrowly ovate, with margins wavy or recurved; corona broad and shallow funnel-shaped, light orange, paling to yellow at base and shading to a darker orange at rim, mouth straight and closely ribbed. Also named

'T.A.Havermeyer'

'Mr Tom' 2 WWY-Y
(Jānis Rukšans, 1987) Jānis Rukšans, 1997
'Green Island' × ?'Patriarch'; sdlg no. 81-14-2
Fl. rounded, 105 mm wide; perianth segments pure white, with brilliant greenish yellow 1A at base, spreading, smooth, overlapping; corona small, vivid yellow 17C, with orange tones near mouth, tightly frilled. Early

'Mr van Noort' 1 Y-Y
(pre-1908)
Hybrid between 'Emperor' and 'Golden Spur'
Fl. large; perianth segments light yellow; corona broad, yellow. AM(Haarlem) 1908

'Mr W.A.Sperling' 1 W-? (b)
(R.A. van der Schoot, pre-1923)

'Mr W.B.Walker' 7
(P.D. Williams, pre-1928)

"Mr Wilmer's Great Double Daffodil"
See "Wilmer's Great Double Daffodil"

'Mr W.P.Milner' 1 W-W
Syn. of 'W.P.Milner'

'Much Afraid' 9
(G.H. Engleheart, pre-1930)

'Much Binding' 1 Y-Y
(H.A. Brown, 1936) J.N. Hancock & Co., 1960
Perianth segments acute, plane; corona straight-sided, yellow, with a darker tone at rim and the rim dentate

'Much the Miller' 1 W-W
(Cartwright & Goodwin, pre-1910)
Perianth segments ovate, lemon white; corona frilled, with rim dentate

'Mudlark' 1 Y-Y
(G.H. Johnstone, pre-1949)

'Muezzin' 2 Y-R
(T.H. Piper, 1955) Unregistered
'Royal Mail' × 'Carbineer' hybrid

'Muffet' 3 W-YYO
(P. Phillips) P. Phillips, 1964
Fl. 95 mm wide; corona lemon yellow, with reddish orange at rim. Mid-season. Resembles 'Corofin' but with the perianth segments more rounded and a narrower band of colour at corona rim

'Muirfield' 1 W-GWW
(Brian S. Duncan) Rathowen Daffodils, 1981
'Empress of Ireland' × 'White Empress'; sdlg no. 306

Fl. forming a double triangle, white, with undertones of green; perianth segments broadly ovate, spreading, somewhat concave at apex, overlapping half; the inner segments with margins incurved; corona cylindrical, expanded in upper third, very lightly ribbed, with olive green at base, mouth obscurely 6-lobed, with rim crenate. Early to mid-season. 2n=28. Resembles a better-formed 'Queenscourt' with the perianth segments more tapering at apex

'Mukana' 2 W-P
(A.O. Roblin) A.O. Roblin, 1956
'Pink Petti' × 'Dawnglow'
Corona copper pink

'Mulata' 3 (a)
(Cartwright & Goodwin, pre-1916)

'Mulatto' 1 Y-WWY
(C.G. van Tubergen, pre-1931)
'Citronella' × 'Roxane'
Perianth segments broadly ovate, blunt, very slightly mucronate, sulphur yellow, smooth, with margins minutely incurving at apex, overlapping half; the inner segments narrower, inflexed, a little twisted; corona ribbed towards mouth, opening sulphur yellow, becoming white, with pale yellow at rim, mouth expanded, lobed, frilled, with rim crenate and a little flanged. 2n=29. AM(Haarlem) 1931, FA(Haarlem) 1937

'Mulberry' 3 W-O
(P.D. Williams, pre-1926)
Perianth segments pure white, corona disc-shaped, deep orange. AM(e) 1926

'Muldoon' 4
(Cartwright & Goodwin, pre-1916)

'Mulga' 1 W-W
(R.H. Bath, pre-1929)

'Mullion' 3 W-YYO
(R.A.Scamp) R.A.Scamp, 1996
'Verona' × 'Fairmile'; sdlg no. 461
Fl. 106 mm wide; perianth segments broad, pure white, deeply overlapping; corona very shallow bowl-shaped, pale yellow, with bright orange at rim, mouth neatly ribbed, with rim dentate. Late

'Mulrany' 2 Y-Y
(J.L. Richardson, pre-1950)
'Braemar' × 'Kildare'
Fl. 115 mm wide; perianth segments very broadly ovate, blunt or rounded at apex, only very slightly mucronate, vivid yellow 12A, spreading, plane, with margins nicked, overlapping half; the inner segments more narrowly ovate, a little inflexed, twisted; corona cylindrical, smooth, with rim regularly crenate and widely rolled. AM(e) 1950

'Mulroy Bay' 1 Y-Y
(Brian S.Duncan, 1983) Brian S.Duncan, 1993
'Golden Jewel' × 'Midas Touch'; sdlg no. 914
Fl. 102 mm wide, deep golden yellow; perianth segments broadly ovate, blunt, prominently mucronate, smooth, with midrib showing, overlapping half; the inner segments more narrowly ovate, square-shouldered at base, a little inflexed, with margins wavy; corona cylindrical, smooth, with mouth slightly expanded and lightly frilled. Early to mid-season

N. multiflorus Lamarck = *N. cupularis*

'Multnomah' 2 Y-O
(Murray W.Evans) Murray W.Evans, 1972
'Paricutin' × 'Armada'
Fl. 110 mm wide

'Mulusine' 5
'Albatross' × *N. triandrus* var. *loiseleurii*

'Mulwa' 2 (a)
(Mrs R.O. Backhouse, pre-1921)

'Mumin' 2 W-P
(Jānis Rukšans, 1986) Jānis Rukšans, 1997
Sdlg no. 82-40-15
Fl. 105 mm wide; perianth segments pure white, plane, smooth, deeply overlapping; corona cylindrical, opening pale yellowish pink 29D, paler towards rim, becoming darker in tone (38D), sometimes with a lilac tinge, mouth slightly expanded, closely frilled. Early. Sunproof

'Mundana' 2 Y-O
(pre-1956)
Corona reddish orange

'Mundra' 2 (a)
(Mrs R.O. Backhouse, pre-1921)
AM(Haarlem) 1930

'Munlochy' 2 W-W
(J.M. de Navarro, pre-1954)
'Chinese White' × 'Murmansk'

'Munna' 2 W-WWR
(A.O. Roblin, 1946) A.O. Roblin, 1956
'Llandaff' × 'Girrawheen'

N. × *munozii-garmendiae* Fernández Casas = *N.* × *susannae*

'Muntham' 2 W-? (b)
(West & Fell, pre-1935)
Perianth segments creamy white; corona buff

'Murchison' 1 W-Y
(H.A. Brown, 1936) J.N. Hancock & Co., 1965
Perianth segments ice white; corona smooth, bright

yellow. Very late. Resembles a larger and later-flowered 'Glenroy'

'Murcia' 3 W-? (b)
(R.O. Backhouse, pre-1933)

'Muriel' 9
(Sir J.A.R. Gore-booth, pre-1908)

'Muriel Bibby' 3 W-YYO
(Mrs R.O. Backhouse, pre-1921)
Fl. 81 mm wide, facing slightly downwards; perianth segments creamy white, with lemon at base, reflexed, irregular, overlapping half; corona bowl-shaped, sulphur yellow, with bright orange at rim, frilled. Mid-season to late

'Muriel Evans' 1 Y-Y
(pre-1949)
Fl. intense golden yellow. Tall

'Muriel Frith' 2 W-? (b)
(West & Fell, pre-1935)
Corona light apricot, with pink at rim

'Murillo' 3 W-YYR
(A.E. Lowe, pre-1927)

'Murlough' 9 W-GYR
(Ballydorn Bulb Farm, 1973) Ballydorn Bulb Farm, 1987
('Cantabile' hybrid) open pollinated
Corona saucer-shaped, opening green, with red at rim, the mid-zone becoming yellow. Dwarf

'Murmansk' 2 W-W
(G.L. Wilson, pre-1948)
'Samite' × 'Slemish'
Perianth segments broadly ovate, blunt or truncate, prominently mucronate, ice white, with shades of green at base, spreading at base, loosely reflexed towards apex, overlapping half; the inner segments more narrowly ovate, more stronglyreflexed at apex, with margins wavy; corona funnel-shaped, smooth, mouth lightly ribbed, even, rim obscurely crenate and slightly flanged

'Murndal' 2 Y-O
(J.N. Hancock & Co., pre-1949)
Perianth segments pale yellow; corona reddish orange

'Murrayfield' 3 W-GYO
(T. Bloomer) Rathowen Daffodils, 1984
('Chinese White' × 'Ballycastle') × 'Woodland Belle'; sdlg no. 279
Fl. forming a double triangle; perianth segments very broadly ovate, blunt or sometimes truncate, slightly mucronate, spreading, overlapping half; the inner segments a little more narrowly ovate, less obviously mucronate, square-shouldered at base, somewhat inflexed, with margins sometimes incurved; corona very shallow bowl-shaped, ribbed, lemon yellow, with green at base and a clearly defined band of bright orange at rim, mouth split in places and overlapping, frilled. Mid-season. Resembles 'Ravenhill' but with a white perianth and a more clearly defined corona rim

'Murreil' 3 W-? (b)
(pre-1926)
AM(Haarlem) 1926

'Murrell Dobell' 1 W-Y
(E. Leeds, pre-1877)
Syn. 'M.Dobell', Pseudonarcissus Bicolor 'Murrell Dobell'. "Absorbed" 'Jeannette', 'Mrs M.Foster' and 'Sims Reeves'

'Murrumbidgee' 1 Y-Y
(J.N. Hancock & Co., 1976) Unregistered

'Musard Orientalis' 8 W-O
Syn. of 'Muzart Orientalis'. Appears to be the earliest form of the cv. name, but Bowles' reference (1934:155) to 'Muzart Orientalis' in Dutch catalogues may pre-date it

'Musarto' W-YYO
Syn. of 'Musartus'

'Musartus' W-YYO
(pre-1633)
Fls 2-3 per stem, star-shaped; corona sulphur yellow, with orange at rim. Syn. 'Musarto'. ?The same as 'Muzart Orientalis'

'Muscadet' 2 W-Y
(J. Gerritsen & Son) J. Gerritsen & Son, 1960
Fl. 100 mm wide; corona pale ivory yellow. Early. Scented. 2n=28. Resembles a taller 'Gervo' of better form. AM(Haarlem) 1960

'Musette' 11a W-YYO
(J. Gerritsen & Son) J. Gerritsen & Son, 1984
'Palmares' × 'Pick Up'; sdlg no. 911
Perianth segments greenish white 157C; corona light greenish yellow 4C, with bronze yellow at base and pale orange 24D at rim. Mid-season

'Musgrove Park' 1 Y-Y
(E.W. Philpott)

'Music' 3 Y-? (a)
(Sir C.H. Cave, pre-1908)

'Music' 2 W-GWW
(Barr & Sons, pre-1915)
Fl. 100 mm wide; corona broad, expanded, pure white, shading to ivory and green at base

'Music' 2 W-PPY
(G.E. Mitsch) G.E. Mitsch, 1979
'Romance' × 'Cool Flame'; sdlg no. LL14/5
Fl. 100 mm wide; perianth segments white, suffused pink; corona salmon rose, with amber at rim, mouth flared and frilled. Mid-season

'Music Hall' 1 W-Y
(J.L. Richardson, pre-1923)
Fl. about 140 mm wide; perianth segments broadly ovate, blunt, only very slightly mucronate, pure white, inflexed, somewhat creased, with margins a little wavy, overlapping one-third; the inner segments with margins more strongly wavy, sometimes twisted or with margins recurved; corona cylindrical, smooth, deep golden yellow, with mouth ribbed, rim widely flanged and deeply and regularly notched and dentate. AM(Haarlem) 1934, FA(Haarlem) 1935

'Musician' 3 W-? (b)
(The Brodie of Brodie, c.1932)
'Mozart' × 'Hades'; sdlg no. 120/A/27

'Musidorus' 9
(G.H. Engleheart, pre-1910)

'Muskegan' 2 W-? (b)
(S.A. van Konynenberg & Co., pre-1950)

'Musket' 2 Y-O
(A. Overton) A. Overton, 1960
Perianth segments rich yellow, smooth; corona shallow, bright reddish orange

'Musketeer' 1 (a)
(W.B. Cranfield, pre-1937)
Perianth segments rich lemon yellow, overlapping; corona buttercup yellow, frilled. Mid-season. 2n=28. Syn. 'Ormolu'. *HC(g) 1936, *AM(g) 1941. Received HC 1936 as sdlg no. 172

'Muslin' 10 W-W
(D. Blanchard, pre-1952)
N. cantabricus var. *foliosus* × *N. romieuxii*

"Mussart his Daffodil"
?The same as 'Muzart Orientalis'

'Mussolini' 1 (a)
(A. Frylink & Sons, pre-1933)
AM(Haarlem) 1933

'Mustang' 2 Y-YOO
(J.O. Sherrard, pre-1943)

'Mustapha' 1 Y-Y
(de Graaff Bros, pre-1923)
Perianth segments acute, rich yellow; corona dark yellow, neatly frilled

'Mustardseed' 2 Y-Y
(A. Gray, pre-1937)
N. asturiensis × *N. poeticus*
See also 'Mustard Seed'

'Mustard Seed' 2 Y-Y
Syn. of 'Mustardseed'

'Muster' 4 W-O
(Jackson's Daffodils) Jackson's Daffodils, 1993
'Glowing Red' × 'Toya'; sdlg no. 18/85
Fl. 100 mm wide; perianth and other petaloid segments ovate, yellowish white 155B; corona segments vivid orange 28B. Early

mutatis = *N. triandrus*

N. muticus Gay = *N. abscissus*

'Mutineer' 1 W-W
(J.S. Leitch) J.S. Leitch, 1967
Fl. 115 mm wide

'Muzara Orientalis' 8 W-O
Syn. of 'Muzart Orientalis'

'Muzart Orientalis' 8 W-O
(pre-1871)
Poetaz
Syn. 'Musard Orientalis', 'Mozart's', 'Muzart's'. ?The same as *N. tazetta* var. *trewianus*, "Mussart his Daffodil", 'Musartus'. Probably the same as 'Mozart'. See also 'Muzara Orientalis'

'Muzart's' 8 W-O
Syn. of 'Muzart Orientalis'

'My Angel' 11a W-YYW
(Jānis Rukšans) Jānis Rukšans, 1997
'April Tears' × 'Canasta'; sdlg no. 85-22-3
Fls 3-5 per stem, 65 mm wide; perianth segments pure white, reflexed, smooth, deeply overlapping; corona deeply split, closely overlying the perianth, brilliant greenish yellow 5B, paling to pure white in upper third, frilled. Late to very late

'Mybird' 2 W-?
(A. Overton) A. Overton, 1960

'My Choice' 2 W-O
(O. Ronalds, pre-1951)
'Hugh Poate' × 'Skylark'
Perianth segments pale yellow, smooth, overlapping; corona pale orange

'My Choice' 2 W-P
(Mrs H.K. Richardson) M.J. Jefferson-Brown, 1975
Corona deep pink. Syn. 'My Lady'

'My Dear' 2 W-? (b)
(R.O. Backhouse, pre-1934)

'My Desire' 2 (a)
(A. Johnson, pre-1937)

'My Dream' 1 Y-Y
(R.H.Glover, pre-1990) Unregistered
'Comal' × ('Warbin' × 'Dream Prince')

'Myfida' 1 W-W
(W.A. Watts, pre-1931)

'My Fondant' 3 W-? (b)
(J.E. Exley, pre-1950)

'My Fortune' 2 Y-Y
(R.H.Glover, pre-1993) Unregistered

'My Gracious' 2 W-P
(J.N. Hancock & Co., 1976) Unregistered
Sdlg no. 49/76H
Corona flared, deep strawberry pink, frilled. Early

'My Joy' 2 W-? (b)
(M. van Waveren & Sons, pre-1942)

'My Lady' 2 W-P
(M.J. Jefferson-Brown) M.J. Jefferson-Brown, 1985
Corona slender, dark pink. Mid-season

'My Lady' 2 W-P
Syn. of 'My Choice'

'Mylor' 2 Y-Y
(The Brodie of Brodie, pre-1930)
'Pilgrimage' × 'Royalist'
Resembles an improved 'Pilgrimage'

'My Love' 2 W-Y
(J.L. Richardson, pre-1948)
'White Sentinel' self pollinated; sdlg no. 234
Fl. 100 mm wide; perianth segments very broadly ovate, blunt or slightly truncate, only very slightly mucronate, pale creamy white, spreading, slightly concave, smooth and of good substance, overlapping half; the inner segments more narrowly ovate, inflexed at base, reflexed at apex, sometimes twisted; corona cylindrical, smooth, opening brilliant greenish yellow 5B, becoming very pale, with greenish lemon at rim, mouth expanded and finely ribbed, split in places and overlapping, with rim dentate and slightly flanged. 2n=28. AM(e) 1957, FCC(e) 1959

'Myms Silver' 3 W-YYO
(Brodie Gardens) Mrs A.M. Allen, 1959
Fl. 95 mm wide; perianth segments creamy white; corona pale yellow. Late

'My My' 2 W-P

(J.L. Richardson) M.J. Jefferson-Brown, 1967
'Salmon Trout' × 'Rose Caprice'
Perianth segments overlapping

'Myna' 2 Y-O
(A.M. Wilson, pre-1948)
'Fortune' hybrid
Perianth segments clear lemon yellow; corona orange

'Myola' 2 W-Y
(T. Morrison) T. Morrison, 1960
Corona opening chrome yellow, becoming dark buff yellow

'Myolanda' 2 W-O
(P. de Jager & Sons) P. de Jager & Sons, 1963
'Pink Fancy' hybrid
Fl. 110 mm wide; perianth segments ivory white; corona pale orange (24D). Mid-season. AM(Haarlem) 1963

'Myomy' 2 W-? (b)
(Mrs Ben Robertson, pre-1953)

'Myosotis' 3 W-? (b)
(Mrs R.O. Backhouse, pre-1921)

'Myra' 2 W-Y
(Mrs R.O. Backhouse, pre-1919)
Corona soft lemon yellow

'Myra Wyanda' 3 W-? (b)
(J.W.A. Lefeber, pre-1943)

'Myriantha' 3 W-WWR
(G.H. Johnstone, 1943) G.H. Johnstone, 1959
'Elspeth' hybrid
Fl. 70 mm wide. Mid-season

'Myril' 3 W-YYR
(J.T. Gray, pre-1949)
Perianth segments broadly ovate, blunt or rounded at apex, slightly mucronate, pure white, spreading, plane, smooth and of good substance, overlapping half; the inner segments slightly narrower, more usually rounded at apex, not noticeably mucronate; corona disc-shaped, closely ribbed, with a broad band of red at rim, with the rim minutely crenate

'Myrin'
(pre-1913)

'Myrmidon' 2 W-? (b)
(Mrs R.O. Backhouse, pre-1921)

'Myrniong' 2 (a)
(H.A. Brown, pre-1936)

'Myrniong' ?-P
(Alister Clark, pre-1948)

'Myroe' 2 (a)
(G.L. Wilson, pre-1937)

'Myrtle' 2 Y-Y
(P.D. Williams, pre-1908)
Fl. clear deep yellow; perianth segments acute

'Myrtle Richardson' 2 W-P
(Brian S.Duncan) Mrs J.M.Baker, 1996
'Verran'? × 'Fellowship'?
Fl. 110 mm wide; perianth segments broadly ovate, acute, plane, smooth; corona broad funnel-shaped, mid-pink, with undertones of lilac, rim entire. Mid-season. Sunproof. Resembles an improved 'Roseate Tern'

'Myrtle Wright' 2 W-? (b or c)
(H.E. Sharp, pre-1930)

'Mystaris' 2 W-WWO
(C.G. van Tubergen) C.G. van Tubergen, 1956
Perianth segments pure white; corona shallow, widely expanded, ivory white, with a narrow band of soft orange at rim, frilled. AM(Haarlem) 1956

'Mysterious' 2 W-W
(G.E. Mitsch, 1972) G.E. Mitsch, 1982
'Silken Sails' × 'Wings of Song'; sdlg no. HH100/1
Fl. 103 mm wide; corona disc-shaped, reflexed. Mid-season

'Mystery' 1 W-Y
(W. Welchman, pre-1913)
Corona pale citron yellow

'Mystery' 2 Y-O
(Unknown origin) M.J. Jefferson-Brown, 1975
Perianth segments gold; corona scarlet-orange. Mid-season

'Mystic' 3 W-GWO
(G.L. Wilson, pre-1923)
'Miss Weisse' × 'Poet'
Fl. 75 mm wide, facing slightly downwards; perianth segments very broadly ovate, rounded at apex, prominently mucronate, creamy greenish white, spreading or a little reflexed, slightly concave, overlapping half; the inner segments a little inflexed, with margins wavy or incurling; corona very shallow bowl-shaped, loosely ribbed, creamy white, with apple green at base and a very narrow band of soft pinkish orange (25B) at rim, frilled. Late. 2n=14. AM(e) 1928

'Mystic' 3 W-YYR
(R.H.Glover, pre-1993) Unregistered

'Mystical' 1 W-W
(L. Buckland, pre-1925)

'Mystic Flame' 2 (a)

(Mrs R.O. Backhouse, pre-1921)

'Mystique' 2 W-W
(J.N.Hancock & Co., 1983) Unregistered
'Chillagoe' × 'Beryl Walker'; sdlg no. 11/83H
Perianth segments acute, milk white; corona opening pale lemon yellow, becoming creamy white, with rim closely and deeply notched, as if fringed. Very early

'My Sweetheart' 3 W-YYR
(John R.Reed, 1986) John R.Reed, 1997
'Hampstead' open pollinated; sdlg no. 81-197-1
Fl. 67 mm wide; perianth segments very broadly ovate, pure white, inflexed; the inner segments almost touching one another; corona bowl-shaped, deep yellow, with intense orange-red at rim. Mid-season

'Myth' 2 W-W
(J.S. Leitch) J.S. Leitch, 1960
Fl. 114 mm wide

'Mythical' 3 (a)
(A.M. Wilson, pre-1937)

'My Valentine' 2 W-Y
(E.W. Philpott)
'Cantatrice' × 'Guardian'
Perianth segments pure white; corona pale lemon

'My Word' 2 W-P
(Mrs E. Murray, 1962) J.N. Hancock & Co., 1979
'Jess Johnson' × 'Pommy'
Fl. 90 mm wide, perianth segments broadly ovate, blunt, only very slightly mucronate, pure white, inflexed, concave, with margins sometimes wavy or incurling, overlapping one-third to a half; the inner segments more strongly inflexed; corona funnel-shaped, finely ribbed, strong yellowish pink 38A, with mouth expanded and lightly frilled, rim crenate with margins minutely dentate. Early. 2n=29

N

'Nabis' 2 W-W
(W. Jackson Sr, 1946) W. Jackson Jr, 1956
'Nimue' × 'Hedi'

'Nabob' 2 ?W-Y
(E. Leeds, pre-1877)
Perianth segments marbled with sulphur yellow; corona large, expanded. Syn. Incomparabilis Sulphureus 'Nabob'. Was "absorbed" into 'Figaro'

'Nabob' 3 (b)
(W.B. Hartland, pre-1907)

'Nabob' 3 W-O
(F.H. Chapman, pre-1931)
Perianth segments pale yellow; corona expanded, reddish orange. Resembles an improved 'Croesus' with a larger and more-disc-like corona

'Nabob' 2 Y-OOY
(Murray W.Evans, 1971) Murray W.Evans, 1982
'Chemawa' × ('Paricutin' × 'Rustom Pasha'); sdlg no. N-55/1
Fl. 90 mm wide. Early to mid-season. Resembles a more refined 'Chemawa' of deeper colour

'Nabowla' 1 W-W
(S.J. Bisdee, pre-1939)
'White Emperor' × 'Beersheba'

'Nacooma' 2 W-P
(S.J. Bisdee, 1948)
'Pink Princess' × 'Roseneath'

'Nacre' 2 Y-P
(Murray W.Evans, 1975) Murray W.Evans, 1986
'Salome' × (['Binkie' × 1 YYW-W] × 'Suede'); sdlg no. S-2/1
Mid-season

'Nada' 2 (a)
(pre-1926)
AM(Haarlem) 1926

'Nada' 3 W-? (b)
(J.T. Gray, pre-1938)
Corona disc-shaped, with red at rim

'Nadia' 3 W-YPP
Syn. of 'Nadia's Memory'

'Nadia's Memory' 3 W-YPP
(G.J.Phillips) J.N.Hancock & Co., 1997
Sdlg no. 76-18-6
Perianth segments broadly ovate; corona cup-shaped, ribbed, intense reddish pink, with creamy yellow at base. Late. Formerly named 'Nadia'

'Nadya' 2 W-Y
(W. Jackson Sr, 1939)
'Veronique' × 'Nimue'

'Naesam' 2 W-W
(R.H. Bath, pre-1923)

'Naevia' 1 W-P
Syn. of 'Noevia'

'Naevis' 2 W-P
(C.E.Radcliff, 1939)
'Pinkeen' × 'Pink o' Dawn'
See also 'Noevta', 'Noevia'

'Nagara' 2 W-Y
(T.H. Piper) T.H. Piper, 1956
'White Sentinel' × 'Kanchenjunga'

'Nagari' 2 W-P
(S.J. Bisdee, 1954)
'Pinkie' × 'Lady Binney'

'Nagasaki' 2 Y-O
(Mrs B.T. Simpson) Mrs B.T. Simpson, 1966
Fl. 102 mm wide; corona reddish orange. Late. Resembles 'Chungking' in colour

'Nagora' 2 W-? (b)
(R.H. Bath, pre-1929)

'Naiad' 5
(G.H. Engleheart, pre-1897)
N. poeticus × *N. triandrus*
FCC 1897

'Nairn' 3 W-YYO
(The Brodie of Brodie, c.1927)
'Bernardino' × 'Sunstar'
Perianth segments very broad, pure white; corona deep red, paling to gold at base

'Nairobi' 2 W-O
(J.L. Richardson, pre-1945)
Fl. 102 mm wide; perianth segments very broadly ovate, blunt or squarish at apex, slightly mucronate, spreading, plane or with margins very slightly wavy and sometimes incurling, smooth and of thick substance, overlapping half; the inner segments more narrowly ovate, a little inflexed; corona bowl-shaped, loosely ribbed, vivid orange 28B, mouth expanded and in places split and overlapping, frilled. Mid-season. AM(e) 1948

'Naivasha' 2 W-P
(Brian S. Duncan) Brian S. Duncan, 1990
'Pismo Beach' × 'High Society'; sdlg no. 1068
Fl. rounded, 112 mm wide; perianth segments very broadly ovate, blunt and prominently mucronate, spreading, shallowly concave, smooth, overlapping half; the inner segments narrower, somewhat inflexed, square-shouldered at base; corona bowl-shaped, smooth, deep rose pink, paler at base and with lilac tones, mouth expanded and frilled, rim crenate. Mid-season to late

'Nakajima' 3 Y-R
(Jackson's Daffodils, 1979) Jackson's Daffodils, 1991
'Kopi' × 'Tia'; sdlg no. 214/79
Fl. forming a double triangle, 110 mm wide; perianth segments broadly ovate, blunt, very slightly mucronate, brilliant greenish yellow 6B, spreading, a little concave, overlapping half; the inner segments more narrowly ovate, square-shouldered at base; corona cup-shaped, smooth, orange-red (30B), with

mouth straight and wavy. Mid-season

'Nakomis' 1 W-? (b)
(R.H. Bath, pre-1927)

'Nakota' 2 W-W
(E.C. Powell, pre-1946)

'Nala' 1 W-Y
(W. Jackson Jr, 1965) Unregistered
'Rowella' × 'Lod'; sdlg no. 110/65

'Namesake' ?-P
(Alister Clark, pre-1948)

'Namoi' 2 W-?
(Alister Clark, 1930) J. Sharp, 1960

'Nampa' 1 Y-W
(G.E. Mitsch) G.E. Mitsch, 1958
'King of the North' × 'Content'
Perianth segments broadly ovate, blunt or rounded at apex, lemon yellow, with slight white mucro and with white at base, slightly reflexed, a little twisted, overlapping half; the inner segments more strongly twisted; corona cylindrical, angled, white, touched lemon yellow at rim, a little frilled, with rim crenate and slightly flanged. Mid-season. 2n=28

'Namraj' 2 Y-YYR
(Tom Bloomer) Rathowen Daffodils, 1988
'Golden Flame' × 'Bunclody'; sdlg no. 349
Perianth segments very broadly ovate, blunt, slightly mucronate, deep yellow, spreading, plain, smooth, with broad and shallow midrib showing, regular, overlapping half; the inner segments only slightly narrower, rounded at base; corona cup-shaped, smooth, golden yellow, with a broad area of dark green at base and a well-defined band of orange-red at rim, mouth a little expanded and lightly frilled. Mid-season. Resembles 'Front Royal' but with the colour at corona rim more clearly defined and of a deeper tone

'Namsos' 2 W-W
(J.L. Richardson, pre-1944)
'Niphetos' × 'Kanchenjunga'
Fl. about 111 mm wide, milk white; perianth segments broad, overlapping; corona widely expanded, frilled, with rim dentate. AM(e) 1949, AM(Haarlem) 1950

'Nana' 2 or 3 W-? (b or c)
(pre-1915)

'Nana Flore Sulphureo Pleno Major'
(pre-1792)

'Nanaval' 2 W-Y
(J.S. Leitch) J.S. Leitch, 1957

'Nancegollan' 7 W-W
(M.P. Williams, pre-1937)
Perianth segments broadly ovate, spreading, with margins wavy, overlapping half; corona cylindrical, lightly ribbed, mouth straight, wavy, with rim crenate

'Nanchisel' 2 Y-O
(R.V. Favell, 1939) R.V. Favell, 1965
Fl. 102 mm wide; perianth segments egg-yolk yellow; corona yellow-orange. Mid-season. Resembles 'Fortune' but with a darker-coloured corona

'Nancy' 2 or 3 W-? (b or c)
(C.B. Blampied, pre-1927)

'Nancy' 2 Y-Y
Syn. of 'Nancy Eliott'

'Nancy Burrell' 1
(?A.M. Wilson, pre-1915)

'Nancy Cumberlege' 2 Y-? (a)
(N.Y. Lower, pre-1929)
'Bernardino' × 'Fortune'

'Nancy Dickinson' 2 W-? (b)
(G. Lewis) D.S. Bell, 1955

'Nancy Eliott' 2 Y-Y
(G. Churcher, pre-1931)
Fl. 89 mm wide; perianth segments pale sulphur, overlapping half; corona broad funnel-shaped, lemon yellow. Mid-season to late. Syn. 'Nancy'

'Nancy Havergal' 2 W-Y
(A.O. Roblin, 1941)
'Nelly' × 'Loila'
Corona bright yellow

'Nancy Love' 9 W-GOR
(Mrs M.S.Yerger) Mrs M.S.Yerger, 1996
Poeticus hybrid open pollinated; sdlg no. A 2-4
Fl. 54 mm wide; the inner shorter than the outer perianth segments; corona cup-shaped, strong orange 26B, with light yellow-green 145B at base and orange-red (35A) at rim. Dwarf. Mid-season

'Nancy Reagan' 2 Y-YYR
(W.H. Roesé) W.H. Roesé, 1985
'Air Marshal' × 'Falstaff'; sdlg no. 3/17/85
Corona colour variable. Mid-season

'Nancy Stair' 1 W-W
(J.T. Gray, pre-1933)

'Nanda' 1 W-W
(Barr & Sons, pre-1923)
Perianth segments pure white, overlapping; corona opening creamy white, becoming paler

in tone, neatly frilled

'Nanda' 2 Y-R
(West & Fell, pre-1938)
Perianth segments deep yellow; corona opening orange, becoming coppery red

'Nanda' 2 W-P
(W. Jackson Jr, 1956) W. Jackson Jr, 1968
'Palin' × 'Ceram'; sdlg no. 95/56

'Nanette' 8 W-?
(pre-1807)

'Nanette' 4 W-W
(J.L. Richardson, pre-1927)
Fl. 54 mm wide, white, facing slightly downwards; perianth and other petaloid segments rounded at apex, sometimes truncate, very slightly mucronate, with midrib showing and with margins incurling, overlapping half; the outer whorl spreading; the inner one-third the length of the outer whorl of petaloid segments and opposite to them, inflexed, sometimes sharply folded along midrib, with cream at base; a loose cluster of short narrow segments at centre

'Nangeela' 1 Y-Y
(West & Fell, pre-1935)
Fl. deep golden yellow

'Nangiles' 4 Y-R
(R.A.Scamp) R.A.Scamp, 1996
'Paricutin' × 'Tamar Fire'; sdlg no. 294
Fl. rounded, 85 mm wide; perianth and other petaloid segments in several whorls, broadly ovate, bright golden yellow; corona segments regularly interspersed, bright red, slightly frilled. Early to mid-season

'Nanhellan' 2 W-P
(G.H. Johnstone, 1954) Mrs A. Johnstone, 1966
'Regency Rose' × 'Wild Rose'
Fl. 102 mm wide; corona coral pink. Late. Resembles 'Chelsea China' but with blunter perianth segments

'Nanjemoy' 1 Y-Y
(E.C. Powell, pre-1946)

'Nanking' 2 Y-R
(J.L. Richardson, pre-1939)
'Marksman' × 'Penquite'
Perianth segments pinkish buff yellow; corona coppery red

'Nannie Netticoat' 2 W-? (b)
(Mrs R.O. Backhouse, pre-1921)

'Nanny Nunn' 3 Y-OOR
(Mrs R.O. Backhouse, pre-1921)
Perianth segments pale creamy yellow, with a darker tone at base, overlapping; corona widely expanded, yellowish orange, with rich orange-red at rim. 2n=21. AM(Haarlem) 1926, *HC(g)(c) 1927, *HC(g) 1936

'Nansidwell' 2 W-P
(R.A. Scamp) R.A. Scamp, 1993
'Dailmanach' × 'Accent'; sdlg no. 166
Fl. 130 mm wide; perianth segments broad, acute, deeply overlapping; corona bright rose pink, paling slightly at base, mouth slightly expanded and neatly frilled. Mid-season

'Nansloe' 1 W-W
(P.D. Williams, pre-1927)

'Nanstallon' 1 Y-Y
(R.A.Scamp) R.A.Scamp, 1996
'Viking' × 'Ristin'; sdlg no. 52
Fl. 112 mm wide, soft primrose yellow; perianth segments ovate, plane, deeply overlapping; corona cylindrical, with mouth a little flared and rim crenate. Early to mid-season

'Nantucket' 2 W-O
(J.L. Richardson) J.L. Richardson, 1959
'Kilworth' × 'Arbar'
Corona very shallow bowl-shaped, reddish orange

'Nantwich' 2 W-? (b)
(E.L. Jones, pre-1949)

'Nanty' 2 (a)
(L. van Leeuwen & Son, pre-1931)
Syn. 'Souvereign'

'Nanty' 6 Y-Y
(Glenbrook Bulb Farm, pre-1992) Unregistered
'Little Beauty' × *N. cyclamineus*; sdlg no. 8/88

N. nanus Spach 13 Section Pseudonarcissus

'Nanus' 2 Y-Y
(pre-1878)
Syn. Incomparabilis Sulphureus 'Nanus'

'Nanus' 2 ?-Y
(pre-1878)
Corona dark yellow, tinged orange. Syn. Incomparabilis Leedsii 'Nanus'

'Nanus' 2? W-Y
Syn. of 'Dove'

'Nanus' 3 Y-Y
Syn. of 'Tall Golden Mary' and 'Dwarf Golden Mary'

'Nanushca' 2 Y-P
(D.S. Bell) D.S. Bell, 1982
'Red Conquest' hybrid × 'Lemonaire'
Fl. 100 mm wide; perianth segments lemon yellow;

corona deep pink, frilled. Mid-season

'Nanus Plenus' 4 Y-Y
(pre-1871)
Fl. rich yellow; the segments closely arranged. Dwarf. Syn. Pseudonarcissus 'Nanus Plenus'

'Nanus Plenus Monstrosus' 4 Y-Y
Fl. rich yellow. Dwarf. Resembles a large flowered 'Nanus Plenus'. Syn. Pseudonarcissus 'Nanus Plenus Monstrosus'

'Naomi' 2 W-YYO
(Mrs R.O. Backhouse, pre-1921)
Perianth segments broadly ovate, blunt, fairly prominently mucronate, yellowish white, a little inflexed, concave and with margins sometimes incurling, overlapping one-third to a half; the inner segments more strongly inflexed and with margins wavy; corona bowl-shaped, smooth, butter yellow, with reddish orange at rim, mouth expanded and a little frilled, rim irregularly and slightly notched. AM(Haarlem) 1929, FA(Haarlem) 1936

'Naomi Lutwyche' 1 W-W
(C.E. Radcliff, 1938)
'Saint Aloysius' × 'Beersheba'

'Napé' 1 W-W
(W. Jackson Sr, 1938)
'Beersheba' × 'Quartz'

'Naples' 2 Y-YOO
(A. Gibson, pre-1951)

'Napoleon' 1 Y-Y
(M. van Waveren & Sons, pre-1930)
Fl. large; corona slightly darker in tone than the perianth

'Napper' 2 W-?
(Alister Clark, 1950) J. Sharp, 1960

'Nar' 1 W-Y
(W. Jackson Sr, 1945)
'Helga' × 'Napé'

'Narang' 1 W-Y
(W. Jackson Jr, 1957) Unregistered
'Tamara' × 'Preamble'; sdlg no. 313/57

"Narcissus of the Sun"
Syn. of 'Soleil d'Or'

'Narla' 1 Y-O
(J.T. Gray, 1940) Parr's Nurseries, 1958
Perianth segments rounded; corona narrow, dark copper orange

'Narmara' 1 Y-Y

(A.O. Roblin) A.O. Roblin, 1956
'Rianga' × 'Fahan'
Fl. deep gold; corona with rim dentate and deeply flanged

'Narok' 4 W-O
(Brian S. Duncan) Brian S. Duncan, 1991
'Monterrico' × 'Doctor Hugh'; sdlg no. 753
Fl. 102 mm wide; perianth and other petaloid segments white; the outer whorl broad, spreading; the inner whorl very slightly narrower and a little inflexed; some smaller segments at centre; corona segments interspersed, deep orange, touched yellow at rim. Mid-season

'Narrabi' 9 W-GYR
Syn. of 'Narrabri'

'Narrabri' 9 W-GYR
(G.H. Engleheart, pre-1927)
Perianth segments very broad, blunt or squarish at apex, sometimes a little truncate, fairly prominently mucronate, reflexed, concave at apex and with margins sometimes incurling, of good substance, overlapping half; the inner segments narrower, roundish, not noticeably mucronate, less strongly reflexed; corona small disc-shaped, tightly ribbed, yellow, with green at base and a very narrow band of red at rim. AM(c) 1928. See also 'Narrabi', 'Narribri'

'Narracott' 2 W-? (b)
(R.O. Backhouse, pre-1938)

'Narrawong' 2 W-OOY
(Heathcote Bulb Nursery, pre-1960) Unregistered
Corona narrow, apricot orange, with yellow at rim

'Narrewarren' 1 W-Y
(J.N. Hancock & Co., c.1955) Unregistered
'Bonnington' × 'Cromarty'

'Narribri' 9 W-GYR
Syn. of 'Narrabri'

'Narrican' 2 Y-O
(C.A. Nethercote, pre-1957) Unregistered
Perianth segments rich yellow, smooth; corona reddish orange, frilled. Tall

'Narvik' 2 Y-O
(J.L. Richardson, pre-1940)
'Carbineer' × 'Porthilly'
Fl. 95 mm wide; perianth segments broadly ovate, blunt, prominently mucronate, golden yellow, spreading, plane, regular, overlapping half; the inner segments a little narrower, slightly inflexed, shouldered at base and sometimes "thumbed", with margins slightly wavy; corona long cup-shaped, deep orange, mouth straight and frilled. Mid-season. 2n=28. *(Gulval)PC(m) 1940, AM(e) 1942,

AM(Haarlem) 1950, FCC(Haarlem) 1956

'Narya' 3 Y-YYR
(Brian S. Duncan) Rathowen Daffodils, 1978
'Merlin' open pollinated; sdlg no. 189
Fl. 94 mm wide; perianth segments mid-yellow; corona deeper in tone than the perianth, with deep red at rim. Mid-season. Resembles a taller and more vigorous 'Montego'

'Naseby' 2 Y-Y
(?New Zealand origin, pre-1997) Unregistered

'Nash' 1 W-? (b)
(A.M. Wilson, pre-1950)

'Nashua' 1 W-W
(E.C. Powell, pre-1949)
'Kenbane' × 'Fortune'

'Nashville' 2 Y-R
(The Brodie of Brodie, pre-1931)
Perianth segmernts deep yellow; corona red. Early

'Nassau' 3 (a)
(de Graaff Bros, pre-1928)
Syn. 'Walter Scott'

'Nasute' 1 W-Y
(A.O. Roblin, 1947)
'Bonnington' × 'Kanchenjunga'

'Natasha' 2 W-Y
(D.J. Cooper) D.J. Cooper, 1959
Fl. 115 mm wide; corona pale creamy yellow. Late

'Natee' 2 W-P
(W. Jackson Jr) W. Jackson Jr, 1966
'Imp' × 'Dallbro'

'Nathalie' 2 W-? (b)
(W.B. Hartland, pre-1914)

'Nathalie' 2 W-O
(G.H. Johnstone, pre-1960) Unregistered

'National' 2 W-Y
(J.G. Weightman, pre-1938)
Perianth segments very broad, of strong substance, overlapping; corona rich buff yellow

'National Emblem' 2 W-OOR
(D.S. Bell) D.S. Bell, 1960
'Idealist' × 'Artist's Model'
Fl. 108 mm wide; corona very shallow, closely overlying the perianth, apricot orange, with a narrow band of red at rim. Mid-season

'Native Dancer' 2 Y-R
(W.M. Spry, pre-1975) Unregistered

'Port Kembla' × 'Malta'
Corona brick red, with overtones of copper. Mid-season to late

'Natividad' 1 W-W
(J.N. Hancock & Co.) J.N. Hancock & Co., 1960
Corona funnel-shaped, with rim rolled

'Nativity' 4 Y-W
(Jānis Rukšans) Jānis Rukšans, 1997
'Pink Paradise' × 'Daydream'; sdlg no. 88-17-2
Fl. rounded, 100 mm wide; perianth and other petaloid segments in numerous whorls, light greenish yellow 4B-5C; the outer whorl plane, smooth, deeply overlapping; the inner whorls interspersed with corona segments; corona segments opening yellow, becoming white. Mid-season

'Natone' 2 W-W
(J.R.Erp) J.R.Erp, 1956
'Brunswick' × 'Carnlough'

'Natrium' 2 (a)
(J.W.A. Lefeber, pre-1945)

'Naughty' 3 W-GYR
(Ken Farmer Nurseries) Ken Farmer Nurseries, 1978
Fl. 75 mm wide; corona yellow, with green at base and orange-red at rim. Mid-season

'Nauplion' 2 W-W
(J.M. de Navarro) J.M. de Navarro, 1968
Sdlg × 'Snowshill'

'Nauset' 2 Y-O
(G. Lewis) D.S. Bell, 1955

'Nausori' 2 Y-R
(D.S. Bell) D.S. Bell, 1971
'Checkmate' × 'Sabre Dance'
Fl. 106 mm wide; perianth segments rich yellow; corona red

'Nauta' 2 Y-YY0
(S.C. Gaspar, pre-1949)
Corona shallow, golden yellow, with reddish orange at rim

'Nautilus' 2 (a)
(Barr & Sons, pre-1923)

'Nautilus' 2 W-W
(C.E. Radcliff, 1930) J.M.Radcliff, 1956
'W.F.Gates' × 'Janet'
Fl. milk white; perianth segments opening creamy white; corona opening pale primrose yellow

'Navahoe' 2 (a)
(R.H. Bath, pre-1933)

'Navajo' 2 Y-O
(Konynenburg & Mark) Konynenburg & Mark, 1963
'Red Goblet' × 'Contrapunt'
Fl. 85 mm wide; perianth segments vivid yellow 9A; corona brilliant orange 29A. Early

'Navarone' 1 W-W
(T. Bloomer) Rathowen Daffodils, 1985
'April Parade' × 'White Empress'; sdlg no. 316
Fl. large. Mid-season

'Navarre' 2 W-? (b)
(R.H. Bath, pre-1931)

'Navarre' 2 Y-O
(L. Buckland, pre-1936)
Corona reddish orange

'Navarre' 1 Y-Y
(Iberian origin) Unregistered
Selection by R.C.Elliott (c.1957) from wild-collected *N. asturiensis*
Perianth segments inflexed, twisted; corona constricted at mid-point, with rim more-or-less finely notched. Dwarf

'Naxos' 2 W-W
(G.H. Engleheart, pre-1923)
Perianth segments overlapping; corona with rim flanged. Tall

'Nazareth' 2 Y-W
(G.E. Mitsch) G.E. Mitsch, 1958
'Binkie' × sdlg K43 ('King of the North' × 'Content')
Mid-season. 2n=28

'Nazareth' 8 W-W
Syn. of 'Yael'

'Nazir' 3 W-? (b)
(R.H. Bath, pre-1931)

'Neahkahnie' 1 W-W
(Murray W.Evans, 1972) Murray W.Evans, 1985
'Empress of Ireland' × 'Celilo'; sdlg no. 0-15
Mid-season. Resembles a smaller-flowered 'Empress of Ireland' of purer white

'Nearula' 3 W-R
(J.L. Richardson, pre-1953)
'Algiers' × 'Mahmoud'
Fl. forming a double triangle; perianth segments broadly ovate, blunt or slightly truncate, prominently mucronate, spreading, a little concave, overlapping one-third to a half; the inner segments more narrowly ovate, shouldered at base, slightly inflexed, with margins incurling; corona almost disc-shaped, ribbed, cerise red, frilled, with rim minutely crenate

'Neatness' 2 Y-Y
(R. Gibson, pre-1927)
Fl. creamy yellow; corona darker in tone. Mid-season

'Nebula' 9
(pre-1908)

'Nebula' 2 (a)
(A.H. Ahrens) J.S. Leitch, 1955

'Nectar' 2 (a)
(P.D. Williams, pre-1933)

'Nectarine' 3 W-? (b)
(W.B. Hartland, pre-1907)

'Nectric' 2 Y-R
(?G. Lewis, pre-1940)
('Scarlet Queen' × 'Fortune') hybrid × 'Golden Treasure'
Perianth segments golden yellow; corona red

'Nedda' 2 (a)
(N.F. Lock, pre-1944)

'Nederburg' 1 Y-O
(Brian S.Duncan) Brian S.Duncan
'Hero' × 'King's Grove'; sdlg no. 1689
Fl. 105 mm wide; perianth segments broadly ovate, blunt, deep golden yellow, spreading, smooth; corona cylindrical, mid-orange, with mouth slightly expanded and rim dentate. Early to mid-season. Sunproof

'Neerim' 2 W-Y
(W. Jackson Jr) W. Jackson Jr, 1966
'Sari' × 'Buncrana'; sdlg no. 40/60

'Neewari' 4 W-P
(Jackson's Daffodils) Jackson's Daffodils, 1989
Murray Evans sdlg × sdlg 309/76; sdlg no. 134/84
Fl. 96 mm wide; perianth and other petaloid segments in three whorls, greenish white (155A); the outer whorl a little reflexed; corona segments pink (28D). Mid-season

'Nefertiti' 2 (a)
(A.H. Ahrens, pre-1949)

N. neglectus Tenore = *N. tazetta* subsp. *lacticolor*

'Negligée' 2 W-? (b)
(A. Overton) A. Overton, 1959

'Neglina' 3 (a)
(A.H. Ahrens, pre-1951)

'Nehalem' 3 W-GWY
(Murray W.Evans) Murray W.Evans, 1975
('Carolina' × ['Rubra' × 'Otranto']) × 'Marshfire'; sdlg

no. G-40
Fl. 108 mm wide. Mid-season

'Neicia' 2 W-? (b)
(Mrs M. Moorby, pre-1949)

'Neienust' 1 W-? (b)
(W. de Ruyter, pre-1942)

'Nelamy' 2 W-GYY
(G.H. Johnstone, pre-1960) Unregistered
'Nelly' × 'May Molony'

'Nelaromi' 2 Y-R
(G.J.Phillips, 1983) G.J.Phillips, 1994
'Cinel' × 'Hiromi'; sdlg no. 78-89-1
Fl. 100 mm wide; perianth segments broadly ovate, deep rich yellow; corona short funnel-shaped, deep orange-red, with mouth frilled. Early

'Neleta'
(W. Jackson Sr, pre-1938)
'Blodwen' hybrid

'Nella' 1 W-? (b)
(E.H. Krelage & Son, pre-1943)

'Nell Barry' 1 Y-Y
(W. Backhouse, pre-1869)
Perianth segments sulphur yellow, incurved at apex, with margins notched; corona darker in tone. Syn. Pseudonarcissus 'Nell Barry'

'Nelle McPherson-Smith' 2 W-R
(L.P. Dettman) L.P. Dettman, 1974
'Glamor' open pollinated
Fl. 94 mm wide

'Nelle Stone' 2 W-Y
(L.P. Dettman) L.P. Dettman, 1968
'Jean Hood' × 'Nevose'

'Nelle Worth' 2 W-P
(L.P. Dettman) L.P. Dettman, 1974
'Glamor' × 'Green Island'
Fl. 96 mm wide

'Nell Gwynne' 2 W-? (b or c)
(J.W. Barr, pre-1930)

'Nellie Roe' 2 Y-YOO
(John T. Williams) John T. Williams, 1992
'Falstaff' × 'Camelot'; sdlg no. 12
Fl. forming a double triangle, 90 mm wide; perianth segments broadly ovate, blunt, brilliant greenish yellow 5B, with white mucro, spreading, plane, with margins slightly incurlng, smooth, regular, overlapping about three-fifths; the inner segments a little more narrowly ovate and less prominently mucronate; corona funnel-shaped, ribbed, opening orange, becoming yellow-orange, with yellow at base, mouth straight, wavy, rim crenate. Mid-season. The corona sometimes predominantly yellow

'Nellore' 2 Y-R
(O. Ronalds, 1950) T. Morrison, 1960
Perianth segments broad; corona cup-shaped, dark red

'Nell's Gift' 9 W-GYR
(Mrs M.S. Yerger) Mrs M.S. Yerger, 1993
N. poeticus var. *recurvus* open pollinated; sdlg no. 79 I 3
Fl. forming a double triangle, 62 mm wide; perianth segments rounded at apex, reflexed; the inner segments narrower; corona almost disc-shaped, vivid yellow 15B, with moderate yellow-green 139C at base and a suffusion of orange-red (33A) at rim. Very late

'Nell Stuart' 1 W-W
(G.L. Wilson, pre-1938)

'Nelly' 3 W-Y
(P.D. Williams, pre-1927)
Fl. 95-98 mm wide; perianth segments broadly ovate, creamy white, slightly inflexed, with margins a little incurling, regular, overlapping half to two-thirds; corona cup-shaped, strongly ribbed, brilliant yellow 7B, with rim sometimes stained light orange, mouth straight, split in places and overlapping, closely frilled, with rim crenate. Mid-season to late. 2n=28. *HC(g) 1931

'Nelly' 9 W-?
Syn. of 'Henny'

'Nelly' 3? W-W
(New Zealand origin) Unregistered

'Nelly Jarrett' 2 W-WWY
(pre-1961) Unregistered
Perianth segments broad, smooth; corona shallow, white, with greenish yellow at rim

'Nelly Kelly' 3 W-? (b)
(G. Lewis) D.S. Bell, 1955

'Nelly Lubbe' 1 W-? (b)
(G. Lubbe & Son, pre-1938)
AM(Haarlem) 1938

'Nel Richardson' 4 W-WWO
(W.J.M. Blom, 1968) W. Blom & Son, 1984
'Anne Frank' × 'Coquille'; sdlg no. 68-F-2
Perianth and other petaloid segments very broadly ovate, prominently mucronate, with midrib showing; the outer whorl reflexed; the inner whorl inflexed, creased, with margins sometimes strongly incurved; a single segment at centre; corona segments one-third the length of the inner whorl, yellowish white, with

a well-defined band of light orange (near to 23B) at rim becoming pinkish. Late. Sweetly scented

'Nelsonian' 2 W-? (b)
(R.P. Cook, pre-1949)

'Nelsonii' 2 W-Y
(E. Leeds, pre-1877)
Hybrid between a variant of *N. bicolor* and *N. poeticus*
Corona straight-sided, sometimes tinged orange on opening. Late. Resembles a much larger-flowered *N. bicolor*. Syn. Nelsonii 'Nelsonii'. This has also been used as a Group name. Was "absorbed" into Nelsonii 'Major'

'Nelson's' 1 Y-Y
(E. Leeds, pre-1877)
Perianth segments sulphur yellow. Very early. Syn. Pseudonarcissus 'Nelson's'

'Neltonia'
(G.H. Johnstone, pre-1960)

'Nemesis' 2 W-Y
(W.F.M. Copeland, pre-1911)
'Minnie Hume' × 'Weardale Perfection'
Fl. 102 mm wide; perianth segments ivory white, deeply overlapping; corona short, very widely expanded, light yellow, with mouth deeply frilled. Mid-season

'Nemo' 3 W-YYO
(J.L. Richardson, pre 1953)
Fl. 89 mm wide; perianth segments creamy white, of good substance, overlapping half; corona widely expanded, ribbed, vivid yellow 9B, shading to vivid orange 28B towards rim, frilled, with rim crenate. 2n=28. *AM(g) 1958

'Nendrum' 3 W-R
(Ballydorn Bulb Farm, 1975) Ballydorn Bulb Farm, 1986
'Corncrake' hybrid × 'Faraway'
Late

'Nene Beauty' 2 W-YYO
(R.H. Bath, pre-1926)
Corona deep yellow, with a broad band of orange at rim. AM(e) 1926

'Nenone' 2 (a)
(Mrs R.S. Cobley, pre-1954)

'Nenyto' 1 W-? (b)
(P. van Deursen, pre-1931)
AM(Haarlem) 1931

N. × *neocarpetanus* Rivas Ponce, C.Soriano & Fernández Casas 13 = *N. cantabricus* de Candolle ×

N. bulbocodium Linnaeus var. *nivalis* (Graells) Baker?.
    var. **neocarpetanus**
    var. **romanensis** U.Plaza

'Neon Light' 2 W-YOO
(Clive Postles) Clive Postles Daffodils, 1995
'Rubh Mor' × 'Loch Brora'; sdlg no. 1-41-84
Fl. 118 mm wide; perianth segments very broadly ovate, pure white, with margins slightly incurving, smooth; corona bowl-shaped, orange, with yellow at base, frilled, with rim crenate. Late

'Nepal' 2 (a)
(A.M. Wilson, pre-1950)

'Neptune' 2 W-Y
(W.F.M. Copeland, pre-1908)
'Minnie Hume' × 'Grandee'
Perianth segments opening yellow and becoming white, of stiff substance, overlapping; corona cylindrical, narrow, rich yellow

'Neptune' 1 W-Y
(J.L. Richardson) J.L. Richardson, 1956
'Spitzbergen' × 'Broughshane'

'Nerada' 2 Y-Y
(J.N.Hancock & Co., 1983) Unregistered
'Toorak Gold' × 'Artist's Model'; sdlg no. 20/83H
Perianth segments roundish, soft primrose yellow; corona disc-shaped, ribbed, orange-yellow. Very early

'Nereides' 1 W-? (b)
(Barr & Sons, pre-1923)

'Nereus' 1 (a)
(Barr & Sons, pre-1923)

'Nericon' 2 Y-Y
(J.N.Hancock & Co., 1980) Unregistered
'Tempura' × Philpott 1 Y-Y; sdlg no. 18/80H
Perianth segments broadly ovate, butter yellow; corona golden yellow. Tall. Early

'Nerida' 2 W-P
(Jackson's Daffodils, 1984) Jackson's Daffodils, 1995
Sdlg 113/75 × 'Vandyke'; sdlg no. 53/84
Fl. 108 mm wide; perianth segments broadly ovate, greenish white (155A); corona funnel-shaped, light yellowish pink 27B, with mouth flared. Early to mid-season

'Nerissa' 2 W-? (b)
(R.H. Bath, pre-1927)

'Nerissa' 2 W-R
(T.H. Piper, 1949) T.H. Piper, 1956
'T.H.Piper' × 'Portia'

'Nero' 1 W-Y
(Barr & Sons, pre-1924)
Fl. 89 mm wide; perianth segments creamy white, flushed primrose yellow at base, twisted, regular, overlapping at base only; corona pale buttercup yellow, with mouth expanded and frilled. Mid-season to late. 2n=28. *C(g) 1930

'Nerrina' 2 (a)
(H.A. Brown, pre-1936)

'Nesta' 2
(Australian origin, pre-1961)
Resembles 'Jean Hood' but with a larger corona

'Nestegg' 2 W-P
(Alister Clark, 1935) J. Sharp, 1960

'Nestor' 8 Y-Y
(pre-1798)
Fl. pale yellow

'Nestor' 2 WWY-Y
(Barr & Sons, pre-1908)
Perianth segments creamy white, flushed canary yellow at base; corona brilliant golden yellow, neatly frilled

'Nestor' 1 W-W
(J.S. Leitch) J.S. Leitch, 1960
Fl. 102 mm wide

'Nestucca' 2 W-? (b)
(Oregon Bulb Farms, pre-1951)

'Nethanya' 3 Y-O
(G.H. Rotteveel & Sons, 1967) G.H. Rotteveel & Sons, 1984
Fl. 95 mm wide; perianth segments primrose yellow; corona marigold orange. Late

'Nether Barr' 2 W-GRR
(Brian S. Duncan) Rathowen Daffodils, 1983
'Irish Splendour' × ('Mahmoud' × ['Bravura' × 'Glenwherry']); sdlg no.716
Fl. rounded, 105 mm wide; perianth segments very broad, deeply truncate, spreading, overlapping half or more; the inner segments narrower, roundish, with margins wavy and sometimes recurved at base; corona shallow, deep orange-red, with green at base, mouth widely expanded, sometimes deeply split and overlapping, loosely frilled. Mid-season

'Netherbow' 2 (a)
(R.H. Bath, pre-1929)

'Netherby Belle' 1 W-W
(G.C. Graham, pre-1949)

'Netherwood Marsh' 3 W-W
(Clive Postles, 1984) Clive Postles Daffodils, 1996
Lea sdlg 2-4-69 × 'Cool Crystal'; sdlg no. 7-52-79
Fl. rounded, 110 mm wide; perianth segments broadly ovate, with margins slightly incurved; corona bowl-shaped, opening yellow, becoming milky white, with mouth lobed and rim crenate. Late

'Netia' 10 W-W
(Sir F.C. Stern) Sir F.C. Stern, 1962
N. cantabricus subsp. *monophyllus* × *N. triandrus* var. *concolor* or variant
Fl. 40 mm wide; perianth segments narrowly ovate, reflexed, with margins deeply incurved, sometimes twisted, separated; corona cup-shaped, ribbed, with mouth straight. Dwarf. Very early. Scented. Resembles 'Dolly'. PC(p) 1962, AM(p) 1965. Div. 5 until 1969

'Netta' 2 W-? (b)
(L. Buckland, pre-1936)

'Nette Fortune' 2 (a)
(K.L. Reynolds, pre-1937)

'Nettleton Circle' 10 Y-Y
(Potterton and Martin) Potterton and Martin, 1993
N. romieuxii open pollinated; sdlg no. 12/79
Fl. 34 mm wide, light greenish yellow 3C; perianth segments narrowly triangular in appearance, a little inflexed, separated; corona broad funnel-shaped, mouth straight or a little incurving, ribbed, sometimes very shallowly 6-lobed, rim irregularly and minutely crenate. Dwarf. Very early

'Netty' 3 W-? (b)
(R.H. Bath, pre-1930)

'Neumatic' 7
(pre-1913)

'Neuralia' 1 W-W
(N.Y. Lower, pre-1933)
'Mrs Robert Sydenham' × 'Conqueror'

'Neva'
(pre-1915)

'Nevada' 3 (a)
(Warnaar & Co., pre-1929)
AM(Haarlem) 1930

N. nevadensis Pugsley 13 Section Pseudonarcissus.

'Nevana' 2 W-P
(W. Jackson Jr, 1956) Unregistered
Sdlg 86/51 × 'Ceram'

'Neville' 1 (a)
(W.A. Watts, pre-1939)

'Nevin' 2 W-? (b or c)
(W.A. Watts, pre-1923)
'Minnie Hume' × 'Weardale Perfection'

'Nevis' 1 W-W
(The Brodie of Brodie, c.1915)
('King of the North' × 'Glory of Noordwijk') × 1 W-W
Fl. opening a pale bicolor, soon becoming ivory or milk white. AM(e) 1924

'Neviski' 1 Y-Y
(G.H. Johnstone, pre-1960) Unregistered
'Nevis' × 'King of the North'

'Nevose' 3 W-W
(A.O. Roblin, 1943)
Perianth segments very broadly ovate in outline, blunt or truncate at apex and slightly mucronate, pure white, spreading, with margins sometimes nicked, overlapping half; the inner segments more narrowly ovate, sometimes inflexed, with margins recurved at base and wavy; corona shallow bowl-shaped, ribbed, creamy white, with mouth wavy and rim crenate. Tall. Mid-season to late. Resembles an earlier-flowered 'Chinese White'

'Nevra' 2 W-W
(G.L. Wilson, pre-1943)

'Nevta' 2 Y-R
(J.M. de Navarro) Rathowen Daffodils, 1988
'Dancing Flame' × 'Loch Hope'; sdlg no. 591
Perianth segments deep golden yellow; corona cup-shaped, deep orange-red, with mouth a little expanded. Mid-season

'New Amsterdam' 2 W-YOO
(de Graaff Bros, pre-1931)
Syn. 'Nieuw Amsterdam'. AM(Haarlem) 1930

'New-Baby' 7 W-Y
(J. Gerritsen & Son) J. Gerritsen & Son, 1963
'Baby Star' sport
Fls up to 4 per stem, 20 mm wide; perianth segments broadly ovate or oblong, squarish at apex, prominently mucronate, greenish white, with a patch of yellow at margin in lower half, spreading, plane, separated; the inner segments ovate, blunt, sometimes a little twisted; corona bowl-shaped, smooth, dark yellow, with rim entire or obscurely crenate. Very late. Resembles 'Baby Star' but with pale perianth segments

'Newcastle' 1 W-Y
(W.J. Dunlop) W.J. Dunlop, 1957
'Niphetos' × 'Kanchenjunga'. AM(e)1957
Fl. 120 mm wide; perianth segments very broadly ovate, blunt, slightly mucronate, pure white, tinged brilliant greenish yellow 6A at base, plane, smooth, regular, overlapping half; the inner segments a little inflexed, with margins wavy; corona cylindrical, smooth, vivid yellow 12A, mouth expanded, ribbed, broadly and shallowly lobed, wavy, with rim minutely notched. AM(e) 1957

'Newcomer' 3 W-P
(Murrey W. Evans, 1979) Estella L. Evans, 1992
'Quasar' × (sdlg × 'Everpink'); sdlg no. W-2/2
Fl. 86 mm wide, rounded; perianth segments prominently mucronate, glistening white; the inner segments with margins slightly wavy; corona cup-shaped, ribbed, deep pink, with mouth lightly frilled. Mid-season

'New Dawn' 2 Y-P
(J.S.B.Lea, 1985) Clive Postles Daffodils, 1995
Lea sdlg 1-18-76 × Lea sdlg 1-13-75; sdlg no. 1-49-80
Fl. rounded, 107 mm wide; perianth segments very broadly ovate, soft butter yellow, plane, smooth; corona cylindrical, salmon pink, with mouth flared and rim crenate. Late. Sunproof

'New Day' 7 Y-W
(G.E. Mitsch) G.E. Mitsch, 1972
'Quick Step' × 'Daydream'; sdlg no. D80/27
Fl. rounded, 80 mm wide; perianth segments lemon gold, with white at base; corona opening lemon, becoming first white then buff. Mid-season

'New Deal' 2 W-O
(Warnaar & Co., pre-1946)

'New Dorothy' 8 W-Y
(pre-1759)

'New Era' 2 (a)
(L. van Leeuwen & Son, pre-1938)

'New Era' 1 Y-W
(G.E. Mitsch) Oregon Bulb Farms, 1958
'Binkie' × ('King of the North' × 'Content')
Corona opening primrose yellow, becoming off white. Resembles an improved 'Spellbinder'

'New Europe' 2 W-? (b)
(H. Zeestratun, pre-1954)

'New Fashion' 2 Y-YOR
(M.E.Brogden) Unregistered

'New Foundling' 8 W-Y
(?W. Twisk, pre-1913)
Perianth segments pure white. AM(Haarlem) 1913

'New Generation' 1 Y-WWY
(J.W.A. van der Wereld, 1978) J.W.A. van der Wereld, 1991
'Lunar Sea' × 'Rus Holland'; sdlg no. K 6515

Fl. 100 mm wide; perianth segments broadly or very broadly ovate, blunt, brilliant greenish yellow 5A, with prominent white mucro, a little reflexed, plane, overlapping one-third to a half; the inner segments more nearly spreading, slightly concave and somewhat twisted, with margins notched; corona cylindrical, opening yellow, becoming pale yellowish white (2D), touched with a darker tone (5 or 6A) at rim, mouth expanded and frilled, rim flanged and irregularly notched. Tall. Mid-season

'New Gold' 2 Y-Y
(G. Lubbe & Son, pre-1950)
AM(Haarlem) 1950

'New Grange' 2 W-W
(J.L. Richardson, pre-1949)

'New Guinea' 2 (a)
(G.L. Wilson, pre-1937)

'Newhaven' 2 W-W
(C.E. Radcliff, 1933)
'Phyllida' × 'White Emperor'

'New Hope' 3 W-YYR
(Warnaar & Co., pre-1953)
Fl. rounded; perianth segments glistening white, plane. AM(Haarlem) 1953

'New Hope' 3 W-Y
(Brogden Bulbs, pre-1996) Unregistered

'New Horizon' 1 Y-Y
(G.H. Johnstone, pre-1949)
'Nevis' × 'King of the North'

'New Idea' 2 W-? (b)
(A. Gibson, pre-1951)

'New Idea' 2 Y-R
(?Australian origin, pre-1996) Unregistered

'New Issue' 1 W-Y
(W.J. Dunlop) M.J. Jefferson-Brown, 1975
'Niphetos' × 'Kanchenjunga'
Corona rich primrose

'Newlaid' 2 W-YYO
(Sir F.C. Stern, pre-1953)
Perianth segments pure white, spreading; corona rich egg yellow, stained deep apricot orange at rim, frilled. Mid-season

'Newland' 3 W-GYY
(J.T.E. Akers) J.L. Akers, 1991
'Valediction' × 'Old Satin'; sdlg no. 52
Fl. 89 mm wide. Late

'New Life' 3 W-Y
(G.W.E.Brogden, pre-1992) Unregistered
'Verona' × 'Motif'; sdlg no. x52/A

'New Light' 2 W-YOY
(J.N. Hancock & Co., 1947) J.N. Hancock & Co., 1964
Perianth segments broad, of strong substance; corona large, widely expanded. Early

'Newlyn' 2 (a)
(The Brodie of Brodie, pre-1930)
'White Sentinel' × 'Gallipoli'

'New Magic' 11a Y-O
(R. & E.Havens) R. & E.Havens, 1996
'Hillstar' × 'Shrike'; sdlg no. Z70/1
Fl. 80 mm wide; perianth segments ovate, yellow; corona deeply split, the six segments opposite and closely overlying the perianth segments, buff orange or sometimes golden yellow. Late. Sunproof. Lightly scented

'New Moon' 3 W-WWO
(G.L. Wilson, pre-1930)
'Mystic' self pollinated
Perianth segments pure white, slightly reflexed; corona shallow, widely expanded, pure white, with a narrow band of pale golden orange at rim. Late

'New Penny' 3 Y-Y
(W.G. Pannill) W.G. Pannill, 1972
'Lemonade' × 'Lemnos'
Fl. 81 mm wide

'Newport' 2 W-YOY
(W.G. Pannill) W.G. Pannill, 1980
('Limerick' × 'Broughshane') × 'Avenger'; sdlg no. 65/67
Fl. 98 mm wide. Mid-season

'New Snow' 2 W-W
(G.E. Mitsch) G.E. Mitsch, 1977
'Silken Sails' × 'Wings of Song'; sdlg no. H100/4
Fl. 100 mm wide, pure white; perianth segments very broad, slightly reflexed; corona with rim broadly crenate. Late. Resembles a larger-flowered 'Wings of Song' with a broader corona

'New Song' 2 W-GYY
(G.E. Mitsch) G.E. Mitsch, 1963
'Green Island' × 'Bithynia'; sdlg no. P32/9
Fl. 102 mm wide, of good form and strong substance; perianth segments very broad, overlapping; corona very shallow bowl-shaped, creamy yellow, suffused apricot yellow. Mid-season

'New Star' 2 W-P
(Mrs H.K. Richardson) M.J. Jefferson-Brown, 1985
'Rose Caprice' hybrid

Fl. of strong substance; perianth segments broad at base, snow white; corona large, expanded, rich glowing salmon pink. Tall. Mid-season

'Newstead' 1 Y-Y
(R.C.A. Tombleson) R.C.A. Tombleson, 1968
Fl. 115 mm wide. Mid-season. Resembles a smaller and later-flowered 'Goldcourt'

'Newtimber' 2 W-GYY
(Sir F.C. Stern, pre-1952)
Corona lemon, with green at base and a slightly darker tone of yellow at rim

'Newton' 8 Y-O
(Unknown origin, pre-1875) Rosewarne EHS, 1961
Fls 5-8 per stem, 46 mm wide; perianth segments acute, vivid yellow 12A, creased at midrib; corona cup-shaped, with mouth incurved, strongly ribbed, yellow-orange (17B). Dwarf. Autumn-flowered. Strongly scented. Resembles a slightly larger-flowered 'Grand Soleil d'Or' with the perianth segments of a slightly darker tone. Perhaps the same as 'Sir Isaac Newton'

'Newton Ferrers' 4 Y-O
(Mrs H.K. Richardson) du Plessis Bros, 1986
'Daybreak' × pink sdlg; sdlg no. 3615
Perianth segments opening very pale yellow, becoming creamy yellow; corona segments bright orange, becoming darker in tone. Mid-season

'New Venture' 11?a Y-Y
(J. Gerritsen & Son) R.W. Ward & Son, 1968
Mid-season

'New Vista' 2 Y-WWP
(V. Brink) V. Brink, 1968
'Content' × 'Frilled Beauty'
Fl. 95 mm wide; perianth segments sulphur yellow, flushed reddish orange; corona opening rose pink, with a darker tone at rim, becoming off white, with pale pink at rim. Mid-season

'New World' 2 Y-YYP
(M.J. Jefferson-Brown) M.J. Jefferson-Brown, 1984
'Rose Caprice' self pollinated
Perianth segments broadly ovate, blunt, mucronate, pale lemon yellow, spreading, overlapping one-third to a half; the inner segments a little narrower, shouldered at base, slightly inflexed at base and reflexed towards apex, with margins wavy; corona deep bowl-shaped, primrose yellow, becoming flushed with pink, with stronger tones of pink at rim, frilled. Mid-season

"New Year Lily"
Syn. of *N.tazetta* subsp. *lacticolor*

'New York' 8 W-O
(A. Frylink & Sons, pre-1928)
Corona soft orange. AM(Haarlem) 1928

'New Zealand' 2 (a)
(L. van Leeuwen & Son, pre-1938)

'Next Door' 2 W-P
(Mrs E. Murray)

'Nexus' 2 W-P
(Jackson's Daffodils) Jackson's Daffodils, 1986
Sdlg 110/70 × 'Dear Me'; sdlg no. 78/78
Perianth segments yellowish white 155D; corona light orange 26C. Mid-season

'Ngaere' 3 W-YYR
(C.E. Radcliff, 1934)
'Silver Plane' × 'Maid of the Mist'

'Ngahere' 3 W-Y
(G.C. Yeates) G.C. Yeates, 1974
Fl. 98 mm wide

'Ngaire' 2 W-Y
(W.E. Weightman, pre-1936)
Perianth segments deeply overlapping; corona lemon yellow, with a darker tone at rim

'Ngaire' 2 (a)
(G.W.E. Brogden) E.A.K. Lee, 1955

'Ngarea' 1 (a)
(D.S. Bell) D.S. Bell, 1955

'Ngareta' 2 W-? (b)
(Mrs M. Moorby) Mrs M. Moorby, 1957
'Kingscourt' × 'Goldcourt'

'Ngauruhoe' 1 W-Y
(R. Hyde) R. Hyde, 1955
'Kingscourt' × 'Goldcourt'

'Niagara' 1 W-W
(G.H. Engleheart, pre-1931)

'Niantic' 9 W-GYO
(E.C. Powell, pre-1946)
'Minuet' × ?'Lord Wellington'
2n=28

'Niblick' 2 Y-O
(J.N. Hancock & Co.) J.N. Hancock & Co., 1955
See also 'Niblik'

'Niblik' 2 Y-O
Syn. of 'Niblick'

'Nicander' 9
(Cartwright & Goodwin, pre-1916)

'Nicastro' 2 W-W
(S.C. Gaspar) R.J. Abernethy, 1960
Fl. 115 mm wide. Mid-season to late

'Nice Day' 3 W-GWW
(Clive Postles Daffodils) Clive Postles Daffodils, 1987
Sdlg 40-77 × 'Cool Crystal'
Late

'Nicephorus' 1 W-W
(R.H. Bath, pre-1933)

'Nicety' 3 (a)
(M.P. Williams, pre-1938)

'Nicholas' 1 (a)
(J.W. Barr, pre-1930)

'Nickel Coin' 3 (a)
(G. Lubbe & Son, pre-1951)
AM(Haarlem) 1951

'Nickey' 2 Y-YYO
(J.S. Leitch) J.S. Leitch, 1964
Fl. 95 mm wide

'Nicola Marianne' 2 W-YYP
(Brian S.Duncan) R.A.Brand, 1993
'Pismo Beach' × 'High Society'; sdlg no. 1156
Perianth segments broadly ovate, blunt, prominently mucronate, spreading, with margins incurling at apex, overlapping half; the inner segments a little narrower, only very slightly mucronate; corona very short funnel-shaped, smooth, opening pink, becoming yellow, with a broad band of light yellowish pink 26D at rim, mouth widely expanded, minutely ribbed, rim slightly rolled and fairly regularly crenate. Mid-season to late. Resembles a taller and improved 'Pismo Beach'

'Nicole' 2 Y-O/YW
(J.W.A. Lefeber) J.W.A. Lefeber, 1984
'Paolo Veronese' × 'Burning Heart'; sdlg no. 7633
Perianth segments very broadly ovate in outline, blunt or squarish at apex, prominently mucronate, opening ivory white, becoming pale yellow, with a slightly darker tone at margins, spreading, overlapping half; the inner segments more narrowly ovate, not noticeably mucronate; corona spreading, with six very deeply overlapping lobes alternate to the perianth segments; the lobes with a broad band of light orange overlying yellow at midrib and tapering to apex, with yellow at base and white at margins, lightly frilled. Very early

'Nicolette' 7
(A.H. Ahrens, pre-1949)

'Nida Senff' 2 (a)
(de Graaff Bros, pre-1937)

'Niello' 1 Y-Y
(J.S. Leitch) J.S. Leitch, 1960
Fl. 108 mm wide

'Niels Larsen' 2 W-O
(pre-1949)
Perianth segments creamy white; corona apricot orange

'Nietta' 2 Y-R
(C.E. Radcliff, 1939)
'Garibaldi' × 'Lilian Murdoch'

'Nieuw Amsterdam' 2 W-YOO
Syn. of 'New Amsterdam'

'Nigel' 2 (a)
(Barr & Sons, pre-1903)

'Nigeria' 2 Y-YYO
(J.L. Richardson, pre-1942)
'Porthilly' × 'Carbineer'
Perianth segments broadly ovate, clear yellow; corona large, golden yellow, shading to orange towards mouth, frilled

'Nightcap' 1 Y-Y
(H.G. Cross) H.G. Cross, 1984
'Mireen' × 'Olympic Gold'; sdlg no. 131-5
Fl. golden yellow; perianth segments broadly ovate, blunt, with white mucro, spreading, concave, with margins minutely incurling, overlapping half; the inner segments shouldered at base, a little inflexed; corona narrow, cylindrical or somewhat funnel-shaped, smooth, with mouth even, rim almost entire, very slightly flanged. Late

'Nightfall' 2 W-P
(Mrs C.O. Fairbairn) J.L. Martin, 1982
Fl. 100 mm wide; corona moderate pink 49B. Resembles a larger 'Dreamlike' with a deeper pink corona

'Nightflight' 1 W-W
(Clive Postles) Clive Postles Daffodils, 1996
Lea sdlg 4-58-73 × 'Panache'; sdlg no. 1-17A-82
Fl. forming a double triangle, 112 mm wide; perianth segments ovate; corona funnel-shaped, with mouth flared and rim dentate. Early

'Night Hawk' 2 Y-O
(G.E.Mitsch, 1986) R. & E.Havens, 1997
('Executive' × 'Golden Aura') × ('Zuni' × 'Vertex'); sdlg no. 2V6/1
Fl. 115 mm wide, of heavy substance; perianth segments broadly ovate, golden yellow, spreading, plane; corona flared, tangerine orange, with rim rolled. Late. Sunproof

'Nightingale' 9 W-GYR
(G.H. Engleheart, pre-1914)

Fl. rounded, 80 mm wide; perianth segments greenish white (155A), of thick substance, glistening, deeply overlapping; corona light orange-yellow 22C, with yellowish green 141C at base and a narrow band of vivid red 45A at rim. AM(e) 1914

'Nightlight' 5 W-W
(Alister Clark, pre-1914)
'Minnie Hume' × *N. triandrus*
Fl. pure white

'Night Music' 4 W-P
(G.E. Mitsch) G.E. Mitsch, 1984
'Pink Chiffon' × sdlg D29/2 ('Carita' × sdlg Z20/ ['Green Island' × 'Accent']); sdlg no. KK33/5
Fl. 85 mm wide; perianth and other petaloid segments in several whorls, white; the two outer whorls almost equal in length, broadly ovate, blunt or somewhat truncate, sometimes prominently mucronate, spreading, with broad midrib showing, overlapping half or more; the inner whorls shorter, inflexed, closely and irregularly arranged, with margins incurled or strongly incurled; corona segments half as long as the inner whorls and clustered among them, broad, pink, with a darker tone at rim, frilled. Mid-season

'Nikita' 2 W-W
(A.H. Ahrens) J.S. Leitch, 1956

'Nikko' 7 Y-Y
(S.J. Bisdee, 1950)
'Sungold' × ? *N jonquilla*

'Nikko' 3 Y ? (a)
(K.D. Smith) K.D. Smith, 1959

'Nile' 1 W-W
(G.E. Mitsch and R. & E.Havens, 1974) G.E. Mitsch and R. & E.Havens, 1985
('Vigil' × 'Empress of Ireland') × 'Panache'; sdlg no. JJ57/10
Perianth segments broadly ovate, slightly inflexed; corona narrow at base and with a greenish cast, rim slightly rolled. Mid-season

'Nilkanta' 1 W-W
(G.L. Wilson, pre-1941)
'Kenbane' × 'Kanchenjunga'
Perianth segments spreading, of waxy substance; corona slender, with rim neatly flanged. See also 'Nil Kanta'

'Nil Kanta' 1 W-W
Syn. of 'Nilkanta'

'Nillumbik' 2 W-YYR
(D.V. West, pre-1927)
Perianth segments creamy white; corona expanded, orange

'Nim' 2 W-R
(A.M. Wilson, pre-1944)
Corona disc-shaped, vermilion red

'Nimbus' 3 W-O
(G.H. Engleheart, pre-1916)
Fls sometimes 2 per stem; perianth segments acute, glistening white, reflexed; corona dark orange. Late

'Nimbus' 2 W-Y
(K.D. Smith) K.D. Smith, 1959

'Nimbus' 2 W-Y
(P.Cleine, 1981) Unregistered
Sdlg no. 26/81C
Perianth segments milk white; corona soft citron yellow, with mouth flared, rim rolled. Early

'Nimitabel' 3 W-GGO
(W.M. Spry, pre-1975) Unregistered
Corona lemon green, with brownish orange at rim. Late

'Nimlet' 2 Y-Y
(D. & J.W. Blanchard, 1964) J.W. Blanchard, 1992
N. rupicola × *N. asturiensis*; sdlg no. 59/3A
Fl. 30 mm wide, pale mid-yellow; perianth segments broadly ovate, blunt, only very slightly mucronate, spreading or a little inflexed, plane or very slightly twisted, overlapping a quarter; corona funnel-shaped, with mouth flared and even, rim crenate. Dwarf. Very early

'Nimrod' 2 Y-Y
(P.D. Williams, pre-1927)
Fl. 114 mm wide, facing slightly downwards; perianth segments clear yellow, with margins a little incurling, slightly creased, overlapping; corona funnel-shaped, golden yellow, with mouth frilled. Mid-season to late. 2n=28. AM(e)(Haarlem) 1930, FCFA(Haarlem) 1936, *HC(g) 1936. ?The same as 'Carlton'

'Nimue' 2 W-W
(W. Jackson Sr, 1934)
'Mary Blewitt' × 'Imbros'

'Nina' 9
(G.H. Engleheart, pre-1914)

'Nina' 2 W-P
(A.O. Roblin, 1959) Unregistered
Sdlg × 'Pink Monarch'

'Ninetta' 2 (a)
(J.S. Leitch) J.S. Leitch, 1956

'Ningana' 2 Y-Y
(W. Jackson Jr, 1965)
('Melissa' × 'Jobi') × sdlg 65/57; sdlg no. 36/65

'Nino' 3 W-R
(P. Phillips) P. Phillips, 1965
Fl. 102 mm wide. Mid-season. Resembles 'Vieva' in colour

'Ninon' 2 (a)
(Warnaar & Co., pre-1926)
AM(Haarlem) 1926

'Ninth Lancer' 1 (a)
(Hon. Sir R.H. Rhodes, pre-1914)

'Ninth Lancer' 2 Y-O
(J.L. Richardson) P. de Jager & Sons, 1959
Fl. 106 mm wide; perianth segments near brilliant yellow 7A, overlapping; corona between strong orange 25A and a darker tone (28A), mouth expanded, widely lobed, slightly frilled, with rim dentate. 2n=28. *AM(g) 1970, *FCC(g) 1971

'Niobe' 3 W-? (b or c)
(W.B. Hartland, pre-1907)

'Niobe' 5
(Sir A.P.W. Thomas, pre-1914)

'Niobe' 3 W-? (b)
(de Graaff Bros, pre-1926)
AM(Haarlem) 1926

'Nion' 8
(H. Prins, pre-1929)

'Niphetos' 2 W-W
(P.D. Williams, pre-1927)
Perianth segments broadly ovate, blunt, prominently mucronate, pure white, spreading, smooth, with midrib showing, margins sometimes incurling, overlapping half; the inner segments slightly more narrowly ovate, shouldered at base, somewaht twisted; corona opening very pale yellow, becoming creamy white, with mouth ribbed and expanded, rim rolled and regularly crenate. 2n=28. AM(e) 1932

'Nipigon' 2 W-? (b)
(Oregon Bulb Farms, pre-1951)

'Nipissing' 2 W-? (b)
(Oregon Bulb Farms, pre-1951)

'Nipper' 3 W-? (b)
(pre-1910)

'Nippit' 2 (a)
(J.E. Exley, pre-1950)

'Nippon' 11b W-Y/W
(W.F. Leenen) W.F. Leenen, 1970
Perianth segments white; corona deeply split, the six segments alternate to the perianth segments, with brilliant yellow 21C in a longitudinal band flanked by white. Dwarf. Early

'Nir'
(Dorit Sandler, pre-1996) Unregistered

'Niree' 1 Y-Y
(W. Jackson Jr, 1954)
'Kalman' × 'Melissa'

'Niree' 3 W-Y
(R.H.Glover, pre-1976) Unregistered
'Nevose' × 'Green Island'
Corona soft yellow. Late. Sometimes measuring Div.2

'Nirimba' 1 W-P
(Jackson's Daffodils, 1981) Jackson's Daffodils, 1992
'Madang' × 'Melancholy'; sdlg no. 93/81
Fl. rounded, 108 mm wide; perianth segments broadly ovate, greenish white (155A); the inner segments more narrowly ovate; corona funnel-shaped, pale yellowish pink 27C, frilled, with rim deeply rolled. Early to mid-season

'Nirvana' 7 W-W
(Barr & Sons, pre-1950)
Fl. pure white. Scented

'Nissa' 2 W-Y
(The Brodie of Brodie, c.1920)
'Kingdom' self pollinated; sdlg no. 13/A/15
Fl. 89 mm wide; perianth segments broadly ovate, blunt, slightly mucronate, spreading, plane, overlapping half; the inner segments a little inflexed, somewhat ribbed; corona funnel-shaped, vivid yellow 9A, with mouth expanded and even, rim shallowly crenate. 2n=28. AM(e) 1928, *AM(g) 1950

'Nita' 2 W-? (b)
(C. Dawson, pre-1907)

'Nita' 2 W-? (b)
(A.H. Ahrens) J.S. Leitch, 1956
Syn. 'Inspiration'

'Nitro' 3 W-O
(Jackson's Daffodils) Jackson's Daffodils, 1987
'Kabi' × 'Envoy'; sdlg no. 119/78
Fl. rounded; perianth segments very broadly ovate, rounded at apex, slightly mucronate, greenish white (155A), spreading, plane, with margins sometimes a little incurling, overlapping half; the inner segments roundish; corona very shallow bowl-shaped, deeply ribbed, strong orange 25A, with mouth frilled. Early

'Nitwit' 4 W-P
(W. Jackson Jr, 1971) Jackson's Daffodils, 1983
'Lawali' × 'Chimeon'; sdlg no. 190/71

N. nivalis Graells = *N. bulbocodium* subsp. *bul-*

bocodium var. *nivalis*

'Nivea' 2 W-W
(D. Bramley) D. Bramley, 1980
'Dallas' hybrid; sdlg no. 72/28
Fl. 101 mm wide. Mid-season. Resembles 'Dallas' but with shorter neck and broader corona

'Niveo-aurantius' 4 W-O
Syn. of 'Orange Phoenix'

'Niveth' 5 W-W
(H. Backhouse, pre-1931)
Fls 2 per stem, 76 mm wide, milk white, facing down; perianth segments broadly ovate, lightly reflexed, overlapping; corona short funnel-shaped. Mid-season to late. 2n=21. *HC(g) 1936. See also 'Nivette'

'Nivette' 5 W-W
Syn. of 'Niveth'

N. niveus Loiseleur-Deslongchamps = *N. papyraceus*

'Niveus'
Syn. of *N. papyraceus*

'Niwin' 2 W-? (b)
(C.A. van der Wereld, pre-1949)

'Nixie' 9 W-YYR
(A.O. Roblin, 1941)
'Minuet' × 'La Fontaine'

'Nizam' 1 W-Y
(A.O. Roblin, 1946) A.O. Roblin, 1956
'Sincerity' × 'Kanchenjunga'

'No. 1' 2 W-Y
(French origin)
Selection by H.E.Buxton (1881) from wild-collected *N.* × *bernardii*
Syn. Bernardii 'No. 1'. ?The same as *N.* × *incomparabilis*

'Nobbie' 2 W-Y
(R. Gibson, pre-1927)

'Nobby' 3 W-YYO
(P.L.A. Pouw) P.L.A. Pouw, 1961
Fl. 110 mm wide, corona vivid yellow 12A, with strong orange 25A at rim. Mid-season

'Nobelex' 2 Y-Y
(H.A. Brown, 1941)
Fl. large; corona disc-shaped, ribbed, opening lemon yellow, becoming orange gold. Very early

'Nob Hill' 2 YYW-Y
(Sidney DuBose) Sidney DuBose, 1990
'Daydream' × 'Sabine Hay'; sdlg no. G26-15

Fl. 95 mm wide; perianth segments yellow, with white at base. Early to mid-season

N. nobilis (Haworth) Schultes f. 13 Section Pseudonarcissus
    var. ***nobilis*** (Pseudonarcissus Nobilis 'Nobilis')
    var. ***leonensis*** (Pugsley) A.Fernandes
    var. ***primigenius*** Fernández Casas & Lainz

N. nobilis Jordan = *N. cupularis*

'Nobilis'
Syn. of *N. nobilis* var. *nobilis*

'Nobilissima' 8 W-Y
(pre-1846)
Corona citron yellow. Possibly the same as 'Nobilissimus'

'Nobilissimo' 4 Y-O
(pre-1798)
Selection from *N. tazetta*
Corona segments orange. Possibly the same as 'Nobilissimus'

'Nobilissimus' 4 W-Y
(pre-1871)
Corona segments yellow. Syn. Tazetta 'Nobilissimus'. See also 'Nobillissimus', 'Noblissimus'. Possibly the same as 'Nobilissimo' and 'Nobilissima' pre-1846

'Nobility' 9 W-O
(pre 1915)
Fl. large. AM(Haarlem) 1915

'Nobility' 3 W-O
(L. van Leeuwen & Son, pre-1920)
Perianth segments creamy white; corona large, shallow, reddish orange. AM(Haarlem) 1920

'Nobillissimus' 4 W-Y
Syn. of 'Nobilissimus'

'Noble' 2 Y-Y
(G.H. Engleheart, pre-1907)
Fl. pale yellow

'Noble Artist' 2 W-YYO
(R. Hyde) R. Hyde, 1955

'Noble Diamond' 3 W-GYR
(A.M. Wilson, pre-1938)

'Nobleman' 2 (a)
(R. Dick, pre-1933)

'Noble Prince' 1 Y-Y
(A. Glover, c.1964) Unregistered
'Golden Beauty' × 'Melissa'

'Noblesse' 1 W-W
(E.M. Crosfield, pre-1909)
Corona long, milk white, tinged pale primrose yellow, mouth expanded, with rim deeply notched

'Noblesse' 2 (a)
(L. Buckland, pre-1936)

'Noblesse' 2 Y-O
(Konynenburg & Mark, 1950) Konynenburg & Mark, 1966
'Pro Domo' × 'Fortuna'
Fl. 98 mm wide; perianth segments canary yellow; corona strong orange 25A. Mid-season

'Noble Star' 3 W-? (b)
(J.L. Richardson, pre-1937)

'Noblissimus' 4 W-Y
Syn. of 'Nobilissimus'

'Nocello' 2 W-GPP
(Brian S. Duncan) Rathowen Daffodils, 1987
'Fragrant Rose' × 'Ken's Favorite'
Corona short bowl-shaped, deep pink, with green at base. Mid-season to late

'Nocturne' 9
(pre-1913)

'Nocturne' 2 W-W
(G.L. Wilson, pre-1942)
'Marmora' × 'Evening'

'Nod' 3 W-R
(A.M. Wilson, pre-1944)
Perianth segments pure white, slightly reflexed; corona clear vermilion red. Late

'Nodding Acquaintance' 7 Y-Y
(G. Temple-Smith) G. Temple-Smith, 1993
'Ristin' × *N. jonquilla*; sdlg no. 10/88
Fls 3 per stem, 75 mm wide, yellow; perianth segments with margins slightly incurved, of good substance; corona slightly darker in tone than the perianth, with mouth straight. Mid-season

'Noddy' 2 W-? (b)
(R.V. Favell) Trenoweth Valley Flower Farm, 1955

'No Doubt' 2 W-YYP
(pre-1961)
Perianth segments pure white; corona large, yellow, with a broad band of deep pink at rim, frilled

'Noel' 9
(G.H. Engleheart, pre-1916)

'Noel Buxton' 2 W-? (b)
(H.R. Meyer, pre-1927)

'Noelle' 5 W-W
(T. Morrison) T. Morrison, 1960
Fls 1-3 per stem

'Noevia' 1 W-P
(W.Jackson Sr, 1939) W.Jackson Jr, 1956
'Pink o' Dawn' × 'Pinkeen'
Syn. of 'Naevia'

'Noevia' 2 W-P
Syn. of 'Naevis'

'Noevta' 2 W-P
Syn. of 'Naevis'

'Nogah' 2 Y-R
(A.O. Roblin, c.1966) Unregistered
'Maranoa' × 'Tegwith'

'Nokomai' 1 (a)
(G.H. Brownlee, pre-1949)

'Nokomis' 1 W-W
(R.H. Bath, pre-1933)

'Nola' 3 W-YYR
(G.W.E. Brogden) M.E. Brogden, 1959

'Nomad'
(E.M. Crosfield, pre-1913)

'Nomad' 2 W-W
(J.S. Leitch) J.S. Leitch, 1968

'Nona' 2 or 3 W-? (b or c)
(pre-1907)

'Nona' 2 W-W
(W. Jackson Sr, 1935)
'Imbros' × 'Mary Blewitt'

'Nona' 2 W-P
(P. & G. Phillips) P. & G. Phillips, 1979
Fl. 110 mm wide. Mid-season

'Nona' 2 W-P
(J.N. Hancock & Co., 1963) Unregistered

'Nonchalant' 3 Y-GYY
(Jackson's Daffodils) Jackson's Daffodils, 1989
'Lemonade' × sdlg 250/78; sdlg no. 208/84
Fl. rounded, 96 mm wide; perianth segments very broadly ovate, truncate, brilliant greenish yellow 3B, with slight white mucro and a touch of white at midrib at apex, spreading, overlapping half or more; the outer segments overlapping one other; the inner segments roundish, less prominently truncate, a little inflexed, with margins slightly wavy; corona short, flared, loosely ribbed, a little darker in tone (6B) than the perianth, with deep green at base, mouth straight,

deeply frilled. Mid-season to late

'Nonotuck' 3 W-YYR
(E.C. Powell, pre-1946)

'Nonpareil' 1 W-? (b)
(pre-1926)

'Nonpareil' 3 W-GYR
(P.D. Williams, pre-1935)
Perianth segments very broadly ovate, rounded at apex, prominently mucronate, spreading, a little concave, with margins slightly incurling, overlapping half; the inner segments narrower, sharply angled at shoulder, a little inflexed, with margins wavy; corona small bowl-shaped, ribbed, bright yellow, shading to green at base and with a band of dark red at rim, mouth loosely frilled, rim ragged, with some deeply overlapping folds. Mid-season

'Non Pareille' 8 W-W
(pre-1807)

'Nonsense' 9
(pre-1914)

'Nonsuch' 2 or 3 ?-R
(pre-1914)

'Nony' 8 W-Y
(Herut Yahel, pre-1982) C.S.Weijers Jr, 1997
Probably *N. papyraceus* × 'Soleil d'Or'
Fls 10-15 per stem, 40 mm wide; perianth segments broadly ovate, blunt, mucronate, yellowish white (155B), spreading, overlapping one-third to a half; the inner segments twisted; corona bowl-shaped, ribbed, brilliant greenish yellow 7C, mouth even or slightly wavy, rim entire. Dwarf. Mid-season to late. Sweetly scented. Syn. 'Bethlehem'

'Noojee' 2 Y-O
(J.N. Hancock & Co., 1953)

'Noon' 2 Y-R
(P.D. Williams) Trenoweth Valley Flower Farm, 1955

'Noonday' 2 W-? (b)
(?A.G. Bull, pre-1912)

'Noonday' 2 Y-O
(O. Ronalds, 1947) T. Morrison, 1960
Perianth segments rich yellow; corona coppery orange

'Noon Gold' 1 Y-Y
(J.N. Hancock & Co., c.1980) Unregistered

'Noontide' 2 (a)
(J.C. Williams, pre-1945)

'Nooreen' 3 (b)
Syn. of 'Noreen'

'Noose' 2 (a)
(A.H. Ahrens) J.S. Leitch, 1955

'No Peer' 2 Y-R
(J.M. Radcliff, 1973) P.J. Radcliff, 1989
Sdlg 1/68 × 'Jaguar'
Fl. 110 mm wide or more; perianth segments very broad, rounded at apex, light yellow 11B, a little reflexed, of good substance, overlapping half; the inner segments narrower and more nearly ovate; corona bowl-shaped, vivid reddish orange 32A, with mouth widely expanded and lightly frilled. Tall. Mid-season. Sunproof

'Nora' 2 or 3 W-W
(pre-1887)
Perianth segments pure white; corona opening primrose yellow, becoming pale creamy white

'Nora' 2 or 3 W-? (b or c)
(C. Dawson, pre-1907)

'Norah Connor' 1 (a)
(G.L. Wilson, pre-1932)

'Norah Pearson' 2 W-Y
(J.R. Pearson & Sons, pre-1910)
'Minnie Hume' × 'Madame de Graaff'
Fl. 95 mm wide; perianth segments pure white, overlapping; corona pale soft citron yellow, frilled. Mid-season. Resembles 'Honourable Mrs J.L.Francklin'.
*HC(g) 1927

'Norah Phillips' 3 W-? (b)
(H.D. Phillips, pre-1926)

'Nora Margaret' 3 (a)
(Mrs R.O. Backhouse, pre-1914)

'Nordia' 2 Y-Y
(Doornbosch Bros, 1954) Doornbosch Bros, 1968
Fl. 100 mm wide; perianth segments creamy yellow; corona vivid yellow 9B. Very early

'Nordic Rim' 3 W-WWY
(G.E. Mitsch, 1982) R. & E. Havens, 1993
'Silken Sails' × 'Merlin'; sdlg no. 2R32/10
Fl. 100 mm wide; perianth segments very broad, rounded at apex, fairly prominently mucronate, pure white, a little reflexed, plane; the inner segments more nearly ovate and spreading, somewhat creased, with margins wavy, almost touching at shoulder; corona very shallow, white, with a broad band of golden yellow at rim, ribbed, with mouth heavily frilled and rim crenate. Late

'Noreen' 3 W-? (b)
(G.C. Graham, pre-1951)

See also 'Nooreen'

'Norellen' 4 W-P
(W. Jackson Jr) W. Jackson Jr, 1968
('Palin' × 'Dawnglow') hybrid; sdlg no. 72/60

'Norfolk' 2 (a)
(Mrs R.O. Backhouse, pre-1921)
Syn. 'Red Prince'. AM(Haarlem) 1928

'Norfolk Beauty' 2 (a)
(R.H. Bath, pre-1931)

'Noriko' 2 W-P
(P. & G. Phillips) P. & G. Phillips, 1975
Fl. 92 mm wide. Mid-season

'Norina' 2 W-? (b)
(J.T. Gray, pre-1951)

'Norla' 2 Y-Y
(J.L. Martin) J.L. Martin, 1973
'Ptolemy' × 'Scorcher'
Fl. 125 mm wide; perianth segments light greenish yellow 4C; corona vivid yellow 14A. Early. See also 'Morla'

'Norma' 1 W-? (b)
(G.H. Engleheart, pre-1907)
Perianth segments cream; corona saffron. Early

'Norma' 2 W-O
(Konynenburg & Mark) Konynenburg & Mark, 1960
'Diva' hybrid × ('Frederike' × 'Mimosa')
Fl. 100 mm wide; perianth segments creamy white; corona strong orange 24A. Mid-season

'Norma' 2 (a)
Syn. of 'Michigan'

'Norma Anderson' 4 Y-R
(C.F. Anderson, 1980) A.W. Chappell, 1990
'Warne' × 'Falstaff'
Fl. 80 mm wide. Early

'Norma Graham' 1
(W.M. Spry, pre-1975) Unregistered
'Blond Giant' × 'Clare'
Fl. golden brown, flushed pink; corona with lemon at rim, frilled

'Norma Jean' 2 Y-Y
(J.S.B. Lea) Clive Postles Daffodils, 1988
Sdlg LI-25-68 × 'Ashmore'; sdlg no. LI-17-75
Fl. 95 mm wide; perianth segments pale yellow, spreading, very smooth; corona short, straight-sided, of a darker yellow than the perianth. Mid-season

'Norman' 2 Y-O
(Miss G. Evelyn, pre-1927)
Corona intense reddish orange. AM(Haarlem) 1933

'Norman Cross' 2 (a)
(R.H. Bath, pre-1933)

'Normandy' 2 Y-O
(R.W. Ward, 1950) R.W. Ward & Son, 1960
Mid-season. Resembles a stronger and more upright 'Armada' with a paler corona

'Normandy' 8
(H. Frylink)

'Norman Harper' 6 Y-Y
(L.P.Dettman, 1973) Unregistered
'Cyclades' hybrid; sdlg no. 13/73

'Norman McLeod' 2 (a)
(Australian origin, 1940) R. Hyde, 1958

'Norman Thomas' 1 W-W
(W.F. Mitchell, pre-1919)
Fl. 140 mm wide; perianth segments broadly ovate, blunt, slightly mucronate, white, touched yellow at midrib, inflexed, smooth, overlapping; the inner segment with margins wavy; corona cylindrical, mouth expanded, split and overlapping, frilled, with rim flanged. Syn. 'Lieutenant N.R.W.Thomas'

'Normanton' 2 W-GPP
(Mrs H.K. Richardson) Mrs J. Abel Smith, 1978
'Infatuation' × 'Debutante'; sdlg no. 125
Fl. 97 mm wide; corona soft pink, with green at base. Mid-season. Resembles a larger-flowered 'Infatuation' with more pink to the corona

'Norna' 1 W-W
(J.T. Gray, 1940) Parr's Nurseries, 1958
Fl. pure white

'Nor-Nor' 2 Y-YYO
(G.L. Wilson, pre-1941)
Fl. 73 mm wide; perianth segments opening yellow, becoming whitish yellow, with brilliant greenish yellow 7C at base, overlapping only slightly; corona vivid yellow 14B, shading to yellow-orange (21A) at rim, mouth ribbed and straight, rim crenate. Dwarf. Sunproof

'Norseman' 1 W-? (b)
(A.M. Wilson, pre-1908)

'Norseman' 2 W-Y
(W.A. Grace, pre-1927)
Mid-season

'Northam' 2 W-W
(M.J.Jefferson-Brown) Mary Lou Gripshover, 1997
Sdlg no. 212B

Fl. star-shaped, 52 mm wide; perianth segments ovate, acute, spreading, a little twisted or with margins recurved, only slightly overlapping; the inner segments slightly inflexed; corona funnel-shaped, opening vivid yellow 15a, with a darker tone at rim, becoming self white, with rim rolled and dentate. Dwarf. Early

'North Anderson' 3 W-R
(Ken Farmer Nurseries) Ken Farmer Nureries, 1978
Fl. 110 mm wide; corona orange-red. Mid-season

'North Cape' 2 W-W
(Barr & Sons, pre-1945)

'Northcote' 2 Y-YYO
(H.A. Brown, 1940) J.N. Hancock & Co., 1960
Corona disc-shaped, with deep orange at rim, with the rim dentate

'Northern Flame' 2 Y-YOR
(T. Bloomer) T. Bloomer, 1972
'Craigywarren' × 'Air Marshal'; sdlg no. 3/35/58
Perianth segments gold; corona with orange-red at rim

'Northern Light' 2 (a)
(G.H. Engleheart, pre-1907)

'Northern Light' 2 W-O
(J.L. Richardson) J.L. Richardson, 1958
'Fermoy' × 'Arbar'
Corona very shallow bowl-shaped, reddish orange

'Northern Minstrel' 1 W-W
(J.W. Barr, pre-1930)

'Northern Queen' 3 W-? (b)
(pre-1910)

'Northern Sceptre' 2 W-YYR
(Ballydorn Bulb Farm) Ballydorn Bulb Farm, 1975
'Northern Light' open pollinated
Fl. 100 mm wide; corona yellow, with a broad band of red at rim. Mid-season

'Northern Spell' 3 W-R
(Ballydorn Bulb Farm) Ballydorn Bulb Farm, 1977
'Merlin' open pollinated

'Northern Star' 1 W-W
(W.F.M. Copeland, pre-1908)

'Northern Star' 1 Y-Y
(Mrs A.O. Meyrick) Mrs B.T. Simpson, 1963
Fl. 115 mm wide, vivid yellow 9A. Late

'Northland' 8 Y-Y
(New Zealand origin, pre-1996) Unregistered

'Northlea' 2 W-Y
(J.N. Hancock & Co., 1953)
Coron bright yellow, with rim rolled

'North Pole' 2 W-Y
(The Brodie of Brodie, c.1910)
'Minnie Hume' × 'Lady Margaret Boscawen'

'North Rim' 2 W-GYP
(Brian S.Duncan) Brian S.Duncan, 1993
'High Society' × 'Fragrant Rose'; sdlg no. 1029
Fl. 96 mm wide; perianth segments very broadly ovate, blunt, slightly mucronate, pure white, spreading, plane, with margins slightly incurving at apex, overlapping half or more; the inner segments more narrowly ovate, more prominently mucronate, slightly inflexed; corona funnel-shaped, yellow, distinctly green at base, with a broad band of deep reddish pink at rim, mouth lobed and lightly frilled, rim crenate. Mid-season to late. Sunproof

'North River' 1 W-Y
(Raymond W.Lewis) Raymond W.Lewis, 1983
'Arctic Gold' open pollinated

'North Star' 1 (a)
(W.B. Hartland, pre-1914)

'North Uist' 1 W-GWW
(G.L. Wilson) E. Longford, 1969
'Glendermott' × 'Empress of Ireland'; sdlg no. 46/15
Fl. 108 mm wide; corona tinged green at base. Mid-season

'Northwest' 1 W-W
(W.G. Pannill) W.G. Pannill, 1983
'Vigil' × 'Empress of Ireland'

'Norton' 5
(N.Y. Lower, pre-1929)

'Norval' 2 W-O
(J.L. Richardson) J.L. Richardson, 1959
'Kilworth' × 'Arbar'
Fl. forming a double triangle, 106 mm wide; perianth segments broadly ovate, somewhat truncate and fairly prominently mucronate, pure white, flushed brilliant yellow 7A at base, spreading or slightly inflexed, plane or with margins slightly incurling, very smooth and of good substance, overlapping one-third to a half; the inner segments a little more narrowly ovate, only very slightly mucronate, with margins very slightly wavy; corona shallow, widely expanded, heavily ribbed, vivid orange (28A), with mouth wavy and rim obscurely crenate. AM(e) 1967

'Norway' 1 W-Y
(H. Bader, pre-1939)
FA(Haarlem) 1939, FCFA(Haarlem) 1940, EFA(Haarlem) 1941

'Norwester' 6 Y-Y
(Mary Lou Gripshover, 1980) Mary Lou Gripshover, 1995
'Small Talk' × *N. cyclamineus*; sdlg no. 73-6
Fl. yellow; perianth segments ovate, with pale mucro, very strongly reflexed, with margins slightly incurved, overlapping at base only; corona cylindrical, a little constricted near mouth, smooth, with mouth slightly flared, rim dentate. Dwarf. Very early. Resembles a larger *N. cyclamineus*

'Norwind' 11a Y-Y
(J. Gerritsen & Son) J. Gerritsen & Son, 1966
Fl. 90 mm wide, pale primrose yellow; perianth segments broadly ovate; corona split to base, the six segments as wide and almost as long as the perianth segments, opposite and closely overlying them, creased, loosely frilled. Mid-season. Resembles a large-flowered 'Cassata'

'Norwood' 3 W-R
(Mrs H.K. Richardson) Mrs J. Abel Smith, 1977
'Matapan' × 'Rockall'; sdlg no. 3895
Fl. 87 mm wide; perianth segments pure white; corona almost disc-shaped, brilliant red. Mid-season. Resembles a larger-flowered 'Matapan'

'Nosegay' 7 Y-O
(R.V. Favell, pre-1946)
'Warlock' × *N. jonquilla*

"Nosegay"
See "The Nosegay"

'Noss Mayo' 6 W-Y
(Rosewarne EHS) du Plessis Bros, 1986
N. cyclamineus × 'Trousseau'; sdlg no.65/63/4
Perianth segments broadly ovate, slightly mucronate, opening creamy white, becoming whiter, strongly reflexed, plane, overlapping one-third to a half; corona cylindrical, smooth or obscurely ribbed, bright clear lemon yellow, with rim crenate and slightly flanged. Early

'Nostradamus' 2 W-O
(F.E. Board) F.E. Board, 1965
'Polindra' × 'Tudor Minstrel'

'Notable' 3 W-GYO
(Ballydorn Bulb Farm, 1967) Ballydorn Bulb Farm, 1979
'Nemo' open pollinated
Fl. 83 mm wide. Early to mid-season

'Noteworthy' 3 W-YYO
(W.G. Pannill) W.G. Pannill, 1992
('Lough Areema' × 'Rose Caprice') × 'Jewel Song'; sdlg no. 73/22
Fl. 100 mm wide. Mid-season

'Notos' 2 (a)
(Mrs R.O. Backhouse, pre-1921)

'Notre Dame' 2 W-GYP
(Brian S. Duncan) Brian S. Duncan, 1992
'Raspberry Ring' × 'Fragrant Rose'; sdlg no. 1186
Fl. rounded, 105 mm wide; perianth segments very broad, somewhat truncate, mucronate, pure white, slightly reflexed, concave, overlapping half; the inner segments narrower, less noticeably mucronate, sometimes inflexed towards apex, with margins wavy; corona long cup-shaped, constricted near mouth, pinkish yellow, with green at base and a broad band of orange-pink (32B) at rim, rim sometimes slightly flanged. Late to very late. Sunproof. AM(e) 1996

'Noumea' 2 Y-O
(H.A. Brown, 1941)
Fl. large; perianth segments rich yellow; corona expanded, bright orange. Mid-season

'Nouvelle' 3 W-YPO
(Ballydorn Bulb Farm, 1969) Ballydorn Bulb Farm, 1987
'Mount Pleasant' × 'Nemo'
Corona saucer-shaped, creamy pink, with yellow tones at base and orange tones at rim. Mid-season

'Nova' 3 W-? (b)
(W.A. Bell, pre-1949)

'Nova Scotia' 2 W-YYO
(Mrs R.O. Backhouse, pre-1921)
Perianth segments creamy yellow; corona shallow, widely expanded, golden yellow, with a broad band of orange at rim, frilled. AM(Haarlem) 1932

'Nova Zembla' 2 Y-O
(pre-1935)
Perianth segments narrow, acute; corona large, widely expanded, reddish orange

'Novelist' 1 Y-Y
(pre-1965) Unregistered
Fl. rich yellow

'Novelty' 2 W-? (b)
(Sir C.H. Cave, pre-1908)
'Lulworth' × *N. poeticus*

'Novelty Crown' 2 W-O
(C.W. Culpepper, pre-1970) Unregistered
Fl. large, rounded; perianth segments white; corona very shallow bowl-shaped, yellow-orange, frilled, with rim crenate

'Novice' 1
(T.B. Green, pre-1936)

'Novice' 2 (a)
(A.H. Ahrens) J.S. Leitch, 1955

'No Way' 3 Y-O
(D. Jackson) Jackson's Daffodils, 1982
'Kopi' × 'Riis'; sdlg no. 123/77
Fl. 88 mm wide. Mid-season

'Nowell' 1 W-W
(R.H. Bath, pre-1929)

'Noweta' 3 W-WWY
(G.E. Mitsch, 1951) G.E. Mitsch, 1963
'Green Island' × 'Chinese White'; sdlg no. M39/4
Fl. rounded, 102 mm wide; perianth segments pure white, deeply overlapping; corona creamy white, with lemon yellow at rim. Mid-season. Resembles a taller and larger-flowered 'Sylvia O'Neill'

'No Worries' 3 W-WWY
(Jackson's Daffodils) Jackson's Daffodils, 1996
Sdlg ?220/79 × sdlg 118/82; sdlg no. 246/88
Fl. 125 mm wide; perianth segments broadly ovate, greenish white (155A); corona bowl-shaped, yellow-white (11D), with light greenish yellow 7D at rim. Mid-season

'Nowra' 2 W-R
(Jackson's Daffodils, 1987) Jackson's Daffodils, 1997
'Potent' × 'Hartz'; sdlg no. 130/87
Fl. 114 mm wide; perianth segments broadly ovate, yellowish white 155D, the inner segments narrower; corona bowl-shaped, bright orange-red. Mid-season

'Nuage' 2 W-W
(G.H. Johnstone, pre-1949)
'Lady-Day' × 'Truth'
2n=28

'Nuance' 3 Y-? (a)
(R. Crews, pre-1949)
Syn. 'Ecstasy'

'Nucleus' 2 (a)
(R. Crews, pre-1949)

'Nugget' 1 Y-Y
(Mrs R.O. Backhouse, pre-1921)

'Nuke' 1 W-P
(Jacksons Daffodils, 1977) Jacksons Daffodils, 1987
Sdlg 163/69 × 'Verran'; sdlg no. 72/77
Perianth segments greenish white 155C; corona dark reddish pink (47B). Early

'Nulli Secundus' 3 W-? (b)
(Alister Clark, pre-1911)

'Numa' 1 W-? (b)
(Barr & Sons, pre-1923)

'Numa Pompilius' 7
(de Graaff Bros, pre-1927)
AM(Haarlem) 1932

'Numen Rose' 2 W-GPP
(Brian S.Duncan) Brian S.Duncan, 1995
'Fragrant Rose' × 'Mentor'; sdlg no. 1199
Fl. 103 mm wide; perianth segments ovate, blunt, spreading; corona funnel-shaped, deep apricot pink, with greenish shades at base, mouth straight, even, with rim entire. Late to very late. Sunproof. Scented

'Nuna' 2 W-?
(Alister Clark, 1935) J. Sharp, 1960

'Nursemaid' 3 W-O
(Mrs R.O. Backhouse, pre-1921)
Perianth segments pure white, overlapping; corona rich reddish orange, neatly frilled

'Nurse Noble' 2 (a)
(V.M. Dickinson, pre-1949)

N. × *nutans* Haworth = ? *N. jonquilla* Linnaeus × *N. triandrus* Linnaeus

'Nuthatch' 6 Y-Y
(M. Fowlds) G.E. Mitsch, 1968
'Fortune's Sun' × *N. cyclamineus*; sdlg no. F168/1
Fl. 57 mm wide, mid-yellow, of strong substance; perianth segments moderately reflexed; corona slightly darker in tone than the perianth. Mid-season

'Nutmeg' 2 W-Y
(Murray W.Evans) Murray W.Evans, 1976
Sdlg × 'Accent'; sdlg no. K-38/1
Fl. 100 mm wide. Mid-season

'Nutwith' 2 Y-? (a)
(A.M. Wilson, pre-1927)
'Hospodar' hybrid

'Nydia' 3 W-W
(R.H. Bath, pre-1927)

'Nylon' 10 W-W
Now treated as Nylon Group

Nylon Group 10 W-W
(D. Blanchard) A.Gray, 1949
2n=28. A group of unselected seedlings raised from crossing *N. cantabricus* var. *foliosus* and *N. romieuxii*. Formerly treated as 'Nylon'

'Nym' 2 W-Y
(W. Jackson Jr) W. Jackson Jr, 1968
'Tudor Minstrel' × 'Faralong'; sdlg no. 74/60

'Nymph' 2 or 3 (b or c)
(W.F.M. Copeland, pre-1908)

'Nymphaea' 2 W-W
Syn. of 'Nymphea'

'Nymphea' 2 W-WWY
(C.E.Radcliff, pre-1936)
'Lemon Star' × 'Mrs W.Moodie'
Perianth segments broadly ovate, overlapping; corona funnel-shaped, with mouth straight. See also 'Nymphaea'

'Nymphette' 6 W-P
(Brian S. Duncan) Rathowen Daffodils, 1978
'Roseworthy' hybrid; sdlg no. 48
Perianth segments broadly elliptic, near to pure white, reflexed; corona cylindrical, constricted near midpoint, coppery pink with lilac tones. Mid-season. 2n=27

'Nynja' 2 Y-Y
(Jackson's Daffodils) Jackson's Daffodils, 1992
'Scipio' × sdlg 11/78; sdlg no. 47/86
Fl. 105 mm wide; perianth segments very broadly ovate, blunt, brilliant greenish yellow 6A, slightly inflexed, concave, overlapping half or more; corona almost as long as the perianth segments, funnel-shaped, darker in tone (14B), with mouth straight and even, rim crenate. Mid-season to late

'Nyora' 2 (a)
(H.A. Brown, pre-1936)

'Nyora' 3 W-YYR
(W. Jackson Jr) W. Jackson Jr, 1968
'Masaka' × 'Jo'; sdlg no. 2/62

'Nysa' 3 W-O
(C. Dawson, pre-1919)
Perianth segments slightly reflexed; corona expanded, closely ribbed, reddish orange

#

'Oadby' 1 Y-Y
(W.A. Noton, 1972) W.A. Noton, 1985
'Golden Rapture' × 'Arkle'; sdlg no. 513
Fl. 116 mm wide, near to vivid yellow 9A, with the perianth greener and the corona richer in tone; perianth segments very broadly ovate, with slight white mucro, inflexed, overlapping one-third to a half; the inner segments more narrowly ovate, twisted; corona cylindrical, broadly and obscurely ribbed, with mouth expanded, rim deeply notched and crenate. Early. 2n=28

'Oakhurst' 1 W-Y
(G.P. Haydon, pre-1910)

Fl. rounded, 102 mm wide; corona ribbed, soft primrose yellow, tinged sulphur yellow at mouth, with mouth widely expanded and rim flanged

'Oakland' 2 Y-Y
(G.E. Mitsch, 1979) R. & E. Havens, 1993
'Camelot' × 'Aurum'; sdlg no. 2015/1
Fl. 100 mm wide, deep golden yellow, of heavy substance; perianth segments ovate, spreading, plane, smooth; corona funnel-shaped, with mouth slightly flared. Mid-season

'Oakura' 6 Y-Y
(Robin Brown) Robin Brown, 1995
'Mite' × *N. cyclamineus*; sdlg no. M/CYC 1
Fl. 56 mm wide, mid-yellow; perianth segments reflexed; corona cylindrical, smooth, with mouth straight and frilled. Dwarf. Early

'Oakvale' 1 W-W
(F.E. Board) F.E. Board, 1965
'Cotterton' × 'Glendermott'; sdlg no. 1101
Mid-season

'Oakwood' 3 Y-Y
(S.J. Bisdee, 1950) E. Longford, 1966
'Carbineer' × 'Keren'
Fl. 89 mm wide; corona yellow, with greenish yellow at base and orange-yellow at rim. Late

'Oamaru' 1 Y-Y
(W.D. Burns, pre-1927)

'Oasis' 9
(W. Welchman, pre-1929)

'Oat Cake' 2 W-GYO
(J.N. Hancock & Co., 1956) J.N. Hancock & Co., 1977
'Del Rose' hybrid; sdlg no. 54/51
Fl. 102 mm wide; corona opening brilliant yellow 13C, becoming creamier in tone (16C), with green at base and orange at rim. Early

'Oba' 3 W-? (b or c)
(W. Jackson Sr, 1938)
'Mountain Pride' × 'Mayflower'

'Oban' 1 W-Y
(J.A. O'More) P. Phillips, 1971
'Samite' × 'Broughshane'
Fl. 109 mm wide

'Obdam' 4 W-W
(C.J. Bakker) C.J. Bakker, 1984
'Ice Follies' sport
Perianth and other petaloid segments white at maturity; the outer whorl often with green beneath; corona segments opening yellow, becoming white

'Obelisk' 11a Y-Y
(J. Gerritsen & Son) J. Gerritsen & Son, 1973
'Flevo' × 'Gold Collar'
Fl. 110 mm wide, very deep yellow

'Obelisk' 2 W-Y
(J.N. Hancock & Co., c.1977) Unregistered

'Oberlin' 2 Y-Y
(W. Jackson Jr, 1955) Unregistered
'Kalman' × 'Melissa'; sdlg no. 89/55

'Oberon' 1 W-W
(G.H. Engleheart, pre-1914)

'Oberon' 5
(Sir A.P.W. Thomas, pre-1930)

'Oberon' 1 (a)
Syn. of 'Maryland'

'Oberon' 3 W-Y
Syn. of 'Eoster'

N. obesus Salisbury 13 Section Bulbocodium. AM 1993

'Obligato' 2 W-P
(G.L. Wilson) F.E. Board, 1962
'Contour' × 'Rosario'; sdlg no. 46-38
Mid-season. Resembles 'Rosario' but with a paler corona

N. obliquus Gussone = N. italicus

N. obliteratus Willdenow = N. broussonetii

'Oboe' 1 W-WWY
(J.N. Hancock & Co., 1966) Unregistered

'Obrana' 3 W-OOR
(D.S. Bell) D.S. Bell, 1962
Fl. 104 mm wide; corona apricot, with red at rim. Mid-season. Resembles a larger-flowered 'Corofin' with the perianth segments more narrowly acute at apex

'Obsession' 2 W-P
(D. Jackson) Jackson's Daffodils, 1982
'Cathlin' × 'Verran'; sdlg no. 188/76
Fl. 98 mm wide; corona pink, with rim slightly dentate

N. × obsoletus Haworth 13 = N. elegans (Haworth) Spach × N. viridiflorus Schousboe

N. obsoletus Spach = N. serotinus

N. obvallaris Salisbury 13 Section Pseudonarcissus ("The Tenby Daffodil"). *AM(g) 1973, AGM 1993

'Obvallaris Maximus' 1 Y-Y
(pre-1873)
Fl. rich golden yellow. Early

'Ocarino' 4 Y-Y
(J.L. Richardson) Mrs H.K. Richardson, 1964
'Gay Time' × 'Spanish Gold'
Fl. 86-95 mm wide; perianth and other petaloid segments in several whorls, light greenish yellow 4C; the outer whorls very broadly ovate, blunt, slightly mucronate, spreading, regular, overlapping half; the centre whorls shorter, strongly inflexed, with margins wavy or incurling; corona segments as long as the centre petaloid segments and interspersed among them, roundish, vivid yellow 13A. Late. 2n=29. AM(e) 1966

'Occasionally' 1 W-Y
(G.E. Mitsch, 1972) Grant Mitsch Novelty Daffodils, 1984
'Wahkeena' × (['Silver Dale' × 'Kanchenjunga'] × 'Preamble'); sdlg no. H122/4
Fl. forming a double triangle, 120 mm wide; perianth segments broadly ovate, blunt, very slightly mucronate, spreading, plane, overlapping one-third to a half; the inner segments more narrowly ovate, more nearly acute, slightly reflexed towards apex, with margins a little wavy; corona funnel-shaped, smooth, lemon yellow, with mouth flared and frilled, rim crenate. Mid-season

'Occident' 3 Y-O
(G.H. Engleheart, pre-1903)
Perianth segments soft canary yellow; corona reddish orange. AM 1903

'Occleston' 4
(T.O. Occleston, pre-1928)

'Ocean Blue' 2 W-WWP
(Brian S.Duncan) Brian S.Duncan, 1997
'Dailmanach' × 'Gracious Lady'; sdlg no. 1492
Fl. forming a double triangle, 113 mm wide; perianth segments broadly ovate, spreading, smooth; corona broad funnel-shaped, opening apple-blossom pink, becoming white, with pink at rim, mouth slightly flared, frilled. Mid-season to late

'Ocean Breeze' 6 W-W
(G.E. Mitsch) G.E. Mitsch, 1979
'Titania' × N. cyclamineus; sdlg no. G91/2
Fl. 64 mm wide, of good substance; perianth segments ovate, slightly mucronate, lightly reflexed, plane, sometimes creased at midrib, overlapping one-third; the inner segments more extensively creased; corona cylindrical, smooth, opening pale yellow, becoming almost white, with mouth flared and a little frilled, rim crenate. Dwarf. Early. Resembles a somewhat smaller 'Ibis' of clearer white

'Oceanid' 5 W-W
(R. Gibson, pre-1927)
PC(e)(NZ) 1929

'Ocean Mist' 1 W-W
(P. Phillips) P. Phillips, 1966
Fl. forming a double triangle, 120 mm wide, pure white. Mid-season. Resembles a larger-flowered 'Cantatrice' with a more widely expanded corona

'Oceano' 2 W-W
(Brian S. Duncan) W.H. Roesé, 1985
'Easter Moon' × 'Knowehead'; sdlg no. 240
Fl. of smooth texture. Mid-season

'Ocean Rain' 11a W-Y
(J.N.Hancock & Co., 1984) Unregistered
'Innisfail' × 'Artist's Model'; sdlg no. 37/84H
Perianth segments creamy white; corona deeply split, the six segments opposite and closely overlying the perianth segments, orange-yellow. Tall. Mid-season

'Ocean Spray' 7 W-W
(G.E. Mitsch) G.E. Mitsch, 1966
('Rubra' × 'Green Island') × *N. rupicola* subsp. *watieri*; sdlg no. V97/3
Fl. rounded, 57 mm wide; corona deep bowl-shaped. Mid-season. 2n=21. Resembles a large-flowered 'Dainty Miss'

'Ocean Wave' 2 W-W
(G. Lewis, pre-1940)
'White Emperor' × 'Tenedos'
Corona pale yellow

'Ochre' 1 Y-Y
(J.N. Hancock & Co., *c.*1978) Unregistered

'Ochree' 3
(C. Bourne, pre-1916)

N. ochroleucus Loiseleur-Deslongchamps = *N. tazetta* subsp. *ochroleucus*

'Oconee' 5 Y-Y
(E.C. Powell, pre-1946)
? × *N. triandrus*

'O'Connell' 3 W-? (b)
(H. Prins, pre-1927)

'Octavia' 3 (a)
(W. Welchman, pre-1910)

'Octavianus' 1 W-W
(de Graaff Bros, pre-1929)

'Octoroon' 2 (a)
(Mrs R.O. Backhouse, pre-1908)

'Odalisque' 3 (a)
(F.H. Chapman, pre-1913)

'Oddity' 2? W-W
(W. Backhouse, pre-1869)
Fl. silver white. Syn. Leedsii 'Oddity'

'Odds On' 4 W-R
(M.J. Jefferson-Brown) M.J. Jefferson-Brown, 1975
'Gay Time' hybrid
Mid-season. Resembles an earlier-flowered 'Gay Time'

'Ode' 9
(F.H. Chapman, pre-1910)

'Odense' 2 W-YYO
(Konynenburg & Mark) Konynenburg & Mark, 1960
'Frederike' × (['Frederike' × 'Mimosa'] × 'Glorious')
Fl. 100 mm wide; corona pale yellow 11D, with light orange (23B) at rim. Mid-season. 2n=28

'Odeon' 2 (a)
(J.L. Richardson, pre-1938)

'Odessa' 2 Y-YYO
(The Brodie of Brodie, *c.*1927)
'Seraglio' × 'Fortune'
Perianth segments pale yellow; corona large, widely expanded, yellow, with orange at rim, with the rim closely and deeply notched, as if fringed. AM(Haarlem) 1936

'Odette' 3 W-? (b)
(Mrs R.O. Backhouse, pre-1921)

'Odile' 7 Y-O
(Roberta C.Watrous, 1966) Roberta C.Watrous, 1989
'Seville' × *N. assoanus*; sdlg no. 621-5
Fl. 38 mm wide; perianth segments ovate, acute, light greenish yellow 8B, slightly reflexed; corona bowl-shaped, vivid yellow 14B. Dwarf. Late

'Odin' 2 W-? (b)
(W. Welchman, pre-1929)

'Odin' 1 Y-Y
(W. Jackson Jr, 1955) Jackson's Daffodils, 1979
'Ristin' × 'Otewa'; sdlg no. 99/72
Fl. 106 mm wide. Early to mid-season

'Odist' 9 W-GYO
(Murray W.Evans, 1973) Murray W.Evans, 1985
('Chinese White' hybrid × [*N. poeticus* var. *recurvus* × 'Carolina']) × ('Falaise' × 'Foxfire'); sdlg no. P-29
Corona with glowing coral orange at rim. Late

'Odo' 2 W-? (b or c)
(pre-1935)

'Odoacer' 8 Y-Y
(pre-1798)
Fl. golden yellow

'Odon Warland' 2 (a)
(de Graaff-Gerharda, pre-1930)
AM(Haarlem) 1930

'Odorata' 8 W-Y
Syn. of 'Odoratus'

'Odoratus' 8 W-Y
(?French origin, pre-1936)
Found by Alec Gray on the Isles of Scilly and named by him
Fls up to 6 or more per stem, small; perianth segments narrowly oval, milk-white, reflexed, separated; corona cup-shaped, smooth, brilliant yellow 13B, with mouth wavy, rim shallowly notched in places. Dwarf. Apricot-scented. Resembles a taller *N. canaliculatus*. Syn. 'Odorata'. Found by Alec Gray on the Isles of Scilly and named by him

***N.* × *odorus* Linnaeus 13** = *N. jonquilla* Linnaeus × *N. pseudonarcissus* Linnaeus (or *N. hispanicus* Gouan?) (Odorus 'Campernelli', Odorus 'Curtisii', Odorus 'Interjectus', "The Great 6-lobed", "The Great Curled Cup", "The Late Great 6-lobed"). 2n=14

'Odulation' 2 Y-O
(Jacksons Daffodils) Jacksons Daffodils, 1986
'Iatros' × sdlg 166/73; sdlg no. 282/78
Perianth segments broadly ovate, blunt, slightly mucronate, brilliant greenish yellow 6C, spreading, with midrib showing, overlapping half; the inner segments a little inflexed, with margin slightly nicked; corona bowl-shaped, smooth or very lightly ribbed, vivid orange 28B, with mouth even, rim minutely crenate. Mid-season

'Odysseus' 3 (a)
(de Graaff Bros, pre-1927)

'Odyssey' 4 W-Y
(W.G. Pannill) W.G. Pannill, 1978
'Snowshill' × 4 W-Y sdlg; sdlg no. 67/57
Fl. 120 mm wide. Mid-season

'Oecumene' 11a Y-Y
(J. Gerritsen & Son) J. Gerritsen & Son, 1970
'Overcollar' × 'Golden Harvest'
Perianth segments golden yellow; corona segments large, golden yellow, with green at base. Early

'Oehoe' 3 W-? (b)
(J.W.A. Lefeber, pre-1944)

'Oenone' 2 W-? (b or c)
(P.D. Williams, pre-1913)

'Oeo' 3 (a)
(G.W.E. Brogden) C.W. Johnson, 1955

'Off Picture' 11a W-YYP
(J.Gerritsen & Son) Unregistered

'Og, King of Basan' 1 W-? (b)
(C. Wolley-Dod, pre-1907)

'Ogee' 1 Y-Y
(W. Jackson Sr, 1939)
'Siward' × 'Crocus'

'Ogeesan Wally' 2 W-O
(L.P. Dettman) L.P. Dettman, 1970
'Buncrana' × 'Dunseverick'

'Ogwen' 2 (a)
(W.A. Watts, pre-1935)

'Ohakea' 1 Y-Y
(A. Gibson, pre-1940)
Fl. bright yellow. PC(e)(NZ) 1940

'Oharabrook' 2 W-P
(Mrs H.K. Richardson) Carncairn Daffodils, 1978
Fl. 95 mm wide; perianth segments greenish white (155A); corona expanded, light yellowish pink 29C, with rim dentate. Late

'Ohau' 3 W-W
(J.A.O'More, 1959) P.D.K. Ramsay, 1984
'Chinese White' × 'Green Island'; sdlg no. 95/59

'Ohio' 2 W-YOO
(J.M. de Navarro) J.M. de Navarro, 1966
'Kilworth' × 'Brahms'
Fl. 92 mm wide; perianth segments very broadly ovate, blunt, slightly mucronate, creamy white, tinged greenish yellow at base, spreading, concave, with margins minutely incurling at apex, smooth, overlapping half; the inner segments sometimes "thumbed" at shoulder, steeply narrowing to base; corona shallow bowl-shaped, ribbed, vivid orange 28B, with vivid yellow 9A at base and a tinge of green in tube, mouth widely expanded, sometimes deeply split and overlapping, lightly frilled, with rim shallowly crenate. Late. 2n=28. Resembles 'Fermoy' but with a more reddish cast to the corona. The corona sometimes predominantly yellow

'Ohisay' 1 W-Y
(T.H. Piper, *c.*1966) Unregistered
'Thera' × 'Lorinna'

'Oh Kaye' 4 W-P
(Glenbrook Bulb Farm, 1983) Glenbrook Bulb Farm,

1997
'Anne of Cleves' × 'Lawali'
Fl. 72 mm wide; perianth segments broadly ovate, greenish white (155C); corona segments near to light yellowish pink 19B, frilled. Mid-season to late

'Ohoke' 2 Y-?
(J.S. Leitch, c.1967) Unregistered

'Ohutu' 4 Y-Y
(Koanga Daffodils, 1985) Koanga Daffodils, 1995
Fl. 100 mm wide; perianth and other petaloid segments broadly ovate, vivid yellow 9B; corona segments opening with green at rim, becoming self yellow and of a slightly darker tone than the petaloid segments. Mid-season

'Oiseau de Feu' 3 W-R
(The Brodie of Brodie, c.1912)
'Will Scarlett' × Engleheart sdlg (late-flowering red Poeticus)

'Oithona' 1 W-W
(W. Jackson Sr, 1939)
'Beersheba' × 'Anthis'

'Okaihau' 6 W-Y
(Robin Brown) Robin Brown, 1995
'Tinkerbell' × *N. cyclamineus*; sdlg no. T/CY 1
Fl. 45 mm wide, facing down; perianth segments reflexed; corona cylindrical, smooth, with mouth straight and frilled. Dwarf. Early

'Okapi' 1 Y-Y
(G.P. Haydon, pre-1910)
?'Princess Mary' hybrid

'Okapi'
(The Brodie of Brodie, c.1917)
'Giraffe' × 'Bernardino'

'Okapi'
(?W. Jackson Jr, pre-1959) Unregistered

'Okato' 2 W-R
(J.A.O'More) P.D.K. Ramsay, 1984
'Basra' × 'Arbar'; sdlg no. 65/70
Mid-season

'Okaw' 3 W-GYR
(V. Brink) V. Brink, 1977
Sdlg no. 62-30
Fl. 91 mm wide; corona greenish yellow, with green at base and a line of red at rim. Mid-season. Resembles a much later and somewhat larger-flowered 'Pride of Erin' with green at corona base

'Okhrida' 3 W-O
(S.J. Bisdee, 1945) S.J. Bisdee, 1956
'Hades' × 'Mr Sparks'

Corona reddish orange

'Oklahoma' 1 W-Y
(Warnaar & Co., pre-1948)
AM(Haarlem) 1948

'OK Ted' 2 Y-O
(Mrs E.Murray) Unregistered
Perianth segments rich golden yellow; corona reddish orange, with mouth slightly flared and frilled. Tall. Mid-season to late

'Olanda' 3 (a)
(Mrs R.O. Backhouse, pre-1921)
Syn. 'Surprise'

'Olathe' 3 W-GYO
(G.E. Mitsch, 1957) G.E. Mitsch, 1968
'Tryst' × 'Moina'; sdlg no. R84/1
Fl. 102 mm wide; perianth segments ivory white; corona pale lemon yellow, with green at base and a band of reddish orange at rim. Mid-season. Resembles a larger-flowered 'Moina' of better substance with a broader band of colour at corona rim

'Olderfleet' 2 W-P
(W.J. Dunlop, c.1964) Unregistered
Perianth segments snow white; corona pink

'Old Faithful' 2 W-O
(T.H. Piper, 1953)
'Rethel' × 'Wonderlight'

'Old Gold' 1
(C.L. Adams, pre-1919)

'Old Gold' 2 (a)
(Mrs M.Moorby) Mrs M.Moorby, 1956

'Oldina' 1 W-? (b or c)
(W. Jackson Jr, 1957) Unregistered
'Tamara' × 'Preamble'

"Old Italian"
Syn. of 'Romanus'

'Old Ivory'
(pre-1939)

'Old Lace' 2 W-W
(D.S. Bell) D.S. Bell, 1959
Fl. 114 mm wide. Mid-season. Resembles 'Chinese White' but with a more widely expanded corona

'Oldpark' 1 W-Y
(W.J. Dunlop, pre-1969)
Corona pale yellow

'Old Satin' 2 Y-Y
(G.E. Mitsch, 1956) G.E. Mitsch, 1967

'Green Island' × 'Chinese White'; sdlg no. R33/2
Fl. 95 mm wide; perianth segments opening white, becoming pale beige yellow; corona shallow, pale lemon yellow, with a darker tone at rim. Mid-season

'Old Scotch' 2 Y-Y
(S.J. Bisdee) S.J. Bisdee, 1956
'Dorado' × 'Osella'

'Old Smoothie' 1 Y-Y
(J.S. Romine, 1972) J.S. Romine, 1984
'Goldcourt' × 'Honeybird'; sdlg no. 72-3
Fl. 90 mm wide. Early. Resembles a smoother 'Goldcourt' with the perianth segments more symmetrically arranged

'Old Sol' 2 Y-O
(J.S. Leitch) J.S. Leitch, 1967
Fl. 115 mm wide; corona reddish orange

'Old Spice' 2 W-Y
(W.G. Pannill) W.G. Pannill, 1985
'Precedent' × 'Pinafore'; sdlg no. 67/56 B
Perianth segments very broad, blunt, overlapping; corona orange-yellow. Mid-season

'Old Stager' 4 W-WWP
(Jackson's Daffodils, 1979) Jackson's Daffodils, 1989
'Rose Rhythm' × 'Kimellen'; sdlg no. 198/79
Fl. 93 mm wide; perianth segments greenish white (155A); corona segments yellowish white (158D), with pale yellowish pink 27C at rim. Early to mid season

'Old Swan' 2 W-W
(J.T.E. Akers) J.L. Akers, 1991
'It's True' × 'Vigil'; sdlg no. 53
Fl. 117 mm wide. Late

'Ole!' 7 Y-Y
(Mrs G. Link) Mrs G. Link, 1989
N. jonquilla × 'Amberglow'
Fl. golden yellow; perianth segments smooth; corona bowl-shaped. Mid-season. Resembles 'Sweetness' but with a shorter coroner

'Ole Lavik' 3 W-? (b)
(J.W.A. Lefeber, pre-1938)

'Olga' 1 W-W
(Barr & Sons, pre-1927)

'Olga' 2 W-GYP
(J.N. Hancock & Co., *c.*1975) Unregistered

'Olhain' 1 W-W
(W.A. Watts, pre-1930)

'Olistina' 2 W-? (b)
(W.A. Grace, pre-1938)

'Olive Dent' 1 (a)
(van der Viel, pre-1948)

'Olive Eye' 3 W-? (b)
(W.F.M. Copeland, pre-1953)

'Olive Graham' 2 (a)
(W.A. Grace, pre-1938)

'Olive Horsham' 2 W-W
(Broadfield's Daffodils, pre-1985) Unregistered
'Easter Moon' × 'Merry Princess'

'Olive Long' 2 W-W
(J.N. Hancock & Co., pre-1949)
Perianth segments pure white; corona flared

'Oliver' 1 W-Y
(O. Ronalds, 1938) M. Gardiner, 1956
'Mrs Ernst H.Krelage' × 'Renown'
Perianth segments broad, pure white; corona light yellow, flanged

'Oliver Cromwell' 1 W-Y
(J. Gerritsen & Son, pre-1922)
FA(Haarlem) 1922

'Oliver Goldsmith' 9 W-GYO
(G.H. Engleheart, pre-1909)
Perianth segments very broad in outline, squarish and truncate at apex, sometimes prominently mucronate, spreading, slightly concave, overlapping half; the inner segments narrower, not noticeably mucronate, spathulate, loosely inflexed, with margins wavy; corona disc-shaped, ribbed, pale lemon yellow, with deep brilliant green at base and a narrow band of bright reddish orange at rim

'Oliver Sheldon' 2 W-? (b)
(J.W.A. Lefeber, pre-1945)

'Olivet' 2 W-W
(G.E. Mitsch) G.E. Mitsch, 1958
'Broughshane' × 'Chinese White'
Mid-season. 2n=28

'Olivia' 3 W-YYR
(Sir C.H. Cave, pre-1913)
'Lulworth' × 'Horace'
Perianth segments pure white, slightly reflexed; corona shallow, ribbed, canary yellow, with a broad and well-defined band of scarlet at rim

'Olivia' 1 W-? (b)
(G. Lewis, 1935) Parr's Nurseries, 1958

'Olivine' 5 W-W
(pre-1926)
Fls often 2 per stem, pure white

'Oloron' 11a W-OOY
(J. Gerritsen & Son) J. Gerritsen & Son, 1986
'Royal Highness' × 'Sovereign'
Perianth segments ivory white; corona segments nasturtium orange, with rich yellow at rim. Mid-season. 2n=28. Resembles 'Sovereign'

'Olwen' 2 W-? (b)
(W.A. Watts, pre-1908)

'Olwen' 3 W-P
(W. Jackson Sr, 1937) W. Jackson Jr, 1956
'Blodwen' × 'Rubra'

'Olwen Williams' 2 W-Y
(J.N. Hancock & Co., pre-1949)
Corona opening pale lemon, becoming creamy yellow

'Olympia' 1 Y-Y
(M. van Waveren & Sons, pre-1900)
Fl. large; perianth segments bright yellow; corona dark golden yellow. 2n=28. AM 1900, AM(p) 1914

'Olympia Alba'
Syn. of 'Olympia Albus'

'Olympia Albus'
(pre-1913)
See also 'Olympia Alba'

'Olympic Fire' 2 Y-R
(Warnaar & Co., pre-1951)
AM(Haarlem) 1951

'Olympic Gold' 1 Y-Y
(J.L. Richardson) Mrs H.K. Richardson, 1962
'Yellow Idol' × 'King's Ransom'
Fl. 114 mm wide, vivid yellow 9A; perianth segments blunt, twisted, slightly inflexed, regular, overlapping; corona ribbed, mouth expanded and frilled, with rim flanged and crenate. Mid-season. Resembles a large-flowered 'Kingscourt'. *AM(e) 1969

'Olympic Torch' 2 W-YYO
(J.O. Sherrard, pre-1948)
Fl. 99 mm wide; perianth segments cream, slightly inflexed, overlapping two-thirds; corona ribbed, vivid yellow 17C, overlaid at rim with strong orange 25B, mouth widely expanded and frilled, with rim crenate. *AM(g) 1958

'Olympus' 1 (a)
(Dutch origin, pre-1913)

'Omagh' 3 W-R
(T. Bloomer) Omagh & District Hort. Soc., 1968
'Mahmoud' × 'Glenwherry'; sdlg no. 5/43/51
Perianth segments smooth; corona expanded, deep red, with deep green at base

'Omaha' 3 W-YYR
(Ballydorn Bulb Farm) Ballydorn Bulb Farm, 1974
'Mr Jinks' × 'Lichfield'
Fl. 100 mm wide

'O'Mahoney' 1 Y-Y
Syn. of 'The O'Mahoney'

'Omar' 2 W-? (b)
(G.H. Furness, pre-1941)

'Omar Khayy·m' 9
(G.H. Engleheart, pre-1914)

'Omaroe' 2 W-Y
(C.E. Radcliff, 1940) J.M.Radcliff, 1956
('Amusing' × 'Niphetos') × 'Pinkenba'
Perianth segments pure white; corona opening chrome yellow, becoming bright yellow ochre

'Omaru' 2 Y-Y
(R.H.Glover, pre-1993) Unregistered

'Omatane' 3 W-Y
(M. Hamilton, 1976) Koanga Daffodils, 1992
Fl. forming a double triangle, 115 mm wide; perianth segments ovate; corona disc-shaped, slightly ribbed, yellow. Tall. Late

'Ombersley' 1 Y-Y
(Clive Postles, 1985) Clive Postles Daffodils, 1996
'Gold Convention' × 'Midas Touch'; sdlg no. 1-7-81
Fl. rounded, 112 mm wide; perianth segments broadly ovate, with margins slightly incurved; corona funnel-shaped, with mouth flared and rim crenate. Mid-season

'Omeath' 1 W-W
(G.L. Wilson, pre-1951)
'Broughshane' × 'Saint Mary'
PC 1952

'Omega' 9
(H. Backhouse, pre-1908)

'Omega' 9 W-YYR
(W.G. Pannill) W.G. Pannill, 1982
'Milan' × 'Smyrna'; sdlg no. C 10
Fl. 65 mm wide. Mid-season

'Omelette' 4
(N.Y. Lower, pre-1930)

'Omen' 2 W-P
(J.T.Gray, 1954) P. Phillips, 1964
Fl. 92 mm wide; corona soft pink, shaded lavender. Mid-season. Resembles 'Rosario' but with a different tone to the corona

'Omigon' 2 W-Y
(A.H. Ahrens) J.S. Leitch, 1957

'Omri' 8 Y-Y
(Herut Yahel, pre-1982) C.S.Weijers Jr, 1997
Probably *N. papyraceus* × *N. tazetta*
Fls up to 12 per stem, 40 mm wide; perianth segments broadly ovate, blunt, prominently mucronate, greenish white 157C/D, spreading, somewhat creased, with margins incurling, overlapping one-third; the inner segments less prominently mucronate, shouldered at base; corona cup-shaped, smooth, brilliant greenish yellow 6C, mouth straight, wavy or somewhat 3-angled, with rim entire. Mid-season to late. Strongly scented. Syn. 'Israel'

'Oms' 2 W-O
(W. Jackson Sr, 1936)
'Blodwen' × 'Rubra'
Corona salmon orange

'On Approval'
(New Zealand origin, pre-1940)

'Onawe' 3 Y-? (a)
(S.C. Gaspar, 1947) R.J. Abernethy, 1957

'On Call' 2 W-WWY
(G.W.E. Brogden) Brogden Bulbs, 1991
'Guiding Light' × 'Bandit'; sdlg no. x93/9
Fl. 103 mm wide; perianth segments broadly ovate, blunt, spreading, very smooth; corona broad cup-shaped, opening light yellow, becoming white, with a wide band of light yellow at rim, mouth even, rim slightly crenate. Mid-season

'Once-in-a-While' 2 W-GPP
(T.D. Throckmorton) T.D. Throckmorton, 1977
'Carita' × 'Salome'; sdlg no. 65/1/2
Fl. 95 mm wide. Mid-season

'Ondine' 1 Y-Y
(J.N. Hancock & Co., 1953)
'Roycroft' × 1 W-Y
Fl. greenish yellow

'Ondine' 2 W-W
(J.L. Richardson) Mrs H.K. Richardson, 1964

'One Desire' 2 W-P
(G.L. Wilson) E. Longford, 1970
'Easter Moon' × 'Passionale'

'On Edge' 3 Y-GYR
(T.D. Throckmorton) T.D. Throckmorton, 1976
'Old Satin' × 'Altruist'; sdlg no. 67/24/4
Perianth segments soft yellow; corona yellow, with deep green at base and a very narrow band of orange-red at rim. Mid-season

'Oneiza' 1 W-? (b)
(Shea, pre-1923)

'Oneonta' 2 Y-Y
(Murray W. Evans, 1958) Murray W. Evans, 1968
Fl. 102 mm wide, pale greenish yellow; corona with greener tones at base. Late. Resembles 'Kilfannan' but with the flower of a different yellow and a larger corona

'Onibi' 3 Y-O
(H.G. Cross, 1974) H.G. Cross, 1984
Sdlg no. 28-4
Fl. forming a double triangle; perianth segments broadly ovate, blunt, soft yellow, with slight white mucro, spreading, concave, smooth, overlapping half; the inner segments square-shouldered at base, a little inflexed; corona bowl-shaped, loosely ribbed, reddish orange, closely frilled. Very late

'Onibla' 2 W-P
(A.O. Roblin, 1942)
'Mitylene' × 'Suda'

'Onkaparinga' 2 Y-O
(W.M. Spry, pre-1975) Unregistered
Late

'Onoke' 2 Y-O
(J.S. Leitch) J.S. Leitch, 1967

'On Parade' 2 Y-YYR
(G. Lewis) D.S. Bell, 1955
Perianth segments very broadly ovate, rounded at apex, rich yellow, with midrib showing; corona disc-shaped, yellow, with a very broad band of red at rim

'Onslaught' 1 W-Y
(W.F.M. Copeland, pre-1913)
Fl. of great substance; corona with rim flanged. Mid-season

'On Target' 2 W-Y
(G.W.E. Brogden) Brogden Bulbs, 1991
'Nola' hybrid × 'Bandit'; sdlg no. x96/3
Fl. 105 mm wide; perianth segments very broad, roundish, smooth; corona broad and shallow bowl-shaped, light lime yellow, with mouth lobed, rim entire. Mid-season

'Onward' 3 (a)
(W. Welchman, pre-1908)

'Onward'
(T. Batson, pre-1915)

'Onward' 4 Y-O
(Mrs H.K. Richardson) M.J. Jefferson-Brown, 1975
'Falaise' × 'Border Chief'
Perianth segments gold; corona scarlet-orange. Mid-

season. Resembles a large and earlier-flowered 'Tahiti'

'Onyx' 3
(Mrs R.O. Backhouse, pre-1908)

'Onyx' 2 W-W
(H.A. Brown, 1949) A. Ladson, 1960
Fl. large, glistening white

'Ooloo-Toora' 2 Y-Y
(A.O. Roblin, 1939)
Sdlg × 'Gloriana'

'Oomph' 2 W-P
(Jackson's Daffodils) Jackson's Daffodils, 1996
'Vahu' × 'Precocious'; sdlg no. 248/87
Fl. 108 mm wide; perianth segments very broadly ovate, greenish white (155A), touching one another at the margins; corona funnel-shaped, moderate yellowish pink 31D, with mouth frilled. Mid-season

'Oona' 1 W-W
(C.O. Fairbairn)

'Oonah' 3 Y-R
(J.R.Erp) J.R.Erp, 1956
'Market Merry' × 'Sunset Fires'

'Oo'naka' 2 W-R
(J.S. Leitch) J.S. Leitch, 1956

'Oops' 2 W-Y
(Jackson's Daffodils) Jackson's Daffodils, 1995
Sdlg 224/79 × sdlg 118/82; sdlg no. 136/87
Fl. 110 mm wide; perianth segments very broadly ovate, greenish white (155A); corona short, brilliant yellow 8A, with mouth even, rim entire. Mid-season

'Opaki' 1 W-Y
(J.S. Leitch) J.S. Leitch, 1968
Fl. 155 mm wide; corona lemon yellow

'Opal' 3 W-? (b or c)
(N.Y. Lower, pre-1916)

'Opal' 2 W-P
(Mrs E. Murray)

'Opalescent' 2 W-PPY
(G.E. Mitsch) G.E. Mitsch, 1972
'Precedent' × 'Carita'; sdlg no. A34/5
Fl. 108 mm wide; perianth segments broadly ovate; corona bowl-shaped, expanded, shaded with lilac pink, merging into apricot amber at rim. Mid-season

'Opalesque' 2 W-P
(J.N. Hancock & Co., 1959) Unregistered

'Opaline' 5
(Cartwright & Goodwin, pre-1910)

'Opalite' 2 W-P
(R.C.A. Tombleson) R.C.A. Tombleson, 1965
Fl. 105 mm wide. Mid-season. Resembles 'Mrs Oscar Ronalds' but with the perianth segments of better form

'Opal Pearl' 2 W-P
(Mrs J. Abel Smith, 1976) Mrs J. Abel Smith, 1986
Sdlg no. V1/01
Corona lilac pink. Early

'Opal Sky' 2 Y-Y
(Mrs G. Link, 1980) Mrs G. Link, 1991
'Canisp' × 'Amberjack'; sdlg no. 1774
Fl. light buffy yellow; perianth segments smooth and of heavy substance, overlapping; corona bowl-shaped, with green at base on opening, becoming self yellow. Early

'Opare' 2 Y-Y
(W. Jackson Jr, 1957) Unregistered
'Aala' × 'Moque'

'Opening Bid' 6 Y-Y
(A. Gray) M.J. Jefferson-Brown, 1975
Fl. gold. Early

'Opera' 9 W-GYO
(G.H. Engleheart, pre-1923)
Fl. rounded; perianth segments overlapping; corona very shallow, with green at base and a broad band of cinnamon orange at rim. AM(e) 1923

'Operetta' 2 W-P
(J.L. Richardson) Mrs H.K. Richardson, 1973
'Debutante' × 'Salome'
Corona expanded, rose pink, with rim dentate

'Ophelia' 1 (a)
(W.B. Hartland, pre-1907)

'Ophelia' 1 W-W
(de Graaff Bros, pre-1913)

'Ophelia' 9
(pre-1915)

'Ophelia' 1 (a)
(D.V. West, pre-1936)

'Ophelia' 2 W-P
(J.L. Richardson) Mrs H.K. Richardson, 1967
'Infatuation' × 'Debutante'
Fl. 90 mm wide; corona bright coral pink. Mid-season. Resembles a small-flowered 'Debutante'

'Ophir' 1 Y-Y
(?Irish origin, pre-1900)

'Ophir' 1 Y-Y
(E.H. Krelage & Son, pre-1931)
'Glory of Leiden' × 'Big Ben'

'Ophir d'Or' 1 (a)
(J. de Groot & Sons, pre-1914)

'Ophir's Gold' 2 (a)
(G.L. Wilson, pre-1938)

'Oporto Yellow' 1 Y-Y
(Spanish origin)
Selection by Peter Barr (*c*.1887) from wild-collected material
Fl. rich yellow; perianth segments ovate, spreading, sometimes inflexed towards apex, twisted, separated; corona cylindrical and narrow at base, flared in upper half, lightly ribbed, with mouth even, rim regularly crenate. Early

'Optima' 2 W-Y
(Mrs R.O. Backhouse, pre-1921)
Perianth segments creamy white; corona large, widely expanded, heavily frilled. AM(Haarlem) 1931, FCC(Haarlem) 1937

'Optimist' 2 W-? (b)
(J.W.A. Lefeber, pre-1938)

'Optimus' 8 Y-O
(pre-1798)

'Opulence' 2 Y-Y
(W.F.M. Copeland, pre-1913)
'King Alfred' × 'Weston'
Fl. golden yellow; perianth segments broad

'Opulence' 1 Y-Y
(R. Dick, pre-1938)
Perianth segments of smooth texture; corona deep yellow, rim flanged

'Opulent' 1 Y-Y
(S.C. Gaspar, pre-1949)
'Sincerity' × 'Royalist'
Perianth segments broadly ovate, sulphur yellow

'Opus' 2 W-W
(J.N.Hancock & Co., 1973) Unregistered
Sdlg no. 83/79H
Fl. rounded, pure white; corona funnel-shaped, with rim dentate. Early

'Oracle' 9 W-OOR
(G.H. Engleheart, pre-1908)
Fl. 67 mm wide; perianth segments white, with cream at base, reflexed, of thick texture, overlapping half; corona very shallow bowl-shaped, buffy orange, shading to dark orange-red at rim. Mid-season to late

'Oracle' 2 W-Y
(J.N. Hancock & Co., 1982) Unregistered

'Oraglow' 2 Y-YOO
(J.N. Hancock & Co., 1955) Unregistered
Perianth segments very broadly ovate in outline, blunt or rounded at apex, only very slightly mucronate, bright yellow, a little inflexed, with margins incurling, overlapping half; the inner segments more narrowly ovate, with margins nicked near apex, square-shouldered at base; corona short cylinder-shaped, lightly ribbed, brilliant reddish orange, with yellow at base, mouth straight, neatly frilled. Late

'Orale' 2 W-Y
(A.H. Ahrens) J.S. Leitch, 1956

'Orama' 2 W-WWO
(J.N. Hancock & Co., 1946)

'Oran' 1 Y-Y
(A.O. Roblin, 1944)
'Dawson City' × 'Saigon'
2n=28

'Oran' 3 W-YYO
(J.L. Richardson, pre-1944)
'Seraglio' × 'Sunstar'
Perianth segments snowy white, of thick and waxy texture; corona almost disc-shaped, pale citron, with a broad band of reddish orange at rim

'Orana' 2 Y-R
(W. Jackson Jr, pre-1950)
'Dunkeld' × 'Redlands'

'Orangeade' 2 O-O
(Mrs B.T.Simpson) Mrs B.T.Simpson, 1966
Fl. 108 mm wide; perianth segments pale orange; corona darker in tone. Mid-season. Resembles 'Buncrana' in form

'Orange and Blaue' 8 W-O
(pre-1777)

'Orange and Lemon' 4
(Cartwright & Goodwin, pre-1916)

ORANGE APPEAL 2 Y-O
Trade designation for 'Loveday'

'Orange Banner' 2 Y-O
Syn. of 'Oranje Vaan'

'Orange Beacon' 2 W-O
(Carncairn Daffodils) Carncairn Daffodils, 1978
'Alicante' × Richardson sdlg 260; sdlg no. 112/60
Fl. 105 mm wide; perianth segments greenish white (155A), of thick texture; corona vivid orange 28B.

Late. Resembles an improved 'Alicante' of clearer colour

'Orange Beauty' 2 Y-Y
(R.H. Bath, pre-1927)
Fl. 89 mm wide, deep yellow, shaded orange; corona funnel-shaped, with rim deeply dentate. AM(Haarlem) 1927

'Orange Beauty' 4
(K.J. Heazlewood)

'Orange Beauty' 4 W-O
(?Australian origin, pre-1996) Unregistered

'Orange Bell' 2 Y-O
(Warnaar & Co., pre-1948)

'Orange Bird' 2 Y-R
(P.D. Williams, pre-1939)
Fl. 105 mm wide; perianth segments brilliant greenish yellow 7A, faintly touched creamy white at midrib, overlapping half; corona bowl-shaped, strong orange 25A, with a slightly lighter tone at rim. 2n=28. *HC(g) 1946, *AM(g) 1947

'Orange Blossom' 8 W-O
(?A. Vis, pre-1913)
Poetaz
Fls 5-6 per stem; corona glowing orange, tinged scarlet, frilled. Tall. Resembles an improved 'Albert Vis'. AM(Haarlem) 1924

'Orange Bowl' 2 W-?
(W. Balch)

'Orange Boy' 2 Y-O
(Mrs R.O. Backhouse, pre-1921)
Fl. large; corona rich reddish orange

'Orange Boy' 2 Y-O
(H.A. Brown, 1939)
Perianth segments bright yellow; corona large, mid-orange. Mid-season

'Orange Bride' 2 W-GOO
Syn. of 'Oranje Bruid'

'Orange Brilliant' 4 Y-O
(Mrs R.O. Backhouse, pre-1921)
Perianth segments deep yellow; corona segments scarlet-orange. AM(e) 1926

'Orange Buffer' 3 (a)
(G.H. Engleheart, pre-1913)

'Orange Button' 3 W-? (b)
(P. van Deursen, pre-1939)
AM(Haarlem) 1939

'Orange Cerise'
(pre-1951)

'Orange Charm' 2 (a)
(M. van Waveren & Sons, pre-1937)
AM(Haarlem) 1937

'Orange Cheer' 2 (a)
(Barr & Sons, pre-1935)
AM(Haarlem) 1935

'Orange Circlet' 2 Y-YOO
(Mrs R.O. Backhouse, pre-1921)
Perianth segments clear primrose yellow, overlapping; corona large, clear orange, with deep orange-yellow at base, expanded, frilled. Mid-season. AM(Haarlem) 1929

'Orange Cocarde' 3 W-O
Syn. of 'Orange Cockade'

'Orange Cockade' 3 W-O
(P. van Deursen, pre-1938)
Syn. 'Orange Cocarde'. AM(Haarlem) 1937

'Orange Cooler' 9 W-GGR
(Mrs M.S. Yerger) Mrs M.S. Yerger, 1991
'Juliet' × 'Quetzal'; sdlg no. 77 E 5
Fl. 50 mm wide; perianth segments roundish; corona disc-shaped, yellow-green (1B), with a darker tone (154A) at base and orange-red (32A) at rim. Late. Scented

'Orange Courier' 2 W-O
Syn. of 'Oranje Koerier'

'Orange Crest' 2 Y-YYO
(J.L. Richardson, pre-1941)
Fl. 102 mm wide; perianth segments brilliant greenish yellow 6B, slightly inflexed, overlapping half; corona short and broad funnel-shaped, vivid yellow 12A, deepening to strong orange 24A at rim, mouth expanded and frilled, with rim crenate. *AM(g) 1953

'Orange Crinoline'
(pre-1949)
2n=28

'Orange Crush' 2 Y-O
(J.N. Hancock & Co., 1946)

'Orange Cup' 8 Y-YYR
(?Tromp Bros, pre-1881)
'Almira' × 'Staaten Generaal'
Perianth segments sulphur yellow; corona sometimes with additional segments, deep yellow, with bright red at rim, frilled

'Orange Cup' 3 (a)
(G.H. Engleheart, pre-1913)

'Orange Decor' 2 Y-YYO
(P. van Deursen, pre-1946)

'Orange Delight' 2 W-O
(R.H. Bath, pre-1927)
Perianth segments creamy white; corona fiery reddish orange

'Orange Delight' 2 W-OOY
(J.W.A. van der Wereld) J.W.A. van der Wereld, 1981
Fl. 100 mm wide; perianth segments ivory white; corona cadmium orange, with buttercup yellow at rim

'Orange Disc' 3 W-? (b)
(A.M. Wilson, pre-1916)

'Orange Doubloon' 4
(W.F.M. Copeland, pre-1923)

'Orange Dream' 2 Y-YYO
(Konynenburg & Mark) Konynenburg & Mark, 1960
'Etude' × ('David Copperfield' × 'Floriment')
Fl. 90 mm wide; perianth segments vivid yellow 9A; corona orange-yellow (17C), with a narrow band of strong orange 25A at rim. Mid-season

'Orange Eye' 3 Y-O
(The Brodie of Brodie, c.1908)
'Princess Mary' × 9 W-R
Perianth segments creamy yellow; corona disc-shaped, apricot orange

'Orange Favourite' 2 (a)
(J.L. Richardson, pre-1949)
AM(Haarlem) 1950

'Orange Festival' 2 W-? (b)
(P. van Deursen, pre-1953)

'Orange Fire' 2 W-O
(Konynenburg & Mark) Konynenburg & Mark, 1960
('Frederike' × 'Mimosa') × ('Dandy Boy'? × 'Red Bird')
Fl. 110 mm wide

'Orange Flag' 2 W-O
(Mrs R.O. Backhouse, pre-1921)
Perianth segments sulphur white; corona widely expanded, rich orange. AM(Haarlem) 1930

'Orange Flame' 2 (a)
(L. van Grieken, pre-1944)

'Orange Flame' 2 Y-O
(Konynenburg & Mark) Konynenburg & Mark, 1960
'Lady Moore' × 'Extase'
Fl. 85 mm wide

'Orange Flute' 2 Y-O
(H.A. Brown, 1942)
Perianth segments broadly ovate, blunt, yellow, with slight white mucro, spreading, plane, overlapping half; the inner segments a little inflexed, with margins wavy or incurling; corona shallow, widely expanded, narrowly ribbed, bright orange, with mouth even, rim minutely crenate. Tall. Late

'Orange Flyer' 2 W-O
(Warnaar & Co, pre-1925)
AM(Haarlem) 1925

'Orange Frill' 3 Y-GYO
(Barr & Sons, pre-1908)
Perianth segments narrow, usually acute, primrose yellow, only very slightly overlapping; corona bright canary yellow, with dull yellowish green at base and a broad band of bright orange at rim, neatly frilled

'Orange Frilled' 2 Y-O
(P. van Deursen, 1943)
AM(Haarlem) 1942

'Orange Gem' 3 W-? (b)
(pre-1913)

'Orange Girl' 2 Y-YOO
(Barr & Sons, pre-1925)
Perianth segments primrose yellow; corona ribbed, bright orange, paling to golden yellow at base, neatly frilled

'Orange Globe' 8 W-O
(van Zonnefeld Bros & Philippo, pre-1917)
Poetaz
Perianth segments creamy white; corona dark orange. AM(Haarlem) 1917

'Orange Glory' 6 Y-O
(de Graaff Bros, pre-1920)
1 Y-Y × N. cyclamineus
Fl. 79 mm wide; perianth segments buttercup yellow, slightly reflexed; corona funnel-shaped, bright golden orange. Mid-season to late. 2n=28. AM 1920, *AM(g) 1936, *HC(g) 1936

'Orange Glow' 2 Y-O
(Mrs R.O. Backhouse, pre-1922)
? × N. cyclamineus
Perianth segments soft yellow; corona rich orange, neatly frilled. 2n=26. AM(e) 1922, AM(Haarlem) 1923, FCC(Haarlem) 1926

'Orange Glow' 6 Y-Y
(pre-1935)

'Orange Hackle' 2 W-O
(G.H. Johnstone, pre-1954)
'Red Hackle' × 'Killifreth'

'Orange Halo' 2 W-YYO
(O.L. Brown) O.L. Brown, 1977
'Autowin' × 'Talana'; sdlg no. 67/42/1
Fl. 105 mm wide; perianth segments yellowish white (11D); corona very shallow bowl-shaped, vivid yellow 12A, with a very broad band of strong orange 25A at rim. Mid-season

'Orange Ice' 11?a W-O
(?New Zealand origin, pre-1997) Unregistered

'Orange Jewel' 3
(C.L. Adams, pre-1913)

'Orange Joy' 2 W-YOO
(G. Lubbe & Son, pre-1948)
AM(Haarlem) 1948

'Orange King' 9 W-?
(pre-1914)

'Orange King' 2 Y-O
(Mrs R.O. Backhouse, pre-1921)
Perianth segments creamy yellow, overlapping; corona large, widely expanded, rich reddish orange. AM(Haarlem) 1926

'Orange Kite' 6 Y-YOO
(Mrs G. Link) Mrs G. Link, 1989
'Bushtit' × 'Red Fox'; sdlg no. 979-A
Corona long, straight-sided, orange, with a broad band of yellow at base. Mid-season. Resembles 'Whip-poor-will' but with a deep orange corona

'Orange Lace' 2 W-O
(G.E. Mitsch, pre-1952)
'John Evelyn' × 'Dick Wellband'; sdlg no. 38C43/1

'Orange Light' 2 Y-O
(Mrs H.K. Richardson) Mrs H.K. Richardson, 1976
'Cathay' × sdlg 475
Fl. 92 mm wide; perianth segments orange-yellow; corona deep orange. Mid-season

'Orange Lodge' 2 W-O
(Brian S. Duncan) Rathowen Daffodils, 1978
'Irish Charm' × 'Norval'; sdlg no. 83
Corona bowl-shaped, deep orange. Mid-season. Sunproof

'Orangeman' 2 W-O
(G.H. Engleheart, pre-1907)
Perianth segments creamy white, reflexed; corona expanded, rich orange

'Orange Marvel' 2 Y-O
(de Graaff Bros, pre-1947)
Perianth segments creamy yellow; corona widely expanded. AM(Haarlem) 1947

'Orange Master' 2 Y-O
(J. Gerritsen & Son, pre-1948)
AM(Haarlem) 1948

'Orange Monarch' 2 W-YOO
(G.A. Uit den Boogaard, pre-1944)

'Orange Nassau' 2 Y-O
Syn. of 'Oranje Nassau'

'Orange Ophelia' 2 W-O
(Mrs R.O. Backhouse, pre-1921)
Perianth segments creamy white. AM(Haarlem) 1932

'Orange Pansy' 2 Y-YYO
(G. Lubbe & Son, pre-1947)
Perianth segments butter yellow; corona shallow, widely expanded. AM(Haarlem) 1947, FCC(Haarlem) 1950

'Orange Perfection' 2 Y-O
(Mrs R.O. Backhouse, pre-1921)
Fl. large; perianth segments narrow, acute; corona narrow, clear reddish orange. AM(Haarlem) 1930

'Orange Phoenix' 4 W-O
(pre-1731)
Perianth and other petaloid segments in many whorls, white or creamy white; the outer whorls broadly ovate, blunt, spreading, not much overlapping; the inner whorls successively a little narrower but not much shorter, inflexed or strongly inflexed, with margins incurved or strongly incurved; corona segments one-quarter the length of the petaloid segments and interspersed among them, orange or pale orange, tightly frilled. Syn. 'Fried Eggs', 'Aurantius Flore Pleno', 'Eggs and Bacon', 'Incomparabilis Plena', 'Niveo-aurantius', Incomparabilis 'Albus Plenus Aurantius'

'Orange Picture' 2 W-? (b)
(de Graaff Bros, pre-1948)

'Orange Pippin' 2 Y-O
(J.N. Hancock & Co., 1946)
Perianth segments bright yellow; corona large, expanded, deep orange, frilled. Early

'Orange Plate' 2 W-O
(S.C. Gaspar, pre-1948)
Perianth segments creamy white; corona disc-shaped, orange

'Orange Post' 3 (a)
(G.H. Engleheart, pre-1914)

'Orange Prince' 8 Y-YYO
(Dutch origin, pre-1907)
Poetaz

Perianth segments soft yellow, overlapping; corona dark golden yellow, flushed orange, with bright orange at rim. FA(Haarlem) 1933

'Orange Prince'
(?Sir A.P.W. Thomas, pre-1915)

'Orange Princess' 2 (a)
(P.D.Williams, pre-1929)

'Orange Progress' 2 Y-O
(J.W.A. Lefeber) J.W.A. Lefeber, 1968
Perianth segments very broadly ovate, truncate, slightly mucronate, a little reflexed, with margins incurling, overlapping one-third to a half; the inner segments with margins wavy; corona funnel-shaped, broad, ribbed, frilled, with rim minutely and irregularly notched and crenate

'Orange Prospect' 2 W-? (b)
(C.G. van Tubergen, pre-1948)
AM(Haarlem) 1948

'Orange Queen' 3 Y-O
(The Brodie of Brodie, c.1908)
'Princess Mary' × *N. poeticus* sdlg; sdlg no. 115/A/04
Perianth segments creamy yellow; corona very shallow bowl-shaped, vivid reddish orange

'Orange Queen' 7 Y-Y
(Dutch origin, pre-1913)
'Rugulosus' sport
Fls 2-4 per stem, vivid yellow 14A; perianth segments ovate or oblong, with fairly prominent white mucro, spreading or slightly inflexed, with broad midrib showing, overlapping a quarter to one-third; the inner segments twisted; corona funnel-shaped, smooth or lightly ribbed, mouth straight, 6-lobed, wavy, with rim crenate. Dwarf or standard. Scented. 2n=14. Syn. 'Aurantiacus'. AM(Haarlem) 1913. ?The same as *N. × infundibulum*

'Orange Queen' 8 W-O
Syn. of 'Orange Wonder'

'Orange Queen' 8
Syn. of 'Flower Wealth'

'Orange Radiance'
(C.L. Adams, pre-1913)

'Orange Red' 2 (a)
(A.H. Ahrens) J.S. Leitch, 1955

'Orange Rim' 2 Y-YYO
(G.E. Mitsch) G.E. Mitsch, 1979
'Aranjuez' × 'Vulcan'; sdlg no. F99/4
Fl. 88 mm wide, soft clear yellow; corona with a narrow band of reddish orange at rim. Mid-season

'Orange Ring' 9
(G.H. Engleheart, pre-1913)

'Orange River' 2 (b)
(H. Backhouse, pre-1908)

'Orange River' 2 Y-O
(H. Leber) H. Leber, 1972
? × 'Texas'
Fl. 115 mm wide

'Orange Ruffle' 2 Y-O
(H.A. Brown, 1938)
Corona large, expanded, orange, with a deeper tone at rim, frilled. Mid-season

'Orangery' 11a W-OOY
(J. Gerritsen & Son) J. Gerritsen & Son, 1957
Perianth segments very broad in outline, blunt or squarish at apex, prominently mucronate, spreading, overlapping one-third to a half; the inner segments narrower, shouldered at base, a little inflexed, with margins wavy; corona split to base, the six segments as wide as the perianth segments, three-quarters their length and opposite and closely overlying them, deeply bi-lobed, with the lobes overlapping, loosely ribbed and frilled, yellow-orange (21A), usually with vivid yellow 9A at rim and shoulder, with white at shoulder on occasion, sometimes self orange. Early to mid-season. 2n=28. AM(Haarlem) 1957

'Oranges and Lemons' 4 Y-O
(W.F.M. Copeland, pre-1931)
Perianth segments pale yellow; corona segments dark bright orange

'Orange Sceptre' 2 W-? (b)
(Mrs R.O. Backhouse, pre-1921)

'Orange Sherbert' 2 Y-YOY
(J.N. Hancock & Co., 1965) Unregistered

'Orange Sherbet' 2 W-O
(Carncairn Daffodils) Carncairn Daffodils, 1978
Fl. 82 mm wide; perianth segments roundish, smooth; corona disc-shaped, clear orange, with a darker tone at base and lighter at rim. Mid-season

'Orange Sir Watkin' 2 (a)
(Mrs R.O. Backhouse, pre-1921)

'Orange Splendour' 2 (a)
(R.H. Bath, pre-1929)

'Orange Splendour' 4 W-O
(J.L. Richardson) G. Zandbergen-Terwegen, 1962
'Falaise' hybrid

'Orange Standard' 2 Y-O
(Waarner & Co, pre-1953)

'Hollywood' × 'El Paso'
AM(Haarlem) 1953

'Orange Star' 8 W-O
(R.A.van der Schoot, pre-1928)
Poetaz
AM(Haarlem) 1928

'Orange Sun' 2 (a)
(Mrs R.O. Backhouse, pre-1921)
AM(Haarlem) 1926

'Orange Tango' 2 Y-YOO
(J.N. Hancock & Co., 1965) Unregistered

'Orange Triumph' 1 Y-Y
(J. Kouwenhoven, pre-1935)
'King Alfred'? × 'Orange Queen'
Fl. orange-yellow. AM(Haarlem) 1934, FA(Haarlem) 1935

'Orange Triumphator' 2 Y-O
(F. Rijnveld & Sons, pre-1948)
Perianth segments yellow; corona almost disc-shaped, scarlet-orange

'Orange Trophy' 2 Y-O
(J.J.W. Beyk) J. van Waardenburg, 1968
Fl. 110 mm wide; perianth segments brilliant yellow 8A; corona strong orange 25A

'Orange Trumpet' 1 Y-O
(W.M.Spry, pre-1987) Unregistered

'Orange Walk' 3 W-OOY
(A.J.R. Pearson, 1978) A.J.R. Pearson, 1992
'Kilworth' × ('Fairy Tale' × 'Corofin'); sdlg no. 79-25-D22
Fl. forming a rounded double triangle, 108 mm wide; perianth segments very broadly ovate, greenish white (157C), spreading, with margins slightly incurling at apex, smooth and of heavy substance; the inner segments more narrowly ovate, angled at shoulder; corona very shallow bowl-shaped, lightly ribbed, strong orange 25B, with a broad and clearly defined band of vivid yellow 14A at rim, mouth straight, more or less even, obsurely crenate. Mid-season to late. Resembles 'Blarney' but with more intense orange to the corona and 'Torcross' but with a more clearly defined corona rim

'Orange Warley' 2 Y-O
(L. Buckland, pre-1939)
'Great Warley' hybrid
Corona frilled

'Orange Wonder' 8 W-O
(R.A.van der Schoot, pre-1928)
Syn. 'Orange Queen'. AM(Haarlem) 1928

'Orangia' 3 W-? (b)
(C. Dawson, pre-1908)

'Oranique' 2 W-YYO
(1963) Unregistered

'Oranje Boven' 1 (a)
(C.G. van Tubergen, pre-1928)
AM(Haarlem) 1928

'Oranje Bruid' 2 W-GOO
(G.A. Uit den Boogaard, pre-1930)
Syn. 'Koh-i-noor', 'Orange Bride'. AM(Haarlem) 1930, FCC(Haarlem) 1946

'Oranje Koerier' 2 W-O
(L. van Leeuwen & Son, pre-1946)
Syn. 'Orange Courier'. AM(Haarlem) 1946

'Oranjemei' 2 (a)
(J.W.A. Lefeber, pre-1949)
AM(Haarlem) 1941

'Oranje Nassau' 2 Y-O
(de Graaff Bros & van Konynenburg & Co., pre-1931)
Perianth segments soft yellow; corona widely expanded, soft orange, frilled. Syn. 'Orange Nassau'. AM(Haarlem) 1930

'Oranje Nassau' 8
Syn. of 'Mannequin'

'Oranje Vaan' 2 Y-O
(D.W. Lefeber & Co., pre-1943)
Corona large, widely expanded, reddish orange. Syn. 'Orange Banner'. AM(Haarlem) 1943

'Orari' 2 W-Y
(?New Zealand origin, pre-1990) Unregistered

'Oratia' 1 Y-Y
(Miss M. Verry) Miss M. Verry, 1965
Fl. 108 mm wide, vivid yellow 13A. Mid-season. Resembles 'Goldcourt'. PC(e)(NZ) 1959

'Orator' 2 Y-O
(G.W.E. Brogden) G.W.E. Brogden, 1966
Fl. 95 mm wide; corona reddish orange. Mid-season

'Oratorio' 2 W-Y
(G.E. Mitsch) G.E. Mitsch, 1959
Sdlg no. P61/3
Fl. rounded; perianth segments very broadly ovate, rounded at apex, slightly mucronate, pure white, spreading, a little concave, with broad midrib showing, overlapping half; the inner segments a little narrower, square-shouldered at base, slightly inflexed; corona short funnel-shaped, pale lemon yellow, with a deeper tone at rim, mouth split in places and

overlapping, lightly frilled, with rim crenate. Mid-season. 2n=28

'Orb' 3 W-? (b)
(E.M. Crosfield, pre-1910)

'Orb' 2 W-Y
(pre-1965) Unregistered
Perianth segments creamy white; corona greenish yellow, becoming whiter with age, heavily frilled, with rim flanged

'Orbit'
(E.M. Crosfield, pre-1914)

'Orbit' 2 Y-R
(J.L. Richardson) G. Zandbergen-Terwegen, 1961
'Ceylon' × 'Narvik'
Fl. 100 mm wide; perianth segments golden yellow. Early. Resembles a stronger-coloured 'Caramba'

'Orbita' 2 W-O
(R.H. Bath, pre-1929)
Perianth segments creamy white; corona scarlet-orange

'Orbitor' 1 W-Y
(J.A. Morris) J.A. Morris, 1964
Fl. 121 mm wide; corona clear yellow. Mid-season

'Orb of Day' 2 W-? (b)
(C.L. Adams, pre-1916)

'Orb of Night' 2 W-? (b)
(C.L. Adams, pre-1916)

'Orcades' 2 W-Y
(S.J. Bisdee, 1942)
'Maid of the Mist' × 'Pinkeen'

'Orchard Pink' 3 W-P
(Mrs J.Abel Smith) Mrs J.Abel Smith, 1995
(Sdlg × ['Chelsea Derby' × 'Leonaine']) × 'Jewel Song'; sdlg no. D44/31
Fl. rounded, 128 mm wide; perianth segments pure white, of great substance, overlapping; corona pink, with highlights of peach pink. Late

'Orchard Place' 3 Y-YYO
(T.D. Throckmorton, 1971) R. & E. Havens, 1989
'Aircastle' × 'Irish Coffee'; sdlg no. 66/12/5
Fl. 90 mm wide; perianth segments light creamy yellow; corona disc-shaped, deeper in tone than the perianth, with cinnamon orange at rim. Late

'Orchard Yellow' 2 (a)
(P.D. Williams, pre-1908)

'Orchid' 11a W-Y
Syn. of 'Buttonhole'

'Oread' 2 or 3 W-? (b or c)
(G.H. Engleheart, pre-1914)

'Oregon' 1 (a)
(de Graaff Bros, pre-1928)
Syn. 'Plato'

'Oregon Beauty' 4 Y-R
(G.E. Mitsch and R. & E.Havens, 1970) G.E. Mitsch and R. & E.Havens, 1989
('Playboy' × 'Paricutin') × 'Enterprise'
Fl. 110 mm wide; perianth segments mid-yellow, regular; corona segments orange-red. Mid-season. Resembles sibling 'Grebe' but with slightly fewer extra segments

'Oregon Bells' 7 W-W
(G.E. Mitsch, 1973) R. & E. Havens, 1992
'Quick Step' × *N. jonquilla*; sdlg no. II134/4
Fl. 55 mm wide, opening yellow and soon becoming white; perianth segments regular; corona mouth even or a little wavy. Dwarf. Very late

'Oregon Gold' 7 Y-Y
(G.E. Morrill) G.E. Morrill, 1973
Sdlg × *N. jonquilla*
Fl. 70 mm wide, golden yellow; corona deeper in tone than the perianth. Scented

'Oregon Green' 7 Y-GYY
(G.E.Mitsch, 1982) R. & E.Havens, 1997
'Coral Light' × *N. jonquilla*; sdlg no. 2R3/1
Fls 1-2 per stem, 65 mm wide, bright clear yellow; perianth segments broadly ovate; corona cup-shaped, very small, with bright green at base. Late

'Oregon Lights' 2 W-O
(R. & E.Havens, 1982) R. & E.Havens, 1997
'Gold Crown' × (['Ardour' × 'Ceylon'] × 'Brer Fox'); sdlg no. bREH26/1
Fl. 100 mm wide; perianth segments ovate, spreading, plane; corona cylindrical, with mouth slightly expanded. Mid-season. Sunproof

'Oregon Music' 2 W-W
(G.E. Mitsch) Grant Mitsch Novelty Daffodils, 1984
'Easter Moon' × 'Broughshane' hybrid; sdlg no. W65/2/4
Fl. 100 mm wide, opening yellowish, becoming clean white; perianth segments broadly ovate, blunt, slightly mucronate, very slightly reflexed, plane, smooth, overlapping half; the inner segments more nearly spreading, with margins wavy; corona funnel-shaped, smooth, with mouth straight, loosely frilled. Mid-season. Resembles sibling 'Gull' but with the perianth less strongly reflexed and the corona mouth more widely expanded

'Oregon Pioneer' 2 Y-P
(R. & E.Havens) R. & E.Havens, 1995

'Widgeon' × 'Pink Silk'; sdlg no. VH19/1
Fl. 105 mm wide; perianth segments broadly ovate, lemon yellow, spreading, plane, smooth and of heavy substance; corona straight-sided, opening lemon yellow, becoming intense pink, with light pink outside. Mid-season. Sunproof

'Oregon Rose' 4 W-P
(R. & E.Havens, 1984) R. & E.Havens, 1994 ('Precedent' × 'Pink Cloud') × 'Music'; sdlg no. TEH85/3
Fl. 95 mm wide; perianth and other petaloid segments in several whorls, broad, white, with overtones of pink; the outer whorls spreading or a little inflexed, concave at apex and with margins narrowly incurling; the centre whorl irregularly arranged, strongly inflexed, with margins deeply incurled or folded inwards; corona segments up to half the length of the petaloid segments and interspersed among them, broad, bright pink, frilled. Late. Sunproof

'Oregon Snow' 2 W-W
(G.E. Mitsch, 1974) R. & E. Havens, 1991
Sdlg Z40/5 (sdlg N6/1 × 'Empress of Ireland') × 'Queenscourt'; sdlg no. JJ56/2
Fl. of heavy substance; corona slightly flared. Mid-season.

'Orestes' 3 W-? (b)
(W.B. Hartland, pre-1907)

'Orestes' 1 (a)
(M. van Waveren & Sons, pre-1930)

'Orford' 2 Y-O
(C.E. Radcliff, 1934)
'W.F.Gates' × 'Golden Legend'

'Organdy' 2 W-P
(Oregon Bulb Farms, pre-1950)

'Organza' 2 (a)
(R. Crews) R. Crews, 1956

'Orgy' 3 W-? (b)
(F.H. Chapman, pre-1923)

'Oriad' 2 Y-YRR
(J.N. Hancock & Co., 1955) Unregistered

'Oriana' 1 W-Y
(Barr & Sons, pre-1904)
Corona soft canary yellow

'Oriana' 2 W-YPO
(J.L. Richardson) Mrs H.K. Richardson, 1964
'Interim' × 'Rose Caprice'
Perianth segments pure white, glistening, overlapping; corona with a broad band of clear pink towards mouth and with orange at rim, frilled, rim dentate

'Oriel' 1 (a)
(A.J. Bliss, pre-1930)

'Orient' 8 W-?
(G.H. Engleheart, pre-1907)
Poetaz
Perianth segments sulphur white; corona with red at rim

N. orientalis Linnaeus = *N. tazetta* subsp. *lacticolor*

'Oriental Pearl' 3 W-? (b)
(Mrs P.M. Davis, pre-1948)

'Oriental Ray' 2 Y-YYO
(pre-1969) Unregistered

'Oriental Silk' 2 Y-W
(G.E. Mitsch and R. & E.Havens, 1977) G.E. Mitsch and R. & E.Havens, 1988
'Surfside' open pollinated; sdlg no. MO20/1
Perianth segments soft lemon yellow, slightly reflexed, smooth. Mid-season

'Oriflamme' 3 W-O
(G.H. Engleheart, pre-1897)
Fl. rounded; perianth segments creamy white; corona scarlet-orange. Mid-season. AM 1898

"Original Pearl"
Syn. of 'White Pearl'

'Orinoco' 2 (a)
(J.L. Richardson, pre-1953)

'Oriole' 1 (a)
(Oregon Bulb Farms, pre-1950)

'Orion' 2 (a)
(W.F.M. Copeland, pre-1908)

'Orion' 1 Y-Y
(H.J. Poole Sr, pre-1927)

'Orion' 2 (a)
(D.V. West, pre-1936)

'Orion' 2 W-O
(J.L. Richardson) J.L. Richardson, 1959
'Kilworth' × 'Arbar'
Fl. 84 mm wide; perianth segments very broadly ovate, blunt, truncate, pure white, spreading, a little concave, smooth, overlapping half; the inner segments more narrowly ovate; corona ribbed, vivid orange 28B, mouth widely expanded, frilled, occasionally split and with shallow overlapping lobes, rim dentate. Mid-season. 2n=28. AM(e) 1962, *AM(g) 1979

'Orissa' 3 Y-YYO
(J.L. Richardson, pre-1943)
'Seraglio' × 'Aviemore'
Perianth segments bright yellow; corona very shallow bowl-shaped, yellow, with a broad band of bright reddish orange at rim

'Orizaba' 3 W-? (b)
(J.L. Richardson, pre-1953)

'Orlando' 1 W-Y
(Sir A.P.W. Thomas, pre-1914)
Perianth segments lightly twisted; corona soft yellow

'Orlando' 2 Y-O
(Trenoweth Valley Flower Farm, pre-1939)

'Orleans' 3 W-? (b)
(P.D. Williams, pre-1939)

'Orlove' 2 (a)
(Mrs R.O. Backhouse, pre-1921)

'Ormanli' 3 W-? (b)
(D. Blanchard, pre-1940)
'Mitylene' × 'Hades'; sdlg no. 28/7B

'Ormeau' 2 Y-Y
(W.J. Dunlop, 1949)
'Pilgrimage' × 'Cromarty'
Fl. 109 mm wide; perianth segments brilliant yellow 7A, overlapping; corona deep golden yellow, with mouth expanded, rim flanged and crenate. 2n=28.
*AM(g) 1967, *FCC(g) 1971, AGM 1993

'Ormley' 2 Y-R
(W. Jackson Jr, 1953)
'Chungking' × 'Magherally'

'Ormolu' 3 W-O
(P.D. Williams, pre-1910)
Perianth segments opening pale lemon, becoming sulphur white; corona shallow, bright reddish orange

'Ormolu' 1 Y-Y
Perianth segments rich lemon yellow, overlapping; corona buttercup yellow, frilled. Mid-season. Syn. of 'Musketeer'

'Ormonde'
(Cartwright & Goodwin, pre-1908)
?The same as 'Ormonde' pre-1914

'Ormonde' 2 W-? (b)
(G.H. Engleheart, pre-1914)
?The same as 'Ormonde' pre-1908

'Ormonde' 3 W-GOR
(O.D. Knight) O.D. Knight, 1981
'Arbar' × 'Corofin'

Fl. 102 mm wide. Mid-season

'Ornament' 3 Y-O
(G.H. Engleheart, pre-1913)
Perianth segments soft primrose yellow; corona ribbed, scarlet-orange

'Ornament' 1 Y-Y
(C.A. van der Wereld) C.A. van der Wereld, 1959
Perianth segments pale yellow; corona darker in tone

N. ornatus Haworth = variant of *N. poeticus* ("The Flat Crowned Saffron Rim")

'Ornatus' 9 W-YYR
(French origin)
Selection from *N. radiiflorus* var. *exertus*, introduced c.1870 by James Walker
Fl. 64 mm wide; perianth segments broadly obovate, blunt, fairly prominently mucronate, pure white, spreading, with margins wavy, separated at base, overlapping at shoulder; the inner segments with margins strongly recurved at base as if spathulate; corona disc-shaped, ribbed, brilliant greenish yellow 6B, with shades of green at base and with a narrow band of red (43B) at rim. Mid-season to late. 2n=14. Syn. Poeticus 'Ornatus'. Mistakenly named "The Flat Crowned Saffron Rim"

'Ornatus Maximus' 9 W-GYR
(Dutch origin, pre-1927)
Fl. rounded; perianth segments white, slightly stained yellow at base, reflexed, plane, overlapping; corona disc-shaped, ribbed, pale greenish lemon, with moss green at base and a narrow band of deep red at rim. 2n=14. Resembles 'Ornatus' but is larger and broader in the perianth and a little earlier in flower. Syn. 'White Fairy'

'Ornatus Praecox' 9

'Orono' 1 W-? (b)
(E.C. Powell, pre-1947)

'Orontes' 1 Y-Y
(H.A. Brown, 1943)
Perianth segments soft primrose yellow; corona large, bright yellow. Early

'Orontes' 2 Y-O
(R.V. Favell, pre-1946)
'Pentreath' × 'Fortune'

'Orotava' 4 Y-Y
(Mrs H.K. Richardson) Mrs H.K. Richardson, 1972
'Falaise' × 'King's Ransom'

'Orpen' 2 (a)
(Miss G. Evelyn, pre-1933)

'Orphan' 2 W-WWO
(J.N. Hancock & Co., pre-1949)
Perianth segments creamy white; corona with orange at rim

'Orphée' 3 Y-YYR
(W. Backhouse, pre-1869)
Perianth segments opening primrose yellow, becoming sulphur yellow; corona with a broad band of scarlet at rim. Syn. Barrii 'Conspicuus Minor'

'Orpheus' 1 W-? (b)
(J.W. Barr, pre-1930)

'Orpheus' 2 W-PPY
(J.L. Richardson) J.L. Richardson, 1961
'Rose of Tralee' self pollinated
Fl. 118 mm wide; perianth segments pure white, smooth, overlapping; corona pink, tinged gold at rim, frilled, with rim slightly flanged. Late. Resembles a smaller-flowered 'Salome'

'Orphir' 1 (a)
(J.W. Barr, pre-1930)

'Orsino' 1 W-? (b)
(Barr & Sons, pre-1923)

'Orthia' 2 W-R
(W. Jackson Sr, 1944)
'Oba' × 'Dawnglow'

'Orthodox' 3 W-? (b)
(F.H. Chapman, pre-1913)

'Ortiz' 1 Y-Y
(S.J. Bisdee) S.J. Bisdee, 1956
'Tarik' × 'Rob Roy'

'Ortona' 3 W-GOO
(J.L. Richardson, pre-1945)
'Mitylene' × 'Coronach'
Perianth segments very broad in outline, blunt or rounded at apex, prominently mucronate, pure white, spreading, plane, of good substance, overlapping half; the inner segments less noticeably mucronate, a little inflexed; corona broad, very shallow, heavily ribbed, intense reddish orange, with green at base. Late. 2n=28

'Ortona' 2 Y-O
(J.N. Hancock & Co., pre-1949)
Perianth segments rich yellow; corona pale orange, frilled

'Orven Francis Dudley' 2 (a)
(J.W.A. Lefeber, pre-1948)

'Orvieto' 2 W-O
(J.L. Richardson) Mrs H.K. Richardson, 1966
'Kilworth' × 'Matapan'
Perianth segments very broadly ovate, pure white; corona reddish orange, frilled

'Orwell' 2 Y-O
(M.P. Williams, pre-1949)
Perianth segments soft yellow; corona rich scarlet-orange

'Oryx' 7 Y-W
(G.E. Mitsch) G.E. Mitsch, 1969
'Aircastle' × *N. jonquilla*; sdlg no. Z2/15
Fls 2-3 per stem, 70 mm wide; perianth segments broadly ovate or oblong, rounded at apex and sometimes somewhat truncate, brilliant to light greenish yellow 3B to C, with slight white mucro, spreading or inflexed, a little concave, with margins incurling, smooth, overlapping half; the inner segments ovate, with margins more strongly incurved; corona bowl-shaped, straight-sided, loosely ribbed, opening light greenish yellow to pale yellow-green 4C to D, becoming near white, with mouth straight, wavy, rim entire. Mid-season. Scented. AM(e) 1990

'Osage' 3 W-W
(E.C. Powell, pre-1949)

'Osaka' 2 Y-O
(Mrs B.T. Simpson) Mrs B.T. Simpson, 1966
Fl. 108 mm wide; corona reddish orange. Late

'Osbert Sitwell' 2 W-Y
(R.V. Favell, pre-1939)
'Silver Coin' × 2 Y-R
Fl. rounded; perianth segments overlapping; corona pinky buff, frilled

'Osborne' 1 (a)
(A.M. Wilson, pre-1948)

'Oscar' 1 Y-Y
(A. Overton) A. Overton, 1960
Fl. golden yellow

'Oscar Louis' 2 (a)
(W. Poupart, pre-1923)

'Oscar's Memory' 2 W-P
(O. Ronalds)
'Wild Rose' × 'Mrs Oscar Ronalds'

'Oscar Wilde' 9
(G. Lubbe & Son, pre-1923)
Syn. 'Shakespeare'

'Osella' 2 Y-Y
(S.J. Bisdee, 1940)
'Golden Queen' × 'Crocus'

'Osiris' 2 W-Y
(Barr & Sons, pre-1903)
'Princess Mary' hybrid × 'King Alfred'
Perianth segments creamy white; corona broad, flared, canary yellow, lightly frilled

'Osiris' 1 Y-Y
(P.L.A. Pouw) P.L.A. Pouw, 1974
'Rembrandt' × 'Golden Sunbeam'
Fl. 120 mm wide. 2n=28

'Oskar Strauss' 2 W-O
(J.W.A. Lefeber) J.W.A. Lefeber, 1960
Fl. 85 mm wide; perianth segments pure white; corona reddish orange. Mid-season

'Oslo' 2 W-W
(A.M. Wilson, pre-1934)
'Nelly' × 'Beersheba'
Fl. pure white; perianth segments of strong substance; corona flared

'Osman' 1 Y-Y
(J.N. Hancock & Co., c.1980) Unregistered

'Osmington' 2 W-R
(J.W. Blanchard) J.W. Blanchard, 1974
Sdlg 51/60a × 'Privateer'; sdlg no. 58/44A
Fl. 95 mm wide; perianth segments broad, smooth; corona bright red. Mid-season

'Osprey' 3 W-Y
(J.C. Williams, 1925)
Fl. about 89 mm wide, of great substance; perianth segments rounded at apex, pure white, with margins wavy; corona short, strongly ribbed, opening citron yellow, soon becoming paler in tone, with mouth widely expanded, rim flanged

'Osprey' 3 W-? (b)
(L. Buckland, pre-1936)
Corona with red at rim

'Osprey' 3 (a)
(Sir A.P.W. Thomas)

'Ossa' 1 (a)
(Hon. Sir R.H. Rhodes, pre-1914)

'Ossa' 1 Y-Y
(The Brodie of Brodie, c.1917)
AM(Haarlem) 1931

'Ossian' 3 W-Y
(E. Leeds, pre-1877)
Fl. large; corona widely expanded. Syn. Burbidgei 'Ossian'

'Ostara' 2 Y-? (a)
(Warnaar & Co, pre-1936)
AM(Haarlem) 1936

'Ostara' 1 W-Y
(W. Jackson Sr, 1944)
'Napé' × 'Oithona'

'Ostende' 2 (a)
(Warnaar & Co, pre-1933)
AM(Haarlem) 1932

'Oswald' 1 (a)
(Sir A.P.W. Thomas, pre-1930)

'Oswega' 2 W-Y
(de Graaff Bros, pre-1948)
Corona lemon yellow. AM(Haarlem) 1948

'Oswell'
(pre-1940)

'Otago' 4 W-Y
(Jackson's Daffodils, 1984) Jackson's Daffodils, 1996
Sdlg 244/75 × Evans sdlg; sdlg no. 107/84
Fl. 110 mm wide, in seven or more whorls; perianth and other petaloid segments greenish white (155a); corona segments two-thirds the length, light greenish yellow 8B. Late

'Otahuna' 1 W-Y
(Hon. Sir R.H. Rhodes, pre-1914)
Perianth segments irregular; corona creamy yellow

'Otaihape' 2 Y-Y
(M.Hamilton) Koanga Daffodils, 1996
Sdlg hybrid
Fl. 115 mm wide; perianth segments ovate, vivid yellow 12A, plane; corona cylindrical, darker in tone (15A) than the perianth, shading to a still darker tone at rim (17B), the rim slightly crenate. Mid-season

'Otakou' 1 W-? (b)
(G.H. Brownlee, pre-1930)

'Otaru' 3 W-O
(Mrs B.T. Simpson) Mrs B.T. Simpson, 1966
Fl. 89 mm wide; corona frilled. Mid-season

'Otekura' 2 Y-? (a)
(R. Crews, pre-1949)
Syn. 'Awatea'

'Otewa' 1 Y-Y
(P. Phillips) P. Phillips, 1964
Fl. 102 mm wide. Mid-season. Resembles 'Bayard' in colour but has the perianth segments of different form and the corona more heavily frilled

'Othello' 1 Y-Y
(Barr & Sons, pre-1905)
Perianth segments primrose yellow, inflexed;

corona rich yellow

'Othello' 2 Y-Y
(de Graaff Bros, pre-1931)
Perianth segments narrow, acute, sulphur yellow; corona large, widely expanded. AM(Haarlem) 1931

'Otira' 2 W-Y
(J.A. Hunter) J.A. Hunter, 1966
Fl. 155 mm wide. Mid-season

'Otonga' 2 Y-Y
(R.C.A. Tombleson) R.C.A. Tombleson, 1964
Fl. 155 mm wide, vivid yellow 12A. Mid-season. PC(e)(NZ) 1958

'Otranto' 3 W-OOR
(J.L. Richardson, pre-1944)
'Seraglio' × 'Red Sun'
Fl. rounded, more than 102 mm wide; perianth segments very broad in outline, rounded or truncate at apex, more or less prominently mucronate, pure white, slightly reflexed, overlapping half; the inner segments narrower, more nearly spreading, with margins wavy; corona shallow, split to base, the six segments in two deeply overlapping whorls of three, alternate to the perianth segments, loosely ribbed, gold, shading to deep red at rim, frilled. Late

'Otterburn' 9 W-YYR
(G. Harrison, 1955) G. Harrison, 1968
'Actaea' hybrid
Fl. 89 mm wide. Mid-season

'Otto' 8 Y-Y
(pre-1798)
Fl. pale yellow

'Otto' 2 Y-YYO
(G. Lewis) D.S. Bell, 1955
Fl. bright yellow; corona with fiery reddish orange at rim

'Ottoman' 8 Y-Y
(pre-1798)
Fl. sulphur yellow

'Ottoman Gold' 2 W-GYR
(Ballydorn Bulb Farm) Ballydorn Bulb Farm, 1986
'Topkapi' × 'Hilford'
Corona deep yellow, with a broad band of red at rim. Mid-season

'Ottowa' 3 W-? (b)
(pre-1930)

'Otway' 1 Y-Y
(J.N. Hancock & Co., 1976) Unregistered

'Ouida' 2 or 3 W-? (b or c)
(R.H. Bath, pre-1913)

'Ouma' 1 Y-Y
(R.A. Scamp) R.A. Scamp, 1993
'Viking' × 'Ristin'; sdlg no. 268
Fl. 105 mm wide, golden yellow; perianth segments broadly ovate, blunt, slightly mucronate, spreading, plane, smooth, overlapping half; the inner segments a little more narrowly ovate, square-shouldered at base, slightly inflexed; corona cylindrical, narrow, smooth, with mouth a little expanded, lightly frilled, rim crenate. Mid-season

'Our Bessie' 2 W-? (b)
(G.P. Haydon, pre-1908)

'Our Bride' 2 W-W
(Tom Forster, 1960s) Unregistered

'Our Darling' 3 W-WWR
(Tom Forster, 1960s) Unregistered
Perianth segments roundish, ice white; corona shallow, white, with a clearly defined band of vivid red at rim, frilled. Mid-season to late

'Our Gift' 2 W-P
(Tom Forster, 1960s) Unregistered
Perianth segments creamy white; corona cylindrical, pink, neatly frilled. Late

'Our Gold' 2 (a)
(A. Gibson, pre-1951)

'Our Joy' 3 W-YYR
(Mrs P.E. Speyer) Mrs P.E. Speyer, 1984
'Lynx' × 'Motif'; sdlg no. 2/56
Fl. 98 mm wide

'Our Mark' 1 Y-Y
(Mrs P.E. Speyer, 1975) Mrs P.E. Speyer, 1986
'Camelot' × 'Royal Gold'; sdlg no. 1/7
Fl. 100 mm wide. Mid-season. Resembles 'Royal Gold' more than 'Camelot'

'Our M.P.' 1 (a)
(G.P. Haydon, pre-1910)

'Our Nellie' 1 W-? (b)
(G.P. Haydon, pre-1910)

'Our Sal' 2 W-GYW
(D.C.MacArthur) D.C.MacArthur, 1997
'Vi Grant' open pollinated; sdlg no. EV5091
Fl. forming a double triangle, 85 mm wide; perianth segments broadly ovate, prominently mucronate, greenish white 155C; the inner segments less noticeably mucronate; corona bowl-shaped, smooth, greenish yellow (154C), with moderate yellow-green at base and yellowish white 155D at rim, mouth lobed and widely flared, with rim crenate. Mid-season

'Our Tempie' 3 W-YYO
(W.G. Pannill) W.G. Pannill, 1980
'Merlin' × 'Hotspur'; sdlg no. 64/84/2
Fl. 90 mm wide. Mid-season

'Outcrop' 1 Y-Y
(J.N. Hancock & Co., c.1978) Unregistered

'Outer Space' 4 W-O
(G.E. Mitsch) G.E. Mitsch, 1974
'Falaise' × 'Roimond'
Fl. 104 mm wide

'Outlaw' 2 W-? (b)
(W. Welchman, pre-1908)

'Outlook' 2 (a)
(Mrs R.O. Backhouse, pre-1921)

'Outlook' 2 W-WWP
(W.G. Pannill) W.G. Pannill, 1983
'Empress of Ireland' × 'Accent'

'Outpost' 1 Y-Y
(G.H. Engleheart, pre-1907)
'Emperor' hybrid
Perianth segments sulphur yellow; corona canary yellow. Resembles an earlier and larger-flowered 'Emperor' of paler colour

'Output' 2 (a)
(J.F. Exley, pre 1950)

'Outrider' 1 Y-Y
(G.H. Engleheart, pre-1930)
Fl. 108 mm wide, golden yellow; perianth segments broadly ovate, blunt, very slightly mucronate, inflexed, twisted, creased, overlapping at base only; corona cylindrical, smooth, frilled, rim widely flanged and deeply notched, with margins recurved. Dwarf to standard. Early to mid-season.
*(Kirton)HC(g) 1935

'Outspan' 2 (a)
(W.F.M. Copeland, pre-1938)

'Outward Bound' 1 W-Y
(G. Lewis) D.S. Bell, 1955
Fl. forming a double triangle; perianth segments very broadly ovate, prominently mucronate, pure white, slightly reflexed, of thick texture, with margins slightly wavy, overlapping half; the inner segments more nearly spreading; corona cylindrical, lemon yellow, with rim widely flanged and regularly crenate

'Ouzel' 6 W-W
(G.E. Mitsch) G.E. Mitsch, 1984
'Dipper' open pollinated; sdlg no. NN01/1
Fl. 92 mm wide; corona opening pale lemon, becoming white. Mid-season. Resembles a larger and whiter 'Dipper'

'Ovation' 2 (a)
(R. Crews, pre-1949)

'Overbury' 1 Y-Y
(J.M. de Navarro) J.M. de Navarro, 1958
'Royalist' × 'Arctic Gold'

'Overcall' 2 Y-R
(D.S. Bell) D.S. Bell, 1970
'Air Marshal' × 'Checkmate'

'Overcollar'
Unregistered
Seed parent of 'Oecumene'

'Overdraft' 3 Y-R
(Jackson's Daffodils) Jackson's Daffodils, 1987
'Kopi' × 'Tia'; sdlg no. 287/79
Fl. forming a double triangle; perianth segments broadly ovate in outline, blunt or rounded at apex, brilliant greenish yellow 6A, with white mucro, with a faint white band at midrib broadening at apex, spreading, plane, overlapping half; the inner segments more narrowly ovate; corona cup-shaped, ribbed, orange-red (30B), mouth straight, even, rim notched. Mid-season

'Overlord' 1 W-Y
(F.E. Board) F.E. Board, 1965
'Glenshesk' × 'Preamble'
Early. Resembles a large-flowered 'Preamble'

'Overseas' 3 Y-?
(C.W. Pierson) C.W. Pierson, 1964
'Potent' × 'Southern Cross'

'Overseer' 1 Y-Y
(G.L. Wilson, pre-1940)
('Lemon Weardale' × 'The Perfect Gentleman') × 'Royalist'
Fl. golden yellow

'Overton's Titbit' 2 W-?
(A. Overton) R.A. Dunn, 1960

'Overtrick' 2 W-W
(Miss M. Verry) Miss M. Verry, 1966
Fl. 113 mm wide. Mid-season. Resembles a slightly green-tinged 'Ave' with larger perianth segments

'Overture' 2 W-? (b)
(G.H. Johnstone, pre-1944)

'Overture' 2 W-P
(C.E. Radcliff, 1945)
'Nautilus' × 'Mrs R.O. Backhouse'

'Overwinnaar' 8 W-O
(pre-1798)

'Ovid' 9
(G.H. Engleheart, pre-1908)

'Ovidius' 2 W-? (b)
(pre-1926)
AM(Haarlem) 1926

'Owaka' 3 W-YOO
(R. Crews) R. Crews, 1960
Fl. 105 mm wide; corona yellow-orange, with golden yellow at base. Mid-season

'Owen' 3 Y-O
(Mrs R.O. Backhouse, pre-1921)
Perianth segments primrose yellow; corona reddish orange. AM(g)(c) 1923, *C(g) 1927

'Owen Bray' 1 (a)
(R.G. Sharp, pre-1930)

'Owen Roe' 2 (a)
(The Brodie of Brodie, pre-1932)

'Owen Roe' 1 Y-Y
(Ballydorn Bulb Farm) Ballydorn Bulb Farm, 1983
'Golden Radiance' open pollinated
Fl. forming a double triangle, 120 mm wide, golden yellow; perianth segments broadly ovate, blunt, slightly mucronate, spreading or a little inflexed, concave, smooth, overlapping one-third; the inner segments more narrowly ovate, with margins incurved; corona cylindrical, smooth, darker in tone than the perianth, with mouth ribbed and flared, even, rim crenate. Mid-season

'Owen Wolley-Dod' 1 (a)
(pre-1907)

'O.W.Holmes' 9
(?G.P. Haydon, pre-1910)

'Owl' 8
(W.F.M. Copeland, pre-1936)

'Owler Bar' 2 Y-Y
(F.E. Board) F.E. Board, 1965
'Chevalier' × 'Galway'; sdlg no. 762
Late

'Owo' 3 W-? (b)
(W. Jackson Sr, 1938)
'Mountain Pride' × 'Mayflower'

'Owston Wood' 1 W-Y
(W.A. Noton) W.A. Noton, 1976
'Newcastle' × 'Ballygarvey'; sdlg no. 500
Fl. 104 mm wide; perianth segments broadly ovate, pure white; corona with rim slightly flanged. Mid-season

'Owyhee' 2 Y-P
(G.E. Mitsch, 1976) R. & E. Havens, 1993
'Milestone' × 'Sugar Maple'; sdlg no. LL8/3
Fl. 95 mm wide; perianth segments broadly ovate, pale yellow, slightly reflexed; corona cylindrical, apricot pink, with mouth frilled. Mid-season. Sunproof. Resembles a less formally arranged 'Irresistible' with the perianth more obviously reflexed

'Oxburgh' 1 W-? (b)
(R.H. Bath, pre-1933)

'Ox Eye' 2
(C.L. Adams, pre-1913)

'Oxford' 3 W-Y
(G.E. Mitsch, 1980) R. & E. Havens, 1993
'Impala' × 'Green Hills'; sdlg no. 2P59/1
Fl. 100 mm wide; perianth segments broadly ovate, slightly reflexed, regular; corona disc-shaped, ribbed, deep yellow, with green prominent in tube, frilled. Late. Scented

N. oxypetalus Boissier = *N. elegans* var. *oxypetalus*

'Oykel' 3 W-Y
(J.S.B. Lea) J.S.B. Lea, 1978
'Loch Assynt' × 'Merlin'
Fl. 95 mm wide; perianth segments pure white; corona citron yellow. Late

'Oz' 12 Y-Y
(W.G. Pannill) W.G. Pannill, 1980
'Jenny' × *N. jonquilla*
Fls 2 per stem, 50 mm wide; perianth segments ovate, blunt, with white mucro, reflexed, with margins wavy, overlapping a quarter; corona cylindrical or somewhat funnel-shaped, with mouth straight and wavy, rim irregularly notched and crenate. Dwarf. Mid-season

'Ozan' 2 W-Y
(P.D. Williams, pre-1916)
Corona tightly ribbed, pale yellow. AM(e) 1916. Div. 3 until 1935

'Ozark' 2 (a)
(R.H. Bath, pre-1929)

'Ozark Star' 1 W-Y
(Mrs M. Ferguson) Mrs M. Ferguson, 1966
'Beersheba' × 'Carlton'
Fl. 118 mm wide; perianth segments opening pale creamy yellow, becoming creamy white; corona opening soft yellow, becoming creamy yellow. Mid-season. Resembles 'Bonython' in form

'Ozone' 2 W-W
(W. Gould Jr) W. Gould Jr, 1992
'Broomhill' × ('Coral Ribbon' × 'Rose Royale'); sdlg no. 84-3-A
Fl. 115 mm wide, white. Mid-season. Resembles 'Broomhill'

P

'Pace' 2 Y-O
Syn. of 'Indonesia'

'Pacelli' 1 (a)
(G. Lubbe & Son, pre-1939)
AM(Haarlem) 1939

'Pacemaker' 2 Y-O
(S.C. Gaspar, pre-1950) R.J.Abernethy, 1961
Fl. 95 mm wide; perianth segments golden yellow; corona deep reddish orange. Early

***N. × pacensis* Fernández Casas 13** = *N. confusus* Pugsley × *N. triandrus* subsp. *pallidulus* (Graells) D.A.Webb

***N. pachybolbus* Durieu de Maisonneuve 13**
Section Tazettae

'Pacific' 1 W-W
(de Graaff-Gerharda, pre-1926)
Perianth segments creamy white, overlapping; corona tinged sulphur yellow. Mid-season. 2n=30.
AM(Haarlem) 1926, *HC(g) 1936, *AM(g) 1946

'Pacific Beauty' 2 W-Y
(David L. Sheppard) David L. Sheppard, 1977
'Muscadet' × 'Hillbilly'; sdlg no. 72-A-1
Fl. 100 mm wide; corona spreading, with mouth split and frilled. Early to mid-season

'Pacific Coast' 8 Y-Y
(E.Lievens) J.E.Lievens, 1994
'Minnow' sport
Fl. 35 mm wide; perianth segments light greenish yellow 5C; corona vivid yellow 9A. Dwarf. Late

'Pacific Dawn' 2 W-? (b)
(Oregon Bulb Farms, pre-1950)

'Pacific Glow' 2 Y-YOO
(J.A. Hunter) J.A. Hunter, 1992
('Air Marshal' × 'Swordsman') × 'Torridon'; sdlg no. 22/80B
Fl. 115 mm wide; perianth segments very broadly ovate, yellow; corona orange, touched yellow at base, with mouth straight, frilled. Early to mid-season

'Pacific Lady' 2 W-R
(R.H.Glover)
'Green Island' × 'Arbar'

'Pacific Mist' 11a Y-YYP
(R. & E.Havens, 1985) R. & E.Havens, 1996
'Milestone' × 'Square Dancer'; sdlg no. UH12/1
Fl. 87 mm wide; perianth segments ovate, clear lemon yellow; corona deeply split, the six segments opposite and closely overlying the perianth segments, light lemon yellow, with pale pink at rim, frilled. Late. Sunproof

'Pacific Princess' 3 W-GWW
(Mrs J. Abel Smith, 1978) Mrs J. Abel Smith, 1989
Mary Isabel' hybrid; sdlg no. F33/92
Mid-season

'Pacific Rim' 2 Y-YYR
(Grant E.Mitsch, 1984) R. & E.Havens, 1994
'Montego' × 'Ringmaster'; sdlg no. TT35/1
Fl. 90 mm wide, of heavy substance; perianth segments broadly ovate, clear yellow, spreading, plane; corona very shallow bowl-shaped, clear yellow, with a band of orange-red at rim. Mid-season. Sunproof

'Pacific Star' 2 W-Y
(J.A. Hunter) J.A. Hunter, 1982
'Easter Moon' × ('Daisy Schäffer' × 'Carnlough')
Fl. 120 mm wide; corona buff yellow. Mid-season

'Pacific Sunset' 4 Y-O
(David L. Sheppard) David L. Sheppard, 1970

'Pactolus'
(Sir A.P.W Thomas, pre-1915)

'Pactolus' 1 Y-Y
(S. Morrison, pre-1936)
Fl. rich yellow

'Paddington' 1 Y-Y
(J.N. Hancock & Co., 1973) Unregistered

'Paddy' 2 W-? (b or c)
(G.L. Wilson, pre-1932)

'Padstow' 3 (a)
(P.D. Williams, pre-1933)

'Padua' 1 W-W
(G.H. Engleheart, pre-1907)

'Padua' 2 Y-O
(pre-1956)
Perianth segments rich yellow; corona yellow-orange

'Padua' 2 W-R
(J.M. de Navarro) J.M. de Navarro, 1958
'Blarney' × 'Helvick'

'Paean' 1 Y-Y
(Jackson's Daffodils) Jackson's Daffodils, 1995
'Scipio' × 'Sasham'; sdlg no. 103/87
Fl. 105 mm wide; perianth segments very broadly ovate, brilliant yellow 7A, plane; corona cylindrical, brighter in tone (12A) than the perianth, with mouth flared. Mid-season

'Pagan'
(W. Backhouse, pre-1869)

'Pageant' 2 Y-R
(A.M. Wilson, pre-1948)
'Fortune' hybrid × 'Senegal'
Corona vivid red

'Pageant' 1 Y-O
(W.M. Spry, pre-1975) Unregistered
'Gat Gordon' × 'Golden'

'Page Lee' 3 Y-YYR
(W.G.Pannill, 1983) W.G.Pannill, 1996
('Goyescas' × 'Ballysillan') × 'Sabine Hay'; sdlg no. 77/23B
Corona yellow, with red at rim. Late

'Page Polka' 2 YYW-W
(Konynenburg & Mark) Konynenburg & Mark, 1964
Fl. 115 mm wide; perianth segments lemon yellow, with white at base. Late

'Pagoda' 2 W-O
(G.L. Wilson, pre-1952)
'Red Hackle' × 'Cairo'
Perianth segments ivory; corona scarlet-orange

'Pahiatua' 1 Y-Y
(Miss M. Verry) Miss M. Verry, 1966
Fl. 108 mm wide, deep yellow; perianth segments smooth. Early. Resembles a larger, taller and earlier-flowered 'Goldcourt' of deeper colour

'Paikatiro' 1 Y-Y
(R. Hyde) R. Hyde, 1959
'Pretoria' × 'Goldcourt'
Fl. golden yellow; perianth segments broadly ovate, deeply overlapping; corona with rim rolled. See also 'Parkatiro'

'Painted Desert' 3 Y-GYO
(T.D. Throckmorton) T.D. Throckmorton, 1974
'Old Satin' × 'Altruist'
Perianth segments rich yellow; corona with green at base and bright red at rim, frilled

'Painted Doll' 2 W-WPP
(Murray W. Evans, 1971) Murray W. Evans, 1985
'Julep' × 'Pontsianna'; sdlg no. 0-44
Corona opening self pink. Late. Resembles a smaller-flowered 'Pontsianna'

'Painted Lady' 2 W-O
(The Brodie of Brodie, c.1933)
('Bernardino' × 'Mrs Ernst H.Krelage') × 'Fortune' × 'Tregoose'
Perianth segments white; corona deep bowl-shaped, vivid reddish orange

'Pakatoa' 3 W-GYR
(G. Lewis) P. Phillips, 1968
Perianth segments broad, pure white, smooth; corona yellow, with green at base and a narrow and distinct band of red at rim, mouth expanded and lobed, with rim dentate

'Pakeha' 2 (a)
(C.E. Buckingham, pre-1936)

'Pakotai' 12 Y-Y
(Robin Brown) Robin Brown, 1995
N. jonquilla × *N. cyclamineus*; sdlg no. J/CYC 121
Fls 2-3 per stem, 47 mm wide, mid-yellow, facing down; perianth segments reflexed; corona cylindrical, smooth, with mouth straight. Dwarf. Early

'Paladin' 1 Y-Y
(The Brodie of Brodie, pre-1908)
Richardson sdlg 985 × 'Arbar'
Corona reddish orange. Late

'Paladin' 2 W-O
(F.E. Board) F.E. Board, 1965
'Santa Maria' × 'Weardale Perfection'; sdlg no. 261/05
Fl. deep yellow; perianth segments slightly twisted

'Palamedes' 8 Y-Y
(pre-1807)
Fl. sulphur yellow

'Palana' 3 W-R
(S.J. Bisdee, 1945)
'Hades' × 'Mr Sparks'

'Palana-Too' 2 W-YYR
(S.J. Bisdee, 1950)
'Flamenco' × 'Hades'

'Palatial' 2 (a)
(H.A. Brown) H.A. Brown, 1956

'Palaverer' 1 W-Y
(G.H. Johnstone) G.H. Johnstone, 1959
'Courtesy' × 'Content'
Fl. 121 mm wide; corona primrose yellow. Early. 2n=28

'Pale Angel' 5
(F.R. Waley, pre-1950)

N. palearensis Romo 13 Section Jonquilla

'Pale Beauty' 2 Y-O
(J.A. O'More) J.A. O'More, 1981
'Red Baron' × 'Dunkeld'; sdlg no. 114/58
Fl. 96 mm wide; perianth segments light greenish yellow 6D; corona vivid orange 28B. Mid-season.

'Pale Enigma' 1 YYW-WWY
(M.G.Temple-Smith, 1984) M.G.Temple-Smith, 1997
Sdlg no. 13/84
Perianth segments broad, brilliant greenish yellow 5B, with white at base; corona straight-sided, somewhat funnel-shaped, white, with a band of yellow at rim. Mid-season. Immature flowers sometimes measuring Div. 2

'Pale Face' 2 or 3 W-? (b or c)
(Cartwright & Goodwin, pre-1916)

'Paleface' 2 W-W
(A. Overton) A. Overton, 1960

'Pale Face' 2 W-? (b)
(W.B. Blanden)

'Paleface' 2 Y-W
(?Australian origin, pre-1990) Unregistered

'Pale Hands' 2 W-P
(Sidney DuBose, 1986) Sidney DuBose, 1996
'Salome' × sdlg E80-3 ('Peace Pipe' × Evans sdlg N58-2 ['Rima' × 'Alpine Glow']); sdlg no. L56-4
Fl. forming a double triangle, 93 mm wide; perianth segments broadly ovate, blunt, slightly mucronate, spreading, plane, smooth, with narrow midrib showing, overlapping half; the inner segments very little narrower, rounded at shoulder, with margins slightly wavy; corona somewhat funnel-shaped, pale pink, touched green at base, with apricot pink at rim, mouth even, rim crenate. Late

'Pale Moon' 2 W-YYO
(G. Lewis) D.S. Bell, 1955
Corona almost disc-shaped, bright yellow, with a very narrow band of reddish orange at rim

'Pale Moon' 1 W-Y
Syn. of 'Casselle'

'Palermo' 2 Y-O
(P.D. Williams, pre-1916)
Perianth segments yellow; corona reddish orange. AM(e) 1916

'Palestine' 2 Y-YOO
(J.L. Richardson, pre-1951)
'Carbineer' open pollinated
Perianth segments deep lemon yellow; corona bright reddish orange, with a sharply defined band of gold at base

'Pale Sunlight' 2 Y-Y
(Carncairn Daffodils) Carncairn Daffodils, 1982
'Green Island' × 'Tobernaveen'; sdlg no. W5/30
Fl. 100 mm wide, light greenish yellow 6D. Mid-season. 2n=28. Resembles 'Aircastle' but with a differently-shaped corona

'Palette' 11a W-YYO
(J. Gerritsen & Son) J. Gerritsen & Son, 1973
'Canasta' hybrid
Fl. 95 mm wide; perianth segments opening yellow, becoming white; corona deeply split, the six segments opposite and closely overlying the perianth segments, opening greenish yellow, becoming deep yellow, with orange at rim. Mid-season to late

'Palid' 2 Y-W
(P. & G. Phillips) P. & G. Phillips, 1975
Fl. 88 mm wide; perianth segments pale lemon; corona opening lemon, becoming white. Mid-season

'Palin' 2 W-P
(W. Jackson Sr, 1947)
'Pinka' × 'Leto'

'Palisade' 2 W-P
(R.C.A. Tombleson) R.C.A. Tombleson, 1966
Late

'Palladio' 2 (a)
(Warnaar & Co., pre-1933)

'Pallas' 8 W-O
(pre-1798)

'Pallas' 2 (a)
(W.F.M. Copeland, pre-1908)

'Pallas' 2 W-Y
(J.S. Leitch) J.S. Leitch, 1958

'Pallas Athene' 2 W-? (b)
(de Graaff Bros, pre-1928)

N. pallens Willkomm = *N. assoanus*

N. pallidiflorus Pugsley 13 Section Pseudonarcissus (Pseudonarcissus Moschatus 'Pallidus Praecox', "The Early Straw Coloured Bastard Daffodil"). FCC 1884
    var. ***pallidiflorus***
        f. ***pallidiflorus***
        f. ***asturicus*** (Barr) Pugsley
    var. ***intermedius*** Pugsley

N. pallidulus Graells = *N. triandrus* subsp. *pallidulus*.

N. pallidus Graells = *N. bulbocodium* var. *pallidus*

N. pallidus Poiret = *N. dubius*

'Pallidus' 2 W-Y
(E. Leeds, pre-1877)
Perianth segments yellowish white. Syn. Incomparabilis Pallidus 'Pallidus'. Was "absorbed" into 'Prince Teck'

'Pallidus' 1 Y-Y
(pre-1884)
Perianth segments sulphur; corona yellow. Syn. Pseudonarcissus 'Pallidus'

'Pallidus Maximus'
(?Thomas Smith, pre-1899)

'Pallidus Praecox'
Syn. of *N. pallidiflorus*

'Palliser' 1 W-Y
(D. Bramley) D. Bramley, 1980
Sdlg no. 70/12
Fl. 105 mm wide. Mid-season

'Palma' 2 W-O
(The Brodie of Brodie, *c.*1924)
'Princess Mary' × 'Gallipoli'

'Palma Giovanni' 11?b W-O
(J.W.A. Lefeber) J.W.A. Lefeber, 1968
'Silvester' hybrid

'Palmares' 11a W-P
(J. Gerritsen & Son) J. Gerritsen & Son, 1973
'Split' × 'Collarosa'
Fl. 90 mm wide; perianth segments broadly ovate, blunt, ivory white, spreading, separated at base, overlapping at mid-point; the inner segments more narrowly ovate; corona split to base, the six segments more than half as long as the perianth segments, opposite to them and inflexed, three-lobed, apricot pink (24D), with a darker tone at rim and at the notches between lobes, spreading or inflexed, loosely frilled, sometimes with a short linear extra growth at the base of the centre lobe or in place of it; the inner segments of corona and perianth joined at margins at base. Mid-season to late. Resembles 'Split' but with a pink corona

'Palm Beach' 1 Y-Y
(W.M. Spry, pre-1975) Unregistered
'Ferny Creek' × 'Golden'
Mid-season

'Palm Day' 2 Y-Y
(A.G. Thompson) A.G. Thompson, 1960

'John Evelyn' × 'Imperator'
Fl. 115 mm wide; perianth segments creamy yellow; corona large, widely expanded, darker in tone than the perianth, frilled. Early. Resembles 'John Evelyn' but with improved texture and a larger corona

'Palmer' 2 Y-O
(C.E. Radcliff) J.M.Radcliff, 1956
'Dunkeld' × 'Royal Mail'

'Palmer's Gold' 1 Y-Y
(L.C.Palmer) M.E.Rollinson, 1994
Sdlgs J63 × K2; sdlg no. 85/82
Fl. forming a double triangle, brilliant yellow 7A; perianth segments very broadly ovate, blunt, with slight white mucro, spreading, plane, overlapping half or more; the inner segments more narrowly ovate, with margins wavy; corona cylindrical, smooth, mouth flared, split and overlapping, intricately frilled, rim flanged. Early to mid-season

'Palmer's Lemon' 1 WWY-Y
(L.C.Palmer) M.E.Rollinson, 1994
'Camelot' × 'Carrickbeg'; sdlg no. 84/63
Fl. forming a double triangle; perianth segments broadly ovate, blunt, only very slightly mucronate, white, touched yellow at base, spreading, somewhat concave, very smooth, overlapping half; the inner segments more narrowly ovate; corona cyindrical, lightly ribbed, yellow, with mouth flared and very slightly frilled, rim flanged and crenate

'Palmer's Snow' 1 W-YWW
(L.C.Palmer) M.E.Rollinson, 1994
'Spindrift' × 'Canisp'; sdlg no. 84/103
Fl. forming a double triangle; perianth segments broadly ovate, only very slightly mucronate, spreading, with margins slightly wavy, overlapping half; the inner segments more narrowly ovate, sometimes nicked at margin; corona cyindrical and smooth in lower two-thirds, expanded and lightly ribbed towards mouth, with greenish yellow in tube, mouth even, rim flanged, almost entire, occasionally notched. Mid-season to late

'Palmerston' 3 W-Y
(W. Backhouse, pre-1869)
Corona canary yellow. Syn. Leedsii 'Palmerston'

'Palmino' 1 Y-Y
(A.H. Ahrens, pre-1949)
'Royalist' × 'Crocus'
AM(e)(NZ) 1959

'Palmira' 8
(pre-1939)

'Palmy Days' 2 Y-O
(W.M. Spry, pre-1967) Unregistered
'Stanley Mann' × 'Golden Valley'

'Palmyra' 3 W-YRR
(G.E. Mitsch) G.E. Mitsch, 1970
'Cadence' × 'Clockface'; sdlg no. Y5/1
Fl. rounded, pure white; corona small, orange-red, with yellow at base. Late

'Palo' 2 W-P
(W. Jackson Jr, 1956) W. Jackson Jr, 1966
Sdlg 86/51 × 'Ceram'; sdlg no. 179/56

'Paloma' 3 W-GYR
(W.H. Roesé, c.1981) Unregistered
'Estrella' × 'Merlin'

'Palomar' 1 (d)
(Oregon Bulb Farms, pre-1951)

'Palomind' 1 Y-Y
(J.W.A. Lefeber) J.W.A. Lefeber, 1968

'Paloona' 2 Y-O
(S.J. Bisdee) S.J. Bisdee, 1956
'Caruna' × 'Royal Mail'

'Pam' 3 W-? (b)
(de Graaff Bros, pre-1937)
AM(Haarlem) 1937

'Pamela' 3 W-? (b)
(J.W. Barr, pre-1930)

'Pamela' 2 (a)
(J. Wilson, pre-1931)
AM(Haarlem) 1931

'Pamela' 1 W-W
(T. Buncombe, pre-1934)

'Pamela' 6 W-Y
(M.P. Williams, pre-1951)
AM(Haarlem) 1956, HC(p) 1985. Some stock sold as 'April Love'

'Pamela' 8 W-O
Syn. of 'Medio Luteo Pamela'

'Pamina' 3 W-? (b)
(N.F. Lock, pre-1944)

'Pamir' 2 Y-O
(D.W. Lefeber & Co.) van Graven Bros, 1955
'Scarlet Elegance' hybrid
Perianth segments bright golden yellow; corona intense scarlet-orange.

'Pamlea' 2 W-W
(J.N. Hancock & Co., c.1962) Unregistered

'Pamlin' 2 W-Y
(de Graaff Bros) de Graaff Bros, 1957
AM(Haarlem) 1957

'Pamplona' 2 Y-R
(J.M. de Navarro) J.M. de Navarro, 1956
('Trevisky' × 'Porthilly') × 'Gibraltar'

'Panacea' ?-P
(Alister Clark, pre-1948)

'Panache' 1 W-W
(G.L. Wilson) F.E. Board, 1962
Sdlg W35-139 ('Courage' × 'Broughshane') × 'Empress of Ireland'; sdlg no. 46-29
Fl. 115 mm wide; perianth segments blunt, with green at base, spreading, regular, overlapping; corona narrow, with mouth expanded, rim flanged and bluntly dentate. Mid-season. 2n=28. FCC(e) 1967

'Pan Am' 2 Y-R
(P. & G. Phillips) P. & G. Phillips, 1979
Fl. 110 mm wide. Mid-season

'Panama' 2 Y-OOR
(A.M. Wilson, pre-1930)
Perianth segments deep yellow, overlapping; corona orange, with red at rim

'Panama' 1 W-Y
(G. Lewis, pre-1950)
Perianth segments of waxy texture; corona lemon yellow

'Panamint' 3 W-YYO
(Oregon Bulb Farms, pre-1951)
'Glad Boy' × 'John Evelyn'

'Pancake Too' 2 W-Y
(C.E. Radcliff, 1931)
'Warflame' × 'Puzzle'

'Panda' 2 W-W
(P.D. Williams, pre-1948)

'Pandion' 2 W-? (b)
(Mrs R.O. Backhouse, pre-1921)

'Pandita' 2 (a)
(J.T. Gray, pre-1949)

'Pandora'
(W. Backhouse, pre-1869)

'Pandora' 3 W-YYO
(C. Dawson, pre-1912)
'Lulworth' × 'Horace'
Fl. facing slightly downwards; perianth segments tinged sulphur yellow; corona shallow, expanded, ribbed, buff yellow, shading to pale orange at rim. AM(Haarlem) 1915

'Pandora' 3 Y-YYO
(?Australian origin) R. Hyde, 1955

'Pango' 8 Y-Y
(A. Gray, pre-1949)
N. dubius × 'John Evelyn'
Fls occasionally 2 per stem, soft yellow; perianth segments broadly ovate, blunt, mucronate, reflexed, with margins incurling, overlapping one-third to a half; the inner segments more narrowly ovate, with margins more deeply incurved; corona cup-shaped, ribbed, darker in tone than the perianth, with mouth straight, wavy, rim entire or slightly notched. The perianth sometimes becoming white at maturity

'Pania' 3 W-O
(J.S. Leitch) J.S. Leitch, 1962
Fl. 92 mm wide; corona reddish orange. Mid-season

N. panizzianus **Parlatore 13 Section Tazettae**
("Paper White Minor")

'Pankin' 2 W-P
(W. Jackson Jr) W. Jackson Jr, 1966
'Lanka' × 'Saint Therese'

'Pankot' 2 W-GWP
(Carncairn Daffodils) Carncairn Daffodils, 1984
'Easter Moon' × 'Rose Caprice'; sdlg no. W9/14
Fl. 94 mm wide; corona pale yellow, with green at base and delicate orange-pink at rim. Late

'Panorama' 2 (a)
(Warnaar & Co., pre-1933)
AM(Haarlem) 1932

'Panshanger' 1 W-P
(C.E. Radcliff, pre-1945)
'Glendevie' × 'Dawnglow'

'Pansie' 3 (a)
(Cartwright & Goodwin, pre-1916)
Perianth segments pure white; corona orange-red

'Pansy' 3 W-O
(pre-1956) Unregistered
Corona reddish orange

'Panther' 3 W-O
(P.D. Williams, pre-1929)
Perianth segments creamy white; corona reddish orange

'Pantomime' 9 W-YYR
(Murray W. Evans, 1970) Murray W. Evans, 1982
N. poeticus var. *recurvus* × 'Dallas'; sdlg no. N-25/1
Fl. 75 mm wide. Late. First registered in 1978 as Div. 3

'Panwakin' 7

(Mrs P.M. Davis, pre-1948)

'Panzer Chief' 2 Y-YYR
(P. & G. Phillips) P. & G. Phillips, 1971
Fl. 105 mm wide

'Paola' 2 Y-R
(J.S. Leitch) J.S. Leitch, 1962
Fl. 89 mm wide. Mid-season

'Paole Veronese' 2 W-OOY
(J.W.A. Lefeber) J.W.A. Lefeber, 1975
Fl. 110 mm wide; perianth segments ivory white; corona light orange (23C), with brownish yellow at rim. Mid-season

'Papanui Queen' 2 W-O
(G. Lewis, pre-1940)
Perianth segments overlapping; corona shallow, widely expanded, reddish orange

'Papawai' 1 W-Y
(J.S. Leitch) J.S. Leitch, 1966
Fl. 108 mm wide; corona lemon yellow

'Paper Sails' 8 W-W
(H.Koopowitz) H.Koopowitz, 1997
Hybrid between *N. papyraceus* sdlgs
Fls 8 per stem, 45 mm wide; perianth segments very broad, slightly inflexed; corona cup-shaped, with mouth incurved and rim entire. Early

'Paper Sol' 8 W-Y
(H. Koopowitz) H. Koopowitz, 1981
'Paper White' × 'Autumn Sol'; sdlg no. NN77
Fls 9 per stem, 36 mm wide; perianth segments ivory white; corona opening lemon yellow, becoming buff. Very early. Scented

'Paper White'
Syn. of *N. papyraceus*

'Paper White Early Snowflake' 8 W-W
Syn. of 'Paper White Grandiflorus'

'Paper White Grandiflora' 8 W-W
?Syn. of 'Paper White Grandiflorus'

'Paper White Grandiflorus' 8 W-W
(pre-1887)
Fl. pure white. Very early. 2n=22. Resembles a large and earlier-flowered 'Paper White'. Syn. ?'Paper White Snowflake', 'Early Snowflake', 'Paper White Early Snowflake', 'Paper White Grandiflora', 'Paper White New Large Flowered', 'Paper White Snowflake Improved', 'Snowflake', Tazetta 'Papyraceus Grandiflorus'

"Paper White Minor"
Syn. of *N. panizzianus*

'Paper White New Large Flowered' 8 W-W
Syn. of 'Paper White Grandiflorus'

'Paper White Snowflake' 8 W-W
(?Barr & Sons, pre-1895)
?Syn. of 'Paper White Grandiflorus'

'Paper White Snowflake Improved' 8 W-W
Syn. of 'Paper White Grandiflorus'

'Papillon' 8
(J.B. van der Schoot & Son, pre-1931)
Syn. 'Candida'

'Papillon Blanc' 11b W-W
(J.W.A. Lefeber, 1940) J.W.A.Lefeber, 1960
Fl. 85 mm wide; perianth segments very broad, prominently mucronate, creamy white, spreading, concave, overlapping half or more; the inner segments narrower, only very slightly mucronate, with margins wavy; corona split to base, the six segments more than half as long as the perianth segments and alternate to them, opening with a longitudinal band of yellow at midrib, becoming self creamy white, darker in tone than the perianth, inflexed, frilled, overlapping, sometimes with a short extra growth at the overlap. Late. 2n=29. AM(Haarlem) 1962. Spelt 'Papillon Blanche' until 1966

'Papillon Blanche' 11b W-W
Syn. of 'Papillon Blanc'

'Papillon Paradiso' 11b W-Y/W
(J.W.A. Lefeber) J.W.A. Lefeber, 1963
Fl. 130 mm wide; perianth segments creamy white; corona segments with yellow and white in longitudinal bands. Mid-season. Resembles a large-flowered 'Lemon Beauty'

'Papoose' 7 W-W
(C.R. Wootton, 1950) C.R.Wootton, 1962
'Evening' × *N. jonquilla*
Fls 2-3 per stem; corona narrow, opening pale creamy yellow, becoming creamy white. Mid-season to late

'Paprika' 3 W-R
(J.L. Richardson, pre-1941)
'Folly' × 'Hades'
Perianth segments acute, snowy white, somewhat reflexed at apex; corona very shallow bowl-shaped, bright brick red

'Papua' 4 Y-Y
(J.L. Richardson) J.L. Richardson, 1961
'Falaise' × 'Kingscourt'
Fl. 91 mm wide; perianth segments near to brilliant greenish yellow 6B, overlapping; corona segments near to strong orange-yellow 17A, with rim entire or very slightly dentate. Mid-season. 2n=27. *AM(g) 1970, *FCC(g) 1971, AGM 1993

***N. papyraceus* Ker Gawler 13 Section Tazettae**
('Paper White', 'Single Paper White'?, Tazetta 'Niveus', Tazetta 'Unicolor', 'Totus Albus Prior', "White Italian"). 2n=22.

N. papyraceus Ker Gawler subsp. *pachybolbus* (Durieu de Maisonneuve) D.A.Webb = *N. pachybolbus*

N. papyraceus Ker Gawler subsp. *panizzianus* (Parlatore) Arcangeli = *N. panizzianus*

N. papyraceus Ker Gawler subsp. *polyanthos* (Loiseleur-Deslongchamps) Ascherson & Graebner = *N. polyanthos*

'Papyraceus Grandiflorus' 8 W-W
Syn. of 'Paper White Grandiflorus'

'Papyrus' 9 W-YYO
(G.H. Engleheart, pre-1926)
Fl. rounded; perianth segments white, with lemon at base, with margins a little wavy, overlapping two-thirds; corona yellow, with reddish orange at rim. AM(c)(m) 1926, FCC(c) 1932

'Paquita' 2 W-W
(P. & G. Phillips) P. & G. Phillips, 1981
Fl. 105 mm wide. Mid-season

'Parable' 4 W-P
(W.G. Pannill) W.G. Pannill, 1978
'Pink Chiffon' × pink sdlg; sdlg no. G 21 A
Fl. 110 mm wide. Mid-season

'Paracelsus' 2 W-? (b)
(F.H. Chapman, pre-1913)

'Paracelsus' 1 Y-Y
(N.J. Walton) N.J. Walton, 1977
'Ulster Prince' × 'Content'; sdlg no. 67/9
Fl. 105 mm wide; perianth segments sulphur yellow; corona lemon yellow. Early. Resembles a paler 'Ulster Prince'

'Parachute' 2 W-? (b)
(P. van der Voet, pre-1939)

'Paraclete' 2 W-YYR
(C.E. Radcliff, 1931)
'Bernardino' × 'Blodwen'

'Paraclete' 1 W-Y
(A.G. Thompson) A.G. Thompson, 1960
'Beersheba' × 'Imperator'
Fl. 102 mm wide; corona pale creamy yellow. Mid-season

'Paracutin' 2 Y-R
Syn. of 'Paricutin'

'Parade' 2 (a)
(D.W. Lefeber & Co., pre-1953)
AM(Haarlem) 1952

'Paradigm' 4 Y-O
(Brian S.Duncan) Brian S.Duncan, 1996
Sdlg 633 ('Gettysburg' × 'Barnsdale Wood') × 'Smokey Bear'; sdlg no. 1470
Fl. rounded, 98 mm wide; perianth and other petaloid segments in several whorls, deep golden yellow, overlapping; the outer whorl roundish in outline, spreading; the inner whorls shorter, broadly ovate, inflexed, concave or with margins incurling, regularly arranged; corona segments shorter still, interspersed among the petaloid segments, deep orange, frilled. Mid-season

'Paradise' 3 W-? (b)
(Mrs R.O. Backhouse, pre-1921)

'Paradise' 2 W-W
(F.E. Board) F.E. Board, 1965
'Vigil' × 'Castle of Mey'
Mid-season

'Parador' 2 Y-O
(J.S. Leitch) J.S. Leitch, 1958

'Paradox' 2 Y-Y
(G.E. Mitsch) G.E. Mitsch, 1970
'Binkie' × 'Lunar Sea'; sdlg no. Y4/1
Fl. pale ivory lemon; corona with a band of a deeper tone at rim. Mid-season

'Paradoxus' 1 W-Y
Syn. of 'Albidus Paradoxus'

'Paragon' 2 (a)
(P.D. Williams, pre-1931)

'Paragon' 2 W-Y
(Konynenburg & Mark) Konynenburg & Mark, 1961
'Flaming Torch' × 'Fortune'
Fl. 120 mm wide; perianth segments ivory white; corona vivid yellow 16A. Late

'Paramaribo' 2 Y-R
(F. Rijnveld & Sons) F. Rijnveld & Sons, 1956
AM(Haarlem) 1956

'Paramount' 2 Y-O
(F.H. Chapman, pre-1926)
'Crimson Brand' hybrid
Perianth segments soft yellow; corona deep orange. AM(e) 1926

'Paraphrase' 2 (a)
(Konynenburg & Mark, pre-1954)

'Parasol' 1 Y-Y
(J.S. Leitch) J.S. Leitch, 1967
Fl. 111 mm wide

'Parata' 2 or 3 W-? (b or c)
(A. Miller, pre-1914)

'Parattah' 2 W-W
(C.E. Radcliff, 1929)
'Czarina' hybrid

'Parca' 1 Y-Y
(W. Jackson Sr, 1944)
'Yugao' × 'Principal'

'Parcival' 2 Y-O
(Konynenburg & Mark) Konynenburg & Mark, 1960
'Amy Belle' × ('Memphis' × 'Gladiator')
Fl. 90 mm wide; perianth segments vivid yellow 9B; corona strong orange 25A. Early

'Parcpat' 7 Y-O
(M.P. Williams, pre-1937)
2n=21

'Pardo' 2 W-? (b)
(R.H. Bath, pre-1931)

'Pardon' ?-P
(Alister Clark, pre-1948)

'Parfait' 3 W-? (b or c)
(pre-1870)

'Parfait' 4 W-P
(Murray W. Evans) Murray W. Evans, 1975
'Pink Chiffon' × 'Accent'; sdlg no. L-43/3
Fl. 100 mm wide. Early to mid-season

'Paricutin' 2 Y-R
(G.E. Mitsch, pre-1952)
'Klingo' × 'Ardour'
Perianth segments golden yellow; corona disc-shaped, bright red. Mid-season. See also 'Paracutin'

'Parigo' 3 W-YYO
(C.A. van Paridon) C.A. van Paridon, 1963
Fl. 106 mm wide; perianth segments ivory white; corona brilliant yellow 12B, with brilliant orange 29A at rim. Late. Resembles a less robust 'Selma Lagerl^f'

'Parilla' 2 (a)
(H.A. Brown, pre-1938)

'Paringa' 1 W-Y
(Jackson's Daffodils, 1980) Jackson's Daffodils, 1993
Sdlg 116/69? × 'Daric'?; sdlg no. 40/80
Fl. 110 mm wide; perianth segments broadly ovate, greenish white (155A); corona funnel-shaped,

brilliant greenish yellow 3B, with mouth flared. Mid-season to late

'Paris' 1 Y-Y
(R.H. Bath, pre-1915)
Fl. rich yellow; corona with rim flanged

'Paris' 2 W-W
(Alister Clark, pre-1950)

'Parisienne' 11a W-O
(J. Gerritsen & Son) J. Gerritsen & Son, 1961
'George's Pink' × 'Dailmanach'; sdlg no. 1/4/84
Fl. 100 mm wide; perianth segments very broadly ovate in outline, squarish or truncate at apex, fairly prominently mucronate, creamy white, reflexed, a little concave, overlapping one-third; the inner segments narrower, more rounded at apex, less strongly reflexed, with margins wavy or recurved; corona split to base, the six segments a quarter to one-third as long as the perianth segments and opposite and closely overlying them, very broad and overlapping, deeply bi-lobed, ribbed, orange, sometimes touched white or yellow at margins, heavily frilled. Mid-season. 2n=28. Resembles a more heavily frilled 'Professor Einstein'. AM(Haarlem) 1967

'Parkatiro' 1 Y-Y
Syn. of 'Paikatiro'

'Park Avenue' 4 W-P
(Brian S. Duncan) Rathowen Daffodils, 1987
Evans sdlg N-22/1 ('Pink Chiffon' × ['Rosegarland' × pink sdlg]) × 'Pink Pageant'; sdlg no. 931
Corona segments deep pink. Mid-season

'Park Beauty' 3 W-? (b)
(P.D. Williams, pre-1942)

'Park Bedder' 1 (a)
(J.E. Exley, pre-1937)

'Parkdene' 2 W-O
(T. Bloomer) Rathowen Daffodils, 1984
('Irish Charm' × sdlg 202) × 'Royal Regiment'; sdlg no. 373
Corona deep orange, with a paler tone at rim on opening. Tall. Mid-season. Resembles a taller and larger-flowered 'Irish Rover' and is more nearly sunproof

'Parkfields Beauty' 2 W-P
(Carncairn Daffodils) Carncairn Daffodils, 1989
('Easter Moon' × 'Rose Caprice') open pollinated; sdlg no. 1/18/76
Fl. 100 mm wide; perianth segments pure white, spreading, smooth, overlapping; corona funnel-shaped, clear pink. Mid-season

'Park Gate' 2 W-P
(Kate Reade) Carncairn Daffodils, 1996

'George's Pink' × 'Dailmanach'; sdlg no. 1/4/84
Fl. 101 mm wide; perianth segments broadly ovate, rounded at apex, slightly mucronate, spreading, plane, overlapping one-third; the inner segments narrower, more nearly acute, shouldered at base, a little inflexed; corona cylindrical, angled, pink, with mouth flared and lightly frilled. Mid-season

'Parkhill' 1 (a)
(G.H. Engleheart, pre-1916)

'Parkhill' 2 W-Y
(L.P. Brumley) T. Morrison, 1960
Fl. large; perianth segments smooth, of good substance; corona pale lemon yellow

'Parkia'
(pre-1915)

N. parkinsonii Steudel = *N.* × *incomparabilis*

'Parkinsonii'
Syn. of *N.* × *incomparabilis*

"Parkinson's Daffodil"
Syn. of 'Plenus Laciniis Pallidis'

'Park Lane' 1 W-P
(W.G. Pannill) W.G. Pannill, 1983
'Rima' × 'Salmon Trout'

'Parkmore' 2 W-W
(G.L. Wilson, pre-1945)
'Niphetos' × 'Scapa'
Fl. 121 mm wide; perianth segments smooth, overlapping; corona cylindrical, opening pale lemon, becoming white, with rim narrowly flanged and frilled. Early. Syn. 'Rona'. AM(e) 1947

'Parkridge' 2 W-R
(T. Bloomer) Rathowen Daffodils, 1984
('Irish Charm' × sdlg 202) × 'Royal Regiment'; sdlg no. 300
Corona deep orange-red. Mid-season. Resembles a larger and more consistent 'Royal Regiment'

'Parkrose' 2 W-P
(Murray W. Evans) Murray W. Evans, 1987
'Quasar' × 'Arctic Char'; sdlg no. V-11/1
Perianth segments pure white; corona expanded, reddish pink, with rim dentate. Mid-season. Resembles a larger and broader-flowered 'Arctic Char' with the perianth of purer white

'Park Royal' 2 Y-YYR
(A. Gibson, pre-1951)
PC(e)(NZ) 1953, AM(e)(NZ) 1957

'Park Springs' 3 W-WWY
(Mrs J. Abel Smith) Mrs J. Abel Smith, 1972

'Ethel' × 'Syracuse'
Fl. 95-105 mm wide, greenish white (155A); perianth segments very broadly ovate, rounded at apex, slightly mucronate, spreading, a little concave, smooth, overlapping half; the inner segments a little narrower, slightly inflexed, with margins wavy; corona shallow funnel-shaped, broad, ribbed, with a tinge of blue-green at base and with pale yellow 11C at rim, minutely frilled. 2n=29. PC(e) 1975, AM(e) 1976, FCC(e) 1979, FCC(e) 1980

'Parleon' 2 W-? (b)
(R.H. Bath, pre-1929)

'Parliament' 2 (a)
(D.W. Lefeber & Co., pre-1954)

'Parmelia' 1 W-W
(J.N.Hancock & Co., 1983) Unregistered
'Moonstruck' × 'Daydream'; sdlg no. 34/83H
Fl. greenish white; perianth segments of good substance, deeply overlapping; corona cylindrical, with rim rolled and dentate. Early to mid-season

'Parmenia' 9
(W.B. Hartland, pre-1907)

'Parnach' 2 W-P
(A.O. Roblin, 1957) Unregistered
'Roseum' hybrid

'Parnassus' 8 Y-Y
(pre-1851)

'Parnassus' 1 W-Y
(R.H. Bath, pre-1910)
Corona lemon yellow

'Parnassus' 4 W-W
(E.W. Cotter) E.W. Cotter, 1968
'Silver Rose' × 'Green Island'

'Parnell's Knob' 1 Y-Y
(W.A. Bender, 1969) W.A. Bender, 1990
'Arctic Gold' × 'Chemawa'; sdlg no. 1
Fl. 100 mm wide; perianth segments broadly ovate, vivid yellow 12A, spreading, smooth; corona funnel-shaped, darker in tone (14A) than the perianth. Early. Resembles 'Arctic Gold'

'Parody' 2 Y-W
(G.E. Mitsch) G.E. Mitsch, 1976
'Daydream' × 'Binkie'; sdlg no. F70/1
Fl. 100 mm wide; perianth segments pale lemon yellow, reflexed; corona opening pale lemon yellow, becoming near white. Mid-season

'Parole' 2 W-? (b)
(M.P. Williams) F.E. Board, 1956

'Parsifal' 2 or 3 W-Y
(The Brodie of Brodie, c.1915)
'Minnie Hume' × 'Cassandra'
Corona pale lemon yellow

'Parsifal' 2 W-R
(J.L. Richardson) Mrs H.K. Richardson, 1962
'Kilworth' × 'Arbar'; sdlg no. 245/10
Fl. 112 mm wide; perianth segments pure white; corona orange-scarlet, with rim dentate

'Parsonage' 2 YYW-PPY
(W.G.Pannill) W.G.Pannill, 1994
('Just So' × 'Daydream') × 'Soft Light'; sdlg no. 79/16/7
Perianth segments yellow, with a band of white at base; corona pink, with a band of yellow at rim. Mid-season

'Parson Jack' 1 Y-Y
(T. Buncombe, pre-1931)

'Parson's Chapel' 2 W-Y
(Curtis Tolley) Curtis Tolley, 1997
'April Love' × 'Churchman'; sdlg no. 89-11

'Parterre' 2 W-Y
(T. Bloomer) Rathowen Daffodils, 1983
?'My Love' hybrid; sdlg no. 220
Fl. 110 mm wide; perianth segments broadly ovate, reflexed; corona constricted near mid-point, lemon yellow. Mid-season

'Parth' 1 W-W
(P.D. Williams, pre-1927)
*C(g) 1927

'Parthenia' 3 W-? (b)
(J.M. de Navarro, pre-1949)
'Warlock' × 'Matapan'
Perianth segments very broad, mucronate, smooth, overlapping half; the inner segments oval; corona ribbed, mouth very widely expanded and a little frilled

'Parthenon' 4 W-O
(Mrs H.K. Richardson) Carncairn Daffodils, 1987
Sdlg no. 3626
Perianth and other petaloid segments yellowish white 155B; corona segments orange (28A), sometimes touched with yellow. Late. Resembles a more brightly coloured 'Acropolis'

'Parthia' 3 W-R
(J.L. Richardson) Mrs H.K. Richardson, 1962
'Kilworth' × 'Arbar'
Fl. 95 mm wide; perianth segments pure white; corona cherry red, with rim dentate

'Partner' ?-P
(Alister Clark, pre-1948)

'Partout' 2 W-Y
(E. Leeds, pre-1877)
Syn. Incomparabilis Albus 'Partout'. Was "absorbed" into 'Albert Victor'

'Partridge' 2 W-P
(G.E. Mitsch) G.E. Mitsch, 1970
'Leonaine' × 'Caro Nome'; sdlg no. Z28/10
Fl. rounded; perianth segments milk white; corona almost disc-shaped, closely ribbed, apricot salmon, heavily suffused with lavender, deeply frilled. Mid-season

'Party Doll' 4 W-P
(W.G. Pannill) W.G. Pannill, 1980
('Wild Rose' × 'Interim') × 'Magic'; sdlg no. 67/26
Fl. 80 mm wide. Mid-season

'Party Dress' 11a W-W
(A.N. Kanouse, 1958) A.N. Kanouse, 1976
'Hillbilly' × 'Mabel Taylor'
Fl. 100 mm wide; perianth segments cream ivory; corona segments darker than the perianth, with a lighter tone at rim, deeply ribbed and frilled. Mid-season. Resembles 'Square Dancer' in form

'Party Frock' 2 W-W
(D.S. Bell) D.S. Bell, 1975
'Ludlow' × 'Debonair'
Fl. 94 mm wide, pure white; corona wide-spreading, deeply frilled. Mid-season

'Party Girl' 4 W-YYP
(David L. Sheppard) David L. Sheppard, 1989
'Gay Song' × ('Accent' × 'Easter Bonnet')
Fl. 90 mm wide; perianth and other petaloid segments in 3-4 whorls, pure white; the outer whorl very broadly ovate, blunt, prominently mucronate, spreading, concave, overlapping half; the inner segments of this whorl a little narrower, more prominently mucronate; the second whorl inflexed, not much shorter, only very slightly mucronate; the inner whorls more strongly inflexed, no shorter than the second whorl, deeply concave or longitudinally folded, with margins wavy or crumpled; corona segments half as long as the second and inner whorls of petaloid segments and regularly arranged beneath them, broad, creamy yellow, with pink at rim, a little frilled, becoming crumpled at centre, more strongly inflexed and more deeply frilled. Late

'Party Pink' 2 W-P
(J.N. Hancock & Co., c.1980) Unregistered

'Party Time' 2 W-PPW
(Brian S.Duncan, 1986) Brian S.Duncan, 1997
'Roseate Tern' × 'Mentor'; sdlg no. 1310A
Fl. rounded, 102 mm wide; perianth segments broadly ovate, blunt, spreading; corona bowl-shaped, broad, opening bright apple blossom pink, the rim becoming white with tints of pink, mouth deeply or very deeply lobed. Mid-season to late. Variably Div. 11

'Parua' 12 Y-Y
(Robin Brown) Robin Brown, 1995
N. jonquilla var. *henriquesii* × *N. cyclamineus*; sdlg no. JH/C 3
Fls 2 per stem, 44 mm wide, mid-yellow, facing down; perianth segments reflexed; corona cylindrical, smooth, with mouth straight and lobed. Dwarf. Very early

'Parvati' 2 Y-O
(J.S. Leitch) J.S. Leitch, 1957

***N. parviflorus* (Jordan) Pugsley 13 Section Pseudonarcissus**

N. parvulus Sweet = *N. assoanus*

'Parwich' 2 (a)
(D.B. Milne, pre-1952)

'Pasadena' 2 W-? (b)
(J.S. Leitch) J.S. Leitch, 1957

'Pascali' 1 W-W
(G.L. Wilson) G.L. Wilson, 1966
(['White Sentinel' × 'Kanchenjunga'] × 'Greenland') × 'Rashee'

'Pasha' 2 Y-?
(A. Overton) A. Overton, 1960

'Passe Bazelman' 8 W-Y
(pre-1759)

'Passe Juno' 8 Y-Y
(pre-1798)
Fl. golden yellow

'Passe Soleil d'Or' 8 Y-Y
(pre-1807)

'Passetout' 8 Y-Y
(pre-1807)

'Passionale' 2 W-P
(G.L. Wilson) F.E. Board, 1956
'Rose of Tralee' × 'Irish Rose'
Fl. 102 mm wide; perianth segments broadly ovate, blunt, mucronate, spreading, plane or very slightly concave, smooth, overlapping half; the inner segments more narrowly ovate, acute, slightly inflexed; corona funnel-shaped, light yellowish pink 36B, mouth expanded, finely ribbed, a little frilled, rim slightly flanged, crenate. 2n=28. AM(e) 1957, *AM(g) 1963, *FCC(g) 1971, *FCC(p) 1976, AGM 1993

'Passport' 2 Y-YYO
(G.W.E. Brogden) G.W.E. Brogden, 1966
Fl. 102 mm wide; corona with a broad band of deep reddish orange at rim. Mid-season

'Pastel' 3 W-? (b)
(P.D. Williams, pre-1910)

'Pastel' 2 W-? (b)
(Mrs M.Moorby) Mrs M.Moorby, 1956

'Pastel Flare' 1 W-P
(Colin Crotty, 1986) Colin Crotty, 1996
'Telita' × 'Eclat'; sdlg no. 110-81
Fl. forming a double triangle, 105 mm wide; perianth segments ovate, slightly mucronate; corona funnel-shaped, yellowish pink, shading to pastel pink at rim, with mouth flared and frilled. Mid-season to late. Sunproof

'Pastel Gem' 2 Y-YPP
(G.E. Mitsch) G.E. Mitsch, 1975
'Leonaine' × 'Daydream'; sdlg no. F25/3
Fl. 94 mm wide; perianth segments pale lemon yellow; corona suffused with pink, paling to lemon yellow at base. Mid-season

'Pasteline' 2 W-P
(G.E. Mitsch) G.E. Mitsch, 1979
('Caro Nome' × 'Accent') × ('Precedent' × 'Carita'); sdlg no. G36/2
Fl. 96 mm wide; corona rich deep pink. Early to mid-season. Resembles an improved and slightly later-flowered 'Dawncrest'

'Pastel Pink' 2 Y-P
(D.S. Bell) D.S. Bell, 1964
? × ('White Sentinel' × 'Seraglio')
Fl. 103 mm wide; perianth segments broadly ovate, blunt, slightly mucronate, lemon yellow, a little inflexed, creased, overlapping half; the inner segments more strongly inflexed, with margins wavy or twisted; corona cylindrical, pink, with mouth widely expanded, rim rolled and very deeply notched and dentate. Mid-season

'Pastel Rose' 2 W-P
(W. Jackson Jr) W. Jackson Jr, 1968
'Nevana' × 'Dallbro'; sdlg no. 69/62

'Pasternak' 1 Y-GYY
(P.L.A. Pouw) P.L.A. Pouw, 1973
'Rembrandt' × 'Golden Sunbeam'
Fl. 110 mm wide

'Pastiche' 2 Y-YWW
(J.L. Richardson, 1976) Clive Postles Daffodils, 1986
'Golden Aura' × 'Daydream'; sdlg no. 891
Perianth segments broadly ovate, blunt, mucronate, smooth, overlapping half; the inner segments very slightly narrower; corona cup-shaped, expanded, loosely frilled. Mid-season

'Pastime' 1 Y-Y
(Murray W. Evans, 1972) Murray W. Evans, 1985
'Fine Gold' × ('Kingscourt' × 'Roundabout'); sdlg no. 0-23/1
Fl. mid-yellow; perianth segments very broad. Mid-season

'Pastorale' 2 Y-WWY
(G.E. Mitsch, pre-1954) G.E.Mitsch, 1965
'Binkie' × ('King of the North' × 'Content'); sdlg no. P5/3
Fl. 108 mm wide; perianth segments broad, pale lemon yellow, slightly reflexed, deeply overlapping; corona opening with a suffusion of buffy apricot, becoming sulphur white, with lemon yellow at rim. Mid-season. Resembles a taller 'Fawnglo' with a reflexed perianth

'Patabundy' 2 Y-R
(Brian S.Duncan) Rathowen Daffodils, 1987
'Patagonia' × 'Bunclody'; sdlg no. 701
Fl. forming a double triangle; perianth segments broadly ovate, blunt, slightly mucronate, deep golden yellow, spreading, a little concave, regular, overlapping half; the inner segments more nearly acute, angular at shoulder, with margins shallowly incurved; corona bowl-shaped, deep orange-red, with mouth straight, frilled. Mid-season. Resembles a sunproof and more consistent 'Bunclody'

'Patacake' 3 W-YYR
(Mrs R.O. Backhouse, pre-1921)
Perianth segments cream

'Patachou' 2 Y-O
(C.M. Grullemans) J.J. Grullemans & Sons, 1956
Perianth segments pale yellow; corona clear pale orange, with a darker tone at rim, frilled

'Patagonia' 2 Y-O
(J.L. Richardson) J.L. Richardson, 1956
'Narvik' × 'Sun Chariot'
Fl. 88 mm wide; perianth segments vivid yellow 9A, overlapping half; corona opening orange-yellow (17B), becoming strong orange 25A, with mouth expanded and rim crenate. 2n=28. *AM(g) 1968

'Patching' 3 W-? (b)
(Sir F.C. Stern, pre-1947)

'Patchit' 3 W-OOR
(P. Phillips) P. Phillips, 1978
Fl. 98 mm wide; perianth segments somewhat reflexed, smooth and of good substance; corona with a broad band of bright red at rim, mouth expanded and frilled. Mid-season

'Pateena' 1 W-?
(K.J. Heazlewood) K.J. Heazlewood, 1970
'Lanena' × 'Bon Rose'

N. patellaris Salisbury = *N. poeticus* var. *majalis*

'Patellaris'
Syn. of *N. poeticus* var. *majalis*

'Patellaris Pleno Albo Cum Croceo' 4 W-YYR
Syn. of Poeticus 'Plenus'

'Pathan' 2 Y-O
(A.M. Wilson, pre-1944)
'Seraglio' × 2 Y-R
Perianth segments overlapping; corona deep reddish orange

'Pathfinder' 2 W-R
(G.H. Johnstone, pre-1944)
'Damson' × 2 W-R

'Patience' 3 W-? (b)
(Sir C.H. Cave, pre-1908)

'Patience' 2 W-?
(C.O. Fairbairn) C.O. Fairbairn, 1960

'Patmos' 1 W-? (b)
(The Brodie of Brodie, *c.*1919)
'Mrs Ernst H.Krelage' × 'Nevis'

'Patois' 9 W-GYR
(Brian S. Duncan) Brian S. Duncan, 1992
'Perdita'? × 'Lisbane'; sdlg no. 1247
Fl. rounded, 78 mm wide; perianth segments very broad in outline, blunt or rounded at apex, prominently mucronate, spreading, plane or concave, overlapping half or more; the inner segments a little narrower, roundish, not obviously mucronate, slightly inflexed; corona broad disc-shaped, closely ribbed, greenish yellow, with green at base and a narrow band of orange-red at rim, mouth split in places and overlapping, wavy, rim minutely notched. Late to very late. Sunproof. AM(e) 1996

'Pat Pittle' 2 W-Y
(L.P. Dettman) L.P. Dettman, 1974
'Chartwell' open pollinated
Fl. 99 mm wide

'Patra' 2 Y-YYO
(J.N. Hancock & Co., 1963) Unregistered

'Patria' 1 W-Y
(Warnaar & Co., pre-1938)
Fl. 121 mm wide; perianth segments creamy white, slightly twisted, overlapping half; corona vivid yellow 9A, with mouth widely expanded and frilled, rim flanged and dentate. Dwarf. AM(Haarlem) 1938, *AM(g) 1956

'Patriarch' 2 W-O
(J.W.A. Lefeber, pre-1945)
Corona shallow, tangerine orange, with mouth frilled

'Patricia' 1 W-W
(J.W. Barr, pre-1930)

'Patricia' 2 W-R
(R.H.Glover, pre-1993) Unregistered

'Patricia' 4 W-R
(Murray W. Evans) Unregistered
Selection from Poeticus 'Plenus'

'Patricia Craig' 2 (a)
(van Zonnefeld Bros & Philippo, pre-1930)

'Patricia Dyson' 2 Y-O
(L. Buckland, pre-1933)

'Patricia Elbert' 1 W-? (b)
(W.F.M. Copeland, pre-1926)

'Patrician' 2 W-? (b or c)
(E.M. Crosfield, pre-1930)

'Patrician' 2 Y-Y
(G.E. Mitsch) G.E. Mitsch, 1974
'Galway' × 'Saint Keverne'; sdlg no. A17/8
Fl. 108 mm wide; perianth segments golden yellow; corona funnel-shaped, slightly deeper in tone than the perianth. Mid-season

'Patricia Reynolds' 1 W-P
(B. Reynolds, 1940) B.Reynolds, 1963
'Le Voleur' × 'Pucelle'
Fl. 102 mm wide; perianth segments smooth; corona narrow, light pink. Mid-season. Resembles 'Penvose' but with a paler corona

'Patrick O'Hagen' 2 Y-O
(Tom Forster, 1960s) Unregistered
Perianth segments soft lemon yellow; corona very broad disc-shaped, apricot orange. Tall. Mid-season

'Patriot' 1 W-? (b)
(W. Welchman, pre-1908)

'Patriot' 2 (a)
(Alister Clark, pre-1939)

'Patroclus'
(Barr & Sons, pre-1915)

'Patrol' 6 Y-R
(P. Phillips) P. Phillips, 1968

'Patron' 2 (a)
(P.D. Williams, pre-1932)

'Patsy' 5
(J.W. Barr, pre-1930)

'Patsy' 1 Y-Y
(Sir F.C. Stern) Sir F.C. Stern, 1960
'Tanagra' × *N. atlanticus*
Fl. pale yellow. Early

'Patterdale' 1 W-W
(G.L. Wilson) E. Longford, 1965
('Nilkanta' × 'Murmansk') × 'Knowehead'
Fl. 108 mm wide; corona tinged green. Resembles 'Chamonix' but with larger perianth segments

'Pattern' 2 W-? (b)
(Alister Clark, pre-1950)

N. patulus **(Loiseleur-Deslongchamps) Baker 13 Section Tazettae**

paucinervis = *N. bulbocodium* subsp. *praecox* var. *paucinervis*

'Paudeen' 1 (a)
(J. Bankhead, pre-1950)

'Paul' 3 W-? (b)
(J. Taylor, pre-1937)

'Paula' 2 W-O
(C.E. Radcliff, 1930)
'Warflame' × 'Ruby'
Corona almost disc-shaped, apricot orange

'Paula Cottell' 3 W-GWW
(A. Gray) A. Gray, 1961
'Samaria' hybrid
Fl. 50 mm wide; perianth segments milk white, of strong substance, overlapping; corona small, creamy white. Dwarf. Late. Scented

'Paula's Mite' 3 W-O
(T.H. Piper, 1945)
'Paula' × 'White Cheerio'

'Paul Bunyan' 1 Y-Y
(G.E. Mitsch, pre-1952)
'Aerolite' × 'Kandahar'; sdlg no. 38C6/1
Perianth segments broad, overlapping; corona with mouth expanded and rim flanged

'Paul Engleheart' 1 W-Y
(W. Backhouse, pre-1869)
Perianth segments sulphur white; corona slender, primrose yellow. Resembles 'Mrs J.B.M.Camm'. Syn. Pseudonarcissus Moschatus 'Paul Engleheart'. ?Syn. of 'Mrs J.B.M.Camm'

'Paulette' 3 W-? (b or c)
(Barr & Sons, pre-1923)
'Maggie May' × *N. poeticus* var. *recurvus*

'Paul Gubranssen' 2 W-O
(J.W.A. Lefeber, pre-1948) J.W.A.Lefeber, 1960
Fl. 80 mm wide; perianth segments pure white; corona reddish orange. Mid-season. Sunproof

'Paulhan' 3 W-YYO
(?Barr & Sons, pre-1913)
Corona widely expanded, clear lemon yellow, with fiery reddish orange at rim

'Pauline' 2 W-O
(West & Fell, pre-1935)
Perianth segments creamy white; corona expanded, orange

'Pauline Frances' 4 Y-Y
(Brian S.Duncan) R.A.Brand, 1993
'Smokey Bear' × 'Sportsman'; sdlg no. 984
Fl. 105 mm wide; perianth segments deep golden yellow; corona segments deep orange gold. Early to mid-season

'Paulinia' 3 W-? (b)
(C. Dawson, pre-1916)

'Paul M.Davis' 2 (a)
(The Brodie of Brodie, pre-1931)

'Paul Rubens' 1 (a)
(Konynenburg & Mark, pre-1953)

'Pavallion' 2 Y-R
(G.J.Phillips, 1975) G.J.Phillips, 1994
'True Orbit' × 'Everglaze'; sdlg no. 70-15-1
Fl. 107 mm wide; perianth segments broadly ovate; corona funnel-shaped, with mouth a little flared and rim almost entire. Mid-season

'Pavane' 3 (a)
(F.H. Chapman, pre-1930)

'Pavane' 2 W-? (b)
(F. Rijnveld & Sons) F. Rijnveld & Sons, 1956
AM(Haarlem) 1956

'Pavlova' 2 W-YYR
(J.W. Barr, pre-1928)
Corona with a broad band of orange-scarlet at rim

'Pavlova' 4 W-Y
(Unknown origin) Lady Cory-Wright, 1959
95 mm wide; corona segments deep yellow. Mid-season

'Pawley's Island' 2 W-YYP
(Brian S.Duncan) Brian S.Duncan, 1995

'Pismo Beach' × 'High Society'; sdlg no. 1263
Fl. forming a double triangle, 102 mm wide; perianth segments very broadly ovate, blunt, slightly mucronate, smooth, spreading; the inner segments more narrowly ovate, angled at shoulder, a little inflexed, with margins wavy; corona short funnel-shaped, deep lemon yellow, with a very broad band of deep apple blossom or peach pink at rim, mouth straight, shallowly 6-lobed, slightly frilled. Mid-season to late

'Pawnee' 1 W-Y
(E.C. Powell, pre-1946)
'Nevis' × 'Bodilly'

'Pawtella' 3 W-? (b)
(W. Jackson Jr, 1953)
'Gyda' × 'Ethni'

'Pawtella' 1 W-P
(K.J. Heazlewood, c.1967) Unregistered
'Rosedale' × 'Pink Bonnington'

'Pax' 2 W-Y
(Mrs R.O. Backhouse, pre-1916)
Corona large, primrose yellow, flushed apricot pink

'Pax' 1 W-W
(A.O. Roblin, pre-1950)
'Zamira' × 'National'

'Paxeen' 1 W-W
(A.O. Roblin, 1947)
'Zamira' × 'National'

'Pay Day' 1 YYW-W
(Elise Havens) G.E. Mitsch, 1976
'Royal Oak' × 'Daydream'; sdlg no. GEJ9/1
Fl. 105 mm wide; perianth segments very broadly ovate, blunt, lemon yellow, with prominent white mucro and with a band of white at base, spreading, plane, overlapping half; the inner segments square-shouldered at base, a little inflexed; corona funnel-shaped, lightly ribbed, opening lemon yellow, becoming white, with mouth flared and more strongly ribbed, frilled, with rim notched and crenate. Late

'Paynim' 1 (a)
(G.L. Wilson, pre-1931)

'P.B.F.' 1 W-? (b)
(pre-1913)

'P.C.Hooft' 2 (a)
(P. van Deursen, pre-1930)

'P.D.'s Seedling'
(P.D. Williams, pre-1913)
Perianth segments tinged pink

'Peabody' 1 W-Y
(W. Backhouse, pre-1869)
Dwarf. Syn. Pseudonarcissus Bicolor 'Peabody'. Was "absorbed" into 'William Robinson'

'Peace' 3 W-? (b or c)
(C. Dawson, pre-1913)

'Peace' 2 W-W
(G.W.E. Brogden) M.E. Brogden, 1959

'Peaceful' 5
(J.W. Barr, pre-1930)

'Peaceful' 2 W-OOY
(G.E. Mitsch, 1960) G.E. Mitsch, 1975
'Artist's Model' × 'Blarney's Daughter'; sdlg no. V1/1
Fl. 94 mm wide; perianth segments milk white; corona bowl-shaped, salmon orange, with yellow at rim. Mid-season

'Peacemaker' 1 W-GWW
(G.H. Johnstone, 1949) G.H.Johnstone, 1959
'Silver Wedding' × 'Kanchenjunga'
Fl. 108 mm wide. Mid-season

'Peace Pipe' 1 W-Y
(Murray W. Evans) Murray W. Evans, 1969
'Effective' hybrid; sdlg no. C-173

'Peach' 3 W-O
(G.H. Engleheart, pre-1897)
Sdlg no. 93
Fl. star-shaped; perianth segments ovate, spreading, some with margins wavy, separated; corona deep cup-shaped, ribbed, apricot orange, paler at base, mouth straight and loosely frilled. Mid-season

'Peach Circle' 9 W-GGP
(Mrs M.S.Yerger) Mrs M.S.Yerger, 1994
'Pinkie' × 'Doily'; sdlg no. 84 G 7
Corona almost disc-shaped, light yellow-green 154D, with a band of light yellowish pink 27A at rim. Dwarf. Very early

'Peaches and Cream' 2 W-YOP
(Oregon Bulb Farms, pre-1950)

'Peaches and Cream' 2 W-O
(Dutch origin, 1975) Unregistered
Mid-season

'Peach Garter' 3 W-WOW
(W.G.Pannill, 1980) W.G.Pannill, 1993
'Silken Sails' × 'Ariel'; sdlg no. 11/93
Corona orange, with white at base and rim. Mid-season

'Peach Melba' 11a Y-O
Syn. of 'Peche Melba'

'Peach Petal' 2 W-P
(H.A. Brown, pre-1949)
Corona creamy white, flushed pink

'Peach Pink' 4 W-P
(D.S. Bell) D.S. Bell, 1983

'Peach Prince' 4 W-O
(Murray W. Evans, 1975) Murray W. Evans, 1985
'Pink Chiffon' × (['Siam' × 'Radiation'] × 'Cordial');
sdlg no. Q-28
Corona segments rich apricot orange. Mid-season

'Peach Seedling'
(H.G. Hawker, pre-1914)

'Peach Tip'
(pre-1913)

'Peach 'Un'' 1 W-P
(J.M.Radcliff) P.J. & K.P.Radcliff, 1993
Sdlg no. 11/93
Fl. forming a double triangle; perianth segments broadly ovate, clear white, smooth, deeply overlapping; corona funnel-shaped, light yellowish pink 27A, with rim flanged. Mid-season. Sunproof

'Peacock' 2 W-WWP
(W.G. Pannill) W.G. Pannill, 1972
'Green Island' × 'Accent'
Fl. 97 mm wide

'Peal o' Bells' 1 W-W
(Mrs R.O. Backhouse, pre-1921)

'Pearl' 3 W-O
(W. Backhouse, pre-1869)
Corona widely expanded, rich yellow, suffused orange. Resembles 'Mary'. Syn. Burbidgei 'Pearl'

'Pearl' 2
(G. Zeestraten, pre-1916)

'Pearl' 3 W-W
(pre-1950)
Corona faintly tinged lemon yellow

"Pearl"
Syn. of 'White Pearl'

'Pearlax' 11a W-Y
Syn. of 'Perlax'

'Pearl Buck' 2 W-W
(C.G. van Tubergen, pre-1948)

'Pearl Diver' 2 or 3 W-? (b or c)
(C. Dawson, pre-1908)

'Pearl Drift' 11a W-W
(Colin Crotty) Colin Crotty, 1996
'Ice Crystal' open pollinated; sdlg no. 10-88
Fl. 97 mm wide; perianth segments broadly ovate; the inner segments smaller and more nearly acute; corona deeply split, the six segments opposite the perianth segments and fairly closely overlying them, opening pale yellow, becoming pure white, the rim deeply lobed and slightly inflexed. Early to mid-season

'Pearl Harbor' 1 W-W
(G.L. Wilson, pre-1952)
'Corinth' × 'Kanchenjunga'; sdlg no. 25/73

'Pearlie' 5 W-W
(Hilda M.C.Jeffrey) Hilda M.C.Jeffrey
'Hawera' open pollinated
Fl. 55 mm wide, milk white; perianth with the inner segments broader than the outer; corona funnel-shaped, with mouth a little flared, rim slightly crenate. Dwarf. Late

'Pearlite' 2 W-? (b or c)
(J. Mallender, pre-1913)

'Pearl Maiden' 5
(Cartwright & Goodwin, pre-1916)

'Pearl Maiden' 3 W-? (b or c)
(L. Buckland, pre-1936)

'Pearl of Dawn' 3 (a)
(Mrs R.O. Backhouse, pre-1921)

'Pearl of Dew' 5 W-W
(The Brodie of Brodie, c.1910)
'Albatross' × *N. triandrus* var. *loiseleurii*; sdlg no. 730/A/05
Fl. glistening white; corona very large, almost disc-shaped. Resembles 'Ariadne' in the form of corona

'Pearl of Gauja' 4 W-Y
(Vitauts Skuja) Vitauts Skuja, 1996
'Pink Paradise' × 'Coral Ribbon'
Fl. 85 mm wide; perianth and other petaloid segments pure white; corona segments interspersed, pale orange-yellow 16D. Late

'Pearl of Kent' 1 W-W
(G.P. Haydon, pre-1906)
'Monarch' × 'Madame de Graaff'
Corona frilled. AM 1906

'Pearl Pastel' 2 W-P
(G.E. Mitsch) G.E. Mitsch, 1972
('Mabel Taylor' × 'Green Island') × 'Caro Nome'; sdlg no. Y43/2
Fl. rounded, 95 mm wide; corona very shallow bowl-shaped, light lemon, shaded with pinkish lavender

'Pearl Round' 2 W-GYY
(J.N. Hancock & Co., 1975) Unregistered

"Pearls"
Collective name for numerous slight variants of 'White Pearl'

'Pearl Schubert' 2 W-Y
(L.P. Dettman) L.P. Dettman, 1972
'Content' open pollinated
Fl. 91 mm wide

'Pearlshell' 11a W-P
(J. Gerritsen & Son) J. Gerritsen & Son, 1969
'Cassata' × 'Poesy'
Perianth segments broadly ovate, somewhat reflexed, overlapping; the inner segments narrower; corona split to base, the six segments about half as long as the perianth segments, opposite to them and joined at margins at base, opening yellow, becoming yellowish pink, ageing to white, spreading or reflexed, frilled. Mid-season to late

'Pearl Wedding' 3 W-WWY
(Mrs J. Abel Smith, 1979) Mrs J. Abel Smith, 1990
'Troutbeck' hybrid; sdlg no. W44/31
Fl. 91 mm wide. Late

'Pearly Dawn' 2 W-P
(J.N. Hancock & Co., 1965) Unregistered
Sdlg no. 87/65H

'Pearly Gem' 2 W-W
(J.T. Gray, pre-1950)

'Pearly King' 1 W-W
(W.A. Noton, pre-1983) Unregistered

'Pearly Queen' 5 W-Y
(de Graaff Bros, pre-1927)
Perianth segments ovate, acute, prominently mucronate, creamy white; corona lemon yellow, with a pearl-like flush, rim notched and crenate. AM(Haarlem) 1930

'Peart' 9 W-GYO
(Murray W. Evans, 1966) Murray W. Evans, 1987
'Milan' × *N. poeticus* var. *recurvus* × 'Carolina'; sdlg no. N-30
Perianth segments roundish, smooth; corona disc-shaped, with reddish orange at rim. Mid-season. Resembles a smoother-flowered 'Milan' of improved quality

'Peaseblossom' 7 Y-Y
(A. Gray, pre-1938)
N. assoanus × *N. triandrus*
See also 'Pease-blossom'

'Pease-blossom' 7 Y-Y
Syn. of 'Peaseblossom'

'Pebble Mill' 1 W-W
(Clive Postles, 1986) Clive Postles Daffodils, 1996
'White Convention' × 'Croila'; sdlg no. 1-18A-82
Fl. forming a double triangle, 115 mm wide; perianth segments ovate, with margins slightly incurved; corona cylindrical, with mouth flared and even. Early

'Pebbles' 2 Y-O
(J.S. Leitch) J.S. Leitch, 1968

'Peblo' 2 Y-O
(J.S. Leitch) J.S. Leitch, 1956

'Peche Melba' 11a Y-O
(J. Gerritsen & Son) J. Gerritsen & Son, 1963
Fl. 90 mm wide; perianth segments light greenish yellow 4C; corona segments two-thirds the length of the perianth segments, ribbed, near to vivid orange-yellow 21A, usually deeply 3-lobed, frilled; a single very narrow extra growth between each corona segment at base. Mid-season to late. Syn. 'Peach Melba

'Pecousic' 1 W-W
(E.C. Powell, pre-1946)
'Mrs Ernst H.Krelage' × 'Winsome'

'Pedestal' 2 W-Y
(E.M. Crosfield, pre-1908)
Perianth segments slender, acute, creamy white, a little ribbed, overlapping one-third; corona rich yellow, with mouth slightly expanded and rim lightly crenate. AM 1912

'Pedlar' 2 W-? (b)
(P.D. Williams, pre-1932)

'Pedro' 1 Y-Y
(P.D. Williams, pre-1927)

'Pedrocita' 2 (a)
(Mrs R.S. Cobley, pre-1937)

pedunculatus = *N. cuatrecasasii*

'Peekaboo' 2 Y-Y
(J.N.Hancock & Co., 1983) Unregistered
Sdlg 8A/76H × 'Artist's Model'; sdlg no. 60/83H
Fl. rounded; perianth segments mid-yellow, glistening; corona expanded, orange-yellow. Early

'Peekoa' 2 Y-R
(J.S. Leitch) J.S. Leitch, 1956

'Peep-Bo' 3 W-? (b)
(G.H. Johnstone, pre-1944)
'Capri' hybrid
2n=14

'Peeping Tom' 6 Y-Y
(P.D. Williams, pre-1948)
N. cyclamineus sdlg?
Fl. 95 mm wide; perianth segments ovate, brilliant yellow 7A, with white mucro, reflexed, finely ribbed, twisted, regular, overlapping up to a quarter; corona cylindrical, narrow, smooth, sometimes slightly constricted at mid-point, much deeper than vivid yellow 12A, paling slightly towards base, mouth ribbed, expanded, obscurely 6-lobed, rim flanged and strongly crenate. Early. 2n=21. Resembles an earlier-flowered 'Bartley'. AM(Haarlem) 1955, *FCC(p) 1976, AGM 1995, Wister Award 1996

'Peep o' Dawn' 1 W-Y
(G.H. Engleheart, pre-1931)
Perianth segments pale creamy white; corona deep primrose yellow, flushed pink

'Peep of Spring' 11a Y-Y
(J. Gerritsen & Son) J. Gerritsen & Son, 1969
'Peeping Tom' × 'Gold Collar'

'Peeress' 1 W-Y
(G.L. Wilson, pre-1935)
'Weardale Perfection' hybrid × 'Carmel'
Corona pale lemon or primrose

'Peer Gynt' 1 Y-Y
(Oregon Bulb Farms, pre-1946)

'Peerless' 8
(Mrs R.O. Backhouse, pre-1921)
AM(Haarlem) 1929

'Peerless' 1 W-Y
(D.V. West, pre-1927)

'Peerless' 2 or 3 W-W
(Australian origin, pre-1937)

"Peerless Daffodil"
See "The Peerless Daffodil"

'Peerless Gold' 1 Y-Y
(G.B. van Rhijn, pre-1937)
AM(Haarlem) 1948

'Peerless Rose' 1 W-P
(C.A. van der Wereld) C.A. van der Wereld, 1968
Fl. 102 mm wide; perianth segments creamy white; corona light yellow 21D, flushed pink, with darker yellow at base and paler yellow (18B) outside

'Pegarah' 2 W-Y
(S.J. Bisdee, 1946)
'Saint Kilian' × 'Courtship'
Corona shallow

'Pegasus' 2 W-? (b)
(Mrs R.O. Backhouse, pre-1921)

'Peg Fraser' 2 Y-Y
(L.P. Dettman) L.P. Dettman, 1978
'Chartwell' × 'Binkie'; sdlg no. 3/73 TT3a 3R
Fl. 81 mm wide; perianth segments light greenish yellow 5D; corona slightly darker in tone (5C). Early. Resembles a paler 'Binkie'

'Peggi' 3 W-YYO
Syn. of 'Peggy'

'Peggie' 2 Y-Y
(R. Gibson, pre-1927)
Perianth segments yellow; corona rich yellow

'Peggotty' 3 W-? (b)
(A.M. Wilson, pre-1913)

'Peggy' 3 W-YYO
(P.D. Williams, pre-1927)
Perianth segments creamy white; corona with yellow-orange at rim, frilled. Tall. AM(Haarlem) 1930. See also 'Peggi'

'Peggy' 3 ?-?O (a or b)
(Sir J.S. Arkwright, pre-1935)

'Peggy' 2 (a)
Syn. of 'Peggy Briscoe'

'Peggy Bauer' 3 W-? (b)
(Mrs R.O. Backhouse, pre-1921)

'Peggy Briscoe' 2 (a)
(Mrs R.O. Backhouse, pre-1921)
Formerly named 'Peggy'

'Peggy Dettman' 2 W-P
(H.T. Dettmann) L.P. Dettman, 1970
Perianth segments broadly ovate, pure white, of good substance; corona deep strawberry pink, with mouth expanded and rim dentate

'Peggy Gordon Taylor' 2 W-? (b)
(W.A. Watts, pre-1936)

'Peggy Low' 5 W-Y
(L.P. Dettman) L.P. Dettman, 1979
'Laura' hybrid; sdlg no. 1M-76
Fl. 55 mm wide; perianth segments ice white, reflexed; corona cup-shaped, brilliant yellow 9C, with mouth somewhat constricted. Mid-season. Resembles a larger 'Laura' with the perianth segments less strongly reflexed

'Peggy O'Shea' 2 Y-Y
(J.N. Hancock & Co., 1962) Unregistered
Fl. golden yellow

'Peggy Pelcher' 2 W-?
(H.T. Dettmann) H.T.Dettmann, 1960

'Peggy Pritchard' 3 W-O
(F.R.Coles) F.R.Coles, 1997
'Mrs David Calvert' open pollinated
Resembles a larger-flowered 'Mrs David Calvert' with the perianth of firmer texture

'Peggy White' 2 W-W
(W.G. Pannill, 1980) W.G. Pannill, 1990
'Easter Moon' × 'Cataract'; sdlg no. 74/41 P
Perianth segments broadly ovate, blunt, only very slightly mucronate, a little reflexed, plane, deeply overlapping; the inner segments spreading, with margins wavy; corona cylindrical, broadly ribbed, mouth a little flared, even, rim minutely crenate. Mid-season

'Peg's Memory' 2 W-P
(L.P.Dettman, 1975) Unregistered
'Peggy Dettman' × 'Pink Treasure'; sdlg no. PP 1/76

'Peg's Pride' 2 Y-Y
(Barr & Sons) T.M. Dorrien Smith, 1969

'Peiping' 2 Y-O
(J.L. Richardson, pre-1939)
'Carbineer' × 'Porthilly'
Perianth segments bright yellow; corona tangerine orange, frilled

'Pekin' 3 W-?
(de Graaff Bros, pre-1935)
Syn. 'Peking'

'Peking' 1 Y-Y
(G. Lubbe & Son, pre-1947)
Fl. large, soft lemon yellow. AM(Haarlem) 1947, FA(Haarlem) 1949

'Peking' 2 W-P
Syn. of 'Siam'

'Peking' 3 W-?
Syn. of 'Pekin'

'Peking' 11b W-O/W
(J.W.A. Lefeber, pre-1991) Unregistered
Perianth segments very broad, prominently mucronate, yellowish white, a little inflexed, concave, overlapping half or more; corona segments two-thirds the length of the perianth segments and alternate to them, with light orange at base and in a longitudinal band to apex, flanked by white, margins wavy or incurling; some short extra growths at overlap of corona segments. Syn. 'Anna Floor'

'Peko' 3 W-YYR
(H.A. Brown, 1941)

'Pekon' 9
(A.M. Wilson, pre-1929)

'Pelayo' 1 Y-Y
(Spanish origin)
Selection by Peter Barr (1888) from wild-collected *N. × johnstonii*

'Peleon' 1 (a)
(pre-1939)

'Pelican' 3 Y-O
(Mrs R.O. Backhouse, pre-1921)
Perianth segments primrose; corona reddish orange. AM(g)(c) 1922

'Pelion' 1 Y-Y
(The Brodie of Brodie, c.1917)
'Don Juan' × 'Cleopatra'

'Pella' 2 W-YYO
(S.J. Bisdee, 1939)
'Waratah' × 'Cheerio'

'Pelleas' 3 W-YYR
(de Graaff Bros, pre-1934)
Perianth segments broad, glistening white

'Pelopidas' 1 W-? (b)
(de Graaff Bros, pre-1927)

'Pelops' 3 W-? (b)
(W.B. Hartland, pre-1907)

'Pelorus' 2 Y-O
(S.C. Gaspar, 1951) R.J. Abernethy, 1961
Fl. 89 mm wide; perianth segments clear yellow; corona reddish orange. Mid-season

'Pelsen' 1 Y-Y
(P. Phillips) P. Phillips, 1966
Fl. 108 mm wide, sulphur yellow. Mid-season. Resembles 'Kanga' in form but not colour

'Pelynt' 3 W-O
(Brian S. Duncan) du Plessis Bros, 1989
'Kildrum' × 'Rockall'; sdlg no. 374
Fl. 102 mm wide; perianth segments ovate, pure white; corona pure orange, with mouth lightly frilled. Late. Resembles 'Rockall' but with a differently coloured corona

'Pem' 2 W-YOR
(W. Jackson Jr, 1969) Unregistered
'Glenburvie' × 'Arbar'; sdlg no. 67/69

'Pembraze' 1 Y-Y
(M.P. Williams, pre-1937)
Fl. dark yellow

'Pembridge' 2 W-R
(A.M.Wilson, c.1930)
Perianth segments creamy white; corona red

'Pembroke' 3 Y-R
(Mrs R.O. Backhouse, pre-1921)
Perianth segments pale yellow, overlapping; corona expanded, rich red

'Penalewey' 2 W-WWY
Syn. of 'Penelewey'

'Penamint' 3 W-? (b)
(de Graaff Bros)
'Glad Boy' × 'John Evelyn'

'Penang' 2 (a)
(G.C. Graham, pre-1949)

'Penara' 2 Y-R
(J.T. Gray, pre-1949)
Perianth segments golden yellow; corona bright red

'Penare' 8
(P.D. Williams, pre-1927)

'Penarth' 2 Y-Y
(R.V. Favell, pre-1939)
'Havelock' × 'Sulphur'

'Penbeagle' 2 Y-Y
(P.D. Williams, pre-1938)
Fl. deep yellow; perianth segments broadly ovate, blunt, mucronate, with margins sometimes incurving near apex, overlapping one-third; the inner segments narrower, often recurved at apex, with margins a little wavy or incurving; corona large, funnel-shaped, lightly ribbed, rim widely flanged and deeply crenate

'Penbearth' 1 Y-Y
Syn. of 'Genuine'

'Penberth' 1 Y-Y
(R.V. Favell, pre-1937)
Fl. 115 mm wide; perianth segments broadly ovate, slightly mucronate, brilliant yellow 12B, inflexed, plane or with margins sometimes incurling, overlapping one-third; the inner segments narrower, more strongly inflexed, twisted; corona cylindrical at base, flared in upper half, smooth, slightly darker in tone (12A) than the perianth, with mouth expanded and 6-lobed, rim rolled and crenate. *HC(g) 1952

'Pencarrow' 2 Y-R
(G. Lewis) D.S. Bell, 1955

'Pencoys' 2 Y-YOO
(P.D. Williams, pre-1936)
Sdlg no. 690

Perianth segments primrose yellow; corona expanded, reddish orange, paling to golden yellow at base

'Pencrau' 2 Y-R
(Mrs C.O. Fairbairn)

'Pencrebar' 4 Y-Y
(H.G. Hawker, pre-1929)
? *N. jonquilla* sdlg
Fls often 2 per stem; perianth and other petaloid segments in 3-4 whorls, vivid yellow 12A; the outer segments in each whorl with prominent white mucro; the outer whorl broadly ovate, truncate, spreading; the inner segments of this whorl a little more narrowly ovate, blunt; the inner whorls inflexed, becoming successively more strongly inflexed towards centre, where they are concave; corona segments shorter than the petaloid segments and interspersed among them, slightly darker in tone (13A), with margins tightly rolled inwards. Scented. 2n=14

'Penda' 2 W-? (b)
(W. Welchman, pre-1929)

'Pendant' 1 W-Y
(A.G. Thompson) A.G. Thompson, 1961
Fl. 115 mm wide, facing down; perianth segments pale creamy white; corona clear yellow. Mid-season. Resembles 'Lapford' but with an improved corona

'Pendeen' 2 Y ? (a)
(The Brodie of Brodie, pre-1930)
'Beacon' hybrid × 'Fortune'

'Pendeford Apricot'
(pre-1927)

'Pendennis' 2 Y-Y
(P.D. Williams, pre-1932)
Resembles a larger and slightly paler 'Penbeagle'

'Pendennis' 3 Y-R
(G. Lewis, pre-1945)

'Pend Oreille' 3 W-Y
(R. & E. Havens, 1982) R. & E. Havens, 1993
'Silken Sails' × 'Verona'; sdlg no. REH45/1
Fl. rounded, 110 mm wide, smooth and of heavy substance; perianth segments very broadly ovate, spreading, plane, smooth; corona cup-shaped, opening butterscotch yellow, becoming whitish yellow, with mouth slightly wavy. Mid-season

'Pendragon' 2 (a)
(Mrs R.S. Cobley, pre-1932)

'Pendrathen' 2 (a)
(A. Gray) T.M. Dorrien Smith, 1956

'Penelewey' 2 W-WWY
(P.D. Williams, pre-1927)
Corona creamy, with golden yellow at rim. AM(e) 1927. See also 'Penalewey'

'Penelope' 2 W-? (b or c)
(H.Backhouse, pre-1914)

'Penelope Aitken' 2 W-W
(Lord Headfort, pre-1954)

'Pengarth' 2 YYW-WWY
(Brian S.Duncan) Dan du Plessis, 1996
'Milestone' open pollinated 'Lunar Sea' open pollinated; sdlg no. 765
Fl. 86 mm wide; perianth segments broadly ovate, deep lemon yellow, with white at base, slightly reflexed; corona opening yellow, quickly becoming white, with lemon yellow at rim, slightly frilled. Early

'Pengelley' 2 W-Y
(P.D. Williams, pre-1927)
Corona buff yellow

'Penghana' 1 W-P
(R.J. Ralph, 1946)
'Pink o' Dawn' × 'Mrs R.O.Backhouse'

'Pengornin' 2 W-Y
(R.V. Favell, 1939) R.M.Favell, 1965
Fl. 102 mm wide; corona pale cream yellow. Mid-season

'Penguin' 2 W-Y
(C. Dawson, pre-1907)
Corona creamy primrose yellow, neatly frilled

'Penguin' 2 W-W
(C.E. Radcliff) D.H. Butcher, 1979
'Easter Moon' × 'Empress of Ireland'; sdlg no. 8/68
Fl. 125 mm wide. Mid-season

'Penguin' 4 W-O
Syn. of 'Chukar'

'Penguin' 2 W-Y
(Heathcote Bulb Nursery, pre-1960) Unregistered
Perianth segments pure white, of good substance; corona large, clear lemon yellow

'Penhallick' 3 W-? (b)
(The Brodie of Brodie, c.1927)
'Harpagon' × 'Sunstar'

'Penhallow' 3 (a)
(P.D. Williams, pre-1927)

'Peninnis' 1 W-? (b)
(G.L. Wilson, pre-1937)

'Penkivel' 2 W-P
(R.A. Scamp) R.A. Scamp, 1992
'Rose Royal' × 'Dailmanach'; sdlg no. 172
Fl. 105 mm wide; perianth segments ovate, smooth; corona smooth, clear bright pink, with rim neatly flanged. Mid-season

'Penlee' 3 W-? (b)
(P.D. Williams, pre-1927)

'Pennance Mill' 2 Y-Y
(R.A. Scamp) R.A. Scamp, 1991
'Saint Keverne' open pollinated; sdlg no. 19
Fl. 100 mm wide; perianth segments broad, brilliant greenish yellow 3A, deeply overlapping; the inner segments a little narrower; corona funnel-shaped, slightly paler in tone than the perianth, with mouth lobed. Early

'Pennant' 3 W-? (b)
(F.H. Chapman, pre-1913)

'Pennant' 1 W-Y
(G.W.E. Brogden) G.W.E. Brogden, 1964
Perianth segments pure white; corona slender, chrome yellow, with rim dentate. Early

'Pennine Way' 1 W-Y
(F.E. Board) F.E. Board, 1965
'Killynure' × 'Preamble'
Perianth segments creamy white; corona orange-yellow. Early

'Pennsylvania' 1 W-? (b)
(W.J. Eldering & Son, pre-1928)

'Pennsylvania' 2 W-O
(J.W.A. Lefeber, 1942) J.W.A. Lefeber, 1960
Fl. 90 mm wide; corona clear orange, with reddish orange at rim. Mid-season

'Penny Ann' 3 (a)
(A. White, pre-1946)

'Pennybridge' 2 W-GPP
(Carncairn Daffodils) Carncairn Daffodils, 1975
'Irish Rose' hybrid; sdlg no. 92/60
Fl. 80 mm wide; corona strong yellowish pink 37A, divided by a band of darker pink from the emerald green at base

'Penny-come-quick' 3 W-YYR
(P.D. Williams, pre-1927)
Fl. 76 mm wide; perianth segments white, overlapping half; corona very shallow bowl-shaped, pale sulphur, with a narrow band of red at rim. Mid-season to late. *AM(m) 1930

'Pennyghael' 2 W-Y
(D.C. MacArthur) D.C. MacArthur, 1985

'Kingscourt' × 'Preamble'; sdlg no. E8324
Perianth segments broadly ovate, prominently mucronate, spreading, with margins wavy, overlapping one-third to a half; the inner segments a little inflexed, somewhat creased, with margins nicked and more strongly wavy; corona long cup-shaped, ribbed, darker in tone (5C) than the perianth, with mouth straight and heavily frilled, the rim deeply notched in places. Mid-season

'Penny Green' 2 Y-W
(J.N. Hancock & Co., 1974) Unregistered

'Penola' 2 Y-O
(J.T. Gray, pre-1936)
Perianth segments yellow; corona disc-shaped, reddish orange

'Penola' 2 W-? (b)
(H.A. Brown, pre-1938)

'Penpol' 7 Y-Y
(P.D. Williams, pre-1935)
2n=21. AM(Haarlem) 1934

'Penquite' 2 Y-O
(P.D. Williams, pre-1930)
Perianth segments deep yellow; corona shallow, expanded, deep coppery orange. AM(e) 1932

'Penrice' 3 W-? (b)
(A.M. Wilson, pre-1931)

'Penril' 6 W-POO
(Brian S. Duncan) du Plessis Bros, 1989
'Roseworthy' × 'Foundling'; sdlg no. 545
Fl. 72 mm wide; perianth segments broadly to very broadly ovate, blunt or rounded at apex, reflexed, plane, overlapping one-third; the inner segments creased and with margins wavy; corona short broad funnel-shaped, ribbed, coppery orange, tinted pink at base, mouth straight, wavy, rim minutely notched and crenate. Dwarf. Mid-season

'Penrose'
(G.L. Wilson, pre-1938)

'Penrose' 1 W-P
(W.M. Spry, pre-1975) Unregistered
'Trousseau' × 'Rosy Pink'
Early

'Penryn' 2 W-W
(M.P. Williams, pre-1949)
Perianth segments large and of smooth texture, overlapping

'Pensilva' 2 (a)
(P.D. Williams, pre-1927)

'Pensioner' 2 W-P
(Brian S.Duncan, 1985) Brian S.Duncan, 1997
'Ken's Favorite' × ('Infatuation' × 'Gem of Antrim'); sdlg no. 1139
Fl. rounded, 118 mm wide; perianth segments broadly ovate, blunt; corona broad bowl-shaped, deep coral pink. Mid-season

'Pensive' 2 W-P
(G.L. Wilson, pre-1950)
Sdlg 27/133 × 'Wild Rose'
Corona flushed pale pink

'Penta' 2 W-P
(W. Jackson Sr, 1940)
'Pinkeen' × 'Buffo'

'Pentavalon' 1 W-P
(S.J. Bisdee, 1942)
'Eskimo' × 'Dawnglow'

'Pentewan' 2 Y-Y
(P.D. Williams, pre-1927)
Fl. 90 mm wide, facing slightly downwards; perianth segments broadly ovate, deep greenish yellow, spreading, lightly creased, overlapping one-third to a half; the inner segments a little narrower and somewhat inflexed; corona cylindrical or somewhat funnel-shaped, loosely ribbed, darker and less green in tone than the perianth, with mouth flared and more closely ribbed, rim notched and dentate. Early. 2n=28. *(Gulval)HC(m) 1935, *(Gulval)AM(m) 1936, FA(Haarlem) 1951. Received FA(Haarlem) 1951 as 'California'

'Penthea' 2 (a)
(A.M. Wilson, pre-1937)

'Pentille' 1 Y-Y
(Mrs H.K. Richardson) du Plessis Bros, 1979
'Yellow Idol' open pollinated; sdlg no. 3497
Fl. 115 mm wide. Late

'Pentreath' 3 Y-O
(P.D. Williams, pre-1937)

'Pentucket' 9 W-GYR
(E.C. Powell, pre-1946)

'Penver' 2 Y-? (a)
(R.V. Favell, pre-1937)
'Killigrew' × 'Hades'

'Penvose' 2 Y-Y
(P.D. Williams, pre-1926)
Fl. 108 mm wide; perianth segments light greenish yellow 5D, slightly reflexed, slightly ribbed, overlapping half; corona slightly ribbed, vivid yellow 12A, with mouth straight, rim flanged and dentate. 2n=28. AM(e) 1939, *AM(g) 1952, *FCC(g) 1953,

AM(Haarlem) 1957

'Penwith' 2 W-Y
(The Brodie of Brodie, c.1926)
'Tenedos' × 'Fortune'
Perianth segments creamy white; corona apricot yellow. AM(e) 1932

'Penybont' 3 W-? (b)
(A.M. Wilson, pre-1950)

'Penyoke' 1 W-Y
(du Plessis Bros) du Plessis Bros, 1976
Sdlg no. 320
Fl. 112 mm wide. Mid-season

'Penza' 2 Y-O
(J.T. Gray, pre-1949)
Corona narrow, reddish orange

'Penzance' 3 W-W
(The Brodie of Brodie, pre-1928)
'Kantara' × 'Naxos'

'Peona' 2 (a)
(R.M. Miller, pre-1949)

'Pepin' 1 W-W
(W. Jackson Sr, 1936)
'White Emperor' × 'Pink o' Dawn'
Fl. pure white

'Pepita' 3 W-O
(G.H. Johnstone, 1939) G.H.Johnstone, 1959
Fl. 64 mm wide. Late. Resembles 'Picador'

'Pepper' 2 Y-O
(J.C. Williams, pre-1933)
N. radiiflorus var. *poetarum* × ('Maximus' × 'Firebrand')
Fl. star-shaped, 75 mm wide; perianth segments ovate, acute, brilliant greenish yellow 6B, spreading or somewhat inflexed, somewhat twisted, with margins incurling, overlapping at base only; corona broad funnel-shaped, ribbed, light orange (21A) paling to base, with a darker tone at rim (23A) flushed strong orange 25A, mouth straight, even, rim notched and crenate. Early. 2n=14. *AM(m) 1935

'Pepys' 6 W-Y
(P.D. Williams, pre-1927)
Fl. 90 mm wide; perianth segments ovate, blunt, fairly prominently mucronate, whitish, strongly reflexed, with margins incurved, overlapping a quarter; the inner segments less prominently mucronate; corona cylindrical, a little constricted at mid-point, lightly ribbed, sulphur yellow, with mouth closely ribbed and a little expanded, rim regularly crenate. AM(e) 1939

'Pequenita' 7 Y-Y
(J.W. Blanchard) J.W. Blanchard, 1985
N. atlanticus × *N. cuatrecasasii*; sdlg no. 56/7C
Fl. primrose yellow; perianth segments very broadly ovate in outline, rounded or squarish at apex, with whitish mucro prominent, a little reflexed, smooth, overlapping one-third to a half; the inner segments more narrowly ovate, only very slightly mucronate, more nearly spreading, with margins wavy; corona cup-shaped, very lightly ribbed, darker in tone than the perianth, with mouth straight or slightly incurved, wavy, rim entire or obscurely crenate. Very early

'Pera' 3 W-R
(The Brodie of Brodie, c.1927)
'Beacon' × 'Sunstar'
Perianth segments broadly ovate, blunt or slightly truncate, slightly mucronate, pure white, spreading or a little reflexed, overlapping one-third to a half; the inner segments a little narrower, more nearly spreading, with margins wavy or incurled; corona almost disc-shaped, ribbed, deep red, with mouth wavy and sometimes folded. Late. AM(e) 1931, FCC(e) 1935

'Perchance' 6 W-YPP
(F.Silcock, 1979) F.Silcock, 1993
2 W-P × *N. cyclamineus*
Fl. with colours slow to mature; perianth segments whitish, strongly reflexed; corona cylindrical, slowly becoming pink, with yellow at base. Late

'Percival' 3 W-? (b)
(G.H. Engleheart, pre-1910)

'Perconger' 6 Y-O
(A. Gray, pre-1941)
Perianth segments yellow; corona pale orange. Dwarf. Early

'Percuil' 6 Y-Y
(R.A. Scamp) R.A. Scamp, 1991
'Saint Keverne' × *N. cyclamineus*; sdlg no. 3
Fl. 74 mm wide, brilliant greenish yellow 4A; perianth segments ovate, blunt, prominently mucronate, reflexed, of thick substance, overlapping one-third; the inner segments a little narrower, more nearly acute, with margins wavy; corona cylindrical, lightly ribbed, with mouth sharply expanded, rim deeply notched and crenate. Dwarf. Very early

'Perdita' 9
(pre-1907)

'Perdita' ?-P
(Alister Clark, pre-1948)

'Perdita' 9 W-GYR
(D.W.Gourlay) Mrs H.K. Richardson, 1963
Fl. 74 mm wide; perianth segments very broadly

ovate, blunt or truncate, prominently mucronate, a little reflexed, concave, overlapping half; the inner segments more nearly spreading, with margins more strongly incurved; corona very shallow bowl-shaped, ribbed, pale yellow, with green at base and red at rim, mouth wavy, obscurely 3-lobed, with the lobes sometimes overlapping, rim minutely dentate. 2n=28

'Perdita's Pride' 9 W-OOR
(Mrs M.S. Yerger) Mrs M.S. Yerger, 1984
'Light's Out' × 'Perdita'; sdlg no. 73 B 6
Fl. 69 mm wide; corona strong orange 25B, with orange-red (31A) at rim. Late. Slightly scented

'Perdita's Prince' 9 W-OOR
(Mrs M.S. Yerger) Mrs M.S. Yerger, 1984
'Lights Out' × 'Perdita'; sdlg no. 73 B 2
Fl. 60 mm wide; corona vivid orange 28B, with orange-red (32A) at rim. Late. Sweetly scented. Resembles 'Perdita' in form and 'Lights Out' in corona colour

'Perdredda' 3 O-R
(Brian S.Duncan) Dan du Plessis, 1996
'Ulster Bank' × 'Altruist'; sdlg no.881
Fl. 90 mm wide; perianth segments very broadly ovate, orange; corona bowl-shaped, red, with rim crenate. Mid-season

'Peregrine' 2 W-W
(P.D. Williams, pre-1907)
Resembles a larger-flowered 'White Queen' of improved substance

'Perena' 2 or 3 W-Y
(pre-1927)
Perianth segments pure white; corona pale greenish citron, frilled, with rim crenate

N. perez-chiscanoi Fernández Casas 13 Section Pseudonarcissus

N. × perezlarae Font Quer 13 = *N. cavanillesii* Barra & López × *N. serotinus* Linnaeus

'Perfeck' 2 Y-Y
(Colin Crotty) Colin Crotty, 1996
'Golden Aura' × 'Camelot'; sdlg no. 81-94
Fl. 67 mm wide, bright yellow; perianth segments very broadly ovate, blunt; corona short funnel-shaped, with mouth slightly wavy. Mid-season

'Perfecta' 8 W-O
(pre-1798)

'Perfecta' 3 W-? (b)
(P. van Deursen, pre-1930)

'Perfect Gentleman' 1 Y-Y
Syn. of 'The Perfect Gentleman'

'Perfection' 9
(W. Welchman, pre-1907)

'Perfection' 4
(R.A. van der Schoot, pre-1931)
'Emperor' sport

'Perfection' 1 W-Y
(D. Bramley) D. Bramley, 1959
Fl. 108 mm wide. Mid-season. Resembles a more vigorous 'Saint Saphorin' with a darker corona

'Perfect Spring' 6 Y-Y
(G.E. Mitsch, 1975) R. & E. Havens, 1990
N. obvallaris × *N. cyclamineus*; sdlg no. KK100/1
Fl. 65 mm wide, deep yellow; perianth segments smooth; corona cylindrical. Dwarf. Very early. 2n=21

'Perfectus' 2 W-Y
(M. van Waveren & Sons, pre-1900)
Perianth segments broadly ovate, blunt, prominently mucronate, greenish white, spreading, plane, with broad midrib showing, overlapping one-third; the inner segments a little narrower, slightly inflexed, with margins wavy; corona shallow, widely expanded, loosely ribbed, canary yellow, faintly tinged orange at rim, a little frilled

'Perfectus' 2 W-P
(Alister Clark, pre-1935)
Perianth segments pure white; corona widely expanded, pink

'Perfectus' 3 Y-Y
Syn. of 'Vanessa'

'Perfume' 3 W-? (b)
(R.H. Bath, pre-1929)

'Perhaps' ?-P
(Alister Clark, pre-1948)

'Perhaps' 2 W-WPP
(J.N. Hancock & Co., 1953)
'Dual Gift' hybrid
Corona suffused pink

'Perhaps' 2 Y-Y
(Ken Farmer Nurseries) Ken Farmer Nurseries, 1978
Fl. 125 mm wide; perianth segments pale yellow; corona bright yellow. Mid-season

'Pericles' 2 Y-Y
(E. Leeds, pre-1877)
Perianth segments pale primrose yellow; corona pale yellow. Syn. Incomparabilis Pallidus 'Pericles'

'Pericles' 1 W-W
(J.L. Richardson) J.L. Richardson, 1958
'Spitzbergen' × 'Cantatrice'
Fl. pure white; perianth segments broadly ovate; corona frilled, with rim flanged

'Peridot' 2 W-GYY
(G.L. Wilson) G.L. Wilson, 1960
Probably ('Nelly' × 'Chinese White') × 'Chinese White'

'Perigo'
?Syn. of 'Perigot'

'Perigot' 3 W-? (b)
(J.W. Barr, pre-1930)
?See also 'Perigo'

'Peril' 3 Y-YYR
(pre-1926)

'Peril' 3 W-O
(A.E. Lowe, pre-1927)

'Perimeter' 3 Y-YYO
(J.L. Richardson) J.L. Richardson, 1956
'Aranjuez' × 'Narvik'
Perianth segments soft yellow; corona with a narrow band of reddish orange at rim

'Peripheral Pink' 2 W-GWP
(G.E. Mitsch and R. & E.Havens, 1971) G.E. Mitsch and R. & E.Havens, 1986
'Precedent' × 'Eclat'; sdlg no. G13/18
Perianth segments broad, smooth, regular; corona with dark clear pink at rim. Mid-season

'Peris' 2 (a)
(W.A. Watts, pre-1913)

'Perker' 1 W-W
(G.P. Haydon, pre-1910)
Fl. small; perianth segments pure white, overlapping; corona opening pale primrose yellow, becoming milk white. Dwarf

'Perky' (1970) 6 W-Y
(G.E.Mitsch, 1964) R. & E.Havens, 1996
'Trousseau' × *N. cyclamineus*; sdlg no. Z39/2
Fl. 80 mm wide; perianth segments ovate, blunt, slightly mucronate, opening greenish white, slowly becoming white, reflexed, with margins incurved, overlapping one-quarter; the inner segments a little twisted; corona cylindrical, very lightly ribbed, vivid yellow 9A, paler at base, mouth a little expanded, even, rim regularly notched and crenate. With occasional secondary stems. AM(e) 1996. The re-use of this epithet is sanctioned under Article 26 of the *Cultivated Code* (1995); to ensure distinction from 'Perky' 1968, the epithet must always be followed by the date of publication, 1970

'Perky' 6 W-W
(G.E. Mitsch) G.E. Mitsch, 1968
'Mitylene' × *N. cyclamineus*; sdlg no. V28/11
Fl. 89 mm wide; corona opening pale lemon yellow, becoming sulphur white. Mid-season. Resembles a smaller-flowered 'Frostkist' of improved substance

'Per Lagerquist' 2 Y-YYO
(Konynenburg & Mark) Konynenburg & Mark, 1960
'Aranjuez' × ('Kimono' × 'Memphis')
Fl. 80 mm wide; perianth segments brilliant yellow 8A; corona orange-yellow (17C), with vivid orange 28B at rim. Mid-season

'Perlax' 11a W-Y
(J. Gerritsen & Son) J. Gerritsen & Son, 1971
'Valdrome' × 'Fondant'
Fl. 80 mm wide; perianth segments ivory white; corona segments opening pinkish yellow, becoming buff yellow. Mid-season to late. Syn. 'Pearlax'

'Perle' 2 W-W
(D.V. West, pre-1927)
Fl. pure white; corona narrow funnel-shaped

'Perle Brillante' 8
(R.A. van der Schoot, pre-1930)

'Perle d'Amour' 8 Y-Y
(pre-1861)
Perianth segments primrose yellow; corona darker in tone

'Perlee' 2 W-W
(Miss M. Verry) Miss M. Verry, 1974
'Truth' × 'Ludlow'
Fl. 95 mm wide

N. perluteus Spach = *N. cupularis*

'Perm' ?-P
(Alister Clark, pre-1948)

'Permanent' 3
(pre-1913)

'Permissive' 2 W-W
(H.R. Barr) H.R. Barr, 1971
'Sea Urchin' × 'Ludlow'
Fl. 118 mm wide; perianth segments broadly ovate, spreading or a little inflexed, overlapping one-third to a half; the inner segments with margins wavy; corona funnel-shaped, strongly 6-angled, opening yellow, becoming white, with mouth very deeply 6-lobed, the lobes opposite the perianth segments and sometimes deeply bi-lobed, frilled, with rim crenate; occa-

sional extra growths at the notches between lobes, short, acute, yellow

'Permit' ?-P
(Alister Clark, pre-1948)

N. peroccidentalis **Fernández Casas 13 Section Bulbocodium**

'Perola' 8
(Cartwright & Goodwin, pre-1916)

'Perosi' 1 Y-O
(J.W.A. Lefeber) J.W.A. Lefeber, 1968

'Perpetuation' 7 YYW-W
(R. & E.Havens) R. & E.Havens, 1995
'Hillstar' × 'Quick Step'; sdlg no. Y91/14
Fls 3 per stem, 70 mm wide; perianth segments broadly ovate, deep lemon yellow, with white at base, spreading, plane; corona bowl-shaped, creamy white, with mouth wavy. Late. Scented

'Perri' 7 Y-O
(J.S. Leitch) J.S. Leitch, 1961
Fls 3-4 per stem, 64 mm wide. Late

'Persephone' 2 W-Y
(J.T. Gray, pre-1933)
Corona pale lemon

'Persephone' 2 W-P
(Alister Clark, 1935) J. Sharp, 1960

'Persepolis' 2 W-W
(Mrs H.K. Richardson) Mrs H.K. Richardson, 1976
'Verona' × 'Stainless'
Fl. 105 mm wide, snow white; corona frilled, with rim dentate. Mid-season

'Perseus' 2 (a)
(W.F.M. Copeland, pre-1913)

'Perseus' 1 W-W
(J.L. Richardson) Mrs H.K. Richardson, 1963
'Broughshane' × 'Brussels'
Fl. pure white; corona with rim rolled. Late

'Persia' 1 Y-Y
(G.L. Wilson, pre-1935)
'Sorley Boy' hybrid
Fl. tinged apricot. Scented

'Persian Orange' 3 W-? (b)
(G.H. Engleheart, pre-1910)

'Persil' 2 W-Y
(C.E. Radcliff, 1940)
'Pinkeen' × 'Dawnglow'

'Persimmon' 2 (a)
(Cartwright & Goodwin, pre-1908)

'Personable' 2 W-P
(Murray W.Evans, 1979) Estella L. Evans, 1992
'Quasar' × (sdlg × 'Everpink'); sdlg no. W-2/1
Fl. 92 mm wide; perianth segments roundish, slightly reflexed, smooth; corona slightly flared, ribbed, intense reddish pink, with mouth lightly frilled. Mid-season

'Personality' 2 W-Y
(G.L. Wilson) G.L. Wilson, 1955
'Zero' × 'Greeting'
Corona lemon, with mouth straight and even

'Persuasion' 2 W-OOY
(G.L. Wilson) M.J. Jefferson-Brown, 1963
'Blarney' hybrid

'Pert' 9 W-GYR
(Mrs M.S. Yerger) Mrs M.S. Yerger, 1993
N. poeticus var. *hellenicus* × 'Lights Out'; sdlg no. 75 H 3-2
Fl. forming a double triangle, 40 mm wide; perianth segments white, streaked greenish yellow at base; the inner segments narrower; corona almost disc-shaped, greenish yellow (154A), with green at base and red (32A) at rim, with a line of white between yellow and red. Dwarf. Very late

'Perth' 2 Y-O
(The Brodie of Brodie, c.1929)
'Beacon' hybrid × 'Fortune'
Perianth segments pale primrose yellow, overlapping; corona yellowish orange, with rim flanged. AM(e) 1933

'Perth's Fair Maid' 2 W-? (b or c)
(Miss A.I. Smith, pre-1934)

'Peru' 1 (a)
(Cartwright & Goodwin, pre-1916)

'Peru' 2 Y-R
(J.L. Richardson) J.L. Richardson, 1958
'Carbineer' × 'Royal Ransom'
Perianth segments pale yellow, of thick substance; corona bowl-shaped, deep red

'Perugia' 2 W-O
(J.M. de Navarro) J.M. de Navarro, 1958
'Fermoy' × 'Carrowmore'
Corona yellow, deeply stained bright reddish orange. Sunproof

'Pet' 4 W-Y
(S.C. Gaspar) R.J. Abernethy, 1957
Corona segments bright yellow

'Petal Pie' 2 W-P
(J.N. Hancock & Co., 1962) Unregistered

'Petaluma' 2 W-P
(J.N.Hancock & Co., 1975) Unregistered
Corona expanded, deep apricot pink. Mid-season

'Pete' 1 Y-Y
(pre-1927)

'Peter Barr' 1 W-W
(Barr & Sons, pre-1902)
'Monarch' × 'Madame de Graaff'
Perianth segments broad, blunt, milk white, inflexed, with margins recurved, overlapping one-third; corona cylindrical, angled, sulphur white, mouth flared, with rim flanged and crenate. Mid-season. FCC 1902

'Peterborough' 2 Y-Y
(F. Rijnveld & Sons, pre-1950)
AM(Haarlem) 1950

'Peter Bosuston' 11a Y-O
(Tom Forster, 1960s) Unregistered
Perianth segments yellow; corona deeply split, the six segments two-thirds the length of the perianth segments and opposite and closely overlying them, vivid deep orange, heavily frilled. Early to mid-season

'Peter Davis' 2 (a)
(P.D. Williams, pre-1931)

'Peter de Groote' 1 (a)
(N. Zandbergen, pre-1938)
AM(Haarlem) 1937

'Peter de Hoogh' 1 (a)
(Konynenburg & Mark, pre-1953)

'Peter Grace' 3 (a)
(W.A. Grace, pre-1936)

'Peter Lower' 8
(N.Y. Lower, pre-1928)
'Yeoman of the Guard' × 'Mandalay'

'Peter Lycett' 2 (a)
(W.F.M. Copeland, pre-1939)
'Mary Copeland' hybrid

'Peterman' 2 Y-OOR
(P. Phillips) P. Phillips, 1966
Fl. 100 mm wide; perianth segments acute; corona funnel-shaped, mid-orange, shading to bright red at rim. Mid-season

'Peterman' 2 Y-? (a)
(E.W. Philpott)

'Peter Pan' 1 W-? (b)
(Hon. Sir R.H. Rhodes, pre-1911)

'Peter Pan' 3 (a)
(A.M. Wilson, pre-1913)

'Peter Piper' 2 Y-O
(R.V. Favell, pre-1939)
Perianth segments bright yellow, of good substance; corona brilliant red

'Peter's Gift' 6 Y-Y
(M.J.Jefferson-Brown) M.J.Jefferson-Brown, 1997
Hybrid between Div. 6 sdlgs
Fl. rich gold; perianth segments fairly broad, spreading or slightly reflexed; corona with rim neatly flanged and dentate. Early

'Pete's Pride' 1 W-P
(P.J.Irwin) P.J.Irwin, 1995
O'More sdlg 76/30 × 'Eiko'; sdlg no. 18
Fl. forming a double triangle, 113 mm wide; perianth segments very broadly ovate, plane; the inner segments more narrowly ovate; corona cylindrical, pink, a little frilled, with rim crenate and slightly flanged. Mid-season. Sunproof

'Pet Finch' 7 Y-O
(M.J. Jefferson-Brown, 1959) M.J. Jefferson-Brown, 1975
'Harrier' × *N. jonquilla*
Perianth segments gold; corona orange. Early. Formerly named 'Goldfinch'

'Petillant' 3 W-YYO
(J. Gerritsen & Son, 1957) J. Gerritsen & Son, 1967
Div. 3 × 'Actaea'
Fl. 85 mm wide; corona with orange (28A) at rim. Late

'Petina' 1 W-P
(W. Jackson Jr) W. Jackson Jr, 1968
'Illinga' × 'Telita'; sdlg no. 6/60
Syn. 'Kara'

'Petit Beurre' 1 Y-Y
(J. Gerritsen & Son) J. Gerritsen & Son, 1971
'Little Gem' hybrid
Fl. 47 mm wide

'Petite' 7 Y-YOO
(G.E. Mitsch) G.E. Mitsch, 1970
('Playboy' × 'Paricutin') × *N. jonquilla*; sdlg no. E39/2
Fl. rounded; perianth segments clear yellow; corona small, light orange, paling to yellow at base. Late

'Petite' 2 W-R
(R.H.Glover, pre-1993) Unregistered

'Petite Pink' 2 W-GPP
(A.W. Chappell) A.W. Chappell, 1991
'Silent Wonder' × 'John's Pink'; sdlg no. SJ-4
Fl. rounded, 50 mm wide; corona salmon pink.

Mid-season

'Petite Prodigy' 9 W-GYR
(Mrs M.S.Yerger) Mrs M.S.Yerger, 1996
Poeticus hybrid open pollinated; sdlg no. 84 F 2
Fl. 50 mm wide; perianth segments broad, roundish, creamy white; the inner segments narrower; corona brilliant greenish yellow 3B, with vivid yellow-green 154A at base and orange-red (32A) at rim. Dwarf. Early

'Petite Rose' 2 W-P
(A.W. Chappell) A.W. Chappell, 1990
'Silent Wonder' × 'John's Pink'; sdlg no. SJ-1
Fl. 50 mm wide; corona bright pink, with a darker tone at rim. Mid-season

'Petit Fleur' 4 Y-PPY
Syn. of 'Petit Four'

'Petit Four' 4 W-PPY
(F. Rijnveld & Sons) F. Rijnveld & Sons, 1961
'Champagne' sport
Fl. up to 110 mm wide; perianth segments blunt, prominently mucronate, greenish white (slightly paler than 1D), spreading or a little reflexed, plane, overlapping a quarter to one-third; the inner segments a little more narrowly ovate; corona cup-shaped, smooth or loosely ribbed, opening light yellow 18B, becoming light yellowish pink 27B, with light yellow 18B at rim, frilled, with rim flanged and crenate; the corona enclosing six shorter segments of the same or a darker colour, sometimes similarly touched yellow at rim, broad, crumpled, lobed, with margins wavy and crenate; the segments each with one lobe longer than the corona, narrowly tubular, tapering, yellow-white. Mid-season. 2n=28. Resembles a Div. 4 'Champagne'. Syn. 'Petit Fleur'. AM(p) 1986

'Petition' 2 W-Y
(G.W.E. Brogden) G.W.E. Brogden, 1964
Fl. 108 mm wide; corona lemon yellow. Mid-season. Resembles a better poised 'Tudor Minstrel'

'Petitpoint' 2 W-? (b)
(Oregon Bulb Farms, pre-1946)

'Petra' 3 W-GGO
(J.L. Richardson) Mrs H.K. Richardson, 1968
'Corofin' open pollinated
Corona yellow-green, with orange at rim and the rim dentate

'Petrarch' 9
(G.H. Engleheart, pre-1896)
'Ornatus' × *N. poeticus* var. *recurvus*
AM 1896

'Petrel' 1 W-W
(Sir C.H. Cave, pre-1908)

'Petrel' 5 W-W
(G.E. Mitsch) G.E. Mitsch, 1970
'Quick Step' × *N. triandrus*; sdlg no. C52/1
Fls up to 7 or more per stem, ivory white; perianth segments broadly oblong in outline, blunt or truncate at apex, slightly mucronate, a little reflexed, plane, overlapping one-third; the inner segments with margins wavy; corona cup-shaped, mouth straight, even, rim obscurely crenate. Late. With occasional secondary stems. Resembles 'Quick Step' but with much broader perianth segments

N. × ***petri-mariae*** **Fernández Casas 13** = *N. pallidiflorus* Pugsley × *N. provincialis* Pugsley

'Petrinia' 3 W-? (b)
(pre-1936)
'Princess Mary' × 'Horace'

'Petrocleus' 2 Y-Y
(Barr & Sons, pre-1923)
'King Alfred' × 'Weardale Perfection'

'Petrona' 2 (a)
(J.T. Gray, pre-1939)

'Petronel' 1 W-W
(G.H. Engleheart, pre-1923)

'Petronella' 2 (a)
(N.F. Lock, pre-1942)

'Petronius' 2 (a)
(Mrs R.O. Backhouse, pre-1921)

'Petrouchka' 3 W-O
(The Brodie of Brodie, *c.*1913)
'Princess Mary' hybrid
Fl. star-shaped; corona disc-shaped, reddish orange

'Petsamo' 1 W-W
(J.L. Richardson, pre-1944)
'Niphetos' × 'Kanchenjunga'
Fl. 108 mm wide; perianth segments very broadly ovate, blunt, slightly mucronate, spreading, with margins a little wavy, overlapping half; the outer segments overlapping one another; the inner segments more narrowly ovate, shouldered at base, a little inflexed, with margins more strongly wavy; corona cylindrical, mouth ribbed and very widely expanded, with rim rolled and crenate. Mid-season. Resembles a smaller but much improved 'Kanchenjunga'. AM(e) 1950

'Petticoat' 1 Y-Y
(P.D. Williams, pre-1910)
Perianth segments overlapping; corona richer in tone than the perianth, regularly and heavily frilled

'Petticoat Lace' 11a W-GWW
(John R.Reed) John R.Reed, 1997
'Panache' × 'Colblanc'; sdlg no. 84-140-2
Fl. 88 mm wide, intense white; perianth segments broadly ovate; corona split to base, the six segments opposite and closely overlying the perianth segments, bi-lobed, with green at base, tightly frilled. Dwarf. Mid-season

'Petticoat Lane' 1 W-W
(G. Lewis, pre-1945)

'Petticoats' 4
(K.D. Smith) K.D. Smith, 1959

'Pettna' 3 Y-O
(J.N. Hancock & Co.)
Corona coppery orange

petunioides = *N. cantabricus* var. *petunioides*

'Petworth' 2 (a)
(Sir F.C. Stern, pre-1948)

'Peveril' 3 W-? (b)
(pre-1907)

'Pewee' 3 W-GWP
(Mrs G. Link) Mrs G. Link, 1966
'Evening' × 'Dunkeld'
Fl. 64 mm wide, of smooth texture and good substance; corona with dark green at base and a narrow band of pink at rim

'Pex' 2 Y-O
(J.S. Leitch) J.S. Leitch, 1958

'Phaenomen' 3 W-Y
(Konynenburg & Mark) Konynenburg & Mark, 1965
Fl. 111 mm wide; perianth segments ivory white; corona pale greenish yellow 9D. Mid-season

'Phalarope' 6 W-Y
(G.E. Mitsch) G.E. Mitsch, 1982
'Titania' × *N. cyclamineus*; sdlg no. JJ81/5
Fl. 82 mm wide; perianth segments ovate, milk white, tinged yellow at base, strongly reflexed, with margins sometimes notched, smooth, overlapping a quarter to one-third; corona cylindrical, smooth, clear lemon yellow, mouth ribbed and flared, even, rim notched and dentate, flanged. Early. Resembles 'Perky' but with the corona more widely flared

'Phaleron' 3 W-? (b)
(The Brodie of Brodie, *c.*1909)
'Princess Mary' × 'Stella Superba'
Perianth segments creamy white

'Phantasy' 1 W-W
(E.M. Crosfield, pre-1910)
Fl. pure white

'Phantom' W-Y
(G.H. Engleheart, pre-1905)
Fl. large. Somewhat resembles 'Grandis' but with the flower facing further down

'Phantom' 11a W-P
(G.E. Mitsch) G.E. Mitsch, 1975
'Accent' × ('Wild Rose' × 'Hillbilly'); sdlg no. D7/2
Fl. 105 mm wide; corona deeply split, the six segments opposite and closely overlying the perianth segments, opening yellowish, becoming buffy pink. Mid-season

'Pharais' 1 W-? (b)
(Slieve Donard Nursery Co., pre-1932)

'Pharaoh' 1 W-Y
(G.P. Haydon, pre-1904)
Fl. very large; perianth segments creamy white; corona expanded, ribbed, canary yellow, lightly frilled

'Phar Lap' 2 W-O
(Tom Forster, 1960s) Unregistered
Corona broad disc-shaped, orange. Tall. Late

'Pharos' 1 (a)
(Sir A.P.W. Thomas, pre-1930)

"Pheasant's Eye"
Syn. of *N. poeticus* var. *recurvus*

'Phebe' 9 W-GYO
(Mrs G. Link) Mrs G. Link, 1975
'Sidelight' × 'Sea Green; sdlg no. 1962/2
Fl. 62 mm wide; corona amber yellow, with cypress green at base and burnt orange at rim. Late. Resembles a more brilliantly coloured 'Sidelight' with a larger corona with the rim closely and deeply notched, as if fringed. 2n=14

'Phenomena' 1 W-? (b)
(de Graaff Bros, pre-1927)

'Philaletus' 2 W-WWY
(G.A. Uit den Boogaard, pre-1954)

'Philanderer' 2 W-O
(F.E. Board) F.E. Board, 1965
'Tudor Minstrel' × Sdlg 100/63
Mid-season

'Philip' 1 (a)
(L. Buckland, pre-1936)

'Philip Hurt' 2 W-O
(?Pyrenean origin)
Selection by C.Wolley-Dod (*c.*1893) from wild-

collected *N.* × *bernardii*
Perianth segments yellowish white; corona deep orange. Late. AM 1896

'Philip Kennedy' 1 Y-Y
(T. Morrison) T. Morrison, 1960
Fl. clear medium yellow; perianth segments broad, smooth; corona with rim flanged

'Philippa Linton' 2 W-? (b)
(Barr & Sons, pre-1926)

'Philippe de Vilmorin' 1 W-W
(G.P. Haydon, pre-1915)
Corona creamy white

'Philip Visser' 1 (a)
(G. Lubbe & Son, pre-1926)
AM(Haarlem) 1926

'Phillipa' 3 W-? (b or c)
(Barr & Sons, pre-1923)

'Phillip Kennedy' 1 Y-Y
(?Australian origin, pre-1997) Unregistered

'Phillipstown' 1 Y-Y
(New Zealand origin, pre-1955)

'Phillip Wise' 2 W-GPP
(Tom Forster, 1960s) Unregistered
Perianth segments roundish, slightly mucronate, pure white, reflexed, plane, overlapping half; the inner segments more nearly spreading, with margins wavy; corona funnel-shaped, short, smooth, salmon pink, with green at base, heavily frilled, with rim deeply notched. Late

'Phillis' 8 ?-O
Syn. of 'Phyllis'

'Phillis Bossence' 2 W-WWY
(L.P.Dettman, 1970) Unregistered
'Arctic Doric' open pollinated; sdlg no. 16/71

'Phillus Chidgey' 2 Y-Y
(L.P. Dettman) L.P. Dettman, 1972
'Yellow Moon' × 'Chromis'
Fl. 98 mm wide; perianth segments broad, soft yellow, overlapping; corona deeper in tone. Early

'Phil May' 1 Y-Y
(Barr & Sons, pre-1904)
Corona darker in tone than the perianth

'Philo' 2 W-P
(W. Jackson Jr) W. Jackson Jr, 1968
'Imp' × 'Dallbro'

'Philomath' 7 Y-Y
(M. Fowlds) G.E. Mitsch, 1970
N. cyclamineus sdlg × *N. jonquilla*; sdlg no. F332/1
Fls 2-3 per stem, bright yellow; perianth segments narrowly ovate, acute, spreading, overlapping at base only; corona somewhat funnel-shaped, ribbed, with mouth straight and rim minutely crenate. Mid-season. Syn. 'Vista'

'Philomel' 5
(H.G. Longford, pre-1927)

'Philon' 3 W-OOR
(G.A. Uit den Boogaard, pre-1949)

'Phil's Gift' 1 Y-Y
(P.Phillips, 1983) John R.Reed, 1995
From Phillips open-pollinated seed; sdlg no. POPS.1
Fl. 98 mm wide, deep yellow; perianth segments ovate, very smooth; corona slightly flared. Early

'Philtaton' 2 W-O
(G.A. Uit den Boogaard, pre-1949)
'John Evelyn' hybrid
See also 'Piltaton'

'Phinda' 2 W-P
(Brian S.Duncan, 1986) Brian S.Duncan, 1996
'Gracious Lady' × sdlg 290 ('Infatuation' × 'Gem of Antrim'); sdlg no. 1290
Fl. 112 mm wide; perianth segments broadly ovate, blunt, spreading, plane; corona cylindrical, slightly ribbed, deep rose pink, with mouth a little flared. Mid-season

'Phineas' 2 Y-Y
(Barr & Sons, pre-1915)
Perianth segments sulphur yellow, tinged canary yellow, inflexed; corona dark golden yellow. AM(e) 1919. See also 'Phineus'

'Phineus' 2 Y-Y
Syn. of 'Phineas'

'Phips Green' 2 Y-WWY
(P. Cleine, *c.*1985) Unregistered
'Daydream' open pollinated
Fl. forming a double triangle; perianth segments broadly ovate, blunt, sulphur yellow, with slight white mucro, a little inflexed, overlapping one-third to a half; the inner segments more narrowly ovate, shouldered at base, more strongly inflexed; corona cylindrical, opening sulphur yellow, becoming white, with a band of bright yellow at rim, mouth ribbed and flared, lightly frilled, rim deeply notched. Mid-season

'Phocea' 2 W-? (b)
(C.G. van Tubergen, pre-1930)
Fl. 95 mm wide; perianth segments creamy white, with margins incurved, overlapping one-third; corona funnel-shaped, sulphur. Mid-season. Syn.

'Corinna'

'Phoebe' 2 W-? (b)
(Mrs R.O. Backhouse, pre-1921)
'Phoebe Too' 1 W-W
(A.O. Roblin, 1959) Unregistered
'Rhana' × 'Cardecu'

'Phoebus' 3 W-? (b)
(J.W. Barr, pre-1930)

'Phoenician' 2 W-W
(G.E.Mitsch & R. & E. Havens, 1984) R. & E.Havens, 1995
'Broomhill' × 'Canisp'; sdlg no. TT23/18
Fl. 105 mm wide, pure white; perianth segments broadly ovate, spreading, plane; corona straight-sided, with mouth wavy. Mid-season

'Phoenix' 3 Y-? (a)
(R. Crews, pre-1949)

'Phryne' 1 W-? (b)
(E.H. Krelage & Son, pre-1920)
AM(Haarlem) 1920, AM(Haarlem) 1921

'Phuket' 11b
(?Dutch origin, pre-1989) Unregistered

'Phyllida' 2 W-Y
(W.F.M. Copeland, pre-1916)
Perianth segments cream; corona large, expanded, deeply ribbed, creamy yellow, neatly frilled. AM(e) 1916

'Phyllida Garth' 5 W-W
(A. Gray, pre-1948)
? × *N. triandrus* var. *loiseleurii*
Fls 3-4 per stem, pure white

'Phyl Lipscombe' 2 Y-YYO
(L.P. Dettman) L.P. Dettman, 1974
'Fireking' × 'Fairy King'
Fl. 79 mm wide

'Phyllis' 8 ?-O
(pre-1880)
Corona yellow-orange. See also 'Phillis'

'Phyllis' 3 W-Y
(G.H. Engleheart, pre-1901)
Corona ribbed, canary yellow, lightly frilled

'Phyllis' 2 W-Y
Syn. of 'Sweetheart'

'Phyllis Lillian' 2 W-W
(Ken Farmer Nurseries) Ken Farmer Nurseries, 1978
Fl. 110 mm wide; corona opening shell pink, becoming white. Mid-season

'Phyllis Miller' 1 Y-Y
(F. Rijnveld & Sons, pre-1947)
Fl. golden yellow; corona darker in tone than the perianth. AM(Haarlem) 1946

'Phyllis Rochford'
(Barr & Sons, pre-1929)

'Phyllis Rowntree' 1 W-W
(W.A. Grace, pre-1936)

'Phyllis Vansittart' 1 W-? (b)
(W.A. Watts, pre-1923)
'Madame de Graaff' × 'Weardale Perfection'

'Phyrene' 2 Y-Y
(W. Jackson Jr, *c.*1973) Unregistered
'Jaslin' × 'Tulendena'

physaloides = *N. poeticus* var. *physaloides*

'Pia' 2 W-OOR
(W. Jackson Jr, 1966) Unregistered
'Jo' × 'Arbar'; sdlg no. 158/66

'Piano Concerto' 2 W-P
(G.E. Mitsch, 1980) R. & E. Havens, 1992
'Easter Moon' × 'Cool Flame'; sdlg no. 2P8/8
Fl. 95 mm wide; perianth segments very broadly ovate, blunt, pure white, smooth; corona clear light pink, with a darker tone at rim, frilled. Mid-season Sunproof. Somewhat resembles a slightly later-flowered 'Silent Pink'

'Picador' 3 W-GOO
(P.D. Williams, pre-1910)
Perianth segments pure white, overlapping; corona very shallow, rich orange

'Picardy' 4 Y-O
(Mrs R.O. Backhouse, pre-1921)
Perianth and other petaloid segments sulphur yellow; corona segments scarlet-orange. Syn. 'Aryan'. AM(Haarlem) 1938

'Picarillo' 2 Y-Y
(B.O. Mulligan, pre-1951)
N. rupicola subsp. *watieri* × *N. pumilus*
Fl. 30-35 mm wide, brilliant greenish yellow 3B; perianth segments ovate or narrowly ovate, acute; corona funnel-shaped, mouth expanded, wavy. AM(a)(r) 1982

'Picaroon' 3 W-? (b)
(W.B. Cranfield, pre-1930)

'Picasso' 3 W-YYO
(Carncairn Daffodils, 1973) Carncairn Daffodils, 1984
'Corofin' × 'Merlin'

Fl. 92 mm wide; corona yellow, with bright orange at rim. Late

'Picatus' 1 (a)
(J.R.Byfield, pre-1936)

'Piccadilly' 3 W-? (b)
(A.M. Wilson, pre-1939)

'Piccio' 3 W-O
(W. Backhouse, pre-1869)
Perianth segments narrow, acute, creamy white; corona stained orange. Syn. Barrii Albidus 'Piccio'. "Absorbed" 'Gazelle'

'Piccolo' 1 Y-Y
(J. Gerritsen & Son) J. Gerritsen & Son, 1967
N. minor × 'Little Gem'
Fl. 45 mm wide; perianth segments brilliant greenish yellow 6B; corona vivid yellow 9A. Early

'Piccolo' 2 Y-Y
(C.O. Fairbairn)

'Pickanjinnie' 1 W-Y
(W.M. Spry, pre-1975) Unregistered
'Early Prince' × 'Stand By'
Tall. Early

'Pickering' 2 W-? (b)
(J,W.A. Lefeber, pre-1943)

'Pick Me' 2 Y-O
(O. Ronalds, 1950) T. Morrison, 1960
Perianth segments rich yellow, smooth; corona reddish orange. Early

'Pick Up' 11a W-YOO
(J. Gerritsen & Son) J. Gerritsen & Son, 1968
Perianth segments opening pale greenish yellow, becoming white; corona strong orange 24A, with a paler tone at base, and with some flecks of yellow and white at rim. 2n=28

'Pickwick' 1 (a)
(G.P. Haydon, pre-1910)

'Pickwick' 2 W-YYO
(G.L. Wilson) Guy L.Wilson Ltd, 1964
'Fairy Tale' × ('Raphoe' × 'Killala')
Corona somewhat funnel-shaped. 2n=28

'Picnic' 2 W-Y
(Murray W. Evans) Murray W. Evans, 1976
Sdlg × 'Accent'; sdlg no. K-38
Fl. 105 mm wide. Mid-season

'Pico Bello' 11b W-O/W
(J.W.A. Lefeber) J.T. Oosten, 1979
Sdlg no. GBS 30

Perianth segments very broadly ovate, squarish at apex and slightly truncate, prominently mucronate, ivory white, spreading, concave and a little creased, overlapping half; the inner segments with margins incurved giving a narrower appearance, shouldered at base, a little inflexed; corona split to base, the six segments spreading, alternate to the the perianth segments, with orange in a broad longitudinal band at midrib flanked by white, twisted or with margins wavy

'Picoblanco' 2 W-W
(Mrs F.M.Gray) Mrs F.M Gray, 1961
N. rupicola subsp. *watieri* sdlg
Fl. 30 mm wide, milk white. Mid-season. Resembles a larger 'Xit'. Scented. Mistakenly registered Div. 3 until 1988

'Picola' 1 W-Y
(H.A. Brown, pre-1938)
Corona lemon yellow, frilled

'Picotee' 1 (a)
(J. Pope, pre-1908)

'Picotee' 2 W-WWO
(G. Errey) G. Errey, 1962
Fl. 102 mm wide; corona with reddish orange at rim. Late

'Picotee Chiffon' 11a W-YWP
(J.Gerritsen & Son) Mrs F.Bullivant, 1997
Sdlg no. GBS 30
Fl. 99 mm wide; perianth segments very broadly ovate, blunt, prominently mucronate, shouldered at base, creamy white, reflexed, plane, overlapping half; the inner segments narrower, inflexed, ribbed, with margins wavy and deeply incurved; corona split to base, the six segments two-thirds the length of the perianth segments, closely overlying and interleaved with them, very deeply bi-lobed, ribbed, pinkish white, with yellow at base and shading to pink (26C) at rim, frilled, with rim often rolled

'Picotee Witch' 2 W-YYR
(Colin Crotty) Colin Crotty, 1992
'Cherryrim' × 'Accent'; sdlg no. 11-76
Fl. 105 mm wide; perianth segments broadly ovate, pure white, overlapping; corona bowl-shaped, creamy yellow, with a broad band of pinkish red at rim, heavily frilled, with rim very deeply crenate. Mid-season

'Picton' 1 W-Y
(J.T. Gray, pre-1950)
Corona lemon yellow, with rim lightly rolled

'Pictorial' 3 Y-O
(C. Goodson, pre-1927)

'Picture' 2 W-O
(J.C. Williams, pre-1945)
Corona very broad, rich apricot, with a deeper tone at rim, with the rim closely and deeply notched, as if fringed

'Picturesque' 2 W-?
(H.A. Brown) J.N. Hancock & Co., 1960

'Piculet' 5 Y-Y
(G.E. Mitsch) G.E. Mitsch, 1969
('Bahram' × 'Ardour') × *N. triandrus* var. *concolor*
Fl. rounded; perianth segments slightly reflexed; corona very shallow bowl-shaped. Mid-season

'Pidget' 9 W-GYR
(Mrs H.K. Richardson) Mrs H.K. Richardson, 1976
'Como' open pollinated
Perianth segments very broad, truncate, a little reflexed, plane, sometimes concave near apex, overlapping half; the inner segments with margins wavy or incurled; corona disc-shaped, closely ribbed, with mouth wavy, rim minutely incised. Dwarf. Late

'Piece of Eight' 1 Y-Y
(T.H. Piper, 1955) Unregistered
'Bulwark' × 'Roundabout'

'Piedmont' 2 W-W
(W.G. Pannill, 1970) W.G. Pannill, 1987
'Easter Moon' × 'Vigil'; sdlg no. D 11 G
Mid-season

'Pieman' 2 W-Y
(Jackson's Daffodils, 1980) Jackson's Daffodils, 1991
'Nala' × 'Lod'; sdlg no. 59/80
Fl. forming a double triangle, 118 mm wide; perianth segments very broadly ovate, blunt, fairly prominently mucronate, greenish white (155A), stained vivid yellow 14B at margins, spreading, plane, smooth and of thick substance, overlapping half; the inner segments square-shouldered at base; corona short funnel-shaped, smooth, vivid yellow 14B, with mouth expanded and even, rim crenate. Mid-season

'Pierette'
(C. Dawson, pre-1907)

'Pierette' 2 Y-YYR
(G. Lewis) D.S. Bell, 1955
Perianth segments deep yellow; corona broad disc-shaped, with bright red at rim

'Pierre' 2 W-YYO
(L. Buckland, pre-1936)

'Pierre Gassend' 2 (a)
(J.W.A. Lefeber, pre-1945)

'Pierrot' 3 W-R
(P.D. Williams, pre-1935)

'Piety' 3 W-W
(A.M. Wilson, pre-1948)

'Pigalle' 2 W-OOY
(J. Gerritsen & Son, pre-1951)
AM(Haarlem) 1951

'Pigeon' 2 W-W
(G.L. Wilson, pre-1952)
'Cushlake' × 'Evening'

'Pigmy' 1 (a)
(W.B. Hartland, pre-1907)

'Piha'
(H.E. Sharp, pre-1915)

'Pikamanu' 3 W-R
(A.B. Davey) A.B. Davey, 1978
'Ellen Mann' × 'Arbar'; sdlg no. 1/5/65
Fl. 88 mm wide. Mid-season. Resembles a much improved 'Ellen Mann'

'Pikiarero' 2 W-W
(A.B. Davey, c.1972) Unregistered

'Pilata' 2 W-W
(J.S. Leitch) J.S. Leitch, 1960
Fl. 115 mm wide. Late

'Pilgrim' 2 W-Y
(G.H. Engleheart, pre-1905)
Perianth segments opening primrose yellow, becoming creamy white; corona ribbed, lemon yellow, lightly frilled

'Pilgrimage' 2 Y-Y
(The Brodie of Brodie, c.1918)
'Pilgrim' × 'Broadford'
Fl. star-shaped, rich yellow; perianth segments broadly ovate, blunt, fairly prominently mucronate, spreading, a little concave and with margins sometimes more strongly incurved in lower half, waxy smooth and of great substance, overlapping one-third; the inner segments slightly inflexed, twisted; corona cup-shaped, smooth, tinged orange, with mouth expanded and loosely frilled. Mid-season. AM(e) 1925

'Pilgrim Father' 2 Y-Y
(The Brodie of Brodie, c.1917)
'Pilgrim' × 'Ben Alder'
Fl. soft yellow

'Pillage' 2 W-W
(J.S. Leitch) J.S. Leitch, 1968

'Pillar Box' 2 Y-OOR
(K.J. Heazlewood) R. Hyde, 1959

'Dunkeld' × 'Royal Mail'
Perianth segments broad, rounded at apex, smooth; corona orange, shading to red at rim, mouth expanded and frilled. Fl. of variable colour

'Pilleth' 2 W-? (b)
(A.M. Wilson, pre-1950)

'Pilot' 3 Y-YYO
(E.M. Crosfield, pre-1909)
Perianth segments primrose yellow; corona expanded, with a narrow band of reddish orange at rim, lightly frilled

'Pilot' 3 W-? (b)
(R.H. Bath, pre-1929)

'Pilot Light' 2 Y-O
(Warnaar & Co., pre-1951)
'Arnhem' × 'Rosslare'
AM(Haarlem) 1951

'Piltaton' 2 W-O
Syn. of 'Philtaton'

'Pilum' 3 W-? (b)
(G.H. Engleheart, pre-1923)

'Pimm' 2 Y-R
(T. Bloomer) Rathowen Daffodils, 1985
'Break of Day' × 'Shining Light'; sdlg no. 291
Perianth segments deep golden yellow, corona bright orange-red. Resembles a richer-coloured 'Shining Light'

'Pimpernel' 2 Y-O
(J. Gerritsen & Son) J. Gerritsen & Son, 1984
'Orange Progress' hybrid
Perianth segments vivid yellow 9A; corona strong orange 30D. Mid-season

'Pinafore' 2 W-W
(G.E. Mitsch, 1955) G.E. Mitsch, 1966
'Green Island' × 'Chinese White'; sdlg no. R33/47
Fl. 102 mm wide; corona with rim rolled. Mid-season

'Pinard' 8 W-O
(pre-1938)
Fls usually 2 per stem; perianth segments creamy white; corona reddish orange

'Pinaroo' 2 W-Y
(Jackson's Daffodils) Jackson's Daffodils, 1993
Sdlg no. 136/85
Fl. forming a double triangle, 115 mm wide; perianth segments broadly ovate, blunt, only very slightly mucronate, greenish white (155A), spreading or a little inflexed, smooth and of thick substance, overlapping half; the inner segments more narrowly ovate, with margins a little wavy; corona funnel-shaped, smooth, vivid yellow 9A, mouth straight and lightly frilled, rim crenate. Early to mid-season

'Pinaster' 2 W-W
(A.H. Ahrens) J.S. Leitch, 1956

'Pinata' 2 Y-R
(J.S. Leitch) J.S. Leitch, 1957

'Pindar' 3 W-GWP
(A.M. Wilson, pre-1930)
Corona with a touch of green at base and with bright pink at rim

'Pineapple Cup' 2 W-Y
(Mrs K.B. Anderson) Mrs K.B. Anderson, 1963
'Tunis' × 'Lord Kitchener'
Fl. 115 mm wide; corona ribbed, opening medium yellow, quickly becoming pale pineapple yellow, with primrose yellow at rim. Early. Resembles an earlier-flowered 'Tunis' with a brighter-coloured corona

'Pineapple Frills' 2 W-Y
(Mrs K.B. Anderson) Mrs K.B. Anderson, 1966
'Pineapple Cup' × 'Gertie Miller'
Fl. 89 mm wide; corona pale pineapple yellow, frilled. Mid-season. Resembles a darker-coloured 'Tunis' with a less deeply frilled corona

'Pineapple Prince' 2 Y-W
(G.E. Mitsch and R. & E.Havens, 1975) G.E. Mitsch and R. & F. Havens, 1987
Sdlg no. KK19/4
Perianth segments deep lemon; corona becoming pure white. Mid-season

'Pinetic'
(?G. Lewis, pre-1940)

'Ping' 2 W-W
(W.M. Spry, pre-1975) Unregistered
'Zero' × Fairbairn sdlg
Tall. Early

'Pinka' 1 W-P
(W. Jackson Sr, 1940) W. Jackson Jr, 1956
'Pink o' Dawn' × 'Mrs R.O.Backhouse'
Corona slender, flushed apricot pink

'Pink Accent' 2 W-P
(D.S. Bell) D.S. Bell, 1982
'Pearlax' × 'Accent'
Fl. 108 mm wide. Mid-season

'Pink-a-dell' 2 W-P
(H.A. Brown, pre-1935)
Corona opening yellow, becoming pink

'Pink Angel' 7 W-GWP
(G.E. Mitsch, 1964) R. Havens, 1980

('Wild Rose' × 'Interim') × *N. jonquilla*; sdlg no. Z46/4
Fls 1-3 per stem, 72 mm wide; perianth segments snow white; corona snow white, with clear green at base and bright pink at rim. Mid-season. Scented

'Pink Art' 2 W-WPP
(D.S. Bell) D.S. Bell, 1968
'Artist's Model' × pink sdlg
Corona broad, almost disc-shaped, pink, with white at base

'Pinkatilla' 2 W-? (b or c)
(J.E. Exley, pre-1938)

'Pink Bairn' 6 W-P
(Mrs C.O.Fairbairn, 1973) F.R.Coles, 1997
Perianth segments broadly ovate in outline, blunt or squarish at apex, slightly mucronate, reflexed, plane, with midrib showing, overlapping half; the inner segments narrower, with margins wavy; corona cylindrical, broad, smooth, with rim deeply rolled

'Pink Beauty' 1 W-YYP
(C.L. Adams, pre-1915)

'Pink Beauty' 2 W-P
(G.L. Wilson) G. Zandbergen-Terwegen, 1957
AM(Haarlem) 1957

'Pink Bell' 2 W-? (b)
(Mrs F.S. Foote, pre-1940)

'Pink Belladonna' 1 W-P
(D.C. Tongs) D.C. Tongs, 1992
'Melancholy' × 'Dear Me'
Fl. rounded, 96 mm wide; perianth segments ovate, greenish white (155A); corona cylindrical, pale yellowish pink, with green in tube, mouth straight. Mid-season

'Pink Blossom' 2 W-P
(O. Ronalds, pre-1955) Unregistered
Perianth segments pure white, smooth; corona bright pink, frilled

'Pink Blush' 2 W-? (b)
(F.H. Chapman, pre-1938)

'Pink Blush' 4 W-P
(W. Jackson Jr, 1970) Unregistered
Sdlg 72/61 × 'Lawali'; sdlg no. 48/70

'Pink Bomb' 2 W-PPR
(G.E. Mitsch and R. & E.Havens, 1971) G.E. Mitsch and R. & E.Havens, 1987
'Precedent' × 'Eclat'; sdlg no. G13/25
Perianth segments broad; corona expanded, deep bright pink, with red at rim. Mid-season

'Pink Bonnet' 2 W-P
(G. Lewis, pre-1956) Unregistered
Fl. large; corona flared and frilled

'Pink Bonningdon' 1 W-P
(C.E. Radcliff, 1945) J.M.Radcliff, 1956
'Bonnington' × 'Dawnglow'
Corona amber pink

'Pink Bowl' 2 W-P
(J.N. Hancock & Co.) J.N. Hancock & Co., 1955
Corona bowl-shaped, flushed creamy pink

'Pink Butterfly' 2 W-? (b)
(Mrs F.S. Foote, pre-1940)

'Pink Camellia' 4 W-P
Syn. of 'Pink Camilla'

'Pink Cameo' 2 W-YPP
(G.H. Johnstone, pre-1953)

'Pink Camilla' 4 W-P
(H.G. Cross, 1974) H.G. Cross, 1984
'Ardbane' × 'Glowing Red'; sdlg no. 53-4
Mid-season. Syn. 'Pink Camellia'

'Pink Candy' 2 W-P
(J.A. O'More) P.D.K. Ramsay, 1983
'Topic' × 'Tarago Pink'

'Pink Caprice' 2 Y-P
(D.S. Bell) D.S. Bell, 1968
'White Sentinel' × 'Seraglio'
Perianth segments lemon; corona soft pink, with rim dentate

'Pinkcarn' 2 W-?
(A. Overton) A. Overton, 1960

'Pink Champagne' 4 W-YPP
(Mrs H.K. Richardson) Mrs H.K. Richardson, 1972
'Marietta' × 'Irani'
Perianth segments overlapping; corona segments rosy pink, with yellow at base

'Pink Charisma' 7 W-GYP
(Eileen E. Frey, 1981) J. & E. Frey, 1993
Sdlg F31/5 × *N. jonquilla*; sdlg no. QEE14/26
Fl. 68 mm wide; perianth segments roundish, reflexed, overlapping a quarter; the inner segments with margins wavy and incurved; corona bowl-shaped, ribbed, opening rich pink, becoming shell pink, with a band of yellow above the green at base, with mouth even. Dwarf. Mid-season to late

'Pink Charm' 2 W-WWP
(P. de Jager & Sons) van Eeden Bros, 1977
Fl. 90 mm wide; perianth segments ivory white; corona yellowish white, with a broad band of chinese coral

at rim. Mid-season

'Pink Chiffon' 4 W-YYP
(A.N. Kanouse) G.E. Mitsch, 1963
'Royal Sovereign' × 'Suda'
Fl. 102 mm wide; perianth and other petaloid segments in two whorls, white; the outer whorl spreading; the inner whorl more or less strongly inflexed; sometimes one or more segments at centre; corona segments tightly clustered at centre, more loosely arranged between the whorls of petaloid segments, creamy yellow, touched with buff pink at rim. Mid-season. 2n=27. Resembles a smaller-flowered 'Pink Cloud'

'Pink Chimes' 5 W-P
(John R.Reed) John R.Reed, 1995
'Roseworthy' × *N. triandrus* var. *concolor*; sdlg no. 83-53-1
Fls 2 per stem, 57 mm wide; perianth segments acute, dull white, with margins slightly wavy; corona cylindrical, long, pure light pink. Dwarf. Mid-season. Sunproof. Resembles a smaller and less formal 'Akepa'

'Pink China' 2 W-P
(R. & E.Havens, 1983) R. & E.Havens, 1994
'Pink Ice' × sdlg HEJ17/?; sdlg no. SEH3/1
Fl. 80 mm wide; perianth segments broadly ovate, rounded at apex, spreading, plane; corona cup-shaped, deep pink. Mid-season. Sunproof

'Pink Cloud' 4 W-P
(Oregon Bulb Farms, pre-1942)

'Pink Cloud' 2 W-PPW
(J.N. Hancock & Co., *c*.1978) Unregistered
Corona bowl-shaped, pink, with white at rim, the outside becoming completely white with age

'Pink Clover' 2 W-P
(Mrs J.Abel Smith) M.W.Baxter, 1996
Sdlg no. D44/35
Fl. 85 mm wide; perianth segments broadly ovate, only very slightly mucronate, pure white, spreading, overlapping one-third to a half; the inner segments with margins incurved; corona broad cup-shaped, loosely ribbed, bright pink (28C), paling to base, mouth straight, more closely ribbed, wavy, with rim more or less entire. Late

'Pink Coat' 2 W-P
(R.C.A. Tombleson) R.C.A. Tombleson, 1964
Fl. 118 mm wide. Mid-season. Resembles a larger 'Mukana' with rounder perianth segments and a brighter pink corona

'Pink Confetti' 2 W-P
(K.J. Heazlewood, *c*.1967) Unregistered
'Rosedale' × 'Mabel Taylor'

'Pink Conquest' 1 Y-P
(D.S.Bell, pre-1986) Unregistered
'Red Conquest' sdlg × 'Hicol'

'Pink Dart' 2 W-P
(G.E. Mitsch, 1978) R. & E. Havens, 1993
('Precedent' × 'Accent') × 'Recital'; sdlg no. NN12/5
Fl. 100 mm wide; perianth segments broadly ovate, slightly reflexed, of heavy substance; corona very shallow, ribbed, intense reddish pink, with mouth frilled. Mid-season. Sunproof

'Pink Dawn' 2 W-P
(Mrs J.Abel Smith) M.W.Baxter, 1996
'Rose Royale' × 'Wellow'; sdlg no. F44/41
Fl. 97 mm wide; perianth segments very broadly ovate, somewhat truncate, mucronate, spreading, creased, overlapping half or more; the inner segments a little narrower, square-shouldered at base; corona cylindrical or somewhat funnel-shaped, loosely ribbed, pink (24C), paler at base, with mouth straight or very slightly flared, frilled. Late

'Pink Declaration' 2 W-P
(G.E. Mitsch and R. & E.Havens, 1971) G.E. Mitsch and R. & E.Havens, 1987
'Precedent' × 'Eclat'; sdlg no. G13/16
Perianth segments broad; corona expanded, deep bright pink, with a deeper tone at rim. Mid-season

'Pink Delight' 2 W-YYP
(Oregon Bulb Farms, pre-1945)

'Pink Delight' 1 W-P
(Mrs C.O. Fairbairn)
Perianth segments broadly ovate, pure white; corona coral pink

'Pink Diamond' 2 W-YYP
(Oregon Bulb Farms, pre-1945)
'Jim' × 'Mrs R.O.Backhouse'

'Pink Dream' 2 W-? (b)
(Mrs F.S. Foote, pre-1941)

'Pink Dresden' 2 W-? (b)
(Oregon Bulb Farms, pre-1946)

'Pink Duet' 4 W-P
(W. Jackson Jr, *c*.1973) Unregistered
'Chimeon' × 'Lawali'

'Pink Easter' 2 W-P
(T.D. Throckmorton) T.D. Throckmorton, 1974
'Easter Moon' × 'Accent'; sdlg no. T/65/20
Fl. forming a double triangle; perianth segments broad; the inner segments smaller; corona apple blossom pink, with greenish tones at base, mouth slightly lobed. Mid-season

'Pinkeen' 2 W-P
(G.L. Wilson, pre-1931)
'Okapi' × 'Tenedos'
Perianth segments very broad, milk white; corona opening soft apricot orange, flushed pink, becoming warm peachy pink

'Pink Elf' 2 W-P
(Mrs J. Abel Smith) Mrs J. Abel Smith, 1992
Fl. 33 mm wide; perianth segments white; corona pink, with a deeper tone at rim. Late

'Pink Elite' 2 W-P
(D.S. Bell) D.S. Bell, 1978
1 Y-Y × 'Hicol'
Fl. 102 mm wide; perianth segments opening white, sometimes becoming yellowish; corona strong pink. Mid-season

'Pinkenba' 2 W-P
(A.O. Roblin, 1942) A.O. Roblin, 1956
'Janet' hybrid × 'Carnlough'
Perianth segments pure white; corona bright pink, frilled

'Pink Era' 2 W-P
(J.A. O'More) P.D.K. Ramsay, 1984
'Vasey' × 'Tarago Pink'; sdlg no. 102/62
Perianth segments milk white, smooth, of good substance; corona funnel-shaped, deep pink, with rim dentate. Late

'Pinkerton' 2 or 3 W-? (h or c)
(Mrs R.O. Backhouse, pre-1910)

'Pinkess' 1 W-P
(W. Jackson Sr, 1939) W. Jackson Jr, 1956
'Pink o' Dawn' × 'Mrs R.O.Backhouse'

'Pinkette' 1 W-? (b)
(Mrs M. Moorby) Mrs M. Moorby, 1957

'Pink Evening' 2 W-YWP
(G.E. Mitsch, 1976) R. & E. Havens, 1990
'Coral Light' × ('Pigeon' × 'Carnmoon'); sdlg no. LL18/5
Fl. 90 mm wide; perianth segments broadly ovate, pure white; corona small bowl-shaped, with deep pink at rim. Late. Varies between Divs 2 and 3

'Pink Fairy' 2 W-P
(S.J. Bisdee, 1939)
'Mary Blewitt' × 'Pink o' Dawn'

'Pink Fancy' 2 W-P
(L. van Leeuwen & Son, pre-1943)
'Mrs R.O.Backhouse' hybrid
Corona opening pale apricot, with a broad band of very pale yellow at rim, soon becoming apricot pink, with a paler tone outside, with rim closely and deeply notched, as if fringed. 2n=28. AM(Haarlem) 1942

'Pink Favourite' 2 W-OOP
Syn. of 'Pink Select'

'Pink Fire' 2 W-P
(G.E. Mitsch and R. & E.Havens, 1975) G.E. Mitsch and R. & E.Havens, 1988
('Precedent' × 'Accent') × 'Spaceship'; sdlg no. KK32/4A
Perianth segments pure white; corona bowl-shaped, deep reddish pink, frilled. Mid-season

'Pink Fizz' 2 W-P
(J.N. Hancock & Co., 1955)

'Pink Flair' 2 W-P
(J.N. Hancock & Co., c.1977) Unregistered

'Pink Flame' 2 W-P
(G.E. Mitsch and R. & E.Havens, 1975) G.E. Mitsch and R. & E.Havens, 1988
('Precedent' × 'Accent') × 'Spaceship'; sdlg no. KK32/2
Perianth segments pure white; corona bowl-shaped, slightly flared, very deep reddish pink, frilled. Mid-season

'Pink Flamingo' 2 W-P
(K.J. Heazlewood)
'Lyetta' × 'Mabel Taylor'

'Pink Flare' 2 W-P
(Murray W. Evans, 1964) Murray W. Evans, 1976
'Rose of Tralee' × 'Rose City'; sdlg no. H-45
Fl. 95 mm wide. Mid-season

'Pink Formal' 11a W-P
(G.E. Mitsch, 1979) R. & E. Havens, 1993
'Recital' × 'Phantom'; sdlg no. 205/3
Fl. 110 mm wide; perianth segments ovate, acute; corona split, the six segments ribbed, mid-apricot pink, heavily frilled. Mid-season. Sunproof

'Pink Frill' 2 W-P
(J.T. Gray, pre-1949)

'Pink Frills' 2 W-GPW
(H.R.Mott) Unregistered
Perianth segments roundish; corona pink, with green at base and flecks of white at rim, frilled. Late

'Pink Frost' 2 W-P
(G.E. Mitsch and R. & E.Havens) Grant Mitsch Novelty Daffodils, 1984
'Lough Maree' × 'Radiation'; sdlg no. Q52/1
Fl. 105 mm wide; perianth segments milk white; corona light pink, with a hint of lavender. Mid-season

'Pink Garden' 2 W-GPP

(W.G. Pannill) W.G. Pannill, 1985
('Wild Rose' × 'Interim') × 'Infatuation'; sdlg no. G 22
Mid-season

'Pink Gem' 2 W-P
(Oregon Bulb Farms, pre-1942)
Corona opening salmon pink, becoming clear pink

'Pink Gin' 4 W-P
(Mrs H.K. Richardson) Mrs H.K. Richardson, 1976
'Marietta' × 'Irani'
Mid-season

'Pink Gin' 2 W-GPP
(G.H. Johnstone, pre-1960) Unregistered

'Pink Gin II'
(?G.H. Johnstone, pre-1959) Unregistered

'Pink Glacier' 11a W-P
(G.E. Mitsch, 1979) R. & E. Havens, 1993
'Recital' × 'Phantom'; sdlg no. 205/1
Fl. 90 mm wide; perianth segments fairly broadly ovate; corona split, the six segments light pink, shading to a deeper tone at rim, spreading, frilled. Mid-season. Sunproof

'Pink Gleam' 2 W-P
Syn. of 'Valana'

'Pink Glory' 2 W-P
(L. van Leeuwen & Son, pre-1948)
? × 'Mrs R.O.Backhouse'
Perianth segments pure white; corona opening light orange-yellow, soon becoming pink. 2n=26

'Pink Glow' 2 W-? (b)
(W.J. Dunlop, pre-1947)

'Pink Goblet' 2 W-? (b)
(Mrs F.S. Foote, pre-1940)

'Pink Halo' 2 W-PPW
(John R.Reed, 1984) John R.Reed, 1997
'Salome' × 'Tangent'; sdlg no. 79-6-1
Fl. forming a double triangle, 100 mm wide; perianth segments ovate, clean white, smooth; corona short cylindrical or somewhat funnel-shaped, deep pink. Mid-season. Sunproof

'Pink Holly' 11a W-P
(R. & E. Havens) R. & E. Havens, 1991
'Space Ship' × sdlg D7/12 ('Accent' × sdlg Q97/2); sdlg no. PEH26/4
Corona split, the six segments clear rosy pink, frilled. Mid-season. The corona deeper in tone than that of 'Phantom'

'Pink Horizon' 3 W-P
(G.L. Wilson, pre-1948)
AM(Haarlem) 1948

'Pink House' 2 W-? (b)
(J.T. Gray, pre-1951)

'Pink Hummer' 7 W-GPP
(Eileen E. Frey, 1981) J. & E. Frey, 1993
Sdlg F31/5 × *N. jonquilla*; sdlg no. QEE4/7
Fl. 65 mm wide; perianth segments opening with pink at base, becoming self white; corona opening rich pink, becoming clear pink, with green at base. Dwarf. Late

'Pink Ice' 2 W-P
(Elise Havens) G.E. Mitsch, 1977
'Precedent' × sdlg A5/12 ('Caro Nome' × 'Accent'); sdlg no. GEJ5/17
Fl. 85 mm wide; perianth segments very broadly ovate, fairly prominently mucronate, ivory white, spreading, a little concave and with margins minutely incurling, smooth, overlapping half; the inner segments a little inflexed; corona bowl-shaped, smooth, salmon pink, with mouth ribbed and straight, frilled, with rim crenate. Mid-season. Resembles a smaller 'Coral Light' with the corona self coloured on opening

'Pinkie' 9 W-WWP
(Mrs R.O. Backhouse, pre-1910)
Perianth segments broad, rounded at apex, slightly mucronate, opening greenish and becoming pure white, spreading or reflexed, overlapping half; the inner segments sometimes twisted, with margins recurved at base and sometimes wavy or incurved in upper part; corona almost disc-shaped, ribbed, opening green, becoming greenish white, with a narrow band of coral pink at rim paling with age

'Pinkie' 2 W-P
(C.E. Radcliff, 1934)
'Pink'un' × 'Mrs Moodie'

'Pinkie Too' 2 W-P
(Ken McCombe) Unregistered
Perianth segments broad, pure white; corona rich pink, with rim dentate. Mid-season

'Pink Isle' 2 W-P
(W.J. Dunlop, pre-1947)
'White Sentinel' × 'Carnlough'
Perianth segments broadly ovate, blunt, slightly mucronate, spreading, plane, overlapping half; the inner segments more narrowly ovate, very slightly inflexed, a little concave; corona cup-shaped, salmon pink, with mouth straight and a little wavy, rim entire. PC 1954

'Pink Jewel' 3 W-GWP
(E.W. Cotter) E.W. Cotter, 1968

'Dallas' × 'Dreamlight'
Fl. rounded, 76 mm wide; perianth segments glistening white, of waxy substance; corona disc-shaped, white, with emerald green at base and a line of bright pink at rim

'Pink Ki' 2 W-P
(E.W. Philpott)

'Pink Lace' 2 W-P
(G.E. Mitsch, pre-1952)
'Shirley Wyness' × 'Pink-a-dell'; sdlg no. J80/1
Perianth segments broadly ovate or somewhat oblong, blunt and very slightly mucronate, spreading, plane, overlapping half; the inner segments more distinctly ovate, a little inflexed, with margins wavy; corona funnel-shaped, lightly ribbed, opening creamy lemon yellow, becoming shell pink in two or three days, fading with age, mouth straight, split in places and overlapping, deeply frilled. Mid-season

'Pink Lace' 2 W-GPP
(Tom Forster, 1960s) Unregistered
Perianth segments roundish; corona large, flared, pure pink, with green at base, heavily frilled. Tall. Late

'Pink Lady' 1 W-WYP
(C.L. Adams, pre-1916)

'Pink Lady' 2 W-? (b or c)
(West & Fell, pre-1936)
Fl. light buff; corona with rim rolled

'Pinklette' 1 W-P
(W. Jackson Sr, 1940)
'Pink o' Dawn' × 'Mrs R.O.Backhouse'

'Pink Lightning' 7 W-GPP
(Eileen E.Frey, 1981) J. & E.Frey, 1994
Sdlg G27/1 × *N. jonquilla*; sdlg no. QEE15/1
Fls 1-2 per stem, 23 mm wide; perianth segments very broadly ovate, reflexed, deeply overlapping; the inner segments with margins slightly wavy; corona opening with an orange cast, becoming very deep pink. Dwarf. Mid-season to late

'Pink Lotus' 2 W-P
(E.W. Cotter) E.W. Cotter, 1968
'Salmon Trout' × 'Roselene'
Corona apricot pink, with a slightly lighter tone at base, with rim rolled

'Pink Maerie' 2 W-P
(Mrs M. Moorby) Mrs M.Moorby, 1963
Perianth segments smooth, overlapping; corona very shallow. Mid-season

'Pink Magic' 2 W-? (b)
(Mrs F.S. Foote, pre-1940)

'Pink Melody' 2 W-? (b)
(Mrs F.S. Foote, pre-1940)

'Pink Mentone' 2 W-? (b)
(pre-1956) Unregistered
Corona apricot, shaded pink outside, with rim closely and deeply notched, as if fringed

'Pink Migration' 4 W-P
(G.E. Mitsch and R. & E.Havens, 1971) G.E. Mitsch and R. & E.Havens, 1987
'Precedent' × 'Pink Cloud'; sdlg no. G70/6
Perianth and other petaloid segments white; the outer whorl broadly ovate, blunt, slightly mucronate, spreading, with margins incurling and midrib showing, overlapping half; the inner whorl shorter, inflexed, with margins tightly incurled; corona segments two-thirds the length of the inner whorl of petaloid segments and opposite and closely overlying them, broad, frilled, sometimes crumpled, clear pink. Late

'Pink Mink' 2 Y-P
(Brian S. Duncan) Rathowen Daffodils, 1978
'Binkie' hybrid × Rathowen sdlg 3341; sdlg no. 89
Perianth segments mid- to pale yellow; corona pale pink. Mid-season. Resembles 'Milestone'

'Pink Mist' 2 W-? (b)
(Oregon Bulb Farms, pre-1945)

'Pink Mitylene' 2 W-P
(The Brodie of Brodie, pre-1943)
'Mitylene' × 'Evening'

'Pink Monarch' 2 W-P
(C.E. Radcliff, 1948)
'Rosario' × 'Rosebowl'
Fl. 118 mm wide; perianth segments very broadly ovate, blunt, very slightly mucronate, pure white, spreading, smooth, overlapping half or more; the inner segments more narrowly ovate, a little inflexed, with margins slightly wavy; corona clear rose pink, loosely frilled, rim flanged and deeply crenate, with the crenations often overlapping

'Pink Morn' 2 W-GWP
(Mrs G. Link) Mrs G. Link, 1988
'Glenside' × 'Tangent'; sdlg no. 1679-B
Fl. 100 mm wide. Mid-season. Resembles a smoother 'Tangent' of better form and heavier substance

'Pink Nautilus' 2 W-P
(C.E. Radcliff, 1938) J.M.Radcliff, 1956
'Nautilus' × 'Pink o' Dawn'
Corona flushed amber pink, with solid amber pink at rim

'Pink o' Dawn' 1 W-P
(C.E. Radcliff, 1931)

'Lemon Star' × 'Mrs Moodie'
Perianth segments broadly ovate, blunt, slightly mucronate, spreading, ribbed, with margins very slightly incurling at apex, overlapping half; the inner segments narrower, of apparently varying width, slightly inflexed; corona bowl-shaped, with mouth expanded and loosely frilled, rim notched and crenate

'Pink of Perfection' 2 W-? (b)
(Alister Clark, pre-1932) J. Sharp, 1960

'Pink Opal' 2 W-? (b)
(J.W. Barr, pre-1930)

'Pink Pacer' 2 W-P
(W.M. Spry, pre-1973) Unregistered
'Pink Promise' × 'Sweetness'
Corona powder pink. Very early. 2n=28

'Pink Pageant' 4 W-P
(Brian S. Duncan) Rathowen Daffodils, 1976
('Falaise' × 'Debutante') × 'Polonaise'; sdlg no. 73
Fl. rounded; perianth and other petaloid segments pure white; the outer whorl very broad, a little truncate and very slightly mucronate, spreading, plane, smooth and of heavy substance, overlapping more than half; the inner segments of the outer whorl very little narrower, rounded at apex, not noticeably mucronate, slightly inflexed; the inner whorl half as long as the outer whorl, regularly arranged, inflexed, with margins folded inwards and tightly incurled; corona segments short, clustered at centre and tightly frilled, more loosely arranged and sometimes continuous between the whorls of petaloid segments, deep pink. Mid-season. 2n=27

'Pink Pageant' 4 W-P
(W. Jackson Jr, 1965) Unregistered
'Chimeon' × 'Lawali'; sdlg no. 5/65

'Pink Panther' 2 W-P
(Mrs J. Abel Smith) Mrs J. Abel Smith, 1974
'Infatuation' × 'Chelsea Derby'; sdlg no. U4/81
Fl. 105 mm wide; corona bright pink. Mid-season. 2n=28

'Pink Parade' 2 W-P
(G.E. Mitsch and R. & E.Havens, 1971) G.E. Mitsch and R. & E.Havens, 1985
'Precedent' × 'Eclat'; sdlg no. G13/42
Corona rich apricot pink. Tall. Mid-season. Resembles 'Pink Valentine' but with a longer corona

'Pink Paradise' 4 W-P
(Brian S. Duncan) Rathowen Daffodils, 1976
('Falaise' × 'Debutante') × 'Polonaise'; sdlg no. 81
Perianth and other petaloid segments broadly ovate, rounded or very sightly truncate at apex, only very slightly mucronate, white, concave, overlapping half; the outer whorl spreading; the inner whorl inflexed; some shorter segments at centre irregularly arranged, broad, strongly inflexed, with margins tightly incurled; corona segments half as long as the centre petaloid segments and clustered among them, more loosely arranged between the surrounding whorls, broad, bright rose pink, heavily frilled. Mid-season. 2n=28

'Pink Paragon' 1 W-P
(S.J. Bisdee) S.J. Bisdee, 1956
Sdlg 120/45 × 'Wild Rose'

'Pink Parasol' 1 Y-YOO
(J.Gerritsen & Son) H.Wijnhout & Son, 1994
Fl. 80 mm wide; perianth segments a little paler than pale greenish yellow 1D; corona light orange 26C or a tone paler (26D), touched yellow at base. Mid-season

'Pink Parfait' 2 W-P
(J.N. Hancock & Co., pre-1974) Unregistered
Perianth segments deep cream; corona widely expanded, pinky buff

'Pink Pearl' 3 W-? (b)
(G.H. Engleheart, pre-1908)

'Pink Pearl' 1 W-P
(de Graaff Bros, pre-1914)
Corona flushed rose pink. AM(Haarlem) 1914

'Pink Pearl' 2 W-P
(H.A. Brown) J.N. Hancock & Co., 1960
'Nelly' × 'Seraglio'
Perianth segments pure white; corona opening creamy buff, becoming clear pink. Mid-season

'Pink Perfection' 2 W-? (b)
(Oregon Bulb Farms, pre-1945)

'Pink Perfume' 2 W-WPP
(G.E. Mitsch, 1965) G.E. Mitsch, 1979
'Flamingo' × 'Accent'; sdlg no. A16/7
Fl. 95 mm wide; perianth segments milk white; corona opening self pink, becoming white at base. Mid-season. Scented

'Pink Perry' 2 Y-P
(Brian S.Duncan) Brian S.Duncan, 1997
'Rose Gold' × 'Sandycove'; sdlg no. 1619
Fl. 100 mm wide; perianth segments broadly ovate, blunt, opening with pinkish tones, becoming honey yellow, spreading; corona cylindrical, warm lilac pink, with mouth even. Mid-season to late

'Pink Petti' 2 W-P
(A.O. Roblin, 1942)
'Mitylene' hybrid

'Pink Petticoat' 2 W-P
(S.J. Bisdee, 1942)
'White Sentinel' × 'Pinkeen'

'Pink Plantation' 2 W-P
(G.E. Mitsch and R. & E.Havens, 1970) G.E. Mitsch and R. & E.Havens, 1986
('Precedent' × 'Carita') × 'Radiation' hybrid; sdlg no. F67/3
Fl. large, of strong substance; perianth segments broad; corona opening rich pink, becoming pale pink, with a slightly darker tone at rim. Mid-season. Resembles a larger-flowered 'Sentinel' with a paler corona

'Pink Platter' 2 W-WPP
(J.A.Hunter) J.A.Hunter, 1997
'Fair Prospect' × 'Caro Nome'; sdlg no. 44/83A
Fl. 112 mm wide; perianth segments ovate, rounded at apex; corona disc-shaped, smooth, with mouth wavy. Mid-season

'Pink Porcelain' 2 Y-P
(D.S. Bell) D.S. Bell, 1960
Fl. 108 mm wide; perianth segments opening white, becoming lemon yellow. Mid-season

'Pink Pride' 2 W-WPP
(W.P. van Eeden) W.P. van Eeden, 1970
'Pink Rim' × 'Lady Kesteven'
AM(Haarlem) 1970

'Pink Princess' 2 W-P
(S.J. Bisdee, 1943)
'White Sentinel' × 'Igerna'

'Pink Prism' 2 W-P
(C.L. Andrews)

'Pink Promise' 2 W-WWP
(G.H. Johnstone, pre-1954)

'Pink Promise' 2 W-P
(O. Ronalds)

'Pink Puff' 4 W-P
(W.G. Pannill) W.G. Pannill, 1990
'Androcles' × 'Alumna'
Mid-season to late

'Pink Punch' 2 W-WWP
(Oregon Bulb Farms, pre-1942)

'Pink Pussy Cat' 2 W-P
(J.N. Hancock & Co., 1967) Unregistered

'Pink Quartz' 2 W-PPW
(J.A. Hunter) J.A. Hunter, 1989
'Tangent' × 'Vascule'; sdlg no. 2/78A
Fl. 114 mm wide; perianth segments broadly ovate, pure white, smooth and of good substance; corona slightly expanding towards mouth, strong pink 49A, with white at rim, frilled. Mid-season to late

'Pink Ray' 2 W-? (b)
(J.T. Gray, pre-1949)

'Pink Reward'
(pre-1960) Unregistered

'Pink Ribbon' 2 W-WWP
(S.J. Bisdee, 1946)

'Pink Rim' 2 W-YYP
(?F. Rijnveld & Sons, pre-1939)
Corona with a distinct band of light pink at rim. 2n=21. AM(Haarlem) 1947

'Pink Robe' 2 W-? (b)
(Mrs F.S. Foote, pre-1940)

'Pink Robe' 2 W-? (b)
(pre-1949)

'Pink Romance' 2 W-P
(C.A. Latta) C.A. Latta, 1964
Fl. 108 mm wide; corona pale pink. Mid-season. Resembles 'Pink Pearl'

'Pink Rosette' 4 W-P
(W. Jackson Jr) W. Jackson Jr, 1968
'Lawali' × sdlg 42/61; sdlg no. 77/65

'Pink Ruffles' 2 W-P
(K.J. Heazlewood) K.J. Heazlewood, 1968
'Mabel Taylor' hybrid

'Pink Sable' 4 W-P
(D.S. Bell) D.S. Bell, 1979
('Papanui Queen' × 'Green Island') × 'Temple Bells' × 'Hicol'
Fl. 110 mm wide; perianth and other petaloid segments pure white; corona segments soft pink. Mid-season

'Pink Sacrifice' 2 W-P
(G.J. Phillips, 1980) G.J. Phillips, 1992
'Fair Prospect' × 'Dear Me'; sdlg no. 75-78-2
Fl. 115 mm wide. Early

'Pink Sapphire' 2 W-P
(J.A. Hunter) J.A. Hunter, 1992
Fl. 100 mm wide; perianth segments broadly ovate; corona cylindrical, with mouth slightly expanded. Early to mid-season

'Pink Satin' 2 W-P
(G.E. Mitsch and R. & E.Havens, 1974) G.E. Mitsch and R. & E.Havens, 1987
('Radiation' × 'Rima') × 'C.E.Radcliff'; sdlg no. JJ22/4A

Very smooth. Early

'Pink Select' 2 W-OOP
(L. van Leeuwen & Son, pre-1947)
Perianth segments broadly ovate, blunt, prominently mucronate, creamy white, spreading, plane, overlapping one-third; the inner segments more narrowly ovate, square-shouldered at base, with margins wavy; corona funnel-shaped, smooth, opening pale yellow, becoming apricot orange, with soft pink at rim, mouth expanded and frilled. 2n=27+1B. Syn. 'Pink Favourite'. AM(Haarlem) 1946

'Pink Sensation' 2 W-P
(G.L. Wilson, pre-1950)
AM(Haarlem) 1950. Received AM(Haarlem) 1950 as 'Rosy Pink'

'Pink Sentinel' 2 W-? (b)
(F.E. Gibbs, pre-1948)

'Pink Shadow' 2 Y-P
(Mrs J. Abel Smith, 1975) Mrs J. Abel Smith, 1992
'Rosedew' × 'Chelsea Derby'; sdlg no J1/71
Fl. 35 mm wide; perianth segments pale lemon yellow; corona bright pink. Late

'Pink Shell' 2 W-P
(G. Lewis) D.S. Bell, 1955

'Pink Silhouette' 2 W-P
(W. Jackson Jr, 1969) Jackson's Daffodils, 1979
'Verran' × 'Egina'; sdlg no. 200/69
Fl. 110 mm wide. Mid-season

'Pink Silk' 1 W-P
(R. Havens) R. Havens, 1980
'At Dawning' × 'Graduation'; sdlg no. NEJ11/1
Fl. forming a double triangle, 95 mm wide, smooth and of good substance; perianth segments very broadly ovate, blunt, slightly mucronate, spreading, plane, smooth, with margins slightly incurling, overlapping half; the inner segments more narrowly ovate, a little inflexed, with margins sometimes wavy; corona funnel-shaped, angled, pale pink at base, shading to bright pink at rim, mouth ribbed and flared, wavy, rim minutely and regularly crenate. Mid-season. Resembles a larger and more brightly coloured 'At Dawning'

'Pink Sister' 2 W-? (b)
(pre-1949)
Fl. pinkish buff

'Pink Sky' 4 W-P
(G.E. Mitsch, 1977) R. & E. Havens, 1991
'Pink Chiffon' × sdlg A6/5 ('Caro Nome' × 'Carita'); sdlg no. MM30/5
Fl. 120 mm wide. Mid-season

'Pink Smiles' 2 W-P
(W.J. Dunlop, pre-1953)
'White Sentinel' × 'Trousseau'
Corona deep amber pink. 2n=28

'Pink Sparkler' 2 W-P
(G.E. Mitsch and R. & E.Havens, 1971) G.E. Mitsch and R. & E.Havens, 1987
'Precedent' × 'Eclat'; sdlg no. G13/15
Perianth segments broad, of strong substance; corona large, bright pink, with a few white flecks. Mid-season

'Pink Special' 2 W-P
(A. Glover, c.1965) Unregistered
'C.E.Radcliff' × 'Salmon Trout'
Perianth segments broadly ovate, blunt, only very slightly mucronate, spreading, plane, overlapping half; the inner segments a little inflexed; corona funnel-shaped, smooth, with mouth expanded and even, rim notched and minutely crenate, slightly rolled

'Pink Sprite' 2 W-P
(G.E. Mitsch) G.E. Mitsch, 1960
('Mitylene' × 'Mrs R.O. Backhouse') × 'Wild Rose'

'Pink Star' 2 W-YPP
(F.A. Saunders) F.A. Saunders, 1966
'Carnlough' × 'Panshanger'
Fl. 95 mm wide; perianth segments broad; corona with creamy yellow at base. Mid-season

'Pink Step' 7 W-P
(G.E. Mitsch and R. & E.Havens, 1972) G.E. Mitsch and R. & E.Havens, 1988
'Quick Step' open pollinated; sdlg no. HO20/7
Fls 2-3 per stem; corona bowl-shaped, pastel pink. Dwarf. Late. 2n=28. Resembles an improved 'Quick Step' with a darker corona

'Pink Sugar' 2 W-? (b)
(A. Gibson, pre-1951)

'Pink Sunrise' 2 W-? (b)
(J.T. Gray, pre-1950)

'Pink Sunset' 2 W-P
(Alfred Clark) Alfred Clark, 1955

'Pink Supreme' 2 W-P
(C.V. Hybrida) Doornbosch Bros, 1958
Perianth segments pure white

'Pink Surprise' 2 W-WPP
(John R.Reed) John R.Reed, 1995
'Precedent' × 'Rainbow'; sdlg no. 81-2-1
Fl. 102 mm wide; perianth segments ovate, slightly reflexed; corona bowl-shaped, light pink. Mid-season. Sunproof

'Pink Swan' 2 W-P
(G.E. Mitsch, 1970) Grant Mitsch Novelty Daffodils, 1984
'Mrs Oscar Ronalds' × 'Debutante'; sdlg no. F27/1
Fl. 110 mm wide. Mid-season

'Pink Sweetie' 3 W-?
(Mrs B.A. Woods) Mrs B.A. Woods, 1968

'Pink Symphony' 2 W-? (b)
(Mrs F.S. Foote, pre-1940)

'Pink Tango' 11a W-P
(G.E.Mitsch & R. & E.Havens, 1975) R. & E. Havens, 1991
Sdlg C53/11 (['Loch Maree' × 'Radiation'] × 'Accent') × 'Phantom'; sdlg no. KK28/1
Fl. of strong colour and heavy substance; perianth segments broadly ovate, clean white, spreading, with margins incurling, overlapping half; the inner segments with margins wavy or more strongly incurved; corona split to base, the six segments half as long as the perianth segments and closely overlying them, ribbed, clear pink, heavily frilled. Mid-season. Resembles a more heavily frilled 'Phantom' of deeper colour

'Pink Tea' 2 W-P
(Murray W. Evans) Murray W. Evans, 1979
'Irish Rose' × ('Cordial' × 'Accent'); sdlg no. P-20
Fl. 110 mm wide. Mid-season

'Pink Terrace' 1 W-P (b)
(C. Goodson) R. Hyde, 1958

'Pink Treasure' 2 W-P
(M. Gardiner)

'Pink Tutu' 2 W-P
(O.David Niswonger) O.David Niswonger, 1993
'Carita' × 'Impact'; sdlg no. 1-88
Fl. 95 mm wide; perianth segments broadly ovate, spreading, twisted; corona bowl-shaped, near to salmon pink, with mouth flared and frilled, rim flanged. Late. Sunproof

'Pink'un' 2 W-YYP
(L. Buckland, pre-1912)
'Maria Magdaline de Graaff' hybrid
Perianth segments pure white; corona widely expanded, canary yellow, with salmon pink at rim

'Pink Valentine' 2 W-WPP
(G.E. Mitsch and R. & E.Havens, 1971) G.E. Mitsch and R. & E.Havens, 1985
'Precedent' × 'Eclat'; sdlg no. G13/23
Perianth segments very broadly ovate, blunt, slightly mucronate, spreading, concave, smooth, overlapping half; the inner segments with margins wavy or more strongly incurved; corona bowl-shaped, ribbed, bright pink, with white at base, frilled. Mid-season

'Pink Valley' 2 W-P
(G.E. Mitsch and R. & E.Havens, 1965) G.E. Mitsch and R. & E.Havens, 1985
'Precedent' × 'Carita'; sdlg no. A34/22
Fl. of heavy substance; perianth segments broadly ovate, blunt, slightly mucronate, a little inflexed, concave, with margins incurling, overlapping half; the inner segments creased, with margins wavy; corona broad bowl-shaped, soft pink, paling to buff pink at rim, mouth expanded and closely ribbed, even, rim crenate. Mid-season

'Pink Velvet' 2 W-P
(P. Phillips) P. Phillips, 1966
Fl. 115 mm wide; corona frilled. Late

'Pink Wax' 2 W-P
(John R.Reed) John R.Reed, 1995
'Ruby Throat' × 'Verran'; sdlg no. 81-112-1
Fl. 97 mm wide; perianth segments broadly ovate, clear white; corona funnel-shaped, pure intense pink. Early. Sunproof

'Pink Whispers' 2 W-P
(Mrs J. Abel Smith) Mrs J. Abel Smith, 1986
'Chelsea China' × 'Fair Prospect'
Corona deep rose pink, with rim dentate. Mid-season

'Pink Wing' 2 W-P
(Murray W. Evans) Murray W. Evans, 1979
('Rose City' × 'Irish Rose') × 'Caro Nome'; sdlg no. P-5
Fl. 97 mm wide. Mid-season

'Pink Wraith' 2 W-? (b)
(Oregon Bulb Farms, pre-1945)

'Pin Money' 7 Y-O
(C.R. Wootton) M.J. Jefferson-Brown, 1975
'Blinkbonny' × *N. jonquilla*
?The same as 'Pinmoney'

'Pinmoney'
(C.R. Wootton, pre-1961) Unregistered
?Syn. of 'Pin Money'

'Pinnacle' 2 W-P
(Alister Clark, 1935) J. Sharp, 1960

'Pinnacle' 2 W-W
(pre-1931)

'Pinnacle' 1 Y-Y
(P. van Deursen, 1947) L. van Hensbergen, 1961
Fl. 120 mm wide; perianth segments brilliant greenish yellow 4A; corona vivid yellow 12A. Mid-season. Resembles a larger-flowered and darker-coloured 'Joseph MacLeod'

'Pinnocchio' 3 Y-GYO
(J.N. Hancock & Co., 1946)
'Diolite' × 'Seraglio'
Corona tightly ribbed, pale yellow, with green at base and orange at rim

'Pinocchio' 2 W-GOO
(R.V. Favell, pre-1946)
'Therapia' hybrid

'Pinque'
(W.Jackson Sr, pre-1936)

'Pinquita' 2 W-P
(Alister Clark, 1937) J. Sharp, 1960

'Pinsk' 2 W-YPP
(C.E. Radcliff, 1943)
'Pinkeen' × 'Dawnglow'

'Pinta' 2 W-P
(S.J. Bisdee, 1946)
'Rosemount' hybrid

'Pintio' 2 Y-O
(J.S. Leitch) J.S. Leitch, 1956

'Pinup' 2 W-?
(A. Overton) A. Overton, 1960

'Pinwheel' 2 Y-Y
(G.E. Mitsch, pre-1952)
'John Evelyn' × 'Fortune'; sdlg no. 37C14/14
Perianth segments light yellow; corona almost disc-shaped, very large, deep yellow. Mid-season

'Pinza' 2 Y-YYO
(J.L. Richardson) Mrs H.K. Richardson, 1962
'Ceylon' × 'Narvik'
Fl. 94 mm wide; perianth segments broadly ovate, blunt, slightly mucronate, vivid yellow 9A, spreading, plane, smooth, regular, overlapping half; the inner segments slightly more narrowly ovate, shouldered at base, a little inflexed; corona cup-shaped, lightly ribbed, vivid orange-yellow 21A at base, shading to a broad band of orange (28A) at rim, mouth more closely ribbed, lightly frilled, with rim slightly flanged. 2n=28. AM(e) 1962, *AM(g) 1966, *FCC(g) 1970, HC(p) 1986, AGM 1993

'Pionbo' 11?b W-R
(J.W.A. Lefeber) J.W.A. Lefeber, 1968

'Pioneer' 1 W-W
(R H. Bath, pre-1929)

'Pioneer' 1 W-Y
(van der Meer Bros, 1930) van der Meer Bros, 1961
Fl. 110 mm wide; perianth segments creamy white; corona deep yellow. Early. 2n=28

'Pioneer' 2 Y-YOO
(J.N. Hancock & Co., 1946)

'Pip' 2 W-? (b)
(A.H. Ahrens) J.S. Leitch, 1955

'Pipe Major' 2 Y-O
(F.E. Board) F.E. Board, 1965
'Kindled' × 'Craigywarren'
Corona reddish orange. Late. 2n=28

'Piper' 2 W-P
(J.S. Leitch) J.S. Leitch, 1966
Fl. 108 mm wide

'Pipers Barn' 7 Y-Y
(A. Gray, pre-1947)
N. jonquilla sdlg
Fl deep butter yellow; perianth segments acute, reflexed. 2n=20

'Piper's End' 3 W-GWW
(Mrs J. Abel Smith) Mrs J. Abel Smith, 1984
'Mary Isabel' hybrid; sdlg no. F33/11
Perianth segments very broad, rounded at apex, deeply truncate, reflexed, a little concave, regular, overlapping half; the inner segments narrower, with margins recurved at base; corona shallow bowl-shaped, with deep green at base, mouth expanded and lightly frilled

'Piper's Gold' 1 Y-Y
(Brian S.Duncan) Brian S.Duncan, 1996
'Goldfinger' open pollinated; sdlg no. 1435
Fl. 105 mm wide, deep golden yellow; perianth segments very broadly ovate, only slightly mucronate, spreading, plane, smooth, overlapping half or more; the inner segments a little narrower, touching each other at the square shoulder at base; corona cylindrical, smooth, darker in tone than the perianth, mouth straight, wavy, with rim very lightly dentate. Late to very late

'Pipes o' Pan' 5 W-W
(A.E. Lowe, pre-1927)

'Pipestem' 2 W-P
(Curtis Tolley) Curtis Tolley, 1997
'Mentor' × 'Pol Voulin'; sdlg no. 89-47
Fl. forming a double triangle, 97 mm wide; perianth segments acute, spreading; corona funnel-shaped, orange-pink (25D), lightly frilled, with rim flanged. Mid-season. Sunproof

'Pipestone' 2 W-R
(Murray W. Evans) Murray W. Evans, 1979
'Accent' × ('Caro Nome' × 'Allurement'); sdlg no. N-51
Fl. 115 mm wide; perianth segments ovate, blunt, fairly prominently mucronate, spreading, with mar-

gins incurling at apex, overlapping one-third to a half; the inner segments a little inflexed, wth margins incurved; corona cylindrical, short, broadly ribbed, red (40C), with a narrow band of yellow at base, mouth straight, more closely ribbed, wavy, with rim crenate. Mid-season

'Piping Time' 6 Y-Y
(F.Silcock, 1979) F.Silcock, 1993
'Jobi' × *N. cyclamineus*
Perianth segments reflexed; corona cylindrical. Mid-season

'Pipit' 7 YYW-W
(G.E. Mitsch) G.E. Mitsch, 1963
'Binkie' × *N. jonquilla*; sdlg no. T6/6
Fls 2-3 per stem, 70 mm wide; perianth segments broadly ovate, pale sulphur yellow, with slight white mucro, paling almost to pure white at base, spreading, with margins incurling, overlapping one-third; the inner segments a little inflexed, with margins wavy or more strongly incurved; corona short funnel-shaped, lightly ribbed, opening pale sulphur yellow, becoming near to pure white, mouth straight, loosely frilled. Mid-season. 2n=21

'Pippa' 9 W-GYR
(A.M. Wilson) D.W. Gourlay, 1957
Corona light yellow, with green at base and red at rim

'Pippin' 3 W-O
(F.H. Chapman, pre-1916)
'Princess Mary' × 'Chaucer'
Perianth segments cream; corona broad, orange. AM(p) 1916

'Pip Pip' 4
(W.F.M. Copeland, pre-1907)

'Pippykin' 7
(R.V. Favell) Treneweth Valley Flower Farm, 1956
'Adela' × *N. jonquilla*

'Piquant' 3 W-O
(Murray W. Evans) Murray W. Evans, 1974
'Blarney' × 'Artist's Model'
Fl. 122 mm wide

'Pique' 2 Y-O
(J.S. Leitch) J.S. Leitch, 1964

'Piraeus' 4 W-R
(Brian S. Duncan) Rathowen Daffodils, 1988
'Monterrico' × 'Doctor Hugh'; sdlg no. 752
Fl. rounded; perianth and other petaloid segments in several whorls, regularly arranged, pure white; the outer whorl often more than six in number; the outer whorls very broad in outline, blunt or rounded at apex and sometimes truncate, prominently mucronate, spreading, plane, overlapping half or more; the inner whorls successively a little shorter, becoming inflexed, with margins incurved; those at centre strongly inflexed, with margins tightly incurled; corona segments very short, clustered among the centre petaloid segments, deep orange-red. Mid-season to late. Resembles 'Acropolis' but with more corona segments visible

'Pirandello' 2 W-R
(S.J. Bisdee, 1945)
'Hades' × 'Red Crusader'

'Pirani' 1 Y-O
(W.M. Spry, pre-1975) Unregistered
'Morning Glory' × 'Golden Valley'
Corona becoming brighter with maturity. Early

'Pirate' 2 (a)
(Mrs R.O. Backhouse, pre-1908)

'Pirate King' 2 W-O
(J.L. Richardson) J.L. Richardson, 1956
'Kilworth' × Arbar'
Fl. 115 mm wide; perianth segments white, touched brilliant yellow 12B or 13B at base, inflexed, overlapping half; corona orange (28A) or vivid orange-yellow 23A, tinged strong orange 25A, with mouth straight and ribbed, rim dentate. 2n=28. AM(e) 1957, *AM(g) 1966

'Pirate's Gold' 2 (a)
(G.L. Wilson, pre-1946)
Syn. 'Killigenz'

'Pirate's Hoard' 2 (a)
(Oregon Bulb Farms, pre-1946)

'Pirate Treasure' 2 W-O
(Tom Forster, 1960s) Unregistered
Perianth segmens broad, creamy white; corona yellow-orange, heavily frilled. Tall. Late

'Pirini' 9 W-YYR
(H. Aldersey, pre-1931)
Fl. 82 mm wide; perianth segments white, separated; corona very shallow bowl-shaped, sulphur, with a narrow band of bright red at rim. Mid-season to late

'Pirouette' 2 W-? (b)
(J. Jacob, pre-1932)

'Pisano' 1 W-? (b)
(J.W. Barr, pre-1930)

N. pisanus Pugsley = *N. pseudonarcissus* var. *pisanus*

'Pismo Beach' 2 W-GWP
(Brian S. Duncan) Rathowen Daffodils, 1978
'Syracuse' × 'Jewel Song'; sdlg no. 267
Fl. rounded, 95 mm wide; perianth segments very

broad in outline, rounded at apex and sometimes truncate, mucronate, spreading, plane, overlapping half; the inner segments only slightly narrower, blunt, a little inflexed; corona shallow bowl-shaped, ribbed, white, with grey-green at base and bright apple blossom pink at rim, mouth widely expanded, split in places and overlapping, rim closely and minutely crenate. Mid-season. 2n=28. Resembles a better-poised 'Syracuse' in form

'Pitcairn' 4 W-R
(Mrs H.K. Richardson) P. & G. Phillips, 1975
'Gay Time' × 'Rockall'; sdlg no. 3715
Fl. 65 mm wide. Resembles 'Acropolis' but with whiter perianth segments

'Pitchroy' 2 W-GWW
(J.S.B. Lea) J.S.B. Lea, 1973
('Easter Moon' × 'Castle of Mey') × 'Fionn'; sdlg no. 1-29-62
Fl. 105 mm wide

'Pitta' 2 W-P
(G.E. Mitsch) G.E. Mitsch, 1976
'Precedent' × 'Debutante'; sdlg no. F34/2
Fl. rounded, 100 mm wide; perianth segments very broadly ovate, blunt, only very slightly mucronate, milk white, a little inflexed, concave, with margins sometimes incurling, overlapping half; the inner segments with margins nicked; corona shallow bowl-shaped, ribbed, light salmon pink, with mouth widely expanded, sometimes deeply split and overlapping, a little frilled, rim broadly crenate. Mid-season. Resembles 'Precedent' but with a greater depth of pink in the corona

'Pittaccus' 8 Y-Y
(pre-1807)

'Pitti Sing' W-P
(Alister Clark, pre-1940)
Perianth segments pure white; corona pink, with rim flanged

'Pittwater' 1 W-?
(W.M. Spry, pre-1975) Unregistered
'Hunter's Moon' × 'Tunis'
Corona cream, with lemon green. Tall. Early

'Piute' 6
(K.L. Reynolds, pre-1944)

'Pivert' 11?a Y-Y
(J. Gerritsen & Son) J. Gerritsen & Son, 1974
Sdlg × 'Majorette'
Fl. 105 mm wide

'Piwakawaka' 2 W-YPP
(David Adams) David Adams, 1994
'Easter Moon' × 'Melancholy'; sdlg no. 84/14A

Fl. forming a double triangle, 138 mm wide; perianth segments broadly ovate, plane; the outer segments overlapping one another; corona funnel-shaped, opening yellow, soon becoming soft pink, with soft yellow at base, the pink deepening in tone with age, lightly frilled. Tall. Mid-season to late. Sunproof

'Pixie' 3 W-YOR
(E.M. Crosfield, pre-1908)
Fl. 76 mm wide, of smooth texture; perianth segments ivory white, overlapping; corona large, very shallow, with canary yellow at base shading to orange-red at rim

'Pixie' 7 Y-Y
(M. Fowlds) G.E. Mitsch, 1959
N. assoanus × ? *N. jonquilla*
Fls up to 5 per stem; perianth segments broad, somewhat obovate, rounded at apex, prominently mucronate, reflexed, plane, overlapping half; the inner segments not noticeably mucronate, a little less strongly reflexed, somewhat concave or with margins wavy; corona bowl-shaped, smooth, with mouth even or very slightly wavy, rim entire

'Pixie Pink' 2 W-P
(J.N.Hancock & Co., 1974) Unregistered
Sdlg no. 49B/82H
Corona cylindrical, deep pink, frilled. Early to mid-season

'Pixie's Parlour' 3 W-Y
(Carncairn Daffodils) Carncairn Daffodils, 1970
'Sylvia O'Neill' hybrid
Perianth segments opening cream, becoming white; corona yellow, with green at base, frilled. Sweet scented

'Pixies Pool' 3 W-GGY
(Carncairn Daffodils) Carncairn Daffodils, 1979
'Cushendall' × 'Sea Green'; sdlg no. 2/65
Fl. 65 mm wide; perianth segments yellowish white 155D; corona tightly ribbed, deep to strong yellowish green 141A-C, with brilliant greenish yellow 6C at rim. Late. Scented. 2n=14. Resembles 'Grace Note' but with rounder and more deeply overlapping perianth segments

'Pixie's Sister' 7 Y-Y
(G.E. Mitsch) G.E. Mitsch, 1966
Hybrid between *N. assoanus* and *N. jonquilla*
Fl. 3-5 per stem, 27 mm wide; perianth segments very broadly ovate, prominently mucronate, spreading, concave, with margins incurling, overlapping half; the inner segments with margins more strongly incurling; corona cup-shaped, smooth, with mouth even or a little wavy, rim entire. Dwarf. Mid-season. Resembles a paler-coloured 'Pixie' with shallower corona and slightly longer flowering period. AGM 1996

'Pizarro' 2 Y-Y
(G.E. Mitsch, 1979) R. & E. Havens, 1993
'Executive' × 'Golden Aura'; sdlg no. 2023/2
Fl. 100 mm wide, of heavy substance; perianth segments broadly ovate, deep yellow, spreading, plane; corona cup-shaped, golden yellow, with mouth slightly flared. Mid-season

'Pizzicato' 2 W-Y
(Konynenburg & Mark) Konynenburg & Mark, 1964
Fl. 105 mm wide; perianth segments ivory; corona pale yellow 11C. Late

'Placid' 3 W-Y
(W. Jackson Jr, 1958) W. Jackson Jr, 1968
'Beirut' × 'Jeb'; sdlg no. 103/58
Perianth segments very broadly ovate, blunt, only very slightly mucronate, pure white, a little inflexed, slightly concave, smooth, overlapping half; the inner segments more narrowly ovate, square-shouldered at base, more strongly inflexed, with margins wavy; corona narrow bowl-shaped, ribbed, soft lemon yellow, with mouth straight, tightly frilled. Mid-season to late

'Placida' 2 (a)
(A.M. Wilson, pre-1927)

'Placid Sea' 3 W-YWY
(J.A.Hunter) J.A.Hunter, 1997
'Placid' × 'Sea Dream'; sdlg no. 11/86C
Fl. 108 mm wide; perianth segments broadly ovate, smooth; corona bowl-shaped, with mouth lobed and wavy. Mid-season

'Plain Jane' 2 W-? (b)
(P.J. Worsley, c.1907)
'Lulworth' × 'Duchess of Brabant'

'Plaisante' 8 W-O
(pre-1851)

'Planet' 3 (a)
(C. Dawson, pre-1907)

'Planet' 3 Y-YYO
(G.E. Mitsch) G.E. Mitsch, 1982
'Kingbird' × 'Moonfire'; sdlg no. LL53/3
Fl. 122 mm wide; perianth segments soft yellow, smooth, overlapping; corona deeper in tone, with orange at rim. Mid-season

'Planet' 4 Y-Y
(G. Zandbergen-Terwegen, pre-1978) Unregistered
'Golden Harvest' sport
2n=28. Closely resembles 'Golden Ducat'

'Planeta' 3 W-? (b or c)
(Barr & Sons, pre-1927)

N. planicorona Spach = *N.* × *gracilis*

'Planicorona'
Syn. of *N.* × *gracilis*

'Plantagenet' 3 W-O
(Mrs R.O. Backhouse, pre-1921)

'Plantation' 1 Y-Y
(Mrs E. Murray)

'Platinal' 3 W-GWW
(J. Gerritsen & Son) J. Gerritsen & Son, 1961
Fl. 70 mm wide, pure white; corona with green at base. Late. Resembles a late-flowered 'Polar Ice'

'Platinum' 3 W-? (b or c)
(G.H. Furness, pre-1934)

'Plato' 9
(Sir C.H. Cave, pre-1916)

'Plato' 1 (a)
(pre-1927)

'Plato' 1 Y-Y
(E.H. Krelage & Son, pre-1929)

'Plato' 1 (a)
Syn. of 'Oregon'

N. platylobus Jordan = *N. pseudonarcissus* var. *platylobus*

'Playaway' 2 W-P
(Alister Clark, 1948) J. Sharp, 1960

'Playboy' 2 Y-O
(G.L. Wilson, pre-1944)
'Carbineer' × 'Rosslare'
Fl. rounded; perianth segments lemon gold, slightly reflexed, of great substance; corona bowl-shaped, flushed orange in upper half. 2n=28

'Playful' 2 W-? (b)
(M.P. Williams, pre-1938)

'Playmate' 1 W-W
(Sir C.H. Cave, pre-1928)

'Playschool' 3 W-YYO
(Carncairn Daffodils, 1969) Carncairn Daffodils, 1987
'Bravura' × 'Bushmills'; sdlg no. 2/11/64
Corona vivid yellow, with yellow-orange at rim, slightly frilled. Late

'Playtime' 2 W-O
(J. Gerritsen & Son) J. Gerritsen & Son, 1968
'Alpine Glow' hybrid

Fl. 110 mm wide; perianth segments ivory white; corona pale orange (24D). Late

'Plaza' 2 Y-W
(Murray W. Evans, 1965) Murray W. Evans, 1975
'Bethny' × 'Binkie' hybrid; sdlg no. I-22
Fl. 100 mm wide; perianth segments lemon. Midseason

'Pleasance' 2 (a)
(J.W. Paardekooper, pre-1940)

'Pleasant' 2 Y-O
(M.P. Williams, pre-1949)

'Pleasantries' 3 W-? (b)
(J.E. Exley, pre-1950)

'Pleasing' 2 Y-Y
(M.P. Williams, pre-1949)
Fl. 89 mm wide; perianth segments brilliant yellow 8A, overlapping half; corona slightly ribbed, vivid yellow 13A, mouth a little expanded, frilled, with rim dentate. *AM(g) 1958

'Pleated Skirts' 5 W-W
(M. Fowlds) G.E. Mitsch, 1970
('John Evelyn' × 'Fortune') × *N. triandrus*
Fls 3-4 per stem; corona flared, ribbed, frilled. Midseason

'Pledge' 1 W-W
(M.J. Jefferson-Brown, c.1978) Unregistered
'Little Beauty' × (*N. cyclamineus* × [*N. cyclamineus* × 'Rockery Beauty'])

'Pleiad' 5
(pre-1907)

'Pleiades' 8 W-R
(H. Selkirk, pre-1914)
'Adonia' × 'Ornatus'
Fls up to 7 per stem

'Pleiades' 8 W-Y
(C.E. Radcliff, 1930)
'Grand Monarque' × 'Osiris'
Fls many per stem; perianth segments white; corona soft yellow

'Pleinpouvoir' 1 Y-Y
(Konynenburg & Mark) Konynenburg & Mark, 1963
'Spellbinder' × 'Binkie'
Fl. 110 mm wide, light greenish yellow 5C. Midseason

'Pleione' 2 W-? (b)
(C. Dawson, pre-1923)
'Lulworth' × 'Horace'

'Plenipo' 4 Y-Y
(G.H. Engleheart, pre-1904)
'Ornatus' × 'Telamonius Plenus'
Fl. sulphur yellow; perianth and other petaloid segments acute, densely arranged. AM(Haarlem) 1912

'Plenissimus' 4 Y-Y
(pre-1629)
Fl. large, sometimes with several centres, sometimes with green segments among the yellow; perianth and other petaloid segments in many whorls, ovate, pale yellow, with margins wavy, not much overlapping; the outer whorls spreading; the inner whorls inflexed or at centre strongly inflexed; corona segments broad, more than half as long as the petaloid segments and interspersed among them, of a deeper yellow, sometimes bi-lobed, frilled; sometimes opening with the outer whorl of the corona continuous, with pale yellow and darker yellow segments intermingled within. Resembles a taller 'Grandiplenus'. Syn. "John Tradescant's Great Rose Daffodil", "Tradescant's Great Rose Double Daffodil", 'A Cent Feuilles', 'Tratus Cantus', Pseudonarcissus Major 'Maximus Grandiplenus', Pseudonarcissus Major 'Plenissimus'. ?The same as 'Maximus Flore Pleno'

'Pleno Flore' 4 Y-Y
Syn. of 'Eystettensis'

'Plentiful' 9
(F. Rijnveld & Sons, pre-1942)

'Plenus' 4 Y-Y
(pre-1629)
Perianth segments sulphur yellow; corona filled with golden yellow segments. Syn. "Gerard's Double Daffodil", "The English Double Daffodil", Pseudonarcissus 'Plenus'

'Plenus' 4 Y-O
(pre-1665)
Perianth and other petaloid segments in several whorls, regularly arranged, ovate or oblong, sulphur or primrose yellow, sometimes green; the outer whorls spreading; the inner whorls a little shorter and inflexed or at centre shorter still and more strongly inflexed; corona segments one-quarter the length of the petaloid segments and interspersed among them, bright orange. Syn. Incomparabilis 'Plenus'

'Plenus' 4 Y-Y
(pre-1831)
?Variant of *N. minor* var. *conspicuus*
Syn. "The Common Deep Yellow Double Daffodil", Pseudonarcissus Lobularis 'Plenus' of Haworth

'Plenus' 4 Y-Y
(pre-1860)
Fl. rich yellow. Strongly scented. Syn. "The Double

Yellow Jonquil", Jonquilla 'Plenus'

'Plenus' 4 W-YYR
(pre-1861)
Perianth and other petaloid segments in several whorls, broad in outline, sometimes squarish at apex, pure white, overlapping; the outer whorls spreading or a little inflexed; the inner whorls successively slightly shorter and more strongly inflexed; corona segments very small, in more than one sometimes near-continuous whorl among the petaloid segments at centre, yellow, usually with red at rim, sometimes with a line of white between the yellow and the red. Very late. Strongly scented. 2n=14. Syn. "Double Pheasant Eye", "Double Poeticus", "The Large Gardenia Flowered Double White Daffodil, ?"Double Border", ?'Gardenia', 'Albus Plenus Odoratus', Poeticus 'Flore Pleno', Poeticus 'Patellaris Pleno Albo Cum Croceo, Poeticus 'Plenus'. A number of different double variants of *N. poeticus* have been recorded, but the identity of the original Poeticus 'Plenus' remains unclear. Two variants currently in cultivation are treated as 'Tamar Double White' and 'Spalding Double White'; any other older names not known to be directly related to either of these are referred to Poeticus 'Plenus'.

'Plenus' 4 Y-Y
(pre-1873)
Perianth and other petaloid segments in several whorls, ovate, acute, light yellow, with margins wavy, separated; the outer whorl spreading; the inner whorls a little inflexed, or at centre strongly inflexed and contorted; corona segments broad, almost as long as the petaloid segments and interspersed among them, rich yellow, somewhat frilled. Syn. "The Dwarf Double Light Yellow", Pseudonarcissus Lobularis 'Plenus'

'Plenus' 4 Y-Y
Syn. of 'Flore Pleno'

'Plenus' 4 Y-Y
Syn. of 'Rip van Winkle'

'Plenus' 4 W-W
Syn. of 'Cernuus Plenus'

'Plenus' 4
Formerly listed as a variant of *N. minor* var. *conspicuus*. ?The same as Pseudonarcissus Lobularis 'Plenus' or Pseudonarcissus Lobularis 'Grandiplenus'

'Plenus' 4
Syn. of 'Double Campernelle'

'Plenus Laciniis Pallidis' 4 Y-Y
(1618)
'Maximus' hybrid
Perianth and other petaloid segments in more than one whorl; the outer whorl a little reflexed, opening greenish, becoming more nearly yellow; the inner whorl(s) with some segments pale yellow and others more golden yellow; the segments at centre shorter, strongly inflexed, some appearing to be tubular. Syn. "The Great Double Yellow Spanish Daffodil", Parkinson's Daffodil, Pseudonarcissus 'Plenus Laciniis Pallidis'

'Plenus Odoratissimus' 4? Y-Y
(pre-1882)
Dwarf. Sweetly scented. Syn. Pseudonarcissus Lobularis 'Plenus Odoratissimus'

'Plimsoll' 1 W-Y
(J.S. Leitch) J.S. Leitch, 1968
Fl. 115 mm wide; corona lemon yellow

'Plough Boy' 1 Y-Y
(Hon. Mrs Petre, pre-1934)

'Plover' 3 (a)
(W.A. Watts, pre-1927)

'Plover' 2 W-P
(G.E. Mitsch) G.E. Mitsch, 1975
'Precedent' × 'Carita'; sdlg no. F33/20
Fl. rounded, 112 mm wide; perianth segments very broadly ovate, blunt, slightly mucronate, a little reflexed, overlapping half or more; the inner segments more nearly spreading, creased, sometimes nicked at margin; corona very broad bowl-shaped, ribbed, soft apricot pink, mouth straight, split in places and overlapping, lightly frilled. Mid-season. Resembles a taller 'High Repute' of more rapid increase with a smaller corona

'Plumeleteer' 6 W-P
(G.E. Mitsch) Grant Mitsch Novelty Daffodils, 1984
Sdlg × *N. cyclamineus*; sdlg no. KK105/6
Fl. 72 mm wide; perianth segments milk white; corona apricot pink, with lighter tones towards rim. Early to mid-season. Resembles 'Carib' but with narrower and whiter perianth segments and a much less widely flared corona

'Plunder' 2 W-Y
(J.S. Leitch) J.S. Leitch, 1967
Fl. 108 mm wide; corona lemon yellow

'Plurry' 2 Y-O
Syn. of 'Abo'

'Plush' 4 W-R
(Murray W. Evans) Murray W. Evans, 1978
Sdlg × 'Hallali'; sdlg no. N-15
Mid-season

'Plutarch' 9
(W.B. Hartland, pre-1914)

'Plutarchus' 8 W-O
(pre-1777)
Early

'Pluto' 9
(G.H. Engleheart, pre-1913)

'Pluto' 2 W-? (b)
(P.D. Williams, pre-1927)

'Plutocrat' 1 (a)
(R. Dick, pre-1933)

'Plutus' 1 Y-Y
(S.J. Bisdee, pre-1939)
'Golden City' × 'Gambrinus'

'Pluvia d'Oro' 1 (a)
(M. van Waveren & Sons, pre-1942)

'Pluvius' 2 Y-O
(Mrs R.O. Backhouse, pre-1921)
Perianth segments narrow, acute; corona clear orange.
AM(Haarlem) 1931

'Plymouth' 3 W-? (b)
(J.W.A. Lefeber, pre-1938)

'Poached Egg' 4 Y-O
Syn. of 'Butter & Eggs'

'Poached Egg' 2 Y-Y
(?Tom Forster) Unregistered
Perianth segments broadly ovate, blunt, prominently mucronate, soft yellow, spreading, plane or with margins somewhat wavy, overlapping half; the inner segments with margins more strongly wavy; corona very shallow, spreading to two-thirds the length of the perianth segments, ribbed, deep yellow, frilled, with rim deeply notched and dentate. Early

'Poatina' 2 W-P
(K.J. Heazlewood) K.J. Heazlewood, 1968
'Rosedale' × 'Mukana'
Fl. 108 mm wide; corona clear pink. Mid-season

'Pocahontas' 2 Y-YYR
(E.C. Powell, pre-1946)
'Bernardino' × 'Fortune'

'Pocatalico' 2 YYW-W
(Curtis Tolley) Curtis Tolley, 1996
'Impresario' × 'Dotteral'; sdlg no. 89-14-7
Fl. forming a double triangle, 102 mm wide; perianth segments ovate, lemon yellow, with a wide band of white at base; corona funnel-shaped, opening yellow, becoming white, with mouth slightly frilled. Early

'Pocono' 2 W-? (b)

(Oregon Bulb Farms, pre-1951)

N. × *poculiformis* Salisbury 13 = *N. dubius* Gouan × *N. moschatus* Linnaeus (Poculiformis 'Montanus', Poculiformis 'Poculiformis', "The White Nonpareil Daffodil")

'Poculiformis'
Syn. of *N.* × *poculiformis*

'Poem' 9
(J. Pope, pre-1903)

'Poesie' 9
(G.H. Engleheart, pre-1914)

'Poesie' 2 W-P
(*c.*1957) Unregistered

'Poesy' 2 W-P
(J. Gerritsen & Son, *c.*1978) Unregistered

'Poet' 9?
(pre-1936)

N. poetarum Haworth = *N. radiiflorus* var. *poetarum*

'Poetaz' 8
(van der Schoot, pre-1936)
N. tazetta × 'Ornatus'

N. poeticus Linnaeus 13 Section Narcissus
("Janette des Contois", "White Lady")
  subsp. *angustifolius* Ascherson & Graebner = *N. radiiflorus*
  subsp. *radiiflorus* (Salisbury) Baker = *N. radiiflorus*
    var. *grandiflorus* Sabine = *N. radiiflorus* var. *poetarum*
    var. *ornatus* hort. = variant of *N. poeticus*
    var. **poeticus**
    var. **hellenicus** (Pugsley) A.Fernandes
    var. **majalis** (Curtis) A.Fernandes (Poeticus 'Patellaris', "The Great White Purple Ringed Daffodil")
    var. **physaloides** Beauverd
    var. **recurvus** (Haworth) A.Fernandes ("Jean(n)ette Blanche", "Pheasant's Eye"). 2n=21. AGM 1993
    var. *tripedalis* Loddiges = *N. ornatus* Haworth
    var. *tripodalis* Salisbury = *N. ornatus* Haworth
    var. **verbanensis** Herbert
    var. *verus* hort. = *N. poeticus* var. *hellenicus*

N. poeticus Hudson = *N.* × *medioluteus*

N. poeticus Smith = *N. poeticus* var. *majalis*

'Poetry' 5 W-Y
(F. Barchard, pre-1916)
Perianth segments creamy white; corona primrose.

AM(r) 1916

'Poet's Corner' 9 W-?
(T.O. Cowan) T.O. Cowan, 1968
Late. PC(e) 1967

'Poet's Dream' 9
(W. Balch, pre-1933)

'Poet's Dream' 2 W-O
(J.W.A. Lefeber, 1955) J.W.A. Lefeber, 1978
Fl. 95 mm wide; perianth segments ivory white; corona strong orange 25A, with a lighter tone (23A) at rim. Early

'Poet's Ransom' 9 W-?
(T.O. Cowan) T.O. Cowan, 1968
'Hexameter' × 'Milan'
Mid-season. PC(e) 1968

'Poet's Reverie' 9 W-?
(T.O. Cowan) T.O. Cowan, 1968
'Hexameter' × 'Milan'
Mid-season. PC(e) 1966

'Poet's Way' 9 W-GYR
(T. Bloomer) Rathowen Daffodils, 1975
'Smyrna' × ?'Lough Areema'; sdlg no. 13/26/57
Perianth segments very broad, acute, slightly mucronate, a little reflexed, plane, overlapping half; the inner segments narrower and more nearly spreading; corona almost disc-shaped, tightly ribbed, yellow, with green at base, and a band of deep red at rim, minutely crenate. Late. Resembles a larger-flowered 'Cantabile' with a more obviously reflexed perianth

'Poet's Wings' 9 W-GYR
(T. Bloomer) Rathowen Daffodils, 1976
'Smyrna' hybrid; sdlg no. 1/31/53
Perianth segments ovate, acute, reflexed; corona yellow, with deep green at base and red at rim. Late

'Pogo' 3 W-GYO
(Mrs G. Link) Mrs G. Link, 1989
Sdlg 14/3BY/1YY × sdlg 3379 × 'Altruist'
Perianth segments medium yellow, smooth, of good substance. Late

'Point Barrow' 1 W-W
(Konynenburg & Mark) Konynenburg & Mark, 1960
Sdlg × 'Mount Hood'
Fl. 100 mm wide; perianth segments creamy white; corona paler in tone. Mid-season

'Point d'Aigu' 1 W-W
(de Graaff Bros, pre-1927)

'Point du Jour' 2 W-? (b)
(F.E. Gibbs, pre-1948)

'Point Duty' 2 Y-YOO
(J.N. Hancock & Co., 1953)

'Pointer' 1 W-? (b)
(L. Buckland, pre-1936)

'Poise' 2 W-? (b)
(Mrs R.S. Cobley, pre-1938)

'Poiteau' 2 W-Y
(W. Backhouse, pre-1869)
Syn. Incomparabilis Albus 'Poiteau'

'Poitiers' 1 (a)
(pre-1913)

'Pokana' 5
(S.J. Bisdee, 1942) S.J. Bisdee, 1956
'Robert Berkeley' × *N. triandrus*

'Pokomoke' 1 W-W
(E.C. Powell, pre-1948)
'White Conqueror' × 'Corinth'

'Poland'
(pre-1940)

'Pola Negri' 2 (a)
(R.H. Bath, pre-1929)

'Polar Bear' 1 W-W
(A.M. Wilson, pre-1944)
Perianth segments acute; corona opening very pale primrose, becoming white

'Polar Circle' 2 W-W
(Carncairn Daffodils) Carncairn Daffodils, 1982
Sdlg × 'Ardbane'; sdlg no. W23/1
Fl. 99 mm wide; perianth segments very broadly ovate, mucronate, somewhat reflexed, overlapping half; the inner segments more narrowly ovate, with margins a little wavy; corona very short funnel-shaped, broad, lightly ribbed, opening yellowish white, with yellow at rim, becoming self white in most climates, mouth straight, with six shallowly overlapping lobes, rim minutely dentate. Mid-season

'Polar Dawn' 2 W-WWY
(J.A. Hunter) J.A. Hunter, 1982
'Easter Moon' × ('Green Island' × 'Personality')
Fl. 105 mm wide; corona with yellow rim at rim. Mid-season

'Polar Dream' 2 W-W
(Jānis Rukšans, 1984) Jānis Rukšans, 1997
'Easter Moon' × 'Empress of Ireland'; sdlg no 79-07-6
Fl. rounded, 110 mm wide, pure white; perianth segments very broad, smooth, overlapping; corona flared, with yellowish green at base, rim slightly

flanged. Very early to early

'Polar Fire' 3 W-O
(J.A. Hunter) J.A. Hunter, 1966
Fl. 111 mm wide; corona reddish orange. Mid-season. Resembles a larger 'Forfar' of improved form

'Polar Flame' 3 W-YOO
(J.A.Hunter, 1987) J.A.Hunter, 1997
'Corofin' × ('Polar Fire' × [Div. 2 sdlg × 'Arbar']); Sdlg no. 40/82C
Fl. 105 mm wide; perianth segments ovate, white, stained yellow at base, smooth; corona bowl-shaped, with mouth tightly frilled. Mid-season

'Polar Gem' 1 W-W
(R.C.A. Tombleson) R.C.A. Tombleson, 1968
Fl. 115 mm wide. Mid-season. Resembles an earlier 'Hikurangi' with the corona more deeply dentate

'Polar Glow' 2 W-PPW
(J.A.Hunter) J.A.Hunter, 1995
('Cascade' × ['Lingering Light' × 'Gisela']) × 'Verran'; sdlg no. 24/82D
Fl. forming a double triangle, 110 mm wide; perianth segments ovate; corona flared, light yellowish pink 36B, with white at mouth, frilled. Mid-season

'Polar Gull' 2 W-GWW
(Mrs G. Link) Mrs G. Link, 1990
'Benediction' × 'April Rose'; sdlg no. 217-Z
Fl. 100 mm wide, perianth segments spreading, plane. Late

'Polar Ice' 3 W-W
(G. Lubbe & Son, pre-1936)
2n=29. AM(Haarlem) 1936

'Polar Ice' 1 W-W
(J.A.Hunter, pre-1997) Unregistered

'Polar Imp' 3 W-W
(E.W. Philpott) E.W. Philpott, 1973
Fl. rounded; perianth segments very broadly ovate, squarish at apex and sometimes truncate, slightly mucronate, pure white, a little reflexed, plane, or sometimes slightly concave near apex, overlapping half or more; the inner segments narrower, more rounded at apex, more nearly spreading, with margins wavy; corona shallow bowl-shaped, ribbed, white, with green at base. Early. Resembles 'Frigid'

'Polaris' 1 W-W
(G.L. Wilson) Guy L.Wilson Ltd, 1966
'Empress of Ireland' × 'Prestige'

'Polar Island' 2 W-W
(J.A.Hunter) J.A.Hunter, 1995
'Penguin' × ('Glendermott' × 'Kotuku'); sdlg no. 34/83F
Fl. forming a double triangle, 115 mm wide; perianth segments ovate; corona with rim flanged and crenate. Mid-season

'Polar Legend' 2 W-W
(J.L. Richardson) Mrs H.K. Richardson, 1964

'Polar Light' 2 W-YYW
(J.A. Hunter) J.A. Hunter, 1966
Fl. 102 mm wide; perianth segments smooth; corona pale primrose yellow. Mid-season

'Polar Monarch' 1 W-W
(J.A. Hunter) J.A. Hunter, 1992
('Bonniform' × 'Kanchenjunga') × ('Glendermott' × 'Kotuku'); sdlg no. 20/82A
Fl. 120 mm wide; perianth segments very broadly ovate; corona with rim flanged. Early to mid-season

'Polar Morn' 3 W-YWW
(J.A. Hunter) J.A. Hunter, 1992
'Polar Imp' × 'Polar Dawn'; sdlg no. 32/81A
Fl. 105 mm wide; corona white, touched yellow at base. Mid-season

'Polar Princess' 2 W-W
(J.A. Hunter) J.A. Hunter, 1990
'Empress of Ireland' × 'Canisp'; sdlg no. 28/80D
Fl. 114 mm wide; perianth segments ovate; corona mouth expanded, with rim slightly rolled. Mid-season

'Polar Sea' 3 W-GWW
(The Brodie of Brodie, c.1926)
Cross no. 259/14 × 'Raeburn'
Fl. pure white; perianth segments acute, of strong substance; corona with rich sea green at base. Late

'Polar Sky' 2 W-WWP
(J.A. Hunter) J.A. Hunter, 1992
'Leonaine' × ('Easter Moon' × ['Daisy Schäffer' × 'Carnlough']); sdlg no. 33/82A
Fl. 110 mm wide; corona white, with pink at rim, mouth slightly expanded. Mid-season to late

'Polar Snow' 2 W-W
(J.A. Hunter) J.A. Hunter, 1982
'Easter Moon' × 'Glendermott'
Fl. 105 mm wide. Mid-season

'Polar Star' 2 W-WWY
(Oregon Bulb Farms, pre-1946)

'Polar Sunrise' 2 W-P
(J.N. Hancock & Co., c.1975) Unregistered

'Polar Sunset' 2 W-YYP
(J.A.Hunter, 1987) J.A.Hunter, 1997
'Precedent' × 'Verran'; sdlg no. 38/82B

Fl. 112 mm wide; perianth segments ovate, very smooth; corona flared, with pale pink at rim, frilled. Mid-season

'Polar Venture' 2 W-W
(J.A. Hunter, 1978) J.A. Hunter, 1989
'Glendermott' × 'Kotuku'; sdlg no. 12/72C
Fl. 122 mm wide; perianth segments broadly ovate, of good substance; corona mouth slightly expanded, with rim slightly rolled

'Polbathic' 2 Y-R
(Brian S. Duncan) du Plessis Bros, 1986
'Vagabond' × 'Battle Cry; sdlg no. 425
Mid-season

'Polcoverack' 3 W-? (b)
(The Brodie of Brodie, pre-1930)
'Mozart' × 'Sunstar'

'Pol Crocan' 2 W-P
(J.S.B. Lea) Clive Postles Daffodils, 1989
Sdlg 2-19-69 × sdlg 29-73; sdlg no. 1-45-77
Fl. rounded, 111 mm wide; perianth segments roundish, pure white, deeply overlapping; corona with mouth slightly flared. Mid-season

'Poldark' 2 Y-R
(J.A. O'More) P. Phillips, 1978
'Indian Summer' × 'Red Baron'; sdlg no. 2AR-25
Fl. 102 mm wide; perianth segments rounded, rich yellow, somewhat ribbed; corona widely expanded. Mid-season. Resembles a deeper-coloured 'Red Baron'

'Poldhu' 2 W-W
(The Brodie of Brodie, pre-1930)
'Imbros' × 'Tenedos'
Fl. greenish white; perianth segments very broad, regular; the inner segments narrower, with margins sometimes wavy or incurving; corona slender, with rim deeply and regularly crenate. AM(e) 1935

'Pol Dornie' 2 W-P
(J.S.B. Lea) J.S.B. Lea, 1978
'Kildavin' × de Navarro sdlg 796 (['Interim' × 'Salmon Trout'] × 'Rosedew'); sdlg no. 1-40-67
Fl. 100 mm wide; corona deep pink. Late

'Polefinder'
(New Zealand origin, pre-1915)

'Polemon' 1 Y-Y
(Barr & Sons, pre-1922)
Perianth segments primrose yellow; corona slender, deep yellow, frilled

'Polestar' 3 W-Y
(G.H. Engleheart, pre-1904)

Perianth segments reflexed; corona large, almost disc-shaped, ribbed, soft canary yellow. Late

'Polglase' 8 W-R
(P.D. Williams, pre-1927)
2n=24

'Polglass' 3 W-GWW
(J.S.B. Lea) J.S.B. Lea, 1980
'Achnasheen' × 'Loch Assynt'; sdlg no. 1-28-72
Fl. 100 mm wide

'Polgrean' 3 W-? (b)
(P.D. Williams, pre-1933)

'Polindra' 2 W-Y
(P.D. Williams, pre-1927)
Fl. 102 mm wide; perianth segments mucronate, creamy white, smooth, overlapping half; corona expanded, brilliant yellow 8A to light greenish yellow 8B, deeply frilled. 2n=28. AM(e) 1937, FCC(e) 1938, AM(Haarlem) 1940, FCC(Haarlem) 1944, *AM(g) 1950

'Politician' 2 Y-Y
(C.E. Radcliff, 1935)
'W.F.Gates' × 'Golden Legend'

'Poljew' 2 (a)
(P.D. Williams, pre-1927)

'Polka Dot' 5 W-W
(Don Bramley) Don Bramley, 1989
'Lunar Ring' × *N. triandrus*; sdlg no. 79/44
Fl. 50 mm wide; perianth segments reflexed; corona cup-shaped, mouth expanded. Mid-season. Resembles 'Rippling Waters' but with broader perianth segments and a more widely expanded corona mouth

'Polka Dot' 3 W-OOR
(Glenbrook Bulb Farm, pre-1992) Unregistered
'Koala' × 'Matapan'; sdlg no. 9/87

'Pollino' 2 W-W
(Mrs B.T. Simpson) Mrs B.T. Simpson, 1966
Fl. 115 mm wide, smooth. Mid-season

'Pollux' 2 (a)
(E. Oostdam, pre-1939)

'Pollux' 5 W-W
(D. & J.W. Blanchard) M.J. Jefferson-Brown, 1968
'Silver Coin' × *N. triandrus* subsp. *pallidulus*
Fl. 64 mm wide, greenish white (155A); perianth segments slightly reflexed, irregular, overlapping; corona ribbed, with mouth straight, rim crenate. PC(e) 1968

'Polly' 2 W-? (b)
(pre-1910)

'Polly' 1 W-? (b)
(Alister Clark) G.E. Mitsch, 1956

'Pollyanna' 3 W-YYR
(S.A. Free) S.A. Free, 1976
'Dresden' hybrid; sdlg no. 69-34
Fl. 100 mm wide; perianth segments creamy white; corona yellow, shading to red at rim. Mid-season

'Polly Eccles' 1 W-? (b)
(W.B. Hartland, pre-1907)

'Polly-Esther' 4 W-O
(Glenbrook Bulb Farm, 1984) Glenbrook Bulb Farm, 1997
'Anne of Cleves' × 'Dimity'
Fl. 85 mm wide; perianth segments ovate, greenish white 155A; corona segments strong orange 25A, frilled. Mid-season to late

'Pollyjoke' 2 Y-? (a)
(G.H. Johnstone, pre-1947)

'Polly Peachum' 3 W-? (b)
(N.F. Lock, pre-1944)

'Polly Perkins' 1 (a)
(G.P. Haydon, pre-1908)

'Polly's Pearl' 8 W-W
H. Koopowitz, 1979
Selection from 'White Pearl'
Fls. up to 20 per stem, 30-40 mm wide; perianth segments broadly or very broadly ovate, blunt, fairly prominently mucronate, spreading or a little reflexed, with margins incurling, overlapping one-third to a half; the inner segments a little inflexed; corona shallow cup-shaped, ribbed, opening cream, quickly becoming white, mouth straight, wavy, with rim entire. Mid-season. 2n=32. Resembles 'Grand Monarque' in form

'Polnesk' 7 Y-Y
(P.D. Williams, pre-1927)
? × *N. jonquilla*
Fls 2-3 per stem, soft yellow. 2n=21

'Polonaise' 3 W-? (b)
(F.H. Chapman, pre-1927)

'Polonaise' 2 W-P
(J.L. Richardson) Rathowen Daffodils, 1974
'Daybreak' × 'Merry Widow'
Perianth segments pure white; corona bowl-shaped, opening raspberry, becoming salmon pink

'Polo Prince' 2 W-W
(R.C.A. Tombleson) R.C.A. Tombleson, 1972
Fl. 104 mm wide

'Polperro' 3 W-? (b or c)
(Lord Rendlesham, pre-1937)

'Polquest' 2 W-W
(M.P. Williams, pre-1949)
'Trevean' hybrid
See also 'Pol Quest'

'Pol Quest' 2 W-W
Syn. of 'Polquest'

'Polrudden' 2 Y-R
(G.H. Johnstone, pre-1946)

'Polsue' 2 (a)
(G.L. Wilson, pre-1947)

'Polvarth' 7
(J.C. Williams, pre-1949)

'Pol Voulin' 2 W-P
(J.S.B. Lea) J.S.B. Lea, 1983
Sdlg 1-40-67 × 'Dailmanach'; sdlg no. 2-14-74
Fl. 115 mm wide

'Polwyn' 9
(P.D. Williams, pre-1927)
AM(Haarlem) 1929

N. polyanthos Loiseleur-Deslongchamps 13
Section Tazettae

'Polybarth' 2 (a)
(pre-1951)

'Polydore' 2 (a)
(R.H. Bath, pre-1933)

'Polydorus' 5
(Barr & Sons, pre-1923)
'Albatross' × *N. triandrus* var. *loiseleurii*

'Polymna' 2 Y-YYO
(Konynenburg & Mark) Konynenburg & Mark, 1963
'Mimosa' × ('Gratia' × 'Daisy Schäffer')
Fl. 100 mm wide; perianth segments light greenish yellow 6D; corona vivid yellow 13A, with strong orange 25A at rim. Mid-season

'Polynesia' 1 W-? (b)
(D.S. Bell) D.S. Bell, 1957

'Polyphant' 2 W-W
(Brian S. Duncan) du Plessis Bros, 1989
'Easter Moon' × 'Empress of Ireland'; sdlg no. 381
Fl. 88 mm wide; corona opening light yellow, becoming pure white. Mid-season

'Polyphonie' 1 (a)
(Konynenburg & Mark, pre-1953)

'Polyphonie' 2 Y-Y
(Konynenburg & Mark) Konynenburg & Mark, 1960
'Rembrandt' × 1 Y-Y
Fl. 120 mm wide; perianth segments brilliant yellow 8A; corona darker in tone (12A). Early

'Polyxena' 5
(Barr & Sons, pre-1923)
'Weardale Perfection' × *N. triandrus*

'Polzeath' 3 (a)
(P.D. Williams, pre-1934)
AM(Haarlem) 1934

'Pomeranza' 11a W-O
(J. Gerritsen & Son) J. Gerritsen & Son, 1973
'Orangery' hybrid
Fl. 90 mm wide

'Pommy' 2 W-P
(Mrs C.O. Fairbairn)

'Pomona' 3 W-GYO
(de Graaff Bros, pre-1930)
Corona yellow, with rim apricot at rim.
AM(Haarlem) 1936

'Pomp' 1 W-Y
(The Brodie of Brodie, c.1909)
'King Alfred' × 'Glory of Noordwijk'

'Pomp' 2 W-P
(J.M. Radcliff, 1953) P. Phillips, 1964
'Karanja' × 'Pink Nautilus'
Fl. 89 mm wide; corona clear pink, with paler tones at base. Mid-season. Resembles an improved 'Pink Nautilus' of cleaner pink

'Pompadour' 2 W-? (b)
(R. Freer, pre-1916)

'Pompadour' 2 W-P
(S.J. Bisdee, 1954)
'Pinkenba' × 'Rose of Sharon'

'Pompeii' 2 W-W
(W.G. Pannill) W.G. Pannill, 1970
'Broughshane' × 'Vigil'

'Pompey' 2 W-? (b)
(Barr & Sons, pre-1923)

'Pompidou' 2 W-P
(J.N. Hancock & Co., 1962) J.N. Hancock & Co., 1977
Sdlg × 'Joss Johnson'; sdlg no. 264/62H

Fl. 95 mm wide; corona strong to moderate yellowish pink 31C-D. Mid-season

'Pom-pom' 4 W-W
(G.L. Wilson) Trenoweth Valley Flower Farm, 1955

'Pona' 1 W-W
(S.J. Bisdee, pre-1939)
'Saint Aloysius' × 'Beersheba'

'Ponatahi' 1 W-W
(J.S. Leitch) J.S. Leitch, 1968

'Ponca' 2 Y-Y
(E.C. Powell, pre-1947)
'Bodilly' × 'Kantara'

'Poncho' 2 Y-O
(J.N. Hancock & Co., 1960) Unregistered

'Ponderosa' 4
(pre-1910)
('Golden Torch' × 'Trenoon') open pollinated

'Ponderosa' 1 Y-Y
(G.L. Wilson) G.L. Wilson, 1964
2n=28

'Pongee' 2 Y-Y
(Murray W. Evans) Murray W. Evans, 1986
(['Binkie' × 1 YYW-W] × ['Daydream' × 'Bethany']) × ('Just So' × ['Bethany' × 'Daydream']); sdlg no. W-5/1
Mid-season

'Ponjeravah' 2 Y-? (a)
(G.H. Johnstone, pre-1950)
'Copper Bowl' hybrid

'Ponjola' 1 Y-Y
(Australian or New Zealand origin, pre-1927)
Corona deeply flanged

N. × *ponsii-sorollae* Fernández Casas 13 = *N. assoanus* Dufour × *N. triandrus* Linnaeus subsp. *pallidulus* (Graells) D.A.Webb

'Pontes' 1 W-Y
(W. Jackson Jr, 1967) Jackson's Daffodils, 1979
Sdlg no. 87/67
Fl. 111 mm wide. Mid-season

'Pontex'
(New Zealand origin, pre-1940)

'Pontiff' 3 W-? (b)
(Mrs R.O. Backhouse, pre-1921)

'Pontresina' 2 W-Y

(J.L. Richardson) J.L. Richardson, 1958
'Green Island' × 'Chinese White'
Fl. 114 mm wide; perianth segments very broad, not prominently mucronate, pure white, spreading, concave and with margins incurling at apex, smooth, regular, overlapping half; the inner segments narrower, shouldered at base; corona very shallow funnel-shaped or almost disc-shaped, opening pale yellow, soon becoming whitish, with green in tube, mouth deeply split and overlapping, usually 3-lobed, frilled. 2n=28. Resembles 'Green Island' in form. AM(e) 1959, *AM(g) 1966

'Pontsianna' 2 W-P
(G.L. Wilson) G.L. Wilson, 1966
'Mondaine' × 'Roseworthy'

'Pooh Bah' 4
(Mrs B.A. Woods) Mrs B.A. Woods, 1968

'Poo Koo' 2 W-P
(P. Phillips) Ken Farmer Nurseries, 1978
Fl. 76 mm wide. Mid-season

'Poolewe' 2 W-P
(J.S.B. Lea) J.S.B. Lea, 1978
'Fionn' × 'Rose Royale'; sdlg no. 1-47-64
Fl. 100 mm wide; corona peach pink. Late

'Pooley Bridge' 2 (a)
(Alister Clark, 1936) J. Sharp, 1960

'Poolijs' 1 W-W
(G. Zandbergen-Terwegen, pre-1937)

'Popcorn' 2 Y-R
(Carncairn Daffodils) Carncairn Daffodils, 1992
From P.Phillips open-pollinated seed
Fl. forming a double triangle, 101 mm wide; perianth segments ovate, a little inflexed, smooth, overlapping half; the inner segments a little more narrowly ovate; corona cylindrical, somewhat constricted towards the mouth, vivid yellowish pink 30C, with green prominent in tube, mouth slightly flared, with rim notched. Mid-season

'Pope's Giant'
(pre-1915)

'Pope's King' 1 Y-Y
(J. Pope, pre-1899)
Fl. yellow; perianth segments with green at midrib below. Early. Resembles a larger-flowered 'Golden Spur'. AM 1899

'Pope's Selene' 2 W-YYR
(pre-1927)
Perianth segments white, of great substance; corona yellow, with scarlet at rim

'Pope's Surprise' 1 W-?
Syn. of 'Surprise'

'Pope the Poet' 9
Syn. of 'The Poet Pope'

'Popinjay' 3 Y-O
(Mrs R.S. Cobley, pre-1937)

'Poplin' 10 Y-Y
(D. & J.W. Blanchard) D. & J.W. Blanchard, 1960
Hybrid from species in the *N. bulbocodium* group
Fl. 38 mm wide, rich yellow. Early. 2n=28. Resembles a yellow-flowered *N. cantabricus*

'Poppea' 8
(pre-1939)

'Poppet' ?-P
(Alister Clark, pre-1948)

'Poppet' 5 W-W
(A. Gray) A. Gray, 1958
N. cyclamineus × *N. triandrus* var. *loiseleurii*
Perianth segments yellowish white; corona milk white. Dwarf

'Poppy's Choice' 4 Y-R
(R.A.Scamp) S.Holden, 1996
'Golden Aura' × 'Menabilly'; sdlg no. 484
Fl. 95 mm wide; perianth and other petaloid segments in several whorls, prominently mucronate, very dark yellow; corona segments interspersed, deep bright red. Mid-season

'Pops Legacy' 1 W-Y
(W.A. Bender, 1975) W.A. Bender, 1985
From P.Phillips open-pollinated seed; sdlg no. 75/57
Perianth segments very broadly ovate, blunt, only very slightly mucronate, greenish white (155A), spreading, a little concave, of heavy substance, overlapping half; the inner segments shorter, more narrowly ovate, square-shouldered at base; corona cylindrical, broad, lightly ribbed, brilliant yellow 8A, paling a little to base, mouth more strongly ribbed, slightly flared, wavy, with rim notched and crenate. Early. Resembles 'Lenz' but with the perianth more rounded

'Porcelain' 2 W-W
(Murray W. Evans) Murray W. Evans, 1980
'Pristine' × 'Moyard'; sdlg no. O-20
Fl. 110 mm wide. Mid-season

'Porcelaine' 3 W-? (b or c)
(N.Y. Lower, pre-1916)

'Porfia' 8 W-?
(pre-1807)

'Porlock' 2 W-? (b)
(Warnaar & Co., pre-1929)
AM(Haarlem) 1930

N. porrigens Jordan = *N. pseudonarcissus* var. *porrigens*.

'Portadown' 1 Y-Y
(W.J. Dunlop) W.J. Dunlop, 1961
Fl. deep gold. 2n=28

'Portaferry' 3 W-O
(W.J. Dunlop, pre-1952)
Perianth segments pure white; corona deep reddish orange. Late

'Portal' 2 W-WPP
(G.E. Mitsch) G.E. Mitsch, 1963
'Rose Ribbon' × 'Caro Nome'; sdlg no. R109/2
Fl. 108 mm wide; perianth segments milk white; corona pale lemon yellow, with a broad band of salmon pink at rim. Mid-season

'Portarlington' 1 Y-Y
(J.L. Richardson, pre-1943)
'Bloemlust' × 'Trenoon'
Fl. forming a double triangle, soft golden yellow; perianth segments very broadly ovate, blunt, only very slightly mucronate, a little reflexed, plane, smooth and of good substance, overlapping half; the inner segments more narrowly ovate, spreading or a little inflexed; corona cylindrical, smooth, mouth broadly ribbed, flared, with rim flanged and crenate. Early to mid-season

'Portavo' 2 W-W
(Carncairn Daffodils, 1965) Carncairn Daffodils, 1978
'Easter Moon' × G.L.Wilson sdlg 45/115; sdlg no. 4/140/60
Fl. 100 mm wide. Mid-season. Resembles a rounder-flowered 'Easter Moon' in colour and texture but with a larger and frilled corona with green at base

N. portensis Pugsley 13 Section Pseudonarcissus

'Portent' ?-P
(Alister Clark, pre-1948)

'Port Erin' 3 W-GGW
(Ballydorn Bulb Farm) Ballydorn Bulb Farm, 1980
'Portstewart' × 'Tryst'
Fl. 75 mm wide; corona with green at base spreading into mid-zone and with white towards mouth. Mid-season

'Portfolio' 1 W-W
(W.G. Pannill) W.G. Pannill, 1980
'Vigil' × 'Empress of Ireland'; sdlg no. 64/119 U
Fl. 110 mm wide; corona with rim rolled

'Porth'
(pre-1935)

'Porthallow' 2 (a)
(R.F. Calvert, pre-1930)

'Porthchapel' 7 Y-O
(R.V. Favell, pre-1953)
Fl. 60 mm wide; perianth segments ovate, blunt, brilliant greenish yellow 6A, with prominent white mucro, spreading or a little reflexed, overlapping at base only; the inner segments more usually spreading, with margins incurling; corona cup-shaped, lightly ribbed, yellow-orange (23A), with mouth wavy, rim broadly and shallowly crenate. 2n=21

'Porthcurno' 2 Y-YYO
(R.V. Favell) R.M. Favell, 1960
Fl. 89 mm wide; perianth segments pale yellow; corona with reddish orange at rim. Early

'Porthgwarra' 2 W-Y
(R.V. Favell, *c.*1939) R.M. Favell, 1965
Fl. 89 mm wide; corona pale creamy yellow. Mid-season

'Porthia' 2 W-? (b)
(de Graaff Bros, pre-1943)
AM(Haarlem) 1942

'Porthilly' 2 Y-O
(P.D. Williams, pre 1927)
Fl. 100 mm wide; perianth segments very broadly ovate, blunt, fairly prominently mucronate, primrose yellow, spreading, with margins incurling at apex, smooth, regular, overlapping one-third to a half; the inner segments more narrowly ovate, shouldered at base, only very slightly mucronate, a little inflexed, with margins sometimes reflexed from midrib; corona short broad funnel-shaped, orange, with mouth straight and lightly frilled, rim notched and crenate. 2n=28. AM(e) 1933, FCC(e) 1936, *(Kirton)AM(g)(m) 1939

'Porthloe' 2 W-? (b or c)
(The Brodie of Brodie, pre-1930)

'Porthminster' 3 W-? (b)
(The Brodie of Brodie, pre-1930)

'Porthos' 1 (a)
(W.B. Hartland, pre-1914)

'Porthtowan' 2 (a)
(The Brodie of Brodie, pre-1938)
Perianth segments very broad in outline, blunt or squarish at apex, mucronate, spreading, plane, overlapping half; the inner segments square-shouldered at base, a little inflexed; corona bowl-shaped, lightly ribbed, with mouth split in places and overlapping,

closely and minutely frilled

'Portia' 1 W-Y
(Barr & Sons, pre-1892)
Perianth segments opening pale primrose yellow, becoming sulphur white, of strong substance; corona darker in tone

'Portia' 3 W-Y
(C.E. Radcliff, 1933)
'Pink'un' × 'Mayflower'
Perianth segments pure white, deeply overlapping; corona shallow, ribbed, pale primrose yellow

'Portia' 1 (a)
Syn. of 'Savannah'

'Port Kembla'
Unregistered
Pollen parent of 'Bessiebelle' and others

'Portland' 2 W-? (b)
(de Graaff Bros, pre-1928)
Syn. 'Prometheus'

'Port Latta' 1 W-P
(K.J. Heazlewood) K.J. Heazlewood, 1968
'Rosedale' × 'Rosario'
Fl. 108 mm wide, of good substance; corona deep pink. Mid-season. Resembles 'Fintona' but with a paler-coloured corona

'Portlight' 3 W-R
(The Brodie of Brodie, c.1933)
'Seraglio' × 'Hades'; sdlg no. 133/E/28
See also 'Port Light'

'Port Light' 3 W-R
Syn. of 'Portlight'

'Port Lightning' 2 (a)
(S.C. Gaspar, pre-1949)

'Portmadock'
(pre-1940)

'Portmarnock' 2 Y-Y
(J.L. Richardson, pre-1938)
('Hospodar' × 'Tredore') × 'Aviemore'
Fl. 127 mm wide; perianth segments broadly ovate, blunt, prominently mucronate, deep golden yellow, spreading, somewhat creased, overlapping half; the inner segments only a little narrower, square-shouldered at base, slightly inflexed; corona funnel-shaped, strongly ribbed towards the mouth, slightly darker in tone than the perianth, with mouth expanded and frilled, rim deeply crenate. Mid-season

'Portnagolan' 2 W-GPP
(Carncairn Daffodils) Carncairn Daffodils, 1988

Sdlg W9/27 × 'Tynan'; sdlg no. 1/73/76
Corona cup-shaped, clear pink, with mouth expanded, rim dentate. Late

'Port Noo' 3 W-Y
(Carncairn Daffodils) Carncairn Daffodils, 1992
'Golden Aura' × 'Aircastle'; sdlg no. 5/4/79
Fl. 80 mm wide, rounded; perianth segments very broad, truncate, only slightly mucronate, yellowish white 155B, spreading, concave, smooth, overlapping half or more; the inner segments roundish; corona shallow bowl-shaped, ribbed, pale greenish yellow 9C, mouth with six deeply overlapping lobes, frilled. Mid-season

'Portobello' 3 W-OOR
(D.S. Bell) D.S. Bell, 1960
'Idealist' × 'Boswell'
Fl. 108 mm wide; perianth segments pure white, smooth and of good substance, overlapping; corona apricot, with a broad band of red at rim. Late. Resembles 'Catherine Howard' but with stronger substance and better colour

'Port Patrick' 3 W-GOR
(Ballydorn Bulb Farm, 1980) Ballydorn Bulb Farm, 1990
'Portstewart' × 'Northern Spell'
Fl. 70 mm wide; perianth segments roundish, very smooth; corona very shallow bowl-shaped, brightly coloured. Late

'Portrait' 2 W-P
(Murray W. Evans) Murray W. Evans, 1984
'Cordial' × 'Caro Nome'; sdlg no. L-30/2
Fl. 105 mm wide. Mid-season

'Portreath' 2 (a)
(The Brodie of Brodie, pre-1938)
Perianth segments very broadly ovate, blunt, slightly mucronate, spreading, concave near apex, overlapping half; the inner segments more narrowly ovate, somewhat creased, with margins wavy; corona deep bowl-shaped, lightly ribbed, mouth expanded, split in places and overlapping, more or less even, with rim crenate

'Portrush' 3 W-W
(G.L. Wilson, pre-1947)
'Silver Coin' × 'Crimson Braid'
Fl. 83 mm wide; perianth segments very broad, blunt or truncate, mucronate, a little reflexed, overlapping half; the inner segments ovate, not noticeably mucronate, spreading, with margins wavy; corona narrow cup-shaped, closely ribbed, with deep green in tube, mouth straight, tightly frilled, with rim minutely crenate. Very late. 2n=28

'Port Said' 3 W-? (b)
(Barr & Sons, pre-1945)

'Portsoy' 3 Y-YYO
(Mrs R.S. Cobley, 1948) Seymour Cobley Ltd, 1968
Perianth segments primrose yellow; corona greenish yellow, with a broad band of orange at rim. Late

'Portstewart' 3 W-W
(Ballydorn Bulb Farm) Ballydorn Bulb Farm, 1971
'Portrush' open pollinated
Fl. 90 mm wide

'Port William' 3 W-GYO
(Ballydorn Bulb Farm) Ballydorn Bulb Farm, 1991
'Portstewart' × 'Northern Spell'
Fl. 92 mm wide; corona saucer-shaped, pale yellow, with very dark emerald green at base and a band of orange at rim. Late

'Posai' 2 Y-P
(D.J. Jackson, 1979) Jackson's Daffodils, 1989
'Daydream' × 'Chino'; sdlg no. 279/79
Fl. 98 mm wide; perianth segments vivid yellow 9B, touched white at base, slightly concave; corona light yellowish pink 19B. Early to mid-season

'Poseidon' 2 W-W
(F.A. Secrett, pre-1948)

'Possum' 3 W-P
(H.G.Cross) H.G.Cross, 1994
'Cascade' × 'Kerstin'; sdlg no. 5263
Fl. 90 mm wide; perianth segments broadly ovate, blunt, only very slightly mucronate, greenish white (157C), slightly reflexed, somewhat creased, overlapping half; corona shallow, very widely expanded, lightly ribbed, pink, paling to faint pink at base, with a narrow band of strong pink at rim, mouth frilled, rim minutely dentate. Mid-season to late. Varies between Divs 3 and 2

'Possum' 2 W-P
(J.N.Hancock & Co., 1975) Unregistered
'Hylena' × 'Verran'; sdlg no. 84/75H
Fl. rounded; corona cylindrical, peach pink, with mouth flared. Mid-season

'Post Horn' 6 Y-Y
(Rosewarne EHS) Cornwall Area Bulb Growers Association, 1985
'Cornet' × 'Priority'; sdlg no. 66-24-2
Perianth segments clear lemon yellow; corona darker in tone. Early

'Post House' 4 W-P
(Brian S. Duncan) Rathowen Daffodils, 1988
Sdlg 8/74 (['Falaise' × 'Debutante'] × 'Polonaise') × sdlg 376 ('Polonaise' × 'Violetta'); sdlg no. 889
Fl. rounded; perianth and other petaloid segments white; the outer whorl very broadly ovate, blunt, slightly mucronate, spreading, plane, with broad midrib showing, overlapping half or more; the inner whorl a little shorter and narrower, irregularly arranged, strongly inflexed, folded inwards along the midrib, with margins incurling, sometimes twisted; corona segments shorter than the petaloid segments at centre and clustered among them, broad, deep pink, more or less heavily frilled. Mid-season to late

'Postmistress' 2 W-R
(G.L. Wilson, pre-1950)
'Folly' × 'Athlone'
Perianth segments pure white, slightly reflexed; corona shallow, bright red. 2n=28

'Potent' 2 W-? (b)
(E.M. Crosfield, pre-1908)

'Potent' 3 W-R
(W. Jackson Jr) Jackson's Daffodils, 1979
('Jo' × 'Masaka') × 'Arbar'; sdlg no. 183/70
Fl. 94 mm wide

'Potentate' 1 Y-Y
(J.R. Pearson & Sons, pre-1913)
Fl. large, clear bright yellow. Tall

'Potential' 1 W-P
(R. & E. Havens, 1982) R. & E. Havens, 1993
('Rima' × 'Graduation') × 'Pink Silk'; sdlg no. REH52/1
Fl. 100 mm wide, smooth; perianth segments broadly ovate, spreading, plane; corona cylindrical, clear mid-pink. Mid-season. Sunproof

'Potheen' 1 (a)
(J.L. Richardson, pre-1923)

'Poto' 1 W-W
(pre-1940)

'Pot o' Gold' 1 (a)
(Mrs F.S. Foote, pre-1941)

'Potomac' 2 W-? (b)
(E.C. Powell, pre-1949)

'Potter' 1 (a)
(G. Lubbe & Son, pre-1927)

'Poudrée' 1 W-W
(Barr & Sons, pre-1927)
Perianth segments inflexed; corona with rim slightly rolled

N. poujastou Barr mss. = *N. pallidiflorus* var. *intermedius*

'Poujastou Blond Doré' 1 Y-Y
(Pyrenean origin)
Selection by Peter Barr (1887) from wild-collected *N.*

pallidiflorus
Fl. pale yellow; perianth segments oblong, almost acute, mucronate, with margins paler in tone, inflexed, somewhat twisted, slightly overlapping; corona a little expanded, with a darker tone at rim, mouth deeply folded, obscurely lobed, rim irregularly and finely dentate. Early. Syn. 'Blond Doré'

'Poulton' 1 Y-Y
(H. Williams) E.W. Cotter, 1957
Fl. rich yellow, of thick substance; perianth segments broad; corona with rim rolled and dentate

'Pounawea' 2 Y-YOO
(R. Crews, 1944) R. Crews, 1958
? × 'Dunkeld'
Fl. 89 mm wide, of good substance; corona with golden yellow at base. Mid-season

'Pour Toi' 2 Y-Y
(Konynenburg & Mark) Konynenburg & Mark, 1963
'Mimosa' hybrid
Fl. 110 mm wide; perianth segments brilliant yellow 9C; corona light greenish yellow 8C. Mid-season

'Powder Pink' 2 W-P
(G.E. Mitsch, 1954) G.E. Mitsch, 1965
'Loch Maree' × 'Dawnglow'; sdlg no. P45/2
Fl. 115 mm wide; perianth segments ivory white, overlapping; corona soft apricot pink, with rim flanged. Mid-season

'Powder Puff' 4
(W.F.M. Copeland, pre-1913)

'Powder River' 2 (a)
(K.L. Reynolds, pre-1944)

'Powder Room' 2 W-P
(Carncairn Daffodils, 1984) Carncairn Daffodils, 1994
'Boudoir' self pollinated; sdlg no. 1/21/78
Fl. forming a double triangle, 100 mm wide; perianth segments very broadly ovate, not prominently mucronate, greenish white 157D, spreading, with margins sometimes incurling at apex, overlapping half; the inner segments more narrowly ovate and a little twisted; corona funnel-shaped, 6-angled, strong yellowish pink, shading to darker pink at base and very dark pink in tube, mouth widely expanded, with rim crenate and widely rolled. Late

'Powerstock' 2 W-O
(J.W.Blanchard, 1986) J.W.Blanchard, 1997
Sdlg 71/22A (sdlg 59/46A × 'Hotspur') × 'Osmington'; sdlg no. 81/10B
Fl. 95 mm wide; perianth segments very broad in outline, blunt or somewhat truncate at apex, slightly mucronate, spreading, a little concave, with margins incurling, smooth, of thick substance, regular, overlapping half; the inner segments narrower, somewhat oblong, a little inflexed; corona almost disc-shaped, broad, ribbed, vivid orange 28B, with mouth split in places and overlapping, a little frilled. Mid-season. Resembles a larger 'Osmington' with a deeper-coloured corona

'Powhatan' 1 Y-Y
(E.C. Powell, pre-1949)
'The Perfect Gentleman' × 'Sunstar'

'Pow Wow' 4
(Cartwright & Goodwin, pre-1916)

'Prado' 1 Y-GYY
(W. Jackson Jr) Jackson's Daffodils, 1979
'Ristin' × sdlg 128/65; sdlg no. 35/72
Fl. 105 mm wide. Early to mid-season

N. praecox Tenore = *N. italicus*

praecox = *N. bulbocodium* subsp. *praecox*

'Praecox' 9 W-GYR
(pre-1900)
N. poeticus sdlg
Fl. star-shaped; perianth segments pure white, reflexed, with margins wavy and strongly incurved, of poor substance, overlapping up to a quarter; corona very shallow bowl-shaped, closely ribbed, yellow, faintly tinged green at base, with a band of orange-red at rim, rim sometimes deeply notched. Early. Resembles a shorter and smaller-flowered 'Praecox Grandiflorus' of later flowering season and less sweet a scent

'Praecox Grandiflorus' 9 W-YYR
(pre-1893)
Selection from *N. poeticus*
Fl. large, somewhat star-shaped; perianth segments pure white, with margins inflexed; corona yellow, suffused crimson, with red at rim. Tall. Early for a Poeticus hybrid. Differs in size from 'Praecox' and has no green tinge at base corona. Is somewhat earlier in flower than 'Ornatus' and more sweetly scented

N. praelongus Jordan = *N. gayi*

praelongus = *N. assoanus* var. *praelongus*

'Praga' 1 W-Y
(J.T. Gray, pre-1949)
Corona lemon yellow

'Praha' 2 W-P
(J.N. Hancock & Co., 1949) J.N. Hancock & Co., 1965
Late

'Prairie Fire' 3 O-R
(Brian S. Duncan) Rathowen Daffodils, 1986
(['Ballintoy' × 'Air Marshal'] × 'Shining Light') × 'Sabine Hay'; sdlg no. 745
Perianth segments evenly flushed apricot orange; corona dark red. Mid-season. Resembles a taller and more robust 'Sabine Hay' with a less rounded flower of smoother texture

'Praline' 4 W-O
(J. Gerritsen & Son) J. Gerritsen & Son, 1977
'Pink Glory' hybrid
Fl. 115 mm wide; perianth segments ivory white; corona pale orange (25D), with a lighter tone (23D) at rim. Late

N. pratensis Jordan = *N. tazetta* subsp. *lacticolor*

N. × *pravianoi* Fernández Casas 13 = *N. nobilis* (Haworth) Schultes f. var. *primigenius* Fernández Casas & Lainz × *N. triandrus* Linnaeus

'Praze' 3 W-? (b)
(P.D. Williams, pre-1927)
'Gold Tray' × 'Cromarty'

'P.R.Barr' 1 Y-Y
(W. Backhouse, pre-1869)
Perianth segments broadly ovate, blunt, prominently mucronate, primrose yellow, inflexed, overlapping one-third; the inner segments slightly twisted; corona cylindrical, lightly ribbed, much darker in tone than the perianth, with mouth flared and loosely frilled, rim notched and crenate. Resembles a small-flowered 'Emperor'. Syn. Pseudonarcissus Lorifolius 'P.R.Barr'

'Preamble' 1 W-Y
(G.L. Wilson, 1946)
'Niphetos' × 'Kanchenjunga'
Fl. forming a double triangle, 115 mm wide; perianth segments very broadly ovate, blunt, slightly mucronate, spreading or a little reflexed, with margins slightly wavy, smooth, overlapping half; the inner segments more narrowly ovate, inflexed at base, reflexed at apex; corona cylindrical, smooth, opening brilliant yellow 9C, becoming lemon, mouth ribbed and expanded, lightly frilled, with rim flanged and crenate. Early. 2n=28. AM(e) 1948, FCC(e) 1949, AM(Haarlem) 1950

'Precedent' 2 W-P
(G.E. Mitsch) G.E. Mitsch, 1960
'Mabel Taylor' × 'Green Island'; sdlg no. P46/2
Fl. 108 mm wide; perianth segments slightly reflexed; corona salmon pink. Mid-season. Resembles a taller 'Carita' with smoother perianth segments and a smaller corona

'Precentor' 1 Y-Y
(Slieve Donard Nursery Co., pre-1931)
Perianth segments somewhat inflexed, only slightly overlapping; corona fairly broad. Very early

'Preceptor' 1 (a)
(R.H. Bath, pre-1931)

'Preciosa' 2 W-W
(Konynenburg & Mark) Konynenburg & Mark, 1962
('Daisy Schäffer' × 'Faveur') × 'Mount Hood'
Fl. 120 mm wide; corona creamy white. Mid-season

'Precious' 3 W-? (b)
(Mrs R.O. Backhouse, pre-1921)

'Precious Pink' 2 W-GWP
(D.S. Bell) Mrs G. Link, 1992
Fl. 90 mm wide; perianth segments roundish, spreading, smooth and of heavy substance, overlapping; corona funnel-shaped, white, with green at base and yellow at rim, with the rim becoming pink before fading with age, mouth wavy. Early

'Precise' 3 W-YYR
(W.G. Pannill) W.G. Pannill, 1985
'Merlin' × 'Autowin'; sdlg no. E 35/1 B
Mid-season

'Precision' 3 W-W
(W.O. Backhouse) M.J. Jefferson-Brown, 1964

'Precision' 3 W-Y
(?Australian origin, pre-1997) Unregistered

'Precocious' 2 Y-O
(pre-1927)
Corona reddish orange. Early

'Precocious' 2 W-P
(G.E. Mitsch, 1966) G.E. Mitsch, 1976
'Precedent' × 'Eclat'; sdlg no. G13/1
Fl. rounded, 98 mm wide, facing slightly downwards; perianth segments very broadly ovate, only slightly mucronate, ivory white, spreading, a little concave and with margins slightly incurling at apex, overlapping half or more; corona bowl-shaped, salmon rose pink, with mouth widely expanded and heavily frilled. Mid-season

'Precocity' 2 or 3 W-? (b or c)
(W.B. Hartland, pre-1907)

'Predator' 1 W-Y
(Jackson's Daffodils) Jackson's Daffodils, 1987
'Lenz' × 'Helsal'; sdlg no. 216/79
Fl. forming a double triangle; perianth segments broadly ovate, greenish white (155A), spreading, plane, overlapping half; the inner segments a little

inflexed; corona cylindrical, narrow, smooth, brilliant greenish yellow 6A, with mouth flared and wavy, rim minutely notched. Mid-season

'Pre-eminent' 1 Y-Y
(G. Lewis)
'Gold Tray' × 'Cromarty'

'Preface' 6 Y-Y
(G.E. Mitsch) G.E. Mitsch, 1956
'Magnificence' × *N. cyclamineus*
Fl. rich golden yellow; perianth segments reflexed; corona with rim flanged. Early

'Preference' 2 Y-? (a)
(G.H. Johnstone, pre-1949)

'Prefix' 6 Y-Y
(G.E. Mitsch) G.E. Mitsch, 1969
'Cibola' × *N. cyclamineus*; sdlg no. Z12/1
Perianth segments broad, reflexed; corona with mouth expanded. Early

'Preislied' 2 Y-Y
(Konynenburg & Mark) Konynenburg & Mark, 1963
(('Cocktail' × 'Red Bird') × ('Fortune' × 'Flaming Torch')
Fl. 115 mm wide; perianth segments light greenish yellow 4C; corona vivid yellow 15B. Early

'Prejudice' 6 Y-Y
(F.A. Saunders) F.A. Saunders, 1969
'Garron' × *N. cyclamineus*

'Prelate' 1 Y-Y
(Hon. Mrs Petre, pre-1934)
Perianth segments ovate, blunt, with slight pale mucro, a little inflexed, with margins wavy, overlapping a quarter to one-third; the inner segments twisted and somewhat creased; corona cylindrical, smooth, with mouth ribbed and flared, rim widely flanged and deeply notched and dentate

'Prelude' 1 Y-Y
(Sir A.P.W. Thomas, pre-1930)

'Prelude' 9 W-GYR
(pre-1955) Unregistered

'Premier' 2 Y-Y
(E.M. Crosfield, pre-1913)
Fl. 108 mm wide; perianth segments clear yellow; corona rich dark yellow. Tall

'Premier' 1 Y-Y
(R.H. Bath, pre-1927)
Fl. 102 mm wide; perianth segments pale lemon yellow, overlapping half; corona pale buttercup yellow, with mouth somewhat expanded. Mid-season to late

'Premiere' 2 W-GPP
(Brian S. Duncan) Brian S. Duncan, 1973
'Pink Isle'? × 'Rose Royale'
Fl. 100 mm wide; perianth segments broadly ovate. 2n=28

'Preolema' 2 Y-YYO
(S.J. Bisdee, 1942) R. Hyde, 1958
'Market Merry' × 'Killigrew'
Syn. 'Preolenna'

'Preolenna' 2 Y-YYO
Syn. of 'Preolema'

'Presence' 4 W-P
(D.S. Bell) D.S. Bell, 1983

'Present to England' 2 (a)
(P.D. Williams, pre-1936)

'President Arthur' 1 Y-Y
(E. Leeds, pre-1877)
Perianth segments inflexed, overlapping. Syn. Pseudonarcissus Major 'President Arthur'

'President Carnot' 1 W-W
(de Graaff Bros, pre-1923)

'President Carter' 1 Y-Y
(D. van Buggenum) de Groot, 1978
Fl. 125 mm wide; perianth segments brilliant greenish yellow 5A; corona vivid yellow 12A, with darker tones at rim and greenish yellow at base. Early

'President Cleveland' 2 (a)
(F. Rijnveld & Sons, pre-1939)

'President Faure' 1 W-Y
(de Graaff Bros, pre-1923)
Fl. 95 mm wide; perianth segments creamy white, twisted, irregular, overlapping at base only; corona pale primrose, mouth frilled and somewhat expanded. Mid-season

'President Garfield' 1 W-Y
(W. Backhouse, pre-1869)
Syn. Pseudonarcissus Bicolor 'President Garfield'. Was "absorbed" into 'Horsfieldii'

'President Harding' 1 W-? (b)
(W.J. Eldering & Son, pre-1930)

'President Harrison' 8
(pre-1907)
Perianth segments pale sulphur; corona darker in tone

'Presidential Pink' 2 W-P
(G.E. Mitsch and R. & E.Havens) G.E. Mitsch and R. & E.Havens, 1985
(['Mabel Taylor' × 'Green Island] × 'Caro Nome') ×

'Space Ship'; sdlg no. LL20/3
Fl. of heavy substance; perianth segments very broad, rounded at apex, only very slightly mucronate, spreading, concave at apex or with margins boldly incurling, overlapping half; the inner segments narrower, square-shouldered at base, slightly inflexed; corona bowl- or short funnel-shaped, broadly ribbed, reddish orange-pink, paler at base, mouth straight, split in places and overlapping, frilled, with rim crenate. Mid-season

'President Lebrun' 1 W-? (b)
(P.D. Williams, pre-1942)
AM(Haarlem) 1943

'President Lincoln' 1 Y-Y
(E. Leeds, pre-1877)
Fl. yellow; perianth segments twisted, sometimes ribbed; corona slightly different in tone. Syn. Pseudonarcissus Major 'President Lincoln'. Was "absorbed" into 'Edward Leeds'

'President Roosevelt' 1 W-W
(van Zonneveld Bros & Philippo, pre-1931)

'President Taft' 3 W-? (b)
(H. Prins, pre-1929)

'President Viger' 2 (a)
(pre-1938)

'President Wentholt' 1 (a)
(M. van Waveren & Sons, pre-1907)

'President Wilson' 1 W-? (b)
(van Zonneveld Bros & Phillipo, pre-1931)

'Presieuse' 8 Y-Y
(pre-1807)

'Presteigne' 1 (a)
(N.Y. Lower, pre-1928)

'Prestige' 1 W-W
(G.L. Wilson, pre-1946)
'Candour' × 'Kanchenjunga'
Fl. 130 mm wide; perianth segments broadly ovate, blunt, slightly mucronate, spreading, plane, smooth, overlapping half; the inner segments more narrowly ovate, a little inflexed, creased and somewhat twisted; corona cylindrical, smooth, opening faint primrose, becoming white, with rim rolled and minutely crenate. AM(e) 1954

'Prestios' 2 Y-Y
(E. Leeds, pre-1877)
Perianth segments sulphur; corona tinged orange. Syn. Incomparabilis Albidus 'Prestios'

'Presto' 3 W-GYR
(Ballydorn Bulb Farm) Ballydorn Bulb Farm, 1978
'Merlin' × 'Fairmile'
Fl. 110 mm wide. Mid-season. Resembles 'Fairmile' but with a broader band of colour at corona rim

'Preston' 2 W-W
(F.D.B. Cobb, pre-1954)

'Preston'
(G.L. Wilson, pre-1962)
'Madame de Graaff' × 'King Alfred'

'Preston Flame' 2 Y-O
(Mrs M. Moorby) Mrs M. Moorby, 1963
F. 95 mm wide; corona intense reddish orange. Mid-season. Resembles a larger-flowered 'Caerleon' with a darker-coloured corona

'Pretender' 2 W-Y
(G.E. Mitsch, 1954) G.E.Mitsch, 1964
('John Evelyn' × 'Fortune') × 'Green Island'; sdlg no. P110/1
Fl. rounded, 100 mm wide; perianth segments with margins somewhat incurved, of heavy substance, deeply overlapping; corona almost disc-shaped, pale lemon yellow, paling to creamy yellow towards base, with shades of grey in tube and flecks of white between the notches at rim, mouth heavily frilled and folded, with some extra segments beneath. Mid-season

'Pretoria' 2 or 3 ?-O
(W.B. Hartland, pre-1914)
Corona scarlet-orange

'Pretoria' 1 Y-Y
(J.L. Richardson, pre-1944)
'Shanghai' × 'Crocus'
Perianth segments broadly ovate, blunt, slightly mucronate, inflexed, concave in upper half, smooth, overlapping one-third to a half; the inner segments more narrowly ovate, with margins sometimes nicked at shoulder; corona cylindrical, lightly ribbed, mouth expanded and more heavily ribbed, rim rolled and more or less deeply notched and crenate. Mid-season

'Pretty Gay' 2 W-P
(J.N. Hancock & Co., c.1982) Unregistered

'Pretty Girl' 2 W-O
(Tom Forster, 1960s) Unregistered
Perianth segments broadly ovate, blunt, fairly prominently mucronate, creamy white, spreading or reflexed, somewhat concave, overlapping half or more; the inner segments spreading, creased, with margins nicked in places; corona very broad disc-shaped, almost as long as the perianth segments and closely overlying them, ribbed, deep tangerine orange, with rim deeply notched and dentate. Mid-season

'Pretty Lady' 4 Y-O
(Th. van der Hulst) Th. van der Hulst, 1989
'Kissproof' × 'Tahiti'
Fl. 95 mm wide; perianth segments light greenish yellow 8B; corona segments orange (28A). Mid-season. Resembles 'Double Fashion'

'Pretty Miss' 7 W-Y
(G.E. Morrill) G.E. Morrill, 1973
'Polindra' × *N. jonquilla*
Fl. 70 mm wide; corona primrose. Scented

'Pretty Polly' 2 W-WWP
(J.L. Richardson) F.D.B. Cobb, 1958
Corona with strong yellowish pink 32D at rim

'Preview' 2 W-? (b)
(A.H. Ahrens) J.S. Leitch, 1955

'Priam' 1 Y-Y
(S.J. Bisdee, 1939)
'Mortlake' × 'Golden City'

'Priamus' 3 Y-? (a)
(P.D. Williams, pre-1934)

'Pride' 6
(F.A. Saunders) F.A. Saunders, 1957

'Pride of Baltimore' 9 W-GGR
(Mrs M.S. Yerger) Mrs M.S. Yerger, 1993
'Hexameter' × 'Lights Out'; sdlg no. 75 M 9
Fl. forming a double triangle, 48 mm wide; perianth segments acute, overlapping; the inner segments narrower and slightly shorter; corona disc-shaped, brilliant yellow-green (154B), with a darker tone at base and a narrow band of orange-red (33A) at rim. Late

'Pride of Cambridge' 2 W-OOY
(R.H. Bath, pre-1930)
Corona dull tomato orange, with a narrow band of yellow at rim. AM(e) 1930

'Pride of Cornwall' 8 W-YYR
(P.D. Williams, pre-1933)
Fls 2-3 per stem, 59 mm wide; perianth segments broadly ovate, blunt or truncate, prominently mucronate, white, tinged yellow at base, concave, overlapping half; the inner segments more narrowly ovate, a little inflexed, with margins incurling; corona bowl-shaped, ribbed, deep orange-yellow, with red at rim, mouth straight, neatly frilled. Scented. 2n=24

'Pride of England' 2 (a)
(G. Zandbergen-Terwegen, pre-1936)

'Pride of Erin' 3 W-YYR
(W.J. Dunlop, pre-1952)
'Sunstar' × 'Isola'
Perianth segments pure white; corona yellow, with crimson-red at rim

'Pride of Guernsey' 2 or 3 W-? (b or c)
(E.H. Wheadon & Sons, pre-1916)

'Pride of Hatton' 2 (a)
(?Mrs D. Duff, pre-1951)

'Pride of Heemstede' 4 Y-Y
(J.B. Roozen, pre-1951)
Syn. 'Fascination'

'Pride of Hillegom' 1 Y-Y
(M. van Waveren & Sons, pre-1931)
AM(Haarlem) 1930

'Pride of Holland' 8 W-O
(R.A.van der Schoot, pre-1931)
Poetaz
AM(Haarlem) 1930

'Pride of Lisse' 1 W-? (b)
(de Graaff-Gerharda, pre-1930)

'Pride of Munster' 1 W-? (b)
(Mrs D. Bucknall, pre-1930)

'Pride of Portugal' 8 W-Y
(pre-1997) Unregistered

'Pride of Texel' 4 Y-Y
(J. Leber, pre-1942)
Resembles an early-flowered 'Telamonius Plenus'.
TGA(Haarlem) 1949

'Pride of the East' 2 (a)
(R.H. Bath, pre-1933)

'Pride of the Market' 2 W-Y
(R.H. Bath, pre-1931)
Fl. 89 mm wide; perianth segments pale cream, overlapping half; corona funnel-shaped, bright orange-yellow. Mid-season to late

'Pride of Virginia' 3 W-O
(P.D. Williams, pre-1930)
Corona deep orange. Tall. AM(Haarlem) 1930

'Priestly' 3 W-? (b)
(van Zonneveld Bros & Philippo, pre-1931)

'Prim' 3 W-GYY
(Sir J.S. Arkwright, pre-1938)
Perianth segments ivory white, with margins slightly wavy; corona shallow, lemon yellow, with deep moss green at base, frilled

'Prima Donna' 2 W-? (b)
(G.H. Engleheart, pre-1908)

'Prima Donna' 8
(R.A. van der Schoot, pre-1931)
AM(Haarlem) 1930

'Primate'
(G.H. Engleheart, pre-1907)

'Primate' 2 W-W
(N.R. McIsaac) N.R. McIsaac, 1982
'Greenland' × 'Newcastle'; sdlg no. 112
Fl. 107 mm wide. Mid-season

'Primatice' 2 or 3 W-? (b or c)
(W.B. Hartland, pre-1907)

'Primavera' 2 (d)
(de Graaff-Gerharda, pre-1925)
AM(Haarlem) 1925

'Primavera' 1 Y-Y
Syn. of 'Galileo'

'Prima Vista' 1 W-Y
(Konynenburg & Mark) Konynenburg & Mark, 1960
Sdlg × ('Gracious' × 'Faveur')
Fl. 120 mm wide; perianth segments greenish white; corona brilliant yellow 12B. Early

'Prime Minister' 1 Y-Y
(Sir A.P.W. Thomas, pre-1915)
Fl. large

'Prime Time' 2 Y-Y
(Eileen E. Frey) G.E. Mitsch, 1979
'Playboy' × 'Daydream'; sdlg no. JEE9/3
Fl. 90 mm wide, clear yellow; corona with a slightly deeper tone at rim, frilled. Mid-season

'Primeur' 1 Y-Y
(P. de Jager & Sons) J.W.A. van der Wereld, 1978
Fl. 95 mm wide; perianth segments much brighter and richer than vivid yellow 12A, overlapping; corona slightly ribbed, darker in tone (14A) than the perianth, mouth expanded and heavily frilled, rim crenate and slightly flanged. Early

primigenius = *N. nobilis* var. *primigenius*

'Primlough' 1 Y-Y
(H.A. Brown) J.N. Hancock & Co., 1960
Fl. primrose yellow

'Primo' 8 W-Y
Syn. of 'Grand Primo Citronière'

'Primo Angers' 8 W-O
(pre-1798)

'Primo Citronier' 8 W-Y
Syn. of 'Grand Primo Citronière'

'Primo Citronière' 8 W-Y
Syn. of 'Grand Primo Citronière'

'Primo de Munk' 8 W-O
(pre-1798)

'Primo des Narcisses' 8 Y-Y
?The same as 'Prino des Narcisses'

'Primo Jeaun' 8 Y-Y
(pre-1777)

'Primo Luteo' 8 Y-Y
?Syn. of 'Grand Primo'

'Primo Madouce' 8 Y-O
(pre-1798)

'Primo Merode' 8 Y-Y
(pre-1798)
?The same as 'Prince de Merode'

'Primo Zelander' 8 Y-Y
(pre-1807)

'Primrose' 5
(P.D. Williams, pre-1913)

'Primrose Beauty' 4 Y-O
W. Blom & Son, 1955
$2n=24$

'Primrose Beauty' 4 Y-Y
An error for 'Primrose Cheerfulness'

'Primrose Cheerfulness' 4 Y-Y
(C. Alkemade, pre-1954)
'Cheerfulness' sport
Fl. pale primrose yellow. Sometimes seen in error as 'Primrose Beauty'

'Primrose Cream' 4 W-Y
(W. Jackson Jr, 1972) Unregistered
'Mrs William Copeland' × 'Lawali'; sdlg no. 27/72

'Primrose Cup' 8 W-Y
(pre-1872)
Corona primrose yellow

'Primrose Dame' 3 Y-Y
(Barr & Sons, pre-1909)
'Honourable Mrs Jocelyn' × *N. poeticus*
Perianth segments creamy primrose yellow; corona deeply ribbed, bright yellow, suffused golden yellow. Resembles a paler-coloured 'Noble'

'Primrose Dame' 5 Y-Y
(P.D. Williams, pre-1915)

Fl. lemon yellow; corona slightly darker in tone

'Primrose Day' 5 Y-Y
(A.E. Lowe, pre-1927)
Fl. primrose yellow

'Primrose Eye' 3 W-? (b)
(Cartwright & Goodwin, pre-1916)

'Primrose Gem' 2 Y-Y
(W. Backhouse, pre-1869)
Perianth segments primrose yellow. Syn. Incomparabilis Albidus 'Primrose Gem'

'Primrose Gem' 5 Y-Y
(W. Backhouse, pre-1869)
Fl. soft primrose yellow. Resembles 'Queen of Spain' in form

'Primrose Gem' 7
(Barr & Sons, pre-1923)

'Primrose Girl' 2 W-WWY
(R.H. Bath, pre-1927)
Perianth segments creamy white; corona opening lemon, becoming white, with a distinct band of deep yellow at rim. Late

'Primrose Glory' 1 W-Y
(R.H. Bath, pre-1934)
PC 1934

'Primrose King' 1 (a)
(C.L. Adams, pre-1910)

'Primrose Knight' 1 (a)
(J.L. Richardson, pre-1927)
Perianth segments very broadly ovate, blunt, slightly mucronate, reflexed in upper half, with margins wavy, overlapping half; the inner segments more narrowly ovate, sometimes twisted; corona cylindrical, smooth, with mouth expanded and even, rim entire or obscurely crenate

'Primrose League' 1 (a)
(G.H. Johnstone, pre-1952)

'Primrose Path' 2 W-P
(Carncairn Daffodils) Carncairn Daffodils, 1983
'Passionale' × 'Rose Caprice'; sdlg no. W8/9
Fl. 100 mm wide; corona buff pink. Mid-season. Primrose-scented

"Primrose Peerless"
Syn. of *N.* × *medioluteus*

'Primrose Perfection' 4
(pre-1913)

'Primrose Phoenix' 4 Y-Y
(pre-1902)
Fl. rounded, primrose yellow; perianth and other petaloid segments in numerous whorls, fairly regular superimposed, ovate or broadly ovate, with white mucro; the outer whorls spreading or a little inflexed, often concave each side of a raised midrib or with margins recurved, overlapping one-third; the inner whorls successively a little shorter and more strongly inflexed, with margins incurled; the centre whorls clustered, strongly inflexed, with margins tightly incurled. AM 1902

'Primrose Queen' 4 Y-Y
(pre-1898)
Fl. large; petaloid and other petaloid segments densely arranged, primrose yellow; corona segments orange-yellow

'Primrose Queen' 2 Y-Y
(C. Dawson, pre-1910)
Perianth segments soft primrose yellow; corona ribbed, bright yellow, lightly frilled. Faintly scented

'Primrose Star' 3 Y-Y
(W. Backhouse, pre-1869)
Perianth segments primrose yellow; corona darker in tone. Syn. Burbidgei 'Primrose Star'. "Absorbed" 'Arabella'

N. primulinus Haworth = *N.* × *intermedius*

N. primulinus Schultes = *N. tazetta*

primulinus = *N. bertolonii* var. *primulinus*

'Primulinus' ?-Y
(?E. Leeds, pre-1877)
Corona citron yellow. Syn. Leedsii 'Primulinus'

'Primulinus'
Syn. of *N.* × *intermedius*

'Primulinus' 1 W-Y
Syn. of 'Dean Herbert'

'Primulinus' 3 Y-R
Syn. of 'Cowslip'

'Primulinus' 3 W-Y
Syn. of 'Romeo'

'Primus' 3 W-? (b)
(F. Rijnveld & Sons, pre-1930)
AM(Haarlem) 1930

'Prince' 3 W-YYR
(A.T. van Graven, pre-1934)
Fl. 89 mm wide; perianth segments broadly ovate, blunt or rounded at apex, slightly mucronate, creamy white, spreading, a little concave, sometimes nicked

near apex, overlapping half; the inner segments more narrowly ovate, a little inflexed; corona very small disc-shaped, closely ribbed, light yellow 12C, with a band of orange-red (33B) at rim. Standard to tall. Late. 2n=28. Syn. 'The Prince'. AM(Haarlem) 1934, *HC(g) 1941, *AM(g) 1944

'Prince Arthur' 2 W-Y
(Barr & Sons, pre-1919)
Perianth segments overlapping; corona primrose yellow, tinged lemon yellow, with mouth expanded

'Prince Bernhard' 1 (a)
(G. Lubbe & Son, pre-1936)
Syn. 'Queen Mary'. AM(Haarlem) 1936

'Prince Bismarck' 3 W-Y
(M. Leichtlin, pre-1884)
Perianth segments sulphur white; corona flared. Syn. Barrii Sulphureus 'Prince Bismarck'

'Prince Charles' 1 (a)
(C. Dawson, pre-1923)

'Prince Charming' 5
(Mrs R.O. Backhouse, pre-1908)

'Prince Charming' 4 W-P
(Oregon Bulb Farms) Oregon Bulb Farms, 1958
Mid-season

'Prince Colibri' 1 W-Y
Perianth segments creamy white; corona large, of strong substance. Dwarf

'Prince de Baden' 8 W-O
(pre-1798)

'Prince de Merode' 8 Y-Y
(pre-1777)
?The same as 'Primo Merode'

'Prince de Metternich' 8
(pre-1890)

'Prince de Soubise' 8 Y-Y
Syn. of 'Prince of Soubise'

'Prince d'Orange' 8 Y-Y
(pre-1798)
Fl. golden yellow

'Prince Fushima' 2 W-WYY
Syn. of 'Prince Fushimi'

'Prince Fushimi' 2 W-WYY
(W. Welchman, pre-1908)
Corona closely ribbed, apricot yellow, paling to ivory white at base, with a tinge of orange at rim. AM(c) 1919. See also 'Prince Fushima'

'Prince George' 1 Y-Y
(E. Leeds, pre-1877)
Syn. Pseudonarcissus Major 'Prince George'

'Prince George' 1 Y-Y
(de Graaff Bros, pre-1890)
Perianth segments soft primrose yellow; corona darker in tone than the perianth

'Prince Hendrik' 1 (a)
(R.A. van der Schoot, pre-1923)

'Prince Igor' 1 Y-Y
(J.O. Sherrard, pre-1943)
Probably 'Royalist' × 'Cromarty'

'Prince Ki' 1 Y-Y
(E.W. Philpott) E.W. Philpott, 1959
'Robert Montgomery' × 'Protos'
Fl. golden yellow. Tall. Early. Resembles a small-flowered 'Regal Coin'

'Prince Llewellyn' 1 (a)
(W.A. Watts, pre-1914)

'Prince of Arragon' 1 Y-Y
(G.P. Haydon, pre-1923)
Perianth segments light yellow, somewhat inflexed; corona golden yellow

'Prince of Asturias' 1 (a)
(W. Welchman, pre-1908)

'Prince of Brunswick' 2 W-GYY
(Ballydorn Bulb Farm, 1966) Ballydorn Bulb Farm, 1976
'Brunswick' × 'Promptitude'
Fl. 98 mm wide; corona opening yellow, becoming primrose. Early

'Prince of Mars' 3 W-? (b)
(Mrs R.O. Backhouse, pre-1921)

'Prince of Netherlands' 1 W-Y
Syn. of 'Prince of the Netherlands'

'Prince of Orange' 1 Y-? (a)
(W. Welchman, pre-1907)

'Prince of Orange' 2 W-O
(de Graaff Bros & van Konynenburg & Co., pre-1925)
Perianth segments pure white, of thick substance, overlapping; corona rich reddish orange. Syn. 'Prins van Orange'. AM(Haarlem) 1925, FCC(Haarlem) 1927

'Prince of Poets' 9 W-?
(L. Buckland, pre-1915)
Corona with red at rim

'Prince of Poets' 9 W-?
(C. Dawson, pre-1927)
'Raeburn' × 'Dactyl'
Fl. rounded; perianth segments ivory white, of thick substance; corona with red at rim

'Prince of Soubise' 8 Y-Y
(pre-1777)
Fl. pale yellow. Syn. 'Prince de Soubise'

'Prince of the Netherlands' 1 W-Y
(J. de Groot & Sons, pre-1913)
See also 'Prince of Netherlands'

'Prince of Wales' 1 W-Y
(W. Backhouse, pre-1869)
Perianth segments sulphur white. Syn. Pseudonarcissus Bicolor 'Prince of Wales'. Was "absorbed" into 'James Walker'

'Prince of Wales' 8
(pre-1885)

'Prince of Wales' 1 Y-Y
(M. van Waveren & Sons, pre-1926)
Perianth segments soft primrose yellow, fairly smooth, overlapping; corona bright yellow

'Prince Orlof' 1 W-? (b)
(J.W.A. Lefeber, pre-1938)

'Princeps' 1 W-Y
(?Italian origin, pre-1830)
Fl. 95 mm wide; perianth segments narrowly ovate, acute, sulphur white, inflexed, twisted, smooth, overlapping at base only; corona narrowly funnel-shaped, loosely ribbed, rich yellow, paler at base, mouth expanded and more strongly ribbed, rim notched and dentate. Early. 2n=14. Syn. ?'Principe Umberto Primo', 'Irish Princeps', 'Princeps Grand Trumpeter'. The same as *N. gayi*?

'Princeps Grand Trumpeter' 1 W-Y
Syn. of 'Princeps'

'Princeps Improved' 1 Y-Y
(pre-1912)
Resembles a larger-flowered 'Princeps' of better poise

'Princeps Maximus' 1 W-Y
(W.B. Hartland, pre-1884)
Perianth segments sulphur white. Late. 2n=14. Syn. 'Don Quixotte'

'Prince Regent' 2 Y-O
(J.L. Richardson, pre-1947)
'Porthilly' × 'Carbineer'
Perianth segments deep golden yellow; corona bright reddish orange

'Prince Romantic' 2 W-O
(Tom Forster, 1960s) Unregistered
Perianth segments snow white; corona expanded, bright apricot orange. Tall. Mid-season

'Prince Royal' 2 Y-O
(J.L. Richardson) Mrs H.K. Richardson, 1964
'Air Marshal' × 'Firecracker'
Perianth segments deep golden yellow; corona bright orange, with mouth frilled. Very late

'Prince Rupert' 1 Y-Y
(Barr & Sons, pre-1913)
Perianth segments acute, creamy yellow, spreading; corona rich butter yellow, frilled

'Prince Siddartha' 1 W-W
(Barr & Sons, pre-1923)

'Princess' 4 Y-Y
(Barr & Sons, pre-1897)
Fl. pale yellow; petaloid and corona segments regularly arranged. Dwarf

'Princess' 1 W-Y
(P.D. Williams, pre-1907)
Corona pale yellow

'Princess Alexandra' 6 W-W
(Rosewarne EHS) W.J.Hosking, 1997
N. cyclamineus × 'Woodgreen'; sdlg no. 65/64/1
Fl. 95 mm wide; perianth segments reflexed, with margins slightly incurling at apex, a little creased, overlapping; corona almost straight-sided, slender, opening pale creamy yellow, quickly becoming cream, frilled. Dwarf. Very early

'Princess Alice' 8 W-O
(W. Backhouse, pre-1869)
Perianth segments creamy white; corona clear yellow. Dwarf. Syn. Tridymus 'Princess Alice'. Was "absorbed" into 'Innocence'

'Princess Alice' 2 W-? (b)
(G.H. Engleheart, pre-1914)

'Princess Anne' 9 W-GYR
(Mrs M.S. Yerger) Mrs M.S. Yerger, 1993
'Dulcimer' open pollinated; sdlg no. 76 A 18
Fl. 62 mm wide; the inner a little shorter than the outer perianth segments; corona almost disc-shaped, brilliant greenish yellow 1A, with yellow-green (151B) at base and a broad band of orange-red (32A) at rim. Late

'Princess Astrid' 2 Y-O
(de Graaff Bros, pre-1927)
Perianth segments clear buttercup yellow; corona orange. AM(Haarlem) 1927

'Princess Badura' 3 W-? (b)
(Mrs R.O. Backhouse, pre-1921)

'Princess Beatrix' 2 W-R
(P. van Deursen, pre-1938)
AM(Haarlem) 1940

'Princess Betty' 2 W-P
(C. Goodson, pre-1927)

'Princess Charming' 1 W-? (b)
(G.H. Johnstone, pre-1954)

'Princess Diana' 6 W-Y
(Rosewarne EHS) W.J.Hosking, 1997
N. cyclamineus × 'Trousseau'; sdlg no. 65/63/1
Fl. 95 mm wide; perianth segments a little reflexed, with margins slightly incurled, overlapping; corona expanded, rich creamy yellow, lightly frilled, with rim flanged. Dwarf. Early

'Princess Elisabeth' 8 W-O
(pre-1925)
Poetaz
Corona reddish orange. AM(Haarlem) 1925

'Princess Elizabeth' 1 (a)
(Slieve Donard Nursery Co., pre-1937)

'Princess Ena' 5 W-Y
(C.G. van Tubergen, pre-1906)
'Grandee' × *N. triandrus*
Fl. 95 mm wide, facing down; perianth segments creamy white, reflexed, overlapping half; corona funnel-shaped, sulphur. Dwarf. Mid-season to late. AM 1906

'Princess Fairal' 2 Y-? (a)
(P. van Deursen, pre-1939)
AM(Haarlem) 1939

'Princess Ida' 1 W-WWY
(C. Smith, pre-1888)
Perianth segments ovate, inflexed, twisted, overlapping at base only; corona narrowly funnel-shaped, yellowish white, with a broad band of bright yellow at rim, mouth expanded and 6-lobed, rim widely flanged and crenate. Somewhat resembles *N. moschatus* in form

'Princess Ida' 1 W-PPY
(J.N. Hancock & Co., *c.*1977) Unregistered
Corona pinkish, with yellow at rim, with the rim rolled

'Princess Ingrid' 8
(A. Vis, pre-1936)
AM(Haarlem) 1936

'Princess Irene' 4 W-Y
(?Australian origin, pre-1997) Unregistered

'Princess Juliana' 1 Y-Y
(de Graaff Bros, pre-1910)
Fl. 102 mm wide, deep golden yellow; perianth segments lemon yellow, irregular, overlapping one-third; corona a little darker in tone than perianth, with mouth expanded, rim widely flanged. Mid-season. FCC(Haarlem) 1914, AM(e) 1914

'Princess Louisa'
?Syn. of 'Princess Louise'

'Princess Louise' 3 W-Y
(W. Backhouse, pre-1869)
Perianth segments acute; corona expanded, tinged scarlet-orange on opening, becoming apricot yellow. Syn. Burbidgei 'Princess Louise'. ?See also 'Princess Louisa'

'Princess Margaret' 1 W-W
(A. Chrystal, pre-1931)
PC(e)(NZ) 1931

'Princess Mary' 2 W-O
(E. Leeds, pre-1877)
Possibly (*N. pseudonarcissus* × *N. poeticus*) × *N. poeticus*
Perianth segments broadly ovate, blunt, prominantly mucronate, creamy white, spreading, somewhat creased, overlapping a quarter; the inner segments more narrowly ovate, not noticeably mucronate, with margins wavy or incurling; corona shallow and very widely expanded, strongly ribbed, yellow, suffused with scarlet-orange, mouth wavy, rim dentate. Syn. 'Princess Mary of Cambridge', Incomparabilis Pallidus 'Princess Mary'. FCC 1884. "Absorbed" 'Fitzjames'

'Princess Mary of Cambridge' 2 W-O
Syn. of 'Princess Mary'

'Princess Maud' 3 W-Y
(C. Smith, pre-1902)
Perianth segments inflexed; corona primrose yellow

'Princess May' W-W
(?Thomas Smith, pre-1899)
Corona slightly stained sulphur

'Princess Metternich' 8 W-Y
(pre-1904)
Corona rich golden yellow

'Princess Miriam' 3 W-YYO
(Mrs R.O. Backhouse, pre-1921)
?'Will Scarlett' hybrid
Perianth segments pure white; corona dark yellow, with orange at rim. AM(Haarlem) 1935

'Princess of Holland' 8 W-O
(A.C. van der Schoot, pre-1925)

Poetaz
Fl. large; perianth segments white; corona deep yellow-orange. Syn. 'Grand Maitre'. AM(Haarlem) 1925

'Princess of Tasmania' 2 W-YYO
(Tom Forster, 1960s) Unregistered
Perianth segments milk white; corona disc-shaped, lightly ribbed, lemon yellow, with bright orange at rim. Tall. Mid-season

'Princess of Wales' 3 W-WWO
(W. Backhouse, pre-1869)
Corona expanded, opening canary yellow, becoming sulphur white, with orange at rim. Syn. Leedsii 'Princess of Wales'

'Princess Rangi' 2 (a)
(W.A. Grace, pre-1938)

'Princess Rick' 2 W-? (b)
(Mrs A.O. Meyrick, pre-1949)

'Princess Rose' 2 W-? (b or c)
(A. Chrystal, pre-1933)

'Princess Royal' 2 W-W
(A.M. Wilson, pre-1944)

'Princess Royale' 8 Y-Y
(pre-1798)
Fl. golden yellow

'Princess Superior'
(pre-1946)
PC(e)(NZ) 1946

'Princess Victoria' 2 Y-? (a)
(W.A. Watts, pre-1923)
'Sir Watkin' × 'Ornatus'
Early

'Princess Yolande' 8 W-Y
(W. Polman-Mooy, pre-1930)
Poetaz
Perianth segments silver white. Syn. ?'Yolande', 'Helena Maria'

'Princess Zaide' 3 W-GWW
(Mrs J. Abel Smith) Mrs J. Abel Smith, 1986
'Mary Isabel' hybrid; sdlg no. F33/26
Perianth segments very broad, rounded at apex and slightly truncate, a little reflexed, plane, with midrib showing, overlapping half; the inner segments more nearly ovate, with margins incurved; corona very shallow bowl-shaped, densely ribbed, with deep green at base, mouth very widely expanded and heavily frilled, rim minutely crenate. Late

'Prince Teck' 2 W-Y
(E. Leeds, pre-1877)
Perianth segments creamy white, overlapping; corona large, expanded, of smooth texture. Syn. Incomparabilis Pallidus 'Prince Teck'. "Absorbed" 'Lady Gray' and 'Pallidus'

'Princeton' 3 W-WWY
(G.E. Mitsch) R. & E. Havens, 1993
'Limpkin' × 'Wedding Band'; sdlg no. TT47/24
Fl. rounded, 110 mm wide; perianth segments very broad, slightly mucronate, pure white, spreading, plane, silken smooth, overlapping half or more; the inner segments not noticeably mucronate, rounded at base; corona disc-shaped, white, with a well-defined band of deep yellow at rim, regularly frilled. Late

'Princette' 3 W-GYR
(Mrs G.Link, 1975) Mrs G.Link, 1995
'Fairy Circle' × *N. jonquilla*; sdlg no. 1670
Fl. 40 mm wide; perianth segments spreading, overlapping; corona cylindrical, light yellow, with green at base and a narrow band of red at rim, mouth a little flared. Dwarf. Mid-season

'Prince Umbria' 2 W-Y
(Barr & Sons, pre-1923)
Perianth segments broadly ovate, blunt, mucronate, spreading, plane, overlapping one-third; the inner segments a little inflexed, with margins slightly wavy; corona deep bowl-shaped, creamy primrose yellow, with mouth expanded, densely frilled. AM(e) 1923

'Principal' 1 Y-Y
(G.L. Wilson, pre-1931)
'Cleopatra' × 'Sorley Boy'
Fl. 102 mm wide; perianth segments broadly ovate, blunt, mucronate, chrome yellow, spreading, irregular, overlapping half; the inner segments a little inflexed, slightly twisted or with margins wavy, more regular; corona cylindrical, smooth, a little darker in tone than the perianth, with rim widely flanged and regularly notched. 2n=28. Resembles an improved 'Dawson City'. AM(e) 1935, FCC(e) 1937

'Principe Umberto Primo' 1 W-Y
?Syn. of 'Princeps'

'Prinity' 11a W-Y
Syn. of 'Printal'

'Prino des Narcisses' 8 Y-Y
(pre-1835)
Early. ?The same as 'Primo des Narcisses'

'Prins Bernhard' 1 (a)
(G. Zandbergen-Terwegen, pre-1936)

'Prins Boudewyn' 3 W-? (b)
(de Graaff Bros, pre-1938)

AM(Haarlem) 1937

'Prins Carnaval' 11b Y-R/Y
(J.W.A. Lefeber, 1950) J.W.A.Lefeber, 1960
Fl. 86 mm wide; perianth segments canary yellow; corona segments with a longitudinal band of red at midrib and yellow at margins. Late

'Prinses Ingeborg' 11?b W-O
(J.W.A. Lefeber, 1950) J.W.A. Lefeber, 1960
Fl. 80 mm wide; perianth segments pure white; corona segments reddish orange. Mid-season

'Prinses Irene' 4
(C.A. van der Wereld, pre-1952)
AM(Haarlem) 1952, TGA(Haarlem) 1955

'Prinses Marijke' 2 W-O
(G. Lubbe & Son, pre-1947)
Perianth segments creamy white; corona shallow, dark orange. AM(Haarlem) 1947

'Prins' Giant' 1 W-? (b)
(H. Prins, pre-1929)

'Prins van Baden' 8 W-O
(pre-1846)

'Prins van Orange' 2 W-O
Syn. of 'Prince of Orange'

'Prins van Vriesland' 8 Y-Y
(pre-1807)
Fl. sulphur yellow

'Printal' 11a W-Y
(J. Gerritsen & Son, 1966) J. Gerritsen & Son, 1976
'Expo' hybrid
Fl. 85 mm wide; perianth segments very broadly ovate, blunt, ivory white, spreading, overlapping half; the inner segments narrower, creased, a little inflexed; corona split, the six segments half as long as the perianth segments and opposite and closely overlying them, bi-lobed, with the lobes overlapping, pale yellow, with a broad band of darker yellow at rim, spreading, very deeply frilled. Early. See also 'Prinity'

'Priority' 1 Y-Y
(G.L. Wilson, pre-1945)
'Magnificence' × 'Hebron'
Corona with rim dentate and widely flanged

'Priory Park' 9 W-YYR
(H. Prins, pre-1929)
Fl. 67 mm wide; perianth segments somewhat reflexed, overlapping; corona almost disc-shaped, greenish lemon, with bright red at rim. Late

'Priscilla' 1 W-Y
(pre-1889)

Corona citron yellow, with lemon yellow at rim

'Priscilla' 2 W-? (b or c)
(J.R. Pearson & Sons, pre-1908)

'Priscilla' 2 Y-R
(G. Lewis, 1945) D.S. Bell, 1958
Perianth segments golden yellow; corona widely expanded, dark flaming red

'Priscilla' ?-P
(Alister Clark, pre-1948)

'Priscilla Bright' 2 W-YYO
(G. Lubbe & Son, pre-1944)
AM(Haarlem) 1944

'Prisk' 7 Y-Y
(M.P. Williams, pre-1937)
Fl. rounded, bright yellow, smooth; corona broad. Dwarf

'Prism' 2 Y-Y
(G.E. Mitsch and R. & E.Havens, 1974) G.E. Mitsch and R. & E.Havens, 1986
'Aircastle' × 'Cool Flame'; sdlg no. JJ3/1
Perianth segments light yellow; corona shallow, deep yellow, tinged rose pink at rim. Late

'Prissy' 5 W-GYO
(Mrs G. Link, 1978) Mrs G. Link, 1991
'Dinkie' × N.triandrus; sdlg no. 773-B
Perianth segments opening with green at base, becoming self white, slightly reflexed, of heavy substance; corona funnel-shaped, with mouth flared. Late. Resembles a larger and later-flowered 'Missy'

'Pristine' 2 W-GWW
(G.L. Wilson) Harry I.Tuggle Jr & W.G.Pannill, 1964
'Broughshane' × 'Greenland'
Fl. 108 mm wide; corona flared, opening cream, becoming white, with green at base, rim rolled. Mid-season

'Privateer' 3 W-O
(J.L. Richardson) J.L. Richardson, 1958
'Kilworth' × 'Arbar'
Perianth segments broadly ovate; corona disc-shaped, tightly ribbed, reddish orange

'Prizewinner' 1 Y-Y
(D. van Buggenum) D. van Buggenum, 1971
'Dutch Master' × 'Gold Medal'
Fl. 110 mm wide

'Probably' 2 W-P
(J.N. Hancock & Co., c.1963) Unregistered
'Pink Pearl' × 'Rose Bay'

'Probity' 2 W-Y
(F.E. Board) F.E. Board, 1965
'Easter Moon' × 'Homage'
Corona lemon yellow

'Problem' 5
(F.H. Chapman, pre-1913)

'Probus' 1 Y-Y
(R.A.Scamp) R.A.Scamp, 1997
'Viking' × 'Ristin'; sdlg no. 57
Fl. 94 mm wide, deep clear golden yellow; perianth segments ovate, plane, overlapping; corona cylindrical, with mouth slightly expanded, rim neatly crenate. Mid-season to late

'Procession' 2 W-WWP
Syn. of 'Foray'

'Procne' 5
(T. Batson, pre-1914)

'Procrustes' 2 W-? (b)
(de Graaff Bros, pre-1928)

'Procyon' Y-Y
(J.A. Hunter, 1977) J.A. Hunter, 1989
'Moon River' × 'Camelot'; sdlg no. 2/71A
Fl. 114 mm wide, vivid yellow 9A; perianth segments broadly ovate, blunt, of good substance; corona cylindrical, mouth straight, with rim dentate. Mid-season

'Prodigal' 2 (a or b)
(J.N. Hancock & Co., pre-1949)

'Producer' 1 Y-Y
(van Zonneveld Bros & Philippo, pre-1942)

'Proema' 1 W-W
Syn. of 'Proemia'

'Proemia' 1 W-W
(W. Jackson Sr, 1944)
'Cameronian' × 'Pepin'
See also 'Proema'

'Professor Baas Bekking' 1 (a)
(G. Lubbe & Son, pre-1931)

'Professor Barnard' 1 Y-Y
(Konynenburg & Mark) Konynenburg & Mark, 1969
'Virtuoso' × sdlg × 'Thor'

'Professor Einstein' 2 W-R
(J.W.A. Lefeber, pre-1946)
Fl. rounded; perianth segments very broad, blunt or truncate, prominently mucronate, pure white, more or less spreading, glistening and of thick substance, with margins sometimes incurling and broad midrib showing, overlapping half; corona very broad disc-shaped, closely ribbed, scarlet-red, with rim notched in places and minutely crenate. Mid-season. 2n=28. AM(Haarlem) 1955, FCC(Haarlem) 1957

'Professor Hammerstein' 2 Y-Y
(J.W.A. Lefeber) J.W.A. Lefeber, 1958
Perianth segments vivid yellow 9B; corona orange-yellow (17C)

'Professor Lorentz' 1 (a)
(W.J. Eldering & Son, pre-1930)

'Professor Parkinson' 2 WWY-YYO
Syn. of 'Doctor James Parkinson'

'Professor Thomson' 3 W-? (b)
(W. Welchman, pre-1910)

'Professor van Rooy' 2 W-? (b)
(de Graaff Bros, pre-1931)
AM(Haarlem) 1930

'Professor Westerdyke' 2 W-W
(pre-1930)
Fl. large; perianth segments overlapping. Tall

'Profile' 2 W-Y
(Murray W. Evans) Murray W. Evans, 1970
'Limerick' × 'Broughshane'
2n=28

'Profusion' 8 W-O
(pre-1908)
Poetaz

'Profusion' 2 W-P
(P. Phillips) P. Phillips, 1971
Fl. 115 mm wide

'Progenitor' 1 Y-O
(W.O. Backhouse) E. Longford, 1967
'Red Curtain' hybrid
Fl. 103 mm wide; corona reddish orange. Mid-season

'Progress'
(J. Pope, pre-1907)

'Progression' 1 Y-Y
(L. van Leeuwen & Son, pre-1927)
Perianth segments soft sulphur yellow; corona golden yellow, with mouth widely expanded. AM(Haarlem) 1927

'Prolific' 1 Y-Y
(C.A. van Paridon, pre-1950)
'Golden Harvest' × 'Godolphin'
AM(Haarlem) 1950, FCC(Haarlem) 1960

'Prologue' 1 W-Y
(G.E. Mitsch, 1952) G.E.Mitsch, 1962
'Foresight' × 'Trousseau'
Corona clear yellow. Very early. 2n=28. Resembles a taller and larger-flowered 'Foresight'

'Promenade' 1 W-? (b)
(Mrs Ben Robertson, pre-1953)

'Prometheus' 3 W-W
(W.B. Hartland, pre-1907)

'Prometheus' 2 W-R
(J.L. Richardson) M.J. Jefferson-Brown, 1969
'Kilworth' × 'Norval'

'Prometheus' 2 W-? (b)
Syn. of 'Portland'

'Prominent' 1 (a)
(M. van Waveren & Sons, pre-1943)

'Promise' 2 W-? (b)
(Oregon Bulb Farms, pre-1942)

'Promisso' 2 W-P
(Alister Clark) Oregon Bulb Farms, 1955
Corona becoming self pink after two to three days

'Promotion' 2 W-YYO
(G. Lubbe & Son, pre-1947)
Perianth segments ivory white; corona with yellow-orange at rim. AM(Haarlem) 1947

'Promptitude' 2 W-Y
(G.L. Wilson, pre-1945)
'Gracious' × 'Diva'
Perianth segments pure white; corona bright lemon yellow. Very early

'Proper Pride' 1 (a)
(Wrigley, pre-1913)

'Property' 2 W-? (b or c)
(Sir C.H. Cave, pre-1928)

'Prophet' 2 W-? (b or c)
(Sir C.H. Cave, pre-1928)

'Prophet' 1 Y-YYP
(H.R. Barr) M.J. Jefferson-Brown, 1975
'Lunar Sea' × 'Maiden's Blush'
Perianth segments pale lemon; corona lemon, with pink at rim. Early. Resembles 'Entrancement' but is paler-coloured and has the additional colour at corona rim. PC(e) 1975

'Propine' 2 W-W
(P.D. Williams, pre-1948)

N. propinquus Salisbury = *N. hispanicus* var. *propinquus*

'Propinquus'
Syn. of *N. hispanicus* var. *propinquus*

'Propriety' 2 W-P
(Murray W. Evans) Murray W. Evans, 1970
'Rose of Tralee' × 'Interim'

'Proserpine' 1 WWY-Y
(Spanish origin)
Selection by Peter Barr (*c*. 1897) from wild-collected material
Perianth segments white, shading to golden yellow at base, twisted; corona rich golden yellow, with mouth expanded

'Proska' 2 Y-Y
(W. Jackson Jr) Jackson's Daffodils, 1979
'Vixi' × 'Gold Script'; sdlg no. 88/70
Fl. 112 mm wide. Early to mid-season

'Prospect' 2 (a)
(R.G. Sharp, pre-1930)

'Prospector' 1 Y-Y
(G.H. Engleheart, pre-1923)
Fl. deep yellow; perianth segments twisted; corona with rim neatly flanged. Mid-season. AM(g)(m)(c) 1926

'Prosperity' 2 (a)
(L. van Leeuwen & Son, pre-1931)

'Prosperity' 1 Y-Y
(Elise Havens) G.E. Mitsch, 1978
'Nazareth' × 'Butterscotch'; sdlg no. FEJ6/4
Fl. 105 mm wide; perianth segments broadly ovate, blunt, clear bright yellow, spreading, plane, overlapping one-third to a half; the inner segments narrower, a little inflexed, with margins slightly wavy; corona cylindrical, smooth, bright yellow, with mouth even, rim flanged and regularly crenate. Mid-season. Resembles a lighter-coloured 'Goldcourt'

'Prospero' 1 Y-Y
(E.M. Crosfield, pre-1909)
Perianth segments ovate, blunt, pale creamy yellow, inflexed, ribbed, overlapping a quarter; the inner segments twisted; corona narrowly funnel-shaped, lightly ribbed, soft primrose yellow, with mouth straight or very slightly expanded, even, rim slightly crenate. Possibly not Div. 5 but Div. 1

'Prospero' 2 (a)
(Sir A.P.W. Thomas, pre-1915)

'Prospero' 3 W-R
(J.L. Richardson) J.L. Richardson, 1958

'Mahmoud' self pollinated
Resembles a larger 'Mahmoud' with a paler corona

'Protege' 2 Y-Y
(Murray W. Evans) Murray W. Evans, 1969

('Trousseau' × 'Pink o' Dawn') × ('Tunis' × 'Trousseau')

'Proteus' 2 W-Y
(Barr & Sons, pre-1913)
Corona soft canary yellow

'Protocol' 6 W-W
(G.E.Mitsch, 1984) R. & E.Havens, 1997
(['Vigil' × 'Empress of Ireland'] × 'Panache')× *N. cyclamineus*; sdlg no. TT29/2
Fl. 82 mm wide; perianth segments narrow, spreading on opening, becoming a little reflexed; corona very narrowly constricted at mid-point, with mouth slightly expanded. Dwarf. Early

'Protos' 1 (a)
(C.E. Radcliff, *c*.1940)
Very early

'Protos' 1 Y-Y
(W. Jackson Sr, 1940) W. Jackson Jr, 1956
'Aurelius' × 'Wattle'

'Prototype' 6 Y-YPP
(Brian S.Duncan) Brian S.Duncan, 1993
'Milestone' open pollinated; sdlg no. 1166
Fl. 79 mm wide; perianth segments broadly ovate, greenish yellow, spreading at base, strongly reflexed in upper half, somewhat twisted, overlapping one-third; corona cylindrical, loosely ribbed, rose pink, with pale pinkish yellow at base, mouth straight. Mid-season

'Proud Prince' 1 Y-Y
(R.C.A. Tombleson) R.C.A. Tombleson, 1971
'Spanish Gold' × 'Faris'
Fl. 115 mm wide

'Proverb' 2 Y-Y
(Angus Wilson) Wallace & Barr, 1959
Fl. 105 mm wide, rich yellow; corona slightly darker in tone. Mid-season. Resembles 'Galway'

'Providence' 2 (a)
(A.H. Ahrens) J.S. Leitch, 1955

N. provincialis Pugsley 13 Section Pseudonarcissus

'Proviso' 2 (a)
(J.E. Exley, pre-1950)

'Provost' 1 Y-Y
(W. Backhouse, pre-1869)
Corona expanded. Syn. Incomparabilis Concolor 'Provost'. Was "absorbed" into 'Autocrat'

'Provost' 1 Y-Y
(G.H. Engleheart, pre-1923)
Fl. golden yellow; perianth segments slightly twisted. AM(e) 1923

'Prowess' 2 W-Y
(G.E. Mitsch) G.E. Mitsch, 1963
'Green Island' × 'Chinese White'

'Proximo' ?-P
(Alister Clark, pre-1948)

'Proxy' 9 W-GYR
(Murray W. Evans, 1970) Murray W. Evans, 1985
N. poeticus var. *recurvus* × 'Dallas'; sdlg no. N-25/3
Very Late. Resembles a smaller and later-flowered 'Array'

'Prudence' 2 or 3 W-W
(C. Dawson, pre-1907)
'Minnie Hume' × *N. triandrus*

'Prudence' 2 W-P
(C.E. Radcliff, 1943) J.M.Radcliff, 1956
'Carmoa' × 'Dawnglow'

'Prudent' 1 (a)
(A.H. Ahrens) J.S. Leitch, 1955

'Prue Leith' 3 Y-YYO
(Clive Postles, 1985) Clive Postles Daffodils, 1995
Richardson sdlg 83 × 'Achduart'; sdlg no. 1-69-80
Fl. forming a double triangle, 80 mm wide; perianth segments ovate, primrose yellow; corona bowl-shaped, yellow, with a very narrow band of orange at rim, rim crenate. Mid-season

'Pruina' 9
(W.A. Milner, pre-1931)

'Prunella' 2 W-? (b)
(Cartwright & Goodwin, pre-1916)

'Prussima' 1 (b)
(C.G. van Tubergen, pre-1946)

'Pryda' 2 Y-W
(G.W.E. & M.E.Brogden, pre-1983) Unregistered

N. pseuditalicus Rouy = *N. italicus*

'Pseudo-juncifolius'
Syn. of *N. jonquilla* var. *minor*

N. pseudonarcissus Linnaeus 13 Section

Pseudonarcissus
　subsp. *abscissus* (Schultes f.) A.Fernandes = *N. abscissus*
　subsp. *albescens* (Pugsley) A.Fernandes = *N. albescens*
　subsp. *alpestris* (Pugsley) A.Fernandes = *N. alpestris*
　subsp. *bicolor* (Linnaeus) Baker = *N. bicolor*
　subsp. *confusus* (Pugsley) A.Fernandes = *N. confusus*
　subsp. *cyclamineus* Baker = *N. cyclamineus*
　subsp. *eugeniae* (Fernández Casas) Fernández Casas
　subsp. *gayi* (Hénon) A.Fernandes = *N. gayi*
　subsp. *leonensis* Pugsley = *N. nobilis* var. *leonensis*
　subsp. *longispathus* (Pugsley) A.Fernandes = *N. longispathus*
　subsp. *macrolobus* (Jordan) A.Fernandes = *N. macrolobus*
　subsp. *major* (Curtis) Baker = *N. hispanicus*
　subsp. *minor* Baker = *N. minor*
　subsp. *moschatus* (Linnaeus) Baker = *N. moschatus*
　subsp. *muticus* Baker = *N. abscissus*
　subsp. *nevadensis* (Pugsley) A.Fernandes = *N. nevadensis*
　subsp. *nobilis* (Schultes f.) A.Fernandes = *N. nobilis*
　subsp. *obvallaris* (Salisbury) A.Fernandes = *N. obvallaris*
　subsp. *pallidiflorus* (Pugsley) A.Fernandes = *N. pallidifloruş*
　subsp. *pisanus* (Pugsley) A.Fernandes = *N. pseudonarcissus* var. *pisanus*
　subsp. *portensis* (Pugsley) A.Fernandes = *N. portensis*
　subsp. ***pseudonarcissus*** ('King Umberto', 'Telamonius', "The Garland", "The Lent Lily"). AGM 1994
　　var. *pseudonarcissus*
　　var. *festinus* (Jordan) Pugsley
　　var. *humilis* Pugsley ('Scoticus')
　　var. *insignis* Pugsley
　　var. *minoriformis* Pugsley
　　var. *montinus* (Jordan) Pugsley
　　var. *pisanus* (Pugsley) A.Fernandes
　　var. *platylobus* (Jordan) Pugsley
　　var. *porrigens* (Jordan) Pugsley
　subsp. ***pugsleyanus*** Barra & López
　subsp. *tortuosus* (Haworth) A.Fernandes = *N. tortuosus*
　　var. *bromfieldii* Syme = *N. obvallaris*
　　var. *cambricus* (Haworth) hort. = *N. obvallaris*
　　var. *concolor* Bromfield = *N. obvallaris*
　　var. *johnstonii* Baker = *N.* × *johnstonii*
　　var. *lorifolius* Gillot = *N. abscissus*
　　var. *toscanus* (Parlatore) Pugsley = *N. obvallaris*

'Psyche' 2 W-? (b)
(Barr & Sons, pre-1913)

'Ptarmigan' 3 W-Y
(G.H. Engleheart, pre-1907)
'Daydream' × *N. jonquilla*; sdlg no. D32/1
Perianth segments lemon; corona almost white, shading to lemon at rim. Mid-season. Resembles a smaller 'Daydream'

'Ptarmigan' 2 Y-WWY
(G.E. Mitsch) G.E. Mitsch, 1975
Fl. 76 mm wide; perianth segments overlapping; corona lemon, with mouth expanded

'Ptolemy' 1 W-Y
(Barr & Sons, pre-1921)
Fl. facing slightly downwards; perianth segments creamy white; corona pale primrose yellow, with mouth expanded frilled

'Publicity' 2 W-YYO
(Sir J.S. Arkwright, pre-1937)
Corona shallow, very pale citron yellow, with clear orange at rim

'Publicity Officer' 4 Y-O
(Mrs H.K. Richardson) M.J. Jefferson-Brown, 1975
'Falaise' × 'Border Chief'
Resembles a taller and slightly smaller-flowered 'Tahiti' of earlier season and more prolific habit

'Publius' 1 (a)
(J. Pope, pre-1908)

'Puccini' 2 (a)
(G.B. de Vroomen & Sons) G.B. de Vroomen & Sons, 1956
AM(Haarlem) 1956

'Pucelle' 2 W-W
(G.H. Engleheart, pre-1930)
Fl. dainty, pure white

'Puck' 3 W-W
(G.H. Engleheart, pre-1907)
Fl. 82 mm wide; perianth segments creamy white, irregular, overlapping half; corona bowl-shaped, pale cream, faintly tinged apricot. Mid-season to late.
AM(Haarlem) 1930

'Puck' 2 W-? (b)
Syn. of 'La Tendresse'

'Pueblo' 7 W-W
(G.E. Mitsch) G.E. Mitsch, 1966
'Binkie' × *N. jonquilla*; sdlg no. T6/5
Fl. 76 mm wide; corona opening lemon yellow, becoming milk white. Mid-season

pugsleyanus = *N. pseudonarcissus* subsp. *pugsleyanus*

N. × ***pugsleyi*** Fernández Casas 13 = *N. alpestris*

Pugsley × *N. assoanus* Dufour

N. × *pujolii* **Font Quer 13** = *N. assoanus* Dufour × *N. dubius* Gouan

'Pukatea' 2 (a)
(Parr's Nurseries, 1947) Parr's Nurseries, 1958

'Pukawa' 7 Y-R
(J.A. O'More) P. Phillips, 1977
'Indian Summer' × *N. jonquilla*
Fl. 46 mm wide; perianth segments golden; corona red

'Pukenui' 4 W-YOO
(M.Hamilton) Koanga Daffodils, 1996
'Blossom' × 'Bandit'; sdlg no. 22-87
Fl. 110 mm wide; perianth and other petaloid segments broadly ovate, white; corona segments yellow-orange (17B), paling to yellow at base. Mid-season

'Pukepapa' 1 Y-Y
(A. Gibson, pre-1927)

'Puk-Puk' 2 W-P
(D.J. Jackson, 1979) Jackson's Daffodils, 1989
'Madang' × 'Tim'; sdlg no. 307/79
Fl. 107 mm wide; perianth segments very broadly ovate, greenish white (155A); corona light yellowish pink 37D, mouth expanded and frilled, with rim rolled. Mid-season to late

N. pulchellus Salisbury = *N. triandrus* var. *pulchellus*

'Pulchellus' 2 W-Y
(E. Leeds, pre-1877)
Fl. facing down on opening; perianth segments overlapping. Syn. Nelsonii 'Pulchellus'

'Pulsar' 2 W-P
(Brian S.Duncan) Brian S.Duncan, 1997
'Dailmanach' × 'Quasar'; sdlg no. 1472
Fl. rounded, 112 mm wide; perianth segments broadly ovate, spreading, plane, smooth; corona cylindrical, broad, deep rose pink, with mouth slightly flared, frilled. Mid-season

'Puma' 2 Y-P
(W.G. Pannill) W.G. Pannill, 1987
'Just So' × 'Bethany'; sdlg no. 70/14
Fl. 89 mm wide. Mid-season

***N. pumilus* Salisbury 13 Section Pseudonarcissus**

N. pumilus Herbert = *N. asturiensis*

N. pumilus Redouté = *N. dubius*

'Punch'
(C. Dawson, pre-1908)

'Punch Bowl' 2 W-?
(pre-1965) Unregistered
Corona expanded, slightly ribbed, opening pale yellow, soon becoming white, with coppery buff at rim

'Punchinello' 3 W-O
(J.L. Richardson, pre-1935)
'Hospodar' × 'Sunstar'
Perianth segments narrow, acute, milk white, reflexed; corona intense reddish orange. Resembles 'Folly'

'Punchline' 7 Y-YYP
(G.E. Mitsch) G.E. Mitsch, 1982
'Quick Step' × 'Silken Sails'; sdlg no. HH109/1
Fls 2-3 per stem, 82 mm wide; perianth segments ivory buff; corona buff yellow, with pink at rim. Mid-season

'Pundit' 1 Y-Y
(J.T. Gray, 1953) P. Phillips, 1966
Mid-season

'Pungel' 3 W-O
(S.J. Bisdee) S.J. Bisdee, 1956
'Limerick' × 'Mr Sparks'

'Punjab' 1 W-W
(R.C.A. Tombleson) R.C.A. Tombleson, 1968

'Punter' 2 W-Y
(Jackson's Daffodils) Jackson's Daffodils, 1996
'Pieman' × 'Calleva'; sdlg no. 23/89
Fl. 110 mm wide; perianth segments ovate, greenish white (155A); the inner segments a little more narrowly ovate; corona cylindrical, brilliant greenish yellow 5A. Early

'Puppet' 5 Y-O
(G.E. Mitsch) G.E. Mitsch, 1970
'Narvik' × *N. triandrus* var. *concolor*
Fls 1-2 per stem; perianth segments somewhat narrow, deep golden yellow; corona bright reddish orange. Mid-season

'Puppy' 6 Y-Y
(M.J. Jefferson-Brown) M.J. Jefferson-Brown, 1984
Fl. rich yellow. Early

'Purbeck' 3 W-YOO
(J.W. Blanchard) J.W. Blanchard, 1971
'Roimond' × 'Arbar'
Fl. 95 mm wide; perianth segments very broadly ovate, rounded at apex, not prominently mucronate, greenish white (155A), slightly reflexed, smooth, regular, overlapping half; the inner segments a little narrower, shouldered at base, with margins very slightly wavy; corona loosely ribbed, strong orange 25A, merging into pale yellow 11c at base, mouth expanded and regularly frilled. Corona with variable pro-

portions of orange and yellow. AM(e) 1970

'Pure Bliss' 6 Y-Y
(Mrs G. Link) Mrs G. Link, 1990
'Dipper' × *N. cyclamineus*; sdlg no. N-78
Fl. 90 mm wide; perianth segments broad, reflexed; corona deeper in tone than the perianth. Early

'Pure Delight' 1 Y-Y
(A.G. Thompson) A.G. Thompson, 1960
'Fortune' × 'Golden Harvest'
Fl 95 mm wide; perianth segments sulphur yellow; corona dark yellow. Mid-season. Resembles 'Kingscourt' in form

'Pure Gold' 2 Y-Y
(P.D. Williams, pre-1907)
Fl. deep golden yellow

'Pure Gold' 1 Y-Y
(Alister Clark, 1930) A. Ladson, 1960
Fl. rich yellow. Very early

'Pure Joy' 2 W-Y
(G.E. Mitsch) G.E. Mitsch, 1971
'Easter Moon' × 'Aircastle'; sdlg no. D34/1
Fl. rounded, 100 mm wide; perianth segments broadly ovate, blunt, pure white, spreading, concave near apex, with broad midrib showing, regular, overlapping half; the inner segments a little inflexed; corona short funnel-shaped, ribbed, pale lemon yellow, with a deeper tone at rim, mouth straight, frilled. Mid-season

'Purer Gem' 2 W-P
(R.H.Glover, pre-1993) Unregistered

'Purest of All' 3 W-? (b or c)
(pre-1939)

'Purissima' 1 W-W
(C.G. van Tubergen, pre-1946)

'Puritan' 1 W-? (b)
(J.C. Williams, pre-1910)

'Puritan' 3 W-? (b or c)
(G.H. Engleheart, pre-1910)

'Puritan Maiden' 2 W-W
(J.R. Pearson & Sons, pre-1915)
2 W-? × 'Florence Pearson'
Perianth segments overlapping; corona pale creamy white, with rim flanged. Mid-season. AM(e) 1923

'Purity' 8 W-W
(pre-1862)
Fl. pure white

'Purity' 3 W-W
(W. Backhouse, pre-1869)
Fl. silver white. Syn. Leedsii 'Purity'. Was "absorbed" into 'Beatrice'

'Purity' 5
(G.H. Engleheart, pre-1914)

'Purity' 1 W-W
(D.V. West, pre-1927)

'Purity' 2 W-W
(G.L. Wilson) M.J. Jefferson-Brown, 1960
(['Evening' × Dava'] × ['Silver Coin' × 'Dava']) × 'Snowline'
Fl. 108 mm wide, snow white; perianth segments broad, notched at apex, slightly inflexed; corona slightly ribbed, with mouth slightly expanded, rim crenate. AM(e) 1960

'Purity' 1 W-Y
Syn. of 'Centenaire'

'Purpureo-cinctus' 9 W-?
(pre-1629)
Syn. "The Dwarf Purple Rimmed", Poeticus 'Purpureo-cinctus'

'Purrdie' 1 W-Y
(Ken Farmer Nurseries) Ken Farmer Nurseries, 1978
Fl. 120 mm wide. Mid-season

'Purrum' 1 W-Y
(I.I. Aldersey, pre-1930)
Fl. 114 mm wide; perianth segments creamy white, twisted, overlapping one-third; corona sulphur yellow, with mouth slightly expanded. Mid-season to late. *AM(g) 1930

'Pursuit' 2 Y-O
(J.S. Leitch) J.S. Leitch, 1957

N. pusillus G.Don = *N. assoanus*

'Puss Puss' 2 W-? (b)
(Mrs R.O. Backhouse, pre-1921)

'Puzzle' 2 Y-O
(L. Buckland, pre-1936)
Corona expanded

'Pyalong' 1 W-Y
(S. Morrison) S. Morrison, 1960
Perianth segments pure white; corona light lemon yellow

'Pydar' 1 (a)
(G.L. Wilson, pre-1949)

'Pydna' 2 W-W
(W. Jackson Sr, 1945)
'Polindra' × 'Pepin'

'Pyenna' 1 W-P
(K.J. Heazlewood) K.J. Heazlewood, 1968
'C.E.Radcliff' × 'Mrs Oscar Ronalds'

'Pygmalion' 2 W-? (b)
(Mrs R.O. Backhouse, pre-1921)
AM(Haarlem) 1932

'Pygmee' 1 Y-Y
(J. Gerritsen & Son) J. Gerritsen & Son, 1984
Perianth segments pale greenish yellow 2D; corona darker in tone (5C) than the perianth. Very early

'Pylades' 1 Y-Y
(Barr & Sons, pre-1915)
Perianth segments lightly twisted, of smooth texture, overlapping

'Pylades' 5 W-W
(pre-1928)
Fls usually 2 per stem; corona short, neatly frilled

'Pylos' 3 W-? (b)
(W.B. Hartland, pre-1907)

'Pyramus' 1 W-Y
(G.P. Haydon, pre-1903)
'Weardale Perfection' × 'Madame de Graaff'
Perianth segments creamy white; corona canary yellow, with rim rolled. AM 1904

N. pyrenaicus Persone = *N. triandrus*

'Pyrite' 2 W-GYY
(Murray W. Evans, 1965) Murray W. Evans, 1977
'Artist's Model' × 'Marshfire'; sdlg no. I-19
Fl. 110 mm wide. Late

'Pyroantha' 2 Y-O
(Mrs R.O. Backhouse, pre-1921)
Perianth segments overlapping; corona yellowish orange. AM(Haarlem) 1928. Received AM(Haarlem) 1928 as 'Mercurius'

'Pyrrha' 3 W-YYR
(G.H. Engleheart, pre-1908)
Perianth segments slightly reflexed; corona almost disc-shaped, widely expanded, ribbed, yellow, with bright scarlet at rim

'Pytchley' 3 W-R
(J.O. Sherrard, pre-1950)

'Pythia' 2 W-? (b)
(R.H. Bath, pre-1933)

'Pzaz' 3 Y-O
(D. Jackson) D. Jackson, 1984
'Dimity' × 'Riis'; sdlg no. 245/78
Fl. 86 mm wide. Mid-season. Syn. 'Urchin'

Q

'Qantasia' 2 Y-W
(D.S. Bell) D.S. Bell, 1974
('White Sentinel' × 'Seraglio') hybrid
Fl. 108 mm wide; corona opening pinkish buff, soon becoming pure white, with rim rolled. Resembles a larger and better-formed 'Binkie'

'Quabaug' 1 W-? (b)
(E.C. Powell, pre-1949)

'Quadroon' 2 (a)
(Mrs R.O. Backhouse, pre-1914)

'Quail' 7 Y-Y
(G.E. Mitsch) G.E. Mitsch, 1974
'Daydream' × *N. jonquilla*; sdlg no. F72/1
Fl. 2-3 per stem, 60 mm wide, rich golden yellow; perianth segments broadly ovate, with prominent whitish mucro, spreading or slightly inflexed, plane, overlapping half; corona funnel-shaped, loosely ribbed, a little darker in tone than the perianth, mouth straight or a little flared, split in places and overlapping, wavy. Mid-season. Scented

'Quaint' 6 Y-O
(P. & G. Phillips) P. & G. Phillips, 1975
Fl. 57 mm wide; perianth segments lemon; corona reddish orange. Mid-season. Resembles 'Jetfire' but with a broader perianth and shorter corona

'Quakeress' 5
(Cartwright & Goodwin, pre-1914)

'Qualco' 4 Y-O
(J.N.Hancock & Co., 1986) J.N.Hancock & Co., 1997
Sdlg no. 15/86H
Perianth and other petaloid segments lemon yellow; the outer whorl ovate; the inner whorls interspersed with bright orange corona segments. Early to mid-season

'Quality' 1 Y-Y
(T. Morrison) T. Morrison, 1960
Perianth segments medium yellow; corona slightly deeper in tone

'Quality Street' 1 W-W
(D.S. Bell) D.S. Bell, 1955
Perianth segments broadly ovate, a little reflexed

'Quambatook' 1 W-YYW
(Tom Forster, 1960s) Unregistered
Corona wide-spreading, bright yellow, with white at rim, closely and deeply notched, as if fringed. Tall. Late

'Quamby' 1 W-Y
(T.H. Piper, 1950) T.H. Piper, 1956
'Lorinna' × 'Nautilus'
Corona lemon yellow

'Quandal' 3 W-YYR
(P. Phillips) P. & G. Phillips, 1975
Fl. 100 mm wide; perianth segments becoming reflexed with age; corona pale yellow, with red at rim. Resembles 'Katinka' but with a whiter perianth and more widely expanded corona

'Quantico' 2 W-Y
(E.C. Powell, pre-1947)
'Florist's Delight' × 'Killigrew'

'Quark' 1 W-W
(Jackson's Daffodils) Jackson's Daffodils, 1993
Sdlg 120/79 × 'Who's Who'; sdlg no. 98/85
Fl. forming a double triangle, 102 mm wide, greenish white (155A); perianth segments ovate; corona funnel-shaped, with mouth straight. Mid-season

'Quartermain' 2 W-GYY
(J.N. Hancock & Co., c1980) Unregistered
Perianth segments very broad, rounded or squarish at apex, slightly mucronate, pure white, spreading, concave, overlapping half or more; the inner segments roundish, inflexed, with margins sometimes nicked near apex; corona broad disc-shaped, ribbed, bright canary yellow, with green at base, mouth wavy, rim minutely dentate. Tall. Late

'Quartz' 1 W-W
(The Brodie of Brodie, c.1920)
'Morven' × 'White Emperor'
Perianth segments broadly ovate, blunt, mucronate, spreading, plane, overlapping one-third; the inner segments narrower, inflexed, twisted; corona cylindrical, smooth, with mouth ribbed and expanded, rim crenate and lightly rolled. Resembles 'White Royalist'. AM(e) 1928

'Quasar' 2 W-PPR
(Murray W. Evans) Murray W. Evans, 1977
'Cordial' × 'Precedent'; sdlg no. M-49
Fl. 90 mm wide; corona strong yellowish pink 32D, shading to orange-red (32B) at mouth. Mid-season. Resembles 'Cool Flame' but with a whiter perianth and more intensely coloured corona

'Quatrain' 9
(F.H. Chapman, pre-1913)

'Que' 2 Y-O
(J.N. Hancock & Co., pre-1988) Unregistered
Perianth segments broadly ovate, blunt or rounded at apex, fairly prominently mucronate, mid-yellow, spreading or a little reflexed, plane, overlapping one-third; the inner segments more usually spreading, with margins wavy; corona funnel-shaped, light orange, with a darker tone at rim, mouth straight, split in places and overlapping, loosely frilled, with rim crenate. Mid-season to late

'Quebec' 1 (a)
(A.M. Wilson, pre-1948)

'Queen' 2 (a)
(L. van Leeuwen & Son, pre-1932)
AM(Haarlem) 1931

'Queen Alexandra' 3 W-YYO
(J. Kendall, pre-1902)
Perianth segments ovate, blunt, spreading, with margins recurved at base, separated or slightly overlapping; the inner segments a little inflexed, twisted; corona shallow, orange-yellow, with a darker tone at rim, with the rim deeply and irregularly notched. AM 1902

"Queen Anne's Daffodil"
Syn. of 'Eystettensis'

"Queen Anne's Double Daffodil"
Syn. of 'Eystettensis'

"Queen Anne's Double Jonquil"
Syn. of 'Flore Pleno'

"Queen Anne's Jonquil"
Syn. of 'Flore Pleno'

'Queen Astrid' 3 W-?
Syn. of 'Koningin Astrid'

'Queen Bee' 1 W-Y
(pre-1927)
Perianth segments snow white; corona light yellow, with mouth expanded, rim flanged

'Queen Bee' ?-P
(Alister Clark, pre-1948)

'Queen Bess' 2 W-Y
(E. Leeds, pre-1877)
Corona expanded, pale yellow. Syn. Incomparabilis Albus 'Magnificus', Incomparabilis Albus 'Queen Bess'. "Absorbed" 'Consul Crawford', 'Harpur Crewe' and 'Roland'

'Queen Catherina' 2 W-Y
(Barr & Sons, pre-1903)
Fls often 2 per stem; perianth segments creamy white, with veins of primrose yellow, reflexed; corona expanded, ribbed, bright yellow, suffused orange

'Queen Christina' 1 W-Y
(Barr & Sons, 1902)
Corona expande, ribbed, soft lemon yellow. AM 1902

'Queen City' 2 W-P
(G.E. Mitsch, 1976) R. & E. Havens, 1992
'Romance' × 'Cool Flame'; sdlg no. LL14/3
Fl. 95 mm wide; perianth segments very broadly ovate, clean white, smooth; corona deep reddish pink, with mouth a little frilled. Mid-season. Sunproof

'Queen Eleanor' 5
(Barr & Sons, pre-1907)

'Queen Elizabeth' 2 (a)
(W.F.M. Copeland, pre-1927)

'Queen Emma' 1 W-? (b)
(M. van Waveren & Sons, pre-1902)
AM 1902

'Queen Emma' 1 (a)
(M. van Waveren & Sons, pre-1938)

'Queen Emma' 2 W-?
Syn. of 'Waldeck Piermont'

'Queen Empress' 1 W-? (b)
(W. Welchman, pre-1913)

'Queen Ermenilde' 2 W-? (b)
(W. Welchman, pre-1927)

'Queen Farida' 2 W-? (b)
(P. van Deursen, pre-1938)
AM(Haarlem) 1938

'Queen Flora' 3 W-? (b)
(de Graaff Bros, pre-1930)
AM(Haarlem) 1930

'Queen Helen' 1 W-? (b)
(Barr & Sons, pre-1923)

'Queenie' 2 W-? (b or c)
(L. Buckland, pre-1939)

'Queenie' ?-P
(Alister Clark, pre-1948)

'Queen Isabella' 1 W-Y
(Barr & sons, pre-1905)
Perianth segments acute; corona creamy yellow, frilled

'Queen Juliana' 1 W-W
(G.L. Wilson, pre-1949)
'Courage' × 'Kanchenjunga'

'Queen Ki' 1 W-Y
(E.W. Philpott) E.W. Philpott, 1959
'Bonnington' × 'Trousseau'
Fl. rounded; corona pale lemon yellow. Early. Resembles 'Trousseau', with a more widely flared corona

'Queen Louise' 4
(C.A. van der Wereld) C.A. van der Wereld, 1955
TGA(Haarlem) 1955, AM(Haarlem) 1955

'Queenly' 3 W-YYO
(The Brodie of Brodie, pre-1936)
Perianth segments white; corona disc-shaped, with soft salmon orange at rim

'Queen Mab' 2 W-Y
(E. Leeds, pre-1877)
Perianth segments sulphur white; corona slightly stained orange. Syn. Incomparabilis Sulphureus 'Marginatus Minor', Incomparabilis Sulphureus 'Queen Mab'. Was "absorbed" into 'Astraea'

'Queen Mab' 6 W-P
(Brian S. Duncan) W.H. Roesé, 1982
'Lilac Charm' hybrid; sdlg no. 178
Fl. 75 mm wide; perianth segments reflexed; corona becoming flared with maturity, soft pink, with rim dentate. Early to mid-season

'Queen Mab' 2 W-WWY
(J.N. Hancock & Co., pre-1988) Unregistered

'Queen Maeve' 9
(T. Collins, pre-1908)

'Queen Mary' 3 W-? (b)
(Miss E. Willmot, pre-1910)

'Queen Mary' 1 (a)
Syn. of 'Prince Bernhard'

'Queen Maud' 3 W-? (b)
(J.W.A. Lefeber, pre-1938)
Syn. 'Sweet Seventeen'

'Queen Maya' 1 W-Y
(C. Dawson, pre-1919)
Perianth segments creamy white, tinged pale sulphur yellow; corona soft canary yellow, with mouth flared and frilled

'Queen of Beauty' 1 W-? (b)
(Barr & Sons, pre-1923)
'Lord Roberts' × 'Loveliness'

'Queen of Bicolors' 1 W-Y
(E.H. Krelage & Son, pre-1925)
Perianth segments broadly ovate, blunt, slightly mucronate, very slightly inflexed, plane or a little concave at apex, sometimes ribbed, overlapping half; the inner segments more narrowly ovate, occasionally a little reflexed and with margins incurved; corona cylindrical, ribbed, canary yellow, with mouth expanded, rim flanged and crenate. 2n=28,43

'Queen of Dawn' 3 Y-R
(Sir C.H. Cave, 1915)
Perianth segments very pale yellow, tinged apricot pink, stained reddish pink at base; corona shallow, fiery scarlet. AM 1917

'Queen of Denmark' 1 W-W
(de Graaff Bros, pre-1927)

'Queen of Diamonds' 9 W-R
(G.L. Wilson, pre-1935)
'Dactyl' × 'Ace of Diamonds'

'Queen of Elfland' 9 W-GGR
(S.J. Bisdee, 1937)
'Silver Salver' × 'Dactyl'

'Queen of England' 9 W-YYR
(?G.H. Engleheart, pre-1922)
Perianth segments overlapping; corona small, yellow, with crimson at rim. Mid-season

'Queen of England' 3? W-W
(W. Backhouse)
Fl. large; corona expanded, opening canary yellow, becoming white. Resembles 'Minnie Hume'. Syn. Leedsii 'Queen of England'. Was "absorbed" into 'Minnie Hume' and 'Duchess of Brabant'

'Queen of Hearts' 3 W-O
(G.H. Engleheart, pre-1911)
Perianth segments large, rounded at apex, deep creamy white; corona widely expanded, rich reddish orange. Tall. AM 1911

'Queen of Holland' 1 (a)
(J.H. Veen, pre-1907)

'Queen of Holland' 8 W-Y
Syn. of 'Queen of the Netherlands'

'Queen of Narcissi' 3 W-YYR
(G. Lubbe & Son, pre-1939)
2n=14. AM(Haarlem) 1939. Received AM 1939 as 'Cottage Maid'

'Queen of Netherlands' 8 W-Y
Syn. of 'Queen of the Netherlands'

'Queen of Poets' 9
(R.H. Bath, pre-1913)

'Queen of Scots' 3 W-O
(G.H. Engleheart, pre-1910)
Perianth segments milk white; corona almost disc-shaped, apricot orange, tinged vermilion

'Queen of Sheba' 1 W-W
(H.G. Longford, pre-1927)

'Queen of Spain' 5 Y-Y
(Spanish origin)
Selection by Peter Barr (1888) from wild-collected material
Fls often 2 per stem. 2n=20,21. Syn. "Villa Cha". A name that cannot now be applied with any certainty to any one of several clones of *N.x johnstonii*

'Queen of Spring' 2 W-? (b)
(J.W.A. Lefeber, pre-1944)

'Queen of Stars' 3 W-YYO
(J.W.A. Lefeber, pre-1941)
Corona yellow, with dark orange at rim

'Queen of the Dale' 2 W-Y
(A.E. Lowe, pre-1927)
'White Queen' × 'Weardale Perfection'

'Queen of the East' 2 W-? (b)
(R.H. Bath, pre-1913)

'Queen of the Netherlands' 8 W-Y
(Dutch origin, pre-1861)
Corona deep yellow. Syn. ?'Reine des Pays Bas', 'Queen of Holland', 'Queen of Netherlands', 'Reine de Pas Bas'

'Queen of the North' 3 W-Y
(Barr & Sons, pre-1908)
Fl. star-shaped, about 80 mm wide, facing slightly downwards; perianth segments narrowly elliptic, mucronate, milk white, slightly stained yellow at base, a little reflexed, with margins wavy or recurved, slightly ribbed, of thin substance, separated; corona cup-shaped, more or less straight-sided, ribbed, becoming pale primrose yellow, with mouth straight, rim lightly dentate. Mid-season. 2n=21. AM(Haarlem) 1921, *(Kirton)AM(g) 1935

'Queen of the South' 1 W-? (b)
(G.H. Engleheart, pre-1923)

'Queen of the West' 1 Y-Y
(W. Polman-Mooy, pre-1907)
Fl. soft lemon yellow; perianth segments narrow, sometimes inflexed and twisted; corona narrow, ribbed, mouth widely flared, rim deeply notched and rolled. AM 1907, FCC 1909

'Queen of the Yellows' 8 Y-Y
(pre-1869)
Fls many per stem, rich golden yellow. Syn. 'Queen of Yellows'

'Queen of Ulster' 1 W-Y
(G.L. Wilson, pre-1923)
'Darius' × 'Weardale Perfection'

'Queen of Whites' 1 W-W
(Barr & Sons, pre-1908)

'Queen of Yellows' 8 Y-Y
Syn. of 'Queen of the Yellows'

'Queen Primrose' 1 W-Y
(G.H. Engleheart, pre-1914)
Perianth segments very pale primrose yellow; corona sulphur yellow, with mouth flared. AM(e) 1914

'Queen Ross' 2 W-? (b or c)
(J.W. Barr, pre-1930)

'Queen Salote' 2 Y-YYR
(C.E. Radcliff, 1931)
'Bernardino' × 'Seville'

'Queen's Counsel' 1 W-W
(J.L. Richardson) J.L. Richardson, 1956
'Killaloe' × 'Broughshane'
Corona with rim dentate and widely flanged

'Queenscourt' 1 W-W
(G.L. Wilson) F.E. Board, 1956
'Courage' × 'Empress of Ireland'
Fl. opening with corona yellow, becoming pure white

'Queen's Flight' 1 Y-Y
(T.H. Piper, c.1966) Unregistered
'Spanish Gold' × ('Melissa' × 'Kingscourt')

'Queen's Guard' 1 W-Y
(Brian S.Duncan) Brian S.Duncan, 1997
'Pontes' open pollinated; sdlg no. 1530
Fl. forming a double triangle, 105 mm wide; perianth segments broadly ovate, acute, spreading, plane; corona cylindrical, mid-yellow, with mouth widely expanded. Early

'Queen Size' 3 W-Y
(G.E. Mitsch) G.E. Mitsch, 1976
'Pretender' × 'Aircastle'; sdlg no. D47/2
Fl. 120 mm wide; perianth segments broadly ovate, blunt, spreading, concave near apex, overlapping up to a half; the inner segments sightly inflexed, with margins wavy and sometimes recurved; corona shallow, widely expanded, closely ribbed, lemon yellow, with mouth split in places and overlapping, tightly frilled. Mid-season. Resembles 'Bit o' Gold' but with a smaller corona

'Queen's Jubilee' 2 W-? (b)
(G. Lubbe & Son, pre-1948)
AM(Haarlem) 1948

'Queen's Lady' 1 W-?
M.J. Jefferson-Brown, 1963

'Queensland' 2 W-P
(G. Barr, 1954) E.B. Champernowne, 1985
Fl. 92 mm wide; perianth segments broadly ovate, blunt, very slightly mucronate, creamy white, spreading, sometimes a little reflexed in upper half, overlapping half; the inner segments narrower, somewhat creased, with margins wavy or incurved; corona funnel-shaped, loosely ribbed, orange-pink (25D), paling to base, with mouth expanded and 6-lobed, lightly frilled, rim slightly flanged. Late. Resembles 'Rose Noble' but with a darker-coloured corona

'Queen Sophia' 2 Y-O
(W. Backhouse, pre-1869)
Perianth segments broadly ovate, sulphur yellow or almost white, sometimes twisted or with margins wavy, overlapping a quarter; the inner segments more narrowly ovate; corona shallow bowl-shaped, heavily stained orange, with a darker tone at rim, loosely frilled. Syn. Incomparabilis Sulphureus 'Queen Sophia'. FCC 1884

'Queen's Taste' 1 Y-Y
(T.H. Piper, c.1966) Unregistered
'Kingscourt' × 'Melissa'

'Queenswood' 2 W-Y
(R.C.A. Tombleson) R.C.A. Tombleson, 1968
Fl. 108 mm wide; corona lemon yellow. Mid-season. Resembles a dwarfer, earlier 'My Love' with a darker corona

'Queen Sybilla' 2 W-YYP
(J.N. Hancock & Co.) J.N. Hancock & Co., 1960
Corona with amber pink at rim, frilled

'Queen Teie' 9
(W. Welchman, pre-1910)

'Queen Victoria' 8 W-Y
(pre-1872)

'Queen Victoria's Jubilee' 8
(pre-1897)

'Queen Wilhelmina' 1 W-? (b)
(pre-1908)

'Queltia Alba' 2 W-Y
Syn. of 'Doctor Gorman'

'Queltia Plene' 4 Y-O
Syn. of 'Butter and Eggs'

'Quench' 1 W-Y
(Jackson's Daffodils, 1975) Jackson's Daffodils, 1986
'Lod' × 'Betrin'; sdlg no. 13/75
Perianth segments greenish white (155A); corona brilliant yellow 7B. Early

'Querida' 2 W-O
(colin Crotty, pre-1994) Unregistered
'Eclat' × 'Gay Time'; sdlg no. 108-81

'Quest' 2 W-W
(G.L. Wilson, pre-1923)

'Quest' ?-P
(Alister Clark, pre-1948)

'Questing' 2 W-YPP
(J.N. Hancock & Co., 1962) Unregistered

'Questionnaire' 1 W-? (b)
(J.R.Byfield, pre-1936)

'Quetta' 3 W-O
(The Brodie of Brodie, c.1925)
'Bernardino' × 'Crimson Braid'
Fl. large; perianth segments very broadly ovate, deeply truncate and slightly mucronate, creamy white, spreading or a little reflexed, with margins sometimes incurling, overlapping half; the inner segments with margins wavy; corona shallow bowl-shaped, closely ribbed, reddish orange, paling to base, with mouth widely expanded and tightly frilled. AM(e)(c) 1930

'Quetzal' 9 W-GYR
(G.E. Mitsch, 1952) G.E. Mitsch, 1965
'Cantabile' × ?'Cushendall'
Fl. 83 mm wide. Late

'Quex' 2 W-W
(F.D.B. Cobb, pre-1953)

'Quezette' 2 W-P
(J.M. Radcliff, 1953) P. Phillips, 1966
Late. Resembles 'Lisdillon' but with a darker-coloured corona and more deeply rolled rim

'Quickfire' 2 Y-YOO
(J.A. Hunter, 1973) J.A. Hunter, 1990
'Swordsman' × 'Air Marshal'; sdlg no. 13/68B
Fl. 103 mm wide, smooth and of good substance; perianth segments ovate, rounded at apex; corona with rim slightly dentate. Mid-season to late

'Quick Fox' 2 Y-YYO
(J.N. Hancock & Co., 1958) Unregistered

'Quicksilver' 2 W-W
(G.L. Wilson, pre-1923)

'Quick Start' 7 W-P
(G.E.Mitsch, 1972) R.E.Havens, 1997
Sdlg Z02/3 ('Quick Step' open pollinated) open pollinated; sdlg no. HO19/1
Fl. rounded, 50 mm wide; perianth segments broadly ovate; corona cup-shaped, mid-pink. Late.

Sunproof

'Quick Step' 7 W-P
(G.E. Mitsch, 1955) G.E. Mitsch, 1965
'Wild Rose' × *N. jonquilla*; sdlg no. P99/20
Fls usually 3 per stem, 70 mm wide; perianth segments ivory white; corona very pale pink. Mid-season. Scented. 2n=28. Corona nearly white in dry climates

'Quiency' 2 W-? (b)
(P.D. Williams, pre-1931)

'Quiet Day' 2 W-GPP
(Carncairn Daffodils) Carncairn Daffodils, 1983
('Irish Rose' × 'Rose Caprice') open pollinated; sdlg no. 1/3/71
Fl. 90 mm wide; corona light yellowish pink 29C, with emerald green at base. Late. 2n=28

'Quiet Waters' 1 W-W
(A.J.R. Pearson) A.J.R. Pearson, 1992
'Stoke Charity' × 'Panache'; sdlg no. 86-28-J35
Fl. 105 mm wide, forming a rounded double triangle, pure white; perianth segments broadly ovate, greenish white (157C), spreading, plane, smooth; corona funnel-shaped, ribbed, slightly whiter than the perianth (157D), with mouth flared and wavy, rim crenate. Mid-season to late

'Quiff' 2 W-W
(G.H. Johnstone, pre-1960)
'Beersheba' hybrid

'Quiljon' 7 W-W
(E.H.G. Thurston, pre-1930)
Fls 2-3 per stem, creamy white; perianth segments only slightly overlapping; corona shallow, with pale green at base, tinged soft pink on opening. *(Kirton)AM(g) 1934

'Quilp' 2 (a)
(P.D. Williams, pre-1908)

'Quilty' 2 W-YYW
(J.N. Hancock & Co., 1946)

'Quince' 12 Y-Y
(A. Gray, pre-1953)
'Cyclataz' self or open pollinated
Fls 2-4 per stem, soft sulphur yellow; perianth segments very broadly ovate, truncate, with white mucro, reflexed, plane, overlapping one-third to a half; the inner segments more narrowly ovate, blunt, less noticeably mucronate, less strongly reflexed, somewhat twisted or with margins wavy; corona cylindrical, short, somewhat angled, mouth ribbed, straight, a little wavy, with rim entire or obscurely notched. Dwarf. 2n=24. Resembles 'Cyclataz' in size and form

'Quinella' 2 Y-YYR
(P. & G. Phillips) P. & G. Phillips, 1975
Fl. 116 mm wide, lemon; corona with a narrow band of red at rim. Mid-season. Resembles a larger-flowered 'Park Royal' with a narrower band of colour at corona rim

'Quinella' 2 Y-WWY
(J.N. Hancock & Co., 1963) Unregistered

'Quinn' 2 W-Y
(P. & G. Phillips) P. & G. Phillips, 1975
Fl. 105 mm wide; perianth segments whitish; corona buff. Mid-season. Resembles a deeper-coloured 'Kintamani'

'Quinney' 1 W-? (b)
(J.W. Barr, pre-1930)

'Quintana' 2 Y-O
(J.S. Leitch) J.S. Leitch, 1957

quintanilhae = *N. bulbocodium* subsp. *quintanilhae*

'Quinton' 3 Y-O
(E.F. Hughes) E.F. Hughes, 1962
Fl. 140 mm wide; perianth segments pale yellow; corona shallow, widely expanded, intense scarlet-orange, lightly frilled. Mid-season

'Quintroon' 3 Y-O
(The Brodie of Brodie, c.1919)
'Princess Mary' × 'Nightingale'
Perianth segments pale yellow; corona disc-shaped, dusky orange

'Quintus' 1 (a)
(J. Pope, pre-1907)

'Quip' 1 W-O
(G.L. Wilson, pre-1938)
Corona opening deep chrome yellow, soon becoming deep reddish orange. Sunproof

'Quirindi' 2 W-? (b)
(J.N. Hancock & Co.) J.N. Hancock & Co., 1959

'Quirinus' 2 Y-O
(G. Lubbe & Son, pre-1939)
Fl. forming double triangle, 95–105 mm wide; perianth segments very broadly ovate, blunt, prominently mucronate, spreading, creased, overlapping one-third to half; the inner segments almost as prominently mucronate, inclined to twist; corona funnel-shaped, ribbed, mouth straight, rim irregularly notched and crenate. 2n=28. AM(Haarlem) 1944, FA(Haarlem) 1950

'Quita' 3 (a)
(Cartwright & Goodwin, pre-1914)

'Quito' 1 (a)
(J.L. Richardson, pre-1953)

'Quitos' 1 Y-Y
(H.A. Brown, 1941)
Fl. forming a double triangle, lemon yellow; perianth segments broadly ovate, blunt, slightly mucronate, inflexed, overlapping half; the inner segments narrower, angled at shoulder, with margins wavy and sometimes incurved; corona cylindrical, smooth, with mouth expanded, lightly frilled, rim crenate. Early

'Quiver' ?-P
(Alister Clark, pre-1948)

'Quivira' 2 Y-O
(G.E. Mitsch) G.E. Mitsch, 1963
('Clackmar' × 'Carbineer') × 'Armada'; sdlg no. R102/1
Fl. 115 mm wide; perianth segments clear dark yellow; corona deep bowl-shaped, brilliant reddish orange. Mid-season. Resembles a large and earlier-flowered 'Paricutin'

'Quota' 1 Y-Y
(J.N. Hancock & Co., 1973) Unregistered

'Quo Vadis' 8 W-YYO
(Dutch origin, pre-1914)
Poetaz
Perianth segments white, stained golden yellow at base; corona with orange at rim. AM(Haarlem) 1914

R

'Ra' 2 Y-ORR
(W. Jackson Jr, 1968) Unregistered
'Vulcan' × 'Dimity'; sdlg no. 178/68

'Raad' 2 W-P
Syn. of 'Aare'

'Rabat' 2 or 3 W-? (b or c)
(pre-1915)

'Rabaul' 1 Y-Y
(H.A. Brown, 1936) J.N. Hancock & Co., 1960
'A.L.Scott' × 'Royalist'
Fl. rounded; perianth segments smooth. Late

'Rabelais' 9
(G.H. Engleheart, pre-1916)

'Rabid' 2 Y-R
(W. Jackson Jr) Jackson's Daffodils, 1979

Sdlg 65/66 × 'Dimity'; sdlg no. 158/73
Fl. 100 mm wide. Mid-season

'Raby' 1 W-? (b)
(N.Y. Lower, pre-1929)

'Racehorse' 1 Y-Y
(G.L. Wilson, pre-1923)
'King Alfred' × 'Monarch'
Early

'Racer' 3 Y-R
(M.P. Williams, pre-1938)

'Raceview' 2 Y-O
(Kate Reade) Carncairn Daffodils, 1996
'Zeus' × 'Bunclody'; sdlg no. 19/3/82
Fl. 85 mm wide; perianth segments broadly ovate, blunt, deep yellow, with slight white mucro, spreading, plane, or a little concave near apex, overlapping one-third to a half; the inner segments a little inflexed; corona long cup-shaped, smooth, orange, with mouth only slightly expanded, rim crenate. Mid-season

'Rachel' 3 (a)
(Mrs R.O. Backhouse, pre-1921)

'Rachel Baker' 2 W-P
(Brian S.Duncan) Mrs J.M.Baker, 1996
'Gracious Lady' × 'Dailmanach'; sdlg no. 1300
Fl. 112 mm wide; perianth segments broadly ovate, spreading, smooth; corona cylindrical, long, apple blossom pink, with mouth expanded. Mid-season. Sunproof

'Rachel Goodson' 2 or 3 W-? (b or c)
(New Zealand origin, pre-1940)

'Rachel Hallowes' 2 (a)
(Mrs R.O. Backhouse, pre-1921)

'Rachel Prentice' 2 W-W
(H.R. Meyer, pre-1927)

'Radar' 2 Y-R
(S.J. Bisdee, 1947)
'Market Merry' × 'Royal Mail'

'Radar' 2 Y-R
(M.P. Williams, pre-1949)
Perianth segments yellow; corona red, with scarlet-red at rim

'Radelma' 8
(pre-1939)

'Rademon' 2 Y-R
(Carncairn Daffodils) Carncairn Daffodils, 1973
'Chungking' × 'Fury'

Fl. 97 mm wide; perianth segments very deep yellow; corona crimson-red, frilled

'Radford' 1 W-O
(V. Brink) V. Brink, 1970
'Sincerity' × 'Lady Kesteven'
Fl. 68 mm wide

'Radiance' 2 W-O
(G.H. Engleheart, pre-1907)
Corona rosy orange

N. radians Lapeyrouse = *N. pseudonarcissus*

'Radiant' 3 W-GYR
(E.M. Crosfield, pre-1908)
Corona spreading, dark golden yellow, with a broad band of orange-red at rim

'Radiant Gem' 8 Y-R
(G.E. Mitsch & R. & E.Havens, 1974) Grant Mitsch Novelty Daffodils, 1984
'Matador' × *N. jonquilla*; sdlg no. JJ77/5
Fl. 3-6 per stem, 50 mm wide; perianth segments broadly ovate, blunt or truncate, prominently mucronate, golden yellow, spreading, somewhat creased, overlapping half; the inner segments a little twisted or with margins wavy or incurling; corona bowl-shaped, ribbed, bright orange-red, mouth straight, wavy. Mid-season. Resembles 'Hoopoe' but with the perianth of a deeper yellow

'Radiant Glory' 3 (a)
(G. Zandbergen-Terwegen, pre-1939)

'Radiant Light' 2 Y-O
(H.A. Brown, pre-1936) J.N. Hancock & Co., 1960

'Radiant Morn' 2 W-? (b)
(R.H. Bath, pre-1933)

'Radiation' 2 W-P
(G.E. Mitsch, pre-1954)
'White Sentinel' × 'Mrs R.O.Backhouse'; sdlg no. G170/1
Corona opening pale yellow, soon becoming clear soft pink, with slight overtones of salmon. Mid-season

'Radiator' 2 W-W
(C. Goodson, pre-1927)

N. radiatus Delile = *N.* × *intermedius*

'Radical' 6 Y-Y
(Rosewarne EHS) M.J. Jefferson-Brown, 1985
'Cornet' × 'Cyclone'; sdlg no. 65/13/1
Fl. rich golden yellow; perianth segments reflexed, overlapping; corona slender, ribbed, with rim rolled and deeply crenate. Resembles a larger 'Bartley' of firmer and smoother substance

N. radiiflorus Salisbury 13 Section Narcissus
    var. *radiiflorus*
    var. *exertus* (Haworth) A.Fernandes
    var. *poetarum* (Haworth) Burbidge & Baker
        ('Poetarum'). 2n=c.14,21
    var. *stellaris* (Haworth) A.Fernandes

N. radinganorum Fernández Casas 13 Section Pseudonarcissus

'Radio' 2 W-? (b)
(de Graaff Bros, pre-1927)

'Radium' 3 Y-O
(Mrs. R.O. Backhouse, pre-1921)
Sdlg no. 25/25
Perianth segments opening pale creamy yellow, becoming pale buff; corona reddish orange, heavily frilled as if in two rows

'Radius' 1 (a)
(Mrs R.O. Backhouse, pre-1921)

'Radjel' 4 Y-R
(R.A.Scamp) R.A.Scamp, 1994
'Paricutin' × 'Tamar Fire'; sdlg no. 298
Fl. rounded, 75 mm wide; perianth and other petaloid segments bright golden yellow, deeply overlapping; corona segments interspersed, dark red, slightly wavy. Early to mid-season. Sunproof

'Radnor' 2 Y-R
(A.M. Wilson, pre-1937)
Sdlg no. 560

'Radom' 2 W-GOR
(V. Brink, 1967) V. Brink, 1979
Sdlg no. 60-4
Fl. 100 mm wide. Mid-season

'Rae' 5
(pre-1910)

'Raeburn' 9 W-GYR
(G.H. Engleheart, pre-1913)
Perianth segments rounded, overlapping; corona very shallow, lemon yellow, with metallic green at base and a broad band of dark crimson at rim. 2n=14

'Rael' 3 W-R
(J.S. Leitch) J.S. Leitch, 1958

'Raewyn Hyde' 2 W-W
(R. Hyde) R. Hyde, 1957

'Raewyn Morris' 2 WWY-O
(J.A. Morris) J.A. Morris, 1963
Fl. 111 mm wide; perianth segments white, with pale yellow at base; corona deep reddish orange. Mid-season. Resembles 'Signal Light'

'Raffael' 1 Y-Y
(P.L.A. Pouw) P.L.A. Pouw, 1973
'Rembrandt' × 'Golden Sunbeam'
Fl. 120 mm wide

'Raffrey' 2 W-WWY
(W.J. Toal) Ballydorn Bulb Farm, 1965
'Broughshane' × 'White Prospect'
Corona widely expanded, rich creamy white, with clear deep yellow at rim. Mid-season

'Ragamuffin' 1 W-W
(W. Jackson Jr) Jackson's Daffodils, 1982
Sdlg 133/61 × 'Mercedes'; sdlg no. 88/74
Fl. 107 mm wide. Mid-season

'Ragbag' 4 W-O
(Glenbrook Bulb Farm, 1983) Glenbrook Bulb Farm, 1997
'Anne of Cleves' × 'Dimity'
Fl. 90 mm wide; perianth segments very broadly ovate, yellowish white (155B); corona segments varying from vivid yellow 12A to yellow-orange (14A), frilled. Mid-season

'Rager' 4 W-O
(Jackson's Daffodils) Jackson's Daffodils, 1992
'Glowing Red' × 'Challenge'; sdlg no. 52/86
Fl. 90 mm wide; perianth and other petaloid segments in 3-4 whorls, very broadly ovate, whitish, spreading, overlapping more than half; the inner whorls successively a little shorter and more inflexed; some segments at centre strongly inflexed, creased at midrib and with margins wavy or deeply incurled; corona segments short, tightly clustered at centre and more loosely interspersed among the inner whorls of petaloid segments, bright orange (23A), frilled. Mid-season

'Ragged Friar' 4
(W.F.M. Copeland, pre-1929)

"Ragged White"
Syn. of *N. tazetta* subsp. *ochroleucus*. ?The same as "Early White"

'Ragnild Hveger' 2 W-? (b)
(de Graaff Bros, pre-1937)

'Rags and Tatters' 4 Y-YYO
(W.F.M. Copeland, pre-1909)
Perianth and other petaloid segments in three whorls, soft lemon yellow; corona disc-shaped, deep yellow, with orange at rim. Mid-season

'Ragtime' 1 Y-Y
(P.L.A. Pouw) P.L.A. Pouw, 1973
'Rembrandt' × 'Golden Sunbeam'
Fl. 100 mm wide

'Ragusa' 2 (a)
(A.H. Ahrens, pre-1949)

'Rahiti' 2 W-Y
(J.N.Hancock & Co., 1983) Unregistered
'Hail Storm' × 'Doris May'; sdlg no. 68/83H
Perianth segments creamy white; corona disc-shaped, ribbed, orange-yellow, frilled. Early to mid-season

'Raider' 2 Y-R
(Mrs R.O. Backhouse, pre-1921)
Perianth segments rich yellow; corona scarlet

'Raigort' 1 Y-Y
(J.L. Martin) J.L. Martin, 1982
'Tarago' × 'Courthill'; sdlg no. T/C 7
Fl. 100 mm wide; perianth segments brilliant yellow 12B; corona slightly darker in tone (12A). Mid-season. Resembles 'Courthill' but with narrower perianth segments

'Rail' 4 W-Y
(G.E. Mitsch) G.E. Mitsch, 1979
'Windblown' × 'Carita'; sdlg no. G71/6
Fl. 110 mm wide; perianth and other petaloid segments ivory white; corona segments lemon. Midseason. Resembles a better-formed 'Windblown'

'Rainbird' 2 W-YYO
(J.N. Hancock & Co., 1949) J.N. Hancock & Co., 1960
Corona pale creamy yellow, with buffy apricot orange at rim, frilled

'Rainbow' 2 W-? (b)
(W.B. Hartland, pre-1907)

'Rainbow' 2 W-WWP
(J.L. Richardson) J.L. Richardson, 1961
'Interim' × 'Rose Caprice'
Fl. rounded, 100 mm wide; perianth segments very broad, blunt, fairly prominently mucronate, pure white, spreading or a little reflexed, somewhat concave, regular, overlapping half; the inner segments narrower, only very slightly mucronate, with margins wavy and incurved; corona funnel-shaped, lightly ribbed, white, with a broad band of orange-pink (25C-26D) at rim, mouth wavy, rim slightly flanged, irregularly notched and crenate. Late. 2n=28. AM(e) 1967, *HC(g) 1990, FCC(e) 1991

'Rainbow's End' 2 W-YWP
(J.A.Hunter) J.A.Hunter, 1995
('Cascade' × ['Lingering Light' × 'Gisela']) × 'Verran'; sdlg no. 24/82A
Fl. forming a double triangle, 115 mm wide; perianth segments ovate; corona funnel-shaped, white, with yellow at base and light yellowish pink 36C at rim, rim crenate. Mid-season

'Raincheck' 3 W-Y
(R.G. Cull) Hokorawa Daffodils, 1992
'Ceres' × 'Calleen'; sdlg no. HC/G71
Corona brilliant greenish yellow 6A. Mid-season

'Rain Dance' 2 W-W
(Murray W. Evans, 1970) Murray W. Evans, 1986
'Celilo' × 'Arctic Doric'
Early. Resembles a whiter and better-formed 'Arctic Doric'

'Raindrop' 5 W-W
(A. Gray, pre-1942)
N. dubius × *N. triandrus* var. *loiseleurii*
Fls up to about 30 mm wide; perianth segments acute, becoming strongly reflexed, overlapping; corona cup-shaped. Dwarf. AM(p) 1955

'Rainga' 1 Y-Y
(A.O. Roblin, 1939)
'Golden City' × 'Renown'

'Rainlover' 3 W-WWY
(R.H. Glover) R.H. Glover, 1972
'Marilyn' × 'Estrella'
Fl. 102 mm wide

'Raiwena' 2 Y-Y
(West & Fell, pre-1937)

'Rajah' 2 Y-Y
(J.L. Gray, pre-1949)
Fl. deep golden yellow

'Rajah' 2 Y-O
(R.C.A. Tombleson) R.C.A. Tombleson, 1969

'Rajah Brook' 3 W-? (b)
(E.H. Williams, pre-1910)

'Rajah Sahib' 1 W-W
(Mrs B.A. Woods) Mrs B.A. Woods, 1968

'Raland' 2 W-Y
(J.S. Leitch) J.S. Leitch, 1957

'Raleigh' 1 Y-Y
(G. Lewis) D.S. Bell, 1955

'Ralph' 2 W-O
(West & Fell, pre-1935)
Corona orange to apricot

'Ralph Bunche' 2 W-Y
(Pouw Bros, pre-1949)
Perianth segments milk white; corona orange-yellow. AM(Haarlem) 1949, FCC(Haarlem) 1950

'Rama' 1 Y-Y
(S.J. Bisdee, pre-1939)

'Renown' × 'Mortlake'

'Ramada' 2 W-GYO
(Brian S. Duncan) Rathowen Daffodils, 1978
'Verona' open pollinated; sdlg no. 84
Fl. 100 mm wide; corona greenish yellow, shading to green at base and salmon orange towards mouth, with a band of yellow at rim. Mid-season. Resembles 'Abalone'

'Ramadhin' 2 Y-O
(S.J. Bisdee, 1950)
'Freycinet' × 'Keren'

'Ramah' 3 W-O
(The Brodie of Brodie, c.1931)
'Sunstar' × 'Hades'

'Ramar' 3 Y-R
(G.J.Phillips, pre-1996) Unregistered

'Rambler' 1 Y-Y
(F. Rijnveld & Sons) F. Rijnveld & Sons, 1959
'Phyllis Miller' × 'Unsurpassable'
Perianth segments mimosa yellow; corona canary yellow. FA(Haarlem) 1960, FA(Haarlem) 1961

'Rame Head' 1 Y-Y
(Brian S. Duncan) du Plessis Bros, 1981
'Kingscourt' open pollinated; sdlg no. 126
Fl. 113 mm wide. Mid-season

'Rameses' 1 (a)
(Barr & Sons, pre-1923)

'Rameses' 2 W-O
(J.L. Richardson) J.L. Richardson, 1960
'Kilworth' × 'Rockall'; sdlg no. 258
Fl. 86 mm wide; perianth segments very broadly ovate, blunt, mucronate, spreading, plane or very slightly concave, smooth, regular, overlapping half; the inner segments usually more narrowly ovate, less prominently mucronate, shouldered at base, with margins sometimes slightly incurling; corona ribbed, vivid orange 28B, with mouth widely expanded and closely frilled, rim minutely and irregularly crenate. Mid-season. 2n=28. PC 1960, AM(e) 1963

'Ramillies' 2 Y-O
(J.L. Richardson, pre-1937)
AM(Haarlem) 1944

'Raminea' 1 Y-Y
(S.J. Bisdee) S.J. Bisdee, 1956
'Kingscourt' × 'Butter King'

'Ramoan' 3 W-GYO
(G.L. Wilson) G.L. Wilson, 1955
('Armoy' × ['Alburnia' × 'Sincerity']) × 'Chinese White'

Perianth segments very broad, rounded or truncate at apex, pure white, spreading, overlapping half; the inner segments narrower, with margins wavy; corona bowl-shaped, pale citron yellow, with green at base and salmon orange at rim, frilled

'Ramona' 2 (a)
(J.R.Byfield, pre-1939)

'Ramona' 2 W-YOO
(G.E. Mitsch) G.E. Mitsch, 1960
'Linn' × 'Green Island'; sdlg no. P70/1
Perianth segments broad, overlapping; corona orange, paling to yellow at base, frilled. Mid-season

'Rampage' 1 Y-Y
(Jackson's Daffidils) Jackson's Daffodils, 1995
'Prado' × sdlg 3/74; sdlg no. 12/87
Fl. 108 mm wide, vivid yellow 9A; perianth segments broadly ovate; corona funnel-shaped, with mouth slightly flared and frilled. Early

'Rampant' 1 (a)
(F.H. Chapman, pre-1923)

'Ramrod' 2 Y-YYO
(J.N. Hancock & Co., 1968) Unregistered

'Ramsay MacDonald' 1 W-? (b)
(G. Lubbe & Son, pre-1930)

'Ranalagh' 1 Y-Y
(G. Lewis) D.S. Bell, 1955
Fl. golden yellow; perianth segments very broad. See also 'Ranelagh'

'Randalstown' 1 Y-Y
(G.L. Wilson, pre-1927)

'Randolph Churchill' 1 Y-Y
(pre-1885)
Perianth segments twisted; corona slender, rich yellow, with rim crenate

'Random Event' 3 W-YOY
(Sidney DuBose, 1978) Sidney DuBose, 1990
'Glenwherry' open pollinated; sdlg no. D55-A5
Fl 90 mm wide. Mid-season

'Random Harvest' 2 Y-R
(D.S. Bell) D.S. Bell, 1955
Corona very broad, widely expanded, deep red

'Random Light' 2 W-O
(J.L. Richardson) Mrs H.K. Richardson, 1973
'Kilworth' × 'Rockall'
Corona bowl-shaped, reddish orange, with rim dentate. Early

'Ranefer' 1 Y-Y
(S.J. Bisdee, 1944)
'Principal' × 'Yscydion'

'Ranelagh' 1 Y-Y
Syn. of 'Ranalagh'

'Ranella' 2 Y-? (a)
(J.T. Gray, pre-1949)
Perianth segments golden yellow; corona with bright red at rim

'Ranfurley' 2 (a)
(D.S. Bell) D.S. Bell, 1957

'Rangatiki' 2 (a)
(A. Gibson, pre-1930) Parr's Nurseries, 1958

'Rangatira' 1 (a)
(Hon. Sir R.H. Rhodes, pre-1912)

'Ranger' 2 W-Y
(A.E. Lowe, pre-1927)

'Ranger Johnson' 1 Y-Y
(Barr & Sons, pre-1903)
Fl. soft yellow; corona of strong substance, ribbed, lightly frilled

'Rangitane' 2 Y-O
(Mrs B.T. Simpson) Mrs B.T. Simpson, 1963
Fl. 102 -108 mm wide; perianth segments vivid yellow 2A; corona vivid orange 28B. Mid-season

'Rangitata' 2 W-R
(K.B. Burns) K.B. Burns, 1960
Fl. 114 mm wide. Mid-season. Resembles 'Sir Heaton Rhodes' but with the perianth segments more rounded and the corona more brightly coloured

'Rangitoto'
(?Sir A.P.W. Thomas, pre-1915)

'Rangoon' 2 W-? (b)
(Mrs R.O. Backhouse, pre-1921)

'Rani' 1 Y-Y
(Jackson's Daffodils) Jackson's Daffodils, 1986
'Akala' × 'Warcom'; sdlg no. 164/79
Perianth segments brilliant yellow 7B; corona vivid yellow 9A. Early to mid-season

'Ranksborough' 1 W-Y
(J.O. Sherrard, pre-1947)

'Ranmoor' 2 W-W
(F.E. Board) F.E. Board, 1965
'Greenland' × 'Knowehead'; sdlg no. 1012
Late

'Ransom' 4 YYW-P
(Jackson's Daffodils) Jackson's Daffodils, 1993
'Tavelle' × 'Daydream'; sdlg no. 154/85
Fl. 90 mm wide; perianth and other petaloid segments brilliant greenish yellow, with a narrow band of yellowish white 155B at base; corona segments pale yellowish pink (16D). Late

'Raoul Wallenberg' 2 Y-Y
(D.P. de Graaf) D.P. de Graaf, 1985
'Ice Follies' sport
Perianth segments primrose yellow; corona canary yellow. Mid-season

'Rapallo' 3 Y-YYR
(J.L. Richardson, pre-1943)
AM(Haarlem) 1943

'Raphaël' 8 W-Y
(A. Vis, pre-1922)
Poetaz
Corona deep golden yellow. Early

'Raphael' 11b W-Y/W
(Dutch origin, pre-1968) Unregistered
Corona segments with yellow and white in longitudinal bands

'Raphoe' 2 W-WWY
(G.L. Wilson, pre-1948)
'Market Merry' open pollinated
Perianth segments white; corona ivory white, with lemon at rim

'Rapier' 3 W-? (b)
(G.H. Engleheart, pre-1923)

'Rapport' 2 Y-WWY
(Murray W. Evans, 1966) Murray W. Evans, 1985
'Binkie' × 'Limeade'; sdlg no. J-5/1
Corona opening sulphur yellow, becoming off white, with pale sulphur yellow at rim. Mid-season

'Rapture' 9
(F.H. Chapman, pre-1913)

'Rapture' 6 Y-Y
(G.E. Mitsch) G.E. Mitsch, 1976
'Nazareth' × *N. cyclamineus*; sdlg no. G78/1
Fl. 79 mm wide; perianth segments ovate, blunt, strongly reflexed, plane, overlapping one-third to a half; the inner segments with margins wavy; corona cylindrical, slightly constricted towards mouth, lightly ribbed, mouth more strongly ribbed and very slightly flared, wavy. Early. Wister Award 1997

'Rapture' 1 Y-Y
(pre-1966) Unregistered

'Rara Koo' 2 W-WWR
(A.O. Roblin, 1943)
Sdlg × 'Market Merry'

'Rare Gem' 2 W-P
(A. Glover, c.1978) Unregistered
'Pink Special' × 'Verran'

'Rareka' 2 W-P
(R. Hyde) R. Hyde, 1959

'Rarity' 3 Y-YYO
(R.H. Bath, pre-1927)

'Rarkmoyle' 2 W-P
(Carncairn Daffodils) Carncairn Daffodils, 1969
'Irish Rose' hybrid
Resembles 'Irish Rose' but is of stronger habit and more rapid increase

'Rascal' 6 Y-O
(D. Bramley) D. Bramley, 1986
Div. 6 sdlg 70/5 × 'Falling Star'; sdlg no. 77/1
Perianth segments reflexed; corona colour fading slightly with age. Early. Resembles a later-flowered 'Rascal' of more consistent colour

'Rasharkin' 1 Y-Y
(W.J. Dunlop, pre-1969) Unregistered

'Rashee' 1 W-W
(G.L. Wilson, pre-1952)
'Cotterton' × 'Broughshane'
Fl. 116 mm wide, pure ice white; perianth segments very broadly ovate, blunt, prominently mucronate, spreading, with margins slightly wavy, overlapping half; the inner segments narrower, inflexed at base, reflexed at apex, with margins incurved; corona cylindrical, smooth, with a touch of moss green at base, mouth ribbed and expanded, rim rolled and almost entire. 2n=28

'Rashid' 2 W-R
(J.A. O'More) J.A. O'More, 1968
'Kilworth' × 'Arbar'

'Rashleigh' 2 W-W
(A.J. Sherriff, c.1966) Unregistered
'Mowbray' × 'Crinalyn'

'Raspberry Creme' 11a W-P
(G.E.Mitsch, 1982) R. & E.Havens, 1996
'Sentinel' × 'Shrike'; sdlg no. 2R6/2
Fl. 100 mm wide; perianth segments broad; corona deeply split, the six segments opposite the perianth segments, bright pink, heavily frilled. Mid-season. Sunproof

'Raspberry Ring' 2 W-GWP
(J.M. de Navarro) J.M. de Navarro, 1977

'Infatuation' × 'Rainbow'
Fl. 95 mm wide; corona blush white, with green at base and raspberry pink at rim. Mid-season

'Raspberry Rose' 2 W-P
(Sidney DuBose, 1984) Sidney DuBose, 1996
'Ken's Favorite' × 'Verran'; sdlg no. H76-24
Fl. rounded, 100mm wide; perianth segments very broad, roundish; the inner segments slightly narrower; corona pink, with mouth a little flared and rim dentate. Mid-season

'Rata' 2 (a)
(C.E. Radcliff, 1932)
'Warflame' × 'Puzzle'

'Rata' 3 W-? (b)
(C.H.E. Rhodes, pre-1933)
AM(e)(NZ) 1931

'Ratanui' 3 (a)
(R. Crews, pre-1949)

'Rathcavan' 2 W-GWW
(G.L. Wilson) G.L. Wilson, 1959
'Portrush' × 'Sylvia O'Neill'
Perianth segments broad, pure white, slightly inflexed, smooth; corona with dark green at base, frilled

'Rathcoole' 2 Y-W
(W.J. Dunlop) W.J. Dunlop, 1962
Resembles an improved 'Binkie'

'Rathgar' 2 W-WWY
(W.J. Dunlop) W.J. Dunlop, 1960
'White Sentinel' × 'Broughshane'
Corona cream, with greenish lemon at rim

'Rathkeel' 2 Y-R
(W.J. Dunlop, pre-1947)
'Seraglio' × 'Marksman'
Perianth segments deep gold; corona crimson-red

'Rathkenny' 1 W-Y
(G.L. Wilson, pre-1938)
Sdlg × 'Vestal Virgin' × 'Kenbane'
Perianth segments greenish white, mucronate, with margins sometimes incurving, overlapping one-third; corona slender, bright chrome yellow, lightly frilled, with rim widely flanged. 2n=28+1B. AM(e) 1938. See also 'Rothkenny'

'Rathlin' 1 (a)
(R.H. Bath, pre-1933)

'Rathlin' 1 W-Y
(T. Bloomer) T. Bloomer, 1964
'Rashee' × 'Empress of Ireland'; sdlg no. 6/19/58
Perianth segments pure white; corona pale

lemon yellow

'Rathlin' 2 Y-Y
Syn. of 'Kilbride'

'Rathmullan' 2 W-W
(W.J. Dunlop) W.J. Dunlop, 1961
'Parkmore' × 'Kanchenjunga'
Corona with rim rolled

'Rathowen' 1 W-?
(T. Bloomer) T. Bloomer, 1964

'Rathowen Dawn' 1 Y-Y
(T. Bloomer) T. Bloomer, 1973
'Arctic Gold' × 'Golden Rapture'; sdlg no. 3/48/65

'Rathowen Fires' 2 Y-?
(T. Bloomer) T. Bloomer, 1973
'Richhill' × 'Vulcan'

'Rathowen Flame' 2 Y-O
(T. Bloomer) T. Bloomer, 1973
'Ballintoy' × 'Air Marshal'; sdlg no. 1/36/58
Perianth segments gold; corona reddish orange

'Rathowen Gold' 1 Y-Y
(T. Bloomer) T. Bloomer, 1973
'Camelot' × 'Arctic Gold'; sdlg no. 1/72/65
Fl. deep gold; corona with rim slightly dentate

'Rathroe' 3 W-R
(G.L. Wilson) G.L. Wilson, 1960
'Gala' hybrid

'Raucus' 4 W-P
(Jackson's Daffodils) Jackson's Daffodils, 1987
Sdlg 66/70 × sdlg 48/71; sdlg no. 28/79
Corona segments light yellowish pink 19B

'Raumati' 2 (a)
(R. Crews) R. Crews, 1956

'Raun' 1 W-W
(D.J. Jackson, 1978) Jackson's Daffodils, 1989
'Glendermott' × 'Mercedes'; sdlg no. 70/78
Fl. 105 mm wide, greenish white (155A); corona frilled, with rim strongly rolled. Mid-season

'Ravana' 1 Y-Y
(S.J. Bisdee, 1939)
'Mortlake' × 'Golden City'

'Rave' 3 Y-O
(W. Jackson Jr) W. Jackson Jr, 1966
'Magherally' × 'Chungking'; sdlg no. 118/57

'Ravel' 2 (a)
(D.J. Cooper) D.J. Cooper, 1957

'Ravelston' 2 W-OOY
(D.S. Bell) D.S. Bell, 1959
'Rosslare' × 'Artist's Model'
Fl. 115 mm wide; corona apricot orange, with golden yellow at rim. Mid-season. Resembles 'Green Island'

'Ravenhill' 3 W-GYO
(T. Bloomer) Rathowen Daffodils, 1984
('Chinese White' × 'Ballycastle') × 'Woodland Belle'; sdlg no. 278
Perianth segments very broadly ovate, blunt, slightly mucronate, spreading, with margins sometimes incurling, overlapping half; the inner segments more narrowly ovate, reflexed in upper half, with margins incurved; corona shallow bowl-shaped, loosely ribbed, yellow, with green at base and a clearly defined band of deep orange at rim, mouth with three lobes deeply overlapping, lightly frilled, rim minutely crenate. Mid-season

'Ravenna' 2 Y-Y
(S.J. Bisdee, 1949)
'Kallista' × 'Osella'

'Ravenna' 3 W-WYY
(de Graaff Bros, pre-1952)
AM(Haarlem) 1952

'Raven Red' 2 Y-O
(Oregon Bulb Farms, pre-1945)

'Ravenshoe' 1 Y-Y
(W.M. Spry, pre-1975) Unregistered
'Kingscourt' × 'Golden Valley'
Corona deep golden yellow. Mid-season

'Ravenswood' 2 (a)
(P.D. Williams, pre-1939)

'Ravisante' 8 Y-Y
(pre-1835)
Early

'Ravish' 2 (a)
(M.P. Williams) M.P. Williams, 1957

'Ravissante' 2 W-W
(F.E. Board) F.E. Board, 1965
'Petsamo' × 'Rashee'
Mid-season

'Rawene' 2 Y-O
(A. Gibson, pre-1951)
'Royal Mail' × 'Narvik'
Perianth segments golden yellow; corona reddish orange. PC(e)(NZ) 1951

'Rawhiti' 2 Y-R
(R. Hyde) R. Hyde, 1955

'Narvik' × 'Magherally'
Perianth segments rounded, of good substance; corona bowl-shaped, dark red

'Raw Silk' 3 Y-WWY
(T.D. Throckmorton) T.D. Throckmorton, 1974
'Easter Moon' × 'Irish Coffee'

'Ray Jesse' 2 W-YYO
(J.N. Hancock & Co., 1963) Unregistered

'Rayma' 2 Y-O
(G. Lewis) D.S. Bell, 1955
Perianth segments deep yellow; corona expanded, scarlet-orange

'Raymond' 2 (a)
(R.H. Bath, pre-1933)

'Rayo' 2 (a or b)
(pre-1933)
'Gloria Mundi' hybrid
Resembles 'Gloria Mundi'

'Rayon' 3 W-? (b)
(R. Crews, pre-1949)

'Rayon de Lune' 2 W-? (b or c)
(G.H. Johnstone, pre-1943)

'Ray Ribbon' 2 W-YRR
(H.A. Brown, 1938)
Mid-season to late

'Ray Smith' 1 Y-Y
(Barr & Sons, pre-1899)
Fl. rich yellow; perianth segments twisted

'Raysun' 2 Y-YYO
(J.N. Hancock & Co.) J.N. Hancock & Co., 1955
Perianth segments rich yellow, deeply overlapping; corona yellow, with a broad band of intense orange at rim

'Razadaz' 1 W-Y
(Jackson's Daffodils, 1987) Jackson's Daffodils, 1997
'Wilbur' × 'Hussy'; sdlg no. 104/87
Fl. 108 mm wide; perianth segments ovate, yellowish white 155B; corona funnel-shaped, vivid yellow 9A, frilled, with rim flanged. Early to mid-season

'R.Berkeley' 1
(?R.G. Berkeley, pre-1933)

'Ready Money' 2 (a)
(T.A.V. Wood, pre-1949)

'Reality' 1 (a)
(W.B. Hartland, pre-1913)

'Reality' 2 (a)
(M.P. Williams, pre-1949)
Fl. smooth; perianth segments overlapping

'Realm' 2 Y-Y
(H.A. Brown) J.N. Hancock & Co., 1955
Corona deeper in tone than the perianth, with rim closely and deeply notched, as if fringed

'Realty' 2 W-O
(F.E. Board) F.E. Board, 1965
'Mazaka' × 'Arbar'

'Reaper' 2 W-?
(Alister Clark) J. Sharp, 1960

'Rearguard' 2 W-Y
(G.H. Engleheart, pre-1901)
Corona rich yellow. AM 1901

'Rearguard' 9
(E.L. Jones, pre-1946)

'Rearquhar' 2 Y-YYO
(D.C.MacArthur) D.C.MacArthur, 1996
Hybrid between Div. 2 Y-O sdlgs; sdlg no. EV86213
Fl. forming a double triangle, 86 mm wide; perianth segments broadly ovate, mucronate, brilliant yellow 7B, spreading; the inner segments narrower and slightly twisted; corona funnel-shaped, angled, vivid yellow 14A, with a slightly creamier tone (13A) at base and strong orange 24A at rim, mouth flared and deeply lobed, rim flanged and crenate. Early. Scented

'Rebecca Anne' 4 W-O
(D.S. Bell) D.S. Bell, 1980
'Temple Maid' × ('Falaise' × 'Masquerade')
Fl. 106 mm wide; perianth and other petaloid segments white; corona segments reddish orange. Midseason

'Rebecca Clarke' 2 Y-O
(A.M. Wilson, pre-1944)
Perianth segments deep yellow, deeply overlapping; corona reddish orange

'Rebecca Syme' 1 W-Y
(W. Backhouse, pre-1869)
Corona slender, citron yellow. Violet-scented. Syn. "The Violet-scented Daffodil", Pseudonarcissus Moschatus 'Rebecca Syme'

'Rebecca West' 2 W-? (b)
(G. Lubbe & Son, pre-1952)

'Rebekah' 4 W-P
(R.A.Scamp) R.A.Scamp, 1997
'Dailmanach' × 'Pink Pageant'; sdlg no. 491
Fl. 100 mm wide; perianth and other pataloid segments in several whorls, white, smooth; the outer

whorl ovate; the inner whorls interspersed with soft pink corona segments. Late. Sunproof

'Rebel' 2 W-? (b)
(Mrs R.O. Backhouse, pre-1921)

'Rebel' 1 Y-Y
(R.H.Glover, pre-1993) Unregistered

'Rebound' 2 (a)
(W.F. Mitchell, pre-1938)

'Recap' 2 W-YYP
(J.N. Hancock & Co.)
'Cameronian' hybrid × 'Maylene'

'Recessional' 9 W-YYO
(F.H. Chapman, pre-1929)
'Socrates' × 'Lullaby'
Corona yellow, with orange at rim, frilled. AM(e) 1929

'Recital' 2 W-P
(G.E. Mitsch) G.E. Mitsch, 1972
'Carita' × 'Tangent'; sdlg no. D29/2
Fl. 112 mm wide; perianth segments broad, overlapping; corona rich deep salmon pink. Mid-season

'Reckless' 3 W-GYR
(Carncairn Daffodils) Carncairn Daffodils, 1987
'Merlin' × Wootton sdlg; sdlg no. W4/20
Perianth segments rounded, overlapping; corona very shallow, tightly ribbed, vivid yellow, with a narrow band of orange-red at rim, mouth split and overlapping. Late. Resembles 'Brave Journey'

'Recompense' ?-P
(Alister Clark, pre-1948)

'Recorder' 1 Y-Y
(A.E. Lowe, pre-1927)

'Recoup' 2 Y-R
(K.J. Heazlewood) K.J. Heazlewood, 1972
'Redeem' × 'Colours'
Fl. 102 mm wide

'Recreation' 2 W-? (b)
(G.H. Johnstone, pre-1949)

'Recruit' 2 (a or b)
(J.N. Hancock & Co., pre-1949)

'Rector' 1 (a)
(pre-1908)

'Reculver' 2 W-? (b)
(F.D.B. Cobb, pre-1954)

N. recurvus Haworth = *N. poeticus* var. *recurvus*

'Red Abbot' 2 W-R
(Mrs R.O. Backhouse, pre-1921)
Perianth segments broadly ovate, blunt and sometimes slightly truncate, slightly mucronate, pure white, with margins a little incurved, ribbed, overlapping one-third; the inner segments narrower, inflexed, with margins wavy; corona short funnel-shaped, intense red, with mouth expanded and lightly frilled

'Red Ace' 2 (a)
(de Graaff Bros, pre-1950)
AM(Haarlem) 1950

'Red Admiral'
(C. Dawson, pre-1907)

'Red Admiral' 2 Y-R
(G. Lewis, 1945) D.S. Bell, 1958
Perianth segments bright yellow; corona dark red

'Red Alert' 2 Y-R
(G.W.E. Brogden, 1979) Brogden Bulbs, 1991
'Orator' × 'Loch Hope'; sdlg no. x78/11
Fl. 100 mm wide; perianth segments broad, rounded at apex, golden yellow, very smooth; corona fiery orange-red, with rim dentate. Mid-season

'Red Alligator' 2 Y-O
(H.R. Barr) H.R. Barr, 1968
'California Gold' × 'Krakatoa'
Fl. 108 mm wide; perianth segments vivid yellow 13A; corona strong orange 24A. Early. Sunproof

'Red and Gold' 4 Y-YYR
(W.F.M. Copeland, pre-1909)
Hybrid between *N. radiiflorus* var. *poetarum* and 'Telamonius Plenus'
Perianth and other petaloid segments in three whorls, rich yellow; corona segments interspersed, deep yellow, with a broad band of bright crimson-red at rim and the rim finely incised

'Red Angel' 3 Y-OOR
(G.H. Rotteveel & Sons, 1967) G.H. Rotteveel & Sons, 1981
Fl. 100 mm wide; perianth segments primrose yellow; corona nasturtium orange, with nasturtium red at rim. Mid-season

'Red April' 2 W-R
(J.L. Richardson, pre-1948)
'Kilworth' × 'Nairobi'
Corona bowl-shaped, red

'Red Aria' 2 O-R
(G.E. Mitsch, 1977) R. & E. Havens, 1989
'Kindled' × 'Feeling Lucky'; sdlg no. MM16/1
Fl. 105 mm wide; perianth segments buff orange; corona almost disc-shaped, widely expanded, bright

orange-red. Mid-season

'Red Armorel' 3 W-? (b)
(G.H. Engleheart, pre-1913)

'Red Arrow' 1 Y-O
(W.O. Backhouse) C.R. Wootton, 1968
'Red Curtain' × 'Brer Fox'
Corona reddish orange. Mid-season. ?Received PC 1967 as 'Sonnet'

'Red Atom' 2 Y-O
(N.R.McIsaac, 1983) N.R.McIsaac, 1996
Sdlg 139 ('Firecracker' × 'Falstaff') × 'Hot Line'; sdlg no. 711
Fl. rounded, about 70 mm wide; perianth segments ovate, vivid yellow 12A, flushed reddish orange, overlapping; corona cup-shaped, vivid orange 28B, with rim dentate. Dwarf. Mid-season. Sunproof

'Red Banner' 2 (a)
(A.H. Ahrens) J.S. Leitch, 1955

'Red Baron' 2 Y-R
(J.A. O'More) J.A. O'More, 1968
'Seraglio' × 'Ivo Fell'

'Red Bay' 2 Y-R
(W.J. Dunlop) du Plessis Bros, 1978
Fl. 110 mm wide; perianth segments deep yellow; corona dark crimson-red. Late

'Red Beacon' 3 W-O
(J.C. Williams, pre-1910)
Fl. 75 mm wide, facing down; perianth segments broadly to very broadly ovate, blunt, fairly prominently mucronate, ivory white, slightly shaded sulphur yellow at base, spreading or reflexed, with midrib showing, of great substance, overlapping one-third to a half; the inner segments more narrowly ovate, somewhat twisted, with margins wavy and sometimes incurling; corona large, shallow, intense reddish orange, with mouth wavy

'Red Beauty' 2 Y-O
(G. Lubbe & Son) G. Lubbe & Son, 1961
Fl. 50 mm wide; perianth segments brilliant greenish yellow 6B; corona strong orange 30D. Mid-season. AM(Haarlem) 1961

'Red Bern' 2 W-? (b)
(W. Balch, pre-1933)

'Red Bird' 2 W-O
(de Graaff Bros, pre-1936)
Perianth segments cream white; corona scarlet-orange. AM(Haarlem) 1936, FCC(Haarlem) 1938

'Red Blodwen' 2 W-R
(W. Jackson Sr, pre-1937) W. Jackson Jr, 1956

'Warflame' × 'Pink'un'

'Red Boy' 2 (a)
(A.H. Ahrens) J.S. Leitch, 1955

'Redbreast' 3 W-? (b)
(G.H. Engleheart, pre-1910)

'Redbreast' 2 W-R
(D.S. Bell) D.S. Bell, 1957
'Idealist' × 'Show Boat'
Corona very shallow bowl-shaped, deep red

'Red Button' 2 Y-O
(Warnaar & Co., pre-1949)
'Aranjuez' × 'Westminster'
AM(Haarlem) 1949

'Red Cameo' 2 Y-R
(M. Hamilton, 1970) P.D.K. Ramsay, 1982
'Rawene' × 'Jaguar'; sdlg no. 12-71
Fl. 100 mm wide; perianth segments broad, rounded at apex, deep yellow, smooth, of good substance; corona bowl-shaped, wide, brick red. Mid-season. Resembles 'Rawene' but with a shallower corona

'Red Cap' 2 W-O
(C. Dawson, pre-1908)
Perianth segments creamy white; corona deep scarlet-orange

'Red Cap'
(J.N. Hancock & Co., pre-1962) Unregistered

'Red Carpet' 3 W-GRR
(T.D. Throckmorton) T.D. Throckmorton, 1977
'Kilworth' × 'Russet'; sdlg no. 66/24/7
Fl. 91 mm wide. Mid-season

'Red Charm' 2 (a)
(G.L. Wilson, pre-1943)

'Red Chief' 3 W-? (b)
(J.C. Williams, pre-1909)
Perianth segments opening creamy white, becoming pure white, overlapping; corona shallow, widely expanded, with a broad band of reddish orange at rim, frilled

'Red Chief' 2 Y-YOO
(J.N. Hancock & Co., pre-1949)
Perianth segments yellow; corona reddish orange, with yellow at base

'Red Circle' 2 (a)
(J.W.A. Lefeber, pre-1944)

'Redcliffs' 2 Y-O
(J.J. Abernethy, 1951) R.J. Abernethy, 1962
Fl. 92 mm wide; perianth segments dark golden

yellow; corona dark reddish orange. Mid-season. Resembles a smaller-flowered 'Teheran'

'Red Clipper'
(pre-1946)

'Red Coat' 2 Y-O
(W. Backhouse, pre-1869)
Perianth segments dark primrose yellow, tinged buff yellow; corona bright reddish orange, with rim neatly crenate. Syn. 'Redcoat'

'Red Coat' 2 Y-R
(J.A. O'More, 1963) P.D.K. Ramsay, 1979
'Red Baron' × ('Marksman' × 'Rustom Pasha'); sdlg no. 43/63
Fl. 100 mm wide. Mid-season

'Redcoat' 2 Y-O
Syn. of 'Red Coat'

'Red Conquest' 1 Y-P
(D.S. Bell) D.S. Bell, 1970
Sdlg × ('White Sentinel' × 'Seraglio')
Fl. opening almost white; perianth segments becoming lemon; corona becoming pale pink

'Red Coral' 2 Y-R
(D.S. Bell) D.S. Bell, 1962
'Nene Beauty' × 'Papanui Queen'
Fl. 110 mm wide; corona very shallow bowl-shaped, pinkish red. Mid-season. Resembles 'Ceylon' but with the perianth segments more rounded and the corona more widely expanded

'Red Cottage' 2 W-YYR
(Carncairn Daffodils) Carncairn Daffodils, 1967
'Sylvia O'Neill' × G.L.Wilson sdlg
Fl. 83 mm wide; perianth segments pure white, overlapping; corona yellow, with bright red at rim. Mid-season. 2n=28. Resembles 'Crown Derby' in colour

'Red Craze' 2 Y-O
(R. Hyde) R. Hyde, 1957

'Red Crest'
(pre-1914)

'Red Crest' 2 (a)
(D.S. Bell) D.S. Bell, 1957

'Red Cross' 2 Y-YOO
(Mrs R.O. Backhouse, pre-1921)
'Will Scarlett' hybrid
Perianth segments primrose yellow, somewhat twisted; corona rich orange, paling to orange-yellow at base. AM(Haarlem) 1922, FCC(Haarlem) 1923

'Red Crusader' 2 W-? (b)
(S.J. Bisdee, 1939) S.J. Bisdee, 1956

'Popinjay' × 'Cheerio'

'Red Cup'
(pre-1936)

'Red Curtain' 1 Y-O
(W.O. Backhouse) W.O. Backhouse, 1956
Perianth segments rich yellow; corona reddish orange

'Red Dawn' 2 W-? (b)
(W. Balch, pre-1933)

'Red Dawn' 2 Y-O
(D.S. Bell) D.S. Bell, 1968
'Jansen' × 'Ceylon'
Perianth segments deep yellow; corona reddish orange

'Red Defiance' 2 Y-O
(R.H. Bath, pre-1932)
Perianth segments broadly oblong, squarish at apex, slightly mucronate, primrose yellow, spreading, creased, overlapping one-third; the inner segments ovate, inflexed and slightly twisted; corona funnel-shaped, three-quarters the length of the perianth segments, loosely ribbed, orange, with mouth straight and a little frilled. Mid-season. 2n=28. AM(c) 1932, *AM(g) 1936

'Red Delight' 2 (a)
(Mrs R.O. Backhouse, pre-1921)

'Red Delight' 3 W-R
(pre-1956) Unregistered
Perianth segments cream; corona scarlet

'Red Demon' 2 Y-R
(D.S. Bell, 1976) D.S.Bell, 1983
'Checkmate' × 'Falstaff'
Fl. 98 mm wide; corona very shallow bowl-shaped, red. Mid-season

'Red Devil' 2 W-R
(Carncairn Daffodils) Carncairn Daffodils, 1973
'Kilworth' × 'Pirate King'
Fl. 98 mm wide

'Red Devon' 2 Y-O
(E.B. Champernowne, pre-1943)
'Fortune' × 'Killigrew'
Fl. 103 mm wide; perianth segments very broadly ovate, blunt, brilliant greenish yellow 6B, with very slight white mucro, spreading, concave, regular, overlapping half; the inner segments more narrowly ovate, notched at shoulder, with margins wavy; corona very short funnel-shaped, lightly ribbed, strong orange 25A, mouth straight, with shallow overlapping lobes, wavy. Slightly scented. 2n=28. AM(Haarlem) 1950, *AM(g) 1968, *FCC(g) 1977, *AM(p) 1985, AGM 1993

'Red Diamond' 3 O-R
(G.E.Mitsch, 1986) R. & E.Havens, 1996
'Red Aria' × 'Sabine Hay'; sdlg no. 2V4/1
Fl. 95 mm wide; perianth segments broadly ovate, heavily suffused with orange, spreading, plane, smooth; corona bowl-shaped, orange-red. Late

'Red Dice' 2 (a)
(Oregon Bulb Farms, pre-1945)

'Red Dirk' 3 (a)
(Mrs R.O. Backhouse, pre-1910)

'Red Disc' 2 Y-YOO
(G.H. Engleheart, pre-1903)
Perianth segments soft yellow; corona very broad, rich reddish orange, with yellow at rim. AM 1903

'Red Disc' 3 Y-YYO
Syn. of 'Concord'

'Redditch' 2 Y-R
(W.M. Spry, pre-1975) Unregistered
'Winsome' × 'Revelry'
Corona flame red

'Red Dot' 2 (a)
(Warnaar & Co., pre-1933)

'Red Dragon' 2 Y-Y
(pre-1936)
'Honourable Mrs Jocelyn' × 'The Bride'

'Red Duster' 2 Y-R
(S.C. Gaspar, 1950) R.J. Abernethy, 1961
Fl. 95 mm wide. Mid-season

'Red Eagle' 3 W-R
(G.H. Engleheart, pre-1905)
Perianth segments creamy white; corona bright scarlet, with rim dentate

'Red Eagle' 2 Y-R
(S.C. Gaspar, 1946) R.J. Abernethy, 1957
Perianth segments yellow, of thick substance; corona expanded, deep red

'Red Eclipse' 3 W-R
(J.M.Radcliff, 1982) P.J. & K.P.Radcliff, 1993
Fl. 104 mm wide; perianth segments broadly ovate, blunt, slightly mucronate, with margins minutely incurling, overlapping one-third to a half; the inner segments more narrowly ovate; corona bowl-shaped, ribbed, orange-red (30A), frilled. Very late

'Redeem' 2 Y-R
(K.J. Heazlewood) K.J. Heazlewood, 1968
'Revelry' × 'Ceylon'
Fl. 102 mm wide; perianth segments dark yellow; corona opening orange, becoming bright red.
Mid-season. Resembles 'Revelry' but with a larger corona

'Red Ember' 3 Y-R
(J.A. O'More, 1971) P.D.K. Ramsay, 1981
'Merry King' × sdlg 52/64; sdlg no. 75/71
Fl. 71 mm wide; corona very shallow bowl-shaped. Late. Varies between Divs 3 and 2

'Red Emperor' 3 W-O
(P.D. Williams, pre-1908)
Perianth segments creamy white, slightly reflexed; corona large disc-shaped, ribbed, scarlet-orange

'Red Empress' 2 (a)
(G. Lewis) D.S. Bell, 1955

'Red Ensign' 3 W-? (b)
(G.H. Engleheart, pre-1907)

'Red Ensign' 2 Y-R
(D.S. Bell) D.S. Bell, 1968
Perianth segments pure yellow, of good substance; corona bowl-shaped, widely expanded, red

'Red Ensign' 2 W-R
(J.L. Richardson, c.1959) Unregistered
'Kilworth' × 'Arbar'

'Red Era' 3 Y-YRR
(J.A. O'More) P.D.K. Ramsay, 1981
'Merry King' hybrid; sdlg no. 74/71
Fl. 70 mm wide. Late

'Red Eric' 2 Y-R
(D.S. Bell) D.S. Bell, 1982
'Court Martial' × 'Checkmate' hybrid
Fl. 102 mm wide. Mid-season

'Red Eve'
(pre-1913)

'Redex' 2 Y-O
(S.J. Bisdee) S.J. Bisdee, 1956
'Market Merry' × sdlg 62/45
Corona reddish orange

'Red Excelsior' 2 Y-O
(de Graaff Bros & van Konynenburg & Co., pre-1927)
Perianth segments soft yellow, with margins incurved; corona large, clear orange, with mouth widely expanded, frilled. AM(Haarlem) 1927

'Red Eye' 3 W-? (b)
(P.D. or J.C. Williams, pre-1913)

'Red Eye' 3 W-? (b)
(Cartwright & Goodwin, pre-1916)

'Redfast' 2 Y-O
(A.J. Bliss, pre-1931)
Fl. 70 mm wide; perianth segments deep primrose, reflexed, overlapping at base only; corona bright orange. Mid-season to late. Syn. 'Kathleen'

'Red Feather' 2 (a)
(T.A.V. Wood, pre-1949)

'Red Fed' 3 ?-R
(pre-1927)
Corona disc-shaped, scarlet

'Red Fern' 3 W-? (b)
(J.W.A. Lefeber, pre-1938)

'Red Fire'
(?Sir A.P.W. Thomas, pre-1915)

'Red Flag' 2 (a)
(G.H. Engleheart, pre-1910)

'Red Flame' 2 Y-R
(J.A. O'More) P.D.K. Ramsay, 1983
'Red Baron' × 'Firecracker'
Perianth segments broadly ovate, smooth; corona rich red

'Red Folly' 2 Y-O
(S.C. Gaspar, 1950) R.J. Abernethy, 1961
Fl. 102 mm wide; perianth segments golden yellow; corona dark reddish orange. Mid-season

'Red Fox' 3 W-? (b)
(Cartwright & Goodwin, pre-1916)

'Red Fox' 3 Y-O
(Murray W. Evans) Murray W. Evans, 1973
'Hades' × 'Paricutin'
Fl. 90 mm wide

'Red Frill' 2 W-?
(T. Morrison) T. Morrison, 1960
Corona widely expanded, with a broad band of reddish orange at rim, frilled

'Red Gauntlet' 3 W-O
(Mrs R.O. Backhouse, pre-1908)
Perianth segments creamy white, flushed pale primrose yellow at base; corona deeply ribbed, reddish orange

'Red Gem' 2 Y-R
(J.A. O'More, 1958) P.D.K. Ramsay, 1980
'Dunkeld' × 'Alamein'; sdlg no. 26/58
Fl. 104 mm wide. Mid-season

'Red Giant' 2 (a)
(Mrs R.O. Backhouse, pre-1921)
AM(Haarlem) 1930

'Red Glory' 2 Y-R
(Mrs R.O. Backhouse, pre-1921)
Perianth segments golden yellow, spreading, overlapping; corona funnel-shaped, red, with mouth expanded. AM(Haarlem) 1927

'Red Glory' 2 Y-R
(G. Lewis, pre-1937)
Perianth segments golden yellow; corona red

'Red Glow' 2 Y-R
(N.R. McIsaac) N.R. McIsaac, 1978
'Naples' × 'Falstaff'; sdlg no. 140
Fl. 87 mm wide; perianth segments deep yellow; corona deep orange-red. Early to mid-season

'Red Goblet' 2 Y-O
(J.L. Richardson, pre-1937)
'Marksman' × 'Penquite'
Fl. rounded, about 102 mm wide; perianth segments very broad, rounded or truncate at apex, slightly mucronate, lemon yellow, with a faint flush of pink radiating from the base, spreading, plane, or a little concave near apex, sometimes creased, overlapping half; the inner segments roundish, a little inflexed; corona deep cup-shaped, incurved at base, ribbed, orange, with mouth straight or somewhat incurved, a little frilled, rim crenate. Mid-season. 2n=28. AM(e) 1941, *AM(g) 1952

'Red Gold' 1 (a)
(Sir A.P.W. Thomas, pre-1930)

'Red Guard' 8 Y-O
(Mrs R.O. Backhouse, pre-1921)
Poetaz
Fl. 54 mm wide; perianth segments apricot yellow suffused with red; corona small, bright orange, flushed red. Tall. AM(e) 1923, AM(Haarlem) 1925, FCC(Haarlem) 1927. Div. 3 until 1930

'Red Hackle' 2 W-YOO
(The Brodie of Brodie, c.1936)
'Folly' × 'Red Abbott'
Fl. 118 mm wide; perianth segments slightly reflexed, overlapping; corona bowl-shaped, ribbed, vivid orange 28B, paling to vivid yellow 15B at base, mouth frilled and widely expanded, rim dentate and slightly flanged. AM(e) 1948, *AM(g) 1952

'Red Hall' 3 W-GRR
(Mrs H.K. Richardson, 1967) Carncairn Daffodils, 1985
Perianth segments pure white; corona very shallow, orange-red. Late. Resembles a more vigorous and more sunproof 'Matapan'

'Red Halo' 2 W-? (b)
(R.H. Bath, pre-1950)

'Red Hand' 2 (a)
(The Brodie of Brodie, pre-1932)

'Red Hawk' 2 Y-R
(G.E. Mitsch, 1957) Elise Havens, 1979
('Campfire' × 'Fortune's Blaze') × 'Armada'; sdlg no. R98/1
Fl. 98 mm wide; perianth segments golden yellow; corona orange-red. Early

'Red Haze' 2 Y-R
(J.A. O'More, 1969) P.D.K. Ramsay, 1981
'Spelter' × 'Tekapo'; sdlg no. 16/69
Perianth segments orange-yellow; corona red

'Red Head' 2 (a)
(A.H. Ahrens) J.S. Leitch, 1955

'Red Heart' 3 W-? (b)
(J.L. Richardson, pre-1923)

'Red Heckle' 3 Y-YYR
(G. Lewis, pre-1955)
Fl. rounded; perianth segments smooth and of heavy substance; corona disc-shaped, with bright red at rim. Resembles a more refined 'Seraglio'

'Red Heel' 2 Y-O
(L. Buckland, pre-1936)

'Redhill' 2 W-R
(P. de Jager & Sons, 1958) G.A. Preyde, 1978
Fl. 95 mm wide; perianth segments very broadly ovate, blunt or truncate, prominently mucronate, ivory white, spreading or slightly reflexed, somewhat concave, with margins occasionally incurling at apex and with midrib showing, overlapping half; the inner segments more narrowly ovate, shouldered at base, more nearly spreading, creased, with margins wavy or rolled inwards; corona bowl-shaped, ribbed, orange-red (30C), mouth expanded, split in places and overlapping, frilled. Early. 2n=28

'Red Hint' 2 Y-R
(?New Zealand origin, pre-1990) Unregistered

'Red Hood' 2 W-? (b)
(C. Goodson, pre-1943)

'Red Hot' 2 O-R
(J.A. O'More) P. & G. Phillips, 1975
'Naples' × 'Home Fires'; sdlg no. 12/60
Fl. 85 mm wide; perianth segments rounded, with rich shades of orange; corona brick red. Early to mid-season

'Red Hugh' 9 W-GRR
(Ballydorn Bulb Farm, 1974) Ballydorn Bulb Farm, 1987
'Cantabile' hybrid open pollinated

Dwarf. Late

'Red Hunter' 2 Y-R
(D.S.Bell, pre-1986) Unregistered
'Huntsman' × 'Rockall'

'Red Hussar' 4
(Mrs R.O. Backhouse, pre-1921)

'Red Idol' 2 Y-R
(Warnaar & Co., pre-1951)
'Aranjuez' × 'Carbineer'
AM(Haarlem) 1951

'Red Ike' 2 (a)
(The Brodie of Brodie, pre-1932)

'Red Imp' 6 Y-O
(D. Bramley) D. Bramley, 1986
'Falstaff' × 'Falling Star'; sdlg no. 78/2
Perianth segments reflexed; corona colour fading with age. Mid-season. Resembles a neater-flowered 'Falling Star' of improved colour, with the perianth segments more strongly reflexed

'Red Indian' 3 W-? (b)
(Mrs R.O. Backhouse, pre-1921)
AM(Haarlem) 1941

'Red Jacket' 2 Y-O
(Curtis Tolley) Curtis Tolley, 1997
'Vulcan' × 'Resplendent'; sdlg no. 89-13
Fl. forming a double triangle, 90 mm wide; perianth segments ovate, vivid yellow 9B; corona funnel-shaped, strong orange 25A, with mouth ribbed. Early to mid-season. Sunproof

'Red Jester' 3 W-YRR
(D.S. Bell) D.S. Bell, 1963
Fl. 108 mm wide. Mid-season. Resembles a larger-flowered 'Corofin' with a more extensive area of red in the corona

'Red Joker' 2 Y-R
(J.A. O'More) P.D.K. Ramsay, 1984
'Naples' × 'Sun Chariot'; sdlg no. 5/66

'Red King' 2 W-? (b)
(Warnaar & Co., pre-1930)

'Red King' 2 (a)
(S.C. Gaspar) R.J. Abernethy, 1957

'Red Knight' 2 W-? (b)
(G.H. Engleheart, pre-1907)

'Red Knight' 2 W-? (b)
(Mrs R.O. Backhouse, pre-1921)
AM(Haarlem) 1929

'Red Lace' 2 (a)
(D.S. Bell) D.S. Bell, 1955

'Red Lacquer' 3 W-? (b)
(Mrs F.S. Foote, pre-1940)

'Red Lady' 3 W-R
(E.M. Crosfield, pre-1913)
Perianth segments pure white; corona red

'Redlake' 2 W-? (b)
(P.D. Williams, pre-1943)

'Red Lake' 3 W-OOR
(E.B. Champernowne, pre-1969) Unregistered

'Redland' 2 Y-O
(H. A. Brown, 1932)
Perianth segments broad, rich yellow, plane; corona rich reddish orange. Mid-season

'Redlands' 2 Y-R
(C.E. Radcliff, 1946) J.M.Radcliff, 1956
'Robigana' × 'Hugh Poate'
Resembles a larger and improved 'Hugh Poate'

'Redlands Too' 2 Y-R
(J.M. Radcliff) J.M. Radcliff, 1987
Sdlg 5/75 × sdlg 33/77; sdlg no. 53/83
Perianth segments very broadly ovate, blunt, yellow, with slight white mucro, spreading, with margins minutely incurling, smooth, overlapping half; the inner segments more narrowly ovate, shouldered at base, with margins a little wavy; corona bowl-shaped, red, with mouth shallowly lobed, rim entire. Mid-season

'Redleap' 2 Y-R
(W.M. Spry, pre-1975) Unregistered
'Torchlight' × 'Delight'
Corona orange-scarlet

'Red Legend' 2 Y-R
(Colin Crotty, 1980) Colin Crotty, 1995
'Falstaff' × 'Red Baron'; sdlg no. 1-75
Fl. forming a double triangle, 106 mm wide; perianth segments ovate, bright deep yellow; corona bowl-shaped, very deep orange-red, with mouth flared and heavily frilled. Early

'Red Letter Day' 2 Y-R
(Tom Forster, 1960s) Unregistered
Perianth segments deep golden yellow; corona cylindrical, brilliant orange-red. Tall. Early to mid-season

'Red Light' 2 W-? (b)
(Mrs R.O. Backhouse, pre-1921)
See also 'Redlight'

'Redlight' 2 W-?
Syn. of 'Red Light'

'Red Lion' 2 W-YOR
(F.H. Chapman, pre-1938)

'Red Lodge' 2 Y-O
(E.W. Cotter) E.W. Cotter, 1968
'Firemaster' × 'Fury'

'Red Lory' 2 Y-R
(G.E. Mitsch) G.E. Mitsch, 1970
('Narvik' × 'California Gold') × ('Playboy' × 'Alamein')
Perianth segments deep yellow; corona bright orange-red, touched yellow at rim. Mid-season

'Red Macaw' 3 (a)
(E.M. Crosfield, pre-1908)

'Red Maestro' 2 Y-ORR
(J.A.O'More, 1970) Koanga Daffodils, 1996
Sdlg 68/60 ('Carrowkeel' × Navarro sdlg 394) × 'Red Hot'; sdlg no. 33/70
Fl. 115 mm wide; perianth segments ovate, brilliant yellow 12B, slightly concave; corona bowl-shaped, orange-red (32B), paling to orange at base. Mid-season

'Red Magic' 3 W-R
(Mrs R.O. Backhouse, pre-1921)
Perianth segments milk white, of thick substance; corona rich scarlet

'Redman' 2 Y-R
(Ballydorn Bulb Farm) Ballydorn Bulb Farm, 1975
'Torero' open pollinated
Fl. 120 mm wide; perianth segments deep gold; corona orange-red, with a paler tone outside. Early

'Red Manfred'
(New Zealand origin, pre-1940)

'Red Mantle' 2 Y-R
(S.J. Bisdee, 1942)

'Red Mantle' 2 Y-R
(D.S. Bell) D.S. Bell, 1979
'Air Marshal' × 'Cresalla'
Fl. 106 mm wide; corona red. Mid-season. Resembles 'Air Marshal' but with a more rounded flower

'Redmarley' 2 Y-O
(Mrs R.O. Backhouse, pre-1921)
Perianth segments pale yellow; corona reddish orange, with rim dentate. Late. Sunproof. AM(Haarlem) 1938. See also 'Red Marley'

'Red Marley' 2 Y-O
Syn. of 'Redmarley'

'Red Marquis' 2 Y-O
(J.J. Abernethy) R.J. Abernethy, 1962
Fl. 95 mm wide; perianth segments soft golden yellow; corona shallow, widely expanded, deep reddish orange. Mid-season

'Red Mars' 2 Y-YYR
(D.S. Bell) D.S. Bell, 1963
'Monica' × 'Diamond King'
Fl. 104 mm wide; perianth segments rich yellow, smooth, overlapping; corona bowl-shaped, yellow, with a broad band of rich red at rim. Mid-season. Resembles 'On Parade' but with a more widely expanded corona

'Red Marshal' 2 W-O
(Mrs H.K. Richardson) Mrs H.K. Richardson, 1976
'Lorenzo' × 'Avenger'
Fl. 90 mm wide; perianth segments rounded, pure white; corona fiery reddish orange, with rim dentate. Mid-season

'Redmayne' 2 Y-R
(J.C. Whibley) J.C. Whibley, 1959

'Red Mecaw' 3 W-O
(pre-1927)
Corona disc-shaped, orange-scarlet

'Red Mission' 2 Y-R
(G.W.E. & M.E.Brogden) G.W.E. & M.E.Brogden, 1980
'Orator' × 'Edition'; sdlg no. T93
Fl. 89 mm wide; corona orange-red. Mid-season

'Red Monarch' 2 W-? (b)
(G.H. Engleheart, pre-1913)

'Red Monarch' 2 W-? (b)
(Mrs R.O. Backhouse, pre-1921)
AM(Haarlem) 1935

'Red Moon' 2 (a)
(Sir F.C. Stern, pre-1951)

'Red Morn' 2 Y-R
(S.J. Bisdee, 1936)
'Red Heel' × 'Bokhara'

'Red Oak' 2 Y-R
(Colin Crotty) Unregistered
Sdlg no. 26-75

'Red Omen' 2 Y-R
(J.A. O'More, 1964) P.D.K. Ramsay, 1984
'Home Fires' × 'Spelter'; sdlg no. 18/64

'Redondo' 2 (a)
(J.L. Richardson, pre-1943)

'Red Orb' 3 W-? (b)
(A.M. Wilson, pre-1916)

'Redoubt' 2 (a)
(L. Buckland, pre-1936)

N. redoutei Rouy = *N. tazetta* subsp. *lacticolor*

N. redoutei Sweet = *N. triandrus* var. *loiseleurii*

'Redpa' 2 Y-R
(A.O. Roblin, *c*.1966) Unregistered
('Sudan' × 'Freycinet') × 'Vulcan'

'Red Pearl' 2 (a)
(Miss K.M. Hinchliff, pre-1935)

'Red Pedestal' 2 (a)
(Miss K.M. Hinchliff, pre-1940)

'Red Planet' 3 W-R
(Mrs R.O. Backhouse, pre-1921)
Corona bright red

'Red Planet' 2 Y-R
(?New Zealand origin, pre-1990) Unregistered

'Redpole' 3 W-? (b)
(N.Y. Lower, pre-1914)
'Yeoman of the Guard' × 'Black Prince'

'Red Poll' 2 Y-R
(Colin Crotty) Unregistered
Sdlg no. 7-75

'Red Poppett'
Unregistered
Pollen parent of 'Kandos'

'Red Prince' 3 W-? (b)
(G.H. Engleheart, pre-1897)

'Red Prince' 2 (a)
Syn. of 'Norfolk'

'Red Prospect' 2 Y-R
(J.L. Richardson) P.D.K. Ramsay, 1984

'Red Punch' 2 (a)
(Oregon Bulb Farms, pre-1945)

'Red Queen' 2 (a)
(Sir A.P.W. Thomas, pre-1930)

'Red Radiance' 2 W-R
(H.A. Brown, pre-1936)
Perianth segments opening yellow, becoming white; corona solid red

'Red Ranger' 2 Y-O
(W.J. Dunlop, pre-1953)
?'Carbineer' × ?'Bahram'
Perianth segments deep yellow; corona crimson-orange

'Red Rascal' 2 Y-R
(Warnaar & Co., pre-1950)
'Bahram' × 'Carbineer'
Perianth segments deep golden yellow; corona bright red. 2n=28. AM(Haarlem) 1954, FCC(Haarlem) 1956

'Red Rebel' 2 (a)
(G.L. Wilson) J. Swain, 1955

'Redress' 2 Y-R
(K.J. Heazlewood) K.J. Heazlewood, 1968
'Penara' × 'Ceylon'
Fl. 115 mm wide; corona bright red. Late. Resembles a slightly larger 'Rawhiti' with a rounder flower

'Red Riband' 2 Y-YYR
(The Brodie of Brodie, c.1935)
'Seraglio' × 'Fortune'
Fl. clear yellow; corona with a broad and well-defined band of bright red at rim. Resembles 'Fortune' in form

'Red Riband' 2 Y-YYR
(J.N. Hancock & Co., pre-1988) Unregistered
Perianth segments broadly ovate, blunt, fairly prominently mucronate, clear yellow, a little inflexed, creased, overlapping half; the inner segments sometimes with a "thumb" at the margin at mid-point; corona cup-shaped, lightly ribbed, yellow, with a band of tomato red at rim, mouth straight, a little frilled, rim minutely notched. Tall. Mid-season

'Red Ribbon' 3 Y-YYO
(pre-1956) Unregistered

'Red Riding Hood' 3 W-R
(Sir C.H. Cave, pre-1923)
'Lulworth' × 'Horace'
Perianth segments creamy white; corona bright red

'Red Rim' 3 W-? (b)
(Cartwright & Goodwin, pre-1910)

'Red Rim' 9 W-YYR
(G.H. Engleheart, pre-1923)
Fl. rounded; perianth segments broad, squarish at apex, prominently mucronate, clear white, spreading, a little concave either side of the midrib, overlapping half; the inner segments narrower, angled at shoulder, only very slightly mucronate, a little inflexed; corona disc-shaped, tightly ribbed, greenish yellow, with a narrow band of orange-red at rim, rim minutely notched and crenate. 2n=14. Syn. 'Red River'. AM(e) 1923, FCC(c)(m) 1926, AM(c) 1928, AM(Haarlem) 1929, FCC(Haarlem) 1930, *(Gulval)AM(m) 1936

'Red River' 9 W-YYR
Syn. of 'Red Rim'

'Red Robe' 2 (a)
(Mrs R.O. Backhouse, pre-1921)

'Red Robert' 2 Y-O
(Barr & Sons) T.M. Dorrien Smith, 1971
Sdlg no. 3402
Fl. 100 mm wide

'Red Robin' 2 (a)
(H.A. Brown, pre-1950)

'Red Rock' 2 (a)
(H.A. Brown, pre-1950)

'Red Rocket' 2 W-O
(?Australian origin, pre-1997) Unregistered

'Red Rooster' 3 W-R
(Brian S. Duncan) Rathowen Daffodils, 1978
'Enniskillen' × 'Don Carlos'; sdlg no. 78
Fl. 105 mm wide; corona tightly ribbed, deep orange-red. Mid-season. Resembles 'Doctor Hugh' but with a more rounded flower and a deeper-coloured corona

'Red Rosette' 2 Y-O
(S.J. Bisdee, 1945)
'Kaoota' × 'Sunset Fires'

'Red Rover' 2 (a)
(R.H. Bath, pre-1929)

'Red Rowan' 2 Y-O
(S.J. Bisdee, 1942)
'Gulliver' × 'Sunset Fires'

'Red Ruff' 3 Y-R
(K.J. Heazlewood) K.J. Heazlewood, 1968
Fl. 102 mm wide; perianth segments pale yellow. Late. Resembles 'Freycinet' but with a paler perianth and more heavily frilled corona

'Red Ruff' 2 Y-R
(R.H.Glover, pre-1989) Unregistered
'Brett' × 'E.M.R.'

'Red Rufus' 2 (a)
(Barr & Sons, pre-1941)

'Red Rum' 2 Y-R
(Mrs H.K. Richardson) Mrs H.K. Richardson, 1973
'Tambourine' × 'Falstaff'
Perianth segments very broadly ovate, blunt, slightly mucronate, spreading, with margins incurled near apex, overlapping half; the inner segments somewhat

round, a little inflexed; corona bowl-shaped, loosely ribbed, with mouth straight, tightly frilled

'Red Ruth' 2 W-? (b)
(E. & J.C. Martin, pre-1916)

'Redruth' 9 W-R
(A.G. Bull, pre-1927)
Corona scarlet

'Red Sahib' 3 (a)
(Cartwright & Goodwin, pre-1916)

'Red Sails' 2 R-O
(S.J. Bisdee) S.J. Bisdee, 1956
Sdlg 35/42 × 'Morello'

'Red Sand' 3 (a)
(Mrs M. Moorby, pre-1949)

'Red Satin' 2 W-R
(J.C. Whibley, 1940) R. Hyde, 1958
Perianth segments of thick and waxy substance; corona red. Very early

'Red Sea' 3 Y-R
(The Brodie of Brodie, c.1922)
Perianth segments very broadly ovate, blunt or squarish at apex, prominently mucronate, creamy yellow, spreading, plane or sometimes creased, with margins incurling at apex, of great substance, overlapping half; the inner segments more narrowly ovate, not noticeably mucronate, a little inflexed, with margins wavy and sometimes nicked; corona shallow bowl-shaped, ribbed, red, with mouth expanded. Mid-season. PR(e) 1927, AM(e) 1928

'Red Seal' 3 W-? (b)
(E.M. Crosfield, pre-1913)

'Red Shadow' 2 Y-YYO
(Mrs R.O. Backhouse, pre-1921)
AM(Haarlem) 1937

'Redshank' 2 (a)
(Mrs R.O. Backhouse, pre-1907)

'Red Sheen' 3 O-R
(R. & E. Havens, 1982) R. & E. Havens, 1993
'Bantam' × 'Kindled'; sdlg no. REH7/1
Fl. 80 mm wide; perianth segments acute, yellow, flushed with orange, slightly reflexed, smooth; corona bowl-shaped, brilliant orange-red, a little frilled. Late. Sunproof. Resembles 'Scarlet Tanager' but with the perianth less rounded

'Red Shield' 2 Y-YYR
(pre-1949)
Perianth segments acute, primrose yellow; corona gold, with red at rim

'Red Shoes' 2 Y-R
(D.S. Bell, c.1955) Unregistered
Perianth segments deep yellow; corona red

'Red Signal' 2 W-? (b)
(G. Zandbergen-Terwegen, pre-1939)

'Red Silk' 3 W-? (b)
(E. & J.C. Martin, pre-1916)

'Redskin' 3 W-? (b)
(Mrs R.O. Backhouse, pre-1921)

'Redskin' 2 (a)
(E.G. Taylor) E.G. Taylor, 1956

'Red Sky' 2 (a)
(A.H. Ahrens) J.S. Leitch, 1955

'Red Snapper' 3 Y-R
(Mrs J. Abel Smith) Mrs J. Abel Smith, 1988
'Pipe Major' × 'Altruist'; sdlg no. S55/11
Very late. Varies between Divs 3 and 2

'Red Snow' 2 W-R
(Mrs R.O. Backhouse, pre-1921)
Corona vivid orange-red, frilled

'Red Socks' 6 Y-R
(Koanga Daffodils, 1985) Koanga Daffodils, 1995
O'More sdlg 2/66 (sdlg 4/60 × *N. cyclamineus*) × O'More sdlg 19/76 ('Sharif' × 'Red Coat'); sdlg no. 21/85
Fl. 70 mm wide; perianth segments ovate, vivid yellow 14A, reflexed; corona funnel-shaped, orange-red (30B), with rim crenate. Dwarf. Mid-season

'Red Spartan' 2 Y-R
(Brian S. Duncan) Rathowen Daffodils, 1983
'Richhill' × 'Bunclody'; sdlg no. 554
Fl. forming a double triangle; perianth segments very broadly ovate, deep golden yellow, with slight white mucro, a little inflexed, shallowly concave, silken smooth, overlapping half; the inner segments more narrowly ovate, roundish at apex; corona long cup-shaped, deep orange-red, with mouth straight and even. Mid-season to late. Resembles 'Richhill' but with a solid red and more nearly sunproof corona

'Red Splendour' 2 Y-O
(R.H. Bath, pre-1943)
Fl. 102 mm wide; perianth segments brilliant yellow 8A, overlapping half; corona strong orange 25A, with mouth expanded and frilled, rim dentate. *AM(g) 1953

'Red Spot' 3 W-O
(A.E. Lowe, pre-1927)
Corona reddish orange

'Red Squaw' 2 (a)
(E.G. Taylor) E.G. Taylor, 1956

'Red Squirrel' 2 Y-O
(G.L. Wilson) G.L. Wilson, 1956
'Klingo' × 'Indian Summer'
Corona deep reddish orange

'Red Star' 2 W-O
(de Graaff Bros, pre-1898)
Perianth segments acute, creamy white, reflexed; corona stained reddish orange

'Red Star' 3 W-R
(Alfred Clark) Alfred Clark, 1955

'Redstart' 2 (a)
(Mrs R.O. Backhouse, pre-1907)

'Redstart' 3 W-GWO
(G.E. Mitsch) G.E. Mitsch, 1959
'Rubra' × 'Sylvia O'Neill'
Corona ivory white, with green at base and coral orange at rim

'Redstone' 2 YYW-P
(G.E. Mitsch) G.E. Mitsch, 1984
('Leonaine' × 'Daydream') × 'Milestone'; sdlg no. KK45/2
Fl. 72 mm wide; perianth segments buff yellow, with white at base; corona pink apricot, near to red. Mid-season

'Red Stream' 2 Y-YRR
(D.S. Bell) D.S. Bell, 1958
Corona broad, very shallow, deep red, paling to gold at base

'Red Sun' 3 W-O
(Mrs R.O. Backhouse, pre-1921)
Resembles an improved 'Red Planet'

'Red Sundew' 2 Y-YRR
(W.F.M. Copeland, pre-1911)
Fl. 108 mm wide; perianth segments rich cream yellow, flushed full yellow at base, overlapping; corona closely ribbed, almost crimson, with yellow at base, mouth heavily frilled. Early. Resembles a more vividly coloured 'Sunrise'

'Red Sunrise' 2 Y-O
(C.W. Culpepper) C.W. Culpepper, 1957
'Fortune' × 'Dick Wellband'
Perianth segments pale yellow; corona reddish orange

'Red Sunset' 3 W-? (b)
(W.F.M. Copeland, pre-1916)

'Red Supreme' 2 Y-R
(Konynenburg & Mark) Konynenburg & Mark, 1962
'Red Goblet' × 'Contrapunt'
Fl. 95 mm wide, of strong substance; perianth segments vivid yellow 12A; corona orange-red (near 32A). Mid-season

'Red Surprise' 3 (a)
(R.H. Bath, pre-1933)

'Red Tartan' 2 Y-O
(Mrs R.O. Backhouse, pre-1921)
Perianth segments primrose yellow; corona rich orange, flushed scarlet, frilled, with rim flanged

'Red Torch' 2 Y-R
(C.E. Radcliff, 1929)
'Torch' × 'Militant'

'Red Treasure' 2 Y-R
(J.A. O'More) J.A. O'More, 1972
'Dunkeld' × 'Sun Chariot'
Fl. 100 mm wide

'Red Triumph' 2 Y-?
(A. Overton) A. Overton, 1960

'Red Trombone' 2 (a)
(Miss K.M. Hinchliff, pre-1937)

'Red Trumpeter' 2 Y-O
(A.E. Lowe, pre-1927)
Corona reddish orange

'Red Turban' 2 Y-R
(G. Lewis) D.S. Bell, 1955
Perianth segments broadly ovate in outline, blunt or rounded at apex, mucronate, a little reflexed, overlapping one-third to a half; the inner segments narrower, more nearly spreading, creased, with margins slightly wavy or incurled; corona bowl-shaped, lightly frilled. Formerly named 'Red Turbin'

'Red Turbin' 2 Y-R
Syn. of 'Red Turban'

'Red Vale' 2 O-O
(Colin Crotty) Unregistered
Sdlg no. 37-76

'Red Valley' 2 Y-? (a)
Syn. of 'Sun Valley'

'Red Velvet'
(?G. Lewis, pre-1940)

'Redwald' 1 W-? (b)
(W. Welchman, pre-1908)

'Red Wheel'
(C. Goodson, pre-1930)

PC(e)(NZ) 1930

'Red White and Blue'
(J.H. Hinsby, pre-1937)

'Red Wing' 3 Y-OOR
(T. Buncombe, 1912)
? 'Lucifer' × ?'Barcarolle'
Fl. star-shaped; perianth segments somewhat obovate, blunt, slightly mucronate, creamy yellow, tinged pink, spreading, creased, overlapping a quarter; the inner segments narrower, ovate; corona almost disc-shaped, ribbed, scarlet, paling to yellow-orange at base. Mid-season

'Redwing' 2 Y-O
(C. Goodson, pre-1927)
Corona reddish orange

'Red Wing' 2 W-? (b)
(J.N. Hancock & Co., pre-1949)
Corona disc-shaped, with crimson-orange at rim

'Red Wing' 2 Y-R
(D.S. Bell) D.S. Bell, 1957
Perianth segments deep yellow; corona broad bowl-shaped, fiery red

'Redwood' 2 Y-O
(R.C.A. Tombleson) R.C.A. Tombleson, 1968

'Redwyn' 2 (a)
(Mrs M.Moorby) Mrs M.Moorby, 1956

'Reed Warbler' 2 W-? (b)
(E.B. Champernowne, pre-1948)

'Reference Point' 2 YYW-Y
(J.S.B. Lea) Clive Postles Daffodils, 1987
'Daydream' × 'Creag Dubh'; sdlg no. LI-18-76
Perianth segments broadly ovate, blunt, yellow, with white mucro and with white at base, spreading, plane, smooth, with broad and pale midrib showing, regular, overlapping half; corona funnel-shaped, amber yellow, mouth slightly expanded and a little wavy, rim densely and minutely notched. Mid-season

'Referendum' 2 W-P
(*c*.1978) Unregistered

'Refined Gold' 1 Y-Y
(J.R. Pearson & Sons, pre-1927)
*HC(g) 1927

'Refinement' 1 Y-Y
(C.G. van Tubergen, pre-1926)
Fl. 102 mm wide, facing down; perianth segments pale lemon yellow, overlapping half; corona buttercup yellow with mouth expanded and rim flanged. Mid-season. AM(Haarlem) 1926

'Reflection' 2 W-P
(G.L. Wilson, pre-1947)
'Raphoe' × 'Wild Rose'

'Reflection' 2 W-YOO
(J.N. Hancock & Co., pre-1949)
Corona deep orange, paling to deep yellow at base, with rim closely and deeply notched, as if fringed

N. reflexus Brotero = *N. triandrus* var. *triandrus*

N. reflexus Loiseleur-Deslongchamps = *N. triandrus* var. *loiseleurii*

'Reflexus' 9
Selection from *N. poeticus*

'Reform' 2 (a)
(Sir C.H. Cave, pre-1908)

'Refrain' 2 W-P
(G.E. Mitsch) G.E. Mitsch, 1982
'Romance' × 'Cool Flame'; sdlg no. LL14/4
Fl. 104 mm wide; perianth segments broadly ovate or very broad, slightly truncate, only very slightly mucronate, spreading, plane, with margins minutely incurling at apex, overlapping half or more; the inner segments narrower, a little inflexed, with margins wavy; corona bowl-shaped, smooth, salmon pink, mouth straight, split in places and overlapping, loosely frilled. Mid-season. Resembles a taller 'Romance' of deeper colour with fewer nicks in the perianth segments

'Refresh' 3 W-R
(P. & G. Phillips) P. & G. Phillips, 1981
Fl. 105 mm wide. Mid-season

'Refreshment' 2 W-Y
(Sir F.C. Stern, pre-1953)
Perianth segments clean white; corona broad, soft rich yellow, with mouth regularly and heavily frilled. Mid-season

'Refulgence' 2 Y-O
(R.H. Bath, pre-1910)
Perianth segments deep yellow. Late

'Regal' 1 (a)
(F.H. Chapman, pre-1923)

'Regal' 1 Y-Y
(A. Overton) A. Overton, 1960

'Regal Bliss' 2 W-GWW
(Brian S. Duncan) Rathowen Daffodils, 1982
'Easter Moon' × 'Knowehead'
Fl. 120 mm wide; perianth segments broadly ovate, mucronate, spreading, plane, regular, overlapping half; the inner segments more narrowly ovate, blunt,

shouldered at base, a little inflexed; corona cylindrical, with mouth slightly expanded and lightly frilled. Mid-season

'Regal Coin' 1 Y-Y
(T. Morrison) T. Morrison, 1960

'Regal Crest' 2 W-GWY
(D.S. Bell) D.S. Bell, 1960
'Papanui Queen' × 'Green Island'
Fl. 105 mm wide; perianth segments broad, rounded, pure white, of good substance, overlapping; corona almost disc-shaped, very broad, white, with green at base and a broad band of buttercup yellow at rim. Mid-season. Resembles 'Green Island' but with the perianth segments more nearly plane

'Regal Gold' 1 Y-Y
(D. Bramley) D. Bramley, 1963
Fl. 121 mm wide, golden yellow. Mid-season. Resembles a darker-coloured 'Kingscourt' with larger perianth segments of stronger substance

'Regalia' 2 W-? (b)
(H. Backhouse, pre-1908)

'Regalia' 2 W-W
(D.S. Bell, 1947) D.S. Bell, 1958

'Regalis' 2 W-YYO
(J.N. Hancock & Co., 1947) J.N. Hancock & Co., 1960
Corona expanded, gold, with a band of orange at rim and the rim dentate

'Regality' 1 (a)
(G. Zandbergen-Terwegen, pre-1936)

'Regality' 3 W-YOO
(F. Rijnveld & Sons) F. Rijnveld & Sons, 1957
AM(Haarlem) 1957

'Regal Pink' 2 W-P
(J.L. Richardson) Mrs H.K. Richardson, 1964
('Rose of Tralee' × 'Lisbreen') × 'Rose Caprice'
Perianth segments roundish; corona soft pink, with rim widely rolled. Resembles a much taller 'Pink Monarch'

'Regal Status' 1 Y-Y
(H.A. Brown, 1943) J.N. Hancock & Co., 1959
Fl. deep yellow; perianth segments broadly ovate, overlapping; corona with rim rolled

'Regan' 3 W-? (b)
(Barr & Sons, pre-1929)

'Regard' 2 (a)
(A.H. Ahrens) J.S. Leitch, 1955

'Regency' 3 W-? (b)
(Barr & Sons, pre-1946)

'Regency' 1 Y-Y
(J.N. Hancock & Co., c.1977) Unregistered
Fl. rich yellow

'Regency Lace' 1 W-W
(G. Lewis) D.S. Bell, 1955
?'Ledbury' × 'Kanchenjunga'
See also 'Regency Lane'

'Regency Lane' 1 W-W
Syn. of 'Regency Lace'

'Regency Rose' 2 W-P
(G.H. Johnstone, pre-1954)

'Regeneration' 7 YYW-W
(R. & E.Havens) R. & E.Havens, 1995
'Hillstar' × 'Quick Step'; sdlg no. Y91/1
Fls 3-5 per stem, 65 mm wide; perianth segments ovate, sharp lemon yellow, spreading, plane; corona bowl-shaped, opening the same colour as the perianth, becoming creamy white, with mouth wavy. Late. Scented

'Regent' 1 Y-Y
(New Zealand origin, pre-1914)
Fl. pale clear yellow. Early

'Regent' 2 Y-Y
(F.H. Chapman, pre-1930)
'Kestrel' × 'Fortune'

'Regent Palace' 4 W-P
(Brian S. Duncan) Rathowen Daffodils, 1988
Richardson sdlg 3509 × 'Polonaise' × 'Valinor'; sdlg no. 968
Perianth and other petaloid segments white; corona segments interspersed, deep pink. Mid-season to late

'Reggae' 6 W-GPP
(Brian S. Duncan) Rathowen Daffodils, 1981
'Roseworthy' × 'Foundling'; sdlg no. 450
Corona deep pink, with green at base. Mid-season. Resembles 'Foundling' but with more strongly reflexed perianth segments and a smaller corona

'Regina' 8 W-?
(pre-1807)

'Regina' 1 W-? (b)
(J. Gerritsen & Son, pre-1934)

'Regina' 3 W-? (b)
(C.A. van der Wereld) C.A. van der Wereld, 1956

'Reginald' 2 (a)
(R.H. Bath, pre-1929)

'Reginald Dixon' 2 Y-O
(F. Rijnveld & Sons, pre-1939)
AM(Haarlem) 1940

'Reginald Foort' 1 (a)
(F. Rijnveld & Sons, pre-1937)
AM(Haarlem) 1937

'Reginald Vance' 2 Y-GYO
(L.P.Dettman, 1975) Unregistered
'Bubbles' × 'Camelot'; sdlg no. 58/77

'Regina Margherita' 1 (a)
(Italian origin, pre-1902)

'Regina Pacis' 1 W-W
(J.W.A. Lefeber, pre-1945)

'Regina Victoria' 1 W-? (b)
(C. Alkemade, pre-1944)

'Regoli' 2 (a)
(R. Hyde) R. Hyde, 1955

'Regularity' 1 W-W
(C.G. van Tubergen, pre-1930)
Fl. 99 mm wide, facing down; perianth segments creamy white, overlapping half; corona pale cream. Mid-season to late

N. regulosus Sweet = *N.* × *odorus*

'Reg Wootton' 2 W-P
(J.A. O'More) J.A. O'More, 1971
'Moorpark' × 'Fintona'
Fl. 125 mm wide

'Rehoboth' 2 W-W
(G.E. Mitsch, 1955) G.E. Mitsch, 1966
'Green Island' × 'Chinese White'; sdlg no. R33/5
Fl. 108 mm wide; corona shallow, of almost Div. 3 proportions. Mid-season

'Reigh Count' 2 (a)
(P.D. Williams, pre-1930)
Sdlg no. 494

'Reine Blanche' 8 W-W
(pre-1829)

'Reine Blanche' 2 W-W
(J.W.A. Lefeber, 1942) J.W.A. Lefeber, 1960
Fl. 70 mm wide; perianth segments pure white; corona widely expanded, white, with a touch of pale green at base, with lemon yellow at rim on opening. Mid-season

'Reine de France' 8?
(pre-1831)

'Reine de Pas Bas' 8 W-Y
Syn. of 'Queen of the Netherlands'

'Reine de Persi' 8 W-W
(pre-1851)

'Reine de Portugal' 8 Y-Y
(pre-1807)
Fl. sulphur yellow

'Reine des fleurs' 8 Y-Y
(pre-1807)

'Reine d'Espagne' 8 W-O
(pre-1807)

'Reine des Pays Bas' 8
(pre-1931)
?Syn. of 'Queen of the Netherlands'

'Rejerrah'
(G.H. Johnstone)

'Rejoice' 3 W-GYR
(W.G. Pannill) W.G. Pannill, 1992
'Bithynia'x 'Merlin'; sdlg no. D 9 C
Fl. 90 mm wide. Late

'Rekuna' 3 W-GYR
(W. Jackson Jr, 1969) Unregistered
'Arbar' × sdlg 208/65; sdlg no. 128/69

'Relda' 2 Y-O
(J.S. Leitch) J.S. Leitch, 1967
Corona reddish orange

'Relentless' 1 Y-P
(Jackson's Daffodils) Jackson's Daffodils, 1992
'Daydream' × 'Lalita'; sdlg no. 189/84
Fl. 97 mm wide; perianth segments very broadly ovate, blunt, obscurely mucronate, brilliant greenish yellow 5B, with a faint band of white at base, spreading, plane, overlapping half; the inner segments narrower, a little inflexed, somewhat creased at midrib; corona funnel-shaped, smooth, pale orange-pink (19D), with mouth flared and lightly frilled. Mid-season to late

'Reliability' 1 (a)
(M. van Waveren & Sons, pre-1942)

'Reliance' 2 W-? (b)
(C. Smith, pre-1907)

'Reliance' 2 W-Y
(M.J. Jefferson-Brown) M.J. Jefferson-Brown, 1975
Corona primrose. Mid-season. Resembles 'Green Island' but with the perianth segments more nearly acute and the larger corona more widely flanged

'Reliance' 2 W-? (b)
Syn. of 'Substance'

'Relief' 2 (a)
(Sir C.H. Cave, pre-1928)

'Relieve' 1 W-W
Syn. of 'Rosamundi'

'Relish' 2 Y-? (a)
(M.P. Williams, pre-1938)

'Relish' 2 W-W
(C.E. Radcliff, 1945)
'Nautilus' × 'Slemish'

'Relko' 2 W-O
(Mrs H.K. Richardson) Mrs H.K. Richardson, 1972
'Kilworth' × 'Arbar'
Perianth segments broadly ovate, ice white; corona very shallow bowl-shaped, orange, with rim dentate

'Remake' 4 Y-Y
(K.J. Heazlewood) K.J. Heazlewood, 1972
'Fiji' × 'Golden Castle'
Fl. 89 mm wide

'Remalia' 2 (a)
(Warnaar & Co., pre-1936)

'Remark' 2 W-PPY
(C.E. Radcliff, 1940)
'Glendevie' × 'Dawnglow'

'Remarquable' 1 Y-Y
(de Graaff Bros, pre-1897)
Perianth segments rich primrose yellow; corona ribbed, dark golden yellow, frilled

'Rembrandt' 1 (a)
(J. de Groot & Sons, pre-1907)

'Rembrandt' 8 W-YYO
(Dutch origin, pre-1920)
Perianth segments pure white; corona golden yellow, with orange at rim

'Rembrandt' 1 Y-Y
(G. Lubbe & Son, pre-1926)
Fl. 108 mm wide; perianth segments broadly ovate, vivid yellow 9B, slightly inflexed, overlapping half; the inner segments somewhat twisted; corona funnel-shaped, smooth at base, lightly ribbed towards mouth, vivid yellow 12A, with rim widely flanged and very deeply dentate, with margins recurved. Early to mid-season. 2n=28. Resembles a large-flowered 'King Alfred' with broader perianth segments. Syn. 'Jacob Maris'. AM(Haarlem) 1926, *AM(g) 1959, *FCC(g) 1965, *AM(p) 1978

'Rembrandt' 3 W-R
?See also 'Rembrant'

'Rembrant' 3 W-R
(A.E. Lowe, pre-1927)
?Syn. of 'Rembrandt'

'Remembered Kiss' 2 W-WWP
(Sidney DuBose, 1982) Sidney DuBose, 1996
Sdlg C43-6 ('Dove Song' × 'Carita') × sdlg D27-1 ('Eminent' × 'Cordial'); sdlg no. I58-13
Fl. 92 mm wide; perianth segments broadly ovate, blunt or rounded at apex, spreading, plane, overlapping half; corona cup-shaped, white, with a broad band of deep pink at rim, frilled. Mid-season

'Remembrance' 2 (a)
(Mrs R.O. Backhouse, pre-1921)

'Remembrance' 1 W-? (b)
(de Graaff Bros, pre-1927)

'Remembrance' 2 W-Y
(C.M. Grullemans) J.J. Grullemans & Sons, 1959
Fl. 115 mm wide; perianth segments creamy white; corona vivid yellow 17B, with light yellow 10C at base. Late

'Remie' 2 W-? (b)
(Oregon Bulb Farms, pre-1951)

'Reminder' 2 W-? (b)
(Alister Clark, 1950) J. Sharp, 1960

'Remis' 2 W-P
(W. Jackson Jr, 1956) W. Jackson Jr, 1966
'Ceram' × sdlg 86/51

N. rempolensis Parlatore = *N. corcyrensis*

rempolensis = *N. tazetta*

'Remuera' 1 W-? (b)
(Sir A.P.W. Thomas, pre-1930)

'Remulus' 7
(de Graaff Bros, pre-1927)

'Remus' 1 Y-Y
(Mrs R.O. Backhouse, pre-1921)

'Rena' 2 Y-Y
(R.J. Mack) E. Dalley, 1989
'Gold Bank' × 'Top Notch'
Fl. 105 mm wide. Early

'Renaissance' 3 W-W
(F.E. Board) F.E. Board, 1965
Richardson cross 2337 × G.L.Wilson sdlg 36/190

'Renate Tebaldi' 1 W-W
(J.W.A. Lefeber) J.W.A. Lefeber, 1958
Fl. creamy white; corona darker in tone than the perianth

'Renato' 4 W-Y
(J.L. Richardson) D.A. Lloyd, 1962
Fl. 102 mm wide; corona segments primrose yellow. Mid-season. Resembles 'Double Event' but with the corona segments more closely frilled

N. renaudii Bavoux = *N. pseudonarcissus*

'Rendezvous' 2 W-? (b)
(D.S. Bell) D.S. Bell, 1959

'Rendlesham' 2 W-? (b)
(Mrs R.O. Backhouse, pre-1921)

'Rendlesham Beauty' 2 W-? (b)
(Mrs R.O. Backhouse, pre-1921)

'Rendlesham Perfection' 2 W-? (b)
(R.F. Calvert, pre-1935)

'Rendlesham Rose' 2 W-P
(Trenoweth Valley Flower Farm, pre-1948)

'Rendova' 2 W-Y
(S.J. Bisdee, 1945) S.J. Bisdee, 1956
'Nissa' hybrid

'René de Chalons' 2 Y-O
(G.A. Uit den Boogaard, pre-1938)
Perianth segments lemon yellow; corona cup-shaped, soft orange, frilled. AM(Haarlem) 1938

'Renee' 1 W-W
(D.V. West, pre-1935)
Corona narrow, with rim flanged

'Renée Donaldson' 2 Y-O
(Warnaar & Co.) Warnaar & Co., 1959
'Westminster' × 'Carbineer'
Fl. 115 mm wide; perianth segments light sulphur yellow; corona shallow, widely expanded, reddish orange. Mid-season. AM(Haarlem) 1960

'Renee Gouma' 2 W-YYR
(L.P. Dettman) L.P. Dettman, 1978
'Diane Barker' × 'Lynette Sholl'; sdlg no. 54/68
Fl. 85 mm wide; perianth segments greenish white (155A); corona brilliant yellow 13C, with green at base and light orange-red (33C) at rim. Mid-season. Resembles an earlier-flowered 'Diane Barker'

'Renegade' 2 Y-O
(J.N. Hancock & Co., pre-1949)

'Renelgin' 1 Y-Y
(S.J. Bisdee, 1943)
'Renown' × 'Elgin'

'Renewal' 3 W-GYO
(V. Brink) V. Brink, 1972
'Mystic' × 'Sylvia O'Neill'
Fl. 65 mm wide

'Renishaw' 2 W-O
(F.E. Board) F.E. Board, 1965
'Nearula' × 'Arbar'; sdlg no. 1281
Late

'Renmark' 9
(pre-1949)

'Renmark' 2 W-YRR
(W.M. Spry, pre-1975) Unregistered
'Margerie' × Ronalds sdlg
Corona chrome yellow, with orange-scarlet at rim.
Late

'Rennoc' 2 W-W
(J.H. Davenport) Mrs E. Milliken, 1974
'Kanchenjunga' hybrid
Fl. 116 mm wide

'Renny' 2 (a)
(C.G. van Tubergen, pre-1948)

'Renocore' 1 W-Y
(J.H. Davenport) Mrs E. Milliken, 1974
'Trostan' hybrid
Fl. 120 mm wide

'Renown' 1 Y-Y
(D.V. West, pre-1923)
Perianth segments primrose yellow; corona deep yellow, frilled

'Renown II' 1 (a)
Syn. of 'Mortlake'

'Renvyle' 1 W-Y
(J.L. Richardson) Mrs H.K. Richardson, 1963
'Broughshane' × 'Cape Horn'
Perianth segments broadly ovate, pure white; corona creamy buff, with rim dentate and slightly rolled

'Repaid' 4 W-P
(K.J. Heazlewood) K.J. Heazlewood, 1972
Fl. 89 mm wide

'Reparation' 1 W-W
(A. Gibson, pre-1951)

'Repartee' 2 Y-W
(G.E. Mitsch) G.E. Mitsch, 1972
'Gleeful' × 'Daydream'; sdlg no. D44/12
Fl. 90 mm wide

'Repeal' 3 W-Y
(K.J. Heazlewood) K.J. Heazlewood, 1968
'Crepello' × 'Nevose'
Fl. 95 mm wide; corona buff yellow, frilled. Mid-season

'Replete' 4 W-P
(Murray W. Evans) Murray W. Evans, 1975
'Pink Chiffon' × 'Accent'; sdlg no. L-43/1
Fl. 105 mm wide; perianth and other petaloid segments white; the outer whorl broadly ovate, blunt, prominently mucronate, spreading, overlapping half; the inner whorls shorter, crumpled, strongly inflexed; corona segments half as long as the inner whorls and interspersed among them, broad, reddish pink, frilled. Mid-season. 2n=28

'Repose' 2 W-WPP
(S.J. Bisdee, 1941)
'White Sentinel' × 'Pink o' Dawn'

'Repose' 2 YYW-YYW
(G.E. Mitsch) G.E. Mitsch, 1982
'Quick Step' × 'Daydream'; sdlg no. HH107/5
Fl. 82 mm wide; perianth segments luminous lemon gold, with white at base; corona apricot buff, paling to cream at rim. Late

'Reprieve' 3 W-GWY
(G.L. Wilson, pre-1947)
'Silver Coin' × 'Crimson Braid'
Perianth segments greenish ivory white; corona primrose white, with soft green at base and lemon at rim, frilled. 2n=28

'Reproof' 2 Y-R
(W. Jackson Jr, pre-1952)
'Chungking' × 'Kai'

'Repton' 1 (a)
(R.H. Bath, pre-1931)

'Reputation' 2 W-? (b)
(J.A. Morris) J.A. Morris, 1957

'Request' ?-P
(Alister Clark, pre-1948)

'Request' 1 W-Y
(J.N. Hancock & Co., pre-1949)
Corona with mouth expanded and rim dentate

'Request' 2 W-W
(K.J. Heazlewood) K.J. Heazlewood, 1971
'Glenshesk' × 'Castle of Mey'
Fl. 115 mm wide

'Requiem' 3 Y-GYO
(Mrs G. Link) Mrs G. Link, 1989
'Tynemouth' × 'Altruist'; sdlg no. 2877-B

Corona bowl-shaped, frilled. Late

N. requienii Roemer = *N. assoanus*

'Research' 2 W-? (b or c)
(Sir C.H. Cave, pre-1928)

'Reserve' 2 Y-O
(G.L. Wilson, pre-1952)
'Carbineer' × 'Bahram'
Corona reddish orange. Late

'Resolute' 2 Y-Y
(G.H. Engleheart, pre-1897)
'Grandee' × variant of *N. poeticus*
Fl. facing down; perianth segments broadly ovate, blunt, prominently mucronate, creamy yellow, tinged with darker yellow at base, slightly inflexed, with margins wavy, with midrib showing, overlapping a quarter; the inner segments more strongly inflexed, twisted; corona cylindrical, short, loosely ribbed, clear yellow, with mouth straight, frilled

'Resolution' 2 (a)
(R.G. Sharp, pre-1930)

'Respect' 2 Y-Y
(J.H. Rijkelijkhuizen) J.H. Rijkelijkhuizen, 1964
Fl. 90 mm wide; perianth segments brilliant greenish yellow 4A; corona vivid yellow 15B. Mid-season. Resembles a dark-coloured 'Carlton'. Syn. 'Respectability'

'Respectability' 2 Y-Y
Syn. of 'Respect'

'Respite' 2 W-P
(G.J. Phillips) Unregistered
Sdlg no. 75-78-2

'Resplendence' 3 W-? (b)
(L. van Leeuwen & Son, pre-1933)

'Resplendent' 2 Y-R
(G.E. Mitsch, 1966) G.E. Mitsch, 1977
('Narvik' × 'California Gold') × 'Flaming Meteor'; sdlg no. B45/14
Fl. 100 mm wide; perianth segments broadly ovate, blunt, rich clear yellow, with slight white mucro, spreading or very slightly reflexed, somewhat concave, smooth, overlapping half; the inner segments more nearly spreading, sometimes creased; corona short funnel-shaped, smooth, vivid orange-red, with mouth straight, tightly frilled. Mid-season

'Resplendent' 9
Syn. of 'Lady Sylvia'

'Ressaldar' 2 (a)
(G.H. Johnstone, pre-1946)

'Restormel' 2 W-? (b)
(P.D. Williams, pre-1933)

'Result' 2 (a)
(J.E. Exley, pre-1950)

'Retainer' 2 W-? (b)
(G.H. Engleheart, pre-1910)

'Rethel' 3 W-YYR
(J.T. Gray, pre-1936)
Perianth segments broad, blunt, overlapping; corona widely expanded. AM(e)(NZ) 1936

'Retreat' 2 Y-R
(W.J. Dunlop) W.J. Dunlop, 1957
'Dunkeld' × 'Bahram'

'Retreat' 3 W-YYR
(Australian origin, pre-1955) Unregistered
Corona disc-shaped, yellow, with deep red at rim

'Retro' 2 W-P
(Alister Clark, 1930) J. Sharp, 1960

'Return' 3 W-? (b)
(pre-1934)
Perianth segments snow white, overlapping

'Return' 2 W-O
(A. Overton) A. Overton, 1960
Perianth segments broad

'Reuter' 1 Y-Y
Syn. of 'Routor'

'Rêve d'Or' 2 Y-? (a)
(Mrs R.O. Backhouse, pre-1921)
AM(Haarlem) 1928

'Réveille' 2
(F.H. Chapman, pre-1916)

'Reveille' 1 W-Y
(T. Bloomer) Rathowen Daffodils, 1978
'Alpine Eagle' × 'Downpatrick'; sdlg no. 4/75/65
Fl. 120 mm wide. Mid-season. Resembles a larger and much stronger 'Downpatrick'

'Reveille' 11?a W-Y
(?Australian origin, pre-1990) Unregistered

'Revelation' 2 W-Y
(W.G. Pannill) W.G. Pannill, 1970
'Bizerta' × 'Festivity'

'Revelite' 2 Y-O
(J.S. Leitch) J.S. Leitch, 1960
Corona reddish orange

'Reveller' 2 W-YOR
(F.H. Chapman, pre-1938)

'Reveller' 2 Y-YYR
(S.J. Bisdee, 1949)
'Market Merry' × 'Dunkeld'

'Revelry' 2 Y-O
(J.L. Richardson, pre-1948)
'Carbineer' × 'Bahram'
Fl. about 100 mm wide; perianth segments broadly ovate, blunt, slightly mucronate, brilliant yellow 8A, spreading, with margins very slightly incurving at apex, smooth and of good substance, regular, overlapping half; the inner segments narrower, shouldered at base, with margins more strongly incurved; corona cup-shaped, strong orange 30D, mouth straight, slightly expanded, lightly frilled, with rim widely crenate. AM(Haarlem) 1949, AM(e) 1951

'Revenge' 1 W-? (b)
(Sir C.H. Cave, pre-1928)

'Revenge' 1 Y-Y
(J.L. Richardson) Mrs H.K. Richardson, 1964
Sdlg 693 open pollinated

'Reverbera' 1 Y-WWY
(J. Gerritsen & Son) J. Gerritsen & Son, 1961
'Citrix' hybrid
Fl. 120 mm wide; brilliant greenish yellow 6C; corona white, with sulphur yellow at rim. Early. Resembles a darker-flowered 'Citrix'

'Reverend A.M.Boeyenga' 2 or 3 (b or c)
(pre-1938)

'Reverend C.A.Gottwaltz' 1 Y-Y
(J. Mallender, pre-1913)
Perianth segments overlapping; corona flared

'Reverend Charles Digby' 5 W-Y
(G.H. Engleheart, pre-1903)
AM 1903

'Reverend C.Wolley-Dod' 2 Y-Y
Syn. of 'Charles Wolley-Dod'

'Reverend D.R.Williamson' 1 Y-Y
(Barr & Sons, pre-1904)
Perianth segments broadly ovate, blunt, soft primrose yellow, inflexed, somewhat ribbed, overlapping one-third; the inner segments more strongly inflexed, twisted; corona cylindrical, smooth at base, ribbed towards mouth, rich golden yellow, with mouth expanded and rim crenate. See also 'Reverend R.D.Williamson'

'Reverend Ewbank' 1 W-? (b)
(R.A. van der Schoot, pre-1923)

'Reverend Frederick Tymons' 1 W-Y
(Irish origin, pre-1922)
Perianth segments spreading or a little inflexed, twisted, separated; corona funnel-shaped, ribbed. Usually dwarf. Very early. Resembles a more richly coloured 'Creagh Castle Seedling'. Thought to be derived from 'Princeps'

'Reverend Gilbert Raynor' 1 W-W
(Barr & Sons, pre-1927)

'Reverend Joseph Jacob' 1 W-? (b)
(R.A.van der Schoot, pre-1931)

'Reverend R.D.Williamson' 1 Y-Y
Syn. of 'Reverend D.R.Williamson'

'Reverend S.E.Bourne'
(pre-1914)

'Reverie' 3 W-? (b)
(Barr & Sons, pre-1933)

'Reverie' 2 YYW-W
(Brian S. Duncan) Rathowen Daffodils, 1979
'Daydream' hybrid; sdlg no. 154
Fl. 86 mm wide; perianth segments deep luminous yellow, with a clearly defined band of pure white at base; corona expanded, becoming pure white. Mid-season. Resembles a smaller 'Daydream' of brighter and more contrasting colours

'Reversa' 3 (d)
(Barr & Sons, pre-1941)

'Reverse Image' 11a Y-W
(John R.Reed) John R.Reed, 1997
'Split' × 'Salem'; sdlg no. 80-110-4
Fl. 92 mm wide; perianth segments broadly ovate, opening light yellow, becoming darker in tone; corona split to base, the six segments narrower than the perianth segments, spreading, dull white. Mid-season

'Review' 2 W-Y
(G.W.E. Brogden) G.W.E. Brogden, 1966
Fl. 108 mm wide; corona biscuit yellow. Mid-season

'Revillee' 2 W-? (b)
(de Graaff Bros, pre-1936)
AM(Haarlem) 1936

'Revival' 4 W-R
(M.J. Jefferson-Brown, pre-1985) Unregistered
'Gaytime' × 'Rockall'

'Revivalist' 2 (a)
(J.E. Exley, pre-1950)

'Revlon' 2 W-ORR
(J.L. Richardson) C.R. Wootton, 1968
'Kilworth' × 'Signal Light'
Fl. 95 mm wide; corona orange-red, paling to base. Mid-season

'Revolute' 6 Y-O
(V. Brink) V. Brink, 1969
'Emperor' × 'Larkelly'

'Rewa' 2 W-O
(N.Y. Lower, pre-1928)
'Bernardino' × 'Fortune'
Fl. rounded; perianth segments very broadly ovate, rounded at apex, prominently mucronate, pure white, spreading, a little concave either side of midrib, overlapping half; the inner segments only very slightly mucronate, with margins wavy and sometimes notched near mid-point; corona broad bowl-shaped, smooth, bright pinkish apricot orange, mouth expanded, split in places and overlapping, loosely frilled, rim minutely ribbed. Mid-season. Resembles 'Bernardino' in colouring and 'Fortune' in form. AM(e) 1931, AM(Haarlem) 1933, *HC(g) 1936, *AM(g) 1946

'Reward' 9 W-GYR
(H.G. Longford, pre-1927)
Perianth segments shining white; corona citron yellow, with green at base and deep red at rim. Late

'Reward' 1 Y-Y
(G.W.E. Brogden) G.W.E. Brogden, 1963
'Galway' × 'Goldena'
Fl. 115 mm wide, deep yellow. Early. Resembles 'Ohakea' in form

'Rex' 1 Y-Y
(C.G. van Tubergen, pre-1929)
Perianth segments primrose yellow; corona lemon yellow, with mouth widely expanded. AM(Haarlem) 1929. Received AM(Haarlem) 1929 as 'Royalty'

'Rexcourt' 1 (a)
(D.H.L. Corrigan, pre-1951)

'Reynella' 2 W-WWP
(H.A. Brown, 1941)

'Reynoldstown' 2 Y-R
(J.L. Richardson, pre-1936)
'Damson' × 'Marksman'
Perianth segments rich deep yellow; corona narrow, deep yellowish scarlet. 2n=28

'Rezare' 2 Y-O
(Brian S. Duncan) du Plessis Bros, 1990
'Patagonia' × 'Bunclody'; sdlg no. 626
Fl. 98 mm wide; perianth segments ovate, acute, very smooth; corona pure orange, with mouth lobed. Mid-season

'Rhamus' 3 W-R
(R.H.Glover, pre-1990) Unregistered
'Rockall' × 'Ida May'

'Rhana' 1 W-W
(A.O. Roblin, 1950)
Sdlg × 'Nizam'

'Rhanakim' 4 W-Y
(?Australian origin, pre-1990) Unregistered

'Rhapsody' 9 W-GYR
(G.H. Engleheart, pre-1913)
Fl. 70 mm wide; perianth segments white, with lemon at base, reflexed, overlapping two-thirds; corona very shallow bowl-shaped, greenish yellow, with green at base and a broad band of bright crimson at rim. Mid-season to late

'Rhapsody' 2 W-W
(W. Jackson Jr, 1964) Unregistered
'Green Valley' × 'Filia'; sdlg no. 57/64
Fl. white; perianth segments broadly ovate, blunt, not prominently mucronate, spreading, with broad midrib showing, overlapping half; the inner segments square-shouldered at base, a little inflexed; corona funnel-shaped, loosely ribbed, tinged green at base, mouth straight, wavy, rim irregularly notched, unevenly and obscurely crenate or almost entire. Mid-season

'Rhayader' 2 W-R
(A.M. Wilson, pre-1937)
Sdlg no. 665
Perianth segments ivory white; corona bright red

'R.H.Beamish' 1 W-Y
(R.H. Beamish, pre-1914)
Corona pale sulphur yellow

'Rhea' 1 W-Y
(Barr & Sons, pre-1904)
Corona golden yellow

'Rhea' 2 W-P
(G.E. Mitsch, 1962) G.E. Mitsch, 1975
'Accent' × 'Flamingo'; sdlg no. X45/4
Fl. 100 mm wide; corona clear pink. Mid-season. Resembles a more vigorous 'Flamingo' of more rapid increase with a broader perianth

'Rheban' 2 W-P
(J.M. Radcliff) P.J. Radcliff, 1989
'Dear Me' × 'Verran'
Fl. 95-100mm wide; perianth segments very broadly ovate, spreading, slightly concave, overlapping half; the inner segments narrower; corona pale purplish pink 56A, with mouth expanded, rim flanged. Mid-season. Sunproof

'Rheban Charm' 1 W-P
(J.M. Radcliff, 1977) P.J. Radcliff, 1989
'Maree' × J.M.Radcliff sdlg 20/58
Fl. 70-80 mm wide; perianth segments broadly ovate, blunt, spreading, of good substance, overlapping half; corona narrow, light yellowish pink 36A, mouth flared and lightly frilled. Mid-season to late. Sunproof

'Rheban Red' 2 Y-O
(J.M. Radcliff) P.J. Radcliff, 1990
Fl. forming a double triangle, 103 mm wide; perianth segments very broadly ovate, blunt, rich golden yellow, spreading and a little concave, regular, overlapping half or more; the inner segments shouldered at base; corona strong reddish orange, with mouth expanded and lightly frilled. Tall. Sunproof. Resembles 'No Peer'

'Rheban White' 1 W-W
(J.M. Radcliff, 1980) P.J. Radcliff, 1980
'Lady Slim' × 'Rashleigh'
Fl. 100 mm wide, pure white; perianth segments broadly ovate, spreading, overlapping half; corona funnel-shaped, with yellow noticeable in tube, lightly frilled, with rim rolled. Mid-season

'Rheingold' 1 Y-Y
(G.H. Engleheart, pre-1923)

'Rheingold' 4 Y-Y
(D.S. Bell) D.S. Bell, 1976
'Papua' × 'Hicol'
Fl. 107 mm wide, yellow, very slightly flushed pink. Mid-season. PC(e)(NZ) 1975

'Rhine' 1 W-Y
Syn. of 'Centenaire'

'Rhine Maiden' 2 W-P
(J.L. Richardson) J.L. Richardson, 1959
'Rosewell' × 'Salmon Trout'
Perianth segments broadly ovate, blunt, only very slightly mucronate, a little reflexed, plane, smooth, with midrib showing, overlapping one-third to a half; the inner segments more narrowly ovate, square-shouldered at base, a little inflexed, with margins slightly wavy and somewhat "thumbed"; corona funnel-shaped, with mouth straight and loosely frilled

'Rhinestone' 1 W-Y
(Brian S. Duncan) Rathowen Daffodils, 1979
'Joybell' × 'Empress of Ireland'; sdlg no. 587
Perianth segments broadly ovate, pure white; corona slightly constricted near mid-point, with mouth expanded and rim rolled. Mid-season. Resembles a deeper-coloured 'Form Master' with a larger corona

'Rhine Wine' 1 W-W
(W.G. Pannill) W.G. Pannill, 1978
'Desdemona' × 'Canisp'; sdlg no. 65/30 B

Fl. 120 mm wide. Mid-season

'Rhitta' 1 Y-Y
(S.J. Bisdee, 1939)
'Mortlake' × 'Golden City'

'Rhoda' 5 W-W
(G.H. Engleheart, pre-1912)

'Rhoda Adamson' 3 W-YYO
(P.D. Williams, pre-1934)

'Rhodesia' 2 W-W
(P. Phillips) P. Phillips, 1966
Fl. 108 mm wide. Mid-season. Resembles 'Zero' but with perianth segments inflexed and corona more widely flared

'Rhonda McLeod' 2 W-P
(L.P.Dettman, 1976) Unregistered
'Pink Treasure' × 'Verran'; sdlg no. P/V 1/77

'Rhondo' 1 Y-Y
(pre-1956) Unregistered
Fl. deep gold

'Rhymster' 9 W-?
(G.H. Engleheart, pre-1902)
Corona with dark scarlet at rim

'Rhythm' 9
(T. Buncombe, pre-1931)

'Rhythm' 1 W-? (b)
(A.H. Ahrens) J.S. Leitch, 1955

'Rialto' 2 Y-R
(Ballydorn Bulb Farm) Ballydorn Bulb Farm, 1974
'Gaucho' × 'Torero'
Fl. 96 mm wide

'Riamena' 2 (a)
(West & Fell, pre-1935)

'Riana' 2 W-P
(C.E. Radcliff, 1943) J.M.Radcliff, 1956
'Mitylene' × 'Rosario'

'Rianne' 2 W-PPY
(W.A. van Schie, 1976) W.A. van Schie, 1986
Perianth segments ivory white; corona with flecks of lemon yellow at rim. Mid-season

'Riband' 3 W-YYO
(Mrs R.O. Backhouse, pre-1921)
Perianth segments very broadly ovate in outline, blunt or squarish at apex, prominently mucronate, spreading, creased, overlapping half or more; the inner segments with margins wavy; corona broad disc-shaped, ribbed, deep yellow, with a broad band of orange at rim

'Ribbonwood' 2 W-G
(W.M. Spry, pre-1975) Unregistered
'Margerie' × Ronalds sdlg
Late

'Riber' 1 W-W
(D.B. Milne, pre-1950)

N. ricasolianus Parlatore = *N. patulus*

'Rich' 2 Y-YYO
(J.L. Richardson, pre-1937)

'Richard' 1 Y-Y
(N.Y. Lower, pre-1931)

'Richard Chandler' 2 Y-Y
(Ken Farmer Nurseries) Ken Farmer Nurseries, 1978
Fl. 129 mm wide. Mid-season

'Richard Cobden' 2 W-? (b)
(de Graaff Bros, pre-1928)

'Richard Crooks' 1 Y-Y
(Konynenburg & Mark) Konynenburg & Mark, 1966
('Lady Moore' × 'Orange Cup') × 'Bird of Dawning'
Fl. 110 mm wide; perianth segments buttercup yellow; corona lemon yellow. Mid-season

'Richard Strauss' 1 W-? (b)
(C.G. van Tubergen, pre-1914)
'Grandis' × *N. triandrus*

'Richard Tauber' 8 W-Y
(A. Vis, pre-1930)
Perianth segments creamy white; corona tightly ribbed, deep yellow. Syn. 'Caruso'. AM(Haarlem) 1931

'Richard Wagner' 2 W-? (b)
(J.W.A. Lefeber, pre-1943)

'Richelda' 7 W-Y
(J.W. Barr, pre-1926)
Fls usually 2 per stem; corona primrose yellow. Scented

'Richelieu' 4
(Mrs R.O. Backhouse, pre-1921)

'Richhill' 2 Y-YYR
(W.J. Dunlop) W.J. Dunlop, 1958
Perianth segments golden yellow; corona yellow, with a broad band of red at rim

'Richmond' 2 W-? (b)
(Mrs R.O. Backhouse, pre-1921)

Syn. 'Rudyard Kipling'

'Richmond Gem' 6 W-Y
E.W. Cotter, 1968
Perianth segments broad, milk white, slightly reflexed; corona large disc-shaped, pale lemon

'Rich Reward' 1 Y-W
(G.E. Mitsch) G.E. Mitsch, 1968
'Lunar Sea' × 'Bethany'; sdlg no. W11/1
Fl. 102 mm wide, deep lemon yellow; perianth segments deeply overlapping; corona somewhat narrow, becoming almost white. Mid-season

'Rich Strike'
Unregistered
Seed parent of 'Ivory Fashion'

'Ricom' 1 Y-Y
(W. Jackson Jr) Jackson's Daffodils, 1979
'Ristin' × 'Comal'; sdlg no. 25/73
Early to mid-season

'Rideau Hall' 3 W-YYO
(G. Lubbe & Son, pre-1939)
Corona buttercup yellow, with orange at rim. AM(Haarlem) 1939, FCC(Haarlem) 1943

'Ridgecrest' 3 W-YYO
(Brian S.Duncan) Brian S.Duncan, 1993
'Merlin' open pollinated; sdlg no. 1249
Fl. rounded, 98 mm wide; perianth segments very broadly ovate; corona shallow bowl-shaped, mid-yellow, with a mottled band of orange and deeper yellow at rim, lightly frilled. Mid-season

'Riding Mill' 3 W-Y
(G. Harrison) G. Harrison, 1968
'Chinese White' × 'Clockface'
Fl. 105 mm wide; corona pale yellow, with a darker tone at rim. Mid-season to late

'Riesenbeck' 2 W-YYO
(J.W.A. Lefeber, pre-1945)
Corona yellow, with orange at rim, frilled

'Riesling' 11a W-WWY
(J. Gerritsen & Son) J. Gerritsen & Son, 1974
'Grapillon' hybrid
Fl. 115 mm wide; corona segments opening soft yellow, slowly becoming creamy white, with vivid yellow 9A in tube and at rim and margins. Mid-season to late

'Rieti' 2 W-YYP
(R.V. Favell, pre-1946)
'Silver Coin' × 'Kilter'

rifanus = *N. romieuxii* subsp. *romieuxii* var. *rifanus*

'Rifleman' 3 W-? (b)
(H.G. Longford, pre-1927)

'Riga' 2 W-W
(Alister Clark, 1930) T. Morrison, 1960
Fl. pure white; corona slightly expanded

'Rigel' 3 W-? (b)
(A.M. Wilson, pre-1937)

'Right Angle' 1 Y-Y
(J.N. Hancock & Co., 1963) J.N. Hancock & Co., 1977
'Chromis' hybrid
Fl. 87 mm wide; perianth segments vivid yellow 12A; corona slightly darker in tone (13A). Early

'Right Royal' 2 Y-R
(Ballydorn Bulb Farm, 1969) Ballydorn Bulb Farm, 1980
'Rialto' open pollinated
Fl. 110 mm wide; perianth segments gold yellow; corona red. Early to mid-season. Resembles a stronger 'Rialto' of improved substance and colour

'Rigi' 2 W-P
(S.J. Bisdee, 1945)
Sdlg × 'Rosario'

'Rigoletto' 3 W-YYO
(The Brodie of Brodie, *c*.1910)
'Princess Mary' × *N. poeticus*
Perianth segments white, with yellow radiating from base; corona disc-shaped, yellow, with deep orange at rim

'Rigoletto' 2 W-Y
(Konynenburg & Mark) Konynenburg & Mark, 1960
Fl. 115 mm wide; perianth segments creamy white; corona brilliant yellow 12B. Late

'Riis' 3 Y-R
(W. Jackson Jr, 1967) Unregistered
'Rave' × 'Dimity'; sdlg no. 195/67

'Rijndam' 1 W-? (b)
(G.B. van Rhijn, pre-1951)

'Rijnveld's Early Sensation' 1 Y-Y
(F.H. Chapman, 1943) F. Rijnveld & Sons, 1956
Fl. 90 mm wide; perianth segments ovate, acute, brilliant greenish yellow 6C, inflexed, with margins a little incurved, overlapping a quarter; the inner segments more strongly inflexed, twisted; corona somewhat funnel-shaped, smooth, much deeper in tone (darker than 12A) than the perianth, mouth expanded, wavy, rim flanged, deeply notched and crenate. Very early. 2n=33. Syn. 'Early Sensation'. *AM(g) 1984, AGM 1993. Trade designation JANUARY

'Rikki' 7 W-Y
(A. Gray) A. Gray, 1962
N. rupicola subsp. *watieri* × *N. poeticus*
Fl. 40 mm wide; perianth segments very broadly ovate, blunt, prominently mucronate, light greenish yellow 8B, slightly reflexed, plane or a little concave, overlapping one-third to a half; the inner segments with margins deeply incurved or wavy; corona very shallow bowl-shaped, ribbed, vivid yellow 12A, with mouth widely expanded. Dwarf. Late. Resembles 'Sun Disc' but with more strongly contrasted colouring

'Rima' 1 W-P
(G.E. Mitsch, pre-1954)
'Kenmare' × 'Dawnglow'; sdlg no. O41/1
Perianth segments pure white, overlapping; corona rose lilac. Mid-season. 2n=28. Div. 2 until 1966

'Rimdeedee' 2 W-WWP
(M.G.Temple-Smith) M.G.Temple-Smith, 1995
'Foundling' × 'Fiddleedee'; sdlg no. 17/86
Corona spreading, white, with a very broad band of pink at rim. Late

'Rimfire' 2 (a)
(J. Bankhead, pre-1950)

'Rimfire' 2 W-? (b)
(pre-1956) Unregistered
Corona expanded, with a broad band of orange-red at rim

'Rimgold' 2 W-WWO
(D.S. Bell)
'Papanui Queen' × 'Green Island'

'Rimini' 2 Y-O
(A. Gibson, pre-1951)

'Rimlock'
(J.J. Brown, pre-1949)

'Rimmon' 3 W-GWY
(Brian S. Duncan) Rathowen Daffodils, 1981
'Woodland Prince' × 'Crepello'; sdlg no. 336
Fl. rounded, 102 mm wide; perianth segments very broad, squarish at apex, slightly mucronate, pure white, a little reflexed, concave at apex, very smooth, overlapping half or more; the inner segments narrower, roundish at apex, not noticeably mucronate, inflexed at base, reflexed at apex; corona very shallow bowl-shaped, ribbed, opening lemon yellow, becoming white, with green or yellow-green at base and a very broad band of golden yellow at rim. Mid-season

'Rim Ride' 3 W-GYO
(W.G. Pannill) W.G. Pannill, 1976
'Precedent' × 'Glenwherry'; sdlg no. D 52
Fl. 100 mm wide. Mid-season

'Rimski' 2 W-YWP
(Brian S. Duncan) Rathowen Daffodils, 1984
'Stainless' × 'Foundling'; sdlg no. 369
Corona with a broad band of apple blossom pink at rim. Mid-season

'Rimster' 2 W-YWP
(Brian S. Duncan) Rathowen Daffodils, 1984
'Roseworthy' hybrid × 'Foundling'; sdlg no. 370
Corona with copper pink at rim. Mid-season. Resembles a dwarf 'Rainbow'

'Rimutaka' 1 Y-Y
(J.S. Leitch) J.S. Leitch, 1968

'Rina' 5
(Barr & Sons, pre-1923)

'Rinadena' 5 W-W
(S.J. Bisdee, pre-1939)
'May Molony' × *N. triandrus*

'Rinegolde' 2 Y-Y
(S.J. Bisdee, 1947)
'Saint Egwin' × 'Golden Image'

'Rinfield' 2 (a)
(G.L. Wilson, pre-1937)

'Ring-a-Ling' 9 W-GOR
(Mrs M.S. Yerger) Mrs M.S. Yerger, 1986
'Lights Out' × 'Ace of Diamonds'; sdlg no. 75 L 1
Corona brilliant orange 25C, with moderate yellow-green 138B at base and orange-red (30A) at rim. Mid-season to late. Resembles 'Ace of Diamonds' but with a disc-shaped corona

'Ring-a-Rosy' 2 W-WWO
(A. Overton, pre-1960) Unregistered
Perianth segments broad; corona widely expanded, with coppery reddish orange at rim, frilled

'Ring Coin' 3 W-? (b)
(A.M. Wilson, pre-1916)

'Ringcraft' 2 W-YYR
(G. Lewis, pre-1945)

'Ringdove' 9 W-GYO
(E.M. Crosfield, pre-1913)
Fl. rounded, 73 mm wide; perianth segments very broad in outline, rounded or somewhat square at apex, prominently mucronate, pure white, spreading, of waxy texture, overlapping half or more; the inner segments only very slightly mucronate, square-shouldered and spathulate at base, with margins wavy; corona small disc-shaped, ribbed, yellow, with green at base and a narrow band of orange at rim. AM(Haarlem) 1927. See also 'Ring Dove'

'Ring Dove' 2 W-? (b)
(W.B. Hartland, pre-1914)

'Ring Dove' 9 W-GYO
Syn. of 'Ringdove'

'Ring Fence' 3 Y-YYR
(Brian S.Duncan) Brian S.Duncan, 1996
'Dateline' × 'Triple Crown'; sdlg no. 1471
Fl. 95 mm wide; perianth segments broadly ovate, acute, slightly mucronate, deep yellow; the inner segments not noticeably mucronate; corona shallow bowl-shaped, golden yellow, with a narrow and sharply defined band of deep red at rim, a little frilled. Mid-season to late

'Ringhaddy' 3 W-GYO
(Ballydorn Bulb Farm, 1977) Ballydorn Bulb Farm, 1989
Fl. 90 mm wide; perianth segments very broad, rounded at apex, plane, overlapping; corona very shallow bowl-shaped. Mid-season to late. Sunproof. Slightly scented

'Ringing Bells' 5 W-W
(G.E. Mitsch & R. & E.Havens) Grant Mitsch Novelty Daffodils, 1984
'Quick Step' × *N. triandrus*; sdlg no. C52/3
Fl. 65 mm wide. Late. Scented. Resembles a slightly larger 'Petrel' of a little less formality

'Ringinglow' 2 Y-Y
(F.E. Board) F.E. Board, 1965
'Ormeau' × 'Arctic Gold'; sdlg no. 484
Mid-season

'Ringleader' 2 W-YYO
(Mrs H.K. Richardson) Mrs H.K. Richardson, 1972
'Kilworth' × 'Arbar'
Perianth segments broadly ovate, smooth; corona almost disc-shaped, deep lemon, with orange at rim and the rim dentate

'Ringleader' 2 Y-YYO
(J.N. Hancock & Co., 1955) Unregistered
Sdlg no. 160/55H
Perianth segments broadly ovate, blunt, prominently mucronate, a little inflexed, smooth, overlapping half; the inner segments with margins sometimes nicked; corona short funnel-shaped, ribbed, yellow, with a broad band of reddish orange at rim, mouth straight, sometimes deeply split and overlapping, rim notched and crenate. Tall. Mid-season

'Ringlet' 3 W-? (b)
(Mrs R.O. Backhouse, pre-1908)

'Ringlet' 3 W-O
(A.H. Ahrens) J.S. Leitch, 1956
Corona deep reddish orange

'Ringmaster' 2 Y-YYO
(J.L. Richardson, pre-1953)
'Aranjuez' × 'Bahram'
Perianth segments very broadly ovate or roundish, mucronate, spreading, a little concave, with margins occasionally slightly incurling, smooth, with midrib sometimes prominent, overlapping half; the inner segments shouldered at base, slightly inflexed; corona bowl-shaped, smooth, slightly deeper in tone than the perianth, with bright orange at rim, mouth widely expanded and a little frilled

'Ringmer' 3 Y-YYO
(N.A. Burr) N.A. Burr, 1988
'Montego' × 'Achduart'; sdlg no. 4.4.76
Perianth segments broadly ovate, blunt, mucronate, deep rich yellow, spreading, very slightly concave, smooth, with midrib showing, of thick substance, regular, overlapping half; corona shallow bowl-shaped, slightly darker in tone than the perianth, with a broad band of orange at rim, mouth widely expanded, frilled. Mid-season

'Ringo' 2 W-WWP
(G.E. Mitsch and R. & E.Havens, 1961) G.E. Mitsch and R. & E.Havens, 1986
'Deodora' × 'Caro Nome'; sdlg no. W7/4
Corona with a well-defined band of bright pink at rim. Mid-season

'Ring of Fire' 2 W-WWR
(Dutch origin, pre-1995) Unregistered

'Ring o' Roses' 2 Y-YYR
(F.H. Chapman, pre-1936)
Perianth segments broadly ovate, blunt, buttercup yellow, overlapping; corona widely expanded, bright yellow, with a broad band of rosy scarlet at rim. Div. 3 until 1965

'Ringstead' 3 W-YYO
(D. & J.W. Blanchard) D. & J.W. Blanchard, 1968
'Hamzali' × 'Matapan'
Fl. 83 mm wide; corona greenish yellow, with reddish orange at rim. Mid-season. Resembles an improved 'Hamzali' with a broader band of colour at corona rim. AM(e) 1968

'Ringway' 3 W-GYR
(Brian S. Duncan) Rathowen Daffodils, 1978
'Merlin' open pollinated; sdlg no. 72
Fl. 93 mm wide; corona deep yellow, with a sharply defined band of deep red at rim. Mid-season

'Ringwood' 3 W-WWO
(J.W. Blanchard, 1976) J.W. Blanchard, 1992
'Purbeck' × 'Kimmeridge'; sdlg no. 71/23A
Fl. rounded, 95 mm wide; perianth segments broadly ovate, spreading, with margins incurving; corona cup-shaped, white, with deep green at base and a well-

defined band of strong orange 25B at rim, mouth straight, frilled, rim crenate. Mid-season. Varies between Divs 3 and 2

'Rinsey' 3 W-W
(P.D. Williams, pre-1934)
'Silver Coin' hybrid
Corona pure white, with green at base and a faint green tinge at rim

'Rio' 2 W-? (b)
(Mrs R.O. Backhouse, pre-1921)

'Rio Bonito' 2 (a)
(A.H. Ahrens, pre-1949)

'Rio Bravo' 2 O-R
(Ballydorn Bulb Farm) Ballydorn Bulb Farm, 1986
'Rio Rouge' × 'Firestorm'
Perianth segments opening with a faint flush of coppery red, becoming yellowish orange. Early

'Rio Dell' 2 YYW-WWY
(W.H. Roesé, c.1980) Unregistered
'Golden Aura' × 'Daydream'

'Rio del Rey' 2 (a)
(A.H. Ahrens, pre-1949)

'Rio d'Oro' 1 Y-Y
(J.L. Richardson) J.L. Richardson, 1956
'Goldcourt' × 'Kingscourt'
Fl. golden yellow; corona with rim flanged and frilled

'Rio Grande' 2 (a)
(A.H. Ahrens, pre-1949)

'Rio Gusto' 2 O-R
(Ballydorn Bulb Farm) Ballydorn Bulb Farm, 1981
'Rio Rouge' × 'Carnbeg'
Perianth segments copper orange; corona cup-shaped, red. Mid-season

'Rio Lobo' 2 O-O
(Ballydorn Bulb Farm, 1980) Ballydorn Bulb Farm, 1991
'Rio Rouge' × 2 O-O sdlg
Fl. 102 mm wide; perianth segments ovate, flushed faint orange, overlapping; the inner segments more broadly ovate; corona wide bowl-shaped, orange, becoming reddish orange with age. Early to mid-season. Sunproof

'Rio Negro' 2 (a)
(A.H. Ahrens, pre-1949)

'Rio Rita' 2 Y-O
(Warnaar & Co., pre-1929)
AM(Haarlem) 1933

'Rio Rondo' 2 O-O
(Ballydorn Bulb Farm) Ballydorn Bulb Farm, 1992
'Rio Rouge' × 2 O-O sdlg
Fl. rounded, 85 mm wide; perianth segments very broad, coppery yellow, plane, smooth; corona shallow, widely expanded, ribbed, reddish orange. Early. Sunproof

'Rio Rouge' 2 O-R
(Ballydorn Bulb Farm) Ballydorn Bulb Farm, 1974
'Foxhunter' × 'Alight' hybrid
Fl. 87 mm wide; perianth segments copper-toned; corona orange-red. Mid-season

'Riot' 2 W-P
(G.E. Mitsch) G.E. Mitsch, 1984
('Precedent' × 'Debutante') × 'Space Ship'; sdlg no. LL38/1
Fl. 93 mm wide; perianth segments white, heavily suffused pink; corona very shallow bowl-shaped, reddish pink, paling to tan at rim, frilled. Mid-season

'Rio Tinto' 2 (a)
(A.H. Ahrens, pre-1938)

'Riotous' 4 Y-Y
(Oregon Bulb Farms, pre-1946)
'Fortune' × 'Spring Glory' sport
2n=28

'Ripe Tomatoes' 4 Y-R
(W.F.M. Copeland, pre-1923)
Corona segments dark red

'Ripon' 5 W-W
(W.A. Grace, pre-1927)

'Ripper' 2 Y-O
(W.M. Spry, pre-1975) Unregistered
'Torchlight' × Ronalds sdlg
Corona dark reddish orange

'Ripple' 7 Y-Y
(Barr & Sons, pre-1949)
'Beersheba' × 'Rugulosus'

'Rippling Waters'
(New Zealand origin, pre-1915)

'Rippling Waters' 5 W-W
(Barr & Sons, pre-1932)
Fls 3 per stem, 83 mm wide, facing down; perianth segments ovate, blunt, only very slightly mucronate, creamy white, touched yellow at base, spreading or a little inflexed, overlapping a quarter to one-third; corona somewhat funnel-shaped, loosely ribbed, creamy white, with yellow at base, mouth straight, split in places and overlapping, wavy, with rim irregularly dentate. Mid-season. 2n=21.
*AM(g) 1946, *AM(g) 1946, *FCC(g) 1947,

*FCC(g) 1947, AGM 1995

'Riptide' 1 Y-W
(D.S. Bell) D.S. Bell, 1971
'David Bell' × 'Dawngold'
Fl. 112 mm wide; perianth segments very deep lemon yellow

'Rip van Winkle' 4 Y-Y
(Irish origin, pre-1884)
Variant of *N. pumilus*?
Fl. about 50 mm wide, pale greenish yellow; perianth and other petaloid segments in several whorls symmetrically superimposed, narrowly ovate and acute, or lanceolate and with prominently incurved mucro, sometimes twisted, with margins tinged green, separated; the outer whorl inflexed; the inner whorls successively more strongly inflexed; corona segments opposite the petaloid segments, a little shorter, clustered at centre, more loosely interspersed among the surrounding whorls, obscurely bi-lobed. Very early. 2n=14,21. Syn. 'Plenus'

'Risdon' 2 (a)
(Alister Clark, 1945) J. Sharp, 1960

'Riseden' 3 Y-Y
(N.A.Burr) N.A.Burr, 1996
'Verwood' × 'Badbury Rings'; sdlg no. 4.11.83
Fl. rounded, 100 mm wide; perianth segments broad, rounded at apex, light greenish yellow 4B, slightly reflexed, overlapping half; the inner segments narrower and more nearly spreading; corona widely expanded, more or less straight-sided, ribbed, vivid yellow 9A, touched orange at rim, with mouth straight and a little frilled, rim crenate. Tall. Mid-season

'Rising Dawn' 2 W-PPR
(G.L. Wilson) Guy L.Wilson Ltd, 1967
('Mabel Taylor' × 'Interim') × 'Irish Rose'
Corona deep pink, with raspberry red at rim. Mid-season. Resembles a robust and more richly coloured 'Pink Rim'

'Rising Fame' 2 (a)
(H.A. Brown, pre-1950)

'Rising Fast' 1 Y-Y
(J.A. Morris) J.A. Morris, 1957

'Rising Light' 2 W-? (b)
(H.R. Meyer, pre-1946)

'Rising Star' 7 W-P
(W.G. Pannill) W.G. Pannill, 1982
Pink sdlg × *N. jonquilla*; sdlg no. 74/26
Fl. 60 mm wide. Mid-season

'Rising Sun' 1
Syn. of 'Lubbe Senior' and of 'The Rising Sun'

'Rising Sun' 2 Y-O
Syn. of 'Bright Dawn'

'Rissalder' 2 Y-?
(G.H. Johnstone, pre-1946)

'Ristin' 1 Y-Y
(W. Jackson Jr, 1965) Jackson's Daffodils, 1979
'Bene' × sdlg 16/59 ('Moque' × 'Anukis'); sdlg no. 1/65
Fl. 105 mm wide. Early. Resembles 'Moque'

'Riston' 3 W-? (b)
(R.H. Bath, pre-1931)

'Rita Barker' 2 W-YPP
(K.B. Burns) K.B. Burns, 1964
Fl. 102 mm wide; corona with creamy yellow at base. Mid-season

'Rita Harley'
(pre-1954)
Corona widely expanded, frilled

'Rita Martin' 2 W-W
(T. Martin, *c*.1984) Unregistered

'Rita May' 2 W-YYO
(L.P.Dettman, 1970) Unregistered
'Most Delicious' × 'Pommy'; sdlg no. 10/71

'Rita Parnell' 3 W-? (b)
(W.A. Grace, pre-1938)

'Rita Pavone' 2 W-Y
(Konynenburg & Mark) Konynenburg & Mark, 1966
'Binkie' × 'Spellbinder'
Perianth segments ivory white; corona straw yellow. Mid-season

'Rita Payne' 2 (a)
(W.A. Grace, pre-1938)

'Ritz' 2 (a)
(M.P. Williams, pre-1949)

'Riva' 2 W-W
(The Brodie of Brodie, *c*.1923)
'Bernardino' × 'Rosary'
Corona flushed pale peach

'Rival'
(pre-1913)

'Rival' 1 (a)
(P. van Deursen, pre-1930)

'Rival' 6 YYG-Y
(G.E. Mitsch) G.E. Mitsch, 1976
'Jenny' open pollinated; sdlg no. EO6/1
Fl. 92 mm wide, glowing yellow, smooth; perianth segments broadly ovate, blunt, with slight white mucro and with green at base, reflexed, with margins slightly wavy, overlapping one-third; the inner segments with margins more strongly wavy; corona cylindrical, lightly ribbed, with mouth flared and rim notched. Mid-season. Somewhat resembles a larger and later-flowered 'Prefix' touched green at base

'Rivalis' 1
(R.H. Bath, pre-1908)

N. rivasmartinezii Fernández Casas 13 Section Jonquilla

'Rivelin' 1 Y-Y
(F.E. Board) F.E. Board, 1965
'Galway' × 'Kingscourt'; sdlg no. 123
Mid-season

'Rivendell' 3 W-GYY
(Brian S. Duncan) Rathowen Daffodils, 1981
'Woodland Prince' × 'Crepello'; sdlg no. 335
Fl. forming a double triangle; perianth segments broadly ovate, blunt, slightly mucronate, with margins very slightly wavy, of good substance and smooth texture, overlapping one-third; the inner segments more narrowly ovate, sometimes folded inwards at apex and seemingly acute, sharply angled at shoulder, with margins more distinctly wavy; corona disc-shaped, ribbed, mid-yellow, with green at base, sometimes paling to white at base on maturity, heavily frilled. Mid-season. Resembles a better-poised 'Syracuse' with a rounder flower

'Riverdale' 1 Y-Y
(J.T. Gray, pre-1949)
Perianth segments broadly ovate, yellow; corona of a slightly deeper tone, with rim rolled

'River Dance' 2 W-Y
(Brian S.Duncan) Brian S.Duncan, 1995
'Vernal Prince' × ('Aircastle' × 'Woodland Prince'); sdlg no. 1311
Fl. rounded, 105 mm wide; perianth segments milk white, with margins slightly incurving at apex, of good substance and smooth texture; corona wide bowl-shaped, deep golden yellow, with mouth wavy. Mid-season to late

'River Gold' 1 Y-Y
(D.S. Bell) D.S. Bell, 1962
'Ranalagh' × 'Val d'Or'
Fl. 108 mm wide, rich gold; corona frilled. Mid-season. Resembles 'Kingscourt' but with the perianth segments more nearly plane

'Riverina' 2 Y-R
(J.N. Hancock & Co., 1970) Unregistered

'Riverlea' 1 Y-Y
(D.S. Bell) D.S. Bell, 1983
'River Gold' open pollinated

'Riverlea Amy' 2 Y-Y
(R. Gibson, pre-1927)

'Riverlea Beauty' 2 W-YYP
(R. Gibson, pre-1927)

'Riverlea Bride' 1 W-W
(R. Gibson, pre-1927)

'Riverlea Perfection' 2 Y-Y
(R. Gibson, pre-1927)

'Riverlea Queen' 2 W-W
(R. Gibson, pre-1927)

'Riverlea Ruby' 2 W-Y
(R. Gibson, pre-1927)
Perianth segments creamy white

'River Queen' 2 W-W
(W.G. Pannill) W.G. Pannill, 1977
'Easter Moon' × 'Vigil'; sdlg no. D 11 C
Fl. 105 mm wide. Early to mid-season

'Riversdale' 1 W-P
(C.E. Radcliff, 1943) J.M.Radcliff, 1956
('Renown' × 'Bernardino') × 'Rosario'

'Riverton' 2 W-GWW
(E.W. Philpott, *c.*1959) Unregistered
'Swanley Peerless' × 'Whitefoord'

'Riverwood' 2 W-PPY
(D.S. Bell) D.S. Bell, 1960
'Greenore' × pink sdlg
Fl. 115 mm wide; corona widely expanded, pink, with golden yellow at rim. Mid-season

'Riviera' 3 W-GWW
(The Brodie of Brodie, pre-1928)

'Rivoli' 6 Y-YOO
Syn. of 'Emperor's Waltz'

'Rivulet' 3 W-? (b)
(G.H. Engleheart, pre-1923)

'Riza' 1 Y-Y
(S.J. Bisdee, 1945)
'Principal' × 'Robert Montgomery'

'R.J.B.' 3 W-YOO
(Broadfield's Daffodils, pre-1989) Unregistered

'Pacific Lady' × 'Dorus'

'R.J.C.Meyer' 2 Y-Y
(H.R. Meyer, pre-1936)

'Roamer' 2 (a or b)
(J.N. Hancock & Co., pre-1949)

'Roanna' 2 W-? (b)
(Mrs R.O. Backhouse, pre-1921)

'Roanoak' 2 Y-YYR
(E.C. Powell, pre-1946)
'Diana Kasner' × 'Copper Bowl'

'Rob' 2 (a)
(A.M. Williams, pre-1952)

'Robanal' 2 W-P
(Mrs A.R. Simmons) Mrs A.R. Simmons, 1980
Sdlg no. 65-6 51
Fl. 90 mm wide. Mid-season

'Rob Berkeley' 1 W-W
(Mrs Berkeley, pre-1922)
Fl. pure white; corona slender, with rim flanged and frilled. AM(e) 1922

'Robbie Jenkins' 3 W-YWW
(Barr & Sons, pre-1907)
Fl. facing down; corona ribbed, ivory white, with buff yellow at base

'Robe' 3 W-? (b or c)
(W.B. Hartland, pre-1908)

'Roberta' 1 W-? (b)
(de Graaff Bros, pre-1954)
2n=28. Syn. 'Mariette'. AM(Haarlem) 1954

'Robert Ascroft' 2 (a)
(F.H. Chapman, pre-1927)

'Roberta Watrous' 7 Y-GYP
(Mrs G. Link) Mrs G. Link, 1979
'Gossamer' × *N. jonquilla*; sdlg no. 1570
Fls 1-2 per stem, 65 mm wide; perianth segments soft lemon; corona flared and frilled. Mid-season. Scented. 2n=21

'Robert Berkeley' 5 W-W
(G.H. Engleheart, pre-1901)
N. triandrus × 'Minnie Hume'
FCC 1901

'Robert Boyle' 1 W-W
(Irish origin, pre-1889)
Fl. becoming sulphur white; perianth segments opening primrose yellow; corona opening lemon yellow

'Robert Bridges' 9
(C.L. Adams, pre-1914)

'Robert Browning' 3 W-? (b)
(G.H. Engleheart, pre-1907)

'Robert Bruce' 1 (a)
(H.G. Longford, pre-1927)

'Robert Burns' 1 (a)
(W.B. Hartland, pre-1913)

'Robert Dettman' 2 W-YYP
(L.P. Dettman) L.P. Dettman, 1982
'Creamed Honey' × 'Salmon Trout'; sdlg no. CH-ST 1
Fl. 95 mm wide; perianth segments yellowish white 155B; corona light yellow 10B, with a broad band of a pinkish tone (20B) at rim. Early

'Robert Lee' 1 W-? (b)
(de Graaff Bros, pre-1928)
AM(Haarlem) 1928

'Robert Montgomery' 1 Y-Y
(C.E. Radcliff, 1931)
'Golden City' × ('King Alfred' × 'Lord Roberts')
Fl. golden yellow

'Robert Ormston Backhouse' 1 Y-R
(W.O. Backhouse, pre-1953)
Corona strong orange 25B. Resembles a smaller 'King Alfred' with an orange corona. PC 1953

'Robert Southwell' 9
(G.H. Engleheart, pre-1913)

'Robert Spencer' 2 W-? (b or c)
(J.W. Barr, pre-1930)

'Robert Sydenham' 1 Y-Y
(M. van Waveren & Sons, pre-1908)
Perianth segments broadly ovate, blunt, only very slightly mucronate, sulphur yellow, spreading, plane or with margins very slightly wavy, overlapping half; the inner segments inflexed at base, reflexed towards apex, with margins wavy; corona funnel-shaped, darker in tone than the perianth, with mouth widely expanded, rim deeply notched and crenate. FCC(Haarlem) 1908

'Robespierre' 2 W-O
(P.D. Williams, pre-1907)
Perianth segments ivory; corona reddish orange. AM 1912

'Robey' 1 Y-Y
(G. Lubbe & Son, pre-1937)
2n=28. AM(Haarlem) 1937

'Robhan Jay' 2 Y-Y
(Ken Farmer Nurseries) Ken Farmer Nurseries, 1978
Fl. 91 mm wide. Early

'Robigana' 2 Y-R
(C.E. Radcliff, 1937)
'Red Torch' × 'Marengo'

'Robin' 3 W-R
(G.L. Wilson, pre-1934)
'Beacon' × 'Dactyl'

'Robin' 1 (a)
(W.O. Backhouse) W.O. Backhouse, 1956

'Robina' 2 W-? (b or c)
(Mrs R.O. Backhouse, pre-1921)

'Robina' 1 Y-Y
(T.H. Piper, 1945) T.H. Piper, 1956
'Bulwark' × 'Duddingston'

'Robin Adair' 2 W-O
(Mrs R.O. Backhouse, pre-1921)
Perianth segments pale yellow; corona pinkish orange

'Robinet' 3 W-? (b)
(G.H. Engleheart, pre-1910)

'Robin Hood' 3 W-YYO
(W. Backhouse, pre-1869)
Corona lemon yellow, with scarlet-orange at rim. Syn. Burbidgei 'Marginatus', Burbidgei 'Robin Hood'

'Robin Hood' 1 Y-Y
(L. van Leeuwen Jr, 1926) F. Rijnveld & Sons, 1958
Corona cylindrical, rich orange-yellow, darker in tone than the perianth, frilled. Mid-season. AM(Haarlem) 1930. Received AM(Haarlem) 1930 as 'Robinhood'

'Robinhood' 1 Y-Y
Syn. of 'Robin Hood'

'Robin Redbreast' 3 W-R
(Mrs R.O. Backhouse, pre-1907)
Corona disc-shaped

'Robinson' 8 W-W
(pre-1880)

'Robin's Pride' 2 W-P
(G.E.Mitsch, 1970) R. & E.Havens, 1994
Sdlg A24/1 ('Leonaine' × 'Carita') × sdlg V38/1 ('Radiation' × ['Mabel Taylor' × 'Interim']); sdlg no. F65/3
Fl. 92 mm wide; perianth segments broadly ovate; corona very shallow bowl-shaped, brilliant reddish pink, heavily frilled. Late. Sunproof

'Robins Roost' 2 W-O
(F.E. Board) F.E. Board, 1965
'Blarney' × 'Arbar'
Corona reddish orange

"Robinus his Daffodil"
Syn. of 'Eystettensis'

'Rob Roy' 1 Y-Y
(A.O. Roblin, pre-1942)
'Royalist' × 'Robert Montgomery'

'Rob Roy' 3 W-R
(J.L. Richardson) M.J. Jefferson-Brown, 1975
'Kilworth' × 'Arbar'
Corona cup-shaped, with mouth straight and almost even

'Robust' 1 (a)
(J.D. van den Burg, pre-1931)
Syn. 'Jane and Mary'. AM(Haarlem) 1931

'Robyn Morris' 2 W-O
(J.A. Morris) J.A. Morris, 1963
Fl. 118 mm wide; perianth segments stained pale yellow at base; corona reddish orange. Mid-season. Resembles a large- flowered 'Pirate King'

'Roca' 1 (a)
(W.O. Backhouse) W.O. Backhouse, 1956

'Rochdale' 1 W-W
(G. Lewis) D.S. Bell, 1955

'Rochelle' 1 W-YYP
(S.J. Bisdee, pre-1943)
'Eskimo' × 'Dawnglow'

'Rochester' 9
(pre-1907)

'Rochester Quinton' 2 W-YOO
(F.H. Chapman, pre-1915)
'Firebrand' × 'Swashbuckler'
Perianth segments tinged green at base; corona slender, reddish orange, with greenish lemon yellow at base and a darker tone of orange towards rim

'Rockabelle'
(The Brodie of Brodie, c.1909)
'Ornatus' × 'W.P.Milner'

'Rockall' 3 W-R
(J.L. Richardson) J.L. Richardson, 1955
'Kilworth' × 'Arbar'
Fl. 112 mm wide; perianth segments very broadly ovate, blunt, slightly mucronate, pure white, spreading, plane or a little concave, smooth and of heavy substance, regular, overlapping one-third to a half; the inner segments more narrowly ovate, a little inflexed, shouldered at base; corona shallow bowl-

shaped, heavily ribbed, orange-red (30C), with mouth split in places and overlapping, loosely frilled. Mid-season. AM(e) 1959, FCC(e) 1965

'Rock Creek' 3 W-YYR
(Brian S.Duncan) Brian S.Duncan, 1995
'Mount Angel' × ('Arctic Flame' × 'Random Light'); sdlg no. 1265
Fl. rounded, 102 mm wide; perianth segments broadly ovate, pure white; corona shallow bowl-shaped, deep yellow, with a broad band of deep orange-red at rim, slightly frilled. Mid-season to late

'Rockery Beauty' 1 W-Y
(W.J. Eldering & Son, pre-1925)
Dwarf. 2n=14. AM(Haarlem) 1925

'Rockery Gem' 1 W-W
(R.A. van der Schoot, pre-1930)

'Rockery White' 1 W-W
(G. Zandbergen-Terwegen, pre-1936)
N. minor var. *conspicuus* sport

'Rocket' 2 W-? (b)
(M.P. Williams, pre-1938)
Fl. smooth and of thick substance; corona ribbed, with a broad band of crimson at rim

'Rock Fire' 2 W-? (b)
(Mrs R.O. Backhouse, pre-1921)

'Rockfire' 2 Y-R
Syn. of 'Rokfire'

'Rock Garden Gem' 6 Y-GYY
(G.E.Mitsch, 1978) R. & E.Havens, 1996
'Atom' open pollinated; sdlg no. 2NO3/2
Fl. 42 mm wide, yellow; perianth segments very broad; corona with green at base. Dwarf. Very early

'Rockhaven' 2 W-Y
(D.S. Bell) D.S. Bell, 1963
'Idealist' × 'Artist's Model'
Fl. 104 mm wide; corona lemon yellow, tinged green. Late

'Rockliff' 1 W-Y
(W.A. Grace, pre-1927)

'Rock 'n' Roll' 11a W-Y
(Jackson's Daffodils) Jackson's Daffodils, 1996
Sdlg 116/77 × 'Cassata'; sdlg no. 179/87
Fl. 114 mm wide; perianth segments broadly ovate, greenish white (155A); corona deeply split, the six segments two-thirds the length of the perianth segments and opposite to them, vivid yellow 9A. Late

'Rockport' 2 W-GWW
(Carncairn Daffodils) Carncairn Daffodils, 1989
(Wootton sdlg × 'Shantallow') open pollinated; sdlg no. 3/76
Fl. 87 mm wide, pure white; perianth segments spreading, plane, smooth, overlapping; corona mouth slightly expanded, even, slightly flushed pink on opening, becoming white. Mid-season

'Rock Sensation' 1 Y-Y
(J. Gerritsen & Son) J. Gerritsen & Son, 1977
'Little Beauty' self pollinated
Fl. 55 mm wide; perianth segments greenish yellow (4D); corona vivid yellow 9A, paling towards base. Early

'Rockville Center' 2 (a)
(L. van Leeuwen & Son, pre-1950)

'Rocky Horror' 11a Y-Y
(J. Gerritsen & Son) J. Gerritsen & Son, 1976
Fl. sulphur yellow; corona segments with a lighter tone at rim. Early

'Rocky Mountains' 2 W-? (b)
(de Graaff Bros, pre-1927)

'Rocliffe' 2 Y-? (a)
Syn. of 'Khalasa'

'Rococo' 6
(F.H. Chapman, pre-1936)

'Rococo' 2 W-O
(C.G. van Tubergen, 1944)
'John Evelyn' × 'Fortune'
Perianth segments very broad in outline, rounded or squarish at apex, slightly mucronate, creamy white, smooth, overlapping half; the inner segments a little narrower, creased, slightly nicked at shoulder; corona very broad and shallow, loosely ribbed, apricot orange, with mouth split and overlapping, deeply frilled. AM(Haarlem) 1946, FCC(Haarlem) 1947

'Rococo' 2 W-O
(pre-1974) Unregistered
Perianth segments ivory white; corona orange, heavily frilled

'Rocquefort' 1 W-Y
(J. Gerritsen & Son, 1956) J. Gerritsen & Son, 1967
Sdlg × 'Beersheba'
Perianth segments creamy white; corona creamy yellow. Late. Resembles a smaller ' Beersheba' in all its parts

'Rodd' 9
(P.D. Williams, pre-1933)

'Rodeo' 2 Y-R
(D.S. Bell) D.S. Bell, 1963
'Pencarrow' × 'Burgundy'

Fl. 108 mm wide. Mid-season. Resembles 'Carbineer' but with a larger corona

'Roderic Dhu' 1 (a)
(H.G. Longford, pre-1927)

'Roderigo' 2 W-Y
(Barr & Sons, pre-1923)
Perianth segments creamy white; corona bright canary yellow

'Rodin' 2 Y-O
(Konynenburg & Mark, 1950) Konynenburg & Mark, 1960
'Aranjuez' × 'Beauty of the Garden'
Fl. 95 mm wide; perianth segments brilliant greenish yellow 6C; corona orange (28A). Early

'Rodinga' 2 Y-Y
(W. Jackson Jr) W. Jackson Jr, 1968
Syn. ?'Anat'

'Rodney' 2 W-? (b)
(T.A.V. Wood, pre-1949)

'Rodney Stone' 1 Y-Y
(T.H. Piper, 1954)
'Derflinger' × 'Roundabout'

'Rodomont' 2 Y-O
(P.D. Williams, pre-1932)
Perianth segments rich yellow. AM(Haarlem) 1932. Div. 3 until 1942

'Rodosto' 3 W-YYO
(The Brodie of Brodie, c.1927)
'Mozart' × Donard sdlg 297
Corona disc-shaped, bright yellow, with a narrow band of deep reddish orange at rim, frilled. AM(Haarlem) 1935

'Rod's Early' 4 W-O
(H.G.Cross, pre-1997) Unregistered

'Roebuck' 1 (a)
(Mrs R.O. Backhouse, pre-1914)

N. × *rogendorfii* Battandier 13 = *N. elegans* (Haworth) Spach × *N. tazetta* Linnaeus

'Roger' 6 Y-Y
(A. Gray, pre-1952)
'Beryl' × 'Nor-Nor'
Fl. of strong substance; perianth segments broadly ovate, creamy yellow, sometimes becoming whitish, spreading, with margins sometimes incurved, overlapping a quarter to one-third; the inner segments somewhat twisted or with margins wavy; corona cup-shaped, ribbed, orange, shading to a darker tone at rim, with mouth even and rim minutely crenate.

Sunproof. 2n=37. Resembles a larger 'Beryl' with colouring midway between that and 'Nor-Nor'

'Rogilla' 2 (a)
(W.A. Grace, pre-1938)

'Rohanta' 2 Y-O
(A.H. Ahrens) D.J. Cooper, 1959
Fl. 89 mm wide; perianth segments golden yellow; corona reddish orange. Early

'Rohnozi' 2 Y-O
(J.L. Martin) J.L. Martin, 1978
'Wansea' × 'Kai'; sdlg no. W/K 9
Fl. 100 mm wide; perianth segments light greenish yellow 6D; corona between very light orange (23D) and a darker tone (24B). Early to mid-season. Resembles 'Wansea' but with rounder perianth segments

'Roiaal' 8 Y-Y
(pre-1807)

'Roi de Perse' 8 W-W
(pre-1777)

'Roi d'Or' 1 Y-Y
(Ballydorn Bulb Farm) Ballydorn Bulb Farm, 1995
'Owen Roe' open pollinated
Fl. 110 mm wide; perianth segments broadly obovate, golden yellow, with margins slightly wavy; corona straight sided, narrower at base, smooth, of a deeper tone than the perianth, with mouth more or less even. Early to mid-season

'Roimond' 2 W-O
(J.L. Richardson, pre-1948)
Fl. rounded; perianth segments very broadly ovate, blunt or squarish at apex, slightly mucronate, reflexed, plane, overlapping one-third to a half; the inner segments more narrowly ovate, more nearly spreading, with margins wavy; corona bowl-shaped, ribbed, opening greenish orange, becoming orange, with mouth more or less even, rim crenate. Tall. Late to very late. Sunproof

'Roi Soleil' 2 (a)
(P.D. Williams, pre-1942)

'Roisterman' 2 W-R
(Brian S. Duncan) Rathowen Daffodils, 1987
'Red Rooster' × 'Shandon'
Perianth segments unstained pure white; corona bowl-shaped, deep red. Mid-season to late. Resembles 'Verve' but is of purer and deeper colour

'Rokfire' 2 Y-R
(R.C.A. Tombleson) R.C.A. Tombleson, 1966
Fl. 115 mm wide. Mid-season. See also 'Rockfire'

'Roland' 2 W-Y
(W. Backhouse, pre-1869)
Corona expanded. Syn. Incomparabilis Albus 'Expansus', Incomparabilis Albus 'Roland'. Was "absorbed" into 'Queen Bess'

'Roland' 9 W-OOR
(G.H. Engleheart, pre-1923)
Corona orange, with crimson at rim. AM 1923

'Roland' 1 Y-Y
(C.E. Radcliff, pre-1948)
'Golden Wealth' × 'Roundabout'

'Roland's Horn' 2 W-Y
(D.N.Y. Olson) D.N.Y. Olson, 1990
'Green Island' open pollinated
Fl. 85 mm wide; perianth segments broadly ovate, blunt or truncate, not prominently mucronate, clear white, strongly reflexed, of good substance, overlapping half or more; the inner segments only a little more narrowly ovate, rounded at shoulder to a narrow base; corona short funnel-shaped, greenish yellow, with mouth straight, rim minutely and closely notched; the corona encircled at about mid-point by an extra growth similarly notched. Late to very late

'Rolf Knie' 1 Y-Y
(J.W.A. van der Wereld) J.W.A. van der Wereld, 1983

'Rolinda' 2 W-O
(de Graaff Bros) de Graaff Bros, 1969

'Rolled Gold' 1 Y-Y
(G.L. Wilson, pre-1941)
'Goldbeater' × 'Penbeagle'

'Rolled Sulphur' 1 W-Y
(A.G. Thompson) A.G. Thompson, 1961
Fl. 102 mm wide; perianth segments creamy white; corona sulphur yellow. Early. Resembles 'Petsamo' in form

'Rollo' 2 Y-? (a)
(J.T. Gray, pre-1949)
Perianth segments deep chrome yellow; corona with rim rolled

'Rollo Meyer' 2 W-? (b)
(H.R. Meyer) Hon. Mrs B.B.Ponsonby, 1956

'Roma' 2 W-? (b)
(Hon. Mrs Petre, pre-1934)

'Roma' 2 W-YYO
(West & Fell, pre-1936)
?The same as 'Roma Wyness'

'Romagna' 4
(Mrs R.O. Backhouse, pre-1921)

'Romaine' 1 W-W
(de Graaff Bros, pre-1939)
AM(Haarlem) 1939

'Roman' 4 W-W
Syn. of 'Romanus'

'Roman Candle' 2 W-P
(Oregon Bulb Farms, pre-1950)
'Tunis' × 'Mrs R.O.Backhouse'

'Romance' 2 Y-YYR
(G.H. Engleheart, pre-1910)

'Romance' 2 (a)
(Mrs R.O. Backhouse, pre-1921)

'Romance' 2 W-P
(J.L. Richardson) J.L. Richardson, 1959
Fl. 92 mm wide; perianth segments roundish, slightly mucronate, creamy white, spreading, somewhat concave or with margins incurving, with midrib showing, overlapping half; corona short funnel-shaped, loosely ribbed, pink (near to 31D), with yellow-pink (24C) at rim, mouth slightly expanded, frilled, deeply and regularly 6-lobed, the lobes themselves bi-lobed, with occasional flecks of white at notch, rim more or less entire. Mid-season. Scented. AM(e) 1966, *AM(p) 1986, *AM(g) 1991, AGM 1995

romanensis = *N*. × *neocarpetanus* var. *romanensis*

'Roman Legion' 2 Y-O
(Tom Forster, 1960s) Unregistered
'John Evelyn' × 'Cuprona'
Perianth segments very soft yellow; corona large, ribbed, yellow-orange, with a deeper tone at rim, frilled. Tall. Early

'Roman Star' 3 (a)
(Mrs R.O. Backhouse, pre-1921)
AM(Haarlem) 1929

'Romantica' 2 O-O
(J. Gerritsen & Son) J. Gerritsen & Son, 1960
Fl. 60 mm wide, rich orange. Mid-season. 2n=29. Resembles a more vigorous 'Sologne' of stronger colouring

'Roman Tile' 2 W-WYP
(G.H. Johnstone) G.H. Johnstone, 1959
'Assent' × 'Ann Abbott'
Fl. 108 mm wide; corona bowl-shaped, rich primrose, with deep pink at rim. Mid-season

'Romanus' 4 W-O
(pre-1576)
Double Tazetta
Corona yellow-orange. Sweetly scented. Syn.

"Double Marsellian", "Double White Polyanthus", "Old Italian", "The Double Roman Narcissus", 'Constantinopolitanus', ?"Double Italian", ?"Double Roman", ?"Double White Sweet Scented", 'Flore Multiplici', 'Italicus Plenus', 'Roman', Tazetta 'Flore Pleno' (in part), Tazetta 'Romanus'

'Romany' 2 W-?
(Alister Clark) J. Sharp, 1960

'Romany Lass' 3 (a)
(Mrs R.O. Backhouse, pre-1921)

'Romany Red' 3 O-R
(Brian S. Duncan) Rathowen Daffodils, 1983
'Altruist' × 'Ulster Bank'; sdlg no. 550
Fl. 100 mm wide; perianth segments peachy orange; corona deep red. Mid-season. Resembles a larger and taller 'Altruist' of deeper colour with the perianth segments more nearly spreading

'Roma Wyness' 2 W-YYO
(West & Fell, pre-1935)
Perianth segments pure white; corona broad disc-shaped, pale primrose, with a broad band of salmon at rim, frilled. ?See also 'Roma'

'Rombarde' 2 W-? (b or c)
(G.H. Engleheart, pre-1923)

'Romeo' 3 W-Y
(W. Backhouse, pre-1869)
Perianth segments creamy white, inflexed; corona canary yellow. Syn. Barrii Albidus 'Primulinus', Barrii Albidus 'Romeo'

'Romeo' 8 Y-O
(C.A. van der Wereld, 1946) C.A. van Paridon, 1962
Fl. 55 mm wide; perianth segments brilliant yellow 10A; corona strong orange 25A. Late. 2n=17. AM(Haarlem) 1962, FCC(Haarlem) 1964

***N. romieuxii* Braun-Blanquet & Maire 13 Section Bulbocodium.**
    subsp. *romieuxii*
        var. *romieuxii*. AM(a) 1938, AGM 1994
        var. *mesatlanticus* Maire. AM 1984
        var. *rifanus* (Emberger & Maire) A.Fernandes
    subsp. *albidus* (Emberger & Maire) A.Fernandes
        var. *albidus*
        var. *zaianicus* (Maire, Weiller & Wilczec) A.Fernandes

'Romina' 1 W-Y
(J.S. Leitch) J.S. Lietch, 1967
Fl. 95 mm wide; corona primrose yellow

'Romney' 3 W-W
(H.R. Bulman, c.1966) Unregistered
'Lunawanna' × 'Bura'

***N.* × *romoi* Fernández Casas 13** = *N. cantabricus* de Candolle × *N. fernandesii* Pedro

'Romola' 2 W-Y
(Barr & Sons, pre-1923)
Perianth segments creamy white, of waxy texture, overlapping; corona rich yellow

'Romona' 2 W-GYO
(J.N. Hancock & Co., c.1977) Unregistered

'Romulus' 1 Y-Y
(Mrs R.O. Backhouse, pre-1921)

'Romulus' 2 W-W
(J.S. Leitch) J.S. Leitch, 1968

'Romulus' 7
Syn. of 'Ronchi'

'Rona' 2 W-W
Syn. of 'Parkmore'

'Rona Gower' 2 W-WWP
(D.S. Bell) D.S. Bell, 1977
'Artist's Model' hybrid self pollinated
Fl. 103 mm wide; corona broad disc-shaped, white, with pink at rim, with the rim flanged and touching the perianth segments. Mid-season

'Ronchi' 7
(de Graaff Bros, pre-1929)
Syn. 'Romulus'

'Rondeau' 9
(F.H. Chapman, pre-1923)

'Rondel' 2 O-O
(P. & G. Phillips) P. & G. Phillips, 1979
Fl. 92 mm wide; perianth segments flushed orange, smooth; corona widely expanded, rich deep orange. Mid-season

'Rondetto' 2 W-P
(J.L. Richardson) Mrs H.K. Richardson, 1968
'Interim' × 'Rose Caprice'
Perianth segments white, of waxy texture; corona pale salmon pink, frilled

'Rondeveau' 2 W-R
(D.S. Bell) D.S. Bell, 1959
Fl. 115 mm wide. Mid-season. Resembles 'Signal Light' but with a whiter perianth and the corona more widely expanded

'Rondino' 3 W-GGP
(A.M. Wilson, pre-1948)
Corona pale, near to olive green, shading to a darker tone at base, with coral pink at rim. Late

'Rondo' 9 W-GYR
(A.H. Ahrens, 1945) R. Hyde, 1958

'Rongotai' 1 Y-Y
(A. Gibson, pre-1949)
'Kingscourt' × 'Goldcourt'

'Ron Hyde' 1 Y-Y
(R. Hyde) R. Hyde, 1957
'Rongotai' × 'Principal'

'Ronlip'
(pre-1959)

'Rooney' 2 (a)
(Mrs R.O. Backhouse, pre-1914)

'Rory's Glen' 2 O-O
(Carncairn Daffodils and A.E.Robinson) Carncairn Daffodils, 1988
'Bunclody' × 'Fire Raiser'
Perianth segments broadly ovate, blunt, deep orange, with white mucro, somewhat inflexed, plane, smooth, of good substance, regular, overlapping half; the inner segments slightly twisted; corona cylindrical, lightly ribbed, orange, mouth straight or a little expanded, wavy. Mid-season

'Rosa' W-W
(Irish origin, pre-1902)
Hybrid between *N. nanus* and *N. triandrus* subsp. *pallidulus*

'Rosa' 2 W-P
(C.E. Radcliff, 1944)
'Rosario' × 'Dawnglow'

'Rosa Bedford' 3 W-? (b)
Syn. of 'Miss Rose Bedford'

'Rosabella' 1 W-P
(de Graaff Bros, pre-1930)
AM(Haarlem) 1930

'Rosa Bonheur' 2 W-Y
(W. Backhouse, pre-1869)
Syn. Incomparabilis Albus 'Rosa Bonheur'. Was "absorbed" into 'Bertie'

'Rosa Dear' 2 W-P
(T.H. Piper, 1955) Unregistered
'Saint Aloysius' × 'Success'

'Rosado' 11a W-P
(J. Gerritsen & Son) J. Gerritsen & Son, 1986
'Articol' hybrid
Perianth segments ivory white; corona segments orange-pink, with bronze green at base. Late. Resembles 'Musette'

'Rosalba' 2 W-? (b or c)
(Cartwright & Goodwin, pre-1910)

'Rosalie' 3 W-? (b)
(R.H. Bath, pre-1927)
Corona slightly tinted orange

'Rosalie Morrill' 2 W-YPP
(G.E. Morrill) G.E. Morrill, 1979
'Precedent' × 'Carita'; sdlg no. 67-7-3
Fl. 100 mm wide; perianth segments yellowish white 155B; corona pink 49B, with pale greenish yellow 1D at base. Mid-season

'Rosalind' 3 W-YYO
(G.H. Engleheart, pre-1902)
Fls facing down; perianth segments reflexed; corona bright yellow, with scarlet-orange at rim. Late

'Rosaline' 2 W-P
(A.O. Roblin, 1948)
'White Sentinel' × 'Pinka'

'Rosaline Murphy' 2 Y-Y
(A. Gray) A. Gray, 1958
N. asturiensis × *N. rupicola* subsp. *watieri*
Fls sulphur yellow. 2n=14. Resembles a much smaller 'Picarillo'

'Rosalynd' 1 W-? (b)
(E.H. Krelage & Son, pre-1921)
AM(Haarlem) 1921

'Rosamond'
(pre-1936)

'Rosamund' 1 W-W
(Barr & Sons, pre-1923)

'Rosamundi' 1 W-W
(W.A. Bell, pre-1949)
Syn. 'Relieve'

'Rosanna' 1 W-P
(C.A. Nethercote) T. Morrison, 1960
Perianth segments pure white; corona delicate pink

'Rosanne' 2 (a)
(J.T. Gray, pre-1950)

'Rosapenna' 2 W-GPP
(Carncairn Daffodils, 1963) Carncairn Daffodils, 1978
'Irish Rose' × G.L.Wilson sdlg; sdlg no. 3/3/57
Fl. 98 mm wide; perianth segments greenish white (155A); corona orange-pink (29B). Late. Resembles an earlier-flowered 'Pennybridge' with a smaller corona

'Rosario' 2 W-P
(C.E. Radcliff, pre-1940)
'Pinkie' × 'Rosary'
Fl. forming a double triangle; perianth segments broadly ovate, blunt, slightly mucronate, spreading, plane, overlapping half; the inner segments more narrowly ovate, slightly inflexed, with margins very slightly wavy; corona funnel-shaped, lightly ribbed, very pale primrose, flushed rosy shell-pink, frilled, rim notched and crenate, narrowly flanged

'Rosary' 1 W-P
(G.H. Engleheart, pre-1926)
Perianth segments creamy white; corona creamy shell pink, in some climates paling almost to white, with mouth widely expanded. Very early. AM(Haarlem) 1926, AM(e) 1926

'Rosas' 2 Y-O
(J.W.A. Lefeber, 1952) J.W.A. Lefeber, 1980
Fl. 110 mm wide; perianth segments primrose yellow, with a darker tone at base; corona strong orange 25A. Early to mid-season

'Rosasharn' 4 W-WWP
(D.S. Bell) D.S. Bell, 1985
Div. 4 sdlg × pink sdlg
Fl. 105 mm wide; perianth segments broad, pure white, smooth; corona segments with bright pink at rim. Mid-season. Resembles 'Presence' but with more numerous corona segments

'Rosaura' 5
(Barr & Sons, pre-1923)

'Rosa van Lima' 2 W-P
(P.D. Williams, pre-1948)
AM(Haarlem) 1948

'Roscarrick' 6 W-P
(Brian S. Duncan) R.A.Scamp & du Plessis Bros, 1989
'Roseworthy' × 'Foundling'; sdlg no. 343
Fl. 96 mm wide; perianth segments ovate, acute, only very slightly mucronate, pure white, reflexed, plane, overlapping a quarter; the inner segments with margins sometimes incurved; corona funnel-shaped, lightly ribbed, deep pink, paler at base, with mouth straight, frilled. Late

'Roscoe' 1 Y-Y
(pre-1965) Unregistered
Perianth segments medium yellow; corona slightly deeper in tone, with rim flanged and dentate

'Roscommon' 1 (a)
(J.L. Richardson, pre-1947)

'Rosdew' 2 W-P
(G.H. Johnstone) G.H. Johnstone, 1959
'Assent' × 'Chelsea China'
Fl. 76 mm wide; corona golden pink. Mid-season

'Roseanna' 2 W-P
(G.L. Wilson) G.L. Wilson, 1955
'Rose of Tralee' × 'Wild Rose'
Perianth segments pure white; corona slender, apricot pink. Dwarf

'Roseanthy' 2 W-P
Syn. of 'Roseworthy'

'Roseate' 2 (a)
(H. Backhouse, pre-1910)

'Roseate Hues' 2 W-YYP
(H.R. Meyer, pre-1944)
Perianth segments sulphur white. AM(Haarlem) 1949

'Roseate Tern' 2 W-P
(J.M. de Navarro) J.M. de Navarro, 1975
(['Templemore' × 'Salmon Trout'] × 'Debutante') × 'Romance'; sdlg no. 483/II
Fl. 90 mm wide; perianth segments very broad, blunt, slightly mucronate, spreading, a little concave, regular, overlapping half; the inner segments narrower; corona bowl-shaped, smooth, pink, with mouth straight, lightly frilled, rim shallowly crenate. Mid-season. Resembles 'Romance' but with wider perianth segments and a paler corona

'Rosebank' 2 W-YPP
(Mrs J. Abel Smith, 1974) Mrs J. Abel Smith, 1989
'Dulcie Joan' hybrid; sdlg no. R2/72
Mid-season

'Rose Bay' 2 W-P
(J.N. Hancock & Co.) J.N. Hancock & Co., 1960

'Rose Bell Butler' 3 W-W
(Mrs J. Butler, pre-1949)

'Rosebery' 2 W-P
(C.E. Radcliff, 1939)
'Princess Betty' × 'Pink o' Dawn'

'Rosebowl' 1 W-P
(C.E. Radcliff, 1943) J.M. Radcliff, 1956
'Dawnglow' hybrid

'Rose Bowl' 2 W-P
(pre-1956) Unregistered
Perianth segments broad, smooth; corona widely expanded, rose pink

'Rose Brocade' 2 W-P
(J.L. Richardson) J.L. Richardson, 1961
'Rose of Tralee' × 'Rose Caprice'
Fl. 102 mm wide; perianth segments of thick texture;

corona rose pink, with mouth slightly expanded, frilled

'Rosebud' 3 W-O
(P.D. Williams, pre-1927)
Perianth segments milk white; corona small, shallow, soft dark orange. AM(Haarlem) 1931

'Rose Caprice' 2 W-GPP
(J.L. Richardson, pre-1952)
'Templemore' × 'Green Island'
Fl. 100 mm wide; perianth segments very broadly ovate, blunt or squarish at apex, slightly mucronate, pure white, spreading, concave either side of the midrib, with margins sometimes notched, of waxy substance, overlapping half; the inner segments a little inflexed, convex either side of the midrib, with margins wavy; corona funnel-shaped, lightly ribbed, apricot pink (24D), with green at base, paler in tone on the outside, a little frilled, with rim narrowly flanged. Mid-season. AM(e) 1955, AM(Haarlem) 1962

'Rose City' 2 W-P
(Murray W. Evans) Murray W. Evans, 1969
'Interim' × 'Radiation'

'Rosecliston' 2 W-P
(The Brodie of Brodie)
'Mitylene' × 'Evening'

'Rose Cottage' 2 W-YYP
(H.R. Barr) H.R. Barr, 1971
'Interim' × 'Maiden's Blush'
Fl. 110 mm wide

'Rosedale' 2 W-P
(H.R. Bulman, 1950) H.R. Bulman, 1956
'Allara' × 'Rosario'

'Rosedale' 1 W-P
(J.M.Radcliff)
'Roseum' × 'Alpine Glow'

'Rose Dawn' 2 W-? (b)
(G.H. Engleheart, pre-1948)

'Rose Day'
(c.1957) Unregistered

'Rosedean' 2 W-P
(E.N. Amoore, pre-1983) Unregistered
Perianth segments broadly ovate, pure white; corona bowl-shaped

'Rosedew' 2 W-? (b or c)
(G.T.C. Pearce, pre-1938)
'White Sentinel' × 'Tenedos'

'Rosedew' 2 W-P

(J.L. Richardson) Mrs H.K. Richardson, 1962
'Rose Caprice' × sdlg 355
Corona clear pink, with rim flanged and dentate

'Rosedown' 5 Y-O
(A. Gray, pre-1949)
N. triandrus × Div. 2 Y-R
Fl. about 75 mm wide; perianth segments bright yellow; corona cup-shaped, reddish orange. Dwarf to standard

'Rose Duet' 4 W-P
(W. Jackson Jr) W. Jackson Jr, 1968
Sdlg 59/59 × 'Lawali'; sdlg no. 78/64

'Roseflush' 1 W-P
(C.E. Radcliff, 1945) J.M.Radcliff, 1956
'Rosario' × 'Dawnglow'

'Rosefrills' 2 W-WWP
(C.E. Radcliff, 1940) J.M.Radcliff, 1956
'Princess Betty' × 'Dawnglow'

'Rose Garden' 4 W-R
(G.E. Mitsch, 1980) R. & E. Havens, 1993
'Gay Time' × 'Green Hills'; sdlg no. 2P68/10
Fl. 95 mm wide; petaloid and corona segments in many whorls, symmetrically arranged; perianth and other petaloid segments pure white; corona segments orange-red. Late. Sunproof. Scented

'Rosegarland' 2 W-YYP
(J.L. Richardson, pre-1941)
'Mitylene' × 'Red Sun'
Corona bowl-shaped, pale primrose, strongly flushed and rimmed rosy shell pink, irregularly frilled

'Rose Garland' ?-?P
(?Mrs J. Hanber, pre-1959) Unregistered

'Rosegem' 2 W-P
(C.E. Radcliff, 1945) J.M.Radcliff, 1956
Syn. 'Rose Gem'

'Rose Gem' 2 W-P
Syn. of 'Rosegem'

'Rose Gold' 1 YYW-GPP
(Brian S. Duncan) Rathowen Daffodils, 1983
'Daydream' × 'Reverie'; sdlg no. 697
Fl. forming a double triangle, 105 mm wide; perianth segments broadly ovate, deep sulphur yellow, with slight white mucro and with a clearly defined band of white at base, spreading, plane, overlapping half; the inner segments only a little narrower, very slightly inflexed; corona funnel-shaped, lightly ribbed, rose pink, with green at base, mouth expanded, lightly frilled, rim notched and crenate. Mid-season. Resembles a 'Milestone' of improved colour and form

'Roselands' 2 W-P
(C.E. Radcliff, 1939)
'Pinkie' × 'Luther'
Corona slender, flushed pale pink

'Roselene' 2 W-P
(F. Hanger, pre-1949)
Fl. 95 mm wide; perianth segments creamy white, overlapping half; corona broad bowl-shaped, salmon pink, with undertones of creamy white. 2n=28. HC 1949, *AM(g) 1953

'Roselight' 2 W-P
(C.E. Radcliff, 1940)
'White Sentinel' × 'Pink o' Dawn'
Corona rich clear pink

'Roselight' 2 W-P
(W.J. Dunlop) W.J. Dunlop, 1961

'Roselip' 2 W-WWP
(C.E. Radcliff, 1943) J.M.Radcliff, 1956
'Pink o' Dawn' hybrid
Corona with cherry pink at rim

'Rosella' 3 W-O
(E.M. Crosfield, pre-1907)
Perianth segments creamy white, overlapping; corona almost disc-shaped, scarlet salmon orange

'Rosella' 2 W-P
(J.S. Leitch) J.S. Leitch, 1960
Fl. 108 mm wide

'Roselle' 2 W-P
(J.N.Hancock & Co., 1973) Unregistered
Sdlg no. 9B/73H

'Rosellen' 1 W-P
(R.J. Ralph, 1945)
('Finn' × 'Pinkeen') × 'Dawnglow'

'Rosemar' 2 W-? (b)
(Mrs M.Moorby) Mrs M.Moorby, 1956

'Rose Marie' 3 W-O
(de Graaff Bros, pre-1927)
Perianth segments overlapping; corona lightly frilled

'Rosemarkie' 2 W-P
(The Brodie of Brodie, c.1932)
'Osiris' × 'Naxos'

'Rosemary' 1 W-Y
(H. Aldersey, pre-1931)
Fl. 83 mm wide, facing somewhat downwards; perianth segments creamy white, inflexed, regular, overlapping at base only; corona deep sulphur yellow, mouth expanded and frilled. Mid-season to late

'Rosemary Anne' 9 W-YYR
(L.P. Brumley) T. Morrison, 1960
Corona with red at rim

'Rosemary Hyde' 2 W-P
(R. Hyde) R. Hyde, 1959
Perianth segments broad, of good substance; corona bowl-shaped

'Rosemerryn' 2 W-P
(R.A.Scamp, 1985) R.A.Scamp, 1996
'Rose Royale' × 'Dailmanach'; sdlg no. 173
Fl. 97 mm wide; perianth segments ovate, acute, chalky white, deeply overlapping; corona funnel-shaped, pale pink, with rim neatly crenate. Mid-season to late. Sunproof

'Rosemont' 1 Y-Y
(J.N.Hancock & Co., 1978) Unregistered
Sdlg no. 100/78H
Early to mid-season

'Rosemorran' 2 W-? (b)
(G.L. Wilson, pre-1951)

'Rosemorran Giant' 1 W-Y
(C. Dawson, pre-1927)
Corona strong lemon yellow

'Rosemount' 2 W-P
(S.J. Bisdee, 1942) S.J. Bisdee, 1956
'Eskimo' × 'Dawnglow'

'Rose Mullion' 2 W-P
(K.J. Heazlewood) K.J. Heazlewood, 1970
'Bon Rose' × 'Salmon Trout'

'Roseneath' 1 W-P
(S.J. Bisdee, 1942) S.J. Bisdee, 1956
'Eskimo' × 'Dawnglow'

'Roseness' 2 W-P
(J.M. de Navarro) J.M. de Navarro, 1976
(['Rose of Tralee' × 'Lisbreen'] × 'Rose Caprice') × (['Templemore' × 'Salmon Trout'] × ['Debutante' × 'Rose Royale']); sdlg no. 303/III
Corona deep pink. Mid-season. Resembles a shorter-stemmed 'Romance' with the inner perianth segments broader and the corona of a deeper colour

'Rosenkavalier' 2 W-? (b)
(D.S. Bell) D.S. Bell, 1955

'Rose Noble' 2 W-?
(G.L. Wilson) G. Zandbergen-Terwegen, 1957
Corona with pink at rim

'Rosenwyn' 1 Y-Y
(Rosewarne EHS, 1974) Rosewarne EHS, 1989
'Dominator' × 'Toorak Gold'

Fl. 110 mm wide; perianth segments brilliant yellow 7A, slightly twisted, overlapping; corona expanded, slightly brighter in tone (12A), with mouth lobed, rim flanged and crenate. Very early

'Rose o' Day' 2 W-YYP
(de Graaff Bros) de Graaff Bros, 1969

'Rose of Brodie' 2 W-GPP
(The Brodie of Brodie, pre-1949)
'Easter Morn' × 'Riva'
Corona opening creamy yellow, becoming rosy pink depending on place and season, with pale green at base and a slightly paler pink at rim, mouth expanded and frilled. Scented

'Rose of Calvary' 2 W-P
(S.J. Bisdee, 1945)
'White Sentinel' × 'Rosario'

'Rose of Cuan' 2 W-? (b)
(The Brodie of Brodie, pre-1953)
Corona opening yellow, quickly becoming white, tinged pink. Div. 1 until 1965

'Rose of May' 4 W-W
(G.L. Wilson, pre-1950)
'Sacrifice' × 'Smyrna'
Fl. rounded, 65 mm wide, pale creamy white; perianth and other petaloid segments in several whorls, very broad, rounded at apex, only very slightly mucronate, overlapping half or more; the outer whorl spreading or a little inflexed, plane; the inner whorls very little shorter, successively more strongly inflexed, with margins incurved, often folded at midrib; the centre segments strongly inflexed, with margins tightly incurled. Late. Scented. AM(Haarlem) 1950, AM(e) 1957

"Rose of May
Variant of Poeticus 'Plenus'?

'Rose of Nashville' 2 W-P
(V. Brink) V. Brink, 1968
'Wild Rose' open pollinated
Fl. 102 mm wide; corona deep rose pink. Mid-season

'Rose of Sharon' 1 W-P
(S.J. Bisdee, 1942) S.J. Bisdee, 1956
'Eskimo' × 'Dawnglow'

'Rose of Tralee' 2 W-P
(J.L. Richardson, pre-1937)
'White Sentinel' self pollinated
Fl. 95 mm wide; perianth segments ovate, blunt, fairly prominently mucronate, pure white, spreading, overlapping one-third; the inner segments a little inflexed, with margins wavy; corona funnel-shaped, smooth, rosy apricot-pink, lightly frilled, with rim crenate and a little flanged. Late. 2n=27.

AM(Haarlem) 1950

'Roseport' 2 W-P
(J.N. Hancock & Co., 1950) J.N. Hancock & Co., 1964
'Kenmare' × 'Pink o' Dawn'
Corona lilac pink. Late

'Roseprincess' 2 W-P
(S.J. Bisdee, 1951)
'Gala' × 'Rosario'

'Rose Quartz' 2 W-GPP
(J.M. de Navarro) J.M. de Navarro, 1976
'Passionale' × ('Rose Caprice' × 'Rose Royale'); sdlg no. 340/III
Fl. 95 mm wide. Mid-season. Resembles a shorter-stemmed 'Passionale' with the inner perianth segments broader and the corona of a deeper pink

'Rose Queen' 2 W-P
(A. Gibson, pre-1949)

'Rose Rhythm' 4 W-P
(W. Jackson Jr, 1970) Unregistered
'Lawali' × sdlg 72/60; sdlg no. 134/70

'Rose Ribbon' 2 W-YYP
(G.E. Mitsch, pre-1954)
'Interim' × 'Mabel Taylor'
Corona flared, pale yellow or cream, with a band of rich salmon rose or rosy orange at rim. Mid-season

'Rose Royale' 2 W-P
(J.L. Richardson) J.L. Richardson, 1958
('Rose of Tralee' × 'Lisbreen') × 'Salmon Trout'
Fl. 102 mm wide; perianth segments very broadly ovate, blunt or squarish at apex, prominently mucronate, ice white, spreading or a little inflexed, plane or with margins slightly incurling near apex, smooth and of thick substance, overlapping half; the inner segments more narrowly ovate, blunt, a little more strongly inflexed, with margins slightly wavy; corona somewhat funnel-shaped, broad, smooth, strong yellowish pink, with lime green in tube and a darker tone of pink at rim, mouth expanded and wavy, with rim only very slightly notched in places. 2n=28. PC(e) 1961, AM(e) 1964, FCC(e) 1972

'Rose Song' 2 W-P
(H.A. Brown, 1941)
Corona salmon pink, frilled. Mid-season

'Rosetta' 3 W-? (b or c)
(Miss F.W. Currey, pre-1910)
'Ann Abbott' × 'Wild Rose'

'Rosetta' 2 W-P
(G.H. Johnstone, 1949) G.H. Johnstone, 1959
Fl. 89 mm wide

'Rosette'
(pre-1908)

'Rosette' 4
(R.A. van der Schoot, pre-1930)
'Argent' sport

'Roseum' 2 W-P
(C.E. Radcliff, 1945) J.M.Radcliff, 1956
'Pinkie' × 'Dawnglow'

'Rosevale' 2 W-P
(S.J. Bisdee, 1945) S.J. Bisdee, 1956
'White Sentinel' × 'Rosario'
Syn. 'Rose Vale'

'Rose Vale' 2 W-P
Syn. of 'Rosevale'

'Roseve' 2 W-GPP
(Mrs G. Link) Mrs G. Link, 1966
'Rosabella' × 'Evening'
Fl. 89 mm wide. Corona buff pink. Mid-season. Resembles an improved 'Rosabella'

'Rosevean' 3 W-? (b)
(G.L. Wilson, pre-1939)

'Rosevears' 2 W-WWP
(S.J. Bisdee, 1941)
'Pinkeen' × 'Pink o' Dawn'

'Rose Victor' 2 W-P
(J.R.Erp, c.1956) Unregistered
'Moorpark' × 'Pink Bonnington'

'Rosewell' 2 W-P
(J.L. Richardson, pre-1952)
'Rose of Tralee' × 'Lisbreen'
Perianth segments pure white; corona apricot pink, with mouth expanded and frilled

'Rosewing' 1 W-P
(K.J. Heazlewood) , 1967
'Roselands' × 'Roseum'

'Rosewood' 2 W-P
(S.J. Bisdee, 1945)
'Avanley' × 'Rosario'

'Rosewood' 2 W-? (b)
(Barr & Sons, pre-1950)

'Rosewood' 1 W-P
(K.J. Heazlewood, c.1972) Unregistered
Sdlg A15 × 'Dear Me'
Fl. 85 mm wide; corona deep pink, with a darker tone at base, rim flanged. Early. Resembles 'Dear Me' but with a deeper-coloured corona

'Roseworthy' 2 W-P
(D. Blanchard, 1948)
'Rose of Tralee' × 'Wild Rose'; sdlg no. 43/37A
Fl. facing down; perianth segments broadly ovate, blunt and mucronate, sometimes truncate, spreading or slightly reflexed, a little concave, with margins incurling, overlapping half; the inner segments narrower and twisted; corona cup-shaped, straight-sided, bright rosy pink, with mouth slightly expanded, frilled. Resembles an improved 'Wild Rose' with a longer stem. *AM(g) 1991. See also 'Roseanthy'

'Roseworthy' 2 W-P
(S.J. Bisdee, 1950)
'Kerabin' × 'Courtship'

'Rosewynne' 2 W-P
(Mrs M. Moorby) Mrs M. Moorby, 1963
Fl. 95 mm wide; perianth segments milk white; corona large disc-shaped, deep pink. Mid-season. Resembles 'New Break'

'Roseyards' 2 W-P
(G.L. Wilson, pre-1953)
'Interim' × 'Evening'
Corona opening clear pink, becoming coppery pink

'Rosey Pink' 2 W-?
Unregistered
See also 'Rosy Pink'

'Rosie' 2 W-P
(M.E.Brogden) Unregistered

'Rosie Bates' 2 W-W
(Ken Farmer Nurseries) Ken Farmer Nurseries, 1978
Fl. 110 mm wide

'Rosie McNabb' 2 W-P
(W.M. Spry, pre-1973) Unregistered
'August Pink' × Fairbairn sdlg
Corona dark pink. Very early

'Rosiera' 2 W-W
(R.H. Bath, pre-1931)

'Rosina' 8 Y-Y
(pre-1850)

'Rosina' 5
(Sir A.P.W. Thomas, pre-1930)

'Rosinate' 2 (a)
(A.H. Ahrens) J.S. Leitch, 1955

'Rosita' 2 (a)
(R.H. Bath, pre-1927)

'Roslyn' 1 W-P
(C.E. Radcliff, 1944) J.M.Radcliff, 1956

'Dawnglow' × 'Rosario'
Perianth segments broadly ovate, blunt, very slightly mucronate, a little inflexed, concave and with margins minutely incurling, overlapping half; the inner segments more narrowly ovate, inflexed at base, reflexed at apex, a little twisted; corona cylindrical, mouth expanded and 6-lobed, loosely frilled, with rim irregularly crenate and widely rolled

'Roslyn' 2 W-? (b)
(de Graaff Bros, pre-1948)
AM(Haarlem) 1948

'Rosny' ?-P
(Alister Clark, pre-1948)

'Rosny' 2 W-P
(C.E. Radcliff)

'Rosque' 2 W-P
(C.E. Radcliff, 1941) J.M.Radcliff, 1956

'Ross' 2 (a)
(C.E. Radcliff, 1942)

'Ross' 2 W-P
(W. Jackson Jr, 1956) W. Jackson Jr, 1968
Sdlg 86/51 × 'Ceram'

'Rossaphin' 1 W-Y
(D. Bramley) D. Bramley, 1963
Fl. 115 mm wide, corona pale creamy yellow. Mid-season. Resembles 'Preamble' but with the perianth segments less acute and the corona of a lighter colour

'Rossarden' 2 W-? (b)
(S.J. Bisdee, 1939)
'Mitylene' × 'Sunstar'

'Rossetti' 1 W-W
(Barr & Sons, pre-1913)

'Rossevan' 1 W-W
(W. Jackson Jr, 1966) Unregistered
'Tranquil' × 'Caprice'; sdlg no. 67/66

'Rossferry' 2 W-GYR
(Ballydorn Bulb Farm) Ballydorn Bulb Farm, 1986
'Gransha' open pollinated
Corona deep yellow, with deep orange-red at rim. Very late

'Rossini' 1 Y-Y
(pre-1896)
Perianth segments pale yellow

'Rossini' 2 W-O
(J.L. Richardson) Mrs H.K. Richardson, 1968
'Kilworth' × 'Rockall'
Corona slightly expanded, reddish orange, frilled. $2n=28$

'Rosslare' 2 Y-YOO
(The Brodie of Brodie, c.1929)
'Seraglio' × 'Fortune'; sdlg no. 167/H/24
Perianth segments clear primrose yellow, deeply overlapping; corona rich reddish orange, golden yellow at base, frilled. AM(e) 1936, AM(Haarlem) 1939

'Rosslyn' 1 Y-Y
(pre-1889)
Corona slender, rich yellow

'Rossmore' 2 Y-O
(J.L. Richardson, pre-1943)
'Marksman' × 'Caerleon'
Perianth segments bright yellow; corona intense reddish orange. Resembles an improved 'Marksman'

'Rostella' 2 W-P
(C.E. Radcliff, 1941) J.M.Radcliff, 1956
'Glendevie' × 'Dawnglow'

'Rosthwaite Cam' 1 W-P
(W.O. Backhouse) E. Longford, 1969
Corona coppery salmon pink. Resembles an improved 'Maiden's Blush' in form with less flare to the corona mouth

'Rostov' 2 W-W
(J.L. Richardson, pre-1944)
'Slemish' × 'Cameronian'
Corona with rim flanged and dentate. Resembles a larger and improved 'Slemish'

'Rostrevor' 1 W-Y
(J.T. Gray, pre-1931)
Perianth segments overlapping; corona lemon yellow. AM(e)(NZ) 1931

'Rosy' 2
(M. van Waveren & Sons, pre-1916)

'Rosy Bill' 2 W-? (b)
(G.L. Wilson) G. Zandbergen-Terwegen, 1959

'Rosy Cloud' 4 W-P
(C.A. van Zanten & Sons) C.A. van Zanten & Sons, 1968
'Mrs R.O.Backhouse' sport
Fl. 110 mm wide; perianth and other petaloid segments ivory white; corona segments between pale yellowish pink 29D and light yellowish pink 36B

'Rosy Dawn' 2 Y-Y
(N. Grakon) N. Grakon, 1980
'Apricot Beauty' × 'Rosa van Lima'
Fl. 110 mm wide; perianth segments greenish yellow (4D); corona vivid to brilliant yellow 14B-C

'Rosy Diamond' 2 W-WWP
(G.L. Wilson) G. Zandbergen-Terwegen, 1950
AM(Haarlem) 1950

'Rosy Glow' 2 W-? (b)
(Oregon Bulb Farms, pre-1946)

'Rosy Morn' 3 W-? (b)
(Mrs R.O. Backhouse, pre-1913)
Fl. 64 mm wide; perianth segments tinged pink

'Rosy Morn' 2 W-? (b)
(Alister Clark, 1930) A. Overton, 1960

'Rosy Pink' 2 W-P
Syn. of 'Pink Sensation'

'Rosy Pink' 2 W-P
(O. Ronalds, pre-1967) Unregistered
See also 'Rosey Pink'

'Rosy Prelude' 2 W-P
(E.F. Hughes) E.F. Hughes, 1962
Fl. 115 mm wide; corona widely expanded, pale pink, with a darker tone at rim, frilled. Early. Resembles an earlier-flowered 'Rosario' of better substance

'Rosy Sunrise' 2 W-P
(F. Rijnveld & Sons) F. Rijnveld & Sons, 1939
Corona pure salmon apricot, with distinct overtones of rose pink, rim closely and deeply notched, as if fringed. AM(Haarlem) 1942, FCC(Haarlem) 1943

'Rosy Trumpet' 1 W-P
(R.O. Backhouse, 1928) de Graaff Bros, 1952
Fl. 82 mm wide; perianth segments narrowly ovate, acute, creamy white, with green flanked by yellow at midrib beneath, inflexed, strongly and symmetrically twisted, separated; corona funnel-shaped, finely ribbed, pink (near to 26C), paling to creamy white at base, mouth straight, wavy, with rim deeply notched. 2n=14

'Rosy Wonder' 2 W-WWP
(P. de Jager & Sons) van Eeden Bros, 1977
Fl. 85 mm wide; perianth segments ivory white; corona pinkish white, with a more or less broad band of strong yellowish pink 32C at rim. Early to mid-season

'Rotarian' 3 Y-R
(T. Bloomer) Rathowen Daffodils, 1982
'Sun Fire' hybrid × ?'Perimeter'; sdlg no. 203
Fl. 90 mm wide; perianth segments honey yellow; corona deep orange-red. Mid-season

'Rotary' 1 Y-Y
(T. Buncombe, pre-1934)

'Rothbury' 2 Y-O
(G. Harrison) G. Harrison, 1968
Sdlg × 'Ceylon'
Mid-season

'Rotherside' 3 W-? (b)
(F.H. Chapman, pre-1913)

'Rothesay' 1 W-? (b)
(C.R. Wootton) C.R. Wootton, 1956
'Trostan' × 'Content'

'Rothkenny' 1 W-Y
Syn. of 'Rathkenny'

'Rothroe'
(The Brodie of Brodie, pre-1943)
'Sunstar' × 'Hades'

'Rotoiti' 2 W-W
(J.S. Leitch) J.S. Leitch, 1967
Fl. 121 mm wide

'Rotoma' 1 W-Y
(J.S. Leitch) J.S. Leitch, 1967
Corona lemon yellow

'Rotonde' 3 W-Y
(Warnaar & Co.) Warnaar & Co., 1962
'Sempre Avanti' × 'Mrs Barclay'
Fl. 105 mm wide; perianth segments ivory white; corona vivid yellow 12A. Mid-season

'Rotopika' 2 Y-O
(S.A. Free) Mrs S.I. Free, 1968

'Rotor' 12 Y-Y
(David Adams) David Adams, 1994
N. asturiensis × *N. cyclamineus*; sdlg no. 85/02A
Fl. star-shaped, 42 mm wide, facing slightly downwards; perianth segments narrow, plane; corona cylindrical, smooth, constricted near mouth, with mouth frilled. Dwarf. Very early

'Rotorua'
(?Sir A.P.W. Thomas, pre-1915)

'Rotorua' 1 W-? (b)
(A. Gibson, pre-1950)

'Rotterdam' 1 Y-Y
(G. Lubbe & Son) G. Lubbe & Son, 1962
Fl. 120 mm wide; perianth segments vivid yellow 9B; corona darker in tone (13A). Mid-season. AM(Haarlem) 1962

'Rotunda' 1 W-? (b)
(G.D. Davison, pre-1913)

'Rouge' 2 Y-O
(G.L. Wilson, pre-1936)

Fl. 102 mm wide; perianth segments broadly ovate, blunt or truncate, light yellow 15D, with pinkish orange overtones, paler at midrib, with slight white mucro, more or less spreading, somewhat creased, with margins incurling, overlapping one-third to a half; the inner segments more heavily creased, with margins wavy; corona bowl-shaped, ribbed, deep orange (near to 28A), mouth straight, tightly frilled, rim crenate. Early. *AM(g) 1952

'Rouge Dragon' 2 W-? (b)
(Sir C.H. Cave, pre-1908)

'Roulette' 2 W-YYO
(G.A. Uit den Boogaard) J.J. Grullemans & Sons, 1959
Fl. 115 mm wide; perianth segments creamy white; corona brilliant greenish yellow 4A, with strong orange 25A at rim. Mid-season. AM(Haarlem) 1959

'Roulette' 2 Y-R
(D.S. Bell, c.1978) Unregistered
'Ceylon' × 'Rupee'
Perianth segments deep yellow, slightly suffused red at base; corona red

'Roumania' 8 W-Y
(?G. van der Weyden Jobson, pre-1914)
Corona canary yellow. AM(Haarlem) 1914

'Roundabout' 1 Y-Y
(C.E. Radcliff, 1941) J.M.Radcliff, 1956
'Fahan' × 'Carbine'

'Roundelay' 7
(pre-1907)

'Roundelay' 2 W-Y
(W.G. Pannill) W.G. Pannill, 1978
'Cascade' × 'Verona'; sdlg no. 64/29
Fl. 85 mm wide. Mid-season

'Roundhead'
(The Brodie of Brodie, c1915)
N. poeticus sdlg × 'Kestrel'
Fl. small, rounded

'Round Hill' 4 W-Y
(W.G. Pannill) W.G. Pannill, 1982
'Moyard' × 'Gay Challenger'; sdlg no. 66/16 A
Fl. 92 mm wide. Mid-season

'Round Island' 3 Y-R
(The Brodie of Brodie, c.1929)
'Hospodar' × ('Beacon' × 'Fortune'); sdlg no. 95/B/24
Perianth segments deep yellow; corona widely expanded, brick red

'Roundle' 2 Y-Y
(G.H. Engleheart, pre-1927)

Fl. 83 mm wide; perianth segments clear lemon, irregular, overlapping one-third; corona clear pale buttercup yellow

'Round Meadow' 3 W-GYY
(W.G. Pannill) W.G. Pannill, 1978
'Green Hills' × 'Tobernaveen'; sdlg no. 64/55
Fl. 98 mm wide. Late

'Round Robin' 2 Y-YYR
(Carncairn Daffodils) Carncairn Daffodils, 1985
'Aircastle' hybrid
Perianth segments broad, creamy yellow, overlapping; corona widely expanded, with a well-defined band of red at rim. Mid-season. Resembles a red-rimmed 'Aircastle'

'Roundstone' 2 W-Y
(J.L. Richardson, pre-1947)
Corona broad, opening pale yellow, becoming cream, with rim rolled

'Roussillon' 11a W-WPP
(J. Gerritsen & Son) J. Gerritsen & Son, 1984
'Pick Up' × 'Pearlshell'; sdlg no. 937
Perianth segments opening pale greenish yellow (4D), becoming white; corona split, the six segments orange-pink, with white at base. Mid-season

'Routor' 1 Y-Y
(G.W. Tarry, 1975) du Plessis Bros, 1989
Sdlg no. G1A
Fl. 102 mm wide, mid-yellow; corona cylindrical. Mid-season to late

'Rovena' 2 (a)
(R.F. Calvert, pre-1937)

'Rovenius' 1 W-? (b)
(J.A. van der Swet & Son, pre-1951)
AM(Haarlem) 1951

'Rover' 1 Y-Y
(H.A. Brown, 1943)
Fl. bright clear yellow. Early

'Rover' 2 Y-YOO
(R.V. Favell, pre-1947)

'Rovers Return' 2 W-WWO
(Tom Forster, 1960s) Unregistered
Perianth segments pure white; corona large disc-shaped, creamy white, with deep orange at rim and the rim dentate. Late

'Rowallane' 1 Y-Y
(G.L. Wilson) G.L. Wilson, 1960
Fl. 100 mm wide; perianth segments brighter than vivid yellow 9A; the inner segments a little shorter; corona very slightly ribbed, vivid yellow 14B, mouth

expanded and lightly frilled. Late. 2n=28

'Rowan' 8
(pre-1914)
Poetaz

'Rowella' 1 W-Y
(W. Jackson Jr, 1954) W. Jackson Jr, 1966
'Tamara' × 'Merri'
Corona lemon yellow

'Rowena' 1 W-W
(Barr & Sons, pre-1904)
Perianth segments narrow, acute, silvery white; corona expanded, flushed peach pink. Early

'Rowena Lee' 1 (a)
(M. van Waveren & Sons, pre-1948)

'Rowena Lee Teagle' 2 W-ORR
(Warnaar & Co.) Warnaar & Co., 1956
'Flamenco' × 'Aflame'
AM(Haarlem) 1957

'Rowner' 2 W-Y
(G. Churcher, pre-1931)
Fl. 89 mm wide; perianth segments creamy white, with lemon at base, regular, overlapping two-thirds; corona broadly funnel-shaped, bright lemon. Mid-season

'Rowsley' 2 Y-O
(J.N. Hancock & Co., pre-1949)
Perianth segments pale yellow; corona pale orange

'Rowsley' 2 W-? (b)
(D.B. Milne, pre-1950)

'Roxana' 3 W-? (b)
(P.D. Williams, pre-1913)

'Roxane' 1 W-W
(C.G. van Tubergen, pre-1927)
Fl. facing slightly downwards; perianth segments milk white, overlapping; corona broad, flared, opening primrose yellow, quickly becoming creamy white, with rim rolled. Mid-season. 2n=28. AM(Haarlem) 1926, FA(Haarlem) 1929, FCC(Haarlem) 1930, *AM(g) 1936

'Roxborough' 2 (a)
(R. Hyde) R. Hyde, 1957

'Roxie' 2 W-P
(Curtis Tolley) Curtis Tolley, 1995
'Dewy Rose' × 'Dailmanach'; sdlg no. T88-6-11
Perianth segments broad; corona funnel-shaped, solid pink, frilled. Mid-season. Sunproof

'Royal' 1 (a)
(G.H. Engleheart, pre-1907)

'Royal Applause' 2 W-YYO
(Tom Forster, 1960s) Unregistered
Perianth segments creamy white; corona disc-shaped, ribbed, bright orange-yellow, with a broad band of orange at rim. Tall. Mid-season to late

'Royal Arch' 2 W-P
(S.A. Free) S.A. Free, 1961
Fl. 108 mm wide. Late. Resembles 'Pensive' but with a shorter and paler-coloured corona

'Royal Armour' 1 Y-Y
(O. Ronalds, c.1967) Rosewarne EHS, 1987
Fl. golden yellow; perianth segments broadly ovate, blunt, slightly mucronate, spreading or inflexed, somewhat creased, overlapping half; the inner segments a little narrower, somewhat twisted or with margins wavy; corona cylindrical, narrow, smooth, with mouth expanded, rim flanged and deeply crenate. Tall. Early. 2n=28

'Royal Aron' 2 Y-R
Syn. of 'Royal Avon'

'Royal Artist' 3 (a)
(W.A. Grace, pre-1936)

'Royal Ascot' 4 Y-R
(D.S. Bell) D.S. Bell, 1983
'Fiji' × 'Ashanti'
Perianth and other petaloid segments yellow; corona segments dark red

'Royal Avon' 2 Y-R
(D.S. Bell) D.S.Bell, 1978
'Ceylon' × 'Rupee'
Fl. 96 mm wide; perianth segments deep yellow, slightly suffused red at base; corona red. Early. Resembles a deeper-coloured 'Rupee'. See also 'Royal Avon'

'Royal Ballet' 2 W-WPP
(Brian S. Duncan) Rathowen Daffodils, 1984
'Simile' × 'Violetta'; sdlg no. 362
Fl. 110 mm wide; perianth segments very broad, rounded at apex, slightly mucronate, pure white, spreading, plane, smooth, overlapping half; the inner segments broadly ovate, square-shouldered at base, a little inflexed; corona funnel-shaped, lilac pink, with white at base, mouth expanded, rim crenate. Mid-season. Sunproof

'Royal Banner' 2 (a)
(A.M. Wilson, pre-1939)

'Royal Beauty' 3 Y-R
(G.H. Rotteveel & Sons) G.H. Rotteveel & Sons, 1980

Perianth segments light greenish yellow 5C; corona orange-red (30C)

'Royal Bengal' 2 Y-R
(G. Lewis) D.S. Bell, 1955
Perianth segments deep yellow; corona dark red

'Royal Blood' 1 Y-Y
(A. Gibson, pre-1927)
Corona expanded, with rim dentate

'Royal Blush' 4 W-P
(K.J. Heazlewood, c.1967) Unregistered
'Mary Copeland' × 'Mabel Taylor'

'Royal Bride' 1 W-W
(J.W.A. Lefeber, pre-1953)
AM(Haarlem) 1952

'Royal Bugler' 2 (a)
(Miss K.M. Hinchliff, pre-1935)

'Royal Cadenza' 2 Y-R
(D.S. Bell, 1968) D.S. Bell, 1978
'Ceylon' × 'Rupee'
Fl. 112 mm wide; perianth segments strong yellow; corona very shallow bowl-shaped, red. Early to mid-season

'Royal Castle'
G.L.Wilson sdlg × 'Goldcourt' × 'King's Ransom'

'Royal Charger' 2 Y-O
(J.L. Richardson, pre-1953)
'Royal Mail' × 'Bahram'
Fl. 102 mm wide; perianth segments broadly ovate, slightly mucronate, brilliant yellow 9C, with margins incurling at apex, overlapping half; the inner segments more narrowly ovate and slightly inflexed; corona cup-shaped, vivid orange 28B, mouth straight, tightly frilled, with rim dentate. AM(e) 1954

'Royal Charm' 2 Y-ORR
(J.L. Richardson) Mrs H.K. Richardson, 1964
'Air Marshal' × 'Jaguar'
Perianth segments deep golden yellow; corona bright orange-red, with a paler tone towards base, rim slightly dentate. 2n=28

'Royal Chief' 2 Y-?
(H.A. Brown) A. Ladson, 1960

'Royal Choice' 1 W-Y
(D. Bramley) D. Bramley, 1964
Fl. 121 mm wide; corona pale creamy yellow. Mid-season. Resembles a larger-flowered 'Trostan' with a darker corona of smoother texture

'Royal City' 1 (a)
(H.A. Brown, pre-1950)

'Royal Coachman' 2 W-GYO
(Murray W. Evans) Murray W. Evans, 1969
'Rose Marie' × 'Carolina'
2n=28

'Royal Command' 2 W-YPP
Syn. of 'Royal Decree'

'Royal Command' 1 Y-Y
(T.H. Piper, c.1966) Unregistered
'Guinea Gold' × ('Melissa' × 'Kingscourt')

'Royal Crown' 1 (a)
(Warnaar & Co., pre-1930)

'Royal Crown' 2 W-O
(Warnaar & Co., pre-1950)
'John Evelyn' hybrid
Perianth segments silver white; corona widely expanded, soft apricot orange, heavily frilled

'Royal Daffodil' 1 Y-Y
(G.L. Wilson) G. Zandbergen-Terwegen, 1965
Fl. golden yellow. Mid-season. Resembles a darker 'Irish Luck'

'Royal Daffodil' 1 Y-Y
Syn. of 'Coronation Fanfare'

'Royal Day' 2 Y-O
(G.H. Rotteveel & Sons, 1946) G.H. Rotteveel & Sons, 1961
Fl. 90 mm wide; perianth segments brilliant greenish yellow 5C; corona orange (28A). Late

'Royal Decree' 2 W-YPP
(M.J. Jefferson-Brown) M.J. Jefferson-Brown, 1985
'Rose Caprice' × 'Rose Royale'
Corona clear rose pink. Mid-season. Syn. 'Royal Command'

'Royal Degree' 4 W-O
(?New Zealand origin, pre-1996) Unregistered

'Royal Delight' 1 Y-Y
(Warnaar & Co., pre-1930)
'Golden Harvest' × 'Magnificence'

'Royal Diamond' 3 W-? (b)
(Mrs R.O. Backhouse, pre-1921)

'Royal Dornoch' 1 Y-Y
(D.C. MacArthur) D.C. MacArthur, 1991
'Sundance' × 'Magnificence'; sdlg no. EV80-52
Fl. 116 mm wide; perianth segments ovate, vivid yellow 12A, with white mucro, spreading, of great substance; corona funnel-shaped, ribbed, darker in tone (14A) than the perianth, mouth widely flared, lobed, rim crenate and flanged. Mid-season. Strongly scented

'Royal Dutch' 2 W-? (b)
(L. van Leeuwen & Son, pre-1938)

'Royal Dutch' 1 Y-Y
(W.F.Leenen, pre-1977) Unregistered
Fl. deep yellow. Mid-season to late

'Royal Eve' 2 W-Y
(J.N. Hancock & Co., 1946) J.N. Hancock & Co., 1964
'Show Princess' × 'White House'
Corona creamy yellow. Late. Resembles a large-flowered 'White House'

'Royal Flame' 2 Y-O
(D.V. West, pre-1935)

'Royal Flush' 1 Y-Y
(G.L. Wilson, pre-1927)
Early

'Royal Flush' 4
'Binkie' × 'Royal Sovereign'

'Royal Gaelic' 2 Y-Y
(G.L. Wilson) E. Longford, 1964
'Goldcourt' sdlg × 'King's Ransom'
Fl. deep golden yellow, faintly flushed apricot orange; corona slightly darker in tone. Early to mid-season

'Royal Gem' 1 Y-Y
(A. Overton) A. Overton, 1960
Fl. clear yellow; perianth segments broad, smooth; corona with rim flanged

'Royal George' 2 W-? (b)
(G.H. Engleheart, pre-1914)

'Royal George' 2 Y-YRR
(D.S. Bell) D.S. Bell, 1963
'Dunkeld' × 'Burgundy'
Fl. 100 mm wide. Mid-season

'Royal Gift' 1 Y-Y
(C.A. Nethercote) T. Morrison, 1960
Fl. rich yellow; corona with rim flanged

'Royal Glimpse' 2 Y-O
(A. Gibson, pre-1951)
'Royal Mail' × 'Rosslare'

'Royal Gold' 1 Y-Y
(de Graaff Bros, pre-1921)
Perianth segments rich yellow, overlapping; corona ribbed, golden yellow, with rim crenate

'Royal Gold' 1 Y-Y
(Warnaar & Co.) Warnaar & Co., 1956
'Rembrandt' × 'Golden Harvest'
2n=29. AM(Haarlem) 1956

'Royal Highness' 11a W-O
(J. Gerritsen & Son) J. Gerritsen & Son, 1977
'Sovereign' × 'Royal Orange'
Fl. 110 mm wide; perianth segments ivory white; corona segments light orange 23B, tinged strong orange 25B, with a much paler tone at rim and with near to white at shoulders, heavily frilled. Early

'Royal Huntsman' 2 W-R
(D.S. Bell) D.S. Bell, 1983
'Huntsman' × 'Rockall' hybrid

'Royal Hussar' 2 W-? (b)
(Mrs R.O. Backhouse, pre-1921)

'Royalist' 1 Y-Y
(N.Y. Lower, pre-1914)
'Cleopatra' × 'Broadford'
Fl. soft clear yellow; perianth segments inflexed

'Royal Jenny' 6 W-W
(J.L. Richardson) E. Longford, 1963
'Broughshane' × 'Jenny'
Fl. 85 mm wide; corona opening creamy yellow, quickly becoming white, with rim rolled. Early to mid-season

'Royal Jester' 2 Y-R
(J.L. Richardson) Mrs H.K. Richardson, 1970
'Patagonia' × 'Firecracker'
Perianth segments deep golden yellow; corona slightly expanded, vivid deep red, with mouth lobed. Sunproof

'Royal Lady' 3 W-Y
(G.H. Engleheart, pre-1914)
Perianth segments pure white, overlapping at base only; corona bright canary yellow, with rim dentate. Tall. Resembles a larger 'Seagull' of stronger substance

'Royal Lancer' 2 (a)
(Mrs R.O. Backhouse, pre-1921)

'Royal Mail' 2 Y-O
(J.L. Richardson, pre-1937)
'Tregoose' × 'Porthilly'
Perianth segments golden yellow; corona vivid reddish orange, frilled. 2n=28. AM(Haarlem) 1942, FCC(Haarlem) 1950

'Royal Marine' 2 W-YOO
(J.S.B. Lea) Clive Postles Daffodils, 1989
'Colley Gate' × 'Ibberton', sdlg no. 1-20-75
Fl. 110 mm wide; perianth segments broadly ovate, prominently mucronate, spreading, plane, smooth, regular, overlapping half; corona shallow cup-shaped, closely ribbed, bright orange, with yellow at base, mouth expanded, rim regularly dentate. Mid-season

'Royal Minstrel' 2 Y-O
(D.S. Bell) D.S. Bell, 1957
'Artist's Model' hybrid
Perianth segments rich yellow; corona disc-shaped, orange

'Royal Model' 2 W-YYO
(Tom Forster, 1960s) Unregistered
Corona disc-shaped, ribbed, bright yellow, rim with a line of bright orange at rim. Tall. Late

'Royal Oak' 1 (a)
(G. Zandbergen-Terwegen, pre-1937)
Syn. 'Handsome'

'Royal Oak' 1 Y-Y
(J.L. Richardson) J.L. Richardson, 1955
('Royalist' × 'Crocus') × 'Goldcourt'
Fl. deep golden yellow; corona with rim rolled and dentate

'Royal Occasion' 2 W-P
(Mrs J. Abel Smith) Mrs J. Abel Smith, 1982
'Knightwick' hybrid; sdlg no. E8/31
Fl. 102 mm wide; perianth segments pure white; corona deep pink. Mid-season

'Royal Orange' 2 W-O
(G.A. Uit den Boogaard, pre-1953)
Perianth segments broadly ovate, blunt, mucronate, with margins slightly incurving, overlapping a little more than half; the inner segments slightly narrower; corona widely expanded, reddish orange, loosely flanged and frilled. 2n=28. AM(Haarlem) 1954. Received AM(Haarlem) 1954 as 'Coronation'

'Royal Palace' 2 Y-O
(J.L. Richardson) Mrs H.K. Richardson, 1968
'Patagonia' × 'Firecracker'
Perianth segments golden yellow; corona deep reddish orange, with mouth expanded, rim dentate

'Royal Palm' 2 Y-R
(S.C. Gaspar) R.J. Abernethy, 1957
Corona ruby red

'Royal Pennant' 4 Y-R
(R.C. Gordon) R.C. Gordon, 1964
Fl. 102 mm wide. Mid-season. Resembles a shorter-necked and stronger 'Scarlet Perfection' with more numerous whorls

'Royal Pink' 2 W-WWP
(P. de Jager & Sons) van Eeden Bros, 1977
Fl. 90 mm wide; perianth segments greenish white 157D; corona yellowish white, with coral pink at rim

'Royal Porcelain' 2 W-WPP
(J.L. Richardson) Mrs H.K. Richardson, 1963
'Rose Caprice' × 'Infatuation'
Perianth segments broadly ovate, of thick and waxy substance; corona pink, paling to white at base, with rim dentate and slightly flanged

'Royal Pride' 2 W-O
(Tom Forster, 1960s) Unregistered
Perianth segments broad, creamy white; corona large, shallow, bright yellow-orange, with rim broadly crenate. Mid-season to late

'Royal Princess' 3 W-WWR
(Mrs J. Abel Smith) Mrs J. Abel Smith, 1985
'Mary Isabel' × ('Hamzali' × 'Aircastle'); sdlg no. F33/01
Fl. pure white; perianth segments very broad, rounded at apex and truncate, slightly reflexed, a little concave, overlapping half; the inner segments narrower, more strongly reflexed, with margins lightly incurved; corona bowl-shaped, loosely ribbed, with a narrow band of orange-red at rim, mouth expanded and frilled. Late

'Royal Ransom' 2 Y-O
(J.L. Richardson, pre-1937)
'Damson' × 'Penquite'
Perianth segments broadly or very broadly ovate in outline, blunt or rounded at apex, slightly mucronate, soft buff yellow, shaded with pink on ageing, spreading, plane, smooth and of great substance, overlapping half; the inner segments more narrowly ovate, only very slightly mucronate, a little inflexed; corona bowl-shaped, lightly ribbed, orange, mouth sometimes deeply split and overlapping, a little frilled. Early to mid-season. AM(Haarlem) 1955

'Royal Red' 2 Y-O
(pre-1949)

'Royal Regiment' 2 W-O
(J.L. Richardson) J.L. Richardson, 1961
'Kilworth' × 'Arbar'
Perianth segments broadly ovate, rounded at apex, not noticeably mucronate, pure white, spreading, concave, overlapping half; the inner segments only a little narrower, somewhat inflexed; corona shallow bowl-shaped, closely ribbed, fiery reddish orange. 2n=28

'Royal Revel' 2 Y-O
(J.L. Richardson) Mrs H.K. Richardson, 1967
'Air Marshal' × 'Firecracker'
Fl. 110 mm wide; perianth segments golden yellow; corona reddish orange, with rim deeply crenate. Mid-season. 2n=28. Resembles a large-flowered 'Air Marshal'

'Royal Robe' 2 W-Y
(H.A. Brown, 1939) J.N. Hancock & Co., 1960
'Walter J.Smith' × 'Fortune'
Corona widely expanded, pale primrose yellow, frilled

'Royal Romance' 2 (a)
(H.A. Brown, pre-1950)

'Royal Rouge' 3 W-? (b)
(H. Backhouse, pre-1910)

'Royal Ruby' 3 W-? (b)
(J.L. Richardson, pre-1923)

'Royal Sceptre' 4 Y-R
(D.S. Bell) D.S. Bell, 1979
'Fiji' × 'Ashanti'
Fl. 110 mm wide; perianth and other petaloid segments strong yellow; corona segments red. Mid-season. Resembles a differently coloured 'Fiji'

'Royal Scot' 2 W-YYO
(R.O. Backhouse, pre-1931)
Perianth segments creamy white, overlapping; corona shallow, bright yellow, with reddish orange at rim

'Royal Seal' 2 W-R
(The Brodie of Brodie, c.1942)
'Red Hackle' × 'Sunstar'; sdlg no. 57/A/37
Perianth segments pure white; corona shallow, sealing-wax scarlet

'Royal Silk' 2 Y-R
(G. Lewis) D.S. Bell, 1955

'Royal Sovereign' 4 W-Y
(W.F.M. Copeland, pre-1908)
Hybrid between 'Minnie Hume' and 'Telamonius Plenus'
Perianth and other petaloid segments ovate, blunt, ivory white, smooth, separated; the outer whorl prominently mucronate, with margins sometimes wavy or incurling; the inner segments of the outer whorl not noticeably mucronate, twisted; the inner whorl shorter, with margins folded inwards; corona segments shorter than the inner whorl of petaloid segments and interspersed among them, bright yellow, frilled. Mid-season. AM(e) 1914

'Royal Spain' 1 (a)
(Miss K.M. Hinchliff, pre-1937)
Syn. 'Los Flamencos'

'Royal Standard'
(F.H. Chapman, c.1911)

'Royal Standard' 2 (a)
(J.L. Richardson, pre-1938)

'Royal Star' 3 W-O
(G.H. Engleheart, pre-1906)
Perianth segments opening creamy white, tinged sulphur yellow, becoming milk white; corona almost disc-shaped, ribbed, opening bright yellowish orange, becoming intense reddish orange. Tall

'Royal Tan' 2 Y-R
(R. Hyde) R. Hyde, 1955

'Royal Torch' 2 (a)
(S.C. Gaspar) R.J. Abernethy, 1957

'Royal Tour' 1 Y-Y
(C.O. Fairbairn) J.L. Martin, 1978
Fl. 103 mm wide; perianth segments brilliant yellow 10A; corona darker in tone (12A). Early to mid-season. Resembles a taller 'Kingscourt' of deeper colour

'Royal Trophy' 3 W-YYR
(W.G. Pannill) W.G. Pannill, 1970
'Tuskar Light' × 'Aircastle'

'Royalty' 2 Y-Y
(G.H. Engleheart, pre-1913)
Fl. 102 mm wide; corona flared, darker in tone than the perianth

'Royalty' 1 Y-Y
Syn. of 'Rex'

'Royal Victory' 1 Y-Y
(G.B. van Rhijn) G.B. van Rhijn, 1961
Fl. 130 mm wide; perianth segments broadly ovate, brilliant yellow 8A, with slight white mucro, a little inflexed, creased, overlapping one-third to a half; the inner segments more strongly inflexed, twisted; corona funnel-shaped, ribbed, darker in tone (13B) than the perianth, with mouth 6-lobed, frilled, rim crenate. Mid-season

'Royal Viking' 1 Y-Y
(Mrs J. Abel Smith) Mrs J. Abel Smith, 1990
'Great Expectations' × 'Ormeau'; sdlg no. A77/42
Fl. 105 mm wide, deep golden yellow. Mid-season

'Royal Visit' 2 Y-R
(?Australian origin, pre-1956) Unregistered
Corona bright red, frilled

'Royal Wedding' 2 W-GWY
(Carncairn Daffodils) Carncairn Daffodils, 1982
'Green Island' × 'Tobernaveen'; sdlg no. W5/20
Fl. 97 mm wide; perianth segments greenish white (155A); corona yellowish white 155B, with light greenish yellow 5D at rim. Mid-season. 2n=29

'Royal White' 1 W-W
(G.L. Wilson, pre-1950)

'Royal Widow' 1 W-W
(pre-1915)

'Royal Windsor' 2 Y-YRR
(Warnaar & Co., pre-1949)
'Bermuda' × 'Carbineer'

Perianth segments canary yellow. AM(Haarlem) 1949. Received AM(Haarlem) 1949 as 'War Paint'

'Royal Yellow' 1 (a)
(G.B. van Rhijn, pre-1937)

'Roycroft' 1 Y-Y
(H.A. Brown, 1941) J.N. Hancock & Co., 1964
Fl. rounded, crocus yellow; perianth segments broadly ovate, smooth and of good substance; corona regularly flanged. Early

'Roysterer' 1 (a)
(W.B. Cranfield, pre-1930)

'Royston' 2 W-? (b)
(Mrs R.O. Backhouse, pre-1921)

'Royton' 2 (a)
(Parr's Nurseries, pre-1947) Parr's Nurseries, 1958

N. × *rozeirae* Fernández Casas 13 (parentage: *N. bulbocodium* Linnaeus × *N. triandrus* subsp. *pallidulus* (Graells) D.A.Webb) = *N.* × *consolationis*

'Rozelle' 1 W-P
(S.J. Bisdee) S.J. Bisdee, 1956
('Eskimo' × 'Dawnglow') × 'Rosario'

'Ruad' 2 Y-? (a)
(W. Jackson Jr, 1957)
'Kai' × 'Ceylon'

'Ruahine' 2 W-W
(R.C.A. Tombleson) R.C.A. Tombleson, 1971
'Hawea' × 'Glenbush'
Fl. 117 mm wide

'Ruanda' 2 W-? (b)
(Mrs R.S. Cobley, pre-1937)

'Ruapehu' 1
(pre-1914)

'Ruapehu' 1 W-W
(A. Gibson, pre-1950)

'Ruapuna' 2 Y-YYR
(R.J. McIlraith) R.J. McIlraith, 1982
'Fooklan' × 'True Colours'; sdlg no. 74/3
Fl. 85 mm wide; perianth segments overlapping; corona pale yellow, shading to red towards mouth, with rim regularly dentate

'Ruatapu' 4 W-Y
(D.S. Bell) D.S. Bell, 1982
Div. 4 sdlg × 'Mount White'
Fl. 105 mm wide. Mid-season

'Rubaiyat' 3 W-? (b or c)

'Crimson Braid' × *N. poeticus* sdlg

'Rubella' 2 W-? (b)
(R.H. Bath, pre-1929)

'Rubella' 2 Y-R
(T.H. Piper, 1953)
'Caerleon' × 'Cotopaxi'

'Rubellite' 8 W-R
(J.C. Williams, pre-1912)
Poetaz
Fl. 64 mm wide; perianth segments pure white; corona sealing-wax red. AM 1912

'Rubena' 2 Y-O
(J.S. Leitch) J.S. Leitch, 1964

'Rubens' 1 Y-Y
(J. de Groot & Sons, pre-1907)

'Rubens' 3 W-O
(A.E. Lowe, pre-1927)
Corona reddish orange

'Rubens' 1 Y-Y
Syn. of 'Willem Maris'

'Rubh Mor' 2 W-O
(J.S.B. Lea) J.S.B. Lea, 1971
Richardson sdlg 257 × 'Borrobol'; sdlg no. 1-56-62
Fl. 130 mm wide; corona orange (28B). Mid-season

'Rubicon' 3 W-? (b)
(F.H. Chapman, pre-1914)

'Rubicon' 2 Y-Y
(Konynenburg & Mark) Konynenburg & Mark, 1960
('Toscanini' × 'Diorama') hybrid
Fl. 115 mm wide; perianth segments brilliant greenish yellow 4A; corona vivid yellow 12A. Mid-season

'Rubicon' 4 Y-O
Syn. of 'Ariake'

'Rubicon Blush' 1 W-P
(J.M.Radcliff) Radcliff Daffodils, 1996
Sdlg 10/79 × sdlg 17/79; sdlg no. 27/90
Fl. 103 mm wide; perianth segments very broadly ovate, blunt, slightly reflexed, a little concave, overlapping half; the inner segments a little inflexed, more distinctly concave or with margins incurved; corona cylindrical, smooth, strong yellowish pink 35C, with mouth ribbed and widely expanded, rim irregularly crenate. Mid-season to late. Sunproof

'Rubicon Orange' 2 W-OOY
(J.M.Radcliff, 1980) Radcliff Daffodils, 1996
Sdlg no. 12/82

Fl. 97 mm wide; perianth segments very broadly ovate, blunt, somewhat inflexed, a little concave, overlapping; corona funnel-shaped, loosely ribbed, strong orange 24A, with a narrow band of vivid yellow 15B at rim, mouth more closely ribbed, straight, wavy. Late. Sunproof

'Rubicon Pink' 1 W-P
(J.M.Radcliff) Radcliff Daffodils, 1996
'Alana' × sdlg 46/77; sdlg no. 24/88
Fl. forming a double triangle, 95 mm wide; perianth segments very broadly ovate, blunt, spreading, with margins incurling at apex, overlapping half; the inner segments slightly inflexed; corona cylindrical, smooth, moderate pink 35D, with mouth ribbed and widely expanded, even, rim deeply and irregularly notched and crenate. Mid-season to late. Sunproof

'Rubina' 4 Y-R
(W.F.M. Copeland, pre-1929)

'Rubini' 3 W-? (b)
(Barr & Sons, pre-1908)

'Rubini' 2 W-O
(R.H. Bath, pre-1927)
Corona scarlet-orange. AM(Haarlem) 1936

'Rubinia' 4 Y-R
(pre-1961) Unregistered
Fl. with redoubling of both perianth and corona

'Rubinstein' 1 (a)
(J.B. van der Schoot, pre-1931)

'Rubio' 3 W-? (b)
(Cartwright & Goodwin, pre-1908)

'Rubra' 2 W-Y
(H.A. Brown, pre-1933)
Perianth segments broad, deeply overlapping; corona shallow, apricot yellow, frilled

'Ruby' 3 W-O
(Sir C.H. Cave, pre-1907)
Fl. rounded; perianth segments very broadly ovate, blunt or truncate, prominently mucronate, creamy white, spreading or slightly reflexed, plane, creased at midrib, overlapping half; corona shallow bowl-shaped, widely ribbed, bright orange, with a darker tone at rim, mouth wavy, rim minutely and irregularly crenate

'Rubyat' 6 Y-R
(Ballydorn Bulb Farm) Ballydorn Bulb Farm, 1989
'Dove Wings' × Div. 3 W-R sdlg
Fl. 98 mm wide; perianth segments narrow, pale yellow, reflexed; corona rich garnet red, with a somewhat paler tone towards base. Mid-season. Sunproof

'Ruby Cup'
(J. Pope, pre-1908)

'Ruby Eye' 3 W-? (b)
(Cartwright & Goodwin, pre-1908)

'Ruby Fell' 2 W-W
(West & Fell, pre-1935)
Perianth segments creamy white; corona opening pale buff, becoming creamy white

'Ruby Gem' 3 (a)
(?C.L. Adams, pre-1914)

'Ruby King' 2 (a)
(de Graaff Bros, pre-1951)
AM(Haarlem) 1951, TGA(Haarlem) 1956

'Ruby Pearl' 3 Y-R
(A.G. Thompson) A.G. Thompson, 1961
Fl. 83 mm wide; perianth segments creamy yellow; corona ruby red. Resembles 'Mahmoud' in form

'Ruby Petre' 2 (a)
(Hon. Mrs Petre, pre-1934)

'Ruby Red' 2 W-R
(John R.Reed) John R.Reed, 1995
Duncan 2 W-P sdlg × 'Spaceship'; sdlg no. 81-176-1
Fl. 97 mm wide; perianth segments ovate; corona wide bowl-shaped, intense pinkish red, in some years paler. Mid-season

'Ruby Romance' 2 W-PPR
(R. & E.Havens, 1986) R. & E.Havens, 1997
'Pink Valentine' × 'Pink Flame'; sdlg no. VH20/1
Fl. 105 mm wide; perianth segments broadly ovate; corona very shallow bowl-shaped, lavender pink, shading to tomato red at rim, frilled. Late. Sunproof

'Ruby Rose' 4 W-R
(Brian S. Duncan) Rathowen Daffodils, 1987
'Pink Paradise' × ('Polonaise' × ['Interim' × 'Rose Caprice'])
Perianth and other petaloid segments white; corona segments interspersed at centre, near ruby red. Late

'Ruby Star' 2 W-P
(R. & E.Havens, 1986) R. & E.Havens, 1997
'Pink Valentine' × 'Pink Flame'; sdlg no. VH20/13
Fl. 95 mm wide; perianth segments broadly ovate, becoming slightly reflexed; corona almost disc-shaped, brilliant reddish pink, with mouth 3-angled, frilled. Late. Sunproof

'Ruby Tail' 2 W-R
(J.L. Richardson) G. Zandbergen-Terwegen, 1959

'Rubythroat' 2 W-P
(G.E. Mitsch) G.E. Mitsch, 1969
'Precedent' × 'Accent'; sdlg no. C35/5
Perianth segments pure white; corona bowl-shaped, rosy reddish pink. Mid-season

'Ruby Wedding' 2 W-P
(Brian S.Duncan) Brian S.Duncan, 1997
'Fragrant Rose' × 'Pol Dornie'; sdlg no. 1322
Fl. 115 mm wide; perianth segments broadly ovate, blunt, spreading; corona cylindrical, very deep pink, with shades of ruby, rim dentate. Mid-season to late. Sunproof

'Ruby Wills' 1 Y-Y
(F.R.Coles) F.R.Coles, 1997
'Tarago' × 'Early Sensation'
Resembles 'Tarago' in robust stem and flower size; resembles 'Early Sensation' in flowering season and pale colour

'Ruddigore' 2 (a)
(Mrs R.O. Backhouse, pre-1921)

'Ruddy Glow' 2 W-R
(Mrs R.O.Backhouse, pre-1921)
Perianth segments creamy white; corona bowl-shaped, scarlet

'Ruddynosey' 1 Y-O
(M.G.Temple-Smith, 1985) M.G.Temple-Smith, 1997
'Trumpet Call' × 'Loch Owskeich'; sdlg no. 15/85
Perianth segments vivid yellow 9A, overlapping; corona funnel-shaped, strong orange 25A, with mouth slightly flared. Mid-season

'Rudi Carrell' 3 Y-YYO
(G.H. Rotteveel & Sons, 1946) G.H. Rotteveel & Sons, 1961
Fl. 95 mm wide; perianth segments light greenish yellow 8C; corona vivid yellow 17B, with orange (28A) at rim. Mid-season

'Rudi Seeliger' 2 W-R
(J.W.A. Lefeber, pre-1968) Unregistered

'Rudolf' 2 Y-?
(C.O. Fairbairn) L.M. Saunders, 1960

'Rudyard Kipling' 9
(G.H. Engleheart, pre-1910)

'Rudyard Kipling' 2 W-?
Syn. of 'Richmond'

'Ruffled Gem' 1 (a)
(W.J. Eldering & Son, pre-1928)

'Ruffled Quilt' 2 W-P
(W.B.Blanden) Unregistered
Perianth segments acute, creamy white; corona funnel-shaped, deep bronze pink, with mouth flared and frilled. Tall. Early

'Ruffles' 3 W-R
(A.H. Ahrens) J.S. Leitch, 1955

'Rufford' 2 W-P
(Mrs J. Abel Smith) Mrs J. Abel Smith, 1975
'Rose of Tralee' × 'Chelsea China'; sdlg no. R2/62
Fl. 90 mm wide; corona apple blossom pink. Mid-season. Resembles a larger-flowered 'Chelsea China' with a rounded perianth

'Rufus' 3 W-? (b)
(P.D. Williams, pre-1907)

'Rufus' 2 Y-R
(R.C.A. Tombleson) R.G.Cull, 1981
'Charity May' hybrid; sdlg no. B30
Fl. 69 mm wide; perianth segments vivid yellow 9A; corona orange-red (30C). Mid-season. Fl. sometimes with a coppery sheen, with perianth segments reflexed

'Rugby' 1 (a)
(Mrs R.O. Backhouse, pre-1921)

N. rugilobus Steudel = *N. bicolor* var. *lorifolius*

'Rugilobus'
Syn. of *N. bicolor* var. *lorifolius*

'Rugosa' 2 W-? (b)
(A.H. Ahrens) J.S. Leitch, 1956

'Rugulosus' 7 Y-Y
(pre-1819)
Fls 2-4 per stem, 57 mm wide, yellow; perianth segments ovate, with prominent white mucro, spreading, plane or with margins incurved; the inner segments a little inflexed, with margins strongly incurved; corona funnel-shaped, lightly ribbed, slightly deeper in tone than the perianth, mouth straight, wavy. Syn. "The Great Wrinkled Cup", *N. rugulosus* Linnaeus, Odorus 'Rugulosus'. *AM(g) 1973, AGM 1993

N. rugulosus Linnaeus = 'Rugulosus'.

'Rugulosus Maximus' 7 Y-Y
Selection from *N.* × *odorus*
Fl. orange-yellow. AM 1906

'Ruin' 2 W-? (b)
(M.P. Williams, pre-1938)

'Rukuhia' 2 Y-Y
(P. & G. Phillips) P. & G. Phillips, 1982
Fl. 98 mm wide. Mid-season. Resembles a later-

flowered 'Golden Aura' with a less rounded perianth

'Rumarcal' 7 Y-Y
(D. & J.W. Blanchard) D. & J.W. Blanchard, 1962
N. rupicola subsp. *marvieri* × *N. calcicola*
Fl. 1-3 per stem, 30 mm wide; perianth segments ovate, blunt, slightly mucronate, vivid yellow 12A, reflexed, overlapping one-third; corona broad cup-shaped, darker in tone (15A) than the perianth, with mouth straight and even, rim widely and shallowly crenate. Dwarf. Early. Sweetly scented. Resembles a larger and improved *N. calcicola*. AM(p) 1962

'Rumba' 2 Y-O
(de Graaff Bros, pre-1950)
AM(Haarlem) 1950

'Rumble' 2 Y-R
(J.S. Leitch) J.S. Leitch, 1956

'Rumpelstiltskin' 1 Y-Y
(G.L. Wilson, pre-1949)
'Trenoon' open pollinated
PC 1949

'Rumpole' 2 Y-Y
(P. & G. Phillips) P. & G. Phillips, 1979
Fl. 92 mm wide. Mid-season

'Runaway' 2 Y-O
(Jackson's Daffodils) Jackson's Daffodils, 1986
'Kopi' × 'Tia'; sdlg no. 285/79
Perianth segments broadly ovate, blunt, vivid yellow 9B, with very slight white mucro, spreading, concave, with midrib showing, overlapping half; the inner segments more narrowly ovate, inflexed; corona cup-shaped, orange (28A), with mouth straight and a little wavy, rim deeply crenate. Mid-season

'Rungis' 11a Y-O
(J. Gerritsen & Son) J. Gerritsen & Son, 1972
'Parisienne' sport
Fl. 90 mm wide; perianth segments light yellow 10B; corona segments spreading, vivid orange 28B, frilled. Mid-season to late. Resembles 'Parisienne' but with a yellow perianth

'Runita' 3 W-W
(G.W.E.Brogden, pre-1992) Unregistered
'Easter Moon' × 'Verona'; sdlg no. x52/1

'Runnymede' 2 W-O
(S.J. Bisdee, 1949)
'Red Crusader' × 'Ivo Fell'

'Rupee' 2 Y-R
(D.S. Bell) D.S. Bell, 1963
Fl. 104 mm wide; corona bowl-shaped, widely expanded, rich red. Early

'Rupert' 1 W-Y
(A. Gray) A. Gray, 1961
N. asturiensis × 'Rockery Gem'
Fl. 50 mm wide; perianth segments milk white; corona brilliant greenish yellow 6B. Mid-season

'Rupert Brooke' 9 W-GYR
(G.H. Engleheart, *c.*1919)
Fl. 45 mm wide, rounded; corona saucer-shaped, ribbed, yellow, with faint green at base and deep orange-red at rim, with a line of white between mid-zone and rim

'Rupert Brooke' 9 W-YYR
(E.W. Cotter) D.S. Bell, 1975
Fl. 70 mm wide; perianth segments with margins wavy; corona disc-shaped, citron yellow, with greenish yellow at base and red at rim, with a line of white between mid-zone and rim on ageing. Syn. 'Masefield'

N. rupicola Dufour 13 Section Apodanthi. AM(a) 1941, AM 1977, AM 1979
    subsp. ***rupicola***. AGM 1994
    subsp. ***marvieri*** (Jahandiez & Maire) Maire & Weiller. AM(a) 1940, AM(p) 1952, AGM 1994
    subsp. ***pedunculatus*** (Cuatrecasas) Lainz = *N. cuatrecasasii*
    subsp. ***watieri*** (Maire) Maire & Weiller. AM(a) 1939

N.* × *rupidulus Fernández Casas 13 = *N. rupicola* Dufour × *N. triandrus* Linnaeus subsp. *pallidulus* (Graells) D.A.Webb.

'Rural Gold' 1 Y-Y
(J.A. Morris) J.A. Morris, 1957

'Rushcliffe' 3 W-Y
(Mrs J. Abel Smith) Mrs J. Abel Smith, 1983
'Ethel' × 'Syracuse'
Corona deep yellow. Early

'Rush Giant' 1
(Hogg & Robertson, pre-1908)

'Rushlight' 2 Y-W
(Angus Wilson) Wallace & Barr, 1957
Fl. 101 mm wide; perianth segments nearest to light greenish yellow 5C, with some tinges of a lighter tone, paling almost to white at base, overlapping; corona ribbed, whitish, with brilliant greenish yellow 5B at rim, the outside almost white at base, flushed light greenish yellow 5C towards mouth, mouth straight, frilled. 2n=28. AM(Haarlem) 1959, *AM(g) 1978

'Rushmore' 2 W-O
(J.W. Blanchard) J.W. Blanchard, 1990
'Hotspur' × 'Osmington'; sdlg no. 77/19A

Fl. 100-105 mm wide; perianth segments lanceolate, white, slightly tinged yellow at base; corona funnel-shaped, reddish orange. Mid-season

'Rus Holland' 1 Y-WWY
(H.T. Dettmann) H.T. Dettmann, 1960
Fl. opening greenish sulphur yellow; corona becoming white, with sulphur yellow at rim, frilled. See also 'Russ Holland'

'Rushworth' 2 Y-O
(J.N. Hancock & Co., c.1978) Unregistered

'Rusina' 2 (a)
(G. Lubbe & Son, pre-1938)
AM(Haarlem) 1938

'Ruskin' 9 W-YYR
(G.H. Engleheart, pre-1910)
Perianth segments overlapping; corona bright yellow, with intense orange-scarlet at rim

'Russet' 3 Y-R
(G.L. Wilson, pre-1947)
'Seraglio' × 'Pera'
Perianth segments primrose yellow, of leathery substance; corona dark crimson-red

'Russ Holland' 1 Y-WWY
Syn. of 'Rus Holland'

'Russian Chimes' 5 W-W
(Grant E.Mitsch, 1967) R. & E.Havens, 1994
'Lemon Drops' open pollinated; sdlg no. CO6/1
Fls 1-2 per stem, 80 mm wide; perianth segments acute; corona mouth flared. Mid-season

'Rusthall' 2 Y-O
(Barr & Sons) Wallace & Barr, 1959
Fl. 90 mm wide; perianth segments primrose yellow; corona reddish orange. Mid-season. Resembles 'Royal Mail'

'Rusthoff' 3 W-? (b)
(Warnaar & Co., pre-1929)
AM(Haarlem) 1929

'Rusticana' 11a Y-Y
(J. Gerritsen & Son) J. Gerritsen & Son, 1981
'Riesling' hybrid
Fl. 100 mm wide, primrose yellow; corona segments with a darker tone at rim. Mid-season

'Rustington' 2 W-Y
(Sir F.C. Stern, pre-1948)
Fl. 102 mm wide; perianth segments overlapping; corona ribbed, cream yellow, with mouth slightly expanded, frilled, with rim crenate

'Rustom Pasha' 2 Y-O
(A.M. Wilson/Miss G.Evelyn, pre-1930)
'Hospodar' × A.M.Wilson sdlg
Fl. 102 mm wide; perianth segments acute, vivid to brilliant yellow 12A-B, overlapping; corona opening strong orange 25A, becoming darker in tone, mouth expanded, with rim deeply dentate. 2n=28.
AM(Haarlem) 1943, *AM(g) 1949, *FCC(g) 1954

'Rusty' 2 (a)
(R.F. Calvert, pre-1937)

'Ruth' 3 W-R
(P.D. Williams, pre-1907)
Corona expanded, crimson

'Ruth 11' 2 W-Y
(L. Buckland, pre-1939)

'Ruth Elder' 3 (a)
(H. Prins, pre-1929)

'Ruth Fox' 4 Y-Y
Syn. of 'Yellow Cheerfulness'

'Ruth Haller' 5 Y-Y
(C.R. Phillips) C.R. Phillips, 1968
N. triandrus × 'Rosabella'; sdlg no. 53/72 A52
Perianth segments pale yellow; corona lemon yellow. Mid-season. Resembles a lighter-coloured 'Lemon Drops' with a shorter corona

'Ruth Ireland' 1 W-? (b)
(R. Dick, pre-1938)
'Stuart' × 'Iolanthe'

'Ruth Murphy' 3 W-GRR
(L.P. Dettman) L.P. Dettman, 1982
'Rockall' × 'Rameses'; sdlg no. R-R 1/76
Fl. 103 mm wide; perianth segments greenish white (155A); corona orange-red (30C). Late. Resembles a larger-flowered 'Rockall'

'Ruth Tunbridge' 2 W-? (b)
(D.V. West, pre-1935)
Corona spreading

'Ruthvose' 2 W-P
(Brian S. Duncan) du Plessis Bros, 1989
'Polonaise' × 'Violetta'; sdlg no. 561
Fl. 110 mm wide; perianth segments spreading; corona bright pink, with mouth expanded. Late

'Rutland' 3 W-R
(W.A. Noton) W.A. Noton, 1976
'Irish Splendour' × 'Rockall'; sdlg no. 617
Fl. 110 mm wide. Mid-season

'Rutland Water' 2 W-W
(W.A. Noton, 1974) W.A. Noton, 1985
'Misty Glen' × 'Easter Moon'

Corona shallow, tinged green at base. Early

'Ruysdael' 1 (a)
(J. de Groot & Sons, pre-1914)

'Ruysdael' 2 Y-O
(Konynenburg & Mark) Konynenburg & Mark, 1960
'Fortune' × 'Pro Domo'
Fl. 85 mm wide; corona vivid reddish orange 32A. Early

'Ryan Son' 3 Y-GYY
(Mrs J. Abel Smith) Mrs J. Abel Smith, 1986
'Silver Howard' × 'Emily'; sdlg no. SE/91
Perianth segments deep primrose yellow; corona yellow, with a deeper tone at rim and the rim dentate. Late. Resembles a larger 'Minster Lodge' of deeper colour

'Rybellin' 3 Y-R
(K.J. Heazlewood, c.1970) Unregistered
'Redeem' × 'Firecracker'

'Rye Royal' 1 W-? (b)
(F.H. Chapman, pre-1927)

'Rylock' 2 Y-R
(R.H.Glover, pre-1993) Unregistered

'Rytha' 2 Y-O
(Mrs H.K. Richardson) du Plessis Bros, 1978
Sdlg no. 270
Fl. 111 mm wide. Early to mid-season

'Ryzende Zon' 8 W-?
(pre-1807)

S

'Saberwing' 5 W-GWW
(G.E. Mitsch) G.E. Mitsch, 1976
'Easter Moon' × *N. triandrus*; sdlg no. F152/5
Fls 1-2 per stem, rounded, 75 mm wide; perianth segments spreading; corona bowl-shaped, smooth, with green at base. Mid-season

'Sabik' 2 W-YYO
(W.F.Leenen, pre-1997) Unregistered
Corona widely flared, rich honey yellow. Mid-season. Scented

'Sabina' 3 W-? (b)
(de Graaff Bros, pre-1936)
AM(Haarlem) 1936. Div. 9 until 1957

'Sabine' 8
(J.B. van der Schoot, pre-1931)

'Sabine Hay' 3 O-R
(D.B. Milne) B.C. James, 1970
Sdlg no. Z.11
Fl. rounded, 85-95 mm wide; perianth segments very broad, truncate, prominently mucronate, light orange (24B), spreading, overlapping half or more; the inner segments less noticeably mucronate; corona disc-shaped, ribbed, orange-red (31A). Mid-season. AM(e) 1974

'Sabine Silk' 3 Y-O
(John R.Reed, 1984) John R.Reed, 1995
'Air Marshal' × 'Sabine Hay'; sdlg no. 79-42-3
Fl. rounded, 89 mm wide; perianth segments broadly ovate, soft yellow, sometimes tinged with orange; corona bowl-shaped, strong dull orange. Mid-season

'Sabine's Sister' 3 O-R
(D.B. Milne, pre-1985) Unregistered
Fl. flushed with colour. Resembles a taller 'Sabine Hay' of smaller flower and lighter colour

N. × *sabinii* Lindley = *N.* × *incomparabilis*

'Sabinii'
Syn. of *N.* × *incomparabilis*

'Sabot Hill' 4 W-Y
(W.G.Pannill) W.G.Pannill, 1994
'Ave' × 'Gay Time'; sdlg no. 66/2
Mid-season to late

'Sabra' 1 Y-Y
(J.N.Hancock & Co., 1976) Unregistered
Sdlg no. 73/76H

'Sabre' 2 Y-R
(G.W.E. Brogden, 1981) Brogden Bulbs, 1991
('Air Marshal' × 'Orator') × 'Falstaff'; x85/9
Fl. 105 mm wide; perianth segments very broad, rounded at apex, deep yellow, smooth and of great substance; corona large cup-shaped, with rim lightly dentate. Early

'Sabre Dance' 2 Y-R
(D.S. Bell) D.S. Bell, 1961
Fl. 108 mm wide; corona dark red. Mid-season. Resembles an 'Alamein' of heavier texture with the perianth segments more rounded and the corona more widely expanded

'Sabrina' 1 W-Y
(Barr & Sons, pre-1903)
Perianth segments creamy white; corona ribbed, pale yellow, frilled

'Sabrina' 3 Y-O
(G.W.E. Brogden) M.E. Brogden, 1957

'Sabrosa' 7 Y-Y
(J.W. Blanchard, 1976) J.W. Blanchard, 1986
N. jonquilla × *N. rupicola* subsp. *watieri*; sdlg no. 71/3D
Fls 2-3 per stem; perianth segments pale yellow; corona darker in. Dwarf. Late. Resembles a slightly larger 'Moncorvo' with a darker-coloured corona

'Sacajawea' 2 Y-YYO
(G.E. Mitsch, pre-1954)
Fl. large; perianth segments deep yellow; corona golden yellow, with a broad band of rich reddish orange at rim, mouth widely expanded. Very early. 2n=28. Resembles an earlier-flowered 'Whitely Gem' of twice the size

'Sacramento' 3 W-W
(J.M. de Navarro, pre-1949)
'Chinese White' × 'Green Island'
Fl. 92 mm wide; perianth segments very broad, rounded at apex, slightly mucronate, creamy white, spreading, plane, smooth, regular, overlapping half; the inner segments narrower, blunt; corona cup-shaped, creamy white, with deep green at base and a darker cream towards mouth, mouth slightly flared and heavily frilled, rim crenate. Mid-season. 2n=28. PC(e) 1960, AM(e) 1964

'Sacrifice' 3 W-R
(H.D. Phillips, pre-1926)
'Seville' × 'Kestrel'
Fl. rounded; perianth segments very broad, blunt, fairly prominently mucronate, spreading, a little concave, with margins sometimes incurling at apex and with broad midrib showing, overlapping half; the inner segments slightly inflexed, shouldered and sometimes recurved at base; corona disc-shaped, closely ribbed, orange-red

'Sacrosanct' 2 Y-YYR
(Jackson's Daffodils, 1985) Jackson's Daffodils, 1995
'Kudos' × 'Dynamic'; sdlg no. 20/85
Fl. 95 mm wide; perianth segments broadly ovate, vivid yellow 12A; corona darker in tone than the perianth, with a clearly defined band of bright orange-red at rim. Early to mid-season

'S.A.de Graaff' 3 W-O
(W. Backhouse, pre-1869)
Corona spreading, stained scarlet-orange. Syn. Barrii Albus 'S.A.de Graaff'

'S.A.de Graaff' 8 Y-Y
(W. Backhouse, pre-1869)
Fls 2-3 per stem; perianth segments opening rich primrose yellow, becoming paler in tone, deeply overlapping; corona darker in tone. Syn. Tridymus 'S.A.de Graaff'. Was "absorbed" into 'Golden Star'

'Sadie' 1 W-Y
(West & Fell, pre-1937)
Corona deep yellow

'Safara' 2 (a)
(A.J. Bliss, pre-1930)

'Safari' 2 Y-O
(Mrs H.K. Richardson) Mrs H.K. Richardson, 1972
'Air Marshal' × 'Vulcan'
Perianth segments golden; corona reddish orange, frilled

'Safe Harbour' 2 W-Y
(D.S. Bell) D.S. Bell, 1965
'Papanui Queen' hybrid
Fl. 107 mm wide; corona very shallow bowl-shaped, pale yellow

'Safety' 2 W-O
(C.O. Fairbairn, pre-1967) Unregistered
Corona broad, deep orange

'Saffron' 2 (a)
(J. Jacob, pre-1913)

'Saffron Queen' 11a W-O
(W.F.Leenen, 1978) Unregistered
Sdlg no. 14/78I
Perianth segments pure white; corona bright orange, frilled. Mid-season to late

'Safona' 2 W-YYO
(J.N.Hancock & Co.) Unregistered
Perianth segments creamy white, overlapping; corona creamy yellow, with orange at rim, frilled. Tall. Early

'Sagacity' 9
(G.H. Engleheart, pre-1930)

'Sagana' 9 W-YYR
(S.J. Bisdee) S.J. Bisdee, 1956
'Chaconne' × 'Sea Green'

'Sage Lady' 2 Y-WWY
(J.N. Hancock & Co., 1976) Unregistered
Sdlg no. 71/76H

'Sagina' 5 W-W
(W.F.M. Copeland, pre-1927)

'Sagittarius' 2 (b or c)
(W.F.M. Copeland, pre-1908)

'Sahalie' 1 Y-Y
(G.E. Mitsch, c.1965) Unregistered
'Camberwell King' × 'Galway'

'Sahara' 2 W-? (b)
(G.H. Engleheart, pre-1913)
'Braemar' × 'Gold Tray'

'Sahara' 1 Y-Y
(G. Lewis, 1945) D.S. Bell, 1958

'Sahib' 9
(pre-1921)

'Sahib' 4 W-P
(W. Jackson Jr) Jackson's Daffodils, 1982
'Lawali' × 'Chimeon'; sdlg no. 68/74
Fl. 90 mm wide. Early to mid-season

'Sai' 2 W-OOR
(W. Jackson Jr, 1967) Unregistered
'Jo' × 'Arbar'; sdlg no. 93/67

'Saigon' 1 Y-Y
(R.O. Roblin, 1939)

'Saigon' 1 W-Y
(J.N. Hancock & Co., 1955) Unregistered

'Sail' 9 W-GGO
(Mrs M.S.Yerger) Mrs M.S.Yerger, 1994
'Quetzal' × 'Ace of Diamonds'; sdlg no. 77 G 7
Fl. 43 mm wide; perianth segments rounded at apex, deeply overlapping; the inner segments narrower; corona almost disc-shaped, light yellow-green 145B, with strong yellow-green 144C at base and orange (28A) at rim. Dwarf. Late

'Sailaway' 2 W-P
(Alister Clark, 1940) J. Sharp, 1960

'Sailboat' 7 W-W
(W.G. Pannill) W.G. Pannill, 1980
'Frostkist' × *N. jonquilla*; sdlg no. G 15 A
Fl. 60 mm wide. Mid-season

'Sailho' 2 W-W
(T.H. Piper, *c*.1966) Unregistered
'Vigil' × 'Rhana'

'Sailing Light' 2 W-YYO
(J.L. Richardson, pre-1953)
'Glenshane' × 'Bahram'
Perianth segments pure white; corona disc-shaped, yellow, with a broad band of orange at rim

'Sailor' 2 W-Y
(The Brodie of Brodie, *c*.1909)
'Minnie Hume' × 'Stella Superba'

'Sainfoin' 1 G-G
(W.M. Spry, pre-1975) Unregistered
'Hunter's Moon' × 'Content'
Fl. lemon green

'Saint Agnes' 8 W-O
(P.D. Williams, pre-1926)
'Chaucer' × *N. tazetta*
Fl. rounded, 60 mm wide; perianth segments pure or creamy white, reflexed, overlapping half; corona shallow bowl-shaped, bright reddish orange. 2n=17. Syn. 'Agnes'. AM(e) 1926, AM(Haarlem) 1930, *AM(g) 1930, FCC(Haarlem) 1932, *(Kirton)AM(m) 1934

'Saint Albans' 1 Y-Y
(W.M. Spry, pre-1975) Unregistered
'Hunter's Moon' × 'Kingscourt'
Fl. lemon yellow. Late

'Saint Alma' 2 W-? (b or c)
(W.A. Grace, pre-1936)

'Saint Aloysius' 1 W-W
(C.E. Radcliff, 1932)
'Pink o' Dawn' × 'Renee'

'Saint Andrew' 1 W-W
(The Brodie of Brodie, *c*.1943)
'Cotterton' × 'Broughshane'; sdlg no. 36/A/38

'Saint Anns' 3 W-R
(Mrs H.K. Richardson) du Plessis Bros, 1978
'Matapan' × 'Toreador'; sdlg no. 304
Fl. 82 mm wide. Mid-season

'Saint Anselm' 2 Y-Y
(A. G. Thompson) A. G. Thompson, 1960
Fl. 108 mm wide. Early. Resembles 'Carlton' but with a much improved perianth

'Saint Anthony' 3 W-WWO
(Mrs R.O. Backhouse, pre-1921)
Fl. 84 mm wide, facing slightly downwards; perianth segments white, with no green beneath, overlapping at base only; corona cup-shaped, pale cream, with bright pale orange at rim, frilled. Late

'Saint Asaph' 1 (a)
(W.A. Watts, pre-1913)

'Saint Bavo' 4 Y-Y
(?D. Heere, pre-1912)
Fl. creamy yellow. AM(Haarlem) 1912

'Saint Bavo' 1 W-W
(C.G. van Tubergen, pre-1914)

'Saint Begha' 2 W-W
(P.D. Williams, pre-1935)

'Saint Bernard' 2 Y-O
(W.F.M. Copeland, pre-1923)
'King Alfred' × 'Bernardino'
Perianth segments pale yellow; corona tinged red

'Saint Brendan' 2 W-W
(G.L. Wilson, pre-1947)
'Niphetos' × 'Kanchenjunga'
Fl. very large; corona with mouth expanded, frilled

'Saint Breock' 8
(P.D. Williams, pre-1927)

'Saint Bride' 1 W-W
(S.J. Bisdee, 1939)
'Saint Aloysius' × 'Beersheeba'

'Saint Bride' 1 W-W
(G.L. Wilson, pre-1943)
('Vestal Virgin' hybrid × 'Kenbane') × 'Samite'

'Saint Brigid' 1 Y-Y
(W. Backhouse, pre-1869)
Fl. soft yellow, at right angles to the stem; perianth segments a little inflexed, twisted, overlapping at base only; corona cylindrical, broad, with rim notched and flanged. Syn. Pseudonarcissus Major 'Saint Brigid'

'Saint Bryde' 2 Y-O
(H.A. Brown, 1939)
Perianth segments brilliant yellow; corona broad disc-shaped, orange. Mid-season

'Saint Budock' 1 Y-Y
(R.A.Scamp) R.A.Scamp, 1996
'Saint Keverne' × 'Golden Aura'; sdly no. 140
Fl. 96 mm wide, rich golden yellow; perianth segments ovate, plane, smooth, deeply overlapping; corona funnel-shaped, with mouth slightly expanded and rim neatly crenate. Mid-season

'Saintbury' 3 W-W
(J.M. de Navarro) J.M. de Navarro, 1959
'Green Island' × 'Chinese White'
Fl. 98 mm wide. Mid-season. Resembles 'Syracuse' but with the inner perianth segments broader and rounder and the corona less heavily frilled

'Saint Buryan' 8 W-YYO
(P.D. Williams, pre-1927)
Fls 1-2 per stem, 63 mm wide; perianth segments creamy white, with yellow at base, reflexed, overlapping half; corona very shallow bowl-shaped, lemon, with reddish orange at rim. Mid-season to late

'Saint Cecelia' 2 W-Y
Syn. of 'Saint Cecilia'

'Saint Cecilia' 1 W-W
(G.H. Engleheart, pre-1901)
Corona ivory, with pink overtones. AM 1901

'Saint Cecilia' 2 W-Y
(S.J. Bisdee, 1941)
'Rewa' × 'Elspeth'
See also 'Saint Cecelia'

'Saint Christopher' 1 (a)
(Barr & Sons, pre-1927)

'Saint Clair' 2 W-Y
(S.J. Bisdee, 1935)
'Militant' × 'Fleetwing'

'Saint Clements' 2 W-? (b)
(R.H. Bath, pre-1929)

'Saint Clement's Bells' 2 W-Y
(Konynenburg & Mark) Konynenburg & Mark, 1964
Fl. 105 mm wide; perianth segments creamy white; corona light yellow 18A. Mid-season

'Saint Columb' 8
(P.D. Williams, pre-1927)

'Saint Crida' 2 W-? (b)
(G.T.C. Pearce, pre-1939)

'Saint David' 1 Y-Y
(G.H. Engleheart, pre-1913)

'Saint Declan' 2 W-W
(S.J. Bisdee) S.J. Bisdee, 1956
'Pona' × 'Dava'

'Saint Dennis' 2? W-W
(G.H. Johnstone, pre-1950)
Sdlg × 'Lady-Day'

'Saint Dilpe' 2 W-W
(Brian S. Duncan) du Plessis Bros, 1987
'Easter Moon' × 'White Star'; sdlg no. 385
Corona short funnel-shaped, mouth expanded and frilled. Mid-season

'Saint Dorothea' 1 W-W
(Slieve Donard Nursery Co., pre-1926)
Fl. broad, pure white; perianth segments overlapping. Resembles a white 'Royalist'

'Saint Dorothea' 2 W-? (b or c)
(R. Dick, pre-1931)

'Saint Dunstan' 1 (a)
(R.H. Bath, pre-1931)

'Saint Duthus' 1 Y-Y
(D.C. MacArthur) D.C. MacArthur, 1992
'Magnificence' × 'Sundance'; sdlg no. EV78341
Fl. 99 mm wide; perianth segments broadly ovate, vivid yellow 9A, with white mucro, spreading, of thick texture; corona funnel-shaped, ribbed, darker in tone (14A) than the perianth, with mouth flared

and lobed, rim flanged and crenate. Mid-season. Scented

'Saint Egwin' 2 Y-Y
(P.D. Williams, pre-1927)
'Merit' hybrid
Fl. 127 mm wide, soft clear yellow; perianth segments broadly ovate, blunt, slightly mucronate, spreading, of waxy substance, overlapping one-third; the inner segments narrower, with margins slightly wavy; corona bowl-shaped, ribbed, loosely frilled. AM(e) 1927, FCC(e) 1936. Received AM 1927 as 'Egwin'

'Saint Elian' 3 W-Y
(S.J. Bisdee, 1938)
?'Pink'un' hybrid

'Saint Elmo' 1 W-W
(pre-1914)

'Saint Elmo' 2 Y-O
(H.A. Brown) J.N. Hancock & Co., 1955
Perianth segments rich yellow; corona yellow-orange

'Saint Elvan' 1 W-W
(R.O. Backhouse, pre-1926)
Perianth segments overlapping; corona slender, soft clear yellow, mouth expanded and frilled

'Saint Elwyn' 1 W-Y
(G.L. Wilson, 1955) L. Major, 1965
'Broughshane' hybrid
Corona greenish yellow. Mid-season. Resembles 'Broughshane' in form

'Saint Enodoc' 1 W-W
(A.M. Wilson, pre-1936)
AM(Haarlem) 1936

'Saint Erbin' 1 W-Y
(Barr & Sons, pre-1925)
Perianth segments inflexed; corona soft primrose yellow, lightly frilled

'Saint Erme' 2 W-Y
(P.D. Williams, pre-1927)
Fl. facing slightly downwards; perianth segments broadly ovate, blunt, only very slightly mucronate, creamy white, a little inflexed, overlapping half; the inner segments more strongly inflexed, twisted; corona funnel-shaped, smooth, sulphur yellow, with mouth 6-lobed and widely expanded. *AM(g) 1933. See also 'Saint Erne'

'Saint Erne' 2 W-Y
Syn. of 'Saint Erme'

'Saint Ewe' 3 W-? (b)
(P.D. Williams, pre-1927)

'Saintfield' 2 W-P
(W.J. Dunlop, pre-1953)
'White Sentinel' × 'Justice'
Perianth segments pure white; corona bowl-shaped, flushed very pale pink

'Saint Finbar' 1 W-WWP
(S.J. Bisdee, 1942) S.J. Bisdee, 1956
'Eskimo' × 'Dawnglow'

'Saint Francis' 1 W-W
(C. Goodson, pre-1930)
AM(e)(NZ) 1930

'Saint Frusquin' 3 W-WWO
(W.M. Spry, pre-1975) Unregistered
'Aldgate' × 'Galilee'
Corona white, with pale orange at rim. Late

'Saint George' 3 W-YOR
(G.H. Engleheart, pre-1909)
Perianth segments creamy white; corona small, shallow, ribbed, with scarlet at rim, neatly frilled

'Saint Germans' 1 W-W
(Barr & Sons, pre-1925)
'Madame de Graaff' × 'Duchess of Westminster'
Fl. 102 mm wide; perianth segments slightly inflexed; corona broad funnel-shaped, creamy primrose yellow, tinged white, with rim widely flanged. Mid-season

'Saint Germans' 2 W-?
Syn. of 'Gayton'

'Saint Gluvias' 8
(P.D. Williams, pre-1927)

'Saint Helens' 2 W-? (b)
(A. Gray, pre-1941)

'Saint Hilary' 5
(Barr & Sons, pre-1923)

'Saint Hilda' 1 W-YWW
(R.O. Backhouse, pre-1924)
Perianth segments broadly ovate, blunt, only very slightly mucronate, spreading, overlapping one-third; the inner segments narrower, a little inflexed, slightly twisted, somewhat creased; corona widely expanded, creamy white, shading to primrose yellow at base, mouth heavily ribbed, with rim crenate

'Saint Hya' 3 W-? (b or c)
(Barr & Sons, pre-1923)

'Saint Hywin' 2 W-W
(R.O. Backhouse, pre-1926)
Perianth segments broadly spathulate, milk white; corona expanded, ribbed, rich creamy white, frilled

'Saint Ilario' 3 W-WWY
(W.F.M. Copeland, pre-1916)
Corona disc-shaped, ribbed, ivory, with faint tones of lemon at rim. Tall. Late. AM(e) 1916

'Saint Issey' 2 Y-Y
(P.D. Williams, pre-1927)
Perianth segments buttercup yellow, overlapping; corona slightly darker in tone, with mouth flared. AM(e) 1938. Div. 1 until 1936

'Saint Ives' 2 Y-Y
(P.D. Williams, pre-1927)
'King Alfred' hybrid
Fl. clear bright yellow, facing slightly downwards; perianth segments overlapping; corona darker in tone than the perianth, frilled. Mid-season. 2n=28. *HC(g) 1932, *HC(g) 1936, *AM(g) 1939

'Saint Joan' 1 W-Y
(pre-1948)

'Saint John's' 8 Y-Y
(Unknown origin) T.A.V. Wood, 1968
Fl. 32-35 mm wide; perianth segments brilliant greenish yellow 7C, slightly reflexed, twisted, with margins notched, regular, overlapping; corona cup-shaped, slightly ribbed, vivid yellow 14A-B, with mouth straight, rim crenate. Mid-season. PC(p) 1968, AM(p) 1969

'Saint John's Beauty' 3 W-Y
(W. Backhouse, pre-1869)
Corona lemon yellow, tinged orange. Syn. Burbidgei 'Saint John's Beauty'. "Absorbed" 'Marvel'

'Saint Just' 3 W-YYO
(P.D. Williams, pre-1927)
Fl. 89 mm wide; perianth segments pale cream, with sulphur at base, of great substance, irregular, overlapping half; corona bowl-shaped, deep sulphur, with a broad band of orange at rim. Mid-season to late

'Saint Justin' 1 (a)
(W.A. Grace, pre-1936)

'Saint Keverne' 2 Y-Y
(M.P. Williams, 1934)
'Royalist' hybrid
Fl. 100 mm wide; perianth segments broadly ovate, blunt, vivid yellow 12A, with white mucro, spreading, plane, with margins sometimes slightly incurling, very smooth, overlapping one-third; the inner segments more narrowly ovate, slightly inflexed, with margins a little wavy; corona cylindrical, smooth or lightly ribbed, darker in tone than the perianth, mouth a little expanded, rim flanged, deeply notched and minutely crenate. 2n=28. AM(e) 1950, FCC(e) 1951, *FCC(p) 1976, *FCC(g) 1978, AGM 1993

'Saint Keyne' 8 W-O
(P.D. Williams, pre-1927)
Fl. 67 mm wide; perianth segments slightly reflexed, overlapping half or more; the inner segments slightly inflexed; corona expanded, reddish orange, with deep orange at base, lightly frilled. 2n=24. *(Gulval)AM(m) 1940

'Saint Kilda' 1 W-W
(Barr & Sons, pre-1945)

'Saint Kilian' 2 W-P
(S.J. Bisdee, 1939)
'Silver Plane' × 'Sunstar'

'Saint Lawrence' 2 (a)
(F.D.B. Cobb, pre-1954)

'Saint Levan' 4 W-Y
(P.D. Williams, pre-1934)
Perianth segments pure white, slightly reflexed, of waxy texture; corona clear lemon yellow

'Saint Louis' 3 Y-YOO
(F. Rijnveld & Sons, pre-1939)
Fl. 115 mm wide; perianth segments brilliant yellow 13B, paling to creamy white at base, reflexed, with margins slightly incurving, overlapping half; corona ribbed, orange (28A), with vivid yellow 15B at base, mouth straight, frilled, rim crenate and minutely dentate. AM(Haarlem) 1943, *AM(g) 1952, *FCC(g) 1953

'Saint Ludguan'
(A.T.Boscawen, pre-1939)
Probably dwarf

'Saint Mabyn' 2 Y-O
(P.D. Williams, pre-1927)
Perianth segments golden yellow, overlapping half; corona yellowish orange, with mouth flared and frilled. Mid-season. *(Gulval)AM(m) 1936

'Saint Maden' 5 Y-Y
(Barr & Sons, pre-1926)
Perianth segments soft creamy yellow; corona slender, slightly darker in tone than the perianth

'Saint Magnus' 1 Y-Y
(D.C.MacArthur) D.C.MacArthur, 1996
Sdlg × 'Sun Dance'; sdlg no. EV86512
Fl. forming a double triangle, 106 mm wide; perianth segments broadly ovate, mucronate, vivid yellow 12A, spreading; corona funnel-shaped, very shallowly ribbed, darker in tone than the perianth, with mouth widely flared and deeply lobed, rim flanged and crenate. Early. Vanilla-scented

'Saint Martin' 2 (a)
(P.D. Williams, pre-1927)

Fl. 70 mm wide, facing slightly downwards; perianth segments very broad, blunt, primrose yellow, regular, overlapping one-third; the inner segments narrower; corona golden or chrome yellow, with sulphur yellow or orange at rim, mouth expanded and frilled. AM(c) 1932, *(Gulval)HC(m) 1935

'Saint Mary' 1 W-W
(G.L. Wilson, pre-1944)
'Quartz' × 'Diva'
Corona mouth expanded. AM(Haarlem) 1956

'Saint Mawes' 2 Y-O
(T. Bloomer) du Plessis Bros, 1985
'Rathowen Flame' × Board sdlg 318; sdlg no. 196
Perianth segments pale lemon yellow; corona very pale orange. Mid-season. Sunproof. Syn. 'Saint Neot'

'Saint Mawgan' 3 W-? (b)
(T.A.V. Wood, pre-1949)

'Saint Melanus' 1 W-W
(Barr & Sons, pre-1923)

'Saint Mellion' 2 W-OOY
(Mrs H.K. Richardson) du Plessis Bros, 1978
'Kilworth' × 'Rockall'; sdlg no. 398
Fl. 110 mm wide. Mid-season

'Saint Merryn' 8 W-?
(P.D. Williams, pre-1927)

'Saint Michael' 2 W-W
(Mrs P.M. Davis, pre-1948)

'Saint Minver' 8
(P.D. Williams, pre-1927)

'Saint Moritz' 2 W-W
(J.L. Richardson) J.L. Richardson, 1958
'Spitzbergen' × 'Broughshane'
Corona heavily frilled, with rim widely flanged

'Saint Neot' 2 W-? (b or c)
(P.D. Williams, pre-1927)

'Saint Neot' 2 Y-O
Syn. of 'Saint Mawes'

'Saint Newlyn' 3 W-? (b)
(A.M. Wilson, pre-1949)

'Saint Nicholas' 3 W-YYR
(Mrs R.O. Backhouse, pre-1921)
Perianth segments blunt, milk white, overlapping; corona shallow, bright golden yellow, with a broad band of scarlet at rim. Late

'Saint Ninian' 3 Y-? (b)
(The Brodie of Brodie, c.1914)

('Mrs Bowley' × 'Virgil') × 'Cossack'
Perianth segments primrose yellow; corona brightly coloured

'Saint Ninian' 3 W-YYR
(The Brodie of Brodie, c.1933)
'Nairn' × 'Killigrew'; sdlg no. 106/A/28

'Saint Olaf' 3 W-W
(G.H. Engleheart, pre-1913)
Fl. 89 mm wide; perianth segments rounded at apex, milk white, deeply overlapping; corona shallow, wide-spreading, opening with pale sulphur yellow at base and rim, becoming creamy white. Scented. 2n=28. AM(Haarlem) 1913, AM 1913

'Saint Omar' 1 W-Y
Syn. of 'Saint Omer'

'Saint Omer' 1 W-Y
(Barr & Sons, pre-1927)
Perianth segments overlapping; corona soft creamy yellow. See also 'Saint Omar'

'Saint Patrick'
(Mrs Lawrenson, pre-1900)

'Saint Patrick' 8 Y-Y
(C. Smith, pre-1908)
Fls 3 per stem; perianth segments soft yellow; corona dark golden yellow

'Saint Patrick's Day' 2 Y-Y
(Konynenburg & Mark) Konynenburg & Mark, 1964
'Ice Follies' × 'Binkie'
Fl. 100 mm wide; perianth segments very broadly ovate, blunt, fairly prominently mucronate, light greenish yellow 4B, spreading, somewhat concave and with margins slightly incurling, overlapping one-third to a half; the inner segments narrower, a little inflexed, ribbed; corona very broad funnel-shaped, heavily ribbed, brilliant greenish yellow 4A, with a band of a darker tone (6A) at rim, mouth straight, often deeply split and overlapping, frilled. Early. 2n=28

'Saint Peter' 1 W-W
(pre-1947)
Corona opening pale yellow, becoming white

'Saint Piran' 7 W-Y
(R.A. Scamp) R.A. Scamp, 1993
'Aircastle' × *N. jonquilla*; sdlg no. 108
Fls usually 2 per stem, rounded, 77 mm wide; perianth segments very broadly ovate in outline, blunt or rounded at apex, slightly mucronate, opening with yellow tones, becoming creamy white, a little inflexed, smooth, overlapping half; the inner segments more nearly roundish, with margins wavy; corona bowl-

shaped, pale lemon yellow, with mouth expanded and lightly frilled. Late

'Saint Ronan's Well' 2 W-? (b)
(The Brodie of Brodie, c.1909)
'Emperor' × Engleheart red Poeticus sdlg
Perianth segments creamy white; corona slightly tinted orange, with mouth expanded

'Saint Ruan' 7 Y-Y
(P.D. Williams, pre-1927)
Fl. rich lemon yellow

'Saint Saphorin' 1 W-Y
(A.H. Ahrens) A.H. Ahrens, 1955
'Sincerity' × 'Trousseau'

'Saint Senara' 3 W-? (b)
(C. Dawson, pre-1923)
'Princess Mary' × *N. poeticus* var. *recurvus*

'Saint Sennans' 2 W-W
(Barr & Sons, pre-1928)
Perianth segments silvery white; corona expanded, ribbed, creamy white

'Saint Teath' 9
(P.D. Williams, pre-1927)

'Saint Therese' 2 W-P
(R.J. Ralph, 1945)

'Saint Tudy' 2 W-? (b or c)
(P.D. Williams, pre-1927)

'Saint Uny' 1 Y-Y
(M.P. Williams, pre-1937)
Fl. yellow, smooth

'Saint Vincent' 2 W-? (b or c)
(pre-1926)
Corona opening light primrose, becoming almost white

'Saint Wendrona' 1 W-Y
(Barr & Sons, pre-1919)
Fl. 95 mm wide, facing down; perianth segments creamy white, inflexed, irregular, overlapping one-third; corona opening sulphur, becoming paler, mouth expanded, neatly frilled. Mid-season

'Saint Winnow' 2 W-W
(P.D. Williams, pre-1925)
AM(e) 1925

'Saki' 1 W-W
(W. Jackson Jr, 1972) Jackson's Daffodils, 1982
Sdlg 54/66 × sdlg 78/65; sdlg no. 108/72
Fl. 114 mm wide. Mid-season

'Sakura' 2 W-OOY
(Jackson's Daffodils) Jackson's Daffodils, 1991
'Dorus' × 'Toya'; sdlg no. 282/82
Fl. 110 mm wide; perianth segments broadly ovate or roundish in outline, blunt and fairly prominently mucronate, greenish white (155A), spreading, a little concave, with broad midrib showing, overlapping half; the inner segments a little narrower, truncate and only very slightly mucronate, shouldered at base, with margins slightly wavy; corona broad disc-shaped, closely ribbed, strong orange 25B, with narrow band of brilliant greenish yellow 6C at rim, mouth with overlapping and sometimes very deeply split lobes, rim crenate. Mid-season

'Salaam' 1 W-W
(G.W E. Brogden) G.W.E. Brogden, 1966
Mid-season

'Salacia' 2 W-GWW
(W. Jackson Jr, 1968) Unregistered
Sdlg 74/68 × 'Empress of Ireland'; sdlg no. 4/68

'Salad Days' 2 W-P
(J.N. Hancock & Co., c.1956) Unregistered
'Felspar' × 'Mabel Taylor'
Perianth segments broadly ovate, smooth; corona rich salmon pink, heavily frilled

'Salade' 1 W-W
(G.H. Engleheart, pre-1923)

'Saladin' 1 W-? (b)
(E.M. Crosfield, pre-1907)

'Saladin' 2 W-W
(A.G. Thompson) A.G. Thompson, 1960
'John Evelyn' × 'Fortune'
Fl. 89 mm wide; corona opening sulphur yellow, becoming white. Mid-season. Resembles an improved 'John Evelyn' with a more widely expanded corona

'Salakee' 2 Y-Y
(R.A.Scamp) R.A.Scamp, 1996
'Ristin' × *N. cyclamineus*; sdlg no. 401
Fl. 73 mm wide, rich golden yellow; perianth segments ovate, acute, plane, deeply overlapping; corona cylindrical, long, smooth, with rim neatly crenate. Dwarf. Early

'Salamanca' 2 Y-? (a)
(F.H. Chapman, pre-1933)
Syn. 'Beau Ideal'

'Salamander' 3 (a)
(G.H. Engleheart, pre-1913)

'Salamaua' 1 W-Y
(J.N. Hancock & Co., 1948) J.N. Hancock &

Co., 1960
Perianth segments creamy; corona with mouth expanded and rim rolled

'Salambo' 2 or 3
(?F.A. Secrett, pre-1933)

'Salamis' 1 W-GWW
(G.H. Johnstone, pre-1960)

'Salarino' 2 W-Y
(Barr & Sons, pre-1919)
Perianth segments inflexed; corona deeply ribbed, lemon yellow

'Salcombe' 2 W-Y
(Brian S. Duncan) du Plessis Bros, 1989
'My Love' × 'Tudor Minstrel'; sdlg no. 281
Fl. 107 mm wide; perianth segments ovate; corona deep golden yellow, with rim dentate. Mid-season

'Salem' 2 Y-W
(G.E. Mitsch) G.E. Mitsch, 1972
'Fawnglo' × 'Lunar Sea'; sdlg no. Y40/1
Fl. 118 mm wide

'Salembo' 2 W-? (b)
(Mrs R.O. Backhouse, pre-1921)
AM(Haarlem) 1928

'Salerno' 2 W-O
(J.J. Richardson, pre 1944)
'Red Sun' × 'Hades'
Perianth segments pure white; corona cup-shaped, red, frilled, with rim dentate. 2n=27

'Sallandia' 2 (a)
(Mrs R.O. Backhouse, pre-1921)

'Sally' 1 (a)
(Sir J.S. Arkwright, pre-1931)

'Sally' 2 W-P
(Graham Miller, pre-1997) Unregistered

'Sally Ann' 9 W-GYR
(L.P. Dettman) L.P. Dettman, 1979
'Sea Green' open pollinated; sdlg no. OTP 3
Fl. 52 mm wide; perianth segments yellowish white (155D); corona pale greenish yellow 2D, with strong yellow-green 145A at base and orange-red (34C) at rim. Late. Resembles a smaller-flowered 'Sea Green'

'Sally Forth' 2 W-YYO
(Albert Davis, 1979) Albert Davis, 1991
'Kilworth' × 'Rockall'; sdlg no. 705/74
Fl. 106 mm wide; perianth segments roundish, prominently mucronate; corona bowl-shaped, vivid yellow 13A, with light yellowish pink 27A at rim, neatly frilled. Mid-season. Resembles 'Ringleader'
but with the perianth segments more nearly roundish

'Sally Horner' 3 W-? (b)
(G. Lewis) D.S. Bell, 1955

'Sally Moon' 2 W-Y
(Albert Davis, 1979) Albert Davis, 1991
'My Love' × 'Irish Mist'; sdlg no. 411/74
Fl. 92 mm wide; perianth segments roundish, prominently mucronate; corona cup-shaped, light greenish yellow 6D, neatly frilled. Mid-season

'Sally Sky' 3 W-YOO
(Albert Davis, 1979) Albert Davis, 1991
'Kilworth' × 'Rockall'; sdlg no. 719/74
Fl. 95 mm wide; perianth segments very broadly ovate, prominently mucronate; corona orange, with vivid yellow 12A at base. Mid-season

'Sally Star' 3 W-YRR
(Albert Davis, 1979) Albert Davis, 1989
'Kilworth' × 'Rockall'; sdlg no. 719/74
Fl. 100 mm wide; perianth segments broad, overlapping; corona very shallow bowl-shaped, orange-red (30B), with vivid yellow 9B at base. Mid-season. Resembles 'Cairntoul' but with a slightly larger perianth of purer white

'Sally Sun' 2 Y-Y
(Albert Davis, 1978) Albert Davis, 1989
'Camelot' × 'Arctic Gold'; sdlg no. 301/74
Fl. 98 mm wide; perianth segments vivid yellow 9B, overlapping; corona pale yellow 12D, with mouth expanded. Mid-season. Resembles 'Golden Joy' but with a rolled rim to a deeper yellow corona

'Salma Riante' 2 W-O
(1940) C. van der Salm, 1965
Fl. 90 mm wide; perianth segments creamy white; corona strong orange 25A. Early

'Salmestone' 2 W-W
(F.D.B. Cobb, pre-1953)

'Salmonetta' 3 W-Y
(G.H. Engleheart, pre-1903)
Perianth segments ovate, pure white; corona expanded, ribbed, opening apricot yellow, becoming tinged with peach pink

'Salmon Leap' 2 W-GWP
(Carncairn Daffodils) Carncairn Daffodils, 1979
('Rosario' × 'Irish Rose') × ('Guardian' × 'Preamble')
Fl. 120 mm wide; perianth segments greenish white 155C; corona with light yellowish pink 29C at rim

'Salmon Queen' 2 W-? (b)
(Oregon Bulb Farms, pre-1945)

'Salmon Spray' 2 W-P
(J L. Richardson) Mrs H.K. Richardson, 1967
'Rose Caprice' × 'Salmon Trout'
Fl. 102 mm wide; perianth segments very broadly ovate, blunt, spreading, creased, overlapping one-third to a half; the inner segments slightly inflexed, with margins a little wavy; corona funnel-shaped, broad, ribbed, opening orange-yellow, with a darker tone at rim, becoming rich pink, paling to greenish white at base, mouth flared, with rim slightly flanged and regularly crenate. Mid-season

'Salmon Trout' 2 Y-P
(J.L. Richardson, pre-1948)
'Rose of Tralee' hybrid
Fl. 108 mm wide; perianth segments very broadly ovate, blunt, prominently mucronate, spreading, plane, or a little concave at apex, smooth and of good substance, overlapping half; the inner segments more narrowly ovate, a little inflexed, with margins slightly wavy; corona cylindrical, smooth, light yellowish pink 27A, mouth ribbed, expanded, only slightly wavy, with rim rolled and very shallowly crenate. 2n=27. PC 1948, AM(e) 1951, FCC(e) 1952, AM(Haarlem) 1962

'Salome' 3 W-? (b)
(The Brodie of Brodie, c.1909)
'Princess Mary' × Engleheart red Poeticus sdlg
Perianth segments creamy white; corona apricot

'Salome' 2 W-PPY
(J.L. Richardson) J.L. Richardson, 1958
'Salmon Trout' × 'Rose Caprice'
Fl. 90 mm wide; perianth segments very broadly ovate, slightly mucronate, spreading, with margins a little incurling, smooth, overlapping half; the inner segments only slightly narrower, rounded at apex and square-shouldered at base, a little inflexed and concave; corona funnel-shaped, only slightly expanding, opening yellow, becoming orange-pink (near 22D), shading to near 24D at base, with brilliant yellow 20A at rim, lightly frilled. 2n=28. AM(Haarlem) 1962, *AM(g) 1971, *AM(p) 1985, Wister Award 1995

'Saloniki' 2 Y-O
(J.W.A. Lefeber, 1946) J.W.A. Lefeber, 1960
Fl. 80 mm wide, deep yellow; corona reddish orange. Late

'Salote' 2 W-P
(J.N. Hancock & Co., 1953)

'Saltash' 2 Y-O
(P.D. Williams, pre-1933)
'Hospodar' hybrid
Perianth segments golden yellow; corona narrow, orange-red, a little frilled, slightly flanged. PC 1940

'Salter' 2 (a)
(Alister Clark, 1930) J. Sharp, 1960

'Saltermill' 1 W-WYY
(Mrs H.K. Richardson) du Plessis Bros, 1976
Sdlg no. 88
Fl. 107 mm wide; corona lemon, with white at base and buff at rim. Early

'Salutation' 3 (a)
(R. Crews, pre-1949)

'Salute' 2 Y-R
(G.W.E. & M.E.Brogden) G.W.E. & M.E.Brogden, 1980
'Orator' × 'Falstaff'; sdlg no. T96
Fl. 95 mm wide. Mid-season

'Salvador' 3 W-YYR
(S.C. Gaspar) R.J. Abernethy, 1957
Perianth segments pure white, of very thick substance; corona disc-shaped, yellow, with a broad band of red at rim

'Salvation Yeo' 1 (a)
(Cartwright & Goodwin, pre-1908)

'Salvator Rosa' 3 W-YYR
(S.J. Bisdee, 1937)
'Margaret H.' × 'Sunstar'

'Salvington' 2 (a)
(Sir F.C. Stern, pre-1951)

'Salvo' 2 Y-O
(A. Robert, 1956) A. Robert, 1966
'Sunkist' × 'Rustom Pasha'
Fl. 95 mm wide; perianth segments clear golden yellow; corona bright reddish orange. Early. Resembles 'Tinker' but with broader perianth segments

'Samantha' 4 W-YPP
(Mrs H.K. Richardson) Mrs H.K. Richardson, 1972
'Marietta' × 'Irani'
Perianth and other petaloid segments white; the outer whorl broad, overlapping; corona segments short, interspersed among the inner whorls of petaloid segments, deep salmon pink. Late. Scented

'Samantha Smith' 2 W-GWP
(Jānis Rukšans) Jānis Rukšans, 1987
'Green Island' × 'Interim'; sdlg no. R-77-01/1
Perianth segments milky white; corona funnel-shaped, white, green at base, with bright apricot pink at rim becoming pure pink. Mid-season

'Samar' 1 W-W
(W. Jackson Sr, 1945) W. Jackson Jr, 1956
'Adri' × 'Syys'

'Samaria' 3 W-WWY
(The Brodie of Brodie, c.1919)
'Ethelbert' hybrid × 'Moonbeam'
Fl. milk white; perianth segments broad, smooth; corona disc-shaped, ribbed, with greenish tones at base and pale yellow at rim. Late. AM(e) 1926

'Samarkand' 2 Y-? (a)
(The Brodie of Brodie, c.1924)
'Ben Alder' × 'Fortune'; sdlg no. 42/A/19

'Samarkand' 1 Y-Y
(H.M.O. Hale, pre-1938)

'Samba' 5 Y-R
(Barr & Sons, pre-1952)
Sdlg × *N. triandrus* var. *concolor*
Fl. about 78 mm wide; perianth segments butter yellow, suffused brick-red at base; corona small, brick-red. Dwarf. 2n=21

'Sam Hunt' 9 W-GYR
(M.F. Butcher) A.W. Chappell, 1990
'Rupert Brooke' × 'Rondo'; sdlg no. P-12
Fl. 55 mm wide; perianth segments roundish; corona disc-shaped. Mid-season

'Samite' 1 W-W
(G.L. Wilson, pre-1930)
'Mrs Ernst H.Krelage' × 'Beersheba'
Fl. 115 mm wide, ivory white; perianth segments of good substance, overlapping half; corona mouth expanded and frilled, with rim crenate. AM(e) 1939, FCC(e) 1940, *HC(g) 1952, *AM(g) 1953

'Samite' 5
(Sir A.P.W. Thomas)

'Sammy Boy' 2 W-O
(H.R. Barr) H.R. Barr, 1972
'Tudor Minstrel' × 'Arbar'
Fl. 120 mm wide

'Sammy Girl' 8 W-P
(H.Koopowitz, 1976) H.Koopowitz, 1997
'Lilac Delight' × 'Avalanche' hybrid
Fls up to 3 per stem, 62 mm wide; perianth segments broadly ovate, overlapping; the inner segments narrower; corona opening cup-shaped, with mouth incurved, becoming flared, clear mid-pink, with mouth wavy. Mid-season

'Samoa' 2 Y-R
(S.C. Gaspar, pre-1949)

'Samoa Red' 2 W-? (b)
(Oregon Bulb Farms, pre-1945)

'Samos' 1 W-W
(The Brodie of Brodie, c.1921)

'Conqueror' × 'The Fawn'

'Samoset' 1 Y-Y
(E.C. Powell, pre-1946)
'Pilgrimage' × 'White Emperor'

'Samothrace' 1 Y-Y
(G.H. Engleheart, pre-1923)

'Samovar' 2 W-? (b)
(R.H. Bath, pre-1929)

'Samsara' 3 Y-YRR
(Clive Postles) Clive Postles Daffodils, 1995
'Achduart' × 'Stanway'; sdlg no. 2-43-82
Fl. 95 mm wide; perianth segments very broadly ovate, clear medium yellow, concave at margins; the inner segments more nearly roundish; corona cup-shaped, small, with rim crenate. Mid-season

'Samson' 1 Y-Y
(de Graaff Bros, pre-1890)
Fl. rich yellow

'Samson' 1 (a)
(R.van der Schoot & Son, pre-1907)

'Samson' 2 Y-Y
(C.E. Radcliff, 1930)
Sdlg × 'Anax'

'Samson' 1 W-Y
Syn. of 'Glory of Sassenheim'

'Samuel Pepys' 2 (a)
(Miss E. Willmott, pre-1907)

'Samurai' 2 Y-R
(D.S. Bell) D.S. Bell, 1968
Perianth segments deep yellow; corona red

'San Carlo' 2 W-Y
(J.L. Richardson) D.A. Lloyd, 1963
Fl. 115 mm wide; corona primrose yellow. Mid-season

'Sancerre' 11a W-Y
(J. Gerritsen & Son) J. Gerritsen & Son, 1974
'Floralie' hybrid
Fl. 110 mm wide; perianth segments broadly ovate, blunt, fairly prominently mucronate, ivory white, spreading, overlapping one-third; the inner segments narrower and somewhat inflexed; corona split to base, the six segments as long as the perianth segments and opposite to them, bi-lobed, with the lobes overlapping, between light greenish yellow 4C and a paler tone (4D), frilled. Mid-season

'Sancho' 2 Y-Y
(pre-1885)

Perianth segments sulphur yellow; corona yellow, tinged orange

'Sancho Panza' 1 (a)
(pre-1890)

'Sancia' 1 W-W
(W. Jackson Sr, 1937) W. Jackson Jr, 1956
'Quartz' × 'Beersheba'

'Sanction' 2 W-P
(G.E. Mitsch) G.E. Mitsch, 1984
'Caro Nome' hybrid × 'Space Ship'; sdlg no. LL20/1
Fl. 115 mm wide; corona deep pink, with orange overtones. Mid-season

'Sanctity' 2 W-W
(G.L. Wilson, pre-1923)

'Sanctuary' 2 W-? (b)
(C.G. van Tubergen, pre-1946)

'Sanda' 7 Y-Y
(de Graaff Bros, pre-1923)
'King Alfred' × 'Rugulosus Maximus'
Fl. 114 mm wide, rich golden yellow; perianth segments very broad, slightly inflexed, overlapping; corona short and broad

'Sanda' 1 W-W
(W. Jackson Jr, 1954)
'Whitemark' × 'Broughshane'
2n=45+1B

'Sanda' 8 W-Y
Fls 3-5 per stem, 76 mm wide; corona solid golden yellow. ?The same as 'Killara'

'Sandalphon' 2 Y-R
(A.M. Wilson, pre-1946)
Perianth segments deep yellow; corona deep red, frilled

'Sanderling'
(C. Dawson, pre-1908)

'Sanderling' 4
(J.L. Richardson) G. Zandbergen-Terwegen, 1959
'Falaise' hybrid

'Sandford' 1 W-Y
(West & Fell, pre-1935)
Perianth segments pure white; corona pale yellow

'Sandgate' 1 W-W
(G.P. Haydon, pre-1913)

'Sandgold' 1 Y-Y
(J.C. Martin) J.C. Martin, 1973
'Charles Draper' × 'Tea Cake'

Fl. 110 mm wide

'Sandow' 1 W-Y
(G.H. Engleheart, pre-1910)
Perianth segments ivory white, tinged sulphur yellow at base; corona rich golden yellow, with mouth flared

'Sand Piper' 5
(C. Dawson, pre-1907)

'Sandpiper' 5 W-Y
(G.E. Mitsch) G.E. Mitsch, 1971
'Bithynia' × *N. triandrus*; sdlg no. C5/2
Fls usually 3 per stem, rounded, 63 mm wide; corona bowl-shaped, small, lemon yellow. Dwarf. Late

'Sandra' 3 W-? (b)
(Mrs R.S. Cobley, pre-1954)

'Sandra Hall' 2 W-? (b)
(Mrs Ben Robertson, pre-1953)

'Sandringham' 3 W-YYO
(R.H. Bath, pre-1933)
Sdlg × 'Green Eyes'
Fl. 76 mm wide; perianth segments white, overlapping two-thirds; corona very shallow bowl-shaped, brilliant yellow 12B, shading to orange (28A) at rim. 2n=21. AM(Haarlem) 1937, *HC(g) 1947

'Sandwell' 7
(Miss J. Smith, pre-1949)

'Sandy Bay' 2 Y-Y
(H.A. Brown, 1937)
Perianth segments lemon yellow; corona becoming orange-yellow at rim, with mouth expanded. Very early

'Sandycove' 2 Y-GWP
(Brian S.Duncan) Brian S.Duncan, 1993
'Pismo Beach' × 'High Society'; sdlg no. 1157B
Fl. 98 mm wide; perianth segments very broadly ovate, blunt, slightly mucronate, opening white, becoming deep creamy yellow, spreading, with margins incurling at apex, overlapping half; the inner segments more narrowly ovate, not noticeably mucro, a little inflexed, with margins incurved; corona deep bowl-shaped, white, tinged green at base, with a broad band of rich coral pink at rim, mouth expanded, rim notched, slightly rolled, irregularly crenate. Late

'Sandygate' 2 W-W
(F.E. Board) F.E. Board, 1965
'Wedding Bell' × 'Empress of Ireland'; sdlg no. 464

'Sandy Lane's Queen' 2 W-? (b)
(Miss K.M. Hinchliff, pre-1940)

'Sandymount' 2 Y-O
(Ballydorn Bulb Farm) Ballydorn Bulb Farm, 1992
'Golden Amber' open pollinated
Fl. rounded, 95 mm wide; perianth segments broad, golden sandy yellow; corona bowl-shaped, pale orange, with a narrow band of a paler tone developing at rim, mouth flared, rim lightly dentate. Early. Sunproof

'San Francisco' 4
(Speelman, pre-1944)

'Sangay' 2 W-R
(C.E. Radcliff, pre-1938)
'Croesus' × 'Blodwen'

'Sangro' 2 (a)
(M.P. Williams, pre-1946)

'Sanguine' 2 Y-OOR
(New Zealand origin, pre-1934)
Perianth segments broad, rich yellow; corona expanded, rich orange, with dark red at rim. Tall. Early

'San Ilario' 3 W-WWO
(W.F.M.Copeland, pre-1910)
'Albatross' hybrid
Fl. of great substance; perianth segments oval, pure white, overlapping; corona shallow, ribbed, pale ivory white, with buff orange at rim. Late. AM(e) 1916, *HC(g) 1927. See also 'Sant' Ilario', 'Sant Ilaris', 'Sant Haris', 'St. Ilario'

'San Marino' 2 W-P
(Oregon Bulb Farms, pre-1951)

'San Michele' 2 Y-R
(G. Lewis) D.S. Bell, 1955
Perianth segments rich yellow; corona dark red

'Sanok' 3 W-? (b)
(J.T. Gray, pre-1937)

'San Paolo' 2 (a)
(J.L. Richardson, pre-1937)

'San Remo' 2 (a)
(G. Lubbe & Son, pre-1938)
AM(Haarlem) 1938

'Sanroma' 2 W-O
(S.J. Bisdee) S.J. Bisdee, 1956
'Rubra' × 'Ivo Fell'

'San Sebastian' 2 Y-R
(J.M. de Navarro, pre-1949)
('Trevisky' × 'Porthilly') × 'Gibraltar'
Fl. 86 mm wide; perianth segments very broad, rounded at apex, slightly mucronate, brilliant yellow 7A, spreading, plane or very slightly concave, overlapping half or more; the inner segments narrower, roundish, not noticeably mucronate, with margins nicked or creased at shoulder; corona cup-shaped, orange-red (32A), regularly and tightly frilled. PC(e) 1958, AM(e) 1970

'Sanslim' 1 W-W
(Mrs C.O. Fairbairn)

'Sansovino' 1 W-W
(J.L. Richardson, pre-1927)
Fl. pure white; perianth segments of great substance; corona with rim widely rolled

'Sans Reproche' 1 W-? (b)
(M. van Waveren & Sons, pre-1942)

'Sansui' 2 Y-YRR
(W. Jackson Jr) Jackson's Daffodils, 1979
'Sunpride' × 'Vulcan'; sdlg no. 21/72
Fl. 117 mm wide. Early to mid-season

'Santa Anita' 1 W-W
(G. Lewis) D.S. Bell, 1955
Fl. pure white; perianth segments of waxy texture; corona expanded, with rim dentate

'Santa Barbara' 5
(Oregon Bulb Farms, pre-1951)

'Santa Claus' 4 W-W
(G,L. Wilson, pre 1950)
'Cushendall' hybrid × 'Smyrna'
Fl. rounded, 75 mm wide, pure white; perianth and other petaloid segments in several whorls, very broad in outline, rounded and truncate at apex, overlapping two-thirds; the outer whorls spreading or a little inflexed; the inner whorls successively slightly shorter and more strongly inflexed, often folded at midrib; a few segments at centre convoluted and strongly inflexed; corona segments minute. Late. Strongly scented. AM(e) 1950, FCC(e) 1958, AM(Haarlem) 1964

'Santa Cruz' 3 W-O
(Mrs R.O. Backhouse, pre-1921)
Perianth segments narrow, acute, pure white; corona slender, reddish orange. AM(Haarlem) 1930

'Santa Fé' 1 W-Y
(G.B. van Rhijn) G.B. van Rhijn, 1958
Perianth segments creamy white; corona canary yellow

'Santakeda' 1 W-W
(R. Hyde) R. Hyde, 1957
Syn. 'Tongariro'

'Santa Lucia' 2 W-W
(J.L. Richardson) J.L. Richardson, 1956

'Broughshane' × 'Ludlow'
Fl. ice white; corona expanded, frilled

'Santa Maria' 1 Y-Y
(Spanish origin)
Selection by Peter Barr (1887) from wild-collected *N. hispanicus*
Fl. rich orange-yellow; perianth segments inflexed, twisted; corona cylindrical or somewhat funnel-shaped, mouth expanded, with rim deeply notched, sometimes distinctly 6-lobed. Early. Variable in form and colour

'Santa Monica' 2 W-YYP
(G. Lewis, 1945) D.S. Bell, 1958

'Santander' 1 W-Y
(Dutch origin, pre-1931)
Perianth segments sulphur white; corona flared. AM(Haarlem) 1931

'Santarini' 2 W-? (b)
(G.H. Johnstone, pre-1954)

'San Tarosa' 1 W-P
(A.O. Roblin, 1946)

'Santa Rosa' 2 W-WWP
(J.L. Richardson) Mrs H.K. Richardson, 1973
'Rose Caprice' × ('Interim' × 'Rose Caprice')
Perianth segments ice white, slightly reflexed; corona widely expanded, greenish white, with a broad band of salmon pink at rim and the rim deeply crenate

'Santawarna' 2 Y-Y
(R.W. Ward & Son) R.W. Ward & Son, 1960
Mid-season. Resembles a stronger-stemmed 'California' with the corona more heavily frilled

'Sant Haris' 3 W-WWO
Syn. of 'San Ilario'

'Santhea'
?Syn. of 'Anthea'

'Santiago' 2 (a)
(Barr & Sons, pre-1937)

'Santiam' 2 Y-YYO
(G.E. Mitsch, pre-1952)
'John Evelyn' × 'Fortune'; sdlg no. 37C41/16
Perianth segments opening pale yellow, becoming cream; corona yellow, with orange at rim, frilled, with the rim closely and deeply notched, as if fringed. Mid-season

'Sant' Ilario' 3 W-WWO
(W.F.M.Copeland, pre-1914)
Syn. of 'San Ilario'

'Sant Ilaris' 3 W-WWO
Syn. of 'San Ilario'

'Santorin' 2 Y-O
(?New Zealand origin, pre-1996) Unregistered

'Santoy' 3 W-O
(J.L. Richardson) C.R. Wootton, 1960
'Mahmoud' × 'Khartum'
Fl. 89 mm wide; corona reddish orange. Mid-season. Resembles a vigorous and large-flowered 'Khartum'

'Sapphire' 5 W-W
(W.F.M. Copeland, pre-1908)
Fl. small, pure white

'Sapphire' 2 or 3 (b or c)
(pre-1927)
Fl. pure white; corona disc-shaped

'Sappho' 9
(G.H. Engleheart, pre-1897)
Sdlg no. 385
Fl. rounded

'Sarabande' 9 W-GOR
(F.H.Chapman, pre-1916)
Perianth segments overlapping. AM(Haarlem) 1936

'Saracen' 3 W-?O
Syn. of 'The Saracen'

'Saragossa' 1 Y-Y
(Spanish origin)
Selection (*c.*1886) from wild-collected material
Fl. varying from pale to full yellow; perianth segments inflexed, twisted, overlapping at base only; corona cylindrical, short, ribbed, with mouth widely expanded, rim flanged and deeply notched. Early. Syn. 'Floribunda', 'Saragossa Daffodil', 'Saragossa Maximus'. Variable in form

'Saragossa Daffodil' 1 Y-Y

'Saragossa Maximus' 1 Y-Y
Syn. of 'Saragossa'

'Sarah' 2 W-Y
(W. Poupart, pre-1914)
'Frilled Beauty' × 'Maiden's Blush'; sdlg no. 3445
Perianth segments broadly ovate, inflexed in upper part, with margins sometimes wavy or recurved, overlapping one-third; corona broad funnel-shaped, with mouth slightly flared and lightly frilled

'Sarah' 2 W-P
(G. Barr, 1955)
'Frilled Beauty' × 'Maiden's Blush'; sdlg no. 3445
Perianth segments broadly ovate, blunt, fairly prominently mucronate, spreading, with margins a little

incurling, overlapping one-third to half; the inner segments a little inflexed, somewhat creased; corona soft pink, lightly frilled, with rim flanged and irregularly crenate

'Sarah Bernhardt' 1 W-W
(P. van Deursen, pre-1930)
AM(Haarlem) 1926

'Sarah Dear' 2 W-P
(R.A.Scamp) George Dear, 1994
'Chenoweth' × 'Kirklington'; sdlg no. S478
Fl. 98 mm wide; perianth segments broadly ovate, pure white, smooth, deeply overlapping; corona soft pale pink, smooth, with rim neatly rolled. Mid-season to late. Sunproof

'Sarah Lancashire' 3 W-? (b or c)
(P.D. Williams, pre-1927)

'Sarah Lancaster' 2 Y-YYR
(J.O. Sherrard, pre-1954)

'Sarah Leycester' 2 (a)
(Mrs R.O. Backhouse, pre-1921)

'Sarah Lowes' 2 Y-YYO
(D.C. MacArthur) D.C. MacArthur, 1985
'Chungking' self pollinated; sdlg no. E8319
Perianth segments broad in outline, blunt or squarish at apex, vivid yellow 9A, spreading, with midrib showing, overlapping half or more; the inner segments narrower, somewhat truncate, a little inflexed; corona narrow, ribbed, strong orange-yellow 17B, shading to light orange (23A) at rim, with flecks of white at rim, mouth straight, closely frilled. Mid-season. Scented

'Sarah Penton' 5
(Barr & Sons, pre-1913)

'Sarah Rachel' 4 Y-Y
(David Adams, pre-1996) Unregistered
4 Y-Y × 'Daydream'; sdlg no. 80/191

'Sarah Tisdale' 1 W-W
(W. Backhouse, pre-1869)
Fl. small, sulphur white; perianth segments somewhat twisted. Syn. Pseudonarcissus Moschatus 'Sarah Tisdale'

'Sarasate' 2 Y-O
(Konynenburg & Mark) Konynenburg & Mark, 1963
'Red Goblet' × 'Contrapunt'
Fl. 100 mm wide; perianth segments vivid yellow 9A; corona orange (28A). Late

'Sarastro' 2 W-W
(The Brodie of Brodie, c1942)
'White Sentinel' hybrid

'Saratoga' 2 W-YYO
(E.C. Powell, pre-1947)
'Killigrew' × 'Twinkle'

'Sarcelle' 2 Y-YRR
(D.S. Bell) D.S. Bell, 1960
'Burgundy' × 'Dunkeld'
Fl. 121 mm wide; corona deep red, with yellow at base. Mid-season. Resembles a large-flowered 'Dunkeld'

'Sarchedon' 9 W-GYR
(G.H. Engleheart, pre-1910)
Fl. 102 mm wide, of strong substance; perianth segments very broadly obovate, truncate, mucronate, pure white, spreading, overlapping one-third; the inner segments narrower, inflexed, with margins wavy; corona disc-shaped, finely ribbed, sulphur yellow, with green at base and a narrow band of scarlet at rim, with mouth split in places and overlapping. Mid-season. 2n=14. Resembles 'Comus'

'Sardius' 3 (a)
(A.M. Wilson, pre-1908)

'Sardonix' 3 W-? (b)
(The Brodie of Brodie, pre-1938)
'Sunstar' × 'Hades'

N. sardous Martelli = *N. tazetta* subsp. *lacticolor*

'Sargasso' 2 Y-YOO
(A.M. Wilson, pre-1933)
Sdlg no. 612
Fl. 95 mm wide; perianth segments brilliant greenish yellow 6C, with margins slightly incurving, overlapping half; corona ribbed, vivid orange 28B, paling to vivid yellow 15A at base, with mouth expanded and frilled, rim crenate. *AM(g) 1952

'Sargent Murphy' 1 Y-Y
?Syn. of 'Sergeant Murphy'

'Sargon' 1 (a)
(A.J. Bliss, pre-1930)

'Sari' 2 W-Y
(W. Jackson Jr, 1950)
'Adeline' × 'Wing Commander'

'Sarina' 2 W-W
(J.N. Hancock & Co., 1973) Unregistered

'Sarita' 1 W-W
(A.H. Ahrens) J.S. Leitch, 1956

'Sarn' 2 W-P
(H.G. Cross) H.G. Cross, 1984

'Cathlin' × 'Rose Royale'; sdlg no. 100-5
Perianth segments greenish white 157D; corona pale yellowish pink 29D, with a darker tone at rim. Mid-season

'Sarnian Belle' 1 W-W
(pre-1887)
Perianth segments twisted; corona slender, pure white

'Sarno' 1 Y-Y
(West & Fell, pre-1935)
'Royalist' hybrid × ('Cleopatra' × 'Golden City')
Perianth segments lemon; corona deep yellow. Syn. 'Walter Smith'

'S.Arnott' 1 W-? (b)
(W.B. Hartland, pre-1907)

'Sarobin' 2 Y-YYR
(D.S. Bell) D.S. Bell, 1960
'Dunkeld' × 'Burgundy'
Fl. 115 mm wide; corona yellow, with a broad band of bright red at rim. Early. Resembles 'Dunkeld' but with the perianth segments more rounded

'Sarong' 2 Y-P
(D.S. Bell) D.S. Bell, 1979
Fl. 107 mm wide; perianth segments lemon; corona pink. Mid-season

'Sarony' 2 (a)
(P.D. Williams, pre-1933)

'Saroya' 1 W-W
(W. Jackson Jr, 1951)
'Laur' × 'Karanja'; sdlg no. 103/51

'Sarre' 1 (a)
(G.P. Haydon, pre-1908)

'Sartoria' 1 W-GWW
(T. Bloomer) Rathowen Daffodils, 1982
'White Venture' × 'White Empress'; sdlg no. 400
Mid-season

'Saseeta' 2 W-R
(J.S. Leitch) J.S. Leitch, 1956

'Sasha' 2 W-YYO
(H. Selkirk, pre-1927)
Corona with apricot orange at rim

'Sasham' 2 Y-Y
(W. Jackson Jr) Jackson's Daffodils, 1979
Sdlg 35/65 × 'Warbin'; sdlg no. 38/72
Fl. 110 mm wide. Early to mid-season

'Saskia' 2 W-? (b)
(M. van Waveren & Sons, pre-1937)

'Saskia' 2 W-YYP
(J.N. Hancock & Co., 1954)

'Sassafras' 2 (a or b)
(pre-1949)

'Sassenheim's Giant' 1 Y-Y
(L. van Leeuwen & Son, pre-1928)
Early

'Sassenheim's Gold' 1 Y-Y
(G. Haver, pre-1933)
AM(Haarlem) 1930. Received AM(Haarlem) 1930 as 'Lorentz'

'Sasso' 9
(A.M. Wilson, pre-1913)

'Sassy' 12 Y-Y
(Glenbrook Bulb Farm, pre-1995) Unregistered
N. jonquilla var. *stellaris* × *N. cyclamineus*; sdlg no. 7/89

'Sasti' 2 (d)
(J.N. Hancock & Co.) J.N. Hancock & Co., 1955

'Satan' 9
(de Graaff Bros, pre-1927)

'Satara' 1 W-Y
(A. Gibson, pre-1927)
Corona creamy yellow

'Sateen' 2 W-YYP
(H.R. Barr) H.R. Barr, 1968
'Spellbinder' × 'Maiden's Blush'
Fl. 94 mm wide; perianth segments very broadly ovate, slightly mucronate, creamy white, a little inflexed, with margins sometimes incurling, overlapping half; the inner segments slightly narrower, shouldered at base; corona expanding and slightly ribbed, opening yellow, flushed pale apricot, becoming paler, mouth 6-lobed, with rim minutely crenate and very slightly flanged. 2n=27. *AM(g) 1974

'Satellite' 2 W-? (b or c)
(A.M. Wilson, pre-1927)

'Satellite' 6 Y-O
(G.E. Mitsch, 1952) G.E. Mitsch, 1962
'Rouge' × *N. cyclamineus*; sdlg no. N104/2
Fl. 75 mm wide; perianth segments ovate, clear yellow, with white mucro, reflexed, creased, overlapping half; corona cylindrical, closely ribbed, reddish orange, sometimes paling to clear yellow at base, with mouth straight and rim closely notched. Dwarf. Early

'Satin Blanc' 7 W-GWW
(Brian S. Duncan) Mrs G. Link, 1992
'Quickstep' open pollinated; sdlg no. 01256

Fl. 2-3 per stem, creamy white, smooth and of good substance; corona bowl-shaped, opening light yellow, frilled. Late. Scented. Resembles a purer white 'Quickstep' with a broader corona

'Satin Doll' 2 W-GYP
(Clive Postles, 1982) Clive Postles Daffodils, 1993
'Rainbow' × 'Dailmanach'; sdlg no. 1-51-77
Fl. 100 mm wide; perianth segments broadly ovate, with margins a little concave; corona funnel-shaped, pale yellow, with a clearly defined band of bright pink at rim, mouth flared, rim rolled. Late. Sunproof

'Satin King' 1 W-W
(G. Lewis) D.S. Bell, 1955

'Satin Lustre' 3 W-GGW
(Murray W. Evans, 1964) Jean E. Driver, 1993
'Frigid' × 'Cushendall' hybrid; sdlg no. H-44
Fl. 79 mm wide; perianth segments broadly ovate, pure white, satin smooth and glistening, overlapping; corona very short cup-shaped, vivid green, with a band of white at rim and the rim dentate. Late

'Satin Pink' 2 W-P
(J.L. Richardson) Warnaar & Co., 1958
Perianth segments ivory white; corona amber pink. AM(Haarlem) 1962

'Satin Prince' 2 Y-R
(G. Lewis) D.S. Bell, 1955

'Satin Queen' 2 W-YYO
(G. Lewis, 1940) G. Lewis, 1956
'White Sentinel' × 'Scarlet Perfection'
Corona expanded, yellow, with a band of orange at rim, frilled

'Satire' 3 W-? (b)
(A.H. Ahrens) J.S. Leitch, 1956

'Satisfaction' 2 W-? (b)
(E.M. Crosfield, pre-1908)

'Satisfaction' 1 W-W
(C.G. van Tubergen, pre-1927)
Fl. 95 mm wide, facing down; perianth segments creamy white, overlapping half; corona pale dull cream, mouth expanded. Mid-season to late

'Satrap' 2 (a)
(Mrs R.O. Backhouse, pre-1921)

'Satsuma' 1 Y-Y
(Murray W. Evans) Murray W. Evans, 1975
'Daydream' × 'New Era'; sdlg no. K-39/1
Fl. 105 mm wide; corona opening yellow, becoming pinkish buff or rich apricot yellow. Mid-season

'Saturday Girl' 2 W-?
(W.M. Spry, pre-1975) Unregistered
'Hunter's Moon' × 'Tunis'
Corona creamy brown. Early

'Saturn' 3 W-? (b)
(G.H. Engleheart, pre-1907)

'Saturn' 2 W-O
(West & Fell, pre-1931)
Mid-season

'Saturn' 3 W-GYO
(Carncairn Daffodils) Carncairn Daffodils, 1978
'Bravura' × 'Bushmills'; sdlg no. 6/11/64
Fl. 96 mm wide; corona yellow, with green at base and a distinct band of orange (28A or B) at rim. Late

'Saturn Five' 6 Y-Y
(David Adams) David Adams, 1992
'Gambas' × *N. cyclamineus*
Fl. 45 mm wide, deep lemon yellow; perianth segments oblong, acute, with prominent white mucro, strongly reflexed, sometimes twisted, overlapping at base only; corona cylindrical and as long as the perianth segments, mouth a little expanded, rim notched. Dwarf. Very early

'Saturnin' 8 Y-Y
(pre-1798)
Fl. sulphur yellow

'Saturnus' 3 W-YYR
(J.L. Richardson, pre-1935)
AM(Haarlem) 1934, FCC(Haarlem) 1936

'Saucy' 3 W-? (b)
(E.M. Crosfield, pre-1908)

'Saucy' 2 W-P
(Murray W. Evans) Murray W. Evans, 1974
('Wild Rose' × 'Rosegarland') × 'Interim'
Fl. 90 mm wide

'Saulcerite' 2 Y-YYO
(Evalds Paupers) Evalds Paupers, 1986
'Kissproof' × 'Armada'; sdlg no. P-75-23
Perianth segments vivid yellow 12A, flushed with pale yellow-orange (20B); corona cup-shaped, expanded, vivid orange-yellow 21A, with vivid orange 28B at rim. Mid-season. Sunproof

'Sava' 1 W-W
(C.E. Radcliff, 1938)
'Beersheba' × 'Paula'

'Savage Pink' 1 W-P
(M.G. Temple-Smith, 1984) M.G. Temple-Smith, 1997
'Savage River' × 'Accent'; sdlg no. 14/84

Corona straight-sided, pink, paling with age. Mid-season

'Savage River' 2 W-P
(Tom Forster, 1960s) Unregistered
'Salmon Trout' × 'Blushing Bride'
Perianth segments smooth; corona deep rose pink, with mouth lightly flared. Tall. Late

'Savaldo' 2 Y-O
(J.W.A. Lefeber) J.W.A. Lefeber, 1968

'Savannah' 1 (a)
(de Graaff Bros, pre-1928)
Syn. 'Portia'

'Savannah' 2 W-Y
(D.S. Bell) D.S. Bell, 1979
'My Love' open pollinated
Fl. 103 mm wide; perianth segments pure white; corona yellow. Mid-season. Resembles 'My Love' but with a more funnel-shaped corona

'Savin' 2 W-? (b)
(Parr's Nurseries, 1947) Parr's Nurseries, 1958

'Savla' 2 W-Y
(?E.C. Powell, pre-1936)

'Savoir Faire' 2 W-GWP
(Brian S. Duncan) Brian S. Duncan, 1992
'Pismo Beach' × 'High Society'; sdlg no. 1038
Fl. rounded, 111 mm wide; perianth segments very broad, blunt, prominently mucronate, spreading, plane, smooth, overlapping half; the inner segments narrower and more nearly ovate; corona bowl-shaped, opening yellow, becoming white, with green at base and a broad band of pink at rim, mouth with six lobes sometimes overlapping, rim rolled. Mid-season to late. Sunproof

'Savonarola' 2 W-?
(The Brodie of Brodie, c.1913)
'Princess Mary' × *N. poeticus*
Perianth segments creamy white, deeply overlapping; corona widely expanded, of strong colour

'Savonarola' 1 W-Y
(The Brodie of Brodie, c.1918)
'Weardale Perfection' × 'White Knight'
Corona very pale yellow

'Savoy' 2 Y-YOO
(G. Lubbe & Sons, pre-1938)
AM(Haarlem) 1938

'Savoy' 2 Y-Y
(N.R. McIsaac) N.R. McIsaac, 1982
'Kingscourt' × 'Barrington'; sdlg no. 77
Fl. 107 mm wide, deep yellow. Early to mid-season.

Resembles 'Kingscourt' but with a shorter corona

'Saxon' 1 Y-Y
(W.M. Spry, pre-1975) Unregistered
'Morning Glory' × 'Stand By'

'Saxonbury' 2 Y-Y
(N.A.Burr) N.A.Burr, 1995
'Viking' × 'Gold Convention'; sdlg no. 1.5.83
Fl. rounded, 118 mm wide; perianth segments very broad, vivid yellow 9A, spreading, a little concave at apex, with broad midrib showing, overlapping half or more; the inner segments very little narrower; corona cylindrical or somewhat funnel-shaped, smooth at base, lightly ribbed towards mouth, deeper in tone (13A) than the perianth, with mouth lightly flared, even, rim crenate. Mid-season

'Saxon Earl' 1 Y-Y
(W. Balch, pre-1940)

'Saxon Maid' 2 W-? (b)
(G.H. Engleheart, pre-1913)
Late

'Saymara' 2 W-Y
(T.H. Piper) T.H. Piper, 1956
'Grayling' × 'Lorinna'
Corona lemon yellow. See also 'Sayonara'

'Sayonara' 2 W-Y
Syn. of 'Saymara'

'Sayonara' 1 Y-Y
(J.N. Hancock & Co., c.1965) Unregistered
'Wilson' × 'Pretoria'

'Scabbard' 3 W-? (b)
(F.H. Chapman, pre-1913)

N. scaberulus Henriques 13 Section Apodanthi

'Scafell' 4
(G.C. Graham, pre-1953)

'Scallywag' 2 W-YYO
(Jackson's Daffodils, 1978) Jackson's Daffodils, 1988
Sdlg 144/70 × sdlg 167/70; sdlg no. 269/78
Perianth segments greenish white (155A); corona brilliant greenish yellow 151D, with vivid orange 28B at rim. Mid-season

'Scandal' 3 W-O
(A.M. Wilson, pre-1930)
Corona disc-shaped, scarlet-orange

'Scapa' 1 W-W
(The Brodie of Brodie, c.1930)
'Quartz' × 'Tenedos'
Fl. 115 mm wide, creamy white; perianth segments

overlapping half; corona with mouth expanded and rim flanged. 2n=28. AM(e) 1939, *AM(g) 1949

'Scaramouche' 3 (a)
(P.D. Williams, pre-1931)

'Scarlatti' 2 W-O
(Konynenburg & Mark) Konynenburg & Mark, 1963
('Frederike' × 'Mimosa') × ('Anaconda' × 'Marian')
Fl. 98 mm wide; corona light orange (23A). Mid-season

'Scarlet Admiral' 3 W-O
(S.J. Bisdee, 1946)
'Mr Sparks' × 'Hades'

'Scarlet Beauty' 2 W-O
(Mrs R.O. Backhouse, pre-1921)
Perianth segments creamy white; corona orange, almost scarlet at rim. AM(e) 1926, AM(Haarlem) 1938

'Scarlet-brigade' 3 (a)
(Mrs P.M. Davis, pre-1948)

'Scarlet Champion' 2 (a)
(G. Zandbergen-Terwegen, pre-1936)

'Scarlet Cheer' 2 (a)
(Mrs R.O. Backhouse, pre-1921)

'Scarlet Chord' 2 Y-R
(G.E. Mitsch, 1981) R. & E. Havens, 1991
Sdlg 2H59/4 ('Chemawa' × 'Brer Fox') × 'Loch Hope'; sdlg no. 2Q15/5
Fl. rounded; per. segments clear yellow; corona bowl-shaped, bright orange-red, with mouth straight. Early

'Scarlet Cockade' 3 W-? (b)
(Mrs R.O. Backhouse, pre-1921)

'Scarlet Comet' 9?
(G.H. Engleheart, pre-1930)
? *N. poeticus* var. *recurvus* sdlg
Resembles 'Folly'

'Scarlet Elegance' 2 Y-YRR
(P.D. Williams, pre-1938)
Fl. 84 mm wide; perianth segments broadly ovate in outline, blunt or slightly truncate, bright lemon yellow, with white mucro, spreading, with margins incurling, overlapping one-third to a half; the inner segments more narrowly ovate, angled at shoulder, with margins wavy; corona cup-shaped, deep red, paling to yellow at base, mouth straight and lightly frilled. Resembles a more intensely coloured 'Killigrew'. Syn. 'Brilliant Star', 'Jupiter', 'Scarlet Elegans', 'Star of the East', 'Star of the West'. FA(Haarlem) 1939

'Scarlet Elegans' 2 Y-YRR
Syn. of 'Scarlet Elegance'

'Scarlet Emblem' 2 Y-O
(pre-1930)
Perianth segments rich yellow; corona rich reddish orange. Tall

'Scarlet Eye' 3 W-O
(G.H. Engleheart, pre-1906)
Perianth segments pure white; corona almost disc-shaped, intense scarlet-orange

'Scarlet Flame' 2 (a)
(F. Rijnveld & Sons, pre-1951)
AM(Haarlem) 1951

'Scarlet Frill' 3 W-YYR
(Barr & Sons, pre-1923)
Perianth segments opening soft creamy yellow, becoming paler; corona ribbed, deep yellow, with orange-scarlet at rim, frilled. Tall

'Scarlet Gem' 8 Y-O
(P.D. Williams, pre-1910)
Poetaz
Fls 4-6 per stem; perianth segments very broadly ovate, blunt and mucronate, rich primrose yellow, inflexed, overlapping two-thirds; the inner segments less prominently mucronate, loosely twisted; corona shallow, widely expanded, ribbed, vivid orange, with green clearly showing in tube, a little frilled. Mid-season. Scented. 2n=17. AM(e) 1914, AM(Haarlem) 1927, FA(Haarlem) 1936, *FCC(g) 1936

'Scarlet Glory' 2 (a)
(Mrs R.O. Backhouse, pre-1921)

'Scarlet Glory' 2 W-? (b)
(de Graaff Bros, pre-1930)
AM(Haarlem) 1930

'Scarlet Glow' 2 (a)
(Mrs R.O. Backhouse, pre-1921)
AM(Haarlem) 1926

'Scarlet Gold' 2 Y-O
(H.P. Zwetsloot, pre-1949)
Perianth segments lemon yellow. AM(Haarlem) 1949

'Scarlet Harvest' 2 Y-R
(D.S. Bell) D.S. Bell, 1957
Perianth segments yellow; corona bowl-shaped, dark red

'Scarlet Heaven' 2 W-P
Syn. of 'Seventh Heaven'

'Scarlet King' 2 (a)
(G. Zandbergen-Terwegen, pre-1937)

'Scarlet Lady' 2 (a)
(H.P. Zwetsloot, pre-1952)

'Scarlet Lancer' 2 Y-O
(Mrs R.O. Backhouse, pre-1908)
Perianth segments pale yellow; corona disc-shaped, reddish orange, tightly frilled. AM(Haarlem) 1931

'Scarlet Leader' 2 Y-O
(Mrs R.O. Backhouse, pre-1921)
Perianth segments cream yellow; corona scarlet-orange, frilled. 2n=28. AM(Haarlem) 1931, FCC(Haarlem) 1938

'Scarlet Monarch' 2 Y-R
(D.S. Bell) D.S. Bell, 1957
Perianth segments very broad, soft yellow; corona very shallow bowl-shaped, strongly shaded red

'Scarlet Orb' 2 (a)
(R.H. Bath, pre-1929)

'Scarlet Perfection' 2 Y-O
(Mrs R.O. Backhouse, pre-1921)
Perianth segments primrose yellow, overlapping; corona rich scarlet-orange. 2n=28. PC 1923, AM(e) 1927, AM(Haarlem) 1932, FCC(Haarlem) 1937

'Scarlet Pimpernel' 2 Y-O
(Barr & Sons, pre-1908)
'Henry Irving' × *N. poeticus*
Perianth segments soft primrose yellow, corona stained reddish orange

'Scarlet Pimpernel' 2 Y-O
(Australian or New Zealand origin, *c*.1927)
Perianth segments yellow; corona almost scarlet

'Scarlet Pimpernel' 2 W-O
(J.W.A. Lefeber) J.W.A. Lefeber, 1956
Perianth segments pure white; corona intense reddish orange

'Scarlet Queen' 2 W-? (b)
(Mrs R.O. Backhouse, pre-1921)

'Scarlet Queen' 2 Y-YYR
(D.V. West, pre-1927) G.E. Mitsch, 1956
Perianth segments broadly ovate, blunt, fairly prominently mucronate, spreading, with margins slightly wavy, overlapping one-third; the inner segments narrower, a little inflexed, creased, with margins more strongly wavy; corona very broad and shallow funnel-shaped, finely ribbed, deep orange, with a broad band of deep red at rim and the rim minutely crenate. Late

'Scarlet Robe' 2 W-? (b)
(S.C. Gaspar, 1939) R.J. Abernethy, 1957

'Scarlet Robe' 2 W-O
(G. Lewis, pre-1940)
Perianth segments creamy white, of great substance; corona reddish orange, slightly frilled

'Scarlet Royal' 2 Y-R
(G. Lubbe & Son, pre-1948)
AM(Haarlem) 1948, FCC(Haarlem) 1951

'Scarlet Runner' 3 W-O
(P.D. Williams, pre-1907)
Corona bright scarlet-orange

'Scarlet Sceptre' 2 (a)
(R.H. Bath, pre-1943)

'Scarlet Splendour' 3 W-? (b)
(G. Zandbergen-Terwegen, pre-1938)

'Scarletta' 3 W-R
(G.H. Engleheart, pre-1904)
Perianth segments creamy white; corona ribbed, intense scarlet

'Scarlet Tanager' 2 Y-R
(R. & E. Havens, 1982) R. & E. Havens, 1992
'Bantam' × 'Kindled'; sdlg no. REH7/3
Fl. 70 mm wide; perianth segments very broad, clear medium yellow, spreading, concave, smooth, overlapping half; the inner segments ovate or roundish, touching at shoulder; corona bowl-shaped, smooth or loosely ribbed, bright orange-red, with mouth straight and even, rim minutely notched. Late

'Scarlet Thread' 3 W-GYR
(J.M. de Navarro) J.M. de Navarro, 1977
'Merlin' × 'Brahms'; sdlg no. 244/III
Fl. 81 mm wide; corona disc-shaped, ribbed, yellow, with green at base and orange-red at rim. Mid-season. Resembles 'Merlin' but with a narrower band of colour at corona rim

'Scarlet Tiger' 2 W-R
(A.M. Wilson, 1945) J.L. Richardson, 1956
Perianth segments pure white, of good substance; corona widely expanded, intense bright red

'Scarlett O'Hara' 2 Y-R
(H.P. Zwetsloot, pre-1950)
2n=28. AM(Haarlem) 1950, FCC(Haarlem) 1953

'Scarlet Wonder' 2 (a)
(de Graaff Bros, pre-1937)

'Scarsdale' 2 W-? (b)
(L. Buckland, pre-1936)
Corona expanded, with red at rim

'Scarslight'
(New Zealand origin, pre-1940)

'Scarva' 2 W-W
(J.L. Richardson, pre-1937)
'Mitylene' × 'Fortune'
Corona faintly tinged with pale greenish lemon. Resembles a larger and whiter 'Mitylene'

'Scarvia'
(pre-1940)

'Sceance' 1 W-W
(E.M. Crosfield, pre-1913)

'Scenario' 2 (a or b)
(pre-1949)

'Scented April' 1 (b)
(V.Brink) V.Brink, 1968

'Scented April' 8 W-YRR
(V. Brink) V. Brink, 1973
'Richard Tauber' self pollinated; sdlg no. 60-4
Fls 2-4 per stem, 66 mm wide; corona very short cup-shaped, opening dull orange, becoming deep orange-red, with yellow at base. Late. Poeticus-scented. Resembles 'Richard Tauber' but with fewer and larger flowers per stem

'Scented Breeze' 2 W-YYP
(Brian S.Duncan) Brian S.Duncan, 1997
'Fragrant Rose' × 'Pol Dornie'; sdlg no. 1323
Fl. 120 mm wide; perianth segments broadly ovate, blunt, spreading; corona cylindrical, creamy yellow, shading to warm pastel pink at rim, with mouth slightly flared. Late. Scented

'Scentella' 4 W-P
(W. Jackson Jr, 1968) Jackson's Daffodils, 1982
'Lawali' × 'Chimeon'; sdlg no. 117/69
Fl. 105 mm wide. Mid-season. Scented

'Sceptre' 3 Y-O
(G.H. Engleheart, pre-1902)
Perianth segments light primrose yellow; corona ribbed, bright reddish orange. Tall

'Sceptre' 1 Y-Y
(D.W. Gourlay) D.W. Gourlay, 1958
'Galway' × 'Kingscourt'
Perianth segments vivid yellow 9B; corona slightly brighter in tone (12A), frilled

'Sceptre Royal' 8 Y-Y
(pre-1851)

'Schapiro' 2 Y-R
(G.L. Wilson) G.L. Wilson, 1963
'Playboy' × ('Indian Summer' × 'Chungking')

'Schenectady' 1 Y-Y
(A.O. Roblin, pre-1942)

'Royalist' × 'Robert Montgomery'

'Schiapparelli' 2 (a)
(J.W.A. Lefeber, pre-1945)

'Schiehallion' 1 (a)
(The Brodie of Brodie, c.1911)
'King Alfred' × 'Weardale Perfection'

'Schiller' 9
(G. Lubbe & Son, pre-1927)

'Scholar' 2 Y-W
(Elise Havens) G.E. Mitsch, 1976
'Bethany' × 'Butterscotch'; sdlg no. FEJ4/3
Fl. 115 mm wide; perianth segments lemon; corona opening lemon, becoming white, with rim rolled. Mid-season

'Schönbrünn' 1 Y-Y
(P. Hopman & Son) P. Hopman & Son, 1984
Perianth segments opening with pale patches at base, becoming self pale greenish yellow 2D; corona much darker in tone

'Schoonoord' 4
(C.A. van der Wereld, pre-1954)

'Schweppes' 2 Y-Y
(Mrs A.R. Simmons) Mrs A.R. Simmons, 1980
Sdlg no. 67-8-03
Fl. 104 mm wide, lemon yellow, with a greenish tinge. Mid-season

'Scillonian Sunset' 2 W-YYO
(W.J.G. Hector) W.J.G. Hector, 1965
Fl. 100 mm wide; corona with rim frilled. Early. Resembles a larger 'Flower Record' in all parts

'Scilly Isles' White' 8 W-W
Syn. of 'Scilly White'

'Scilly White' 8 W-W
(pre-1865)
?Variant of *N.tazetta* subsp. *ochroleucus*
Fls ± 10 per stem, 35-40 mm wide; perianth segments broadly ovate, prominently mucronate, spreading, with apex incurved, somewhat concave, overlapping half; corona cup-shaped, obscurely ribbed, opening pale greenish yellow, becoming creamy white, mouth straight, even or a little wavy, rim entire, occasionally notched. Early to mid-season. Scented. 2n=32. Resembles 'Grand Primo Citronière' but with a paler corona. Syn. ?'Sicily White', 'Scilly Isles' White'

'Scimitar' 2 W-GYY
(J.N.Hancock & Co., 1983) J.N.Hancock & Co., 1997
Sdlg 120/78H × sdlg 125/78H; sdlg no. 131/83H
Perianth segments broadly ovate, pure white, plane;

corona bowl-shaped, expanded, citron yellow, with rim crenate. Late

'Scintilla' 2 W-R
(de Graaff Bros, pre-1944)
EFA(Haarlem) 1943

'Scintillant' 2 W-WWR
(C.E. Radcliff, 1931)
'Pink'un' × 'Harpagon'

'Scio' 2 Y-Y
(G.E. Mitsch) G.E. Mitsch, 1969
'Playboy' × 'Daydream'; sdlg no. B36/6
Perianth segments lemon gold, deeply overlapping; corona opening deeper in tone, becoming amber in tone. Mid-season

'Scipio' 2 Y-Y
(W. Jackson Jr) Jackson's Daffodils, 1980
'Manuella' × 'Camelot'; sdlg no. 137/73
Fl. forming a double triangle, 105 mm wide; perianth segments very broadly ovate, blunt, with slight white mucro, spreading, plane, with margins sometimes incurling at apex, smooth, overlapping half; the inner segments more narrowly ovate, a little inflexed; corona cup-shaped, smooth, slightly darker in tone than the perianth, with mouth straight and loosely frilled, rim entire. Mid-season

'Scolboa' 2 W-O
(Carncairn Daffodils) Carncairn Daffodils, 1973
'Enniskillen' × Richardson sdlg
Fl. 86 mm wide; corona shallow, orange-red

'Scolopax' 6
(A.M. Wilson, pre-1948)

'Scootles' 9 W-GYR
(Mrs M.S. Yerger) Mrs M.S. Yerger, 1993
N. poeticus var. *hellenicus* × 'Lights Out'; sdlg no. 75 H 1-3
Fl. forming a double triangle, 35 mm wide; perianth segments broad; the inner segments narrower; corona bowl-shaped, brilliant greenish yellow 3B, with brilliant yellow-green 142B at base and red (41A) at rim. Dwarf. Very late

'Scopas' 2 Y-Y
(W.A. Grace, pre-1927)

'Scope' 1 W-GWW
(W. Jackson Jr) Jackson's Daffodils, 1979
Sdlg 80/60 × 'Empress of Ireland'; sdlg no. 162/70
Fl. 116mm wide; perianth segments pure white, smooth, of good substance, deeply overlapping; corona opening slightly creamy, soon becoming white, with green at base, rim dentate and slightly rolled. Mid-season. Syn. 'Hope'

'Scorcher' 3 W-? (b)
(Alister Clark, pre-1911)

'Scorcher' 2 Y-R
(C. Goodson, pre-1927)

'Scorcher' 2 Y-O
(E.C. Genat, 1952) G. Errey, 1962
Fl. 115 mm wide; perianth segments brilliant greenish yellow 6A; corona strong orange 24A. Early. 2n=28. Resembles an earlier- flowered 'Armada'

'Scoreline' 1 Y-Y
(Brian S. Duncan) Rathowen Daffodils, 1977
'Kingscourt' open pollinated; sdlg no. 20
Fl. deep yellow. Mid-season. Resembles an improved 'Bayard' with the perianth more rounded

'Scorpion' 2 Y-R
(A.M. Wilson, pre-1930)
Corona intense red

'Scotch Gold' 1 Y-Y
(The Brodie of Brodie, pre-1952)
Yellow sdlg × 'Maviston'
Fl. opening gold, becoming almost orange

'Scotch Mist' 3 W-WWY
(G.H. Johnstone, pre-1949)
Corona with a narrow band of lemon yellow at rim

'Scotch Quarter' 1 Y-Y
(John R.Reed, 1985) John R.Reed, 1997
'Golden Jewel' × 'Dream Prince'; sdlg no. 85-7-1
Fl. rounded, 90 mm wide, clear yellow; perianth segments broadly ovate, very smooth; the inner segments almost touching one another; corona funnel-shaped. Mid-season

'Scotch Rose' 2 W-P
(The Brodie of Brodie, *c*.1939)
'Rosary' hybrid
2n=28

'Scoticus' 1 Y-Y
(pre-1819)
Perianth segments narrowly ovate, sulphur yellow; corona yellow, with mouth widely expanded, rim deeply crenate. Treated by Haworth in 1819 as *N. festalis* var. *scoticus* and in 1831 as *N. lobularis* var. *scoticus*

'Scoticus'
Syn. of *N. pseudonarcissus* var. *humilis*

'Scoticus Plenus' 4 Y-Y
(pre-1827)
Selection from *N. pseudonarcissus*
Perianth and other petaloid segments in 3-4 whorls, ovate, acute, pale yellow, with margins somewhat

wavy; the outer whorl spreading or a little inflexed; the inner whorls successively a little shorter and becoming more inflexed; corona segments not much shorter than the inner whorls and closely overlying them, oblong, rich yellow, a little frilled, those at centre contorted. ?The same as 'Gallicus Major Flore Pleno'

'Scotney Castle' 1 Y-Y
(N.A. Burr) N.A. Burr, 1985
'Arctic Gold' × 'Arkle'
Fl. clear rich lemon yellow; perianth segments broadly ovate, blunt, with very slight white mucro, spreading, plane, overlapping half; the inner segments narrower, square-shouldered at base, inflexed, with margins incurved and slightly wavy; corona funnel-shaped, slightly darker in tone than the perianth, with mouth slightly expanded and a little frilled, rim notched and crenate. Tall. Early. Resembles a larger-flowered 'Arctic Gold' of paler colour

'Scottia' 2 (a)
(Warnaar & Co., pre-1930)
AM(Haarlem) 1930

'Scotty' 1 W-Y
(W.M. Spry, pre-1975) Unregistered
'Lochin' × 'Golden'
Corona chrome yellow

'Scout' 2 W-? (b)
(C. Dawson, pre-1907)

'Scout' 2 W-? (b)
(West & Fell, pre-1938)

'Scoutmaster' 2 W-? (b)
(F.H. Chapman, pre-1913)
'King Alfred' × 'Minnie Hume'

'Scrabo' 2 Y-O
(The Brodie of Brodie, c.1936)
'Damson' × 'Invergordon'
Perianth segments soft yellow; corona broad disc-shaped, deep reddish orange

'Scrambled Eggs' 4 W-Y
(W.F.M. Copeland, pre-1931)
Perianth and other petaloid segments creamy white; corona segments interspersed, apricot yellow, paling to yellow at base

'Scrooby' 1 Y-Y
(pre-1914)

'Scud' 3 W-W
(T.H. Piper) T.H. Piper, 1956
'Beersheba' × 'Nona'

'Sculptor' 1 (a)
(R.H. Bath, pre-1931)

'Scute' 2 W-W
(?G.H. Johnstone, pre-1950)
'White Sentinel' × 'Ischia'

'Scythia' 4
(pre-1926)

'Seabank' 2 W-O
(The Brodie of Brodie, c.1931)
Sdlg 118/A/20 × 'Hades'
Perianth segments white, of thick substance; corona light orange

'Seabird' 3 W-? (b)
(G.H. Engleheart, pre-1901)
AM 1901

'Sea Bird' 3 W-GYY
(pre-1913)
Perianth segments white, with pale green at base, with margins wavy; corona ribbed, orange-yellow, with dark green at base. AM 1901

'Seabreeze'
(pre-1913)

'Sea Breeze' 2 or 3 W-? (b or c)
(pre-1915)

'Sea Breeze' 1 W-W
(Oregon Bulb Farms, pre-1945)

'Seabrook' 2 (a)
(S.C. Gaspar) S.C. Gaspar, 1955

'Seacraft' 1 (a)
(G.H. Engleheart, pre-1927)

'Sea Dream' 3 W-GWW
(J.A. O'More) J.A. O'More, 1968
'Nelly' × 'Chinese White'
Perianth segments very broadly ovate or roundish, only very slightly mucronate, spreading, very smooth, overlapping half; the inner segments more narrowly ovate; corona shallow bowl-shaped, strongly ribbed, with mouth straight and frilled, rim dentate

'Seadrift' 2 W-? (b)
(W. Welchman, pre-1913)

'Seadrift' 1 W-W
(J.S. Leitch) J.S. Leitch, 1960

'Sea Eagle' 1 W-W
(J.L. Richardson, pre-1953)
'Glendalough' × 'Truth'

'Seafarer' 1 W-W
(J.L. Richardson) Mrs H.K. Richardson, 1963
'Empress of Ireland' × 'Early Mist'
Fl. ivory white; corona frilled

'Sea Fever' 1 W-W
(D.S. Bell, 1968) D.S. Bell, 1978
('Kilsheelan' × 'Broughshane') × 'Empress of Ireland'
Fl. 109 mm wide, pure white; corona expanded, frilled, with rim dentate. Mid-season. Resembles 'Empress of Ireland' but with a different profile at corona rim

'Seafire' 3 W-GYO
(K. McCombe) J.N. Hancock & Co., 1979
'Hokitiki' open pollinated
Fl. 90 mm wide; corona brilliant yellow 12B, with light yellow-green 154D at base and strong orange 30D at rim. Early

'Seafoam' 3 W-? (b)
(W. Welchman, pre-1908)

'Seafoam' 2 W-W
(G.E. Mitsch) G.E. Mitsch, 1978
'Easter Moon' × 'Carnmoon'; sdlg no. F139/2
Fl. rounded, 92 mm wide, very smooth; perianth segments very broad, a little reflexed, with broad midrib showing, overlapping half; the inner segments narrower, more nearly spreading, loosely creased; corona short funnel-shaped, less pure in tone than the perianth, with mouth straight and closely frilled. Mid-season. Resembles a shorter 'Easter Moon' with a whiter perianth and more closely frilled corona

'Seaford' 2 W-W
(J.L. Richardson) Mrs H.K. Richardson, 1963
('Templemore' × 'Ludlow') × 'Vahsel Bay'
Corona slender, with rim slightly flanged

'Seafret' 2 W-W
(R.V. Favell, pre-1946)

'Seafury' 1 Y-Y
(G.B. van Rhijn) G.B. van Rhijn, 1958

'Sea Gift' 7 Y-Y
(A. Gray, pre-1935)
Found in a Cornish garden

'Sea Green' 9 W-GYR
(G.H. Engleheart, pre-1930)
Fl. rounded, 60 mm wide; perianth segments very broad, rounded at apex, prominently mucronate, spreading or very slightly reflexed, plane, smooth, of good substance, regular, overlapping half or more; the inner segments roundish, somewhat truncate, only very slightly mucronate, spreading; corona broad disc-shaped, loosely ribbed, yellow, with pale green at base and a clearly defined narrow band of bright red at rim, with the rim minutely crenate. 2n=14. AM(e) 1930

'Seagull' 3 W-Y
(G.H. Engleheart, pre-1893)
'Ornatus' × 'Empress'
Fl. up to 127 mm wide; perianth segments broadly ovate in outline, blunt or rounded at apex, fairly prominently mucronate, pure white, spreading or a little inflexed, with margins incurling and sometimes wavy, separated at base, sometimes overlapping at mid-point; corona bowl-shaped, ribbed, canary yellow, with pale orange at rim soon fading to yellow, loosely frilled. Resembles sibling 'Albatross' but with no contrasting colour at corona rim at maturity. Syn. 'Sea-gull'

'Sea-gull' 3 W-Y
Syn. of 'Seagull'

'Seaham' 1 W-W
(C.E. Radcliff, 1943) J.M.Radcliff, 1956
'Bonnington' × 'Tain'

'Seahorse' 1 Y-Y
(G.P. Haydon, pre-1910)
Fl. deep yellow. Resembles a later-flowered and more refined 'King Alfred'

'Sea Horse' 1 Y-Y
Syn. of 'Sea Horse'

'Sea King' W-W
(pre-1905)
Corona cylindrical. Resembles *N.* × *johnstonii*

'Sea King' 2 Y-? (a)
(E. & J.C. Martin, pre-1916)
Corona suffused with red

'Sealark' 2 W-WWO
(Mrs J.U. Yonge, pre-1944)
'Mrs R.O.Backhouse' × 'Madame de Graaff'
Corona creamy white, with pale apricot orange at rim, frilled

'Sealed Orders' 3 W-GRR
(J.M. de Navarro) J.M. de Navarro, 1977
'Arctic Flame' × 'Leonora'
Fl. 93 mm wide; perianth segments broadly ovate, pure white; corona bowl-shaped, red, with green at base. Mid-season. Resembles 'Don Carlos' but with whiter perianth segments and shorter corona

'Sea Legend' 2 W-W
(Jackson's Daffodils, 1981) Jackson's Daffodils, 1991
'Immaculate' × 'Rhapsody'; sdlg no. 88/81
Fl. rounded, 98 mm wide, greenish white (155A); perianth segments very broad, blunt, slightly mucronate, spreading, glistening, with midrib

showing, overlapping half or more; the inner segments more nearly ovate, square-shouldered at base; corona cylindrical, with green showing in tube, mouth straight and loosely frilled. Mid-season

'Sealight' 9 W-GGR
(Mrs M.S. Yerger) Mrs M.S. Yerger, 1984
'Lights Out' × 'Sea Green'; sdlg no. 73 A 1
Fl. 60 mm wide; perianth segments strongly reflexed; corona brilliant yellow-green 154B, with orange-red (32A) at rim. Late. Spicily scented

'Sealing Wax' 3 W-? (b)
(J.C. Williams, pre-1913)

'Sealing Wax' 2 Y-O
(Barr & Sons) Wallace & Barr, 1957
Fl. 90 mm wide; perianth segments broad, blunt, brilliant greenish yellow 6B; corona slightly ribbed, strong orange 25A, paling slightly to base, mouth very slightly expanded, frilled. 2n=28. *AM(p) 1978

'Sea Lord' 2 Y-R
(D.S. Bell) D.S. Bell, 1968
'Monica' × 'Diamond King'
Fl. rounded; corona very shallow bowl-shaped, deep red

'Sea Mew' 2 W-? (b)
(P.D. Williams, pre-1910)

'Sea Mist' 1 W-W
(G.H. Engleheart, pre-1923)

'Sea Mist' 3 W-W
(J.A. O'More) P.D.K. Ramsay, 1983
'Portrush' × 'Altyre'

'Sean' 2 Y-Y
(W. Jackson Jr, 1969) Unregistered
'Gold Script' × 'Vixi'; sdlg no. 53/69

'Sea Nymph' 1 W-W
(Mrs R.O. Backhouse, pre-1921)
Corona suffused with shell pink

'Sea Pearl' 2 W-P
(R.C.A. Tombleson) R.C.A. Tombleson, 1970
'Wirruna' hybrid

'Seaplane' 2 W-? (b or c)
(W. Balch, pre-1933)

'Sea Princess' 3 W-GYY
(Mrs J. Abel Smith) Mrs J. Abel Smith, 1984
'Mary Isabel' hybrid; sdlg no. F33/94
Corona greenish beige yellow

'Searchlight' 3 (a)
(F.H. Chapman, pre-1913)

'Searchlight' 1 (a)
(R.A. van der Schoot, pre-1929)
AM(Haarlem) 1929

'Searchlight' 2 W-? (b)
(E. & J.C. Martin, pre-1930)

'Searchlight' 2 W-W
(G.H. Johnstone) G.H. Johnstone, 1959
'Zero' × ('Silver Coin' × 'Beersheba')
Fl. 108 mm wide. Mid-season

'Sea Road' ?-O
(?Australian origin) Unregistered

'Sea Rose' 2 W-P
(Mrs H.K. Richardson) Mrs H.K. Richardson, 1976
'Enchantress' × 'Romance'
Fl. 94 mm wide; corona deep rose pink. Mid-season

'Seascape' 3 W-GYY
(F.H. Chapman, pre-1913)
Perianth segments snow white, overlapping; corona pale citron yellow

'Sea Scout' 2 (a)
(W. Balch, pre-1933)

'Sea Shell' 2 W-Y
(G.H. Engleheart, pre-1908)
?'Beacon' hybrid
Fl. facing slightly downwards; perianth segments pure white, deeply overlapping; corona expanded, pale sulphur yellow, faintly shaded orange, with rim almost entire. Mid-season. 2n=28. AM(e) 1922, *HC(g) 1936, *AM(g) 1944

'Seaspray' 1 W-W
(S.A. Free) Mrs S.I. Free, 1968

'Sea Sprite' 9 W-GGR
(Mrs M.S. Yerger) Mrs M.S. Yerger, 1990
'Sea Green' open pollinated
Fl. 54 mm wide; perianth segments spreading; the inner segments slightly shorter; corona disc-shaped, brilliant yellow-green 154B, with a much darker tone (144C) at base and a broad band of orange-red (32A) at rim. Late. Strongly scented

'Seastar' 2 Y-YYO
(J.L. Martin) J.L. Martin, 1982
'Kai' × 'Carbineer'; sdlg no. K/Car.1
Fl. 100 mm wide; perianth segments vivid yellow 9B; corona darker in tone (13A), with vivid orange 28B at rim. Mid-season. Resembles 'Hugh Poate' but with a deeper-coloured corona

'Sea Swallow' 2 W-WWY
(Hon. Sir R.H. Rhodes, pre-1914)
'Seagull' sport

'Seaton' 3 W-YYO
(Mrs H.K. Richardson) du Plessis Bros, 1981
'Syracuse' × 'Cascade'; sdlg no. 3546
Fl. 106 mm wide. Mid-season

'Sea Urchin' 2 W-Y
(G.L. Wilson, pre-1935)
'White Nile' × 'Tenedos'
2n=28

'Seawald' 1 W-Y
(Barr & Sons, pre-1920)
Perianth segments creamy white; corona canary yellow, with rim flared

'Seaway' 1 W-W
(J.S. Leitch) J.S. Leitch, 1967

'Sea White' 9 W-W
(W.A.Bender, 1976) W.A.Bender, 1996

'Seawitch' 1 W-W
(J.S. Leitch) J.S. Leitch, 1966

'Sebastian'
(pre-1913)

'Sebastopol' 2 W-Y
(J.L. Richardson, pre-1945)
'Bloemlust' × ?'Crocus'; sdlg no. 1823
Perianth segments very broadly ovate, blunt, only very slightly mucronate, pure white, spreading, concave at apex, of great substance, overlapping half; the inner segments more narrowly ovate, a little inflexed; corona clear deep lemon yellow, with mouth expanded and ribbed, even, rim widely rolled, deeply notched and crenate. Mid-season. 2n=29

'Sebilla Bisschop' 8 W-?
(pre-1807)

'Seborga' 1 W-Y
(A.M. Wilson, pre-1913)
Corona lemon yellow

'Seconde Citroniere' 8 W-Y
Syn. of 'Secunde Citronier'

'Seconde Zeelander' 8 Y-O
(pre-1798)

'Secret' 2 W-? (b or c)
(Sir C.H. Cave, pre-1928)

'Secretary'
(?G.P. Haydon, pre-1914)

'Secretary Voors' 1 (a)
(G. Lubbe & Son, pre-1938)
AM(Haarlem) 1938

'Secret Circle' 9 W-GYR
(Mrs M.S. Yerger) Mrs M.S. Yerger, 1984
N. poeticus sdlg × 'Red Rim'; sdlg no. 74 C 1-1
Fl. 53 mm wide; corona vivid yellow 9B, with green at base and deep orange-red (34A) at rim, with the rim dentate. Mid-season

'Secret Love' 1 W-P
(J.N.Hancock & Co., 1983) Unregistered
'Beryl Hancock' × 'Jolly Roger'; sdlg no. 17/83H
Perianth segments broadly ovate, smooth; corona cylindrical, opening apricot orange, becoming apricot pink, with rim closely and deeply notched, as if fringed. Early

'Secret Ring' 9 W-GYR
(Mrs M.S. Yerger) Mrs M.S. Yerger, 1986
'Quetzal' open pollinated; sdlg no. 75 I 4
Perianth segments white; corona brilliant yellow 13B, with strong yellow-green 144C at base and orange-red (32A) at rim, with a line of white between midzone and rim at maturity. Late. Resembles a smaller 'Quetzal'

'Secunde Citronier' 8 W-Y
(pre-1777)
Syn. 'Seconde Citroniere'

'Security' 2 Y-Y
(F.E. Board) F.E. Board, 1965
'Kindergold' × 'Saint Keverne'
Early

'Sedan' 2 (a)
(Barr & Sons, pre-1942)

'Sedate' 2 W-P
(P. Phillips) P. Phillips, 1967
Fl. forming a double triangle; perianth segments spreading; the inner segments sometimes inflexed; corona funnel-shaped, pure pink, mouth flared, with rim dentate. 2n=28

'Sedgeley Beacon' 2 (a)
(T.A.V. Wood, pre-1949)

'Seductive' 3 W-? (b)
(Mrs P.M. Davis, pre-1948)

'Seebach' 2 W-? (b)
(J.W.A. Lefeber, pre-1945)

'Seeker' 1 Y-Y
(J.N. Hancock & Co., *c.*1978) Unregistered

segimonensis = *N. cuatrecasasii* var. *segimonensis*

'Segovia' 3 W-Y
(Mrs F.M.Gray) Mrs F.M. Gray, 1962
N. rupicola subsp. *watieri* sdlg?

Fl. 50 mm wide; perianth segments very broadly ovate, blunt, prominently mucronate, a little reflexed, plane or with margins somewhat incurving, overlapping one-third to a half; the inner segments more narrowly ovate, more sharply reflexed, slightly twisted and with margins strongly incurved; corona discshaped, ribbed, brilliant to light greenish yellow 6C-8B, with mouth wavy, rim minutely crenate. Dwarf. Resembles 'Xit' in form. AGM 1996

'Segura' 3 W-? (b)
(G.A. Uit den Boogaard, pre-1950)

'Seiko' 2 W-R
(P. & G. Phillips) P. & G. Phillips, 1981
Fl. 100 mm wide. Mid-season

'Selbourne' 1 W-Y
(C.E. Radcliff, 1939)
'Bonnington' × 'Beersheba'

'Selda' 2 W-? (b or c)
(Sir J.S. Arkwright, pre-1931)

'Selecta' 1 (a)
(C.G. van Tubergen, pre-1931)

'Select Lynn' 3 Y-O
(Warnaar & Co.) Warnaar & Co., 1962
Perianth segments brilliant greenish yellow 6C; corona brilliant orange 29A. Early

'Selene' 2 or 3 W-Y
(P.D. Williams, pre-1913)
Corona shallow, creamy primrose

'Selene' 2 (a)
(A.H. Ahrens) J.S. Leitch, 1956

'Seleucus' 1 (a)
(W.A. Grace, pre-1936)

'Selia' 3 ?-G (a)
(W. Jackson Sr, 1937) W. Jackson Jr, 1956
'Mountain Pride' × 'Mayflower'
Corona small, deep green

'Selina' 3 W-? (b)
(C. Dawson, pre-1908)

'Selina' 1 W-W
(E.M. Crosfield, pre-1913)

'Selina Malone' 1 W-Y
(G.H. Engleheart, pre-1923)
Corona clear soft lemon, with mouth expanded

'Sella' 2 Y-O
(J.T. Gray, pre-1949)
Perianth segments yellow; corona spreading, reddish orange, with rim frilled

'Sellada' 2 W-P
(S.J. Bisdee) S.J. Bisdee, 1956
'Carnlough' × Sdlg 156/42

'Selma' 1 W-? (b)
(J.W. Barr, pre-1930)

'Selma' 8
(pre-1951)
'Geranium' × 'Martha Washington'

'Selma Lagerl^f' 2 W-YYO
(J.W.A. Lefeber, pre-1938)
Perianth segments creamy white; corona large discshaped, with a broad band of orange at rim. AM(Haarlem) 1943

'Selsey' 3 W-? (b)
(Sir F.C. Stern, pre-1949)

'Seltan' 2 W-P
(G.L. Wilson) G.L. Wilson, 1960
'Pink o' Dawn' × 'Irish Rose'

'Selwyn' 4 W-Y
(D.S. Bell, 1970) D.S. Bell, 1982
('Papanui Queen' × 'Green Island') × 'Temple Bells'
Fl. 105 mm wide. Mid-season. Resembles a taller 'Temple Bells'

'Semantha' 1 W-W
(P. Phillips) P. Phillips, 1966
Fl. 100 mm wide; perianth segments broad; corona with mouth flared. Mid-season. Resembles 'Prestige' but with a whiter flower and narrower corona. See also 'Sementha'

'Semaphore' 2 Y-O
(c.1927)
Corona expanded, dark orange

'Semaphore' 2 W-? (b)
(H.A. Brown, pre-1936)

'Semele' 3 (a)
(J.W. Barr, pre-1930)

'Sementha' 1 W-W
Syn. of 'Semantha'

'Sementha' 1 W-W
(?New Zealand origin, pre-1997) Unregistered

'Semi-Buttonhole' 1 W-Y
(Dutch origin, pre-1916)
Perianth segments broadly ovate, slightly inflexed, plane, overlapping a quarter; the inner segments narrower, more strongly inflexed, with margins wavy;

corona funnel-shaped, with mouth very deeply lobed and the lobes overlapping, frilled

'Seminole' 1 W-W
(E.C. Powell, pre-1946)
'Maharajah' × 'Kantara'

'Seminole Chief' 1 (a)
(A.M. Wilson, pre-1948)

N. semipartitus Link = *N.* × *odorus*?

'Semipartitus' 2 Y-Y
(E. Leeds, pre-1877)
Perianth segments pale primrose yellow; corona sulphur yellow, with rim deeply crenate. Syn. Incomparabilis Pallidus 'Semipartitus'

'Semi-partitus Plenus' 4 Y-Y
(pre-1902)
Fl. soft lemon yellow, with numerous whorls of segments. Syn. Incomparabilis 'Semi-partitus Plenus'

'Semiramis' 3 W-? (b)
(G.H. Engleheart, pre-1910)

'Semiramis' 2 ?-YYR (a)
(pre-1927)
Corona disc-shaped, yellow, with scarlet at rim

'Semiramis' 2 W-Y
(Konynenburg & Mark, 1951) Konynenburg & Mark, 1964
'Golden Harvest' × 'Rembrandt'
Fl. 100 mm wide; perianth segments greenish white; corona light yellow 11B

'Semo' 1 Y-Y
(W. Jackson Sr, 1934)
'Renown' × 'Marcos'

'Semper Avanti' 2 W-O
Syn. of 'Sempre Avanti'

'Sempre Avanti' 2 W-O
(de Graaff Bros, pre-1938)
Perianth segments sulphur white; corona broad and shallow, pure orange. 2n=28. AM(Haarlem) 1938. Received AM(Haarlem) 1938 as 'Semper Avanti'

'Senator' 3?
(pre-1913)

'Senator' 1 (a)
(W. Sutherland, pre-1933)

'Senator Wallace' 2 W-? (b)
(J.W.A. Lefeber) W. Blom & Son, 1955

'Sender Wallace'
Unregistered
Pollen parent of 'Abadan'

'Senegal' 2 Y-R
(A.M. Wilson, pre-1948)
'Fortune' hybrid
Perianth segments deep yellow; corona broad, red

'Seneschal' 2 W-? (b)
(G.H. Engleheart, pre-1907)

'Senior Ball' 2 W-WPP
(Grant E.Mitsch, 1975) R. & E.Havens, 1994
(['Caro Nome' × 'Accent'] × ['Precedent' × 'Carita']) × (['Radiation' × 'Mabel Taylor'] × 'Interim'); sdlg no. KK10/1
Fl. 120 mm wide, of heavy substance; perianth segments ovate, somewhat acute; corona disc-shaped, brilliant pink, paling to white at base, frilled. Midseason. Sunproof

'Seniority' 2 W-Y
(D. Bramley) D. Bramley, 1966
Fl. 115 mm wide; corona creamy yellow. Early. Resembles a large and earlier-flowered 'Saint Saphorin' with a shorter corona

'Senlac' 2 (a)
(A.J. Bliss, pre-1930)

'Sennen' 2 (a)
(R.F. Calvert, pre-1930)

'Sennocke' 5 Y-Y
(F.R. Waley, pre-1948)
N. triandrus × ? *N. pallidiflorus*
Perianth segments narrowly ovate, pale yellow, spreading or reflexed, separated; corona cylindrical, smooth, darker in tone than the perianth, mouth straight or very slightly flared, with rim broadly and shallowly crenate. PC(p) 1984

'Senorita' 2 W-Y
(R.O. Backhouse, pre-1932)
Perianth segments milk white, with margins slightly wavy, overlapping; corona large, ribbed, bright yellow

'Sensation' 3 W-YYO
(W. Backhouse, pre-1869)
Perianth segments pure white, reflexed; corona canary yellow, with scarlet-orange at rim. Syn. Barrii Albus 'Beauty', Barrii Albus 'Sensation'

'Sensation' 2 W-R
(pre-1949)
Perianth segments creamy white; corona scarlet, frilled

'Sensation' 8 ?-YYO
Syn. of 'Gardeners' Pride'

'Senta' 3 W-? (b)
(N.F. Lock, pre-1944)

'Sentiment' 2 W-WWP
(A.C. McKillop, pre-1949)
'Rewa' × 'White Sentinel'
Corona shallow, ivory, with pinkish buff at rim

'Sentinel' 1 W-Y
(Barr & Sons, pre-1899)
Perianth segments pure white, spreading; corona clear yellow, with rim flanged

'Sentinel' 2 W-P
(G.E. Mitsch) G.E. Mitsch, 1972
'Precedent' × 'Carita'; sdlg no. A34/3
Fl. 108 mm wide; corona almost disc-shaped, very broad, apricot salmon to pink. Mid-season. 2n=28

'Sentinel' 1 (a)
Syn. of 'Golden Sentinel'

'Sentinel' 7
Syn. of 'Amoy'

'Sentry' 3 Y-YYR
(F.H. Chapman, pre-1913)
Resembles a smaller 'Frank Miles' in form

'Sentry' 7 Y-Y
Syn. of 'Little Sentry'

'Seoma' 2 Y-? (a)
(J.S. Leitch) J.S. Leitch, 1962

'Seonnac' 2 Y-YYO
(D.C. MacArthur) D.C. MacArthur, 1985
Perianth segments broadly ovate in outline, blunt or rounded at apex, only very slightly mucronate, brilliant yellow 12B, spreading, concave either side of raised midrib, overlapping half; the inner segments narrower, slightly inflexed, ribbed, with margins slightly wavy; corona cylindrical, short, ribbed, vivid yellow 14A, shading to light orange (23A) in places at rim, with mouth straight, closely frilled. Late. Scented

'Seoul' 2 Y-O
(G.E. Mitsch, pre-1954)
'Damson' × 'Fortune'; sdlg no. 38C19/4
Perianth segments rich yellow; corona orange, with a deeper tone at rim. Mid-season

'Sepoy' 2 Y-R
(T.H. Piper, 1952) T.H. Piper, 1956
'Maranoa' × 'Chungking'

'September Cloud' 2 W-O
(Tom Forster, 1960s) Unregistered
Perianth segments very broadly ovate in outline, rounded and sometimes split at apex, only very slightly mucronate, creamy white, somewhat reflexed, overlapping half or more; the inner segments more nearly spreading, with margins a little wavy; corona broad disc-shaped, heavily ribbed, apricot orange, mouth split in places and overlapping, closely frilled, with rim notched and minutely crenate. Tall. Late

'September Morn' 1 W-P
(D.S. Bell) D.S. Bell, 1958
Fl. 108 mm wide. Mid-season. Resembles 'Salmon Trout'

'Sepulchre' 1 Y-Y
(W.G. Pannill) W.G. Pannill, 1972
'Fine Gold' × 'Enmore'
Fl. 112 mm wide

'Sequin' 3 W-Y
(G.H. Engleheart, pre-1900)
Perianth segments snow white; corona broad, almost disc-shaped, golden yellow

'Serac' 1 W-W
(C.G. van Tubergen, pre-1935)
AM(Haarlem) 1934

'Seraglio' 3 Y-YYO
(The Brodie of Brodie, pre-1926)
'Mozart' × 'Gallipoli'; sdlg no. 40/A/17
Fl. 90 mm wide; perianth segments very broad in outline, rounded or squarish at apex, only very slightly mucronate, creamy yellow, spreading, loosely creased, of great substance, overlapping half; the inner segments roundish, slightly truncate, inflexed; corona shallow bowl-shaped, ribbed, bright yellow, with a broad band of orange at rim, mouth deeply split in places and overlapping, expanded, frilled. Mid-season. AM(e) 1926, AM(Haarlem) 1930, FCC(Haarlem) 1936, *HC(g) 1936

'Serang' 2 W-? (b)
(D.S. Bell) D.S. Bell, 1957
Div. 1 until 1961

'Serape' 3 Y-YYO
(Murray W. Evans) Murray W. Evans, 1977
'Aircastle' × 'Showboat'; sdlg no. M-55
Fl. 115 mm wide; corona yellow, with reddish orange at rim. Mid-season

'Seraph' 1 Y-Y
(E. Leeds, pre-1877)
Perianth segments sulphur yellow; corona richer in tone, with rim crenate. Early. Syn. Pseudonarcissus Major 'Seraph'. Was "absorbed" into 'Morning Star'

'Seraph' 9 W-GYR
(G.E. Mitsch) G.E. Mitsch, 1976
'Quetzal' × 'Smyrna'; sdlg no. D95/10
Fl. rounded, 64 mm wide; perianth segments deeply overlapping; corona yellow, with green at base and orange-red at rim. Late. Resembles a much smaller 'Angel Eyes' with a more rounded flower

'Seraphin' 1 W-Y
Fl. large; perianth segments creamy white, twisted; corona soft lemon yellow, with mouth expanded and frilled. Late. Syn. of 'Seraphine'

'Seraphine' 1 W-Y
(Barr & Sons, pre-1908)
('Weardale Perfection' × *N. moschatus*)?
Fl. large; perianth segments creamy white, twisted; corona soft lemon yellow, with mouth expanded, rim broadly crenate. See also 'Seraphin'

'Seraphine' 1 Y-Y
(C.G. van Tubergen, pre-1926)
Fl. 89 mm wide, delicate sulphur yellow; perianth segments regular, overlapping half; corona broad, darker in tone than the perianth, with mouth a little expanded. Mid-season. AM(Haarlem) 1926, *AM(g) 1930

'Serapis' 3 W-?
(C. Dawson, pre-1923)
'Lulworth' × 'Horace'

'Serena' 11?a W-Y
(?New Zealand origin, pre-1997) Unregistered

'Serena Beach' 4 W-Y
(Brian S. Duncan) Brian S. Duncan, 1992
'Gay Song' × 'Dallas'; sdlg no. 983
Fl. 120 mm wide; perianth and other petaloid segments in three whorls regularly superimposed, very broadly ovate, blunt, some with prominent mucro, pure white, a little inflexed, overlapping half or more; the inner whorls successively slightly shorter and more strongly inflexed, with margins incurling; one or more very short segments at centre; corona segments very short, clustered at centre, crumpled, deep lemon yellow. Mid-season

'Serenade' 2 (a)
(R.H. Bath, pre-1929)

'Serenade' 2 W-? (b)
(A.H. Ahrens) J.S. Leitch, 1956

'Serena Lodge' 4 W-Y
(Brian S. Duncan) Brian S. Duncan, 1992
'Smokey Bear' × 'Sportsman'; sdlg no. 1081
Fl. 105 mm wide; perianth and other petaloid segments broadly ovate, milk white; the outer whorl prominently mucronate, spreading, a little concave, very smooth, overlapping half or more; the inner whorl a little shorter, without apparent mucro; the three outer segments of the inner whorl truncate, inflexed, of irregular surface; the three inner segments strongly inflexed, with margins tightly incurled; some longer segments intermingled; corona segments half as long as the inner whorl of petaloid segments and clustered among them at centre, broad, deep buff yellow, frilled. Mid-season to late

'Serendipity' 5 Y-Y
(W.G. Pannill) W.G. Pannill, 1972
'Fair Colleen' × *N.* × *intermedius*
Fl. 79 mm wide; perianth segments pale yellow

'Serene' 2 (a)
(pre-1926)
AM(Haarlem) 1926

'Serene' 3 W-W
(K.L. Reynolds, pre-1937)

'Serene Sea' 3 Y-Y
(G.E.Mitsch, 1984) R. & E.Havens, 1996
'Limpkin' × 'Wedding Band'; sdlg no. TT47/1A
Fl. 110 mm wide, becoming creamy yellow; perianth segments broadly ovate, spreading, plane, of heavy substance; corona funnel-shaped, ribbed, expanded. Late

'Serenity' 1 W-? (h)
(Sir A.P.W. Thomas, pre-1930)

'Serenity' 1 W-W
(?G.L. Wilson, pre-1936)

'Sergeant Murphy' 1 Y-Y
(J.L. Richardson, pre-1927)
Fl. golden yellow. Resembles a larger and taller 'King Alfred'. ?See also 'Sargent Murphy'

'Serifos' 1 Y-Y
(G.H. Johnstone, pre-1960) Unregistered
'Constantine' × 'King of the North'

'Seriki'
Unregistered
Pollen parent of 'Ajana'; in parentage of 'Delight'

N. serioflorens Schur = ? *N. radiiflorus* var. *stellaris*

'Serius' 2 W-O
(G.H. Johnstone, pre-1960) Unregistered
'White Sentinel' × 'Hades'

'Serola' 2 Y-R
K.J. van der Veek, 1986
Perianth segments primrose yellow; corona orange-red (30C). Mid-season

N. serotinus Linnaeus 13 Section Serotini
   var. *serotinus*
   var. *deficiens* (Herbert) Baker
   var. *emarginatus* Chabert

N. serotinus Haworth = *N. bulbocodium* var. *serotinus*

N. serotinus Jordan = *N. abscissus* var. *serotinus*

N. serratus Haworth = *N. pseudonarcissus*

'Serratus' 1 W-Y
(pre-1884)
Perianth segments whitish; corona deep yellow. Syn. Pseudonarcissus 'Serratus'

'Servador' 3 W-O
(P.D. Williams, pre-1927)
Perianth segments pale cream; corona deep orange. Very tall

'Servia' 8 Y-Y
(?G. van der Weyden Jobson, pre-1914)
Perianth segments pale yellow; corona large, darker in tone. AM(Haarlem) 1914

'Sesame' 3 Y-GYO
(E.W. Cotter) E.W. Cotter, 1968
'Tryst' hybrid

'Sesotris' 2 Y-Y
(E.M. Crosfield, pre-1923)
Perianth segments pale soft yellow; corona bright yellow, suffused yellowish orange

'Seti I' 2 (a)
(O. Pease, pre-1927)

'Setting Sun' 1 Y-Y
(C. Goodson, pre-1927)

'Setting Sun' 2 W-O
(D.S. Bell) D.S. Bell, 1960
'Papanui Queen' × 'Invergordon'
Fl. 102 mm wide; perianth segments creamy white; corona dark reddish orange. Mid-season. Resembles 'Papanui Queen' but with a redder corona

'Sevenoaks' 12 W-W
(F.R. Waley) F.R. Waley, 1973
N. triandrus × *N. bulbocodium* var. *citrinus*
Fl. 26 mm wide

'Seven Sisters' 2 Y-Y
?Syn. of 'Seven Stones'

'Seven Stones' 2 Y-Y
(P.D. Williams, pre-1937)
Tall. Mid-season. Of the same deep yellow as 'Trenoon', if not deeper. Syn. ?'Seven Sisters'

"Seventeen Sisters"
Syn. of *N. tazetta*

'Seventh Armoured' 1 Y-Y
(G.L. Wilson) E. Longford, 1969
'Arctic Gold' × 'Bastion'

'Seventh Heaven' 2 W-P
(D.S. Bell) D.S. Bell, 1957
Syn. 'Scarlet Heaven'

'Severn' 1 Y-Y
(D.R. Acheson, pre-1933)
'White Knight' × 'Royalist'
Fl. soft yellow

'Seville' 2 W-O
(P.D. Williams, pre-1908)
Sdlg × 'Lulworth'
Fl. rounded, 76 mm wide; perianth segments snowy white, slightly reflexed, deeply overlapping; corona disc-shaped, ribbed, rich orange. AM 1912

'Seville Dancer' 11a W-WYO
(J.Gerritsen & Son) Mrs E.Bullivant, 1995
Sdlg no. GBS 18
Fl. 100 mm wide; perianth segments broadly ovate, blunt, mucronate, a little reflexed, creased, overlapping one-third to a half; the inner segments more nearly spreading, sometimes truncate, not noticeably mucronate, with margins wavy or incurled; corona deeply split, the six segments one-third the length of the perianth segments and opposite to them, brilliant greenish yellow 6A, with yellowish white at base and light orange (21A) in upper part, spreading, frilled, with rim notched and dentate. Mid-season. Sunproof. Resembles a paler 'Tongues of Flame'

'Sevingstone'
(pre-1913)

'Sextant' 6 W-GWW
(Brian S. Duncan) Rathowen Daffodils, 1981
'Stainless' × 'Foundling'; sdlg no. 479
Perianth segments broadly ovate, mucronate. Mid-season. $2n=28$

'Seymour' ?-P
(Alister Clark, pre-1948)

'Seymour Cobley' 2 W-Y
(Mrs R.S. Cobley, 1948) Seymour Cobley Ltd, 1968
Corona lemon yellow. Mid-season

'Shackleton' 3 W-? (b)
(pre-1925)
FCC(Haarlem) 1925

'Shadeen' 2 W-P
(G.L. Wilson, pre-1952)

Sdlg 21/32 × 'Evening'; sdlg no. 27/146
Corona creamy buff, with pinkish tones

'Shadow' 1 W-? (b)
(W. Welchman, pre-1908)

'Shadow' 2 W-GWW
(Murray W. Evans) Murray W. Evans, 1977
'Desdemona' × 'Knockbane'; sdlg no. N-72
Fl. 115 mm wide. Mid-season. Resembles 'Williamsbury' but with green at corona base

'Shadow King' 2 G-G
(W.M. Spry, pre-1975) Unregistered
'Hunter's Moon' × Ronalds sdlg
Fl. creamy lemon green

'Shadow Mist' 2 W-WWP
(Sidney DuBose, 1982) Sidney DuBose, 1996
'Misty Glen' × 'My Word'; sdlg no. G55-1
Fl. 90 mm wide; corona white, with pink at rim. Early

'Shadrach' 3 W-YYR
(Glenbrook Bulb Farm, 1985) Glenbrook Bulb Farm, 1997
'Colour Parade' × 'Koala'
Fl. 105 mm wide; perianth segments very broadly ovate, yellowish white (155D); corona disc-shaped, vivid yellow 9A, with orange-red (30A) at rim, frilled. Mid-season

'Shady' 5 W-Y
(A. Gray) A. Gray, 1962
Fl. 75 mm wide; corona light greenish yellow 4B. Dwarf. Late. Resembles 'Dawn' but with better poise and stronger substance

'Shady Lady' 2 W-P
(Sidney DuBose, 1979) Sidney DuBose, 1996
'Celilo' × 'Cool Flame'; sdlg no. E32-2
Fl. 100 mm wide; corona true medium pink, frilled. Mid-season

'Shagreen' 3 W-GWW
(The Brodie of Brodie, c.1942)
'Cushendall' × 'Silver Salver'
Corona disc-shaped

'Shah' 7 Y-Y
(Barr & Sons, pre-1949)
'Dawson City' × 'Rugulosus Maximus'
Fl. very smooth, deep golden yellow; perianth segments overlapping; corona funnel-shaped, mouth 6-lobed, slightly frilled, rim reflexed. 2n=28

'Shakespeare' 1 Y-Y
(de Graaff Bros, pre-1897)
Perianth segments sulphur yellow; corona deep golden yellow. Resembles an improved 'Samson'

'Shakespeare' 9
Syn. of 'Oscar Wilde'

'Shako' 3 (a)
(pre-1914)

'Shako' 3 W-? (b)
(A.H. Ahrens) J.S. Leitch, 1956

'Shaldon' 2 W-Y
(H.P. Heemskerk, 1957) Groeneveld & Lindhout, 1967
? × 'Carlton'
Fl. 100 mm wide; perianth segments creamy white; corona pale yellow 11D. Mid-season

'Shalimar' 2 W-W
(Mrs P.M. Davis, pre-1948)

'Shalley' 2 W-? (b)
(D.W. Lefeber & Co.) G.B. de Vroomen & Sons, 1955

'Shalom' 1 W-Y
(J.N. Hancock & Co., 1968) J.N. Hancock & Co., 1979
'Trousseau' × 'Broadlea'; sdlg no. 22/68H
Fl. 90 mm wide; corona brilliant greenish yellow 6C, with rim flanged. Early. Resembles a larger-flowered 'Beryl Hancock'

'Shaman' 2 W-W
(Jackson's Daffodils) Jackson's Daffodils, 1986
Sdlg 159/70 × 'Rhapsody'; sdlg no. 239/79
Perianth segments greenish white 155C; corona darker in tone (155A)

'Shamgar' 1 W-? (b)
(A.H. Ahrens) D.J. Cooper, 1956

'Shamrock' 1 W-? (b)
(Sir C.H. Cave, pre-1908)

'Shan'
(W. Jackson Jr, 1943)
'Chruseos' × 'Trenoon'

'Shanach' 9 W-YYR
(G.L. Wilson, pre-1939)
'Dactyl' hybrid
Corona citron yellow, with red at rim

'Shandon' 2 W-GOO
(Brian S. Duncan) Rathowen Daffodils, 1979
'Kilworth' × 'Don Carlos'; sdlg no. 40
Fl. 107 mm wide; corona deep orange, with green at base. Mid-season. Sunproof. Resembles 'Don Carlos' but with a wider and more deeply lobed corona. 2n=28

'Shandy' 2 Y-Y
(W. Jackson Jr, c.1960) Unregistered
Sdlg × 'Farmington'

'Shanes Castle' 1 Y-Y
(Carncairn Daffodils, 1968) Carncairn Daffodils, 1978
'Maviston' × 'Pretoria'; sdlg no. 5/62
Fl. 109 mm wide; perianth segments brilliant greenish yellow 6B; corona very slightly darker in tone (6A). Late. Resembles a stronger-stemmed 'Golden Rapure' of better substance

'Shangani' 2 Y-YYR
(Brian S.Duncan) Brian S.Duncan, 1996
'Triple Crown' × 'Burning Bush'; sdlg no. 1498
Fl. rounded, 96 mm wide; perianth segments very broadly ovate, golden yellow; corona short funnel-shaped, slightly ribbed, golden yellow, with a band of deep orange-red at rim. Late

'Shanghai' 2 Y-Y
(Warnaar & Co., pre-1933)
Fl. soft yellow

'Shangri-La' 1 Y-Y
(J.W.A. Lefeber, 1943) J.W.A. Lefeber, 1960
Fl. 95 mm wide. Mid-season

'Shannon' 2 W-W
(J.L. Richardson, pre-1937)
'White Emperor' × 'Beersheba'
Fl. about 105 mm wide; perianth segments very broadly ovate in outline, blunt or squarish at apex, slightly mucronate, spreading, plane, of great substance, overlapping half; the inner segments more narrowly ovate, square-shouldered at base, only very slightly mucronate, inflexed at base, reflexed at apex; corona cylindrical, smooth, with mouth expanded and even, rim rolled and crenate. Mid-season. AM(e) 1942

'Shantallow' 3 W-GWY
(G.L. Wilson) G.L. Wilson, 1956
'Tryst' × 'Chinese White'
Fl. rounded; perianth segments very broad in outline, squarish at apex and shallowly truncate, mucronate, pure white, a little reflexed, overlapping half or more; the inner segments rounded at apex, more nearly spreading, with margins wavy; corona bowl-shaped, ribbed, usually opening moss green, quickly becoming whitish, with green at base and faint greenish lemon at rim. 2n=14

'Shantung' 2 Y-Y
(Oregon Bulb Farms, pre-1950)

'Shapely' 2 Y-Y
(G.E. Mitsch) G.E. Mitsch, 1977
('Mitylene' × *N. cyclamineus*) open pollinated;
sdlg no. E07/4
Fl. 91 mm wide; perianth segments soft clear lemon yellow; corona clear lemon yellow. Early

'Sharessa' 2 W-W
(J.A. Morris) J.A. Morris, 1957

'Sharia' 2 W-? (b)
(A.H. Ahrens) D.J. Cooper, 1957

'Sharif' 2 Y-R
(J.A. O'More) J.A. O'More, 1968
(Sdlg × 'Fortune') × 'Magherally' × sdlg × 'Clackrattle'

'Sharman Crawford' 1 Y-Y
(E. Leeds, pre-1877)
Perianth segments sulphur yellow, with streaks of a darker tone. Syn. Pseudonarcissus Major 'Sharman Crawford'

'Sharnden' 1 Y-Y
(N.A. Burr) N.A. Burr, 1992
'Camelot' × 'Golden Aura'; sdlg no. 2.1.73
Fl. 114 mm wide, vivid yellow 9A; perianth segments very broadly ovate, blunt, with slight white mucro, spreading, concave, with margins incurling and midrib showing, regular, overlapping half; the inner segments rounded at base, only very slightly mucronate, slightly inflexed, more nearly plane; corona funnel-shaped, smooth, heavier in texture than the perianth and appearing to be darker in tone, with mouth expanded and wavy, rim crenate. Late

'Sharon' 1 W-W
(S.J. Bisdee, pre-1939)
'White Emperor' × 'Beersheba'

'Sharon' 2 Y-R
(J.S. Leitch) J.S. Leitch, 1959

'Sharon Elizabeth' 2 W-P
(L.P.Dettman, 1975) Unregistered
'Jill Bolte' × 'Cherry Pie'; sdlg no. JB/CP 1/75

'Sharrow' 3 W-W
(S.J. Bisdee, 1945)
'Nelly' × 'Saint Cecilia'

'Sharrowvale' 2 W-P
(F.E. Board) F.E. Board, 1965
'Saintfield' × 'Irish Rose'; sdlg no. 634
Late

'Sharwood' 2 Y-Y
(W. Jackson Sr, 1950)
'Acca' × 'Guilmette'

'Shasta' 2 W-? (b or c)
(W.A. Watts, pre-1935)

'Shaun' 2 Y-O
(R.H.Glover, pre-1989) Unregistered
'Arab Pasha' × 'Kasia'

'Shawn' 2 W-W
(J.S. Leitch) J.S. Leitch, 1968

'Shayle' 3 W-R
(?New Zealand origin, pre-1990) Unregistered

'She' 2 W-P
(M.J. Jefferson-Brown) M.J. Jefferson-Brown, 1978
Perianth segments very broadly ovate, blunt or slightly truncate, very slightly mucronate, spreading, plane, with midrib showing, overlapping half; the inner segments shouldered at base, somewhat twisted or with margins wavy; corona long cup-shaped, smooth, mouth very shallowly lobed and occasionally split, a little expanded, wavy, with rim slightly flanged

'Shearwater' 3 W-Y
(P.D. Williams, pre-1907)
Fl. 107 mm wide; corona widely expanded, citron

'Shearwater' 2 W-WWY
(G.E. Mitsch) G.E. Mitsch, 1980
'Aircastle' × 'Homage'; sdlg no. D21/4
Fl. rounded; perianth segments broad, opening white, becoming ivory white, overlapping; corona opening pale lemon, becoming almost white, with lemon at rim. Mid-season. Resembles 'Limpkin' but with a more distinctly coloured corona rim

'Sheba' 3 W-R
(P.D. Williams, pre-1908)
Perianth segments spreading; corona crimson

'Sheelagh Rowan' 2 W-W
(A.J.R. Pearson) A.J.R. Pearson, 1989
'Stoke Charity' × 'Panache'; sdlg no. 86/22/J35
Fl. forming a double triangle, 130 mm wide; perianth segments very broad, off-white, spreading, smooth and of very thick substance, overlapping half; the inner segments a little twisted or with margins wavy; corona cylindrical, of a purer white than the perianth, with green at base, mouth flared, with six shallow overlapping lobes, lightly frilled, rim obscurely crenate. Mid-season to late

'Sheena' 3 W-YYR
(J.T. Gray, pre-1936)

'Sheerabba' 1 W-W
(G.H. Johnstone, pre-1959) Unregistered
?'Beersheba' × ?'Ann Abbott'

'Sheer Gold' 2 Y-Y
(Brian S. Duncan) Rathowen Daffodils, 1987
'Golden Level' hybrid open pollinated; sdlg no. 930
Mid-season

'Sheer Joy' 6 W-W
(Brian S. Duncan, 1982) Brian S. Duncan, 1992
'Joybell' × 'Lilac Charm'; sdlg no. 778
Perianth segments narrowly ovate, reflexed; corona cylindrical, long, opening pale buff yellow tinged lilac pink, becoming almost pure white, with rim rolled. Early to mid-season

'Sheerline' 2 W-W
(Brian S. Duncan) Rathowen Daffodils, 1987
'Broomhill' × 'Ave'; sdlg no. 670
Corona cylindrical, with mouth expanded. Mid-season

'Sheeroe' 1 W-W
(G.L. Wilson, pre-1927)
'Madame de Graaff' hybrid

'Sheeroe' 2 Y-R
(G.L. Wilson) G.L. Wilson, 1960
('Carbineer' × 'Porthilly') × 'Spry'

'Sheffield' 1 W-W
(F.E. Board) F.E. Board, 1965
'Templepatrick' × 'Empress of Ireland'; sdlg no. 1094
Mid-season

'Sheherasade' 2 Y-Y
(Mrs R.O. Backhouse, pre-1921)
AM(Haarlem) 1930

'Sheik' 2 W-R
(Carncairn Daffodils) Carncairn Daffodils, 1978
'Kilworth' × 'Richardson sdlg 260; sdlg no. 105
Fl. 100 mm wide; perianth segments greenish white (155A); corona orange-red (30B). Mid-season. Resembles a Div. 2 'Rockall'

'Sheila' 3 W-? (b)
(Sir J.A.R. Gore-Booth, pre-1916)

'Sheilah' 9 W-GYO
(Mrs G. Link, 1964) Mrs G. Link, 1975
'Tannahill' × 'Thomas Hardy'; sdlg no. 2157
Fl. 75 mm wide. Late. Resembles a larger and smoother 'Thomas Hardy' of improved colouring

'Sheldrake' 2 (a)
(Sir C.H. Cave, pre-1928)
Selected from *N. papyraceus*
Perianth segments somewhat inflexed, concave, overlapping half or, when the inner segments are more reflexed, at base only; corona cup-shaped, ribbed, mouth straight, wavy, rim crenate. Sweetly scented. Resembles a smaller, less uniform and less free-flowering 'Yael'

'Sheleg' 8 W-W
(Herut Yahel, pre-1980) Unregistered
Selection from *N. papyraceus*

Perianth segments somewhat inflexed, a little concave, overlapping half; corona cup-shaped, mouth ribbed, straight, wavy, with rim crenate. Sweetly scented. Resembles a smaller and less floriferous 'Yael'. Syn. 'Jerusalem'

'Shelford' 1 Y-Y
(J.N.Hancock & Co., 1980) Unregistered
'Jobi' open pollinated; sdlg no. 109/80H
Fl. rounded; perianth segments mid-yellow; corona cylindrical, deep yellow. Late

'Shell Bay' 2 W-P
(D. & J.W. Blanchard) D. & J.W. Blanchard, 1974
('Green Island' × 'Roseworthy') × 'Debutante'
Fl. 105 mm wide; corona with green at base. Mid-season

'Shellbourne' 1 W-Y
(H.A. Brown, 1938) J.N. Hancock & Co., 1960
Corona deep cream, tightly frilled

'Shelley' 9
(G.H. Engleheart, pre-1907)
Syn. of 'Los Angeles'

'Shelley Anne' 4 Y-Y
(Mrs W.A. Jones) Mrs W.A. Jones, 1968

'Shelley Louise' 2 W-GOR
(D.C. MacArthur) D.C. MacArthur, 1989
'Passionale' sdlg × sdlg EV83/212
Fl. 104 mm wide; perianth segments greenish white (155A), plane, overlapping; corona pale orange (29C), shading to orange-red (31C) at rim, with brilliant yellow-green 150C at base, rim neatly rolled. Late

'Shelly' 3 W-O
(S.A. Free) S.A. Free, 1961
Fl. 102 mm wide; corona pale orange. Mid-season

'Shelly Baker' 2 W-P
(Brian S.Duncan) Mrs J.M.Baker, 1996
?'Verran' × ?'Fellowship'; sdlg no. 1552
Fl. 90 mm wide; perianth segments ovate, pure white, smooth; corona funnel-shaped, pure pink, with slight undertones of salmon pink, with mouth a little expanded. Mid-season

'Shemada' 2 W-P
(J.N.Hancock & Co., 1974) J.N.Hancock & Co., 1997
Sdlg no. 45/82H
Fl. forming a double triangle; perianth segments spreading; corona funnel-shaped, deep pink, with rim neatly crenate. Early to mid-season

'Shenandoah' 2 W-WWP
(J.M. de Navarro) J.M. de Navarro, 1975

'Waterville' × 'Romance'; sdlg no. 846
Fl. 87 mm wide. Resembles 'Rainbow' but with a whiter perianth and paler corona rim

'Shephard' 3 W-OR
(pre-1968) Unregistered

'Shepherds' Delight' 2 Y-R
(A.M. Wilson, pre-1950)
'Khamseen' × 'Fortune'
Corona slightly expanded, vivid red

'Shepherd's Hey' 7 Y-Y
(Rosewarne EHS, 1977) Rosewarne EHS, 1987
'Seraglio' × *N. fernandesii*; sdlg no. 71/326/1
Fls 2-3 per stem; perianth segments very broadly ovate in outline, blunt or squarish at apex, brighter and darker in tone than vivid yellow 9A, spreading or a little reflexed, with margins wavy or incurved, deeply overlapping; the inner segments with margins more strongly waved; corona bowl-shaped, ribbed, darker in tone than the perianth. Mid-season. Scented

'Shepherds' Warning' 2 Y-R
(A.M. Wilson, pre-1950)
'Khamseen' × 'Fortune'
Perianth segments deep yellow; corona red, frilled

'Sheppy' 1 Y-Y
(G.L. Wilson, pre-1949)
'Hebron' × 'Goldcourt'
Corona somewhat narrow, straight-sided, with rim flanged and dentate

'Sheraton' 3 Y-R
(Jackson's Daffodils) Jackson's Daffodils, 1992
Sdlg 267/78 × 'Tia'; sdlg no. 197/84
Fl. 98 mm wide; perianth segments very broadly ovate in outline, blunt or obscurely truncate, only very slightly mucronate, brilliant greenish yellow 6A, a little inflexed, concave and with margins incurling at apex; the inner segments square-shouldered at base and touching one another, more strongly inflexed; corona cup-shaped, closely ribbed, orange-red (30B), with mouth straight and a little frilled.

'Sherbet' 2 W-P
(Murray W. Evans) Murray W. Evans, 1987
'Quasar' × 'Arctic Char'; sdlg no. V-11/2
Perianth segments smooth; corona rich salmon pink, mouth flared, with rim slightly dentate. Mid-season

'Sherborne' 4 Y-Y
(D.A. Lloyd) J.W. Blanchard, 1989
'Camelot' × 'Beauvallon'; sdlg no. 75/34A
Fl. 103 mm wide; perianth and other petaloid segments in three or more regularly superimposed whorls, brilliant greenish yellow 6B-C; the two outer whorls spreading, broadly ovate, prominently mucronate, concave, overlapping half; the inner

whorls shorter, more narrowly ovate, inflexed; corona segments shorter than the inner whorls of petaloid segments and interspersed among them, strong orange-yellow 17A, with rim wavy and entire. AM(e) 1989

'Sherbrooke' 2 Y-Y
(H.A. Brown, 1941)
'Royalist' × 'Trenoon'

'Shergol' 2 Y-Y
(W.A. Grace, pre-1927)

'Sheridan' 2 (a)
(Barr & Sons, pre-1949)

'Sherlock' 1 Y-Y
(L.P. Dettman) L.P. Dettman, 1984
'Content' × 'Clare'; sdlg no. 18/78
Fl. 101 mm wide; perianth segments greenish yellow (154C); corona darker in tone (3A). Early

'Sherman' 2 W-? (b)
(de Graaff Bros, pre-1929)

'Sherpa' 1 W-W
(Brian S. Duncan) Rathowen Daffodils, 1986
'Dunmurry' × 'Panache'; sdlg no. 401
Perianth segments very broad in outline, blunt or rounded at apex, fairly prominently mucronate, spreading, plane, smooth and of good substance, overlapping half; the inner segments more nearly ovate, less obviously mucronate, inflexed and somewhat twisted; corona narrowly funnel-shaped, with mouth widely expanded and even, rim rolled and crenate. Mid-season

'Sherry' 2 W-? (b)
(Oregon Bulb Farms, pre-1950)

'Sherwood' 1 Y-Y
(H.A. Brown, 1943)

'Sherwood' 1 Y-Y
(C.R. Wootton) C.R. Wootton, 1962
'Cromarty' × 'Crocus'
Fl. 115 mm wide, soft yellow. Early. Resembles an early-flowered 'Royalist'

'Sherwood Memory' 2 W-W
(W.E. Weightman) A.F. Grieve, 1955

'Sherwood Queen' 2 W-? (b)
(A.F. Grieve) A.F. Grieve, 1957

'Sherwood Surprise' 1 W-W
(pre-1926)
Corona very long, opening primrose, becoming white

'Sherwood Vanity' 3 Y-R
(W.E. Weightman, pre-1936)
Perianth segments broad, citron yellow; corona expanded, bright red, frilled

'She's Apples' 11a Y-Y
(Jackson's Daffodils) Jackson's Daffodils, 1992
Sdlg 116/77 × 'Cassata'; sdlg no. 92/87
Fl. 105 mm wide; perianth segments broadly ovate in outline, rounded at apex or somewhat truncate, spreading, overlapping half; corona split to base, the six segments half as long as the perianth segments and of the same width, opposite and closely overlying them, darker in tone (vivid yellow 13A), densely frilled

'Sheviock' 2 Y-O
(T. Bloomer) du Plessis Bros, 1987
('Ballintoy' × 'Air Marshal') × 'Shining Light'; sdlg no. 339
Fl. rounded; perianth segments very broadly ovate, rounded at apex, fairly prominently mucronate, spreading, plane, very smooth, overlapping half; the inner segments square-shouldered at base; corona bowl-shaped, narrowly ribbed, orange, with mouth expanded and minutely frilled. Late. Sunproof

'Shield' 1 W-? (b)
(W. Welchman, pre-1908)

'Shieldaig' 2 Y-YYO
(J.S.B. Lea) J.S.B. Lea, 1964
'Narvik' × 'Air Marshal'; sdlg no. 1-114-54
Perianth segments dark yellow; corona with reddish orange at rim. Mid-season

'Shikellamy' 2 Y-O
(W.A. Bender, 1980) W.A. Bender, 1990
Probably 'Hiromi' open pollinated; sdlg no. 80/59
Fl. 100 mm wide; perianth segments vivid yellow 12A, spreading, smooth, overlapping; corona strong orange 25A, with rim rolled. Early to mid-season. Resembles 'Hiromi' but is taller by 100 mm

'Shillong' 1 W-W
(J.N. Hancock & Co., pre-1974) Unregistered

'Shiloh' 2 Y-YYR
(W.G. Pannill) W.G. Pannill, 1994
'Loch Hope' × 'Javelin'; sdlg no. 75/9B
Mid-season

'Shilric' 2 Y-R
(W. Jackson Sr, 1938)
('Fortune' × 'Beacon') × 'Flamwen'

'Shimmer' 6 Y-O
(G.E. Mitsch, 1964) G.E. Mitsch, 1977
(['Market Merry' × 'Carbineer'] × 'Armada') × *N. cyclamineus*; sdlg no. A52/5
Fl. 87 mm wide; perianth segments amber yellow,

reflexed; corona reddish orange. Early. Resembles an earlier-flowered 'Jetfire' with a broader perianth and less brightly coloured corona

'Shimmer' 2 W-W
(G.H. Johnstone, pre-1960) Unregistered
'Snow Crystal' × 'Slemish'

'Shimna' 1 W-W
(Ballydorn Bulb Farm) Ballydorn Bulb Farm, 1991
'April Love' × 'Spelga'
Fl. 110 mm wide; perianth segments ovate, deeply overlapping; corona constricted near mouth, with yellow-green showing at base, mouth flared, rim dentate. Mid-season

'Shindig' 2 Y-YYR
(Brian S.Duncan) Brian S.Duncan, 1997
'Triple Crown' × 'Burning Bush'; sdlg no. 1598
Fl. 102 mm wide; perianth segments very broadly ovate, mid-yellow, spreading; corona shallow bowl-shaped, slightly ribbed, deeper in tone than the perianth, shading to deep red in upper third. Late

'Shine On' 2 W-WWY
(Colin Crotty) Colin Crotty, 1996
'Sun Child' × 'Spot On'; sdlg no. 76-88
Fl. rounded, 104 mm wide; perianth segments very broadly ovate, blunt, pure white; corona short funnel-shaped, opening yellow, becoming whitish, with green in tube and bright yellow at rim, neatly wavy. Mid-season to late

'Shin Falls' 1 Y-Y
(D.C.MacArthur) D.C.MacArthur, 1996
'Magnificence' × 'Sun Dance'; sdlg no. EV621
Fl. forming a double triangle, 122 mm wide; perianth segments ovate, mucronate, vivid yellow 9A, slightly reflexed; corona funnel-shaped, angled, more orange in tone than the perianth, with mouth flared and lobed, rim rolled and crenate. Very early. Scented

'Shingerra' 11?a W-Y
(?Dutch origin, pre-1970) Unregistered

'Shining Gold' 1 Y-Y
(F. Rijnveld & Sons, 1948) F. Rijnveld & Sons, 1961
Fl. 118 mm wide; perianth segments vivid yellow 9B; corona a little brighter in tone (12A). Late. Resembles a paler 'Burgemeester'. AM(Haarlem) 1961

'Shining Light' 2 Y-R
(F.E. Board) F.E. Board, 1965
'Dunkeld' × 'Revelry'; sdlg no. 572
Perianth segments broadly ovate, pale yellow, reflexed; corona red, with a darker tone at rim, with the rim dentate. Mid-season

'Shining Sun' 1 (a)
(Slieve Donard Nursery Co., pre-1932)

'Shining Waters' 2 W-W
(G.L. Wilson, pre-1937)
'Niphetos' × 'Zero'

'Shintaro' 1 W-Y
(R.C.A. Tombleson) R.C.A. Tombleson, 1967
Fl. 108 mm wide. Mid-season. Resembles an earlier-flowered 'Preamble' with a darker corona

'Shipmate' 2 W-P
(G.L. Wilson, pre-1948)
?'Fortune' hybrid
Corona shallow bowl-shaped, opening pale primrose cream, becoming buff cream

'Shipshape' 4 W-Y
(G.E. Mitsch, c.1976) Unregistered
'Pink Chiffon' × 'Carita'; sdlg no. E22/4
Corona segments cream and buff. Mid-season

'Shiralee' 2 W-O
(H.A. Brown, 1946) J.N. Hancock & Co., 1965
Perianth segments broad, of good substance; corona long, opening creamy yellow, becoming buff yellow, frilled. Mid-season to late

'Shirin' 1 Y-Y
(W. Jackson Sr. 1937)
'Halfa' × 'Fi-krye'

'Shirin' 2 W-W
(J.S. Leitch) J.S. Leitch, 1960
Fl. 102 mm wide

'Shirland' 5 W-W
(W.A. Grace, pre-1927)

'Shirley' 5 W-Y
(W.F.M. Copeland, pre-1915)
'Lady Margaret Boscawen' × *N. triandrus* var. *loiseleurii*
Fls usually 2 per stem; perianth segments creamy white; corona expanded, pale primrose yellow

'Shirley Ann' 2 W-WWP
M. Gardiner, 1956
Corona with pink at rim

'Shirley Deane' 2 W-WWY
(D.S. Bell, c.1965) Unregistered
'Papanui Queen' × 'Green Island'
Perianth segments pure white; corona with a broad band of lemon at rim

'Shirley Hale' 3 W-Y
(Ken Farmer Nurseries) Ken Farmer Nurseries, 1978
Fl. 95 mm wide

'Shirley Hibberd' 1 Y-Y
(W. Backhouse, pre-1869)
Perianth segments slightly twisted; corona large, expanded, deep yellow, darker in tone than the perianth. Syn. Pseudonarcissus Major 'Shirley Hibberd'

'Shirley Neale' 2 W-YOY
(H.A. Brown) G.E. Mitsch, 1956
?'Rubra' hybbrid
Perianth segments white; corona expanded, orange, with buff at base and lemon at rim

'Shirley Temple' 4 W-W
Syn. of 'Snowball'

'Shirley Wyness' 2 W-YYP
(West & Fell, pre-1935)
Corona lemon, with rim with buff pink at rim, heavily frilled as if in more than one whorl

'Shock-headed Peter' 4 W-Y
(W.F.M. Copeland, pre-1909)
Perianth and other petaloid segments in three whorls, ovate, creamy white; corona segments rich orange-yellow, frilled. Mid-season

'Shockwave' 2 Y-O
(Jackson's Daffodils, 1983) Jackson's Daffodils, 1995
Sdlg 124/75 × 'Colorful'; sdlg no. 49/83
Fl. 107 mm wide; perianth segments roundish, vivid yellow 12A, with a slight flush of red, somewhat concave; corona bowl-shaped, orange (28A). Early to mid-season

'Shogun' 1 W-? (b)
(A.J. Bliss, pre-1930)

'Shona' 2 W-? (b)
(Mrs M. Moorby, pre-1949)

'Shona' 1 Y-W
(?Australian origin, pre-1997) Unregistered

'Shooting Star' 2 (a)
(G. Zandbergen-Terwegen, pre-1945)

'Shore Acres' 1 W-W
(P. & G. Phillips) P. & G. Phillips, 1982
Fl. 95 mm wide. Mid-season

'Shorecliffe' 2 W-P
(Brian S.Duncan) Brian S.Duncan, 1993
'Gracious Lady' × ('Infatuation' × 'Gem of Antrim'); sdlg no. 1136
Fl. 93 mm wide; perianth segments very broadly ovate, blunt, slightly mucronate, pure white, a little inflexed, plane, regular, overlapping half; corona funnel-shaped, deep pink, with mouth wavy. Mid-season. Sunproof

'Shortcake' 2 W-P
(Murray W. Evans) Murray W. Evans, 1984
'Rose City' × 'Chiquita'; sdlg no. Q-19/1
Fl. 95 mm wide

'Shoshone' 2 W-? (b or c)
(K.L. Reynolds, pre-1944)

'Shot Silk' 5 W-W
(de Graaff Bros, pre-1931)
Fls 3 per stem, somewhat star-shaped, creamy white; corona long. 2n=21. AM(Haarlem) 1931

'Shot Tower' 2 W-P
(Alister Clark, 1939) J. Sharp, 1960
Corona opening bronzy pink, becoming pink, with mouth expanded and frilled, rim rolled

'Show Band' 2 W-WWP
(Brian S. Duncan) Brian S. Duncan, 1993
'Pismo Beach' × 'High Society'; sdlg no. 1087
Fl. rounded, 110 mm wide; perianth segments very broadly ovate, blunt, fairly prominently mucronate, pure white, a little reflexed, plane, overlapping half or more; the inner segments roundish, spreading; corona broad and shallow bowl-shaped, ribbed, white, with a broad band of deep pink at rim, mouth split in places and overlapping, a little frilled. Tall. Late

'Showbiz' 3 W-OOW
(T.D. Throckmorton, 1971) Grant Mitsch Novelty Daffodils, 1987
'Green Island' × 'Russet'; sdlg no. 66/18/7
Perianth segments broad, rounded at apex; corona yellow-orange, with white at rim, mouth flared and frilled. Mid-season

'Show Bizz' 2 W-R
(R.H.Glover, pre-1993) Unregistered

'Showboat' 2 W-YYR
(Murray W. Evans) Murray W. Evans, 1970
'Bithynia' × ('Seraglio' × 'Gracious')
Corona almost disc-shaped, yellow, with salmon red at rim

'Show Bride' 3 W-? (b)
(J.W.A. Lefeber, pre-1939)
Syn. 'Edelweiss'

'Showcase' 2 Y-O
(D.S. Bell) D.S. Bell, 1964
('Scarlet Perfection' × 'White Sentinel') × 'Narvik'
Corona spreading, closely overlying the perianth, reddish orange, with rim rolled. Resembles 'Artist's Model' in form

'Show Countess' 2 W-W
(J.N. Hancock & Co., 1946)

('Hebron' × 'Ecstatic') × 'Truth'
Fl. pure white, of thick substance. Early to mid-season. 2n=28

'Showday' 2 Y-R
(D.S. Bell) D.S. Bell, 1983
'Checkmate' × 'Falstaff'

'Showgirl' 2 W-O
(F. Rijnveld & Sons) F. Rijnveld & Sons, 1967
Fl. 102 mm wide; perianth segments ivory white; corona shallow, widely expanded, orange (28A). Early. Resembles 'Oranje Bruid' but with a more heavily frilled corona

'Show Glow' 2 W-W
Syn. of 'Showglow'

'Showglow' 2 W-W
(J.N. Hancock & Co., c.1977) Unregistered
Perianth segments pure white; corona opening creamy white, becoming white, frilled. See also 'Show Glow'

'Showman' 2 W-Y
Warnaar & Co., 1963
Fl. 127 mm wide; corona pale lemon yellow. Mid-season. Resembles an improved 'Smaragd'. AM(Haarlem) 1966

'Show Mist' 1 W-? (b)
(A.H. Ahrens) J.S. Leitch, 1933

'Show Off' 9 W-OOR
(Mrs M.S.Yerger) Mrs M.S.Yerger, 1994
'Dulcimer' open pollinated; sdlg no. 76 A 4
Fl. forming a double triangle, 45 mm wide; perianth segments acute; the inner segments rounded at apex; corona almost disc-shaped, strong reddish orange 31B, with orange-red (34C) at rim. Mid-season

'Show Princess' 2 W-W
(J.N. Hancock & Co.) J.N. Hancock & Co., 1955

'Showtime' 2 Y-Y
(R.G. Cull) Hokorawa Daffodils, 1968

'Show Valley' 2 W-W
(J.N. Hancock & Co.) J.N. Hancock & Co., 1955

'Shrew' 8 W-Y
(A. Gray, pre-1950)
N. tazetta subsp. *lacticolor* × *N. minor*

'Shrewsbury' 1 (a)
(Barr & Sons, pre-1945)

'Shri' 3 W-? (b)
(W. Jackson Sr, 1947)
'Selia' × 'Gyda'

Fl. rounded, 102 mm wide; perianth segments very broad, rounded at apex, slightly mucronate, spreading, with margins sometimes incurling or wavy and often nicked, overlapping two-thirds; the inner segments roundish; corona small bowl-shaped, closely frilled

'Shrike' 11a W-P
(G.E. Mitsch) G.E. Mitsch, 1984
('Accent' × sdlg G97/20) × sdlg 97/2 ('Wild Rose' × 'Hillbilly'); sdlg no. LL34/3
Fl. 93 mm wide; perianth segments broadly ovate, spreading, overlapping one-third to a half; the inner segments somewhat twisted; corona split to base, the six segments about two-thirds the length of the perianth segments and opposite to them, squarish at apex, narrowing to base, closely ribbed, rose pink, spreading or a little inflexed, bi-lobed, with the lobes overlapping, heavily frilled. Mid-season

'Shrimp' 5 Y-Y
(A. Gray) A. Gray, 1955
N. triandrus × *N. assoanus*
Fl. pale yellow; corona proportionately somewhat large. Dwarf

'Shriner' 2 W-Y
(Murray W. Evans) J. Gerritsen & Son, 1972
'Wahkeena' × ('Content' × 'Flora's Favourite'); sdlg no. A-56
2n=28

'Shriner' 2 Y-O
Fl. 105 mm wide. Syn. of 'Marimba'

'Shropshire Lass' 3 W-GYO
(Frank Verge, 1979) Frank Verge, 1994
'Aircastle' hybrid; sdlg no. p-6-6
Fl. 90 mm wide; perianth segments rounded at apex, spreading, smooth, overlapping; corona shallow, deep yellow, with a narrow band of orange at rim. Very late

'Shrove' 3 W-? (b)
(F.H. Chapman, pre-1914)
'Princess Mary' × 'Horace'
Corona large, shallow, tinted mother-of-pearl pink

'Shuttlecock' 2 (a)
(Sir C.H. Cave, pre-1928)

'Shuttlecock' 6 W-O
(Brian S. Duncan) Rathowen Daffodils, 1977
'Merlin' hybrid; sdlg no. 91
Fl. 100 mm wide; perianth segments broadly ovate, blunt, prominently mucronate, pure white, strongly reflexed, plane, overlapping half or more; the inner segments without apparent mucro; corona broad disc-shaped, heavily ribbed, bright deep orange, frilled. Mid-season

'Shy Face' 2 W-GWP
(Carncairn Daffodils, 1965) Carncairn Daffodils, 1982
Erp sdlg 93/50 × Radcliff sdlg 85/94; sdlg no. 1/89/60
Fl. 92 mm wide; perianth segments greenish white (155A); corona with orange-pink (29B) at rim. Mid-season. 2n=29

'Shykoski' 4 W-Y
(Jackson's Daffodils) Jackson's Daffodils, 1991
'Tavelle' × sdlg 116/77; sdlg no. 116/83
Fl. rounded, 95 mm wide; perianth and other petaloid segments very broad in outline, blunt or slightly truncate at apex, pure white, of thick texture, overlapping half or more; the outer whorl a little inflexed; the inner whorl slightly shorter, more strongly inflexed; some shorter segments at centre very strongly inflexed, with margins deeply incurled; corona segments shorter than the petaloid segments at centre, crumpled and clustered among them, more loosely arranged between the surrounding whorls, opening bright yellow, becoming creamy white. Mid-season to late

'Shy Lady' 2 W-WWP
(Jackson's Daffodils) Jackson's Daffodils, 1986
'Iridescent' × 'Verran'; sdlg no. 190/75
Perianth segments greenish white (155C); corona of a slightly darker tone (155A), with light yellowish pink 29C at rim. Mid-season

'Shylock' 1 (a)
(Barr & Sons, pre-1923)

'Siam' 2 W-P
(F. Rijnveld & Sons, pre-1939)
? × 'Mrs R.O.Backhouse'
Corona opening apricot, gradually becoming soft pink. Syn. 'Peking'

'Sibella' 3 W-GYR
(D.F. Lee) D.F. Lee, 1979
Sdlg no. 67/0/28
Fl. 84 mm wide; corona vivid yellow 12A, with brilliant yellow-green 149A at base and orange-red (30A) at rim. Late. Resembles a rather more robust 'Merlin' or 'Corofin' with the green at base more pronounced

'Siberia' 2 W-W
(J.L. Richardson, pre-1943)
'Cameronian' × 'Slemish'
Corona widely expanded, heavily frilled, with rim dentate

'Siberian Pink' 4 W-P
(G.E. Mitsch, 1977) R. & E. Havens, 1991
'Quick Step' × 'Ocarino'; sdlg no. MM36/2
Fl. 110 mm wide, of heavy substance. Mid-season

'Sibling' 1 W-W
(P. Phillips) P. Phillips, 1968

N. sibthorpii Haworth = *N. obvallaris*

'Sicily' 1 Y-Y
(G.H. Engleheart, pre-1914)
Perianth segments creamy sulphur, with margins incurved, overlapping half; corona pale buttercup yellow, with mouth expanded

'Sicily' 2 W-? (b)
(Alister Clark, 1940) T. Morrison, 1960
Perianth segments pure white, of strong substance; corona with rich pink at rim, frilled. Tall

'Sicily White' 8
2n=21. ?Syn. of 'Scilly White'

N. siculus Parlatore = *N. patulus*

'Sidar' 2 W-WYY
(J.S. Leitch) J.S. Leitch, 1959

'Siddington' 3 Y-YYO
(W. Backhouse, pre-1869)
Fls often 2 per stem; perianth segments broadly ovate, blunt, prominently mucronate, light yellow, spreading or a little inflexed, with margins slightly wavy or incurled, overlapping a quarter; the inner segments more narrowly ovate, more strongly inflexed, twisted and with margins often deeply incurled; corona broad cup-shaped, ribbed, darker in tone than the perianth, with a broad band of reddish orange at rim, lightly frilled, with rim crenate

'Side-car' 2 W-O
(W.M. Spry, pre-1975) Unregistered
'Jean Hood' × 'Delight'
Corona disc-shaped, reddish orange

'Sidelight' 9 W-GOR
(G.L. Wilson, pre-1940)
'Dactyl' × 'Ace of Diamonds'
Fl. rounded, smooth, of solid substance; perianth segments pure white; corona rich red. Syn. 'Dierdre'

'Sidenta' 2 W-? (b)
(W.A. Grace, pre-1938)

'Sidewinder' 2 Y-R
(N.H. Anglo) N.H. Anglo, 1986
'Loch Hope' × 'Loch Owskeich'
Perianth segments dark butter yellow; corona orange-red, with mouth slightly expanded, rim neatly dentate. Mid-season

'Sidhe' 5 Y-Y
(A. Gray, pre-1944)
Fls several per stem, 60 mm wide, sulphur yellow; perianth segments becoming paler; corona small

'Sidley' 3 W-GYY
(T. Bloomer) Rathowen Daffodils, 1982
'Shantallow' × 'Woodland Prince'; sdlg no. 383
Fl. 70 mm wide; perianth segments broadly ovate in outline, blunt or rounded at apex, prominently mucronate, pure white, spreading, overlapping half; the inner segments more narrowly ovate, more nearly acute, only very slightly mucronate, a little inflexed; corona short funnel-shaped, closely ribbed, pale yellow, with green at base and a broad band of darker yellow at rim, mouth straight, tightly frilled. Mid-season

'Sidney' 9
(G.H. Engleheart, pre-1907)

'Sidney Fell' 1 Y-Y
(pre-1955) Unregistered
'Halfa' × 'Royalist'
Perianth segments lemon yellow; corona deep yellow

'Sidney Gower' 1 Y-Y
(D.S. Bell) D.S. Bell, 1982
'David Bell' hybrid
Fl. 103 mm wide. Mid-season. Later-flowered than 'David Bell'. Syn. 'S.W.Gower'

'Sidney Mott' 2 (a)
(H.R. Meyer) H.R. Meyer, 1927

'Sidney Torch' 2 Y-YOO
(F. Rijnveld & Sons, pre-1951)
2n=28. AM(Haarlem) 1951

'Sidon' 2 (a)
(J.T. Gray, pre-1950)

'Sidonia' 2 W-? (b)
(de Graaff Bros, pre-1930)
AM(Haarlem) 1930

'Sid Vale' 2 W-? (b or c)
(Sir C.H. Cave, pre-1928)

'Siege' 1 W-? (b)
(C.W. Pierson, 1945) R. Hyde, 1958

'Siegfried' 1 Y-Y
(de Graaff Bros, pre-1924)
Fl. 102 mm wide; perianth segments rich sulphur yellow, with margins recurved, overlapping; corona rich golden yellow, with mouth expanded and deeply frilled. Mid-season. *C(g) 1927, *HC(g) 1936

'Sieglinde' 3 W-? (b)
(N.F. Lock, pre-1944)

'Sierra Gem' 2 (a)
(Oregon Bulb Farms, pre-1946)

'Sierra Glow' 3 W-? (b)
(Oregon Bulb Farms, pre-1950)

'Sierra Gold' 7 Y-Y
(de Graaff Bros, pre-1927)

'Sierra Madre' 4
(Oregon Bulb Farms, pre-1950)

'Sierra Snow' 2 W-W
(Oregon Bulb Farms, pre-1946)

'Siesta' 2 W-R
(D.S. Bell) D.S. Bell, 1959
'Show Boat' × 'Galveston'
Fl. 115 mm wide. Mid-season. Resembles 'Signal Light' but with a shorter and more brightly coloured corona

'Sie-Tao' 2 W-R
(W. Jackson Sr, 1932)
'Eucharis' × 'Silver Plane'

'Sigismund' 5 W-W
(G.H. Engleheart, pre-1912)
Fl. white, tinged green; perianth segments broad. Tall

'Signal' 3 W-? (b)
(F.H. Chapman, pre-1910)

'Signal Hill' 2 W-? (b)
(Oregon Bulb Farms, pre-1951)

'Signaller' 1 Y-Y
(E.W. Philpott)

'Signal Light' 2 W-O
(J.L. Richardson, pre-1948)
'Monaco' × 'Flamenco'
Fl. 98 mm wide; perianth segments very broadly ovate, blunt, prominently mucronate, creamy white, spreading, plane, overlapping half; the inner segments somewhat roundish, only very slightly mucronate, a little inflexed, with margins slightly wavy; corona broad and shallow bowl-shaped, loosely ribbed, orange (23A), flushed with a darker tone (25A), with mouth split in places and overlapping, frilled, rim crenate. Mid-season. PC 1948, AM(e) 1954, AM(Haarlem) 1960, *HC(g) 1968

'Signify' 3 (a)
(R. Hyde) R. Hyde, 1955

'Signorina' 2 W-GYP
(Brian S. Duncan) Brian S. Duncan, 1993
'Fellowship' × 'High Society'; sdlg no. 1162
Fl. 63 mm wide; perianth segments very broadly ovate, blunt, only very slightly mucronate, pure white, veined green at base, spreading, slightly concave, overlapping more than a half; corona funnel-

shaped, slightly ribbed towards mouth, chrome yellow, with emerald green at base and a broad band of deep raspberry pink at rim, mouth straight, frilled. Dwarf. Late

'Sigrid' 2 W-Y
(E.H. Krelage & Son, pre-1930)
'Lady Margaret Boscawen' × 'Mrs Ernst H.Krelage'
AM(Haarlem) 1931

'Sigrid Undset' 3 W-YOO
(J.W.A. Lefeber, pre-1941)
Fl. 99 mm wide; perianth segments creamy white, slightly inflexed, overlapping half; corona ribbed, strong orange 25A, paling to vivid yellow 12A at base, with mouth slightly expanded and frilled, rim crenate. *HC(g) 1958

'Sigurd' 1 W-? (b)
(J.T. Gray, pre-1933)

'Sigval' 1 W-W
(W. Jackson Sr, 1944)
Glyce' × 'Syys'

'Sihouette' 2 W-P
(W.Jackson Jr, pre-1975) Unregistered
'Verran' × 'Egina'

'Silba'
(New Zealand origin, pre-1940)

'Silence' 2 (a)
(Mrs R.S. Cobley, pre-1932)

'Silence d'Or' 2 (a)
(P.D. Williams, pre-1931)

'Silene'
(pre-1913)

'Silent Beauty' 3 W-YYR
(T. Bloomer) T. Bloomer, 1964
'Enniskillen' × ('Isola' × 'Chinese White'); sdlg no. 1/22/55
Corona disc-shaped, deep yellow, with a broad band of deep red at rim

'Silent Charm' 3 W-YYR
(T. Bloomer) T. Bloomer, 1962
'Corofin' × 'Hamzali'; sdlg no. 3/78/58
Corona deep yellow, with a broad band of very deep red at rim, with the rim dentate

'Silent Cheer' 3 W-YYR
(T. Bloomer) T. Bloomer, 1964
'Bravura' × 'Glenwherry'; sdlg no. 2/69/51
Corona yellow, with a broad band of deep red at rim

'Silent Glow' 3 W-R
(T. Bloomer) T. Bloomer, 1964
'Mahmoud' × 'Matapan'; sdlg no. 9/26/52

'Silent Grace' 3 W-YYR
(T. Bloomer) T. Bloomer, 1964
'Corofin' × 'Hamzali'; sdlg no. 6/78/58

'Silent Morn' 3 W-YYO
(T. Bloomer) T. Bloomer, 1964
'Chinese White' × 'Ballycastle'
Perianth segments broad; corona yellow, with a broad band of orange at rim. 2n=28

'Silent Pink' 2 W-P
(G.E. Mitsch, 1980) R. & E. Havens, 1992
'Easter Moon' × 'Cool Flame'; sdlg no. 2P8/11
Fl. forming a double triangle, 100 mm wide; perianth segments very broadly ovate, blunt, pure white, with margins a little incurling at apex, very smooth, overlapping half; the inner segments narrower, with margins wavy; corona funnel-shaped, smooth, soft pink, shading to a slightly darker tone at rim, mouth straight, loosely frilled, with rim almost entire. Mid-season. Sunproof. Resembles 'Easter Moon' in form

'Silent Valley' 1 W-GWW
(T. Bloomer) T. Bloomer, 1964
'Rashee' × 'Empress of Ireland'; sdlg no. 1/18/58
Fl. forming a double triangle, snow white; perianth segments broadly ovate, blunt, slightly mucronate, spreading, smooth and of heavy texture, overlapping one-third to a half; the inner segments more narrowly ovate, reflexed in upper half; corona cylindrical, smooth, with mouth expanded and very slightly wavy, rim entire. 2n=28

'Silent Waters' 2 W-W
Syn. of 'Still Waters'

'Silent Wonder' 3 W-YYO
(T. Bloomer) T. Bloomer, 1964
'Corofin' × 'Hamzali'; sdlg no. 23/78/58
Corona deep yellow, with pinkish orange at rim

'Siletz' 2 Y-W
(G.E. Mitsch) G.E. Mitsch, 1972
'Fawnglo' × 'Lunar Sea'; sdlg no. Y40/1
Fl. 115 mm wide; perianth segments clear soft lemon yellow; corona somewhat narrow, opening yellow, becoming almost white, touched lemon at rim, frilled. Mid-season

'Silhouette' 2 W-RRY
(D.S. Bell) D.S. Bell, 1964
'Mannequin' × 'Garland'
Fl. 102 mm wide; corona shallow, red, with a narrow band of golden yellow at rim. Resembles 'Blarney's Daughter' but with the perianth segments more rounded and the corona more widely expanded

'Silk Cut' 2 W-GWW
(Brian S. Duncan) Rathowen Daffodils, 1986
'Easter Moon' × 'Silent Valley'; sdlg no. 622
Perianth segments acute, slightly reflexed; corona of a purer white than the perianth. Mid-season

'Silken Sails' 3 W-WWY
(G.E. Mitsch) G.E. Mitsch, 1964
'Green Island' × 'Chinese White'; sdlg no. M33/10
Fl. 115 mm wide; perianth segments somewhat acute, pure white, very smooth, deeply overlapping; corona almost disc-shaped, greyish white, with a narrow band of lemon yellow at rim becoming near white. Mid-season. Resembles a larger-flowered 'Chinese White' of better poise

'Silken Thomas' 2 Y-WWY
(D.N.Y. Olson) D.N.Y. Olson, 1978
'Gold Script' × 'Spanish Gold'; sdlg no. 78/2
Fl. 110 mm wide; perianth segments pale golden yellow, with buff white at base; corona buff, with a narrow band of gold at rim. Resembles 'Gold Script' but with narrower perianth segments

'Silken Wings' 2 Y-P
(Grant E.Mitsch) R. & E.Havens, 1994
'Memento' × 'Lorikeet'; sdlg no. UU5/1
Fl. 100 mm wide, smooth and of heavy substance; perianth segments very broadly ovate, lemon yellow, slightly reflexed; corona apricot pink, with mouth flared and rim flanged. Mid-season. Sunproof

'Silkoline' 2 W-? (b)
(de Graaff Bros, pre-1948)

'Silk Purse' 2 W-W
(W.G. Pannill) W.G. Pannill, 1985
'Pristine' × 'Panache'; sdlg no. I 59 C
Mid-season

'Silk Sonata' 2 W-P
(J.N.Hancock & Co., 1976) Unregistered
'Greta' × 'My Word'; sdlg no. 48/76H
Corona narrow at base, flared, rich pink, frilled. Early

'Silk Stocking' 3 Y-GWY
(T.D. Throckmorton) T.D. Throckmorton, 1977
'Gossamer' × 'Aircastle'; sdlg no. 65/2/4
Fl. 102 mm wide; corona white, with greenish tones at base and yellow at rim. Mid-season. Resembles a rounder-flowered 'Lalique'

'Silkwood' 3 W-W
(Clive Postles) Clive Postles Daffodils, 1993
'Cool Crystal' × sdlg L2-4-69; sdlg no. 2-52-79
Fl. 111 mm wide; perianth segments broadly ovate, pure white, convex; corona bowl-shaped, opening creamy white, becoming white, with rim dentate. Late

'Silky Peach' 2 W-GPP
(J.N.Hancock & Co., 1982) Unregistered
'Love in Idleness' × 'Artist's Model'; sdlg no. 134/82H
Perianth segments milk white; corona widely expanded, apricot pink, with green at base, rim broadly crenate. Late

'Siloam' 2 W-W
(A.M. Wilson, pre-1948)

'Silonyx' 1 Y-Y
(de Graaff Bros, pre-1923)

'Silvan' 2 W-YYO
(H.A. Brown, 1947)
Corona funnel-shaped, deep golden yellow, with rich orange at rim, frilled. Mid-season to late

'Silvana' 1 W-W
(A.H. Ahrens) J.S. Leitch, 1956

'Silvania' 10 Y-Y
Syn. of 'Golden Bells'

'Silvanite' 1 W-Y
(de Graaff Bros, pre-1923)
Perianth segments broadly ovate, blunt, very slightly mucronate, a little inflexed, with margins slightly wavy, overlapping half; the inner segments narrower, more strongly inflexed, somewhat twisted; corona cylindrical, smooth, with rim flanged and crenate

'Silver & Gold' 4 W-Y
(A.E.Barnaart & Co., pre-1889)
Perianth segments almost white; corona segments chrome yellow. Early, as compared with other Div. 4 daffodils. Resembles a larger "Gerard's Double Daffodil"

'Silver Arrow' 1 W-W
(G.H. Engleheart, pre-1933)

'Silver Bar' 1 W-W
(Miss F.W. Currey, pre-1890)
Fl. sulphur white; perianth segments opening pale primrose yellow; corona opening lemon yellow

'Silver Barge' 1 W-W
(E. & J.C. Martin, pre-1916)

'Silver Beam' 2 W-W
(C.E. Radcliff, 1932)
'Pedestal' × 'Mrs Moodie'

'Silver Beauty' 2 W-W
(C. Goodson, pre-1927)

'Silver Bell' 1 W-W
(W. Welchman, pre-1908)

'Silver Bells' 5 W-W
(G.E. Mitsch) G.E. Mitsch, 1962
('Daisy Schäffer' × 'Polindra') × *N. triandrus*; sdlg no. O106/1
Fl. 70 mm wide; perianth segments strongly reflexed; corona somewhat flared. 2n=22

'Silver Bells' 1 W-Y
Variant of *N. tortuosus*?
Perianth segments ovate, milk white, faintly green at midrib beneath, very strongly inflexed, somewhat creased, only slightly overlapping; corona cylindrical, somewhat ribbed, pale greenish yellow (4D), with mouth ribbed and flared, wavy, rim notched. Dwarf. The same as *N. tortuosus*?

'Silver Birch' 2 W-? (b or c)
(T. Buncombe, pre-1938)

'Silver Blaze' 2 W-W
(C.G. van Tubergen, pre-1927)

'Silver Blaze' 2 W-GWW
(Brian S. Duncan) Rathowen Daffodils, 1978
'Easter Morn' × 'Empress of Ireland'; sdlg no. 114
Perianth segments broadly ovate or almost triangular in appearance, very slightly mucronate, spreading, plane, or slightly concave at apex, smooth, with midrib sometimes showing, regular, overlapping half; the inner segments more narrowly ovate; corona with deep green at base, mouth expanded and frilled. Mid-season

'Silver Bowl' 2 W-? (b or c)
(J.L. Richardson, pre-1937)

'Silver Braid' 1 W-? (b)
(G.P. Haydon, pre-1910)

'Silver Bugle' 2 W-W
(P.D. Williams, pre-1939)
Fl. 108 mm wide; perianth segments waxy white, overlapping half; corona opening light yellow 10B, soon becoming white, mouth expanded. *AM(g) 1949

'Silver Chalice' 3 W-? (b)
(P.D. Williams, pre-1938)

'Silver Charm' 1 W-W
(R. Crews, pre-1949)

'Silver Chief' 1 W-W
(W.A. Noton) W.A. Noton, 1985
'Panache' × sdlg 515
Corona slender. Late

'Silver Chimes' 8 W-W
(E. & J.C. Martin, pre-1914)
'Scilly White' × *N. triandrus*

Fls 5-7 per stem, 50 mm wide; perianth segments broadly ovate, prominently mucronate, spreading, overlapping one-third; the inner segments more narrowly ovate; corona cup-shaped, lightly ribbed, creamy white, mouth straight and very slightly wavy, rim obscurely crenate. Dwarf. Late. Scented. 2n=28+1B. AM(c) 1922, AM(Haarlem) 1950, FCC(Haarlem) 1953. Div. 5 until 1965

'Silver Circle' 3 W-W
(G.H. Johnstone, pre-1941)
2n=28

'Silver Circle' 1 W-W
(J.N. Hancock & Co., 1955) Unregistered
Fl. opening cream, becoming white; corona with a brighter white at rim

'Silver Cloud' 5
(G.H. Engleheart, pre-1916)

'Silver Cloud' 3 W-GGW
(J.L. Richardson) Mrs H.K. Richardson, 1964
'Dallas' × 'Bryher'
Perianth segments roundish, slightly inflexed; corona disc-shaped, green, with a band of white at rim

'Silver Coin' 3 W-W
(P.D. Williams, pre-1935)
Perianth segments opening light primrose, becoming white; corona tightly ribbed, creamy

'Silver Convention' 1 W-W
(J.S.B. Lea) J.S.B. Lea, 1978
?(Sdlg 1-4-64 × sdlg 1-25-62); sdlg no. 29-36-71
Fl. 110 mm wide. Mid-season. 2n=28

'Silver Coral' 2 W-W
(D.S. Bell) D.S. Bell, 1969
Perianth segments broad, pure white, of strong substance; corona opening with a flush of shell pink, becoming pure white

'Silver Corn'
(pre-1940)

'Silver Crest' 3 W-? (b or c)
(Barr & Sons, pre-1908)

'Silver Crown' 3 W-Y
(Albert Davis, 1981) Albert Davis, 1995
'Green Island' × 'Verona'; sdlg no. 519/77
Fl. 98 mm wide; perianth segments very broadly ovate, overlapping; corona bowl-shaped, vivid yellow 15A, with a slightly lighter tone (15B) at base, mouth frilled, rim crenate. Late

'Silver Crystal' 3 W-GWW
(Brian S. Duncan) Rathowen Daffodils, 1983
'Cool Crystal' × 'Monksilver'; sdlg no. 665

Fl. pure white; perianth segments broadly or very broadly ovate in outline, blunt or rounded at apex, fairly prominently mucronate, spreading, slightly concave, very smooth, overlapping half; the inner segments more narrowly ovate, truncate, with margins wavy and folded inwards from midrib; corona shallow bowl-shaped, ribbed, with moss green at base, a little frilled. Mid-season

'Silver Cycle' 6
(R.O. Backhouse, pre-1927)

'Silverdale' 2 W-W
(R.H. Bath, pre-1929)
Div. 3 until 1938

'Silverdale' 1 W-W
(G.E. Mitsch) G.E. Mitsch, 1956
'Beersheba' × 'Kandahar'
Fl. ivory white; perianth segments broad, slightly reflexed, overlapping; corona slender. Mid-season

'Silver Dawn' 2 W-W
(R.H. Bath, pre-1915)
Corona widely expanded, opening pale citron yellow, becoming white

'Silver Dew' 5
(Cartwright & Goodwin, pre-1910)
'Minnie Hume' × *N. triandrus* var. *loiseleurii*

'Silver Dew' 3 W-? (b)
(New Zealand origin) Parr's Nurseries, 1958

'Silver Dial' 2 W-W
(C. Goodson, pre-1927)

'Silver Dream' 2 W-W
(Frank Verge) Frank Verge, 1975
'Glenocum' × 'Newcastle'; sdlg no. D.6.5
Fl. 80 mm wide

'Silver Fairy' 3 W-? (b or c)
(C.L. Adams, pre-1910)

'Silver Falls' 2 W-W
(R. & E.Havens, 1981) R. & E.Havens, 1994
'Graduation' × (sdlg A39/1 × 'Panache'); sdlg no. QEJ4/1
Fl. 110 mm wide, smooth; perianth segments broadly ovate, spreading, plane; corona cylindrical, opening ivory white, becoming white, with mouth wavy. Mid-season

'Silver Fleece' 5 W-W
(Barr & Sons, pre-1923)
Fls usually 2 per stem, snow white; perianth segments ovate, blunt, spreading, with margins slightly wavy, overlapping one-third; the inner segments a little inflexed, with margins more strongly wavy; corona cup-shaped, lightly ribbed, neatly frilled

'Silver Flood' 5
(Cartwright & Goodwin, pre-1908)

'Silver Fox' 2 W-W
(G.H. Engleheart, pre-1923)
Perianth segments spreading; corona large, expanded. Tall

'Silver Frill' 2 W-? (b or c)
(Hon. Sir R.H. Rhodes, pre-1936)

'Silver Gem' 3 W-? (b or c)
(W. Balch, pre-1931)
PC(e)(NZ) 1931

'Silver Ghost' 2 W-W
(Mrs R.S. Cobley, pre-1937)
Fl. large, pure white

'Silver Giant' 1 W-? (b)
(R.A. van der Schoot, pre-1923)

'Silver Gift' 1 W-W
(de Graaff Bros, pre-1921)

'Silver Gift' 1 W-W
(pre-1956) Unregistered
Fl. snow white

'Silver-gilt' 2 W-? (b)
(G.H. Johnstone, pre-1943)

'Silver Glory' 1 W-W
(de Graaff Bros, pre-1923)

'Silver Gull' 2 W-W
(T. Morrison) T. Morrison, 1960
Corona narrow, opening lemon, becoming white

'Silver Heels' 1 W-W
(Hon. Sir R.H. Rhodes, pre-1911)

'Silver Helmet' 5
(W.F.M. Copeland, pre-1910)

'Silverhouse' 2 W-P
(G.H. Johnstone, 1948) G.H. Johnstone, 1959
'Evening' × 'Ann Abbott'
Fl. 102 mm wide; corona pale pink. Mid-season

'Silver Howard' 3 Y-Y
(G.H. Johnstone) Mrs J. Abel Smith, 1971
'Green Howard' × ('Silver Coin' × 'Peggy')
Fl. 89 mm wide, greenish yellow. Late

'Silverine' 1 W-W
(Oregon Bulb Farms, pre-1946)

"Silver Jonquil"
Variant of *N.* × *gracilis*

'Silver Jubilee' 1 W-? (b)
(R. & G. Cuthbert, pre-1938)

'Silver Jubilee' 2 W-?
Syn. of 'Carlow'

'Silver King' 3 W-Y
(E. Leeds, pre-1877)
Corona canary yellow. Resembles 'Fanny Mason'. Syn. Leedsii 'Silver King'. Was "absorbed" into 'Fanny Mason'

'Silver Kiwi' 2 W-W
(G.W.E. Brogden Bulbs, 1975) Brogden Bulbs, 1991
'Verona' hybrid; sdlg no. P.83/6
Perianth segments roundish, with margins a little incurling, smooth, with a silver sheen, of thick substance; corona shallow bowl-shaped, ribbed, with rim dentate. Mid-season to late

'Silver Lagoon' 2 W-W
(W.A. Noton) W.A. Noton, 1976
'Homage' × 'Verona'; sdlg no. 623
Fl. 90 mm wide. Mid-season

'Silver Lamp' 5
(Cartwright & Goodwin, pre-1916)

'Silverlea' 2 W-? (b or c)
(J.T. Gray, pre-1936)

'Silver Leopard' 3 W-WWY
(Mrs H.K. Richardson) Mrs H.K. Richardson, 1972
'Syracuse' open pollinated
Fl. large; perianth segments waxy white, slightly reflexed; corona pale cream, tinged buff at rim, with the rim deeply dentate. 2n=28

'Silver Light' 2 W-W
(N.Y. Lower, pre-1937)

'Silverling' 7
(G.H. Johnstone, pre-1946)
N. triandrus sdlg

'Silver Lining' 2 W-W
(G.L. Wilson, pre-1948)
AM(Haarlem) 1948

'Silver Link' 2 W-Y
(J.N. Hancock & Co., 1949) J.N. Hancock & Co., 1960
Corona widely expanded, pale yellow, frilled

'Silver Maid' 1 W-W
(Cartwright & Goodwin, pre-1916)

'Silvermere' 2 W-W
(Brian S. Duncan) Rathowen Daffodils, 1981
'Easter Moon' × 'Empress of Ireland'; sdlg no. 324
Mid-season. Resembles a more consistent 'Ben Hee' with the corona whiter than the perianth

'Silvermine' 3 W-W
(G.L. Wilson, pre-1937)
Corona disc-shaped, with a tinge of green at base

'Silver Minx' 1 W-Y
(Jackson's Daffodils) Jackson's Daffodils, 1993
'Tamarus' × sdlg 27/77; sdlg no. 121/84
Fl. forming a double triangle, 115 mm wide; perianth segments broadly ovate, blunt, fairly prominently mucronate, greenish white (155A), slightly stained vivid yellow 12A at base, spreading, plane, smooth, overlapping one-third to a half; the inner segments with margins a little wavy; corona cylindrical, angled, vivid yellow 12A, with rim crenate and widely flanged. Early

'Silver Mist' 3 W-? (b or c)
(Mrs R.O. Backhouse, pre-1907)
Sdlg no. 511

'Silver Mist' 2 W-W
(W.A. Noton) W.A. Noton, 1976
'Stainless' × 'Knowehead'; sdlg no. 511
Fl. 90 mm wide. Mid-season

'Silver Monarch' 2 W-W
(J.A. Hunter, 1986) J.A. Hunter, 1997
('Easter Moon' × 'Glendermott') × ('Glendermott' × 'Kotuku'); sdlg no. 17/81C
Fl. 110 mm wide; perianth segments ovate, smooth; corona slightly flared, with mouth wavy. Mid-season

'Silver Moon' 3 W-W
(Barr & Sons, pre-1907)
N. poeticus × *N. radiiflorus*
Perianth segments very broad, rounded at apex, slightly twisted; corona tightly ribbed, pure white. Tall. Late

'Silver Moon' 2 W-O
(C.M. Grullemans) J.J. Grullemans & Sons, 1959
Fl. 110 mm wide; perianth segments creamy white; corona yellow-orange (16A). Mid-season. 2n=28. Syn. 'Moonsilver'

'Silvern' 1 W-Y
(de Graaff Bros, pre-1923)
Fl. large; perianth segments silvery white, slightly twisted; corona soft primrose yellow

'Silvern Isle' 2 W-W
(R.H. Bath, pre-1929)

'Silver Paper' 2 or 3 W-? (b or c)
(Cartwright & Goodwin, pre-1916)

'Silver Pearl' 3 W-? (b or c)
(W. Welchman, pre-1927)

'Silver Penny' 3 W-O
(E. & J.C. Martin, pre-1913)
Perianth segments ivory white; corona mid-orange. Resembles 'Gold Eye' in form

'Silver Phantom' 3 W-GWY
(Mrs J. Abel Smith) Mrs J. Abel Smith, 1987
'Mary Isabel' hybrid; sdlg no. F33/27
Perianth segments roundish, smooth, of good substance; corona disc-shaped. Late. Resembles a larger-flowered 'Sea Princess'

'Silver Phoenix'
(pre-1884)

'Silver Pink' 2 W-Y
(de Graaff Bros, pre-1935)
Perianth segments creamy white; corona amber yellow. AM(Haarlem) 1935. ?Syn. of 'Ernest H.Wilson'

'Silver Plane' 3 W-Y
(A.E. Lowe, pre-1927)
Perianth segments broadly ovate, blunt, fairly prominently mucronate, pure white, spreading or a little inflexed, with margins creased, overlapping one-third; the inner segments narrower, more strongly inflexed, with margins wavy; corona broad disc-shaped, ribbed, with mouth 6-lobed and rim minutely dentate. Somewhat resembles 'White Sentinel' but with the corona more obviously disc-shaped. AM(e) 1928. Div. 2 until 1937

'Silver Plate' 11a W-W
(J. Gerritsen & Son) J. Gerritsen & Son, 1969
'Split' hybrid
Corona segments opening yellow, becoming white

'Silver Poppy' 5
(Cartwright & Goodwin, pre-1910)

'Silver Princess' 3 W-W
(W.J. Dunlop, pre-1953)
'Silver Salver' × 'Dreamlight'
Perianth segments pure white; corona very shallow, creamy white, faintly tinged green at base

'Silver Queen' 4
(pre-1907)

'Silver Radiance' 5
(Cartwright & Goodwin, pre-1908)

'Silver Realm' 1 W-W
(R.P. Cook, pre-1949)

'Silver Ripples' 2 W-W
(G. Lewis) D.S. Bell, 1955

'Silver Rose' 4 W-Y
(W.F.M. Copeland)
Fl. of good substance; perianth and other petaloid segments broad, creamy white; corona segments interspersed, opening chrome yellow, becoming buffy primrose yellow

'Silver Rupee' 1 W-W
(J.R. Pearson & Sons, pre-1927)

'Silver Salver' 3 W-GWW
(The Brodie of Brodie, c.1916)
'Moonbeam' × *N. poeticus*
Fl. pure white; corona disc-shaped, tinged pale emerald green at base. Late. AM(e) 1922, AM(Haarlem) 1925

'Silver Sand' 3 W-WWY
(pre-1963) Unregistered
Perianth segments very broadly ovate, blunt, prominently mucronate, spreading or a little inflexed, concave, with margins loosely incurling and midrib showing, overlapping half; the inner segments slightly narrower, more nearly acute, more strongly inflexed; corona small bowl-shaped, ribbed, white, with pale yellow at rim, mouth flared and frilled. 2n=28

'Silver Scorn' 1 W-Y
(G. Lewis, pre-1936)

'Silver Scroll' 5
(Cartwright & Goodwin, pre-1910)

'Silver Sheen' 3 W-? (b or c)
(Mrs R.S. Cobley, pre-1937)

'Silver Sheet'
(Mrs R.S. Cobley, pre-1937)

'Silver Shell' 11a W-W
(J. Gerritsen & Son) J. Gerritsen & Son, 1983
'Cassata' × 'Colblanc'
The outer perianth and corona segments recurved; the inner segments inflexed; corona segments as long as the perianth segments and at apex broader, sometimes opening yellowish, with rim deeply bi-lobed and overlapping, lightly frilled. Early

'Silversmith' 2 W-W
(W.A. Noton, 1973) W.A. Noton, 1985
'Arpege' × 'Easter Moon'
Perianth segments broadly ovate, blunt, spreading, a little concave, overlapping half; the inner segments more narrowly ovate, shouldered at base; corona cup-shaped, ribbed, tinged green at base, with mouth straight and regularly frilled. Late. Resembles a

smaller-flowered and more refined 'Arpege'

'Silver Snow' 3 W-W
(W.G. Pannill) W.G. Pannill, 1987
'Noweta' × 'Tobernaveen'; sdlg no. 65/34
Late

'Silver Soleil d'Or'
(pre-1885)

'Silver Song' 2 W-W
(Slieve Donard Nursery Co., pre-1933)
Perianth segments pure white; corona ivory white, shading to a slightly deeper tone at rim

'Silver Spangle' 3 W-Y
(F.H. Chapman, pre-1912)
'Lulworth' × 'Horace'
Perianth segments roundish; corona shallow, ribbed, soft yellow. AM 1912

'Silver Spell' 3 W-GWW
(Mrs H.K. Richardson, c.1975) Unregistered
'Shagreen' × 'Dallas'
2n=14

'Silver Spray' 1 W-W
(G.L. Wilson, pre-1951)

'Silverspring' 1 W-Y
(J.L. Richardson, pre-1923)
Perianth segments pure white; corona opening pale primrose, becoming almost cream

'Silver Spur' 1 W-Y
(W.B. Hartland, pre-1897)
Syn. 'Sulphur Spur'

'Silver Standard' 2 W-W
(C.G. van Tubergen, pre-1944)
Perianth segments broadly ovate, blunt, only very slightly mucronate, a little inflexed, somewhat creased, overlapping half; the inner segments more narrowly ovate, more strongly inflexed, more thickly creased, a little twisted; corona shallow, widely expanded, heavily ribbed, opening faint sulphur yellow, becoming white, closely frilled. 2n=28. AM(Haarlem) 1944

'Silver Star' 3 W-Y
(W. Backhouse, pre-1869)
Corona citron yellow. Syn. Barrii Albus 'Silver Star', Barrii Albus 'Stellatus'

'Silver Star' 2 W-YWW
(Mrs R.O. Backhouse, pre-1921)

'Silver Strand' 1 W-W
(R.H. Bath, pre-1910)

'Silver Stream' 1 W-W
(de Graaff Bros, pre-1923)

'Silverstream' 2 W-W
(D.S. Bell) D.S. Bell, 1957
Fl. pure white

'Silver Surf' 2 W-W
(Brian S. Duncan) Rathowen Daffodils, 1978
'Easter Moon' × 'Empress of Ireland'; sdlg no. 122
Fl. pure white; perianth segments broadly ovate, blunt, slightly mucronate, slightly reflexed, plane, overlapping half; the inner segments a little narrower, less noticeably mucronate, with margins very slightly wavy; corona bowl-shaped, smoothly 6-angled, pinkish white, loosely frilled. Mid-season. 2n=28

'Silver Swan' 5 W-W
(A.R. Goodwin, pre-1908)
'Minnie Hume' × *N. triandrus* var. *loiseleurii*

'Silver Tassie' 2 W-W
(Mrs R.S. Cobley, pre-1935)

'Silver Thaw' 3 W-W
(Murray W. Evans, 1967) Murray W. Evans, 1978
('Duke of Windsor' × 'Green Island') × 'White o' Morn'; sdlg no. K-37
Fl. 100 mm wide. Mid-season

'Silverthorne' 3 W-W
(R.A.Scamp) R.A.Scamp, 1997
'Cool Crystal' × 'Delos'; sdlg no. 440
Fl. 105 mm wide, pure white; perianth segments ovate, slightly reflexed, very smooth, deeply overlapping; corona shallow bowl-shaped, with rim neatly crenate. Mid-season

'Silver Tide' 1 W-W
(G. Lewis) F.A. Saunders, 1959

'Silvertips' 3 (a)
(Mrs R.S. Cobley, 1937)

'Silverton' 1 W-W
(G.H. Engleheart, pre-1923)

'Silverton' 5 W-W
(G.E. Mitsch, 1967) R. Havens, 1980
'Quick Step' × *N. triandrus*; sdlg no. C52/17
Fl. 50 mm wide, ivory white. Late. Resembles a smaller 'Petrel'

'Silvertone' 1 W-Y
(E.W. Philpott) E.W. Philpott, 1959
Corona pale yellow. Early. Resembles 'Caramel' but with larger perianth segments and longer corona

'Silver Top' 1 W-Y
(G.B. van Rhijn) G.B. van Rhijn, 1963
Fl. 120 mm wide; perianth segments greenish white; corona vivid yellow 9B. Mid-season

'Silver Tower' 2 W-GWW
(J.N. Hancock & Co., 1973) Unregistered

'Silver Trumpet' 5
(W.F.M. Copeland, pre-1908)

'Silver Trumpet'
Syn. of *N. moschatus*

'Silver Twink' 4
(J.C. van der Meer, pre-1943)
AM(Haarlem) 1943

'Silver Vase' 5
(J.W. Barr, pre-1930)

'Silver Water' 5
(Cartwright & Goodwin, pre-1914)

'Silver Wedding' 1 W-W
(G.L. Wilson, pre-1938)
'Halfa' × 'Beersheba'
Fl. greenish white, facing down; perianth segments broadly ovate, blunt, slightly mucronate, a little inflexed, with margins slightly wavy, smooth, overlapping half; the inner segments more narrowly ovate, shouldered at base, inflexed at base, reflexed at apex, a little twisted; corona cylindrical, smooth, with rim rolled and obscurely crenate. AM(e) 1938

'Silver White' 1 W-W
(H.A. Brown, pre-1950)

'Silver Wing' 4
(pre-1927)

'Silverwings' 8
(Sutton & Sons, pre-1898)
'Paper White Grandiflora' hybrid

'Silverwood' 3 W-W
(Brian S. Duncan) Rathowen Daffodils, 1988
'Verona' × 'Monksilver'; sdlg no. 894
Fl. rounded; perianth segments very broadly ovate, rounded at apex and a little truncate, slightly mucronate, pure white, spreading or a little reflexed, concave at apex, smooth, overlapping half; the inner segments a little narrower, more deeply truncate, more nearly spreading and plane; corona bowl-shaped, closely ribbed, opening pure white, becoming yellowish white, with greenish grey in tube, mouth expanded and lightly frilled. Mid-season to late. AM(e) 1996

'Silvester' 11b W-R/W
(J.W.A. Lefeber) J.W.A. Lefeber, 1958
? × 'Buttonhole' hybrid
Perianth segments whitish; corona segments with red and white in longitudinal bands

N. silvestris Lamarck = *N. pseudonarcissus*

'Silvia' 5 Y-Y
(F.H. Chapman, pre-1913)
Fl. soft primrose yellow, tinged lemon yellow

'Silvia' 5
(Sir C.H. Cave, pre-1927)

'Silviana' 8 Y-Y
(pre-1798)
Fl. pale yellow

'Silvius' 2 W-Y
(W.M. Spry, pre-1975) Unregistered
'Oliver' × 'Carnlough'
Corona lemon yellow

'Silvo' 1 W-? (b)
(J.L. Richardson, pre-1927)

'Silvretta' 1 Y-Y
(J. Gerritsen & Son, 1949) J. Gerritsen & Son, 1961
Fl. 110 mm wide, greenish yellow (4D); corona with a narrow band of a darker tone (6B) at rim. Late. 2n=29. Resembles an earlier-flowered 'Citrix'

'Silwa'
(New Zealand origin, pre-1940)

'Simano' 2 Y-R
(J.S. Leitch) J.S. Leitch, 1957

'Simbo' 1 Y-Y
(S.J. Bisdee, 1943)
'Crocus' × 'Robert Montgomery'

'Simile' 2 W-GPP
(J.L. Richardson) Brian S. Duncan, 1973
'Rose Caprice' × 'Rose Royale'
Fl. 120 mm wide

N. similis Steudel = *N. jonquilla*

'Simla' 2 W-YYO
(N.Y. Lower, pre-1929)
'Bernardino' × 'Seville'
Perianth segments only slightly overlapping; corona expanded, lemon yellow, with a broad band of orange at rim. Mid-season. *C(g) 1936

'Simon' 2 Y-Y
(A. Sandys-Winsch) A. Sandys-Winsch, 1956
'Penquite' × 'Elgin'
Fl. orange-yellow

'Simone' 2 W-P
(J.N.Hancock & Co., 1974) Unregistered
Perianth segments pure white; corona funnel-shaped, deep pink, deeply frilled. Mid-season

'Simone Martini' 2 W-O
(J.W.A. Lefeber) J.W.A. Lefeber, 1968
'Redmarley' hybrid

'Simple' 3 W-WWO
(Mrs R.O. Backhouse, pre-1921)
Fl. 76 mm wide, facing down; perianth segments overlapping one-third; corona cup-shaped, cream, with orange at rim. Mid-season to late

'Simple Simon' 2 Y-? (a)
(G.H. Johnstone, pre-1950)

"Simplex"
Syn. of *N. jonquilla*

'Simplicity' 2 or 3 W-? (b or c)
(E.H. Wheadon & Sons, pre-1916)

'Simplicity' 3 W-W
(T. Bloomer) T. Bloomer, 1964
'Chinese White' × 'Bryher'; sdlg no. 8/81/58

'Simply Bloomfield' 2 Y-Y
(Carncairn Daffodils) Bangor Horticultural Society, 1993
'Golden Aura' × 'Aircastle'
Perianth segments broadly ovate in outline, blunt or truncate, pale yellow, spreading or sometimes inflexed, with midrib showing, overlapping half; the inner segments square-shouldered at base and more often inflexed; corona short funnel-shaped, loosely ribbed, vivid yellow 12A, mouth straight, split in places and overlapping, frilled, with rim minutely and closely dentate. Mid-season

'Simply Stunning' 1 Y-Y
(John R.Reed) John R.Reed, 1997
'Arkle' × 'Dream Prince'; sdlg no. 90-12-1
Fl. rounded, 102 mm wide; perianth segments very broadly ovate, deep yellow, overlapping; the inner segments touching one another; corona funnel-shaped, slightly darker in tone than the perianth, with mouth flared. Early

'Simson' 2 (a)
(G. Lubbe & Son, pre-1937)
AM(Haarlem) 1937

'Sims Reeves' 1 W-Y
(E. Leeds, pre-1877)
Syn. Pseudonarcissus Bicolor 'Sims Reeves'. Was "absorbed" into 'Murrell Dobell'

'Simvu' 1 W-W
(S.J. Bisdee, 1943)
'White Emperor' × 'Dawnglow'

'Sinai' 2 Y-O
(Daniel Bellinger) Daniel Bellinger, 1997
'Gala King' × 'Altruist'; sdlg no. 87-20-2
Fl. rounded, 98 mm wide; perianth segments ovate, pale yellow, flushed with a darker tone at base, slightly reflexed, plane, smooth and of thick substance; corona bowl-shaped, fiery orange, with a slightly darker tone at rim. Late. Sunproof

'Sinbad' 3 W-YYO
(W. Polman-Mooy, pre-1913)
Perianth segments ivory white; corona widely expanded, deep yellow, shading to reddish orange at rim

'Sincerity' 1 W-Y
(N.Y. Lower, pre-1930)
'Lord Roberts' × 'White Knight'
Fl. forming a double triangle, 114 mm wide, facing slightly downwards; perianth segments broadly ovate, blunt, fairly prominently mucronate, greenish white, spreading, with margins a little wavy, overlapping half; the inner segments narrower and more nearly acute, a little inflexed, with margins more strongly wavy; corona cylindrical, primrose yellow, with mouth expanded, rim rolled and irregularly notched. AM(e) 1938, FCC(e) 1940

'Sinclair Lewis' 2 (a)
(F. Rijnveld & Sons, pre-1940)

'Sindbad' 1 (a)
(Sir C.H. Cave, pre-1928)

'Sindbad' 2 (a)
(A.H. Ahrens) J.S. Leitch, 1955

'Sindbad' 1 Y-Y
Syn. of 'Galileo'

'Sindy' 2 W-R
(J.S. Leitch) J.S. Leitch, 1956

'Singapore' 2 Y-YYO
(Miss G. Evelyn, pre-1930)
Perianth segments bright lemon yellow; corona with reddish orange at rim

'Singing Pub' 3 W-O
(Brian S.Duncan) Brian S.Duncan, 1997
Sdlg no. 1813
Fl. rounded, 115 mm wide; perianth segments very broadly ovate, spreading, plane; corona very shallow bowl-shaped, closely ribbed, deep orange. Late. Syn. 'Singin' Pub'

'Singin' Pub' 3 W-O
Syn. of 'Singing Pub'

'Single Cloth of Gold' 1 Y-Y
Syn. of 'Golden Plover'

"Single Orange Phoenix"
Syn. of 'Mary Anderson'

'Single Paper White'
?Syn. of *N. papyraceus*

'Sinope' 1 W-? (b)
(C. Dawson, pre-1923)

'Sinopel' 3 W-WWY
(P. de Jager & Sons) P. de Jager & Sons, 1974
Fl. 85 mm wide; perianth segments broadly ovate, truncate, slightly mucronate, ivory white, spreading, with margins incurled to give an oblong appearance, overlapping one-third; the inner segments more nearly acute, with margins wavy; corona very shallow bowl-shaped, ribbed, greenish white, with a band of deep yellow at rim

'Sinora' 8
(pre-1939)

'Sinquist' 3 W-? (b)
(J.W.A. Lefeber, pre-1945)

'Sintram' 2 (a)
(A.J. Bliss, pre-1931)
'Mrs C. Bowley' × *N. abscissus*
Fl. 76 mm wide, facing down; perianth segments pale sulphur, irregular, overlapping half; corona cylindrical, bright lemon, suffused with orange. Mid-season to late

'Sioux' 2 Y-R
(G.E. Mitsch, 1966) G.E. Mitsch, 1976
('Narvik' × 'California Gold') × 'Flaming Meteor'; sdlg no. B45/26
Fl. 100 mm wide; perianth segments deep gold; corona orange-red. Early to mid-season. 2n=28. Resembles a larger 'Chemawa' of greater substance with a less noticeably yellow rim

'Sir Accola' 1 (a)
(W. Jackson Sr, pre-1939)
?Syn. of 'Sir Accolon'

'Sir Accolon' 1 Y-Y
(W. Jackson Sr, 1935)
'Sir Gawaine' × 'Sir Bors'
?See also 'Sir Accola'

'Sir Agravine' 1 Y-Y
(W. Jackson Sr, 1931)
'Golden City' × 'Renown'

'Sir Bedivere' 1 W-W
(J. Mallender, pre-1913)

'Sir Bedivere' 2 (a)
(?T. Buncombe, pre-1913)

'Sir Blink' 2 Y-O
(J.N. Hancock & Co., *c*.1968) Unregistered
Perianth segments yellow; corona short, orange-red, rim dentate. Sunproof

'Sir Bors' 1 Y-Y
(W. Jackson Sr, 1931)
'Golden City' × 'Victor'

'Sir Charles Dilke' 1 Y-Y
(W. Backhouse, pre-1869)
Fl. soft primrose yellow; perianth segments somewhat inflexed. Syn. Pseudonarcissus Major 'Sir Charles Dilke'

'Sir Christopher Wren' 2 Y-?Y
(W. Backhouse, pre-1869)
Perianth segments sulphur yellow; corona large, expanded. Syn. Incomparabilis Sulphureus 'Sir Christopher Wren'. Was "absorbed" into 'Magog'

'Sirdar' 2 W-Y
(Mrs R.O. Backhouse, pre-1908)
Perianth segments silvery white, overlapping; corona deeply ribbed, light creamy yellow, frilled. Tall

'Sir Dighton Probyn' 1 W-Y
(C.G. van Tubergen, pre-1914)
Perianth segments sulphur white; corona expanded, deep yellow. AM(Haarlem) 1914

'Sir Douglas Haig' 2 Y-Y
(pre-1930)
Fl. large, rich deep yellow, of strong substance

'Sire' 1 (a)
(A. Overdevest, pre-1952)

'Sir Echo' 1 Y-W
(pre-1978) Unregistered
(*N. asturiensis* × 'Mitzy') × *N. asturiensis* sdlg

'Sir Edmund' 1 W-? (b)
(H. Daines) H. Daines, 1955

'Sir Edmund Hillary' 1 W-W
(F.D.B. Cobb, pre-1954)

'Sir Edward Carson' 3 W-W
(de Graaff Bros, pre-1916)

'Sirella' 3 W-R
(G.L. Wilson) Guy L. Wilson Ltd, 1964
('Flamenco' × 'Delice') hybrid

'Siren' 1 W-W
(G.H. Engleheart, pre-1897)

Sdlg no. 480
Perianth segments creamy white, spreading; corona cylindrical, yellow-white

'Siren' 5 W-W
(G.H. Engleheart, pre-1897)
White Div. 1 × *N. triandrus*; sdlg no. 628
Corona long

'Sirene' 1 W-W
(de Graaff Bros, pre-1923)

'Sirene' 3 W-? (b)
(J. Pope, pre-1923)

'Sirene' 11?a Y-Y
(J. Gerritsen & Son, 1953) J. Gerritsen & Son, 1963
Fl. 90 mm wide; perianth segments light greenish yellow 5C; corona vivid yellow 13A. Early. Resembles an improved 'Flaneur'

'Sir Ernest Shackleton' 1 W-W
(C.G. van Tubergen, pre-1914)

'Sir Ernest Shackleton' 1 W-Y
(M. van Waveren & Sons, pre-1930)

'Sir Fergus' 2 W-? (b)
(G.C. Graham, pre-1949)

'Sir Francis Drake' 1 Y-Y
(J. Kendall, pre-1902)
Early. Resembles a paler and earlier-flowered 'Emperor' of darker colour. AM 1902

'Sir Frederick' 3 W-Y
(G.H. Engleheart, pre-1914)
Corona clear yellow. Resembles 'Duchess of Westminster'

'Sir Gaherus' 1 Y-Y
(W. Jackson Sr, 1933)
'Golden City' × 'Renown'

'Sir Galahad' 3 W-Y
(P.D. Williams, pre-1910)
Perianth segments broadly ovate, blunt, only very slightly mucronate, pure white, spreading, overlapping half; the inner segments a little inflexed; corona broad bowl-shaped, loosely ribbed, soft primrose yellow, frilled

'Sir Gareth' 1 Y-Y
(W. Jackson Sr, 1933)
'Renown' × 'Golden City'

'Sir Gawain' 1 W-Y
(Barr & Sons, pre-1920)
Perianth segments slightly reflexed, overlapping; corona primrose yellow, with mouth expanded

'Sir Gawaine' 1 Y-Y
(W. Jackson Sr, 1933)
'Golden City' × 'Renown'
Fl. rich yellow

'Sir Graelent' 1 Y-Y
(W. Jackson Sr, 1936)
'Sir Bors' × 'Aurelius'

'Sir Guyan' 3 W-? (b)
(pre-1935)

'Sir Guyan' 3 Y-Y
Syn. of 'Sir Guyton'

'Sir Guyton' 3 Y-Y
(A.E. Lowe, pre-1927)
See also 'Sir Guyan'

'Sir Harry Veitch' 1 (a)
(M. van Waveren & Sons, pre-1916)

'Sir Heaton Rhodes' 2 W-O
(G. Lewis) D.S. Bell, 1955
Perianth segments very broadly ovate, blunt, prominently mucronate, spreading or a little reflexed, concave, overlapping half; the inner segments inflexed, with margins nicked, with broad midrib showing; corona bowl-shaped, ribbed, with mouth split in places and overlapping, closely frilled

'Sir Henry Campbell-Bannerman' 1 Y-Y
(pre-1908)
Perianth segments acute, yellow; corona deep yellow. AM(Haarlem) 1908

'Sir Henry Deterding' 1 W-?
Syn. of 'Henry Deterding'

'Sir Henry Irving' 1
Syn. of 'Henry Irving'

'Sir Herbert' 2 (a)
(H.F. Fletcher, pre-1935)

'Sir Horace Plunkett' 1 Y-Y
(Sir J.A.R. Gore-Booth, 1908)
Fl. large, golden yellow

'Sir Hugh' 2 W-? (b)
(H.F. Fletcher, 1935)

'Sirikit' 2 W-YYP
(Mrs B.T. Simpson) Mrs B.T. Simpson, 1963
Fl. 95 mm wide; corona lemon yellow. Early. Resembles 'Carnlough' but with colours unfading

'Sir Isaac Newton' 8 Y-O
(pre-1861)

Syn. Tazetta 'Sir Isaac Newton'. ?The same as 'Newton' 8 Y-O

'Sirius' 2 W-YYO
(Mrs Lawrenson, pre-1897)
'Princeps' × *N. radiiflorus* var. *poetarum*; sdlg no. 2
Perianth segments oblong, blunt, prominently mucronate, somewhat inflexed, with margins wavy, separated; the inner segments not noticeably mucronate, with margins more stongly wavy or twisted; corona short funnel-shaped, ribbed, greenish yellow, with a broad band of reddish orange at rim, mouth straight, wavy, rim crenate. Early

'Sirius' 2 W-YYR
(J.L. Richardson) Mrs H.K. Richardson, 1963
'Kilworth' × 'Cairo'
Corona disc-shaped, primrose yellow, with deep red at rim, with the rim dentate

'Sir Ivor' 1 Y-Y
(Mrs H.K. Richardson) Mrs H.K. Richardson, 1972
'Argosy' open pollinated
Fl. deep gold; perianth segments very smooth; corona slightly expanded, with rim dentate

'Sir John French' 1 (a)
(J.L. Richardson, pre-1916)

'Sir John Suckling' 9
(A.R. Goodwin, pre-1908)

'Sir Knight' 2 W-GRR
(T. Bloomer) T. Bloomer, 1962
'Red Hackle' × 'Arbar'; sdlg no. 4/40/54
Perianth segments broadly ovate; corona orange-red

'Sir Lancelot' 3 W-YYR
(Barr & Sons, pre-1908)
Perianth segments snowy white; corona expanded, ribbed, bright canary yellow, with bright madder scarlet at rim, with the rim notched

'Sir Nigel' 1 Y-Y
(J.T. Gray, pre-1940)
Fl. very large, deep golden yellow

'Sirocco' 3 W-W
(The Brodie of Brodie, *c*.1930)
'Mystic' × 'Dactyl'
Perianth segments pure white

'Sirocco' 2 Y-O
(J.J. Abernethy) R.J. Abernethy, 1957
Perianth segments deep golden yellow; corona dark reddish orange, with rim slightly dentate

'Sir Percy' 2 Y-O
(Konynenburg & Mark) Konynenburg & Mark, 1960

('Bertha Aten' × 'Red Bird') × 'Rustom Pasha'
Fl. 85 mm wide; perianth segments brilliant yellow 8A; corona vivid orange 28B. Mid-season

'Sir Philip Sidney' 9
(G.H. Engleheart, pre-1914)

'Sir Redvers Buller' 1 W-? (b)
(S.A. van Konynenberg & Co., pre-1907)

'Sir Robert' 2 W-? (b)
(W.A. Watts, pre-1939)

'Sir Robert Peel' 1 W-Y
(W. Backhouse, pre-1869)
Corona with rim flanged. Syn. Pseudonarcissus Bicolor 'Sir Robert Peel'. Was "absorbed" into 'Horsfieldii'

'Sir Roger' 1 Y-Y
(W. Balch, pre-1933)

'Sir R.Peel' 1 W-Y
Syn. of 'Sir Robert Peel'

'Sir Samuel' 2 W-P
(W.M. Spry, pre-1973) Unregistered
'Dorothy Strom' × 'Longeray'
2n=28

'Sir Stafford Northcote' 1 W-W
(W. Backhouse, pre-1869)
Corona long, pale sulphur. Syn. Pseudonarcissus Moschatus 'Sir Stafford Northcote'

'Sir Stanley Maude' 1 Y-Y
(C.E. Kitchin, pre-1927)
Fl. 95 mm wide; perianth segments creamy sulphur, inflexed, overlapping half; corona rich lemon yellow, with mouth expanded. Mid-season

'Sir Walter Raleigh' 1 W-? (b)
(Miss F.W. Currey, pre-1908)
Div. 2 until 1931

'Sir Walter Scott' 8 W-Y
(pre-1881)
Syn. Tazetta 'Sir Walter Scott'

'Sir Walter Scott' 9
(G.H.Engleheart, pre-1897)
Sdlg no. 362
Corona broad disc-shaped

'Sir Watkin' 2 Y-Y
(W. Pickstone, pre-1868)
Fl. 112 mm wide; perianth segments broadly ovate, blunt or truncate, fairly prominently mucronate, light greenish yellow 3C, spreading or a little inflexed, overlapping one-third or less; the inner segments

more nearly acute, with margins wavy or recurved; corona funnel-shaped, more or less strongly ribbed, vivid yellow 12A, slightly tinged orange, with mouth straight, often deeply 6-lobed and overlapping, frilled, rim minutely and irregularly crenate. 2n=21. Syn. "Giant Daffodil", "Mountain Daffodil", "Star Narcissus", "The Welsh Peerless", 'Watkin', Incomparabilis Giganteus 'James Dickson', Incomparabilis Giganteus 'Sir Watkin'. FCC 1884

'Sir Watkin, Double' 4 Y-O
Syn. of 'Double Sir Watkin'

'Sir W.Harcourt' 1 Y-Y
(W. Backhouse, pre-1869)
Fl. rich yellow. Resembles a Div. 1 'Edward Hart'. Syn. Pseudonarcissus Major 'Sir W.Harcourt'

'Sir Wilfred Laurier'
(C.G. van Tubergen, pre-1908)

'Sir William' 2 (a)
(G.T.C. Pearce, pre-1939)

'Sir William Harcourt' 1 Y-Y
Syn. of 'Sir W.Harcourt'

'Sir Winston Churchill' 4 W-O
(Unknown origin) H.A. Holmes, 1966
'Geranium' sport
Fls averaging 4 per stem, rounded, 60 mm wide; perianth and other petaloid segments in several whorls, white; the outer whorl very broad, truncate, some with prominent mucro, spreading, overlapping half or more; the inner whorls inflexed, sometimes touched yellow or orange at midrib, with margins wavy or incurled; the centre whorl short, strongly inflexed, with margins tightly incurled; corona segments shorter than the centre whorl and clustered among them, orange. Mid-season. Strongly scented. 2n=17. TGA(Haarlem) 1966, *AM(g) 1988

'Sir Wroth' 3 W-? (b)
(J.W. Paardekooper, pre-1931)

'Siskin' 3 Y-? (a)
(G.H. Engleheart, pre-1923)

'Siskin' 2 W-Y
(A.O. Roblin, 1947)

'Siskin' 2 YYW-W
(E.G.B.Jarman) E.G.B.Jarman, 1978
'Daydream' × 'Majorca'; sdlg no. 41
Fl. 100 mm wide; perianth segments lemon yellow, with white at base; corona becoming white, with a less pure tone outside. Mid-season. Resembles 'Chiloquin' but with a shorter corona

'Siskiyou' 2 W-? (b)
(Oregon Bulb Farms, pre-1951)

'Sister' 2 W-Y
(Mrs R.O. Backhouse, pre-1921)
Corona widely expanded, sulphur yellow, frilled. AM(Haarlem) 1930

'Sister Dora' 2 W-? (b or c)
(J.R. Pearson & Sons, pre-1923)

'Sister Mary' 2 W-? (b)
(E.H.G. Thurston, pre-1930)

'Sister Reinalde' 2 W-YYO
(J.W.A. Lefeber) W. Blom & Son, 1955

'Sister Sue' 2 (a)
(E.H.G. Thurston, pre-1930)

'Sister Taylor' 1 W-W
(W.A. Grace, pre-1936)

'Sita' 2 Y-YRR
(S.J. Bisdee, 1943) R. Hyde, 1958
'Invergordon' × 'Sunset Fires'

'Siva' 5
(pre-1913)

'Siva' 2 (a)
(W.A. Grace, pre-1938)

'Siwah' 2 Y-O
(P. van Deursen, pre-1953)
Perianth segments clear yellow. Very early

'Siward' 1 Y-Y
(W. Jackson Sr, 1928)
'Orange Warley' × 'Golden Gate'

'Six of Spades' 2 (a)
(Mrs R.S. Cobley, pre-1944)

'Sixty-seventh Brigade' 2 (a)
(W.A. Watts, pre-1926)

'Skater's Waltz' 6 Y-Y
(G.E. Mitsch and R. & E.Havens, 1971) G.E. Mitsch and R. & E.Havens, 1988
'Vulcan' × *N. cyclamineus*; sdlg no. G59/5
Perianth segments moderately reflexed; corona funnel-shaped, yellow, slightly tinged orange. Dwarf. Early

'Skeena' 2 W-Y
(V. Brink) V. Brink, 1967
'Tunis' × 'Mabel Taylor'
Fl. 89 mm wide; corona yellow, flushed with buff. Mid-season. Resembles 'Greeting' but with broader and longer perianth segments and a more widely

expanded corona

'Skelmersdale Gold' 1 Y-Y
(A. Gray, 1970) Broadleigh Gardens, 1986
N. asturiensis sdlg?; sdlg no. 176B
Early

'Skerry' 2 Y-Y
(Carncairn Daffodils) Carncairn Daffodils, 1991
'Golden Aura' × 'Aircastle'; sdlg no. 4/4/79
Fl. 89 mm wide, light greenish yellow 3C; perianth segments very broadly ovate, fairly prominently mucronate, paling almost to white at midrib, inflexed, slightly concave, smooth, overlapping half; corona shallow funnel-shaped, lightly ribbed, slightly paler than 3C at the mid-zone, mouth straight and lightly frilled, rim irregularly crenate. Mid-season

'Skerryvore' 2 (a)
(M. van Waveren & Sons, pre-1950)

'Sketrick' 1 Y-Y
(Ballydorn Bulb Farm, 1980) Ballydorn Bulb Farm, 1996
'Arctic Gold' × 'Viking'
Fl. 88 mm wide, golden yellow; perianth segments broadly ovate, smooth; corona funnel-shaped, with mouth flared, rim flanged and almost entire. Early

'Skiathos' 2 W-GWW
(J.M. de Navarro) J.M. de Navarro, 1975
'Verona' × 'Stainless'; sdlg no. 101/III
Fl. 92 mm wide. Mid-season. Resembles 'Ice Queen' but with the inner perianth segments broader

'Skiffle' 7 Y-Y
(A. Gray) A. Gray, 1957
N. asturiensis × *N. calcicola*
Fls 1-2 per stem, bright yellow. Corona shallow bowl-shaped, closely frilled. Dwarf. Early

'Skim' 9 W-GYR
(Mrs M.S.Yerger) Mrs M.S.Yerger, 1994
'Proxy' open pollinated; sdlg no. 85 L
Fl. forming a double triangle, 43 mm wide; perianth segments rounded at apex, reflexed, overlapping; the inner segments narrower; corona disc-shaped, light greenish yellow 8B, with moderate yellow-green 138B at base and orange-red (32A) at rim. Late

'Skipper' 9 W-YYO
(Mrs M.S.Yerger) Mrs M.S.Yerger, 1994
'Lights Out' open pollinated; sdlg no. 76 P 3
Fl. forming a double triangle, 52 mm wide; perianth segments white; corona bowl-shaped, greenish yellow (154B), with a darker tone at base and vivid reddish orange 30A at rim. Late

'Skipton' 2 Y-Y
(pre-1956) Unregistered

Corona large, widely expanded

'Skookum' 3 Y-Y
(Murray W. Evans, 1965) Murray W. Evans, 1976
'Green Island' × 'Actaea'; sdlg no. I-12
Fl. 95 mm wide; perianth segments yellow; corona primrose yellow. Late

'Skyblaze' 8 W-R
(J.C.Williams, pre-1927)
Resembles a somewhat larger and slightly earlier-flowered 'Glorious'

'Skyglow' 9 W-YYR
(Mrs M.S. Yerger) Mrs M.S. Yerger, 1986
'Lights Out × 'Sea Green'; sdlg no. 73 A 2
Corona brilliant yellow 13B, with orange-red (32A) at rim. Late. Spicily scented. Resembles 'Lights Out' but with the corona colours muted

'Skylark' 2 Y-? (a)
(L. van Leeuwen & Son, pre-1942)

'Skylark' 2 Y-O
Syn. of 'Song Lark'

'Skyline' 2 W-Y
(Sir J.S. Arkwright, pre-1936)
Corona lemon yellow

'Skylon' 7 Y-YRR
(T.A.V. Wood, pre-1951)
Fls 2 per stem, 66 mm wide; perianth segments broadly ovate, blunt, yellow, with white mucro, slightly reflexed, plane, overlapping half; the inner segments with margins wavy; corona shallow cup-shaped, ribbed, orange-red, with a band of yellow at base, mouth expanded, even, rim minutely crenate. Dwarf. Late. 2n=22

'Skymaster' 2 Y-YYO
(de Graaff Bros, pre-1947)
Perianth segments apricot yellow; corona with a broad band of orange at rim. AM(Haarlem) 1946

'Sky Pilot' 2 Y-R
(D.S. Bell) D.S. Bell, 1960
'Rosslare' hybrid
Fl. 115 mm wide. Mid-season. Resembles 'Ceylon'

'Sky Ray' 2 Y-YYR
(W.G. Pannill) W.G. Pannill, 1983
'Balalaika' × 'Ringmaster'

'Sky Rocket' 2 Y-O
(J.J. Grullemans & Sons) J.J. Grullemans & Sons, 1956

'Sky Scraper' 3 W-? (b)
(Warnaar & Co., pre-1931)

AM(Haarlem) 1930

'Slaney' 3 Y-Y
(Carncairn Daffodils) Carncairn Daffodils, 1988
'Aircastle' hybrid
Fl. 97 mm wide; perianth segments soft yellow; corona slightly deeper in tone than the perianth, with some green showing in the tube. Mid-season

'Sleeping Beauty' 2 W-P
(D.S. Bell) D.S. Bell, 1957
Corona bright pink

'Sleepy Lagoon' 2 W-OOY
(D.S. Bell) D.S. Bell, 1957
'Artist's Model' × 'Technicolour'
Perianth segments pure white, smooth; corona disc-shaped, deep reddish orange, with gold at rim

'Sleigh Bells' 2 Y-W
(C.M. Grullemans) J.J. Grullemans & Sons, 1959

'Slemish' 2 W-W
(G.L. Wilson, pre-1930)
'Findhorn' × 'Beersheba'
Fl. forming a double triangle; perianth segments broadly ovate, blunt, very slightly mucronate, opening greenish white, becoming pure white, spreading, plane, overlapping half; the inner segments narrower, twisted or with margins strongly wavy; corona cylindrical, smooth, ivory white, with mouth expanded, rim rolled and broadly crenate. AM(e) 1935, AM(Haarlem) 1938, FCC(e) 1939. Div. 1 until 1938

'Slender'
(K.J. Heazlewood, c.1967) Unregistered
'Barrington Gold' × 'Vigi'

'Sleveen' 2 W-W
(G.L. Wilson) G.L. Wilson, 1960
'Guardian' × 'Greenland'
Fl. 102 mm wide, creamy white; perianth segments overlapping; corona with mouth lobed, expanded and slightly frilled, rim dentate and very slightly reflexed

'Slieve Bernagh' 1 Y-Y
(Slieve Donard Nursery Co., pre-1930)
'Magnificence' hybrid
AM(e) 1930

'Slieveboy' 1 Y-Y
(G.L. Wilson, pre-1953)
'Royalist' × 'Gold Digger'
Fl. 102 mm wide; perianth segments very broadly ovate, slightly mucronate, vivid yellow 12A, smooth, overlapping half; the inner segments more narrowly ovate, a little twisted; corona straight-sided, rich deep golden yellow, with mouth ribbed and expanded, rim reflexed and regularly dentate. *AM(g) 1970

'Slieve Donard' 1 Y-Y
(G.H. Engleheart, pre-1927)
Fl. large, deep golden yellow. Tall

'Slievenamon' 1 Y-Y
(J.L. Richardson, pre-1927)
Early

'Slieverue' 1 W-W
(J.L. Richardson, pre-1938)
'White Emperor' × 'Beersheba'
Corona somewhat narrow, with rim rolled

'Sligachan' 1 W-W
(D.C. MacArthur) D.C. MacArthur, 1985
'Ludlow' × ('Braniel' × 'Preamble'); sdlg no. E831
Fl. small; perianth segments broadly ovate, blunt, slightly mucronate, spreading, plane, overlapping one-third; the inner segments a little narrower, slightly inflexed, sometimes twisted; corona large cup-shaped, with mouth straight and a little frilled. Early

'Sligo' 2 Y-Y
(J.L. Richardson, pre-1943)
'Royalist' × 'Crocus'
2n=28. Closely resembles a much later-flowered 'Galway'

'Slimkow' 1 W-W
(C.O. Fairbairn)

'Slim Whitman' 2 W-OOY
(D.P. de Graaf, 1978) D.P. de Graaf, 1988
'Ice Follies' sport
Perianth segments ivory white; corona nasturtium orange, with sulphur yellow at rim

'Slipstream' 6 Y-Y
(Brian S.Duncan) Brian S.Duncan, 1997
N. cyclamineus × 'King's Ransom'; sdlg no. 1610
Fl. 73 mm wide, deep golden yellow; perianth segments ovate, reflexed; corona cylindrical, with mouth flared and frilled. Dwarf. Very early to early

'Slocum' 2 W-? (b)
(A.H. Ahrens) J.S. Leitch, 1956

'Sloeblossom' 2 W-W
(Sir F.C. Stern, pre-1953)
Perianth segments snow white; corona creamy white. Mid-season

'Slowcoach' 3 W-GYO
(Brian S. Duncan) Rathowen Daffodils, 1979
'Arbar' × 'Don Carlos'; sdlg no. 15
Fl. 102 mm wide; corona bowl-shaped, deep orange, with a band of yellow near base shading to green at base. Mid-season

'Sly Fox' 2 W-O
(J.N.Hancock & Co., 1983) Unregistered
Sdlg 77/77H × sdlg 2Y-O; sdlg no. 51/83H
Fl. rounded; perianth segments creamy white; corona cylindrical, short, brilliant orange. Tall. Early

'Sly Puss'
(Alister Clark, pre-1948)

'Small Fry' 1 Y-Y
(Rosewarne EHS, 1969) Geest Horticultural Group, 1981
'M.J.Berkeley' × *N. asturiensis*; sdlg no. 64/19/1
Fl. 60 mm wide; perianth segments dark bright yellow; corona deeper in tone. Very early

'Small Talk' 1 Y-Y
(G.E. Mitsch) G.E. Mitsch, 1965
Fl. 45 mm wide, golden yellow. Early. Resembles a deeper-coloured 'Wee Bee' with narrower perianth segments

'Smaragd' 2 W-? (b)
(G.A. Uit den Boogaard, pre-1937)

'Smarple' 10 W-W
(Glenbrook Bulb Farm, 1985) Glenbrook Bulb Farm, 1997
N. bulbocodium var. *conspicuus* × *N. cantabricus* var. *foliosus*
Fl. 40 mm wide; perianth segments very narrow, acute, yellowish white 158C, slightly twisted; corona slightly darker in tone, with mouth widely flanged. Dwarf. Very early

'Smasher' 1 Y-W
(Mrs C.O. Fairbairn)

'Smash Hit' 4 Y-Y
(M.E.Brogden, pre-1997) Unregistered
('Papua' × 'Camelot') open pollinated; sdlg no. 141/2

'Smeroe' 2 Y-OOW
(de Graaff-Gerharda, pre-1924)
Fl. facing slightly downwards; perianth segments clear sulphur yellow, overlapping; corona expanded, suffused bright rich orange, with a narrow band of white at rim. Mid-season. AM(Haarlem) 1924, FCC(Haarlem) 1925, *AM(g) 1936

'Smiler' 1 W-? (b)
(G. Lubbe & Son, pre-1937)
AM(Haarlem) 1937

'Smiles' 2 W-WWP
(G.E. Mitsch) G.E. Mitsch, 1962
'Green Island' × 'Glenshane'; sdlg no. N50/3
Fl. rounded, 102 mm wide; perianth segments very broadly ovate, spreading, with margins incurling at apex, overlapping half; the inner segments slightly inflexed, shouldered at base, with margins wavy; corona short funnel-shaped, broad, ribbed at base, smoother towards mouth, opening pale lemon, becoming almost white, with coral pink at rim, mouth straight, with six overlapping lobes, frilled. Mid-season. Resembles 'Caro Nome' in form but with a distinctive corona

'Smiling Maestro' 2 Y-R
(G.E. Mitsch) G.E. Mitsch, 1964
'Paricutin' × 'Armada'; sdlg no. R106/3
Fl. 127 mm wide; perianth segments rich yellow; corona shallow, widely expanded. Mid-season. Resembles a smaller and later-flowered 'Paricutin'

'Smiling Mary' 3 W-? (b)
(J.W.A. Lefeber, pre-1938)

'Smiling Morn' 2 W-P
(G.L. Wilson, 1950) L. Major, 1965
Corona deep pink. Late

'Smiling Princess' 1 (a)
(J. Jonkheer, pre-1944)

'Smiling Queen' 2 W-YOO
(J.W.A. Lefeber, pre-1949)

'Smokering' 2 W-WWY
(D.S. Bell) D.S. Bell, 1965
'Papanui Queen' × 'Green Island'
Fl. 105 mm wide; corona shallow, with golden yellow at rim, frilled, with rim crenate. Resembles 'Green Island' but with the corona more widely expanded

'Smokey Bear' 4 Y-O
(Brian S. Duncan) Rathowen Daffodils, 1978
'Papua' × 'Vagabond'; sdlg no. 274
Perianth segments broadly ovate, blunt, fairly prominently mucronate, orange-yellow, spreading, plane, overlapping half; a number of orange-yellow petaloid segments at centre half as long as the perianth segments, irregularly arranged, inflexed, with margins tightly incurled; corona segments broad, crumpled and clustered at centre, wavy and more loosely arranged between the surrounding whorls of petaloid segments, orange. Mid-season

'Smooth Gold' 2 (a)
(Mrs A.O. Meyrick, pre-1949)

'Smooth Sails' 3 W-W
(R. & E.Havens, 1982) R. & E.Havens, 1994
'Silken Sails' × 'Verona'; sdlg no. REH45/2
Fl. 100 mm wide; perianth segments broadly ovate; corona bowl-shaped, opening creamy white and becoming white, with mouth frilled. Late

'Smuggler' 2 W-O
(J.N.Hancock & Co., 1983) Unregistered

'Tangaloa' × 'Orange Monarch'; sdlg no. 105/83H
Perianth segments creamy white; corona large disc-shaped, orange, very heavily frilled. Mid-season

'Smyrna' 9 W-GOO
(The Brodie of Brodie, c.1926)
'James Hogg' × 'Ace of Diamonds'
Fl. rounded; perianth segments very broad, pure white, of good substance, deeply overlapping; corona proportionately large, bright reddish orange, paling towards base, with base moss green. Earlier-flowered than most Poeticus daffodils. AM(e) 1933

'Snaefell' 2 W-W
(D.N.Y. Olson) D.N.Y. Olson, 1979
Fl. 108 mm wide; corona opening pale pinkish buff, becoming white. Mid-season. Resembles 'Hawea' but with a narrower and more cylindrical corona

'Snapdragon' 2 (a)
(E.B. Champernowne, pre-1947)

'Snaphammer' 3 W-? (b)
(G.H. Engleheart, pre-1923)

'Snapshot' 2 W-O
(P. Phillips) P. Phillips, 1968

'Sneeuwprinses' 3 W-YYO
(J.W.A. Lefeber, pre-1944)
2n=27. Syn. 'Snow Princess'

'Sneezy' 1 Y-Y
(A. Gray) A. Gray, 1956
N. asturiensis × *N. obvallaris*

'Snigo' 2 Y-R
(C.E. Radcliff, 1938)
'Rata' × 'Lillian Murdoch'

'Snipe' 6 W-W
(A.M. Wilson, pre-1948)
'W.P.Milner' × *N. cyclamineus*
Perianth segments narrowly ovate, acute, opening pale yellow, soon becoming white, reflexed, with margins inward-rolling, separated; corona cylindrical, lightly ribbed, opening brilliant yellow 8A, becoming yellowish white, with mouth expanded, rim notched and crenate. AM(p) 1953, AM(Haarlem) 1959

'Snocat' 1 W-W
(D.W. Gourlay) D.W. Gourlay, 1959
'Knockdolian' hybrid; sdlg no. 422
Fl. pure white; perianth segments spreading; corona with golden yellow in tube. Early

'Snook' 6 Y-Y
(Glenbrook Bulb Farm, 1987) Glenbrook Bulb Farm, 1997

N. nevadensis × *N. cyclamineus*
Fl. 47 mm wide; perianth segments narrowly ovate, brilliant yellow 13C, with slight white mucro, strongly reflexed, overlapping at base only; corona cylindrical at base, flared in upper third, smooth or somewhat angled, very slightly darker in tone than the perianth, lightly frilled, with rim dentate. Dwarf. Early

'Snoopie' 6 W-GPP
(Brian S. Duncan) Rathowen Daffodils, 1979
'Lilac Charm' × ('Interim' × 'Aosta'); sdlg no. 266
Fl. 85 mm wide; perianth segments very broadly ovate, truncate, reflexed, overlapping half; the inner segments more narrowly ovate, blunt, with margins a little wavy; corona deep bowl-shaped, ribbed, bright rose pink, with green at base, mouth expanded, with rim minutely crenate. Mid-season. 2n=28

'Snouter'
Unregistered
Seed parent of 'Conrad Weiser'

'Snowball' 4 W-W
(W. Welchman, pre-1907)

'Snowball' 4 W-W
(G.A. Uit den Boogaard, pre-1937)
Perianth segments broadly ovate in outline, blunt or truncate at apex, fairly prominently mucronate, pure white, spreading or a little inflexed, concave or with margins incurling, overlapping half; the inner segments with margins wavy and sometimes nicked; corona segments one-third as long as the perianth segments, opening pure white, becoming ivory white, inflexed and closely overlapping at first, more spreading later, and more loosely arranged. Scented. AM(Haarlem) 1938, FCC(Haarlem) 1944. Received AM(Haarlem) and FCC(Haarlem) 1938 and 1944 as 'Shirley Temple'

'Snowbank' 1 W-W
(W.J. Eldering & Son, pre-1928)
AM(Haarlem) 1937

'Snowbell' 5 W-GWW
(G.H. Johnstone, pre-1944)

'Snow Bird' 2 W-W
(Miss M. Verry) Miss M. Verry, 1974
'Vigil' × 'Empress of Ireland'
Fl. 104 mm wide

'Snow Bird' 5
Syn. of 'Snowbird'

'Snowbird' 5
(P.D. Williams, pre-1908)
Fls 2 per stem; perianth segments acute, slightly reflexed; corona cup-shaped. See also 'Snow Bird'

'Snowbird' 5 W-W
(Mrs R.O. Backhouse, pre-1921)

'Snowbird' 4 W-W
(Dutch origin, pre-1995) Unregistered
'Ice Follies' sport

'Snow Born' 1 W-W
(J.N.Hancock & Co., 1982) Unregistered
'Limeade' × 'Jean Ladson'; sdlg no. 88/82H
Fl. creamy white; perianth segments overlapping; corona cylindrical, with mouth expanded and rim rolled. Mid-season to late

'Snowbound' 1 W-W
(J.N. Hancock & Co.) , 1962
Fl. opening cream, quickly becoming pure glistening white; perianth segments acute

'Snowbound' 1 W-W
(P. Phillips) P. Phillips, 1968

'Snowboy' 4
(pre-1950)

'Snow Bunting' 7 W-Y
(P.D. Williams, pre-1935)
Perianth segments opening yellow, becoming white. 2n=21

'Snowcan' 1 W-W
(D.H.L. Corrigan, pre-1949)

'Snowcap' 2 W-W
(T.H. Piper, 1952)
'Astrid' × 'Pink o' Dawn'

'Snowcem' 1 W-W
(G.H. Johnstone) G.H. Johnstone, 1959
Fl. 102 mm wide. Early. Resembles a smaller-flowered 'Jennifer Ruth'

'Snowcliffe'
(New Zealand origin, pre-1940)

'Snow Cloud' 3 (b)
(F.H. Chapman, pre-1913)

'Snowcloud' 1 W-W
(G.W.E. Brogden) G.W.E. Brogden, 1968

'Snowcraft' 1 W-W
(S.A. Free) S.A. Free, 1961
Fl. 102 mm wide. Mid-season

'Snow Crest' 2 W-W
(Barr & Sons, pre-1908)
$N. \times poculiformis \times N. poeticus$
Corona closely ribbed, heavily ruffled

'Snowcrest' 3 W-GWW
(Mrs H.K. Richardson) Mrs H.K. Richardson, 1972
'Verona' open pollinated
Corona white, with emerald green at base and faint lemon at rim, frilled. 2n=28

'Snow Crown' 1 W-W
(The Brodie of Brodie, pre-1928)
'White Emperor' × 'Beersheba'

'Snow Crystal' 2 W-W
(G.H. Johnstone, pre-1949)

'Snowdean' 2 W-W
(E.N. Amoore, 1950) P. & G. Phillips, 1975
Fl. 110 mm wide; corona opening primrose, becoming white. Early to mid-season. 2n=28. Resembles 'Carnlough' but with a whiter corona often irregularly split and overlapping at mouth

'Snowdon' 5 W-?
(Mrs R.O. Backhouse, pre-1921)

'Snowdon' 5
(H. Prins, pre-1929)

'Snow Dream' 2 W-W
(W.J. Dunlop, pre-1953)
'Niphetos' × 'Truth'
Perianth segments roundish, pure white, smooth, of thick substance; corona opening cream, soon becoming white, with rim rolled. Early

'Snowdrift' 2 W-W
(G.H. Engleheart, pre-1907)
Fl. pure white

'Snowdrift' 5
(pre-1925)
AM(Haarlem) 1925

'Snowdrift' 1 Y-GYY
Syn. of 'Marieke'

'Snowdrift' 2 W-W
Syn. of 'Bald Eagle'

'Snowdrop' 5 W-W
(G.H. Engleheart, pre-1893)
$N. triandrus$ subsp. $pallidulus \times N. triandrus$
Fls sometimes 2 per stem, clear white; perianth spreading; corona cylindrical. Resembles a white and somewhat larger 'Mrs George Cammell'. FCC 1897

'Snow Eagle' 2 W-W
(J.N. Hancock & Co., 1961) Unregistered

'Snow Elf' 1 W-W
(de Graaff Bros, pre-1907)

'Snowfall' 2 W-W
(G.L. Wilson, pre-1950)
Fl. ice white

'Snowfield' 1 W-W
(G.H. Engleheart, pre-1923)

'Snowfire' 4 W-R
(Mrs H.K. Richardson) Carncairn Daffodils, 1976
'Falaise' × 'Rockall'; sdlg no. 206
Fl. 90 mm wide; perianth and other petaloid segments greenish white (155A); corona segments red (40A). Mid-season. Scented. Resembles a taller 'Acropolis' with fewer whorls of segments

'Snowflake' 1 W-W
(de Graaff Bros, pre-1888)
Corona tinged apricot yellow on opening, becoming pure white

'Snowflake' 8
(French origin, pre-1927)

'Snowflake' 5 W-W
(pre-1933)
Fls 1-3 per stem, pure white

'Snowflake' 8 W-W
Syn. of 'Paper White Grandiflorus'

'Snow Flurry' 2 W-W
(Mrs F.S. Foote, pre-1941)

'Snow Frills' 2 YYW-W
(G.E. Mitsch) G.E. Mitsch, 1977
'Rushlight' × 'Daydream'; sdlg no. F84/1
Fl. 90 mm wide; perianth segments broadly ovate, blunt, soft lemon yellow, with slight white mucro and a band of white at base, reflexed, overlapping half; the inner segments square-shouldered at base, somewhat creased, with margins wavy; corona funnel-shaped, opening lemon yellow, becoming almost white, with mouth straight, heavily frilled. Mid-season. Resembles a less rounded 'Daydream' with a narrower and whiter corona

'Snow Frolic' 1 W-W
(Miss M. Verry) Miss M. Verry, 1975
'Vigil' × 'Empress of Ireland'; sdlg no. 1C/17
Fl. 118 mm wide; corona narrow at base, tinged green

'Snow Gem' 3 W-O
(C.W. Culpepper, pre-1957)
'Firetail' × 'Franciscus Drake'
Corona reddish orange. 2n=28

'Snow Gleam' 1 W-GWW
(Brian S. Duncan) Rathowen Daffodils, 1977
'Joybell' × 'Empress of Ireland'; sdlg no. 95
Perianth segments broadly ovate, pure white; corona constricted near mid-point, pure white, with green at base, rim flanged. Mid-season. 2n=28

'Snow Glory' 1 W-W
(R.H. Bath, pre-1927)

'Snow Glow' 2 W-W
(J.N. Hancock & Co.) J.N. Hancock & Co., 1955
Perianth segments pure white; corona opening creamy white, soon becoming pure white, frilled

'Snow Goose' 1 W-W
(J.L. Richardson, pre-1952)
'Spitzbergen' × 'Truth'
Fl. snow white; perianth segments of thick substance; corona frilled, with rim dentate

'Snow King' 1 W-W
(pre-1892)
Fl. snow white. Early

'Snow King' 9 W-YYR
(E.M. Crosfield, pre-1909)
Fl. large; perianth segments broad, squarish at apex, slightly mucronate, spreading, somewhat creased, of great substance, overlapping one-third to a half; the inner segments narrower and ovate, a little inflexed, with margins wavy or sometimes recurved at base; corona small disc-shaped, vivid yellow, with a narrow band of red at rim. Tall. Syn. 'Christina Rosetti'. AM(Haarlem) 1927

'Snow Leopard' 2 W-W
(G.L. Wilson) E. Longford, 1967
Sdlg 45/56 ('Courage' × 'Empress of Ireland') × 'Glendermott'
Fl. 108 mm wide

'Snow Light' 1 W-W
(J.A. O'More) P.D.K. Ramsay, 1980
'Ardbane' × 'Petsamo'; sdlg no. 10/70
Fl. 100 mm wide. Mid-season

'Snow Lily' 5 W-W
(Barr & Sons, pre-1923)
Fl. rounded, snowy white; perianth segments overlapping; corona ribbed

'Snowline' 2 W-W
(G.L. Wilson, pre-1953)
'Niphetos' × 'Zero'
Fl. 127 mm wide, opening pale lemon, soon becoming white; perianth segments broad, smooth, overlapping. AM(e) 1953

'Snow Magic' 3 W-W
(Carncairn Daffodils) Carncairn Daffodils, 1973
'Chinese White' × 'Easter Moon'
Fl. 91 mm wide; perianth segments broadly ovate,

snow white; corona small, with olive green at base, frilled. Late

'Snow Maid'
Unregistered
Pollen parent of 'Coonamble'

'Snow Maiden' 5
(Barr & Sons, pre-1923)

'Snow Maiden' 2 W-W
(G.L. Wilson) E.G. Hayes, 1958
Fl. 93 mm wide; corona widely expanded, creamy white, frilled

'Snowman' 1 W-W
(J. Bankhead, pre-1950)

'Snowmantle' 2 W-W
(G.L. Wilson, pre-1940)
('Eskimo' × 'Tenedos') × 'Slemish'

'Snow Nymph' 5
(Barr & Sons, pre-1923)
'Albatross' × *N. triandrus* var. *loiseleurii*

'Snow Peak' 2 W-W
(R.J. McIlraith) R.J. McIlraith, 1982
'Cantru' × 'First Frost'; sdlg no. 71/4
Fl. 108 mm wide; perianth segments white; corona white or creamy white, frilled. Early to mid-season

'Snow Pearl' 8 W-W
(E. Zinkowski) E. Zinkowski, 1981
'Paper White' sport
Fls about 11 per stem, 25 mm wide. Early to mid-season. Resembles a smaller-flowered 'Paper White'

'Snow Pink' 2 W-P
(Murray W. Evans) Murray W. Evans, 1972
('Shirley Wyness' × 'Interim') hybrid
Fl. 88 mm wide

'Snow Princess' 2 W-W
(J.N. Hancock & Co., pre-1949)
Fl. pure white; corona flushed pink at base. 2n=27

'Snow Princess' 3 W-? (b)
Syn. of 'Sneeuwprinses'

'Snow Queen' 1 W-W
(pre-1908)
AM(Haarlem) 1908

'Snow Queen' 5
(E.M. Crosfield, pre-1908)

'Snow Queen' 2 W-W
(R.A. van der Schoot, pre-1931)
Perianth segments overlapping; corona expanded, opening with pale buff yellow at rim, soon becoming self creamy white. Mid-season. 2n=28. *C(g) 1936, *AM(g) 1939, *FCC(g) 1947. Div. 3 until 1936

'Snow Queen' 3 W-?
Syn. of 'Winter Queen'

'Snow Ring' 9
(pre-1913)

'Snowscape' 1 W-W
(G.H. Engleheart, pre-1923)
Fl. 89 mm wide, facing slightly downwards; perianth segments creamy white, inflexed, overlapping half; corona narrow at base, opening pale cream, becoming creamy white, mouth expanded, with rim dentate and widely flanged. Mid-season to late

'Snowsheen' 1 W-? (b)
(M.E. Brogden) M.E. Brogden, 1956

'Snowshill' 2 W-W
(J.M. de Navarro, pre-1949)
'May Molony' × 'Chinese White'
Fl. 95 mm wide; perianth segments very broadly ovate, blunt, slightly mucronate, spreading, plane, with margins sometimes incurling at apex; the inner segments more narrowly ovate, shouldered at base; corona ribbed, with a touch of deep green at base, mouth expanded, regularly and loosely frilled. 2n=28. AM(e) 1957, AM(e) 1963, *AM(g) 1988

'Snow Shoe' 9 W-GYR
(G.H. Engleheart, pre-1908)
Perianth segments reflexed, with margins wavy; corona bright canary yellow, with crimson at rim. AM 1908. See also 'Snowshoe'

'Snowshoe' 9 W-GYR
Syn. of 'Snow Shoe'

'Snowsong' 3 W-W
(E.W. Cotter) E.W. Cotter, 1968
Div. 3 white sdlg × 'Bryher'
Fl. pure white; corona with sage green at base

'Snow Sprite' 4 W-Y
(Barr & Sons, pre-1913)
Fl. rounded, 76 mm wide; perianth and other petaloid segments white; the outer whorl very broad in outline, rounded and sometimes truncate at apex, slightly mucronate, snow white, spreading, with margins a little wavy, overlapping half; the inner segments somewhat inflexed; segments at centre shorter, inflexed; corona segments very short, interspersed among the centre petaloid segments, pale primrose yellow. Late. Scented. AM(Haarlem) 1926. See also 'Snowsprite'

'Snowsprite' 4 W-Y
Syn. of 'Snow Sprite'

'Snow Star' 2 W-W
(Mrs P.M. Davis, pre-1948)

'Snowstorm' 1 W-W
(H. Backhouse, pre-1910)

'Snow Storm' 7 W-W
(G.E. Morrill) G.E. Morrill, 1977
'Bithynia' × *N. jonquilla*; sdlg no. 66-5-1
Fls 1-2 per stem, 64 mm wide; perianth segments greenish white (155A), somewhat reflexed; corona yellowish white 155B. Scented

'Snowvale' 3 W-W
(K.J. Heazlewood, c.1967) Unregistered
'Vigilant' × 'Whitefoord'

'Snow Valley' 2 W-W
(J.N. Hancock & Co., pre-1962) Unregistered
Fl. pure white; perianth segments deeply overlapping; corona with rim rolled

'Snow-white' 1 W-W
(L. van Leeuwen & Son, pre-1928)

'Snow-White' 3 W-W
(?H. Fell, pre-1948)
Perianth segments pure white; corona widely expanded, opening buffy apricot yellow

'Snow White' 1 W-W
(C.O. Fairbairn) C.O. Fairbairn, 1960

'Snowy' 2 W-W
(C.E. Radcliff, 1946) J.M.Radcliff, 1956
'Slemish' × 'Nautilus'

'Snowy Egret' 2 W-W
(C.R. Runyan, pre-1952)

'Snowy Morn' 1 W-GWW
(W. & J. Munro) W. & J. Munro, 1985
'White Prince' × 'Passionale'; sdlg no. 73/11/7
Fl. forming a double triangle, 115 mm wide, of strong substance; perianth segments broadly ovate, blunt, slightly mucronate, spreading, smooth, overlapping half; the inner segments narrower; corona funnel-shaped, with green at base, rim slightly rolled. Mid-season. PC(e)(NZ) 1984, FCC(e)(NZ) 1992

'Snowy River' 2 W-GWW
(A.W. Chappell) A.W. Chappell, 1990
'Egmont Snow' open pollinated; sdlg no. D-2-2
Fl. 110 mm wide; perianth segments roundish; corona with mouth slightly flared. Tall. Mid-season

'Snug' 1 W-W

(A. Gray) A. Gray, 1957
N. alpestris sdlg
Perianth segments white; corona cream

'Soar' 2 Y-Y
(Mrs G. Link) Mrs G. Link, 1973

'Sobar' 3 W-R
(R.H.Glover, pre-1990) Unregistered
'Yin Nell' × 'Rockall'

'Sobersides' 1 Y-Y
(Jackson's Daffodils, 1983) Jackson's Daffodils, 1993
'Warcom' × sdlg 3/74; sdlg no. 5/83
Fl. forming a double triangle, 107 mm wide, vivid yellow 9A; perianth segments very broadly ovate, blunt, slightly inflexed, smooth and of thick substance, overlapping half or more; the inner segments square-shouldered at base and almost touching one another; corona cylindrical, smooth, with mouth flared and more or less even, rim minutely crenate. Early to mid-season

'Sobig' 2 Y-O
(P. & G. Phillips) P. & G. Phillips, 1975
Fl. 114 mm wide; perianth segments broad, rounded at apex; corona large, bowl-shaped, deep reddish orange. Mid-season. Resembles a larger and smoother 'Court Martial' of thicker substance

'Sobriety' 2 W-Y
(J.N. Hancock & Co., c.1975) Unregistered

'Socialite' 3 W-YYR
(W.G. Pannill) W.G. Pannill, 1983
'Merlin' × 'Hotspur'

'Society' 1 Y-Y
(P. Phillips) P. Phillips, 1968

'Society Belle' 2 W-GYP
(Brian S. Duncan) Rathowen Daffodils, 1987
'High Society' × 'Fragrant Rose'; sdlg no. 985
Fl. rounded; perianth segments very broadly ovate, blunt, slightly mucronate, square-shouldered at base, pure white, spreading, with margins sometimes incurling at apex, smooth, overlapping half; the inner segmemnts very little narrower, a little inflexed; corona short funnel-shaped, lightly ribbed, yellow, sometimes fading to white, with green at base sometimes fading to yellow, with a broad band of deep pink at rim, mouth widely expanded, more closely ribbed, a little frilled, rim minutely crenate. Mid-season to late. Resembles a more deeply coloured 'High Society'

'Sockeye' 2 W-WWP
(Colin Crotty) Unregistered
Sdlg no. 33-75

'Socotra' 2 Y-GYO
(D.N.Y. Olson) D.N.Y. Olson, 1988
'Rupee' × 'Kazan'; sdlg no. 319/1
Fl. 95 mm wide; perianth segments broad, mucronate, light to medium yellow, inflexed; corona cylindrical, incurved at base, medium yellow, shading to deep reddish orange at rim, lightly frilled. Very early. Sunproof. Resembles a neater 'Rupee'

'Socrates' 9 W-YYR
(G.H. Engleheart, pre-1890)
Fl. 61 mm wide; perianth segments pure white, overlapping two-thirds; corona almost disc-shaped, lemon, with a broad band of deep scarlet at rim, with the rim dentate. Mid-season to late. AM 1911

'Socrates' 1 Y-Y
Syn. of 'Herman Gorter'

'Sodium' 9 W-?
(F.H. Chapman)
'Acme' × *N. poeticus*

'Soestdijk' 2 W-YOW
(J.W.A. Lefeber) J.W.A. Lefeber, 1975
Fl. 100 mm wide; perianth segments ivory white; corona brilliant orange 25C, with base yellow and rim whitish

'So Fair' 2 W-P
(J.N. Hancock & Co., 1963) Unregistered

'Sofina' 8
(pre-1939)

'Soft Breeze' 2 (a)
(Mrs Ben Robertson, pre-1950)

'Soft Light' 2 Y-P
(W.G. Pannill) W.G. Pannill, 1970
'Fawnglo' × 'Fintona'

'Softly' 2 W-P
(J.N.Hancock & Co., 1969) Unregistered
'First Frost' hybrid; sdlg no. 80/69H
Perianth segments broadly ovate, milk white; corona long cup-shaped, becoming soft peach pink, with mouth lightly flared. Early

'Soft Moonlight' 1 W-? (b)
(W.M. & A.P. Spry) , 1956

'Soft Rain' 2 YYW-Y
(Sidney DuBose, 1981) Sidney DuBose, 1996
'Limeade' × 'Camelot'; sdlg no. G49-2
Fl. 100mm wide; perianth segments opening self yellow, becoming white at base. Late

'Soft Touch' 6 Y-O
(G.E. Mitsch, 1965) J. & E. Frey, 1982

(['Market Merry' × 'Carbineer'] × 'Armada') × *N. cyclamineus*; sdlg no. A52/7
Fl. 80 mm wide; corona light orange

'Soho' 11a Y-Y
(?Dutch origin, pre-1995) Unregistered
Perianth segments broadly ovate, rounded at apex, creamy yellow, with whitish mucro, spreading, overlapping half; the inner segments more narrowly ovate, blunt, a little inflexed; corona split to base, the six segments three-quarters the length of the perianth segments, opposite and closely overlying them, deep golden yellow, heavily frilled. Late

'Soirée' 2 W-? (b)
(Konynenburg & Mark, pre-1953)

'Soirée' 2 W-Y
(G.L. Wilson) Konynenburg & Mark, 1961
Fl. 110 mm wide; perianth segments ivory white; corona darker in tone than brilliant yellow 10B. Mid-season

'Sol' 1 Y-Y
(G.H. Engleheart, pre-1894)
Sdlg no. 4
Perianth segments soft pale yellow; corona deep rich yellow

'Sol' 1 Y-Y
(W. Jackson Jr, 1968) Unregistered
'Jobi' × 'Farmington'; sdlg no. 21/68

'Solace' 2 (a)
(A.H. Ahrens) J.S. Leitch, 1955

'Solange' 2 W-R
(W. Jackson Sr, 1937)
'Rubra' × 'Blodwen'

'Solange' 2 W-? (b)
(C.G. van Tubergen, pre-1946)

'Solar Flare' 2 Y-YYO
(J.A. Hunter) J.A. Hunter, 1973
'Carbineer' hybrid
Fl. 103 mm wide

'Solar Flare' 3 Y-R
'Carbineer' hybrid
Syn. of 'Solar Tan'

'Solar Glow' 2 W-P
(R.C. Gordon) R.C. Gordon, 1964
Mid-season. Resembles 'Kenmare' but with perianth of purer white and corona of richer pink

'Solario' 2 W-Y
(J.L. Richardson, pre-1927)
Perianth segments of thick substance; corona deep

yellow, with rim widely rolled. 2n=28

N. solaris Spach = *N. cupularis*

'Solar Mist' 2 Y-R
(D.S. Bell) D.S. Bell, 1957
'Monica' × 'Diamond King'
Perianth segments deep yellow

'Solar Star' 3 W-? (b)
(A.M. Wilson, pre-1937)
'Folly' hybrid; sdlg no. 224

'Solar Tan' 3 Y-R
(Brian S. Duncan) Rathowen Daffodils, 1984
'Ulster Bank' × 'Achduart'; sdlg no. 656
Fl. forming a double triangle; perianth segments broadly ovate in outline, blunt or sometimes truncate, deep golden yellow, with very slight white mucro, spreading, concave, smooth, sometimes creased at midrib, overlapping half; the inner segments more narrowly ovate; corona bowl-shaped, ribbed, deep orange-red, mouth straight, with six shallow lobes each obscurely bi-lobed. Mid-season. Syn. 'Solar Flare'

'Solar Wind' 4 W-Y
(J.A.Hunter) J.A.Hunter, 1995
'Blossom' × 'Virma'; sdlg no. 13/81A
Fl. rounded, 95 mm wide; perianth and other petaloid segments white, touched greenish yellow at base; the outer whorl ten in number, broadly ovate, regularly arranged, overlapping half; the inner whorls irregularly arranged within the corona, with margins deeply incurved; corona half as long as the petaloid segments, light greenish yellow 8B, deeply split and overlapping, frilled; numerous corona segments interspersed among the petaloid segments within the corona, tightly frilled. Early to mid-season

'Sol City' 8 Y-Y
(G.J. Phillips, 1976) G.J. Phillips, 1987
'Soleil d'Or' × 'Malvern City'; sdlg no. 72-6-1
Fls one or sometimes 2-3 per stem; perianth segments yellow; corona deep golden yellow, almost orange. Mid-season

'Soldier' 2 Y-? (a)
(The Brodie of Brodie, *c.*1929)
'Knipp' × 'Fortune'

'Soldier Brave' 2 Y-R
(M.J. Jefferson-Brown) M.J. Jefferson-Brown, 1985
Perianth segments broad, blunt, mucronate, deep golden yellow, deeply overlapping; the inner segments slightly narrower, acute; corona short funnel-shaped, opening orange, becoming red, with mouth flared, rim regularly and deeply notched, flanged. Very late. Sunproof

'Soledad' 2 W-W
(Mrs H.K. Richardson) Carncairn Daffodils, 1978
'Verona' × 'Stainless'; sdlg no. 127
Fl. 97 mm wide, greenish white (155A). Mid-season. Resembles a larger and stronger 'Stainless' with more rounded perianth

'Soleil Brillant' 4
(pre-1768)
Perianth and other petaloid segments in many whorls

'Soleil Brillant' 8 Y-O
Syn. of 'Soleil Brilliant'

'Soleil Brilliant' 8 Y-O
(Dutch origin, pre-1913)
Perianth segments dark golden yellow. Syn. 'Soleil Brillant', ?'Soleil d'Brilliant'. AM(Haarlem) 1913

'Soleil d'Brilliant'
?Syn. of 'Soleil Brilliant'

'Soleil d'Or' 8 Y-Y or O
(pre-1731)
Possibly derived from *N. bertolonii*
Perianth segments yellow; corona rich golden yellow or orange. 2n=20,30. Resembles a smaller-flowered 'Grand Soleil d'Or' with a less vividly coloured corona. Syn. "Narcissus of the Sun", 'Golden Sun', 'Le Soleil d'Or'

'Soleil Levant' 8 W-?
(pre-1807)

'Sole Mio' 1 Y-Y
(D. Zandbergen, pre-1930)
AM(Haarlem) 1930

'Sole Ponente' 1 Y-Y
(Konynenburg & Mark) Konynenburg & Mark, 1960
'Rembrandt' hybrid
Fl. 110 mm wide; perianth segments vivid yellow 9A; corona darker in tone (13B). Early

'Solesmes' 9
(A.M. Wilson, pre-1931)

'Solfatare' 2 (a)
(G.H. Engleheart, pre-1907)

'Solferino' 1 Y-Y
(C.G. van Tubergen, pre-1930)
Fl. pale sulphur yellow; perianth segments overlapping; corona large, with a slightly darker tone at rim, mouth flared, with rim crenate. Mid-season. 2n=29. AM(Haarlem) 1920, *AM(g) 1936

'Solferique' 2 W-P
(Brian S. Duncan) Rathowen Daffodils, 1988

'Violetta' open pollinated; sdlg no. 682
Perianth segments very broadly ovate in outline, blunt or rounded at apex, some prominently mucronate, pure white, spreading, shallowly concave, of good substance, overlapping half; the inner segments a little inflexed; corona funnel-shaped, narrow at base, smooth, deep copper pink, with mouth widely expanded, loosely frilled. Mid-season to late. Resembles an improved 'Fair Prospect'

'Solidarity' 4 W-Y
(D.S. Bell) D.S. Bell, 1984
Resembles 'Ruatapu' but with more corona segments. Mid-season

'Solid Gold' 1 Y-Y
(Slieve Donard Nursery Co., pre-1931)
Fl. clear golden yellow; perianth segments broad, spreading, smooth, overlapping; corona slender, with rim neatly flanged. AM(e)(c) 1931, FCC(e) 1936

'Solidity' 1 (a)
(J. Bankhead, pre-1950)

'Solid Petal'
(pre-1950)

'Solidset'
(pre-1913)

'Solight' 2 W-YOO
(J.N. Hancock & Co., 1947) J.N. Hancock & Co., 1964
Sdlg × 'Pink-a-dell' × 'Rosslare'
Perianth segments broad, pure white, of strong substance, deeply overlapping; corona dark orange, with pale lemon yellow at base. Late

'Solihull' 2 Y-O
(Kate Reade) Carncairn Daffodils, 1997
'Bunclody' × 'Safari'; sdlg no. 5/2/82
Fl. 105 mm wide; perianth segments broadly ovate, blunt, yellow, with paler mucro, spreading, overlapping one-third to a half; the inner segments a little narrower, slightly inflexed; corona cylindrical, short, clear deep orange, with mouth expanded and lightly frilled, rim slightly dentate. Mid-season

'Soliloquy' 1 W-W
(C.R. Wootton) C.R. Wootton, 1956

'Solinus' 2 W-P
(W. Jackson Jr) W. Jackson Jr, 1966
'Illinga' × 'Pink Monarch'; sdlg no. 57/57

'Solita' 4 Y-O
(J.L. Richardson) G. Zandbergen-Terwegen, 1962
'Falaise' hybrid
Fl. 92 mm wide; perianth and other petaloid segments light greenish yellow 4C; corona segments vivid reddish orange 32A

'Solitaire' 2 Y-Y
(A.G. Thompson) A.G. Thompson, 1960
'John Evelyn' × 'Porthilly'
Fl. 76 mm wide; corona rich yellow, heavily frilled. Mid-season

'Solitude' 1 W-GWW
(J.N. Hancock & Co., 1947) J.N. Hancock & Co., 1964
Fl. ice white; corona with a green glow at base. Late. Resembles an improved 'Josephine'

'Solleret' 7 Y-Y
(G.H. Engleheart, pre-1923)
Fl. rich golden yellow; perianth segments overlapping; corona large. Tall. Richly scented. AM(e) 1929

'Solo' 1 Y-Y
(D. Heere, pre-1908)
'Golden Spur' hybrid
AM(Haarlem) 1912

'Solo' 2
(W.F.Leenen, pre-1991) Unregistered

'Sologne' 2 Y-O
(J. Gerritsen & Son, pre-1944)
Corona reddish orange. AM(Haarlem) 1944

'Solomon' 9
(F.H. Chapman, pre-1928)

'Solon' 8 Y-Y
(pre-1798)
Fl. sulphur yellow

'Solon' 2 W-? (b)
(Mrs R.O. Backhouse, pre-1921)

'Soloptic' 2 (a)
(P.D. Williams, pre-1930)

'Solorodo' 2 Y-R
(J.S. Leitch) J.S. Leitch, 1956

'Solo Star' 2 W-Y
(P. de Jager & Sons) P. de Jager & Sons, 1966
'Polindra' × 'Jules Verne'
Fl. 100 mm wide; perianth segments ivory white; corona pale yellow 11D. Early

'Sol Rex' 2 Y-O
(J.N. Hancock & Co.) J.N. Hancock & Co., 1955
Perianth segments yellow; corona clear orange. Early

'Soltar' 6 Y-Y
(A. Gray, 1951) A. Gray, 1961
Fl. 70 mm wide, deep golden yellow. Very early.

Weatherproof. Resembles an earlier-flowered 'Le Beau' of stronger substance

'Solva' 1 (a)
(A.M. Wilson, pre-1950)

'Solveig' 1 W-Y
(Barr & Sons, pre-1932)
Perianth segments creamy white; corona soft creamy lemon yellow

'Solveig's Song' 5 Y-Y
(R.B. Wallis) R.B. Wallis, 1992
N. bulbocodium var. *tenuifolius* × *N. triandrus* subsp. *pallidulus*
Fls usually one per stem, 52 mm wide, usually at right angles to the stem; perianth segments lanceolate, blunt, brilliant greenish yellow 4A, spreading, twisted, with margins wavy, smooth, with midrib showing, regular, separated; corona funnel-shaped, lightly ribbed, darker in tone (5A) than the perianth, with mouth even and slightly incurved, rim almost entire. Dwarf. Mid-season to late. PC 1997. Other plants not answering to this colour description have been circulated under this name

'Solvera' 2 Y-O
(H. Leber) H. Leber, 1973
Fl. 110 mm wide

'Somali' 2 Y-YOO
(J.L. Richardson, pre-1950)
'Rosslare' open pollinated
Perianth segments bright yellow; corona widely expanded, reddish orange, paling to gold at base. Late

'Sombrero' 10 Y-Y
(James S. Wells) James S. Wells, 1993
'Julia Jane' × 'February Gold'; sdlg no. 83-52-2
Fl. 35 mm wide, pale yellow; perianth segments lanceolate, separated; corona very broad funnel-shaped, lightly and narrowly ribbed, mouth more or less even, with rim minutely crenate. Dwarf. Early

'Some Day' 2 Y-R
(G.W.E. Brogden) Brogden Bulbs, 1991
'Orator' × 'Torridon'; sdlg no. x97/2
Fl. 100 mm wide; perianth segments broad, deep yellow tinged with gold, very smooth and of good substance, deeply overlapping; corona deep red, with rim neatly dentate. Early to mid-season

'Somerby' 1 Y-Y
(W.A. Noton) W.A. Noton, 1976
'Arctic Gold' × 'Golden Rapture'; sdlg no. 548
Fl. 110 mm wide. Mid-seaon

'Somers' 2 W-Y
(R. Gibson, pre-1927)

'Somerset' 1 Y-Y
(W.T. Ware, pre-1915)
Fl. 114 mm wide; perianth segments acute, with margins wavy; corona with rim flanged

'Somerset' 1 Y-Y
(C.E. Radcliff, 1937)
Sdlg × 'Gambrinus'

'Somerset' 3 W-? (b)
(A.M. Wilson, pre-1938)

'Somerset Maugham' 3 W-Y
(Konynenburg & Mark) Konynenburg & Mark, 1966
'Orange Queen' × 'Extase' hybrid
Fl. 110 mm wide; perianth segments ivory white; corona orange-yellow. Late

'Somerville' 3 W-? (b)
(G.A. Uit den Boogaard, pre-1950)

'Sometime' 2 W-P
(J.N. Hancock & Co., 1954) J.N. Hancock & Co., 1977
'Del Rose' × 'Maylene'; sdlg no. 197/49
Fl. 95 mm wide; corona light yellowish pink 29C at base, shading to strong yellowish pink 32D at rim. Mid-season

'Somner' 2 (a)
(C.E. Radcliff, 1939)

'Sompting' 3 W-? (b)
(Sir F.C. Stern, pre-1948)

'Sonata' 9 W-GYR
(G.H. Engleheart, pre-1910)
Fl. 73 mm wide; perianth segments narrow, acute, white, with lemon at base, somewhat reflexed, overlapping two-thirds; corona almost disc-shaped, sulphur yellow, greenish at base, with a well-defined narrow band of bright red at rim. Late. 2n=14. AM 1911, *AM(g)(m) 1931, *(Kirton)AM(g)(m) 1934

'Sonatine' 1 W-? (b)
(C. Alkemade, pre-1944)

'Songbird' 2 W-? (b)
(Mrs F.S. Foote, pre-1940)

'Songket' 2 W-GWP
(Brian S. Duncan) Brian S. Duncan, 1992
'Pismo Beach' × 'High Society'; sdlg no. 1157A
Fl. rounded, 90 mm wide; perianth segments very broadly ovate, blunt, slightly mucronate, pure white, spreading, plane, glistening, overlapping half or more; the inner segments more narrowly ovate; corona funnel-shaped, white, with emerald green prominent at base and a wide band of coral pink at

rim, mouth slightly flared, wavy. Late. Sunproof

'Song Lark' 2 Y-O
(O. Ronalds, pre-1939)
'Militant' × 'Fortune'
Perianth segments broad, deep yellow, smooth; corona large, deep reddish orange. Syn. 'Skylark'

'Song of Songs' 3 W-W
(T.H. Piper, c.1966) Unregistered
'Swanley Peerless' × 'Nevose'

'Songster' 3 W-? (b or c)
(W.A. Watts, pre-1916)
'Mrs Thomson' × 'Ornatus'

'Songster' 7 YYW-Y
(G.E. Mitsch) G.E. Mitsch, 1971
'Quick Step' × 'Daydream'; sdlg no. DO11/1
Fl. rounded, 77 mm wide; perianth segments yellow, with a well-defined band of white at base; corona coppery yellow. Late

'Songster' 2 W-YPP
(G.H. Johnstone, pre-1960) Unregistered

'Sonia' 2 W-W
Syn. of 'Sonietta'

'Sonia Round' 2 W-YYO
(J.N. Hancock & Co.) J.N. Hancock & Co., 1977
'Coolibah' hybrid; sdlg no. 129/57
Fl. 98 mm wide; corona vivid yellow 14A, with a lighter tone (12A) at base and strong orange 25A at rim, with the rim deeply dentate. Early to mid-season

'Sonia Sloan' 2 W-OOY
(C.O. Fairbairn) L.P. Dettman, 1971
Fl. 79 mm wide. 2n=29

'Sonietta' 2 W-W
(G.H. Johnstone, pre-1951)
Syn. 'Sonia'

'Sonja' 2 Y-O
(P.D. Williams, pre-1930)
Perianth segments pale yellow; corona shallow, widely expanded. AM(Haarlem) 1930

'Sonneclair' 1 W-Y
(J. Gerritsen & Son, 1950) J. Gerritsen & Son, 1963
Corona clear yellow. Mid-season. Resembles a more vigorous 'Queen of Bicolors'

'Sonnet' 9
(G.H. Engleheart, pre-1907)

'Sonnet' 1 W-Y
(T.H. Piper, 1952)
'Grayling' × 'Lorinna'

'Sonnet'
?Syn. of 'Red Arrow'

'Sonnet' 9 W-YYR
(M.J. Jefferson-Brown, c.1973) Unregistered
'Cantabile' hybrid

'Sonnevanck' 1 Y-Y
(H. Leber) H. Leber, 1972
'Golden Harvest' hybrid
Fl. 125 mm wide

'Sonnica' 2 W-O
(de Graaff Bros, pre-1943)
AM(Haarlem) 1943

'Sonora' 1 W-W
(Barr & Sons, pre-1929)

'Sonora' 1 W-W
(D.V. West, pre-1931)

'Sookie' 2 W-P
(J.N. Hancock & Co., 1974) Unregistered
Sdlg no. 85/79H
Fl. rounded; perianth segments deeply overlapping; corona cylindrical, opening amber pink, becoming rich true pink, with mouth slightly flared and rim dentate. Tall. Mid-season to late

'Soothsayer' 2 W-Y
(F.E. Board) F.E. Board, 1965
'Wedding Bell' × 'Greenland'
Corona lemon yellow. Mid-season

'Sophia' 2 W-Y
(pre-1927)
Perianth segments rounded at apex; corona shallow, orange-yellow, frilled. AM(Haarlem) 1927

'Sophia' 2 YYW-Y
(Mrs H.K. Richardson) du Plessis Bros, 1980
'Golden Aura' × 'Daydream'; sdlg no. 892
Fl. 90 mm wide. Late

'Sophia Dix' 2 (a)
(J.A. van der Zwet & Sons, pre-1950)
AM(Haarlem) 1950

'Sophie' 2 W-WWY
(J.N. Hancock & Co., 1967) Unregistered

'Sophie Girl' 2 W-P
(Mrs J. Abel Smith) Mrs J. Abel Smith, 1984
'Chelsea Derby' × 'Leonaine'
Corona damson pink

'Sophie of Lethien' 2 or 3 W-Y
(?A. Parker, pre-1936)
Corona apricot yellow

'Sophonisba'
(?G.P. Haydon, pre-1914)

'Sophy Primrose' 3 (a)
(W. Polman-Mooy, pre-1913)

'Soprano' 2 W-GPP
(Brian S. Duncan) Brian S. Duncan, 1992
'High Society' × 'Valinor'; sdlg no. 1159
Fl. forming a double triangle, 105 mm wide; perianth segments very broadly ovate, blunt, mucronate, spreading, plane, overlapping half; corona shallow bowl-shaped, ribbed, opening rich rose pink, becoming paler lilac pink, with green at base, mouth slightly expanded, even. Late. Sunproof

'Sora' 2 Y-Y
(Mrs G. Link) Mrs G. Link, 1973
'Goldcourt' × 'Rustom Pasha'
Fl. 112 mm wide

'Soraya' 3 Y-O
(S.J. Bisdee) S.J. Bisdee, 1956
'Market Merry' × 'Freycinet'

'Sorbet' 11b W-Y/OW
(W.F. Leenen, 1966) W.F. Leenen, 1977
'Nippon' hybrid
Fl. 100 mm wide; perianth segments very broad, truncate, prominently mucronate, spreading, a little creased, overlapping half or more; corona split, the six segments half to three-quarters the length of the perianth segments and alternate to them, ovate or oblong, deeply bi-lobed, buttercup yellow, with flecks of orange at apex and with patches of white at margins, slightly inflexed, with margins incurling, overlapping, with a short extra growth at base beneath. Late. 2n=28

'Sorbonne'
(Alister Clark, pre-1948)

'Sorcerer' 3 W-? (b)
(F.H. Chapman, pre-1910)

'Sorcerer' 3 W-YYR
(Carncairn Daffodils) Carncairn Daffodils, 1982
'Matapan' × 'Tulyar'; sdlg no. 111/60
Fl. 98 mm wide; perianth segments yellowish white 155D; corona vivid yellow 9A, with a narrow band of orange-red (32A) at rim. Mid-season. Resembles a taller and larger 'Merlin'

'Sordello' 8
(P.D. Williams, pre-1915)

'Sorello' 3 W-WWO
(The Brodie of Brodie, pre-1929)
'Dactyl' × 'Mystic'
Resembles a larger 'Marco' with a narrower band of colour at corona rim

'Sorley Boy' 1 Y-Y
(G.L. Wilson, pre-1927)
('Monarch' × 'King Alfred') hybrid
Fl. very large, of great substance. Mid-season to late

'Sorrento' 2 (a)
(P.D. Williams, pre-1938)

'Soubrette' 2 W-Y
(Murray W. Evans) Murray W. Evans, 1974
'Blarney' × ('Siam' × 'Green Island')
Fl. 80 mm wide

'Soubrette' 11a W-Y
(J. Gerritsen & Son, c.1975) Unregistered
'Canasta' hybrid

'Souffre Royale' 8 Y-Y
(pre-1798)
Fl. sulphur yellow

'Soult' 2 Y-Y
(P.D. Williams, pre-1927)

'Soundness' 1 W-Y
(P. van Deursen, pre-1939)
'Roxane' hybrid
AM(Haarlem) 1939

'Sousan' 1 Y-Y
(J.S. Leitch) J.S. Leitch, 1957

'Southease' 2 W-GYY
(N.A. Burr) N.A. Burr, 1986
'Homage' × 'Irish Minstrel'; sdlg no. 3.2.75
Perianth segments very broad, prominently mucronate, becoming white, of thick texture, overlapping half; the inner segments ovate, more nearly acute, somewhat creased; corona bowl-shaped, ribbed, yellow, with green at base, mouth straight, tightly frilled. Mid-season. Later in flower than sibling 'Lydwells'

'Southern Beauty' 2
(pre-1913)

'Southern Cross'
(W.Balch, pre-1929)
PC(e)(NZ) 1929

'Southern Cross' 2 W-Y
(P. van Deursen, pre-1930)
Perianth segments soft yellow; corona large, shallow, butter yellow. AM(Haarlem) 1930

'Southern Gem' 2 W-W
(P.D. Williams, pre-1913)
Fl. forming a double triangle, about 80 mm wide,

facing slightly downwards; perianth segments oblong, very prominently mucronate, milk white, a little inflexed, with margins wavy and sometimes recurved from midrib, a little ribbed and of thin substance, fairly regular, overlapping a quarter; the inner segments more nearly ovate, only very slightly mucronate, more strongly inflexed and with margins more noticeably wavy; corona cup-shaped, ribbed, opening rich primrose yellow, gradually becoming yellow-white, frilled, with rim slightly flanged, crenate and irregularly notched. 2n=21. AM(g)(c) 1914

'Southern Light' 2 (a)
(O. Ronalds) M. Gardiner, 1956

'Southern Lights' W-P
(Campbell Duncan, pre-1955) Unregistered
'Beechwood' hybrid
Corona with a purplish tone

'Southern Maid' 3 W-? (b)
(J.T. Gray, pre-1933)

'Southern Plane' 2 W-W
(W. Balch, pre-1933)
Perianth segments broad, blunt, overlapping; corona opening pale lemon yellow, soon becoming white

'Southern Queen' 2 W-? (b)
(Sir A.P.W. Thomas, pre-1927)

'Southern Queen' 1 W Y
(D.V. West, pre-1936)
Corona creamy yellow

'Southern Seas' 2 W-W
(D.S. Bell) D.S. Bell, 1960
Fl. 105 mm wide, pure white; corona opening lemon, becoming white. Mid-season. Resembles 'Ludlow' but with smoother and more rounded perianth segments

'Southern Star' 3 W-YYR
(G.H. Engleheart, pre-1897)
Fl. 114 mm wide; perianth segments ovate, blunt, slightly mucronate, spreading or a little recurved, with margins slightly wavy, overlapping a quarter; corona shallow, yellow, with a broad band of orangered at rim, rim crenate. FCC 1897

'Southgate' 1 Y-Y
Syn. of 'Southgrove'

'South Georgia' 3 W-?
(W.M. Spry, pre-1975) Unregistered
'Margerie' × Ronalds sdlg
Corona chrome yellow and orange, frilled. Late

'Southgrove' 2 W-P
(F.E. Board) F.E. Board, 1965

'Irish Rose' × 'Rose Caprice'; sdlg no. 1296
Late. See also 'Southgate'

'South Lodge' 1 Y-Y
(E.W. Philpott)

'South Pacific' 2 W-Y
(Oregon Bulb Farms, pre-1950)

'South Pole' 1 W-? (c)
(E.H. Krelage & Son, pre-1913)
Corona clear sulphur yellow and white, with rim rolled. FCC(Haarlem) 1912

'South Pole' 1 W-W
(J.L. Richardson) J.L. Richardson, 1958
'Spitzbergen' × 'Broughshane'
Fl. snow white; perianth segments slightly reflexed in upper part; corona with rim widely rolled

'South Saxon'
(?F.H. Chapman, pre-1913)

'South Street' 2 Y-O
(W.A. Noton) W.A. Noton, 1994
Wootton sdlg × 'Border Chief'; sdlg no. N13/81
Fl. 108 mm wide; perianth segments broadly ovate, blunt, vivid yellow 9A, with slight white mucro, spreading, concave, with margins incurling at apex, regular, overlapping half; the inner segments square-shouldered at base, somewhat ribbed, with margins sometimes wavy; corona cylindrical, lightly ribbed, orange (23A), mouth straight and more strongly ribbed, rim very slightly flanged, obscurely and irregularly crenate. Mid-season

'Southward' 2 W-YYO
(S.A. Free) S.A. Free, 1960
'Green Island' × 'Boswell'
Fl. rounded, 102 mm wide; perianth segments very broad in outline, rounded at apex and slightly truncate, milky white, spreading, plane, smooth, overlapping half or more; the inner segments somewhat inflexed; corona bowl-shaped, yellow, with a broad band of reddish orange at rim, a little frilled, with rim notched. Late. Resembles 'Boswell' but with better texture and a larger corona

'Southwick' 3 W-R
(W.G. Pannill) W.G. Pannill, 1983
'Accolade' × 'Merlin'

'Southwind' 1 W-Y
(J.S. Leitch) J.S. Leitch, 1967
Fl. 102 mm wide; corona lemon yellow

'Souvenir' 7 Y-Y
(P.L.A. Pouw Bros, 1920) van Graven Bros, 1962
Fl. 36 mm wide; perianth segments vivid yellow 12A; corona slightly darker in tone (13A). Mid-season

'Souvenir' 2 (a)
(R.H. Bath, pre-1929)

'Souvenir' 2 W-OOY
(Tom Forster, 1960s) Unregistered
Perianth segments reflexed; corona flared, bronze orange, with a band of gold at rim and the rim dentate

'Souvereign' 2 (a)
Syn. of 'Nanty'

'Sovereign' 8
(M. van Waveren & Sons, pre-1916)

'Sovereign' 1 Y-Y
(D.V. West, pre-1927)
Fl. light yellow

'Sovereign' 11a W-O
(J. Gerritsen & Son) J. Gerritsen & Son, 1973
'Orangery' hybrid
Fl. 115 mm wide; perianth segments very broadly ovate, rounded at apex, fairly prominently mucronate, ivory white, tinged yellow beneath, concave, overlapping half or more; corona split to base, the six segments seven-eighths the length of the perianth segments and of the same width, opposite and closely overlying them, joined to them at the margins at base, deeply bi-lobed, with the lobes overlapping, strong orange 24A, sometimes with a narrow band of paler orange at rim, loosely frilled; the inner segments heavily ribbed and tightly frilled. Mid-season. Resembles a larger-flowered 'Orangery'

'Sovereign Gold' 1 (a)
(J.R. Pearson & Sons, pre-1913)

'Sovereign Star' 2 Y-O
(W.O. Backhouse) E. Longford, 1963
Fl. 110 mm wide; perianth segments lemon yellow; corona deep orange. Early to mid-season

'Space Age' 2 Y-Y
(Murray W. Evans, 1955) G.E. Mitsch, 1965
'Polindra' × 'Playboy'
Fl. 108 mm wide, clear mid-yellow. Mid-season

'Space Cadet' 2 Y-R
(D.S. Bell) D.S. Bell, 1960
Fl. 115 mm wide. Resembles 'Illuminate' but with a more widely expanded corona.

'Space Ship' 2 W-P
(G.E. Mitsch) G.E. Mitsch, 1974
(['Precedent' × 'Carita'] × ['Radiation' × 'Mabel Taylor']) × 'Interim'; sdlg no. F67/2
Fl. 105 mm wide; perianth segments rounded at apex, milk white; corona very shallow bowl-shaped, deep salmon pink or sometimes darker. Mid-season

'Space Shuttle' 11b W-O/YW
(J.W.A. Lefeber, 1970) J.W.A. Lefeber, 1981
'Papillon Blanc' × 'Burning Heart'
Fl. forming a double triangle, 90 mm wide; perianth segments broadly oblong, truncate, fairly prominently mucronate, white, spreading, lightly creased, overlapping one-third; the inner segments more heavily creased, with margins wavy; corona split, the six segments one-eighth to half as long as the perianth segments and alternate to them, narrowly oblong, notched or more deeply split at apex, with a broad longitudinal band of strong orange 25B at midrib radiating to variable lengths from base, flanked by light greenish yellow 5C, with white at margins and sometimes at apex, with margins curled inwards, separated or slightly overlapping; some short malformed extra growths between the segments. Early to mid-season

'Spade Guinea' 3 W-? (b)
(E. & J.C. Martin, pre-1916)

'Spahi'
(J. Pope, pre-1907)

'Spalding Beauty' 2 W-? (b)
(G. Lubbe & Son, pre-1953)
AM(Haarlem) 1953

'Spalding Double White' 4 W-YYR
Fl. rounded, about 70 mm wide; perianth and other petaloid segments in three whorls opposite one another, broadly ovate in outline, rounded at apex, white, with green at base, overlapping a quarter to one-third; the two outer whorls of about the same length, slightly inflexed; the centre whorl with fewer than six segments, only slightly shorter, more strongly inflexed; corona segments in near-continuous whorls between the whorls of petaloid segments, greenish yellow, with a narrow band of scarlet at rim, sometimes with a line of white between the yellow and the scarlet. Late. Scented. Syn. 'Double White'. See also note under Poeticus 'Plenus'

'Spalding Gold' 1 Y-Y
(pre-1930)
Fl. rich golden yellow; perianth segments overlapping

'Spalding Queenie' 4 W-W
Syn. of 'Daphne'

'Spandrel' 1 Y-Y
(G.H. Johnstone, pre-1953)

'Spangle' 2 W-GYO
(M.J. Jefferson-Brown) M.J. Jefferson-Brown, 1985
Corona widely expanded, pale citron yellow, with bluish green at base and a narrow band of pinkish orange at rim. Mid-season

'Spaniards Inn' 4 W-P
(Brian S. Duncan) Dan du Plessis, 1993

'Spanish Beauty' 1 W-Y
(J.W. Barr, pre-1930)
Perianth segments tinged golden yellow at base base; corona rich orange-yellow

'Spanish Flag' 2 W-O
(Mrs R.O. Backhouse, pre-1921)
Perianth segments creamy; corona shallow, wide-spreading, rich reddish orange, with splashes of gold

'Spanish Gold' 1 Y-Y
(J.L. Richardson, pre-1948)
'Kingscourt' × 'Goldcourt'
Fl. gold; perianth segments of waxy substance; corona with mouth expanded and rim flanged. Resembles a darker-coloured 'Kingscourt'

'Spanish Lady' 2 Y-O
(D. Bramley) D. Bramley, 1963
Fl. 95 mm wide. Early. Resembles 'Carbineer' but with perianth segments of darker yellow and corona of richer orange

'Spanish Main' 1 Y-Y
(W.O. Backhouse) E. Longford, 1969

'Spanish Moon' 1 W-W
(G.L. Wilson) E. Longford, 1965
'White Prince' × (['Gracious' × 'Tain'] × ['Silver Coin' × 'Dava']) × 'Glendermott'
Fl. 108 mm wide. Mid-season. Resembles a whiter 'Empress of Ireland' with more rounded perianth segments

'Spanish Sun' 1 Y-Y
(Warnaar & Co.) van Graven Bros, 1973
Fl. 105 mm wide

'Spanish War' 1 Y-Y
(Warnaar & Co., c.1973) Unregistered

'Spark' 3 W-? (b)
(G.L. Wilson, pre-1907)

'Spark'
(G.H. Engleheart, pre-1908)

'Sparkle' 2 (a)
(Oregon Bulb Farms, pre-1950)

'Sparkler' 2 Y-YOO
(G.H. Engleheart, pre-1914)
Perianth segments rich yellow; corona expanded, golden yellow at base, shading to bright scarlet-orange at rim. AM(c)(m) 1916

'Sparkling Diamond' 2 (a)
(G. Zandbergen-Terwegen, pre-1937)

'Sparkling Eye' 8 W-GOO
(R.A. van der Schoot, pre-1931)
Poetaz
Perianth segments sulphur white; corona orange. 2n=17. AM(Haarlem) 1930

'Sparkling Gem' 3 W-?
(T. Bloomer) T. Bloomer, 1970
'Corofin' × 'Hamzali'; sdlg no. 12/78/58

'Sparkling Jewel' 3 W-YYR
(T. Bloomer) T. Bloomer, 1970
'Corofin' × 'Hamzali'; sdlg no. 10/58/78

'Sparkling Light' 2 (a)
(G. Zandbergen-Terwegen, pre-1937)

'Sparkling Tarts' 8 Y-O
(G.E. Mitsch and R. & E.Havens, 1974) G.E. Mitsch and R. & E.Havens, 1987
'Matador' × *N. jonquilla*; sdlg no. JJ77/20
Mid-season. Scented. Resembles 'Falconet' but with a more distinctly coloured corona

'Sparkling Waters' 2 W-Y
(T. Bloomer) T. Bloomer, 1964
'Castlecoole' × ('Blarney' × 'Sylvia O'Neill'); sdlg no. 6/54/58
Perianth segments pure white; corona lemon yellow

'Sparrow' 6 W-Y
(G.E. Mitsch) G.E. Mitsch, 1982
'Trousseau' × *N. cyclamineus*; sdlg no. JJ83/2
Fl. 70 mm wide; corona lemon

'Sparrow Hawk' 2 Y-R
(G.E. Mitsch, 1957) R. Havens, 1979
('Market Merry' × 'Carbineer') × 'Armada'; sdlg no. R100/4
Fl. 98 mm wide. Early

'Sparta' 3 W-? (b)
(P.D. Williams, pre-1910)

'Sparta' 1 Y-Y
(The Brodie of Brodie, c.1919)
'White Emperor' × 'White Maximus'
Fl. pale yellow; corona slightly darker in tone than the perianth

'Spartacus' 2 (a)
(Mrs R.O. Backhouse, pre-1921)

'Spartan' 1 W-Y
(W.G. Pannill) W.G. Pannill, 1970
'Newcastle' × 'Statue'

'Spar White' 1 W-W
(Cartwright & Goodwin, pre-1916)

N. spathulatus Haworth = *N. tazetta*

'Spathulatus' 9 W-?
(pre-1831)
Corona small, rim saffron. Syn. "The Lesser Saffron Rim", Poeticus 'Spathulatus'

'Spear Chief' 2 W-O
(W.M. Spry, pre-1975) Unregistered
'Gregalach' × 'Hades'

'Spearhead' 2 Y-Y
(W.M. Spry, pre-1975) Unregistered
'Torchlight' × 'Golden Valley'
Fl. golden yellow. Tall

'Special Envoy' 2 Y-Y
(J.S.B. Lea) Clive Postles, 1991
'Meldrum' × 'Gold Convention'; sdlg no. 8-21-78
Fl. 96 mm wide; perianth segments ovate, concave at margins, very smooth; corona funnel-shaped, with mouth flared. Early

'Special Reward' 2 W-P
(A. Glover, c.1965) Unregistered
'Rosaline' × 'Bon Rose'

'Specimen' 1 W-W
(Sir C.H. Cave, pre-1928)

'Spectacular' 2 Y-YYO
(C.M. Grullemans) J.J. Grullemans & Sons, 1957
Perianth segments sulphur yellow, veined with a darker tone; corona orange-yellow, with pale orange at rim, frilled. Syn. 'Spectaculator'

'Spectaculator' 2 Y-YYO
Syn. of 'Spectacular'

'Spectator' 2 W-YYO
(G.A. Uit den Boogaard, pre-1954)
AM(Haarlem) 1957

'Spectrum' 3 W-? (b)
(W.B. Hartland, pre-1908)

'Spectrum' 3 W-R
(D.S. Bell) D.S. Bell, 1963
'Mannequin' × 'Garland'
Corona deep red. Late. Resembles 'Masquerade' in colour

'Speculant' 2 (a)
(Mrs R.O. Backhouse, pre-1921)
AM(Haarlem) 1930

'Spelga' 2 W-W
(Ballydorn Bulb Farm) Ballydorn Bulb Farm, 1975
'Dunseverick' hybrid open pollinated
Fl. 125 mm wide. Mid-season

'Spellbinder' 1 Y-WWY
(G.L. Wilson, pre-1944)
'King of the North' × 'Content'
Fl. 100-115 mm wide; perianth segments broadly ovate, blunt, prominently mucronate, brilliant greenish yellow 6B, paler at base, spreading, somewhat twisted, overlapping one-third to a half; the inner segments a little reflexed, more strongly twisted; corona cylindrical, smooth, opening paler than brilliant greenish yellow 6B, with whitish base, becoming almost pure white, with a line of greenish yellow at rim, remaining yellow on the outside, mouth expanded and frilled, rim flanged, deeply and irregularly notched. 2n=28,29. Syn. 'Spellbound'. AM(e) 1948, AM(Haarlem) 1950, *AM(g) 1971, *AM(p) 1978, *FCC(g) 1980, *FCC(p) 1985, AGM 1993

'Spellbound' 1 W-? (b)
(D.S. Bell) D.S. Bell, 1955

'Spellbound' 1 Y-W
Syn. of 'Spellbinder'

'Spelter' 2 Y-O
(J.L. Richardson, pre-1951)
'Royal Mail' × 'Red Goblet'
AM(Haarlem) 1954

'Spencer Tracy' 2 W-O
(J.W.A. Lefeber, pre-1943)
Perianth segments pure white; corona broad, golden orange, heavily frilled. AM(Haarlem) 1944, FCC(Haarlem) 1949

'Spendthrift' 2 W-? (b)
(J.N. Hancock & Co.) J.N. Hancock & Co., 1955

'Spenser' 9 W-?
(G.H. Engleheart, pre-1901)
AM 1901

'Sperrin' 1 Y-Y
(T. Bloomer) T. Bloomer, 1964
'Kingscourt' × 'Standard Bearer'; sdlg no. 1/8/58

'Sperrin Gold' 1 Y-Y
(Brian S. Duncan) Rathowen Daffodils, 1986
'Golden Jewel' open pollinated; sdlg no. 750
Fl. deep golden yellow; perianth segments very broadly ovate, rounded at apex or somewhat truncate, not obviously mucronate, the colour paling at base, spreading, slightly concave, sometimes with midrib raised, overlapping half; the inner segments a little inflexed, slightly creased; corona cyindrical, lightly ribbed, with mouth straight and wavy, rim crenate. Dwarf. Mid-season to late

'Spey Bay' 3 W-O
(Brian S. Duncan) Rathowen Daffodils, 1981
'Merlin' × 'Norval'; sdlg no. 497
Mid-season

'Sphere' 2 Y-R
(A. Overton) A. Overton, 1960
'Mrs E.E.Morbey' × 'Metaphor'

'Sphinx' 2 (a)
(H.A. Brown, pre-1936)

'Spica' 2
(?A.Wilson, pre-1902)
'Horsfieldii' hybrid
Perianth segments ovate, reflexed, overlapping a quarter; the inner segments a little twisted; corona long cup-shaped, ribbed, with mouth straight

'Spica' 2 W-? (b)
(A.M. Wilson, pre-1946)

'Spice' 2 W-? (b)
(Oregon Bulb Farms, pre-1950)

'Spiced Lemon' 9 W-GYR
(Mrs M.S. Yerger) Mrs M.S. Yerger, 1989
'Quetzal' × 'Ace of Diamonds'; sdlg no. 77 G 3
Fl. 65 mm wide; perianth segments rounded at apex; corona very shallow bowl-shaped, vivid greenish yellow 2A, with strong yellow green 144B at base and a very narrow band of orange-red (32A) at rim. Mid-season. Sweetly scented

'Spice Island' 2 W-P
(T.D. Throckmorton) T.D. Throckmorton, 1974
'Easter Moon' × 'Rose Caprice'

'Spick and Span' 2 Y-YYO
(G.L. Wilson, pre-1950)

'Spider' 6 Y-Y
(G.E. Morrill) G.E. Morrill, 1979
'Little Gem' × *N. cyclamineus*; sdlg no. 74-2-3
Fl. 42 mm wide, brilliant yellow 7A. Resembles 'Atom' but with the perianth segments narrower and less strongly reflexed

'Spike Milligan' 11a Y-Y
(Reg Nicholl) Reg Nicholl, 1997
'Perky' × 'Kingsize'; sdlg no. 19/89
Fl. star-shaped, 95 mm wide; perianth segments ovate, blunt, vivid yellow 9A, with slight white mucro, spreading, separated; corona split to base, the six segments almost as long as the perianth segments, opposite and closely overlying them, bi-lobed, spathulate, brighter in tone (7C) than the perianth, frilled. Mid-season

'Spinado' 3 W-? (b)
(P.D. Williams, pre-1928)

'Spindletop' 3 W-Y
(W.G. Pannill) W.G. Pannill, 1972
'Blarney' × 'Aircastle'
Fl. 91 mm wide

'Spindrift' 5
(F.H. Chapman, pre-1910)
'White Lady' × *N. triandrus*
Fl. 95 mm wide

'Spindrift' 2 W-P
(H.A. Brown, 1938)
Perianth segments pure white; corona deep shell pink.
Late

'Spindrift' 1 W-W
(D.S. Bell) D.S. Bell, 1968
White sdlg × 'Empress of Ireland'
Corona frilled, with rim flanged

'Spinet' 9
(F.H. Chapman, pre-1927)

'Spinnaker' 2 W-? (b)
(G.H. Engleheart, pre-1907)

'Spinnaker' 1 W-W
(T.H. Piper, 1953)
'White Knight' × 'Cantatrice'

'Spinnaker' 1 W-Y
(J.N. Hancock & Co., 1961) Unregistered

'Spinning Fire' 2 Y-R
(G.E. Mitsch, 1975) Grant Mitsch Novelty Daffodils, 1985
Sdlg A53/1 ('Paricutin' hybrid) × 'Falstaff'; sdlg no. KK66/1
Fl. 105 mm wide; perianth segments clear yellow; corona bright rich orange-red. Mid-season

'Spin Off' 3 W-YOO
(J.N. Hancock & Co., 1963) J.N. Hancock & Co., 1977
'Gay Comedy' × 'Arbar'; sdlg no. 221/63H
Fl. 106 mm wide; corona yellow-orange (17B), with vivid yellow 12A at base and strong orange 25A at rim. Early to mid-season

'Spinoza' 1 W-? (b)
(de Graaff Bros, pre-1928)

'Spinster' 2 (a)
(F.H. Chapman, pre-1915)

'Spionella' 5
(E.H.G. Thurston, pre-1930)

N. spiralis Parlatore = *N. tazetta* subsp. *lacticolor*

'Spirit of Dunblane' 1 Y-Y
(D.C.MacArthur) D.C.MacArthur, 1996
'Royal Dornoch' × 1 Y-Y sdlg; sdlg no. G513
Fl. 113 mm wide; perianth segments broadly ovate, mucronate, vivid yellow 12A, slightly reflexed, overlapping half; corona cylindrical, angled, more orange in tone than the perianth, with a tone paler than the perianth at base, mouth widely flared, wavy, rim rolled and crenate. Very early

'Spirit of Love' 2 W-WWP
(John B.Johnson) John B.Johnson, 1994
'Wings of Song' × 'Mrs R.O.Backhouse'; sdlg no. 61
Fl. 93 mm wide; perianth segments ovate, blunt, mucronate, spreading, overlapping one-third; the inner segments with margins wavy or recurved; corona funnel-shaped, loosely ribbed, opening apricot yellow, becoming pinkish white, with a band of pink at rim narrower on the outside, mouth straight and more closely ribbed, frilled. Mid-season

'Spirit of Rame' 3 W-YYR
(R.A. Scamp) R.A. Scamp, 1993
'Corofin' × 'Crenver'; sdlg no. 126
Fl. 98 mm wide; perianth segments very broadly ovate, truncate, slightly mucronate, pure white, spreading, smooth, overlapping half; the inner segments narrower, less noticeably mucronate, square-shouldered at base, with margins wavy; corona small, almost disc-shaped, ribbed, bright yellow, with a band of deep red at rim, lightly frilled. Mid-season

'Spirk' 1 W-W
(G.L. Wilson, pre-1936)

'Spitfire' 3 (a)
(G.H. Engleheart, pre-1916)

'Spitfire' 2 Y-YYR
(D.S. Bell) D.S. Bell, 1959
Fl. 115 mm wide. Mid-season. Resembles 'Seraglio' but with a broader band of colour at the rim of a more widely expanded corona

'Spitzbergen' 1 W-Y
(J.L. Richardson, pre-1943)
'Cameronian' × 'Slemish'
Fl. about 120 mm wide; perianth segments broad, sulphur white, with margins wavy, overlapping; corona greenish yellow (4D), with rim flanged and dentate. 2n=28. AM(e) 1947

'Splash' 2 Y-O
(G.H. Johnstone, 1948) G.H.Johnstone, 1959
Fl. 92 mm wide. Mid-season

'Splendens' 2 Y-Y
(E. Leeds, pre-1877)

Corona yellow, stained orange. Syn. Incomparabilis Sulphureus 'Splendens'

'Splendid' 1 (a)
(L. van Leeuwen & Son, pre-1933)

'Splendor' 2 Y-R
(R.H.Glover, pre-1993) Unregistered

'Splendour' 1 (a)
(G.H. Engleheart, pre-1916)

'Splendour' 2 W-YYO
(C.M. Grullemans) J.J. Grullemans & Sons, 1959

'Split' 11a W-W
(J. Gerritsen & Son) J. Gerritsen & Son, 1957
Fl. opening pale yellow, becoming ivory white

'Split Image' 2 W-P
(Brian S.Duncan, 1986) Brian S.Duncan, 1996
'Broadway Rose' × Bloomer sdlg 290 ('Infatuation' × 'Gem of Antrim'); sdlg no. 1137
Fl. rounded, 110 mm wide; perianth segments very broadly ovate, pure white; corona widely expanded, bowl-shaped, deep bright strawberry pink, split and lobed to half its length. Mid-season to late

'Splurge' 9 W-YYR
(Mrs M.S. Yerger) Mrs M.S. Yerger, 1991
'Poet' × 'Milan'; sdlg no. 76 K 1
Fl. 60 mm wide; the inner shorter than the outer perianth segments; corona closely ribbed, brilliant greenish yellow 2B, with orange-red (32A) at rim. Mid-season

'Spofforthiae' 3 W-YOO
(W. Herbert, pre-1843)
N. × *incomparabilis* × *N. radiiflorus* var. *stellaris*
Perianth segments broadly ovate, fairly prominently mucronate, pale greenish white, spreading, with margins incurling, overlapping one-third; corona bowl-shaped, orange, paling to yellow at base, mouth widely expanded, lobed and wavy, with rim crenate

'Spofforthiae Spurius' 3 W-Y
(W. Herbert, pre-1843)
N. × *incomparabilis* × *N. radiiflorus* var. *stellaris*
Perianth segments ovate, yellowish white, with margins incurved and wavy, separated; corona short funnel-shaped, loosely ribbed, golden yellow, mouth straight and rim dentate

'Spook' 1 W-W
(J.T.Gray, 1951) P. Phillips, 1964
Mid-season

'Sporting Life' 2 Y-R
(D.S. Bell) D.S. Bell, 1965
Corona tinged bright red. Early. Resembles a larger-

flowered 'Ceylon' with more rounded perianth segments

'Sporting Prince' 1 Y-Y
(J.L. Richardson, pre-1952)
'Kingscourt' × 'Goldcourt'

'Sportsman' 1 Y-Y
(G.L. Wilson, pre-1927)
Fl. golden yellow; corona with rim flanged and dentate

'Sportsman' 2 Y-R
(Brian S. Duncan) Rathowen Daffodils, 1979
'Ceylon' × ?'Battle Cry'; sdlg no. 373
Fl. rounded, 95 mm wide; perianth segments very broadly ovate in outline, blunt or a little truncate at apex, golden yellow, with slight white mucro, slightly reflexed, smooth, overlapping half; the inner segments spreading; corona bowl-shaped, ribbed, very deep orange-red, with mouth straight and lightly frilled. Mid-season. Resembles a taller and more rounded 'Barnsdale Wood'

'Spot Light' 2 Y-R
(C. Goodson, pre-1927)

'Spotlight' 2 W-Y
(D.S. Bell) D.S. Bell, 1959
'Polindra' × 'Broughshane'
Fl. 115 mm wide; corona apricot yellow. Mid-season. Resembles 'Polindra' but with a proportionately longer corona

'Spot On' 2 W-Y
(Colin Crotty, 1981) Colin Crotty, 1995
'Eminent' × 'Lysander'; sdlg no. 19-76
Fl. rounded, 110 mm wide; perianth segments ovate, pure white, slightly concave, overlapping; corona broad disc-shaped, mid-yellow, shading to deep yellow at mouth, heavily frilled. Mid-season

'Spranston' 5 W-W
(W.A. Grace, pre-1927)

'Spread Eagle' 1 Y-Y
(W.B. Hartland, pre-1910)
'Honourable Mrs Jocelyn' × *N. poeticus*

'Spreyton' 1 Y-Y
(C.E. Radcliff, 1938)
'Loxton' × 'Gambrinus'

'Sprig' 2 (a)
(P.D. Williams, pre-1930)

'Sprightly' 1 Y-Y
(Barr & Sons, pre-1902)
Fl. rich golden yellow. Early

'Spring' 1 W-? (b)
(Barr & Sons, pre-1907)

'Spring' 4 W-R
(J.L. Richardson) G. Zandbergen-Terwegen, 1962
Mid-season. Resembles 'Acropolis'

'Spring Beauty' 3 Y-O
(Warnaar & Co., pre-1936)

'Springbok' 2 Y-Y
(pre-1927)
Fl. rich golden yellow

'Spring Break' 2 W-P
(W.G. Pannill, 1976) W.G. Pannill, 1996
('Interim' × 'Carita') × 'Rose Royale'; sdlg no. 70/43
Mid-season

'Spring Bride' 2 W-R
(H.P. Zwetsloot, pre-1948)
AM(Haarlem) 1948

'Springdale' 1 W-Y
(Barr & Sons, pre-1929)
Perianth segments creamy white, overlapping; corona slender, soft primrose yellow

'Springdale' 7 W-Y
(W.G. Pannill) W.G. Pannill, 1983
'Cascade' × *N. jonquilla*

'Spring Dawn' 2 W-Y
(Rosewarne EHS) O.A. Taylor & Sons, 1986
'Rijnveld's Early Sensation' × 'Finland'; sdlg no. 63/3/11
Perianth segments creamy white, slightly twisted; corona expanded, bright lemon, frilled. Very early

'Spring Diamond' 11b W-O/W
(J.W.A. Lefeber) P.Q.M. Pennings, 1988
('Papillon Blanc' × 'Barrett Browning') × 'Papillon Blanc'; sdlg no. 200
Fl. 95 mm wide; perianth segments broadly ovate, deeply truncate, slightly mucronate, spreading, creased or with margins infolding, overlapping half; the inner segments with margins wavy; corona split, the six segments two-thirds the length of the perianth segments and alternate to them, broad, rounded at apex, with a narrow longitudinal band of orange at midrib becoming narrower still in mid-zone and broadening again at apex, flanked by canary yellow at base and itself becoming canary yellow towards apex, with ivory white at margins, spreading, with margins sometimes incurling, overlapping; sometimes with a long "thumb" at margin at base. Mid-season. Resembles 'Brilliant Star'

'Springdream' 1 W-W
(C.A. van der Wereld) C.A. van der Wereld, 1961

Selection from *N. nanus*
Fl. 70 mm wide, ivory white. Dwarf. Mid-season. AM(Haarlem) 1961

'Spring Drops' 5 W-W
(Jānis Rukšans) Jānis Rukšans, 1997
'April Tears' × 'Canasta'; sdlg no. 85-22-4
Fls 3-5 per stem, 72 mm wide, facing slightly upwards; perianth segments pure white, slightly reflexed, smooth, deeply overlapping; corona funnel-shaped, creamy white, a little frilled. Late to very late

'Spring Fair' 2 Y-O
(D.S. Bell) D.S. Bell, 1959
'Ivo Fell' × 'Encore'
Fl. 108 mm wide; corona shaded reddish orange. Very early. Resembles 'Ivo Fell' but with the perianth of a richer yellow

'Spring Fashion' 2 W-P
(Mrs H.K. Richardson) Rathowen Daffodils, 1977
'Romance' × 'Daybreak'; sdlg no. 196
Perianth segments pure white; corona coral pink. Mid-season

'Spring Festival' 11a Y-Y
Syn. of 'Golden Orchid'

'Spring Festival' 3 W-YYR
(M.Boyd) Unregistered
Fl. rounded; perianth segments broadly ovate, blunt, fairly prominently mucronate, pure white, spreading, with margins incurled at apex or slightly wavy, overlapping half; the inner segments only very slightly mucronate, shouldered at base, a little inflexed, with margins more heavily waved; corona shallow bowl-shaped, ribbed, soft yellow, with a well-defined band of intense red at rim, mouth only a little frilled. Tall. Late

'Spring Fever' 2 Y-O
(Warnaar & Co.) Warnaar & Co., 1957
AM(Haarlem) 1957

'Springfield' 2 Y-O
(W.M. Spry, pre-1975) Unregistered
'Golden Coin' × 'Hades'
Corona reddish orange

'Spring Fling' 2 Y-R
(S.A. Free, 1969) Mrs S.I. Free, 1986
'Pillar Box' hybrid; sdlg no. 69/99
Corona orange-red (30C). Mid-season

'Spring Gem' 3 W-? (b)
(Warnaar & Co., pre-1933)

'Spring Glory' 1 W-Y
(J. de Groot & Sons, pre-1914)
Perianth segments broadly ovate, blunt, very slightly mucronate, a little inflexed, with margins sometimes recurved, overlapping one-third to a half; the inner segments more strongly inflexed, with margins slightly wavy; corona bright yellow, with mouth widely expanded, rim very deeply notched and dentate, with margins recurved. Early. 2n=29. FA(Haarlem) 1921

'Spring Glory' 1 Y-Y
(pre-1950)
Fl. clear yellow; corona darker in tone than the perianth

'Spring Gold' 2 Y-Y
(T. Bloomer) T. Bloomer, 1970
'Stout Lad' × 'Standard Bearer'; sdlg no. 2/26/58
Corona with rim dentate

'Spring Greeting' ?-P
(Alister Clark, pre-1948)

'Springgreeting' 2 W-? (b)
(F. Rijnveld & Sons, pre-1950)
AM(Haarlem) 1950

'Spring Greetings' 2 W-R
(J.A. Morris) J.A. Morris, 1965
Fl. 105 mm wide. Mid-season. Sunproof. Resembles 'Signal Light' but with purer white perianth segments of stronger substance

'Spring Grove' 2 W-Y
(A.G. Bull, pre-1927)
Corona creamy yellow

'Spring Hills' 1 Y-Y
(O.W. Fay) O.W. Fay, 1959
'Milanion' × 'Kingscourt'
Fl. golden yellow. Early

'Springlo' 2 Y-O
(R.C.A. Tombleson) R.C.A. Tombleson, 1971
'Air Marshal' hybrid
Fl. 100 mm wide

'Spring Love' 2 W-? (b)
(Oregon Bulb Farms, pre-1950)

'Spring Lustre' 3 W-YYO
(J.A.Hunter, 1986) J.A.Hunter, 1997
'Verona' × 'Rockall'; sdlg no. 43/81B
Fl. rounded, 94 mm wide; perianth segments broadly ovate, very smooth; corona bowl-shaped, with a broad band of orange at rim, mouth wavy. Mid-season

'Spring Magic' 2 W-R
(T. Bloomer) T. Bloomer, 1970
('Fermoy' × 'Arbar') × Richardson sdlg 260; sdlg no. 3/14/60
Corona ribbed, deep red

'Springmaid' 2 W-? (b)
(Oregon Bulb Farms, pre-1950)

'Spring Melody' 1 W-GWW
(J.N. Hancock & Co., 1954)

'Spring Mist' 2 W-? (b)
(Oregon Bulb Farms, pre-1950)

'Spring Morn' 2 Y-YPP
(G.E. Mitsch, 1972) Grant Mitsch Novelty Daffodils, 1984
'Euphony' open pollinated; sdlg no. HO13/8
Fl. forming a double triangle, 92 mm wide; perianth segments very broadly ovate, blunt, soft lemon yellow, with slight white mucro and with a touch of white at base, spreading or a little reflexed, somewhat concave, smooth, overlapping one-third to a half; the inner segments square-shouldered at base, more nearly spreading, with margins wavy; corona funnel-shaped, broadly ribbed, whitish pink, with undertones of lemon yellow, becoming darker pink at rim, mouth closely ribbed and a little expanded, frilled, rim notched and minutely crenate. Mid-season

'Spring Morning' 1 Y-Y
(pre-1966) Unregistered

'Springmount' 2 W-Y
(W.J. Dunlop, pre-1949)
Perianth segments pure white; corona deep golden yellow

'Spring Parade' 1 W-? (b)
(A.H. Ahrens) J.S. Leitch, 1956

'Spring Peeper' 6 Y-Y
(Helen A.Grier) Helen A.Grier, 1964
'Peeping Tom' × 'March Sunshine'
Fl. 83 mm wide, clear lemon yellow; corona darker in tone. Very early. Resembles a more vigorous 'Charity May'

'Spring Present' 3 W-O
(J.W.A. Lefeber, 1944) J.W.A. Lefeber, 1960
Fl. 65 mm wide; corona reddish orange. Very early

'Spring Queen' 2 W-Y
(A.C. Paardekooper) A.C. Paardekooper, 1965
Fl. 115 mm wide; perianth segments creamy white; corona lemon yellow. Mid-season

'Spring Rose' 4
(N.H. Onderwater, pre-1954)

'Spring Shower' 2 W-O
(D.S. Bell) D.S. Bell, 1963
'Mannequin' × 'Garland'
Fl. 111 mm wide; corona intense carrot orange. Late.

Resembles 'Masquerade' in form

'Spring Snow' 9 W-GOO
(Mrs M.S.Yerger) Mrs M.S.Yerger, 1996
'Lights Out' × 'Ace of Diamonds'; sdlg no. L 7
Fl. rounded, 55 mm wide; perianth segments broad, pure white, of heavy substance, overlapping; corona disc-shaped, yellow-orange (24B), with vivid yellowish green 134A at base and a darker tone of orange (28A) at rim. Late

'Spring Song' 1 W-? (b)
(Slieve Donard Nursery Co., pre-1933)

'Spring Song' 2 W-WWP
(G.E. Mitsch) G.E. Mitsch, 1958
'Mabel Taylor' × 'Pink Lace'; sdlg no. P47/5
Corona nearly white, with clear pink at rim, closely frilled. Mid-season

'Spring Song' 1 W-W
(C.R. Wootton, c.1965) Unregistered
'Ardclinis' × 'Trousseau'

'Spring Star' 3 Y-O
(D.W. Lefeber & Co.) D.W. Lefeber & Co., 1955

'Springston Charm' 2 W-W
(L.J. Chambers) L.J. Chambers, 1980
'Empress of Ireland' × 'Easter Moon'; sdlg no. 70/24
Fl. forming a double triangle, 130 mm wide; perianth segments broadly ovate, blunt, spreading, overlapping half; the inner segments a little inflexed; corona funnel-shaped, with mouth straight, loosely frilled. Mid-season. PC(e)(NZ) 1975, FCC(e)(NZ) 1991

'Springston Gem' 2 W-W
(L.J. Chambers) L.J. Chambers, 1980
'Empress of Ireland' × 'Easter Moon'; sdlg no. 66/124
Fl. 110 mm wide. Mid-season

'Springston Jewel' 2 W-R
(L.J. Chambers) L.J. Chambers, 1984
'Rameses' × 'Masquerade'; sdlg no. 67/169
Mid-season

'Spring Success' 1 Y-Y
(J.H. Rijkelijkhuizen) J.H. Rijkelijkhuizen, 1966
Fl. 120 mm wide; perianth segments canary yellow; corona buttercup yellow. Dwarf. Early

'Spring Surprise' 9 W-GOR
(Mrs M.S. Yerger) Mrs M.S. Yerger, 1991
'Praecox Grandiflorus' × 'Lights Out'; sdlg no. 75 Q 4
The inner shorter than the outer perianth segments. Dwarf. Late

'Spring Swirl' 9 W-GYR
(Mrs M.S. Yerger) Mrs M.S. Yerger, 1991
'Praecox Grandiflorus' × 'Lights Out'; sdlg no. 75 P 4
The inner shorter than the outer perianth segments. Late

'Spring Tears' 5 W-W
(Jānis Rukšans) Jānis Rukšans, 1997
'April Tears' × 'Canasta'; sdlg no. 85-22-2
Fls 3-5 per stem, 60 mm wide, pure white, facing slightly downwards; perianth segments plane, overlapping; corona short. Dwarf. Late to very late

'Spring Tide' 1 W-Y
(?New Zealand origin, pre-1990) Unregistered

'Springtime' 3 W-? (b)
(F. Roozen, pre-1938)
AM(Haarlem) 1938

'Spring Tonic' 3 Y-GYR
(T.D. Throckmorton) T.D. Throckmorton, 1974
'Old Satin' × 'Altruist'

'Spring Valley' 3 W-GYY
(Carncairn Daffodils) Carncairn Daffodils, 1984
Sdlg × 'Bizerta'; sdlg no. 1/6/69
Fl. 92 mm wide; corona chrome yellow, with green at base

'Springwood' 2 W-GWW
(Brian S. Duncan) Rathowen Daffodils, 1986
'Easter Moon' × 'Silent Valley'; sdlg no. 598
Fl. forming a double triangle; perianth segments broadly ovate, spreading, overlapping half; the inner segments more narrowly ovate; corona cup-shaped, of a brighter white than the perianth, with a hint of blue, mouth slightly expanded and lightly frilled. Tall. Mid-season. Resembles a larger and taller 'Silk Cut'

'Sprinter' 11a Y-Y
(J. Gerritsen & Son) J. Gerritsen & Son, 1980
'Moonbird' hybrid
Fl. 100 mm wide; perianth segments light greenish yellow 4B; corona segments vivid to brilliant yellow 9A-C, tinged orange. Mid-season. Resembles 'Flyer' but with the corona more heavily tinged orange

'Sprite' 3 W-? (b or c)
(J. Mallender, pre-1914)

'Sprite' 2 W-W
(G.W.E. Brogden) G.W.E. Brogden, 1963
Early

'Sprite' 1 W-W
(?A. Gray, c.1972) Unregistered
Corona white or very pale primrose

'Spritely' 2 W-P
(T.H. Piper)
'Nina' × 'Dear Me'

'Spritzig' 2 W-W
(J.N.Hancock & Co.) J.N.Hancock & Co., 1997
Sdlg 3/70H × 'Immaculate'; sdlg no. 107/82H
Fl. forming a double triangle, pure white; perianth segments plane; corona cylindrical, with mouth slightly flared, rim crenate. Late

'Spry' 2 Y-R
(G.L. Wilson, pre-1950)
'Indian Summer' × 'Carbineer'
Perianth segments clear yellow; corona almost blood red

'Spun Gold' 2 (a)
(Mrs R.S. Cobley, pre-1932)

'Spun Honey' 4 Y-Y
(G.E. Mitsch) G.E. Mitsch, 1979
'Gay Time' × 'Daydream'; sdlg no. HH102/5
Fl. 108 mm wide; perianth and other petaloid segments clear lemon; corona segments interspersed, of a deeper tone. Late

'Spur' 1 Y-Y
Syn. of 'Golden Spur'

N. spurius Haworth = *N. hispanicus* var. *spurius*

'Spurius'
Syn. of *N. hispanicus* var. *spurius*

'Spurius Coronatus' 1 Y-Y
(pre-1884)
Perianth segments spreading; corona large, widely expanded, darker in tone than the perianth. Syn. 'Coronatus', Pseudonarcissus Major 'Spurius Coronatus'. At one time identified (probably wrongly) with 'General Gordon'

'Spurius Henry Irving' 1 Y-Y
Syn. of 'Henry Irving'

'Spurius Yellow King'
Syn. of 'Ard Righ'

'Sputnik' 6 W-YYP
(Brian S. Duncan) Rathowen Daffodils, 1978
'Interim' × 'Joybell'; sdlg no. 148
Corona yellow, with a sharply defined band of pink at rim, mouth expanded. Much smaller than either parent. Mid-season

'Spycatcher' 2 W-OOY
(J.N.Hancock & Co., 1983) Unregistered
Perianth segments rounded, regular; corona widely expanded, warm orange, with yellow at rim. Early

'Square Dancer' 11a Y-Y
(A.N. Kanouse, 1956) A.N. Kanouse, 1976
'Hillbilly' × 'Mabel Taylor'
Fl. 100 mm wide; perianth segments golden yellow; corona segments of a deeper tone, ribbed and frilled. Mid-season

'Squatter' 2 Y-O
(G.W.E. Brogden) G.W.E. Brogden, 1963
Fl. 102 mm wide; perianth segments soft yellow; corona reddish orange, with a paler tone at base

'Squib' 2 Y-? (a)
(G.H. Johnstone, pre-1950)

'Squire' 1 Y-Y
(Mrs J. Abel Smith) Mrs J. Abel Smith, 1969
'Kingscourt' × 'Brabazon'
Fl. golden yellow. 2n=28

'Srinigar' 2 Y-Y
(W.A. Grace, pre-1927)

'S.T.'
(pre-1913)

'Staaten Generaal' 8 W-Y
(pre-1862)
Resembles 'Chinese Sacred Lily'. Syn. Tazetta 'Staaten Generaal'. See also 'Staten General'. ?The same as 'States-General'

'Stability' 2 W-Y
(G.L. Wilson, pre-1923)
'Princess Mary' × 'Vestal Virgin'
Perianth segments spreading, of good substance, overlapping; corona pale primrose. Very late

'Stadium' 2 W-Y
(J.L. Richardson, pre-1948)
Fl. 115 mm wide; perianth segments broadly ovate, blunt, mucronate, greenish white (1D), spreading, plane, with margins slightly incurving, regular, overlapping half; the inner segments somewhat twisted or inflexed; corona very short funnel-shaped, smooth or slightly ribbed, vivid yellow 9B, with mouth widely expanded and frilled, rim deeply notched and crenate, with margins flanged. 2n=28. *AM(g) 1953, AM(Haarlem) 1967

'Stafford' 7 Y-O
(A. Gray) A. Gray, 1956
N. rupicola × N. poeticus
Perianth segments very broad, rounded at apex, mucronate, spreading or very slightly reflexed, plane, smooth, with broad midrib showing, overlapping half; the inner segments a little narrower, with margins sometimes rolling inward; corona disc-shaped, ribbed, with mouth widely expanded. Resembles an earlier-flowered 'Bobbysoxer'

'Stainless' 2 W-W
(G.L. Wilson) G.L. Wilson, 1960
('Nelly' × 'Chinese White') × ('Evening' × 'Foyle')
Fl. 95 mm wide; perianth segments very broadly ovate in outline, blunt or truncate at apex, slightly mucronate, spreading, with midrib showing, overlapping half; the inner segments narrower, a little inflexed, with margins wavy; corona shallow bowl-shaped, broad, ribbed, bluish white, with mouth even, rim crenate. 2n=28. *AM(g) 1978

'Stalingrad' 2 (a)
(D. Cobb, pre-1943)

'Stalwart' 1 (a)
(Sir A.P.W. Thomas, pre-1930)

'Stamboul' 3 W-YYR
(The Brodie of Brodie, c.1929)
'Mozart' × 'Gallipoli'
Perianth segments of thick substance; corona large, bright yellow, with a broad band of bright red at rim

'Stampede' 2 Y-YYO
(G.W.E. Brogden) G.W.E. Brogden, 1963
Fl. 102 mm wide; perianth segments deep yellow; corona yellow, with a very broad band of reddish orange at rim. Mid-season

'Standard' 1 Y-Y
(C.G. van Tubergen, pre-1927)
Fl. 120 mm wide; perianth segments pale lemon, overlapping one-third; corona buttercup yellow, with mouth expanded. Mid-season

'Standard' 2 W-O
(G.B. de Vroomen & Sons) G.B. de Vroomen & Sons, 1958
AM(Haarlem) 1960

'Standard Bearer' 1 (a)
(H.G. Longford, pre-1927)

'Standard Bearer' 1 Y-Y
(J.L. Richardson) J.L. Richardson, 1956
('Royalist' × 'Crocus') × 'Goldcourt'
Corona slender, with rim dentate and widely rolled

'Standard Value' 1 Y-Y
(P. Geerlings, pre-1949)
2n=28

'Standby' 2 (a)
(E.T. England, pre-1938)

'Stand By' 1 W-Y
Syn. of 'Dependable'

'Standfast' 9
(G.H. Engleheart, pre-1930)

'Standfast' 1 Y-Y
(T. Bloomer) Rathowen Daffodils, 1982
'Arctic Gold' × 'Camelot'; sdlg no. 66
Fl. 92 mm wide, deep golden yellow. Mid-season.
2n=29+1B

'Standfast' 1 Y-Y
(A.M. Wilson, pre-1957) Unregistered
Fl. clear yellow; corona with mouth slightly flared

'Standfirm' 1 W-Y
(J.J. Abernethy) R.J. Abernethy, 1957
Corona pale yellow

'Standing' 3 W-? (b)
(Mrs R.O. Backhouse, pre-1921)
AM(Haarlem) 1938

'Stanfield' 1 Y-Y
(pre-1891)

'Stanfield' 2 Y-O
(P. de Jager & Sons) P. de Jager & Sons, 1963
'Walt Disney' × 'Armada'
Fl. 120 mm wide; perianth segments brilliant yellow 12B; corona strong orange 24A. Early. AM(Haarlem) 1963

'Stanford' 3 W-YYO
(D.S. Bell) D.S. Bell, 1963
Fl. 92 mm wide; corona with a broad band of reddish orange at rim. Mid-season. Resembles 'Catherine Howard' but with a shallower corona. PC(e) 1970

'Stanley' 2 W-Y
(W. Backhouse, pre-1890)
Corona straight-sided

'Stanley Mann' 2 Y-R
(West & Fell, pre-1938)
Corona scarlet, frilled

'Stanley Park' 2 Y-Y
(Mrs J.Abel Smith) M.W.Baxter, 1996
'Trifine' × 'Westhorpe'
Fl. forming a double triangle, 110 mm wide; perianth segments very broadly ovate, blunt, vivid yellow 12A, spreading, somewhat concave; the inner segments a little narrower and slightly inflexed, with margins wavy; corona funnel-shaped, ribbed, darker in tone (14A) than the perianth, mouth straight, split in places and overlapping, frilled, with rim slightly rolled and regularly crenate. Very late

'Stanley Richards' 2 W-W
(H.R. Meyer, pre-1927)

'Stansbatch' 2 (a)
(A.M. Wilson, pre-1950)

'Stansfield' 1 Y-Y
(W. Backhouse, pre-1869)
Perianth segments sulphur yellow, spreading; corona darker in tone. Pseudonarcissus 'Stansfield'

'Stanway' 3 Y-ORR
(Clive Postles Daffodils, 1979) Clive Postles Daffodils, 1986
Sdlg × 'Pipe Major'; sdlg no. 2-37-74
Corona shallow. Late. Varies between Divs 3 and 2

'Stanza' 9
(G.H. Engleheart, pre-1914)

'Stapleford Park' 1 W-W
(W.A. Noton) W.A. Noton, 1977
'Vigil' × 'Panache'; sdlg no. 614
Fl. 112 mm wide. Late

'Stapleton' 9
(N.Y. Lower, pre-1929)

'Starbeam' 3 W-ORR
(D.S. Bell) D.S. Bell, 1963
Fl. 102 mm wide; perianth segments broad, pure white, smooth; corona neat, intense red, with apricot orange at base. Resembles a larger-flowered 'Corofin' with a wider extent of red in the corona

'Starboard Light' 3 W-? (b)
(E.M. Crosfield, pre-1914)
Late

'Starbright' 3 (a)
(Oregon Bulb Farms, pre-1946)

'Starbrook' 3 Y-O
(R. & E.Havens, 1982) R. & E.Havens, 1996
'Paricutin' × *N. jonquilla*; sdlg no. REH31/1
Fl. star-shaped, 75 mm wide; perianth segments narrow, bright yellow, slightly overlapping; corona cup-shaped, tangerine orange, with mouth even. Mid-season. Sunproof

'Star Burst' 4 Y-O
R.W. Ward & Son, 1971
'Tahiti' × 'Variant'
Fl. 99 mm wide

'Stardance' 3 W-? (b)
(de Graaff Bros, pre-1948)

'Stardom' 3 Y-R
(M.E.Brogden, pre-1993) Unregistered
'Kiwi Invader' × 'Achduart'

'Stardust' 3 W-W
(G.L. Wilson, pre-1942)
Corona shallow, fluted, frilled

'Starfall' 2 W-P
(G.E. Mitsch) Grant Mitsch Novelty Daffodils, 1984
Sdlg × 'Eclat'; sdlg no. KK22/3
Fl. 102 mm wide; corona apricot pink, with reddish tones at base. Mid-season

'Star Ferry' 1 W-P
(Jackson's Daffodils, 1982) Jackson's Daffodils, 1992
'Madang' × 'Melancholy'; sdlg no. 198/82
Fl. rounded, 108 mm wide; perianth segments ovate, greenish white (155A); corona funnel-shaped, light yellowish pink 27A, with mouth frilled and rim rolled. Mid-season

'Starfinder' 2 (a)
(Australian origin) Parr's Nurseries, 1958

'Starfire' 7 Y-O
(R. Hyde) R. Hyde, 1959
N. jonquilla var. *minor* × 'Karapiro'
Fls usually one per stem; perianth segments rich deep yellow, smooth; corona small, bright reddish orange. Scented

'Starfire' 2 Y-R
(W.M. Spry, pre-1975) Unregistered
'Stanley Mann' × 'Golden Valley'
Corona dark orange-red. Tall. Early

'Starfish' 3 (a)
(de Graaff Bros, pre-1897)

'Star Flight' 2 Y-O
(J.A. Hunter) J.A. Hunter, 1982
'Air Marshal' × 'Swordsman'
Fl. 103 mm wide; corona yellow-orange. Mid-season

'Stargazer' 2 W-W
(Mrs P.M. Davis, pre-1948)

'Stargazer' 1 Y-GYY
Syn. of 'Marieke'

'Star Glow' 2 W-R
(Brian S. Duncan) Brian S. Duncan, 1992
'Leonora' × 'Doctor Hugh'; sdlg no. 1240
Fl. forming a double triangle, 108 mm wide; perianth segments broadly ovate, truncate, slightly mucronate, pure white, very slightly reflexed, with margins a little incurling at apex, overlapping half; the inner segments spreading or slightly inflexed; corona bowl-shaped, slightly ribbed, orange-red, with a very much darker tone in the tube, lightly frilled. Mid-season to late

'Star King' 3 W-? (b)
(de Graaff Bros, pre-1948)

'Starlet' 9 W-GYR
(Murray W. Evans) Murray W. Evans, 1970

N. poeticus var. *recurvus* × 'Dallas'; sdlg no. N-25/4
Corona very shallow. Very Late. Resembles an earlier-flowered *N. poeticus* var. *recurvus* with the perianth segments broader, smoother and less strongly reflexed

'Starlight' 8 W-R
(J. Veitch & Sons, pre-1907)
Corona disc-shaped, scarlet

'Starlight' 4 Y-Y
(Nuyens Bros) Nuyens Bros, 1958
?'Glory of Heemstede' sport
Fl. light greenish yellow 4C. AM(Haarlem) 1958

'Starlight Express' 3 W-R
(Mrs J. Abel Smith, 1978) Mrs J. Abel Smith, 1988
'Dragoman' × 'Rockall'; sdlg no. K33/11
Mid-season

'Starliner' 2 W-YYO
(J.J. Abernethy) R.J. Abernethy, 1962
Fl. 115 mm wide; corona greenish lemon yellow, with orange at rim. Mid-season to late. Resembles an improved and larger-flowered 'Brightmark'

'Starling' 3 W-? (b)
(Sir C.H. Cave, pre-1908)

'Starmount' 2 W-W
(W.G. Pannill) W.G. Pannill, 1970
'Easter Moon' × 'Vigil'

'Star Music' 6 Y-Y
(Eileen E.Frey, 1979) J. & E.Frey, 1994
'Wee Bee' × *N. cyclamineus*; sdlg no. PEF9/4
Fl. 60 mm wide, golden yellow; perianth segments ovate, blunt, strongly reflexed, overlapping at base only; corona cylindrical, with mouth slightly expanded and rim notched. Dwarf. Very early

"Star Narcissus"
Syn. of 'Sir Watkin'

'Star of Bethlehem' 8
(pre-1928)

'Star of Fire' 9
(W.B. Hartland, pre-1907)

'Star of Gold' 6
(J.W. Barr, pre-1930)

'Star of Hope' 3 W-YYR
(Slieve Donard Nursery Co., pre-1926)
Fl. rounded; perianth segments roundish, very broad; corona disc-shaped, yellow, shading to bright red at rim

'Star of Silver' 2 W-W
(C. Goodson, pre-1927)

'Star of Strathearn' 2 W-GWW
(D.N.Y. Olson) D.N.Y. Olson, 1990
('Greenland' × 'Empress of Ireland') × 'Immaculate'
Fl. 95 mm wide, clean white; perianth segments very broadly ovate, only very slightly mucronate, inflexed, plane, with margins nicked, smooth and of good substance, with midrib showing, overlapping half; the inner segments more narrowly ovate; corona cylindrical, narrowly ribbed, with mouth expanded and closely frilled, rim crenate. Late

'Star of the East' 2 W-? (b)
(The Brodie of Brodie, c.1911)
'Princess Mary' × 'Praecox Grandiflorus'
Perianth segments overlapping; corona small

'Star of the East' 2 Y-YRR
Syn. of 'Scarlet Elegance'

'Star of the South'
(pre-1915)

'Star of the South' 2 (a)
Parr's Nurseries, 1958

'Star of the West' 2 Y-YRR
Syn. of 'Scarlet Elegance'

'Star of Venus' 2 W-Y
(Tom Forster, 1960s) Unregistered

'Staroma' 9 W-GYR
(Mrs M.S. Yerger) Mrs M.S. Yerger, 1989
'Hexameter' × 'Lights Out'; sdlg no. 75 M 8
Fl. forming a double triangle, 57 mm wide; perianth segments broadly ovate, acute; corona very shallow bowl-shaped, greenish yellow (154C), with strong yellow-green 143C at base and orange-red (32A) at rim. Late. Citrus scented

'Star Parade' 2 Y-YYR
(G. Lewis) D.S. Bell, 1955

'Star Plane' 2 W-? (b or c)
(C. Goodson, pre-1933)

'Starry Bright' 2 (a)
(A.M. Wilson, pre-1932)
AM(Haarlem) 1931

'Stars' 8 W-Y
Syn. of 'Minor Monarque'

'Starshell' 3 (a)
(Hon. Mrs Petre, pre-1934)

'Starshine' 2 W-P
(Sidney DuBose, 1985) Sidney DuBose, 1996
'Easter Moon' × 'Arctic Char'; sdlg no. J10-3
Fl. 108 mm wide, of heavy substance; perianth segments broadly ovate in outline, blunt or squarish at apex, a little reflexed, plane, overlapping half; the inner segments narrower, more nearly acute, spreading, with margins slightly wavy; corona straight-sided, ribbed, pink, with a darker tone at rim, mouth wavy. Late

'Starship' 2 Y-R
(Brian S. Duncan) Rathowen Daffodils, 1987
'Patagonia' × 'Bunclody'
Corona deep orange-red. Mid-season. Sunproof

'Star Signal' 2 W-YYO
(J.N. Hancock & Co.) J.N. Hancock & Co., 1955
Corona yellow, with rich orange at rim, frilled

'Star Song' 6 Y-Y
(Eileen E.Frey, 1983) J. & E.Frey, 1994
'Atom' × 'Tiny Tot'; sdlg no. TEF30/3
Fl. 50 mm wide, golden yellow; perianth segments broadly ovate, strongly reflexed, overlapping at base only; corona cylindrical, mouth slightly expanded. Dwarf. Very early

'Starstream' 6 W-Y
(H. Koopowitz) H. Koopowitz, 1981
'Beryl' × 'Ambergate'; sdlg no. A573/2
Fl. 90 mm wide; corona bright yellow. Mid-season. Resembles 'Surfside' but with strongly reflexed and smoother perianth segments and a shorter corona of brighter colour

'Star Striker' 2 Y-WYY
(J.N.Hancock & Co.) Unregistered
Fl. soft lemon yellow; corona cylindrical, with white at base. Early to mid-season

'Starthroat' 2 W-GYW
(G.E. Mitsch, 1972) G.E. Mitsch, 1982
'Pigeon' × 'Tryst'; sdlg no. HH83/3
Fl. 90 mm wide, of heavy substance; perianth segments very broad in outline, blunt or truncate at apex, slightly mucronate, a little inflexed, somewhat concave, with margins sometimes narrowly incurling, overlapping half; the inner segments more strongly inflexed; corona bowl-shaped, ribbed, shaded yellow at base, with vivid emerald green prominent at base, mouth expanded and loosely frilled, rim minutely crenate. Late

'Startime' 2 Y-O
(J.S. Leitch) J.S. Leitch, 1967
Fl. 115 mm wide; corona reddish orange

'Startler' 2 W-? (b)
(J. Bankhead, pre-1950)

'Startle Startle' 2 W-W
(L.P. Dettman, 1963) L.P. Dettman, 1974
'Promptitude' self pollinated; sdlg no. 11/63

Fl. 79 mm wide, of good substance; perianth segments greenish white 157D; corona darker in tone (157A). Mid-season. Resembles 'The Little Gentleman' in form

'Star Tracker' 2 Y-W
(G.W.E. Brogden, 1979) Brogden Bulbs, 1991
'Gold Bank' × 'Daydream'; sdlg no. x74/G11
Fl. 110 mm wide; perianth segments ovate, blunt, soft creamy yellow, plane, smooth; corona funnel-shaped, opening the same colour as the perianth, becoming white, with rim flanged. Mid-season to late

'Star Trek' 3 W-GYR
(T.D. Throckmorton) T.D. Throckmorton, 1976
'Old Satin' × 'Altruist'; sdlg no. 67/24/9
Fl. 105 mm wide; corona lime lemon, with deep green at base and vermilion scarlet at rim. Mid-season

'Starvell' 2 W-Y
(R.P. Cook, pre-1949)
Perianth segments pure white; corona expanded, greeny lemon, shading to darker tones at base, frilled

'Star War' 2 Y-R
(T. Bloomer) Rathowen Daffodils, 1984
'Break of Day' × 'Shining Light'; sdlg no. 295
Perianth segments deep golden yellow; corona deep orange-red. Mid-season

'Star Wish' 3 W-GYR
(T.D. Throckmorton) T.D. Throckmorton, 1977
'Old Satin' × 'Altruist'; sdlg no. 67/24/8
Fl. 87 mm wide; corona greenish yellow, with green at base and red at rim. Mid-season. Resembles a more rounded 'Star Trek' with the corona more widely expanded and a narrower band of red at rim

'State Express' 2 Y-GOO
(Brian S. Duncan) Rathowen Daffodils, 1983
'Richhill' × 'Bunclody'; sdlg no. 555
Fl. 110 mm wide; perianth segments very broadly ovate, blunt, slightly mucronate, spreading, concave at apex, overlapping half; the inner segments more narrowly ovate, angled at shoulder, a little inflexed, plane, somewhat creased; corona cup-shaped slightly constricted near mouth, orange, with green prominent at base, mouth expanded and neatly frilled, rim flanged and dentate. Mid-season to late

'State Fair' 3 Y-GYR
(T.D. Throckmorton) T.D. throckmorton, 1977
'Old Satin' × 'Altruist'; sdlg no. 67/24/6
Fl. 100 mm wide; corona bright lemon, with deep green at base and red at rim. Mid-season

'Stateliness' 2 W-W
(G.L. Wilson, pre-1923)
Perianth segments waxy white; corona opening warm peach yellow, becoming almost cream. Late

'Stately' 1 Y-Y
(A. Overton) A. Overton, 1959
Fl. 102 mm wide

'Stately Lily' 2 W-? (b)
(C.L. Adams, pre-1916)

'Statendam' 1 Y-Y
(de Graaff Bros, pre-1929)
Syn. 'Etat General'. AM(Haarlem) 1929

'Staten General' 8 W-Y
Syn. of 'Staaten Generaal'

'States-General' 8 W-Y
(pre-1849)
Perianth segments very broadly ovate or roundish, fairly prominently mucronate, spreading, with margins sometimes incurling, with broad midrib showing, overlapping half; corona bowl-shaped, lemon yellow, mouth wavy, rim entire. Syn. 'Etat General'. ?The same as 'Staaten Generaal'

'Statesman' 2 Y-Y
(J.T. Gray, pre-1949)
Fl. large, deep yellow

'Statesman' 2 W-? (b)
(J. Bankhead, pre-1950)

'Statesman' 2 Y-O
(H.A. Brown)
Corona pale orange, with a deeper tone at rim, neatly frilled

'Statira' 8 Y-Y
(pre-1798)
Fl. sulphur yellow

'Statue' 2 W-Y
(J.L. Richardson, pre-1938)
'Mitylene' × 'Fortune'
Fl. 124 mm wide; perianth segments fairly broad, smooth; corona funnel-shaped, brilliant greenish yellow 6C, frilled. AM(e) 1947, PC(e) 1947

'Statuesque' 2 W-? (b or c)
(F.H. Chapman, pre-1916)

'Statuesque' 2 Y-Y
(G.E. Mitsch, 1963) G.E. Mitsch, 1979
'Playboy' × 'Daydream'; sdlg no. B36/18
Fl. 105 mm wide; perianth segments pale lemon, with white at base; corona deeper in tone, with mouth flared. Mid-season

'Stavangar' 1 Y-Y
(J.N. Hancock & Co.)
Fl. bright yellow

'Staveley' 1 (a)
(J.O. Sherrard, pre-1950)

'Stay Sail' 2 W-? (b)
(E.M. Crosfield, pre-1916)

'Staythorpe' 2 W-WWP
(Mrs J. Abel Smith) Mrs J. Abel Smith, 1985
'Lady Jowitt' × 'Famille Rose'
Corona frilled. Early

'Steadfast' 2 W-Y
(G.H. Engleheart, pre-1906)
Fl. of strong substance; perianth segments overlapping; corona rich yellow. Late. *C(g) 1927

'Steenbok' 3 W-YYR
(Brian S.Duncan, 1986) Brian S.Duncan, 1996
'Mount Angel' × 'Doctor Hugh'; sdlg no. 1216
Fl. rounded, 104 mm wide; perianth segments broadly ovate, blunt; corona shallow bowl-shaped, slightly ribbed, yellow, with deep red at rim, frilled. Mid-season to late

'Stella' 2 W-Y
(W. Backhouse, pre-1869)
Fl. star-shaped; perianth segments ovate, acute, fairly prominently mucronate, spreading or a little inflexed, sometimes twisted or with margins wavy or incurled, separated or only slightly overlapping; corona long cup-shaped, ribbed, with mouth straight, loosely frilled. Early or very early. Syn. Incomparabilis Albus 'Stella'

'Stella' 2 W-YYP
(Tom Forster, 1960s) Unregistered
Corona expanded, creamy yellow, with a broad band of pink at rim, lightly frilled. Mid-season to late

'Stella Benson' 3 W-? (b)
(J. Wilson, pre-1941)

'Stella Graham' 2 Y-W
(L.P. Dettman) L.P. Dettman, 1974
'Ellimatta' × 'Creamed Honey'
Fl. 101 mm wide

'Stella Maris' 2 Y-O
(D.S. Bell) D.S. Bell, 1955
Perianth segments deep golden yellow, overlapping; corona bowl-shaped, tinged bright reddish orange

'Stella Maxima' 2 W-Y
Syn. of 'Stella Superba'

'Stella Nova' 2 Y-R
(D.S. Bell) D.S. Bell, 1968
'Ceylon' × 'Rupee'

'Stella Polaris' 8
(Dutch origin, pre-1930)

'Stella Pratt' 2 Y-YYO
Syn. of 'Stella Tidd-Pratt'

N. stellaris Haworth = *N. radiiflorus* var. *stellaris*

stellaris = *N. jonquilla* var. *stellaris*

'Stellaris' 9 W-GYO
(pre-1884)
Perianth segments broadly ovate, prominently mucronate, pure white, reflexed, with margins wavy and incurled; corona very shallow bowl-shaped, greenish yellow, with green at base and a narrow band of orange at rim, tightly frilled. Late. Syn. 'Marvel'

'Stella Superba' 2 W-Y
(Dutch origin, pre-1899)
Fl. star-shaped; perianth segments narrowly ovate, blunt or acute, only very slightly mucronate, spreading, often twisted, or with margins incurved at apex and recurved at base, overlapping at base only; corona bowl-shaped, ribbed, bright yellow, with mouth split in places and overlapping, tightly frilled. Tall. Syn. 'Albus Stella'. AM 1901

'Stellata Pratt' 2 Y-YYO
Syn. of 'Stella Tidd-Pratt'

'Stella Tidd-Pratt' 2 Y-YYO
(Mrs R.O. Backhouse, pre-1921)
Fl. star-shaped; perianth segments ovate, blunt, only very slightly mucronate, light primrose yellow, spreading, with margins sometimes wavy, overlapping at base only; the inner segments twisted; corona long cup-shaped, deep yellow, shading to orange, with mouth straight, closely frilled. Syn. 'Stellata Pratt'. See also 'Stella Pratt'

'Stella Turk' 6 Y-Y
(A. Gray) A. Gray, 1958
N. cyclamineus × *N. calcicola*
Fl. deep yellow. Dwarf. Resembles *N. cyclamineus* in form but with shorter perianth segments and corona

'Stellatus' ?-Y
(?E.Leeds, pre-1877)
Syn. Incomparabilis Albus 'Stellatus'

'Stellatus' 1 Y-Y
Syn. of 'Morning Star'

'Stellatus' 2 Y-Y
Syn. of 'Cupid'

'Stellatus' 2 Y-O
Syn. of 'Sun-light'

'Stellatus' 2 Y-Y
Syn. of 'Sun-ray'

'Stellatus' 2 Y-?Y
Syn. of 'Gil Blas'

'Stellatus' 3 W-Y
Syn. of 'Amy'

'Stellatus' 3 W-Y
Syn. of 'Dandy'

'Stellatus' 3 Y-Y
Syn. of 'Lass o' Gowrie'

'Stellatus' 3 W-W
Syn. of 'Io'

'Stellatus Albus' 3? W-Y
(British origin, pre-1879)
Corona citron yellow. Syn. Barrii 'Stellatus Albus'. ?The same as 'Silver Star'

'Stellatus Sulphureus' 3 Y-Y
(British origin, pre-1883)
Syn. Barrii 'Stellatus Sulphureus'. ?The same as 'Amy'

N. stelliflorus Schur = *N. radiiflorus* var. *stellaris*

N. × *stenanthus* Fernández Casas 13 = *N. bulbocodium* Linnaeus var. *nivalis* (Graells) Baker × *N. confusus* Pugsley

'Stentor' 1 Y-Y
(G.B. van Rhijn, pre-1953)

'Step Child' 6 YYW-GPP
(John R.Reed, 1987)
John R.Reed, 1997
'Milestone' × 'Foundling'; sdlg no. 81-60-2
Fl. 88 mm wide; perianth segments ovate, deep golden yellow, smooth; corona funnel-shaped, dull strawberry pink, with green at base. Dwarf. Mid-season. Sunproof

'Step Forward' 7 Y-W
(G.E. Mitsch) G.E. Mitsch, 1970
'Quick Step' × 'Daydream'; sdlg no. D80/1
Fls 2-3 per stem; perianth segments bright yellow; corona opening soft yellow, becoming white. Mid-season

'Stephanie' 2 Y-GGR
(A.M. Wilson, pre-1948)
Fl. rounded; perianth segments creamy primrose, of thick substance; corona disc-shaped, greenish, with intense red at rim

'Stephanie Margaret' 3 W-YYR
(L.P.Dettman, 1970) Unregistered

'Lynette Sholl' × 'Diane Barker'; sdlg no. 15/70

'Stephen Haynes' 2 Y-Y
(L.P. Dettman) L.P. Dettman, 1975
'Coope' × 'Bowls'; sdlg no. 9/71
Fl. 97 mm wide; perianth segments vivid yellow 12A; corona light orange-yellow 23C. Early to mid-season

'Stephen Phillips' 9
(G.H. Engleheart, pre-1913)

'Steppe' 2 W-? (b)
(Alister Clark, 1930) J. Sharp, 1960

'Stepping Stone' 2 W-P
(Alister Clark, 1935) J. Sharp, 1960

'Stereo' 3 W-GWW
(Jackson's Daffodils) Jackson's Daffodils, 1989
'Sea Dream' × sdlg 212/75; sdlg no. 202/81
Fl. rounded, 97 mm wide, greenish white (155A); perianth segments very broad in outline, blunt or truncate at apex, slightly mucronate, spreading, plane, overlapping half or more; the inner segments more nearly ovate; corona short, ribbed, with dark green at base, mouth straight, frilled. Mid-season

'Sterill' 2 Y-R
(H. Selkirk, pre-1927)

'Sterling' 1 Y-Y
(R.L. Thornton, pre-1930)

'Sterling' 1 Y-Y
(G.L. Wilson) G. Zandbergen-Terwegen, 1956
AM(Haarlem) 1956, FCC(Haarlem) 1961

'Sterrenkyker' 8 W-O
(pre-1798)

'Steuben' 1 W-W
(Murray W. Evans, 1968) Mrs T.D. Throckmorton, 1979
('Zero' × 'Beersheba') × 'Empress of Ireland'; sdlg no. N32/2
Fl. milk white; corona with greenish tones at base. Early to mid-season

'Stevens' Market Favourite' 8
Syn. of 'Market Favourite'

'Steward' 2 Y-OOR
(G.W.E. Brogden) G.W.E. Brogden, 1968
Fl. 102 mm wide; perianth segments deep yellow

'Steyning' 2 W-YYO
(Sir F.C. Stern, pre-1948)
Corona disc-shaped, yellow, with a line of orange at rim

'Stheno' 2 (a)
(A.M. Wilson, pre-1916)

'St. Ilario' 3 W-WWO
Syn. of 'San Ilario'

'Still Flight' 6 Y-Y
(F.Silcock, 1979) F.Silcock, 1993
'Jobi' × *N. cyclamineus*
Fl. deep yellow; perianth segments strongly reflexed; corona cylindrical. Early

'Still Waters' 2 W-W
(G.H. Engleheart, pre-1931)
'Beacon' hybrid
Perianth segments ice white; corona pinkish white.
Syn. 'Silent Waters'

'Stillwood' 2 W-P
(K.J. Heazlewood, *c.*1967) Unregistered
'Sellada' × 'Roseum'

'Stilton' 9 W-YYR
(E.B. Champernowne, pre-1909)
2n=28

'Stimulus' 2 (a)
(R. Crews) R. Crews, 1956

'Stinger' 2 Y-YYR
(T.D. Throckmorton) T.D. Throckmorton, 1974
'Irish Coffee' × 'Aircastle'
Perianth segments pale yellow; corona yellow, with a slightly lighter tone at base and a very narrow band of red at rim. Mid-season

'Stint' 5 Y-Y
(M. Fowlds) G.E. Mitsch, 1970
('Fortune's Sun' × 'Cheerio') × *N. triandrus*, sdlg no. 297/1
Fls 2-3 per stem; perianth segments pale lemon yellow; corona slightly darker in tone

'Stirling' 1 Y-Y
(J.L. Richardson, *c.*1956) Unregistered
'Beacon' × 'Pilgrimage' hybrid

'Stirling Silver' 5
(H. Backhouse, pre-1910)

'Stirrup Cup' 3 Y-O
(T.D. Throckmorton) T.D. Throckmorton, 1974
'Old Satin' × 'Russet'

'Stockade' 1 Y-Y
(A.M. Wilson) D.W. Gourlay, 1957
Fl. clear yellow; corona with mouth slightly flared

'Stocken' 3 W-? (b)
(A.M. Wilson, pre-1950)
2n=21

'Stocken' 7 Y-Y
Unregistered
Name given for catalogue purposes to a wild-collected variant of an unidentified species, possibly allied to *N. willkommii*

'Stocksfield' 1 W-Y
(G. Harrison) G. Harrison, 1968
Sdlg × 'Preamble'
Fl. 115 mm wide; corona deep golden yellow. Mid-season. Resembles 'Preamble' but with perianth segments of stronger substance and a darker-coloured corona

'Stockwell' 1 (a)
(G.P. Haydon, pre-1910)

'Stoic' 2 W-? (b)
(J.L. Richardson, pre-1939)

'Stoic' Y-O
(C.O. Fairbairn, pre-1940)
Perianth segments old gold; corona cup-shaped, with rounded sides, orange

'Stoke' 5 Y-Y
(P.D. Williams, pre-1934)

'Stoke Charity' 2 W-W
(A.J.R. Pearson, 1970) A.J.R. Pearson, 1987
'Easter Moon' × 'Rashee'; sdlg no. 72/16/C14
Perianth segments broadly ovate, milk white, a little inflexed, concave; the inner segments slightly narrower, with margins wavy; corona narrow funnel-shaped, lightly ribbed, opening pinkish white, becoming chalk white, with mouth straight and wavy, rim shallowly notched and irregularly crenate. Mid-season. PC(e) 1981

'Stoke Doyle' 2 W-W
(A.J.R.Pearson) A.J.R.Pearson, 1994
'Stoke Charity' × 'Panache'; sdlg no. 87-71-J35
Fl. forming a double triangle, 105 mm wide; perianth segments broadly ovate, blunt, slightly mucronate, greenish white (157C), spreading, plane, satin smooth and of great substance, overlapping two-thirds; the inner segments only a little narrower, reflexed at apex; corona cylindrical, broad, lightly ribbed, greenish white 157D, with rim crenate and evenly rolled. Mid-season to late

'Stokensia' 2 (a)
(F.A. Saunders) F.A. Saunders, 1955

'Stoker' 3 W-? (b)
(W. Balch, pre-1933)

'Stolberg' 2 W-W
(C.G. van Tubergen, pre-1914)
Fl. facing slightly downwards; perianth segments pure white, overlapping; corona opening pale primrose yellow, becoming creamy white, frilled. Mid-season. FCC(Haarlem) 1914, *HC(g) 1930, *HC(g) 1936

'Stonechat' 3 Y-R
(G.H. Engleheart, pre-1907)
Fl. star-shaped; perianth segments yellow, overlapping; corona scarlet

'Stonechat' 2 (b)
(pre-1950)

'Stonecote' 3 (a)
(A.M. Wilson, pre-1950)

'Stoneleigh' 2 W-? (b)
(J.R.Byfield, pre-1936)

'Stonewall' 2 YYW-WWY
(H. Koopowitz) H. Koopowitz, 1979
'Binkie' × ('Ambergate' × 'Caracas'); sdlg no. C172/3
Fl. 118 mm wide, slow to develop mature colouring; perianth segments pale lemon, with white at base; corona white, with lemon at rim

'Stoplight' 2 W-? (b)
(Warnaar & Co, pre-1943)

'Storeen' 9 W-YYO
(P.D. Williams, pre-1928)

'Storm Cloud' 1 W-Y
(R.J. Abernethy, 1975) R.J. Abernethy, 1991
Sdlg no. 167
Fl. very smooth; corona funnel-shaped, with rim flanged. Early to mid-season

'Stormcock' 1 Y-Y
(E.B. Champernowne, pre-1933)
Early

'Stormer' 2 W-? (b)
(Mrs R.O. Backhouse, pre-1921)

'Storm King' 1 W-Y
(D.S. Bell) D.S. Bell, 1968
'Glacier' × 'Ulster Queen'
Fl. pure white; corona frilled, with rim dentate

'Stormont' 1 W-W
(W.J. Dunlop) W.J. Dunlop, 1956
'Ardclinis' × 'Kanchenjunga'
Fl. pure white, of thick and waxy substance. Resembles a taller, larger and improved 'Ardclinis'

'Stormtide' 1 W-? (b)
(D.S. Bell) D.S. Bell, 1955

'Stormy Weather' 1 W-Y
(D.S. Bell) D.S. Bell, 1957
Perianth segments opening cream, becoming pure white, of thick substance, overlapping; corona golden, frilled

'Stornoway' 1 (a)
(Barr & Sons, pre-1927)

'Stourbridge' 2 Y-YOO
(J.S.B. Lea) J.S.B. Lea, 1974
'Loch Stac' × 'Majorca'; sdlg no. 1-14-61
Fl. 92 mm wide; perianth segments vivid yellow 12A; corona vivid orange 28B, paling to yellow at base, with rim dentate. Mid-season. Sunproof

'Stout Heart'
(A.E. Grindrod, pre-1915)
Resembles a small-flowered 'Great Warley'

'Stout Lad' 2 Y-Y
(G.L. Wilson, pre-1941)
'Faithful' hybrid
Fl. 95 mm wide; perianth segments light greenish yellow 4B, with margins slightly incurving, overlapping half; corona vivid yellow 13A, mouth a little expanded, frilled, rim slightly reflexed, dentate. *AM(g) 1953

'Stowaway' 2 (a or b)
(J.N. Hancock & Co., pre-1949)

'Strabane' 2 W-P
(W.J. Dunlop) W.J. Dunlop, 1965

'Strabo' 3 W-R
(Mrs R.O. Backhouse, pre-1921)

'Stradella' 2 W-GWW
(Miss M. Verry) Miss M. Verry, 1966
Fl. 113 mm wide. Mid-season. Resembles a larger-flowered 'Ave' with broader perianth segments and the corona more widely expanded

'Stradivarius' 2 W-Y
(K.J. van der Veek) K.J. van der Veek, 1984
Perianth segments ivory white; corona vivid yellow, with a darker tone at rim

"Straffan Snowdrop"
Syn. of N. × bernardii

'Straight' 1 W-Y
(P. van Deursen, pre-1938)
Fl. 108 mm wide; perianth segments creamy white, with margins incurving, overlapping one-third; corona vivid yellow 9A, smooth, mouth expanded and frilled, rim reflexed and dentate. 2n=28. AM(Haarlem) 1938, *AM(g) 1956, *FCC(g) 1962

'Straight Arrow' 6 Y-R
(G.E. Mitsch, 1977) R. & E. Havens, 1993
'Jetfire' open pollinated; sdlg no. MO10/2
Fl. 80 mm wide; perianth segments broadly ovate, blunt, very slightly mucronate, bright yellow, strongly reflexed, creased, overlapping half or more; the inner segments a little less strongly reflexed, more heavily creased; corona cylindrical, ribbed, deep orange-red, with mouth straight and only a little frilled, rim crenate. Early. Sunproof. Somewhat resembles a deeper-coloured 'Jetfire'

'Straight Bat' 2 W-W
(F.E. Board) M.J. Jefferson-Brown, 1965
Resembles an earlier-flowered 'Glendermott' with the perianth segments more nearly spreading and plane and the corona rim less widely flanged

'Straight Flush' 2 Y-O
(J.L. Richardson) F.E. Board, 1955
'Narvik' × 'Ceylon'

'Stralmak'
(New Zealand origin, pre-1940)

N. stramineus Spach = *N. tazetta*

'Strand Palace' 2 Y-O
(Barr & Sons, pre-1933)
Perianth segments sulphur yellow; corona yellow-orange, frilled. AM(Haarlem) 1932

'Stranger' 3 W-WWO
(J.N. Hancock & Co., pre-1949)
Perianth segments cream; corona cream, with orange at rim

'Strangford' 3 W-GYR
(Ballydorn Bulb Farm) Ballydorn Bulb Farm, 1970
'Fermoy' hybrid

'Stratford' 1 W-Y
(H. Daines) H. Daines, 1975
'Cromarty' × 'Trousseau'; sdlg no. 10/64
Fl. 102 mm wide. Early

'Stratherin' 1 Y-Y
(pre-1964) Unregistered
Perianth segments yellow; corona deeper in tone, frilled. ?The same as 'Strathern'

'Strathern' 1 Y-Y
(C.E. Radcliff, 1939)
'The Gift' × 'Golden Legend'
?See also 'Stratherin'

'Strathern' ?-P
(?E.W. Philpott, pre-1959) Unregistered

'Strathfoyle' 3 W-OOR
(W.J. Dunlop) W.J. Dunlop, 1962

'Strathkanaird' 1 Y-Y
(J.S.B. Lea) J.S.B. Lea, 1959
'Kingscourt' × Richardson sdlg 658; sdlg no. 1-16-53
Fl. up to 140 mm wide; perianth segments broadly ovate, blunt, very slightly mucronate, canary yellow, spreading or slightly reflexed, plane, smooth, overlapping one-third; the inner segments more narrowly ovate, more noticeably reflexed; corona smooth, vivid yellow, with mouth expanded and frilled, rim slightly flanged. Mid-season. Resembles an earlier-flowered 'Kingscourt' with the inner perianth segments more rounded

'Strathmore' 1 Y-Y
(J.S.B. Lea) J.S.B. Lea, 1981
'Arctic Gold' × 'Otewa'; sdlg no. 23-14-71
Fl. 110 mm wide, rich gold

'Strathrowan' 1 Y-Y
(G.L. Wilson) E. Longford, 1965
('Milanion' × 'Bastion') × 'Spanish Gold'
Fl. 102 mm wide, deep yellow; perianth segments very broad; corona slightly darker in tone. Mid-season. Resembles an improved 'Irish Luck' of richer colouring

'Strathspey' 2 W-GWW
(J.J. Abernethy) R.J. Abernethy, 1961
?'Artist's Model' hybrid
Fl. 95 mm wide; perianth segments pure white; corona very shallow, white, shading to greenish lemon at base, frilled. Mid-season

'Stratosphere' 7 Y-O
(G.E. Mitsch) G.E. Mitsch, 1968
'Narvik' × *N. jonquilla*; sdlg no. V30/10
Fls 1-3 per stem, 60-65 mm wide, opening self golden yellow; perianth segments broadly ovate, blunt, fairly prominently mucronate, spreading or slightly reflexed, plane, overlapping one-third to a half; the inner segments more nearly ovate, spreading or a little inflexed, with margins sometimes wavy or incurled; corona bowl-shaped, smooth, becoming strong yellow-orange (17A), with mouth wavy and rim shallowly crenate. Mid-season. Scented. Resembles a taller and lighter-coloured 'Bunting'. Wister Award 1985, AM(e) 1990. The orange corona dependent on climate

'Stratus' 1 (a)
(G.H. Engleheart, pre-1923)

'Strawberries and Cream' 4
(W.F.M. Copeland, pre-1923)

'Strawberry Ice' 2 W-GWP
(W.G. Pannill) W.G. Pannill, 1985

('Wild Rose' × 'Interim') × 'Just So'; sdlg no. 68/1 D
Fl. small. Mid-season

'Strawberry Pie' 2 W-R
(John R.Reed, 1986) John R.Reed, 1997
'Old Satin' × 'Eclat'; sdlg no. 81-45-1
Fl. rounded, 96 mm wide; perianth segments broadly ovate, slightly inflexed, overlapping; the inner segments spreading; corona almost disc-shaped, broad, deep pinkish red, or in some seasons paler and more nearly pink, sometimes flecked white near rim. Late. Sunproof

'Strawberry Rim' 2 W-GWP
(G.E. Mitsch, 1960) R. Havens, 1980
('Mabel Taylor' × 'Interim') × 'Caro Nome'; sdlg no. W7/2
Fl. 90 mm wide. Mid-season. Resembles 'Coral Ribbon' but with a less rounded perianth and shallower corona

'Strawberry Shortcake' 3 W-P
(John R.Reed) John R.Reed, 1997
'Pismo Beach' × 'Everpink'; sdlg no. 84-171-1
Fl. forming a double triangle, 88 mm wide, facing down; perianth segments very broad, slightly inflexed, smooth and of waxy texture; corona bowl-shaped, intense strawberry pink. Mid-season. Sunproof

'Strawberry Soda' 2 W-P
(G.E. Mitsch and R. & E.Havens, 1976) G.E. Mitsch and R. & E.Havens, 1986
'Rose Prelude' × ('Caro Nome' × 'Carita'); sdlg no. LL17/3
Early

'Strawberry Wine' 2 W-P
(Colin Crotty) Unregistered
Sdlg no. 18-75

'Straws' 8 W-Y
Syn. of 'Minor Monarque'

"Straw White"
Syn. of *N. tazetta* subsp. *ochroleucus*

'Stray' 6 W-WWP
(Carncairn Daffodils) Carncairn Daffodils, 1983
'Foundling' × 'Lilac Charm'
Fl. 90 mm wide; corona greenish white, with pale pink at rim. Mid-season. Resembles a pink-rimmed 'Dove Wings'

'Stray Pink' 2 W-P
(C.E. Radcliff) G.L. Wilson, 1956
Fl. facing slightly downwards; corona rose pink, with rim neatly flanged

'Streamline' 3 (a)

(A.M. Williams, pre-1948)

'Strega' 4 Y-Y
(Mrs H. Oxton) Mrs H. Oxton, 1982
'Gay Time' × 'Daydream'; sdlg no. 1-1-79
Fl. 90 mm wide; perianth and other petaloid segments light greenish yellow 7D; the outer whorl broadly ovate, with prominent white mucro, spreading, a little concave, smooth, overlapping; the inner whorl not much shorter, sometimes nicked at shoulder, with the outer segments inflexed and the inner segments more sharply inflexed; a single segment at centre with margins tightly rolled inwards; corona segments in two whorls, one-third to a half as long as the petaloid segments, brilliant yellow 7A; the outer whorl split to base, with the six segments between the whorls of petaloid segments; the inner whorl continuous, funnel-shaped, smooth, frilled at mouth, with some overlapping lobes. Late

'Strephon' 1 Y-Y
(Carncairn Daffodils) Carncairn Daffodils, 1982
'Daydream' × 'Moonspell'; sdlg no. 9/69
Fl. 110 mm wide, vivid yellow 9A-B. Early

'Stresa' 1 W-W
(P. van Deursen, pre-1938)
'Imperator' × 'Roxane'

'Stretto' 3 W-? (b)
(W.A. Grace, pre-1938)

N. striatellus Spach = *N. triandrus*

'Strigil' 2 Y-Y
(G.H. Engleheart, pre-1930)
Fl. 86 mm wide; perianth segments sulphur, suffused lemon yellow, overlapping half; corona pale buttercup yellow, with mouth expanded. Mid-season to late. *AM(g) 1930

'Strike' 2 Y-Y
(Ken Farmer Nurseries) Ken Farmer Nurseries, 1978
Fl. 95 mm wide, gold

'Strike Me' 2 W-?
(A. Overton) A. Overton, 1960

'Striking' 9
(de Graaff Bros, pre-1927)
AM(Haarlem) 1935

'Strines' 2 Y-Y
(F.E. Board) F.E. Board, 1965
'Golden Torch' × 'Kingscourt'; sdlg no. 410
Fl. 127 mm wide; perianth segments brilliant greenish yellow 5A, slightly reflexed, nicked, overlapping; corona somewhat funnel-shaped, slightly ribbed, brilliant yellow 7A, mouth straight and a little frilled, with rim crenate and slightly flanged. Early. 2n=28.

AM(e) 1969, *FCC(e) 1979

'Stringbow' 2 W-Y
Syn. of 'Strongbow'

'Striver' ?-P
(Alister Clark, pre-1948)

'Stromboli' 3 W-? (b)
(N.Y. Lower, pre-1913)

'Stromboli' 2 W-O
(J.L. Richardson) J.L. Richardson, 1959
'Kilworth' × 'Arbar'
2n=28

'Strongbow' 2 W-Y
(G.H. Engleheart, pre-1898)
Perianth segments snow white; corona expanded, rich yellow. AM 1899, AM 1903. See also 'Stringbow'

'Strongheart' 1 W-W
(Mrs F.S. Foote, pre-1941)

'Stronghold' 1 Y-Y
(G.L. Wilson, pre-1938)
Fl. golden yellow

'Strophe' 3 W-? (b or c)
(W.B. Hartland, pre-1913)

'Stuart' 1 W-? (b)
(pre-1938)

'Student Prince' 2 W-P
(Brian S. Duncan) Rathowen Daffodils, 1977
Sdlg × 'Passionale'; sdlg no. 65
Fl. 114 mm wide; corona rose pink. Mid-season

'Study' 2 (a)
(Sir C.H. Cave, pre-1928)

'Stunning' 2 W-P
(W.G. Pannill) W.G. Pannill, 1992
('Pink Lace' × 'Interim') × ('Green Island' × 'Accent'); sdlg no. I 43 C
Fl. 88 mm wide. Mid-season

'Sturdy'
(?Thomas Smith, pre-1899)
Dwarf

'Sturry' 2 (a)
(F.D.B. Cobb, pre-1954)

'Styleman' 1 Y-Y
(R.C.A. Tombleson) R.C.A. Tombleson, 1970
'Spanish Gold' × 'Faris'

'Stylish' 2 O-O

(P. & G. Phillips) P. & G. Phillips, 1975
Fl. 84 mm wide; perianth segments broadly ovate or somewhat oblong, light orange (23B), with prominent whitish mucro, slightly reflexed, plane, overlapping one-third to a half; the inner segments narrower, more nearly ovate, less noticeably mucronate; corona bowl-shaped, lightly ribbed, strong orange 25A, with a paler tone at base, mouth straight, shallowly 6-lobed, with rim crenate. Mid-season

'Stylish' 1 W-Y
(?New Zealand origin, pre-1996) Unregistered

'Stylist'
(New Zealand origin, pre-1940)

'Stylita' 3 W-? (b)
(G. Haver, pre-1938)
AM(Haarlem) 1938

'Styx' 3 (a)
(de Graaff Bros, pre-1927)

'Suada' 2 Y-Y
(P.L.A. Pouw & Sons) P.L.A. Pouw & Sons, 1980
'Carlton' × 'Pluvius'
Fl. 115 mm wide; perianth segments brilliant greenish yellow 6C; corona brilliant yellow 21C. Early to mid-season

'Suave' 3 Y-Y
(T.D. Throckmorton) T.D. Throckmorton, 1976
'Aircastle' × 'Irish Coffee'; sdlg no. T66/12/1
Fl. rounded, 100 mm wide; perianth segments very broad, truncate, only very slightly mucronate, opening whitish, becoming creamy yellow, a little reflexed, smooth, overlapping half or more; the inner segments narrower, blunt, more nearly spreading; corona shallow, spreading, narrowly ribbed, opening greyish yellow, with buff yellow at rim, becoming slightly deeper in tone than the perianth, with rim minutely crenate. Late

N. subalbidus Loiseleur-Deslongchamps = *N. italicus*

N. subcrenatus Haworth = *N. tazetta* subsp. *lacticolor*

'Subcrenatus' 8 W-O
Syn. of 'Bazelman Medius'

'Sublime' 2 W-P
(Mrs R.O. Backhouse, pre-1921)
Perianth segments narrow, acute; corona soft pink. AM(Haarlem) 1931

N. subluteus Haworth = *N. aureus*.

***N. subnivalis* Fernández Casas 13 Section Bulbocodium**

'Substance' 2 W-? (b)
(L. van Leeuwen & Son, pre-1931)
Syn. 'Reliance'

'Subzero' 1 W-W
(J.N.Hancock & Co., 1978) Unregistered
'Empress of Ireland' × 1 W-W sdlg; sdlg no. 102/78H
Fl. ice white. Late

'Success' 2 W-WWP
(C.E. Radcliff, 1941)
'Luther' × 'Nautilus'

'Successor' 1 Y-Y
(de Graaff Bros, pre-1943)

'Succour' 2 W-?
(A. Overton) A. Overton, 1960

'Suda' 2 W-Y
(The Brodie of Brodie, c.1921)
'Nevis' × 'Lord Kitchener; sdlg no. 2/A/16
Perianth segments broadly ovate, blunt, prominently mucronate, pure white, spreading, with margins incurling at apex and recurved at base, of good substance, overlapping one-third to a half; the inner segments somewhat inflexed, with margins wavy; corona funnel-shaped, opening primrose yellow, becoming pinkish yellow, with mouth widely expanded and even, rim shallowly crenate. AM(e) 1927

'Suda Bay' 2 Y-GOO
(Carncairn Daffodils) Carncairn Daffodils, 1984
Wootton sdlg × ('Sunkist' × 'Magherally'); sdlg no. W16
Fl. 88 mm wide; perianth segments deep yellow. Early

'Sudan' 2 Y-R
(J.L. Richardson, pre-1938)
'Tregoose' × 'Hades'
Perianth segments deep greenish lemon yellow; corona ruby red. 2n=28

'Suede' 2 Y-W
(Murray W. Evans) Murray W. Evans, 1972
'Daydream' × 'Bethany'
Fl. 95 mm wide

'Suez' 2 W-Y
(R.O. Backhouse, pre-1932)
Perianth segments overlapping; corona large, golden yellow, stained yellowish orange

'Suffragette' 3 W-YYO
(R.G. Cull) Hokorawa Daffodils, 1992
'Dresden' open pollinated; sdlg no. HC/200
Corona brilliant greenish yellow 5B, with a broad band of strong orange 25A at rim. Mid-season

'Suffren' 4 Y-Y
(A.J. Bliss, pre-1931)
'Emperor' × 'Telamonius Plenus'
Fl. 76 mm wide, bright buttercup yellow. Mid-season to late

'Suffride' 1 (a)
(de Graaff Bros, pre-1923)

'Suffusion' 1 W-Y
(J.N.Hancock & Co.) Unregistered

'Sugar and Spice' 3 W-YYO
(A.J.R.Pearson) A.J.R.Pearson, 1994
'Dell Chapel' × 'Corozal'; sdlg no. 89-69-L15
Fl. forming a rounded double triangle, 95 mm wide; perianth segments broadly ovate, rounded at apex, greenish white (145D), spreading, plane, silken smooth and of great substance, overlapping two-thirds; corona bowl-shaped, straight-sided, ribbed, light greenish yellow 5D, shading to a slightly darker tone (5C) at base, with a band of strong orange (24A to 28A) at rim, mouth frilled and sometimes lobed. Mid-season to late

'Sugar Bird' 2 W-P
(Brian S.Duncan) Brian S.Duncan, 1997
'Dailmanach' × 'Gracious Lady'; sdlg no. 1326
Fl. rounded, 110 mm wide; perianth segments broadly ovate; corona bowl-shaped, broad, pink, with overtones of lilac, paling towards rim, with mouth slightly flared. Mid-season

'Sugarbush' 7 W-YYW
(A. Gray, pre-1954)
N. jonquilla × ('John Evelyn' × 'Red Cross')
Fls 1-2 per stem, 65 mm wide, opening yellow; perianth segments broadly ovate, prominently mucronate, becoming ivory white, spreading or a little inflexed, with margins incurling, overlapping half; the inner segments more nearly roundish, less noticeably mucronate, with margins deeply incurved; corona bowl-shaped, broadly ribbed, becoming between brilliant yellow 8A and light greenish yellow 8B, with creamy white at rim, mouth very shallowly lobed, wavy, with rim minutely notched. Mid-season. 2n=21. *AM(p) 1986

'Sugar Glow' 2 W-Y
(J.N.Hancock & Co., 1984) Unregistered
Sdlg no. 9/84H
Perianth segments pure white, slightly reflexed; corona long cup-shaped, constricted near mouth, soft yellow. Tall. Early

'Sugar Loaf' 4 W-P
(Murray W. Evans, 1968) Murray W. Evans, 1980
'Pink Chiffon' × 'Accent'; sdlg no. L-43/5
Fl. 105 mm wide

'Sugar Maple' 2 YYW-P
(G.E. Mitsch) G.E. Mitsch, 1977
'Leonaine' × 'Daydream'; sdlg no. F25/1
Fl. 87 mm wide; perianth segments deep lemon, with white at base, overlapping; corona salmon pink, with some white at base and with a deeper pink towards rim. Mid-season

'Sugar Plum' ?-P
(Alister Clark, pre-1948)

'Suhaili' 3 W-OOW
(R.W. Ward) R.W. Ward & Son, 1969
'Blarney' × 'Heaven'

'Suilven' 2 (a)
(A.M. Wilson, pre-1916)

'Suilven' 3 W-W
(J.S.B. Lea) J.S.B. Lea, 1956
'Chinese White' × 'Green Island'
Perianth segments very broad, rounded and sometimes nicked at apex, mucronate, spreading, plane, with midrib showing, overlapping half; the inner segments narrower, shouldered at base; corona bowl-shaped, white, with dark green at base, loosely frilled. Mid-season. PC(e) 1957

'Suisgill' 4 W-PPY
(J.S.B.Lea) J.S.B.Lea, 1983
Sdlg 2-61-62 × sdlg 1-40-67; sdlg no. 23-31-72
Fl. 112 mm wide

'Suitor' 2 (a or b)
(J.N. Hancock & Co., pre-1949)

N. sulcicaulis Spach = *N. corcyrensis*

'Sulis' 3 W-WWR
(C.E. Radcliff, 1933)
'Silver Plane' × 'Blodwen'

'Sulivan' 1 W-? (b)
(J.W. Barr, pre-1930)

'Sulpherino' 8 Y-Y
(pre-1807)
Fl. sulphur yellow; corona a little darker in tone

'Sulphre Kroon' 4 W-Y
(pre-1798)
Perianth and other petaloid segments silver white; corona segments sulphur yellow. 2n=14. Syn. 'Sulphur Crown', 'Sulphur Kroon'. ?The same as 'Sulphur Phoenix'

'Sulphur' 1 Y-Y
(P.D. Williams, pre-1927)
'Maximus' hybrid
Perianth segments broadly ovate, blunt, only very slightly mucronate, chrome yellow, slightly inflexed, somewhat twisted, with margins incurling, overlapping one-third; the inner segments narrower and more strongly twisted; corona primrose yellow, with rim widely flanged and deeply notched and dentate. Early. *AM(c)(g) 1927, *AM(m) 1935, *AM(g) 1936. Also named 'Lamorna'

'Sulphur Beauty' 1 W-W
(den Older, pre-1908)
Corona opening creamy white, becoming white. FCC(Haarlem) 1908

'Sulphur Bride' 2 W-W
(J. Vink, pre-1949)

'Sulphur Crown' 4 W-Y
Syn. of 'Sulphre Kroon'

'Sulphurea Major' 8 Y-Y
(pre-1798)
Fl. sulphur yellow

'Sulphurea Nova' 8 Y-Y
(pre-1798)
Fl. sulphur yellow

'Sulphurescens' 1 W-Y
Syn. of 'Michael Foster'

'Sulphureus' 3 W-Y
(W. Backhouse, pre-1869)
Perianth segments becoming sulphur white. Syn. Barrii Sulphureus 'Sulphureus'. "Absorbed" Barrii Albidus 'Albidus'

'Sulphureus' 2 Y-Y
(E. Leeds, pre-1877)
Perianth segments sulphur yellow; corona darker in tone. Syn. Incomparabilis Sulphureus 'Sulphureus'

'Sulphureus' 3 Y-YYR
(pre-1879)
Perianth segments primrose yellow; corona citron yellow, with cinnabar red at rim

'Sulphureus' 8 Y-O
(pre-1885)
Perianth segments sulpur yellow; corona widely expanded, light orange

'Sulphureus Delicatus' 3 Y-Y
(pre-1880)
Perianth segments pale primrose yellow; corona widely expanded, darker in tone. Syn. Burbidgei 'Sulphureus Delicatus'

'Sulphureus Model' 3 ?-YYO
Syn. of 'Model'

'Sulphureus Stellatus' 3 W-YYR
Syn. of 'Sulphur Star'

'Sulphur Eye' 3 W-Y
(The Brodie of Brodie, c.1909)
? × 'Ornatus'
Fl. rounded; corona disc-shaped, pale yellow

'Sulphur Frills' 1 W-? (b)
(R.H. Bath, pre-1931)

'Sulphur Gem' 1 (a)
(J.R. Pearson & Sons, pre-1916)

'Sulphur Giant' 1 (a)
(de Graaff Bros, pre-1928)

'Sulphur Gold' 1 Y-Y
(D.S. Bell) D.S. Bell, 1962
'Broughshane' × 'Ardclinis'
Fl. 104 mm wide, sulphur yellow. Early. Resembles 'Kingscourt' but with the perianth segments more nearly acute

'Sulphurine' 8 Y-Y
(pre-1861)
Poetaz
Perianth segments citron yellow; corona dark yellow. AM(Haarlem) 1913

'Sulphurine' 1 Y-Y
(de Graaff Bros) de Graaff Bros, 1961
Fl. 115 mm wide; perianth segments light greenish yellow 4B; corona pale buttercup yellow. Late

'Sulphur King' 1 Y-Y
(R.H. Bath, pre-1923)

'Sulphur Kroon' 4 W-Y
Syn. 'Sulphre Kroon'

'Sulphur Monarch' 1 Y-Y
(J.A.Hunter) J.A.Hunter, 1995
'Temple Gold' × 'King's Ransom'; sdlg no. 2/82B
Fl. 110 mm wide, sulphur yellow; perianth segments ovate; corona flared, with mouth frilled. Early to mid-season. AM(e)(NZ) 1997

'Sulphur Orange' 8 W-O
(Dutch origin, pre-1922)
Poetaz
Perianth segments sulphur white; corona orange

'Sulphur Phoenix' 4 W-Y
(pre-1820)
Perianth and other petaloid segments in many whorls, white or yellowish white, ovate, slightly overlapping; the outer whorls spreading, with margins recurved, fairly regularly arranged; the inner whorls successively shorter, inflexed; the centre whorls twisted and more strongly inflexed; corona segments very short, interspersed among the petaloid segments, sulphur yellow. 2n=14. Syn. ?'Sulphur Kroon', 'Codlings and Cream', 'Codlins and Cream', 'Lemon Phoenix', Incomparabilis 'Albus Plenus Sulphureus'

'Sulphur Prince' 1 Y-Y
(The Brodie of Brodie, c.1925)
'Ben Alder' × 'White Knight'
Fl. large, soft yellow; perianth segments overlapping; corona slightly darker in tone than the perianth. Mid-season. 2n=28. *HC(g) 1936, *AM(g) 1939

'Sulphur Queen' 2 (a)
(Cartwright & Goodwin, pre-1908)

'Sulphur Queen' 4
(pre-1930)

'Sulphur Queen' 5 Y-Y
(C.G. van Tubergen) C.G. van Tubergen, 1956
Fls 2 per stem; perianth segments sulphur yellow; corona creamy yellow

'Sulphur Spur' 1 W-? (b)
Syn. of 'Silver Spur'

'Sulphur Star' 3 W-YYR
(W. Backhouse, pre-1869)
Perianth segments sulphur white; corona primrose yellow, with scarlet at rim. Syn. Burbidgei 'Sulphur Star', Burbidgei 'Sulphureus Stellatus'

'Sultan' 8 W-O
(pre-1846)

'Sultan' 1 Y-Y
(G.L. Wilson, pre-1931)
'Ceopatra' × 'Darius'
Fl. large, soft yellow; perianth segments very broad, smooth, overlapping; corona slender

'Sultana' 5
(?Sir C.H. Cave, pre-1914)

'Sultry' 2 W-? (b or c)
(J.R. Pearson & Sons, pre-1937)

'Sumatra' 2 Y-O
(Warnaar & Co., pre-1939)
'Fortune' × 'Tregoose'
AM(Haarlem) 1939

'Sumgent' 1 W-Y
(P. Phillips) P. Phillips, 1967
Corona buff yellow. Mid-season. Resembles a larger-flowered 'Trousseau' with the corona more widely expanded and of a darker colour with the rim deeply dentate

'Summer' 2 Y-O/Y
(J.W.A. Lefeber, c.1972) Unregistered
'Papillon Blanche' × 'Professor Einstein'

'Summercourt' 2 W-WWP
(T.A.V. Wood, pre-1949)
Corona opening pale lemon yellow, becoming white, with buff pink at rim

Summercups Group
Commercial name for a group of several different cultivars specially retarded for late flowering

'Summerfield' 2 W-RRY
(F.E. Board) F.E. Board, 1965
'Blarney's Daughter' × 'Arbar'; sdlg no. 542
Late

'Summer Fiesta' 2 W-P
(J.N. Hancock & Co., c.1966) Unregistered
'Wonder Bird' × 'Princess Betty'
Corona peach pink, frilled

'Summerleas' 1 W-WPP
(S.J. Bisdee, 1942) S.J. Bisdee, 1956
'Eskimo' × 'Dawnglow'

'Summer Love' 2 W-YYW
(C.M. Grullemans) J.J. Grullemans & Sons, 1959
Fl. 125 mm wide; perianth segments creamy white; corona light greenish yellow 8B, with creamy white at rim. Mid-season

'Summer Solstice' 3 Y-R
(Brian S. Duncan) Brian S. Duncan, 1997
'Triple Crown' × 'Burning Bush'; sdlg no. 1520
Fl. rounded, 95 mm wide; perianth segments broadly ovate, deep golden yellow, plane, smooth; corona slightly flared, ribbed, deep red. Late

'Summer-time' 3 W-GYR
(G.H. Johnstone, pre-1954)

'Summer Wine' 2 W-P
(J.N. Hancock & Co.) Unregistered
Corona funnel-shaped, true pink, mouth expanded and neatly frilled. Tall. Early

'Summit' 2 W-O
(G.A. Uit den Boogaard) G.A. Uit den Boogaard, 1958
Perianth segments creamy white; corona shallow, pale orange. AM(Haarlem) 1958, FCC(Haarlem) 1960

'Summit' 1 Y-Y
(J.N. Hancock & Co., 1955) Unregistered
'Shanghai' hybrid
Fl. bright yellow; corona mouth expanded and frilled

'Sumner' 11b Y-O/Y
(J.W.A. Lefeber, 1968) J.W.A. Lefeber, 1978
Fl. 90 mm wide; perianth segments greenish yellow (4D); corona segments with a longitudinal band of strong orange 25A at midrib flanked by primrose yellow. Early to mid-season

'Sumo Jewel' 6 Y-Y
(R.A. Scamp) D. Woodman, 1993
'Arctic Gold' × *N. cyclamineus*; sdlg no. 213
Fl. 80 mm wide, deep yellow; perianth segments ovate, reflexed, slightly twisted, overlapping a quarter or less; corona cylindrical, long, angled, constricted near mouth, with rim notched and flanged. Dwarf. Early

'Sumptuous' 1 W-Y
(G.E. Mitsch, 1957) G.E. Mitsch, 1967
'Paul Bunyan' × 'Content'; sdlg no. R55/1
Fl. 121 mm wide; perianth segments milk white; corona clear yellow

'Sun 'n' Snow' 1 Y-W
(G.E. Mitsch) G.E. Mitsch, 1970
(['Shirley Wyness' × 'Pink-a-dell'] × 'Dawnglow') × 'Lunar Sea'

'Sunapee' 3 Y-YYR
(Murray W. Evans) Murray W. Evans, 1969
'Carbineer' × 'Ardour'
Perianth segments very broadly ovate, blunt or truncate, mucronate, creamy yellow, spreading, with margins slightly incurling at apex; the inner segments very slightly inflexed; corona shallow bowl-shaped, lightly ribbed, golden yellow, with orange at rim

'Sun Aura' 2 W-YYO
(J.N. Hancock & Co., c.1966) Unregistered
'Fortune' hybrid × 'Ivo Fell'
Corona yellow, with bright reddish orange at rim, frilled

'Sun Ball' 4 Y-Y
(Murray W. Evans) Murray W. Evans, 1976
'Falaise' hybrid × 'Dawnlight'; sdlg no. L-42
Fl. 105 mm wide; perianth and other petaloid segments yellow; corona segments deeper in tone. Mid-season. Resembles a later-flowered 'Fiji' of more symmetrical form

'Sun Bath' 2 Y-O
(J.N. Hancock & Co.) J.N. Hancock & Co., 1955
Perianth segments golden yellow; corona widely expanded, orange

'Sunbather' 2 Y-R
(Carncairn Daffodils) Carncairn Daffodils, 1984
'Vulcan' × 'Spelter'; sdlg no. W24/12
Fl. 90 mm wide; perianth segments orange-yellow; corona orange-red. Early to mid-season

'Sunbeam' 1 (a)
(W.B. Hartland, pre-1890)

'Sunbeam' 3 W-O
(Mrs R.O. Backhouse, pre-1907)
Fl. small; perianth segments ovate, creamy white, tinged sulphur yellow at base; corona shallow, bright reddish orange. Resembles 'Sunrise'

'Sunbeam' 1 Y-Y
(C.G. van Tubergen, pre-1947)
Fl. pale yellow

'Sunbeam' 1 Y-Y
(A. Gibson) R. Hyde, 1959

'Sunbeater' 2 (a)
(Mrs Ben Robertson, pre-1953)

'Sun Beauty' 2 Y-?
(T. Bloomer) T. Bloomer, 1972
'Richhill' × 'Vulcan'; sdlg no. 4/84/65

'Sunbird' 2 Y-Y
(G.E. Mitsch) G.E. Mitsch, 1967
('King of the North' × 'Content') × 'Binkie'; sdlg no. P5/14
Fl. 115 mm wide, bright yellow. Mid-season. Resembles 'Bethany' in form

'Sunblaze' 2 W-? (b)
(Slieve Donard Nursery Co., pre-1927)

'Sunbreak' 2 Y-? (a)
(G.L. Wilson, pre-1940)
'Killigrew' × 'Porthilly'

'Sunbright' 2 (a)
(G. Zandbergen-Terwegen, pre-1937)

'Sunburst' 1 (a)
(R.H. Bath, pre-1927)

'Sunburst' 2 Y-? (a)
(L. Buckland, pre-1936)
Corona with red at rim

'Sunburst' 4 Y-Y
(Oregon Bulb Farms) Oregon Bulb Farms, 1955
Fl. large; perianth and other petaloid segments in several whorls, pale sulphur yellow; corona segments interspersed, rich yellow. Tall. 2n=28

'Sunburst' 11a Y-Y
Syn. of 'Brandaris'

'Sunbury' 1 (a)
(J.T. Gray, pre-1949)

'Sun Chariot' 2 Y-O
(J.L. Richardson, pre-1943)
Fl. 114 mm wide; perianth segments broadly ovate, blunt, fairly prominently mucronate, vivid yellow 12A, spreading, plane, with margins minutely incurling, regular, overlapping one-third; the inner segments more narrowly ovate, a little inflexed; corona short funnel-shaped, orange, paler at base, with mouth straight and regularly frilled. Early to mid-season. Sunproof. AM(e) 1951, AM(Haarlem) 1954, FCC(Haarlem) 1956, *AM(g) 1963

'Sun Child' 2 W-GWY
(Colin Crotty) Colin Crotty, 1990
'Eminent' × 'Lysander'; sdlg no. 10-76
Fl. 86 mm wide; perianth segments roundish, somewhat truncate, fairly prominently mucronate, pure white, spreading, smooth, overlapping half; the inner segments more nearly ovate, square-shouldered at base; corona shallow, ribbed, white, with green at base and a wide band of rich yellow at rim, closely frilled. Mid-season

'Sun City' 1 Y-Y
(Mrs J. Abel Smith) Mrs J. Abel Smith, 1983
'Squire' × 'Arctic Gold'
Fl. deep golden yellow

'Suncollar' 11a Y-Y
(J. Gerritsen & Son) J. Gerritsen & Son, 1984
'Obelisk' hybrid
Perianth segments brilliant yellow 8A; corona segments darker in tone (9A). Early

'Suncrest' 2 Y-YYO
(Barr & Sons) Wallace & Barr, 1957
Fl. 85 mm wide; perianth segments brilliant greenish yellow 6B; corona slightly ribbed, vivid yellow 14B, flushed strong orange 25A towards mouth, mouth slightly expanded, frilled, with rim dentate

'Sun Dance' 1 Y-Y
(G.L. Wilson, pre-1936)
'Magnificence' × 'Fortune'
Div. 2 until 1938

'Sundart' 3 W-? (b)
(Barr & Sons, pre-1937)

'Sunday Chimes' 5 W-W
(G.E. Mitsch and R. & E.Havens, 1972) G.E. Mitsch and R. & E.Havens, 1985
'Pigeon' × *N. triandrus*; sdlg no. 2H85/2
Fls usually 2 per stem, of waxy texture; perianth segments ovate, blunt, fairly prominently mucronate, strongly reflexed, with margins sometimes incurling at apex, overlapping half; the inner segments less strongly reflexed, with margins sometimes wavy or recurved; corona cup-shaped, lightly ribbed, with green in tube, mouth straight, wavy, rim almost entire. Late

'Sunday Silence' 3 W-YYO
(Mrs J. Abel Smith, 1978) Mrs J. Abel Smith, 1990
'Verona' hybrid; sdlg no. R33/91
Fl. 93 mm wide. Late

'Sunderland' 1 Y-Y
(C.E. Radcliff, 1938)
'Loxton' × 'Ossa'

'Sundew' 2 Y-Y
(Barr & Sons, pre-1915)
Perianth segments broadly ovate, blunt, prominently mucronate, primrose yellow, spreading, plane, overlapping half; the inner segments narrower, a little inflexed, twisted; corona bowl-shaped, smooth, deep yellow, loosely frilled

'Sundew' 2 W-? (b or c)
(P.D. Williams, pre-1927)

'Sundial' 2 or 3 W-? (b or c)
(Barr & Sons, pre-1908)

'Sundial' 7 Y-Y
(A. Gray) A. Gray, 1955
N. rupicola × *N. poeticus*
Fl. 35 mm wide; perianth segments very broadly ovate, blunt, brilliant yellow 8A, with slight white mucro, reflexed, overlapping half; the inner segments with margins incurved; corona very shallow bowl-shaped, ribbed, darker in tone (12A) than the perianth, with mouth wavy, rim entire. Early. 2n=14. Resembles a shorter, smaller and much earlier-flowered 'Bobbysoxer'

'Sun Disc' 7 Y-Y
(A. Gray, pre-1946)
N. rupicola sdlg
Fl. rounded, 50 mm wide, self yellow or with perianth paler than corona; perianth segments very broad in outline, rounded or squarish and sometimes truncate at apex, prominently mucronate, a little reflexed, smooth, of good substance, overlapping half; the inner segments narrower, with apex rounded or retuse, not noticeably mucronate, more nearly spreading, with margins somewhat incurved; corona disc-shaped, ribbed, lightly frilled. Dwarf. AGM 1996

'Sundown' 4
(?Cartwright & Goodwin, pre-1914)

'Sundown' 2 (a)
(Mrs R.O. Backhouse, pre-1921)

'Sundown' 2 W-?
(D.J. Cooper) D.J. Cooper, 1963
Fl. 115 mm wide, creamy white; corona with patches of orange-yellow. Late. Resembles 'Melitza'

'Sundowner' 2 Y-O
(J.N.Hancock & Co.) J.N.Hancock & Co., 1997
'Cove' × 'Artist's Model'; sdlg no. 8/84H
Perianth segments ovate, bright yellow, spreading; corona bowl-shaped, expanded, brilliant orange, with mouth ribbed and frilled. Mid-season

'Sun Dream' 2 Y-Y
(G.H. Rotteveel & Sons) G.H. Rotteveel & Sons, 1982
Perianth segments brilliant yellow 7A; corona orange-yellow (15A)

'Sunella' 5 Y-Y
(Mrs G.Link) Mrs G.Link, 1995
'Pink Sprite' × *N. triandrus*; sdlg no. 480
Fls sometimes 3 per stem, 50 mm wide; perianth segments ovate, acute, sulphur yellow, somewhat reflexed, more or less plane, deeply overlapping; corona bowl-shaped, ribbed, slightly deeper in tone than the perianth, with rim 12-notched. Dwarf. Mid-season. Scented

'Sun Fire' 3 Y-R
(T. Bloomer) T. Bloomer, 1962
'Therm' × 'Chungking'; sdlg no. 3/36/50
Perianth segments deep yellow; corona deep red. 2n=28

'Sunfirm' 2 (a)
(Mrs R.O. Backhouse, pre-1921)

'Sunfish' 1 (a)
(W.F.M. Copeland, pre-1908)

'Sun Flame' 3 Y-R
(T. Bloomer) T. Bloomer, 1970
'Chungking' × 'Sun Fire'; sdlg no. 2/16/57

'Sunflower' 1
(G.H.Engleheart, pre-1897)

'Sunflower' 2 (a)
(P.D. Williams, pre-1907)

'Sunflower' 2 W-O
(J.N. Hancock & Co., c.1977) Unregistered
Corona closely overlying the perianth, orange, with rim regularly dentate. Late

'Sun Frolic' 3 W-R
(H.A. Brown) J.N. Hancock & Co., 1955
Perianth segments cream; corona bright red

'Sungazer' 2 Y-?
(R.C.A. Tombleson) R.C.A. Tombleson, 1972
'Vulcan' × 'Narvik'
Fl. 124 mm wide

'Sungazer' 2 Y-R
(R.H.Glover, pre-1993) Unregistered

'Sun Gem' 2 YYW-W
(G.E. Mitsch, 1974) G.E. Mitsch, 1984
Sdlg no. JO14/1
Fl. rounded, 82 mm wide; perianth segments very broadly ovate, blunt, rich lemon yellow, touched white at base, reflexed, overlapping half; the inner segments square-shouldered at base, with margins wavy; corona somewhat funnel-shaped, lightly ribbed, opening buff yellow, becoming almost white, with mouth flared and even, rim irregularly and minutely notched. Dwarf to standard. Mid-season

'Sungleam' 2 Y-O
(Barr & Sons, pre-1925)
Fl. star-shaped; perianth segments sulphur; corona ribbed, scarlet-orange

'Sun Gleam' 3 Y-R
(T. Bloomer) T. Bloomer, 1972
'Chungking' × 'Air Marshal'; sdlg no. 13/67/58
Fl. 92 mm wide; perianth segments broad, deep yellow, smooth, of heavy substance; corona small, deep red, with mouth straight

'Sun Glory' 3 W-? (b)
(Mrs R.O. Backhouse, pre-1921)

'Sunglow' 2 W-? (b)
(L. van Leeuwen & Son, pre-1930)
AM(Haarlem) 1930

'Sungod' 1 Y-Y
(pre-1927)

'Sungold' 2 Y-Y
(S.J. Bisdee, 1941)
Sdlg × 'Fahan'

'Sun Gold' 1 Y-Y
(D.S. Bell) D.S. Bell, 1957
Fl. golden yellow; corona with rim rolled

'Sunheat' 4 Y-O
(Th. van der Hulst) Th. van der Hulst, 1989
'Mary Bohannon' × 'Tahiti'
Fl. 115 mm wide; perianth segments brilliant greenish yellow 6B; corona segments vivid orange 28B. Early

'Sunhill' 2 Y-Y
(H. Leber) H. Leber, 1972
? × 'John Evelyn'
Fl. 105 mm wide

'Sunion' 3 (a)
(Mrs R.O. Backhouse, pre-1921)
Syn. 'Jason'

'Sun King' 2 (a)
(H.G. Longford) H.G. Longford, 1933

'Sun King' 3 Y-R
(D.S.Bell, pre-1986) Unregistered

'Sunkist' 2 Y-O
(G.L. Wilson, pre-1935)
Sdlg 15/7 × 'Cornish Fire'
Perianth segments golden yellow; corona clear reddish orange, frilled. Sunproof

'Sunkist' 2 W-? (b)
(P.D. Williams, pre-1937)
AM(Haarlem) 1937

'Sun Lane' 1 W-W
(E.W. Philpott) E.W. Philpott, 1959
Mid-season. Resembles an improved 'Quartz'

'Sunleigh' 2 (a)
(Mrs M. Moorby) Mrs M. Moorby, 1956

'Sun-light' 2 Y-O
(E. Leeds, pre-1877)
Fl. star-shaped; corona stained orange. Syn. Incomparabilis Leedsii 'Stellatus', Incomparabilis Leedsii 'Sun-light'. "Absorbed" 'Sun-ray'

'Sunlight' 8 Y-Y
(van Zonneveld Bros & Philippo, pre-1922)
Poetaz
Perianth segments yellow; corona orange-yellow

'Sunlit' 2 W-? (b)
(G.L. Wilson, pre-1939)

'Sunlit Hours' 2 Y-Y
(G.E. Mitsch, 1952) G.E. Mitsch, 1963
'Saint Issey' × 'Galway'; sdlg no. N115/1
Fl. 121 mm wide, bright yellow. Early. Resembles a larger and paler-flowered 'Saint Issey' with a longer corona

'Sunlover' 2 Y-O
(W.F. Leenen) W.F. Leenen, 1982
'Ipi Tombi' hybrid
Perianth segments brilliant greenish yellow 7C; corona strong orange 30D, frilled

'Sun Magic' 3 Y-R
(T. Bloomer) T. Bloomer, 1970
'Richhill' × 'Doubtful'
Perianth segments mid-yellow; corona deep red

'Sunmaid' 2 W-YYO
(S.A. Free, 1965) S.A. Free, 1976
Sdlg no. 65-65
Fl. 100 mm wide; corona buff, with apricot at rim. Mid-season

'Sunmaster' 2 Y-Y
(G. Lubbe & Sons) G. Lubbe & Sons, 1978
Fl. 140 mm wide; perianth segments brilliant greenish yellow 6A; corona vivid yellow 12A. Mid-season

'Sunnal' 2 Y-Y
(N.R. McIsaac) N.R. McIsaac, 1978
'Squatter' × 'Kingscourt'; sdlg no. 99
Fl. 108 mm wide; perianth segments deep yellow; corona gold. Early to mid-season

'Sunnette' 2 (a)
(Mrs M. Moorby) Mrs M. Moorby, 1957

'Sunningdale' 2 Y-O
(Warnaar & Co., pre-1951)
'Aranjuez' × 'Westminster'
AM(Haarlem) 1951

'Sunny' 3 W-? (b)
(Warnaar & Co., pre-1926)
AM(Haarlem) 1926

'Sunny Boy' 2 (a)
(Warnaar & Co., pre-1938)

'Sunny Boy' 2 Y-Y
(G.H. Rotteveel & Sons) G.H. Rotteveel & Sons, 1962
Fl. 105 mm wide; perianth segments brilliant greenish yellow 5B; corona light orange-yellow 16C. Early

'Sunny Brook' 2 W-O
(de Graaff Bros, pre-1938)
AM(Haarlem) 1938

'Sunny Charm' 2 Y-R
(T. Bloomer) T. Bloomer, 1972
'Royal Charger' × 'Border Chief'; sdlg no. 2/29/58
Perianth segments deep yellow; corona deep red

'Sunny Day' 2 Y-Y
(G.H. Rotteveel & Sons) G.H. Rotteveel & Sons, 1982
Perianth segments light greenish yellow 4C to pale yellow-green 4D; corona vivid yellow 12A

'Sunny Delight' 2 Y-Y
(Eileen E. Frey) J. & E. Frey, 1982
'Playboy' × 'Chiloquin'; sdlg no. JEE8/9
Fl. 97 mm wide

'Sunny Future' 2 YYW-GWW
(Eileen E.Frey, 1974) J. & E.Frey, 1996
'Playboy' × 'Daydream'; sdlg no. JEE9/6
Fl. 100 mm wide; perianth segments lemon yellow, with white at base; corona opening lemon yellow, with soft apricot at rim, becoming white, with green at base. Mid-season

'Sunny Girl' 2 W-YYO
Syn. of 'Beaucaillou'

'Sunny Isle' 3 W-YYO
(Mrs R.O. Backhouse, pre-1921)
Perianth segments slightly reflexed; corona very shallow, bright yellow, with a broad band of scarlet-orange at rim

'Sunny Jim' 3 W-? (b)
(W. Polman-Mooy, pre-1923)

'Sunny Lad' 2 Y-?
(pre-1960) Unregistered
Perianth segments rich yellow. Tall. Early

'Sunny Lass' 3 W-YYR
(C. Dawson, pre-1919)
Corona expanded, bright yellow, with a broad band of scarlet at rim

'Sunny Maiden' 6 Y-GYY
(Eileen E.Frey, 1980) J. & E.Frey, 1996
'Wee Bee' × *N. cyclamineus*; sdlg no. PEF9/1
Fl. 48 mm wide, bright yellow; perianth segments reflexed; corona cylindrical, with green at base, mouth very slightly expanded, frilled. Dwarf. Very Early

'Sunnymead' 2 W-? (b)
(Barr & Sons, pre-1946)

'Sunny Miss' 7 Y-O
(W.G. Pannill) W.G. Pannill, 1985
'Tuskar Light' × *N. jonquilla*; sdlg no. D 76
Mid-season

'Sunny Morn' 3 Y-?
(T. Bloomer) T. Bloomer, 1972
'Lemonade' × 'Doubtful'

'Sunny Ring' 2 W-WWY
(Jānis Rukšans, 1985) Jānis Rukšans, 1997
'Knowehead' × 'Bit o' Gold'
Fl. 104 mm wide; perianth segments pure white, concave, deeply overlapping; corona opening cylindrical, becoming funnel-shaped, pure white, with a distinct and narrow band of vivid greenish yellow 2A at rim, tightly frilled. Early

'Sunnyside' 2 Y-Y
(W.G. Pannill) W.G. Pannill, 1972
'Fine Gold' × 'Saint Keverne'
Fl. 96 mm wide

'Sunny Song' 2 Y-GYY
(Eileen E.Frey, 1974) J. & E.Frey, 1996
'Playboy' × 'Chiloquin'; sdlg no. JEE8/8
Fl. 85 mm wide, lemon yellow; perianth segments roundish; corona with green at base. Mid-season

'Sunny Thoughts' 2 Y-Y
(Eileen E. Frey) G.E. Mitsch, 1979
'Playboy' × 'Chiloquin'; sdlg no. JEE8/2
Fl. 90 mm wide; perianth segments golden yellow, overlapping; corona deeper in tone. Mid-season. Resembles a slightly larger-flowered 'Scio' with a more deeply frilled corona

'Sunny Trace' 3 W-? (b)
(Mrs R.O. Backhouse, pre-1921)
Sdlg no. 2/25

'Sun Orb' 1 (a)
(Barr & Sons, pre-1929)

'Sun Orbit' 2 Y-R
(R.H.Glover, pre-1993) Unregistered

'Sunpath' 1 (a)
(G.H. Engleheart, pre-1927)

'Sun Pink' 2 Y-WPP
(G.E. Mitsch and R. & E.Havens, 1970) Grant Mitsch Novelty Daffodils, 1984
'Leonaine' × 'Daydream'; sdlg no. F25/10
Fl. 88 mm wide; perianth segments deep lemon yellow. Mid-season

'Sunpool' 2 Y-O
(H.A. Brown, 1936) J.N. Hancock & Co., 1955
Perianth segments rich yellow; corona large, deep orange-red, mouth widely flared, with rim deeply rolled. Early-mid-season

'Sunpride' 2 Y-O
(S.C. Gaspar, 1950) R.J. Abernethy, 1960
Fl. 102 mm wide; perianth segments bright golden yellow; corona bowl-shaped, deep reddish orange, with a lighter tone at base. Mid-season

'Sun Prince' 2 Y-O
(J.L. Richardson, pre-1951)
'Sudan' open pollinated
Perianth segments clear gold; corona deep orange. Resembles a smaller 'Sun Chariot'

'Sunproof' 2 (a)
(G. Zandbergen-Terwegen, pre-1937)

'Sunproof Orange' 2 Y-O
(G.L. Wilson, pre-1935)
Sdlg 15/7 × P.D. Williams Y-R sdlg
Perianth segments rich gold; corona deep tangerine orange. Sunproof. 2n=28

'Sun Queen' 2 (a)
(S.C. Gaspar) R.J. Abernethy, 1957

'Sun-ray' 2 Y-Y
(E. Leeds, pre-1877)
Perianth segments narrow, acute. Syn. Incomparabilis Concolor 'Stellatus', Incomparabilis Concolor 'Sunray'. Was "absorbed" into 'Sun-light'

'Sunray' 2 Y-YYO
(P.D. Williams, pre-1930)
Perianth segments clear yellow; corona gold, shading to bright reddish orange at rim. AM(Haarlem) 1930, AM(e) 1932

'Sunray' 2 Y-YYR
(R.H.Glover, pre-1989) Unregistered
'Emblaze' × 'Falstaff'

'Sunraysia' 2 Y-O
(W.M. Spry, pre-1975) Unregistered
'Bahram' × 'Golden Coin'

'Sun Reveller' 2 Y-R
(E.F. Hughes) E.F. Hughes, 1962
Fl. 108 mm wide; perianth segments medium yellow; corona intense scarlet. Mid-season

'Sunrider' 2 Y-? (a)
(F.E. Board) F.E. Board, 1956
'Royalist' × 'Bastion'

'Sunridge' 2 Y-OOY
(H.A. Brown, 1939) J.N. Hancock & Co., 1955
Perianth segments bright yellow; corona short, deep reddish orange, with yellow at rim. Early

'Sunrise' 3 W-YYO
(Mrs R.O. Backhouse, pre-1901)
Fl. 70 mm wide, facing slightly downwards; perianth segments obovate in outline, blunt or squarish at apex, mucronate, white, with a suffusion of yellow at base and along midrib sometimes extending almost to apex, spreading, more or less plane, a little ribbed and of thin substance, somewhat irregular in form, overlapping one-third to a half; the inner segments narrower, ovate, more regular in form, only very slightly mucronate, a little inflexed, with margins wavy; corona shallow bowl-shaped, slightly ribbed, rich orange-yellow, shading to clear mid-orange at rim, mouth split in places and overlapping, rim dentate and sometimes notched. 2n=14. FCC(Haarlem) 1912, AM(c) 1914, *AM(m) 1927, EFA(Haarlem) 1928, *AM(g) 1936

'Sunrising' 2 W-?
(G.H. Johnstone, pre-1960) Unregistered
('White Sentinel' × 'Hades') × 'Latonia'

'Sun Salute' 2 Y-O
(H.A. Brown, 1932) J.N. Hancock & Co., 1960
Corona bright orange, with mouth expanded and frilled

'Sun Salver' 2 Y-R
(Ballydorn Bulb Farm) Ballydorn Bulb Farm, 1976
'Gaucho' open pollinated
Fl. 110 mm wide; perianth segments golden; corona orange-red. Mid-season. Resembles 'Rialto' but with a brighter-coloured corona

'Sunset' 8 Y-O
(Barr & Sons, pre-1889)
Hybrid between *N. jonquilla* and *N. tazetta*
Fls 3 or more per stem; perianth segments ovate, canary yellow, more or less spreading, sometimes twisted or with margins incurved or wavy, overlapping a quarter; corona shallow cup-shaped, ribbed, rich orange, with mouth straight and closely ribbed. Dwarf. AM 1899

'Sunset Fires' 3 W-R
(S.J. Bisdee, 1936) S.J. Bisdee, 1956
Sdlg × 'Lillian Murdoch'
Perianth segments soft yellow; corona almost disc-shaped, ribbed, rich orange-red, with rim lightly frilled. Tall

'Sunset Glory' 2 (a)
(J. Gerritsen & Son, pre-1944)

'Sunset Glow' 2 Y-O
(Mrs R.O. Backhouse, pre-1921)
Perianth segments soft yellow; corona shallow, widely expanded, dark orange. AM(Haarlem) 1930

'Sunset Gold' 1 (a)
(Sir A.P.W. Thomas, pre-1930)

'Sunset Pink' 2 W-P
(K.J. Heazlewood, c.1967) Unregistered
'Lanena' × 'Wild Rose'

'Sunset Serenade' 11b W-Y/W
(J.W.A. Lefeber) J.J. Grullemans & Sons, 1959
Fl. rounded, 95 mm wide; perianth segments very broad, squarish at apex, prominently mucronate, a little reflexed, concave near apex, overlapping half or more; the inner segments almost as broad, truncate, spreading, with margins wavy; corona split to base, the six segments about half as long as the perianth segments and alternate to them, broadly ovate, with vivid yellow 13A at base and in a broad longitudinal band at midrib, with overtones of orange and with patches of white at margins in upper half, inflexed, somewhat twisted, with margins deeply incurled, deeply overlapping; with some short extra growths at base. Mid-season

'Sunset Sonata' 2 Y-YOO
(J. & E.Frey, 1983) J. & E.Frey, 1996
'Sunny Thoughts' × 'Vulcan'; sdlg no. TEF2/10
Fl. rounded, 75 mm wide; perianth segments very broadly ovate, bright yellow, spreading, plane, regular, overlapping half; the inner segments slightly truncate, a little inflexed; corona cylindrical or narrowly funnel-shaped, light orange, paling to yellow at base, shading to bright orange at rim, mouth only slightly expanded, wavy. Dwarf to standard. Mid-season

'Sun's Eye' 3 W-? (b)
(G.H. Engleheart, pre-1907)

'Sunshade' 2 W-Y
(C. Goodson, pre-1927)

'Sunshafts' 2 Y-Y
(S.J. Bisdee, 1943)
'Saint Egwin' × 'Crocus'

'Sunshine' 1 W-Y
(G.P. Haydon, pre-1907)
'Glory of Leiden' × Nelsonii 'Aurantius'
Corona rich dark yellow

'Sunshine' 2 Y-Y
(A.E. Lowe, pre-1927)

'Sunshine Susie' 2 W-P
(S.J. Bisdee, 1938) R. Hyde, 1958
'Mitylene' × 'Pink o' Dawn'

'Sunsilk' 2 Y-Y
(P. Phillips) P. Phillips, 1968

'Sunsplash' 3 Y-YYR
(Mrs G. Link) Mrs G. Link, 1991
'Tynemouth' × 'Altruist'; sdlg no. 2877
Perianth segments spreading, of thick substance, overlapping; corona bowl-shaped. Late

'Sun Spot' 3 (a)
(?W.A. Watts, pre-1913)
?The same as 'Sunspot'

'Sunspot' 3 (a)
(W.A. Watts, pre-1923)
?See also 'Sun Spot'

'Sunspot' 4 Y-O
(R.C. Gordon) R.C. Gordon, 1964
Mid-season

'Sunstar' 3 W-R
(Mrs R.O. Backhouse, pre-1921)
?'Will Scarlett' hybrid
Perianth segments milk white, of strong substance; corona dark crimson, with orange at base. Late. 2n=28. AM(Haarlem) 1928, AM(e) 1929

'Sunstar' 2 Y-Y
(C. Goodson, pre-1927)

'Sunstone' 1 Y-Y
(A.E. Lowe, pre-1927)

'Sunstroke' 2 O-R
(John R.Reed) John R.Reed, 1995
'Red Haze' × 'Stylish'; sdlg no. 83-108-5
Fl. 74 mm wide; perianth segments uniformly suffused orange; corona deep orange-red. Early

'Suntan' 1 Y-Y
(C.E. Radcliff, 1940)
'Princess Betty' × 'Dawnglow'

'Suntan' 2 Y-?
(J.S. Leitch) J.S. Leitch, 1960
Fl. 102 mm wide

'Sun Test' 2 (a)
(J.E. Exley, pre-1938)

'Suntide' 2 Y-O
(J.N. Hancock & Co.) J.N. Hancock & Co., 1960
Corona shallow, orange, with rim rolled

'Suntime' 1 Y-Y
(H. Leber) H. Leber, 1972
Fl. 130 mm wide

'Suntory' 3 Y-GYR
(Brian S. Duncan) Rathowen Daffodils, 1987
Corona narrow, ribbed, golden yellow, with very deep green at base and orange-red at rim. Mid-season

'Suntrail' 2 (a)
(Mrs P.M. Davis, pre-1948)

'Suntrap' 2 Y-YYR
(Brian S.Duncan) Brian S.Duncan, 1997
Sdlg no. 1812
Fl. 96 mm wide, deep golden yellow; perianth segments broadly ovate, spreading, plane, smooth; corona broad funnel-shaped, with a broad band of deep orange-red at rim, mouth slightly ribbed and expanded. Mid-season to late. Sunproof

'Sun Up' 2 Y-R
(A. Gibson, pre-1927)

'Sun Valley' 2 Y-O
(C.A. van Paridon) C.A. van Paridon, 1958
'Scarlet Perfection' × 'Fortune'
Perianth segments greenish yellow; corona orange (28A). AM(Haarlem) 1958. Received AM(Haarlem) 1958 as 'Red Valley'

'Sunwell' 1 Y-Y
(A.E. Lowe, pre-1927)

'Sun White' 1 W-W
(H. A. Brown, 1931)
Fl. pearly white, very smooth; corona cylindrical, with mouth straight. Very late. Syn. 'Sunwhite'

'Sunwhite' 1 W-W
Syn. of 'Sun White'

'Sun-Yat-Sen' 2 W-? (b)
(F.H. Chapman, pre-1927)

'Superb' 8 W-Y
(pre-1759)

'Superb' 1 (a)
(G.H. Engleheart, pre-1916)

'Superb' 2 Y-P
(Mrs C.O. Fairbairn, pre-1960) Unregistered

'Superba' 1 (a)
(de Graaff Bros, pre-1927)
?Syn. of 'Aubrey'

'Superbe' 8 W-O
Syn. of 'Medio Luteo Superbe'

'Superbissima' 8 Y-Y
(pre-1851)

'Super Bowl' 2 W-GYR
(Brian S.Duncan, 1985) Brian S.Duncan, 1996
Richardson sdlg 3517 ('Roseworthy' self pollinated × ?) × 'Raspberry Ring'; sdlg no. 1155
Fl. rounded, 92 mm wide; perianth segments very broad, only very slightly mucronate, pure white, spreading, plane; the inner segments narrower, not noticeably mucronate; corona bowl-shaped, widely expanded, lemon yellow, with olive green at base and a broad band of pinkish red at rim, mouth slightly lobed. Mid-season to late

'Superbus' 1 Y-Y
(E. Leeds, pre-1851)
'Major' or 'Maximus' hybrid
Fl. very deep yellow; perianth segments ovate, spreading or a little inflexed, overlapping a quarter to one-third; corona cylindrical, with mouth ribbed, rim deeply notched and crenate, widely flanged. Syn. Pseudonarcissus Major 'Superbus'. Was "absorbed" into 'Distinction'

'Superbus' 2 or 3 W-W
(E. Leeds, pre-1877)
Perianth segments inflexed; corona opening lemon yellow, becoming sulphur white. Syn. Leedsii 'Superbus'

'Superfine' 1 W-? (b)
(A.M. Williams, pre-1948)

'Supérieure' 8 W-O
(pre-1850)

'Superior' 2 (a)
(C.G. van Tubergen, pre-1944)

'Superior Rank' 2 Y-Y
(D.S. Bell) D.S. Bell, 1960
Fl. 108 mm wide, bright gold. Mid-season. Resembles 'Saint Egwin' but with a differently shaped corona

'Superlative' 2 W-W
(J.A. Morris) J.A. Morris, 1960
Fl. 121 mm wide. Mid-season. Resembles 'Early Mist'

'Supernova' 2 Y-R
(D.S. Bell) D.S. Bell, 1965
'Ceylon' × 'Rupee'
Mid-season. Resembles a larger-flowered 'Alamein' with the perianth segments more rounded

'Super Star' 2 Y-Y
(J.J. Grullemans & Sons) P.Q.M. Pennings, 1983
Fl. forming a double triangle; perianth segments very broadly ovate, fairly prominently mucronate, stained yellow, shading to a darker tone at base, a little reflexed, concave, overlapping half; the inner segments more nearly spreading, creased; corona shallow funnel-shaped, broad, ribbed, with mouth deeply split in places and overlapping, frilled

'Super Stars' 8 W-Y
(W.R.P. Welch, pre-1980) Unregistered
Selection from 'Minor Monarque'
Very early. Resembles a 'Minor Monarque' of improved substance and greater vigour with broader perianth segments

'Supertex' 2 Y-O
(J.N. Hancock & Co., 1968) Unregistered

'Support' 1 W-? (b)
(A.H. Ahrens) J.S. Leitch, 1955

'Suppose' 2 W-P
(J.N. Hancock & Co., 1953)
'Pink Pearl' × 'Rose Bay'
Perianth segments pure white; corona opening cream, becoming bright pink

'Suprema' 8 W-?
(pre-1807)

'Supremacy' 1 Y-Y
(Cartwright & Goodwin, pre-1910)
'King Alfred' × 'Reverend D.R. Williamson'
Fl. pale yellow; perianth segments acute

'Suprematie' 3 W-?
Syn. of 'Wisbech Gem'

'Supreme' 2 Y-O
(F. Rijnveld & Sons, pre-1947)
Corona dark orange, with a deeper tone at rim, tightly frilled. AM(Haarlem) 1947

'Supreme Beauty' 2 (a)
(A.E. Linn, pre-1949)

'Supreme Bowl' 2 (a)
(A.E. Linn, pre-1949)

'Supreme Buff Queen' 3 W-? (b)
(A.E. Linn, pre-1949)

'Supreme Coin' 2 (a)
(A.E. Linn, pre-1949)

'Supreme Command' 1 W-W
(G. Lewis) D.S. Bell, 1955
Corona with rim flanged and dentate

'Supreme Empire' 2 W-P
(G.E. Mitsch and R. & E. Havens, 1975) G.E. Mitsch and R. & E. Havens, 1987
'Sentinel' × 'Eclat'; sdlg no. KK15/1
Perianth segments very broad, somewhat truncate, slightly mucronate, pure white, reflexed, of heavy substance, overlapping half or more; the inner segments narrower, less strongly reflexed, with margins wavy; corona spreading, very broad, closely ribbed, deep reddish pink, with mouth tightly frilled. Mid-season

'Supreme Flower' 2 (a)
(A.E. Linn, pre-1949)

'Supreme Gold' 2 (a)
(A.E. Linn, pre-1949)

'Supreme Grace' 2 (a)
(A.E. Linn, pre-1949)

'Supreme Joyce' 3 W-? (b)
(A.E. Linn, pre-1949)

'Supreme Lady' 2 W-? (b)
(A.E. Linn, pre-1949)

'Supreme Lassie' 2 (a)
(A.E. Linn, pre-1949)

'Supreme Leader' 1 W-? (b)
(A.E. Linn, pre-1949)

'Supreme Louise' 3 W-? (b)
(A.E. Linn, pre-1949)

'Supreme Maid' 2 (a)
(A.E. Linn, pre-1949)

'Supreme Neatness' 2 (a)
(A.E. Linn, pre-1949)

'Supreme Orange Cup' 2 Y-O
(A.E. Linn, pre-1949)

'Supreme Orange Sun' 2 (a)
(A.E. Linn, pre-1949)

'Supreme Princess' 2 W-? (b)
(A.E. Linn, pre-1949)

'Supreme Queen' 2 (a)
(A.E. Linn, pre-1949)

'Supreme Red Beacon' 2 (a)
(A.E. Linn, pre-1949)

'Supreme Red Beam' 2 (a)
(A.E. Linn, pre-1949)

'Supreme Red Gown' 2 (a)
(A.E. Linn, pre-1949)

'Supreme Red Letter' 2 (a)
(A.E. Linn, pre-1949)

'Supreme Red Spark' 2 (a)
(A.E. Linn, pre-1949)

'Supreme Ribbon' 3 (a)
(A.E. Linn, pre-1949)

'Supreme Royal Red' 2 (a)
(A.E. Linn, pre-1949)

'Supreme Sensation' 2 W-? (b)
(A.E. Linn, pre-1949)

'Supreme Success' 2 (a)
(A.E. Linn, pre-1949)

'Supreme Wonder' 2 (a)
(A.E. Linn, pre-1949)

'Surcoat' 2 W-? (b or c)
(G.H. Engleheart, pre-1914)

'Sure Fire' 2 Y-YOR
(H.A. Brown, 1936)
Perianth segments bright yellow; corona orange, with yellow at base, shading to signal red at rim. Early to mid-season

'Surewin' 4 W-R
(Jackson's Daffodils) Jackson's Daffodils, 1993
Div. 4 × 'Gay Side'; sdlg no. 58/85

Fl. 95 mm wide; perianth and other petaloid segments in five or six whorls, broadly ovate, greenish white (155A); corona segments short, interspersed among the petaloid segments, orange-red (30C). Early to mid-season

'Surf' 2 W-? (b or c)
(Mrs R.S. Cobley, pre-1937)

'Surf' 3 W-W
Syn. of 'Surfdale'

'Surfbird' 3 Y-Y
(G.E. Mitsch, 1968) G.E. Mitsch, 1980
'Aircastle' × 'Homage'; sdlg no. D21/8
Fl. 102 mm wide; perianth segments opening white, becoming buff beige; corona opening pale lemon, becoming somewhat paler. Mid-season. Resembles 'Limpkin' but with yellower perianth and longer corona

'Surfdale' 3 W-W
(C. de Berry) C. de Berry, 1960
Fl. 95 mm wide; corona opening creamy yellow, becoming white. Late. Resembles 'Chinese White'. Syn. 'Surf'. PC(e)(NZ) 1959

'Surfer Girl' 3 W-W
(M.E.Brogden, pre-1993) Unregistered
'Sea Dream' × 'Verona'

'Surfside' 6 W-Y
(G.E. Mitsch) G.E. Mitsch, 1972
'Oratorio' × *N. cyclamineus*; sdlg no. C33/2
Fl. 98 mm wide; perianth segments ovate, truncate, fairly prominently mucronate, milk white, reflexed, smooth, overlapping half; corona cylindrical, broadly ribbed, soft lemon yellow, ageing to ivory white, with mouth flared and frilled, rim notched and crenate

'Surge' 2 Y-O
(P. & G. Phillips) P. & G. Phillips, 1975
Fl. 89 mm wide; perianth segments orange-yellow; corona orange. Mid-season

'Surpassante' 8 W-Y
(pre-1759)

'Surpassante Reine' 8 Y-Y
(pre-1798)
Fl. sulphur yellow

'Surplice' 1 W-W
(D.H.L. Corrigan, pre-1949)

'Surprise' 2 W-Y
(E. Leeds, 1877)
Perianth segments creamy white. Syn. Incomparabilis Albus 'Surprise'. "Absorbed" 'Jane Kolle'

'Surprise' 1 Y-Y
(J. Pope, pre-1904)
Fl. golden yellow; corona broad, regularly frilled. AM 1904. ?The same as the 'Surprise' described as 1W-?

'Surprise' 1 W-?
(J.Pope, pre-1904)
Corona expanded

'Surprise' 3 (a)
Syn. of 'Olanda'

'Surrey' 2 Y-R
(Brian S. Duncan) Rathowen Daffodils, 1988
'Shining Light' × 'Torridon'; sdlg no. 648
Perianth segments golden yellow; corona deep orange-red. Early to mid-season

'Surrey Gold' 2 Y-Y
(D.S. Bell) D.S. Bell, 1957
'Goldcourt' × 'Pre-eminent'
Fl. golden yellow; perianth segments broad; corona frilled

'Surrey Maid' 1 W-Y
(D.S. Bell) D.S. Bell, 1975
'Surrey Gold' open pollinated
Fl. 113 mm wide. Mid-season. Resembles 'Surrey Gold' but with a white perianth

'Surtsey' 2 Y-R
(Murray W. Evans) Murray W. Evans, 1972
'Zarah Leander' × 'Porthilly'
Fl. 95 mm wide

'Surveyor' 1 Y-Y
(E.W. Cotter) E.W. Cotter, 1968
'Glenfalloch' × 'Arctic Gold'
Fl. rich yellow; perianth segments broad, of leathery texture; corona with rim rolled and dentate

'Survivor' 2 (a)
(Alister Clark, 1925) J. Sharp, 1960

'Susan'
(P.D. Williams, pre-1913)

'Susan' 2 W-W
(R.H.Glover, pre-1993) Unregistered

'Susan Blatch' 2 (a)
(G.L. Wilson, pre-1950)

'Susan Elizabeth' 9 W-YYR
(Mrs M.S.Yerger) E.Charles Nelson, 1996
Sdlg no. 75 0-1
Fl. 66 mm wide; perianth segments oval, white, tinged yellow at base, slightly reflexed; the inner segments more heavily tinged yellow at base; corona orange-yellow, with red at rim. Late

'Susani' 3 (a)
(Miss K. Spurrell, pre-1908)

'Susan Jennifer' 3 W-GOO
(A.G. Thompson) A.G. Thompson, 1965
'Blarney' × 'Kansas'
Fl. 89 mm wide; corona apricot orange. Mid-season. Resembles 'Kansas' but with green at corona base

'Susan Morris' 1 W-? (b)
(J.A. Morris) J.A. Morris, 1955

'Susanna' 3 W-? (b)
(P.D. Williams, pre-1937)

N. × *susannae* Fernández Casas 13 = *N. cantabricus* de Candolle subsp. *monophyllus* (Durieu de Maisonneuve) A.Fernandes × *N. triandrus* subsp. *pallidulus* (Graells) D.A.Webb. PC 1996
    var. ***susannae***
    var. ***toletanus*** Fernández Casas & Luceño

'Susannah' 2 W-?
(W.M. Spry, pre-1975) Unregistered
'Mrs Oscar Ronalds' × 'Pink Blossom'
Corona cream honey, with pink at rim, frilled. Late

'Susan Pearson' 7 Y-O
(R.V. Favell, pre-1954)
'Hades' × *N. jonquilla*
Perianth segments rich yellow; corona disc-shaped, reddish orange. Closely resembles 'Suzy'

'Susette' 3 W-O
(C. Dawson, pre-1922)
'Lulworth' × 'Horace'
Perianth segments reflexed; corona almost disc-shaped, ribbed, pale scarlet-orange

'Susie'
(G.H. Johnstone, pre-1960) Unregistered
'Tunis' × 'Mrs R.O.Backhouse'

'Susie's Blush' 2 W-P
(S.J. Bisdee, 1947)
'Sunshine Susie' × 'Rosario'

'Suspense' 9 W-GYR
(G.E. Mitsch, 1968) G.E. Mitsch, 1979
'Quetzal' × 'Smyrna'; sdlg no. D94/7
Fl. rounded, 80 mm wide. Late

'Susy Lee' 2 Y-YYR
(G. Lewis) D.S. Bell, 1955

'Sutter's Gold' 5
(Oregon Bulb Farms, pre-1951)

'Sutton Court' 1 Y-R
(W.O. Backhouse) E. Longford, 1966

'Red Curtain' × 'Brer Fox'
Fl. 108 mm wide; perianth segments very broad; corona orange-red. Early

'Suvla' 2 W-Y
(The Brodie of Brodie, c.1923)
('Minnie Hume' × 'Bombastes') × sdlg SS9 (pollen from Engleheart)
Corona lemon, with a somewhat paler tone at base

'Suwanee' 2 Y-YOR
(E.C. Powell, pre-1946)
'Expectation' × 'Fortune'

'Suzie Dee' 6 Y-Y
(Brian S.Duncan) Brian S.Duncan, 1994
'Elfin Gold' × *N. cyclamineus*; sdlg no. 1483
Perianth segments ovate, blunt, prominently mucronate, vivid yellow 9A, reflexed, with margins slightly wavy, overlapping a quarter; the inner segments more narrowly ovate, only very slightly mucronate, with margins more strongly wavy; corona cylindrical, smooth, deeper in tone than the perianth, nearest to vivid yellow 12 or 13A, mouth lightly ribbed, very slightly flared, shallowly notched and 6-lobed. Dwarf. Very early

'Suzie's Sister' 6 Y-Y
(Brian S.Duncan, pre-1997) Unregistered
'Elfin Gold' × *N. cyclamineus*; sdlg no. 1483B
Fl. 75 mm wide, yellow; perianth segments ovate, mucronate, reflexed, ribbed, overlapping one-third; the inner segments less strongly inflexed; corona cylindrical, ribbed, darker in tone than the perianth, with mouth straight and rim entire. Dwarf to standard. Early

'Suzon' W-Y
(P.D. Williams, pre-1913)
Fl. 83 mm wide; perianth segments narrow, pure white; corona small, pale lemon yellow, with a greenish tinge

'Suzy' 7 Y-O
(R.V. Favell, pre-1954)
'Hades' × *N. jonquilla*
Fls 2-3 per stem, 62 mm wide; perianth segments ovate or broadly ovate, blunt or truncate, slightly mucronate, brilliant yellow 8A, spreading, a little concave, overlapping one-third; the inner segments narrower, with margins incurling; corona shallow bowl-shaped, ribbed, strong orange 26A, with mouth expanded and only a little frilled, rim notched and crenate. Mid-season to late. Scented. 2n=21. Closely resembles a 'Susan Pearson' of more rapid increase. AM(Haarlem) 1954, FCC(Haarlem) 1956, AM(e) 1963, *AM(g) 1977, *FCC(g) 1979, AGM 1993

'Suzy Marie' 2 W-P
(D.S. Bell) D.S. Bell, 1984

Sdlg × 'Fintona'
Fl. 108 mm wide. Mid-season

'Svelte' 2 Y-O
(D. Jackson) Jackson's Daffodils, 1982
'Iatros' × 'Blandfordia'; sdlg no. 147/77

'Svengali' 1 W-Y
(Barr & Sons, pre-1929)

'Sven Hedin' 3 W-? (b)
(J.W.A. Lefeber, pre-1943)

'Svenska Bojan' 2 Y-YOO
(D.C. MacArthur) D.C. MacArthur, 1985
'Chungking' self pollinated; sdlg no. E837
Perianth segments broadly ovate, rounded at apex, vivid yellow 9A, with very slight white mucro, spreading, plane, somewhat creased, irregular, overlapping half; the inner segments narrower at apex, a little inflexed, with margins creased or nicked at shoulder; corona narrow bowl-shaped, ribbed, vivid orange 28B, with vivid yellow 17B at base and with flecks of yellow at rim, irregularly and closely frilled. Late

'Svetlana' 2 W-O
(C.R. Wootton) , 1965
'Templemore' × 'Green Island'

'Swain' 1 Y-Y
(Murray W. Evans) Murray W. Evans, 1982
'Arctic Gold' × 'Galway' hybrid; sdlg no. N-46/1
Fl. 110 mm wide. Early

'Swaledale' 2 Y-Y
(Jan Dalton) Jan Dalton, 1989
'Daydream' hybrid; sdlg no. 756/1
Fl. 90 mm wide; perianth segments smooth, overlapping; corona cylindrical, becoming peachy buff, with mouth slightly flared, rim crenate. Mid-season. Resembles 'Daydream' in form and colour of perianth but with the segments more nearly acute

'Swallow' 3 W-? (b or c)
(W. Welchman, pre-1927)

'Swallow' 6 YYW-W
(G.E. Mitsch) G.E. Mitsch, 1976
'Nazareth' × *N. cyclamineus*; sdlg no. G78/3
Fl. 80 mm wide; perianth segments opening pale yellow, becoming deeper in tone, with white at base, reflexed; corona becoming lighter in tone than the perianth. Early

'Swallowcliffe' 6 Y-O
(J.W. Blanchard) J.W. Blanchard, 1986
'Cattistock' × *N. cyclamineus*; sdlg no. 76/29A
Perianth segments narrowly ovate, blunt, deep golden yellow, reflexed; corona cylindrical, pale orange. Dwarf. Early

'Swallow Hotel' 4 W-YPP
(Brian S.Duncan) Brian S.Duncan, 1997
'Pink Pageant' × 'High Society'; sdlg no. 1400
Fl. 100 mm wide; perianth and other petaloid segments in several whorls, white; the outer whorl broadly ovate, somewhat acute; the inner whorls of variable length and form; corona segments regularly interspersed among the inner whorls of petaloid segments, apricot pink, paling to yellow at base, frilled. Mid-season to late

'Swallownest' 1 Y-Y
(F.E. Board) F.E. Board, 1965
'Kingscourt' × 'Wexford'; sdlg no. 340
Perianth segments very broadly ovate, blunt, with slight white mucro, spreading, plane, with margins incurling at apex, overlapping one-third to a half; corona funnel-shaped, smooth, with mouth lobed and frilled, rim flanged and crenate

'Swallowtail' 6
(C.F. Coleman) C.F. Coleman, 1969

'Swallowtail' 2 W-? (b)
(pre-1955) Unregistered

'Swallow Wing' 6 W-WWP
(Brian S.Duncan, 1986) Brian S.Duncan, 1997
'Mary Kate' × 'Swing Wing'; sdlg no. 1380
Fl. 85 mm wide; perianth segments ovate, variably reflexed according to weather conditions, slightly overlapping; corona funnel-shaped, opening pink, with creamy yellow at base, becoming white, with pink at rim, mouth straight, rim entire. Late

'Swamp Fox' 2 Y-O
(W.G. Pannill) W.G. Pannill, 1984
'Miralgo' × 'Ambergate'; sdlg no. 66/24
Fl. 87 mm wide. Mid-season

'Swanaven' 1 W-W
(T.H. Piper, c.1966) Unregistered
'Swanlough' × 'Ave'

'Swan Ballet' 1 W-W
(T.H. Piper, c.1966) Unregistered
'Achi' × 'Rhana'

'Swandaya' 2 Y-R
(J.S. Leitch) J.S. Leitch, 1956

'Swandean' 2 W-WWY
(Sir F.C. Stern, pre-1948)
Fl. 95 mm wide; perianth segments creamy white, overlapping; corona ribbed, pale cream, tinged brilliant yellow 13B at rim, mouth slightly expanded, frilled, with rim dentate. *AM(g) 1958

'Swanhilda' 3 W-? (b)
(Barr & Sons, pre-1913)

'Swan Hill' 1 W-Y
(W.M. Spry, pre-1975) Unregistered
'Hunter's Moon' × 'Kingscourt'
Corona pale lemon yellow

'Swan Lake' 1 W-W
(D.S. Bell) D.S. Bell, 1955

'Swanley Peerless' 2 W-W
(West & Fell, pre-1935)
Perianth segments broad; corona disc-shaped, ribbed, opening pale lemon, becoming white

'Swanley Perfection' 1 W-Y
(D.V. West, pre-1927)
Perfection segments creamy white; corona deep yellow

'Swanlough' 1 W-W
(T.H. Piper, pre-1957) Unregistered
('Swanley Perfection' × 'Lorinna') × ('Beersheba' × 'Carnlough')

'Swan Neck' 1? W-W
(?W.B. Hartland, pre-1886)

'Swannie' 2 W-P
(R.H.Glover, pre-1989) Unregistered
'Pink Special' × 'Vahu'

'Swan of Avon' 1 W-W
(J.M. de Navarro, pre-1949)
'Glenshesk' × 'Glacier'
PC(e) 1975

'Swansdown' 4 W-W
(The Brodie of Brodie, c.1938)
'Mitylene' × 'Smyrna'
Perianth segments very broadly ovate in outline, blunt or truncate at apex, only very slightly mucronate, pure white, spreading, overlapping; corona segments numerous, clustered, short, broad, creamy white, frilled, with margins minutely dentate. Late. 2n=26. PC(e) 1940, AM(Haarlem) 1951

'Swansea' 2 W-? (b)
(C.A. Latta) C.A. Latta, 1956

"Swan's Neck Daffodil"
See "The Swan's Neck Daffodil"

'Swan Song' 2 W-YYO
(H.A. Brown) J.N. Hancock & Co., 1955
Corona large, disc-shaped, lemon, with orange at rim

'Swanston' 1 W-? (b)
(A.M. Wilson, pre-1941)

'Swanvale' 1 W-W
(R.A.Scamp) R.A.Scamp, 1996

'Pitchroy' × 'White Star'; sdlg no. 442
Fl. 100 mm wide, pure white; perianth segments broadly ovate; corona cylindrical, with mouth slightly flared. Late

'Swanwick' 9 W-GOR
(V. Brink) V. Brink, 1979
'Actaea' × 'Dulcimer'; sdlg no. 62-4
Fl. 70 mm wide. Mid-season

'Swarthmoor' 2 Y-YWY
(Reg Nicholl) Reg Nicholl, 1991
'Chiloquin' × 'Delectable'; sdlg no. 8/85
Fl. 72 mm wide; perianth segments very broadly ovate, rounded at apex, fairly prominently mucronate, brilliant greenish yellow 7C, with white at base, spreading, with margins incurling at apex, smooth, overlapping half; corona funnel-shaped, light orange-yellow 16C, with a band of a slightly darker tone (16B) at rim, mouth ribbed and expanded, densely frilled. Mid-season

'Swashbuckler' 2 Y-? (a)
(F.H. Chapman, pre-1910)
'King Alfred' × 'Minnie Hume'
Perianth segments broad and roundish; the inner segments ovate and acute

'Swastika' 1 Y-Y
(G.H. Engleheart, pre-1923)
Fl. rich orange-yellow

'Swedish Fjord' 2 YYW-W
(G.E. Mitsch, 1975) R. & E. Havens, 1988
('Playboy' × 'Daydream') × 'Chiloquin'; sdlg no. KK42/1
Perianth segments yellow, with white at base; corona becoming white, frilled. Mid-season. Resembles a larger 'Chiloquin' with a slightly shorter corona

'Sweepstake' 9
(W.B. Hartland, pre-1914)
Resembles an improved 'Heroine' with less red to the corona

'Sweet Acre' 2 W-P
(H.A. Brown, 1938)
Corona constricted near mouth, shell pink, with mouth expanded. Late

'Sweet Adare' 1 W-Y
(C. Dawson, pre-1925)
Perianth segments inflexed; corona short, expanded, creamy sulphur yellow, frilled. Resembles 'Carmenta'

'Sweet Blanche' 7 W-W
(R.A.Scamp) R.A.Scamp, 1995
'Grand Prospect' × *N. jonquilla*; sdlg no. 220
Fl. 98 mm wide, opening pale lemon yellow, becoming white; perianth segments narrow, acute, smooth, overlapping; corona short cup-shaped, with rounded sides, ribbed. Mid-season. Scented. With many secondary stems

'Sweetbriar' 2 W-? (b)
(Mrs F.S. Foote) Mrs F.S. Foote, 1940

'Sweet Caroline' 2 W-P
(J.N. Hancock & Co., 1964) Unregistered

'Sweet Charity' 2 W-YYO
(W.F. Leenen) W.F. Leenen, 1971
Fl. 110 mm wide; perianth segments ivory white; corona light yellow (21D), shading to pale orange at mouth. Mid-season to late. Scented

'Sweet Cicely' 2 W-Y
(J.W. Barr, pre-1927)
Corona lemon yellow. Tall

'Sweet Delight' 9 W-GYR
(Mrs M.S. Yerger) Mrs M.S. Yerger, 1984
N. poeticus sdlg × 'Milan'; sdlg no. 74 B 1
Fl. 63 mm wide; perianth segments slightly reflexed. Early to mid-season

'Sweet Dorothy' 2 W-Y
(pre-1921)
Perianth segments overlapping; corona creamy yellow, frilled

'Sweet Dream' 9 W-GYR
(Mrs M.S. Yerger) Mrs M.S. Yerger, 1984
N. poeticus sdlg × 'Milan'; sdlg no. 74 B 3-2
Fl. 53 mm wide; corona brilliant greenish yellow 4A, with green at base and orange-red (30C) at rim. Early to mid-season. Strongly scented

'Sweet Dreams' 2 W-P
(Ken McCombe) Unregistered
Perianth segments smooth; corona peach pink, frilled. Late

'Sweetedge' 2 W-?
(A. Overton) A. Overton, 1960

'Sweet Emma' 2 W-P
(J.N. Hancock & Co., 1959) Unregistered

'Sweet Fantasy' 9 W-GYR
(Mrs M.S. Yerger) Mrs M.S. Yerger, 1987
(Div. 9 × 'Milan') open pollinated; sdlg no. 76 K 2
Perianth segments broad, slightly reflexed, of thick substance, deeply overlapping; the inner segments narrower; corona shallow bowl-shaped, ribbed, light greenish yellow 5C, with deep yellowish green 141A at base and orange-red (33A) at rim. Early. Scented

'Sweet Georgia' 2 W-GPP
(J.S.B. Lea, 1980) Clive Postles, 1992

'Dailmanach' × Lea sdlg 1-40-67; sdlg no. 1-13-75
Fl. rounded, 102 mm wide; perianth segments ovate, pure white; corona cylindrical, very deep pink, with rim flanged. Late. Sunproof

'Sweet Harmony' 2 W-WWY
(F. Rijnveld & Sons) F. Rijnveld & Sons, 1956
Corona deeply lobed. AM(Haarlem) 1956

'Sweetheart' 2 W-Y
(Barr & Sons, pre-1901)
Corona ribbed, canary yellow, lightly frilled. Wrongly named 'Phyllis' in Barr catalogue 1905

'Sweetheart' 2 W-YYO
(J.W.A. Lefeber) J.W.A. Lefeber, 1956
Perianth segments pure white; corona widely expanded, apricot yellow, frilled

'Sweet Honey' 1 Y-Y
(J.W. Barr, pre-1927)
Corona soft canary yellow, lightly frilled, with rim flanged

'Sweet Hope' 9 W-YYR
(Mrs M.S. Yerger) Mrs M.S. Yerger, 1986
N. poeticus sdlg × 'Milan'; sdlg no. 74 B 2
Perianth segments slightly reflexed; corona disc-shaped, greenish yellow (154B), with a darker tone (145A) at base and red (35A) at rim, with a line of white appearing between mid-zone and rim at maturity. Mid-season. Resembles 'Ornatus' in form but with the disc-like corona of 'Milan'

'Sweetie-pie' 3 W-GYY
(A.J.R.Pearson) A.J.R.Pearson, 1997
'Tryst' × 'Fairmile'; sdlg no. 93-61-N47
Fl. rounded, 73 mm wide; perianth segments very broad, slightly mucronate, greenish white 155C, plane, of thick and waxy substance; the inner segments almost as broad, not noticeably mucronate; corona bowl-shaped, ribbed, brilliant greenish yellow 7C, with deep yellowish green 141A at base, mouth somewhat 6-angled, with rim crenate. Late

"Sweeties"
Syn. of *N. jonquilla*

'Sweet Lass' 2 Y-R
(pre-1951)

'Sweet Lemon'
(J. Pope, pre-1913)

'Sweet Luck' 2 W-O
(G.W.E. Brogden)

'Sweet Maid' 3 W-YYR
(J.W. Barr, pre-1926)
Perianth segments snow white; corona yellow, with a broad band of scarlet at rim

'Sweet Marjoram' 2 Y-GYP
(D.S. Bell) D.S. Bell, 1984
'Alfresco' × 'Hicol'
Fl. 105 mm wide; corona frilled. Mid-season

'Sweetmeat' 3 W-? (b)
(F.H. Chapman, pre-1913)

'Sweet Melody' 3 W-YOO
(Mrs R.O. Backhouse, pre-1921)
Perianth segments very broadly ovate, rounded at apex, more or less prominently mucronate, creamy white, spreading, overlapping half; the inner segments a little inflexed, with margins lightly wavy; corona very shallow, broad, lightly ribbed, yellowish orange, with golden yellow at base, shading to vermilion orange at rim, with mouth split and overlapping, irregularly frilled

'Sweet Memory' 2 W-P
(D.S. Bell) D.S. Bell, 1963
2n=27. Resembles 'Salmon Trout' but with a shorter corona

'Sweet Music' 4 W-GWW
(G.E. Mitsch, 1951) G.E. Mitsch, 1965
'Cushendall' × 'Cantabile'; sdlg no. M19/1
Fl. 76 mm wide, pure white. Late.

'Sweet Nancy' 7 Y-Y
(Barr & Sons, pre-1919)
Fl. 75 mm wide; perianth segments soft yellow, overlapping; corona short, bright yellow. Scented

"Sweet Nancy"
Variant of *N. poeticus*

'Sweet Nell' 2 W-Y
(Barr & Sons, pre-1923)
'Maggie May' × *N. poeticus* var. *recurvus*
Perianth segments very broadly ovate, rounded at apex, prominently mucronate, spreading, a little concave, overlapping half; the inner segments narrower, inflexed, with margins creased and often incurved; corona small bowl-shaped, heavily ribbed, soft primrose yellow, with mouth split in places and overlapping, frilled

'Sweetness' 7 Y-Y
(R.V. Favell, pre-1939)
Fls occasionally 2 per stem, 65 mm wide; perianth segments broadly ovate, acute, vivid yellow 9A, with white mucro, spreading, plane, smooth and of heavy substance, overlapping one-third; the inner segments with margins incurved; corona cup-shaped, of thick substance, darker in tone (14B) than the perianth, with mouth straight and wavy, rim lightly crenate. Scented. 2n=21. *AM(g) 1973, *FCC(g) 1983,

Wister Award 1993, AGM 1993

'Sweet Orange' 2 Y-O
(R. & E.Havens, 1982) R. & E.Havens, 1997
'Gold Crown' × (['Ardour' × 'Ceylon'] × 'Brer Fox'); sdlg no. REH26/2
Fl. 105 mm wide; perianth segments ovate, soft lemon yellow, spreading, plane; corona bright tangerine orange, with mouth flared and rim rolled. Mid-season. Sunproof

'Sweet Peggy' 3 W-? (b)
(E.M. Crosfield, pre-1927)

'Sweet Pepper' 7 Y-O
(R.V. Favell, pre-1939)
'Hades' × *N. jonquilla*
Corona deep red. 2n=21. AM(Haarlem) 1957

'Sweet Prince' 1 YYW-WWY
(Murray W. Evans, 1965) Murray W. Evans, 1978
'Daydream' × ('Lunar Sea' × 'Galway'); sdlg no. I-17
Fl. 100 mm wide; perianth segments broadly ovate, blunt, brilliant greenish yellow 6B, with slight white mucro and with white at base, inflexed, somewhat concave, smooth, overlapping half; corona cylindrical, smooth, creamier in tone (8B), with a darker tone outside and with vivid yellow 9A at rim, mouth slightly expanded, rim flanged and regularly crenate. Mid-season

'Sweet Promise' 9 W-GGR
(Mrs M.S. Yerger) Mrs M.S. Yerger, 1986
Sdlg no. 75 F 2
Perianth segments white; the inner segments narrower, inflexed; corona almost disc-shaped, yellow-green, with a darker tone at base and orange-red (30A) at rim. Mid-season. Sweetly scented

'Sweet Repose' 4 W-Y
(J.L. Richardson) G.L'E. Wallace, 1961
'Falaise' × 'Rose Caprice'
Fl. 102 mm wide; corona segments chrome yellow. Mid-season. Resembles 'Acropolis'

'Sweet Reproach' 2 W-O
(Tom Forster, 1960s) Unregistered
Fl. rounded; perianth segments milk white; corona large disc-shaped, soft yellow-orange, with a deeper tone at rim, frilled. Tall

'Sweet Rosalind' 2 W-? (b)
(Mrs R.O. Backhouse, pre-1921)

'Sweet Rose' 9 W-GGP
(Mrs M.S. Yerger) Mrs M.S. Yerger, 1986
N. poeticus var. *hellenicus* open pollinated; sdlg no. 75 G 3
Corona light yellow-green 154D, with a much darker tone (151B) at base and moderate yellowish pink 31D at rim. Mid-season to late

'Sweet Sensation' 2 W-? (b)
(Warnaar & Co., 1950) Warnaar & Co., 1966
'High Life' × 'Princess Beatrix'

'Sweet Seventeen' 9
(R.H. Bath, pre-1923)

'Sweet Seventeen' 3 W-?
Syn. of 'Queen Maud'

'Sweet Sixteen' 2 W-WWO
(pre-1927)
Perianth segments pure white; corona cream, with reddish orange at rim

'Sweet Somerset' 9 W-GYR
(Mrs M.S. Yerger) Mrs M.S. Yerger, 1986
N. poeticus sdlg × 'Milan'; sdlg no. 74 B 3-1
Perianth segments broadly ovate, truncate, white, with a band of green at midrib beneath, spreading, with midrib showing, overlapping one-third; corona bowl-shaped, green-yellow (150C), with yellow-green (151A) at base and a narrow band of deep orange-red (34A) at rim, mouth wavy. Mid-season. Scented. Resembles 'Milan' but with the flower less precisely forming a double triangle

'Sweet Spice' 9 W-GYR
(Mrs M.S. Yerger) Mrs M.S. Yerger, 1988
'Dulcimer' open pollinated; sdlg no. 76 A 7
Fl. rounded; perianth segments ovate, very smooth, of good substance, regular, overlapping; corona shallow bowl-shaped, greenish yellow (154D), with brilliant yellow-green 149A at base and orange-red (30B) at rim. Dwarf. Very late. Scented

'Sweet Sue' 3 W-YYO
(A.J.R.Pearson) A.J.R.Pearson, 1994
'Dell Chapel' × 'Corozal'; sdlg no. 88-60-L15
Fl. rounded, 100 mm wide; perianth segments broadly ovate, blunt, only very slightly mucronate, white (1D), spreading, slightly concave, a little creased at midrib, smooth, glistening and of great substance, overlapping two-thirds; corona bowl-shaped, straight-sided, lightly ribbed, vivid yellow 9A, with a line of vivid orange 28B at rim, frilled, with rim crenate. Mid-season to late

'Sweet Surprise' 9 W-GYO
(Mrs M.S. Yerger) Mrs M.S. Yerger, 1984
N. poeticus sdlg × 'Milan'; sdlg no. 74 B 3-4
Fl. 60 mm wide; perianth segments acute; corona ribbed. Early to mid-season. Strongly scented

'Sweet Talk' 2 W-WWP
(Oregon Bulb Farms, pre-1950)

'Sweet Treat' 7 Y-GYY
(Eileen E. Frey, 1976) Eileen E. Frey, 1988
'Bantam' × *N. assoanus*; sdlg no. LEE1/2
Perianth segments very broad, rounded at apex, light yellow, a little reflexed, with midrib showing, overlapping half; the inner segments narrower; corona bowl-shaped, darker in tone, with green at base. Very late

'Sweet Victory' 9 W-GGO
(Mrs M.S. Yerger) Mrs M.S. Yerger, 1986
N. poeticus var. *hellenicus* open pollinated; sdlg no. 75 G 2
Perianth segments white; the inner segments narrower; corona light yellow-green 145D, with light orange 29B at rim. Late

'Sweet Whisper' 2 W-P
(J.N.Hancock & Co.) Unregistered
Perianth segments roundish; corona cylindrical, bright pink, frilled. Late

'Swell Time' 4 W-Y
(?New Zealand origin, pre-1996) Unregistered

'Swettry' 5
(P.D. Williams, pre-1931)

'S.W.Gower' 1 Y-Y
Syn. of 'Sidney Gower'

'Swift' 6 W-Y
(G.E. Mitsch) G.E. Mitsch, 1972
'Trousseau' × *N. cyclamineus*; sdlg no. Z39/3
Fl. 87 mm wide; perianth segments ivory white, reflexed; corona long, opening pale lemon, becoming paler still. Early

'Swift Arrow' 6 Y-Y
(G.E. Mitsch, 1977) R. & E. Havens, 1991
Sdlg B45/12 (sdlg P50/1 × 'Flaming Meteor') × *N. cyclamineus*; sdlg no. 2N41/1
Perianth segments ovate in outline, blunt or truncate at apex, clear deep yellow, with slight white mucro, strongly reflexed, overlapping half or more; the inner segments with margins wavy or incurling; corona cylindrical, lightly angled, slightly deeper in tone than the perianth segments, sometimes with undertones of orange, mouth flared, rim notched. Early. Resembles a slightly earlier-flowered 'Warbler' with more yellow than green at base of perianth and corona

'Swiftsure' 1 Y-Y
(T.H. Piper, 1954)
'Butter King' × 'Derflinger'

'Swing' 2 (a)
(A.H. Ahrens) J.S. Leitch, 1955

'Swing Time' 1 W-P
(J.N.Hancock & Co., 1986) J.N.Hancock & Co., 1997
'Verran' hybrid; sdlg no. C/86
Perianth segments ovate, plane; corona funnel-shaped, pink, with mouth expanded. Early to mid-season

'Swing Wing' 6 W-GPP
(Brian S. Duncan) Rathowen Daffodils, 1982
'Roseworthy' × 'Foundling'; sdlg no. 476
Perianth segments pure white, reflexed; corona intense pink, with green at base, mouth slightly expanded. Mid-season

'Swiss Chimes' 5 W-W
(Grant E.Mitsch, 1972) R. & E.Havens, 1994
'Pigeon' × *N. triandrus*; sdlg no. HH85/6
Fls 2-3 per stem, 70 mm wide; perianth segments very broad, somewhat reflexed; corona with mouth flared and wavy. Late. Resembles a later-flowered 'Church Bells'

'Swiss Miss' 2 W-P
M.J. Jefferson-Brown, 1964

'Swods Gem' 2 Y-Y
(Brian S. Duncan) Leone Y. Low, 1989
'Golden Aura' open pollinated; sdlg no. 806
Perianth segments broad, golden yellow, of thick substance; corona bowl-shaped, in some years darker in tone than the perianth, with rim crenate. Early. Resembles an earlier-flowered 'Golden Aura' of brighter colouring with the corona more widely flared

'Sword Play' 3 W-O
(F.E. Board) F.E. Board, 1965
'Mazaka' × 'Arbar'; sdlg no. 555
Corona reddish orange. Late. Resembles a large-flowered 'Mazaka'

'Swordsman' 2 Y-O
(J.A. Hunter) J.A. Hunter, 1967
'Marksman' × 'Narvik'
Fl. 99 mm wide. Mid-season. Resembles a larger-flowered 'Marksman' of stronger substance and colouring

'S.Y.B.' 3 (a)
(pre-1913)

'Sybarite'
(E.M. Crosfield, pre-1914)

'Sybil' 2 W-Y
(R.H. Bath, pre-1907)
Fl. 95 mm wide; perianth segments somewhat inflexed, irregular, overlapping one-third; corona broad funnel-shaped, pale lemon yellow, with a darker tone at rim, frilled. AM(g) 1926, *AM(g) 1931

'Sybil Dulce' 3 W-? (b)
(J.T. Gray, pre-1939)

'Sybil Forster' 1 W-W
(J. Mallender, pre-1913)
Fl. 98 mm wide; perianth segments pure white; corona cylindrical, opening creamy white, becoming ivory white. Mid-season. See also 'Sybil Foster'

'Sybil Foster' 1 W-W
Syn. of 'Sybil Forster'

'Sybil Thorndike' 2 (a)
(R.H. Bath, pre-1933)

'Sycamore' 8 W-Y
(H. Prins, pre-1919)
Poetaz
Corona rich golden yellow. AM(Haarlem) 1919

'Sycorax' 2 Y-Y
(W. Backhouse, pre-1869)
Perianth segments narrow, acute. Syn. Incomparabilis Concolor 'Sycorax'. Was "absorbed" into 'Lass o' Gowrie'

'Sycorax' 6 Y-Y
(Barr & Sons, pre-1907)
Perianth segments canary yellow, reflexed; corona rich golden yellow, with rim flared

'Sycorax' 6
(de Graaff Bros, pre-1914)

'Sycorax' 4 Y-O
(pre-1927)
Fl. compact; perianth and other petaloid segments soft yellow; corona segments clear orange. AM(Haarlem) 1927

'Sydenham' 1 Y-Y
(W.J. Dunlop) W.J. Dunlop, 1965

'Sydling' 5 W-GWW
(J.W. Blanchard) J.W. Blanchard, 1977
(*N. triandrus* var. *loiseleurii* × 'Hamzali') self pollinated; sdlg no. 64/41A
Fls up to 3 per stem, 85 mm wide; corona short, with green at base, slightly frilled. 2n=21

'Sydney Mitchell' 2 (a)
(The Brodie of Brodie, pre-1931)

'Syenna' 5
(Mrs R.O. Backhouse, pre-1921)

'Sylko' 2 W-W
(Mrs M. Moorby, pre-1949)

'Syllmar' 2 W-WWY

(D.J. Cooper) D.J. Cooper, 1959
Fl. 95 mm wide; corona shallow, widely expanded, creamy white, with lemon yellow at rim. Mid-season

'Sylph' 1 W-W
(G.H. Engleheart, pre-1907)

'Sylph' 1 Y-Y
(G.E. Mitsch) G.E. Mitsch, 1979
Sdlg A52/ hybrid; sdlg no. FO15/1
Fl. 57 mm wide; perianth segments lemon yellow, spreading; corona narrow, slightly deeper in tone. Early

'Sylphide' 1 W-? (b)
(C.G. van Tubergen, pre-1929)
AM(Haarlem) 1929

'Sylvan Hill' 1 W-W
(Ballydorn Bulb Farm) Ballydorn Bulb Farm, 1984
'Churchman' × 'Courage' hybrid
Fl. 105 mm wide. Early to mid-season

'Sylvania' 9
(de Graaff Bros, pre-1928)
Syn. 'Mephistopheles'

'Sylvan Lake' 1 W-Y
(D.N.Y. Olson, 1971) D.N.Y. Olson, 1988
'Bonnington' × 'My Love'; sdlg no. 59/1
Fl. large. Mid-season

'Sylvan Pink' 2 W-? (b)
(Mrs F.S. Foote, pre-1940)

'Sylvene' 1 W-W
(D.V. West, pre-1936)
Corona narrow, cream

'Sylvester' 1 W-W
(C.G. van Tubergen, pre-1927)

'Sylvestris Stellatus' 4 Y-Y
Syn. of 'Eystettensis'

'Sylvette' 7
(D.J. Cooper) D.J. Cooper, 1956

'Sylvia' 3 W-Y
(W. Backhouse, pre-1869)
Perianth segments sulphur white. Syn. Barrii Albidus 'Sylvia'. Was "absorbed" into 'Gog'

'Sylvia' 3? W-W
(G.P. Haydon, pre-1904)
Fl. small, facing down; perianth segments pure white, twisted; corona small, flushed peach pink

'Sylvia' 2 W-W
(A.M. Wilson, pre-1927)

Fl. 114 mm wide, white, facing down; perianth segments inflexed, overlapping half; corona funnel-shaped, with creamy white at base. Mid-season to late. *AM(g) 1930

'Sylvia Gower' 2 Y-O
(J.N. Hancock & Co., 1949) J.N. Hancock & Co., 1960
Perianth segments rich yellow; corona deep orange, frilled

'Sylviane' 8 Y-Y
(pre-1792)
Fl. pale yellow

'Sylvia O'Neill' 2 W-? (b)
(G.L. Wilson, pre-1940)

'Sylvia O'Neill' 3 W-WWY
(G.L. Wilson, pre-1940)
'Silver Plane' × 'Silver Coin' hybrid
Perianth segments very broadly ovate in outline, blunt or rounded at apex, mucronate, spreading, slightly concave, overlapping half; the inner segments a little inflexed, twisted; corona bowl-shaped, strongly ribbed, with pale lemon at rim, mouth straight and loosely frilled, rim minutely crenate

'Sylvia Sharman' 2 Y-YOO
(H.A. Brown, 1939) J.N. Hancock & Co., 1960
Perianth segments rich yellow; corona wide disc-shaped, scarlet-orange, with rich yellow at base, regularly frilled

'Symbol' 1 (a)
(R.H. Bath, pre-1929)

'Symbol' 2 Y-YYO
(G.W.E. Brogden) G.W.E. Brogden, 1969

'Symbolic' 2 W-? (b)
(A.H. Ahrens) J.S. Leitch, 1955

'Symmetry' 3 W-YYO
(G.H. Engleheart, pre-1903)
Perianth segments cream; corona yellow, with orange at rim. AM 1903

'Symmetry' 1 (a)
(J. Hall, pre-1930)

'Sympathy' 1 W-W
(J.N. Hancock & Co., 1954)

'Symphonette' 2 Y-Y
(G.E. Mitsch) G.E. Mitsch, 1975
'Playboy' × 'Daydream'; sdlg no. B36/31
Fl. 103 mm wide, soft lemon yellow; perianth segments broadly ovate, blunt, slightly mucronate, with a band of white at base, spreading, slightly concave

at apex, overlapping half; the inner segments narrower, square-shouldered at base, a little inflexed; corona funnel-shaped, with mouth even, rim rolled and crenate. Mid-season

'Symphony' 9
(G.H. Engleheart, pre-1913)

'Symphony' ?-P
(Alister Clark, pre-1948)

'Symposium' 9 W-GYO
(G.H. Engleheart, pre-1923)
Perianth segments very broad, overlapping; corona almost disc-shaped, with a narrow band of orange at rim

'Symptom' 3 W-O
(Jackson's Daffodils, 1977) Jackson's Daffodils, 1987
'Kabi' × 'Envoy'; sdlg. no. 160/77
Fl. rounded; perianth segments very broad, blunt, prominently mucronate, pure white, spreading, with margins sometimes minutely incurling at apex, smooth and of great substance, overlapping half or more; the inner segments more nearly ovate, somewhat truncate, only very slightly mucronate; corona very shallow bowl-shaped, closely ribbed, bright reddish-orange, with mouth a little frilled. Mid-season

'Synstar' 1 Y-Y
(R.H.Glover, pre-1993) Unregistered

'Syntax' 2 Y-Y
(R.C.A. Tombleson) R.C.A. Tombleson, 1966
Fl. 111 mm wide. Late. Resembles an earlier-flowered 'Gold Script' with narrower perianth segments

'Syphax' 7 Y-Y
(J.C. Williams, pre-1914)
'King Alfred' × ? *N. jonquilla*
Fl. rich golden yellow; perianth segments fairly narrow; corona lightly frilled. AM(g)(c) 1914

'Syra' 2 W-W
(G.H. Engleheart, pre-1927)
Corona shaded cool green at base. Resembles a more star-shaped 'Tenedos'

'Syracuse' 3 W-WWY
(J.L. Richardson) J.L. Richardson, 1958
'Green Island' × 'Chinese White'
Fl. 108 mm wide; perianth segments broadly ovate, somewhat truncate, slightly mucronate, spreading, a little creased, overlapping half; the inner segments more narrowly ovate, shouldered at base, slightly inflexed, with margins wavy; corona bowl-shaped, small, ribbed, pale cream, with a deeper tone at mouth and touches of pale greenish yellow at rim, frilled. Mid-season. Resembles a large 'Altyre'. AM(e) 1961

'Syr Daffyd'
(Mann, pre-1907)

N. syriacus Boissier = *N. tazetta* subsp. *lacticolor*

'Syrian Prince' 3 W-? (b)
(Mrs R.O. Backhouse, pre-1921)

'Syrian Rose' 1 Y-WWY
(D.N.Y. Olson, 1969) D.N.Y. Olson, 1987
'Maravel' × 'Spellbinder'; sdlg no. 11/21
Fl. 103 mm wide; perianth segments broadly ovate, pale yellow, with prominent white mucro, slightly inflexed, with margins wavy, overlapping half; corona cylindrical, lightly ribbed, buff-white, with a narrow band of bright golden yellow at rim, mouth expanded and more or less even, rim deeply notched and crenate. Early to mid-season. Resembles a larger-flowered 'Spellbinder' with a more brightly coloured perianth

'Syringa' 3 W-? (b)
(G.H. Engleheart, pre-1914)

'Syver' 1 Y-Y
(W. Jackson Sr, 1944)
'Semo' × 'Djaro'

'Syys' 1 W-W
(W. Jackson Sr, 1938) W. Jackson Jr, 1956
'Quartz' × 'Beersheba'

T

'Tabard' 1 W-? (b)
(G.H. Engleheart, pre-1914)

'Tabasco' 2 (a)
(G.L. Wilson) F.A.L. Harrison, 1956

'Tabitha' 2 W-P
(J.N.Hancock & Co., 1974) Unregistered
Perianth segments brilliant white; corona flared, deep bronze pink, frilled. Late

'Tableau' 3 W-? (b)
(Oregon Bulb Farms, pre-1950)

'Tablecloth' 1 W-W
(A. Overton) A. Overton, 1959
Fl. 114 mm wide

'Tablet'
(?P. Phillips, pre-1984) Unregistered

'Tabor' 2 W-? (b)
(Slieve Donard Nursery Co., pre-1932)

'Tabs' 3 Y-R
(K.B. Burns) K.B. Burns, 1964
Fl. 89 mm wide. Mid-season. Resembles 'Tamino' but with a larger corona

'Tace' 2 (a)
(G.H. Engleheart, pre-1923)

'Tacitus' 8 Y-Y
(pre-1798)
Fl. golden yellow

'Tacity' 2 W-YYR
(W. Jackson Jr) W. Jackson Jr, 1966
'Ethni' × 'Kalang'; sdlg no. 108/58
Corona dark yellow

'Taco' 3 W-R
(W.G. Pannill) W.G. Pannill, 1980
'Kilworth' × 'Avenger'; sdlg no. 62/57
Fl. 110 mm wide. Mid-season

'Taco Tio' 2 Y-R
(Ben Hager) Ben Hager, 1990
('Carnbeg' × 'Gypsy') × 'Alamo'; sdlg no. D125 Y/R
Fl. 110 mm wide

'Tacunda' 2 W-O
(Mrs R.O. Backhouse, pre-1921)
Perianth segmens sulphur white; corona widely expanded, frilled. AM(Haarlem) 1931

'T.A.Dorrien Smith' 1 W-Y
(W. Backhouse, pre-1869)
Perianth segments sulphur white, overlapping; corona rich yellow, of thick texture. Syn. 'Dorrien Smith', Pseudonarcissus Bicolor 'T.A.Dorrien Smith'

'Taffeta' 10 W-W
(D. Blanchard, pre-1952)
N. cantabricus var. *foliosus* × *N. romieuxii*
Fl. opening greenish yellow, becoming ice white; perianth segments lanceolate, with a broad band of strong green from base to apex beneath, strongly inflexed, separated; corona as long as the perianth segments, funnel-shaped, with mouth very slightly wavy, rim minutely, shallowly and irregularly crenate. $2n=28$

'Taffy'
(Mann, pre-1907)

'Taffy' 2 Y-W
(Elise Havens) G.E. Mitsch, 1976
'Nazareth' × 'Butterscotch'; sdlg no. FEJ6/3
Fl. 115 mm wide; perianth segments yellow, slightly tinged buff, overlapping; corona opening yellow, strongly shaded with buff, becoming white. Mid-season

'Taffytus' 1 Y-Y
(J.L. Richardson, pre-1927)
Fl. bright yellow

'Tagalie' 1 W-? (b)
(Cartwright & Goodwin, pre-1916)

'Taghboy' 2 Y-Y
(G.L. Wilson) G.L. Wilson, 1960
('Bastion' × 'Goldcourt') × ('Golden Torch' × 'Trenoon')

'Tagore' 2 W-? (b)
(Mrs R.O. Backhouse, pre-1921)

'Tahati'
(?Irish origin, pre-1927)

'T.A.Havermeyer' 3 W-YOO
Syn. of 'Mr Theo A.Havemeyer'

'Tahima' 2 W-Y
(W.A. Grace, 1945) R. Hyde, 1958
Corona becoming peach yellow

'Tahiti' 2 W-? (b)
(Australian or New Zealand origin, c.1927)

'Tahiti' 4 Y-O
(J.L. Richardson) J.L. Richardson, 1956
Fl. 108 mm wide; perianth and other petaloid segments very broad in outline, rounded or truncate at apex, bright greenish yellow 6C, with slight white mucro, overlapping half; the outer whorl spreading or a little inflexed, concave; the inner whorl more strongly inflexed and more deeply concave; some shorter petaloid segments at centre strongly inflexed, with margins folded inwards or strongly incurled; corona segments shorter than the petaloid segments and interspersed among them, orange, touched with yellow, frilled. Mid-season. 2n=28. PC 1956, FCC(Haarlem) 1961, AM(Haarlem) 1961, FCC(e) 1961, AGM 1995

'Tahni' 2 Y-O
(J.N.Hancock & Co.) Unregistered
Perianth segmens roundish, mid-yellow; corona small, bright orange. Late

'Tahoe' 2 Y-R
(W.G. Pannill) W.G. Pannill, 1972
'Matlock' × 'Paricutin'
Fl. 97 mm wide

'Tahuanui' 1 (a)
(R. Hyde) R. Hyde, 1957

'Taieri' 2 Y-? (a)
(J.T. Gray, pre-1949)
Perianth segments yellow; corona reddish orange in upper half

'Taihoa' 2 W-Y
(G.C. Yeates) G.C. Yeates, 1970

'Taillight' 2 (a)
(W.A. Grace, pre-1938)

'Tain' 1 W-W
(The Brodie of Brodie, c.1930)
Cross 221/20 × 'Beersheba'
Fl. pure white; corona cylindrical, with rim notched. Resembles a later-flowered 'Beersheba' with broader perianth segments

'Tai Nui'
(pre-1915)

'Tainui' 1 W-?
(G.C. Yeates) G.C. Yeates, 1972
Fl. 97 mm wide

'Taipan' 1 W-Y
(W. Jackson Jr) W. Jackson Jr, 1970
'Rowella' × 'Lod'

N. × *taitii* Henriques 13 = *N. pseudonarcissus* Linnaeus × *N. triandrus* subsp. *pallidulus* (Graells) D.A.Webb

'Tajmahal' 2 W-W
(A.M. Wilson, pre-1944)

'Tajo' 4
(R.A. van der Schoot, pre-1931)
Syn. 'Modesty'

'Takahe' 4 Y-O
(G.E. Mitsch, 1970) G.E. Mitsch, 1983
('Playboy' × ['Klingo' × 'Ardour']) × 'Enterprise'; sdlg no. F133/11
Fl. 102 mm wide; perianth and other petaloid segments pale yellow; corona segments orange. Mid-season. Resembles a larger 'Grebe'

'Takanini' 1 (a)
(R. Hyde) R. Hyde, 1957

'Taker' 2 W-P
(Alister Clark, 1940) J. Sharp, 1960

'Takone' 2 (a)
(S.J. Bisdee, 1945)

'Takone' 1 Y-Y
(W. Jackson Jr, 1955)
'Tompion' × 'Melissa'

'Takoradi' 4 W-W
(J.L. Richardson) Mrs H.K. Richardson, 1963

'Falaise' × 'Broughshane'
Fl. ice white. 2n=28

'Tal'
(Dorit Sandler, pre-1996) Unregistered

'Talahi' 2 W-YYR
(H.R. Bulman, c.1967) Unregistered
'Nancy Havergal' × 'Red Crusader'

'Talamba' 3 W-? (b)
(Mrs R.O. Backhouse, pre-1921)

'Talana' 2 Y-YOO
(C.W. Pierson, 1945) R. Hyde, 1958
Perianth segments rich yellow; corona disc-shaped, broad, scarlet-orange, with rich yellow at base, frilled

'Talavera' 3 Y-R
(The Brodie of Brodie, c.1932)
'Beacon' hybrid
Perianth segments sulphur yellow, overlapping; corona red

'Talbingo' 2 W-O
(W.M. Spry, pre-1975) Unregistered
'Torchlight' × 'Delight'

'Talbot' 1 W-? (b)
(F.H. Chapman, pre-1927)

'Talent' 2 W-W
(G.W.E. Brogden) G.W.E. Brogden, 1964
Fl. 115 mm wide. Mid-season

'Talisker' 2 W-Y
(D.N.Y. Olson) D.N.Y. Olson, 1989
'Stormy Weather' × 'Malaspina'; sdlg no. 292/10
Fl. 98 mm wide; perianth segments broad, rounded at apex, slightly mucronate, very smooth; corona bowl-shaped, with fairly straight sides, honey yellow, frilled. Early to mid-season. Sunproof. Resembles 'Premier'

'Talisman' 3 W-? (b)
(F.H. Chapman, pre-1913)

'Talisman' 1 Y-Y
(A.E. Lowe, pre-1927)

'Talisman' 2 Y-Y
(G.L. Wilson) C.R. Wootton, 1958
Fl. golden yellow

'Talisman' 3 W-?
Syn. of 'Atherton'

'Talitha' 2 W-Y
(D.S. Cooper) D.S. Cooper, 1959
Fl. 102 mm wide; corona cream yellow, tinged lime green. Mid-season

'Talkback' 6 O-R
(P. & G. Phillips) P. & G. Phillips, 1981
Fl. 90 mm wide. Mid-season

'Talland' 2 Y-O
(G.L. Wilson) L. Major, 1965
'Armada' × 'Bahram'
Corona strong orange 25A. Tall. Mid-season. 2n=28. Resembles a deeper-coloured 'Foxhunter'

'Tallboy' 2 W-? (b)
(D.R. Acheson, pre-1936)

'Tallchief' 1 Y-Y
(C.R. Wootton, 1952) C.R. Wootton, 1962
'Principal' × 'Crocus'
Fl. 115 mm wide; perianth segments pale yellow, faintly flushed apricot orange on opening; corona rich yellow. Mid-season

'Tall Golden Mary' 3 Y-Y
(E. Leeds, pre-1877)
Perianth segments becoming primrose yellow. Syn. Barrii 'Tall Golden Mary', Incomparabilis 'Nanus', Incomparabilis Concolor 'Nanus'. Was "absorbed" into 'Golden Mary'

'Tall Ship' 1 W-Y
(G.W. Tarry) Carncairn Daffodils, 1992
'Dunmurry' × 'Stormy Weather'; sdlg no. 1/36/82
Fl. 112 mm wide; perianth segments very broad, blunt, prominently mucronate, spreading, overlapping half; the inner segments more nearly ovate; corona chrome yellow, with rim rolled. Early

'Tall Timber' 1 W-Y
(G. Lewis) D.S. Bell, 1955

'Tall Timber' 2 Y-YOR
(M.E. Brogden) Unregistered

'Tallulah' 2 (a)
(Mrs R.O. Backhouse, pre-1921)

'Tally Ho' 4
(Cartwright & Goodwin, pre-1916)

'Tallyho' 2 W-R
(J.L. Richardson) Mrs H.K. Richardson, 1963
'Kilworth' × 'Signal Light'

'Talma' 1 Y-Y
Syn. of 'Minister Talma'

'Talone' 1 W-P
(C.E. Radcliff, 1941) J.M. Radcliff, 1956
'Glendevie' × 'Dawnglow'

'Talpura' 1 W-W
(H.R. Bulman, c.1967) Unregistered
'Primlough' × 'Mowbray'

'Talwyn' 1 Y-Y
(Rosewarne EHS, 1971) Rosewarne EHS, 1989
'Dutch Master' × 'Saint Keverne'
Fl. 110 mm wide; perianth segments brilliant greenish yellow, overlapping; corona expanded, vivid yellow 14B, with mouth lobed, rim flanged and crenate. Early

'Tam' 1 Y-Y
(A.O. Roblin, 1943)
'Nautilus' × 'Grayling'

'Tamahere' 2 Y-R
(D.S. Bell) D.S. BEll, 1983
'Checkmate' × 'Falstaff'
Perianth segments very broad, deep yellow

'Tamaki' 2 W-P
(R.H.Glover, pre-1993) Unregistered

'Tamale' 2 (a)
(A.M. Wilson) L.A. Hagen, 1957

'Tamale Pie' 2 Y-O
(Ben Hager, 1978) Ben Hager, 1990
'Cinel' × ('Ambergate' × 'Velvet Robe'); sdlg no. D47
Fl. 110 mm wide; perianth segments deep yellow. Early

'Tamar' 1 Y-Y
(P.D. Williams, pre-1933)

'Tamar' 2 W-P
(Campbell Duncan, 1950)
'Pink-a-Dell' × ('Carmoa' × 'Mrs R.O.Backhouse')

'Tamara' 1 W-Y
(W. Jackson Sr, 1944) W. Jackson Jr, 1956
'Hothu' × 'Tain'

'Tamara' 2 Y-Y
(Rosewarne EHS, 1969) Rosewarne EHS, 1980
'Trenance' × 'Rijnveld's Early Sensation'; sdlg no. 64/48/1
Fl. 110 mm wide; perianth segments brilliant yellow 7B; corona vivid yellow 9A. Very early. Resembles an earlier-flowered 'Trenance' with the perianth segments narrower and more heavily creased and the corona mouth more widely expanded

'Tamara' 2 W-?
Syn. of 'Birkasha'

'Tamarack' 1 Y-Y
(Curtis Tolley) Curtis Tolley, 1997
'Comal' × 'Ormeau'; sdlg no. 88-10-3

Fl. forming a double triangle, 102 mm wide; perianth segments acute, vivid yellow 9B; corona cylindrical, darker in tone (9B), with mouth even. Mid-season

'Tamar Double White' 4 W-Y
(pre-1880)
Fl. rounded, about 70 mm wide; perianth and other petaloid segments in 3-4 whorls opposite one another, broadly ovate in outline, rounded or squarish at apex, white, sometimes touched green at apex, sometimes with a touch of yellow near base shading to dark green at base, with midrib prominent, overlapping a quarter to one-third; the outer whorl a little inflexed; the inner whorls not much shorter, successively more strongly inflexed; the centre whorl often with fewer than six segments, very strongly inflexed, with margins strongly incurved; corona segments minute, of irregular length and shape, yellow, sometimes with green at base, sometimes with white at apex. Late. Scented. Syn. 'Double White', 'Tamar Valley White'. See also note under Poeticus 'Plenus'

'Tamar Fire' 4 Y-R
(Mrs H.K. Richardson) du Plessis Bros, 1976
'Tonga' × 'Vulcan'; sdlg no. 3756
Fl. 70 mm wide; perianth and other petaloid segments in three whorls, very broadly ovate, blunt or rounded at apex, yellow, more or less concave, overlapping half or more; the outer whorl with prominent white mucro, a little inflexed; the second whorl only a little shorter, more strongly inflexed; the centre whorl shorter still, strongly inflexed, irregularly arranged, with margins deeply incurled; corona segments half the length of the centre petaloid segments and clustered among them, broad, red, frilled. Mid-season. 2n=28. Resembles a more durable 'Tonga'

'Tamarind' 2 (a)
(R.H. Bath, pre-1931)

'Tamar Lad' 2 Y-O
(Brian S.Duncan) Dan du Plessis, 1996
'Ulster Bank' × 'Altruist'; sdlg no. 842
Fl. 94 mm wide; perianth segments broadly ovate, deep yellow; corona shallow bowl-shaped, very deep reddish orange, lightly frilled. Mid-season

'Tamar Lass' 3 O-O
(Brian S.Duncan) Dan du Plessis, 1996
'Ulster Bank' × 'Altruist'; sdlg no. 880
Fl. 95 mm wide; perianth segments very broadly ovate, light orange; corona shallow bowl-shaped, orange, with mouth lobed and rim crenate. Mid-season

'Tamaroa' 9 W-GGR
(V. Brink) V. Brink, 1967
'Shanach' × 'Dulcimer'
Fl. 57 mm wide; corona opening green, becoming

paler in tone, with deep red at rim. Late. Resembles a larger and later-flowered 'Cantabile'

'Tamar Snow' 2 W-GWW
(Brian S. Duncan) du Plessis Bros, 1986
'Easter Moon' × 'White Star'; sdlg no. 512
Fl. white; corona with green at base. Mid-season

'Tamarus' 1 W-Y
(W. Jackson Jr) Jackson's Daffodils, 1979
Sdlg 61/64 × 'White Prince'; sdlg no. 49/71
Fl. 121 mm wide. Early to mid-season

'Tamar Valley White' 4 W-Y
Syn. of 'Tamar Double White'

'Tamatea' 2 W-Y
(J.S. Leitch) J.S. Leitch, 1968

'Tambi' 2 W-? (b)
(A.M. Wilson, pre-1930)

'Tambora' 2 (a)
(de Graaff Bros, pre-1930)

'Tambora' 2 Y-R
Syn. of 'Tambora Gold'

'Tambora Gold' 2 Y-R
(H.G. Cross) H.G. Cross, 1984
Sdlg no. 53-6
Perianth segments broad, rich yellow; corona small, orange-red, frilled. Very early. Syn. 'Tambora'

'Tambourine' 2 W-? (b)
(F.H. Chapman, pre-1914)

'Tambourine' 2 Y-O
(J.L. Richardson) Mrs H.K. Richardson, 1962
'Teheran' × 'Ceylon'
Perianth segments golden; corona bowl-shaped, deep reddish orange

'Tambov' 3 W-? (b)
(A.M. Wilson, pre-1949)
Fl. slightly tinged yellow

'Tamerlane' 2 Y-O
(J.C. Williams, pre-1914)
'Firebrand' × 'King Alfred'
Perianth segments lemon yellow, deeply overlapping; corona large, expanded, rich reddish orange

'Tami' 2 W-OOR
(W. Jackson Jr) W. Jackson Jr, 1971
'Jeb' × 'Arbar'; sdlg no. 93/66
Fl. 105 mm wide. Mid-season

'Taminate' 2 Y-R
(S.C. Gaspar) S.C. Gaspar, 1955

Perianth segments deep yellow; corona shallow, ribbed, dark red

'Tamino' 2 Y-O
(The Brodie of Brodie, c.1936)
'Tredore' × 'Penquite'
Fl. 102 mm wide; perianth segments very broadly ovate, blunt, prominently mucronate, light greenish yellow 8B, spreading, plane, smooth, overlapping half; the inner segments more narrowly ovate, a little inflexed, with margins slightly wavy, sometimes twisted at apex; corona bowl-shaped, lightly ribbed, strong orange 30D, with mouth straight, rim irregularly crenate. AM(e) 1943

'Tammy' 2 W-YYO
(J.N. Hancock & Co., 1955) Unregistered
Corona expanded

'Tamora' 1 W-W
(Barr & Sons, pre-1914)
Fl. 95 mm wide, facing slightly downwards; perianth segments broadly ovate, blunt, mucronate, a little inflexed, plane, overlapping one-third; the inner segments narrower, inflexed at base, reflexed at apex, slightly twisted; corona cylindrical, creamy white, with mouth ribbed and widely expanded, rim deeply notched and crenate. Mid-season to late

'Tamoretta' 4 W-O
(J.L. Richardson) Mrs H.K. Richardson, 1969
'Falaise' × 'Arbar'
Perianth and other petaloid segments white; corona segments interspersed, bright reddish orange

'Tampa' 2 W-? (b)
(Mrs R.O. Backhouse, pre-1921)
Syn. 'Tosca'

'Tampico' 3 W-O
(J.L. Richardson, pre-1943)
'Warlock' × 'Forfar'
Fl. forming a double triangle; perianth segments broadly ovate, blunt, slightly mucronate, milk white, spreading, a little concave along midrib, overlapping half; the inner segments considerably narrower, a little inflexed, with margins sometimes creased or with a slight "thumb" in lower half; corona bowl-shaped, ribbed, brick orange, with mouth expanded and frilled. Mid-season

'Tamsin' 1 Y-Y
(W. Jackson Jr, 1955) Unregistered
'Shan' × 'Haldor'

'Tamsyn' 1 Y-Y
(Rosewarne EHS, 1969) Rosewarne EHS, 1980
'Saint Keverne' × 'Joseph MacLeod'; sdlg no. 65/70/1
Fl. 105 mm wide; perianth segments vivid yellow 9A; corona darker and brighter in tone. Early. Resembles

an earlier-flowered 'Saint Keverne' with the perianth segments more heavily creased and a longer corona

'Tanager' 1 W-? (b)
(Mrs G. Link, pre-1953)
'Mrs Ernst H.Krelage' × 'Fortune'

'Tanagra' 1 Y-Y
(A. Gray, pre-1946)
N. asturiensis × *N. obvallaris*
Perianth segments broadly ovate, blunt, slightly mucronate, inflexed, plane, overlapping a quarter; the inner segments only a little narrower; corona narrowing towards mouth, angled, with mouth ribbed and expanded, rim closely and deeply notched and crenate, sometimes appearing to be fringed

'Tanah' 2 W-Y
(Dofferhof, 1943) Groenveld & Lindhout, 1967
'Fortune' × 'Blazing Sword'
Fl. 93 mm wide; perianth segments creamy white; corona brilliant yellow 12B. Mid-season. Resembles a taller 'John Evelyn' with a less heavily frilled corona

'Tanais' 2 Y-OOR
(W. Jackson Jr, 1964)
'Dimity' × sdlg 187/53; sdlg no. 24/64

tananicus = *N. cantabricus* subsp. *tananicus*

'Tanawai' 1 W-W
(J.S. Leitch) J.S. Leitch, 1968
Fl. 111 mm wide

'Tancred'
(C. Dawson, pre-1908)

'Tandarra' 2 W-? (b)
(H.A. Brown, pre-1936)

'Tane' 2 Y-Y
(J.S. Leitch) J.S. Leitch, 1968

'Tanera' 2 Y-O
(J.S.B. Lea) J.S.B. Lea, 1959
'Carbineer' × 'Mexico'; sdlg no. 7-53-52
Fl. 127 mm wide; perianth segments very broadly ovate, blunt, only very slightly mucronate, deep golden yellow, spreading, plane, or a little concave at apex, smooth, regular, overlapping one-third to a half; the inner segments narrower, very slightly inflexed; corona bowl-shaped, smooth, dark reddish orange, with mouth split in places and overlapping, minutely frilled. Mid-season. Resembles a larger and more deeply coloured 'Carbineer'. PC 1959

'Tangaloa' 2 W-YYO
(J.N. Hancock & Co., 1971) Unregistered

'Tangata' 3 W-Y
(C.E. Radcliff, 1933)
'Pink'un' × 'Mayflower'

'Tangee' 2 (a)
(Oregon Bulb Farms, pre-1945)

'Tangent' 2 W-P
(G.E. Mitsch) G.E. Mitsch, 1969
'Green Island' × 'Accent'; sdlg no. Z20/1
Fl. rounded; perianth segments overlapping; corona cup-shaped, deep coral rose. Mid-season.

'Tangerine' 3 W-O
(G.H. Engleheart, pre-1907)
Corona bright scarlet-orange

'Tangerine' 2 Y-O
(H.A. Brown, 1931)
Corona tangerine orange, with mouth widely flared. Early

'Tangerine' 2 Y-O
Syn. of 'Flamboyant'

'Tangible' 2 W-? (b)
(Warnaar & Co., pre-1930)
AM(Haarlem) 1930

'Tangie' 2 W-W
(W.M. Spry, pre-1975) Unregistered
'Chinese White' × Ronalds sdlg
Corona frilled. Late

'Tangiers' 2 (a)
(H.G. Longford, pre-1933)

'Tangiers' 2 Y-YOO
(S.C. Gaspar) R.J. Abernethy, 1957
Perianth segments deep yellow, of good substance; corona reddish orange, paling to golden yellow at base, with rim dentate

'Tangine' 2 W-P
(J.L. Martin) J.L. Martin, 1973
'Pink-a-dell' × 'Pink Bonnet'
Fl. 96 mm wide

'Tangiwai' 3 W-? (b)
(R. Hyde) R. Hyde, 1955

'Tanglewood' 3 Y-R
(W.G. Pannill) W.G. Pannill, 1992
'Ambergate' × 'Altruist'; sdlg no 69/1
Fl. 89 mm wide. Mid-season

'Tangmere' 2 (a)
(Sir F.C. Stern, pre-1953)

'Tango' 3 (a)
(W. Welchman, pre-1923)

'Tango' 2 W-? (b)
(A.H. Ahrens) J.S. Leitch, 1956

'Tania' 5 Y-Y
(Sir F.C. Stern) Sir F.C. Stern, 1963
N. cantabricus subsp. *monophyllus* × *N. triandrus* var. *concolor*
Fl. 31 mm wide, light yellow; perianth segments ovate, blunt, mucronate, spreading, plane, separated; the inner segments narrower, somewhat oblong; corona cup-shaped, lightly ribbed, mouth straight or slightly incurved, more or less even, sometimes somewhat 3-angled, with rim regularly crenate. Dwarf. Early. Scented. Syn. 'Tania Stern'

'Tania Stern' 5 Y-Y
Syn. of 'Tania'

'Tanina' 2 W-P
(S.J. Bisdee) S.J. Bisdee, 1956
'Courtship' × 'Rosario'

'Tanist' 1 Y-Y
Syn. of 'Golden Plover'

'Tanith' 1 W-? (b)
(W. Jackson Jr, 1956) Unregistered
'Preamble' × 'Tamara'

'Tanjil' 2 W-?
(C.A. Nethercote) T. Morrison, 1960
Perianth segments broad; corona with a broad band of deep reddish orange at rim

'Tanloch' 1 W-? (b)
(?R. Hyde, pre-1959) Unregistered

'Tannaghmore' 1 W-Y
(T. Bloomer) T. Bloomer, 1973
'Rashee' × 'Empress of Ireland'; sdlg no. 1/19/58
Corona lemon yellow

'Tannahill' 9 W-R
(The Brodie of Brodie, c.1929)
'Dactyl' × 'Ace of Diamonds'
Corona flat, deep crimson scarlet

'Tannhauser' 2 Y-YYO
(F. Rijnveld & Sons, pre-1950)
'Reginald Dixon' × 'Aranjuez'
AM(Haarlem) 1950

'Tansley' 3 W-? (b)
(D.B. Milne, pre-1952)

'Tantalis' 2
(van Zonneveld Bros & Philippo, pre-1930)

'Tantalus' 2 W-Y
(W.A. Watts, pre-1914)

'Minnie Hume' × 'Weardale Perfection'
Corona soft yellow, frilled. Tall. Early. AM(c) 1914

'Tantara' 3 W-R
(T.D. Throckmorton) T.D. Throckmorton, 1974
'Green Island' × 'Russet'

'Tantivy' ?-P
(Alister Clark, pre-1948)

'Tantrum' 3 W-R
(G.L. Wilson, pre-1947)
('Clava' × 'Hades') × 'Coronach'
Corona clear dark red, with a ruby tone

'Tanya' 2 (a)
(M.E. Brogden) M.E. Brogden, 1956

'Tanzey' 2 W-OOY
(M.E. Brogden, pre-1995) Unregistered
('Motif' × 'Avenger') × 'Crimpelene'; sdlg no. 155/9

'Tanzy' 2 W-R
(J.S. Leitch) J.S. Leitch, 1962
Fl. 95 mm wide. Mid-season

'Tao' 3 Y-O
(Jackson's Daffodils) Jackson's Daffodils, 1996
'Odulation' × 'Pzaz'; sdlg no. 204/87
Fl. 102 mm wide; perianth segments very broadly ovate, brilliant greenish yellow 6B; corona cup-shaped, strong orange 25A. Mid-season

'Taoroa' 4 W-P
(M. Hamilton) Koanga Daffodils, 1992
Fl. 110 mm wide; perianth and other petaloid segments white; the inner whorls successively more inflexed; corona segments about three-quarters the length of the petaloid segments and interspersed among them, light orange 29B. Late

'Tapanui' 2 Y-R
(D.S. Bell) D.S. Bell, 1983
'Playboy' × 'Ashanti'
Corona red, with rim becoming rolled

'Tap Dance' 11a Y-Y
(A.N. Kanouse) Mrs A.N. Kanouse, 1990
'Daydream' × 'Lemon Ice'
Fl. rounded, 65 mm wide; perianth segments light lemon yellow, with a paler tone at apex; the inner segments slightly narrower; corona deeply split, the six segments two-thirds the length of the perianth segments, opposite and closely overlying them and a little darker in tone. Mid-season

'Tapestry' 2 Y-Y
(G.E. Mitsch) G.E. Mitsch, 1960
'John Evelyn' × 'Dick Wellband'; sdlg no. 38C43/1
Perianth segments pale yellow; corona almost disc-

shaped, large, ribbed, deeper in tone than the perianth, frilled. Mid-season

'Tapin' 1 W-Y
(J.L. Richardson, pre-1927)
'Cleopatra' × 'White Knight'
Perianth segments broadly ovate in outline, blunt or rounded at apex, only very slightly mucronate, pure white, slightly reflexed, plane, overlapping half; the inner segments more narrowly ovate, square-shouldered at base, more strongly recurved, with margins a little wavy; corona cylindrical, smooth, pale primrose yellow, with rim rolled and obscurely crenate. Mid-season

'Tapiola' 3 (a)
(D.S. Bell, 1947) D.S. Bell, 1958

'Tapua' 2 Y-R
(G.W.E. Brogden) M.E. Brogden, 1959

'Tara' 2 (a)
(J.L. Richardson, pre-1938)
'Mozart' × 'Penquite'
AM(Haarlem) 1943

'Taradale' 2 W-ORR
(D. Bramley) D. Bramley, 1986
'Foremost' × 'Rockall'; sdlg no. 75/58
Perianth segments deeply overlapping; corona shallow. Mid-season. Resembles a large and earlier-flowered 'Foremost' of more refined colour

'Tarago' 1 Y-Y
(O. Ronalds) T. Morrison, 1960
Fl. rich yellow

'Tarago Pink' 2 W-P
(O. Ronalds) O. Ronalds, 1955
Corona very deep pink, frilled

'Taran' 1 W-W
(W. Jackson Sr, 1944)
'Kanchenjunga' × 'Tain'
Perianth segments broadly ovate, blunt, only very slightly mucronate, spreading; the inner segments a little inflexed or with margins wavy; corona cylindrical, narrow, smoothly angled, with mouth expanded

'Taransay' 2 Y-Y
(D.C. MacArthur) D.C. MacArthur, 1992
Sdlg no. EV88/95
Fl. 94 mm wide; perianth segments very broadly ovate, prominently mucronate, brilliant yellow 9C, glistening; corona funnel-shaped, angled, darker in tone (12A) than the perianth at base, shading to a still darker tone (14A or B) at rim, mouth straight and lobed. Mid-season

'Tarantella' 9 W-YYR
(S.J. Bisdee) S.J. Bisdee, 1956
'Chaconne' × 'Sea Green'

'Taranto' 2 W-Y
(The Brodie of Brodie, c.1928)
'Great Warley' × 'Mrs Ernst H.Krelage'
Perianth segments pure white; corona yellow

'Tara Ranee' 3 W-O
(E.M. Crosfield, pre-1914)
Corona reddish orange. AM(Haarlem) 1915

'Tara Rose' 2 W-P
(Mrs H.K. Richardson) Mrs H.K. Richardson, 1972
'Rose Caprice' × 'Rose Royale'
Corona constricted near mouth, bright coral pink, with mouth expanded, rim dentate. Resembles 'Salmon Spray'

'Tararua' 1 W-W
(D. Bramley) D. Bramley, 1964
Fl. 115 mm wide. Mid-season. Resembles a smoother-textured 'Lochin' with the flower opening pure white and the corona rim more evenly rolled

'Tarata' 2 (a)
(G.W.E. Brogden) G.W.E. Brogden, 1957

'Taratoa' 2 (a)
(S.C. Gaspar, 1948) R.J. Abernethy, 1957

'Tarawa' 2 Y-R
(?New Zealand origin, pre-1997) Unregistered

'Tarawera' 2 Y-R
(Sir A.P.W. Thomas, pre-1930)

'Tarday' 4 Y-Y
(David Adams) David Adams, 1996
Sdlg 80/19B (4 Y-Y × 'Daydream') × 'Tahiti'; sdlg no. 85/27A
Fl. rounded, 105 mm wide, light yellow; perianth and other petaloid segments broadly ovate, plane; the inner whorl more nearly acute, inflexed; corona segments in two whorls, interspersed among the petaloid segments, one-third their length and of a slightly darker tone. Mid-season to late

'Tardiva' 9 W-R
(H. Prins, pre-1929)
Perianth segments pure white; corona scarlet. Late

'Tardree' 1 W-GPP
(Carncairn Daffodils) Carncairn Daffodils, 1987
Sdlg × 'Tynan'; sdlg no. 60/76
Perianth segments pure white; corona straight-sided, light yellowish pink 29C, tinged mauve. Mid-season

'Tardus' 3 W-WWY
(D. Jackson) Jackson's Daffodils, 1982

'Verona' × sdlg 186/70; sdlg no. 226/75
Fl. 90 mm wide. Mid-season

'Taree' 1 Y-Y
(A.O. Roblin, 1959)
'Kingscourt' × 'Goldcourt'

'Targe' 1 (a)
(A.M. Wilson, pre-1950)

'Target' 3 ?-YYO (a)
(The Brodie of Brodie, c.1909)
'Princess Mary' × 'Chaucer'
Fl. rounded; perianth segments creamy; corona disc-shaped, yellow, with a broad band of reddish orange at rim

'Target' 3 W-? (b)
(K.D. Smith) K.D. Smith, 1959

'Target' 2 Y-?
Syn. of 'Colombo'

'Target' 2 Y-O
(G.H. Johnstone, pre-1960) Unregistered
'Marksman' hybrid

'Tarifa' 2 Y-O
(J.M. de Navarro) J.M. de Navarro, 1959
'Ballyclare' × 'Revelry'
Fl. 102 mm wide; corona vivid reddish orange. Late. Resembles an earlier-flowered 'Border Chief' with narrower perianth segments

'Tarik' 1 Y-Y
(S.J. Bisdee, 1941)
'Loxton' × 'Robert Montgomery'

'Tarinna' 1 W-W
(S.J. Bisdee, pre-1939)
'Mary Blewitt' × 'Beersheba'

'Tarkaro' 1 Y-Y
(S.A. Free) S.A. Free, 1966
Fl. 115 mm wide. Mid-season

'Tarlatan' 10 W-W
(D. Blanchard, pre-1952)
$N.\ cantabricus$ var. $foliosus \times N.\ romieuxii$
Fl. opening greenish yellow, becoming ice white; perianth segments lanceolate (broader than in 'Taffeta' or 'Jessamy'), with very faint longitudinal lines of green beneath, strongly inflexed, separated; corona as long as the perianth segments, funnel-shaped, with mouth somewhat incurved, rim shallowly crenate. 2n=28

'Tarlee' 2 Y-? (a)
(Mrs E. Murray) Mrs E. Murray, 1959

'Taro' 1 Y-Y
(J.S. Leitch) J.S. Leitch, 1956

'Taroona' 2 Y-P
(J.R.Erp) J.R.Erp, 1956
'Moorpark' × 'Pink Bonnington'
Corona deep apricot pink

'Tarquin' 1 (a)
(A.M. Wilson, pre-1908)

'Tarquinius Superbus' 2 W-? (b)
(de Graaff Bros, pre-1927)

'Tarraleah' 1 W-Y
(C.E. Radcliff, 1935)
'Renown' × 'White Emperor'

'Tarring' 2 (a)
(Sir F.C. Stern, pre-1947)

'Tart' 9 W-R
(G.E. Mitsch) G.E. Mitsch, 1976
'Quetzal' × 'Smyrna'; sdlg no. D94/4
Fl. 68 mm wide; corona orange-red. Late

'Tartan' 3 W-O
(R. Crews, 1945) R. Crews, 1958
? × 'Matapan'
Late. Resembles 'Matapan'

'Tartar' 2 (a)
(A.M. Wilson, pre-1930)

'Tartarin' 7 Y-Y
(A.J. Bliss, pre-1931)
'M.J.Berkeley' × $N.\ jonquilla$
Fl. 70 mm wide, pale buttercup yellow; perianth segments inflexed, overlapping at base only; corona funnel-shaped. Mid-season to late

'Tarwin' 1 (a)
(R.H. Bath, pre-1931)

'Tarzan' 2 W-O
(de Graaff Bros, pre-1948)
AM(Haarlem) 1948

'Tasberg' 4 W-W
(H.G. Cross, 1975) H.G. Cross, 1992
'Pontresina' × 'White Lion'; sdlg no. 57
Fl. 105 mm wide; perianth and other petaloid segments in several whorls, yellowish white 155B; the two outer whorls of more or less equal length, very broad, prominently mucronate, spreading, plane or somewhat concave, overlapping half or more; the inner whorls shorter, strongly inflexed, with margins more or less strongly incurling; corona segments about one-third the length of the outer petaloid segments, interspersed among those at centre, opening pale greenish yellow 10D, becoming whitish yellow

(158D), frilled, with margins notched. Late

'Tascharm' 4 W-P
(H.G.Cross, 1978) H.G.Cross, 1994
'Precedent' × Jackson sdlg 192/69; sdlg no. 84-8
Fl. 95 mm wide; perianth and other petaloid segments in three whorls, broadly ovate, blunt, only very slightly mucronate, greenish white; the two outer whorls of more or less equal length, spreading, a little concave, smooth, overlapping half or more; the centre whorl shorter, strongly inflexed, with margins strongly incurled; corona segments half as long as the outer petaloid segments, tightly clustered at centre, more loosely arranged among the petaloid segments, roundish, orange-pink, paling to yellow-pink at base, frilled. Late

'Tasfire' 4 W-R
(H.G. Cross, 1975) H.G. Cross, 1986
'Northern Light' × 'Acropolis'; sdlg no. 125-5
Perianth and other petaloid segments in four whorls, broadly ovate in outline, blunt or truncate at apex, prominently mucronate, yellowish white 155D, a little inflexed, with margins incurling, overlapping half or more; the inner whorls successively more inflexed, with margins more strongly incurling; a few shorter segments clustered at centre, strongly inflexed; corona segments very short, interspersed, almost continuous, red, frilled. Late

'Tasflame' 4 Y-O/Y
(H.G. Cross, 1978) H.G. Cross, 1992
'Hot Stuff' × 'Fiji'; sdlg no. S298
Fl. 110 mm wide; perianth and other petaloid segments of more or less equal length, broadly ovate, blunt, brilliant yellow 7B, with white mucro, plane, creased at midrib, overlapping half or more; the outer whorl spreading; the inner whorl inflexed; a few narrow segments at centre strongly inflexed, twisted; corona segments almost half as long as the petaloid segments, clustered among them at centre, more loosely arranged between the surrounding whorls, strong orange 25B, with longitudinal bands of yellow, frilled. Late. Sunproof

'Tasgem' 4 Y-Y
(H.G. Cross) H.G. Cross, 1984
'Camelot' × ('Kingscourt' × 'Fiji'); sdlg no. 103-7
Perianth and other petaloid segments in three whorls, broadly ovate, blunt, vivid yellow 12A, with white mucro, a little inflexed, with margins incurling at apex, overlapping half; the inner whorls successively slightly shorter and more inflexed; a few narrow segments clustered at centre, short, twisted, strongly inflexed; corona segments almost as long as the inner whorls of petaloid segments, loosely arranged opposite and among them, broad, rounded, deeper in tone (14B). Late

'Tasgleam' 4 W-P
(H.G. Cross) H.G. Cross, 1984
'Precedent' × Jackson sdlg 192/69; sdlg no. 104-7
Perianth and other petaloid segments in two to three whorls, broadly ovate, greenish white 157D, with paler mucro, a little inflexed, concave, sometimes creased at midrib, overlapping more or less half; the inner whorls successively slightly shorter and more strongly inflexed; some segments at centre shorter still, narrow, twisted, strongly inflexed; corona segments one-third the length of the inner petaloid segments and interspersed among them, orange-pink (24C), frilled. Late

'Tasgold' 4 Y-Y
(H.G. Cross) H.G. Cross, 1984
'Camelot' × sdlg 111-1 ('Kingscourt' × 'Fiji'); sdlg no. 54-9
Perianth segments in several whorls, very broadly ovate, blunt, pale golden yellow, with white mucro, a little inflexed, concave, overlapping half; the inner whorls successively slightly shorter and more strongly inflexed; some segments clustered at centre; corona segments almost as long as the inner whorls of petaloid segments, clustered round the segments at centre, more loosely arranged among the surrounding whorls, of a richer yellow, with margins wavy. Mid-season

'Tashkend' 2 Y-Y
(The Brodie of Brodie, c.1924)
'Ben Alder' × 'Fortune'
Corona rich golden yellow, frilled, with rim flanged. AM(e) 1930

'Tasjoy' 4 W-O/Y
(H.G. Cross) H.G. Cross, 1985
Sdlg no. 78-8
Perianth and other petaloid segments in three whorls of more or less equal length, broadly ovate in outline, blunt or truncate at apex, greenish white (155A), with paler mucro, a little inflexed, slightly concave and with margins sometimes incurling at apex, overlapping half; the inner whorls successively a little narrower, more strongly inflexed and more deeply concave; a few short segments at centre, crumpled, strongly inflexed; corona segments one-third the length of the petaloid segments and interspersed among them, broad, strong orange 25A, with pale yellow 20C at margins, wavy. Late

'Taslass' 4 W-Y
(H.G. Cross, 1974) H.G. Cross, 1984
'Gideon' × 'White Lion'; sdlg no. 78-4
Fl. rounded, of strong substance; perianth and other petaloid segments in three whorls, very broadly ovate, rounded at apex, greenish white (155A), with paler mucro, spreading or a ittle inflexed, somewhat concave, overlapping half or more; the inner whorls successively shorter, a little narrower and more strongly inflexed; some segments at centre crumpled and very

strongly inflexed; corona segments shorter still, clustered among the petaloid segments, pale yellow 8D, with brilliant yellow 10A at rim, tightly frilled. Mid-season

'Taslea' 4 W-P
(H.G. Cross) H.G. Cross, 1986
'Tropic Isle' × ('Precedent' × Jackson sdlg 192/69); sdlg no. 5273
Perianth and other petaloid segments broadly ovate, blunt, creamy white, with paler mucro, a little inflexed, overlapping half; the outer whorls of about the same length and width; some shorter and narrower segments at centre strongly inflexed, with margins folded inwards; corona segments half as long as the outer whorls and loosely arranged between them, more tightly clustered among the segments at centre, broad, amber pink, with a darker tone at rim, frilled. Mid-season

'Taslove' 4 W-P
(H.G. Cross) H.G. Cross, 1986
('Precedent' × Jackson sdlg 192/69) × 'Fair Prospect'; Sdlg no. 5121
Perianth and other petaloid segments very broad, blunt or slightly truncate, minutely mucronate, creamy white, concave, of heavy substance, overlapping half; the outer whorl a little inflexed, with margins incurling at apex; the inner whorl shorter, more strongly inflexed, with margins more heavily incurling; corona segments half as long as the outer whorl, loosely arranged between the whorls, more tightly clustered at centre, broad, pale yellowish pink 29D, shading to deep orange-pink (170A) at rim, wavy or frilled. Late

'Tasma' 4 Y-O
(K.J. Heazlewood) R. Hyde, 1959
'Mary Copeland' × 'Dunkeld'
Fl. opening greenish yellow; perianth and other petaloid segments becoming yellow; corona segments becoming orange

'Tasman' 1 Y-Y
(C.E. Radcliff, 1935)
'The Gift' × 'Billali'

'Tasman' 1 W-? (b)
(C.A. Latta) C.A. Latta, 1957

'Tasman' 2 (d)
Syn. of 'Monogram'

'Tasman Ltd' 2 W-?
(Tom Forster, 1960s) Unregistered
Mid-season

'Tasmiss' 4 W-Y
(H.G. Cross, 1974) H.G. Cross, 1986
'Gay Time' × Jackson sdlg 221-69; sdlg no. 95-4

Perianth and other petaloid segments in several whorls, broadly ovate, blunt or truncate, greenish white 157D, a little inflexed, plane, sometimes creased at midrib, overlapping half; the inner whorls successively slightly shorter, more strongly inflexed; the centre whorl with margins folded inwards; some mis-shapen segments at centre strongly inflexed, with margins rolled inwards; corona segments very short, clustered among the petaloid segments at centre, more loosely arranged among the surrounding whorls, vivid yellow 14A, frilled. Mid-season

'Taspride' 4 Y-Y
(H.G. Cross, 1977) H.G. Cross, 1992
('Kingscourt' × 'Fiji') × 'Fiji'; sdlg no. S286
Fl. 95 mm wide; perianth and other petaloid segments in three whorls; the two outer whorls of about equal length, broadly or very broadly ovate, blunt or somewhat truncate, brilliant yellow 7A with white mucro, a little inflexed, with margins sometimes slightly incurling, smooth, overlapping half; the centre whorl strongly inflexed, with margins heavily incurled; corona segments half to three-quarters the length of the perianth segments, broad, vivid yellow 14A, some clustered at centre, strongly inflexed and closely frilled, some loosely interspersed among the petaloid segments, more nearly spreading, with margins wavy. Late

'Tasrose' 4 W-P
(H.G. Cross) H.G. Cross, 1985
'Precedent' × Jackson sdlg 192/69; sdlg no. 11-0
Perianth and other petaloid segments in several whorls, broadly ovate, greenish white (157C), with paler mucro, a little inflexed, concave, with midrib showing, overlapping half or more; the inner whorls successively a little shorter and more strongly inflexed; the segments at centre very strongly inflexed, folded or with margins wavy; corona segments half the length of the petaloid segments, crumpled and tightly clustered among the petaloid segments at centre, more loosely interspersed among the surrounding whorls, orange-pink, wavy. Mid-season

'Tasse d'Or' 7 Y-Y
(Barr & Sons, pre-1925)
Perianth segments bright yellow, spreading; corona ribbed, rich yellow, neatly frilled

'Tassie Fair' 2 Y-O
(Tom Forster, 1960s) Unregistered
Perianth segments soft yellow; corona deep orange, with rim rolled and broadly crenate. Tall. Early to mid-season

'Tassie Queen' 2 W-O
(Tom Forster, 1960s) Unregistered
Perianth segments pure white; corona widely expanded, opening lemon yellow, becoming apricot orange

and deepening in tone with age, frilled. Tall. Mid-season

'Tasso' 9
(G.H. Engleheart, pre-1897)

'Tasty' ?-P
(Alister Clark, pre-1948)

'Tasvention' 4 W-O
(H.G. Cross, 1976) H.G. Cross, 1991
'Northern Light' × 'Acropolis'; sdlg no. 59-70
Fl. 105 mm wide; perianth and other petaloid segments in several regularly superimposed whorls, very broadly ovate in outline, blunt or somewhat truncate at apex, not noticeably mucronate, white, spreading, with margins incurling, smooth, overlapping half or more; the inner whorls successively slightly shorter and becoming inflexed, folded at midrib or with margins strongly incurled; some segments clustered at centre, mis-shapen, strongly inflexed, with margins tightly rolled inwards; corona segments short, interspersed, reddish orange, sometimes flecked with yellow. Late. Resembles a slightly earlier-flowered 'Ulster Bride' with creamier white perianth segments

'Tat' 2 Y or W-? (a or b)
(pre-1915)

'Tatatoa' 2 Y-Y
(S.C. Gaspar, pre-1948)

'Tatcho Pal' 1 W-Y
(H. Aldersey, pre-1931)
Fl. 102 mm wide; perianth segments creamy white, with sulphur at base, regular, overlapping half; corona butercup yellow, with mouth almost straight, frilled. Mid-season. *AM(g) 1931

'Tater-du' 5 W-Y
(R.A.Scamp) R.A.Scamp, 1994
'Penril' × *N. triandrus*; sdlg no. 374
Fls usually 2-3 per stem, 70 mm wide; perianth segments broadly ovate or oblong, fairly prominently mucronate, opening creamy yellow, becoming creamy white, reflexed, slightly twisted, overlapping; corona bowl-shaped, broad, ribbed, lemon yellow. Dwarf. Mid-season

'Tatong' 1 W-? (b)
(W. Balch, pre-1933)

'Tatua' 2 W-OOR
(G.H. Yarrall, 1947) A.G. Scott, 1958
Fl. 102 mm wide; perianth segments broad, opening creamy white, becoming ivory white. Mid-season

'Tatura' 2 Y-R
(C.E. Radcliff, 1943) J.M.Radcliff, 1956

'Lybster' × 'Cheerio'

'Tauloch' 1 W-W
(A. Gibson, pre-1957)
PC(e)(NZ) 1957

'Taumata' 1 (a)
(Sir A.P.W. Thomas, pre-1930)

'Taupiri' 1 W-W
(C.A. Latta) C.A. Latta, 1964
Early

'Taupo' 2 W-? (b)
(A. Gibson, pre-1950)
Corona shallow, soft pinkish buff

'Tauranga' 1 (a)
(R. Hyde) R. Hyde, 1957

'Taurus' 2 W-W
(J.A. Hunter, 1977) J.A. Hunter, 1990
('Greenland' × 'Glendermott') × 'Kokutu'; sdlg no. 9/72A
Fl. 105 mm wide; perianth segments broadly ovate; corona mouth expanded, with rim slightly rolled. Mid-season to late

'Tauto' 2 Y-Y
(J.L. Martin) J.L. Martin, 1978
'Kingscourt' × 'Royal Tour'; sdlg no. RT/K 1
Fl. 100 mm wide; perianth segments brilliant greenish yellow 3A; corona vivid yellow 13A. Early. Resembles an earlier-flowered 'Camelot' of improved form

'Tavel' 1 W-GPP
(J. Gerritsen & Son) J. Gerritsen & Son, 1975
'Pink Beauty' hybrid
Fl. 110 mm wide; perianth segments ivory white; corona light yellowish pink 29C, with yellow-green at base. Mid-season

'Tavelle' 4 W-Y
(W. Jackson Jr, 1967) Unregistered
Sdlg no. 254/67

'Tavistock' 3 W-? (b)
(J.C. Williams, pre-1945)

'Tawa' 2 W-O
(J.S. Leitch) J.S. Leitch, 1966
Fl. 102 mm wide

'Tawanui' 3 W-? (b)
(R. Crews) R. Crews, 1956

'Tawasentha' 3 W-YYR
(S.J. Bisdee, 1938)
'Sunstar' hybrid

'Tawdry' 4
(Cartwright & Goodwin, pre-1916)

'Tawny Gold' 1 Y-Y
(de Graaff Bros) de Graaff Bros & van Konynenburg & Co., 1960
Fl. 127 mm wide; perianth segments vivid yellow 9B; corona very slightly darker in tone (9A). Mid-season

'Tawny Lad' 2 Y-O
(Mrs H.K. Richardson) Mrs H.K. Richardson, 1976
('Firecracker' × 'Spelter') × 'Flamboyant'
Perianth segments broadly ovate, blunt or truncate, vivid yellow 13A, with white mucro, touched vivid yellow 14B at margins, spreading or a little reflexed, smooth, overlapping one-third to a half; the inner segments a little narrower, with margins wavy, nicked at shoulder; corona short funnel-shaped, broad, smooth, deep orange, with mouth wavy, rim notched and crenate and slightly flanged. 2n=28

'Taxation' 2 W-O
(W. Jackson Jr) Jackson's Daffodils, 1980
Sdlg 229/67 × 'Rockall'; sdlg no. 100/74
Fl. 93 mm wide; perianth segments white, touched orange at base, smooth, of good substance; the inner segments slightly smaller; corona bright orange

'Tayene' 2 W-R
(C.E. Radcliff, 1931)
'Warflame' × 'Puzzle'

N. tazetta Linnaeus 13 Section Tazettae ("Kashmir Local", "Seventeen Sisters")
  subsp. *tazetta*
    var. *chrysanthus* (de Candolle) hort.= *N. bertolonii*
    var. *neglectus* (Tenore) hort.= *N. tazetta* subsp. *lacticolor*
    var. *praecox* (Tenore) hort.= *N. italicus*
    var. *syriacus* (Boissier) hort.= *N. tazetta* subsp. *lacticolor*
  subsp. *aureus* (Loiseleur-Deslongchamps) Baker = *N. aureus*
  subsp. *bertolonii* (Jordan) Baker = *N. bertolonii*
  subsp. *canariensis* (Herbert) Baker = *N. canariensis*
  subsp. *corcyrensis* (Herbert) Baker = *N. corcyrensis*
  subsp. *cupularis* (Salisbury) Baker = *N. cupularis*
  subsp. *dubius* (Gouan) Baker = *N. dubius*
  subsp. **gussonei** (Rouy) A.Fernandes
  subsp. **lacticolor** Baker ('Bazelman Minor', 'Chinese Grand Emperor', 'Chinese Sacred Lily', 'Crenulatus', 'Grand Emperor', ?'Grand Emperor of China', "China Lily", "Good Luck Lily", "Joss Lily", "Lien Chu Lily", "New Year Lily", "Water Fairy Flower", "Water Nymph Flower"). 2n=30. HC 1974
    var. *tenorii* (Parlatore) hort.
    var. *trewianus* (Ker Gawler) hort. ('Basselman Major', 'Bazelman Major', ?'Muzart Orientalis', Tazetta 'Trewianus', "Bossleman's Narcissus")
  subsp. **ochroleucus** (Loiseleur-Deslongchamps) Baker ("Ragged White", "Straw White")
  subsp. *pachybolbus* (Durieu de Maisonneuve) Baker = *N. pachybolbus*
  subsp. *panizzianus* (Parlatore) Baker = *N. panizzianus*
  subsp. *papyraceus* (Ker Gawler) Baker = *N. papyraceus*
  subsp. *patulus* (Loiseleur-Deslongchamps) Baker = *N. patulus*
  subsp. *polyanthos* (Loiseleur-Deslongchamps) Baker = *N. polyanthos*

N. tazetta-poeticus Grenier & Godron = *N.* × *medioluteus*

"TCD Maximus"
Syn. of Pseudonarcissus Major 'Maximus'

'Tchaikowsky' 2 Y-YYO
(Konynenburg & Mark) Konynenburg & Mark, 1960
'Aranjuez' × ('Kimono' × 'Memphis')
Fl. 105 mm wide; perianth segments brilliant yellow 8A; corona orange-yellow (17C), with strong orange 25B at rim. Mid-season

'Tea Cake' 2 W-YYO
(H.A. Brown, 1938) J.N. Hancock & Co., 1955
Perianth segments broad, creamy white; corona large, almost disc-shaped, gold, with bright reddish orange at rim

'Teal' 1 Y-W
(G.E. Mitsch) G.E. Mitsch, 1975
'Handcross' × 'Salem'; sdlg no. F76/1
Fl. 105 mm wide; perianth segments broad, rich lemon yellow; corona quickly becoming pure white. Early to mid-season

'Tealia' 5
(pre-1961) Unregistered

'Tean' 7 Y-O
(Barr & Sons, pre-1939)
Resembles 'Lintie'

'Te Anau' 2 W-W
(A. Gibson, pre-1951)

'Te Anga' 1 W-W
(J.S. Leitch) J.S. Leitch, 1967

'Te-ao-roa' 1 W-W
(pre-1926)

Fl. pure white

'Tearaway' 2 Y-P
(Jackson's Daffodils) Jackson's Daffodils, 1989
'Daydream' × 'Pink Silhouette'; sdlg no. 141/84
Fl. rounded, 100 mm wide; perianth segments very broad in outline, blunt or somewhat truncate at apex, light greenish yellow 4B, with slight white mucro, paler at midrib and apex and faintly touched white at base, spreading, plane, overlapping half; the inner segments a little inflexed; corona broad funnel-shaped, smooth, light yellowish pink 19B, with a slightly darker tone at rim, mouth frilled, rim somewhat rolled. Mid-season

'Teardrop' 5 ?-W
(The Brodie of Brodie, c.1910)
'Albatross' × *N. triandrus*
Corona small, white

'Tearie'
(pre-1955)

'Te Aroha' 4 Y-Y
(D.S. Bell) D.S. Bell, 1979
'Papua' × 'Hicol'
Fl. 105 mm wide; perianth and other petaloid segments yellow; corona segments interspersed, darker in tone

'Tearose Phoenix' 4 Y-Y
Syn. of 'Tea Rose Phoenix'

'Tea Rose Phoenix' 4 Y-Y
See also 'Tearose Phoenix'

'Te Awatea' 1 Y-Y
(Hon. Sir R.H. Rhodes, pre-1912)
Fl. pale yellow

'Tebessa' 3 W-R
(J.L. Richardson, pre-1944)
'Hades' × 'Forfar'

'Tebourba' 3 W-R
(J.L. Richardson, pre-1944)
'Hades' × 'Forfar'
Fl. rounded; corona disc-shaped, deep red. Sweetly scented. 2n=28

'Technicolour' 2 W-OOY
(G. Lewis) D.S. Bell, 1955
Perianth segments pure white, of thick substance; corona disc-shaped, apricot orange, with yellow at rim

'Tecoma' 2 Y-O
(H.A. Brown, 1932)
Perianth segments rich golden yellow; corona large, soft orange, with a darker tone at rim. Tall. Very early. 2n=28

'Tecumseh' 1 W-Y
(E.C. Powell, pre-1946)
'Van Waveren's Giant' × 'Lord Kitchener'

'Tedder' 2 W-P
(David Adams, pre-1996) Unregistered
Sdlg no. 77/O15A

'Tedstone' 1 W-W
(M.J. Jefferson-Brown) M.J. Jefferson-Brown, 1985
Fl. large. Mid-season

'Teen-age' 2 W-? (b)
(A.H. Ahrens) J.S. Leitch, 1955

'Teetotum' 2 W-YYR
(G.H. Johnstone, pre-1944)
'Silver Coin' hybrid

'Tegwith' 3 Y-R
(A.O. Roblin) A.O. Roblin, 1956
'Market Merry' × 'Dunkeld'

'Tehachapi' 2 W-? (b or c)
(K.L. Reynolds, pre-1944)

'Te Haka' 1 Y-Y
(D.S. Bell) D.S. Bell, 1979
'Golden Fortune' × 'Red Conquest'
Fl. 108 mm wide, sulphur yellow. Mid-season

'Tehana' 2 Y-R
(O.R. Marshall, 1957) Mrs N. Hurford, 1987
Sdlg no. 61/34
Fl. 108 mm wide; perianth segments broadly ovate, blunt, slightly mucronate, deep yellow, spreading, plane, or somewhat creased to one side of midrib, overlapping one-third to a half; the inner segments more narrowly ovate, slightly inflexed; corona deep bowl-shaped, lightly ribbed, red, shading to a deeper tone at rim, with mouth slightly expanded and more strongly ribbed, closely frilled

'Teheran' 2 Y-O
(J.L. Richardson, pre-1944)
'Aranjuez' self pollinated
Fl. 81 mm wide; perianth segments very broadly ovate, blunt, vivid to brilliant yellow 12A-B, with white mucro, spreading, slightly concave, overlapping half; the inner segments more narrowly ovate, a little inflexed; corona shallow bowl-shaped, closely ribbed, vivid orange 28B, with a lighter tone (24A) at base, mouth widely expanded, split in places and overlapping, frilled, with rim crenate. Mid-season. *HC(g) 1963

'Tehidy' 3 Y-YYR
(R.A.Scamp) R.A.Scamp, 1997

'Aircastle' × 'Montego'; sdlg no. 334
Fl. 92 mm wide, pale lemon yellow; perianth segments ovate, slightly concave, overlapping; corona bowl-shaped, with a well-defined band of bright red at rim and the rim neatly crenate. Mid-season to late

'Tekapo' 2 O-O
(A. Gibson, pre-1951)
Fl. bright reddish orange; perianth segments opening rich apricot; corona sometimes flushed yellow. Early

'Tekim' 3 Y-YYR
(D.J. Jackson, 1978) Jackson's Daffodils, 1989
'Lichfield' × sdlg 183/70; sdlg no. 186/78
Fl. 95 mm wide; perianth segments rounded, greenish white (155A), of glistening substance; corona vivid yellow 9A, with a very narrow band of red (40B) at rim. Mid-season to late

'Te Kuri'
(New Zealand origin, pre-1940)

'Telamon' 2 (a)
(Barr & Sons, pre-1923)

N. telamonius Link = *N. pseudonarcissus*

'Telamonius'
Syn. of *N. pseudonarcissus* subsp. *pseudonarcissus*

'Telamonius Grandiplene' 4 Y-Y
(pre-1829)
Petaloid segments with streaks of green

'Telamonius Plenus' 4 Y-Y
(pre-1620)
Fl. 100 mm wide; perianth and other petaloid segments ovate, light greenish yellow 4B, with white mucro, flushed with a slightly darker tone (4A) and becoming darker still at base, often with green beneath, inflexed, twisted or with margins wavy or recurved, separated; corona funnel-shaped, smooth, vivid yellow 14B, slightly paler at base, sometimes touched with green at apex, more or less deeply split, the six segments opposite the perianth segments and bi-lobed, more or less spreading, with rim rolled; the corona filled with petaloid and corona segments in alternate whorls; the petaloid segments longer than the darker corona segments. Early. 2n=14,27,28. Syn. "Guernsey Cabbage Daffodil", "Wilmer's Great Double Daffodil", "Wilmot's Double Daffodil", ?'Centifolio', 'Van Sion', 'Vincent Sion', Pseudonarcissus 'Telamonius Plenus'. *AM(p) 1978

'Telegraph Hill' 2 W-? (b)
(Oregon Bulb Farms, pre-1951)

'Telema' 3 W-? (b)
(Mrs R.O. Backhouse, pre-1921)

'Telemetry' 7 YYW-W
(R. & E.Havens) R. & E.Havens, 1995
'Symphonette' × *N. jonquilla*; sdlg no. VH86/1
Fls 2-3 per stem, 75 mm wide, of heavy substance; perianth segments ovate, soft lemon yellow, becoming white at base at maturity, spreading, plane; corona long, straight-sided, opening soft lemon yellow, becoming white, with mouth wavy. Late

'Telephus' 2 (a)
(C. Dawson, pre-1923)

'Telestar' 2 Y-YYO
(J.S. Leitch) J.S. Leitch, 1968

'Telex' 2 (a)
(Warnaar & Co., pre-1936)

'Telford' 1 Y-Y
(J.N.Hancock & Co., 1982) Unregistered
'Daydream' hybrid; sdlg no. 53/82H
Fl. glowing sulphur yellow; corona funnel-shaped, frilled. Tall. Early to mid-season

'Telita' 1 W-P
(J.R.Erp) J.R.Erp, 1956
'Rosque' × 'Karanja'

'Telluride' 1 W-W
(W.G.Pannill, 1983) W.G.Pannill, 1996
'Panache' × 'Cataract'; sdlg no. 77/27D
Mid-season

'Telopea' 2 W-YOO
(West & Fell, pre-1935)
Perianth segments creamy white; corona scarlet-orange, paling to gold at base

'Telstar' 1 W-W
(L. Major) L. Major, 1962
Fl. milk white, of strong and almost waxy substance. Mid-season. Resembles 'Trousseau'

'Te Manui' 2 W-W
(R.G. Cull) Hokorawa Daffodils, 1978
'Green Island' × 'Easter Moon'; sdlg no. 72/4
Fl. 106 mm wide. Mid-season. Resembles 'Pristine' but with a differently shaped corona

'Te Matai' 2 Y-Y
(Mrs A.R. Simmons) Mrs A.R. Simmons, 1980
Fl. 108 mm wide, lemon. Early to mid-season

'Temco' 2 Y-R
(J.S. Leitch) J.S. Leitch, 1958

'Temecula' 2 (a)
(K.L. Reynolds, pre-1944)

'Temeraire' 2 Y-Y
(S.C. Gaspar) R.J. Abernethy, 1957
'Balmoral' × 'Kingscourt'
Fl. deep golden yellow. See also 'Temeriare'

'Temeriare' 2 Y-Y
Syn. of 'Temeraire'

'Te Moana' 11a W-Y
(?New Zealand origin, pre-1997) Unregistered

'Temora' 2 Y-O
(J.N. Hancock & Co., 1946)

'Tempe' 2 Y-Y
(W. Jackson Jr, 1966) Unregistered
'Tulendena' × 'Jaslin'; sdlg no. 43/66

'Tempest' 2 (a)
(Mrs R.O. Backhouse, pre-1921)

'Templar' 1 W-W
(Warnaar & Co., pre-1950)

'Temple Bar' 2 Y-R
(D.S. Bell) D.S. Bell, 1984
('Checkmate' × 'Falstaff') open pollinated
Fl. 114 mm wide. Mid-season. Resembles a larger-flowered 'Checkmate'

'Temple Bells' 4 W-Y
(D.S. Bell) D.S. Bell, 1957
'Mrs William Copeland' × 'Mary Copeland'
Perianth and other petaloid segments white; corona segments interspersed, yellow

'Temple Cloud' 4 W-P/W
(J.W.Blanchard) J.W.Blanchard, 1994
'Dailmanach' × 'Clouds Hill'; sdlg no. 83/21A
Fl. 105 mm wide; perianth and other petaloid segments very broadly ovate, overlapping half or more; the outer whorl spreading, plane, with the three outer segments fairly prominently mucronate; the inner whorl shorter, inflexed, with margins incurling; corona segments half as long as the inner whorl, clustered at centre, inflexed, pink, with patches of white at margin, frilled. Mid-season

'Temple-fire' 3 (a)
(A.M. Wilson, pre-1948)

'Temple Gift' 2 W-YYO
(D.S.Bell) M.J.Brown, 1995
Fl. rounded, 105 mm wide; perianth segments broadly ovate, yellowish white 155B; corona funnel-shaped, light greenish yellow (2C), shading to brilliant orange 25C at mouth, with mouth straight, rim flanged and dentate. Tall. Late

'Temple Gold' 1 Y-Y
(D.S. Bell) D.S. Bell, 1968
'Dawn Gold' × 'Dawn Shower'
Fl. large, deep golden yellow; perianth segments broad, smooth; corona frilled

'Temple Guiting' 1 Y-Y
(J.M. de Navarro, pre-1949)
'Principal' × 'Spellbinder'
Fl. greenish yellow

'Temple Joy' 2 Y-OOR
(D.S.Bell) M.J.Brown, 1994
'Playboy' × 'Ashanti'
Fl. forming a double triangle, 100 mm wide; perianth segments ovate, brilliant greenish yellow 7C, plane; corona cup-shaped, ribbed, yellow-orange (21B), with orange-red (30C) in upper part, mouth flared and frilled, rim flanged and dentate. Mid-season

'Temple Legacy' 1 W-Y
(D.S.Bell, 1981) M.J.Brown, 1994
Fl. rounded, 110 mm wide; perianth segments broadly ovate, greenish white (155A); corona funnel-shaped, light greenish yellow 4B, with mouth flared and wavy, rim flanged and dentate. Mid-season

'Temple Lemon' 1 Y-Y
(D.S.Bell) M.J.Brown, 1995
Fl. forming a double triangle, 98 mm wide, light greenish yellow 4C; perianth segments ovate, plane; corona cylindrical, with mouth flared and wavy, rim flanged and crenate. Early

'Temple Maid' 4 W-O
(D.S. Bell, 1965) D.S. Bell, 1975
'Falaise' × 'Temple Bells'
Fl. 109 mm wide; perianth and other petaloid segments creamy white; corona segments interspersed, orange. Mid-season

'Templemore' 2 W-W
(J.L. Richardson, pre-1938)
'White Sentinel' × 'Forfar'
Fl. 115 mm wide, greenish white; perianth segments very broad, smooth, overlapping; corona opening pale primrose yellow, quickly becoming white, with mouth slightly expanded. AM(e) 1943

'Temple Mount' 2 W-GWW
(D.S. Bell) D.S. Bell, 1984
'Verona' hybrid open pollinated
Fl. 113 mm wide. Mid-season. Resembles a larger-flowered 'Verona'

'Templepatrick' 2 W-W
(W.J. Dunlop) W.J. Dunlop, 1957
'Courage' × 'Zero'
Fl. snow white

'Temple Perfecta' 4 W-Y
(D.S.Bell) M.J.Brown, 1995
Fl. 110 mm wide; perianth and other petaloid segments in three whorls, yellowish white 155D; the centre whorl incurved, concave; corona segments irregularly interspersed, light yellow 10C, frilled. Mid-season

'Temple Splendour' 1 W-W
(D.S.Bell, 1978) M.J.Brown, 1994
'Glacier' hybrid; sdlg no. 36
Fl. rounded, 115 mm wide; perianth segments broadly ovate, yellowish white 155D; corona funnel-shaped, a little darker in tone (155B) than the perianth, with mouth flared and frilled, rim flanged and dentate. Mid-season

'Templeton Beauty' 1 Y-Y
(D.S. Bell) D.S. Bell, 1979
'Red Conquest' × 'Golden Fortune'
Fl. 102 mm wide, sulphur lemon; corona with rim rolled. Resembles 'Red Conquest' but with a differently coloured corona

'Templeton Bell' 11a W-Y
(D.S.Bell) J.A.Hunter, 1997
Fl. 137 mm wide; perianth segments ovate, very smooth; corona split, frilled. Early to mid-season

'Templeton Pride' 4 W-R
(D.S.Bell, pre-1986) Unregistered
'Falaise' × 'Masquerade'

'Templeton Red' 3 Y-R
(D.S.Bell, 1976) D.S.Bell, 1983
Sdlg 163/79 ('Mannequin' × 'Garland') × 'Ashanti'
Fl. rounded, 100 mm wide. Mid-season

'Templeton Rose' 4 W-P
(D.S. Bell) D.S. Bell, 1983
Pink Div. 4 hybrid

'Temple White' 1 W-W
(D.S. Bell) D.S. Bell, 1985
Fl. 105 mm wide. Mid-season. Resembles 'Morning Light' but with the perianth segments more rounded

'Temple Yellow' 2 Y-Y
(D.S.Bell, 1978) M.J.Brown, 1994
Fl. 103 mm wide; perianth segments ovate, mucronate, brilliant greenish yellow 6A; corona cylindrical, vivid yellow 14A, mouth straight, wavy, rim slightly flanged. Late

'Temptation' 2 W-W
(G. Lubbe & Son, pre-1950)
AM(Haarlem) 1950

'Tempter' 2 (a or b)
(J.N. Hancock & Co., pre-1949)

'Temptress' 2 W-? (b)
(Oregon Bulb Farms, pre-1946)

'Tempura' 2 Y-Y
(J.N. Hancock & Co., 1954)
Perianth segments mucronate, sulphur yellow, deeply overlapping; corona large, deep yellow. Early

'Tenalga' 2 W-R
(A.O. Roblin, pre-1946)
('Token' × 'Saint Cecilia') × 'Matapan'

"Tenby Daffodil"
See "The Tenby Daffodil"

'Tender Moment' 7 W-GYP
(Eileen E.Frey, 1981) J. & E.Frey, 1994
Sdlg F31/5 × *N. jonquilla*; sdlg no. QEE14/43
Fls 1-2 per stem, 75 mm wide; perianth segments broadly ovate, blunt, spreading, with margins incurling, overlapping half; the inner segments a little inflexed, with margins more deeply incurling, sometimes twisted; corona cup-shaped, constricted near mouth, creamy yellow, shading to darker yellow at base, with green at base and a wide band of pink at rim. Late

'Tendresse' 11a W-P
(J. Gerritsen & Son, 1970) J. Gerritsen & Son, 1981
'Pearl Shell' hybrid
Fl. 90 mm wide; perianth segments ivory white; corona segments pale orange-pink (24D). Early

'Tendrine' 7
Syn. of 'Trendrine'

'Tenedos' 2 W-Y
(G.H. Engleheart, pre-1923)
Perianth segments broad, creamy white, overlapping one-third; the inner segments a little narrower, acute, somewhat ribbed, with margins slightly incurved; corona creamy lemon yellow, with rim rolled and crenate. AM 1924, AM(Haarlem) 1925

'Tenella' 3 W-? (b)
(C. Dawson, pre-1907)

'Teneo' 2 (a)
(S.C. Gaspar) R.J. Abernethy, 1957

'Teneriffe' 2 W-? (b)
(Mrs R.O. Backhouse, pre-1921)

'Teneriffe' 11a W-O
(J.L. Richardson) J.H. Rijkelijkhuizen, 1965
Fl. 98 mm wide; perianth segments creamy white; corona segments strong orange 25A

'Teniers' 1 W-Y
(J. de Groot & Sons, pre-1914)
Perianth segments overlapping; corona bright yellow

'Tennyson' 9 W-YYR
(P.D. Williams, pre-1907)
Corona lemon yellow, with dark madder red at rim

'Ten of Diamonds' 9 W-GGR
(Mary Lou Gripshover) Mary Lou Gripshover, 1993
'Dactyl' × Evans sdlg; sdlg no. 73-22-8
Fl. rounded, 62 mm wide; perianth segments broad, spreading; corona disc-shaped, green, with red at rim. Very late

N. tenorii Parlatore = *N. tazetta* var. *tenorii*

'Tenor Royal' 2 W-? (b)
(R. Hyde) R. Hyde, 1955

'Tension' 3 W-R
(P. Phillips) P. Phillips, 1968
Perianth segments very broad, smooth; corona widely expanded, ribbed, rich orange-red, frilled

'Tenterfield' 1 Y-Y
(Mrs J. Abel Smith) Mrs J. Abel Smith, 1985
'Arctic Gold' × 'Squire'; sdlg no. D33/91
Corona narrow, frilled. Early

'Tentrelle' 2 W-P
(J.N. Hancock & Co., 1956) Unregistered

N. tenuiflorus Schultes = *N. italicus*

N. tenuifolius Salisbury = *N. bulbocodium* subsp. *bulbocodium* var. *tenuifolius*

N. × *tenuior* Curtis 13 = *N. jonquilla* Linnaeus × *N. poeticus* Linnaeus (assumed)

'Teona' 2 (a)
(Barr & Sons) T.M. Dorrien Smith, 1958

'Tepena' 2 (a)
(West & Fell, pre-1938)

'Tepena' 4 Y-O
(K.J. Heazlewood, c.1970) Unregistered
'Mary Copeland' × 'Hollandia'

'Tepo' 2 Y-Y
(West & Fell, pre-1938)
Perianth segments primrose; corona pale yellow

'Te Poi' 2 Y-Y
(D.S. Bell, 1969) D.S. Bell, 1979
Fl. 107 mm wide; corona bowl-shaped. Mid-season

'Tepolo' 11b W-O/W

Syn. of 'Trepolo'

'Tequila' 4 Y-O
(J.N.Hancock & Co., 1986) J.N.Hancock & Co., 1997
('Falaise' × 'Ceylon') × 'Jezebel'; sdlg no. L/86H
Perianth and other petaloid segments bright yellow; corona segments bright orange. Early to mid-season

'Te Ra' 3 W-R
(A.E. Lowe, pre-1927)

'Teraplane' 2 W-? (b)
(S.C. Gaspar) R.J. Abernethy, 1957

'Terarco' 2 W-W
(R.H.Glover, pre-1993) Unregistered

'Ter Borgh' 1 W-W
(van Zonneveld Bros & Philippo, pre-1931)

'Terence' 9
(G.H. Engleheart, pre-1907)

'Terence' 2 Y-Y
(W.A. Grace, pre-1927)

'Teresa' 3 W-? (b)
(C. Dawson, pre-1923)
'Lulworth' × 'Horace'

'Teresa Draper' 1 Y-Y
(L.P. Dettman) L.P. Dettman, 1982
'Arctic Gold' × 'Ghana'; sdlg no. AG 1/81
Fl. 97 mm wide; perianth segments vivid yellow 9A; corona darker in tone (14A). Mid-season. Resembles 'Arctic Gold' but with the perianth segments plane and the corona straight-sided

'Teressken' 1 (a)
(Barr & Sons, pre-1923)

'Terminator' 2 Y-R
(Jackson's Daffodils) Jackson's Daffodils, 1995
Sdlg no. 15/89
Fl. 110 mm wide; perianth segments broadly ovate, vivid yellow 12A, with a flush of red; corona cylindrical, orange-red. Early

'Terminus' 1 (a)
(G. Lubbe & Son, pre-1938)
AM(Haarlem) 1938

'Tern' 3 W-GWW
(G.E. Mitsch, 1952) G.E. Mitsch, 1965
'Cushendall' × 'Cantabile'
Fl. 95 mm wide; corona milk white, with vivid green at base, frilled. Late. Resembles a vigorous 'Cushendall'

'Terna' 2 W-P
(W. Jackson Sr, 1944)
'Dawnglow' × 'Pinkess'

'Terracotta' 2 W-GYO
(Brian S.Duncan) Brian S.Duncan, 1993
'Raspberry Ring' × 'Fragrant Rose'; sdlg no. 1056
Fl. 102 mm wide; perianth segments very broad, blunt, fairly prominently mucronate, white, touched green at base, spreading or a little reflexed, slightly concave, with margins incurling, overlapping half; the inner segments more nearly spreading, somewhat creased; corona broad cup-shaped, loosely ribbed, pinkish yellow, with yellow-green at base, shading to a broad band of vivid orange 28B at rim, mouth slightly wavy, rim crenate and minutely flanged. Mid-season to late

'Terragona' 1 Y-Y
(D.S. Bell) D.S. Bell, 1979
'Iberia' self pollinated
Fl. 110 mm wide. Mid-season. Resembles an improved 'Iberia'

'Terrain' 2 W-Y
(J.S. Leitch) J.S. Leitch, 1967
Corona lemon yellow

'Terra Nova' 8
(New Zealand origin, pre-1933)

'Terrapin' 3 Y-YYR
(Brian S.Duncan) Brian S.Duncan, 1997
'Dateline' × 'Triple Crown'; sdlg no. 1644
Fl. 102 mm wide, mid-yellow; perianth segments broadly ovate, spreading; corona shallow bowl-shaped, with a line of deep red at rim, mouth wavy. Late

'Terrica' 1 Y-Y
(J. Hall, pre-1930)

'Terrific' 2 Y-R
(P. Phillips) P. Phillips, 1966
Fl. 112 mm wide; corona widely expanded, orange-red. Late. Resembles an earlier-flowered 'Traffic Light' with a differently coloured corona

'Terrific' 2 Y-Y
(Tom Forster, 1960s) Unregistered
Corona broad disc-shaped, ribbed, bright lemon yellow. Mid-season

'Terrington' 2 W-? (b)
(R.H. Bath, pre-1933)

'Teruel' 2 Y-R
(J.M. de Navarro, pre-1952)
'Market Merry' × 'Alamein'
Fl. forming a double triangle; perianth segments broadly ovate, blunt, prominently mucronate, spreading, plane, with margins incurling at apex, smooth, with midrib showing, overlapping half; the inner segments a little narrower, more rounded at apex and only slightly mucronate, shouldered at base; corona bowl-shaped, smooth, mouth with overlapping lobes, expanded and frilled, rim deeply notched and crenate

'Terwee' 3 (a)
(G. Lubbe & Son, pre-1944)
AM(Haarlem) 1944

'Terwegen' 4 Y-R
(F. Zandbergen) F. Zandbergen, 1971
'Tahiti' × 'Orbit'
Fl. 105 mm wide

'Terzet' 2 W-O
(Konynenburg & Mark) Konynenburg & Mark, 1960
'Carolina' × ('Geranium' × 'Aranjuez')
Fl. 95 mm wide; corona yellow-orange (23A). Mid-season

'Tessa' 1 (a)
(F.H. Chapman, pre-1927)

'Tessie' 2 W-W
(F.G. Lawson, pre-1947)

'Tessie Moule' 5
(Barr & Sons, pre-1923)

'Testament' 2 W-YPP
(M.J. Jefferson-Brown) M.J. Jefferson-Brown, 1985
Fl. large, of smooth texture. Mid-season. Resembles a 'Passionale' of stronger substance with the corona more widely expanded

'Testify' 2 Y-O
(P. Phillips) P. Phillips, 1971
Fl. 120 mm wide

'Teston' 2 Y-R
(R.J. Ralph, 1945)
'Marengo' × 'Rouge'

'Tête-à-Tête' 12 Y-Y
(A. Gray, pre-1949)
'Cyclataz' open pollinated
Fls 2-3 per stem, 65 mm wide; perianth segments ovate, brilliant yellow 8A, with slight white mucro, spreading or a little reflexed, plane, overlapping a quarter; the inner segments with margins wavy; corona cylindrical, short, broadly angled, slightly constricted near mouth, darker in tone (more vivid than 14B) than the perianth, mouth straight or slightly expanded, 6-lobed, with rim crenate. Dwarf. Very early. 2n=24+1B. AM(p) 1956, FCC(p) 1962,

*AM(g) 1973, *FCC(g) 1974, AGM 1993

'Tetecta'
Unregistered
In parentage of 'Immaculate'

'Tetee' 1 W-Y
(J.L. Martin) J.L. Martin, 1973
'Tangine' × 'Tringa'
Fl. 103 mm wide

'Tetherstones' 3 W-WWR
(D.S. Bell) D.S. Bell, 1968
'Hampstead' × 'Masquerade'
Fl. rounded; perianth segments very broad in outline, rounded or squarish at apex, mucronate, spreading, a little concave, overlapping half; the inner segments roundish; corona almost disc-shaped, broad, ribbed, creamy white, with a broad band of red at rim, mouth deeply split in places and overlapping, lightly frilled

N. teticaulis Haworth = *N. tazetta* Linnaeus × ? *N. jonquilla* Linnaeus

'Tetis' 1 Y-Y
(?de Graaff Bros, pre-1913)
Corona sulphur yellow. AM(Haarlem) 1913

'Tetlow' 2 Y-O
(J.N. Hancock & Co., 1955) Unregistered

'Tetoki' 2 Y-Y
(J.S. Leitch) J.S. Leitch, 1960
Fl. 108 mm wide

'Tewkesbury' 2 W-W
(D.A.B. Harries) D.A.B. Harries, 1969

'Texas' 4 Y-O
(Mrs R.O. Backhouse, pre-1921)
Perianth and other petaloid segments in many whorls, broadly ovate, blunt, slightly mucronate, overlapping one-third; the outer whorls more or less spreading, plane; the inner whorls clustered at centre, inflexed, with margins incurled; corona segments half the length of the petaloid segments and interspersed among them, bright orange, frilled. 2n=21. Syn. 'Marvel'. AM(Haarlem) 1927, FA(Haarlem) 1936, FCFA(Haarlem) 1938

"Texas Star"
Syn. of *N.* × *intermedius*

'Textile' ?-P
(Alister Clark, pre-1948)

'T.G.Sharpe' 1 W-? (b)
(F.H. Chapman, pre-1914)

'Thackeray' 1 Y-Y

(E.H. Krelage & Son, pre-1912)
Fl. large, golden yellow; corona with rim neatly rolled. AM(Haarlem) 1912

'Thackeray' 9 W-GYR
(Brian S. Duncan) Rathowen Daffodils, 1979
'Milan' × 'Cantabile'; sdlg no. 153
Perianth segments prominently mucronate; corona closely overlying the perianth, primrose, with green at base and bright red at rim. Late

'Thakeham' 2 W-? (b)
(Sir F.C. Stern, pre-1948)

'Thale' 1 W-W
(W. Jackson Sr, 1944)
'Trostan' self pollinated

'Thalia' 8 Y-Y
(pre-1798)
Fl. sulphur yellow

'Thalia' 5 W-W
(M. van Waveren & Sons, pre-1916)
Fls 3-4 per stem, pure white, facing slightly downwards; perianth segments ovate or oblong, blunt, fairly prominently mucronate, spreading or a little inflexed, separated; the inner segments more usually ovate, twisted or with margins wavy; corona long cup-shaped, ribbed, mouth straight, wavy, rim crenate. Late. 2n–21. AM(Haarlem) 1919, FA(Haarlem) 1921. Formerly wrongly listed as Div. 8

'Thamar' 1 (a)
(E.H. Krelage & Son, pre-1930)
AM(Haarlem) 1930

'Thamar's Delight' 1 W-? (b)
(G.L. Wilson, pre-1938)

'Thanet' 3 W-YYR
(C.E. Radcliff, 1946) J.M.Radcliff, 1956
'Jordan' × 'Veronique'
Corona lemon yellow, with red at rim

'Thanksgiving' 8 Y-Y
(pre-1969) Unregistered

'Tharnia' 2 Y-R
(A.O. Roblin, 1943)
'Killigrew' × 'Invergordon'

'The Admiral' 3 W-YYR
(Mrs R.O. Backhouse, pre-1921)
Corona large disc-shaped, yellow, with a very broad band of bright crimson at rim. Mid-season to late

'The Alliance' 6 Y-Y
(Rosewarne EHS) M.J. Jefferson-Brown, 1985
N. cyclamineus × 'Saint Keverne'; sdlg no. 65/65/1

Perianth segments ovate, with fairly prominent white mucro, reflexed, plane, overlapping a quarter to one-third; the inner segments only very slightly mucronate; corona cylindrical, widely ribbed, mouth more closely ribbed and a little flared, wavy, rim closely and minutely notched and dentate. Dwarf. Very early. Syn. 'Alliance', 'Alliance Party'. *AM(g) 1987

'The Allies' 8 W-R
(A.E. Lowe, pre-1927)
Fls 4-6 per stem; perianth segments creamy white; corona disc-shaped, red

'The Amber Witch' 2 (a)
(W. Welchman, pre-1908)

'Theano' 2 W-Y
(G.L. Wilson) F.A.L. Harrison, 1959
'Guardian' hybrid
Perianth segments ivory white; corona creamy yellow. Tall

'The Ashes' 2 W-? (b or c)
(W.E. Weightman, pre-1938)
Perianth segments fairly narrow, acute, pure white; corona shallow, frilled

'The Atom' 3 (a)
(W.A. Watts, pre-1913)

'The Banshee' 1 W-W
(de Graaff Bros, pre-1910)
Fl. pure white

'The Baroness' 2 W-? (b)
(R.H. Bath, pre-1923)

'The Benson' 2 Y-Y
(T.D. Throckmorton) T.D. Throckmorton, 1975
'Easter Moon' × 'Irish Coffee'
Perianth segments pale yellow; corona darker in tone. Mid-season

'The Bishop'
(pre-1914)

'The Bishop' 2 W-R
(S.J. Bisdee, 1942)
'Glendwin' × 'Elspeth'

'The Boggart' 1 (a)
(G.H. Engleheart, pre-1923)

'The Bride' 9 W-R
(Barr & Sons, pre-1905)
Perianth segments snow white; corona very small, scarlet

'The Bride' 2 W-WWP
(pre-1955) Unregistered

Corona slender, with pink at rim

'The Bridesmaid' 1 W-W
(Australian or New Zealand origin, c.1927)

'The Cardinal' 1 W-W
(C. Goodson, pre-1927)

"The Castlewellan Daffodil"
Syn. of 'Countess of Annesley'

'The Cid'
(pre-1914)

'Thecla' 2 W-YYO
(J.T. Gray, pre-1949)
Corona citron, with a broad band of deep tangerine at rim, in some seasons with tangerine to base

'The Colonel' 1 Y-Y
(J. Mallender, pre-1913)
Corona with rim flanged

'The Colonist' 1 Y-Y
(pre-1914)

"The Common Deep Yellow Double Daffodil"
Syn. of Pseudonarcissus Lobularis 'Plenus' of Haworth

'The Commonwealth' 1 Y-Y
(W. Welchman, pre-1908)
Fl. 121 mm wide, deep yellow; perianth segments smooth; corona with rim rolled

'The Coplow'
(J.O. Sherrard, pre-1949)

"The Cowslip Cupped"
Syn. of *N.* × *intermedius*

'The Czar' 2 W-? (b)
(Barr & Sons, pre-1923)
'Gaiety' × 'Lord Roberts'

'Theda' 2 W-? (b)
(R.H. Bath, pre-1927)

'The Deemster' 1
(pre-1913)

"The Derwydd Daffodil"
Syn. of "Thomas' Virescent Daffodil"

'The Doctor' 1 Y-Y
(W. Polman-Mooy, pre-1913)
Fl. 121 mm wide, clear yellow; perianth segments ovate, blunt, fairly prominently mucronate, inflexed at base, recurved at apex, with margins more or less tightly incurling, overlapping at base only; corona

cylindrical, broad, strongly ribbed, with mouth expanded and even, rim deeply notched. Mid-season

'The Don' 1 W-Y
(R.H. Bath, pre-1913)
'Weardale Perfection' × 'Madame de Graaff'
Perianth segments overlapping; corona pale lemon yellow

"The Double Purple Ring Daffodil"
Syn. of 'Medio Purpureus Multiplex'

"The Double Roman Narcissus"
Syn. of 'Romanus'

"The Double White Daffodil"
Syn. of 'Albus Multiplex'

"The Double White Trumpet Daffodil"
Syn. of 'Cernuus Plenus'

"The Double White Trumpet Daffodil with the Divisions of the Perianth in Duplicate"
Syn. of 'Cernuus Bicinctus'

"The Double Yellow Daffodil of Cyprus"
Syn. of 'Cyprius Flore Pleno Luteo Polyanthos'

"The Double Yellow Jonquil"
Syn. of Jonquilla 'Plenus'

'The Dove' 3 W-W
(C. Smith, pre-1907)
Corona opening pale creamy yellow, becoming milk white

"The Drooping White Spanish Daffodil"
Syn. of *N. moschatus*

'The Duchess'
(pre-1938)

'The Duchess' 1 W-P
(J.N.Hancock & Co., 1983) Unregistered
Sdlg no. 145/83H

"The Dwarf Double Light Yellow"
Syn. of Pseudonarcissus Lobularis 'Plenus'

"The Dwarf Purple Rimmed"
Syn. of 'Purpureo-cinctus'

"The Dwarf Saffron Rimmed"
Syn. of 'Croceo-cinctus'

'The Earl' 1 Y-Y
(C.L. Adams or G.H.Engleheart, pre-1908)
Fl. 108 mm wide, deep yellow. Early

"The Early Straw Coloured Bastard Daffodil"

Syn. of *N. pallidiflorus*

'The Emperor' 1 Y-Y
Syn. of 'Emperor'

'The Empress' 1 W-Y
Syn. of 'Empress'

"The English Double Daffodil"
Syn. of Pseudonarcissus 'Plenus'

"The Fair Maid of Erin"
Syn. of 'Colleen Bawn'

'The Fawn' 2 W-W
(Mrs R.O. Backhouse, pre-1908)
'Minnie Hume' × 'Weardale Perfection'
Perianth segments of waxy substance, overlapping; corona almost white, tightly ribbed

'The First' 1 Y-Y
(van Zonneveld Bros & Philippo, 1921)
Fl. pale yellow. AM(Haarlem) 1921, EFA(Haarlem) 1928

"The Flat Crowned Saffron Rim"
Syn. of *N. ornatus* Haworth

'The Ford' 2 W-? (b or c)
(E.H.G. Thurston, pre-1935)

'The Fuchsia' 2 W-? (b)
(W.B. Hartland, pre-1914)

"The Garland"
Syn. of *N. pseudonarcissus* subsp. *pseudonarcissus*

'The Geisha' 3 W-Y
(Barr & Sons, pre-1916)
'Lulworth' × 'Horace'
Perianth segments silver white; corona expanded, ribbed, apricot yellow, with lemon yellow at base and patches of white and lemon at rim

'The Geraldine' 3 W-O
(G.H. Engleheart, pre-1907)
Perianth segments white, shaded pale sulphur yellow at base; corona intense scarlet-orange

'The Ghost' 5
(Mrs R.O. Backhouse, pre-1908)

'The Gift' 1 Y-Y
(L. Buckland, pre-1936)

'The Golden Butterfly' 2 Y-Y
Syn. of 'Golden Butterfly'

'The Golden Image' 2 Y-Y
Syn. of 'Golden Image'

"The Great 6-lobed"
Syn. of *N.* × *odorus*

"The Great Curled Cup"
Syn. of *N.* × *odorus*

"The Great Double French Daffodil"
Syn. of 'Gallicus Major Flore Pleno'

"The Great Double Purple Ringed Daffodil of Constantinople"
Syn. of 'Chalcedonicus Fimbriatus Multiplex Polyanthos'

"The Great Double Yellow Spanish Daffodil"
Syn. of 'Plenus Laciniis Pallidis'

"The Greatest White Spanish Daffodil"
Syn. of 'Albicans'

"The Great Late Flowering White Daffodil with a Long Cup"
?Syn. of *N.* × *incomparabilis*

"The Great Spanish Beauty"
Syn. of 'Mrs George Cammell'

"The Great Tortuose White Spanish Daffodil"
Syn. of *N. tortuosus*

"The Great White"
Syn. of 'Doctor Gorman'

"The Great White Purple Ringed Daffodil"
Syn. of *N. poeticus* var. *majalis*

"The Great Wrinkled Cup"
Syn. of 'Rugulosus'

'The Grey Mare' 1 W-W
(G.P. Haydon, pre-1910)
Perianth segments slightly inflexed, corona ribbed, with mouth expanded

'The Hesperides' 3 W-? (b)
(W. Welchman, pre-1913)

"The Jasmine Jonquil"
Syn. of 'Compressus' pre-1799

'The King' 1 (a)
(G.H. Engleheart, pre-1916)

'The Knave' 6 W-Y
(C.F. Coleman, pre-1957) Unregistered

'The Knight' 1 Y-Y
(R.H. Glover, pre-1993) Unregistered

"The Large Gardenia Flowered Double White Daffodil"
Syn. of Poeticus 'Plenus'

'Thelastris' 3 W-? (b)
(A.H. Ahrens, pre-1949)

"The Late Great 6-lobed"
Syn. of *N.* × *odorus*

'The Leek' 2 W-Y
(G.P. Haydon, pre-1905)
Fl. facing down; perianth segments creamy white, inflexed; corona straight-sided, rich yellow

"The Lent Lily"
Syn. of *N. pseudonarcissus* subsp. *pseudonarcissus*

"The Lesser 3-lobed"
Syn. of 'Trilobus'

"The Lesser Clipt Trunk Daffodil"
?Syn. of *N. minor*

"The Lesser French Double Bastard Daffodil"
Syn. of 'Eystettensis'

"The Lesser Saffron Rim"
Syn. of 'Spathulatus'

'The Little Gentleman' 6 Y-Y
(C.A. Nethercote, pre-1948)
Fl. 66 mm wide, vivid yellow 9A; perianth segments ovate, acute, with slight white mucro, spreading, with margins a little wavy, slightly overlapping; corona cylindrical, smooth or lightly ribbed, slightly darker in tone than the perianth, with mouth expanded and deeply 6-lobed, rim crenate. Dwarf. Mid-season. See also 'Little Gentleman'

'Thelma' 9 W-YYR
(M. van Waveren & Sons, pre-1911)
Perianth segments oblong, squarish at apex, sometimes slightly truncate, only very slightly mucronate, snow white, spreading, plane, overlapping one-third to a half; the inner segments narrower, angled from shoulder to a narrow base, with margins wavy; corona disc-shaped, small, ribbed, yellow, with a narrow band of red at rim. Mid-season

'Thelma Dyer' 2 W-P
(A. Gibson) A. Gibson, 1965
Fl. 95 mm wide. Mid-season

'Thelma Flemming' 3 W-? (b)
(J. Flemming, pre-1938)

'Thelma Gower' 2 W-P
(A. Gibson, pre-1949)
PC(e)(NZ) 1949. Received PC(NZ) 1949 as 'Apple Blossom'

'Thelrosia' 2 W-P
(R. Hyde) R. Hyde, 1963
Fl. 102 mm wide. Mid-season. Resembles a smaller-flowered 'Thelma Gower' with a paler corona

'The Marquis' 1 Y-Y
(R.H. Bath, pre-1914)
Fl. 89 mm wide, deep yellow; perianth segments broadly ovate, blunt, slightly mucronate, a little inflexed, with margins wavy, overlapping half; the inner segments more strongly inflexed, sometimes twisted; corona cylindrical, smooth, darker in tone than the perianth, with mouth expanded and lightly frilled, rim narrowly flanged. Mid-season

'The Martian' 2 W-O
(G.H. Engleheart, pre-1910)
Corona heavily stained vermilion orange

'Themis' 3 W-? (b)
(A.M. Wilson, pre-1944)

'The Missus' ?-P
(Alister Clark, pre-1948)

'Themistocles' 2 W-Y
(E. Leeds, pre-1877)
Perianth segments sulphur. Syn. Incomparabilis Albidus 'Themistocles'. Was "absorbed" into 'Lorenzo'

'The Moonstone' 5 W-W
Syn. of 'Moonstone'

'The Muse' 9
(Cartwright & Goodwin, pre-1914)

"The Narrow Cupped"
Syn. of *N.* × *infundibulum*

"The Nosegay"
Syn. of 'Grand Monarque'

'The Nun' 5
(G.H. Engleheart, pre-1913)

'Theo' 1 Y-Y
(C.E. Radcliff, 1930)
'Michael' × 'Mrs W.Moodie'

'Theodora' 2 W-Y
(R. Parrett) R. Parrett, 1968
Fl. 102 mm wide; perianth segments ivory white; corona widely expanded, opening pale lemon yellow, becoming creamy yellow, frilled. Late

'Theodora Maria' 2 (a)
(P.J. Ruigrok, pre-1946)

'Theodore' 2 W-? (b)
(G.H. Engleheart, pre-1907)

"The Old English Double White Daffodil"
Syn. of 'Cernuus Plenus'

'The O'Mahoney' 1 Y-Y
Selection from *N. pseudonarcissus*
Syn. 'O'Mahoney'

'Theorum' 1 W-Y
(Jackson's Daffodils) Jackson's Daffodils, 1989
'Helsal' × sdlg 116/74; sdlg no. 70/81
Fl. 103 mm wide; perianth segments very broadly ovate, blunt or somewhat truncate, fairly prominently mucronate, greenish white (155A), reflexed, plane, smooth and of thick substance, overlapping half; the inner segments more nearly spreading at base, reflexed at apex, with margins wavy; corona funnel-shaped, light greenish yellow 3C, with mouth lightly frilled and rim rolled. Early

'The Pearl' 2 or 3 W-? (b or c)
(Sir A.P.W. Thomas, pre-1914)
Fl. facing slightly downwards. Tall

'The Pearl' 4 W-W
(G. Zeestraten, pre-1914)
'Sulphur Queen' sport
Fl. star-shaped, creamy white; perianth segments long, slender, acute. AM(Haarlem) 1915

'The Pearl' 8 W-W
(pre-1933)
Fl. large

"The Peerless Daffodil"
Syn. of 'Albus'

'The Perfect Gentleman' 1 Y-Y
(C.L. Adams, pre-1923)
Corona with rim dentate. Syn. 'Perfect Gentleman'

'The Pet' 3 W-Y
(W. Backhouse, pre-1869)
Fl. small; perianth segments pure white. Syn. Burbidgei 'The Pet'

'The Poet Pope' 9
(pre-1906)
Syn. 'Pope the Poet'

'The President' 2 W-YYR
(pre-1926)
Perianth segments creamy white; corona disc-shaped, yellow, with a narrow band of scarlet at rim

'The President' 1 Y-Y
(R.H. Bath, pre-1927)
'King Alfred' hybrid
Fl. soft yellow

'The Prime Minister' 1 W-? (b)
(W.A. Watts, pre-1923)

'The Prince' 2 W-? (b)
(West & Fell, pre-1936)

'The Prince' 3 W-YYR
Syn. of 'Prince'

'The Quaker' 1 W-W
(Cartwright & Goodwin, pre-1916)

'The Queen'
(pre-1914)

'The Queen' 1 W-Y
(D.V. West, pre-1936)
Perianth segments pure white, of great substance; corona light canary yellow

'Thera'
Unregistered
Seed parent of 'Ohisay'

'Therapia' 3 W-YYO
(The Brodie of Brodie, c.1922)
Perianth segments very broadly ovate, rounded at apex, very slightly mucronate, spreading, plane, sometimes lightly creased, overlapping one-third to a half; the inner segments somewhat truncate, a little inflexed, the margins slightly wavy and sometimes "thumbed" at or below mid-point; corona almost disc-shaped, broad, ribbed, bright yellow, with a very broad band of orange at rim, frilled. Mid-season. AM(e) 1927, AM(Haarlem) 1930, FCC(Haarlem) 1933

'Theresa Baxter' 2 W-P
(W.B. Blanden)

'Thérèse' 2 W-? (b)
(de Graaff Bros, pre-1930)

'The Rising Sun' 1 Y-Y
(W. Welchman, pre-1906)
Syn. 'Rising Sun'. AM 1906

'The Rival' 2 Y-YYO
(C. Smith, pre-1906)
Perianth segments pale primrose yellow; corona bright yellow, with bright scarlet-orange at rim, frilled

'The Rival' 2 (a)
(J.H. Braithwaite, pre-1930)

'Therm' 3 Y-R
(G.L. Wilson, pre-1938)
'Varna' × 'Cornish Fire'
Corona shallow, almost ruby red

'Theron' 1 W-W
(J.L. Richardson) J.L. Richardson, 1956
'Killaloe' × 'Broughshane'
Perianth segments broadly ovate, milk white; the inner segments slightly reflexed; corona narrow, with rim rolled

'The Rural' 1 Y-Y
(D.C.MacArthur) D.C.MacArthur, 1993
1 Y-Y × 'Sundance'; sdlg no. EV215
Fl. 116 mm wide; perianth segments broadly ovate, prominently mucronate, vivid yellow 9A, convex, with broad midrib showing, overlapping one-third to a half; corona funnel-shaped, angled, brilliant yellow 13B at base, deepening to vivid yellow 14A at rim, mouth flared and deeply frilled, rim flanged and crenate. Early. Wind resistant. Scented

'The Ryton' 1 W-? (b)
(pre-1913)

'The Sahib' 3 W-YYR
(G.H. Engleheart, pre-1916)
Corona disc-shaped, yellow, with deep red at rim

'The Sapper' 3 W-? (b)
(Mrs R.O. Backhouse, pre-1921)
AM(Haarlem) 1930

'The Saracen' 3 W-?O
(G.P. Haydon, pre-1909)
Fl. 115 mm wide; perianth segments narrow, acute; corona cylindrical, ribbed, golden yellow, suffused orange. Late. Syn. 'Saracen'

"The Scilly White"
Syn. of 'Scilly White'

'The Scout' 2 ?-Y
(West & Fell, pre-1937)
Corona very shallow bowl-shaped, deep citron

'Theseus' 1 (a)
(de Graaff Bros, pre-1927)

'Theseus' 7 Y-Y
(pre-1927)
Perianth segments soft butter yellow; corona ribbed, slighter darker in tone. Sweetly scented

'The Sheriff' 2 Y-Y
(W.A. Grace, pre-1927)

'Thesis' 1 Y-Y
(G.H. Johnstone, pre-1960) Unregistered

'The Sisterhood' 3 W-Y
(C. Smith, pre-1901)
Fls 2-3 per stem; corona pale buffy primrose yellow

"The Six-angled Clipt Trunk Daffodil"
Syn. of 'Hexangularis'

'The Skipper' 1 W-? (b)
(Cartwright & Goodwin, pre-1910)

"The Slender Flat Crowned"
Syn. of *N.* × *gracilis*

"The Small Clipt Trunk Daffodil"
?Syn. of *N. asturiensis*

"The Small Early White Daffodil with a Long Cup"
?Syn. of *N.* × *incomparabilis*

"The Small Gardenia Flowered Double White Daffodil"
Variant of "The Large Gardenia Flowered Double White Daffodil"

'The Spider'
(pre-1914)

'The Squire' 2 W-? (b)
(C. Smith, pre-1907)

'The Star' 2 W-? (b)
(R.A. van der Schoot, pre-1923)
FA(Haarlem) 1927

'The Star' 3 W-O
Syn. of 'The Sun'

'The Stork' 2 W-WWP
(S.J. Bisdee, 1941)
'Astrid' × 'Kyema'

'The Sun' 3 W-O
(C. van Zonneveld, pre-1926)
AM(Haarlem) 1926. Received AM(Haarlem) 1926 as 'The Star'

"The Swan's Neck Daffodil"
Syn. of *N. moschatus*

'Theta'
(pre-1913)

"The Tenby Daffodil"
Syn. of *N. obvallaris*

'The Tetrarch' 1 (a)
(Cartwright & Goodwin, pre-1916)

'Thetis' 1? W-W
(de Graaff Bros, pre-1910)

'Thetis' 9 W-R
(G.H. Engleheart, pre-1923)

Corona rich red

'The Triad' 5
(Sir A.P.W. Thomas, pre-1930)

"The Trine Narcissus"
Syn. of 'Tridymus'

"The Turkie Daffodil with a Double Crown"
Syn. of 'Medio-luteus Corona Duplici'

'The Twins' 8 W-Y
(J. de Groot & Sons or Barr & Sons, pre-1899)
Fls usually 2 per stem; perianth segments creamy white; corona rich yellow, of strong substance. Violet scented

'The Usurper' 6 Y-Y
Syn. of 'Englander'

"The Violet-scented Daffodil"
Syn. of 'Rebecca Syme'

'The Wanderer' 1 (a)
(Barr & Sons, pre-1927)

"The Welsh Peerless"
Syn. of 'Sir Watkin'

"The White Nonpareil Daffodil"
Syn. of *N.* × *poculiformis*

'The Wolf' 3 Y-R
(pre-1937)
Perianth segments deep yellow; corona small, vivid red. Late

'The Wrekin'
(The Brodie of Brodie, c.1910)
'Horsfieldii' × 'Weardale Perfection'

'Thimani' 2 W-O
(J.S. Leitch) J.S. Leitch, 1967

'Thimble' 5 Y-Y
(M.J. Jefferson-Brown) M.J. Jefferson-Brown, 1960
Fl. pale lemon yellow; perianth segments darker in tone. Mid-season

'Think Big' 1 Y-Y
(J.N. Hancock & Co., c.1979) Unregistered

'Thira' 2 W-W
(The Brodie of Brodie, c.1921)
'Kingdom' × 'White Emperor'
Corona with rim flanged

'Thisbe' 3 W-YYR
(C. Smith, pre-1902)
Perianth segments reflexed; corona expanded, canary

yellow, with salmon red at rim

'Thisbe' 2 W-YWW
(W. Jackson Jr) Jackson's Daffodils, 1979
('Snowfall' × 'Joningham') × 'Empress of Ireland'; sdlg no. 118/70
Fl. 113 mm wide. Mid-season

'Thistle' 2 W-? (b or c)
(W.F.M. Copeland, pre-1908)

'Thistle Dew' 2 W-Y
(G.E. Mitsch, 1948) G.E. Mitsch, 1963
'Bodily' × 'Gold Crown'; sdlg no. J3/1
Fl. 115 mm wide; perianth segments pure white, overlapping; corona somewhat flared, clear lemon yellow. Mid-season

'Thomas Baker' 2 W-YRR
(L.P. Dettman, 1978) L.P. Dettman, 1986
'Rockall' × 'Rameses'; sdlg no. R1-79
Fl. 80 mm wide; perianth segments yellowish white 155D; corona red (41A), with brilliant yellow 12B in lower half. Late. Resembles a later and smaller-flowered 'Ruth Murphy'

'Thomas Beccles'
(pre-1885)

'Thomas Hardy' 9 W-R
(G.L. Wilson, pre-1934)
Thought to be a hybrid between 'Ace of Diamonds' and 'Dactyl'
Fl. rounded; corona solid red

'Thomas Hay' 2 (a)
(Mrs R.O. Backhouse, pre-1921)

'Thomas I'Anson'
(pre-1914)

'Thomas King-Harmon' 1 (a)
(H.R. Meyer, pre-1946)

'Thomas Lodge' 9
(A.R. Goodwin, pre-1908)

'Thomas M.Absolon' 3 W-Y
Syn. of 'Thomas Moore Absolon'

'Thomas Mark' 2 Y-YOO
(J.W.A. Lefeber) W. Blom & Son, 1955

'Thomas Moore' 1 Y-Y
(E. Leeds, pre-1877)
Perianth segments pale yellow; corona slender, rich yellow, with rim crenate. Syn. Pseudonarcissus Major 'Mooreanus', Pseudonarcissus Major 'Thomas Moore'. "Absorbed" 'General Gordon'

'Thomas Moore Absolon' 3 W-Y
(W. Backhouse, pre-1869)
Corona citron yellow, with rim flared. Syn. 'T.M.Absolon', Burbidgei 'Grandiflorus Expansus', Burbidgei 'Thomas Moore Absolon'. Was "absorbed" into 'Mary'

'Thomas Sherriff' 2 W-WWY
(T. Sherriff, 1953) Mrs E. Milliken, 1964
Fl. 108 mm wide; corona creamy white, with lemon yellow at rim. Mid-season. Resembles 'Green Island' but with the corona of a slightly different colour. PC(e)(NZ) 1963

'Thomas Spanswick' 1 Y-Y
(E. Leeds, pre-1877)
Fl. rich clear yellow. Syn. Pseudonarcissus Major 'Thomas Spanswick'

"Thomas' Virescent Daffodil"
Double variant of *N. obvallaris*?
Syn. "The Derwydd Daffodil"

'Thomsonii' 1 Y-Y
(W.M. Thomson, pre-1942)
Dwarf

'Thoona' 2 Y-Y
(H.A. Brown) J.N. Hancock & Co., 1955
Perianth segments deep golden yellow; corona ribbed, deep yellow

'Thor' 1 W-? (b)
(H. Backhouse, pre-1913)

'Thor' 3 W-? (b)
(A.H. Ahrens) J.S. Leitch, 1956

'Thora' 2 W-Y
(J.R. Pearson & Sons, pre-1913)
Fl. facing slightly downwards; perianth segments slightly reflexed; corona large, opening lemon yellow, becoming soft buffy apricot yellow

'Thorbecke' 1 W-? (b)
(van Zonneveld Bros & Philippo, pre-1931)

'Thorbecke' 2 W-O
(J.W.A. Lefeber, 1950) J.W.A. Lefeber, 1960
Fl. 102 mm wide; perianth segments creamy white; corona rich reddish orange. Mid-season

'Thordis' 2 W-W
(J.R. Pearson & Sons, pre-1923)

'Thoresby' 3 W-YYO
(Mrs J. Abel Smith) Mrs J. Abel Smith, 1975
'Hamzali' × 'Aircastle'; sdlg no. Q4/12
Fl. 104 mm wide; corona disc-shaped, yellow, with reddish orange at rim. Mid-season. Resembles a

larger-flowered 'Hamzali' with a deeper-coloured corona

'Thorfinn' 1 (a)
(J.T. Gray, pre-1933)

'Thorkel' 1 Y-Y
(J.R. Pearson & sons, pre-1923)

'Thorla' 3 W-? (b)
(J.T. Gray, pre-1951)

'Thorne' 2 (a)
(F.D.B. Cobb, pre-1953)

'Thoroughbred' 1 Y-Y
(G.L. Wilson, pre-1937)
'King of the North' × 'Sorley Boy'

'Thorwaldsen' 1 W-? (b)
(R.A. van der Schoot, pre-1923)

'Thoughtful' 5 Y-Y
(A. Gray, pre-1951)
? × *N. triandrus* var. (loiseleurii}
Fls 1-3 per stem, 84 mm wide, sulphur yellow; perianth segments ovate, blunt, with white mucro, spreading, overlapping a quarter; corona broad funnel-shaped, ribbed, with mouth straight, even, rim irregularly notched and crenate. Fls larger when only one per stem, with corona more widely expanded. 2n=21

'Thrasher' 2 W-P
(G.E. Mitsch) Grant Mitsch Novelty Daffodils, 1984
Sdlg × 'Space Ship'; sdlg no. LL39/5
Fl. 108 mm wide; corona rose pink

'Three Cheers' 11a Y-W
(A.N. Kanouse) A.N. Kanouse, 1978
'Daydream' × 'Lemon Ice'; sdlg no. Reverse 1
Fl. 95 mm wide; perianth segments soft lemon; corona segments opening soft lemon, becoming creamy white, with a slightly darker tone at base, frilled. Early to mid-season

'Three Oaks' 1 W-Y
(John R.Reed) John R.Reed, 1997
'Bravoure' × 'Pops Legacy'; sdlg no. 86-21-1
Fl. rounded, 89 mm wide, facing up; perianth segments broadly ovate, spreading; corona flared, light yellow, with rim slightly rolled. Mid-season

'Three of Diamonds' 3 W-GWO
(Mary Lou Gripshover, 1975) Mary Lou Gripshover, 1993
'Cushendall' × 'Knave of Diamonds'; sdlg no. 69-38
Fl. 50 mm wide; perianth segments broadly or very broadly ovate, reflexed, with broad midrib showing, overlapping half; corona disc-shaped.

Mid-season to late

'Three Trees' 1 W-Y
(A.E. Robinson) Carncairn Daffodils, 1991
'Newcastle' × 'Cool Harmony'; sdlg no. 6/38/79
Fl. 98 mm wide; perianth segments broadly ovate, blunt, slightly mucronate, greenish white (155A), spreading, very smooth, overlapping one-third to a half; corona cylindrical, somewhat constricted near mouth, light greenish yellow 4B, with mouth flared and rim dentate. Mid-season

'Thrice' 11a W-P
(Grant E. Mitsch, 1984) R. & E. Havens, 1994
'Decoy' × 'Mission Impossible'; sdlg no. TT4/2
Fl. 80 mm wide; perianth segments ovate; corona deeply split, the three segments opposite the inner perianth segments, bright pink. Mid-season. Sunproof

'Thriller' 2 Y-O
(J.N. Hancock & Co., pre-1949)
Perianth segments pale yellow; corona orange

'Thriller' 2 Y-R
(C.G. van Tubergen, pre-1952)
AM(Haarlem) 1952

'Thrombara'
(?G. Lubbe & Son, pre-1950)

'Throstle' 2 W-? (b)
(A.M. Wilson, pre-1948)

'Thrumpton' 1 Y-Y
(Mrs J. Abel Smith) Mrs J. Abel Smith, 1984
'Brabazon' × 'Maraval'
Fl. soft sulphur lemon; corona with rim rolled. Early

'Thubui' 1 W-W
(W. Jackson Sr, 1935)
'Callirhoe' × 'Beersheba'
Fl. pure white

'Thumberlena' 5
(A.H. Ahrens) J.S. Leitch, 1956

'Thunderbird' 1 Y-Y
(J.S. Leitch) J.S. Leitch, 1967

'Thunderbolt' 2 (a)
(Sir C.H. Cave, pre-1928)

'Thunderbolt' 1 Y-O
(M.J. Jefferson-Brown) M.J. Jefferson-Brown, 1975
'Uncle Remus' hybrid
Perianth segments gold; corona reddish orange

'Thunderbolt' 2 Y-R
(W.M. Spry, pre-1975) Unregistered

'Winsome' × Ronalds sdlg

'Thunderer' 1 W-? (b)
(G.H. Engleheart, pre-1916)

'Thurleston' 1 (a)
(M.H. Tribe, pre-1937)

'Thurso' 1 W-W
(The Brodie of Brodie, c.1935)
'Beersheba' × 'Askelon'
Corona frilled

'Thwaite' 3 O-R
(Jan Dalton) Jan Dalton, 1997
Milne sdlg 68/8 × 'Achduart'; sdlg no. 833/1
Mid-season

'Thyl'
Unregistered
Pollen parent of 'Hymyr'

'Thylacine' 2 Y-R
(Jackson's Daffodils) Jackson's Daffodils, 1989
'Cowboy' × 'Colorful'; sdlg no. 114/84
Fl. 112 mm wide; perianth segments broadly ovate, blunt, vivid yellow 9A; corona cup-shaped, orange-red (30C). Mid-season

'Thyone' 3 W-WWP
(A.M. Wilson, pre-1939)
'Dulcimer' × 'Mystic'
Perianth segments white; corona with pink at rim

'Tia' 3 Y-R
(W. Jackson Jr) Jackson's Daffodils, 1979
Sdlg 152/65 × sdlg 101/65; sdlg no. 120/71
Fl. 110 mm wide; perianth segments broad, smooth, corona intense red, with mouth expanded and frilled, rim finely dentate. Mid-season. Sunproof

'Tiara'
(pre-1913)

'Tiara' 5 W-W
(Oregon Bulb Farms, pre-1946)

'Tiare Moana' 2 W-GYP
(D.S. Bell) D.S. Bell, 1979
'Iridescent' × ('Fontinalis' × 'Barbara Allen')
Fl. 102 mm wide; corona very shallow bowl-shaped, with green at base and pink at rim, frilled. Early to mid-season

'Tiawan' 3 (a)
(Barr & Sons, pre-1948)

'Tiberias' 2 W-Y
(S.J. Bisdee, 1939)
'White Nile' × 'Bodilly'

'Tibet' 2 W-W
(G.L. Wilson, pre-1942)
'Tunis' × 'Askelon'
Fl. 95 mm wide, pale creamy white; perianth segments very broadly ovate, slightly mucronate, a little inflexed, plane, overlapping half; the inner segments with margins incurved or wavy; corona short funnel-shaped, smooth, opening yellow, sometimes retaining more colour than the perianth, mouth expanded and frilled, rim flanged and deeply notched. Scented. 2n=28. AM(Haarlem) 1950, *AM(g) 1964

'Ticcidew' 2 W-YYR
(G.H. Johnstone, pre-1943)

'Tick' 2 W-P
(A. Overton) A. Overton, 1960
Ticket' × 'Perfectus'

'Ticket'
(pre-1951)

'Tickle' 2 W-P
(P. Phillips) P. Phillips, 1964
Fl. 105 mm wide; corona opening pink, becoming richer in tone. Mid-season

'Tidal Wave' 3 W-? (b or c)
(H. Backhouse, pre-1908)

'Tidbit' 2 W-WWP
(Oregon Bulb Farms, pre-1946)

'Tiddler' 1 W-WYY
(A. Gray) A. Gray, 1962
N. asturiensis sdlg
Fl. 70 mm wide; perianth segments milk white; corona vivid yellow 9A. Late. Resembles 'Cowley' but with a more deeply coloured corona

'Tiddleywinks' 3 W-? (b)
(M.P. Williams, pre-1949)

'Tidd-Pratt' 1 Y-O
(W.O. Backhouse, pre-1953)
Corona strong orange 25A. PC 1953

'Tidebrook' 3 W-W
(N.A.Burr) N.A.Burr, 1994
'Verona' × 'Angel'; sdlg no. 2.33.80
Fl. 98 mm wide, pure white; perianth segments very broad, blunt, slightly mucronate, spreading, concave, overlapping half; the inner segments narrower, square-shouldered at base, with margins a little wavy; corona very short funnel-shaped, widely expanded, closely ribbed, with light green in tube, mouth straight, split in places and deeply overlapping, densely frilled. Mid-season to late

'Tideswell' 1 W-W
(D.B. Milne, pre-1950)

'Tidy Ann' 2 W-P
(J.N. Hancock & Co., 1964) Unregistered

'Tiercel' 2 W-? (b or c)
(P.D. Williams, pre-1927)

'Tiercel' 1 Y-Y
(W. Jackson Jr) Jackson's Daffodils, 1979
Sdlg no. 64/73
Fl. 100 mm wide. Early to mid-season

'Tiernan' 1 Y-Y
(Barr & Sons, pre-1923)
'Madame de Graaff' × 'Monarch'

'Tiffany' 10 Y-Y
(D. & J.W. Blanchard) D. & J.W. Blanchard, 1960
Hybrid between species in the *N. romieuxii* and *N. cantabricus* groups
Fl. 75 mm wide, pale lemon yellow. Early. Resembles a much larger *N. romieuxii* of paler colour with a more tightly frilled corona

'Tiffany Jade' 3 Y-YYR
(R.A.Scamp) S.Holden, 1996
'Aircastle' × 'Montego'; sdlg no. 373
Fl. 97 mm wide; perianth segments broadly ovate, soft lemon yellow; corona shallow, closely ribbed, yellow, with a band of dark red at rim and the rim dentate. Mid-season

'Tigard' 2 W-O
(G.E. Mitsch, 1960) G.E. Mitsch, 1975
'Kilworth' × 'Signal Light'; sdlg no. V25/1
Fl. 90 mm wide; perianth segments ivory white; corona bowl-shaped, reddish orange. Mid-season

'Tiger' 2 Y-YYR
(The Brodie of Brodie, c.1910)
'Pope's King' × *N. poeticus*
Fl. yellow; corona with red at rim

'Tiger Boo' 2 W-Y
(Ken Farmer Nurseries) Ken Farmer Nurseries, 1978
Fl. 100 mm wide; corona orange-yellow. Mid-season

'Tiger Lily' 2
(Mrs R.O. Backhouse, pre-1921)

'Tiger Moth' 6 W-P
(Brian S. Duncan) Rathowen Daffodils, 1981
'Roseworthy' × 'Foundling'; sdlg no. 446
Perianth segments broadly ovate, slightly mucronate, reflexed, overlapping half; the inner segments a little narrower, with margins folded inwards; corona cylindrical, short, ribbed, deep pink, with mouth straight and wavy, rim crenate. Mid-season. Resembles '

Cha Cha' but with a narrower corona of darker colour

'Tiger Tim' 7 Y-Y
(L.P. Dettman) L.P. Dettman, 1970

'Tigress' 2 W-? (b)
(F.H. Chapman, pre-1927)

'Tikah' 2 W-O
(S.J. Bisdee, 1946)
'Hades' × 'Mr Sparks'

'Tiki' 2 Y-Y
(A.H. Ahrens) J.S. Leitch, 1956
Syn. 'Lemon Heart'

'Tiki Gold' 1 Y-Y
(D.S. Bell) D.S. Bell, 1983
Fl. golden yellow

'Tilberthwaite' 2 W-? (b)
(R.O. Backhouse, pre-1936)

'Tilburg Princess' 1 W-W
(J.N. Hancock & Co., 1975) J. Beekman, 1985
Sdlg no. 1/75 B
Fl. 95 mm wide. Late. Resembles 'Vigil' but with the corona mouth more widely expanded

'Tildarg' 2 Y-O
(Carncairn Daffodils) Carncairn Daffodils, 1992
'Pale Sunlight' × Wootton sdlg; sdlg no. 3/10/82
Fl. rounded, 92 mm wide; perianth segments roundish, only very slightly mucronate, whitish yellow, spreading, a little concave, with margins sometimes incurling at apex, overlapping half or more; the inner segments a little inflexed, rounded at base; corona widely expanded, lightly ribbed, light orange, mouth minutely and closely ribbed, split in places and overlapping, a little frilled. Late. Fl. of variable colour

'Tilla Durieux' 3 W-GYR
(Mrs R.O. Backhouse, pre-1921)
Corona small, with deep red at rim, frilled. AM(Haarlem) 1927

'Tillamook' 2 W-O
(Murray W. Evans) Murray W. Evans, 1977
Sdlg × 'Accent'; sdlg no. L-29
Fl. 115 mm wide. Mid-season

'Tilland' 2 Y-Y
(Mrs H.K. Richardson) du Plessis Bros, 1989
'Carrickbeg' open pollinated; sdlg no. 882
Fl. 103 mm wide, deep golden yellow; perianth segments smooth; corona cylindrical, with mouth slightly expanded. Late

'Tillicum' 2 W-P
(Murray W. Evans) Murray W. Evans, 1969
('Shirley Neale' × 'Chinese White') × ('Green Island' × 'Chinese White')

'Tillingham' 3 W-? (b)
(pre-1914)

'Tillington' 3 W-? (b)
(Sir F.C. Stern) Sir F.C. Stern, 1956

'Tilly' 2 W-GYO
(A.M. Wilson, pre-1944)
Corona disc-shaped, shading to apricot-orange at rim, with clear lemon at base

'Tilly Koenen' 2 W-? (b)
(J.W.A. Lefeber, pre-1949)

'Tilsin' 1 W-W
(J.T.Gray, 1949) P.Phillips, 1964
Fl. 108 mm wide. Mid-season. Resembles 'Beersheba' but with broader perianth segments and the corona rim more deeply rolled

'Tim'
(?W. Jackson Sr, pre-1948)

'Timandaw' 3 Y-R
(W. Jackson Jr) W. Jackson Jr, 1970
Sdlg 118/57 × 'Dimity'; sdlg no. 120/65
Perianth segments soft yellow; corona bright red. Resembles 'Dimity'

'Ti-Maru Audacious' 1 Y-Y
(C. Goodson, pre-1927)

'Ti-Maru Berenice' 3 W-W
(C. Goodson, pre-1927)

'Ti-Maru Bingen' 2 Y-Y
(C. Goodson, pre-1927)
Perianth segments pale yellow

'Ti-Maru Bon-Bon' 2 W-Y
(C. Goodson, pre-1927)

'Ti-Maru Bulbul' 3 W-R
(C. Goodson, pre-1927)

'Ti-Maru Burley' 2 Y-Y
(C. Goodson, pre-1927)

'Ti-Maru Concerta' 2 Y-Y
(C. Goodson, pre-1927)

'Ti-Maru Corinna' 2 Y-Y
(C. Goodson, pre-1927)

'Ti-Maru Delaven' 2 W-Y
(C. Goodson, pre-1927)

'Ti-Maru Delight' 2 W-O
(C. Goodson, pre-1927)
Perianth segments creamy white; corona reddish orange

'Ti-Maru Glandore' 2 W-Y
(C. Goodson, pre-1927)

'Ti-Maru Gold Peter' 2 Y-Y
(C. Goodson, pre-1927)

'Ti-Maru Gold Star' 1 Y-Y
(C. Goodson, pre-1927)

'Ti-Maru Ibex' 1 W-Y
(C. Goodson, pre-1927)

'Ti-Maru Jasmin' 2 Y-Y
(C. Goodson, pre-1927)

'Ti-Maru Jewel' 2 W-O
(C. Goodson, pre-1927)
Corona reddish orange

'Ti-Maru Lady' 2 W-? (b)
(C. Goodson, pre-1938)

'Ti-Maru Musang' 2 W-YYO
(C. Goodson, pre-1927)
Corona with reddish orange at rim

'Ti-Maru Nikora' 2 W-W
(pre-1927)

'Ti-Maru Odill' 2 W-Y
(C. Goodson, pre-1927)

'Ti-Maru Ohau' 2 W-Y
(C. Goodson, pre-1927)

'Ti-Maru Onyx' 2 W-O
(C. Goodson, pre-1927)
Corona salmon orange

'Ti-Maru Orion' 2 W-Y
(C. Goodson, pre-1927)
Corona pale creamy yellow

'Ti-Maru Oselot' 2 Y-Y
(C. Goodson, pre-1927)

'Ti-Maru Panda' 2 Y-Y
(C. Goodson, pre-1927)

'Ti-Maru Pride' 1 Y-Y
(C. Goodson, pre-1927)

'Ti-Maru Pronto' 2 Y-Y

(C. Goodson, pre-1927)

'Ti-Maru Queen' 1 W-Y
(C. Goodson, pre-1927)

'Ti-Maru Ricardo' 2 W-Y
(C. Goodson, pre-1927)

'Ti-Maru Rona' 2 W-Y
(C. Goodson, pre-1927)

'Ti-Maru Rosa' 2 W-Y
(C. Goodson, pre-1927)
Corona pale creamy yellow

'Ti-Maru Sonata' 2 Y-Y
(C. Goodson, pre-1927)

'Ti-Maru Talaro' 2 W-W
(C. Goodson, pre-1927)

'Ti-Maru Tapir' 1 Y-Y
(C. Goodson, pre-1927)

'Ti-Maru Tinsel' 5 W-W
(C. Goodson, pre-1927)

'Ti-Maru Toro' 1 Y-Y
(C. Goodson, pre-1927)

'Ti-Maru Varvet' 2 W-O
(C. Goodson, pre-1927)
Corona reddish orange

'Ti-Maru Victory'
(C. Goodson, pre-1940)

'Ti-Maru Walroona' 2 W-Y
(C. Goodson, pre-1927)

'Timberman' 2 W-Y
(F.Silcock, 1976) F.Silcock, 1993
'First Frost' × 'Chillagoe'
Corona cup-shaped, with mouth even or very slightly frilled. Early

'Timbuktu' 3 Y-Y
(W.G.Pannill) W.G.Pannill, 1994
'Daiquiri' × 'Alumna'; sdlg no. 77/25F
Mid-season to late

'Time Bell' 2 Y-O
(J.N. Hancock & Co., 1959) Unregistered
Corona reddish orange

'Timely' 3 W-GYR
(W. Jackson Jr) Jackson's Daffodils, 1979
Sdlg 168/61 × 'Arbar'; sdlg no. 177/70
Fl. 92 mm wide. Mid-season

'Times Square' 2 W-R
(J.J. Grullemans & Sons) J.J. Grullemans & Sons, 1956

'Timko' 2 Y-R
(J.S. Leitch) J.S. Leitch, 1960
Fl. 108 mm wide

'Timolin' 3 Y-GYR
(Carncairn Daffodils) Carncairn Daffodils, 1985
'Sunapee' × 'Aircastle'; sdlg no. 2/18/74
Perianth segments lemon yellow; corona cup-shaped, yellow, with dark green at base and red at rim. Mid-season

'Timon' 9 W-GYR
(G.H. Engleheart, pre-1910)
Fl. 51 mm wide; perianth segments overlapping half; corona almost disc-shaped, primrose yellow, with dark cinnabar red at rim, frilled. Late

'Timorous' 9
(G.H. Engleheart, pre-1930)

'Timos' 2 Y-Y
(W. Jackson Jr, 1967) Unregistered
'Lyetta' × sdlg 38/60; sdlg no. 150/67

'Timothy' 9
(A.M. Wilson, pre-1930)

'Timpenny' 2 W-W
(J.N.Hancock & Co., 1983) Unregistered
Sdlg 13/75H × sdlg 7/70J; sdlg no. 49/83H
Fl. rounded; corona very shallow, opening pale primrose yellow, becoming white. Tall. Early

'Tina Marie' 2 W-P
(S.A. Free) S.A. Free, 1968

'Tincleton' 5 W-W
(D. & J.W. Blanchard) D. & J.W. Blanchard, 1960
Fls 2 per stem, 80 mm wide. Mid-season. Resembles 'Frosty Morn' but with one fewer flowers per stem, a smoother perianth and a more widely expanded corona

'Tinderbox' 2 Y-R
(Brian S.Duncan) Brian S.Duncan, 1997
'Red Spartan' × 'Ulster Bank'; sdlg no. 1658
Fl. rounded, 105 mm wide; perianth segments broadly ovate, blunt, deep golden yellow, spreading; corona slightly constricted at mid-point, rich orange-red, with mouth expanded, rim crenate. Mid-season to late. Sunproof

'Tinerfé' 2 W-O
(J.W.A. Lefeber) J.W.A. Lefeber, 1976
Fl. 120 mm wide; perianth segments ivory white; corona strong orange 25B, with dark brownish orange

at base. Early to mid-season

'Tinge' 2 W-W
(A. Overton) A. Overton, 1960

'Tingent' 2 W-? (b)
(P.D. Williams, pre-1931)

'Tingford' 3 W-GWY
(Mrs J. Abel Smith) Mrs J. Abel Smith, 1987
'Mary Isabel' hybrid
Perianth segments rounded at apex, pure white; corona very shallow bowl-shaped. Late

N. tingitanus Fernández Casas 13 Section Bulbocodium

'Tinker' 2 Y-O
(G.L. Wilson, pre-1937)
'Damson' × 'Rustom Pasha'
Perianth segments deep gold; corona scarlet-orange. 2n=28. AM(Haarlem) 1948

'Tinkerbell' 6 W-Y
(Miss M. Verry) Miss M. Verry, 1971
'Assini' × *N. cyclamineus*
Fl. 72 mm wide, at an acute angle to the stem; perianth segments reflexed; corona opening primrose yellow, becoming a little paler, with rim flanged. Dwarf. Early

'Tinkerbell' 2 Y-Y
(Ken McCombe) Unregistered
'Julius Caesar' hybrid
Perianth segments yellow, deeply overlapping; corona somewhat funnel-shaped, rich golden yellow, with mouth flared and frilled. Mid-season

'Tinkle Bell' 3 W-GYY
(Barr & Sons, pre-1909)
N. × *medioluteus* × *N. poeticus*
Perianth segments pure white; corona small, sulphur yellow, with yellowish olive green at base. Tall. Late. Scented. Resembles a smaller-flowered 'Greenheart' of improved form

'Tinnell' 1 W-Y
(Mrs H.K. Richardson) du Plessis Bros, 1978
Sdlg no. 377
Fl. 104 mm wide

'Tino Rossi' 2 Y-O
(J.W.A. Lefeber) W. Blom & Son, 1955
Perianth segments creamy yellow; corona broad, orange, frilled

'Tinsel'
(E.M. Crosfield, pre-1913)
?'Ethelbert' hybrid
Fl. 86 mm wide

'Tinsel' 3 W-WWY
(G.L. Wilson, pre-1940)
('Silver Plane' × 'Distingué') × 'Silver Coin'
Fl. white; corona shallow, with gold at rim

'Tintagel' 2 W-? (b or c)
(The Brodie of Brodie, pre-1930)
'Nevis' × 'Tenedos'

'Tintara' 1 W-W
(A.J. Bliss, pre-1930)

'Tintern' 2 W-? (b)
(Barr & Sons, pre-1947)

'Tintern' 1 W-Y
(J.N. Hancock & Co., c.1960) Unregistered
Perianth segments spreading, smooth, of heavy substance; corona soft yellow, with mouth straight

'Tintex' 2 W-? (b)
(Alister Clark, 1930) J. Sharp, 1960

'Tinting' 2 W-P
(J.N. Hancock & Co.) J.N. Hancock & Co., 1960
Corona buff pink, frilled

'Tintorello' 9 W-YYR
(S.J. Bisdee) S.J. Bisdee, 1956
'Chaconne' × 'Sea Green'

'Tintoretto' 4 Y-R
(W.F.M.Copeland, pre-1914)
Fl. loosely arranged; perianth and other petaloid segments deep primrose yellow; corona segments rich orange-red or with a broad band of red at rim. Mid-season

'Tintoretto' 1 Y-Y
(C.G. van Tubergen, pre-1938)
AM(Haarlem) 1939

'Tiny'
(The Brodie of Brodie, c.1910)
'Mrs C.Bowley' × *N. poeticus* sdlg; sdlg no. 557/A/05

'Tiny' 5
(W.A. Watts, pre-1939)

'Tiny Kiwi' 2 W-R
(Ken Farmer Nurseries) Ken Farmer Nurseries, 1978
Fl. 70 mm wide; corona orange-red. Mid-season

'Tiny Tim' 3 W-W
(Oregon Bulb Farms, pre-1946)

'Tiny Tot' 1 Y-Y
(M. Fowlds, c.1958) G.E. Mitsch, 1975
Sdlg × *N. cyclamineus* × *N. asturiensis*; sdlg no. 268/2
Fl. star-shaped, 35 mm wide, clear yellow; perianth

segments narrow. Early. Resembles a paler-coloured 'Small Talk'

'Tioga' 2 W-Y
(E.C. Powell, pre-1946)
'Robert Sydenham' × 'Pilgrim'

'Tippeny' 2 W-Y
(W.M. Spry, pre-1975) Unregistered
'Aldgate' × 'The Bride'
Corona lemon yellow

'Tipperary Tim' 1 Y-Y
(J.C. Williams, pre-1929)
Fl. deep yellow; perianth segments overlapping. Late

'Tippet' ?-P
(Alister Clark, pre-1948)

'Tipster' 2 W-Y
(J.S. Leitch) J.S. Leitch, 1968

'Tiptoe' 5
(Mrs F.S. Foote, pre-1940)

'Tiptop' 2 (a)
(C.G. van Tubergen, pre-1938)

'Tirana' 2 W-? (b)
(J.T. Gray, pre-1950)

'Tiri' 2 (a)
(Sir A.P.W. Thomas, pre-1930)

'Tiriara' 2 Y-O
(J.C. Whibley) J.C. Whibley, 1962
Fl. 127 mm wide; perianth segments deep yellow; corona deep reddish orange. Mid-season. Resembles 'Rawene' but with the perianth segments more rounded and more richly coloured

'Tiritomba' 11a Y-O
(J. Gerritsen & Son) J. Gerritsen & Son, 1974
Fl. 90 mm wide; perianth segments very broad, squarish at apex, prominently mucronate, greenish yellow (2C), spreading, overlapping half; the inner segments narrower, ovate or roundish, angled at shoulder; corona split to base, the six segments more than twice as long as the perianth segments, opposite and closely overlying them and of the same width, bi-lobed, with the lobes overlapping, opening yellow, becoming strong orange 25A-B, ribbed near mouth and deeply frilled, overlapping at shoulder. Early

'Tiroran' 2 Y-YYO
(D.C.MacArthur) D.C.MacArthur, 1994
'Chungking' hybrid × 2 Y-R; sdlg no. EV6187
Fl. 83 mm wide; perianth segments ovate, mucronate, vivid yellow 12A, spreading, concave; corona cup-shaped, large, ribbed, orange-yellow (15A) with a broad band of strong orange 25A at rim, mouth straight, lobed, rim flanged and crenate. Dwarf. Late. Sunproof

'Tirpitz' 1 W-Y
(S.C. Gaspar) R.J. Abernethy, 1962
'Opulent' self pollinated
Fl. 108 mm wide; perianth segments pure white; corona lemon yellow. Mid-season. Resembles an improved 'Sincerity'

'Tirranna' 2 W-R
(C.E. Radcliff, 1938)
'Helles' × 'Blodwen'

'Tisa' 2 W-O
(D.J. Jackson, 1978) Jackson's Daffodils, 1989
'Toya' × sdlg 167/70; sdlg no. 203/78
Fl. 108 mm wide; perianth segments very broadly ovate, greenish yellow 155A; the inner segments a little narrower; corona very deeply split, with the six lobes overlapping, vivid orange 28B. Mid-season

'Tishomingo' 2 W-GOO
(Brian S. Duncan) W.H. Roesé, 1986
'Syracuse' × 'Jewel Song'; sdlg no. 515
Corona apricot orange, with green at base. Mid-season to late

'Tita' 2 Y-O
(P.D. Williams, pre-1907)
Perianth segments soft sulphur yellow; corona large, reddish orange, with a darker tone at rim, frilled. AM(g)(c) 1914

'Titaan' 2 Y-O
(J.W.A. Lefeber) J.W.A. Lefeber, 1975
Fl. 120 mm wide; perianth segments brilliant yellow 7A; corona light orange (24B-25B), with a darker tone at base. Late

'Titan' 2 Y-YYO
(W. Backhouse, pre-1869)
Fl. large; corona with orange at rim. Syn. Incomparabilis Leedsii 'Grandiflorus', Incomparabilis Leedsii 'Titan'. "Absorbed" 'Winslow'

'Titan' 1 Y-Y
Syn. of 'Charlemagne'

'Titania' 3 W-P
(Barr & Sons, pre-1913)
'Maggie May' × *N. poeticus* var. *recurvus*

'Titania' 2 W-W
(C.E. Radcliff, 1929)
'White Queen' hybrid

'Titania' 8
(pre-1939)

'Titania' 6 W-W
(J.L. Richardson) J.L. Richardson, 1958
'Trousseau' open pollinated
Fl. 84 mm wide, pale creamy white; perianth segments rounded at apex, slightly reflexed, overlapping; corona cylindrical, ribbed, with mouth expanded and frilled, rim crenate and minutely dentate. AM(e) 1960

'Titanic' 1 W-Y
(The Brodie of Brodie, c.1910)
'Lady Margaret Boscawen' × 'Glory of Noordwijk'

'Titanic' 2 W-YYO
(Tom Forster, 1960s) Unregistered
Corona disc-shaped, bright orange-yellow, with orange at rim, frilled. Early to mid-season

'Titch' 1 Y-Y
(H.A. Brown, pre-1946)
Fl. bright rich yellow. Very early. 2n=29

'Titley' 2 (a)
(A.M. Wilson, pre-1950)

'Titmouse' 2 W-YYO
(Mrs G. Link) Mrs G. Link, 1958
'Alight' × 'Coverack Perfection'
Perianth segments pure white; corona chrome yellow, with nasturtium orange at rim

'Titoki' 1 (a)
(J.H. Braithwaite, 1937) Parr's Nurseries, 1958

'Tittle-Tattle' 7 Y-GYY
(C.R. Wootton, pre-1953)
'Gulliver' × ? *N. jonquilla*
Fl. 2-3 per stem; perianth segments clear yellow; corona shallow, yellow, tinged golden orange. Late. Scented. 2n=21

'Titus'
(J. Pope, pre-1908)

'Tityus' 1 W-? (b)
(Barr & Sons, pre-1923)

'Tiverton' 2 Y-ORR
(O.R. Marshall) O.R. Marshall, 1963
Fl. 118 mm wide; perianth segments deep golden yellow; corona intense red, paling towards base. Early. Resembles a more intensely coloured 'Playboy'

'Tivoli' 2 Y-R
(Warnaar & Co., pre-1951)
AM(Haarlem) 1951

'Tiwihi' 2 Y-R
(J.S. Leitch) J.S. Leitch, 1957

'Tizer' 2 (a)
(P.D. Williams) J.E. Exley, 1938

'T.M.Absolon' 3? W-Y
Syn. of 'Thomas Moore Absolon'

'Tmei' 2 W-? (b)
(W. Jackson Sr, 1935)
'Mary Blewitt' × 'Holmdale'

'Tobago' 4 W-O
(J.L. Richardson) Mrs H.K. Richardson, 1968
'Falaise' × 'Arbar'
Fl. rounded; perianth and other petaloid segments in several whorls, neatly arranged, pure white, overlapping; the outer whorl very broad, blunt, fairly prominently mucronate, spreading or a little inflexed, plane; the inner whorls successively slightly shorter, only very slightly mucronate, more strongly inflexed, with margins wavy; some petaloid segments at centre very strongly inflexed, with margins tightly incurled; corona segments very short, the majority clustered among the petaloid segments at centre, orange, with reddish orange at rim. Late

'Tobernaveen' 3 W-GWW
(G.L. Wilson) G.L. Wilson, 1960
('Nelly' × 'Chinese White') × 'Chinese White'
Perianth segments very broad, rounded or sometimes squarish at apex, truncate, slightly mucronate, spreading, plane, regular, overlapping half; the inner segments narrower, a little inflexed, with margins sometimes wavy or a little incurled; corona shallow, lightly ribbed, mouth expanded and loosely frilled

'Tobin Bronze' 2 W-O
(Tom Forster, 1960s) Unregistered
Perianth segments very broadly ovate or somewhat oblong, blunt or slightly truncate, slightly mucronate, more or less spreading, smooth, overlapping half; the inner segments more narrowly ovate, a little inflexed; corona very broad and shallow, closely ribbed, opening soft orange, becoming yellow-orange, frilled, with rim dentate. Tall. Late

'Tobruk' 2 (a)
(J.L. Richardson, pre-1941)

'Tobruk' 3 W-GRR
(J.L. Richardson, pre-1944)
'Clava' × 'Coronach'
Corona small disc-shaped, intense red, with green at base

'Toby' 2 Y-R
(M.P. Williams) G. Zandbergen-Terwegen, 1957
AM(Haarlem) 1960

'Toby' 6 W-Y
Syn. of 'Toby the First'

'Toby the First' 6 W-Y
(Rosewarne EHS) M.J. Jefferson-Brown, 1993
N. cyclamineus × 'Trousseau'; sdlg no. 65/83/2
Fl. facing down; perianth segments ovate, reflexed, separated; corona cylindrical, long, opening bright primrose yellow, becoming creamy buff yellow, with mouth expanded and rim notched. Dwarf. Early. Syn. 'Toby', 'Tony'

'Toccata' 2 ?-R (a)
(A.M. Wilson, pre-1944)
Corona red, frilled

'Togo' 4
(Mrs B.A. Woods) Mrs B.A. Woods, 1968

'Tohunga' 2 (a)
(J.H. Braithwaite, pre-1930)

'Toison d'Or' 8 Y-O
(pre-1798)

'Toitoi' 2 (a)
(W.E. Weightman, pre-1936)

'Token' 2 W-O
(C.E. Radcliff, 1942) J.M.Radcliff, 1956
'Atanga' × 'Paula'
Corona almost disc-shaped, scarlet-orange

'Tokiu' 2 (a)
(R. Dick, pre-1938)
'Damson' × 'Killigrew'
Perianth segments broad; corona shallow, expanded

'Tokonui' 2 Y-R
(S.A. Free) Mrs S.I. Free, 1971
Fl. 108 mm wide; perianth segments broadly ovate, smooth; corona with mouth flared

'Tokoroa' 3 W-? (b)
(R. Hyde) R. Hyde, 1957

'Toledo' 2 (a)
(Barr & Sons, pre-1941)

toletanus = *N.* × *susannae* var. *toletanus*

'Tolgus' 2 Y-Y
(P.D. Williams, pre-1927)

'Tolkien' 1 Y-Y
(P.L.A. Pouw & Sons) P.L.A. Pouw & Sons, 1983
'Rembrandt' × 'Golden Sunbeam'

'Tollard Royal' 1 W-? (b)
(J.W. Barr, pre-1931)

'Tollard Royal' 1 Y-Y
(D. & J.W. Blanchard) D. & J.W. Blanchard, 1958

('Magog' × 'Hebron') × 'Kingscourt'

'Tollymore' 2 W-P
(Ballydorn Bulb Farm) Ballydorn Bulb Farm, 1984
'Theano' × 'Tullyroyal'
Fl. 95 mm wide; corona pure deep pink. Dwarf. Early to mid-season

'Tollymore' 1 Y-WWY
(Tom Forster, 1960s) Unregistered
Perianth segments broadly ovate, blunt, greenish yellow, touched with white at base and along midrib to white mucro, spreading, overlapping one-third to a half; the inner segments shouldered at base, a little inflexed, with margins sometimes nicked; corona cylindrical, opening rich greenish yellow, becoming greenish white with a well-defined band of yellow at rim, mouth flared and frilled. Tall. Mid-season

'Tolosa' 2 Y-R
(J.M. de Navarro) J.M. de Navarro, 1956
('Trevisky' × 'Porthilly') × 'Gibraltar'

'Tolvan' 2 W-R
(P.D. Williams, pre-1927)
Perianth segments pure white; corona red

'Tolwin' 1 W-Y
(W. Jackson Sr, 1935)
'Renown' × 'Callirhoe'

'Tom' 1 Y-Y
(de Graaff Bros, pre-1908)
Fl. large, yellow; corona darker in tone than the perianth. AM(Haarlem) 1908

'Tom' 8
(Herut Yahel, pre-1991) Unregistered

'Tomasina' 1 Y-Y
(G.H. Johnstone) G.H. Johnstone, 1959
'Trenithon' × 'Golden Torch'
Fl. 102 mm wide. Mid-season. Resembles a large 'Peeping Tom'

'Tom Hood' 9 W-GYR
(pre-1910)
Perianth segments somewhat oblong, truncate, prominently mucronate, spreading, plane, overlapping one-third to a half; the inner segments narrower, ovate, somewhat spathulate; corona disc-shaped, minutely ribbed, yellow, with a narrow band of red at rim, with rim minutely and densely notched

'Tom Houston' 2 W-? (b or c)
(W.A. Grace, pre-1938)

'Tom Jones' 3 Y-ORR
(T.D. Throckmorton) T.D. Throckmorton, 1974
'Old Satin' × 'Altruist'

'Tomlyn' 1 Y-Y
(W. Jackson Sr, 1944)
'Principal' × 'Matoome'

'Tom Marshall' 2 (a)
(Barr & Sons, pre-1936)

'Tommy' 3 (a or b)
(pre-1914)

'Tommy Atkins' 1 W-W
(?G.P. Haydon, pre-1914)

'Tommy Handley' 3 Y-O
(Beyk & Co., pre-1949)

'Tommy Lawton' 3 W-YYO
(F. Rijnveld & Sons) F. Rijnveld & Sons, 1957 AM(Haarlem) 1957

'Tommy Townshend' 1 W-? (b)
(Barr & Sons, pre-1923)

'Tomphubil' 2 W-WWP
(J.M. de Navarro, 1973) Rathowen Daffodils, 1985
('Waterville' × 'Romance') × 'Highland Wedding'; sdlg no. 392
Perianth segments broadly ovate, pure white, spreading, overlapping half; the inner segments more narrowly ovate, a little inflexed, with margins slightly wavy; corona short funnel-shaped, lightly ribbed, pure white, with a well-defined band of pure bright shell pink at rim, mouth straight and 6-lobed, frilled, with rim crenate and margins minutely dentate. Mid-season. Resembles 'Rainbow' but with a whiter perianth and a clearer-pink corona rim

'Tompion' 1 Y-Y
(W. Jackson Sr, 1944) W. Jackson Jr, 1956
'Semo' × 'Djaro'

'Tom Thumb' 3 W-? (b)
(A.M. Wilson, pre-1944)

'Tom Tit' 3 Y-O
(G.H. Engleheart, pre-1907)
Perianth segments lemon yellow; corona scarlet-orange. See also 'Tomtit'

'Tomtit' 3 Y-O
Syn. of 'Tom Tit'

'Tom Ward' 2 W-O
(L.P.Dettman, 1975) Unregistered
'Rockall' × 'Rameses'; sdlg no. R/R 2/76

'Tonga' 2 Y-OOR
(T.H. Piper, 1952)
'Royal Mail' × 'Sun Chariot'

'Tonga' 4 Y-R
(J.L. Richardson) J.L. Richardson, 1958
Falaise' × 'Ceylon'
Fl. rounded, 79 mm wide; perianth and other petaloid segments very broad, rounded at apex, light greenish to brilliant yellow 8B-A, deeply overlapping; the outer whorl prominently mucronate, spreading or slightly inflexed, with margins incurling at apex; the inner whorls very little shorter, successively more strongly inflexed, with margins deeply incurled; corona segments very short, clustered among the petaloid segments at centre, orange-red (32A). AM(e) 1961

'Tongahoe' 3 W-YOO
(M.E. Brogden) M.E. Brogden, 1956
Perianth segments very broad, rounded at apex; corona very shallow bowl-shaped, large, reddish orange, paling to orange-yellow at base, frilled

'Tongala' 1 Y-Y
(J.N. Hancock & Co., pre-1949)
Fl. yellow; corona deeper in tone than the perianth, with rim slightly rolled

'Tongariro' 2 Y-YYO
(Sir A.P.W. Thomas, pre-1930)
Perianth segments pale yellow; corona with scarlet-orange at rim. ?The same as 'Tongarri'

'Tongariro' 1 W-W
Syn. of 'Santakeda'

'Tongarri' 2 Y-YYO
?The same as 'Tongariro'

'Tongues of Flame' 11a W-GYO
(J.Gerritsen & Son) Mrs E.Bullivant, 1995
Sdlg no. GBS 12
Fl. 100 mm wide; perianth segments very broadly ovate, blunt, mucronate, spreading, somewhat creased, overlapping half; the inner segments a little inflexed, with margins wavy or incurled; corona deeply split, the six segments one-third the length of the perianth segments and opposite and closely overlying them, squarish at apex, primrose yellow, with apple green at base, shading to strong orange at rim, tightly frilled, with rim dentate. Mid-season. Sunproof

'Tonic' 9 W-GYR
(Murray W. Evans, 1970) Murray W. Evans, 1985
('Frigid' × 'Jade') × 'Dallas'; sdlg no. N-20/1
Perianth segments broad, deeply overlapping. Very late

'Tonkin' 2 (a)
(Oregon Bulb Farms, pre-1951)

'Tonto' 3 W-R
(Oregon Bulb Farms, pre-1950)

'Tony' 7
(J.W. Barr, pre-1930)

'Tony' 6 W-Y
Syn. of 'Toby the First'

'Tony' 2 W-WWP
(pre-1956) Unregistered
Corona whitish, with salmon pink at rim

'Tony de Ridder' 3 W-? (b)
(G. Lubbe & Son, pre-1943)

'Tony John' 1 Y-Y
(R.H.Glover, pre-1993) Unregistered

'Tony Shergold' 1 Y-Y
(J.L. Martin) J.L. Martin, 1973
Sdlg × 'Kingscourt'
Fl. 100 mm wide

'Tooboorac' 1 Y-Y
(T. Morrison) T. Morrison, 1960

'Toofin' 9
(A.M. Wilson, pre-1938)

'Too Late' 3 W-YYR
(W.G.Pannill, 1972) W.G.Pannill, 1996
'Kingfisher' × 'Gay Challenger'; sdlg no. 66/16
Very late

'Toongabbie' 2 Y-O
(H.A. Brown, 1937) J.N. Hancock & Co., 1955
? × 'Fortune'; sdlg no. 71/37/33
Perianth segments yellow; corona pale orange, with an indistinct broad band of a deeper tone at rim and another narrower band about one-third the length of the corona below the rim

'Toora' 2 (a)
(H.A. Brown, pre-1936)

'Toorak' 2 W-Y
(C.E. Radcliff, 1933)
'Pedestal' × 'White Empress'

'Toorak Gold' 2 Y-Y
(J.N. Hancock & Co., 1945) J.N. Hancock & Co., 1964
'Malvern Gold' hybrid
Perianth segments broadly ovate, bright yellow, with white mucro, spreading, of heavy substance, overlapping one-third; corona short, smooth, deep golden yellow, mouth broadly but not deeply lobed, with rim rolled. Tall. Early. 2n=28. Resembles an improved 'Malvern Gold'

'Toorak Pride' 2 Y-Y
(J.N.Hancock & Co.) Unregistered
'Toorak Gold' hybrid
Fl. rounded, intense golden yellow; corona funnel-shaped, with rim neatly rolled and broadly crenate. Tall. Very early

'Toorop' 1 (a)
(G. Lubbe & Son, pre-1927)

'Tooter' 1 W-Y
(W.M. Spry, pre-1975) Unregistered
'Full Moon' × 'Hereami'
Corona frilled. Mid-season

'Tooth Fairy' 3 W-YYO
(R.G.Cull) Hokorawa Daffodils, 1994
'Calleen' × 'Sunmaid'; sdlg no. HC/D111
Corona light greenish yellow 3C, with strong orange 24A at rim. Mid-season

'Toots' 2 O-R
(C.R. Phillips) C.R. Phillips, 1968
'Royal Ransom' × 'Erie'; sdlg no. 76/68B B53
Perianth segments orange; corona red. Early. Resembles 'Jezebel' but with the perianth segments nearer to red and less strongly reflexed

'Tootsie' 2 W-P
(J.N.Hancock & Co., 1976) Unregistered
Sdlg 78/65H × 'My Word'; sdlg no. 47/76H
Corona funnel-shaped, true pink. Early to mid-season

'Topaz' 2 W-O
(G.H. Engleheart, pre-1907)
Corona reddish orange

'Topaz' 2 or 3 W-? (b or c)
(M. van Waveren & Sons, pre-1942)

'Topaz' 7 W-Y
(M. van Waveren & Sons) P. de Jager & Sons, 1956

'Topaz Treasure' 9 W-GYO
(Mrs M.S. Yerger) Mrs M.S. Yerger, 1991
'Felindre' × 'Bon Bon'; sdlg no. 78 D 7
Fl. forming a double triangle, 60 mm wide; perianth segments slightly reflexed, deeply overlapping; the inner segments narrower; corona disc-shaped, vivid yellow 15B, with strong yellow-green 143C at base, shading to orange (28A) at rim. Late

'Topeka' 1 W-W
(R.A. van der Schoot, pre-1930)

'Topeka' 1 W-W
(S.C. Gaspar) R.J. Abernethy, 1960
Fl. 121 mm wide. Mid-season. Resembles a smaller-flowered and more refined 'Kanchenjunga'

'Topex'
(pre-1958) Unregistered

'Topflight' 1 Y-Y
(T.H. Piper, c.1966) Unregistered
'Goldbridge' × 'Melissa'

'Top Flight' 2 Y-O
(J.N.Hancock & Co., 1982) Unregistered
'Scorcher' × Ted Armstrong 2Y-R; sdlg no. 26/82H
Perianth segments golden yellow, deeply overlapping; corona cup-shaped, brilliant orange, with mouth expanded. Tall. Early

'Top Gallant' 3 W-Y
(Ballydorn Bulb Farm, 1971) Ballydorn Bulb Farm, 1986
'Fairmaid' × Div. 3 W-GWY sdlg
Corona rich yellow. Tall. Late

'Top Hit' 11a Y-Y
(J. Gerritsen & Son) J. Gerritsen & Son, 1974
'Grand Seigneur' × 'Baccarat'
Corona segments yellow, sometimes with orange at rim, with the rim closely and deeply notched, as if fringed

'Topic' 2 W-P
(The Brodie of Brodie, pre-1947)
'Mitylene' × 'Fortune's Queen'

'Topkapi' 2 W-OOY
(Ballydorn Bulb Farm) Ballydorn Bulb Farm, 1975
'Blarney' open pollinated
Fl. 45 mm wide; corona orange, with golden yellow at rim. Mid-season

'Toplan' 2 Y-? (a)
(West & Fell, pre-1938)
Perianth segments lemon yellow; corona spreading

'Toplight' 1 W-? (b)
(R.A. van der Schoot, pre-1930)
AM(Haarlem) 1930

'Topmark' 1 W-W
(G.W.E. Brogden) G.W.E. Brogden, 1969

'Topmost' 1 Y-Y
(R.C.A. Tombleson) R.C.A. Tombleson, 1966
Fl. 108 mm wide. Late. Resembles a smaller-flowered 'Spanish Gold' with broader perianth segments

'Top Notch' 2 Y-Y
(G.E. Mitsch) G.E. Mitsch, 1970
'Playboy' × 'Daydream'; sdlg no. B37/7
Perianth segments soft lemon yellow, with white at base, spreading, smooth, deeply overlapping; corona opening lemon yellow, becoming buff and amber. Mid-season

'Top-notcher' 1 Y-Y
(G.H. Johnstone, pre-1960) Unregistered

'Top of the Hill' 3 W-GWY
(Ballydorn Bulb Farm) Ballydorn Bulb Farm, 1981
'Crebilly' × 'Ballymartin'
Fl. 82 mm wide. Mid-season. Resembles an improved 'Crepello'

'Topolino' 1 W-Y
(J. Gerritsen & Son) J. Gerritsen & Son, 1965
Fl. 65 mm wide; perianth segments ovate, blunt, only slightly mucronate, opening creamy yellow, becoming almost white, spreading, somewhat twisted or with margins wavy, overlapping at base only; corona cylindrical, smooth, vivid yellow 9B, paling at base to the colour of the perianth, mouth flared, with six deep lobes recurved at margins or slightly overlapping, frilled, rim dentate. Dwarf. Early. 2n=14. Resembles a taller and earlier-flowered 'Little Beauty' or a larger *N. nanus*

'Topper' 2 (a)
(A.H. Ahrens) J.S. Leitch, 1955

'Toppop' 2 Y-YYO
(W.F. Leenen) W.F. Leenen, 1980
'Mancia' × 'Ipi Tombi'
Fl. 105 mm wide; perianth segments light greenish yellow 7D; corona brighter in tone (3A), with a broad band of yellow-orange at rim. Early

'Toprank' 1 Y-Y
(S.A. Free) S.A. Free, 1963
Fl. 115 mm wide, deep yellow. Mid-season

'Topsail' 2 W-? (b)
(G.H. Engleheart, pre-1907)

'Topscore' 2 (a)
(P.D. Williams, pre-1949)

'Top Secret' 2 W-O
(W.H. Roesé) W.H. Roesé, 1973
'Rameses' × 'Limerick'
Fl. 100 mm wide

'Top Shelf' 2 Y-Y
(J.N. Hancock & Co., c.1978) Unregistered

'Topspot' 1 W-W
(G.W.E. Brogden, 1981) Brogden Bulbs, 1991
'Guiding Light' × ('Empress of Ireland' × 'Canisp'); sdlg no. x91/5
Fl. forming a double triangle, 95 mm wide; clean white; perianth segments very broadly ovate, plane, very smooth; corona cylindrical, narrow, with mouth flared and even, rim dentate. Mid-season

'Topsy' 3 W-YYO
(W. Backhouse, pre-1869)
Corona with orange at rim. Syn. Burbidgei 'Topsy'. Was "absorbed" into 'Model'

'Topsy' 3 W-? (b)
(C. Dawson, pre-1907)
'Lulworth' × 'Horace'

'Topsy' 2 W-R
(J.S. Leitch) J.S. Leitch, 1960
Fl. 89 mm wide

'Topsy Jane' 3 W-WWO
(Frank Verge) Frank Verge, 1972
'Irish Minstrel' × 'Deodora'
Fl. 114 mm wide

'Tor' 1 Y-Y
(G.L. Wilson, pre-1934)
'Michael' × 'Mrs Ernst H.Krelage'
Fl. rich yellow, of strong substance. Tall. Late

'Tora' 3 W-? (b)
(G.H. Engleheart, pre-1910)

'Tora' 2 W-R
(W. Jackson Jr, 1959) Unregistered
'Capella' × sdlg 62/54; sdlg no. 19/59

'Torana' 2 W-W
(G.C. Yeates) G.C. Yeates, 1968
PC(e)(NZ) 1972

'Torch' 2 Y-YOO
(G.H. Engleheart, pre-1897)
'Maximus' × *N. radiiflorus* var. *poetarum*
Fl. star-shaped; perianth segments narrowly ovate, blunt, slightly mucronate, spreading or a little inflexed, heavily twisted, separated; corona long cup-shaped, yellow, with a broad suffusion of reddish orange from the rim, with mouth straight, closely frilled. AM 1902

'Torch Bearer' 2 Y-Y
(Ballydorn Bulb Farm) Ballydorn Bulb Farm, 1975
'Golden Torch' hybrid
Fl. 120 mm wide. Mid-season

'Torchdance' 2 Y-Y
(M.P. Williams, pre-1954)

'Torchfire' 2 Y-R
(W.H. Roesé) W.H. Roesé, 1982
'Burning Torch' × 'Heathfire'; sdlg no. 72/15/1
Fl. 103 mm wide. Early to mid-season

'Torchlight' 3 Y-O
(G.H. Engleheart, pre-1902)
Perianth segments pale primrose yellow, overlapping; corona expanded, golden orange, tinged scarlet-orange. AM 1902

'Torchlight' 2 Y-R
(O. Ronalds, pre-1951)

'Torcross' 3 W-OOY
(Brian S. Duncan) Rathowen Daffodils, 1986
'Irish Rover' × ('Mahmoud' × ['Bravura' × 'Glenwherry']); sdlg no. 596
Fl. 110 mm wide; perianth segments very broad in outline, rounded at apex and a little truncate, slightly mucronate, pure white, spreading, glistening, overlapping half; the inner segments ovate, angular at shoulder, a little inflexed, with margins minutely incurled; corona bowl-shaped, narrow, closely ribbed, rich orange, with a band of rich yellow at rim, mouth with six deeply overlapping lobes, lightly frilled. Tall. Mid-season. Resembles 'Leonora' but with a wider perianth of purer white

'Toreador' 3 W-OOR
(G.H. Engleheart, pre-1909)
Perianth segments fairly smooth; corona almost disc-shaped, with a broad band of intense scarlet at rim

'Toreador' 1 Y-? (a)
(D.V. West, pre-1936)
Perianth segments sulphur yellow; corona yellow, with a distinct band of another tone or colour at rim

'Toreador' 2 Y-O
(pre-1950)
Perianth segments deep yellow; corona intense reddish orange, frilled

'Toreador' 3 W-R
(J.L. Richardson) J.L. Richardson, 1961
'Kilworth' × 'Arbar'
Fl. 88 mm wide; perianth segments white, shading to near vivid yellow 13A at extreme base, with margins slightly incurving, overlapping; corona ribbed, orange-red (near 30C), with near strong orange 25B at base, mouth straight and slightly frilled, rim slightly dentate. Mid-season. 2n=28

'Torello' 1 Y-Y
(J.S. Leitch) J.S. Leitch, 1967

'Torero' 3 W-? (b)
(C.G. van Tubergen, pre-1929)

'Torero' 2 Y-O
(G.L. Wilson) F.A.L. Harrison, 1959
Corona widely expanded, opening deep reddish orange, becoming darker in tone. Tall. Wind resistant

'Torfrida' 3 W-YYO
(W. Welchman, pre-1926)

Corona with reddish orange at rim. Tall

'Torianne' 2 W-W
(R.A.Scamp) S.Holden, 1997
'Ben Hee' × 'Brierglass'; sdlg no. 439
Fl. 98 mm wide, pure white; perianth segments broadly ovate, slightly concave; corona funnel-shaped, neatly frilled. Mid-season to late

'Torina' 2 W-? (b)
(Mrs R.O. Backhouse, pre-1921)

'Torina' 2 Y-YOO
(S.C. Gaspar, pre-1961) Unregistered
Perianth segments broadly ovate, soft golden yellow; corona deep reddish orange, paling to yellow at base, frilled

'Torlonia' 2 W-? (b)
(D.J. Cooper) D.J. Cooper, 1957

'Tornado' 4
(J. Bankhead, pre-1950)

'Tornamona' 2 W-W
(G.L. Wilson, pre-1945)
'White Sentinel' × ('Askelon' × 'Samite')
Fl. 115 mm wide, snow white; perianth segments broadly ovate, blunt, slightly mucronate, spreading, plane, overlapping one-third; the inner segments more narrowly ovate, a little inflexed; corona deep cup-shaped, with rim slightly flanged and regularly crenate. AM(Haarlem) 1950, AM(e) 1954

'Toronto' 2 W-? (b)
(M. van Waveren & Sons, pre-1949)

'Torpedo' 1 (a)
(Sir C.H. Cave, pre-1908)

'Torquay' 2 Y-O
(G.H. Johnstone, pre-1953)

'Torque' 2 Y-O
(J.N. Hancock & Co., c.1977) Unregistered

'Torr Head' 9 W-GYR
(Ballydorn Bulb Farm, 1974) Ballydorn Bulb Farm, 1987
'Cantabile' hybrid open pollinated
Corona disc-shaped, lightly frilled. Late

'Torrid' 2 Y-O
(Mrs R.O. Backhouse, pre-1921)
Perianth segments soft yellow; corona widely expanded, deep reddish orange

'Torrid' 2 W-O
(J.N. Hancock & Co., pre-1949)
Corona bright orange. Late

'Torridge' 1 (a)
(T. Buncombe, pre-1931)

'Torridon' 2 Y-O
(J.S.B. Lea) J.S.B. Lea, 1964
Sdlg 2-17-54 ('Spry' × Navarro sdlg) × 'Vulcan'; sdlg no. 1-41-63
Fl. 90-95 mm wide; perianth segments broadly ovate, rounded at apex, only very slightly mucronate, brilliant yellow 7A, slightly inflexed, smooth, somewhat concave, overlapping half; the inner segments a little narrower, more nearly plane; corona deep cup-shaped, somewhat straight-sided, smooth or slightly ribbed, vivid orange 28B, with mouth straight and a little frilled. Mid-season. AM(e) 1977

'Torrish' 3 W-Y
(J.S.B. Lea) J.S.B. Lea, 1964
'Suilven' × 'Hamzali'; sdlg no. 1-48-57
Corona citron yellow. Late. Resembles 'Suilven' in form

'Torso' 2 W-? (b)
(F.H. Chapman, pre-1913)
'Almira' × 'Will Scarlett'

N. tortifolius Fernández Casas 13 Section Tazettae

'Tortrix' 1 W-W
(T. Batson, pre-1914)

N. tortuosus Haworth 13 Section Pseudonarcissus
(Pseudonarcissus Moschatus 'Tortuosus', ?'Silver Bells', "The Great Tortuose White Spanish Daffodil")

'Tortuosus Tenuifolius' 1 W-W
Syn. of 'Hartland's Leda'

'Torver' 2 Y-W
(Reg Nicholl) Reg Nicholl, 1991
'Daydream' × 'Chiloquin'; sdlg no. 14/86
Fl. forming a double triangle, 102 mm wide; perianth segments ovate, brilliant greenish yellow 3A; corona slightly flared, with mouth frilled. Mid-season

'Tosca' 8
(pre-1939)

'Tosca' 1 W-Y
(A. Gray) Broadleigh Gardens, 1969
N. asturiensis × 'Little Beauty'
Fl. 54 mm wide; perianth segments cream white, overlaid with light greenish yellow 8B at base, plane or slightly twisted, overlapping at base only; corona slightly ribbed, light greenish yellow 8B, flushed with a darker tone at rim, mouth expanded, with rim dentate. Mid-season. Resembles a deeper-coloured 'Little Beauty'

'Tosca' 2 W-?
Syn. of 'Tampa'

'Toscanini' 2 W-WWP
(L. van Leeuwen & Son, pre-1953)
Perianth segments pure white; corona ivory white, with a broad band of apricot pink at rim

N. toscanus Parlatore = *N. obvallaris*

'Totara' 1 Y-Y
(D. Bramley) D. Bramley, 1980
'Mellow Dawn' × 'Palmino'; sdlg no. 69/22
Fl. 100 mm wide. Mid-season. Resembles a larger and more deeply coloured 'Mellow Dawn'

'Totem' 1 W-W
(J.S. Leitch) J.S. Leitch, 1967
Fl. 102 mm wide

'Toto' 12 W-W
(W.G. Pannill) W.G. Pannill, 1983
'Jenny' × *N. jonquilla*
Fls star-shaped, 1-3 per stem, 55 mm wide; perianth segments narrowly ovate, a little reflexed, overlapping at base only; corona cylindrical or somewhat funnel-shaped, with mouth straight, rim flanged and dentate. Dwarf. AGM 1997

'Tottenham Yellow' 1 Y-Y
(T.S. Ware, pre-1869)
Corona mid-yellow, darker in tone than the perianth.
Syn. Pseudonarcissus Major 'Tottenham Yellow'

'Totten Tot' 6 Y-Y
(James S. Wells) James S. Wells, 1990
'Tiny Tot' × *N. cyclamineus*; sdlg no. 85-21
Fl. 15 mm wide, bright clear yellow, facing down; perianth segments ovate, with white mucro, strongly reflexed, plane or with margins a little incurved, overlapping; corona cylindrical, lightly ribbed, with mouth expanded, rim deeply notched and crenate. Dwarf. Early

'Totus Albus Prior'
Syn. of *N. papyraceus*

'Toucan' 2 Y-R
(G.E. Mitsch) G.E. Mitsch, 1975
('Armada' × 'Paricutin') × 'Falstaff'; sdlg no. H74/5
Fl. 110 mm wide; perianth segments golden yellow, somewhat reflexed; corona flared, orange-red. Early to mid-season

'Touché' 1 W-Y
(W.F. Leenen) W.F. Leenen, 1983

'Touch of Silver' 2 W-GWW
(W.A. Noton) Unregistered

'Touchstone' 3 W-OOR
(E.M. Crosfield, pre-1913)
Fl. 102 mm wide; perianth segments rounded at apex, ivory white, overlapping; corona small, shallow, pale orange, shading to orange-red at rim. Tall

'Toujours' 1 Y-Y
(F.E. Board) F.E. Board, 1965
'Kingscourt' × 'Spellbinder'
Fl. 109 mm wide; perianth segments very broadly ovate, lemon yellow, with white mucro, spreading, with margins sometimes recurved, regular, overlapping half; the inner segments with margins more often and more strongly recurved; corona funnel-shaped, smooth, golden yellow, mouth lightly ribbed, straight, wavy, with rim irregularly and shallowly notched and crenate. Late

'Toulo' 2 (a)
(West & Fell, pre-1938)

'Touloch' 1 W-? (b)
(R. Hyde) R. Hyde, 1955

'Tourist' 2 Y-R
(G.W.E. Brogden, c.1973) Unregistered

'Tourmente' 11?a Y-Y
(J. Gerritsen & Son) J. Gerritsen & Son, 1981
'Flyer' × 'Colblanc'
Fl. 90 mm wide; perianth segments primrose yellow; corona segments buttercup yellow, with greenish yellow at base. Early to mid-season

'Tournament' 4 W-R
(Murray W. Evans) Murray W. Evans, 1970
'Falaise' × 'Lady Kesteven' hybrid

'Toute Jolie' 2 W-? (b)
(J.W.A. Lefeber, pre-1952)

'Towai' 12 Y-Y
(Robin Brown) Robin Brown, 1995
N. jonquilla var. *henriquesii* × *N. cylamineus*; sdlg no. JH/C 1
Fls 2 per stem, 44 mm wide, mid-yellow, hanging almost vertically; perianth segments reflexed; corona cylindrical, smooth, with mouth straight and lobed. Dwarf. Very early

'Towhee' 2 W-Y
(Mrs G. Link) Mrs G. Link, 1958
'Mrs Ernst H.Krelage' × 'Fortune'
Corona chrome yellow

'Town Crier' 2 W-Y
(G.H. Johnstone, pre-1949)
'Carlton' × 'Godolphin'

'Townshend Boscawen' 1 Y-Y
(W. Backhouse, pre-1869)
Fl. large. Syn. Pseudonarcissus Major 'Townshend Boscawen'. "Absorbed" 'Marie Louise'

'Town Talk' 2 W-YOY
(D.S. Bell, 1965) D.S. Bell, 1978
('Papanui Queen' × 'Sir Heaton Rhodes') × 'Arbar'
Fl. 110 mm wide; corona orange, with yellow at base and light yellow at rim. Mid-season. Resembles 'Arbar' but with a differently coloured corona

'Toya' 2 W-O
(W. Jackson Jr, 1970) Unregistered
'Red April' × 'Arbar'; sdlg no. 144/70

'Toyota' 3 W-WWO
(J.N. Hancock & Co., 1955) Unregistered
Perianth segments broadly ovate, blunt, slightly mucronate, sparkling white, spreading, overlapping half; the inner segments rounded at apex, somewhat spathulate at base, a little inflexed, with margins wavy or incurled, sometimes recurved in lower half; corona bowl-shaped, small, ribbed, white, with apricot orange at rim, mouth split and overlapping. Tall. Late. Scented

'Traboe' 3 W-YYO
(P.D. Williams, pre-1926)
Corona deep yellow, with orange at rim. AM(e) 1926

'Tracery' 3 W-? (b)
(W. Welchman, pre-1913)

'Tracery' 3 Y-YYO
(T.D. Throckmorton) T.D. Throckmorton, 1974
'Old Satin' × 'Arbar'

'Tracey' 6 W-W
(Miss M. Verry) Miss M. Verry, 1968
Fl. facing down at first, at right angles to the stem at maturity; perianth segments ovate, strongly reflexed, overlapping one-third to a half; the inner segments somewhat twisted or with margins wavy; corona cylindrical, opening lemon yellow, becoming milk white, with mouth widely expanded and even, rim notched and crenate and slightly rolled

'Trader Horn' 2 (a)
(C.W. Johnston) E.A.K. Lee, 1955

"Tradescant's Great Rose Double Daffodil"
Syn. of 'Plenissimus'

'Tradewind' 1 W-W
(D.S. Bell) D.S. Bell, 1955
'Metropolis' × 'Empress of Ireland'
Fl. pure white; perianth segments broad; corona frilled

'Tradition' 1 W-Y
(M.J. Jefferson-Brown) M.J. Jefferson-Brown, 1965
Fl. 108 mm wide; perianth segments mucronate, white, flushed brilliant yellow-green 154B, inflexed, twisted, overlapping; the inner segments slightly narrower; corona brilliant greenish yellow 6B, with rim flanged and crenate. Mid-season. AM(e) 1965

'Trafalgar' 2 Y-YYO
(Sir A.P.W. Thomas, pre-1914)
Fl. large; corona widely expanded, with a broad band of reddish orange at rim

'Trafalgar' 1 W-W
(W.A. Milner, pre-1916)

'Traffic Light' 2 W-O
(C.O. Fairbairn, pre-1962) Unregistered
Corona widely expanded, amber orange. Tall

'Trailblazer' 2 Y-W
(V. Brink) V. Brink, 1969
'Frilled Beauty' × 'Content'

'Trailblazer' 3 W-GYO
(K. McCombe, c.1985) Unregistered
('Forfar' × 'Rouge') × 'Seafire'
Fl. rounded; perianth segments very broad in outline, blunt or squarish at apex, fairly prominently mucronate, pure white, spreading or a little inflexed, concave, gllistening, overlapping half; the inner segments more nearly ovate, shouldered at base, more strongly inflexed, with margins sometimes wavy; corona bowl-shaped, narrow, pale lemon yellow, with green at base and a band of bright tangerine orange at rim. Late

'Tra La' ?-P
(Alister Clark, pre-1948)

'Tramore' 2 W-Y
(J.L. Richardson, pre-1940)
'Bodilly' × 'Crocus'
Perianth segments broadly ovate; corona lemon yellow, with mouth widely expanded, rim dentate. PC(e) 1940, AM(Haarlem) 1948

'Tranquil' 5 W-W
(W.A. Grace, pre-1927)

'Tranquil' 1 W-W
(W. Jackson Jr, 1954) W. Jackson Jr, 1968
'Bonnington' × 'Taran'
Perianth segments almost triangular in appearance, spreading, smooth; the inner segments more rounded; corona narrow, with mouth flared

'Tranquil Dawn' 2 W-WPP
(J.A. Hunter) J.A. Hunter, 1992
'Precedent' × 'Verran'; sdlg no. 38/82C

Fl. 120 mm wide; corona pink, touched white at base, with rim flanged and dentate. Mid-season

'Tranquility' 3 W-O
(W. Welchman, pre-1908)
Perianth segments broadly ovate, blunt, prominently mucronate, creamy white, overlapping one-third; the inner segments narrower, sometimes truncate, with margins slightly wavy; corona widely expanded and deeply split, the six lobes alternate to the perianth segments, ribbed, overlapping, soft orange, with a distinct band of a paler tone at rim, lightly frilled. Resembles 'Emperor of India' but with the corona of a softer tone

'Tranquility' 2 W-Y
(G. Lewis, 1945) D.S. Bell, 1958

'Tranquility' 3 W-YOO
(pre-1956) Unregistered
Corona orange, with yellow at base

'Tranquil Morn' 3 W-W
(G.E. Mitsch) G.E. Mitsch, 1962
'Green Island' × 'Chinese White'; sdlg no. R33/9
Fl. 120 mm wide; perianth segments pure white, somewhat reflexed, overlapping; corona small, almost disc-shaped, touched lemon yellow on opening, becoming self white, with pearl grey at base. Mid-season. 2n=28. Resembles a larger and better-poised 'Chinese White'

'Transcend' 2 W-WWO
(J.A.Hunter) J.A.Hunter, 1997
'Corofin' × 'Pure Joy'; sdlg no. 58/83A
Fl. 111 mm wide; perianth segments ovate, very smooth; corona bowl-shaped, with a broad band of orange at rim, mouth wavy. Mid-season

'Transkei King' 2 Y-WWY
(H. Koopowitz) H. Koopowitz, 1979
'Binkie' × 'Ambergate'; sdlg no. B4 72/3
Fl. 98 mm wide; perianth segments deep lemon yellow; corona white, with yellow at rim. Mid-season. Resembles 'Dotteral' but with a frilled and shallower corona

'Transmitter' 4 Y-R
(Mrs H.K. Richardson) du Plessis Bros, 1978
'Falaise' × 'Heath Fire'; sdlg no. 99
Fl. 95 mm wide; perianth and other petaloid segments yellow; the outer whorl broadly ovate, blunt or truncate, with white mucro, spreading, smooth; the second whorl almost as long and broad, inflexed, creased; the centre whorls successively shorter and narrower, with margins folded inwards; corona segments shorter than the second and centre whorls of petaloid segments and lying between them, red, with streaks of yellow at the margins at base, frilled. Mid-season

'Transparente' 8 W-O
(pre-1798)

'Trappist' 1 W-W
(The Brodie of Brodie, c.1912)
'Mrs H.D.Betteridge' × 'King Alfred'
Perianth segments pure white; corona opening pale lemon, becoming white, rim evenly rolled

'Trasna' 3 W-GOR
(Ballydorn Bulb Farm) Ballydorn Bulb Farm, 1970
'Fermoy' hybrid

'Tratus Cantus' 4 Y-Y
Syn. of 'Plenissimus'

'Traumerei'
(pre-1960) Unregistered

'Travatore' 2 W-O
(Konynenburg & Mark) Konynenburg & Mark, 1960
'Bertha Aten' × 'Dandy Boy'

'Traveller' 2 Y-YYO
(G.W.E. Brogden, c.1969) Unregistered

'Travers Morrison' 1 Y-Y
(Alister Clark) T. Morrison, 1960
Perianth segments smooth; corona with rim flanged

'Travertine' 11a W-GWW
(J. Gerritsen & Son) J. Gerritsen & Son, 1975
'Cassata' × 'Echo'
Fl. 105 mm wide; corona marble white, with green at base. Early to mid-season. Resembles 'Cassata' but with the flower white on opening

'Traviata' 2 W-? (b)
(G.H. Johnstone, pre-1941)

'Trawalla' 1 Y-Y
(H.A. Brown, pre-1933)
Fl. large, rich golden yellow. Mid-season

'Treasure' 2 Y-Y
(C.G. van Tubergen, pre-1920)
'King Alfred' hybrid
Fl. 92 mm wide, facing slightly downwards; perianth segments rich lemon yellow, overlapping half; corona bright pale buttercup yellow, mouth somewhat expanded, frilled, with rim flanged. Mid-season. AM(Haarlem) 1920, AM(e) 1925, *C(g) 1936. Div. 1 until 1938

'Treasure' 1 Y-Y
(G. Lewis, pre-1946)
'Gold Tray' × 'Cromarty'
Fl. dark bronze yellow, of smooth texture. Mid-season

'Treasure' 1 Y-Y
Syn. of 'Babylon's Treasure'

'Treasure Chest' 1 Y-Y
(D.S. Bell) D.S. Bell, 1957
Fl. golden yellow

'Treasure Gold' 2 Y-Y
(D.S. Bell) D.S. Bell, 1958
('Chief Ruler' × 'Goldcourt') × 'Golden Beauty'
Fl. 115 mm wide. Mid-season. Resembles 'Galway'

'Treasure Island' 2 W-? (b)
(J.L. Richardson, pre-1939)
'Hera' × 'Sunstar'

'Treasure Ring' 1 Y-Y
(D.S. Bell) D.S. Bell, 1957
Fl. dark golden yellow; corona frilled, with rim rolled

'Treasure Roll' 1 Y-Y
(D.S. Bell) D.S. Bell, 1958
Fl. 115 mm wide. Mid-season. Resembles a more richly coloured 'Kingscourt' with the corona rim more heavily rolled

'Treasure Trove' 1 W-W
(G.P. Haydon, pre-1913)
Syn. 'Castaway'

'Treasure Trove' 1 Y-Y
(G. Lewis, pre-1962) Unregistered

'Treasure Valley' 2 Y-YYP
(R. & E. Havens) R. & E. Havens, 1992
'Spun Honey' × sdlg LL20/2 ([('Mabel Taylor' × 'Green Island') × 'Caro Nome'] × 'Space Ship'); sdlg no. TEH80/2
Fl. 90 mm wide, deep lemon yellow; perianth segments very broad, rounded, smooth; the inner segments less broad; corona with a broad band of coral pink at rim, slightly frilled. Late. Sunproof

'Treasure Waltz' 2 Y-Y
(G.E. Mitsch and R. & E.Havens, 1972) G.E. Mitsch and R. & E.Havens, 1988
'Leprechaun' × *N. cyclamineus*; sdlg no. H131/1
Perianth segments spreading; corona straight-sided, deep yellow, with orange undertones, slightly frilled. Very early

'Treath' 9
(P.D. Williams, pre-1930)

'Treavon' 2 W-? (b)
(P.D. Williams, 1928)

'Trebah' 2 Y-Y
(R.A. Scamp) R.A. Scamp, 1993
'Saint Keverne' × 'Golden Aura'; sdlg. no. 129

Fl. 96 mm wide, dark golden yellow; perianth segments broadly ovate, rounded at apex, very slightly mucronate, spreading, plane, overlapping half; the inner segments a little narrower, shouldered at base, slightly inflexed; corona cylindrical, loosely ribbed, with mouth straight and frilled, rim neatly dentate. Mid-season

'Trebella' 5 W-Y
(M.G.Temple-Smith, 1987) M.G.Temple-Smith, 1997
'Beryl' × *N. triandrus*; sdlg no. 38/87
Fls 3 per stem, facing down; perianth segments opening yellow, becoming white, reflexed; corona cup-shaped, brilliant greenish yellow 3A. Mid-season to late

'Trebelsue' 2 (a)
(P.D. Williams, pre-1930)

'Trebilcock' 2 (a)
(P.D. Williams, pre-1930)

'Treble Chance' 10 Y-Y
(Moroccan origin) Potterton and Martin, 1993
Selection from J.C.Archibald's wild-collected *N. romieuxii*; sdlg no. JCA805 xxx
Fl. 35 mm wide, pale greenish yellow 1D; perianth segments very narrowly triangular in appearance, spreading or a little inflexed, widely separated; corona wide-spreading, lightly ribbed, with mouth straight, rim irregularly and obscurely crenate. Dwarf. Very early. Resembles 'Yellow Pet'

'Treble Two' 7 Y-GYY
(R.A.Scamp) R.A.Scamp, 1995
'Aircastle' × *N. jonquilla*; sdlg no. 222
Fls up to three per stem, rounded, 75 mm wide, golden yellow; perianth segments very deeply overlapping; corona cup-shaped, small, with rounded sides, with green at base, rim neatly crenate. Mid-season to late. With many secondary stems

'Treburley' 2 W-YYP
(Brian S. Duncan) du Plessis Bros, 1989
'May Queen' × 'Polonaise'; sdlg no. 573
Fl. 110 mm wide; perianth segments milk white; corona with pink at rim, mouth expanded and frilled. Late

'Trecarne' 2 W-? (b)
(R.H. Bath, pre-1933)

'Trecarrel' 2 W-O
(G.L. Wilson, 1951) L. Major, 1965
Mid-season. Resembles 'Arbar'

'Tredethy' 2 (a)
(P.D. Williams, pre-1930)

'Tredinnick' 2 W-P
du Plessis Bros, 1987
Sdlg no. S37/58
Corona cup-shaped. Late

'Tredore' 3 Y-O
(P.D. Williams, pre-1927)
Perianth segments rounded, soft sulphur yellow, overlapping; corona shallow, intense reddish orange. 2n=28. AM(Haarlem) 1930

'Treen' 2 Y-OOR
(R.V. Favell, 1939) R.V. Favell, 1965
Fl. 89 mm wide; corona reddish orange, with red at rim. Mid-season. Resembles a red-rimmed 'Fortune'

'Treena' 6 W-Y
Syn. of 'Trena'

'Treesa' 3 (a)
(P.D. Williams, pre-1930)

'Treffry' 3 W-O
(P.D. Williams, pre-1930)
Perianth segments ivory white; corona orange

'Trefoil'
(C.L. Adams, pre-1913)

'Trefusis' 1 Y-Y
(R.A.Scamp) R.A.Scamp, 1994
'Arctic Gold' × 'Ristin'; sdlg no. 134
Fl. rounded, 92 mm wide, rich golden yellow; perianth segments broadly ovate, blunt, slightly mucronate, spreading, smooth, overlapping half; the inner segments narrower, a little inflexed; corona narrow, smooth, with mouth ribbed and flared, rim notched and crenate. Early to mid-season

'Tregadillet' 2 W-P
(Brian S. Duncan) du Plessis Bros, 1989
'Polonaise' × 'Violetta'; sdlg no. 562
Fl. 110 mm wide; corona very deep pink, with mouth expanded and frilled. Late

'Treganny'
(pre-1940)

'Tregantle' 2 W-Y
(P.D. Williams, pre-1937)
Perianth segments broad, corona pale primrose. Tall. Mid-season

'Tregarne' 3 W-? (b)
(P.D. Williams, pre-1928)

'Tregarrick' 2 Y-OOR
(J.S.B. Lea) du Plessis Bros, 1985
Sdlg no. 3/10/64
Perianth segments broadly ovate, blunt, spreading or somewhat inflexed, with broad midrib showing, overlapping half; the inner segments shouldered at base; corona funnel-shaped, orange, shading to red at rim, with mouth flared. Mid-season

'Tregarthen Perfection' 2 W-? (b)
(G.L. Wilson, pre-1952)

'Tregasson' 2 (a)
Syn. of 'Tregassow'

'Tregassow' 2 (a)
(P.D. Williams, pre-1928)
See also 'Tregasson'

'Tregeare' 2 Y-Y
(Brian S. Duncan) du Plessis Bros, 1990
'Golden Aura' open pollinated; sdlg no. 652
Fl. 93 mm wide, golden yellow; corona with rim slightly dentate. Late

'Tregellas' 2 (a)
(P.D. Williams, pre-1930)

'Tregenna' 2 (a)
(P.D. Williams, pre-1930)

'Tregoise' 2 Y-R
(pre-1933)
Corona red, frilled

'Tregolls' 1 (a)
(P.D. Williams, pre-1930)

'Tregoose' 2 Y-O
(P.D. Williams, pre-1927)
Fl. 114 mm wide; perianth segments very broadly ovate, rounded at apex, fairly prominently mucronate, spreading, plane, overlapping one-third to a half; the inner segments more narrowly ovate, blunt, not noticeably mucronate, a little inflexed, with margins slightly wavy and sometimes nicked near mid-point; corona bowl-shaped, loosely ribbed, reddish orange, irregularly frilled. Mid-season. AM(e) 1927, AM(Haarlem) 1931

'Tregowris' 3 W-? (b or c)
(P.D. Williams, pre-1928)

'Tregye' 3 (a)
(P.D. Williams, pre-1927)

'Trehane' 6 Y-Y
(R.A. Scamp) R.A. Scamp, 1991
'Saint Keverne' × *N. cyclamineus*; sdlg no. 212
Fl. 78 mm wide; perianth segments broadly ovate, brilliant greenish yellow 3A, reflexed, overlapping; corona narrowly funnel-shaped, ribbed, slightly paler in tone than the perianth, with mouth a little expanded, neatly frilled. Dwarf. Early

'Trelan' 3 W-YYR
(P.D. Williams, pre-1928)
Perianth segments pure white, of great substance; corona citron yellow, with deep red at rim

'Trelane'
(New Zealand origin, pre-1940)

'Trelask' 2 W-? (b)
(P.D. Williams, pre-1930)

'Trelawne' 2 Y-O
(G.L. Wilson, 1952) L. Major, 1965
'Armada' × 'Bahram'
Corona dark orange. Mid-season. Resembles 'Foxhunter'

'Trelawny' 2 W-? (b)
(Lord Rendlesham, pre-1937)

'Trelay' 3 Y-OOR
(P. Phillips) P. Phillips, 1972
Fl. 107 mm wide; perianth segments broad, rich yellow, smooth; corona orange, paler at base, shading to red at rim, with mouth expanded and rim neatly dentate

'Treliever' 2 W-? (b)
(P.D. Williams, pre-1930)

'Trelill' 2 W-W
(P.D. Williams, pre-1927)
Fl. creamy white

'Trelowarren' 2 W-? (b)
(G.L. Wilson, pre-1951)

'Trematon' 2 Y-O
(T. Bloomer) du Plessis Bros, 1986
'Break of Day' × 'Ardour'; sdlg no. 245
Mid-season

'Tremingie' 6 Y-Y
Syn. of 'Trewirgie'

'Tremont' 1 W-Y
(H.A. Brown, pre-1938)
Corona lemon, frilled

'Trena' 6 W-Y
(Miss M. Verry) Miss M. Verry, 1971
'Assini' × *N. cyclamineus*
Fl. 82 mm wide, facing slightly downwards; perianth segments ovate or broadly ovate, blunt, slightly mucronate, reflexed, creased, with margins a little incurling at apex, overlapping one-third to a half; corona somewhat funnel-shaped, smooth, vivid yellow 9A, paler at base, with mouth flared and more or less even, rim very shallowly notched and obscurely crenate. Dwarf. Early. 2n=21. FCC(e)(NZ) 1979, AM(e) 1996. See also 'Treena'

'Trenah' 1 W-? (b)
(W. Jackson Jr, 1957) Unregistered
'Preamble' × 'Tamara'

'Trenance' 2 Y-Y
(R.V. Favell, pre-1939)
Fl. bright golden yellow

'Trend' 4 W-P
(D.S. Bell) D.S. Bell, 1980
'Double Event' × 'Sleeping Beauty'
Fl. 103 mm wide; perianth and other petaloid segments white; corona segments interspersed, pink. Mid-season. Resembles 'Double Event' but with differently coloured corona segments

'Trend' 4 Y-Y
Syn. of 'Angkor'

'Trendrine' 7
(P.D. Williams, pre-1928)
Syn. 'Tendrine'

'Trendsetter' 2 Y-O
(J.S.B. Lea) M.J. Jefferson-Brown, 1975
'Nanking' × 'Ambergate'
Perianth segments gold, flushed orange; corona reddish orange

'Trenithon' 1 Y-Y
(G.H. Johnstone, pre-1950)
2n=28. See also 'Trenython'

'Trenode' 1 Y-Y
(Mrs H.K. Richardson) du Plessis Bros, 1989
Sdlg no. 893
Fl. 101 mm wide; perianth segments ovate, very smooth; corona with rim slightly rolled. Late

'Trenoon' 2 Y-Y
(P.D. Williams, pre-1930)
Fl. dark golden yellow; perianth segments broadly ovate, blunt, slightly mucronate, spreading or a little inflexed, with margins minutely incurling at apex, overlapping one-third to a half; the inner segments more strongly inflexed, twisted or with margins wavy; corona funnel-shaped, with mouth ribbed and expanded, rim crenate and slightly rolled

'Trenowth' 3 W-GYR
(P.D. Williams, pre-1927)

'Trent' 3 (a)
(pre-1947)
AM 1947

'Trentino' 2 (a)
(R.H. Bath, pre-1930)

Sdlg no. 33/24

'Trenton' 1 (a)
(J.T. Gray, pre-1950)

'Trenython' 1 Y-Y
Syn. of 'Trenithon'

'Trepolo' 11b W-O/W
(J.W.A. Lefeber) J.W.A. Lefeber, 1968
'Brilliant Star' hybrid
Fl. 85 mm wide; perianth segments very broadly ovate, truncate, very prominently mucronate, spreading, with raised midrib, overlapping half; the inner segments less noticeably truncate or mucronate, square-shouldered at base; corona split to base, the six segments two-thirds the length of the perianth segments and alternate to them, oblong, narrow, squarish at apex, twisted and with margins incurved or more tightly incurled, with a broad longitudinal band of orange flanked by white, sometimes with a small extra growth between the segments at base. Mid-season. See also 'Tepolo'

'Treringey'
(G.H. Johnstone, pre-1960) Unregistered

'Tresamble' 5 W-W
(P.D. Williams, pre-1930)
Fls 2-3 per stem, forming a double triangle, 90 mm wide; perianth segments ovate, blunt or truncate, prominently mucronate, ivory white, spreading, slightly twisted, overlapping one-third to a half; the inner segment more narrowly ovate, more nearly acute, with margins wavy or incurved; corona funnel-shaped, lightly ribbed, pale cream, mouth straight, loosely frilled, rim irregularly and minutely dentate. 2n=21. AM(Haarlem) 1947, FCC(Haarlem) 1950, TGA(Haarlem) 1956, *AM(g) 1958, *AM(p) 1976

'Tresco' 2 Y-R
(M.P. Williams, pre-1949)
Perianth segments lemon yellow; corona red

'Tresillian' 2 (a)
(P.D. Williams, pre-1930)

'Tresithick' 2 Y-Y
(M.P. Williams, pre-1949)

'Treskerby' 3 Y-R
(P.D. Williams, pre-1927)
'Beacon' × 'Tamerlane'
Perianth segments creamy yellow; corona deep red.
*AM(g)(m) 1927

'Treskewes' 5 Y-Y
(P.D. Williams, pre-1928)
'King Alfred' × *N. triandrus*

Fl. 79 mm wide, facing down; perianth segments bright lemon, somewhat reflexed, separated; corona funnel-shaped, bright lemon. Mid-season to late

'Treslong' 2 (a)
(G.A. Uit den Boogaard, pre-1944)

'Trespasser' 2 Y-O
(S.A. Free) Mrs S.I. Free, 1971
Fl. 102 mm wide

'Tress' 3 W-O
(L. Buckland, pre-1926)
FCC 1926

'Tresserve' 1 Y-Y
(Heere Bros, pre-1912)
'Golden Spur' × 'Emperor'
Perianth segments canary yellow, inflexed; corona expanded, ribbed, rich yellow, frilled. AM(Haarlem) 1912, FA(Haarlem) 1921

'Trethvas' 3 W-O
(G.H. Johnstone, 1956) Mrs A. Johnstone, 1966
'Kilworth' × 'Caralsa'
Fl. 108 mm wide; corona orange (28A). Late. Resembles 'Caralsa' but with a whiter perianth and a brighter-coloured corona

'Trevalsoe' 2 (a)
(P.D. Williams, pre-1928)

'Trevarth' 3 W-? (b)
(P.D. Williams, pre-1930)

'Trevean' 1 (a)
(G.L. Wilson, pre-1951)

'Trevecca' 3 W-W
(P.D. Williams, pre-1928)
Perianth segments pure white; corona creamy

'Trevedron' 9
(The Brodie of Brodie, pre-1930)

'Trevelmond' 2 W-YPP
(T. Bloomer) du Plessis Bros, 1986
'Passionale' × sdlg 375
Late

'Trevemper' 2 Y-Y
(G.H. Johnstone) G.H. Johnstone, 1959
'Frontispiece' × ('Constantine' × 'King of the North')
Fl. 146 mm wide. Early

'Trevennick' 2 W-W
(P.D. Williams, pre-1928)

'Treverbyn' 2 W-W
(P.D. Williams, pre-1928)

'Treverva' 6 Y-Y
(R.A. Scamp) R.A. Scamp, 1991
'Foresight' × *N. cyclamineus*; sdlg no. S2
Fl. 78 mm wide, at an acute angle to the stem; perianth segments ovate, acute, reflexed, more or less strongly twisted, overlapping at base only; corona cylindrical, narrow, brilliant greenish yellow 4A, slightly darker in tone than the perianth, neatly frilled, with rim flanged. Dwarf. Very early

'Treveth' 2 (a)
(P.D. Williams, pre-1928)

'Treviddo' 2 W-GWP
(R.A.Scamp) R.A.Scamp, 1994
'Chenoweth' × 'Rainbow'; sdlg no. S324
Fl. 95 mm wide; perianth segments broadly ovate, slightly concave, deeply overlapping; corona slightly expanded, white, with green at base and clear pink at rim, frilled. Mid-season. Sunproof

'Trevilley' 2 W-? (b)
(G. Matthews, pre-1951)

'Trevilvas'
(G.H. Johnstone, pre-1950)

'Trevisky' 2 Y-O
(P.D. Williams, pre-1930)
Perianth segments broadly ovate, blunt, prominently mucronate, primrose yellow, spreading, smooth, regular, overlapping one-third; the inner segments more narrowly ovate; corona funnel-shaped, short, reddish orange, with mouth straight and wavy, rim notched. AM(Haarlem) 1931, AM(e) 1932

'Trevithian' 7 Y-Y
(P.D. Williams, pre-1927)
'Pilgrim' × 'Jonquil' [sic]
Fls 2-3 per stem, 71 mm wide; perianth segments very broad, rounded at apex, clear primrose yellow, with prominent white mucro, spreading, somewhat concave, smooth, overlapping half; the inner segments a little narrower, less obviously mucronate, with margins incurled or wavy, shouldered at base; corona short and broad funnel-shaped, lightly ribbed, darker in tone than the perianth, mouth straight, occasionally split and overlapping, wavy, with rim minutely crenate. Mid-season. Scented. 2n=21. AM(Haarlem) 1931, *AM(g)(m) 1931, *FCC(g) 1936, FA(Haarlem) 1938, AGM 1995

'Trevitvas' 2 Y-Y
(G.H. Johnstone, pre-1960) Unregistered
'Trenoon' × 'Hebron'

'Trevone' 3 W-YYO
(R.V. Favell, pre-1946)
'Silver Coin' × 'Beacon'

'Trevose' 2 W-W
(The Brodie of Brodie, pre-1930)
'White Emperor' hybrid

'Trevothen' 2 W-? (b or c)
(The Brodie of Brodie, pre-1930)

'Trewarvas' 2 W-Y
(R.A. Scamp) R.A. Scamp, 1991
'Newcastle' × 'Irish Minstrel'; sdlg no. 28
Fl. 114 mm wide; perianth segments ovate, blunt, clear white; corona smooth or slightly ribbed, rich golden yellow, with mouth a little expanded. Late

'Trewergie' 6 Y-Y
Syn. of 'Trewirgie'

'Trewhiddle Bicolor' 1 W-Y
(Shilson, pre-1909)
Fl. small, neat. Early

N. trewianus Ker Gawler = *N. tazetta* var. *trewianus*

'Trewianus'
Syn. of *N. tazetta* var. *trewianus*

'Trewidland' 2 W-P
(Brian S. Duncan) du Plessis Bros, 1987
Richardson sdlg 3341 × 'Passionale'; sdlg no. 183
Perianth segments very smooth; corona with mouth expanded. Late

'Trewinard' 3 (a)
(P.D. Williams, pre-1928)

'Trewince' 2 Y-Y
(P.D. Williams, pre-1927)
Fl. 102 mm wide, facing down; perianth segments clear primrose, irregular, overlapping one-third; corona pale buttercup yellow, mouth expanded and somewhat frilled. Mid-season

'Trewinnard' 3 (a)
(E. & J.C. Martin, pre-1930)

'Trewirgie' 6 Y-Y
(P.D. Williams, pre-1928)
Perianth segments a little reflexed; corona long, with rim slightly flanged. See also 'Trewergie', 'Tremingie'

'Trewithen' 1 Y-Y
(G.H. Johnstone, pre-1949) Mrs J. Abel Smith, 1971
'Golden Torch' × 'Acclaim'
Fl. 114 mm wide, mid-yellow, of smooth texture. 2n=28

'Trewithiel' 1 Y-Y
(Sir A.P.W. Thomas, pre-1930)
Perianth segments pale yellow, slightly twisted;

corona darker in tone, with rim flared and deeply notched. Tall

'Trewithy'
(pre-1940)

'Treyew' 2?
(?B.J. Carter, pre-1947)

'Triabunna' 4 Y-R
(K.J. Heazlewood) K.J. Heazlewood, 1970
'Redeem' × 'Hollandia'

N. triandrus Linnaeus 13 Section Ganymedes
("Ganymede's Cup"). AM 1984, AGM 1994
    var. *calathinus* (de Candolle) hort. =
        N. triandrus var. *loiseleurii*
  subsp. *capax* (Salisbury) D.A. Webb =
        N. triandrus var. *loiseleurii*
    var. *cernuus* (Salisbury) Baker = *N. triandrus*
        subsp. *pallidulus*
  subsp. ***triandrus***
    var. ***triandrus*** ("Angel's Tears")
    var. *albus* (Haworth) Baker = *N. triandrus* var. *triandrus*
    var. *aurantiacus* hort.= *N. triandrus* var. *concolor*. 2n=14
    var. ***concolor*** (Haworth) Link. 2n=14 AM(a) 1938
    var. ***loiseleurii*** (Rouy) A.Fernandes. AM(e) 1920
    var. *mutatis* Coutinho = *N. triandrus*
    var. ***pulchellus*** (Salisbury) Baker
  subsp. ***pallidulus*** (Graells) D.A.Webb

N. triandrus Curtis = *N. triandrus* subsp. *pallidulus*

'Trianon' 3 W-Y
(Konynenburg & Mark, 1952) Konynenburg & Mark, 1962
'Bertha Aten' × ('Fortune' × 'Memphis')
Fl. 120 mm wide; corona creamy apricot yellow. Mid-season

'Triavial' 1 Y-Y
(Mrs G. Link) Mrs G. Link, 1988

'Tribune' 3 W-O
(Mrs R.O. Backhouse, pre-1921)
Fl. 76 mm wide, facing down; perianth segments creamy white, reflexed, overlapping half; corona bowl-shaped, rich bright reddish orange. Late

'Tribune' 4 Y-Y
(Mrs H.K. Richardson) M.J. Jefferson-Brown, 1975
Perianth segments yellow; corona deeper in tone. Mid-season

'Tribute' 2 W-? (b)
(R. Crews, pre-1949)

'Tribute' 2 W-R
(?J.L. Richardson)
'Kilworth' × 'Arbar'

'Tribute' 4 Y-Y
(c.1973) Unregistered

'Trice' 2 (a)
(P.D. Williams, pre-1930)

'Tricia' 3 W-WWR
(H.A. Brown, 1938)

'Tricia' 2 W-O
(T.H. Piper, 1945) T.H. Piper, 1956
'White Cheerio' × 'Blodwen'

'Tricky' 5
(pre-1913)

'Tricollet' 11a W-O
(J. Gerritsen & Son) J. Gerritsen & Son, 1969
Sdlg × 'Joli-Coeur'
Perianth segments very broadly ovate, blunt, only very slightly mucronate, spreading, slightly concave, creased, with margins incurving, overlapping half or more; the inner segments triangular in appearance, inflexed; corona split, the three segments each half to two-thirds the length of the inner perianth segments and opposite to them, square at apex, with two deep lobes overlapping at rim, ribbed, deep orange, sometimes touched white near margins, lightly frilled. Mid-season to late. 2n=29

'Tricolour' 2 W-? (b)
(R.V. Favell, pre-1946)

'Tricycle' 5
(F.R. Waley, pre-1950)
N. triandrus × *N. cyclamineus*

'Trident' 3 W-YYR
(Antipodean origin, pre-1958) M.J. Jefferson-Brown, 1975
Perianth segments broadly ovate, blunt, fairly prominently mucronate, snow white, spreading, plane, with margins sometimes a little incurling, smooth and of thick texture, overlapping one-third to a half; the inner segments shouldered at base, somewhat inflexed, with margins more strongly incurling; corona shallow, ribbed, bright yellow, with a broad and well-defined band of dark red at rim. Tall. Mid-season. Syn. 'Bellavista', 'Bella Vista'

'Tridia' 2 W-? (b)
(A.H. Ahrens) J.S. Leitch, 1955

'Tridymus' 8 Y-Y
(pre-1884)
Fls 1-3 per stem; perianth segments ovate, whitish

yellow, more or less spreading, overlapping a quarter to one-third; corona cylindrical or somewhat funnel-shaped, bright yellow, with mouth ribbed and straight, lightly frilled. Syn. "The Trine Narcissus", Tridymus 'Tridymus'. This has also been used as a Group name

'Trieste' 2 (a)
(A. Gibson, pre-1950)

'Trifect' 1 W-W
(D. Jackson) Jackson's Daffodils, 1983
Sdlg × 'Mercedes'; sdlg no. 19/78
Fl. 105 mm wide. Early to mid-season

'Trifine' 2 Y-O
(G.H. Johnstone) Mrs J. Abel Smith, 1970
('Dunkeld' × 'Fortune') × 'Armada'
Fl. 126 mm wide; perianth segments slightly brighter than brilliant greenish yellow 6A, overlapping; corona slightly ribbed, near to strong orange 25A, paler towards base, with mouth expanded and frilled, rim dentate and slightly flanged. 2n=28

'Trifle' 5 Y-Y
(D. Blanchard, pre-1948)
'White Knight' × *N. triandrus* var. *loiseleurii*

'Trifo' 2 W-P
(R.H.Glover, pre-1990) Unregistered
'Cathlin' × 'Dorothy B.'

'Trigo' 3 W-GYR
(F.H. Chapman, pre-1930)
Perianth segments creamy white

'Trigonometry' 11a W-P
(G.E.Mitsch, 1979) R. & E.Havens, 1995
'Recital' × 'Phantom'; sdlg no. 205/2
Fl. 105 mm wide; perianth segments broadly ovate, of heavy substance; corona deeply split, the six segments opposite and closely overlying the perianth segments, deep creamy pink, a little frilled. Mid-season. Sunproof

'Trilby' 1 W-Y
(D.V. West, pre-1935)

'Triller' 7 Y-O
(G.E. Mitsch) G.E. Mitsch, 1979
'Vulcan' × *N. jonquilla*; sdlg no. G58/1
Fl. 65 mm wide; perianth segments golden yellow; corona opening pale orange, becoming rich reddish orange. Mid-season

'Trilliarch' 2 (a)
(W.A. Grace, pre-1938)

'Trillick' 3 W-GYR
(Brian S. Duncan) Rathowen Daffodils, 1978

'Enniskillen' × 'Omagh'; sdlg no. 254
Fl. 95 mm wide; corona yellow, with green at base and a broad band of red at rim. Mid-season

N.* × *trilobus Linnaeus = *N. bicolor* Linnaeus × *N. jonquilla* Linnaeus

'Trilobus' 7 Y-Y
(pre-1629)
Fl. full yellow. Syn. "The Lesser 3-lobed", Odorus 'Trilobus'

'Trilobus Plene' 4 Y-Y
Syn. of 'Eystettensis'

'Trilogy' 5 W-Y
(W.F.M. Copeland, pre-1909)
Fls 3 per stem, facing down; perianth segments spreading; corona cylindrical, constricted at base, clear yellow, with mouth straight

'Trilune' 11a W-Y
(J. Gerritsen & Son) J. Gerritsen & Son, 1983
'Tricollet' hybrid
Corona deeply split, with three segments only. Mid-season

'Trim' 7 Y-O
(P.D. Williams, pre-1943)
Perianth segments acute, bright golden yellow; corona rich orange

'Trimdon' 1 (a)
(A.M. Wilson, pre-1948)

'Trimon' 5 W-W
(A.W. Tait, pre-1899)
N. cantabricus subsp. *monophyllus* × *N. triandrus*
Fl. creamy white; perianth segments with green showing through from a longitudinal band of colour beneath; corona with mouth slightly flared. AM 1899

'Trimpley Gem' 3 W-? (b or c)
(Cartwright & Goodwin, pre-1913)

'Trinculo' 5 W-W
(D. Blanchard, pre-1948)
'Irish Pearl' × *N. triandrus* var. *loiseleurii*

'Tringa' 1 W-Y
(T. Morrison) T. Morrison, 1960
Corona lemon yellow

'Tringy' 2 W-? (b or c)
(P.D. Williams, pre-1930)

'Trinidad' 2 W-O
(J.L. Richardson, pre-1940)
'Invergordon' × 'Penquite'

'Trinity' 4
(E.G. Hebblethwaite, pre-1936)

'Trinity Bells' 5 Y-Y
(S.J. Bisdee, pre-1939)
'Pedestal' × *N. triandrus*

"Trinity College (Dublin) Maximus"
Syn. of Pseudonarcissus Major 'Maximus'

'Trinket' ?-P
(F.H. Chapman, c.1910)

'Trinket' 3 W-? (b)
(M.P. Williams, pre-1938)

'Triomphator' 3 W-? (b)
(de Graaff-Gerharda, pre-1925)
AM(Haarlem) 1925

'Triomphe des Jaunes' 8 Y-Y
(pre-1850)

'Tripartite' 11a Y-Y
(R.L. Brook) R.L. Brook, 1980
'April Tears' × 'Baccarat'; sdlg no. 280/1
Fls 2-3 per stem, 65 mm wide, shining greenish yellow; perianth segments broadly ovate, blunt, becoming paler in tone with maturity, with slight white mucro, spreading or a little reflexed, plane, with margins a little incurling, smooth, with midrib showing, overlapping one-third to a half; corona split to two-thirds its length, the six segments one-third to a half as long as the perianth segments and opposite and closely overlying them, bi-lobed, becoming deeper in tone with maturity, with shades of honey yellow at base, rim entire or irregularly crenate. Late. Slightly scented

N. tripartitus Schultes f. = *N.* × *intermedius*

'Tripaway' 2 W-P
(R.H.Glover, pre-1989) Unregistered
'Mirra Donna' × 'Sprightly'

N. tripedalis Loddiges = *N. ornatus* Haworth

'Triple Crown' 3 Y-GYR
(Brian S. Duncan) Rathowen Daffodils, 1987
'Sunapee' × 'Achduart'; sdlg no. 962
Fl. rounded; perianth segments very broad, rounded at apex, slightly mucronate, deep golden yellow, a little reflexed, concave at apex, overlapping half; the inner segments narrower, roundish, more nearly spreading; corona shallow bowl-shaped, ribbed, deep golden yellow, with emerald green at base and a narrow band of red at rim, mouth expanded and minutely frilled. Mid-season

'Triple Phase' 3 Y-R

(David Adams) David Adams, 1994
'Chungking' × 'Pzaz'; sdlg no. 84/19E
Fl. forming a double triangle, 105 mm wide; perianth segments ovate, deep yellow, plane; the inner segments a little narrower; corona cup-shaped, orange-red, with mouth frilled. Tall. Early to mid-season. Resembles an improved 'Chungking'

'Triplex' 4 W-W
(F.H. Chapman, pre-1929)
'Moonbeam' × *N. poeticus*
Fl. snow white; perianth segments very broad in outline, blunt or truncate at apex, prominently mucronate, overlapping half; the inner segments a little inflexed, with margins wavy; segments at centre in two whorls of three, half the length of the perianth segments and opposite to them, broadly ovate, heavily creased; the outer whorl spreading; the inner whorl a little inflexed. AM(e) 1929, AM(Haarlem) 1938

N. tripodalis Salisbury = *N. ornatus* Haworth.

'Tripoli' 2 Y-YRR
(J.L. Richardson, pre-1944)
'Porthilly' × 'Bahram'
Perianth segments soft yellow; corona bright cherry red, paling to gold at base, heavily frilled

'Tripper' ?-P
(Alister Clark, pre-1948)

'Triqueter'
(pre-1885)

'Trispin' 3 W-YYO
(P.D. Williams, pre-1927)

'Tristan' 2 W-YYP
(W.M. Spry, pre-1975) Unregistered
'Sweetness' × 'Stella'
Corona chrome yellow, with pink at rim, frilled

'Tristar' 11?a W-W
(Jānis Rukšans, pre-1997) Unregistered

'Tristesse' 5 W-W
(D. Blanchard, pre-1948)
'White Knight' × *N. triandrus* var. *loiseleurii*
Corona long

'Tristram' 5 Y-Y
(Barr & Sons, pre-1923)

'Tristram' 1? W-W
(G.L. Wilson, pre-1936)

'Tristram' 2 Y-Y
(Mrs H.K. Richardson) Mrs H.K. Richardson, 1976
'Golden Aura' × 'Camelot'
Perianth segments mid-yellow; corona buff yellow,

with rim slightly dentate. Mid-season. 2n=29

'Tritaz' 8
(M.H. Tribe, pre-1937)

'Tritoma' 2 W-? (b)
(G.H. Engleheart, pre-1913)

'Triton' 1 W-? (b)
(Barr & Sons, pre-1923)

'Triton' 2 W-Y
(W. Jackson Jr, 1969) Unregistered
'Filia' × 'Killymoon'; sdlg no. 10/69

'Triumph' 8 W-Y
(R.van der Schoot & Son, pre-1906)
Poetaz
Fls about 3 per stem, large; perianth segments snow white, overlapping; corona golden yellow

'Triumph' 1 Y-Y
(J.N. Hancock & Co., 1976) Unregistered

'Triumphant' 8 Y-?
(pre-1759)
?The same as 'Triumphant Jaune'

'Triumphante Jaune' 8 Y-Y
(pre-1798)
Fl. golden yellow. ?The same as 'Triumphant'

'Triumphant Nosegay' 8 W-Y
(pre-1759)

'Triumphator' 1 W-? (b)
(pre-1927)

'Trivet' 3 W-W
(P.D. Williams, pre-1934)

'Trivial' 1 Y-Y
(Mrs G. Link) Mrs G. Link, 1988
'Tiny Tot' × 'Divine'; sdlg no. 1-75-A
Fl. 40 mm wide; corona frilled. Tall. Early to mid-season. Weatherproof. Resembles 'Tiny Tot' but with a more heavily frilled corona

'Trixie' 3 W-? (b)
(A.H. Ahrens) J.S. Leitch, 1956

'Trocadero' 1 W-Y
(G. Lubbe & Son, pre-1938)
AM(Haarlem) 1938

'Trogon' 2 Y-R
(G.E. Mitsch) G.E. Mitsch, 1979
('Narvik' × 'California Gold') × ('Playboy' × 'Alamein') × 'Falstaff'; sdlg no. G63/4
Fl. 93 mm wide; perianth segments rounded at apex, deep yellow, deeply overlapping; corona bright orange-red, mouth flared and frilled. Early to mid-season

'Troilus' 1 Y-Y
(pre-1886)
Perianth segments sulphur yellow; corona rich yellow. Dwarf. Early. See also 'Trollius'

'Trojan' 2 Y-Y
(West & Fell, pre-1935)
Corona frilled

'Trojan Boy' 2 W-? (b or c)
(Cartwright & Goodwin, pre-1908)

'Trollius' 1 Y-Y
Syn. of 'Troilus'

'Trombone' 1 (a)
(G. Lubbe & Son, pre-1940)
AM(Haarlem) 1940

'Trompet Marin' 10
Syn. of 'Trumpet Marin'

"Trompette de Meduse"
Syn. of *N. bulbocodium*

'Trona' 3 W-GWW
(Murray W. Evans, 1968) Murray W. Evans, 1987
'Limberlost' × 'Lostine'; sdlg no. L-64
Corona expanded and frilled. Late. Resembles a taller and larger 'Lostine' of smoother substance

'Troon' 2 W-W
(Brian S. Duncan) Rathowen Daffodils, 1978
'Easter Moon' × 'Empress of Ireland'; sdlg no. 117
Fl. pure white. Mid-season. Resembles 'Inverpolly' but with the perianth segments of improved form

'Trophy' 1 Y-Y
(A.E. Lowe, pre-1927)

'Trophy' 1 W-? (b)
(R.L. Thornton)

'Tropical Heat' 2 Y-R
(Brian S.Duncan) Brian S.Duncan, 1996
'Garden News' × sdlg 769 ('Bunclody' × 'Barnsdale Wood'); sdlg no. 1324
Fl. 104 mm wide; perianth segments broadly ovate, blunt, deep golden yellow, plane, smooth; corona narrowly funnel-shaped, with mouth slightly flared and frilled. Mid-season to late

'Tropical Showers' 2 W-Y
(W.J.G. Hector) W.J.G. Hector, 1965
Fl. 103 mm wide; corona shallow, widely expanded, lemon yellow, frilled. Early

'Tropicana' 4 Y-Y
(D.S. Bell) D.S. Bell, 1982
'Fiji' × 'Ashanti'
Fl. 115 mm wide, lemon yellow. Mid-season. Resembles a fuller-flowered 'Fiji'

'Tropic Delight' 9 W-YYR
(Mrs M.S. Yerger) Mrs M.S. Yerger, 1989
'Stilton' open pollinated; sdlg no. 77 I 2
Fl. 60 mm wide; perianth segments broad; the inner segments narrower and longer; corona bowl-shaped, vivid yellow 15A, with orange-red (33A) at rim. Late. Strongly citrus scented

'Tropic Isle' 4 W-P
(G.E. Mitsch) G.E. Mitsch, 1975
'Pink Chiffon' × 'Accent'; sdlg no. E21/3
Fl. 90 mm wide; perianth and other petaloid segments of equal length, broadly ovate, blunt, slightly mucronate, white, somewhat concave either side of midrib, overlapping half or more; the outer whorl spreading; the inner whorl inflexed, sometimes with margins abruptly folded inwards; some short petaloid segments at centre strongly inflexed, with margins tightly incurled; corona segments shorter than the centre petaloid segments and clustered among them, more loosely arranged between the surrounding whorls, broad, salmon pink, frilled. Mid-season

'Tropic Star' 2 W-O
(Warnaar & Co., pre-1938)

'Tropic Sun' 2 (a)
(Mrs R.O. Backhouse, pre-1921)
AM(Haarlem) 1926

'Tropic Surprise' 9 W-GGR
(Mrs M.S. Yerger) Mrs M.S. Yerger, 1991
'Dactyl' open pollinated; sdlg no. 79 C 7
Fl. 57 mm wide; perianth segments acute, overlapping; corona brilliant yellow-green 154B, with a darker tone (145A) at base and orange-red (31A) at rim. Very late.

'Tros'
(?Barr & Sons, pre-1915)

'Trostan' 1 W-Y
(G.L. Wilson, pre-1938)
'King Alfred' × 'Askelon'
Perianth segments very broadly ovate, blunt, fairly prominently mucronate, a little reflexed, creased, overlapping half; the inner segments narrower, spreading at base, reflexed at apex, with margins wavy; corona cylindrical, smooth, pale yellow, rim widely flanged and deeply crenate. 2n=28

'Troubadour'
(C. Dawson, pre-1908)

'Troubadour' 2 W-P
(Oregon Bulb Farms) Oregon Bulb Farms, 1958
Perianth segments pure white; corona opening rich pink, becoming paler. Tall. Early

'Troupial' 2 W-P
(G.E. Mitsch) G.E. Mitsch, 1968
('Radiation' × 'Interim') × 'Rima'; sdlg no. V109/1
Fl. 115 mm wide; corona deep salmon pink, with a paler tone at base. Mid-season

'Trousseau' 1 W-Y
(P.D. Williams, pre-1934)
Brodie sdlg × 'Tunis'
Fl. 120 mm wide; perianth segments broadly ovate, fairly prominently mucronate, milk white, spreading, plane, somewhat creased, overlapping one-third; the inner segments a little inflexed; corona funnel-shaped, lightly ribbed, opening soft yellow, becoming rich buff rosy cream, with the flanged rim notched and crenate. 2n=28. PC 1939, AM(e) 1945, FCC(e) 1947, AM(Haarlem) 1957

'Troutbeck' 3 W-GWW
(Mrs J. Abel Smith) Mrs J. Abel Smith, 1977
'Blanc de Chine' × 'Kincorth'; sdlg no. B3/91
Fl. 89 mm wide; corona disc-shaped, with emerald green at base

'Trouvaille' 2 W-? (b)
(G.A. Uit den Boogaard, pre-1937)

'Trouville' 2 W-W
(Mrs H.K. Richardson) Mrs H.K. Richardson, 1974
'Verona' × 'Stainless'
Fl. 95 mm wide; perianth segments broadly ovate, pure white; corona very shallow, opening pale lemon, soon becoming white, with green at base, frilled. Resembles 'Pontresina'

'Trowutta' 2 W-W
(C.E. Radcliff, 1939)
'Astrid' × 'Maid of the Mist'

'Troy' 2
(Mrs R.O. Backhouse, pre-1921)

'Troy' 1 W-W
(J.S. Leitch) J.S. Leitch, 1968

'Troytown' 2 Y-R
(G.H. Johnstone, pre-1943)
'Fortune' hybrid

'Tru' 3 W-WWY
(D.J. Jackson, 1977) Jackson's Daffodils, 1989
Sdlg 212/69 × 'Bandit'; sdlg no. 245/77
Fl. 100 mm wide, greenish white (155A); perianth segments rounded at apex; corona disc-shaped, with brilliant greenish yellow 6A at rim. Mid-season to late

'Truan' 2 Y-R
(P.D. Williams, pre-1930)
Perianth segments deep yellow; corona narrow, almost ruby red

'Truce' 1 W-? (b)
(G.C. Graham, pre-1951)

'Truculent' 3 W-WWY
(Jackson's Daffodils) Jackson's Daffodils, 1993
Sdlg 220/78 × sdlg 118/82; sdlg no. 386/88
Fl. 108 mm wide, greenish white (155A); perianth segments very broadly ovate; corona bowl-shaped, with a well-defined narrow band of brilliant yellow 7B at rim. Early to mid-season

'Trudy' 3 W-O
(G.H. Johnstone, 1942) G.H.Johnstone, 1959
'Elspeth' hybrid
Fl. 95 mm wide. Late

'Trudy Louise' 2 W-WWP
(J.N. Hancock & Co., c.1980) Unregistered

'Trudy May'
Unregistered
Seed parent of 'Classic Touch'

'True Charm' 2 W-? (b or c)
(G.H. Engleheart, pre-1931)

'True Colours' 2 Y-O
(J.N. Hancock & Co., 1959) Unregistered
Perianth segments smooth, of good substance, overlapping; corona long, deep reddish orange, with mouth straight

'True Form' 1 W-W
(J.N. Hancock & Co., 1959) Unregistered
Fl. sparkling white; perianth segments broad, prominently mucronate; corona cylindrical, with mouth straight, rim notched

'Truelove' 3 W-R
(M.P. Williams, pre-1938)

'True Orbit' 2 Y-R
(D.S. Bell) D.S. Bell, 1965
'Monica' × 'Diamond King'
Mid-season. Resembles 'Alamein' but with narrower perianth segments

'Truganini' 2 Y-O
(Tom Forster, 1960s) Unregistered
Perianth segments very broadly ovate, blunt, only very slightly mucronate, spreading or somewhat reflexed, creased, overlapping half; the inner segments a little narrower, more usually spreading; corona disc-shaped, very broad, heavily ribbed, bright apricot orange, with mouth closely frilled. Tall. Mid-season

'Truism' 1 W-W
(Murray W.Evans, 1982) Estella L.Evans, 1992
'Neahkahnie' × ('Panache' × ['Petsamo' × 'Zero']); sdlg no. Z-3/1
Fl. 120 mm wide; perianth segments triangular in appearance, smooth; corona cylindrical, narrow, slightly ribbed towards mouth. Mid-season. Resembles a less purely white 'Ghost'

'Trump' 11a W-Y
(M.E.Brogden, pre-1996) Unregistered
'Bandit' × 'Colblanc'; sdlg no. 135/4

'Trump Card' 1 W-Y
(J.L. Richardson, pre-1930)
Perianth segments ivory white, of thick substance; corona constricted near mouth, primrose, with mouth expanded

'Trumper' 2 Y-Y
(W.M. Spry, pre-1975) Unregistered
'Aldgate' × 'Golden Valley'
Perianth segments yellow; corona darker in tone

'Trumpet-call' 1 W-Y
(A.G. Thompson) A.G. Thompson, 1961
Fl. 115 mm wide; perianth segments creamy white. Resembles 'Ballygarvey' in form

'Trumpet Call' 1 Y-O
(C.O. Fairbairn)

'Trumpeter' 1 Y-Y
(T. Buncombe, pre-1934)

'Trumpeter' 1 Y-Y
(G.L. Wilson) M.J. Jefferson-Brown, 1975
Fl. primrose gold. Mid-season. 2n=28. Resembles 'Slieveboy' but with the perianth segments more nearly spreading and plane

'Trumpeter' 1 Y-Y
(R.W. Ward, pre-1989)

'Trumpeter' 1 Y-Y
(R.W. Ward, pre-1989) Unregistered
Perianth segments broadly ovate, blunt and slightly mucronate, slightly inflexed, plane, regular, overlapping half; the inner segments more narrowly ovate, acute, more prominently mucronate; corona broad funnel-shaped, smoothly 6-angled, mouth ribbed, expanded, regularly and deeply lobed, with rim flanged

'Trumpet Major' 1 Y-Y
Syn. of 'Maximus'

'Trumpet Marin' 10
(pre-1629)
Selection from *N. bulbocodium*

Syn. 'Trompet Marin', 'Trumpet Merin', 'White Trompet Marin'

'Trumpet Merin' 10
Syn. of 'Trumpet Marin'

'Trumpet Sulphur' 1 Y-Y
(pre-1841)
Fl. sulphur yellow

'Trumpet Warrior' 1 YYW-WWY
(G.E. Mitsch, 1980) R. & E. Havens, 1990
'Chiloquin' × 'Arctic Gold; sdlg no. 2P33/1
Fl. forming a double triangle, 120 mm wide; perianth segments broadly ovate in outline, blunt or somewhat truncate at apex, slightly mucronate, deep lemon yellow, with white at base, spreading, plane, overlapping half; the inner segments square-shouldered at base, slightly inflexed, with margins a little wavy; corona cylindrical, smooth, pure white, with yellow at rim, with the rim notched and crenate and widely flanged. Mid-season

'Trumpington' 1 Y-Y
(J.N. Hancock & Co.) J.N. Hancock & Co., 1977
Sdlg × 'Kingscourt'
Fl. 100 mm wide; perianth segments vivid yellow 12A; corona slightly deeper in tone (13A). Mid-season

'Truro' 2 W-W
(E. & J.C. Martin, pre-1931)

'Trusty' 1 Y-Y
(P. & G. Phillips) P. & G. Phillips, 1981
Fl. 110 mm wide, pale lemon. Mid-season

'Truth' 2 W-W
(G.L. Wilson, pre-1936)
'Naxos' × Sdlg × 'Beersheba'
Fl. 121 mm wide; perianth segments broad, pure white, very smooth, overlapping; corona ribbed, with pale yellow at base, and with rim slightly reflexed. AM(e) 1940, AM(Haarlem) 1956

'Truvius' 1 Y-Y
(W. Jackson Jr) Jackson's Daffodils, 1979
Sdlg 28/64 × 'Ristin'; sdlg no. 23/71
Fl. 88 mm wide. Early to mid-season

'Tryad' 3 Y-Y
(Jackson's Daffodils) Jackson's Daffodils, 1989
'Lemonade' × sdlg 94/74; sdlg no. 180/81
Fl. rounded, 98 mm wide; perianth segments very broad in outline, blunt or rounded at apex, very slightly mucronate, light greenish yellow 3D, slightly reflexed, plane, overlapping half or more; the inner segments more nearly ovate, with broad midrib showing; corona bowl-shaped, short, ribbed, vivid yellow 9A, with a deeper tone at rim, mouth straight and frilled. Mid-season

'Trydens' 2 W-? (b)
(Mrs R.O. Backhouse, pre-1921)

'Tryst' 2 W-W
(G.L. Wilson, pre-1944)
'Silver Coin' × 'Armoy'
Corona faintly tinged primrose

'Tsjaikowski' 3 W-O
(J. Gerritsen & Son, c.1975) Unregistered

'Tua Heeta' 2 (a)
(Mrs R.O. Backhouse, pre-1921)

'Tuamarina' 4 W-P
(D.S. Bell) D.S. Bell, 1983

'Tuba' 1 W-W
(Baartman & Koning, pre-1942)

N. tubaeflorus Salisbury = *N. poeticus*

'Tubal' 1 Y-Y
(P. Phillips) P. Phillips, 1978
Fl. 94 mm wide, pale lemon. Early to mid-season. Resembles a paler 'Ristin'

'Tuba Maxima' 1 (a)
(C.A. van Paridon)
AM(Haarlem) 1950

'Tubertina' 2 (a)
(Konynenburg & Mark, pre-1953)

'Tubertina' 2 W-?
(Konynenburg & Mark) Konynenburg & Mark, 1960

N. tubulosus Jordan = *N. abscissus* var. *tubulosus*

'Tucaman' 2 Y-Y
(Colin Crotty) Colin Crotty, 1996
'Daydream' × 'Camelot'; sdlg no. 49-88
Fl. rounded, 110 mm wide, glistening; perianth segments very broadly ovate, pure yellow, deeply overlapping; corona straight-sided, of a slightly deeper tone than the perianth, faintly touched white at base, with mouth flared and slightly wavy. Mid-season

'Tucana' 1 W-Y
(J.A. Hunter, 1980) J.A. Hunter, 1990
'Otira' × 'Tudor King'; sdlg no. 21/74A
Fl. 105 mm wide; perianth segments ovate; corona narrow funnel-shaped, creamy yellow, only slightly expanded. Mid-season to late

'Tuckahoe' 3 W-GYR
(W.G. Pannill) W.G. Pannill, 1980

'Corofin' × 'Hotspur'; sdlg no. 64/36 C
Fl. 90 mm wide. Mid-season

N. × *tuckeri* Barra & López = *N. fernandesii* Pedro × *N. hedraeanthus* (Webb & Heldreich) Colmeiro

'Tudor' 1 (a)
(P.D. Williams, pre-1910)

'Tudor' 2 W-? (b)
(pre-1957)

'Tudor Chief' 2 (a)
(A. Gibson, pre-1951)

'Tudor Dance' 1 W-Y
(Mrs H.K. Richardson) Mrs H.K. Richardson, 1977
'My Love' open pollinated
Fl. 102 mm wide; perianth segments pure white; corona deep lemon yellow, with rim dentate and slightly rolled. Early to mid-season. Resembles a much larger 'My Love'

'Tudor Grove' 2 W-Y
(Mrs H.K. Richardson) Rathowen Daffodils, 1982
'Salome' open pollinated; sdlg no. 147
Fl. 130 mm wide; corona deep yellow. Mid-season

'Tudor King' 1 W-Y
(J.L. Richardson, pre-1953)
'Ardclinis' × 'Kanchenjunga'
Perianth segments pure white; corona deep lemon yellow, with rim flanged and dentate

'Tudor Legend' 2 W-Y
(J.L. Richardson) Mrs H.K. Richardson, 1964
'Broughshane' × 'Cape Horn'
Perianth segments very broadly ovate; corona lemon yellow, with rim flanged and dentate

'Tudor Love' 2 W-Y
(J.L. Richardson) Mrs H.K. Richardson, 1973
'Irish Minstrel' × 'My Love'
Corona canary yellow, with rim dentate. Resembles 'Tudor Minstrel'

'Tudor Melody' 2 W-Y
(J.L. Richardson) Mrs H.K. Richardson, 1964
From two 'Rose of Tralee' hybrids
Corona constricted near mouth, lemon yellow, with mouth expanded, rim slightly flanged and dentate

'Tudor Minstrel' 2 W-Y
(J.L. Richardson, pre-1948)
('Mitylene' × 'Penquite') × 'Cardigan'
Fl. 130 mm wide; perianth segments broadly ovate, mucronate, creamy white, overlaid with brilliant greenish yellow 6B, plane or a little concave, smooth, overlapping half; the inner segments more narrowly ovate, sometimes truncate; corona funnel-shaped, lightly ribbed, vivid yellow 12A, with mouth straight, frilled. AM(e) 1950, FCC(e) 1956, *AM(g) 1963, *AM(p) 1978

'Tudor Myth' 6 W-W
(J.L. Richardson) E. Longford, 1964
'Trousseau' × 'Jenny'
Fl. 89 mm wide. Mid-season. Resembles a more creamy-coloured 'Royal Jenny' of smoother texture with the corona rim less widely rolled

'Tudor Prince' 1 Y-Y
(H.A. Brown, 1955) J.N. Hancock & Co., 1955
Fl. clear mid-yellow; perianth segments very broad, spreading, smooth, overlapping; corona broad. Mid-season

'Tudor Rose' 8
(Mrs R.S. Cobley, pre-1937)

'Tudor Rose' 2 W-P
(J.N. Hancock & Co., pre-1974) Unregistered
Corona deep pink, frilled

'Tudor Rose' 2 W-Y
(?J.L. Richardson) Unregistered

'Tuesday's Child' 5 W-Y
(D. Blanchard) M.J. Jefferson-Brown, 1964
'Interim' × *N. triandrus* var. *loiseleurii*
Fls more than one per stem, 76 mm wide; perianth segments ovate, blunt, only very slightly mucronate, greenish white (157C), reflexed, slightly concave, with margins sometimes wavy or incurling, overlapping half; the inner segments with margins more often and more strongly wavy; corona long cup-shaped, very broadly ribbed, brilliant to light greenish yellow 5B-C, with mouth straight and wavy, rim entire or occasionally minutely notched. 2n=21. AM(e) 1969, AGM 1995

'Tui' 2 W-YYO
(S.C. Gaspar, pre-1948)
Perianth segments pure white; corona disc-shaped, golden yellow, with a broad band of reddish orange at rim, dentate

'Tui' 2 W-W
(A.H. Ahrens) J.S. Leitch, 1956

'Tuinui' 2 (a)
(W.A. Grace, pre-1938)

'Tulendena' 1 Y-Y
(W. Jackson Jr, 1955) W. Jackson Jr, 1966
'Moque' × 'Jobi'

'Tulita Miner' 2 W-YYO
(de Graaff Bros, pre-1935)
Fl. star-shaped; perianth segments whitish; corona

large, orange-yellow, with a narrow band of orange at rim

'Tulla' 2 Y-O
(J.N. Hancock & Co., 1962) Unregistered
Perianth segments very deep yellow; corona widely expanded, deep orange

'Tullamore' 2 W-Y
(J.L. Richardson, pre-1943)
'Cromarty' × 'Crocus'

'Tullia' 3 W-? (b)
(de Graaff Bros, pre-1929)
'Hothu' × 'Tain'

'Tullia' 1 W-W
(W. Jackson Sr, 1944)
'Hothu' × 'Tain'

'Tullus Hostilius' 7 Y-Y
(de Graaff Bros, pre-1927)
Perianth segments ovate, blunt, slightly mucronate; corona with rim entire

'Tullybeg' 3 W-GYR
(Ballydorn Bulb Farm) Ballydorn Bulb Farm, 1979
'Merlin' open pollinated
Fl. 85 mm wide, of good substance; perianth segments pure white. Late

'Tullycore' 2 W-P
(W.J. Toal, 1959) Ballydorn Bulb Farm, 1967
'Interim' × 'Salmon Trout'
Fl. 120 mm wide; corona pink, with green at base. Mid-season

'Tullygarley' 2 Y-R
(W.J. Dunlop) W.J. Dunlop, 1959
?'Carbineer' × ?'Porthilly'
Perianth segments broad, deep golden yellow, smooth; corona shallow, dark crimson. Mid-season

'Tullygirvan' 2 W-W
(Carncairn Daffodils) Carncairn Daffodils, 1976
'Blarney' × 'Irish Rose'; sdlg no. 2/7/63
Fl. 103 mm wide; perianth segments greenish white (157B); corona opening buff, becoming yellowish white 158D, with mouth even

'Tullyglass' 2 W-WWY
(J.L. Richardson) W.J. Dunlop, 1956
'Greenore' × 'Green Island'
Perianth segments pure white, of thick substance; corona opening pale primrose, soon becoming almost white, flushed greenish lemon at rim

'Tullynakill' 2 W-P
(Ballydorn Bulb Farm, 1974) Ballydorn Bulb Farm, 1989

'Tullycore' open pollinated
Fl. 102 mm wide; perianth segments very broadly ovate, deeply overlapping; corona bowl-shaped, expanded, pure rich pink, with rim dentate. Mid-season. Sunproof

'Tullynog' 4 W-O
(Carncairn Daffodils, 1975) Carncairn Daffodils, 1989
'Egg Nogg' × 'Tullycore'; sdlg no. 5/3/70
Fl. 100 mm wide; perianth and other petaloid segments in several whorls, pure white, regularly arranged; corona segments deep orange, in some seasons becoming pink. Late

'Tullyroe' 2 W-R
(G.L. Wilson) G.L. Wilson, 1960
2n=28

'Tullyrose' 2 W-P
(W. Toal or Ballydorn Bulb Farm, pre-1970) Unregistered
'Interim' × 'Rose Caprice'

'Tullyroyal' 2 W-P
(Ballydorn Bulb Farm) Ballydorn Bulb Farm, 1975
'Tullycore' open pollinated
Fl. 125 mm wide; corona slightly flared, clear pink, with a darker tone at base. Mid-season

'Tulsa' 2 Y-O
(J.T. Gray, pre-1949)
Corona spreading, deep reddish orange

'Tulyar' 3 W-R
(J.L. Richardson, pre-1952)
'Coronach' × 'Limerick'
Fl. 90 mm wide; perianth segments very broad, blunt or truncate, mucronate, with margins sometimes slightly incurling, overlapping half; the inner segments narrower, roundish, blunt; corona almost disc-shaped, tightly ribbed, opening slightly lighter than orange-red (32A), becoming darker in tone, with mouth widely expanded and frilled, rim very slightly dentate. AM(e) 1958

'Tumasha' 2 W-?
(A. Overton) A. Overton, 1960

'Tumbiumbi' 1 W-W
(J.N.Hancock & Co., 1987) J.N.Hancock & Co., 1997
Sdlg no. 8/87H
Perianth segments ovate, blunt, spreading; corona cylindrical, with mouth straight, rim slightly crenate. Mid-season

'Tumbler' 3 Y-O
(J.S. Leitch) J.S. Leitch, 1966
Fl. 95 mm wide

'Tummel' 2 W-P
(Alister Clark, 1940) J. Sharp, 1960

'Tundie' 2 W-GOO
(A.M. Wilson, pre-1944)
Perianth segments overlapping; corona deep apricot, with green at base

'Tundra' 2 W-W
(J. Bankhead, pre-1950)

'Tungamah' 2 Y-O
(J.N. Hancock & Co., pre-1949)
Corona deep reddish orange

'Tungi' 2 W-Y
(W. Jackson Sr, 1944)
'Thubui' × 'Dawnglow'

'Tunis' 2 W-WWY
(P.D. Williams, pre-1927)
'King Alfred' hybrid
Fl. 115 mm wide, ivory or milk white; perianth segments broadly ovate, blunt, fairly prominently mucronate, a little inflexed, with margins slightly wavy or recurved, somewhat irregular, overlapping a quarter to one-third; corona cylindrical, with pale amber yellow at rim, mouth expanded and a little frilled, rim irregularly notched and crenate. Mid-season. 2n=28

'Tupare' 1 W-Y
(G.C. Yeates) G.C. Yeates, 1972
'Beau Vite' × 'Polindra'
Fl. 103 mm wide. AM(e)(NZ) 1975

'Turakina' 1 W-Y
(D.S. Bell) D.S. Bell, 1983
'My Love' hybrid
Corona bright yellow, or sometimes buff (near to 11C)

'Turangi' 2 Y-Y
(J.S. Leitch) J.S. Leitch, 1967
Fl. 108 mm wide

'Turenne' 11a Y-Y
(J. Gerritsen & Son) J. Gerritsen & Son, 1983
'Floralie' hybrid
Fl. forming a double triangle; perianth segments ovate, inflexed; the inner segments narrower and more strongly inflexed; corona as broad as or broader than the perianth segments and two-thirds their length, bi-lobed

N. × *turgaliensis* Dorda Alcaraz & Fernández Casas 13 (parentage: *N. bulbocodium* Linnaeus subsp. *bulbocodium* var. *conspicuus* (Haworth) Baker × *N. jonquilla* Linnaeus) = *N.* × *abilioi*

N. turgidus Salisbury = *N. bulbocodium*

'Turica' 3 W-? (b)
(D. Blanchard, pre-1948)

'Turin' 3 W-GOO
(P.D. Williams, pre-1927)
Perianth segments of good substance; corona disc-shaped, reddish orange, with yellow-green at base. 2n=28. AM(e) 1927

'Turk' 1 Y-O
(John R.Reed) John R.Reed, 1995
Selection from Evans sdlg Q20 ('Arctic Gold' × 'Brer Fox') × 'Sutton Court'; sdlg no. 81-30-7
Fl. 104 mm wide; perianth segments broadly ovate, light yellow; corona narrowly funnel-shaped, deep orange. Mid-season. Sunproof

'Turkish Delight' 2 W-? (b or c)
(Sir C.H. Cave, pre-1928)

'Turkish Delight' 2 W-P
(J.N. Hancock & Co., 1965) Unregistered

'Turkish Patrol' 2 Y-R
(G. Lewis) D.S. Bell, 1955
Perianth segments deep yellow; corona expanded, deep red

'Turn About' 2 W-? (b)
(A.H. Ahrens) J.S. Leitch, 1955

'Turncoat' 6 W-O
(Brian S. Duncan) Rathowen Daffodils, 1984
'Richill' × 'Foundling'; sdlg no. 341
Fl. 57 mm wide; perianth segments white, becoming flushed with coppery pink at base, reflexed; corona opening red, becoming orange and later coppery pink. Mid-season

'Turning Point' 2 YYW-WWY
(M.E.Brogden, pre-1997) Unregistered
'Star Tracker' × Silcock sdlg; sdlg no. 354/P5

'Turntable' 2 Y-GWY
(Mrs H.H. Simmons) Mrs H.H. Simmons, 1976
'White Spire' × 'Green Island'
Fl. 105 mm wide; perianth segments opening white, becoming greenish yellow. Mid-season

'Turon' 1 Y-Y
(S. Morrison) T. Morrison, 1960
Fl. golden yellow

'Turtle' 3 W-O
(Mrs R.O. Backhouse, pre-1921)
Fl. 59 mm wide; perianth segments white, with lemon at base, reflexed, overlapping two-thirds; corona very shallow bowl-shaped, orange, with

reddish orange at rim, frilled

'Tuscan' 2 Y-YYO
(A.M. Wilson, pre-1927)
'Fleetwing' × 'Hospodar'
Fl. 114 mm wide, facing slightly downwards; perianth segments bright sulphur, overlapping at base only; corona funnel-shaped, lemon yellow, tinged orange at rim. Mid-season. *C(g) 1931

'Tuscan Bonnet' 1 W-Y
(pre-1896)
Perianth segments pale creamy white; corona pale canary yellow

'Tuscan Hills' 1 Y-Y
(D.N.Y. Olson) D.N.Y. Olson, 1993
'Spanish Gold' × 'Valley Gold'; sdlg no. 82/75/2
Fl. forming a double triangle, 120 mm wide, medium yellow; perianth segments broadly ovate, acute, with white mucro, spreading, overlapping half; the inner segments with margins wavy; corona cylindrical, smooth, with mouth expanded and lightly frilled, rim deeply notched. Mid-season

'Tuscany' 2 W-? (b)
(Mrs R.O. Backhouse, pre-1921)

'Tuscarora' 1 Y-Y
(W.A. Bender) W.A. Bender, 1990
('Slieveboy' × ['Kingscourt' × ?'Shah']) × 'Gold Convention'; sdlg no. 225
Fl. 102 mm wide; perianth segments very broadly ovate, brilliant greenish yellow 5A, spreading, smooth, overlapping; corona cylindrical, narrow, constricted near mid-point, vivid yellow 12A, with mouth slightly expanded, rim rolled. Early

'Tuskar Light' 2 W-YYR
(J.L. Richardson, pre-1937)
'Mitylene' × 'Sunstar'
Perianth segments pure white; corona large, pale lemon yellow, with clear red at rim

'Tutanekai' 2 (a)
(R. Hyde) R. Hyde, 1957
Syn. 'Gold Standard'

'Tutankhamun' 2 W-GWW
(Mrs J. Abel Smith) Mrs J. Abel Smith, 1972
'Ave' × 'Empress of Ireland'; sdlg no. L3/82
Fl. forming a double triangle, 126 mm wide, greenish white 155C; perianth segments very broad in outline, blunt or rounded at apex, variably mucronate, spreading, plane, overlapping half; the inner segments narrower, a little inflexed, somewhat twisted or with margins wavy, angular at shoulder; corona ribbed, with brilliant yellow-green 154B at base, mouth expanded and wavy, rim shallowly rolled and more or less entire. Mid-season. 2n=28. PC(e) 1974,

AM(e) 1975

'Tu Tu' 5 W-W
(Mrs G. Link) Mrs G. Link, 1979
'Green Hills' × *N. triandrus*; sdlg no. 2470
Fls 1-2 per stem, 70 mm wide; perianth segments slightly reflexed, overlapping; corona almost disc-shaped, heavily ribbed, with green at base on opening. Mid-season.

'Twain's Gold' 8 Y-Y
(L.S. Hannibal) L.S. Hannibal, 1990
Hybrid between 'Fortune' and a selection from wild-collected *N. tazetta*
Fls 3-4 per stem; perianth segments yellow; corona cup-shaped, orange-yellow. Mid-season

'Tweedle Dee' 5 Y-Y
(J.N. Hancock & Co., 1979) Unregistered

'Tweedsmouth' 9 W-YYR
(G. Harrison) G. Harrison, 1968
Sdlg × 'Actaea'

'Tweeny' 2 W-Y
(A. Gray, pre-1950)
Div. 2 × *N. rupicola* subsp. *watieri*
Corona citron yellow. Dwarf. Very late

'Twelve Gauge' 2 YYW-WWY
(R.G.Cull) Hokorawa Daffodils, 1996
'Lemon Haze' × 'Daydream'
Fl. 97 mm wide. Mid-season

'Twenty-four Karat' 1 Y-Y
(Murray W. Evans, 1968) T.D. Throckmorton, 1979
'Galway' hybrid × 'Arctic Gold'; sdlg no. N46/2
Fl. 102 mm wide, facing slightly upwards, smooth; perianth segments spreading and plane. Early to mid-season

'Twentyniner' 2 Y-Y
(L.P. Dettman) L.P. Dettman, 1975
'Dalai' × 'Kingscourt'; sdlg no. 3/71
Fl. 81 mm wide; perianth segments vivid yellow 9A; corona darker in tone (14A). Early. Resembles 'Dalai' but with a more deeply coloured perianth

'Twerp' 1 W-P
(Jackson's Daffodils) Jackson's Daffodils, 1996
'Valiant' × 'Vivacious'; sdlg no. 81/87
Fl. 113 mm wide; perianth segments broadly ovate, greenish white (155A); corona funnel-shaped, light yellowish pink 27A, with mouth flared. Early to mid-season

'Twicer' 2 Y-YOO
(D. Jackson) Jackson's Daffodils, 1982
'Yoone' × 'True Orbit'; sdlg no. 198/75
Fl. 116 mm wide. Mid-season

'Twilight' 1 W-W
(W. Welchman, pre-1908)

'Twilight' 2 W-Y
(J.N. Hancock & Co., 1949) J.N. Hancock & Co., 1960
Corona pale lemon yellow

'Twilight Zone' 2 YYW-WWY
(G.W.E. Brogden, 1979) Brogden Bulbs, 1991
'Gold Bank' × 'Daydream'; sdlg no. x74/G22
Fl. 110 mm wide; perianth segments ovate, acute, mid-lemon yellow, with a broad band of white at base, plane, smooth; corona cylindrical, becoming white, with the upper half light lemon yellow, mouth straight and wavy, rim crenate. Early to mid-season

'Twillo' 4 W-Y
(Jackson's Daffodils) Jackson's Daffodils, 1986
Sdlg × 'Mount Somers'; sdlg no. 28/78
Corona opening light greenish yellow 5D, becoming paler (4D). Early to mid-season

'Twin' 9 W-YYR
(G.H. Engleheart, pre-1930)
Fls 1-2 per stem, 67 mm wide; perianth segments white, with lemon at base, overlapping half; corona almost disc-shaped, lemon, with bright red at rim. Late. *AM(m) 1930

'Twink' 4 Y-O
(de Graaff Bros, pre-1925)
Perianth and other petaloid segments in three whorls, broadly ovate, blunt or squarish at apex, pale primrose yellow, flushed white, with margins wavy or twisted, overlapping at base only; the outer whorl a little inflexed; the second whorl only a little shorter, more strongly inflexed; the centre whorl half the length of the second, strongly inflexed, with margins incurled; corona segments short, clustered among the petaloid segments, glowing orange, frilled. Early. 2n=21. AM(Haarlem) 1926

'Twinkle' 3 Y-R
(Mrs R.O. Backhouse, pre-1921)
Perianth segments yellow, suffused pink at base; corona deep cherry red. AM(Haarlem) 1929

'Twinklepink' 5 ?-P
(V. Brink) V. Brink, 1968
'Pink Fancy' × 'Thalia'
Fl. 70 mm wide; perianth segments strongly reflexed; corona strong salmon pink. Late

'Twinkletoes' 1 W-W
(W.M. Spry, pre-1975) Unregistered
'Snow Maid' × Fairbairn sdlg
Very early

'Twinkling Eye' 2 (a)
(G. Zandbergen-Terwegen, pre-1937)

'Twinkling Star' 2 (a)
(G. Zandbergen-Terwegen, pre-1937)

"Twin Sisters"
Syn. of $N. \times medioluteus$

'Twiscob' 3 W-? (b)
(A.M. Wilson, pre-1950)

'Two Step' 11a W-W
(A.N. Kanouse, 1956) A.N. Kanouse, 1976
'Hillbilly' × 'Mabel Taylor'
Fl. 92 mm wide; corona segments lightly frilled. Mid-season. Somewhat resembles 'Doll Dance'

'Twotees' 11b W-P/W
(H.G. Cross, 1981) H.G. Cross, 1991
'Precedent' × 'Romance'; sdlg no. 5301
Fl. 95 mm wide; perianth segments very broad in outline, blunt or rounded at apex, not prominently mucronate, yellowish white 158D, spreading, plane, with margins slightly incurling, overlapping half; the inner segments slightly inflexed, somewhat concave; corona split to base, the six segments half as long as the perianth segments and more-or-less alternate to them, squarish at apex, with a broad longitudinal band of yellow-pink (22D) at midrib shading to dusky pink (41D) at apex, flanked by white, spreading or a little inflexed, lightly frilled. Late

'Twotone' 2 Y-Y
(R.C.A. Tombleson) R.C.A. Tombleson, 1964
Fl. 115 mm wide; corona slightly darker in tone than the perianth. Mid-season

'Tycho' 2 (a)
(pre-1940)

'Tyee' 2 W-P
(Murray W. Evans) Murray W. Evans, 1973
'Propriety' × ('Interim' × 'Wild Rose')
Fl. 108 mm wide

'Tykky-dew' 2 W-GWP
(A.J.R.Pearson) A.J.R.Pearson, 1995
Sdlg 72-11-C23 ('Cloneen' × 'Interim') × 'Foundling'; sdlg no. 87-62-K37
Fl. 110 mm wide; perianth segments fairly narrow, greenish white, strongly reflexed, smooth; corona cup-shaped, with rounded sides, smooth, white, with shades of bluish pink on ageing, with green at base and a narrow band of pink at rim, with the rim lightly crenate. Mid-season. Syn. 'Dawn Sky'

'Tynan' 2 W-P
(Carncairn Daffodils) Carncairn Daffodils, 1973
'Pink o' Dawn' × 'Rose Royale'
Fl. 92 mm wide; perianth segments slightly reflexed;

corona cylindrical, slightly frilled

'Tyndall' 2 W-P
(C.E. Radcliff, 1946) J.M.Radcliff, 1956
('Pinkeen' × 'Dawnglow') × 'Roselands'

'Tynedale' 3 W-O
(G. Harrison) G. Harrison, 1968
'Red Hackle' × 'Mahmoud'
Fl. 92 mm wide; corona deep orange. Mid-season. Resembles a large-flowered 'Mahmoud'

'Tyneham' 3 W-R
(J.W. Blanchard) J.W. Blanchard, 1974
Sdlg 46/102A ('Red Hackle' × 'Conbeg') × 'Avenger'; sdlg no. 61/38A
Fl. 95 mm wide; perianth segments broad; corona red, heavily frilled. Mid-season. Resembles 'Hotspur' but with a shorter and more heavily frilled corona

'Tynemouth' 3 W-Y
(G. Harrison) G. Harrison, 1968
'Chinese White' × 'Clockface'

'Typhoon' 2 Y-? (a)
(G.H. Johnstone, pre-1944)

'Tyrant' 1 W-W
(J.S. Leitch) J.S. Leitch, 1968

'Tyrella' 1 Y-Y
(Ballydorn Bulb Farm, 1975) Ballydorn Bulb Farm, 1996
'Golden Aura' × 'Viking' hybrid
Fl. 90 mm wide, deep golden yellow; perianth segments broad, smooth; corona flared, with rim more or less entire. Early to mid-season

'Tyrian Rose' 2 W-GPP
(Brian S.Duncan) Brian S.Duncan, 1992
'Fragrant Rose' × 'Ken's Favorite'; sdlg no. 995
Fl. 104 mm wide; perianth segments broadly ovate, glistening white, spreading, plane; corona funnel-shaped, broad, slightly ribbed, bright deep pink, with green at base, mouth lobed. Mid-season. Sunproof

'Tyro' 2 (a)
(Mrs R.O. Backhouse, pre-1921)

'Tyrod' 1 Y-Y
(W. Jackson Jr) Jackson's Daffodils, 1980
'Warbin' × 'Otewa'; sdlg no. 51/72
Fl. 115 mm wide. Early to mid-season

'Tyrol' 9
(F. Rijnveld & Sons, pre-1939)

'Tyrol' 1 W-W
(J.L. Richardson) J.L. Richardson, 1958

'Killaloe' × 'Truth'

'Tyrone' 2 (a)
(S.C. Gaspar, 1946) R.J. Abernethy, 1957

'Tyrone Gold' 1 Y-Y
(Brian S. Duncan) Rathowen Daffodils, 1986
'Golden Jewel' × 'Midas Touch'; sdlg no. 729
Fl. deep golden yellow, smooth; perianth segments broadly ovate, blunt, with prominent white mucro, spreading, plane, overlapping half; the inner segments rounded at apex, only very slightly mucronate, inflexed at base, recurved at apex, somewhat twisted; corona cylindrical, smooth, with mouth ribbed and widely expanded, wavy, rim obscurely crenate. Early to mid-season

'Tyros' 2 W-R
(R.H.Glover, pre-1993) Unregistered

'Tyrrheus' 1 W-? (b)
(Barr & Sons, pre-1923)

'Tyson's Corner' 3 W-GYR
(W.G. Pannill, 1972) W.G. Pannill, 1988
'Larry' × ('Milan' × 'Snow Gem'); sdlg no. 72/13
Fl. 85 mm wide. Late

'Tyson's Kid' 9 W-GYR
(Mrs M.S.Yerger) Mrs M.S.Yerger, 1994
'Dulcimer' open pollinated; sdlg no. /6 A 23
Fl. forming a double triangle, 40 mm wide; perianth segments rounded at apex, deeply overlapping; the inner segments narrower, with margins infolded; corona cup-shaped, brilliant greenish yellow 1B, with light yellowish green 135D at base and orange-red (30A) at rim. Dwarf. Late

U

'Uam Var' 1 W-Y
(The Brodie of Brodie, c.1911)
'Madame de Graaff' × 'Lord Roberts'

'Ubero' 2 (a)
(W.A. Grace, pre-1938)

'Uckfield' 1 (a)
(G.P. Haydon, pre-1910)

'Ucluelet Gem' 5
(C.T.Hilton, pre-1947)
2n=21. See also 'Ucluluet Gem'

'Ucluluet Gem' 5
Syn. of 'Ucluelet Gem'

'Ufo' 3 Y-YOO
(W.F. Leenen) W.F. Leenen, 1980
Fl. 105 mm wide; perianth segments greenish yellow (4D); corona orange, with yellow at base, and with green prominent in tube. Mid-season

'Uganda' 2 W-? (b)
(R.H. Bath, pre-1931)

'Uki' 2 Y-Y
(T.H. Piper, c.1966) Unregistered
'Golden Cockerel' × 'Khem'

'Ukraine'
(The Brodie of Brodie, c.1917)
'Cossack' × 'Socrates'

'Ulala' 2 W-? (b)
(Mrs M. Moorby) Mrs M. Moorby, 1957

'Ulic' 2 (a)
(P.D. Williams, pre-1931)

'Ulla' 2 (a)
(E.M. Crosfield, pre-1934)

'Ullswater' 1 W-W
(G.L. Wilson) E. Longford, 1969
'Rashee' × 'White Prince'

'Ulrico' 1 W-? (b)
(Barr & Sons, pre-1929)

'Ulster Bank' 3 Y-R
(Brian S. Duncan) Rathowen Daffodils, 1978
'Carbineer' × 'Air Marshal'; sdlg no. 303
Fl. rounded, 95 mm wide; perianth segments very broad, rounded at apex, deep golden yellow, with slight white mucro, sometimes flushed orange at base, spreading, plane, of thick and waxy texture, overlapping half or more; the inner segments narrower, roundish, sometimes truncate; corona bowl-shaped, finely ribbed, fiery orange-red, with mouth widely expanded and even. Mid-season

'Ulster Beauty' 2 W-WWY
(W.J. Dunlop, pre-1952)
'Gracious' × 'Trousseau'
Corona white, with lemon at rim

'Ulster Bride' 4 W-O
(H.G. Cross) H.G. Cross, 1985
'Northern Light' × 'Acropolis'; sdlg no. 116-6
Perianth and other petaloid segments in four whorls regularly superimposed, very broadly ovate, blunt, prominently mucronate, clear white, slightly inflexed, somewhat concave, with midrib showing, overlapping half; the inner whorls successively shorter and becoming more strongly inflexed, with margins incurled or strongly incurled; corona segments short, clustered at centre and more loosely interspersed among the surrounding petaloid segments, vivid orange 28B, frilled. Late

'Ulster Bullion' 2 Y-Y
(Ballydorn Bulb Farm) Ballydorn Bulb Farm, 1984
'Golden Clarion' × 'Galway'
Fl. 115 mm wide, deep yellow. Early to mid-season

'Ulster Chieftain' 2 W-YOR
(T. Bloomer) T. Bloomer, 1964
'Kilworth' × ('Red Hackle' × 'Glenwherry'); sdlg no. 4/12/57

'Ulster Contrast' 2 W-O
(T. Bloomer) T. Bloomer, 1964
'Arbar' × 'Bravura'; sdlg no. 1/16/52

'Ulster Knight' 2 W-R
(T. Bloomer) T. Bloomer, 1964
('Red Hackle' × 'Arbar') × Richardson sdlg 202; sdlg no. 1/57/58
Perianth segments broadly ovate; corona red

'Ulster Lass' 1 W-W
(D.S. Bell) D.S. Bell, 1982
'Glacier' × 'Ulster Queen'
Fl. 105 mm wide. Mid-season

'Ulster Love' 2 W-P
(John R.Reed) John R.Reed, 1995
'Valinor' × 'Verran'; sdlg no. 85-40-1
Fl. forming a double triangle, 90 mm wide; perianth segments ovate, smooth; corona deep pink, with a paler tone outside. Mid-season to late. Sunproof

'Ulster Maiden' 2 W-R
(T. Bloomer) T. Bloomer, 1964
'Blarney' × 'Arbar'; sdlg no. 10/29/52

'Ulster Prince' 1 Y-Y
(G.L. Wilson, pre-1950)
'Hebron' × 'Mortlake'
Fl. 102 mm wide; perianth segments brilliant greenish yellow 5B, overlapping half; corona slightly ribbed, vivid yellow 12A, with mouth expanded and frilled, rim flanged and dentate. Early. *AM(g) 1959, *FCC(g) 1968, AGM 1993

'Ulster Princess' 2 W-R
(T. Bloomer) T. Bloomer, 1964
'Fermoy' × 'Arbar'; sdlg no. 21/22/53
Corona deep red, with green at base

'Ulster Queen' 1 W-W
(G.L. Wilson) Mrs H.K. Richardson, 1962
'Empress of Ireland' × 'Vigil'; sdlg no. 47/4
Perianth segments very broadly ovate, of thick substance; corona frilled

'Ulster Standard' 1 ?-Y
(T. Bloomer) T. Bloomer, 1964
'Cargan' × 'Standard Bearer'; sdlg no. 2/25/58

'Ulster Star' 2 W-R
(T. Bloomer) T. Bloomer, 1964
('Fermoy' × 'Arbar') × Richardson sdlg 260; sdlg no. 1/17/60
Perianth segments slightly inflexed; corona bowl-shaped

'Ultima' 2 W-R
(W. Jackson Jr, 1970) Unregistered
Sdlg 9/62 × 'Arbar'; sdlg no. 52/70

'Ultima Thule'
(pre-1915)

'Ultimus' 2 Y-O
(C.G. van Tubergen, pre-1947)
2n=28+4B

'Ulverstone Star' 2 W-W
(R.H.Glover, pre-1989) Unregistered
'Panache' × 'Heralding'

'Ulysses' 1 W-? (b)
(C. Dawson, pre-1923)

'Uma' 1 W-? (b)
(W. Jackson Jr, 1956) Unregistered
'Tamara' × 'Preamble'

'Umbra' 1 W-? (b)
(T. Batson, pre-1913)

'Umbria' 2 W-Y
(J.M. de Navarro, pre-1952)
'Green Island' × 'Galilee'

'Umbriel' 4 W-YOO
(W.F.M. Copeland, pre-1909)
Perianth and other petaloid segments in 4 to 5 whorls, creamy; corona segments bright orange with yellow at base, frilled

'Umfolozi' 2 (a)
(A.M. Wilson, pre-1936)

'Umona' 1 W-? (b)
(A.M. Wilson, pre-1916)

'Umpqua' 2 (a)
(Oregon Bulb Farms, pre-1951)

'Una' 2 W-YYO
(G.H. Engleheart, pre-1899)
Fl. facing slightly downwards; perianth segments ovate, mucronate, creamy white, a little inflexed, with margins recurved in lower half, overlapping only slightly; corona straight-sided, slightly expanding, loosely ribbed, bright lemon yellow, tinged apricot at rim, with mouth straight and lightly frilled

'Una' 3? ?-O (a or b)
(pre-1936)
'Silver Plane' hybrid

'Una' 2 Y-O
A. Ladson, 1960
Perianth segments primrose yellow; corona opening pale in tone, becoming light orange

'Una Bremner' 2 Y-OYY
(D.C. MacArthur) D.C. MacArthur, 1985
'Rouge' × 'Chungking'; sdlg no. E822
Perianth segments very broad in outline, blunt or rounded at apex, slightly mucronate, light greenish yellow 4C, spreading, overlapping half; the inner segments narrower, a little inflexed, somewhat creased, with margins wavy; corona flared, ribbed, vivid yellow 13A, shading to yellow-orange (17B) at base, frilled. Mid-season. Scented

'Una Dunbar' 3 Y-? (a)
(Mrs R.O. Backhouse, pre-1921)

'Unaware' 3 W-R
(P. Phillips) P. Phillips, 1978
Fl. 102 mm wide; corona red. Early to mid-season. Resembles 'Arbar' but with a smaller and darker-coloured corona

'Uncas' 2 Y-YOO
(Murray W. Evans) Mrs J.B. Capen, 1989
'Paricutin' × ('Ardour' × 'Rustom Pasha'); sdlg no. G-9
Fl. 99 mm wide; perianth segments pale sulphur yellow, corona somewhat flared, smooth, intense reddish orange, paling to yellow at base, with a spot of green at centre, mouth only a little wavy. Mid-season. Sunproof

'Uncial'
(pre-1915)

'Uncle Ben' 1 Y-O
(Mrs J. Abel Smith) Mrs J. Abel Smith, 1980
'Charioteer' × 'Uncle Remus'; sdlg no. G7/32
Fl. 89 mm wide; corona frilled. Early. Resembles an 'Uncle Remus' of improved form

'Uncle Duncan' 1 Y-O
(A.J.R. Pearson) A.J.R. Pearson, 1991
Sdlg 72-8-C16 × sdlg 70-10-C16; sdlg no. 85-3-J17
Fl. forming a double triangle, 95 mm wide; perianth segments plane, smooth; corona funnel-shaped, with apple green noticeable in tube, mouth neatly ribbed, with rim rolled. Mid-season. Sunproof

'Uncle Remus' 1 Y-O
(W.O. Backhouse) M.J. Jefferson-Brown, 1975
Perianth segments gold; corona deep scarlet-orange. Resembler a smaller and more prolific 'Brer Fox'

'Uncle Robert' 1 W-W
(E.M. Crosfield, pre-1908)
Fl. large; perianth segments inflexed; corona creamy white, with mouth expanded and frilled

'Uncle Roland' 2 W-P
(Evalds Paupers) Evalds Paupers, 1986
'Debutante' × 'Accent'; sdlg no. P-78-59
Perianth segments pure white; corona funnel-shaped, light yellowish pink 27B. Very late

'Undaunted' 1 Y-Y
(T.H. Piper, 1954)
'Carbine' × 'Roundabout'

'Undertone' 2 Y-P
(Brian S. Duncan) Rathowen Daffodils, 1977
'Binkie' hybrid × Richardson sdlg 3341; sdlg no. 86
Fl. 115 mm wide; perianth segments lemon yellow; corona light salmon pink. Mid-season

'Undine' 3 W-W
(G.H. Engleheart, pre-1903)
Perianth segments snow white, inflexed; corona straight-sided, deeply ribbed, creamy white

'Ungava' 1 W-W
(Mrs B.T. Simpson) Mrs B.T. Simpson, 1966
Fl. 115 mm wide, of smooth texture. Late. Resembles 'Vigil'

'Unicolor'
Syn. of *N. papyraceus*

N. unicolor Tenore = *N. papyraceus*

'Unicorn' 1 (a)
(G.D. Davison, pre-1911)

'Unicorn' 1 W-Y
(J.N. Hancock & Co., 1973) Unregistered

'Unicum' 2 Y-O
(G.B. de Vroomen & Sons) G.B. de Vroomen & Sons, 1958
Perianth segments brilliant greenish yellow 6C; corona strong orange 30D

'Unionist' 2 Y-R
(J.N. Hancock & Co., 1960) Unregistered

'Union Jack' 2 W-? (b)
(G. Lewis) D.S. Bell, 1955

'Unique' 1 W-? (b)

(R.H. Bath, pre-1907)

'Unique' 4 W-Y
(J.L. Richardson) G. Zandbergen-Terwegen, 1961
'Falaise' hybrid
Fl. rounded, 105 mm wide; perianth and other petaloid segments in three whorls, broadly ovate, blunt, only very slightly mucronate, creamy white, overlapping half; the outer whorl spreading, plane; the second whorl inflexed, concave or with margins incurling; the centre whorl strongly inflexed, with margins tightly incurled; corona segments short, clustered among the centre petaloid segments, broad, brilliant yellow 7B, frilled. Mid-season. 2n=28. AM(Haarlem) 1961, AM(e) 1979, FCC(e) 1980

'Unitoi' 1 Y-Y
(Barr & Sons, pre-1927)
Fl. rounded; perianth segments soft yellow; corona straight-sided, dark yellow, with rim flared

'Unity' 1 Y-P
(Murray W. Evans) Murray W. Evans, 1980
('Daydream' × 'Lunar Sea') × 'Rima'; sdlg no. N-91
Fl. 105 mm wide. Early to mid-season

'Unity Hope' 2 W-? (b or c)
(pre-1927)

'Universe' 1 (a)
(F.D.B. Cobb) G. Zandbergen-Terwegen, 1957

'Unley' 2 (a)
(H.A. Brown, pre-1938)

'Uno' 1 W-W
(M. van Waveren & Sons, pre-1953)

'Unpainted' 1 W-W
(A.O. Roblin, c.1956) Unregistered
'Samar' × 'Broughshane'

'Unrivalled' 2 W-? (b)
(Mrs R.O. Backhouse, pre-1921)
Perianth segments sulphur white. AM(Haarlem) 1930

'Unspoilt' 2 W-W
(J.L. Richardson, pre-1949)

'Unsurpassable' 1 Y-Y
(G. Lubbe & Son, pre-1923)
Fl. 108 mm wide; perianth segments broadly ovate, blunt, slightly mucronate, brilliant greenish yellow 6B, inflexed, with margins strongly recurved, overlapping a quarter; corona cylindrical, smooth, vivid yellow 14B, with mouth expanded and frilled, rim widely flanged, deeply notched and crenate. Very early. 2n=27+1B. Syn. 'Insurpassable'. AM(Haarlem) 1923, FCC(Haarlem) 1926, *AM(p) 1975

'Up' 2 W-O
(P. Phillips) P. & G. Phillips, 1975
Fl. 111 mm wide. Mid-season. Resembles a taller 'Professor Einstein' with a differently coloured corona of less regular outline

'Upcott' 2 W-? (b)
(Mrs R.O. Backhouse, pre-1921)

'Up Front' 1 Y-Y
(G.E. Mitsch) G.E. Mitsch, 1963
'King of the North' × 'Content'; sdlg no. M49/13
Fl. luminous lemon yellow; corona flared and frilled. Mid-season

'Uphaz' 1 Y-Y
(S.J. Bisdee, 1943)
'Golden City' × 'Sorley Boy'

'Upkeep' 2 W-Y
(J.N. Hancock & Co., 1948) J.N. Hancock & Co., 1965
'Truth' × 'Ivo Fell'
Perianth segments pure white, of thick substance, deeply overlapping; corona short, bright yellow, with mouth straight. Mid-season. Resembles a more refined 'Polindra'

'Upper Broughton' 2 W-P
(Mrs J. Abel Smith) Mrs J. Abel Smith, 1980
'Stainless' × 'Jewel Song'; sdlg no. E0/51
Fls 87 mm wide; corona pale or very pale pink, with a darker tone at rim. Late. Resembles 'Stainless' but with a differently coloured corona

'Up Periscope' 2 W-YWY
(K. McCombe) J.N. Hancock & Co., 1979
'Green Island' hybrid × 'Emerald'
Fl. 100 mm wide. Late

'Upper Ten' 2 W-? (b)
(Mrs R.O. Backhouse, pre-1921)
AM(Haarlem) 1938

'Upright' 1 (a)
(G.L. Wilson, pre-1947)

'Upshot' 3 W-PPR
(Murray W. Evans, 1979) Estella L. Evans, 1992
'Quasar' × (sdlg × 'Everpink'); sdlg no. W-2/3
Fl. 103 mm wide, rounded; perianth segments broad, reflexed; corona cup-shaped, ribbed towards mouth, deep reddish pink, paling at base at maturity, with mouth expanded and very slightly frilled. Mid-season

'Upshot' 1 Y-Y
(P.Cleine, pre-1981) Unregistered
Sdlg no. 4/81C
Fl. bright sulphur yellow; perianth segments broadly ovate; corona funnel-shaped, rim neatly rolled and dentate. Early

'Upstart' 1 (a)
(T. Batson, pre-1913)

'Up-to-Date' 2 (a)
(G. Zandbergen-Terwegen, pre-1937)

'Uptown' 2 W-P
(Jackson's Daffodils, 1976) Jackson's Daffodils, 1987
Sdlg 22/69 × 'Vahu'; sdlg no. 133/76
Fl. forming a double triangle; perianth segments very broadly ovate, blunt, with margins incurling at apex, very slightly mucronate, yellowish white 155D, spreading, overlapping half; the inner segments more narrowly ovate, with margins sometimes wavy; corona funnel-shaped, narrow at base, ribbed, orange-pink (28D), with mouth widely expanded, rim shallowly rolled and minutely crenate. Mid-season

'Upward' 2 (a)
(A.H. Ahrens) J.S. Leitch, 1956

'Urach' 2 W-? (b)
(W.A. Grace, pre-1938)

'Urangan' 2 W-Y
(C.E. Radcliff, 1932)
'Bernardino' × 'Seville'

'Urania' 3 (a)
(C.G. van Tubergen, pre-1944)

'Uranus' 2 W-? (b)
(G. Lubbe & Son, pre-1943)

'Urbane' 2 W-YOY
(Murray W. Evans) Murray W. Evans, 1979
'Marshfire' × 'Hotspur'; sdlg no. N-36
Fl. 95 mm wide. Mid-season

'Urchin' 2 W-P
(Brian S. Duncan) Rathowen Daffodils, 1981
'Roseworthy' × ?'Foundling'; sdlg no. 448
Corona frilled. Mid-season. 2n=28. Resembles 'Foundling' but with a frilled corona of bronze pink

'Urchin' 3 Y-O
Syn. of 'Pzaz'

'Ursa' 2 W-WPP
(J.M. Radcliff, 1947) P. Phillips, 1966
Fl. 115 mm wide; corona soft pink, paling to base. Mid-season. Resembles 'Cantatrice' in form

'Ursula' 2 (a)
(pre-1907)

'Ursula' 2 W-YYP
(J.N. Hancock & Co., 1968) Unregistered

'Ursus' 2 W-? (b)
(J.W.A. Lefeber, pre-1941)

'Usan' 2 W-Y
(W. Jackson Sr, 1940)
'Nimue' × 'Pinkeen'

'Useful' 3 W-? (b)
(Warnaar & Co., pre-1930)

'Utah' 2 (a)
(F. Rijnveld & Sons, pre-1939)

'Utgard' 1 W-? (b)
(P.D. Williams, pre-1948)

'Utiku' 6 Y-Y
(M.Hamilton) Koanga Daffodils, 1993
'Ristin' × *N. cyclamineus*; sdlg no. 15-86
Fl. 84 mm wide; perianth segments very broadly ovate, blunt, vivid yellow 12A, spreading at first, soon becoming strongly reflexed, overlapping half; the outer segments overlapping one another; the inner segments square-shouldered at base; corona cylindrical, very lightly ribbed, darker in tone (15A) than the perianth, with mouth slightly flared, even, rim minutely crenate. Early

'Utopia' 3 W-? (b)
(F. Rijnveld & Sons, pre-1939)
?'Pickwick' × 'Ornatus'
AM(Haarlem) 1940

V

'Vacuna' 1 W-Y
(Barr & Sons, pre-1913)
Corona pale yellow, with rim lightly flanged

'Vaga' 1 Y-Y
(W. Jackson Sr, 1944)
'Chromis' × 'Vuster'

'Vagabond' 1 (a)
(Sir C.H. Cave, pre-1928)

'Vagabond' 2 Y-R
(J.L. Richardson) Rathowen Daffodils, 1975
Perianth segments deep golden, slightly suffused orange at the base; corona deep orange-red. Early to mid-season

'Vagabond' 1 Y-Y
(A.J. Sherriff, c.1966) Unregistered
Sdlg × 'Melissa'

'Vagabond' 2 Y-O
(J.N. Hancock & Co., pre-1988) Unregistered

'Vagabond Prince' 2 (a)
(Warnaar & Co., pre-1938)

'Vago' 2 Y-Y
(W. Jackson Jr) W. Jackson Jr, 1971
sdlg 65/57 × 'Haka'; sdlg no. 7/66
Fl. 108 mm wide. Mid-season

'Vagrant'
(C. Dawson, pre-1908)

'Vahsel Bay' 2 W-W
(J.L. Richardson) J.L. Richardson, 1956
'Spitzbergen' × 'Killaloe'
Fl. pure white; corona with mouth expanded, frilled

'Vahu' 2 W-P
(W. Jackson Jr) Jackson's Daffodils, 1979
'Cathlin' × 'Verran'; sdlg no. 30/70
Fl. 115 mm wide; perianth segments very broadly ovate, blunt, slightly mucronate, white, touched greenish yellow at base, spreading, somewhat concave, with margins incurling at apex, overlapping half; the inner segments more narrowly ovate; corona funnel-shaped, ribbed, orange-pink (25D), mouth slightly expanded and deeply 6-lobed, regularly frilled, with rim entire and slightly rolled. Mid-season. Resembles an improved 'Verran' with a deeper-pink corona

'Vain' 3 W-YYO
(R.H.Glover, pre-1993) Unregistered

'Vainqueur' 2 Y-YOO
(J.N. Hancock & Co., pre-1965) Unregistered
Perianth segments rich yellow; corona disc-shaped, ribbed, gold, flushed orange towards mouth

'Vaity' 2 W-P
(W. Jackson Jr, c.1978) Unregistered
'C.E.Radcliff' × 'Remis'

'Vakara Pasaka' 6 W-WWP
(Jānis Rukšans) Jānis Rukšans, 1986
'Jenny' × 'Chiffon'; sdlg no. R-79-18/1
Perianth segments pure snow, reflexed in some seasons; corona cup-shaped, with a well-defined band of orange-pink (32D) at rim. Early

'Valana' 2 W-P
(W. Jackson Jr) W. Jackson Jr, 1968
'Dallbro' × 'Karanja'; sdlg no. 118/62
Syn. 'Pink Gleam'

'Valaria' 1 W-W
(W. Jackson Jr, 1957) Unregistered
'Joningham' × 'Ammon'; sdlg no. 80/57

'Valda' 2 W-? (b)
(A.M. Wilson, pre-1948)

'Val d'Incles' 3 W-W
(Brian S. Duncan) Rathowen Daffodils, 1987
'Verona' × 'Cool Crystal'; sdlg no. 695
Fl. rounded; perianth segments very broad, rounded at apex, slightly mucronate, slightly reflexed, overlapping half; the inner segments a little narrower, more nearly spreading, with margins minutely incurled and slightly wavy; corona bowl-shaped, ribbed, with mouth lightly frilled, rim minutely crenate. Late

'Valdis' 2 W-GPP
(W. Jackson Jr) Jackson's Daffodils, 1979
'Remis' × 'C.E.Radcliff'; sdlg no. 8/70
Fl. 113 mm wide. Early to mid-season

'Val d'Or' 1 Y-Y
(D.S. Bell) D.S. Bell, 1955
Perianth segments very broadly ovate, ribbed; the inner segments more narrowly ovate; corona narrow, with mouth expanded, rim notched and reflexed

'Valdrome' 11a W-Y
(J. Gerritsen & Son) J. Gerritsen & Son, 1965
Perianth segments ovate, blunt, yellowish white, heavily tinged yellow at base also at midrib beneath, spreading, overlapping one-third; corona split to base, the six segments as wide and almost as long as the perianth segments and opposite and closely overlying them, bi-lobed, with the lobes overlapping, ribbed, vivid yellow, loosely frilled. Tall. Mid-season

'Valdura' 3 W-? (b)
(R.H. Bath, pre-1931)

'Vale' 1 (a)
(G.L. Wilson, pre-1942)

'Valecare' 1 W-Y
(G. Lewis) D.S. Bell, 1955

'Valediction' 3 W-GWW
(Mrs H.K. Richardson) Mrs H.K. Richardson, 1976
'Verona' × 'Benediction'
Corona with rim dentate. Mid-season

'Valencia' 4 Y-O
(de Graaff Bros, pre-1927)
Fl. large; perianth and other petaloid segments in many whorls, clear yellow; corona segments orange. AM(Haarlem) 1927, FCC(Haarlem) 1933

'Valencia' 1 W-Y
(West & Fell, pre-1936)
Corona soft yellow. Mid-season

'Valentia' 2 (a)
(J.M. de Navarro) J.L. Richardson, 1957

'Valentine' 3 W-? (b)
(Sir C.H. Cave, pre-1908)

'Valentine' 2 W-R
(M.P. Williams, pre-1949)
Fl. large; corona with green at base

'Valentine's Day' 2 Y-Y
(G.H. Johnstone, pre-1949)
'Magnificence' hybrid

'Valentino' 1 (a)
(J.W. Barr, pre-1930)

'Valentio' 5
(Barr & Sons, pre-1923)

'Valeria' 3 W-YYO
(G.H. Engleheart, pre-1903)
Perianth segments pure white; corona deep yellow, with orange at rim. AM 1903

'Valerie' 1 Y-Y
(R.H. Bath, pre-1934)

'Valerie' 2 Y-YYO
Perianth segments yellow; corona yellow with orange rim. Syn. of 'Valerie May'

'Valerie May' 2 Y-YYO
(H.A. Brown, 1944) J.N. Hancock & Co., 1960
Syn. 'Valerie'. AM 1944, FCC 1945

'Valerie Tempest' 4
(R. Tempest, pre-1932)
'Empress' sport

'Valescure' 1 (a)
(A.M. Wilson, pre-1930)

'Valet' 2 W-Y
(R.H. Bath, pre-1929)
Fl. 102 mm wide; perianth segments opening very pale sulphur white, quickly becoming creamy white, with lemon at base, with margins incurving, irregular, overlapping one-third; corona deep lemon yellow, with mouth widely expanded. Mid-season to late

'Valet' 2 W-Y
(J.J. Abernethy) R.J. Abernethy, 1960
Fl. 115 mm wide; perianth segments pure white; corona dark buff lemon yellow, frilled. Mid-season. Resembles an improved 'Bread and Cheese'

'Valetta' 1 W-W
(The Brodie of Brodie, c.1920)
'Morven' × 'Loch Lomond'
Fl. pure white; corona frilled, with rim lightly flanged. AM(e) 1926

'Valhalla' 4 Y-Y
(W.F.M. Copeland, pre-1909)
Fl. large; perianth and other petaloid segments in four whorls, broad, soft sulphur yellow; corona segments darker in tone. Early

'Valhalla' 3 W-O
(J.L. Richardson) Mrs H.K. Richardson, 1962
'Kilworth' × 'Rockall'
Fl. 111 mm wide; corona reddish orange, with rim dentate. Late

'Valiant' 1 Y-Y
(G.L. Wilson, pre-1913)
Fl. of strong substance; perianth segments spreading, with margins slightly wavy; corona with rim dentate. Tall

'Valiant' 2 W-GPP
(W. Jackson Jr, 1970) Unregistered
'Cathlin' × 'Verran'; sdlg no. 119/70

'Valiant Chief' 2 W-Y
(W.M. Spry, pre-1975) Unregistered
'Full Moon' × 'Clinton'
Corona chrome yellow

'Valiant Spark' 2 Y-O
(W. Blom & Son) W. Blom & Son, 1959
Fl. 94 mm wide; perianth segments rich golden yellow; corona bright reddish orange. Very early. 2n=28. Resembles a less vibrantly coloured 'Fortune'

'Valight' 1 Y-Y
(R.H.Glover, pre-1993) Unregistered

'Valinda' 3 W-YYO
(C.A. Nethercote, pre-1949)
Perianth segments broad, smooth; corona shallow, with pale orange at rim. Tall

'Valinor' 2 W-P
(Brian S. Duncan) Rathowen Daffodils, 1978
'Polonaise' × 'Violetta'; sdlg no. 248
Fl. 112 mm wide; perianth segments broadly ovate, blunt or a little truncate, only very slightly mucronate, spreading, overlapping half; the inner segments slightly inflexed; corona funnel-shaped, short, ribbed, deep pink, with shades of violet, mouth widely expanded, lightly frilled. Mid-season. 2n=28. Resembles a larger-flowered 'Violetta' with whiter and smoother perianth segments

'Valkyrie' 2 W-W
(H. Backhouse, pre-1914)

'Valkyrie' 3 W-W
(P.D. Williams, pre-1914)
'Silver Coin' hybrid
Corona tightly ribbed, white, with a faint green tinge at rim

'Vallee' 2 W-? (b or c)
(W.A. Grace, pre-1938)

'Vallem' 11a Y-Y
(Colin Crotty, pre-1994) Unregistered
Sdlg no. 53-81

'Valley Belle' 2 W-P
(Curtis Tolley) Curtis Tolley, 1997
'Portrait' × 'Dailmanach'; sdlg no. 88-7-10
Fl. forming a double triangle, 86 mm wide; perianth segments acute; corona funnel-shaped, dark orange-pink, lightly frilled. Mid-season

'Valleydale' 2 (a)
(Mrs M. Moorby) Mrs M. Moorby, 1957

'Valley Dew' 2 W-WWP
(Colin Crotty, 1980) Colin Crotty, 1992
'Cherryrim' × 'Kilworth'; sdlg no. 40-75
Fl. 96 mm wide; perianth segments broadly ovate, pure white, smooth, overlapping; corona bowl-shaped, white, with a broad band of deep pink at rim, slightly frilled

'Valley Flame' 2 Y-O
(Colin Crotty) Unregistered
Sdlg no. 52-75

'Valley Forge' 1 YYW-Y
(W.G. Pannill) W.G. Pannill, 1985
'Burnished Gold' × 'Daydream'; sdlg no. I 48
Perianth segments yellow, with sulphur white at base; corona tinged pale lemon yellow, becoming white in cooler conditions. Mid-season

'Valley Gold' 1 (a)
(J.R. Pearson & Sons, pre-1938)

'Valley Gold' 1 Y-Y
(E.W. Cotter) E.W. Cotter, 1968
'Arctic Gold' × 'Glenfalloch'
Fl. deep gold; corona with rim rolled and dentate

'Valley Lace' 2 W-O
(colin Crotty) Unregistered
Sdlg no. 2-79

'Valley Lode' 2 Y-Y
(Colin Crotty, 1980) Colin Crotty, 1992
'Golden Aura' × 'Camelot'; sdlg no. 54-75
Fl. 98 mm wide, deep golden yellow; perianth

segments roundish, very smooth, overlapping; corona funnel-shaped, with mouth straight and rim entire. Mid-season. Resembles a large-flowered 'Golden Aura' and a more smoothly textured 'Camelot'

'Valley Rose' 2 W-WRR
(Colin Crotty) Unregistered
Sdlg no. 38-75

'Valley Stream' 2 (a)
(L. van Leeuwen & Son, pre-1950)

'Valley Sun' 2 W-Y
(Colin Crotty) Colin Crotty, 1992
'Irish Mist' × 'Dunmurry'; sdlg no. 55-81
Fl. 98 mm wide, rounded; perianth segments pure white, with margins somewhat incurving at apex at first, smooth, overlapping; corona deep golden yellow, with mouth flared and obscurely lobed. Mid-season

'Valmai' 2 W-?
(A. Overton) A. Overton, 1960

'Valona' 8
(pre-1939)

'Valona' 2 Y-YOO
(J.T. Gray, pre-1949)
Perianth segments broad, smooth, of thick substance; corona large, reddish orange, paling to rich yellow at base

'Valona' 2 Y-O
(J.S. Leitch) J.S. Leitch, 1964
Fl. 95 mm wide

'Valor' 2 Y-Y
(K.D. Smith) K.D. Smith, 1959

'Valorous' 2
(Mrs R.O. Backhouse, pre-1921)

'Valour' 2 (a)
(W. Welchman, pre-1927)

'Valparaiso' 2 Y-? (a)
(J.L. Richardson) J.L. Richardson, 1956
'Krakatoa' × 'Mexico'

'Valpeen' 2 W-Y
(R.C.A. Tombleson) R.C.A. Tombleson, 1968
Fl. 121 mm wide; corona lemon yellow. Mid-season. Resembles a larger 'Queenswood' with a darker corona

'Valuation' 3 W-O
(Mrs R.O. Backhouse, pre-1921)
Perianth segments sulphur white; corona tightly frilled. AM(Haarlem) 1930

'Value' 1 (a)
(Sir C.H. Cave, pre-1928)

'Value' 2 W-YPP
(W. Jackson Jr) Jackson's Daffodils, 1979
'Kuprina' × 'Verran'; sdlg no. 189/70
Fl. 94 mm wide. Mid-season

'Valvalet' 1 W-W
(J.N. Hancock & Co., c.1966) Unregistered
'Eve Daly' × 'Show Valley'
Corona white, with pale cream outside, rim dentate

'Valvua' 2 Y-Y
(P. Phillips) P. Phillips, 1966
Fl. 105 mm wide. Mid-season. Resembles a larger-flowered 'Smooth Gold' with the corona rim more strongly rolled

'Vambrace' 2 W-? (b or c)
(G.H. Engleheart, pre-1923)

'Vamp' 2 W-GPP
(W. Jackson Jr) Jackson's Daffodils, 1979
Sdlg 176/66 × 'Verran'; sdlg no. 163/73
Fl. 104 mm wide. Mid-season

'Vamphire' 2 Y-YYO
(West & Fell, pre-1936)
Perianth segments deep yellow; corona with red at rim

'Vampire' 2 W-? (b)
(N.Y. Lower, pre-1933)

'Vana' 1 W-Y
(J.N. Hancock & Co., 1957) Unregistered
'Shan' × 'Melissa'
Fl. forming a double triangle; perianth segments more or less broadly ovate, blunt, slightly mucronate, pure white, spreading, with broad midrib showing, overlapping one-third; the inner segments a little inflexed, with margins wavy; corona narrowly funnel-shaped, smooth, soft lemon yellow, with mouth flared and lightly frilled, rim crenate. Tall. Late

'Vandal' 1
(A.M. Wilson, pre-1908)

'Vandar' 2 W-P
(G.J.Phillips) G.J.Phillips, 1994
'Voltage' × 'Dailmanach'; sdlg no. 82-17-1
Fl. 110 mm wide; perianth segments very broadly ovate; corona pink, with mouth flared and rim slightly dentate. Mid-season

'Van den Brande' 8?
(pre-1844)

'Van den Broeke' 1 W-? (b)
(G. Lubbe & Son, pre-1931)

'Vanderbilt' 1 (a)
(P. van Deursen, pre-1947)

'Vanderbilt' 1 Y-Y
(?Australian origin, pre-1997) Unregistered

'Van der Helst' 1 W-Y
(J. de Groot & Sons, pre-1914)
Fl. large; perianth segments spreading; corona slender, rich yellow, frilled

'Van der Hoop' 1 (a)
(G. Lubbe & Son, pre-1923)
AM(Haarlem) 1923

'Van der Scheer' 1 (a)
(Warnaar & Co., pre-1930)

'Van Dieman' 1 Y-Y
(S.J. Bisdee, pre-1939)
'Golden City' × 'Renown'

'Van Doorne's Favoriet' 2 W-Y
(Warnaar & Co.) Warnaar & Co., 1962
Fl. 115 mm wide; perianth segments ivory white; corona vivid yellow 9A. Mid-season. Resembles 'Stadium' but with a shallower corona

'Van Dyck' 1 Y-Y
(pre-1890)
Corona expanded, rich golden yellow

'Van Dyk' 8 W-O
Syn. of 'Medio Luteo Van Dyk'

'Vandyke' 2 W-YPP
(W. Jackson Jr) Jackson's Daffodils, 1979
Sdlg 22/58 × sdlg 64/63; sdlg no. 105/72
Fl. 108 mm wide. Mid-season

'Vanella' 1 W-W
(E.M. Crosfield, pre-1910)

'Vanessa' 3 Y-Y
(W. Backhouse, pre-1869)
Fl. rounded; perianth segments broadly ovate, becoming primrose yellow, with white at midrib and mucro, spreading, overlapping one-third; corona bowl-shaped, clear yellow, with mouth 6-lobed. Syn. Burbidgei 'Perfectus', Burbidgei 'Vanessa'

'Vanessa' 3 W-OOR
(D.S. Bell) D.S. Bell, 1959
'Nina' × ('Keera' × 'Bon Rose')
Fl. 112 mm wide; corona very shallow bowl-shaped, apricot, with pure red at rim. Mid-season. Resembles a larger-flowered 'Corofin' with a broader band of colour at corona rim

'Vanguard' 2 (a)
(G.H. Engleheart, pre-1923)

'Vanguard' 1 Y-Y
(D.S. Bell) D.S. Bell, 1957
'Treasure Island' × 'Pre-eminent'

'Van Helden' 8 W-Y
(pre-1846)

'Vanilla' 1 W-Y
(R.van der Schoot & Son, pre-1910)
Scented

'Vanilla Ice' 2 W-? (b)
(Alister Clark, 1930) J. Sharp, 1960

'Vanity' 9
(G.H. Engleheart, pre-1910)

'Vanity' 1 W-W
(T.H. Piper, c.1966) Unregistered
'Ave' hybrid

'Vanity Fair' 1 W-W
(Sir C.H. Cave, pre-1928)

'Vanity Fair' 2 W-YYO
(D.S. Bell) D.S. Bell, 1959
'Idealist' × 'Artist's Model'
Fl. 115 mm wide; corona closely overlying the perianth, apricot yellow, with reddish orange at rim. Mid-season

'Vanity Queen' 2 W-? (b)
(A. Gibson, pre-1950)

'Van Kempen' 1 (a)
(P. van Deursen, pre-1932)
AM(Haarlem) 1932

'Vanora' 5
(Barr & Sons, pre-1923)
'Lady Audrey' × *N. triandrus* var. *loiseleurii*

'Vanquisher' 2 W-O
(Mrs R.O. Backhouse, pre-1921)
Fl. of strong substance; perianth segments narrow, acute, sulphur white; corona widely expanded, clear orange

'Van Rijn' 1 (a)
(G. Lubbe & Son, pre-1927)

'Van Sion' 4 Y-Y
Syn. of 'Telamonius Plenus'

'Vantage' 3 W-? (b)
(Warnaar & Co., pre-1930)

'Vantage' 2 W-WPP
(Murray W. Evans) Murray W. Evans, 1970
('Shirley Wyness' × 'Interim') hybrid

'Vantage' 2 W-GPP
Syn. of 'Vascule'

'Vanto' 2 Y-YOO
(J.L. Martin) J.L. Martin, 1973
'Kai' × 'Fortune'
Fl. 97 mm wide

'Van Tromp' 1 Y-Y
(S.J. Bisdee) S.J. Bisdee, 1956
'Dawson City' × 'J.P.'

'Van Waveren's Giant' 1 Y-Y
(M. van Waveren & Sons, pre-1900)
'Emperor' hybrid
Fl. large; perianth segments primrose yellow, inflexed; corona expanded, ribbed, richer in tone then the perianth. Tall. 2n=28. FCC 1900, FCC(Haarlem) 1908

'Van Waveren's Glory' 1 (a)
(M. van Waveren & Sons, pre-1942)

'Van Waveren's Rapture' 1 (a)
(M. van Waveren & Sons, pre-1949)

'Van Weerden-Poelman' 1 (a)
(G. Lubbe & Son, pre-1925)
AM(Haarlem) 1925

'Van Wereld's Favourite' 1 W-Y
(C.A. van der Wereld, pre-1936)
2n=28. AM(Haarlem) 1934, FCC(Haarlem) 1951

'Vapor Trail' 1 W-W
(Murray W. Evans, 1969) Murray W. Evans, 1985
'Celilo' × ('Petsamo' × 'Zero'); sdlg no. L-32/1
Early

N. varduliensis Fernández Casas & Uribe-Echebarría 13 Section Pseudonarcissus

'Varela'
(pre-1914)

N. varians Gussone = *N. tazetta* subsp. *lacticolor*

'Variant' 2 Y-R
(J.L. Richardson) G. Zandbergen-Terwegen, 1959

'Variety' 1
(G.P. Haydon, pre-1907)

'Variety Girl' 2 W-YYO
(C.M. Grullemans) J.J. Grullemans & Sons, 1959
Fl. 105 mm wide; perianth segments white, flushed pale green; corona pale yellow 11D, with light orange (23A) at rim flecked white

'Variiformis' 1 W or Y-Y
(pre-1629)
Fl. variable of form and colour; perianth segments varying from white to yellow; corona varying from sulphur to deep yellow. Some variants resemble *N. nobilis*. Syn. Pseudonarcissus 'Variiformis'

'Varlet' 2 W-GPP
(W. Jackson Jr) Jackson's Daffodils, 1979
Sdlg 176/66 × 'Verran'; sdlg no. 162/73
Fl. 102 mm wide. Mid-season

'Varna' 3 Y-YOO
(The Brodie of Brodie, c.1925)
'Beacon' × 'Fortune'
Perianth segments broadly ovate or somewhat oblong in outline, blunt or rounded at apex, slightly mucronate, sulphur yellow, spreading, plane, somewhat irregular, overlapping one-third to a half; the inner segments more narrowly ovate, a little inflexed, with margins wavy; corona bowl-shaped, ribbed, bright reddish orange, with golden yellow at base, mouth even, with rim almost entire. AM(e) 1933

'Varrius' 2 W-YYR
(W. Jackson Jr) W. Jackson Jr, 1966
'Capella' × sdlg 62/54; sdlg no. 89/58

'Vasanta' 2 (a)
(C. de Berry, pre-1936)

'Vasco' 2 W-W
(R.H. Bath, pre-1933)

'Vasco' 2 W-YPP
(W. Jackson Jr, 1968) Jackson's Daffodils, 1979
'Cathlin' × sdlg 180/61; sdlg no. 187/68
Fl. 112 mm wide. Early to mid-season

N. vasconicus Fernández Casas = *N. jacetanus* subsp. *vasconicus*

'Vascule' 2 W-GPP
(W. Jackson Jr) Jackson's Daffodils, 1979
'Pompadour' × 'Dallbro'; sdlg no. 109/70
Fl. 114 mm wide; corona deep pink, with green at base, with rim rolled and dentate. Mid-season. Syn. 'Vantage'

'Vasey' 2 W-YYP
(?J.A.O'More, pre-1955)
Perianth segments roundish; corona yellow, with buff pink at rim

'Vaticaan' 1 W-Y
(?J.J. Grullemans & Sons, 1970) P.Q.M.Pennings, 1988
Sdlg no. 213
Fl. 135 mm wide; perianth segments greenish white 157D; corona light greenish yellow 3C, with brilliant greenish yellow 5B at rim. Mid-season to late. Resembles 'Las Vegas'

'Vauban' 2 Y-O
(A.M. Wilson, pre-1914)
Perianth segments deep yellow; corona widely expanded

'Vaucluse' 2 W-? (b)
(Alister Clark, 1935) J. Sharp, 1960

'Vaudeville' 9
(F.H. Chapman, pre-1930)

'Vaunter' 2 Y-? (a)
(de Graaff Bros, pre-1948)

'Vaviko' 2 Y-Y
(J.S. Leitch) J.S. Leitch, 1960
Fl. 108 mm wide

'Vectis' 2 W-GPP
(W. Jackson Jr) Jackson's Daffodils, 1979
Sdlg 175/65 × 'Verran'; sdlg no. 43/71
Fl. 108 mm wide. Early to mid-season

'Veda' 1 W-P
(W. Jackson Jr, 1953)
'Palin' × 'Rosario'

'Vedete' 2 W-P
(J.N. Hancock & Co., pre-1967) Unregistered
Corona shallow bowl-shaped, pale pink, frilled

'Vedette' 2 Y-? (a)
(A.M. Wilson, pre-1927)
'Beacon' × 1 Y-Y

'Vedette' 1 W-W
(D.S. Bell) D.S. Bell, 1959
Fl. 108 mm wide. Mid-season. Resembles a Div. 1 'Cantatrice'

'Veery' 7 Y-Y
(M. Fowlds) G.E. Mitsch, 1968
('Bodilly' × 'Fortune') × *N. jonquilla*; sdlg no. F188/3
Fl. 76 mm wide, clear deep yellow; corona ribbed. Mid-season. Resembles 'Trevithian' but with a darker-coloured and more widely expanded corona

'Vega' 2 W-W
(J.R. Pearson & Sons, pre-1910)
'Minnie Hume' × 'Madame de Graaff'

Perianth segments acute, ivory white, lightly inflexed; corona opening yellow, becoming white. *C(g) 1927

'Vela' 2 W-? (b)
(M. van Waveren & Sons, pre-1943)

'Velask' 2 W-GPP
(W. Jackson Jr) Jackson's Daffodils, 1979
'Remis' × 'C.E.Radcliff'; sdlg no. 6/70
Fl. 117 mm wide. Early to mid-season

'Velasques' 2 Y-O
(J.W.A. Lefeber, c.1977) Unregistered

'Velasquez' 2 (a)
(J. Berbee, pre-1945)

'Velia' 2 W-YPP
(W. Jackson Jr) Jackson's Daffodils, 1979
'Cathlin' × 'Verran'; sdlg no. 112/70
Fl. 106 mm wide. Early to mid-season

'Velikij Poczin' 2
(Latvian origin, pre-1956)

'Vellum' 9
(F.H.Chapman, pre-1928)

'Velma' 2 W-? (b)
(A.H. Ahrens) D.J. Cooper, 1956

'Velocity' 6 Y-R
(R. & E.Havens, 1984) R. & E.Havens, 1995
'Jetfire' × 'Gypsy'; sdlg no. TEH53/2
Fl. 80 mm wide; perianth segments acute, yellow, with undertones of orange, strongly reflexed; corona cylindrical, long, bright orange-red. Dwarf. Early. Sunproof. Resembles 'Jetfire' but with stronger undertones of orange in the perianth

'Velocity' 2 Y-YYO
(J.N.Hancock & Co., 1978) Unregistered
'Innisfail' × 'Air Marshal'; sdlg no. 91/78H
Perianth segments acute, yellow, overlapping; corona cylindrical, short, yellow, with a broad band of rich orange at rim. Mid-season to late

'Velutina' 3 (a)
(G.A. Uit den Boogaard, pre-1951)

'Velveteen' 2 Y-Y
(A.M. Wilson, pre-1937)
'Carbineer' hybrid
Perianth segments broadly or very broadly ovate, blunt, slightly mucronate, spreading, a little creased, regular, overlapping half; the inner segments more narrowly ovate, slightly inflexed; corona very short funnel-shaped, ribbed, with rim notched and crenate. *(Kirton)AM(g)(m) 1941

'Velvet Robe' 2 Y-R
(G.E. Mitsch, 1956) G.E. Mitsch, 1966
'Playboy' × 'Paricutin'; sdlg no. R63/2
Fl. rounded, 108 mm wide; perianth segments rich golden yellow, deeply overlapping; corona very shallow bowl-shaped, large, deep orange-red. Mid-season. Resembles a larger and later-flowered 'Paricutin' with a paler corona

'Vena' 1 W-W
(pre-1927)

'Venango' 2 W-? (b)
(Oregon Bulb Farms, pre-1951)

'Vendee' 2 W-? (b)
(A.M. Wilson, pre-1931)

'Vendetta' 2 W-? (b)
(J.O. Sherrard, pre-1943)
'May Molony' × 'Ediba'

'Veneration' 1 W-YPP
(W. Jackson Jr) Jackson's Daffodils, 1979
'Telita' hybrid × 'Verran'; sdlg no. 12/71
Fl. 110 mm wide. Early to mid-season

'Venetia' 5 W-W
(H. Backhouse, pre-1910)
'Minnie Hume' × *N. triandrus* var. *loiseleurii*
Fls 1-2 per stem, 92 mm wide, facing down; perianth segments ovate, blunt, slightly mucronate, spreading or a little inflexed, plane or with margins wavy or incurved, overlapping one-third to a half; the inner segments more narrowly ovate, with margins sometimes recurved in lower half; corona long cup-shaped, loosely ribbed, with mouth straight or somewhat incurved, rim crenate. AM 1913, *HC(g) 1927, AM(c) 1927

'Venetia's Dream' 11a W-Y
(Juris Svarcs) Juris Svarcs, 1992
'Poet's Dream' × 'Sancerre'; sdlg no. 84-52-01
Fl. 105 mm wide; perianth segments broadly ovate, prominently mucronate, greenish white (155A), with a greenish tint at base, a little reflexed; the inner segments somewhat inflexed, square-shouldered and narrowly spathulate at base; corona split, the six segments two-thirds the length of the perianth segments, opposite to them and joined at margins in lower third, bi-lobed, vivid yellow 12A, spreading, with margins wavy. Mid-season

'Venezuela' 2 W-R
(J.L. Richardson) J.L. Richardson, 1956
'Kilworth' × 'Arbar'
Late

'Vengeance' 2 Y-R
(A.M. Wilson, pre-1949)

Perianth segments deep yellow; corona vivid red

'Venice' 1 W-W
(G.H. Engleheart, pre-1907)

'Venice' 2 W-W
(J.M. de Navarro) J.M. de Navarro, 1958

'Venilia' 3 W-? (b)
(Barr & Sons, pre-1923)

'Venlo' 2 (a)
(J.T. Gray, pre-1950)

'Venn' 2 W-Y
(R.V. Favell, pre-1946)
'Merit' × 'Tolgus'

'Venosa' 2 W-W
(West & Fell, pre-1935)
Fl. pure white. Div. 3 until 1948

'Venta' 2 W-GPP
(W. Jackson Jr) Jackson's Daffodils, 1979
'Cathlin' × 'Verran'; sdlg no. 154/70
Fl. 100 mm wide. Mid-season

'Ventura' 2 W-? (b)
(A. Gibson) R. Hyde, 1958

'Venturer' 1 Y-Y
(Warnaar & Co., pre-1933)

'Venus' 2 W-W
(E. Leeds, pre-1877)
Fl. facing down; corona opening creamy yellow with a tinge of orange, becoming milk white. Syn. Leedsii 'Galanthiflorus Minor', Leedsii 'Venus'

'Venus' 2 W-W
(W.F.M. Copeland, pre-1907)
Corona opening pale lemon yellow, becoming milk white

'Venus' 2 W-YYO
(C.M. Grullemans) J.J. Grullemans & Sons, 1959

'Vera' 3 W-O
(Dutch origin, pre-1930)

'Vera Best' 2 (a)
(J.E. Exley, pre-1950)

'Vera Bray' 2 W-? (b or c)
(R.G. Sharp, pre-1930)

'Veracity' 2 W-W
(F.E. Board) F.E. Board, 1965
'Topic' × 'Vigil'

'Veragua' 2 W-? (b)
(W.A. Grace, pre-1938)

'Vera Lynn' 2 Y-YYO
(G. Lubbe & Son, pre-1954)
AM(Haarlem) 1954

'Vera Lynn' 2 W-WWY
(Tom Forster, 1960s) Unregistered
'Walter J.Smith' hybrid
Corona disc-shaped, parchment white, with soft yellow at rim, frilled. Mid-season

'Vera Pura' 5 ?-W
(L. Buckland, pre-1939)

'Vera West' 2 Y-YYO
(West & Fell, pre-1935)
Perianth segments lemon yellow, deeply overlapping; corona cup-shaped, with rounded sides, deep yellow, with orange at rim, frilled

N. verbanensis (Herbert) Pugsley = *N. poeticus* var. *verbanensis*

'Verdant' 1 Y-GYY
(Brian S. Duncan) Rathowen Daffodils, 1979
'Joybell' × 'Empress of Ireland'; sdlg no. 586
Perianth segments greenish primrose; corona cylindrical, slightly constricted near mid-point, darker in tone than the perianth, with green at base, mouth expanded and lightly frilled, rim flanged and crenate. Mid-season

'Verdant Meadow' 3 W-GWW
(G.E. Mitsch, 1973) R. & E. Havens, 1990
'Dallas' × 'Delightful'; sdlg no. II95/1
Fl. 70 mm wide, pure white; perianth segments broadly ovate, blunt, slightly mucronate, spreading, plane, smooth, overlapping half or more; the inner segments a little inflexed, with margins recurved at base and wavy or incurled near apex; corona bowl-shaped, small, closely ribbed, with bright green at base, mouth straight, split in places and overlapping, frilled. Very late

'Verdelli' 1 Y-Y
(S.J. Bisdee, pre-1943)
'White Emperor' × 'Sorley Boy'

'Verdi' 1 W-?
Syn. of 'Giuseppe Verdi'

'Verdi' 2 W-P
(R.H.Glover, pre-1993) Unregistered

'Verdin' 7 Y-W
(G.E. Mitsch) G.E. Mitsch, 1965
'Binkie' × *N. jonquilla*; sdlg no. T6/3

Fls 1-3 per stem, 25 mm wide; perianth segments broadly ovate, sometimes squarish at apex, soft lemon yellow, touched white at base and along midrib to mucro, spreading, plane or with margins incurling, overlapping a quarter; the inner segments with margins wavy; corona short funnel-shaped, loosely ribbed, opening yellow, becoming white, with mouth straight and frilled. Mid-season. 2n=21. Resembles a paler and slightly later-flowered 'Dickcissel' and a darker and more rounded 'Pipit'

'Verdoy' 2 W-PPW
(Brian S.Duncan) Brian S.Duncan, 1997
'Verran' × 'Algarve'; sdlg no. 1540
Fl. 100 mm wide; perianth segments very broadly ovate, slightly mucronate, pure white, spreading, glistening; corona broad funnel-shaped, lilac pink, with lilac overtones, whitish at rim, mouth slightly expanded. Early to mid-season

'Verdun' 1 Y-Y
(J.N. Hancock & Co., 1946)

'Vere' 3 (a)
(P.D. Williams, pre-1927)

N. vergellensis Parlatore = *N. patulus*

'Verger' 3 W-R
(P. van Deursen, pre-1930)
2n=28. AM(Haarlem) 1930, FA(Haarlem) 1936, EFA(Haarlem) 1948

'Verity' 2 W-? (b)
(J.L. Richardson, pre-1937)

'Verlene' 1 W-Y
(Miss M. Verry, 1953) Miss M.Verry, 1965
Sdlg no. 1B/16
Fl. 115 mm wide; corona brilliant greenish yellow 6A. Mid-season. Resembles a larger-flowered 'Sincerity' with a darker corona and a less strongly rolled corona rim. PC(e)(NZ) 1959

'Vermeil' 3 W-? (b)
(G.H. Engleheart, pre-1907)

'Vermilion' 3 W-OOY
(Murray W. Evans, 1964) Murray W. Evans, 1975
'Artist's Model' × 'Marshfire'; sdlg no. I-19/1
Fl. 120 mm wide; corona salmon orange, with yellow at rim. Mid-season

'Vermont' 1 W-? (b)
(de Graaff Bros, pre-1928)
Syn. 'Lohengrin'

'Verna' 2 or 3 W-? (b or c)
(Cartwright & Goodwin, pre-1916)

'Vernal' 2 W-WWY
(G.E. Mitsch) G.E. Mitsch, 1982
'Oratorio' × 'Pretender'; sdlg no. B32/4
Fl. 100 mm wide; corona white, with lemon at rim, frilled. Mid-season. Resembles a larger 'Dessert' of better quality

'Vernal Prince' 3 W-GYY
(T. Bloomer) Rathowen Daffodils, 1982
'Shantallow' × 'Woodland Prince'; sdlg no. 306
Fl. 100 mm wide; perianth segments very broad in outline, squarish or rounded at apex, prominently mucronate, pure white, very sightly reflexed, plane, smooth, overlapping half; the inner segments broadly ovate, blunt or truncate, less noticeably mucronate, more nearly spreading, with margins wavy; corona bowl-shaped, narrow, deep lemon yellow, deepening in tone towards the rim, with dark green prominent at base, deeply frilled. Mid-season

'Vernay' 3 W-? (b)
(Mrs R.O. Backhouse, pre-1921)

'Vernedale' 3 W-GWW
(Brian S. Duncan) Rathowen Daffodils, 1981
Dunlop sdlg × 'Verona'; sdlg no. 500
Corona whiter than perianth. Mid-season

'Vernie' 3 W-W
(J.L. Richardson) Brian S.Duncan, 1973
'Verona' self pollinated
Fl. 95 mm wide, pure white

'Vernon' 1 Y-Y
(W. Poupart, pre-1914)

'Verona' 1 W-W
(G.H. Engleheart, pre-1907)

'Verona' ?-P
(Alister Clark, pre-1948)

'Verona' 3 W-W
(J.L. Richardson) J.L. Richardson, 1958
'Green Island' × 'Chinese White'
Fl. rounded, 95-100 mm wide; perianth segments very broad, rounded at apex, only very slightly mucronate, spreading, plane, with margins sometimes minutely incurling at apex, smooth, with broad midrib showing, regular, overlapping half or more; the inner segments a little narrower; corona very shallow bowl-shaped, ribbed, creamy white, with green prominent in tube, mouth split in places and overlapping, loosely frilled, rim minutely crenate. Mid-season. 2n=28. AM(e) 1960, FCC(e) 1961, *AM(g) 1970, *FCC(g) 1971, AGM 1993

'Veronica' 2 W-P
(de Graaff Bros, pre-1927)

'Veronique' 2 W-W
(W. Jackson Sr, 1932)
'Eucharis' × 'Silver Plane'
Corona very shallow bowl-shaped, ribbed, frilled

'Verran' 2 W-P
(W. Jackson Jr, 1965) Jackson's Daffodils, 1979
'Kootara' × 'Egina'; sdlg no. 150/65
Fl. 98 mm wide; perianth segments very broadly ovate in outline, blunt or rounded at apex, slightly mucronate, pure white, spreading, plane, with midrib showing, overlapping half or more; the inners segments only a little narrower, squarish at shoulder, slightly inflexed, with margins a little wavy and sometimes nicked; corona cylindrical, smooth, delicate pink, with mouth flared, rim minutely and closely notched and crenate. Mid-season. Resembles 'Egina'

'Verran Rose' 2 W-GPP
(John R.Reed) John R.Reed, 1995
'Erlirose' × 'Verran'; sdlg no. 81-99-5
Fl. 96 mm wide, somewhat upward-facing; perianth segments broadly ovate, a little concave at margins, deeply overlapping; the inner segments almost touching one another; corona funnel-shaped, light pink, with mouth lobed and slightly flared. Late. Sunproof

'Verree' 1 W-Y
(Miss M. Verry) Miss M. Verry, 1974
'Verlene' × 'Ballygarvie'
Fl. 105 mm wide. Resembles a 'Ballygarvie' of improved substance

'Versa' 6 Y-W
(S.P. Haycock) S.P. Haycock, 1985
'Jenny' open pollinated; sdlg no. NY-W-1
Perianth segments pale yellow; corona opening with yellow at rim. Mid-season

'Vers Libre' 9 W-GYR
(Brian S. Duncan) Rathowen Daffodils, 1984
'Cantabile' × 'Milan'; sdlg no. D.295
Fl. 80 mm wide; perianth segments very broadly ovate in outline, blunt or rounded at apex, fairly prominently mucronate, pure white, spreading, overlapping half; the inner segments more narrowly ovate, a little inflexed, with margins slightly wavy; corona disc-shaped, ribbed, buff yellow, with olive green at base and a clearly defined band of brick red at rim. Tall. Late

'Vertex' 2 Y-R
(G.E. Mitsch) G.E. Mitsch, 1977
Sdlg A53/1 ('Paricutin' hybrid) × 'Falstaff'; sdlg no. G67/1
Fl. 110 mm wide; perianth segments broadly ovate, blunt, golden yellow, with slight white mucro, spreading, sometimes a little concave or with margins incurling, silken smooth, overlapping one-third to a half; the inner segments narrower, sometimes creased, with

margins wavy; corona short funnel-shaped, lightly ribbed, fiery orange-red, with mouth straight and a little frilled. Mid-season. Resembles a larger 'Loch Hope'

verus = *N. poeticus* var. *hellenicus*

'Verva' 2 W-P
(J.N. Hancock & Co., 1959) Unregistered

'Verve' 2 W-YYO
(Murray W. Evans) Murray W. Evans, 1978
'Marshfire' × 'Hotspur'; sdlg no. N-36/1
Fl. 97 mm wide; corona yellow, with a more or less broad zone of deep orange in upper part

'Verwood' 2 Y-O
(pre-1926)
Perianth segments rich golden yellow; corona intense reddish orange

'Verwood' 3 Y-YYO
(J.W. Blanchard, 1971) J.W.Blanchard, 1997
'Lemonade' × sdlg 59/33C; sdlg no. 66/13C
Fl. 100 mm wide; perianth segments rounded at apex, medium yellow; the inner segments more nearly acute; corona bowl-shaped, darker in tone than the perianth, with a narrow band of pale orange at rim, rim slightly crenate. Mid-season. Resembles a larger-flowered 'Ferndown' with a less deeply crenate corona rim

'Veryan' 1 Y-Y
(Rosewarne EHS, 1972) Rosewarne EHS, 1989
'Unsurpassable' × 'Malvern City'; sdlg no. 68/128/1
Fl. 113 mm wide; perianth segments brilliant greenish yellow 6A, overlapping; corona expanded, vivid yellow 9A, with rim flanged and crenate. Early

'Vespa' 2 W-W
Syn. of 'Glencoe'

'Vesper' 2 Y-Y
(W.A. Grace, pre-1927)

'Vesper' 2 Y-W
Syn. of 'Chelan'

'Vesta' 2 W-?Y
(E. Leeds, pre-1877)
Perianth segments sulphur white; corona large, expanded. Syn. Incomparabilis Albidus 'Vesta'. Was "absorbed" into 'Magog'

'Vesta' 5
(Mrs R.O. Backhouse, pre-1907)

'Vesta'
(?Barr & Sons, c.1914)

'Vesta' 2 (a)
(F.W. Parkinson, pre-1936)

'Vesta' 2 W-?
(A. Overton) A. Overton, 1960

'Vesta' 1 W-?
Syn. of 'Medford'

'Vestal'
(C. Dawson, pre-1908)

'Vestal' 2 W-W
(D.S. Cooper) D.S. Cooper, 1959
Fl. 95 mm wide. Early

'Vestal Virgin' 1 W-W
(H. Backhouse, pre-1908)
'Madame de Graaff' × 'Weardale Perfection'
Perianth segments broadly ovate, inflexed, with margins wavy, overlapping one-third; the inner segments more narrowly ovate, twisted; corona cylindrical, smoothly angled, with rim neatly rolled

'Vestan' 1 W-W
(W.F.M. Copeland, pre-1927)

'Vesta Tilley' 3 W-? (b)
(J.W.A. Lefeber, pre-1941)

'Vestcourt' 2 Y-Y
(R. Hyde) R. Hyde, 1959
'Golden Vest' × 'Goldcourt'

'Vestian'
(pre-1934)

'Vestral' 2 W-W
(D.J. Cooper, c.1959) Unregistered

'Vestris' 2 W-? (b)
(R.H. Bath, pre-1931)

'Vesuvius' 2 W-O
(Mrs Lawrensen, pre-1901)
Perianth segments broadly ovate, blunt and sometimes split at apex, fairly prominently mucronate, sulphur white, spreading, a little concave, overlapping half; the inner segments a little inflexed, with margins wavy; corona bowl-shaped, straight-sided, ribbed, glowing reddish orange, with mouth frilled. Late

'Vesuvius' 2 W-O
(Ken McCombe) Unregistered
'Estrellita' hybrid
Perianth segments roundish; corona very shallow, bright orange, frilled. Late

'Veta' 2 or 3 W-? (b or c)
(pre-1915)

'Veuve Cliquot' 2 Y-Y
(S.J. Bisdee, 1939)
'Nautilus' × 'Pinkeen'

'Vi' 1 W-Y
(W.M. Spry, pre-1975) Unregistered
'Golden' × 'Ina Marshall'
Corona cream. Late

'Vibella' 3 W-YYO
(H.A. Brown, 1945) J.N. Hancock & Co., 1964
Corona disc-shaped, ribbed. Very late

'Vi Boone' 2 W-P
(Daniel Bellinger) Daniel Bellinger, 1997
'Raspberry Ring' × 'Little Princess'; sdlg no. 87-19-1
Fl. rounded, 90 mm wide; perianth segments very broadly ovate, smooth and of thick substance, deeply overlapping; the outer segments overlapping one another; corona bowl-shaped, opening raspberry pink, becoming deep salmon pink, with mouth deeply lobed. Late. Sunproof

'Vibrant' 2 W-YYO
(Murray W. Evans, 1971) Murray W. Evans, 1987
'Showboat' × ('Fermoy' × 'Flamenco'); sdlg no. N-98
Corona disc-shaped. Mid-season

'Vicar of Lulworth' 2 W-O
Syn. of 'Lulworth'

'Vice-President' 2 W-P
(G.E. Mitsch and R. & E.Havens, 1976) G.E. Mitsch and R. & E.Havens, 1987
('Mabel Taylor' × 'Green Island') × 'Caro Nome'; sdlg no. LL20/10
Perianth segments pure white; corona rich rose pink. Mid-season

'Vice-Regal' 3 W-? (b)
(W.A. Grace, pre-1938)

'Viceroy' 2 W-? (b)
(Sir C.H. Cave, pre-1908)

'Viceroy' 1 Y-Y
(G.H. Johnstone) G.H. Johnstone, 1959
'Acclaim' × 'Frontispiece'
Fl. 115 mm wide. Early

'Vickie Linn' 6 Y-P
(John R.Reed, 1987) John R.Reed, 1997
'Little Princess' × 'Milestone'; sdlg no. 81-101-1
Fl. rounded, 75 mm wide; perianth segments broadly ovate, soft yellow, reflexed; corona funnel-shaped, strong reddish pink. Dwarf. Early to mid-season

'Vicksburg' 1 W-W
(Brian S. Duncan) J.R. Reed, 1985
'Ave' × 'Empress of Ireland'; sdlg no. 124
Perianth segments greenish white (157C), flushed pale green at base; corona with olive green at base. Mid-season. Resembles a large-flowered 'Ave'

'Vicksburg' 6 Y-O
Syn. of 'Flower Waltz'

'Vicland' 2 W-? (b)
(P.D. Williams, pre-1948)
AM(Haarlem) 1948

'Victor' 2 (a)
(E.M. Crosfield, pre-1913)

'Victor' 1 Y-Y
(West & Fell, 1936) A. Ladson, 1960

'Victor Borge' 1 W-Y
(Konynenburg & Mark) Konynenburg & Mark, 1960
Sdlg × 'Daisy Schäffer'
Fl. 100 mm wide, ivory white; corona vivid yellow 9A. Early

'Victor Gould' 1 (a)
(J.E. Exley, pre-1938)

'Victor Hugo' 1 W-? (b)
(W.J. Eldering & Son, pre-1928)
EFA(Haarlem) 1928

'Victoria' 1 W-Y
(?M. Vos, pre-1897)
Fl. 84 mm wide; perianth segments ovate, fairly prominently mucronate, creamy white, with green and yellow at midrib beneath, inflexed, overlapping one-third; the inner segments somewhat twisted or with margins wavy; corona cylindrical, lightly ribbed, vivid yellow 9A to 12A, mouth expanded, sometimes with six deeply overlapping lobes, frilled, with rim crenate. 2n=14,22,28. Syn. ?'Dutch Victoria'. AM 1897

'Victoria Los Angelos' 2 W-O
(J.W.A. Lefeber, 1950) J.W.A. Lefeber, 1960
Fl. 34 mm wide. Late

'Victorious' 2 W-Y
(R.V. Favell, pre-1954)
Corona pale lemon yellow, with a darker tone at rim. 2n=28

'Victor J.Hurley' 1 W-Y
(West & Fell, pre-1938)
Corona lemon yellow

'Victory' 2 W-Y
(J.C. Williams, pre-1907)
Perianth segments creamy white, overlapping; corona pale lemon

'Victory' 2 W-R
(J.L. Richardson) M.J. Jefferson-Brown, 1961
'Kilworth' × 'Arbar'

'Victory Light' 2 Y-O
(Warnaar & Co., pre-1951)
'Westminster' × 'Carbineer'
AM(Haarlem) 1951

'Vida' 2 Y-Y
(J.S. Leitch) J.S. Leitch, 1964
Fl. 95 mm wide

'Vieni d'Amour' 2 W-Y
(Konynenburg & Mark) Konynenburg & Mark, 1963
Fl. 115 mm wide; perianth segments greenish white; corona vivid yellow 13A. Late

'Vienna View' 2 (a)
(A. Gibson, pre-1951)

'Vienna Woods' 9 W-R
(G.E. Mitsch, 1968) R. & E. Havens, 1992
'Quetzal' × 'Smyrna'; sdlg no. D94/8
Fl. 70 mm wide; perianth segments broad, rounded, pure white, slightly reflexed; corona disc-shaped, orange-red. Late

'Viennese Rose' 4 W-P
(Mrs H.K. Richardson) Mrs H.K. Richardson, 1976
'Marietta' × 'Irani'
Fl. 85 mm wide; perianth and other petaloid segments white; corona segments pink. Mid-season. 2n=29

'Viennese Waltz' 6 W-Y
(G.E. Mitsch, 1975) R. & E. Havens, 1991
Sdlg Z70/3 × *N. cyclamineus*; sdlg no. KK106/7
Perianth segments strongly reflexed; corona cylindrical, cream yellow, with pink undertones, usually with some extra segments within. Dwarf. Very early

'Vieva' 3 W-R
(J.T. Gray, pre-1949)
Fl. rounded; perianth segments very broad in outline, rounded or squarish at apex, prominently mucronate, spreading, plane, overlapping half or more; the inner segments with midrib showing and with margins slightly wavy; corona disc-shaped, heavily ribbed, deep brick red

'Vigi' 1 Y-Y
(W. Jackson Sr, 1939)
'Chruseos' × 'Vuster'
Fl. deep yellow

'Vigil' 1 W-W
(G.L. Wilson, pre-1947)
'Courage' × 'Kanchenjunga'
Fl. 127 mm wide, ice white; perianth segments ovate and acute, slightly mucronate, spreading, plane or a little twisted, smooth and of good substance, overlapping one-third; the inner segments more narrowly ovate, more strongly twisted; corona cylindrical, smooth, with mouth expanded and a little frilled, rim notched and crenate and loosely flanged. 2n=28. AM(e) 1956, *AM(g) 1978, AGM 1993

'Vigilance' 2 (a)
(A.M. Wilson, pre-1937)

'Vigilant' 2 W-W
(K.J. Heazlewood, c.1967) Unregistered
'Vigil' × 'Truth'

'Vigilante' 1 W-W
(Brian S. Duncan) Rathowen Daffodils, 1977
'Vigil' open pollinated
Fl. pure white; corona cylindrical, with mouth expanded, rim dentate. Early to mid-season. 2n=28. Resembles 'Vigil' but with broader perianth segments

'Vigo' 2 W-? (b)
(de Graaff Bros, pre-1942)
AM(Haarlem) 1942

'Vigorous' 2 Y-O
(R.V. Favell, pre-1946)
'Killigrew' × 'Pentreath'

'Vigour' 1 Y-Y
(C.G. van Tubergen, pre-1929)
Fl. 114 mm wide; perianth segments lemon yellow, twisted, irregular, overlapping one-third; corona bright buttercup yellow, with mouth somewhat expanded. Mid-season

'Vi Grant' 2 W-GWW
(D.C. MacArthur) D.C. MacArthur, 1991
2 W-W × 'Misty Glen'; sdlg no. EV84-513
Fl. 101 mm wide, greenish white (155A); perianth segments ovate, spreading; corona narrowly funnel-shaped, ribbed, with yellowish green (151A) at base, mouth flared and frilled, rim crenate and slightly flanged. Mid-season. Slightly scented

'Viki' 2 W-R
(J.S. Leitch) J.S. Leitch, 1956

'Viking' 5
(C. Dawson, pre-1907)

'Viking' 1 Y-Y
(J.L. Richardson) J.L. Richardson, 1956
'Goldcourt' × 'Kingscourt'
Fl. 115 mm wide; perianth segments broadly ovate,

blunt or a little truncate, vivid yellow 9A, with slight white mucro, spreading, plane, overlapping half; the inner segments somewhat narrower, shouldered at base, slightly reflexed in upper half, with margins wavy; corona funnel-shaped, lightly ribbed, of a richer tone (13A) than the perianth, with mouth flared and lightly frilled, rim notched and crenate. Mid-season. 2n=28. AM(e) 1960, *AM(g) 1967, AGM 1995

'Vikiwi' 1 Y-Y
(R.J. Abernethy) R.J. Abernethy, 1991
'Mangere' × 'Viking'; sdlg no. 466
Fl. very smooth and of heavy substance; corona funnel-shaped, with rim flanged. Mid-season

'Vilbia' 3 W-? (b)
(J.T. Gray, pre-1949)
Corona disc-shaped, with a band of red at rim

'Vilene' 3 W-? (b)
(de Graaff Bros, pre-1938)
AM(Haarlem) 1938. Div. 9 until 1957

"Villa Cha"
Syn. of 'Queen of Spain'

'Village Beauty' 3 W-YYR
(W. Polman-Mooy, pre-1922)
Fl. 83 mm wide; perianth segments creamy white, with cream at base, overlapping half; corona funnel-shaped, rich lemon yellow, with scarlet at rim. Mid-season. AM(Haarlem) 1921

'Village Maid' 1 W-? (b)
(Barr & Sons, pre-1908)

'Villa Maria' 4 W-WWP
(D.S. Bell) D.S. Bell, 1983

'Villa Rosea' 4 W-P
(D.S. Bell) D.S. Bell, 1982
Sdlg × 'Accent'
Fl. 102 mm wide. Mid-season

'Villa Royale' 4 Y-YYR
(D.S. Bell) D.S. Bell, 1985
'Fiji' × 'Ashanti'
fl. 98 mm wide. Mid-season. Resembles 'Royal Sceptre' but with the segments at centre more tightly arranged

'Villette' 3 W-? (b)
(J.W. Barr, pre-1930)

'Vilna' 2 W-W
(A.M. Wilson, pre-1944)
Corona opening very pale primrose, becoming white

'Vinaka' 1 Y-Y

(J.N.Hancock & Co., 1980) Unregistered
Sdlg 38/61H × Fairbairn 2Y-Y; sdlg no. 13/80H
Fl. deep golden yellow; corona funnel-shaped, with rim broadly crenate. Very early

'Vincennes' 11a Y-O
(J. Gerritsen & Son) J. Gerritsen & Son, 1969
Sdlg × 'Orange Master'

'Vincenti' 3 W-Y
Syn. of 'Duchess of Brabant'

'Vincenti Delicata' 3 W-Y
Syn. of 'Ianthe'

'Vincenti Delicatus' 3 W-Y
Syn. of 'Ianthe'

'Vincenti Gloriosa' 3 W-Y
Syn. of 'Fanny Mason'

'Vincenti Gloriosus' 3 W-Y
Syn. of 'Fanny Mason'

'Vincenti Katherine Spurrell' 3 W-Y
Syn. of 'Katherine Spurrell'

'Vincenti Minnie Hume' 3 W-Y
Syn. of ' Minnie Hume'

'Vincenti Miriam Barton' 3 Y-Y
Syn. of 'Miriam Barton'

'Vincenti Stellatus' W-Y
(pre-1883)
Perianth segments narrow, acute; corona canary yellow

'Vincent Sion' 4 Y-Y
Syn. of 'Telamonius Plenus'

'Vincent Square' 2 W-? (b)
(P.D. Williams, pre-1927)

'Vincent Van Gogh' 1 Y-Y
(G.L.A. Pouw) N. Blokker, 1977
'Rembrandt' × 'Golden Sunbeam'
Fl. 110 mm wide; perianth segments brilliant yellow 8A; corona darker in tone (12A)

'Vinetta' 2 W-? (b)
(J.T. Gray, pre-1938)

'Vinka' 2 W-P
(P. Phillips) P. Phillips, 1971
Fl. 102 mm wide

'Vinsky' 3 (a)
(A.M. Wilson, pre-1950)

'Vintage' 5 Y-Y
(F.H. Chapman, pre-1917)
'King Alfred' × *N. triandrus* var. *loiseleurii*
Fl. facing down, citron yellow. AM 1917

'Vintner' 2 ?-R (a)
(A.M. Wilson, pre-1944)
Perianth segments slightly reflexed; corona bowl-shaped, red

'Viola' 3 W-GYY
(C. Dawson, pre-1919)
'Princess Mary' × 'Horace'
Perianth segments ivory white; corona ribbed, lemon yellow, with greenish tones at base

'Violate' 2 W-? (b)
(W.A. Bell, pre-1949)

'Violet Dawson' 1 W-Y
(Mrs G. Link, 1982) Mrs G. Link, 1993
'Glencairn' open pollinated; sdlg no. 97-77
Fl. 91 mm wide; perianth segments broadly ovate, clear white, of smooth and thick substance, deeply overlapping; corona narrowly funnel-shaped, narrow at base, of heavy substance, lemon yellow, with mouth slightly frilled. Tall. Mid-season. Varies between Divs 1 and 2

'Violet May' 2 Y-R
(F.A. Saunders) F.A. Saunders, 1969

'Violetta' 2 W-GPP
(Brian S. Duncan) Rathowen Daffodils, 1975
'Roseworthy' × 'Minerva'; sdlg no. 25
Perianth segments broadly ovate, slightly mucronate, glistening white, spreading or a little inflexed, plane or a little concave, with margins very slightly incurling at apex, smooth, overlapping half; the inner segments more narrowly ovate; corona funnel-shaped, loosely ribbed, vivid pink, tinted violet, with mouth a little frilled, rim notched and crenate. Mid-season. 2n=28

'Violetta Elvin' 2 W-O
(D.S. Bell, pre-1961) Unregistered
Fl. large; perianth segments broad, pure white, smooth; corona shallow, widely expanded, reddish orange. Tall

'Violin' 2 W-P
(Brian S. Duncan) Rathowen Daffodils, 1976
'Roseworthy' × 'Minerva'; sdlg no. 47
Corona narrow, vivid pink, with violet undertones. Mid-season. Resembles 'Violetta' but with the corona more tightly ribbed and frilled

'Viota' 2 Y-R
(J.S. Leitch) J.S. Leitch, 1958

'Viotta' 2 W-? (b)
(de Graaff Bros, pre-1944)

'Vireo' 7 Y-GYY
(G.E. Mitsch) G.E. Mitsch, 1962
'Seraglio' × *N.assoanus*; sdlg no. P85/1
Fl. rounded, 64 mm wide, soft clear yellow; corona small, with vivid deep green at base. Late

'Virgil' 9 W-GYO
(G.H. Engleheart, pre-1894)
Perianth segments broadly ovate, white, sometimes flushed shell pink, somewhat reflexed, overlapping a quarter; corona sulphur yellow, with greenish base, shading to orange at rim. AM 1900

'Virgilia' 2 W-? (b)
(C. Dawson, pre-1923)

'Virgin' 5
(G.H. Engleheart, pre-1914)

'Virgineus' 8 W-W
(Spanish origin)
Selection by Peter Barr (1887) from wild-collected *N. tazetta*
Fl. pure white

'Virginia' 1 W-YYO
(pre-1927)
Corona funnel-shaped, creamy yellow, with pale apricot orange at rim, lightly frilled. AM(Haarlem) 1927

'Virginia' 9 W-?
(H.G. Longford, pre-1927)

'Virginia Hale' 2 (a)
(The Brodie of Brodie, pre-1931)

'Virginia Walker' 1 W-W
(W.G. Pannill) W.G. Pannill, 1992
'Panache' × 'Cataract'; sdlg no. 74/48
Fl.101 mm wide. Mid-season

'Virginia Waters' 3 W-GWY
(R.A.Scamp) R.A.Scamp, 1995
'Verona' × 'Fairmile'; sdlg no. 400
Fl. 90 mm wide; perianth segments very broadly ovate, pure white, deeply overlapping; corona almost disc-shaped, white, with green at base and bright lemon yellow at rim, neatly frilled. Mid-season to late

'Virginia Wright' 1 Y-Y
(M. van Waveren & Sons, pre-1943)

'Virgin Snow' 2 W-W
(M. van Waveren & Sons, pre-1953)
Syn. 'Ballet Dancer'

'Virgo' 2 (a)
(A.H. Ahrens) J.S. Leitch, 1955

N. viridiflorus Schousboe 13 Section Jonquilla

'Virlie' 2 W-YPP
(W. Jackson Jr) Jackson's Daffodils, 1979
'Remis' × 'C.E.Radcliff'; sdlg no. 7/70
Fl. 120 mm wide. Early to mid-season

'Virma' 1 W-YPP
(W. Jackson Jr) Jackson's Daffodils, 1979
Sdlg 113/63 × 'Verran'; sdlg no. 107/70
Fl. 102 mm wide. Mid-season

'Virtue' 2 Y-Y
(G.L. Wilson, pre-1942)
'Hebron' × 'Crocus'
Perianth segments brilliant yellow 12B; corona very slightly darker in tone (12A), with rim dentate. AM(e) 1950

'Virtuoso' 3 W-? (b)
(R. Crews, pre-1949)
Syn. 'Captivation'

'Virtuoso' 2 W-WWP
(Colin Crotty) Unregistered
Sdlg no. 21-75

'Visa' 3 Y-R
(P. & G. Phillips) P. & G. Phillips, 1981
Fl. 100 mm wide. Mid-season

'Viscount' 2 W-YYO
(S.A. Free) S.A. Free, 1961
Fl. 102 mm wide; corona with dark orange at rim. Mid-season

'Viscount' 2 Y-OOY
(J.N. Hancock & Co., c.1975) Unregistered

'Viscount Bledisloe' 2 W-W
(G. Lewis, pre-1949)
'Alroi' × 'Kanchenjunga'

'Viscountess' 1 Y-Y
(pre-1914)
Fl. pale sulphur yellow. Resembles a more robust 'Countess of Desmond'

'Viscountess Allenby' 3 W-? (b)
(Mrs R.O. Backhouse, pre-1921)

'Viscountess Bledisloe' 1 W-W
(G. Lewis, pre-1949)
'Alroi' × 'Kanchenjunga'

'Viscountess Falmouth' 5 W-W
(G.H. Engleheart, pre-1903)

AM 1903

'Viscountess Northcliffe' 5 W-W
(Mrs R.O. Backhouse, pre-1921)
Corona cylindrical, lightly ribbed, with mouth slightly flared, frilled

'Vishnu' 1 W-W
(pre-1913)

'Vision' 2 W-P
(P. Phillips) P. Phillips, 1963
Fl. 102 mm wide; corona deep pink. Mid-season. Resembles a larger-flowered 'Roseum' with whiter perianth segments and a darker-coloured corona

'Visitor' 1 W-W
(Sir C.H. Cave, pre-1928)

'Visitor' 2 W-WWO
(Alister Clark) H. Dettmann, 1960
Corona soon becoming apricot at rim

'Visor' 3 W-? (b)
(G.H. Engleheart, pre-1923)

'Vista' 7 Y-Y
Syn. of 'Philomath'

'Vista' 2 W-YYP
(J.N.Hancock & Co., 1980) Unregistered
'Isabella' × 'Verran'; sdlg no. 70/80H
Perianth segments broadly ovate; corona funnel-shaped, pale lemon yellow, with a clearly defined band of true pink at rim, with the rim dentate. Mid-season

'Vista' 1 Y-Y
(R.H.Glover, pre-1993) Unregistered

'Vistula' 2 W-? (b)
(Mrs R.O. Backhouse, pre-1921)

'Vital' 2 W-YPP
(W. Jackson Jr) Jackson's Daffodils, 1979
'Cathlin' × 'Verran'
Fl. 114 mm wide. Mid-season

'Vita Nova' 3 W-? (b)
(A.M. Wilson, pre-1938)

'Vivace' 3 W-? (b)
(G.A. Uit den Boogaard, pre-1946)

'Vivacious' 2 W-GPP
(W. Jackson Jr) Jackson's Daffodils, 1979
'Remis' × 'C.E.Radcliff'; sdlg no. 159/71
Fl. 108 mm wide. Mid-season

'Vivaldi' 2 W-O
(J.N.Hancock & Co.) Unregistered

'Artist's Model' × 'Avenger'; sdlg no. 54/84H
Fl. rounded; corona disc-shaped, ribbed, bright orange. Late

'Vivandière' 3 W-YYO
(P.D. Williams, pre-1907)
Perianth segments ivory white; corona disc-shaped, yellow, with scarlet-orange at rim

'Vivanne' 2 (b)
(Mrs M. Moorby) Mrs M. Moorby, 1957

'Vivarino' 11?b Y-O
(J.W.A. Lefeber) J.W.A. Lefeber, 1968

'Vivex' 2 Y-YYR
(Konynenburg & Mark, 1950) Konynenburg & Mark, 1961
'Aranjuez' × 'Beauty of the Garden'
Fl. 90 mm wide; perianth segments light greenish yellow 8C; corona brilliant yellow 13B, with a narrow band of orange-red (32A) at rim. Early

'Vivian' 2 W-Y
(W. Backhouse, pre-1869)
Perianth segments sulphur white, twisted; corona widely expanded, yellow. Syn. Barrii Albidus 'Expansus', Barrii Albidus 'Vivian'. FCC 1879

'Vivian Burbidge' 1 (a)
(W.B. Hartland, pre-1913)

'Vivian Gosnell' 1 W-W
(pre-1907)
Fl. 102 mm wide; perianth segments white, twisted; corona almost pure white, with rim flanged

'Vivian Romanof' 2 (a)
(J.W.A. Lefeber, pre-1954)

'Vivid' 3 W-O
(G.H. Engleheart, pre-1902)
Perianth segments cream; corona very shallow bowl-shaped, broad, reddish orange

'Vivid' 2 Y-?
(C.O. Fairbairn) C.O. Fairbairn, 1960

'Vivid Crown' 2 W-? (b)
(G. Lubbe & Son, pre-1944)
AM(Haarlem) 1944

'Vivien' 1 W-W
(J.W. Barr, pre-1930)

'Vivien Leigh' 2 W-W
(M. van Waveren & Sons, pre-1953)
AM(Haarlem) 1953

'Vivinette'
(?A.M. Wilson, pre-1915)

'Viv Lumsden' 2 W-GYO
(D.C. MacArthur) D.C. MacArthur, 1989
2W-YOO sdlg × ('Mahmoud' hybrid × 'Verger'); sdlg no. EV88-92
Fl. 104 mm wide; perianth segments broad, yellowish white 155A, of good substance, overlapping; corona disc-shaped, brilliant yellow 13B, with yellow-green (151B) at base and strong orange 25A at rim touched with white, mouth deeply split, with overlapping lobes. Mid-season

'Vixen' 2 W-? (b)
(Mrs R.O. Backhouse, pre-1921)
AM(Haarlem) 1929

'Vixen' 2 W-P
(R.H.Glover, pre-1993) Unregistered

'Vixi' 2 Y-Y
(W. Jackson Jr, 1957) W. Jackson Jr, 1968
'Hymis' × 'Galway'; sdlg no. 270/57
Fl. deep yellow

'Viyella' 3 W-? (b)
(A.H. Ahrens) J.S. Leitch, 1956

'Vizir' 1 W-Y
(J. Mallender, pre-1910)
Perianth segments inflexed; corona pale sulphur yellow, with rim flanged

'Vladimir' 2 Y-Y
(Barr & Sons, pre-1923)
'Gaiety' × 'Lord Roberts'
Perianth segments dark primrose yellow, overlapping; corona large, darker in tone, neatly frilled

'Vlammenspel' 2 Y-? (a)
(J.W.A. Lefeber) J.J. Grullemans & Sons, 1959

'Vltava' 2 W-W
(A.M. Wilson, pre-1948)

'V.M.Warren' 1 W-? (b)
(G.P. Haydon, pre-1908)

'Voana' 2 Y-R
(C.E. Radcliff) J.M.Radcliff, 1956
'Carbineer' × 'Rosslare'

'Vocalist' 2 W-W
(J.R.Byfield, pre-1936)

'Vocation' 2 W-P
(Brian S. Duncan) Rathowen Daffodils, 1976
'Interim' × 'Aosta'; sdlg no. 27
Perianth segments pure white; corona tightly ribbed, deep reddish copper pink. Mid-season. Resembles a

larger-flowered 'Aosta' with perianth segments broader at base

'Voda' 2 Y-Y
(W. Jackson Jr, c.1964) Unregistered
'Hymis' × 'Galway'

'Voda' 3 W-R
(W. Jackson Jr, 1964) Unregistered
'Kin' × 'Arbar'; sdlg no. 62/64
Perianth segments somewhat narrow; corona very small, bright red

'Vogue' 2 W-? (b)
(F.H. Chapman, pre-1931)
'Lowdham Beauty' × 'Crimson Braid'

'Vogue' 2 W-OOY
(C.M. Grullemans) J.J. Grullemans & Sons, 1959
Fl. 120 mm wide; perianth segments creamy white; corona pale orange (24D), with a narrow band of pale yellow at rim. Early

'Volante' 2 (a)
(P.D. Williams, pre-1948)

'Volare' 2 W-GWP
(Murray W. Evans, 1968) Murray W. Evans, 1978
'Everpink' × ('Caro Nome' × ['Mabel Taylor' × Rosario']) × 'Interim'
Corona white, with green at base and a broad band of deep pink at rim. Mid-season. Resembles 'Heart Throb' but with broader perianth segments and a deeper colour at corona rim

'Volatile' 2 Y-R
(J.N. Hancock & Co., 1967) Unregistered

'Volcanic Action' 2 Y-R
(G. Lewis) D.S. Bell, 1955
Perianth segments deep yellow; corona closely overlying the perianth, bright red

'Volcano' 4 Y-O
(Barr & Sons, pre-1908)
'Ornatus' × 'Telamonius Plenus'
Perianth and other petaloid segments sulphur yellow; corona segments bright orange, tinged scarlet. FCC(Haarlem) 1912

'Volcano' 2 Y-O
(J.J. Abernethy) R.J. Abernethy, 1961
Fl. 102 mm wide; perianth segments bright golden yellow, slightly reflexed; corona bowl-shaped, intense reddish orange. Mid-season

'Volendam' 2 (a)
(R.O. Backhouse, pre-1937)
AM(Haarlem) 1937

'Volenti' 1 W-W
(R.H. Bath, pre-1929)

'Volga' 2 W-W
(J.L. Richardson, pre-1945)
'Cameronian' × 'Slemish'
Perianth segments broadly ovate; corona with rim flanged and dentate

'Volkersz' 1 Y-Y
Syn. of 'Ingenieur K.Valkersz'

'Volkerz' 1 Y-Y
Syn. of 'Ingenieur K.Volkersz'

'Voltage' 2 W-P
(W. Jackson Jr) Jackson's Daffodils, 1979
Sdlg 154/66 × 'Verran'; sdlg no. 22/74
Fl. 97 mm wide. Early to mid-season

'Voltaire' 2 W-YYR
(pre-1927)
Perianth segments creamy white; corona light yellow, with red at rim

'Volterra' 2 Y-O
(J.N. Hancock & Co., 1950) J.N. Hancock & Co., 1960
Perianth segments deep yellow; corona bright reddish orange

'Volturno' 2 W-YYO
(J.L. Richardson, pre-1945)
 Unknown parentage
Perianth segments pure white; corona very shallow bowl-shaped, deep yellow, suffused with colour from a broad band of reddish orange at rim. 2n=28

'Volumnia' 1 W-W
(Barr & Sons, pre-1913)

'Volunteer' 1 Y-Y
(D.V. West, pre-1935)
Fl. rich yellow. Late

'Voluptuary' 2 (a)
(Mrs R.O. Backhouse, pre-1921)

'Volutus' 1 Y-Y
Syn. of 'J.G.Baker'

'Vona'
(A.M. Wilson, pre-1914)

'Vonda' 2 W-P
(W. Jackson Jr) W. Jackson Jr, 1968
Sdlg 248/57 × sdlg 117/57; sdlg no. 70/64

'Vondel' 9
(G. Lubbe & Son, pre-1927)

'Vonie' 3 Y-R
(D.P. de Graaf) D.P. de Graaf, 1988
Perianth segments canary yellow; corona orange-red (30B or C), with a paler tone at base

'Voodoo' 6 Y-Y
(M.G. Temple-Smith) M.G. Temple-Smith, 1987
N. cyclamineus × 'Ristin'; sdlg no. 2/83
Perianth segments very broadly ovate, with slight white mucro, strongly reflexed, with margins inward rolling, smooth, with faint midrib showing, overlapping almost half; the inner segments more narrowly ovate, a little less strongly reflexed; corona cylindrical, smooth at base, lightly ribbed towards mouth, mouth flared, deeply 6-lobed, even, rim notched and crenate. Early. Resembles 'Abracadabra' and 'Alacabam'

'Vortex' 2 W-YYO
(J.N. Hancock & Co., 1963) Unregistered

'Votary' ?-P
(Alister Clark, pre-1948)

'Votive Candle' 6 W-W
(A. Gray) A. Gray, 1967
N. cyclamineus × 'Rockery Gem'
Fl. 70 mm wide, milk white. Mid-season. Resembles a more robust 'Pepys' with a more widely expanded corona

'Voyageur' 2 W-W
(A.H. Ahrens) J.S. Leitch, 1956

'Vrony' 4 W-O
(J.L. Richardson, 1955) R.W. Ward & Son, 1966
Perianth and other petaloid segments creamy; corona segments rich orange. Mid-season. Resembles a large-flowered and vigorous 'Acropolis'

'Vulcan'
(G.H. Engleheart, pre-1907)

'Vulcan' 1 W-Y
(H.J. Poole Sr, pre-1927)

'Vulcan' 2 Y-O
(J.L. Richardson) J.L. Richardson, 1956
'Carbineer' × 'Ceylon'
Fl. 94 mm wide; perianth segments broadly ovate, blunt, only very slightly mucronate, vivid yellow 9A, spreading, plane, regular, overlapping half; the inner segments only a little narrower; corona cup-shaped, smooth, vivid or strong orange (28B or 25A), tinged with a lighter tone (21A) towards base, mouth straight or slightly expanded, very lightly frilled, with rim irregularly crenate. Sunproof. 2n=28. AM(e) 1962, *AM(g) 1966, *FCC(g) 1969, AGM 1993

'Vulcan's Fire' 2 Y-R

(D.S. Bell) D.S. Bell, 1958
'Jansen' × 'Diamond King'
Fl. 115 mm wide; corona rich red. Mid-season. Resembles an 'Alamein' of stronger substance with more rounded perianth segments and a more richly coloured corona

'Vulcanus' 3 (a)
(de Graaff Bros, pre-1927)

N. vulgaris Coutinho = *N. bulbocodium* subsp. *bulbocodium*

'Vuster' 1 Y-Y
(W. Jackson Sr, 1938)
'Golden Legend' × 'Wattle'

'Waban' 2 W-Y
(E.C. Powell, pre-1946)
'Bernardino' × 'Tenedos'

'Wachuset' 2 W-W
(E.C. Powell, pre-1946)
'Pilgrimage' × 'Beersheba'

'Wadavers' 2 W-GWW
(R.A.Scamp) R.A.Scamp, 1995
'Pitchroy' × 'Canisp'; sdlg no. 310
Fl. 100 mm wide, pure white; perianth segments broadly ovate, deeply overlapping; corona smooth, with green at base, mouth neatly expanded and frilled. Mid-season

'Waffle' 2 Y-O
(J.S. Leitch) J.S. Leitch, 1964
Fl. 108 mm wide; corona reddish orange

'Wagga Wagga' 1 Y-Y
(L.P. Dettman, 1967) L.P. Dettman, 1978
'Caramel' × 'Dutch Girl'; sdlg no. 12/67
Fl. 123 mm wide; perianth segments pale greenish yellow 2D; corona brilliant yellow 7A. Early. Resembles a larger-flowered 'Caramel' with the corona more widely expanded

'Waggon Wheels' 2 W-YYO
(New Zealand origin, pre-1955) Unregistered
Fl. rounded; corona disc-shaped, yellow, with a line of orange at rim

'Wagner's Rheingold' 1 Y-Y
(J. Kouwenhoven, pre-1931)
Fl. golden yellow; perianth segments broad, ribbed; corona large, ribbed, with mouth flared, rim rolled

1095

and notched. AM(Haarlem) 1931, EFA(Haarlem) 1932, FCEFA(Haarlem) 1933

'Wagtail' 2 W-Y
(P.D. Williams, pre-1910)
Corona clear yellow

'Wag-the-Chief' 9 W-GYR
(Mrs M.S. Yerger) Mrs M.S. Yerger, 1982
N. poeticus var. *hellenicus* × 'Lights Out'
Fl. 32 mm wide. Late

'Wahine' 2 W-? (b or c)
(W.E. Weightman, pre-1936)

'Wahkeena' 2 W-Y
(Murray W. Evans, 1955) G.E. Mitsch, 1965
'Polindra' × 'Frolic'
Fl. 115 mm wide, perianth segments broad; corona clear lemon yellow. Mid-season. 2n=28. Resembles 'Descanso' in colour

'Waif' 6 W-P
(Carncairn Daffodils) Carncairn Daffodils, 1983
'Foundling' × 'Lilac Charm'
Fl. 90 mm wide. Mid-season. Resembles 'Foundling' but with a longer and more widely expanded corona

'Waiheke' 1 W-Y
(J.S. Leitch) J.S. Leitch, 1967
Fl. 108 mm wide, corona primrose yellow

'Waihola' 2 Y-YOO
(S.C. Gaspar, 1951) R.J. Abernethy, 1962
Fl. 89 mm wide; perianth segments deep yellow; corona reddish orange, with rich yellow at base. Mid-season. Resembles a smaller and more brightly coloured 'Samoa'

'Waikato' 2 W-W
(J.T. Gray, pre-1949)

'Waikato Queen' 2 W-? (b)
(J.H. Braithwaite, pre-1930)

'Waimakariri' 11a W-Y
(David Adams) David Adams, 1996
'Ebony' open pollinated; sdlg no. 84/115N
Fl. 80 mm wide; perianth segments blunt, spreading; the inner segments narrower; corona split to base, the six segments in two whorls of three opposite the perianth segments, whitish yellow, shading to a darker tone at base and rim, deeply frilled; the inner segments narrower. Early to mid-season

'Waimate' 1 Y-Y
(G. Lewis) D.S. Bell, 1955

'Waimea' 2 W-? (b)
(F.A. Saunders) F.A. Saunders, 1955

'Wainui' 2 Y-O
(J.J. Abernethy, 1952) R.J. Abernethy, 1962
Fl. 108 mm wide; perianth soft golden yellow; corona bright reddish orange. Mid-season. Resembles a large-flowered and vigorous 'Alamein'

'Wairarapa' 2 W-? (b)
(J. Flemming, pre-1938)

'Wairarapa' 2 Y-Y
(D. Bramley) D. Bramley, 1978
'Mellow Dawn' × 'Golden Horn'; sdlg no. 68/11
Fl. 98 mm wide, deep yellow. Mid-season. Resembles a Div. 2 'Golden Horn' with a rounder and smoother flower

'Wairau' 2 W-WYW
(F.A. Saunders) F.A. Saunders, 1968
Fl. 108 mm wide; corona lemon yellow, with creamy white at base, frilled. Late

'Waireka' 2 W-W
(D. Bramley) D. Bramley, 1980
'Pallas' hybrid; sdlg no. 72/27
Fl. 90 mm wide. Mid-season. Resembles 'Pallas' but with a cream corona

'Wairere' 1 W-W
(D. Bramley) D. Bramley, 1980
'Whitemost' hybrid, sdlg no. 72/36
Fl. 108 mm wide. Mid-season. Resembles a larger 'Whitemost' with the perianth segments more broadly ovate

'Wairoa Belle' 3 Y-YYR
(C.L. Andrews)

'Wairuna Star' 2 Y-OOR
(D.N.Y. Olson) D.N.Y. Olson, 1988
'Checkmate' × 'Heathcliffe'; sdlg no. 77/29
Fl. 92 mm wide; perianth segments ovate, rounded at apex, medium yellow, overlapping; corona funnel-shaped, with the lower half orange and the upper half red, mouth expanded, with rim closely and deeply notched, as if fringed. Early. Sunproof. Resembles 'Heathcliffe' in strength of colour but with a differently shaped corona

'Waitara' 1 W-? (b)
(A. Overton) A. Overton, 1959

'Waitati' 1 W-? (b)
(J.A. Morris) J.A. Morris, 1955

'Waitemata'
(?Sir A.P.W. Thomas, pre-1915)

'Waitomo' 1 W-W
(C.A. Latta) C.A. Latta, 1960
Fl. 105 mm wide. Mid-season. Resembles 'Beersheba'

but with narrower perianth segments

'Wajang' 11a W-OOY
(J. Gerritsen & Son) J. Gerritsen & Son, 1984
Sdlg × 'Pick Up'; sdlg no. 833
Perianth segments ivory white; corona segments strong orange 25A, with patches of lemon yellow at rim. Mid-season

'Wakatipu' 2 W-? (b)
(A. Gibson, pre-1950)

'Wakefield' 2 W-W
(W.G. Pannill) W.G. Pannill, 1976
'Easter Moon' × 'Glendermott'; sdlg no. 62/24
Fl. 101 mm wide

'Wake Up' 2 Y-Y
(V. Brink, 1964) V. Brink, 1977
'Garden Princess' hybrid; sdlg no. 59/60
Fl. 102 mm wide, opening deep orange-yellow, becoming golden yellow. Early. Resembles a larger and earlier-flowered 'Garden Princess'

'Walana' 2 W-P
(H.G. Cross) H.G. Cross, 1985
'Precedent' × 'Verran'
Perianth segments very broadly ovate, mucronate, spreading, a little concave, with margins slightly incurling at apex, overlapping half; the inner segments narrower, square-shouldered at base, a little inflexed; corona flared, lightly ribbed, tinged salmon pink, flushed yellow at base, mouth lobed, split in places and overlapping, loosely frilled, with rim minutely crenate. Mid-season

'Walbottle' 2 Y-O
(G. Harrison) G. Harrison, 1971
Sdlg × 'Ceylon'
Fl. 102 mm wide

'Waldeck Piermont' 2 W-? (b)
(J.W.A. Lefeber, pre-1939)
Syn. 'Queen Emma'

'Walden Pond' 3 Y-Y
(T.D. Throckmorton, 1975) Grant Mitsch Novelty Daffodils, 1987
Sdlg 66/16 ('Oasis' × 'Green Island') × sdlg 66/12 ('Aircastle' × 'Irish Coffee'); sdlg no. 70/2/7
Fl. luminous yellow; corona small, very shallow bowl-shaped. Late. Resembles 'Golden Pond' but with a lighter-coloured corona

'Waldheim' 1 W-Y
(T.H. Piper) T.H. Piper, 1956
'Grayling' × 'Lorinna'
Corona lemon yellow

'Waldock' 1 Y-Y
(Frank Wilson, 1979) Frank Wilson, 1991
'Dutch Master' × (['Moonstruck' × 'Goldcourt'] × ['Sundance' × 'Dungiven']); sdlg no. K 94
Fl. forming a double triangle, 130 mm wide; perianth segments broadly ovate, with white mucro, spreading; the inner segments more narrowly ovate, somewhat creased, with margins wavy; corona funnel-shaped, smooth, darker in tone than the perianth, with mouth expanded, rim irregularly notched and widely rolled. Very early

'Waldorf Astoria' 4 W-P
(Brian S. Duncan) Rathowen Daffodils, 1987
'Pink Pageant' × sdlg 241 ('Passionale' × 'Polonaise'); sdlg no. 634
Fl. 105 mm wide; perianth and other petaloid segments in three whorls successively slightly shorter, very broad, somewhat truncate, only very slightly mucronate, very deeply overlapping; the outer whorl reflexed, plane, with margins slightly incurled; the second whorl more nearly spreading, with margins incurved, sometimes loosely folded along midrib; the centre whorl inflexed, with margins tightly infolded, sometimes twisted; corona segments half the length of the petaloid segments, opposite and interspersed among them, pink (shading from 25D to C). Late. AM(e) 1996

'Walesby' 2 W-P
(Mrs J. Abel Smith, 1972) Mrs J. Abel Smith, 1985
'Rose of Tralee' hybrid; sdlg no. T7/51
Corona deep pink. Mid-season

'Walhalla' 2 W-OOY
Syn. of 'Duke of Windsor'

'Walkover' 3 W-? (b)
(pre-1955)

'Walk͵re' 2 W-W
(Konynenburg & Mark) Konynenburg & Mark, 1964
Fl. 105 mm wide. Late

'Wallace' 3 W-Y
(E. Leeds, pre-1877)
Corona primrose yellow. Syn. Burbidgei 'Wallace'. Was "absorbed" into 'Guinever'

'Wallowa' 2 W-? (b)
(Oregon Bulb Farms, pre-1951)

'Wall Street' 2 (a)
(Barr & Sons, pre-1954)

'Walma' 3 W-? (b)
(H.A. Brown, pre-1936)

'Walo' 9
(A.M. Wilson, pre-1908)

'Walreddon' 2 (a)
(E.B. Champernowne, pre-1943)

'Walt Disney' 2 Y-O
(J.W.A. Lefeber, pre-1944)
Perianth segments rich yellow; corona orange. AM(Haarlem) 1944

'Walter Breedveld' 2 W-? (b)
(J.W.A. Lefeber, pre-1942)

'Walter Evans' 9
(N.Y. Lower, pre-1936)

'Walter Fitch' 3 W-? (b or c)
(pre-1936)

'Walter Hampden'
(pre-1939)

'Walter J.Smith' 2 W-WWY
(H.A. Brown, pre-1935)
Fl. large; perianth segments broadly ovate or somewhat oblong, blunt, prominently mucronate, a little reflexed, pure white, plane, overlapping half; the inner segments narrower, more nearly spreading, with margins wavy; corona disc-shaped, broad, loosely ribbed, greenish creamy white, with lemon yellow at rim, mouth closely ribbed and frilled, rim irregularly notched. Mid-season to late

'Walter Scott' 3 (a)
Syn. of 'Nassau'

'Walter Smith' 1 Y-Y
Syn. of 'Sarno'

'Walton Castle' 2 W-? (b)
(F.G. Lawson, pre-1947)

'Waltraute' 2 Y-YYR
(N.F. Lock, pre-1944)
Perianth segments yellow; corona bowl-shaped, darker in tone, with red at rim

'Walt Whitman' 9
(G.H. Engleheart, pre-1913)

'Waltzing Lily' 2 (a)
(Alister Clark, pre-1933)

'Walwyn' 1 W-Y
(pre-1920)
Perianth segments acute; corona slender, pale primrose yellow

'Wamphray' 2 Y-O
(D.C. MacArthur) D.C. MacArthur, 1992
2 Y-R × 2 Y-O; sdlg no. EV806
Fl. 93 mm wide; perianth segments broadly ovate, slightly mucronate, vivid yellow 9A, glistening; corona funnel-shaped, ribbed, opening strong orange 25B, soon becoming darker in tone (25A), with mouth flared and lobed. Early. Sunproof. Scented

'Wampum' 4 W-P
(Jackson's Daffodils) Jackson's Daffodils, 1997
Sdlg 211/78 × sdlg 122/83; sdlg no. 398/88
Fl. 108 mm wide; perianth and other petaloid segments broadly ovate, yellowish white 155B; corona segments pink, becoming darker in tone with age. Mid-season to late

'Wanda' 2 W-? (b or c)
(Cartwright & Goodwin, pre-1916)

'Wanda' 6 Y-Y
(de Graaff Bros, pre-1949)
Fl. dark yellow. AM(Haarlem) 1949

'Wanda Blenska' 2 W-O
(J.W.A. Lefeber) J.W.A. Lefeber, 1960
Corona rich pink-orange. Early

'Wanderer' 2 Y-Y
(J.S. Leitch) J.S. Leitch, 1968

'Wandering Ways' 2 (a)
(R. Hyde, pre-1951)

'Wandin Beauty' 2 W-W
(A. Overton) A. Overton, 1959
Corona opening pale pink, becoming white, with rim deeply dentate

'Wandin Gem' 1 W-Y
(A. Overton, pre-1960) Unregistered
Corona flanged. Early

'Wandin Giant' 1 Y-Y
(S. Morrison) T. Morrison, 1960

'Wandin Glory' 1 Y-Y
(S. Morrison, 1950) T. Morrison, 1960
Fl. rich yellow; corona frilled. Early

'Wandin Gold' 1 (a)
(S. Morrison, pre-1936)

'Wandin Queen' 2 W-Y
(S. Morrison, 1950) T. Morrison, 1960
Corona opening lemon yellow, becoming creamy yellow with tinges of buff yellow

'Waneta' 2 W-? (b)
(E.C. Powell, pre-1948)

'Wang' 1 Y-Y
(C.E. Radcliff, 1931)
'Golden City' × 'Gertrude Nethercote'

'Wanganui' 2 (a)
(W.A. Grace, pre-1938)

'Wangold' 1 Y-Y
(J.L. Martin) J.L. Martin, 1973
Sdlg × 'Kingscourt'
Fl. 91 mm wide

'Wanlo' 1 (a)
(West & Fell, pre-1938)

'Wannabe' 4 W-P
(Jackson's Daffodils, 1985) Jackson's Daffodils, 1997
'Chios' hybrid; sdlg no. 103/85
Fl. 100 mm wide; perianth segments ovate, yellowish white 155B, spreading, plane; corona segments orange-pink (29B), with yellow at base. Late

'Wannon' 1 (a)
(West & Fell, pre-1935)

'Wansea' 2 Y-YYO
(J.L. Martin) J.L. Martin, 1968
'Ivo Fell' × 'Shanghai'
Fl. 42 mm wide; perianth segments lemon yellow; corona golden yellow, shading to dark orange at rim. Mid-season

'Wansford' 2 W-? (b)
(R.H. Bath, pre-1931)

'Wantsum' 1 (a)
(G.P. Haydon, pre-1908)

'Wapiti' 11?a Y-Y
(Mrs H.H. Simmons) Mrs H.H. Simmons, 1976
'Hillbilly's Sister' × 'Paricutin'
Fl. 100 mm wide; perianth segments yellow; corona segments opening orange-yellow, becoming yellow. Mid-season

'Wapley' 2 (a)
(A.M. Wilson, pre-1950)

'War Ace' 2 W-O
(G.A. Nethercote) T. Morrison, 1960
Perianth segments creamy white; corona orange

'Waratah' 2 W-R
(West & Fell, pre-1929)
PC(e)(NZ) 1929

'Waratah' 2 Y-YYR
(pre-1949)
Perianth segments primrose yellow; corona with scarlet at rim

'Warbin' 1 Y-Y
(W. Jackson Jr, 1965) Jackson's Daffodils, 1979
'Bene' × ('Moque' × 'Anukis'); sdlg no. 3/65

Fl. 105 mm wide

'War Bird' 2 (a)
(H.A. Brown, pre-1950)

'Warbler' 6 Y-Y
(G.E. Mitsch) G.E. Mitsch, 1984
Sdlg B45/12 ('Flaming Meteor' hybrid) × *N. cyclamineus*; sdlg no. NN41/2
Fl. 70 mm wide; perianth segments broadly ovate, blunt, only very slightly mucronate, deep yellow, tinged green at base, strongly reflexed, overlapping half; the inner segments somewhat creased and with margins wavy; corona cylindrical, smoothly angled, slightly deeper in tone than the perianth, tinged orange at rim, mouth flared and loosely frilled, rim with deep crenations sometimes overlapping. Mid-season

'Warbleton' 2 Y-YOO
(N.A. Burr) N.A. Burr, 1990
'Vulcan' × 'Loch Lundie'; sdlg no. 1.4.78
Fl. forming a double triangle, 95 mm wide; perianth segments broadly ovate, blunt, fairly prominently mucronate, spreading, a little concave at apex, smooth, with broad midrib showing, regular, overlapping half; the inner segments more nearly roundish, plane, rounded at shoulder; corona cylindrical, smooth, mouth ribbed, straight, wavy or lightly frilled, with rim notched and crenate. Early to mid-season

'War Cloud' 1 W-O
(Hon. Sir R.H. Rhodes, pre-1912)
Perianth segments creamy white; corona golden orange, with mouth expanded. ?The same as 'War Cloud' 2 W-O

'War Cloud' 2 W-O
(A.E. Lowe, pre-1927)
Perianth segments pure white; corona widely expanded, golden orange. ?The same as 'War Cloud' 1 W-O

'Warcom' 1 Y-Y
(W. Jackson Jr, 1972) Unregistered
'Warbin' × 'Comal'; sdlg no. 24/72
Fl. rich golden yellow; perianth segments broadly ovate, smooth, deeply overlapping; corona with green at base, rim dentate and slightly flanged. Mid-season

'War Cry' 2 Y-YOO
(H.A. Brown, 1937) J.N. Hancock & Co., 1960
Perianth segments yellow; corona ribbed, orange, with yellow at base

'War Dance' 3 O-R
(Brian S.Duncan) Brian S.Duncan, 1993
('Altruist' × 'Ulster Bank') × (['Richhill' × 'Masai King'] × 'Bunclody); sdlg no. 1046

Fl 90 mm wide; perianth segments flushed apricot orange; corona shallow bowl-shaped, ribbed, rich orange-red, with mouth neatly lobed. Mid-season

'Warden' 2 W-? (b)
(G.H. Engleheart, pre-1907)

'Wareham' 2 W-? (b)
(Barr & Sons, pre-1949)

'Warflame' 2 W-R
(D.V. West, pre-1935)
Perianth segments off-white, twisted; corona large, opening greenish orange, becoming intense orange-red

'War Hawk' 2 (a)
(R.O. Backhouse, pre-1932)

'Warialda' 1 Y-Y
(W.M. Spry, pre-1973) Unregistered
'Welcome' × 'Irish Maximus'
Tall. Very early

'Warkworth' 3 W-YYO
(G. Harrison) G. Harrison, 1971
'Otterburn' × 'Signal Light'
Fl. 89 mm wide

'Warleggan' 2 Y-Y
(G.W. Tarry) du Plessis Bros, 1989
'Red Squirrel' × 'Zanzibar'; sdlg no. G5D
Fl. 95 mm wide, bright yellow. Late

'Warleigh' 2 Y-P
(T. Bloomer) du Plessis Bros, 1987
('Rose Caprice' × 'Binkie' hybrid) × 'Polonaise'; sdlg no. 432
Corona funnel-shaped, light pink, with mouth widely expanded. Mid-season to late. Resembles 'Camelford'

'Warleyensis' 1 Y-Y
(Miss E. Willmott, pre-1906)
AM 1906

'Warley Magna' 1 W-W
(G.H. Engleheart, pre-1902)
AM 1902

'Warley Scarlet' 3 W-YYR
(G.H. Engleheart, pre-1904)
Perianth segments broadly ovate, mucronate, creamy white, spreading, with margins usually incurving, slightly overlapping in lower third; the inner segments narrower, reflexed; corona large, shallow, closely ribbed, with lower half saffron yellow and upper half orange-red, closely frilled. AM 1904

'Warliana' 2 W-Y
(L. Buckland, pre-1926)
Corona intense orange-yellow

'Warlock' 2 W-YYO
(P.D. Williams, pre-1927)
'Chaucer' hybrid
Perianth segments very broadly ovate, prominently mucronate, opening cream, becoming white, stained yellow at base, spreading, overlapping one-third; the inner segments more nearly oblong; corona bowl-shaped, clear rich yellow, shading to bright orange at rim, with mouth split in places and overlapping, lightly frilled. Tall. Mid-season. 2n=28. *AM(g) 1930, *AM(g) 1936, *FCC(g) 1939

'War Lord' 2? W-O
(S.M. Mitchell, pre-1942)
'Havelock' × 'Hades'

'War Lord' 1 Y-Y
(R.C.A. Tombleson) R.C.A. Tombleson, 1968
Fl. 121 mm wide. Mid-season. Resembles an earlier-flowered and slightly paler 'Kingscourt'

'Warma' 2 W-P
(A.O. Roblin, 1947)
'Pink o' Dawn' × 'Pinkess'

'Warm Day' 2 O-O
(Kate Reade) Carncairn Daffodils, 1996
'Stylish' × 'Rory's Glen'; sdlg no. 1/6/86
Fl. 75 mm wide; perianth segments broadly ovate, rounded at apex, opening yellow-orange, becoming reddish orange, with white mucro, spreading, plane, opening ribbed, becoming smoother, overlapping half; corona cup-shaped, very deep reddish orange, with mouth straight and rim dentate. Mid-season. Resembles 'Rory's Glen' in colour

'Warmington' 3 W-W
(J.S.B. Lea) Clive Postles Daffodils, 1988
Sdlg no. L4-52-77
Fl. 105 mm wide, pure white; perianth segments very broadly ovate, blunt or truncate, mucronate, spreading, plane or somewhat concave, with margins incurling, smooth, with midrib showing, regular, overlapping half; the inner segments more narrowly ovate, with margins a little wavy; corona very short funnel-shaped, closely ribbed, with mouth expanded and wavy, rim minutely notched and crenate. Late

'Warm Springs' 2 Y-YYO
(G.A. Uit den Boogaard, pre-1945)

'Warmunda' 1 W-? (b)
(G.B. de Vroomen & Sons, pre-1934)

'Warne' 4 Y-O
(pre-1987) Unregistered
Perianth and other petaloid segments opening rich

yellow, becoming somewhat paler; corona segments deep orange

'Warning' 9
(W.F. Mitchell, pre-1939)

'War Paint' 2 Y-YYR
(G. Lewis, pre-1939)
Fl. forming a double triangle, 115 mm wide; perianth segments very broadly ovate, blunt, very slightly mucronate, spreading, plane, with margins incurling at apex, overlapping half or more; the inner segments a little narrower, somewhat creased, with margins incurved or twisted; corona shallow, widely expanded, ribbed, yellow, with a broad band of bright red at rim, mouth even, with rim minutely and densely notched

'War Paint' 2 Y-YRR
Syn. of 'Royal Windsor'

'War Queen' 1 Y-Y
(A.E. Lowe, pre-1927)

'Warragul Gem' 2 W-Y
(M. Gardiner) M. Gardiner, 1961
Fl. 140 mm wide; corona bright rich lemon yellow. Mid-season

'Warrantina' 2 W-R
(S.J. Bisdee, 1938)
'Margaret H.' × 'Sunstar'

'Warrawee' 2 W-W
(C.E. Radcliff, 1932)
'Pedestal' × 'Mrs W.Moodie'

'Warren' 1 Y-Y
(A.O. Roblin) , 1966
'Chromis' × 'Kingscourt'

'Warrington' 1 Y-Y
(W. Balch, pre-1933)

'Warrior' 3 W-O
(G.H. Engleheart, pre-1908)

'Warrior' 3 Y-O
(pre-1926)
Perianth segments pale yellow; corona reddish orange

'Warrior' 1 W-? (b)
(D.V. West, pre-1936)

'Warrior' 1 (a)
(Sir A.P.W. Thomas, pre-1937)

'Warrior' 2 Y-O
(J.L. Richardson) M.J. Jefferson-Brown, 1961
'Prince Regent' × 'Ceylon'

'Warspite' 3 W-YYO
(Mrs R.O. Backhouse, pre-1921)
Perianth segments very broad, pure white, with broad midrib showing, overlapping half; the inner segments more nearly ovate, square-shouldered at base; corona disc-shaped, orange-yellow, with a broad band of strong orange 25A at rim, mouth ribbed and widely expanded, split in places and overlapping, frilled. AM 1924

'War Step' 2 Y-YYR
(G. Lewis) D.S. Bell, 1955
See also 'Warstep'

'Warstep' 2 Y-YYR
Syn. of 'War Step'

'Warwick' 1 Y-Y
(de Graaff Bros, pre-1923)
'King Alfred' hybrid
Fl. rich butter yellow; corona a little darker in tone than the perianth

'Wasco' 2 Y-WWY
(Murray W. Evans) Murray W. Evans, 1987
('Daydream' × sdlg J-18) × ('Daydream' × 'Gypsy Princess'); sdlg no. V-3/1
Corona expanded, frilled. Mid-season

'Washington' 1 W-Y
(de Graaff Bros, pre-1923)

'Wasp' 1 (a)
(Cartwright & Goodwin, pre-1916)

'Watauga' 3 W-? (b)
(J.R. Pearson & Sons, pre-1948)

'Watcha' 1 Y-Y
(Jackson's Daffodils) Jackson's Daffodils, 1986
'Warbin' × 'Comal'; sdlg no. 34/78
Perianth segments vivid yellow 9B; corona very slightly darker in tone (9A). Early

'Watchfire' 3 W-O
(G.H. Engleheart, pre-1902)
'Princess Mary' × *N. poeticus* sdlg
AM 1902

'Watchful' 9
(G.H. Engleheart, pre-1930)

'Watchlight' 2 (a)
(de Graaff Bros, pre-1948)

'Watchman' 1 Y-Y
(R. Gibson, pre-1927)

'Watercolor' 2 W-P
(W. Gould Jr) W. Gould Jr, 1980

'Easter Moon' × 'Rose Royale'; sdlg no. 69-6-9-1
Fl. 110 mm wide. Early to mid-season

"Water Fairy Flower"
Syn. of *N.tazetta* subsp. *lacticolor*

'Waterfall' 2 or 3 W-? (b or c)
(Mrs R.O. Backhouse, pre-1914)

'Waterfall' 5 W-W
(G.H. Engleheart, pre-1927)
Fl. 76 mm wide, creamy white, facing down; perianth segments overlapping a quarter; corona funnel-shaped. Mid-season to late

'Waterford' 3 W-? (b)
(Mrs R.O. Backhouse, pre-1921)

'Watergate' 2 W-O
(J.W.A. Lefeber) J.W.A. Lefeber, 1977
Fl. 130 mm wide; perianth segments ivory white; corona light orange (23C), with a paler tone at rim

'Water Lily' 2 W-W
(G.H. Engleheart, pre-1907)

'Water Lily' 4
(E. & J.C. Martin, pre-1930)

'Waterloo' 2
(pre 1915)

'Waterloo' 1 W-? (b)
(Cartwright & Goodwin, pre-1916)

'Waterloo' 1 (a)
(G.H. Engleheart, pre-1921)

'Waterloo' 1 W-Y
(H.J. Poole Sr, pre-1927)
Perianth segments creamy white

'Water Music' 2 Y-W
(Elise Havens) G.E. Mitsch, 1975
'Nazareth' × 'Butterscotch'; sdlg no. FEJ6/1
Fl. forming a double triangle, 110 mm wide; perianth segments broadly ovate, blunt, only very slightly mucronate, soft pale lemon yellow, spreading or very slightly reflexed, plane, overlapping half; the inner segments more narrowly ovate, a little creased, slightly inflexed at base, reflexed in upper half; corona funnel-shaped, lightly ribbed, opening lemon yellow, becoming white, with mouth flared and frilled. Mid-season

'Water Nymph' 5
(Cartwright & Goodwin, pre-1908)

"Water Nymph Flower"
Syn. of *N.tazetta* subsp. *lacticolor*

'Waterperry' 7 W-YPP
(R.V. Favell, pre-1953)
Fls up to 3 per stem, 70 mm wide; perianth segments ovate, prominently mucronate, ivory white, spreading, creased, overlapping a quarter to one-third; the inner segments a little inflexed, square-shouldered at base, somewhat twisted or with margins wavy; corona cylindrical or narrowly funnel-shaped, smooth, flushed pale shell pink, with creamy yellow at base, shading to a darker tone of pink at rim, with mouth straight and lightly ribbed, wavy, rim crenate. Mid-season. Scented. 2n=21. *HC(p) 1986

'Watership Down' 2 W-W
(Clive Postles) Clive Postles Daffodils, 1990
'Burntollet' × 'Canisp'; sdlg no. 1-50-76
Fl. 98 mm wide, pure white; perianth segments ovate, smooth; corona slightly flared, with rim neatly dentate. Early

'Water Sprite' 3 W-? (b or c)
(G.H. Engleheart, pre-1907)

'Waterton' 3 W-? (b)
(pre-1907)

'Waterville' 2 W-W
(J.L. Richardson, pre-1943)
'White Sentinel' × 'Seraglio'
Perianth segments pure white, of waxy substance; corona very shallow bowl-shaped, almost white, faintly tinged green, with a stronger tinge of green at base and rim

'Waterway' 5
(G.H. Engleheart, pre-1923)

'Waterway' 2 W-?
(J.L. Richardson) D.A.B. Harries, 1963

'Waterwitch' 2 W-W
(G.H. Engleheart, pre-1907)
Syn. 'Water Witch'

'Water Witch' 2 W-W
Syn. of 'Waterwitch'

N. watieri Maire = *N. rupicola* subsp. *watieri*

'Watkin'
Syn. of 'Sir Watkin'

'Watling' 2 Y-Y
(K.B. Burns) K.B. Burns, 1964
Fl. 108 mm wide, lemon yellow; corona darker in tone. Mid-season

'Watteau' 1 W-Y
(de Graaff Bros, pre-1922)
Perianth segments creamy white, slightly twisted;

corona ribbed, pale sulphur yellow, flushed shell pink, with rim broadly crenate

'Wattle' 1 Y-Y
(West & Fell, pre-1935)
Fl. lemon yellow

'Wau' 1 Y-Y
(J.N. Hancock & Co., pre-1949)
Corona tightly frilled. Late

'Waubra' 2 Y-O
(J.N. Hancock & Co., pre-1949)
Perianth segments golden yellow; corona pale orange, with a deeper tone at rim, with rim closely and deeply notched, as if fringed. Early

'Wave Crest' 5
(G.H. Engleheart, pre-1910)

'Wavelength' 3 W-YYR
(Brian S.Duncan) Brian S.Duncan, 1997
'Mount Angel' × ('Cul Beag' × 'Doctor Hugh'); sdlg no. 1649
Fl. rounded, 103 mm wide; perianth segments very broadly ovate, pure white, spreading; corona shallow bowl-shaped, golden yellow, with a well-defined band of red at rim, mouth slightly ribbed. Mid-season to late

'Wavelet' 5 W-W
(G.H. Engleheart, pre-1923)
Fl. 95 mm wide, creamy white, facing down; perianth segments overlapping a quarter; corona cup-shaped. Mid-season to late

'Waveney Tribute' 2 W-YOO
(T. Bloomer) T. Bloomer, 1964
'Fermoy' × 'Arbar'; sdlg no. 2/39/54

'Waverley' 2 W-Y
(The Brodie of Brodie, c.1910)
'Emperor' × *N. poeticus*
Perianth segments very broad, creamy white, deeply overlapping; corona large, yellow

'Waverley' 2 W-W
(G.L. Wilson) C.R. Wootton, 1958
'Tryst' hybrid
Fl. becoming pure white; corona opening creamy yellow

'Wavertree' 1 Y-Y
International Registration Authority, 1997
Selection by F.R.Waley (pre-1987) from wild-collected *N. asturiensis*
Fl. vivid yellow; perianth segments oblong or narrowly ovate, acute, not prominently mucronate, inflexed or strongly inflexed, with margins sometimes wavy or incurving, separated or only very slightly overlapping; corona as long as the perianth segments, cylindrical, sometimes slightly constricted at mid-point, smooth, of thicker substance than the perianth and appearing to be darker in tone, with mouth flared and deeply 6-lobed, rim deeply and closely notched. Dwarf. Formerly named 'Giant'

'Wax Eye' 3 W-Y
(Colin Crotty, 1981) Colin Crotty, 1992
'Eminent' × 'Lysander'; sdlg no. 29-76
Fl. rounded, 102 mm wide; perianth segments pure white, smooth, deeply overlapping; corona pale yellow, with a darker tone at base and rim and with strong green noticeable in tube, frilled. Late

'Waxin' 1 Y-Y
(J. Gerritsen & Son) J. Gerritsen & Son, 1977
'Echo' hybrid
Fl. 100 mm wide. Early to mid-season

'Waxwing' 1 W-Y
(P.D. Williams, pre-1910)

'Waxwing' 5 W-W
(M. Fowlds) G.E. Mitsch, 1967
'Honey Bells' × 'Green Island'; sdlg no. F293/8
Fl. 85 mm wide, ivory white, of almost waxy texture. Mid-season

'Wayalinah' 2 W-P
(S.J. Bisdee, 1946)
'Pink o' Dawn' × 'Rosario'

'Wayfarer' 2 Y-R
(J.S. Leitch) J.S. Leitch, 1957

'Wayward' 2 W-? (b)
(Barr & Sons, pre-1950)

'Wazir' 2 (a)
(A.M. Wilson, pre-1950)

'W.C.Sharp' 2 W-? (b or c)
(R.G. Sharp, pre-1930)

'W.D.Burns' 1 (a)
(Mrs W.D. Burns, pre-1933)

'W.D.Drury' 1 W-Y
(pre-1907)
Perianth segments inflexed; corona canary yellow

'W.Dent'
(pre-1935)

'Wealden Fire' 2 Y-O
(N.A.Burr, 1984) N.A.Burr, 1995
'Drumrunie' × 'Bunclody'; sdlg no. 2.3.79
Fl. 113 mm wide; perianth segments very broadly ovate, blunt, slightly mucronate, vivid yellow 9A,

with the inner segments flushed orange, spreading, plane, overlapping half; the inner segments a little more narrowly ovate; corona cup-shaped, lightly ribbed, strong orange 25A, with mouth straight, rim notched and crenate. Mid-season

'Weardale' 1 W-Y
Syn. of 'Weardale Perfection'

'Weardale Perfection' 1 W-Y
(W. Backhouse, pre-1869)
Fl. up to 127 mm wide; perianth segments broadly or very broadly ovate, blunt, only very slightly mucronate, milk white or pale sulphur, touched with the corona colour at base, inflexed, with margins wavy, somewhat creased or with broad midrib showing, of good substance, overlapping one-third; the inner segments twisted; corona cylindrical, lightly ribbed, primrose yellow, paling a little at base, mouth expanded, rim broadly and irregularly crenate and a little flanged. Resembles a larger and paler-flowered 'Empress' with the corona mouth more widely expanded. FCC 1894. Received FCC 1894 as 'Weardale'

'Wearmouth' 1 W-? (b)
(G.P. Haydon, pre-1908)

'Weatherstones' 5 W-W
(D.H.L. Corrigan, pre-1949)
Fls up to 3 per stem, pure white

'Weatray' 1 (a)
(J.T. Gray, 1935) Parr's Nurseries, 1958

N. webbii Parlatore = *N. jonquilla*

'Webster' 9 W-GYR
(Brian S. Duncan) Rathowen Daffodils, 1981
'Milan' × 'Cantabile'; sdlg no. 505
Fl. 67 mm wide; perianth segments rounded at apex, prominently mucronate. Mid-season to late

'W.E.Cleverdon' W-? (b or c)
(West & Fell, pre-1935)

'Wedderburn' 1
(T.Morrison, pre-1960) Unregistered

'Wedding Band' 3 Y-WWY
(T.D. Throckmorton) T.D. Throckmorton, 1977
'Aircastle' × 'Chinese White'; sdlg no. 66/12/6
Fl. 90 mm wide; perianth segments opening white, becoming yellow, with a lighter tone at margins; corona white, with green at base and the colour of the perianth at rim. Mid-season

'Wedding Bell' 2 W-W
(W.J. Dunlop, pre-1950)
'Gracious' × 'Zero'
Fl. pure white

'Wedding Day' 1 W-W
(G.H. Engleheart, pre-1931)

'Wedding Gift' 2 W-W
(G.L. Wilson, 1951) H.I. Tuggle Jr, 1961
'Justice' × 'Guardian'
Fl. 102 mm wide. Mid-season. Resembles 'Guardian'

'Wedding Gown' 1 W-W
(A.M. Wilson) Mrs R. McConnel, 1956

'Wedding March' 2 W-? (b or c)
(R.H. Bath, pre-1937)
AM(Haarlem) 1937

'Wedding Ring' 3 W-OOR
(G. Lewis, pre-1936)
Perianth segments broad, mucronate, overlapping half; corona very large, widely expanded, ribbed, orange, with red at rim, heavily frilled. AM(e)(NZ) 1936

'Wedding Ring' ?-P
(Alister Clark, pre-1948)

'Wedding Ring' 2 W-? (b)
Syn. of 'Flaming Halo'

'Wedding Veil' 3 W-? (b or c)
(pre-1910)

'Wedmore' 1 (a)
(A.M. Wilson, pre-1930)
AM(Haarlem) 1937

'Wee Bee' 1 Y-Y
(Dutch origin, pre-1948)
Perianth segments ovate, with white mucro, inflexed, symmetrically twisted, overlapping at base only; corona cylindrical, smooth, a little constricted near mid-point, smooth, darker in tone than the perianth, with mouth flared, rim deeply notched. Dwarf. Resembles 'Bagatelle' and 'Little Gem'

'Weebud' 3 W-? (b)
(Mrs R.O. Backhouse, pre-1921)

'Weegeena' 2 W-W
(C.E. Radcliff, 1939) J.M.Radcliff, 1956
'Maid of the Mist' × 'Portia'

'Wee Macgreegor' 3
(J. Mallender, pre-1910)
Fl. small; corona disc-shaped, brightly coloured

'Weena' 2 W-? (b)
(A.H. Ahrens, pre-1949)

'Wee One' 2 Y-R
(M.E.Brogden, pre-1996) Unregistered
'Orator' × 'Salute'; sdlg no. 115/1

'Weeresteijn' 1 Y-Y
(J.H. Rijkelijkhuizen) J.H. Rijkelijkhuizen, 1975
'Carlton' hybrid
Fl. 140 mm wide; perianth segments brilliant yellow 7b; corona darker in tone (12A). Early

'Weeta' 1 W-W
(W. Jackson Jr, c.1957) Unregistered
'Ammon' × 'Merri'

'Weetapoona' 2 W-Y
(S.J. Bisdee, pre-1939)
'Jean Hood' × 'Blodwen'

'Wega' 2 W-? (b)
(Papendrecht-Vandervoet, pre-1939)

'Weiner Blut' 2 W-O
(pre-1972) Unregistered

'Weipa' 1 W-Y
(Jackson's Daffodils) Jackson's Daffodils, 1991
Sdlg no. 204B/82
Fl. forming a double triangle, 110 mm wide; perianth segments very broadly ovate, blunt, fairly prominently mucronate, greenish white (155A), spreading, a little concave, smooth and of thick substance, overlapping half; the inner segments more narrowly ovate, slightly inflexed; corona cylindrical, broadly angled, light greenish yellow 3C, with mouth widely expanded and lightly frilled, rim rolled and crenate. Early to mid-season

'Weisshorn' 1 W-W
(J.L. Richardson, pre-1952)
'Carmel' open pollinated × 'Broughshane'
Corona with mouth widely expanded and rim flanged

'Weka' 2 W-Y
(J.S. Leitch) J.S. Leitch, 1967
Corona large, widely expanded, lemon yellow

'Welbeck' 1 Y-Y
(Mrs J. Abel Smith, 1964) Mrs J. Abel Smith, 1975
'Kingscourt' × 'Ios'; sdlg no. T/81
Fl. 110 mm wide, golden yellow. Early to mid-season

'Welcome' 2 W-Y
(R.Gibson, pre-1927)

'Welcome' 2 (a)
(J.R.Pearson & Sons, pre-1927)

'Welcome' 2 W-Y
(G.W.E. & M.E.Brogden) G.W.E. & M.E.Brogden, 1980

('Green Island' × 'Landmark') × 'Verona'; sdlg no. T63
Fl. 108 mm wide

'Welcome Inn'
(O. Ronalds, pre-1979) Unregistered
2n=28

'Welcome Nugget' 1 (a)
(D.S. Bell) D.S. Bell, 1955

'Weld Cona' 2 (a)
(G. Lewis) D.S. Bell, 1955
Syn. 'Wild Cona'

'Welfare' 2 W-P
(Tom Forster, 1960s) Unregistered

'Welkin' 1 Y-Y
(O. Ronalds) A. Overton, 1960

'Well-born' 2 W-W
(G.L. Wilson, pre-1948)
'Niphetos' × 'Truth'

'Wellesley' 2 W-? (b)
(S.L. Danby, pre-1936)

'Wellington' 2 Y-Y
(E. Leeds, pre-1877)
Tall. Syn. Incomparabilis Concolor 'Wellington'. Was "absorbed" into 'Incomparabilis'

'Wellington' 2 Y-R
(Australian or New Zealand origin, c.1927)

'Wellington' 2 Y-R
(C. Goodson, pre-1930)

'Wellington'
(G. Lewis)
'Tamerlane' × 'Gloria Mundi'
AM(e)(NZ) 1928

'Wellingtonia' 2 Y-O
(H.A. Brown, 1936) J.N Hancock & Co., 1960

'Wellow' 2 W-P
(Mrs J. Abel Smith) Mrs J. Abel Smith, 1979
'Chelsea Derby' × 'Rose Caprice'; sdlg no. Q6/11
Fl. 95 mm wide; corona bright pink, with a deeper tone at rim. Late

'Wellshott' 2 W-? (b)
(Alister Clark, 1930) J. Sharp, 1960

'Wellwisher' ?-P
(Alister Clark, pre-1948)

'Well Worth' 7 Y-Y
(W.G. Pannill) W.G. Pannill, 1977

'Aircastle' × *N. jonquilla*; sdlg no. G 17
Fl. 75 mm wide, beige. Late

"Welsh Peerless"
See "The Welsh Peerless"

'Welvan' 3 W-GYY
(W. Jackson Jr, 1969) Unregistered
'Arbar' × sdlg 79/60; sdlg no. 175/69

'Wembley' 2 Y-Y
(D. van Egmond & Sons) D. van Egmond & Sons, 1963
Fl. 111 mm wide; perianth segments greenish yellow (4D); corona vivid yellow 13A, with a darker tone at rim. Mid-season

'Wen' 1 W-W
(A.O. Roblin, c.1966) Unregistered
'Taran' × 'Rhana'

'Wenckebach' 2 (a)
(E. Oostdam, pre-1939)

'Wendover' 7 W-Y
(W.G. Pannill) W.G. Pannill, 1978
'Silken Sails' × *N. jonquilla*; sdlg no. G5
Fl. 75 mm wide; perianth segments white; corona yellow, becoming white with age. Mid-season

'Wendy' 2 W-Y
(The Brodie of Brodie, pre-1920)
Perianth segments acute, overlapping; corona expanded, ribbed, buffy apricot yellow

'Wendy' 2 W-W
(R.H.Glover, pre-1993) Unregistered

'Wendy Dunne' 2 W-P
(L.P.Dettman, 1977) Unregistered
'Isobel Chaplin' × 'Ann Cameron'; sdlg no. IC/AC 6/78

'Wendy-Stewart' 2 W-P
(L.P. Dettman) L.P. Dettman, 1982
'Peggy Dettman' open pollinated; sdlg no. P/D 1/81
Perianth segments greenish white (155A); corona pale yellowish pink 27D. Mid-season

'Wendy Walsh' 2 Y-GYP
(Carncairn Daffodils) Carncairn Daffodils, 1988
('Shantallow' × 'Irish Rose') × 'Tynan'; sdlg no. 1/52/76
Fl. 90 mm wide; perianth segments broadly ovate, blunt, mucronate, opening white, becoming soft yellow, reflexed, plane, with margins sometimes nicked, smooth, regular, overlapping half; the inner segments more narrowly ovate; corona cup-shaped, lightly ribbed, with a well-defined band of pink at rim, mouth expanded. Late

'Wenjen' 3 W-YYR
(Campbell Duncan) Campbell Duncan, 1956
'Seraglio' self pollinated

'Wenonah' 1 W-? (b)
(G.H. Furness, pre-1934)

'Wenonah' 3 W-W
(S.J. Bisdee, 1935)
'Fay' × 'Silver Plane'
Div. 2 until 1948

'Wensley' 1 (a)
(D.B. Milne, pre-1950)

'Wentworth' 2 W-GWW
(Brian S. Duncan) Rathowen Daffodils, 1978
'Ave' × 'Empress of Ireland'; sdlg no. 125
Fl. white; corona with olive green at base. Mid-season. Resembles a larger-flowered and stronger-stemmed 'Inverpolly' with green in the corona

'Weregild' 2 W-O
(Warnaar & Co., pre-1930)
AM(Haarlem) 1930

'Werrington' 1 (a)
(A.M. Williams, pre-1951)

'Westbrook' 2 W-W
(F.D.B. Cobb, pre-1953)

'Westbury' 4 W-P
(Brian S. Duncan) Rathowen Daffodils, 1987
('Falaise' × 'Debutante') × ('Polonaise' × ('Polonaise' × 'Violetta'); sdlg no. 815
Perianth and other petaloid segments white; corona segments interspersed at centre, delicate lilac pink. Mid-season to late

'West End' 4 W-P
Syn. of 'Blushing Maiden'

'Westerdunes' 2 W-W
(F.E. Board) F.E. Board, 1965
'Easter Moon' × 'Homage'; sdlg no. 1362
Late

'Westerhope' 3 Y-O
(G. Harrison) G. Harrison, 1968
Sdlg × 'Chungking'
Fl. 95 mm wide; corona dark orange. Mid-season. Resembles 'Chungking' but with the perianth of smoother texture

'Western Flame' 3 Y-YRR
(W.F.M. Copeland, pre-1910)
Fl. rounded; perianth segments glistening sulphur yellow, of great substance, deeply overlapping; corona strongly ribbed, glowing orange-red, with a broad

band of lemon yellow at base

'Western Lady' 1 W-? (b)
(G.H. Engleheart, pre-1916)

'Western Star' 2 W-Y
(Oregon Bulb Farms, pre-1950)

'Westgate' 3 W-?
(J.L. Richardson, pre-1944)
'Seraglio' × 'Hades'
Perianth segments very broad, truncate and prominently mucronate, spreading, with margins wavy, overlapping half; the inner segments narrower, more deeply truncate, with margins more strongly wavy; corona shallow bowl-shaped, ribbed, with a broad band of a contrasting colour at rim, mouth split in places and overlapping, tightly frilled

'Westholme' 2 W-GYY
(Brian S. Duncan) Rathowen Daffodils, 1986
'Woodland Prince' × 'Eminent'; sdlg no. 714
Corona lemon yellow. Mid-season. Resembles 'Eminent' but with a whiter perianth and longer corona

'Westhorpe' 2 Y-R
(Mrs J. Abel Smith) Mrs J. Abel Smith, 1971
'Armada' × 'Carbineer'
Fl. 102 mm wide; perianth segments golden yellow; corona orange-red. Mid-season. Sunproof

'Westminster' 2 Y-? (a)
(P.D. Williams, pre-1933)
AM(Haarlem) 1933, FCC(Haarlem) 1939

'West Moors' 1 W-W
(J.W. Barr, pre-1926)
Fl. sulphur white; corona neatly frilled

'Weston' 1 Y-Y
(R. Dick, pre-1933)
Fl. clear golden yellow

'Westonville' 2 (a)
(F.D.B. Cobb, pre-1953)

'West Point' 2 W-? (b)
(Warnaar & Co., pre-1938)
AM(Haarlem) 1937

'Westport' 1 Y-Y
(Mrs E. Murray) Mrs E. Murray, 1959

'Westralian' 2 (a)
(The Brodie of Brodie, pre-1927)

'Westray' 1 Y-Y
(J.T. Gray, pre-1949)
Corona with rim rolled and dentate

'West Sands' 1 Y-Y
(J.N. Hancock & Co., 1946)

'West View' 2 or 3 W-? (b or c)
(pre-1915)

'West Virginia' 2 W-W
(Mrs C.E. Fitzwater) Mrs C.E. Fitzwater, 1984
'Easter Moon' × 'Panache'; sdlg no. 43/4
Mid-season

'Westward' 4 W-Y
(J.L. Richardson) G. Zandbergen-Terwegen, 1962
'Falaise' hybrid
Perianth and other petaloid segments ivory white; corona segments vivid yellow 9B. AM(Haarlem) 1962

'West Wind' 7 Y-Y
(A. Gray) A. Gray, 1958
N. rupicola subsp. *watieri* × *N. jonquilla*
Fl. pale yellow

'Westwood' 2 G-G
(W.M. Spry, pre-1975) Unregistered
'Hunter's Moon' × Ronalds sdlg
Perianth segments pale green; corona buff lemon green, frilled. Late

'Wetherby' 3 W-YYR
(Brian S. Duncan) Unregistered Rathowen Daffodils, 1983
'Merlin' × 'Silent Beauty'; sdlg no. 411
Fl. 106 mm wide; perianth segments very broadly ovate, somewhat truncate, slightly mucronate, spreading, concave, with margins minutely incurling at apex, smooth, overlapping half; the inner segments narrower, rounded at apex, with margins a little wavy; corona very shallow bowl-shaped, faintly ribbed, yellow, with a broad band of bright orange-red at rim, frilled, with rim dentate and in places more deeply notched. Mid-season. 2n=28. Resembles a smoother 'Silent Beauty' of more consistency as a show flower

'Wewak' 2 Y-OYO
(J.N. Hancock & Co., 1947)
'Trenoon' hybrid
Corona yellow, with orange at base and rim

'Wexford' 2 Y-Y
(J.L. Richardson, pre-1948)
'Braemar' × 'Crocus'
Fl. soft golden yellow; perianth segments broadly ovate, prominently mucronate, spreading, with margins incurling at apex, smooth, overlapping half; the inner segments more narrowly ovate, inflexed at base, slightly reflexed at apex; corona cylindrical, smooth, with mouth ribbed and widely flared, lightly frilled, rim notched and crenate

'W.F.Fitch' 2 W-? (b)
(H.R. Meyer, pre-1927)

'W.F.Gates' 2 Y-Y
(D.V. West, pre-1933)
Fl. soft yellow

'Whakatane' 2 W-W
(R. Hyde) R. Hyde, 1957

'Whang-Hi' 6 Y-O
(C.F. Coleman, 1948) C.F. Coleman, 1960
Fl. 72 mm wide; perianth segments broadly ovate, strongly reflexed, overlapping; corona bowl-shaped, ribbed. Dwarf to standard. Resembles a larger and more colourful 'Beryl'

'Whariti' 2 Y-YOR
(S.A. Free) S.A. Free, 1964
Fl. 108 mm wide; perianth segments deep yellow; corona orange, shading to rich yellow at base and bright red at rim. Mid-season

'W.H.Booth' 1 (a)
(J. Flemming, pre-1949)

'Wheadon's Delight' 2 W-? (b)
(E.H. Wheadon & Sons, pre-1916)

'Wheal Bush' 4 Y-Y
(R.A.Scamp) R.A.Scamp, 1997
'Saint Keverne' × 'Tamar Fire'; sdlg no. 438
Fl. 100 mm wide; perianth and other petaloid segments in several whorls, ovate, dark golden yellow; corona segments darker in tone, slightly frilled. Mid-season

'Wheal Coates' 7 Y-O
(R.A.Scamp) R.A.Scamp, 1996
'Pinza' × *N. jonquilla*; sdlg no. 416
Fl. rounded, 62 mm wide; perianth segments broadly ovate, dark golden yellow, deeply overlapping; corona shallow bowl-shaped, bright orange, with rim neatly crenate. Mid-season

'Wheal Honey' 1 W-Y
(R.A.Scamp) R.A.Scamp, 1997
'Burntollet' × 'Ben Aligin'; sdlg no. 456
Fl. 110 mm wide; perianth segments broadly ovate, pure white, plane, smooth; the inner segments almost overlapping one another; corona cylindrical, bright canary yellow, neatly frilled. Mid-season to late

'Wheal Jane' 2 W-W
(R.A.Scamp) R.A.Scamp, 1997
'Pitchroy' × 'Canisp'; sdlg no. 245
Fl. 115 mm wide, pure white; perianth segments ovate, deeply overlapping; corona funnel-shaped. Mid-season to late

'Wheal Kitty' 7 W-W
(R.A. Scamp) R.A. Scamp, 1993
'Handcross' × *N. jonquilla*; sdlg. no. 219
Fl. 72 mm wide, opening yellowish white, becoming pure white; perianth segments sometimes twisted, deeply overlapping; corona smooth, with rim neatly flanged. Dwarf. Early

'Wheatear' 3 W-GRR
(P.D. Williams, pre-1907)

'Wheatear' 6 Y-WWY
(G.E. Mitsch) G.E. Mitsch, 1976
('Mitylene' × *N. cyclamineus* sdlg) hybrid; sdlg no. E57/5
Fl. 100 mm wide; perianth segments reflexed; corona opening yellow, becoming pure white, with yellow at rim. Mid-season

'Wheel of Fortune' 2 Y-Y
(W.F.M. Copeland, pre-1923)
Fl. broad, pale lemon yellow; perianth segments overlapping; corona large, with rim dentate

'Whelp' 2 (a)
(P.D. Williams, pre-1914)

'Whelp' 3 W-YYO
(P.D. Williams, pre-1915)
Perianth segments acute; corona mid-yellow, with a very narrow band of orange at rim

'Whenuapai' 1 W-? (b)
(New Zealand origin) R. Hyde, 1958

'Whero' 2 Y-R
(G.W.E. Brogden) G.W.E. Brogden, 1959

'Wherwell' 3 W-? (b)
(P.D. Williams, pre-1928)

'Whetstone' 1 W-W
(G.E. Mitsch and R. & E.Havens, 1974) G.E. Mitsch and R. & E.Havens, 1987
('Vigil' × 'Empress of Ireland') × 'Panache'; sdlg no. JJ57/5
Corona narrow, constricted near mid-point. Mid-season

'Whetstone Tribute' 7 W-P
(G.E.Mitsch, 1972) R. & E.Havens, 1996
'Quick Step' open pollinated; sdlg no. HO20/20
Fls 1-2 per stem, 57 mm wide; perianth segments ovate; corona cup-shaped, light pink, with mouth slightly wavy. Late. Sunproof. Scented

'Whimbrel' 2 W-WOO
(A.M. Wilson, pre-1938)
Corona soft apricot orange, paling towards base. Div. 3 until 1944

'Whimsey' 2 Y-Y
(J.N. Hancock & Co., 1965) Unregistered

'Whimsy' 4
(G.C. Graham, pre-1951)

'Whinfire' 2 (a)
(J.W. Barr, pre-1930)

'Whipcord' 7 Y-O
(J.W.Blanchard, 1985) J.W.Blanchard, 1996
'Falstaff' × N. cordubensis; sdlg no. 80/1G
Fls 1-2 per stem, 60 mm wide; perianth segments broadly ovate, rich butter yellow, with white mucro, spreading, with margins incurving, overlapping half; the inner segments a little inflexed, with margins wavy; corona short funnel-shaped, widely expanded, deep orange, paling to base, with mouth lobed and even. Very early. Sunproof

'Whipcracker' 2 W-O
(N.H. Anglo) N.H. Anglo, 1986
'Irish Rover' × 'Don Carlos'
Perianth segments of heavy substance; corona with rim lightly dentate. Mid-season to late. Resembles 'Irish Rover' but with a larger corona

'Whipped Cream' 4
(?W.A. Watts, pre-1913)

'Whippersnapper' 2 W-Y
(R.G. Cull) Hokorawa Daffodils, 1992
'Ceres' open pollinated; sdlg no. HC/Z1
Corona brilliant yellow 13C. Mid-season

'Whip-poor-will' 6 Y-Y
(Mrs G. Link) Mrs G. Link, 1979
'Bushtit' open pollinated; sdlg no. 1970/3
Fl. 100 mm wide, deep yellow, of heavy substance and smooth texture. Mid-season. Resembles a much larger and better-poised 'Bushtit' of deeper colouring

'Whirlaway' 3 Y-GYO
(T.D. Throckmorton) T.D. Throckmorton, 1976
'Gossamer' × 'Aircastle'; sdlg no. 65/2/8
Perianth segments soft beige yellow; corona yellow, with olive green at base and pinkish orange at rim. Mid-season. Resembles 'Lalique' but with a more colourful corona

'Whirligig' 4 W-O
(W.F.M. Copeland, pre-1909)
Perianth and other petaloid segments creamy white, regularly arranged; corona segments rich orange. Early

'Whirlowdale' 1 W-Y
(F.E. Board) F.E. Board, 1965
'Preamble' × 'Kanchenjunga'; sdlg no. 504
Early

'Whirlwind' 1 W-W
(G.L. Wilson, pre-1938)
'Beersheba' × 'Kanchenjunga'
Corona ribbed and frilled

'Whiro Kina' 1 W-W
(G.L. Wilson, 1954) G.B. Cull, 1964
Fl. 108 mm wide; corona opening pale lemon yellow. Early. Resembles an earlier-flowered 'Bridal Robe' of stronger substance with the perianth segments more nearly spreading and plane

'Whisky' 1 Y-Y
(D. Bramley) D. Bramley, 1980
'Mellow Dawn' × 'Palmino'; sdlg no. 69/25
Fl. 102 mm wide. Mid-season. Resembles a smoother and rounder-flowered 'Palmino' of deeper colour

'Whisper' 3 W-GYY
(P.D. Williams, pre-1914)
Perianth segments ivory white; corona citron yellow, with pale green at base. Late

'Whisper' 5 W-Y
(M.J. Jefferson-Brown) M.J. Jefferson-Brown, 1960
'Orange Glory' × 'Dawn'
Perianth segments narrow, opening primrose yellow, becoming white, smooth; corona smooth, pale yellow. Late. Resembles a taller and more robust 'Dawn' with a longer corona

'Whispering Winds' 2 W-GPP
(G.E.Mitsch, 1979) R. & E.Havens, 1996
Sdlg A49/1 (sdlg Q36/4 × 'Carita') × 'Eclat'; sdlg no. 2K22/3
Fl. 100 mm wide; perianth segments broadly ovate, spreading, plane; corona shallow, apricot pink, with green at base and a deeper pink at rim, closely frilled. Mid-season. Sunproof

'Whistler' 1 Y-Y
(M. van Waveren & Sons, pre-1926)
Fl. 140 mm wide; perianth segments broadly ovate, blunt, fairly prominently mucronate, sulphur yellow, spreading, somewhat creased, overlapping one-third to a half; the inner segments narrower, square-shouldered at base, a little inflexed, with margins wavy; corona funnel-shaped, darker in tone than the perianth, with mouth ribbed and widely expanded, sometimes deeply split and overlapping, rim very widely flanged, deeply and irregularly notched and crenate. AM(Haarlem) 1930

'Whistler' 2 Y-O
(?de Graaff Bros, pre-1928)
Perianth segments narrow, acute; corona large, dark orange. AM(Haarlem) 1928

'Whit' 9 W-GWP
(Mrs M.S.Yerger) Mrs M.S.Yerger, 1994

Evans sdlg N-25 × 'Dreamland'; sdlg no. 80 A 1
Fl. 40 mm wide; perianth segments very deeply overlapping; the inner segments narrower; corona cup-shaped, yellow-white, with light yellow-green 138D at base and moderate yellowish pink 39C at rim, with the rim closely notched. Dwarf. Early

'Whitbourne' 3 W-GYR
(M.J. Jefferson-Brown) M.J. Jefferson-Brown, 1975
Mid-season to late. Resembles 'Merlin' but with the perianth segments broadly ovate and with green at corona base

'Whiteabbey' 2 W-GWW
(Ballydorn Bulb Farm) Ballydorn Bulb Farm, 1986
'Churchman' × 'Spelga'
Fl. of strong substance; perianth segments broadly ovate; corona flared. Mid-season

'Whiteadder' 4 Y-Y
(Mrs M.G. Mitchell Innes, 1955) Mrs M.G. Mitchell Innes, 1968
?*N. pseudonarcissus* sport
Fl. 50-65 mm wide, pale yellow, strongly suffused with lime green, with some older flowers appearing to be entirely green; perianth and other petaloid segments in several whorls, successively narrower towards centre. Mid-season to late. Resembles a larger and later-flowered 'Rip van Winkle' more heavily suffused with green. ?The same as 'Greenstar'

'White Admiral' 1 W-W
(Mrs R.O. Backhouse, pre-1908)

'White Ajax' 1 W-W
Syn. of 'White Trumpet'

'White Angel' 4
(van Graven Bros, pre-1954)

'White Artist' 3 W-YYR
(S.C. Gaspar) S.C. Gaspar, 1955
Perianth segments pure white, of thick substance; corona disc-shaped, deep yellow, with a band of bright red at rim, rim dentate

'White Ash' 1 W-W
(J. Gerritsen & Son) J. Gerritsen & Son, 1968
'Roquefort' × *N. minor* sdlg
Fl. 80 mm wide; perianth segments ivory white; corona creamy white. Early

'White Australia' 1 W-W
(West & Fell, pre-1935)
'Swanley Perfection' × 'White Emperor'

'White Banner' 2 W-? (b)
(C.G. van Tubergen, pre-1945)

'Whitebeam' 2 W-? (b or c)
(P.D. Williams, pre-1931)

'White Beauty' 1 W-W
(The Brodie of Brodie, pre-1929)

'White Bell' 1 W-W
(P.D. Williams, pre-1923)

'White Belle' 3 W-W
(T. Bloomer) T. Bloomer, 1970
'Verona' × 'Cascade'

'Whitebridge' 1 W-W
(The Brodie of Brodie, c.1932)
'Corinth' × 'Naxos'

'White Butterfly' 2 W-W
(The Brodie of Brodie, c.1936)
'Alburnia' × 'Evening'

'White Butterfly' 11b W-Y/OW
Syn. of 'Marie-José'

'White Caps' 6 W-Y
(G.E. Mitsch, 1958) G.E. Mitsch, 1968
'Mitylene' × *N. cyclamineus*; sdlg no. T35/10
Fl. 64 mm wide; corona lemon yellow. Mid-season. Resembles a smaller-flowered and more robust 'Dove Wings' with the perianth segments more strongly reflexed

'White Castle' 1 W-W
(G.L. Wilson, pre-1948)
AM(Haarlem) 1950

'White Charm' 2 W-W
(J.A. O'More) J.A. O'More, 1971
'Beersheba' × 'Carnlough'
Fl. 108 mm wide

'White Cheerio' 2 W-R
(C.E. Radcliff, 1946) J.M. Radcliff, 1956
('Puzzle' × 'Warflame') × 'Atanga'

'White Chevron' 1 W-W
(W.B. Cranfield, pre-1927)

'White Chief' 1 W-W
(M.J. Jefferson-Brown) M.J. Jefferson-Brown, 1975
Early to mid-season. 2n=28

'White China' 4 W-W
(D.S. Bell) D.S. Bell, 1983
Sdlg × 'Accent'

'White Christmas' 1 W-W
(H.A. Brown, 1942)
Fl. large; perianth segments plane, smooth; corona pearl white. Late

'White Christmas' 2 W-W
Syn. of 'White Xmas'

'White Circle' 3 W-GWY
(G.L. Wilson) G.L. Wilson, 1960
'Tryst' × 'Bryher'

'White City' 3 W-W
(Mrs R.O. Backhouse, pre-1910)
Fl. opening creamy white; perianth segments becoming pure white, somewhat inflexed, of strong substance; corona small, usually becoming pure white. AM(Haarlem) 1925, FA(Haarlem) 1926

'White City' 1 W-W
(West & Fell, pre-1936)

'White Cliffs' 5 W-W
(A.E. Lowe, pre-1927)

'White Cloud' 5 W-W
(H. Backhouse, pre-1913)
'Minnie Hume' × *N. triandrus* var. *loiseleurii*

'White Coat' 1
(C.L. Adams, pre-1913)

'White Cockade' 4 W-Y
(W.F.M. Copeland, pre-1915)
Perianth and other petaloid segments creamy white; corona segments short, densely arranged among the few petaloid segments at centre, citron yellow

'White Colossus' 2 W-Y
(C.G. van Tubergen, pre-1923)
Fl. 81 mm wide; perianth segments overlapping half; corona creamy yellow, flushed orange, with mouth expanded. Mid-season

'White Conqueror' 1 W-W
(Mrs R.O. Backhouse, pre-1921)
Corona opening very faintly tinged lemon, becoming white. Early. *C(g) 1927

'White Convention' 1 W-W
(J.S.B. Lea) J.S.B. Lea, 1983
'Pitchroy' × 'Panache'; sdlg no. 4-58-73
Fl. 105 mm wide

'White Coral' 5 W-W
(W.F.M. Copeland, pre-1922)
Fl. 76 mm wide, creamy white, facing down; perianth segments overlapping half; corona cup-shaped, with mouth widely expanded, frilled. Mid-season to late. AM(e) 1922

'White Countess' 2 W-? (b or c)
(P.D. Williams, pre-1913)

'White Court' 1 W-W
(D.S. Bell) D.S. Bell, 1968
Fl. pure white

'White Crest' 1 W-W
(G.L. Wilson, pre-1950)

'White Cross' 2 W-? (b)
(C.G. van Tubergen, pre-1914)

'White Cross' 2 W-W
(Ballydorn Bulb Farm, 1970) Ballydorn Bulb Farm, 1983
'Glandore' × 'Theano'
Fl. 105 mm wide; corona with olive green at base. Mid-season

'White Crown' 1 W-W
(E.H. Krelage & Son, pre-1942)

'White Crystal' 2 W-W
(Mrs J. Abel Smith) Mrs J. Abel Smith, 1986
'Desdemona' × 'Jennifer Ruth'

'White Cycle'
(pre-1938)

'White Dame' 1 W-W
(G.L. Wilson, pre-1922)
?'Madame de Graaff' × 'Lola'
Perianth segments broadly ovate, not prominently mucronate, spreading or a little inflexed, with margins sometimes wavy, overlapping one-third; the inner segments more narrowly ovate, ribbed, with margins twisted; corona funnel-shaped, with mouth ribbed and widely expanded, rim flanged and irregularly crenate. FCC(e) 1922

'White Damson' 2 W-O
(J.L. Richardson, pre-1946)
Perianth segments pure white; corona reddish orange

'White Delight' 2 W-W
(R.H. Bath, pre-1923)
Perianth segments creamy white, overlapping; corona expanded, tinged pale creamy yellow. Mid-season. *C(g) 1936

'White Diamond' 1 W-W
(Mrs J. Abel Smith) Mrs J. Abel Smith, 1982
'Desdemona' × 'Jennifer Ruth'; sdlg no. G9/61
Fl. 112 mm wide, pure white. Early. 2n=28

'White Dove' 1 W-W
(Miss K. Spurrell, pre-1907)

'White Dream' 1 W-WWY
(J.W.A. Lefeber) N. Vonderbank & Son, 1988
Sdlg no. 62
Fl. becoming ivory white; corona opening with pale primrose yellow at rim. Mid-season

'White Duchess' 2 W-W
(Cartwright & Goodwin, pre-1916)

'White Duchess' 2 W-? (b or c)
(F.H. Chapman, pre-1937)
AM(Haarlem) 1937

'White Duchess' 11b W-YYW
(J.W.A. Lefeber, 1942) J.W.A. Lefeber, 1960
Fl. 75 mm wide; corona segments with a longtudinal band of lemon yellow at midrib and white at margins. Late

'White Eagle' 3 W-YYO
(Barr & Sons, pre-1907)
Perianth segments reflexed; corona lemon yellow, tinged orange and with orange at rim. Late

'White Eagle' 2 W-Y
(Barr & Sons, pre-1931)
Perianth segments pure white, overlapping; corona expanded, creamy primrose yellow

'White Elephant' 9
(G.H. Engleheart, pre-1898)

'White Elf' 1 W-W
(R.H. Bath, pre-1923)

'White Emblem' 2 W-W
(II. de Graaff & Sons, pre-1927)
Fl. silvery white. Tall. Early. FA(Haarlem) 1927

'White Emperor' 1 W-W
(G.H. Engleheart, pre-1913)
'J.B.M.Camm' × 'Madame de Graaff'
Fl. 95-105 mm wide; perianth segments broadly ovate, blunt, mucronate, creamy white, a little inflexed, slightly concave, overlapping one-third; the inner segments narrower, inflexed at base, reflexed in upper half, slightly twisted; corona funnel-shaped, opening pale cream, becoming creamy white, with mouth finely ribbed and rim narrowly rolled. Midseason. 2n=28. AM 1913. Varies between Divs 1 and 2

'White Empire' 1 W-W
(J.L. Richardson, pre-1949)
'Cameronian' × 'Broughshane'
Fl. pure white

'White Empress' 2 or 3 W-? (b or c)
(Mrs R.O. Backhouse, pre-1914)

'White Empress' 1 W-W
(T. Bloomer) T. Bloomer, 1970
'Rashee' × 'Empress of Ireland'; sdlg no. 10/18/58
Fl. 96 mm wide, ice white; perianth segments very broadly ovate, blunt, prominently mucronate, somewhat inflexed, a little creased, overlapping half; the inner segments more narrowly ovate, acute; corona cylindrical, smooth, touched green at base, frilled, with rim rolled and irregularly notched. 2n=28

'White Ensign' 3 W-Y
(G.H. Engleheart, pre-1904)
Perianth segments very broadly ovate, squarish at apex, prominently mucronate, slightly reflexed, plane, overlapping half; the inner segments truncate, with no noticeable mucro, more nearly spreading; corona very shallow bowl-shaped, closely ribbed, citron yellow. AM 1904

'White Ermine' 2 W-GWW
(Brian S. Duncan) Rathowen Daffodils, 1978
'Easter Moon' × 'Knowehead'; sdlg no. 232
Perianth segments very broadly ovate, mucronate, spreading, plane, smooth, of thick substance, overlapping half; the inner segments more narrowly ovate, not apparently mucronate; corona cylindrical, with mouth lightly flared, a little frilled, rim crenate. Midseason. Resembles 'Broomhill' but with a larger corona with green at base

'White Excelsior' 1 W-W
(P. van Deursen, pre-1930)
AM(Haarlem) 1928

'White Eye' 3 W-? (b)
(P.D. Williams, pre-1908)

'White Fairy' 9 W-GYR
Syn. of 'Ornatus Maximus'

'White Falcon' 2 W-Y
(Barr & Sons, pre-1908)
Fls often 2 per stem; perianth segments inflexed; corona large, ribbed, pale creamy yellow

'White Fang' 2 or 3 W-?
(Mrs R.O. Backhouse, pre-1914)

'White Feather' 5
(Cartwright & Goodwin, pre-1910)

'White Flag' 2 or 3 W-? (b or c)
(pre-1915)

'White Flame' 3 W-W
(J.L. Richardson) Mrs H.K. Richardson, 1973
'Pontresina' open pollinated
Corona disc-shaped, frilled. Resembles 'Verona'

'White Fleck' 2 Y-R
(A.H. Ahrens) J.S. Leitch, 1957

'White Foam' 2 or 3 W-? (b or c)
(Cartwright & Goodwin, pre-1916)

'Whitefoord' 2 W-W
(C.E. Radcliff, 1940) J.M.Radcliff, 1956
'Nymphea' × ?'Mrs W.Moodie'

'White Fox' 2 W-W
(G.H. Engleheart, pre-1930)
Fl. ivory white

'White Frank' 3 W-W
(G.H. Engleheart, pre-1914)

'White Frill' 2 W-Y
(F.A. Saunders) F.A. Saunders, 1969

'White Frills' 1 W-W
(M.E.Brogden) Unregistered

'White Frost' 1 W-W
(G.L. Wilson, pre-1927)
Sdlg × 'White Dame'
Fl. pure white

'White Gem' 3 W-? (b or c)
(J. Mallender, pre-1933)

'White Gem' 2 W-W
(T. Bloomer) T. Bloomer, 1962
'Rashee' × 'Empress of Ireland'; sdlg no. 12/18/58

'White Giant' 1 W-W
(R.H. Bath, pre-1923)

'White Giant' 8 W-O
(R.A. van der Schoot, 1929)
Poetaz
AM(Haarlem) 1929

'White Glen' 2 W-W
(J.A.O'More, 1973) J.A.Hunter, 1997
'Easter Moon' × 'Empress of Ireland'; sdlg no. 46/73
Fl. 108 mm wide; perianth segments ovate, smooth; corona flared, with mouth wavy. Mid-season

'White Glory' 1 W-W
(The Brodie of Brodie, pre-1928)
'Vestal Virgin' × 'Nevis'

'White Glory' 2 W-W
(Unknown origin) A. Ladson, 1960

'White Goddess' 2 W-W
(W.A. Noton) W.A. Noton, 1976
'Homage' × 'Stainless'; sdlg no. 587
Fl. 96 mm wide. Mid-season

'White Gold' 2 W-Y
(C.W. Culpepper, c.1973) Unregistered
2n=28

'White Grace' 1? W-W
(?J. Kouwenhoven, pre-1913)
AM(Haarlem) 1913

'White Guard' 3 W-W
(R.O.Backhouse, pre-1927)
Fl. rounded; perianth segments very broad in outline, rounded or squarish at apex and sometimes truncate, only very slightly mucronate, spreading, concave, overlapping half or more; the inner segments more often truncate, sometimes also notched at apex, inflexed, with margins incurling; corona bowl-shaped, very small, ribbed

'White Guard' 1 W-W
(pre-1938)

'Whitehall' 2 W-W
(Sir A.P.W. Thomas, pre-1930)

'White Harmony' 2 W-W
(Oregon Bulb Farms, pre-1946)

'White Hart'
(pre-1913)

'White Hart' 2 W-W
(G.H. Johnstone, pre-1949)

'White Haven' 1 W-W
(S.J. Bisdee) S.J. Bisdee, 1956
'Tain' × 'Cantatrice'

'White Hawk' 3 W-Y
(Barr & Sons, pre-1909)
Fl. facing slightly downwards; corona expanded, ribbed, canary yellow

'Whitehead' 2 W-W
(W.J. Dunlop, pre-1953)
'White Sentinel' × 'Kanchenjunga'
Fl. forming a double triangle; perianth segments very broadly ovate, blunt, not noticeably mucronate, spreading, with margins sometimes nicked, overlapping half; the inner segments more narrowly ovate, square-shouldered at base, more obviously mucronate; corona short funnel-shaped, opening cream, soon becoming pure white, with mouth straight and wavy. 2n=28

'White Heart' 5 W-W
Syn. of 'Lemon Heart'

'White Heather' 1 W-? (b)
(W.B. Hartland, pre-1907)

'White Helmet' 3 W-? (b or c)
(W.B. Hartland, pre-1907)

'White Heron'
(?Sir A.P.W. Thomas, pre-1915)

'White Heron' 1 W-W
(R. Crews, pre-1949)

'White Hill' 2 W-W
(Ballydorn Bulb Farm, 1975) Ballydorn Bulb Farm, 1986
'Stainless' × 'Candour' hybrid
Mid-season. Resembles an improved 'Stainless'

'White Hills' 1 W-W
(J.N. Hancock & Co., c.1966) Unregistered
Fl. large, smooth; corona flared

'White Horse Eagle' 3 W-W
(P. van Deursen, pre-1930)
AM(Haarlem) 1931

'White Horse of Kent'
(pre-1913)

'White House' 2 W-Y
(The Brodie of Brodie, c.1931)
'Nissa' × 'Tenedos'
Fl. large; perianth segments broad, deeply overlapping; corona smooth, very pale lemon yellow

'White Hunter' 1 W-W
(W.G. Pannill) W.G. Pannill, 1972
'Brussels' × 'Empress of Ireland'
Fl. 107 mm wide

'White Hybrid' 8
(pre-1934)

'White Ideal' 1 W-W
(J.H. Rijkelijkhuizen) J.H. Rijkelijkhuizen, 1980
Fl. 115 mm wide; perianth segments ivory white; corona opening pale yellow, becoming ivory white. Early to mid-season

'White Island' 3 W-W
(D.R. Acheson, pre-1938)

"White Italian"
Syn. of *N. papyraceus*

'White Ivory' 1 W-W
(L. Buckland, pre-1936)
Fl. ivory white

'White Jade' 2 W-W
(Mrs F.S. Foote, pre-1940)

'White Jade' 2 W-W
(A.C. McKillop, pre-1946)

'White Jasmine' 8 W-W
(E.H.G.Thurston, pre-1938)
'Paper White' hybrid
Fl. pure white

'White Jewel' 1 W-W
(de Graaff Bros) de Graaff Bros & van Konynenburg & Co., 1960
Fl. creamy white; corona slightly darker in tone than the perianth. Mid-season. AM(Haarlem) 1960

'White Ki' 1 W-W
(E.W. Philpott, c.1966) Unregistered

'White King' 2 W-Y
(J. Mallender, pre-1914)
Perianth segments acute; corona large, flared, very pale primrose yellow, lightly frilled. AM(e) 1915

'White Knight' 1 W-W
(de Graaff Bros, pre-1907)
?'Madame de Graaff' self pollinated
Fl. opening soft sulphur yellow, becoming creamy white, facing down; corona cylindrical, slender. 2n=14. AM(Haarlem) 1915, AM(e) 1916

'White Label' 1 W-W
(W.G. Pannill) W.G. Pannill, 1970
'Glenshesk' × 'Vigil'

'White Lace' 2 W-W
(G.L. Wilson, pre-1948)

'White Lady' 3 W-Y
(G.H. Engleheart, pre-1897)
'Ornatus' × *N. triandrus* subsp. *pallidulus*; sdlg no. 44
Fl. forming a double triangle, 86 mm wide; perianth segments ovate, blunt, pominently mucronate, spreading, somewhat lax, with margins wavy, lightly creased, overlapping a quarter to one-third; the inner segments more nearly acute, less obviously mucronate, with margins more strongly wavy and recurved at base; corona cup-shaped, ribbed, pale creamy yellow, mouth straight, with 6 overlapping lobes, frilled, rim minutely notched and crenate. Scented. 2n=21. AM 1898

"White Lady"
Syn. of *N. poeticus*

'White Lamb' 2 or 3 W-? (b or c)
(Cartwright & Goodwin, pre-1916)

'White Lance' 6 W-WPP
(V. Brink) V. Brink, 1968
'High Sierra' × 'Peeping Tom'

'White Laus Tibi' W-?
(pre-1548)

'Whiteley Gem' 2 Y-O
(The Brodie of Brodie, c.1934)
'Hospodar' × 'Fortune'
Fl. facing slightly downwards; perianth segments broadly ovate, deep yellow, spreading, overlapping

one-third to a half; the inner segments more narrowly ovate; corona cylindrical, reddish orange, paling to base, with rim flanged and crenate. Early. Sunproof. 2n=28. AM(e) 1929, AM(c) 1930, AM(Haarlem) 1931, *(Gulval)AM(m) 1934, AM(f) 1934

'Whitelight' 2 (b or c)
(Australian or New Zealand origin, c.1927)

'White Lion' 4 W-WYY
(de Graaff-Gerharda, pre-1949)
'Mary Copeland' × 'John Evelyn'
Fl. 92 mm wide; perianth and other petaloid segments in two whorls, broadly or very broadly ovate, creamy white; the outer whorl spreading or a little inflexed, truncate and with margins incurled at apex, with broad midrib showing; the inner whorl only slightly shorter, more strongly inflexed, with margins wavy; some separate petaloid segments at centre very strongly inflexed, with margins tightly incurled; corona segments short, clustered or sometimes continuous at centre, more loosely interspersed among the surrounding whorls of petaloid segments, ribbed, light yellow 11B, tinged brilliant yellow 13B, with creamy white at base, frilled, with rim crenate. Mid-season. 2n=28. AM(Haarlem) 1939, FCC(Haarlem) 1944, AM(Haarlem) 1953, *HC(g) 1956, *AM(g) 1958, *FCC(g) 1968, *AM(p) 1975, AGM 1993

'White Lodge' 1 W-W
(A.O. Roblin, 1940) A.O. Roblin, 1956
'Cora' × 'White Emperor'

'White Magic' 2 W-GWW
(G.L. Wilson, pre-1943)
Fl. white; corona with green at base

'White Magnolia' 2 W-W
(C.W. Culpepper, pre-1973) Unregistered

'White Maid' 2 or 3 W-? (b or c)
(Cartwright & Goodwin, pre-1916)

'White Maiden' 2 W-W
(N.Y. Lower, pre-1916)
'Felspar' × 'White Knight'
Fl. facing slightly downwards; perianth segments pure white, deeply overlapping; corona expanded, opening pale creamy sulphur yellow, with white at rim, becoming creamy white. Mid-season. *HC(g) 1936

'White Majesty' 1 W-W
(T. Bloomer) T. Bloomer, 1970
'Rashee' × 'Empress of Ireland'; sdlg no. 2/18/58
Corona with deep green at base, with rim dentate and widely rolled. 2n=28

'White Mantle' 2 W-W
(F.H. Chapman, pre-1928)

'White Marble' 5
(F.H. Chapman, pre-1927)

'Whitemark' 1 W-W
(C.E. Radcliff, 1943) J.M.Radcliff, 1956
'Tain' × 'Whitefoord'

'White Marvel' 4 W-W
(G. Zandbergen-Terwegen, pre-1950)
'Tresamble' sport
Fl. 87 mm wide; perianth segments oblong or broadly ovate, blunt, mucronate, ivory white, a little reflexed, plane or sometimes twisted, overlapping one-third to a half; the inner segments spreading or a little inflexed; corona cup-shaped, broad, smooth, with mouth straight and lightly frilled; many petaloid or corona segments of the same length as the corona closely packed within it, tightly frilled, with some slightly longer petaloid segments interspersed. Tall. Early. 2n=21. AM(Haarlem) 1953, FCC(Haarlem) 1954, *AM(p) 1976

'White Maximus' 1 W-Y
(G.H. Engleheart, pre-1914)
Perianth segments creamy white, lightly twisted; corona pale creamy yellow, frilled. AM(e) 1914

'White Melody' 2 W-W
(T. Bloomer) T. Bloomer, 1970
'Glenbush' × 'Empress of Ireland'; sdlg no. 4/20/58

'White Mere' 2 W-Y
(G.H. Engleheart, pre-1915)
Perianth segments smooth; corona slender, pale primrose yellow

'White Minor' 1 W-W
(Irish origin, pre-1886)
Fl. small, pure white

'Whitemire' 2 W-W
(The Brodie of Brodie, pre-1934)
 Probably 'Nevis' self pollinated × 'Naxos'

'White Mischief' 3 W-W
(T. Bloomer) T. Bloomer, 1964

'White Mist' 2 W-W
(W.A. Noton) W.A. Noton, 1976
'Homage' × 'Verona'; sdlg no. 612
Fl. rounded, 92 mm wide; perianth segments broad, overlapping; corona disc-shaped. Mid-season. Resembles 'Homage'

'White Model' 5
(G.H. Engleheart, pre-1914)
'Defiance' × 'Madame de Graaff'

'White Monarch' 1 W-W
(G.L. Wilson, pre-1948)

Sdlg × 'Kanchenjunga'
AM(Haarlem) 1948, FCC(Haarlem) 1953

'Whitemont' 2 W-W
(K.J. Heazlewood, c.1967) Unregistered
'Mowbray' × 'Truth'
Probably the same as 'Whitemore'

'Whitemore' 1 W-W
(K.J. Heazlewood, c.1967) Unregistered
'Mowbray' × 'Truth'
Syn. ?'Whitemont'

'Whitemost' 1 W-W
(D. Bramley) D. Bramley, 1964
Fl. 115 mm wide, pure white. Mid-season

'White Mountain' 1 W-W
(G. Lewis) D.S. Bell, 1955
'Flying Cloud' × 'Kanchenjunga'

'White Mouse' 1 W-W
(P.J. van der Ploeg, pre-1952)

'White Mystery' 3 W-W
(T. Bloomer) T. Bloomer, 1970
'Verona' × 'Cascade'

'White Myth' 1 Y-Y
(A.O. Roblin, pre-1940)
'White Emperor' × 'Honey Boy'

'White Nectarine' 3 W-WWY
(W.F.M. Copeland, pre-1909)
White Div. 1 sdlg × *N. poeticus*
Perianth segments pure white, regular, overlapping; corona widely expanded, pure white, tinged lemon yellow at rim

'Whiteness' 5
(G.H. Engleheart, pre-1930)

'White Nile' 2 W-W
(The Brodie of Brodie, c.1916)
Fl. 100 mm wide; perianth segments broadly ovate, blunt, only very slightly mucronate, spreading or a little inflexed, concave near apex, overlapping half; the inner segments only a little narrower, more strongly inflexed, somewhat creased, with margins wavy and sometimes nicked; corona cylindrical, smooth, opening yellow, becoming yellowish white, with a darker tone at rim, mouth flared and frilled, rim notched and crenate, with margins flanged. Mid-season. 2n=29. AM(e) 1922, AM(m)(c) 1925, *(Gulval)AM(m) 1936

'White Nun' 2 or 3 W-? (b or c)
(W.T. Ware, pre-1914)

'Whiteoaks' 1 W-W
(G. Lewis) D.S. Bell, 1955

'White o' Morn' 3 W-W
(Murray W. Evans) Murray W. Evans, 1969
'Chinese White' × ('Rubra' × 'Sylvia O'Neill')

'White Orchid' 11a W-W
(?Dutch origin, pre-1970) Unregistered

'White Owl' 3 W-? (b or c)
(Barr & Sons, pre-1908)
'Scilly White' × 'Minnie Hume'
Fls 2-3 per stem, large; perianth segments white; corona narrow funnel-shaped, cream. Late

'White Owl' 8 W-W
(New Zealand origin, pre-1950)
Fls 2-3 per stem, creamy white. 2n=35

'White Palace' 1 W-W
(G.L. Wilson, pre-1948)

'White Park' 2 W-W
(G.L. Wilson, pre-1950)
'Greeting' × 'Chinese White'

'White Peacock' 2 W-? (b or c)
(G.H. Furness, pre-1934)

'White Pearl' 8 W-W
(?Dutch origin, pre-1861)
Fl. large; perianth segments pure white; corona opening citron yellow, becoming white. 2n=22. Resembles a much later-flowered 'Paper White Grandiflora'. Syn. "Original Pearl", "Pearl", "Pearls". The corona variably more yellow than white. ?The same as 'Louis le Grand', 'White Perfection'

'White Pearl' 2 W-W
(W.F.M. Copeland, pre-1907)
Perianth segments milk white; corona broad, creamy white, with mouth expanded, neatly frilled. AM 1916

'White Pennant' 2 W-W
(G.H. Engleheart, pre-1913)
Perianth segments narrow. AM(e) 1916

'White Perfection' 8 W-W
(pre-1885)
Corona sulphur white. ?The same as 'White Pearl'

'White Phantom' 1 W-W
(Carncairn Daffodils) Carncairn Daffodils, 1975
'Cotterton' × 'Broughshane'; sdlg no. M58
Fl. 120 mm wide, yellowish white (155B); corona with rim rolled. Early to mid-season

'White Plains' 2 W-W
(W.G. Pannill) W.G. Pannill, 1982
'Glendermott' × 'Starmount'; sdlg no. J 3

Fl. 87 mm wide. Mid-season

'White Plume' 2 W-W
(G.L. Wilson) G.L. Wilson, 1957
'Tryst' × 'Chinese White'
Perianth segments somewhat reflexed; corona long cup-shaped, with lime green at base, frilled

'White Prince' 1 W-W
(G.L. Wilson, pre-1952)
('Quartz' × 'Tenedos') × 'Guardian'
Fl. ice white; perianth segments ovate, blunt, somewhat twisted or with margins wavy, overlapping one-third; the inner segments more definitely twisted; corona cylindrical, smooth, with rim flanged and irregularly and shallowly crenate

'White Princess' 1 W-W
(J. Pope, pre-1908)

'White Princess' 1 W-W
(Mrs J. Abel Smith) Mrs J. Abel Smith, 1978
'Purity' × 'Vigil'; sdlg no. J6/32
Fl. 101 mm wide; corona with rim dentate. Late. Resembles a larger-flowered 'Purity'

'White Prophet' 1 W-W
(Cartwright & Goodwin, pre-1916)

'White Prospect' 1 W-W
(J.L. Richardson, pre-1948)
'Cameronian' × 'Droughtshane'
Fl. 112 mm wide; perianth segments very broadly ovate in outline, blunt or rounded at apex, spreading, overlapping half; the inner segments a little narrower, inflexed and slightly twisted; corona cylindrical, slightly ribbed, with mouth expanded, rim widely flanged and broadly crenate. AM(e) 1958

'White Queen' 2 W-W
(G.H. Engleheart, pre-1898)
'Minnie Hume' × 'Madame de Graaff'
Perianth segments pure white; corona opening pale citron yellow, becoming milk white, closely frilled. Resembles 'Sir Watkin' in form. FCC 1898

'White Queen' 4 W-W
(pre-1898)
Fl. milk white. Resembles 'Sulphur Phoenix' in form

'White Ray' 2 W-W
(pre-1949)
Corona opening very pale lemon, gradually becoming white

'White Robe' 2 or 3 W-? (b or c)
(W.T. Ware, pre-1914)

'White Robigana' 3 W-? (b)
(S.J. Bisdee, 1938) S.J. Bisdee, 1956

'Silver Plane' × 'Portia'

'White Rock' 1 W-W
(E.G. Taylor) E.G. Taylor, 1956

'White Rose' 5 W-W
(H. Backhouse, pre-1913)
'Minnie Hume' × *N. triandrus* var. *loiseleurii*

'White Rose' 4 W-W
Syn. of 'Engleheart's White Rose'

'White Sail' 4 W-W
(C.A. van der Wereld, pre-1946)
N. poeticus sdlg
2n=14. AM(Haarlem) 1946, TGA(Haarlem) 1952, FCC(Haarlem) 1953

'White Sapphire' 2 W-W
(J.A.Hunter) J.A.Hunter, 1995
'Polar Snow' × ('Glendermott' × 'Kotuku'); sdlg no. 16/82G
Fl. forming a double triangle, 110 mm wide; perianth segments ovate; corona with rim flanged and crenate. Mid-season

'White Satin' 1 W-W
(Murray W. Evans) Murray W.Evans, 1976
'Yosemite' × ('Beersheba' × 'Zero'); sdlg no. L-71
Fl. 105 mm wide. Mid-season

'White Sea' 2 W-? (b)
(G.L. Wilson, pre-1928)

'White Sentinel' 2 W-Y
(G.H. Engleheart, c.1915)
'Beacon' hybrid
Perianth segments broadly ovate, yellowish white, spreading, with margins incurling, overlapping half; the inner segments a little inflexed, with margins slightly wavy; corona funnel-shaped, lightly ribbed, tinged pale yellow, slightly frilled, rim crenate and sometimes a little flanged. 2n=28. Resembles 'Mitylene' but with a yellower corona. AM(e) 1926

'White Sergeant' 1 W-? (b)
(pre-1907)

'White Shadows' 2 W-W
(Oregon Bulb Farms, pre-1950)

'White Shepherdess' 1 W-W
(C.L. Adams, pre-1916)

'White Shoulders' 2 W-? (b)
(Oregon Bulb Farms, pre-1950)

'White's Hybrid' 8 W-YYR
(van Zonneveld Bros & Philippo, 1928)
Poetaz

Fls 3-4 per stem; perianth segments very broad in outline, blunt or truncate at apex, creamy white, spreading, creased, overlapping half; the inner segments more nearly ovate, rounded at base; corona shallow bowl-shaped, orange-yellow, with some green showing below the stamens and with a very narrow band of red at rim. Mid-season. 2n=24. AM(Haarlem) 1928, FA(Haarlem) 1928, *HC(g) 1936, *AM(g) 1939

'White Silk' 3 W-? (b)
(E. & J.C. Martin, pre-1931)

'White Sister' 1 W-W
(G.L. Wilson, pre-1927)

'White Slave' 3 W-WYY
(J.C. Williams, pre-1907)
Perianth segments overlapping; corona expanded, ribbed, pale citron yellow, shading to sulphur white at base, frilled. Tall

'White Snow'
(pre-1914)

'White Spire' 2 W-W
(G.E. Mitsch) G.E. Mitsch, 1958
'Daisy Schäffer' × 'Chinese White'
Mid-season. 2n=28

'White Splendour' 2 W-? (b or c)
(pre-1939)

'White Splendour' 1 W-W
(L. van Leeuwen & Son, pre-1946)
Perianth segments ivory white; corona creamy white. AM(Haarlem) 1946

'White Spray' 2 W-W
(J.A. O'More) J.A. O'More, 1968
('Bodilly' × 'Clonmel') × 'Petsamo'

'White Sprite' 3 W-W
(T. Bloomer) T. Bloomer, 1964
'Chinese White' × 'Bryher'; sdlg no. 7/81/58
Perianth segments pure white, slightly reflexed; corona touched green at base

'White Stag' 1 W-W
(W.A. Noton) W.A. Noton, 1976
'Panache' × 'Empress of Ireland'; sdlg no. 527
Fl. 108 mm wide. Mid-season

'White Standard' 9 W-?
(G.H. Engleheart, pre-1909)
Perianth segments pure white; corona with crimson at rim

'White Star' 3 W-GYY
(J.C. Williams, pre-1910)

'Princess Mary' × 'Horace'
Fl. 83 mm wide, facing down; perianth segments white, with sulphur at base, reflexed, regular, separated; corona small, very shallow bowl-shaped, lemon yellow, with a greenish tone at base. Mid-season to late

'White Star' 1 W-W
(T. Bloomer) T. Bloomer, 1970
'Rashee' × 'Empress of Ireland'; sdlg no. 7/18/58
Fl. 115 mm wide; perianth segments very broadly ovate, blunt, mucronate, snow white, spreading or very slightly reflexed, plane, smooth, of thick substance, regular, overlapping one-third; the inner segments one-third narrower, acute; corona smooth, with green at base, mouth widely expanded and a little frilled, rim widely rolled, very slightly crenate. 2n=28. AM(e) 1981, AM(e) 1982

'White Stranger' 3 W-? (b or c)
(pre-1927)

'White Superior' 1 W-W
(de Graaff Bros, pre-1940)
AM(Haarlem) 1940

'White Surf' 1 W-W
(G.L. Wilson, pre-1950)
AM(Haarlem) 1954

'White Surprise' 3 W-W
(T. Bloomer) T. Bloomer, 1964
'Chinese White' × 'Bryher'; sdlg no. 5/81/58
Perianth segments pure white, of great substance; corona with deep green at base, heavily frilled

'White Swan' 1 W-? (b)
(W. Welchman, pre-1908)

'White Sylph' 2 or 3 W-? (b or c)
(C.L. Adams, pre-1916)

'White Tartar' 1 W-W
(G.L. Wilson, pre-1948)
AM(Haarlem) 1948, FCC(Haarlem) 1950

'White Tea' 2 W-GWW
(Clive Postles) Clive Postles Daffodils, 1994
'Croila' × Lea sdlg 4-58-73; sdlg no. 4-18A-82
Fl. rounded, 90 mm wide; perianth segments very broadly ovate; corona funnel-shaped, with mouth wavy. Early

'Whitethroat' 3 W-W
(A.M. Wilson, pre-1948)

'White Tie' 3 W-W
(T.D. Throckmorton) T.D. Throckmorton, 1978
'Aircastle' × 'Irish Coffee'; sdlg no. 66/12/3
Fl. 96 mm wide; corona with gold tints. Mid-season

'White Tower' 1 W-W
(A. Johnson) A. Johnson, 1955

'White Trader' 2 W-W
(D.S. Bell) D.S. Bell, 1964
Fl. 56 mm wide. Resembles 'Ludlow' but with a larger corona

'White Triumphator' 1 W-W
(G.L. Wilson, pre-1938)
Fl. silvery white; corona with rim dentate. 2n=28. AM(Haarlem) 1938

'White Trompet Marin' 10
Syn. of 'Trumpet Marin'

'White Trophy' 1 W-W
(de Graaff Bros, pre-1940)
AM(Haarlem) 1940

'White Trumpet' 1 W-W
(pre-1936)
Syn. 'White Ajax'

'White Trumpet' 1 ?-W
(C.E. Radcliff)

'White Venture' 1 W-W
(T. Bloomer) T. Bloomer, 1970
'Rashee' × 'Empress of Ireland'; sdlg no. 5/18/58
Corona with deep green at base, frilled, with rim dentate

'Whitewater' 4
(Oregon Bulb Farms, pre-1951)

'White Wave' 2 W-W
(G.L. Wilson, pre-1927)
AM(Haarlem) 1954

'White Wax' 1 W-W
(P.D. Williams, pre-1908)
Perianth segments pure white; corona slender, frilled

'Whiteway' 2 W-? (b)
(A.H. Ahrens) J.S. Leitch, 1955

'Whiteways' 4 W-W
(D.S. Bell, pre-1983) Unregistered
'Mount White' open pollinated
Fl. pure white

'White Wedding' 2 W-W
(T. Bloomer) T. Bloomer, 1970
'Rashee' × 'Empress of Ireland'; sdlg no. 6/17/58

'White Wedgwood' 7 W-W
(de Graaff Bros, pre-1927)
Perianth segments broadly ovate, blunt, only slightly mucronate; corona with rim entire or very slightly notched

'Whitewell' 2 W-Y
(W. Polman-Mooy, pre-1910)
Perianth segments acute to rounded at apex, creamy white, reflexed, overlapping; the inner segments a little inflexed; corona neat, ribbed, chrome yellow, tinged orange, with rim crenate. Tall. 2n=21. AM(Haarlem) 1915

'White Whirl' 3 W-? (b or c)
(A. Frylink & Sons, pre-1931)

'White Wine' 1 W-W
(D.S. Bell) D.S. Bell, 1971
'Big Ben' × 'Petsamo'
Fl. 106 mm wide, pure white; corona frilled. Early

'White Wing' 2 W-Y
Syn. of 'White Wings'

'White Wings' 2 W-Y
(G.H. Engleheart, 1898)
Fl. rounded; corona expanded, clear yellow. AM 1898. See also 'White Wing'

'White Witch' 5 W-W
(Mrs R.O. Backhouse, pre-1908)
N. triandrus sdlg
Fl. pure white. See also 'Whitewitch'

'Whitewitch' 5 W-W
Syn. of 'White Witch'

'White with Green Eye' 9 W-GYY
(pre-1950)
Fl. large; perianth segments pure white; corona small

'White Wolf' 5
(The Brodie of Brodie, c.1907)
'Madame de Graaff' × *N. triandrus*

'White Wonder' 2 W-W
(de Graaff Bros, pre-1923)

'White Wonder' 1 W-W
(?Australian origin, pre-1997) Unregistered

'Whitewort' 2 W-? (b or c)
(P.D. Williams, pre-1931)

'White Xmas' 2 W-W
(D.S. Bell) D.S. Bell, 1955
Syn. 'White Christmas'

'White Xmas' 1 W-W
(J.N. Hancock & Co., c.1977) Unregistered
Fl. very large. Late

'Whitiora' 1 W-W
(C.A. Latta) C.A. Latta, 1960
Fl. 108 mm wide. Late

'Whitney' 2 W-W
(Mrs B.T. Simpson) Mrs B.T. Simpson, 1966
Mid-season

'Whittier' 9
(A.M. Wilson, pre-1908)

'Whittington' 1 Y-Y
(F.E. Board) F.E. Board, 1965
'Goldsborough' × 'Wexford'

'Whitton' 2 W-W
(A.M. Wilson, pre-1949)

'Whitwell' 2 W-P
(W.A. Noton) W.A. Noton, 1977
'Roselight' × 'Passionale'; sdlg no. 570
Fl. 89 mm wide. Mid-season

'Whiz-bang' 4 Y-Y
(Jackson's Daffodils, 1987) Jackson's Daffodils, 1997
('Nala' × 'Tavelle') × sdlg 285/77; sdlg no. 143/87
Fl. 108 mm wide; perianth and other petaloid segments broadly ovate, brilliant greenish yellow 7C; corona segments slightly darker in tone, frilled. Mid-season to late

'Whoa' 2 W-GYO
(T.D. Throckmorton) T.D. Throckmorton, 1977
'Kilworth' × 'Russet'; sdlg no. 66/24/3
Fl. 115 mm wide; corona green-yellow, with green at base and bright orange at rim. Mid-season

'Whoopi' 2 W-YPP
(J.N.Hancock & Co.) J.N.Hancock & Co., 1997
'My Word' hybrid; sdlg no. 5/89H
Perianth segments ovate, plane; corona funnel-shaped, deep pink, with mouth flared. Early

'Who's Who' 2 W-W
(Jackson's Daffodils) Jackson's Daffodils, 1986
Sdlg 159/70 × 'Rhapsody'; sdlg no. 240/79
Perianth segments greenish white 155C; corona slightly darker in tone (155A). Mid-season

'Whykets' 2 W-GYY
(L.P. Dettman) L.P. Dettman, 1984
'Daisy Schäffer' open pollinated; sdlg no. 11/70
Fl. 100 mm wide; perianth segments yellowish white 155B; corona brilliant greenish yellow 5A. Early. Resembles 'Daisy Schäffer' but with narrower perianth segments and with green at corona base

'Why Not' 1 Y-Y
(T.H. Piper, c.1966) Unregistered
'King's Ransom' × 'Khem'

'Wibbern' 2 W-W
(G.L. Wilson, pre-1937)
Resembles 'Sea Shell'

'Wicklow' 2 W-? (b)
(J.L. Richardson, pre-1938)

'Wideawake' 7 Y-Y
(Roberta C.Watrous) Roberta C.Watrous, 1964
'Seville' × *N. assoanus*
Perianth segments occasionally seven in number, pale yellow; corona bright yellow. Mid-season

'Wide Wing' 9 W-GYR
(G.H. Engleheart, pre-1923)
Perianth segments very broad, squarish at apex, prominently mucronate, paper white, slightly reflexed, plane, with broad midrib showing, overlapping half or more; the inner segments narrower, spreading, with margins wavy and sometimes incurling; corona disc-shaped, tightly ribbed, greenish yellow, with green at base and a well-defined narrow band of yellowish red at rim. Late. AM(e) 1923, AM(c) 1928, AM(Haarlem) 1929, AM(p) 1930

'Widgeon' 2 Y-P
(G.E. Mitsch) G.E. Mitsch, 1975
'Daydream' hybrid; sdlg no. HO1/1
Fl. 100 mm wide; perianth segments soft lemon, tinged buff; corona with pink overlying pale lemon. Mid-season

'Wieland Wagner' 2 W-Y
(Konynenburg & Mark) Konynenburg & Mark, 1960
('Gracious' × 'Faveur') hybrid
Fl. 110 mm wide; perianth segments white, tinged green; corona light greenish yellow 5C. Mid-season

'Wien' 2 Y-O
(C.A. van Paridon) C.A. van Paridon, 1963
Perianth segments pale yellow; corona pale orange

'Wiener Blut' 2 W-O
(P.L.A. Pouw) Warnaar & Co., 1963
Fl. 102 mm wide; corona reddish orange. Mid-season. Resembles an earlier-flowered 'Crusader' of better form. AM(Haarlem) 1963

'Wigmore' 2 Y-R
(A.M. Wilson, pre-1948)
'Pathan' hybrid
Fl. rounded; perianth segments light yellow; corona red, frilled

'Wigram' 1 (a)
(R. Hyde) R. Hyde, 1957

'Wihareja' 2 Y-R
(C.E. Radcliff, 1939)

'Margaret H.' × 'Lillian Murdoch'

'Wilber' 1 W-Y
(W. Jackson Jr, pre-1977) Unregistered

'Wilbur' 1 W-Y
(W. Jackson Jr, 1969) Unregistered
'Maweena' × 'Lod'; sdlg no. 116/69

'Wildarra' 2 W-W
(H.R. Bulman, c.1967) Unregistered
'Grayling' × 'Ludlow'

'Wild Carnival' 2 Y-O
(W.F. Leenen) W.F. Leenen, 1982
'Ipi Tombi' hybrid
Perianth segments brilliant greenish yellow 7C; corona vivid orange 23B, heavily frilled

'Wild Cona' 2 (a)
Syn. of 'Weld Cona'

'Wildfire' 3 W-GOR
(Sir C.H. Cave, pre-1908)
'Princess Mary' × 'Gloria Mundi'
Perianth segments white, tinged pale sulphur yellow; corona rich orange, shading to brick red at rim

'Wild Fire' 6 Y-O
(L.P. Dettman) L.P. Dettman, 1977
'Vulcan' × 'Spelter'; sdlg no. 25/75
Fl. 93 mm wide, perianth segments vivid yellow 14A, with a coppery sheen; corona orange (28A). Early to mid-season

'Wild Oats' 2 W-W
(Jackson's Daffodils) Jackson's Daffodils, 1987
'Waikato' × sdlg 152/70; sdlg no. 188/80
Fl. forming a double triangle, greenish white (155A); perianth segments very broadly ovate, blunt, only very slightly mucronate, a little reflexed, plane, overlapping half or more; the inner segments more nearly spreading, with margins wavy; corona cylindrical, short, smooth, mouth finely ribbed and very slightly flared, even or a little wavy. Mid-season

'Wild Rose' 2 W-P
(The Brodie of Brodie, c.1936)
'Mitylene' × 'Evening'
Perianth segments pure white; corona rose pink, or deeper in tone in some seasons. Mid-season. 2n=28. PC 1946

'Wild West' 2 Y-O
(Grant E.Mitsch, 1976) R. & E.Havens, 1994
('Firecracker' × sdlg R63/2) × (['Playboy' × 'Paricutin'] × 'Vulcan'); sdlg no. LL48/4
Fl. 105 mm wide; perianth segments ovate, bright yellow; corona very widely expanded, bright tangerine orange, with rim rolled. Mid-season. Sunproof

'Wild Women' 1 Y-Y
(Glenbrook Bulb Farm, 1984) Glenbrook Bulb Farm, 1997
'Ansett' × 'Ristin'
Fl. 95 mm wide; perianth segments ovate, vivid yellow 9A, spreading; corona cylindrical, narrow, slightly brighter in tone (12A) than the perianth, with mouth straight and very slightly frilled. Early

'Wildwood' 2 W-? (b)
(R. Glendenning, pre-1947)
Syn. 'J.W.Winson'

'Wilf Carter' 4 Y-O
(Tom Forster, 1960s) Unregistered
Perianth and other petaloid segments yellow; corona segments as long as the petaloid segments and interspersed among them, bright orange. Tall. Mid-season

'Wilfred Danby' 2 Y-YYR
(W.A. Grace, pre-1938)

'Wilhelmina' 1 (a)
(J. de Groot & Sons, pre-1900)
AM 1900

'Wilkin' 2 Y-YYO
(West & Fell, pre-1935)
Perianth segments yellow, slightly reflexed; corona rich yellow, shading to a broad band of reddish orange at rim

'Willamette' 2 W-Y
(G.E. Mitsch, pre-1954)
'Tunis' × 'Mitylene'; sdlg no. 39C134/1
Fl. large; perianth segments smooth; corona clear yellow. Very tall. Mid-season

'Will Carlton' 9
(G.P. Haydon, pre-1910)

'Willem de Zwijger' 1 (a)
Syn. of 'William the Silent'

'Willem Maris' 1 Y-Y
(G. Lubbe & Son, pre-1926)
Fl. clear pale golden yellow. AM(Haarlem) 1926. Received AM(Haarlem) 1926 as 'Rubens'

'Willem Mengelberg' 1 (a)
(A. Frylink & Sons, c.1931)
Syn. ?'Mengelberg'. AM(Haarlem) 1933

'Willemstad' 2 W-O
(F. Rijnveld & Sons, pre-1949)
Corona reddish orange, frilled. AM(Haarlem) 1951

'Willet' 6 Y-Y
(G.E. Mitsch) G.E. Mitsch, 1966
'Mitylene' × *N. cyclamineus*; sdlg no. T35/8

Fl. 89 mm wide; perianth segments broadly ovate, reflexed, plane, overlapping one-third to a half; the inner segments more narrowly ovate, with margins sometimes wavy; corona cylindrical, constricted at base and towards mouth, very slightly darker in tone than the perianth, with mouth expanded and frilled. Early. Resembles a smaller and earlier-flowered 'Charity May' with less strongly reflexed perianth segments and a longer and narrower corona

'William'
(pre-1936)

'William Backhouse' 2 W-Y
(W. Backhouse, pre-1869)
Corona clear yellow. Resembles 'Pulchellus'. Syn. Nelsonii 'William Backhouse'

'William Barnes' 9 W-?
(D. Blanchard, pre-1949)
'Ringdove' × 'John Masefield'

'William Baylor Hartland' 1 W-Y
(W.B. Hartland, pre-1901)
'Ione' × 'Horsfieldii'
Fl. rounded; perianth segments overlapping; corona soft golden yellow. Early. Syn. 'Cedric'

'William Beatty' 1 Y-Y
(J. Hall, pre-1942)
Fl. deep yellow, corona with mouth expanded and frilled

'William Buchanan'
(pre-1913)

'William Bull' 2 W-Y
(E. Leeds, pre-1877)
Perianth segments tinged sulphur yellow. Syn. Incomparabilis Albus 'William Bull'

'William Clay' 1 (a)
(R. & G. Cuthbert, pre-1938)

'William Davey' 2 W-? (b)
(G.A. Uit den Boogaard, pre-1951)
AM(Haarlem) 1951

'William Dent' 2 W-? (b)
(Mrs R.O. Backhouse, pre-1921)

'William Farmer' 2 Y-Y
(Ken Farmer Nurseries) Ken Farmer Nurseries, 1978
Fl. 120 mm wide. Mid-season. 2n=28

'William Forster' 2 W-Y
(pre-1905)
AM 1905. See also 'William Foster'

'William Foster' 2 W-Y
Syn. of 'William Forster'

'William Goldring' 1 W-Y
(E. Leeds, pre-1877)
Fl. facing down; perianth segments inflexed, nicked and uneven at apex; corona primrose yellow. Syn. Pseudonarcissus Moschatus 'William Goldring'

'William Herschel' 2 W-O
(G. Lubbe & Son, pre-1943)
Corona orange, heavily frilled. AM(Haarlem) 1943

'William Hovell' 2 W-O
(Tom Forster, 1960s) Unregistered
Perianth segments very broad, slightly mucronate, pure white, spreading or a little reflexed, overlapping half; the inner segments more usually spreading, creased; corona broad disc-shaped, very closely ribbed, creamy orange. Late

'William Ingram' 2 W-O
(W. Backhouse, pre-1869)
Corona primrose yellow, conspicuously stained scarlet-orange. Syn. Barrii Albus 'Milneri', Barrii Albus 'William Ingram', Incomparabilis Albidus 'Milnerii', Incomparabilis Albus 'Milneri'

'William Miles' 2 (a)
(pre-1915)

'William of Normandy' 7
(W. Welchman, pre-1927)

'William of Orange' 2 W-? (b)
(W.B. Hartland, pre-1907)

'William Park's Favorite' 2 Y-Y
(J.W.A.Lefeber) Kapiteyn Bros, 1994
Fl. 135 mm wide; perianth segments very broad, truncate, yellowish white (150D), spreading, overlapping one-third to a half; the inner segments narrower and a little shorter, with margins nicked; corona very widely expanded, ribbed, sometimes deeply split, vivid yellow 14A, heavily frilled. Mid-season

'William Penn' 1 W-? (b)
(W.J. Eldering & Son, pre-1930)

'William Pitt' 2 (a)
(de Graaff Bros, pre-1937)
AM(Haarlem) 1937

'William Poupart' 1 (a)
(Barr & Sons, pre-1927)

'William Rex' 8 W-O
(pre-1835)

'William Robinson' 1 W-Y
(E. Leeds, pre-1877)

Perianth segments sulphur white. Syn. Pseudonarcissus Bicolor 'William Robinson'. "Absorbed" 'Peabody'

'William Rufus' 2 (a)
(Mrs R.O. Backhouse, pre-1910)

'Williamsburg' 2 W-W
(W.G. Pannill) W.G. Pannill, 1970
'Easter Moon' × 'Vigil'
Fl. forming a double triangle; perianth segments broadly ovate, blunt, spreading, somewhat creased, overlapping half; the inner segments more narrowly ovate, a little inflexed; corona funnel-shaped, ribbed, with mouth straight and frilled

'Williams's Glory' 9
(P.D. Williams, pre-1942)

'William Stukeley' 2 W-? (b)
(pre-1955) Unregistered

'William the Conqueror' 1 (a)
(G.H. Engleheart, pre-1916)

'William the Lion' 2 (a)
(G.H. Engleheart, pre-1913)

'William the Silent' 1 Y-Y
(A. Frylink & Sons, pre-1933)
2n=28. Syn. 'Willem de Zwijger'. AM(Haarlem) 1933, FCC(Haarlem) 1937, FA(Haarlem) 1944

'William Wilks' 2 Y-Y
(de Graaff Bros, pre-1885)
Perianth segments very broadly ovate or somewhat roundish, mucronate, primrose yellow, spreading, with margins nicked, with midrib showing, overlapping one-third to a half; the inner segments only a little narrower, slightly inflexed; corona cylindrical or somewhat funnel-shaped, broad, ribbed, orange-yellow, mouth lobed and flared, rim crenate

'Willie Barr' 1 Y-Y
Syn. of 'J.W.H.Barr'

N. willkommii (Sampaio) A.Fernandes 13 Section Jonquilla. AM 1995

'Willonyx'
(pre-1913)

'Will-o'-the Wisp' 3 W-GRR
(P.D. Williams, pre-1907)
Corona suffused crimson, with green at base

'Willowbank' 2 W-? (b)
(D.S. Bell) D.S. Bell, 1957

'Willowby' 2 (a)
(S.C. Gaspar) R.J. Abernethy, 1957

'Willowfield' 3 W-R
(W.J. Dunlop, pre-1952)
'Sunstar' × 'Isola'
Perianth segments pure white; corona deep crimson

'Willow Green' 1 W-Y
(Mrs J. Abel Smith) Mrs J. Abel Smith, 1977
'Brabazon' × 'Preamble'; sdlg no. 03/01
Fl. 108 mm wide; corona deep lemon, with rim rolled. Early. Resembles 'Preamble' but with the perianth segments less white and the corona unfading

'Will Rogers' 3 W-? (b)
(P.D. Williams, pre-1934)

'Will Scarlett' 2 W-O
(G.H. Engleheart, pre-1898)
N. abscissus × *N. radiiflorus* var. *poetarum*
Fl. 79 mm wide; perianth segments ovate, blunt, creamy white, reflexed, often twisted, with margins strongly waved or recurved, separated; corona bowl-shaped, broad, ribbed, opening bright rich orange, often fading, with mouth expanded and deeply six-lobed. Mid-season to late. 2n=14. FCC 1898

'Will Shakespear' 3 W-? (b)
(H.G. Longford, pre-1927)

'Willy' 1 Y-Y
(G.B. de Vroomen & Sons, pre-1934)

'Willy Dunlop' 2 W-Y
(W.J.M. Blom, 1968) W. Blom & Son, 1984
'Ballygarvey' × 'Salome'; sdlg no. 68-9-9
Perianth segments broadly ovate, only slightly mucronate, pure white, flushed yellow at base, spreading; corona cylindrical, smooth, golden yellow, with rim flanged. Mid-season to late

"Wilmer's Great Double Daffodil"
Syn. of 'Telamonius Plenus'

'Wilmot' 2 W-W
(C.E. Radcliff, 1939) J.M.Radcliff, 1956
('Mary Blewitt' × 'Blodwen') × 'Niphetos'

"Wilmot's Double Daffodil"
Syn. of 'Telamonius Plenus'

'Wilruna' 2 W-R
(A.O. Roblin, 1946)
'Jean Hood' × 'Lady Derby'

'Wilshire' 4
(L. Wilshire) L. Wilshire, 1955

'Wilson' 1 W-Y
(den Older Bros, pre-1927)

Corona pale creamy yellow. FA(Haarlem) 1927, EFA(Haarlem) 1928

'Wilson's Seedling' 3 Y-O
(A.M. Wilson, 1913)
'Beacon' × Div. 9 sdlg
Perianth segments fairly broadly ovate, blunt, creamy yellow, tinged pinkish orange, with prominent white mucro, a little creased, with margins slightly wavy, overlapping one-third to a half; the inner segments narrower, with margins more strongly wavy; corona disc-shaped, small, deeply ribbed, pale orange, shading to rich orange at rim

'Wilson's Victory' 2 (a)
(A.M. Wilson, pre-1938)

'Wimaway' 2 Y-WWY
(J.N.Hancock & Co., 1979) J.N.Hancock & Co., 1997
'Chartwell' × 'Daydream'; sdlg no. 57/79H
Perianth segments ovate, bright yellow, plane, deeply overlapping; corona becoming creamy white, with yellow at rim, mouth flared and wavy. Mid-season

'Wimba' 1 W-Y
(J.N. Hancock & Co., c.1978) Unregistered

'Wimblington' 3 W-? (b or c)
(R.H. Bath, pre-1933)

'Wimborne Beauty' 1 W-W
(J.W. Barr, pre-1930)

'Wimple' 3 W-R
(A.M. Wilson, pre-1953)
Perianth segments of waxy substance; corona bright scarlet, frilled. Late

'Win All' 3 Y-YYR
(J.L. Richardson, pre-1938)
AM(Haarlem) 1938

'Wincanton' 2 Y-R
(New Zealand origin, pre-1955) Unregistered
Perianth segments golden yellow; corona scarlet

'Winchester' 2 Y-YOO
(Barr & Sons, pre-1954)
$2n=28$

'Winchester' 2 W-YYO
(Tom Forster, 1960s) Unregistered
Perianth segments pure white; corona broad disc-shaped, ribbed, bright yellow, with orange at rim. Mid-season

'Winchester Pride' 2 W-YPP
(L.C.Palmer) M.E.Rollinson, 1994
'Barnard Castle' × 'Dailmanach'; sdlg no. 23/88

Perianth segments very broadly ovate, blunt, only very slightly mucronate, spreading, plane, overlapping half; the inner segments more narrowly ovate, angled at shoulder, a little inflexed; corona funnel-shaped, narrowly ribbed, pink, with yellow in tube, mouth expanded and even, rim minutely crenate. Mid-season

'Wincobank' 2 Y-Y
(F.E. Board) F.E. Board, 1965
'Ormeau' × 'Arctic Gold'; sdlg no. 482

'Windarra' 1 W-Y
(H.A. Brown, pre-1936)
Corona frilled

'Windblown' 4 W-Y
(Oregon Bulb Farms, pre-1946)
$2n=29$

'Wind Chimes' 7 YYW-P
(G.E. Mitsch, 1968) G.E. Mitsch, 1979
'Quick Step' × 'Daydream'; sdlg no. D80/17
Fl. 81 mm wide; perianth segments yellow, with white at base; corona bowl-shaped, pinkish buff, sometimes near white in dry areas. Scented. Resembles 'Songster' but with a shorter corona and often with more than one flower per stem

'Windermere' 9 W-?
(pre-1914)

'Windermere' 3 (a)
(R.H. Bath, pre-1933)

'Windermere' 1 W-Y
(H.A. Brown, pre-1936) J.N. Hancock & Co., 1960
Corona lemon yellow

'Windfall' 2 W-? (b)
(Sir C.H. Cave, pre-1908)

'Windfall' 2 Y-YYO
(G.E. Mitsch) G.E. Mitsch, 1972
('Narvik' × 'California Gold') × ('Playboy' × 'Alamein'); sdlg no. X42/1
Fl. 100 mm wide, golden yellow; corona shading to orange at rim, with mouth frilled. Mid-season

'Windhover' 3 W-GYR
(R.E. Jerrell, 1974) R.E. Jerrell, 1987
'Green Island' × 'Glenwherry; sdlg no. 68-29-1
Perianth segments of good substance; corona shallow, widely expanded. Mid-seson. Resembles a taller and stronger-stemmed 'Oykel'

'Windjammer' 1 Y-Y
(W.J. Dunlop) M.J. Jefferson-Brown, 1964

'Windmill' 1 (a)
(The Brodie of Brodie, pre-1913)
'M.J.Berkeley' × 'King Alfred'

'Windmill' 2 (a)
(N.Y. Lower, pre-1930)

'Windrush' 2 (a)
(J.M. de Navarro, pre-1949)

'Wind Song' 2 Y-YYP
(T.D. Throckmorton) T.D. Throckmorton, 1974
'Chinese White' × 'Irish Coffee'

'Windsor' 1 Y-Y
(The Brodie of Brodie, c.1936)
'Hebron' hybrid; sdlg no. 20/A/31
Fl. clear yellow

'Windsor' 1 W-Y
(H.A. Brown, 1938) J.N. Hancock & Co., 1955
'Sincerity' × 'Windermere'
Perianth segments broad, pure white, smooth, of good substance; corona pale gold, with rim dentate. Late

'Windsor Castle' 2 (a)
(P.D. Williams, pre-1937)
AM(Haarlem) 1937

'Windsor Court' 4 W-Y
(W.G. Pannill) W.G. Pannill, 1992
'Snowshill' × 'Bromley'; sdlg no. 67/57 E
Fl.103 mm wide. Late

'Windswept' 4 Y-Y
(Oregon Bulb Farms, pre-1946)

'Windward' 2 W-W
(A.M. Wilson, pre-1937)
Perianth segments acute; corona ribbed

'Windwheel' 2 Y-YYO
(pre-1949)
Perianth segments pale yellow, deeply overlapping; corona pale citron, with reddish orange at rim

'Winfrith' 2 W-W
(D. & J.W. Blanchard) D. & J.W. Blanchard, 1966
Fl. forming a double triangle, 110 mm wide; perianth segments very broadly ovate, blunt, more or less prominently mucronate, spreading, slightly concave, smooth, overlapping half; the inner segments more narrowly ovate, shouldered at base, a little inflexed, with margins slightly wavy; corona straight-sided, smooth, with green at base, mouth expanded and lightly frilled, with rim crenate. Mid-season. Resembles a whiter 'Snowshill' with the corona more definitely frilled. PC(e) 1966

'Winfro' 2 W-Y
(J.N. Hancock & Co., 1957) Unregistered

'Wingadee' 2 W-O
(W.M. Spry, pre-1967) Unregistered
'Jean Hood' × 'My Choice'
Corona apricot orange, with a lighter tone at rim. Early. 2n=28

'Winganna' 1 W-P
(S.J. Bisdee) S.J. Bisdee, 1956
'Rosario' × 'Mastercraft'

'Wingatui' 2 (a)
(S.C. Gaspar) R.J. Abernethy, 1957

'Wing Commander' 2 W-Y
(S.J. Bisdee, 1945)
'Nelly' × 'Whitefoord'

'Winged Easter' 2 W-GWW
(T.D. Throckmorton) T.D. Throckmorton, 1975
'Easter Moon' × 'Waxwing'
Corona opening with tints of opalescent pink, becoming white, with green at base

'Winged Flight' 3 W-GYR
(Murray W. Evans, 1970) Jean E. Driver, 1993
N. poeticus var. *recurvus* × 'Dallas'; sdlg no. N-25
Fl. 96 mm wide; perianth segments pure white, strongly reflexed, of smooth texture, glistening, overlapping; corona spreading. Late. Sunproof

'Winged Victory' 6 W-Y
(C.F. Coleman) C.F. Coleman, 1961
'Jenny' × 'Salmon Trout'
Perianth segments broadly ovate, yellowish white (4D), reflexed, with margins wavy, overlapping one-third; the inner segments twisted; corona cylindrical at base, flared in upper part, ribbed, yellow (3C, streaked with 3B, paling to 4D at rim), mouth even, with rim notched. Early. *HC(g) 1990, *AM(g) 1991

'Wingeen' 2 Y-R
(C.E. Radcliff, 1931)
'Warflame' × 'Puzzle'

'Wingham' 3 W-? (b)
(F.D.B. Cobb, pre-1954)

'Wingletang' 8 Y-Y
(Rosewarne EHS) Rosewarne EHS, 1982
'French Sol' × 'Autumn Sol'; sdlg no. 69/305/1
Fls about 10 per stem, 45 mm wide; perianth segments brilliant yellow 7A; corona opening orange-yellow (14A), becoming darker in tone (17B). Very early. Resembles a much earlier-flowered 'Newton' with a wider perianth

'Winglow' 2 W-P
(J.N. Hancock & Co., 1947) J.N. Hancock & Co., 1964
Corona medium pink, with rim rolled. Mid-season

'Wingold' 2 Y-O
(pre-1935)
Perianth segments yellow; corona reddish orange, frilled

'Wings of Beauty' 2 W-?
(T. Bloomer) T. Bloomer, 1964

'Wings of Freedom' 6 Y-Y
(G.E.Mitsch, 1978) R. & E.Havens, 1994
(Sdlg P50/1 × 'Flaming Meteor') × *N. cyclamineus*; sdlg no. 2N41/3
Fl. 75 mm wide, bright yellow. Early. A little smaller than siblings 'Swift Arrow' and 'Warbler'. Dwarf

'Wings of Grace' 2 W-?
(T. Bloomer) T. Bloomer, 1964

'Wings of Morning' 2 W-?
(T. Bloomer) T. Bloomer, 1964

'Wings of Song' 3 W-GWW
(G.E. Mitsch, 1954) G.E. Mitsch, 1965
'Chinese White' × ('Rubra' × 'Sylvia O'Neill'); sdlg no. P16/2
Perianth segments pure white, reflexed; corona opening as if bluish grey, becoming white, with green at base, frilled. Mid-season

'Wings of Spring' 9 W-GYR
(Mrs M.S. Yerger) Mrs M.S. Yerger, 1990
'Praecox Grandiflorus' × 'Lights Out'; sdlg no. 75 P 1
Fl. 60 mm wide; perianth segments ovate, acute, reflexed; the inner segments a little shorter; corona brilliant yellow 7A, with light yellow-green 145B at base and orange-red (33A) at rim. Late. Strongly scented

'Winiata' 2 W-W
(M.Hamilton) Koanga Daffodils, 1996
'Modulux' × ('Snowcrest' × 'Angel')
Fl. rounded, 115 mm wide; perianth segments very broadly ovate, plane; corona cylindrical, with mouth lobed. Late

'Winifred' 2 (a)
(Dutch origin, pre-1903)

'Winifred' 3 W-? (b or c)
(D.V. West, pre-1936)

'Winifred van Graven' 3 W-YYR
(van Graven Bros, pre-1954)
2n=28

'Winifred Walker' 1 W-W
(G. Lubbe & Son, pre-1926)
AM(Haarlem) 1926

'Winjeel' 2 Y-WWY
(J.N.Hancock & Co., 1979) Unregistered
'Chartwell' × 'Daydream'; sdlg no. 58/79H
Fl. rounded; perianth segments sulphur yellow, deeply overlapping; corona funnel-shaped, becoming creamy white, with yellow at rim, frilled. Tall. Mid-season

'Winkburn' 3 W-YYO
(Mrs J. Abel Smith) Mrs J. Abel Smith, 1977
'Hamzali' × 'Aircastle'; sdlg no. Q4/93
Fl. 86 mm wide; corona yellow, with a narrow band of orange at rim. Mid-season. Resembles 'Hamzali'

'Winkfield's Dower' 1 Y-Y
(G.L. Wilson, pre-1927)
'King Alfred' × 'Lord Roberts'
Fl. 105 mm wide; perianth segments sulphur yellow, inflexed, twisted, overlapping one-third; corona chrome yellow, with mouth expanded, rim crenate. *(Gulval)AM(m) 1940

'Winkie' 2 W-P
(Oregon Bulb Farms, pre-1950)

'Winkipop' 2 Y-Y
(Broadfield's Daffodils) Unregistered

'Winkist' 2 W-P
(S.J. Bisdee, 1953)
'Pink Petticoat' × 'Mabel Taylor'

'Winna' 2 W-Y
(W.M. Spry, pre-1975) Unregistered
'Morning Glory' × 'Stand By'
Corona broad, lemon yellow

'Winnaleah' 3 W-? (b)
(S.J. Bisdee, 1942)
'Market Merry' × 'Sunset Fires'

'Winner' 3 (a)
(A.M. Wilson, pre-1948)

'Winnibelle' 2 Y-O
(S.J. Bisdee, 1948) S.J. Bisdee, 1956
Sdlg 167/42 × 'Red Morn'

'Winnie' 2 W-WWP
(L. Buckland, pre-1936)
Perianth segments pure white; corona spreading, with delicate pink at rim

'Winnie Garlick' 2 W-O
(L.P. Dettman, pre-1952)

'Winnie Weedon' 9 W-YYR
(G.H. Engleheart, pre-1938)
Fl. rounded, 76 mm wide; perianth segments very broad, roundish, truncate, prominently mucronate, a little reflexed, concave, overlapping half; the inner segments narrower, spreading or somewhat inflexed; corona disc-shaped, tightly ribbed, bright yellow, with a band of red at rim and the rim minutely crenate. Late

'Winning Way' 2 Y-Y
(M.E.Brogden, pre-1997) Unregistered
'Thunderbird' × ('Iberia' × 'Gold Bank')

'Winnipeg' 2 Y-YYO
(S.C. Gaspar, 1946) R.J. Abernethy, 1957
Perianth segments rich yellow; corona very shallow bowl-shaped, deep yellow, with a broad band of reddish orange at rim

'Winona' 2 (a)
(R.H. Bath, pre-1927)

'Winona' 2 Y-YYO
(S.C. Gaspar, 1950) R.J. Abernethy, 1960
Fl. 108 mm wide; corona golden yellow, shading to reddish orange at rim. Mid-season. Resembles 'Aranjuez'

'Winooka' 2 W-P
(S.J. Bisdee, 1947)
'Pink o' Dawn' × 'Rosario'

'Winscott' 2 W-? (b)
(R.O. Backhouse, pre-1938)

'Winsley' 2 W-P
(C.E. Radcliff, 1941) J.M.Radcliff, 1956
'Nautilus' × 'Shirley Wyness'

'Winslow' 2 Y-Y
(E. Leeds, pre-1877)
Perianth segments rich yellow; corona tinged orange. Syn. Incomparabilis Leedsii 'Winslow'. Was "absorbed" into 'Titan'

'Winslow' 1 W-W
(R.H. Bath, pre-1931)

'Winsome' 3 W-O
(E.M. Crosfield, pre-1913)

'Winsome' 2 or 3 W-W
(G.L. Wilson, pre-1926)
Fl. creamy white; perianth segments overlapping; corona with rim rolled

'Winsome' 2 or 3 W-? (b or c)
(West & Fell, pre-1931)

'Winsome' 3 W-YYO
(G.H. Johnstone, 1944) G.H. Johnstone, 1959
'Elspeth' hybrid
Fl. 89 m wide. Late

'Winsome' 2 W-Y
(?New Zealand origin, pre-1990) Unregistered

'Winsome Girl' 2 W-? (b)
(A. Gibson, 1930) Parr's Nurseries, 1958

'Winsome Winifred' 2 Y-WWO
(H. Koopowitz) H. Koopowitz, 1984
'Binkie' × ?'Lilac Delight'; sdlg no. C373/5
Fl. 94 mm wide; perianth segments lemon yellow; corona opening pink, with a deeper tone at rim, becoming white, with orange at rim, with the rim crenate. Mid-season

'Winston' 1 (a)
(Miss K.M. Hinchliff, pre-1943)

'Winston' 2 Y-Y
(T. MacLaren) Holland Bulb Co. (Australia), 1959
'Gambrina' × 'Golden City'

'Winter' 1 W-Y
(G.H. Johnstone, pre-1942)
'Halfa' hybrid
Fl. 102 mm wide; perianth segments rounded at apex, sulphury white, smooth, overlapping; corona light greenish yellow 4C, with rim dentate and strongly flanged. AM(e) 1944

'Winter Bells' 8 W-Y
(E.W. Cotter)
'Silver Chimes' × 'White Owl'
Fls usually about 9 per stem. Scented. Resembles 'Grand Monarch'

'Winter Cheer' 2 Y-? (a)
(The Brodie of Brodie, pre-1932)
'Fortune' × 'Killigrew'

Wintercups Group
Commercial name for a group of several cultivars specially forced for early flowering

'Winter Evening' 2 W-P
(R. & E.Havens, 1985) R. & E.Havens, 1997
'Pink Easter' × 'Music'; sdlg no. UH17/6
Fl. 105 mm wide; perianth segments broadly ovate, white, sometimes with pink undertones, spreading, plane; corona funnel-shaped, pure soft pink, slightly frilled. Mid-season. Sunproof

'Winter Glow' 1 (a)
(Mrs R.S. Cobley, pre-1932)

'Winter Gold' 1 Y-Y
(Barr & Sons, pre-1928)
'Goldseeker' hybrid
Fl. 83 mm wide, facing slightly downwards; perianth segments oblong, fairly narrow, acute, vivid yellow, with darker overtones, spreading or a little inflexed, somewhat twisted, overlapping up to a quarter; the inner segments more nearly ovate, with margins wavy; corona cylindrical, lightly ribbed, of the same colour as the dark overtones in the perianth, with mouth somewhat expanded, frilled, rim flanged and deeply and irregularly notched. Early. *(Gulval)AM(m) 1936, *AM(g) 1936

'Winterhope' 2 Y-Y
(J.N. Hancock & Co., c.1980) Unregistered

'Winterhude' 2 W-Y
(S.J. Bisdee, 1946)
'Maid of the Mist' × 'Polindra'

'Winter Joy' 2 (a)
(L. van Leeuwen & Son, pre-1931)

'Winter Mist' 3 W-W
(W.A. Noton) W.A. Noton, 1976
'Easter Moon' × 'Monksilver'; sdlg no. 622
Fl. 88 mm wide. Late

'Wintermoon' 1 W-Y
(W.M. Spry, pre 1973) Unregistered
'Early Prince' × 'Stand By'
Corona lemon yellow. Early

'Winter Pride' 8 W-O
(W. Polman-Mooy, pre-1930)
Poetaz
Fl. large; corona clear orange. AM(Haarlem) 1930, FA(Haarlem) 1931

'Winter Princess' 2 W-W
(D.N.Y. Olson) D.N.Y. Olson, 1989
'Saint Saphorin' × 'Greenland'; sdlg no. 214
Fl. 100 mm wide; perianth segments mucronate, plane, overlapping; corona opening lemon yellow, rapidly becoming pure white, with mouth slightly expanded, rim rolled. Early

'Winter Queen' 3 W-? (b)
(J.W.A. Lefeber, pre-1939)
Syn. 'Snow Queen'

'Winterset' 2 W-W
(Oregon Bulb Farms, pre-1951)

'Winterset' 2 Y-O
Syn. of 'Ivoson'

'Winter Snow'
(pre-1914)

'Winter Storm' 2 W-W
(Curtis Tolley) Curtis Tolley, 1997
'Williamsburg' × 'Panache'; sdlg no. 90-4-D
Fl. forming a double triangle, 90 mm wide; perianth segments ovate; corona funnel-shaped, frilled, with rim rolled. Mid-season

'Winter Waltz' 6 W-P
(G.E. Mitsch and R. & E.Havens, 1975) G.E. Mitsch and R. & E.Havens, 1988
('Precedent' × 'Accent') × *N. cyclamineus*; sdlg no. KK109/2
Corona funnel-shaped, opening buff, becoming pinkish apricot. Dwarf. Early

'Winton' 4
(West & Fell, pre-1935)

'Winwick' 1 W-W
(G.H. Johnstone, pre-1953)
'Winter' × 'Brunswick'
Fl. pure white

'Winwood' 1 (a)
(A.H. Ahrens) J.S. Leitch, 1956

'Wiper Three' 2 Y-P
(David Adams) David Adams, 1996
Sdlg 76/05B ('Qantasia' × 'Daydream') × 'Dailmanach'; sdlg no. 86/115H
Fl. forming a double triangle, 115 mm wide; perianth segments ovate, blunt, whitish yellow, plane; the inner segments more nearly acute at apex; corona funnel-shaped, smooth, yellowish pink, on the outside resembling the perianth in colour, frilled, with rim flanged and crenate. Mid-season to late. Sunproof

'Wirri' 1 W-P
(W. Jackson Jr, pre-1950)
'Duna' × 'Rosario'

'Wirruna' 1 W-P
(S.J. Bisdee) S.J. Bisdee, 1956
'Rosario' × 'Mastercraft'

'Wisbech Gem' 3 W-? (b)
(J.W.A. Lefeber, pre-1939)
Syn. 'Suprematie'

'Wisdom' 3 W-W
(M.P. Williams, pre-1938)
'Silver Coin' sdlg

'Wisecrack' 3 W-? (b)
(G.H. Johnstone, pre-1943)

'Wishing Well' 7 Y-W
(G.E. Mitsch, 1968) R. Havens, 1979
'Quick Step' × 'Daydream'; sdlg no. D80/50
Fl. 80 mm wide; perianth segments lemon yellow;

corona white, frilled. Late

'Wistful' 5
(G.H. Engleheart, pre-1923)

'Wistful' 2 W-? (b)
(Alister Clark, 1929) J. Sharp, 1960

'Witchcraft' 2 W-O
(D.S. Bell) D.S. Bell, 1960
'Mannequin' × 'Garland'
Fl. 115 mm wide; corona apricot yellow, shaded with orange. Mid-season. Resembles an improved 'Artist's Model'

'Witch Doctor' 3 W-YYO
(Ballydorn Bulb Farm, 1972) Ballydorn Bulb Farm, 1983
'Merlin' hybrid
Fl. 90 mm wide; corona golden yellow, with dark orange at rim. Mid-season. Sunproof. Resembles 'Merlin' but with a differently-coloured corona

'Witchery' 3 W-? (b)
(G.H. Engleheart, pre-1923)

'Witchery' ?-P
(Alister Clark, pre-1948)

'Witch Hunt' 3 W-GOR
(Ballydorn Bulb Farm) Ballydorn Bulb Farm, 1993
'Witch Doctor' open pollinated
Fl. rounded, 95 mm wide; perianth segments broadly ovate, plane, deeply overlapping; corona saucer-shaped, small, orange, with green at base and a broad band of deep red at rim. Mid-season to late. Sunproof. Resembles 'Witch Doctor' but with more highly contrasting colours

'Withypool' 2 Y-O
(D.A. Lloyd) D.A. Lloyd, 1963
Fl. 108 mm wide; perianth segments pale yellow; corona marigold orange. Mid-season. Resembles 'Air Marshal' with a paler perianth and a larger and shallower corona

'Witte Duif' 8 W-W
(pre-1851)

'Witte Hoefnagel' 8 W-O
(pre-1798)

'Wittenburg' 2 W-?
(H. Leber) H. Leber, 1972
Fl. 115 mm wide

'Witte van Ryne' 8 W-W
(pre-1851)

'Wizard' 3 W-? (b)
(Cartwright & Goodwin, pre-1916)

'Wizard' 1 W-Y
(D.V. West, pre-1936)
Perianth segments snowy white; corona canary yellow, with rim flanged

'Wizard' 2 W-Y
(Murray W. Evans) Murray W. Evans, 1976
('Effective' × 'Festivity') open pollinated; sdlg no. L-9
Fl. 97 mm wide; corona chrome yellow. Mid-season

'Wladimir' 2 W-? (b)
(J.W.A. Lefeber, pre-1945)

'Woburn Lemon' 2 Y-Y
(C.E. Buckingham, pre-1938)
Fl. lemon yellow, tinged green

'Woburn Mascot' 1 W-? (b)
(C.E. Buckingham, 1940) J.A.O'More, 1957

'Woburn Masterpiece'
(pre-1940)

'Woburn Primrose' 2 W-? (b)
(C.E. Buckingham, pre-1936)

'Woburn Ruby' 2 (a)
(C.E. Buckingham, pre-1936)

'Woburn Silver' 2 W-? (b or c)
(C.E. Buckingham, pre-1936)

'Woburn Wonder' 2 W-? (b)
(C.E. Buckingham, pre-1933)
Fl. rounded; perianth segments very broad, rounded at apex, fairly prominently mucronate, spreading, a little concave, overlapping more than half; the inner segments a little inflexed, creased; corona shallow, broad, heavily ribbed, lightly frilled

'Wodan' 2 W-YYO
(G.A. Uit den Boogaard, pre-1944)

'Wogen' 1 W-W
(J.N. Hancock & Co., pre-1962) Unregistered
Fl. large; perianth segments broad, smooth; corona flared, with rim crenate

'Wolf' 3 (a)
(A. Gray, pre-1935)

'Wolley Dod' 2 Y-Y
(W. Backhouse, pre-1869)
Fl. yellow; perianth segments large, spreading; corona cylindrical, short, darker in tone than the perianth. Syn. Backhousei 'Wolley Dod'. "Absorbed" 'F.Du Cane Godman'. Formerly listed in the

Pseudonarcissus Group

'Wombat' 1 Y-Y
(T. Morrison) T. Morrison, 1960

'Wonder' 3 W-? (b)
(Mrs R.O. Backhouse, pre-1921)
AM(Haarlem) 1930

'Wonder Bird' 2 W-P
(J.N. Hancock & Co.) J.N. Hancock & Co., 1955
Corona bowl-shaped, pale pink, frilled

'Wonderland' 2 Y-YYO
(W.F.M. Copeland, pre-1910)
Hybrid between 'Emperor' and *N. poeticus*
Fl. large, of strong substance; perianth segments yellowish buff, overlapping; corona cylindrical, broad, very deep yellow, touched orange at rim, frilled

'Wonderous' 1 W-Y
(J.N.Hancock & Co., 1983) Unregistered
'Moonstruck' × 'Chillagoe'; sdlg no. 3/83H
Perianth segments greenish white, deeply overlapping; corona cylindrical, deep lemon yellow, with rim dentate. Tall. Very early

'Wonga' 1 Y-Y
(T. Morrison) T. Morrison, 1960
Fl. soft yellow; corona with rim flanged

'Wontok' 2 W-WWP
(Jackson's Daffodils, 1983) Jackson's Daffodils, 1993
Sdlg 192/75 × 'Cherryrim'; sdlg no. 128/78
Fl. 105 mm wide greenish white (155A); perianth segments broadly ovate; the inner segments more narrowly ovate; corona cylindrical, with light yellowish pink 29C at rim and the rim flanged. Mid-season

'Woodbine' 1 W-? (b)
(M.P. Williams, pre-1938)

'Woodbourne' 1 (a)
(A. Gibson) R. Hyde, 1958

'Woodcock' 6 Y-Y
(M.P. Williams, pre-1949)
Fl. about 115 mm wide; perianth segments ovate, mucronate, vivid yellow 9B, plane or a little twisted, smooth, semi-transparent, overlapping one-third; the inner segments more definitely twisted; corona cylindrical and lightly ribbed, a little constricted near mouth, mouth slightly expanded and frilled, rim notched and very lightly flanged. 2n=29. AM(e) 1951, AM(Haarlem) 1957

'Woodfield' 1 W-Y
(E.W. Cotter) E.W. Cotter, 1968
'Samite' × 'Cameronian'

'Woodford' 1 W-W
(R.C.A. Tombleson) R.C.A. Tombleson, 1968
Fl. 119 mm wide. Mid-season. Resembles a smaller and earlier-flowered 'Empress of Ireland' with the corona rim more deeply crenate

'Woodgreen' 2 W-WYY
(W.J. Dunlop) W.J. Dunlop, 1956
Fl. 109 mm wide; perianth segments creamy white, overlapping; corona flushed light greenish yellow 4C, with creamy white at base and a darker tone of yellow (6C) at rim, mouth slightly expanded, rim flanged and dentate. Early. 2n=28

'Woodland Beauty' 3 W-R
(T. Bloomer) T. Bloomer, 1964
'Mahmoud' × 'Matapan'; sdlg no. 6/76/58
Corona disc-shaped, deep red

'Woodland Belle' 3 W-YYR
(T. Bloomer) T. Bloomer, 1964
'Irish Charm' × Richardson sdlg 202; sdlg no. 1/4/60
Perianth segments broad, glistening white; corona deep yellow, with a broad band of red at rim

'Woodland Charm' 3 W-R
(T. Bloomer) T. Bloomer, 1964
'Bravura' × 'Mahmoud'; sdlg no. 1/46/51
Perianth segments pure white, slightly reflexed; corona very deep red

'Woodland Elf' 3 W-YYR
(T. Bloomer) T. Bloomer, 1964
'Corofin' × 'Hamzali'; sdlg no. 14/78/58
Perianth segments pure white, slightly reflexed; corona expanded, deep yellow, with a broad band of deep red at rim

'Woodland Gem' 3 W-YYR
(T. Bloomer) T. Bloomer, 1970
'Corofin' × 'Hamzali'; sdlg no. 13/78/58
Corona deep yellow, with a broad band of deep red at rim

'Woodland Glade' 3 Y-GYR
(Mrs J.Abel Smith) M.W.Baxter, 1996
'Altruist' × 'Minster Lodge'; sdlg no. F77/41
Fl. 78 mm wide; perianth segments very broadly ovate, somewhat rounded at apex, light greenish yellow 3D, with white mucro, slightly reflexed; the inner segments more distinctly rounded at apex, only very slightly mucronate, more nearly spreading; corona very shallow bowl-shaped, ribbed, vivid yellow 9A, with green at base and a narrow band of orange-red (33A) at rim, mouth wavy. Late

'Woodland Grace' 3 W-GWY
(T. Bloomer) T. Bloomer, 1962
'Chinese White' × 'Bryher'; sdlg no. 6/81/58
Corona white, with green at base and clear lemon at

rim, tightly frilled, with rim deeply dentate

'Woodland Jewel' 3 W-R
(T. Bloomer) T. Bloomer, 1970
'Mahmoud' × 'Matapan'; sdlg no. 1/76/58
Perianth segments slightly reflexed; corona red

'Woodland Knight' 3 W-YYR
(T. Bloomer) T. Bloomer, 1964
'Irish Charm' × Richardson sdlg 202; sdlg no. 1/2/60

'Woodland Prince' 3 W-Y
(T. Bloomer) T. Bloomer, 1964
'Blarney' × 'Sylvia O'Neill'; sdlg no. 3/48/51
Fl. 90 mm wide; perianth segments broad, cream, smooth and of good substance, overlapping; corona slightly ribbed, light greenish yellow 7D, flushed with a darker tone (13A) at rim, mouth expanded and frilled. 2n=28

'Woodland Princess' 3 W-Y
(T. Bloomer) T. Bloomer, 1964
'Chinese White' × 'Matapan'; sdlg no. 9/35/52

'Woodland Splendour' 3 W-R
(T. Bloomer) T. Bloomer, 1970
'Bravura' × 'Arbar'; sdlg no. 3/32/52
Corona red, with rim dentate

'Woodland Sprite' 3 W-Y
(T. Bloomer) T. Bloomer, 1970
'Blarney' × 'Sylvia O'Neill'; sdlg no. 9/48/51

'Woodland Star' 3 W-R
(T. Bloomer) T. Bloomer, 1962
'Bravura' × 'Glenwherry'; sdlg no. 11/69/51
Corona deep red. 2n=28

'Woodlea' 1 W-P
(C.E. Radcliff, 1945) J.M. Radcliff, 1956
'Rosario' × 'Dawnglow'
Corona rosy apricot

'Woodley Vale' 2 Y-Y
(R.A. Scamp) R.A. Scamp, 1995
'Arctic Gold' × 'Ristin'; sdlg no. 50
Fl. 108 mm wide, deep golden yellow; perianth segments broadly ovate, very smooth, deeply overlapping; corona with mouth a little expanded and neatly frilled. Mid-season

'Wood Nymph' 2 W-? (b or c)
(Cartwright & Goodwin, pre-1915)

'Wood Nymph' 5 W-W
(G.E. Mitsch) G.E. Mitsch, 1975
'Honey Bells' × 'Silver Bells'; sdlg no. D50/1
Fl. 72 mm wide, ivory white. Late

'Woodpecker' 2 W-? (b)
(M.P. Williams) M.P. Williams, 1955

'Wood's Colt' 6 Y-Y
(Donna C. Dietsch) Donna C. Dietsch, 1997
'Mite' open pollinated; sdlg no. 89/6
Fl. 37 mm wide, mid-yellow; perianth segments narrow, acute, spreading at base, sharply reflexed at apex, separated; corona cylindrical, with mouth lobed and flared. Dwarf. Early

'Woodside' 2 Y-? (a)
(New Zealand origin, pre-1955) Unregistered
Resembles an improved 'Fortune'

'Woodsie' 2 Y-Y
(pre-1949)
Perianth segments broad, clear yellow, of strong substance; corona widely expanded, rich bright yellow, frilled

'Woods Pink' 2 W-GWP
(W.G. Pannill) W.G. Pannill, 1987
'Interim' × pink sdlg; sdlg no. PL 2 B
Mid-season

'Woodstar' 5 Y-YWW
(G.E. Mitsch, 1969) G.E. Mitsch, 1984
N. triandrus × *N. jonquilla*; sdlg no. E42/1
Fls 5-6 or more per stem, 44 mm wide; perianth segments ovate, blunt, prominently mucronate, soft lemon yellow, strongly reflexed, plane, overlapping half; the inner segments less strongly reflexed, with margins wavy; corona cup-shaped, smooth, whitish, with lemon yellow at base, mouth straight and even, rim entire. Late. Resembles 'Fairy Chimes' but with white in the corona

'Woodstock' 2 W-? (b)
(J.L. Richardson, pre-1945)

'Woodswallow' 2 W-? (b)
(Alister Clark, pre-1930)

'Woodthrush' 6 W-Y
(G.E. Mitsch) G.E. Mitsch, 1972
'Oratorio' × *N. cyclamineus*; sdlg no. C33/3
Fl. 90 mm wide

'Woodvale' 2 W-WWY
(W.J. Dunlop, pre-1947)
'May Molony' × 'Justice'
Perianth segments pure white; corona white, flushed with pale greeny lemon at rim. PC 1949

'Wood White' 2 or 3 W-? (b or c)
(pre-1910)

'Woolaroo' 4 W-P
(Jackson's Daffodils, 1985) Jackson's Daffodils, 1997
'Chios' hybrid; sdlg no. 12/85

Fl. 97 mm wide; perianth and other petaloid segments ovate, yellowish white 155B; corona segments opening yellow, becoming orange-pink, with white at base. Early

'Woolsthorpe' 2 W-GYY
(Mrs J. Abel Smith) Mrs J. Abel Smith, 1992
'Verona' × 'Thoresby'; sdlg no I44/32
Fl. rounded, 36 mm wide. Late

'Woomera' 2 Y-YYO
(J.N. Hancock & Co., 1947) J.N. Hancock & Co., 1964
'Carbineer' × 'Aranjuez'
Perianth segments bright yellow; corona clear yellow, with salmon orange at rim. Early

'Woomerang' 2 Y-YYO
(Tom Forster, 1960s) Unregistered
Fl. rounded; perianth segments bright yellow; corona disc-shaped, ribbed, deep yellow, with orange at rim. Early to mid-season.

'Woonan' 2 Y-R
(W. Jackson Jr) W. Jackson Jr, 1966
Sdlg 41/52 × sdlg 4/52; sdlg no. 92/58

'Woorak' 1 (a)
(A.O. Roblin, 1944) A.O. Roblin, 1956

'Worcester' 2 W W
(M.J. Jefferson-Brown) M.J. Jefferson-Brown, 1975
Perianth segments spreading or slightly reflexed; corona opening pale cream, becoming white, with rim dentate

'Wordsworth' 9 W-GYR
(W. Balch, pre-1931)
Corona disc-shaped, brilliant greenish yellow 2B, with strong yellow-green 143A at base and a narrow band of orange-red (30A) at rim, with a line of white between the yellow and the red. AM(e)(NZ) 1931

'Workman' 2 Y-O
(G.L. Wilson, pre-1940)
R.O.Backhouse Y-R sdlg × 'Fortune'
Perianth segments rich yellow; corona reddish orange. Late

'Work of Art' 7 W-P
(Sidney DuBose) Sidney DuBose, 1997
('Cordial' × 'Canby') × *N. jonquilla*; sdlg no. P38-411
Fls 2-4 per stem, very smooth; perianth segments pure white; corona deep rose pink. Scented

'World's Favorite' 1 (?d)
(?W.H. McNairy, pre-1959)

'Worlington' 1 Y-Y
(Miss K.M. Hinchliff, pre-1930)

Perianth segments ovate, vivid yellow 9B, inflexed, somewhat twisted, creased, overlapping one-third; the inner segments more strongly twisted; corona cylindrical, slightly darker in tone (12A) than the perianth, with mouth flared, rim notched and crenate. 2n=28. *AM(g) 1939

'Worthwhile' 1 W-W
(W.A. Noton) W.A. Noton, 1976
'Empress of Ireland' × 'Vigil'; sdlg no. 509
Fl. 110 mm wide. Mid-season

'Wot' 2 Y-GYO
(L.P. Dettman) L.P. Dettman, 1979
'Vulcan' × 'Spelter'; sdlg no. 24/76
Fl. 86 mm wide; perianth segments brilliant yellow 13B; corona vivid orange-yellow 21B, with green at base and a broad band of orange (28A) at rim. Early to mid-season. Resembles 'Louise Alexandra' but with the perianth segments more nearly spreading and more deeply overlapping

'Wotan' 2 Y-YOO
(J.N. Hancock & Co., c.1977) Unregistered

'Woven Gold' 2 Y-O
(R.H. Bath, pre-1928)
*C(g) 1936

'W.P.Milner' 1 W-W
(W. Backhouse, pre-1869)
Fl. 60 mm wide, opening pale sulphur yellow, becoming creamy white, facing down; perianth segments ovate, acute, fairly prominently mucronate, a little inflexed, twisted or with margins wavy, separated; corona cylindrical, slightly constricted at mid-point, smooth or lightly ribbed, sometimes remaining yellowish, with mouth expanded and frilled, rim notched and dentate. Dwarf. Early. 2n=14. Syn. 'Milneri', 'Mr Milner', Pseudonarcissus Moschatus 'Mr W.P.Milner'. AM(r) 1914, HC(g) 1977

'Wraith' 3 (a)
(G.H. Furness, pre-1934)

'Wren' 4 Y-Y
(G.L. Wilson) G. Zandbergen-Terwegen, 1959
Resembles a more vigorous and somewhat larger 'Pencrebar' of a slightly different in colour

'Wrestler' 1 Y-Y
(R.A. van der Schoot, pre-1930)
Perianth segments pale buttercup yellow, reflexed; corona darker in tone, with rim rolled and crenate. Mid-season. 2n=28. *AM(g) 1936

'W.R.Hughes' 2 Y-YOO
(West & Fell, pre-1935)
Perianth segments lemon, overlapping; corona expanded, ribbed, deep orange. Resembles a later-

flowered 'Marshal Tweedie'

'W.T.Grant' 1 W-? (b)
(J.W. Barr, pre-1930)

'Wulfstan' 1 (a)
(C. Dawson, pre-1916)

'Wurley' 2 Y-R
(K.J. Heazlewood) K.J. Heazlewood, 1968
'Firecracker' × 'Redeem'

'Wyalla' 1 Y-Y
(J.T. Gray, pre-1950)
Corona with rim slightly rolled

'Wyana' 2 W-R
(J.S. Leitch) J.S. Leitch, 1956

'Wyandot' 1 Y-Y
(Mary Lou Gripshover, 1986) Mary Lou Gripshover, 1997
'Small Talk' open pollinated; sdlg no. 80-35
Fl. 34 mm wide; perianth segments ovate, blunt, spreading, plane, overlapping up to a quarter; the inner segments a little narrower, slightly inflexed, with margins incurved; corona cylindrical, with rim flared and regularly crenate. Dwarf. Early

'Wybalena' 4 W-O
(K.J. Heazlewood) K.J. Heazlewood, 1968
'Glowing Red' × 'Stromboli'
Perianth and other petaloid segments in three whorls, broadly ovate, obscurely mucronate, clean white, a little concave, with margins wavy or incurling, smooth, overlapping half; the outer whorl spreading; the second whorl a little inflexed; the centre whorl shorter, strongly inflexed, with margins deeply incurled; corona segments shorter still, clustered among the petaloid segments at centre, light orange, frilled. 2n=27

'Wychavon' 2 W-YRR
(J.S.B. Lea, 1981) Clive Postles, 1991
'Rockall' hybrid × 'Ohio'; sdlg no. 1-46-76
Fl. 102 mm wide; perianth segments broadly ovate, brilliant white, very smooth; corona bowl-shaped, with mouth lobed and rim dentate. Tall. Mid-season. Sunproof

'Wye' 1 W-Y
(D.R. Acheson, pre-1936)
Perianth segments acute, pure white; corona slender, ribbed, lemon yellow, with rim rolled

'Wy'East' 1 W-W
(Murray W. Evans, 1981) Estella L. Evans, 1992
'Neahkahnie' × 'Cataract'; sdlg no. Y-3/2
Fl. 105 mm wide; perianth segments very broadly ovate, plane, smooth; the inner segments almost touching one another; corona cylindrical, regularly ribbed in upper third, with mouth slightly flared. Mid-season

'Wye Mills' 9 W-GYO
(Mrs M.S. Yerger) Mrs M.S. Yerger, 1993
N. poeticus sdlg open pollinated; sdlg no. 75 J 2-7
Fl. forming a double triangle, 16 mm wide; perianth segments rounded at apex; the inner segments more nearly acute. Dwarf. Late

'Wyena' 3 W-? (b)
(W. Jackson Jr, 1954)
Sdlg 61/50 × 'Ethni'

'Wymondham' 2 W-P
(W.A. Noton, 1967) W.A. Noton, 1977
'Fintona' × 'Passionale'; sdlg no. 543
Fl. 88 mm wide. Mid-season

'Wynken' 7 W-W
(Roberta C. Watrous, pre-1972) Delia Bankhead, 1997
'Mitzy' × *N. jonquilla*; sdlg no. 662/2
Fls usually 2 per stem, star-shaped, 47-50 mm wide, greenish white (155A); perianth segments acute, somewhat reflexed, separated; corona cylindrical, with rim slightly flared and crenate. Dwarf. Early to mid-season

'Wynne' 2 W-Y
(K.J. Heazlewood) K.J. Heazlewood, 1970
'Nymph' × 'Gwyn'

'Wynstay' 2 W-YYO
(H.A. Brown, pre-1938)
Corona yellow, with orange at rim, frilled

'Wynyard' 2 W-WWY
(Tom Forster, 1960s) Unregistered
Corona very broad disc-shaped, opening rich creamy yellow, becoming white, with creamy lemon yellow at rim, frilled. Late

'Wyree' 1 W-W
(K.J. Heazlewood) K.J. Heazlewood, 1970
'Empress of Ireland' × 'Brookfield'

'Wysiwyg' 1 W-W
(Jackson's Daffodils, 1987) Jackson's Daffodils, 1997
'Anitra' × 'Mercedes'; sdlg no. 15/87
Fl. 110 mm wide, yellowish white 155B; perianth segments ovate; corona funnel-shaped, with mouth straight and even. Early

'Wyunna' 2 Y-O
(H.A. Brown, pre-1936)
Perianth segments pale yellow; corona light orange

X

'Xana' 1 Y-Y
(Spanish origin) Marilynn Howe, 1997
Selection by Marilynn Howe from wild-collected *N. asturiensis*; collection no. MH93-18
Fl. forming a double triangle, 38 mm wide, clear butter yellow; perianth segments spreading; corona with mouth slightly flared, frilled. Dwarf. Early

'Xanadu' 2 Y-R
(A.M. Wilson, pre-1948)
Perianth segments clear yellow; corona deep red, frilled

'Xanthine' 2 (a)
(G. Lubbe & Son, pre-1940)
AM(Haarlem) 1940

'Xanthin Gold' 1 Y-Y
(Brian S. Duncan) Rathowen Daffodils, 1987
'Olympic Gold' open pollinated; sdlg no. 922
Fl. deep golden yellow. Mid-season. Resembles a larger and taller 'Bayard'. Syn. 'Banquet'

'Xenophon' 8 Y-O
(Mrs R.O. Backhouse, pre-1914)
Poetaz
Fls 2 per stem; perianth segments yellow; corona reddish orange. AM(c) 1922

'Xenophon' 1 Y-Y
Syn. of 'Alexander Moissi'

'Xerxes' 8 W-O
(Mrs R.O. Backhouse, pre-1907)
Poetaz
Corona deep orange. AM(Haarlem) 1925

'Xit' 3 W-W
(A. Gray, pre-1948)
N. rupicola subsp. *watieri* × Div. 2 W-W
Fl. 46 mm wide; perianth segments broadly ovate, prominently mucronate, pure white, somewhat reflexed, concave, smooth, overlapping one-third; the inner segments more nearly ovate, with margins wavy; corona disc-shaped, strongly ribbed, greenish white, with green at base, mouth even or a little wavy, rim entire or minutely notched. Resembles 'Segovia' in form

'Xunantunich' 2 YYW-WWY
(A.J.R. Pearson) A.J.R. Pearson, 1992
'Daydream' × ('Camelot' × 'Daydream'); sdlg no. 85-45-J19
Fl. forming a double triangle, 118 mm wide; perianth segments broadly ovate, blunt, brilliant greenish yellow 5A, with a prominent band of white at base, spreading, plane, smooth, overlapping more than half; corona cylindrical at base, ribbed and widely flared in upper half, creamy white (2C), with brilliant greenish yellow 5A at rim, mouth slightly lobed, rim crenate. Mid-season to late. Resembles 'Daydream' but with the perianth segments narrower and of a deeper colour

'X.Y.Z.'
(pre-1913)

Y

'Yael' 8 W-Y
(Herut Yahel, pre-1982) C.S.Weijers Jr, 1997
Fls 5-11 per stem, 30 mm wide; perianth segments ovate, blunt, mucronate, greenish white (155A), spreading or a little inflexed, somewhat concave or with margins incurling at apex, overlapping one-third; corona cup-shaped, smooth, pale greenish yellow 1D, mouth wavy, rim entire or very slightly notched. Tall. Mid-season to late. Strongly scented. Syn. 'Nazareth'

'Yael' 2 W-YYR
(W. Jackson Jr, 1967) Unregistered
'Jo' × 'Arbar'; sdlg no. 181/67

'Yahoo' 2 W-O
(Tom Forster, 1960s) Unregistered
Fl. rounded; corona long cup-shaped, bright orange, neatly frilled. Late

'Yahtzee' 2 W-Y
(J.N.Hancock & Co., 1983) Unregistered
Perianth segments broad; corona disc-shaped, deeply ribbed, yellow. Late

'Yale' 2 W-YYO
(G.E.Mitsch, 1984) R. & E.Havens, 1995
'Limpkin' × 'Wedding Band'; sdlg no. TT47/2
Fl. rounded, 95 mm wide, of heavy substance; perianth segments very broadly ovate, creamy white, smooth; corona almost disc-shaped, mid-yellow, with a narrow band of orange at rim, rim dentate. Late. Sunproof

'Yallourn' 1 (a)
(Alister Clark, 1940) J. Sharp, 1960

'Yalta' 3 W-YYR
(J.L. Richardson, pre-1945)

'Yama' 3 (a)
(P.D. Williams, pre-1934)

'Yamba' 2 Y-Y
(H.A. Brown, 1943)
Perianth segments yellow, slightly reflexed; corona deeper in tone, with rim closely and deeply notched, as if fringed. Late

'Yamhill' 2 W-YYW
(Murray W. Evans, 1968) Murray W. Evans, 1978
'Oneonta' × 'Protege'; sdlg no. K-7
Fl. 105 mm wide. Mid-season

'Yamolf' 7 Y-Y
(A. Gray, pre-1950)

'Yanchep' 2 W-Y
(J.N.Hancock & Co., 1982) J.N.Hancock & Co., 1997
Sdlg no. 40/82H
Perianth segments ovate, plane; corona cylindrical, lemon yellow, with rim neatly crenate. Early to mid-season

'Yanco' 1 Y-Y
(D. Jackson) Jackson's Daffodils, 1983
'Warbin' × 'Comal'

'Yanderra' 2 Y-R
(W. Jackson Jr) W. Jackson Jr, 1968
'Vanity' × sdlg 37/53; sdlg no. 24/61

'Yandoo' 1 Y-Y
(J.N.Hancock & Co., 1979) Unregistered
1 Y-Y sdlg × Fairbairn 2 Y-Y; sdlg no. 11/79H
Perianth segments deep golden yellow; corona darker in tone and neatly frilled. Tall. Very early

'Yani' 3 W-R
(W. Jackson Jr) W. Jackson Jr, 1968
'Beirut' × 'Ethni'; sdlg no. 168/61

'Yankee Clipper' 2 Y-YYO
(Warnaar & Co., pre-1939)
'Fortune' × 'Scarlet Leader'
Fl. 112 mm wide; perianth segments light greenish yellow 5C, overlapping half; corona ribbed, vivid orange-yellow 21A, shading to vivid orange 28B at rim, with mouth expanded and frilled, rim dentate. 2n=28. AM(Haarlem) 1939, *AM(g) 1959

'Yantara' 1 W-YPP
(C.E. Radcliff, 1942) J.M.Radcliff, 1956
'Shirley Wyness' × 'Dawnglow'

'Yappa' 1 Y-Y
(A.O. Roblin, c.1966) Unregistered
'Kalman' × ('Tain' × 'Butta')

'Yarck' 1 Y-Y
(J.N. Hancock & Co., pre-1974) Unregistered

'Yarley' 1 Y-Y
(W. Jackson Jr, 1964) Unregistered
'Haka' × 'Letti'; sdlg no. 4/64

'Yarra' 1 W-Y
(J.N. Hancock & Co., 1950) J.N. Hancock & Co., 1960
Perianth segments ivory white; corona deep yellow, with rim flanged

'Yasmin' 2 Y-O
(S.J. Bisdee, 1949)
'Carbineer' × 'Red Mantle'

'Yasmin' 2 W-Y
Syn. of 'Zanazan'

'Yazz' 7 W-P
(W.G. Pannill, 1980) W.G. Pannill, 1991
Pink sdlg × *N. jonquilla*; sdlg no. 74/26 B
Mid-season to late

'Yearling' 2 (a)
(J.E. Exley, pre-1950)

'Yeats' 9 W-GOO
(A.E. Robinson) Carncairn Daffodils, 1992
'Como' × 'Andrew Marvel'; sdlg no. 3/19/78
Fl. 70 mm wide; perianth segments broadly ovate, truncate, prominently mucronate, concave, overlapping half; the inner segments a little more narrowly ovate, slightly inflexed, with margins wavy or incurling; corona disc-shaped, closely ribbed, orange, with green at base and a darker tone of orange at rim. Late

'Yeavering Bell' 1 W-W
(G. Harrison) G. Harrison, 1968
'Cantatrice' hybrid × 'Broughshane'
Fl. 118 mm wide. Mid-season. Resembles a more vigorous 'Cantatrice'

'Yeka' 2 (a)
(de Graaff Bros, pre-1927)

'Yelena' 2 W-P
(J.N.Hancock & Co., 1975) Unregistered
Corona funnel-shaped, true pink, with rim rolled. Late

'Yelka' 1 Y-Y
(A.O. Roblin, 1947)
'Rainga' × 'Osella'

'Yelkin' 1 W-W
(J.N. Hancock & Co., c.1975) Unregistered

'Yellingbo' 1 Y-Y
(C.A. Nethercote) T. Morrison, 1960
Fl. clear soft yellow. Early

'Yellow Ajax' 1 Y-Y
Syn. of 'Yellow Trumpet'

'Yellow Aster' 2 Y-Y
(L. Buckland, pre-1918)

'Yellow Beauty' 1 Y-Y
(Barr & Sons, pre-1929)
Perianth segments narrow, acute, soft yellow; corona canary yellow, with mouth flared and frilled. Mid-season. 2n=28. *HC(g) 1936

'Yellow Bird' 2 Y-Y
(R.A. van der Schoot, pre-1931)
Perianth segments very broadly ovate, rounded at apex, only very slightly mucronate, sulphur yellow, spreading, overlapping half; the inner segments more narrowly ovate, a little inflexed, with margins wavy; corona funnel-shaped, broad, dark yellow, tightly frilled, with rim slightly flanged. Mid-season. *AM(g) 1936

'Yellow Boy' 2 Y-Y
(A.E. Lowe, pre-1927)

'Yellow Butterfly' 8 Y-O
(Mrs O.L.Fellers) Mrs Betty Barnes, 1981
'Matador' × 'Golden Dawn'
Fl. 50 mm wide; perianth segments pale lemon; corona orange. Mid-season. 2n=34. Resembles 'Golden Dawn' but with a larger and paler perianth

'Yellow Carpet' 2 (a)
(Mrs R.S. Cobley, pre-1954)

'Yellow Charm' 2 (a)
(R.H. Bath, pre-1950)

'Yellow Cheerfulness' 4 Y-Y
(Eggink Bros, 1937)
'Cheerfulness' sport
Fls. several per stem, 19 mm wide; perianth segments very broadly ovate or roundish, slightly or sometimes fairly prominently mucronate, light greenish yellow 6D, spreading or reflexed, plane, overlapping half; the inner segments more usually spreading, with margins wavy; corona segments half as long as the perianth segments, clustered at centre, vivid yellow 9A, with orange-yellow at rim, inflexed or strongly inflexed. Late to very late. Scented. 2n=24. AM(Haarlem) 1937, FCC(Haarlem) 1942, AM(e) 1946, *AM(p) 1976, AGM 1995. Received AM 1946 as 'Ruth Fox'

'Yellow Cloud' 1 (a)
(de Graaff Bros & van Konynenburg & Co., pre-1937)
Syn. 'Yellow Perfection'

'Yellow Cup' 8 W-Y
(pre-1881)

'Yellow Dale' 1 Y-Y
(J.A. O'More) P.D.K. Ramsay, 1983
'Cromarty' × 'Kingscourt'

'Yellow Dawn' 2 Y-O
(de Graaff Bros) de Graaff Bros, 1962
Fl. 102 mm wide; perianth segments brilliant yellow 12B; corona strong orange 25A, frilled. Early. AM(Haarlem) 1962

'Yellow Dazzler' 1 Y-Y
(de Graaff Bros) de Graaff Bros & van Konynenburg & Co., 1958
Perianth segments narrow, acute, lemon yellow; corona narrow, golden yellow. 2n=28. AM(Haarlem) 1958

'Yellow Diamond' 2 or 3 W-? (b or c)
(W.F M. Copeland, pre-1913)

'Yellow Duke' 2 (a)
(M. van Waveren & Sons, pre-1953)

'Yellow Dune' 8
(A. Vis, pre-1931)

'Yellow Eclipse' 1 Y-Y
(pre-1926)

'Yellow Eye' 3 W-? (b)
(Cartwright & Goodwin, pre-1908)

'Yellow Favourite' 8
(J. Valkering & Sons, pre-1942)

'Yellow Festivity' 2 Y-Y
(G.E. Mitsch) R. Havens, 1980
'Festivity' sport
Fl. 115 mm wide; perianth segments light yellow; corona somewhat deeper in tone. Mid-season

'Yellow Fever' 7 Y-Y
(Rberta C.Watrous, 1984) Delia Bankhead, 1997
6 Y-Y × *N. jonquilla*; sdlg no. 801/5
Fls 2 per stem, 32-38 mm wide, vivid yellow 9A; perianth segments mucronate, very slightly reflexed, plane, overlapping one-third; corona cylindrical, lightly ribbed, with mouth a little expanded, rim slightly crenate. Dwarf. Early

'Yellow Flag' 2 Y-Y
(C. Goodson, pre-1927)

'Yellow Gem' 8
(A. Vis, pre-1943)

'Yellow Gem' 5 Y-Y
(C.G. van Tubergen) C.G. van Tubergen, 1956
N. triandrus var. *loiseleurii* sdlg
Fls 2-3 per stem, large, sulphur yellow; corona broad

'Yellow Giant' 2 Y-Y
(Barr & Sons, pre-1918)
Perianth segments pale yellow; corona expanded, golden yellow

'Yellow Gift' 1 Y-Y
(J.A. O'More, 1963) R.G. Cull, 1977
'Cromarty' × 'Kingscourt'; sdlg no. 42/58
Fl. 110 mm wide. Late. Resembles a more consistent 'Cromarty' of better form and deeper colour

'Yellow Girl' 2 Y-Y
(A.E. Lowe, pre-1927)

'Yellow Gleam' 1 Y-Y
(C.A. van der Wereld) C.A. van der Wereld, 1963
Fl. 100 mm wide, brilliant greenish yellow 5B. Mid-season. AM(Haarlem) 1963

'Yellow Glory' 2 (a)
(K.D. Smith, pre-1951)

'Yellow God' 1 Y-Y
(S.J. Bisdee, 1939)
'Loxton' × 'His Excellency'

'Yellow Hammer' 2 (a)
(A.R. Goodwin, pre-1908)

'Yellow Hammer' 1 Y-Y
Syn. of 'Knut Hamsun'

'Yellow Harvest' 4 Y-Y
(J. Barnhoorn, 1970) J. Barnhoorn, 1980
'Golden Harvest' sport
Perianth segments vivid greenish yellow 2A; corona vivid yellow 12A

'Yellow Horn' 1 Y-Y
(G. Vink & Son, pre-1953)
'Golden Surprise' × 'King Alfred'

'Yellow Idol' 1 Y-Y
(J.L. Richardson, pre-1951)
'Pretoria' × 'Cromarty'
Fl. medium yellow; perianth segments very broadly ovate; corona with rim dentate

'Yellow Image' 1 Y-Y
(J.L. Richardson) J.L. Richardson, 1961
'Golden Idol' open pollinated
Fl. 110 mm wide, golden yellow; corona with rim dentate and slightly rolled

'Yellow Imperator' 1 Y-Y
(S.G. Gaspar, pre-1931)
'Golden Spur' × 'King Alfred'
AM(Haarlem) 1931

'Yellow Jacket' 5
(Mrs R.O. Backhouse, pre-1921)

'Yellow Jacket' 7 Y-Y
(P.D. Williams, pre-1925)
Perianth segments yellow, tinged orange; corona yellow. AM(e)(p) 1925

'Yellow King' 1 Y-Y
Syn. of 'Ard Righ'

'Yellow Marvel' 1 (a)
(van Zanten Bros, pre-1944)

'Yellow Mead' 2 (a)
(P.D. Williams, pre-1932)

'Yellow Moon' 2 Y-Y
(The Brodie of Brodie, c.1935)
'Jubilant' × 'Saint Egwin'
Fl. large, luminous yellow

'Yellow Orb' 2 Y-Y
(C. Goodson, pre-1927)

'Yellow Parade' 2 Y-Y
(H. 't Mannetje) H. 't Mannetje, 1961
Fl. 100 mm wide; perianth segments brilliant greenish yellow 6C; corona vivid yellow 12A. Mid-season

'Yellow Perfection' 1 Y-Y
(P.D. Williams, pre-1936)

'Yellow Perfection' 1
Syn. of 'Yellow Cloud'

'Yellow Pet' 10 Y-Y
(Moroccan origin) Ray Cobb, 1991
Selection from J.C. Archibald's wild-collected *N. romieuxii*; from collection no. JCA805
Perianth segments narrowly triangular in appearance, shorter than the corona, yellow, obscurely veined green, spreading; corona more-or-less spreading, pale greenish yellow 1-2D, mouth even or a little wavy, rim irregularly crenate and becoming slightly rolled with age. Dwarf. Early. Resembles a 'Julia Jane' of paler colour, and a 'Joy Bishop' with the corona less markedly lobed

'Yellow Phoenix' 4 Y-O
Syn. of 'Butter and Eggs'

'Yellow Poet' 3 (a)
(G.H. Engleheart, pre-1913)

'Yellow Poppy' 2 Y-YYO
(Cartwright & Goodwin, pre-1914)
Perianth segments very broadly ovate, irregular in width, blunt or squarish at apex, prominently mucronate, spreading, pale primrose yellow, somewhat creased, with midrib showing, overlapping half;

the inner segments narrower, a little inflexed, with margins more strongly wavy and sometimes nicked or indented; corona bowl-shaped, straight-sided, ribbed, bright yellow, with a narrow band of yellowish orange at rim. Mid-season. 2n=21. AM(Haarlem) 1920, *HC(g) 1936, *AM(g) 1947

'Yellow Primo' 8 Y-Y
(pre-1861)
Perianth segments primrose yellow; corona darker

'Yellow Prince' 8 Y-O
(pre-1872)
2n=30

'Yellow Prince' 2 Y-Y
(Barr & Sons, pre-1910)
Fl. rounded; perianth segments pale primrose yellow, overlapping; corona cup-shaped, rich yellow, neatly frilled

'Yellow Prince' 1 (a)
(pre-1927)

'Yellow Prince'
(G. Lewis, pre-1940)

'Yellow Princeps' 1 (a)
(G. H. Engleheart, pre-1907)

'Yellow Princess' 1 (a)
(G. Haver, pre-1933)

'Yellow Prize' 7 Y-Y
(R.A. van der Schoot, pre-1931)
Fls sometimes 2 per stem; perianth segments clear rich lemon yellow, overlapping; corona shallow, expanded, pale buttercup yellow. Mid-season. 2n=28. *AM(g) 1936, AM(Haarlem) 1938. Div. 2 until 1936

'Yellow Queen' 1 (a)
(J. de Groot & Sons, pre-1907)

'Yellow Queen' 1
Syn. of 'Yellow Superb'

'Yellow River' 1 Y-Y
(H.J. Wentink, 1960) H.J. Wentink, 1988
'Goblet' × 'Gold Medal'; sdlg no. 103
Fl. 100 mm wide; perianth segments brilliant greenish yellow 6C; corona vivid yellow 9A. Mid-season. Resembles 'Gold Medal'

'Yellow Sea' 1 Y-Y
(E.G. Taylor) E.G. Taylor, 1956
'King Alfred' hybrid
Fl. rich yellow; perianth segments of thick substance

'Yellow Silk' 5 Y-Y
(de Graaff Bros & van Konynenburg & Co.) de Graaff Bros & van Konynenburg & Co., 1960
'Shot Silk' sport
Fl. brilliant greenish yellow 4A. Late. AM(Haarlem) 1960

'Yellow Spray' 8
(R.A. van der Schoot, pre-1930)

'Yellow Spring' 2 Y-Y
(G.A. Uit den Boogaard) E. Nieuwenhuis, 1964
Fl. large; perianth segments canary yellow. Tall. Early. Resembles 'Carlton' but with a darker corona

'Yellow Standard' 2 Y-Y
(Barr & Sons, pre-1918)
Perianth segments narrow, acute, citron yellow; corona rich golden yellow. *C(g) 1927

'Yellow Star' 2 Y-Y
(J. Kouwenhoven, pre-1931)

'Yellow Star' 1 Y-GYY
Syn. of 'Marieke'

'Yellowstone' 3 (a)
(E. Oostdam, pre-1939)

'Yellowstone' 1 Y-W
(Murray W. Evans) Murray W. Evans, 1969
'Content' × ('King of the North' × 'Content')

'Yellow Straight' 2 Y-Y
(G. Lubbe & Son, 1950) G. Lubbe & Son, 1960

'Yellow Sun' 2 Y-Y
(G. Lubbe & Son, pre-1940)
AM(Haarlem) 1940, FCC(Haarlem) 1946, FA(Haarlem) 1948, EFA(Haarlem) 1949. Div. 1 until 1948

'Yellow Sunset' 1 (a)
(G.L. Wilson, pre-1948)

'Yellow Sunset' 1 Y-Y
(C. Culpepper, pre-1974) Unregistered

'Yellow Superb' 1 (a)
(G. Haver, pre-1933)
Syn. 'Yellow Queen'

'Yellow Surprise' 1 Y-Y
(M. Veldhuyzen van Zanten & Sons) M. Veldhuyzen van Zanten & Sons, 1977
Fl. 130 mm wide; perianth segments brilliant greenish yellow 7C; corona slightly brighter in tone (12B). Early

'Yellowtail' 2 W-Y
(Murray W. Evans) Murray W. Evans, 1977
'Glenmanus' × ('Rose Marie' × ['Trousseau' × ?'Pink

o' Dawn']); sdlg no. K-17
Fl. 98 mm wide. Mid-season

'Yellowthroat' 2 W-Y
(G.E. Mitsch) G.E. Mitsch, 1972
'Oratorio' × 'Accent'; sdlg no. C32/2
Fl. 105 mm wide; corona large, orange-yellow, paling to ivory at base. Mid-season

'Yellow Tresamble' 5 Y-Y

'Yellow Triumphator' 1 (a)
(A.C. Paardekooper, pre-1948)
AM(Haarlem) 1948, FCC(Haarlem) 1955

'Yellow Trophy' 1 (a)
(P. van Deursen, 1932)
AM(Haarlem) 1932

'Yellow Trumpet' 1 Y-Y
(pre-1914)

'Yellow Underwing' 2 (a)
(P.D. Williams, pre-1930)
AM(Haarlem) 1930

'Yellow Warbler' 5 Y-Y
(G.E. Mitsch, pre-1954)
'Fortune' × *N. triandrus*; sdlg no. G65/2
Fls 2-3 per stem, light yellow, facing down. Mid-season. Resembles an earlier-flowered and paler-coloured 'Lemon Drops'

'Yellow White Emperor' 1 Y-Y
(pre-1933)
'White Emperor' hybrid
Fl. bright deep golden yellow

'Yellow Wings' 6 Y-Y
(K.van der Veek) K.van der Veek, 1994
Fl. 85 mm wide; perianth segments brilliant greenish yellow 6A; corona close to vivid yellow 9A. Early

'Yellow Wonder' 1 Y-Y
(L. Buckland, pre-1936)
Fl. large, rich deep yellow, of strong substance; corona flared

'Yellow Xit' 3 W-Y
(A. Gray) A. Gray, 1968
'Xit' sport

'Yellow Yorlin' 2 Y-Y
(G.L. Wilson, pre-1941)
'Bokhara' × 'Cheerio'
Fl. buttercup yellow; corona shallow bowl-shaped

'Yelmo' 1 Y-Y
(W. Jackson Jr) W. Jackson Jr, 1970
'Tulendena' × 'Jaslin'; sdlg no. 213/66

Fl. 105 mm wide

'Yenbar' 2 Y-O
(J.N. Hancock & Co.) J.N. Hancock & Co., 1955
Perianth segments bright yellow; corona reddish orange

'Yenda' 2 W-Y
(J.N. Hancock & Co., c.1977) Unregistered

'Yen How' 1 (a)
(G.L. Wilson, pre-1930)

'Yeo' 2 W-? (b)
(N.Y. Lower, pre-1931)

'Yeo' 2 Y-O
(H.A. Brown, 1932)
Corona widely expanded, rich lemon yellow, with deep orange at rim. Tall

'Yeodene' 2 (a)
(H.A. Brown, 1939) J.N. Hancock & Co., 1960

'Yeoman'
(C. Dawson, pre-1908)

'Yeoman' 1 W-? (b)
(G.H. Brownlee, pre-1930)

'Yeoman' 2 Y-Y
(J.J. Abernethy, 1950) R.J. Abernethy, 1961
Fl. 102 mm wide, deep yellow. Mid-season

'Yeoman of the Guard' 3 W-? (b)
(G.H. Engleheart, pre-1913)

'Yes Please' 2 W-P
(F.E. Board) M.J. Jefferson-Brown, 1965
'Rose of Tralee' × 'Interim'
Fl. 101 mm wide; perianth segments ovate, blunt, fairly prominently mucronate, somewhat inflexed, overlapping a quarter; the inner segments with margins incurved at apex; corona cylindrical, smooth, rich pink, paler towards base, with mouth a little expanded, lightly frilled, rim notched and crenate. Resembles 'Interim' in the perianth and 'Passionale' in the corona

'Yester' 2 W-Y
(pre-1985) Unregistered

'Yeti' 1 W-YWY
(P.L.A. Pouw & Sons) P.L.A. Pouw & Sons, 1973
'Van Wereld's Favourite' × 'Beersheba'
Fl. 115 mm wide

'Yeti'
(J.N. Hancock & Co., pre-1962) Unregistered

'Yindee' 6 W-W
(A. Gray) A. Gray, 1957
Fl. milk white; corona with mouth slightly expanded

'Yin-Nell' 3 W-R
(A.O. Roblin, pre-1936)
'Jean Hood' × 'Forfar'

'Yippee' 2 Y-P
(Campbell Duncan) Campbell Duncan, 1956
'Shirley Wyness' × 'Rosario'

'Yma' 1 W-P
(S.J. Bisdee) S.J. Bisdee, 1956
('Eskimo' × 'Dawnglow') × 'Kerabin'

'Yolande' 2 Y-O
(A.M. Wilson, pre-1910)

'Yolande' 8
(pre-1933)
?The same as 'Princess Yolande'

'Yolande' 2 W-P
(W. Jackson Jr, 1966) Unregistered
'Kimi' × 'Egina'; sdlg no. 20/66

'Yolla' 2 Y-Y
(C.E. Radcliff, 1939)
'Trenoon' × 'Kallista'

'Yonder' 2 Y-R
(J.R.Erp, 1948)
'Killigrew' × 'Rosslare'

'Yoone' 2 Y-ORR
(W. Jackson Jr, 1968) Unregistered
'Rave' × 'Dimity'; sdlg no. 14/68

'Yootha' 2 W-W
(P. & G. Phillips) P. & G. Phillips, 1979
Fl. 103 mm wide. Mid-season

'Yootha' 2 W-YOW
(J.N. Hancock & Co., 1959) Unregistered

'Yoprim' 8 Y-Y
(Mrs K.B. Anderson) Mrs K.B. Anderson, 1984
'Avalanche' open pollinated; sdlg no. 71-8 A1
Fl. 50 mm wide; perianth segments cream; corona bright yellow. Early

'Yorick' 1 Y-Y
(C. Dawson, pre-1922)
Perianth segments canary yellow; corona rich yellow. Early

'Yorkey' 1 W-P
(Jackson's Daffodils, 1979) Jackson's Daffodils, 1991

'Value' × 'C.E.Radcliff'; sdlg no. 84/79
Fl. 107 mm wide; perianth segments very broadly ovate, blunt, slightly mucronate, greenish white (155A), spreading or a little inflexed, smooth, overlapping half; the inner segments more narrowly ovate, with margins wavy; corona cylindrical, narrow, smooth, light yellowish pink 27A, with mouth expanded and slightly frilled. Early

'Yorkist' 4 W-W
(Mrs R.S. Cobley, pre-1932)
Fl. pure white

'York Minster' 1 Y-Y
(J.S.B. Lea, 1981) Clive Postles, 1991
Sdlg 2-19-68 × 'Glen Farclas'; sdlg no. 1-14-76
Fl. forming a double triangle, 102 mm wide; perianth segments ovate; corona funnel-shaped, deep orange, paling to yellow at base, with mouth flared. Mid-season

'Yorktown' 2 W-GOO
(J.M. de Navarro) J.M. de Navarro, 1977
'Arctic Flame' × 'Leonora'; sdlg no. 508/III
Late. Resembles 'Arctic Flame' but with a deeper-coloured corona

'Yornup' 2 Y-Y
(H.A. Brown, 1939)
Perianth segments broad, lemon yellow; corona expanded, opening lemon yellow, becoming bright orange-yellow. Very early. 2n=27

'Yosemite' 1 (a)
(Shea, pre-1913)

'Yosemite' 2 W-W
(Murray W. Evans) Murray W. Evans, 1969
'Radiation' × ('Trousseau' × 'Pink o' Dawn')

'Yoshiko' 2 W-P
(Brian S. Duncan) Brian S. Duncan, 1992
'Gracious Lady' × ('Infatuation' × 'Gem of Antrim'); sdlg no. 1135
Fl. 114 mm wide; perianth segments broadly ovate, only very slightly mucronate, spreading, overlapping half; the inner segments with margins somewhat wavy; corona funnel-shaped, broad, deep rose pink, with rim deeply dentate. Mid-season to late

'Young American' 1 YYW-WWY
(R. & E. Havens, 1974) R. & E. Havens, 1988
'Daydream' × 'Arctic Gold'; sdlg no. JEJ2/6
Perianth segments very broadly ovate, blunt, deep lemon yellow, with slight white mucro and with a band of white at base, spreading, slightly concave, with margins sometimes incurling at apex, overlapping half; the inner segments slightly inflexed, with margins wavy; corona funnel-shaped, smooth, opening yellow, becoming white, with lemon yellow at

rim, mouth ribbed, straight or very slightly flared, even, with rim crenate. Mid-season

'Young Blood' 2 W-R
(Brian S. Duncan) Rathowen Daffodils, 1983
'Irish Rover' × 'Doctor Hugh'; sdlg no. 666
Perianth segments broadly ovate, blunt or somewhat truncate, spreading, a little concave, overlapping half; the inner segments slightly inflexed; corona bowl-shaped, ribbed, with mouth wavy, rim crenate. Mid-season to late. Div. 3 until 1988

'Young Idea' 7 W-Y
(M.J. Jefferson-Brown, pre-1987) Unregistered

'Young Joy'
(pre-1940)

'Young Love' 2 W-PPY
(Grant E.Mitsch, 1976) R. & E.Havens, 1994
('Precedent' × 'Carita') × 'Partridge'; sdlg no. LL27/1
Fl. 100 mm wide; perianth segments broadly ovate, acute; corona disc-shaped, pink, with undertones of lavender blue and a band of yellow at rim, frilled. Mid-season. Sunproof

'Young Nick' 11a Y-Y
(Colin Crotty) Colin Crotty, 1995
'Gold Phantom' open pollinated; sdlg no. 36-81
Fl. forming a double triangle, 104 mm wide; perianth segments ovate, bright yellow; corona deeply split, the six segments opposite and closely overlying the perianth segments, darker in tone than the perianth, deeply lobed, with rim frilled. Mid-season

'Young Oliver' 3 Y-Y
(Mrs J.Abel Smith) M.W.Baxter, 1996
'Lemonade' hybrid; sdlg no. E88/13
Fl. 93 mm wide; perianth segments roundish, truncate, light greenish yellow, paler at midrib at apex, spreading, concave, with margins incurling, overlapping half; corona broad and shallow, ribbed, vivid yellow 9A, paler at base, with mouth straight and frilled. Late

'Your Grace' 2 W-W
(A.J.R. Pearson) A.J.R. Pearson, 1991
'Easter Moon' × 'Cloneen'; sdlg no. 87-81-K39
Fl. 125 mm wide; perianth segments ovate, only very slightly mucronate, milk white, reflexed, plane or a little concave, smooth and of good substance, with broad midrib showing, regular, overlapping half; the inner segments more usually plane; corona funnel-shaped, narrowly ribbed, pinkish white, with sage green noticeable in tube, mouth lightly ribbed, straight, split in places and overlapping, a little frilled, with rim minutely crenate. Mid-season to late. Resembles 'Cloneen' but with the perianth segments longer, smoother and more sharply reflexed and the corona of a different shape

'Youth' 1 Y-Y
(C.G. van Tubergen, pre-1931)
Perianth segments broadly ovate, blunt, only slightly mucronate, spreading, creased, with margins incurled, overlapping one-third; the inner segments more narrowly ovate, more nearly acute, a little inflexed, somewhat twisted; corona with rim very widely flanged and deeply notched. AM(Haarlem) 1931, FA(Haarlem) 1933, FCC(Haarlem) 1934

'Yo Yo' 3 W-W
(G.L. Wilson, pre-1947)

'Ypres' 3 W-OOR
(Mrs R.O. Backhouse, pre-1921)
Corona orange and vermilion. PC 1922

'Ypsilante' 9 W-YYR
(E.M. Crosfield, pre-1927)
Fl. 85 mm wide; perianth segments overlapping half; corona very shallow bowl-shaped, brilliant yellow 12B, with green at base and a well-defined narrow band of orange-red (32A) at rim. 2n=14. *AM(g) 1949. ?The same as 'Ypsilanti' of pre-1913

'Ypsilanti'
(pre-1913)
?Syn. of 'Ypsilante'

'Ysbryn' 1 Y-Y
(S.J. Bisdee, 1942)
'Golden Queen' × 'Fahan'

'Yscydion' 1 Y-Y
(S.J. Bisdee, pre-1939)
'Golden City' × 'Gambrinus'

'Yseult' 5
(Barr & Sons, pre-1923)

'Yucatan' 2 W-? (b)
(J.L. Richardson, pre-1953)

'Yuen' 2 W-YYR
(H.G. Cross) H.G. Cross, 1984
'Evenlode' × 'White Lion'; sdlg no. 99-5
Fl. rounded; corona lemon yellow. Late

'Yugao'
Unregistered
Seed parent of 'Parca'

'Yukon' 1 Y-Y
(G.H. Engleheart, pre-1923)
?'Weardale Perfection' hybrid
Fl. deep yellow; corona tinged apricot orange

'Yum-Yum' 3 W-WWY
(Jackson's Daffodils) Jackson's Daffodils, 1986
'Sea Dream' × 'Josiana'; sdlg no. 232/77

Fl. rounded; perianth segments very broad in outline, rounded or squarish at apex, slightly mucronate, greenish white 155C, spreading, plane, overlapping two-thirds; the inner segments more usually rounded at apex, not noticeably mucronate, a little creased and with midrib showing; corona bowl-shaped, small, slightly creamier in tone that the perianth, with very pale yellow at rim, frilled. Late

'Yungfrau' 1 W-W
Syn. of 'Dent Blanche'

'Yuriel' 1 Y-Y
(W. Jackson Jr, 1956) Unregistered
'Melissa' × 'Jobi'; sdlg no. 54/56

'Yurla' 2 W-R
(W. Jackson Jr) W. Jackson Jr, 1966
'Capella' × 'Wyena'

'Yuulong' 2 Y-Y
(J.N. Hancock & Co., pre-1949)
Perianth segments broad, rich yellow; corona expanded, deeper in tone than the perianth, with rim closely and deeply notched, as if fringed

'Yves' 2 Y-Y
(W. Jackson Jr, 1966) Unregistered
Sdlg 65/67 × 'Haka'; sdlg no. 76/66

'Yvonne' 2 W-? (b)
(Mrs R.O. Backhouse, pre-1921)

'Yvonne' 2 Y-Y
(J.N. Hancock & Co., 1948)

Z

'Zabarat' 3 Y-YYR
(Mrs H.K. Richardson) Mrs H.K. Richardson, 1972
'Merlin' open pollinated
Fl. golden yellow; corona with crimson at rim, rim dentate

'Zabrina' 2 W-? (b)
(C.G. van Tubergen, pre-1948)

'Zactlee' 1 Y-Y
(A. Overton) A. Overton, 1960
'Mortlake' × 'Gold Salute'
Fl. rich yellow; corona with rim flanged

'Zadara' 2 Y-R
(J.S. Leitch) J.S. Leitch, 1957

'Zagreus' 1 (a)
(Barr & Sons, pre-1915)

'Zahrat' 1 (a)
(R.H. Bath, pre-1933)

zaianicus = *N. romieuxii* var. *zaianicus*

'Zaida' 2 Y-?
Syn. of 'Laida'

'Zaidee' 9
(P.D. Williams, pre-1948)

'Zaire' 8 Y-Y
(pre-1798)
Fl. sulphur yellow

'Zaire' 1 W-W
(W. Jackson Jr, 1950)
'Fiesta' × 'Kanchenjunga'

'Zalmonah' 5 W-W
(W.F.M. Copeland, pre-1927)

'Zalophus' 4
(J.L. Richardson) Mrs H.K. Richardson, 1964

'Zambesi' 2 Y-O
Syn. of 'Zambezi'

'Zambezi' 2 Y-O
(Mrs H.K. Richardson) Mrs H.K. Richardson, 1972
'Air Marshal' × 'Jaguar'
Perianth segments golden yellow; corona orange, with rim dentate. See also 'Zambesi'

'Zamira' 2 W-W
(A.O. Roblin, 1938)
'Darby' × 'Maid of the Mist'

'Zampa' 3 W-? (b)
(W.A. Grace, pre-1938)

'Zampatti' 2 Y-YYO
(W.F.Leenen) J.N.Hancock & Co., 1997
Sdlg no. 38/76
Perianth segments ovate, lemon yellow, plane; corona bowl-shaped, very broad, ribbed and frilled. Late

'Zanazan' 2 W-Y
(J.N.Hancock & Co., 1986) J.N.Hancock & Co., 1997
Sdlg no. B/86H
Fl. rounded; perianth segments deeply overlapping; corona ribbed, opening bright yellow, becoming chrome yellow, frilled. Late. Syn. 'Yasmin'

'Zandy' 4 W-O
(J.L. Richardson, 1954) R.W. Ward & Son, 1966
Perianth segments creamy white; petaloid segments

pale orange. Mid-season. Resembles a vigorous 'Mary Copeland'

'Zane' 2 Y-O
(J.N.Hancock & Co., 1982) Unregistered
'Ablaze' × 'Redeem'; sdlg no. 63/82H
Perianth segments deep yellow; corona cup-shaped, vivid orange. Tall. Early to mid-season

'Zanette' 2 W-P
(J.N. Hancock & Co., 1949) J.N. Hancock & Co., 1961
Fl. creamy white; corona suffused pink

'Zanglo' 2 W-P
(J.L. Martin) J.L. Martin, 1973
'Roselands' × 'Banongill' hybrid
Fl. 100 mm wide

'Zania' 4 Y-Y
(C.E. Radcliff, 1942)
Sdlg × 'Telamonius Plenus'

'Zanita' 7 Y-GYY
(A.M. Wilson, pre-1951)
Fls 2-3 per stem; perianth segments bright citron yellow; corona slightly deeper in tone, with green at base. Late. Sweetly scented. PC(e) 1973

'Zannitt' 2 Y-R
(C.E. Radcliff, 1943) J.M.Radcliff, 1956
'Aviemore' × 'Market Merry'

'Zante' 1 W-?
(The Brodie of Brodie, c.1916)
'Marina' × 'Hypatia'
Perianth segments white; corona salmon

'Zanzibar' 3 W-YYR
(Mrs R.O. Backhouse, pre-1921)
Fl. 89 mm wide; corona expanded, golden yellow, with a broad band of deep scarlet at rim

'Zanzibar' 2 Y-R
(J.L. Richardson) J.L. Richardson, 1959
'Benghazi' × 'Firecracker'
Perianth segments golden yellow; corona crimson, frilled

'Zaphod' 3 W-OOR
(Glenbrook Bulb Farm, 1983) Glenbrook Bulb Farm, 1997
'Icon' × 'Matapan'
Fl. 80 mm wide; perianth segments ovate, yellowish white 155D, spreading; corona disc-shaped, yellow-orange (15A), with orange-red (30C) at rim, lightly frilled. Mid-season to late

'Zapollo' 2 W-Y
(P.B.van Eeden) J.N.M.van Eeden, 1994

Fl. 110 mm wide; perianth segments greenish white (155A) or with hints of yellow (1D); corona brilliant yellow 13B, paling to pale greenish yellow 2D at base. Late

'Zara' 3 W-? (b)
(N.Y. Lower, pre-1931)

'Zarah Leander' 2 Y-R
(R. Rijnveld & Sons, pre-1942)
AM(Haarlem) 1942

'Zariba' 2 Y-? (a)
(A.M. Wilson, pre-1937)

'Zealot' 1 (a)
(Cartwright & Goodwin, pre-1916)

'Zealot' 1 W-?
(J.S. Leitch) J.S. Leitch, 1968

'Zedcom' 1 Y-Y
(G.J. Phillips, 1981) G.J. Phillips, 1992
'Enzed' × 'Comal'; sdlg no. 76-83-1
Fl. 105 mm wide; perianth segments broadly ovate, smooth; corona funnel-shaped, with mouth flared. Early

'Zeeda' 1 W-W
(J.S. Leitch) J.S. Leitch, 1958

'Zeeland' 2 W-Y
(de Graaff Bros, pre-1930)
Fl. 108 mm wide; perianth segments creamy white, with pale sulphur at base, overlapping two-thirds; corona bowl-shaped, brilliant yellow 12B, shading to vivid orange-yellow 21A at rim, mouth expanded. 2n=28. AM(Haarlem) 1930, *HC(g) 1946, *AM(g) 1947

'Zeelander' 8
(pre-1820)
?The same as 'Zeylander'

'Zeila' 2 W-? (b)
(S.J. Bisdee, 1945)
'Nelly' × 'Whitefoord'

'Zeiss' 1 W-W
(J.N. Hancock & Co.) M. Gardiner, 1956
Corona opening very pale lemon, soon becoming delicate milk white

'Zelah' 1 W-W
(T. Bloomer) du Plessis Bros, 1979
'Rashee' × 'Empress of Ireland'; sdlg no. 44
Fl. 131 mm wide. Mid-season

'Zelene' 2 Y-YYR
(G. Lewis, 1935) Parr's Nurseries, 1958

'Zelma' 1 W-GWW
(J.N. Hancock & Co., 1963) Unregistered

'Zelza' 3 W-? (b)
(J.L. Richardson, pre-1939)
'Varna' hybrid

'Zema' 2 W-W
(A.O. Roblin, 1944)
'Nautilus' × 'Slemish'

'Zemidar' 2 (a)
(A.M. Wilson, pre-1950)

'Zena' 2 or 3 W-? (b or c)
(pre-1913)

'Zena' 2 W-? (b)
(Barr & Sons, pre-1954)

'Zenda' 1 W-Y
(P. Phillips, 1968) P. Phillips, 1978
Fl. 105 mm wide; corona pale lemon. Mid-season

'Zenith' 3 W-YYR
(G.H. Engleheart, pre-1904)
Perianth segments creamy white, slightly reflexed, overlapping; corona almost disc-shaped, canary yellow, with scarlet at rim, frilled. AM 1904

'Zennor' 2 Y-O
(P.D. Williams, pre-1927)

'Zenobia' 3 W-? (b)
(A.M. Wilson, pre-1908)

'Zenobia' 2 W-R
(A.H. Ahrens) R. Hyde, 1959
Perianth segments roundish; corona orange-vermilion, with mouth expanded

'Zeolite' 4 W-W
(Murray W. Evans, 1971) Murray W. Evans, 1986
Richardson sdlg 3447 (4 W-Y) × 'Knowehead'
Mid-season

'Zephyr' 8 W-O
(pre-1798)

'Zephyr' 5
(W.F.M. Copeland, pre-1908)

'Zephyr' 2 Y-O
(J.L. Richardson) G. Zandbergen-Terwegen, 1957
Perianth segments brilliant yellow 12B; corona light orange (24B), with a darker tone at rim. AM(Haarlem) 1957

'Zephyrus' 5 W-W
(G.H. Engleheart, pre-1912)

Perianth segments narrow, slightly reflexed

'Zera' 3 W-?
(C. Dawson, pre-1923)

'Zero' 2 W-W
(G.L. Wilson, pre-1935)
'White Frost' × 'Naxos'
Fl. ice white; perianth segments broadly ovate, only very slightly mucronate, spreading, plane, overlapping half; the inner segments a little inflexed at base, somewhat twisted and reflexed at apex, creased; corona cylindrical, smooth, with mouth ribbed and widely expanded, rim shallowly notched in places, minutely crenate

'Zest' 1 W-Y
(G.E. Mitsch, pre-1952)
'Beersheba' × 'Kandahar'; sdlg no. 36C2/2
Perianth segments overlapping; corona opening pale yellow, becoming cream. Mid-season

'Zeta'
(G.H. Johnstone, pre-1959) Unregistered

'Zeta' 1 W-P
(W. Jackson Jr, 1967) Unregistered
'Kimi' × 'Ross' hybrid; sdlg no. 196/67

'Zetland' 2 Y-O
(J.N. Hancock & Co.) Unregistered
Perianth segments soft yellow; corona orange. Tall. Early

'Zeus' 1 W-? (b)
(Barr & Sons, pre-1923)

'Zeus' 2 Y-O
(Carncairn Daffodils) Carncairn Daffodils, 1978
'Vulcan' × 'Chungking'; sdlg no. 2A 1/70
Fl. 100 mm wide; perianth segments vivid yellow 9A; corona orange (28A). Mid-season. Resembles 'Vulcan' but with an improved perianth

'Zeylander' 8 Y-?
(pre-1759)
?The same as 'Zeelander'

'Zie' 2 W-P
(?Australian origin, pre-1997) Unregistered
Corona bowl-shaped, soft pink, with a darker tone at rim, with the rim crenate. Late

'Ziegfeld' 2 Y-O
(J.N. Hancock & Co., 1973) Unregistered

'Zillah' 2 W-? (b)
(Mrs R.O. Backhouse, pre-1921)

'Zillion' 1 Y-Y

(Jackson's Daffodils, 1985) Jackson's Daffodils, 1995
Sdlg 9/72 × 'Akala'; sdlg no. 22/85
Fl. 115 mm wide; perianth segments broadly ovate, vivid yellow 9A; corona cylindrical, narrow, darker in tone (14A) than the perianth, with mouth flared and frilled. Early

'Zina' 1 W-P
(A.O. Roblin, 1957) Unregistered
Sdlg × 'Rosario'

'Zincali' 3 W-? (b)
(J.T. Gray, pre-1933)

'Zinetta' 3 W-? (b)
(R. Crews, pre-1949)

'Zinga' 3 Y-YYR
(J.T. Gray, pre-1939)
Corona disc-shaped, with red at rim

'Zingara' 3 W-YYR
(Mrs R.O. Backhouse, pre-1903)
Perianth segments white, tinged sulphur yellow at base; corona widely expanded, brilliant yellow, with orange-scarlet at rim. AM 1903

'Zion Canyon' 2 W-GYP
(Brian S.Duncan) Brian S.Duncan, 1993
'Pismo Beach' × 'High Society'; sdlg no. 1378
Fl. 102 mm wide; corona funnel-shaped, yellow, with green at base, shading to lilac pink at mouth, with mouth widely expanded. Late

'Zionist' 1 W-W
(J.L. Richardson, pre-1927)
'King Alfred' × 'Madame de Graaff'
Fl. ivory white; perianth segments broadly ovate, slightly mucronate, slightly inflexed, with margins incurling at apex, overlapping one-third to a half; the inner segments more strongly inflexed, with margins somewhat wavy; corona cylindrical, opening pale yellow, a little frilled, with rim widely rolled and irregularly notched. AM(e) 1928

'Zip' 6 Y-Y
(G.E. Mitsch, 1966) G.E. Mitsch, 1976
'Wee Bee' × *N. cyclamineus*; sdlg no. C47/1
Fl. 62 mm wide, clear golden yellow. Early

'Zip' 1 Y-R
(W.M. Spry, pre-1975) Unregistered
'Port Kembla' × 'Red Poppett'
Corona orange-red, with brick red at rim, frilled. Late

'Zircon' 2 W-Y
(Oregon Bulb Farms, pre-1945)

'Ziska' 1 Y-Y
(W. Jackson Jr) Jackson's Daffodils, 1979

Sdlg 22/64 × 'Warbin'; sdlg no. 5/71
Fl. 102 mm wide. Early to mid-season

'Zita' 2 W-? (b or c)
(J. W. Barr, pre-1930)

'Ziva' 8 W-W
(Herut Yahel, pre-1975) C.S.Weijers Jr, 1997
Selection from 'Paper White Grandiflora'
Fls 10-18 per stem, 40 mm wide, yellowish white 155B; perianth segments broadly ovate, spreading or a little inflexed, overlapping half; corona cup-shaped, with mouth wavy. Very early to mid-season. Strongly scented

'Zodiac' 1 W-? (b)
(A.H. Ahrens) J.S. Leitch, 1955

'Zoë' 5 Y-Y
(Mrs R.O. Backhouse, pre-1907)
Perianth segments pale primrose yellow; corona long, lemon yellow

'Zoe' 2 W-? (b)
(D.V. West, pre-1936)

'Zoe' 3 W-Y
(W. Jackson Jr, 1968) Unregistered
'Arbar' × sdlg 79/60; sdlg no. 179/68

'Zoe' 2 W-W
(J.N. Hancock & Co., 1976) Unregistered

'Zohra' 2 W-O
(J.T. Gray, 1933) Parr's Nurseries, 1958
Perianth segments creamy white; corona shallow, deep reddish orange

'Zombie' 11a W-Y
(Jackson's Daffodils) Jackson's Daffodils, 1992
Sdlg 116/77 × 'Dolly Mollinger'; sdlg no. 11/87
Fl. rounded, 105 mm wide; perianth segments very broadly ovate, blunt, fairly prominently mucronate, greenish white (155A), plane, overlapping half or more; corona split to base, the six segments three-quarters the length of the perianth segments, opposite and closely overlying them and joined to them at margins from base to shoulder, deeply bi-lobed, with the lobes overlapping, smooth, vivid yellow 9A, deeply frilled

'Zonar' 2 W-P
(J.N. Hancock & Co., 1971) Unregistered

'Zonda' 2 Y-R
(C.E. Radcliff, 1939)
'Kubelik' × 'Fortune'

'Zorba' 2 W-Y
(J.N. Hancock & Co., 1965) Unregistered

'Zoria' 2 W-? (b)
(Barr & Sons, pre-1926)

'Zorina' 2 W-Y
(S.J. Bisdee, 1945)
'Nelly' × 'Whitefoord'

'Zoroastre' 8 W-?
(pre-1807)

'Zouave' W-YYR
(E.M. Crosfield, pre-1913)
Fl. 95 mm wide; corona shallow, pale yellow, with a broad band of orange-red at rim

'Zouave' 1 (a)
(A.F. Calvert, pre-1929)

'Zuella' 2 Y-ORR
(N.R. McIsaac) N.R. McIsaac, 1982
'Crescendo' × 'Falstaff'; sdlg no. 107
Fl. 104 mm wide; perianth segments deep yellow; corona bright orange-red, paling to orange at base

'Zufra' 2 Y-YYO
(W. Jackson Jr, 1967) Unregistered
'Vanity' × sdlg 38/59

'Zuiderkruis' 2 W-Y
(Konynenburg & Mark, pre-1953)
'Anaconda' × 'Marian'

'Zulema' 8 Y-O
(pre-1850)
Perianth segments sulphur yellow

'Zulu' 2 Y-R
(G.E. Mitsch) G.E. Mitsch, 1982
('Playboy' × 'Paricutin') × 'Zanzibar'; sdlg no. II70/1
Fl. 97 mm wide; perianth segments deep yellow; corona deep orange-red. Mid-season

'Zumdish' 4 W-O
(Jackson's Daffodils) Jackson's Daffodils, 1992
Evans sdlg × 'Career'; sdlg no. 53/83
Fl. 87 mm wide; perianth and other petaloid segments in several whorls, broadly ovate, blunt, yellowish white (4D), plane, overlapping half; the outer whorl prominently mucronate; the inner whorls successively a little shorter, more inflexed and more concave; the petaloid segments at centre irregularly arranged, strongly inflexed, with margins tightly incurled; corona segments half as long as the petaloid segments, clustered among them at centre, more loosely arranged among the surrounding whorls, orange (28A), frilled. Early to mid-season

'Zuni' 2 Y-R
(G.E. Mitsch, c.1976) Unregistered
Sdlg P50/1 ('Narvik' × 'California Gold') × 'Flaming Meteor'; sdlg no. B45/31
Perianth segments very broadly ovate, blunt, golden yellow, spreading, concave near apex, smooth, overlapping half; the inner segments a little inflexed, somewhat creased or with margins wavy; corona funnel-shaped, broad, ribbed, fiery orange-red, mouth straight, split in places and overlapping, heavily frilled. Early

'Zurich' 3 (a)
(G. Lubbe & Son, pre-1938)
AM(Haarlem) 1938

'Zut' 2 Y-R
(J.S. Leitch) J.S. Leitch, 1956

'Zuwela' 1 (a)
(A.F. Calvert, pre-1928)

'Zwanenburg' 1 W-W
(C.G. van Tubergen, pre-1914)
'Empress' × 'Madame de Graaff'

'Zwanendrift' 3 W-? (b)
(J.W.A. Lefeber, pre-1941)

'Zygos' 3 W-? (b)
(P. Lower, pre-1931)

'Zyph' 2 (a)
(P.D. Williams, pre-1931)
Sdlg no. 224

'Zystos' 2 Y-R
(P.D. Williams, pre-1931)
Sdlg no. 645
Perianth segments pale yellow; corona red, frilled

'Zywice' 2 (a)
(The Brodie of Brodie, pre-1931)

'Zyxomma' 1 W-W
(W.B. Cranfield, pre-1931)

'Zyxst' 2 (a)
(The Brodie of Brodie, pre-1931)

EARLY DIVISIONS AND GROUPS

The group names in the synonymy of many of the earlier daffodils in the Register are listed below. They were part of a scheme of classification drawn up by the Royal Horticultural Society's Daffodil Conference of 1884 when "New Daffodils" as opposed to the species were brought under review for the first time. It was resolved that these and all future new garden varieties should carry "fancy" names in the modern language, not pseudo-botanic names in Latin form.

The newly named daffodils were listed in groups and divisions to show their affinities with J.G.Baker's classification of the species (1869, amended 1875; 1884, amended 1888). Some of the groups paralleled Baker's, some more were devised by the Conference committee (on the initiative of T.Moore and Peter Barr). The groups were put into Baker's three divisions: Magnicoronati, Mediicoronati and Parvicoronati.

Baker's three divisions were later subsumed in a scheme of seven put forward by the RHS in 1908 and in the 12-division scheme adopted in 1910 that remained current until 1950. The group names were for the most part abandoned after the Conference, though some re-emerged as division names in the 1910-1950 scheme.

Division 1 Magnicoronati
Pseudonarcissus Group
Pseudonarcissus Abscissus Group
Pseudonarcissus Lobularis Group
Pseudonarcissus Nobilis Group
Pseudonarcissus Major Group
Pseudonarcissus Bicolor Group
Pseudonarcissus Lorifolius Group
Pseudonarcissus Moschatus Group

Division 2 Mediicoronati
Calthinus Group
Incomparabilis Concolor Group
Incomparabilis Leedsii Group
Incomparabilis Sulphureus Group
Incomparabilis Albidus Group
Incomparabilis Pallidus Group
Incomparabilis Albus Group
Incomparabilis Giganteus Group
Barrii Group
Barrii Sulphureus Group
Barrii Albidus Group
Barrii Albus Group
Leedsii Group
Humei Group
Backhousei Group
Poculiformis Group
Macleayi Group
Nelsonii Group
Bernardii Group
Tridymus Group
Odorus Group

Division 3 Parvicoronati
Burbidgei Group
Poeticus Group
Gracilis Group
Tazetta Group

ORIGINATORS AND REGISTRANTS

Hybridizers, introducers and registrants appearing in the Register are listed here. The RHS would welcome information about any whose names have been inadvertently omitted or whose entries are incomplete or incorrect. Others included in the list are botanists, writers and field workers.

b	born
c.	circa
crd	commenced raising daffodils
d	died
rd	raised daffodils

If two or more locations are given, they are in chronological order and, unless otherwise stated, in the same country, county or state as the preceding location.

British county or conurbation names are those obtaining in the person's lifetime, hence in some cases Herefordshire is given rather than the new name Hereford & Worcester. County names that have been completely obliterated in recent boundary changes are for information followed by the new name in brackets, eg Radnorshire (now Powys).

Abel Smith See **Smith**, Mrs J.Abel
Abernethy, J.J.
b 1908, crd 1936, d 1975. Dunedin, New Zealand; Christchurch
Abernethy, R.J.
b 1934, crd 1949. Christchurch, New Zealand; Mosgiel
Acheson, Dr D.R.
Berkeley, Gloucestershire, England; Clevedon, Somerset
Adams, C.Lemesle
crd c.1905, d 1919. Wolverhampton, Staffordshire, England
Adams, David
b 1946, crd 1975. Christchurch, New Zealand
Agee, Elmo L.
Bluefield, West Virginia, USA
Ahrens, Alexander Henry
crd 1929, d 1954. Masterton, New Zealand
Akers, James L.
b 1937, crd 1980. Wrenthorpe, West Yorkshire, England
Akers, J.T.E.
b 1902, crd 1955, d 1986. Altofts, West Yorkshire, England
Aldersey, Hugh
crd c.1899, d 1930. Aldersey, Cheshire, England
Alkemade, C.
Established 1870. Noordwijk, Holland

Alkemade, C.P.
Noordwijk, Holland
Allen, Mrs A.M.
South Mymms, Middlesex, England
Allen, James
Shepton Mallet, Somerset, England
Allen, Leslie T.
b 1926, crd 1975. Lamberhurst, Kent, England
Amisfield
Straffan, Co.Kildare, Republic of Ireland
Amoore, E.N.
Auckland, New Zealand
Anderson, C.F.
Christchurch, New Zealand
Anderson, Mrs Kenneth B.
b 1908, crd 1946. La Canada, California, USA
Anderson, Mrs N.V.
crd 1939. Mangatoki, New Zealand
Anderson, R.
Hadfield, Cheshire, England
Andrews, C.L. (Clarrie)
b 1905, d 1983. Brightwater, New Zealand
Anglo, N.H.
b 1963, crd 1976. West Harrow, Middlesex, England
Archibald, J.C.
Ffostrasol, Dyffed, Wales
Arkwright, Sir John S.
b 1872, crd 1919, d 1954. Presteigne, Radnorshire (now Powys), Wales. Knighted 1934
Avery, Dr J.W.
d c.1967. Darfield, New Zealand
Avery, Rev. W.W.
d 1954. Eltham, New Zealand; Ashburton
Avon Bulbs
See **Stagg**

Baars, S.
Baartman & Koning
Backhouse, Charles James
b 1848. Wolsingham, Durham, England
Backhouse, Henry
b 1849, crd 1895, d 1936. Darlington, Durham, England; Bournemouth, Hampshire
Backhouse, Mrs R.O. (Sarah Elizabeth)
b 1857, crd 1888, d 1921. Hereford, Herefordshire, England
Backhouse, Robert Ormston
b 1854, crd 1888, d 1940. Hereford, Herefordshire, England
Backhouse, William
b 1807, crd 1855/6, d 1869. Wolsingham, Durham, England

Backhouse, William Ormston
  b 1885, d 1962. Rio Negro, Argentina; Hereford, Herefordshire, England
Bader, H.
  crd c.1932. Holland
Bailey, Charles E.
  b 1880, d 1945. Portland, Oregon, USA
Baker, J.G.
  b 1834, d 1920. Keeper of the Herbarium, Royal Botanic Gardens, Kew. Drew up first version of the modern classification system
Baker, Mrs J.M.
  Shepton Mallet, Somerset, England
Bakker, C.J.
  Obdam, Holland
Bakker, N.
  Holland
Balch, W.
  crd 1922, d 1949. Christchurch, New Zealand
Ballydorn Bulb Farm
  See **Harrison**
Bangor Horticultural Society
  Bangor, Co. Down, N.Ireland
Bankhead, Delia
  b 1932, crd 1982. Hillsboro, Virginia, USA; Hendersonville, N.Carolina; Reston, Virginia
Bankhead, J.
  Portrush, Co.Antrim, N.Ireland
Barchard, Francis
  crd c.1898. Uckfield, Sussex, England
Barnaart, A.E., & Co.
  Vogelenzang, Holland
Barnes, Mrs Betty
  Natchez, Mississippi, USA
Barnhoorn, J.
  rd c.1960-1990. Sassenheim, Holland
Barr & Sons
  See **Barr**, Peter
Barr, George R.
  d 1981. Burwash, Sussex, England; Mayfield, Sussex. Partner in Barr & Sons; co-founder 1956 of Wallace and Barr, Tunbridge Wells, Kent, England
Barr, Herbert Rawnsley
  b 1903, crd 1956, d 1987. Groombridge, Sussex, England. Partner in Barr & Sons; co-founder 1956 of Wallace & Barr, Tunbridge Wells, Kent, England
Barr, James William
  d 1950. Three Legged Cross, Dorset, England; Spalding, Lincolnshire. Partner in Barr & Sons, later in Barr & Wellband, Spalding, Lincolnshire
Barr, Peter
  b 1826, crd 1890, d 1909. Co-founder 1860 of Barr & Sugden; founder 1882 of Barr & Son, later (1886) Barr & Sons. Covent Garden, London, England. Nurseries at Tooting, London, 1882-1888; Long Ditton, Surrey, 1889-1910; Taplow, Buckinghamshire, 1911-1955; also at Gulval, Cornwall. Barr & Sons succeeded 1956 by Wallace & Barr
Bartlett, A.W.
  Bright, Victoria, Australia
Barton Nurseries
  Emneth, Norfolk, England
Bath, Messrs R.H.
  Established 1894, crd 1910. Wisbech, Cambridgeshire, England
Batson, Thomas
  b 1846, rd 1896-1918. Beaworthy, Devon, England
Baughn, Mrs R.N.
  b 1892, d 1986. Conway, Arkansas, USA
Baxter, Michael W.
  b 1944, crd 1984. Birch Green, Hertfordshire, England
Beamish, R.H.
  Glounthane, Co.Cork, Republic of Ireland
Beekman, J.
  Sassafras, Victoria, Australia
Beerhorst, R.H. & Son
Beery, Betty
  b 1912, crd 1962, d 1994. Frankfort, Ohio, USA
Bell, David S.
  crd 1944/5, d 1987. Christchurch, New Zealand; Templeton
Bell, Robert
  Ballarat, Victoria, Australia
Bell, W.A.
  crd 1927. Gisborne, New Zealand
Belle & Teeuwen
  rd 1926-1960. Lisse, Holland
Bellinger, Daniel
  Wadsworth, Ohio, USA
Bender, Dr William A.
  b 1914, crd 1966, d 1997. Chambersburg, Pennsylvania, USA
Berbee, J.
  Lisse, Holland
Berghuis, H.
  rd 1920-?1930. Holland
Berkeley Nurseries
  Aldie, Virginia, USA
Bernard, L.
Berry, S.Stillman
  Redlands, California, USA
Best, C.R.
  Australia
Beyk & Co.
  crd 1970. Sassenheim, Holland
Beyk, J.J.W.
  crd 1930. Holland
Bisdee, Stephen J.
  crd 1935. Bagdad, Tasmania, Australia
Blakeman, A.F.
Blampied, C.B.
  crd 1910. St Martin, Guernsey, Channel Islands
Blanchard, Douglas
  b 1887, crd 1927, d 1968. Blandford, Dorset,

England. In partnership from 1954 with J.W.Blanchard

Blanchard, John W.
b 1930, crd 1954. Blandford, Dorset, England. In partnership until 1968 with D.Blanchard

Blanden, W.B.
Windsor Gardens, S. Australia, Australia

Bliss, Arthur J.
b 1860, crd 1923, d 1931. Morwellham, Devon, England

Blokker, N.
rd 1945-1960. St Maarten, Holland

Blom, Walter J.M.
rd 1910-1950. Aerdenhout, Holland

Blom, Walter, & Son
crd c.1950. Hillegom, Holland; also at Cranleigh, Surrey, England; Leavesden, Hertfordshire; Milton Ernest, Bedfordshire

Bloomer, Tom
b 1905, crd 1950, d 1989. Rathowen Daffodils, Dergmoney, Co.Tyrone, N.Ireland (1971-73)

Board, Fred(erick) E.
crd 1948, d 1966. Matlock, Derbyshire, England; Darley Dale

Bonnie Brae Gardens
See **Driver**

Boscawen, Rev. A.T.
b 1862, d 1939. Ludgvan, Cornwall, England

Bourne, Rev. Christopher
b 1884, rd 1910-1914. Bletchley, Buckinghamshire, England

Bowles, E.A.
b 1865, d 1954. Enfield, Middlesex, England. Author of *A Handbook of Narcissus* (1934)

Boyd, M.

Bradbury, Malcolm S.
b 1940, crd 1976. Witham, Essex, England

Bradley, H.H.B.
New South Wales, Australia

Braithwaite, J.H.
d 1959. Epsom, New Zealand

Bramley, Don
b 1923, crd 1947, d 1992. Carterton, New Zealand; Taradale

Brand, R.A.
Winchmore Hill, London, England

Breed, C.
b 1938 crd 1960. Noordwijkerhout, Holland

Brewster, A.S.
d 1980. Feilding, New Zealand

Brink, Venice
d 1985. Nashville, Illinois, USA

Broadfield's Daffodils
Ulverstone, Tasmania, Australia

Broadleigh Gardens
See **Skelmersdale**, also **Stagg**

Brodie, The Brodie of
b 1868, crd 1898, d 1943. Forres, Grampian, Scotland

Broeze, C.B.

crd 1950. Holland

Brogden, G.W.E.
b 1894, crd 1935, d 1993. Hawera, New Zealand; Normanby; Marton. In partnership with M.E.Brogden from c.1968; trading with him as Brogden Bulbs 1989-1993

Brogden, M.E.
crd c.1953. Normanby, New Zealand. In partnership with G.W.E.Brogden from c.1968; trading as Brogden Bulbs from 1989 (with G.W.E.Brogden until 1993)

Brook, Richard L.
b 1942, crd 1969. Wakefield, West Yorkshire, England

Brookdale Nurseries
See **Mauger**

Brown, H.A.
b 1871, crd 1917, d 1956. Ballarat, Victoria, Australia; Fern Tree Gully; Mount Macedon

Brown, Michael J.
b 1954, crd 1978. Loburn, New Zealand

Brown, Opal L.
Milton-Freewater, Oregon, USA

Brown, Robin
b 1924, crd 1976. Papatoetoe, New Zealand

Brownlee, George H.
crd 1925, d 1967. Dunedin, New Zealand

Brumley, Louis P.
b 1906, d 1954. Leongatha, Victoria, Australia; Canterbury

Brunting, C., & Co.

Buchanan, W.
Bearsden, Glasgow, Scotland

Buckingham, C.E.
d 1941. Lower Hutt, New Zealand

Buckland, Leonard
crd c.1900, d 1930. Camperdown, Victoria, Australia

Budden, Henry
b 1842, d 1902. New Zealand nurseryman exhibiting 200 daffodil varieties in 1896

Bull, A.G.
d 1960. Christchurch, New Zealand

Bull, A.W.
Kimbolton, Cambridgeshire, England

Bull, H.B.J.
Auckland, New Zealand

Bullivant, Mrs E.
Zeals, Wiltshire, England

Bulman, H.R.
Legana, Tasmania, Australia

Buncombe, Rev. Thomas
crd 1906, d 1941. Black Torrington, Devon, England

Burbidge, F.W.
b 1847, d 1905. Curator, Trinity College Garden, Dublin. Author of *The Narcissus: its History and Culture* (1875)

Burn, N.
Christchurch, New Zealand

Burns, K.B.
  d 1975. Timaru, New Zealand
Burns, W.D.
  d 1927. Oamaru, New Zealand
Burns, Mrs W.D.
  Oamaru, New Zealand
Burr, Noel A.
  b 1930, crd 1969. Groombridge, Kent, England; Buxted, East Sussex
Butcher, David H.
  b 1904, crd 1970, d 1979. Broadfield, New Zealand; Christchurch
Butcher, M.F.
  b 1909, crd 1970, d 1988. Christchurch, New Zealand
Butler, Mrs J.
Buxton, E.H.
  Titchfield, Hampshire, England; Snape, Suffolk
Byfield, J.R
  Tasmania, Australia

Caledonia Nursery
  See **Smith,** C
Calvert, Albert F.
  crd 1928, d 1945. London NW3, England. Author of *Daffodil Growing for Pleasure and Profit* (1929)
Calvert, Roderick Frank
  rd 1929-1939, d 1953. Coverack, Cornwall, England. Proprietor Carnsulan Nurseries
Cammell, George Henry
  b 1851, crd *c.*1883, d 1903. Hathersage, Derbyshire, England
Capen, Mrs John Brewster (Elizabeth Taintor)
  b 1906, crd *c.*1950, d 1993. Boonton, New Jersey, USA; Montville, Connecticut; Vinal Haven, Maine
Carncairn Daffodils
  See **Reade**
Carne-Ross
Carnsulan Nurseries
  see **Calvert,** R.F.
Carter, B.J.
  Truro, Cornwall, England
Carter, N.
  Invercargill, New Zealand
Cartwright and Goodwin
  Established 1911, closed 1931. Kidderminster, Worcestershire, England
Cascade Daffodils
  See **Karnstedt**
Casper
Cave, Sir Charles H., Bt.
  b 1861, crd 1897, d 1932. Sidmouth, Devon, England. Succeeded 1922 to baronetcy
Challies, G.A.
  d 1995. Beckenham, New Zealand
Chambers, L.J.
  b 1909, crd 1964, d 1984. Springston, New Zealand

Champernowne, Messrs E.B.
  Buckland Monachorum, Devon, England
Chapman, F.Herbert
  b 1870, crd 1904, d 1945. Peasmarsh, Sussex, England; Rye, Sussex
Chatard, Mrs F.
  Baltimore, Maryland, USA
Chappell, A.W.
  b 1926, crd 1946, d 1993. Christchurch, New Zealand
Chatto, Beth
  Elmstead Market, Essex, England
Christie, J.A.
Chrystal, A.
  d 1936. Eltham, New Zealand
Churcher, Major George
  Lindfield, Sussex, England
Ciggaar, P.
  Holland
C.J.Dobbe Export
  rd 1960-1990. Noordwijkerhout, Holland
Clark, Alfred
  d 1961. Ashburton, New Zealand
Clark, Alister
  b 1864, crd 1898, d 1949. Bulla, Victoria, Australia. Proprietor Glenara Daffodils
Cleine, Phillip
Clive Postles Daffodils
  See **Postles**
Clay, Sampson
  Darley Dale, Derbyshire, England
Cobb, F.D.B.
  crd 1940, d 1967. Margate, Kent, England
Cobb, Ray
  Wollaton, Nottinghamshire, England
Cobley, Mrs R.S.
  Bideford, Devon, England
Cobley, R. Seymour
  Bideford, Devon, England. Founder Seymour Cobley Ltd., Spalding, Lincolnshire; also at Inverurie, Grampian, Scotland
Coey, James
  See Donard Nursery Company
Coleman, Cyril F.
  b 1892, crd 1933, d 1980. Cranbrook, Kent, England
Coles, F.R.
  Mitcham, Victoria, Australia
Colley, J.E.
  Leeds, Yorkshire, England
Comer, Mrs Mavis Mary
  Kaikoura, New Zealand
Cook, R.P.
  crd 1935, d 1974. Riwaka, New Zealand
Cookson, Norman C.
  Wylam-on-Tyne, Northumberland, England
Cooper, D.J.
  crd 1946, d 1966. Masterton, New Zealand
Copeland, William F.M.
  b 1872, crd *c.*1893, d 1953. Stone, Staffordshire,

England; Southampton, Hampshire
Cornwall Area Bulb Growers Association
Truro, Cornwall, England
Corrigan, D.H.L.
crd 1920, d 1963. Tauranga, New Zealand
Cory-Wright, Lady (Felicity)
Knebworth, Hertfordshire, England
Cotter, Edward W.
d 1977. Christchurch, New Zealand
Cotter, Mrs Christina
d 1977. Christchurch, New Zealand
Cowan, C.W.
Penicuick, Lothian, Scotland
Cowan, T.O.
Cranfield, William Bathgate
crd 1898, d 1948. Enfield Chase, Middlesex, England
Crawford, Mrs Sharman
Crellin, Miss A.M.
Crews, R.
crd 1930, d 1964. Owaka, New Zealand
Crosfield, Ernest M.
rd 1898-1915, d 1925. Frodsham, Cheshire, England; Wrexham, Denbighshire, Wales; Cossington, Somerset, England; Chepstow, Monmouthshire, Wales
Cross & Co.
Wisbech, Cambridgeshire, England
Cross, Harold G.
b 1920, crd 1962, d 1997. Hagley, Tasmania, Australia; Geilston Bay
Crotty, Colin
b 1937, crd 1974. Geraldine, New Zealand
Crouch, G.S.
Wrotham, Kent, England
Cull, R.G.
b 1938, crd 1965. Hokorawa Daffodils, Foxton, New Zealand
Culpepper, Charles W.
b 1888, crd 1927, d 1980. Arlington, Virginia, USA
Culpin, Frederick
d 1930. Spalding, Lincolnshire, England
Currey, Miss Fanny W.
b 1848, d 1917. Lismore, Co.Waterford, Republic of Ireland. Proprietor The Warren Gardens
Cuthbert, R. & G.
Southgate, London, England; Goff's Oak, Hertfordshire
Cuthbertson, W.B.
?Edinburgh, Lothian, Scotland
C.V.Hybrida
Schoorl, Holland

Daffodil Mart, The
See **Heath**
Daffodil Society, The
United Kingdom
Daines, Horace

d 1976. Morrinsville, New Zealand
Daisy Hill Nursery
Newry, Co. Down, N.Ireland. Established 1887 by Thomas Smith
Daley, U.L
Gisborne, Victoria, Australia
Dalley, E.
b 1928, crd 1966. Marton, New Zealand
Dalton, Jan
b 1949, crd 1973. Richmond, N.Yorkshire, England
Danby, S.L.
Thames, New Zealand
Darnley, Lord
b 1886. Cobham, Kent, England
Davenport, J.H.
b 1909, crd 1932. Geraldine, New Zealand
Davey, Arthur B.
d 1988. Stoke, New Zealand
Davey, J.H.
?Ballarat, Victoria, Australia
Davies, H.
Davis, Albert
Margate, Kent, England
Davis, Mrs Paul M.
crd 1924, d 1962. Nashville, Tennessee, USA
Davison, G.D.
crd 1894. Norwich, Norfolk, England; Great Yarmouth, Norfolk
Davison, Muriel
b 1941, crd 1970. Wyndham, New Zealand
Dawson, Charles
crd c.1900. Gulval, Cornwall, England; Bures, Suffolk; Lymington, Hampshire
Dear, George
Streatham, London, England
de Berry, C.
crd 1937, d 1978. Dunedin, New Zealand; Lower Hutt
de Goede, Chr. J.
Haarlem, Holland
de Graaf, D.P.
rd 1950-1970. Den Helder, Holland
De Graaff Bros
Established 1762, crd 1872. Lisse, Holland; Noordwijk
De Graaff Bros & S.A.Van Konynenburg
Noordwijk, Holland. Later trading as Grakon
de Graaff, Jan
Founded 1928 Oregon Bulb Farms, crd 1921, d 1989. Gresham, Oregon, USA
de Graaff, S.A.
b 1840, crd c.1876, d 1911. Leiden, Holland
De Graaff-Gerharda
Established 1927. Lisse, Holland
de Groot, P.J.
Noordwijk, Holland; Hillegom
de Jager, P., & Sons
Established 1870, crd 1936. Heiloo, Holland, also Anna Paulowna; Marden, Kent, England

Dekker, C., Jr
Limmen, Holland
de Mol, Dr W.E.
b 1888, d 1957. Holland. Pioneer research into split-corona daffodils
de Navarro, J.M.
b 1896, crd 1944, d 1979. Broadway, Worcestershire, England
de Navarro, M.A.
b 1944. Broadway, Worcestershire, England
Dennis, D.J.A.
b 1920. Terang, Victoria, Australia
Den Older Bros
Leiden, Holland
Dent, W.
Moulton, Lincolnshire, England
De Ruyter Bros
Oegstgeest, Holland
Dettmann, Hugh Twyford
b 1889, d 1979. Kyneton, Victoria, Australia
Dettman, Lieutenant-Colonel Lindsay Price
b 1917, d 1989. Diamond Creek, Victoria, Australia. Proprietor Ellimatta Daffodil Nursery
de Vroomen, G.B, & Sons
Established 1895, crd 1895. Warmond, Holland
Dick, R.
d 1939. Weston, New Zealand
Dickinson, V.M.
Dunedin, New Zealand
Dietsch, Donna C
b 1945, crd 1985. Columbus, Ohio, USA
Digby, Rev. C.T.D.
Warham, Norfolk, England
Divers, W.H.
Surbiton, Surrey, England
Dobbe
See **C.J.Dobbe Export**
Dofferhof, N.
crd 1980. Sassenheim, Holland
Donard Nursery Company
Established 1904. Newcastle, Co.Down, N.Ireland. James Coey (1863-1921) proprietor from 1912; William Slinger (1878-1961) Proprietor from 1922. Renamed Slieve Donard Nursery Company c.1928
Doornbosch Bros
rd 1945-1965. Sassenheim, Holland
Dorrien Smith
See **Smith**
Dorwin, C.K.
d 1997. Goleta, California, USA
Doyne, C.M.
Driver, Jean E. (Jeanie McKillop)
Corbett, Oregon, USA. Proprietor Bonnie Brae Gardens
Dryden, Mrs K.N. (Kath)
b 1925, crd 1975. Sawbridgeworth, Hertfordshire, England
DuBose, Sidney
Stockton, California, USA

Dudman, Stanley
London NW11, England
Duff, Mrs D.
Duindam, J.
Dukelow, W. J. E.
Omagh, Co. Tyrone, N.Ireland
Duncan, Brian S.
b 1934, crd 1964. Rathowen Daffodils (1973-1988), Dergmoney, Co.Tyrone, N.Ireland; founded 1989 Brian Duncan Daffodils
Duncan, Dr Campbell
crd 1940s. Hobart, Tasmania, Australia
Dunlop, W.J. (Willy)
crd 1937, d 1990. Ballymena, Co.Antrim, N.Ireland; Broughshane, Co.Antrim
Du Plessis Bros
Retired 1990. Landulph, Cornwall, England. Proprietor Tamar Valley Daffodils
du Plessis, Dan
Landulph, Cornwall, England
Dye, Charles
b 1905, crd 1948, d 1984. Thorpe Saint Andrew, Norfolk, England
Dyer, Henry E.
b 1898, d 1985. Christchurch, New Zealand

Edmunds, E.
Edwards, Alan M.
Westhumble, Surrey, England
Eggink Bros
rd 1930-1980. Voorschoten, Holland
Eldering, W.J., & Son
Established 1853, crd 1900. Overveen, Holland; Sassenheim
Ellimatta Daffodil Nursery
See **Dettman**
Elliott, A.C.
Handsworth, Birmingham, England
Ellis, Mrs Vyner
Minsterworth, Gloucestershire, England
England, E.T.
Edgbaston, Birmingham, England
Engleheart, Rev. George Herbert
b 1851, crd c.1882, d 1936. Appleshaw, Hampshire, England; Dinton, Hampshire
Erp, John R.
crd 1940s. Howrah, Tasmania, Australia
Errey, G.
Esseveld, J.M.
rd 1950-80. Sassenheim, Holland
Evans, Estella L.
b 1915, crd 1947. Corbett, Oregon, USA
Evans, Murray W.
b 1912, crd 1953, d 1988. Corbett, Oregon, USA
Evelyn, Miss G.
Presteigne, Radnorshire (now Powys), Wales
Exley, John Edwin
b 1874, crd 1906. Calverley, Yorkshire, England
Exton, Arthur

Spalding, Lincolnshire, England

Fairbairn, Group Captain C.O.
b 1893, crd 1923, d 1959. Skipton, Victoria, Australia

Fairbairn, Mrs C.O. (Irene)
b 1899, crd 1923, d 1974. Skipton, Victoria, Australia

Farmer, Ken
d 1985. Ken Farmer Nurseries, Rotorua, New Zealand

Favell, Dr R.V.
d 1936. St Buryan, Cornwall, England

Fay, Orville
Northbrook, Illinois, USA

Fell, Hubert
See West, David V.

Fellers, Mrs O.L.
Natchez, Mississippi, USA

Fenn, Peter
b 1936, crd 1974. Farnham, Surrey, England

Ferguson, Mrs M.
Fayetteville, Arkansas, USA

Fernández, Professor Abilio
b 1906, d 1994. Taxonomist. Director, Botanical Garden, Coimbra, Portugal

Ffitch, Ronald A.
b 1929, crd 1980. Rainham, Essex, England

Fitzwater, Mrs C.E.
crd c.1960. Huntington, West Virginia, USA

Fleming, James
Rangataua, New Zealand

Fletcher, Major H.F.
St Asaph, Denbighshire, Wales

Foote, Mrs F.Stuart
crd mid 1930s. Grand Rapids, Michigan, USA

Forster, Tom
d c.1985. Tasmania, Australia

Foster, Professor Sir Michael
b 1836, d 1907. Professor of Physiology, University of Cambridge. Chairman of the first Daffodil Conference, London 1884

Fountain, R.
New Zealand

Fowlds, Matthew
b 1880, d 1972. Salem, Oregon, USA

Fowler, Mrs Angela
Gravesend, Kent, England

Free, S.A.
b 1904, crd 1935, d 1968. Palmerston North, New Zealand

Free, Mrs S.I.
b 1920, crd 1943. Palmerston North, New Zealand

Freer, Dr R.
Rugeley, Staffordshire, England

Frey, Eileen
b 1940, crd c.1960. Canby, Oregon, USA

Frey, Jerald
Canby, Oregon, USA

Fry, Barbara
d 1997. Senior Recorder, Rosewarne Experimental Horticultural Station, Cornwall, England. Design and furtherance of breeding programmes for the improvement of commercial daffodils

Frylink, Adrian
Babylon, New York, USA

Frylink, A., & Sons
Established 1866, crd c.1900. Sassenheim, Holland

Frylink, H.

Furness, G.H.
Burnham-on-Sea, Somerset, England

Gardiner, Murray
b 1910, crd 1940s. Warragul, Victoria, Australia

Gaspar, Sydney C.
b 1890, crd 1928, d 1954. East Tairei, New Zealand

Geerlings, Peter
Noordwijkerhout, Holland

Geest Horticultural Group
Spalding, Lincolnshire, England

Gee Tee Bulb Co.
Genat, E.C.

Gerritsen, J., & Son
Established 1900, crd 1900. Voorschoten, Holland. Family firm under whose name Jack P.Gerritsen later registered his daffodils

Gerritsen, Jack P.
b 1909, crd 1920s, d 1992. Voorschoten, Holland. Registered daffodils under the name of the family firm, J. Gerritsen & Son

Gibbs, F.E.
Hayes, Middlesex, England; Ickham, Kent

Gibson, Alan
crd 1918, d 1977. Marton, New Zealand

Gibson, J
d 1927. New Plymouth, New Zealand

Gibson, Robert
b c.1845, crd 1899, d 1931. Manaia, New Zealand

Glenara Daffodils
See **Clark, A.**

Glenbrook Bulb Farm
Claremont, Tasmania, Australia

Glendenning, R.

Glover, A.

Glover, Ross Henry
b 1909, d 1988. Ulverstone, Tasmania, Australia

Goddard, John H.J.
b 1930, crd 1993. Banstead, Surrey, England

Goldsmith, Jack
b 1908, d 1987. Waterford, Co.Waterford, Republic of Ireland. Foreman to Mr J.L. and Mrs H.K.Richardson

Gooding, H.J.
Tresco, Isles of Scilly, England

Goodson, C.
d 1954. Hawera, New Zealand
Goodwin, Arthur R.
Kidderminster, Worcestershire, England
Goodwin, Horace
b 1919, crd *c.*1979. Halesowen, West Midlands, England
Gordon, R.C.
b 1916, crd 1947. Taihape, New Zealand
Gore-Booth, Sir Josslyn A.R., Bt.
b 1869, crd *c.*1901, d 1944. Lissadell, Co.Sligo, Republic of Ireland. Succeeded 1900 to the baronetcy
Gould, William, Jr
b 1919, crd 1965. Greer, South Carolina, USA; Laurel, Maryland; Mount Pleasant, South Carolina
Gourlay, David W.
Tockington, Gloucestershire, England; Sutton-cum-Lound, Nottinghamshire
Gower, S.
Christchurch, New Zealand
Grace, W.A.
crd 1912, d 1962. Wanganui, New Zealand
Graham, Gerald C.
d 1943. Hastings, New Zealand; Havelock North
Grakon
Noordwijk-Binnen, Holland. Formerly De Graaff Bros & S.A.van Konynenburg
Grant Mitsch Novelty Daffodils
See **Mitsch**, also **Havens**
Gray, Alec
b 1895, crd 1927, d 1986. St Mary's, Isles of Scilly, England; Truro, Cornwall; Camborne, Cornwall
Gray, Mrs F.M.
Camborne, Cornwall, England
Gray, John
Benhall, Suffolk, England
Gray, John T.
crd 1920, d 1969. Dunedin, New Zealand; Palmerston North
Grey, Countess (M.)
Alnwick, Northumberland, England
Grier, Helen A.
b 1916, crd 1929, d 1997. Fullerton, California, USA; Yorba Linda, California
Grieve, A.F.
Grindrod, A.E.
d 1938. Auckland, New Zealand
Gripshover, Mary Lou
b 1935, crd 1969. Columbus, Ohio, USA; Franklin, Tennessee; Milford, Ohio
Groeneveld & Lindhout
rd 1950-1995. Noordwijk, Holland
Grullemans, C.M.
rd 1945-1960. Holland
Grullemans, J.J., & Sons
Established 1839, crd 1927. Lisse, Holland
Grullemans Van Berghem, Mrs J.
crd 1960. Holland
Guilcher
St Peter Port, Guernsey, Channel Islands

Habershon, Major C.B.
d 1954. Aston-on-Clun, Shropshire, England
Hager, Ben
Stockton, California, USA
Haggitt, Mrs A.B.
Hall, Granville
b 1924, crd 1956. Gloucester County, Virginia, USA
Hall, James
Auckland, New Zealand
Hamilton, Max
b 1928, crd 1956. Utiku, New Zealand; Hamilton. Founded Koanga Daffodils in partnership with P.D.K. Ramsay
Hammond, H.M.
d 1982. New Zealand
Hanber, Mrs J.
Hancock, J.N., & Co.
crd 1950. Fern Tree Gully, Victoria, Australia; Kalorama, Victoria; Menzies Creek, Victoria
Hanger, F.
Hanger, Mrs F.E.W.
Hannibal, L.S.
Fair Oaks, California, USA
Harries, D.A.B.
Prestbury, Gloucestershire, England
Harrison, Sir Frank (F.A.L.)
b 1910, crd 1945. Ballydorn Bulb Farm, Killinchy, Co.Down, N.Ireland
Harrison, Gordon
Ponteland, Northumberland, England
Harrison, L.F.
Hart, Benjamin
b 1833, crd *c.*1880, d 1917. Lawrence, New Zealand. Instigator of ìDaffodil Dayî *c.*1900
Hart, H.
crd 1903. Lawrence, New Zealand
Hartland, William Baylor
b 1836, d 1912. Ballintemple, Co.Cork, Republic of Ireland
Harwood, Martin
b 1947. Chobham, Surrey, England
Hatch, Miles B.
Sumner, Washington, USA
Havens, Mrs Elise
b 1942, crd 1964. Hubbard, Oregon, USA. Continuing with R.Havens the business of Grant Mitsch Novelty Daffodils
Havens, Richard
b 1940, crd 1970. Hubbard, Oregon, USA. Continuing with Mrs Elise Havens the business of Grant Mitsch Novelty Daffodils
Haver, G.
crd 1960. Sassenheim, Holland
Hawker, Captain Henry Gore

crd *c*.1910. Ermington, Devon, England
Haworth, A.H.
b 1768, d 1833. Cottingham, Yorkshire, England; Chelsea, London. Author of *A Monograph on the Subordo V. of Amaryllideae containing the Narcissineae* (1831)
Haycock, Stephen P.
Annandale, Virginia, USA
Haydon, Rev. George Philip
b 1846, crd 1898, d 1913. Hatfield, Yorkshire, England; Westbere, Kent
Heath, Brent C.
b 1945, crd *c*.1977. Gloucester, Virginia, USA. Proprietor The Daffodil Mart
Heathcote Bulb Nursery
See **Morrison**
Heazlewood, K.J.
Whitemore, Tasmania, Australia
Hebblethwaite, E.G.
Malvern, Herefordshire, England
Hector, W.J.G.
Heemskerk, P.
crd 1960. Hillegom, Holland
Heere Bros
rd 1960-1970. Beverwijk, Holland
Heere, D.
Wijk-aan-Duin, Holland
Helmus, G.
rd 1960-1970. Sassenheim, Holland
Hemerik, G.F.
Leiden, Holland
Henkes, G.A.
Wassenaar, Holland
Hennis
Akersloot, Holland
Henry, Roger
Falmouth, Cornwall, England
Herbert, Rev. William
b1778, d 1847. Spofforth, Yorkshire, England
Hewitt & Co.
Solihull, Birmingham, England
Hilton, Dr C.T.
d 1957. Port Alberni, British Columbia, Canada
Hinchliff, Miss Katherine Mary
b 1861, crd 1921, d 1947 or 1948. Instow, Devon, England
Hinsby, J.H.
crd 1890s, crd 1920s, d 1945. Taroona, Tasmania, Australia
Hogg & Robertson
Rush, Co.Dublin, Republic of Ireland
Hokorawa Daffodils
see **Cull,** R.G.
Holden, Steven
b 1959. Rustington, West Sussex, England
Holmes, H.A.
Hoog, Michael H.
b 1933, d 1992. Haarlem, Holland
Hopkirk, Alexander
crd c1921, d 1950. Cambridge, New Zealand

Hopman, P., & Son
rd 1945-1995. Hillegom, Holland
Horsefield, John
b 1792, d 1854. Prestwich, Lancashire, England
Hough, Mr & Mrs R.A.
Menheniot, Cornwall, England
Howe, Marilynn
b 1943, crd 1978. Oregon, USA; Culver City, California
Hughes, E.F.
Miller's Flat, New Zealand; Tapanui
Hunter, John Alexander
b 1935, crd 1949. Nelson, New Zealand
Hurford, Mrs Nola
Blenheim, New Zealand
Hybrida
See **C.V.Hybrida**
Hyde, Ron
crd 1940, d 1985. Marton, New Zealand; Tikitiki

Innes, Mrs M.G.Mitchell
Chirnside, Berwickshire, Scotland
International Registration Authority
International Registration Authority for the genus *Narcissus,* Royal Horticultural Society, London, England
IRA
See **International Registration Authority**
Irwin, Peter John
b 1943, crd 1983. Titahi Bay, New Zealand; Te Horo
Ismay, A.L.
Fulton, Missouri, USA
Izzard, J.P.
Gardener to Rev. Canon H.Rollo Meyer

Jackson, David
b 1936, crd 1970. Jackson's Daffodils, Geeveston, Tasmania, Australia
Jackson, William, Jr
b 1908, crd 1930s, d 1975. Dover, Tasmania, Australia. Continued business of W.Jackson Sr
Jackson, Dr William, Sr
b 1865, crd early 1920s, d 1949. Dover, Tasmania, Australia. Business continued by W.Jackson Jr
Jackson's Daffodils
See **Jackson,** David
Jacob, Rev. Joseph
b 1859, d 1926. Whitewell, Shropshire, England. Author of *Daffodils* (1910)
James, E.
Jarman, E.G.B. (Eddie)
b 1933, crd 1965. Ramsden Bellhouse, Essex, England; Wadebridge, Cornwall
Jeffrey, Hilda M.C.
b 1918. Winton, New Zealand
Jefferson-Brown, Michael
b 1930, crd 1943. Westcliffe-on-Sea, Essex,

England; Over, Cambridgeshire; Whitley Bay, Northumberland; Whitbourne, Herefordshire; Martley; Hanley Swan
Jerrell, Robert E.
b 1927, crd 1942. Orinda, California, USA; Loubressac, Lot, France
Jezerniczky, Lajos
b 1925, crd 1965. Balatonszemes, Hungary
Johnson, A.
Eltham, New Zealand
Johnson, C.W.
Johnson, John B.
Four Marks, Hampshire, England
Johnston, George T.
d 1987. Gisborne, New Zealand
Johnstone, Major George H.
b 1882, crd 1928, d 1960. Grampound Road, Cornwall, England
Jones, E.L.
crd 1929. Oamaru, New Zealand; Lower Hutt
Jones, J.W.
Woking, Surrey, England
Jones, Mrs W. Aubrey
Jonkheer, J.

Kanouse, A.N.
d 1980. Olympia, Washington, USA
Kanouse, Mrs A.N.
Olympia, Washington, USA
Kapiteyn Bros
Breezand, Holland
Kaptein, C.
Karnstedt, David
b 1939, crd 1970. St Paul, Minnesota, USA; Cloverdale, Oregon. Proprietor Cascade Daffodils
Keasey, Gilman
b 1900, crd 1963. Corvallis, Oregon, USA
Kendall, John
b c.1828, d 1890. Newton Poppleford, Devon, England
Ken Farmer Nurseries
See **Farmer**
Kerkhof, J.
crd c.1965. Breezand, Holland
Kieft, G.
Kiernan, Patrick
Edgeworthstown, Co.Longford, Republic of Ireland
Killara Bulbs
See **Temple-Smith**
Kitchin, C.E.
Bridgwater, Somerset, England
Klein, Major Francis J., Sr
Hampton, Virginia, USA
Knight, O.D.
Yaxham, Norfolk, England
Koanga Daffodils
See **Hamilton,** also **Ramsay**
Konynenburg & Mark
Established 1919, crd 1938. Noordwijk, Holland
Koopman-Laan
't Zand, Holland
Koopowitz, Dr Harold
b 1940, crd 1968. Orange County, California, USA
Kouwenhoven, J.
crd c.1930. Warmond, Holland
Krelage, E.H., & Son
Established 1811, rd 1900-1920. Haarlem, Holland

Ladson, Alf
crd 1944. Wandin, Victoria, Australia
Latta, Rev. C.A.
Hamilton, New Zealand
Laumonier
Lawrenson, Mrs Alice Louisa
d 1900. Howth, Co.Dublin, Republic of Ireland
Lawson, F.G.
Lea, John S.B.
b 1911, crd 1948, d 1984. Stourport-on-Severn, Worcestershire, England
Leber, J.
Den Burg, Holland
Lee, Donald F.
Welwyn Garden City, Hertfordshire, England
Lee, E.A.K
Stratford, New Zealand
Leeds, Edward
b 1802, crd c.1843, d 1077. Longford Bridge, Lancashire, England
Leenen, W.F.
crd 1970. Warmond, Holland; Sassenheim
Lefeber, D.W., & Co.
Hillegom, Holland
Lefeber, Jac
Bellevue, Washington, USA
Lefeber, J.W.A.
Established 1910, crd 1912. Lisse, Holland; Noordwijkerhout
Leichtlin, Max
b 1831, d 1910. Karlsruhe, Germany; Baden-Baden
Leitch, J.S.
crd 1947. Masterton, New Zealand
Lemmers, Wim
b 1931, rd 1953-1994. Hillegom, Holland; Lisse
Leng, Basil
Lewis, George S.
crd 1920/25, d 1962. Christchurch, New Zealand
Lewis, Mrs Raymond W.
North, Virginia, USA
Lewis, Raymond W.
b 1915, crd 1968, d 1988. North, Virginia, USA
Lewis, R.Lincoln
Eltham, New Zealand
Liefting, Nic
Breezand, Holland

Lievens, J.E.
Anna Paulowna, Holland
Lievens, E.
Anna Paulowna, Holland
Link, Mrs Goethe (Helen)
b 1912, crd 1940. Brooklyn, Indiana, USA
Linn, A.E.
d 1953. Hawera, New Zealand
Lissadell Gardens
See **Gore-Booth**
Lloyd, David A.
b 1915, crd 1950, d 1995. St John's Wood, London, England; Warmington, Oxfordshire
Lock, N.F.
b 1885, d 1972. Exeter, Devon, England; Budleigh Salterton, Devon; Blandford Forum, Dorset
Long, Mrs Doris
b 1895, d 1964. Trenoweth Valley Flower Farm, Cornwall, England
Longbottom, Eric
See **Longford,** Eric
Longford, Eric
Leeds, Yorkshire, England. Formerly known as Eric Longbottom
Longford, H.G.
Abingdon, Berkshire, England
Low, Leone Y.
b 1935, crd 1984. Yellow Springs, Ohio, USA
Lowe, Arthur E.
crd 1895, d c.1925. Tai Tapu, New Zealand. Gardener to Sir Robert Heaton Rhodes
Lower, Dr Nynian Yeo
b 1872, crd 1908, d 1926. Presteigne, Radnorshire (now Powys), Wales
Lower, Peter
d 1996. Malvern, Herefordshire, England; Harpenden, Hertfordshire; Teignmouth, Devon; Dawlish, Devon
Lubbe, G., & Son
crd c.1904. Oegstgeest, Holland; Lisse

MacArthur, Dugald C.
b 1926, crd 1956. Troon, Ayrshire, Scotland; Dornoch, Sutherland
MacHardy, J.
Mack, R.J.
Marton, New Zealand
Major, Leslie
Launceston, Cornwall, England
Mallender, Joseph
crd 1886, d 1945. Worksop, Nottinghamshire, England; Scrooby, Nottinghamshire
Mander, J.H.
Mann, Stanley
Ballarat, Victoria, Australia
Mannetje, H.'t
rd 1940-1970. Hillegom, Holland
Manser, L.F.
b 1931, crd 1965. Matfield, Kent, England

Marchand, L.
Henderson, New Zealand
Markham, W.
Marshall, O.R.
d 1979, Blenheim, New Zealand
Martin, E.
b 1856, crd 1900, d 1941. Truro, Cornwall, England.
Martin, James Coleman
Higherlawn Gardens, Truro, Cornwall, England; Bosvigo Gardens, Truro, Cornwall. Son of E. Martin
Martin, J.L.
b 1901, d 1986. Warrnambool, Victoria, Australia
Matthews, G.
Mauger, W., & Son
Guernsey, Channel Islands. Proprietor Brookdale Nurseries
McCandless, J.K.
Coleraine, Co. Londonderry, N.Ireland.
McCombe, Ken
Airey's Inlet, Victoria, Australia
McConnel, Mrs R.
Colmonell, Ayrshire, Scotland
McIlraith, Robert J.
Mount Waverley, Victoria, Australia
McIntyre, T.J.
New Zealand
McIsaac, Noel R.
b 1935, crd 1952. Wellington, New Zealand; Papatoetoe; Pukekohe
McKillop, Dr A.C.
crd 1933. Christchurch, New Zealand
McLenaghan, D.S.
crd 1951. Christchurch, New Zealand; Geraldine
McLennan, John Frederick
b 1948, crd 1980. Otaki, New Zealand
McNairy, L.G.
d c.1979. Arlington, Virginia, USA
Meyer, Rev. Canon H.Rollo
b 1868, crd 1909, d 1953. Watton-at-Stone, Hertfordshire, England; Little Gaddesden, Hertfordshire
Meyrick, Mrs A.O.
d 1961. Palmerston North, New Zealand
Millar, R.McCheyne
b 1875, crd 1919, d 1965. Wanganui, New Zealand; Wellsford
Miller, A.
Miller, Graham
Ellerslie, Victoria, Australia
Milliken, Mrs H.M. (E.)
d 1987. Geraldine, New Zealand; Temuka
Milne, Dennis B.
d 1979 or 1980. South Darley, Derbyshire, England
Milner, G.
Stourbridge, Worcestershire, England

Milner, William A.
b 1854, crd c.1896, d 1931. Sheffield, Yorkshire, England
Milward, Mrs M.W.
Mitchell, W.F.
b 1877, crd 1911, d 1949. Leek Wootton, Warwickshire, England
Mitsch, Grant E.
b 1907, crd 1934, d 1989. Grant Mitsch Novelty Daffodils, Canby, Oregon, USA
Money, A.
Money, J.
Falmouth, Cornwall, England
Monkton, T.J.
Cheltenham, Gloucestershire, England
Moore, Major-General D.G.
Moore, Mrs D.G.
Moorby, Mrs Margory J.W.
b 1899, crd 1929, d 1996. Okoia, New Zealand
Mooyman, G.J.
Anna Paulowna, Holland
Mott, H.R.
Morrill, George E.
d 1985. Oregon City, Oregon, USA
Morris, J.A.
d 1974. Dunedin, New Zealand
Morrish, S.A.
Cantley, Norfolk, England
Morrison, Scott
crd 1892, d 1942. Essendon, Victoria, Australia; Wandin, Victoria
Morrison, Travers
b 1900, d 1967. Heathcote Bulb Nursery, Wandin, Victoria, Australia
Morris, J.A.
Dunedin, New Zealand
Mulligan, B.O.
Munro, Doug
d 1989. Ringwood, Victoria, Australia
Munro, Judy D.
crd 1964. Waikari, New Zealand; Riwaka
Munro, Welly
crd 1964. Waikari, New Zealand; Riwaka
Murray, Mrs Allan (Evelyn)
b 1900, d 1997. Langley, Victoria, Australia; Kyneton, Victoria

Neave, Sir Arundell T.C.
b 1916, d 1992. Liss, Hampshire, England
Nelson, Rev. John Gudgeon
b 1818, crd 1860, d 1882. Aldborough, Norfolk, England. Noted amateur grower. A group of Div. 2 daffodils with cylindrical coronas named in his honour
Nelson, Dr E. Charles
Outwell, Norfolk, England
Nethercote, Charles Alfred
b 1866, crd 1890, d 1949. Kew, Victoria, Australia; Wandin, Victoria
Nicholl, Reg
b 1929, crd 1970. Rainham, Essex, England
Nieuwenhuis, E.
crd 1890. Lisse, Holland
Nijssen, A.& P., Bros
rd 1920-1940. Santpoort, Holland
Niswonger, O. David
b 1925, crd 1975. Cape Girardeau, Missouri, USA
Noton, W.A. (Tony)
b 1923, crd 1962. Oakham, Rutland, England; Whissendine; Exton
Nuyens Bros
crd c.1950. Breezand, Holland

Oakwood Daffodils
See **Reed**
Occleston, T.O.
Oldham, D.T.
Launceston, Tasmania, Australia
Olson, Douglas N.Y.
b 1923, crd 1961, d 1995. Gore, New Zealand; Otaki
O'More, J.A. (Jim)
b 1911, crd 1939, d 1996. Johnsonville, New Zealand; Newlands
O'Neill, J.A.
Tauranga, New Zealand; Te Kuiti
Onderwater, L.
rd up to 1965. Holland
Onderwater, N.H.
Holland
Oostdam, E.
rd 1925-1935. Noordwijkerhout, Holland
Oosten, J.T.
Holland
Oregon Bulb Farms
See **de Graaff,** Jan
Oudshoorn, C.W.
Holland
Overdevest, A.
Wassenaar, Holland
Overton, Arthur
b 1898, d 1959. Wandin, Victoria, Australia
Owen, Mrs Margaret
Shrewsbury, Shropshire, England
Oxton, Mrs Hylda
b 1913, crd c.1970, d 1989. Layer-de-la-Haye, Essex, England

Paardekooper, A.C.
Palmer, Hon. Lewis
Headbourne Worthy, Hampshire, England
Palmer, L.C.
d 1991. Winchester, New Zealand
Pannill, William G.
Martinsville, Virginia, USA
Papendrecht-Vandervoet
crd 1930. Sassenheim, Holland
Parker, J.S.
crd 1906. Bitton, Gloucestershire, England

Parker, Tom
See **Tom Parker Farms**
Parkinson, F.W.
b 1888, d 1939. Camberwell, Victoria, Australia
Parkinson, John
b 1567, d 1650. London, England. Author of *Paradisi in Sole Paradisus Terrestris* (1629)
Parrett, R.
Parr's Nurseries
crd 1940. Auckland, New Zealand; Hobsonville
Parsons, R.E.
Parton, Mrs M.
Bickley, W.Australia, Australia
Paupers, Evalds
Riga, Latvia
Payne, Paul A.
Postwick, Norfolk, England
Pearce, Rev. G.T.C.
Rock, Cornwall, England
Pearson, Lieutenant-Colonel A.J.R. (John)
b 1936, crd 1962. Little Totham, Essex, England; founded 1987 Hofflands Daffodils
Pearson, J.Duncan
b 1860, crd 1887, d 1932. Lowdham, Nottinghamshire, England
Pearson, J.R., & Sons
Established 1782. Lowdham, Nottinghamshire, England
Pease, Ormiston
Pennings, P.Q.M.
crd 1970. De Zilk, Holland
Petre, Hon. Mrs
Norwich, Norfolk, England
Philippo, A., & Sons
Hillegom, Holland
Philippo, W.A.
Phillips, Dr Charles R.
crd c.1958. Frederick, Maryland, USA
Phillips, Graham J.
b 1945, crd 1967. Hamilton, New Zealand
Phillips, H.D.
Olton, Birmingham, England
Phillips, Phil
crd 1943, d 1984. Otorohanga, New Zealand
Philpott, Rev. E.W.
Aldgate, South Australia, Australia
Pierson, C.W.
d 1952. Te Aroha, New Zealand
Piper, Tom H.
b 1891, crd 1940, d 1993. Ulverstone, Tasmania, Australia
Pitt, R.M.
b 1849, d 1935. Wentworth Falls, New South Wales, Australia
Polman-Mooy, W.
crd c.1893. Haarlem, Holland
Pollock, R.
Cobraine, Co. Derry, N.Ireland
Ponsonby, Hon. Mrs B.B.
Longhope, Hertfordshire, England

Poole, H.J. Sr.
d 1946. Lower Hutt, New Zealand. Proprietor Waterloo Nursery
Pope, John
d 1914. King's Norton, Warwickshire, England
Postles, Clive
b 1937, crd 1974. Purshull Green, Hereford & Worcester, England
Potterton & Martin
Nettleton, Lincolnshire, England
Poupart, William
b 1847, d 1936. Twickenham, Middlesex, England
Pouw, G.L.A.
Roelofarendveen, Holland
Pouw, P.L.A., & Sons
Rijpwetering, Holland
Powell, Edwin C.
b 1870, crd 1925, d 1953. Rockville, Maryland, USA
Preyde, G.A.
rd 1940-1990. Breezand, Holland
Prins, H.
Wisbech, Cambridgeshire, England
Prins, J.
Andijk-West, Holland
Prins, Joh. F.
Lisse, Holland
Pugsley, H.W.
b 1868, d 1947. Wimbledon, Surrey, England. Author of monographs on *N. poeticus* (1915) and *N. pseudonarcissus* (1933)
Pye, A.
New Zealand

Radcliff, Crawford Ernest
b 1879, crd 1922, d 1949. Hobart, Tasmania, Australia
Radcliff, J.M.
b 1908, crd 1936, d 1992. Devonport, Tasmania, Australia
Radcliff, P.J.
b 1936, crd 1985. Lower Barrington, Tasmania, Australia
Rahaman, L.
Newtownabbey, Co. Antrim, N.Ireland
Ralph, R.J
Hobart, Tasmania, Australia
Ramsay, P.D.K.
Pukekohe, New Zealand; Hamilton. Founded Koanga Daffodils in partnership with Max Hamilton
Ramsbottom, James K.
b 1891, d 1925. Scientist at the Royal Horticultural Society. Pioneered hot-water treatment for the control of eel-worm in daffodils
Randall, Erle
Cherington, Gloucestershire, England
Rathowen Daffodils
See **Bloomer,** also **Duncan**

Rawson, Rev. A.
b c.1819, d 1891. Windermere, Westmorland (now Cumbria), England
Reade, Kate
b 1923, crd 1957. Founded Carncairn Daffodils 1956 with Major R.H.Reade. Broughshane, Co.Antrim, N.Ireland
Reed, John R.
Buchanan, Michigan, USA; Niles, Michigan. Proprietor Oakwood Daffodils
Rees, G.N.
Nixa, Missouri, USA
Reeve, H.E.
b 1906, crd 1940s, d 1969. Dover, Tasmania, Australia
Rend, Mrs Doris
Easton, Maryland, USA
Rendlesham, Lord
Mawnan, Cornwall, England
Reynolds, Kenyon L., later Rev. Father Bede
Pasadena, California, USA
Rhodes, C.H.E.
Wanganui, New Zealand
Rhodes, Hon. Sir Robert Heaton
b 1861, d 1956. Tai Tapu, New Zealand. Knighted 1920
RHS(Victoria)
Royal Horticultural Society of Victoria, Australia
Richardson, Mrs Helen K.
b 1903, d 1978. Waterford, Co.Waterford, Republic of Ireland
Richardson, J.Lionel
b 1890, crd 1911, d 1961. Waterford, Co.Waterford, Republic of Ireland
Rijk, G.
Holland
Rijkelijkhuizen, J.H.
rd 1950-1990. Hillegom, Holland
Rijnveld, F., & Sons
rd 1925-1971. Hillegom, Holland
River Gardeners Association
River, Kent, England
Robert, A.
St. Saviour, Jersey, Channel Islands
Robertson, Mrs Ben M.
b 1906, crd 1950. Taylors, South Carolina, USA
Robinson, A.
Robinson, Arthur E.
b 1923, crd 1969. Enfield, Middlesex, England
Roblin, A.O.
crd 1935. Kempton, Tasmania, Australia; West Ulverstone, Tasmania
Roesé, William H.
b 1927, crd 1958. La Habra, California, USA; Santa Maria
Rollinson, M.E.
b 1932, crd 1988. Washdyke, New Zealand
Romine, Jack S.
crd c.1967, d 1992. Walnut Creek, California, USA

Ronalds, Oscar
b 1873, crd 1920s, d 1955. Gippsland, Victoria, Australia
Roozen, Frans
Haarlem, Holland
Roozen, J.B.
Heemstede, Holland
Rosewarne Experimental Horticultural Station
Camborne, Cornwall, England
Rotteveel, G.H., & Sons
rd up to 1988. Noordwijk, Holland
Rowlands, B.
d 1942. Murrumbeena, Victoria, Australia
Ruigrok, R.J.
Lisse, Holland
Rukšans, Jānis
b 1946, crd 1978. Riga, Latvia; Rozula
Runyan, Clifford R.
Cincinnati, Ohio, USA
Rupers, Barbara
b 1935, crd 1967. Salem, Oregon, USA

Salisbury, R.A.
b 1761, d 1829. Chapel Allerton, Yorkshire, England; Mill Hill, London. Drew up and named the first daffodil groups, viz. Ajax, Corbularia, Ganymedes and others
Salter, David
Williton, Somerset, England
Sandler, Dorit
Bet Dagen, Israel
Sandys-Winsch, Captain A.
Brundall, Norfolk, England
Saunders, Rev. F.A.
d 1985. Masterton, New Zealand
Scamp, R.A.
b 1943, crd 1969. Falmouth, Cornwall, England
Schlitt, Jack
Portland, Oregon, USA
Schoorl, L.J.C.
rd 1950-1975. Lisse, Holland
Scowen, C.R.L.
Secrett, F.A.
b 1886, d 1964. Twickenham, Middlesex, England; Walton-on-Thames, Surrey; Kenwyn Valley, Cornwall; Milford, Surrey
Segers, Johan
b 1843, crd 1890, d 1925. Lisse, Holland
Selkirk, Henry
crd c.1894. Killara, New South Wales, Australia
Seymour Cobley Ltd
See **Cobley**
Shailer, H.B.
d 1948. Palmerston North, New Zealand
Sharp, Humphrey Ewing
b 1844, crd c.1901, d 1925. Oratia, New Zealand
Sharp, J.
b 1885, d 1972. Bulla, Victoria, Australia
Sharp, R.Gordon

Oratia, New Zealand
Shepherd, F.W. (Fred)
d 1991. Truro, Cornwall, England
Sheppard, David L.
crd *c.*1944, d 1996. Mount Lehman, British Columbia, Canada
Sherrard, Lieutenant-Colonel James Ormsby
d 1960. Newbury, Berkshire, England
Sherriff, A.J
Whitemore, Tasmania, Australia
Sherriff, T.
Shilson
Silcock, Fred
Mount Macedon, Victoria, Australia
Simmons, Mrs A.R.
crd 1960. Timaru, New Zealand; Rotorua; Te Puke
Simmons, Mrs H.H.
Seattle, Washington, USA
Simpson, Mrs B.T.
d 1980. Palmerston North, New Zealand
Skelmersdale, Lady
b 1948, crd 1990. Broadleigh Gardens, Bishops Hull, Somerset, England (from 1972)
Skuja, Vitauts
Sigulda, Latvia
Slee, T.
d 1938. Huntly, New Zealand
Slieve Donard Nursery Company
See **Donard Nursery Company**
Slinger, William
See **Donard Nursery Company**.
Smith, Major A.A.Dorrien
b 1876, d 1955. Tresco, Isles of Scilly, England
Smith, Augustus
b 1804, d 1872. Tresco, Isles of Scilly, England. Instigator of the Scillonian daffodil industry
Smith, Miss A.I.
Perth, Tayside, Scotland
Smith, Charles, & Son
crd *c.*1890. Guernsey, Channel Islands
Smith, Mrs J.Abel (Barbara)
b 1914, d 1995. Letty Green, Hertfordshire, England
Smith, Kenneth D.
Staten Island, New York, USA
Smith, Commander T.M.Dorrien
Tresco, Isles of Scilly, England
Smith, Thomas
see **Daisy Hill Nursery**
Snazelle, Theodore E.
b 1941, crd 1962. Clinton, Mississippi, USA
Spalding Bulb Co.
Established *c.*1922. Spalding, Lincolnshire, England
Speyer, Mrs P.E. (Pearl)
b 1945, crd 1971. Springston, New Zealand; Christchurch
Spotts, Robert
b 1937, crd 1975. Oakley, California, USA; Stockton, California
Spry, A.P. (Mrs Michael Spry)
The Basin, Victoria, Australia
Spry, W.Michael
d 1987. The Basin, Victoria, Australia
Spurrell, Miss Katherine
d 1912. Bessingham, Norfolk, England
Stagg, Walter
d 1992. Broadleigh Gardens, Sampford Arundel, Somerset, England (to 1972); Avon Bulbs, Bathford, Somerset, later Bradford-on-Avon, Wiltshire (1979-1987)
Steenvoorden, L.
Noordwijk, Holland
Sterling, Robert
Bangor, Co.Down, N.Ireland
Stern, Colonel Sir Frederick
crd 1933, d 1967. Goring-by-Sea, Sussex, England. Knighted 1956
Stevens, J.H.
Sidmouth, Devon, England
Stevens & Son
Woolbrook Nurseries, Sidmouth, Devon, England
Stewart, Wilson
Longparish, Hampshire, England
Stijnman, C.J.
Warmond, Holland
Stralewei, V.O.F.
rd 1980 1995. Breezand, Holland
Stronach, Frank
b 1921, crd 1958, d 1996. Hobart, Tasmania, Australia
Stuart, Dr Charles
b 1825, d 1902. Chirnside, Berwickshire, Scotland
Stuart, D. & M.
Ohura, New Zealand
Summerell, B.L.
Morrinsville, New Zealand
Summerell, M. Lou
Morrinsville, New Zealand
Summers, W.L.
b 1871, d 1958. Blackwood, South Australia, Australia
Sutherland, Dr W.
Lawrence, New Zealand; Waitara; Hamilton
Svarcs, Juris
Ogre, Latvia
Swain, John
Bristol, England
Sydenham, Robert
b 1848, d 1913. Birmingham, England. Driving force behind foundation in 1898 of the Midland Daffodil Society (later the Daffodil Society)

Tait, Alfred Wilby
b 1847, d 1917. Oporto, Portugal
Tamar Valley Daffodils
See **Du Plessis Bros**

Tarry, George W.
b 1920. Ness, South Wirrall, England
Taylor, E.G.
New Zealand
Taylor, H.
Invergowrie, Angus, Scotland
Taylor, O.A., & Sons
Holbeach, Lincolnshire, England
Temple-Smith, Michael Geoffrey
Riverside, Tasmania, Australia. In partnership with Geoffrey Temple-Smith at Killara Bulbs
Temple-Smith, Geoffrey
Blackman's Bay, Tasmania, Australia. In partnership with Michael Temple-Smith at Killara Bulbs
Tesselaar Group
Silvan, Victoria, Australia
Thomas, Professor Sir Algernon P.W.
b 1857, d 1937. Mount Eden, New Zealand. Knighted 1937
Thomas, H.
Thomas, Norman R.W.
d 1969. Auckland, New Zealand
Thompson, A.G.
Garforth, Yorkshire, England
Thomson, Greg
crd 1991. Castle Forbes Bay, Tasmania, Australia
Thomson, Dr William Malcolm
d 1942. Hawera, New Zealand
Thoolen International
crd 1960. Heemstede, Holland
Thornton, Miss R.
Brockhall, Northamptonshire, England
Thornton, R.L
b 1894, crd c.1930, d 1969. Auckland, New Zealand
Throckmorton, Dr Tom D.
Des Moines, Iowa, USA. Creator of the daffodil colour-coding system introduced in 1975
Throckmorton, Mrs J.B.
Des Moines, Iowa, USA
Thurston, E.H.G.
Chandlers Ford, Hampshire, England
Ticknor, William O.
Falls Church, Virginia, USA; Tyner, North Carolina
Titheradge, George S.
b 1848, d 1916. Coburg, Victoria, Australia
Toal, W.J.
Belfast, Co.Antrim, N.Ireland
Tolley, Curtis
b 1923, crd 1972. Pinch, West Virginia, USA
Tom Parker Farms
Philleigh, Cornwall, England
Tombleson, R.C.A.
d 1983. Gisborne, New Zealand
Tongs, D.C.
Ulverstone, Tasmania, Australia
Townley, David
b 1929, crd 1990. Saffron Walden, Essex, England

Trenoweth Valley Flower Farm
Established 1935, crd 1936. St Keverne, Cornwall, England
Trevena, H.T.
d 1943. Otago Harbour, New Zealand
Tribe, M.H.
Kingsbridge, Devon, England
Tromp Bros
rd c.1945-1970. Lisse, Holland
Tuggle, Harry I. Jr
d 1970. Martinsville, Virginia, USA
Turnhout, Messrs
Tunley, Joyce
Middlesborough, Yorkshire, England
Tymons, Rev. Frederick
Baskin Hill, Co.Dublin, Republic of Ireland

Uit Den Boogaard, G.A.
b 1882, crd 1930, d 1943. Warmond, Holland

Valkering, J., & Sons
rd c.1920-1995. Limmen, Holland
Valois, M.
Van Buggenum Bros
rd 1975-1995. Beverwijk, Holland
van Buggenum, D.
rd 1940-1970. Hillegom, Holland
van den Berg, P.J., & Sons
Egmond Binnen, Holland
van der Berg, Jac J.
Noordwijkerhout, Holland
van den Berg-Hytuna, A.P.
Anna Paulowna, Holland; Breezand
van der Brug, L.
Holland
van der Bruggen, N.
d 1970. Holland
van den Burg, J.D.
Lisse, Holland
van der Hulst, Th.
Sassenheim, Holland
van der Meer, J.C.
b 1880, d 1970. Noordwijk, Holland
van der Ploeg, P.J.
Holland
Van der Poel Bros
Lisse, Holland
van der Salm, C.
crd c.1990. Lisse, Holland
van der Schoot, A.C.
Established 1917. Hillegom, Holland; London, England; West Malling, Kent.
van der Schoot, J.B.
Established 1917, rd up to 1950. Hillegom, Holland.
van der Schoot, R., & Son
Established 1830, crd 1890, succeeded 1917 by A.C., J.B. and R.A van der Schoot. Hillegom, Holland
van der Schoot, R.A.

Established 1917, rd up to 1935. Hillegom, Holland.

van der Veek, K.J.
b 1937, crd 1977. Burgerbrug, Holland

Van der Viel & Co.
Holland

van der Viel, J.W.A.
Holland

Vandervliet, M.A.
Mont Cochon, Jersey, Channel Islands

van der Voet, P
Sassenheim, Holland

Vandervoort, C. A.
Established 1919. Noordwijk, Holland; Sassenheim

van der Wereld, C.A.
rd 1930-1940. Roelof-Arendsveen, Holland; Breezand

van der Wereld, J.W.A., & Sons
crd 1950. Breezand, Holland

van der Weyden Jobson, G

Van der Zalm Bros
Noordwijk, Holland

van der Zwet, J.A., & Sons
Roelof-Arendsveen, Holland

van Deursen, P.
Established 1887, crd c.1906. Sassenheim, Holland; Heemskerk

van Dijk, J.M.
rd up to 1993. Hillegom, Holland

van Dobben De Bruyn, C.S., Jr
crd c.1940. Noordwijk, Holland

Van Eeden Bros
Noordwijkerhout, Holland

Van Eeden Goohof
crd 1990. Noordwijkerhout, Holland

van Eeden, J.N.M.
rd 1970-1980. Noordwijkerhout, Holland

van Eeden, P.B.
crd 1925. Noordwijk, Holland

van Eeden, W.P.
crd 1960. Holland

van Egmond, D., & Sons
rd 1940-1970. Hillegom, Holland

van Gent, J.A.
Voorhout, Holland

van Graven, A.T.
crd 1950. De Zilk, Holland

Van Graven Bros
crd 1970. Hillegom, Holland

van Grieken, L.
rd 1930-1950. Lisse, Holland

van Hage, C.M.
Great Amwell, Hertfordshire, England

van Hensbergen, Leo
rd 1950-1970. Holland

van Konynenburg, S.A., & Co.
rd 1920-1975. Noordwijk, Holland

van Konynenburg, Dominicus
b 1895, d 1978. Founded c.1922 Spalding Bulb Co., Spalding, Lincolnshire, England

van Leeuwen, L., & Son
Established 1888, rd 1908-1935. Sassenheim, Holland

Van Meerbech & Co.
Holland

van Oosten, J.Th.
rd 1960-1970. Holland

van Paridon, C.A.
rd 1940-1970. Noordwijkerhout, Holland

Van Paridon's Bloembollenbedrijf
crd 1970. Breezand, Holland

van Reeuwijk, N.
crd c.1975. Holland

van Reisen, P., & Sons
Established 1878. Voorhout, Holland

van Rhijn, G.B.
Noordwijk, Holland

van Rijn, A.
Petten, Holland

van Schie, W.A.
rd 1960-1970. Noordwijkerhout, Holland

van Slogteren, Professor Dr E.
b 1888, d 1968. Pioneer research into daffodil pests and diseases. Director, Bulb Research Centre, Lisse, Holland

Van 't Hof & Blokker
rd 1950-1990. Limmen, Holland

van Tubergen, C.G.
Established 1868, crd 1891. Haarlem, Holland

van Velzen, J.
Zoeterwoude, Holland; Wervershoof

van Waardenburg, J.
Holland

van Waveren, N., & Sons
Established 1822, crd 1890. Hillegom, Holland

van Zanten, C.A.
Holland

Van Zonnefeld Bros & Philippo
Established 1879, crd 1900. Sassenheim, Holland

Veen, J.H.
Haarlem, Holland

Veitch, James, & Sons
Chelsea, London, England

Veldhuyzen van Zanten, M., & Sons
rd 1940-1965. Lisse, Holland

Verdegaal, G.A
rd 1945-1985. Noordwijkerhout, Holland

Verduyn, J.

Verge, Frank B.
b 1926, crd 1963. Seal Chart, Kent, England

Verry, Miss Mavis
b 1911, crd 1947. Te Kuiti, New Zealand

Vink, G.
rd 1960-1970. Noordwijk, Holland

Vis, Albert
crd 1930. Limmen, Holland

Vonderbank, N., & Son
crd c.1980. Breezand, Holland

Voges, John, & Co.
Established 1882. Hillegom, Holland
Vos, M.
b 1834, d 1903. Holland

Waley, Frank R.
b c.1893, d 1987. Sevenoaks, Kent, England
Walker, James
b 1837, d 1911. Ham Common, Surrey, England
Walker, J.M.
b 1896, crd c.1940, d 1963. Te Kuiti, New Zealand
Walker, John
Winton, Dorset, England
Wall, John
Wisley, Surrey, England; Hamilton, Lanarkshire, Scotland
Wallace, G. L'E.
Wallace & Barr
See **Barr,** G., also **Barr,** H.R.
Wallis, Mrs Rannveig
Lower Beeding, Sussex, England
Walls, A.W.A.
Otaki, New Zealand
Walton, N.J.
Altrincham, Cheshire, England
Ward, Michael J.
Killiney, Co.Dublin, Republic of Ireland
Ward, Rodney W.
b 1904, crd 1929. St Mary's, Isles of Scilly, England
Ware, T.S.
b c.1824, d 1901. Tottenham, London, England
Ware, Walter T.
b 1855, crd c.1900, d 1917. Wisbech, Cambridgeshire, England; Inglescombe, Somerset; Wisbech, Cambridgeshire
Warnaar & Co.
Established 1882, crd 1907. Sassenheim, Holland
Warren Gardens
See **Currey**
Waterloo Nursery
See **Poole**
Watrous, Mrs Roberta C.
Washington DC, USA
Watson, Mrs J.
Watts, W.A.
crd 1900, d 1957. St Asaph, Denbighshire, Wales. Proprietor The Welsh Bulb Fields
Wayne, Gerard H.
b 1930, crd 1965. Beverly Hills, California, USA
Webster, C.E.
b 1861, crd 1920s, d 1936. Hobart, Tasmania, Australia
Weightman, J.G.
crd c.1912, d 1942. Feilding, New Zealand
Weightman, W.E.
crd 1912, d 1942. Awahuri, New Zealand

Weijers, C.S., Jr
Hillegom, Holland
Welch, William R.P.
b 1958, crd 1972. Carmel Valley, California, USA
Welchman, William
b 1854, crd 1902, d 1936. Upwell, Norfolk, England
Wells, James S.
b 1915, crd 1980. Red Bank, New Jersey, USA
Welsh Bulb Fields
See **Watts**
Wentink, H.J.
crd 1970. Egmond Binnen, Holland
West & Fell
See **West,** David V.
West, David V.
b 1864, crd 1905, d 1932. Casterton, Victoria, Australia. In partnership with Hubert Fell
Wheadon, E.H., & Sons
Guernsey, Channel Islands
Wheeler, Willis H.
b 1906, crd 1947, d 1996. Arlington, Virginia, USA; Gainesville, Florida
Whibley, J.C.
d 1984. Palmerston North, New Zealand
Wijnhout, H., & Son
crd 1955. Hillegom, Holland
Wilks, W.
b 1843, d 1923. Shirley, Surrey, England
Williams, Alfred Martyn
b 1897, d 1982. Launceston, Cornwall, England
Williams, John Charles
b 1861, crd 1893, d 1939. Gorran, Cornwall, England
Williams, John T.
b 1924, crd 1972. Maghull, Merseyside, England
Williams, Michael Percival
b 1903, crd 1935, d 1963. St Keverne, Cornwall, England
Williams, Percival Dacres
b 1865, crd 1895, d 1935. St Keverne, Cornwall, England
Willmott, Miss Ellen
b 1858, d 1934. Great Warley, Essex, England
Wilshire, L.
New Zealand
Wilson, A.
crd 1890. Canterbury, New Zealand; Dunedin
Wilson, Alexander M.
b 1868, crd 1900, d 1953. East Keal, Lincolnshire, England; Shovell, Somerset; Presteigne, Radnorshire (now Powys), Wales
Wilson, Angus
rd 1940s-1950s
Wilson, Guy Livingstone
b 1885, crd 1906, d 1962. Broughshane, Co.Antrim, N.Ireland
Wilson, G.L. (Marden)
Established 1961. Marden, Kent, England

Wister, Dr John C.
crd 1921, d 1982. Swarthmore, Pennsylvania, USA
Wolfhagen, W.W.
Tasmania, Australia
Wolley-Dod, Rev. Charles
b 1826, crd *c.*1880 d 1904. Malpas, Cheshire, England
Wood, Miss A.E.
Hampton Bishop, Herefordshire, England
Wood, T.A.V.
Cuddra, Cornwall, England; Boscovy, Cornwall
Woodman, D.
Mawnan Smith, Cornwall, England
Woods, Mrs B.A.
Wootton, C.Reginald
b 1897, d 1970. Bloxwich, Staffordshire, England
Wormald, Hugh
b 1885, d 1946. East Dereham, Norfolk, England
Worsley, Philip John
b 1834, crd 1891, d 1917. Clifton, Gloucestershire, England

Yahel, Mrs Herut
Rishon le Zion, Israel
Yates, Arthur
Exeter, New South Wales, Australia
Yeates, G.C.
b 1904, crd 1956, d 1987. New Plymouth, New Zealand
Yerger, Mrs Merton S. (Meg)
b 1914, crd 1973. Princess Anne, Maryland, USA
Yonge, Mrs J.U.
Young, F.W.
Coleraine, Londonderry, N.Ireland
Young, G.S.
Wellington, New Zealand

Zandbergen, D.
Holland
Zandbergen, Matthew
b 1903, d 1990. Sassenheim, Holland
Zandbergen, N.
crd *c.*1920. Rijnsburg, Holland
Zandbergen-Terwegen, G.
Established 1918, crd 1918. Sassenheim, Holland
Zeestraten, G.
Oegstgeest, Holland; Greenhurst, New York, USA
Zeestraten, H.
Holland
Zinkowski, Edward
Rosemead, California, USA
Zwetsloot, Hugo P.
rd 1960-1980. Lisse, Holland; Sassenheim
Zwetsloot, P.Th.